ISBN 978-0-484-67631-1
PIBN 10821819

FB &c Ltd, Dalton House, 60 Windsor Avenue, London, SW19 2RR.
Company number 08720141. Registered in England and Wales.

For support please visit www.forgottenbooks.com

NEUMAN AND BARETTI'S

DICTIONARY

OF THE

SPANISH AND ENGLISH LANGUAGES;

WHEREIN

THE WORDS ARE CORRECTLY EXPLAINED, AGREEABLY TO THEIR DIFFERENT MEANINGS,

AND

A GREAT VARIETY OF TERMS,

RELATING TO THE

ARTS, SCIENCES, MANUFACTURES, MERCHANDISE, NAVIGATION, AND TRADE, ELUCIDATED.

SECOND AMERICAN, FROM THE FOURTH LONDON EDITION,

CAREFULLY REVISED, AND ENLARGED BY THE ADDITION OF MANY THOUSAND WORDS EXTRACTED FROM THE WRITINGS OF THE MOST CLASSICAL SPANISH AND ENGLISH AUTHORS, MANY OF WHICH ARE NOT TO BE FOUND IN ANY OTHER DICTIONARY OF THOSE LANGUAGES; AND ALSO GREAT ADDITIONS FROM THE DICTIONARIES OF CONNELLY AND HIGGINS, THE SPANISH ACADEMY, &c. &c.

IN TWO VOLUMES.

VOL. I.

SPANISH AND ENGLISH.

STEREOTYPED AT THE BOSTON TYPE AND STEREOTYPE FOUNDRY.

BOSTON:

HILLIARD, GRAY, LITTLE, AND WILKINS.

1827.

PREFACE.

Dictionaries have certainly not received those improvements, either in plan or execution, which their increased utility has rendered essentially necessary. The difficulty of their execution sufficiently accounts for this tardiness in their advancement; and the most ignorant reader may often discover an error in what relates to his own particular branch of knowledge, although he may be very unequal to appreciate the merits of any other subject. But the study, or rather the mode of acquiring a knowledge of languages, has made as little progress as the compilation of dictionaries. Grammarians have multiplied divisions, and involved themselves in the subordinate details of grammar, without considering the general and necessary principles of speech, the dependence of oral language on the organs of the voice, or the analogies between the modes of thinking, the sentiment, and the language of a particular people. Hence it is, that persons often labour for years to become familiar with the subdivisions and classifications of words, when a knowledge of what may be truly called the spirit of a language, might be acquired in a few hours, and all other knowledge respecting it would follow as a consequence of imbibing its spirit. Whoever considers words as the efforts of the mind to communicate its ideas and feelings, will soon discover the universal principles of language, and the great similarity of all tongues. With a knowledge of these general elements, it is easy to recognise, and even to feel, the spirit of any particular language or dialect; and hence, the study of different languages becomes not only simple and easy, but really instructive, as it presents incomparably the most faithful pictures of all mental operations, of ideas and passions, as influenced by religion, laws, and civil polity, or climate. Some linguists, indeed, are contented with knowing the grammatical distinctions and the names of a coat or a book in several languages, without any regard to the extension of useful knowledge, and forgetting that a mere vocabulary may be acquired by a mechanical effort of the memory, independent of judgment. Such vocabularists make no discoveries in the arts or sciences; they never extend the actual boundaries of our knowledge, still less do they meliorate their own minds, give to their reason an absolute ascendency over their passions, or expand their benevolent, at the expense of their selfish feelings. To obviate such pedantry and lettered uselessness, has been one of the chief objects of the present edition of this Spanish and English Dictionary, which, it is hoped, contains not only many thousand more words than are to be found in the most copious vocabularies, but also much practical and useful information, correct data from which the nature and operations of the human mind in Spain and in England may be deduced; more facts, principles and terms, now used in the sciences, arts, manufactures, and commerce, than in any similar dictionary hitherto published, and likewise more of the modern words in the polite or familiar conversation of both countries.

When it is remembered that words are the representatives of ideas, and that the language of any people is nearly a perfect picture of what passes or exists in their minds, it will be evident that a complete dictionary must be a faithful epitome of their intellectual labours; their idiomatic phrases being but abridged metaphors, or modes of saying one thing and meaning another, the polite metaphors of the first age become the vulgarisms of the second, the obsolete language of the third, and the nervous expression of the fourth. In this manner, taste, fashion, or the progress of civilization, and the effect of external circumstances, modulate all living languages; and every generation has its circle of what is esteemed polite phraseology, in defiance of all critical dogmas, or the more serious denunciations of censors and moralists. This continued succession of popular phrases (for the words of conversation in one age generally form but a very small part of any cultivated language), contributes to augment the interest of well-digested dictionaries, which thereby enable the writer of taste and reflection to select the best, the most harmonious, the purest, and most moral phraseology that the language of successive ages affords. To the divine, the moralist, and the metaphysician, it is no less important; as, words being the offspring of ideas and things, the existence of the former is the most unequivocal demonstration of that of the latter. For instance, the French have very justly and naturally a term signifying a man or a woman with a bad breath, (*Punais* and *Punaise*;) the Spanish and English, being generally devoid of this quality, have no corresponding term, and are without any such word. This, however, is not the only difference between the languages and people of those countries. With every French thought and word something of colour and stage effect is associated; it is the spirit of the people and of their language, while that of Spain and England is metaphysical, or mere abstract truth and reason. On the other hand, it must be admitted, that the philanthropic observer of men and manners will view, with profound regret, the superabundance of Spanish epithets injurious to women, and feel perhaps disposed to consider the virtue of females as the fairest criterion of national morality. However this may be, there is evidently more wisdom in raising than depreciating the moral qualities of those who necessarily teach the first rudiments of knowledge, and certainly modulate the character of all mankind. Contrary also to the vulgar and even traditional opinion in Britain, there is, in fact, no radical and appropriate Spanish term, which exclusively and forcibly conveys the same idea as the English word *jealousy*. Nevertheless the Spaniards have evinced great wisdom in carefully guarding their language and sentiments from the deteriorating influence of French corruption. In this respect, their conduct presents a noble example to the modern English, who really seem to be almost ashamed of their mother tongue, and to have nearly forgotten that their radical language is as old, and incomparably better than that of France. The fashionable and vulgar foplings of the day have expelled the *s* and *t* final almost entirely from their jargon, and given an Anglo-Gallic pronunciation to plain English words, that is more analogous to the hideous accents of unfortunate maniacs than the tones of rational beings. Happily this practice is still confined to the ignorant and comparatively illiterate; but, however pity may be extended to the prude and the coquette, whose imbecile affectation may abandon the definite and modest term *shift*, for the silly, vague, and not very delicate one *chemise* (*camis* from χαμίσιον would be genuine English); it is impossible to have any other feeling than that of ineffable contempt for the wretched animal, who in the British metropolis has lost his hat to find a *chapeau*. Such things require the admirable pen of Cadalso, in his *Eruditos a la Violeta*. This absurdity is, indeed, become so enormous and offensive, as to astonish and perplex strangers, while it excites the liveliest regret in the minds of reflecting natives. It has been attempted to palliate this disgrace, by alleging that the English language is chiefly derived from the French. Some etymologists, it is true, have read English through French spectacles, and indulged their indolence, or masked their ignorance, by producing parallel words from the French. As to Horne Tooke, the most visionary and illogical of all etymologists, whatever is correct or good in his work, all his pretended discoveries of the *Επεα πτεροεντα*, may be traced to what Spanish writers (Aldrete, Mayans, &c.) have related of the manner in which the Goths corrupted the Latin in Spain; his ribaldry and blasphemy are his own; but his errors have been exposed with equal truth and eloquence by Professor Dugald Stewart. There is, however, no notion more erroneous or unfounded, than that of the English tongue being derived from the French, to which it, correctly speaking, owes nothing whatever. The most cursory investigation must satisfy every enquirer, that the grand basis of the English is the Anglo-Saxon, mixed with Latin and Greek, which were popular languages in England at two different periods of the dark ages. Some barbarous law terms, and a few, but very few, other words, have been borrowed from the French, while the genius and spirit of the language still bear the noble features of their Saxon and classic origin. This was universally admitted, till Bolingbroke, and his follower Pope, introduced the French style into prose and rhyme; the former moralized to obliterate the remembrance of his treason, and the latter rhymed solely in imitation of Boileau. Their example has been adopted by Gibbon, who aped Voltaire; but it is the elephant imitating the monkey; his infidelity and occasional obsecnity betray his extreme want of morality and judgment, and suit the Gallic tinsel of his monotonous jargon. In the voluminous writings of Gibbon, it is perhaps impossible to find one sentence of pure English; and the foreigner, who wishes to have a correct knowledge of the language, will, it is hoped, never read a page either of Bolingbroke or Gibbon in their English form. Between the Spanish and English there is much more similarity than between the French and English; and this Dictionary will furnish satisfactory evidence, that both nations adopted the same Latin words, with the same significations, into their vernacular dialects. Several of those words are marked *disused* in both countries, some others are printed in capitals, while whole families of words are still used, as *indagar*, from *indagare*, to indagate. The judicious traveller, who has studied anatomy and physiognomy, and visited the inhabitants in the valleys of Aragon and other northern provinces of Spain, and who has also observed the natives of the Isle of Wight, and the inhabitants in the valleys of the South Downs, will be at no loss to discover the most unequivocal evidence of indentity of origin, and instantly conclude, that a branch of the same race of Saxons (the Getæ), who invaded the south-west of England, must also have extended themselves to Spain. The physical traits of similarity are as striking as those of the ancient Greeks, whose descendants still appear in the valleys of Granada. The inquisitive reader may perhaps feel disposed to pursue this subject much farther than it is here expedient. A writer in the Archæologia, published by the Society of Antiquaries of London, has traced the first inhabitants of Britain to the Iberians; but it is easier to frame ingenious theories than to collect facts and make correct observations. The Saxon race is much less equivocal.

In order to facilitate the acquisition of English, it may here be proper to notice its significant terminations, which somewhat exceed a hundred. The terminations or affixes *an*, *in*, *ine*, and *ana*, have a possessive import, and signify belonging to, as *partizan* is belonging to a party; *ee* annexed to a verb mark its personal object, patient, or result; *er* to adjectives signifies before or superior; but when *er*, *or*, and *our*, are added to words signifying action, they denote the person who acts; as from love, lover: they also become abstract nouns or general names of things, as from the Saxon mopð, death, we have murther or murder, and *ure* was formerly written *our*, as *plesour*, now pleasure, from the Latin *placeo*, and not the French *plaisir*. *Ess* and *ix* are the only feminine terminations, as *ster* is used to both sexes; the Saxon *ric* or *rick* marks possession or dominion; *en* was the Saxon plural, still used in children, &c.; it also signifies made or consisting of, as gold*en*; and finished, as prov*en*, prov*ed*; to shorten, *i. e.* to *make* shorter: the difference between *ed* of the past tense, and *en* of the participle, is, that in the former the action is considered, in the latter its effects on the object; *ght* is the same as *ed*, finished, and the latter in adjectives often becomes *id*; the adjective affixes *ant*, *ent*, and substantive ones *ance*, *ence*, and *end*, denote being or state, as abundant is the quality of being or existing in abundance; and fri*end* from ꝼreonde, loving; hence the cause of its being still pronounced *frend*; *ing* and *ion* simply indicate the existence of quality or action, and *ment* or *mony* is of the like import; *ile*, *al*, and *ar*, are adjective terminations expressing quality or disposition; when *al* is added to a verb, it is the same as *ing* or *ion*; *able* and *ible* signify having or possessing any quality or power; *ic*, *ick*, *ique*, *esque*, imply kind, division, or similarity; *ical* is *al* and *ic*; *ch* and *ish* have the same meaning, but the latter is generally a diminutive; *ule*, *ulous*, *incle*, and *et*, are also diminutives; *oon* is an augmentative; *y* is derived from the Saxon ʒ, and corresponds to the Latin *ia*; *ly*, *like*, and *ably*, indicate similarity; *ary*, *ery*, and *ory*, express sort or kind; *kin*, *kind*, *ling*, and *let*, denote family or relation, but the two latter are also diminutives; *ous*, *eous*, *wise*, and *ways*, express kind or manner of the word to which they are affixed; *on* makes a personal substantive of similarity, as patron from *pater*, father; *full* or *ful* are self-evident; *less* means want or dismissal; *age* and *ish* imply act, effect, or result, but *age* also signifies space of time and price; *ise* or *ize* are verbal terminations; *ism* denotes collection of effects or classes of action; *ist* and *ite*, personal agent; *ive*, *if*, mean causing or producing; *ate*, *ated*, *ating*, *ation*, *ator*, *atory*, and *ace*, all imply action or agent; *el* or *le*, annexed to verbs, make them frequentatives, as to prate, to prattle, &c. *ad* or *ade* means mass or heap; *cide* and *cidal* are to kill; *ard* denotes nature, species, kind, or manner; *ward* means looking to, or in the direction of; *hearted* is applied to the feelings or passions, *headed* to the mind and judgment; *stead* and *step* indicate place; *dom*, condition of existence; *head*, *hood*, and *chief*, mean principal and state; *ship*, *skip*, or *scape*, also denote head or chief; *ce*, *cy*, *ity*, *tude*, and *th*, are affixes to nouns of generality; *fy* is to make, *faction*, the act of making, and sometimes the thing made, as petrifaction; *ign* expresses quality; *ow* is of the kind; *some* and *sum* mean quantity; and the *s*, so much abused by Gallic affectation, is properly an adverbial affix, as backward is the quality of an action, backwards the manner of it; *stall* and *still* are to place; *tide* and *time* are synonymous; *w* is interchangeable with *g*, as guile and wile. As to the prefixes, they are chiefly Latin or Greek prepositions, and have nothing peculiar. *Un* is of Saxon origin, and is not merely a negative, but means to reverse the action of the verb to which it is prefixed. *En* in composition becomes *em*, *in*, *ig*, *il*, *im*, or *ir*, according to the letter which immediately follows it. Many writers confound the prefixes *en* and *in*, although the latter properly signifies situation or place, and is also a negative; thus, to *in*quire, means to seek in or search the place, and to *en*quire only signifies to ake search. Farther explanations on this head may be found in the grammars of Lowth, Grant, and Allen, and the Analytical Introduction of Booth.

The Spanish terminations are easily acquired. It was observed by Mayans, that many Spanish substantives and adjectives are Latin ablative cases singular, or accusatives plural, as *ars*, arte, artes; *prudens*, prudente, prudentes. The *d*, *l*, *n*, *r*, *s*, *x*, and *z*, are the only consonants, which can terminate a word, though *b*, *c*, *d*, *g*, *l*, *m*, *n*, *p*, *r*, *s*, *t*, *x*, and *z*, may end a syllable; *c*, *l*, *n*, *r*, in few words admit of being doubled, and also the vowels *a*, *e*, *i*, and *o*, but more rarely. The organs of speech render *b*, *p*, *v*, and *f*, and, *c*, *g*, *j* and *q* interchangeable in both languages; in English *s* and *z* are commutable in verbal terminations. The Latin *t* is almost always changed in Spanish for *c* or *z*, as *gratia*, gracia, *ratio*, razon; the Latin mutes are likewise omitted, as *scientia*, ciencia; in other cases an *e* is prefixed for the sake of euphony, as *species* makes especie. The Latin adjectives in *bilis* obey the same law in Spanish and English, and make *ble*; *au* is changed to *o*, as *aurum*, oro; *i* to *e*, as *infirmus*, enfermo; *u* to *o*, as *musca*, mosca; *ovum*, huevo; *f* is converted into *h*, as *facere*, hacer; *m* into *n*, as *lympha*, linfa; Latin infinitives become Spanish by dropping the final *e*, as *ponere*, poner, *dormire*, dormir, *stare*, estar; some words are also augmented, by that spirit of magnanimity which animates every Spaniard, and which was judiciously observed by Smith in his Theory of Moral Sentiments; as from *spes* comes esperanza, *cor*, corazon; and, as a proof of their delicacy and temperance, *comedere* is reduced to comer. These literal mutations will be evident to the classical reader, and to others any further notice of them would be useless.

It remains to say something of the great and numerous additions to the volumes now submitted to the public. Above ten whole sheets have been added to the recent editions of this Dictionary, which, with the additional matter gained by compressing the definitions so as to have few short lines, and a greater length of page, as well as other alterations in the mode of printing, augment the contents to nearly twenty sheets more than the preceding editions. In the Spanish-English, there are above 3000 *entirely new articles* introduced; in the English-Spanish above 12,000. Besides these additions, in both parts, it will be found that very few of the old definitions have been allowed to pass, without either correction or the addition of many new and appropriate synonyms, several thousand of which are not to be found in any Spanish or English dictionary yet published, or indeed in any dictionary of two languages, which has fallen under the observation of the writer. The corrections have been made after carefully consulting the writings of father Isla, Capmany, Jovellanos, &c. and some Spanish living authors of established reputation. In some words the reader will observe definitions in both parts diametrically opposite to what are given in almost all other dictionaries; he is not therefore to conclude that they are wrong, but to examine facts, when he may perhaps discover their general accuracy, and that they are derived from diligent research. It rarely happens, as in the present case, that compilers of dictionaries are equally well acquainted with words and with things: it is the want of the latter, and more arduous kind of knowledge, which occasions the defectiveness of all dictionaries. In this edition, it is believed, more terms of science, arts, manufactures, and commerce, have been introduced than were ever before attempted in a dictionary of two languages, and even more than exist in any English dictionary extant.

Important political circumstances have recently happily combined to promote an extended intercourse between England and Spain—both European and American. The prejudices of religion, which had hitherto interdicted the dissemination of our literature, are rapidly vanishing before the edicts of a more liberal government in the old country, whilst the separation of Spanish Ameri from its parent state cannot but infuse new life into our commercial enterpris and bring us more immediately in contact with a country, the natural resourc of which are boundless; and with a people, who have manifested the stronge desire to cultivate the friendship, and to repose the fullest confidence in th known integrity and honour, of the British nation. That this copious Dictio ary of the languages of these countries may be the medium of facilitating th communication, and of promoting the best interests of each, is not only th earnest desire, but is also the certain anticipation, of the Editors.

Lastly, the Editors regret, from particular circumstances, they are not pe mitted to return publicly their thanks to many Spanish and other gentleme who have generously assisted their researches, either by the loan of books, c by written communications. To James Edwards, Esq. of Binstead, Isle o Wight, they are however happy in having this opportunity of making thei grateful acknowledgments for the very handsome manner in which he favoure them with some valuable books from his well-chosen library, and which the believe to be only a small testimony of his friendship to literature, and of hi zeal for the diffusion of useful knowledge.

EXPLANATION OF THE CONTRACTIONS, &c.

The *sm. sf.* mean substantives masculine and feminine; *s.* implies that the word is of both genders; *va vn. vr.* verbs active, neuter, and reflective or reciprocal; *a.* adjective; *ad.* adverb; *pron.* pronoun; *pa.* participle active. The contractions in parentheses are the first syllables of terms of science and arts, or name of provinces where the word is most used, as (Anat.) Anatomy, (And.) Audalusia, (Ant.) Antiquated, (Ar.) or (Arag.) Aragon, (Arq.) Architecture, (Art.) Artillery, (Aum.) Augmentative, (Bot.) Botany, (Met.) Metaphor or Metaphorical; and so of the others. Verbs active, neuter, or reciprocal are not repeated, but marked thus, AFIRMAR, *va.—vn.—vr.* When a word is substantive, adjective, and adverb, it is marked thus, MAL, *sm.—a.—ad.* The masculine and feminine terminations O, and A, and diminutives ICO, ICA; ILLO, ILLA; ITO, ITA; UELO, UELA, cannot be misunderstood. The words printed in capitals, like ADULTERATEE, are such as have been derived from the Spanish, but which have hitherto either eluded the researches of *English* etymologists, or been erroneously ascribed to another source: the number might have been increased had it been more essential. In the Second Volume the English words are accented so as to convey some idea of their pronunciation. Thus, when a vowel is doubled and pronounced short, the accent is placed on the first, as in *bréeches*, pronounced *breches;* when pronounced long, the accent is on the latter vowel, as in *breéding; beárlike*, pro. barelike; *beástlike*, pro. beestlike; *blóod*, pro. blud; *bloóm*, pro. blume, &c.

DICCIONARIO NUEVO

DE LAS

LENGUAS ESPAÑOLA É INGLESA.

Español é Inglés—Spanish and English.

A In the Spanish language, has but one sound, and is pronounced as the open English *a* in *master*.

A'. *prep.* which signifies, to, in, at, according to, on, by, for, and of; as *voy á Madrid*, I am going to Madrid; *á la Inglesa*, in the English fashion; *á oriente*, in the east: *jugar á los naypes*, to play at cards: *á las ocho*, at eight o'clock: *á prueba de bombas*, bomb-proof: *á ley de Castilla*, according to the law of Castile: *el vino á pie*, he came on foot: *quien á hierro mata, á hierro muere*, he who kills by the sword, dies by the sword; *dos á dos*, two by two: *á como vale la fánega? á treinta reales*, for how much a bushel? for thirty reals; *este libro va á Pedro*, this book is for Peter: *este vaso huele á vino*, this glass smells of wine: *real de á ocho*, piece of eight, V. *Real*.

A' coalesces with the masculine article *el*, and instead of *á el*, as anciently used, *al* is now written, as *al rey*, to the king; *al papa*, to the pope. This prepositive article is also used before the infinitive mode of verbs, as *al amanecer*, at the break of day; *al parecer*, apparently. *A'* is equivalent to the limit or end of any place or time, *á la cosecha pagaré*, I shall pay at harvest-time; *desde aqui á S. Juan*, from this to St. John's day; *me llegaba el agua á la garganta*, the water was up to my throat. Occasionally it implies towards or opposite, as, *se fue á ellos, volvió la cara á tal parte*, being towards or opposite them, he turned his face to such a part.

A' sometimes signifies the motive or principle, as, *á instancia de la villa*, at the request of the city: *á que proposito?* to what purpose? It also serves to express distributive numbers; as, *á perdiz por barba*, a partridge a-head. It is likewise a mere explicative in some phrases joined to a pronoun, as, *á mi me consta la verdad*, I know the truth, or, the truth is evident to me; *yo me culpo á mi*, I blame myself, or, I take blame to myself; *tu te alabas á ti*, thou praisest thyself; *vamos á pasear*, let us take a walk. Before the infinitive mode, and at the beginning of a sentence, it has sometimes a *conditional* sense, as, *á decir verdad*, if I must speak the truth.

A'. This preposition governs almost all parts of speech, whether substantives, adjectives, pronouns, or verbs; *á los hombres*, to men: *de bueno á malo*, from good to bad: *á mi, á ti, á vosotros*, to me, to thee, to you: *á jugar*, to play. It sometimes points out the person in whom the action of the verb terminates, and is placed before the accusative case, as *amo á Pedro*, I love Peter.

A' is still used in some phrases instead of *por*, *en*, *sin*, *para* and *la*; and in obsolete writings for *con* and *de*. In composition it serves to convert substantives and adjectives into verbs, as *abocar* from *boca*, *ablandar* from *blando*, &c. Formerly it was prefixed to many words, as *abazar*, *amatar*, &c. but being redundant these words are now written *bazar*, *matar*, &c.

A' is frequently used adverbially, as, *á deshora*, unseasonably; *á diferencia de esto*, contrary to this; *á proposito de eso*, in consequence of that; *á la verdad*, truly; *á lo menos*, at least; *á sabiendas*, knowingly; *á veces*, sometimes; *á vista de ojos*, evidently, at a glance.

AA. Contraction for *authors*; and *A*. for highness, or for approval.

AARÓN, *sm.* V. *Barba*.

A'BA, *sf.* A small measure for lands of about two yards.

ABÁBA, *sf.* Red poppy, corn-rose. Papaver rhoeas *L.* V. *Amapola*.

ABABÓL, *sm.* (Ar.) V. *Amapola*.

ABACERÍA, *sf.* A chandler's shop, where oil, vinegar, &c. are sold.

ABACÉRO, RA, *s.* A retailer of provisions, oil, vinegar, &c.

ABACIÁL, *a.* Belonging to an abbot.

A'BACO, *sm.* (Arq.) Abacus, highest moulding on the capital of a column.

ABÁD, *sm.* 1. An abbot. 2. A curate. *Abad bendito*, abbot having almost episcopal jurisdiction.

ABÁDA, *sf.* The female rhinoceros.

ABADÉJO, *sm.* 1. Cod-fish: properly Poor-jack. Gadus pollachius *L.* 2. Yellow wren. Motacilla trochilus *L.* 3. (Ant.) Spanish fly; blister beetle.

ABADÉNGO, GA, *a.* Belonging to an abbot.

ABÁDES, *sm. pl.* Spanish flies, cantharides.

ABADÉSA, *sf.* An abbess.

ABADÍA, *sf.* 1. An abbey. 2. Abbacy. 3. A curate's house.

ABADIÁDO, *sm.* (Ant.) Abbey-lands.

ABALÁDO, DA, *a.* Spongy, tumid, soft.

Abalanzádo, da, *a.* 1. Balanced. 2. Audacious.

Abalanzár, *va.* 1. To balance, to counterpoise. 2. To weigh, to compare. 3. To dart, to impel.—*vr.* 1. To rush on with impetuosity. 2. To venture.

Abaldonár, *va.* 1. To debase, to revile, to undervalue, to reproach. 2. (Ant.) To abandon.

Abaleár, *va.* To fan or winnow corn; to cleanse it from the chaff.

Aballár, *va.* (Ant.) 1. To strike down. 2. To carry off. 3. To move. 4. (Pint.) V. *Rebazar.*

Aballestár, *va.* (Naút.) To haul a cable.

Abalórios, *sm. pl.* Bugles, glass beads.

Abanderádo, *sm.* A standard-bearer.

Abanderizadór, ra, *s.* A factious person; a ringleader.

Abanderizár, *va.* To cabal; to stir up disturbances

Abandonádo, da, *a.* Abandoned, profligate, despondent.

Abandonamiénto ó Abandóno, *sm.* 1. The act of abandoning. 2. Lewdness, debauchery.

Abandonár, *va.* To abandon, to desert.—*vr.* To despond, to despair; to give one's self up to.

Abanicár, *va.* To fan.

Abanicázo, *sm.* Stroke with a fan.

Abaníco, *sm.* 1. A fan. 2. A sprit-sail. *En abanico,* Fan-formed, like a fan.

Abaníllo, *sm.* 1. Small fan. 2. A ruff, ruffle, fold.

Abaníno, *sm.* (Ant.) Ruffle, frill, ruff.

Abaniquéro, *sm.* A fan-maker.

Abáno, *sm.* A large fan.

Abánto, *sm.* A bird belonging to the family of vultures.

Abaratár, *va.* To abate, to beat down the price.

Abárca, *sf.* A piece of coarse leather tied on the soles of the feet, and worn by Spanish peasants.

Abarcádo, da, *a.* Having the feet supported by pieces of dry skin.

Abarcadór, ra, *s.* Embracer, undertaker, clasper.

Abarcadúra ó Abarcamiénto, *s.* An embrace.

Abarcár, *va.* 1. To clasp, to embrace. 2. To contain; to undertake. 3. (Mont.) To go round and inspect. *Abarcar el viento,* To go round cattle, game, a hill, &c. with the wind in the face.

Abarcón, *sm.* An iron ring.

Abarloár, *vn.* (Naút.) To bear up, to haul the wind.

Abarquillár, *va.* To build boats and gondolas.

Abarracárse, *vr.* To withdraw into barracks.

Abarrádo, da, *a.* Striped, clouded.

Abarraganárse, *vr.* To live in concubinage.

Abarrancadéro, *sm.* 1. A deep, heavy road. 2. A precipice. 3. (Met.) Difficult business.

Abarrancamiénto, *sm.* Act of making or falling into cavities or ruts; embarrassment.

Abarrancár, *va.* To break up a road; to dig holes.—*vr.* To fall into a pit; to become embarrassed.

Abarrár, *va.* V. *Acibarrar.*

Abarráz, *sm.* (Bot.) Louse-wort. V. *Yerba piojera.*

Abarrenár, *va.* (Ant.) V. *Barrenar.*

Abarréra, *sf.* (Murc.) V. *Regatona.*

Abarrísco, *ad.* Indiscriminately, promiscuously.

Abarrotár, *va.* 1. To tie down, to bind with cords. 2. (Naút.) To trim the hold, to stow the cargo.

Abarróte, *sm.* (Naút.) A small package for filling up the cavities in the stowage of a cargo.

Abastadaménte, *ad.* Abundantly, copiously.

Abastánte, *ad.* (Ant.) V. *Bastante.*

Abastár, *va.* (Ant.) V. *Abastecer* and *Bastar.*

Abastecedór, ra, *s.* A caterer, purveyor or provider.

Abastecér, *va.* To provide necessaries, to purvey.

Abastecimiénto, *sm.* 1. The office of a purveyor. 2. Provisions.

Abastionár, *va.* To construct bastions, to furnish with bastions.

Abásto, *sm.* 1. The supply of a town with provisions. 2. (Met.) Any thing abundant. 3. Small embroideries.

Abatanár, *va.* To beat or full cloth.

Abáte, *sm.* (An Italian term.) An abbé wearing a short cloak.

Abáte, *interj.* Take care! Stand out of the way

Abatidaménte, *ad.* meanly, basely.

Abatído, da, *a.* mean, base.

Abatimiénto, *sm.* 1. Overthrow, destruction. 2. Discouragement, lowness of spirits. 3. Humble, obscure condition. *Abatimiénto del rumbo,* (Naút.) The leeway of a ship.

Abatír, *va.* 1. To throw down, to overthrow. 2. To humble, to debase.—*vn.* To descend, to stoop.—*vr.* 1. To be disheartened. 2. (Naút.) To have leeway.

Abaxadór, *sm.* 1. Stable-boy in mines. 2. An abater, he that takes down.

Abaxamiénto, *sm.* Dejection, humbling.

Abaxár, *va.* (Ant.) V. *Baxar.*

Abáxo, *ad.* Under, underneath, below. *Venirse abaxo,* To fall, to tumble.

Abcíon, *sf.* (Ant.) V. *Accion.*

Abdicación, *sf.* Abdication.

Abdicár, *va.* 1. To abdicate. 2. To revoke, to annul.

Abdicativaménte, *ad.* Exclusively, independently.

Abdicatívo, va, *a.* Exclusive, independent.

Abdómen, *sm.* Abdomen.

Abecé, *sm.* The alphabet; the letters or elements of speech.

Abecedário, *sm.* 1. A spelling-book. 2. A table of contents.

Abedúl, *sm.* The common birch-tree.

Abéja, *sf.* A bee. *Abéja maéstra guia ó madre,* The queen or queen-bee. *Abéja machiega,* Breeding-bee.

Abejár, *sm.* A bee-hive. V. *Colmenar.*

Abejár, *a.* *Uva abejar,* A grape of which bees are very fond.

Abejarrón ó Abejórro, *sm.* A horse-fly.

Abejarúco ó Abejerúco, *sm.* 1. The bee-eater, a bird. Merops apiaster *L.* 2. (Met.) A mean, despicable fellow.

Abejéra, *sf.* Balm-mint, or bee-werth. Melissa officinalis *L.*

Abejéro, *sm.* 1. A keeper of bee hives. 2. V. *Abejaruco.*

Abejíca, lla, ta, ó Abejuéla, *sf.* A little bee.

Abejón, *sm.* 1. A bee which makes no honey; a drone. 2. A rustic play of buzzing in and striking the ear.

Abejoncíllo, *sm.* A small wild bee, a small drone.

Abellacádo, da, *a.* Mean spirited; accustomed to act with meanness.

Abellacárse, *vr.* To be mean; to degrade one's self.

Abellár, *sm.* V. *Colmenar.*

Abemolár, *va.* 1. (Mús.) To compose in B-flat. 2. To soften, to quiet.

Abenúz, *sm.* Eben tree, the tree which yields ebony wood.

Abeñóla ó **Abeñúla**, *sf.* (Ant.) Eye-lash.

Aberengenádo, da, *a.* Having the colour of the egg-plant or mad-apple, lilac.

Abernúncio, *interj.* Far be it from me.

Abenozéra, *sf.* The strawberry-tree. Arbutus unedo *L.*

Aberrugádo, da, *a.* Full of warts.

Abertéro, ra, *a.* V. *Abridéro.*

Abertúra, *sf.* 1. The act of opening; beginning, commencement. 2. An opening, chink. 3. Openness of mind; plain dealing. 4. A leak. 5. (Mús.) Overture.

Abetérno (ó *ab æterno*, Lat.) From all eternity.

Abéte, *sm.* 1. Hook for holding cloth. 2. V. *Abéto.*

Abéto, *sm.* The silver-tree; the yew-leaved fir. Pinus picea *L.*

Abetunádo, da, *a.* Resembling bitumen.

Abeurréa, *sf.* Mark used to designate property in land.

Abezána, *sf.* Several yokes of oxen ploughing together.

Abezár, *va.* V. *Avezar.*

Abezón, *sm.* Dill. Anetum graveolens *L.*

Abiertaménte, *ad.* Frankly, openly.

Abiérto, ta, *a.* 1. Open, free, clear. 2. Sincere, candid.

Abigarrádo, da, *a.* Variegated.

Abigarrár, *va.* To cloud or paint with a diversity of colours, without order or union.

Abigeáto, *sm.* (For.) Theft of cattle.

Abigéo, *sm.* A thief or stealer of cattle.

Abigotádo, da, *a.* A person wearing long whiskers.

Abiñádes, *sm.* 1. Narcissus or daffodil. 2. A precious stone of the colour of the daffodil.

Abinício, (ó *ab initio*, Lat.) From the beginning.

Abintestáto, *a.* (Lat.) Intestate.—*sm.* Process of a judge in cases of no will.

Abióta, *sf.* The buffalo snake. Boa constrictor [L.

Abismáles, *s.* Clasp nails.

Abismár, *va.* To depress, to humble, to destroy.

Abísmo, *sm.* 1. Abyss. 2. That which is immense, or incomprehensible. 3. Hell.

Abispón, *sm.* A hornet.

Abitadúra, *sf.* A turn of the cable around the [bits.

Abitáque, *sm.* A rafter or joist, the fourth part of a girder.

Abitár, *va.* *Abitar el cable*, To bite the cable.

Abítas, *sm. pl.* Bits. *Abitas del Molinete*, Carrick-bits.

A'bito, *sm.* Habit, dress. V. *Habito.*

Abitónes, *sm. pl.* Top-sail sheet, bits.

Abizcochádo, da, *a.* In the form of a biscuit; biscuit-like.

Abjuración, *sf.* Abjuration.

Abjurár, *va.* To abjure, to recant upon oath.

Ablandár, *va.* 1. To soften. 2. To loosen. 3. To assuage, to mitigate.—*vn.* To grow mild or temperate: applied to the weather.

Ablandatívo, va, *a.* Of a softening quality.

Abláno, *sm.* The hazel-tree.

Ablatívo, *sm.* Ablative; the sixth case of Latin nouns.

Ablución, *sf.* 1. Ablution. 2. The water with which Roman Catholic priests purify the chalice at mass.

Abnegación, *sf.* Abnegation, self-denial.

Abnegár, *va.* To renounce, to deny one's self any thing.

Abobádo, da, *a.* Stultified, simple, silly.

Abobamiénto, *sm.* Stupefaction, stupidity.

Abobár, *va.* 1. To stupify. 2. V. *Embobar.*—*vr.* To grow stupid.

Abocádo, *a.* Mild, agreeable; applied to wine.

Abocamiénto, *sm.* A meeting, an interview.

Abocár, *va.* 1. To take or catch with the mouth. 2. *Abocar la artillería*, to bring the guns to bear. 3. *Abocar un estrécho*, To enter the mouth of a channel or strait.—*vr.* To meet by agreement, in order to treat upon, or settle an affair.

Abocardádo, da, *a.* Wide-mouthed, like the wide end of a trumpet.

Abochornár, *va.* 1. To swelter, to overheat. 2 To provoke by abusive language.

Abocinádo, *a.* Bent; applied to an elliptic arch, the two faces of which are nearly the same.

Abocinár, *vn.* (Vulg.) To fall upon the face.

Abofeteadór, ra, *s.* Buffeter, one who insults.

Abofeteár, *va.* 1. To slap one's face. 2. To insult.

Abogacía, *sf.* Profession of a lawyer or advo- [cate.

Abogadeár, *vn.* To play the advocate; used in contempt.

Abogádo, *sm.* A lawyer; an advocate.

Abogádo, da, *s.* A mediator; a mediatrix, lawyer's wife.

Abogadór, *sm.* V. *Muñidor.*

Abogár, *vn.* 1. To follow the profession of a lawyer, to plead. 2. To intercede in behalf of another.

Abohetádo, da, *a.* Inflated, swollen.

Aboléngo, *sm.* 1. Ancestry. 2. Inheritance coming from ancestors.

Abolénza, *sf.* (Ant.) Baseness, meanness, low- [ness.

Abolición, *sf.* Abolition.

Abolír, *va.* To abolish, to annul, to revoke.

Abolládo, *a.* y *s.* V. *Alechugado.*

Abolladúra, *sf.* 1. Inequality, indent. 2. Embossed work, relievo.

Abollár, *va.* 1. To emboss. 2. To annoy with an unpleasant discourse. 3. To stun and confound.

Abollón, *sm.* A bud or germ, in particular of [the vine.

Abollonár, *va.* To emboss.—*vn.* To bud; applied in particular to the vine.

Abólo, la, *s.* (Ant.) V. *Abuelo.*

Abolório, *sm.* V. *Aboléngo.*

Abolsádo, da, *a.* Puckered; folded in the form of a purse.

Abomináble, *a.* Detestable, abominable.

Abominableménte, *ad.* Detestably.

Abominación, *sf.* Abomination, detestation.

Abominár, *va.* To detest, to abhor.

Abonádo, da, *a.* 1. Creditable, rich. o Fit, and disposed for any thing; commonly understood in an ill sense. *Testigo abonado*, An irrefragable witness.

Abonadór, óra, *s.* A person who is bail or surety for another.

Abonamiénto, *sm.* V. *Abóno.*

Abonanzár, *vn.* To clear up, applied to the [weather.

Abonár, *va.* 1. To bail, to insure. 2. To improve,

or meliorate. 3. To make good an assertion. 4. To manure lands. 5. To give one credit.—*vr.* To subscribe to any work, to pay in advance for any thing.—*vn.* V. *Abonanzar*.

Abonador *sm.* He who is surety for another.

Abondáncia, *sf.* V. *Abundancia*.

Abondár, *vn.* (Ant.) To be sufficient or enough.

Abóno, *sm.* 1. Security given for a person, or the performance of a contract. 2. Dung, manure. 3. A receipt in full or part.

Abordadór, *sm.* 1. He that boards, one that approaches. 2. An intruder, who accosts a person with an air of impudence.

Abordáge, *sm.* (Naút.) The act of boarding a ship.

Abordár, *va.* 1. To board a ship. 2. To run foul of a ship. 3. To put into a port.

A'bórdo, *ad.* On board.

Abórdo, *sm.* (Met.) Address, attack, shock or force in execution.

Abordonár, *vn.* To walk, supported by a staff.

Aborracháðo, **da**, *a.* 1. High coloured. 2. Inflamed, fiery.

Aborrascár, *va.* To raise tempests.

Aborrecedór, **ra**, *s.* A detester, a disliker.

Aborrecér, *va.* 1. To hate, to abhor. 2. To relinquish, to desert; in the last sense it is chiefly applied to birds, which desert their eggs or young ones. 3. To adventure or spend money.

Aborrecíble, *a.* Hateful, detestable.

Aborrecibleménte, *ad.* Hatefully, detestably.

Aborrecimiénto, *sm.* Abhorrence, detestation, dislike.

Aborrescér, **Aborrér**, *va.* (Ant.) V. *Aborrecer*.

Abórso, *sm.* (Ant.) V. *Aborto*.

Abortamiénto, *sm.* Abortion.

Abortár, *va.* To miscarry.

Abortívo, **va**, *a.* 1. Abortive. 2. Producing abortion.

Abórto, *sm.* 1. A miscarriage. 2. A monster.

Abortón, *sm.* 1. The abortion of a quadruped. 2. The skin of a lamb born before its time.

Aborujárse, *vr.* To be muffled or wrapped up.

Abotagárse, *vr.* To be swollen, to be inflated.

Abotinádo, **da**, *a.* Made in the form of half-gaiters, closing at the instep.

Abotonadór, *sm.* An iron instrument used for buttoning gaiters or spatterdashes.

Abotonár, *va.* To button, to fasten with buttons.—*vn.* 1. To bud, to germinate. 2. To form a button; applied to eggs boiled with the white obtruding.

Abovedádo, **da**, *a.* Arched, vaulted.

Abovedár, *va.* To arch, to vault, to shape as a vault.

Aboyádo, **da**, *a.* A term applied to a farm rented, with the necessary stock of oxen for ploughing the ground.

Aboyár, *va.* (Naút.) To lay down buoys.

A'bra, *sf.* 1. A bay; a cove or creek. 2. A dale or valley. 3. A fissure or crack in mountains.

Abracíjo, *sm.* An embrace, a hug.

Abrahonár, *va.* (Vulg.) To hold one fast by the garment.

Abrasadaménte, *ad.* Ardently, eagerly.

Abrasadór, **ra**, *s.* 1. One who burns or consumes. 2. One who inflames by the heat of passion.

Abrasamiénto, *sm.* 1. The act of burning. 2. The state of inflammation. 3. The excessive heat of passion.

Abrasár, *va.* 1. To burn, to reduce to ashes; to parch the ground. 2. To dissipate, to squander. 3. To provoke.—*vr.* To be agitated by any violent passion. *Abrasarse vivo*, To be inflamed with passion; to feel extremely hot. *Abrasarse las pazarillas*, To be burning hot.

Abrasiládo, **da**, *a.* Of the colour of Brazil wood.

Abrazadéra, *sf.* 1. A ring put around a thing to prevent its cracking. 2. A cleat. 3. A piece of timber which fastens the plough-tail to the plough.

Abrazadór, **ra**, *s.* 1. One that embraces. (Cant.) A thief-taker. 2. A hook which serves to keep up the pole of a draw-well. 3. (Ant.) One who seduces others into gambling-houses.

Abrazamiénto, *sm.* Embracing.

Abrazár, *va.* 1. To embrace, to hug, to caress. 2. To surround, to encircle. 3. To embrace the opinion of another. 4. To take to one's charge. 5. To comprise, to contain.

Abrázo, *sm.* A hug, an embrace.

A'brego, *sm.* A south-west wind.

Abrenúncio, *int.* (Lat.) A word used to show our detestation of something.

Abrevadéro, *sm.* A watering-place for cattle.

Abrevádo, *a.* Softened in water; applied to skins.

Abrevadór, *sm.* 1. He who waters cattle or land. 2. Watering-place.

Abrevár, *va.* To water cattle or lands.

Abreviación, *sf.* Abbreviation. V. *Compendio*.

Abreviadór, **ra**, *s.* 1. An abridger, who abridges or contracts writings. 2. A breviator; an officer employed in expediting the Pope's bulls.

Abreviár, *va.* To abridge, to contract.

Abreviatúra, *sf.* Abbreviation. *En abreviatura*, Briefly, expeditiously.

Abreviaturía, *sf.* Office of a breviator.

Abribonárse, *vr.* To act the scoundrel; to stroll about, to rove idly.

Abridéro, *sm.* A sort of peach, which, when ripe, opens easily, and drops the stone.

Abridéro, **ra**, *a.* Of an aperitive nature; easily opened.

Abridór, *sm.* 1. (Bot.) A species of the peach-tree. 2. One who opens. *Abridora*, she who opens. *Abridor de láminas*, An engraver. 3. Iron used for opening ruffs or plaits.

Abrigáda, *sm.* Sheltered place.

Abrigáño, *sm.* A shelter for cattle.

Abrigár, *va.* To shelter, to protect; to patronise. *Abríguese vm. con ello*, (Fam.) Defend or protect yourself with it.

Abrígo, *sm.* Shelter, protection; aid, support.

Abríl, *sm.* April; the fourth month of the year. *Estar hecho un abril, ó parecer un abril*, To be gay, florid, handsome.

Abrillantár, *vn.* To sparkle like diamonds, to shine.

Abrimiénto, *sm.* 1. The act of opening. 2. An opening.

Abrír, *va.* 1. To open; to unlock. 2. To remove obstacles. 3. To engrave. 4. To expand as flowers; to distend. *Abrir á chasco*, To jest, to mock. *Abrir el dia*, To dawn. *Abrir el ójo*, To be alert or watchful. *Abrir la mano*, to accept bribes or gifts; to be generous. *Abrir los ojos á uno*, To undeceive, to disabuse.—*vr.* 1. To be open, to tear, applied to clothes. 2. To extend itself. 3. (Met.) To communicate, to disclose a secret.

Abrochadór, *sm.* An instrument used by tailors to button on clothes.

Abrochadúra ó Abrochamiénto, *s.* The act of lacing or buttoning on.

Abrochár, *va.* To button on, to fasten with hooks and eyes, to clasp or button on.

Abrogación, *sf.* Abrogation; the act of repealing a law. [void.

Abrogár, *va.* To abrogate, to annul, to make

Abrójo, *sm.* 1. (Bot.) Caltrops. Tribulus terrestris *L.* 2. (Mil.) A caltrop; a crowfoot. 3. Caltrop fixed on a whip and used by the flagellants to flog the shoulders.—*pl.* Hidden rocks in the sea. [Worm-eaten.

Abromádo, da, *a.* 1. Dark, hazy, foggy. 2.

Abromárse, *vr.* To be worm-eaten.

Abroquelárse, *vr.* 1. To cover one's self with a shield or buckler. 2. To use means of defence in support of one's character or opinion.

Abrótano, *sm.* (Bot.) Southernwood. Artemisia abrotanum *L.*

Abrotonár, *vn.* (Naút.) To scud a-hull.

Abrumadór, ra, *s.* A teazer; an oppressor.

Abrumár, *va.* 1. To crush, to overwhelm. 2. To cause great pains or trouble.

Abrutádo, da, *a.* Brutish, ungovernable in manners and habits.

Absência, *sf.* (Ant.) V. *Ausencia.*

Abscéso, *sm.* An abscess.

Abscondér, *va.* (Ant.) V. *Esconder.*

Absíntio, *sm.* (Ant.) V. *Axenjo.*

Absolución, *sf.* The act of pardoning or forgiving; absolution.

Absolúta, *sf.* Dogma, universal proposition.

Absolutaménte, *ad.* Absolutely; without limits or restrictions.

Absolúto, ta, *a.* 1. Absolute, independent. 2. Unconditional; without restriction. 3. Imperious, domineering.

Absolutório, *sm.* An absolutory sentence.

Absolvedéras, *s.* The facility of giving absolu-

Absolvedór, *sm.* He that absolves. [tion.

Absolvér, *va.* 1. To absolve. 2. To acquit. 3. (Ant.) to fulfil.

Absortár, *va.* To strike with amazement, to suspend the mind with wonder and admiration.

Absórto, ta, *a.* Amazed, absorbed in thought.

Absorvéncia, *sf.* The act of absorbing.

Absorvér, *va.* 1. To absorb, to imbibe. V. *Empapar.* 2. To hurry along by the violence of

Abstémio, mia, *a.* Abstemious. [passion.

Abstenérse, *vr.* To abstain, to forbear.

Abstergénte ó Abstersívo, va, *a.* Abstergent, abstersive.

Abstergér, *va.* To cleanse; to dispel some purulent matter.

Abstersión, *sf.* Abstersion.

Abstinéncia, *sf.* Forbearance, abstinence; the act of refraining from certain enjoyments. *Dia de abstinencia*, A day of abstinence or

Abstinénte, *a.* Abstinent. [fasting.

Abstinenteménte, *ad.* Abstemiously.

Abstracción, *sf.* 1. Abstraction, the act of abstracting, and state of being abstracted. 2. Retirement from all intercourse with the world.

Abstractivaménte, *ad.* Abstractively, separately.

Abstractívo, va, *a.* Abstractive, having the power or quality of abstracting.

Abstrácto, ta, *a.* Abstracted; abstract.

Abstraér, *va.* 1. To abstract or form ideas of some general quality simply in itself, without regard to any other particular attribute. 2. To pass over in silence. 3. To refrain from. 4. To differ in opinion.—*vr.* To withdraw the intellect from material or sensible objects, in order to employ it in the contemplation of those of the mind. [rated.

Abstraído, da, *a.* Abstracted; retired, sepa-

Abstrúso, sa, *a.* Abstruse, difficult.

Absuélto, ta, *pp. irreg.* Absolved; free.

Absurdidád, Absurdo, *s.* Absurdity; an action or expression contrary to the dictates of reason. [dad.

Abtoridád y Abtoridát, *sf.* (Ant.) V. *Autori-*

Abtuál, *a.* (Ant.) V. *Actual.*

Abubílla, *sf.* (Orn.) Hoop or hoopoop. Upupa epops *L.*

Abuchornárse, *vr.* To be muffled or wrapt up.

Abuéla, lo, *s.* Grandmother, grandfather, ancestor.

Abuhádo y Abuhetádo, da, *a.* (Ant.) Pale, discoloured and swollen.

Abulénse, *a.* Native or belonging to Avila.

Abultádo, da, *a.* 1. Increased. 2. Bulky, large.

Abultár, *va.* To increase, to enlarge.—*vn.* To be bulky or large.

Abundáncia, *sf.* Abundance, plenty.

Abundánte, *a.* Abundant, plentiful.

Abundanteménte, *ad.* Abundantly, plentifully.

Abundár, *vn.* To abound, to have plenty.

Abuñuelár, *va.* To make something in the shape of a fritter.

Aburár, *va.* To burn.

Abureládo, da, *a.* Of a greyish colour.

Aburrimiénto, *sm.* Uneasiness of mind; despondency, dejection.

Aburrír, *va.* 1. To vex, to perplex. To venture, to hazard. *Aburriré mil libras esterlinas en esta flota*, I will hazard a thousand pounds in this convoy. 2. To relinquish. V. *Abortar.*

Aburujádo, da, *a.* 1. Pressed together. 2. Perplexed, entangled in difficulties.

Aburujár, *va.* To press or heap together.

Abusár, *va.* To abuse or misapply a thing, to turn it to a bad purpose. [tion.

Abusión, *sf.* 1. Abuse. 2. Divination, supersti-

Abusivaménte, *ad.* Abusively.

Abusívo, va, *a.* Abusive.

Abúso, *sm.* The abuse or ill use of a thing.

Abyacéncia, *sf.* (Ant.) Adjacency.

Abyécto, ta, *a.* (Ant.) Abject, vile.

Acá, *ad.* This way, this side. *De quándo acá?* Since when? *Acá no se estila*, That's not the custom here. *Ven acá*, Come along. *Acá y allá*, Here and there. *Acá*, Hey, used in calling.

Acabáble, *a.* What may be finished.

Acabadaménte, *ad.* (Ant.) 1. Perfectly. 2. (Iron.) Imperfectly, badly.

Acabádo, da, *a.* 1. Perfect, consummate. 2. (Iron.) Old, ill dressed, dejected. *Es acabada cosa*, Low, mean thing.

Acabadór, ra, *s.* Finisher, completer.

Acabalár, *va.* To complete, to finish.

Acaballadéro, *sm.* The time and place when horses cover mares. [mare. 2. Having a bubo.

Acaballádo, da, *a.* 1. Covered; applied to a

Acaballár, *va.* To cover a mare.
Acaballeráдо, da, *a.* Gentlemanlike.
Acaballerár, *va.* 1. To render genteel. 2. To act or behave as a gentleman.
Acabamiénto, *sm.* End, completion; death.
Acabár, *va.* 1. To finish, to conclude. *Acaba ya*, Determine, resolve. 2. To harass. 3. To obtain.—*vn.* 1. To terminate in any thing, as a sword, which ends in a point. 2. To die; to extinguish.—*vr.* To grow weak or feeble. *Es cosa de nunca acabarse*, It is an endless affair. *Acaba de llegar*, He is just arrived.
Acabdilladaménte, *ad.* (Mil.) Orderly.
Acabdilladór, *sm.* (Ant.) Commander, general. [lour.
Acabelládo, da, *a.* Of a bright chesnut colour.
Acabestrillár, *vn.* To fowl with a stalking-horse or ox, that approaches the game, and shelters the fowler. [an end of the matter.
Acabosíto, *ad.* (Joc.) That's enough; there is
Acabronádo, da, *a.* Bold, unembarrassed.
Acachárse, *vr.* To stoop down, to crouch.
Acacheteár, *va.* To tap, to pat, to strike.
Acácia, *sf.* 1. A shrub of the thorn kind. 2. The inspissated juice of acacia.
Acadêmia, *sf.* 1. Academy, university, literary society. 2. A naked figure designed from nature.
Académico, *sm.* An academician, a member of an academy.
Académico, ca, *a.* Belonging to an university or literary society, academic or academical.
Acaecedéro, ra, *a.* Incidental.
Acaecér, *vn. def.* To happen, to come to pass.
Acaecimiénto, *sm.* Event, incident.
Acál, *sm.* A canoe.
Acallár, *va.* 1. To quiet, to still, to silence. 2. To mitigate, to soften, to assuage.
Acaloñár, *va.* (Ant.) To accuse, to calumniate.
Acaloramiénto, *sm.* Ardour, heat; agitation.
Acalorár, *va.* 1. To give heat, to warm. 2. To inflame, to overheat. 3. To urge on. 4. To forward, to promote.—*vr.* To grow warm in debate.
Acalumniár, *va.* (Ant.) V. *Calumniar*.
Acamádo, da, *a.* Laid flat. *Mieses acamadas*, Corn laid by heavy rains or storms.
Acambrayádo, da, *a.* Linens or muslins which have the appearance of cambrick.
Acamelládo, da, *a.* Camel-like; any thing which bears a resemblance to the camel.
Acampaménto, *sm.* (Mil.) Encampment, camp.
Acampár, *va.* To encamp.
Acámpo, *sm.* Portion of common given to graziers or herds for pasture.
Acamuzádo, da, *a.* Shamois-coloured. V. *Agamuzado*.
Acána, *sf.* A hard reddish wood, which grows in the island of Cuba.
Acanaládo, da, *a.* 1. What passes through a narrow passage or channel. 2. Striated, fluted.
Acanaládos, *sm. pl.* The ridge of a horse's back.
Acanaladór, *sm.* An instrument used to cut grooves in timber.
Acanalár, *va.* 1. To make a canal or channel. 2. To flute, to groove.
Acandiládo, da, *a. Sombrero acandilado*, A hat cocked with sharp points, such as is worn in several poor-houses in Spain.

Acaneládo, da, *a.* Of a cinnamon-colour.
Acanelár, *va.* V. *Acanalar*.
Acangrenárse, *vr.* To become gangrenou to mortify.
Acanilládo, da, *a.* Applied to any sort cloth, which forms furrows from the uneve ness of its threads.
Acantaleár, *va.* (Vulg.) To hail large ha stones. [four gallon vesse
Acantarár, *va.* To measure by *cantaras*,
Acantiládo, da, *a. Costa acantilada*, A cle coast, free from rocks and shoals.
Acánto, *sm.* (Bot.) 1. Prickly thistle; bra ursin. 2. (Arq.) Acanthus leaf.
Acantonamiénto, *sm.* Cantonment.
Acantonár, *va.* To send troops into canto ments. [with sharp-pointed cane
Acañavereár, *va.* To prick and wound the fles
Acañoneár, *va.* To cannonade.
Acaparrárse, *vr.* To take refuge under an other's cloak.
Acaparrosádo, da, *a.* Of a copperas colour of a colour between blue and green. [hai
Acapizárse, *vr.* (Vulg.) To seize or pull th
Acaponádo, da, *a.* Capon-like; that which re sembles a capon or eunuch.
Acarár, *va.* To compare, to confront.
Acardenalár, *va.* To pinch, to make livid, t beat black and blue.—*vr.* To be covered wit livid spots.
Acareamiénto, *sm.* Comparing, confronting.
Acareár, *va.* (Ant.) V. *Carear*. [and caresses
Acariciadór, ra, *s.* A fondler; one who fondles
Acariciár, *va.* To fondle, to caress, to cherish.
Acarón, *ad.* (Gal.) Together, near. V. *Junto*.
Acarrárse, *vr.* To shelter one's self from the heat of the sun; applied to sheep.
Acarreadór, ra, *s.* A carrier.
Acarreadúra y Acarreamiénto, *s.* Carriage, the act of carrying.
Acarreár, *va.* 1. To carry or convey something in a cart, or other carriage. 2. (Met.) To occasion, to cause.
Acarréo, *sm.* Carriage, the act of carrying. *Cosas de acarreo*, Goods or effects conveyed by land-carriage for another person's account.
Acarréto, *sm. Hilo de acarreto*, Pack-thread. V. *Acarréo*.
Acáso, *sm.* Chance, casualty, unforeseen event.
Acáso, *ad.* By chance, by accident. *Acáso?* How? How now? [ship.
Acastilláge, *sm.* (Naút.) The upper works of a
Acastoráдо, da, *a.* Beavered; applied to what resembles the texture of beaver.
Acatáble, *a.* (Ant.) Venerable.
Acatamiénto, *sm.* 1. Esteem, veneration, respect. 2. Acknowledgment. 3. Presence, view.
Acatár, *va.* 1. To respect, to revere. 2. To acknowledge. 3. To inspect.
Acatarrárse, *vr.* To catch cold.
Acatárse, *vr.* (Ant.) To be afraid, to dread.
A'cates, *sm.* V. *A'gata*.
Acaudaládo, da, *a.* Rich, wealthy, opulent.
Acaudalár, *va.* 1. To hoard up riches. 2. To acquire a name or reputation. [troops.
Acaudilladór, *sm.* Chief, or commander of
Acaudillár, *va.* To head or command troops.
Accedénte, *p.* Acceding; he who accedes, in state treaties.

Accedér, vn. To accede or become accessory to a treaty or agreement concluded by others.

Accénso, sa, pp. ir. (Ant.) Kindled, inflamed.

Accesíble, a. 1. Accessible. 2. Attainable. 3. Of easy access.

Accesión, sf. 1. Accession; the act of acceding. 2. Access or paroxysm of a fever.

Accéso, sm. 1. Access. 2. Carnal communication. 3. A mode of acquiring property, accession.

Accesórias, sf. pl. Out-buildings, such as coach-houses, stables, &c.

Accesoriaménte, ad. Accessorily.

Accesório, ria, a. Accessory, additional. *Obras accesorias*, (Fort.) The outworks of a fortress.

Accidentádo, da, a. Affected with fits, or who labours habitually under them.

Accidentál, a. Accidental, casual, contingent.

Accidentalménte y Accidentariaménte, ad. Accidentally, casually.

Accidentárse, vr. To be seized with a fit, or suddenly affected with a disease.

Accidentázo, sm. (Aum.) A severe fit of illness.

Accidénte, sm. 1. An accidental, not essential, quality of a thing. 2. An unforeseen event. 3. A sudden fit of illness.

Acción, sf. 1. Action, operation. *Accion de gracias*, Act of thanking, thanksgiving. 2. Faculty of doing something. 3. Lawsuit. 4. Gesticulation. 5. Engagement. 6. Subject of an epic or dramatic poem. 7. (Pint.) Position, posture. 8. (Comer.) Stock, capital in a company or undertaking; fund, share.

Accionár, vn. To accompany a discourse with various motions of the body; to gesticulate.

Accionísta, sm. A stock-holder, a share-holder in a company's stock.

Acebadamiénto, sm. A disease contracted by beasts in drinking water after being surfeited with barley.

Acebadár, va. V. *Encebadar*.

Acebédo, sm. A plantation of holly-trees.

Acébo, sm. (Bot.) Holly-tree. Ilex aquifolium *L.*

Acebuchál, sm. A plantation of wild olive-trees.

Acebuchál, a. Belonging to wild olives.

Acebúche, sm. (Bot.) The wild olive-tree. Olea sylvestris *L.*

Acebuchéno, na, a. Belonging to the wild olive.

Acebuchína, sf. Fruit of the wild olive-tree.

Acechadór, ra, s. 1. A thief lying in ambush. 2. An intruder who pries into other people's affairs.

Acechár, va. 1. To way-lay, to lie in ambush. 2. To pry into other people's affairs.

Acéche, sm. A black earth, of which ink is made.

Acécho, sm. The act of way-laying, or laying in ambush.

Al acécho ó en acécho, ad. In wait, in ambush.

Acechón, na, s. (Joc.) V. *Acechadór*. *Hacér la acechona*, To scrutinize, to inquire with care, to be inquisitive.

Acecinár, va. To salt meat, and dry it in the air or smoke.—vr. To grow old, dry, and withered.

Acedaménte, ad. Sourly, bitterly.

Acedár, va. 1. To sour, to make sour. 2. To displease, to disquiet.

Acedéra, sf. (Bot.) Sorrel. Rumex acetosa *L.* *Acedera de Indias*, (Bot.) Indian sorrel.

Acederílla, sf. (Bot.) Wood-sorrel. Rumex acetosilla *L.*

Acedía, sf. 1. Acidity. 2. Squeamishness. 3. Asperity of address. 4. (Ictiol.) A flounder. Pleuronectes flesus *Block*.

Acédo, da, a. 1. Acid, sour. 2. Harsh, unpleasant.

Acedúra, sf. V. *Acedia*.

Acéfalo, la, a. Headless; applied to a sect or society which wants a head.

Aceleración, sf. 1. Acceleration. 2. (Astr.) In regard to the fixed stars, the difference between the *primum mobile* and the solar revolution.

Aceleradaménte, ad. Speedily, swiftly.

Aceleramiénto, sm. V. *Aceleración*.

Acelerár, va. To accelerate, to perform any thing with expedition.

Acélga, sf. (Bot.) Beet. Beta vulgaris *L.* *Cara de acelga amarga*, A nick-name given to a pale-faced person.

Acémila, sf. 1. A mule, a beast of burthen. 2. (Ar.) Tax paid for mules.

Acemilár, a. Belonging to mules and muleteers.

Acemilería, sf. 1. The stable or place where mules are kept. 2. Royal stable for mules.

Acemiléro, sm. A muleteer, who conducts and takes care of mules.

Acemiléro, ra, a. Belonging to mules, in particular to the king's mules.

Acemíta, sf. Bread made of fine bran.

Acemíte, sm. 1. Pollen, fine bran. 2. (Ant.) Superfine flour. 3. Grits. 4. (And.) Potage made of parched half ground wheat.

Acendér ó Accendér, va. 1. To kindle, to set on fire. 2. To inflame, to incite. 3. To foment disturbances, to sow discord.

Acendrádo, da, a. 1. Purified. 2. Refined, immaculate.

Acendrár, va. 1. To purify or refine metals. 2. To free from stain or blemish.

Acensuadór, sm. (Ant.) V. *Censualista*.

Acensuár, va. To farm or lease out for a certain rent.

Acénto, sm. 1. Accent, a modulation of the voice. 2. Accent, a character placed over a syllable, to mark the modulation of the voice. 3. (Poét.) Voice, word, verse.

Acentuación, sf. Accentuation.

Acentuár, va. To accentuate, to pronounce the words with the proper accent.

Acéña, sf. A water-mill.

Aceñéro, sm. The tenant or keeper of a water-mill.

Acepár, vn. To take root.

Acepción, sf. Acceptation or meaning in which a word is taken. *Acepción de persónas*, A partiality shown to one person in preference to another, without regard to merit.

Acepilladúra, sf. 1. The act of planing or smoothing with a plane. 2. The shavings of timber cut off with a plane.

Acepillár, va. 1. To plane. 2. To clean clothes with a brush. 3. To polish the manners.

Aceptáble, a. Acceptable, worthy of acceptance.

Aceptableménte, ad. Acceptably.

Aceptación, sf. 1. Acceptation. 2. Approbation. 3. Acceptance of a bill of exchange. *Aceptación de herencia*, Acceptance of an inheritance. *Aceptación de persónas*, V. *Acepcion*.

Aceptadór, ra, s. Accepter.

Aceptánte, pa. He who accepts.

Aceptár, va. To accept, to admit what is given

or offered. *Aceptár persónas*, To favour some persons in preference to others. *Aceptar una letra*, To accept a bill.—*vr.* To be pleased or gratified.

Acépto, ta, *a.* Acceptable, agreeable.

Acéquia, *sf.* A canal, channel, trench or drain, for watering lands or other purposes.

Acequiádo, da, *a.* Intersected by canals or channels.

Acequiadór, *sm.* Canal-maker.

Acequiár, *va.* To make canals or drains.

Acequiéro, *sm.* A person appointed to make and preserve canals or channels, a dyke-reeve.

A'cer, *sm.* (Bot.) Maple-tree.

Acéra, *sf.* 1. A foot-path on the side of a street or road. 2. The front stones which form the face of a wall.

Acerádo, da, *a.* 1. Steeled, made of steel. 2. Strong.

Acerár, *va.* 1. To steel, to point or edge with steel. 2. To impregnate liquors with steel. 3. To strengthen.

Acerbaménte, *ad.* Harshly, rudely.

Acerbidád, *sf.* 1. Acerbity, asperity. 2. Rigour, cruelty.

Acérbo, ba, *a.* 1. Acerb; rough to the taste, such as unripe fruit. 2. Severe, cruel.

Acérca, *prep.* About, relating to. *Acerca de lo que hemos hablado*, In regard to what we have said.

Acercamiénto, *sm.* (Ant.) Approaching, approximating.

Acercáno, na, *a.* V. *Cercano.*

A' Cercén, *ad.* V. *Cercen.*

Acercár, *va.* To approach, to place a person or thing close to another.

Aceríco y Aceríllo, *sm.* 1. A pin-cushion. 2. A small pillow put on the bolster of a bed.

Aceríno, na, *a.* Made of steel, or belonging to steel.

Acernadár, *va.* To cover with ashes.

Acéro, *sm.* 1. Steel. *Acero colado*, Cast steel. 2. Edged or pointed small arms, especially all kinds of swords.—*pl. Espada de buenos aceros*, A sword of well tempered steel. *Comer con buenos aceros*, To eat with a keen appetite. *Acéros*, (Met.) Spirit, courage.

Aceróla, *sf.* The fruit of the parsley-leaved hawthorn or azarole.

Aceról o, *sm.* (Bot.) The parsley-leaved hawthorn. Cratægus azarolus *L.*

Acerrár, *va.* (Cant.) To seize, to grasp.

Acerrimaménte, *ad.* Strenuously.

Acérrimo, ma, *a. sup.* Most strenuous, very vigorous and strong.

Acertadaménte, *ad.* Opportunely, fitly, seasonably.

Acertádo, da, *a.* Fit, proper. *Su conducta fue acertada*, He conducted himself with propriety.

Acertadór, ra, *s.* One who hits right upon any thing.

Acertájo, *sm.* V. *Acertijo.*

Acertár, *va.* 1. To hit upon the right point, to hit the mark. 2. To hit by chance; to meet or find. 3. To conjecture right. 4. To cut round or make the cloth even.—*vn.* 1. To turn out true. 2. To happen unexpectedly. 3. To take root, as plants.

Acertíjo, *sm.* A riddle, a puzzling question.

Acervuélo, *sm.* A sort of small pack-saddle used for riding.

Acervár, *va.* (Ant.) To heap, to accumulate.

Acérvo, *sm.* 1. A heap, a pile. 2. The totality of tithes, or of an inheritance.

Acetábulo, *sm.* 1. Acetabulum, cruet; a Roman apothecary's measure. 2. (Anat.) The articulation of the ischium.

Acetár, *va.* V. *Aceptár.*

Acetósa, *sf.* (Bot.) V. *Acedera.*

Acetosílla, *sf.* (Bot.) Gilliflower. Oxalis acetosella *L.*

Acétre, *sm.* A small bucket, with which water is taken out of jars or wells. 2. The holy-water-pot used in Roman catholic churches.

Acetúna, *sf.* (Ant.) V. *Aceytuna.*

Acevilár, *va.* (Ant.) To debase, to vilify.

Aceytáda, *sf.* (Vulg.) Oil spilled.

Aceytár, *va.* To oil, to rub with oil.

Acéyte, *sm.* 1. Oil; any unctuous liquor drawn from olives, almonds, nuts, fish, &c. 2. Resin which distils from the fir-tree. *Aceyte de palo*, Balsam copaiba. *Aceyte abetinote*, Oil or juice of spruce fir.

Aceytéra, *sf.* 1. An oil-jar, oil-cruet, oil-horn. *Aceyteras*, phials for oil and vinegar.

Aceyterázo, *sm.* A blow given with an oil-jar or oil-flask.

Aceytéro, ra, *s.* 1. An oil-man, oil-seller. 2. A horn, or any vessel for holding oil.

Aceytóso, sa, *a.* Oily, containing oil.

Aceytúna, *sf.* Olive, the fruit of the olive-tree. *Acetunas zapatéras*, Olives which stand a long time in pickle.

Aceytunáda, *sf.* The season for gathering olives.

Aceytunádo, da, *a.* Of an olive colour.

Aceytunéro, *sm.* A person who gathers, carries, or sells olives.

Aceytúno, *sm.* (Bot.) Olive-tree. Olea Europæa *L.*

A'cha, *sf.* V. *Hácha.*

Achacadízo, za, *a.* (Ant.) Feigned, fraudulent.

Achacár, *va.* 1. To impute. 2. To frame an excuse.—*vr.* To ascribe a thing or action to one's self.

Achacosaménte, *ad.* Sickly.

Achacóso, sa, *a.* Sickly, unhealthy; hectic.

Achaflanár, *va.* To lower one end of a table, plank, or board; to form a declivity.

Achaparrádo, da, *a.* Of the size of a shrub. *Hombre achaparrado*, A short and lusty man.

Acháque, *sm.* 1. Habitual indisposition. 2. Monthly courses. 3. Excuse, pretext; secret accusation. 4. Vice or common weakness; a failing. 5. Composition with a smuggler. 6. Subject, matter. 7. (For.) Mulct, penalty.

Achaquéro, *sm.* He who farms the fines laid on masters of sheep-walks by the board of *Mesta.*

Achaquiénto, ta, *a.* V. *Achacóso.*

Achaquíllo y íto, *sm.* (dim.) A slight complaint.

Achár, *va.* V. *Hallár.*

Acharolár, *va.* To paint in imitation of varnish.

Achicádo, da, *a.* Diminished, lessened. V. *Aniñado.*

Achicadór, ra, *s.* 1. Diminisher, reducer. 2. Skeet for baling boats.

Achicadúra, *sf.* Diminution, reduction.

Achicár, *va.* 1. To diminish. 2. To bale a boat, or drain a mine. *Achicar un cabo*, To shorten a rope.

Achicharrár, *va.* To fry meat too much; to overheat.

Achichínque, *sm.* A miner, whose business is to drain the mines of water.

Achicória, *sf.* (Bot.) Succory, wild endive. Cichorium intybus sive sylvestre *L.* [rit.

Achinár, *va.* To intimidate, to terrify, to dispi-

Achineládo, da, *a. Zapato achinelado*, A shoe made like a slipper.

Achióte y Achóte, *sm.* (Bot.) The heart-leaved bixa, or anotta. Bixa orellana *L.*

Achocár, *va.* 1. To throw one against the wall. 2. To break or knock asunder. 3. To hoard money. [sages.

Achorizádo, da, *a.* Slashed; made into sau-

Achuchár y Achucharrár, *va.* To crush with a blow, or with the weight of a thing.

Achuládo, da, *a.* Waggish, frolicsome.

A'cia, *ad.* V. *Hácia.*

Aciágo, ga, *a.* Unfortunate, melancholy.

Aciál y Aciár, *sm.* Barnacle; an instrument which farriers put upon the nose of a horse, to make him stand quiet.

Aciáno, *sm.* V. *Estrellamar.*

Acíbar, *sm.* 1. The juice pressed from the aloes. 2. Aloes tree. 3. (Met.) Harshness, bitterness, displeasure.

Acibarár, *va.* 1. To put the juice of aloes into any thing; to make bitter. 2. (Met.) To imbitter, to cause displeasure. [against another.

Acibarrár, *va.* (Ant.) To dash one thing

Acicaladór, ra, *s.* 1. A polisher, burnisher. 2. A tool used for burnishing.

Acicaladúra, *sf.* Acicalamiénto, *sm.* The act and effect of burnishing.

Acicalár, *va.* To polish, to burnish;—*vr.* (Met.) To dress in style, to set one's self off to advantage.

Acicáte, *sm.* A long-necked Moorish spur, with a rowel at the end of it.

Acíche, *sm.* A two-edged tool, used by tilers for cutting and adjusting tiles.

A'cido, *sm.* (Quim.) Acid. *Acido muriatico*, Muriatic acid, spirits of salt.

A'cido, da, *a.* Acid, sour.

Aciérto, *sm.* 1. The act and effect of hitting; a good hit. *Con acierto*, with effect. 2. Prudence, dexterity. 3. Chance, casualty.

Aciguatádo, da, *a.* Jaundiced; pale as persons affected with the jaundice. [dice.

Aciguatárse, *vr.* To be seized with the jaun-

Acijádo, da, *a.* Of the colour of the blackish earth called *acije* or *acécha.*

Acíje, *sm.* V. *Acécha.*

Acijéso, sa, *a.* Brownish; participating in the nature of the blackish earth called *acécha.*

Acimbóga, *sf.* The citron-tree. Citrus medica *L.*

Acimentárse, *vr.* To establish or fix one's self in any place.

Ación, *sf.* Stirrup-leather.

Acionéro, *sm.* A maker of stirrup-leathers.

Acipádo, da, *a.* Well milled; a term applied to broad cloth and other woollens.

Aciprés, *sm.* (Ant.) V. *Cipres.*

Aciráte, *sm.* A landmark which shows the limits and boundaries of fields.

Acitára, *sm.* A thin wall, a partition-wall.

Acitrón, *sm.* A citron dried and made into sweet meat; a preserved citron. [debase.

Acivilár, *va.* (Ant.) To vilify, to humble, to

Aclamación, *sf.* Acclamation, the act of shouting with joy. *Elegir por aclamacion*, To elect by acclamation.

Aclamadór, ra, *s.* Acclaimer, praiser.

Aclamár, *va.* 1. To shout with joy, to applaud. 2. To cry up. 3. To call in the hawk.—*vr.* To complain, to be aggrieved.

Aclaración, *sf.* Illustration, explanation.

Aclarár, *va.* 1. To clear from obscurity, to make bright. 2. To illustrate, to explain. 3. To widen; to thin.—*vn.* To clear up, to recover brightness. [table, &c.

Aclocádo, da, *a.* Stretched, seated at a fire,

Aclocárse, *vr.* 1. To brood, to hatch eggs. 2. To stretch one's self at full length on the ground, bench, &c.

Acobardár, *va.* To intimidate, to terrify.

Acobdár, *va.* V. *Acodár.*

Acoceadór, ra, *s.* A horse or mare that kicks.

Acoceamiénto, *sm.* The act and effect of kick-

Acoceár, *va.* To kick, to wince or winch. [ing.

Acochárse, *vr.* To squat, to stoop down.

Acochinár, *va.* 1. To murder, to assassinate. 2. (Met.) To prevent or obstruct the regular course of a suit at law; to hush up.

Acocotár, *va.* To kill by a blow upon the poll.

Acodadúra, *sf.* Flexure of the arm; the act of bending the elbow.

Acodalár, *va.* (Arq.) To put lintels or transoms in a wall to support a window or niche.

Acodár, *va.* 1. To lean the elbow upon. 2. To lay layers of vines, or other plants in the ground, that they may take root. 3. To square timber.

Acoderárse, *vr.* To put a spring on a cable.

Acodiciár, *va.* To stimulate, to urge on.—*vr.* To be provoked to anger, to be inflamed with passion.

Acodillár, *va.* 1. To double or bend any thing to an elbow or angle. 2. To sink down under a burthen. *Acodillár con la carga*, (Met.) Not to be able to fulfil one's engagements.

Acódo, *sm.* A shoot, or knot of a layer.

Acogér, *va.* 1. To admit one into our house or company; to receive. 2. (Met.) To protect, to give an asylum.—*vr* 1. To take refuge, to resort to. 2. To embrace the opinion of another. 3. To make use of a pretext for dissimulation.

Acogída, *sf.* 1. Reception, the act and effect of receiving. 2. The concurrence of a multitude of things in the same place.

Acogído, *sm.* 1. Collection of breeding mares given to the owner of the principal steed, to keep them at a certain price. 2. Temporary admission of flocks into pasture-ground.

Acogimiénto, *sm.* V. *Acogída.*

Acogollár, *va.* To cover delicate plants with straw, or any thing affording shelter. [plants.

Acogolladúra, *sf.* Moulding or earthing up

Acogombrár, *va.* To dig up the ground about plants; to cover them with earth. [poll.

Acogotádo, da, *a.* Killed by a blow on the

Acogotár, *va.* To kill by a blow on the poll.

Acolalán, *sm.* An insect in Madagascar like a bug.

Acolár, *va.* To arrange or unite two coats of arms under the same crown, shield, &c.

Acolchár, *va.* To quilt; to put silk or cotton between two pieces of cloth, and stitch them together. [a mass priest. 2. An assistant,

Acolíto, *sm.* 1. Acolyte, acolothist, assistant to

Acolladéras, *sm. pl.* (Naút.) Laniards. *Acolladéras de los obenques*, The laniards of the shrouds.
Acolladádo, da, *a.* *Pázaros acollarados*, Birds having about their necks a ring of feathers of a different colour.
Acollarár, *va.* 1. To yoke or harness horses, oxen, &c. 2. To couple hounds.
Acombár, *va.* To bend, to crook.
Acomendadór, *sm.* (Ant.) Protector, aider.
Acomendár, (Ant.) V. *Encomendar.*
Acometedór, ra, *s.* An assistant, an aggressor.
Acometér, *va.* 1. To attack, to assault. 2. To undertake, to attempt. 3. To tempt, to bribe.
Acometída y Acometimiento, *s.* An attack, an assault. *Acometimiénto de calentura*, A fit, or access of the fever.
Acomodáble, *a.* Accommodable.
Acomodación, *sm.* Accommodation.
Acomodadaménte, *ad.* Commodiously, suitably.
Acomodádo, da, *a.* 1. Convenient, fit. 2. Rich, wealthy. 3. Fond of accommodation. 4. Moderate. *A' précio acomodado*, At a moderate price.
Acomodadór, ra, *s.* The person that accommodates; boxkeeper in the theatre.
Acomodamiénto, *sm.* Accommodation; the act and effect of accommodating.
Acomodár, *va.* 1. To accommodate, to arrange things. 2. To put in a convenient place. 3. To reconcile. 4. To provide, to furnish.—*vn.* To fit, to suit, to be convenient.—*vr.* To conform one's self to the opinion, temper, or capacity of another.
Acomodatício, cia, *a.* Figurative, metaphorical. *Sentido acomodaticio*, The figurative sense.
Acomódo, *sm.* 1. Accommodation, employ. 2. Fate, destiny.
Acompañádo, da, *a.* 1. Accompanied, attended. 2. An assistant judge, surgeon, physician, &c.
Acompañadór, ra, *s.* An attendant; companion.
Acompañamiénto, *sm.* 1. Attendance, assistance. 2. Retinue. 3. (Mús.) Accompaniment.
Acompañánte, *a.* Accompanying.
Acompañár, *va.* 1. To accompany, to attend. 2. To join or unite. 3. (Mús.) To sing or play in concert with others.—*vr.* To hold a consultation, to consult with others.
Acompasádo, da, *a.* Measured by the compass.
Acomplexionádo, da, *a.* Of a good or bad complexion or constitution.
Acomulár, *va.* V. *Acumulár.*
Acomunalár, *vn.* To communicate, to treat with.
Aconchabárse, *vr.* (Ant.) V. *Acomodarse.*
Aconchadíllo, *sm.* (Ant.) Kind of ragout or stewed meat.
Aconchár, *va.* To fit out; a term applied in particular to galleys.
Acondicionádo, da, *a.* Of a good or bad condition. *Hombre bien ó mal acondicionado*, A man of a good or bad disposition. *Géneros bien ó mal acondicionados*, Goods in a good or bad condition.
Acondicionár, *va.* To dispose, to affect, to constitute.—*vr.* To acquire a certain quality or condition.
Acongojár, *va.* To vex, to oppress, to afflict.
Aconíto, *sm.* (Bot.) Aconite, wolf's-bane.
Aconsejáble, *a.* Capable or susceptible of advice
Aconsejadór, ra, *s.* An adviser, counsellor.
Aconsejár, *va.* To advise, to counsel.—*vr.* To take advice, to be advised.
Acomsonantár, *va.* To make use of consonants where they should not be used.
Acontár, *va.* 1. To count, to enumerate, to calculate. 2. To prop, or support with props. 3. (Naút.) To shore.
Acontecedéro, ra, *a.* That which may happen.
Acontecér, *v. impers.* To happen, to fall out, to come to pass. *Hacer y acontécer*, common phrase, signifying the promises of any good or benefit; also a threat, a menace.
Acontecimiénto, *sm.* Event, incident, casualty.
Acopádo, da, *a.* Having the form of a cup or vase.
Acopár, *vn.* To form a round head in the shape of a cup; applied to trees and plants.
Acopetádo, da, *a.* Formed in the shape of a toupee.
Acopiamiénto, *sm.* The act and effect of gathering.
Acopiár, *va.* To gather, to store up.
Acópio, *sm.* Act and effect of gathering, storing.
Acopládo, da, *a.* Fitted, adjusted.
Acoplár, *va.* 1. To adjust, or fit pieces of timber-work. 2. To settle or adjust differences. 3. To yoke beasts to a cart or plough.—*vr.* To make up matters, to be agreed.
Acoquinár, *va.* To intimidate, to terrify, to dispirit.
Acorár, *va.* To afflict, to depress with grief. V. *Sofocar.*
Acorchárse, *vr.* 1. To dry up and shrivel from the loss of sap. 2. To become torpid.
Acordableménte, *ad.* V. *Acordadamente.*
Acordación, *sf.* Remembrance; the act of calling to recollection.
Acordáda, *sf.* V. *Carta acordada.*
Acordadaménte, *ad.* By common consent, jointly, with mature deliberation.
Acordádo, da, *a.* 1. Agreed. 2. Done with mature deliberation. *Lo acordado*, decree of a tribunal, enforcing the observance of prior proceedings.
Acordánza, *sf.* (Ant.) V. *Memoria.*
Acordár, *va.* 1. To determine or resolve by common consent. 2. To remind. 3. To tune musical instruments, to dispose figures in a picture. 4. To deliberate.—*vn.* 1. To agree, to be agreed. 2. To remember, to recollect.—*vr.* 1. To come to an agreement. 2. To weigh, to consider maturely. 3. To threaten. *Tu te acordarás de mi*, You shall remember me.
Acórde, *a.* 1. Conformable, correspondent. 2. Coinciding in opinion. 3. Accord, harmony either of sounds or colours.
Acordelár, *va.* To measure with a cord; to draw a right line by a wall or street, in order to make it straight.
Acordeménte, *ad.* By common consent.
Acordonádo, da, *a.* 1. Surrounded. 2. Made in the form of a cord or rope.
Acorneadór, ra, *s.* A horned beast, fighting with its horns.
Acorneár, *va.* To fight or strike with the horns.
Acóro, *sm.* (Bot.) Sweet-smelling flag, sweet cane, sweet grass. Acorus calamus *L.*
Acorralár, *va.* 1. To shut up cattle or sheep in pens. 2. To intimidate. 3. To silence.
Acorrucárse, *vr.* V. *Acurrucarse.*
Acortadízos, *sm. pl.* Shreds cut off, clippings, parings.
Acortamiénto, *sm.* (Astr.) Difference in the dis-

tance from the centre of the globe to the ecliptic and centre of a planet in its orbit.

ACORTÁR, *va.* 1. To shorten, to abridge. 2. To obstruct. *Acortar la vela*, (Naút.) To shorten sail.—*vr.* 1. To shrivel, to be contracted. 2. To be bashful; to fall back.

ACORULLÁR, *va.* (Naút.) To bridle the oars.

ACORVÁR, *va.* To double, to bend.

ACORZÁR, *va.* 1. To dress a child in short clothes. 2. V. *Acortar.*

ACOSADÓR, RA, *s.* A pursuer, persecutor.

ACOSAMIÉNTO, *sm.* Persecution, molestation.

ACOSÁR *va.* 1. To pursue close, to follow eagerly. 2. To vex, to molest.

ACOSTÁDO, DA, *a.* 1. Stretched, laid down. 2. Having a certain pay or salary.

ACOSTAMIÉNTO, *sm.* 1. The act of stretching or lying down. 2. A certain pay, a fixed salary.

ACOSTÁR, *va.* To lay down; to put one in bed. *va.* y *vr.* 1. To incline to one side, to lie down. 2. To be disposed, to adhere. 3. To approach. 4. (Naút.) To stand in shore. 5. (Naút.) To lie along; to have a list. *Acostarse con*, To sleep with.

ACÓSTICA, *sf.* Acoustics; the doctrine or theory of hearing and sounds.

ACOSTUMBRADAMÉNTE, *ad.* Customarily, according to custom.

ACOSTUMBRÁR, *va.* To accustom, to use, to inure.—*vn.* To be accustomed.

ACOTACIÓN, *sf.* 1. Limit; the act of setting bounds. 2. (Met.) Annotation, quotation.

ACOTÁDA, *sf.* Citation, quotation.

ACOTAMIÉNTO, *sm.* Limitation; quotation; annotation.

ACOTÁR, *va.* 1. To limit, to set bounds. *Acótome á Dios*, Let God fix my end, leave me to God; used at sports to express confidence in the actual safety of the place. 2. To lop off the branches of a tree. 3. To quote, to make annotations. 4. To accept for a certain price. 5. To witness, to attest. *Acoto ésterbas*, including all obstacles; used at juvenile games.—*vr.* (Ant.) To shelter one's self, to obtain safety.

ACOTÍLLO, *sm.* A large hammer used by smiths.

ACÓYGA, *pres. sub. irr.* (Ant.) of *Acoger.*

ACOYTÁR, *va.* (Ant.) V. *Cuydar* and *Procurar.*

ACOYUNDÁR, *va.* To yoke oxen to a draught.

A'CRE, *a.* 1. Acrid or sour to the taste. 2. (Met.) Rough, rude.

ACRECENTADÓR, RA, *s.* One that increases.

ACRECÉNCIA Y ACRECENTAMIÉNTO, *s.* Increase, augmentation, accretion.

ACRECENTÁR Y ACRECÉR, *va.* To increase, to augment.—*Derecho de acrecer*, The right of accretion in cathedral chapters, where a distribution is made according to the present residence of the prebendaries.

ACRECIMIÉNTO, *sm.* Increase. V. *Aumento.*

ACREDITÁDO, DA, *a.* Accredited, distinguished.

ACREDITÁR, *va.* 1. To assure, to affirm a thing for certain. 2. To give credit, to procure credit. 3. To prove.—*vr.* To acquire credit.

ACREEDÓR, RA, *s.* 1. A creditor. 2. (Met.) A meritorious person.

ACREÉR, *vn.* (Ant.) To lend upon pawn.

A'CREMÉNTE, *ad.* Sourly, with acrimony.

ACRESCÉR, (Ant.) V. *Acrecer.*

ACRIANZÁDO, DA, *a.* (Ant.) Educated, instructed.

ACRIBADÚRA, *sf.* Sifting.—*pl.* Siftings; the remains of grain which has been sifted.

ACRIBÁR, *va.* 1. To sift. 2. (Met.) To pierce like a sieve.

ACRIBILLÁR, *va.* 1. To pierce like a sieve. 2. (Met.) To molest, to torment. *Los acreedores me acribillan*, My creditors torment me.

ACRIMINACIÓN, *sf.* Crimination; the act of accusing or impeaching.

ACRIMINADÓR, RA, *s.* An informer, accuser, impeacher.

ACRIMINÁR, *va.* 1. To exaggerate a crime or fault. 2. (Ant.) To accuse, to impeach. 3. (For.) To aggravate.

ACRIMÓNIA, *sf.* 1. Sourness, acidity. 2. (Met.) Asperity of expression, acrimony. 3. (Met.) Vehemence in talking.

ACRISOLÁR, *va.* 1. To refine, to purify gold or other metals in a crucible. 2. (Met.) To clear up a thing by means of witnesses and proofs.

ACRISTIANÁR, *va.* To christen, to baptize.

ACRITÚD, *sf.* V. *Acrimónia.*

ACROMIÓN, *sf.* Acromion, the upper process of the spine of the scapula or shoulder-blade.

ACRONÍCTO, TA, *a.* Acronical; applied to the rising of a star when the sun sets, or its setting when the sun rises.

ACRÓSTICO, CA, *a.* *Versos acrosticos*, Verses, the initial, middle, or final letters of which, according to their order, placed separately, form names, mottos, &c.

ACRÓTERA Y ACROTERIA, *sf.* 1. A small pedestal placed at the extremities of pediments, and serving also to support figures, &c. 2. The highest part of columns or buildings.

ACROTÉRIO, *sm.* The superior of the three parts of which the frontispiece of a building is composed.

A'CROY, *sm.* A gentleman of the king's household.

A'CTA, *sf.* Act.—*pl.* 1. The acts or records of communities, chapters, councils. 2. *Actas de los santos*, The lives of the saints.

ACTÍMO, *sm.* The twelfth part of a measure called *punto*; there are 1728 *actimos* in a geometric foot.

ACTITADÉRO, RA, *a.* (For.) Actionable, fit for a process.

ACTITÁR, *va.* 1. To enact. 2. To make judicial acts; to sue.

ACTITÚD, *sf.* (Pint.) Attitude, motion, posture.

ACTIVAMÉNTE, *ad.* Actively, in an active manner.

ACTIVIDÁD, *sf.* 1. Activity, the power or faculty of acting. 2. Quickness in performing.

ACTÍVO, VA, *a.* Active, diligent. *Voz activa*, Suffrage, the right of electing.

A'CTO, *sm.* 1. Act or action. 2. Act or part of a play. 3. Thesis defended in universities. 4. Carnal communication. *En acto*, In the act. *Actos*, (Ant.) V. *Autos.*

ACTÓR, *sm.* 1. Performer, player. 2. (Ant.) Author. 3. Plaintiff, claimant. 4. Proctor, attorney.

ACTÓRA, *sf.* Plaintiff, she who seeks justice.

ACTRÍZ, *sf.* Actress.

ACTUACIÓN, *sf.* Actuation, operation.

ACTUÁDO, DA, *a.* 1. Actuated. 2. Skilled, experienced.

ACTUÁL, *a.* Actual, present.

ACTUALIDÁD, *sf.* 1. Actuality, the actual or pre-

present state of things. 2. (Fil.) Action or determination of the form with respect to matter.
ACTUALIZÁR, *va.* To realize.
ACTUALMÉNTE, *ad.* Actually, now, at present.
ACTUÁNTE, *sm.* Propugner of a thesis in colleges.
ACTUÁR, *va.* 1. To digest. 2. (Met.) To consider, to weigh maturely. 3. To perform judicial acts, to proceed. 4. To instruct; to support a thesis.
ACTUÁRIO, *sm.* An actuary, register, or officer appointed to write down the acts or proceedings of a court or meeting.
ACTUÓSO, SA, *a.* (Rar.) Active, diligent, careful, solicitous.
ACUBÁDO, DA, *a.* Resembling or belonging to a pail or bucket.
ACUCHARÁDO, DA, *a.* Spoonlike, or having the figure of a spoon.
ACUCHILLÁDAS, *sf. pl.* Different coloured, oblong pieces in cloths.
ACUCHILLÁDO, DA, *a.* 1. Slashed, stabbed. 2. (Met.) Experienced, skilful by long practice.
ACUCHILLADÓR, RA, *s.* A quarrelsome person, a bully.
ACUCHILLÁR, *va.* 1. To cut or hack, to give cuts with a sabre. 2. (Ant.) To murder.—*vr.* To fight with knives or swords.
ACUCIÁR Y ACUDICIAR, *va.* 1. (Ant.) To stimulate, to hasten. 2. V. *Codiciar.*
ACUDIMIÉNTO, *sm.* Aid, assistance.
ACUDÍR, *vn.* 1. To assist, to succour, to support. 2. To yield, to produce; to be docile. 3. To have recourse. (Prov.) *La casa quemada, acudir con el agua.* (To come with the water when the house is burnt down.) After meat mustard.
ACUÉNTO, *ad. No me está acuento,* That does not suit me.
ACUERDÁDO, DA, *a.* Constructed by line or rule.
ACUÉRDO, *sm.* 1. Result of the deliberation of a tribunal, assembly, or meeting; resolution, agreed. 2. Body of the members of a tribunal assembled in the form of a court. 3. Opinion, advice. 4. (Pint.) Harmony of colours. *De acuérdo,* Unanimously, by common consent. *Ponerse de acuerdo,* To agree unanimously. *Acuérdos de reino,* Remonstrances made by the states of the realm.
ACUERNÁR, *vn.* To strike with the horns.
A'CUÉSTAS, *ad.* On the back, on the shoulders.
ACUITÁR, *va.* (Ant.) To afflict, to oppress.—*vr.* To grieve.
ACULÁDO, DA, *a.* Retired.
ACULÁR, *va.* (Vulg.) To force one into a corner; to oblige one to retreat.
ACULEBRINÁDO, DA, *a.* Made in the form of a culverin; applied to cannon which from their length resemble culverins.
ACULLÁ, *ad.* On the other side, yonder; opposite.
ACUMULACIÓN, *sf.* 1. Accumulation. 2. Act of filing records.
ACUMULADÓR, RA, *s.* 1. Accumulator. 2. An officer appointed to file the records of a court.
ACUMULÁR, *va.* 1. To accumulate, to heap together, to treasure up. 2. To impute, to upbraid with a fault. 3. To file records.
ACUMULATIVAMÉNTE, *ad.* (For.) By way of prevention; by way of precaution; jointly.
ACUÑACIÓN, *sf.* Coining, milling; the act of coining or milling.

ACUÑADOR, RA, *s.* Coiner.
ACUÑÁR, *va.* 1. To coin. 2. To wedge, or fasten with wedges. *Acuñar dinéro,* (Met.) To hoard up money. (Prov.) *Hermano ayuda y cuñado acuña,* Brothers and sisters in law are always at variance.
ACURRUCÁRSE, *vr.* To muffle one's self up in clothes.
ACURRULLÁR, *va.* (Naút.) To take down the sails of a galley.
ACUSACIÓN, *sf.* Accusation, impeachment.
ACUSADÓR, RA, *s.* Accuser, informer, impeacher.
ACUSÁR, *va.* 1. To accuse, to charge with a crime. 2. To acknowledge the receipt of a letter. 3. To take charge of.—*vr.* To acknowledge sins to a confessor.
ACUSATÍVO, *sm.* Accusative; the fourth case in the declension of nouns.
ACUSATÓRIO, RIA, *a.* Belonging to an accusation.
ACÚSE, *sm.* At cards, a certain number estimated to win so much.
ACUTÁNGULO, *a.* (Geom.) With acute angles.
A'DA, *sf.* A small apple of the pippin kind.
ADAFÍNA Ó ADEFÍNA, *sf.* Sort of stewed meat or fricassee, formerly used by the Jews in Spain.
ADÁGIO, *sm.* Adage, proverb.
ADAGUÁR, *va.* (Ant.) V. *Abrevar.*
ADÁLA, *sf.* (Naút.) Pump-deal.
ADALÍD, *sm.* A band of armed men headed by a commander. *Adalid mayor,* A quartermaster general.
ADAMADÍLLO, LA, *a.* Nice, delicate, pretty.
ADAMÁDO, DA, *a.* Damsel-like; applied to effeminate men.
ADAMÁR, *va.* (Ant.) To love violently.—*vr.* To become as delicate in the face as a lady.
ADAMASCÁDO, DA, *a.* Damask-like; woven or made in imitation of damask.
ADAPTÁBLE, *a.* Capable of being adapted.
ADAPTACIÓN, *sf.* Act of fitting one thing to another.
ADAPTADAMÉNTE, *ad.* In a fit manner.
ADAPTÁDO, DA, *a.* Adapted, fitted.
ADAPTÁR, *va.* To adapt, to fit, to apply one thing to another.
ADARAGUÉRO, *sm.* (Ant.) Man that uses a shield.
ADARÁXA, *sf.* (Arq.) Projecting stones, left to continue a wall.
ADÁRCE, *sm.* Salt froth of the sea dried on canes.
ADÁRGA, *sf.* A shield of an oval form, made of leather.
ADARGÁRSE, *vr.* To cover and defend one's self with a shield.
ADARGÁZO, *sm.* A blow given with a shield.
ADARGUÍLLA, *sm.* A small shield.
ADÁRME, *sm.* Half a drachm, the sixteenth part of an ounce. *Por adármes,* Very sparingly.
ADÁRVE Y ADARBE, *sm.* 1. The flat top of a wall. 2. A wall, a rampart.
ADATÁR, *va.* To place parcels to account under a certain date.
ADATÓDA, *sf.* (Bot.) The willow-leaved Malabar nut-tree.
ADÁZA, *sf.* (Bot.) Common panic.
ADECENAMIÉNTO, *sm.* Act of assembling or forming by ten and ten.
ADECENÁR, *va.* To form people into bodies by ten and ten.

Adefésio, *sm.* Extravagance, folly; not to the purpose.
Adefuéra, *ad.* V. *Por Defuera.*
Adefuéras, *s. pl.* (Vulg.) Out-buildings, buildings on the outside of the town, or adjacent to it.
Adehála, *sf.* Gratuity given over and above the stipulated price or wages.
Adehesádo, *sm.* Place converted into pasture.
Adehesamiénto, *sm.* Act of turning land to pasture, pasturage.
Adehesár, *va.* To convert land into pasture.
Adelantadaménte, *ad.* Beforehand; by way of anticipation.
Adelantadíllo, *a.* Red wine made of the first ripe grapes.
Adelantádo, *sm.* An appellation formerly given to the governor of a province.
Adelantádo, da, *a.* 1. Anticipated, advanced. Bold, forward. 2. Early, when applied to fruit or plants.
Adelantadór, ra, *s.* One that advances, extends, amplifies.
Adelantamiénto, *sm.* 1. Progress; the act of pushing forwards. 2. Anticipation. 3. The dignity of a governor, and the district of his jurisdiction.
Adelantár, *va.* 1. To advance, to accelerate. 2. To anticipate, to pay beforehand. 3. (Met.) To meliorate, to improve. 4. (Ant.) To push forward. 5. To get a-head, to win a race.—*vr.* 1. To take the lead, to get the start of. 2. (Met.) To excel, to outdo.
Adelánte, *ad.* 1. Farther off; higher up. 2. Henceforward; in future, or for the future. (Prov.) *Quién adelante no mira, atrás se queda,* Look before you leap.
Adélfa, *sf.* (Bot.) Rose-bay, Nerium oleander L.
Adelfál, *sm.* Plantation of rose-bay trees.
Adelgazádo, da, *a.* Made slender, or thin.
Adelgazadór, ra, *s.* One that makes thin or slender.
Adelgazamiénto, *sm.* Act of making slender.
Adelgazár, *va.* 1. To attenuate, to make thin or slender. 2. To lessen, to diminish. 3. To refine. 4. (Met.) To discuss with subtilty.—*vr.* To become slender.
Adeliñár, *va.* (Ant.) To amend. V. *Aliñar.*
Adéma y Adéme, *s.* (Min.) The timber, or plank-lining, with which the sides of mines are secured.
Ademadór, *sm.* (Min.) A workman or miner employed in lining the sides of mines with boards.
Ademán, *sm.* 1. A gesture or motion of the muscles, by which approbation or dislike is expressed. 2. (Pint.) Attitude. *En ademan,* In the attitude or posture of performing something.
Ademár, *va.* (Min.) To line or secure the sides of mines with planks, or timber.
Además, *ad.* Moreover; too much.
Adenología, *sf.* (Anat.) Adenology, description of the glands.
Adénos, *sm.* A sort of cotton which comes from Aleppo.
Adenóso, sa, *a.* Glandulous.
Adentál, *ad.* (Ant.) Singly.
Adentellár, *va.* To bite, to catch with the teeth. *Adentellar una pared,* To leave toothing-stones or bricks, to continue a wall.
Adéntro, *ad.* Within; inwardly. *De botones adentro,* In my heart. *Ser muy de adentro,* To be intimate in a house.
Adequación, *sf.* Fitness; the state of being adequate.
Adequadaménte, *ad.* Fitly, properly; to the purpose.
Adequádo, da, *a.* Adequate, fit, idoneous; to the purpose.
Adequár, *va.* To fit, to accommodate, to proportion.
Aderezár, *va.* 1. To dress, to adorn. 2. (Ant.) To prepare. 3. To clean, to repair. 4. (Ant.) To direct; to dispose. *Aderezar la comida,* To dress victuals.
Aderézo, *sm.* 1. Act and effect of dressing and adorning. 2. Gum, starch, and other ingredients, used to stiffen cloth with. *Aderézo de mesa,* A service for the table; applied to oil, vinegar, and salt. *Aderezo de diamantes,* A set of diamonds. *Aderezo de caballo,* Trappings or caparisons of a saddle-horse. *Aderezo de casa,* Furniture. *Aderezo de espada,* Hilt, hook, and other appendages of a sword.
Adérra, *sf.* (Arag.) A rope, made of rush or a sort of sedge, used for pressing the husks of grapes.
A'deshóra, *ad.* 1. Unseasonably, untimely; at irregular hours. 2. (Ant.) Suddenly.
Adestrádo, da, *a.* 1. Instructed; broke in. 2. (Blas.) On the dexter side of the scutcheon: it is also applied to the principal figure in a scutcheon, on the right of which is another.
Adestradór, ra, *s.* 1. Instructor, teacher. 2. Censor, critic.
Adestrár, *va.* 1. To guide, to lead. 2. To teach, to instruct. 3. To perform in a skilful manner.—*vr.* To exercise one's self.
Adeudádo, da, *a.* 1. Indebted. 2. Obliged.
Adeudár, *va.* 1. To pay duty. 2. (Ant.) To contract debts. 3. (Ant.) To oblige.—*vr.* To be indebted.
Adevinár, *va.* (Ant.) V. *Adivinar.*
Adherencia, *sf.* 1. Adhesion. 2. Alliance, kindred. 3. Adherence to a sect or party.
Adherénte, *a.* Adherent.
Adheréntes, *sm. pl.* Ingredients, tools, or instruments necessary for a thing.
Adherír, *vn.* To adhere to a sect or party; to espouse an opinion.
Adhesión, *sf.* Adhesion; the act of adhering.
Adiádo, da, *a.* *Vino al dia adiado,* He arrived or came on the day appointed.
Adiáfa, *sf.* (Ant.) Feast given on the arrival of a fleet in port.
Adiamantádo, da, *a.* Adamantine; hard as a diamond.
Adiár, *va.* (Ant.) To fix a day.
Adición, *sf.* 1. Addition or additament. 2. Remark or note put to accounts. *Adicion de la herencia,* Acceptance of an inheritance. 3. Addition, the first rule of arithmetic.
Adicionadór, ra, *s.* One that makes additions.
Adicionár, *va.* To make additions.
Adícto, ta, *a.* Addicted, inclined, or devoted to a thing.
Adiestrár, *va.* V. *Adestrár.*
Adiéso, *ad.* (Ant.) At the moment, instantly.
Adietár, *va.* To diet; to put to a diet.
Adívas, *sf. pl.* V. *Adivas.*

Adinerádo, da, *a.* Rich, wealthy.
Adinteládo, da, *a.* Falling from an arch gradually into a straight line.
Adipóso, sa, *a.* Fat. V. *Seboso.*
Adír, *va.* (Ant.) To distribute. *Adir la herencia*, To accept an inheritance.
Aditaménto, *sm.* Addition; additament.
Adíva ó Adíve, *sm.* Jackal, an animal resembling a dog of the pointer kind. Canis aureus *L. Adivas*, A swelling in the glands under the ears of horses, much resembling the strangles.
Adivinación, *sf.* Divination.
Adivinádo, da, *a.* Foretold.
Adivinadór, ra, *s.* A diviner, one who foretells events.
Adivinamiénto, *sm.* V. *Adivinación.*
Adivinánza, *sf.* 1. Enigma. 2. V. *Adivinación.*
Adivínar, *va.* 1. To foretell future events. 2. To guess, conjecture, anticipate or divine what is to happen. 3. To unriddle an enigma or difficult problem.
Adivíno, na, *s.* 1. Diviner, soothsayer. 2. One that divines what is to happen.
Adjetivación, *sf.* 1. Act of uniting one thing to another. 2. Construction.
Adjetivár, *va.* 1. To unite one thing to another. 2. To construct the different parts of speech.
Adjetívo, *sm.* (Gram.) Adjective.
Adjudicación, *sf.* Adjudication, act of adjudging.
Adjudicár, *va.* To adjudge.—*vr.* To appropriate to one's self.
Adjunción, *sf.* 1. Adjunction. 2. An assembly of judges.
Adjúnta, *sf.* Letter enclosed in another.
Adjúnto, ta, *a.* United, joined, annexed.
Adjúnto, *sm.* V. *Adjetivo*, and *Aditamento. Adjuntos*, A body of judges commissioned or appointed jointly to try a cause.
Adjurár, *va.* (Ant.) To conjure.
Adminiculár, *va.* (For.) To increase the power and efficacy of a thing by adding collateral aids.
Adminículo, *sm.* Collateral aid, additional help.
Administración, *sf.* 1. Administration, the act of administering a thing. 2. Office of an administrator. *En administracion*, In trust; applied to places in which the occupant has no property.
Administradór, ra, *s.* Administrator. *Administrador de órden*, A knight, who administers for another, incapable of doing it himself.
Administrár, *va.* 1. To administer, to govern; to take care of. 2. To serve an office.
Administratório, ria, *a.* Belonging to an administration or administrator.
Admiráble, *a.* Admirable.
Admiráble, *sm.* A hymn in Roman Catholic churches in praise of the eucharist, at the time it is reserved in the tabernacle.
Admirablemente, *ad.* Admirably.
Admiración, *sf.* 1. Admiration; act of admiring; wonder. 2. Point of admirtion. *Es una admiracion*, It is a thing worthy of admiration.
Admiránte, *pa.* He who admires.
Admirár, *va.* 1. To cause admiration. 2. To admire.—*vr.* To be seized with admiration.
Admirativaménte, *ad.* In an admiring manner.
Admiratívo, va, *a.* Marvelling, admiring, wondering.
Admisíble, *a.* Admissible.
Admisión, *sf.* Admission.

Admitír, *va.* 1. To receive, to give entrance. 2. To accept. 3. To admit, to permit. *Bien admitido*, Well received. *El asunto no admite dilacion*, The affair admits of no delay.
Admonición, *sf.* Admonition, warning, counsel, advice.
Admonitór, *sm.* Monitor, in some religious communities.
Adnáta, *sf.* (Anat.) The external white membrane of the eye.
Adó, *ad.* V. *Adonde.*
Adobádo, da, *a.* Pickled.
Adobádo, *sm.* 1. Pickled pork. 2. Any sort of dressed meat.
Adobadór, ra, *s.* Dresser, preparer.
Adobár, *va.* 1. To dress or make any thing up. 2. To pickle pork or other meat. 3. To cook. 4. To tan hides. 5. (Met.) To prepare or dispose the mind.
Adóbe, *sm.* A brick not yet baked.
Adobería, *sf.* 1. A brick-field. 2. V. *Teneria.*
Adóbo, *sm.* 1. Repairing, mending. 2. Pickle, sauce. 3. Paint for ladies. 4. Ingredients for dressing leather or cloth.
Adocenár, *va.* 1. To count or sell by dozens. 2. To despise, to contemn.
Adoctrinár, *va.* V. *Doctrinar.*
Adolecér, *vn.* 1. To be seized with illness. 2. To labour under disease.—*va.* To produce pain or disease.
Adolescéncia, *sf.* Adolescence; youth.
Adolescénte, *sm.* A person being in the state of adolescence.
Adónde, *ad.* Whither? to what place? *Adonde quiera*, To whatever place you please.
Adónico y Adónio, *sm.* A Latin verse consisting of a dactyle and a spondee.
Adopción, *sf.* Adoption; the act of taking another man's child for his own.
Adoptadór, ra, *s.* Adopter; one that adopts.
Adoptánte, *pa.* Adopting, one who adopts.
Adoptár, *va.* 1. To adopt. 2. To embrace an opinion. 3. To graft.
Adoptívo, va, *a.* Adoptive.
Adoquiér y Adoquiéra, *ad.* (Ant.) Where you please.
Adoquín, *sm.* Long stone used to bind the flags round fountains.
Adór, *sm.* The time assigned for watering land.
Adoráble, *a.* Adorable; worthy of adoration.
Adoración, *sf.* Adoration; the act of adoring.
Adoradór, ra, *s.* Adorer; worshipper; one that adores.
Adorár, *va.* 1. To adore; to reverence with religious worship. 2. To love excessively. 3. To kiss the Pope's hand, as a mark of respect and reverence.
Adoratório, *sm.* A name given by the Spaniards to the temples of idols in America.
Adormecedór, ra, *a.* Soporiferous; that which causes drowsiness or sleep.
Adormecér, *vr.* 1. To cause drowsiness or sleep. 2. To calm, to mitigate.—*vr.* 1. To fall asleep. 2. To grow benumbed, torpid. 3. (Met.) To grow or persist in vice.
Adormecimiénto, *sm.* Drowsiness, slumber.
Adormidéra, *sf.* (Bot.) Poppy. Papaver somniferum *L.*
Adormitárse, *vr.* V. *Dormitar.*

Adornadór, ra, *s.* Adorner.
Adornár, *va.* 1. To beautify, to embellish. 2. To adorn with talents. *Ella está adornada de todas las prendas y circunstancias que pide su caracter y sexo,* She is adorned with all the talents and endowments suitable to her character and sex.
Adornísta, *sm.* Painter of ornaments.
Adórno, *sm.* 1. Ornament, decoration. 2. Furniture.
Adquiridór, ra, *s.* Acquirer. (Prov.) *A' buen adquiridor, buen expendedor,* After a gatherer comes a scatterer.
Adquirír, *va.* To acquire, to obtain.
Adquisición, *sf.* 1. Acquisition, the act and effect of acquiring. 2. Goods or effects obtained by purchase or gift, and not by inheritance.
Adra, *sf.* Turn, time, successive order.
Adráles, *sm. pl.* Hurdles which are put in carts.
Adréde, *ad.* Purposely; on purpose.
Adriático, *a. Mar Adriatico,* the Adriatic Sea.
Adrizár, *va.* (Naút.) To right. *Adrizar un navio,* To right a ship.
Adrubádo, da, *a.* (Ant.) Gibbous; protuberant; swelling into inequalities.
Adscribír, *va.* To appoint a clergyman to the service of a church.
Aduána, *sf.* 1. A custom-house. 2. (Met.) A house much frequented. *Pasar por todas las aduanas,* To undergo a close examination. 3. (Cant.) Brothel, receptacle for thieves and stolen goods.
Aduanár, *va.* 1. To enter goods at the custom-house. 2. To pay the duty.
Aduanéro, *sm.* Customhouse-offices.
Aduár, *sm.* 1. An ambulatory village of Arabs. 2. A cottage of gypsies.
Aducár, *sf.* A coarse sort of silk stuff formerly used.
Aduendádo, da, *a.* Resembling a ghost; walking about like a ghost.
Adufázo, *sm.* Blow with a timbrel, or tabourine.
Adúfe, *sm.* Timbrel or tabourine. V. *Pandero.*
Aduféro, ra, *s.* Timbrel or tabourine-player.
Adujár, *va.* (Naút.) To coil a cable.
Adújas ó Adujádas, *sf. pl.* (Naút.) Flakes of a coiled cable.
Adúla, *sf.* 1. A piece of ground which has no particular irrigation allotted to it. 2. V. *Dula.*
Adulación, *sf.* Adulation, flattery.
Aduladór, ra, *s.* Flatterer.
Adulár, *va.* 1. To flatter. 2. To crouch, to cringe.
Adulatório, ria, *a.* Adulatory, flattering.
Aduleár, *vn.* To bawl, to cry out.
Aduléro, *sm.* Herd or driver of horses or mules.
Adulteración, *sf.* Adulteration; adulterating.
Adulteradór, ra, *s.* One who adulterates.
Adulterár, *va.* 1. To adulterate; to corrupt or falsify. 2. (Ant.) To commit adultery.
Adulterinaménte, *ad.* In an adulterous manner.
Adulteríno, na, *a.* 1. Adulterous; begotten in adultery. 2. Adulterated, falsified, forged.
Adultério, *sm.* Adultery.
Adultéro, ra, *s.* Adulterer; adulteress; a person guilty of adultery.
Adúlto, ta, *a.* Adult, state of manhood.
Adulzár, *va.* 1. To sweeten. 2. To soften. *Adulzar los metales,* To render metals more ductile.
Adumbración, *sf.* Adumbration, shade in a picture.
Adunación, *sf.* Adunation, the act of uniting, and the union itself.
Adunár, *va.* To unite, to join.
Adúr, Adúras, y Adúro, *ad.* (Ant.) V. *Apénas.*
Adustión, *sf.* (Med.) Adustion, an excessive inflammation of the blood.
Adustívo, va, *a.* That which has the power of adusting or burning up.
Adústo, ta, *a.* 1. Adust; that which is adusted or burnt up. 2. Exposed to the scorching heat of a meridian sun. 3. (Met.) Gloomy, untractable.
Advéna, *sm.* A foreigner.
Advenedízo, za, *s.* 1. A foreigner who comes to establish himself in a country. 2. (Ant.) A Mahometan proselyte, converted to the Roman Catholic religion.
Advenimiénto, *sm.* Arrival; advent.
Adventája, *sf.* (For. Arag.) A jewel or piece of furniture, which the surviving husband or wife takes out of the estate of the deceased consort before the division of the inheritance be made.
Adventício, cia, *a.* 1. Adventitious; accidental. 2. (For.) Acquired by industry or right of inheritance, independent of a paternal fortune.
Adverbiál, *a.* Adverbial, belonging to an adverb.
Adverbialménte, *ad.* Adverbially.
Advérbio, *sm.* Adverb; one of the parts of speech, joined to the verbs or adjectives, for the purpose of qualifying and restraining the latitude of their signification.
Adversaménte, *ad.* Adversely; unfortunately.
Adversário, *sm.* Adversary; opponent; antagonist.—*pl.* Notes and annotations in a common-place book; a common-place book.
Adversatívo, va, *a.* (Gram.) Adversative: an adversative particle is that which expresses some difference and opposition between that which precedes and follows.
Adversidád, *sf.* Adversity, calamity.
Advérso, sa, *a.* 1. Adverse, calamitous, afflictive. 2. Opposite, placed in a contrary direction; averse.
Advertência, *sf.* 1. Advertence; attention to; regard to. 2. Advice. 3. Advertisement to the reader.
Advertidaménte, *ad.* Advisedly, deliberately.
Advertído, da, *a.* 1. Noticed. 2. Skilful, intelligent; acting with deliberation and design.
Advertimiénto, *sm.* V. *Advertencia.*
Advertír, *va.* 1. To advert, to take notice of, to observe. 2. To instruct, to advise. 3. To perceive.
Adviénto, *sm.* Advent; the name of one of the holy seasons, comprehending the four weeks before Christmas.
Advocación, *sf.* 1. Appellation given to a church, chapel, or altar, dedicated to the holy virgin, or a saint. 2. Profession of a lawyer.
Advocatório, ria, *a. Carta advocatoria ó convocatoria,* A letter of convocation calling an assembly.
Adyacénte, *a.* Adjacent; applied to islands lying near a continent, or principal island; things contiguous.
Adyutório, *sm.* (Ant.) Aid, support, succour.
Aechadéro, *sm.* The place where grain is winnowed or separated from the chaff.

Aechadór, ra, *s.* Winnower; sifter of corn.
Aechadúras, *sf. pl.* The refuse of grain, chaff.
Aechár, *va.* To winnow, to sift, to separate grain from the chaff.
Aécho, *sm.* Winnowing, cleansing.
Aéreo, rea, *a.* 1. Aerial; consisting of or belonging to air. 2. (Met.) Airy, fantastic; destitute of solidity or foundation.
Aerifórme, *a.* (Quim.) Aeriform, state of air.
Aerología, *sf.* Aerology, the doctrine of air.
Aerománcia, *sf.* Aeromancy, the art of divining by the air.
Aeromántico, *sm.* Professor or student of aeromancy.
Aerometría, *sf.* Aerometry, art of measuring the air.
Aescondídas y á Escondídas, *ad.* Privately; in a secret manner.
Afabilidád, *sf.* Affability; easiness of manners; civility of address.
Afáble, *a.* Affable; agreeable; courteous.
Afableménte, *ad.* Affably, courteously.
Afáca, *sf.* (Bot.) Yellow vetch. Vicia lutea *L.*
Afagásmo, *sm.* A sort of tax or duty.
Afamádo, da, *a.* 1. Famed, celebrated. 2. Hungry.
Afán, *sm.* 1. Anxiety, solicitude, eagerness, in pursuit of worldly affairs. 2. (Ant.) Toil, fatigue.
Afanadaménte, *ad.* Anxiously, laboriously.
Afanadór, ra, *s.* Anxious pursuer of riches.
Afanár, *va.* 1. To toil, to labour; to be over-solicitous. 2. (Ant.) To be engaged in corporal labour. (Prov.) *Afanar, afanar y nunca medrar;* Much toil and little profit.
Afanóso, sa, *a.* Solicitous; laborious; painful.
Afascalár, *va.* To stack, to build ricks of corn.
Afaycionádo, da, *a.* (Ant.) V. *Agestado.*
Afeadór, ra, *s.* One that deforms, disfigures, or makes ugly.
Afeamiénto, *sm.* 1. Deformation; defacing. 2. Ugliness. 3. Calumny, censure.
Afeár, *va.* 1. To deform, to deface. 2. (Met.) To decry, to find fault with, to censure.
Afección, *sf.* 1. Affection; inclination, fondness. 2. (Fil.) Properties of a thing. 3. Right of bestowing a benefice.
Afectación, *sf.* Affectation; the act of making an artificial appearance.
Afectadaménte, *ad.* Affectedly; formally.
Afectádo, da, *a.* Affected, formal, conceited.
Afectádor, ra, *s.* One that affects, or acts in an affected manner.
Afectár, *va.* 1. To feign, to study outward appearance with some degree of hypocrisy. 2. To unite benefices or livings. 3. To aim at, to endeavour after with anxiety.
Afectíllo, *sm.* (Dim.) Slight affection.
Afectívo, va, *a.* Proceeding from or belonging to affection; affective.
Afécto, *sm.* 1. Affection, love, kindness. 2. Passion, sensation. 3. Pain, disease. 4. (Pint.) Lively representation. *Afectos desordenados,* Inordinate desires.
Afécto, ta, *a.* 1. Affectionate. 2. Inclined, disposed. 3. Reserved; applied to benefices, the collation whereof is reserved to the Pope. 4. Subject to some charge or obligation for lands, rents.
Afectuosaménte, *ad.* Affectionately.
Afectuóso, sa, *a.* Affectionate, kind, gracious.

Afélio, *sm.* Aphelion, that part of a planet's orbit which is the most remote from the sun.
Afelpáda, da, *a.* Shaggy, villous. *Palletes afelpados,* (Naút.) Cased mats.
Afeminación, *sf.* Effemination; emasculation.
Afeminadaménte, *ad.* Effeminately, womanly.
Afeminadíllo, la, *a.* Somewhat effeminate.
Afeminamiénto, *sm.* V. *Afeminación.*
Afeminár, *va.* 1. To effeminate, to emasculate, to unman. 2. To debilitate, to enervate, to melt into weakness.
Afëresis, *sf.* Aphæresis; a figure in grammar that takes away a letter or syllable from the beginning of a word, as *Conia* for *Ciconia.*
Afermoseár, *va.* (Ant.) V. *Hermosear.*
Aferradór, ra, *s.* One that grapples or grasps.
Aferramiénto, *sm.* Grasping, grappling; the act of seizing or binding. *Aferramiento de las velas,* (Naút.) The furling of the sails.
Aferrár, *va.* 1. To grapple, to grasp, to seize. 2. (Naút.) To furl, to hand the sails. 3. (Naút. Ant.) To moor.—*vr.* 1. To grasp one another strongly. 2. (Met.) To persist obstinately in an opinion.
Aferravélas ó Acerravélas, *sf. pl.* Furling-lines; rope-bands.
Afervorizár, *va.* V. *Enfervorizar.*
Afeytadaménte, *ad.* Affectedly, artificially.
Afeytadór, ra, *s.* (Ant.) Barber, hair-dresser.
Afeytár, *va.* 1. To shave. 2. To paint, to set off a person with paints or colours. 3. To clip the box, wall-trees, &c. in a garden. 4. To cut the tails and manes of horses and mules; to trim them. 5. (Ant.) To decorate, to adorn.
Aféyte, *sm.* Paint; an artificial colour laid on a thing in order to beautify it.
Afianzár, *va.* 1. To bail, to give security for another. 2. To prop, to support, to secure with stays, ropes, &c.
Afiár, *va.* (Ant.) To promise or give parole for the safety of another, like the ancient knights.
Afición, *sf.* 1, Affection; inclination for a person or thing. 2. Earnestness, eagerness.
Aficionadaménte, *ad.* Affectionately.
Aficionádo, da, *s.* An amateur; a devotee.
Aficionár, *va.* To affect, to cause or inspire affection.
Aficioncílla, *sf.* (Dim.) Sneaking kindness, distant regard; slight affection.
Afiladéra, *sf.* Whetstone, sharpening-stone.
Afiladúra, *sf.* Sharpening, whetting.
Afilamiénto, *sm.* Attenuating, act of thinning.
Afilár, *va.* 1. To whet, to sharpen by attrition. 2. To render keen. *Afilar las uñas,* To make an extraordinary effort of genius or skill.—*vr.* To grow thin and meagre.
Afiligranádo, da, *a* 1. Filigree-like, resembling filigree. 2. (Met.) Applied to persons who are slender, slim of body, and small featured.
Afillár, *va.* (Ant.) To adopt, to make him a son who was not by birth.
Afilón, *sm.* 1. Whetstone. 2. An instrument made of steel, used by comb-makers for edging or whetting their tools.
Afín, *s.* (Ant.) Relation by affinity.
Afinación, *sf.* 1. Completion; the act of finishing, and the state of being finished. 2. Refining. 3. Tuning of instruments.
Afinadaménte, *ad.* Completely, perfectly.
Afinádo, da, *a.* Well-finished, perfect, complete

Afinadór, ra, *s.* 1. Finisher; one that finishes a thing well. 2. Key with which stringed instruments are tuned.

Afinadúra y Afinamiénto, *s.* 1. Refining; the act of finishing. 2. Refinement; perfection.

Afinár, *va.* 1. To complete, to finish, to polish. 2. To tune musical instruments. *Afinar los metales,* To refine metals. *Afinar la voz,* To tune the voice.

Afincádo, da, *a.* Wished for with anxiety; vehemently desired.

Afinidád, *sf.* 1. Affinity; relation by marriage. 2. (Met.) Analogy; relation to; connexion with.

Afíz, *sm.* Horse-medicine made up of juniper-berries.

Afirmación y Afirmativa, *sf.* Affirmation; assertion.

Afirmadaménte, *ad.* Firmly.

Afirmadór, ra, *s.* One that affirms.

Afirmamiénto, *sm.* 1. Affirmation. 2. (Ant. Arag.) Agreement with a servant on his entering the service.

Afirmár, *va.* 1. To make fast, to secure. 2. To affirm, to assure for certain. *Afirmar una carta,* At cards, to give one card a fixed value.—*vn.* To inhabit, to reside, to sojourn.—*vr.* 1. To fix one's self in the saddle or stirrup. 2. To maintain firmly; to advance steadily.

Afirmativaménte, *ad.* Affirmatively; positively.

Afirmatívo, va, *a.* Affirmative; opposed to negative.

Afistolár, *va.* To render fistulous; applied to a wound.

Afíxo, xa, *a.* (Gram.) Affix; applied to letters added to a word.

Aflechátes, *sm. pl.* (Naút.) Ratlings or ratlines.

Aflegir, *va.* (Ant.) V. *Afligir.*

Aflicción, *sf.* Concern, affliction, sorrow, grief.

Aflictívo, va, *a.* Afflictive; that which causes pain and grief. *Pena aflictiva,* corporal punishment.

Aflícto, ta, *a.* (Poet.) Afflicted.

Afligidaménte, *ad.* Grievously, with affliction.

Afligír, *va.* To afflict, to put to pain, to grieve, to torment.

Afloreádo, *a.* V. *Floreado.*

Afloxamiénto y Afloxadúra, *s.* Laxation; act of loosening or slackening; the state of being relaxed.

Afloxár, *va.* 1. To loosen, to slacken, to relax. 2. To debilitate. 3. (Pint.) To soften the colour in shading. 4. (Naút.) *Afloxar los obenques,* To ease the shrouds.—*vn.* 1. To grow weak; to abate. 2. To grow cool in fervour or zeal; to lose courage.

Afluéncia, *sf.* Affluence, plenty, abundance.

Afluénte, *a.* 1. Affluent, copious, abundant. 2. Loquacious; having a flow of words.

Afolládo, da, *a.* Wearing large or wide trousers.

Afollár, *va.* To blow with bellows; to ill-treat.

Afondár, *va.* 1. To put under water. 2. (Naút.) To sink.—*vn.* (Naút.) To founder; to go to the bottom.

Aforádo, *a.* Privileged person.

Aforadór, *sm.* Gauger, or gager.

Aforamiénto, *sm.* 1. Gauging. 2. Duty on foreign goods.

Aforár, *va.* 1. To gauge, to measure vessels or quantities. 2. To examine goods for the purpose of determining the duty to be paid on them. 3. To give or take lands or tenements under the tenure of melioration.

Aforísma, *sf.* A swelling in the arteries of beasts.

Aforísmo, *sm.* Aphorism, brief sentence, maxim.

Aforístico, ca, *a.* Aphoristical.

Afóro, *sm.* Examination and valuation of wine and other commodities for the payment of duties; gauging.

Aforrár, *va.* 1. To line, to cover the inside of cloths. 2. (Ant.) To emancipate a slave. 3. (Naút.) To sheathe. 4. (Naút.) *Aforrar un cabo,* To serve a cable.

Afórro, *sm.* 1. Lining. 2. (Naút.) Sheathing. 3. (Naút.) Waist of a ship.

Afortunádo, da, *a.* 1. Fortunate. 2. Hard, strong. *Tiempo afortunado,* Blowing weather.

Afortunár, *va.* To make happy.

Afosárse, *vr.* (Mil.) To defend one's self by making a ditch.

Afrancesádo, da, *a.* Frenchified; imitating with affectation the French.

Afrancesár, *va.* To Gallicize, to give a French termination to words.—*vr.* To Frenchify, to imitate the French.

Afratelárse, *vr.* To fraternize.

Afraylár, *va.* (And.) To lop off the branches of trees.

Afrécho, *sm.* (And. y Extrem.) Bran, the husks of corn ground.

Afrenillár, *vn.* (Naút.) To bridle the oars.

Afrénta, *sf.* 1. Any dishonour or reproach; outrage; an insult offered to the face. 2. Infamy resulting from the sentence passed upon a criminal. 3. Courage, bravery, valour.

Afrentár, *va.* To affront; to insult to the face.—*vr.* To be affronted; to be put to the blush.

Afrentosaménte, *ad.* Ignominiously; disgracefully.

Afrentóso, sa, *a.* Ignominious; insulting.

Afretár, *va.* To hog and clean the bottom of a row galley.

A'frico, *sm.* The wind that blows off the African coast; south-west wind. V. *A'brego.*

Afrisonádo, da, *a.* Resembling a Friesland draught-horse.

Afrontadaménte, *ad.* Face to face.

Afrontár, *va.* 1. To put one thing opposite to another. 2. To confront. 3. To reproach one with a crime to his face.—*vn.* To face.

Afuér, *ad.* Upon the word of a gentleman.

Afuéra, *ad.* 1. Abroad; out of the house or place. 2. Openly, in public. 3. Besides; moreover. *Afuéra Afuéra,* Stand out of the way; clear the way. *En afuéra,* Except, besides.

Afuéras, *sm. pl.* Environs of a place.

Afuéros, *sm. pl.* Foreign duties.

Afufár y Afufarse, *vn.* y *r.* To flee, to run away, to escape. *No pudo afufarlos,* He could not escape them.

Afúste, *sm.* A gun-carriage. *Afúste de mortero,* A mortar-bed.

Agacháda, *sf.* Submission; temporizing.

Agachadíza, *sf.* (Orn.) A snipe; a small bird. *Hacer la agachadiza,* To stoop down, to conceal one's self.

Agachárse, *vr.* 1. To stoop, to squat, to crouch. 2. To let a misfortune pass unnoticed.

Agalbanádo, da, *a.* V. *Galbanero.*
Agálla, *sf.* (Bot.) Gall-nut. *Agalla de Cipres,* Cypress gall. *Quedarse de la agalla, ó colgado de la agalla;* To be deceived or disappointed in his hopes.—*pl.* 1. Glands in the inside of the throat. 2. Gills of fishes. 3. Distemper of the glands under the cheeks, or in the tonsils. 4. Wind-galls in the pasterns of a horse. 5. Beaks of a shuttle.
Agalládo, da, *a.* Steeped in an infusion of galls.
Agallón, *sm.* A large gall-nut. *Agallónes, pl.* 1. Strings of large silver-beads hollowed like gall-nuts. 2. Wooden beads put to rosaries.
Agalluéla, *sf.* (Dim.) A small gall-nut.
Agamitár, *va.* To imitate the voice of a fawn.
Agamuzádo, da, *a.* Shamois-coloured; having the colour of a shamois-skin.
Agarbádo, da, *a.* V. *Garboso.*
Agarbanzár, *vn.* To bud, to put forth young shoots.
Agarbárse, *vr.* To cower, to squat like a hare.
Agaréno, *sm.* A descendant of Agar; a Mohammedan.
Agárico, *sm.* (Bot.) Agaric; a fungous excrescence growing on the trunks of larch-trees.
Agarradéro, *sm.* (Naút.) Anchoring-ground.
Agarrádo, da, *a.* 1. Seized. 2. Miserable, stingy. [2. Catchpole, bum-bailiff.
Agarradór, ra, *s.* 1. One that grasps or seizes.
Agarrafár, *va.* (Vulg.) To grasp; to grapple hard in a scuffle.
Agarráma, *sf.* V. *Garrama.*
Agarránte, V. *Agarrador.*
Agarrár, *va.* 1. To grasp, to seize, to lay hold of. 2. To obtain. *Agarrarse de un pelo,* To grasp at a hair, to support an opinion or furnish an excuse.
Agárro, *sm.* Grasp, the act of seizing.
Agarrochadór, *sm.* Pricker, stabber, goader.
Agarrochár y Agarrocheár, *va.* To prick with a pike or spear; to goad.
Agarrotár, *va.* To tie and compress bales with ropes and cords.
Agasajadór, ra, *s.* One that receives and treats with impassioned kindness.
Agasajár, *va.* 1. To receive and treat kindly. 2. To regale.
Agasájo, *sm.* 1. Graceful and affectionate reception. 2. A friendly present. 3. Refreshment or collation served up in the evening.
A'gata, *sf.* Agate, a precious stone.
A'gatas, *ad.* All fours. *Andar á gatas,* To go on all fours.
Agavánza, *sf.* (Bot.) Hip-tree, dog-rose. Rosa canina *L.*
Agavillár, *va.* To bind or tie up the corn in sheaves.—*vr.* (Met.) To associate with a gang of sharpers.
Agazapár, *va.* (Joc.) To nab or catch a person. —*vr.* To hide one's self; not to be seen.
A'ge, *sm.* Habitual or chronic disease.
Agzár, *vn.* To cry like a partridge which is closely pursued.
Agenár, *va.* (Ant.) V. *Enagenar.*
Agéncia, *sf.* 1. Agency, the office of an agent. 2. Diligence; activity.
Agenciár, *va.* To solicit; to endeavour eagerly to obtain a thing. [cious.
Agenciéso, sa, *a.* 1. Diligent, active. 2. Offi-

Agengíbre, *sm.* V. *Gengibre.*
Agéno, na, *a.* 1. Foreign, strange; remote. 2 Ignorant. 3. (Met.) Improper. *Ageno de verdad,* Void of truth.
Agénte, *sm.* 1. Agent, actor. 2. Solicitor, attorney. *Agente de negocios,* Broker.
Agenúz, *sm.* (Bot.) Field fennel flower. Nigella arvensis *L.*
Agéo, *sm.* *Perro de ageo,* Setting-dog used for partridges.
Ageráto, *sm.* (Bot.) Sweet milfoil or maudlin. Achillea ageratum *L.*
Agermanárse, *vr.* To enter the society of gipsies.
Agestádo, da, *(Bien ó mal.) a.* Well or ill faced or featured.
Agéste, *sm.* North-west wind.
Agí, *sm.* A sort of sauce made in America of the agi-pepper.
Agiblíbus, *s.* Application and industry used to obtain the conveniences of life.
Agíble, *a.* Feasible; practicable.
Agigantádo, da, *a.* Giantlike, gigantic.
A'gil, *a.* Nimble, ready, expedite.
Agilidád, *sf.* Agility, nimbleness, activity.
Agilitár, *va.* To render nimble; to make active.
A'gilménte, *ad.* Nimbly, readily, actively.
Agío y Agiotage, *sm.* (Com.) Exchange of paper money for coin or coin for bills.
Agiotádor, *sm.* Bill-broker, stock-broker.
Agiotísta, *sm.* Money-changer, bill-broker.
Agironár, *va.* To put gussets or coloured triangular pieces in cloths.
Agitáble, *a.* Capable of agitation.
Agitación, *sf.* Agitation; the act of agitating.
Agitanádo, da, *a.* Gipsy-like, resembling gipsies.
Agitár, *va.* 1. To ruffle. 2. To discuss.
Aglutinánte, *a.* Uniting parts together.
Aglutinatívo, va, *a.* Agglutinative.
Agnación, *sf.* Consanguinity; relation by blood.
Agnádo, da, *a.* (For.) Consanguineous; near of kin; related by blood.
Agnatício, cia, *a.* Consanguineous; belonging to consanguinity.
Agnición, *sf.* Agnition or recognition of a person on the stage. [tree.
Agnocásto, *sm.* (Bot.) Agnus castus, or chaste-
Agnoménto, *sm.* (Ant.) V. *Cognomento ó Sobrenombre.*
Agnus Dei, *sm.* Agnus Dei; a relic or emblematic figure of a lamb, blessed by the Pope.
Agobiár, *va.* 1. To bend the body down to the ground. 2. (Met.) To oppress.—*vr.* To vow.
Agolár, *va.* (Naút.) To hand the sails.
Agolpárse, *vr.* To crowd, to assemble in crowds.
Agonáles, *a. pl.* Games in honour of Janus.
Agóne, (in) (Lat.) *ó en la agonia de la muerte,* In agony; in the struggle of death.
Agonía, *sf.* 1. Agony; the pangs of death. 2. Any violent pain of body or mind. 3. An anxious or vehement desire.
Agonísta, *sm.* (Ant.) A dying person.
Agonizánte, *sm.* 1. One that assists a dying person. 2. A monk of the order of St. Camillus, who is bound to assist dying persons. 3. (Met.) Anxiously desirous. 4. In universities, he who assists students in their ex-

mination for a degree. 5. (Ant.) Dying; in the agony of death.

Agonizár, *va.* 1. To assist dying persons. 2. To desire anxiously; to wish with continued eagerness. 3. (Met.) To annoy, to pester; to importune intolerably. *Estar agonizando*, To be in the agony of death.

Agóra, *ad.* V. *Ahora.*

Agorár, *va.* To divine, to prognosticate; to augur.

Agorería, *sf.* Auguration; divination.

Agoréro, **ra**, *s.* Augur or augurer; diviner.

Agorgojárse, *vr.* To be destroyed by grubs.

Agostadéro, *sm.* Summer pasture where cattle graze in August.

Agostár, *va.* 1. To be parched with heat. 2. (Arag.) To turn up or plough the land in August; to fallow. 3. To pasture cattle on stubbles in August.

Agostéro, *sm.* 1. A boy appointed to assist and wait upon reapers in the field. 2. A religious mendicant who begs corn in August.

Agostízo, **za**, *a.* A person born in August; a colt foaled in that month.

Agósto, *sm.* 1. August, the eighth month in the year. 2. Harvest-time. 3. Harvest; the corn gathered and inned.

Agotár, *va.* 1. To drain off waters or other liquors. 2. (Met.) To beat one's brains; to strike out something. 3. To run out a fortune; to mispend it.

Agóte, *sm.* (Nav.) He who is of one generation; a race so called.

Agracéjo, *sm.* An olive which falls before it is ripe.

Agracéño, **ña**, *a.* Resembling verjuice, or the juice pressed from sour grapes.

Agracéra, *sf.* Vessel to hold verjuice—*a.* Applied to grapes which never ripen.

Agraciádo, **da**, *a.* Graceful, genteel, handsome.

Agraciár, *va.* 1. To adorn or embellish a thing or person. 2. To grant a favour. 3. To communicate divine grace.

Agradáble, *a.* Agreeable, pleasing.

Agradár, *va.* To please, to gratify, to render acceptable.—*vr.* To be pleased.

Agradecér, *va.* 1. To acknowledge a favour. 2. To reward, to recompense.

Agradecído, **da**, *a.* 1. Acknowledged. 2. Grateful, thankful.

Agradecimiénto, *sm.* Gratitude, gratefulness; the act of acknowledging a favour conferred.

Agrádo, *sm.* 1. Affability, agreeableness; the quality of pleasing. 2. Will, pleasure. *Esto no es de mi agrado*, That does not please me.

Agradúlce, *a.* That which is between sweet and sour. V. *Agridulce.*

Agramadéra, *sf.* Brake, an instrument for dressing flax or hemp.

Agramadór, **ra**, *s.* One that dresses flax or hemp with a brake.

Agramár, *va.* To dress flax or hemp with a brake.

Agramiládo, **da**, *a.* Painted like bricks in size and colour.

Agramilár, *va.* To point and colour a brick wall.

Agramíza, *sf.* 1. The stem or stalk of hemp. 2. Refuse of hemp which has been dressed.

Agrandár, *va.* To increase, to make larger.

Agranujádo, **da**, *a.* Filled or covered with grain.

Agravación, *sf.* Aggravation; the act of aggravating.

Agravadór, **ra**, *s.* Oppressor.

Agravamiénto, *sm.* (Canon.) Censure; threatening excommunication.

Agravanteménte, *ad.* Grievously.

Agravár, *va.* 1. To oppress with taxes and other public burthens; to aggrieve. 2. To aggravate; to render more intolerable. 3. To exaggerate; to make larger.

Agravatório, **ria**, *a.* (For.) Compulsory, aggravating.

Agraviadaménte, *ad.* (Ant.) 1. Injuriously, insultingly. 2. Efficaciously, strongly.

Agraviadór, **ra**, *s.* One that gives offence, or aggravates.

Agraviár, *va.* 1. To wrong, to injure. 2. (Ant.) To load, to burthen.—*vr.* To be aggrieved.

Agrávio, *sm.* 1. Offence, injury, insult. 2. (Ant.) Appeal.

Agráz, *sm.* 1. Verjuice; the juice expressed from unripe grapes. 2. An unripe grape. 3. (Bot.) Maple. *En agraz*, *ad.* Unseasonably; unsuitably.

Agrazáda, *sf.* Verjuice-water.

Agrazár, *vn.* To have a sour taste, to become like verjuice.—*va.* To disgust.

Agrazón, *sm.* 1. Wild grape; a bunch of grapes which does not ripen. 2. (Bot.) Gooseberry bush. 3. Vexation, displeasure, resentment.

Agregación, *sf.* 1. Aggregation; the act of collecting into one mass. 2. The state of being thus collected.

Agregádo, **da**, *a.* Aggregated.

Agregádo, *sm.* Aggregate; the collection of many particulars into one whole.

Agregár, *va.* 1. To aggregate, to collect and unite persons or things. 2. To collate, to nominate.

Agresión, *sf.* (Ant.) Aggression, attack, assault.

Agresór, **ra**, *s.* Aggressor, assaulter; one that commits the first act of hostility.

Agréste, *a.* 1. Rustic, clownish, illiterate. 2. Propagated by nature without cultivation.

Agréte, *sm.* Sourness with a mixture of sweet.

Agréte, *a.* Sourish.

Agriaménte, *ad.* Sourly; with asperity or harshness.

Agriár, *va.* 1. To make sour or tart. 2. (Met.) To make peevish, to irritate, to exasperate.

Agricultór, **ra**, *s.* Husbandman or woman.

Agricultúra, *sf.* Agriculture, husbandry.

Agridúlce, *a.* Between sweet and sour.

Agrifólio, *sm.* (Bot.) Holly-tree. Ilex aquifolium *L.*

Agrilládo, **da**, *a.* Chained; put in irons.

Agrillárse, *vr.* V. *Grillarse.*

Agríllo, **la**, *a.* (Dim.) Sourish, tartish.

Agrimensór, *sm.* Surveyor; a measurer of land; a director of buildings.

Agrimensúra, *sf.* Art of surveying land.

Agrimónia, *sf.* (Bot.) Agrimony, liverwort. Agrimonia *L.*

Agrío, **ría**, *a.* 1. Sour, acrid. 2. (Met.) Rough, craggy; applied to a road full of stones and brambles. 3. (Met.) Sharp, rude, unpleasant.

Una respuesta agria, A smart reply. 4. Brittle, apt to break, unmalleable, inductile; applied to metals. 5. Harsh, graceless; applied to colours.

Agrío, *sm.* The acid or acrid juice of fruits. *Agrios*, orchard or plantation of sour fruit-trees.

Agrión, *sm.* (Alb.) Nerve or tumor in the joint of a horse's knee.

Agripalma, *sf.* (Bot.) Motherwort.

Agrisetádo, da, *a.* Flowered, like silks.

Agropíla, *sm.* German bezoar.

Agrupár, *va.* To group, to dispose and unite figures in a picture.

Agrúra, *sf.* 1. Acidity; the sour juice of certain fruits. 2. A group of trees which yield fruit of a sourish taste.

A'gua, *sf.* 1. Water. 2. (Quim.) Liquor distilled from herbs, flowers, or fruit. *Agua de azahar*, Orange flower water. 3. Lustre of diamonds. 4. (Naút.) Leak. *Agua ardiente*, Brandy. *Agua fuerte*, Aqua fortis. *Agua regia*, Aqua regia. *Agua bendita*, Holy water. *Agua va*, A notice to passengers that water is going to be thrown. *Agua viva*, running water.—*pl.* 1. Mineral waters in general. 2. Clouds in silk and other stuffs. 3. Urine. 4. Tide. *Aguas muertas*, Neap-tides. *Aguas vivas*, Spring-tides. *Entre dos aguas*, Between wind and water; in doubt, perplexed.

A'gua Abáxo, *ad.* Down the stream.

A'gua Arríba, *ad.* 1. Against the stream. 2. (Met.) Up hill; with great difficulty.

Aguacáte, *sm.* 1. (Bot.) Vegetable marrow, an American fruit, resembling a large pea. 2. Emerald, shaped as a pear.

Aguacéro, *sm.* A short heavy shower of rain.

Aguácha, *sf.* (Bax. Arag.) A pool of stagnant and corrupted water.

Aguachírle, *sf.* 1. Small inferior wine, consisting of the washings of the wine-press. 2. Slipslop; any bad liquor.

Aguacibéra, *sf.* (Agr. Arag.) A piece of ground sowed when dry, and afterwards irrigated.

Aguacíl, *sm.* A constable. V. *Alguacil.*

Agúada, *sf.* 1. (Naút.) Water-provisions on board a ship. *Hacer aguada*, To water. 2. (Naút.) Port or place whither ships go to water. 3. (Pint.) Sketch, outline.

Aguadéras, *sf. pl.* 1. Frames in which jars of water are carried by horses. 2. The four largest and principal feathers of a hawk.

Aguadéro, *sm.* 1. Watering-place for cattle. 2. (Naút.) Watering-port for ships.

Aguadíja, *sf.* Limpid humour in pimples or sores.

Aguádo, da, *a.* 1. Watered. 2. Drinking no liquor but water.

Aguadór, *sm.* 1. Water-carrier, who carries water to the houses. 2. (Mil.) *Aguador del real*, Sutler. 3. Bucket of a water-wheel.

Aguadúcho, *sm.* 1. Water-course, rush of water. 2. Place where earthen vessels with drinking water are kept.

Aguadúra, *sf.* Disease in horses arising from a surfeit of water.

Aguáge, *sm.* (Naút.) Rapid current of sea-water.

Aguájas, *sf. pl.* Ulcers above the hoofs of horses.

Aguamaníl, *sm.* Water jug of metal or earth for a wash-hand stand.

Aguamános, *sm.* Water for washing the hands. *Dar aguamanos*, To procure water for washing the hands.

Aguameládo, da, *a.* Washed or rubbed over with water and honey.

Aguamíel, *sf.* Hydromel, honey and water.

Aguanáfa, *sf.* (Mur.) Orange-flower water.

Aguaniéve, *sf.* 1. (Orn.) Bird of the family of magpies. 2. Sleet, small hail or snow: in this sense, it is properly two words, *agua nieve.*

Aguanosidád, *sf.* Aqueous humours in the body; serosity.

Aguanóso, sa, *a.* Aqueous; extremely moist.

Aguantár, *va.* 1. To sustain, to suffer, to bear; to maintain. 2. (Naút.) To carry a stiff sail.

Aguánte, *sm.* 1. Fortitude, firmness; vigour in bearing labour and fatigue. 2. Patience, sufferance. 3. (Naút.) *Navio de aguante*, A ship that carries a stiff sail.

Aguañón, *sm.* Constructor of hydraulic machines.

Aguapié, *sm.* Small wine. V. *Aguachirle.*

Aguár, *va.* 1. To mix water with wine, vinegar, or other liquor. 2. (Met.) To disturb or interrupt pleasure.

Aguardáda, *sf.* Expectation; the act of expecting.

Aguardár, *va.* 1. To expect, to wait for, to await. 2. To grant time, *e. g.* to a debtor.

Aguardentería, *sf.* Liquor shop where brandy is sold by retail.

Aguardentéro, ra, *s.* Keeper of a liquor-shop; retailer of brandy and strong liquors.

Aguardiénte, *sm.* Brandy.

Aguárdo, *sm.* Place where a fowler or sportsman waits to fire at the game.

Aguarrás, *sf.* Spirit of turpentine used in varnishing.

Aguárse, *vr.* 1. To be inundated with water. 2. To get stiff after much fatigue; applied to horses or mules.

Aguatócha, *sf.* Fire-engine.

Aguatócho, *sm.* 1. Fire-engine. 2. Small quagmire.

Aguaviéntos, *sm.* (Bot.) Yellow sage-tree.

Aguaxáque, *sm.* A sort of ammoniac gum.

Aguaytadór, ra, *s.* (Bax.) Spy; one sent to watch the motions and conduct of others.

Aguaytamiénto, *sm.* The act of spying.

Aguaytár, *va.* To search or discover by close examination or artifice.

Aguáza, *sf.* 1. Aqueous humour. 2. Juice extracted from trees by incision.

Aguazál, *sm.* V. *Pantano.*

Aguazárse, *vr.* To be covered with water.

Aguázo (*pintura de*), Painting drawn with gum-water of a dull, cloudy colour.

Aguazóso, sa, *a.* Aqueous; extremely moist.

Aguazúr, *sm.* (Mur.) Kind of dark green large leaved barilla plant.

Aguciár, *va.* To desire or solicit with eagerness.

Agudaménte, *ad.* 1. Sharply, lively. 2. Acutely, ingeniously.

Agudéza, *sf.* 1. Keenness or sharpness of instruments. 2. Acuteness, force of intellect. 3. Witty saying. 4. Acidity of fruit and plants.

Agudíllo, lla; to, ta, *a.* (Dim.) A little sharp, witty, or sprightly.

Agúdo, da, *a.* 1. Sharp-pointed, keen-edged. 2. (Met.) Acute, witty. 3. (Met.) Dangerous,

e. g. an acute disease. 4. Brisk, ready, active.

Agüelo, la, *s.* (Ant.) Grand father or mother.

Agüera, *sf.* (Agr. Arag.) Channel or trench for conveying water to a piece of ground.

Agüero, *sm.* Augury, prognostication.

Aguerrido, da, *a.* Inured to war.

Aguerrir, *va.* To accustom to war.

Aguijáda, *sf.* 1. Spur, goad. 2. Stimulation, excitement, pungency.

Aguijadór, ra, *s.* One that goads or stimulates.

Aguijadúra, *sf.* Stimulation; the act of exciting.

Aguijár, *va.* 1. To prick, to spur, to goad. 2. To incite, to stimulate.—*vn.* To march, or go fast.

Aguijatório, ria, *a.* (For.) Stimulating; applied to an order from a superior to an inferior court.

Aguijón, *sm.* 1. Sting of a bee, wasp, &c. 2. Prick, spur, goad. *Dar ó tirar coces contra el aguijon*, To kick against the spur or goad.

Aguijonázo, *sm.* Thrust with a goad.

Aguijoneár y Aguijonár, *va.* V. *Aguijár.*

Aguijoncíllo, *sm.* (Dim.) Petty exciter.

Águila, *sf.* 1. Eagle. *Ve mas que un aguila*, He is more sharp-sighted than an eagle. 2. A gold coin with an eagle of the reign of Charles V. 3. Principal standard of the ancient Romans. 4. (Astr.) A northern constellation.

Aguiláldo, *sm.* V. *Aguinaldo.*

Aguileño, ña, *a.* 1. Aquiline; when applied to the nose, hooked. 2. Resembling or belonging to an eagle.

Aguilílla, *sf.* A little eagle; an eaglet.

Aguilúcho, *sm.* 1. Eaglet, a young eagle. 2. Hobby. Falco subbuteo *L.*

Aguinaldo, *sm.* New-year's gift, Christmas-box.

Aguisár, *va.* (Ant.) 1. To dress, to arrange, to adjust. 2. To cook or provide provisions.

Agüíta, *sf. Dim. de agua*, A little rain or mist.

Agúja, *sf.* 1. Needle, bodkin. 2. Spire of an obelisk or pyramid: steeple. 3. Sort of paste, pointed at both ends. 4. Needle-fish, horn-fish. 5. Needle-shell. 6. Hand of a watch; style of a dial. 7. Rod in a bee-hive. *Agúja de marear*, (Naút.) A mariner's compass. *Agúja de camara*, (Naút.) A hanging compass. *Agúja capotera*, (Naút.) Sailing-needle. *Agúja de relinga*, (Naút.) Boltrope-needle. *Agúja de hacer medias*, Knitting-needle. *Agúja de pastor*, (Bot.) Shepherd's needle, Venus' comb. Scandix pecten *L.*—*pl.* 1. Ribs of the fore-quarter of an animal. 2. Distemper of horses affecting the legs, neck, and throat. 3. A sort of cotton stuff, made at Aleppo. *Vino de agujas*, Wine of a sharp, acrid taste.

Agujár, *va.* To prick with a needle.

Agujázo, *sm.* Prick with a needle.

Agujerázo, *sm.* A large or wide hole.

Agujereár y Agujerár, *va.* To pierce, to bore, to make holes.

Agujeríco, íllo, y uélo, *sm.* (Dim.) A small hole.

Agujéro, *sm.* 1. Hole in clothes, walls, &c. 2. Needle-maker, needle-seller. 3. Pin-case; needle-case.

Agujéta, *sf.* String or strap of leather; a lace.—*pl.* 1. Drink-money given to post-boys or drivers of mail-coaches. 2. Pains felt in consequence of fatigue.

Agujetería, *sf.* Shop where leather straps, laces, or girths, called *agujetas*, are made or sold.

Agujetéro, ra, *sm.* Maker or seller of *agujetas* or laces.

Agujón, *sm.* (Aum.) A large needle.

Aguosidád, *sf.* Lymph, a transparent colourless liquor in the human body.

Aguóso, sa, *a.* Aqueous.

Agustíno, na, y Agustiniáno, na, *s.* Monk or nun of the order of St. Augustin.

Aguzadéra, *sf.* Whetstone.

Aguzadéro, *sm.* Haunt of wild boars, where they turn up the ground and whet their tusks.

Aguzadúra, *sf.* Whet; the act of whetting or sharpening a tool or weapon.

Aguzaniéve, *sf.* Wagtail, a small bird.

Aguzár, *va.* 1. To whet or sharpen a tool or weapon. 2. (Met.) To stimulate, to excite. *Aguzar el ingenio*, To sharpen the wit. *Aguzar las orejas*, To cock up the ears, to listen quickly, to attend to. *Aguzar la vista*, (Met.) To sharpen the sight.

Aguzonázo, *sm.* V. *Hurgonazo.*

Ah! *(Interj. de dolor.)* Ah! an interjection of grief.

Ahajár, *va.* V. *Ajár.*

Ahebrádo, da, *a.* Composed of parts like threads or fibres.

Ahechár, *va.* V. *Aechár.*

Aheleár, *va.* To give gall to drink, to make bitter.—*vn.* To taste very bitter like gall.

Ahembrádo, da, *a.* Effeminate. V. *Afeminado.*

Aherrojamiénto, *sm.* Chaining, putting in irons.

Aherrojár, *va.* To chain, to put in chains or irons.

Aherrumbrárse, *vr.* 1. To become ferruginous, to have the taste and colour of iron. 2. To be full of scoria.

Ahervorárse, *vr.* To be heated; applied to wheat and other sorts of grain.

Ahí, *ad.* There, in that place; in that. *De por ahi*, About that; indicating a common trifling thing.

Ahidalgádo, da, *a.* Gentlemanlike, noble.

Ahijádo, da, *s.* 1. Godchild. 2. One protected or peculiarly favoured.

Ahijadór, *sm.* One who puts a young animal to be nourished by others.

Ahijár, *va.* 1. To adopt as a child. 2. (Among shepherds) To put every lamb with its dam. 3. (Met.) To impute to one what he is not guilty of.—*vn.* 1. To beget children. 2. To bud, to shoot out.

Ahilárse, *vr.* 1. To grow or be faint for want of nourishment. 2. To grow sour; applied to leaven and bread. 3. To be weak; applied to plants. 4. To mould or become mouldy. *Ahilarse el vino*, To turn and grow ropy; applied to wine.

Ahílo, *sm.* Faintness; weakness for want of food.

Ahínco, *sm.* Earnestness, eagerness, with which a thing is solicited or done.

Ahirmár, *va.* (Carp.) V. *Afirmar.*

Ahitár, *va.* To surfeit; to overload the stomach.—*vr.* To be surfeited; to have an indigestion.

Ahitéra, *sf.* Violent or continued indigestion.

Ahíto, ta, *a.* 1. One that labours under an indigestion. 2. (Met.) Disgusted; tired of a person or thing.

Ahíto, *sm.* Indigestion; surfeit.

Ahobachonádo, da, *a.* Dull, slovenly; lazy.

Ahocinárse, *vr.* To run or flow precipitately, like torrents or floods through narrow passages.

Ahogadéro, *sm.* 1. Strangling rope used by

hangmen. 2. Crowd of people, or place difficult to breathe in. 3. Necklace. 4. Throat-band; a part of the headstall of a bridle or halter.

Ahogadízo, za, *a.* Harsh, unpalatable; applied to sour fruit. *Carne ahogadiza*, Flesh of animals suffocated, or drowned.

Ahogádo, da, *a.* Stifled, suffocated. *Carnero ahogado*, Stewed mutton. *Dar mate ahogado*, To pin up the king at the game of chess; (Met.) To insist upon things being done without delay. *Estar ahogado ó verse ahogado*, To be overwhelmed with business.

Ahogadór, ra, *s.* Suffocater.

Ahogamiénto, *sm.* Suffocation; the act of suffocating. *Ahogamiénto de la madre*, Hysterics, an hysteric fit.

Ahógar, *va.* To choak, to throttle, to kill by stopping the breath. 2. (Met.) To oppress. 3. (Met.) To quench, to extinguish. 4. To water plants to excess. 5. (Naut.) To founder, to go to the bottom. [affliction.

Ahógo, *sm.* Oppression, anguish, pain, severe

Ahoguíjo, *sm.* Squinancy; a quinsy.

Ahoguío, *sm.* Oppression in the breast which hinders breathing with freedom.

Ahojár, *vn.* To eat the leaves of trees; applied to cattle.

Ahombrádo, da, *a.* Masculine; applied to a woman of masculine features and manners.

Ahondár, *va.* To sink, to deepen.—*vn.* 1. To penetrate far into a thing. 2. (Met.) To proceed or advance in the knowledge of things.

Ahóra, *ad.* Now, at present, actually. *Ahóra ahóra*, Just now. *Ahora ahora empezó el sermon*, The sermon began this moment. *Por ahora*, For the present. *Ahora bien*, Well, granted, nevertheless.

Ahóra, *conj. dis.* Whether, or. *Ahora sigas por la iglesia, ahora emprendas la carrera de las armas, ahora sirvas al rey en su palacio, siempre te serán útiles las estudios*, Whether you follow the church, or the military profession, or serve the king in his palace, studies will always be useful to you.

Ahorcádo, *sm.* Hanged man. [tioner.

Ahorcadór, *sm.* Hangman, the public execu-

Ahorcadúra, *sf.* The act of hanging. [ged.

Ahorcajárse, *vr.* To sit a-stride, or stride-leg-

Ahorcár, *va.* 1. To hang, to kill by suspending by the neck. 2. To lay aside clothes, to wear them no longer. *Ahorcar los habitos*, To abandon the ecclesiastical garb for another profession. *Que me ahorquen si lo hago*, Hang me if I do.—*vr.* To be vexed or irritated.

Ahormár, *va.* 1. To fit or adjust to a form. 2. To wear clothes or shoes until they fit easy. 3. (Met.) To bring one to a sense of his duty.

Ahornár, *va.* To put into an oven to be baked. —*vr.* To be scorched or burnt in the oven without being baked inwardly; applied to bread or baked meat.

Ahorquilládo, da, *a.* Forked; in the shape of a fork.

Ahorquillár, *va.* To stay, to prop up with forks.—*vr.* To become forked.

Ahorrádo, da, *a.* Unembarrassed; free from impediments.

Ahorrádor, ra, *s.* Liberator, emancipator.

Ahorramiénto, *sm.* Emancipation, enfranchisement.

Ahorrár, *va.* 1. To enfranchise, to emancipate. 2. To economize. 3. To shun labour, danger, or difficulties. 4. Among graziers, to give the elder shepherds leave to keep a certain number of sheep in the pastures.

Ahorratívo, va, *a.* Frugal, thrifty, saving. *Andar ó ir á la ahorrativa*, To be on the saving hand, to go frugally to work.

Ahorratíva y Ahórro, *s.* 1. Parsimony, frugality. 2. Saving: that which is saved or spared.

Ahótas, *ad.* (Ant.) V. *A' la verdad.*

Ahoyadór, *sm.* One that makes holes for the purpose of planting.

Ahoyadúra, *sf.* The act of making holes in the ground. [trees.

Ahoyár, *va.* To make holes in the ground for

Ahuchadór, ra, *s.* Hoarder; a churl.

Ahuchár, *va.* To hoard up any thing saved.

Ahuecamiénto, *sm.* Excavation; the act of cutting into hollows, or forming hollows.

Ahuecár, *va.* 1. To excavate, to hollow, to scoop out. 2. To loosen a thing which was close pressed; to render wool spungy by combing or beating it.—*vr.* To grow haughty; to be proud or elated; to be puffed up with pride. [A sea-fish.

Ahumáda, *sf.* 1. Signal given with smoke. 2.

Ahumár, *va.* To smoke, to cure in smoke.—*vn.* To smoke, to emit smoke.

Ahún, Ahúnque, V. *Aún, Aúnque.* [shaped.

Ahusádo, da, *a.* Formed as a spindle, spindle-

Ahusár, *va.* To make a thing as slender as a spindle.—*vr.* To taper; to be shaped like a spindle. [ens away.

Ahuyentadór, ra, *s.* One that drives or fright-

Ahuyentár, *va.* 1. To drive away, to put to flight. *Ahuyentar los pazaros ó las moscas*, To scare away birds or flies. 2. (Met.) To overcome a passion, to banish care.

Aí, *ad.* V. *Allí.*

Aijádo, *sf.* Goad. V. *Aguijáda.*

Aínas, *ad.* (Vulg.) Well-nigh; almost.

Aínde, *ad.* (Ant.) V. *Adelante.*

Airadaménte, *ad.* Angrily; in an angry manner. [grow angry.

Airárse, *vr.* To put one's self in a passion; to

Aisládo, da, *a.* Insulated; embarrassed.

Aislár, *va.* 1. To surround with water. 2. To insulate.

Ajáda, *sf.* A sauce, made of bread steeped in water, garlic, and salt.

Ajamiénto, *sm.* Disfiguration; the act of disfiguring; deformity.

Ajár, *sm.* Garlic-field; plantation of garlic.

Ajár, *va.* 1. To spoil, to mar, to tarnish. 2. To abuse, to treat with injurious language. *Ajar la vanidad á alguno*, To pull down one's pride.

Ajázo, *sm.* A large head of garlic.

Ajéro, *sm.* Vender of garlic.

Ajéte, *sm.* 1. Young or tender garlic. 2. Sauce made of garlic.

Ajiacéyte, *sm.* Mixture of garlic and oil.

Ajicóla, *sf.* Glue made of cuttings or scraps of gloves, or leather boiled with garlic.

Ajilimóge ó Ajilimógili, *sm.* Sauce of pepper and garlic made for stewed meat.

Ajíllo, *sm.* Tender young garlic.

Ajipuérro, *sm.* Leek. V. *Puerro.*

A'jo, *sm.* 1. (Bot.) Garlic. 2. Garlic-sauce for meat. 3. (Met.) Paint for ladies. 4. (Met.) Affair discussed or treated upon by many. *Revolver el ajo ó el ruido,* To stir up new disturbances. *Ajo blanco,* dish made of bruised garlic, bread, oil, and water.

Ajobár, *va.* To carry upon one's back loads of great weight. [2. A heavy load.

Ajóbo, *sm.* 1. The act of carrying heavy loads.

Ajofáyna, *sf.* V. *Aljofayna.*

Ajólio, *sm.* Sauce made of oil and garlic.

Ajónje, *sm.* Birdlime; a glutinous substance extracted from the low carline thistle.

Ajonjéra ó Ajongéro, *sf.* (Bot.) The low carline thistle. Carlina acaulis *L.*

Ajónjoli y Aljónjoli, *sm.* (Bot.) The oily purging grain. Sesamum orientale *L.*

Ajoquéso, *sm.* Dish made of garlic and cheese.

Ajorár, *va.* To carry off by violence.

Ajórcas, *sf.* V. *Axórcas.*

Ajordár, *va.* (Arag.) To bawl, to cry out.

Ajornaládo, da, *a.* Hired to labour for daily wages.

Ajornalár, *va.* To hire by the day.

Ajuágas, *sf. pl.* Spavin; a disease in horses.

Ajuanetádo, da, *a.* Having bony protuberances on the joints of the feet.

Ajuár, *sm.* 1. Apparel and furniture which a bride brings to her husband. 2. Household furniture.

Ajudiádo, da, *a.* Jewish, resembling Jews.

Ajuiciádo, da, *a.* Judicious, prudent.

Ajuiciár, *va.* To proceed with judgment and prudence.

Ajuntamiénto, (Ant.) V. *Juntamiénto.*

Ajuntár, V. *Juntar.*

Ajustadaménte, *ad.* Justly, exactly, rightly.

Ajustádo, da, *a.* Exact, right, well fitted; stingy. *Es un hombre ajustado,* He is a man of strict morals.

Ajustadór, *sm.* Close waistcoat, jacket.

Ajustamiénto, *sm.* 1. Adjustment, agreement. 2. Settling or liquidation of accounts. 3. Writing which contains the settlement of accounts.

Ajustár, *va.* 1. To regulate, to adjust. 2. To make an agreement. 3. To reconcile. 4. To examine and audit accounts. 5 To settle and liquidate a balance. 6. To press close, to oppress. 7. To fit or adjust clothes.—*vr.* 1. To come to an agreement, to settle matters. 2. To conform one's opinion to that of another. 3. To approach, to draw near a place or thing.

Ajúste, *sm.* 1. Proportion of the constituent parts of a thing. 2. Agreement, contract.

Ajusticiár, *va.* To execute a malefactor, to put him to death.

A'l, *art.* 1. An article formed by a syncope of the preposition *á* and the article *el,* and placed before nouns, &c.; *e. g. El juez debe castigar al delinquente,* The judge ought to punish the delinquent. 2. An Arabic article corresponding to the Spanish articles *el* and *la* in compound words; *e. g. Alfaharero,* a potter. 3. Used in verbs of motion instead of the Latin preposition *ad: e. g. Voy al rio,* I go to the river. 4. Used with the infinitive of divers verbs; *e. g. Alamanecer,* At the dawn of day.

Al, *Pron. indec.* (Ant.) Other, contrary, V. *Otro* and *Demas. Por al,* V. *Por tanto.*

A'la, *sf.* 1. Wing; aisle. 2. Row or file. 3. (Fort.) Flank. 4. Brim of the hat. 5. Auricle, the external fleshy part of the ear. *A'las del Corazon,* (Anat.) Auricles of the heart. 6. Fin of a fish. *A'la de mezanza,* (Naút.) A driver.—*pl.* (Naút.) Upper-studding sails. *Alas de gavia,* Main-top-studding sails. *Alas de velacho,* Fore-studding sails. *Alas de sobremezana,* Mizen-top-studding sails. *Alas de proa,* Head of the ship. *A'las,* Protection; boldness arising from protection: (Poet.) Velocity.

Alá, *sm.* Alla or Allah, an Arabic word, signifying God.

Alá, *int.* Holla; a word used in calling. V. *Allá.*

Alabádo, *sm.* Hymn sung in praise of the sacrament when it is put into the tabernacle.

Alabadór, ra, *s.* Praiser, applauder.

Alabancióso, sa, *a.* Boastful, vainly ostentatious.

Alabandína, *sf.* Manganese, a semi-metal.

Alabánza, *sf.* Praise, the act of praising.

Alabár, *va.* To praise, to applaud.—*vr.* To praise one's self, to display one's own worth.

Alabárda, *sf.* 1. Halberd, a kind of battle-axe. 2. Serjeant's place, from a halberd having formerly been borne by serjeants.

Alabardázo, *sm.* A blow with a halberd.

Alabardéro, *sm.* Halberdier, armed with a halberd.

Alabastrádo, da, *a.* Resembling alabaster.

Alabastrína, *sf.* A thin sheet or plate of alabaster.

Alabastríno, na, *a.* Made of or like alabaster.

Alabástro, *sm.* Alabaster; gypsum.

A'labe, *sm.* 1. Branch of an olive-tree bent down and reaching to the ground. 2. Flier of a water-mill, which serves to set it in motion.

Alabeárse, *vr.* To warp, to grow bent or crooked.

Alabéga, *sf.* (Bot.) Sweet basil. Ocymum basilicum *L.*

Alabéo, *sm.* Warping; the act of warping, and the state of being warped.

Alabésa, *sf.* A sort of pike formerly used, and so called from its being made in Alaba.

Alabiádo, da, *a.* Lipped or ragged; applied to uneven coined money.

Alacéna y Alhacéna, *sf.* 1. Cupboard. 2. (Naút.) Locker, a small box in the cabin and sides of a ship.

Alácha, *sf.* Shad, may-fish. Clupea alosa parva *L.*

Alaciár, *vn.* V. *Enlaciar.*

Alacrán, *sm.* 1. Scorpion, a small poisonous animal. 2. Ring of the mouth-piece of a bridle. 3. Stop or hook fixed to the rocker of organ-bellows, which serves to put them in motion. 4. Chain or link of a sleeve button.

Alacranádo, da, *a.* 1. Bit by a scorpion. 2. (Met.) Infected with some vice.

Alacranéra, *sf.* (Bot.) Mouse-ear, scorpion-grass. Myosotis scorpioides *L.*

Aláda, *sf.* Fluttering; motion of the wings.

Aladáres, *sm. pl.* Locks of hair which hang over the temples.

Aládo, da, *a.* Winged; that which has wings.

Aladráda, *sf.* Furrow or small trench made by the plough.

Aladrár, *va.* To plough.

Aládro, *sm.* 1. Plough. 2. Ploughed land.

Aladróque, *sm.* (Mur.) A fresh anchovy before it is put into pickle.

Alafía, *sf.* (Bax.) Pardon. *Pedir alafia,* To implore mercy and pardon.

A'laga, *sf.* A species of yellow wheat.
Alagaréro, *sm.* Party of horse making an excursion into an enemy's country. V. *Algaréro.*
Alagartádo, da, *a.* Variegated; having a variety of colours similar to the skin of a lizard.
Alaíca, *sf.* (Arag.) Winged ant or pismire.
Alája, Alajár, &c. V. *Alhája, Alhajár*, &c.
Alajú, *sm.* Paste made of almonds, walnuts, honey, &c.
Aláma, *sf.* Gold or silver cloth.
Alamár, *sm.* Laced or embroidered button-hole.
Alambicádo, da, *a.* 1. Distilled. 2. (Met.) Given with a sparing hand, as if coming out of an alembic or still.
Alambicár, *va.* 1. To distil. 2. To investigate closely. *Alembicar los sesos*, To screw one's wits, to hammer one's brains.
Alambíque, *sm.* Alembic, still. *Por alambíque*, Sparingly, in a penurious manner.
Alambór, *sm.* (Ant. Fort.) Inside slope or talus of a ditch. V. *Escarpa.*
Alámbre, *sm.* 1. Copper. 2. Copper-wire. 3. Bells belonging to a flock of sheep. 4. File on which papers are strung.
Alaméda, *sf.* 1. Grove of poplar trees. 2. Public walk with rows of trees.
Alamín, *sm.* 1. Clerk of the market appointed to inspect weights and measures. 2. (And.) Architect, surveyor of buildings. 3. (Nav.) Farmer appointed to superintend irrigation or distribution of water.
Alamína, *sf.* A fine paid by the potters of Sevilla for exceeding the number of vessels to be baked at once in an oven. [&c.
Alaminálgo, *sm.* Office of a clerk, surveyor,
Alamíre, *sm.* Musical sign.
A'lamo, *sm.* (Bot.) Elm-tree. *A'lamo blanco*, White poplar. Populus alba *L. A'lamo temblon*, Aspen-tree, trembling poplar-tree. Populus tremula *L. A'lamo negro*, Black poplar-tree. Populus nigra *L.*
Alampárse, *vr.* To long, to show an anxious desire, especially in regard to eating and drinking.
Alamúd, *sm.* A bolt for fastening a door.
Alanceadór, *sm.* One who throws, casts, or darts. [or spear.
Alanceár, *va.* To dart, to wound with a dart
Alandál, Alánia, V. *Alhandal, Alhania.*
Alandreárse, *vr.* To become dry, stiff, and blanched; used of silk worms.
Aláno, na, *s.* Mastiff of a large kind.
Aláno, *a.* Belonging to the *Alans* or Vandals of the 5th century.
Alanzáda, *sf.* Acre of ground. V. *Aranzada.*
Alanzár, *va.* To throw lances; as in the ancient chivalrous games.
Alaquéca, *sf.* Stone brought from the Indies and applied externally to stem blood.
Alaquéques, *sm. pl.* Those who ransom slaves or captives.
Alár, *sm.* 1. Part of the roof which overhangs the wall. 2. Snare of horse-hair for catching partridges.
Alár, *va.* (Naút.) To hawl. V. *Alhar.*
Alára *(huévo en)*, Egg laid before its time; an egg without a shell. [raquiénto.
Alaráqua, Alaraquiénto, V. *Alharáco, Alha-*
Alárbe, *sm.* Clown; an unmannerly person.

Alárde, *sm.* 1. Review of soldiers. 2. Examination of the swarm, made by the bees, on leaving and returning to the hive. 3. Glory, ostentation, vanity. *Hacer alárde*, (Met.) To boast or brag of something.
Alardóso, sa, *a.* Ostentatious, boastful.
Alargadór, ra, *s.* One who enlarges, delays, protracts, or lengthens out a thing.
Alargamiénto, *sm.* The act of lengthening out, delaying, or protracting; enlargement.
Alargár, *va.* 1. To lengthen out, to make longer. 2. (Met.) To protract, to put off. 3. To increase a marked number or quantity. 4. To reach or hand a thing to another who is more distant. 5. To resign, to make over: yet in this sense *largar* is more used. 6. To advance; to send before. *Alargar la conversacion*, To spin out a conversation. *Alargar el salario*, To increase or augment the pay. *Alargar el cabo*, (Naút.) To pay out the cable.—*vr.* 1. To be prolonged; applied to time. *Se alargan los dias*, The days grow longer. 2. (Naút.) To sheer off.
Alarguéz, *sm.* (Bot.) Dog-rose, hip-tree. Rosa canina *L.*
Alaría, *sf.* A flat iron instrument used by potters to finish and polish their work.
Alarída, *sf.* Hue and cry, shouting of a multitude of people.
Alarído, *sm.* Outcry, shout.
Alarifázgo ó Alarifádgo, *sm.* Office of an *Alarífe* or architect and surveyor of buildings.
Alarífe, *sm.* Architect, surveyor of buildings, builder.
Alaríxes, *sf. pl.* A large sort of grapes.
Alárma, *sf.* (Mil.) Alarm, a sudden attack.
Alarmár, *va.* To alarm, to call to arms.
Alastrár, *va.* 1. To throw back the ears; applied to horses and mules. V. *Amusgar.* 2. (Naút.) To ballast. *Alastrar un navío*, To ballast a ship.—*vr.* To squat close to the ground to prevent being seen; applied to game.
Alatérno, *sm.* (Bot.) Mock-privet. [game.
Alatón, *sm.* 1. Latten, brass. 2. (Bot.) The fruit of the nettle or lote-tree.
Alatonéro, *sm.* (Bot.) Nettle or lote-tree Celtis orientalis *L.*
Alátron, *sm.* Froth or spume of saltpetre.
Alaváneo, *sm.* V. *Lavanco.*
Alavénse y Aláves, sa, *a.* Native of Alava.
Alaxór, *sm.* Ground rent or duty for the site of a house. [horse.
Alazán, na, *a.* Sorrel-coloured; applied to a
Alázo, *sm.* Stroke with the wings.
Alazór, *sm.* (Bot.) Bastard saffron. Carthamus cœruleus *L.*
A'lba, *sf.* 1. Dawn of day. 2. Alb or surplice worn by priests at the celebration of the mass.
Albáca, *sf.* (Bot.) Sweet basil. V. *Albahaca.*
Albacéa, *sm.* Testamentary executor. [cutor.
Albaceázgo, *sm.* Office of a testamentary exe-
Albacóra, *sm.* 1. A sea fish much resembling a tunny. 2. An early fig of the largest kind. V. *Breva.*
Albáda, *sf.* Music which young men in the country give their sweethearts at the break of day.
Albahàca, *sf.* (Bot.) Sweet basil. Ocymum basilicum *L. Albahàca aquática*, a sort of winter

thistle. *Albahaca salváge ó silvestre*, Stone or wild thistle.
ALBAHAQUÉRO, *sm.* A flowerpot with sweet basil.
ALBAHAQUÍLLA DEL RIO, *sf.* (Bot.) Cullen. Psoralea glandulosa *L.*
ALBALÁ, *s.* 1. Cocket, a warrant of entry. 2. A quittance, certificate. *Albala de guia*, A passport.
ALBANÉGA, *sf.* Net for enclosing the hair, or [catching partridges.
ALBAÑAL Y ALBAÑAR, *sm.* Sewer, common sewer; now corrupted to *shore*.
ALBAÑIL, *sm.* Mason, bricklayer.
ALBAÑILERÍA, *sf.* Masonry, trade, craft, and performance of a mason or bricklayer.
ALBAQUÍA, *sf.* Remnant; in collecting tithes, an odd portion which does not admit of division, as six or seven head of cattle.
ALBÁR, *a.* White, whitish. *Conejo albar*, A white rabbit. *Pino albar*, A white pine. This adjective is confined to a few nouns only.
ALBARÁN, *sm.* 1. Bill advertising that apartments are to let. 2. Note of hand or other private instrument.
ALBARAZÁDA, *sf.* A marble-coloured grape.
ALBARAZÁDO, DA, *a.* 1. Affected with the white leprosy. 2. Pale, pallid, declining from the natural complexion to a white colour.
ALBARÁZO, *sm.* White leprosy.
ALBÁRCA, *sf.* V. *Abarca.*
ALBARCOQUÉRO, *sm.* (Bot.) Apricot-tree.
ALBÁRDA, *sf.* 1. Pack-saddle for beasts of burthen. *Bestia de albárda*, Beast of burthen. 2. Broad slice of bacon with which fowls are covered when they are roasted.
ALBARDÁDO, DA, *a.* Applied to animals having a different coloured skin at the loins.
ALBARDÁR, *va.* 1. To put a pack-saddle on beasts of burthen. 2. To cover with large slices of bacon fowls which are to be roasted.
ALBARDÉLA, *sf.* Small saddle to tame colts.
ALBARDERÍA, *sf.* 1. A street, place, or shop where pack-saddles are made and sold. 2. The trade of a pack-saddle maker.
ALBARDÉRO, *sm.* Pack-saddle maker.
ALBARDÍLLA, *sf.* 1. Small pack-saddle. 2. The upper tire of masonry which covers the wall. 3. Border of a garden bed. 4. Small saddle made use of to tame colts. 5. Wool which grows on the back of sheep or lambs. 6. Earth which sticks to a ploughshare when the ground is wet. 7. Batter of eggs, flour, and sugar, with which hogs' tongues and feet are covered.—*pl.* Ridges of earth raised on the sides of deep foot-paths.
ALBARDÍN, *sm.* (Bot.) Matweed. Lygeum spartum *L.*
ALBARDÓN, *sm.* Pannel, a kind of pack-saddle.
ALBARDONCÍLLO, *sm.* A small pack-saddle.
ALBARÉJO Y ALBARÍGO, *sm.* (Mancha.) A sort of wheat which is very white.
ALBARICÓQUE, *sm.* (Bot.) Apricot. Prunus armeniaca *L.*
ALBARÍLLO, *sm.* 1. A tune played on the guitar, for country dances. 2. (Andal.) A small kind of apricots.
ALBARÍNO, *sm.* A composition of white paint formerly used by women.
ALBARRÁDA, *sf.* 1. A dry wall, fence, enclosure. 2. Ditch for defence in war.

ALBARRÁNA, *sf.* (Bot.) *Cebolla albarrana*, Squill. Scilla maritima *L.* *Torre albarrana*, A sort of watch-tower.
ALBARRÁZ, *sm.* (Bot.) Lousewort, stavesacre. Delphinium staphisagria *L.*
ALBATÁRA, *sf.* (Med.) Carbuncle in the urethra.
ALBATÓZA, *sf.* A small covered boat.
ALBAYALDÁDO, DA, *a.* Covered with ceruse or white lead.
ALBAYÁLDE, *sm.* White-lead, ceruse.
ALBÁYDA, *sf.* (Bot.) The shrubby gypsophila. Gypsophila perfoliata *L.*
ALBAZÁNO, NA, *a.* Of a dark chesnut colour.
ALBÁZO, *sm.* An ancient military term, implying an assault or attack at day-break.
ALBEÁR, *va.* To whiten. V. *Blanqueár.*
ALBÉDRIO, *sm.* 1. Free will possessed by man to choose what is good or bad. 2. Free will directed by caprice, and not by reason.
ALBELLÓN, *sm.* V. *Albañal.*
ALBÉNDA, *sf.* Hangings of white linen.
ALBENDÉRA, *sf.* 1. Woman who makes hangings of white linen. 2. A gadding idle woman.
ALBENGÁLA, *sf.* a sort of light crape or gauze worn in the turbans of the Moors in Spain.
ALBÉNTOLA, *sf.* A slight net, made of a very thin thread, for catching small fishes.
ALBÉRCA, *sf.* 1. Pool or pond where cattle drink. 2. (Castilla Vieja.) Sink, conduit for carrying off dirty water.
ALBÉRCHIGA ó ALBÉRCHIGO, *s.* (Bot.) Peach. Amygdalus Persica *L.*
ALBERCÓN, *sm.* (Aum.) A large pool or pond.
ALBERENGÉNA, *sf.* (Bot.) Mad-apple, egg-plant. Solanum melongena *L.*
ALBERGADÓR, RA, *s.* A lodging-house keeper.
ALBERGÁR, *va.* 1. To lodge. 2. To keep a lodging-house.—*vr.* To take a lodging.
ALBÉRGUE, *sm.* 1. Lodging-house. 2. Den for wild beasts. 3. Hospital or charity-school for orphans. 4. Place, space.
ALBERGUERÍA, *sf.* (Ant.) 1. Inn. 2. Hospital for travellers. V. *Posáda.*
ALBERGUÉRO, *sm.* (Ant.) Innkeeper.
ALBERICÓQUE, V. *Albaricóque.*
ALBÉRO, *sm.* 1. Whitish earth. 2. A cloth for cleaning plates and dishes.
ALBERQUÉRO, *sm.* One who takes care of the pond or pool where flax is steeped.
ALBERQUÍLLA, *sf.* (Dim.) A little pool or pond.
ALBEYTÁR, *sm.* Farrier, a veterinarian, a horse-doctor.
ALBEYTERÍA, *sf.* Veterinary art, farriery.
ALBICÁNTE, *a.* That which whitens or blanches.
ALBIGÉNSE, *sm.* Belonging to the sect of Albigenses, which sprang up in Albis in France, at the beginning of the 13th century.
ALBIHÁR, *sm.* (Bot.) Ox-eye. Buphthalmum *L.*
ALBÍLLA, *a.* Applied to an early white grape.
ALBÍLLO, *a.* Applied to the wine of a white grape.
ALBÍN, *sm.* Bloodstone; a sort of iron ore of a brown colour. Hæmatites.
ALBÍNA, *sf.* A marshy piece of ground covered with nitre in the summer season.
ALBÍNO, NA, *a.* A term applied to white people begotten by a white man and a negro or mulatto woman.
ALBÍS, (Met.) *Quedarse in albis*, To be frustrated in one's hopes, to be disappointed.

Albitána, *sf.* (Naút.) Apron. *Albitána del codaste*, (Naut.) Inner post.
A'lbo, ba, *a.* White, in a superior degree.
Albógue, *sm.* 1. A sort of pastoral flute, much used in Biscay. 2. A sort of martial music, played with two plates of brass resembling the *crotalum* of the ancients; a cymbal.
Alboguéro, ra, *s.* One who makes *albogues*, or pastoral flutes; or plays on them.
Albohól, *sm.* (Bot.) A species of bind-weed.
Albóndigas, *sf. pl.* Balls made of forced meat chopped small with eggs and spice.
Albondiguílla, *sf.* (Dim.) A small ball of forced meat.
Albór, *sm.* (Poet.) Whiteness; the state of being white.
Alboráda, *sf.* 1. Twilight, the first dawn of day. 2. (Mil.) Action fought at the dawn of day. 3. Music. V. *Albada*.
Alboreár, *vn.* To dawn, to begin to grow light.
Albórga, *sf.* A sort of sandal made of mat-weed.
Albornía, *sf.* A large glazed earthen jug.
Albornóz, *sm.* 1. A sort of coarse woollen stuff. 2. Cloak which forms part of the Moorish dress.
Alboronía, *sf.* Fried tomates, pumpkins and pimento, much used by labouring people.
Alboróque, *sm.* Regalement given at the conclusion of a bargain.
Alborotadaménte, *ad.* Noisily, confusedly.
Alborotádo y Alborotadízo, za, *a.* Of a restless disposition, turbulent.
Alborotadór, ra, *s.* Disturber, a violator of peace, one that causes tumults.
Alborotapuéblos, *sm.* 1. Disturber, mover of sedition. 2. (Fam.) A good natured person who always proposes feasts in companies and parties.
Alborotár, *va.* To disturb, to vex, to excite disturbances.
Alboróto, *sm.* Noise, disturbance, tumult, riot.
Alborozadór, ra, *s.* Promoter of mirth or merriment.
Alborozár, *va.* To exhilarate, to promote mirth or merriment.
Alborózo, *sm.* Joy, merriment, gaiety, rejoicing.
Albrícias, *sf. pl.* Reward given for some good news. *Ganar las albricias*, To obtain a reward for some good news.
Albudéca, *sf.* (Bot.) Pompion, pumpkin, gourd. Cucurbita pepo *L.*
Albuféra, *sf.* A lake formed by the tide.
Albugíneo, nea, *a.* Albugineous, albumenous, resembling the white of an egg, or white of the eye.
Albuhéra, *sf.* 1. Fresh water lake. 2. (Extrem.) Lake formed by water from the mountains.
Albúr, *sm.* 1. Dace, a river-fish. Cyprinus leuciscus. 2. A sort of game at cards.
Albúra, *sf.* Whiteness, state of being white.
Alburéro, *sm.* A player at the game *albures*.
Alburés, *sm. pl.* A game at cards played in the Spanish West Indies.
Alcabála, *sf.* 1. Excise, a duty per cent. paid on all saleable commodities. *Alcabála del viento*, Duty paid on goods sold by chance. *El caudal de Fulano está en alcabala de viento*, He lives upon what he earns without possessing any property. 2. A net. V. *Xábega*.
Alcabalatório, *sm.* Book of rates of the *alcabala*.
Alcabaléro, *sm.* One who farms or collects the *alcabala*; a tax-gatherer.
Alcabór, *sm.* Flue of a chimney.
Alcabúz, *sm.* Arquebuse, a hand-gun.
Alcacél ó Alcacér, *sm.* Green corn.
Alcachófa, *sf.* 1. (Bot.) Artichoke, the head of an artichoke. 2. Instrument serving to stop a flux of blood. 3. Fluted mallets used by rope-makers.
Alcachofádo, da, *a.* Resembling an artichoke.
Alcachofádo, *sm.* Dish of artichokes.
Alcachofál, *sm.* Ground where artichokes are reared.
Alcachofázo, *sm.* Blow with an artichoke.
Alcachoféra, *sf.* Artichoke.
Alcacíl, *sm.* (Bot.) Cardoon. Cynara cardunculus *L.*
Alcaház, *sm.* A large cage.
Alcahazáda, *sf.* A number of birds shut up in a cage.
Alcahazár, *va.* To shut up in a cage.
Alcahuéte, ta, *s.* 1. Pimp, procurer, bawd. 2. One that receives persons in his house who want concealment.
Alcahueteár y Alcahuetár, *va.* To bawd, to procure women.
Alcahuetería, *sf.* 1. Bawdry; the practice of procuring women. 2. The act of receiving and hiding persons who want concealment.
Alcahuetíllo, la, *s.* A little pimp, a little bawd.
Alcahuetón y Alcahuetázo, *sm.* (Aum.) A great pander, a great bawd.
Alcalaíno, na, *a.* Native of Alcala de Henares, Complutensian.
Alcaldáda, *sf.* 1. An inconsiderate action of an *Alcalde*. 2. Any word said, or action performed, with an air of authority.
Alcálde, *sm.* 1. Justice of peace or judge who administers justice in a town. 2. He who leads off a country dance. 3. Ringleader. *Tener al padre alcalde*, To enjoy the protection of a judge, or other man in power. 4. Game at cards.
Alcaldeár, *vn.* (Joc.) To play the alcalde.
Alcaldésa, *sf.* The wife of an *alcalde*.
Alcaldía, *sf.* Office and jurisdiction of an *alcalde*.
Alcali, *sm.* (Quim.) Alkali.
Alcalíno, na, y Alcalizádo, da, *a.* Alkaline, alkalized, that which has the qualities of alkali.
Alcám, *sm.* (Bot.) Coloquint, bitter apple, bitter gourd. Cucumis colocynthis *L.*
Alcamonías, *sf. pl.* 1. Various kinds of aromatic seeds used in the kitchen, as anise, caraway, cumin, and other stimulants. 2. V. *Alcahuete*.
Alcána, *sf.* 1. A place where shops are kept for the sale of goods. 2. V. *Alheña*.
Alcánce, *sf.* 1. The act of following and overtaking a person. 2. Balance of an account. 3. Arm's length, distance of the length of an arm. 4. Range of fire-arms. 5. Capacity, ability. 6. An extraordinary courier sent after an ordinary messenger to overtake him. 7. Wound which horses give themselves by striking their fore-legs with their feet in travelling. *Ir á los alcances*, To be at one's heels. *No poderle dar un alcance*, To be unable to get sight of one.
Alcánces, *sf. pl.* Profits, gains by any thing.
Alcancía, *sf.* 1. Money-box. 2. Cavalcade, a procession on horseback. 3. Earthen-ware balls filled with ashes and used in cavalry sports, by catching them on shields. 4. (Mil.)

Stink-pot; inflamed combustible balls thrown among the enemy.
ALCANCIÁZO, *sm.* Blow with a money-box or ball.
ALCÁNDARA, *sf.* Perch or roost of a falcon.
ALCÁNDIA, *sf.* (Bot.) Millet, Turkey millet. Holcus sorghum *L.*
ALCANDIÁL, *sm.* Ground sown with millet.
ALCANFÓR, *sm.* Camphor, a gum obtained from the camphor-tree. Laurus camphora *L.*
ALCANFORÁDA, *sf.* Camphor-tree.
ALCANFORÁDO, DA, *a.* Camphorated, impregnated with camphor.
ALCÁNTARA, *sf.* A wooden cover for velvet webs in the loom.
ALCANTARÍLLA, *sf.* 1. A small bridge. 2. A sink, a drain. 3. A sewer or conduit under ground.
ALCANTARILLÁDO, *sm.* Work made in the form of an arch or vault under ground.
ALCANTARÍNO, NA, *a.* Reformed barefooted Franciscan.
ALCANZADÍZO, ZA, *a.* That which is within reach, which may be easily reached. *Hacerse alcanzadizo,* (Met.) To affect ignorance, to feign not to understand something.
ALCANZÁDO, DA, *a.* Necessitous, wanting.
ALCANZADÓR, RA, *s.* Pursuer, one who follows and overtakes another.
ALCANZADÚRA, *sf.* 1. A tumour in the heel or pastern of a horse. 2. Wound or contusion arising from a horse's cutting the foreheel with the hind shoe.
ALCANZAMIÉNTO, *sm.* V. *Alcance.*
ALCANZÁR, *va.* 1. To follow or pursue people until they are found out. 2. To reach a thing, to extend the hand to take it. 3. To obtain, to possess power of obtaining a thing desired. 4. To comprehend. 5. To be creditor of a balance. 6. To know a long while. *Yo alcancé á Pedro, quando empecé á estudiar;* I knew Peter when I began my studies.—*vn.* 1. To come in for a share. 2. To suffice, to be sufficient. 3. To reach; applied to a ball. 4. *Alcanzar en dias,* To survive.—*vr.* To wound the pasterns with the feet, as horses do in travelling. *Alcanzarsele poco á alguno, ó no alcanzarsele mas,* To be of a weak understanding.
ALCAPÁRRA Y ALCAPÁRRO, *s.* (Bot.) 1. Caper-bush. Capparis *L.* 2. Caper, the bud of the caper-bush.
ALCAPARRÁDO, DA, *a.* Dressed with capers.
ALCAPARRÁL, *sm.* Ground planted with caper-bushes.
ALCAPARRÓN, *sm.* (Aum.) A large caper.
ALCAPARRÓSA, *sf.* Earnest, ratifying a bargain.
ALCARAHUÉYA, *sf.* (Bot.) Caraway-seed. Carum carvi *L.*
ALCARAVÁN, *sm.* (Orn.) Bittern. Ardea stellaris *L.*
ALCARAVANÉRO, *sm.* A hawk trained to pursue the bittern.
ALCARAVÉA Y ALCAROVÉA, *sf.* (Bot.) V. *Alcarahueya.*
ALCARCÉÑA, *sf.* (Bot.) Officinal tare, bitter vetch. Ervum ervilia *L.*
ALCARCHÓFA, *sf.* V. *Alcachofa.*
ALCARCÍL, *sm.* V. *Alcacil.*
ALCARRACÉRO, RA, *s.* 1. Potter who makes or sells pitchers and earthen-ware. 2. Shelf on which earthen-ware is placed.
ALCARRÁZA, *sf.* Pitcher or jug not glazed, in which water is put to be kept cool.
ALCARRÉÑO, NA, *a.* Belonging to Alcarria.
ALCATÍFA, *sf.* 1. A sort of fine carpets. 2. Layer of rubbish put under bricks or tiles in flooring. 3. Roof of a house.
ALCATRÁZ, *sm.* 1. Pelican. Pelecanus onocrotalus *L.* 2. A sea-fish taken on the coast of India.
ALCAUCÍL, *sm.* Wild artichoke. V. *Alcacil.*
ALCAYÁTA, *sf.* A hooked nail; a hook.
ALCAYATÁZO, *sm.* Blow with a hook or hooked nail.
ALCAYCERÍA, *sf.* Market-place for raw silk.
ALCÁYDE, *sm.* 1. Governor of a castle or fort. 2. Jailer, the keeper of a jail.
ALCAYDÉSA, *sf.* Wife of a governor or jailer.
ALCAYDÍA, *sf.* 1. Office or place of a governor, and the district of his jurisdiction. 2. Ancient duty paid for the passage of cattle.
ALCAZÁR, *sm.* 1. Palace, castle. 2. Fort, fortress. 3. (Naút.) Quarter-deck.
ALCAZÚZ, *sm.* V. *Regaliza.*
A'LCE, *sm.* At cards, portion cut off after being shuffled.
ALCEDÓN, *sm.* Halcyon, or king's fisher, a bird which breeds on the sea-coast. Alcedo *L.*
ALCHIMÍA, *sf.* Alchemy. V. *Alquimia.*
ALCÍNO, *sm.* (Bot.) Wild basil. Clinopodium vulgare *L.*
ALCIÓN, *sm.* Halcyon. V. *Alcedón.*
ALCÓBA, *sf.* 1. Alcove; a recess. 2. Bed-room. 3. Case in which the tongue of a balance moves to regulate the weight.
ALCOBÁZA, *sf.* (Aum.) A large alcove.
ALCOBÍLLA Y ALCOBÍTA, (Dim.) A small alcove.
ALCOHÉLA, *sf.* V. *Endibia.*
ALCOHÓL, *sm.* 1. Antimony, a mineral substance. 2. Alcohol, highly rectified spirit of wine.
ALCOHOLÁDO, DA, *a.* Being of a darker colour around the eyes than the rest of the body.
ALCOHOLADÓR, RA, *s.* One employed in rectifying spirits, or who paints and dyes with antimony.
ALCOHOLÁR, *va.* 1. To paint or dye with antimony. 2. To rectify spirits. 3. To reduce to an impalpable powder.—*vn.* To pass in a tilt or carrousel the adverse party of combatants.
ALCOHOLÉRA, *sf.* Vessel for antimony or alcohol.
ALCOHOLIZÁR, *va.* To alcoholise. V. *Alcoholar.*
ALCOMENÍAS, (Ant.) V. *Alcamonias.*
ALCÓN, *sm.* Falcon. V. *Halcón.*
ALCORÁN, *sm.* Alcoran, the book of the Mohammedan precepts and credenda.
ALCORANÍSTA, *sm.* One who expounds the Alcoran, or the law of Mohammed.
ALCORNOCÁL, *sm.* Plantation of cork-trees.
ALCORNÓQUE, *sm.* 1. (Bot.) Cork-tree. Quercus suber *L.* 2. (Met.) A person of rude, uncouth manners.
ALCORNOQUÉÑO, ÑA, *a.* Belonging to the cork-tree.
ALCOROVÍA, *sf.* V. *Alcaravea.*
ALCORÓQUE, *sm.* (Ant.) Cork-wood clogs or soles.
ALCÓRZA, *sf.* 1. A paste for sweetmeats made of sugar and starch. 2. A piece of sweetmeat. *Parece hecho de alcorza,* He looks as if he was made of sweet-meat; a chicken.
ALCORZÁR, *va.* To cover with a paste of sugar and starch.
ALCOTÁN, *sm.* Lanner, a bird of prey. Falco lanarius *L.*
ALCOTÁNA, *sf.* Pick-axe.
ALCOTANCÍLLO, *sm.* Lanneret, a young lanner.
ALCOTONÍA, *sf.* (Ant.) Cotton-cloth. V. *Cotonia.*

Alcrebíte, *sm.* Sulphur, brimstone, V. *Azufre.*
Alcrívis, *sm.* A small tube at the back of a forge through which runs the pipe of the bellows.
Alcróco, *sm.* (Ant.) V. *Azafran.*
Alcubílla, *sf.* Reservoir of an aqueduct.
Alcucéro, ra, *s.* One who makes and sells oil-bottles, cruets, and phials, which in Spain are commonly made of tin.
Alcucílla, *sf.* A small oil-bottle, an oil-cruet.
Alcúñar y Alcurnía, *sf.* (Ant.) Family, lineage, race.
Alcúza, *sf.* Oil-bottle which contains the oil for daily use.
Alcuzáda, *sf.* A cruet with oil; as much oil as fills a cruet.
Alcuzázo, *sm.* Blow given with an oil-bottle.
Alcuzcúz y Alcuzcúzu, *sm.* Flour, water, and honey, made into balls, and esteemed by the Moors.
Alcuzéro, ra, *a.* Belonging to an oil-bottle.
Alcuzón, *sm.* (Aum.) A large oil-bottle.
A'lda, *sf.* V. *Halda.*
Aldába, *sf.* 1. Knocker, a hammer on the door for strangers to strike. 2. A cross-bar to secure doors and windows. *Caballo de aldaba,* A steed, a horse for state or war.
Aldabáda, *sf.* 1. Rap given with the knocker. 2. Sudden fear or apprehension of approaching danger; stings of conscience.
Aldabázo, *sm.* Violent rap with the knocker.
Aldabeár, *va.* To rap or knock at the door with the knocker.
Aldabías, *sf. pl.* Beams horizontally placed on two walls, on which a hanging partition is raised.
Aldabílla, *sf.* A small knocker or rapper.
Aldabón, *sm.* 1. A large knocker or rapper. 2. An iron handle of trunks or chests.
Aldéa, *sf.* A small village, a hamlet, a large farm.
Aldeanaménte, *ad.* In the village style; rustic.
Aldeaniégo, ga, *a.* Belonging to a hamlet.
Aldeáno, na, *s.* Villager, an inhabitant of a village.
Aldeár, *va.* V. *Haldear.*
Aldebarán, *sm.* (Astr.) Aldebaran or bull's-eye, a fixed star in the sign of Taurus.
Aldehuéla y Aldeílla, *sf.* A little village, a small hamlet.
Aldeórrio, *sm.* 1. A small, nasty and unpleasant village. 2. A town whose inhabitants are as rude as peasants.
Aldíza, *sf.* A sort of small reed without knots, of which brooms are made at Toledo.
Aldrán, *sm.* One who sells wine to shepherds in pastures.
Aldúdo, da, *a.* V. *Haldudo.*
Aleación, *sf.* The art of alloying metals.
Aleár, *vn.* 1. To move the wings, to flutter. 2. (Met.) To move the arms quickly. 3. (Met.) To recover from sickness, to regain strength after great fatigue or labour.—*va.* To alloy, to mix precious metals with alloy.
Alebrárse, Alebrastrárse, y Alebrestárse, *vr.* 1. To squat, to lie close to the ground as hares do. 2. To be timorous, to cower.
Alebronárse, *vr.* To be dispirited, or discouraged.
Aléce, *sm.* A ragout made of the livers of a large fish, called *mulo,* caught on the coast of Valencia.
Alechugádo, da, *a.* Curled or contracted like the leaf of a lettuce.

Alechugár, *va.* To curl or contract like the leaf of a lettuce.
Alectória, *sf.* Alectoria, stone engendered in the liver, ventricle, or gall-bladder of a cock.
Aléda, *sf.* The first wax, or the refuse of wax in a bee-hive.
Aledáño, ña, *a.* Contiguous, adjacent; a limit.
Alefangínas, *sf. pl.* Purgative pills made of cinnamon, nutmeg, the juice of aloes, and other spices.
Alefrís, *sm.* 1. A rabbet or joint made by paring two pieces of wood so that they wrap over one another. 2. (Naút.) To groove timbers so as to receive the ends of planks.
Alegación, *sf.* Allegation, production of instruments, quotation.
Alegár, *va.* To allege, to affirm, to quote, to maintain, to plead.
Alegáto, *sm.* Allegation, declaration showing the ground of complaint of the plaintiff.
Alegoría, *sf.* Allegory, a figurative discourse.
Alegoricaménte, *ad.* Allegorically.
Alegórico, ca, *a.* Allegorical, not literal.
Alegorizár, *va.* To turn into allegory, to allegorise.
Alegrádo, da, *a.* Delighted, rejoiced. *Me he alegrado mucho de ver á mi hermano,* I was much delighted at seeing my brother.
Alegradór, ra, *s.* 1. One who produces mirth and merriment; a jester. 2. Twisted slip of paper to burn.
Alegrár, *va.* 1. To cause mirth, to make merry. 2. (Met.) To enliven, to beautify. *Alegrar las luces,* To snuff the candles.—*vr.* 1. To rejoice, to be merry. 2. To grow merry and rosy by drinking.
Alégre, *a.* 1. Merry, joyful, content. 2. (Met.) gay, showy, fine; applied to inanimate things. *Un cielo alegre,* A clear beautiful sky. 3. Brilliant, pleasing; applied to colours. 4. Lucky, fortunate, favourable.
Alegreménte, *ad.* Merrily.
Alegría, *sf.* 1. Mirth, merriment, jocularity, pleasure. 2. (Bot.) Bhenne. Sesamum orientale *L.* 3. Paste made of sesamum and honey.—*pl.* Rejoicings, public festivals.
Alegrón, *sm.* 1. Sudden, unexpected joy. 2. Flash, a sudden and short blaze.
Alejamiénto, *sm.* Elongation, removal to a distance.
Alejár, *va.* To remove to a greater distance, to separate one thing from another.
Alejúr, *sm.* V. *Alajú.*
Alelárse, *vr.* To become stupid.
Alelí, *sm.* (Bot.) The winter gilliflower, of various colours: also a general name for violets.
Alelúya, *sf.* 1. Allelujah, a word of spiritual exultation, Praise the Lord. 2. Joy, merriment. 3. Easter time. *Al aleluya nos veremos,* We shall see each other at Easter. 4. Small pictures with the word *aleluya* printed on them, and thrown among the people on Easter-eve. 5. (Bot.) Gilliflower.
Aleluyádo, da, *a.* Happy, merry, joyful.
Aléma, *sf.* The allotted quantity of water for irrigating a piece of ground.
Alemána, *sf.* An ancient Spanish dance.
Alemanísco, ca, *a.* Germanic; applied to cloth made in Germany.

Alesegamiénto, *sm.* An agreement relative to pasture.

Alesguár, *va.* To agree, or conclude an agreement, respecting sheep-walks or pasturage.

Alentáda, *sf.* Interval between two respirations, a continued respiration.

Alentadaménte, *ad.* Bravely, gallantly.

Alentádo, da, *a.* 1. Spirited, courageous, valiant. 2. (Ant.) Bold, daring.

Alentár, *vn.* To respire, to breathe, to draw breath.—*va.* To animate, to encourage, to inspirit.

Alepínes, *sf. pl.* Bombazeens.

Aléra, *sf.* (Ar.) 1. Level place where horses tread out the corn. 2. Right of pasturage near a treading-place.

Alérce, *sm.* (Bot.) Larch-tree. Pinus larix *L.*

Aléro, *sm.* The projecting part of a roof which overhangs a wall; eaves.—*pl.* 1. Pieces of leather in old coaches which cover the body, and hang down to the steps. 2. Snares for partridges.

Alérta, *sm.* (Mil.) Watch-word.

Alérta ó Alertaménte, *ad.* Vigilantly, attentively, carefully. *Estar alerta*, To be on the watch. *Alerta á la buena guardia á proa*, (Naút.) Look out well there afore.

Alertár, *va.* To render vigilant, to put one on his guard.

Alérto, ta, *a.* Vigilant, alert, guarded.

Alésna, *sf.* Awl, a pointed instrument.

Alesnádo, da, *a.* Awl-shaped, pointed like an awl.

Aléta, *sf.* 1. A small wing. 2. Fin of a fish. *Aletas*, (Naút.) Fashion pieces.

Aletáda, *sf.* Motion of the wings.

Aletázo, *sm.* Stroke of the wing.

Aleteár, *vn.* To flutter, to take short flights with great agitation of the wings, to flit.

Aléto, *sm.* (Orn.) The Peruvian falcon. Falco Peruvianus *L.*

Aletón, *sm.* (Aum.) A large wing.

Aletría, *sm.* A kind of paste. V. *Fidéos.*

Aleudárse, *vr.* (Ant.) To become fermented, applied to dough.

Aléve, *a.* Treacherous, perfidious.

Alevósa, *sf.* A tumour under the tongue of cows.

Alevosaménte, *ad.* Treacherously, perfidiously.

Alevosía, *sf.* Treachery, perfidy, breach of trust.

Alevóso, sa, *a.* Treacherous, perfidious.

Alexifármaco, ca, *a.* Alexipharmic, antidotal, possessing the power of destroying or expelling poison.

Alexíjas, *sf. pl.* Soup made of barley peeled, cleaned, and roasted. *Tiene cara de alexijas*, He looks half-starved.

Alfabéga, *sf.* V. *Albahaca.*

Alfabético, ca, *a.* Alphabetical.

Alfabetísta, *sm.* One that studies the alphabet and orthography.

Alfabéto, *sm.* Alphabet, the letters or elements of words.

Alfadía, *sf.* Bribe.

Alfagío, *sf.* 1. Piece of wood for making windows and doors. 2. (Naút.) Batten. 3. (Manuf.) Cross-bars on which clothes are hung.

Alfahár, Alfaharéro, V. *Alfar, Alfarero.*

Alfaharería, V. *Alfarería.*

Alfajór, *sm.* V. *Alajú.*

Alfálfa ó Alfálfe, *s.* (Bot.) Lucern. Medicago sativa *L.*

Alfalfár, *sm.* A piece of ground sown with lucern.

Alfána, *sf.* A large, strong and spirited horse.

Alfanéque, *sm.* 1. The white eagle. Falco albus *L.* 2. Tent or booth.

Alfánge, *sm.* Hanger, cutlass.

Alfangéte, *sm.* A little hanger, a small cutlass.

Alfanjázo, *sm.* A cut or wound with a cutlass.

Alfanjón y Alfonjonázo, *sm.* A large hanger or cutlass.

Alfáque, *sm.* Sand-bank on the sea-coast or at the mouth of a harbour.

Alfár, *sm.* Pottery, a place where earthenware is made.

Alfár, *va.* To raise the forehead too much; applied to a horse.

Alfaráces, *sm. pl.* Horses on which the light cavalry of the Moors was mounted.

Alfárda, *sf.* 1. (Arag.) Duty paid for the irrigation of lands. 2. A beam which supports a certain part of a building.

Alfardéro, *sm.* A collector of the duty for watering lands.

Alfardílla, *sf.* 1. Silk, now called galloon. 2. A small duty for watering lands.

Alfardón, *sm.* 1. Hoop or ring at the end of an axle-tree. 2. Duty paid for watering lands.

Alfaréro, *sm.* Potter, one whose trade is to make earthen-ware.

Alfárge, *sm.* 1. The lower stone of an oil-mill. 2. Ceiling of a room adorned with carved work.

Alfargía, *sf.* V. *Alfagía.*

Alfárma, *sf.* (Arag.) (Bot.) Wild rue. V. *Alhargama.*

Alfayáte, *sm.* (Ant.) A tailor.

Alfeñicárse, *vr.* To affect peculiar delicacy and nicety.

Alfeñíque, *sm.* 1. A sugar-paste made with oil of sweet almonds. 2. (Met.) A person of a delicate complexion.

Alferecía, *sf.* 1. Epilepsy, a convulsive disorder. 2. An ensign's commission.

Alférez, *sm.* 1. Ensign, cornet. 2. *Alferez de navio*, Ensign of the navy.

Alfeyzár, *sm.* The aperture in a wall at the inside of a door or window.

Alficóz, *sm.* (Bot.) The serpent cucumber. Cucumis flexuosus *L.*

Alfíl, *sm.* Bishop, at the game of chess.

Alfilér y Alfilél, *sm.* Pin used by women to fasten their clothes. *Alfileres*, Pin-money, the money allowed to married ladies for their private expenses. *Con todos sus alfileres ó de veinte y cinco alfileres*, In full dress; dressed in style.

Alfilerázo, *sm.* 1. Prick of a pin. 2. A large pin.

Alfiletéro, *sm.* Pin-case, needle-case.

Alfiléte ó Alfiletéte, *sm.* Paste made of coarse flour of wheat or peeled barley.

Alfolí, *sm.* 1. Granary. 2. Magazine of salt.

Alfoliéro y Alfolinéro, *sm.* Keeper of a granary or magazine.

Alfómbra, *sf.* 1. Floor-carpet. 2. Field adorned with flowers. 3. (Med.) Eruptions on the skin.

Alfombrár, *va.* To carpet, to spread with carpets.

Alfombráza, *sf.* A large carpet.

Alfombréro, ra, *s.* Carpet-maker
Alfombrílla, *sf.* 1. A small carpet. 2. (Med.) Efflorescence or breaking out in the skin.
Alfóndega ó Alfóndiga, *sf.* (Ant.) V. *Alhondiga.*
Alfonsearse, *vr.* (Bax.) To jest or joke with each other; to ridicule each other in a jocular style.
Alfonsí, *sm.* A sort of maravedi.
Alfónsigo, *sm.* 1. Pistachio, the fruit of the pistachio-tree. 2. Pistachio-tree. Pistacia vera *L.*
Alfonsín, no, na, *a.* Belonging to the kings called Alphonso, or Ildefonsus.
Alfonsína, *sf.* A solemn act held in the church of the Alphonsine college of Alcalá, where several positions either theological or medical are publicly discussed.
Alfórja, *sf.* Saddle-bag, portmanteau. *Hacerle á alguno la alforja,* To fill one's saddle-bag with provisions.
Alforjéro, *sm.* 1. Maker or seller of saddle-bags. 2. A lay-brother of some religious orders who goes about begging bread. 3. One who carries for others the bag with provisions. 4. Sportsman's dog taught to guard the bag of game.
Alforjílla, Alforjíta y Alforjuéla, *sf.* A small saddle-bag, a small wallet or knapsack.
Alfórza, *sf.* Plait made in a petticoat.
Alfroníтro, *sm.* V. *Alatron.*
A'lga, *sf.* (Bot.) Sea-wreck. Zostera marina *L.*
Algadonéra, *sf.* (Bot.) Cudweed, graphalium.
Algalába, *sf.* (Bot.) Briony, white briony, wild hops. Bryonia alba *L.*
Algália, *sf.* 1. Civet, a perfume extracted from the civet-cat. 2. Catheter, a hollow instrument for extracting the urine.
Algaliár, *va.* (Ant.) To perfume with civet.
Algára, *sf.* 1. The thin integument which covers an egg, onion, &c. 2. Foraging or marauding party of cavalry.
Algarabía, *sf.* 1. The Arabic tongue. 2. (Met.) Any unintelligible gibberish or jargon. 3. (Met.) A confused noise of several persons all speaking at once. 4. (Bot.) Centaury. Centaurea salmantica *L.*
Algaráda, *sf.* 1. A loud cry. 2. A sudden attack. 3. A sort of battering ram or catapult used by the ancients.
Algaréro, ra, *a.* Prating, chattering, loquacious. *La muger algarera nunca hace larga tela,* A prating woman works but little.
Algarráda, *sf.* 1. The act of driving bulls into the pinfold for the bull-feast. 2. (Ant.) Catapult, battering ram.
Algarróba, *sf.* (Bot.) The smooth tare, the smooth-podded tare. Ervum tetraspermum. *L.*
Algarrobál, *sm.* A piece of ground planted with carob-trees.
Algarróbo y Algarrobéra, *s.* (Bot.) Carob-tree, or St. John's bread. Ceratonia siliqua *L.*
Algáyda, *sf.* A ridge of shifting sand.
Algáydo, da, *a.* Thatched, covered with straw or rushes. *Casas algaydas,* Thatched-houses.
Algazára, *sf.* 1. Huzza, cry of Moors rushing forth from ambush. 2. The confused noise of a multitude.
Algebéna, *sf.* (Mur.) An earthen jug.
A'lgebra, *sf.* 1. Algebra, a branch of the higher mathematics. 2. Art of replacing dislocated members.
Algebrísta, *sm.* 1. Algebraist, a person that understands or practises algebra. 2. One who understands and practises the art of setting dislocated members.
Algecería, *sf.* Place for preparing or selling gypsum, or plaster of Paris.
Algecéro, ra, *s.* Plasterer.
Algénte, *a.* Extremely cold.
Algerifre, *sm.* (Ant.) Large fishing-net.
Algéz, *sm.* Gypsum in its crude state.
Algezár, *sm.* Pit of gypsum or sulphate of lime. V. *Yesar.*
Algezón, *sm.* Gypsum, plaster of Paris.
Algíbe, *sm.* Cistern, a receptacle of water.
Algibéro, *sm.* One who takes care of cisterns.
Algimifrádo, da, *a.* Dressed, painted.
A'lgo, *pro.* Somewhat, something.
A'lgo, *ad.* Somewhat. *La medida es algo escasa,* The measure is somewhat short. *Algo ó nada,* All or nothing. *Ser algo que,* To be worth something. *Algo,* property, faculty.
Algodón, *sm.* 1. (Bot.) The cotton-plant. Gossypium herbaceum *L.* 2. Cotton-wool. *Algodones,* Cotton for an ink-stand.
Algodonádo, da, *a.* Filled with cotton.
Algodonál, *sm.* A cotton-plantation.
Algodonéro, ra, *s.* A dealer in cotton.
Algorín, *sm.* A partition of boards in oil-mills for receiving the olives which are to be ground.
Algorítmo, *sm.* Algorithm, an Arabic word signifying the science of numbers.
Algóso, sa, *a.* Weedy, full of sea-weeds.
Algrínal, *sm.* Veil worn by ladies. V. *Alquinal.*
Alguacíl, *sm.* 1. An inferior officer of justice, a bumbailiff; a market-clerk. 2. The short-legged spider. 3. High constable. *Alguacil de campo ó del campo,* Guard or watchman of corn-fields or vineyards.
Alguacilázgo, *sm.* The place or office of an alguacil.
Alguarín, *sm.* 1. A small room on the ground floor in which any thing is kept. 2. Bucket in which flour falls from the millstones
Alguáza, *sf.* Hinge.
Alguién, *pro.* Somebody, some person.
Algún, *pro. Algun tiempo,* Sometime. V. *Alguno.*
Algúno, na, *a.* Some person, some thing, any one. *Ha venido alguno,* Did any one come. *Alguna vez,* Sometimes, now and then.
Algun tánto, *ad.* Somewhat, a tittle.
Alhabéga, *sf.* V. *Albahaca.*
Albadída, *sf.* (Quim.) Burnt copper from which the saffron of copper is extracted.
Alhagár, *va.* To furnish, to supply with furniture.
Alhája, *sf.* 1. Showy furniture, pompous ornament. 2. A thing of great value, a jewel. (Prov.) *Quien trabaja tien alhaja,* He that labours spins gold; the hand of industry maketh rich.
Alhajár, *va.* 1. To adorn. 2. To furnish.
Alhajuéla, *sf.* A little toy.
Alhamél, *sm.* 1. A beast of burthen. 2. Porter, carrier.
Alhandál, *sm.* Coloquint, bitter apple.
Alharáca, *sf.* Clamour, vociferation proceeding from anger, complaint, admiration, &c.
Alharaquiénto, ta, *a.* Noisy, clamorous.

Alhármaga y Alhárma, sm. (Bot.) Wild rue. Peganum harmala L.

Alelí. V. Alelí.

Alheña, sf. 1. (Bot.) Privet, primpriat. Ligustrum vulgare L. 2. Flower of privet. 3. Privet ground to powder. 4. Smut in corn. Rubigo.

Alheñarse, vr. To grow smutty, to be mildewed; applied to corn. V. Arroyarse.

Alhócigo, sm. V. Alfónsigo.

Alhoja, sf. A species of small birds, resembling a lark.

Alholva, sf. (Bot.) Fenugreek. Trigonella Fœnum Græcum L.

Alhóndiga, sf. A public granary, where corn is bought and sold. V. Pósito.

Alhondiguéro, sm. The keeper of a public granary.

Alhóndiga, sf. Royal Moorish tent.

Alhórra, sf. Eruption in the skin of new-born children.

Alhóstigo, sm. V. Alfónsigo.

Alhóz, sm. Limit or lot of land in a district.

Alhucéma, sf. (Bot.) Lavender. Lavandula spica L.

Aliabiérto, ta, a. Open-winged; a term applied to birds that have the wings expanded.

Aliacás y Aliacrán, sm. Jaundice. V. Ictericia. [the jaundice.

Aliacanádo, da, a. Jaundiced, infected with

Aliádo, da, a. y s. Allied; ally.

Aliága, sf. (Bot.) Furze, gorse, whim. Ulex Europæus L.

Aliagár, sm. Place covered with furze.

Aliánza, sf. 1. Alliance, league, coalition. 2. Agreement, convention. 3. Affinity, an alliance contracted by marriage.

Aliára, sf. Goblet or cup made of cow-horns.

Aliaría, sf. (Bot.) Garlic hedge-mustard, jack by the hedge. Erysimum alliaria L.

Aliárse, vr. To be allied, leagued, or coalesced.

Alias, ad. (Lat.) Otherwise, in another manner.

Alica, sf. (Dim.) A small wing.

Alica, sf. Pottage made of spelt, wheat, and other pulse.

Alicaído, da, a. 1. With fallen wings. 2. Weak, extenuated. 3. Uncocked. Sombrero alicaido, An uncocked hat.

Alicántara, sf. A small lizard, in Sierra Morena, whose bite is said to be mortal.

Alicánte, sm. A kind of poisonous snake.

Alicantína, sf. Artifice, stratagem, cunning. Tiene muchas alicantinas, He is full of delusive stratagems.

Alicatádo, sm. Work inlaid with Dutch tiles.

Alicátes, sm. pl. Pincers with very small points, used by watch-makers.

Aliciénte, sm. Attraction, incitement.

Alicionár, va. To give a lesson, to teach.

Alidáda, sf. Geometrical ruler, a cross-staff.

Alidónia, sf. Stone in the intestines of a swallow.

Alienár, va. (Ant.) V. Enagenar.

Aliénde, ad. (Ant.) V. Allende.

Aliénto, sm. 1. Breath, respiration. 2. Vigour of mind, spirit, valour. 3. Smell, scent. Yo fui allá de un aliento, I went thither in a whiff, without drawing breath.

Aliér, sm. (Naút.) 1. Rower on board a galley. 2. Marine stationed on board a ship.

Alifáfe, sm. 1. A callous tumour growing on the hind part of a horse's hock. 2. Habitual ailment or complaint. [bright.

Alifár, va. To polish, to burnish, to make

Alifára, sf. Collation, luncheon.

Aligación, sf. Alligation, the act of tying together. Regla de aligacion, Rule of alligation; in arithmetic. [gether.

Aligamiénto, sm. Act of tying or binding to-

Aligár, va. 1. To tie, to unite. 2. (Met.) To oblige; to lie down.

Aligeramiénto, sm. Alleviation; lightening.

Aligerár, va. 1. To lighten. 2. (Met.) To alleviate, to ease. 3. To hasten. 4. Aligerar un caballo, To make a horse move light and free in the forehand.

Aligéro, ra, a. (Poét.) Winged, quick, fast.

Alijadór, sm. 1. One who lightens. 2. (Naút.) Lanchon alijador, Lighter, a craft used in unloading ships. 3. He who separates the seed from cotton wool.

Alijár, va. 1. (Naút.) To lighten. Alijar un navio, To lighten a ship. 2. To separate the wool or down of cotton from the seed with the hand or with a gin.

Alíjo, sm. 1. (Naút.) Lightening of a ship. Embarcacion de alijo, (Naút.) Lighter. 2. Alleviation. [fish.

Alílla, sf. (Dim.) 1. A small wing. 2. Fin of a

Alimáña, sf. 1. Animal which devours game, as the fox, wild-cat, &c. 2. (Ant.) V. Animal.

Alimentación, sf. Alimentation, act of nourishing.

Alimentár, va. 1. To feed, to nourish. 2. To supply a person with the necessaries of life.

Alimentário y Alimentísta, s. One who enjoys a certain allowance for maintenance.

Alimentício, cia, a. Relating to aliment.

Aliménto, sm. 1. Aliment, nourishment, food, nutriment. 2. (Met.) Incitement, encouragement, incentive.

Alimentóso, sa, a. Alimentary, that which has the power of nourishing; nutritious.

Alimpiár, va. (Ant.) V. Limpiar.

Alindádo, da, a. Affectedly nice or elegant.

Alindár, va. 1. To fix or mark limits or boundaries. 2. To embellish, to adorn. Alindar el ganado, To drive the cattle to pasture as far as the limits extend. V. Lindar.

Alínde, sm. Mercury prepared for mirrors.

Aliñadór, ra, s. 1. One who adorns, or embellishes. 2. (Ant.) Executor, administrator.

Aliñár, va. 1. To arrange, to adorn, to set off. 2. To dress or cook victuals. 3. To season.

Alíño, sm. 1. Dress, ornament, decoration, cleanliness. 2. Apparatus, preparation for the performance of something.

Alionín, sm. The blue-feathered duck.

Alión, sm. Marble. V. Mármol.

Alípede, a. (Poét.) One with winged feet; swift, nimble.

Alípte, sm. (Ant.) An attendant appointed to rub over with unctuous matter and perfume those who came out of the bath.

Aliquánta (parte), Aliquant number, or that part of a number which never divides it exactly; as 5 is an aliquant of 12. [ed.

Aliquebrádo, da, a. Broken-winged; deject-

Aliquóta (parte), Aliquot number, or that

part of a number which exactly measures it without any remainder; as 4 is an aliquot part of 12.

ALIRÓNES, *sm. pl.* (Mur.) Wings of fowls stripped of their feathers.

ALISADÓR, RA, *s.* 1. Polisher. 2. An instrument used to make wax-candles round and tapering on a strong even table. [ing.

ALISADÚRA, *sf.* Planing, smoothing, or polish-

ALISADÚRAS, *sf. pl.* Shavings, cuttings of stone or any other thing made smooth. [lish.

ALISÁR, *va.* To plane, to make smooth, to po-

ALISÁR Y ALISÉDA, *s.* Plantation of alder-trees.

ALÍSMA, *sf.* (Bot.) Water-plantain.

ALÍSO, *sm.* (Bot.) Alder-tree. Betula alnus *L.*

ALISTÁDO, DA, *a.* 1. Enlisted. 2. Striped.

ALISTADÓR, *sm.* 1. A recruiting officer. 2. One who keeps accounts.

ALISTAMIÉNTO, *sm.* Enrolment, conscription.

ALISTÁR, *va.* 1. To enlist, to enrol. 2. To get ready, to prepare.

ALITERACIÓN, *sf.* V. *Paronomasia.*

ALIVIADÓR, RA, *s.* 1. One who eases. 2. A spindle that serves to raise or lower the running mill-stone, and acts as a lever.

ALIVIÁR, *va.* 1. To lighten, to make less heavy, to ease. 2. (Met.) To mitigate grief or sorrow. 3. To hasten, to move with swiftness.

ALÍVIO, *sm.* 1. Alleviation, ease. 2. Mitigation of pain or sorrow.

ALIXÁR, *sm.* An uncultivated, low stony ground.

ALIXARÁR, *va.* To divide waste lands to be cultivated.

ALIXARÉRO, *sm.* One who takes a part or lot of waste lands to cultivate it.

ALIXARIÉGO, GA, *a.* Belonging or relating to uncultivated land.

ALJÁBA, *sf.* Quiver, a case for arrows.

ALJÁMA, *sf.* (Ant.) Assembly of Moors; synagogue.

ALJAMÍA, *sf.* (Ant.) 1. Corrupted Arabic, spoken by the Moors. 2. Moorish name of the Spanish language. 3. (And.) Synagogue.

ALJÁRFA Ó ALJÁRFE, *sf.* A tarred net with small meshes.

ALJOFÁR, *sm.* 1. Pearl of an irregular shape. 2. (Met. Poét.) Drops of water or dew; also the tears and teeth of ladies.

ALJOFARÁR, *va.* 1. To adorn with pearls. 2. To convert something into the shape and colour of pearls.

ALJOFÁYNA Y ALJAFÁNA, *sf.* An earthen jug.

ALJOFÍFA, *sf.* Cloth for washing and cleaning floors.

ALJOFIFÁR, *va.* To rub with a cloth, to mop.

ALJÓNGE, *sm.* V. *Ajonje.*

ALJONGÉRA, *sf.* V. *Ajongera.*

ALJONGÉRO, *a.* Belonging or relating to the carline thistle, from which birdlime is extracted.

ALJONJOLÍ, *sm.* V. *Alegria.*

ALJÚBA, *sf.* A moorish garment, formerly worn by Christians in Spain.

ALKÁLI, *sm.* Alkali or alcali, a salt extracted from a plant called by the Arabs *kali*, by the Spaniards *sosa*, and by the English *glasswort.* Solsola *L.*

ALKALÍNO, NA, *a.* Alkaline. V. *Alcalino.*

ALKALIZÁR, *va.* To alkalize, to render alkaline.

ALKÉRMES, *sm.* A celebrated confection made by the Arabs of pearls, *lapis lazuli*, aloes wood, and cinnamon, with kermes and gold-leaf.

ALLÁ, *ad.* There, in that place; thither, or to that place; anciently; in other times. *Allá va con Dios,* (Naút.) About ship, tack about.

ALLANADÓR, *sm.* 1. Leveller. 2. Goldbeater's paper which contains the beaten gold-leaves.

ALLANAMIÉNTO, *sm.* 1. Levelling, the act of making even. 2. (Met.) Affability, suavity.

ALLANÁR, *va.* 1. To level, to make even. 2. To remove, surmount, or overcome difficulties. 3. To pacify, to subdue. *Allanar la casa,* To enter a house by force under the authority of a search-warrant. *Allanar el camino,* To pave the way for obtaining something.—*vr.* 1. To abide by a law or agreement. 2. To tumble down, to fall to ruin.

ALLARÍZ, *sm.* A sort of linen manufactured at *Allariz* in Galicia.

ALLEGADÍZO, ZA, *a.* Collected without choice.

ALLEGÁDO, DA, *a.* Near, proximate. [persons.

ALLEGÁDOS, *sm. pl.* 1. Friends, allies. 2. Partial

ALLEGADÓR, RA, *s.* One who gathers or collects. *A' padre allegador hijo expendedor,* After a gatherer comes a scatterer.

ALLEGAMIÉNTO, *sm.* Collecting, uniting.

ALLEGÁR, *va.* 1. To collect, to gather, to unite. 2. To approach, to draw near. 3. (Ant.) To know carnally. 4. To solicit, to procure.

ALLÉNDE Y ALLÉNT Ó ALLÉN, *ad.* (Ant.) On the other side. *Allende de.* V. *Ademas.*

ALLÍ, *ad.* 1. There, in that place. *Allí mismo,* In that very place. *De allí,* Thence, from that place. 2. The moment of time when any thing has happened.

ALLO, *sm.* (Mex.) V. *Guacamayo.*

ALLÓZA, *sf.* A green almond.

ALLÓZO, *sm.* (Bot.) The wild almond-tree Amygdalus communis *L.*

ALLUDÉL, *sm.* Earthenware water-pipe.

A'LMA, *sf.* 1. Soul, the immaterial spirit of man. 2. Human being. *No parece, ni se ve un alma en la plaza;* There is not a soul in the market-place. 3. That which imparts spirit or vigour to a thing. *Un buen general es el alma de un exercito,* A good general is the soul of an army. 4. Motto. 5. The principal part of a thing. *Vamos al alma del negocio,* Let us come to the main point of the business. 6. (Naút.) Body of a mast. 7. Conscience. *En mi alma,* Upon my soul. 8. Mould for casting statues. 9. Spirit, gallantry. *Alma mia, mi alma,* My dear, my love. *Alma de cántaro,* An ignorant, insignificant fellow. *El alma me da,* My heart tells me. *Dar el alma,* To expire. *Alma de Dios,* He who is bountiful.

ALMACAÉRO, *sm.* A member of the company of fishermen on the river of Seville.

ALMACÉN, *sm.* 1. Storehouse, warehouse. 2. Magazine of military or warlike stores. 3. Naval arsenal or dock-yard. 4. (Naút.) *Almacen de agua,* A water-cask. 5. (Naút.) *Almacen de una bomba de agua,* The chamber of a pump.

ALMACENÁR, *va.* To store, to lay up, to hoard.

ALMÁCIGA, *sf.* 1. Mastich, a gum obtained by incision from the mastich-tree, or Pistacia lentiscus *L.* 2. Piece of ground where any thing is sown to be afterwards transplanted.

Almaciguár, *va.* To perfume any thing with mastich.

Almácigo, *sm.* 1. Collection of plants growing on a seed-bed. 2. Mastich-tree Pistacia lentiscus *L.* V. *Lentisco.*

Almacigueño, ña, *a.* Relating to mastich, of the nature of mastich.

Almadána, éna, ó ína, *sf.* A large heavy hammer.

Almadén, *sm.* (Ant.) Mine or mineral.

Almadía, *sf.* 1. Canoe used in India. 2. Raft.

Almadiádo, da, *a.* Fainting, languid.

Almadiéro, *sm.* A raft-pilot.

Almadrába, *sf.* 1. Tunny-fishery. 2. Net used in the tunny-fishery. 3. (Ant.) Place where bricks are made

Almadrabéro, *sm* 1. Tunny-fisher. 2. V. *Tejero.*

Almadráque, *sm.* (Ant.) 1. A quilted cushion. 2. A mattress.

Almadréña, *sf.* Wooden shoes or sabots made of one piece, and used in the mountains of Leon and Castile.

Almagacén, *sm.* Magazine. V. *Almacen.*

Almaganéta, *sf.* V. *Almadana ó Almadena.*

Almagésto, *sm.* Almagesta, a mathematical work written by Ptolemy.

Almágra, *sf.* (Ant.) V. *Almagre.*

Almagrál, *sm.* Place abounding in ochre.

Almagrár, *va.* 1. To tinge or colour with ochre. 2. (Among Boxers,) To draw the first blood.

Almágre, *sm.* Ochre.

Almaizár ó Almaizál, *sm.* 1. A gauze veil worn by Moors on festive occasions. 2. A belt or sash worn in some places by priests and subdeacons.

Almajanéque ó Almajanéquis, *sm.* A sort of battering ram used by the ancients.

Almaláfa, *sf.* A long robe resembling a surtout, worn by Moorish men and women.

Almanác ó Almanáque, *sm.* Almanack, calendar. *Hacer almanaques,* (Met.) To muse, to be pensive.

Almanaquéro, *sm.* A maker and vender of almanacks.

Almancébe, *sm.* (Ant.) A fishing boat used on the river of Seville.

Almandína, *sf.* (Min.) Almandine, a precious stone of the ruby kind. Rubinus alabundicus *L.*

Almánta, *sf.* 1. Space between the rows of vines and olive-trees. 2. Space between two furrows. *Poner á almanta,* To plant vines irregularly.

Almaráda, *sf.* A triangular poniard without an edge.

Almárcha, *sf.* A town situated on a low marshy ground.

Almário, *sm.* V. *Armario.*

Almarjál, *sm.* 1. Plantation of glass-wort. 2. Low marshy ground where cattle use to graze.

Almárjo, *sm.* (Bot.) Glass-wort. Salicorni *L.*

Almáro, *sm.* (Bot.) Common clary. Salvia horminum *L.*

Almarraés, *sm. pl.* Instruments with which cotton wool is separated from the seed.

Almarrája ó Almarráza, *sf.* A glass phial with holes, formerly used in sprinkling water.

Almártaga, Almártega y Almártiga, *sf.* 1. Litharge. 2. A sort of halter. 3. Massicot made up with linseed-oil boiled with orange peel.

Almastigádo, da, *a.* Containing mastich.

Almática, *sf.* (Ant.) V. *Dalmática.*

Almatréro, *sm.* A fisherman fishing with shad-fish nets.

Almatríche, *sm.* An aqueduct for irrigating land.

Almázara, *sf.* (Mur. y Gran.) Oil-mill.

Almazaréro, *sm.* Oil-miller.

Almazarrón, *sm.* V. *Almagre.*

Alméa, *sf.* 1. (Bot.) The star-headed water-plantain. Alisma damasonium *L.* 2. The bark of the storax-tree. Styrax officinalis *L.*

Almeár ó Almiár, *sm.* A stack of hay, corn, or straw, made in the open air.

Almecína, *sf.* (And.) Fruit of the lote.

Almecíno, *sm.* (And.) V. *Almez.*

Alméja, *sf.* Muscle, a kind of shell-fish.

Almélga, *sf.* (Extrem. y And.) A furrow opened with a plough to direct others by.

Alména, *sf.* 1. A turret on the ramparts of ancient fortresses. 2. A two pound weight, with which saffron is weighed in several parts of India.

Almenádos, *sm. pl.* Embattled turrets.

Almenáge, *sm.* A series of turrets around a rampart.

Almenár, *va.* To crown a rampart or castle with turrets.

Almenára, *sf.* 1. (Ant.) V. *Velador.* 2. A fire lighted in beacons and light-houses. 3. (Arag.) A channel which conveys back the overplus water in irrigation.

Alméndra, *sf.* 1. Almond, the fruit of the almond-tree. 2. (Among jewellers) A diamond of an almond-shape. 3. (Mur.) A ball of silk of the best quality, which contains but one silk-worm.

Almendráda, *sf.* 1. Almond milk, an emulsion made of blanched and pounded almonds and sugar. 2. Any emulsion to induce sleep. (Met.) *Dar una almendrada,* To say something pleasing or pretty.

Almendrádo, da, *a.* Almond-like, that which resembles an almond in figure and size.

Almendrál, *sm.* A plantation of almond-trees.

Almendréra, *sf.* (Arag.) V. *Almendro.*

Almendréro, ra, *a.* *Plato almendrero,* A dish in which almonds are served up.

Almendríca, ílla, ó íta, *sf.* (Dim.) A small almond.

Almendrílla, *sf.* A lock-smith's file made in the shape of an almond. *Almendrillas,* Almond-shaped diamond ear-rings.

Almendríllo, *sm.* A tough sort of wood of a species of almond-trees, of which ropes are made for draw-wells.

Alméndro, *sm.* Almond-tree. Amygdalus communis *L.*

Almendrúco y Almendrolón, *sm.* A green almond which still preserves its downy husk.

Almenílla, *sf.* 1. A small turret. 2. Ancient fringe for the dresses of men and women.

Alméte, *sm.* 1. Helmet, ancient armour for the head. 2. A soldier wearing a helmet.

Almezí ó Almezía, *sf.* A kind of old-fashioned dress

Alméz ó Almézo, *sm.* The lote or Indian nettle-tree. Celtis *L.*

Alméza, *sf.* (Bot.) The fruit of the lote or Indian nettle-tree.

Almíbar, *sm.* Simple sirup. *Almíbares*, Preserved fruit.

Almibarádo, da, *a.* (Met.) Soft, endearing; applied to words.

Almibarár, *va.* 1. To preserve fruit in boiled sugar. 2. (Met.) To conciliate with soft and endearing words.

Almicantarádas, *sf. pl.* (Astr.) Circles, parallel to the horizon, imagined to pass through all the degrees of the meridian, and indicating the altitude and depression of the stars.

Almicantarát, *sf.* V. *Almicantaradas.*

Almidón, *sm.* Starch, a glutinous matter.

Almidonádo, da, *a.* 1. Starched, dressed with starch. 2. (Met.) Dressed with affected nicety; spruce, beauish.

Almidonár, *va.* To starch.

Almijaréro, *sm.* Porter, in the mines of Almaden, who is charged with examining those going in and out, and supplying the former with a light.

Almílla, *sf.* 1. An under waistcoat, with or without sleeves. 2. A short military jacket formerly worn by pikemen. 3. Scarf which joins two timbers together. 4. Pork-chop.

Almiránta, *sf.* (Naút.) 1. The admiral's or commodore's ship. 2. The admiral's lady.

Almirantázgo, *sm.* (Naút.) 1. Board of admiralty. 2. Admiralty-court. 3. Admiral's dues. 4. Precinct of the jurisdiction of an admiral.

Almiránte, *sm.* 1. Admiral, a commander of a fleet. *Almirante generál*, Lord high-admiral. *Contra-almirante*, Rear-admiral. 2. (Andal.) Swimming-master, one who teaches to swim. 3. A beautiful shell, belonging to the species of rhomb-shells, or *Voluta.*

Almirantía, *sf.* Rank and office of an admiral.

Almiréz, *sm.* A brass mortar in which any thing is pounded with a pestle.

Almirón, *sm.* (And.) V. *Achicoria.*

Almizclár, *va.* To perfume with musk.

Almízcle, *sm.* Musk, a highly perfumed drug taken from the musk deer. Moschus moschiferus *L.*

Almizcléña, *sf.* (Bot.) Grape hyacinth, or grape flower. Hyacinthus muscari *L.*

Almizcléño, ña, y ro, ra, *a.* That which smells of musk.

Almizcléra, *sf.* Musk-rat.

Almistéca, *sf.* V. *Almáciga.*

A'lmo, ma, *a.* (Poét.) 1. That which cherishes or supports. 2. (Poét.) Venerable, holy.

Almocadén, *sm.* In ancient times the commander of a troop of militia, now called captain.

Almocáfre, *sm.* A gardener's hoe.

Almocáti, *sm.* (Ant.) Marrow; brain.

Almocatrácia, *sf.* (Ant.) A duty laid on broadcloth and woollens.

Almocéda, *sf.* Impost on water for irrigation.

Almocráte, *sm.* Sal ammoniac.

Almodí, *sm.* V. *Almudí.*

Almodróte, *sm.* 1. A sauce for the egg-plant or mad-apple. Solanum melongena *L.* 2. Hodgepodge, a confused mixture of various ingredients.

Almofár, *sm.* A part of the ancient armour reclining on the helmet.

Almofía, *sf.* V. *Aljofayna.*

Almofréz, *sm.* A friese bag for coarse clothes; a seaman's canvas bag.

Almogána, *sf.* (Naút.) The hindermost piece of timber in the stern of a ship.

Almogávar y Almogarávе, *sm.* A chosen expert soldier in predatory warfare. *Almogávares*, A sort of light troops in the ancient militia of Spain, chiefly employed to make frequent incursions into the Moorish dominions.

Almogavaría, *sf.* (Ant.) A company of light troops of the ancient militia.

Almoháda, *sf.* 1. Pillow or bolster stuffed with wool, feathers, or hair, to rest the head on; pillow-case. 2. Fire-pillow, a pyrotechnical composition used on board of fire ships. 3. (Naút.) A piece of timber, on which the bowsprit rests, called a pillow. 4. Bed of a cannon, a piece of timber on which the breech of a cannon rests. *Hacer la cuenta con la almohada*, To take time for weighing any thing maturely. *Almohada para arrodillarse*, A cushion to kneel upon.

Almohadílla, *sf.* 1. A small bolster or pillow. 2. Working case, house-wife. 3. A little cushion in the harness of draught horses or mules. 4. Stone projecting out of a wall. 5. A callous excrescence on the back of mules where the saddle is put. *Cantar á la almohadilla*, To sing alone, and without being accompanied by musical instruments.

Almohadilládo, da, *a.* In the form of a cushion.

Almohadón, *sm.* A large cushion.

Almoháyтре y Almojátre, *sm.* Sal ammoniac.

Almoháza, *sf.* Curry-comb, an iron instrument for currying horses.

Almohazádo, da, *a.* Curried.

Almohazadór, *sm.* Groom, a stable-boy who curries horses.

Almohazár, *va.* To curry or rub a horse.

Almojába, *sf.* Smoked tunny fish.

Almojábana, *sf.* 1. Cake made of cheese and flour. 2. Paste made of butter, eggs, and sugar.

Almóna, *sf.* 1. (And.) Soap manufactory. 2. (Ant.) A public magazine, storehouse. 3. Shad-fishery.

Almóndiga ó Almondiguílla, V. *Albóndiga.*

Almonéda, *sf.* Auction, a public sale.

Almonedeár, *va.* To sell by auction.

Almoradúx, *sm.* 1. (Bot.) Sweet marjoram. Origanum majorana *L.* 2. V. *Sándalo.*

Almóri ó Almúri, *sm.* A sweet-meat or cake.

Almoronía, V. *Alboronia.*

Almorránas, *sf. pl.* Hemorrhoids, or piles.

Almorréfa, *sf.* A Mosaic tile floor.

Almórtas, *sf. pl.* (Bot.) Blue or chickling vetch. Lathyrus sativus *L.*

Almorzáda, *sf.* V. *Almuerza.*

Almorzádo, da, *a.* One who has breakfasted.

Almorzadór, *sm.* Breakfast case, which contains plates and all other things necessary for serving up a breakfast.

Almorzár, *va.* To breakfast.

Almotacén, *sm.* 1. Officer of polise who inspects weights and measures. 2. Clerk of the market. 3. A revenue in Toledo, consisting of a third part of the fines imposed by the magistrates.

Almotacenázgo, *sm.* The office of an inspector of weights and measures, or of a clerk of the market.

Almotacenía, *sf.* Custom or duty to the market clerk.

Almotazáf y Almutazáf, *sm.* The weigher of wool.

Almoxarifázgo, Almoxarifádgo, ó Almoxarifálgo, *sm.* A duty on goods imported or exported.

Almoxarífe, *sm.* 1. Officer who formerly collected the king's taxes. 2. Customhouse officer.

Almozárabe, *sm.* A Christian who lived subordinate to the Moors.

Almúd, *sm.* A measure of grain and dry fruit, being the twelfth part of a *fanega*. *Almúd de tierra*, (Mancha.) About half an acre of ground.

Almudáda, *sf.* A piece of ground which takes half a *fanega* of grain for sowing it.

Almudéro, *sm.* A police officer who keeps the standard measures of dry things.

Almudí ó Almudín, *sm.* 1. (Arag. y Mur.) V. *Alhóndiga*. 2. (Arag.) A measure containing six *cahices* or bushels.

Almuérdago, *sm.* (Mur. y Gran.) Bird lime.

Almuérza, *sf.* The portion of grain or fruits held between the two hands.

Almuérzo, *sm.* 1. Breakfast. 2. Cupboard.

Almutazáf, *sm.* (Ar.) V. *Almotacen*.

Alnádo, da, *s.* A step-child, begotten in a former marriage.

Aloária, *sf.* A sort of vault.

Alobadádo, da, *a.* 1. Bit by a wolf. 2. Labouring under morbid swellings.

Alobunadíllo, lla, *a.* Resembling a wolf a little.

Alobunádo, da, *a.* Resembling a wolf in colour.

Alocadaménte, *ad.* Rashly, inconsiderately.

Alocádo, da, *a.* Foolish, acting rather madly.

Alodiál, *a.* Allodial, not feudal.

Alódio, *sm.* Allodium, a possession not held by tenure of a superior lord.

Alóe, *sm.* 1. (Bot.) Aloes-tree. 2. Aloes.

Alojamiénto, *sm.* 1. Lodging, temporary habitation. 2. (Naút.) Steerage, or the room in a ship where the crew sleep.

Alojár, *va.* To lodge, to let lodgings.—*vr.* To lodge, to reside in lodgings.

Alomádo, da, *a.* Having a curved back like a pig; applied to horses.

Alomár, *va.* 1. To distribute equally the strength of a horse, by communicating to his back part of the force of his forehand. 2. To turn up with the plough some earth for covering the seed.—*vr.* To grow strong and vigorous; applied to a stonehorse.

Alón, *sm.* The wing of a fowl or bird stripped of its feathers.

Alón! *int.* Taken from the French *allons*, which signifies, Let us go.

Aloncíllo, *sm.* A little wing.

Alóndra, *sf.* (Orn.) Lark. Alauda *L.*

Alongár, *va.* To dilate, to extend.

Alopécia, *sf.* (Med.) A sort of leprosy, which causes the hair to fall off the head.

Alopiádo, da, *a.* Composed of opium.

Alóque, *a.* Applied to clear white wine or a mixture of red and white.

Aloquín, *sm.* A stone wall which surrounds the wax-chandler's place where wax is bleached.

Alósa, *sf.* (Ict.) Shad. Clupea alosa *L.*

Alósna, *sf.* (Bot.) Wormwood. Artemisia absinthium *L.*

Alotár, *va.* (Naút.) V. *Arrizar*. *Alotár las ancles*, (Naút.) To stow the anchors.

Alotín, *sm.* V. *Almena*.

Alóxa, *sf.* A common beverage made of water, honey, and spice; metheglin.

Aloxería, *sf.* A place where metheglin is prepared and sold.

Aloxéro, *sm.* 1. One who prepares or sells metheglin. 2. A box near the pit in the theatres of Madrid, where the justice sits to keep order.

Alpañáta, *sf.* A piece of cordovan or shamois, which potters make use of to smooth their work.

Alparcería, *sf.* V. *Aparcería*.

Alpargáta, *sf.* A sort of shoes or sandals made of hemp. *Compañía de la alpargata*, (Arag.) A set of ragamuffins, or unprincipled associates.

Alpargatádo, da, *a.* Wearing hempen sandals.

Alpargatár, *va.* To make hempen sandals.

Alpargatázo, *sm.* Blow with a hempen sandal.

Alpargáte, *sm.* Sandal made of plaited cords.

Alpargatería, *sf.* A manufactory of hempen sandals, also the shop where they are sold.

Alpargatéro, *sm.* A manufacturer of hempen sandals.

Alpargatílla, *sf.* 1. A small hempen sandal. 2. (Met.) A crafty designing fellow, who endeavours to wheedle something out of another.

Alpechín, *sm.* Water which oozes from a heap of olives.

A'lpes, *sm. pl.* The Alps.

Alpicóz ó Alpicáz, *sm.* (Murc.) Cucumber.

Alpíste, *sm.* 1. Canary-seed, the seed of canary-grass. Phalaris canariensis *L.* 2. *Quedarse alpiste*, To be disappointed.

Alpistéla ó Alpistéra, *sf.* A cake made of flour, eggs, sesamum, and honey or melted sugar.

Alpistéro, *sm.* A sieve for sifting canary-seed.

Alquería, *sf.* House in a farm-yard where ploughs and other tillage tools are kept.

Alquérmes, *sm.* A sweetmeat.

Alquérque, *sm.* Place in oil mills for laying the bruised olives.

Alquéz, *sm.* A wine measure containing 12 *cántaras*, or about 24 gallons.

Alquicél ó Alquicér, *sm.* 1. A Moorish garment resembling a cloak. 2. A sort of carpets with which benches, tables, &c. were covered.

Alquifól, *sm.* (Min.) Alquifou, or potter's ore; it is an ore of lead; sulphuretted galena is also so called.

Alquiladízo, za, *a.* That which may be let or hired.

Alquiladór, ra, *s.* One who lets coaches on hire.

Alquilár, *va.* To give or take on hire.—*vr.* To serve for stipulated wages.

Alquiláte, *sm.* Duty paid in Murcia on the sale of goods or fruits.

Alquilér, *sm.* 1. Wages or hire paid for the use of any thing. 2. Act of hiring or letting.

Alquilón, na, *a.* That which can be let or hired, such as coaches, horses, &c.

Alquilóna, *sf.* Char-woman, a woman hired occasionally for odd work.

Alquimia, *sf.* 1. Alchymy, the pretended art of transmuting metals. 2. Brass, latten, or any other gold-coloured metal, worked according to the rules of alchymy.

Alquimíla, *sf.* (Bot.) Ladies' mantle. Alchemilla *L.*

Alquimísta, *sm.* Alchymist, one who pursues or professes the science of alchymy.

Alquinál, *sm.* A veil or head-dress for women.
Alquitára, V. *Alambique.*
Alquitarár, *va.* To distil, to draw by distillation, to let fall in drops.
Alquitíra, *sf.* Tragacanth, a gum which exudes from the Astragalus tragacantha *L.*
Alquitrán, *sm.* 1. Tar or liquid pitch, a resin extracted by fire from the pitch-pine, or Pinus resinosa *L.* (Naút.) Stuff for paying a ship's bottom, composed of pitch, grease, resin, and oil: it is also used as a combustible matter. (Met.) *Es un alquitran*, He is a hot, passionate man, all fire and tow.
Alquitranádo, *sm.* (Naút.) Tarpawlin or tarpaulin, a tarred hempen cloth, which serves to cover the hatches. *Cabos alquitranados*, (Naút.) Black or tarred cordage.
Alquitranár, *va.* To tar, to pay with tar.
Alrededóres, *sm. pl.* Environs of a place.
Alróta, *sf.* A very coarse sort of tow.
Alsíne, *sf.* (Bot.) Scorpion-grass, mouse-ear. Myosotis scorpioides *L.*
A'lta, *sf.* A sort of dance formerly common in Spain. 2. Public exercise of fencing at school. 3. Return of the effective men of a regiment or company of soldiers.
Altabáque, *sm.* A small basket in which women keep their needle-work.
Altabaquíllo, *sm.* (Bot.) Small bindweed. Convolvulus arvensis *L.*
Altaménte, *ad.* 1. Highly. 2. Strongly, firmly. 3. (Met.) In a distinguished manner.
Altamía, *sf.* (Ant.) A glass made in the shape of a cup.
Altamísa, *sf.* V. *Artemisa.*
Altanería, *sf.* 1. The towering flight of some birds. 2. Sport, consisting in flying hawks at other birds. 3. (Met.) Haughtiness, loftiness.
Altanéro, ra, *a.* Soaring, towering; applied to birds of prey. 2. (Met.) Haughty, lofty, arrogant, vain, proud.
Altár, *sm.* 1. The table in Christian churches where the communion is administered. *Altar de alma, ó de anima*, A privileged altar. 2. (Astr.) A southern constellation not visible in our hemisphere. 3. The place where offerings to heaven are laid.
Altaréro, *sm.* One who is employed in making or adorning altars for great feasts or festivals.
Altaríco, *sm.* A little altar.
Altéa, *sf.* (Bot.) Common mallow. Malva sylvestris *L.*
Alterabilidád, *sf.* Alterableness; mutability.
Alterábles, *a.* Alterable, that may be changed.
Alteración, *sf.* 1. Alteration; the act of altering, and the state of being altered. 2. Unevenness of the pulse. 3. Strong emotion of anger, or other passion. 4. Disturbance, tumult, seditious commotion.
Alterádo, da, *a.* Alterative. *Caldo alterado*, Medicated or alterative broth.
Alteradór, ra, *s.* One who alters.
Alterár, *va.* 1. To alter, to change. 2. To disturb, to stir up commotion. *Alterár la moneda*, To raise or lower the value of coin, either in weight or alloy.
Alteratívo, va, *a.* Alterative.
Altercación, Altercádo, *s.* An altercation, debate, or controversy.
Altercadór, ra, *s.* One who argues or debates a question in an obstinate manner.
Altercár, *va.* To contend, to dispute obstinately.
Alternación, *sf.* Alternation, the reciprocal succession of things.
Alternadaménte, *ad.* V. *Alternativamente.*
Alternádo, *a.* (Bot.) Alternate; applied to the leaf which is higher than that in front.
Alternár, *va.* To alternate, to perform by turns, to change one thing for another.—*vn.* To alternate, to succeed reciprocally. *Los gustos y los pesares alternan*, Pleasures and sorrows alternate.
Alternatíva, *sf.* 1. Alternative, choice of two things, so that if one be rejected, the other must be taken. 2. The right of archbishops and bishops to dispose of prebends and benefices alternately with the Pope in their dioceses.
Alternativaménte, *ad.* Alternatively.
Alternatívo, va, *a.* Alternative, alternate.
Altérno, na, *a.* (Poét.) Alternate.
Altéza, *sf.* 1. Height, elevation. 2. Highness, a title given to princes, and in Spain to the board of Castile, tribunal of inquisition, exchequer, &c.
Altibáxo, *sm.* (Esg.) 1. A downright blow. 2. (Ant.) A kind of flowered velvet.—*pl.* 1. Uneven ground. 2. (Met.) Vicissitudes of human affairs; vulgarly, the ups and downs in life.
Altíllo, la, *a.* A little high.
Altíllo, *sm.* Hillock; a little hill or height.
Altilóqüo, qüa, (Rar.) Altiloqüénte, (Poét.) *a.* Using high-sounding, pompous language.
Altimetría, *sf.* Altimetry; the art of taking or measuring altitudes or heights.
Altísimo, ma, *a.* Extremely lofty or high.
Altísimo, *sm.* The Most High; God.
Altisonánte y Altísono, na, *a.* Altisonant, high-sounding, pompous in sound.
Altitonánte, *ad.* (Poét.) Thundering, high-sounding.
Altitúd, V. *Altúra.*
Altivaménte, *ad.* In a haughty, arrogant manner.
Altivárse, *vr.* To grow or be arrogant and haughty.
Altivéz, *sf.* Haughtiness, arrogance, pride.
Altívo, va, *a.* Haughty, proud.
A'lto, ta, *a.* 1. High, elevated, (Naút.) *Alta mar*, high seas. 2. Tall, lofty. 3. (Met.) Arduous, difficult. 4. (Met.) Eminent, excellent. 5. Enormous, atrocious. 6. Deep. 7. Late; applied to moveable feasts. *Altas por Abril son las pasquas*, Easter falls late in April.
A'lto, *sm.* 1. Height. 2. Story, a flight of rooms. *Casa de tres altos*, A house three stories high. 3. (Naút.) Depth or height of a ship. 4. High land, high ground. 5. (Milic.) Halt. 6. (Mús.) Notes put over the base.
A'lto, *int.* 1. V. *Alón.* 2. *Altó ahi*, Stop there. 3. *Alto de aqui*, Move off.
A'lto, *ad.* 1. Loud. 2. *De lo alto*, From above. 3. *Se me pasó por alto*, I forgot. 4. *Por alto*, By stealth; by particular favour. *Metió los generos por alto*, He smuggled the goods.
Altozáno, *sm.* A height or little hill.
Altramúz, *sm.* (Bot.) Lupine. Lupinus *L.* *Altramúces*, Lupines which are mixed with ivory beads, and used as black balls in giving votes in cathedral chapters, especially in Castile.
Altúra, *sf.* 1. Height, the elevation above the

surface of the earth. 2. Height, one of the three dimensions of a solid body. 3. Summit of mountains. 4. Altitude, the elevation of the pole, or of any of the heavenly bodies. *Estar en grande altura*, To be raised to a high degree of dignity, favour, or fortune. *Altúras*, The heavens. *Dios de las alturas*, God, the Lord of the heavens. [by the lee.

ALTÁR ó TOMÁR POR LA LÚA, (Naút.) To bring

ALÚBIA, *sf.* (Bot.) French bean, kidney bean. Phaseolus vulgaris *L.*

ALUCINACIÓN, ALUCINAMIÉNTO, *s.* Hallucination. [error.

ALUCINÁR, *va.* To blind, to deceive, to lead into

ALUCÓN, *sm.* (Orn.) Aluco owl. Strix aluco *L.*

ALÚDA, *sf.* (Entom.) Winged emmet or pismire. Formica *L.* [tort.

ALUDÉL, *sm.* (Quim.) Cucurbite, a kind of re-

ALUDÍR, *vn.* To allude, to have reference to.

ALUÉÑE, *ad.* (Ant.) Distant, far off.

ALUFRÁR, *va.* (Vulg.) To discover, to descry, to discern at a distance.

ALUMBRÁDO, DA, *a.* 1. Aluminous, relating to alum, or consisting of alum. 2. Flustered with wine.

ALUMBRÁDO, *sm.* Illumination, festal lights. *Alumbrádos*, Illuminati, a sect.

ALUMBRADÓR, RA, *s.* Link-boy, or girl; one who lights or gives light.

ALUMBRAMIÉNTO, *sm.* 1. Illumination, the act of supplying with light. 2. Illusion, deceit, false appearance. 3. Child-birth. *Alumbramiento bueno ó feliz*, A happy child-birth.

ALUMBRÁR, *va.* 1. To light, to supply with light. 2. To restore sight to the blind. 3. To enlighten, to instruct, to adorn with knowledge. 4. (Among dyers) To dip cloth into alum-water. 5. To open the ground about the roots of vines, that the winter rain may penetrate to the roots. *Dios alumbre á vd. con bien, ó Dios de á vd. feliz parto*, God grant you a safe delivery.

ALÚMBRE, *sm.* Alum, a mineral salt of an acid taste. *Alumbre catino*, A kind of alkali drawn from the plant glass-wort. *Alumbre de rasuras*, Salt of tartar. *Alumbre zucarino*, Alum and the white of an egg formed into a paste.

ALUMBRÉRA, *sf.* Alum-mine. *Alumbrera artificial*, Alum-works.

ALUMINÓSO, SA, *a.* Aluminous, relating to alum, or consisting of alum.

ALÚMNO, NA, *s.* Foster-child, disciple.

ALÚN, V. *Alumbre.*

ALUNÁDO, DA, *a.* 1. Lunatic. 2. Spasmodic; applied to a horse which labours under a contraction of the nerves. 3. Long tusked; applied to a boar whose tusks have grown semicircular. 4. Tainted; applied to salt pork.

ALUQUÉTE, *sm.* (Ant.) A match, V. *Pajuela.*

ALUSIÓN, *sf.* Allusion, a hint, an implication.

ALUSÍVO, VA, *a.* Allusive, hinting at something.

ALUSTRÁR, *va.* To give lustre to any thing.

ALUTACIÓN, *sf.* Layer or stratum of grains of gold, which is found in some mines of that ore.

ALUVIÓN, *sf.* A great swell of waters. [mic.

A'LVAREZ, *sm.* The son of *A'lvaro*: a patrony-

ALVEÁRIO, *sm.* (Anat.) The inward cavity of the ear. [river.

A'LVEO, *sm.* 1. Source of a river. 2. Bed of a

ALVEÓLO, *sm.* 1. Socket of the teeth. 2. Seed vessel, the cavity in which the seeds of plants are lodged. [vetch or tare. Vicia sativa *L.*

ALVÉRJA Y ALVERJÁNA, *sf.* (Bot.) Common

ALVIDRIÁR, *va.* To glaze earthen-ware.

A'LZA, *sf.* 1. (Among shoe-makers) A piece of leather put round the last to make the shoe wider. 2. (Among rope-makers) An instrument used in rope-walks to keep up the rope-yarn in the act of spinning it. 3. Advance in the price of any thing.

ALZACUÉLLO, *sm.* A black collar bound with linen, which clergymen wear round their necks.

ALZÁDA, *sf.* 1. A town, village, &c. situated on an eminence. 2. Appeal. *Juez de alzadas*, A judge in appeal causes. 3. Height; stature.

ALZADAMÉNTE, *ad.* By large parcels, wholesale.

ALZÁDO, *sm.* A plan of a building which shows its front and elevation. 2. Fraudulent bankrupt. *Alzádos*, Spare stores; things laid by for some future use.

ALZADÚRA, *sf.* Elevation; the act of raising up.

ALZAMIÉNTO, *sm.* 1. The act of raising up. 2. Bidding a higher price at an auction.

ALZAPÁÑO, *sm.* A hook fastened to the wall, to keep up a curtain.

ALZAPRÍMA, *sf.* 1. A lever. 2. (Naút.) A hand-spike. *Dar alzaprima*, (Met.) To deceive, to ruin by artifice.

ALZAPRIMÁR, *va.* 1. To raise by means of a lever or fulcrum. 2. (Naút.) To move with hand-spikes.

ALZAPUÉRTAS, *sm.* A player who acts no other part but that of a dumb servant.

ALZÁR, *va.* 1. To raise, to lift up; to erect, to construct. 2. To repeal a decree of excommunication, to recall from banishment. 3. To carry off. 4. To hide, to conceal, to lock up. 5. To cut the cards. 6. (Among printers) To gather the printed sheets for the bookbinder. 7. To fallow, to plough for the first time. 8. (Naút.) To heave, to hoist. *Alzar cabeza*, To recover from a calamity or disease. *Alzar de codo ó el codo*, To drink much wine or liquor. *Alzar de obra*, To cease working. *Alzar de eras*, To finish the harvesting of grain in the farm yards. *Alzar figura*, To assume an air of importance. *Alzar el dedo*, To raise the two fore fingers in asseveration or affirmation of any thing. *Alzar la casa*, To quit a house, to move out of it. *Alzar velas*, (Naút.) To set the sails: (Met.) To decamp, to move off bag and baggage.—*vr.* 1. To rise in rebellion, to form an insurrection. 2. To appeal. *Alzarse con el dinero*, To run away with the money. *Alzarse con el banco*, To make a fraudulent bankruptcy.

A'MA, *sf.* A mistress of the house. *Ama de llaves*, A house-keeper. *Ama de leche*, Nurse.

AMABILIDÁD, *sf.* Amiability, affability.

AMÁBLE, *a.* Amiable, pleasing, lovely.

AMABLEMÉNTE, *ad.* Amiably, lovely.

AMÁCA, V. *Hamaca.* [L.

AMACÉNA, *sf.* (Bot.) A damson plum. Prunus

AMACOLLÁRSE, *vr.* To throw out shoots or stalks.

AMADÓR, RA, *s.* A lover, a sweetheart.

AMADOÚRI, *sm.* A sort of cotton brought from Alexandria. [hamadryads.

AMADRÍAS ó AMADRIÁDES, *sf. pl.* Wood-nymphs;

Amadrigárse, *vr.* 1. To burrow; to get into the burrow. 2. (Met.) To live retired; to decline all intercourse with the world.

Amadrinár, *va.* 1. To couple, to yoke together horses or mules. 2. (Naút.) To join one thing to another, in order to strengthen it.

Amadroñádo, da, *a.* Resembling strawberries. *Rosario amadroñado*, A rosary, the beads of which resemble strawberries.

Amaestrádo, da, *a.* 1. Taught, tutored, instructed. *Caballo amaestrado*, A horse completely broken in. 2. Artfully contrived.

Amaestrár, *va.* To teach, to instruct, to break in.

Amagamiénto, *sm.* V. *Amágo.*

Amagár, *va.* 1. To lift up the hand or arm in a threatening attitude. 2. (Met.) To manifest a desire of doing or saying something.—*vr.* (Ar.) To crouch, to stoop.

Amágo, *sm.* 1. The act of threatening: a threat. 2. Symptom or indication of disease.

A'mago, *sm.* 1. The unpleasant taste of honey gathered from blighted flowers. 2. (Met.) Squeamishness; distaste.

Amajadár, *va.* 1. To retire for shelter into a sheep-fold. 2. To secure sheep in a fold.

Amálgama, *sf.* Amalgam; mixture of metals.

Amalgamación, *sf.* Amalgamation; the act of uniting metals with quicksilver.

Amalgamár, *va.* To amalgamate.

Amamantár, *va.* To suckle; to nurse at the breast.

Amambrucéa, *sf.* A sort of cotton stuff.

Amancebádo, da, *a.* Attached, excessively devoted.

Amancebamiénto, *sm.* Concubinage; the act of living with a woman not married.

Amancebárse, *vr.* To live in concubinage.

Amancillár, *va.* 1. To stain, to defile, to pollute. 2. To offend, to injure. 3. (Met.) To tarnish one's reputation.

Amanecér, *va.* (Poét.) To illustrate, to enlighten.—*vn.* 1. To dawn, to begin to grow light. 2. To arrive at the break of day. *Al amanecer*, At the break of day. 3. (Met.) To begin to appear, or to show itself.

Amanerádo, da, *a.* Applied to painters mannerists.

Amanojár, *va.* To gather by handfuls; to make up into handfuls.

Amansadór, ra, *s.* One that tames, mitigates, or pacifies.

Amansamiénto, *sm.* The act of taming.

Amansár, *va.* 1. To tame, to domesticate. 2. (Met.) To soften, to mitigate, to pacify.

Amantár, *va.* To cover with a blanket or any loose garment.

Amánte, *p.* y *s.* Loving; lover.

A'mantenénte, *ad.* Firmly, with all one's might.

Amántes, *sm. pl.* (Naút.) Runners, ropes which form part of the running rigging of a ship.

Amantillár, *va.* (Naút.) To top the lifts, to hoist one end of the yard-arms higher than the other.

Amantíllos, *sm. pl.* (Naút.) Lifts.

Amanuénse, *sm.* Amanuensis.

Amañár, *va.* To do a thing cleverly, or with skill and address, to be handy.—*vr.* To accustom one's self to do things cleverly, or with skill and address.

Amáños, *sm. pl.* 1. Tools or implements for the execution of a work. 2. (Met.) Means and preparations for performing a thing.

Amapóla, *sf.* (Bot.) Poppy. Papaver *L. Amapola morada*, Corn-poppy, corn-rose. Papaver rhœas *L.*

Amár, *va.* 1. To love, to regard with affection. 2. (Met.) To have a tendency to; applied to inanimate things.

Amaracíno, *a. Ungüento amaracino*, A sort of ointment made of marjoram.

Amaráco. V. *Mejorana.*

Amaránto, *sm.* (Bot.) Amaranth. Amaranthus *L.*

Amargádo, da, *a.* Embittered.

Amargaléja, *sf.* The bitter or wild plum.

Amargaménte, *ad.* Bitterly.

Amargár, *va.* 1. To make bitter. 2. (Met.) To exasperate, to offend.—*vn.* To be bitter or acrid.

Amárgo, ga, *a.* Bitter.

Amárgos, *sm. pl.* 1. Sweet-meats made up of bitter almonds. 2. Bitters, drops made of bitter herbs and other ingredients.

Amargón, *sm.* (Arag. Bot.) Dandelion, lion's tooth. Leontodon taraxacum *L.*

Amargór, *sm.* Bitterness, a bitter taste or flavour.

Amargosaménte. V. *Amargamente.*

Amargóso, sa, *a.* Bitter. V. *Amargo.*

Amarguíllo, lla, *a.* Bitterish, somewhat bitter. It is also used as a substantive.

Amargúra, *sf.* Bitterness. V. *Amargor.*

Amaricádo, da, *a.* Effeminate.

Amarillázo, za, *a.* Of a pale yellow colour.

Amarillear, *vn.* To incline to yellow; to grow yellow.

Amarilléjo, ja; **íto, ta**, *a.* Yellowish, a little yellow.

Amarillénto, ta, *a.* Inclining to yellow.

Amarilléz, *sf.* The yellow colour of the body.

Amarillo, lla, *a.* Yellow; gold colour.

Amarillo, *sm.* Jaundice; a disease incident to silk worms when young, chiefly occasioned by southerly winds.

Amariposádo, da, *a.* Butterfly-like.

Amáro, *sm.* (Bot.) Bitterwort. Teucrium marum *L.*

Amárra, *sf.* 1. A cable. 2. (Manej.) Martingale. *Amárra*, (Naút.) A word of command, corresponding to the English belay, lash, or fasten. *Amarras fixas*, Moorings. *Amarras de popa*, Stern-fasts. *Amarras de proa*, Head-fasts. *Amarras de traves*, Breast-fasts. *Tener buenas amarras*, (Met.) To have powerful friends or interest.

Amarradéro, *sm.* 1. A post or pillar to which any thing is made fast. 2. (Naút.) A birth, the place where a ship is moored. 3. (Naút.) A safe mooring place.

Amarrár, *va.* To tie, to make fast, to lash. *Amarrar un cabo de labor*, To belay a running rope. *Amarrar un baxel entre viento y marea*, To moor a vessel between wind and tide. *Amarrar un baxel con codera sobre el cable*, To moor a ship with a spring on the cable. *Amarrár con reguera*, To moor by the stern.

Amarrazónes, *sm. pl.* (Naút.) Ground-tackle.

Amarrído, da, *a.* Dejected, gloomy, melancholy.

Amartelár, *va.* 1. To court, to make love to a lady. 2. To love, to have a particular regard for a person.

Amartillár, *va.* 1. To hammer, to give strokes with a hammer. 2. To cock a gun or pistol.

Amasadéra, *sf.* A trough in which the dough for bread is kneaded.

Amasadór, ra, *s.* One who works dough into bread.

Amasadúra, *sf.* Kneading, act of kneading.

Amasamiénto, *sm.* The act of uniting or joining.

Amasár, *va.* 1. To knead, to work dough. 2. (Met.) To arrange matters well for the attainment of some purpose.

Amasíjo y Amasadíjo, 1. A quantity of flour kneaded for making bread. 2. The act of kneading, or the preparation for it. 3. A quantity of mortar or plaster. 4. (Met.) Medley, a mixture of heterogeneous things which cause confusion. 5. A task. 6. An agreement or compact made for some evil design. 7. The place where the dough for bread is made.

Amatísta, *sf.* (Min.) Amethyst, a precious stone of a violet colour.

Amatório, ria, *a.* Amatory, relating to love.

Amatúris, *sm.* A kind of Indian linen.

Amaynár, *va.* 1. (Naút.) To strike or lower the sails. 2. To relax in some desire.

Amaytinár, *va.* To observe attentively, to watch with close attention.

Amazóna, *sf.* An amazon; a masculine woman.

Amarorcádo, da, *a.* Pennached; applied to flowers terminating in different colours.

Ambáges, *sm. pl.* 1. Circuit. 2. (Met.) Ambages, circumlocution or multiplicity of words used to describe or explain a thing. [ties.

Ambagióso, sa, *a.* Ambiguous, full of ambigui-

A'mbar, *sm.* Amber. Succinum *L.* *A'mbar gris*, Ambergris. *Es un ámbar*, It is brilliant; applied to liquors. [found in the Atlantic.

A'mbara, *sm.* (Ict.) Amberfish, a large fish

Ambarár, *va.* (Ant.) To perfume with amber.

Ambaríña, *sf.* (Bot.) Sweet centaury or sultan flower. Centaurea moschata *L.*

Ambarílla, *sf.* (Bot.) Muskmallow. Hibiscus abelmoschus *L.*

Ambaríno, na, *a.* Relating to amber.

Ambición, *sf.* 1. Ambition, a desire of preferment or honour. 2. Covetousness.

Ambicionár, *va.* To crave, to pursue with anxious desire.

Ambiciosaménte, *ad.* Ambitiously. [ous.

Ambicióso, sa, *a.* Ambitious, aspiring; covet-

Ambidéxtro, tra, *a.* Ambidextrous, having the use of either hand with equal facility.

Ambiénte, *a.* Ambient, surrounding; going

Ambiénte, *sm.* The ambient air. [round.

Ambigú, *sm.* A French word, signifying an entertainment composed of cold and warm dishes, set all at once on the table.

Ambiguaménte, *ad.* Ambiguously. [ty.

Ambigüedád, *sf.* Ambiguity, doubt, uncertain-

Ambíguo, gua, *a.* Ambiguous, doubtful.

A'mbito, *sm.* Circuit, circumference.

Amblár, *va.* (Ant.) To amble; to pace.

Ambléo, *sm.* A short thick wax-candle with one wick only.

Ambligónio, *sm.* Ambligonium. V. *Triangulo.*

A'mbos, bas, *pro.* Both. *A'mbos ó A'mbas á dos*, Both or both together.

Ambracán, *sm.* A sea-fish of an enormous size.

Ambrollár, *va.* To confound, to perplex.

Ambrósia, *sf.* 1. Ambrosia, the imaginary food of the gods. 2. (Met.) Any delicious viand or liquor. 3. A sweet gentle purging draught. 4. (Bot.) *Ambrosia Campestre*, Buckthorn.

Ambrosiáno, na, *a.* Belonging to St. Ambrose.

Ambulánte, *a.* Ambulatory.

Ambulatívo, va, *a.* Of a roving turn.

Amebéo, *sm.* A dialogue in verse.

Amedrentadór, ra, *s.* One that threatens, frightens, discourages.

Amedrentár, *va.* To frighten, to deter, to discourage.

Amélga, *sf.* A ridge between two furrows thrown up by the plough.

Amelgádo, *sm.* A little hillock to mark the boundaries of a field.

Amelgár, *va.* 1. To open furrows with the plough. 2. To throw up earth to mark boundaries. [amellus *L.*

Amélo, *sm.* (Bot.) Golden star-wort. Aster

Amelonádo, da, *a.* Shaped like a melon.

Amen, *sm.* A Hebrew word, signifying at the end of a prayer, *So be it.* *Voto de amen*, A partial vote, given without the least previous discussion or inquiry. *Sacristan de amen*, One who blindly adheres to the opinion of another. *Amen de*, (Vulg.) Besides; except.

Amenáza, *sf.* A threat, a menace.

Amenazadór, ra, *s.* One who threatens.

Amenazár, *va.* To threaten, to menace.

Aménes ó Amiénes, *sm. pl.* Amiens, a sort of stuff manufactured at *Amiens* in France, also called *burato* in some parts of Spain. *Amenes figurados, lisos, rayados ó listados*; Flowered, plain, striped Amiens.

Amenguár, *va.* 1. To diminish. 2. To defame.

Amenidád, *sf.* 1. Amenity; pleasant and delicious view of verdant fields. 2. (Met.) The florid variety of elegant language.

Amenizár, *va.* 1. To render pleasant or agreeable. 2. (Met.) To adorn a speech with erudition and pleasing sentiments. [ed.

Améno, na, *a.* Pleasant, delicious; ornament-

Aménte, *a.* V. *Demente.*

Améos, V. *Amí.*

Amerár, *va.* To mix wine or other liquor with water.—*vr.* To soak or enter gradually into the ground, or through a building, as water.

Amercendeár, *va.* To bestow favours, to do good, to favour.

Ametaládo, da, *a.* Having the colour of brass.

Ametísta y Ametísto. V. *Amatista.*

Amí, *sm.* (Bot.) Royal cumin, bishop's weed. Ammi majus *L.*

A'mia, *sf.* A large sea-fish of the order *Thoracici.* Scomber amia *L.*

Amiánto ó Amiánta, *s.* (Min.) Amianthus, a filamentous fossil.

Amicíssimo, ma, *a. sup.* Most friendly.

A' miédo, *ad.* For fear. V. *De miedo.*

Amiénto, *sm.* A leather strap, with which the helmet is tied under the chin.

Amíga, *sf.* (And.) A school for girls.

Amigáble, *a.* 1. Friendly, amicable. 2. (Met.) Fit, suitable.

Amigableménte, *ad.* Amicably.

Amígo, ga, *s.* A friend.

Amígo, ga, *a.* Friendly; illicit lover.

Amiguíllo, la, *s.* A little friend; a term commonly used to express contempt.

Amilanár, *va.* To frighten, to terrify.

Amillaramiénto, *sm.* Assessment of a tax.

Amillarár, *va.* To assess a tax.

Amillonádo, da, *a.* Liable to pay a tax called *millones*, which is levied on wine, vinegar, oil, meat, soap, and tallow-candles.

Aminár, *va.* V. *Minar.*

Amistád, *sf.* 1. Amity, friendship. 2. A connexion founded upon a carnal intercourse. 3. Civility, favour. *Hacer amistad á alguno*, To treat one with kindness. 4. (Rar.) Inclination, desire.

Amistár, *va.* y *r.* To reconcile, to bring about a reconciliation.

Amistosaménte, *ad.* In a friendly manner.

Amistóso, sa, *a.* Friendly, amicable.

Amíto, *sm.* Amice, a square piece of linen with a cross in the middle, which forms the undermost part of a priest's garment when he officiates at the mass.

Amnistía ó Amnestía, *sf.* Amnesty, an act of oblivion published by a sovereign.

A'mo, ma, *s.* 1. Master or mistress of a house. 2. *Amo*, Proprietor, owner. 3. Foster-father. 4. Overseer. 5. *Ama*, A nurse. V. *Ama.*

Amoblár, *va.* V. *Moblar.*

Amodíta, *sf.* A sort of small serpent, otherwise called a horned serpent.

Amodorrádo, da, *a.* Heavy with sleep.

Amodorrárse, *vr.* To be drowsy, to grow heavy with sleep.

Amogotádo, da, *a.* Steep with a flat crown; applied by seamen to a mountain descried at sea.

Amohecérse, *vr.* To grow mouldy or rusty.

Amohinár, *va.* y *r.* To put out of humour, to irritate.

Amojamádo, da, *a.* Dry and clean, like a smoked tunny-fish.

Amojonadór, *sm.* One who marks the limits of lands, who sets landmarks.

Amojonamiénto, *sm.* The act of setting landmarks.

Amojonár, *va.* To set landmarks, to mark roads with mounds of earth or stone.

Amoladéra, *sf.* Whetstone; grindstone.

Amoladór, *sm.* 1. Grinder, whetter. 2. An unskilful coachman, a bad driver.

Amoladúra, *sf.* The action of whetting, grinding, or sharpening by attrition. *Amoladúras*, The small sand which falls from the whetstone at the time of whetting or grinding.

Amolár, *va.* To whet, grind, or sharpen an edged tool by attrition.

Amoldadór, *sm.* One who moulds or fits.

Amoldár, *va.* 1. To mould, to cast in a mould. *Amoldar las agujas*, To polish or finish needles. 2. (Met.) To adjust according to the rules of reason, to bring one to his duty. 3. (Ant.) To brand or mark cattle.

Amolladór, ra, *s.* One who lets pass a winning card having a superior one.

Amollár, *va.* 1. (Naút.) To ease off, to ease away. 2. To play an inferior card to a winning one, having a superior card in one's hand, in the game of *reversy*.

Amolletádo, da, *a.* Having the shape of a loaf of bread.

Amómo, *sm.* (Bot.) Stone-parsley, bone-wort. Sison amomum *L.*

Amondongádo, da, *a.* Sallow, coarse. *Muger amondongada*, A coarse-featured black woman.

Amonedár, *va.* To coin, to stamp metals for money.

Amonestación, *sf.* 1. Advice, admonition, warning. 2. Publication of marriage-bans.

Amonestadór, ra, *s.* Monitor; one that admonishes.

Amonestár, *va.* 1. To advise, to admonish. To publish bans of marriage.

Amoníaco, *sm.* Ammoniac.

Amontár, *vn.* To fly or take to the mountains.

Amontonadór, ra, *s.* One that heaps or accumulates.

Amontonamiénto, *sm.* Accumulation; the act of accumulating.

Amontonár, *va.* 1. To heap or throw things together without order or choice. 2. (Pint.) To group a crowd of figures in a painting.—*vr.* To fly into a passion; to grow angry or vexed, and not listen to reason.

Amór, *sm.* 1. Tenderness, affection, love. 2. The object of love. 3. A word of endearment. *Amor mio ó mis amores*, My love. *Por amor de Dios*, for the love of God; an expression of eager solicitation, as charity, &c. *Amor mio ó mis amores*, (Bot.) Sea-daffodil. Pancratium maritimum *L.* *Amor de hortelano*, (Bot.) Goose-grass, cleavers. Galium aparine *L.* *Al amor de la lumbre*, Close to the fire, so that it warms without burning.—*pl.* 1. Amours, criminal love. 2. (Bot.) Burdock. Arctium lappa *L.* *De mil amores*, *ad.* With all my heart.

Amoradúx, *sm.* (Bot.) V. *Mejorana.*

Amoratádo y Amorëtádo, da, *a.* Livid; inclining to the colour of mulberries.

Amorcíllo, *sm.* Slight love, kindness.

Amorgádo, da, *a.* Stupified from eating the husks of pressed olives: applied to fish.

Amoricónes, *sm. pl.* (Bax.) Looks, gestures, and actions, expressive of love and fondness.

Amorío, *sm.* Friendship. V. *Enamoramiento.*

Amoriscádo, da, *a.* Resembling the Moors.

Amormádo, da, *a.* Applied to horses having the glanders.

Amorosaménte, *ad.* Lovingly; amorously.

Amoróso, sa, *a.* 1. Affectionate, kind, loving. 2. Lovely, pleasing. 3. Gentle, mild, serene. *La tarde está amorosa*, It is a charming evening. 4. Tractable, easy, facile.

Amorrár, *vn.* 1. To hold down the head; to muse. 2. To return no answer to what is asked or said; to remain silent with down cast looks.

Amortajár, *va.* To shroud a corpse, to wrap it up in a winding-sheet.

Amortecérse, *vr.* To faint, to be in a swoon.

Amortecimiénto, *sm.* Swoon; fainting.

Amortiguación, Amortiguamiénto, *s.* Mortification, the act of deadening.

Amortiguár, *va.* 1. To mortify, to deaden. 2. To temper, to mollify. 3. To soften colours that they be not too glaring.

Amortización, *sf.* Mortmain, the state of being inalienable; the action by which property is rendered inalienable.

Amortizár, *va.* To render an estate inalienable by transferring it to an ecclesiastical community.

A'mos, A'mas, *pron.* (Ant.) V. *Ambos.*

Amoscár, *va.* To flap flies, to frighten them away with a flap.—*vr.* 1. To shake off the flies. 2. To become irritated.
Amosquilládo, da, *a.* Applied to cattle when tormented with flies, that thrust their heads under the evergreen oaks, furze, &c.
Amostachádo, da, *a.* Wearing whiskers.
Amostazárse, *vr.* To fly into a violent passion; to be vexed.
Amotinadór, ra, *s.* Mutineer; one that stirs up a mutiny or revolt.
Amotinamiénto, *sm.* The act of stirring up a sedition; mutiny.
Amotinár, *va.* 1. To excite rebellion. 2. (Met.) To perturbate the mind; to disorder the mental faculties.
Amovér, *va.* To depose, to remove.
Amovíble, *a.* That which can be moved at will; a term applied to ecclesiastical livings.
Ampa, V. *Hampa.*
Ampára, *sf.* 1. Seizure of chattels or moveable property. 2. (Ant.) V. *Amparo.*
Amparadór, ra, *s.* Protector; favourer.
Amparár, *va.* 1. To shelter, to favour, to protect. 2. (For. Arag.) To make a seizure of chattels or moveable property; to sequestrate. *Amparar en la posesion,* (For.) To maintain in possession.—*vr.* 1. To claim or enjoy protection. 2. To preserve; to recover.
Ampáro, *sm.* 1. Favour, protection, sanction. 2. Refuge, asylum. 3. (Ant.) Breastwork, parapet.
Amphíbio, V. *Anfibio.*—Amphiscios, V. *Anfiscios.*
Amphisbéna, V. *Anfisbena.*
Amphiteátro, V. *Anfiteatro.*
Ampláménte, *ad.* Amply, copiously.
Ampliación, *sf.* Ampliation, enlargement; the act of ampliating or enlarging.
Ampliadór, ra, *s.* Amplifier, one that enlarges.
Ampliaménte, *ad.* Amply, largely, copiously.
Ampliár, *va.* To amplify, to enlarge.
Ampliatívo, va, *a.* Amplifying; having the power of ampliating or enlarging.
Amplificación, *sf.* Amplification, enlargement.
Amplificadór, ra, *s.* Amplifier.
Amplificár, *va.* 1. To amplify, to enlarge. 2. To use the figure of speech termed *amplification.*
Ámplio, lia, *a.* Ample, extensive; dilated.
Amplitúd, *sf.* 1. Amplitude, extent, greatness. 2. (Naút.) *Amplitud magnética,* Magnetic amplitude, or an arch of the horizon contained between the sun and the centre thereof, at the east or west point of the compass. 3. (Astr.) An arch of the horizon intercepted between the true east and west point thereof, and the centre of the sun or star at their rising or setting.
Ámplo, la, *a.* V. *Amplio.*
Ampo de la niéve, Whiteness. This expression is used comparatively; *e. g. Blanco como el ampo de la nieve,* White as the driven snow.
Ampólla, *sf.* 1. A blister formed by raising the cuticle from the cutis. 2. A phial, a cruet. 3. A small bubble of water, formed either by the fall of rain or boiling.
Ampollár, *va.* 1. To blister, to raise blisters. 2. To make hollow, to excavate.—*vr.* To rise in bubbles by the force of the wind.
Ampollár, *a.* Resembling a blister.
Ampolléta, *sf.* (Dim.) 1. A small phial. 2. An hour-glass, a glass filled with sand, which, running through a narrow hole, marks the time. 3. (Naút.) Watch-glass, by which the watch on board ships is regulated.
Amprár, *va.* (Arag.) To borrow; to ask of another the use of something for a time.
Amuchachádo, da, *a.* Boyish, childish.
Amuchiguár, *va.* (Ant.) To augment, to multiply.
Amugamiénto, *sm.* V. *Amojonamiento.*
Amugerádo, da, *a.* Effeminate, having the face, actions, and sentiments of a woman.
Amugeramiénto, *sm.* V. *Afeminacion.*
Amugronadór, ra, *s.* One who trains vine shoots.
Amugronár, *va.* To carry the large shoot of a vine under the earth in order that its extremity may spring up far enough from the original stock.
Amulárse, *vr.* To become sterile.
Amulatádo, da, *a.* Of a tawny complexion, resembling that of a Mulatto.
Amuléto, *sm.* Amulet, hung about the neck for preventing or curing a disease.
Amunicionár, *va.* To supply with ammunition.
Amúra, *sf.* 1. (Naút.) Tack of a sail. *Amura mayor,* Main tack. *Amura del trinquete,* The fore-tack. 2. (Naút.) A word of command. *Amura á babor,* Aboard larboard-tacks. *Amura á estribor,* Aboard starboard-tacks. *Amura trinquete,* Aboard fore-tacks. *Cambiar la amura,* To stand on the other tack.
Amurádas, *sf. pl.* (Naút.) Spirketing, or spirket-rising, the range of planks between the water ways and the lower edge of the gun-ports of a ship of war.
Amurár, *va.* (Naút.) To haul the tack aboard.
Amurcár, *va.* To strike with the horns; applied to a bull.
Amúrco, *sm.* Blow or stroke with the horns.
Amusgár, *va.* 1. To throw back the ears, as a sign of biting or wincing in horses and mules. *Amusgár las orejas,* (Met. Ant.) To listen. 2. To contract the eyes to see better.
Ána, *sf.* 1. Ell, a measure smaller than a yard. 2. An animal of the fox kind in the Indies. 3. Medical prescription, signifying equal parts.
Anabaptísta ó Anabatísta, *sm.* Anabaptist, a sectary, who holds that children ought not to be baptized until they have attained the age of reason.
Anacalífa, *sm.* A poisonous animal of Madagascar.
Anacálo, la, *s.* (Ant.) A baker's servant.
Anacarádo, da, *a.* Of a pearly white colour.
Anacardél, *sm.* A kind of Madagascar serpent.
Anacardína, *sf.* Confection, or sweet-meat, made of anacardium or cashew-nut.
Anacárdo, *sm.* (Bot.) Cashew-tree. Anacardium occidentale *L.*
Anacoréta, *sm.* Anchorite, a recluse, an hermit.
Anacorético, ca, *a.* Relating or belonging to a recluse or hermit.
Anacósta, *sf.* A sort of woollen stuff.
Anacreóntico, ca, ó Anacreóncio, *a.* Anacreontic.
Anacronísmo, *sm.* Anachronism, an error in computing time, whereby an event is placed at an earlier or later period than it actually happened.

A'NADE, *sm.* y *f.* Duck. Anas boschas *L.*
ANADEÁR, *vn.* To waddle, to shake from side to side in walking, like ducks.
ANADÉJA, *sf.* (dim.) A duckling.
ANADÍNO, NA, *s.* A young duck.
ANADÓN, *sm.* V. *A'nade.*
ANADONCÍLLO, *sm.* A grown duckling.
ANAFÁYA, *sf.* A sort of cloth formerly manufactured in Valencia.
ANÁFE, *sm.* A portable furnace or stove.
ANÁFORA, *sm.* Anaphora, a figure, when several periods of a speech are begun with the same word.
ANAGÁLIDE, *sf.* Pimpernel. Anagallis arvensis [*L.*
ANAGÍRIS, *sf.* (Bot.) Stinking beantrefoil. Anagyris fœtida *L.*
ANAGLÍFOS, *sm. pl.* Vases, vessels, or other works adorned with sculpture in *basso relievo*, so that the figures seem standing out from the ground.
ANAGÓGIA Y ANAGÓGE, *sf.* The mystic sense of the holy Scripture.
ANAGOGICAMÉNTE, *ad.* In an anagogical manner.
ANAGÓGICO, CA, *a.* Anagogetical.
ANAGRÁMA, *sf.* Anagram, a transposition of the letters of a name, word, or sentence, by which another word or sentence is formed.
ANÁL, V. *Anual*, *Añal*, and *Anales.*
ANALÉCTICO ó ANALÉPTICO, *sm.* (Med.) Restorative.
ANÁLES, *sm. pl.* Annals or historical accounts digested in the order of years.
ANÁLISIS, *sf.* 1. Analysis; a solution of any thing, whether corporeal or mental, to its first elements. 2. Mathematical, or critical, or chemical analysis.
ANALÍSTA, *sm.* 1. Annalist, a writer of annals. 2. Student of geometry and algebra.
ANALITICAMÉNTE, *ad.* Analytically.
ANALÍTICO, CA, *a.* Analytical, that which resolves any thing into first principles.
ANALIZÁR, *va.* To analyze.
ANALOGAMÉNTE, V. *Analógicamente.*
ANALOGÍA, *sf.* 1. Analogy, resemblance or relation which things bear to each other. 2. Second part of grammar.
ANALOGICAMÉNTE, *ad.* Analogically.
ANALÓGICO, CA, ANÁLOGO, GA, *a.* Analogical or analogous.
ANÁNAS, *sm.* (Bot.) Ananas, pine-apple. Bromelia ananas *L.*
ANAPÉLO, *sm.* (Bot.) Wolf's-bane. V. *Napelo.*
ANAPÉSTO, *sm.* A Latin verse, consisting of two short syllables and a long one.
ANAQUÉL, *sm.* Shelf or board fixed against or supported in book-cases, &c. on which any thing may be placed.
ANARANGEÁR, *va.* To pelt with oranges.
ANARANJÁDO, DA, *a.* Orange-coloured.
ANARQUÍA, *sf.* Anarchy.
ANÁRQUICO, CA, *a.* Anarchial, confused, without [rule.
ANASÁRCA, *sf.* (Med.) Anasarca, a dropsy.
ANASCÓTE, *sm.* Says, a kind of woollen stuff like serge.
ANASTASIA, *sf.* V. *Artemisa.*
ANASTÓMOSIS, *sf.* (Anat.) The inosculation of vessels, or the conjunction of their extremities, by means whereof they communicate with each other, as vein with vein.

ANASTRÓFE, *sm.* (Ret.) Anastrophe, an inversion of words, whereby those which should have been precedent are postponed.
ANÁTA, *sf.* Annats, the first fruits or emoluments which a benefice or employ produces. *Media anata*, The annats of the half year.
ANATÉMA, *s.* 1. Anathema, a curse pronounced by ecclesiastical authority; excommunication. 2. (Ant.) A person anathematized or excommunicated.
ANATEMATÍSMO, *sm.* V. *Excomunion.*
ANATEMATIZÁR, *va.* 1. To anathematize, to excommunicate. 2. To curse, to imprecate.
ANATÍSTA, *sm.* Officer for the half-year's annats.
ANATOCÍSMO, *sm.* Anatocism, the accumulation of interest upon interest.
ANATOMÍA, *sf.* 1. Anatomy, the art of dissecting the human body. 2. Doctrine of the structure of the human body. 3. (Pint.) Skeleton, by which painters and sculptors study the structure of the human frame.
ANATOMICAMÉNTE, *ad.* Anatomically.
ANATÓMICO, CA, *a.* Anatomical.
ANATOMÍSTA, *sm.* Anatomist, professor of anatomy.
ANATOMIZÁR, *va.* 1. To anatomize or dissect an animal body. 2. (Pint.) To form and draw, with the utmost exactness, the bones and muscles in statues and figures.
ANAVAJÁDO, DA, (Ant.) Having knife scars.
A'NCA, *sf.* Croup, the buttocks of a horse. *A' ancas ó á las ancas*, Behind. *A' ancas ó á las ancas de fulano*, With the assistance of Mr Such-a-one.
ANCÁDO, *sm.* (Alb.) A distemper, consisting in a painful contraction of the nerves and muscles.
ANCHAMÉNTE, *ad.* Widely, largely.
ANCHÁNIA, *sf.* (Among merchants and traders.) The width of stuff or cloth.
ANCHÉTA, *sf.* Venture, goods which a person, not engaged in trade, sends or carries on his own account to India.
ANCHICÓRTA, *sf.* (Joc.) A short broad sword.
A'NCHO, CHA, *a.* Broad, wide, extended in breadth. *Ponerse muy ancho*, (Met.) To look big; to be elated with pride. *Vida ancha*, A loose life.
ANCHÓVA Y ANCHÓA, *sf.* Anchovy. Clupea encrasicolus *L.*
ANCHÓR ó ANCHO, *sm.* V. *Anchura.*
ANCHUÉLO, LA, *a.* Somewhat wide.
ANCHÚRA, *sf.* Width, breadth. *A' mis anchuras ó á sus anchuras*, At large, at full liberty. *Vivo á mis anchuras*, I live just as I choose.
ANCHURÓSO, SA, *a.* Large, wide, spacious.
ANCHÚSA, *sf.* (Bot.) Alkanet. Anchusa tinctoria *L.*
ANCIANÁR, *vn.* (Poét.) V. *Envejecer.*
ANCIANÍA, *sf.* (Ant.) In the military orders of friars, the dignity and jurisdiction of the four oldest fathers in the convent.
ANCIANIDÁD, *sf.* 1. Old age. 2. Antiquity.
ANCIÁNO, NA, *a.* Old, stricken in years.
A'NCLA, *sf.* Anchor. *Zafar el ancla para dar fondo*, To clear the anchor for coming to. *El ancla viene al baxel*, The anchor comes home. *El ancla ha soltado el fondo*, The anchor is

a-trip. *Pescar una ancla,* To drag for an anchor. *Alotar las anclas,* To stow the anchors. *Argansa de ancla,* An anchoring. *Caña del ancla,* The shank of the anchor. *Cepo del ancla,* The anchor-stock. *Cruz del ancla,* The crown of the anchor. *Orejas del ancla,* The flukes of the anchor. *Uñas del ancla,* The anchor arms. *Pico del ancla,* The bill of the anchor. *Al ancla ó anclado,* At anchor. *Ancla de la esperanza,* Sheet-anchor. *Ancla del ayuste ó de uso,* The best bower-anchor. *Ancla sencilla ó de leva,* The small bower-anchor. *Ancla del creciente,* The flood-anchor. *Ancla del menguante,* The ebb-anchor. *Ancla de la mar hacia fuera,* Sea-anchor. *Ancla de la tierra ó playa,* Shore-anchor. *Anclas de servidumbre,* Bower-anchors.

Ancladéro, *sm.* (Naút.) Anchor-smith.

Ancláge, *sm.* 1. The act of casting anchor. 2. Anchor-ground, or anchoring-ground. *Derecho de anclage,* Anchorage.

Anclár, *vn.* To anchor.

Anclóte, *sm.* Stream-anchor.

Anclotíllo, *sm.* Kedge-anchor.

Ancón, *sm.* An open road, a bay.

Áncora. V. *Ancla. Echar áncoras,* To cast anchor. *Llevar áncoras,* To weigh anchor. *Estar en áncoras ó sobre las ancoras,* To lie at anchor.

Ancoráge, *sm.* V. *Anclage.*

Ancorár, V. *Anclar.* [painters.

Ancórca, *sf.* A pale yellow earth used by

Ancorería, *sf.* Anchor forge.

Ancoréro, *sm.* Anchor-smith. [L.

Ancúsa, *sf.* (Bot.) Bugloss. Borago officinalis

Andabáta, *sm.* A gladiator who fought hoodwinked.

Andabóra, *sf.* V. *Parar.*

Andáda, *sf.* A thin hard baked cake without crumb. *Andádas,* The traces of game marked on the ground. [learn to walk.

Andadéras, *sm. pl.* Go-carts, in which children

Andadéro, ra, *a.* Accessible, of easy access.

Andádo, *sm.* Step-son; a son-in-law.

Andádo, da, *a.* 1. Beaten, much frequented; applied to a road. 2. Worse for use, threadbare. 3. Usual, customary.

Andadór, ra, *s.* 1. A good walker. 2. Messenger of a court. 3. (Naút.) A fine sailer; a swift sailing vessel. 4. Inferior minister of justice.

Andadóres, *pl.* 1. Leading strings. 2. Alleys or small walks in a garden.

Andadúra, *sf.* 1. Gait, the act and manner of walking. 2. Amble, an easy pace of a horse.

Andália, *sf.* Sandal.

Andalúz, za, *a.* Native of Andalusia.

Andámio, *sm.* 1. Scaffold. 2. (Ant.) Platform of a rampart. 3. Gait, manner of walking. 4. (Naút.) Stage; gangboard.

Andána, *sf.* 1. Row, rank, line. 2. (Naút.) *Andana de los cañones de un costado,* A tier of guns; also a broadside. 3. (Naút.) *Andana de rizos,* The reefs in the sails of ships.

Andaníños, *sm. pl.* Leading strings.

Andantésco, ca, *a.* That which belongs to knighthood, or knight errants.

Andánza, *sf.* Occurrence, event.

Andár, *vn.* 1. To go, to walk, to move along. 2 To act, to proceed, to behave, to transact. 3. To elapse. 4. To go, move or act; applied to machines. *Andar en cuerpo,* To go abroad without a cloak or surtout. *Andar del cuerpo,* To go to stool. *Andar por decir ó por hacer una cosa,* To be determined to say or do a thing. *Andar á caza de gangas,* To waste one's time in fruitless pursuits. *Andar en carnes,* To go stark naked. *Andar de zeca en meca,* To be roving and wandering about. *Todo se andará,* Every thing will be looked into. *Es preciso andar con el tiempo,* It is necessary to conform to the times. *Andar en dares y tomares ó en dimes y diretes,* To be in cross purposes; to deal in *ifs* and *ands.* *Andar en buena vela,* (Naút.) To keep the sails full. *Andar todo,* (Naút.) To bear up the helm. *A' mejor andar,* At best, at most. *A' peor andar,* At worst. *A' mas andar,* In full speed. *Andar el mundo al reves,* To reverse the order of nature, to do any thing contrary to the manner it ought to be.

Andár, *interj.* Well, never mind. *Anda,* Stand out of the way. *Anda hijo,* Come along, child.

Andaráge, *sm.* The wheel of a well, to which the rope and bucket are fastened. [tion.

Andariégo, ga, *a.* Restless, of a roving disposi-

Andarín, *sm.* A fast walker. *Andarines,* An Italian paste of the size of lentils, used for soups. [cilla alba L.

Andarío, *sm.* (Orn.) The white wagtail. Mota-

Andarivél, *sm.* (Naút.) A girt line.

A'ndas, *sf. pl.* A bier, a hearse. [China.

Andátis, *sf.* A sort of stuff manufactured in

Andén, *sm.* 1. A shelf. V. *Anaquel.* 2. A path round the draw well for the horse, which puts the wheel in motion.

Andéro, *sm.* One who carries the shafts of a bier on his shoulders. [makers.

Andilú, *sm.* A burnishing stick used by shoe-

A'ndito, *sm.* A gallery which surrounds the whole or a considerable part of a building.

Andóla, *sf.* An unmeaning expletive used by poets.

Andolína ó Andorína, *sf.* V. *Golondrina.*

Andórga, *sf.* *Llenar la andorga,* To fill the belly, to eat much.

Andorína, *sf.* (Naút.) A truss, a parrel.

Andorréro, ra, y Andórra, *s.* (Vulg.) Street-walker.

Andósco, ca, *a.* Two years old; applied to ewes. [clothes.

Andrajéro, *sm.* Ragman, who deals in old

Andrájo, *sm.* 1. Rag of worn clothes. 2. (Met.) A despicable thing or person. *Hacer andrajos,* To tear to rags.

Andrajosaménte, *ad.* Raggedly.

Andrajóso, sa, *a.* Ragged, dressed in tatters.

Andriána, *sf.* A kind of gown formerly worn

Andrína, *sf.* A sloe. V. *Endrina.* [by women.

Andríno, *sm.* (Bot.) Sloe-tree, black thorn. Prunus spinosa L.

Andrógino y Andrógeno, *sm.* Hermaphrodite, an animal uniting both sexes.

Andrómina, *sf.* (Bax.) Trick, fraud, artifice.

Androséno, *sm.* (Bot.) St. John's wort. Hypericum ascyron L. [habited by Arabs.

Anduár, *sm.* A kind of ambulatory village in-

Andulários, *sm. pl.* A long and wide gown.

Anduléncia, *sf.* (Joc.) Occurrence, event.

ANDÚLLO, *sm.* 1. Carot of tobacco. 2. V. *Pandéro.*
ANDURRIÁLES, *sm. pl.* By-roads, retired places.
ANÉA, *sf.* (Bot.) Great cat's tail, reed mace. Typha latifolia *L.*
ANEÁGE, *sm.* Alnage, ell measure.
ANEÁR, *va.* 1. To measure by ells. 2. (Burgos.) To rock in a cradle.
ANEBLÁR, *va.* To cloud, to darken, to obscure.
ANEGACIÓN, *sf.* Overflowing, inundation.
ANEGADÍZO, ZA, *a.* Liable to be overflowed.
ANEGÁDO, DA, *a.* Overflowed. *Navio anegado,* (Naút.) A water-logged ship.
ANEGAMIÉNTO, *sm.* V. *Anegacion.*
ANEGÁR, *va.* To inundate, to submerge.—*vr.* To be inundated.
ANEGOCIÁDO, DA, *a.* Overwhelmed with business.
ANÉGRAS Y ANÁGROS, *s. pl.* A corn-measure in some parts of Spain.
ANÉMONE, *sf.* (Bot.) Anemone or wind flower.
ANEMOSCÓPIO, *sm.* Anemoscope, a machine invented to foretel the changes of the wind.
A'NEQUÍN Ó DE ANEQUÍN, *ad.* So much a head; applied to the shearing of sheep.
ANEURÍSMA, *sf.* 1. A disease of the arteries, in which they become excessively dilated. 2. An extraordinary dilatation of an artery.
ANEXÁR, *va.* To annex, to join, to unite.
ANEXIDÁDES, *sf. pl.* Annexes, things annexed.
ANEXIÓN, *sf.* Annexion, union, conjunction.
ANÉXO, XA, *a.* Annexed, joined.
ANÉXO, *sm.* A benefice or church depending on another as its principal or head.
ANFÍBIO, BIA, *a.* Amphibious.
ANFIBOLOGÍA, *sf.* Amphibology, words or sentences of a double or doubtful meaning.
ANFIBOLÓGICO, CA, *a.* Amphibological, doubtful.
ANFÍBRACO, *sm.* Amphibrachys, a foot in Latin verse.
ANFICÉFALO, *sm.* A bed with two bolsters opposite to each other.
ANFÍMACRO, *sm.* Amphimacer, a foot in Latin verse.
ANFIÓN, *sm.* Opium.
ANFISBÉNA Y ANFISIBÉNA, *sf.* Amphisbena, an amphibious serpent with a tail as big as its head, and which moves backwards or forwards with the same facility.
ANFÍSCIOS, *sm. pl.* Amphiscii, people of the torrid zone, whose shadows at different times fall north and south.
ANFITEÁTRO, *sm.* Amphitheatre, a circular building.
ANFRACTUOSIDÁDES, *sf. pl.* (Anat.) Anfractuosities, convolutions of the brain or cerebrum.
ANGARÍLLAS, *sf. pl.* 1. Hand-barrow, in which mortar, stones, &c. are carried. 2. Baskets hung to a horse's or mule's side. 3. Cruet-stands. 4. V. *Aguaderas.*
ANGARILLÓN, *sm.* A large wicker basket; a large hand-barrow.
ANGARIPÓLA, *sf.* A kind of coarse striped linen. *Angaripólas,* Gaudy ornaments on clothes.
A'NGARO, *sm.* Light, fire or smoke, used as a signal.
A'NGEL, *sm.* 1. Angel, a spiritual being. 2. A sort of fish much resembling a ray. 3. (Art.) Barshot. *Manga de A'ngel,* Sleeve of a coat ruffled or plaited like a woman's ruffle. *A'ngel custodio ó de la guarda,* Guardian angel. *A'ngel de guarda,* Protector, patron. *A'ngel patudo,* Nickname of a person more malicious than commonly supposed.

ANGÉLICA, *sf.* (Bot.) Angelica. Angelica *L.* *Angélica carlina,* (Bot.) Carline thistles, ash-weed. Carlina acaulis *L.*
ANGELICÁL Y ANGÉLICO, CA, *a.* Angelical or angelic.
ANGELICALMÉNTE, *ad.* In an angelic manner.
ANGELÍCO Y ÍTO, *sm.* (Dim.) A little angel; child.
ANGELÓN, *sm.* (Aum.) Great angel. *Angelon de retablo,* Nickname given to one disproportionately corpulent and besotted.
ANGELÓTE, *sm.* 1. A large figure of an angel placed on altars. 2. A fat, good-natured child.
ANGÉO, *sm.* A coarse sort of linen made in *Anjou.*
ANGÍNA, *sf.* Quinsy, a tumid inflammation in the throat.
A'NGLA, *sf.* A cape.
ANGOSTAMÉNTE, *ad.* Narrowly.
ANGOSTÁR, *va.* To narrow, to contract.
ANGOSTÍLLO, LLA, *a.* A little narrow.
ANGÓSTO, TA, *a.* Narrow, close, strait. *Venir angosto,* To fall short of one's expectations, ambition, or merit.
ANGOSTÚRA, *sf.* 1. Narrowness. 2. A narrow pass. 3. Distress.
A'NGRA, *sf.* A small bay, a cove.
ANGUARÍNA, *sf.* A loose coat hanging down to the knees.
ANGUÍLA, *sf.* (Ict.) Eel. Muræna anguila *L.* *Anguila de cabo,* (Naút.) A port rope with which sailors are flogged on board the galleys. *Anguilas,* Slips or planks on which the keel of a ship slides when launching into the water.
ANGUILÁZO, *sm.* A lash or stroke with a port rope.
ANGUILÉRO, RA, *s.* Basket or pannier for eels.
ANGUÍNA, *sf.* (Alb.) The vein of the groins.
ANGULÁR, *a.* Angular, having angles. *Piedra angular,* The corner stone in a building.
ANGULARMÉNTE, *ad.* With angles.
ANGULÉMA, *sf.* A sort of coarse linen manufactured at *Angoulême* of hemp or tow. *Angulemas,* (Bax.) Fulsome flatteries.
A'NGULO, *sm.* Angle. *A'ngulo óptico,* The visual angle. *A'ngulos de un picadero,* The corners of a riding house.
ANGULÓSO, SA, *a.* Angular, cornered.
ANGÚRRIA, V. *Sandía.*
ANGÚSTIA, *sf.* Anguish, affliction.
ANGUSTIADAMÉNTE, *ad.* Painfully.
ANGUSTIÁDO, DA, *a.* 1. Painful, afflicted with pain. 2. (Met.) Narrow-minded, miserable.
ANGUSTIÁR, *va.* To cause anguish, to afflict.
ANHELÁR, *vn.* 1. To breathe with difficulty. 2. To desire anxiously, to wish eagerly. *Anhelar honores,* To aspire at honours.
ANHÉLITO, *sm.* Respiration.
ANHÉLO, *sm.* A vehement desire; anxiousness.
ANHELÓSO, SA, *a.* Anxiously desirous.
ANHEMÉLES, *sm. pl.* (And.) Horses or other beasts of burthen destined for the conveyance of goods to the sea-side.
ANHÍNA, *sf.* (Orn.) An aquatic bird of prey in Brasil, called the darter. Plotus *L.*
ANIÁGA, *sf.* (Mur.) The yearly wages of a ploughman or labourer.
ANIDÁR, *vn.* 1. To nestle, to make a nest. 2. (Met.) To dwell, to inhabit, to reside. 3. To cherish, to shelter. *Andar anidando,* To prepare for lying in; applied to women great with child.
ANIEBLÁR, *va.* To darken, to obscure. V. *Anublar.*
ANIFÁLA, *sf.* Bread made of bran.

Anillár, *va.* To form rings or circles in work, used by cutlers.
Anilléjo y Anilléte, *sm.* A small ring.
Anillo, *sm.* 1. A ring of gold, silver, &c. worn on the finger. 2. (Naút.) Hank or grummet. *Venir como anillo al dedo*, To come in the very nick of time. 3. (Arq.) Astragal.
A'nima, *sf.* 1. Soul. V. *Alma* 2. (Art.) The bore or diameter of the chase of a gun. *A'nimas*, Ringing of bells at a certain hour, generally at sun-setting, which admonishes the faithful to pray for the souls in purgatory. *A' las ánimas me volví á casa*, At sunsetting I returned home.
Animación, *sf.* Animation.
Animadór, ra, *s.* One who animates, animator.
Animadversión, *sf.* Observation, remark, stricture.
Animadverténcia, *sf.* Admonition, advice.
Animál, *sm.* 1. A living creature, an animal. 2. In contempt, we say that an ignorant and stupid person is—un *animal*.
Animál, *a.* Animal, relating to an animal.
Animaládo, da, *a.* Animalized.
Animalázo, *sm.* A large or big animal.
Animaléjo, ico y íllo, *sm.* A small animal, animalcule.
Animalón y Animalóte, *sm.* A large or big animal.
Animalúcho, *sm.* An ugly, hideous animal.
Animár, *va.* 1. To animate, to enliven, to incite. 2. To give power or vigour to inanimate things.
A'nime ó Goma Anime, *sf.* A resin resembling myrrh.
Animéro, *sm.* One who asks charity for the souls in purgatory.
A'nimo, *sm.* 1. Soul, the immaterial spirit of man. 2. Courage, valour, fortitude. 3. Mind, intention, will. 4. Thought, attention. *Hacer buen ánimo*, To bear up under adversities.
Animosaménte, *ad.* In a spirited manner, courageously.
Animosidád, *sf.* Valour, courage; boldness.
Animóso, sa, *a.* Brave, spirited.
Aniñadaménte, *ad.* In a childish, puerile manner.
Aniñárse, *vr.* To grow childish, to act in a childish manner.
Aniquiláble, *a.* Annihilable, that may be annihilated.
Aniquilación, *sf.* Annihilation, reducing or reduced to nothing.
Aniquiladór, ra, *s.* Destroyer, one who annihilates.
Aniquilamiénto, *sm.* V. *Aniquilacion*.
Aniquilár, *va.* To annihilate, to destroy, to put out of existence.—*vr.* To decline, to decay; to humble.
Anís, *sm.* (Bot.) Anise. Pimpenella anisum *L.* *Anises*, Anise seeds preserved in sugar. *Llegar á los anises*, To come the day after the feast.
Anisádo, da, *a.* Applied to spirits tinctured with anise.
Anisíllo, *sm.* (Dim.) Small anise.
Aniversário, ria, *a.* Annual, yearly, anniversary, returning with the revolution of the year.
Aniversário, *sm.* 1. Anniversary, a day celebrated every year. 2. A mass or service yearly performed for the soul of a person deceased, on the day of his or her death. *Libro de aniversarios*, An obituary of the persons for whom anniversaries are to be performed.
Annabáses, *sm. pl.* Blankets or coverlets manufactured in Holland, and at Rouen.
Annójo, (Mur.) V. *Añojo*
A'no, *sm.* Anus, the orifice of the fundament.
Anóche, *ad.* Last night.
Anochecér, *vn.* To grow dark. *Anochecérle á uno en alguna parte*, To be benighted somewhere. *Al anochecer*, At night-fall.—*vr.* To grow dark. *Yo amanecí en Madrid, y anochecí en Toledo*, I was in Madrid at dawn, and in Toledo at dusk.
Anodinár, *va.* To administer or apply anodyne medicines.
Anodíno, na, *a.* Anodyne, that which has the power of mitigating pain.
Anomalía, *sf.* Anomaly, irregularity, deviation from rules.
Anomalidád, *sf.* Irregularity.
Anómalo, la, *a.* (Gram.) Anomalous.
Anón, *sm.* (Bot.) The annona-tree, the custard apple-tree. Annona *L.*
Anóna, *sf.* 1. Annona or custard-apple, the fruit of the annona-tree. In some parts it is called *guanava*. 2. Store of provisions.
Anonadación, *sf.* 1. Annihilation, the act or state of being reduced to nothing. 2. Self contempt.
Anonadár, *va.* 1. To annihilate, to reduce to nothing. 2. (Met.) To diminish or lessen in a considerable degree.—*vr.* To humble or abase one's self to a low degree.
Anónimo, ma, *a.* Anonymous.
Anotación, *sf.* Annotation, note.
Anotadór, ra, *s.* Commentator, annotater.
Anotár, *va.* To write notes, to comment.
Anotomía, *sf.* V. *Anatomía*.
A'nque, V. *Aúnque*.
Anquéta. *Estar de media anqueta*, To be incommodiously seated.
Anquiboccíno, na, y Anquiboyúno, na, *a.* Having a croup like an ox; applied to horses and mules.
Anquiséco, ca, *a.* Lean crouped; applied to horses and mules.
A'nsar, *sm.* A goose. Anas anser *L.*
Ansarería, *sf.* The place where geese are reared.
Ansaréro, *sm.* A goose-herd.
Ansaríno, na, *a.* (Poét.) Belonging or relating to geese.
Ansaríno, *sm.* A gosling.
Ansarón, *sm.* A large goose.
A'nser, V. *A'nsar*.
Ansí, V. *Así*.
A'nsia, *sf.* Anxiety, anguish, ardent desire.
Ansiadaménte, *ad.* Anxiously, earnestly.
Ansiár, *va.* To desire anxiously, to wish for ardently.
Ansiedád, (Ant.) V. *Ansia*.
Ansína, V. *Así*.
Ansiosaménte, *ad.* Anxiously, earnestly, ardently.
Ansióso, sa, *a.* 1. Anxious, having a longing desire. 2. Attended with anxiety, or great uneasiness.
Ant. *prep.* y *ad.* V. *Ante* and *antes*.
A'nta, *sf.* Tapir, a kind of elk found in Brasil and Paraguay. Tapir *L.*
Antáceo, *sm.* (Ict.) A large fish of the family of sturgeons, from which *isinglass* is prepared. Acipenser huso *L.*
Antagállas *sf. pl.* (Naút.) Sprit-sail reef-bands.

Antagonísta, *sm.* Antagonist, an opponent who contends with another.
Antamílla, *sf.* (Burg.) V. *Altamía.*
Antána. *Llamarse antana,* To unsay, to retract, to deny what one said before.
Antañázo, *ad.* (Bax.) A long time since.
Antaño, *ad.* (Bax.) Last year. (Prov.) *En los nidos de antaño no hay pázaros hogaño,* Time must be seized by the forelock.
Antapóca, *sf.* A security which a debtor gives to his creditor.
Antártico, ca, *a.* Antarctic, belonging to the South pole.
A'nte, *sm.* 1. A dressed buck or buffalo skin. 2. (Ant.) The first course or number of dishes set at once on the table.
A'nte, *prep. Ante mi,* Before me, in my presence. *Ante todas cosas ó ante todo,* Before all things, above all.
Anteádo, da, *a.* Buff-coloured, of a pale yellow colour.
Anteanteanóche, *ad.* Three nights ago.
Anteanteáyer, *ad.* Three days ago.
Anteantíer, *ad.* (Ant.) V. *Anteanteayer.*
Anteáyer, *ad.* The day before yesterday.
Antebrázo, *sm.* The fore arm.
Antecáma, *sf.* A carpet laid along side of a bed.
Antecámara, *sf.* 1. Ante-chamber, a room which leads to the chief apartment. 2. (Naút.) The steerage.
Antecamarílla, *sf.* A room leading to the king's ante-chamber.
Antecapílla, *sf.* The space before the entry to a chapel.
Antecedénte, *sm.* 1. Antecedent, that which goes before. 2. The first proposition of an enthymeme. 3. A noun to which a relative is subjoined.
Antecedenteménte, *ad.* Previously, antecedently.
Antecedér, *va.* To precede.
Antecesór, ra, *s.* Predecessor, one that held a place or employment before another. *Antecesóres,* Ancestors.
Antechínos, *sm. pl.* (Arq.) Fluted mouldings.
Antéco, ca, *a.* Applied to the Anteoci or inhabitants of the same meridian at the same distance on each side the equator.
Antecogér, *va.* 1. To bring any person or thing before one. 2. To gather in fruit before the due time.
Antecolúmna, *sf.* (Arq.) A column placed in the front of porticos.
Antecóro, *sm.* The entrance which leads to the choir.
Antecrísto, *sm.* Antichrist.
Antedáta, *sf.* A date anticipated in letters and other writings.
Antedatár, *va.* To antedate, to date earlier than the true time, or before the proper time.
Ante díem, (Lat.) The preceding day, the day before. *De antedia,* (Ant.) Yesterday, prior, before.
Anteiglésia, *sf.* 1. The portico at the entrance of a church. 2. The parochial church of some towns in Biscay. 3. The district belonging to a parish.
Antelación, *sf.* Preference.
Antelucáno, na, *a.* About the dawn of day.

Antemáno, *ad. De antemano,* Before hand.
Antemeridiáno, na, *a.* Done or passed in the forenoon.
Antemúlas, *sm.* 1. Keeper or driver of mules. 2. Foremost muleteer.
Antemurál, *sm.* 1. A fort, rock, or mountain, which serves for the defence of the body of a fortress. 2. (Met.) A safeguard, defence.
Antemurálla y Antemúro, V. *Antemural.*
Anténa, *sf.* (Naút.) A lateen yard.
Antenállas, *sf. pl.* Pincers.
Antenóche, *ad.* The night before last. 2. (Ant.) Before night-fall.
Antenómbre, *sm.* A title prefixed to a proper name, but not to a family name, and equivalent to Sir in the English, as *Don Pedro, Sir Peter,* &c.
Anteójo, *sm.* A spy glass. *Anteójo de larga vista,* A telescope. *Anteójo de puño,* Opera glass.—*pl.* 1. Spectacles. 2. Pieces of felt or leather cut round, and put before the eyes of vicious horses.
Ante ómnia, (Voz Latina,) Before all things; above all.
Antepagár, *va.* To pay before hand.
Antepasádo, da, *a.* Passed; elapsed; applied to time.
Antepasádos, *sm. pl.* Ancestors, forefathers, predecessors.
Antepécho, *sm.* 1. Breastwork, parapet, battlement. 2. Footstep of a coach. 3. Poitrel, or harness, for the breast of a draught horse. 4. Breast roller of a loom for weaving tapestry. 5. The part of a ribbon frame or loom, which passes from the right to the left, to the point in which the weaver's strap is placed. *Antepéchos,* (Naút.) The iron hawse of the head.
Antepenúltimo, ma, *a.* Antepenult.
Anteponér, *va.* 1. To prefer. 2. To place before.
Antepórtico, *sm.* Vestibule or porch at the entrance of a building.
Antepuérta, *sf.* A curtain or screen placed before a door.
Antequíno, *sm.* (Arq.) V. *Esgucio.*
Antéra, *sf.* (Bot.) Anther, the roundish head which contains the prolific pollen on the stamens of flowers.
Anteriór, *a.* That which precedes in time or place; anterior.
Anterioridád, *sf.* Anteriority, priority; the state of being before; preference.
Anteriorménte, *ad.* Previously.
A'ntes, *prep.* Before, beforehand. *A'ntes de los Marqueses van los Duques,* The Dukes go before the Marquises.
A'ntes, *ad.* First, rather, better. *Haga vm. esto ántes,* Do this first. *Quisiera ántes esto que aquello,* I would rather have this than that. *A'ntes morir que pecar,* Better to die than to sin. It also denotes preference of time or place. *A'ntes bien,* Rather. *A'ntes del dia,* Before day or at day-break. *A'ntes con ántes,* As soon as possible. *De ántes,* Of old, in ancient times. *Las cosas de ántes son muy diferentes de las de ahora,* The affairs of ancient times widely differ from those of the present day.
Antesacristía, *sf.* An apartment which leads to the sacristy.

Antesála, *sf.* An apartment which leads to the principal hall of a building. *Hacer antesala*, To dance attendance in an ante-chamber.

Antestatúra, *sf.* A small entrenchment of palisadoes and sand-bags, run up in haste, to dispute with the enemy a tract of ground, part of which is already in his possession.

Antetémplo, *sm.* Portico.

Antevér, *va.* To foresee.

Antevíspera, *sf.* The day before yesterday.

Anti, An inseparable preposition, signifying against, as *antipapa*, antipope.

Antía, *sf.* (Ict.) The mutton fish. Labrus anthias *L.*

Anticardenál, *sm.* A schismatic cardinal.

Anticipación, *sf.* Anticipation, the act of taking up something before its time.

Anticipáda, *sf.* An unexpected thrust or blow.

Anticipadaménte, *ad.* Prematurely, by way of anticipation.

Anticipadór, ra, *s.* One who anticipates or conceives beforehand; anticipator.

Anticipamiénto, *sm.* V. *Anticipación.*

Anticipánte, *pa.* Anticipated; applied by physicians to a fit of the fever which returns before the stated period.

Anticipár, *va.* To anticipate, to do something before the time appointed.

Anticrítico, *sm.* Anticritic, an opponent to a critic.

Antidorál, *a.* (For.) V. *Remuneratorio.*

Antidotário, *sm.* 1. A book in which the composition of medicines is described and directed; a dispensatory. 2. The place in an apothecary's shop for cordials and other medicines, against poison.

Antídoto, *sm.* 1. Antidote, a medicine given to expel poison. 2. (Met.) A preventive or preservative against vice or error.

Antiér, *ad.* The day before yesterday; a contraction of *ántes de ayer.*

Antifáto, *sm.* Black coral.

Antifáz, *sm.* A veil which covers the face.

Antífona, *sf.* An anthem.

Antifonál ó **Antifonário**, *sm.* A book of anthems which contains all that are sung during the year.

Antifonéro, *sm.* Precentor, he who chants anthems and leads the choir.

Antífrasis, *sf.* Antiphrasis, the use of words opposite to their proper meaning.

Antígo, ga, *a.* (Ant.) Old, ancient.

Antiguálla, *sf.* 1. A monument of antiquity, such as ruins of ancient buildings, &c. 2. Antiquity, ancient account. 3. Ancient custom out of use.

Antiguaménte, *ad.* Anciently, formerly.

Antiguamiénto, *sm.* The act of making old.

Antiguár, *vn.* To obtain seniority, as member of a tribunal, college, &c.—*va.* 1. To antiquate; to make obsolete. 2. To abolish the ancient use of a thing.

Antigüedád, *sf.* 1. Antiquity. 2. Ancient times, the days of yore.

Antigüísimo, ma, *a. sup.* Very ancient.

Antíguo, gua, *a.* Stricken in years, old; having long held an employment or place.

Antíguo, *sm.* 1. An antique or ancient production of the fine arts of Greece or Rome. 2. An aged member of a college or community; an ancient. *Antiguos*, The ancients; the illustrious men of antiquity.

Antilogía, *sf.* An apparent contradiction between two sentences or passages of an author.

Antimoniál, *a.* Antimonial, relating or belonging to antimony.

Antimónio, *sm.* Antimony, a mineral. *Antimonio de agujas*, Purified antimony, so called from its fibrous or needly appearance.

Antinomía, *sf.* Antinomy, a contradiction between two laws, or between two articles of the same law.

Antinóo, *sm.* Antinous, a northern constellation.

Antipápa, *sm.* An anti-pope, a pope who is not canonically elected.

Antipapádo, *sm.* The unlawful dignity of anti-pope.

Antipára, *sf.* 1. A screen placed before another to cover it. 2. A gaiter which covers merely the fore part of the legs and feet.

Antiparástasis, *sf.* (Ret.) A figure, by which one, charged with a crime, asserts, that what he is accused of is praise-worthy.

Antipásto, *sm.* A foot of Latin verse consisting of four syllables, the first and last of which are short, and the second and third long.

Antipátes, *sm.* A sort of black coral; also a precious black stone.

Antipatía, *sf.* Antipathy, a natural contrariety to any thing, so as to shun it involuntarily.

Antipático, ca, *a.* That which has a natural contrariety or aversion from any thing.

Antiperístasis, *sf.* The action of two contrary qualities, one of which, by its opposition, heightens the other.

Antíphona. V. *Antifona.*

Antiphonéro. V. *Antifonero.*

Antipóca, *sf.* (For. Arag.) A writing or deed by which the obligation is acknowledged to pay a certain rent.

Antipocár, *va.* 1. (For. Arag.) To acknowledge, in a public instrument, the obligation to pay a certain rent. 2. (Bax. Arag.) To resume the performance of a duty which has been suspended for some time.

Antípodas, *sm. pl.* 1. Antipodes, people living on the opposite side of the globe, so that their feet are opposed to ours. 2. (Met.) Persons of contrary dispositions, sentiments, or manners.

Antipódia y **Antipódio**, *s.* An extraordinary dish added to the usual or regular meal.

Antipontificádo, *sm.* V. *Antipapádo.*

Antiptósis, *sf.* (Gram.) A figure in grammar by which one case is put for another.

Antipútrido, da, *a.* Antiseptic, antiputrescent.

Antiquádo, da, *a.* Antiquated; obsolete, out of use.

Antiquário, *sm.* Antiquary, a man studious of antiquity.

Antiquisimaménte, *ad. sup.* Very anciently.

Antiquísimo, ma, *a. sup.* Very ancient.

Antirríno, *sm.* (Bot.) Snap-dragon. Antirrhinum *L.*

Antíscios, *sm. pl.* (Astr.) Two points of the heavens equally distant from the tropics.

Antispódio, *sm.* (Farm.) A composition prepared by apothecaries, to supply the place of *spodium.*

Antistrófa, *sf.* 1. Antistrophe, a figure wherein two terms or things mutually depend on each other. 2. A dance much used among the ancients.

Antítesis, *sf.* 1. (Gram.) A figure whereby one letter is substituted in the room of another. 2. (Ret.) A contrast or opposition in the words of a discourse.

Antítipo, *sm.* Antitype, a figure, image, or symbol.
Antiyér, *ad.* V. *Anteayer.*
Antojadizaménte, *ad.* Capriciously, longingly.
Antojadízo, za, *a.* Longing, capricious.
Antojamiénto, *sm.* A longing, an earnest or vehement desire.
Antojánza, *sf.* V. *Antojo.*
Antojárse, *vr.* To long, to desire earnestly. *Antojársele á uno alguna cosa*, To desire or judge without reflection.
Antojéra, *sf.* 1. A spectacle-case. 2. An eye-flap for horses and mules.
Antojéro, *sm.* Maker or vender of spectacles.
Antójo, *sm.* 1. A vehement desire, a longing. 2. A surmise formed without any sufficient foundation. 3. Spectacles, telescope. 4. Eye-flap for mules, and horses.
Antojuélo, *sm.* A slight desire of a thing.
Antoniáno y Antoníno, *sm.* A monk of the order of St. Anthony the abbot.
Antonomásia, *sf.* (Ret.) Antonomasia, a figure by which a title is put for a proper name; thus we say, The Orator, for Cicero.
Antonomástico, ca, *a.* Belonging or relating to antonomasia.
Antór, *sm.* (For. Arag.) Vender or seller of stolen goods, bought *bona fide.*
Antórcha, *sf.* (Poét.) Torch, flambeau, taper.
Antorchéro, *sm.* A candlestick for tapers, &c.
Antória, *sf.* The action of discovering the first seller of stolen goods. [nabar.
A'ntras, *sm.* Vermilion; native or factious cin-
A'ntro, *sm.* (Poét.) Antre, cavern, den, grotto.
Antropófago, *sm.* A man-eater, cannibal.
Antropología, *sf.* Anthropology, the doctrine of the nature and structure of man.
Antruejár, *va.* To wet with water, or play some other carnival trick.
Antruéjo, *sm.* The three last days of the carnival.
Antruído, *sm.* (Ant.) V. *Antruejo.*
Antuvión, *sm.* (Joc.) A sudden, unexpected stroke or attack. *De antuvion*, Unexpectedly. *Fulano vino de antuvion*, Such-a-one came unexpectedly.
Anuál, *a.* Annual, lasting only a year. *Plantas anuales*, (Bot.) Annual plants. [nual.
Anualidád, *sf.* State or quality of being an-
Anualménte, *ad.* Annually.
Anubáda, *sf.* An ancient tax paid in Spain.
Anubarrádo, da, *a.* Clouded; applied chiefly to linens and silks.
Anubládo, da, *a.* 1. Overcast, clouded, covered with gloom. 2. (Speaking of colours) Somewhat more obscure than the rest.
Anublár, *va.* 1. To cloud, to darken the light of the sun with clouds. 2. (Met.) To cloud or obscure merit.—*vr.* 1. To be blasted, withered, or mildewed; applied to corn and other plants. 2. (Met.) To miscarry, to be disconcerted; speaking of plans or projects.
Anudádo, da, *a.* Knotted.
Anudár, *va.* 1. To knot, to complicate with knots. 2. To join, to unite.—*vn.* To wither, to fade, to waste or pine away. *Anudarse la voz*, (Met.) To throb from passion or grief, not to be able to speak.
Anuéncia *sf.* Condescendence, compliance.

Anuénte, *a.* Condescending, courteous.
Anuláble, *a.* That which can be annulled.
Anulación, *sf.* Cessation, abrogation.
Anuladór, ra, *s.* One who makes null or void
Anulár, *va.* To annul, to make void.
Anulár, *a.* Annular, having the form of a ring *Dedo anular*, The ring-finger or fourth finger.
Anulatívo, va, *a.* Derogatory, having the power of making void.
Anulóso, sa, *a.* Composed of many rings, or having the form of them.
Anunciación, *sf.* Annunciation; the angel's salutation of the blessed Virgin.
Anunciáda, *sf.* 1 An order of monks instituted in 1232, by seven Florentine merchants. 2. A religious order for women, instituted by Jane, queen of France, after her divorce from Louis XII. 3. An order of knights, instituted by Amadeus VI. duke of Savoy.
Anunciadór, ra, *s.* One who announces.
Anunciár, *va.* 1. To announce, to bring the first tidings of an event. Seldom used in this sense. 2. To prognosticate, to forebode.
Anúncio, *sm.* Omen, presage.
A'nuo, ua, *a.* V. *Anual.*
Anvérso, *sm.* Obverse; applied to the head side in coins and medals.
A'nvir, *sm.* (South Amer.) A red liquor expressed from the fermented leaves of tobacco: its exhalations are intoxicating, and taste very pungent. V. *Mo.*
Anzoládo, da, *a.* Hooked in.
Anzoléro, *sm.* (Arag.) One whose trade it is to make fish-hooks.
Anzuelíto, *sm.* A small fish-hook.
Anzuélo, *sm.* 1. Fish-hook. 2. (Met.) Allurement, incitement. 3. A kind of fritters made in the shape of a hook. *Caer en el anzuelo*, To be taken in, to be tricked or defrauded. *Roer el anzuelo*, To escape a danger. *Tragar el anzuelo*, To swallow the bait. [L.
Aña, *sf.* Stink-fox. Canes Vulpes Americanus
Añáda, *sf.* 1. The good or bad season which happens in a year. 2. Moiety of arable land.
Añadidúra, *sf.* Addition, additament. *Añadidura á los pesos en la venta de cosas*, Over-weight allowed in the sale of goods.
Añadír, *va.* 1. To add. 2. To exaggerate.
Añaféa, *Papél de añafea*, Brown paper.
Añafíl, *sm.* A musical pipe used by the Moors.
Añafiléro, *sm.* A player on the *añafil.*
Añagáza, *sf.* 1. A bird-call, lure, or decoy, for catching birds. 2. (Met.) Allurement, enticement to mischief.
Añál, *a.* Annual. *Cordero añal*, A lamb that is one year old: a yearling.
Añal, *sm.* 1. An annual offering on the tomb of a person deceased. 2. (Ant.) Anniversary.
Añaléjo, *sm.* An ecclesiastical almanack, pointing out the regulation of the divine office or service.
Añascár, *va.* (Bax.) To collect by degrees, small things of little value. [val.
Añáza y Añacéa, *sf.* An annual feast or festi-
Añéjar, *va.* To make old.—*vr.* To grow old, to become stale; applied to wine and eatables.
Añéjo, ja, *a.* Old, stale.
Añícos, *sm. pl.* A number of years. *Ya tiene sus añicos*, He is of a good round age. *Hacer*

añicos, To break into small bits. *Hacerse añicos*, To take too much exercise, to overheat one's self.

AÑÍL, *sm.* 1. (Bot.) The Indigo-plant. Indigofera anil *L.* 2. The mass extracted from the leaves, and stalks, of the indigo-plant. 3. A blue colour.

AÑINÉRO, *sm.* Skinner, a dealer in lamb-skins.

AÑÍNES, *sm.* Coarse tow. [lambs.

AÑÍNOS, *sm. pl.* The fleecy skins of yearling

AÑIRÁDO, DA, *a.* Dyed blue.

AÑO, *sm.* 1. A year, twelve months. 2. A long space of time more than what is regular or necessary. 3. The companion or partner who falls to one's lot, in family diversions, the first day of the year. *Mal año*, Surely, without doubt. *Mal año para el*, The deuce take him. *Años*, The birth-day of a person. *Dar los años*, To keep the birth-day. *Estar en años*, To be in years.

AÑOJÁL, *sm.* Piece of land cultivated some years and then allowed to rest.

AÑÓJO, JA, *s.* A yearling calf.

AÑÓRA Y AÑORÍA, *sf.* A draw-well.

AÑÓSO, SA, *a.* Old, stricken in years.

AÑUBLÁDO, DA, *a.* Blindfolded.

AÑUBLÁR. V. *Anublar*.

AÑUBLÁRSE, *vr.* To be afflicted with grief in the midst of prosperity and joy.

AÑÚBLO, *sm.* Mildew: a disease incident to grain. V. *Tizon*.

AÑUDÁDO, DA, *a.* Knotted.

AÑUDADÓR, RA, *s.* One who knots or ties.

AÑUDÁR, *va.* 1. V. *Anudar*. 2. To make fast, to unite, to tie close. *Añudar los labios*, To impose silence.

AÑUSGÁR, *va.* 1. To choke, to stifle. 2. To vex, to annoy.—*vn.* To be vexed or displeased.

AOCÁDO, DA, *a.* Hollowed. V. *Ahuecar*.

AOJÁDO, DA, *a.* Bewitched.

AOJADÓR, RA, *s.* A conjurer, one who bewitches.

AOJADÚRA Y AOJAMIÉNTO, *s.* Witchcraft, the act of bewitching.

AOJÁR, *va.* To fascinate, to charm, to bewitch.

AÓJO, *sm.* The act of bewitching.

AÓRTA, *sf.* (Anat.) Aorta, the great artery, which rises immediately out of the left ventricle of the heart. [egg.

AOVÁDO, DA, *a.* Formed in the shape of an

AOVÁR, *vn.* To lay eggs; applied to fowls.

AOVILLÁRSE, *vr.* To grow or be contracted into the shape of a clew.

APABILÁR, *va.* To prepare the wick of a wax-candle, so that it may be in readiness for being lighted.—*vr.* 1. To die away; applied to the light of a candle which is going out. 2. (Met.) To sink under the hand of death.

APACENTADÉRO, *sm.* Pasture, grazing ground.

APACENTADÓR, *sm.* A herdsman; a pastor.

APACENTAMIÉNTO, *sm.* 1. The act of tending grazing cattle. 2. Pasture.

APACENTÁR, *va.* 1. To tend grazing cattle. 2. To graze, to feed cattle. 3. (Met.) To teach, to instruct spiritually. 4. (Met.) To inflame the passions; to incite desires.

APACIBILIDÁD, *sf.* Affability, mildness of manners, meekness of temper.

APACÍBLE, *a.* 1. Affable, meek, mild of temper. 2. Pleasant, calm, moderate. *Tiempo apacible*, (Naút.) Moderate weather. *Semblante apacible*, A serene countenance. *Sitio apacible*, A pleasant place.

APACIBLEMÉNTE, *ad.* Mildly, gently, agreeably.

APACIGUADÓR, RA, *s.* Pacificator, peace-maker.

APACIGUAMIÉNTO, *sm.* Pacification, the act of appeasing or making peace.

APACIGUÁR, *va.* To appease, to pacify, to quiet.—*vn.* (Naút.) To grow moderate; applied to the wind and sea.

APADRINADÓR, RA, *s.* Patron, defender, protector; one who supports or cherishes.

APADRINÁR, *va.* To support, to favour, to patronize, to protect.

APAGÁBLE, *a.* Extinguishable; that which may be quenched.

APAGÁDO, DA, *a.* Humble-minded, submissive, pusillanimous.

APAGADÓR, *sm.* 1. One who quenches or extinguishes. 2. Extinguisher, a hollow cone put upon a candle to quench it. 3. A small bit of cloth put on the jack of a harpsichord to deaden the echo of the chords.

APAGAMIÉNTO, *sm.* Extinction, the act of quenching.

APAGAPÉNOLES, *sm. pl.* (Naút.) Leech-ropes, leech-lines.

APAGÁR, *va.* 1. To quench, to extinguish. 2 (Met.) To efface, to destroy. 3. (Pint.) To soften colours which are too bright or glaring. *Apagar la cal*, To slack lime. *Apagar la sed*, To quench the thirst. *Apagar la voz*, To put a mute on the bridge of stringed musical instruments for the purpose of lowering the sound.

APAGULLÁR, *va.* 1. To strike an unexpected blow. 2. To take by surprise.

APAINELÁDO, DA, *a.* Made in imitation of half an ellipsis; applied to an arch.

APALABRÁR, *va.* 1. To appoint a meeting for conferring on some subject or other. 2. To treat by word of mouth.

APALAMBRÁR, *va.* (Ant.) To set on fire. *Apalambrárse de sed*, To be parched with thirst.

APALANCÁR, *va.* 1. To lift or move with a lever. 2. To supplant.

APALEÁDO, DA, *a.* Cudgelled, caned.

APALEADÓR, RA, *s.* One who cudgels or canes.

APALEAMIÉNTO, *sm.* Basting, drubbing; beating.

APALEÁR, *va.* 1. To cane, to baste, to drub. 2. To beat out the dust with a cane or stick. 3. To move and shovel grain to prevent its being spoiled. *Apalear el dinero*, To heap up money with shovels; to be excessively rich.

APALMÁDA, *a.* (Blas.) Palm of the hand stretched out in a coat of arms.

APANCÓRA, *sf.* The common crab. Cancer mænas *L.*

APANDILLÁR, *va.* To form parties; to divide into factions.—*vr.* To be divided into parties at play.

APANTANÁR, *va.* 1. To make a reservoir or *pantano*. 2. To fill a reservoir with water.

APANTUFLÁDO, DA, *a.* Wearing shoes made in the slipper fashion.

APAÑÁDO, DA, *a.* Resembling woollen cloth in body and texture.

APAÑADÓR, RA, *s.* 1. One who grasps or seizes with the hand. 2. A pilferer.

Apañadúra, sf. The act of seizing, grasping, or snatching away.

Apañamiénto. V. *Apaño.*

Apañar, va. 1. To grasp or seize with the hand. 2. (Met.) To take or carry away. 3. To filch. to pilfer. 4. To dress, to set off, to make up. 5. To patch, to mend.—vr. To submit to, to reconcile one's self to do any thing.

Apáño, sm. 1. The act of disposing of a thing in a fit manner. 2. A patch or other way of mending a thing.

Apañuscadór, ra, s. One who rumples a thing by pressing or squeezing it rudely.

Apañuscár, va. To rumple; to crush or contract into inequalities.

Apapagayádo, da, a. Parrot-like, that which resembles a parrot.

Apapagayárse, vr. To be dressed in green; to be of a parrot colour.

Aparadór, sm. 1. Buffet, sideboard. 2. Dresser in the kitchen. 3. Workshop of an artizan. 4. Wardrobe. *Estar de aparador,* To be decked out or dressed in style for receiving visits.

Aparár, va. 1. To stretch out the hands or skirts of clothes for catching or receiving any thing thrown by another. 2. (Among gardeners) To dig and heap the earth round plants which are somewhat grown. 3. (Among shoemakers) To close the upper and hind-quarters of a shoe. 4. (Ant.) To couple male and female animals. 5. *Aparár un navio,* (Naút.) To dub a ship.

Aparatádo, da, a. Prepared, disposed.

Aparáto, sm. 1. Apparatus, preparation, disposition. 2. Pomp, ostentation, show. 3. Circumstance or token which precedes or accompanies something. *Hay aparatos de llover,* It looks as if it were going to rain. *El mal viene con aparatos de ser grave, ó con malos aparatos,* The disease is attended with indications of danger.

Aparatóso, sa, a. Pompous, showy, ushered in with great preparations.

Aparcería, sf. Partnership in a farm.

Aparcéro, sm. 1. Partner in a farm. 2. An associate in general.

Apareár, va. To match, to suit one thing to another.—vr. To be coupled in pairs by two and two.

Aparecér, vn. y vr. To appear unexpectedly, to make a sudden appearance. [ing.

Aparecimiénto, sm. Apparition, act of appear-

Aparejádo, da, a. Prepared, fit, ready.

Aparejadór, ra, s. 1. One who prepares or gets ready. 2. Overseer of a building, who instructs and directs the workmen, and distributes the materials. 3. (Naút.) Rigger.

Aparejár, va. 1. To prepare, to get ready. 2. To saddle or harness horses or mules. 3. (Naút.) To rig a ship. 4. (Pint.) To size a piece of linen or board on which something is to be painted. 5. To prepare the timber and stones for a building.

Aparéjo, sm. 1. Preparation, disposition. 2. Harness. 3. Sizing of a piece of linen or board on which something is to be painted. 4. (Naút.) Tackle and rigging employed on board a ship. *Aparejo de amante y estrella,* Runner and tackle. *Aparejo de amura,* Tack-tackle. *Aparejo de bolinear,* Bow-line tackle. *Aparejo de combés,* Luff-tackle. *Aparejo de estrelleras de combés,* Winding-tackle. *Aparejo de estrique,* Garnet, a tackle wherewith goods are hoisted in and out of the hold. *Aparejo de peñol,* Yard-tackle. *Aparejo de pescante,* Fish-tackle. *Aparejo de polea,* Burton, a small tackle used in hoisting things in and out of a ship. *Aparejo real,* Main-tackle. *Aparejo de virador,* Top-tackle. *Aparejo de rolin,* Rolling-tackle. *Aparejo del tercio de las vergas mayores,* Quarter-tackle.

Aparéjos, pl. 1. The apparatus, tools, implements, or instruments, necessary for a trade. 2. (Pint.) The materials necessary for priming, burnishing, and gilding.

Aparejuélo, sm. A small apparatus. *Aparejuelos,* (Naút.) Small-tackle. *Aparejuelos de portas,* Port-tackle. *Aparejuelos de rizos,* Reef-tackle. *Aparejuelos de socayre,* Jigger-tackle.

Aparentádo, da, a. (Ant.) Related, allied.

Aparentár, va. To make a false show. *El rico aparenta pobreza y el vicioso la virtud,* The rich man affects poverty, and the vicious virtue. [venient, seasonable, fit.

Aparénte, a. 1. Apparent, but not real. 2. Con-

Aparenteménte, ad. Apparently. [ing.

Aparición, sf. Apparition, the act of appear-

Apariéncia, sf. 1. Appearance, outside. 2. Mark, vestige. 3. (Ant.) Probability. *Caballo de apariencia,* A stately horse.—pl. 1. Phenomena discovered by astronomical observations. 2. Scenes and decorations of the stage.

Aparrádo, da, a. Crooked or spreading like vines; applied to trees and plants.

Aparroquiádo, da, a. Belonging to a parish, as an inhabitant or parishioner.

Aparroquiár, va. To bring or attract customers to a shop. [division of a passage.

Apartadéro, sm. Parting-place, cross roads,

Apartadíjo, sm. A small part, share, or portion of a certain whole. *Hacer apartadijos,* To divide a whole into shares.

Apartadízo, sm. A small room, separated or taken from another apartment, of which it made a part.

Apartadízo, za, a. Shy, retired, untractable.

Apartádo, da, a. 1. Separated. 2. Distant, remote, retired.

Apartádo, sm. 1. A retired room, separate from the rest of the apartments of a house. 2. A smelting-house, where gold is separated from silver. 3. A small box, at the post-office, into which such private letters are put as are to be kept separate from the rest.

Apartadór, ra, s. 1. One who divides or separates. 2. A sorter of different sorts of wool or of rags in paper-mills. *Apartado de ganado,* One who steals sheep or cattle. *Apartador de metales,* One who smelts ores.

Apartamiénto, sm. 1. Separation, the act of separating. 2. Formal renunciation of a claim, right, or action. 3. (Ant.) Divorce. 4. (Ant.) Apartment *Apartamiento de ganado,* The act of stealing cattle. *Apartamiento meridiano,* (Naút.) Departure, meridian distance or difference in the latitude.

Apartár, va. 1. To part, to separate, to divide. 2. To dissuade one from a thing. 3. To remove a thing from the place where it was. 4. To sort letters.—vr. 1. To withdraw from a place. 2. To be divorced. 3. To desist from a claim, action, or plea.
Apárte, sm. Break in a line, space marking a [paragraph.
Apárte, ad. 1. Apart, separately. 2. Aside on the stage. *Dexar aparte*, To lay aside.
Aparvár, va. 1. To arrange the corn for being threshed. 2. To heap, to pile, to throw together.
Apascentár, va. (Ant.) V. *Apacentar*.
Apasionadaménte, ad. Passionately.
Apasionádo, da, a. 1. Passionate. 2. Affected with pain. 3. Devoted to a person or thing.
Apasionár, va. To excite or inspire a passion.—vr. To be taken with a person or thing to excess.
Apático, ca, a. Apathetic, indifferent.
Apatuscár, va. To do things in a bungling manner, with precipitation and confusion.
Apatúsco, sm. 1. (Joc.) Ornament, dress, array. 2. A thing done in a bungling manner, with precipitation and confusion.
Apaysádo, da, a. Resembling a landscape; applied to a painting more broad than high.
Apazóte, sm. (Bot.) American basil. Ocimum americanum *L.*
Apéa, sf. (Cast.) A rope with which the fore-feet of horses are tied when grazing.
Apeadéro, sm. 1. A block or step, with the aid of which a person mounts a horse or mule. 2. A house provisionally taken by a person coming from abroad, until he can provide himself with a permanent habitation
Apeadór, sm. A land surveyor.
Apeamiénto, sm. V. *Apeo*.
Apeár, va. 1. To alight from a horse, mule, or carriage. 2. To measure lands, tenements, or buildings. 3. To scoat or scotch a wheel, to stop a wheel by putting a stone or piece of wood under it. 4. To prop a building in order to take down a structure contiguous to it. 5. To take a thing down from its place. 6. (Met.) To dissuade. 7. (Met.) To remove difficulties, to surmount obstacles. 8. To displace from an office, to degrade. 9. (Ant.) To walk. *Apear el rio*, To wade or ford a river. *Apear una caballeria*, To shackle a horse or mule.—vr. (Met.) *Apearse por la cola, ó por las orejas*, To give some absurd answer.
Apechugár, va. 1. To push with the breast, to come breast to breast. 2. (Met.) To undertake a thing with spirit and boldness, without considering the danger which the enterprise may be attended with.
Apedazár, va. To patch, to mend, to repair.
Apedernaládo, da, a. Flinty, as hard as flint.
Apedreár. V. *Apedrear*.
Apedreadéro, sm. A place where boys assemble to throw stones at each other.
Apedreádo, da, a. 1. Stoned, pelted. 2. *Cara apedreada*, A face pitted with the small pox.
Apedreadór, sm. One who throws stones, or [pelts.
Apedreamiénto, sm. Lapidation.
Apedreár, va. To stone, to throw stones, to kill with stones.—vn. 1. To hail. 2. (Met.) To talk in a rude uncouth manner, or with asperity.—vr. To be injured by hail; applied to grain, vines, &c. &c.
Apedréo, sm. Lapidation, the act of stoning.
Apegadaménte, ad. Studiously, devotedly.
Apegamiénto, sm. 1. Adhesion, the act and state of sticking to something. 2. (Met.) Attachment.
Apegár, vn. (Ant.) To adhere, to stick to something.—vr. To be much taken with a thing.
Apégo, sm. Attachment, a particular affection, or inclination for a thing.
Apelación, sf. Appeal, the act of removing a cause from an inferior to a superior court. *Médico de apelacion*, A physician whose advice is taken in dangerous cases. *No haber ó no tenér apelacion*, To be despaired of, to be given over by the physicians.
Apelado, da, pp. Appealed.
Apeládo, da, a. Of the same coat or colour; applied to mules or horses.
Apelambrár, va. To steep skins or hides in pits or vats filled with lime-water, that the hair [may come off.
Apelánte, a. Appellant.
Apelár, vn. 1. To appeal, to transfer a cause from an inferior to a superior court. 2. To have recourse to, to seek remedy for some urgent necessity or distress. 3. To be of the same colour, applied to the hair of horses or mules. *Apelar un tiro de caballos de coche*, to match a set of coach horses. *Apelar el enfermo*, To escape from the jaws of death in a fit of sickness.
Apelatívo, a. *Nombre apelativo*, An appellative name, which belongs to a whole class of beings.
Apeldár, vn. (Joc.) To flee, to set off, to run [awry.
Apélde, sm. 1. Flight, escape. 2. The first ringing of a bell before day-break in convents of the Franciscan order.
Apeligrádo, da, a. In danger, exposed to dan-[ger.
Apeligrár, va. To endanger, to expose to dan-[ger.
Apeliótes, sm. North-east wind.
Apellár, va. (Among curriers) To grease and curry skins and hides, to dress leather.
Apellidádo, da, a. Named.
Apellidamiénto, sm. The act of giving a name, or of calling one by his name.
Apellidár, va. 1. To call one by his name. 2. To proclaim, to raise shouts of acclamation. 3. (Ant.) To convene.
Apellído, sm. 1. Surname, family name. 2. A peculiar name given to things. 3. A nick-name; epithet. 4. The assembling of troops.
Apelluzgádo, da, a. Modelled, formed.
Apelluzgár, va. To model, to mould.
Apelmazár, va. To compress, to render less spongy or porous.
A'pélo, ad. Apropos, to the purpose. *Venir a pelo*, To come to the point.
Apenachádo, da, a. Adorned with plumes, [wearing plumes.
Apénas, ad. 1. Scarcely, hardly, with a deal of trouble. 2. No sooner than, as soon as.
Apendéncia, sf. (Ant.) Appurtenance.
Apendíce, sm. Appendix, supplement, addi-[tion.
Apeñuscár. V. *Apañuscar*.
Apéo, sm. 1. Boundary, limit of lands or tenements. 2. Frame with props, stays, &c. put under the upper parts of a building, while the lower parts are repairing.

Apeonár, *vn.* To walk swiftly, to run like partridges and other birds.

Aperadór, *sm.* 1. One who has the care of a farm, and the agricultural implements. 2. A cartwright, who builds and repairs carts and wagons.

Aperár, *va.* To carry on the trade of a cartwright, to build and repair carts and wagons.

Apercibído, da, *a.* Provided.

Apercibimiénto, *sm.* 1. The act of providing or getting ready. 2. Arrangement, adjustment. 3. Order, advice. 4. Summons.

Apercibír, *va.* 1. To prepare, to provide, to get ready. 2. To warn, to advise. 3. To summon.

Aperción, *sf.* Act of opening. V. *Abertura.*

Apercollár, *va.* 1. (Bax.) To seize one by the collar. 2. (Met.) To snatch away a thing in haste, and, as it were, by stealth. 3. (Bax.) To assassinate, to kill in a treacherous manner.

Aperdigádo, da, *a.* 1. Broiled, toasted. 2. Condemned and burnt by the inquisition; by way of derision.

Aperdigár, *va.* V. *Perdigar.*

Aperitívo, va, *a.* Aperitive, that which has the power and quality of opening.

Apernadór, *sm.* A dog which seizes the game by the legs or hams.

Apernár, *va.* To seize by the hough or ham; applied to dogs.

Apéro, *sm.* 1. The whole of the agricultural implements used on a farm. 2. The whole of the tools and implements necessary for a trade. 3. A sheep-cot, or sheep-fold.

Aperreádo, da, *a.* Harassed. *Andar aperreado*, To be harassed or fatigued.

Aperreadór, ra, *s.* One that is importunate, an intruder.

Aperreár, *va.* To throw one to the dogs to be torn to pieces.—*vr.* To toil and beat about; applied to hounds and pointers.

Apersonárse, *vr.* (Ant.) To appear genteel.

Apertúra. V. *Abertura.*

Apesadumbrádo, da, *a.* Concerned, vexed.

Apesadumbrár, *va.* To vex, to cause trouble and affliction.

Apesaradaménte, *ad.* Mournfully, grievously.

Apesarár. V. *Apesadumbrar.*

Apesgamiénto, *sm.* The act of sinking under a load or burthen.

Apesgár, *va.* To overload, to press down under a load or burthen.—*vr.* To grow dull or heavy; to be aggrieved.

Apestádo, da, *a.* Pestered. *Estar apestado de alguna cosa*, To have plenty of a thing, even to loathing and satiety. *La plaza está apestada de verduras*, The market-place is full of greens.

Apestár, *va.* 1. To infect with the plague or pestilence. 2. To cause or produce an offensive smell. In this sense it is commonly used as a neuter verb in the third person; *e. g. Aquí apesta*, There is here an offensive smell. 3. (Met.) To corrupt, to turn from a sound into a putrid state. 4. To pester, to cause displeasure. *Fulano me apesta con su afectacion*, He sickens me with his affectation.

Apetecedór, ra, *s.* One who desires or longs for a thing.

Apetecér, *va.* To long for a thing, to desire it earnestly.

Apetecíble, *a.* Desirable, that which is worthy of being wished for.

Apeténcia, *sf.* Appetite, hunger.

Apetíte, *sm.* (Raro.) Sauce, relish to excite the appetite.

Apetíto, *sm.* 1. Appetite, desire of food. 2. That which excites desire.

Apetitóso, sa, *a.* Pleasing to the taste. 2. (Ant.) Pursuing sensual pleasures.

Apeynazádo, da, *a.* Made of cross-pieces.

Apezuñár, *vn.* To tread firm on the hoof.

Apiadadór, ra, *s.* One who pities or commiserates.

Apiadárse, *vr.* To pity, to commiserate, to treat with compassion.

Apiaradéro, *sm.* A shepherd's account of the number of sheep which compose his flock.

Apicarádo, da, *a.* Roguish, knavish, impudent.

A'pice, *sm.* 1. Apex, summit, the utmost height or highest point. 2. The smallest part of a thing. 3. (Met.) The most intricate or most arduous point of a question. *A'pices*, Anthers or small roundish knobs, which grow on the tops of the stamens in the middle of flowers. *Estar en los ápices*, To have a complete and minute knowledge of a thing.

Apiladór, *sm.* One who piles the wool up at the sheep-shearing time.

Apilár, *va.* To pile or heap up, to put one thing upon another.

Apimpollárse, *vr.* To shoot, to germinate.

Apiñádo, da, *a.* Pyramidal, pine-shaped.

Apiñadúra y Apiñamiento, *s.* The act of pressing together.

Apiñár, *va.* To press things close together, to join, to unite.

A'pio, *sm.* (Bot.) Celery. Apium *L.* *A'pio montano*, (Bot.) Common lovage. Ligusticum levisticum *L.* *A'pio de risa*, (Bot.) Crow-foot. Ranunculus *L.*

Apiolár, *va.* 1. To gyve a hawk. 2. To tie hares or other game together by the legs. 3. (Met.) To seize, to apprehend. 4. To kill, to murder.

Apíque, *ad.* Almost, nearly.

Apisonár, *va.* To ram down earth or other things with a rammer.

Apitonamiénto, *sm.* 1. Putting forth the tenderlings. 2. Passion, anger.

Apitonár, *vn.* 1. To put forth the tenderlings; a term applied to deer, and other horned animals. 2. To bud, to germ.—*va.* To pick, as hens do their eggs, that the chickens may come out.—*vr.* To treat each other with abusive language.

Aplacáble, *a.* Placable, easy to be appeased, meek, gentle.

Aplacación y Aplacamiénto, *s.* Act of appeasing.

Aplacadór, ra, *s.* One who appeases.

Aplacár, *va.* To appease, to pacify.

Aplacíble, *a.* V. *Agradable.*

Aplaciénte, *a.* That which pleases.

Aplanadéro, *sf.* A roller for levelling the ground.

Aplanadór, *sm.* A leveller, one who makes even.

Aplanamiénto, *sm.* The act of levelling.

Aplanár, *va.* 1. To level, to make even. 2. To terrify, or astonish by some unexpected novaity.—*vr.* To tumble down to the ground; applied to a building.

APLANCHÁDO, DA, *a.* Ironed, smoothed with an iron.

APLANCHÁDO, *sm.* A parcel of linen which is to be ironed, or has been ironed. 2. Act of smoothing or ironing linen.

APLANCHADÓRA, *sf.* A woman whose trade it is to iron and get up linen.

APLANCHÁR, *va.* To iron linen, or to smooth it with a hot iron.

APLANTILLÁR, *va.* To adjust or fit a stone, a piece of timber, or a board, according to the model.

APLASTÁDO, DA, *a.* Caked.

APLASTÁR, *va.* 1. To cake, to flatten or crush a thing, to make it lose its shape. 2. To confound an opponent, so that he does not know what to say or to answer.

APLAUDÍDO, DA, *a.* Applauded.

APLAUDÍR, *va.* To applaud, to praise with shouts of acclamation.

APLÁUSO, *sm.* Applause, approbation, praise.

APLAYÁR, *vn.* To overflow.

APLAZAMIÉNTO, *sm.* Convocation, act of convening.

APLAZÁR, *va.* 1. To convene, to call together. 2. To invest. 3. To concert, to regulate.

APLEBEYÁR, *va.* (Ant.) To render vile, or servile like plebeians.

APLEGÁR, *va.* (Arag.) To join one thing to another.

APLICÁBLE, *a.* Applicable, that which may be applied.

APLICACIÓN, *sf.* 1. Application, the act of applying or state of being applied. 2. Attention given or paid to a thing, assiduity. *Aplicacion de bienes ó hacienda,* The act of adjudging estates or other property.

APLICÁDO, DA, *a.* Studious, intent on a thing.

APLICÁR, *va.* 1. To apply, to put one thing to another. 2. (Met.) To apply some thoughts or ideas to a subject under discussion. 3. (Met.) To attribute or impute a word or fact. 4. (For.) To adjudge.—*vr.* 1. To study or devote one's self to any thing. 2. To earn a living.

APLOMÁDO, DA, *a.* 1. Of the colour of lead. 2. (Met.) Heavy, dull, lazy.

APLOMÁDO, *sm.* 1. (Among bookbinders) A composition of lead-glance, glue, and water, with which books are marbled. 2. Lead ore, minerals impregnated with lead.

APLOMÁR, *va.* 1. To overload, to crush with too much weight. 2. To raise a wall perpendicularly, by means of a plummet and line.—*vn.* To stand erect, to stand in a perpendicular position.—*vr.* To tumble, to fall to the ground.

A'POCA, *sf.* Receipt, acquittance, discharge.

APOCADAMÉNTE, *ad.* 1. In a scanty manner. 2. Abjectly.

APOCÁDO, DA, *pp.* Lessened, diminished.

APOCÁDO, DA, *a.* 1. Pusillanimous, mean-spirited, cowardly. 2. Narrow-hoofed; speaking of a horse. 3. (Ant.) Of mean, low extraction.

APOCADÓR, RA, *s.* One who lessens or diminishes.

APOCALÍPSIS Y APOCALÍPSI, *sm.* Apocalypse.

APOCAMIÉNTO, *sm.* Abjectness of mind, meanness of spirit.

APOCÁR, *va.* 1. To lessen, to diminish. 2. (Met.) To cramp, to contract.—*vr.* To humble one's self, to undervalue one's self.

APÓCEMA ó APÓCIMA. V. *Pócima.*

APOCOPÁR, *va.* To make use of the figure called *apocope,* to take away the last letter or syllable of a word.

APÓCOPE, *sf.* 1. (Gram.) A figure, where the last letter or syllable of a word is taken away. 2. (Cir.) Amputation of any part of the body.

APOCRIFAMÉNTE, *ad.* Apocryphally, uncertainly, on a false foundation.

APÓCRIFO, FA, *a.* Apocryphal, fabulous, of doubtful or uncertain authority.

APODADÓR, *sm.* A wag, one who ridicules, scoffs, or gives nick-names.

APODÁR, *va.* 1. To give nick-names, to scoff, to ridicule. 2. (Ant.) To compare one thing with another. 3. (Ant.) To appraise.

APODENCÁDO, DA, *a.* Pointer-like, resembling a pointer, or setting dog.

APODERÁDO, DA, *a.* 1. Empowered, authorised. 2. Powerful.

APODERÁDO, *sm.* An attorney, agent.

APODERÁR, *va.* 1. (Ant.) To give possession of a thing. 2. To empower, to authorise.—*vr.* 1. To possess one's self of a thing. 2. (Ant.) To become powerful or strong.

APÓDO, *sm.* Nick-name, a name given in jest or contempt.

APÓFISIS, *sf.* (Med.) Apophysis, the prominent part of some bones; the same as process.

APÓGRAFO, *sm.* Transcript or copy of some book or writing.

APOGÉO, *sm.* Apogæon, apogee, or apogæum; a point in the heavens, in which the sun or a planet is at the greatest distance possible from the earth in its whole revolution.

APOLILLÁDO, DA, *a.* Moth-eaten.

APOLILLADÚRA, *sf.* A hole eaten by moths in clothes, and other things made of wool.

APOLILLÁR, *va.* To gnaw or eat clothes, or other things; applied to moths.—*vr.* To be moth-eaten.

APOLINÁR Y APOLÍNEO, NEA, *a.* (Poét.) Belonging to Apollo.

APOLOGÉTICO, CA, *a.* Apologetic or apologetical, that which is said or written in defence of a thing.

APOLOGÍA, *sf.* Apology, defence, excuse.

APOLÓGICO, CA, *a.* That which relates or belongs to an apologue.

APOLOGÍSTA, *sm.* One who pleads in excuse or favour, he that apologises, an apologist.

APÓLOGO, *sm.* Apologue, a fable or story contrived to convey some moral truth.

APÓLOGO, GA, *a.* V. *Apologico.*

APOLTRONÁDO, DA, *a.* Intimidated, frightened; fixed, motionless.

APOLTRONÁRSE, *vr.* To grow lazy, to loiter.

APOMAZÁR, *va.* 1. To glaze printed linens with pumice-stone for the purpose of painting on them. 2. (Among silversmiths) To burnish gold or silver with pumice-stone.

APOMÉLI, *sf.* A decoction prepared of honeycomb dissolved in vinegar and water.

APONÉR, *va.* (Ant.) To impute. V. *Imponer.*

APOPLEGÍA, *sf.* Apoplexy, a sudden privation of all sensation by disease.

APOPLÉTICO, CA, *a.* Apoplectic.

APORCADÚRA, *sf.* The act of raising earth around celery, or other plants.

APORCÁR, *va.* To cover garden plants with earth

for the purpose of rendering them ripe and mellow.

A' Porfía, *ad.* With strife and contention.

Aporísma, *sm.* Echymosis, an extravasation of blood between the flesh and skin, caused in bleeding, when the opening in the vein is made larger than in the skin.

Aporismárse, *vr.* To become an echymosis.

Aporraceár, *va.* To pommel, to give repeated blows.

Aporrár, *vn.* To stand mute, to remain silent on an occasion when silence may be injurious.—*vr.* To become importunate or troublesome.

Aporreádo, da, *pp.* 1. Cudgelled. 2. Dragged along.

Aporreamiénto, *sm.* The act of beating or pommelling.

Aporreánte, *pa.* Cudgeller; applied to bad fencers.

Aporreár, *va.* To beat or cudgel.—*vr.* To study with close and intense application; to apply one's self to intellectual labour. *Aporrearse en la jaula,* To engage in fruitless toils; to drudge to no purpose.

Aporréo, *sm.* The act of beating or pommelling.

Aporrillárse, *vr.* To get swellings in the articulations; a term applied to horses.

Aporrílllo, *ad.* (Bax.) Abundantly, plentifully.

Aportadéras, *sf. pl.* A sort of chests, wider at the top than at the bottom, in which provisions are carried on a horse or mule.

Aportadéro, *sm.* A place where a ship or person may stop.

Aportár, *vn.* 1. To make a port, to arrive at a port. 2. To reach an unexpected place.

Aportelládo, *sm.* (Ant.) Formerly an officer of justice, a member of the council of large towns, that administered justice to the people of the neighbouring villages.

Aportillár, *va.* 1. To make an opening or breach in a rampart or wall. 2. To break down, to break open.—*vr.* To tumble down; to fall into ruins.

A'pos, *sm.* Shore bird, sea swallow, sand martin. Hirundo riparia *L.*

Aposentadór, ra, *s.* One who lets lodgings. *Aposentadór,* Quarter-master who prepares quarters for troops. *Aposentador de camino,* An officer of the king's household, who goes before the royal family to provide and prepare convenient houses for their reception.

Aposentamiénto, *sm.* 1. The act of lodging or taking up a temporary habitation. 2. (Ant.) A room.

Aposentár, *va.* To lodge; to give or afford a temporary dwelling.—*vr.* To take a lodging or temporary habitation; to take up residence at night.

Aposentíllo, *sm.* A small room.

Aposénto, *sm.* 1. A room or apartment in a house. 2. A temporary habitation; an inn. 3. A box or seat in the play-house. *Casas de aposento,* Houses in Spain which are obliged to lodge persons of the king's household. *Aposento de corte,* The apartment or habitation destined for the king's servants. *Huésped de aposento,* A lodger belonging to the king's household.

Aposesionárse, *vr.* To take possession of a thing; to possess one's self of a thing.

Aposición, *sf.* (Gram.) Apposition, a figure, when two or more substantives are put together in the same case, without any copulative conjunction between them.

Aposiópesis, *sf.* (Ret.) A figure of speech, by which a speaker affects to say nothing on a subject, at the same time he really speaks of it.

Apósito, *sm.* Any external medicinal application.

Apospélo, *ad.* 1. Against the grain. 2. Contrary to the natural order.

Apósta y Apostadaménte, *ad.* Designedly, on purpose.

Apostadéro, *sm.* 1. A place where soldiers or other persons are stationed. 2. (Naút.) A station for ships.

Apostadór, *sm.* Bettor, one that wagers.

Apostál, *sm.* (Ast.) A convenient fishing place in a river.

Apostaléos, *sm. pl.* Planks from 5 to 7 inches thick.

Apostár, *va.* 1. To bet, to lay a wager. 2. To distribute horses on the road to relieve others, to place relays. 3. To post soldiers or other persons in a place. 4. (Ant.) To dress, to adorn. *Apostárlas ó apostárselas,* To contend; to defy, or bid defiance.—*vr.* To emulate, to rival, to stand in competition, to endeavour to equal or excel.

Apostasía, *sf.* Apostasy, departure from the religion formerly professed.

Apóstata, *sm.* Apostate, one that has forsaken his religion.

Apostatár, *vn.* To apostatise, to forsake one's religion.

Apostelár, *va.* To write short notes. V. *Apostillar.*

Apostéma, *sf.* An apostume, abscess, tumor.

Apostemár, *va.* To swell and corrupt into matter; to form an abscess.—*vr.* To get an abscess; to be troubled with a purulent humour.

Aposteméro, *sm.* Bistoury, a chirurgical instrument for opening abscesses.

Apostemílla, *sf.* A small abscess.

Apostemóso, sa, *a.* Relating to abscesses.

Apostílla, *sf.* A brief note put to a book or writing.

Apostillár, *va.* To put brief notes to a book or writing.—*vr.* To break out in pimples or pustules.

Apóstol, *sm.* Apostle, missionary. *Apóstoles,* (Naút.) Hawse pieces.

Apostoládo, da, *a.* 1. The dignity or office of an apostle. 2. The congregation of the apostles. 3. The images or pictures of the 12 apostles.

Apostolicaménte, *ad.* Apostolically.

Apostólico, ca, *a.* 1. Apostolical, that which in any manner belongs to the apostles. 2. Apostolic, that which belongs to the Pope, or derives from him apostolical authority.

Apóstolos, *sm. pl.* (Ant. For.) Dimissory apostolical letters.

Apóstre, *ad.* (Ant.) V. *Postreramente.*

Apostrofár, *va.* To apostrophize, to address one; to apply to another by words.

Apóstrofe, *sm.* (Ret.) A diversion of speech to another person than the speech appointed did intend or require.

Apóstrofo, *sm.* The contraction of a word by the use of a comma; as, *l'amistad* for *la amistad;* but this contraction is now disused.

Apostúra, *sf.* (Ant.) 1. Gentleness, neatness in

...2. (Ant.) Good order and disposition ...ings.

...RAGES. V. *Barraganetes*.

... *ad*. Abundantly, largely.

...MA, *sm*. Apothegm, a short, remarkable ...ing.

...OSIS, *sf*. Apotheosis, deification.

...ARIO, *sm*. (Ar.) V. *Boticario*.

...OME, *sm*. (Alg.) The remainder or differ...ce of two incommensurable qualities.

...DERO, *sm*. Prop, support.

...URA, *sf*. Flow of the milk which comes ...of the breast when nurses give suck to ...dren.

...AR. *va*. 1. To favour, to protect, to patro... 2. To bear upon the bit; spoken of ...s which hang down their heads. *Apoy... las espuelas*, To spur. 3. To confirm, to ...ort or prove. *Apoya esta sentencia con ...xto de la escritura*, He confirms this ...nce by a text of Scripture.—*vn*. To rest ... *La columna apoya sobre el pedestal*, The ...mn rests on the pedestal.—*vr*. To lean ...a person or thing. *Apoyarse en los es...s*. To bear upon the stirrups.

... *sm*. 1. Prop, stay, support. 2. (Met.) ...tection, patronage. *Apoyo de la vejez de ...*, One who supports the aged or alle...tes the oppressed.

...CIABLE, *a*. 1. Valuable, respectable, worthy ...steem. 2. That which can fetch a price; ...rsetable.

...CIACIÓN, *sf*. Estimation, valuation.

...CIADAMÉNTE, *ad*. In a valuable, respecta... manner.

...CIADÓR, RA, *s*. Estimator, appraiser; a ...son appointed to set a price upon a thing.

...CIÁR, *va*. To appreciate, to estimate, to ... [upon a thing.

...TATÍVO, VA, *a*. Relating to the value set

...CIO, *sm*. 1. Appraisement, the value set ...on a thing. 2. Esteem, approbation.

...EHENDÉR, *va*. 1. To apprehend, to seize, to ...hold of one. 2. To fancy, to conceive, to ...m an idea of a thing. *Aprehender la po...sion*, To take possession. *Aprehender los ...es*, To seize or distrain goods.

...EHENSIÓN, *sf*. 1. The act of seizing, appre...ding, or taking up a criminal. 2. Percep...n, acuteness; a ready and witty saying. 3. ...prehension, fear. 4. The act of putting the ...'s arms or seal on a house, until the rights ...e different claimants are discussed, or ... true owner appears.

...HENSÍVO, VA, *a*. Apprehensive, quick to ...erstand, fearful.

...HENSÓR, RA, *s*. One who apprehends.

...HENSÓRIO, RIA, *a*. Apprehending, seizing.

...MIADÓR, RA, *s*. One who compels or forces ...do a thing.

...MIÁR, *va*. 1. To press, to urge, to con... 2. To compel, to oblige.

...MIO, *sm*. 1. Pressure, constriction. 2. Ju...al compulsion.

...NDÉR, *va*. 1. To learn; to acquire know...ge of a thing by study. 2. (Ant.) To ...re, to apprehend.

...NDÍZ, ZA, Y APRENDIGÓN, *s*. Apprentice, ...prentice.

APRENDIZÁGE, *sm*. Apprenticeship, the years which an apprentice is to pass under a master to learn a trade.

APRENSADÓR, *sm*. Presser, calenderer.

APRENSÁR, *va*. 1. To dress cloth in a press, to calender. 2. To vex, to crush, to oppress. 3. (Naút.) To stow wool, cotton, &c. on board a ship. [tor.

APRESADÓR, RA, *s*. 1. Privateer, cruiser. 2. Cap-

APRESAMIÉNTO, *sm*. Capture, prize.

APRESÁR, *va*. 1. To seize, to grasp. 2. (Naút.) To take or capture an enemy's ship.

APRESTÁR, *va*. To prepare, to make ready.

APRÉSTO, *sm*. Preparation for a thing.

APRESURACIÓN, *sf*. The act of making haste.

APRESURADAMÉNTE, *ad*. Hastily.

APRESURÁDO, DA, *a*. 1. Brief, hasty. 2. Acting with precipitation.

APRESURAMIÉNTO, *sm*. V. *Apresuracion*.

APRESURÁR, *va*. To accelerate, to hasten.

APRETADAMÉNTE, *ad*. Tightly, closely.

APRETADÉRA, *sf*. A strap or rope to tie or bind any thing with. *Apretadéras*, Pressing remonstrances.

APRETADÉRO, *sm*. Truss or bandage by which ruptures are restrained from relapsing.

APRETADÍLLO, LLA, *a*. Somewhat constrained, rather hard put to it. *Apretadillo está el enfermo*, The patient is in great danger.

APRETÁDO, DA, *a*. 1. Mean, miserable, narrow-minded, illiberal. 2. Hard, difficult, dangerous.

APRETADÓR, *sm*. 1. One who presses or beats down. 2. An under-waistcoat without sleeves. 3. A sort of soft stays without whalebone for children. 4. A net for tying up the hair. 5. A coarse sheet wrapt round mattresses, to keep them even and tight. 6. An instrument which serves for tightening things, and pressing them down; a rammer. [ing down.

APRETADÚRA, *sf*. Compression, the act of press-

APRETAMIÉNTO, *sm*. 1. Crowd, great concourse of people. 2. Conflict. 3. Avarice, narrowness.

APRETÁR, *va*. 1. To compress, to tighten, to press down. 2. To distress, to afflict with calamities. 3. To act with more energy and vigour than usual. 4. To urge earnestly. 5. To darken that part of a painting which is too bright and glaring. *Apretar las soletas*, To run away. *Apretar con uno*, To attack a person. *Apretar la mano*, To correct with a heavy hand, to punish severely.

APRETÓN, *sm*. Pressure, the act of pressing. 2. Struggle, conflict. 3. A sudden violent looseness of the body. 4. A short but rapid race. 5. The act of throwing a thicker shade on one part of a piece of painting.

APRETÚRA, *sf*. 1. A crowd, a multitude pressing against each other. 2. Distress, conflict, anguish. 3. A narrow, confined place.

APRIÉSA, *ad*. In haste, in a hurry.

APRIÉTO, *sm*. Crowd; conflict.

APRIMÍR, *va*. 1. To compress, to force into a narrower compass, to depress. 2. To restrain, to crush, to subdue.

APRÍSA, *ad*. Swiftly, promptly.

APRISÁR, *va*. To hasten, to hurry, to push forwards. [cot.

APRISCADÉRO Y APRÍSCO, *sm*. Sheepfold, sheep-

APRISIÉRA *preterpluper*. (Ant.) from *Aprender*.

Aprisionadaménte, *ad.* Narrowly, contractedly, with little breadth or wideness.
Aprisonádo, *a.* (Poét.) Bound, subjected.
Aprisonár, *va.* To confine, to imprison.
Apró, *sm.* V. *Pro.*
Aproár, *vn.* (Naút.) To turn the head of a ship towards any part.—*va.* To benefit.
Aprobación, *sf.* Approbation.
Aprobadór, ra, *s.* Approver, one who approves.
Aprobánte, *sm.* 1. A probationer; one who proves his qualifications for an office. 2. Approver.
Aprobár, *va.* To approve, to like, to be pleased with.
Aprobatívo, va, *a.* Approbative, approving.
Apróches, *sm.* Approaches, the several works made by besiegers for advancing and getting nearer to a fortress. *Contra-aproches*, Counter-approaches. *Las trincheras se llaman lineas de aproches*, the trenches are called lines of approach.
Aprón, *sm.* (Ict.) A small fresh-water fish, resembling a gudgeon.
Aprontár, *va.* To prepare hastily, to get ready with expedition and despatch.
Aprónto, *sm.* A speedy expeditious preparation.
Aporpiación, *sf.* Appropriation, assumption, the act of appropriating or assuming a thing.
Apropiadaménte, *ad.* Conveniently, fitly, properly.
Apropiadór, *sm.* Appropriator.
Apropiár, *va.* 1. To appropriate, to assume. 2. To assimilate, to bring to a resemblance. 3. To accommodate, to apply.—*vr.* To appropriate any thing to one's self, to encroach.
Apropinquación, *sf.* Approach, the act of approaching.
Apropinquárse, *vr.* To approach, to draw near.
Apropriár. V. *Apropiar.*
Aprovecér, *vn.* To make progress.
Aprovechábile, *a.* Profitable, that which may be rendered useful or serviceable.
Aprovechadaménte, *ad.* Usefully, profitably.
Aprovechádo, da, *pp.* Improved; taken advantage of.—*a.* Sparing, parsimonious.
Aprovechamiénto, *sm.* 1. Profit, utility, advantage. 2. Progress made in an art or science, proficiency. 3. Land, commons, houses, &c. belonging to a town or city. V. *Propios.*
Aprovechár, *vn.* To make progress, to advance, to become useful.—*va.* 1. To profit of a thing, to employ it usefully. 2. (Ant.) To protect, to favour. 3. (Ant.) To meliorate.—*vr.* To avail one's self of a thing, to take advantage of a thing.
Aproximación, *sf.* Approximation.
Aproximár, *va.* To approximate, to approach.
Aptaménte, *ad.* Conveniently, fitly, aptly.
Aptitúd, *sf.* Aptitude or fitness for obtaining or exercising an employment.
A'pto, ta, *a.* Apt, fit, idoneous, able to perform a thing.
Apuésta, *sf.* A bet, a wager. *Ir de apuesta*, To undertake the performance of a thing in competition with others.
Apuésto, ta, *a.* 1. (Ant.) Elegant, genteel. 2. (Ant.) Opportune, fit.
Apuésto, *sm.* Epithet, title. V. *Apostura.*
Apulgarár, *va.* To force with the thumb.—*vr.* (Baxo.) To contract black spots from having been doubled up when moist; spoken of linen.
Apunchár, *va.* (Among comb-makers) To cut out the teeth of a comb.
Apuntación, *sf.* 1. Annotation, the act of noting down. 2. The act of marking musical notes with exactness.
Apuntádo, da, *a.* 1. Pointed, marked. 2. *El cañon está apuntado muy baxo*, (Art. y Naút.) The gun dips.
Apuntadór, *sm.* 1. Observer, one who notes or marks. 2. (Naút.) Gunner, who points the guns. 3. *Apuntadór de comedias*, A prompter, one who helps the players, and suggests the word to them when they falter.
Apuntalár, *va.* 1. To prop, to support with props. 2. (Naút.) To shore a vessel.
Apuntamiénto, *sm.* 1. Observation, remark. 2. Abstract, summary, heads of a law-suit pointed out by the report in a court of justice; a judicial report.
Apuntár, *va.* 1. To aim, to take aim. 2. To point out, to mark, to indicate. 3. To put down in writing any remarkable idea read or heard. 4. To touch lightly upon a point. 5. To fix or fasten provisionally a board or other thing. 6. To begin to appear or show itself. *El dia se apunta*, The day peeps or begins to appear. 7. To sharpen edged tools. 8. To prompt or help players, by suggesting the word to them when they falter. 9. To offer. *Apuntar y no dar*, To promise readily and not perform.—*vr.* 1. To begin to turn, to be pricked; applied to wine. 2. (Bax.) To be half seas over, or half drunk.
Apúnte, *sm.* V. *Apuntamiento.*
Apúnto, *sm.* The words suggested by a prompter on the stage.
Apuñadár, *va.* (Arag.) To strike with the fist.
Apuñár, *va.* (Ant.) To seize with the fist.
Apuñeár, *va.* V. *Apuñadar.*
Apuñeteár, *va.* To strike repeatedly with the hand clenched.
Apuración, *sf.* (Ant.) Indagation, investigation.
Apuradaménte, *ad.* 1. At the nick of time. 2. Punctually, exactly. 3. Radically.
Apuradéro, (Ant.) *sm.* Inquiry, disquisition which ascertains the true nature of a thing.
Apurádo, da, *a.* 1. Poor, destitute of means, exhausted. 2. Evident. 3. Excellent.
Apuradór, *sm.* 1. A refiner, purifier. 2. One who spends or consumes. 3. One who gleans and picks up olives left by the first reapers.
Apuramiénto, *sm.* Research, inquiry, verification.
Apurár, *va.* 1. To purify, to depurate. 2. To clear up, to verify, to investigate minutely. 3. To consume, to drain, to exhaust. *Apurar á uno*, To tease and perplex one.—*vr.* To grieve, to be afflicted.
Apúro, *sm.* 1. Want, indigence. 2. Anguish, affliction.
Apurrír, *va.* (Burg.) To hand or deliver a thing to another.
Aquá, *ad.* (Ant.) V. *Acá.*
Aquadrillár, *va.* To form or head parties.
Aquário, *sm.* Aquarius, one of the 12 signs of the Zodiac.

Aquarteládo, da, *a.* Quartered, divided into quarters.

Aquartelamiénto, *sm.* The quartering of troops, and the place where they are quartered.

Aquartelár, *va.* 1. To quarter troops, to distribute them into quarters. 2. (Naút.) *Aquartelar las velas*, To flat in the sails.

Aquartillár, *vn.* To bend in the quarters under a heavy load; applied to beasts of burthen.

Aquático y Aquátil, *a.* Aquatic, that which inhabits or grows in the water.

Aquedár, *va.* (Ant.) To detain.—*vr.* V. *Dormirse.*

Aqüedúcto, *sm.* 1. Aqueduct, a conduit of water. 2. Canal which runs from the ear to the mouth. It was anciently written *Aqueducho.*

Aquejamiénto, *sm.* (Ant.) Acceleration.

Aquejár, *va.* 1. To complain, to lament. 2. To fatigue, to afflict. 3. (Ant.) To stimulate, to incite. 4. (Ant.) To pin up closely.

Aquél, lla, llo, *pron. demonst.* He, she, that.

Aquén y Aquénde, *ad.* (Ant.) Here, thither.

Aqüéo, ea, *a.* Aqueous, watery. *Humor aqueo*, Aqueous humour which runs from the eye.

Aquerenciárse, *vr.* To be fond of a place; a term applied to cattle.

Aquése, sa, so, A demonstrative pronoun, relating to a person or thing somewhat distant.

Aquestár, *va.* To conquer, to acquire.

Aquéste, ta, to, *pron. demonst.* (Ant.) This, that.

Aqüéste, *sm.* (Ant.) Question, dispute.

Aquí, *ad.* 1. Here, in this place. 2. To this place. 3. Now, at present. 4. Then, on that occasion. *Aquí de Dios*, Assist me, O God. *Aquí fué ello*, Here did it happen. *He aquí*, Look here, behold. *De aquí adelante*, Henceforth. *De aquí para allí*, To and fro, up and down. *De aquí*, From this.

Aquiescéncia, *sf.* (For.) Acquiescence, consent.

Aquietár, *va.* To quiet, to appease.—*vr.* To grow calm, to be quiet.

Aquila álba, *sf.* Corrosive sublimate mixed with fresh mercury.

Aquilatár, *va.* 1. To assay gold and silver. 2. To examine closely, to find out the truth of a thing.

Aquiléa, *sf.* (Bot.) Milfoil, yarrow. Achillea millefolium *L.*

Aquiléña, *sf.* (Bot.) Columbine. Aquilegia vulgaris *L.*

Aquilífero, *sm.* (Among the Romans) The standard-bearer, he who carried the Roman eagle.

Aquilíno, na, *a.* Aquiline, resembling an eagle; when applied to the nose, hooked. V. *Aguileño.*

Aquilón, *sm.* (Poét.) 1. Due north-wind. 2. The north point.

Aquilonál y Aquilonár, *a.* Northern, northerly. *Tiempo aquilonal*, (Met.) The winter season.

Aquitíbi, *sm.* Nickname of priests hired for processions.

Aquosidád, *sf.* Aquosity, wateriness.

Aquóso, sa, *a.* Aqueous, watery.

A'ra, *sf.* 1. Altar, the place where offerings are made to heaven. 2. The consecrated stone, on which a consecrated linen cover is laid during the celebration of the mass. 3. (Among Plumbers) A cistern head. *Amigo hasta las aras*, A friend until death.

Arabésco, *sm.* (Pint.) Arabesk, whimsical ornaments of foliage in painting.

Arábiga, *sf.* A stone resembling spotted ivory.

Arábigo, ga, y Arábico, ca, *a.* Arabic, Arabian.

Aracadér, *sm.* A flat fish in the seas of Brasil.

Aráda, *sf.* (Agr.) Ploughed ground; husbandry.

Arádo, *sm.* 1. A plough. 2. Ploughed ground.

Aradór, *sm.* 1. A ploughman. 2. A hand-worm, flesh-worm, ring-worm.

Aradorcíco, *sm.* A small hand-worm.

Arádro, *sm.* (Arag.) V. *Arádo.*

Aradúra, *sf.* 1. Aration, the act or practice of ploughing. 2. Quantity of land which a yoke of oxen can conveniently plough in the course of a day.

Aragán, *sm.* Idler. V. *Haragan.*

Aragonésa. *Uva Aragonesa*, A large black grape, very frequent in Aragon.

Arambél, *sm.* (Ant.) 1. Drapery, furniture of a room or bed. 2. (Met.) Rag, tatter, or piece hanging from cloths.

Arámbre, *sm.* (Ant.) V. *Alambre.*

Aránia, *sf.* A piece of ploughed ground fit for sowing.

Arána, *sf.* (Ant.) Imposition, trick, deception.

Aranáta, *sf.* An animal of the shape and size of a dog, a native of America.

Arancél, *sm.* 1. The fixed rate and price of provisions or other things. 2. The regulations by which the rate and price of bread and other things are fixed.

Arancíl, *sm.* Price current, tariff. V. *Arancel.*

Arandáno, *sm.* (Bot.) Bilberry. Vaccinium myrtillus *L.*

Arandéla, *sf.* 1. The pan of the socket of a candlestick. 2. A guard around the staff of a lance. 3. Nave-box of a gun carriage. 4. *Arandelas*, (Naút.) Half ports, square boards with a hole in the middle, to which a piece of canvass is nailed, to keep the water out when the cannon is in the port-hole.

Arandíllo, *sm.* Pad, or small hoop, used by women, which in Castile is called *Caderillas.*

Araniégo, *a.* Taken in a net, which is called *arañuela;* applied to a young hawk.

Aranzáda, *sf.* An acre of ground: in the opinion of some Spanish linguists, it is as much land as a pair of oxen can plough in a day.

Aráña, *sf.* 1. (Entom.) Spider. 2. (Ict.) Sting-bull, common weaver, sea-spider. Trachinus draco *L.* 3. Chandelier, girandole. 4. Play among boys. 5. (Ant.) Net for catching birds. 6. (Naút.) Crow-foot. *Es una araña*, He is an industrious man. 7. (Mur.) V. *Arrebatiña.*

Arañadór, ra, *s.* One who scratches.

Arañamiénto, *sm.* The act of scratching.

Arañar, *va.* 1. To scratch. 2. To scrape, to gather by penurious diligence. *Arañar riquezas*, To gather riches with great eagerness. *Arañarse con los codos*, To rejoice in other people's misfortunes. *Arañar la cubierta*, To make great exertions, to get clear of danger.

Arañázo, *sm.* A long deep scratch.

Arañéro, *a.* V. *Zahareño.*

Aráño, *sm.* A scratch, any slight wound.

Arañón, *sm.* Sloe, the fruit of the black thorn.

Arañuélo y Arañuéla, *s.* 1. A small species of spiders very destructive in corn fields, vines, &c. 2. A very slight net for catching birds.

Arapénde, *sm.* Ancient measure of 120 square feet.

Arár, *va.* 1. To plough the land. 2. (Naút.) *Arar con el ancla*, To drag the anchor. *No me lo harán creer quantos aran y cavan*, No man shall ever make me believe it.

Aratório, ria, *a.* Belonging to a husbandman.

Arbellón, *sm.* Gutter for drawing off the water from roads and bridges.

Arbélo, *sm.* (Geom.) A curvilinear figure, composed of three segments of a circle, and three acute angles.

Arbitána. V. *Albitana.*

Arbitrábles, *a.* Arbitrary, depending upon the will.

Arbitración, *sf.* (Ant.) Arbitration.

Arbitradór, *sm.* Arbiter, arbitrator, umpire.

Arbitrál, *a.* V. *Arbitrario.*

Arbitraménto, Arbitramiénto, y Arbitráge, *sm.* The award of an arbitrator.

Arbitrár, *va.* 1. To adjudge, to award as an arbitrator. 2. (Ant.) To discover, to find out. 3. To judge after one's own feelings and sentiments. 4. To strike out means and expedients.

Arbitrariaménte, *ad.* In an arbitrary manner.

Arbitrário, ria, Arbitratívo, va, *a.* Arbitrary, that which depends upon the will.

Arbitratório, ria, *a.* That which belongs or relates to arbitrators.

Arbítrio, *sm.* 1. Free and uncontrolled will and pleasure. 2. Means, expedients. 3. Arbitration, bond, compromise. 4. *Arbitrio de juez*, The discretionary power of a judge in cases not clearly decided by the law. 5. *Arbitrios*, Duty or taxes imposed on wine, vinegar, oil, meat, and other provisions exposed for sale.

Arbitrísta, *sm.* Schemer, projector, contriver.

A'rbitro, *sm.* Arbiter, arbitrator.

A'rbol, *sm.* (Bot.) 1. A tree. 2. (Naút.) Mast, V. *Palo.* 3. In some machines, the upright post which serves to give them a circular motion. 4. Drill, a pointed instrument used for making holes in metal. 5. Body of a shirt without sleeves. 6. Upright post, around which winding stairs turn. *A'rbol de amor*, (Bot.) Judas-tree. Cercis siliquastrum *L.* *A'rbol de clavo*, Clove-tree. Eugenia caryophillata *L.* *A'rbol del coral*, Coral-tree. Erythrina Corallodendron *L.* *A'rbol del paraiso, ó árbol paraiso*, Flowering ash. Fraxinus ornus *L.* *A'rbol marino*, (Ict.) A fish much resembling the star-fish, but larger.

Arboládo, da, *a.* 1. Planted with trees. 2. Masted. *Arbolado en la hoya*, Masted hoy-fashion.

Arboladúra, *sf.* (Naút.) A general name for masts, yards, and all sort of round timber. *Maestre de arboladura*, A master mast-maker.

Arbolár, *va.* To hoist, to set upright. *Arbolar el navio*, (Naút.) To mast a ship.—*vr.* *Arbolarse el caballo*, To rear on the hind feet, as horses.

Arbolário, *sm.* V. *Herbolario.*

Arboláso, *sm.* (Aum.) A large tree.

Arbolecíllo y Arbolecíco, *sm.* (Dim.) A small tree.

Arboléda, *sf.* Grove, plantation of trees.

Arboléjo, *sm.* A small tree.

Arboléte, *sm.* Branch of a tree put on the ground, to which bird-catchers fasten their lime-twigs.

Arbolísta, *sm.* Arborist, a naturalist who makes trees his study.

Arbollón, *sm.* Flood-gate, sluice, dam, conduit, channel.

Arbor, *sm.* (Ant.) V. *A'rbol.*

Arbóreo, rea, *a.* Relating or belonging to trees.

Arborizádo, da, *a.* Arborescent, resembling trees and foliage; applied to dendrites or stones having the appearance of foliage.

Arbotánte, *sm.* Arch of stone or brick raised against a wall to support a vault. *Arbotánte de pie de campana*, (Naút.) Bell-crank, the place where the ship's bell is hung.

Arbústo y Arbusta, *s.* A shrub.

A'rca, *sf.* 1. Chest, a large wooden box. *Arcas*, Coffer, iron chest for money. *Hacer arcas*, To open the coffers or treasury chest. 2. (In glass houses) The tempering oven, in which glass-ware, just blown, is put to cool or anneal. 3. Sepulchral urn, a tomb. 4. Head of a spout or pipe, through which water runs down into a drain. *Arca de noé*, (Met.) Lumber chest. *Arca de fuego*, (Naút.) Fire-chest, a small box, filled with gun-powder, combustibles, pebbles, nails, &c. used to annoy an enemy who attempts to board a ship. *Ser arca cerrada*, To be yet unknown; applied to persons and things. *Sangrar á uno de la vena del arca*, To drain one of his money. *Arca de agua*, Reservoir. *Arcas*, Cavities of the body under the ribs.

Arcabucéar, *va.* 1. To shoot with the cross-bow. 2. To shoot a criminal by way of punishment.

Arcabucería, *sm.* 1. A troop of archers. 2. Number of cross bows. 3. Manufactory of bows and arrows.

Arcabucéro, *sm.* 1. Archer. 2. Manufacturer of bows and arrows.

Arcabúz, *sm.* Arquebuse, a fire-arm, a hand-gun.

Arcabuzázo, *sm.* A shot from a gun, and the wound it causes.

Arcacíl, *sm.* (Bot.) A species of artichoke. Cynara sylvestris *L.*

Arcáda, *sf.* 1. Violent motion of the stomach, which excites vomiting. 2. Arcade or row of arches in bridges, and other buildings.

A'rcade, *a.* 1. Native of Arcadia, Arcadian. 2. Belonging to the Roman academy of polite literature, called *arcades.*

Arcadór, *sm.* (Ant.) V. *Arqueador.*

Arcadúz, *sm.* 1. Conduit or pipe for the conveyance of water. 2. Bucket or jar for raising water out of a draw-well. 3. (Met.) Channel for enforcing a claim, obtaining a place, &c. *Llevar una cosa por sus arcaduces*, To conduct an affair through its proper channel.

Arcaduzár, *va.* To convey water through conduits.

Arcaísmo, *sm.* Archaism, the mixture of ancient or antiquated words with modern language.

Arcám, *sm.* A very venomous serpent, spotted black and white, which is found in the country of Turkestan.

Arcángel, *sm.* Archangel.

Arcanidád, *sf.* A profound secret of great moment.

Arcáno, na, *a.* y *s.* Secret, recondite, reserved.

Arcár, *va.* (Among Clothiers) To beat the wool with a bow of one or two cords.

A'rcaz, *sm.* 1. A large chest. 2. (Arag.) A bier, on which the dead are carried to be buried.

Arcáza, *sf.* A large chest.

A'rce, *sm.* (Bot.) Maple-tree. Acer *L.*

Arcedianáto, *sm.* Archdeaconship; archdeaconry.

Arcediáno, *sm.* Archdeacon.

Arcén, *sm.* 1. Border, brim, edge. 2. Stone laid round the brim of a well.

Arquéro, *sm.* Archer.

Archiducádo, *sm.* Dignity of an archduke, and an archduchy, or the territory belonging to an archduke.

Archiducál, *a.* That which belongs or relates to an archduke or archduchy.

Archidúque, *sm.* Archduke.

Archiduquésa, *sf.* Archduchess.

Archiláud, *sm.* A musical instrument shaped and stringed as a lute, but of a larger size.

Archipámpano, *sm.* (Joc.) A word used to express an imaginary dignity or authority.

Archipiélago, *sm.* Archipelago, a part of the sea crowded with islands.

Archivár, *va.* To deposit a thing or writing in an archive.

Archivéro y Archivísta, *sm.* Keeper of an archive, master of the rolls.

Archívo, *sm.* 1. Archives, the place where public records are kept. 2. (Met.) A person who is entrusted with the most profound secrets, a confidant.

Arcílla, *sf.* Argil, white pure earth, alumina.

Arcillóso, sa, *a.* Clayish, argillaceous.

Arciprestádgo ó Arciprestázgo, *sm.* The dignity of an archpriest.

Arcipréste, *sm.* Archpriest, the first or chief presbyter.

A'rco, *sm.* 1. Arch, a part of a circle not more than the half. 2. Bow, a weapon for throwing arrows. 3. Fiddle bow. 4. Hoop, any thing circular with which something else is bound, particularly casks and barrels. 5. (Naút.) Bow of a ship. *Arco del cielo ó dè San Martin*, Rainbow.

A'rcola, *sf.* A sort of coarse linen.

Arcón, *sm.* 1. A large chest. 2. A great arch.

A'rctico, ca, *a.* Arctic, northern. V. *A'rtico.*

Arcuádo, da, *a.* Gauged or gaged. V. *Arqueado.*

A'rda, *sf.* Squirrel. V. *Ardilla.*

Ardaleádo, da, *pp.* Made thin or clear.

Ardaleár, *va.* To thin, to make thin.

Ardáses, *sf. pl.* The coarser sort of Persia silk.

Ardasínas, *sf. pl.* The finer sort of Persia silk.

Arderón, *sm.* A kind of serpent.

Ardentía, *sf.* 1. Heat. 2. (Naút.) Phosphoric sparkling of the sea when it is much agitated.

Ardeóla, *sf.* A small kind of heron.

Ardér, *vn.* 1. To burn, to flame, to blaze. 2. To be agitated by the passions of love, hatred, anger, &c. *Arderse en pleytos*, To be entangled in lawsuits.

Ardéro, ra, *a.* Squirrel hunter; applied to dogs.

Ardíd, *sm.* Stratagem or artifice.

Ardído, da, *a.* 1. Heated; applied to grain, olives, tobacco, &c. thrown into a state of fermentation. 2. (Ant.) Bold, intrepid, valiant.

Ardiénte, *a.* 1. That which burns. *Calentura ardiente*, A burning fever. 2. Ardent, passionate, active.

Ardiénte, *sm.* A luminous exhalation in marshy places, called, by the vulgar, Will o' the wisp, or Jack with the lantern.

Ardienteménte, *ad.* Ardently.

Ardílla, *sf.* Squirrel. Sciurus vulgaris *L.*

Ardimiénto, *sm.* 1. (Ant.) Conflagration. 2. (Met.) Valour, intrepidity, undaunted courage.

Ardínculo, *sm.* (Albeyt.) An inflamed swelling or ulcer on the backs of animals.

Ardíte, *sm.* An ancient coin of little value, formerly current in Spain. *No vale un ardite*, It is not worth a doit.

Ardór, *sm.* 1. Great heat. 2. (Met.) Valour, vivacity, spirit, vigour.

Ardoróso, sa, *a.* Fiery, restless; applied to a horse.

Arduaménte, *ad.* In a difficult, arduous manner.

Arduidád, *sf.* Extreme difficulty.

A'rduo, dua, *a.* Arduous, difficult.

A'rea, *sf.* 1. Area, the surface contained between any lines or boundaries. 2. A bright circle which surrounds the sun, moon, or stars; a halo.

Aréna, *sf.* 1. Sand, particles of stone not joined. 2. Place where wrestlers and gladiators fought. *Edificar sobre arena*, To build upon sand. *Sembrar en arena*, To labour in vain. *Arena de hóya*, Pit sand. *Arena movediza*, (Naút.) Quick-sand. *Arénas*, Gravel formed in the kidneys.

Arenáceo, ea, *a.* Arenaceous, gravelly.

Arenál, *sm.* A sandy ground, a sandy beach.

Arenaléjo y Arenalíllo, *sm.* 1. A small sandy piece of ground. 2. Small, fine sand.

Arenár, *va.* To cover with sand.

Arencón, *sm.* (Aum.) V. *Arenque.*

Arenéro, *sm.* One who deals in sand.

Arénga, *sf.* Harangue, speech, popular oration.

Arengár, *vn.* To harangue, to deliver in public a speech or oration.

Areníca y Arenílla, *sf.* Small, fine sand.

Areníllas, *pl.* (In gunpowder mills) Saltpetre refined, and reduced to grains as small as sand.

Arenísco, ca, y **Arenóso**, sa, *a.* Sandy, abounding with sand.

Arénque, *sm.* Herring. Clupea harengus *L.* *Arénque ahumado*, A red herring.

Areómetro, *sm.* Areometer, an instrument for measuring the density and gravity of spirituous liquors.

Areopagíta, *sm.* Judge of the supreme court of judicature in Athens.

Areópago, *sm.* The supreme court of judicature in Athens.

Arésta, *sf.* (Ant.) 1. Coarse tow. 2. V. *Espina.*

Arestín, *sm.* Frush, a disease in horses, consisting in a scabby incrustation of the heel up to the pastern.

Arestinádo, da, *a.* Afflicted with the disease called the frush.

Arfáda, *sf.* (Naút.) The pitching of a ship.

Arfár, *va.* (Naút.) To pitch; applied to a ship.

Arfíl. V. *Alfil.*

Argadíjo y Argadíllo, *sm.* 1. Reel. V. *Devanadéra.* 2. (Met.) A blustrous, noisy, restless person. 3. Large basket made of twigs of osier. 4. (Ant. y Met.) Structure of the human body.

Argádo, *sm.* Prank, trick, artifice.

Argálla, *sf.* V. *Algalia.*

Argalléra, *sf.* A kind of saw for cutting grooves.

Argamandél, *sm.* Rag, tatter.

Argamandíjo, *sm.* (Joc.) Collection of trifling implements used in trade or business. *Dueño* *ó señor del argamandijo*, Powerful lord and master.

Argamása, *sf.* Mortar, a cement for building.

Argamasár, *va.* 1. To make mortar. 2. To cement with mortar.

Argamasón, *sm.* A large piece of mortar found among the ruins of a building.

Argamúla, *sf.* (Bot.) Starwort. V. *Amelo.*

A'rgana, *sf.* A machine resembling a crane, for raising stones and other weighty things. *A'rganas*, 1. Baskets or wicker vessels in which fruit or other things are carried on a horse. 2. Large nets in which forage is carried.

Arganél, *sm.* A small brass ring, used in the composition of an astrolabe.

Argañéo, *sm.* (Naút.) Anchor-ring, a large ring in the anchor to which the cable is fastened.

A'rgano, *sm.* An ancient warlike machine.

A'rgel, *a.* 1. This adjective is applied to a horse whose right hind foot only is white. 2. (Met.) Unlucky, unfortunate.

Argelíno, na, *a.* Algerine, belonging to Algiers.

Argéma, *sm.* A thin pellicle or skin formed in the pupil of the eye.

Argémone, *sm.* (Bot.) Prickly or horned poppy. Argemone mexicana *L.*

Argén, *sm.* (Blas.) Argent, white or silver colour.

Argént, *sm.* (Ant.) V. *Plata.*

Argentádo, da, *a.* 1. This term was formerly applied to a shoe pierced with holes, through which the fine white colour of the stuff was seen with which it was lined. 2. *Voz argentada*, A clear, sonorous voice.

Argentadór, *sm.* One who silvers or covers superficially with silver.

Argentár, *va.* To plate or cover with silver; to give an argent colour.

Argentário y Argentéro, *sm.* 1. (Ant.) Silver-smith. 2. (Ant.) Master of the mint.

Argentería, *sf.* 1. Embroidery in gold or silver. 2. (Met.) Expression which has more brilliancy than solidity.

Argentifodína, *sf.* Silver mine.

Argentína, *sf.* (Bot.) Satin cinquefoil; tormentil cinquefoil. Potentilla argentea *L.*

Argénto, *sm.* 1. (Poét.) Silver. 2. *Argento vivo sublimado*, Sublimate. V. *Soliman.*

Argílla, *sf.* V. *Arcilla.*

Argirítas, *sm. pl.* Marcasites, which are found in silver mines.

Argirogónia, *sf.* Philosopher's stone.

Argólla, *sf.* 1. Large iron ring; a staple. *Argollas de cureña*, Draught hooks of a gun-carriage. *Argollas de amarra*, Lashing-rings. 2. Pillory; a public punishment in putting a ring round the neck.

Argolléta, Argollíca, y Argollíta, *sf.* A small staple; an iron ring of a small size.

Argollón, *sm.* A very large iron ring; a large staple.

A'rgoma, *sf.* (Bot.) Prickly broom or cytisus. Spartium spinosum *L.*

Argomál, *sm.* Plantation of cytisus.

Argomón, *sm.* Large prickly broom.

Argonáutas, *sm. pl.* 1. Argonauts, the companions of Jason, who embarked on board the *Argo for Colchis*, to obtain the golden fleece. 2. *Argonautas de San Nicolas*, The name of a military order at Naples.

A'rgos, *sm.* 1. Argo, the celebrated ship of the Argonauts. 2. (Met.) An able, clever person.

Argoudán, *sm.* A kind of cotton, manufactured in different parts of India.

Arguanáque, *sm.* Gum ammoniac.

Argúcia, *sf.* Subtilty, which degenerates into sophistry.

Argüe, *sm.* 1. Machine for moving large weights; windlass. 2. Machine for drawing fine gold wire.

Arguellárse, *vr.* To be emaciated; to be in a bad state of health.

Arguéllo, *sm.* Faintness, want of health.

Arguénas, *sf. pl.* V. *Angarilas.*

Argüír, *sm.* To argue, to dispute.—*va.* To give signs, to make a show of something. *Argüirle á uno su conciencia*, To be pricked by one's conscience.

Argullía y Argúllo, *s.* (Ant.) V. *Orgullo.*

A'rguma. V. *Argoma.*

Argumentación, *sf.* Argumentation.

Argumentadór, ra, *s.* Arguer, a reasoner.

Argumentár. V. *Argüir.*

Argumentíllo, *sm.* A slight argument.

Arguménto, *sm.* 1. Objection started against the opinion of another. 2. In the universities, the person who argues or disputes is sometimes called so. 3. Summary of the points treated on in a work. 4. Indication, sign, token.

Argumentóso, sa, *a.* Ingenious, laborious.

Arguyénte, *pa.* Arguer; arguing.

A'ria, *sf.* 1. Tune or air. 2. Verses to be set to music, the last of which in each stanza generally rhymes.

Aribár, *va.* To reel yarn into skeins.

Aríbo, *sm.* Reel for making skeins.

Aricár, *va.* To plough across the ground sown with corn; to clear it of weeds.

Aridéz, *sf.* Drought, want of rain.

A'rido, da, *a.* 1. Dry, wanting moisture. 2. (Met.) Dry, barren; applied to style or conversation.

Ariéte, *sm.* 1. A little ram. 2. (Ant.) An old coin of Castile. 3. V. *Adarme.*

A'ries, *sm.* Aries, or ram, one of the twelve signs of the zodiac.

Ariéta, *sf.* Arietta, a short air, song or tune.

Ariéte, *sm.* Battering-ram, an ancient warlike machine for battering walls.

Arietíno, na, *a.* Resembling the head of a ram.

Aríja, *sf.* Mill-dust, that part of the flour which flies about the mill.

Aríjo, ja, *a.* Light, easily tilled; applied to soil.

Arîllo, *sm.* A small hoop. *Arillos*, Ear-rings.

Arímez, *sf.* Part of a building which juts or stands out.

Arindájo, *sm.* (Orn.) Jay. Corvus glandarius *L.*

Arisáro, *sm.* (Bot.) Wake-robin. Arum arisarum *L.*

Arísco, ca, *a.* 1. Fierce, rude, untractable, stubborn; applied to brutes. 2. (Met.) Harsh, unpolished, churlish.

Arismética, *sf.* Arithmetic. V. *Aritmética.*

Arisprièto, *sm.* Species of wheat, with a blackish beard, which yields more flour than the white. It is also called *arisnegro* and *rubion.*

Arísta, sm. 1. Awn, beard of corn, sharp prickles growing upon the ears of corn. 2. Edge of a rough piece of timber in naval architecture. *Aristas*, Salient angles formed by the meeting of two cylindrical vaults of equal height, which cross each other.

Aristárco, sm. 1. A severe censurer of another's writings. 2. The third spot of the moon.

Aristíno. V. *Arestin*.

Aristocrácia, sf. Aristocracy, a form of government which places the supreme power in the nobles.

Aristocrático, ca, a. Aristocratical.

Aristolóquia, sf. (Bot.) Birthwort. Aristolochia *L.*

Aristóso, sa, a. Having many prickles on the ear; spoken of corn.

Aristotélico, ca, a. Belonging to the doctrine of Aristotle.

Aritmética, sf. Arithmetic.

Aritmético, sm. Arithmetician.

Aritmético, ca, a. Arithmetical.

Arlequín, sm. Harlequin, a buffoon who plays tricks to amuse the populace, a jack pudding.

Arlít, sm. A sort of cumin, which forms a considerable branch of trade in the East Indies.

Arlinsánse, sm. A sort of linen.

A'rlo, sm. (Bot.) Berberry or pipperidge bush. Berberis vulgaris *L.*

Arlóta ó Alróta, sf. Tow of flax or hemp, which falls from it while it is dressing.

A'rma, sf. Arms, all sorts of weapons for attack and defence. *Arma, arma, ó á las armas*, To arms. *Arma arrojadiza*, A missile weapon. *Arma de fuego*, Fire-arms. *Arma blanca*, Side-arms for cutting or thrusting.—*pl.* 1. Troops, armies. 2. Ensigns armorial, coat of arms. *Armas y dineros buenos manos quieren*, (Prov.) Arms and money ought to be put into wise hands. *Hombre de armas*, A military man. *Maestro de armas*, A fencing-master. *Pasar por las armas*, To be shot as a criminal. *Rendir las armas*, To lay down the arms. 3. (Met.) Means, power, reason.

A'rma, sf. Alarm or arms. *Arma falsa*, False alarm; this expression is used instead of *falsa alarma*. *Tener el pueblo en arma*, To keep the people in alarm.

Armación, sf. Concert of flutes.

Armáda, sf. Fleet, squadron. *Armada de barlovento*, (Naút.) The fleet stationed to the windward.

Armadéra, sf. (Naút.) The principal timbers of a ship.

Armadía, sf. Raft, a frame or float made by laying pieces of timber across each other.

Armadíjo, sm. Trap or snare for catching game.

Armadílla, sf. A small squadron of men of war.

Armadíllo, sm. Armadillo, a small four-footed animal, covered with hard scales like armour. Dasypus *L.*

Armádo, da, pp. 1. Armed. 2. Gold or silver placed on other metal.

Armádo, sm. A man armed with a coat of mail.

Armadór, sm. 1. Owner, one who fits out privateers. 2. Privateer, cruiser. 3. One who recruits sailors for the whale and cod-fishery. 4. Jacket.

Armadúra, sf. 1. Armour. 2. The compages of the integral parts of a thing. 3. Skeleton. 4. Frame of a roof. *Armadura del tejado*, The shell of a building. *Armadura de una mesa*, The frame of a table.

Armajál, sm. (Mur.) Fen, moor, bog.

Armajára, sf. (Mur.) A plot of ground well dug and dunged for rearing garden plants.

Armaménto, sm. Armament, warlike preparation. *Armamento naval*, A naval armament.

Armandíjo, sm. V. *Armadijo*.

Armár, va. 1. To arm with offensive or defensive weapons. 2. To square with one's opinion. 3. To set a snare for catching animals. 4. To place one thing above another. 5. To set up a person in business. *Armar la cuenta*, To make up an account. *Armarla*, To cheat at cards. *Armarla con queso*, To decoy. *Armar navío, ó baxel*, To fit out a ship. *Armar pleyto ó ruido*, To stir up disturbances; to kick up a dust. *Armar una casa*, To frame the timber-work of the roof of a house.—*vr.* To prepare one's self for war. *Armarse de paciencia*, To prepare one's self to suffer.

Armário, sm. 1. A press, a kind of wooden case or frame for clothes and other things. 2. A niche, made of brick, in which bees lodge themselves for want of hives.

Armatóste, sm. 1. An unwieldy machine or piece of furniture, which is more cumbersome than convenient. 2. A trap, a snare, V. *Armadijo*.

Armatrínche, sm. (Joc.) Trifle, an insignificant thing.

Armazón, sm. 1. Armour; breast armour. V. *Armadura*. 2. Carcass of a ship. 3. Fishing-tackle. 4. A wooden frame for supporting bells either in the foundry or belfry. *No tener mas que la armazon*, To be only skin and bone.

Armelína, sf. Ermine skin.

Armélla, sf. Staple or ring made of iron or other metal. *Armellas*, (Naút.) Pieces of iron doubled in the shape of a Π with two large points, that they may be nailed to any part of a ship.

Armelluéla, sf. A small staple or ring.

Armería, sf. 1. Building, where various sorts of arms are kept either for curiosity, ostentation, or use. 2. Trade of an armourer or gun-smith. 3. (Ant.) Heraldry.

Arméro, sm. 1. Armourer or gun-smith. 2. Keeper of arms or armours.

Armígero, ra, a. (Poét.) Warlike.

Armilár, a. *Esfera armilár*, Armillary sphere.

Armílla, sf. Principal part of the base of a column.

Armíño, sm. Ermine, a small animal, having a white pile, and the tip of the tail black, and furnishing a valuable fur. Mustela Erminea *L.* *Armiños*, (Blas.) Figures of a white field interspersed with black spots.

Armipoténte, a. Mighty in war.

Armisticio, sm. Armistice, suspension of hostilities.

Armoisín, sm. A thin silk or taffety manufactured in Italy and in the East Indies.

Armonía, sf. 1. Harmony, just proportion of sound. 2. Concord or correspondence of one thing with another. *Hacer ó causar armonía*, To excite admiration, to produce novelty. 3. Friendship. *Correr con armonía* To live in peace.

Armoníaco, sm. Gum ammoniac.

ARMÓNICO, CA, *a.* Harmonic, harmonical, adapted to each other, musical.
ARMONIOSAMÉNTE, *ad.* Harmoniously.
ARMONIÓSO, SA, *a.* 1. Harmonious, sonorous, pleasing to the ear. 2. (Met.) Adapted to each other, having the parts proportioned to each other.
ARMUÉLLE, *sm.* (Bot.) Orach. Atriplex *L.*
A'RNA, *sf.* Bee-hive.
ARNÁCHO, *sm.* (Bot.) Rest-harrow. Ononis arvensis *L.*
ARNÉS, *sm.* 1. Coat of mail or steel net-work for defence; armour. 2. Store-room for the accoutrements of cavalry. *Arnéses*, Necessary tools, utensils, furniture used in a house, trade, or kitchen. *Arneses de caballo*, Trappings and furniture of a horse.
ARNÍLLA, *sf.* A small bee-hive.
A'RO, *sm.* 1. Hoop of wood, iron or other metals; iron staple. 2. (Bot.) V. *Yaro.*
ARÓCA, *sf.* A sort of linen somewhat more than three quarters wide.
ARÓMA, *s.* 1. Flower of the Aromatic myrrh-tree. 2. Peculiar odour. 3. A general name given to all gums, balsams, woods, and herbs of strong fragrance.
AROMATICIDÁD, *sf.* An aromatic or fragrant quality, perfume.
AROMÁTICO, CA, *a.* Aromatic, fragrant.
AROMATIZACIÓN, *sf.* Act of making aromatic.
AROMATIZÁR, *va.* To aromatize, to perfume.
ARÓMO, *sm.* (Bot.) The aromatic myrrh-tree.
ARÓZA, *sm.* Foreman in iron-works or forges.
A'RPA, *sf.* A harp.
ARPÁDO, *a.* Serrated, toothed.
ARPADÓR, *sm.* Harp-player, harper.
ARPADÚRA, *sf.* V. *Araño.*
ARPÁR, *va.* 1. To tear clothes to pieces, to rend and reduce to tatters. 2. To claw, to tear with nails, claws or talons.
ARPÉLLA, *sf.* (Orn.) Harpy. Falco rufus *L.*
ARPÉO, *sm.* (Naút.) Grappling iron.
ARPÍA, *sf.* 1. (Poét.) Bird of prey represented by poets as having the face of a woman, and long claws; a harpy. 2. A ravenous woman; an ugly, scolding shrew.
ARPILLÉRA, *sf.* Sack-cloth, coarse linen made of tow.
ARPÍSTA, *sm.* Player on the harp by profession.
ARPONÁDO, DA, *a.* Harpooned, like a harpoon.
ARPÓN, *sm.* Harpoon, a harping-iron.
ARPONÉRO, *sm.* Harpooner, he who throws the harpoon.
ARQUEÁDA, *sf.* Stroke with the fiddle-bow, whereby sounds are produced from the strings of a musical instrument.
ARQUEÁDO, *a.* Arched.
ARQUEADÓR, *sm.* 1. Ship-gauger, an officer whose business it is to measure the dimensions of ships. 2. One who forms arches. 3. Wool-beater.
ARQUEÁGE, *sm.* The gauging of a ship.
ARQUEAMIÉNTO, *sm.* V. *Arqueo.*
ARQUEÁR, *va.* 1. To arch, to form in the shape of an arch. 2. (Among Clothiers) To beat the dust out of the wool so as to make it fit for use. 3. (Naút.) To gauge or measure the dimensions of ships. *Arquear las cejas*, To arch the eye-brows as a sign of admiration; to admire.—*vr.* To grow hog-backed.

ARQUÉO, *sm.* 1. The act of bending any thing into the form of an arch. 2. (Naút.) The tonnage, dimensions, or burthen of a ship.
ARQUERÍA, *sm.* Series of arches.
ARQUÉRO, *sm.* 1. One whose trade is to make arches, hoops, or bows for arrows. 2. Treasurer, cashier. 3. Bowman, archer.
ARQUÉTA, *sf.* A little chest, a small trunk.
ARQUETÍPO, *sm.* Archetype.
ARQUETÓN, *sm.* A large trunk.
ARQUETONCÍLLO, *sm.* A trunk or chest of a middling size.
ARQUIBÁNCO, *sm.* A bench or seat with drawers.
ARQUIEPISCOPÁL, *a.* Archiepiscopal. V. *Arzobispal.*
ARQUÍLLA, *sf.* A little chest.
ARQUÍLLO, *sm.* A small arch.
ARQUIMÉSA, *sf.* Scrutoire, a case of drawers for writing, with a desk.
ARQUISINAGÓGO, *sm.* Principal in the synagogue.
ARQUÍTA, *sf.* A small chest.
ARQUITÉCTO, *sm.* Architect, a professor of the art of building.
ARQUITECTÓNICO, CA, *a.* Architectonic.
ARQUITECTÚRA, *sf.* Architecture, art of building.
ARQUITRÁBE, *sm.* Architrave, that part of a column which lies immediately upon the capital, and is the lowest member of the entablature.
ARRABÁL, *sm.* 1. Suburb. 2. (Joc.) The posteriors. *Arrabáles*, Suburbs or extremities of a large town.
ARRABALÉRA, *sf.* V. *Rabera.*
ARRÁBIO, *sm.* Cast iron. V. *Hierro.*
ARRACÁDA, *sf.* Ear-ring. *Arracádas.* (Met.) Young children hanging about a widow.
ARRACADÍLLA, *sf.* A small ear-ring.
ARRACÍFE, *sm.* 1. Causeway, paved road. 2. (Naút.) Reef, ridge of hidden rocks lying close under the surface of the water.
ARRACIMÁRSE, *vr.* To be clustered together like a bunch of grapes.
ARRAÉZ, *sm.* Captain or master of a Moorish ship.
ARRALÁR, *vn.* V. *Ralear.*
ARRAMBLÁR, *va.* 1. To cover with sand and gravel; applied to torrents and rivulets which overflow the adjacent country. 2. To sweep away, to drag along.
ARRANCÁDA, *sf.* Sudden departure, violent sally.
ARRANCADÉRA, *sf.* Large bell worn by those animals which guide the rest of the flocks.
ARRANCADÉRO, *sm.* 1. The thickest part of the barrel of a gun. 2. Starting-point, course or route.
ARRANCÁDO, DA, *a.* *Boga arrancada*, (Naút.) Strong uniform rowing. *De boga arrancada*, With long strokes of oars.
ARRANCADÓR, RA, *s.* Extirpator, one who roots out, a destroyer.
ARRANCADÚRA Y ARRANCAMIÉNTO, *s.* (Ant.) The act of pulling up by the roots.
ARRANCÁR, *va.* 1. To pull up by the roots. 2. To pull out a nail, to draw out a tooth. 3. To carry off with violence. 4. To force up phlegm, bile, &c. 5. To start and pursue one's course. 6. To run away from a place. *Arrancar la espada*, To unsheath the sword. *Arrancarsele á uno el alma*, To die broken-hearted. *Arranca pinos*, Nickname for little persons.
ARRANCASIÉGA, *sf.* 1. Poor corn, half mowed and

half pulled up by the roots. 2. A quarrel or dispute attended with injurious language.

Arrancharse, *vr.* To mess together; applied to soldiers and crews of ships.

Arranciárse, *vr.* To grow rancid.

Arránque, *sm.* 1. Extirpation, the act of pulling up by the roots. 2. Sudden and violent fit of passion. *Un hombre de mucho arranque*, A man of hasty temper. 3. Sudden and unexpected event. 4. Arch-stone of a vault supported by imposts and pillars. *Carbon de arranque*, Charcoal made of the roots of trees. *Arranque del caballo*, The start of a horse.

Arrapár, *va.* To snatch away, to carry off.

Arrapiézo y Arrápo, *sm.* 1. Tatter or rag hanging down from old and torn clothes. 2. (Met.) A mean, worthless, despicable person.

Arras, *sf. pl.* 1. Thirteen pieces of money, which the bridegroom gives to the bride, as a pledge, in the act of marriage. 2. Dowry, a sum of money assigned by a husband to his wife, for her maintenance after his death, which, according to the Spanish laws, cannot exceed the tenth part of his fortune. 3. *Arras de la bodéga*, (Naút.) Wings of the hold. 4. (Orn.) Macaco. Psittacus ara *Buff.*

Arrasár, *va.* 1. To level, to make even, to smooth the surface of a thing. 2. To demolish, to destroy. *Arrasar un vaso de algun licor*, To fill a glass with liquor up to the brim. *Arrasar un bazel*, (Naút.) To cut down a vessel, to cut away part of her dead works.—*vn.* To clear up, to grow fine; applied to the weather.

Arrastradaménte, *ad.* 1. Imperfectly, in an imperfect manner. 2. Painfully, wretchedly.

Arrastradéras, *sf. pl.* (Naút.) Lower studding-sails.

Arrastradéro, *sm.* (Naút.) A place on the sea-coast, gently sloping towards the sea, where ships are careened; a careening place.

Arrastrádo, da, *a.* Dragged along. *Andar arrastrado*, To live in the utmost misery and distress. [along the ground.

Arrastramiénto, *sm.* The act of dragging

Arrastránte, *sm.* Claimant of a degree in colleges. V. *Bayétas.*

Arrastrár, *va.* 1. To drag along the ground. 2. To bring one over to our opinion. 3. *Arrastrar la causa, el pleyto, los autos, &c.* To move a lawsuit into another court. 4. *Arrastrar bayetas*, To wear a long student's gown in the university. 5. To lead a trump at cards. *Hacer alguna cosa arrastrando*, To do a thing against one's will, to do it ill.

Arrastre, *sm.* 1. The act of leading a trump at cards. 2. The act of dragging a long gown in some universities. 3. Ceremonious visit.

Arráte, *sm.* A pound of sixteen ounces.

Arraziáque, Arrezaca, ó Arrezaco. V. *Arraque.* [L.

Arrayán, *sm.* (Bot.) Myrtle. Myrtus bœtica

Arrayanál, *sm.* Plantation of myrtles.

Arraygádas, *sf. pl.* (Naút.) Foot-hook shrouds.

Arraygár, *va.* 1. To root, to fix the root. 2. To give security in land.—*vr.* 1. To establish one's self in a place, to fix one's residence or abode. 2. To be of long continuance; as a custom, habit.

Arráygo, *sm.* Landed property. *Es hombre de arraygo*, He is a man of considerable landed property.

A'rre, A word used by drivers of horses, mules, &c. to make them go on. *Arre borrico*, Go on, ass.

Arreár, *va.* To drive horses, mules, &c., to make them go on.—*vr.* To be a muleteer.

Arrebañadór, ra, *s.* Gleaner, gatherer.

Arrebañadúra, *sf.* The act of gleaning, gathering, picking up, or scraping together.

Arrebañár, *va.* To glean, to gather, to scrape together, to pick up.

Arrebatadaménte, *ad.* Precipitately, headlong, in an inconsiderate manner.

Arrebatádo, da, *a.* 1. Rapid, violent, impetuous. 2. Precipitate, rash, inconsiderate. *Muerte arrebatada*, A sudden death. *Hombre arrebatado*, A rash, inconsiderate man.

Arrebatadór, ra, *s.* One who snatches away, or takes any thing by violence.

Arrebatamiénto, *sm.* 1. The act of carrying away by violence or precipitation. 2. Fury, rage, extreme passion. 3. Rapture, ecstasy.

Arrebatár, *va.* 1. To carry off, to take away by violence and force. 2. To snatch and seize things with hurry and precipitation. 3. To attract the attention, notice, &c.—*vr.* To be led away by passion. 2. To be made or brought to perfection by means of fire. 3. To assemble at the sound of the alarm-bell. *Arrebatarse el pan*, is said of bread which is scorched from the excessive heat of the oven. *Arrebatarse las mieses*, is said of crops which are got in more early than usual on account of uncommon hot weather. *Arrebatarse el caballo*, is said of a horse which is overheated.

Arrebatíña, *sf.* The act of carrying off a thing precipitately out of a crowd.

Arrebáto, *sm.* (Ant.) Surprise, a sudden and unexpected attack made upon an enemy.

Arreból, *sm.* 1. The red appearance of the sky or clouds. 2. Rouge, red paint for ladies.

Arrebolár, *va.* To paint red.—*vr.* To lay on rouge.

Arreboléra, *sf.* 1. A woman who sells rouge. 2. Alkanet, a plant of which vegetable rouge is made. 3. (Ant.) A small pot or saucer with red paint.

Arrebollárse, *vr.* To precipitate one's self, to fall headlong.

Arrebozáda, *sf.* Swarm of bees.

Arrebozár, *va.* To overlay meat with a jelly. —*vr.* 1. To muffle or wrap one's self up. 2. To be clustered around the bee-hive; spoken of bees.

Arrebózo, *sm.* V. *Rebozo.*

Arrebujadaménte, *ad.* Confusedly, with disorder or confusion.

Arrebujár, *va.* To gather up any pliable thing, as cloth, &c. without order: to throw together with confusion.—*vr.* To cover and roll one's self in the bed-clothes. [L.

Arrecáfe, *sm.* Cardoon. Cynara carduncculus

Arreciár, *vn.* To increase, to augment.—*vr.* To grow stronger, to recover one's strength.

Arrecífe, *sm.* 1. Causeway, a road paved with stone. 2. Reef, a ridge of hidden rocks lying close under the surface of the water.

Arrecíl, *sm.* A sudden flood.
Arrecírse, *vr.* To have one's limbs benumbed with excessive cold, to grow stiff with cold.
Arrecogér. V. *Recoger.*
Arredondeár, *va.* To round. V. *Redondear.*
Arredór, *ad.* (Ant.) V. *Al rededor.*
Arredramiénto, *sm.* The act of removing to a greater distance.
Arredrár, *va.* 1. To remove to a greater distance. 2. To terrify, to cause dread.
Arrédro, *ad.* Backwards. It is generally used to drive away Satan.
Arregazádo, da, *a.* Having the point turned up. *Nariz arregazada ó arremangada*, A cocked nose.
Arregazár, *va.* To truss, to tuck up the skirts of clothes.
Arregladaménte, *ad.* Regularly; according to rule.
Arregládo, *a.* Regular, moderate.
Arreglamiénto, *sm.* Regulation, instruction in writing.
Arreglár, *va.* 1. To regulate, to reduce to order. 2. To adjust the administration of provinces, and enact laws for them.—*vr.* To conform to law, rule, or custom.
Arréglo, *sm.* Rule, order. *Con arréglo*, Conformably, according to.
Arregostárse, *vr.* To relish or have a taste for a thing, to be attached to it.
Arrejacár, *va.* To plough across a piece of ground sown with corn to clear it of weeds.
Arrejáda, *sf.* (Agr.) Paddle of a plough.
Arrélde y Arrél, *sm.* 1. Weight of four pounds. 2. Bird of a very small size.
Arrellanárse, *vr.* 1. To sit at ease, to incline one's seat for greater ease. 2. (Met.) To make one's self comfortable.
Arremangádo, da, *a.* Lifted upward. *Ojos arremangados*, Uplifted eyes.
Arremangár, *va.* To tuck up the sleeves or petticoats.—*vr.* To be fully resolved actually to perform something.
Arremángo, *sm.* The act of tucking up the clothes.
Arremedadór, ra, *s.* Mimic, a ludicrous imitator of another's actions or manners.
Arremembrár, *va.* (Ant.) To remember.
Arremetedór, *sm.* Assailant, aggressor.
Arremetér, *va.* 1. To assail, to attack with impetuosity and fury. 2. To seize briskly, such as a sword, lance, &c. 3. To shock or offend the sight.
Arremetída, *sf.* 1. Attack, assault, invasion. 2. Start of horses from a barrier, or other place.
Arremolinádo, da, *a.* Whirled, turned round.
Arrempujár, *va.* 1. To move or detain a thing with violence or force. 2. To drive away, to shove off from a place.
Arremuésco, *sm.* 1. Caress, a demonstration of love or friendship. 2. Movement of the lips expressive of contempt or scorn.
Arrendáble, *a.* Rentable, that which can be rented.
Arrendación, *sf.* The act of renting, or taking at a certain rent.
Arrendadéro, *sm.* An iron ring fastened to the manger, to which horses are tied.
Arrendádo, da, *a.* Obedient to the reins; applied to horses and mules.
Arrendadór, *sm.* 1. Renter, tenant or lessee, who holds lands, houses, &c. 2. V. *Arrendadero.*
Arrendadorcíllo, *sm.* A petty renter or tenant.
Arrendájo, *sm.* 1. (Orn.) The mocking-bird, an American bird which imitates all the notes and sounds it hears. 2. Mimic, buffoon, a person who imitates the words and actions of others.
Arrendamiénto, *sm.* The act of renting or letting to a tenant.
Arrendánte, *sm.* Tenant, occupant who pays rent.
Arrendár, *va.* 1. To rent, to hold by paying rent, to let to a tenant for rent. 2. To bridle a horse. 3. To tie a horse by the reins of a bridle, or the strings of a headstall. 4. To mimic, to imitate as a buffoon, to ridicule by a burlesque imitation. 5. To thin plants which stand too thick. *Arrendar á diente*, To rent or let on condition of allowing commonage.
Arrendatário, ria, *s.* 1. One who lets for rent, a lessor. 2. Lessee.
Arréo, *sm.* Dress, ornament, decoration. *Arréos*, Appendages, dependencies.
Arréo, *ad.* (Vulg.) Successively, uninterruptedly. *Llevar arreo*, To carry on one's shoulders.
Arrepápalo, *sm.* A sort of fritters or buns.
Arrepásate acá compádre, A boyish play of running and touching each other before reaching a certain station. *Arrepásate* is a compound word from *Arre* and *pasar.*
Arrepentídas, *sf. pl.* Penitents, women who, sensible of their faults and errors, shut themselves up in convents to do penance.
Arrepentimiénto, *sm.* Repentance, penitence.
Arrepentírse, *vr.* To repent, to express sorrow for having said or done something.
Arrepistár, *va.* (In paper-mills) To grind or pound rags into a fine pulp.
Arrepísto, *sm.* The act of grinding or pounding rags, in paper-mills, into a fine pulp.
Arreptício, cia, *a.* Possessed or influenced by the devil.
Arrequesonárse, *vr.* To agitate or churn milk in order to separate the butter from it.
Arrequífe, *sm.* Singeing iron for burning or taking off the down which remains on cotton goods.
Arrequíves, *sm. pl.* 1. Ornaments. 2. Circumstances of a case. 3. Requisites.
Arrestádo, da, *pp.* y *a.* 1. Confined, imprisoned. 2. Intrepid, bold, audacious.
Arrestár, *va.* To arrest, to confine, to imprison. *vr.* To be bold and enterprising, to engage with spirit in an enterprise or undertaking.
Arrésto, *sm.* 1. Spirit, boldness, in undertaking an enterprise. 2. (Mil.) Prison, arrest.
Arretín, *sm.* V. *Filipichin.*
Arrexáco, *sm.* V. *Vencejo.*
Arrexáque, *sm.* 1. Fork with three prongs bent at the point. 2. (Orn.) Swift, martinet. Hirundo apus *L.*
Arrezáfe, *sm.* A place full of thistles, brush-wood, and brambles.
Arriáda, *sf.* Swell of waters, flood, overflowing.
Arriáno, na, *a.* Adherent to the tenets of Arius.
Arriár, *va.* (Naút.) 1. To lower, to strike. *Arriar la bandera*, To strike the colours. *Arriar las vergas y los masteleros*, To strike the yards and top-masts. 2. *Arriar un cabo*, To pay out the cable. *Arriar en banda*, To pay out

the whole cable. *Arriar la gavia*, To let go the main top-sail. 3. To destroy by floods, or a sudden fall of rain.

ARRIÁTA Y ARRIÁTE, *s.* 1. (Jard.) A border in gardens, where herbs, flowers, &c. are planted. *Arriátes*, Treillage or trellis, a contexture of pales, wood, or osier, around beds or walks in a garden. 2. A causeway, a paved road.

ARRIÁZ Y ARRIÁS, *sm.* (Ant.) Guard of a sword.

ARRÍBA, *ad.* 1. Above, over, up. 2. (Naút.) Aloft. 3. (Naút.) At the top of the mast-head. 4. (Met.) A high post or station in which a person is placed with respect to others. 5. In the hands of the king. *La consulta está arriba*, The business is laid before the king. *Está decretado de arriba*, It is decreed by high authority. *Arriba dicho*, Above-mentioned. *De arriba abáxo*, From top to bottom. *No arriba de seis varas*, Not above six yards. *Ir agua arriba*, (Naút.) To work up the river. *De arriba*, From heaven.

ARRIBÁDA, *sf.* 1. (Naút.) The arrival of a vessel in a port. 2. (Naút.) *Arribada de un bazel á sotavento*, The falling off of a vessel to leeward. *Llega el baxel de arribada*, The ship put into port by stress of weather.

ARRIBÁGE, *sm.* Arrival.

ARRIBÁR, *va.* (Naút.) 1. To put into a harbour in distress. 2. To fall off to leeward. 3. *Arribar todo*, To bear away before the wind. *Arribar á escota larga*, To bear away large. *Arribar sobre un bazel*, To bear down upon a ship. 4. (Met.) To recover, to grow well from a disease or calamity. 5. (Met.) To attain one's end, to accomplish one's desire.

ARRÍBO, *sm.* Arrival.

ARRICÉTE Y ARRIÉTE, *sm.* Shoal, sand-bank.

ARRICÍSES, *sm. pl.* The saddle-straps, to which the stirrup-leathers and girths are fastened.

ARRIÉDRO. V. *Arredro y Átrás*.

ARRIÉNDO. V. *Arrendamiento*.

ARRIERÍA, *sf.* The trade of a driver of mules, or other beasts of burthen.

ARRIERÍCO, ÍLLO, Y ÍTO, *sm.* One who carries on the trade of mule-driving in a petty way.

ARRIÉRO, *sm.* Muleteer, he who drives mules or other beasts of burthen, carrying goods from one place to another.

ARRIESGADAMÉNTE, *ad.* Dangerously, in a hazardous manner.

ARRIESGÁDO, DA, *a.* 1. Perilous, attended with hazard. 2. Dangerous to be dealt with. *Hombre arriesgado*, A dangerous man.

ARRIESGÁR, *va.* To risk, to hazard, to expose to danger.—*vr.* To be exposed to danger.

ARRIMADÉRO, *sm.* Scaffold, stage for having a view of something; a stick or support to lean upon.

ARRIMADÍLLO, *sm.* Room adorned with carpets, [and other nice furniture.

ARRIMADÍZO, *a.* y *sm.* 1. That which is designed to be applied to any thing. 2. (Met.) Parasite, sponger, one who meanly hangs upon another for subsistence. 3. (Met.) Support, prop.

ARRIMÁDO, DA, *pp.* V. *Arrimar*. *Tener arrimado ó arrimados*, To be possessed by evil spirits.

ARRIMADÓR, *sm.* A block put at the back part of a fire to burn gradually with the help of small wood.

ARRIMADÚRA, *sf.* Approach, the act of approach- [ing.

ARRIMÁR, *va.* 1. To approach, to draw near, to join one thing to another. 2. (Naút.) To stow the cargo, to trim the hold. 3. To lay a thing aside, to give up the use of a thing. 4. To lay down a command. 5. To displace, to dismiss. 6. *Arrimar el clavo*, To prick or hurt a horse at the time of shoeing him. *Arrimar el clavo á uno*. (Met.) To impose, to deceive.—*vr.* 1. To lean upon a thing, to be supported by it. 2. To join others for the purpose of forming a body with them. 3. (Met.) To come to the knowledge of a thing. 4. *Arrimarse el punto de la dificultad*, To come to the point. 5. *Arrimarse al parecer de otro*, To espouse another's opinion.

ARRÍMES, *sm.* In the game of bowls, the mark for the balls to arrive at.

ARRÍMO, *sm.* 1. Approximation, the act of joining one thing to another. 2. Staff, stick, crutch. 3. (Met.) Protection or support of a powerful person. 4. (Among Builders) An insulated wall which has no weight to support. *Hacer el arrimon*, (Joc.) To stagger along a wall, supported by it, in a state of intoxication. *Estar de arrimon en acecho de alguno*, To stand watch over somebody.

ARRINCONÁR, *va.* 1. To put a thing in a corner. 2. (Met.) To remove one from a trust or place he held, to withdraw one's favour or protection.—*vr.* To retire or withdraw from intercourse with the world.

ARRISCADAMÉNTE, *ad.* Boldly, audaciously.

ARRISCÁDO, DA, *a.* 1. Forward, bold, audacious, impudent. 2. Brisk, easy, free. *Caballo arriscado*, A high-mettled horse. 3. (Ant.) Broken or craggy ground.

ARRISCADÓR, *sm.* Gleaner of olives, one who picks up the olives which drop on the ground at the time of gathering them from the trees.

ARRISCÁRSE, *vr.* 1. To hold up the head with an affected briskness. 2. To be proud, haughty, arrogant.

ARRITRÁNCA, *sf.* A sort of wide crupper for mules, and other beasts of burthen.

ARRIZÁR, *va.* (Naút.) 1. To reef, to take in reefs in the sails. 2. To stow the boat on deck. *Arrizar el anclar*, To stow the anchor. *Arrizár la artillería*, To house the guns. 3. (On board the galleys) To tie or lash one down.

ARRÓBA, *sf.* 1. A Spanish weight of twenty-five pounds, containing each sixteen ounces. 2. A Spanish measure, containing thirty-two pints. *Echar por arrobas*, (Met.) To exaggerate, to make hyperbolical amplifications.

ARROBADÍZO, ZA, *a.* Feigning ecstasy and rapture.

ARROBÁDO, (Por.) *ad.* By wholesale.

ARROBADÓR, *sm.* One who treats by Arrobes.

ARROBAMIÉNTO, *sm.* 1. Ecstatic rapture or elevation of the mind to God. 2. Amazement, astonishment, high admiration.

ARROBÁR, *va.* 1. (Ant.) To weigh or measure by Arrobes. 2. To make even, to plane.—*vr.* To be in a state of rapturous amazement, to be out of one's senses.

ARROBÉRO, RA, *s.* One who makes and provides bread for a religious community.

ARROBÍTA, *sf.* The weight of an Arrobe in a small [compass.

ARRÓBO, *sm.* V. *Arrobamiento*.

Arrocéro, *sm.* A grower of, or dealer in rice.

Arrocinádo, da, *a.* Stupid like an ass.

Arrocinárse, *vr.* To become dull and stupid.

Arrodeládo, da, *a.* Bearing a target, shield, or buckler.

Arrodelárse, *vr.* To be armed with a shield or buckler.

Arrodilladúra y Arrodillamiénto, *s.* The act of kneeling or bending the knee.

Arrodillár, *vn.* To bend the knee down to the ground.—*vr.* To kneel, to touch the ground with the knee.

Arrodrigonár y Arrodrigár, *va.* To prop vines.

Arrogación, *sf.* 1. Arrogation, the act of claiming in a proud manner. 2. Adoption of a child which has no father, or is independent of him.

Arrogadór, *sm.* One who claims in a proud manner.

Arrogáncia, *sf.* 1. Arrogance, haughtiness, loftiness. 2. Stately carriage of a high-mottled horse.

Arrogánte, *a.* 1. High-minded, spirited. 2. Haughty, proud, assuming.

Arrogantemênte, *ad.* Arrogantly, in an arrogant manner.

Arrogár, *va.* To arrogate, to claim in a proud manner.—*vr.* To appropriate to one's self, to claim unjustly, for instance, the jurisdiction.

Arrógio, *sm.* V. *Arroyo.*

Arrojadamênte, *ad.* Audaciously, boldly.

Arrojadíllo, *sm.* Handkerchief, or other piece of silk or linen, which women tie around the head to keep it warm.

Arrojadízo, za, *a.* 1. That which can be easily cast, thrown, or darted. 2. Spirited, bold, courageous.

Arrojádo, da, *a.* 1. Rash, inconsiderate, forward. 2. Bold, intrepid.

Arrojadór, *sm.* Thrower, caster.

Arrojár, *va.* 1. To dart, launch, or fling any thing. 2. To shed a fragrance, to emit light. 3. To shoot, to sprout. 4. (Naút.) To drive or cast on rocks or shoals; applied to the wind. 5. To make red hot; as an oven. 6. To turn away or dismiss in an angry manner. —*vr.* 1. To throw one's self forward with impetuosity. 2 (Met.) To venture upon an enterprise in an inconsiderate manner.

Arrójo, *sm.* Boldness, intrepidity.

Arrolladór, *sm.* Roller, a kind of cylinder used for moving weighty things.

Arrollár, *va.* 1. To roll up, to enwrap. 2. To carry off, to sweep away; applied to a storm or torrent. 3. (Met.) To defeat, to rout an enemy. 4. (Met.) To confound an opponent, to render him unfit for returning an answer. 5. *Arrollar á un niño*, To dandle a child. 6. (Ant.) To lull to rest.

Arromadizárse, *vr.* To catch cold.

Arromanzár, *va.* To translate into the common or vernacular Spanish language.

Arromár, *va.* To blunt, to dull the edge or point.

Arrompér, *va.* To break up the ground for sowing.

Arrompído, da, *a.* Broken up, ploughed.

Arrompído, *sm.* A piece of ground newly broken up for culture.

Arrompimiénto, *sm.* The act of breaking up ground for culture.

Arronzár, *va.* (Naút.) To haul or pull a cable or hawser, without the aid of the capstern, windlass, or tackle.

Arropádo, da, *a.* Covered with must; applied to wine.

Arropamiénto, *sm.* 1. The act of clothing or dressing. 2. Dress or clothes.

Arropár, *va.* 1. To cover the body with clothes, to dress. *Arropate que sudas*, Cover yourself as you sweat; ironically addressed to a person who has done little and affects to be fatigued. 2. *Arropar el vino*, To mix wine in a state of fermentation with boiled wine, to give it a body. 3. *Arropar las viñas*, To cover the roots of vines with dung and earth.

Arrópe, *sm.* 1. Must or new wine boiled or prepared at the fire. 2. A kind of decoction made by apothecaries in imitation of must. 3. Conserve made of boiled honey. *Arrope de moras*, Mulberry sirup.

Arropéas, *sf. pl.* Irons, fetters. In Asturia they are called *farropeas*, and in Gallicia *ferropeas.*

Arropéra, *sf.* Vessel for holding must, sirup, &c.

Arropía, *sf.* (And.) Cake made of flour, honey, and spice.

Arropiéro, *sm.* (And.) Maker or seller of sweet cakes.

Arrostrár, *va.* 1. To set about or perform a thing in a cheerful manner. 2. *Arrostrar á los peligros, á los trabajos, á la muerte*, To encounter dangers, fatigues, death.—*vr.* To close with the enemy, to fight him face to face.

Arroxár, *va.* To make red hot.

Arroyáda y Arroyadéro, *s.* The valley, through which a rivulet runs.

Arroyár, *va.* To overflow or inundate sown ground.—*vr.* To be smutted; spoken of wheat, and other grain and plants.

Arroyíco y Arroyuélo, *sm.* Rill, a small brook, a little streamlet.

Arróyo y Arroyáto, *sm.* Rivulet, a small river.

Arróz, *sm.* Rice. Oryza sativa *L.*

Arrozál, *sm.* Field sown with rice.

Arrozár, *va.* To ice a liquid in a slight manner, to congeal it a little.

Arruár, *vn.* To grunt like a wild boar.

Arrufádo, da, *pp.* Sheered, incurvated. *Navio muy arrufado*, (Naút.) A moon-sheered ship.

Arrufadúra, *sf.* (Naút.) Sheer of a ship.

Arrufaldádo, da, *a.* 1. Having the clothes tucked up. 2. (Ant.) V. *Arrufianado.*

Arrufár, *va.* To incurvate, to form the sheer of a ship.

Arrufianádo, da, *a.* Having the sentiments and manners of a ruffian; impudent.

Arrúfo, *sm.* V. *Arrufadura.*

Arrúga, *sf.* 1. Wrinkle, a corrugation or contraction into furrows. 2. Rumple, or rude plait in clothes.

Arrugación y Arrugamiénto, *s.* Corrugation, the act and effect of wrinkling.

Arrugár, *va.* 1. To wrinkle, or contract into wrinkles. 2. To rumple, to fold, to make plications in paper, clothes, &c. *Arrugar la frente*, To knit the brow.—*vr.* To die.

Arrugía, *sf.* A cavity dug in the ground to discover gold.

Arrugón, *sm.* Prominent decoration of carved work.

Arruinadór, ra, *s.* Ruiner, demolisher.

Arruinamiénto, *sm.* Ruin, destruction, the act of ruining or destroying.

Arruinár, *va.* 1. To throw down buildings, to demolish. 2. (Met.) To destroy, to cause great mischief.
Arrulladór, ra, *s.* 1. A person who lulls babes to rest. 2. Flatterer, cajoler.
Arrullár, *va.* 1. To lull babes to rest. 2. To court, to coo and bill.
Arrúllo, *sm.* 1. The cooing and billing of pigeons or doves. 2. Lullaby, a song to lull babes to rest.
Arrumáco, *sm.* 1. Caress, the act of endearment, profession of love or friendship. 2. Motion of the lips expressive of contempt.
Arrumáge, *sm.* (Naút.) Stowage of a ship's cargo.
Arrumár, *va.* (Naút.) To stow the cargo.
Arrumazón, *sm.* 1. (Naút.) The act and effect of stowing. 2. Horizon overcast with clouds.
Arrumbádas, *sf. pl.* Wales of a row-galley.
Arrumbadór, ra, *s.* 1. One who heaps or piles. 2. (Naút.) Steersman.
Arrumbár, *va.* 1. To put any thing away in a lumber-room as useless. 2. (Met.) To refute one in the course of conversation. 3. To decant wine, to pour it off gently into another vessel.—*vr.* (Naút.) To resume and steer the proper course.
Arrumbelár, *a.* V. *Arramblar.*
Arrumuéco, *sm.* V. *Arrumaco.*
Arrunflárse, *vr.* To have a flush of cards of the same suit.
Arsenál, *sm.* Arsenal, dock-yard.
Arsenicál, *a.* (Quím.) Arsenical, relating to arsenic.
Arsénico, *sm.* Arsenic, a ponderous mineral substance, which facilitates the fusion of metals, and proves a violent corrosive poison.
Artaléjo, *sm.* A little pie.
Artaléte, *sm.* A sort of tart.
Artanita, *sf.* (Bot.) Sow-bread. Cyclamen europæum *L.*
Artár, *va.* (Ar.) V. *Precisar.*
Arte, *sf.* 1. Art. a collection of rules and precepts by which any thing is performed. 2. Trade, all that is accomplished by the skill and industry of man. 3. Caution, skill, artfulness. 4. Book which contains the rudiments of an art. 5. Grammar. *De arte,* (Ant.) So, that. *No tener arte ni parte en alguna cosa,* To have neither art nor part in a thing; to have nothing to do with the business. *Arte tormentaria,* Art of artillery or military engineery. *Ártes mecanicas,* Mechanical arts, occupations, or handicrafts. *Ártes liberales,* Liberal arts. *Las bellas ártes,* The fine arts. *Ártes,* Management; manage.
Arte, *sm.* y *f.* Used in both genders. *Maestro en artes,* Master of arts.
Artecíllo, lla, *s.* Petty art or trade.
Artefácto, *sm.* Mechanical work performed according to the rules of art.
Artéjo, *sm.* Joint or knuckle of the fingers.
Artemísa ó **Artemísia**, *sf.* (Bot.) Mug-wort. Artemisia vulgaris *L.*
Arténna, *sf.* An aquatic fowl of the size of a goose, found in the island of Tremiti in the Adriatic gulph.
Artéra, *sf.* An iron instrument for marking bread before it is baked.
Arteraménte, *ad.* (Ant.) Artfully, cunningly.
Artéria, *sf.* 1. (Anat.) Artery, a cylindrical canal which conveys the blood from the heart to all parts of the body. *Artérias de la madera,* Veins formed in wood and timber by the various ramifications of the fibres. *A'spera arteria, ó traquiarteria,* The wind-pipe. 2. (Ant.) Sagacity, cunning.
Arteriál, *a.* Arterial, belonging to the arteries.
Arterióla, *sf.* Small artery.
Arterióso, sa, *a.* V. *Arterial.*
Artéro, ra, *a.* (Ant.) Dexterous, cunning, artful.
Artésa, *sf.* 1. Trough in which dough of bread is worked. 2. Canoe, a boat hewn out of the trunk of a tree.
Artesáno, *sm.* Artisan, artist, manufacturer.
Artesílla, *sf.* 1. A small trough. 2. A sort of festive exercise on horseback. 3. A trough into which the water is poured out of the bucket of a draw-well.
Artesón, *sm.* 1. A round kitchen trough, in which dishes, plates, &c. are washed and scoured. 2. Ceiling carved in the shape of a trough; ornamented vaulting.
Artesonádo, da, *a.* Shaped in the form of a trough; applied to ceilings.
Artesoncíllo, *sm.* A small trough.
Artesuéla, *sf.* A small kneading-trough.
Artética, *sf.* Arthritis, gout, disease of the joints.
Artético, ca, *a.* Afflicted with the arthritis.
A'rtico, ca, *a.* (Ast.) Arctic, northern.
Articulación, *sf.* 1. Articulation, the juncture of moveable bones in animal bodies. 2. Clear and distinct pronunciation of words and syllables.
Articuladaménte, *ad.* Distinctly, articulately.
Articulár, *va.* 1. To articulate, to pronounce words clearly and distinctly. 2. To form the interrogatories which are put to witnesses examined in the course of law proceedings.
Articulár y **Articulário**, ria, *a.* Belonging to the joints.
Artículo, *sm.* 1. Article, a particular part of a writing. 2. Plea put in before a court of justice. 3. Question or query of an interrogatory. 4. (Gram.) Part of speech, as *the, an.* 5. Joint or juncture of moveable bones in animal bodies. *Formar articulo,* To start an incidental question in the course of a lawsuit. *Artículo de la muerte,* Point of death.
Artífice, *sm.* 1. Artificer, artisan, artist. 2. Inventor, contriver.
Artificiál, *a.* Artificial, made by art, not natural. *Fuegos artificiales,* Fire-works.
Artificialménte, *ad.* Artificially.
Artificiár, *va.* To act or do a thing in an artful manner.
Artifício, *sm.* 1. Art with which a thing is performed, workmanship. 2. (Met.) Artifice, cunning. 3. Machine which facilitates the performance of something.
Artificiosaménte, *ad.* 1. Artificially. 2. Artfully.
Artificióso, sa, *a.* 1. Skilful, ingenious. 2. Artful, crafty, cunning.
Artíga, *sf.* Land newly broken up for cultivation.
Artigár, *va.* To break and level land before cultivation.
Artillár, *va.* To mount cannon in a ship.
Artillería, *sf.* 1. That branch of military art which teaches the use of cannon. 2. Artillery, cannon, piece of ordnance. *Parque de*

artilleria, Park of artillery. *Tren de artilleria*, Train of artillery. *Poner ó asestar toda la artilleria*, (Met.) To set all engines at work for obtaining something; to leave no stone unturned.

Artilléro, *sm.* 1. Professor of the art of artillery. 2. Gunner, artillery-man.

Artimáña, *sf.* 1. Trap, snare, gin for catching game. 2. Device, stratagem, artifice.

Artimón, *sm.* (Naút.) Mizen-mast; sail of a galley.

Artísta, *sm.* 1. Artist; artisan, tradesman. 2. He who studies the fine arts, logic, poetry, &c.

Artizádo, da, *a.* Skilful, dexterous, versed in some art or trade.

Artizár, *va.* (Ant.) To work with skill.

Artólitos, *sm.* A concave stone of the nature of a sponge.

Artródia, *sf.* A kind of articulation which connects one bone with the socket of another.

Artúña, *sf.* An ewe whose lamb has perished.

Artúro, *sm.* (Astr.) Great bear, a constellation.

A'rula, *sf.* A small altar.

Aruñár, V. *Arañar.*

Aruñázo, *sm.* A large scratch. V. *Arañazo.*

Aruñón, *sm.* 1. Scratcher. 2. Pick-pocket.

Arúspice y Arúspex, *sm.* Augurer, soothsayer.

Aruspicína, *sf.* Divining from the intestines of animals.

Arvéja, *sf.* (Bot.) Vetch, tare. Lathyrus aphaca *L.*

Arvejál, *sm.* Field sown with vetches or tares.

Arvéjo, *sm.* (Bot.) Bastard chick-pea, or Spanish pea. Cicer arietinum *L.*

Arvejón, *sm.* (Bot.) Chickling-vetch. Lathyrus sativa *L.*

Arxicayádo, da, *a.* Oxygenated, impregnated or combined with oxygen.

Arxicávo, *sm.* Oxygen, of the Spanish chemists.

A'rza, *sf.* (Naút.) Fall of a tackle.

Arzobispádo, *sm.* Archbishopric.

Arzobispál, *a.* Archiepiscopal.

Arzobíspo, *sm.* Archbishop.

Arzólla, *sf.* (Mur.) V. *Almendruco.*

Arzón, *sm.* Fore and hind bow of a saddle.

A's, *sm.* 1. Ace. 2. Roman copper coin.

A'sa, *sf.* 1. Handle of a vessel. 2. Gum benzoin. V. *Asafétida.* 3. Vault made in the form of the handle of a basket. *Amigo del asa, ó ser muy del asa*, A bosom friend. *Dar ó tomar asa*, To afford or borrow a pretence. *En asas*, Having the hands in the girdle and the elbows turned out.

A' sabiéndas, *ad.* Willingly, knowingly.

Asaborír, *va.* (Ant.) V. *Saborear.*

Asación, *sf.* The act of roasting.

Asadéro, ra, *a.* That which is fit for roasting.

Asádo, da, *a.* Roasted; dressed.

Asadór, *sm.* 1. Spit, a long prong on which meat is driven to be turned before the fire. 2. Jack, an engine which turns the spit. *Parece que come asadores*, He walks as stiff as if he had swallowed a spit. 3. *Asador de bomba*, (Naút.) The pump-hook.

Asadorázo, *sm.* Stroke or blow with a spit.

Asadorcíllo, *sm.* Small spit.

Asadúra, *sf.* Entrails of an animal.

Asadúra y Asaduría, *sf.* Toll paid for cattle.

Asadurílla, *sf.* Small entrails.

Asaeteadór, *sm.* Archer, bow-man.

Asaeteár, *va.* To attack, wound, or kill with arrows.

Asaetinádo, da, *a.* Like satin; applied to cloths.

Asafétida, *sf.* Asafœtida, a gum-resin brought from the East Indies.

Asalariár, *va.* To give a fixed salary or pay.

Asaltadór, *sm.* 1. Assailant, assailer, assaulter. 2. Highwayman.

Asaltár, *va.* 1. To form an assault, to storm a place. 2. To assail, to surprise, to attack unexpectedly.

Asálto, *sm.* 1. Assault or storm formed against a place. 2. Assault, the act of offering violence or injury to a person. 3. (Met.) A sudden gust of passion.

Asambléa, *sf.* 1. Assembly, meeting, congress, committee. 2. In the order of Malta, a tribunal established in every grand priory of the order. 3. Assembly, a beat of the drum directing the soldiers to join their companies, or to assemble in the alarm-place.

Asár, *va.* To roast, to dress meat by turning it round at the fire.—*vr.* To be excessively hot.

Asarabácara, *sf.* (Bot.) Wild ginger or nard, common asarabacca. Asarum europæum *L.*

Asargádo, da, *a.* Serge-like, made in imitation of serge.

Asarína, *sf.* (Bot.) Bastard asarum. Pseudo asarum *L.*

A'saro, *sm.* V. *Asarabacara.*

Asasinár, (Ant.) V. *Asesinar.*

Asatívo, va, *a.* Dressed or boiled in its own juice, without any other fluid.

Asáz, *ad.* (Ant.) Enough, abundantly.

Asbestíno, na, *a.* Belonging to asbestos.

Asbésto, *sm.* 1. Asbestos, a fossil which may be split to threads and filaments, incombustible by fire, which merely whitens it. 2. A sort of incombustible cloth made of the filaments of asbestos.

Ascalónia, *sf.* A seed onion.

Ascendéncia, *sf.* A line of ascendants, as fathers, grandfathers, &c. from whom a person descends.

Ascendénte, *sm.* 1. An ascendant. 2. Horoscope, the configuration of the planets at the hour of birth.

Ascendér, *vn.* 1. To ascend, to mount. 2. To be promoted to a higher dignity or station.

Ascendiénte, *sm.* y *f.* 1. An ascendant. 2. Ascendency, influence, power.

Ascensión, *sf.* 1. Ascension, the act of mounting or ascending. 2. Feast of the ascension of Christ. 3. Exaltation to the papal throne. 4. Rising point of the equator.

Ascensionál, *a.* (Astr.) That which belongs to the ascension of the planets, right or oblique.

Ascénso, *sm.* Promotion to a higher dignity or station.

Ascéta, *sm.* Hermit.

Ascético, ca, *a.* Ascetic, employed wholly in exercises of devotion and mortification.

A'schia, *sf.* Grayling or umber, a delicate fresh-water fish found in rapid streams with stony bottoms.

A'scios, *sm. pl.* Ascii, people who, at certain times of the year, have no shadow at noon; such are the inhabitants of the torrid zone.

Ascíro, *sm.* (Bot.) St. Peter's wort, St. Andrew's cross. Hypericum elatum *L.*

Asclepiáda, *sf.* (Bot.) Swallow-wort. Asclepias *L.*

Asclepiadéo, *sm.* A kind of Latin verse of four feet, containing a spondee, a choriambus, and two dactyles.

A'sco, *sm.* Nauseousness, loathsomeness, quality of raising disgust, and turning the stomach. *Es un asco*, It is a mean, despicable thing. *Hacer ascos*, To excite loathsomeness, to disease the stomach.

Ascondrijo, *sm.* (Ant.) V. *Escondrijo.*

A'scua, *sf.* Red hot coal.

A scuas! *interj.* (Joc.) How it pains! *Estar en ascuas*, To be upon thorns. *Estar hecho un ascua ó echar ascuas*, To be high coloured by agitation or anger.

Ascúso, *ad.* (Ant.) V. *A' Escondidas.*

Aseadaménte, *ad.* Cleanly, elegantly.

Aseádo, da, *a.* Clean, elegant, neatly finished.

Aseár, *va.* To set off, to decorate, to adorn, to embellish.

Asechadór, *sm.* Ensnarer, way-layer.

Asechamiénto, ó Asechánza, *s.* 1. Way-laying. 2. Artifice, trick, stratagem.

Asechár, *va.* To way-lay, to watch insidiously.

Asechóso, sa, *a.* Inclined to insidious artifices.

Asécla, *sm.* Follower.

Asecución, *sf.* V. *Consecucion.*

Asecuración, *sf.* 1. Certainty, security, safety. 2. Insurance, exemption from hazard obtained by the payment of a certain sum.

Asedádo, da, *a.* Silky, that which resembles silk in softness and smoothness.

Asedár, *va.* To work flax and hemp so as to make it feel like silk.

Asediadór, ra, *s.* One who besieges, or blockades.

Asediár, *va.* To besiege, to lay siege to a strong place or fortress.

Asédio, *sm.* Siege, the act of besieging a fortified place.

Aseglarárse, *vr.* To secularize; applied to the clergy who relax in their duty for the pleasures of the world.

Asegundár, *va.* To repeat with little or no intermission of time.

Aseguración, *sf.* 1. Security, safety. 2. Insurance, a contract for insuring from hazards and dangers.

Aseguradór, *sm.* Insurer, underwriter.

Aseguramiénto, *sm.* V. *Aseguracion.*

Asegurár, *va.* 1. To secure, to insure. 2. To preserve, to shelter from danger. 3. To bail, to give security. 4. (Naút.) To insure against the dangers of the seas. *Asegurar las velas*, To secure the sails. *Asegurarse de la altura*, To ascertain the degree of latitude in which we find ourselves.

Asemblár, *va.* (Ant.) To resemble.

Asemejár, *va.* To assimilate, to bring to a likeness or resemblance.—*vr.* To resemble, to be like another person or thing.

Asendereádo, da, *a.* Beaten, frequented; applied to roads.

Asendereár, *va.* 1. To persecute, to pursue with repeated acts of vengeance and enmity. 2. To open a path.

Asengladúra, *sf.* (Naút.) A day's run, the way a ship makes in 24 hours.

Asénjo y Aséncio, (Ant.) V. *Axenjo.*

Asénso, *sm.* Assent, the act of giving one's consent.

Asentación, *sf.* (Ant.) Adulation, flattery.

Asentáda, *sf.* A stone ranged in its proper place. *De una asentada*, At once, at one sitting. *A' Asentadas.* V. *A' Asentadillas.*

Asentadéras, *sf. pl.* (Fam.) Buttocks, the seat.

A' Asentadíllas, *ad.* Sitting on horseback, like a woman, with both legs on one side.

Asentádo, da, *a.* 1. Seated, planted. 2. Clear, serene. *En hombre asentado, ni capuz tundido, ni camison curado*, (Prov.) Self do, self have.

Asentadór, *sm.* A stone-mason, a stone-cutter.

Asentadúra y Asentamiénto, *s.* 1. (For.) Possession of goods given by a judge to the claimant or plaintiff for non appearance of the respondent or defendant. 2. Establishment, settlement, residence. 3. (Ant.) Session, act of sitting. 4. Site.

Asentár, *va.* 1. To place on a chair, bench, or other seat; to cause to sit down. *Asentar el rancho*, To stop in any place or station to eat, sleep, or rest. 2. To suppose, to take for granted. 3. To affirm, to assure. 4. To adjust, to make an agreement. 5. To note, to take down in writing. 6. To fix a thing in any particular place. 7. (For.) To put a claimant or plaintiff in possession of the goods claimed for non-appearance of the respondent or defendant. 8. To assess, to charge with any certain sum. *Asentar bien su baza*, To establish one's character or credit. *Asentar casa*, To set up house for one's self. *Asentar con maestro*, To bind one's self prentice to a master. *Asentar plaza*, To enlist in the army.—*vn.* 1. To fit, to sit well, as clothes. 2. To sit down, to take a seat. 3. To settle, to establish a residence or domestic state.—*vr.* 1. To settle, to subside, as liquors. 2. To perch or settle after flying; applied to birds. 3. To sink, to give way under the weight of a work, as a foundation.

Asentír, *vn.* To coincide in opinion with another, to be of the same mind.

Asentísta, *sm.* A contractor, one who contracts to supply the navy or army with provisions, ammunition, &c. *Asentista de construccion*, (Naút.) Contractor for ship-building.

Aseñoreár, *va.* (Ant.) V. *Señorear.*

Aséo, *sm.* Cleanness, cleanliness, neatness.

Aséqui, *sm.* (Mur.) Duty on every 40 head of cattle.

Asequíble, *a.* Attainable, that which may be obtained or acquired.

Aserción, *sf.* Assertion, affirmation.

Aserradéro, *sm.* 1. Saw-pit where timber and other things are sawed. 2. Horse or wooden machine on which timber or other things are sawed.

Aserradízo, za, *a.* Proper to be sawed.

Aserrádo, da, *a.* Serrate, serrated, dented like a saw; applied to the leaves of plants.

Aserradór, *sm.* Sawer or sawyer, one whose trade is to saw timber into boards or beams.

Aserradúra, *sf.* Sawing, the act of cutting timber with the saw. *Aserradúras*, Saw-dust.

Aserrár, *va.* To saw, to cut timber with the

saw. *Aserrar piedras en un molino*, To saw stones in a saw-mill.

Asertivaménte, *ad.* Affirmatively.

Asertívo, va, *a.* Assertive. V. *Afirmativo.*

Asérto, *sm.* V. *Ascrcion.*

Asertório, V. *Juramento.*

Asesár, *vn.* To become prudent, to acquire prudence and discretion.

Asesinár, *va.* 1. To assassinate, to murder treacherously. 2. To betray the confidence of another, to be guilty of a breach of trust.

Asesináto, *sm.* 1. Assassination, the act of assassinating. 2. Treachery, deceit, fraud.

Asesíno, *sm.* 1. Assassin, one who kills treacherously. 2. Impostor, cheat, one who practises fraud, and betrays the confidence of another. 3. Small spot of black silk which ladies put near the corner of the eye.

Asesór, ra, *s.* 1. A counsellor, adviser, conciliator. 2. Assessor, a lawyer appointed to assist the ordinary judge with his advice in the conduct of law proceedings.

Asesoráse, *vr.* To take the assistance of counsel, used of a judge who takes a lawyer to assist him.

Asesoría, *sf.* 1. The office or place of an assessor. 2. The pay and fees of an assessor. 3. Tavern where wine is sold by small quantities.

Asestadéro, *sm.* (Arag.) Place where a short sleep is taken after dinner.

Asestadór, *sm.* Gunner who points the cannon.

Asestadúra, *sf.* Aim, the act of pointing the cannon, or taking aim.

Asestár, *va.* 1. To aim, to point, to take aim. 2. (Met.) To try to do some mischief to others.

Asetadór, *sm.* An instrument for polishing iron.

Aseveración, *sf.* Asseveration, solemn affirmation.

Aseveradaménte, *ad.* V. *Afirmativamente.*

Aseverár, *va.* To asseverate, to affirm with great solemnity, as upon oath.

Asfálta, *sm.* Asphaltum, a kind of bitumen.

Asfodélo, *sm.* Asphodel. V. *Gamon.*

A'sga, *pres. subjunct. irreg.* of *Asir.*

A'sgo. V. *Asco.*

Así, *ad.* 1. So, thus, in this manner. 2. Therefore, so that, also, equally. *Así bien*, As well, as much so, equally. *Así que*, So that, therefore. *Es así, ó no es así*, Thus it is, or it is not so. *Así fuera yo santo, como fulano es docto*, If I were as sure of being a saint, as he is learned. 3. Followed immediately by *como*, is equivalent to, in the same manner or proportion, as *Así como la modestia atrae, así se huye la disolucion;* In the same proportion that modesty attracts, dissoluteness deters. But when the particle *como* is in the second part of the sentence, *así* is equal to, so much. *Así, así*, So so; middling. *Así que llegó la noticia*, As soon as the news arrived. *Así que así*, It matters not, whether this or that way. *Así que asú ó asado*, Let it be as it will. *Así me estoy*, It is all the same to me. *Como así*, Even so, just so, how so.

A'sia, *sf.* A stone in Asia resembling pumice.

Asidéro, *sm.* 1. Handle. 2. (Met.) Occasion, pretext. *Asideros*, (Naút.) Ropes with which vessels are hauled along the shore.

Asidílla, *sf.* V. *Asidero.*

Asído, da, *pp.* 1. Seized, grasped, laid hold of. 2. Fastened, tied, attached. *Fulano está asido á su propia opinion*, He is wedded to his own opinion.

Asíduo, dúa, *a.* Assiduous, constant in application.

Asiénto, *sm.* 1. Chair, bench, stool, or other seat. 2. Seat in a tribunal or court of justice. 3. Spot on which a town or building is or was standing. 4. Solidity of a building resulting from the reciprocal pressure of the materials upon each other. 5. Bottom of a vessel. 6. Sediment or lees of liquors. 7. Treaty. 8. Contract for supplying an army, town, &c. with provisions, &c. 9. Entry, the act of registering or setting down in writing. 10. Judgment, prudence, discretion. 11. District of the mines in South America. 12. List, roll. 13. Sort of pearls, flat on one side and round on the other. *Hombre de asiento*, A prudent man. *Asientos de popa*, (Naút.) Stern seats in the cabin. *Asiento del estómago*, Indigestion, crudity. *Asiento de molino*, Bed or lowest stone in a mill. *Dar ó tomar asiento en las cosas*, To let things take a regular course. *Asientos*, posteriors, nates, seat; bindings at the wrists and necks of shirts.

Asignáble, *a.* That which may be assigned.

Asignación, *sf.* 1. Assignation, the act of assigning. 2. Distribution, partition. 3. Destination.

Asignár, *va.* To assign, to mark out, to determine, to ascribe, to attribute.

Asignatúra, *sf.* Catalogue of the lectures delivered in universities in the course of a year.

Asílla, *sf.* 1. A small handle. 2. A slight pretext.—*pl.* 1. Clavicles, the collar bones of the breast. 2. Small hooks or keys employed in the different parts of an organ.

Asílo, *sm.* 1. Asylum, sanctuary, place of shelter and refuge. 2. (Met.) Protection, support, favour. 3. (Ant.) A sea-insect which pursues the tunny fish.

Asiméсmo, *ad.* V. *Asimismo.*

Asimiénto, *sm.* 1. Grasp, the act of seizing or grasping. 2. Attachment, affection.

Asimilár, *vn.* To resemble, to be like, to have likeness to.

Asimilatívo, va, *a.* Assimilating, that which has the power of rendering one thing like another.

Asimísmo, *ad.* Exactly so, in the same manner.

Asimpládo, da, *a.* Having the air of a simpleton, or silly person.

Asín y Asína, *ad.* (Ar.) V. *Así.*

Asinár, *va.* (Ant.) V. *Asignar.*

Asinárias, *sf. pl.* Birds, in Brasil, which are very ugly, and whose voice resembles the braying of an ass.

Asiníno, na, *a.* Asinine, belonging to an ass.

Asír, *va.* To grasp or seize with the hand.—*vn.* To strike or take root.—*vr.* To dispute, to contend, to rival. *Asirse de alguna cosa*, To avail one's self of an opportunity to do or say something.

Asisía, *sf.* (For.) Part of law proceedings containing the depositions of witnesses.

Asisón, *sm.* (Extrem.) Bird belonging to the family of *francolins.*

Asisténcia, *sf.* 1. Actual presence. 2. Reward or recompense gained by personal attendance. 3. Assistance, favour, aid. *Asisténcia de Sevilla*, Appellation given to the chief magistracy of Seville. *Asistencias*, Allowance made to any one for his subsistence, maintenance, or support.

Asisténta, *sf.* 1. The wife of the chief magistrate of Seville. 2. Servant maid who waits on the maids of honour at court, and also on religious women of any of the military orders in their convents.

Asisténte, *sm.* 1. Assistant, he who assists. 2. The chief officer of justice at Seville.

Asistír, *vn.* 1. To be present, to assist. 2. To live in a house or frequent it much.—*va.* 1. To accompany one in the execution of some public act. 2. To serve or act provisionally in the room of another. 3. To attend a sick person.

Ásma, *sf.* Asthma, diseased respiration.

Asmadéro, ra, *a.* (Ant.) Discerning, intellectual.

Asmár, *va.* (Ant.) To consider ; to estimate ; to compare.

Asmático, ca, *a.* Asthmatic, troubled with the asthma.

A'sna, *sf.* A she ass. *A'snas*, Rafters or secondary timbers let into the great or ridge-beam of the roof of a house.

Asnáda, *sf.* A brutal action.

Asnádos, *sm. pl.* Large pieces of timber, with which the sides and shafts in mines are secured.

Asnál, *a.* 1. Asinine, relating to an ass. 2. Brutal.

Asnáles, *sm. pl.* Stockings larger and stronger than the common sort.

Asnalménte, *ad.* 1. Foolishly. 2. Mounted on an ass.

Asnázo, *sm.* 1. A large jack-ass. 2. (Met.) A brutish ignorant fellow.

Asnería, *sf.* (Joc.) Stud of asses.

Asnéro, *sm.* (Ant.) Ass-keeper.

Asníco, ca, *s.* 1. A little ass. 2. Andiron, irons at the end of a fire-grate in which the spit turns.

Asnílla, *sf.* Stanchion or prop which supports a ruinous building.

Asníllo, lla, *s.* A little ass. *Asnillo*, Grasshopper, field-cricket.

Asníno, na, *a.* (Joc.) Asinine, resembling an ass.

A'sno, *sm.* 1. Ass, an animal of burthen. 2. (Met.) A dull, stupid, heavy fellow. *Asno de muchos, lobos le comen*, (Prov.) Every body's business is nobody's business. *El hijo del asno dos veces rozna al dia*, (Prov.) Birds of a feather flock together. *No se hizo la miel para la boca del asno*, (Prov.) It is not for asses to lick honey; we should not throw pearls before swine.

Asobarcádo, *sm.* A porter.

Asobarcár, *va.* To lift a weighty thing up from the ground with one hand.

Asobinárse, *vr.* To fall down with a burthen so that the head comes between the fore feet; applied to beasts of burthen.

Asocarronádo, da, *a.* Crafty, cunning, waggish.

Asociación y Asociamiénto, *sf.* Association, the act of associating.

Asociádo, *sm.* Associate who accompanies another with equal authority to execute a commission.

Asociár, *va.* To take an associate.—*vr.* To associate or unite with another.

Asohóra, *ad.* (Ant.) Suddenly, unexpectedly.

Asolación y Asoladúra, *sf.* Desolation, devastation.

Asoladór, ra, *s.* Destroyer, one who desolates.

Asolamiénto, *sm.* Depopulation, destruction.

Asolanár, *va.* To parch or dry up ; applied to easterly winds.

Asolár, *va.* To level with the ground, to destroy, to devastate.—*vr.* To settle and get clear ; applied to liquors.

Asoleár, *va.* To sun, to expose to the sun.—*vr.* To be sun-burnt, or discoloured by the sun.

Asolvamiénto, *sm.* Stoppage, the act of stopping

Asolvárse, *vr.* To be stopped ; spoken of pipes, canals, &c. through which water is running.

Asomáda, *sf.* 1. Appearance, apparition, the act of appearing for a short time. 2. (Ant.) The spot whence any object is first seen or descried.

Asomádo, da, *a.* Fuddled, half seas over.

Asomár, *vn.* 1. To begin to appear, to become visible. *Asoma el dia*, The day begins to peep. 2. (Naút.) To loom.—*va.* To show a thing, to make it appear. *Asomé la cabeza á la ventana*, I put my head out of the window. —*vr.* To be flustered with wine.

Asombradízo, za, *a.* Fearful, timid, easily frightened.

Asombradór, *sm.* Terrifier, one who frightens.

Asombramiénto, *sm.* V. *Asombro*.

Asombrár, *va.* 1. To frighten, to terrify. 2. To astonish, to cause admiration. 3. (Poét.) To shade, to darken, to obscure.—*vr.* To take fright ; applied to a horse.

Asómbro, *sm.* 1. Dread, fear, terror. 2. Amazement, astonishment, high degree of admiration.

Asombróso, sa, *a.* Wonderful, astonishing, amazing.

Asómo, *sm.* 1. Mark, token, sign, indication. 2. Supposition, conjecture, surmise. *Ni por asomo*, Not in the least, by no means.

Asonádia, *sf.* (Ant.) Tumultuous hostility.

Asonáncia, *sf.* 1. Assonance, consonance. 2. Harmony or connexion of one thing with another.

Asonantár, *va.* (Poét.) To mix assonant with consonant verses, in Spanish poetry, which is inadmissible in modern verse.

Asonánte, *a.* Assonant, last word in a Spanish verse whose accented vowel is the same as the preceding, as *milónes, azótes*.

Asonár, *vn.* 1. To be assonant, to accord. 2. (Ant.) To unite in riots and tumultuous assemblies.

Asordár, *va.* (Ant.) To deafen with noise.

Asosiégo, (Ant.) V. *Sosiego*.

Asotanár, *va.* To vault, to make vaults or arched cellars.

A'spa, *sf.* 1. Cross, a frame formed by two cross sticks in the shape of an X. 2. Reel, a turning frame, on which yarn is wound into skeins or hanks. 3. Wings of a wind-mill. *Aspa de cuenta*, A clock-reel. *Aspa de San Andres*, Coloured cross on the yellow cloaks of penitents by the Inquisition.

Aspádo, da, *a.* 1. Having the arms extended in the form of a cross, by way of penance or mortification. 2. (Met.) Having one's arms confined, and their movements obstructed, by tight clothes.

Aspadór, *sm.* Reel, a revolving wheel on which yarn is wound. [thread or silk.
Aspadór, ra, *s.* Reeler, one who reels yarn,
Aspaláto, *sm.* (Bot.) Rosewood. Aspalathus *L.*
Aspálto, *sm.* 1. Asphaltos. 2. V. *Espalto.*
Aspamiénto. V. *Aspaviento.*
Aspár, *va.* 1. To reel, to gather yarn off the spindle, and form it into skeins. 2. To crucify. 3. (Met.) To vex or mortify. *Asparse á gritos*, To hoot, to cry out with vehemence.
Aspaviénto, *sm.* 1. Dread, fear, consternation. 2. Astonishment, admiration, expressed in confused and indistinct words. *Aspavientos*, Boasts, brags, bravadoes.
Aspécto, *sm.* 1. Sight, appearance. 2. Aspect, countenance. 3. Situation or position of a building. 4. Relative position of stars and planets. *A' primer aspecto, ó al primer aspecto*, At first sight. *Tener buen ó mal aspecto*, To have a good or bad aspect.
A'speramente, *ad.* Rudely, in a harsh manner.
Aspereár, *vn* To imbitter, to render rough and acrid to the taste.—*va.* (Ant.) To exasperate, to irritate.
Asperéte, *a.* V. *Asperillo.*
Asperéza, *sf.* 1. Asperity, the quality of being harsh to the taste and hearing. 2. Roughness, ruggedness, inequality, or unevenness of the ground. 3. Austerity, sourness, rigour, or harshness of temper.
Aspérges, *sm.* A Latin word, used for *aspersion* or sprinkling. *Quedarse asperges*, To be frustrated or disappointed in one's expectations.
Asperiéga, *sf.* A sour apple of the pippin kind.
Asperíllo, lla, *a.* Tart, sourish, like unripe fruit. [vant.
A'spero, *sm.* A silver coin current in the Le-
A'spero, ra, *a.* 1. Rough, rugged, uneven. 2. (Met.) Harsh and unpleasing to the taste or ear. 3. (Met.) Severe, rigid, austere. *Aspera artéria.* V. *Traquiarteria.*
Asperón, *sm.* Grindle-stone or grind-stone.
Aspersión, *sf.* Aspersion, the act of sprinkling.
Aspersório, *sm.* Instrument with which holy water is sprinkled in the church.
A'spid y A'spide, *sm.* 1. Aspic, a small kind of serpents. Coluber aspis *L.* 2. Sort of culverin. 3. (Met.) Person of a very choleric temper.
Aspiración, *sf.* 1. Aspiration, the act of aspiring, or desiring something high. 2. Pronunciation of a vowel with full breath. 3. (Mús.) A short pause which gives only time to breathe.
Aspiradaménte, *ad.* With aspiration.
Aspiránte, *pa.* Aspirant.
Aspirár, *va.* 1. To inspire the air, to draw in the breath. 2. To aspire, to wish ardently for an employment or dignity. 3. To pronounce with full breath.
Asqueár, *va.* To consider with disgust or dislike, to disdain.
Asquerosaménte, *ad.* Nastily, nauseously.
Asquerosidád, *sf.* Nastiness, filthiness.
Asqueróso, sa, *a.* 1. Nasty, filthy, nauseously impure. 2. Loathsome, fastidious, squeamish.
A'sta, *sf.* 1. Lance, a long spear with a sharp point. 2. Part of the deer's head which bears the antlers. 3. Handle of a pencil, brush. 4. (Naút.) Staff or light pole erected in different parts of the ship, on which the colours are displayed. *Asta de bandera de popa*, Ensign-staff. *Asta de bandera de proa*, Jack-staff. *Asta de tope*, Flag-staff. *Asta de bomba*, Pump-spear. *Astas*, Horns of animals, as bulls, &c. *Darse de las astas*, To snap and carp at each other.
Astáco, *sm.* Lobster, crayfish or crawfish.
Astádo ó Astéro, *sm.* Roman pikeman or lancer.
Astér, *sm.* (Bot.) Star-wort.
Astería, *sf.* 1. Star-stone, a kind of precious stone. 2. Cat's eye, a sort of false opal.
Asterísco, *sm.* 1. Asterisk, a mark in printing in the form of a small star. 2. (Bot.) Oxeye. Buphthalmum *L.* [tion.
Asterísmo, *sm.* (Ant.) Asterism, a constella-
Astíl, *sm.* 1. Handle of an axe, hatchet, &c. 2. Shaft of an arrow. 3. Beam of a balance. 4. Any thing which serves to support another.
Astilíco, *sm.* A small handle.
Astílla, *sf.* 1. Chip of wood, splinter of timber. 2. (Ant.) Reed or comb of a loom. 3. *Astilla muerta de un baxel*, (Naút.) The dead rising of the floor-timbers of a ship. *De tal palo, tal astilla*, (Prov.) A chip of the same block.
Astillár, *va.* To chip, to cut into small pieces.
Astilláze, *sm.* 1. Crack, the noise produced by a splinter being torn from a block. 2. (Met.) The damage which results from an enterprise to those who have not been its principal authors and promoters.
Astilléjos, *sm. pl.* (Astr.) Castor and Pollux, two brilliant stars in the sign Gemini.
Astilléro, *sm.* 1. Rack on which lances, spears, pikes, &c. are placed. 2. One who makes reeds or combs for looms. 3. *Astillero de construccion*, Ship-wright's yard, dock-yard. 4. (Ant.) Bottom of the ship. *Poner en astillero*, (Met.) To place one in an honourable post.
Astillíca y Astillíta, *sf.* A small chip.
Astrágalo, *sm.* 1. (Arq.) Astragal, a little round member, in form of a ring, serving as an ornament at the tops and bottoms of columns. 2. (Artil.) A kind of ring or moulding on a piece of ordnance, at about half a foot distance from the mouth, serving as an ornament to the piece. 3. (Bot.) Milk-vetch.
Astrál, *a.* That which belongs to the stars, or bears a relation to them.
Astráncia, *sf.* (Bot.) Master-wort.
Astricción y Astringéncia, *sf.* Astriction, compression.
Astrictívo, va, *a.* Astrictive, styptic.
Astrícto, ta, *a.* 1. Contracted, compressed. 2. Determined, resolved. [stars.
Astrífero, ra, (Poét.) Starry, sideral, full of
Astringénte, *a.* Astringent. [press.
Astringír, *a.* To astringe, to contract, to com-
A'stro, *sm.* 1. Luminous body of the heavens, such as the sun, moon, and stars. 2. Illustrious person of uncommon merit.
Astrolábio, *sm.* Astrolabe, an instrument chiefly used for taking the altitude of stars at sea. [telling things by the stars.
Astrología, *sf.* Astrology, the practice of fore-
Astrológico, ca, y Astrólogo, *a.* Astrological, that which belongs to astrology.
Astrólogo, *sm.* Astrologer, one who professes to foretel future events by the stars.

Astronomía, *sf.* Astronomy, a mixed mathematical science teaching the knowledge of celestial bodies, their magnitudes, motions, distances, periods, eclipses, and order.
Astronómico, ca, *a.* Astronomical, that which belongs to astronomy.
Astrónomo, *sm.* Astronomer, one who studies the celestial motions.
Astrosaménte, *ad.* Slovenly, in a coarse, sluttish manner.
Astróso, sa, *a.* 1. Indecent, sordid, base, vile. 2. (Ant.) Unfortunate.
Astúcia, *sf.* Cunningness, craftiness, slyness.
Asturión, *sm.* Pony, a small horse.
Astutaménte, *ad.* Cunningly, in a sly artful manner.
Astúto, ta, *a.* Cunning, sly, crafty.
Asubiár, *vn.* (Burg.) To guard against the rain.
Asuéto, *sm.* Holyday for schoolboys and students; vacation.
Asulcár, V. *Surcar.*
Asumir, *va.* To ascend, to assume any dignity. —*vr.* V. *Arrogarse.*
Asunción, *sf.* 1. Assumption, the act of taking any thing to one's self. 2. Elevation to a higher dignity. 3. Ascent of the Holy Virgin to heaven.
Asúnto, *sm.* Subject, the matter treated upon.
Asuramiénto, *sm.* Ustion, the act of burning, and the state of being burnt.
Asurárse, *vr.* 1. To be burnt in the pot or pan; applied to meat. 2. To be parched with drought; applied to fields.
Asurcár, *va.* To furrow sown land for the purpose of rooting out the weeds.
Asúrez, *sm.* The son of Suero, ancient patronymic, usual in Spain.
Asúso, *ad.* (Ant.) Upwards; above.
Asustár, *va.* To frighten, to terrify.—*vr.* To be frightened or struck with fear.
Ata, *prep.* (Ant.) V. *Hasta.*
Atabacádo, da, *a.* Having the colour of tobacco.
Atabál, *sm.* 1. Kettle-drum. 2. *Atabalero.*
Atabaleár, *vn.* To imitate the noise of kettle-drums. [drum.
Atabalíco ó Atabalíllo, *sm.* A small kettle-
Atabaléro, *sm.* Kettle-drum player.
Atabanádo, da, *a.* Having white spots about the head, neck, and flanks; applied to horses.
Atabardilládo, da, *a.* Applied to diseases of the nature of spotted fevers.
Atábe, *sm.* A small vent or spiracle left in waterpipes.
Atabernádo, da, *a.* Retailed in taverns; applied to wine and other liquors.
Atabladéra, *sf.* Roller, machine for levelling the soil.
Atablár, *va.* To level land sown with corn by means of a levelling board (on which the driver stands), drawn by two horses, like a harrow.
Atacadéra, *sf.* Rammer used in splitting stones with gunpowder.
Atacádo, da, *pp.* 1. Attacked. 2. (Met.) Irresolute, not constant in purpose, not determined. 3. (Met.) Close, miserable, narrow-minded. *Calzas atacadas*, Breeches formerly worn in Spain, which covered the legs and thighs. *Hombre de calzas atacadas*, A strict observer of old customs, and rigid in his proceedings.
Atacadór, *sm.* 1. Aggressor, he that invades or attacks. 2. Ramrod or rammer, an instrument with which the charge is forced into guns.
Atacadúra y Atacamiénto, *s.* Stricture, act and effect of tightening.
Atacár, *va.* 1. To fit clothes tight to the body, to lace them very close. 2. To force the charge into fire-arms with a ramrod. 3. To attack, to assault. *Atacár bien la plaza*, (Joc.) To cram or stuff gluttonously.
Atachonádo, da, *a.* (Ant.) Buttoned, laced.
Atadéras, *sf. pl.* Garters.
Atadéro, *sm.* 1. Cord or rope, with which something may be tied. 2. The place where a thing is tied. *No tener atadero*, To have neither head nor tail; applied to a speech or discourse. [cel.
Atadízo, *sm.* An ill-shaped little bundle or par-
Atadíto, ta, *a.* Somewhat cramped or contracted.
Atádo, *sm.* Bundle, parcel. *Atado de cebollas*, A string of onions. [rassed.
Atádo, da, *a.* Pusillanimous, easily embar-
Atadór, *sm.* 1. He who ties. 2. A man who binds sheaves of corn; a binder.
Atadúra, *sf.* 1. Alligation, the act of tying together. 2. (Ant.) Tie, fastening. 3. (Met.) Union, connexion. *Ataduras de galeotes y presos*, A number of prisoners tied together, to be conducted to the galleys.
Atafagár, *va.* 1. To stupify, to deprive of the use of the senses. 2. (Met.) To tease, to molest by incessant importunity.
Atafetanádo, da, *a.* Resembling tiffany, a light thin silk. [saddle.
Atahárre, *sm.* The broad crupper of a pack
Atahórma, *sf.* (Orn.) Osprey, a kind of sea-eagle. Falco ossifragus *L.*
Ataifór ó Ataiforíco, *sm.* (Ant.) Round table; deep plate.
Atairár, *va.* To cut mouldings in the pannels and frames of doors and windows.
Atáire, *sm.* Moulding in the pannels and frames of doors and windows.
Atajadízo, *sm.* Partition of boards, linen, &c. by which a place or ground is divided into separate parts. *Atajadizo de la caxa de agua*, (Naút.) The manger-board.
Atajadór, *sm.* 1. One that intercepts or stops a passage, or obstructs the progress of another. 2. (Ant. Mil.) Scout. 3. *Atajador de ganado*, A sheep thief.
Atajár, *vn.* To go the shortest way: to cut off part of the road.—*va.* 1. To overtake flying beasts or men, by cutting off part of the road, and thus getting before them. 2. To divide or separate by partitions. 3. To intercept, stop, or obstruct the course of a thing. 4. *Atajar ganado*, To steal sheep. 5. *Atajar la tierra*, To reconnoitre the ground.—*vr.* To be confounded with shame, dread, or reverential fear.
Atájo, *sm.* 1. Cut by which a road or path is shortened. 2. Partition, division. 3. A separate part of a flock. 4. Ward or guard, made by a weapon in fencing. 5. Expedient, conveniency. *No hay atajo sin trabajo*, There is no conveniency without some inconveniency.

6. Obstruction. *Salir al atajo*, To interrupt another's speech, and anticipate in a few words what he was going to say in many.

Atál, *a.* (Ant.) V. *Tal.*

Ataladrár, *va.* (Ant.) To bore. V. *Taladrar.*

Atalánta, *sf.* (Ant.) Fixed and coagulated sulphur.

Atalantár, *va.* To stun, to stupify.—*vn.* To agree, to accord, to be pleased.

Ataláya, *sf.* 1. Watch-tower, which overlooks the adjacent country and sea-coast. 2. Height, whence a considerable track of country may be overlooked. 3. Guard, placed in a watch-tower to keep a watchful eye over the adjacent country and sea-coast.

Atalayadór, ra, *s.* 1. Guard or sentry stationed in a watch-tower. 2. (Met.) Observer; investigator.

Atalayár, *va.* 1. To overlook and observe the country and sea-coast from a watch-tower or eminence. 2. To spy or pry into the actions of others.

Atalvína, *sf.* V. *Talvina.*

Atambién, *ad.* V. *Tambien.*

Atamiénto, *sm.* 1. Pusillanimity, meanness of spirit. 2. Embarrassment, perplexity.

Atán, *ad.* (Ant.) V. *Tan.*

Atanásia, *sf.* 1. (Bot.) Tansy. Tanacetum vulgare *L.* 2. (Imprent.) A sort of types, between Pica and English Roman.

Atancárse, *vr.* To be embarrassed or perplexed; to stop short.

Atánes, *ad.* (Ant.) V. *Hasta.*

Atanór, *sm.* (And.) A siphon or tube for conveying water.

Atanquía, *sf.* 1. Depilatory, a sort of ointment, made up of unslaked lime, oil, &c. to take away hair; mixture of orpiment and lime. 2. Refuse of silk which cannot be spun.

Atánto, (Ant.) V. *Tanto.*

Atañér, *v. imp.* (Ant.) To belong, to appertain.

Atapár, *va.* (Ant.) V. *Tapar.*

Atáque, *sm.* 1. Attack. 2. Trenches, made to cover troops, which besiege a place. 3. Fit of the palsy, an apoplectic fit. 4. (Met.) Verbal dispute.

Ataquíza, *sf.* The act of provining or laying a branch of a vine in the ground to take root.

Ataquizár, *va.* To provine or lay a branch of a vine in the ground to take root.

Atár, *va.* 1. To tie, to bind, to fasten. 2. (Met.) To deprive of motion, to stop. *Atar bien su dedo*, To take care of one's self, to be attentive to one's own interest. *Al atar de los trapos*, At the close of the accounts. *Loco de atar*, A fool, that should wear a strait-waistcoat. *Atatela al dedo*, Tie it to the finger; said to ridicule a person led by visionary expectations.—*vr.* 1. To be embarrassed or perplexed, to be at a loss how to extricate one's self from some difficulties. 2. To confine one's self to some certain subject or matter *Atarse á la letra*, To stick to the letter of the text. *Atarse las manos*, To tie one's self down by promise.

Ataracéa y Ataráce, *s.* Marquetry, chequered work, wood, or other matter inlaid or variegated.

Ataraceár, *va.* To chequer, to inlay or variegate.

Atarantádo, da, *a.* 1. Bit by a tarantula. 2. Having a tremelous head and hand, as if bit by a tarantula. 3. (Met.) Surprised, astonished, amazed.

Atarazána ó Atarazanál, *s.* 1. Arsenal, a public dock-yard. 2. Shed in rope-walks, for the spinners to work under cover. 3. Cellar, where wine is kept in casks.

Atarazár, *va.* To bite or wound with the teeth.

Atárde, *ad.* (Ant.) In the evening. V. *Tarde.*

Atareádo, da, *a.* Busied, occupied; tasked.

Atareár, *va.* To task, to impose a task.—*vr.* To labour or work with great application.

Atarquinár, *va.* To bemire, to cover with mire.—*vr.* To be bemoiled, to be covered with mire.

Atarragár, *va.* To fit a shoe to a horse's foot before it is nailed.

Atarrajár, *va.* To form the thread of a screw, to make a screw with a screw-plate.

Atarugádo, da, *a.* (Fam.) Abashed, ashamed.

Atarugamiénto, *sm.* (Vulg.) Act and effect of wedging.

Atarugár, *va.* 1. To fasten or straiten with wedges. 2. To stop with wedges. 3. (Met.) To silence one, so that he does not know what to answer.

Atarxéa, *sf.* 1. A small vault made of brick, over the pipes of an aqueduct, to prevent them from receiving any hurt. 2. A small sewer or drain for carrying off the filth of houses.

Atasajádo, da, *a.* Stretched across a horse.

Atasajár, *va.* To cut meat into small pieces, and dry it by the sun, in imitation of hung-beef.

Atascadéro, *sm.* 1. A deep miry place, in which carriages, horses, &c. stick fast. 2. (Met.) Obstruction, impediment.

Atascár, *va.* 1. (Naút.) To stop or fother a leak. 2. (Met.) To throw an obstacle in the way of some undertaking to prevent its being carried into effect.—*vr.* 1. To stick in a deep miry place. 2. (Met.) To stop short in a speech or discourse, without being able to proceed.

Ataúd, *sm.* 1. Coffin in which dead bodies are put into the ground. 2. (Ant.) A measure for corn.

Ataudádo, da, *a.* Made in the shape of a coffin.

Atauxía, *sf.* Damaskening, the art or act of adorning gold, silver, or steel, with inlaid work of various colours.

Atauxiádo, da, *a.* Worked damaskening fashion.

Ataviár, *va.* To dress out, to trim, to adorn, to embellish.

Atavillár, *va.* (Arag.) To unfold a piece of cloth so that the selvages are open to view on both sides.

Atavío, *sm.* The dress and ornament of a person.

Ataxéa y Ataxía, *sf.* V. *Atarxea*

A'te, *prep.* (Ant.) V. *Ante.*

Atediárse, *vr.* To be disgusted or displeased, to consider with disgust.

Ateísmo, *sm.* Atheism or disbelief of God.

Ateísta, *sm.* Atheist, one who denies the existence of God.

Atemorizár y Atemorár, *va.* To terrify, to strike with terror.

Atémpa, *sf.* Pasture in plains and open fields.

Atemperación, *sf.* The act and effect of tempering.

ATEMPERÁR, *va.* 1. To temper, to form metals to a proper degree of hardness. 2. To soften, to mollify, to assuage. 3. To accommodate, to modify.

ATEMPLÁR, *va.* (Ant.) V. *Templar.* [by turns.

ATEMPORÁDO, DA, *a.* (Ant.) Alternate, serving

ATENACEÁR ó ATENAZÁR, *va.* To tear off the flesh with pincers.

ATENCIÓN, *sf.* 1. Attention, the act of being attentive. 2. Civility, complaisance. 3. (In the wool-trade) A contract of sale, whereby the price of wool is not determined, but left to be regulated by what is paid by others. *En atencion*, Attending; in consideration.

ATENDÉR, *vn.* 1. To attend or be attentive, to fix the mind upon a subject. 2. To expect, to wait or stay for.

ATENEDÓR, *sm.* (Ant.) Partisan, sectarian.

ATENÉR, *vn.* 1. To walk at the same pace with another. 2. To guard, to observe.—*vr.* To stick or adhere to one for greater security.

ATENTACIÓN, *sf.* Procedure contrary to the order and form prescribed by the laws.

ATENTADAMÉNTE, *ad.* 1. Prudently, considerately. 2. Contrary to law.

ATENTÁDO, DA, *a.* 1. Discreet, prudent, moderate. 2. Done without noise, and with great circumspection.

ATENTÁDO, *sm.* 1. Proceeding of a judge not warranted by the law. 2. Excess, transgression, offence.

ATENTAMÉNTE, *ad.* 1. Attentively, with attention. 2. Civilly, politely.

ATENTÁR, *va.* 1. To attempt to commit any crime. 2. To try with great circumspection. 3. To encamp.—*vr.* To proceed with the utmost circumspection in the execution of an enterprise.

ATÉNTO, TA, *a.* 1. Attentive, bent upon a thing. 2. Polite, civil. *Atento*, In consideration.

ATENUACIÓN, *sf.* Attenuation, the act of making thin or slender. [diminish, to lessen.

ATENUÁR, *va.* To render thin and slender; to

ATÉO, *sm.* V. *Ateista.*

ATERCIANÁDO, DA, *a.* Afflicted with a tertian or intermitting fever. [velvet.

ATERCIOPELÁDO, DA, *a.* Velvet-like, resembling

ATERICIÁRSE. V. *Atiriciarse.*

ATERILLÁDO, DA, *a.* Crumbled or sifted fine.

ATERIMIÉNTO, *sm.* Act of growing stiff with cold.

ATERÍRSE, *vr.* To grow stiff with cold.

ATERRAMIÉNTO, *sm.* 1. Ruin, destruction. 2. Terror, communication of fear.

ATERRÁR, *va.* 1. To destroy, to pull or strike down; to prostrate. 2. To terrify, to appal, to cause terror or dismay.—*vr.* (Naút.) To stand in shore, to keep the land on board.

ATERRONÁRSE, *vr.* To clod, to gather into concretions, to coagulate.

ATERRORIZÁR, *va.* To frighten, to terrify.

ATESÁR, *va.* 1. To harden or stiffen a thing. 2. (Naút.) To haul taught.

ATESORÁR, *va.* 1. To treasure or hoard up riches. 2. To possess many amiable qualities and perfections.

ATESTACIÓN, *sf.* Attestation, certificate.

ATESTÁDO, DA, *a.* Attested, witnessed.

ATESTÁDOS, *sm. pl.* Certificates, testimonials.

ATESTADÚRA, *sf.* 1. The act of cramming, or stuffing. 2. Must, poured into pipes and butts, to supply the soakage. [stuffing.

ATESTAMIÉNTO, *sm.* The act of cramming or

ATESTÁR, *va.* 1. To cram, to stuff. 2. To fill up pipes or butts of wine. 3. To attest, to witness.

ATESTIGUACIÓN, *sf.* Deposition upon oath.

ATESTIGUÁR, *va.* To depose, to witness, to attest, to affirm as a witness. *Atestiguar con alguno*, To cite or summon one as a witness.

ATETÁDO, DA, *a.* Mammillated, mammiform.

ATETÁR, *va.* To suckle, to give suck.

ATETILLÁR, *va.* To dig a trench around the roots of trees, leaving the soil against their trunks. [ening.

ATEZAMIÉNTO, *sm.* The act and effect of black-

ATEZÁR, *va.* To blacken, to make black.—*vr.* To grow black.

ATIBORRÁR, *va.* 1. To stuff or pack up close with locks of wool, tow, &c. 2. To cram with victuals.

A'TICISMO, *sm.* 1. Atticism, a concise manner of speech, used by the Athenians. 2. Nice, witty and polite joke.

A'TICO, CA, *a.* 1. Attic, elegant, poignant; applied to wit and humour. 2. Superior to objection or confutation. *Testigo ático*, An irrefragable witness. 3. Upper part of a building.

ATICÚRGA, *sf.* Base of an attic column.

A' TIÉNTAS, *ad.* In the dark, at random.

ATIESÁR, *va.* To make hard or stiff.

ATÍFLE, *sm.* An instrument in the shape of a trevet, which potters place between earthen vessels, to prevent them from sticking to each other in the kiln or oven. [the skin of a tiger.

ATIGRÁDO, DA, *a.* Tiger-coloured, resembling

ATILDADÚRA, *sf.* 1. Dress, attire, ornament. 2. Culture of the mind, good breeding. 3. Punctuation.

ATILDÁR, *va.* 1. To put a dash or stroke over a letter. 2. To censure the speeches and actions of others. 3. To deck, to dress, to adorn.

ATINADAMÉNTE, *ad.* 1. Cautiously, judiciously, prudently. 2. Pertinently, appositely, to the purpose.

ATINÁR, *vn.* 1. To touch the mark, to reach the point. 2. To hit upon a thing by conjecture.

ATINCÁR, *sm.* Tincal; when refined, it is the Borax of commerce.

ATIPLÁR, *va.* To raise the sound of a musical instrument.—*vr.* To grow very sharp or acute; applied to the sound of a musical instrument.

ATIRANTÁR, *va.* To fix collar beams in a building.

ATIRICIÁRSE, *vr.* To grow jaundiced, to be infected with the jaundice.

ATISBADÓR, RA, *s.* A person who pries into the business and actions of others.

ATISBADÚRA, *sf.* The act of prying into the business and actions of others. [closely.

ATISBÁR, *va.* To scrutinize, to pry, to examine

ATISUÁDO, DA, *a.* Tissue-like, made tissue-fashion. [cites.

ATIZADÉRO, *sm.* Exciter, the thing which ex-

ATIZADÓR, RA, *s.* 1. One who stirs up or incites others. 2. Poker, an instrument to stir the fire. 3. (In Oil-mills) The person who puts the olives under the mill-stone. 4. (In Glass-houses) He who supplies the furnace with wood or coals.

Atizár, *va.* 1. To stir the fire with a poker. 2. (Met.) To stir up or rouse and incite the passions. *Atizar la lámpara ó el candil*, To raise the lamp wick, and fill it with oil. *Atizar la lámpara*, (Joc.) To fill the glasses. *Pedro por que atiza? Por gozar de la ceniza*, (Prov.) Why does Peter sow? Because he expects to reap.

Atizonár, *va.* To join bricks and stones close together, and fill up the chinks in a wall with mortar and brick bats.—*vr.* To be smutted; applied to grain.

Atlánte, *sm.* He who bears the weight of government, in allusion to Atlas. *Atlantes*, (Arq.) Figures or half figures of men, sometimes used instead of columns.

Atlántico, ca, *a.* Atlantic. *Mar Atlantico*, The Atlantic Ocean.

A'tlas, *sm.* 1. Atlas, a collection of maps. 2. (Anat.) The first *vertebra* or joint of the neck. 3. (Com.) A kind of rick silk manufactured in the East Indies.

Atléta, *sm.* Wrestler, he who wrestles.

Atlético, ca, *a.* Athletic, belonging to wrestling; robust.

Atmósfera, *sf.* Atmosphere, the air which encompasses the earth. and carries off vapours.

Atmosférico, ca, *a.* Atmospherical, belonging to the atmosphere.

Atoár, *va.* (Naút.) To tow or haul a vessel through the water by the help of a rope.

Atobár, *va.* To astonish, to cause admiration.

Atócha, *sf.* (Bot.) Feathergrass, bass-weed. Stipa tenacissima *L.*

Atochál ó Atochár, *sm.* A field where bass-weed grows.

Atochár, *va.* To fill with bass-weed.

Atocinádo, da, *a.* (Vulg.) Corpulent, fat, fleshy.

Atocinár, *va.* 1. To cut up a pig into parts fit for salting and drying. 2. (Met.) To assassinate or murder in a perfidious manner.—*vr.* (Vulg.) To swell with anger and rage, to be exasperated.

A'tole, *sm.* A liquor much drank in Mexico, extracted from Indian corn in its milky state, and mixed with other ingredients.

Atolladéro, *sm.* 1. A deep miry place. 2. (Met.) Obstacle, impediment, obstruction.

Atollár, *vn.* To fall into the mire, to stick in the mud.—*vr.* (Met.) To be involved in great difficulties.

Atolondramiénto, *sm.* Stupefaction, the act and effect of stupifying.

Atolondrár, *va.* To stun, to stupify, to render stupid.—*vr.* To be stupified, to grow dull or stupid.

Atomecérse ó Atomescérse, (Ant.) V. *Entumirse.*

Atomísta, *sm.* Atomist, one who holds the *atomical* philosophy, or the system of atoms.

Atomístico, ca, *a.* Atomical, consisting of atoms.

A'tomo, *sm.* 1. Atom, such a small particle as cannot be physically divided. 2. Any thing extremely small. *No exceder en un átomo*, To stick closely to one's orders and instructions. *Reparár en un átomo*, To remark the minutest actions. *Atomos*, Minute parts seen by a solar ray in any place.

Atondár, *va.* To spur a horse.

Atónito, ta, *a.* Astonished, amazed.

Atontadaménte, *ad.* Foolishly, in a stupid manner.

Atontamiénto, *sm.* The act of stupifying, and state of being stupified.

Atontár, *va.* To stun, to stupify.—*vr.* To be stupid, to grow stupid.

Atóra, *sf.* (Ant.) Law of Moses.

Atorár, *vn.* 1. To stick in the mire. 2. To fit closely the bore of a cannon; applied to a ball.

Atordecér, *va.* (Ant.) V. *Aturdir.*

Atormecér, (Ant.) V. *Adormecer.*

Atormentadaménte, *ad.* Anxiously, tormentingly.

Atormentadór, ra, *s.* Tormentor, one who torments or gives pain.

Atormentár, *va.* 1. To torment, to give pain 2. (Met.) To cause affliction, pain, or vexation. 3. To rack or torment by the rack, to obtain a confession of the truth.

Atorozonárse, *vr.* To suffer gripes or colic; applied to saddle horses.

Atortolár, *va.* To confound, to intimidate.—*vr.* To be frightened or intimidated, like a turtle.

Atortorár, *va.* (Naút.) To frape a ship, to strengthen the hull with ropes tied round it.

Atortujár, *va.* (Vulg.) To squeeze, to make flat by pressing.

Atorzonárse, *vr.* To be griped, to be troubled with pains in the bowels.

Atosigadór, *sm.* Poisoner, one who poisons.

Atosigamiénto, *sm.* The act of poisoning, and state of being poisoned.

Atosigár, *va.* 1. To poison, to infect with poison. 2. (Met.) To harass, to oppress.

Atóti, *sm.* An American plant.

Atrabancár, *va.* To huddle, to perform any thing in a hurry, without considering whether it be ill or well done.

Atrabánco, *sm.* The act of huddling, or doing a thing with precipitation and hurry.

Atrabilário, ria, y Atrabilióso, sa, *a.* Atrabilarious, melancholy.

Atrabílis, *sf.* The state of being atrabilarious; black bile.

Atracár, *va.* 1. (Naút.) To overtake another ship, to come up with her. 2. To cram, to fill with food and drink beyond satiety.—*vr.* 1. To be stuffed with eating and drinking. 2. (Naút.) *Atracarse al costado*, To come along-side of a ship.

Atracción, *sf.* Attraction, the act or power of attracting.

Atractívo, va, *a.* Attractive, having the power of attracting.

Atractívo, *sm.* Charm, something fit to gain the affections.

Atractríz, *sf.* The power of attracting.

Atraér, *va.* 1. To attract, to draw to something. 2. To allure, to invite, to make another submit to one's will and opinion.—*vr.* (Ant.) V. *Juntarse* and *Extenderse.*

Atrafagádo, da, *a.* Much occupied; laborious.

Atrafagár, *vn.* (Bax.) To toil, to exhaust one's self with fatigue.

Atragantárse, *vr.* 1. To stick in the throat or wind-pipe. 2. (Met.) To be cut short in conversation.

Atraidoradaménte, *ad.* Treacherously, in a treacherous manner.

Atraidoráδo, da, *a.* Treacherous, faithless, perfidious.

Atraillár, *va.* 1. To leash, to bind with a string. 2. To follow game, being guided by a dog in leash.

Atraimiénto, *sm.* The act of attracting, and state of being attracted. [er of dying black.

Atramentóso, sa, *a.* That which has the pow-

Atrampárse, *vr.* 1. To be caught in a snare. 2. To be choaked, to be stopped or blocked up. 3. To be involved in difficulties.

Atrancár, *va.* 1. To bar a door. 2. To step out, to take long steps. 3. (Met.) To read so fast as to skip over passages, to omit some sentences.

Atrapár, *va.* 1. To overtake, to lay hold of one who is running away. 2. To impose upon, to deceive.

Atrás, *ad.* 1. Backwards, towards the back. 2. Past, in time past. *Hacerse atrás,* To fall back. *Quedarse atrás,* To remain behind. *Volverse atrás,* (Met.) To retract, to unsay. *Hacia atrás,* Far from that, quite the contrary.

Atrasádo, da, *a. Atrasado de medios,* Short of means, poor.

Atrasádos, *sm. pl.* Arrears, sums which remain behind unpaid though due.

Atrasár, *va.* 1. To leave another behind: in this sense seldom used. 2. To obstruct another person's fortune or advancement. 3. To protract or postpone the execution or performance of something. *Atrasar el relox,* To retard the motion of a watch.—*vr.* 1. To remain behind. 2. To be in debt.

Atráso, *sm.* 1. Backwardness. 2. Loss of fortune or wealth. 3. Arrears of money.

Atravesádo, da, *a.* 1. Squint-eyed, looking obliquely. 2. Cross-grained, perverse, troublesome. 3. Mongrel, of a mixed or cross breed.

Atravesádo, *sm.* One of the muscles of the neck. [peace.

Atravesadór, *sm.* Disturber, a violator of

Atravesáño, *sm.* Cross-timber, timber which crosses from one side to another. *Atravesaño firme de colchar,* (Naút.) A cross-piece for belaying ropes. *Atravesaños de los propaos,* Cross-pieces of the breast-work. *Atravesaños de las latas,* Carlines or carlings, two pieces of timber lying fore and aft from one beam to another, directly over the keel.

Atravesár, *va.* 1. To lay a beam, piece of timber, or plank, athwart a place. 2. To run through with a sword, to pass through the body. 3. To cross or pass over. 4. (Bax.) To bewitch by a spell or charm. 5. To bet, to stake at a wager. 6. To lay a trump on a card which has been played. 7. (Naút.) To lie to. *Atravesar el corazon,* (Met.) To move to compassion. *Atravesar los géneros,* To buy goods by wholesale in order to sell them by retail. *Atravesar todo el pais,* To overrun or traverse the whole country. *No atravesar los umbrales,* Not to darken one's door.—*vr.* 1. To be obstructed by something thrown in the way. 2. To interfere in other people's business or conversation. 3. To have a dispute. 4. (Naút.) To cross the course of another vessel under her head or stern.

Atravesía, *sf.* (Ant.) V. *Travesía.*

Atrazadéras, *sf. pl.* (Ant.) Shifts, tricks.

Atrazár, *va.* (Ant.) To practise shifts. It is still used vulgarly in Aragon.

Atreguadaménte, *ad.* Madly, rashly.

Atreguádo, da, *a.* Rash, foolish, precipitate, or deranged.

Atresnalár, *va.* To collect sheaves of corn into heaps, that they may be carried and stacked.

Atrevérse, *vr.* 1. To be too forward from want of judgment or respect. 2. To dare, to venture.

Atrevidaménte, *ad.* Audaciously. [ture.

Atrevidíllo, lla, *a.* Somewhat audacious.

Atrevidísimo, ma, *a.* Most audacious.

Atrevído, da, *a.* Forward, audacious, bold.

Atrevído, *sm.* A muscle of the shoulder blade.

Atrevimiénto, *sm.* Boldness, audaciousness.

Atriaquéro, *sm.* (Ant.) A manufacturer and retailer of treacle. Apothecaries were formerly called so.

Atribución, *sf.* 1. The act of attributing something to another. 2. Attribúte, attribution.

Atribuír, *va.* To attribute, to ascribe as a quality, to impute as to a cause.—*vr.* To assume, to arrogate to one's self.

Atribulár, *va.* To vex, to afflict.—*vr.* To be vexed, to suffer tribulation.

Atributár, *va.* (Ant.) To impose tribute.

Atributívo, va, *a.* Attributive.

Atribúto, *sm.* Attribute, the thing attributed to another; a quality adherent.

Atricapílla, *sf.* (Orn.) The Epicurean warbler. Motacilla ficedula *L.*

Atricéses, *sm. pl.* The staples or iron rings to which the stirrup-straps are fastened.

Atrición, *sf.* 1. Attrition, grief for sin arising from the fear of punishment, and a sense of the deformity and odiousness of sin. 2. (Alb.) Contraction of the principal nerve in a horse's fore-leg.

Atríl, *sm.* A stand for the missal, and other church-books in Roman catholic churches.

Atriléra, *sf.* An ornamental cover laid over the stand of the missal, or other church-books, while divine service is performed.

Atrincheramiénto, *sm.* Intrenchment. *Atrincheramiéntos de abordage,* (Naút.) Close quarters, breast-works on board of merchant ships, from behind which the crew defend themselves in case of the ship being boarded by an enemy.

Atrincherárse, *vr.* To intrench, to cover one's self from the enemy by means of trenches.

A'trio, *sm.* 1. Porch, a roof supported by pillars between the principal door of a palace and the stair-case. 2. Portico, a covered walk before a church door.

Atristár, *va.* (Ant.) V. *Entristecer.* [sin.

Atríto, ta, *a.* Feeling attrition, sorrowful for

A'tro, ra, *a.* (Poét.) Dark, black, obscure.

Atrocemente, *ad.* (Ant.) V. *Atrozmente.*

Atrochár, *vn.* To go by bye and cross paths.

A' tróche móche, *ad.* Helter-skelter, in a hurry, and without order.

Atrocidád, *sf.* 1. Atrocity or atrociousness, enormous wickedness. 2. Excess. *Es una atrocidad lo que come, lo que trabaja,* He eats or works to excess.

Atrofía, *sf.* Atrophy, a gradual wasting of the body for want of nourishment.

Atrófico, ca, *a.* Affected with atrophy.
Atrompetádo, da, *a.* Trumpet-like, having the shape of a trumpet. *Tiene narices atrompetadas*, His nostrils are as wide as the mouth of a trumpet. [prudence or reflection.
Atronadaménte, *ad.* Precipitately, without
Atronádo, da, *a.* Acting in a precipitate, imprudent manner. [a thundering noise.
Atronadór, ra, *s.* Thunderer, one who makes
Atronadúra, *sf.* V. *Alcanzadura.*
Atronamiénto, *sm.* 1. The act of thundering. 2. Stupefaction caused by a blow. 3. Crepane or ulcer in the feet or legs of horses, generally occasioned by a blow.
Atronár, *va.* 1. To make a great noise in imitation of thunder. 2. To stun, to stupify.—*vr.* To be thunderstruck.
Atronerár, *va.* To make embrasures in a wall.
Atropádo, da, *a.* Grouped, clumped; applied to trees and plants. [order.
Atropár, *va.* To assemble in groups without
Atropelladaménte, *ad.* Tumultuously, confusedly. [hasty, precipitate manner.
Atropelládo, da, *a.* Speaking or acting in a
Atropelladór, ra, *s.* Trampler, one who overturns or tramples under foot. [under foot.
Atropellamiénto, *sm.* Conculcation, trampling
Atropellár, *va.* 1. To trample, to tread under foot. 2. *Atropellar las leyes*, To act in defiance of the law. 3. To insult with abusive language. 4. *Atropellar al caballo*, To overwork a horse.—*vr.* To hurry one's self too much in speech or action.
Atróz, *a.* 1. Atrocious, enormous; cruel. 2. Huge, vast, immense. *Estatura atroz*, Enormous stature. [mast.
Atrozár, *va.* (Naút.) To truss a yard to the
Atrozménte, *ad.* 1. Atrociously. 2. Excessively, to excess. *Trabajar atrozmente*, To work to excess.
Atruhanádo, da, *a.* Scurrilous, acting the buffoon, using low jests.
Attelábe, *sm.* A sea-spider.
Atuéndo, *sm.* (Ant.) Pomp, ostentation.
Atufadaménte, *ad.* Peevishly, morosely.
Atufár, *va.* To vex, to plague.—*vr.* To be on the fret; applied to wine and other liquors in a state of fermentation.
Atumno, (Ant.) V. *Otoño.*
Atún, *sm.* Tunny or tunny-fish. Scomber thynnus *L. Pedazo de atun*, An ignorant stupid fellow. *Por atun y ver al duque*, (Prov.) To kill two birds with one stone.
Atunára, *sf.* Place for the tunny-fisheries.
Atunéra, *sf.* 1. A fishing-hook used in the tunny-fishery. 2. A net with which the tunny-fish is caught.
Atunéro, *sm.* A fisherman engaged in the tunny-fishery, a fishmonger who deals in tunny-fish.
Aturár, *va.* 1. To stop or shut up closely. 2. (Ant.) To endure, to bear; to procrastinate.
Aturdimiénto, *sm.* Perturbation of the mind; dullness, drowsiness.
Aturdír, *va.* 1. To perturb or perturbate, to confuse. 2. To stupify with wonder or admiration. [lence.
Aturrullár, *va.* To confound, to reduce to si-
Atusadór, *sm.* 1. Hair-dresser, who cuts the hair. 2. One who trims box, and other plants in a garden.
Atusár, *va.* 1. To cut the hair even, to comb it smooth and even. 2. To shear or trim the box, and other plants in a garden.—*vr.* To trim and dress one's self with too much care and affectation. [lected in a furnace.
Atutía, *sf.* Tutty, a sublimate of calamine col-
A'tutiplén, *ad.* (Bax.) Abundantly, plentifully.
Aúca, *sf.* A goose. V. *Oca.*
Auctorizár, (Ant.) V. *Autorizar.* [ness.
Audácia, *sf.* Audacity, boldness, audacious-
Audáz, *a.* Forward, bold, daring, audacious.
Audiéncia, *sf.* 1. Audience, a hearing given by men in power to those who have something to propose or represent. 2. Audience-chamber, the room in which an audience is given. 3. A court of oyer and terminer, whose jurisdiction is more limited than that of the *chancillerias*, or chanceries. 4. Law-officers appointed by a superior judge to institute some judicial inquiry. 5. *Audiencia de los grados en Sevilla*, A court of appeal in Seville. 6. *Audiencia pretorial en Indias*, A court of judicature in India, which in some respects is not subordinate to the viceroy.
Auditívo, va, *a.* 1. Having the power of hearing. 2. Invested with the right of giving an audience.
Auditór, *sm.* 1. Auditor, a hearer. 2. A judge. *Auditor de la nunciatura*, A delegate of the Nuncio, appointed to hear and decide appeal causes respecting complaints against bishops. *Auditor de rota*, One of the twelve prelates who compose the *Rota* at Rome, a court which inquires into and decides appeal-causes in ecclesiastical matters, which are carried thither from all Roman Catholic provinces and kingdoms. [tor.
Auditoría, *sf.* The place and office of an audi-
Auditório, *sm.* Auditory, an audience.
Auditório, ria, *a.* Auditory. V. *Auditivo.*
A'uge, *sm.* 1. Great elevation in point of dignity or fortune. 2. (Astr.) Apogee of a planet or star.
Augmentár, (Ant.) V. *Aumentar.*
Auguración, *sf.* Auguration, the act of prognosticating by the flight of birds.
Augurál, *a.* Augurial, belonging to augury.
Augurár. V. *Agorar.*
Augúres, *sm. pl.* Augurs, persons who pretend to predict future events by the flight of birds.
Augústo, ta, *a.* August, great, grand, magnificent.
A'ula, *sf.* 1. Hall where lectures are given on a science or art. 2. The court or palace of a sovereign.
Aulága, *sf.* V. *Aliaga.*
A'ulico, ca, *a.* Belonging to a court or palace. *Consejo áulico*, Aulic counsel.
Aulladéro, *sm.* A place where wolves assemble at night and howl.
Aulladór, ra, *s.* Howler.
Aullár, *vn.* To howl, to yell, to utter cries in distress.
Aullído y Aúllo, *sm.* Howl, the cry of a wolf or dog; a cry of horror or distress.
Aumentáble, *a.* Augmentable.
Aumentación, *sf.* Augmentation, increase.

Aumentadór, ra, *s.* Enlarger, amplifier; one who augments, increases, or amplifies.

Aumentár, *va.* To augment, to increase, to enlarge.

Aumentatívo, va, *a.* Increasing, enlarging.

Auménto, *sm.* Augmentation, increase, enlargement. *Auméntos*, Promotion, advancement, an increase of fortune and riches.

Aún, *ad.* 1. Yet, as yet, nevertheless, notwithstanding. V. *Todavia y Tambien.* 2. Still, farther, even. *Esto es estimable aun con estas circunstancias*, It is estimable even with all these circumstances.

Aun desquartelado, (Naút.) Abaft the beam; applied to a wind which blows pretty large.

Aúna, *ad.* Jointly, to the same end or purpose.

Aunár, *va.* 1. To unite, to assemble 2. To incorporate, to mix.—*vr.* To be united or confederated for one end.

Aúnque, *ad.* Though, notwithstanding.

Aúpa, Up, up; a word used to animate children to get up.

Aúra, *sf.* 1. A bird of Mexico. 2. (Poét.) A gentle breeze. *Aúra popular*, (Met.) Popularity, state of being favoured by the people.

Aurelianénse, *a.* Belonging to or made at Orleans.

Aúreo, *sm.* 1. An ancient gold coin of the reign of king Ferdinand. 2. (Among Apothecaries) A weight of four scruples or ninety-six grains of a pound troy.

Aúreo, rea, *a.* Golden, gilt. *Aúreo número*, Golden number, the lunar cycle, or cycle of the moon, comprehending nineteen solar years and seven intercalary months.

Auréola, *sf.* Glory, a circle of rays which surrounds the heads of images or of saints in pictures.

Auricálco, *sm.* Aurichalcum, formerly a mixture of gold and silver; brass.

Aurícula, *sf.* 1. Auricle, one of the two appendages of the heart, or of the two muscular caps which cover the two ventricles thereof. 2. (Bot.) The bear's-ear.

Auriculár, *a.* Within the sense or reach of hearing. *Testigo auricular*, An auricular witness.

Aurífero, ra, *a.* (Poét.) Auriferous, containing or producing gold.

Auríga, *sm.* 1. (Poét.) A coachman. 2. (Astr.) Wagoner, one of the Northern constellations.

Auróra, *sf.* 1. The first dawn of day. 2. (Poét.) The origin or first appearance of a thing. 3. A beverage made up of the milk of almonds and cinnamon water. 4. (Naút.) The morning watch-gun. 5. *Aurora boreal*, A luminous meteor seen in the northern latitudes. *Color de aurora*, A colour made up of white, red, and blue.

Aurragádo, da, *a.* Badly tilled and cultivated; applied to land.

Aurúspice. V. *Arúspice.*

Auséncia, *sf.* 1. Absence, the state of being absent. 2. The time of being absent. *Servir ausencias y enfermedades*, To perform the functions of absent or sick persons. *Tener alguno buenas ó malas ausencias*, To be ill or well spoken of in one's absence.

Ausentárse, *vr.* To absent one's self from a person or place.

Ausénte, *a.* Absent, distant from a person or place.

Auspício, *sm.* 1. Auspice, or presage drawn from birds. 2. (Met.) Prediction of future events. 3. Protection, favour, patronage.

Austeraménte, *ad.* Austerely.

Austeridád, *sf.* Austerity, severity, rigour.

Austéro, ra, *a.* Austere, severe, rigorous.

Austrál y Austríno, na, *a.* Austral, southern.

Aústro, *sm.* South wind.

Aután, *ad.* (Ant.) V. *Tanto. Beber de autan*, To drink as often as invited.

Auténtica, *sf.* 1. A certificate. 2. (Ant.) An attested copy.

Autenticádo, da, *pp.* Authenticated, attested.

Autenticación, *sf.* The act of rendering authentic or genuine.

Auténticamente, *ad.* Authentically, in an authentic manner.

Autenticár, *va.* To attest, to legalize, to render authentic.

Autenticidád, *sf.* Authenticity, genuineness.

Auténtico, ca, *a.* Authentic, genuine.

Autíllo, *sm.* (Dim.) 1. A particular act or decree of the Inquisition, distinguished from a general sentence. 2. (Orn.) A bird, belonging to the family of owls. Strix aluco *L.*

Autívo, va, *a.* (Ant.) V. *Activo.*

Aúto, *sm.* 1. A judicial decree or sentence. 2. A writ, warrant. 3. An edict, ordinance. *Auto de fe*, A sentence given by the Inquisition, and read and published to a criminal on a public scaffold. 4. (Ant.) Act, action. *Auto definitivo*, Definitive act, which has the force of a sentence. *Auto sacramental*, An allegorical or dramatical piece of poetry on some religious subject represented as a play. *Aútos*, The pleadings and proceedings in a law-suit. *Estar en los autos*, To know a thing profoundly.

Autógene, *sm.* (Bot.) Daffodil.

Autógrafo, *sm.* Autograph, first copy, archetype.

Autómato, *sm.* Automaton, a machine which has the power of motion within itself.

Autór, ra, *s.* 1. Author, the first cause or inventor of a thing. 2. One that composes a literary work. 3. Manager of a theatre. 4. (For.) Plaintiff or claimant.

Autoría, *sf.* The employment of a manager of a theatre.

Autoridád, *sf.* 1. Authority or power derived from a public station, merit, or birth. 2. Ostentation, pompous display of grandeur. 3. Words cited from a book or writing, in support of what has been said or asserted.

Autoritativaménte, *ad.* In an authoritative manner, with due authority.

Autoritatívo, va, *a.* Arrogant, assuming an improper or undue authority.

Autorizáble, *a.* That which can be authorised.

Autorización, *sf.* Authorisation, the act of authorising.

Autorizadaménte, *ad.* In an authoritative manner.

Autorizádo, da, *a.* Respectable, commendable.

Autorizádo, da, *pp.* Authorised.
Autorizadór, *sm.* He who authorises.
Autorizamiénto, *sm.* V. *Autorizacion.*
Autorizár, *va* 1. To authorise, to give power or authority to do something. 2. To attest, to legalise. 3. To prove an assertion by passages extracted from the work of an author. 4. To exalt the lustre and merit of a thing.
Autumnál, *a.* (Rar.) Autumnal, belonging to autumn.
Auxiliadór, ra, *s.* Auxiliary, helper, assistant.
Auxiliár, *va.* 1. To aid, to help, to assist. 2. To attend a dying person.
Auxiliár, *a.* Auxiliar, helping, assistant *Tropas auxiliares*, Auxiliary troops.
Auxiliatório, ria, *a.* (For.) Auxiliary.
Auxilio, *sm.* Aid, help, assistance.
A'va-Áva, *sf.* (Bot.) A plant so called by the inhabitants of Otaheite, from the leaves of which they extract an intoxicating liquor.
Avacádo, da, *a.* Cow-like, resembling a cow; applied to a horse big-bellied, and of little spirit.
Avadárse, *vr.* 1. To become fordable; applied to rivers. 2. (Met.) To subside; applied to passion.
Avahár, *va.* 1. To warm with the breath, or with steam and vapour. 2. To wither; applied to plants.
Avalár, *vn.* (Gal.) To shake, to tremble; applied to the ground or earth.
Avalentádo, da, *a.* Bragging, vainly boasting, puffing.
Avaliár y Avaluár, *va.* (Ant.) V. *Valuar.*
Avalío, *sm.* (Ant.) Valuation, estimation.
Avallár, *va.* To enclose a piece of ground with pales or hedges.
Avállo, *sm.* 1. A slight shock. 2. An earthquake.
Avalorár, *va.* 1. To estimate, to value. 2. (Met.) To inspirit, to animate.
Avalóte, *sm.* Commotion, insurrection.
Avaluación, *sf.* Valuation, rate, assessment.
Avambrázo, *sm.* Piece of ancient armour that served to cover the arm from the elbow to the wrist.
Avampiés, *sm.* (Ant.) Instep of boots, or spatterdashes.
Avánce, *sm.* 1. (Mil.) Advance, attack, assault. 2. (Among Merchants) An account of goods received and sold. 3. A balance in one's favour.
Avandícho y Avantdícho. (Ant.) V. *Sobredicho.*
Avanguárda y Avanguárdia, *sf.* (Mil.) V. *Vanguardia.*
Avantál, *sm.* Apron.
Avantalíllo, *sm.* A small apron.
Avánte, *ad.* 1. (Naút.) A-head. *Hala avante*, Pull a-head. 2. V. *Adelante.*
Avantrén, *sm.* Limbers of a gun-carriage.
Avanzádo, da, *a.* Advanced. *Avanzado de edad, ó de edad avanzada*, Advanced in years, stricken in years.
Avanzár, *vn* 1. To advance, to attack, to engage. 2. To have a balance in one's favour. —*va.* To advance, to push forward.
Avánzo, *sm.* 1. (Among Merchants) An account of goods received and sold. 2. A balance in one's favour.
Aváos, *ad.* (Vulg.) Clear the way, out of the way.

Avaraménte, *ad.* Avariciously, in a covetous manner.
Avareár, (Ant.) V. *Varear.*
Avarícia, *sf.* Avarice, cupidity, covetousness.
Avariciár, *va.* y *n.* (Ant.) To covet, to desire anxiously.
Avarienteménte, *ad.* Greedily, covetously.
Avarientéz, *sf.* (Ant.) V. *Avaricia.*
Avariénto, ta, *a.* Avaricious, covetous.
Aváro, ra, *a.* Avaricious, covetous.
Avarráz, V. *Albarraz.*
Avasallár, *va.* To subdue, to subject.—*vr.* To become subject, to become a vassal.
A've, *sf.* 1. Bird, a general name for the feathered kind. 2. Fowl. *Ave de rapiña*, A bird of prey. *Ave brava ó silvestre*, A wild bird. *Ave fria*, A kind of wild pigeon: (Met.) An insipid spiritless person; usually applied to women. *Todas las aves con sus pares*, (Prov.) Birds of a feather flock together. *Es un ave*, He is as light as a feather. *Ave nocturna*, (Met.) One who rambles about in the night-time.
Avechúcho, *sm.* 1. (Orn.) Sparrow-hawk. Falco nisus *L.* 2. (Met.) Ragamuffin, a paltry fellow, despicable in his mean appearance, as well as in his sentiments.
Avecíca, Avecílla, y Avecíta, *sf.* A small bird.
Avecinár, *va.* To bring near. V *Avecindar.*—*vr.* To come near, to approach.
Avecindamiénto, *sm.* 1. Acquisition of the rights of a denizen or freeman. 2. The act of residing in a place, invested with the rights of a denizen.
Avecindár, *va.* To admit to the privileges of a denizen, to enrol in the number of the citizens of a place.—*vr.* 1. To acquire the rights and privileges of a denizen or citizen. 2. To approach, to join.
Avejentádo, da, *a.* Appearing old, without being really so.
Avejentár, *vn.* y *r.* To look old, to appear older than one really is from sickness, grief, hard labour, &c.
Avelár, *vn.* (Naút.) To set sail.
Avelenár, (Ant.) V. *Envenenar.*
Avellána, *sf.* Filbert, the fruit of a species of the hazel or nut-tree. *Avellana I'ndica, ó de la India ó nuez ungüentaria*, Myrobalan, or Indian nut, at present only used in perfumes.
Avellanádo, da, *a.* Of the colour of nuts.
Avellanár, *sm.* A plantation of hazels or nut-trees.
Avellanárse, *vr.* To shrivel, to grow as dry as a nut.
Avellanéra, *sf.* V. *Avellano.*
Avellanéro, ra, *s.* A dealer in nuts and filberts.
Avellaníca, *sf.* A small nut.
Avellàno, *sm.* (Bot.) A hazel or nut-tree. Corylus avellana *L.*
Ave María, *sf.* Ave Mary, the angel's salutation of the Holy Virgin. *Al ave Maria*, At the fall of night. *En un ave Maria*, In an instant.
Avéna, *sf.* (Bot.) 1. Oats. Avena *L.* 2. (Poét.) A pastoral pipe, made of the stalks of corn, and used by shepherds.
Avenádo, da, *a.* 1. Belonging or relating to oats. 2. Lunatic, liable to fits of madness with lucid intervals.
Avenál, *sm.* A field sown with oats.

Avenamiénto, *sm.* The act of draining or drawing off water.

Avenár, *va.* To drain or draw off water.

Avenáte, *sm.* Water-gruel, oatmeal and water boiled together.

Avenenár, *va.* To poison. V. *Envenenar.*

Avenéncia, *sf.* 1. Agreement, compact, bargain. 2. Conformity, union, concord. *Mas vale mala avenencia, que buena sentencia,* (Prov.) A bad composition is better than a good lawsuit.

Avenentéza ó Aveninténza, *sf.* (Ant.) Occasion, opportunity.

Avenáceo, cea, *a.* Oaten, belonging to, or made of oats.

Avenida, *sf.* 1. A sudden impetuous overflow of a river or brook. 2. (Met.) A conflux or concurrence of several things. 3. (Arag.) Agreement, concord. *Avenidas,* Avenues or roads meeting in a certain place.

Avenido, da, *a.* Agreed. *Bien ó mal avenidos,* Living on good or bad terms.

Avenidór, ra, *s.* (Ant.) Mediator, one that interferes between two parties to reconcile them.

Avenír, *va.* To reconcile parties at variance, to accommodate matters in dispute.—*vr.* 1. To settle differences on friendly terms, to get reconciled. 2. To join, to unite.

Aventadéro, *sm.* (Ant.) A winnowing place.

Aventádo, da, *a.* *Escotas aventadas,* Flowing sheets.

Aventadór, *sm.* 1. Winnower, one who separates chaff from grain by means of the wind. 2. A wooden fork with three or four prongs, used for winnowing the corn, by throwing the straw and chaff in the air. 3. A fan or kind of round mat, used by poor people for blowing the fire; it also serves in the room of a dust-pan, to carry out the sweepings of houses.

Aventadúra, *sf.* Wind-gall, a disease in horses, *Aventadura de estopa,* (Naút.) A leak.

Aventája, *sf.* 1. Advantage, profit. 2. (For. Arag.) Part of the personal estate or chattels of a person deceased, which his or her surviving consort takes before a division of the furniture is made.

Aventajadaménte, *ad.* Advantageously, conveniently, opportunely.

Aventajádo, da, *a.* 1. Advantageous, profitable, convenient. 2. Beautiful, excellent. 3. Having additional pay; applied to common soldiers.

Aventajár, *va.* 1. To acquire or enjoy advantages. 2. To meliorate, to improve. 3. To surpass, to excel.

Aventár, *va.* 1. To move or agitate the air, to blow. 2. To toss or throw something in the wind, such as corn, to winnow it. 3. To expel, to drive away. 4. (Naút.) To work out the oakum: spoken of a ship.—*vr.* 1. To be filled with wind, to be inflated or puffed up. 2. To escape, to run away. 3. (Extrem.) To be tainted; applied to meat.

Aventário, *sm.* (Alb.) Nostril of an animal through which the air passes.

Aventúra, *sf.* 1. Adventure, event, incident. 2. Casualty, contingency, chance. 3. (Ant.) Hazard, risk. 4. Duty formerly paid to lords of the manor.

Aventúra, *ad.* Peradventure.

Aventurádo, da, *pp.* Risked.

Aventurádo, da, *a.* *Bien ó mal aventurado,* Fortunate or unfortunate.

Aventurár, *va.* To venture, to hazard, to risk, to endanger.

Aventuréro, *sm.* Adventurer, a knight-errant.

Aventuréro, ra, *a.* 1. Voluntary; undisciplined; applied to recruits and soldiers. 2. Adventurer; applied to a person who voluntarily goes to market to sell any articles. 3. V. *Advenedizo.*

Avér, V. *Habér.*

Averámia, *sf.* A kind of duck.

Averár, *va.* (Ant.) To aver, certify, or affirm.

Averdugádo, da, *a.* Having many pimples or scars in the face.

Avergonzár y Avergoñar, *va.* To abash, to make ashamed, to put to the blush.

Avería, *sf.* 1. Damage sustained by goods or merchandise; detriment received by ships and their cargoes. *Avería gruesa,* General average. *Avería particular,* Particular average. *Avería ordinaria,* Usual average. 2. (In the Indian Trade) A certain duty laid on merchants and merchandise. 3. A collection of birds; an aviary.

Averiádo, da, *a.* Averaged, damaged.

Averiárse, *vr.* To make average, to sustain damage.

Averiguáble, *a.* Investigable, what may be verified or ascertained.

Averiguación, *sf.* Investigation, the act of searching or finding out the truth. *Averiguacion judicial,* A judicial inquiry, an inquest.

Averiguadaménte, *ad.* Certainly, surely.

Averiguadór, ra, *s.* A searcher or examiner, one who investigates.

Averiguamiénto, *sm.* (Ant.) V. *Averiguacion.*

Averiguár, *va.* To inquire, to investigate, to search out. *Averiguárse con alguno,* To bring one to reason. *Averíguelo várgas,* It is difficult to investigate.

Averío, *sm.* 1. Beast of burthen. 2. Flock of birds

Avérno, *sm.* (Poét. Mit.) Hell.

Aversár, *va.* (Ant.) To manifest aversion; to be repugnant.

Aversión, *sf.* 1. Aversion, opposition, repugnance, dislike. 2. Fear, apprehension.

Avérso, sa, *a.* Averse, hostile; perverse.

Avertír, (Ant.) V. *Apartar.*

Avés, *ad.* V. *Apénas.*

Avestrúz, *sm.* (Orn.) Ostrich. Struthio *L.*

Avezár, *va.* (Ant.) V. *Acostumbrar.*

Aviádo, *sm.* (New Spain) One supplied with money, and other articles, to work a silver-mine.

Aviadór, *sm.* 1. He who supplies others with money and other articles to work some silver-mines. 2. He who provides provisions and other things for a journey. 3. (Naut.) The smallest auger, used by calkers.

Aviár, *va.* 1. To provide provisions and other articles for a journey. 2. To hasten the execution of a thing.

Aviciár, *va.* 1. (Ant.) To render vicious. 2. To give a luxuriant bloom and verdure to plants and trees

A'vido, da, *a.* (Poét.) Greedy, covetous.
Avieĵarse, *vr.* To grow old. V. *Avejentarse.*
Aviénto, *sm.* A fork with two or three prongs, used for separating the straw from the grain. V. *Bieldo.*
Aviesamente, *ad.* Sinistrously, perversely.
Aviésas, *ad.* (Ant.) Adverse, contrary, perversely.
Aviéso, sa, *a.* 1. Fortuitous, irregular, out of the way. 2. (Met.) Mischievous, perverse.
Avigorár, *va.* To invigorate, to animate or inspire with vigour and spirit.
Avilantéz y Avilantéza, *sf.* Forwardness, boldness, audaciousness.
Avillanádo, da, *a.* Having the manners of a peasant, clownish, mean.
Avillanárse, *vr.* To grow mean or abject, to degenerate.
Avillár, *va.* (Ant.) V. *Envilecer.*
Avinagrádo, da, *pp.* 1. Soured. 2. (Met.) Harsh of temper, crabbed, peevish.
Avinagrár, *va.* To sour, to make acid.
Aviñónes, sa, *a.* y *s.* Native of, or made at, Avignon.
Avío, *sm.* 1. Preparation, provision. 2. (In South America) Money and other articles advanced for working silver-mines.
Avión, *sm.* (Orn.) Martin, martinet, martlet, or window-swallow. Hirundo urbica *L.*
Avirádo, da, *a.* (Ant.) V. *Convenido.*
Avisación, *sf.* (Ant.) V. *Aviso.*
Avisadaménte, *ad.* Prudently.
Avisádo, da, *a.* 1. Prudent, cautious. 2. Expert, sagacious, skilful. *Mal avisado*, Ill advised, injudicious.
Avisadór, *sm.* Adviser, admonisher.
Avisár, *va.* 1. To inform, to give notice. 2. To advise, to counsel, to admonish.
Avíso, *sm.* 1. Information, intelligence. 2. Prudence, care, attention. *Estar ó andar sobre aviso*, To be on one's guard. 3. (Naút.) Advice-boat, a light vessel sent with despatches from one place to another.
Avíspa, *sf.* Wasp, a stinging insect. Vespa *L.*
Avispádo, da, *pp.* Stung, pricked.—*a.* Lively, brisk, vigorous, vivacious.
Avispár, *va.* 1. To spur, to drive with the spur, to urge forward with the spur and whip. 2. To investigate, to observe closely.—*vr.* To fret, to be peevish.
Avispéro, *sm.* 1. Nest made by wasps. 2. Comb or cavities in which the wasps lodge their eggs.
Avispón, *sm.* A large wasp.
Avistár, *va.* To descry at a distance, to see far off.—*vr.* To have an interview or meeting to transact some business.
Avitár, *va.* (Naút.) To bit the cable.
Avitónes, *sm. pl.* (Naút.) V. *Abitones.*
Avituallár, *va.* (Mil.) To victual, to supply with victuals or provisions.
Avivadaménte, *ad.* In a lively manner, briskly.
Avivadór, ra, *s.* 1. One that enlivens or inspirits. 2. A plane, with which timber work is fluted. 3. (Mur.) Paper full of pin-holes, which is laid over the eggs of silk-worms, that the young worms or larvæ may creep through it.
Avivár, *va.* 1. To quicken, to enliven, to encourage. *Avivar el paso*, To hasten on step. 2. To heat, to inflame. 3. To viv the eggs of silk-worms. 4. To heighten t brightness of colours.—*vn.* To revive, cheer up, to grow gay or gladsome. *Aviv el ojo*, To be watchful.
Avizorár, *va.* To watch with care and atte tion, to spy, to search narrowly.
A'vo, *sm.* One of the parts into which a fra tion is subdivided.
Avocación y Avocamiénto, *s.* (For.) Avoc tion, business; the act of calling aside.
Avocár, *va.* 1. (For.) To remove a lawsu from an inferior to a superior court. 2. *Av car la artillería*, To point the ordnanc *Avocarse con alguno*, To be agreed, to be the same mind or opinion. V. *Abocar.*
Avol, *a.* (Ant.) V. *Vil.*
Avucásta, *sf.* Widgeon, a kind of wild duc Anas penelope *L.*
Avucástro, *sm.* (Ant.) Troubler or import nate person.
Avutárda, *sf.* Bustard, a wild turkey. Ot tarda *L.*
Avutardádo, da, *a.* Bustardlike.
Ax, *interj.* V. *Ay.*—*sm.* V. *Axe*
Axada, (Ant.) V. *Azada.*
Axamar, (Ant.) V. *Llamar.*
Axanar, (Ant.) V. *Allanar.*
Axaquéfa, *sf.* (Ant.) Cave, cellar.
Axár, (Ant.) V. *Hallar.*
Axaráfe, *sm.* (Ant.) Olive plantation.
A'xe, *sm.* An habitual complaint.
Axéa, *sf.* A sort of brush-wood, used for firin in the environs of Toledo.
Axébe, (Ant.) V. *Alumbre.*
Axedréa, *sf.* (Bot.) Winter-savory. Saturo hortensis *L.*
Axedréz, *sm.* 1. Chess, a game. 2. (Naút Netting.
Axedrezádo, da, *a.* Chequered, diversified l alternate colours, like a chess-board.
Axenábe, *sm.* (Bot.) Wild or hedge mustard
Axénjo, *sm.* (Bot.) Wormwood.
Axenúz, *sm.* (Bot.) The fennel flower. Nigel arvensis *L.*
Axí, *sm.* (Bot.) The red Indian dwarf pepper
Aximéz, *sm.* (Andal.) An arched window wi a pillar or mullion in the centre to suppo it.
Axióma, *sm.* Axiom, a proposition evident first sight.
Axórcas, *sf. pl.* Gold or silver rings, worn l Moorish women about the wrists or ankles
Axuár, *sm.* 1. Articles of dress and furnitu which a bride brings with her at the time marriage. 2. Household furniture.
Axufáyna, *sf.* (Ant.) A basin or deep dish.
Ay! *interj.* An exclamation of pain or gri *Ay de mi!* Alas, poor me!
Ayánque, *sm.* (Naút.) The main haliard.
Ayéno, na, *a.* (Ant.) V. *Ageno.*
Ayér, *ad.* 1. Yesterday. 2. Lately, not lo ago. *De ayer acá*, From yesterday to th present moment.
Aymé, *int.* (Ant.) V. *Ay de mi.*
A'yo, ya, *s.* Tutor or governess, a person wl has the care of the education of children.
Ayontár, (Ant.) V. *Juntar.*

Ayrázo, *sm.* Blast, a violent gust of wind.

A'yre, *sm.* 1. Air, the element which encompasses the terraqueous globe. 2. Wind. 3. Briskness of the motion of a horse. 4. (Met.) Gracefulness of manners and gait. *Esto no es del ayre de vm*, That is not in your manner. 5. Aspect, countenance, figure of the face. 6. Musical composition. *Ayres naturales*, The native air; (Met.) Mien of the inhabitants of a country. *Beber los ayres y los vientos*, To desire anxiously. *Creerse del ayre*, To be apt to believe, to be credulous. *Hablar al ayre*, To talk idly. *Que ayres traen á vm. por aca?* What good wind brings you here? *Tomar el ayre*, To take a walk. *De ayre, ad.* In a pleasing manner. *De buen ó mal ayre*, In a pleasing or peevish manner. *En el ayre*, In an expeditious manner.

Ayreárse, *vr.* 1. To take the air, to expose one's self to the air. 2. To cool one's self, to obstruct perspiration.

Ayrecíco, llo, y to, *sm.* (Dim.) A gentle breeze.

Ayrón, *sm.* (Aum.) 1. Violent gale. 2. Ornament of plumes. 3. (Orn.) The crested crane.

Ayrosaménte, *ad.* Gracefully.

Ayrosidád, *sf.* Graceful deportment, elegant mien.

Ayróso, sa, *a.* 1. Airy, exposed to the wind; windy. 2. Graceful, genteel. 3. Successful.

Ayúda, *sf.* 1. Help, aid, assistance. *Ayúda de parroquia*, Chapel of ease. 2. An injection, a clyster. 3. Syringe with which clysters are injected. *Ayuda de costa*, A gratification paid over and above the salary.—*sm.* Deputy or assistant of one of the high officers at court. *Ayuda de cámara*, A valet de chambre. *Ayuda de cámara del rey*, Groom of the bed-chamber. *Dios y ayuda*, This cannot be done but with the assistance of God. *Ayuda de oratorio*, Clergyman in an oratory who performs the office of sacristan. *Ayuda de cocinero*, (Naút.) The cook's shifter. *Ayuda de dispensero*, (Naút.) The steward's mate. *Ayuda de virador*, (Naút.) A false preventer.

Ayudadór, ra, *s.* Assistant, helper; one who assists the chief shepherd or herdsman.

Ayudánte, *sm.* 1. (Mil.) Adjutant, aid-de-camp. 2. *Ayudante de cirujano*, A surgeon's mate.

Ayudár, *va.* To aid, to help, to favour. *Ayudar á misa*, To serve the priest at mass.—*vr.* To adopt the most proper measures for obtaining success.

Ayunadór, ra, *s.* One who fasts.

Ayunár, *va.* To fast, to abstain from food; to keep the canonical fast. *Ayunar al traspaso*, To fast from holy Thursday to the next following Saturday after ringing the *gloria*. *Ayunar despues de harto*, To fast after a good repast.

Ayúnas (En), *ad.* 1. Fasting, without eating. 2. Without knowledge. *Quedar en ayunas*, To be ignorant of an affair, to know nothing of the matter.

Ayúno, *sm.* Fast, abstinence from food.

Ayúno, na, *a.* 1. Fasting, abstaining from food. *Estoy ayuno*, I have not yet broken my fast. 2. Abstaining from certain pleasures. 3. Ignorant of a subject or topic of conversation. *En ayuno*, (Ant.) V. *En ayunas*.

Ayúnque, *sm.* Anvil. V. *Yunque*.

Ayuntadór, ra, *s.* One who unites, joins, or assembles.

Ayuntamiénto, *sm.* 1. Union, junction. 2. (Ant.) Carnal copulation. 3. Body of magistrates of cities and towns, composed in Spain of a *Corregidor* or *Alcalde*, and *Regidores*; the first corresponding to Mayors, and the latter to Aldermen in England. *Casa de ayuntamiento*, Town-house, Guildhall, senate-house.

Ayuntár, *va.* (Ant.) V. *Juntar y Añadir*.

Ayúnto, *sm.* (Ant.) V. *Junta*.

Ayúso, *ad.* (Ant.) V. *Abaxo*.

Ayustár, *va.* (Naút.) To bend two ends of a cable or rope. *Ayustar con costura*, To bend with a splice. *Ayustar con gorupo*, To bend with a knot and seizing.

Ayúste, *sm.* (Naút.) Bending or splicing whereby two ends of a rope or cable are joined.

A'z, *sm.* V. *Haz*.

A'za, *sf.* V. *Haza*.

Azabachádo, da, *a.* Jetty, black as jet, or of the colour of jet.

Azabáche, *sm.* (Min.) Jet, a black shining fossil. Succinum nigrum *L.* *Azabáches*, Trinkets made of jet.

Azábara, *sf.* (Bot.) The Barbadoes aloe. Aloe perfoliata *L.*

Azábra, *sf.* A small coasting vessel in the Cantabrian Seas.

Azacán, *sm.* 1. (Ant.) Water-carrier. 2. V *Odre*.

Azacáya, *sf.* Conduit of water, a water-pipe.

Azáche, *a.* Of an inferior quality; applied to silk.

Azáda, *sf.* (Agr.) Spade.

Azadáda, *sf.* Blow with a spade.

Azadíca y Azadílla, *sf.* A small spade.

Azadón, *sm.* Pick-axe, mattock. *Azadon de peto*, Handspike or lever armed with a kind of chissel to introduce it between roots or stones.

Azadonáda, *sf.* Blow or stroke with a pick-axe. *A' tres azadonadas sacar agua*, (Met.) To obtain easily the object of one's wishes.

Azadonár, *va.* To dig or break up the ground with a spade or pick-axe.

Azadonázo, *sm.* Stroke with a mattock.

Azadoncíllo, *sm.* A small pick-axe.

Azadonéro, *sm.* 1. Digger, one that opens the ground with a spade. 2. (Mil.) Pioneer.

Azafáta, *sf.* Lady of the queen's wardrobe.

Azafáte, *sm.* A low, flat-bottomed basket.

Azafrán, *sm.* (Bot.) Saffron. Crocus *L.* *Azafran bastardo y azafran romí ó romin*, (Bot.) Bastard saffron, dyers' safflower. Carthamus tinctorius *L.* *Azafran del timon*, (Naút.) After-piece of the rudder. *Azafran del tajamar*, (Naút.) Fore-piece of the cut-water. *Azafran de Venus*, (Quim.) Crocus martis, the calx or oxyd of metals of a saffron colour.

Azafranádo, da, *pp.* Saffron-like, of the colour of saffron.

Azafranál, *sm.* A plantation of saffron.

Azafranár, *va.* To tinge or dye with saffron, to impregnate with saffron.

Azafranéro, *sm.* Dealer in saffron.

Azagadór, *sm.* The path for cattle.

Azagáya, *sf.* Javelin, a spear or half pike formerly used both by foot and horse

Azagayáda, *sf.* Cast of a javelin.
Azaguán, *sm.* (Ant.) V. *Zaguan.*
Azahár, *sm.* Orange or lemon flower. *Agua de azahar*, Orange-flower water. *Azahar brabo*, Narrow-leaved blue lupine. Lupinus angustifolius *L.*
Azaléja, *sf.* (Ant.) Towel.
Azalón, *sm.* (Orn.) A small bird, an enemy to the crow and fox.
Azambóa, *sf.* (Bot.) V. *Zamboa.*
Azambóo, *sm.* (Bot.) The zamboa-tree, a kind of quince-tree.
Azanória, *sf.* (Bot.) Carrot. V. *Zanahoria.*
Azanoriáte, *sm.* 1. Preserved carrots. 2. (Met. Arag.) Fulsome, affected compliments.
Azáña, **Azañería**, V. *Hazaña, Hazañeria, &c.*
Azár, *sm.* 1. Unforeseen disaster, an unexpected accident. 2. Unfortunate card or throw at dice. 3. Obstruction, obstacle, impediment. *Tener azar con alguna cosa*, To have an antipathy against a thing.
Azárbe, *sm.* (Mur.) Trench or drain which carries off the overplus of irrigation-waters.
Azarcón, *sm.* 1. Bluish ashes or earth made of calcined lead. 2. A high orange colour. 3. Earthen pot or boiler.
Azaría, *sf.* A kind of coral.
Azárja, *sf.* Instrument for winding raw silk.
Azarnéfe, *sm.* (Ant.) Orpiment. V. *Oropimente.*
Azarosaménte, *ad.* Unfortunately.
Azaróso, **sa**, *a.* Unlucky, unfortunate.
Azaróte, *sm.* Styptic, glue for closing wounds.
Azáya, *sf.* Instrument used for reeling silk.
Azaynadaménte, *ad.* Perfidiously, viciously; applied to horses.
Azcón y Azcona, *sm.* y *f.* (Ant.) A dart.
Azconílla, *sf.* A small dart.
Azemár, *va.* (Ant.) To instruct, to adorn.
A'zimo, **ma**, *a.* Unleavened.
Azimút, *sm.* (Astr.) Azimuth, the assumed vertical circle which passes through the centre of a planet.
Azimutál, *a.* Relating to the azimuth.
Aznácho, *sm.* (Bot.) Tree resembling a pine.
Azóe, *sm.* (Quim.) Azot, or nitrogen.
Azófar, *sm.* Latten. V. *Laton.*
Azofáyfa, *sf.* V. *Azufayfa.*
Azogadaménte, *ad.* In a quick and restless manner.
Azogamiénto, *sm.* 1. The act of overlaying something with quicksilver. 2. The act of slaking lime. 3. State of restlessness and agitation.
Azogár, *va.* To overlay with quicksilver. *Azogar la cal*, To slake lime.—*vr.* 1. To undergo a salivation. 2. To be in a state of agitation, to be at a loss how to act.
Azógue, *sm.* 1. (Min.) Quicksilver. Hydrargyrum *L.* *Es un azogue*, He is as restless as quicksilver. *Azogues*, Quicksilver ships, the ships which carry the quicksilver from Spain to South America. 2. A market-place.
Azoguéjo, *sm.* A small market-place.
Azoguería, *sf.* (New Spain) The place where quicksilver is incorporated with metals.
Azoguéro, *sm.* 1. Dealer in quicksilver. 2. (New Spain) A workman who incorporates quicksilver, salt, and other materials, with pounded silver ore, to extract the silver.
Azolár, *va.* To model timber with an adz, to cut away the superfluous parts.
Azolvár, *va.* (Ant.) To stop or obstruct water conduits.
Azomár, *va.* (Ant.) To incite or stimulate animals to fight.
Azór, *sm.* (Orn.) Goshawk. Falco palumbarius *L.*
Azorádo, *a.* *Navio azorado*, A ship which sails heavy on account of her cargo being ill stowed.
Azoráfa, *sf.* (Ant.) V. *Girafa.*
Azoramiénto, *sm.* Trepidation, the act of trembling with fear.
Azorár, *va.* 1. To frighten, to terrify, to confound; applied to birds which are pursued by the goshawk. 2. To incite, to irritate.
Azorramiénto, *sm.* Great heaviness of the head.
Azorrárse, *vr.* To be dull or drowsy from a great heaviness of the head.
Azotacálles, *sm. pl.* Street-loungers, idlers who are constantly walking the streets.
Azotádo, *sm.* 1. A criminal who is publicly whipped. 2. He who lashes himself by way of mortification.
Azotadór, **ra**, *s.* Whipper, one who inflicts lashes with a whip.
Azotár, *va.* 1. To whip, to lash. 2. *Azotar las calles*, To lounge about the streets. 3. (Met.) *Azotar el ayre*, To beat the air, to act to no purpose. 4. (Naút.) *Azotar con paleta*, To inflict the punishment called *cobbing* on board English ships, which consists in being struck on the breech with a *cobbing-board*. 5. (Naút.) *Azotar la ampolleta*, To flog the glass, when the steersman turns it before the sand has entirely run out.
Azotáyna ó Azotína, *sf.* (Joc.) A drubbing, a sound flogging.
Azotázo, *sm.* A severe lash or blow on the breech.
Azóte, *sm.* 1. Whip, an instrument of correction with which lashes are inflicted. 2. Lash given with a whip. 3. (Met.) Calamity, affliction. *Pena de azotes*, A public whipping inflicted by the hangman. *Mano de azotes, ó vuelta de azotes*, The number of lashes which a delinquent or criminal is to receive.
Azotéa, *sf.* The flat roof of a house, a platform.
Azre, *sm.* (Bot.) Maple-tree.
Azúa, *sf.* Beverage prepared by the Indians with the flour of Indian corn.
Azúcar, *sm.* Sugar, a sweet juice extracted from the sugar-cane. *Azúcar de pilon*, Loaf-sugar. *Azúcar de lustre*, Double loaves, fine powdered sugar. *Azúcar mascabado*, Single loaves. *Azúcar negro*, Coarse brown sugar. *Azúcar piedra ó cande*, Sugar-candy. *Azúcar terciado ó pardo*, Clayed sugar. *Azúcar de plomo*, Calcined sugar of lead. *Azúcar y canela*, Sorrel-grey; a colour peculiar to horses.
Azucarádo, **da**, *a.* 1. Sugared. 2. Sugary, having the taste of sugar. 3. (Met.) Affable, pleasing. *Palabras azucaradas*, Soothing, artful words.
Azucarádo, *sm.* A kind of paint for ladies.
Azucarár, *va.* To sugar, to sweeten; to soften.
Azucaréro, *sm.* 1. Sugar-dish, sugar-basin. 2. Confectioner.

AZUCARILLO, *sm.* Sweetmeat of flour, sugar, and rose-water.

AZUCÉNA, *sf.* (Bot.) White lily. Lilium candidum *L.* *Azucenas*, the military order of the lily, founded by king Ferdinand of Aragon.

AZÚD, *sf.* A dam with a sluice or flood-gate, by which water is conveyed into the canals for irrigating lands.

AZÚDA, *sf.* Persian wheel, consisting of earthen pitchers fixed along the sides of a wheel, each of which is filled and emptied by a revolution; these machines are constructed near rivers or wells to raise water for irrigation.

AZUÉLA, *sf.* Addice, a carpenter's tool used in trimming a piece of timber. *Azuela de construccion*, A ship-wright's adze. *Azuela curva*, A hollow adze.

AZUFAÝFA, *sf.* Jujub or jujubes, the fruit of the jujub-tree. Rhamnus zizyphus *L.*

AZUFÁYFO Y AZUFÉYFO, *sm.* Jujub or jujube-tree.

AZUFRÁDO, DA, *pp.* y *a.* 1. Whitened or fumigated with sulphur. 2. Sulphureous, containing sulphur.

AZUFRADÓR, *sm.* A small stove for bleaching wool with the fumes or smoke of sulphur.

AZUFRÁR, *va.* To bleach, to fumigate with sulphur.

AZÚFRE, *sm.* Sulphur, brimstone. *Azúfre vivo*, Native sulphur.

AZUFRÓSO, SA, *a.* Sulphureous, containing sulphur.

AZÚL, *a.* Blue. *Azul celeste*, Sky blue. *Azul obscuro*, Dark blue. *Azul de Prusia*, Berlin or Prussian blue. *Azul subido*, Bright blue. *Azul Turqui ó Turquesado*, Turkish or deep blue. *Azul verdemar ó de costras*, Sea-blue, resembling sea green. *Darse un verde con dos azules*, To be highly entertained with a very pleasing amusement.

AZÚL, *sm.* Lapis lazuli; a mineral.

AZULÁQUE, *sm.* V. *Zulaque*.

AZULÁR, *va.* To dye or colour blue.

AZULÉA, *sf.* Bluishness.

AZULEÁR, *vn.* To have a bluish cast.

AZULEJÁDO, DA, *a.* (Ant.) Covered with bluish tiles.

AZULÉJO, *sm.* 1. Dutch glazed tile painted with various colours. 2. (Bot.) Blue bottle, corn-flower. Centaurea cyanus *L.*

AZULÍNO, NA, *a.* Of an azure colour, inclining to azure.

AZUMÁR, *va.* To dye the hair.

AZÚMBAR, *sm.* (Ant.) V. *Alisma*.

AZUMBRÁDO, DA, *a.* Measured by *azumbres*.

AZÚMBRE, *sf.* Measure of liquids which makes the eighth part of an *arobe*, and about half a gallon English measure.

AZUQUÉRO, *sm.* (And.) V. *Azucarero*.

AZÚR, *a.* Azure, the blue colour in coats of arms.

AZÚT, *sf.* Dam raised across a river to change its course.

AZUTÉA, *sf.* Terrace. V. *Azotea*.

AZUTÉRO, *sm.* Sluice-master, he who has the care of dams, sluices, and flood-gates; dyke-reeve.

AZUZADÓR, RA, *s.* Instigator.

AZUZÁR, *va.* 1. To set on dogs, to incite them to fight. 2. To irritate, to provoke, to stir up.

B IS the second letter of the Spanish alphabet, the sound and use of which is frequently confounded with that of the consonant *V*, even in writing, except before *L* and *R*, which are always preceded by *B*. *B.* stands for Blessed; *B. A.* for Bachelor of Arts; and *B. C.* for *Basso Continuo*, or thorough bass.

B mol, in music, B-flat. *B quadrádo*, B-sharp.

BÁBA, *sf.* Drivel, slaver, spittle running from the mouth.

BABABUÍ, *sm.* The mocking bird. V. *Arrendajó*.

BABÁDA, *sf.* Thigh-bone.

BABADÉRO Y BABADÓR, *sm.* Bib, a small piece of linen put under the chins of infants when feeding.

BABÁNCA, *sm.* (Ant.) V. *Bobo*.

BABÁRA, *sf.* 1. A Landau or Berlin, an oblong coach. 2. A kind of country dance.

BABÁZA, *sf.* 1. Frothy humour running from the mouth. 2. Aloe. 3. A viscous worm of the snail kind, without a shell. Limax *L.*

BABAZÓRRO, *sm.* (Arag.) Clown, a coarse ill-bred man.

BABEÁR, *vn.* To drivel, to slaver.

BABÉO, *sm.* The act of drivelling or slavering.

BABÉRA, *sf.* 1. Fore part of the helmet which covers the cheeks, mouth, and chin. 2. A foolish, silly fellow.

BABÉRO, *sm.* V. *Babador*.

BABERÓL, *sm.* V. *Babera*.

BABÍA, *sf.* *Estár en babia*, To be absent in mind, heedless, inattentive.

BABICAÍDO, DA, *a.* Slavered, covered with saliva fallen from the mouth.

BABIÉCA, *sm.* *Es un babieca*, He is an ignorant, stupid fellow.

BABÍLLA, *sf.* Thin skin about the flank or chambrel of a horse.

BABILÓNIA, *sf.* *Es una babilonia*, There is such a crowd, it is all uproar and confusion.

BABILÓNICO, CA, *a.* Belonging to Babylon; confused.

BABÓR, *sm.* (Naút.) Larboard, the left-hand side of a ship, standing with the face towards the head. *A' babor el timon*, A-port the helm. *A' babor todo*, Head a-port. *De babor á estribor*, Athwart ship.

BABÓSA, *sf.* 1. A viscous worm of the snail kind without a shell. Limax *L.* 2. Aloe. 3. An old onion which is transplanted, and produces others. 4. A young onion.

BABOSEÁR, *va.* To drivel, to slaver, to cover with spittle.

BABOSÍLLA, *sf.* A small viscous worm of the snail kind.

BABOSÍLLO, LLA; UÉLO, LA, *a.* Somewhat drivelling or slavering.

BABÓSO, SA, *a.* Drivelling, slavering.

Báca, *sf.* 1. Berry, *Baca de laurel*, Bay-berry. 2. Breach in a dyke or dam. *Bacas*, (Ant.) Quick tune on the guitar.
Bacáda, *sf.* (Ant.) V. *Caida.*
Bacalláo, *sm.* Ling, poor jack, cod-fish. Gadus morhua et molva *L.*
Bacanáles, *sf. pl.* Bacchanals, feasts of Bacchus.
Bacánte, *sf.* Bacchante, priestess of Bacchus; lewd drinking person.
Bácara ó Bacáris, *sf.* (Bot.) Great flea-bane. Baccharis *L.*
Bacári, *a.* Covered; applied to the oval shields covered with leather, and used in the wars against the Moors.
Bacéra, *sf.* (Bax.) Obstruction in the milt, a swelling of the belly.
Bacéta, *sf.* The stock or four remaining cards in the game of *Reversi.*
Báche, *sm.* 1. A deep miry hole in a road. 2. A place where sheep are shut up to sweat previously to their being shorn. V. *Sudadero.*
Báchico, ca, *a.* Relating or belonging to Bacchus.
Bachillér, *sm.* 1. Bachelor, one who has obtained the first degree in the sciences and liberal arts. 2. Babbler, prater, one who talks much, and not to the purpose.
Bachilléra, *sf.* Forward, loquacious woman.
Bachillér, ra, *a.* Garrulous, loquacious.
Bachilleráto, *sm.* Bachelorship, the degree and function of a Bachelor.
Bachillereár, *vn.* To babble, to prattle, to talk much and not to the purpose.
Bachilleréjo, *sm.* A talkative little fellow.
Bachillería, *sf.* Babbling, prattling.
Bachilleríllo, lla; co, ca; to, ta, *a.* Loquacious, talkative. V. *Bachillerejo.*
Bacía, *sf.* 1. A metal basin used for several purposes; 2. Barber's basin.
Bacíga, *sf.* A game played with three cards.
Bacín, *sm.* A large pan or basin which serves as a close-stool.
Bacína, *sf.* Poor-box in which alms are collected.
Bacináda, *sf.* Filth thrown from the basin of a close-stool.
Bacinéjo, *sm.* A small close-stool.
Bacinéro y Bacinéra, *s.* The person who carries about the poor-box in a church, and collects the alms.
Bacinéta, *sf.* 1. A small poor-box in which alms are collected. 2. *Bacineta de arma de fuego*, The pan of a gun-lock.
Bacinéte, *sm.* 1. A head-piece, formerly worn by soldiers, in the form of a helmet. 2. Cuirassier, a horseman formerly armed with a cuirass.
Bacinica ó Bacinílla, *sf.* A small earthen close-stool for children.
Báculo, *sm.* 1. Walking stick, a staff. *Báculo de Jacob*, Jacob's staff, a mathematical instrument which serves to take heights and distances. *Báculo de peregrino*, Pilgrim's staff. *Báculo pastoral*, Bishop's crosier. 2. (Met.) Support, relief, consolation.
Báda. V. *Abada.*
Badajáda, *sf.* 1. A stroke of the clapper against the bell. 2. Foolish language, idle talk.
Badájo, *sm.* 1. Clapper or tongue of a bell. 2. An idle talker, a foolish prattling fellow.
Badajázo *sm.* (Aum.) A large clapper.
Badajeár, *vn.* (Ant. Vulg.) To babble, to talk much nonsense.
Badajuélo, *sm.* (Dim.) A small clapper.
Badál, *sm.* 1. Muzzle, a fastening for the mouth of animals, which hinders them to bite. *Echar un badal á la boca*, To stop one's mouth. 2. Shoulder and ribs of butcher's meat. 3. (Cir.) Instrument for opening the mouth.
Badána, *sf.* A dressed sheep-skin. *Zurrar la badana*, To dress a sheep-skin: (Met.) To give one a hiding or flogging.
Badázas, *sf. pl.* (Naút.) Keys of the bonnets; ropes with which the bonnets are laced to the sails. V. *Barjuleta.*
Badéa, *sf.* 1. Pompion or pumpkin. Cucurbita pepo *L.* 2. (Met.) A dull, insipid being.
Badén, *sm.* Channel made by a sudden fall of water.
Badiána, *sf.* (Bot.) Indian aniseed, badiana. Illicium anisatum *L.*
Badíl, *sm.* Fire-shovel.
Badilázo, *sm.* Blow with a fire-shovel.
Badína, *sf.* Pool of water in the roads.
Badómia, *sf.* Nonsense, absurdity.
Baduláque, *sm.* 1. Ragout of stewed livers and lights. 2. A stupid person of little sense or reason.
Bafaneár, *vn.* To boast, to exaggerate.
Bafanería, *sf.* Romancing, gasconading.
Bafanéro, *sm.* Boaster, bragger.
Bága, *sf.* 1. A rope or cord with which the loads of beasts of burthen are fastened. 2. A little head of flax with its seed.
Bagáge, *sm.* 1. Beast of burthen. 2. Baggage carried by beasts of burthen.
Bagagéro, *sm.* Driver, he who conducts beasts of burthen or baggage.
Bagár, *vn.* To yield the seed; applied to flax.
Bagása, *sf.* V. *Carcavera.*
Bagatéla, *sf.* Trifle.
Bagázo, *sm.* (And.) The remains of grapes, olives, palms, &c. which have been pressed.
Bagílla, *sf.* Service, the dishes, plates, and other vessels necessary for serving up a dinner.
Bágre, *sm.* A delicious fish in the American seas and rivers. Silurus bagre *L.*
Baguillito, *sm.* (Ant.) A small staff.
Baharí, *sm.* (Orn.) Sparrow-hawk. Falco nisus *L.*
Bahía, *sf.* Bay, an arm of the sea stretching into the land.
Báho, *sm.* 1. Steam, the smoke and vapour of any thing moist and hot. 2. (In Cloth Manufactories) A tenter with hooks which serve to bring the cloth to a certain breadth.
Bahorrína, *sf.* 1. Collection of filthy things mixed with dirty water. 2. Rabble.
Bahúno, na, *a.* Vile, low, contemptible, worthless.
Bahurréro, *sm.* (Ant.) Sportsman who catches birds in nets or snares.
Bajóca, *sf.* 1. (Mur.) Green kidney-beans. 2. (Mur.) A dead silk-worm.
Bála, *sf.* 1. Ball, bullet, shot. *Balas roxas*, Red-hot balls. *Balas encazonadas*, Case-shot. *Balas enramadas ó encadenadas*, Chain-shot. *Balas de metralla*, Grape-shot. 2. Bale of goods. 3. Bale of paper, containing ten reams. 4. Small hollow ball of wax filled with water, and used to play tricks during the carnival. 5. Printer's ball with which the ink is applied to the form

Baláda ó Baláta, *sf.* Ballad, a song.
Baladí, *a.* Mean, despicable, worthless.
Baladór, ra, *s.* Animal that bleats.
Baládre, *sm.* (Bot.) Rose-bay, Nerium oleander *L.*
Baladrón, *sm.* Boaster, bragger, bully.
Baladronáda, *sf.* Boast, brag, fanfarenade.
Baladronear, *vn.* To boast, to brag.
Balagár, *sm.* Long straw or hay preserved for winter fodder.
Bálago, *sm.* 1. V. *Balagar.* 2. Hay-rick. 3. Thick spume of soap, of which wash-balls are made up. *Sacudir ó menear el balago,* To give a sound drubbing.
Balaguéro, *sm.* Rick of straw.
Baláncе, *sm.* 1. Fluctuation, vibration, motion of a body from one side to another. 2. Equilibrium or equipoise of a rider on horseback. 3. Balance of accounts. 4. (Ant.) Doubt. 5. Rolling of a ship.
Balanceár, *vn.* 1. To balance, to vibrate, to fluctuate, to roll. 2. (Met.) To waver, to be unsettled.—*va.* 1. To weigh, to examine. 2. To settle accounts.
Balancéro. V. *Balanzario.*
Balancía, *sf.* 1. (And.) Water-melon. 2. Scale, a vessel suspended by a beam against another. 3. A kind of white grape.
Balancín, *sm.* 1. Splinter-bar of a carriage, swing-bar of a cart. 2. Iron beam for striking coins and medals. 3. (Ant.) Poy, a rope-dancer's pole. *Balancines,* (Naút.) Lifts, ropes belonging to the yard-arms, and serving to raise or lower the yards. *Balancines de la brúxula,* (Naút.) Brass rings by which the compass is suspended in the binnacle.
Balándra, *sf.* (Naút.) Bilander, a small vessel which carries but one mast.
Balandrán, *sm.* A loose surtout worn by priests when they are at home.
Balánte, *pa.* (Poét.) Bleating. In cant, a sheep.
Balánza, *sf.* 1. Scale, a vessel suspended by a beam against another. 2. Balance, a pair of scales. 3. A kind of fishing net. 4. (Met.) Comparative estimate, judgment. *Fiel de balanza de la romana,* Needle of the balance. *Andar en balanza,* (Met.) To be in danger of losing one's property or place. 5. Gallows, in cant.
Balanzár, *va.* V. *Balancear.*
Balanzário, *sm.* Balancer, he who weighs and adjusts the coins in the mint.
Balánzo, *sm.* V. *Balance.*
Balanzón, *sm.* Copper pan used by silversmiths.
Baláo, *sm.* (Ict.) A kind of sprat of the size of a pilchard.
Balár, *vn.* To bleat as a sheep. *Andar balando por alguna cosa,* To be gaping after something.
Baláta, *sf.* (Ant.) Ballet, an historical dance.
Balasór, *sm.* Balassor, a stuff made of the bark of trees, which comes from China.
Balaústra y Balaustría, *sf.* Flowers of the wild pomegranate.
Balaustráda y Balustrería, *sf.* Balustrade, a row of small pillars called balusters.
Balaustrádo, da, y Balaustrál, *a.* Made in the form of balusters, or adorned with balusters.
Balaústre, *sm.* Small pillars, with which balustrades are formed. *Balaústres de navio,* (Naút.) Head rails of a ship.

Balax, *sm.* Balass or spinel ruby.
Balázo, *sm.* A shot.
Balbucéncia, *sf.* Stuttering speech, difficulty of utterance.
Balbuciénte, *a.* Stammering, stuttering.
Balcón, *sm.* Balcony, a frame of wood, iron, or stone before the window of a room.
Balconáge y Balconería, *sm.* Range of balconies.
Balconázo, *sm.* A large balcony.
Balconcíllo, *sm.* A small balcony.
Bálda, *sf.* (Ant.) Trifle, a thing of little value. *A' la balda,* Living in a heedless imprudent manner.
Baldaquí ó Baldaquíno, *sm.* Canopy supported by the columns over the holy Sacrament, and Pope's head in processions.
Baldár, *va.* 1. To cripple, to take away the use of a limb. 2. To break a set of books, or other things, by taking away one or more of them. 3. To trump or win a trick in a game at cards. 4. To obstruct, or hinder.
Bálde, *sm.* Bucket used on board of ships.
Bálde (De) *ad.* Gratis, for nothing, without a recompense. *En balde,* In vain, to no purpose, ineffectually.
Baldeár, *vn.* (Naút.) To throw water on the deck and sides of a ship, for the purpose of cleaning them.
Baldéro, ra, *a.* (Ant.) Idle. V. *Baldio.*
Baldés, *sm.* A piece of dressed skin, soft and pliable.
Baldío, día, *a.* 1. Untilled, uncultivated; applied to land. *Campos baldios,* Commons. 2. Idle, lazy. *Hombre baldio,* Vagrant, vagabond.
Báldo, da, *a.* Unfurnished with a card of the same suit, which has been played by another.
Baldón, *sm.* Censure, reproach, insult.
Baldonár ó Baldoneár, *va.* To insult with abusive language, reproach.
Baldósa, *sf.* A fine square tile.
Baldráque, *sm.* (A cant word) Trifle, fiddle-faddle.
Baldrés, *sm.* (Ant.) V. *Baldés.*
Baleárico, ca, ó Baleário, ria, *a.* Balearic, belonging to the Baleares, or isles of Majorca, Minorca, &c.
Balería, *sf.* A large quantity of balls, bullets, or shot heaped together.
Baléta, *sf.* A small bale.
Balhurría, *sf.* (Cant.) Low people.
Balído, *sm.* Bleating, the cry of a sheep.
Balíja, *sm.* 1. Portmanteau or portmantle, a bag in which clothes are carried. 2. Mail, the post-man's bag in which the letters are conveyed. 3. Post or postboy who carries letters from one place to another.
Balijón, *sm.* A large portmantle.
Balitadéra, *sf.* Call, an instrument made of reeds for calling fawns.
Ballár, *va.* (Ant.) V. *Cantar.*
Balléna, *sf.* 1. Whale, Balæna *L.* 2. Train-oil, oil drawn by coction from the blubber or fat of the whale. 3. Whale-bone. 4. (Astr.) One of the northern constellations.
Ballenáto, *sm.* Cub, the young of a whale.
Ballenér, *sm.* A sort of a vessel which has the shape of a whale.
Ballésta, *sf.* Cross-bow, an ancient missive weapon. *A' tiro de ballesta,* (Met.) At a great distance.

Ballestázo, *sm.* Blow given or received from any thing thrown from a cross-bow.
Ballesteadór, *sm.* Cross-bower, arbalist.
Ballesteár, *va.* To shoot with a cross-bow.
Ballestéra, *sf.* Loop-holes through which cross-bows were discharged.
Ballestería, *sf.* 1. Archery, the art of an archer, or of shooting with a bow and arrow. 2. Number of cross-bows, or persons armed with cross-bows. 3. Place where cross-bows are kept, or arbalists quartered.
Ballestéro, *sm.* 1. Archer, arbalist, cross-bower. 2. Cross-bow maker. 3. King's archer or armourer, whose business it is to keep the arms of the royal family in order. *Ballestero de maza*, Mace-bearer. *Ballesteros de corte*, The king's porters, and the porters of the privy council, were formerly so called.
Ballestílla, *sf.* 1. Small cross-bow. 2. Instrument for bleeding cattle, but which is at present called *fleam*. 3. Cross-staff, an instrument for taking heights. 4. (Naút.) Fore-staff, an instrument used for taking the altitude of the sun, stars, &c.
Ballestón, *sm.* Large cross-bow, arbalet.
Ballestrínque, *sm.* (Naút.) Clove-hitch, by which one rope is fastened to another.
Ballíco, *sm.* (Bot.) Red or perennial darnel, rye-grass. Lolium perenne *L.*
Ballueca, *sf.* (Bot. Arag.) Wild oats. Avena fatua *L.*
Balón, *sm.* 1. Large foot-ball, with which the game of that name is played. 2. The game of foot-ball. 3. Balloon. 4. Large bale. 5. (Naút.) State-vessel in Siam. 6. Bale of paper containing 24 reams.
Baloncíta, *sf.* Saveall.
Balóta, *sf.* Ballot, a little ball used in voting.
Balotáda, *sf.* Ballotade, leap of a horse in which he shows the shoes of his hinder feet.
Balotár, *va.* Ballot, to choose by ballot without open declaration of the vote.
Bálsa, *sf.* 1. Pool, a lake of standing water. 2. (Naút.) Raft or float for conveying goods or persons across a river. 3. (Andal.) Half a butt of wine. 4. (In Oil-mills.) The room where the oil is kept. *Estar como una balsa de aceyte*, To be as quiet as a pool of oil; spoken of a place or country.
Balsameríta, *sf.* A small smelling bottle for balsam.
Balsamía, *sf.* (Ant.) Fabulous tale.
Balsámico, ca, *a.* Balsamic.
Balsamína, *sf.* (Bot.) Balm.
Balsamíta mayor, (Bot.) Costmary. Balsamita vulgaris *L. Balsamita menor*, (Bot.) Maudlin tansy. Tanacetum annuum *L.*
Bálsamo, *sm.* 1. Balsam of balm. *Bálsamo de Maria*, Balsam of Tolu. *Es un bálsamo*, It is a balsam; applied to generous wine and other delicious liquors. 2. (Med.) The purest and soundest part of the blood.
Balsár, *sm.* A marshy piece of ground with brambles.
Balseár, *va.* To cross rivers on floats or frames of timber joined together.
Balséro, *sm.* Ferry-man.
Balsílla, *sf.* A small float or raft.
Balsopéto, *sm.* 1. A large pouch carried near the breast. 2. (Bax.) Bosom, the inside of the breast.
Bálteo, *sm.* (Ant.) Officer's belt.
Baluárte, *sm.* 1. (Fort.) Bastion, a mass of earth raised in the angles of a polygon, with flanks, faces, and a gorge. 2. (Met.) Defence, support. *Eso es el baluarte de la fe y de la religion*, This is the bulwark of faith and religion.
Balúmba y Balúma, *sf.* Bulk or quantity of things heaped together.
Balúmbo y Balúme, *sm.* A heap of things which take up much room.
Bálza, *sf.* Banner, standard.
Bambalína, *sf.* Scene, the hanging of the theatre adapted to the play.
Bambaleár y Bambaneár, *vn.* V. *Bambolear.*
Bambalína, *sf.* The upper part of the scenes in theatres, which are fixed.
Bambaroteár, *vn.* To bawl, to cry out.
Bambárria, *sm.* 1. (Bax.) A fool, an idiot. 2. An accidental but successful hit or stroke at billiards.
Bambóche, *sm.* A landscape representing banquets or drunken feats, with grotesque figures. *Es un bamboche, ó parece un bamboche*, A thick short person with a red bloated face.
Bamboleár ó Bamboneár, *vn.* To reel, to stagger, to totter, to dangle.
Bamboléo y Bamboneo, *sm.* Reeling, staggering.
Bambólla, *sf.* Ostentation, boast, vain show.
Bán, *sm.* A sort of fine muslin brought from China.
Banána, *sf.* The fruit of the plantain tree.
Banásta, *sf.* A large basket made of twigs or laths. *Meterse en banasta*, To meddle with things which do not concern one.
Banastéro, *sm.* 1. Basket-maker or dealer in baskets. 2. (Cant.) Jailer.
Banásto, *sm.* A large round basket.
Bánca, *sf.* 1. Form, a long wooden seat without a back. 2. *Banca de plaza*, A table for selling fruit. 3. A sort of washing box in which women place themselves when they are washing at the brink of a brook or river. 4. Basset, a game of chance at cards.
Bancál, *sm.* 1. An oblong plot of ground for raising pulse, roots, and fruit-trees. 2. Terrace in a garden. 3. Carpet thrown over a form or bench by way of ornament.
Bancaléro, *sm.* Carpet-manufacturer.
Bancaría. V. *Fianza bancaria.*
Bancarróta, *sf.* Bankruptcy, the failure of a merchant, tradesman, &c. who declares himself insolvent.
Bancáza y Bancázo, *s.* A large form or bench.
Bánco, *sm.* 1. Form or bench without a back. 2. A strong bench with four legs for the use of carpenters; *e. g. Banco de acepillar*, A planing bench. 3. Athwart, or bench of rowers. 4. A bank, a place where money is laid up to be called for occasionally. 5. Company of persons concerned in managing a joint stock of money. 6. The cheeks of the bit of a bridle. *Banco de arena*, A sand bank. *Banco de hielo*, A field of ice. *Banco de rio*, Sand-bank in a river. *Banco pinjado*, An ancient warlike machine for battering. *Pasar banco*, To flog the sailors on board a galley. *Razon de pie de banco*, An absurd reason, a groundless motive.

Bánda, *sf.* 1. Sash worn by military officers when on duty. 2. Ribbon worn by the knights of the military orders. 3. Band or body of troops. 4. Party or number of persons confederated by a similarity of designs or opinions. 5. Bank, border, edge; side of a ship. *La banda del norte*, The north side. *A' la banda*, (Naút.) Heeled or hove down. *En banda*, (Naút.) A-main. *Arriar en banda*, To let go a-main. *Caer, ó estar en banda*, To be a-main. *Dar á la banda*, To heel. *Bandas del tajamar*, (Naút.) The cheeks of the head.

Bandáda, *sf.* Flock of birds flying together.

Bandárria, *sf.* (Naút.) An iron maul with a wooden handle, used for driving large nails and pegs into the planks or timbers of a ship.

Bandeár, *va.* To traverse, to pass, to cross from one side to another; to band.—*vn.* To form parties, to unite with a band.—*vr.* To conduct one's self with prudence for earning a livelihood, to shift for one's self.

Bandéja, *sf.* A silver waiter.

Bandéra, *sf.* 1. A pair of colours of a regiment of infantry. 2. Infantry, soldiers who serve on foot. 3. Flag or colours which distinguish the ships of the different nations. *Bandera de popa*, (Naút.) The ensign. *Bandera de proa*, (Naút.) The jack. *Bandera de quadra*, The royal standard. *Bandera blanca, ó de paz*, The flag of truce. *Vuelo de la bandera*, The flag of the ensign. *Arriar la bandera*, To strike the colours. *Salir con banderas desplegadas*, To get off with flying colours. *Asegurar la bandera*, To fire a cannon-shot with ball at the time of hoisting the colours. *Dar la bandera*, (Met.) To submit to the superior talents or merits of another. *Levantar banderas*, (Met.) To put one's self at the head of a party.

Banderéta, *sf.* A small flag. *Banderétas*, (Mil.) Camp-colours.

Banderíca ó Banderílla, *sf.* 1. A small flag, a banner. 2. A small dart with a bannerol, which dexterous bull-fighters thrust into the shoulders and neck of a bull. *Poner á uno una banderilla*, (Met.) To taunt, to ridicule, to revile.

Banderilleár, *va.* To put small flags on bulls, at bull feasts.

Banderilléro, *sm.* He who sticks bannerets in a bull's neck.

Banderizár, *va.* V. *Abanderizár*.

Banderízo, za, *a.* Factious, given to party or [faction.

Banderólas, *sf. pl.* Bannerols, camp-colours.

Bandíbula, *sf.* Mandible or jaw, the bone of the mouth in which the teeth are fixed.

Bandído, *sm.* 1. Banditto, highwayman. 2. Fugitive pursued with judicial advertisements.

Bandín, *sm.* Seat in a row-galley.

Bandíta, *sf.* A small band.

Bándo, *sm.* 1. Edict or law solemnly published by superior authority. 2. Faction, party. *Echar bando*, To publish a law or edict.

Bándola, *sf.* 1. A small musical instrument with four strings resembling a lute. 2. (Naút.) Jurymast, a mast set up occasionally at sea, in the room of a mast lost.

Bandoléra, *sf.* Bandoleer. *Dar ó quitar la bandolera*, To admit or dismiss one from the king's life-guards in Spain.

Bandoléro, *sm.* Highwayman, robber, free-booter.

Bandosidád, *sf.* (Ant.) V. *Parcialidad.*

Bandújo, *sm.* (Ant.) Large sausage.

Bandúllo, *sm.* (Vulg.) Belly, the whole of the bowels or intestines.

Bandúrria, *sf.* A musical instrument resembling a fiddle.

Bánes, *sm.* A sort of stuff manufactured in [Burgundy.

Banóva, *sf.* (Arag.) Bed-quilt, bed-cover.

Banquéra, *sf.* 1. Small open bee-house. 2. Frame on which bee-hives are placed in a bee-house.

Banquéro, *sm.* Banker. V. *Cambista.*

Banquéta, *sf.* 1. A stool with three legs. 2. (Fort.) Banquette or footbank behind the parapet. *Banquetas de crueña*, Gun-carriage beds. *Banquetas de calafate*, (Naút.) Calking stools.

Banquéte, *sm.* Banquet, a splendid repast. *Banquete casero*, A family feast.

Banqueteár, *vn.* To banquet, to feast.

Banquíllo, *sm.* A little stool without a back.

Bánzos, *sm. pl.* Cheeks or sides of an embroidering or quilting frame.

Báña, *sf.* V. *Bañadero.*

Bañadéra, *sf.* (Naút.) Skeet, a narrow oblong ladle or scoop for wetting the sails, decks, and sides of a ship, or for baling a boat.

Bañadéro, *sm.* Pool, or puddle, in which wild boars wallow or bathe themselves.

Bañádo, *sm.* V. *Bacin.*

Bañadór, ra, *s.* One who bathes. *Bañador*, Tub or vat with liquid wax, into which wax-chandlers dip the wicks for forming wax-candles.

Bañár, *va.* 1. To bathe, to immerse or wash in water. 2. To water, to irrigate. *El rio baña las murallas de la ciudad*, The river washes the walls of the town. 3. To candy biscuits, plums, &c. with melted sugar, which forms an incrustation when cold. 4. (Pint.) To wash over a painting with a second coat of bright or transparent colours. 5. To overlay with something shining or pellucid. *Bañarse en agua rosada*, To bathe in rose-water, to be highly pleased. 6. To extend or enlarge.

Bañéro, *sm.* Owner or keeper of baths.

Bañíl, *sm.* A small pool in which deer bathe themselves. [or bathes in them

Bañísta, *sm.* He who drinks the mineral waters

Báño, *sm.* 1. Bath; the act of bathing in water, wine, or other liquor. 2. Bagnio, the house or place where people bathe, a large tub or trough for bathing. 3. Incrustation or coat made with sugar over sweetmeats, or with wax over any thing. 4. Coat of bright paint put over another. 5. Varnish; the art of glazing or putting varnish on a picture. 6. Prison in which Moors confine their prisoners until they are ransomed. 7. (Quim.) Bath for retaining an uniform heat from the fire; as *Baño de arena*, Sand-bath; *Baño de María*, Balneum Mariæ.

Bañuélo, *sm.* (Dim.) A little bath.

Báos, *sm. pl.* (Naút.) Beams, the main cross timbers, stretching from side to side. *Baos de las cubiertas altas*, The beams of the upper deck. *Bao maestro*, The midship beam. *Baos del sollado*, Orlop beams. *Baos del saltillo de proa*, The collar-beams. *Baos de los palos*,

Trestle trees. *Baos y crucetas de los palos,* Cross and trestle trees.

Baptísmo, *sm.* V. *Bautismo.*

Baptistério, *sm.* Baptistery.

Baptizár, (Ant.) V. *Bautizár.*

Báque, *sm.* 1. (Ant.) The blow which a body gives in falling. 2. A water-trough in glass-houses.

Baquería, *sf.* (Ant.) A cow-house for cattle in winter; a stable.

Baquéta, *sf.* 1. Ramrod, the stick with which the charge is forced into fire-arms. 2. Switch used in a riding-house, in breaking in young horses. *Mandar á baqueta, ó á la baqueta,* To command imperiously. *Tratár á baqueta,* To treat a person in a haughty manner.—*pl.* 1. Drum-sticks, sticks with which drums are beaten. 2. Gantlet, a military punishment. 3. Rods of holly-wood, used in beating wool.

Baquetázo, *sm.* Violent fall, great blow given by the body when falling. *Tropecé y dí un baquetazo,* I tripped and fell violently.

Baqueteár, *va.* To inflict the punishment of the gantlet. *Baquetear la lana,* To beat wool.

Baquetílla, *sf.* A little rod.

Báquico, ca, *a.* Bacchanal, relating to Bacchus.

Baradéro, *sm.* (Naút.) Skeed or skid. *Baradéro de baxa mar,* A muddy place in which vessels stick at low water.

Baradúra, *sf.* (Naút.) The grounding of a vessel.

Barahúnda, *sf.* Hurly-burly, a great bustle or confusion.

Barahúste, *sm.* V. *Balaustre.*

Barahustíllos, *sm. pl.* Small balusters.

Barája, *sf.* 1. A complete pack of cards. 2. (Ant.) A quarrel. *Meterse en barajas,* To seek a quarrel. *Entrarse en la baraja,* Not to enter upon a hand, to give a game up: (Met.) To relinquish a claim, to desist from a pretension.

Barajadúra, *sf.* 1. Shuffling of cards. 2. Dispute, difference.

Barajár, *va.* 1. To shuffle the cards, to change their position with regard to each other. 2. To bar a cast at dice. 3. (Met.) To jumble things together. *Barajar un negocio,* To entangle or perplex an affair. *Barajarle á alguno una pretension,* To frustrate one's pretensions. *Barajar una proposicion,* To reject a proposal. —*vn.* To wrangle, to contend.

Baránda, *sf.* Railing of timber, iron, or brass, around altars, fonts, balconies, &c. *Barandas de los corredores de popa de un navío,* Stern-rails. *Echar de baranda,* (Met.) To exaggerate something, to boast.

Barandádo, *sm.* Series of balusters, balustrade.

Barandál, *sm.* The under-piece of a balustrade, in which the rails or balusters are fixed.

Barandílla, *sf.* A small balustrade, a small railing.

Barangáy, *sm.* An Indian vessel, worked with oars.

Barár, *vn.* (Naút.) To strike aground, to be stranded. *Barar en la costa,* (Naút.) To run on shore.

Baráta, *sf.* 1. Barter, exchange, low price, or little value of things exposed for sale. V. *Baratura.* 2. An after game in backgammon. 3. (Ant.) A fraudulent barter. *A' la barata,* Confusedly, disorderly. *Mala barata,* Profusion, prodigality.

Baratadór, *sm.* 1. (Ant.) Barrator, impostor, deceiver. 2. Barterer.

Baratár, *va.* 1. (Ant.) To barter, to traffic by exchanging one commodity for another. 2. (Ant.) To make fraudulent barters, to cheat, to deceive. 3. (Ant.) To give or receive a thing under its just value.

Baratás, *sm.* A kind of sea-mouse.

Barateár, *vn.* (Ant.) To cheapen; to sell at an under price.

Baratería, *sf.* (Ant.) Barratry, fraud, deception.

Baratéro, *sm.* He who by art or force obtains money from the fortunate gamesters.

Baratíjas, *sf. pl.* Trifles, things of small value.

Baratíllo, lla. *a.* Cheap, of little value.

Baratíllo, *sm.* 1. Trumpery or trifles sold in a public place. 2. A place where petty pedlers sell things of little value about the fall of night.

Baratísta, *sm.* (Ant.) Barterer, trafficker.

Baráto, ta, *a.* 1. Cheap, bought or sold for a low price. *De barato,* Gratuitously, gratis. 2. (Met.) Easy.

Baráto, *sm.* 1. Money given by the winners at a gaming table to the by-standers as part of the gain. 2. (Ant.) Fraud, deceit. 3. (Ant.) Plenty, abundance. 4. Cheapness, low price. *Hacer barato,* To sell under value in order to get rid of goods. *Dar de barato,* (Met.) To grant for argument's sake, a thing to be so. *Lo barato es caro,* The cheapest goods are dearest. *Ni juega, ni da barato,* To act with indifference, without taking a part with, or engaging in a faction.

Báratro, *sm.* (Poét.) Hell.

Baratúra, *sf.* Cheapness, lowness of price, little value set upon things.

Baraúnda, *sf.* Noise, great confusion.

Baraústre, *sm.* V. *Balaustre.*

Bárba, *sm.* 1. Chin, the part of the face where the beard grows. 2. Beard, the hair which grows on the lips and chin. 3. The first swarm of bees which leaves the hive. 4. The roof of the bee-hive, where the new swarm begins to work. *Barba cabruna,* (Bot.) Yellow goat's beard. Tragopogon pratense *L.* *Barba de aaron,* (Bot.) Indian turnip. Arum esculentum *L.* *Barba de cabra,* (Bot.) Queen of the meadows. Spiræa ulmaria *L.* *Amarrado á barba de gato,* (Naút.) Moored by the head. *Temblar la barba,* To shake with fear. *Barba á barba,* Face to face. *A' barba regado,* In great plenty. *Por barba,* A head, a piece. *A' polla por barba,* Every man his bird.—*sm.* Player who acts the parts of old men on the stage.—*pl.* (Naút.) 1. Hause or hawse, the position of the cable of a ship, when she is moored by the head, with two anchors out, on the starboard and larboard bow. 2. Slender roots of trees or plants; fibres, filaments. 3. A disease under the tongue of horses. *Barbas enredadas,* A foul-hawse. *Barbas de ballena,* Whalebone. *Barbas honradas ó hombre de respeto,* A respectable man. *Decir á uno en sus barbas alguna cosa,* To tell a man a thing to his face. *Echarlo á las barbas,* To reproach a man with something. *Hacer la barba,* To shave, to take off the beard; (Met.) To speak ill of somebody. *Mentir por la barba,* To tell a lie in a barefaced manner. *Pelarse las barbas,*

(Met.) To fly into a violent passion. *Subirse á las barbas*, To fly into one's face. *Tener buenas barbas*, To have a graceful mien: applied to a fine woman. *Echar á la buena barba*, To induce one to pay for what he and his companions have eaten and drank. *Andar, estar, ó traher la barba sobre el hombro*, To wear the face on the shoulder, to be alert, to live watchful and careful. *Tener pocas barbas*, To be young or inexperienced.

Barbacána, *sf.* 1. (Fort.) Fausse braye, an elevation of earth about three feet high, which runs along the foot of the rampart towards the field. 2. A low wall around a church-yard.

Barbáda, *sf.* 1. Beard of a horse, or that part of the mandible which bears the curb of the bridle. 2. Curb, or iron chain made fast to the upper part of the branches of the bridle, and running under the beard of the horse. 3. (Ict.) Pout, or whiting pout. Gadus barbatus *L.* *Agua de la Barbada*, Barbadoes water, a liquor distilled from the sugar-cane.

Barbadaménte, *ad.* (Bar.) Strongly, vigorously.

Barbadíllo, lla, *a.* 1. Having little beard. 2. Having slender filaments, applied to plants.

Barbádo, da, *a.* Bearded, having a beard.

Barbádo, *sm.* 1. Man grown up. 2. Vine transplanted with the roots. 3. Shoots issuing from the roots of trees.

Barbaja, *sf.* (Bot.) V. *Barba cabruna*. *Barbájas*, (Agr.) The hairy filaments of the roots of plants.

Barbajóve, *sm.* (Bot).) Lady's finger.

Barbánca, *sf.* Confusion, noise, uproar.

Barbár, *vn.* 1. To get a beard. 2. Among bee-masters, to rear or keep bees. 3. To begin to strike root; applied to plants.

Bárbara, *sf.* *Sánta bárbara*, (Naút.) Powder room or magazine on board of ships of war.

Bárbaraménte, *ad.* 1. In a cruel barbarous manner. 2. Rudely, without culture in point of learning and manners.

Barbarésco, ca, *a.* Belonging or peculiar to barbarians.

Barbáricaménte. V. *Bárbaramente*.

Barbaridád, *sf.* 1. Barbarity, fierceness, cruelty. 2. Rashness, temerity. 3. Rudeness, want of culture in point of manners or learning. 4. Barbarous expression or action.

Barbárie, *sf.* Barbarousness, impurity of language, incivility of manners; rusticity.

Barbarísmo, *sm.* 1. Form of speech, contrary to the purity of language; barbarism. 2. Crowd of barbarians. 3. Barbarousness.

Barbarizár, *va.* To make barbarous, wild, or cruel.

Bárbaro, ra, *a.* 1. Barbarous, fierce, cruel. 2. Rash, bold, daring. 3. Rude, ignorant, unpolished.

Bárbaro, *sm.* A Barbary horse.

Barbaróte, *sm.* A great savage or barbarian.

Barbáto, ta, *a.* Bearded, applied to a comet.

Barbáza, *sf.* A long beard.

Barbeár, *vn.* To reach with the beard or lips.

Barbechár, *va.* To plough the ground and prepare it for sowing.

Barbechazón ó Barbechión, *sm.* (Among Farmers) The fallowing time.

Barbechéra, *sf.* 1. Series of different successive ploughings. 2. Fallowing time or season. 3. Act and effect of ploughing or fallowing.

Barbécho, *sm.* 1. First ploughing of the ground, in order to plough it again. 2. Ground ploughed in order to be sown. *Como en un barbecho, ó por un barbecho*, With too much confidence or assurance.

Barbéra, *sf.* A barber's wife.

Barbería, *sf.* 1. Trade of a barber. 2. Barber's shop.

Barberíto, íllo, *sm.* A spruce little barber.

Barbéro, *sm.* 1. Barber, one who shaves, or takes off the beard. 2. (Ict.) Mutton-fish. Labrus anthias *L.*

Barbéta, *sf.* 1. (Naút.) Rackline. 2. (Naút.) Ring-rope, a rope occasionally tied to the ringbolts of the deck. *Batería á barbeta*, Barbet-battery, having neither embrasures nor merlons, and where the cannon fire over the parapet.

Barbiblánco, ca, *a.* Having a beard grey or white with age.

Barbíca y íta, *sf.* A small beard.

Barbicácho, *sm.* Riband or band tied under the chin.

Barbicáno, na, *a.* Having a grey beard.

Barbiespéso, sa, *a.* One who has a thick beard.

Barbihécho, cha, *a.* Fresh shaved.

Barbilampíño, ña, *a.* Having a thin beard.

Barbilíndo, da, *a.* Well shaved and trimmed.

Barbílla, *sf.* 1. A small beard. 2. Point of the chin. 3. Morbid tumour under the tongue of horses and cattle.

Barbilléra, *sf.* 1. Tuft of tow, put between the staves of a cask or vat to prevent it from leaking. 2. Bandage put under the chin of a dead person to keep the mouth shut.

Barbilúcio, cia, *a.* Smooth-faced, pretty, genteel.

Barbinégro, gra, *a.* Black-bearded.

Barbiponiénte, *a.* 1. Having the beard growing; applied to a boy or lad. 2. (Met.) Beginning to learn any art or profession.

Barbiquéjo, *sm.* 1. Handkerchief, with which the Indians muffle the chin. 2. (Naút.) Bobstay, a strong rope which keeps the bowsprit downwards to the stem.

Barbirúbio, bia, *a.* Red-bearded, having a red beard.

Barbirúcio, cia, *a.* Having a black and white beard.

Barbiteñído, da, *a.* Having a painted beard.

Barbizaéño, ña, *a.* Having a rough beard.

Bárbo, *sm.* (Ict.) Barbel, a river fish. Cyprinus barbus *L.*

Barbón, *sm.* 1. An old man of a grave and austere aspect. 2. A man with a thick, strong beard. 3. A lay brother of the Carthusian order.

Barboquéjo, *sm.* 1. A piece of rope put into a horse's mouth instead of a bridle, to guide him and keep him from biting. 2. Hind part of the under-jaw of a horse.

Barbotár, *va.* To mumble, to mutter.

Barbóte, *sm.* Fore part of a helmet. V. *Babera*.

Barbúdo, da, *a.* Having a long beard. *A' la muger barbuda de léjos la saluda*, (Ref.)

Flee a woman with a beard as you would a bear.

Barbúdo, *sm.* Vine transplanted with the roots.

Barbúlla, *sf.* Loud, confused noise, made by people all talking together at the same time.

Barbullár, *va.* To talk loud and fast, with disorder and confusion.

Barbullón, na, *a.* Talking loud, fast, and confused.

Bárca, *sf.* (Naút.) 1. Boat, barge. *Barca chata para pasar gente*, A ferry-boat. *Barca longa*, A fishing boat. 2. (Met.) Fortune, chance of life. *Conduce bien su barca*, He steers his course well.

Barcáda, *sf.* 1. Passage in a ferry-boat from one side of the river to the other. 2. A boat full of persons or goods. *Barcada de lastre*, A boat-load of ballast.

Barcáge, *sm.* 1. Fare paid at a ferry for passing over water. 2. Ferry, passage-boat for carrying goods or persons over in a boat.

Barcáza, *sf.* A large ferry-boat.

Barcázo, *sm.* A large barge.

Barcélla, *sf.* Measure for grain.

Barcéo, *sm.* Dry bass or sedge for making mats, ropes, &c.

Barcína, *sf.* 1. Net, made of bass or sedge, for carrying straw. 2. Large truss of straw.

Barcinár, *va.* To load a cart or waggon with sheaves of corn, in order to carry them to the threshing-place.

Barcíno, na, ó **Barcéno, na**, *a.* Ruddy, approaching to redness, pale-red; reddish gray.

Bárco, *sm.* (Naút.) Boat, barge; bark. *Barco aguador*, A watering boat. *Barco chato*, A flat-bottomed boat. *Barco de la vez*, A passage-boat.

Barcolóngo y Barcoluéngo, *sm.* An oblong boat with a round head.

Barcón y Barcóte, *sm.* A large boat.

Bárda, *sf.* 1. Ancient armour of horses to cover them from arrows and javelins. 2. Straw, brushwood or fence wood, laid on fences, mud-walls, &c. to preserve them. *Aun hay sol en bardas*, There are even still hopes of attaining it.

Bardádo, da, *a.* Caparisoned with a defensive armour; applied to a horse.

Bardágo, *sm.* (Naút.) Loof-hook-rope.

Bardaguéra, *sf.* A sort of sedge used in making ropes for draw-wells.

Bardál, *sm.* Mud-wall, covered at the top with straw, brush or fence-wood. *Salta bardales*, A nick-name given to bold mischievous boys.

Bardána, *sf.* (Bot.) Common burdock. Arctium lappa *L. Bardána menor*, (Bot.) Lesser burdock. Xanthium strumarium *L.*

Bardánza, *sf.* *Andar de bardanza*, To go here and there.

Bardár, *va.* To cover the tops of fences, mud, or other walls, with straw or brushwood.

Bardáxa y Bardáxe, *sm.* V. *Sodomita.*

Bardílla, *sf.* Small brushwood.

Bárdo, *sm.* Bard, poet.

Bardóma, *sf.* Filth, dirt, mud.

Bardoméra, *sf.* (Mur.) Weeds or small wood carried off by currents.

Barfól, *sm.* A coarse stuff, which comes from the coast of Gambia.

Bárga, *sf.* 1. The steepest part of a declivity. 2. Hut covered with straw, or thatched.

Bargánte, (No), *ad.* V. *No Embargante.*

Baríga, *sf.* A sort of silk which the Dutch bring from India.

Baríllo, *sm.* An inferior sort of silk, which the Portuguese bring from the East Indies.

Baríto, *sm.* A precious stone of a blackish colour.

Barítono, *sm.* Voice of a low pitch, between a tenor and a base.

Barjuléta, *sf.* 1. Knapsack, haversack, a travelling bag carried on the shoulders. 2. A sort of double purse used in some chapters of Aragon for distributing the dividends of the incumbents. *Ladroncillo de agujeta, despues sube á barjuleta*, (Prov.) A young filcher becomes an old robber.

Barloár, *vn.* (Naút.) To grapple for the purpose of boarding.

Barlóas, *sf. pl.* (Naút.) Relieving tackles, or relieving tackle pendants.

Barloventeár, *vn.* 1. (Naút.) To ply to windward, to beat about. 2. (Met.) To rove about, to wander up and down.

Barlovénto, *sm.* (Naút.) Weather-gage, the point from whence the wind blows. *Costa de barlovento*, The weather-shore. *Costado de barlovento*, The weather-side. *Ganar el barlovento*, To get to windward, to gain the wind.

Barnabítas, *sm. pl.* Members of the religious community of St. Paul.

Barníz, *sm.* 1. Varnish, a liquid laid on paintings, wood, metal, &c. to make them shine. 2. Paint or colours laid on the face. 3. Gum of the juniper tree. 4. Printer's ink.

Barnizár, *va.* To varnish, to cover with something shining.

Báro, ra, *a.* Thin, loose.

Barómetro, *sm.* Barometer, an instrument for measuring the weight of the atmosphere, or the height of mountains.

Barón, *sm.* A degree of nobility of more or less eminence in different countries. *Barones del timon*, (Naút.) Rudder pendants and chains.

Baronál, *a.* Baronial, relating to a baron.

Baronésa, *sf.* Baroness, a baron's lady.

Baronía, *sf.* Barony, honour or lordship which gives title to a baron.

Barosánemo, *sm.* Aerometer, an instrument for measuring the air.

Barqueár, *vn.* To cross in a boat, to go to and fro in a boat.

Barquéro, *sm.* Waterman, ferryman.

Barquéta, *sf.* A small boat.

Barquichuélo, *sm.* (Dim.) Small bark or boat.

Barquílla, *sf.* 1. A little boat. 2. *Barquilla de la corredera*, (Naút.) The log, a triangular piece of wood fastened to the log-line, which serves to measure the ship's way. 3. Thin boat-formed or conical pastry cake.

Barquilléro, *sm.* 1. One who makes or sells wafers. 2. Iron mould for making wafers.

Barquíllo, *sm.* 1. Cock-boat, a small boat used on rivers and near a sea-coast. 2. Paste made to close letters. 3. A thin pastry cake rolled up in the form of a tube or cone. 4. A mould with holes used by wax-chandlers.

Barquín ó Barquinéra, *s.* Large bellows for iron-works or furnaces.
Barquinéro, *sm.* Bellows-maker.
Barquíno, *sm.* Wine-bag. V. *Odre.*
Bárra, *sm.* 1. Iron crow or lever. 2. Bar or ingot of gold, silver, &c. 3. Rock or sand-bank at the mouth of a harbour. 4. List or gross spun thread in cloth, left as a mark of defective manufactory. 5.(Among Wax-chandlers) A plate with holes for framing small wax-candles. 6. (In Horse-mills) Bar, set in motion by the staves of the trundle. 7. The fleshy part of a horse's jaw, which has no teeth. 8. (In Heraldry) The third part of a shield. *Estirar la barra,* (Met.) To make the utmost exertions for attaining some purpose. *Tirar la barra,* (Met.) To enhance the price. *De barra á barra,* From one point to another. *Bárras,* (Among Pack-saddle Makers) The arched trees of a pack-saddle. *Barras de cabrestante y molinete,* (Naút.) The bars of the capstern and windlass. *Barras de escotillas,* (Naút.) Bars of the hatches. *Barras de portas,* (Naút.) Gun-port bars. *Estar en barras,* (Met.) To be on the point of settling an affair. *Sin daño de barras,* (Met.) Without injury or danger.
Barrabasáda, *sf.* Embarrassment, perplexity; plot, intrigue.
Barráca, *sf.* Hut for soldiers, or for fishermen on the sea-coast.
Barrachél, *sm.* Head-constable, the principal *alguacil.*
Barráco, *sm.* V. *Verraco.* 1. A boar. 2. Spume thrown up by must when it is in a state of fermentation. 3. An ancient kind of ship-guns now disused. 4. Snag, a tooth which grows over another.
Barrádo, da, *a.* 1. (Among clothiers) Corded, or having stripes rising above the ground; striped. 2. (Blas.) Barred.
Barragán, *sm.* 1. (Ant.) Companion. 2. (Ant.) Bachelor, an unmarried man. 3. Barracan, a strong kind of camlet. 4. (Ant.) Man of spirit and courage.
Barragána, *sf.* 1. (Ant.) A concubine. 2. Married woman or lawful wife, who (being of inferior birth) does not enjoy the civil rights of the matrimonial state.
Barraganería, *sf.* 1. Unmarried state. 2. Concubinage.
Barraganía, *sf.* (Ant.) V. *Amancebamiento.*
Barraganétes, *sm. pl.* (Naút.) Top-timbers.
Barrál, *sm.* A large bottle containing an *arroba* or 25 pints of water, wine, &c.
Barránca, *sf.* A deep break or hole made by mountain-floods, or heavy falls of rain.
Barránco, *sm.* 1. V. *Barranca.* 2. (Met.) Great difficulty or embarrassment which obstructs the attainment of some purpose.
Barrancóso, sa, *a.* Broken, uneven, full of breaks and holes.
Barráque. V. *Traque Barraque.*
Barraqueár, *va.* To grunt like a boar.
Barraquílla, *sf.* A little hut.
Barraquíllo, *sm.* (Ant.) A short light field-piece.
Barreár, *va.* 1. To daub, to smear, to paint coarsely. 2. (Ant.) To bar, to barricade.
Barreár, *va.* 1. To bar, to barricade, to fortify with timbers, fascines, pales, stakes, &c. 2. (Arag.) To cancel a writing. 3. To secure or fasten a thing with a bar of iron, or other metal.—*vn.* To glance along a knight's armour without piercing it; applied to a lance—*vr.* 1. V. *Atrincherarse.* 2. To wallow, to roll in mud, mire, or any other thing filthy; applied to wild boars.
Barréda, *sf.* V. *Barrera.*
Barredéras, *sf. pl.* (Naút.) Studding sails.
Barredéro, *sm.* Mop, pieces of cloth fixed to a pole to wipe any place.
Barredéro, ra, *a.* Sweeping along any thing met with.
Barredúra, *sf.* Act of sweeping.—*pl.* 1. Sweepings, filth swept away. 2. Remains, residue, that which is left of grain or other things.
Barréna, *sf.* 1. Auger, borer, gimlet. 2. A strong iron with a sharp point, to make holes in rocks or stones which are to be blown up with gunpowder. *Barrena de diminucion,* A taper auger. *Barrena de guia,* A centre bit.
Barrenádo, da, *pp.* 1. Bored. 2. (Met.) *Barrenado de cascos,* Crack-brained, crazy, wanting right reason.
Barrenadór, *sm.* (Naút.) Auger.
Barrenár, *va.* 1. To bore, to pierce, to make holes with a borer or gimlet. *Barrenar un navío,* (Naút.) To sink a ship. 2. (Met.) To defeat one's intentions, to frustrate one's designs.
Barrendéro, ra, *s.* Sweeper, dustman.
Barrenéro, *sm.* In the mines of Almaden, the boy that serves with the boring tools.
Barréno, *sm.* 1. A large borer or auger. 2. Hole made with a borer, auger, or gimlet. 3. (Met.) Vanity, ostentation. *Dar barreno,* (Naút.) To bore and sink a ship.
Barréña, *sf.* (Ant.) V. *Barreño.*
Barréño, *sm.* Earthen pan.
Barreñón, *sm.* Large earthen pan.
Barreñoncíllo, *sm.* Small earthen pan.
Barrér, *va.* 1. To sweep, to clean with a broom. 2. (Met.) To cut off the whole, not to leave any thing of what there was in a place. *Barrer un navío de popa á proa,* (Naút.) To rake a ship fore and aft.
Barréra, *sf.* 1. Clay-pit. 2. Inner circular paling within which bull-feasts are performed. 3. Mound or heap of earth from which saltpetre is extracted. 4. Cup-board with shelves where crockery-ware is kept. 5. Parapet. 6. Barrier, turnpike. *Salir á barrera,* (Met.) To expose one's self to public censure.
Barréro, *sm.* 1. Potter. 2. (Extr.) Height, eminence, a high ridge of hills. 3. Clay-pit; place full of clay and mud.
Barréta, *sf.* 1. Small bar. 2. Lining of a shoe. 3. Helmet, casque. *Barrétas,* Pieces of iron which hold the bows of a saddle together.
Barreteár, *va.* 1. To secure or fasten a thing with bars. 2. To line the inside of a shoe.
Barretéro, *vn.* In mining, one who works with a crow, wedge, or pick.
Barretíllo, *sm.* Small helmet or casque.
Barretón, *sm.* Large bar.
Barretoncíllo, *sm.* Small bar.
Barriáda, *sf.* Suburb, district or ward of a city.
Barríca, *sf.* Keg, a small barrel.

Barricáda, *sf.* Barricado; a collection of barrels or beams to form a cover like a parapet.
Barrído, *sm.* Sweep, the act of sweeping.
Barríga, *sf.* 1. Abdomen, belly, that part of the human body which contains the bowels. 2. Pregnancy, state of being pregnant. 3. Middle part of a vessel where it swells out into a larger capacity. *Tener la barriga á la boca,* To be very big with child. *Volverse la albarda á la barriga,* To be frustrated in one's wishes and expectations.
Barrigón, *sm.* A big belly.
Barrigúdo, da, *a.* Big-bellied.
Barriguílla, *sf.* A little belly.
Barríl, *sm.* 1. Barrel, a round wooden vessel of different dimensions. 2. Jug, a large earthen vessel with a gibbous or swelling belly and narrow neck. 3. (Naút.) Water-cask.
Barriléjo, *sm.* A small barrel.
Barrilería, *sf.* A number of barrels collected in one place.
Barriléte, *sm.* (Naút.) Mouse. *Barrilete de estay,* The mouse of a stay. *Barrilete de remo,* The mouse of an oar. *Barrilete de virador,* The mouse of a voyal. *Barrilete de banco,* (Carp.) Hold-fast, a tool used by joiners, which serves to keep the stuff steady on the bench when worked.
Barrilíco, íllo y íto, *sm.* Keg, a small barrel.
Barrílla, *sf.* 1. A little bar. 2. (Bot.) Barilla, salt-wort, an herb which is burnt to ashes, and afterwards used for making glass, soap, &c. or yielding soda.
Barrillár, *sm.* Barilla-pits, where the *barilla* is burnt, and at their bottom collected in a stony mass, which is called *rocheta:* it is the barilla ashes of commerce.
Bárrio, *sm.* 1. One of the districts or wards into which a large town or city is divided. 2. Suburb. *Andar de barrio, ó vestido de barrio,* To wear a plain simple dress.
Barrióndo, da, *a.* Sharp, sour.
Barriscár, *va.* To lump, to sell or buy in the gross.
Barríta, *sf.* 1. A small bar. 2. A small keg.
Barrizál, *sm.* Place full of clay and mud. *Barrizal de olleros,* A potter's clay-pit.
Bárro, *sm.* 1. Clay, a mass formed of earth and water. 2. Vessel of different shapes and colours, made of sweet-scented clay, for drinking water. 3. Lock of wool put into the comb. *Dar ó tener barro á mano,* To have money or the necessary means to do any thing.—*pl.* 1. Red pustules or pimples in the faces of young persons. 2. Fleshy tumours growing on the skin of horses or mules.
Barrócho, *sm.* V. *Birlocho.*
Barróso, sa, *a.* 1. Muddy, full of mire. *Camino barroso,* Muddy-road. 2. Pimpled, full of pimples called *barros.* 3. Of a pale-yellow; applied to oxen.
Barróte, *sm.* 1. Iron bar with which tables are made fast. 2. Ledge of timber laid across other timbers. *Barrótes,* Battens, scantlings or ledges of stuff, which serve for many purposes on board a ship. *Barrotes de las escotillas,* Battens of the hatches.
Barrotínes, *sm. pl. Barrotines de los baos,* (Naút.) Carlings or Carlines, *Barrotines, ó baos de la toldilla,* (Naút.) Carline knees, or the beams of the stern.
Barruéco, *sm.* Pearl of unequal form, and not perfectly round.
Barrumbáda, *sf.* Great expense made by way of ostentation.
Barruntadór, ra, *s.* Conjecturer, one who guesses by signs and tokens.
Barruntamiénto, *sm.* The act of conjecturing or guessing by signs and tokens.
Barruntár, *va.* To foresee or conjecture by signs or tokens.
Barrúnto, *sm.* Conjecture, the act of conjecturing.
Bartúlos, *sm. pl.* Affairs or business.
Barulé, *sm.* The upper part of the stockings rolled up over the knee, as was anciently the fashion.
Barzón, *sm.* 1. Idle walk. 2. The strap with which oxen are yoked to the plough-beam.
Barzoneár, *vn.* To loiter or rove about without any certain design.
Bása, *sf.* 1. Basis or pedestal of a column or statue. 2. (Met.) Basis or foundation of a thing. *Basa cula,* Locker of the thumb-plate in a stocking frame.
Basaménto, *sm.* (Arq.) Basement.
Basár ó Bazár, *sm.* Turkish market-place.
Báscas, *sf. pl.* Squeamishness, inclination to vomit.
Bascosidád, *sf.* Uncleanliness, nastiness, filth.
Báscula, *sf.* Lever, pole, staff.
Báse, *sf.* 1. Base, basis. 2. Chief or ground colour, the principal colour used in dying any stuff. *Base de distincion,* Focus of glasses spherically convex on both sides.
Basílica, *sf.* 1. Royal or imperial palace. 2. Public hall where courts of justice hold their sittings. 3. Large and magnificent church.
Basilicón, *sm.* Basilicon, an ointment prepared of resin, wax, and oil of olives.
Basílio, lia, *a.* Basilian, monk or nun of the order of St. Basil.
Basilísco, *sm.* 1. Basilisk, a kind of serpent. 2. Ancient kind of ordnance.
Báso, sa, (Ant.) V. *Bazo.*
Basqueár, *va.* To be squeamish or inclined to vomit.
Basquílla, *sf.* Disease in sheep arising from a plenitude of blood.
Basquíña, *sf.* Upper petticoat worn by Spanish women, especially when they go abroad.
Básta, *ad.* Enough; halt, stop.
Básta, *sf.* Stitch made by tailors to keep clothes even, before they are sewed. *Bástas,* Stitches put into a mattress at certain distances through wool, cotton, or some other soft substance, to form a quilt.
Bastáge, *sm.* Porter who carries burthens for hire.
Bástago y Bástiga. V. *Vástago.*
Bastánte, *a.* Sufficient, enough.
Bastantaménte, *ad.* Sufficiently.
Bastantéro, *sm.* In the chancery of Valladolid, and other Spanish courts of justice, an officer appointed to examine into the powers presented, whether they are sufficient, and drawn up in a lawful form.
Bastár, *vn.* 1. To suffice, to be proportioned to something. 2. To abound to be plentiful.

Bastárda, *sf.* 1. Bastard file. 2. Piece of ordnance. 3. (Naút.) Main-sail of a galley.

Bastardeár, *vn.* 1. To degenerate, to fall from its kind; applied to animals and plants. 2. (Met.) To fall from the virtue of our ancestors, or the nobleness of our birth.

Bastardélo, *sm.* (Arag.) Draft-book of a notary, which contains the minutes or first draughts of acts, deeds, instruments, &c.

Bastardía, *sf.* 1. Bastardy, state of being born out of wedlock. 2. (Met.) Speech or action unbecoming the birth or character of a gentleman.

Bastardílla, *sf.* (Ant.) A kind of flute or musical instrument.

Bastárdo, da, *a.* Bastard, spurious, degenerating from its kind and original qualities.

Bastárdo, *sm.* 1. A son born out of wedlock. 2. A short, thick bodied, and very poisonous snake. 3. *Basterdo de un racamento*, (Naút.) Parrel-rope.

Báste, *sm.* (Arag.) V. *Basto.*

Basteár, *va.* To baste, to stitch loosely, to sew slightly.

Bastecér y Bastescér. (Ant.) V. *Abastecer.*

Bastéro, *sm.* One who makes or retails pack-saddles.

Bastída, *sf.* (Ant.) An ancient warlike engine for covering approaches.

Bastidór, *sm.* Frame for stretching linen, silk, &c. which is to be painted, embroidered, or quilted. *Bastidóres,* (Naút.) Frames for canvas bulkheads, provisional cabins, and other temporary compartments.

Bastílla, *sf.* Hem, the edge of cloth doubled and sewed to keep the threads from spreading or ravelling.

Bastimentár, *va.* To victual, to supply with provisions.

Bastiménto, *sm.* 1. Supply of provisions for a city or army. 2. (Ant.) Building, structure. 3. Thread with which a mattress is quilted. 4. (Naút.) Vessel. *Bastimentos,* First fruits, in the order of Santiago or St. James.

Bastión, *sm.* Bastion.

Básto, *sm.* 1. Pack-saddle for beasts of burthen. 2. Ace of clubs in several games of cards. *Bástos,* Clubs, one of the four suits at cards. 3. Home-spun, unmannerly clown.

Básto, ta, *a.* 1. Coarse, rude, unpolished. 2. (Ant.) Supplied with provisions.

Bastón, *sm.* 1. Cane or stick with a head or knob to lean upon. 2. Truncheon, a staff of command. 3. (Met.) Military command. 4. (Among silk-weavers) The roller of a silk frame which contains the stuff. 5. Carrot of snuff, generally weighing about three pounds. 6. (Arq.) Fluted moulding. *Dar baston,* To stir the must with a stick to prevent its becoming ropy. *Bastones,* (Blas.) Bars in a shield.

Bastonázo y Bastonáda, *s.* **Bastinádo**, stroke or blow given with a stick or cane.

Bastoncíllo, *sm.* 1. Small cane or stick. 2. Narrow lace which serves for trimming clothes.

Bastoneár, *va.* To stir must with a stick to prevent its becoming ropy.

Bastonéro, *sm.* 1. Master of the ceremonies at a ball, steward of a feast. 2. Assistant jail-keeper.

Basúra, *sf.* 1. Sweepings, filth swept away. 2. Dung, the excrements of animals used to manure the ground.

Basuréro, *sm.* 1. He who carries dung to the field. 2. Dust-pan. 3. Dung-yard, dung-hill.

Báta, *sf.* 1. Night-gown, a loose gown, used by gentlemen for an undress. 2. Refuse of silk.

Batacázo, *sm.* Violent contusion received from a sudden or unexpected fall on the ground.

Batahóla, *sf.* Hurly-burly, bustle, clamour.

Batálla, *sf.* 1. Battle, the contest, conflict or engagement of one army with another. 2. (Ant.) Centre of an army in contradistinction to the van and rear. 3. Fencing with foils. 4. (Met.) Struggle or agitation of the mind. 5. (Pint.) Battle-piece, a painting which represents a battle. 6. Just, tournament. *Campo de batalla,* Field of battle. *Cuerpo de batalla de una esquadra,* The centre division of a fleet. *En batalla,* (Mil.) With an extended front.

Batalladór, ra, *s.* 1. Combatant, a fighting person; warrior. 2. Fencer with foils.

Batallár, *vn.* 1. To fight, to be engaged in battle. 2. To fence with foils. 3. (Met.) To contend, to argue, to dispute.

Batallóla, *sf.* V. *Batayolas.*

Batallón, *sm.* Battalion, a division of infantry.

Batallóso, sa, V. *Belicoso.*

Batán, *sm.* Fulling-mill where cloth is fulled or cleansed from oil and grease. *Batanes,* A boyish play of striking the soles of the feet, hands, &c.

Batanádo, da, *a.* Fulled, milled.

Batanár, *va.* To full cloth.

Bataneár, *va.* To bang or beat, to handle roughly.

Batanéro, *sm.* Fuller, a clothier.

Batáta, *sf.* (Bot.) Spanish potatoe, or sweet potatoe of Malaga. Convolvulus batatas *L.*

Batatín, *sm.* (Bot.) Common potatoe. Solanum tuberosum *L.*

Batáya, *sf.* (Ant.) V. *Batalla.*

Batayólas, *sf. pl.* (Naút.) Rails. *Batayolas de los empalletados,* (Naút.) Quarter-netting rails. *Batayolas de las cofas,* (Naút.) Top-rails. *Batayolas del pasamano,* (Naút.) Gang-way rails.

Batéa, *sf.* 1. Painted tray or hamper of japanned wood which comes from the East Indies. 2. Trough for bathing the hands or feet. 3. Boat made in the form of a trough.

Batéar, V. *Bautizar.*

Bateguéla, *sf.* A small hamper or tray.

Batél, *sm.* Small vessel.

Bateléjo, íco, íllo, y íto, *sm.* Yawl, a small boat.

Batéo, *sm.* Baptism.

Batér, (Ant.) V. *Batir.*

Batería, *sm.* 1. Battery, a number of pieces of ordnance arranged to play upon the enemy; also the work on which they are placed. *Bateria á barbeta,* A barbet battery. *Bateria en terrada,* A sunk battery. *Bateria á rebote,* A ricochet battery. *Bateria cruzante,* Cross battery. *Bateria de cocina,* Kitchen-furniture. 2. (Naút.) Tier or range of guns on one side of a ship. *Bateria entera de una banda,* (Naút.) A broad-side. *Navio de bateria floreada,* (Naút.) A ship which carries her ports at a proper height out of the water. 3. (Met.) Repeated importunities that a person may do what is solicited. 4. Battery, the act and effect of battering. 5. (Met.) Any thing which makes a strong impression on the mind.

Batéro, ra, *s.* Mantua-maker, one whose trade is to make gowns.

Batída, *sf.* 1. A hunting party for chasing wild animals. 2. Noise made by huntsmen to cheer the hounds and rouse the game.

Batidéra, *sf.* 1. Beater, an instrument used by plasterers and bricklayers for beating and mixing mortar. 2. An instrument used by glass-makers for stirring the sand and ashes in melting pots in glass-houses.

Batidéro, *sm.* 1. Collision, the clashing of one thing against another. 2. Uneven ground, which renders the motion of carriages unpleasant. *Guardar los batideros,* To drive carefully in broken roads: (Met.) To guard against inconveniencies. 3. (Naút.) Wash-board. *Batidero de una vela,* Foot-tabling of a sail. *Batidero de proa,* Wash-board of the cut water.

Batído, da, *a.* 1. Changeable; applied to silks, the warp of which is of one colour, and the woof or weft of another. 2. Beaten, as roads.

Batído, *sm.* Batter of flour and water for making the host, wafers, or biscuits.

Batidór, *sm.* 1. Scout, one who is sent to explore the position of the enemy, and the condition of the roads. 2. Ranger, one who rouses the game in the forest. 3. One of the Life-guards, who rides before a royal coach. *Batidor de cañamo,* A hemp-dresser. *Batidor de oro ó plata,* A gold or silver beater, he who makes gold or silver leaves.

Batiénte, *sm.* 1. Jamb or post of a door. 2. Portcell. 3. *Batiente de la bandera,* (Naút.) Fly of an ensign. 4. *Batiente de un dique,* Apron of a dock.

Batifúlla, (Ant.) V. *Batihoja.*

Batihója, *sm.* 1. Gold-beater. 2. Artisan who works iron and other metal into sheets. 3. Warp of cloth which crosses the woof.

Batimiénto, *sm.* (Ant.) 1. The act and effect of beating. 2. The thing beaten.

Batiportár, *va.* (Naút.) To house a gun on board a ship, to secure it by tackles and breechings.

Batipórtes, *sm. pl.* Port-cells.

Batír, *va.* 1. To beat, to dash, to strike two bodies together. 2. To demolish, to rase, to throw down. 3. To move in a violent manner. 4. (In Paper-mills) To fit and adjust the reams of paper already made up. 5. To strike or fall on without injury, spoken of the sun or wind. *El cierzo bate á Madrid,* The north-wind blows on Madrid. *Batir banderas,* To salute with the colours: (Naút.) To strike the colours. *Batir el campo,* (Mil.) To reconnoitre the enemy's camp. *Batir moneda,* To coin money. *Batir las olas,* To ply the seas. *Batir hoja,* To beat metals into leaves or plates.—*vr.* 1. To lose courage, to decline in health or strength. V. *Abatirse.* 2. (Met.) *Batirse el cobre,* To toil hard for useful purposes.

Batísta, *sf.* Batist, cambric or lawn.

Batojár, *va.* To beat down the fruit of a tree.

Batucár, *va.* To beat liquors and other things in a violent manner to and fro, to mix things by long and frequent agitation.

Batuquério, *sm.* Agitation, disturbance

Baturríllo, *sm.* 1 Hotch-potch, salmagundi, a medley altogether suitable. 2. (Met.) Mixture of unconnected and incongruous ideas either in conversation or writing.

Baúl, *sm.* 1. Trunk, a kind of chest for clothes. 2. Belly. *Llenar el baul,* (Vulg.) To fill the paunch.

Baulíllo, *sm.* A small trunk.

Bauprés, *sm.* (Naút.) Bow-sprit. *Botalon del bauprés,* The bow-sprit boom.

Bausán, na, *s.* 1. Effigy or human figure made of straw, or other matter. 2. Fool, idiot. 3. (Naút.) Bow-sprit. 4. Down, downy hair.

Bautismál, *a.* Baptismal, belonging to baptism.

Bautísmo y Bautízo, *sm.* Baptism.

Bautistério, *sm.* Baptistery, the place where the sacrament of baptism is administered.

Bautizár, *va.* 1. To baptize. 2. (Naút.) To duck seamen in those seas where they have not been before. *Bautizar un baxel,* To give a name to a ship. *Bautizar el vino,* To mix water with wine.

Bauzadór, ra, *s.* V. *Embaucador.*

Baxá, *sm.* Bashaw, a Turkish governor.

Báxa, *sf.* 1. Diminution of price. 2. A dance introduced into Spain by the natives of Lower Germany, as *Alta* was by those of the Upper. 3. Ticket of admission in an hospital. 4. (Mil.) Head of casualties in a muster roll. *Dar baxa,* (Mil.) To discharge from service. *Dar de baxa,* (Mil.) To make a return of the casualties which have happened in a corps.

Baxáda, *sf.* 1. Inclination of an arch with regard to the horizon. 2. Descent, the act of descending, and the road or path by which a person descends.

Baxádo, da, *pp.* Descended. *Baxado del cielo,* Dropped from heaven, uncommonly excellent.

Baxamár, *sf.* Low water.

Baxaménte, *ad.* Basely, lowly, meanly.

Baxár, *vn.* 1. To descend, to go down. 2. To lessen, to diminish.—*va.* 1. To lower, to take from a higher to a lower place. *Baxar la cuesta,* To go down hill. 2. To bow, to bend downwards. 3. To lower the price, to abate the price in selling. 4. To lessen the value of a thing. *Baxar de punto,* To decay, to decline. 5. To humble, to bring down. *Le baxaré los brios,* I will pull down his courage. *Baxar los humos,* To become more humane. *Baxar los ojos,* To be ashamed. *Baxar la cabeza,* To obey without objection. *Baxarse de la querella,* (For.) To give up a law-suit, to relinquish a claim. *Baxar la tierra,* (Naút.) To lay the land. *Baxar por un rio,* (Naút.) To drop down a river. *Baxar las velas,* (Naút.) To lower the sails.

Baxél, *sm.* (Naút.) Vessel; a general name for all ships, barges, hoys, lighters, boats, &c. *Baxel desaparejado,* A ship unrigged or laid up in ordinary. *Baxel boyante,* A light ship. *Baxel de baxo bordo,* A low-built ship. *Baxel marinero,* A good sea-boat. *Baxel velero,* A swift sailer.

Baxeléro, *sm.* Owner or master of a vessel.

Baxéro, ra, *a.* That which is under; as, *Sábana baxera,* The under sheet.

Baxéte, *sm.* 1. Person of a low stature. 2. Voice between a tenor and a base.

Baxéza, *sf.* 1. A mean act, an unworthy action.

2. A low, deep place. *Baxeza de animo*, Lowness of spirits, weakness of mind. *Baxeza de nacimiento*, Meanness of birth.

BAXÍLLO, *sm.* Wine-pipe in a vintner's shop.

BAXÍO, XÍA, *a.* (Ant.) V. *Baxo.*

BAXÍO, *sm.* 1. A shoal, sand-bank, shallow, or flat. 2. (Met.) Decline of fortune or favour. 3. Abatement.

BÁXO, XA, *a.* 1. Low, not high. 2. (Met.) Humble, despicable, abject. 3. Bent downwards. 4. Dull, faint, not bright; applied to colours. 5. Mean, coarse, vulgar; applied to language. *Baxa de ley*, Of a base quality; applied to metals. *Baxo de la mar*, (Naút.) Shoal or sand-bank.

BÁXO, *ad.* 1. Under, underneath, below. V. *Abaxo y Debaxo.* 2. In an humble, submissive manner. 3. *Por lo baxo*, Cautiously, in a cautious, prudent manner. 4. *Baxo mano*, Underhand, privately, secretly.

BÁXO, *sm.* 1. Base, a voice or note which is an eighth lower than the tenor. 2. Player on the base-viol or bassoon. 3. Low situation or place. *Baxo relieve*, (Esc.) Bas-relief, figures raised above the field or ground. 4. *Baxo monte*, Coppice, a wood which contains only shrubs and low wood. 5. *Quarto baxo*, Ground-floor. *Báxos*, Hoofs of fore and hind feet of horses; under petticoats of women.

BAXÓN, *sm.* 1. Bassoon, a wind instrument of musick. 2. A player on the bassoon.

BAXONCÍLLO, *sm.* Counter-base.

BAXUÉLO, LA, *a.* Somewhat low. [*Baxeza.*

BAXÚRA, *sf.* (Ant.) 1. A hollow place. 2. V.

BÁYA, *sf.* 1. Berry, the fruit of various vegetables. 2. Pole used as a partition to separate horses in a stable. 3. Scoff, jest.

BAYÁL, *a.* Not steeped or soaked; applied to flax.

BAYÁL, *sm.* Lever composed of two pieces of timber, one of which is straight and the other bent, fastened together with an iron ring, and used in raising mill-stones.

BAYÉTA, *sf.* Baize or bays, a kind of cloth of an open texture, a sort of flannel. *Bayeta de alconcher*, Colchester baize. *Bayeta fazuela*, Lancashire baize. *Bayeta miniquina*, Long baize. *Bayeta del sur ó cien kilos*, White list baize. *Arrastrar bayetas*, To claim a degree in superior colleges, the claimants whereof are obliged to visit the college in wide loose gowns with a train of baize. *Arrastrar bayetas*, (Met.) To enforce a claim with care and assiduity.—*pl.* 1. Pall, the black covering thrown over the dead. 2. (In Paper-mills) Felts used in the manufacture of paper.

BAYETÓNES, *sm. pl.* Coatings. *Bayetones moteados*, Spotted coatings. *Bayetones de nubes*, Clouded coatings. *Bayetones rayados*, Striped coatings.

BÁYLA, *sf.* 1. (Ant.) V. *Bayle.* 2. (Ict.) Sea-trout. *Ser dueño ó amo de la bayla*, (Ar.) To be the principal or chief of any business.

BAYLADÉRO, RA, *a.* (Ant.) Applied to music fit for dancing.

BAYLADÓR, RA, *s.* 1. Dancer. 2. (Cant.) Thief.

BAYLADORCÍLLO, ÍLLA, *s.* A little dancer.

BAYLÁR, *vn.* 1. To dance, to move in measure. 2. To move in a rapid, lively manner. 3. To move by a short brisk gallop; applied to horses. *Baylar el agua delante*, To dance attendance, to wait with suppleness and obsequiousness. *Baylar sin son*, To dance without music; to be too eager for performing any thing to require a stimulus.

BAYLARÍN, NA, *s.* 1. Dancer, caperer, one who dances in a frolicsome manner. 2. A fiery high-mettled horse, which prances and bounds in a restless manner.

BÁYLE, *sm.* 1. Dance, a motion of one or many in concert. 2. Ball, rout. 3. Farce, a Spanish interlude between the second and third act. 4. *Bayle de boton gordo*, A rustic dance or hop among the lower classes of the people. *Bayle de cuenta*, Dance with a fixed number of steps and figures. 5. Bailiff, a judge or justice. *Bayle general*, Chief justice of the exchequer.

BAYLECÍTO, *sm.* A little dance or hop.

BAYLÉTE, *sm.* Cavalcade, a procession on horseback.

BAYLÍA Y BAYLIÁZGO, *s.* 1. District of the jurisdiction of a *Bayle* or Bailiff. 2. District of a commandery in the order of the knights of Malta.

BAYLIÁGE, *sm.* A commandery or dignity in the order of Malta, the incumbent whereof is called *Baylio.*

BÁYO, *sm.* Y *a.* 1. A bay horse. 2. Brown butterfly used in angling with a fishing-rod.

BAYÓCO, *sm.* 1. Copper coin current in Rome, Naples, and other parts of Italy. 2. (Mur.) Fig, either not yet ripe, or which has withered and fallen before it was ripe.

BAYÓNA, (Arda), *sf.* The little care an exhibition or festival gives to those whom it costs nothing, compared with those whom it costs much.

BAYONÉTA, *sf.* Bayonet, a short sword fixed at the end of a musket. *Bayoneta calada*, A fixed bayonet. [net.

BAYONETÁZO, *sm.* Thrust or stroke with a bayo-

BAYÓQUE. V. *Bayóco.*

BAYÚCA, *sm.* Tippling-house.

BAYSÁRE, *sm.* Large sea-fish, resembling a sea-calf.

BAYVÉL, *sm.* (In Masonry and Joinery.) BEVEL, a kind of square, one leg of which is frequently crooked.

BÁZA, *sf.* Trick at cards, a number of cards regularly laid up and won by one of the players. *No dexar meter baza*, Not to suffer another to put in a single word. *Tener bien sentada su baza*, To have one's character well established.

BAZÁO, *sm.* Fine sort of cotton brought from Jerusalem.

BÁZO, *sm.* Spleen or milt, one of the viscera which is found in the left hypochondres.

BÁZO, ZA, *a.* Brown inclining to yellow. *Pan bazo*, Brown bread.

BAZÓFIA, *sf.* 1. Offal, waste meat which is not eaten at the table. 2. Refuse, any thing of no value.

BAZUCÁR, *va.* To stir liquids by shaking the vessel in which they are contained.

BAZUQUÉO, *sm.* The act of stirring liquids by shaking the vessel.

Bé, The cry of sheep and lambs when they bleat; name of the second letter, *B.*
Beáta, *sf.* 1. Woman who wears a religious habit, and is engaged in works of charity. 2. Female hypocrite, affecting piety and religion.
Beatería, *sf.* Act of affected piety and religion.
Beatério, *sm.* House inhabited by pious women.
Beatíco, ca, *s.* A little hypocrite, affecting piety.
Beatificación, *sf.* Beatification, the act whereby the Pope declares that a person deceased is in heaven, and may be reverenced as blessed.
Beatificaménte, *ad.* Beatifically.
Beatificár, *va.* 1. To beatify, or declare the blessed state of a person deceased; applied to the Pope. 2. To render a thing respectable.
Beatífico, ca, *a.* (Tool.) Beatific, beatifical.
Beatílla, *sf.* A sort of fine thin linen.
Beatísimo, ma, *a. sup. Beatísimo padre*, Most holy father; applied to the Pope.
Beatitúd, *sf.* 1. Beatitude, blessedness, the state of the blessed in celestial enjoyment. 2. Title given to the Pope.
Beáto, ta, *a.* 1. Happy, blessed; beatified. 2. Wearing a religious habit without being a member of a religious community.
Beáto, ta, *s.* 1. A pious person devoted to works of charity and virtue, and abstaining from public diversions. 2. One who lives in pious retirement, and wears an humble, religious dress.
Beatóno, na, y Beatón, *s.* Hypocrite, pretended saint.
Bebedéro, *sm.* 1. Drinking vessels for birds and other domestic animals. 2. Place whither fowls resort to drink. *Bebedéros*, Stripes of cloth used by tailors for lining the inside of clothes.
Bebedéro, ra, ó Bebedízo, za, *a.* Potable, drinkable, such as may be drunk.
Bebedízo, *sm.* 1. Philter or love potion superstitiously administered to excite love. 2. Physical potion for brutes, drench.
Bebédo, da, *a.* Drunk, intoxicated.
Bebedór, ra, *s.* Tippler, toper.
Bebér, *va.* 1. To drink, to swallow any liquid. 2. To pledge, to toast. *Beber á la salud de alguno*, To drink to another's health. *Sin comerlo ni beberlo*, To suffer an injury without having had any part in the cause or motive of it. *Beber de codos*, To drink at leisure and luxuriously. *Beber las palabras, los accentos, los semblantes y acciónes á otro*, To listen with the greatest care, to swallow or adopt the speech, accent, features, and actions of another. *Beber los pensamientos á alguno*, To anticipate one's thoughts. *Beber los vientos*, To solicit with much eagerness. *Le quisiera beber la sangre*, I would drink his heart's blood. *Beber como una cuba*, To drink as a fish. *Beber el caliz*, To drink the cup of bitterness.
Bebéres, *sm. pl.* (Ant.) Opportunities for drinking often, as at feasts or invitations.
Beberrón, *sm.* Tippler, maltworm, low drunkard.
Bebída, *sf.* 1. Drink, beverage, potion. 2. The short time allowed to workmen and day-labourers to drink and refresh themselves in the intervals of labour.
Bebído, da, *s.* 1. An intoxicated person. *Bien bebido*, Half drunk. 2. Drench or physical potion for brutes. 3. (Ant.) V. *Bebida.*

Bebistrájo, *sm.* An irregular and extravagant mixture of drinks.
Beborroteár, *va.* To sip, to drink by small draughts.
Bebrâge, *sm.* Beverage. V. *Brebage.*
Béca, *sf.* 1. Part of a student's dress in the shape of an oar, which is worn over the gown. *Bécas*, Stripes of velvet, satin, &c. with which the fore part of cloaks is lined by way of ornament. 2. Tippet worn by the dignitaries of the church. 3. Foundation, a revenue settled and established for the maintenance of students.
Becabúnga, *sf.* (Bot.) Brook-lime. Veronica becabunga *L.*
Becáda, *sf.* (Orn.) Wood-cock.
Becafígo, *sm.* (Orn.) Fig-pecker, epicurean warbler. Motacilla ficedula *L. Becafigo raro*, (Orn.) Great red-pole, or red-headed linnet. Fringilla cannabina *L.*
Becardón, *sm.* (Arag.) Snipe.
Becérra, *sm.* 1. (Bot.) Snap-dragon. 2. Earth and stones swept down by mountain floods.
Becerríllo, lla; to, ta, *s.* (Dim.) 1. Calf, the young of a cow. 2. Tanned and dressed calf-skin.
Becérro, ra, *s.* 1. A yearling calf. 2. Calf-skin tanned and dressed. 3. Register in which are entered the privileges and appurtenances of cathedral churches and convents. 4. Manuscript bound in calf-skin, and found in the archives of *Simancas*, containing an account of the origin and titles of the Spanish nobility. *Becerro marino*, A sea-calf.
Becoquín, *sm.* Cap tied under the chin.
Bedél, *sm.* 1. Beadle, an officer in universities, whose business it is to inspect the conduct of the students. 2. Apparitor of a court of justice.
Bedelía, *sf.* The place and employment of a beadle.
Bedélio, *sm.* Bdellium, an aromatic gum.
Bedíja, *sf.* Flock, a small lock of wool.
Bedijéro, ra, *s.* A person who picks up and gathers the locks of wool which are dropped on the ground during the shearing.
Bedúro, *sm.* V. *Bequadrado.*
Béfa, *sf.* 1. Irrision; the act of deriding, scoffing, or laughing. 2. Garland, a wreath of flowers.
Befabemí, *sm.* Musical sign.
Befár, *va.* 1. To mock, to scoff, to ridicule. 2. To move the lips, and endeavour to catch the chain of the bit; applied to horses.
Befedád, *sf.* (Ant.) The deformity of bandy-legged.
Beféz, *a.* (Ant.) V. *Bazo.*
Béfo, *sm.* 1. Lip of a horse or other animal. 2. Thick, projecting under lip, and bandy legs.
Begárdo, da, *s.* Heretic of the 13th century who pretended to be impeccable.
Begín, *sm.* 1. Common puff-ball, fuzz-ball. Lycoperdon bovista *L.* 2. (Met.) Peevish, wayward child, which puts itself out of humour from any slight motive.
Beguería, *sm.* The district and jurisdiction of a *Beguer* or magistrate in Catalonia and Majorca.
Beguíno, na, *s.* Heretic of the 14th century, pretending to be without sin.
Behetría ó Bienfetría, *sf.* 1. A town whose inhabitants are invested with the right of electing their own magistrates. 2. Confusion, disorder.

Lugar de behetria, (Met.) A place where a perfect equality prevails without the least distinction of rank.

Beíto, (Ant.) V. *Benito*.

Bejucál, *sm.* A place where reeds grow in considerable quantities.

Bejúco, *sm.* 1. Thin or pliable reed or cane growing in India. 2. Filaments growing on some trees in America.

Bejuquíllo, *sm.* 1. A small gold chain brought from India, and worn by women about the neck. 2. Root of an Indian plant called ipecacuanha.

Bel, la, *a.* V. *Bello*.

Beldád, *sf.* Beauty; at present only applied to exalt the beautifulness of women.

Beledín, *sf.* Sort of cotton stuff of a middling quality.

Beléño, *sm.* 1. (Bot.) Hen-bane. Hyoscyamus niger *L.* 2. Poison.

Belérico, *sm.* (Bot.) Myrobalan. Hernandia sonora *L.*

Bélfo, fa, *a.* Blob-lipped or blubber-lipped, having a thick under lip. *Diente belfo*, Snag tooth, a tooth which stands beyond the rest.

Bélfo, *sm.* Thick under lip of a horse.

Belhéz, *sf.* A large jar in which oil or wine is kept.

Belhézo, *sm.* 1. A large jar. 2. (Ant.) Furniture.

Bélico, ca, *a.* Warlike, military, relating to war.

Belicóso, sa, *a.* 1. Warlike, martial. 2. Quarrelsome, irascible, easily irritated.

Belicosidád, *sf.* Warlike state.

Belígero, ra, *a.* (Poét.) Warlike, belligerous.

Beligeránte, *a.* Belligerent.

Belítre, *a.* (Vulg.) Low, mean, vile, of vulgar sentiments and manners; roguish.

Bellacáda, *sf.* 1. A nest of rogues, a set of villains. 2. (Bax.) Knavery, roguery.

Bellacaménte, *ad.* Knavishly, roguishly.

Belláco, ca, *a.* 1. Artful, sly. 2. Cunning, roguish, deceitful.

Belláco, *sm.* Rogue, a villain, a swindler.

Bellaconázo, *sm.* Great knave, an arrant rogue.

Bellacuélo, *sm.* Artful, cunning little fellow.

Belladáma ó Belladóna, *sf.* (Bot.) Deadly nightshade. Atropa belladona *L.*

Bellaménte, *ad.* Prettily, gracefully.

Bellaqueár, *vn.* To cheat, to swindle, to play knavish, roguish tricks.

Bellaquería, *sf.* Knavery, roguery, the act of swindling or deceiving.

Belléza, *sf.* 1. Beauty, an assemblage of fine features and graces. 2. Decoration or ornament, which sets off the front of buildings. *Decir bellezas*, To say fine things.

Béllo, lla, *a.* Beautiful, handsome, perfect. *Bella pedreria*, Fine jewels. *Bello principio*, An excellent beginning. *De su bella gracia*. Of one's own accord. *Por su bella cara no se le concederá*, It will not be granted for his pretty face's sake, or without any peculiar cause or motive.

Bellório, ia, *a.* Mouse coloured; applied to the coat of horses.

Bellorita, *sf.* (Bot.) Common daisy. Bellis perennis *L.*

Bellóta, *sf.* 1. Acorn, the fruit of an oak, but particularly of the ever-green oak. 2. Balsam or perfume box, in the shape of an acorn, to carry balsam or perfumes. *Bellota marina*, Centre-shell, a shell in the shape of an acorn.

Bellóte, *sm.* Large round-headed nail.

Belloteár, *vn.* To be fed with acorns; applied to swine.

Bellotéra, *sf.* Season for gathering acorns, and feeding swine with them.

Bellotéro, ra, *s.* One who gathers or sells acorns.

Bellotéro, *sm.* (Ant.) Any tree which bears acorns.

Bellotíca, illa, ita, *sf.* Small acorn.

Belórtas, *sf. pl.* The iron rings or screws with which the bed of the plough is fastened to the beam.

Bemól, *sm.* (Mús.) B-flat.

Bemoládo, *a.* Having B-flat.

Bén, *sm.* (Ant.) V. *Bien*.

Bén ó Behén, *sf.* Fruit of the size of a filbert, which yields a precious oil by expression.

Benaláque, *sm.* House or hut in a vineyard.

Benarríza, *sf.* A very saveury bird of the family of Ortolans.

Bendecír, *va.* 1. To devote something to the service of the church; to consecrate. *Bendecir la bandera*, To consecrate the colours. 2. To bless, to praise, to exalt. *Dios te bendiga*, God bless thee.

Bendición, *sf.* Benediction, the act of blessing. *Echar la bendicion*, (Met.) To give up a business, not to have any thing more to do with it. *Es una bendicion ó es bendicion*, (Vulg.) It does one's heart good to see what a plenty there is. *Miente que es una bendicion*. (Iron.) It is a blessing to hear how he lies. *Hijo y fruto de bendicion*, A child begotten in wedlock.

Bendícho, cha, *pp. irreg.* (Ant.) of *Bendecir*.

Bendíto, ta, *pp.* of *Bendecir*.

Bendíto, ta, *a.* 1. Sainted, blessed. 2. Simple, silly. *Es un bendito*, He is a simpleton, or silly mortal. *El bendito*, V. *Alabado*.

Benecír y Benedecír, *va.* (Ant.) V. *Bendecir*.

Benedícite, (Lat.) Permission solicited by ecclesiastics with this word.

Benedícta, *sf.* Benedict, an electuary made up of various powders, herbs, purging roots, and stomachics, mixed with honey.

Benefactór, *sm.* Benefactor. V. *Bienhechor*.

Benefatoría, *sf.* (Ant.) V. *Behetria*.

Beneficéncia, *sf.* Beneficence, active goodness.

Beneficación, *sf.* Benefaction.

Beneficiádo, *sm.* The incumbent of a benefice which is neither a curacy nor prebend, but a sinecure.

Beneficiadór, ra, *s.* Administrator or administratrix, who improves or meliorates.

Beneficiál, *a.* Relating to benefices or ecclesiastical livings.

Beneficiár, *va.* 1. To do good. 2. To cultivate and meliorate the ground, to work and improve mines. 3. (Ant.) To confer an ecclesiastical benefice. 4. To purchase a place or employ. *Beneficiar una compañia de caballeria*, To buy the commission of a captain of horse. *Beneficiar los efectos, libranzas y otros creditos*, To resign and make over effects, credits, and other claims.

Beneficiário, *sm.* Beneficiary, he that is in

possession of a benefice which he holds in subordination to another.

Beneficio, *sm.* Benefit, favour, or advantage, conferred on or received from another. 2. (Ant.) Paint. 3. Right belonging to one either by law or charter. 4. Labour and culture; applied to the ground, trees, mines, &c. 5. Utility, profit; a benefice. *Beneficio curado*, Benefice to which a curacy is annexed. 6. Purchase of public places, employs, or commissions in the army. 7. Act of resigning and making over credits and demands for sums not equal to their amount. *Beneficio de inventario*, Benefit of inventory, the effect whereof is, that the heir is not obliged to pay debts to a larger amount than that of the inheritance. *No tener oficio, ni beneficio*, To have neither profession nor property; applied to vagabonds.

Beneficióso, sa, *a.* Beneficial, advantageous, profitable.

Benéfico, ca, *a.* Beneficent, kind, doing good.

Benemeréncia, *sf.* (Rar.) Meritorious service.

Benemérito, ta, *a.* Meritorious, deserving of reward.

Beneplácito, *sm.* Good-will, approbation, permission.

Benevoléncia, *sf.* Benevolence, good-will, kindness.

Benévolo, la, *a.* Benevolent, kind.

Bengála, *sf.* (Ant. Burgos.) Muslin.

Benignaménte, *ad.* Kindly, favourably.

Benignidád, *sf.* 1. Benignity, graciousness, kindness, piety. 2. Mildness of the air or weather.

Benígno, na, *a.* 1. Benign, gracious, pious. 2. Mild, temperate, gentle.

Beníno, *sm.* Pimple, a small red pustule in the face.

Beníto, ta, *s.* Benedictine friar or nun.

Benivoléncia, *sf.* (Ant.) V. *Benevolencia*.

Benjuí, *sm.* Benzoin or Benjamin, a gum-resin.

Benqueréncia, *sf.* (Ant.) V. *Bienquerencia*.

Beodéz, *sf.* (Ant.) Drunkenness, intoxication.

Beódo, da, *a.* Drunk, drunken.

Bequadrádo, *sm.* (Mús.) B quadrate.

Béque, *sm.* (Naút.) 1. Head of the ship. 2. Privies for the sailors made in the head-gratings.

Bequéso, *sm.* (Orn.) Wood pecker. Picus *L.*

Berám, *sf.* Coarse cotton stuff which is brought from the East Indies.

Berbéna, *sf.* V. *Verbena*.

Berberís ó Bérbero, *sm.* (Bot.) Barberry, berberry, piperedge-bush.

Berbí, *sm.* A sort of woollens.

Berbiquí, *sm.* A carpenter's breast-bit for boring.

Bercería, *sf.* Green-market, where cabbage and other vegetables are sold.

Bercéro, ra, *s.* Green-grocer.

Berengéna, *sf.* (Bot.) Egg-plant, mad-apple. Solanum melongena *L.*

Berengenádo, da, *a.* Having the colour of a mad-apple.

Berengenál, *sm.* A mad-apple plantation. *Meterse en un berengenal*, To involve one's self in difficulties.

Berengenázo, *sm.* Blow given with a mad-apple.

Bergamóta, *sf.* 1. Bergamot, a sort of pear. 2. Snuff scented with the essence of bergamot.

Bergamóte ó Bergamóto, *sm.* (Bot.) Bergamot-tree.

Bergánte, *sm.* Brazen-faced villain, a ruffian.

Bergantín, *sm.* (Naút.) Brig or brigantine, a two-masted vessel.

Bergantinéjo, *sm.* Small brig.

Bergantón, na, *s.* (Aum.) Brazen-faced, impudent person.

Bergantonázo, *sm.* Most impudent ruffian.

Berílo y Beríl, *sm.* 1. Beryl, a precious stone of a green colour. 2. Edge of some shoal or sand-bank.

Berlína, *sf.* Landau or Berlin, an open carriage, with a front and back seat.

Berlínga, *sf.* 1. Pole driven perpendicularly into the ground, at the top of which is fastened a rope, and carried to another pole, which serves to hang clothes upon to be dried. 2. (Naút.) Round timber of six inches in diameter.

Bérma, *sf.* (Fort.) Berm, a small space of ground at the foot of the rampart towards the moat, to prevent the earth from falling into the ditch.

Bermejeár, *vn.* To be of a reddish colour, to incline towards red.

Bermejízo, za, *a.* Reddish.

Berméjo, ja, *a.* Of a bright reddish colour.

Bermejón ó Bermillón, (Ant.) V. *Bermellon*.

Bermejuéla, *sf.* (Ict.) Rochet, a small river fish.

Bermejuélo, la, *a.* A little reddish.

Bermejúra, *sf.* Ruddy colour.

Bermellón, *sm.* Vermilion, or cinnabar, a red and ponderous mineral, being an oxide of quicksilver.

Bermudiána, *sf.* (Bot.) Bermudian lily-plant. Sisyrinchium *L.*

Bernandínas, *sf. pl.* Fanfaronades, false boasts.

Bernárdo, da, *s.* Bernardine religious.

Bernegál, *sm.* Bowl, a wide-mouthed cup or vessel to hold liquids.

Bernía, *sf.* 1. Rug, a coarse nappy woollen cloth, of which coverlets are made for mean beds. 2. Cloak made of rug.

Berníz, *sm.* V. *Barniz*.

Bérra, *sf.* (Bot.) Water parsnep. Sium latifolium *L.*

Berráza, *sf.* 1. V. *Berra*. 2. Common water-cress.

Berreár, *vn.* To cry like a calf, to low, to bellow.

Berreguetár, *vn.* (In games at Cards) To cheat, to play slight-of-hand tricks like sharpers.

Berrénche, *sm.* Courage; great petulancy.

Berrenchín, *sm.* 1. Foaming, grunting, and blowing of a wild boar at the rutting time. 2. Cry of angry wayward children.

Berrendéarse, *vr.* 1. (And.) To grow yellow; applied to wheat nearly ripe. 2. To be stained or tinged with two different colours.

Berréndo, da, *a.* 1. Stained or tinged with two different colours. 2. (And.) Ripe wheat which gets a yellow colour. 3. (Mur.) Applied to a silk-worm which has a duskish brown colour.

Berréra ó Berrizál, *sf.* V. *Berraza*.

Berrído, *sm.* The cry and bellowing of a calf, or other animal.

Berrín, *sm.* Child or person in a violent passion.

…rro. sm. (Bot.) Water-cresses. Sisymbrium nasturtium L. Andar á la flor del berro, To …d' and wander about

…cál, sm. Place full of rocks.

…queña, a. Piedra berroqueña, Granite, a …rd stone composed of large concretions, …erally of an ash colour with black spots, …red variegated with black and white.

…ruéco, sm. 1. Rock. 2. Pin, a small horny …uration of the membranes of the eye.

…úga, sf. Wart, a horny protuberance …wing on the flesh.

…gáza, sf. Large wart.

…góso, sa, a. Warty, full of warts. [ons.

…scia, sf. Sort of stuff manufactured at Ly-

…za, sf. (Bot.) Cabbage. Brassica L. Berza …perro, (Bot.) Wild mercury, dog's cab- … Theligonum cynocrambe L. Berza flo- …, Cauliflower. Berza crespa, Savoy-cab- … Estár en berza, To be in the blade, …ed to grain.

…áza, sf. A large head of cabbage.

…dór, ra, a. Kissing; kisser.

…amános, sm. 1. Levee or court-day, when …obility assemble at court, to kiss the king's … 2. Salute, performed with the hand.

…na, sf. First furrow opened in the ground …h a plough.

…ar. va. 1. To kiss any thing with the lips, as …ark of fondness or respect. 2. To touch … another closely; applied to inanimate …gs. A besar, (Naút.) Home, or block on … Besar el azote, (Met.) To kiss the rod, … receive a chastisement with patience and …gnation. Llegar y besar, No sooner said … done. Besar la mano, ó los pies, Ex- …ssions of courtesy and respect—vr. To …identally strike heads or faces together.

…o y Besíto, sm. A little kiss. Besicos de …nja, (Bot.) A kind of convolvulus.

… sm. 1. Kiss, a salute given with the lips. … Violent knock of persons or things against …h other. 3. (Among Bakers) Kissing …t, where one loaf touches another. Beso … monja, A delicious kind of sweet-meat. … un beso al jarro, (Vulg.) To toss about … pot, to drink freely.

…tezuéla, sf. A little beast.

…tia, sf. 1. Beast, a quadruped. Bestia de al- …rda. A beast of burthen. Bestia de silla, A …ddle mule. Gran bestia, An elk, a large and …ely animal of the stag kind. 2. (Met.) Dunce, idiot, rude ill-bred fellow.

…tiáge, sm. An assembly of beasts of bur- …en.

…tiál, a. Bestial, brutal, belonging to a beast.

…tialidád, sf. V. Brutalidad.

…tialménte, ad. In a brutal manner.

…tiécica, élla, íta, y Bestiezuéla, sf. A …tle beast.

…tión, sm. Large beast.

…tóla, sf. Paddle, or paddlestaff, for clean- …g the coulter of the plough.

…turín, sm. Bistouri.

…ucadór, sm. Kisser, one who kisses.

…ucár, va. To give many kisses.

…ucón, sm. (Aum.) Hearty kiss.

…ugáda, sf. A lunch or luncheon, or supper …f sea breams.

Besúgo, sm. (Ict.) Sea bream, or red gilt head, a fish frequent in the Bay of Biscay. Sparus pagrus L. Ojo de besugo, Squint-eyed. Ya te veo besugo, (Met.) I can anticipate your design. [breams.

Besuguéra, sf. A pan for dressing besugos or

Besuguéro, sm. 1. Fishmonger who sells breams. 2. (Ast.) Fishing-hook and tackle for catching breams.

Besuguéte, sm. (Ict.) Red sea bream. Sparus erythinus L.

Besuquéo, sm. Embracing kiss.

Béta, sf. (Arag.) Any bit or line of thread. Beta de la madera, The grain of the wood. Betas, (Naút.) Pieces of cordage for serving all sorts of tackle.

Betarrága y Betarráta, sf. (Bot.) Beet-root. Beta vulgaris L.

Betlemítas, sm. pl. Bethlemites, a religious order established in America.

Betónica, sf. (Bot.) Betony. Betonica L.

Betúm, Betume, y Betumen, sm. (Ant.) V. Betun.

Betún, sm. 1. Bitumen, a kind of fossil pitch. 2. Cement, made chiefly of lime and oil. 3. (Naút.) Stuff with which the masts and bottoms of ships are payed. Betun de colmena, Coarse wax, found at the entrance of the hive.

Betunár, va. To pay or cover any thing with pitch, tar, resin, &c.

Beúna, sf. (Arag.) A gold coloured wine, made of a grape of the same name.

Beút, sm. A kind of sea-fish.

Bexína, sf. (Ant.) V. Alpechin.

Bexinéro, sm. (And.) One who separates the lees or watery sediment from the oil.

Beyupúra, sf. A large kind of fish, caught off the coast of Brasil.

Bezaártico, ca, a. V. Bezoárdico.

Bezánte, sm. (Blas.) Round figure like a piece of money on a shield.

Bezár y Bezaár, sf. Bezoar, a stone, formerly esteemed as an antidote.

Bézo, sm. 1. Blubber-lip, a thick lip. 2. (Ant.) A lip in general. 3. Proud flesh growing around a wound.

Bezoár, sm. V. Bezár. [with bezoar.

Bezoárdico, ca, a. Bezoardic, compounded

Bezón, sm. Battering-ram.

Bezóte, sm. A ring which the Indians wear in their under lip by way of ornament.

Bezúdo, da, a. Blubber-lipped, or blop-lipped.

Biambónas, sf. pl. A stuff made in China of the bark or rind and covering of plants.

Biása, sf. A kind of coarse silk, which the Dutch bring from the Levant.

Biázas, sf. pl. Saddlebags made of leather.

Bíbaro, sm. Beaver, castor. Castor fiber L.

Bíbero, sm. A sort of linen, which comes from Galicia.

Bíblia, sf. Bible, the sacred volume in which are contained the revelations of God.

Bíblico, ca, a. Biblical, relating to the bible.

Bibliófilo, sm. Book-lover, book-worm.

Bibliografía, sf. Bibliography, a knowledge of manuscripts and books.

Bibliógrafo, sm. Bibliographer, one who possesses much knowledge of manuscripts and books.

Bibliomanía, *sf.* Book-madness, an extravagant passion for books.

Biblióttafo, *sf.* One who lends his books to no [person.

Bibliotéca, *sf.* Library.

Bibliotecário, *sm.* Librarian.

Bíca, *sf.* (Ict.) A sea fish, resembling a bream.

Bicérra, *sf.* A kind of wild or mountain goat. Capra ibex *L.*

Bichéro, *sm.* (Naút.) A long pole with a hook fixed at the end, a boat-hook. *Asta de bichero*, The shaft of a boat-hook. *Gancho de bichero*, The hook of a boat-hook.

Bícho, cha, *s.* 1. A general name for small grubs or insects. 2. *Bicho*, (Met.) A little fellow, of a ridiculous figure and appearance. *Mal bicho*, A mischievous urchin. 3. Slut, bitch; a term of reproach to women.

Bicóca, *sf.* 1. Sentry box. 2. A small borough or village. 3. Thing of little esteem or value.

Bicoquéte, *sm.* A bonnet or head dress formerly worn.

Bicoquín, *sm.* Cap. V. *Becoquin.*

Bicórne, *a.* (Poet.) Bicornuous, having two horns.

Bícos, *sm. pl.* Small gold points or lace, formerly put on velvet bonnets by way of ornament.

Bidénte, *sm.* 1. Two-pronged spade, used in breaking up the ground. 2. Sheep. 3. (Bot.) A sort of hemp, called water hemp.

Biélda, *sf.* Pitch fork with 6 or 7 prongs and a rack used in gathering and loading straw.

Bieldár, *va.* To winnow corn, to separate the grain from the chaff by means of a wooden fork with two or three prongs.

Biéldo y Biéleo, *sm.* Winnowing fork with two or three prongs.

Bién, *sm.* 1. Supreme goodness, an attribute peculiar to God alone. 2. Object of esteem or love. 3. Good, utility, benefit. 4. (Ant.) Property, estate. *El bien de la patria*, The public welfare. *Bienes*, Property, fortune, riches. *Bienes de fortuna*, Worldly treasures. *Decir mil bienes*, To praise, to commend.

Bién, *ad.* 1. Well, right. *Ha vivido bien*, He has lived in a just and upright manner. 2. Happily, prosperously. *El enfermo va bien*, The patient is in a fair way of doing well. 3. Willingly, readily. 4. Heartily. *Comió bien*, He dined heartily. *Caminó bien*, He walked at a great rate. 5. Well, well; it is all well; said in a threatening tone. 6. As well as, in the same manner as. 7. *Bien que*, Although. 8. *Bien si*, But if. 9. *Ahora bien*, Now, this being so. *Bien está*, Very well. 10. *Mas bien*, Rather. *Si bien me acuerdo*, To the best of my recollection. *Hay bien de eso*, There is plenty of that. *Y bien, y que tenemos con eso*, Well, and what of that. Joined to adjectives or adverbs it is equivalent to *very*, as *bien rico*, very rich; and to verbs, *much*, as, *El bebió bien*, He drank much. *Ser bien*, To be good, useful, or convenient. *De bien, á bien ó por bien*, Willingly, amicably.

Biénal, *a.* Biennial, of the continuance of two years.

Bienandánza, *sf.* Felicity, prosperity, success.

Bienaventuradaménte, *ad.* Fortunately, happily.

Bienaventurádo, da, *a.* 1. Blessed, enjoying the blessings of heaven. 2. Fortunate, successful. 3. (Iron.) Simple, silly, harmless.

Bienaventuránza, *sf.* 1. Beatitude, enjoyment of celestial bliss. 2. Prosperity, human felicity. *Bienaventuranzas*, The eight beatitudes of heaven mentioned in the Scriptures.

Bienestár, *sm.* Well-being, possessing and enjoying all the comforts of life.

Bienfechor, ra, (Ant.) V. *Bienhechor.*

Bienestánte, *sm.* He who possesses ease and affluence; well-being.

Bienfortunádo, da, *a.* Fortunate, successful.

Biengranáda, *sf.* (Bot.) Curl-leaved goosefoot. Chenopodium botrys *L.*

Bienhabládo, da, *a.* Well and civilly spoken.

Bienhechór, ra, *s.* Benefactor, one who confers benefits and favours upon another.

Bienío, *sm.* Term of two years.

Bienquerér, *va.* To wish the good of another, to esteem.

Bienquerér, *sm.* Esteem, attachment.

Bienquísto, ta, *a.* Generally esteemed and respected.

Bienvenída, *sf.* Welcome, kind reception of a new comer.

Bienvísta, *sf.* (Ant.) 1. Prudence, sound judgment. 2. Good appearance.

Biésza, *sf.* The thin film which sticks to the inside of the shell of an egg.

Biérzo, *sm.* A sort of linen, manufactured at *Bierzo.* [forms.

Bifórme, *a.* Biformed, compounded of two

Bifrónte, *a.* Double-fronted or double-faced.

Bíga, *sf.* The traces or harness of two horses.

Bigamía, *sf.* 1. Bigamy, the crime of having two wives at once. 2. Second marriage.

Bígama, *sm.* 1. Bigamist, one who has two wives living. 2. He who has married a widow. 3. A widower, who has married again.

Bigardeár, *vn.* To be a bigamist; to dissemble.

Bigardía, *sf.* Jest, fiction, dissimulation.

Bigárdo, *sm.* An opprobrious appellation given to a friar of loose morals and irregular conduct.

Bígarro, *sm.* A large sea snail.

Bigarrádo, da, *a.* V. *Abigarrado.*

Bigáto, ta, *a.* Ancient coin which had the impression of a chaise and two horses.

Bignónia, *sf.* (Bot.) Trumpet-flower.

Bigornéta, *sf.* A small anvil.

Bigórnia, *sf.* Anvil, an iron block, or large piece of iron, on which smiths forge their metal.

Bigóta, *sf.* (Naút.) Dead-eye. V. *Vigota.*

Bigotázo, *sm.* Large whiskers.

Bigóte, *sm.* Whisker, the hair growing on the upper lip and cheeks unshaven, mustachio. *Hombre de bigote*, (Met.) A man of spirit and vigour. *Tener bigotes*, (Met.) To be firm and undaunted; to be obstinate, to be a bigot.

Bigotéra, *sm.* 1. Leather cover for whiskers or mustachios. 2. Ornament of ribbons, worn by women on the breast. 3. Folding-seat put in the front of a chariot. *Pega una bigotera*, To play one a trick. *Bigotéras*, Face, mien. *Tener buenas bigoteras*, To have a pleasing face or graceful mien; applied to women.

Bíja, V. *Achiote.*

Bilánder, *sm.* (Naút.) Bilander, a small merchant vessel.

...BAÍNO, NA, *a.* Native of Bilboa.

...BILITÁNO, NA, *a.* Native of Calatayud.

...IAR, *a.* Biliary, relating to the vessels which ...ain bile.

...GÜE, *s.* Double-tongued, deceitful.

...OSO, SA, *a.* Bilious, abounding in bile.

...IS, *sf.* Bile, a thick yellow bitter liquid.

...LAR, *sm.* Game of billiards, or billiard-table.

...ALDA ó BILLÁRDA, *sf.* A kind of children's ...

...ETE, *sm.* Billet, small paper note. *Billete ...banco*, A bank note.

...TICO, *sm.* A small billet, a love-letter.

...DÓR, *sm.* V. *Algebrista.*

...TA, *sm.* 1. Ring made of a twisted yellow ... 2. Flying report. 3. (Naút.) Burr, a ... of iron ring used for various purposes ...board of ships. 4. A sport among country ...ple, somewhat resembling cricket.

...TO, *sm.* Bat having a crooked head.

...OTEÁR, *vn.* To ramble about the streets.

...OTÉRA, *sf.* A woman who makes it her busi-...ness to ramble about the streets and gossip.

...IS, *sf.* A kind of Brasil wood.

...ESTRE, *a.* Of two months' duration.—*sm.* Two months' leave of absence or furlough.

...DÉRA, *sf.* Instrument with teeth used by ...husbandmen to take away weeds from ground.

...ADÓR, *sm.* Digger, he who digs the same ...und again.

...AR, *va.* To dig or plough a piece of ground ...second time.

...ARIO, *sm.* 1. A number which consists of ...two unities. 2. Time, consisting of two equal ...tions.

...ATÉRAS, *sf. pl.* (Naút.) Beckets, strops or ends ...ropes, wooden brackets or hooks, used to ...fine ropes and tackles to their places, and ...prevent them from being fouled.

...AZÓN, *sm.* The act of digging or ploughing ...piece of ground a second time.

...CULO, LA, *a.* Binocular, having two eyes, ...mploying both eyes at once.

...ZA, *sf.* Pellicle, a thin skin on the inside of ...the shell of an egg; any thin membrane.

...RAFÍA, *sf.* Biography.

...RAFO, *sm.* Biographer, a writer of lives.

...OMBO, *sm.* Screen.

...ARTÍDO, DA, *a.* (Poét.) Bipartite, divided ...into two correspondent pieces or parts.

...PÉDAL, *a.* Bipedal, two feet in length; hav-...ing two feet.

...EDO, *sm.* Biped, an animal with two feet.

...VITÓRTES, *sm. pl.* (Naút.) Quarter gallery ...ces.

...BIQUÍ, *sm.* Borer, an instrument used by ...carpenters and cabinet-makers to make holes.

...ADA, *sf.* *Birada de borda*, (Naút.) Tack, ...the act of putting the ship about.

...ADÓR, *sm.* (Naút.) Top rope. *Birador de ...astelero sencillo ó doble*, A single or double ...top rope. *Birador de cubierta*, Voyal.

...RAR, *va.* (Naút.) 1. To wind, to twist. 2. To ...tack, to put or go about. *Birar el cabrestante*, ...To heave at the capstern. *Birar para proa*, To heave a-head. *Birar para popa*, To heave ...astern. *Birar el cable*, To heave taught. *Birar de borda*, To tack or go about. *Birar de borda tomando por avante*, To put the ship to windward. *Birar de bonde en redondo*, To put the ship to leeward. *Birar por las aguas de otro bazel*, To tack in the wake of another ship. *Bira, bira!* Heave cheerly.

BIRAZÓNES, *sm. pl.* Land and sea breezes, which blow alternately.

BIRIBÍS Y BISBIS, *sm.* Biribi, a sort of game.

BIRICÚ, *sm.* Sword-belt.

BIRÍLLA, *sf.* Ornament of gold or silver, formerly worn in shoes.

BÍRLA, V. *Bolo.*

BIRLADÓR, *sm.* One who knocks down at a blow: used in the game of nine-pins.

BIRLÁR, *va.* 1. At the game of nine-pins, to throw a bowl a second time from the same place. 2. To knock down at one blow, to kill at one shot. 3. To snatch away an employment which another was aiming at. 4. To dispossess.

BIRLÍ, *Por arte de birli birloque*, (loc. fam.) To have done any thing by occult and extraordinary means.

BÍRLO, *sm.* (Ant.) Bowl for playing.

BIRLÓCHA, *sf.* Paper kite.

BIRLÓCHO, *sm.* High open carriage with four wheels and two seats.

BIRLÓN, *sm.* Large middle pin in the game of nine-pins.

BIRLÓNGA, *sf.* Mode of playing in the game at cards called ombre. *A' la birlonga*, In a negligent, careless manner.

BIRÓLA, *sf.* 1. Brass cap or ferrule fixed on the end of canes or walking-sticks. 2. Goad, a pointed instrument with which oxen are driven forward by the drivers. 3. *Birola de chavetas*, (Naút.) Forelock-ring. 4. *Birolas de pantales*, (Naút.) Hoops of the stanchions between decks.

BIRRÉTA, *sf.* Cardinal's red cap.

BIRRÉTE, *sm.* Cap. V. *Gorro ó Bonete.*

BIRRETÍNA, *sf.* Grenadier's cap.

BÍSA, *sf.* (Bot.) An oriental plant.

BISABUÉLO, LA, *s.* Great grandfather or grandmother.

BISÁGRA, *sf.* 1. Hinge, the joint upon which a door or gate turns. 2. Piece of box-wood, with which shoe-makers polish and finish the soles of shoes. *Bisagras y pernos*, Hooks and hinges. *Bisagras de la porteria*, (Naút.) Port hinges.

BISAGÜÉLO, LA, (Ant.) V. *Bisabuelo.*

BISÁLTO, *sm.* (Bot.) Pea. Pisum sativum *L.*

BISÁRMA, *sf.* (Ant.) Halberd.

BISÉL, *sm.* The basil edge of the plate of a looking-glass, or of the crystal door of a shrine in which relics are kept.

BISESTÍL, *a.* (Ant.) V. *Bisiesto.*

BISIÉSTO, *a.* Belonging to a leap year, which consists of 366 days, and happens every four years. *Mudar bisiesto ó de bisiesto*, To change one's ways and means, to alter one's course.

BISÍLABO, BA, *a.* Consisting of two syllables.

BISLÍNGUA, *sf.* (Bot.) Double tongue, or narrow-leaved butcher's broom. Ruscus hypoglossum *L.*

BISNIÉTO, TA, (Ant.) V. *Biznieto.*

BISÓJO, JA, *a.* Squint-eyed, looking obliquely.

BISÓNTE, *sm.* Bison, a large quadruped of the

family of oxen, having a bunch on its back, and chiefly found in the forests of Poland. Bos bison *L.*

BISOÑÁDA Y BISOÑERÍA, *sf.* A rash and inconsiderate speech or action, done without the least knowledge or experience.

BISÓNO, ÑA, *a.* 1. Raw, undisciplined; applied to recruits or new levied soldiers. 2. Novice, tyro. 3. Unbacked horse, not yet broken in or tamed for use.

BISPÁL, (Ant.) V. *Episcopal.*

BÍSPO, *sm.* (Ant.) V. *Obispo.*

BISPÓN, *sm.* Roll of oil cloth, a yard in length, used by sword cutlers.

BÍSTOLA, *sf.* (Manch.) V. *Arrejada.*

BISTÓRTA, (Bot.) Bistort or snake-weed. Polygonum bistorta *L.*

BISTRÉTA, *sf.* Payment made before the money becomes due.

BISÚNTO, TA, *a.* That which is dirty or greasy.

BISURCÁDO, DA, *a.* Bifurcated, forked.

BITÁCORA, *sf.* (Naút.) Binnacle or bittacle, a box in the steerage of a ship, wherein the compass is placed. *Lámpara ó lántias de la bitacora,* A binnacle lamp.

BITADÚRA, *sf.* (Naút.) Cable bit, a turn of the cable around the bits.

BÍTAS, *sf. pl.* (Naút.) Bits, large pieces of timber placed abaft the manger, to belay the cable, when the ship rides at anchor. *Forro de bitas,* Lining of the bits. *Contrabitas,* Standards of the bits. *Bita de molinete,* Knight-head of the windlass.

BITCHEMÁRE, *sm.* Fish on the coast of China which is salted and cured like cod.

BITÓNES, *sm. pl.* (Naút.) Pins of the capstern.

BITÓQUE, *sm.* (And.) Bung, a wooden stopper for the bung-hole of a cask. *Tener ojos de bitoque.* (Vulg.) To squint.

BITÓR, *sm.* (Orn.) Rail, a bird called the king of the quails.

BITÚMEN, *sm.* V. *Betun.*

BITUMINÓSO, SA, *a.* Bituminous, containing bitumen.

BIVÁR, *sm.* Gander.

BIVÉRIO, *sm.* V. *Vivar.*

BÍXA, *sf.* (Bot.) Anotto, a sort of reddish yellow die.

BÍZA, *sf.* (Ict.) Fish belonging to the family of tunnies. Scomber pelamis *L.*

BIZARRAMÉNTE, *ad.* Courageously, gallantly.

BIZARREÁR, *vn.* To act in a spirited and gallant manner.

BIZARRÍA, *sf.* 1. Gallantry, valour, fortitude of mind. 2. Liberality, generosity, splendour.

BIZÁRRO, RRA, *a.* 1. Gallant, brave, high-spirited. 2. Generous, liberal, high-minded.

BIZÁZAS, *sf. pl.* Saddle-bags made of leather.

BIZCÁCHA, *sf.* An animal with a long tail in the kingdom of Peru, the flesh of which resembles that of a rabbit.

BIZCÁR, *va.* To squint, to turn the eyes obliquely.

BÍZCO, CA, *a.* V. *Bisojo.*

BIZCOCHÁDA, *sf.* Soup made of biscuit boiled in milk with sugar and cinnamon.

BIZCOCHÁR, *va.* To make or bake biscuit.

BIZCOCHÉRO, *sm.* 1. Biscuit-cask, a cask in which biscuit is carried on board a ship. 2. One who makes or sells biscuits.

BIZCOCHÍLLO Y BIZCOCHÍTO, *sm.* A small biscuit.

BIZCÓCHO, *sm.* 1. Biscuit, or sea-biscuit, a kind of hard dry bread. 2. Paste made of fine flour, eggs, and sugar. 3. Whiting made of the plaster of old walls.

BIZCOCHUÉLO, *sm.* Small biscuit.

BIZCOTÉLA, *sf.* Biscuit lighter and thinner than the common sort.

BÍZMA, *sf.* Comforting cataplasm or poultice.

BIZMÁR, *va.* To apply a cataplasm or poultice.

BÍZNA, *sf.* Zest, membrane which quarters the kernel of a walnut.

BIZNÁGA, *sf.* (Bot.) Mountain parsley or Spanish carrot, the sprigs whereof are used as toothpicks. Daucus visnaga *L.*

BIZNIÉTO, TA, *s.* Great grandson, great granddaughter.

BLÁGO, (Ant.) V. *Bordon.*

BLÁNCA, *sf.* 1. Copper coin of the value of half a maravedi. *No tener blanca, ó estar sin blanca,* Not to have a doit to bless one's self with. 2. (Orn.) Magpie. 3. *Blanca morfea,* Alphos, a white scurf, tetter, or ring-worm.

BLANCÁZO, (Vulg.) V. *Blanquecino.*

BLANCHÉTE, *sm.* (Ant.) 1. A little white lap-dog originally from Malta. 2. White selvage.

BLÁNCO, CA, 1. White. *Hijo de la gallina blanca,* (Bax.) A lucky fellow. 2. (Naút.) Untarred.

BLÁNCO, *sm.* 1. White star, or any other remarkable white spot in horses. 2. First white sheet pulled at a printing-press, after the form is got ready. 3. Mark to shoot at with a gun, bow, or cross-bow. *Dar en el blanco,* To hit the mark. 4. (Met.) Object of our desire, a thing we wish for or aim at. 5. Mixture of whiting, lime, &c. to size or lay the first coat for painting. *Blanco de estuco,* Stucco whiting, made of lime and pounded marble. 6. Blank left in writing. *Cédula ó patente en blanco,* A blank paper to be filled up by the person to whom it is sent. *Labor blanca,* Plain work. *Tela ó ropa blanca,* Linon. *Armas blancas,* Side-arms, to thrust and cut with. *De punta en blanco,* Point blank. *Dexar en blanco alguna cosa,* To pass over a thing in silence. *Hombre blanco, ó muger blanca,* An honest man, or an honest woman. *El blanco del ave,* The breast of a fowl. *Quedarse en blanco,* To be frustrated in one's expectations, to be left in the lurch.

BLANCÓR Y BLANCÚRA, *s.* Whiteness, freedom from colour. *Blancura del ojo,* (Alb.) A white spot or film on the eye.

BLANDÁLES, *sm. pl.* (Naút.) Backstays. V. *Brandales.*

BLANDAMÉNTE, *ad.* Softly, mildly, gently, sweetly.

BLANDEADÓR, RA, *s.* One who softens, or renders soft and mild.

BLANDEÁR, *va.* 1. To soften, to render mild. 2. To make one change his opinion. 3. To brandish, to flourish.—*vn.* 1. To slacken, to yield, to be softened. 2. To tread tenderly. 3. *Blandear con otro,* To fall in with another's opinion.—*vr.* To be unsteady, to move from one place to another.

Blandéngue, *sm.* A soldier armed with a lance, who defends the limits of the province of Buenos Ayres.

Blandéo, *sm.* The good or bad quality of the soil of forests and pasture lands.

Blandéza, (Ant.) V. *Delicadeza.*

Blandiénte, *a.* Having a tremulous motion from one side to another.

Blandíllo, lla, *a.* Somewhat soft.

Blandimiénto, *sm.* (Ant.) Adulation, flattery.

Blandír, *va.* 1. To brandish a sword, pike, lance, &c. 2. (Ant.) To flatter.—*vr.* To quiver, to move with a tremulous agitation from one side to another.

Blándo, da, *a.* 1. Soft, pliant, smooth to the touch. 2. (Met.) Mild, gentle, grateful, pleasing. *Blando de boca*, Tender-mouthed; applied to a horse: (Met.) Indiscreet, talkative. *Blando de carona*, (Met.) Soft, not bearing fatigue or labour: (Met.) Fond of women, apt to fall in love with every woman one meets with. *Blando de corazon*, Tender-hearted. *Hombre blando*, A gentle, mild man. *Llevar blanda la mano*, To carry a gentle hand, to reprimand with mildness, to punish with mercy. *Tiempo blando*, Mild, moderate weather.

Blandón, *sm.* 1. Wax taper with one wick. 2. A large church candlestick in which wax tapers or flambeaux are placed. 3. Soft side of a stone. 4. Light of the stars.

Blandoncíllo, *sm.* A small candlestick for wax tapers.

Blandúcho, cha, y Blandújo, ja, *a.* (Bax.) Flabby, loose, soft, not firm.

Blandúra, *sf.* 1. Softness, the quality of being soft. 2. Daintiness, delicacy. 3. (Met.) Gentleness of temper, sweetness of address. 4. Lenitive or emollient application. 5. Soft, endearing language. 6. White paint used by women. 7. Mild temperature of the air.

Blandurílla, *sf.* A sort of fine soft pomatum.

Blanqueación, *sf.* The act of blanching or whitening. [whitens.

Blanqueadór, ra, *s.* One who blanches or

Blanqueadúra, *sf.* Whiteness, the state of being white; whitening.

Blanquéo y Blanqueamiénto, *sm.* 1. The act of making white or bleaching. 2. Whitewash. *El blanqueo del lienzo*, The bleaching of linen.

Blanqueár, *va.* 1. To bleach, to whiten; to white-wash. 2. To give coarse wax to bees in winter. *Blanquear cera*, To bleach wax. —*vn.* To show whiteness.

Blanquecedór, *sm.* An officer employed in the mint, to blanch, clean, and polish the coin.

Blanquecér, *va.* To blanch coin, to give gold, silver, and other metals, their due colours.

Blanquecíno, na, *a.* Whitish, inclining to white.

Blanquería, *sm.* Bleaching place, bleach-field.

Blanquéro, *sm.* Tanner, one whose trade is to tan and dress leather.

Blanquéta, *sf.* (Ant.) Coarse blanket.

Blanquéte, *sm.* White paint used by women.

Blanquíbolo, (Ant.) V. *Albayalde.*

Blanquición y Blanquecimiénto, *s.* The act of blanching the metal before it is coined.

Blanquílla, *sf.* 1. Doit, a very small coin. 2. Sort of long yellowish plum. 3. White grape.

Blanquíllo, lla. *a.* Whitish, somewhat white.

Blanquimiénto, *sm.* The act of blanching coin or wrought metal, by boiling it with water, and salt of tartar. [clay.

Blanquizál, *sm.* (Agr.) Whitish clay, pipe

Blanquízco, ca, *a.* Inclining to white.

Bláo, *a.* (Blas.) Azure, faint blue.

Blasfemáble, *a.* Blamable, culpable, faulty.

Blasfemadór, ra, *s.* Blasphemer. [ously.

Blasfemaménte, *ad.* Blasphemously, impi-

Blasfemár, *vn.* 1. To blaspheme. 2. To curse, to make use of imprecations.

Blasfematório, ria, *a.* Containing blasphemy.

Blasfémia, *sf.* 1. Blasphemy, the use of impious and irreverent language in speaking of God. 2. Gross verbal insult offered to a person.

Blasfémo, ma, *a.* Blasphemous. [mous.

Blasmár, *va.* (Ant.) To vilify, to make infa-

Blasón, *sm.* Heraldry, blazon, the art of drawing or explaining coats of arms. 2. Figures and devices which compose coats of arms or armorial ensigns. 3. Honour, glory. *Hacer blason*, To blazon.

Blasonadór, ra, *s.* Boaster, bragger.

Blasonánte, *pa.* Vain-glorious; boaster.

Blasonár, *va.* 1. To blazon, to draw or explain armorial ensigns. 2. To make a pompous display of one's own merits. *Blasonar del arnes*, To crack and boast of achievements never performed.

Blávo, va, *a.* (Ant.) Yellowish grey and reddish colour.

Blédo, *sm.* Strawberry blite. Blitum virgatum *L.*

Blénno, *sm.* (Ict.) Hake, blenny. Blennius *L.*

Blínno, *sm.* A kind of fish.

Blindáge, *sm.* (Mil.) Blind, a covering made by the besiegers of a strong place, to protect themselves from the enemy's fire; it consists of branches of trees, sand bags, wool-packs, &c.

Blónda, *sf.* Broad lace made of silk. *Escofieta de blonda*, Head dress made of silk lace.

Blondína, *sf.* Narrow silk lace.

Blóndo, da, *a.* Having a fair complexion or flaxen hair.

Bloqueár, *va.* (Mil.) To form a blockade. *Bloquear un puerto*, (Naút.) To block up a port.

Bloquéo, *sm.* Blockade. [Boa *L.*

Bóa, *sf.* Large serpent, found in Calabria.

Boaláge, *sm.* (Ar.) Pasturage of black cattle.

Boarréte, *sm.* Storm or tempest at sea.

Boáto, *sm.* 1. Ostentation, pompous show. 2. Shout of acclamation.

Bobáda, *sf.* V *Bobería.* [dolt.

Bobálias, *sm.* (Bax.) A very stupid fellow, a

Bobalicón y Bobázo, *sm.* Great blockhead.

Bobaménte, *ad.* 1. Without trouble or care. 2. Foolishly, stupidly. *Está comiendo su renta bobamente*, He spends his income in a foolish manner.

Bobatél, *sm.* (Fam.) V. *Bobo.*

Bobático, ca, *a.* Silly, foolish, stupid.

Bobeár, *va.* 1. To act or talk in a foolish and stupid manner. 2. To waste one's time in trifles, to loiter about.

Bobería, *sf.* Foolish speech or action; foolery.

Bóbilis, *ad. De bóbilis bóbilis*, (In Cant Language) Without pain or merit.

Bobíllo, lla; to, ta, *s.* 1. A little dolt or fool. 2. Big-bellied jug with one handle. 3. Frill or lace formerly worn by women around the tucker.

Bobínas, *sf. pl.* Bobbins, a large sort of spools used in ribbon looms.

Bobísimamente, *ad.* Most foolishly.

Bóbo, ba, *s.* 1. Dunce, idiot, ass; one who has little capacity or understanding. 2. Sort of ruff formerly worn by women around the neck. 3. (Ant.) Stage Buffoon. 4. (Orn.) Booby. Pelecanus sula *L. El bobo si es callado, por sesudo es reputado,* (Prov.) A fool that talks little may pass for a wise man. *A' bobas,* Foolishly.

Bobón, na, *s.* Big dolt, great fool.

Boboncíllo, lla, *s.* A little dolt.

Bobóte, *sm.* Great idiot or simpleton.

Bóca, *sf.* 1. Mouth, the aperture in the face at which the food is received. 2. Entrance, opening, hole. 3. Pincers with which cray-fish hold something. 4. Thin or cutting part of edge-tools. 5. Taste, flavour, relish; one who eats. *Instrumento de boca,* Wind-instrument. 6. (Ict.) Shrimp. *Boca de escorpion,* Calumniator. *Boca del estómago,* Pit of the stomach. *Boca de fuego,* Piece of ordnance. *Boca de lobo,* (Met.) Dark dungeon: (Naút.) Lubbers' hole. *Boca de lobo del tamborete,* Cap hole for the top-mast. *Boca de la escotilla,* Hatchway. *Boca de risa,* Smiling countenance. *Boca de rio ó de puerto,* Mouth of a river or of a harbour. *Andar de boca en boca,* To be the talk of the town. *Cerrar ó tapar á uno la boca,* To stop one's mouth. *Coserse la boca,* To shut one's mouth. *Boca de oro,* Mellifluous tongue. *Boca de gacha,* Nickname of a person who mumbles his words, sputtering, and speaking unintelligibly. *A' boca de jarro,* A hearty draught, drinking without a glass or measure. *Decir alguna cosa con la boca chica,* To offer a thing for mere ceremony's sake. *Andar con la boca abierta,* To go gaping about. *Guardar la boca,* Not to commit any excess in eating or drinking; to be silent. *Hablar por boca de ganso,* To exaggerate maliciously other people's reports. *Irse de boca,* To speak much without reflection. *La boca hace juego,* To be as good as one's word. *No decir esta boca es mia,* To keep a profound silence. *No tener boca para negar ó decir no,* Not to dare to say no. *Punto en boca,* Mum, mum, not a word. *Tener buena ó mala boca,* To talk well or ill of others. *A' boca de invierno,* About the beginning of winter. *A' boca de noche,* At the fall of night.—*Boca á boca, ad.* By word of mouth. *Boca con boca,* Face to face. *A' boca de costal,* Profusely, without rule or measure. *A' boca llena,* Perspicuously, openly. *A' pedir de boca,* According to one's desire. *De manos á boca,* Unexpectedly. *De boca,* Verbally, not really; used of boasting or threatening.

Bocacálle, *sf.* Entry, end or opening of a street.

Bocacáz, *sm.* Opening left in the wear or dam of a river, sluice, or flood-gate.

Bocací y Bocacín, *sm.* Fine glazed buckram, much used by tailors.

Bocáda, *sf.* (Ant.) A mouthful.

Bocadeár, *va.* To divide into bits or morsels.

Bocadíllo, *sm.* 1. Scrap. 2. Thin, middling sort of linen. 3. Narrow ribbon or lace, tape, inkle. 4. Lunch or luncheon given to labourers in the field about ten in the morning.

Bocadíto, *sm.* Small bit or morsel.

Bocádo, *sm.* 1. Morsel, a mouthful of food. 2. Bite, a wound made with the teeth. 3. Part of a thing torn off with the teeth or pincers. 4. Poison given in eatables. 5. Mouth-piece of a bridle. 6. *Bocado sin hueso,* Profitable employment without labour; a sinecure. *Con el bocado en la boca,* With a full stomach. *Contarle á uno los bocados,* To watch how another eats. *No tener para un bocado,* To be in extreme distress.—*pl.* 1. Slices of quinces, apples, pumpkins, &c. made up into conserves. 2. (Naút.) Wads of great guns, hause-plugs.

Bocál, *sm.* 1. Pitcher, an earthen vessel with a narrow mouth. 2. Mouth-piece of a trumpet or other wind instrument. 3. (Naút.) The narrows of a harbour.

Bocamánga, *sf.* That part of a sleeve which is near the wrist.

Bocanáda, *sf.* A mouthful of wine or other liquor. *Bocanada de gente,* Mob, a tumultuous rout. *Bocanada de viento,* A sudden blast of wind. *Echar bocanadas,* To boast of one's valour, noble birth, &c. *Echar bocanadas de sangre,* To throw up mouthfuls of blood; to vaunt of noble blood.

Bocarán, *sm.* Fine sort of buckram.

Bocáza, *sf.* A large wide mouth.

Bocezár, *va.* V. *Bocezar.*

Bocél, *sm.* 1. Brim, lip, or upper edge of a vessel. 2. A fluted moulding. 3. Fluting plane, an instrument for fluting mouldings.

Bocelár, *va.* To make fluted mouldings.

Boceléte, *sm.* Small moulding plane.

Bocelón, *sm.* Large moulding plane.

Bocéra, *sf.* Crumbs, or other remains of eating or drinking, sticking to the outside of the lip.

Bocezár, *va.* To move the lips from one side to another, as horses and other animals do when they eat.

Bócha, *sf.* 1. Bowl, a wooden ball for playing at bowls. 2. Fold or double in clothes, where they do not fit well, but purse up. *Juego de las bochas,* The game at bowls. *Pan de bochas,* White bread.

Bochár, *va.* To throw a ball so that it hits another, in the game at bowls.

Bocházo, *sm.* Stroke of one bowl against another.

Bóche, *sm.* Cherry-pit or chuck-hole. V. *Bote.*

Bochín, *sm.* (Ant.) Hangman.

Bochísta, *sm.* A good bowler, or player at bowls.

Bochórno, *sm.* 1. Hot, sultry weather, scorching heat. 2. Blush, the colour of the cheeks raised by shame or passion.

Bocín, *sm.* Round piece of bass mat put about the nave of a cart, as a cap of defence.

Bocína, *sm.* 1. Sort of large trumpet, a bugle-horn. *Bocina de cazador,* A huntsman's horn. 2. Speaking-trumpet. V. *Vocina.* 3. A kind of shell. 4. Constellation called *ursa minor,* or the lesser bear.

Bocinár, *va.* (Ant.) To sound the trumpet, bugle-horn, or huntsman's horn.

Bocinéro, *sm.* Trumpeter.

Bocinílla, *sf.* Small speaking trumpet.
Bocólica, *sf.* Exquisite or delicious eating.
Bocón, *sm.* 1. A wide-mouthed person. 2. Braggart, a talkative boaster.
Bóda, *sf.* Marriage, the feast by which it is solemnized, a wedding. *Boda de hongos*, A beggar's wedding. *Perrito de todas bodas*, (Met.) Parasite who runs from wedding to wedding. *Aun ahora se come el pan de la boda*, (Prov.) The honey-moon is not yet over. *De tales bodas tales costras ó tortas*, (Prov.) A bad beginning a bad end.
Bóde, *sm.* A he-goat.
Bodéga, *sm.* 1. Wine vault, a cellar. 2. Abundant vintage or growth of wine. 3. Store-room, warehouse, magazine. 4. (Naút.) Hold, the whole space in a ship between the floor and the lower deck, where goods and stores are stowed. *Bodega de popa*, After-hold. *Bodega de proa*, Fore-hold.
Bodegón, *sm.* 1. Mean chop-house or cook's shop. 2. Sign of a cook's shop or eating-house. 3. Tippling-house, a low inn. *Bodegon de puntapie*, Stall where cow-heels and black puddings are sold. *Echar el bodegon por la ventana*, To put one's self into a violent passion. *En que bodegon hemos comido juntos?* Out of which platter did we eat together? A rebuke for too much familiarity.
Bodegoncíllo, *sm.* Low chop-house.
Bodegoneár, *va.* To run from one tippling-house to another, to frequent mean eating-houses.
Bodegonéro, ra, *s.* One who keeps a low chop-house or tippling-house. [of a cellar.
Bodeguéro, ra, *s.* Butler, one who has the care
Bodeguílla, *sf.* Small cellar or vault.
Bodián, *sm.* Sea-fish resembling a tench.
Bodígo, *sm.* A small loaf made of the finest flour, and presented as an offering in the church.
Bodíjo, *sm.* Unequal match, a hedge-marriage performed with little ceremony or solemnity.
Bodocál, *a.* Applied to a kind of black grapes.
Bodocázo, *sm.* Stroke of a pellet shot from a cross-bow.
Bodóllo, *sm.* Pruning-knife, pruning-hook.
Bodóque, *sm.* 1. Pellet, a small ball of clay shot from a cross bow. 2. Dunce, idiot. 3. Extremities of the ribs of mutton. *Hacer bodoques*, To be reduced to dust, to be dead.
Bodoquéra, *sf.* 1. Mould in which pellets are formed. 2. Cradle, or that part of the stock of a cross bow where the pellet is put. 3. Strings with which the cord of a cross bow is tied.
Bodoquíllo, *sm.* Small pellet or bullet of clay.
Bodorrío, *sm.* (Vulg.) V. *Bodijo*.
Bódrio, *sm.* 1. Soup, broken meat, and garden stuff, given to the poor at the doors of convents. 2. Any hodge-podge ill dressed, any medley of broken meat.
Boe, *sm.* (Ant.) V. *Buey*.
Boémio, *sm.* Sort of short cloak formerly worn in Spain.
Boezuélo, *sm.* Stalking ox, which serves to screen fowlers engaged in the pursuit of birds.
Bofáda, *sf.* Ragout or fricassee made of the livers and lungs of animals.
Bófes, *sm. pl.* Lungs. *Echar los bofes*, To strain one's lungs.
Boféna, *sf.* (Ant.) V. *Bofes*.
Boféta y Bofetán, *s.* A sort of thin stiff linen.
Bofetáda, *sf.* Slap, buffet, box, a blow on the face given with the hand. *Dar una bofetada*, (Met.) To treat with the utmost contempt.
Bofetón, *sm.* 1. Violent blow upon the face. 2. Stage decoration representing one or two folding doors. [face.
Bofetoncíllo, *sm.* A slight box or slap on the
Bofórdo, *sm.* (Ant.) A short lance or spear.
Bóga, *sf.* 1. (Ict.) Ox-eyed cackerel. Sparus boops *L.* 2. Act of rowing. 3. (Naút.) Rower, one who rows: in this sense when it signifies a man, it is a masculine substantive. 4. (Extr.) Small two-edged knife in the shape of a poniard. 5. White branch about which silk-worms work their cones. *Boga arrancada*, (Naút.) All hands rowing together with all their strength. *Boga larga*, A long stroke, *Dar la boga*, To give the stroke. *Boga avante*, Stroke's man.
Bogáda, *sf.* 1. Rowing stroke. 2. Bucking of clothes with lye.
Bogadór, *sm.* Rower, one who rows.
Bogánte, *pa.* (Poét.) Rower; rowing.
Bogár, *vn.* To row. *Bogar á quarteles*, To row by divisions. *Bogar á barlovento*, To row abroad. *Bogar á sotavento*, To row to leeward.
Bogavánte, *sm.* 1. (Naút.) Stroke's-man of a row galley. 2. Lobster of a large size.
Bogéta, *sf.* (Ict.) A kind of herring.
Bogigánga, *sf.* (Ant.) A company of strolling players.
Bohémio, *sm.* 1. Short cloak formerly worn by the guard of archers. 2. V. *Gitano*.
Bohéna ó Bohéña, *sf.* (Ant.) 1. V. *Bofes*. 2. Pork sausages.
Bohonéro, *sm.* V. *Buhonero*.
Bohordár, *va.* To throw wands, called *bohordos*, in tournaments.
Bohórdo, *sm.* 1. Blade of flag, a water-plant. 2. Wands, the hollow end of which is filled with sand, and which tilters throw at one another in tournaments. 3. Stalk of a cabbage run into seed. 4. Prancing of a horse.
Boíl, *sm.* Ox-stall, a stand for oxen.
Boitríno, *sm.* A kind of fishing net.
Bója, (Ant.) V. *Buba*.
Bókas, *sf.* Sort of cotton stuff brought from the East Indies, and is either blue or white.
Bol, *sm.* Armenian bole, a sort of red earth, chiefly used by gilders. Bolus *L.*
Bóla, *sf.* 1. Ball, a round body of any matter. 2. Game of throwing bullets or bowls. 3. Lie, falsehood. 4. (Naút.) Truck, acorn; a round piece of wood at the end of the ensign staffs and vanes. *Escurrir la bola*, To take French leave, to run away. *Ruede la bola*, Take things easy. *Pie con bola*, Just enough, as much as is wanted, neither too much nor too little.
Boláda, *sf.* Throw or cast of a ball or bowl.
Boládo, *sm.* Cake of clarified sugar used in Spain for drinking water.
Bolantín, *sm.* Fine sort of pack-thread.
Bolarménico, *sm.* V. *Bol*.
Bolázo, *sm.* Violent blow with a bowl.
Bolchàca ó Bolchaco, *s.* Purse, pocket.

Boléa, *sf.* Swing-tree bar of a carriage, to which the traces are made fast.

Boleár, *vn.* 1. To play at billiards for mere amusement, and without staking money. 2. To throw wooden or iron balls for a wager. 3. (Mur.) To boast, to lie extravagantly.—*va.* 1. To dart, to launch. 2. *Bolear el sombrero,* To fix the hat on the head.

Boléo, *sm.* The road or place where balls are thrown.

Boléro, *sm.* Child eloping from its parents or school.

Boléta, *sf.* 1. Ticket giving the right of being admitted into a place. 2. Billet or ticket which directs soldiers where they are to lodge. 3. Ticket or warrant for receiving money or other things. 4. Small paper with tobacco sold at chandlers' shops.

Boletár, *va.* To roll up tobacco in small bits of paper for the purpose of selling them.

Boletín, *sm.* 1. Warrant given for the payment of money. 2. Ticket for the quartering of soldiers. 3. Ticket granting free admittance at a theatre or other place of amusement.

Bolíche, *sm.* 1. Jack, a small ball which serves as a mark for bowl-players. 2. All the small fish caught at once in a drag net near the shore. *Juego de boliche,* Pigeon-holes, a game played on a convex table with a ball; troll-madam. *Boliches,* (Naút.) Fore-top bowlines, and top-gallant bowlines.

Bolichéro, ra, *s.* One who keeps a pigeon-hole, or troll-madam table.

Bolílla, *sf.* A small ball.

Bolíllo, *sm.* 1. Jack, a small ball or bowl. 2. Bobbin, a small pin of box or bone used in making bone lace. 3. Mould or frame on which the cuffs of linen or gauze, worn on the sleeves of counsellors of state and inquisitors, are starched and made up.—*pl.* 1. Paste nuts, small balls made of sweet paste. 2. Starched cuffs worn by counsellors of state and inquisitors.

Bolín, *sm.* Jack, a small ball. V. *Boliche.*

Bolína, *sf.* 1. (Vulg.) Noise and clamour of a scuffle or dispute. 2. (Naút.) Bowline, a rope fastened to the leech or edge of a square sail, to make it stand close to the wind. *Bolina de barlovento,* Weather bow-line. *Bolina de sotavento ó de revés,* Lee bow-line. *Bolina de trinquete,* Fore-bowline. *Dar un salto á la bolina,* To ease or check the bowline. *Presentar la bolina,* To snatch the bowline. *Navegar de bolina,* To sail with bowlines hauled. *Ir á la bolina,* To sail with a side wind. *Navio buen bolinador,* A good plyer, a ship which makes great progress against the direction of the wind. *Echar de bolina,* (Met.) To make fanfaronades, or idle boasts.

Bolineár, *va.* To haul up the bowline in light winds.

Bolinéte, *sm.* (Naút.) A moveable capstern on the deck, in which the whipstaff moves.

Bolísa, *sf.* Embers, hot cinders.

Bólla, *sf.* Duty on woollen and silks retailed for home consumption, levied in Catalonia.

Bolladúra, *sf.* V. *Abolladura.*

Bollár, *va.* 1. To put a leaden seal on cloths to indicate their fabric. 2. To imboss, to raise figures.

Bolléro, ra, *s.* Pastry-cook, seller of sweet cakes.

Bollíco y Bollíto, *sm.* Small loaf made of flour, sugar, milk, and eggs.

Bollído, da, *a.* Boiled. V. *Cocido.*

Bollir, (Ant.) V. *Bullir.*

Bóllo, *sm.* 1. Small loaf or cake made of sugar, flour, milk, and eggs. 2. Bruise made in metal or any similar matter. *Bollo maimon,* A sort of cake filled with sweet-meats. 3. Morbid swelling. 4. *Bóllos,* Ancient head-dress of women, consisting of large buckles. 5. (In Peru,) Bars of silver extracted from the ore by means of fire or quicksilver. *Bollos de relieve,* Embossed or raised work.

Bollón, *sm.* 1. Brass-headed nail used in coaches and furniture. 2. Button which shoots from a plant, especially from a vine-stock.

Bollonádo, da, 1. Adorned with brass-headed nails. 2. Furnished with shoots, buds, or buttons.

Bolluélo, *sm.* V. *Bollico.*

Bolo, *sm.* 1. One of the nine pins or pieces of wood, which are set up on the ground to be knocked down by a bowl. 2. Round or oblong cushion on which women make lace. 3. Large piece of timber, in which the shafts and rests of a winding stair-case are fitted. *Diablos son bolos,* (Prov.) Contingencies cannot be depended upon. *Es un bolo,* He is an idiot, an ignorant, stupid fellow. *Juego de bolos,* A game at nine pins.

Bolónes, *sm. pl.* (Naút.) Square bolts or mortar-bed pintles, which serve to fasten the cheeks to the bed.

Bolónio, *sm.* An ignorant, rattle-brained fellow.

Bólsa, *sf.* 1. Purse. 2. Purse-net made of silk or worsted, with running strings to draw the mouth together. 3. Pouch or net used by sportsmen to put the game in. 4. Bag in which public papers and despatches are carried by ministers and secretaries of state. 5. Bag for the hair. 6. Bag lined with furs or skins to keep the feet warm. 7. (In a Gold-mine) The vein which contains the purest gold. 8. (In Surgery) A morbid swelling. 9. Scrotum. 10. *Bolsa de pastor,* (Bot.) Shepherd's purse. Thlaspi bursa pastoris *L. Bolsa de dios,* Alms, charity. *Bolsa real, sf.* Royal exchange. V. *Lonja. Bolsa rota,* Spendthrift. *Castigar en la bolsa,* To fine. *Dar ó echar otro nudo á la bolsa,* To become extremely frugal, to lessen one's expense. *Page de bolsa,* A minister's servant who carries the official papers. *Tener como en la bolsa alguna cosa,* To be as sure of a thing as if it were in one's pocket. *Tener ó llevar bien herrada la bolsa,* To have the purse well lined; to have money.

Bolseár, *vn.* (Arag.) To purse up, to pucker; applied to clothes, hangings, and other things.

Bolsería, *sf.* (Ant.) Manufactory of purses.

Bolséro, *sm.* Cashier, treasurer.

Bolsíca y Bolsíta, *sf.* Small purse.

Bolsíco, *sm.* Poke, pocket.

Bolsíllo, *sm.* 1. Small purse. *Buen bolsillo ó gran bolsillo,* A large capital, or great sum of money. *Bolsillo secreto,* The king's private purse. 2. Pocket. *Hacer bolsillo,* To make money.

Bolso, *sm.* Purse of money, a money bag.

Bolsón, *sm.* Large purse.—*pl.* 1. Large bars of iron put in vaults or arches to secure the building. 2. (In Oil-mills) Large planks or boards with which the oil-reservoir is lined from the bottom to the edge. 3. Stones on which an arch or vault is sprung.

Bolúla, *sf.* V. *Bululú.*

Bómba, *sf.* 1. Pump, an engine for raising water from wells, ships, or other deep places. *Bomba de guimbalete*, (Naút.) Common pump. *Bomba de rosario ó de cadena*, Chain-pump. *Bomba de proa*, Head-pump. *Bomba de mano*, Hand-pump. *Bomba de carena*, Bilge-pump. *Bomba libre*, Pump in good trim. *Cargar la bomba*, To fetch the pump. *Dar á la bomba*, To pump ship. *La bomba está atascada*, The pump is foul or choked. *La bomba llama*, The pump sucks. *La bomba está arentada*, The pump blows. *Bomba de fuego ó de baho*, Steam-engine. *Bomba de apagar incendios*, Fire-engine. 2. Bomb, a hollow iron ball or shell filled with gunpowder, and furnished with a vent for a fusee or wooden tube full of combustible matter, to be thrown out from a mortar. *Bomba incendiaria*, Carcass, an iron shell with holes, filled with combustibles, and thrown out from mortars. *Estar á prueba de bomba*, To be bomb-proof. 3. *Bomba ó manga marina*, A water-spout.

Bombárda, *sf.* 1. Ancient thick piece of ordnance called a bombard. 2. (Naút.) Bomb-ketch or bomb-vessel, a ship fitted out for throwing bombs and shells.

Bombardeár ó Bombeár, *va.* To bombard, to throw bombs into a place; to discharge bombs.

Bombardéo, *sm.* Bombardment.

Bombardéro, *sm.* Bombardier, an artilleryman charged with throwing bombs.

Bombasí, *sm.* Bombazeen, dimity.

Bombázo, *sm.* Report of a bomb which bursts.

Bómbo, *sm.* 1. Humming of bees, wasps, and other insects. 2. Large drum.

Bon, na, (Ant.) V. *Bueno y hacienda.*

Bonachón, na, *s.* y *a.* Good-natured, easy person.

Bonancíble, *a.* Moderate, calm, fair, serene; applied to the weather at sea.

Bonánza, *sf.* 1. Fair weather at sea. *Ir en bonanza*, (Naút.) To sail with fair wind and weather. 2. Prosperity, success. *Ir en bonanza*, (Met.) To go on prosperously, to do well.

Bonázo, za, *a.* (Fam.) Good-natured, kind.

Bondád, *sf.* 1. Goodness, the qualities which render a thing good. 2. Suavity or mildness of temper.

Bondadóso, sa, *a.* Kind, generous, bountiful.

Bondón, *sm.* Bung, a stopple which is put into the bung-hole of a barrel.

Bonétas, *sf. pl.* (Naút.) Bonnets, pieces of canvas laced to the sails, to make more way in light winds.

Bonetáda, *sf.* Salute or salutation made by taking off the hat or bonnet.

Bonéte, *sm.* 1. Cap, bonnet. 2. Secular clergyman who wears a bonnet, in contradistinction to a monk who wears a hood or cowl. 3. Bonnet, a kind of out-works of a fortress. *Tirarse los bonetes*, To pull caps. *Bravo ó gran bonete*, (Iron.) A great dunce. 4. (Ant.) Wide-mouthed phial for conserves.

Boneteria, *sf.* 1. Shop where caps and bonnets are made or sold. 2. Trade of a cap or bonnet maker.

Bonetéro, ra, *s.* 1. Cap and bonnet maker or retailer. 2. (Bot.) Prickwood, gatheridge, or spindle-tree. Euonymus europæus *L.*

Bonetíllo, *sm.* 1. Small cap or bonnet. 2. Ornament in the shape of a bonnet, which women wear over their head-dress.

Bonicaménte, *ad.* Prettily, neatly.

Boníco, ca, *a.* Pretty good, passable. *Andar á las bonicas*, (Met.) To take things easily, to do them at ease, not to burthen one's self with business. *Jugar á las bonicas*, To play at ball by dodging it from one hand into another.

Bonificár, *va.* 1. To credit, to place to one's credit. 2. To meliorate, to improve.

Bonificatívo, va, *a.* (Ant.) That which makes any thing good, or makes up for it.

Boníllo, lla, *a.* 1. Somewhat handsome. 2 (Ant.) Somewhat great, large, or big.

Bonína, *sf.* (Bot.) A kind of chamomile.

Bonitaménte, *ad.* (Fam.) V. *Bonicamente.*

Boníto y Bonítalo, *sm.* Sea-fish resembling a tunny. Scomber pelamis *L.*

Boníto, ta, *a.* (Dim. of *bueno.*) 1. Pretty good, passable. 2. Affecting elegance and neatness. 3. Graceful, beautiful. 4. Soft, effeminate.

Bonvarón, *sm.* (Bot.) Common groundsel. Senecio vulgaris *L.*

Bónzo, *sm.* In China and other heathen nations, one who professes a life of austerity and seclusion from the rest of the world, in convents or deserts.

Boñíga, *sf.* Cow-dung.

Boñigáres, *sm. pl.* Round white figs.

Boópe, *sm.* A kind of whale found off the coast of Brasil.

Boótes, *sm.* Bootes, a northern constellation.

Bóque, *sm.* He-goat.

Boqueáda, *sf.* Act of opening the mouth, a gasp. *A' la primera boqueada*, Immediately, without delay. *La ultima boqueada*, The last gasp.

Boqueár, *vn.* 1. To gape, to open the mouth wide. 2. To breathe one's last, to expire. 3. (Met.) To end, to terminate.—*va.* To pronounce, to utter a word or expression.

Boquéra, *sf.* 1. Opening or sluice made in a canal for irrigating lands. 2. Opening made in inclosures to let in the cattle. 3. Eruption on the corners of the lips, which hinders the mouth from being freely opened. 4. Ulcer in the mouth of beasts.

Boquerón, *sm.* 1. Wide opening, a large hole. 2. (Ict.) Anchovy. Clupea encrasicolus *L.*

Boquéte, *sm.* Narrow entrance of a place.

Boquiabiérto, ta, *a.* Having the mouth open; walking about gaping.

Boquiáncho, cha, *a.* Wide-mouthed.

Boquiangósto, ta, *a.* Narrow-mouthed.

Boquiconejúno, na, *a.* A rabbit-mouthed horse; hare-lipped.

Boquidúro, ra, *a.* Hard-mouthed.

Boquifrésco, ca, *a.* Fresh-mouthed; applied to horses which have a soft salivous mouth.

Boquifruncído, da, *a.* Having the mouth contracted.

Boquihendído, da, *a.* Large-mouthed.

Boquihundído, da, *a.* Having the mouth sunk in from age or want of teeth.

Boquílla, *sf.* 1. Little mouth. 2. Opening of a pair of breeches at the knees. 3. A small opening in a canal for irrigating lands. 4. Chisel for mortising. 5. Mouth-piece of a musical instrument, such as a trumpet, French horn, &c.

Boquimuélle, *a.* 1. Tender-mouthed; applied to a horse. 2. Unwary, easily imposed upon.

Boquín, *sm.* Coarse sort of baize.

Boquinaturál, *a.* Well-mouthed, neither too tender nor too hard; applied to a horse.

Boquinégro, *sm.* A blackish sort of snails.

Boquirasgádo, da, *a.* Deep-mouthed; spoken of a horse.

Boquiróto, ta, *a.* Loquacious, garrulous.

Boquirúbio, bia, *a.* Simple, artless, easily imposed upon.

Boquiséco, ca, *a.* Dry-mouthed; applied to a horse.

Boquisumído, da, *a.* V. *Boquihundido.*

Boquíta, *sf.* Small mouth.

Boquituérto y Boquitorcído, da, *a.* Wry-mouthed, distorted with crying.

Borbollár y Borbollonear, *vn.* To boil, to rise up in bubbles by ebullition.

Borbollón ó Borbotón, *sm.* 1. Ebullition, the act of boiling up with heat. 2. (Met.) Flow of language, hastily and incorrectly uttered. *A' borbollónes,* In bubbling or impetuous manner, in hurry and confusion.

Borbotár, *vn.* To boil up in bubbles.

Borceguí, *sm.* A kind of half boot which comes up to the middle of the leg.

Borceguinería, *sf.* A shop where buskins or half boots are made or sold.

Borceguinéro, ra, *s.* Maker or retailer of buskin or half boots.

Borcellár, *sm.* (Ant.) Brim of a vessel.

Bórda, *sf.* 1. Hut, cottage. 2. (Naút.) Gunnel or gun-wale, the upper part of a ship's side from the half-deck to the forecastle. 3. (Ant.) Brim, edge.

Bordáda, *sf.* (Naút.) Board, tack. *Dar una bordada,* To tack, to make a tack. [taffety.

Bordadíllo, *sm.* Double flowered taffeta or

Bordádo, da, *pp.* Embroidered.

Bordádo, *sm.* Embroidery. *Bordado de pasado,* Plain embroidery, of one colour only, without light or shade.

Bordadór, ra, *s* Embroiderer.

Bordadúra, *sf.* 1. Embroidery, figures raised upon a ground with a needle; variegated needle-work. 2. (Blas.) Border which surrounds the inside of an escutcheon.

Bordár, *va.* 1. To embroider, to raise figures on any stuff with silk, gold, or silver thread. 2. To perform any thing according to art. *Bayla que lo borda,* He dances charmingly. *Bordar á tambor,* To embroider with a lace point, in a small circular frame or in a regular frame with a tambour needle; to tambour.

Bórde, *sm.* 1. Border, the outer part or edge of a thing. 2. Brim, the upper edge of a vessel. 3. Bastard, child begotten out of matrimony. 4. Shoot or bud of a vine. *A' borde,* (Ant.) On the brink; on the eve.

Bordeár, *vn.* (Naút.) To ply to windward.

Bordél, (Ant.) V. *Burdel.*

Bordióna, *sf.* (Ant.) V. *Ramera.*

Bórdo, *sm.* 1. Border, the outer part or edge of a thing. 2. Ship or vessel. *Fue á bordo,* (Naút.) He was aboard ship. 3. Board, the side of a ship. *Bordo con bordo,* Board and board, side by side; when two ships are close to each other. *Bordo sobre bordo,* Hank for hank, when two ships tack together, and ply to windward. *Bordo á la tierra,* To stand in shore. *Bordo á la mar,* To stand off. 4. (Naút.) Board, tack. *Bordo corto,* A short board. *Bordo largo,* A long board. *Buen bordo,* A good board. *Dar bordos,* (Naút.) To tack: (Met.) To go frequently to and fro. *Correr sobre el mismo bordo con el enemigo,* (Naút.) To run on the same tack as the enemy.

Bordón, *sm.* 1. Pilgrim's staff. 2. Base of a stringed musical instrument. 3. Base of an organ. 4. Vicious repetition of certain words in a discourse. 5. Burthen of a song. 6. (Met.) Staff, guide or support of another. *Bordones,* (Naút.) Shores, outriggers.

Bordoncíco y Bordoncíllo, *sm.* A small staff.

Bordoneár, *vn.* 1. To try the ground with a staff or stick. 2. To strike with a staff or cudgel 3. To rove or wander about to avoid working. 4. To play well on the thorough bass.

Bordonería, *sf.* Vicious habit of wandering about in an idle manner, on a pretence of devotion.

Bordonéro, ra, *s.* Vagrant, vagabond.

Bordúra, *sf.* (Blas.) V. *Bordadura.*

Boreál, *a.* Boreal, northern, belonging to the north-wind and the northern region.

Bóreas, *sm.* Boreas, the north-wind.

Borgóña, *sf.* Burgundy wine.

Borgoñóta, *sf.* Sort of ancient helmet. *A' la Borgoñóta,* In the Burgundy fashion.

Bórla, *sf.* 1. Tassel, bunch of silk, gold, or silver lace. 2. Doctor's bonnet in universities, decorated with a tassel.

Borlílla y Borlíta, *sf.* Small tassel.

Borlón, *sm.* 1. Large tassel. 2. Napped stuff, made of thread and cotton yarn.

Bórne, *sm.* 1. The end of a lance. 2. Tree of the oak kind. [chor.

Borneadéro, *sm.* (Naút.) Birth of a ship at an-

Borneadízo, za, *a.* Pliant, flexible.

Borneár, *va.* 1. To bend, turn, or twist. 2. (Arq.) To model and cut the pillars all round. *Bornear la verdad,* To comment, to explain or expound the truth. *Bornear las palabras,* To turn words into different senses.—*vn.* 1. To edge, to sidle. 2. To warp, to turn. *El navío bornea,* (Naút.) The ship swings or turns round her anchor.

Bornéo, *sm.* 1. Act of turning or winding a thing. 2. (Naút.) Swinging round the anchor.

Bornéra, *sf.* A blackish sort of a mill-stone.

Bornéro, ra, Ground by a black mill-stone; applied to wheat.

Borní, *sm.* (Orn.) Lanner, a kind of falcon. Falco lanarius *L.*

Boróna, *sf.* A sort of grain resembling maize or Indian corn.

Borofía, *sf.* Dish made of apples, pumpkins, and green pepper, chopped together.

Bórra, *sf.* 1. Yearling ewe. 2. Goat's hair, with which the pannels of saddles, cushions, &c. are stuffed. 3. Nap raised on cloth by shearers. 4. Dregs or lees of oil, the refuse of any thing; hairy wool. 5. Tax or duty on sheep. 6. (Met.) Useless words or expressions, without any sense or meaning. *Acaso es borra?* Do you think that to be nothing else but chit-chat and idle talk?

Borrácha, *sf.* Leather bag or bottle for wine.

Borrachear, *vn.* To be often drunk.

Borrachéra, Borrachería, y Borracháda, *sf.* 1. Drunkenness; act of drinking to excess. 2. Drunken feast, where excesses in eating and drinking are committed. 3. Indian tree, the seed whereof, mixed with water, and drank, intoxicates. 4. (Met.) Madness, great folly.

Borrachéz, *sf.* 1. Intoxication. 2. Perturbation of the judgment or reason.

Borrácho, cha, *a.* 1. Drunk, intoxicated. 2. (Met.) Inflamed by passion. *Al borracho fino, ni el agua basta, ni el vino,* (Prov.) A complete drunkard is never satisfied either with wine or water. 3. Coloured, applied to biscuit baked with wine; or to fruits and flowers of a violet or purple colour. [drunkard, a tippler.

Borrachón y Borrachonázo, *sm.* Great

Borrachuéla, *sf.* (Bot.) Bearded darnel. Lolium temulentum *L.* Its seeds, mixed with bread-corn, intoxicate.

Borrachuélo, *sm.* Little tippler.

Borradór, *sm.* 1. Rough draft of a writing in which corrections are made. 2. Waste-book in which merchants or tradesmen make their daily entries.

Borragear, *vn.* To scribble, to write without care on any certain subject.

Borrájo, *sm.* (And. y Extr.) V. *Rescoldo.*

Borrár, *va.* 1. To blot or efface a writing. 2. (Met.) To cloud, to darken, to obscure. *Borrar la plaza,* To abolish a place or employ.

Borrásca, *sf.* 1. Storm, tempest, violent squall of wind. 2. (Met.) Hazard, danger, obstruction.

Borrascóso, sa, *a.* Stormy, boisterous.

Borráz, *sm.* V. *Atincar.*

Borrája, *sf.* (Bot.) Borage. Borago officinalis *L.*

Borregáda, *sf.* Large flock of sheep or lambs.

Borrégo, ga, *s.* 1. Lamb not yet a year old. 2. (Met.) Simpleton, a soft, ignorant fellow. *No hay tales borregos,* There is no evidence of its truth.

Borreguéro, *sm.* Shepherd, he who tends lambs.

Borreguíllo, lla, *s.* (Dim.) Little lamb.

Borrén, *sm.* Pannel of a saddle.

Borrína, *sf.* Kind of engine for raising water to a certain height.

Borricáda, *sf.* 1. Drove of asses. 2. Cavalcade or procession on asses by way of amusement. 3. (Met.) Silly or foolish word or action.

Borríco, ca, *s.* 1. Ass. 2. Fool. *Es un borrico,* He can bear great labour and fatigue. *Puesto en el borrico,* (Met.) Determined to do some business or other. *Poner á alguno sobre un borrico,* To threaten any one with a whipping.

Borricón y Borricóte, *sm.* 1. Large jack-ass. 2. (Met.) Plodder, dull, heavy, and laborious man. 3. (Among Sawyers) Horse, a three-legged machine on which sawyers saw their timber.

Borriquéro, *sm.* One who keeps or tends asses.

Borriquéte de proa, *sm.* (Naút.) Fore-topmast.

Borriquíllo, lla; y to, ta, *s.* A little ass.

Borriquíllos, *pl.* Cross-bars of the frame of a table.

Bórro, *sm.* 1. Wether not yet two years old. 2. Dolt of slow understanding. 3. Duty laid on sheep.

Borrón, *sm.* 1. Blot or stain of ink on paper. 2. Rough draft of a writing. 3. First sketch of a painting. 4. Blemish which tarnishes or defaces. 5. Unworthy action which disgraces one's character and reputation.

Borronázo, *sm.* Great blot or blur.

Borroncíllo, *sm.* Small blot or stain.

Borróso, sa, *a.* 1. Full of dregs and lees. 2. Done in a bad and bungling manner. *Letra borrosa,* Letter badly written, and full of blots and corrections.

Borróso, *sm.* Bungler, a petty tradesman.

Borrufálla, *sf.* (Vulg. Ar.) Bombast, a pompous show of empty sounds or words.

Borrumbáda, *sf.* V. *Barrumbada.*

Borujón, *sm.* Knob, protuberance.

Borúsca, *sf.* Withered leaf which falls off the tree.

Bosár, *va.* 1. To run over, to overflow. 2. To vomit. 3. (Met.) To utter lofty words.

Boscáge, *sm.* 1. Tuft, clump, or cluster of trees or plants. 2. (Pint.) Boscage, landscape with trees, thickets, and animals.

Bósforo, *sm.* Strait or channel by which two seas communicate with each other.

Bósque, *sm.* Tract of land planted with trees and brushwood.

Bosquecíllo, *sm.* Small wood, a coppice.

Bosquejár, *va.* 1. To make a sketch of a painting. 2. To design or project a work without finishing it. 3. To explain a thought or idea rather in an obscure manner. 4. To make a rough model of a figure or *basso-relievo* in wax, clay, plaster of Paris, or any other soft matter.

Bosquéjo, *sm.* 1. Sketch of a painting. 2. Any kind of work unfinished. 3. Unfinished writing or composition. *Estar in bosquejo,* To be in an imperfect or unfinished state.

Bostár, *sm.* Ox-stall, or stand for oxen.

Bostezadór, *sm.* Person who yawns repeatedly.

Bostezár, *vn.* To yawn, to have the mouth opened involuntarily.

Bostézo, *sm.* Yawn, oscitation.

Bóta, *sf.* 1. Small leather bag to carry wine. 2. Butt or pipe with hoops, to contain wine or other liquids. 3. Boot, a leather covering for the feet and legs. 4. (Ant.) Marriage, wedding. 5. (Naút.) Water-cask. *Bota fuerte,* Jack-boot, a wide strong boot. *Estar con las botas puestas,* Ready to perform any thing that may be required.

Botadór, *sm.* 1. Driver, one who drives or impels. 2. Punch, an iron instrument for driving out nails. 3. Crow's bill or pelican, an iron instrument used by dentists to draw teeth. 4. (Naút.) Starting pole used to shove off a boat from the shore.

Botafuégo, *sm.* Linstock, a wooden staff with a match at the end of it, used by gunners in firing cannon.

Botagueña, *sf.* (Cast.) Sausage made of the haslets of pigs.

Botalón, *sm.* (Naút.) Boom, a long pole used in setting up studding or stay-sails. *Botalon del foque*, Jib-boom. *Botalones*, Fire-booms.

Botámen, *sm.* (Naút.) All the casks on board a ship, which contain wine and water.

Botána, *sf.* 1. Plug or stopple used to stop up bung-holes. 2. Cataplasm or plaster put on a wound to heal it. 3. Scar remaining after a wound is healed.

Botánica, *sf.* Botany, the science of plants, or natural history of vegetables.

Botánico, ca, *a.* Botanic or botanical.

Botánico ó Botanísta, *sm.* Botanist, one skilled in the science of plants, or who professes botany.

Botanománcia, *sf.* Superstitious divination by herbs.

Botántes, *sm. pl.* (Naút.) Shores, out-riggers.

Botár, *va.* 1. To cast, to throw, to fling, to launch. 2. To vow, to make vows. *Botar á Dios*, To vow to God. *Botar al agua alguna embarcacion*, (Naút.) To launch a ship. *Botar en vela*, To fill the sails. *Botar afuera los botalones*, To bear off the booms.

Botaráte, *sm.* Thoughtless, blustering person.

Botarél, *sm.* (Arq.) Buttress, a mass of stone which supports the spring of arches or vaults.

Botárga, *sf.* 1. Sort of wide breeches formerly worn, gaskins. 2. Motley dress of a harlequin. 3. Harlequin, buffoon. 4. Kind of large sausages. 5. (Ar.) V. *Dominguillo*.

Botaséla, *sf.* (Mil.) Signal given with a trumpet for the cavalry to saddle.

Botavánte, *sm.* (Naút.) Pike used by seamen to defend themselves against an enemy who attempts to board.

Botavára, *sf.* (Naút.) A small boom or pole which crosses the sail of a boat in a diagonal direction. *Botavara de congreja*, Gaff-sail boom.

Bóte, *sm.* 1. Thrust with a pike, lance, or spear. 2. Rebound of a ball on the ground. 3. Gallipot, a small glazed earthen vessel. 4. Toilet-box, in which women keep paint, pomatum, &c. 5. Chuck-farthing, a play in which the money falls with a chuck into the hole beneath. 6. Canister, a tin vessel for tea or coffee. *Bote de tabaco*, Snuff-canister. 7. (Naút.) Boat, an open vessel commonly worked by oars. *Bote de lastre*, Ballast-lighter. *Bote de maestranza ó minueta*, Shipwright's boat. *Bote en piezas de armazon*, Boat in frame. *Estar de bote en bote*, To be full of people; spoken of a boat. *De bote y voleo*, Instantly.—*pl.* 1. (In places where the wool is washed) Heaps of wool piled up separately. 2. Bounds made by a horse without malice.

Botecário, *sm.* (Ant.) A certain war-tax.

Botecíco y Botecíllo, *sm.* 1. Small pot. 2. Skiff.

Botélla, *sf.* Bottle, a glass or crystal vessel with a narrow neck; also the quantity of wine or other liquor contained in a bottle. *Hemos bebido tres botellas*, We drank three bottles.

Botellér, *sm.* (Ant.) V. *Botillero*.

Botequín, *sm.* (Naút.) Small boat.

Botería, *sf.* In ships, collection of leather bags of wine.

Botéro, *sm.* One who dresses and makes leather bags and leather bottles for wine.

Botéza, *sf.* V. *Embotamiento*.

Botíca, *sf.* 1. Apothecary's shop where medicines are prepared and sold. 2. Potion or medicine given to a sick person. 3. Shop in general. 4. (Ant.) Furnished house or lodging.

Boticáge, *sm.* Rent paid for a shop.

Boticário, *sm.* Apothecary, one who makes up or sells medicines.

Botíga, *sf.* (Arag.) Shop, a place where any thing is sold.

Botiguéro, *sm.* Shop-keeper, one who attends an open shop.

Botiguílla, *sf.* A small petty shop.

Botíja, *sf.* Earthen jar with a short and narrow-neck. *Botija para aceyte*, An oil-jar.

Botijéro, *sm.* One who makes or sells jars.

Botijílla ó Botijuéla, *sf.* A small jar.

Botílla, *sf.* 1. A small wine-bag. 2. Woman's half boot.

Botillería, *sf.* 1. Ice-house, where iced creams, jellies, sweetmeats, and liqueurs, are prepared or sold. 2. (Naút.) Steward's room and stores. 3. (Ant.) Ancient war-tax.

Botilléro, *sm.* One who prepares or sells iced liquors and jellies.

Botíllo, *sm.* A small wine-bag, a leather bottle.

Botín, *sm.* 1. Buskin, a half-boot formerly worn by players on the stage. 2. Spatterdash. 3. Booty taken by soldiers in an enemy's camp or country. 4. (Naút.) Lashing.

Botinéro, *sm.* A soldier who takes care of and sells the booty.

Botiníco, y íllo, *sm.* A little buskin or half-boot.

Botiquería, *sf.* Perfumer's shop, where perfumes are sold.

Botiquín, *sm.* Travelling medicine-chest.

Botivoléo, *sm.* Act of recovering a ball which has just touched the ground.

Bóto, ta, *a.* 1. Blunt, round at the point. 2. (Met.) Dull of understanding.

Bóto, *sm.* Large gut filled with butter, and thus preserved and carried to market.

Botón, *sm.* 1. Button, bud, or gem, put forth by vines and trees in the spring. 2. Bit of wood or bone, covered with silk, thread, cloth, or other stuff. *Boton de metal dorado ó plateado*, A gilt or plated button. 3. (Esgr.) Tip of a foil made roundish, and covered with leather. 4. Button or knob of doors and windows, to pull them after one. *Boton de cerradura*, The button of a lock. 5. Annulet of balusters, and also of keys, serving for an ornament. 6. (Mont.) Piece of wood which fastens a fowling-net. *Boton de fuego*, Cautery in the form of a button, wherewith any thing is cauterized. *Boton de oro*, (Bot.) Upright crow-foot. Ranunculus acris *L.* *Contarle los botones á uno*, (Esgr.) To give one as many thrusts as and where he pleases. *De botones adentro*, Internally.

Botonadúra, *sf.* Set of buttons for a suit of clothes.

Botonázo, *sm.* (Esg.) Thrust given with a foil.
Botoncíco, llo, y to, *sm.* (Dim.) A small button.
Botonéro, ra, *s.* Button-maker; button-seller.
Botonería, *sf.* Button-maker's shop.
Botór, *sm.* (Ant.) Venereal tumour.
Botóso, sa, *a.* (Ant.) V. *Boto.*
Botrítes, *sm.* A kind of burnt cadmia in the form of a bunch of grapes which adheres to the upper part of the furnace.
Boucán, *sm.* Measure of liquids in Italy, containing about four pounds.
Boulíngrin, *sm.* Bowling green.
Bovíge y Bovático, *sm.* Duty formerly paid on horned cattle in Catalonia.
Bóveda, *sf.* 1. Arch or vault. 2. Cave or cavern, a subterraneous habitation, in the form of a vault or arch. 3. A subterraneous vault for the dead in churches. *Hablar en boveda,* To speak big, to brag. *Boveda de jardin,* Bower.
Bovedár, *va.* To vault or cover with ashes.
Bovedílla, *sf.* A small vault made of plaster, in the roof of a house. *Bovedillas,* (Naút.) Counters, arched parts of a ship's poop. *Bovedillas costaleras,* Arches two feet wide, more or less. *Subirse á las bovedillas,* (Met.) To be nettled, to be in a passion.
Bovíno, na, *a.* Belonging to black cattle.
Bóx, *sm.* 1. (Bot.) Box-tree. Buxus *L.* 2. Round piece of box, on which shoemakers close their work. 3. (Naút.) Act of doubling a point or head-land.
Bóxa, *sf.* (Mur.) Southern-wood. V. *Abrótano.*
Boxár, *va.* 1. To sail round an island, and measure the circumference thereof. 2. To scrape off the rough integuments, stains, and moisture of leather, that it may the better take the colour.—*vn.* To measure around, to contain.
Boxeár, *va.* (Naút.) V. *Boxar.*
Boxedál, *sm.* Plantation of box-trees.
Boxéo y Bóxo, *sm.* (Naút.) Act of sailing round an island or head-land.
Boy, (Ant.) V. *Buey.*
Bóya, *sf.* 1. (Naút.) Buoy, a barrel, block, or piece of cork, fastened to an anchor to serve as a signal for sailors. 2. Piece of cork fastened to a fishing-net to keep it from sinking. 3. (Ant.) Butcher. 4. (Ant.) Hangman, public executioner. *Boya de barril,* Nun-buoy. *Boya cónica,* Can-buoy. *Boya de palo,* Wooden-buoy. *Boya de cable,* Cable-buoy. *Echar afuera la boya á la mar,* To stream the buoy. *La boya nada á la vista,* The buoy floats in sight.
Boyáda, *sf.* Drove of oxen or bullocks.
Boyál, *a.* Relating to black cattle.
Boyánte, *pa.* 1. Buoyant, light, sailing well; applied to a ship. 2. (Met.) Fortunate, successful.
Boyar, *vn.* (Naút.) To be a-float; applied to a ship which was on shore.
Boyár, *sm.* (Naút.) Kind of Flemish bilander.
Boyázo, *sm.* Large ox or bullock.
Boyéra, *sf.* Ox-stall, a stand for oxen.
Boyéro, *sm.* Ox-herd, or ox-driver.
Boyezuélo, *sm.* A young or small ox.
Boyúno, na, *a.* Belonging to black cattle.
Boza, *sf.* (Naút.) One end of a rope made fast in a bolt-ring, till the other brings the tackle to its place. *Bózas,* (Naút.) Stoppers, short ends of cables used to suspend or keep something in its place. *Bozas de la uña del ancla,* Shank painter. *Bozas de cable ó cubiertas,* Cable-stoppers. *Bozas de combate ó de las vergas,* The stoppers of the yards. *Bozas de los obenques,* The stoppers of the shrouds.
Bozál, *sm.* 1. Muzzle, a sort of bag made of bass-weed, to prevent beasts of burthen from browsing on the road or injuring corn-fields. 2. Muzzle with bells, worn by horses and mules when travelling. 3. Muzzle for dogs, to prevent their biting; for calves, to prevent their sucking.
Bozál, *a.* 1. Muzzled; applied to negroes lately imported, and also to inhabitants of the less polished provinces of Spain, newly arrived in Madrid. 2. Novice, inexperienced in trade or business. 3. Wild, not broken in; applied to horses.
Bozaléjo, *sm.* A small muzzle.
Bózo, *sm.* 1. Down, which precedes the beard. 2. Headstall, a part of the halter which goes round the mouth and head of a horse.
Brabánte, *sm.* Brabant or Flemish linen.
Brabéra, *sf.* Air-hole, ventilator.
Brábio, *sm.* Prize obtained at public games.
Braceáda, *sf.* Violent extension of the arms.
Braceáge, *sm.* 1. Act of beating the metal for coining in the mint. 2. (Naút.) Act of tying any thing with braces. 3. Depth of water.
Braceár, *vn.* To move or swing the arms.—*va.* (Naút.) To brace. *Bracear las vergas,* To brace the yards.
Bracéro, *sm.* 1. Gentleman-usher, one who hands a lady about. 2. Labourer who hires himself for some work by the day. 3. A strong-armed man.
Bracéte, *sm.* A small arm.
Bracíl, *sm.* (Ant.) Armour of the arm composed of various pieces.
Bracíllo y Bracíto, *sm.* 1. The fleshy part of the arm; a little arm. 2. Branch of the mouth-bit of a bridle for a horse or mule.
Bráco, ca, *a.* (Ant.) 1. Pointing or setting; applied to a pointer. 2. Broken-nosed, flat-nosed.
Brafonéra, *sf.* (Ant.) 1. Piece of ancient armour which covered the upper part of the arm. 2. In clothes, a roller which girded the upper part of the arms; a plaited sleeve.
Brága, *sf.* Child's clout. *Brágas,* Gaskins, a kind of wide breeches; breeches in general. *Calzarse las bragas,* To wear the breeches; applied to an imperious wife, who lords it over her husband. *Viose el perro en bragas de cerro y no conoció su compañero,* (Prov.) Set a beggar on horseback and he will ride to the devil.
Bragáda, *sf.* 1. The flat of the thigh in beasts, from the flank to the hough. 2. *Bragada de una curva,* (Naút.) The throat of a knee. *Madera de bragada,* Compass-timber.
Bragádo, da, *a.* 1. Having the flanks of a different colour from the rest of the body. 2. (Met.) Ill-disposed, being of depraved sentiments.
Bragadúra, *sf.* 1. Part of the human body where it begins to fork. 2. Fork of a pair of breeches, which makes them wide and easy. 3. Flat of the thigh in beasts, from the flank to the hough.
Bragázas, *sf. pl.* 1. Wide-breeches. 2. (Met.) Husband who suffers his wife to wear the breeches.

Braguéro, *sm.* 1. Truss, a bandage for keeping up a rupture or hernia. 2. *Braguero de cañon*, (Naút.) Breeching of a gun, the rope with which it is lashed to the ship's side, to prevent its recoiling too much. *Braguero de una vela*, Bunt of a sail. 3. Piece put into some part of clothes to render them stronger.

Braguéta, *sf.* 1. Opening of the fore-part of a pair of breeches. 2. (In Architecture) Kind of quarter or projecting mould. *Hidalgo de bragueta*, He who enjoys the privilege of a *hidalgo*, or gentleman, for having got seven male children without one intervening female.

Braguetéro, *sm.* (Vulg.) Lecher, one given to women.

Braguetón, *sm.* Large opening in the fore-part of the breeches.

Braguíllas, *sf. pl.* 1. Little breeches. 2. A child breeched for the first time. 3. Ugly, dwarfish person.

Brahonéra y Brahón, (Ant.) V. *Brafonera.*

Bráma, *sf.* Rut, the season of the copulation of deer and other wild beasts.

Bramadéra, *sf.* 1. Rattle. 2. Call or horn, used by shepherds to rally and conduct the flock. 3. Horn, used by the keepers or guards of vineyards and olive plantations, to frighten away the cattle.

Bramadéro, *sm.* Rutting-place, where deer, and other wild beasts, meet in rutting time.

Bramadór, ra, *s.* 1. Roarer, bawler; a noisy person. 2. (In Poetry) Inanimate things, emitting a sound like roaring or groaning.

Bramánte, *sm.* 1. Pack-thread, a strong thread made of hemp. 2. A sort of linen.

Bramár, *vn.* 1. To roar, to groan. 2. (Met.) To roar, to storm, to be boisterous; applied to the wind and sea. 3. (Met.) To fret, to be in a passion, to be sorely vexed.

Bramído, *sm.* 1. Cry uttered by wild beasts. 2. Clamour of persons enraged, and in a passion. 3. Tempestuous roaring of agitated elements.

Bramíl, *sm.* Painted line used by sawyers and carpenters to mark the place where boards or timbers are to be cut or sawed.

Bramóna, *sf. Soltar la bramona*, To break out into injurious expressions, to use foul language; chiefly applied to gamblers.

Bran de Inglaterra, *sm.* An ancient Spanish dance.

Bránca, *sf.* 1. Gland of the throat. 2. (Ant.) Point. *Brancas*, Claws, talons, &c.

Brancáda, *sf.* Drag-net or sweep-net, used at the mouth of rivers, or in the arms of sea.

Brancaursína, *sf.* (Bot.) Bear's breech, brank ursine. Acanthus spinosus *L.*

Bránchas, *sf. pl.* Gills of a fish.

Bránco, ca, *a.* (Ant.) V. *Blanco.*

Brandáles, *sm. pl.* (Naút.) Back stays, strong ropes which serve to support and sustain the top-masts and top-gallant masts. *Brandales del mastelero de gavia*, The main-top-back stays. *Brandales volantes*, Shifting back-stays.

Brandecér, *va.* To soften. V. *Ablandar.*

Brandembúrgo, *sm.* Large and wide-riding coat.

Brandís, *sm.* Great coat. *Brandises*, Collars of ladies' night gowns which extend to the neck.

Brándo, *sm.* Tune ada ted to a dance.

Bránza, *sf.* Staple or ring to which the chains of galley-slaves are fastened.

Bráña, *sf.* (Gal.) 1. Summer pasture. 2. Dung, withered leaves, and other remains of fodder, found on summer pasture-grounds.

Braquíllo, lla, *s.* Small pointer.

Braquilógia, *sf.* Brachylogy, laconism.

Brásas, *sf. pl.* Cinders, live coals almost burnt to ashes. *Ir, correr, ó pasar como gato por brasas*, To run as light as a cat on burning coals. *Estar hecho unas brasas*, To be all in a blaze; red faced. *Estar en brasas ó como en brasds*, (Met.) To be uneasy or restless.

Brasár, V. *Abrasar.*

Braseríco, llo y to, *sm.* A small pan to hold coals; a chafing-dish.

Braséro, *sm.* 1. Brasier, a pan to hold coals. 2. Place where criminals are burnt.

Brasíl, *sm.* 1. (Bot.) Brasiletto. Cæsalpina brasiliensis *L.* 2. Brasil-wood, used by dyers 3. Rouge, a red paint used by ladies.

Brasiládo, da, *a.* 1. Of a red or Brasil-wood colour; ruddy.

Brasiléño, ña, *a.* Brasilian.

Brasiléte, *sm.* An inferior sort of Brasil-wood, of a paler red than the fine sorts.

Brasmológia, *sf.* The science which treats of the flux and reflux of the sea, and investigates its causes.

Braúlis, *sf.* Cloth or stuff with white and blue stripes, which comes from the coast of Barbary.

Bráva, *sf.* (Naút.) Heavy swell of the sea.

Bravaménte, *ad.* 1. Bravely, gallantly. 2. Cruelly, inhumanly, barbarously. 3. Finely, extremely well. *Escribe bravamente*, He writes extremely well. 4. Plentifully, copiously. *Hemos comido bravamente*, We have made a hearty dinner.

Braváta, *sf.* Bravado, boast or brag, an arrogant menace, intended to frighten and intimidate.

Bravàto, ta, *a.* (Ant.) Boasting, impudent.

Braveadór, ra, *s.* Bully, hector.

Braveár, *va.* To bully, to hector, to menace in an arrogant manner.

Bravéra, *sf.* Vent or chimney of certain ovens.

Bravéza, *sf.* 1. (Ant.) Bravery, valour. 2. (Ant.) Vigour. 3. Fury of the elements.

Braviar, (Ant.) V. *Bramar.*

Bravíllo, lla, *a.* Rather wild, not yet tamed.

Bravío, vía, *a.* 1. Ferocious, savage, wild, untamed. 2. Wild, propagated by nature, not cultivated; applied to plants. 3. Coarse, unpolished; applied to manners.

Bravío, *sm.* Fierceness or savageness of wild beasts.

Brávo, va, *a.* 1. Brave, valiant, strenuous. 2. Bullying, hectoring. 3. Savage, wild, fierce; applied to beasts. 4. (Met.) Severe, untractable. 5. (Met.) Rude, unpolished, uncivilized. 6. Sumptuous, expensive. 7. Excellent, fine. *Brava cosa*, (Irón.) Very fine indeed! *El ama brava es llave de su casa*, (Prov.) A severe mistress makes the servants honest.

Bravosidád, *sf.* V. *Gallardía.*

Bravúra, *sf.* 1. Ferocity, fierceness; applied to wild beasts. 2. Bravado, boast, brag.

Bráza, *sf.* 1. Fathom, a measure of length, containing six feet. 2. (Naút.) Brace which is tied to the yards. *Brázas*, (Naút.) Braces, the ropes belonging to the yards of a ship. *Brazas de barlovento*, Weather-braces. *Brazas de sotavento*, Lee-braces. *Brazas de la cebadera*, Sprit-sail braces. *Afirmar las brazas de barlovento*, To secure the weather-braces. *Halar sobre las brazas*, To haul in the braces.

Brazáda, *sf.* Movement of the arms by stretching them out, or lifting them up.

Brazádo, *sm.* An arm-full, as much as can be taken in the arms at once. *Un brazado de leña*, An arm-full of fire-wood. *Un brazado de heno*, A truss of hay.

Brazáge, *sm.* Number of fathoms, depth of water. V. *Braceage.*

Brazál, *sm.* 1. (Ant.) Brachial muscle. 2. Ancient piece of armour, which covered the arms. 3. Bracelet. 4. Ditch or channel for conveying water from a river or canal to irrigate lands. 5. Bracer, a wooden instrument for playing balloons. 6. (Naút.) Rail. *Brazales de proa*, Head-rails. *Brazal del medio de proa*, The middle rail of the head.

Brazalête, *sm.* 1. Bracelet, an ornament for the arms. 2. Ancient iron piece of armour. *Brazalêtes*, (Naút.) Brace pendants.

Brazár, *va.* (Ant.) To embrace. V. *Abrazar.*

Brazázo, *sm.* Large or long arm.

Brázo, *sm.* 1. Arm, the limb which reaches from the shoulder to the hand. 2. (Met.) Bough or branch of a tree. 3. (Met.) Valour, strength, power. 4. Each end of a beam or balance. *Brazo de araña*, Curved branch of a girandole or lustre. *Brazo de mar*, Arm of the sea. *Brazo de silla*, Arm of a chair. *Brazo á brazo*, Arm to arm, with equal weapons. *A' brazo partido*, With the arms only, without weapons; with main force, arm to arm. *Brazos del reyno*, States of the realm; that is, the prelates, nobility, and corporations. *A' fuerza de brazos*, By dint of merit and labour. *Con los brazos abiertos*, With open arms, cheerfully. *Cruzados los brazos*, With the arms folded, idle. *Dar los brazos á uno*, To embrace one. *Hecho un brazo de mar*, With great show or pomp. *Ser el brazo derecho de alguno*, To be one's right hand, or confidant.

Brazólas, *sf. pl.* (Naút.) Coamings of the hatchways.

Brazuélo, *sm.* 1. Small arm. 2. Shoulder or forethigh of beasts. V. *Bracillo.*

Bréa, *sf.* 1. Pitch; artificial bitumen composed of pitch, resin, and grease mixed together. 2. Coarse canvas for wrapping up wares; sackcloth.

Breár, *va.* 1. To pitch. 2. To vex, to plague, to thwart. 3. (Met.) To cast a joke upon one.

Brebáge, *sm.* 1. Beverage, a drink made up of different ingredients. 2. (Naút.) Grog.

Bréca, *sf.* Bleak or blay, a river fish much like the *Besugo.*

Brécha, *sf.* 1. Breach made in the ramparts of a fortress by the fire of battering ordnance. 2. Opening or aperture made in a wall or building. 3. (Met.) Impression made upon the mind by persuasion or self-conviction. *Batir en brecha*, To batter a breach in a fortification. (Met.) To persecute one, and cause his destruction.

Brécoho, *sm.* V. *Escaro.*

Brédo, *sm.* V. *Bledo.*

Bréga, *sf.* 1. Strife, contest, affray. 2. (Met.) Pun, jest, or trick played upon one. *Dar brega*, To play a trick.

Bregádo, da, *a.* (Ant.) Very elaborate.

Bregár, *vn.* 1. To contend, to struggle. 2. (Met.) To struggle with troubles, difficulties, and dangers.—*va.* To work up dough on a board or table with a rolling-pin or roller. *Bregar el arco*, To bend a bow.

Bregučro, *sm.* (Ant.) A wrangler.

Brén, *sm.* Bran. V. *Salvado.*

Bréncа, *sf.* (Bot.) Maidenhair. Adiantum capillus Veneris *L.* V. *Culantrillo.*—*pl.* 1. Sluice posts, the posts of a water or flood-gate. 2. Filaments, the three cristated capillaments of saffron.

Bréña, *sf.* Craggy, broken ground, full of brakes and brambles.

Breñál ó Breñár, *sm.* Place full of briers and brambles.

Breñóso, sa, *a.* Craggy, full of briers and brambles.

Bréque, *sm.* Small river fish. V. *Breca.* *Ojos de breque*, Weak or bloodshot eyes.

Brésca, *sf.* (Arag.) Honey-comb.

Brescadíllo, *sm.* A small tube made of gold or silver.

Bretadór, *sm.* Call, whistle or pipe to call birds.

Bretáña, *sf.* A sort of fine linen, manufactured in Britanny.

Bréte, *sm.* 1. Fetters, shackles, irons for the feet. 2. Indigence, perplexity. *Estar puesto en un brete*, To be hard put to. 3. Kind of food in India, consisting of a masticated leaf in the shape of a heart, and of a spicy juice.

Bretón, *sm.* Young sprouts of cabbage.

Bréva, *sf.* 1. Early fig, the first fruit of the fig-tree. 2. Early large acorn. *Mas blando que una breva*, More pliant than a glove; brought to reason.

Brevál, *sm.* (Ast. Bot.) Early fig-tree. Ficus *L.*

Bréve, *sm.* 1. Apostolic brief, granted by the pope or his legates. 2. (Ant.) Card of invitation, ticket, memorandum in a pocket-book. 3. Brief, in music.

Bréve, *a.* Brief, short, concise. *En breve*, Shortly, in a little time.

Brevecíco, íllo, íto, *a.* Somewhat short or concise.

Brevedád, *sf.* Brevity, shortness, conciseness.

Breveménte, *ad.* Briefly, concisely.

Brevéte, *sm.* V. *Membrete.*

Brevéza, *sf.* (Ant.) V. *Brevedad.*

Breviário, *sm.* 1. Breviary, which contains the daily service of the church of Rome. 2. Brevier, a small letter used in printing. 3. (Ant.) Memorandum-book. 4. (Ant.) Abridgment, epitome.

Brezál, *sm.* Place planted with heaths.

Brézo, *sm.* 1. (Bot.) Heath, ling. Erica *L.* 2. (Ant.) Bed upon thorns.

Briága, *sf.* Rope made of bass-weed, tied round the shaft or beam of a wine-press.

Briál, *sm.* Rich silken petticoat, worn by ladies.

Bríba, *sf.* Truantship, idleness, neglect of business or duty. *A' la briba*, In an idle, lazy, and negligent manner.

Bribár, *vn.* To lead a vagabond life, to rove and loiter about.

Bríbia, *sf.* 1. A beggar's tale, to move compassion. *Echar la bribia*, To go a begging. 2. V. *Biblia*.
Bribón ó Bribión, **na**, *s.* y *a.* Vagrant, impostor.
Briboncáda, *sf.* Beggar's trick, mean cunning.
Bribonázo, *sm.* Great cheat, impudent impostor.
Bribonícillo, *sm.* Little gull, young impostor.
Bribonéar, *vn.* V. *Bribar*.
Briboneríá, *sf.* Life of a vagrant or vagabond, a beggar's trade.
Bribonzuélo, *sm.* V. *Briboncillo*.
Brícho, *sm.* Spangle, used in embroidery.
Brída, *sf.* 1. Reins of a bridle; a bridle complete. 2. Horsemanship, the art of managing a horse by means of a bridle. 3. (Met.) Curb, restraint, check. *A' la brida*, Riding a bur-saddle with long stirrups.
Bridár, *va.* 1. To put a bridle to a horse, to bridle. 2. To curb, to check, to restrain.
Bridón, *sm.* 1. Horseman riding a bur-saddle with long stirrups. 2. Horse accoutred with a bur-saddle and long stirrups. 3. Small bridle used for want of a larger one.
Bríga, *sf.* (Ant.) V. *Poblacion*.
Brigáda, *sf.* Brigade, a certain number of battalions and squadrons, under the orders of a brigadier or general of brigade.
Brigadiér, *sm.* 1. Brigadier or general of brigade 2. *Brigadier en la real armada*, Officer of the navy, who commands a division of a fleet.
Brígola, *sf.* Ram, a machine used in ancient times for battering walls.
Brilladór, **ra**, *a.* Brilliant, sparkling, radiant.
Brilladúra y **Brillantéz**, *sf.* Brilliancy. V. *Brillo*.
Brillánte, *a.* V. *Brillador*.
Brillánte, *sm.* Diamond cut in triangular faces.
Brillár, *vn.* 1. To shine, to emit rays of light, to sparkle. 2. (Met.) To outshine in talents, abilities, or merits.
Bríllo, *sm.* Brilliancy, lustre, splendour.
Brín, *sm.* 1. Fragments of the capillament of saffron. 2. Sail-cloth. 3. Strong sort of linen of which tents are made.
Brincadór, **ra**, *s.* One who leaps, jumps, or hops.
Brincár, *vn.* 1. To leap, to jump. 2. (Met.) To step over others in point of promotion. 3. (Met.) To omit something on purpose, and pass to another. 4. (Met.) To fret, to fly into a passion. *Está que brinca*, He is in a great passion; he is quite mad with anger.
Bríncho, *sm.* A mode of playing at a game of cards, called *Reversi*.
Bríncia, *sf.* Peel or outward coat of an onion.
Bríneo, *sm.* 1. Leap, jump. 2. (Ant.) Small jewel formerly worn by ladies in their head-dress, which moved to and fro with quick motion.
Brindár, *vn.* 1. To drink one's health, to toast. 2. To pledge, or invite one to drink.
Brindéles de chapines, *pl.* Tapes or ribbons with which clogs are tied.
Bríndis, *sm.* Act of drinking the health of another; a toast.
Bringabála, *sf.* (Naút.) Brake or handle of a pump.
Brinquíllo ó **Brinquíño**, *sm.* 1. Gewgaw, a small trinket. 2. Sweetmeat which comes from Portugal. *Estar ó ir hecho un brinquiño*, To be as spruce and trim as a game cock.
Brío, *sm.* 1. Strength, force, vigour. 2. (Met.) Spirit, resolution, courage, valour. *Es un hombre de brios*, He is a man of mettle. *Baxar los brios á alguno*, To pull down one's spirits, to humble.
Brióles, *sm. pl.* (Naút.) Bunt-lines, small-lines fastened to the foot of square-sails to draw them up to the yard.
Briolín, *sm.* (Naút.) Slab-line, fastened to the foot rope of the main-sail and fore-sail, which serves to draw them up a little, that the steersman's view may not be obstructed by them.
Brionía, *sf.* (Bot.) Briony. Bryonia alba *L.*
Briosaménte, *ad.* In a spirited manner, courageously.
Bríoso, **sa**, *a.* Vigorous, full of spirit, high-minded.
Brísa, *sf.* 1. Breeze from the north-east. 2. *Brisa carabinera*, A violent gale. 3. Skin or peel of pressed grapes. V. *Orujo*.
Brísca, *sf.* A game at cards.
Briscádo, **da**, *a.* Mixed with silk; applied to gold and silver twist.
Briscár, *va.* To embroider with gold or silver twist mixed with silk.
Británica, *sf.* (Bot.) Water dock. Rumex aquaticus *L.*
Brivísco, **ca**, *a.* (Ant.) V. *Biblico*.
Bríza, *sf.* (Naút.) V. *Brisa*.
Brizár, *va.* (Ant.) To rock the cradle.
Brízna, *sf.* Fragment, small remain; splinter.
Briznóso, **sa**, *a.* Full of fragments or scraps.
Brízo, *sm.* 1. (Ant.) Cradle which is rocked. 2. A species of sea-urchin. Echinus *L.*
Bróca, *sf.* 1. Reel on which embroiderers wind their twist, silk, or thread. 2. Drill, an instrument for boring holes in iron. 3. Shoemakers' tack or round nail to fasten the sole to the last. 4. Button.
Brocadél ó **Brocatél**, *sm.* Brocade, a rich silk stuff.
Brocadíllo, *sm.* Brocade with gold or silver flowers.
Brocádo, *sm.* Gold or silver brocade.
Brocádo, **da**, *a.* Embroidered, like brocade.
Brocadúra, *sf.* Bite of a bear.
Brocál, *sm.* 1. Stone laid round the brim of a well. 2. Metal rim of the scabbard of a sword. 3. *Brocal de bota*, Mouth-piece of a leathern bottle for wine.
Brocamantón, *sm.* Crotchet of diamonds worn by ladies on their breast.
Brocárdico, *sm.* Axiom at law.
Brocatél, *sm.* 1. Ordinary kind of stuff made of hemp and silk. 2. Spanish marble of a yellow ground, with white veins.
Brocáto, *sm.* (Ar.) V. *Brocado*.
Brócha, *sf.* 1. Painter's brush, pencil. 2. (Ant.) Jewel. 3. (Ant.) Button, clasp. 4. Cogged dice, used by gamblers and sharpers.
Brochádo, **da**, *a.* Relating or belonging to brocade.
Brochadúra, *sf.* Set of clasps, or hooks and eyes, formerly worn in coats and cloaks.
Bróche, *sm.* Clasp, hooks and eyes.
Brochíca y **Brochuéla**, *sf.* Small clasp.
Brochón, *sm.* 1. Large clasp. 2. Washing-brush used by plasterers to white-wash walls.
Brochúra, *sf.* Act of putting a book in boards.
Brócula, *sf.* Drill for piercing iron or other metal.
Bróculi, *sm.* Broccoli, a sort of cabbage. Brassica oleracea *L*

Bródio, *sm.* Hotch-potch, a pottage of bread and meat given to beggars at the door.
Brodísta, *sm.* Poor scholar or student who comes to the doors of convents, and other religious communities, for his portion of *brodio*, or hotch-potch.
Bróma, *sf.* 1. Rubbish mixed with mortar to fill up the chinks of the foundations of walls. 2. Water-gruel made of oatmeal boiled in water. 3. Any thing weighty. 4. A person dull and tiresome in conversation. *Es una broma*, He is a stupid, unpleasant fellow. 5. (Naút.) Ship worm which perforates the bottoms of ships. Teredo navalis *L.*
Bromádo, da, *a.* Worm-eaten; applied to the bottom of a ship.
Bromár, *va.* To gnaw, like the ship-worm.
Brómo, *sm.* (Bot.) Wild-oats. Avena fatua *L.*
Brónce, *sm.* 1. Bronze, a yellow metal, chiefly composed of copper. 2. Trumpet made of brass. 3. Any thing strong and hard. *Ser un bronce*, To be indefatigable. *Tener un corazon de bronce*, To have a heart as hard as steel.
Bronceádo, *sm.* The act and effect of bronzing.
Bronceadúra, *sf.* V. *Bronceado.*
Broncear, *va.* 1. To give a bronze or brass colour. 2. To adorn with pieces of brass, latten, or gilt copper. [bronze.
Broncería, *sf.* Collection of things made of
Bróncha, *sf.* 1. Kind of poniard. 2. (Ant.) Jewel. 3. (Ant.) Plasterer's washing brush.
Broncísta, *sm.* A worker in bronze.
Bróncо, ca, *a.* 1. Rough, coarse, unpolished. 2. (Met.) Rude, unmannerly, clownish. 3. Harsh, rough to the ear; applied to musical sounds.
Bronquedád, *sf.* 1. Harshness, roughness of sound. 2. Rudeness of manners. 3. Unmalleability, in metals. [quarrel.
Bronquína, *sf.* (Bax.) Dispute, contention,
Broñír, *va.* V. *Bruñir.*
Broquél, *sm.* 1. Shield or buckler of wood, iron, &c. 2. (Met.) Support, protection. *Raja broqueles*, Bully, bragger, boaster.
Broquelázo, *sf.* Stroke with a shield or buckler.
Broqueléro, *sm.* 1. One who makes shields or bucklers. 2. He that wears shields or bucklers. 3. Wrangler, one inclined to dispute.
Broqueléte, *sm.* A small buckler.
Broquelíllo, *sm.* 1. Small shield. 2. Sort of small ear-rings worn by women.
Broslár, *va.* (Ant.) To embroider. V. *Bordar.*
Brosquíl, *sm.* Sheep-fold or sheep-cot.
Bróta, *sf.* Bud or germ of a vine.
Brotádo, da, *a.* Budded.
Brotadúra, *sf.* Budding, the act of shooting forth buds and germs.
Brótano, *sm.* (Bot.) Southern-wood. V. *Abrótano.*
Brotánte, *sm.* (Arq.) V. *Arbotante.*
Brotár, *va.* 1. To bud, to put forth young shoots or germs. 2. To break out, to appear; applied to the small-pox and other eruptions.
Bróte y Bróto, *sm.* 1. Germ of vines, bud of trees. 2. Fragment, crumb, chip.
Brotón, *sm.* 1. Large clasp for a kind of wide coat, which is called *sayo*. 2. (Ant.) Shoot, tender twig. 3. Sprout of cabbage.
Bróza, *sf.* 1. Remains of leaves, bark of trees, and other rubbish. 2. Thicket, brush-wood, on mountains. 3. Useless stuff spoken or written. 4. Printer's brush, to brush off the clogged ink from the types. *Gente de toda broza*, People without trade or employment. *Servir de toda broza*, To do all sorts of work.
Brozár, *va.* (Among Printers) To brush the types.
Brozóso, sa, *a.* Full of rubbish.
Bruchéro, *sm.* Brushmaker.
Brúces ó Brúzas, *sf. pl.* The upper lips. *Caer, ó dar de bruces*, To fall headlong to the ground. *De bruces, ó á bruces, ad.* With the face to the ground.
Bruéta, *sf.* Wheel-barrow.
Brugidór, *sm.* Glaziers' nippers used in paring off the corners or edges of glass.
Brugír, *va.* To pare off the corners and edges of panes of glass already cut with the diamond.
Brúgo, *sm.* A sort of grub.
Brúja, V. *Arena.*
Brulóte, *sm.* 1. (Naút.) Fire-ship, a vessel loaded with combustible matters, or artificial fire-works. 2. Warlike machine of the ancients for throwing darts or fire-arrows.
Brúma, *sf.* 1. V. *Broma.* 2. Winter-season. 3. Mist arising from the surface of the sea.
Brumadór, ra, *s.* (Ant.) V. *Abrumador.*
Brumál, *a.* Brumal, belonging to the winter season.
Brumamiénto, *sm.* Weariness, lassitude, the state of being spent with labour or fatigue.
Brumár, *va.* (Ant.) V. *Abrumar.*
Brumazón, *sm.* Thick fog or mist at sea.
Brúno, *sm.* The whitest and finest wax, which wax-chandlers use to polish or varnish tapers and wax-candles.
Brunéla, *sf.* (Bot.) Self-heal. Prunella vulgaris *L.*
Brunéta, *sf.* 1. Sort of black cloth. 2. (Ant.) Unwrought silver.
Brunéte, *sm.* (Ant.) Coarse black cloth.
Brúno, na, *a.* Of a brown dark colour.
Brúno, *sm.* (Ast.) 1. A little black plum. 2. Plum-tree.
Bruñído, da, *a.* Burnished.
Bruñidór, ra, *s.* 1. Burnisher, an instrument used in burnishing. 2. Tool of box-wood, used in finishing the seams of leather breeches. 3. One that burnishes or polishes.
Bruñimiénto, *sm.* Act and effect of polishing.
Bruñír, *va.* 1. To burnish. 2. To put on rouge.
Brúsca, *sf.* 1. (Naút.) Bevel, sweep, or rounding of masts, yards, &c. on board a ship. 2. Brush-wood, small-wood.
Brúscate, *sm.* A sort of hash made of milt, lamb's livers, chopped up with eggs, and stewed in a pan with almond-milk, herbs, and spice.
Brúsco, *sm.* 1. (Bot.) Kneeholly, butcher's broom or prickly pettigree. Ruscus aculeatus *L.* 2. Trifling remains not minded on account of their little value; as, loose grapes dropping at the vintage; fruit blown from the tree, &c. 3. Refuse of wool at the shearing time.
Brúsco, ca, *a.* Rude, peevish, forward.
Bruséla, *sf.* 1. (Bot.) Lesser periwinkle. Vinca minor *L.* 2. *Bruselas*, Sort of broad pincers used by silversmiths.
Bruséles, *sm. pl.* Pin or slice used by apothecaries to mix their drugs.
Brutál, *a.* Brutal, brutish, acting like brutes.
Brutalidád, *sf.* 1. Brutality, the quality of brutes. 2. Brutal action.

Brutalménte, *ad.* Brutally, in a brutal or brutish manner.

Brutésco, ca, *a.* (Ant.) Grotesque. V. *Grutesco.*

Brutéz y Brutéza, *sf.* (Ant.) V. *Brutalidad.*

Brutéza, *sf.* Roughness, want of polish; applied to stones.

Brúto, *sm.* 1. Brute, a creature without reason. 2. (Met.) An ignorant, rude, and immoral person.

Brúto, ta, *a.* Coarse, unpolished, in a rough state. *En bruto*, In a rough state, not polished, not wrought. *Diamante en bruto*, A rough diamond. *Madera en bruto*, (Naút.) Rough timber.

Brúxa, *sf.* (Vulg.) Witch. *Es una bruxa, ó parece una bruxa*, She looks like a witch. *Parece que la han chupado bruxas*, She looks as pale and lean as if she had been sucked by witches.

Bruxeár, *vn.* 1. To practise witchcraft. 2. To rove about in the night-time.

Bruxería, *sf.* Witchcraft.

Brúxo, *sm.* Sorcerer, conjurer, wizard.

Brúxula, *sf.* 1. (Naút.) Sea-compass. 2. Small hole which serves as a direction to point a gun. *Mirar por brúxula*, (Met.) To pry into other people's affairs and actions, and examine them closely.

Bruxuleár, *va.* 1. (At Cards) To examine one card after another, for the purpose of knowing one's hand. 2. (Met.) To discover by conjectures the nature and issue of an event.

Bruxuléo, *sm.* 1. Act of examining the cards, held at a game, one after another. 2. Scrutation, close examination. 3. Guess, conjecture.

Brúza, *sf.* Round brush for cleaning horses and mules. *Brúzas*, (In Woollen Manufactories) Brushes with which the bur of cloth is laid down one way to show the grain. *De bruzas*, V. *De bruces.*

Bú, *sm.* Word used by nurses to frighten children into silence.

Búa, *sf.* Pustule, a pimple with matter which breaks out on the skin. *Búas*, (Ant.) V. *Búbas.*

Buár, *va.* To place boundaries, to limit.

Buárda, *sf.* Sky-light, a window placed horizontally in the ceiling of a room.

Buáro y Buarillo, *sm.* Buzzard, a bird of prey.

Búba, *sf.* (Ant.) Pustule, small tumour. *Búbas*, Buboes.

Búbalo, *sm.* (Ant.) V. *Bufalo.*

Bubático, ca, *a.* Having buboes or glandular tumours.

Bubílla, *sf.* Small pustule, a pimple.

Bubón, *sm.* Large morbid tumour, full of matter.

Bubóso, sa, *a.* Afflicted with a disease in the groin.

Bucarán, *sm.* (Arag.) Fine glazed buckram.

Bucaríto, *sm.* Small earthen vessel of scented or odoriferous earth.

Búcaro, *sm.* Vessel made of fine odoriferous earth.

Buceár, *va.* To dive, to go under water in search of any thing.

Bucelário, *sm.* (Ant.) Vassal or servant who boarded in a house.

Bucéo, *sm.* Diving, the act of going under water in search of any thing.

Bucéro, *a.* Black nosed; applied to a hound or setting dog.

Búces, (De), *ad.* V. *De Bruces.*

Búcha, *sf.* Large chest or box. V. *Hucha. Bucha pescadera*, (Naút.) Buss, a vessel employed in the herring fishery.

Buchár, *va.* To hide or conceal.

Búche, *sm.* 1. Craw or crop, the first stomach of birds and fowls. 2. Maw or stomach of quadrupeds. 3. Mouthful of water or any other liquor. 4. Young sucking ass. 5. Purse, wrinkle, or pucker in clothes which do not fit well. 6. Breast, the place where secrets are pretended to be kept. 7. (Fam.) Human stomach. *Ha llenado bien el buche*, (Vulg.) He has stuffed his budget well. *Hacer el buche*, (In Cant Language) To eat. *Hacer el buche á otro*, To make one dine heartily. *Buche de almizcle*, Musk bag of the musk deer; also a little bag to put perfume in.

Buchecíllo, *sm.* Little craw.

Buchéte, *sm.* Cheek puffed with wind.

Bucinadór, *sm.* Trumpeter.

Bucinár, *va.* To publish or proclaim any thing at the sound of a trumpet.

Búcle, *sm.* Buckle, hair crisped and curled.

Búco, *sm.* (Ant.) 1. (Naút.) Ship, vessel. V. *Buque.* 2. Buck, a male goat. 3. Opening, aperture.

Bucólica, *sf.* 1. Pastoral or rural poetry. 2. (Joc.) Food.

Bucólico, ca, *a.* Bucolic, relating to pastoral poetry.

Bucosidád, *sf.* (Naút.) Tonnage, burthen. V. *Buque.*

Budiál, *sm.* Marsh, fen.

Budión, *sm.* (Ict.) Peacock fish. Labrus pavo *L.*

Buéga, *sf.* (Arag.) Landmark.

Buén, *a.* V. *Bueno.* Used only before a substantive, as *Buen hombre*, A good man. *Buen alma*, A good soul.

Buéna, *sf.* Property, fortune.

Buenabóya, *sm.* Seaman who engages spontaneously to serve on board a galley.

Buenaménte, *ad.* Freely, spontaneously, conveniently. *De buenamente*, Of one's own accord.

Buenandánza, *sf.* The good fortune of any one.

Buenaventúra, *sf.* 1. Fortune, good luck. V. *Ventura.* 2. Prediction of fortune-tellers.

Buéno, na, *a.* 1. Good or perfect in its kind. *La buena de la Catalina*, The good Catharine. *El bueno del cura*, The good curate. 2. Simple, plain, without cunning or craft. 3. Fit or proper for something. 4. Sociable, agreeable, pleasant. *Tener buen dia en buena compañia*, To spend a pleasant day in agreeable company. 5. Great, strong, violent. *Buena calentura*, A strong fever. 6. Sound, healthy. 7. Useful, serviceable. 8. (Iron.) Strange, wonderful, notable; used before the verb *ser*, as, *Lo bueno es que quiera enseñar á su maestro*, The best of it is, that he wishes to teach his master. *Buenos dias*, Good day; a familiar salute. *Buenas noches*, Good night. *Buenas tardes*, Good evening. *Adonde bueno? De don de bueno?* Where are you going? Where do you come from? *Buenas artes y buenas letras*, The fine arts and belles lettres. *De bueno á bueno, ó de buenas á buenas*, Freely, willingly, gratefully. *A' buenas*, Willingly.

Buéno, *ad.* Enough, sufficiently. *Bueno ó bueno está*, Enough, no more.

Buenparecér, *sm.* Good counsel; pleasing aspect.

Buenpasár, *sm.* Independent situation, comfortable subsistence.

Buéña, *sf.* Black pudding.

Buéras, *sf. pl.* (Mur.) Pustules or pimples breaking out about the mouth.

Buéso, *sm.* (Ant.) One ridiculously dressed.

Buéy, *sm.* 1. Ox, bullock. 2. *Buey marino*, Sea-calf. 3. *Buey de caza*, Stalking ox. *A' paso de buey*, At a snail's gallop. *Buey de agua*, Great body of water issuing from a conduit or spring.

Bueyázo, *sm.* Large or big ox.

Bueyecíllo, *sm.* Little ox.

Bueyezuélo, *sm.* Stalking ox.

Bueyúno, na, *a.* Belonging to black cattle.

Buf. *interj.* Poh, poh.

Búfa, *sf.* 1. Breaking wind without noise. 2. Jest, joke.

Bufádo, da, *a.* Bursting with a noise; applied to glass drops blown extremely thin.

Búfala y Búfalo, *s.* Buffalo, a kind of wild ox.

Bufár, *vn.* 1. To puff and blow with anger. 2. To snort, to blow through the nose as a high-mettled horse.

Buféte, *sm.* Desk or writing table.

Bufetíllo, *sm.* Small desk or writing table.

Bufí, *sm.* Kind of watered camblet.

Bufído, *sm.* 1. Blowing of an animal, snorting of a horse. 2. Expression of anger and passion.

Búfo, *sm.* Harlequin or buffoon on the stage.

Búfo, fa, *a.* *Opera bufa*, Comic opera.

Bufón, *sm.* Merry-andrew, jack-pudding.

Bufonáda, *sf.* 1. Buffoonery, a low jest. 2. Sarcastic taunt, ridicule.

Bufonázo, *sm.* Great buffoon.

Bufoncíllo, *sm.* Little merry-andrew.

Bufoneárse, *vr.* To jest, to turn into ridicule.

Bufonería, *sf.* V. *Bufonada y Buhonería.*

Bufós, *sm. pl.* Ancient head-dress of women.

Bugáda, *sf.* Buck, the lye in which clothes are washed.

Bugacéta, *sf.* (Naút.) A small vessel.

Bugálla, *sf.* Gall-nut growing on oak leaves.

Buge, *sm.* Iron ring fixed in the inside of each end of the nave-hole, which keeps it from straining and wearing.

Bugelláda, *sf.* Kind of paint for ladies.

Bugía, *sf.* 1. Wax-taper, a slender wax-candle. 2. Candlestick in which a wax-taper is put.

Bugiér, *sm.* Gentleman usher of the king's household. V. *Uzier.*

Bugiería, *sf.* Office at court where the wax-candles are kept, and given out for the use of the palace.

Buglósa, *sf.* (Bot.) Wild bugloss. Lycopsis arvensis *L.*

Bugúla, *sf.* (Bot.) Alkanet, a species of bugloss.

Buhárda, *sf.* 1. Window in the roof, garret-window. 2. Garret, a room on the highest floor of the house.

Buhardílla, *sf.* Small garret.

Buhárro, *sm.* (Orn.) Eagle-owl. Strix bubo *L.*

Buhedal, *sm.* Pool of stagnant water.

Buhédo, *sm.* Marl, a kind of calcareous earth.

Buhéra, *sf.* Embrasure, loop-hold. V. *Tronera.*

Buhéro, *sm.* Owl-keeper.

Búho, *sm.* Owl. *Es un buho*, He is an unsocial man; he shuns all intercourse with others.

Buhonería, *sf.* Pedler's box, in which small wares are carried, and sold about the streets.

Buhonéro, *sm.* Pedler or hawker who goes about selling small wares.

Buír, *va.* To polish, to burnish.

Bujalazór y Bujarasól, *sm.* Fig, the inside pulp of which is of a reddish colour.

Bujarrón, *sm.* V. *Sodomita.*

Búla, *sf.* 1. Bull, an instrument despatched out of the papal chancery, and sealed with lead. *Echar las bulas á uno*, (Met.) To impose a burthen or troublesome duty. *Tener bula para todo*, To take the liberty of acting at pleasure, according to one's own fancy. 2. (Ant.) Bubble on water.

Bulár, *va.* To mark or brand with a red-hot iron.

Bularcámas, *sf. pl.* (Naút.) Breast-hooks, compass timbers, which serve to strengthen the stem of a ship.

Bulário, *sm.* Collection of papal bulls.

Búlbo, *sm.* (Bot.) Bulb, a kind of onion with several coats. *Bulbo castáño*, (Bot.) Earth-nut, pig-nut. Bunium bulbo-castanum *L.*

Bulbóso, sa, *a.* Bulbous, containing bulbs, consisting of many layers.

Búlda, *sf.* V. *Bula.*

Buldería, *sf.* (Ant.) Injurious expression.

Buléro, *sm.* One who is charged with distributing bulls of crusades, and collecting the alms of charity given for them.

Buléto, *sm.* Brief or apostolic letter granted by the pope, or his legate and nuncio.

Búlla, *sf.* Shout or loud cry of one or more persons. 2. Crowd, mob. *Meterlo á bulla*, To carry off the matter with a joke. 3. V. *Bolla.*

Bulladór, *sm.* Cheat, swindler.

Bulláge, *sm.* Crowd, a multitude confusedly pressed together.

Bullar, *va.* (Naút.) V. *Bollar.*

Bullebúlle, *sm.* Busy-body, a person of lively and restless disposition.

Bullecer, (Ant.) V. *Bullir y Alborotar.*

Bullício, *sm.* 1. Noise and clamour raised by a crowd. 2. Tumult, uproar, sedition.

Bulliciosaménte, *ad.* In a noisy, tumultuous manner.

Bullicióso, sa, *a.* 1. Lively, restless, noisy, clamorous. 2. Seditious, turbulent. 3. (Poét.) Boisterous, applied to the sea.

Bullidór, ra, *a.* V. *Bullicioso.*

Bullír, *vn.* 1. To boil, to be agitated by heat, as water and other liquids. 2. (Met.) To be lively or restless. 3. (Met.) To be industrious and active in business. *Bullirle á uno alguna cosa*, To be earnestly desirous of a thing.—*va.* To move a thing from one place to another; to manage a business.

Bullón, *sm.* 1. Kind of knife. 2. Dye bubbling up in a boiler.

Bultíllo, *sm.* Little lump or tumour.

Búlto, *sm.* 1. Bulk, any thing which appears bulky. 2. Protuberance, tumour, swelling. 3 Bust, image of the human head and neck. 4. Pillow, bolster. *Coger ó pescar el bulto*, (Met.) To lay hold of one, to seize one. *Figura ó imágen de bulto*, Figure or image in sculpture *Menear, ó tocar á otro el bulto*, To give one a nice drubbing. *Ser de bulto*, To be bulky. *A' bulto*, By the bulk. *Comprar las cosas á bulto*, To buy wholesale, or by the lump.

Bululu, *sm.* (Ant.) Strolling comedian, who alone represented in old times a comedy or farce, changing his voice according to the different characters.

Bunéto, *sm.* Hedge-sparrow.

Búnio, *sm.* Sort of earth-nut or pig-nut.

Buñoléro, ra, *s.* One that makes or sells bunns.

Buñuélo, *sm.* Bunn or fritter made of a paste of flour and eggs, and fried in oil. *Es buñuelo?* Is it nothing? observed to those inconsiderate persons, who would have things done without the necessary time.

Bupréste, *sm.* Sort of Spanish fly.

Búque, *sm.* 1. (Naút.) Bulk, capacity, or burthen of a ship. 2. Hull of a ship. 3. Vessel, ship.

Buráto, *sm.* 1. Sort of woollen stuff much worn for mourning, and clergymen's dress. 2. Transparent veil of a light silk stuff, worn by women.

Búrba, *sf.* African coin of small value.

Burbalúr, *sm.* Whale of a large kind.

Burbúja, *sf.* Bubble, a small bladder of water, filled and expanded with air.

Burbujeár, *vn.* To bubble, to rise in bubbles.

Burbujíta, *sf.* Small bubble.

Búrcho, *sm.* (Naút.) Sort of large sloop or barge.

Búrdas, *sf. pl.* (Naút.) Back-stays.

Burdégano, *sm.* (Ant.) Mule, offspring of a horse and she-ass.

Burdél, *sm.* Brothel.—*a.* (Ant.) Libidinous.

Burdeléro, ra, *s.* V. *Alcahuete.*

Burdinállas, *sf.* (Naút.) Sprit-top-sail-stay.

Búrdo, da, *a.* Coarse, common, ordinary.

Buréles, *sm. pl.* (Naút.) Wooden rollers with a point for different uses. *Bureles de hierro para engarzar motones*, Splicing fids. V. *Pasador. Burel*, (Blas.) Bar, being the ninth part of a shield.

Buréngue, *sm.* (Mur.) Mulatto slave.

Buréo, *sm.* 1. Court of justice, in which matters are tried relative to persons of the king's household. 3. Entertainment, amusement, diversion. *Entrar en buero*, To meet for the purpose of inquiring into or discussing a subject.

Búrga, *sf.* Hot spring of mineral waters used for bathing.

Burgalés, *sm.* 1. Ancient coin made at Burgos. 2. Wind blowing from Burgos.

Burgés, *sm.* Native or inhabitant of a village.

Búrgo, *sm.* Borough. *Búrgo-maestre*, Burgomaster, the chief magistrate of the cities in Germany.

Buriél, *a.* Reddish, between dark red and black.

Buriél, *sm.* 1. Kersey, a coarse cloth. 2. Rope-walk, manufactory for cordage.

Buríl, *sm.* Burine, graver, a tool used in graving. *Buríl de punta*, Sharp-pointed burine. *Buríl chaple redonda*, Curved burine.

Buriláda, *sf.* 1. Line or stroke of a burine. 2. Grains of silver taken out by an assayer, to try whether it is standard silver.

Buriladúra, *sf.* 1. Act of engraving with a graver. 2. Print or picture engraved.

Burilár, *va.* To engrave, to grave, to picture by incisions made with a burine or graver.

Burjáca, *sf.* Leather-bag carried by pilgrims or beggars.

Búrla, *sf.* 1. Sneer, an expression of derision or contempt. 2. Trick, a slight fraud or deceit. *Burla burlando le dixo buenas claridades*, Between joke and earnest he told him some plain truths. *Búrlas*, Falsities advanced in a jocular style. *Dexadas las burlas*, Setting jokes aside. *Hablar de burlas*, To speak in jest. *Hombre de burlas*, Empty jester. *No es hombre de burlas*, He is a plain honest man. *Decir algunas cosas entre burlas y veras*, To say something between joke and earnest. *De burlas*, In jest.

Burladór, ra, *s.* 1. Wag, jester, scoffer. 2. Earthen vessel, so contrived that the liquor runs out through hidden holes when it is put to the lips. 3. Hidden or concealed squirt, which throws out water on those who come near.

Burlár, *va.* 1. To ridicule, to mock, to scoff. 2. To play tricks, to deceive. 3. To frustrate one's views, to destroy one's hopes.

Burlería, *sf.* 1. Fun, pun, artifice. 2. Romantic tale. 3. Deceit, illusion. 4. Derision, reproach.

Burlésco, ca, *a.* Burlesque, jocular, ludicrous.

Burlésco, *sm.* (Rar.) Wag, jester, scoffer.

Burléta, illa, y íta, *sf.* Little trick, fun, or joke.

Burlón, na, *s.* Great wag, jester, or scoffer.

Búrra, *sf.* A she-ass. *Caer de su burra*, To fall from one's hobby-horse, to become sensible of one's errors.

Burráda, *sf.* 1. Drove of asses. 2. Stupid or foolish action or saying.

Burrageár, *va.* V. *Borragear.*

Burrájo, *sm.* Dry stable-dung to heat ovens.

Burrázo, za, *s.* Large or big ass.

Burréro, *sm.* 1. Ass-keeper, who sells asses' milk for medicine. 2. Jack-ass-keeper.

Burríllo, *sm.* (Fam.) V. *Añalejo.*

Búrro, *sm.* 1. Ass. 2. Stupid, ignorant being. *Es un burro cargado de letras*, He is an unmannerly clown with all his learning. 3. Horse on which sawyers saw boards or timber. 4. Wheel which puts the machine in motion that twists and reels silk. *Es un burro en el trabajo*, He works and drudges like an ass. *Burros de la mesana*, (Naút.) Mizen-bow-lines.

Burrúcho, *sm.* Young or little ass.

Burrumbáda, *sf.* V. *Barrumbada.*

Burújo, *sm.* 1. Skin or dregs of pressed olives or grapes. 2. Lump of pressed wood, or any other matter.

Burujon y Burullón, *sm.* 1. Large knob or lump. 2. Protuberance in the head caused by a stroke.

Burujoncíllo, *sm.* Little knob or protuberance.

Busárdas, *sf. pl.* (Naút.) Breast-hooks, compass-timbers, which serve to strengthen the stem.

Búsca, *sf.* 1. The act of searching a registry or office for some papers or writings. 2. Terrier, or other dog, which starts, rouses, or springs the game. 3. Troop of huntsmen, drivers, and terriers, that overrun a forest to rouse the game.

Buscadór, ra, *s.* Searcher, investigator.

Buscamiénto, *sm.* Search, research, inquiry

Buscapiés *sm.* 1. Squib running about between

people's feet. 2. (Met.) Word dropped in the course of conversation to come at the bottom of something.

BUSCÁR, *va.* To seek, to search, to endeavour to find out. *Buscar tres pies al gato y el tiene quatro*, To pick a quarrel. *Quien busca halla*, He that seeks will find. *Buscar el vivo á una pieza, ó cañon*, To take the calibre of a gun.

BUSCARRUÍDOS, *sm.* Restless, quarrelsome fellow.

BUSCAVÍDAS, *sm.* A person prying into the actions of others.

BÚSCO, *sm.* (Ant.) Track of an animal.

BUSCÓN, NA, *s.* 1. Searcher. 2. Cheat, pilferer, filcher, petty robber.

BUSÍLIS, *sm.* (In Cant Language,) The point in question where the difficulty lies. *Dar en el busilis*, To hit the mark.

BÚSO, *sm.* Hole. V. *Agujero.*

BÚSTO, *sm.* 1. Bust, a figure representing the human head and neck. 2. Tomb.

BUTIFÁRRA, *sf.* 1. Sort of sausage made in Catalonia. 2. Gaskins, long wide breeches like trousers.

BUTÍLLO, LLA, *a.* Of a pale yellowish colour.

BUTIÓNDO, DA, *a.* (Ant.) V. *Hediondo.*

BUTÍRO, *sm.* (Ant.) Butter. V. *Manteca.*

BUTÓRIO, *sm.* (Orn.) Bittern. Ardea stellaris *L.*

BUTRÍNO, *sm.* Fowling-net for catching birds.

BUTRÓN, *sm.* Net for birds. V. *Buytron.*

BUXÉDA, BUXEDÁL, ó BUXÉDO, *s.* Plantation of box-trees.

BUXERÍA, *sf.* Gewgaw, bauble, toy of little value.

BUXÉTA, *sf.* 1. Box made of box-wood. 2. Perfume-box.

BUXETÍLLA, *sf.* Small perfume-box.

BUXÉTO, *sm.* Burnisher, a polishing stick used by shoemakers to give a gloss to their work.

BÚXO, *sm.* Wooden frame on which painters fix their canvass to paint on.

BÚY, *sm.* (Ant.) V. *Buey.*

BÚYO, *sm.* 1. Hut, shepherd's cottage. 2. Buffalo snake. Boa constrictor *L.*

BÚYTRE, *sm.* (Orn.) Vulture. Vultur *L.* *Mas vale pázaro en mano que buytre volando*, (Prov.) A bird in the hand is worth two in the bush.

BUYTRÉRA, *sf.* Place where fowlers feed vultures.

BUYTRÉRO, *sm.* Vulture-fowler, one whose business is to feed and chase birds.

BUYTRÓN, *sm.* 1. Basket made of osiers to catch fish. 2. Partridge-net. 3. Furnace where silver-ores are smelted to extract the ore. 4. Snare or inclosure into which game is driven.

BÚZ, *sm.* Kiss, given out of respect and reverent regard. *Hacer el buz*, To do homage or pay respect in a servile manner.

BUZANO, *sm.* 1. (Ant.) Diver. 2. Kind of culverin.

BUZO, *sm.* 1. Diver, one that goes under water in search of things dropped into the sea or rivers. 2. An ancient kind of ship. *De buzos*, V. *De bruces.*

BUZÓN, *sm.* 1. Conduit, canal. 2. Hole through which letters are thrown into the post-office. 3. Lid or cover of cisterns, ponds, jars, &c. 4. (In Foundries) Hook, to take off the lids of melting-pots. 5. Sluice of the water-course at a mill. 6. Ancient kind of battering-ram.

C Is the third letter of the alphabet, and before *e* and *i* has generally the sound of the English *th* in *thick*, or the soft *z* in *zeal*; before *a*, *o*, *u*, *l*, and *r*, it sounds like *k*. It is also a numeral, as, C. 100; IƆ. 500, and CIƆ. 1000. The Spanish Academicians consider *ch* as a distinct letter, double in figure but simple in value, and therefore place it after all the other words beginning with a *c*. In this work it is retained in the place usual in English. *Ch* has always the soft sound in Spanish, the same as in the English word *church*, except in words derived from Greek or Hebrew, as *Christo*, *Melchisedech*, &c. where it is pronounced as *k*; but in such words the *h* is often omitted, or the orthography changed, as in *mecanica*, *querubin*, *quimica*, &c.

CÁ, *part.* (Ant.) Because, for, the same as.

CAB ADELANTRE, *ad.* (Ant.) In future, henceforward.

CÁB ó CABE, *sm.* Corn-measure of different capacity in different provinces.

CABÁCO, *sm.* 1. End or small piece of wood. 2. (Naut.) End of round timber, which remains when masts are made.

CABÁL, *a.* 1. Just, exact; applied to weight or measure. 2. Perfect, complete. *Al cabal*, Perfectly, justly. 3. Falling to one's share or dividend. *Por su cabal*, With all his might, most earnestly. *Por sus cabales*, Exactly, perfectly, to the very point; according to rule and order; for its just price, according to what it is worth.

CABÁLA, *sf.* 1. Cabala, mystical knowledge of the celestial bodies. 2. Secret science of the Hebrew rabbins. 3. Cabal, intrigue.

CABALÉRO, *sm.* (Ant.) Horseman, a soldier on horseback.

CABALGÁDA, *sf.* 1. People on horseback making an incursion into a country. 2. Cavalcade, a procession on horseback. 3. Booty or spoils taken by an incursion into an enemy's country.

CABALGADÓR, *sm.* 1. Horseman who goes in procession. 2. (Ant.) Mounting-block, whence people mount on horseback.

CABALGADÚRA, *sf.* Sumpter, a beast of burthen.

CABALGÁR, *vn.* 1. To parade on horseback, to go in a cavalcade. 2. To mount on horseback.—*va.* 1. To cover a mare; applied to a stone-horse. 2. *Cabalgar la artilleria*, To mount cannon on their carriages.

CABALGÁR, *sm.* (Ant.) Harness.

CABALHUÉSTE, *sm.* Kind of saddle.

CABALÍSTA, *sm.* Cabalist, one skilled in the traditions of the Hebrews.

CABALÍSTICO, CA, *a.* Cabalistic, relating to the cabala.

CABÁLLA, *sf.* Horse-mackerel. Scomber hippos *L.*

Caballáda, *sf.* Stud of horses or mares.
Caballáge, *sm.* 1. Place where mares and she-asses are served by stone-horses, or jack-asses. 2. Money paid for that service.
Caballár, *sm.* Mackerel. Scomber scombrus *L.*
Caballár, *a.* Belonging to or resembling horses.
Caballéjo, *sm.* 1. Little horse, nag. 2. Wooden frame for shoeing unruly horses.
Caballeráto, *sm.* Right of laymen to enjoy ecclesiastical benefices by virtue of the pope's dispensation. 2. The benefice enjoyed by virtue of the said dispensation. 3. Privilege of gentleman or esquire, in Catalonia, granted by the Spanish monarch, and giving a middle rank between the nobility and citizens.
Caballereár, *vn.* To set up for a gentleman.
Caballerésco, ca, *a.* Belonging to, or having the appearance of a gentleman.
Caballeréte ó ito, *sm.* Spruce young gentleman.
Caballería, *sf.* 1. Saddle-horse, saddle-mule. *Caballería menor*, Jack-ass. 2. Cavalry, horse-troops. 3. Art of managing a horse, and mounting on horseback. 4. Military order, as *Calatrava*, &c. 5. Assembly of knights of military orders. 6. Institution and profession of knights. 7. Body of the nobility of a province or place. 8. Service rendered by knights and nobles. 9. Share of spoils given to a knight, according to his rank and merit. 10. Lot or measure of land. 11. Pre-eminence and privileges of knights, nobleness of mind. *Libros de caballería*, Books of knight errantry. *Caballería andante*, The profession of knight-errantry. *Andarse en caballerías*, (Met.) To make a fulsome show of superfluous compliments.
Caballeríza, *sf.* 1. Stable, a house for beasts. 2. Number of horses, mules, &c. standing in a stable.
Caballerízo, *sm.* Head groom of a stable. *Caballerizo del rey*, Equerry to the king. *Caballerizo mayor del rey*, Master of the horse to the king.
Caballéro, *sm.* 1. Knight, member of a military order. 2. Horseman, soldier on horseback. 3. Nobleman. 4. Cavalier, a sort of fortification. 5. Old Spanish dance. 6. (Orn.) Red-legged horseman, gambet. Tringa gambetta. *L.* 7. *Caballero andante*, Knight-errant who wanders about in quest of adventures; poor reduced gentleman strolling from place to place. 8. *Ir caballero*, To go on horseback. 9. *Caballero de sierra ó de la sierra*, Ranger of a forest or mountain. *A' caballero*, Above, in a superior degree. *Armar á caballero*, To arm one's self as a knight. *Meterse á caballero*, To assume or affect the character of a gentleman or a knight. *Caballero pardo*, (Ant.) Upstart knight; gentleman by creation not family.
Caballerosaménte, *ad.* Generously, nobly, in a gentlemanlike manner.
Caballeróso, sa, *a.* 1. Noble, generous, genteel. 2. Gentlemanlike, having the manners and deportment of a gentleman.
Caballeróte, *sm.* Graceless, unpolished gentleman.
Caballéta, *sf.* Field-cricket. Gryllus campestris *L.*
Caballéte, *sm.* 1. Ridge of a house forming an acute angle. 2. Horse, an instrument of torture. 3. Brake, an instrument for dressing hemp and flax. 4. Ridge between two furrows, raised by a ploughshare. 5. Cover over the funnel of a chimney, made of tiles in a pyramidical form. 6. Bridge of the nose. 7. Gallows of a printing-press. *Caballete de aserrar*, Sawyer's trestle or horse. *Caballete de colchar cabos*, (Naút.) Rope-laying trussel, a stake-head. *Caballete de pintor*, Painter's easel.
Caballíco y ito, *sm.* 1. Little horse, pony. 2. Stick or cane on which children ride, a rocking-horse.
Caballillo, *sm.* (Ant.) Small ridge.
Cabállo, *sm.* 1. Horse, a quadruped used for riding, draught, and carriage. *Caballo padre*, Stone-horse, a stallion. *Caballo de montar, ó silla*, Saddle-horse. *Caballo de albardo*, Pack-horse. *Caballo castrado, ó capado*, Gelding. *Caballo de coche*, Coach-horse. *Caballo frison*, Draught-horse, Flanders-horse. *Caballo de guerra*, Charger. *Caballo de aldaba ó de regalo*, Sumpter or state horse. *Caballo de arcabuz*. Horse that stands the fire. *Caballo de caza*, Hunter. *Caballo de brida y de corredor*, Racer, a race-horse. *Caballo rabon*, Docked horse, a short-tailed horse. *Caballo desorejado*, Cropped horse. *Caballo de escuela*, Horse well broken in at the manege. *Caballo de vara*, Shaft-horse. *Caballo aguilillo*, Peruvian horse very swift. *Hacer mal á un caballo*, To break in a horse, to make him answer to spur and bridle. *Sacar bien su caballo*, (Met.) To extricate one's self decently out of a difficulty. *Caballo de buena boca*, (Met.) A person who accommodates himself readily to every thing whether good or bad. *Caballo de frisia*, (Mil.) Chevaux-de-frise, a military instrument. *Caballo de palo*, (Joc.) Any vessel to go to sea in; (Vulg.) Rack for criminals. *Caballo marino*, River horse. Hippopotamus *L.*: Pipe-fish, sea-horse. Syngnathus hippocampus *L.* 2. Figure on horseback, equivalent to the queen, at cards. 3. Trestle, bench on which planks or boards are laid for masons and plasterers to work on. 4. Knight in the game of chess. *A' caballo*, On horseback. *Caballos*, Horse, cavalry, soldiers mounted on horseback. 5. Bubo, tumor in the groin. 6. Thread which ravels others. *Huir á uña de caballo*, To have a hair-breadth escape; to extricate one's self from any difficulty by prudence and energy.
Caballón, *sm.* 1. Large, clumsy horse. 2. Ridge of ploughed land between two furrows.
Caballóna, *sf.* Queen in the game of chess.
Caballuélo, *sm.* (Dim.) Little horse.
Caballúno, na, *a.* Belonging to a horse.
Cabalménte, *ad.* Exactly, completely, perfectly.
Cabalúste, *sm.* Kind of saddle.
Cabáña, *sf.* 1. Shepherd's hut, cottage, or cabin. 2. Flock of ewes or breeding sheep. 3. Drove of asses for carrying corn. 4. (Extr.) Weekly allowance of bread, oil, vinegar, and salt, for shepherds. 5. Line drawn on a billiard-table, within which the players must play. 6. Landscape representing a shepherd's hut or cottage, with fowls, and other domestic animals. 7. *Cabaña real*, A meeting of the owners of

travelling flocks, who compose the council of *mesta*.
CABAÑÁL, *sm*. Road for flocks of sheep and droves of cattle.
CABAÑÉRO, *sm*. (Ant.) Shepherd; drover.
CABAÑÉRO, RA, *a*. Belonging to the drove of mules and asses which go with a flock of sheep.
CABAÑÍL ó CABAÑÁL, *a*. V. *Cabañero*.
CABAÑÍL, *sm*. Herd or keeper of mules and asses, which are kept for carrying corn.
CABAÑUÉLA, *sf*. Small hut or cottage. *Cabañuelas*, Festival of the Jews of Toledo.
CABÁZA, *sf*. Large or wide cloak with hood and sleeves, worn in bad weather.
CABDAL, V. *Caudal*.
CABDILLÁR, *va*. V. *Acaudillar*.
CÁBE, *sm*. Stroke given by balls, in the game of *argolla*, whereby the player gains a point. *Dar un cabe al bolsillo, á la hacienda, &c.* (Met.) To give a shake to one's purse, to hurt one in his business, fortune, &c. *Cabe de pala ó paleta*, Opportunity, fortunate moment to attain any object.
CABE, *prep*. (Ant.) V. *Cerca ó Junto*.
CABECEÁR, *vn*. 1. To nod with sleep, to hang the head on one side or another. 2. To shake the head, as a sign of disapprobation. 3. To raise or lower the head; applied to horses. 4. To incline to one side; applied to a load which is not well balanced. 5. (Naút.) To pitch.—*va*. 1. In writing to give some letters the necessary thick stroke. 2. (Among Bookbinders) To put the head-band to a book. 3. to garnish cloth with edgings of tape or lace. 4. To cauterise a vein. 5. To head wine, by adding some old to give it strength.
CABECÉO, *sm*. Act of nodding or shaking the head.
CABECÉQUIA, *sm*. (Ar.) Inspector of watering sluices, guardian of water-courses.
CABECÉRA, *sf*. 1. Upper end of a hall or table. 2. Bolster or pillow at the head of a bed. *Estar ó asistir á la cábecera del enfermo*, To nurse or attend a sick person. 3. Beginning of an instrument or other writing. 4. Executor, trustee. 5. Office of an executor or trustee. 6. Captain. 7. Capital of a kingdom, or of a province. 8. V. *Viñeta*.
CABECÉRO, *sm*. 1. Lintel, the upper part of a door-frame. 2. Head of a branch of a noble family. 3. Compress.
CABECIÁNCHO, CHA, *a*. Broad or flat headed; applied to nails.
CABECÍLLA Y ÍTA, *sf*. 1. Small head. 2. Wrong-headed person, full of levity, indiscretion, and whims.
CABELLÁZO, *sm*. Large bush of hair.
CABELLÉJO, *sm*. Little hair.
CABELLÉRA, *sf*. 1. Long hair spread over the shoulders. 2. False hair. 3. Tail of a comet.
CABELLO, *sm*. Hair of the head. *Llevar á uno de un cabello*, To lead one by the nose. *No faltar en un cabello*. Not to be wanting in the least thing. *No monta un cabello*, It is not worth a rush. *Hender un cabello en el ayre*, To split a hair, to be wonderfully acute. *En cabello*, In a dishevelled manner. *Asirse de un cabello*, To catch at a hair, to adopt any pretext.—*pl*. 1. Large sinews in mutton, which, by much boiling, are split into small fibres. 2. Fibres, the slender filaments of plants. *Cabellos de ángel*, Conserve of fruit cut into small threads. *Estar colgado de los cabellos*, To be in anxious expectation of the issue of a critical affair. *Tomar la ocasion por los cabellos*, (Met.) To profit by the occasion. *Traer alguna cosa por los cabellos*, (Met.) To appropriate a thing to one's self in a violent manner. *Arrancarse los cabellos*, To pull or tear one's hair. *Arrastrar á uno por los cabellos*, To drag one away by the hair.
CABELLÚDO, DA, *a*. Having long and thick hair.
CABELLÚDO, *sm*. Kind of sea-fish.
CABELLUÉLO, *sm*. Thin and short hair.
CABÉR, *vn*. 1. To be able or capable to contain. 2. To have room, place, or right of admission. 3. To be entitled to a thing. 4. To fall to one's share. *Honra y provecho no caben en un saco*, (Prov.) Honour and money are seldom found together. *No caber de gozo*, To be overjoyed. *No caber de pies*, To have no room to stand. *No caber en el mundo*, To be elated with excessive pride, to be puffed up with vanity. *No caber en si*, To be full of one's own merits. *Todo cabe*, It is all possible; it may well be so. *Todo cabe en fulano*, He is capable of any thing. *No cabe mas*, Nothing more to be desired; any thing that has arrived at its ultimate point.—*va*. To contain, to comprise, to include.
CABÉRO, *sm*. Maker of handles for working tools.
CABESTRÁGE, *sm*. 1. Halter, and other head-tackling for beasts. 2. Money paid to a driver for conducting cattle to market. 3. Act of tying a beast with a halter or collar.
CABESTRÁNTE, *sm*. V. *Cabrestante*.
CABESTRÁR, *va*. To halter, to bind with a halter.—*vn*. To fowl with a stalking-ox.
CABESTREÁR, *vn*. To follow one willingly who leads by a halter or collar; applied to beasts.
CABESTRERÍA, *sf*. Shop where halters and collars are made and sold.
CABESTRÉRO, *sm*. One who makes or retails halters and collars.
CABESTRÉRO, RA, *a*. being so tame as to be led by a halter.
CABESTRÍLLO, *sm*. 1. Sling suspended from the neck, in which a sore arm or hand is carried. 2. Kind of hoop, which keeps the cheeks of a saw tight. 3. Gold or silver chain, formerly worn by women about their necks. *Buey de cabestrillo*, Stalking-ox.
CABÉSTRO, *sm*. 1. Halter, put on the head of an animal to lead it with. 2. Bell-ox, a tame bullock with a bell round his neck, to lead the rest of a drove of black cattle. *Traer alguno de cabestro*, To lead one by the nose. 3. (Ant.) Chain. V. *Cabestrillo*. 4. Pimp to his own wife.
CABÉZA, *sf*. 1. Head, that part of the body, which contains the brain, face, &c. 2. Part of the head which comprehends the cranium and forehead. 3. Precious stone of an irregular shape. 4. A person. 5. Source or spring of water. 6. Chapter of a book or treatise. 7. Judgment, talents. 8. Beginning of a thing, *e. g.* of a book. 9. End or extremity of a thing, *e. g.* of a beam, or a bridge. 10. Head of a nail. 11. Head of cattle. *Cabeza mayor*,

Head of black cattle. *Cabeza menor*, Head of sheep, goats, &c. 12. Chief governor or commander. *Cabeza de la iglesia*, A title of the Pope. 13. Title-page of a book. 14. Diameter of a column. 15. Principal town of a province. 16. Head of a process. *Cabeza de aguas*, High water. *Cabeza de un muelle*, Pier or mole head. *Cabeza de ajos*, Head of garlic. *Cabeza de monte*, Top of a mountain. *Cabeza de perro*, (Bot.) Snap-dragon. *Cabezas*, Principal parts of a vessel; an equestrian game. *Cabeza torcida*, Wrongheaded fellow. *Cabeza redonda*, (Met.) Blockhead. *A' un volver de cabeza*, In an instant. *Dar de cabeza*, To decline in one's fortune, power, or authority. *Es mala cabeza*, He is a man of bad principles. *Hablar de cabeza*, To speak without ground or foundation. *Hacer cabeza*, (Ant.) To face the enemy. *Llevar en la cabeza*, To be frustrated in one's views and expectations. *Meter la cabeza en el puchero*, To follow another's dictates, whether right or wrong. *No tener ó no llevar pies ni cabeza alguna cosa*, To have neither head nor tail. *Otorgar de cabeza*, (Ant.) To give a nod of approbation. *Perder la cabeza*, To lose one's senses, to be at a loss how to act. *Poner las cosas pies con cabezas*, To jumble things together in a confused manner. *Sacar de su cabeza alguna cosa*, To strike out a thing. *Tener una cabeza de hierro, ó de bronce*, To be indefatigable in business. *Mala cabeza, ó tener mala cabeza*, (Met.) Without judgment or reflection; weak-minded. *De cabeza*, From memory.

Cabezáda, *sf.* 1. Stroke or butt given with the head. 2. Halter, collar. 3. Headstall of a bridle. 4. Pitching of a ship. 5. (Among Bookbinders,) Head-band of a book. 6. Instep of a boot. *Dar cabezadas*, To nod, to fall asleep. *Darse de cabezadas*, To screw one's wits in the investigation of a thing without success.

Cabezáge, *sm.* (Ant.) Poll-tax. *A' cabezage*, Per head, so much a head.

Cabezál, *sm.* 1. Head-piece in a powder-mill. 2. Small square pillow. 3. Compress, a bolster of folded linen laid on a wound. 4. Long round bolster which crosses a bed. 5. Post of a door. *Cabezáles de coche*, Standards of the fore and hind parts of a coach, to which the braces are fastened. 6. Mattress or piece of cloth on which peasants sleep on benches or stones at the fire.

Cabezaléjo, íco, íllo, y íto, *sm.* 1. Little pillow or bolster. 2. Small compress.

Cabezaléro, ra, *s.* (Ant.) V. *Albacea.*

Cabézo, *sm.* 1. Summit of a hill. 2. Shirt collar.

Cabezón, *sm.* 1. Register of the different taxes paid to government, and of the names of the contributors. 2. Collar of a shirt. 3. Opening of a garment for the head to pass through. 4. Cavesson or noseband, used in taming or breaking in a horse. *Llevar por los cabezones*, To drag along by the collar. *Entra por la manga, y sale por el cabezon*, (Prov.) Applied to those favourites who assume authority and dominion, and originating in the ancient ceremony of adoption, by passing the person through a wide sleeve of a shift.

Cabezórro, *sm.* Large, disproportioned head.

Cabezúdo, *sm.* (Ict.) Chub. *Cyprinus cephalus L.*

Cabezúdo, da, *a.* 1. Large-headed, having a big head. 2. Headstrong, obstinate

Cabezuéla, *sf.* 1. Small head. 2. Blockhead, dolt, simpleton. 3. Coarse flour. 4. Rose-bud, from which rose water is distilled. 5. Little glass-tube in a velvet-loom. 6. (Bot.) Eryngo. *Eryngium tricuspidatum L.*

Cabezuélo, *sm.* Little head or top of any thing.

Cabíal, *sm.* Caviare, the salted eggs of a sturgeon.

Cabída, *sf.* Space or capacity of any thing. *Tener cabida con una persona*, To be in high favour, to have a strong influence over one.

Cabído, *sm.* Knight of the order of Malta, who has the right to claim a commandery.

Cabído, *a.* (Ant.) Esteemed, well received.

Cabildáda, *sf.* (Bax.) Hasty, ill-grounded resolution or proceeding of a chapter or other ecclesiastic body.

Cabildánt, *sm.* He who has a vote in a chapter.

Cabildeár, *vn.* To hold a chapter.

Cabildéro, *a.* Belonging to a chapter.

Cabíldo, *sm.* 1. Chapter of a cathedral or collegiate church. 2. Session of a court of justice. 3. Meeting of a chapter, and the place where the meeting is held.

Cabílla, *sf.* (Naút.) Wooden pin with which the outside planks of vessels are fastened.

Cabíllo, *sm.* Small end of a rope.

Cabimiénto, *sm.* 1. Right of claiming a commandery in the order of Malta. 2. V. *Cabida.*

Cabío, *sm.* Lintel of a door.

Cabíto, *sm.* V. *Cabillo. Cabitos*, Small lines.

Cabizbáxo, xa, *a.* 1. Down in the mouth, crestfallen. 2. Thoughtful, pensive, melancholy.

Cabizcaído, da, *a.* Applied to persons who hang their head on their breast.

Cabiztuérto, ta, *s.* Wry-headed; hypocritical.

Cáble, *sm.* Cable, a strong rope fastened to the principal anchor of a ship. *Cable de esperanza*, Sheet-cable, the largest on board a ship.

Cábo, *sm.* 1. End or extremity of any thing. 2. Cape, headland, or promontory. 3. Place, seat. 4. Requisite. 5. Lowest card in the game called *reversi*. 6. Paragraph, article, head. 7. Chief, head, commander. 8. Haft, handle. 9. Cordage. *Cabo de armeria*, (Nav.) The original mansion of a noble family. *Cabo de año*, The religious offices performed on the anniversary of a person's death. *Cabo de barro*, Chiselled dollar of Mexico; last payment or balance of an account. *Cabo de forzados*, Keeper or overseer of galley slaves. *Cabo de esquadra*, Corporal. *Cabo de ronda de alcabalas*, Tide-waiter, custom-house officer. *Coger todos los cabos*, (Met.) To weigh all the circumstances of a case. *Cabos negros en las mugeres*, Black hair, eyes, and eye-brows of a woman. *Cabos blancos*, (Naút.) Untarred cordage. *Dar cabo*, (Naút.) To throw out a rope for another to take hold of. *Al cabo*, At last. *Dar cabo á alguna cosa*, To perfect or complete a thing; to destroy a thing. *De cabo*, Again, once more, encore. *De cabo á rabo*, From head to tail. *Estar al cabo de algun negocio*, To be thoroughly acquainted with the nature of an affair. *Estar alguno al cabo ó muy al cabo*, To be at death's door. *No tener cabo ni cuenta una cosa*, To have neither head nor tail; applied to a perplexed business. *Por cabo ó por el cabo*, Lastly. *Por ningun cabo*, By no means. *Volver á coger el cabo*, To resume the thread of a discourse.

CABORÁL, *sm.* (Ant.) Captain.

CABOTÁGE, *sm.* (Naút.) 1. Coasting-trade, 2. Pilotage.

CÁBRA, *sf.* 1. Goat. Capra *L.* 2. Engine formerly used to throw stones. 3. *Cabra montes*, Wild goat. Capra ibex *L. La cabra siempre tira al monte*, What is bred in the bone will not come out of the flesh; or Cat after kind.—*pl.* 1. Red marks on the legs caused by fire. 2. Small white clouds floating in the air. *Echar cabras ó las cabras*, To play for who will pay the reckoning. *Echar las cabras á otro*, To throw the blame upon another.

CABRAHIGADÚRA, *sf.* Caprification.

CABRAHIGÁL ó CABRAHÍGAR, *sm.* Grove or plantation of wild fig-trees.

CABRAHIGÁR, *va.* To improve or meliorate a fig-tree; that is, to string up some male figs, and hang them on the branches of the female fig-tree, to make it produce better fruit.

CABRAHÍGO, *sm.* The male wild fig-tree, or its fruit which does not ripen.

CÁBRE, *sm.* (Ant.) V. *Cable.*

CABREÍA, *sf.* (Ant.) Wooden machine for throwing stones.

CABRÉO, *sm.* Register, especially of the privileges and charters of cathedral churches.

CABRERÍA, *sf.* Herd of goats.

CABRÉRO, *sm.* Goat-herd, a keeper of goats.

CABRESTÁNTE, *sm.* 1. (Naút.) Capstan, a large windlass for heaving up the anchor. 2. Machine for moving and raising weighty things, such as stones for building.

CABRÍA, *sf.* 1. Axle-tree. 2. (Naút.) Sheers, a machine used for setting up and taking out masts for want of hulks. 3. Crane.

CABRIÁL, *sm.* Beam. V. *Viga.*

CABRÍLLA, *sf.* 1. Little goat. 2. (Ict.) Prawn. Cancer squilla *L.*—*pl.* 1. (Astr.) Pleiades, a northern constellation. 2. Stones thrown obliquely on the water, called duck and drake. 3. Marks on the legs occasioned by fire.

CABRILLEÁR, *vn.* To throw stones along the surface of water.

CABRÍO, *sm.* Rafter, beam, or other timber, used in building.

CABRÍO, *a.* Resembling goats.

CABRIÓLA, *sf.* 1. Caper made in dancing, by moving the feet several times across each other before they reach the ground. 2. Nimble leap, hop, or jump. [jump.

CABRIOLÁR ó CABRIOLEÁR, *vn.* To caper, to

CABRIOLÉ, *sm.* 1. Kind of cloak used by ladies. 2. Narrow riding coat without sleeves.

CABRÍTA, *sf.* 1. Little she-kid. 2. (Ant.) Kid-skin dressed. 3. (Ant.) Ancient engine to cast stones.

CABRITÉRO, *sm.* 1. Dealer in kids. 2. One who dresses or sells kid-skins.

CABRITÍLLA, *sf.* A dressed or tanned lamb or kid-skin. [a goat.

CABRITÍLLO Y CABRÍTO, *sm.* Kid, the young of

CABRITÚNO, NA, *a.* (Ant.) Of the goat kind.

CABRÓN, *sm.* 1. Buck, he-goat. 2. One who consents to the adultery of his wife.

CABRONÁDA, *sf.* (Bax.) Infamous action which a man permits against his own honour.

CABRONÁZO, *sm.* (Aum.) One who prostitutes his own wife.

CABRONCÍLLO, CÍTO, Y ZUÉLO, *sm.* 1. Easy husband. 2. Fetid herb resembling the celtic spikenard.

CABRÚNO, NA, *a.* Resembling a goat.

CABSA, *sf.* (Ant.) V. *Causa.*

CABÚ, *sm.* Barren ground.

CABUJÁDA, *sm.* Hunting-saddle.

CABUJÓN, *sm.* Rough, unpolished ruby.

CABÚYA, *sf.* 1. Sort of sedge or grass, of which cords are made in America. 2. (Ant.) Cord or rope made of the aloes-plant.

CÁCA, *sf.* 1. Excrements of a child. 2. Word used by children who wish to go to stool.

CACAHUÁL Y CACAOTÁL, *sm.* Plantation of chocolate trees.

CACAHUÁTE, *sm.* (Bot.) American earth-nut.

CACÁO, *sm.* 1. (Bot.) Chocolate-tree. Theobroma cacao *L.* 2. Cocoa, the fruit of the chocolate-tree.

CACAREADÓR, RA, *s.* 1. Cock that crows, a hen that cackles, 2. Boaster, braggart.

CACAREÁR, *vn.* 1. To crow, to cackle. 2. To exaggerate one's own actions, to brag, to boast.

CACARÉO, *sm.* 1. Crowing of a cock, cackling of a hen. 2. Boast, brag. [pan.

CACEÁR, *va.* To toss or shake something in a

CACÉRA, *sf.* 1. Canal, channel, or conduit of water. 2. Sort of pig-nuts.

CACERÍA, *sf.* 1. Hunting or fowling party. 2. (Pint.) Landscape representing field sports.

CACERÍLLA, *sf.* Small drain or canal.

CACERÍNA, *sf.* Cartridge box or pouch in which carabineers carry powder and ball.

CACERÓLA, *sf.* Stewing pan.

CACÉTA, *sf.* Small pan used by apothecaries.

CÁCHA, *sf.* Handle of a knife. *Hasta las cachas*, full to the brim.

CACHÁDA, *sf.* Stroke of one top against another, when boys play at tops.

CACHARÁDO, *sm.* kind of linen.

CACHÁR, *va.* (Ant. Cast.) To break in pieces.

CACHÁRRO, *sm.* 1. Coarse earthen pot; also a piece of it. 2. (Met.) Any useless, worthless thing. [(dias) Rum.

CACHÁZA, *sf.* 1. Inactivity, tardiness. 2. (In-

CACHÉRA, *sf.* Coarse shagged cloth or baize.

CACHÉTAS, *sf. pl.* Teeth or wards in a lock.

CACHÉTE, *sm.* 1. Cheek, the side of the face below the eye. 2. Fist, a blow given with the hand clenched. *Cachetes de un navio*, (Naút.) Bow of a ship.

CACHETÉRO, *sm.* Short and broad knife with a sharp point, used by assassins.

CACHETÚDO, DA, *a.* Plump cheeked, full of flesh.

CACHICÁN, *sm.* Overseer of a farm. [horn.

CACHICUÉRNO, NA, *a.* Having a handle or haft of

CACHIDIÁBLO, *sm.* 1. Hobgoblin. 2. Disguised in a devil's mask. 3. Having an odd and extravagant appearance. [cheeks.

CACHIFOLLÁR, *va.* To puff or blow with the

CACHIGORDÉTE, TA; Y ÍTO, TA, *a.* Squat, thick and plump.

CACHILLÁDA, *sf.* (Bax.) Litter, number of young brought forth by an animal at once. [rivers

CACHIPÓLLA, *sf.* White butterfly on the banks of

Cachipórra, *sf.* 1. Stick with a big knob used by country people. 2. Vulgar exclamation.
Cachipórro, *sm.* (Joc.) Chub-face.
Cachivácne, *sm.* 1. Broken crockery ware, or other old trumpery, laid up in a corner. 2. (Met.) A despicable, useless, worthless fellow.
Cácho, *sm.* 1. Slice, piece; applied to lemons, oranges, or melons. 2. Game of chance at cards. 3. (Ict.) Red surmullet. Mullus barbatus *L.*
Cácho, cha, *a.* Bent, crooked, inflected. V. *Gacho.*
Cachólas, *sf. pl.* (Naút.) Cheeks of the masts.
Cachónes, *sm. pl.* Breakers, waves broken by the shore, or by the rocks and sand-banks.
Cachónda, *a.* *Perra cachonda,* A bitch which is hot or proud. *Cachondas,* (Ant.) Slashed trowsers formerly worn.
Cachondéz, *sf.* (Ant.) Lust, carnal desire.
Cachópo, *sm.* 1. Gulph of the sea between rocks. 2. Trunk or stump of a tree which is dry.
Cachorrénas, *sf. pl.* (And.) Sort of soap, made of oil, orange, bread, and salt.
Cachorríllo y íto, *sm.* 1. A little cub or whelp. 2. A young man; in contempt. 3. A little pistol.
Cachórro, ra, *s.* 1. Grown whelp or puppy; young of animals. 2. Pocket pistol.
Cachúcho, *sm.* 1. Oil-measure containing the sixth part of a pound. 2. Cartridge. 3. (Ant.) Clumsy earthen-pot. 4. Place for each arrow in a quiver.
Cachuéla, *sf.* Fricassee made of the livers and lights of rabbits.
Cachuélo, *sm.* (Ict.) Small river fish resembling an anchovy.
Cachuléra, *sf.* (Mur.) Cavern or place where any one hides.
Cachúmbo, *sm.* Kind of hard cocoa wood, of which rosaries, &c. are made.
Cachúnde, *sf.* Paste made of musk, and other aromatics, which the Chinese carry in their mouth to strengthen the stomach.
Cachupín, *sm.* A Spaniard who goes and settles in the Indies.
Cacicázgo, *sm.* Dignity and territory of a Cacique or Indian prince.
Cacíllo y Cacíto, *sm.* Small saucepan.
Cacíque, *sm.* Prince or nobleman among the Indians.
Cáco, *sm.* 1. Pick-pocket. 2. A coward.
Cacofonía, *sf.* Cacophony, a harsh or unharmonious sound.
Cacoquímia, *sf.* Cacochymy, depraved state of the humours of the human body.
Cacoquímico, ca, *a.* Cacochymical.
Cacoquímio, *sm.* He who suffers melancholy, which makes him pale and sorrowful.
Cáda, *part.* Every, every one. *Cada uno,* Each one. *Cada vez,* Every time. *Cada dia,* Every day. *A' cada palabra,* At every word. *Dar á cada uno,* To give to every one. *Cada qual,* Every one. *Cada vez que* Every time that. *Cada y quando,* Whenever, as soon as.
Cadahálso, *sm.* (Ant.) Wooden shade projecting from a wall.
Cadalécho, *sm.* Bed made of branches of trees, and much used in the huts of Andalusia.
Cadálso, *sm.* 1. Scaffold raised for the execution of malefactors. 2. Temporary gallery or stage, erected for shows or spectators. 3. (Ant.) Fortification or bulwark made of wood.
Cadañál y Cadañégo, ga, *a.* Yearly, annual.
Cadañéro, ra, *a.* Annual, which lasts a year. *Muger cadañera,* A woman who bears every year.
Cadárzo, *sm.* Coarse, entangled silk, which cannot be spun with a wheel.
Cadascúno, na, *a.* (Ant.) V. *Cada uno.*
Cadáver, *sm.* Corpse, a dead body.
Cadavéra, *sf.* 1. Corpse or dead body. 2. Skull, the bones of the head freed from the flesh.
Cadavérico, ca, *a.* Cadaverous, of a pallid colour.
Cadéjo, *sm.* 1. Entangled skein of thread. 2. Entangled hair. 3. Many threads put together to make tassels.
Cadéna, *sf.* 1. Chain, a series of links fastened one to another. 2. (Met.) Tie caused by passion or obligation. 3. Mortice, a hole cut into wood that another piece may be put into it. 4. (Met.) Series of events. 5. Number of malefactors chained together to be conducted to the galleys. 6. Bar of iron, with which a wall is strengthened. 7. Frame of wood put round the hearth of a kitchen. 8. Treadle of a ribbon-weaver's loom. 9. Turning handle which moves a wheel. *Cadena de rocas,* Ledge or ridge of rocks. *Cadena de puerto,* Boom of a harbour. *Estar en la cadena,* To be in prison. *Balas de cadena,* Chain-shot. *Renunciar la cadena,* To give up all one's effects to get out of prison.
Cadenádo, *sm.* Padlock. V. *Candado.*
Cadéncia, *sf.* 1. Cadence, fall of the voice, flow of verses or periods. 2. (In Dancing) Correspondence of the motion of the body with the music. *Hablar en cadencia,* To affect the harmonious flow of rhyme when speaking in prose.
Cadenciádo, da, y óso, sa, *a.* Belonging to a cadence.
Cadenéta, *sf.* Lace or needle-work wrought in form of a chain.
Cadenílla y íta, *sf.* Small chain. *Cadenilla y media cadenilla,* Pearls distinguished by their size.
Cadénte, *a.* 1. Decaying, declining, going to ruin and destruction. 2. Having a correct modulation in delivering prose or verse.
Cadér, *vn.* (Ant.) V. *Caer.*
Cadéra, *sf.* Hip, the joint of the thigh.
Caderíllas, *sf. pl.* Hoops worn by ladies in full dress.
Cadéte, *sm.* Cadet, a volunteer in the army.
Cadillár, *sm.* Place abounding with burdock.
Cadíllo, *sm.* (Bot.) Common burdock. Arctium lappa *L.* *Cadillos,* First threads or fag end of a web, or the loose threads of the end of a warp.
Cadíz, *sm.* Kind of coarse stuff.
Cádmia, *sf.* Calamine. V. *Calamina.*
Cádo, *sm.* Ferret hole. V. *Huronera.*
Cadóce, *sm.* (Ict.) Gudgeon. Cyprinus gobio *L.*
Cadóso ó Cadózo, *sm.* (Ant.) Hole or deep place in a river.
Caducaménte, *ad.* In a weak, doting manner.
Caducár, *vn.* 1. To dote, to have the intellect impaired by old age. 2. To be worn out by

service and use. *Caducar el legado ó el fidei-comiso*, To become extinct; applied to a legacy or fiduciary estate.

Caduceadór, *sm.* King at arms, who proclaims war and peace.

Caducéo, *sm.* Herald's staff; caduceus.

Caducidád, *sf.* (For.) State or quality of being worn out with labour, or debilitated by age.

Cadúco, ca, *a.* 1. Worn out with fatigue, senile, enfeebled by age, decrepit. 2. Perishable, of short duration. *Mal caduco*, Epilepsy.

Caduquéz, *sf.* Weakness, last stage of life, senility.

Caedízo, za, *a.* Ready to fall, being of short duration, or little consistence. *Hacer caediza una cosa*, To let a thing fall designedly. *Peras caedizas*, Pears dropping from the tree.

Caedúra, *sf.* (Among Weavers) Loose threads dropping from the weaver's loom when weaving.

Caér, *vn.* 1. To fall to the ground, to tumble down. *Caer á plomo*, To fall flat. 2. To lose one's situation, fortune, or influence. 3. To fall into an error or danger. 4. (Met.) To deviate from the right road, or to take the wrong one. 5. (Met.) To fall or become due; as, instalments or payments of debts. 6. To fall to one's lot. 7. To befall, to happen to, to come to pass. 8. To die. *Caer á esta parte*, To be situated on this side. *Caer á la mar*, (Naút.) To fall overboard. *Caer á sotavento*, To drive to leeward. *Caer en la cuenta*, To bethink one's self. *No caer en las cosas*, Not to comprehend a thing. *Caer de sueño*, To fall asleep. *Caer bien á caballo*, To sit well on horseback. *Este color cae bien con este otro*, This colour is well matched with the other. *Caer de la gracia de alguno*, To lose one's favour. *Caer en cama, ó en la cama*, To become sick. *Caer en alguna cosa*, To obtain knowledge of a thing. *Caer en falta*, To fail in the performance of one's engagements. *Caer en gracia, ó en gusto*, To please, to be agreeable. *Caer la balanza*, To be partial. *Caerse á pedazos*, To be very fatigued, or very foolish. *Caerse de ánimo*, To be dejected. *Caerse de risa*, To burst out into laughter. *Caerse en flor*, To die in the bloom of age. *Al caer de la hoja*, At the fall of the leaf, about the end of autumn. *Dexarse caer alguna cosa en la conversacion*, To drop something in the course of conversation. *Caer el color*, To fade. *Caer en nota*, To be disgraced or scandalized. *Caer en ello*, To understand or comprehend a thing. *Estar al caer*, About falling, ready to fall. *Caérsele á uno alguna cosa de la boca*, To use frequently, to repeat. *Caérsele á uno la cara de vergüenza*, To blush deeply with shame.—*va.* To throw down, to cause one to fall.

Cáfa, *sf.* Cotton stuff of various colours and kinds.

Cafárd, *sm.* Kind of cloth made at Damascus.

Cafaréo, *sm.* Abyss.

Café, *sm.* 1. Coffee, berry of the coffee-tree. Coffea *L.* 2. Coffee, decoction of roasted coffee-berries. 3. Coffee-house.

Cafetán ó Caftán, *sm.* Embroidered garment worn by the chief Turkish officers.

Cafetéra, *sf.* 1. Coffee-pot in which coffee is made. 2. Coffee-service.

Cafetéro, *sm.* One who makes or sells coffee, a coffee-man.

Cáfila, *sm.* 1. Multitude of people, animals, or other things. 2. Caravan, a troop of merchants or pilgrims travelling together in Arabia and Persia.

Cáfre, *a.* 1. Savage, inhuman; belonging or relating to the Cafrees. 2. (Mur.) Clownish, rude, uncivil.

Cága-aceyte, *sm.* A little bird whose excrements are of an oily substance.

Cagachín, *sm.* Kind of gnat or fly, which stains the clothes of its captor with its dung as soon as it is taken.

Cagáda, *sf.* 1. Excrement. 2. Ridiculous action, or unfortunate issue.

Cagadéro, *sm.* Place where people resort to for the purpose of exonerating the belly.

Cagadíllo, *sm.* A sorry little fellow.

Cagádo, *sm.* A mean-spirited, chicken-hearted fellow.

Cagafiérro, *sm.* Scoria, dross of iron.

Cagajón, *sm.* Dung of mules, horses, or asses.

Cagalaólla, *sf.* One who goes dressed in trowsers and a mask dancing in processions.

Cagalár, *sm.* Tripe.

Cagaléra, *sf.* Looseness of the body, diarrhœa.

Cagamélos, *sm.* Kind of mushroom.

Cagár, *va.* 1. To exonerate the belly. 2. (Met.) To soil, stain, or defile a thing.

Cagarópa, *sm.* V. *Cagachin.*

Cagarráche, *sm.* 1. One who washes the olives in an oil-mill. 2. Bird of the family of starlings, with long legs, and of a dark grey and white colour.

Cagárria, *sf.* Kind of mushroom, called St. George's agaric. Agaricus georgii *L.*

Cagarrúta, *sf.* Dung of sheep and goats.

Cagatório, *sm.* V. *Cagadero.*

Cagón, na, *s.* 1. Person afflicted with a diarrhœa, or looseness. 2. Cowardly, timorous person.

Caguí, *sm.* (Naút.) Kaag, a Dutch vessel with one mast, a kind of bilander.

Cahíz, *sm.* 1. Nominal measure sometimes of twelve *fanegas*, or about 12 English bushels. 2. V. *Cahizada.*

Cahizáda, *sf.* Tract of land which requires about one *cahiz* of grain to be properly sown.

Caída, *sf.* 1. Fall, the act of falling. 2. Declivity, descent. 3. Any thing which hangs down as hangings, curtains, &c. *Caida de la proa*, (Naút.) Casting or falling off. *Caida de una vela*, Depth or drop of a sail. *Ir ó andar de capa caida*, (Met.) To decline in fortune and credit. *A' la caida de la tarde*, At the close of the evening. *A' la caida del sol*, At sunset.—*pl.* 1. That part of a head-dress which hangs down loose. 2. Coarse wool cut off the skirts of a fleece.

Caídos, *sm. pl.* 1. Rents or annual payments become due, and not paid. 2. Arrears of taxes.

Caimán, *sm.* Alligator, an American crocodile.

Caimiénto, *sm.* 1. Lowness of spirits, want of bodily strength. 2. Fall, the act of falling.

Caíque, *sm.* (Naút.) Kind of skiff or small boat.

Cal, *sf.* Burnt lime-stone, of which mortar is

made. *Cal viva*, Quick or unslaked lime. *Ser de cal y canto*, (Met.) To be as strong as if built with lime and stone.

CÁLA, *sf*. 1. (Naút.) Small bay. 2. Small piece cut out of a melon, or other fruit, to try its flavour. 3. Hole made in a wall to try the thickness of it. 4. Probe, an instrument with which surgeons search a wound. 5. Injection, made of soap, oil, and salt, to open the bowels. *Hacer cala y cata*, To examine a thing for the purpose of ascertaining its quantity and quality.

CALABACÉRA, *sf*. Pumpkin. V. *Calabaza*.

CALABACÉRO, *sm*. Retailer of pompions or pumpkins.

CALABACÍCA, ÍLLA Y ÍTA, *sf*. Small pompion.

CALABACÍLLA, *sf*. 1. Piece of wood turned in the shape of a gourd, around which a tassel of silk or worsted is formed. 2. Ear-ring in the shape of a pear.

CALABACÍN, *sm*. A small, young, tender pumpkin.

CALABACINÁTE, *sm*. Fried pumpkins.

CALABACÍNO, *sm*. Dry gourd or pumpkin scooped out, in which wine is carried; a calabash.

CALABÁZA, *sf*. 1. (Bot.) Pompion, pumpkin or gourd. Cucurbita *L*. 2. Calabash. *Calabaza vinatera*, Bottle gourd, which, when dry, is used for carrying wine or drink. 3. Small button joining the ring of a key. *Dar calabazas*, To reprove, to censure; to give a denial; applied to a woman who rejects a proposal of marriage. *Tener cáscos de calabaza*, To be silly, ignorant, or stupid. *Nadar sin calabazas*, To swim without pumpkins; not to need the support of others, to stand on one's own bottom.

CALABAZÁDA, *sf*. 1. Knock with the head against something. *Darse calabazadas*, (Met.) To labour in vain for the purpose of ascertaining something. 2. Liquor drunk out of a calabash.

CALABAZÁR, *sm*. Piece of ground sown or planted with pompions.

CALABAZÁTE, *sm*. Preserved pumpkin candied with sugar. 2. Piece of a pumpkin steeped in honey or treacle. 3. Knock of the head against a wall.

CALABAZÓNA, *sf*. Large winter pumpkin.

CALABÓBOS, *sm*. Small, gentle, continued rain.

CALABOZÁGE, *sm*. Fee paid by prisoners to the jailer.

CALABÓZO, *sm*. 1. Dungeon, a close subterraneous prison. 2. Pruning-hook or pruning-knife.

CALABRIÁDA, *sf*. (Ant.) 1. A mixture of different things. 2. A mixture of white and red wine.

CALABRÓTE, *sm*. (Naút.) Stream-cable.

CALACÁNTO, *sm*. (Bot.) Flea-bane.

CALÁDA, *sf*. 1. Rapid flight of birds of prey. 2. Introduction. 3. (Ant.) Narrow, craggy road. 4. Reprimand. *Dar una calada*, To reprimand.

CALÁDO, *sm*. Open work in metal, wood, or linen. *Caládos*, Lace with which women's jackets were adorned. *Calado de agua*, (Naút.) Draught of water.

CALADÓR, *sm*. 1. One who pierces or perforates. 2. (Naút.) Caulking-iron, an iron chisel used by caulkers in working oakum into the seams or shakes of ships. 3. Probe, a surgeon's instrument.

CALÁDRE, *sf*. A bird belonging to the family of larks.

CALAFÁTE Y CALAFATEADÓR, *sm*. Caulker, a workman employed in caulking ships.

CALAFATEADÚRA, *sf*. Caulking.

CALAFATERÍA, *sf*. The act of caulking.

CALAFATEÁR Y CALAFETEÁR, *va*. (Naút.) To fill up the seams or shakes of a ship with oakum, pitch, &c. to caulk or calk.

CALAFETÍN, *sm*. Calker's boy or mate.

CALAFRÁGA, *sf*. (Bot.) Saxifrage. Saxifraga *L*.

CALÁGE, *sm*. (Arag.) Chest, trunk, or coffer.

CALAGÓZO, *sm*. Bill or hedging hook.

CALAGRÁÑA, *sf*. Kind of grape only fit for eating.

CALAGUÁLA, *sf*. A thick red root common in Peru.

CALAGURRITÁNO, NA, *a*. Belonging to the city of Calahorra.

CALAHÓRRA, *sf*. A public office where bread is distributed in times of scarcity.

CALALÚZ, *sm*. (Naút.) Kind of East Indian vessel.

CALAMÁCO, *sm*. Calimanco, woollen stuff, with a glossy surface. *Calamacos floreádos*, Flowered calimancoes. *Calamacos lisos*, Plain calimancoes. *Calamacos rayados*, Striped calimancoes.

CALAMÁR, *sm*. (Ict.) Sea-sleeve, calamary, a fish which, when pursued, emits a black liquor, and thus effects its escape. Sepia loligo *L*.

CALÁMBRE, *sm*. Spasm, cramp, an involuntary contraction of the fibres and muscles.

CALAMBÚCO, *sm*. (Bot.) Calambac wood, the aromatic aloes.

CALAMÉNTO Ó CALAMÍNTA, *s*. (Bot.) Mountain-balm or calamint. Melissa officinalis *L*.

CALAMIDÁD, *sf*. Misfortune, calamity.

CALAMÍNA Ó PIEDRA CALAMINÁR, *sf*. Calamine, zinc ore, or lapis calaminaris, a mineral which, when mixed with copper, forms brass.

CALAMÍTA, *sf*. 1. Loadstone. 2. V. *Calamite*.

CALAMÍTE, *sm*. Kind of small green frog, which resides among reeds, and does not croak.

CALAMITOSAMÉNTE, *ad*. unfortunately, disastrously.

CALAMITÓSO, SA, *a*. Calamitous, unfortunate, wretched.

CÁLAMO, *sm*. 1. Reed. *Cálamo aromático*, Sweet cane, sweet flag. Acorus calamus *L*. 2. Pen. *Cálamo currente*, (Voz. Lat.) Off hand, in haste. 3. Sort of flute.

CALAMOCÁNO, *a*. *Estar ó ir calamocano*, To be somewhat fuddled: it is also applied to old men who begin to droop.

CALAMÓCO, *sm*. Icicle hanging from the eaves of a house.

CALAMÓN, *sm*. 1. (Orn.) Purple water-hen, or gallinule. Fulica porphyrio *L*. 2. Round-headed nail. 3. Stay which supports the beam of an oil-mill.

CALAMÓRRA, *sf*. (Bax.) The head.

CALAMORRÁDA, *sf*. Butt, a stroke with the head of horned cattle.

CALAMORRÁR, *va*. To strike with the head, as horned animals.

CALANDRÁJO, *sm*. 1. Rag hanging down from a garment. 2. Ragamuffin; a mean, paltry fellow.

CALÁNDRIA, *sf*. 1. (Orn.) Buntin, calendar lark. Alauda calendra *L*. 2. Calender, a press in which clothiers smooth their cloth.

CALÁNIS, *sm*. (Bot.) V. *Cálamo aromático*.

CALÁÑA, *sf*. 1. Pattern, sample. 2. Character, quality. *Es hombre de buena ó mala calaña*, He is a good or ill-natured man. *Es una cosa de mala calaña*, It is a bad thing.

Calapatíllo, *sm.* Maggot or worm prejudicial to corn and fruit.

Calár, *va.* 1. To penetrate, to pierce. 2. (Met.) To discover a design, to comprehend the meaning or cause of a thing. 3. To put, to place. 4. To imitate net or lace work in linen or cotton. *Calar el timon,* (Naút.) To hang the rudder. *Calar el palo de un navio,* (Naút.) To step a mast. *Calar el can de un arma de fuego,* To cock a gun. *Calar el melon, ó la sandia,* To cut a piece of a melon to try its flavour. *Calar el puente,* To let down a draw-bridge. *Calar la bayoneta,* (Mil.) To fix the bayonet. *Calar la cuerda,* (Mil.) To apply the match to a cannon. *Calar las cubas,* To gage a barrel or cask. *Calar el sombrero en la cabeza hasta las cejas,* To press the hat down to the eyebrows.—*vn.* To sink into the water. *Calar tantos pies,* (Naút.) To draw so many feet water.—*vr.* 1. To enter, to introduce one's self. 2. To stoop, to dart down on prey. *Calarse el falcon sobre las aves,* To dart or pounce on the game; spoken of a hawk.

Calár, *a.* Calcareous, abounding with limestone.

Calavéra, *sf.* 1. Skull, the bones of the head. 2. (Met.) Blockhead, stupid fellow, dolt.

Calaveráda, *sf.* Ridiculous, foolish, or ill-judged action.

Calaverreár, *vn.* To act in a foolish manner, to proceed without judgment.

Calaverílla y **Calaveríta**, *sf.* 1. Little skull. 2. (Met.) Little crazy fellow. [or chesnuts.

Calbóte, *sm.* (Extrem.) Bread made of acorns

Calcamár, *sm.* Sea-fowl on the coast of Brasil.

Calcañál ó **Calcañár**, *sm.* Heel-bone, the hindermost part and basis of the foot. *Tener el seso en los calcañares,* To have one's brains in the heels; to be stupid.

Calcáñeo, *sm.* The heel.

Calcañuélo, *sm.* A disease of bees.

Cálce, *sm.* 1. One of the iron plates nailed round the felloes of wheels. 2. (Naút.) Top. 3. (Ant.) Cup, a chalice. 4. (Ant.) Small canal to convey water for irrigation.

Calcedónia, *sf.* Chalcedony, a precious stone.

Cálces, *sm.* (Naút.) Mast-head.

Calcéta, *sf.* 1. Under stocking, generally made of thread. 2. (Met.) Fetters or shackles worn by criminals.

Calcetería, *sf.* 1. Hosier's shop where thread stockings are sold. 2. Trade of a hosier.

Calcetéro, ra, *s.* One who makes, mends, or sells thread stockings.

Calcetón, *sm.* Large stocking worn under boots.

Cálcide ó **Cálcides**, *sf.* Kind of pilchards.

Calcílla, *sf.* Small stocking. [sand.

Calcína, *sf.* Mortar, a mixture of lime and

Calcinación, *sf.* Calcination, pulverizing by fire. [ble by means of fire.

Calcinár, *va.* To calcine, to render bodies fria-

Calcografía, *sf.* Chalcography, art of en-

Calcógrafo, *sm.* Engraver. [graving.

Calculáble, *a.* Calculable.

Calculación, *sf.* Calculation, the act of reckoning, the result of arithmetical operations.

Calculadór, *sm.* Calculator, accomptant.

Calculár, *va.* To calculate, to reckon, to compute, to cast up.

Cálculo, *sm.* 1. Calculo, computation, the result of an arithmetical operation. 2. (Med.) Calculus, a stone in the bladder. 3. Small stone used by the ancients in forming arithmetical operations.

Cálda, *sf.* 1. Warmth, heat. 2. Act of warming or heating. *Cáldas,* Hot baths.

Caldária, *Ley Caldaria,* Water ordeal, by which the innocence of a person accused was considered as being fully proved, by his drawing his arm unscalded out of a caldron of boiling water.

Caldeár, *va.* 1. To weld iron, and render it fit to be forged. 2. To warm, to heat.

Caldéo, *sm.* The language of Chaldea.

Caldéra, *sf.* Caldron, a pot, kettle, or boiler. *Caldera de xabon,* Soap boiler; place where soap is made and sold. *Caldera de pero botero,* (Vulg.) Davy's locker, hell.

Calderáda, *sf.* A caldron full, a copper full.

Calderería, *sf.* 1. Brazier's shop, where caldrons and coppers are made and sold. 2. Trade of a brazier.

Calderéro, *sm.* 1. Brazier, one who makes and sells copper and brass ware. 2. Tinker, who goes about mending or brazing vessels. 3. (Among Wool-washers) One that is charged with keeping the fire constantly burning under the copper or boiler.

Calderéta, *sf.* 1. Small caldron, a kettle, a pot, *Caldereta de agua bendita,* Holy-water pot. 2. Kettle full. *Caldereta de pescado guisado,* Kettle full of stewed fish.

Calderíco y **Calderíllo**, *s.* (Dim.) A small kettle.

Calderílla, *sf.* (Dim.) 1. Holy-water pot. 2. Copper coin, worth 2, 4, and 8 maravedis. 3. The lowermost part of a well where the water is collected, and which has the shape of a caldron.

Caldéro, *sm.* 1. A caldron or boiler in the form of a bucket, a copper. 2. *Caldero hornillo,* Pan, stove. *Caldero de brea,* (Naút.) Pitch kettle. *Caldero del equipage,* (Naút.) Mess kettle.

Calderón, *sm.* 1. Large caldron or kettle. 2. Mark of a thousand Ɔ. 3. (Imprent.) Paragraph ¶. 4. (Mús.) Sign denoting a suspension of the instruments.

Calderuéla, *sf.* 1. Small kettle. 2. Small pot or dark lanthorn, used by sportsmen to drive partridges into the net.

Caldíllo y **Caldíto**, *sm.* Sauce of a ragout or fricassee, light broth.

Cáldo, *sm.* Water in which meat has been boiled, broth. *Caldos,* Wine, oil, and all spirituous liquors exported by sea. *Caldos sulcidos,* Pressed juice of herbs. *Revolver caldos,* (Met.) To excite disturbances, to stir up commotions. *Caldo alterado,* Alterative broth, generally made of veal, partridges, frogs, vipers, and various herbs.

Caldóso, sa, *a.* Having plenty of broth.

Caldúcho, *sm.* (Bax.) Plenty of broth ill-seasoned and without substance, hog-wash.

Calecér, *va.* V. *Calentar.*

Calecíco, *sm.* Small chalice.

Calefacción, *sf.* Calefaction, the act of warming one's self, the state of being warmed.

Calefactório, *sm.* Stove or place in convents, designed for people to warm themselves.
Calembúo, *sm.* Kind of Indian tree.
Caléncas, *sf.* Kind of East India calico.
Caléndа, *sf.* Martyrology, a book which treats of the acts of the saints of the day. *Calendas*, Calends, first day of every month.
Calendár, *va.* (Ant.) To date.
Calendário, *sm.* 1. Almanac, calendar. 2. Date. *Hacer calendarios*, (Met.) To make almanacs; to muse, to be thoughtful. [torm.
Calendáta, *sf.* (Ant.) Date. An Arragon law
Caléndula, *sf.* (Bot.) Wild marygold. Calendula arvensis *L. Caléndula alpina*, (Bot.) Leopard's bane. Arnica montana *L.*
Calentadór, *sm.* 1. One who warms or heats. 2. Warming-pan. 3. Watch of too large a size.
Calentamiénto, *sm.* 1. Calefaction, the act of warming or heating. 2. Disease incidental to horses, and occasioned by hard working.
Calentár, *va.* 1. To warm, to heat. 2. To roll and heat a ball in one's hand before it is played. 3. (Met.) To urge, to press forward, to despatch speedily. *Calentar á alguno las orejas*, To chide or reprove one severely. *Calentar á alguno el asiento ó la silla*, To become tiresome by making too long a visit. *Calentar el horno*, (In Cant Language) To overheat one's noddle, to drink too much spirituous liquor.—*vr.* 1. To be hot or proud; applied to beasts. 2. To dispute warmly, to be hurried along by the ardour of debate. *Calentarsele á uno la boca*, To speak incoherently from excessive ardour. [take a bit of a warning.
Calentón, *sm. Darse un calenton*, (Fam.) To
Calentúra, *sf.* 1. A fever. 2. Warmth, gentle heat. *Calentura de polla por comer gallina*, A pretended sickness, to be well treated and excused from work. *El negocio no le da frio ni calentura*, He takes the business extremely coolly, or with great indifference.
Calenturiénto, ta, *a.* Feverish or feverous; tending to produce a fever.
Calenturílla, *sf.* Slight fever.
Calenturón, *sm.* Violent fever. [ry.
Calepíno, *sm.* (Vulg.) Vocabulary, dictiona-
Calér, *v. impers.* (Ant.) To behove.
Caléra, *sf.* Lime-kiln.
Calería, *sf.* House, place, or street, where lime is burnt and sold. [of lime.
Caléro, ra, *a.* Calcareous, having the nature
Caléro, *sm.* One who breaks and burns limestone. [wheels, and drawn by two mules.
Calésa, *sf.* Calash, a Spanish chaise with two
Caleséro, *sm.* Driver of a calash.
Calesín, *sm.* Single horse chaise.
Calesinéro, *sm.* Owner or driver of a single horse chaise.
Caléta, *sf.* (Naút.) Cove, creek, a small bay.
Calétre, *sm.* 1. Understanding, judgment, discernment. 2. (In abusive Language) The head.
Cáli, *sm.* (Quim.) V. *Alcali.*
Calibíta, *sm.* Inhabitant of a hut.
Calibrár, *va.* To examine the caliber of a ball or fire-arm.
Calíbre, *sm.* 1. Dimensions and diameter of a ball. 2. Caliber or dimensions of the bore of a cannon or other fire-arm. 3. Diameter of a column. *Ser de buen ó mal calibre*, To be of a good or bad quality.
Cálice, (Ant.) V. *Cáliz.*
Caliche, *sm.* Pebble or small piece of limestone accidentally introduced into a brick or tile at the time of its being burnt. [India.
Calicúd ó Calicút, *sf.* Silk stuff imported from
Calidád, *sf.* 1. Quality, the nature or property of a thing relatively considered. 2. Importance or consequence of a thing. 3. Conditions or terms of an agreement. 4. (Ant.) Heat, warmth. *Dineros son calidad*, (Met.) Money is superior to nobility. *Calidades*, Conditions in playing a game.
Calidéz, *sf.* Heat.
Cálido, da, *a.* 1. Hot, piquant. *Es cálida la pimienta*, The pepper is hot. 2. Crafty, artful.
Calientár, V. *Calentár.*
Caliénte, *a.* Warm, hot, scalding. *Hierro caliente*, Red hot iron. *Tener la sangre caliente*, (Met.) To face dangers with great spirit. *En caliente*, Piping hot, on the spot, immediately, instantaneously.
Caliéta, *sf.* Kind of mushroom growing at the foot of the juniper tree.
Califa, *sm.* Calif or caliph, successor; a title assumed by the princes successors of Moham-
Califáto, *sm.* The dignity of caliph. [med.
Calificación, *sf.* 1. Qualification. 2. Judgment, censure. 3. Proof.
Calificádo, da, *a.* Qualified, authorized.
Calificadór, *sm.* 1. One who is qualified to say and do something. 2. *Calificador del santo oficio*, Officer of the Inquisition, appointed to examine books and writings.
Calificár, *va.* 1. To qualify, to render a thing fit for the purpose to which it is intended. 2. To authorize, to empower. 3. To certify, to attest. 4. To illustrate, to ennoble.—*vr.* To prove one's noble birth and descent according to law. [the Roman soldiers.
Calíga, *sf.* A kind of leather half boots worn by
Caliginidád, V. *Obscuridad.*
Caliginóso, sa, *a.* 1. Dark, cloudy. 2. Intricate, difficult to be understood.
Calílla, *sf.* A slight injection, made of soap, oil, and salt, to relieve the bowels.
Calimáco, *sm.* V. *Calamaco.* [sembling lead.
Calín, *sm.* Kind of metallic composition re-
Calína, *sf.* Thick vapour, resembling a mist or fog. [Indies.
Calipédes, *sm.* A tardigrade animal of the
Cáliz, *sm.* 1. Chalice, a cup used in acts of worship. 2. Bitter cup of grief and affliction. 3. Calix, the outward cover of the petals of flowers.
Calízo, za, *a.* Calcareous, limy. [ly.
Calla callándo, *ad.* Privately, secretly, tacit-
Calláda, *sf.* Dish of tripe. [noise, privately.
De Calláda, ó á las Calládas, *ad.* Without
Calladaménte, *ad.* Silently, tacitly, secretly, privately, in a reserved manner.
Calladário, *sf.* Red or black cotton stuff, which comes from Bengal.
Calládo, da, *a.* 1. Silent, reserved. 2. Discreet.
Callamiénto, *sm.* Act of imposing or keeping silence. [low voice.
Callandíco, ca, y Callandíto, ta, *a.* In a
Callár, *vn.* 1. To keep silence, to be silent, not

to utter a syllable. 2. To omit speaking of a thing, to pass it over in silence; to cease singing, spoken of birds. 3. To dissemble, to pretend not to have heard what was said. 4. (Poét.) To abate, to become moderate, to grow calm; applied to the wind or sea. *Callar su pico*, To hold one's tongue, to pretend not to have heard or seen any thing of the matter in question. *Buen callar se pierde*, Check thy own vices and proclaim not those of others. *Matalas callando*, By crafty silence he obtains his ends. *La muger y la pera, la que calla es buena.* (Prov.) A silent woman and a silent plum are best. *Quien calla otorga*, (Prov.) Silence implies consent. *Calle el que dió y hable el que tomó*, (Prov.) Let the giver be silent, and the receiver loud with gratitude. *Cortapicos y callares*, Be silent; an advice to children not to be talkers, or to ask improper questions.—*vr.* (Ant.) To be silent.

CÁLLE, *sf.* 1. Street, paved way between two rows of houses. 2. Pretext or pretence. 3. (Joc.) Gullet. *Calle de árboles*, Alley or walk in a garden. *Boca de calle*, Entrance of a street. *Calle de hombres*, Street crowded with people. *Calle mayor*, Main or leading street. *Calle pasagera*, Thoroughfare. *Calle sin salida*, Blind alley without a thoroughfare. *Calle traviesa*, Cross-street. *Alborotar la calle*, To cause an uproar in the street, to disturb the public tranquillity. *Azotar la calle*, To walk the streets, to loiter about. *Calle hita*, To go from house to house. *Dexar á uno en la calle*, To strip one of his all. *Echar algun secreto en la calle*, To proclaim a secret in the streets. *Hacer calle*, To make way, to clear the passage; (Met.) To overcome difficulties. *Llevarse de calles alguna cosa*, (Met.) To carry every thing before one. *Quedar en la calle*, To be in the utmost distress. *Ser buena una cosa solo para echada á la calle*, Not to be worth keeping. *Calles públicas*, The public streets.

CALLEÁR, *va.* To clear the walks in the vineyard of the loose branches which run across them.

CALLÉJA, *sf.* V. *Callejuéla*.

CALLEJEÁR, *va.* To walk the streets, to loiter about the streets.

CALLEJÉRO, RA, *s.* Street walker, one who loiters about the streets.

CALLÉJO Y CALLÉVO, *sm.* (Burg.) Pit made by sportsmen, into which the game falls when pursued.

CALLEJÓN, *sm.* 1. Narrow lane between two walls. 2. Narrow pass between mountains. *Callejon de combate*, (Naút.) Orlop-gang-way.

CALLEJONCÍLLO, *sm.* A little narrow passage.

CALLEJUÉLA, *sf.* 1. Lane or narrow passage, with houses on each side, which runs across the main streets. 2. (Met.) Shift, subterfuge, evasion. *Dar pan y callejuela*, To help one in his flight. *Todo se sabe, hasta lo de la callejuela*, In time every thing comes to light.

CALLEMANDRA, *sf.* Kind of woollen stuff with a glossy surface, like calamanco.

CALLIÁLTO, TA, *a.* Having swelling welts or borders, applied to horse shoes.

CALLÍZO, *sm.* V. *Callejon y Callejuela.*

CÁLLO, *sm.* 1. Hard or callous substance raised on the hands or feet, a corn, a wen. 2. Extremity of a horse's shoe. *Cállo*, Tripes, the intestines of black cattle, calves, and sheep. *Hacer ó tener callos*, (Met.) To harden the hands by labour.

CALLÓN, *sm.* 1. Big corn or wen. 2. (Among Shoemakers) Rubber, a whetstone for smoothing the blades of awls.

CALLOSIDÁD, *sf.* Callosity, callousness.

CALLÓSO, SA, *a.* Callous, having a hard thick skin. [cocoa trees.

CALLOÚ, *sm.* Wine extracted from palms and

CÁLMA, *sf.* 1. (Naút.) A calm; settled still weather. 2. (Met.) Suspension of business, cessation of pain. *Tierras cálmas*, Flat, bleak country, without trees. *En calma*, (Naút.) Smooth sea. [dyne.

CALMÁNTE, *p. y s.* Mitigating; narcotic, ano-

CALMÁR, *vn.* 1. To fall calm, to be becalmed. 2. (Met.) To be pacified or appeased.

CALMÓSO, SA, *a.* 1. Calm. 2. (Met.) Tranquil.

CALOCÁR, *sm.* Kind of white earth or clay.

CALÓCHA, *sf.* Clog, or wooden shoe.

CALOFRIÁDO, DA, *a.* Chilly, shivering with cold.

CALOFRIÁRSE Y CALOSFRIÁRSE, *vr.* To be chilly, to shudder or shiver with cold, to be feverish.

CALOFRÍO Y CALOSFRÍO, *sm.* Indisposition, attended with shivering and an unnatural heat.

CALÓMA, *sf.* (Naút.) Singing out of sailors when they haul a rope.

CALONGÍA, *sf.* House of canons. V. *Canongía.*

CALONIÁR, *va.* To fine, to impose a pecuniary penalty.

CALÓÑA, *sf.* 1. V. *Calumnia*. 2. Fine or pecuniary punishment for calumniating.

CALÓR, *sm.* 1. Heat, a sensation excited by fire 2. (Met.) Warmth, ardour, fervour; applied to sentiments and actions. 3. Brunt of an action or engagement, where the conflict is most violent or severe. *Dar calor á la empresa*, To encourage an undertaking. *Dar calor*, (Among Tanners) To raise the colour of a hide by heating it over the fire. *Gastár el calor natural en alguna cosa*, (Met.) To pay more attention to a business or affair than it is worth.

CALORÓSO, SA, *a.* V. *Caluroso.*

CALÓSTRO, *sm.* Colostrum, the first milk given by the female after bringing forth her young.

CALÓTO, *sm.* A metal, brought from Pompayan, in America, to which the vulgar attribute peculiar virtues, and therefore frequently mix it with the tongue of bells.

CALPÍXQUE, *sm.* Rent-gatherer, a steward.

CALSÉCO, CA, *a.* (Ant.) Cured with lime.

CALUMBRECÉRSE, *vr.* (Ant.) To grow mouldy.

CALÚMNIA Y CALÚNIA, *sf.* Calumny, false charge, slander. *Afianzar de calumnia*, (For.) To oblige the accuser to prove his allegations under the legal penalties.

CALUMNIADÓR, RA, *s.* Calumniator, a slanderer.

CALUMNIÁR, *va.* To calumniate, to slander, to accuse falsely. [slanderous manner.

CALUMNIOSAMÉNTE, *ad.* In a calumnious or

CALUMNIÓSO, SA, *a.* Calumnious, slanderous.

CALUROSAMÉNTE, *ad.* Warmly, ardently.

CALURÓSO, SA, *a.* 1. Warm, hot. 2. Heating, communicating or exciting heat.

CÁLVA, *sf.* 1. Bald crown of the head, bald pate

2. Game among country people, in which they knock one stone against another. *Calva de almete,* Crest of a helmet.

CALVÁR, *va.* 1. To hit a stone in the game of *Calva.* 2. (Ant.) To impose upon one, to deceive.

CALVÁRIO, *sm.* 1. (Met. y Fam.) Debts, tally, score. 2. Place where the bones of the dead are deposited, a charnel-house. 3. Calvary, hill or elevation on which are crosses representing the stations at Mount Calvary.

CALVATRUÉNO, *sm.* 1. Baldness, extending over the whole head. 2. (Met.) Blockhead.

CALVÁZA, *sf.* Large bald pate.

CALVÉRO, CALVIJÁR, Y CALVITÁR, *sm.* Piece of barren ground situated among fruitful lands.

CALVÉTE, *sm.* Little bald pate, when a small part of the head only is bald.

CALVÉZ, *sf.* Baldness, want of hair on the head.

CALVÍLLA, *sf.* Little baldness.

CALVINÍSTA, *sm.* Calvinist, a follower of Calvin.

CÁLVO, VA, *a.* 1. Bald, without hair on the head. 2. Barren, uncultivated; applied to ground situated among fruitful lands. *Tierra calva,* Barren soil, without any trees or other plants.

CÁLVE, *sf.* (Bot.) Alkanet or orchanet.

CÁLZAS, *sf. pl.* 1. Long loose breeches, trousers. 2. Hose, stockings. *Calzas acuchilladas,* Slashed trousers. *Calzas bermejas,* Red stockings, formerly worn by noblemen. *Calza de arena,* Bag filled with sand, with which malefactors were formerly chastised. *Medias calzas,* Short stockings, which were formerly worn, and reached only up to the knees. *En calzas y jubon,* (Met.) In an odd or imperfect state. *Echarle una calza á alguno,* To point out a person, to be guarded against. *Meter en una calza,* (Met.) To screw up a person, to put him on his mettle. *Tomar las calzas de villadiego,* To make a precipitate flight or escape. *Hombre de calzas atacadas,* (Met.) A rigid observer of old customs.

CALZÁDA, *sf.* Causey or Causeway, a paved high-way.

CALZADÉRA, *sf.* Hempen cord for fastening the *abarcas,* a coarse kind of shoes.

CALZADÍLLO Ó CALZADÍTO, *sm.* Small shoe.

CALZÁDO, *sm.* 1. All sorts of shoes, sandals, or other coverings of the feet. 2. Horse which has got four white feet. *Calzádos,* All articles serving to cover the legs and feet. *Tráeme los calzados,* Bring me my stockings, garters, shoes.

CALZADÓR, *sm.* 1. Leather or horn used to draw up the hind quarters of tight shoes. 2. *Entrar con calzador,* (Met.) To find great difficulties in entering a place.

CALZADÚRA, *sf.* 1. Act of putting on the shoes. 2. Felloe of a cart wheel. 3. Drink money, given to shoemakers for fitting on new shoes.

CALZÁR, *va.* 1. To put on shoes. 2. To strengthen with iron or wood. 3. To scoat or scotch, to stop a wheel by putting a stone or piece of wood under it before. 4. To carry a ball of a determinad size; applied to fire arms. *Calzar las herramientas,* To put a steel edge to iron tools. *Calzar las espuelas,* To put on spurs. *Calzar espuelas al enemigo,* To pursue the enemy with the utmost vigour. *Calzar los guantes,* To put on gloves. *Calzar las mesas,* To secure tables by putting bits of thin boards under them to make them stand fast. *Calzar el ancla,* (Naút.) To shoe the anchor. *Calzar los árboles,* To cover the roots of trees with fresh earth. *Calzar ancha,* (Met.) Not to be very nice and scrupulous. *Calzárse á alguno,* (Met.) To govern or manage a person. *Calzarse los estribos,* To thrust the feet too far into the stirrups. *El que primero llega, ese la calza,* (Prov.) First come first served.

CALZATRÉPAS, *sf.* (Ant.) Snare, trap.

CÁLZO, *sm.* V. *Calce. Cálzos,* (Naút.) Boat-scantlings, skids.

CALZÓN, *sm.* Ombre, a game at cards.—*pl.* 1. Breeches, small clothes. *Calzones marineros,* Trowsers, long breeches worn by sailors. 2. (Naút.) Goose-wings: to make goose-wings of the main and fore-sail, is to haul and furl them in such a manner, that while the bunt is reefed to the yard, the foot and wings may still catch the wind.

CALZONÁZO, *sm.* Big pair of breeches. *Es un calzonazo,* (Met.) He is a weak soft fellow.

CALZONCÍLLOS, *sm. pl.* 1. Linen drawers worn under breeches. 2. Ombre, a game at cards.

CÁMA, *sf.* 1. Bed, couch, a place of repose. *Cama con ruedas,* A truck-bed. 2. Bed-hangings and furniture. 3. Seat or couch of wild beasts, *e. g.* the form of a hare, the burrows of rabbits, &c. 4. Chest or body of a cart. 5. *Cama del arado,* The piece of wood in a plough which connects the plough-share with the beam, the sheath. 6. *Cama del melon,* The part of a melon which touches the ground. 7. Piece of wood which strengthens the posts of a wine press. 8. (Ant.) The grave. 9. Slice of meat put upon another to be both dressed together. 10. Every lay of tallow or wax put on candles when making. 11. Branch of a bridle to which the reins are fastened. 12. Piece of cloth cut slopewise, to be joined to another, to make a round cloak. 13. (Among Gardeners) Layer of dung and earth for raising plants. 14. (In Mints) Box or case wood which contains the dye. 15. (In Conchology) Stratum or layer of small shells. *Hacer cama,* To keep one's bed, to be confined to one's bed on account of sickness. *Hacer la cama,* To make up the bed. *Hacerle la cama á alguno ó á alguna cosa,* (Met.) To pave the way for a person or thing.

CAMÁDA, *sf.* Brood of young animals, a litter. *Camada de ladrones,* Den of thieves, a nest of rogues.

CAMAFÉO, *sm.* Cameo, a gem on which figures are engraved in basso-relievo.

CAMÁL, *sm.* 1. Hempen halter. 2. Chain for slaves.

CAMALEÓN, *sm.* Chameleon. Lacerta Chamæleon *L. Camaleon blanco,* (Bot.) White carline thistle. Carlina acaulis *L. Camaleon negro,* (Bot.) Black carline thistle. Calina corymbosa *L.*

CAMALEOPÁRDO, *sm.* Cameleopard, an animal taller than a camel, and spotted like a leopard.

CAMAMÍLA, *sf.* (Bot.) Chamomile. V. *Manzanilla.*

Camándula, *sf.* Chaplet or rosary of one or three decades. *Tener muchas camándulas,* (Iron.) To make use of many tricks and artifices, to shuffle.

Camandulénse, *a.* Belonging to the religious order of Camandula, or reformed Benedictine.

Camanduléro, ra, *a.* y *s.* Full of tricks and artifices, dissembling, hypocritical.

Camanónca, *sf.* Kind of stuff formerly used for linings.

Cámara, *sf.* 1. Hall or principal apartment of a house. 2. Alcove, part of a chamber separated by an estrade. 3. Granary, a storehouse of threshed corn. 4. Stool, evacuation by stool. 5. (Naút.) Cabin of a ship. 6. *Cámara alta,* (Naút.) Roundhouse of a ship. 7. Chamber in a mine. 8. Chamber of great guns and other fire-arms. 9. Residence of the king and court. *Cámara del rey,* The room in which the king holds a levee for the gentlemen of the bed-chamber; exchequer; or royal academy. *Cámara alta ó de los pares,* The house of lords. *Cámara baxa ó de los comunes,* The house of commons. *Cámara de ciudad, villa, ó lugar,* (Ant.) V. *Concejo ó Ayuntamiento. Cámara de Castilla,* Supreme council, which consists of the president or governor of that of Castile and other ministers. Philip II. in 1588, erected it into a council. *Moza de cámara,* Chamber-maid.

Camaráda, *sf.* 1. Comrade, partner, companion. 2. Society or company of people united; assembly. 3. (Ant.) Battery. *Camaradas de rancho,* Messmates. *Camaradas de navío,* Shipmates.

Camarága, *sm.* Granary rent, hire for a granary.

Camaranchón, *sm.* Garret, the uppermost room in a house, where lumber is kept.

Camaréra, *sf.* 1. Head waiting-maid in great houses. 2. Keeper of the queen's wardrobe.

Camarería, *sf.* Place and employment of a valet de chambre.

Camaréro, *sm.* 1. Valet de chambre, the first man-servant in great houses. 2. Steward or keeper of stores. 3. Lord chamberlain.

Camaréta, *sf.* Small bed-chamber.

Camariénto, ta, *a.* Troubled with a diarrhœa, or looseness of body.

Camarílla, *sf.* 1. Small room. 2. (In public Schools) The room where boys are flogged.

Camarín, *sm.* 1. Place behind an altar where the images are dressed, and the ornaments destined for that purpose are kept. 2. Closet. 3. A lady's dressing-room. 4. (Ant.) Conclave.

Camarína, *sf.* Copse, short wood, a low shrub.

Camarísta, *sm.* 1. Minister of state, and member of the privy council of Castile and the Indies. 2. (Ant.) Guest who has a room to himself, without having any intercourse with the rest of the family. 3. Maid of honour to the queen and the *infantas* of Spain.

Camaríta, *sf.* Small chamber or room.

Camarléngo, *sm.* (Ar.) Lord of the bed-chamber.

Camarón, *sm.* (Ict.) Shrimp. Cancer crangon *L.*

Camaronéro, *sm.* One who catches or sells shrimps.

Camaróte, *sm.* (Naút.) Room on board a ship, a birth.

Camasquínce, *sm.* Nickname jocularly applied to any person.

Camástro, *sm.* Poor miserable bed.

Camastrón, *sm.* Sly artful fellow.

Camastronázo, *sm.* Great impostor, hypocrite, or dissembler.

Camatónes, *sm. pl.* (Naút.) Iron fastenings by which the shrouds are attached to a ship's sides.

Cambaláche, *sm.* Traffic by exchange, barter.

Cambalacheár, Cambalechár y **Camalachár**, *va.* To barter, to exchange one thing for another.

Cambaléo, *sm.* An ancient company of comedians consisting of five men and a woman.

Cámbas, *sf. pl.* Pieces put into a cloak, or other round garment, to make it hang round.

Cambayás, *sf. pl.* Kind of cotton stuff which comes from Bengal.

Cambiáble, *a.* Fit to be bartered or exchanged.

Cambiadór, *sm.* 1. One who barters or traffics by exchanging one thing for another. 2. Trader in money, a banker; money-changer.

Cambiamiénto, *sm.* Change, alteration.

Cambiánte, *a.* Bartering, exchanging.

Cambiánte, *sm.* Variety of hues exhibited by cloth of various colours, according to the manner in which the light is reflected. *Cambiante de letras,* A banker.

Cambiár, *va.* 1. To barter, to exchange one thing for another. 2. To change, to alter. *Cambiar de mano,* To change from the one side to the other; applied to horses. 3. To give or take money on bills, to negotiate bills and exchange them for money. 4. To transfer, to make over, to remove. *Cambiar las velas,* (Naút.) To shift the sails. *Cambiar la comida,* (Better *vomitar la comida*) To bring up the victuals. *Cambiar el seso,* (Ant.) To lose one's senses. 5. To carry on the business of a banker.—*vr.* To be translated or transferred.

Cambíja, *sf.* 1. Reservoir, basin of water. 2. Perpendicular line intersecting another. 3. Square, an instrument made to measure and describe right angles.

Cambíl, *sm.* (Ant.) An old kind of medicine.

Cámbio, *sm.* 1. Barter, exchange of one thing for another. 2. Giving or taking of bills of exchange. 3. Rise and fall of the course of exchange. 4 Public or private bank. 5. Compensation. 6. Certain humour contained in the small veins of an animal. 7. Return of a favour, recompense. *Cambio seco,* Usurious contract; accommodation bill. *Dar ó tomar á cambio,* To lend or borrow money on interest. *Cambio por letras,* Trade in bills of exchange.

Cambísta, *sm.* Banker, trader in money.

Cambíunte, *sm.* A kind of camblet.

Cámbra, *sf.* (Ant.) V. *Cámara ó Quarto.*

Cambráy, *sm.* Cambric, kind of fine linen, first manufactured at Cambray.

Cambrayádo, da, *a.* Resembling cambric.

Cambrayón, *sm.* Coarse cambric.

Cambrón, *sm.* (Bot.) Buckthorn. Rhamnus catharticus *L.*

Cambronál, *sm.* Thicket of briers, brambles, and thorns.

Cambronéra, *sf.* (Bot.) Thorn, brambles. *Cambronéra Africana,* (Bot.) African buckthorn

Camarú, *sm.* (Bot.) American myrtle tree.

Camaúx, *sm.* 1. Child's cap tied close to its head to keep it straight. 2. Mask, veil.

Camedáfne, *sf.* (Bot.) Mezereon, spurge-olive, or dwarf-bay. Daphne mezereum *L.*

Camédrio ó Camédros, *sm.* (Bot.) Speedwell, or mountain germander. Veronica chamædrys *L.*

Camédris, *sm.* (Bot.) Germander. *Camédris de agua*, Water germander. Teucrium scordium *L.*

Cameléa, *sf.* (Bot.) Widow wail, a shrub.

Cameléte, *sm.* Kind of great gun. [farfara *L.*

Cameleúca, *sf.* (Bot.) Colt's-foot. Tussilago

Camélina, *sf.* (Bot.) Purging flax.

Caméllа, *sf.* 1. She-camel. 2. Ridge in ploughed land. 3. Pail into which camels, cows, and other animals, are milked; a milk-pail. 4. Yoke, fastened to the head of an ox.

Camelléjo, *sm.* 1. Small camel. 2. Small piece of ordnance, used in former times.

Camellería, *sf.* 1. Stable or stand for camels. 2. Employment of a camel-driver.

Camelléro, *sm.* Keeper or driver of camels.

Caméllo, *sm.* 1. Camel, a large quadruped and beast of burthen, having a lump on its back. 2. Ancient short cannon of 16 pounds caliber. 3. Engine for setting ships a-float, in places where there is but little water.

Camello-pardál, *sm.* V. *Camaleopardo.*

Camellón, *sm.* 1. Ridge turned up by the plough or spade. 2. Long wooden trough, out of which cattle drink. 3. Carpenter's horse. 4. Bed of flowers in a garden. 5. Camblet. *Camellones listados*, Cambleteens.

Camelóte, *sm.* Camblet.

Camemóro, *sm.* (Bot.) Cloud-berry.

Camepítios, *sm.* (Bot.) Common ground-pine.

Camerhododéndros, *sm.* (Bot.) Dwarf rosebay.

Caméro, *sm.* 1. Upholsterer, one who makes beds and other furniture. 2. One who lets out beds on hire.

Caméro, *a.* Belonging to a bed or mattress.

Camiar, V. *Cambiár y Vomitar.*

Camilla, *sf.* 1. Small bed. 2. Bed on which women repose after child-birth, and on which they receive compliments. 3. Horse, on which linen is aired and dried at the fire. *Camilla baxa*, Low frame, on which cloth shearers put their work.

Caminada, (Ant.) V. *Jornada.*

Caminadór, *sm.* Good walker.

Caminánte, *sm.* Traveller, walker.

Caminár, *vn.* 1. To travel, to walk. 2. To move along; applied to rivers and other inanimate things. *Caminar con pies de plomo*, (Met.) To act with prudence. *Caminar derecho*, (Met.) To act with uprightness and integrity.

Camináta, *sf.* 1. Long walk for the sake of exercise. 2. Excursion into the country.

Camíno, *sm.* 1. Beaten road for travellers, high road. 2. Journey from one place to another. 3. Turn of a boat, or cart, for removing goods from one place to another. 4. (Met.) Profession, station, calling. 5. (Met.) Manner, mode, or method of doing a thing. 6. High road. *Camino cubierto*, (Fort.) Covert-way. *Camino de herradura*, Path, a narrow road, fit only for people on foot or horseback. *Camino carretero*, Road for carriages and wagons. *Camino de santiago*, (Astr.) Galaxy, the milky-way. *Camino real*, High road: (Met.) The readiest and surest way of obtaining one's end. *De un camino ó de una via dos mandados*, (Prov.) To kill two birds with one stone. *Ir fuera de camino*, (Met.) To be out of one's latitude, to act contrary to reason. *Ir su camino*, To pursue one's course, to persist or persevere in one's views. *No llevar alguna cosa camino*, To be without foundation and reason. *Procurar el camino*, To clear the way. *Salir al camino*, To go to meet a person; (Met.) To go on the high-way to rob. *De camino*, In one's way, going along. *Fui á Madrid y de camino hice una visita*, I went to Madrid and in my way thither I paid a visit.

Cámio, *sm.* (Ant.) V. *Cambio.*

Camísa, *sf.* 1. Shirt, shift; the under linen garment of men and women. 2. Alb or surplice worn by priests and deacons. 3. Thin skin of almonds and other fruit. 4. Slough of a serpent. 5. Side of a rampart towards the field. 6. Stock of counters used at a game at cards. 7. (Ant.) Catamenia. 8. Rough-casting or plastering of a wall before it is white-washed. *Camisa alquitranada, embreada, ó de fuego*, (Naút.) Fire-chemise, a piece of canvas thickened by means of a melted composition of pitch, sulphur, rosin, tallow, and tar, and covered with saw-dust, used in branders and fire-ships. *Camisa de una vela*, (Naút.) The body of a sail. *Tomar la muger en camisa*, To marry a woman without money. *Estás en tu camisa?* Are you in your senses? *Jugar hasta la camisa*, To play the shirt off one's back. *Meterse en camisa de once varas*, To interfere in other people's affairs. *Vender hasta la camisa*, To sell all to the last shirt. *Saltar de su camisa*, (Met.) To jump out of one's skin.

Camiséta, *sf.* (Ant.) Short shirt or shift with wide sleeves.

Camisílla, *sf.* Small shirt.

Camisóla, *sf.* 1. Ruffled shirt. 2. Frock worn by the rowers in a galley.

Camisón, *sm.* 1. Long and wide shirt. 2. Frock worn by labourers and workmen.

Camisóte, *sm.* Armour for the body worn in ancient times.

Camíta, *sf.* Small bed.

Camomíla, V. *Manzanilla.*

Camón, *sm.* 1. Large bed. 2. Frame of lath which serves to form an arch. *Camon de vidrios*, Partition in a large apartment made by a glass frame.—*pl.* 1. Felloes of cart wheels, shod with ever-green oak instead of iron. 2. Incurvated pieces of timber in the wheels of corn mills.

Camoncíllo, *sm.* State stool in a drawing room; a cricket richly garnished.

Camórra, *sf.* (Vulg.) Quarrel, dispute. [son.

Camorrísta, *s.* (Bax.) Noisy quarrelsome per-

Camóte, *sm.* (Bot.) Spanish potato. Convolvulus batatas *L.*

Campál, *a.* Belonging to the field, and encampments. *Batalla campal*, Pitched battle fought between two armies.

Campamento, *sm.* Encampment.

Campána, *sf.* 1. Bell, a hollow body of mixed metal, formed to sound. 2. (Met.) Parish-church, parish. *Esta tierra está debaxo la campana de tal parte*, That land is situated in the parish of, &c. 3. Any thing which has the shape of a bell. 4. Bottom of a well made in the form of a bell. 5. Chimney, the funnel of which is bell-shaped. 6. (In Woollen Manufactories) Iron hoop, corded crosswise, serving to keep up the yarn from the bottom of the copper when put into the dye. 7. Glass vessel, wider at the top than at the bottom, like an inverted bell. *Campana de vidrio*, A bell-shaped glass vessel, with which gardeners cover delicate plants. *Campana de buzo*, Diving bell. *Campana de rebato*, Alarm-bell. *A' campana herida ó á campana tañida*, At the sound of the bell. *Oir campanas y no saber donde*, To have heard of a fact, but not to be well informed of its true nature and complexion. *No haber oido campanas*, Not to be informed of the most common things.

Campanáda, *sf.* Sound produced by the clapper striking against the bell. *Dar campanada*, (Met.) To cause scandal, to make a noise.

Campanário, *sm.* 1. Belfry, the place where the bells are rung. 2. (Joc.) Noddle, head. 3. Rack in velvet-looms.

Campaneár, *va.* 1. To ring the bell frequently. 2. To divulge, to noise about. *Allá se las campanean*, (Met.) Not to be willing to interfere in affairs foreign to one's self.

Campanéla, *sf.* Sudden circular motion with the feet in dancing.

Campanéo, *sm.* 1. Bell-ringing, chime. 2. Cantonment.

Campanéro, *sm.* 1. Bell-founder, a person who casts bells. 2. Bellman, he who rings bells.

Campanéta, *sf.* Small bell.

Campánil, *a.* *Metal campanil*, Bell-metal.

Campanílla, *sf.* 1. Small bell. 2. Small bubble. 3. (Anat.) Epiglottis. 4. Little tassel serving as an ornament for ladies' gowns. 5. (Naút.) Cabin-bell. 6. (Bot.) Bell-flower. Narcissus bulbocodium *L.* 7. *Campanillas de otoño*, (Bot.) Snowflake, garden daffodil. Leucojum autumnale *L.* *Tener muchas campanillas*, (Met.) To be loaded with honours and titles.

Campanillázo, *sm.* 1. Strong, violent ringing of bells. 2. Signal given with the bell.

Campanilleár, *va.* To ring a small bell often.

Campanilléro, *sm.* Bellman, one who claims the attention of the public by ringing his bell.

Campaníno, *sm.* Kind of marble.

Campánte, *pa.* Excelling, surpassing.

Campanúdo, da, *a.* 1. Wide, puffed up, bell-shaped; applied to clothes. 2. Campaniform; spoken of flowers which have the shape of bells. 3. Pompous, lofty, high-sounding; applied to the style.

Campánula, *sf.* (Bot.) Bell-flower. Narcissus bulbocodium *L.*

Campáña, *sf.* 1. Flat, level country. 2. Campaign, that space of time during which an army keeps the field, without going into quarters. *Campaña naval*, (Naút.) Cruize. *Víveres de campaña*, (Naút.) Sea provisions, stores. *Salir ó correr la campaña*, To reconnoitre the enemy's camp or motions. *Estar ó hallarse en campaña*, To make a campaign.

Campár, *vn.* 1. To encamp, to be encamped. 2. To excel in abilities, arts, and sciences. *Campar con su estrella*, To be fortunate or successful.

Campeadór, *sm.* (Ant.) Warrior who excelled in the field; thus the celebrated *Cid*, Ruy Diaz de Vivar, was called *Cid campeador*.

Campeár, *vn.* 1. To be in the field. 2. To frisk about in the fields or lawns; applied to brutes. *Campear de sol á sombra*, To be at work from morning to night. 3. To be eminent, to excel.

Campejár, *vn.* (Ant.) V. *Campear*.

Campeón, *sm.* 1. Champion, one eminent for warlike exploits. 2. Second, he who accompanies another in a duel.

Campéro, ra, *a.* Exposed to wind and weather in the open field.

Campéro, *sm.* 1. Friar who superintends the management of a farm. 2. One who inspects and overlooks another's lands and fields. 3 Pig brought up and fed in the fields.

Campés, (Ant.) V. *Campestre*.

Campesíco, *sm.* Small field.

Campesíno, na, y Campestre, *a.* Rural, campestrial, belonging to the country, resembling the country.

Campíllo y Campiéllo, *sm.* Small field.

Campíña, *sf.* Flat tract of arable land.

Cámpo, *sm.* 1. Tract of flat and even country. 2. Field, space, range of material or immaterial things. 3. Crops, trees, plantations. 4. Ground of silks and other stuffs; field. 5. Camp. 6. Ground on which an army is drawn up. 7. Ground of a piece of painting. *Estan perdidos los campos*, The crops have failed. *Campo raso y abierto*, Plain and open country. *Campo volante*, A flying camp. *Campo de batalla*, Field of battle. *Descubrir campo ó el campo*, To reconnoitre the enemy's camp; (Met.) To inquire how the matter stands. *Hacer campo*, To clear the way; (Ant.) To engage in close combat. *Hacerse al campo*, To retreat, to flee from danger. *Dexar el campo abierto, libre, &c.* To decline any pretension or undertaking where there are competitors. *Hombre de campo ó del campo*, One who cultivates the ground, and leads a country life. *Ir á campo traviesa*, To cross the field, to make a short cut. *Partir el campo y el sol*, To mark the ground of the combatants. *Dar campo á la fantasía*, To give a free range to one's fancy. *Quedar en el campo*, To come off victorious in an engagement or dispute. *Salir al campo*, To go out to fight a duel. *Campo á campo*, (Mil.) Force to force.

Camuésa, *sf.* Pippin, an apple of an excellent flavour. *Camuésa blanca*, White pippin.

Camuéso, *sm.* 1. (Bot.) Pippin-tree. 2. Simpleton, fool.

Camúñas, *sf. pl.* All seeds, except wheat, barley, and rye.

Camúza, *sf.* Chamois, goat. V. *Gamuza*.

Camuzón, *sm.* Large chamois skin.

Can, *sm.* 1. (Ant.) Field. 2. (Ant.) Dog. 3. (Poét.) Dog-star. V. *Canícula*. 4. (Ant.) Ace in dice. 5. (Ant.) Trigger of guns and other fire-arms. 6. Ancient piece of ordnance. *Can rostro*, (Ant.) Pointer or setting dog. *Can de levantár*, Dog which starts the game. *Can de busca*, Terrier. *Can que mata al lobo*, Wolf-dog. *De hombre que no habla y de can que no ladra, guardate mucho, porque de ordinario son traidores;* (Prov.) Beware of the man who does not talk, and of the dog which does not bark, for commonly they are both traitors. *Cánes*, (In Architecture) Modillons, brackets, corbels.

Cána, *sf.* Long measure, containing about two ells. *Cánas*, Grey hairs. *Peynar canas*, To grow old. *No peynar muchas canas*, To die young. *Tener canas*, To be old; it is also applied to things.

Canabálla, *sf.* (Naút.) Kind of fishing-boat.

Canál, *sm.* 1. Channel through which water passes. 2. (In Woollen Manufactories) Pole which runs across the copper. 3. Trough for cattle to drink out. 4. Gutter which conveys the rain from the roof of a house to the ground. 5. (Among Weavers) Comb of the loom. 6. Any passage of the body. 7. Hemp after it has been once hackled. 8. (Naút.) Channel. *Canal de la mancha*, (Naút.) British Channel. 9. Bar of a hot-press. *Canal de tocino*, A hog killed, cleaned, and gutted. *Canal de un brulote*, (Naút.) Train-trough of a fire-ship. *Abrir en canal*, (Met.) To reproach bitterly, to reprimand severely.

Canaládo, da, *a.* V. *Acanalado.*

Canaléja, *sf.* 1. Small trough for cattle to drink out. 2. (In Corn-mills) Small channel through which the grain is conveyed from the hopper to the mill-stones.

Canaléra, *sf.* (Arag.) Gutter.

Canaléte, *sm.* Paddle, a small ore for canoes.

Canalíta, *sf.* Small channel or canal.

Canalízo, *sm.* Narrow channel between two islands or sand-banks.

Canálla, *sf.* 1. Mob, rabble, multitude, populace. 2. (Ant.) Pack of hounds.

Canallúza, *sf.* Roguery, vagrancy.

Canalón, *sm.* Large gutter or spout.

Canapé, *sm.* Couch or long seat furnished with a mattress to sit or lie on with ease.

Canário, ria, *s.* 1. Canary-bird. 2. Kind of quick dance, set to music, introduced into Spain by natives of the Canaries. 3. (Naút.) Kind of barge used in the Canary Islands.

Canásta, *sf.* 1. Basket, hamper. 2. Olive-measure, used in Seville, which contains half a *fanega.*

Canastílla, *sf.* 1. Small basket. 2. Present made to ladies of honour, and also to counsellors, on bull-feast days. 3. Swaddling-cloth.

Canastíllo, *sm.* 1. Small tray, made of twigs of osier, to carry sweetmeats. 2. Small basket.

Canásto y Canástro, *sm.* Large basket.

Cancabúz, *sm.* Veil for covering the face.

Cáncamos, *sm. pl.* (Naút.) Bolt-rings, to which the breeches and tackle of the guns are fixed. *Cáncamos de argolla*, Ring-bolts. *Cáncamos de gancho*, Hook-bolts. *Cáncamos de ojo*, Eye-bolts.

Cancamúrria, *sf.* (Bax.) Sadness, melancholy.

Cancamúsa, *sf.* Trick or fraud made use of to deceive one. *Ya le entiendo la cancamusa*, I am aware of the device.

Cáncana, *sf.* Form or stool on which boys are chastised in public schools.

Cancanílla, *sf.* 1. Play-thing to play a trick with. 2. (Ant.) Deception, fraud.

Cáncano, *sm.* (Vulg.) Louse.

Cancél, *sm.* 1. Wooden screen at the doors of churches and halls to obstruct the cold, wind, or idle curiosity. 2. Glass-case in a chapel behind which the king stands without performing the genuflexions during the celebration of mass; (Ant.) chancel. 3. Limits or extent of a thing.

Canceladúra y Cancellación, *sf.* Cancellation, the act of expunging or annulling writing.

Cancelár, *va.* To cancel, to expunge, or annul a writing. *Cancelar de la memoria*, (Met.) To efface from the memory.

Cancelaría y Cancelería, *sf.* Papal chancery, the court or board at Rome, whence all apostolic grants and licenses are expedited.

Canceláreo, *sm.* Chancellor in universities, who grants all the degrees which are solicited and approved of by the academical college.

Cancellér, *sm.* (Ant.) 1. Lord Chancellor. 2. Ancient name of schoolmasters in collegiate churches.

Cancellería, *sf.* (Ant.) Chancery.

Cáncer, *sm.* 1. Cancer, virulent incurable ulcer. 2. One of the twelve signs of the zodiac.

Cancerárse, *vr.* 1. To be afflicted with a cancer. 2. To turn to a cancer, as wounds, which are of a malignant nature.

Canceróso, sa, *a.* Cancerous.

Canchelágua ó Canchalágua, *sf.* A medicinal herb, a species of gentian of Peru.

Cancílla, *sf.* Wicker-door or wicker-gate.

Cancillér, *sm.* Chancellor. *Gran canciller de las Indias*, High chancellor of the Indies.

Cancillerésco, ca, *a.* Belonging to the writing characters used in chancery business.

Cancillería, *sf.* (Ant.) V. *Chancilleria.*

Canción, *sf.* 1. Song, a composition of verses set to music. 2. Poem of one or more equal stanzas. *Volver á la misma cancion*, To return to the old tune, to repeat the old story over again.

Cancioncílla, *sf.* Canzonet, a little song.

Cancionéro, *sm.* Song-book, a collection of songs.

Cancionísta, *sm.* Author or singer of songs.

Cáncro, V. *Cancer.*

Candadíllo y Candadíto, *sm.* Small padlock.

Candádo, *sm.* 1. Padlock, a lock hung before a door, trunk, &c. 2. Pendant, ear-ring. *Echár ó poner candado á los labios*, (Met.) To keep a secret, to be silent. *Candados*, Cavities around the frog of horses' feet.

Cándamo, *sm.* Ancient rustic dance.

Candár, *va.* (Ant.) To lock.

Cándara, *sf.* Frame of laths for sifting sand, earth, and gravel.

Cánde, *a.* V. *Azucar.*

Candeál, *a.* Siliginose, made of fine wheat.

Candéda, *sf.* Flower or blossom of the walnut-tree.

Candéla, *sf.* 1. Candle. 2. Flower or blossom of the chesnut-tree. 3. Candlestick. 3. Inclination of the balance-needle to the thing weighed. 5. Light, fire. *Arrimarse á la candela*, To draw near the fire. *Acabarse la candela*, (Met.) To be near one's end. *Acabarse la candela ó candelilla en almonedas y subhastas*, To sell by inch of candle, to knock down a thing to the highest bidder at public auctions, the candle being burnt. *Estar con la candela en la mano*, To be dying; it being customary in Spain, in similar cases, to put a *blessed* candle in the hand of a dying person. *La muger y la tela no la cates á la candela*, (Prov.) Neither a wife nor cloth should be examined by candlelight.

Candelábro, *sm*. Candlestick. V. *Candelero*.

Candeláda, *sf*. Sudden blaze from straw or brushwood.

Candelária, *sf*. 1. Candlemas, or the feast of the Blessed Virgin, which in Roman Catholic countries is celebrated with many lights in churches. 2. (Bot.) Mullein. Verbascum lychnitis *L*. V. *Gordolobo*.

Candelerázo, *sm*. 1. Large Candlestick. 2. Stroke or blow given with a candlestick.

Candelería, *sf*. Tallow and wax-chandler's shop.

Candeléro, *sm*. 1. Candlestick. *Candelero con muchos brazos*, Chandelier, a candlestick with many branches. 2. (Ant.) Wax or tallow chandler. 3. Lamp, a light made with oil and a wick. 4. Fishing-torch, commonly made of pine, or of the bark of a birch-tree. *Poner ó estar en el candelero*, (Met.) To be high in office, to hold an exalted station. *Candelero de ojo*, (Naút.) Eye-stanchion, or iron stay with a ring. *Candelero ciego*, Blind stanchion or iron stay without a ring. *Candeléros*, (Naút.) Stanchions or crotches, pieces of timber which support the waist-trees. *Candeleros del toldo*, Awning-stanchions. *Candeleros de los portalones*, Entering-rope stanchions. *Candeleros de trincheras y parapetos*, Quarter-netting stanchions.

Candeletón, *sm*. Large stanchion.

Candelíca y Candelílla, *sf*. Small candle.

Candelílla, *sf*. 1. (In Surgery) Bougie put into the urinary passage to keep it open. 2. Blossom of white poplars, asps and other trees. *Hacer la candelilla*, To stand on the hands and head, with the feet straight upwards, as boys do in play. *Le hacen los ojos candelillas con el vapor del vino*, His eyes sparkle with the fumes of wine. *Muchas candelillas hacen un cirio pasqual, ó muchos pocos hacen un mucho*, (Prov.) Light gains make a heavy purse.

Candelízas, *sf. pl*. (Naút.) Brails, small ropes reeved through a block, and made use of in furling the two courses and the mizen. *Candelizas de barlovento*, Weather-braces. *Candelizas de sotavento*, Lee-braces. *Cargar las mayores sobre las candelizas*, To brail up the courses.

Candencía, *sf*. Incandescence, white heat in any body.

Candénte, *a*. Incandescent, tending to a white heat, like heated iron.

Candiál, *a*. Making fine flour; applied to wheat.

Cándidaménte, *ad*. In a sincere, candid manner.

Candidáto, *sm*. Candidate, one who solicits a place.

Candidéz, *sf*. 1. Whiteness, white colour. 2. Candour, sincerity, purity of mind. 3. Simplicity.

Cándido, da, *a*. 1. White, snowy, grey, pale. 2. Candid, without cunning or malice. 3. Simple.

Candiél, *sm*. Beverage used in Andalusia, made of white wine, yolk of eggs, sugar, and nutmeg.

Candíl, *sm*. 1. A kitchen or stable lamp composed of two egg-shaped iron cups, placed over each other, the upper is moveable and contains the oil, the under, the droppings, and is attached to a hooked iron rod. 2. Lamp, with oil and a wick to give light. 3. Cock of a hat. 4. Long irregular fold in women's petticoats. 5. Fishing-torch. V. *Candelero*. *Puede arder en un candil*, It would burn in a lamp; applied to generous wine, and also to persons of brilliant parts. 6. Top of a stag's horn. *Escoger una cosa á moco de candil*, To examine closely, to choose after a close examination. *Bayle de candil*, A low hop by the light of a poor lamp.

Candiláda, *sf*. 1. (Ant.) Small lamp full of oil. 2. Oil spilt from a lamp. 3. Spot of lamp-oil.

Candilázo, *sm*. Blow or stroke given with a lamp.

Candiléja, *sf*. 1. Inner part of a lamp which contains the oil. 2. (Bot.) Deadly carrot. Thapsia villosa *L*.

Candiléjo, *sm*. Small lamp.

Candiléra, *sm*. (Bot.) Bastard mullein. Verbascum lychnitis *L*.

Candilón, *sm*. Large open lamp. *Estar con el candilon en los hospitales*, To attend a dying person. In the hospitals of Spain, it is customary to stand near the bed of the dying person, with the cross in one hand and a large lamp in the other.

Candióta, *sf*. 1. Barrel or keg for carrying wine to and fro in vintage time. 2. Large earthen jar, the inside of which is pitched, and wherein wine is fermented and preserved.

Candiotéro, *sm*. One whose trade it is to make barrels, called *candiotas*.

Candónga, *sf*. 1. Mean, servile civility, intended to deceive one under the appearance of kindness and friendship. 2. Merry, playful trick. *Dar candonga ó chasco*, To play a carnival trick. 3. Old mule no longer fit for service.

Candóngo, *sm*. Wag who turns the actions of others into ridicule. *Seda de candongo ó de candongos*, (Mur.) The finest silk reeled up into three small skeins.

Candongueár, *va*. To jeer, to sneer, to turn into ridicule.

Candonguéro, *sm*. Wag, one that is ludicrously mischievous; satirist.

Candór, *sm*. 1. Supreme whiteness. 2. (Met.) Candour, purity of mind, ingenuousness.

Canecer, *vn*. V. *Encanecer*.

Canecíllo, *sm*. (Arq.) Corbel, modillon.

Canéla, *sf*. (Bot.) Cinnamon, the second bark of an aromatic tree in Ceylon. Laurus cinnamomum *L*. *Agua de canela*, Cinnamon-water.

Caneládo, da, *a*. V. *Acanelado*.

Canélo, *sm*. Cinnamon tree.

Canelón, *sm*. 1. Gutter. V. *Canalon*. 2. Sweetmeat, in the centre whereof is a slice of cinnamon or lemon. 3. Icicle, a shoot of ice hanging down. *Canelónes*, End of a cat of nine-tails, which is thicker and more twisted than the rest.

Canéz, *sf*. Hair hoary or gray with age; old age.

Canfór y Canfora. V. *Alcanfor.*

Cánge, *sm.* Exchange of prisoners of war.

Cangeár, *va.* To exchange prisoners of war.

Cangilón, *sm.* 1. Earthen jar or pitcher to carry wine or water. 2. Oblong earthen jar fastened to the rope of a draw-well, or to a wheel for lifting water, and put in motion by means of a horse or mule. 3. Metal tankard for carrying wine or water.

Cangréja, *a. Vela cangreja,* (Naút.) Boom-sail, brig-sail, or gaff-sail.

Cangréjo, *sm.* 1. (Ict.) Craw-fish, crab. 2. Truckle cart.

Cangrejuélo, *sm.* Small craw-fish.

Cangréna, *sf.* Gangrene, a mortification.

Cangrenárse, *vr.* To be afflicted with a gangrene or mortification.

Cangrenóso, sa, *a.* Gangrenous, mortified.

Cangróso, sa, *a.* (Ant.) Cancerous.

Cánia, *sf.* (Bot.) Nettle. V. *Ortiga.*

Canícula, *sf.* (Astr.) Dog-star. *Canicula marina,* (Ict.) Lesser spotted dog-fish. Squalus catulus *L.*

Caniculáres, *sm. pl.* Dog-days.

Caníido, *sm.* Kind of parrot found in the West Indies.

Caníjo, ja, *a.* y *s.* Weak, infirm, sickly. *Fulano es un canijo,* He is a weak, puny being.

Caníl, *sm.* Coarse bread, dog's bread. V. *Colmillo.*

Canílla, *sf.* 1. (Anat.) *Canilla de pierna,* Shin bone. *Canilla de brazo,* Arm-bone. 2. Any of the principal bones of the wing of a fowl. 3. Small wooden pipe forced into a cask or barrel to draw off liquor. 4. Quill, put into a shuttle, on which the woof is wound. 5. Unevenness or inequality of the woof in point of thickness or colour. *Irse como una canilla ó de canilla,* To labour under a violent diarrhœa; (Met.) To let the tongue run like the clapper of a mill.

Canilládo, da, *a.* V. *Acanillado.*

Canilléra, *sf.* 1. Ancient armour for the shin-bone. 2. Woman who distributes skeins of thread to be wound on spools.

Canilléro, *sm.* 1. Hole made in a cask or vat to draw off the liquid it contains. 2. Weaver's quill-winder.

Canína, *sf.* Excrement of dogs.

Caninaménte, *ad.* In a passionate, snarling manner.

Caninéro, *sm.* One who gathers the excrements of dogs for the use of tan-yards.

Caninéz, *sf.* Inordinate appetite or desire of eating.

Caníno, na, *a.* Canine, relating to or resembling dogs. *Hambre canina,* Canine appetite; violent, inordinate hunger. *Dientes caninos,* Dog-teeth, the teeth between the incisors and grinders. *Muscu'o canino,* Canine muscle of the upper lip, which serves to draw it up.

Caniquí, *sf.* 1. Fine muslin which is brought from the East Indies. 2. Kind of glass phial.

Cáno, na, *a.* Hoary, gray-headed with age. 2. (Met.) Deliberate, prudent, judicious.

Canóa, *sf.* Canoe, a boat used by the Indians, and made by hollowing out the trunk of a tree.

Canoéro, *sm.* One who conducts or steers a canoe.

Canói, *sm.* Basket used by the Indians when they go on a fishing party.

Canoíta, *sm.* Small canoe.

Cánon, *sm.* 1. Canon, the decision of an ecclesiastical council relative to the doctrines or discipline of the church. 2. Whole of the books which compose the Holy Scriptures. 3. Fee paid as a mark of acknowledgment of superiority in a higher lord. 4. Catalogue, list. *Cánones,* Canons or canonical law.

Canonésa, *sf.* Canoness, a woman who lives in a religious house, and observes its rules, without having taken the vows of a monastic life.

Canónge, (Ant.) V. *Canónigo.*

Canongía, *sf.* Prebend or benefice of a canon.

Canongíble, *a.* Relating to canons and canonical prebends.

Canonía, (Ant.) y **Canonicáto.** V. *Canongía.*

Canónicaménte, *ad.* Canonically, conformably to the laws of the church.

Canónico, ca, *a.* Canonical, conformable to the canons or ecclesiastical laws. *Iglesia ó casa canónica,* House or monastery of regular canons. 2. V. *Canónicamente.*

Canónigo, *sm.* Canon or prebendary. *Canónigo reglar,* A canon of Pamplona and of the Premonstratensian or Norbertinian order of religious.

Canonísta, *sm.* Canonist, a professor or student of the canon law.

Canonizáble, *a.* Worthy of canonization.

Canonización, *sf.* Canonization, the act of declaring a saint.

Canonizár, *va.* 1. To canonize, to declare one a saint. 2. (Met.) To applaud or praise a thing. 3. (Met.) To prove any thing good or bad.

Canópo, *sm.* Miner, one who digs for metals.

Canóro, ra, *a.* 1. Canorous, musical, tuneful. 2. Shrill, loud.

Canóso, sa, *a.* Hoary, gray-headed with age.

Cánque, *sm.* Kind of cotton stuff brought from China.

Cansadaménte, *ad.* Importunely, in a troublesome, tiresome manner.

Cansádo, da, *pp.* Wearied, exhausted, impaired. *Una pelota cansada,* A spent ball. *Una vista cansada,* An impaired eye-sight. *Una lamina cansada,* A worn-out copper-plate.—*a.* 1. Tiresome, troublesome. 2. Performed with much pain or fatigue.

Cansádo, *sm.* Troublesome person who tires and fatigues others.

Cansáncio y Cansamiénto, *sm.* Weariness, lassitude, state of being exhausted with fatigue.

Cansár, *va.* 1. To weary, to tire, to fatigue, to molest, to harass. 2. To exhaust land.—*vr.* To tire one's self, to be fatigued.

Canséra, *sf.* Fatigue, weariness. *Fulano es una cansera,* He is a pestering fellow.

Cánso y Cansóso, (Ant.) V. *Cansado.*

Cantáble, *a.* 1. Tunable, harmonious, musical. 2. Pathetic, affecting.

Cantáda, *sf.* Cantata, a musical composition, consisting of recitations, and songs, sung by one.

Cantadór, *sm.* V. *Cantor.*

Cantaléta, *sf.* Pun, jest, joke. *Dar cantaleta,* To deride, to laugh at, to turn to ridicule.

Cantár, *sm.* Song set to music to be sung. *Cantares,* Canticles or Song of Solomon. *Cantares de gesta,* Old metrical romances, detailing the actions of heroes.

Cantár, *va.* 1. To sing or utter harmonious modulations of the voice. 2. To recite and relate in a poetical manner. 3. (Met.) To creak, to make a harsh, grinding noise; applied to carts. 4. To divulge a secret. 5. (At Cards) To announce the trump. *Cantar el gobierno del timon,* (Naút.) To cond or con, to order the steersman how to steer the ship. *Cantar á libro abierto*, To sing off-hand. *Cantar de plano*, To make a plain and full confession. *Cantar la victoria*, (Met.) To triumph. *Cantarle á uno la petra*, (Met.) To have a foretoken of a change of weather by pains in a diseased part of the body. *Cantar misa*, To say mass. *Ese es otro cantar*, That is another kind of speech. *Cantar en tinaja*, (Met.) To be fond of one's own praise.

Cántara, *sf.* 1. Large narrow-mouthed pitcher. V. *Cantaro*. 2. Wine measure which contains one *arroba* of eight *azumbres*, about 32 pints.

Cantarál, *sm.* Kind of press or cupboard with many drawers.

Cantarcico ó Cantarcillo, *sm.* Little song.

Cantaréra, *sf.* Shelf to put jars, pitchers, and other water vessels on.

Cantáridа, *sf.* 1. Cantharides, Spanish flies. Meloe vesicatorius *L.* 2. Blistering-plaster. 3. Blister, a collection of water under the skin.

Cantarillo, lla, *s.* 1. Small jar or pitcher. 2. (Bot.) Oval-leaved androsace. Androsace marima *L.*

Cantarín, *sm.* Continual singer, one who is constantly singing.

Cantarína, *sf.* A woman who sings on the stage.

Cántaro, *sm.* 1. Large narrow-mouthed pitcher. 2. Wine measure of different sizes in the kingdom of Aragon. 3. Vessel into which the votes are put at an election. *Entrar ó estar en cántaro*, To stand a chance of obtaining a place. *Estar en cántaro*, To be proposed for an office. *Llover á cántaros*, To rain heavily, to pour. *Moza de cantaro*, Water-girl, who carries water for the use of the house; fat, bulky woman. *Volver las nueces al cántaro*, To renew a contest.

Cantatríz, *sf.* V. *Cantarina*.

Cantázo, *sm.* Wound given by flinging a stone at one.

Cantéles, *sm. pl.* Ends of old ropes put under casks on board a ship, to make them lie fast.

Cantéra, *sf.* 1. Quarry, a place where stones are dug. 2. (Met.) Talents or genius evinced by a person. *Levantar una cantera*, To cause disturbances, to raise commotions.

Cantereár, *va.* To hang up flitches of bacon, that the brine may run off them.

Cantería, *sf.* 1. Art of hewing stone, the trade of a stone-cutter. 2. (Ant.) Quarry. 3. (Ant.) Parcel of hewn stone.

Cantéro, *sm.* 1. Stone-cutter, one whose business is to hew stones. 2. Part of a hard substance which can be easily separated from the rest; *e. g. cantero de pan*, Crust of bread. *Cantero de heredad*, (Arag.) Piece of ground.

Canterón, *sm.* Large tract of land.

Cantía, *sf.* (Ant.) V. *Quantia*.

Cántica, *sf.* (Ant.) V. *Cantar*.

Canticár, *va.* (Ant.) V. *Cantar*.

Canticio, *sm.* Constant or frequent singing.

Cántico, *sm.* Canticle, the Song of Solomon.

Cantidád, *sf.* 1. Quantity, that property of a thing which may be counted, weighed, or measured. 2. Length of time used in pronouncing a syllable. *Cantidad continua*, (Filos.) Continued quantity. *Cantidad discreta*, (Filos.) Distinct or separate quantity, as of numbers, grains, &c.

Cántiga, *sf.* V. *Cantar*.

Cantil, *sm.* Steep rock.

Cantiléna, *sf.* V. *Cantinela*.

Cantíllo, *sm.* Small rock, little stone.

Cantimarónes, *sm. pl.* (Naút.) Kind of boats.

Cantimplóra, *sf.* 1. Syphon, a crooked tube or pipe for drawing off water or other liquor. 2. Vessel for cooling liquors.

Cantína, *sf.* 1. Cellar where wine or water is kept for use. 2. Case, containing one or two flasks, which are used to cool wine on a journey or march. *Cantinas*, canteens, small tin chests set in cork wood, and covered with leather, for carrying wine and other liquors on a march or journey.

Cantinéla, *sf.* 1. Ballad, a short song. 2. Irksome repetition of a subject. *¿Ahora se viene cón esa cantinela?* Does he come again with that old story?

Cantinéro, *sm.* Butler, servant intrusted with liquors and plate.

Cantíña, *sf.* A vulgar song in Galicia.

Cantizál, *sm.* Stony ground, place full of stones.

Cánto, *sm.* 1. Stone. 2. Game of throwing the stone. 3. Act of singing. 4. End, edge, or border of a thing. *Canto de mesa*, Extremity of a table. *De canto*, On the edge or end. *El ladrillo está de canto, y no de plano*, The brick is put on its edge, and not on the flat part. 5. (Ant.) Canticle. V. *Cantico*. 6. Art of music. 7. Canto, a part of an epic poem. 8. (Extr. y And.) Hard crust of a loaf. 9. Thickness of a thing. *A' ó al canto*, Imminent, very near. *Con un canto á los pechos*, With the utmost pleasure, with the greatest alacrity.

Cantón, *sm.* 1. Corner, exterior angle formed by two lines. 2. (Blas.) Part of an escutcheon.

Cantonáda, *sf.* (Arag.) Corner. *Dar cantonada*, To laugh at a person on turning a corner.

Cantonár, *va.* V. *Acantonar*.

Cantoneárse, *vr.* V. *Contonearse*.

Cantonéo, V. *Contoneo*.

Cantonéra, *sf.* 1. Square plate nailed to the outside corner of a chest, trunk, or box, to strengthen it. 2. Woman of the town.

Cantonéro, ra, *a.* Standing idle at the corner of a street.

Cantór, ra, *s.* 1. Singer, one whose profession is to sing. 2. One who composes hymns or psalms. 3. Small kind of singing bird.

Cantorcíllo, *sm.* Petty, worthless singer.

Cantoría, *sf.* (Ant.) Musical canto; singing.

Cantorrál, *sm.* Piece of stony ground, place full of stones.

Cantúdas, *sf. pl.* Large coarse knives for the poorer classes of the people.

Cantueso, *sm.* (Bot.) French lavender. Lavandula stœchas *L.*

Cantуría, *sf.* 1. Vocal music. 2. Musical composition. 3. Method of performing musical compositions. *Esta composicion tiene buena ó mala canturia*, That piece of music is well or ill performed.

Cantusár, *va.* To enchant. V. *Encantusar*.

Canúdo, da, *a.* Hoary, gray; ancient.

Cáña, *sf.* 1. Cane, reed. Arundo *L.* 2. Stem, stalk. *La caña del trigo*, Stem of corn. 3. (Bot.) Indian reed used for walking-sticks. Canna indica *L.* 4. (Anat.) Bone of the arm or leg. 5. Subterraneous passage or communication in mines. 6. Shaft of a column or pillar. 7. Marrow, the oleaginous substance found in bones. 8. Tournament. *Caña del pulmon*, (Anat.) Windpipe, the passage of the breath. *Caña de la media*, Leg of a stocking. *Caña del timon*, (Naút.) Tiller, a strong piece of wood fastened to a ship's rudder, which serves to steer her. *Caña de pescar*, Fishing-rod. *Caña de vaca*, Shinbone of beef. *Caña dulce ó de azúcar*, (Bot.) Sugar-cane. Saccharum officinarum *L.* *Caña de un cañon*, Chase of a gun. *Cañas de cebadera*, (Naút.) Sprit-sail sheet-blocks. *Hubo toros y cañas*, (Met.) There was the devil to pay. *Pescador de caña, mas come que gana;* (Prov.) An angler eats more than he gets. *Cañas;* Equestrian exercises of throwing canes.

CAÑÁDA, *sf.* 1. Glen or dale between two mountains. 2. *Cañada real*, Sheep-walk for the travelling flocks which pass from the mountainous and colder parts of Spain to the flat and warmer parts of that country. 3. (Astur.) Measure of wine.

CAÑADÍCAS ó CAÑADÍTAS, *sf. pl.* Small measures for wine.

CAÑAFÍSTOLA, *sf.* Cassia fistula, the fruit of the cassia-tree.

CAÑAFÍSTOLO, *sm.* (Bot.) Purging cassia-tree. Cassia fistula *L.*

CAÑAHÉJA Y CAÑAHÉRLA, *sf.* (Bot.) Fennel-giant, or gigantic fennel. Ferula communis *L.*

CAÑAL, *sm.* 1. Wear or wier for fishing, made of canes or reeds. 2. (Ant.) Plantation of canes or reeds. 3. Small sluice, or channel, for catching fish. 4. Conduit of water.

CAÑALIÉGA, *sf.* (Ant.) Wear or wier for fishing.

CÁÑAMA, *sf.* Assessment of taxes, paid by a village or other place. *Casa cañama*, House exempt from taxes. *Cogedor de cañama*, Tax-gatherer.

CAÑAMÁR, *sm.* Field sown with hemp-seed.

CAÑAMÁZO, *sm.* 1. Tow of hemp. 2. Coarse canvas made of the tow of hemp. 3. Painted or checkered stuff for table carpets, made of hemp.

CAÑAMÉÑO, ÑA, *a.* Hempen, made of hemp.

CAÑAMIEL, *sm.* (Bot.) Sugar-cane. V. *Caña dulce.*

CAÑAMÍZ, *sm.* Kind of Indian vessel.

CAÑAMÍZA, *sf.* Stalk of hemp. V. *Agramiza.*

CÁÑAMO, *sm.* 1. (Bot.) Hemp. Cannabis *L.* *Cáñamo silvestre*, Bastard hemp, which grows wild in the fields. 2. Cloth made of hemp. 3. (Poét.) Slings, nets, rigging, and other things, made of hemp.

CAÑAMÓN, *sm.* Hemp-seed.

CAÑÁR, *sm.* 1. Plantation of canes or reeds. 2. Wear for catching fish.

CAÑARÉJA, *sf.* V. *Cañaheja.*

CAÑARIÉGO, GA, *a.* *Pellejos cañariegos*, Skins of sheep which die on the road when travelling.

CAÑARRÓYA, *sf.* (Bot.) Pellitory, wall-wort. Parietaria officinalis *L.*

CAÑAVÉRA, *sf.* (Bot.) Common reed-grass. Arundo donax *L.*

CAÑAVERÁL, *sm.* Plantation of canes or reeds.

CAÑAVERER ó CAÑAVERÁR, V. *Acanaverear.*

CAÑAVERÍA, *sf.* Place where reed-grass or reeds grow.

CAÑAVERÉRO, *sm.* Retailer of canes or reeds.

CAÑAVÉTE, *sm.* 1. Penknife. 2. Small locust, a grashopper.

CAÑÁZO, *sm.* Hostile blow given with a cane. *Dar cañazo*, (Met.) To shock by a scandalous expression.

CAÑERÍA, *sf.* Conduit of water, a water pipe.

CAÑÉRO, *sm.* 1. Conduit-maker, director of water-works. 2. Angler, one who fishes with a rod, hook, and line.

CAÑILAVÁDO, DA, *a.* Small limbed; applied to horses and mules.

CAÑÍLLA ó CAÑÍTA, *sf.* Small cane or reed.

CAÑIVÉTE, *sm.* Small knife, or penknife.

CAÑÍZA, *sf.* Kind of coarse linen.

CAÑIZÁL, *sm.* V. *Cañaveral.*

CAÑÍZO, *sm.* 1. Hurdle, a frame made of canes or reeds, for rearing silk-worms. 2. Hurdle, used by hatters for shearing hats.

CÁÑO, *sm.* 1. Tube, pipe, or cylinder, made of wood, glass, or metal. 2. Common sewer. 3. Spring; spout through which spring water runs. 4. Cellar or other place for cooling water. 5. (Ant.) Mine. 6. (Ant.) Subterraneous passage. 7. (Ant.) Warren or burrow. V. *Vivar. Caños ó cañónes del órgano*, Tubes or pipes of an organ.

CAÑOCÁZO, *sm.* (Ant.) Coarse flax.

CAÑÓN, *sm.* 1. Tube or pipe, hollow and cylindrical. 2. (In Glass-houses) Tube or pipe for blowing glass. 3. Quill, the hard strong feather of the wings of fowls, of which pens are made. 4. Down, or soft feathers of fowls. 5. Hollow folds in clothes. 6. Strongest part of the beard, next to the root. 7. Cannon, great gun. *A' boca de cañon*, At the mouth of a cannon. *Cañon de batir*, Battering piece of ordnance. *Cañon de campaña*, Field-piece. *Cañon de cruzia*, Gun of a row-galley. *Cañon de proa*, (Naút.) Bow-chase. *Cañon reforzado*, A reinforced cannon. 8. *Cañon de candalero*, Tube of a candlestick. 9. *Cañon de chimenea*, Funnel, the shaft of a chimney, the passage for the smoke. 10. *Cañon de escalera*, Well of a staircase; that is, the cavity in which it stands from the top to the bottom. 11. One of the four spindles of the bar of a velvet loom. *Cañones*, Bits of a horse's bridle.

CAÑONÁZO, *sm.* 1. Large piece of ordnance. 2. Cannon-shot.

CAÑONCÍCO, ÍLLO, Y ÍTO, *sm.* Small cannon.

CAÑONEÁR, *va.* To cannonade.—*vr.* To cannonade each other.

CAÑONÉO, *sm.* Cannonade.

CAÑONÉRA, *sf.* 1. Embrasure through which a cannon is pointed. 2. Large tent.

CAÑONERÍA, *sf.* The whole of the pipes of an organ.

CAÑÓTA SUAVE, *sf.* (Bot.) Yellow-seeded soft grass. Holcus saccharatus *L.*

CAÑUCÉLA ó CAÑUÉLA, *sf.* Small cane or reed. *Cañuela descollúda*, (Bot.) Large fescue-grass. Festuca elatior *L.*

CAÑUTÁZO, *sm.* (Bax.) Information, private accusation, suggestion, whisper, tale. *Fue con su cañutazo*, He went to carry his tale.

CAÑUTERÍA, *sf.* V. *Cañonería.*

CAÑUTÍLLO, *sm.* 1. Small tube or pipe. 2. Bugle, small glass tubes of different colours, stitched to the tassels and flounces of women's gowns, to make them appear more brilliant. *Cañutillo de hilo de oro ó de plata para bordar*, Quill of gold or silver twist for embroidery.

Cañúto, *sm.* 1. Part of a cane from knot to knot. 2. Pipe made of wood or metal. 3. Pin-case. 4. Blast, gust. V. *Soplo*. 5. Informer, tale-bearer. V. *Soplon*. [Swietenia mahogani *L.*

Caóba ó Caóbana, *sf.* (Bot.) Mahogany tree.

Cáos, *sm.* 1. Chaos, the confused mass of the universe before the creation. 2. Confusion.

Cóstra, *sf.* (Ant.) V. *Claustro*.

Caoúp, *sm.* Caoup, an American tree with leaves like an apple-tree, and fruit like an orange.

Cápa, *sf.* 1. Cloak, a large outer garment without sleeves, worn by gentlemen over the rest of their clothes. 2. Tegument, cover, layer. 3. Coat or hair of a horse. 4. (Met.) Cloak, pretence, or pretext. 5. Property, fortune. V. *Caudal*. 6. Large quadruped in America, which brays like an ass, resembles a large hog in shape, and feeds upon fish. 7. (Among Bell-founders) Third mould used in casting bells. 8. Coat of paint put over another. *Capa del cielo*, (Met.) Canopy of heaven. *Capa de rey*, (Ant.) Kind of linen. *Capa magna*, Pontifical cope worn by bishops when they officiate. *Capa pluvial*, A pluvial or choir cope worn by prelates in processions. *Capa del timon*, (Naút.) Rudder-coat, or tarred canvass, put on the head of the rudder, near the helm-port. *Capa de fogonaduras*, (Naút.) Mast-coat, or tarred canvass, put about the mast near the partners. *Capa de los costados, fondos, palos y vergas*, (Naút.) Coat of tar, pitch, resin, tallow, and other materials, with which the sides of a ship's bottom, masts, and yards, are payed or covered, to preserve them from the weather. *Capa y sombrero*, (Naút.) Hat-money, allowance per ton to the captain on his cargo. *Capa rota*, (Met.) Emissary sent in a disguised manner to execute some important commission. *Andar ó ir de capa caida*, To be down in the mouth, or crest-fallen. *Defender una cosa á capa y espada*, To defend a thing with all one's might. *Echar la capa al toro*, (Met.) To expose one's self to danger. *Estar ó estarse á la capa*, (Met.) To have a good or sharp look-out. *Gente de capa parda*, Common country-people, whose chief dress is a brown frieze cloak. *Hombre de buena capa*, A man of genteel address. *Gente de capa negra*, Townsmen of a decent appearance and situation in life. *Ministro de capa y espada*, Counsellor by brevet, though not brought up to the bar. *Puerto de arrebata capas*, Windy place where cloaks are troublesome. *Quitar ó quitarse la capa*, To gamble the shirt off one's back. *Sacar bien su capa*, (Met.) To disengage one's self from arduous difficulties. *Tirar á uno de la capa*, To pull any one by the cloak, to warn him of an impending danger. *A la capa*, (Naút.) Lying-to. *De capa y gorra*, In a plain manner.

Capacéte, *sm.* Helmet, casque.

Capácha, *sf.* 1. Frail, hamper. V. *Capacho*. 2. Frail-basket. 3. (Vulg.) The religious order of St. John of God.

Capacházo, *sm.* Blow given with a basket.

Capachéro, *sm.* He who carries things in baskets.

Capácho, *sm.* 1. Frail, hamper, large basket. 2. *Capacho de albañil*, Bricklayer's hod, in which mortar is carried. 3. (In Oil-mills) Bass-frail, through which the oil is filtered. 4. Mendicant hospitaller, who collects charity for the sick. 5. (Orn.) Common owl, barn-owl. Strix flammea *L.*

Capacidád, *sf.* 1. Capacity, the power of receiving and containing a thing. 2. Extent of a place. 3. Opportunity or means of executing a thing. 4. (Naút.) Bulk or burthen of a ship. 5. (Met.) Talent, genius, mental ability.

Capáda, *sf.* 1. Any thing wrapt up and carried in a person's cloak. 2. Lark. V. *Alondra*.

Capádo, da, *pp.* Castrated.

Capadór, *sm.* 1. One whose business is to geld or castrate. 2. Instrument used in gelding or castrating.

Capadúra, *sf.* 1. Act of gelding or castrating. 2. Scar which remains after castration.

Capár, *va.* 1. To geld, to castrate. 2. (Met.) To curtail, to diminish one's authority, income, &c.

Caparazón, *sm.* 1. Carcass of a fowl stripped of all its flesh. 2. Caparison, a sort of cover put over the saddle of a horse. 3. Cover of a coach, or other things, made of oil cloth. 4. (Mur.) Frail made of bass, in which horses feed when out of the stable.

Capárra, *sf.* 1. Sheep-louse. V. *Garrapata*. 2. Earnest, money given to confirm a bargain. 3. V. *Alcaparra*.

Caparílla, *sf.* A small tick, which molests bees.

Caparrón, *sm.* (Ant.) Bud of a vine or tree.

Caparrósa y Caparros, *s.* Copperas, green vitriol, sulphat of iron.

Capatáz, *sm.* 1. Overseer, a superintendent. 2. One who is charged with receiving the marked metal which is to be coined in the mint 3. Steward who superintends a farm. 4. Warden of a company or guild.

Capáz, *a.* 1. Capacious, able to hold other things. 2. Ample, spacious, roomy, wide. 3. (Met.) Fit, apt, suitable. 4. (Met.) Learned, ingenious, capable. *Capaz de prueba*, Capable of trial; what may be proved. *Hacerse capaz de alguna cosa*, (Met.) To render one's self master of a thing, to acquire a complete knowledge of it.

Capáza, *sf.* (Arag.) V. *Capacho*.

Capazménte, *ad.* Capaciously, amply; with capacity.

Capázo, *sm.* 1. Large frail or basket made of bass. 2. Blow given with a basket.

Capazón, *sm.* Very large frail made of bass.

Capcióso, sa, *a.* Captious, insidious, artful.

Capciosaménte, *ad.* Insidiously, captiously.

Capeadór, *sm.* Cloak-stealer.

Capeár, *va.* 1. To strip or rob one of a cloak in any inhabited place. 2. (Naút.) To try, or lay to. 3. To challenge a bull with one's cloak.

Capél, *sm.* (Arag.) Pod or ball of a silk-worm.

Capéla, *sf.* Star of the first magnitude in the left shoulder of the constellation Auriga.

Capelardiénte, *sf.* V. *Capilla ardiente*.

Capelláda, *sf.* Toe-piece put to the forepart of a shoe.

Capellán, *sm.* 1. Chaplain, a clergyman who is preferred to an ecclesiastical benefice. 2.

Clergyman who says mass in a private family. *Capellan de navio*, Chaplain of the navy. *Capellan de regimiento*, Chaplain of a regiment.
Capellanía, *sf.* Foundation or revenue settled and established by some person, and erected into an ecclesiastical benefice by the bishop.
Capellár, *sm.* Moorish cloak, worn in Spain.
Capelléta, *sf.* (Ant.) Hood, a cover for the head.
Capellína, *sf.* 1. Head-piece of a helmet, or casque. 2. Hood worn by country-people. 3. (Ant.) Trooper armed with a helmet.
Capélo, *sm.* 1. Duty, or dues, received in ancient times by bishops from their clergy. 2. (Ant.) Hat. V. *Sombrero*. 3. Red hat, or cap of a cardinal. [cloak.
Capéo, *sm.* Act of challenging a bull with a
Capéon, *sm.* Yearling or young bull challenged with a cloak.
Capéro, *sm.* Priest who carries the cope, or pluvial, in cathedral and collegiate churches.
Caperóles, *sm. pl.* (Naút.) V. *Coronamiento*.
Caperucíta ó Caperucílla, *sf.* Small hood.
Caperúza, *sf.* Cap ending in a point which inclines towards the back part of the head. *Caperuza de chimenea*, Covering of the top of a chimney, which consists of bricks or tiles set up in a pyramidal form. *Caperuza de fogon*, (Naút.) Hood of the caboose or cookroom. *Caperuza de palo*, Hood of a masthead when the ship is unrigged. *Dar en caperuza*, (Met.) To frustrate or disconcert one's views and designs.
Caperuzón, *sm.* Large hood.
Capialzádo, *sm.* Arch, sloping on the outside, and indented on the inside.
Capibára, *sm.* A kind of fish.
Capíchola, *sf.* Kind of silk stuff.
Capidéngue, *sm.* Small cloak, worn by ladies.
Capiéllo, *sm.* (Gal. y Ant.) V. *Capillo*.
Capigorrísta, *sm.* (Bax.) V. *Capigorron*.
Capigorrón, *sm.* 1. Vagabond who strolls and roves idly about; a parasite. 2. (Extr.) Student who has taken the minor orders, and will not take any more.
Capíl, *sm.* Little cap or hood.
Capilár, *a.* Capillary; applied to the small veins and arteries of the human body, or strait tubes.
Capílla, *sf.* 1. Hood to cover and defend the head. 2. Cowl, the hood of a monk or friar. 3. Chapel. 4. Band of musicians, paid to play and sing in a chapel. 5. Chapter or assembly of collegians, to treat on the affairs of their college. 6. (Among Printers) Proof, the rough draught of a sheet when first taken. 7. Portable chapel for military corps. *Caza de capilla*, (Naút.) Chest for chapel ornaments. *Capilla ardiente*, Room where a dead body lies in state, lighted up or set off with many lights. *Estar en la capilla*, To prepare for death; spoken of criminals who are in the chapel of a prison, previous to their being carried to the place of execution: (Fam.) To await with impatience the issue of an affair.
Capilláda, *sf.* A hoodful of any thing.
Capilléja y Capillíta, *sf.* Small chapel.
Capilléjo, *sm.* 1. Small hood. 2. Skein of silk for sewing.
Capillér ó Capilléro, *sm.* Clerk or sexton who has the care of a chapel; a church-warden

Capilléta, *sf.* 1. Small chapel. 2. Hood w[orn] by the knights of Calatrava.
Capíllo, *sm.* 1. Child's cap. 2. Fee paid to c[ler]gymen for baptizing a child. 3. Lining under the toe-piece of a shoe. 4. Hood [of a] hawk. 5. Bud or germ of a rose. 6. Net [for] catching rabbits. 7. Colander through w[hich] wax is strained. 8. (Ant.) Kind of cowl w[hich] served the peasantry for hat and cloak. [*Ca*]*pillo de hierro*, Helmet. *Seda dé todo capi*[*llo*], Coarse sort of silk.
Capillúdo, da, *a.* Resembling the hood [or] cowl of a monk.
Capinegót, *sm.* Riding coat without sleeves.
Capirón, *sm.* (Ant.) Covering for the head.
Capirotáda, *sf.* Sort of American paste, m[ade] up of herbs, eggs, garlic, and spice.
Capiróte, *sm.* 1. Ancient cover for the h[ead], at present only worn by doctors in the univ[er]sities. 2. Sort of half gown worn by some [of] the collegians of Salamanca. 3. Sharp-poin[ted] white or black cap, worn in processions. [4. *Ton*]*to de capirote*, Blockhead, ignorant fool. [4.] *Capirote de colmena*, Cover of a bee-h[ive] when it is full of honey. 5. V. *Papiróte*.
Capiroténo, *a.* Accustomed to carry a ho[od]; applied to a hawk.
Capisáyo, *sm.* Garment which serves both [as] a cloak and riding coat.
Capiscól, *sm.* (In Toledo) Precentor; s[ub]chanter.
Capiscolía, *sf.* Office and dignity of a prec[en]tor.
Capíta, *sf.* Small cloak.
Capitación, *sf.* Poll-tax.
Capitál, *sm.* 1. Sum of money put out at int[er]est. 2. Fortune of a husband at the time of [his] marriage. 3. Capital stock of a merchant [or] trading company. 4. (Fort.) Line dra[wn] from the angle of a polygon to the point [of] the bastion and the middle of the gorge.— Principal or chief city of a country.
Capitál, *a.* 1. Belonging or relating to t[he] head. *Remedio capital*, Remedy good for t[he] head. 2. Principal, capital, essential. *Enemi*[*go*] *capital*, Principal enemy. *Error capital*, Ca[pi]tal error. *Letra capital*, Capital letter. *Pec*[*ca*]*dos capitales*, Capital sins. *Pena capit*[*al*], Capital punishment.
Capitalísta, *sm.* Capitalist, possessor of fun[ds].
Capitalménte, *ad.* Capitally, mortally.
Capitán, *sm.* 1. Captain, a military officer wh[o] commands a company. 2. Commander-in-chi[ef] of an army. 3. Ringleader of a band of ro[b]bers. 4. *Capitan á guerra*, The mayor or chi[ef] magistrate of a place, invested with a power [to] direct military affairs. 5. *Capitan de bander*[*a*], (Naút.) Captain of the fleet. *Capitan de fr*[*a*]*gata*, He who has the command and rank [of] a lieutenant-colonel. *Capitan de navio*, [He] who has the command and rank of colon[el]. *Capitan de guardias de corps*, A captain [of] the king's life-guards. *Capitan general*, Con[m]mander-in-chief of an army, of a fleet, or lord-lieutenant of a county or province. *Cap*[*i*]*tan de puerto*, (Naút.) Port-captain. *Capita*[*n*] *del puerto*, (Naút.) Harbour-master, wat[er] bailiff. *Capitan de gallinas de un navio d*[*e*] *guerra*, (Naút.) Poulterer of a man of wa[r].

Capitan de maestranza en los arsenales, (Naút.) Store-keeper in a dock-yard. *Capitan de llaves en las plazas de armas*, Town-major in strong places. 6. (In the Wool Trade) Overseer who superintends the washing of wool.

Capitána, *sf.* Admiral's ship.

Capitanázo, *sm.* Great warrior; an able general.

Capitaneár, *va.* 1. To have the command in chief of an army. 2. To head a troop of people, though they be not military men.

Capitanía, *sf.* 1. Commission and employment of a captain. 2. Company of officers and soldiers commanded by a captain. 3. Military government of a province. 4. Chief authority, power, command.

Capitél, *sm.* 1. Spire over the dome of a church. 2. (Arq.) Capital, head or uppermost part of a column or pilaster.

Capítol, *sm.* (Ant.) V. *Capítulo y cabildo*.

Capitolíno, na, *a.* Belonging or relating to the Capitol.

Capitólio, *sm.* Capitol, a celebrated public building at Rome.

Capitón, *sm.* (Ict.) Pollard, chub. Cyprinus cephalus L.

Capitóso, sa, *a.* Obstinate, capricious, whimsical.

Capítula, *sf.* Part of the prayers read at divine service.

Capitulación, *sf.* 1. Agreement or convention relative to some important affair. *Capitulacion de matrimonio*, Articles of intermarriage, matrimonial contract. 2. (Mil.) Surrender of a place on certain terms and conditions.

Capitulár, *sm.* One who has the right of voting in a civil or ecclesiastical community.

Capitulár, *a.* Belonging or relating to a chapter.

Capitulár, *va.* 1. To conclude an agreement, to draw up the articles of a contract. 2. (Mil.) To capitulate, to settle the terms on which a place is to be surrendered. 3. (For.) To impeach, to accuse by public authority.—*vn.* To sing prayers at divine service.

Capitulário, *sm.* Book which contains the prayers to be read or sung at divine service.

Capitularménte, *ad.* According to the rules or laws of a chapter.

Capituléro, *sm.* y *a.* Capitular; capitulary.

Capítulo, *sm.* 1. Chapter, meeting or assembly of a cathedral for the election of prelates, or to deliberate on other ecclesiastical matters. 2. Meeting or assembly of any secular community or corporation. 3. Chapter, the division or section of a book or other writing. 4. Charge preferred against a person for neglect of duty. 5. *Capítulos matrimoniales*, Articles of intermarriage; conditions of the matrimonial contract. *Dar un capítulo*, (Met.) To lecture or reprimand severely. *Ganar ó perder capítulo*, (Met.) To carry or lose one's point.

Capnítis, *sf.* Sort of cadmia.

Capnománte, *sm.* Fortune-teller by the help of smoke.

Cápo, *sm.* (Ant.) V. *Cabo*.

Capóc, *sm.* Bark of the capoc-tree, which produces very fine cotton.

Capoládo, *sm.* 1. Minced meat, or meat cut into small pieces and dressed. 2. Act of cutting or tearing into ends and bits.

Capolár, *va.* 1. To mince or chop meat into very small bits. 2. (Mur.) To behead, to decapitate.

Capón, *sm.* 1. Castrated person or brute. 2. Capon, a castrated cock fattened for use. 3. Fillip on the head, a jerk of the finger let go from the thumb. 4. (Gal.) Fagot, a bundle of brushwood for fuel. 5. (Naút.) Anchor-stopper at the cat-head. 6. *Capon de galera*, Kind of salmagundi made on board of row-galleys, and composed chiefly of biscuit, oil, vinegar, and garlic. *Capon de ceniza*, Stroke on the forehead with a dust-bag.

Capóna, *sf.* Sort of Spanish dance. *Llave capona*, Key worn by a lord of the bed-chamber, who is such by brevet only, and without performing the duty of that office.

Caponádo, da, *pp.* Tied together, such as branches of vines.

Caponár, *va.* 1. To tie up the branches of vines, that they may not obstruct the tilling of the ground. 2. To cut, to curtail, to diminish.

Caponéra, *sf.* 1. Coop, pen, or inclosure to fatten capons and other poultry. 2. (Met.) Place where one lives well at other people's expense. 3. (Fort.) Caponier, a passage under a dry moat to the outworks. *Estar metido en caponera*, To be locked up in a jail.

Caporál, *sm.* 1. Chief, ringleader. 2. (Ant.) Commander of a division of ships.

Capóta, *sf.* (Manuf.) Head of the teasel or fuller's thistle, used to raise the nap on woollen cloth.

Capóte, *sm.* 1. Sort of cloak with a round lined cape, commonly made of coarse camblot, to keep off the rain. 2. (Met.) Austere, angry look or mien. 3. Thick cloud or mist hanging over a mountain. 4. (In some Games at Cards) Capot, when one player wins all the tricks. *Dar capote*, (Met.) To leave a guest or visitor without a dinner, for coming late. *Á mi capote*, In my opinion, according to my way of thinking. *Capote de centinela*, A sentinel's great-coat, or watch-coat.

Capotéro, *sm.* One who make or sells cloaks.

Capotíllo, *sm.* Short cloak worn by women. *Capotillo de dos faldas*, Short, loose jacket fast before and behind, and open on both sides.

Capotón, *sm.* Large wide coat.

Capotúdo, da, *a.* Frowning. V. *Ceñudo*.

Caprícho, *sm.* 1. Caprice, whim, fancy. 2. (Mús.) Irregular but pleasing composition. 3. (Pint.) Invention or design of a painting. *Hombre de capricho*, Queer, whimsical fellow.

Caprichosaménte, *ad.* In a capricious or obstinate manner.

Caprichóso, sa, *a.* 1. Capricious, whimsical, obstinate. 2. Fanciful, full of imagination and invention.

Caprichúdo, da, *a.* Obstinate, stubborn.

Capricórnio, *sm.* 1. Capricorn, the tenth sign of the zodiac. 2. Cuckold, one that is married to an adulteress.

Caprimúlga, *sf.* Goat-sucker, a kind of owl.

Capríno, na, *a.* (Poét.) Goatish. V. *Cabruno*.

Capsário, *sm.* One who guards the clothes of persons who are going to bathe.

CÁPSULAS, *sf. pl.* Seminal capsules of plants.

CAPTÁR, *va.* To captivate, to engage the benevolence of another, to win by soft and endearing words.

CAPTIVÁR, *va.* V. *Cautivar.*

CAPTIVIDÁD, *sf.* V. *Cautividad.*

CAPTÚRA, *sf.* Capture, seizure, the apprehension of a criminal, or caption of a debtor.

CAPTURÁR, *va.* To apprehend, to take up, to arrest.

CAPÚCHA, *sf.* 1. Circumflex (^), an accent used to regulate the pronunciation. 2. Hood of a woman's cloak.

CAPUCHÍNA, *sf.* 1. Capuchin nun who follows the rules of the order of St. Francis, and goes barefooted. 2. (Bot.) Indian cress, nasturtium. Tropæolum *L.* *Capuchinas,* (Naút.) Crotches and knees.

CAPUCHÍNO, *sm.* Capuchin monk, of the order of St. Francis, who is barefooted, and wears his beard.

CAPUCHÍNO, NA, *a.* Relating or appertaining to Capuchin friars or nuns. *Chupa capuchina,* Waistcoat with a back of an inferior stuff.

CAPÚCHO, *sm.* Cowl or hood forming part of a monk's dress.

CAPULÍN, *sm.* (Bot.) An American fruit resembling a cherry.

CAPULLÍTO, *sm.* Small pod of a silk worm.

CAPÚLLO, *sm.* 1. Pod of a silk-worm. 2. Flax knotted at the end, which knot resembles the pod of a silk-worm. 3. Germ or bud of roses and other flowers. 4. Coarse stuff made of spun silk. *Seda de capullos,* Ferret-silk, grogram yarn. 5. Shell of an acorn.

CAPUMPÉBA, *sf.* (Bot.) Name of a Brasil plant.

CAPÚZ, *sm.* 1. (Ant.) Kind of long morning-gown formerly worn. 2. (Ant.) Old-fashioned cloak.

CAPUZÁR, *va.* *Capuzar un bazel,* (Naút.) To sink a ship by the head.

CAQUÉXIA, *sf.* (Med.) Cachexy, deranged constitution.

CAQUÍMIA, *sf.* An imperfect metallic substance.

CAR, *sf.* (Naút.) Extreme end of the mizen-yard and mizen.

CAR, *ad.* (Ant.) V. *Porque.*

CÁRA, *sf.* 1. Face, visage, countenance, the cast of the features. *Fulano me recibió con buena cara,* He received me with a cheerful countenance. *Fulana me mostró mala cara,* I was received by her with a frown. 2. Cover of melted sugar for pastry. 3. Presence of a person. 4. Surface of a thing. *Cara de acelga,* Pale, sallow face. *Cara de pasqua,* Smiling, cheerful countenance. *Cara de pocos amigos,* Churlish look, froward countenance. *Cara de vaqueta ó de bronze,* Brazen face. *Cara de viernes santo,* Lean, meagre face. *Cara de carton,* Wrinkled face. *Cara empedrada ó apedreada,* A face pitted by the small pox. *Hacer la cara,* (In Tar Manufactories) To make an incision in a pine-tree in order to extract the resin. *Càra de cebo,* Pale face. *A' cara descubierta,* Openly, plainly. *Andar con la cara descubierta,* To act in a plain and open manner; to proceed with frankness and without evasion or reserve. *A' primera cara,* At first sight. *Dar á alguno con las puertas en la cara,* To shut the door in one's face. *Dar en cara,* (Met.) To reproach, to upbr *Dar el sol de cara,* To have the sun in o face. *Decirselo en su cara,* (Met.) To tell to his face. *Hacer cara,* To face an ene *Hombre de dos caras,* Double dealer, an sidious artful fellow. *La cara se le dice,* face betrays him. *Lavar la cara á algu* (Met.) To flatter, to please with blandi ments. *Lavar la cara á alguna cosa,* brush up, to clean; *e. g.* a painting, house coach. *No conocer la cara al miedo ó á la cessidad,* To be a stranger to fear or distr *No sabe en donde tiene la cara,* He does know his profession or duty. *No tener c para hacer ó decir alguna cosa,* Not to h the face or courage to say a thing. *No vol la cara atrás,* (Met.) To pursue with sp and perseverance. *Volver á la cara las labras injuriosas,* To retort or return abus language. *Salir á la cara el contento, la fermedad, la vergüenza,* Satisfaction, infir ty, shame, to be expressed in the face. *Ca á cara,* Face to face. *De cara,* Opposite, o against, regarding in front.

CARÁBA, *sf.* (Naút.) Kind of vessel used in Archipelago.

CÁRABE, *sm.* Amber.

CARABÉLA, *sf.* 1. (Naút.) Long, narrow, thr masted vessel. 2. Large basket or tray carry provisions in.

CARABELÓN, *sm.* (Naút.) Brig or brigantine.

CARABÍNA, *sf.* 1. Fowling-piece. 2. Carbine carabine, a small firelock used by caval *Carabina rayada,* Rifle carabine.

CARABINÁZO, *sm.* Report of a carabine, eff of a carabine shot.

CARABINÉRO, *sm.* 1. Carabinier, a horse-soldi armed with a carabine. 2. (In the Spani service) Kind of light horse attached to eve regiment of cavalry.

CÁRABO, *sm.* 1. (Ict.) Sort of crab or cockle. (Orn.) Large horn owl. 3. (Ant.) Kind vessel. V. *Caraba.* 4. Kind of setting do 5. Earth beetle. Carabus *L.*

CARÁCHE, *sm.* Kind of scab incident to Per vian sheep.

CARACÓA, *sf.* Small row-barge used in the Ph lippine islands.

CARACÓL, *sm.* 1. Small cone in a clock or watc round which the chain is wound. 2. Snail. slimy animal, some of which have shells o their backs. *Caracol marino,* Periwinkle. Winding stair-case. 4. Oblique pace in th manege. *Hacer caracoles,* (Met.) To car cole, to go to and fro. *No se le da un caraco* It does not matter, it is not worth a rush.

CARACÓLA, *sf.* A small whitish-shell snail.

CARACOLEÁR, *vn.* To CARACOLE.

CARACOLÉJO, *sm.* Small snail, or shell of a snai

CARACOLÉRO, RA, *s.* One who gathers and sell snails.

CARACÓLI, *sm.* Kind of metallic composition re sembling pinchbeck.

CARACOLÍLLA, *sf.* Small snail-shell.

CARACOLÍLLO, *sm.* 1. Small snail. 2. (Bot. Snail-flowered kidney bean. Phaseolus cara calla *L.* 3. Sort of purple-coloured thread *Caracolillos,* Sort of shell-work wrought o the edgings of clothes by way of ornament.

Caracolíto, *sm.* Small snail.
Caracón, *sm.* (Ant.) Kind of small vessel.
Carácter, *sm.* 1. Character, distinctive quality of persons and things. 2. Adventitious quality impressed by a post or office. 3. Letter used in writing or printing. 4. Mark put upon sheep.
Característicamente, *ad.* In a characteristic manner.
Característico, ca, *a.* Characteristic.
Caracterizádo, da, *a.* Distinguished for eminent qualities or talents. *Es hombre muy caracterizado*, He is a man endowed with uncommon talents.
Caracterizár, *va.* 1. To characterize, to distinguish a person or thing by peculiar qualities. *Le caracterizáron de sabio*, He was classed among wise men. 2. To confer a distinguished employment, dignity, or office. 3. To mark, to point out.
Caracúcho, cha, *a.* (Ant.) Mouse-coloured.
Caradelánte, (Ant.) V. *En adelante.*
Caráดo, da, *a.* Faced. This adjective is always joined to the adverbs *bien* or *mal*; *e. g. Bien carado*, Pretty faced; *Mal carado*, Ill faced.
Caragách, *sm.* Kind of cotton.
Caramanchón, *sm.* Garret. V. *Camaranchon.*
Caramángeza, *sf.* Chinese medicinal drug.
Carámba, *interj.* (Vulg.) Hah, strange!
Carámbano, *sm.* Icicle, a shoot of ice broken off from a large piece.
Carambóla, *sf.* 1. Manner of playing at the billiard table. 2. Method of playing the game at cards, called *Revesino.* 3. (Met.) Device or trick to cheat or deceive. 4. East India fruit.
Carambolear, *vn.* To play the *carambola.*
Carambolero, *sm.* Player at *carambola.*
Carambú, *sm.* (Bot.) Willow herb.
Caramél, *sf.* (Ict.) Kind of pilchard.
Caraméla, *sf.* (Ant.) V. *Caramillo.*
Caramélo, *sm.* Kind of lozenge made of sugar, oil of sweet almonds, and other ingredients.
Caraménte, *ad.* 1. Dearly, at an high price. 2. Bitterly, severely.
Caramiéllo, *sm.* Kind of hat formerly worn.
Caramillár, *vn.* To play on the flagelet.
Caramilléras, *sf. pl.* Pot-hooks.
Caramíllo, *sm.* 1. Flagelet, a small flute. 2. (Bot.) Glasswort, saltwort. Salsola kali *L.* 3. Heap of things confusedly jumbled together. 4. Deceit, fraudulent trick. 5. Pickthanking, tale-carrying. *Armar un caramillo*, To raise disturbances, to excite dissension.
Caramúyo, *sm.* Kind of sea-snail. Nerita *L.*
Caramuzál, *sm.* Transport vessel used by the Moors.
Caránque, *sm.* Kind of flat fish in the West Indies.
Carantamáula, *sf.* 1. Hideous mask or visor. 2. (Met.) Ugly, hard-featured person.
Carantóña, *sf.* 1. Hideous mask or visor. 2. Old coarse woman who paints and dresses in style, in order to please. *Carantóñas*, Caresses, soft words, and acts of endearment to wheedle or coax a person.
Carantoñéro, *sm.* Flatterer, wheedler, cajoler.
Caráña, *sf.* Kind of resinous American gum.
Caráos, *sm.* Act of drinking a full bumper to one's health.
Carápa, *sf.* Oil of a nut, the fruit of an American tree, which is said to cure the gout.

Carapúza, V. *Caperuza.*
Caraqueño, ña, *a.* Belonging to Caraccas.
Caraschúlli, *sm.* Indian shrub resembling a caper-bush.
Carátula, *sf.* 1. Mask made of pasteboard. 2. Cover for the face to defend it from bees, musquitoes, &c. 3. (Met.) Band of players.
Caratuléro, *sm.* One whose trade is to make or sell masks.
Caráuz, *sm.* (Ant.) V. *Caraos.*
Cárava, *sf.* (Ant.) Meeting of country people on festive occasions.
Caravána, *sf.* 1. (Naút.) Sea-campaign performed by the knights of Malta. 2. Caravan, a company of traders travelling together, for security, through deserts. *Hacer ó correr caravanas*, (Met.) To take a variety of steps for obtaining some end.
Caravéla, *sf.* Kind of light vessel easily navigated.
Caravenéra, *sf.* Caravansary, a large public building for the reception and accommodation of caravans.
Caravéro, *sm.* Loiterer, one who neglects his duty for the purpose of frequenting *caravas.*
Caráy, *sm.* Tortoise-shell. V. *Carey.*
Caráza, *sf.* Broad large face.
Cárbaso, *sm.* 1. (Ant.) Kind of fine flax. 2. (Poét.) Sail of a ship. 3. An ancient short petticoat coming only to the knee.
Carbón, *sm.* 1. Charcoal, coal made by burning wood under a cover of earth or turf. 2. *Carbon de piedra*, Pit-coal. 3. Black pencil. V. *Carboncillo.* 4. (Ant.) Blot, stain, spot. V. *Mancha.*
Carbonáda, *sf.* 1. Broiled chop or steak. 2. Kind of pancake made of milk, eggs, and sugar, and afterwards fried in butter.
Carbonadílla, *sm.* Small *carbonada.*
Carboncíllo, *sm.* 1. Small coal. 2. Black crayon made of rosemary wood, heath, hazel, or willow, burnt in an iron tube, and quenched in ashes.
Carbóncol, *sm.* V. *Carbunclo.*
Carbonéra, *sf.* Place where charcoal is made and preserved for use.
Carbonería, *sf.* Coal-yard, coal-shed.
Carbonéro, *sm.* 1. Charcoal-maker, collier, a digger of coals. 2. Dealer in coals. 3. (Naút.) Ship employed in the coal trade.
Carbonizádo, da, *a.* Carbonated, impregnated or united with carbon.
Carbúnclo y Carbúnco, *sm.* 1. Carbuncle, a precious stone resembling a ruby. 2. Red pustule or pimple.
Carbuncóso, sa, *a.* Of the nature of a carbuncle, or resembling it.
Carbúnculo y Carbúncula, *s.* V. *Carbunclo.*
Carcajáda, *sf.* Loud laughter, horse-laugh.
Carcamál, *sm.* Nick-name of old people, especially of old women.
Carcañál ó Carcañár, *sm.* Heel-bone. V. *Calcañar.*
Carcápuli, *sm.* 1. (Bot.) Indian yellow orange of Java and Malabar. 2. (Bot.) The large carcapulla-tree in America, which produces a sweet fruit resembling a cherry.
Cárcava, *sf.* 1. Inclosure, mound, hedge, ditch. 2. (Ant.) Pit or grave for interring the dead

Carcavár ó Carcavear, *va.* To fortify a camp.
Carcavéra, *sf.* Vulgar prostitute about ditches.
Carcávo, *sm.* (Ant.) The cavity of the abdomen.
Carcavón, *sm.* Large and deep ditch.
Carcáx y Carcáxa, *sf.* 1. Kind of fire-engine. 2. Ribbon with a case at the end, in which the cross is borne in a procession. 3. Quiver. 4. Ornament of the ankle worn by the Moors. V. *Azorca.*
Cárcel, *sf.* 1. Prison, a building in which criminals are confined. 2. (Among Carpenters) Wooden cramp used to keep glued planks fast together, that they may join well. 3. (Cast.) Two small cart-loads of fire-wood. 4. Cheek of a printing-press. *Cárceles,* (Among Weavers) Cog-reeds of a loom.
Carceláge y Carceráge, *sm.* Prison-fees.
Carcelería, *sf.* 1. Imprisonment. 2. Bail or security given for the appearance of a prisoner set at liberty. 3. (Ant.) Whole number of persons confined in a jail.
Carceléro, *sm.* Jail-keeper. *Fiador carcelero,* One who is bail or surety for a prisoner.
Carcerár, *va.* To imprison.
Carcóa, *sf.* Row-barge used in some parts of [India.
Cárcola, *sf.* Treadle, a piece of wood moved by the weaver's foot to raise and lower the stays of the loom.
Carcóma, *sf.* 1. Wood-louse, an insect which gnaws wood and timber. 2. Dust made by the wood-louse. 3. (Met.) Grief, anxious concern. 4. (Met.) One who runs by degrees through his whole fortune. 5. (Med.) Cariosity or rottenness of a bone.
Carcomér, *va.* 1. To gnaw, to corrode; applied to the wood-louse. 2. To consume a thing by degrees. 3. (Met.) To impair, gradually, health, virtue, &c.—*vr.* To decay, to decline in health, virtue, &c.
Carcomído, da, *a.* 1. Worm-eaten, consumed. 2. (Met.) Decayed, declined, impaired.
Cárda, *sf.* 1. Teazel, or teasel, the head of a thistle for raising the wool on cloth before it goes to the shearer. 2. Card, an instrument with which wool is combed, and prepared for spinning. 3. (Met.) Severe reprimand or censure. 4. (Naút.) Small vessel built snow-fashion. *Gente de la carda, ó los de la carda,* Idle street-walkers; wicked licentious people.
Cardadór, *sm.* Carder, one who combs wool.
Cardadúra, *sf.* Act of carding or combing wool.
Cardaestámbre, *sm.* (Ant.) V. *Cardador.*
Cardámino de prados, *sm.* (Bot.) Meadow-cresses, lady's smock. Cardamine pratensis *L.*
Cardamómo, *sm.* (Bot.) Cardamomum, a medicinal seed. Amomum cardamomum *L.*
Cardamóuri, *sf.* Kind of drug used for dying.
Cardár, *va.* 1. To card or comb wool, to render it fit for spinning. 2. To raise the wool on cloth with a teasel. *Cardarle á uno la lana,* (Met.) To win a large sum at play. *Cardarle á alguno la lana,* (Met.) To reprimand severely.
Cardelína, *sf.* (Orn.) Goldfinch, thistle finch. Fringilla carduelis *L.*
Cardenál, *sm.* 1. Cardinal, an eminent dignitary of the Roman Catholic Church. 2. (Orn.) Virginian nightingale, cardinal grosbeak. Loxia cardinalis *L.* 3. Weal or discoloration made by a lash or blow.
Cardenaláto, *sm.* Dignity of a cardinal.
Cardenalía, *sf.* (Ant.) V. *Cardenaláto.*
Cardenalício, cia, *a.* Belonging or appertaining to a cardinal.
Cardéncha, *sf.* 1. (Bot.) Fuller's thistle. Dipsacus fullonum *L.* 2. Card or comb, an instrument for carding or combing of wool.
Cardenchál, *sm.* Place where fuller's thistles grow.
Cardenillo, *sm.* 1. Verdigrise, rust of copper 2. Verditure, a green paint made of verdigrise
Cárdeno, na, *a.* Of a dark purple colour.
Cardéro, *sm.* Card-maker.
Cardiáca, *sf.* (Bot.) Mother-wort.
Cardiáco, ca, *a.* Cardiac, cordial; having the quality of invigorating.
Cardíal, *a.* (Ant.) Cardiacal, cardiac.
Cardialgía, *sf.* (Med.) Cardialgy, or heart-burn
Cardiálgico, ca, *a.* Belonging to cardialgy.
Cardíco ó Cardíto, *sm.* Small thistle.
Cardíllo, *sm.* (Bot.) Golden thistle. Scolymus maculatus *L. Cardillo de comer,* (Bot.) Perennial or star-thistle. Scolymus hispanicus *L*
Cardinál, *a.* Cardinal, principal, fundamental *Vientos cardinales,* Winds from the 4 cardinal points. *Virtudes cardinales,* Cardinal virtues, justice, prudence, fortitude, and temperance. *Numeros cardinales,* Cardinal numbers, absolute numbers, opposed to ordinal or relative numbers.
Cárdine, *sm.* Hinge, a joint on which a door or gate turns. *Cárdines,* Poles, the extremities of the axis of the earth.
Cardíta, *sf.* Small vessel.
Cardizál, *sm.* Land covered with thistles.
Cárdo, *sm.* 1. Artichoke. V. *Alcachofa.* 2. *Cardo silvestre ó borriqueño,* (Bot.) Wild artichoke. Carduus leucanthus *L.* 3. *Cardo aljonjero,* Sow-thistle, cardoon. Cynara carduncului *L.* 4. *Cardo hortense,* (Bot.) Chard. Culcus acarna *L.* 5. *Cardo corredor,* (Bot.) Sea-holly, field eringo. Eryngium campestre *L.* 6. *Cardo bendito ó santo,* (Bot.) Holy-thistle. Centaurea benedicta *L.* 7. *Cardo marino,* (Bot.) Globe-thistle. Carduus crispus *L.* 8. *Cardo huso,* (Bot.) Black chameleon thistle. Atractilis humilis *L. Cardo setero,* Thistle surrounded with mushrooms.
Cardón, *sm.* (Bot.) 1. Fuller's thistle. Dipsacus fullonum *L.* 2. The act and effect of carding.
Cardoncíllo, *sm.* Kind of small thistle. [wool.
Cardúcha, *sf.* Large iron comb for combing
Cardúme ó Cardúmen, *sm.* Shoal or multitude of fishes.
Carduza, *sf.* (Ant.) V. *Cardu.*
Carduzadór, *sm.* Carder. V. *Cardador.*
Carduzál, *sm.* V. *Cardizal.* [To shear cloth.
Carduzár, *va.* 1. To card or comb wool. 2. (Ant.)
Careár, *va.* 1. To confront criminals, to bring them face to face. 2. To compare. 3. To tend a drove of cattle, or flock of sheep.—*vr.* To assemble or meet for the purpose of treating on business.
Carecér, *vn.* To want, to be in need of something
Careciénte, *a.* (Ant.) Wanting.
Carecimiénto, V. *Carencia.*
Caréna, *sf.* (Naút.) 1. Careening or repairing of a ship. *Media carena,* Boot-hose-topping.

Carena mayor, Thorough repair. 2. (Poét.) Ship. 3. (Ant.) Forty days' penance on bread and water. *Dar carena*, (Met.) To blame, to find fault with, to reprimand; to banter, to joke.

Carenáge, *sm.* V. *Carenero.*

Carenár, *va.* To careen a ship, to pay a ship's bottom. *Aparejo de carenar*, Careening jeer.

Caréncia, *sf.* Want, need, the state of being deprived or in want of a thing.

Carenéro, *sm.* Careening-place.

Caréo, *sm.* 1. Confrontation, the act of bringing criminals or witnesses face to face. 2. Comparison, the act of comparing. 3. (Fort.) Front of a bastion or fortress.

Caréro, ra, *a.* Being in the habit of selling things dear.

Carestía, *sf.* 1. Scarcity, want. 2. Dearness or high price originating from scarcity.

Caréta, *sf.* 1. Mask made of pasteboard. 2. Wire-cover of the face worn by bee-keepers when they smother or examine the hives. 3. V. *Judía.*

Caréto, ta, *a.* Having the forehead marked with a white spot or stripe; applied to horses.

Caréy, *sm.* Tortoise-shell.

Caréza, *sf.* V. *Carestía.*

Cárga, *sf.* 1. Load, burthen; cargo. 2. Charge of a cannon or other fire-arms. *Carga de balas encaxonadas*, Case-shot. *Carga muerta*, Overloading, dead load. 3. Corn measure in Castile, containing four *fanegas*, or bushels. 4. Medical preparation for curing sprains and inflammations in horses and mules. 5. Impost, duty, toll, tax. *Carga real*, King's tax, land tax. 6. (Met.) Burthen of the mind. 7. (Ant.) Discharge of cannon and other fire-arms. *Carga cerrada*, Volley, a general discharge. *Carga concejil*, Municipal office which all the inhabitants of a place must serve in their turn. *Dar á uno una carga cerrada*, To scold or reprimand one severely. *Dar con la carga en tierra, ó en el suelo*, (Met.) To sink under fatigue and distress. *Echar la carga á otro*, (Met.) To throw the blame upon another. *Llevar los soldados á la carga*, (Mil.) To lead soldiers to the charge. *Volver á la carga sobre el enemigo*, To return to the charge. *Ser alguna cosa de ciento en carga*, To be a thing of little value. *Navío de carga*, (Naút.) Ship of burthen, a merchantman. *A' carga cerrada*, Boisterously, inconsiderately, without reflection. *A' cargas*, Abundantly, in great plenty. *A' cargas le vienen los regalos*, He receives loads of presents. *A' cargas va el dinero*, He spends a world of money.

Cargádas, *sf. pl.* Game at cards, in which he that wins the greatest number of tricks loses as well as he who wins no trick.

Cargadéras, *sf. pl.* (Naút.) Down-hauls, brails. *Cargadera de una vela de estay*, Down-haul of a stay-sail. *Cargaderas de las gavias*, Top-sail brails. *Aparejo de cargadera de racamente*, Down-haul tackle.

Cargadéro, *sm.* Place where goods are loaded or unloaded, shipped or unshipped. [tracted.

Cargadílla, *sf.* Increase of a debt newly con-

Cargádo, *sm.* A Spanish step in dancing, putting the right foot in the place of the left.

Cargádo, da, *a.* Loaded, full. *Cargado de espaldas*, Round-shouldered, stooping. *Estar cargado de vino*, To be top-heavy, or half-seas over.

Cargadór, *sm.* 1. Freighter, a merchant who ships and exports goods for other markets. 2. Rammer, a stick with which the charge is forced into guns. 3. He that loads great guns. 4. (Ant.) In New-Spain, he who is hired to conduct a cargo from one place to another.—*pl.* 1. (Naút.) Tackles. V. *Palanquines.* 2. Plates of copper or pallets used in gilding.

Cargaménto, *sm.* (Naút.) Cargo, freight of a ship.

Cargár, *va.* 1. To load, or carry a load; applied to men and beasts. 2. To charge the enemy, to attack the enemy with spirit and vigour. 3. To ship goods for foreign markets. *Cargar á flete*, To ship goods on freight. 4. To load or charge a gun. 5. To overload or overburthen. 6. To charge in account, to book. 7. To impose or lay on taxes. 8. To impute, to arraign, to impeach. 9. To crowd. *Cargar delantero*, (Met.) To be top-heavy or fuddled. *Cargar arriba una vela*, (Naút.) To clue up a sail. *Cargar la consideracion*, (Met.) To reflect with consideration and maturity. *Cargar la mano*, (Met.) To pursue a thing with eagerness: (Met.) To reproach with severity; to extort. *Cargar los dados*, To cog dice. *Cargar sobre uno*, To importune, tease, or molest.—*vr.* 1. To incline with the whole body towards a point or place. *El viento se ha cargado al norte*, The wind has veered to the north. 2. To charge one's own account with the sums received. 3. To maintain, to support or take a charge upon one's self.

Cargazón, *sf.* 1. Cargo or lading of a ship. 2. *Cargazon de cabeza*, Heaviness of the head. 3. *Cargazon de tiempo*, Cloudy, thick weather.

Cárgo, *sm.* 1. Burthen, loading. 2. (Madrid) Load of stones which weighs forty *arrobas*. 3. Total amount of debts and demands, statement of debtors and creditors. 4. (Met.) Employment, dignity, office. *Cargo concejil*, A municipal office. 5. (Met.) Obligation to perform something. 6. (Met.) Command or direction of a thing. 7. Fault or deficiency in the performance of one's duty. 8. *Cargo de conciencia*, Remorse, sense of guilt. *Hacer cargo á alguno de una cosa*, To charge one with a fault. *Hacer cargo de alguna cosa*, To make one's self acquainted with a thing. *Ser en cargo*, To be debtor.

Cargóso, sa, *a.* (Ant.) Grievous, weighty, injurious. [load.

Cárgue, *sm.* 1. Loading a vessel. 2. License to

Carguerío. V. *Cargamento.* [ment.

Carguéro, ra, *a.* Having an office or employ-

Carguílla y Carguíta, *sf.* Small or light load.

Carguío, *sm.* Cargo of merchandise.

Cariá, *sf.* (Arq.) 1. Fust, the body of a column. 2. V. *Caries.* [tenance.

Cariacédo, da, *a.* Having a sour-looking coun-

Cariacontecído, da, *a.* Sad, mournful, expressive of grief.

Cariacuchilládo, da, *a.* Having the face marked with cuts or gashes.

Cariádo, da, *a.* Carious, rotten.

CARIAGUILEÑO, ÑA, *a.* Long-visaged, with an aquiline or hooked nose.
CARIAMPOLLÁDO, DA, *a.* Roundfaced, plump-cheeked.
CARIÁNCHO, CHA, *a.* Broad-faced.
CARIÁTIDE, *sf.* Caryates or caryatides, columns or pilasters under the figures of women dressed in long robes.
CARÍBE, *sm.* Cannibal, man-eater, a savage, barbarous fellow.
CARIBÍTO, *sm.* A river fish of the bream species.
CARIBÓBO, BA, *a.* Having a stupid, sheepish look.
CARÍCAS, *sf. pl.* (Arag.) Sort of kidney beans.
CARICATÚRA, *sf.* Caricature.
CARÍCIA, *sf.* Caress, act of endearment.
CARICIOSAMÉNTE, *ad.* In a fondling or endearing manner.
CARICIÓSO, SA, *a.* Fondling, endearing, caressing.
CARICUÉRDO, DA, *a.* Having a serene or composed mien.
CARIDÁD, *sf.* 1. Charity, kindness, good-will, benevolence. 2. Alms, relief given to the poor. 3. Refreshment of bread and wine, which confraternities cause to be given to travellers at the church-door.
CARIDELANTÉRO, RA, *a.* Brazen-faced, impudent.
CARIDOLIÉNTE, *a.* Having a mournful countenance, expressive of grief.
CARIDÓSO, SA, *a.* V. *Caritativo.*
CÁRIES, *sf.* 1. Caries or cariosity, rottenness of the teeth or bones. 2. Pellicle or thin skin which surrounds the bone.
CARIESCRÍTO, *a.* Corrugated, shrivelled; applied to a melon.
CARIEXÊNTO, TA, *a.* Brazen-faced, impudent.
CARIFRUNCÍDO, DA, *a.* Having a face contracted into wrinkles by age or affliction.
CARIGÓRDO, DA, *a.* Having a full or plump face.
CARILÁRGO, GA, *a.* Long-visaged.
CARÍLLA, *sf.* 1. Little or small face. 2. Mask used by bee-keepers. V. *Careta.* 3. Silver coin in Aragon worth 18 *dineros*, or deniers, having the king's image on one side. 4. V. *Llana.*
CARILLÉNO, NA, *a.* Plump-faced, having a full face.
CARÍLLO, LLA, *a.* Dear, bearing a high price. 2. Dear, beloved.
CARILÚCIO, CIA, *a.* Having a shining or glossy face.
CARILLÚDO, DA, *a.* Plump-cheeked.
CARÍNA, *sf.* 1. (Arq.) Building raised by the Romans in the form of a ship. 2. (Bot.) Hard shells of fruits.
CARINCURÍNI, *sm.* An Indian tree.
CARINÉGRO, GRA, *a.* Being of a swarthy complexion.
CARINÍNFO, FA, *a.* Having a womanish face; applied to man.
CARIÑÁNA, *sf.* (Ant.) Ancient head-dress like a nun's veil.
CARÍÑO, *sm.* 1. Love, fondness, tenderness. 2. Soft or endearing expression. 3. Anxious desire of a thing.
CARIÑOSAMÉNTE, *ad.* In a fond or affectionate manner.
CARIÑÓSO, SA, *a.* 1. Affectionate, endearing, benevolent. 2. Anxiously desirous, longing.
CARIOFILÁTA, *sf.* (Bot.) Herb bennet, common avens. Geum urbanum *L.*
CARIÓSO, SA, *a.* (Ant.) Carious, liable to corruption.
CARIÓTA, *sf.* (Bot.) Wild carrot. Daucus lucidus *L.*
CARIPÁNDO, DA, *a.* Idiot-like, stupid-faced.
CARIPARÉJO, JA, *a.* y *s.* Resembling, having a similar face; likeness.
CARIRAÍDO, DA, *a.* Brazen-faced, impudent.
CARIREDÓNDO, DA, *a.* Round-faced.
CÁRIS, *sm.* Kind of ragout or fricassee much used among the Indians.
CARISÉA, *sf.* Kind of kersey.
CARÍSMA, *sm.* (Teol.) Divine gift or favour.
CARISTÍA, *sf.* 1. A small bird so called. 2. (Ant.) V. *Carestia.*
CARÍTA, *sf.* Little or small face.
CARITATÉRO, *sm.* A distributor of charity.
CARITATIVAMÉNTE, *ad.* In a charitable manner.
CARITATÍVO, VA, *a.* Charitable, of a humane and benevolent disposition.
CARLÁN, *sm.* (Arag.) He who owns the duties and jurisdiction of a district.
CARLÁNCA, *sf.* A mastiff's collar made of strong leather, and stuck full of nails, to serve as a defence against wolves. *Tener muchas carlancas,* To be very cunning or crafty.
CARLANCÓN, *sm.* (Met.) Person very subtle and crafty.
CARLANÍA, *sf.* Dignity and district of the jurisdiction of a *carlan*, an ancient magistrate in Aragon.
CARLEÁR, *vn.* To pant. V. *Jadear.*
CARLÍN, *sm.* An ancient silver coin of the reign of Charles V.
CARLÍNA, *sf.* (Bot.) Carline thistle. Carduus acaulis *L.*
CARLÍNGA, *sf.* (Naút.) Step of a mast.
CARLOÉK, *sm.* Kind of isinglass imported from Archangel.
CARMÉL, *sm.* (Bot.) Ribwort, plantain, rib-grass. Plantago lanceolata *L.*
CARMELÍTA, *s.* Carmelite, a religious man or woman of the Carmelite order.
CARMELITÁNO, NA, *a.* Belonging to the Carmelite order.
CÁRMEN, *sm.* 1. (Granada) Country-house and garden. 2. Carmelite order.
CARMENADÓR, *sm.* Teaser, one who scratches cloth for the purpose of raising the nap.
CARMENADÚRA, *sf.* Act of teasing or scratching cloth, in order to raise the nap.
CARMENÁR, *va.* 1. To prick or card wool. 2. To scratch cloth, for the purpose of raising the nap. 3. To pull out the hair of the head. V. *Repelar.* 4. To win another's money at play.
CÁRMES, *sm.* Kermes, the cochineal insect.
CARMESÍ, *sm.* 1. Cochineal powder. 2. Bright red, somewhat darkened with blue; purple.
CARMESÍN Y CARMÉSO, (Ant.) V. *Carmesí.*
CARMÍN, *sm.* 1. Carmine, a bright red or crimson pigment, made of cochineal and Roman alum. *Carmin bazo,* Pale rose colour. 2. (Bot.) Wild rose or dog-rose. Rosa canina *L.*
CARMINÁR, *va.* To expel wind.
CARMINATÍVO, *sm.* Carminative; a remedy used for expelling wind.
CARNÁDA, *sf.* Bait; a piece of meat used as a lure to catch fish or ensnare wolves.
CARNÁGE, *sm.* 1. Salt beef. 2. (Ant.) Carnage, slaughter.
CARNÁL, *a.* 1. Carnal, fleshy; proceeding from the flesh, or belonging to it. 2. Sensual, lustful, lecherous. 3. (Met.) Worldly; opposed to spiritual. 4. United by kindred.

Carnál, *sm.* Time of the year in which meat may be eaten; opposed to Lent and other fast days.

Carnalidád, *sf.* Carnality, lustfulness.

Carnalménte, *ad.* Carnally, sensually.

Carnavál, *sm.* Carnival, the feast held before Shrovetide, V. *Carnestoléndas.*

Carnáza, *sf.* 1. Fleshy part of a hide or skin. 2. Meal, consisting of an abundance of meat.

Cárne, *sf.* 1. Flesh, the fibrous and soft part of the animal body. 2. Meat; flesh intended and used for food, in contradistinction to fish. 3. Pulpous and fleshy part of fruit. 4. A boyish play with a hollow bone. *Carne de membrillo,* Pulp of quinces, boiled, cooled, and preserved. *Carne de pelo,* Flesh of small quadrupeds, as hares, rabbits, &c. *Carne de pluma,* Flesh of all sorts of fowls. *Carne momia,* Mummy, a dead body preserved by means of aromatics and balsams; (Fam.) Flesh of meat without bones; (Pint.) V. *Espalto. Carne nueva,* Meat sold at Easter, when the Lent is over, and meat is new to the people. *Carne sin hueso,* (Met.) Employment of much profit and little trouble. *Carne y sangre,* Flesh and blood, near kindred. *Echar carnes,* To grow fat. *Hacer carne,* (Ant.) To resent. *Ni es carne ni pescado,* (Met.) He is neither fish nor flesh; an insipid fellow. *Poner toda la carne en el asador,* (Met.) To hazard or stake one's all. *Ser uña y carne,* (Met.) To be hand and glove, to be intimate or familiar. *Tomar la muger en carnes,* To take a wife in her smock. *Temblar las carnes,* (Met.) To shudder with fear or horror. *En carnes,* Naked. *Carne de grajo,* (Met.) Brown, meagre woman. *Tener carne de perro,* To have much fortitude or resolution.

Carnecería y Carnescería, (Ant.) V. *Carnicería.*

Carnecica, lla, y ta, *sf.* Small excrescence of flesh rising in some part of the body.

Carnéo, ea, (Ant.) That which has flesh.

Carneráda, *sf.* Flock of sheep.

Carneráge, *sm.* Tax or duty laid on sheep.

Carnerário, *sm.* Charnel-house.

Carnereamiénto, *sm.* Poundage, penalty for the trespass of sheep.

Carnereár, *va.* To fine the proprietor of sheep which have done damage.

Carneréro, *sm.* Shepherd. V. *Pastor.*

Carneríl, *sm.* Sheep-walk, pasture for sheep.

Carnéro, *sm.* 1. Sheep, a cloven-footed quadruped which bears wool. 2. (Arag.) Sheep-skin dressed or tanned. 3. Family vault, burying-place, charnel-house. 4. (Ant.) Larder. *Carnero adalil, ó carnero manso para guia,* Bell-weather. *Carnero de simiente,* Ram kept for breeding. *Carnero ciclan,* Ridgil or ridgling. *Carnero marino,* (Ict.) White shark, Squalus carcharias *L. Carnero verde,* Hashed mutton. *No hay tales carneros,* There is no such thing.

Carnerúno, na, *a.* Resembling or belonging to sheep.

Carnestoléndas, *sf. pl.* Three carnival days before Shrove-tide, or Ash-wednesday.

Carnicería, *sf.* 1. Shambles, slaughter-house. 2. Carnage, havock, slaughter. *Hacer carnicería,* To cut away a great quantity of proud flesh. *Parece carnicería,* It is as noisy as the shambles.

Carnicéro, *sm.* 1. Butcher, one that kills animals to sell their flesh. 2. One who delights in blood and carnage. 3. Pasture-ground for fattening cattle. 4. (Fam.) Person who eats much meat.

Carnicéro, ra, *a.* 1. Carnivorous or flesh-eating; applied to animals. 2. Belonging to shambles. *Libra carnicera,* Pound for butcher's meat, which is generally double the weight of the pound for dry goods, and varies from 24 to 32 ounces.

Carnicól, *sm.* Hoof of cloven-footed animals. V. *Taba.*

Carnívoro, ra, *a.* Carnivorous, flesh-eating; applied to animals.

Carníza, *sf.* (Bax.) 1. Refuse of meat. 2. Cats' or dogs' meat.

Carnók, *sm.* Coomb, an English measure of grain or seed, containing four Winchester bushels.

Carnosidád, *sf.* 1. Proud flesh, growing on the lips of a wound, or a fleshy excrescence of any part of the body. 2. Fatness, an abundance of flesh and blood.

Carnóso, sa, y Carnúdo, da, *a.* 1. Fleshy, full of flesh. 2. Full of marrow; pulpous, applied to fruit.

Cáro, ra, *a.* 1. Dear, high-priced. 2. Dear, beloved, affectionate. *Caro bocado,* (Met.) A dear morsel. *Lo barato es caro,* Cheap things are dearest. *Tener en caro,* To estimate highly.

Cáro, *ad.* Dearly, at a high price, at too great a price.

Caróbo, *sm.* 1. Weight of the 24th part of a grain. 2. Kind of Turkish vessel.

Carócas, *sm. pl.* Caresses, endearing actions or expressions.

Carócha, *sf.* Seed or eggs, which the queen or mother bee deposits in the cells of a bee-hive.

Carochár, *va.* To lay and hatch eggs; applied to the queen bee.

Carólus, *sm.* Ancient Flemish coin, formerly current in Spain.

Caróna, *sf.* 1. Inward part of the saddle, which touches the animal's back. 2. Part of the animal's back on which the saddle lies. *Esquilar la carona,* To shear the back of a mule, which is the general custom in Spain. *Á carona,* (Ant.) Immediate to the skin or back.

Caroñóso, sa, *a.* (Ant.) Old, galled and cast off; applied to beasts of burthen.

Caroquéro, ra, *s.* Wheedler, flatterer; caressing.

Carosiéra, *sf.* 1. (Bot.) Species of the palm-tree. 2. Date, the fruit of that species of the palm-tree.

Carótas, *sf. pl.* Rolls of tobacco ground to powder.

Carótidas, *sf. pl.* The carotid arteries.

Carózo, *sm.* Pellicle, or thin skin, which covers the grains of a pomegranate.

Cárpa, *sf.* 1. (Ict.) Carp, a fresh-water fish. Cyprinus carpio *L.* 2. Part of a bunch of grapes which is torn off. 3. (Anat.) Metacarpus, a bone of the arm.

Carpanél, *sm.* Arch made in a semi-elliptic form.

Cárpe, *sm.* (Bot.) Horn-beam-tree, wych-hasel. Carpinus betulus *L.*

Carpedál, *sm.* Plantation of horn-beam-trees.

Carpentáno, na, V. *Carpetano.*

Carpenteár, *va.* V. *Arrejacár.*

Carpentería, *sf.* V. *Carpintería.*

Carpéta, *sf.* 1. Table-carpet, or other covering of a table. 2. Port-folio, a leather case in which papers are kept. 3. (Ant.) Small curtains hung before the doors of taverns. 4. (Arag.) Cover of a letter.

Carpetáno, na, *a.* Belonging to the kingdom of Toledo, formerly called *Carpetania.*

Carpintear, *va.* To do carpenter's or joiner's work.

Carpintería, *sf.* 1. Trade and business of a carpenter. 2. Shop or place where that trade is carried on.

Carpintéro, *sm.* Carpenter, joiner. *Carpintero de blanco,* Joiner who makes utensils of wood. *Carpintero de prieto ó carretas,* Cart-wright, wheel-wright. *Carpintero de obras de afuera,* Carpenter who timbers or roofs houses. *Carpintero de ribera ó de navío,* Ship-carpenter, ship-wright. *Maestro carpintero de remos,* Master oar-maker. *Segundo carpintero,* Carpenter's mate.

Carpión, *sm.* Large carp, resembling a trout.

Carpír, *vn.* To tear, to scrape, scratch, and scold.

Cárpo, *sm.* (Ant.) Wrist.

Carpobálsamo, *sm.* Fruit of the tree which yields the balm of Gilead.

Carpófago, *sm.* One who lives on fruit.

Carquésa ó Carquésia, *sf.* (In Glass-houses) Annealing furnace for tempering or cooling plate-glass.

Carquésa ó Carquéja, *sf.* (Bot.) Rest-harrow, green-weed. Genista tridentata *L.*

Carráca, *sf.* 1. Large and slow sailing ship of burthen. 2. Rattle, an instrument used instead of bells the three last days of the holy week.

Carráco, ca, *a.* Old, withered, decrepit.

Carracón, *sm.* 1. Ship of burthen of the largest size. 2. Large rattle. 3. Animal worn out with age and fatigue.

Carrál, *sm.* Barrel, butt, vat, pipe for transporting wine in carts or wagons.

Carraléja, *sf.* Black-beetle with yellow stripes, which, when lightly pressed, yields an oily substance that is much used by farriers.

Carraléro, *sm.* Cooper, one who make barrels or wooden vessels for liquids.

Carráncllo, *sm.* A blue-feathered bird, very common in Estremadura. [solemn.

Carrancúdo, da, *a.* Starched, stiff, affected,

Carránque, *sm.* A Peruvian bird like a crane.

Carrásca, *sf.* (Bot.) Kermes-oak. Quercus coccifera *L.*

Carrascál, *sm.* Plantation of kermes-oaks.

Carrásco, *sm.* (Bot.) Evergreen oak-tree. Quercus ilex *L.* [tree.

Carrascón, *sm.* (Bot.) Large evergreen oak-

Carraspáda, *sf.* Beverage made of red wine, honey, and spice, and used by common people on Christmas holidays.

Carraspánte, *a.* Harsh, acrid, strong.

Carraspéra, *sf.* Sore throat, attended with hoarseness.

Carraspíque, *sf.* (Bot.) Rock-cress, naked-stalked candy tuft. Iberis nudicaulis *L.*

Carrasquéño, ña, *a.* 1. Harsh, sharp, biting; applied to things. 2. Rough, rude, sullen; applied to persons.

Carrear y Carrejar, (Ant.) V. *Acarrear.*

Carréra, *sf.* 1. Quick movement of man or beast from one place to another. 2. Race-ground, on which horses run a race. 3. High-road, leading from one town to another. 4. (In Madrid) A street, as, *La carrera de San Francisco,* St. Francis-street. 5. Alley, a walk in a garden; an avenue leading to a house, planted with trees, in the form of a street. 6. Row of things, ranged in a line. 7. Range of iron teeth in cards for combing wool. 8. Line made by dividing and separating the hair. 9. Girder, the largest piece of timber in a floor, next to the beams. 10. Stitch in a stocking, which has broken or fallen. 11. Course and duration of life. 12. Profession of arms or letters; course or mode of action. 13. Street or high-road destined for any public procession. 14. Spanish step in dancing V. *Carrerilla. Carrera de cordelería,* Rope-walk. *Carrera de Indias,* Trade from Spain to South America. *Estar en carrera,* To be in the way of earning a livelihood. *Poner á uno en carrera,* To provide one with an employment. *No poder hacer carrera con alguno,* Not to be able to bring one to reason. *A carrera abierta,* At full speed. *De carrera,* Swiftly, inconsiderately, rashly. *Partir de carrera,* (Met.) To act in a rash and inconsiderate manner.

Carrerílla, ta, *sf.* 1. Small race or course. 2. Rapid motion with the heel and toe, back and forward, in a Spanish dance. 3. (Mús.) Rise or fall of an octave.

Carréta, *sf.* 1. Long narrow cart, drawn by oxen. 2. *Carreta cubierta,* Gallery of a siege, or the covered passage to the walls of a fortress.

Carretáda, *sf.* 1. Cart-full, cart-load. 2. Great quantity of any thing. *A' carretadas,* Copiously, in abundance.

Carretáge, *sm.* Cartage, trade with carts.

Carréte, *sm.* 1. Small reed for winding off silk or gold and silver twist. 2. Fishing pulley, or wheel, which gives line to a fish until it is exhausted with fatigue.

Carretear, *va.* 1. To convey or transport in a cart. 2. To drive a cart.—*vr.* To draw unevenly; applied to horses which are put to a cart.

Carretél, *sm.* 1. Wheel or pulley of a fishing-line. 2. (Naút.) Log-reel. 3. (Naút.) Spun-yarn-winch. 4. Rope-walk reel. 5. *Carretel de carpintero,* Carpenter's marking-line.

Carretéra, *sf.* High, public road.

Carretería, *sf.* 1. Number of carts. 2. Trade of a carman. 3. Cartwright's yard.

Carretéro, *sm.* 1. Cartwright, one whose trade is to make carts and wagons. 2. Carman, driver of a cart. *Voz de carretero,* Harsh, loud, and unpleasant voice. *Jurar como un carretero,* To swear like a carman. 3. (Astr.) Wagoner, a northern constellation.

Carretíl, *sm.* (Ant.) Cart-road.

Carretílla, *sf.* 1. Small cart. 2. Go-cart, in which children learn to walk. 3. Squib, cracker. 4. Small wheel. V. *Rodaja.* 5. Wheel-barrow. *De carretilla,* By custom; without reflection or attention. *Saber de carretilla,* To know by heart.

Carretón, *sm.* 1. Small cart in the shape of an open chest. 2. Go-cart, for children to learn to walk. 3. (Ant.) Gun-carriage. 4. *Carreton*

de lámpara, Pulley for raising or lowering lamps. 5. (Toledo) Stage for religious plays.
CARRETONÉRO, *sm.* Driver of a cart.
CARRICÓCHE, *sm.* 1. (Ant.) Cart with a box like a coach. 2. Old-fashioned coach. 3. Muck-cart, dung-cart.
CARRÍCOLA, *sf.* Kind of phaeton.
CARRICURÉÑA, *sf.* Carriage of a light field-piece with shafts, to be drawn without a limber.
CARRIÉGO, *sm.* 1. Osier basket in the shape of a jar, used for fishing. 2. Large rough basket used in bleaching flax-yarn.
CARRÍL, *sm.* 1. Rut, the track of a coach or cart-wheel. 2. Narrow road where one cart only can pass at a time. 3. Furrow opened by the plough.
CARRILLÁDA, *sf.* Oily or medullar substance of a hog's cheek. *Carrillada de vaca ó carnero*, (Ext.) Cow or sheep's head without the tongue.
CARRILLÁR, *va.* (Náút.) To hoist light things out of the hold by means of a tackle.
CARRÍLLO, *sm.* 1. Small cart. 2. Cheek, the fleshy part of the face from the eye to the jaw-bone. 3 (Naút.) Tackle for hoisting light things out of the hold. *Carillos de monja boba, de trompetero*, &c. Bluffy-cheeked. *Correr carillos*, Horse-racing.
CARRILLÚDO, DA, *a.* Plump or round cheeked.
CARRIÓLA, *sf.* 1. Truckle-bed which runs on wheels. 2. Small chariot; curricle.
CARRIZÁL, *sm.* Land which is full of reed-grass.
CARRIZO, *sm.* (Bot.) Common reed-grass. Arundo phragmites *L.*
CÁRRO, *sm.* 1. Cart, a carriage with two wheels for transporting luggage and other heavy things. *Varas del carro*, Shafts of a cart. *Guardacantones de un carro*, Wheel-iron of a cart. *Estacas del carro*, Staves or rails of the body of a cart. *Arquillo del carro*, Hoops which compose the top of a cart, and support the tilt. *Toldo del carro*, Tilt, the cloth thrown over the hoops of a cart. 2. Carriage of a coach without the body. 3. (Astr.) The greater bear; a northern constellation. *Carro menor*, The lesser bear. 4. *Carro de exequiel*, Sort of woollen stuff manufactured in Languedoc. 5. *Carro de oro*, Brussels camblet. 6. *Carro triunfal*, Triumphal car. 7. (Naút.) Manufactory for cables and other ship cordage. 8. Measure for wood. *Medio carro de leña*, A cord of wood. *Untar el carro*, (Met.) To bribe. *Cogerle á uno el carro*, To be unlucky or ill-fated.
CARRÓCHA, *sf.* Seminal substance in bees and other insects.
CARROCHÁR, *vn.* To shed the seminal substance; applied to bees and other insects.
CARROCÍLLA, *sf.* Small coach.
CARROCÍN, *sm.* Chaise, curricle.
CARROMÁTO, *sm.* Kind of low cart with two wheels.
CARROMETÉRO, *sm.* Carter, charioteer.
CARROÑA, *sf.* Carrion, putrid flesh unfit for use.
CARROÑÁR, *va.* To infect a flock of sheep with the scab.
CARRÓÑO, ÑA, *a.* Putrified, putrid, rotten.
CARRÓZA, *sf.* 1. Large coach; superb state coach. 2. (Naút.) Awning, a cover, sail or tarpawling, spread over a boat, or part of a ship, to keep off the weather. 3. (Naút.) Kind of cabin made on the quarter-deck of a ship, of tarred boards.
CARRUÁGE, *sm.* All sorts of carriages or vehicles for transporting persons or goods.
CARRUAGÉRO, *sm.* Carrier, carter, wagoner.
CARRÚCHA, *sf.* V. *Garrucha.*
CARRÚCO, *sm.* Small cart used in mountainous parts of the country for transporting salt.
CARRUJÁDO, DA, *a.* Corrugated, contracted into wrinkles. V. *Encarrujado.*
CARSÁYA ó CRESÓ, *s.* Kersey, an English woollen stuff.
CÁRTA, *sf.* 1. Letter, a written message, an epistle. 2. (Ant.) Public order. 3. Royal ordinance published or issued by the privy council. 4. (Ant.) Writing-paper. 5. Map. 6. *Carta de marear*, Sea chart. *Carta plana*, Plain chart. 7. Order, directions. 8. Playing cards. *Carta blanca*, Letter or commission with a blank for the name to be inserted at pleasure; full powers given to one to act as he thinks proper. *Carta acordada*, Letter from a superior to an inferior court. *Carta abierta*, Open order, addressed to all persons without exception. *Carta canta*, Written evidence. *Carta cuenta*, Bill or account of sale. *Carta credencial ó de creencia*, Credentials. *Carta de credito*, Letter of credit. *Carta de dote*, Articles of intermarriage. *Carta de encomienda*, Letter of safe conduct through the kingdom. *Carta de espera ó moratoria*, Letter of respite, given to a debtor. *Carta de guia*, Passport. *Carta de exâmen*, License granted to a person to exercise his trade or profession. *Carta de horro*, Letters of enfranchisement. *Carta de libre*, Guardian's discharge. *Carta de naturaleza*, Letters of naturalization. *Carta de pago*, Receipt, discharge. *Carta de pago y lasto*, Acquittance given to a person who has paid money for another that is the chief debtor. *Carta de sanidad*, Bill of health. *Carta de venta*, Bill of sale. *Carta forera*, (Ant.) Judicial despatch or decree; royal grant of privileges. *Carta pastoral*, Pastoral letter or mandate issued by a bishop. *Carta plomada*, Deed or other writing having a seal of lead affixed to it. *Carta receptoria*, Warrant, voucher. *Carta de vecindad*, Burgher-brief. *Carta requisitoria*, Letters requisitorial. *No ver carta*, To have a bad hand. *Pecar por carta de mas ó de menos*, To have either too much or too little. *Perder con buenas cartas*, (Met.) To fail of success, although possessed of merit and protection. *Venir con malas cartas*, (Met.) To attempt to enforce an ill-grounded claim; to be without the necessary documents.
CARTABÓN, *sm.* 1. Square, rule, or instrument used by carpenters, joiners, and other workmen, to measure and form their angles. *Echar el cartabon*, (Met.) To adopt proper measures for attaining one's end. *Cartabon de cola*, Small square piece of glue. 2. Quadrant, a gunner's square, or instrument for elevating and pointing guns.
CÁRTAMA Y CÁRTAMO, *s.* Wild saffron.
CARTAPÁCIO, *sm.* 1. Memorandum-book. 2. Book in which scholars put down the dictates of the masters or professors. 3. Portfolio, a leather case for letters and other writ-

ings. *Razon de cartapacio*, (Ant.) Far-fetched and groundless argument.

CARTAPÉL, *sm.* 1. Memorandum filled with useless and trifling matter. 2. (Ant.) Edict, ordinance. [vere reprehension.

CARTÁZO, *sm.* Letter or paper containing a se-

CARTEÁR, *vn.* To play some low cards, in order to try how the game stands.—*va.* 1. (Naút.) To steer by the sea-chart. 2. (Ant.) To turn over the leaves of a book.—*vr.* To be in the habit of an epistolary correspondence with each other.

CARTÉL, *sm.* 1. Edict or other writing posted up in public places. 2. Agreement made by belligerent powers relative to the exchange of prisoners. 3. (Ant.) Challenge sent in writing. 4. (Naút.) Cartel-ship or flag of truce.

CARTÉLA, *sf.* 1. Slip of paper, piece of wood, or other materials on which a memorandum is made. 2. Bracket or stay on which carved work rests. 3. Iron stay, which supports a balcony, projecting far beyond a wall.

CARTELEÁR, *va.* (Ant.) To publish libels.

CARTELÓN, *sm.* Long edict.

CARTÉRA, *sf.* 1. Port-folio, pocket-book. 2. Letter-case. 3. Flap, the piece that laps over the pocket-hole of a coat.

CARTERIÁNA, *sf.* Sort of silk which comes from Milan.

CARTÉRO, *sm.* Letter-carrier.

CARTÉTA, *sf.* Kind of game at cards.

CARTIBÁNAS, *sf. pl.* Pieces of paper glued to the leaves of a book to facilitate the binding.

CARTÍCA, *sf.* Small letter or note.

CARTIÉRO, *sm.* (Ant.) Quarter of a year.

CARTILAGINÓSO, SA, *a.* Cartilaginous.

CARTILÁGO Y CARTILÁGEN, *sm.* (Anat.) 1. A cartilage. 2. Parchment, a skin dressed for writing.

CARTÍLLA ó CARTÍTA, *sf.* 1. Small or short letter or note. 2. Small prayer-book, in which children are taught to read. 3. Certificate of a clergyman being duly ordained or invested with sacerdotal power. *Cosa que no está en la cartilla*, A thing which is rather strange or uncommon. *Leerle á uno la cartilla*, (Met.) To give one a lecture, and teach him how to behave. *No saber la cartilla*, (Met.) To be extremely ignorant.

CARTÓN, *sm.* 1. Pasteboard. 2. Kind of iron ornament, imitating the shape of the leaves of plants. 3. Cartoon; a painting or drawing made on strong paper. *Parece de carton*, He is as stiff as a poker. *Estar hecho un carton*, To be as thin as a whipping-post.

CARTUCHÉRA, *sf.* Cartridge-box; a pouch or case in which soldiers carry their cartridges.

CARTÚCHO, *sm.* 1. Cartouch, a case or bag filled with gun-powder and grape-shot. *Cartucho de fusil*, Musket cartridge. 2. Small target. V. *Targeta.*

CARTULÁRIO, *sm.* Cartulary, archives or registry in which records and other writings are kept.

CARTULÍNA, *sf.* Piece of pasteboard or parchment, which embroiderers put under their flowers of silk, gold, or silver twist, to raise them. [St. Bruno.

CARTÚXA, *sf.* Carthusian order, instituted by

CARTUXÁNO, NA, *a.* Carthusian.

CARTÚXO, *sm.* 1. Carthusian monk. 2. Kind of skin first used by Carthusian monks.

CARÚNCULA, *sf.* 1. Small protuberance of flesh. 2. Crustaceous excrescence formed on an ulcer or wound.

CARVÁLLO, *sm.* (Bot.) Kind of ever-green oak with rough leaves. Quercus gramuntia *L.*

CARVÍ, *sm.* 1. (Bot.) Carraway. Carum carvi *L.* 2. Carraway-seed.

CÁSA, *sf.* 1. House, edifice. 2. Family residing in a house. 3. Line or branch of a family. 4. Checkers of a chess or draught-board. *Casa a malicia, ó de malicia*, House which has no upper story, for the purpose of being exempted from court-lodgers. *Casa de aposento*, House obliged to lodge persons belonging to the king's household. *Casa de campo ó de placer*, Country house. *Casa de contratacion de las Indias en Cadiz*, The India-house in Cadiz. *Casa de coyma*, (Ant.) Gaming-house. *Casa de locos*, Mad-house: (Met.) Noisy or riotous house. *Casa de moneda*, Mint. *Casa de posada*, Lodging-house, where lodgers may have bed and board. *Casa de tia*, (Joc.) Jail. *Casa fuerte*, (Ant.) House surrounded with a moat. *Casa llana*, (Ant.) Country-house without a moat or defence. *Casa pública*, Brothel, bawdy-house. *Casa de sanidad*, Office of the board of health. *Casa solariega*, Ancient mansion-house of a family. *Apartar casa*, To take a separate house. *Levantar la casa*, To move into another house. *Estar de casa*, To have a free access, to visit frequently, and in a familiar manner. *Franquear la casa*, To grant a free access to one's house. *Guardar la casa*, To stay at home. *Hacer su casa*, (Met.) To raise or aggrandize one's own family. *No tener casa ni hogar*, To have neither house nor home. *Poner casa*, To establish a house, to begin housekeeping. *Ponerle á una casa*, To furnish a house for another. *Ser muy de casa*, To be very intimate in a house, to be on familiar terms. *En casa de tia, pero no cada dia*, (Prov.) We may visit our relations yet without being troublesome. *Pues ya que se quema la casa calentemonos*, (Prov.) Since the house is set on fire, let us warm ourselves. *Casa del Señor*, Church or temple. *Casa santa*, Church of the Holy Sepulchre at Jerusalem. *Casa robada*, Empty house.

CASÁCA, *sf.* Coat, an upper garment made to fit close to the body, with sleeves and skirts. *Casaca de muger*, A woman's jacket. *Volver casaca*, To become a turn-coat, to forsake one's party and principles.

CASACIÓN, *sf.* Abrogation; the act of annulling or repealing a law.

CASACÓN, *sm.* Great-coat, worn over other clothes to keep off the cold and rain.

CASÁDA, *sf.* (Ant. Arag.) Ancient family mansion. [of an age to be married.

CASADÉRO, RA, *a.* Marriageable, fit for marriage,

CASADÍLLA, *sf.* A young bride. [peals.

CASADÓR, *sm.* (Ant.) One who annuls or re-

CASÁL, *sm.* (Ant.) Country-house of an ancient family. [country-house.

CASALÉRO, *sm.* (Ant.) One who resides in his

CASAMÁTA, *sf.* (Fort.) Casemate, a kind of bomb-proof vault or arch in the flank of a bastion.

Casamentéro, ra, *s.* Match or marriage maker.

Casamiénto, *sm.* 1. Marriage, marriage-contract between a man and woman. 2. (Game of Basset) Act of betting money on a card. 3. Portion, a wife's fortune.

Casamúro, *sm.* (Fort. Ant.) Single wall without a terre-plain. [house.

Casapuérta, *sf.* Porch, a wide entrance of a

Casaquílla, *sf.* Kind of short and loose jacket with sleeves, worn over other clothes.

Casár, *sm.* 1. Hamlet, a small village. 2. Country-house for labourers to sleep in.

Casár, *vn.* To marry, to take a wife or husband, to enter into the conjugal state.—*va.* 1. To marry, to join a man and woman in marriage; applied to clergymen. 2. (Met.) To sort things so as to match one another. 3. To repeal, to abrogate, to annul. *Casar la pension,* To relieve a benefice from all incumbrances, by paying the annats at once. *Antes que te cases mira lo que haces,* Look before you leap. *Casarse con su opinion,* To be wedded to one's opinion.

Casatiénda, *sf.* Tradesman's shop.

Casázo, *sm.* (Fam. Aum.) Great event, &c.

Cásca, *sf.* 1. Husks of grapes after the wine has been pressed out. 2. Bad wine or liquor of any kind. 3. Bark for tanning leather. 4. Kind of sweet bread.

Cascabél, *sm.* 1. Bell used for hawks, cats, or dogs, and also for beasts of burthen. 2. Button at the end of the breech of a cannon. 3. Rattlesnake. Crotalus *L.* *Echar á uno el cascabel,* (Met.) To throw off a burthen, and lay it on another. *Echar ó soltar el cascabel,* (Met.) To drop a hint in the course of conversation, to see how it takes. *Ser un cascabel,* (Met.) To be a crazy or rattlebrained fellow. *Tener cascabel,* (Met.) To be uneasy or unhappy in one's mind.

Cascabeláda, *sf.* 1. Jingling with small bells. 2. Inconsiderate speech or action. 3. (Ant.) Noisy feast.

Cascabeleár, *va.* To feed one with vain hopes; to induce one to act on visionary expectations.—*vn.* To act with levity, or little forecast and prudence.

Cascabelíllo, *sm.* Kind of small black plum.

Cascabíllo, *sm.* 1. Hawk's bell. V. *Cascabel.* 2. Chaff, the husk which contains wheat or other grain. 3. Husk of an acorn.

Cascaciruélas, *sm.* Mean, despicable fellow.

Cascáda, *sf.* Cascade, water-fall. *Cascádas,* Small plaits or folds in the drapery of paintings.

Cascádo, da, *pp.* Broken, burst, decayed, infirm. *Vidrio cascado,* (Met.) Singer who has lost his voice. *Estar muy cascado,* To be in a precarious state of health. *Cascados,* Small broken pieces of land. [asunder.

Cascadúra, *sf.* Act of bursting or breaking

Cascajál ó Cascajar, *sm.* 1. Place full of gravel and pebbles. 2. Place on which the husks of grapes are thrown.

Cascájo, *sm.* 1. Gravel; sand mixed with small stones. 2. Fragments of broken vessels and old furniture. 3. Covering of siliquous plants and kernels. 4. (Met.) Copper coin. 5. Bit of a bridle. *Estar hecho un cascajo,* To be very old and infirm.

Cascajóso, sa, *a.* Abounding with gravel or pebbles. [pound a thing slightly.

Cascamajár, *va.* (Arag.) To break, bruise, or

Cascamiénto, *sm.* Act of breaking or bruising.

Cascanuéces, *sm.* Nut-cracker.

Cascapiñónes, *sm.* One who shells hot pine-nuts and cleans the seed.

Cascár, *va.* 1. To crack, burst, or break into pieces. 2. To beat or strike with the hand, stick, or other weapon. *Cascar á uno las liendres,* (Met.) To dress one's jacket, to give one a fine drubbing.—*vr.* To be broken into pieces.

Cáscara, *sf.* 1. Rind, peel, or husk, of various fruits and other things. 2. Bark of trees. 3. Lanaquenet, a game at cards. *Ser de la cáscara amarga,* (Met.) To be ill-tempered, or of a harsh, ill-natured disposition.

Cáscaras, *int.* (And.) O! exclamation expressive of astonishment or admiration.

Cascaréla, *sf.* Lansquenet, a game at cards.

Cascarílla ó Cascárita, *sf.* 1. Small thin bark. 2. Peruvian bark. [do navalis *L.*

Cascarója, *sf.* Ship-worm, ship-piercer. Tere-

Cascarón, *sm.* 1. Egg shell of a fowl or bird. 2. Arch or vault which contains the fourth part of a sphere. 3. Niche where the sacrament is placed for adoration in Roman Catholic churches. 4. Trick won in the game of lansquenet. *Aún no ha salido del cascaron, y ya tiene presuncion,* (Prov.) He is yet a chicken, and assumes the man.

Cascárron, na, *a.* Rough, harsh, rude. *Vino cascarron,* Wine of a rough flavour. *Voz cascarrona,* Harsh, unpleasant tone of voice. [shell.

Cascarúdo, da, *a.* Having a thick large rind or

Cascaruléta, *sf.* (Vulg.) Noise made by the teeth in consequence of chucking under the chin.

Cásco, *sm.* 1. Skull, cranium, the bone which incloses the brain. 2. Potsherd, fragments of a pot or other earthen vessel. 3. Quarter of an orange, lemon, or pomegranate. 4. Coat or tegument of an onion. 5. Helmet or head-piece of ancient armour. 6. Cask, pipe, vat, or other wooden vessel in which wine is preserved. 7. *Casco de un navio,* (Naút.) Hull of a ship. *Casco y quilla ó á riesgo,* Act of lending or borrowing money on the bottom of a ship; bottomry. 8. Crown of a hat. 9. Printer's ball, with which the ink is applied to the forms. 10. Sheep-skin stripped of the wool. 11. Hoof of a horse. *Casco de casa,* Shell of a house. *Casco de lugar,* Dimensions of the ground on which a house is built. *Quitar ó raer del casco,* (Met.) To dissuade or divert one from a pre-conceived opinion. *Cáscos,* Heads of sheep or bullocks without the tongues and brains. *Lavar á uno los cascos,* (Met.) To flatter, to tickle one's vanity. *Levantarle á uno de cascos,* (Met.) To fill one's head with idle notions of grandeur. *Romper los cascos,* (Met.) To disturb, to molest. *Tener los cascos á la gineta,* (Met.) To be on the high horse. *Tener malos cascos,* (Met.) To be crazy or hair-brained.

Cascóte, *sm.* Rubbish, ruins of buildings, fragments of matter used in building.

Cascotería, *sf.* Wall or work made of rubbish

Cascúdo, da, *a.* Large hoofed; applied to horses.
Cascun, (Ant.) V. *Cada uno.*
Caseación, *sf.* (Ant.) Coagulation of milk to form cheese. [cheese.
Caseóso, sa, *a.* Caseous, cheesy, belonging to
Casera, *sf.* House-keeper, a woman-servant that has the care of a family.
Caseraménte, *ad.* Homely, in a plain manner.
Casería, *sf.* 1. Messuage, a building in the country for the residence of those who take care of a farm. 2. Economical management of a house. 3. (Ant.) Brood of chickens. [town.
Caserío, *sm.* A series of houses; village or
Caserna, *sf.* 1. (Mil.) Barracks. 2. Magazine or lodgement which is bomb-proof.
Caséro, ra, *s.* Landlord or steward of a house.
Caséro, ra, *a.* Domestic, homely, in a family way. *Bayle casero,* Family-dance. *Muger casera,* A woman much attached to her family concerns, a good housewife. *Fulana está muy casera,* She dresses in a very plain and homely manner. *Exemplo casero,* Domestic example. *Remedio casero,* Domestic medicine. *Pan casero,* Household bread. *Lienzo casero,* Homespun linen.
Caserón, *sm.* (Aum.) Great house-owner.
Caséta, *sf.* 1. Small house. 2. Peasant, rustic.
Cási, *ad.* Almost, nearly, somewhat more or less. *Cási que, ó casi casi,* Very nearly.
Cásia, *sf.* (Bot.) Cassia. Laurus cassia *L.*
Casíca, Casílla, ó Casíta, *sf.* Small house, cabin.
Casíllas, *sf. pl.* 1. Points or houses of a backgammon table. 2. Square or checkers of a chess or draft-board. *Sacarle á uno de sus casillas,* (Met.) To molest, tease, or harass.
Casillér, *sm.* (In the Royal Palace) Person appointed to empty the close-stools.
Casíllo, *sm.* 1. Trifling or slight cause. 2. (Iron.) A momentous affair, matter of consequence.
Casímbas, *sf. pl.* Pails or buckets for taking out the water made by a ship, which the pumps are unable to discharge.
Casimíro y Casimíras, *s. pl.* Kerseymeres.
Casimódo, (Ant.) V. *Quasimodo.*
Casína, *sf.* 1. Farm-house occupied by soldiers to check the progress of an enemy. 2. Cottage.
Cáso, *sm.* 1. Event, occurrence. 2. Contingency, casualty, unexpected accident. 3. Occasion, opportunity. 4. Case stated to lawyers, physicians, or other persons, to demand their advice. 5. (Gram.) Inflexion or termination of nouns. *Caso de conciencia,* Case of conscience. 6. Peculiar figure of written characters. *En caso de eso,* In that case. *En todo caso,* At all events. *Estar ó no estar en el caso,* To comprehend or not comprehend something. *Hacer caso de una persona,* To esteem or respect a person. *Hacer ó no alguna cosa al caso,* To be material or immaterial. *Ser ó no ser al caso,* To be or not to be to the purpose. *Vamos al caso,* Let us come to the point. *No estoy en el caso,* I do not understand the matter. *Caso que,* In that case. *Dado caso, ó demos caso,* Supposing that. *De caso pensado,* Deliberately. *Caso negado,* Proposition admitted only to be refuted.
Caso, sa, *a.* V. *Nulo.*

Casoortán, *sm.* (Ict.) Fish in the West Ind of an exquisite flavour.
Casório, *sm.* Inconsiderate marriage, contra ed without judgment and prudence.
Cáspa, *sf.* Dandruff, scurf or dirt which stic to the head. [head of the dandr
Caspéra, *sf.* (Ant.) Comb for cleansing t
Cáspita, *int.* Expressive of admiration or wo der.
Caspóso, sa, *a.* (Ant.) Full of dandruff.
Casquetázo, *sm.* Blow given with the hea
Casquéte, *sm.* 1. Helmet, the head-piece ancient armour. 2. Concave covering of t head, made of linen, leather, silk, or pap 3. Helmet shell; a kind of sea-shell. 4. Cat plasm, composed of pitch and other ingre ents to take the scurf off the heads of childr
Casquiblándo, da, *a.* Soft-hoofed; spoken horses which are soft in the hoof.
Casquiderramádo, da, *a.* Wide-hoofed; sa of horses which have a broad hoof.
Casquíjo, *sm.* Gravel, sand and pebbles.
Casquílla, *sf.* Cell in which the queen bee r sides.
Casquíllo, *sm.* 1. Small steel helm. 2. Ir socket with which a spear is shod. 3. Poi of an arrow shod with iron.
Casquilúcio, cia, *a.* Gay, frolicsome.
Casquimuléño, ña, *a.* Narrow-hoofed, lil mules. [acting with levit
Casquiváno, na, *a.* Impudent, inconsiderat
Cásta, *sf.* 1. Cast, race, generation, lineag particular breed. 2. Kind or quality of a thin *Hacer casta,* To get a particular breed o horses or other animals.
Castaménte, *ad.* Chastely, in a chaste manne
Castáña, *sf.* 1. (Bot.) Chesnut, the fruit of th chesnut-tree. 2. Bottle, jug, or jar, in the sha of a chesnut. 3. Hair tied up behind in th form of a bottle. *Castaña pilonga ó apilad* Dried chesnut, seasoned and kept for pottag *Castaña regoldana,* Wild or horse chesnut
Castañál ó Castañar, *sm.* Grove or plant tion of chesnut-trees.
Castañázo, *sm.* Blow given or received by chesnut being flung at a person. [tatio
Castañédo, *sm.* (Astu.) Chesnut-grove or pla
Castañéra, *sf.* (Astu.) Country aboundin with chesnut-trees.
Castañéro, ra, *s.* Dealer in chesnuts.
Castañéta, *sf.* 1. Noise made with the fingers dancing the *fandango* and *bolero,* two cel brated Spanish dances. 2. Castanet. V. *Castañuela.*
Castañetázo, *sm.* 1. Blow given with a cast net. 2. Sound or crack of a chesnut whi bursts in the fire. 3. Crack given by the join
Castañeteádo, *sm.* Rattling sound of cast nets in dancing.
Castañeteár, *vn.* 1. To rattle the castanets dancing. 2. To crackle; applied to kn which make slight cracks in walking. 3. T cry; applied to partridges.
Castáño, *sm.* (Bot.) Chesnut-tree. Fagus ca tanea *L.* *Castaño de Indias,* Indian chesnu tree.
Castañuéla, *sf.* 1. Castanet, small concav shells of ivory or hard wood, which dance rattle in their hands on dancing the *fanda*

ge, bolero, or other Spanish dances. 2. (Bot.) Prickly ox-eye. Buphthalmum spinosum. *L.* *Estar como una castañuela,* To be very gay. *Castañuelas,* (Naút.) Cleats, pieces of wood fastened to the yard-arms to prevent the ropes from sliding off the yards. *Castañuelas de muescas,* Notched cleats. *Castañuelas de ponton,* Pontoon cleats.

Castañuélo, la, *a.* Being of a light chesnut-colour; applied to horses.

Castellán, *sm.* Governor or warden of a castle. *Castellan de amposta,* (Arag.) Governor of a castle belonging to the Knights of Malta.

Castellanía, *sf.* District belonging to a castle.

Castellano, *sm.* 1. Ancient Spanish coin. 2. Fiftieth part of a mark of gold. 3. Mule got by a jack-ass and a mare; the foremost mule in a cart or wagon. 4. Spanish language.

Castellano, na, *a.* Belonging to Castile.

Castellár, *sm.* 1. (Ant.) Building or ruins of an ancient castle. 2. (Bot.) Tutsan, park-leaves. Hypericum androsæmum *L.*

Castidád, *sf.* Chastity, freedom from obscenity.

Castiéllo, *sm.* (Ant.) V. *Castillo.*

Castificadór, *sm.* One that renders chaste, or inspires others with principles of chastity.

Castificár, *va.* To render chaste.

Castigación, *sf.* 1. Castigation. 2. Correction of errors of the press.

Castigadaménte, *ad.* Correctly.

Castigadéra, *sf.* 1. Rope with which a bell is tied to a mule, or other beast of burthen. 2. Small cord with which the ring of a stirrup is tied to the girth. [chastises.

Castigadór, ra, *s.* One who reproaches or

Castigamiénto ó Castigaménto, *sm.* (Ant.) V. *Castigo.*

Castigár, *va.* 1. To chastise, to punish. 2. To treat in a barbarous manner. 3. (Ant.) To advise, to inform. 4. (Met.) To correct proof-sheets or writings.—*vr.* (Ant.) To mend.

Castígo, *sm.* 1. Chastisement, punishment. 2. Censure, animadversion, reproach. 3. (Ant.) Example, instruction. 4. Alteration or correction made in a work.

Castilláge, *sm.* V. *Castilleria.*

Castilléjo, *sm.* 1. Small castle. 2. Go-cart in which children learn to walk.

Castillería, *sf.* 1. Toll paid on passing through a district which belongs to a castle. 2. (Ant.) Government of a castle.

Castíllo, *sm.* 1. Castle, a fortified building. 2. Whole of the mounting of a velvet loom. 3. Cell of the queen-bee. 4. *Castillo de proa,* (Naút.) Fore-castle, *Castillo roquero,* Castle built on a rock. *Hacer castillos en el ayre,* (Met.) To build castles in the air, to form chimerical projects. *Jugar á Castillo ó Leon,* To play Castle or Lion, to toss up a coin and bet on what side it may fall.

Castilluélo, *sm.* Small castle.

Castízo, za, *a.* Of a noble descent, of a good breed. *Caballo castizo,* Blood horse. *Estilo castizo,* Simple, easy style. [easy. V. *Castizo.*

Cásto, ta, *a.* 1. Pure, chaste, honest. 2. Simple,

Castór, *sm.* 1. Beaver, an amphibious quadruped. Castor *L.* *Cástor y Pólux,* (Naút.) Castor and Pollux, St. Elm's fire, or Jack with a lantern, an *ignis fatuus,* which sometimes appears on the masts and yards of ships in stormy weather. [cloth.

Castorcíllo, *sm.* Kind of rough serge like

Castóreo, *sm.* Castoreum, a liquid matter, found in the inguinal region of the beaver.

Cástra, *sf.* Act of pruning or lopping off the superfluous branches of trees or plants.

Castradéra, *sf.* Iron instrument with which honey is taken out of the hive.

Castradór, *sm.* One that performs the act of gelding or castrating.

Castradúra, *sf.* 1. Act of gelding or castrating. 2. Scar which remains after an animal has been castrated. [ing.

Castrametación, *sf.* Castrametation, encamp-

Castrapuércas, *sm.* Sow-gelder's whistle.

Castrár, *va.* 1. To geld, to castrate. 2. To cut away the proud flesh about a wound. 3. To prune or lop off the superfluous branches of trees or plants. 4. *Castrar las colmenas,* To cut the honey-combs out of bee-hives.

Castrazón, *sf.* 1. Act of cutting honey-combs out of the hives. 2. Castrating or gelding season. [season.

Castrénse, *a.* Belonging to the military pro-

Cástro, *sm.* 1. (Ant.) Place where an army is encamped. 2. (Gal. y Ast.) Ruins of ancient fortified places. 3. Game played by boys, consisting in small stones being arranged in the form of a camp. 4. Act of taking honey-combs out of hives.

Castrón, *sm.* Castrated he-goat.

Casuál, *a.* Casual, accidental. [event

Casualidád, *sf.* Casualty, an unforeseeen

Casualménte, *ad.* Casually, accidentally.

Casúcha, *sf.* Poor, miserable hut. [casuarius *L.*

Casuél, *sm.* (Orn.) Cassowary, emeu. Struthio

Casuísta, *sm.* Casuist, one that studies or settles cases of conscience.

Casúlla, *sf.* Vestment worn by priests over the alb and stole when they say mass.

Casulléro, *sm.* One who makes *casullas,* and other vestments for the performance of divine service.

Cáta, *sf.* 1. Act of trying a thing by the taste. *Dar á cata,* To give upon trial. *Echar cata,* To make a careful inquiry. 2. (Ant.) Plummet for measuring heights.

Cáta, *ad.* Mark, beware.

Catábre, *sm.* (Naút.) Sheep-shank. [&c.

Catacáldos, *sm.* Taster of wine, liquors, soup,

Cataclísmo, *sm.* Deluge, inundation.

Catacúmbas, *sf. pl.* Catacombs, subterraneous grottoes for the burial of the dead.

Catadór, *sm.* Taster, one who tries by taste.

Catadúpa, *sf.* Water-fall, cataract. V. *Catarata.*

Catadúra, *sf.* 1. Act of trying by the taste. 2. Gesture, face, countenance. 3. Mode of guarding or inspecting criminals.

Cataléjo, *sm.* Telescope. [cine.

Catalicón, *sm.* Catholicon, an universal medi-

Catalína y Catalinílla, *sf.* Small kind of parrot.

Catálnica, *sf.* Parrot. V. *Cotorra.*

Catálogo, *sm.* Catalogue, a list or enumeration of persons or things.

Catalúfa, *sf.* Kind of floor carpet. [tion.

Catamiénto, *sm.* (Ant.) Observation, inspec-

Catán, *sm.* Indian sabre or cutlass.

Catananca, *sf.* (Bot.) Lion's foot.

Cataplasma, *sf.* Cataplasm or poultice.

Catapucia, *sf.* (Bot.) Lesser or caper-spurge. Euphorbia lathyris *L.*

Catapulta, *sf.* Catapult; an ancient warlike engine used to throw stones.

Catár, *va.* 1. To taste, to try by the taste. 2. To view, to inspect, to inquire, to investigate. to examine. 3. To judge, to form an opinion. 4. To esteem, to respect. 5. To bear in mind. 6. To cut the combs out of bee-hives. *Quando menos se cata*, When a person thinks least of it.

Catarañá, *sf.* (Orn.) Sheldrake, a bird resembling a teal. Anas tadorna *L.*

Cataráta, *sf.* 1. Cataract, a disease of the eye, consisting in an inspissation of the crystalline humour. *Batir las cataratas*, To remove cataracts: (Met.) Not to understand clearly and distinctly the nature of things. 2. Cataract, water-fall. *Catarata del cielo*, Heavy fall of rain.

Cataribéra, *sm.* 1. Man-servant appointed to follow the hawk on horseback, and bring it down with its prey. 2. (Joc.) Lawyer appointed to examine into the proceedings of magistrates, charged with the administration of justice.

Catarrál, *a.* Catarrhal, inflammatory.

Catárro, *sm.* Cold, a disease caused by cold.

Catarróso, sa, *a.* Catarrhal, catarrhous, troubled with a cold.

Catártico, ca, *a.* Cathartic, purging.

Catástro, *sm.* General tax laid chiefly on land, and assessed according to the circumstances of the contributors.

Catástrofe, *sf.* 1. Catastrophe, the turn which unravels the plot of a play, and brings on its conclusion. 2. Unfortunate event, pregnant with ruin and destruction.

Cataviénto, *sm.* (Naút.) Dog-vane.

Catavíno, *sm.* 1. Small jug or cup used to taste wine in cellars. 2. Small hole made at the top of large wine-vessels for tasting the wine contained in them.—*pl.* 1. One whose employment is to try wine by the taste, and inform the buyers of its quality. 2. Tipplers who run from tavern to tavern, to drink in luxury and excess.

Cateár, *va.* To inquire after, to investigate, to discover.

Catecísmo, *sm.* Catechism, a book containing the Christian doctrine explained.

Catecúmeno, na, *s.* Catechumen, one who is yet in the first rudiments of Christianity.

Cátedra, *sf.* 1. Seat or chair in which professors or masters instruct their pupils in the sciences and arts. 2. Office and functions of a professor or teacher of the sciences and arts. *Pedro regentó la cátedra tantos años*, Peter filled the professor's seat so many years. 3. See, the seat of pontifical or episcopal power.

Catedrál, *sf.* Cathedral, the head or episcopal church of a diocese.

Catedralidád, *sf.* Dignity of a cathedral church.

Catedrár y Catedreár, *vn.* To obtain a professor's chair in an university.

Catedrático, *sm.* 1. Professor in an university who publicly delivers lectures on the sciences and arts. 2. Contribution formerly paid by the inferior clergy to the bishops and prelates in Roman Catholic countries.

Catedrílla, *sf.* Small or poor chair.

Categoría, *sf.* Class, rank; an order of ideas, predicament. *Ser hombre de categoría*, To be a man of estimable qualities and talents.

Categóricamente, *ad.* In a categorical, positive, or decisive manner.

Categórico, ca, *a.* Categorical, absolute, decisive.

Catequísmo, *sm.* Catechism, a form of instruction by means of questions and answers concerning religion.

Catequísta, *sm.* Catechist, one who instructs by questions and answers in religious matters.

Catequizánte, *pa.* He who catechises.

Catequizár, *va.* 1. To catechise, to instruct in the Christian faith by means of questions and answers. 2. (Met.) To persuade, to bring one to an opinion or resolution to which he is adverse.

Catérva, *sf.* Confused multitude of persons, animals, or things.

Catéto, *sf.* (Arq.) Perpendicular line which intersects the volute by passing through its centre.

Caticiégo, ga, *a.* Pur-blind, short-sighted.

Catimarón, *sm.* Indian raft.

Catíno, (Ant.) V. *Cazuela.*

Catíte, *sm.* Loaf of the best refined sugar.

Cativación, Cativamiénto, Cativazon, y Cativério, (Ant.) V. *Cautiverio.*

Catívo, (Ant.) V. *Cautivo.*

Cáto, *sm.* Japan earth, a gum or resin obtained by the decoction of some vegetable substance in water.

Católicamente, *ad.* In a catholic manner.

Catolicísmo, *sm.* The whole body of the Roman Catholic church and its belief.

Católico, ca, *a.* 1. General or universal. 2. True, infallible. 3. Catholic, an appellation peculiar to the king of Spain. *El Rey católico*, His catholic majesty. 4. *No estar muy católico*, Not to be in good health.

Católico, *sm.* 1. One who professes the Roman Catholic religion. 2. (Quím.) Chemical furnace fit for all kinds of chemical operations.

Catolicón, *sm.* V. *Catalicon.*

Catóptrica, *sf.* Catoptricks, that part of optics which treats of vision by reflexion.

Catóptrico, ca, *a.* Catoptrical, relating to vision by reflexion.

Catórce, *a.* Fourteen, the cardinal number of four added to ten.

Catorcéna, *sf.* The conjunction of 14 unities.

Catorcéno, na, *a.* Fourteenth, the ordinal of fourteen, the fourth after the tenth. V. *Paño.*

Cátre, *sm.* Small bedstead for one person only. *Catre de mar*, Hammock or cot. *Catre de tixera á la inglesa*, Field-bed.

Catricófre, *sm.* Press-bed which shuts up in a case or trunk.

Cattequí, *sm.* Kind of blue cotton stuff imported from Surat.

Catúres, *sm.* (Naút.) Kind of armed vessel of Bantam.

Catucálide, *sf.* (Bot.) Bastard or fool's parsley, cicely, lesser hemlock. Æthusa cynapium *L.*

Caúce, *sm.* Drain, an open channel for conveying water to fields and gardens.

Caucéra, *sf.* V. *Cacera.*

Cauchíl, *sm.* Small basin or reservoir of water.

Caucíon, *sf.* 1. Security given for the performance of an agreement. *Caucion juratoria*, Oath taken by a poor person to return to prison, when called on, having no bail. 2. Caution, warning, foresight, prevention.

Caucionár, *va.* To guard against an evil or loss.

Caucionéro, *sm.* (Ant.) One who becomes surety or bondsman for another.

Caúda, *sf.* Train or tail of a bishop's robe when he performs divine service.

Caudál, *sm.* 1. Property, fortune, wealth; especially as far as it consists in money. 2. Capital or principal sum. 3. (Met.) Plenty, abundance. *Hacer caudal de alguna cosa*, To hold a thing in high estimation.

Caudál, *a.* Rich, wealthy. *Aguila caudal*, The red-tailed eagle.

Caudalíto, *sm.* Middling fortune.

Caudalóso, sa, *a.* 1. Carrying much water; spoken of rivers. 2. (Ant.) Rich, wealthy.

Caudatário, *sm.* Clergyman whose business is to carry the train of a bishop's robe when he officiates at divine service.

Caudáto, ta, *a.* 1. Having a tail; applied to a comet. 2. Bearded, hairy.

Caudíllo, *sm.* 1. Commander of a troop of armed men. 2. Chief or director of a company or body of the people.

Caudón, *sm.* V. *Alcaudon*.

Caulículos ó Caulícolos, *sm. pl.* Ornaments of the capital of columns of the Corinthian order.

Caúro, *sm.* North-west wind.

Caúsa, *sf.* 1. Cause, the first principle which produces a thing. 2. Motive or reason of doing a thing. 3. Affair in which one takes a share or interest. 4. Law-suit. 5. Criminal cause or information. *Causa pública*, Public good or welfare.

Causadór, ra, *s.* One who causes.

Causál, *sm.* Ground on which something is done. [effect.

Causalidád, *sf.* Connexion between cause and

Causánte, *p.* y *sm.* 1. He who causes. 2. (For.) The person from whom a right is derived.

Causár, *va.* 1. To cause, to produce. 2. To sue, to enter an action. 3. To occasion.

Causídico, *sm.* Advocate, counsellor. [suits.

Causídico, ca, *a.* Forensic, belonging to law-

Causón, *sm.* Burning fever which lasts several hours, but is not attended with any bad consequences.

Caústico, *sm.* 1. Caustic, a corrosive or burning application. 2. Ray of reflected light which unites with others in one point.

Cautaménte, *ad.* Cautiously, with precaution.

Cautéla, *sf.* 1. Precaution and reserve with which a person proceeds in some business. 2. Artfulness, craft, cunning.

Cautelár, *va.* To take the necessary precaution, to proceed with prudence.

Cautelosaménte, *ad.* In a cautious manner.

Cautelóso, sa, *a.* Cautious, acting with prudence.

Cautério, *sm.* 1. Cautery, caustic medicine; burning with a hot iron. 2. Corrective or preventive remedy.

Cauterización, *sf.* Cauterization, the act of burning with a hot iron, or applying caustic medicines.

Cauterizadór, *sm.* He who cauterizes.

Cauterizár, *va.* 1. To cauterize, to burn with a hot iron, or apply caustic medicines. 2. To correct or reproach with severity.

Cautivár, *va.* 1. To take or make prisoners of war. 2. To imprison, to deprive of liberty. 3. (Met.) To captivate, to charm, to subdue.

Cautivério y Cautividád, *s.* Captivity, the state of being taken prisoner of war.

Cautívo, va, *s.* Captive, a prisoner of war.

Caúto, ta, *a.* Cautious, wary.

Cáva, *sf.* 1. Digging and earthing of vines. 2. Cellar where wine and water are kept for the use of the royal family. 3. (Ant.) Ditch. 4. (Ant.) Subterraneous vault. *Vena cava*, Large vein which receives the refluent blood, and conveys it to the heart.

Cavadízo, za, *a.* Dug out of a pit; chiefly applied to sand.

Caváddo, da, *a.* Hollow, concave.

Cavadór, *sm.* 1. Digger, one who digs or turns up the ground with a spade. 2. Grave-digger.

Cavadúra, *sf.* Hole dug into the ground; act of making hollow. [ridges.

Cavallíllo, *sm.* Water-furrow between two

Cavár, *va.* 1. To dig or turn up the ground. 2. To paw; applied to horses. 3. (Met.) To think intensely or profoundly.—*vn.* To penetrate.

Cavérna, *sf.* 1. Cavern, a hollow place under ground. 2. Hollow inside or depth of wounds.

Cavernílla, *sf.* Small cavern.

Cavernóso, sa, *a.* Full of caverns.

Caví, *sf.* A Peruvian root, called *oca*, dried and dressed.

Cavidád, *sf.* Cavity, hollowness, hollow.

Cavídos, *sm.* Portuguese measure of length.

Cavilación, *sf.* Cavillation, a disposition to make captious objections.

Cavilár, *va.* To cavil, to raise frivolous or captious objections.

Cavílla, *sf.* Iron-pin, tree-nail.

Cavíllar, *sf.* 1. (Bot.) Sea-holly. Eryngium maritimum *L.* 2. (Naút.) Tree-nail, wooden pin. 3. (Naút.) Belaying pin to which the running rigging is fastened.

Cavilladór, *sm.* Tree-nail maker.

Cavillár, *va.* To use tree-nails. *Cavillar un baxel*, To drive tree-nails into a ship.

Cavilosaménte, *ad.* In a captious or cavillous manner.

Cavilosidád, *sf.* Captiousness.

Cavilóso, sa, *a.* Captious, cavillous, apt to raise frivolous objections.

Cávo, va, *a.* 1. (Ant.) Concave. 2. Having only twenty-nine days; spoken of a month.

Cáxa, *sf.* 1. Box or case made of wood, metal, or stone. 2. Coffin. V. *Ataud*. 3. Chest in which money is kept. 4. Warehouse. 5. Drum. 6. Printer's case, divided into square cells, which contain the types. 7. Room in a post-office where the letters are sorted according to their different places of destination. 8. Portable writing-desk. 9. The well or cavity in which a stair-case is raised. 10. Wooden case of an organ. *Caxa de escopeta*, Stock of a fire-lock. *Caxa de brasero*, Pan in which coals are kept; a brazier for warming a room. *Caxa de coche*, Body of a coach. *Caxa de* agua. (Naút.) Manger of a ship. *Caza de balas,* (Naút.) Shot-locker. *Caza de bombas,* (Naút.) Pump-well of a ship. *Caza de lastre,* (Naút.) Ballast-case. *Caza de consulta,* (For.) Counsellor's brief. *Caza de cartuchos,* (Mil.) Cartridge-box. *Caza de mar,* (Naút.) Sea-chest. *Caza de hueso roto,* Cradle for a broken limb. *Libro de caza,* (Among Merchants) Cash-book. *Caza de farol del pañol de pólvora,* (Naút.) Light-room. *Meter las vergas ó entenas en caza,* (Naút.) To place the yards or lateen yards in a horizontal position. *Echar con cazas destempladas,* To dismiss from service, to turn away in a harsh manner. *Estar en caza,* To equilibrate, to be in equipoise. *El pulso está en su caza,* (Med.) The pulse is even and natural. *Notario de caza,* (Arag.) Notary public of the city of Zaragoza.

Caxa-méngala, *sf.* Kind of linen manufactured in China.

Caxéras, *sf. pl.* (Naút.) Cavities or holes in blocks, which contain the sheaves whereupon the running tackle moves.

Caxéro, *sm.* 1. Cashier, cash-keeper. 2. Basin of water or reservoir close to the principal locks in irrigation canals. 3. (Ant.) Pedler, hawker. V. *Buhonero.*

Caxéta, *sf.* 1. Snuff-box. 2. Poor's box. *Caxetas,* (Naút.) Braided cordage.

Caxetín, *sm.* Very small box.

Caxísta, *sm.* Compositor who arranges and adjusts the types in printing.

Caxita y Caxuéla, *sf.* Small box.

Cáxo, *sm.* (Among Bookbinders) Notch or groove for the pasteboards in which books are bound.

Caxón, *sm.* 1. Box or chest in which goods are conveyed from one place to another. 2. Chest of drawers; drawer under a table. 3. Mould for casting the pipes of an organ. 4. Space between the shelves of a book-case. 5. Tub in which wet cloth is laid. 6. Wooden shed for selling provisions. *Ser de cazon,* To be a matter of course, or a common and usual thing. *Ser un caxon de sastre,* (Met.) To have one's brain full of confused ideas. *Caxones de cámara,* (Naút.) Lockers in the cabins of ships.

Cayáda, *sf.* V. *Cayado.*

Cayadílla, *sf.* (Dim.) Small shepherd's hook.

Cayádo, *sm.* 1. Shepherd's hook. 2. Crosier, the pastoral staff of a bishop. 3. Walking-staff of old persons.

Cayánte, *sm.* Kind of stuff manufactured in Lisle.

Cayelác, *sm.* Sweet-scented wood which grows in Siam.

Cayepút, *sm.* Cajeput oil, a green, fragrant, and volatile-oil prepared from the Melaleuca leucadendron *L.*

Caymán, *sm.* 1. Cayman, alligator, the American crocodile. Lacerta alligator *L.* 2. (Met.) Crafty, wily, artful fellow.

Cáyos, *sm. pl.* Rocks, shoals, or islets in the sea.

Cayóte, *sm.* (Bot.) Citron. V. *Cidra.*

Cayóu, *sm.* Cashew-nut.

Cayrél, *sm.* 1. Head of false hair or wig worn by women to embellish their head-dress. 2. Furbelow, a kind of flounce with which women's garments are trimmed. 3. Silk-threads to which wig-makers fasten the hair of which wigs are composed.

Cayreládo, da, *a.* Adorned with flounces.

Cayrelár, *va.* To adorn with flounces.

Cayúco, *sm.* (Naút.) Small fishing-boat used in some parts of America.

Caz, *sm.* Canal, trench or ditch, made close to rivers for the purposes of irrigation.

Cáza, *sf.* 1. Chace, hunting, fowling, all sorts of field sports. 2. Game. 3. (Naút.) Chase, a vessel pursued at sea by another. 4. Chase, the act of pursuing another vessel. 5. (Ant.) Thin linen resembling gauze. *Caza mayor,* Hunting, the act of chasing wild boars, stags, wolves, &c. *Caza menor,* Shooting or fowling, the act of chasing hares, rabbits, partridges, &c. *Andar en caza de alguna cosa,* (Met.) To go in pursuit of a thing. *Levantar la caza,* To rouse or start the game. *Dar caza,* (Naút.) To chase or give chase to a vessel. *Ponerse en caza,* (Naút.) To manœuvre in order to escape from another vessel. *Espantar la caza,* (Met.) To injure one's claim by an untimely application.

Cazábe, *sm.* Bread made in Havannah of the root of the cassavi or cassada-plant. Jatropha manihot *L.*

Cazadéro, *sm.* Place for pursuing game.

Cazadór, ra, *s.* 1. Huntsman, sportsman. 2. Animal which gives chase to another. 3. (Naút.) Vessel which gives chase to another. 4. (Met.) One who prevails upon another, and brings him over to his party. *Cazador de alforja,* One who sports with dogs, snares, and other similar devices.

Cazamóscas, *sm.* (Orn.) Fly-catcher, a bird. Muscicapa *L.*

Cazár, *va.* 1. To chase, to hunt, to fowl, to sport, to go in pursuit of game. 2. (Met.) To attain or gain a difficult point by dexterity and skill. 3. (Met.) To gain one's friendship by caresses and deceitful tricks. 4. (Naút.) To give chase to a ship. 5. *Cazar una vela,* (Naút.) To tally a sail, to haul the sheet aft. *Cazar moscas,* (Met.) To waste one's time in idle amusements. *Cazar con perdigones de plata,* To kill with silver shot; applied to those who buy game, instead of killing it.

Cazcalleár, *vn.* To run to and fro with affected assiduity and diligence, without performing any thing valuable or important.

Cazcárrias, *sf. pl.* Splashings of dirt on clothes.

Cazcarriénto, ta, *a.* Splashed, bemired.

Cázo, *sm.* 1. Copper sauce-pan with an iron handle. 2. Copper or iron ladle for taking water out of a large earthen vessel. 3. (Ant.) Back part of the blade of a knife.

Cazoléja ó Cazoléta, *sf.* 1. Small sauce-pan. 2. Pan of a musket-lock.

Cazoléro, *sm.* Mean person who does women's work in the kitchen. V. *Cominero.*

Cazoléta, *sf.* 1. Pan of a musket-lock. 2. Boss or defence of a shield. 3. Shell of a sword. 4. Kind of perfume.

Cazolílla, *sf.* Small earthen pan.

Cazolón, *sm.* Large earthen pot or stew-pan.

Cazón, *sm.* 1. (Ict.) Tope, Sweet William. Squalus galeus *L.* 2. (Ant.) Brown sugar.

Cazonál, *sm.* Fishing-tackle for the tope-fishery.

Cazonéte, *sm.* (Naút.) Toggel, a wooden pin

from five to six inches long, with a notch in the middle, used to fasten the end of a port-rope.

Cebúdo, da, *a.* Having a thick back; spoken of knives.

Cazuéla, *sf.* 1. An earthen pan or vessel to dress meat in. 2. Meat dressed in an earthen pan. 3. Kind of pit in the play-houses in Spain, reserved for the ladies, and where no gentlemen are admitted. 4. *Cazuela mozi ó moxil,* (Murc.) Tart made of cheese, bread, apples, and honey. 5. Pan for baking tarts and pies. V. *Tartera.*

Cazumbrár, *va.* To join staves together with hempen cords, and tighten them with the strokes of a mallet.

Cazúmbre, *sm.* Hempen cord with which the staves of wine-casks are joined and tightened.

Cazumbrón, *sm.* Cooper, one who makes barrels, pipes, and all sorts of casks in general.

Cazúr, *sm.* (Bot.) Unleaved Aralia. Aralia nudicaulis *L.*

Cazúrro, ra, *a.* 1. Silent, taciturn. 2. (Ant.) Making use of low language.

Cé, *interj.* Hark, here, come hither. *Por ce ó por be,* In one way or other.

Céa, *sf.* (Anat.) Thigh-bone. V. *Cia.*

Ceático, ca, *a.* Affected with rheumatic pains in the thigh or hip. V. *Ciático.*

Cebáda, *sf.* (Bot.) Barley. Hordeum vulgare *L. Cebáda ladilla,* (Bot.) Common long-eared barley. Hordeum distichon *L.*

Cebadál, *sm.* Field sown with barley.

Cebadázo, za, *a.* Made of barley; applied to bread.

Cebadéra, *sf.* 1. Kind of bag or cloth in which the feed is given in the field to working cattle. 2. (Naút.) Sprit-sail.

Cebadería, *sf.* (Ant.) Barley-market.

Cebadéro, *sm.* 1. Place where game or fowls are fed. 2. One whose business is to breed and feed hawks. 3. Mule which on a journey carries barley for the rest. 4. Bell-mule which takes the lead in a herd of mules. 5. Painting which represents domestic fowls in the act of feeding. 6. Entrance of a tile-kiln. 7. Dealer in barley.

Cebadílla, *sf.* 1. (Bot.) Sneeze-wort. Achillea ptarmica *L.* 2. Hellebore powdered, and used as snuff.

Cebádo, *a.* (Blas.) Applied to the picture of a wolf with a lamb or kid in its mouth.

Cebadúra, *sf.* Act of feeding.

Cebár, *va.* 1. To feed animals. 2. To fatten fowls, and other domestic animals. 3. (Met.) To keep up a fire by adding fuel to it. 4. (Met.) To drive in with force, as nails into wood. 5. (Met.) To excite and cherish a passion or desire. 6. To prime, to put powder into the pan of a gun. 7. To let off a rocket or squib. 8. *Cebar un anzuelo,* To bait a fish-hook.—*vr.* To be firmly bent upon a thing.

Cebellína, *sf.* Sable. Mustela zibellina *L.*

Cebíca, *sf.* V. *Cibica.*

Cébo, *sm.* 1. Food given to animals; fodder. 2. Fattening of fowls and other animals. 3. Bait or lure for wolves and birds of prey. 4. (Met.) That which excites or foments a passion. 5. Kind of monkey. V. *Cefo.* 6. Cart-grease. *Cebo de pescar,* Bait for fishing. 7. Gunpowder for the priming of guns.

Cebólla, *sf* 1. (Bot.) Onion. Allium cepa *L.* 2. Any bulbous tunicated root. *Cebolla albarrana,* (Bot.) Squill. Scilla maritima *L. Cebolla ascalonia,* (Bot.) Shallot, Ascalonian garlic. Allium ascalonium *L.*

Cebolláno, *sf.* (Bot.) A large myrobalan, resembling onions.

Cebollár, *sm.* Plot of ground sown with onions

Cebolléro, ra, *s.* Dealer in onions.

Cebollétta, *sf.* A tender onion.

Cebollíno, *sm.* (Bot.) Chive or sive. Allium schœnoprasum *L.*

Cebollón, *sm.* A large onion.

Cebollúdo, da, *a.* Ill-shaped; applied to persons

Cebón, *sm.* A fat bullock or hog. *Cebónes de Galicia,* Stall-fed bullocks.

Ceboncíllo, *sm.* A young fat pig.

Cébra, *sf.* Zebra, a kind of ass. Equus zebra *L.*

Cebratána, *sf.* 1. A long wooden tube or pipe. V. *Cerbatana.* 2. (Art.) Piece of ordnance resembling a culverin.

Cebúrro. V. *Mijo ceburro.*

Cecear, *va.* 1. To pronounce the *s* in the same manner as the *c,* which is a considerable fault in the Spanish pronunciation. 2. To call one by the word *ce-ce.*

Ceceo, *sm.* The act of pronouncing the *s* in the same manner as the *c.*

Ceceóso, sa, *a.* Committing the fault of pronouncing the *s* in the same manner as the *c.*

Cécha, *sf.* Kind of vessel for drinking water.

Ceciál, *sm.* Cod or other fish cured and dried in the air.

Cécias, *sm.* North-west wind.

Cecína, *sf.* Hung beef, or salt beef, dried by the air or smoke. *Echar en cecina,* To salt and dry meat.

Cecinár, *va.* To make hung beef. V. *Acecinar.*

Cedacería, *sf.* Shop where sieves are made or sold.

Cedacéro, *sm.* One who makes or sells sieves.

Cedacíllo y Cedacíto, *sm.* A small sieve. *Cedacito nuevo tres dias en estaca,* (Prov.) A new broom sweeps clean.

Cedázo, *sm.* Hair-sieve or strainer. *Ver ó mirar por tela de cedazo,* To see through a hair-sieve; that is to see readily other people's faults, but not one's own.

Cedazuélo, *sm.* A small hair-sieve or strainer.

Cedénte, *pa.* Ceding, granting.

Cedér, *va.* To grant, to resign, to yield, to deliver up.—*vn.* 1. To submit. 2. To happen, to turn out ill or well. 3. To abate, to grow less.

Cedízo, za, *a.* Tainted; applied to meat.

Cédo, *ad.* (Ant.) Immediately. V. *Luego.*

Cedría, *sf.* Resin, distilled from the cedar.

Cedríde y Cédrio, *sm.* Fruit of the cedar-tree.

Cedríno, na, *a.* Belonging to the cedar-tree.

Cédro, *sm.* (Bot.) Cedar. Pinus cedrus *L.*

Cédula, *sf.* 1. Slip of parchment or paper written or to write upon. 2. Order, bill, decree. 3. Lot. 4. Schedule; warrant. *Cédula de aduana,* A permit. *Cédula de abono,* Order to remit a tax to a town or province. *Cédula de cambio,* Bill of exchange. *Cédula de inválidos,* Warrant for the reception of invalids *Cédula real,* Royal letters patent. *Cédula de comunion ó confesion,* Card or certificate of one having taken the sacrament. *Cédula ante*

dien, Secretary's summons or notice of meeting to the members of a society. *Echar cédulas*, To draw or cast lots.
CEDULÁGE, *sm.* Fees or dues paid for the expedition of decrees or grants.
CEDULÍLLA ó ITA, *sf.* A small scrap or slip of paper.
CEDULÓN, *sm.* A long edict, a large libellous bill or paper. *Poner cedulones*, To post up edicts or libels.
CEFÁLICA, *sf.* Cephalic vein. [head.
CEFÁLICO, CA, *a.* Cephalic, belonging to the
CÉFALO, *sm.* (Ict.) Mullet, a kind of perch.
CÉFIRO, *sm.* Zephyr, the West wind; poetically, any soft gentle breeze.
CÉFO, *sm.* A large kind of monkey, a native of the northern parts of Africa. Simia cephus *L.*
CEGADÓR, RA, *s.* (Ant.) Flatterer, sycophant.
CEGÁJEZ, *sf.* (Ant.) Weakness of sight.
CEGÁJO, *sm.* A he-goat two years old.
CEGAJÓSO, SA, *a.* Blear-eyed; having the eyes dim with rheum or water.
CEGÁR, *vn.* To grow blind.—*va.* 1. To blind, to make blind, to deprive of sight. 2. (Met.) To darken or obscure the light of reason. 3. To shut a door or window. *Cegar los conductos los pasos, ó caminos*, To stop up channels, passages, or roads. *Cegar una via de agua*, (Naút.) To fother a leak.
CEGARRÍTA, *sm.* One who contracts the eye to see at a distance. *A' cegarritas ó á ojos cegarritas*, Having the eyes shut.
CEGÁTO, TA, *a.* Short sighted.
CEGATÓSO, SA, *a.* V. *Cegajoso.*
CEGUECÍLLO ó CEGUEZUÉLO, *sm.* Little blind fellow.
CEGUEDÁD, *sf.* 1. Blindness, privation of sight. 2. (Met.) Ignorance, intellectual darkness.
CEGUÉRA, *sf.* 1. Infirmity or disorder in the eye. 2. Absolute blindness.
CEGUERÍES, *sm.* Kind of martens.
CEGUINUÉLA, *sf.* (Naút.) Whip staff of the helm. V. *Pinzote.*
CEGÚTA, *sf.* (Ant.) V. *Cicuta.*
CÉJA, *sf.* 1. Eye-brow, the hairy arch over the eye. 2. Edging of clothes. 3. (In stringed instruments) Bridge on which the cords rest. 4. Summit of a mountain. 5. Circle of clouds round a hill. *Dar entre ceja y ceja*, (Met.) To tell one to his face unpleasant truths. *Hasta las cejas*, Full up to the eyes. *Quemarse las cejas*, (Met.) To study with the most intense application; literally, to burn one's eye-brows.
CEJADÉRO, *sm.* Rope or traces of harness fastened to the swing-tree of a carriage or wagon.
CÉJAR, *vn.* 1. To retrograde, to go backward. 2. (Met.) To slacken, to relax.
CEJIJÚNTO, TA, *a.* Having eye-brows which join one another.
CÉJO, *sm.* 1. Thick mist or fog which usually arises from rivers. 2. (Ant.) Frown, a look of displeasure.
CEJUÉLA, *sf.* A small eye-brow.
CELÁDA, *sf.* 1. Ancient piece of armour which covered the head. *Celada Borgeñona*, Burgundy helmet, which covered the head, and left the face free. 2. Ambuscade, ambush. 3. Artful trick to deceive one. 4. Part of the key of the cross-bow. 5. Horse soldier formerly armed with a cross-bow. 6. (Naút.) Decoy or stratagem used by a small ship of war to bring an inferior vessel within gun-shot.
CELADÍLLA, *sf.* Small helmet.
CELADÓR, RA, *s.* 1. Curator, one who in congregations and churches takes care that every thing is right and regular. 2. Monitor, in schools.
CELADÚRA, *sf.* Enamel. V. *Esmalte.*
CELÁGE, *sm.* 1. Colour of the clouds, originating from the reflected rays of the sun. 2. Small cloud moving before the wind. 3. Painting which represents the rays of the sun breaking through the clouds. 4. Presage, prognostic. 5. Sky-light, upper part of a window. *Celáges*, Light swiftly-moving clouds.
CELÁR, *vn.* y *a.* 1. To fulfil the duties of an office with care. 2. To watch any person's motions from fear. 3. To cover, to conceal. 4. V. *Rezelar.* 5. To engrave, to cut in wood.
CÉLDA, *sf.* 1. Cell, the apartment of a religious person in a convent. 2. Small cavities or divisions in bee-hives, which contain the honey. 3. (Naút.) Small cabin on board a ship. 4. Small room.
CELDÍLLA ó CELDÍTA, *sf.* Small cell.
CELEBÉRRIMO, MA, *a. sup.* Most celebrated.
CELEBRACIÓN, *sf.* 1. Celebration, solemn performance. 2. Praise, applause, acclamation.
CELEBRADÓR, *sm.* One who applauds or praises a thing or person.
CELEBRÁNTE, *sm.* A priest in the act of celebrating the mass, or preparing to say it.
CELEBRÁR, *va.* 1. To celebrate, to perform in a solemn manner. *Celebrar misa*, To say mass. 2. To praise, to applaud, to commend. 3. To revere, to respect, to venerate.
CÉLEBRE, *a.* 1. Celebrated, famous, renowned. 2. (Met.) Gay, facetious, agreeable in conversation. [celebrity.
CÉLEBREMENTE, *ad.* Facetiously, merrily; with
CELEBRIDÁD, *sf.* 1. Celebrity, a transaction splendidly solemn. 2. Celebriousness, renown, fame. 3. Pomp, magnificence, or ostentation, with which a feast or event is celebrated.
CELEBRÍLLO, *sm.* Cerebel, the hind part of the brain.
CELÉBRO, *sm.* 1. Skull which contains the brain. 2. Brain, the soft substance contained within the skull. 3. Collection of vessels and organs in the head from which sense and motion arise. 4. (Met.) Fancy, imagination.
CELEMÍN, *sm.* Dry measure, which is the 12th part of a *fanega*, and makes about an English peck. [full.
CELEMINÁDA, *sf.* (Ant.) A celemin, or peck-
CELEMINÉRO, *sm.* (Ant.) Ostler who measures out the grain in inns.
CELERÁDO Y CELERÁRIO, (Ant.) V. *Malvado.*
CELERÁRIO, *sm.* (Ant.) Usurer, one who lends money at interest.
CELERIDÁD, *sf.* Celerity, velocity, swift motion.
CELÉSTE, *a.* 1. Celestial, belonging to the heavenly regions. 2. Relating to the seat of the blessed. 3. Sky-blue.
CELESTÍAL, *a.* 1. Celestial, belonging to the heavenly regions. 2. (Met.) Perfect, agreeable, delightful, excellent.
CELESTIALMÉNTE, *ad.* Celestially; perfectly.
CÉLFO, *sm.* V. *Cefo.*

Célia, sf. (Ant.) Beverage made of wheat.
Celíaca, sf. 1. Celiac artery, which conveys the blood to the lower belly. 2. Kind of diarrhœa.
Celíaco, ca, a. Relating to the lower belly. *Fluxo celiaco*, Flux or considerable looseness of the body.
Celibáto y Celíbe, sm. 1. Celibacy, the state of a single life. 2. One who leads a single life.
Célico, ca, a. Celestial, heavenly.
Celidónia, sf. 1. (Bot.) Celandine, swallow-wort, tether-wort. Chelidonium majus *L.* 2. Swallow-stone, a small stone with various impressions.
Celindráte, sm. Ragout made with coriander-seed.
Celíta, sf. Fish caught in the straits of Gibraltar.
Célla, sf. V. *Celda*.
Cellísca, sf. A common prostitute.
Cellísco, ca, a. Decrepit, wasted and worn out with age and infirmities.
Cellísca, sf. V. *Ventisca*.
Céllo, sm. Hoop.
Celosía, sf. Lattice of a window.
Celóso, sa, a. 1. Light and swift-sailing; applied to small vessels. 2. Crank, unable to carry sails; spoken of vessels and boats.
Celsitud, sf. 1. Celsitude, elevation, grandeur. 2. Highness, a title, now expressed *alteza*.
Céltico, ca, a. Celtic, belonging to the Celts.
Célula, sf. A small cell or cabinet.
Celulílla, sf. A very small cell or cabinet.
Cervellína, sf. Hart's-horn.
Cementación, sf. Cementation.
Cementár, va. V. *Cimentar*.
Cementério ó Cemetério, sm. V. *Cimenterio*.
Céna, sf. 1. Act of supping. 2. Supper. 3. Scene, stage. *Jueves de la cena*, Maundy Thursday, Thursday before Good Friday. *Mas mató la cena que sanó Avicena*, (Prov.) Suppers have killed more than Avicenas ever cured. *Cena del rey*, (Nav. y Ar.) Tax paid for the king's table, called *yantar* in Castile.
Cenácho, sm. Basket or hamper made of bass-weed for carrying fruit and greens.
Cenáculo, sm. The cenatory hall in which our Lord administered the last supper to his disciples.
Cenadéro, sm. (Ant.) A place for supping.
Cenadór, sm. 1. One who is fond of suppers, or who sups to excess. 2. Summer-house in a garden, an arbour. *Cenador chinesco*, Chinese temple.
Cenagál, sm. Quagmire, a marshy place full of mud and dirt. *Meterse en un cenagal*, (Met.) To be involved in an unpleasant arduous affair.
Cenagóso, sa, a. Muddy, miry.
Cenár, va. To sup, to eat the evening meal. *Cenar á escuras*, To sup in the dark for the purpose of saving the candle; to be miserly.
Cencéño, ña, a. 1. Lean, thin, slender. 2. (Ant.) Pure, simple. *Pan cenceño*, Unleavened bread.
Cencérra, sf. 1. Bell worn by the leading mule. V. *Cencerro*. 2. Clack of a mill, which strikes the hopper, and promotes the running of the corn. 3. *Señor cencerra*, Mr. Rattlehead; an appellation given by the students of the great college of Alcalá to the collegian who arrived last. 4. The meat between the throttle and the ribs of that part of mutton which is commonly called the saddle.
Cencerráda, sf. Noise made with bells and horns at the door of an old bridegroom or widower the night of his marriage.
Cencerreár, vn. 1. To jingle continually; applied to wether, mule, or horse bells. 2. To play on an untuned guitar, which sounds ill and hard. 3. To make a dreadful noise, such as knockers, bolts, windows, and doors, strained or moved by the wind.
Cencerréo, sm. Noise made by wether, mule, or horse bells. [or horse bells.
Cencerríl, a. Resembling the noise of wether
Cencerrílla y Cencerríllo, s. A small wether, horse, or mule bell.
Cencérro, sm. 1. Bell worn by the leading mule, which serves as a guide for the rest to follow. 2. Ill-tuned guitar. 3. (Orn.) Wood-crow. Corvus *L.* *No quiero perro con cencerro*, I do not want a dog with a bell; that is, I do not like to engage in a business that is more troublesome than profitable. *Á cencerros tapados*, Privately, by stealth. *Irse á cencerros tapados*, To take French leave, to sneak off.
Cencerrón, sm. A small bunch of grapes which remains after the vintage. [to land.
Cencído, da, a. Untilled, uncultivated; applied
Céncris ó Céncro, sm. Kind of serpent with white spots, resembling millet.
Cendál, sm. 1. Light thin stuff made either of silk or thread. 2. Furbelow, flounce, or trimming of gowns or other garments. 3. (Poét.) Garter. *Cendáles*, Cotton for an ink-stand.
Cendéa, sf. (Navar.) Meeting of the inhabitants of several villages to deliberate on some public business.
Cendolílla, sf. (Ant.) A forward girl, acting with little judgment.
Céndra, sf. Paste made of boiled pot-ash, burnt marrow of rams' horns, and other ingredients, which is used to clean silver. *Ser una cendra*, (Met.) To be as lively as a cricket.
Cendrár, va. (Ant.) V. *Acendrar*.
Cenéfa, sf. 1. Frame of a picture. 2. Printed or painted border of any kind of stuff. 3. Valance, fringes and drapery hanging round the tester and head of a bed. 4. Middle piece of a priest's garment, called *casulla*, which divides it into two parts. 5. (Poét.) Bank of a river or lake, the brim of a pond. 6. *Cenefa de un toldo*. (Naút.) Centre of an awning.
Ceniciéro, sm. Ash-hole, the place where ashes are put.
Ceniciénto, ta, a. Ash-coloured.
Cenít, sm. (Astron.) Zenith, the point over our head, opposite the Nadir.
Ceníza, sf. 1. Ashes, the substance to which all bodies are reduced by burning. 2. Coarse ashes, which remain in the strainer when the lye is made. V. *Cernada*. 3. Ashes, the remains of the dead. *Cenizas azules*, Blue paint extracted from various fossils by burning them; the most perfect of which is the lapis lazuli. *Cenizas de ultramar* Ultramarine. *Dar con los huevos en la ceniza*, (Met.) To overset an affair which was in a way of doing well. *Dia de ceniza, ó miércoles de ceniza*, Ash-Wednesday. *Hacer ceniza ó cenizas alguna*

cosa, (Met.) To be reduced to nothing, to come to nothing. *Poner á uno la ceniza en la frente,* (Met.) To reproach any one with a thing which must make him blush or ashamed.

Cenízo, *sm.* (Bot.) Summer and winter savory. Satureia hortensis *L.*

Cenízo, za, *a.* V. *Ceniciento.*

Cenizóso, sa, *a.* Covered with ashes.

Cenóbio, *sm.* (Ant.) V. *Monasterio.*

Cenobíta, *sm.* One who professes a monastic life.

Cenobítico, ca, *a.* (Ant.) Living in communities; cenobitical.

Cenopégias, *sf. pl.* The feast of the tabernacles among the Jews.

Cenogíl, *sm.* Garter.

Cenória, *sf.* (Ant.) V. *Zanahoria.*

Cenotáfio, *sm.* Cenotaph; a monument erected in memory of a person whose remains are buried in another place.

Censál, *s.* y *a.* (Arag.) V. *Censo y Censual.*

Censalísta, *sm.* (Ar.) V. *Censualista.*

Censatário y Censéro, *sm.* One who pays an annuity out of his estate to another person.

Cénso, *sm.* 1. Money which the proprietors of lands or houses yearly receive for the use of their property. Rent, revenue, tax. 2. Poll-tax, formerly in use among the Romans. 3. *Censo de la poblacion,* Enumeration of the inhabitants of a province or country. *Censo al quitar,* Rent paid by a tenant at pleasure. *Censo de por vida,* Annuity for one or more lives. *Censo de agua en Madrid,* Money paid in Madrid for the water which the inhabitants receive for their houses and gardens.

Censór, *sm.* 1. One appointed by public authority to examine new books and publications, whether they contain any thing contrary to religion and good manners. 2. Critic, reviewer of literary compositions. 3. Censorious person, who finds fault with the actions of others without reason.

Censoría, *sf.* Office of censor.

Censoríno, *a.* Censorian.

Censuál, *a.* Belonging to lawful interest, on money advanced or sunk in useful undertakings.

Censualísta, *sm.* A person in whose favour an annuity has been imposed, and who has the right to enjoy it until his death.

Censuário, *sm.* (Ant.) V. *Censualista.*

Censúra, *sf.* 1. A critical review of literary productions. 2. Censure, blame. 3. Reproach without foundation. 4. Spiritual punishment. 5. Register, list. 6. The office of Roman censor.

Censuráble, *a.* Censurable, worthy of censure, or liable to be censured.

Censuradór, *sm.* One who censures.

Censurár, *va.* 1. To review, to criticise. 2. To censure, to blame, to find fault with. 3. To record, to enter into a list or register. 4. To correct, to reprove.

Centauréa ó Centaúra, *sf.* (Bot.) Centaury. Centaurea *L.*

Centaúro, *sm.* 1. Centaur, a poetical being, supposed to be composed of a man and horse. 2. (Astr.) Archer, a southern constellation.

Centélla, *sf.* 1. Lightning, the flash which attends thunder. 2. Flash struck out of a flint with steel. 3. Remaining spark of passion or discord. *Ser vivo como una centella ó ser una centella,* To be all fire and tow, to be all life and spirit.

Centelladór, ra, *a.* Brilliant.

Centelllánte, *a.* Sparkling, flashing.

Centellár y Centelleár, *vn.* To sparkle, to emit rays of light, to throw out sparks.

Centelléo, *sm.* Spark, scintillation.

Centellíca ó íta, *sf.* A small flash or spark.

Centellón, *sm.* (Aum.) A large spark or flash.

Centéna, *sf.* 1. Centenary, the number of a hundred. 2. (Ant.) Stubbles of rye. 3. Hundredth, the ordinal of hundred.

Centenádas, *ad.* *A centenadas ó á centenares,* By hundreds.

Centenál, *sm.* Field sown with rye. 2. Centenary, the number a hundred.

Centenár, *sm.* V. *Centenal.*

Centenár, *sm.* V. *Centena y Centenario.*

Centenário, ria, *a.* Centenary, secular, happening but once in a century.

Centenário, *sm.* A feast which is celebrated every hundred years.

Centenázo, za, *a.* Belonging to rye. *Paja centenaza,* Rye-straw.

Centéno, *sm.* (Bot.) Rye. Secale *L.*

Centéno, na, *a.* A numeral adjective, which signifies hundred.

Centenóso, sa, *a.* Mixed with rye.

Centésimo, ma, *a.* Centesimal, hundredth.

Centilacion, *sf.* (Ant.) V. *Brillo.*

Centíllo, *sm.* V. *Cintillo.*

Centilóquio, *sm.* A work divided into a hundred parts or chapters, as Ptolemy's book on astronomy.

Centimáno, na, *a.* (Poét.) Having a hundred hands.

Centinéla, *sf.* 1. (Mil.) Sentry or sentinel; a soldier posted on guard either in camp or garrison. 2. (Met.) One who observes closely or pries into another's actions. *Centinela avanzada,* Advanced guard. *Centinela á caballo,* Vedet, a sentinel on horseback. *Centinela perdida,* Forlorn hope, a soldier on guard close to the enemy's camp; also a small body of troops detached on some desperate service. *Hacer centinela, ó estar de centinela,* To stand sentry, to be on guard.

Centinódia, *sf.* (Bot.) Knot-grass. Polygonum aviculare *L.*

Centiplicádo, *ad.* A hundred times more.

Centiplicár, *va.* V. *Centuplicar.*

Centólla, *sf.* (Ict.) Center-fish, a kind of turtle with spotted scales.

Centón, *sm.* 1. Coarse covering of warlike machines in ancient times. 2. Cento, a literary composition formed by joining scraps from other authors.

Centrádo, da, *a.* (Blas.) Applied to a globe placed on the centre.

Centrál y Centricál, *a.* Central, relating or belonging to the centre.

Céntrico, *a.* *Punto céntrico,* Object, end of one's views. V. *Centro.*

Centrífugo, ga, *a.* Centrifugal, that which flies back or recoils from the centre.

Centrípeto, ta, *a.* Centripetal, tending towards the centre.

Céntro, *sm.* 1. Centre, the middle point in a figure, equally remote from its extremities. 2.

Height and depth of a thing. 3. (Met.) The main or principal object of one's desires and exertions. 4. (Bot.) Disk, on the central part of flowers. *Estar en el centro de la batalla,* To be in the centre of the action. *Estar en su centro,* (Met.) To be satisfied with one's fate, *El mando es el centro á que aspira la ambicion,* Command is the point to which ambition aspires.

Centuplicár, va. To centuplicate; to make a hundred-fold.

Céntuplo, pla, a. Hundred-fold.

Centúria, sf. 1. Century, a period of one hundred years. 2. (Among the Romans) Company of 100 soldiers, commanded by a centurion.

Centurión, sm. (In Rome) Centurion, a military officer who commanded 100 men.

Cenzálo, sm. (Ent.) Gnat. Culex *L.*

Cenzáya, sf. 1. A governess of children. 2. Nursery-maid.

Ceñár, vn. To frown, to look angry.

Ceñído, da, a. 1. Moderate, not extravagant in point of pleasure or expense. 2. Ringed, encircled with rings; applied to bees and other insects.

Ceñidór y Ceñidúra, s. Belt, girdle.

Ceñíglo, sm. (Bot.) Goose-foot, summer-cypress. Chenopodium *L.*

Ceñír, va. 1. To gird, to surround; to put on a belt or girdle. 2. To environ, to hem in. 3. (Met.) To reduce, to abbreviate, to contract. *Ceñir espada,* To wear or carry a sword. *Ceñir el viento,* (Naút.) To haul the wind.—*vr.* To reduce one's expenses.

Céño, sm. 1. A supercilious look, a frowning or ruffled countenance. 2. Ring or ferrule put round any thing. 3. (Alb.) Circle round the upper part of a horse's hoof. 4. (Poét.) A mournful or gloomy aspect of the sea.

Ceñóso, sa, a. 1. Hoof surrounded with elevated rings; applied to horses. 2. V. *Ceñudo.*

Ceñúdo, da, a. Frowning, supercilious.

Céo, sm. (Ict.) Doree or dory. Zeus faber *L.*

Cépa, sf. 1. That part of the trunk of a tree which joins the root, and stands in the ground. 2. Stock of a vine. 3. (Met.) Stock or origin of a family. 4. (Met.) Bud or root of the horns and tails of some animals. 5. Root of the wool. 6. First foundation of columns, pilasters, or arches.

Cepacabállo, sm. (Bot.) Cardoon. Cynara carduneulus *L.*

Cepádgo, sm. (Ant.) Jail fees.

Cepejón, sm. The highest and largest branch of a tree torn from the trunk.

Cepilladúras, sf. pl. Shavings pared off with a plane.

Cepillár, va. To plane. V. *Acepillar.*

Cepíllo, sm. 1. Plane, an instrument used to smooth the surface of boards. 2. Brush, an instrument made of bristles for cleaning clothes. 3. Poor-box, a small chest in which alms are put. *La cuña que afianza el hierro cortante del cepillo,* The wedge which keeps the iron of a plane tight.

Cepíta, sf. A small poor-box.

Cépo, sm. 1. Block on which an anvil is put. 2. Stocks, a wooden machine with holes for confining the neck and legs of offenders by way of punishment; on board of ships these stocks are called *bilboes.* 3. Kind of reel or turning frame, on which silk is wound before it is twisted. 4. Trap or snare for catching wolves. 5. Charity-box put up in churches and other public places. 6. V. *Cefo.* 7. (Ant.) The stocks with which a great gun is made fast in the carriage. *Cepo del ancla,* (Naút.) Anchor-stock. *Cepo de maniguetes,* (Naút.) Cross-piece of the kevil. *Cepo de molinete,* (Naút.) Knighthead of the windlass. *Cepos,* Notched cleats or timbers fixed across other timbers to strengthen or secure them where they are pierced. *Cepos quedos,* No more of that; said to make a person change the topic of conversation.

Cepón, sm. A large trunk of a tree, an old vine stock.

Cepórro, sm. An old vine pulled up by the roots.

Cequí ó Cequín, sm. A gold coin, formerly used by the Moors in Spain; at present current in Venice and other parts of Italy.

Céra, sf. 1. Wax, a thick tenacious matter gathered by bees. 2. Tapers and candles made of wax. 3. Foot-path in the street. V. *Acera.* *Cera aleda,* The first coarse wax with which bees bedaub the inside of the hive. *Cera virgen,* Virgin wax. *Cera de los oidos,* Ear-wax. *Hacer de alguno cera y pábilo,* (Met.) To mould one like wax, to make him say or do what one pleases. *No hay mas cera que la que arde,* (Met.) To have spent the last of one's fortune. *Ser una cera, ó como una cera, ó hecha una cera,* (Met.) To be as pliable as wax, to be of a pliant or gentle disposition. *Melar las ceras,* To fill the combs with honey. *Céras,* The whole cells of wax and honey formed by bees.

Cerachátes, sf. pl. Wax-stones, a kind of yellow agate. V. *Cerites.*

Cerafólio, sm. (Bot.) Common chervil. Scandix cerefolium *L.*

Cerapéz, sf. Cerate, a plaster made of wax and pitch.

Cerasína, sf. Beverage made of rice. [serpent.

Cerásta, Ceráste, ó Cerástes, s. Horned

Cerástio de Granada, sm. (Bot.) Mouse-ear. Cerastium *L.*

Ceratófilon, sm. (Bot.) Horn-wort, or pond weed. Ceratophylum *L.*

Cerbatána, sf. 1. Tube made of wood or metal, through which pellets of clay are blown by way of amusement. 2. Acoustic trumpet for deaf people, to help the hearing. 3. Ancient culverin of a very small caliber.

Cerbélo, (Ant.) V. *Cerebelo.*

Cérca, sf. 1. Inclosure, hedge, or wall, which surrounds a garden, park, or corn-field. 2. (Ant.) District belonging to a city or other place. 3. (Ant.) Yard. *Las cercas,* (Among Painters) Objects placed in the fore ground of a painting.

Cérca, ad. 1. Near at hand, not far off, close by. 2. With regard to, relating or belonging to. 3. *En cerca,* Round about. *Tener buen ó mal cerca,* To admit, or not admit of a close examination. *Tocar de cerca,* (Met.) To be nearly allied to, or near akin.

Cercádo, *sm.* A garden or field inclosed or surrounded with a fence; an inclosure.
Cercadór, *sm.* One who incloses or surrounds.
Cercadúra, *sf.* (Ant.) Inclosure, walls, fence.
Cercamiénto, *sm.* (Ant.) Act of inclosing.
Cercanaménte, *ad.* Nigh, at a small distance.
Cercanía, *sf.* Proximity, neighbourhood, vicinity.
Cercáno, na, *a.* Near, close by.
Cercár, *va.* 1. To inclose, to surround with a hedge or wall. 2. (Mil.) To invest a town, to block up a fortress. 3. To crowd about a person. 4. (Ant.) To bring or put near. V. *Acercar.* *Cercado de desdichas y trabajos,* Involved in troubles and distress.
Cercén ó Á Cercén, *ad.* At the root.
Cercenadaménte, *ad.* In a clipping manner.
Cercenadéra, *sf.* Clipping-knife used by wax-chandlers.
Cercenadór, *sm.* One who pares, or clips and lops off, the ends or extremities of things.
Cercenadúra, *sf.* Act of clipping, paring, or lopping off.
Cercenár, *va.* 1. To lop off the ends or extremities. 2. To reduce, to lessen; applied to expenses.
Cercéra, *sf.* Air-tube which reaches from the ceiling of a vault up to the surface of the ground, to extract the foul air.
Cercéta, *sf.* 1. (Orn.) Widgeon, garganey, a kind of small wild duck. Anas querquedula *L.* 2. (Among Sportsmen) The first pearl which grows about the bur of a deer's horn; an antler. 3. (Ant.) Tail of a horse.
Cércha, *sf.* A wooden rule for measuring convex objects.
Cerchár. V. *Acodar.*
Cerchón, *sm.* V. *Cimbria.*
Cercíllo, *sm.* 1. (Ant.) Ear-ring. V. *Zarcillo.* 2. Tendril of the vine. V. *Tixereta.* 3. (Ant.) Hoop. V. *Zarcillo.*
Cércio ó Cerción, *sm.* An Indian mocking-bird, belonging to the family of starlings, which imitates the human voice.
Cerciorár, *va.* To assure, to ascertain, to affirm.
Cérco, *sm.* 1. Hoop or ring which surrounds a thing. 2. (Mil.) Blockade of a place. 3. Circular motion. 4. Circle, a private assembly. 5. Frame or case of a door or window. *En cerco,* Round about. *Poner cerco á una plaza,* To block up a place. *Levantar el cerco,* To raise a blockade. *Entrar en cerco, ó venir al cerco,* To use superstitious rites or customs. *Echar cerco,* To surround game with dogs. *Cerco de puerta ó ventana,* The frame of a door or window. *Cerco del sol y de la luna,* Halo, coloured circle, round the sun or moon. *Hacer un cerco,* To strike or draw a circle.
Cercopitéco, *sm.* Kind of long-tailed monkey.
Cérda, *sf.* 1. Strong hair growing in a horse's tail or mane. 2. Corn just cut down, and formed into sheaves, to be carried to the threshing floor. 3. Bundle of flax broken, but not yet hackled. 4. Sow. *Cerda de puerco,* Hog's bristles. *Ganado de cerda,* Herd of swine. *Cerdas,* Snares for birds.
Cerdámen, *sm.* Handful of bristles.
Cerdána, *sf.* Kind of dance in Catalonia.
Cerdázo, *sm.* 1. A large hog or pig. 2. (Ant.) Hair-sieve. V. *Cedazo.*
Cerdeár, *vn.* 1. To be weak in the fore-quarters on account of a dangerous wound; applied to bulls. 2. To emit a harsh and inharmonious sound; applied to musical instruments. 3. To decline a request or demand by subterfuges and evasions.
Cerdíllo ó Cerdito, *sm.* A small hog or pig.
Cérdo y Cerdúdo, *sm.* Hog or pig. *Cerdo de muerte,* A pig which is a twelve-month old, and fit to be killed. *Cerdo de vida,* A pig which is not yet old or fat enough to be killed.
Cerdóso, sa, y Cerdúdo, da, *a.* Bristly, full of bristles: it is also applied to men whose breasts are covered with hair.
Cerebélo, *sm.* (Anat.) Cerebellum, the hind part of the brain or little brain.
Cerébro. V. *Celebro.*
Cerecílla, *sf.* V. *Guindilla.*
Cerecíta, *sf.* A small cherry.
Ceremónia, *sf.* 1. Rite, religious ceremony; outward form in religion. 2. Form of civility; an affected compliment paid to a person. *Guardar ceremonia,* To stick to the ancient ceremonies and established customs of a society or community. *El lo hace de pura ceremonia,* He does it out of mere compliment or ceremony. *De ceremonia,* With all ceremony or pomp.
Ceremoniál, *sm.* A book of the ceremonies used on public occasions.
Ceremoniál, *a.* Ceremonial, that which relates to ceremony.
Ceremoniáticaménte, *ad.* Ceremoniously, in a ceremonious manner.
Ceremoniático, ca, *a.* Ceremonious, adhering to ceremonies, full of affected politeness.
Ceremoniosaménte, *ad.* According to the outward rites and ceremonies.
Ceremonióso, sa, *a.* Ceremonious, fond of ceremonies, polite.
Céreo, *sm.* (Bot.) Torch-thistle. Cactus *L.*
Cerería, *sf.* 1. Wax-chandler's shop. 2. Office in the royal palace where the wax-candles are kept for the use of the royal family.
Ceréro, *sm.* 1. Wax-chandler. 2. Idle vagrant.
Ceréro, *a.* Idle, loitering from street to street.
Ceréza, *sf.* Cherry. *Cereza garrafal,* The large heart cherry.
Cerezál, *sm.* Plantation of cherry-trees.
Cerézo, *sm.* (Bot.) Cherry-tree. Prunus cerasus *L.*
Cergázo, *sm.* (Bot.) Rock-rose. Cistus *L.*
Ceribón ó Ceribónes, *sm.* (Ant.) Act of an insolvent debtor surrendering his whole estate to his creditors. *Hacer caribones,* (Ant.) To make very submissive and affected compliments.
Ceriflór, *sm.* (Bot.) Honey-wort. Cerinthe *L.*
Cerílla, *sf.* 1. Thin wax-tapers rolled up in a globular form. 2. Ball made of wax and other ingredients, much used by women in former times as a kind of paint. 3. Wax-tablet. 4. Wax of the ear.
Cerimónia, (Ant.) V. *Ceremonia.*
Cerítes, *sm.* Wax-stone, or yellow agate.
Cerméña, *sf.* A small early kind of delicious pear, called the Muscadine pear.
Cerméño, *sm.* (Bot.) Muscadine pear-tree.
Cernáda, *sf.* 1. Coarse ashes which remain in

the mixture after the lye is put on. 2. Size laid on a piece of canvass to prepare it for painting. 3. Plaster of ashes and other ingredients used by farriers in the cure of horses.

Cernadéro, *sm.* 1. Coarse linen which serves as a strainer for the lye to buck clothes with. 2. (Ant.) Thread and silk skeins for making ribbons.

Cernedéro, *sm.* 1. Apron worn by persons employed in sifting flour, to prevent their clothes from being covered with the dust. 2. Place destined for sifting flour.

Cernedór, *sm.* One who sifts flour with a sieve.

Cernéjas, *sf. pl.* Fetlocks of a horse growing behind the pastern joints.

Cernér, *va.* To sift, to bolt, to separate the bran and coarse flour from the fine meal.—*vn.* 1. To bud and blossom. 2. To drizzle, to fall in very small drops.—*vr.* 1. To waggle, to waddle, to move from side to side. 2. To soar; spoken of birds.

Cernícalo, *sm.* (Orn.) Kestrel, wind-hover. Falco tinnunculus *L. Coger ó pillar un cernícalo*, To be fuddled, to be half seas over.

Cernidíllo, *sm.* 1. Thick mist or small rain. 2. A short and waddling gait.

Cernído, *sm.* 1. The act of sifting. 2. The flour sifted.

Cernidúra, *sf.* The act of sifting.

Cernír, *va.* 1. V. *Cerner.* 2. To examine, to purify.

Céro, *sm.* Cipher, an arithmetical mark, which standing for nothing itself, increases the value of the other figures, as 10, ten. *Ser un cero*, To be a mere cipher.

Ceroferário, *sm.* Acolothist, who carries the light in the service of the Roman Catholic church.

Ceróllo, lla, *a.* Applied to grain reaped rather green and soft.

Cerón, *sm.* Dregs of pressed wax formed into a cake.

Ceróte, *sm.* 1. Shoemaker's wax, consisting of pitch and bees-wax. 2. Panic, fear. 3. Cerate, a plaster made of wax and other ingredients.

Cerotéro, *sm.* Piece of an old hat, used by artificial fire-work-makers to wax the twine or packthread for sky rockets.

Ceróto, *sm.* A soft cerate made of oil and wax.

Ceróva, *sf.* Crops of corn which begin to grow yellow.

Cerquíllo, *sm.* 1. A small circle or hoop. 2. The seam or welt of a shoe. 3. Tonsure of a monk or other religious persons.

Cerquíta, *sf.* (Dim.) Small inclosure.

Cerquíta, *ad.* At a small distance, nigh or near in point of time or place.

Cerráda, *sf.* 1. The strongest part of a hide or skin which covers the back-bone of an animal. 2. (Ant.) Shutting or locking up of a thing. *Hacer cerrada*, To commit a gross fault or palpable mistake.

Cerradéro, ra, *a.* 1. Staple or iron loop which receives the bolt of a lock. 2. (Ant.) Purse-strings. *Echar la cerradera*, To lend a deaf ear, to refuse.

Cerradízo, za, *a.* That which may be locked or fastened.

Cerrádo, da, *a.* 1. Close, reserved, dissembling. 2. Secreted, concealed. 3. Obstinate, inflexible. *Cerrado como pie de mulato*, As stubborn as a mule. *Cerrados los ojos*, Without examination. *A puerta cerrada*, Privately, secretly.

Cerradór, *sm.* 1. Porter or door-keeper, one who takes care of a door. 2. Tie, fastening. 3. Bond, obligation.

Cerradúra, *sf.* 1. The act of shutting or locking up. 2. Lock, an instrument composed of springs and bolts, used to fasten doors or chests. *Cerradura de golpe*, Spring lock. 3. Park or piece of ground surrounded with a wall, hedge, or fence; an inclosure.

Cerradurílla ó íta, *sf.* (Dim.) A small lock.

Cerrája, *sf.* 1. Lock of a door. 2. (Bot.) Common sow-thistle. Sonchus oleraceus *L. Todo es agua de cerrajas*, It is all good for nothing; literally, It is all sow-thistle water.

Cerrajeár, *vn.* To carry on the trade of a lock-smith, to make locks.

Cerrajería, *sf.* 1. Trade of a lock-smith. 2. Shop or forge where lock-smiths' work is made.

Cerrajéro, *sm.* Locksmith, one who makes locks, keys, bolts, &c.

Cerramiénto, *sm.* 1. The act of shutting or locking up. 2. Inclosure, the act of inclosing, or ground inclosed. 3. The finishing of the roof of a building. 4. Partition walls which separate the different rooms of a house. 5. (Ant.) Conclusion of an argument; inference.

Cerrár, *va.* 1. To shut up the inlets or outlets of a place, to obstruct a passage. 2. To fit a door or window in its frame or case. 3. To lock a door, to fasten it with a bolt or latch. 4. To include, to contain. 5. To fence or inclose a piece of ground. 6. (Met.) To terminate or finish a thing. 7. To stop up, to obstruct. 8. To prohibit, to forbid, to interdict. 9. To engage the enemy. *Cerrar la carta*, To fold up a letter. *Cerrar la cuenta*, To close an account. *Cerrar la boca*, (Met.) To be silent. *Cerrar la mollera*, (Met.) To begin to get sense. *Cerrar la oreja*, (Met.) Not to listen to one's proposals. *Cerrar la puerta*, (Met.) To give a flat denial. *Cerrar los ojos*, To die; to sleep: (Met.) Blindly to submit to another's opinion. *Al cerrar del dia*, At the close of the day, at night-fall. *A' cierra ojos*, (Met.) Blindly, inconsiderately.—*vr.* 1. To remain in one's opinion firm and unshaken. *Cerrarse de campiña*, To adhere obstinately to an opinion. 2. To grow firm and hard; applied to the bones of children. 3. To be shut or locked up. 4. To grow cloudy and overcast; spoken of the sky. 5. To close up; applied to the ranks and files of a body of troops. *Cerrarse todas las puertas*, To be guarded on all sides, or against any thing which may happen.

Cerraurjál, *sm.* (Ant.) Water conduit.

Cerrazón, *sm.* Dark and cloudy weather which precedes tempests.

Cerrejón, *sm.* Hillock, a small hill or eminence.

Cerréño, ra, *a.* 1. Running wild from one hill or eminence to another. 2. (Ant.) Haughty, lofty.

Cerríl, *a.* 1. Mountainous, rough, uneven; applied to a country or ground. 2. Wild, untamed; applied to cattle. *Puente cerril*, A small narrow bridge, intended merely for cattle. 3. (Met.) Rude, unpolished, unmannerly.

Cerrillár, *va.* To mill coined metal, or mark it at the edge.

Cerríllo, *sm.* A little eminence. *Cerrillos*, The dies for milling coined metal.

Cerrión, *sm.* 1. Icicle, a shoot of ice hanging down. 2. Fresh cheese.

Cérro, *sm.* 1. High land, which is in general craggy, rugged, and rocky. 2. Neck of an animal. 3. Back bone, or the ridge it forms. 4. Flax or hemp which is hackled and cleaned. *Cerro enriscado*, A steep and inaccessible mountain. *En cerro*, Nakedly, barely. *Pasar ó traer la mano por el cerro*, (Met.) To flatter, to cajole. *Cómo por los cerros de Ubeda*, (Fam.) Foreign to the purpose, totally different.

Cerrojíllo, *sm.* 1. (Orn.) A wagtail, warbler. Motacilla provincialis *L.* 2. A small bolt.

Cerrójo, *sm.* Bolt, a short piece of iron to fasten a door or window. *Tentar cerrojos*, (Met.) To try all ways and means to succeed in one's undertakings. [tow.

Cerrón, *sm.* Kind of linen in Galicia made of

Cerrumádo, **da**, *a.* Having weak or defective quarters; applied to horses.

Cerrúmas, *sf. pl.* Weak or defective quarters in horses.

Certámen, *sm.* 1. (Ant.) Duel; battle. 2. Controversy, disputation.

Certamente, (Ant.) V. *Ciertamente*.

Certería, *sf.* (Ant.) Dexterity. V. *Tino*.

Certéro, **ra**, *a.* Dexterous or skilled in shooting and fowling.

Certéza, *sf.* Certainty, that which admits no doubt.

Certidúmbre, *sf.* 1. V. *Certeza*. 2. (Ant.) Security, obligation to fulfil any thing.

Certificación, *sf.* 1. Certificate, an instrument attesting the truth of some fact or event. 2. Return of a writ. 3. Certainty, security.

Certificadór, *sm.* One who certifies.

Certificár, *va.* 1. To assure, to affirm, to certify. *Certificar el pliego ó la carta*, (In the Post-office) To assure that a letter will arrive where it is directed. 2. To prove by means of a public instrument.

Certificatório, **ria**, *a.* That which certifies, or serves to certify.

Certinidád y **Certitúd**, (Ant.) V. *Certeza*.

Cerúleo, **lea**, *a.* Sky-blue or light blue.

Cerúma, *sf.* V. *Cerrumas*.

Cervál, *a.* Belonging to a deer, or resembling it. *Miedo cerval*, Great timidity.

Cervário, **ria**, *a.* V. *Cerval*.

Cervática, *sf.* V. *Langoston*.

Cervatíco ó **Cervatíllo**, *sm.* A small deer.

Cerváto, *sm.* A young deer, not yet full grown.

Cervecería, *sf.* 1. Brewhouse. 2. Alehouse where beer is sold.

Cervecéro, *sm.* One who brews or sells beer.

Cervéda, *sf.* Extremity of the ribs of pork.

Cervéza, *sm.* Beer or ale, a liquor prepared from malt and hops.

Cervicabra, *sf.* Gazelle, an animal which partakes both of the figure of the deer and of the goat.

Cervicúdo, **da**, *a.* 1. High or thick necked. 2 (Ant.) Obstinate, stubborn.

Cervigullo, *sm.* Nape, the joint of the neck behind.

Cervíno, **na**, *a.* Resembling a deer, or belonging to it.

Cerviólas, *sf. pl.* (Naut.) Cat-heads. V. *Serviolas*.

Cervíz, *sf.* Nape, the hind part of the neck. *Hombre de dura cerviz*, A stubborn obstinate man. *Ser de dura cerviz*, To be incorrigible. *Bajar la cerviz*, (Met.) To humble one's self. *Levantar la cerviz*, (Met.) To be elated, to grow proud.

Cervúno, **na**, *a.* Resembling or belonging to a deer; being of the colour of a deer.

Cesácio ó **Cesación á Divinis**, *s.* (Latin.) Suspension from religious functions. [stop.

Cesación y **Cesamiénto**, *s.* Cessation, pause,

Cesár, *vn.* To cease, to give over.

César, *sm.* Name of the Roman Emperor. *O' Cesar ó nada*, Neck or nothing.

Cesáreo, **rea**, *a.* Imperial, belonging to an emperor or empire. *Operacion cesárea*, The Cesarian operation, by which a child is cut out of the womb of the mother.

Cése, *sm.* Cease; a mark put against the names of military men who are pensioners on the civil list, that their pay should cease.

Cesíble, *a.* That which may be ceded.

Cesíon, *sf.* Cession, or transfer of goods or estates made in one's favour; resignation. *Cesion de bienes*, Surrender of the whole estate of an insolvent debtor into the hands of his creditors.

Cesionário y **Cesonário**, **ria**, *s.* One in whose favour a transfer is made.

Césped ó **Céspede**, *sm.* 1. That part of the rind of a vine where it has been pruned. 2. Sod, or turf covered with grass. *Cesped francés*, (Bot.) Common thrift, sea-gilly flower. Statice armeria *L.*

Cespedéra, *sf.* Field where green sods are cut.

Césta, *sf.* Basket, pannier. *Llevar la cesta*, (Met.) To pander, to procure women for the lust of others.

Cestáda, *sf.* A basket-full.

Cestería, *sf.* Place where baskets are made or sold.

Cestéro, *sm.* One that makes or retails baskets.

Cestílla ó **Cestíta**, *sf.* A small basket.

Cestíco ó **Cestíllo**, *sm.* A little basket.

Césto, *sm.* Maund, a hand basket. *Estar hecho un cesto*, To be overcome by sleep or liquor. *Quien hace un cesto hará ciento*, (Prov.) He that steals a pin will steal a pound; literally, He that makes one basket will make a hundred. *Ser alguno un cesto*, To be ignorant and rude.

Cestón, *sm.* 1. A large pannier or basket. 2 (Mil.) Gabion, a wicker basket filled with earth, and used in trenches and redoubts to cover troops from the enemy's fire.

Cestonáda, *sf.* Range of gabions to cover troops from the fire of the enemy.

Cestro, (Ant.) V. *Sistro*.

Cesúra, *sf.* Cesura, a figure or a pause in poetry.

Cetáceo, **cea**, *a.* Cetaceous, of the whale kind.

Céiti, *sm.* An old Galician coin, which made the sixth part of a Spanish maravedi.

Cétra, *sf.* A leather shield formerly used by the Spaniards.

Cétre, *sm.* A small brass or copper bucket. V. *Acetre.*

Cetrería, *sf.* 1. Falconry, the art of taming, teaching, and keeping falcons, and other birds of prey. 2. Fowling with falcons.

Cetréro, *sm.* 1. Verger, he that carries a staff and cloak before the bishop, dean, or chapter. 2. Falconer, sportsman.

Cetrífero, *sm.* One who bears a sceptre.

Cetríno, na, *a.* 1. Citrine, lemon-coloured, of a pale yellow. 2. (Met.) Jaundiced, melancholy.

Cétro, *sm.* 1. Sceptre, the ensign of royalty borne in the hand. 2. (Met.) Reign of a prince. 3. Verge borne by dignified canons on solemn occasions. 4: Wand or staff borne by the deputies of confraternities in their feasts and meetings. 5. Perch or roost for birds.

Ceúma, *sf.* (Ret.) Zeugma, a figure in Rhetoric.

Cevíl, *a.* (Ant.) Vile, despicable. V. *Civil.*

Cevilidád, *sf.* (Ant.) Misery, meanness. V. *Civilidad.*

Céyba, *sf.* (Bot.) 1. Sea-weed or sea-moss. 2. Large tree in the Indies, with a poisonous juice.

Chá, *sf.* 1. (In New Spain) Tea, the leaf of a shrub which grows in China, and several parts of Africa. 2. A very thin and light kind of stuff used by the Chinese.

Chabacanaménte, *ad.* In a bungling manner.

Chabacána, *sf.* An insipid kind of plum.

Chabacanería, *sf.* Want of cleanliness and elegance. [finished.

Chabacáno, na, *a.* Coarse, unpolished, ill-

Chabéta ó Chavéta, *sf.* Forelock-key. *Perder la chabeta,* (Met.) To lose one's senses.

Chabnám, *sf.* Sort of muslin, called also *rosee.*

Chacál, *sm.* Jackall, an animal of the size of a fox. Canis aureus *L.*

Chacáry, *sf.* Kind of cotton stuff.

Cháchara, *sf.* Chit-chat, idle prate; garrulity. *Todo eso no es mas que chachara,* That is all mere chit-chat.

Chacharreár, *vn.* To prate to no purpose.

Chacharéra, *sf.* Forward, talkative woman.

Chacharrería, *sf.* Verbosity, verbiage, garrulity. [talker.

Chacharéro y Chacharón, *sm.* Prater, idle

Chácho, *sm.* 1. Stake at the game of *ombre.* 2. Word of endearment to children.

Chacína, *sf.* (Extrem.) Pork seasoned with spice for sausages and balls.

Chacolí, *sf.* A light red wine of a sourish taste, which is made in Biscay.

Chacoloteár, *vn.* To move and clap, as a horse-shoe does for want of nails.

Chacoloteo, *sm.* The clapping of a horse-shoe for want of nails.

Chacóna, *sf.* Tune of a Spanish dance of that name.

Chacóta, *sf.* Noisy mirth. *Echar á chacota alguna cosa,* To carry a thing off with a joke. *Hacer chacota de alguna cosa,* To turn a thing into ridicule. [scoff.

Chacoteár, *vn.* To indulge in noisy mirth, to

Chacotéro, *sm.* A wag, a merry-andrew.

Chacotéro, ra, *a.* Waggish, ludicrous, acting the merry-andrew.

Chácra, *sf.* An Indian rustic habitation without order or neatness.

Chacuáco, *sm.* Clown; a coarse ill-bred man.

Chafaldétes, *sm.* (Naút.) Clue lines.

Chafálla, *sf.* An old tattered suit of clothes.

Chafallár, *va.* To botch, to mend or patch in a clumsy manner.

Chafállo, *sm.* Coarse patch, place mended in a botching and clumsy manner.

Chafallón, na, *s.* A botching tailor.

Chafár, *va.* 1. To make velvet or plush lose its lustre by pressing or crushing the pile. 2. (Met.) To cut one short in his discourse, so that he does not know what to say.

Chafaróte, *sm.* A short broad Turkish sword.

Chafarrináda, *sf.* 1. Blot or stain in clothes. 2. (Met.) Spot in reputation and character.

Chafarrinár, *va.* To blot, to stain.

Chafarrinón, *sm.* Blot, stain. *Echar un chafarrinon,* (Met.) To disgrace one's family by some mean or dishonourable action.

Chafarconéas, *sf. pl.* Kind of printed or coloured linen.

Chaflán, *sm.* Bevel, obtuse angle.

Chaflanár, *va.* To form a bevel, to cut a slope.

Chalán, na, *s.* 1. Dealer, trader. 2. Jobber, regrater, forestaller.

Chalaneár, *va.* 1. To buy and sell, as a dealer and chapman. 2. To forestall, to regrate.

Chalanería, *sf.* Artifice and cunning used by dealers in buying and selling.

Chaléco, *sm.* An inside waistcoat.

Chalón ó Chalún, *sm.* Shalloon, a kind of woollen stuff.

Chalúpa, *sf.* (Naút.) Sloop, a small light vessel, a long boat.

Chamaleón, *sm.* V. *Camaleon.*

Chamarásca, *sf.* A brisk fire, made of brushwood, but of short duration.

Chamaráz, *sf.* (Bot.) Water-germander. Teucrium scordium *L.*

Chamarilléro, *sm.* 1. Broker who deals in old pictures and furniture. 2. Gambler.

Chamarillón, *sm.* A bad player at cards.

Chamaríz, *sm.* (Orn.) (And.) Blue tit-mouse. Parus cæruleus *L.*

Chamarón, *s.* (Orn.) Long-tailed titmouse. Parus caudatus *L.*

Chamárra, *sf.* Garment made of sheep skins, or of very coarse frieze.

Chamarréta, *sf.* A short loose jacket with sleeves.

Chambérga, *sf.* 1. A long and wide cassock with facings and sleeves of the same stuff, or of the colour of the lining. 2. A regiment raised in Madrid during the minority of Charles the IId. 3. Kind of Spanish dance accompanied by a merry song. 4. A narrow silk girdle.

Chambérgo, ga, *a.* Slouched, uncocked; applied to a round hat worn by the regiment of *Chamberga,* and ever since a round uncocked hat has retained that name.

Chamelóte, *sm.* Camblet. *Chamelote de aguas,* Clouded camblet. *Chamelote de flores,* Flowered camblet.

Chamelotína, *sf.* Kind of coarse camblet.

Chamelotón, *sm.* Coarse camblet.

Chamberlúco, sm. Kind of close jacket with a collar, formerly worn by women.

Chamicéra, sf. A piece of wood scorched and made black by fire.

Chamicéro, ra, a. Belonging to scorched wood.

Chamíza, sf. Kind of wild cane or reed.

Chamízo, sm. A piece of wood half burnt.

Chamórra, sf. (In the jocular style) A shorn head.

Chamorráda, sf. Butt given with a shorn head.

Chamorrár, va. To cut the hair off with shears.

Chamórro, ra, a. Shorn, bald, without hair. *Trigo chamorro*, (Bot.) Beardless wheat. Triticum sativum aristis carens *L.*

Champáda, sf. A large stately tree in Malaga.

Champán, sf. Kind of American vessel of about seventy or eighty tons burthen.

Champión, (Ant.) V. *Gladiator*.

Champurrár, va. 1. To mix one liquor with another. 2. (Met.) To speak with an unconnected mixture of words of different languages.

Chamuscádo, da, a. Tipsy, flustered with wine; addicted to some vice.

Chamuscádo, da, pp. Singed; tinged, inclined.

Chamuscár, va. To singe or scorch the outside of a thing.

Chamúsco, sm. V. *Chamusquina.*

Chamuscón, sm. A large singe or scorch.

Chamusquína, sf. 1. The act of scorching or singeing. 2. (Met.) Scolding, wrangling, high words. *Oler á chamusquina*, (Met.) To come from hot words to hard blows.

Chanceár, vn. To jest, to joke.—*vr.* To indulge in jests and jokes.

Chancellár, va. V. *Cancelar*.

Chancellér, (Ant.) V. *Canciller*.

Chancéro, ra, a. Jocose, merry, given to jests.

Cháncharras Mángharras, sf. pl. (Bax.) *No andemos en chancharras mancharras*, Let us not go about the bush, or make use of subterfuges and evasions.

Chancíca ó Chancílla, sf. A little fun or jest.

Chancillerésco, ca, a. Belonging to the court of chancery.

Chancillería, sf. 1. Chancery, the supreme tribunal of equity and justice. 2. The office and dignity of a chancellor. 3. The rights and fees of a chancellor.

Chancíta, sf. A little fun.

Chancléta, sf. Slipper. V. *Chinela*. *Andar en chancleta*, To go slipshod.

Chánclos, sm. pl. 1. Pattens, pieces of wood with an iron ring, worn under the shoes by women to keep them from dirt. 2. Strong leather clogs worn over shoes to preserve gentlemen's feet from moisture and dirt.

Chanfáyna, sf. 1. Ragout of livers and lights. 2. A trifling worthless thing.

Chanflón, na, a. 1. Made in a coarse and clumsy manner; applied to things and persons. 2. Finished in a bungling manner; applied to counterfeit money. [larger.

Chanflon, sm. Money beaten out to appear

Changóte, sm. An oblong bar of iron.

Chantár, va. V. *Vestir*.

Chántre, sm. Precentor, a dignified canon of a cathedral church. [centor.

Chantría, sf. The office and dignity of a pre-

Chánza, sf. Joke, jest, fun, *chanzas pesadas*, A sarcastic taunt.

Chanzonéta, sf. 1. Joke, jest. 2. A little merry song, a ballad.

Chanzonetéro, sm. Sonnetteer, a petty poet.

Cháos, sm. V. *Caos*.

Chápa, sf. 1. A thin metal plate which serves to strengthen or adorn the work it covers. 2. Rosy cheek, blush. 3. Rouge, paint used by ladies. 4. A small bit of leather laid by shoemakers under the last stitches to prevent the bindings giving way. 5. *Chapas de freno*, The two bosses or pieces put on each side of the bit of a bridle. 6. Transom and trunnion plates in gun carriages. *Hombre de chapa*, A man of judgment, abilities, and merit.

Chapadaménte, ad. (Ant.) Perfectly, elegantly.

Chapaléta, sf. (Naút.) A kind of valve made of strong leather, which is put at the bottom of a ship's pump, and serves as an *embolus* or sucker.

Chapár, va. (Ant.) To plate, to coat.

Chapárra, sf. 1. Species of oak. V. *Chaparro*. 2. A coach with a low roof.

Chaparráda, sf. V. *Chaparrón*. [trees.

Chaparrál, sm. Plantation of ever-green oak-

Chapárro, sm. (Bot.) Ever-green oak-tree. Quercus ilex *L.*

Chaparrón, sm. A violent shower of rain.

Chapeár, va. To adorn or garnish with metal plates.—*vn.* V. *Chacolotear*.

Chapeléta de una bomba, sf. (Naút.) The clapper of a ship's pump. *Chapeletas de los imbornales*, (Naút.) The clappers of the scupper holes. [the head, like a bonnet or hat.

Chapeléte, sm. (Arag.) An ancient cover for

Chapelína, sf. An ancient small gold coin.

Chapélo y Chapéo, (Ant.) V. *Sombrero*.

Chapería, sf. Ornament consisting of a number of metal plates.

Chaperón, sm. Ancient hood or cowl.

Chapéta ó Chapílla, sf. A small metal plate, *Chapeta*, Red spot on the cheek.

Chapetón, sm. An European settler in Peru.

Chapetonáda, sf. A disease incident to Europeans who settle in Peru, before they are accustomed to the climate of that country.

Chapín, sm. Clog with a cork sole lined with Morocco leather, worn by women to keep their shoes clean. *Chapin de la reyna*, Tax of 150 millions of maravedis formerly levied in Spain on the occasion of the king's marriage.

Chapinázo, sm. Stroke or blow given with a clog or patten.

Chapinería, sf. Shop where clogs and pattens are made and sold. [sell clogs and pattens.

Chapinéro, sm. One whose trade is to make and

Chapiníto, sm. A small clog.

Chapitél, sm. 1. The upper part of a pillar rising in a pyramidal form. 2. A small moveable brass plate over the compass. 3. V. *Capitel*.

Cháple, sm. Graver, the tool used in engraving.

Chapodár, va. To cut or lop off the branches of trees and vines.

Chapóte, sm. Kind of black glue or wax in America, which is said to be used for cleaning the teeth.

Chapoteár, va. To wet with a spunge or wet cloth.

—vn. To paddle in the water so as to splash or scatter it about.

Chapuceár, va. To botch, to bungle, to perform clumsily.

Chapuceramente, ad. In a coarse or clumsy manner.

Chapucería, sf. A clumsy performance.

Chapucéro, sm. 1. Blacksmith, who makes nails, trevets, shovels, and other iron work. 2. Bungler, botcher, one who performs his work in a clumsy manner.

Chapucéro, ra, a. Rough, unpolished, rude.

Chapúz, sm. 1. The act of ducking one, or putting his head under water. 2. A clumsy performance. V. *Chapucería*. *Chapúces*, (Naút.) Mast spars.

Chapuzár, va. 1. To duck, to put one's head under water. 2. To paddle with the oars.—vn. To dive, to plunge suddenly into water.

Chaquéte, sm. Game resembling back-gammon.

Chaquíra, sf. Kind of pearl-white glass beads, much esteemed by the Peruvians, and sold to them by the Spaniards.

Charádrio, sm. (Orn.) Common roller. Coracias garrula. L. V. *Gálgulo*.

Charánchas, sf. pl. (Naút.) Battens used as supporters on board a ship.

Charanguéro, ra, a. Showy, tawdry colours.

Charanguéro, sm. Pedler, hawker.

Chárca, sf. Pool of water collected on purpose to make it congeal to ice.

Chárcanas, sf. Kind of stuff made of silk and cotton.

Chárco, sm. Pool of standing water. *Pasar el charco*, To cross the seas. *Hacer charcos en el estómago*, To drink too much water.

Chárla, sf. 1. (Orn.) Bohemian chatterer, silktail. Ampelis garrulus *L.* 2. Idle chit-chat or prattle.

Charladór, ra, s. V. *Charlatan*.

Charlár, vn. To prattle, to babble, to prate.

Charlatán, na, s. Prater, babbler, idle talker.

Charlataneár, vn. V. *Charlar*.

Charlatanería, sf. Garrulity, loquacity, charlatanry.

Charlatanísmo, sm. The conduct and proceedings of a prater, verbosity.

Charmílla, sf. (Bot.) Hornbeam tree. Carpinus betulus *L.*

Charnéca, sf. (Bot.) Mastic-tree. Pistacea lentiscus *L.*

Charnecál, sm. Plantation of mastic trees.

Charnéla, sm. Hinge of a box.

Charnéta, sf. (Ant.) Iron plate.

Charól, sm. Varnish, a matter laid on wood or metal to make it shine.

Charolár, va. To varnish.

Charolísta, sm. Gilder, varnisher, or japanner.

Chárpa, sf. Belt with a hook at the end on which fire-arms are hung.

Charpár, va. To scarf, to lap one thing over another.

Charquíllo, sm. A small pool or puddle.

Charráda, sf. Speech or action of a clown.

Charradaménte, ad. Clownishly, tastelessly.

Charretéra, sf. 1. Stripe of cloth or leather, used under the foot to fasten trousers or gaiters. 2. Epaulet, a gold, silver, or silk tassel, worn by military men on the shoulder.

Charríote, sm. V. *Carro*.

Chárro, ra, s. 1. A clownish, coarse, ill-bred person. 2. Peasant of Salamanca.

Chárro, ra, a. Gaudy, loaded with ornaments in a tasteless and paltry manner.

Chás, sm. A low word, denoting the noise made by the cracking of wood or tearing of linen.

Chásco, sm. 1. Fun, joke, jest. 2. An unexpected contrary event or disappointment. 3. Lash, the thong or point of the whip. *Dar chasco*, To play a merry trick.

Chasqueár, va. To crack with a whip or lash.—vn. 1. To crack as timber does at the approach of dry weather. 2. To play a waggish trick.

Chasquí, sm. (Peru) Post-boy or messenger on foot.

Chasquído, sm. 1. Crack of a whip or lash. 2. Crack, the noise made by timber when it breaks into chinks or splits.

Cháta, sf. 1. (Bot.) Round-leaved Egyptian or hairy cucumber. Cucumis chate *L.* 2. (Naút.) A flat-bottomed boat. *Chata alijadora*, Lighter. *Chata de arbolar*, Sheer-hulk. *Chata de carenar*, Careening-hulk.

Chato, ta, a. Flat. *Nariz chata*, A flat nose. *Embarcacion chata*, A flat-bottomed vessel.

Chavarí, sm. Kind of linen.

Chavéta, sf. 1. Forelock key. V. *Chabéta*. 2. Forelock plate.

Chavónis, sf. A kind of muslin.

Chaúl, sm. A kind of blue silk stuff manufactured in China, resembling European grogram.

Cháza, sf. 1. Point where the ball is driven back or where it stops, in a game at balls. 2. (Naút.) Birth on board a ship. *Hacer chaza*, To walk on the hind feet; applied to a horse that rears.

Chazadór, sm. A person employed to stop the ball and mark the game.

Chazár, va. 1. To stop the ball before it reaches the winning point. 2. To mark the point whence the ball was repulsed or driven back.

Chelés, sm. pl. A kind of cotton stuff of different colours.

Chelín, sm. Shilling, an English coin, worth about four and one half *reales de vellon*.

Chéno, na, a. (Ant.) Full. V. *Lleno*.

Chequíllo, lla, to, ta, a. dim. (Ant.) V. *Chiquillo*.

Cheremía y Cheremílla, (Ant.) V. *Chirimia*.

Chérna, sf. (Ict.) Ruffle, a fish resembling a salmon. Perca cernua *L.*

Cherquénola, sf. Kind of stuff made in the East Indies of silk and bark.

Cherubín, sm. (Ant.) V. *Querubin*.

Chérva, sf. (Bot.) Great spurge, Palma Christi. Ricinus communis *L.*

Chevrón, sm. (Blas.) Chevron, a piece representing two rafters of a house joined, and without a division.

Chevronádo, da, a. (Blas.) Coat charged with chevrons.

Chía, sf. 1. A short black mantle, formerly worn in mournings. 2. Cowl, made of fine cloth, and worn by the nobility by way of distinction. 3. A white medicinal earth.

Chiár, vn. To chirp or chirrup like birds. V. *Piar*.

Chíba, sf. Goat. V. *Cabra*.

Chibál, sm. Herd of goats.

Chibalétes, sm. Chest of drawers with a desk for writing. V. *Escritorio*.
Chibáta, sf. (And.) Shepherd's club or staff.
Chibáto, sm. Kid between six and twelve months old.
Chibetéro y Chibitál, sm. Fold or pen where kids are put.
Chíbo, sm. 1. Kid, a he-goat not yet twelve months old. 2. Pit, a place for the lees of oil which glides from the press.
Chíbon, sm. 1. A young cock-linnet. 2. Sort of gum which is brought from America.
Chibón, sm. Kind of monkey. V. *Cafo*.
Chicáda, sf. Herd of sickly kids.
Chicarréro, sm. V. *Zapatillero*.
Chícha, sf. 1. Children's meat. 2. Beverage made of Indian corn. *Ser cosa de chicha y nabo*, To be of little importance. *Tener pocas chichas*, To be very lean.
Chícharo, sf. (Bot.) Pea. Pisum sativum *L.*
Chicharra, sm. Frothworm, harvest-fly. Cicada spumaria *L.* *Es una chicharra*, A prattling, chattering person. *Cantar la chicharra*, To be scorching hot.
Chicharrár, va. V. *Achicharrar*.
Chicharréro, sm. A hot place or climate.
Chicharro, sm. 1. (Ict.) A young tunny-fish. 2. (Ict.) Horse-mackerel. Scomber trachurus *L.* 3. Roll of tobacco kindled at one end and smoked at the other.
Chicharrón, sm. Dried morsel of lard fried in a frying-pan.
Chichería, sf. Tavern where the beverage called *chicha* is sold.
Chichisveadór, sm. Gallant, wooer. [love.
Chichisveár, va. To woo, to court, to sue for
Chichisvéo, sm. Court and attendance paid to a lady; cicisbeo.
Chichón, sm. 1. Lump on the head occasioned by a knock or blow. 2. Bruise. V. *Abolladura*. [lump.
Chichoncíllo ó Chichoncíto, sm. Small
Chichóta, sf. A complete or perfect thing or business, so that nothing is wanting.
Chíco, ca, a. Little, small. *Chicho con grande*, Both great and small.
Chíco, Chíca, s. A little boy or girl.
Chicoleár, va. To joke or jest.
Chicoléo, sm. Joke, jest in gallantry.
Chicória, sf. V. *Achicoria*.
Chicorrotíco, ca; llo, lla; to, ta, a. Very little or small.
Chicorrotín, a. Very small.
Chicóte, ta, s. 1. A fat strong boy or girl; used to express affection. 2. (Naút.) End of a rope or cable.
Chicozapóte, sm. An American fruit resembling a peach both in colour and taste.
Chicuélo, la, s. A little child.
Chífla, sf. 1. Whistle, a small wind-instrument. 2. (With Book-binders) Paring knife with which skins are made thin.
Chiflacayóte, sm. A large kind of pumpkin in America.
Chifladéra, sf. Whistle.
Chifladúra, sf. Whistling.
Chiflár, va. (With Book-binders) To pare leather for covering books.—vn. 1. To whistle, to raise a sound with a small wind-instrument. 2. To mock, to jest. 3. To tipple, to drink to excess.
Chíflo, sm. 1. Whistle. 2. Call, an instrument used by bird catchers to decoy birds into their snares. 3. (Naút.) Priming-horn used by the gunners of the navy. 4. (Naút.) Tide. *Aguas chiflas*, Neap-tide.
Chifléte y Chiflo, sm. V. *Chifla*.
Chiflído, sm. Sound of a whistle or call.
Chilacayóte, sm. (Bot.) American or bottle gourd. Cucurbita lagenaria *L.*
Chíle, sf. (Bot.) Small American red pepper. Capsicum annuum *L.*
Chiléra, sf. (Naút.) Row-lock-hole.
Chilindrína, sf. Trifle; a thing of little value.
Chilindrón, sm. 1. Kind of game at cards. 2. Assemblage, collection. 3. Cut in the head.
Chílla, sf. Call for foxes, hares, or rabbits. *Clavo de chilla*, Tack, a sort of nail. *Tablas de chilla*, Thin boards. *Chillas*, Kind of East India cotton stuff.
Chilládo, sm. Roof, consisting of shingles or thin boards.
Chilladór, ra, s. Person who shrieks or screams; a thing that creaks.
Chillár, vn. 1. To scream, to shriek; to creak, as a cart-wheel. 2. To imitate the notes of birds. 3. To hiss; applied to things frying in a pan.
Chilléras, sf. pl. (Naút.) Shot-lockers in which balls are kept on board a ship.
Chillído, sm. 1. Squeak or shriek; a shrill disagreeable sound. 2. Bawling of a woman or child.
Chíllo, sm. Call. V. *Chilla*.
Chillón, sm. 1. Bawler, screamer, shrieker. 2. Common crier. 3. Nail, tack. *Chillon real*, Spike or long nail used to fasten large timbers or planks. *Clavo chillon*, Tack or small nail.
Chílo, sm. Chyle. V. *Quilo*.
Chimenéa, sf. 1. Chimney; a fire-place with a funnel, through which the smoke ascends. 2. (Met.) Head. *Se le subió el humo á la chimenea*, The vapour has mounted to his head; spoken of one affected with drink.
Chiméra, sf. Chimera, a vain and wild fancy.
Chimia y Chímica, sf. Chemistry. V. *Química*.
Chimísta, sm. (Ant.) Chemist.
Chino, sm. Kind of antispasmodic used in South America.
China, sf. 1. Pebble, a small stone. 2. A medicinal root brought from China. 3. Porcelain, china; a fine sort of earthenware. 4. China silk or cotton stuff. *Media China*, Cloth coarser than that from China. 5. Boyish play of shutting the hands, and guessing which contains the pebble.
Chinár, vn. V. *Rechinar*.
Chinárro, sm. A large pebble.
Chinateádo, sm. Stratum or layer of pebbles or small stones.
Chinázo, sm. A large pebble.
Chincharrázo, sm. Thrust or cut with a sword in an affray.
Chincharréro ó Chinchorréro, sm. Place swarming with bugs.
Chínche, sm. Bug, a fetid insect. Cimex *L.* *Caer ó morir como chinches*, To die like rotten sheep; literally, like bugs.

CHINCHÉRO, *sm.* Bug-trap made of twigs.
CHINCHÍLLA, *sf.* A small quadruped in Peru resembling a squirrel, well known for its fur.
CHINCHÓN, *sm.* V. *Chichon.*
CHINCHORRERÍA, *sf.* 1. (Ant.) Lying jest. 2. Whisper, mischievous tale.
CHINCHORRÉRO, RA, *s.* Insidious tale-teller.
CHINCHÓRRO, *sm.* 1. Fishing-boat used in America. 2. Kind of fishing-net.
CHINCHÓSO, SA, *a.* Peevish, fastidious.
CHINÉLA, *sf.* 1. Slipper. 2. Kind of pattens or clogs worn by women in dirty weather.
CHINILLA ó CHINÍTA, *sf.* A small pebble.
CHÍNO, NA, *s.* Chinese, any thing which is from China; applied particularly to a species of dogs. Canis familiaris turcicus *L. ¿Somos chinos?* Do you think me a simpleton?
CHÍO CHÍO, *sm.* Chirping of sparrows.
CHIQUÉRO, *sm.* 1. Hog-sty, a place where hogs are kept. 2. (Extr.) Hut for goats and kids.
CHIQUICHÁQUE, *sm.* 1. (Vulg.) One whose trade is to saw wood and timber. 2. Noise made by things rubbing against each other.
CHIQUÍLLO, LLA, *s.* A small child.
CHIQUÍTICO, CA; CHIQUITÍLLO, LLA; CHIQUIRRÍTICO, CA; CHIQUIRRITÍLLO, LLA, ITO, TA: CHIQUITÍN Y CHIQUIRRITÍN, *a.* (Dim.) Very small, or little.
CHIQUÍTO, TA, *a.* Little, small. *Hacerse chiquito,* (Met.) To dissemble or conceal one's knowledge on power. [corner.
CHIRIBÍTIL, *sm.* A narrow and low little hole or
CHIRICÁYTA, *sf.* (Mur.) Kind of gourd.
CHIRIMÍA, *sf.* Clarion, a musical wind-instrument.—*sm.* Clarion-player.
CHIRIMÓYA, *sf.* A kind of American pear.
CHIRINÓLA, *sf.* 1. Game played by boys. 2. Trifle, a thing of little importance or value.
CHIRIPEÁR, *vn.* (Joc.) To prattle; to clatter.
CHIRIVÍA, *sf.* 1. (Bot.) Parsnip. Pastinaca sativa L. 2. (Orn.) Wagtail. V. *Aguzanieve.*
CHÍRLA, *sf.* Muscle. V. *Almega.*
CHIRLADOR, RA, *s.* A clamorous prattler, a talkative person.
CHIRLÁR, *vn.* To prattle, to talk much and loud.
CHÍRLO, *sm.* A large wound in the face; the scar it leaves when cured.
CHIROMÁNTICO, *sm.* Chiromancer, professor of chiromancy.
CHIRRIÁDO, *sm.* V. *Chirrido.*
CHIRRIADÓR, RA, *a.* 1. Hissing like hog's lard, oil, or dripping, in which something is fried. 2. Creaking, as a door.
CHIRRIÁR, *vn.* 1. To hiss, as hog's lard or oil in which something is fried. 2. To creak as a door or cart. 3. To sing out of tune or time.
CHIRRICHÓTE, *sm.* A presumptuous man. *Chirrichótes,* A nick-name for French priests who travel in Spain.
CHIRRÍDO, *sm.* Chirping of birds.
CHIRRÍO, *sm.* The creaking noise made by carts and wagons.
CHIRRIÓN, *sm.* A strong muck or dung cart which creaks very loudly; one-horse cart.
CHIRRIONÉRO, *sm.* One who drives a dung-cart.
CHIRUMBÉLA, *sf.* V. *Churumbela.*
CHIRÚRGICO. V. *Quirurgico.*
CHISGARAVÍS, *sm.* An insignificant noisy fellow, who meddles and interferes in every thing.

CHISGUÉTE, *sm.* A small draught of wine.
CHISMÁR, *va.* (Ant.) To tattle. V. *Chismear.*
CHÍSME, *sm.* 1. Tale or story which is intended to excite discord and quarrels. 2. Variety of lumber of little value.
CHISMEÁR, *va.* To tattle, to carry tales.
CHISMÓSO, SA, *a.* Tattling, tale-bearing, propagating injurious rumours.
CHÍSPA, *sf.* 1. Spark emitted by some igneous body. 2. A very small diamond. 3. (Rar.) A short gun. 4. Small particle. V. *Migaja.* 5. Penetration, acumen. *Fulano tiene chispa,* Such a one is very acute. *Ser una chispa,* To be all life and spirit. *Echar chispas,* (Met.) To be in a violent passion.
CHISPÁS! *interj.* Fire and tow.
CHISPÁZO, *sm.* 1. The act of a spark flying off from the fire, and the damage it does. 2. (Met.) Tale or story carried from one to another with a view of breeding discord.
CHISPEÁR, *vn.* 1. To sparkle, to emit sparks. 2. To rain gently or in small drops.
CHISPÉRO, *sm.* Smith who makes kitchen utensils.
CHISPÉRO, RA, *s.* Emitting a number of sparks.
CHÍSPO, *sm.* (Bax.) V. *Chisguete.*
CHISPORROTEÁR, *vn.* To hiss and crackle as burning oil or tallow mixed with water.
CHISPORROTÉO, *sm.* Sibilation, hissing, crackling.
CHISPÓSO, SA, *a.* Sparkling, emitting sparks.
CHISTÁR, *vn.* To mumble, to mutter. *No chistó palabra,* He did not open his lips.
CHÍSTE, *sm.* 1. A fine witty saying. 2. Fun, joke, jest. *Dar en el chiste,* To hit the nail on the head. [men keep their fish
CHISTÉRA, *sf.* A narrow basket in which fisher-
CHISTÓSO, SA, *a.* Gay, cheerful, lively, facetious.
CHÍTA, *sf.* 1. The ankle-bone in sheep and bullocks. 2. Game with this bone. *No vale una chita,* It is not worth a rush. *Tirar á dos chitas,* To have two strings to one's bow. *Dar en la chita,* (Met.) To hit the nail on the head. *Caga chitas,* (Vulg.) Nick-name to deformed wandering persons.
CHÍTES, *sm.* Kind of cotton stuff.
CHITICÁLLA, *sm.* One who keeps silence, and divulges not what he sees.
CHITICALLÁR, *va.* To keep silence. *Ir ó andar chiticallando,* To go on one's tip-toes, not to make a noise.
CHÍTO, *sm.* A piece of wood, bone, or other substance, on which the money is put in the game of *chito. Irse á chitos,* To lead a debauched life, to run from pleasure to pleasure.
CHITO ó CHITÓN, *interj.* Hush! not a word! Mum! Mum! *Con el rey y la inquisicion chiton,* (Prov.) Towards the king and inquisition be silent and respectful.
CHO! *interj.* A word used by the drivers of mules or horses to make them stop.
CHÓCA, *sf.* 1. Part of the game given to a hawk. 2. Stick or paddle with which soap-boilers stir the lie of barilla or ashes when they make soap.
CHOCADÓR, RA, *s.* One that irritates or provokes.
CHOCÁLLO, (Ant.) V. *Zarcillo.*
CHOCÁNTE, *a.* Provoking, irritating.
CHOCÁR, *vn.* 1. To strike, to dash against one

another. 2. To fight, to combat.—*va.* To provoke, to vex, to disgust.
CHOCARREÁR, *vn.* To joke, to jest, to act the buffoon.
CHOCARRERÍA, *sf.* 1. Buffoonery, low jests, scurrilous mirth. 2. Deceiving, cheating at play. V. *Fullería.*
CHOCARRÉRO, *sm.* 1. Buffoon, one who practises indecent raillery, or gross jocularity. 2. Cheat, or sharper at play. V. *Fullero.*
CHOCARRÉRO, RA, *a.* Practising indecent raillery.
CHOCARRÉSCO, CA, *a.* (Ant.) V. *Chocarrero.*
CHÓCHA ó CHOCHAPERDIZ, *sf.* (Orn.) Woodcock. Scolopax rusticola *L.*
CHOCHEÁR, *vn.* To dote, to have the intellect impaired by age.
CHOCHÉRA ó CHOCHÉZ, *sf.* Dotage, the speech and action of a dotard.
CHOCHÍLLA, *sf.* A small hut, a low cottage.
CHÓCHO, CHA, *a.* Doting, having the intellect impaired by age.
CHÓCHO, *sm.* 1. (Bot.) Lupine. V. *Altramuz.* 2. A sweetmeat or confection with a bit of cinnamon in the middle of it. *Chóchos,* All sorts of sweetmeats given to children.
CHOCLÁR, *vn.* 1. (In the Spanish game of *Argolla*) To drive the ball right out by the rings. 2. (Ant.) To bolt into a room.
CHÓCLO, *sm.* V. *Chanclo.*
CHOCLÓN, *sm.* (In the Spanish game of *Argolla*) The driving of a ball through the rings.
CHÓCO, *sm.* (Viz. y Gal.) The small cuttle-fish. Sepia sepiola *L.* V. *Xibia.*
CHOCOLÁTE, *sm.* Chocolate, a paste composed of cocoa-nut, sugar, and cinnamon; beverage.
CHOCOLATÉRA, *sf.* Chocolate-pot, in which the chocolate is boiled and beat up.
CHOCOLATÉRO, *sm.* One who grinds or makes chocolate.
CHOCOLOTEÁR, *vn.* V. *Chacolotear.*
CHÓDE, *sm.* Paste made of milk, eggs, sugar, and flour.
CHÓFA, *sf.* Falsehood, lie, false assertion.
CHOFEÁR, *va.* To utter falsehoods. V. *Mentir.*
CHOFÉRO, *sm.* V. *Chofista.*
CHÓFES, *sm. pl.* Lungs. V. *Bofes.*
CHOFÉTA, *sf.* Chafing-dish, a vessel for making any thing warm, a portable grate for coals.
CHOFÍSTA, *sm.* 1. One who lives upon livers and lights. 2. One that tells or asserts falsehoods.
CHÓLLA, *sf.* 1. Skull or upper part of the head. 2. (Met.) Faculty, powers of the mind, judgment. *No tiene cholla,* He has not the brains of a sparrow.
CHÓPA, *sf.* 1. (Ict.) Kind of sea-bream having a black spot on its tail. Sparus melanurus *L.* 2. (Naút.) Top-gallant poop, or poop-royal.
CHÓPO, *sm.* (Bot.) Black poplar-tree. Populus nigra *L.*
CHÓQUE, *sm.* 1. Shock, the striking or dashing of one thing against another. 2. (Mil.) Skirmish, a slight engagement. 3. Difference, dispute, contest. *Choques de henchimientos,* (Naút.) Filling pieces. *Choques de entremises,* (Naút.) Faying-chocks.
CHOQUEZUÉLA, *sf.* (Anat.) The whirlbone of the knee in the knee-pan.
CHÓRCA, *sf.* Pit or hole dug in the ground. V. *Hoyo.*

CHÓRCHA, *sf.* V. *Chochaperdiz.*
CHORDÓN, *sm.* Raspberry-jam. V. *Churdon.*
CHORICÉRO, *sm.* One who sells sausages.
CHORÍZO, *sm.* Pork-sausage, a gut filled with minced meat, salt, and spice.
CHORLÍTO, *sm.* 1. (Orn.) Curlew or grey plover, Scolopax arquata *L.* 2. (Orn.) Redshank, Scolopax calidris *L.*
CHORREÁDO, *sm.* Satin.
CHORREÁR, *vn.* 1. To fall or drop from a spout; applied to liquids. 2. (Met.) To come successively, or one by one; applied to things and persons. *Esta noticia está chorreando sangre,* This piece of news is piping-hot.
CHORRÉRA, *sf.* 1. Spout or place from whence liquids drop. 2. Mark left by water or other liquids. 3. Ornament which was formerly appended to military crosses or badges of military orders. 4. Frill of a shirt.
CHORRETÁDA, *sf.* Water or other liquid rushing from a spout. *Hablar á chorretadas,* (Met.) To speak fast and thick.
CHORRÍLLO Y CHORRÍTO, *sm.* 1. A small spout of water or any other liquid. 2. The continual coming in and out-going of money. *Irse por el chorrillo,* (Met.) To drive with the current, to conform to custom.
CHÓRRO, *sm.* 1. Water, or any other liquid, issuing from a spout or other narrow place. 2. A strong and coarse sound emitted by the mouth. 3. Hole made in the ground for playing with nuts. *Soltar el chorro,* (Met.) To burst out into laughter. *A' chorros,* Abundantly, copiously.
CHORRÓN, *sm.* Hackled or dressed hemp.
CHOTACÁBRAS, *sf.* (Orn.) Goat-sucker. Caprimulgus *L.*
CHOTÁR, *va.* (Ant.) To suck. V. *Mamar.*
CHÓTO, *sm.* A sucking kid.
CHOTÚNO, NA, *a.* 1. Sucking; applied to young goats or kids. 2. Poor, starved; applied to lambs. *Oler á chotuno,* To stink like a goat.
CHÓVA, *sf.* (Orn.) Jay, chough. Corvus glandarius *L.*
CHÓYA, *sf.* (Orn.) Jackdaw. Corvus monedula *L.*
CHÓZ, *sm.* Sound which is the effect of a blow or stroke. *Esta especie me ha dado choz,* I was struck with amazement at this affair.
CHÓZA, *sf.* Hut, a shepherd's cottage.
CHÓZNO, NA, *s.* Great grandson or great granddaughter.
CHOZUÉLA, *sf.* A small hut or cottage.
CHUBÁRBA, *sf.* (Bot.) Stone-crop. Sedum album *L.*
CHUBÁSCO Y CHUBÁZO, *sm.* (Naút.) Squall, a violent gust of wind and rain.
CHÚCA, *sf.* The concave part of a ball which is used by boys for playing.
CHUCÁLLO, (Ant.) V. *Zarcillo.*
CHUCÉRO, *sm.* (Mil.) Pikeman, a soldier armed with a pike.
CHÚCHA, *sf.* Opossum, an American animal of the order Feræ. Didelphis *L.*
CHUCHEÁR, *va.* 1. To fowl with calls, gins, and nets. 2. To whisper. V. *Cuchichear.*
CHUCHERÍA, *sf.* 1. Gewgaw, bauble, a pretty trifle without value. 2. Tid-bit which is nice but not expensive. 3. Mode of fowling with calls, gins, and nets.

Chuchéro, *sm.* Bird-catcher.
Chúcho, *sm.* 1. (Orn.) Long eared owl. Strix otus *L.* 2. A word used to call a dog.
Chuchuméco, *sm.* A sorry, contemptible little fellow.
Chuchurrár, *va.* 1. To press and squeeze a thing so as to make it lose its shape. 2. To bruise, to pound with a pestle.
Chúco, *sm.* (Extr.) Francis.
Chuéca, *sf.* 1. Pan or hollow of the joints of bones. 2. A small ball with which country-people play at crickets. 3. Fun, trick.
Chuecázo, *sm.* Stroke given to a ball.
Chúfa, *sf.* 1. (Bot.) The edible cyperus. Cyperus esculentus *L.* 2. (Ant.) Rodomontade, an empty boast. *Echar chufas*, To hector, to act the bully.
Chufár ó **Chufeár**, *vn.* 1. To mock, to burlesque. 2. To hector, to bully.
Chuféta, *sf.* 1. Jest, joke. 2. Small pan with feet and a handle, used to hold live coals.
Chufléta, *sf.* Taunt, jeer, contemptuous scoff.
Chufletear, *vn.* To sneer, to taunt, to show contempt.
Chufletéro, ra, *a.* Taunting, sneering.
Chuláda, *sf.* 1. Droll speech or action, pleasant conversation. 2. Contemptuous word or action.
Chuleár, *va.* 1. To jest, to joke. 2. To sneer, to taunt, to ridicule.
Chulería, *sf.* A pleasing manner of acting and speaking.
Chuléta, *sf.* Veal steak, or mutton-chop, fried or broiled.
Chulíllo, lla, y to, ta, *s.* A comical little wag.
Chúlla, *sf.* (Arag.) Slice of bacon.
Chúlo, la, *s.* 1. Punster, jester, merry-andrew. 2. An artful, sly, and deceitful person. 3. Butcher's mate or assistant. 4. Bullfighter's assistant, ready to assist him if he should be in danger. 5. V. *Pícaro*.
Chumacéra, *sf.* (Naút.) Cloth put on the side of a boat to prevent the oars from wearing it.
Chumár, *va.* (Vulg.) To drink. V. *Beber*.
Chúmbo, ó **higo de chumbo**, *sm.* Indian fig.
Chúnga, *sf.* Jest, joke. *Estar de chunga*, To be merry, or in good humour.
Chúpa, *sf.* Waistcoat.
Chupadéra, *sf.* (Anat.) The emulgent vein which brings down the urine.
Chupadéro, ra, *a.* Sucking, drawing out milk or other liquids with the lips; absorbent.
Chupádo, da, *a.* Lean, emaciated.
Chupadór, ra, *s.* 1. One who sucks or draws out with the lips. 2. A child's coral.
Chupadúra, *sf.* The act and effect of sucking.
Chúpa-flores, Chúpa-miel, Chúpa-romeros, *s.* (Orn.) Humming-birds. Trochili *L.*
Chupalandéro, *sm.* A kind of snail that lives on trees and plants.
Chupamelóna, *sf.* (Joc.) A coxcomb.
Chupár, *va.* 1. To suck, to draw out with the lips. 2. To imbibe moisture; applied to vegetables. 3. (Met.) To spunge, to hang meanly and artfully upon others for subsistence. *Chuparse los dedos*, To eat with much appetite. *Chupar la sangre*, (Met.) To quit another's property with cunning and deceit.
Chupatívo, va, *a.* Of a sucking nature, having the power to suck.
Chupéta, illa, y íta, *sf.* A short waistcoat.
Chupéte, *sf.* *Ser alguna cosa de chupete*, To possess great delicacy and good taste.
Chupeteár, *va.* To suck, to use suction; to kiss the skin of children.
Chupetín, *sm.* A man's inner garment or doublet.
Chupetón, *sm.* Suction.
Chupón, *sm.* 1. Sucker, a young twig shooting from the stock. 2. The act of sucking. 3 Doublet. V. *Chupetin*.
Chupón, na, *a.* One who with cunning and deceit deprives another of his money.
Chupóda, *sf.* A mean, blood-sucking strumpet.
Churdón, *sm.* Raspberry-jam.
Chúrla ó **Chúrlo**, *s.* Bag in which cinnamon and other spices are brought from the East Indies.
Chúrra, *sf.* The little pin-tailed grouse. Tetrao alchata *L.*
Chúrre, *sm.* Thick dirty grease.
Churretáda. V. *Chorretada*.
Churretóso, sa, *a.* Gushing, spouting; applied to fluids.
Churribúrri, *sm.* 1. A low fellow. 2. Rabble.
Churriénto, ta, *a.* Greasy.
Churrilléro, ra, *s.* (Ant.) V. *Charrullero*.
Chúrro, ra, *a.* Applied to sheep that have coarse wool in consequence of being fed in plains. V. *Riberiégo*.
Churrulléro, *sm.* 1. Tattler, prattler, gossip. 2. Deserter.
Churrupeár, *vn.* (Bax.). To sip, to drink by small draughts.
Churrús, *sm.* Kind of silk stuff interwoven with a little gold and silver.
Churruscárse, *vr.* To be scorched, to begin to be burnt, as bread, stewed meat, &c.
Churrúsco, *sm.* Bread which is too much toasted, or which begins to burn.
Churumbéla, *sf.* Wind instrument resembling a hautboy or clarion.
Churúmo, *sm.* Juice or substance of a thing. *Hay poco churumo*, There is little cash.
Chus ni mus, (Bax.) *No decir chus ni mus*, Not to say a word.
Chuscáda, *sf.* Pleasantry, drollery, buffoonery.
Chúsco, ca, *a.* Pleasant, droll, merry.
Chúsma, *sf.* 1. The crew and slaves of a row-galley. 2. Rabble, mob.
Chuzeár, *va.* V. *Cuchuchear*.
Chuzázo, *sm.* 1. Pike, a long weapon for a foot soldier. 2. Blow or stroke given with a pike.
Chúzo, *sm.* (Naút.) Pike used on board a ship to keep off the enemy at boarding. *Chuzos*, Copiousness, abundance of any thing. *A' chuzos*, Abundantly; impetuously. *Echar chuzos*, To brag.
Chuzón, na, *s.* 1. A crafty, artful, cunning person. 2. Wag, punster, jester. 3. A large pike.
Cía, *sf.* Hip-bone.
Ciabóga, *sf.* (Naút.) The act of tacking or putting a row-galley about with one side of the oars. *Hacer ciaboga*, to turn the back, to flee.
Ciaescúrre, *sf.* The act of putting about and backing a row-galley.

Ciánco, *sm.* (Ant.) Hip-bone. V. *Cia.*
Ciáno, *sm.* (Bot.) The blue bottle. Cyanella *L.*
Cianqueár ó Cianqueár, *va.* (Ant.) To draw the hip-bone well in a painting.
Ciár, *va.* 1. (Naút.) To hold water, to back a row-galley, to stop with the oars. 2. (Ant.) To retrograde. 3. (Met.) To slacken in the pursuit of an affair.
Ciática, *sf.* Sciatica, lumbago, or hip-gout.
Ciático, ca, *a.* Sciatical, afflicting the hip.
Cibário, ria, *a.* Concerning all species of food or provisions; chiefly applied to regulations relative to that subject.
Cibdad, Cibdáde, y Cibdát, (Ant.) V. *Ciudad.*
Cibéleo, lea, *a.* (Poét.) of Cybele, belonging to Cybele.
Cibéra, *sf.* 1. Quantity of wheat which is put at once into the hopper. 2. All sorts of seeds or grain fit for animal subsistence. 3. Coarse remains of grain and fruit, the substance of which has been extracted by chewing. 4. Every operation which engages the powers of imagination and fancy. 5. Hopper in a corn-mill, the box into which corn is put to be ground.
Cibíca, *sf.* Clouts, the iron plates nailed to the end of the axle-tree, or any other implement exposed to friction.
Cibicón, *sm.* A large kind of clouts.
Cíbolo, la, *s.* A quadruped called the Mexican bull.
Cicateár, *vn.* To be sordidly parsimonious.
Cicatería, *sf.* Niggardliness, avarice, sordid parsimony.
Cicateríllo, lla, *s.* A sordid or avaricious little person. It is also used as an adjective.
Cicatéro, ra, *a.* Niggardly, sordid, parsimonious.
Cicateruélo, *sm.* An avaricious or niggardly little fellow, a little miser.
Cicatricílla, *sf.* A small scar, the mark of a slight wound.
Cicatríz, *sm.* 1. Cicatrice, the scar remaining after a wound. 2. (Met.) Impression which remains in the mind of some feeling or passion.
Cicatrización, *sf.* Cicatrization, the act of healing a wound.
Cicatrizál, *a.* Belonging to a cicatrice or scar.
Cicatrizár, *va.* To heal a wound, to apply such medicines to wounds as skin them.
Cicatrizatívo, va, *a.* That which has the power of cicatrizing, or of healing and skinning a wound.
Cicerón, *sm.* Mixture of meal, honey, water, and other ingredients.
Cicércha, *sf.* Small kind of chick pea.
Ciceroniáno, na, *a.* Ciceronian; applied to style.
Cicilaón, *sm.* (Bot.) Bitter vetch. Orobus *L.*
Ción, *sm.* An intermittent fever.
Cicláda, *sf.* Kind of undress for ladies.
Ciclán, *sm.* A male animal which has but one testicle.
Ciclár, *va.* To clean, to polish, to burnish.
Cíclo, *sm.* Cycle, a round of time, a space in which the same revolution begins again, a periodical space of time.
Cíclope, *sm.* Cyclops.

Cicúta, *sf.* 1. (Bot.) Hemlock. Conium *L.* Cicuta aquatica, (Bot.) Water-hemlock. Cicuta virosa *L.* *Cicuta de España*, Spanish hemloc[k]. 2. Pipe or flute made of reed, a flagelet.
Cídra, *sf.* 1. Fruit which has the smell, tast[e] and shape of a lemon. 2. (Ant.) Conser[ve] made of citrons.
Cidracayóte, *sm.* (Bot.) The American gour[d]. Cucurbita citrullus, folio colocynthidis *L.*
Cidrál, *sm.* Plantation of citron trees.
Cidría, *sf.* V. *Cedria.*
Cídro, *sm.* (Bot.) Citron-tree. Citrus *L.*
Cidroníla, *sf.* (Bot.) Common balm. Melis[sa] officinalis *L.*
Ciegaménte, *ad.* Blindly, without sight.
Ciégo, ga, *a.* 1. Blind, deprived of sight. [2.] (Met.) Swayed by some violent passion. *Ciego de ira*, Blind with passion. 3. Choaked [or] shut up; applied to a passage. 4. Lar[ge] black pudding. V. *Mercon.* *A' ciegas*, Blin[d]ly, in the dark.
Cieguecíco, ca; llo, lla; to, ta, y Ci[e]guezuélo, la, *a. y s.* A little blind pe[r]son.
Ciélo, *sm.* 1. Heaven, the expanse of the sk[y], atmosphere. 2. Habitation of God and pu[re] souls departed. 3. The supreme power, t[he] sovereign of heaven. 4. Climate. *Este es* [un] *cielo benigno*, This is a mild climate. *España goza de benigno cielo*, Spain enjoys a salub[ri]ous air. *Mudar cielo*, To change the air. [5.] Roof, ceiling. *El cielo del toldo de un bo[te]* (Naút.) The roof of a boat's awning. *Cielo raso*, Flat roof. *El cielo de la cama*, Tester [or] cover of a bed. *El cielo del coche*, The ro[of] of a coach. *El cielo de la boca*, The roof [of] the palate. *Estar hecho un cielo*, To be sple[n]did, to be most brilliant. *Tomar el cielo c[on] las manos*, (Met.) To be transported wi[th] rapture or passion.
Cién, *a.* One hundred; it is always used b[e]fore substantives instead of *ciento*, as, *Cien doblones*, A hundred pistoles.
Ciénaga, *sf.* A miry place. V. *Cenegal.*
Ciencabézas, *sf.* (Bot.) Common eryng[o]. Eryngium campestre *L.*
Ciéncia, *sf.* 1. Science, an art attained by pr[e]cepts or built on principles. 2. Knowledg[e], certainty. *A' ciencia y paciencia*, By one's knowledge and permission. *Cierta cienci[a]*, Complete knowledge.
Ciéno, *sm.* Mud, mire, a marshy ground.
Ciént, (Ant.) V. *Cien y ciento.*
Ciental y Cientañál, *a.* (Ant.) Centenar[y] consisting of 100 years.
Ciénte, *a.* (Ant.) Learned, knowing, skilful.
Cienteménte, *ad.* (Ant.) In a knowing, sur[e] and prudent manner.
Científicamente, *ad.* Scientifically, in a scien[tific] manner.
Científico, ca, *a.* Scientific.
Ciénto, *a.* One hundred.
Ciénto, *sm.* 1. A hundred. *Un ciento de huevos*, A hundred of eggs. 2. A hundred-weight. V. *Quintal.*—*pl.* 1. Tax assessed at so much per cent. 2. Piquet, a game at cards.
Cientopiés, *sm.* Wood-louse, millepedes, hog louse. Oniscus asellus *L.*
Ciérne, *sf.* (Ant.) Blossom of vines and corn

En cierne, In blossom. *Estar en cierne*, (Met.) To be in its infancy.
Cierra España, The war-hoop of the ancient Spaniards.
Cierro, *sm.* The act and effect of enclosing.
Ciertamente, *ad.* Certainly.
Cierto, ta, *a.* 1. Certain, doubtless. 2. Used in an indeterminate sense, as, *Cierto lugar*, A certain place; but in this case it always precedes the substantive. *Ciertos son los toros*, The story is true; it is a matter of fact. *Me dan por cierto que*, I have been credibly informed that. *Por cierto*, Certainly, surely; in truth.
Cierva, *sf.* Hind, the female to a stag.
Ciervo, *sm.* Deer, hart, stag.
Ciervo volante, *sm.* Stag-beetle. Lucanus cervus L.
Cierzo, *sm.* A cold northerly wind. *Tener ventana al cierzo*, (Met.) To be haughty, lofty, elated with pride.
Cifac ó Cifaque, *sm.* (Ant. Anat.) The peritoneum.
Cifra, *sf.* 1. A secret or occult manner of writing, intelligible to those only who have a key to it. 2. Intertexture of letters engraved on seals or painted on coaches. 3. Contraction, abbreviation. 4. An arithmetical mark. *En cifra*, Briefly, shortly, in a compendious manner: obscurely, mysteriously.
Cifrar, *va.* 1. To cipher, to cast up accounts. 2. To write in ciphers. 3. To abridge or shorten a discourse.
Cigarra, *sf.* Balm-cricket. Cicada L.
Cigarral, *sm.* (Toledo) Orchard or fruit-garden.
Cigarro, *sm.* A small roll of tobacco, kindled at one end and smoked at the other.
Cigarrón, *sm.* 1. A large roll of tobacco for smoking. 2. A large balm-cricket.
Cigatera, *sf.* Prostitute that submits to every thing.
Cigoñal, *sm.* Machine in the shape of a stork's neck, with which water is drawn up out of wells by the help of a crank or draw-beam.
Cigoñino, *sm.* (Orn.) A young stork.
Cigoñuela, *sf.* (Orn.) A small bird resembling a stork.
Ciguatera, *sf.* (America) Kind of jaundice, occasioned by eating diseased fish.
Ciguato, ta, *a.* V. *Aciguatado*.
Cigúda, *sf.* (Ant.) V. *Cicuta*.
Ciguente, *sm.* Kind of white grape.
Cigüeña, *sf.* 1. (Orn.) White stork, a bird of passage. Ardea ciconia L. 2. Crank of a bell, to which a cord is fastened to ring it. 3. *Cigüeña de piedra de amolar*, The iron winch of a grind-stone. 4. *Cigüeña de cordeleria*, (Naút.) A laying-hook or winch.
Cigüeñal, *sm.* V. *Cigoñal*.
Cigüeño, *sm.* 1. A male stork. 2. (Joc.) Tall, slender, and silly-looking person.
Cigüeñuela, *sf.* Small crank of a bell.
Cigüeñuelo de la caña del timon, (Naút.) The goose-neck of the tiller.
Cigzaque, *sm.* (Mil.) Zigzag, line of approach made in the form of a Z.
Cija, *sf.* 1. Dungeon, dark narrow prison. 2. (Ant.) Granary.

Cilantro, *sm.* (Bot.) Coriander. Coriandrum sativum L. V. *Culantro*.
Cilicio, *sm.* 1. Hair-cloth, very rough and prickly. 2. A cilicium, or hair covering for the body, in ancient times frequently worn as penance. 3. Girdle or band made of bristles or netted wire, with projections or points, and worn in mortification of the flesh. 4. (Mil.) Hair cloth laid on a wall to preserve it.
Cilíndrico, ca, *a.* Cylindric or Cylindrical; in the form of a cylinder.
Cilindro, *sm.* Cylinder, a body which has two flat surfaces and one circular; a roller.
Cilla, *sf.* Granary for tithes and other grain.
Cillazgo, *sm.* Store-house fees paid by the persons concerned in the tithes which are kept in a granary.
Cillerero, *sm.* Steward, provider.
Cilleriza, *sf.* A nun who has the direction of the domestic affairs of the convent.
Cillero, *sm.* 1. Keeper of a granary or store-house where tithes are kept. 2. Vault, cellar, store-room.
Cima, *sf.* 1. Summit of a mountain or hill. 2. Top of trees. 3. Heart and tender sprouts of cardoons. 4. End or extremity of a thing. *Á la por cima*, (Ant.) Lastly, to conclude. *Por cima*, At the uppermost part, at the very top. *Dar cima*, To conclude happily.
Cimacio, *sm.* Moulding which is half convex and half concave. *Cimacio del pedestal*, Cornice of a pedestal.
Cimar, *va.* (Ant.) To clip or cut the tops of dry things, as plants, hedges.
Cimarrón, na, *a.* Wild, unruly; applied to men and beasts.
Cimbalaria, *sf.* Ivy-wort; a plant which grows on old walls.
Cimbalillo, *sm.* A small bell.
Címbalo, *sm.* Cymbal, a musical instrument used by the ancients.
Címbara, *sf.* (And.) A large sickle, used to cut away low shrubs and other plants.
Cimbel, *sm.* 1. Decoy-pigeon, which serves to lure others. 2. Rope with which decoy-pigeons are made fast.
Cimborio ó Cimborrio, *sm.* Cupola. V. *Cúpula*.
Cimbornales, *sm. pl.* (Naút.) Scupper-holes. V. *Imbornales*.
Cimbra, *sf.* 1. A wooden frame for constructing an arch. 2. *Cimbra de una tabla*, (Naút.) The bending of a board.
Cimbrado, *sm.* Quick movement in a Spanish dance.
Cimbrar y Cimbrear, *va.* To brandish a rod or wand. *Cimbrar á alguno*, To give one a drubbing.—*vr.* To bend, to vibrate.
Cimbreño, ña, *a.* Pliant, flexible; applied to a rod or cane which doubles easily.
Cimbreo, *sm.* Bending or moulding of a plank.
Cimbria, *sf.* V. *Cimbra*.
Cimbronazo, *sm.* Blow or stroke given with a foil. V. *Cintarazo*.
Cimentado, *sm.* Refinement of gold.
Cimentador, *sm.* (Ant.) He who lays the foundation of any thing.
Cimental, (Ant.) V. *Fundamental*.
Cimentar, *va.* 1. To lay the ground-work or

foundation of a building. 2. (Met.) To establish the fundamental principles of religion, morals, and sciences. 3. To refine or purify metals.

Cimentéra, *sf.* (Ant.) The art of laying the ground-work or foundation of a building.

Cimentério, *sm.* Cemetery, church-yard.

Ciméra, *sf.* Crest of a helmet.

Ciméro, *sm.* A very dark place.

Ciméro, ra, *a.* Placed at the height of some elevated spot.

Cimiénto, *sm.* 1. Ground-work or foundation of a building. 2. (Met.) Basis, origin. *Cimiento real,* A composition of salt, vinegar, and brick-dust, for purifying gold.

Cimíllo, *sm.* Decoy-pigeon, which serves to call and ensnare others.

Cimitárra, *sf.* Cimeter, a short curved sword.

Cimitério ó Cimintério, *sm.* V. *Cimenterio.*

Cimórra, *sf.* Glanders, a disease in horses, consisting in a morbid running from the nostrils.

Cinábrio, *sm.* 1. Kind of gum, distilled from a tree in Africa. 2. Cinnabar. 3. Vermilion or artificial cinnabar, made of mercury and sulphur sublimed.

Cinamómino, *sm.* An aromatic ointment, the chief ingredient of which is taken from the bead-tree.

Cinamómo, *sm.* (Bot.) The bead-tree. Melia azedarach *L.*

Cínca, *sf.* *Hacer cinca en el juego de bolos,* To gain five points in the game of nine-pins.

Cincél, *sm.* Chisel, an edged tool.

Cinceladór, *sm.* Engraver, sculptor, stone cutter.

Cinceladúra, *sf.* Fretwork; embossment.

Cincelár, *va.* To cut with a chisel, to engrave, to emboss.

Cincelíto, *sm.* Small chisel.

Cínch ó Cinck, *sm.* Zink, spelter.

Cíncha, *sf.* Girth, a band by which the saddle or burthen is fixed upon a horse. *Ir rompiendo çinchas,* To drive on full speed.

Cinchadúra, *sf.* The act of girthing.

Cinchár, *va.* To girth, to bind with a girth.

Cinchéra, *sf.* 1. Girth-place, the spot where the girth is put on a mule or horse. 2. Vein which horses or mules have in the place where they are girthed. 3. Disorder incident to horses and mules, which affects the place where they are girthed.

Cíncho, *sm.* 1. Belt or girdle used by labourers to keep their bodies warm. 2. The iron hoop which goes round the felloes of a wheel. 3. Vessel made of bass-weed, in which cheese is moulded and pressed. 4. Disorder which affects the hoofs of horses. V. *Ceño.*

Cinchón, *sm.* A broad girdle.

Cinchuéla, *sf.* 1. A small girth. 2. A narrow riband.

Cínco, *sm.* An arithmetical character, by which the number five is denoted.—*a.* Five.

Cincoañál, *a.* Five years old; applied to beasts.

Cinco en ráma, *sf.* (Bot.) Cinquefoil. Potentilla reptans *L.*

Cincomesíno, na, *a.* Five months old.

Cincuénta, *sm.* Fifty.

Cincuentañál, *a.* (Ant.) Fifty years old.

Cincuentáyna, *sf.* (Ant.) A woman 50 years old.

Cincuenténo, na, *s.* Fiftieth.

Cincuésma, *sf.* (Ant.) Pentecost, the 50th day after Easter.

Cinéreo y Cinerício, (Ant.) V. *Ceniciento.*

Cíngaro, ra, *s.* Gipsy. V. *Gitano.*

Cingladúra, *sf.* (Naút.) One day's run or sailing.

Cinglár, *va.* 1. (Naút.) To sail with a fair wind and full sails. 2. To brandish a rod or wand.

Cíngulo, *sm.* 1. Girdle or band with which a priest's alb is tied up. 2. (Ant.) A military badge. 3. Ring or list at the top and bottom of a column.

Cínico, ca, *a.* Cynic, cynical; satirical.

Cínico, *sm.* 1. Philosopher of the sect of Diogenes. 2. Spasm which causes convulsions, similar to those of a dog when mad.

Cínife, *sm.* The long-shanked buzzing gnat.

Cinocéfalo, *sm.* Kind of monkey or baboon.

Cinosúra, *sf.* Cynosure, the polar star in the tail of the Lesser Bear.

Cinquéno, na, *a.* (Ant.) V. *Quinto.*

Cinquéño ó Cinquíllo, *sm.* Game at cards played among five persons.

Cínta, *sf.* 1. Ribbon or riband; tape. 2. A strong net used in the tunny fishery. 3. The lowest part of the pastern of a horse. 4. *Cintas de navio,* (Naút.) Wales. *Cintas galimas,* (Naút.) Bow-wales or harpings. 5. (Ant.) Girdle. V. *Cinto.* 6. First course of floor tiles. *Andar ó estar con las manos en la cinta,* To be idle. *En cinta,* Under subjection; liable to restraint. *Espada en cinta,* With the sword on one's side. *Estar en cinta,* To be pregnant, or with child.

Cintadéro, *sm.* That part of the crossbow to which the string is made fast.

Cintagórda, *sf.* Coarse hempen net for the tunny fishery.

Cintájos ó Cintarájos, *sm. pl.* Knot or bunch of ribands.

Cintár, *va.* To adorn with ribands.

Cintarázo, *sm.* 1. Stroke or blow given with the flat part of a broad-sword. 2. Chastisement given to a horse with the stirrup-leather.

Cintareár, *va.* To strike with the flat part of a broad-sword.

Cinteádo, da, *a.* Adorned with ribands.

Cintería, *sf.* (Ant.) Trade in ribands.

Cintéro, *sm.* 1. One who weaves or sells ribands. 2. (Ant.) Harness-maker. 3. (Ant.) Belt, girdle. 4. (Arag.) Truss. 5. Rope with a running knot thrown on a bull's head.

Cintílla, *sf.* A small riband.

Cintíllo, *sm.* 1. Hat-band. 2. Ring set with precious stones.

Cínto, *sm.* Belt, girdle. V. *Cintura y Cingulo.*

Cintrél, *sm.* Rule or line placed in the centre of a dome to adjust the ranges of brick or stone.

Cintúra, *sf.* 1. Waist, the small part of the body where a girdle is worn. 2. (Ant.) Small girdle to bind the waist. *Meter en cintura,* (Met.) To keep one in a state of subjection. 3. Narrow part of a chimney. V. *Canal.*

Cinturíca, ílla ó íta, *sf.* A small girdle.

Cinturón, *sm.* A broad-sword belt.

Ciñidéro, *sm.* (Ant.) V. *Ceñidor.*

Cipéro, *sm.* (Bot.) Cyperus or sedge. Cyperus *L.*

Cipion, *sm.* (Ant.) A walking-stick.

Cipolíni, *sm.* Kind of greenish marble.

Cíppos, *sm. pl.* 1. Mile-stones. 2. Finger-posts.

Cipréś, *sm.* (Bot.) Cypress-tree. Cupressus sempervirens *L.* *Baya del ciprés*, The cypress nut or berry.
Cipresál, *sm.* Grove or plantation of cypress-trees.
Cipresíno, na, *a.* Resembling or belonging to cypress.
Ciquiricáta, *sf.* Caress, act of endearment; flattery.
Ciráto, *sm.* A hill or small height.
Circénse, *a.* Belonging to a circus.
Círco, *sm.* 1. Circus, a spacious place in ancient Rome, for exhibiting games or other public amusements to the people. 2. (Orn.) The moor-buzzard. Falco Æruginosus *L.*
Circonscribír, *va.* (Ant.) V. *Circunscribir.*
Circuír, *va.* To surround.
Circúito, *sm.* 1. Circuit, the space enclosed in a circle. 2. Circumference of that space.
Circulación, *sf.* Circulation. *Circulacion de la sangre*, Circulation of the blood.
Circulánte, *a.* That which circulates.
Circulár, *a.* Circular, round like a circle; circumscribed by a circle. *Carta circular*, A circular letter, a letter directed to several persons who are concerned in some common affair.
Circulár, *va.* To circulate, to go from hand to hand, as money.
Circularménte, *ad.* Circularly, in the form of a circle.
Círculo, *sm.* 1. Circle, a plane figure comprehended under one line, which is called the circumference. 2. A superstitious ring or circle. 3. District. 4. Figure of speech, wherein a sentence begins and ends with the same words. *Círculos del imperio*, Circles of the German empire, provinces or districts.
Circumpolár, *a.* Circumpolar, near the pole.
Circuncidánte, *sm.* He who circumcises.
Circuncidár, *va.* 1. To circumcise, to cut the prepuce. 2. (Met.) To diminish, to curtail or modify any thing.
Circuncisión, *sf.* 1. Circumcision, the act of circumcising. 2. A religious festival.
Circuncíso, sa, *a.* Circumcised.
Circundár, *va.* To surround, to encircle.
Circunferéncia, *sf.* Circumference, the periphery of the circle.
Circunferenciál, *a.* Belonging to the circumference, surrounding.
Circunferencialménte, *ad.* In a circular or surrounding manner.
Circunfléxo, *sm.* Circumflex; an accent (ˆ), composed of the acute and grave.
Circunfléxo, xa, *a.* Oblique; bent round.
Circunlocución, *sf.* Circumlocution.
Circunlóquio, *sm.* The act of expressing in a number of words that which may be said in a few.
Circunscribír, *va.* To circumscribe, to enclose in certain lines or limits.
Circunscriptívo, va, *a.* Circumscriptive; surrounding or enclosing a superficies.
Circunspeccíon, *sf.* Circumspection, prudence, general attention. *Para estar bien con todos se requiere circunspeccion*, To be on good terms with every one requires a deal of circumspection.
Circunspécto, ta, *a.* Circumspect, cautious.
Circunstáncia, *sf.* 1. Circumstance, something appendant or relative to a fact. *Refirió el caso con todas sus circunstancias*, He gave a full and minute account of the case. 2. Incident, event. 3. Condition, state of affairs. *En las circunstancias presentes*, In the actual state of things.
Circunstanciádo, da, *a.* 1. According to circumstances. 2. Circumstantial, minute.
Circunstántes, *sm. pl.* By-standers, persons present.
Circunvalación, *sf.* Circumvallation; the act of surrounding a place. *Linea de circunvalacion*, (Fort.) Line of circumvallation.
Circunvalár, *va.* 1. To surround, to encircle. 2. (Fort.) To surround with trenches or intrenchments.
Circunvecíno, na, *a.* Neighbouring, adjacent, contiguous.
Circunvenír, *va.* (Ant.) To circumvent, to overwhelm by deceitful artifices.
Circunvolucíon, *sf.* Circumvolution; the act of rolling round.
Ciriál, *sm.* A large candlestick used in churches.
Ciremónia, *sf.* (Ant.) V. *Ceremonia.*
Cirinéo, *sm.* Mate, assistant.
Círio, *sm.* A thick and long wax candle or taper. *Cirio pascual*, Paschal candle to which five pieces of incense are attached in the form of a cross.
Círro, *sm.* (Cir.) 1. Schirrus, an indurated gland, or other morbid induration in the animal body. 2. Tuft of mane hanging down over a horse's face. 3. Fibre of the roots of plants.
Cirróso, sa, *a.* 1. Scirrhous, affected with a morbid induration. 2. Fibrous. *Raices cirrosas*, Fibrous roots.
Ciruéla, *sf.* Prune, a stone fruit of different qualities. Prunum *L.* *Ciruéla pasa*, A dried plum; a prune. *Ciruéla verdal*, A green gage. *Ciruéla de frayle*, The long green plum.
Ciruelár, *sm.* A large plantation of plum-trees.
Ciruelíca, ílla, y íta, *sm.* A small plum.
Ciruelíco, íllo, y íto, *sm.* A dwarf plum-tree.
Ciruélo, *sm.* (Bot.) Plum-tree. Prunus domestica *L.*
Cirugía, *sf.* Surgery, the art of curing wounds and sores by manual operations.
Cirujáno, *sm.* Surgeon, one who cures sores and wounds by manual operations. *Primer cirujano de navio*, Surgeon of a ship. *Segundo cirujano de navio*, Surgeon's mate.
Cirurgía, *sf.* (Ant.) V. *Cirugía.*
Cisalpíno, na, *a.* Cisalpine, belonging to the country between Rome and the Alps.
Císca, *sf.* Kind of reed with which huts and cottages are roofed.
Ciscár, *va.* To besmear, to make dirty.—*vr.* To ease nature. *Ciscarse de miedo*, To dirty one's self from fear.
Císco, *sm.* Coal-dust; a coal broken into very small pieces.
Cisión, *sf.* Incision. V. *Cisura ó Incision.*
Císma, *sm.* 1. Schism, a separation or division in the church. 2. Disturbance in a community.
Cismático, ca, *a.* 1. Schismatic; inclining to or practising a schism. 2. Author or abetter of disturbances in a community.

Cismontáno, na, *a.* Living on this side of the mountains.

Císne, *sm.* 1. (Orn.) Swan, a large water-fowl. Anas cygnus *L.* 2. A constellation in the northern hemisphere. 3. (Met.) A good poet or musician. 4. (Cant.) Prostitute.

Cispadáno, na, *a.* Belonging to the country between Rome and the Po.

Cisquéro, *sm.* A small linen bag with coal-dust, used by painters and draftsmen to mark their designs or sketches.

Cistél ó Cistér, *sm.* Cistertian order instituted by St. Bernard.

Cisterciénse, *a.* Cistertian, belonging to the order of St. Bernard.

Cistérna, *sf.* 1. Cistern, a receptacle of water for domestic use. 2. Reservoir, an enclosed fountain.

Cisterníca, íllà, y íta, *sf.* A small cistern.

Cisúra, *sf.* Incisure, incision.

Cíta, *sf.* 1. Assignation, an appointed meeting of two or more persons. 2. Quotation of the passage of a book.

Citación, *sf.* 1. Quotation; a passage adduced out of an author as evidence or illustration. 2. Summons, citation, judicial notice.

Citadór, ra, *s.* One who cites.

Citáno, *sm.* V. *Zutano.*

Citár, *va.* 1. To make an appointment of meeting a person at a fixed time to treat on business. 2. To quote, to cite a passage from an author. 3. To summon before a judge; to give judicial notice.

Cítara, *sf.* 1. Cithara or cithern, a musical instrument resembling a guitar. 2. Partition wall of the thickness of a common brick. 3. Body of troops covering the flanks of those who are advancing to charge the enemy.

Citarísta, *s.* One who plays on the cithern.

Citarístico, ca, *a.* (Poét.) Belonging to poetry adapted to the cithara.

Citarizár, *vn.* (Ant.) To play on the cithara.

Citatório, ria, *a.* Applied to a summons to appear in a tribunal of justice.

Citeriór, *a.* *España citerior,* The higher or north-eastern part of Spain.

Citíso, *sm.* (Bot.) Shrub-trefoil. Cytisus *L.*

Círo, *sm.* A word used to call dogs.

Citocredénte, *a.* Credulous.

Cítola, *sf.* 1. (In Corn-Mills) Clack or clapper, a piece of wood which strikes the hopper, and promotes the running of the corn. 2. V. *Citara.*

Citoléro, ra, *s.* (Ant.) V. *Citarista.*

Citória, *sf.* (Ant.) V. *Citacion.*

Citóte, *sm.* Summons, a judicial citation or notice.

Cítra, *ad.* (Ant.) On this side.

Citramontáno, na, *a.* On this side of the mountains.

Citríno, na, *a.* Lemon-coloured. V. *Cetrino.*

Cítum, *sm.* Beverage made of barley.

Ciudád, *sf.* 1. City, a large place enjoying more privileges than a common town. 2. Corporation.

Ciudadanaménte, *ad.* Civilly, in the manner of a citizen.

Ciudadáno, *sm.* 1. Liveryman of a city. 2. Citizen, freeman who enjoys the privileges of a city. 3. Inhabitant of a city; rank of the community. 4. (Ant.) A degree of nobi[lity] inferior to that of *caballero,* and superio[r to] the condition of a tradesman.

Ciudadáno, na, *a.* Belonging to a city o[r] citizens; citizen-like.

Ciudadéla, *sf.* (Fort.) Citadel, a small fortr[ess] situated on a commanding ground to def[end] a town.

Cívico, ca, *a.* Civic. V. *Doméstico.*

Civíl, *a.* 1. Civil, polite, courteous. 2. Ci[vil,] not military, not ecclesiastical. 3. (Ant.) [Of] a low rank or extraction. 4. In law, civil, [not] criminal.

Civilidád, *sf.* 1. Civility, politeness, urban[ity.] 2. (Ant.) Misery, distress.

Civilización, *sf.* 1. Civilization. 2. Act of j[us]tice by which a criminal process is conver[ted] into a civil cause.

Civilizár, *va.* To civilize.

Civilménte, *ad.* 1. In a civil or polite man[ner.] 2. According to the common law. 3. (A[nt.]) Poorly, miserably, meanly.

Cizálla, *sf.* Fragments or filings of gold, [sil]ver, or other metal.

Clamár, *va.* 1. (Ant.) To call. V. *Llamar.* [2.] To cry out in a mournful tone. 3. (Met.) [To] show a want of something; applied to ina[ni]mate substances, as, *La tierra clama [por] agua,* The ground wants water.

Clamór, *sm.* 1. Outcry, scream, shriek. 2. Sou[nd] or peal of passing bells. 3. (Ant.) The pu[blic] voice.

Clamoreár, *va.* To implore or solicit ass[ist]ance in a mournful manner.—*vn.* To toll [the] passing-bell. [b[ell.]

Clamoréo, *sm.* Sound or peal of the passi[ng]

Clamoróso, sa, *a.* Clamorous, plaintive soun[d.]

Clamóso, sa, *a.* That which calls out, or solic[its.]

Clandestinaménte, *ad.* In a clandestine m[an]ner. [and reserv[ed.]

Clandestinidád, *sf.* The quality of being cl[andestine]

Clandestíno, na, *a.* Clandestine, secret, priv[ate.]

Clánga, *sf.* V. *Planga.*

Claóstra, *sf.* V. *Claustro.*

Clára, *sf.* A short interval of fair weather [on] a rainy day. *Me aproveché de una clara p[ara] salir,* I availed myself of a fair moment to [go] abroad. *Clara de huevo,* White of an e[gg.] *Cláras,* Pieces of cloth ill woven, throu[gh] which the light can be seen. *A' la clara.* [*A'*] *las claras,* Clearly, evidently. [r[oof.]

Clarabóya, *sf.* Sky-light; a window in [the]

Claramént y Claramiént, (Ant.) V. *Cla[ra]mente.*

Claraménte, *ad.* Clearly, openly, manifes[tly.]

Clarár, *va.* (Ant.) V. *Aclarar.*

Claréa, *sf.* Ramboose, a beverage made of wh[ite] wine, sugar, cinnamon, and the yolk of an e[gg.]

Clareár, *vn.* To dawn, to grow light.—*vr.* To be transparent, translucent, not opaq[ue.] 2. (Met.) To be cleared up by conjecture[s or] surmises. *Clarearse de hambre,* To g[row] lean and thin with hunger.

Clarecér, *vn.* To dawn, to grow light.

Claréte, *a.* Being of the colour of claret; [ap]plied to wine.

Claridád y Claréza, *sf.* 1. Clarity, brightn[ess,] splendor. 2. Clearness, distinctness, free[dom] from obscurity and confusion; applied to id[eas.]

3. Freedom and resolution in communicating one's thoughts. *Yo le dixe dos claridades*, I told him my mind very clearly. 4. Glory of the blessed. 5. (Met.) Celebrity, fame. *Salir á puerto de claridad*, (Met.) To get well over an arduous undertaking.

Clarificacíon, *sf.* Clarification, the art of making any thing free from impurities.

Clarificár, *va.* 1. To brighten, to illuminate, to supply with light. 2. To clarify, to purify, or clear from obscurities. *Clarificár la sangre*, To purify or cleanse the blood.

Clarificatívo, va, *a.* Purificative or purificatory; having power or tendency to make pure.

Claríſico, ca, *a.* (Ant.) Clarified, resplendent.

Clarílla, *sf.* (And.) Lye, a liquor impregnated with ashes, or any other alkaline salt.

Clariménte, *sm.* Ancient lotion used by the ladies for beautifying the face.

Claríɴ, *sm.* 1. Trumpet, a kind of musical wind-instrument. 2. (In Organs) Stop or instrument by which the different sounds are regulated. 3. Trumpeter, one who sounds a trumpet. 4. Fine and transparent cambric, used for ruffles.

Clarinádo, da, *a.* Applied to animals with bells in their harness.

Clarináta, *sf.* (Joc.) Tall shrill-voiced person.

Clarinéro, *sm.* Trumpeter, one whose business is to blow the trumpet.

Clarinéte, *sm.* 1. Clarinet, a straight wind instrument. 2. Player on the clarinet.

Clarión, *sm.* Crayon, a roll of paste of various colours for drawing or designing.

Clarísa, *sf.* Nun of the order of St. Clair.

Cláro, ra, *a.* 1. Clear, bright, transparent. 2. Pellucid, transparent. 3. Light, not deeply tinged. *Azul claro*, A light blue. 4. Evident, manifest, indisputable. *Es una verdad clara*, It is an undeniable truth. 5. Open, frank, ingenuous. 6. (Ant.) Celebrated, illustrious. 7. (Met.) Sagacious, quick of thought.

Cláro, *sm.* 1. Light, clearness; that which affords clearness. 2. Break in a discourse or writing. 3. Rays of light falling on a painting or picture. *Claro y obscuro*, Drawing with one colour only. 4. Opening or space between the columns of a building or other things. 5. Clearness or thinness of cloth and stuff. 6. Sagacity, acuteness of mind. 7. (Naút.) A clear spot in the sky. *Poner ó sacar en claro*, (Met.) To render manifest or evident; to place a point in its true light. *Vamos claros*, (Met.) Let us be clear and correct. *Pasar la noche de claro en claro*, To have not a wink of sleep all the night. *Pasar de claro en claro*, To run a thing over or through from one part to another. *Pasarse de claro en claro alguna cosa*, (Met.) To be forgotten. *De claro en claro*, Evidently, manifestly. *Claro, ó Por lo claro*, Clearly, manifestly.

Claról, *sm.* Inlaid work; applied chiefly to furniture.

Claróɴ, *sm.* (Ant.) V. *Resplandor*.

Cláse, *sf.* 1. Class or rank of the people, order of persons. 2. Division of school-boys, classed according to their attainments. 3. A set of beings or things. *Cláses de navio*, (Naút.) Rates of ships. *Primera clase*, A first-rate ship.

Clásico, ca, *a.* 1. Classical, classic; relating to antique authors. 2. Principal, remarkable, of the first order or rank. *Error clásico*, A gross error or mistake.

Claudicacíon, *sf.* Claudication, the act and habit of halting or limping.

Claudicár, *vn.* 1. To claudicate, to halt or limp. 2. (Met.) To act or proceed in a bungling and inconsiderate manner, without rule or order.

Clauquilladór, *sm.* (Ant. Arag.) Custom-house sealer.

Clauquillár, *va.* (Ant.) To put the custom-house seal on bales of goods.

Claústra, *sf.* (Ant.) V. *Claustro*.

Claustrál, *a.* 1. Claustral, relating to cloisters. 2. Claustral, applied to monks of the orders of St. Benedict and St. Francis.

Claustréro, *a.* (Ant.) Applied to the members of a cloister.

Claustríco, íllo, *sm.* A small cloister.

Claústro, *sm.* 1. Cloister, piazza, or gallery which runs around the court of a convent, and joins the different parts of the building. 2. Assembly or meeting of the principal members of an university. 3. (Anat.) Womb. 4. (Ant.) Room, chamber.

Cláusula, *sf.* 1. Period; a single part of a discourse. 2. Clause; an article or particular stipulation.

Clausulár, *va.* To close a period, to terminate a speech.

Clausulílla, *sf.* A little clause.

Clausúra, *sf.* 1. Cloister, the inner recess of a convent. 2. Confinement, retirement. *Guardar clausura, ó vivir en clausura*, To lead a monastic or retired life.

Cláva, *sf.* 1. Club, a heavy stick. 2. (Naút.) Scupper, or scupper-hole.

Clavádo, da, *a.* 1. Exact, precise. *El relox está clavado á las cinco*, It is just five by the clock. *Venir clavada una cosa á otra*, To fit exactly. 2. Nailed, armed or furnished with nails. 3. Belonging or relating to a club, especially to that of Hercules.

Clavadúra, *sf.* The act of driving a nail to the quick of a horse's foot in shoeing.

Clavár, *va.* 1. To nail, or drive a nail into a thing; to fasten with nails. 2. To stick, to prick; to introduce a pointed thing into another. *Se clavó un alfiler*, He pricked himself with a pin. *Me clavé una espina*, I pricked myself with a thorn. *Clavar á un caballo*, To prick a horse in shoeing. *Clavarle á uno el corazon alguna cosa*, To be extremely affected by something. *Clavar la artillería*, To spike or nail up guns. *Clavar los ojos á la vista*, To stare, to look with fixed eyes. 3. To cheat, to deceive. 4. To set in gold or silver. 5. (Mil.) To ground. *Clavar las armas*, To ground the arms.

Clavário, *sm.* 1. Treasurer, cashier. 2. A certain dignitary of the church of Valencia.

Clavazóɴ, *sm.* 1. Set or parcel of nails. 2. (Naút.) Assortment of the different nails used in the construction of ships.

Cláve, *sf.* 1. Key-stone, which binds and closes the sweep of an arch. *Echar la clave*, (Met.) To close a speech, to terminate an affair. 2. Key to any work or writing, to develope the characters of which it treats. 3. (In Music) Tune to which every composition, whether long or short, ought to be fitted. 4. Chime or concord of bells. 5. (Ant.) Key. V. *Llave.* 6. Harpsichord. V. *Clavicordio.*

Clavecímbano ó Clavicímbalo, (Ant.) V. *Clavicordio.*

Clavél, *sm.* (Bot.) Pink, a flower. *Clável de muerto,* (Bot.) Common marigold.

Clavelína, *sf.* (Bot. Arag.) Pink, a flower.

Clavellína, *sf.* 1. (Bot.) Jamaica pepper-tree. 2. (Bot.) Spanish carnation, a flower. 3. (Ant.) Stopple, made of tow, and put into the vent-hole of a great gun.

Clavelón, *sm.* 1. (Bot.) A large pink. 2. *Clavelon de Indias,* (Bot.) Indian pink.

Clavéque, *sm.* Stone resembling a diamond, but of little value; a false diamond.

Clavéra, *sf.* 1. Mould for nail heads. 2. Hole in a horse-shoe for fastening the latter to the hoof. 3. (Extrem.) Boundary where land-marks are set up.

Clavería, *sf.* 1. Office and dignity of the key-bearer in the military orders of Calatrava and Alcantara. 2. Management and administration of foreign property.

Clavéro, ra, *s.* 1. Keeper of the keys, treasurer, cashier. 2. (Bot.) Clove-tree, which produces the aromatic spice called cloves. 3. Key-bearer, the knight of the orders of Calatrava and Alcantara, who takes care of the castle, convent, and archives.

Clavéte, *sm.* Tack, a small nail.

Claveteár, *va.* 1. To nail, to garnish with brass or other nails. 2. To point or tag a lace.

Clavicórdio, *sm.* Harpsichord, a musical instrument with brass or iron strings.

Clavícula, *sf.* (Anat.) Clavicle, the collar-bone.

Clavigéra, *sf.* (Arag.) Cut or opening made in mud walls to let in the water.

Clavigéro, *sm.* Bridge of a harpsichord, in which the pegs are fastened.

Clavíja, *sf.* 1. Pin, peg, or tack of wood or iron, thrust into a hole for rolling or winding something around. 2. Peg of a stringed musical instrument. 3. *Clavija maestra,* The fore axle-tree pintle. *Apretar á uno la clavija,* (Met.) To push home an argument.

Clavíllo ó Clavíto, *sm.* 1. A small nail. 2. *Clavillo de hebilla,* Rivet of a buckle.

Claviórgano, *sm.* An organized harpsichord; a very harmonious musical instrument, composed of strings and pipes, like an organ.

Clávo, *sm.* 1. Nail, an iron spike with a head and point. *Clavo trabadero,* Bolt with a key on the opposite side. *Clavo plateado,* Tinned nail, a nail dipped in lead or solder. 2. Corn, a hard and painful excrescence on the feet. 3. Spot in the eye. 4. Lint, linen scraped into a soft woolly substance, to be put in wounds or on sores. 5. Clove, a valuable spice brought from the East Indies. 6. (Naút.) Rudder of a ship. 7. (Met.) Severe pain or grief, which thrills the heart. 8. Tumour between the hair and the hoof of a horse. 9. Head-ache. V. *Xaqueca. De clavo pasado,* Franticly, utterly abandoned. *Dar en el clavo,* (Met.) To hit the mark. *Echar un clavo en la rueda de la fortuna,* (Met.) To fix one's fortune. *No importa un clavo,* It does not matter a pin. *Sacar un clavo con otro clavo,* (Met.) To cure one excess by another. *Hacer clavo,* To s[illegible] applied to mortar.

Clemátide, *sf.* (Bot.) Traveller's-joy, the [illegible] right Lady's bower Clematis angustifolia

Clemáncia, *sf.* Clemency, mercy.

Cleménte, *a.* Clement, unwilling to punish

Clementeménte, *ad.* Mercifully, meekly.

Clementínas, *sf. pl.* Collection of the can[ons] published by Pope Clement the Fifth.

Clemesí, Clemesína, ó Clemesíno, na, (Ant.) V. *Carmesí.*

Clepsídra, *sf.* Water-clock, an hour-gla[ss] serving to measure time by the fall of a c[er]tain quantity of water.

Clerecía, *sf.* 1. Clergy. 2. Meeting or asse[m]bly of clergymen.

Clericál, *a.* Clerical, belonging to the cler[gy]

Clericalménte, *ad.* In a clerical manner.

Clericáto, *sm.* State and dignity of a cler[gy]man. *Clericato de cámara,* The clergy e[m]ployed in the palace of the pope.

Clericatúra, *sf.* State of a clergyman.

Clérigo, *sm.* A clergyman. *Clérigo de cá[ma]ra,* Roman Catholic clergyman employed [in] the government of the papal dominions. *[Clé]rigo de corona,* Roman Catholic clergy[man] who has received the tonsure. *Clérigo [de] misa,* A presbyter. *Clérigo de misa y [olla],* A priest who is only fit for choir duty. *[Clé]rigo menor,* A priest of the minor order.

Clerigoíllo, *sm.* A little petty clergyman [a] term of contempt.

Clerizón, *sm.* Chorister, a singing-boy belon[g]ing to a cathedral.

Clerizónte, *sm.* 1. One who wears a m[an's] clerical dress without being ordained. 2. [Ill] dressed priest.

Cléro, *sm.* Clergy, a body of men set apar[t] [by] due ordination for the service of God. *[Clero] secular,* Secular clergy, who do not make [the] three solemn vows of poverty, obedien[ce] and chastity. *Clero regular,* Regular cl[er]gy, who profess a monastic life, and ma[ke] the above vows.

Clibanário, ria, *a.* (Ant.) Belonging to a p[or]table oven.

Clíbano, *sm.* A small moveable oven.

Cliénte, *sm.* Client, a person under the p[ro]tection and tutorage of another. [clie]

Clientéla, *sf.* Clientship, the condition o[f]

Cliéntulo, la, *s.* V. *Cliente.*

Clíma, *sm.* 1. Climate; a space upon the surf[ace] of the earth between the circles, parallel [to] the equator. 2. The particular quality o[f a] region in point of air, seasons, soil. &c.

Climatérico, ca, *a.* Climacteric, or climac[te]rical, containing a number of years, at [the] end of which some great change is suppo[sed] to befal the body. *Estar climaterico al[gu]no,* To be ill-humoured.

Clímax, *sf.* Climax, rhetorical figure.

Climéno de españa, *sm.* (Bot.) Chickling, everlasting pea.

Clín, *sm.* (Ant.) V. *Crin. Tenerse á las clin[es],* (Met.) To make every effort not to decl[ine] in rank or fortune.

Clinopódio, *sm.* (Bot.) Large wild basil.

Clistél ó Clistér, *sm.* Clyster, an inject[ion] into the rectum. V. *Ayuda.*

Clisteléra, *sf.* Person who administers clysters.
Clisterizár, *va.* To administer clysters.
Clivóso, sa, *a.* Declivous, gradually descending.
Clo, Clo, *sm.* Clucking of a hen when she is hatching or calling her chickens. [&c.
Cloáca, *sf.* Sewer, a conduit for dirty water,
Clocár, *va.* To cluck. V. *Cloquear.*
Clochél, *sm.* (Ant.) V. *Campanario.*
Cloclear, *sm.* To cackle like a turkey-cock.
Clóque, *sm.* 1. (Naút.) Grapnel, a grappling iron, with which, in battle, one ship fastens on another. V. *Cocle.* 2. Harpoon.
Cloqueár, *va.* 1. To cluck, to make a noise like a hen that hatches or calls her chickens. 2. To angle, to fish with a rod, hook, and line.
Cloquéra, *sf.* The state of hatching in fowls.
Cloquéro, *sm.* A person who has the management of the harpoon in the tunny-fishery.
Clóris, *sf.* (Orn.) Greenfinch.
Clóso, sa, *a.* (Ant.) V. *Cerrado.*
Clúcia donosa, *sf.* (Bot.) The balsam-tree.
Cluéca, *a.* Clucking and hatching; applied to a hen.
Cluéco, ca, *a.* Decrepit, worn out with age.
Cneoróń, *sm.* (Bot.) Widow-wail.
Coa, *sf.* (Ant.) V. *Cola.*
Coaccióń, *sf.* Coaction, compulsion. [ther.
Coacervár, *va.* To coacervate, to heap toge-
Coactívo, va, *a.* Coactive, having the force of restraining or compelling; compulsive.
Coadjútor, ra, *s.* 1. Coadjutor, fellow-helper, an assistant. 2. Coadjutor, a person elected or appointed to a prebend without enjoying the benefit thereof until the death of the incumbent.
Coadjutoría, *sf.* 1. Coadjuvancy, help, assistance. 2. Right of survivorship of a coadjutor. 3. Office or dignity of a coadjutor.
Coadministradór, *sm.* One who governs a diocese by virtue of a bull, or by appointment of a bishop.
Coadunacióń, *sf.* Coadunition, the conjunction of different substances into one mass. [ther.
Coadunár, *va.* To mix or jumble things toge-
Coadyudadór, *sm.* (Ant.) V. *Coadyuvador.*
Coadyutór, *sm.* (Ant.) V. *Coadjutor.*
Coadyutório, ria, *a.* (Ant.) That which assists.
Coadyuvadór, *sm.* Fellow-helper, assistant.
Coadyuvár, *va.* To help, to assist.
Coagulacióń, *sf.* Coagulation, concretion.
Coagulánte, *a.* That which coagulates.
Coagulár, *vn.* To coagulate, to condense, to become concrete.
Coágulo, *sm.* 1. Coagulum, coagulated blood. 2. That which causes or produces coagulation.
Coálla, *sf.* (Orn.) Woodcock. V. *Chochaperdiz y Codorniz.* [in loving.
Coamánte, *a.* (Ant.) A partner or companion
Coapóstol, *sm.* Co-apostle, a fellow-labourer in the propagation of the Gospel.
Coaptacióń, *sf.* Coaptation, the adjustment of parts to each other.
Coaptár, *va.* To fit, to adjust. [any thing.
Coarrendadór, *sm.* A joint partner in renting
Coartacióń, *sf.* (For.) Obligation to be ordained within a certain time to enjoy a benefice.
Coartáda, *sf.* Alibi. *Probar la coartada*, To prove an alibi.
Coartár, *va.* To limit, to restrict, to restrain.
Cobált, *sm.* Cobalt, a grayish semimetal.
Cobanillo, *sm.* A small basket used by vintners during the vintage.
Cobárde, *a.* Cowardly, timid, fearful.
Cobardeár, *vn.* To be a coward; to be timid or fearful.
Cobardeménte, *ad.* In a cowardly manner.
Cobardía, *sf.* Cowardice, want of valour and fortitude.
Cobdeár, *vn.* (Ant.) V. *Codear.*
Cobdícia y Cobdíza, *sf.* (Ant.) V. *Codicia.*
Cobegéra, *sf.* (Ant.) V. *Encubridora.*
Cobertéra, *sf.* 1. Pot-lid, an iron, wood, or earthen cover of a pot. 2. (Met.) Bawd, procuress. *Cobertéras*, The two middle feathers of a hawk's tail, which are covered when the hawk is perched.
Cobertéro, *sm.* (Ant.) Cover or top of any thing.
Cobertízo, *sm.* 1. A small roof jutting out from the wall to shelter people from the rain. 2. A covered passage.
Cobertór, *sm.* Coverlet, quilt.
Cobertúra, *sf.* 1. Cover, covering. 2. Act of a grandee of Spain of covering himself the first time he is presented to the king.
Cobíja, *sf.* 1. The part of the roof which projects from the wall to throw off the rain. 2. (Ant.) A small cloak for women: it is still used in Estremadura.
Cobijadúra, *sf.* (Ant.) The act of covering.
Cobijár, *va.* To cover, to overspread, to shelter.
Cobijéra, *sf.* (Ant.) Chambermaid.
Cobíl, *sm.* (Ant.) Corner, angle.
Cóbra, *sf.* (Ant. y Extr.) A number of mares (not less than 5,) for treading out the corn.
Cobradéro, ra, *a.* That which may be recovered.
Cobrádo, da, *a.* 1. Recovered, received. 2. (Ant.) Complete, undaunted.
Cobradór, *sm.* Receiver or collector of rents and other money. *Perro cobrador*, Kind of dog that fetches game out of the water.
Cobramiénto, *sm.* (Ant.) 1. Recovery, restoration. 2. (Ant.) Utility, profit, emolument.
Cobránza, *sf.* 1. Recovery or collection of money. 2. Act of fetching the game which is killed or wounded.
Cobrár, *va.* 1. To recover, to collect or receive what is due. 2. To recover what is lost. 3. To fetch the game that is wounded or killed. 4. To gain affection or esteem. *Cobrar animo ó corazon*, To take courage. *Cobrar fuerzas*, To gather strength.—*vr.* 1. To recover, to return to one's self. 2. To gain celebrity or fame.
Cóbre, *sm.* 1. Copper, a red coloured metal. 2. Kitchen furniture. 3. (Ant.) String of onions or garlic. 4. *Cobre de cecial*, A pair of cods dried in the sun. *Batir el cobre*, (Met.) To pursue with spirit and vigour.
Cobréño, ña, *a.* (Ant.) Made of copper.
Cobrimiénto, *sm.* (Ant.) V. *Encubrimiento.*
Cobrír, *va.* (Ant.) V. *Cubrir.*
Cobrízo, za, *a.* Coppery, containing copper.
Cóbro, *sm.* 1. V. *Cobranza.* 2. (Ant.) Receptacle, place of safety. 3. (Ant.) Expedient, reason, means of attaining any end.
Cóca, *sf.* 1. Plant in Peru which the inhabit-

ants suck. 2. Seed resembling the berry of laurel. 3. (Naút.) Sort of small vessel. 4. (Gal.) Figure of a large serpent borne at festivals. 5. (Naút.) Turn or twist of a cable. 6. Kind of a red gum. 7. (Ant.) Head.

Cocár, *va.* 1. To make grimaces or wry faces. 2. (Met.) To coax, to gain by wheedling and flattering.

Cocarár, *va.* To gather or collect the leaves of cocoa.

Coccíneo, nea, *a.* Of a purple colour.

Cocción, *sf.* Coction, the boiling of any thing.

Cóce, *sf.* (Ant.) A kick. V. *Coz.*

Cocеadór, ra, *s.* One that kicks.

Coceadúra y Coceamiénto, *s.* Act of kicking.

Coceár, *va.* 1. To kick. V. *Acocear.* 2. (Met.) To repugn, to resist. 3. (Ant.) To trample, to tread under foot.

Cocedéro, ra; y Cocedízo, za, *a.* Easily boiled. [and baked.

Cocedéro, *sm.* Place where bread is kneaded

Cocedór, *sm.* A person whose business is to boil must and new wine.

Cocedréra, *sf.* A large feather-bed.

Cocedúra, *sf.* The act of boiling.

Cocér, *va.* 1. To boil, to dress victuals. 2. To bake bricks, tiles, or earthen-ware. 3. To digest.—*vn.* To boil; to ferment.—*vr.* To suffer intense and continued pain.

Cócha, *sf.* A small reservoir of water.

Cochámbre, *sm.* A greasy, dirty, and stinking thing.

Cochambrería, *sf.* (Bax.) Heap of nasty and filthy things.

Cochambróso, sa, *a.* Nasty, filthy, stinking.

Cochárro, *sm.* A wooden dish, cup, or platter.

Cochárse, *vr.* (Ant.) To hasten, to accelerate.

Cochástro, *sm.* A little sucking wild boar.

Cóche, *sm.* 1. Coach, carriage with four wheels for pleasure or state. *Echar coche,* To set up a coach. *Maestro de coches,* A coach-maker. *Coche de colleras,* Coach drawn by mules harnessed with collars. *Coche de estribos,* Coach with steps to the doors. 2. (Naút.) Kind of coasting barge.

Cocheár, *vn.* To drive a coach.

Cochecíllo y Cochecíto, *sm.* A small coach.

Cochéra, *sf.* 1. Coach-house, a place where coaches are kept. 2. Coachman's wife.

Cocheríl, *a.* (Joc.) Relating or belonging to coachmen.

Cocheríllo, *sm.* A little coachman.

Cochéro, *sm.* 1. Coachman. 2. (Ant.) Coachmaker. 3. Wagoner, a northern constellation.

Cochéro, ra, *a.* That which is easily boiled.

Cochiéllo ó Cochíllo, (Ant.) V. *Cuchillo.*

Cochifríto, *sm.* Fricassee made of lamb, mutton, or kid.

Cochína, *sf.* Sow.

Cochináda, *sf.* 1. Herd of swine. 2. A mean dirty action.

Cochináta, *sf.* (Naút.) Rider, a piece of timber to strengthen a vessel.

Cochineár, *vn.* To be dirty, to be hoggish.

Cochinílla, *sf.* 1. Wood-louse, a small insect found in damp places under flags and tiles. 2. Cochineal, an insect reared on Indian figtrees, from which a red colour is extracted.

Cochiníllo, *sm.* 1. A little pig. 2. An amphibious animal in Brasil resembling a pig. 3. *Cochinillo de Indias,* Guinea-pig.

Cochíno, na, *a.* Dirty, nasty, filthy.

Cochíno, *sm.* Pig. V. *Puerco.*

Cochío, ía, *a.* (Ant.) Easily boiled.

Cochiquéra, *sf.* Hogsty.

Cochíte Hervíte, (Fam.) Applied to any thing done hastily or precipitately.

Cócho, cha, *a.* (Ant.) V. *Cocido.*

Cochúra, *sf.* 1. Act of boiling. 2. Dough made for a batch of bread.

Cocído, da, *a.* 1. Boiled, baked. 2. (Met.) Skilled, experienced. *Estar cocido en alguna cosa,* To understand business well.

Cocído, *sm.* Boiled meat.

Cocimiénto, *sm.* 1. Coction, decoction. 2. (Med.) Draught or poultice, made of herbs. 3. With Dyers, a bath or mordant preparatory to dying. 4. A quick, lively sensation. V. *Escozor.*

Cocína, *sf.* 1. Kitchen, the room in a house where the victuals are dressed. 2. Pottage made of greens and other ingredients. 3. Broth. *Cocina de boca,* Kitchen in which only the meat for the king and royal family is dressed.

Cocinár, *va.* 1. To cook or dress victuals. 2. (Met.) To meddle or interfere in other people's affairs.

Cocinéro, ra, *s.* Cook, one who professes to dress victuals for the table.

Cocinílla ó Cocinita, *sf.* A small kitchen.

Cócle, *sm.* (Naút.) Grapnel, a grappling iron with which in fighting one ship fastens on another.

Cóclea, *sf.* 1. An ancient machine for raising water. 2. An endless screw. 3. The inner cavity of the ear.

Cocleár, *va.* To strike and catch with a harpoon.—*vn.* To cluck or hatch. V. *Cloquear.*

Cocleária, *sf.* (Bot.) The sea scurvy-grass. Cochlearia officinalis *L.*

Cóco, *sm.* 1. (Bot.) Cocoa-tree; Indian palmtree. Cocos nucifera *L.* 2. Cocoa-nut. 3. Chocolate-cup made of the cocoa-nut. 4. Worm or grub bred in seeds and fruit. 5. Bugbear for frightening children. *Ser un coco, ó parecer un coco,* To be an ugly-looking person. *Cócos,* Beads made of cocoa-nuts for rosaries. *Hacer cocos,* (Met.) To flatter, to wheedle, to gain one's affections; to make signs or manifest affection.

Cocóbolo, *sm.* (Bot.) A species of the cocoatree, the wood of which is of a ruddy colour, and much used by cabinet-makers.

Cocodrílo, *sm.* Crocodile, an amphibious and voracious animal of the lizard kind.

Cocolíste, *sm.* Fever or disease peculiar to New Spain.

Cocóso, sa, *a.* Worm-eaten, gnawed by grubs.

Cocóte, *sm.* (Arag.) Occiput. V. *Cogote.*

Cocotríz, *sm.* V. *Cocodrilo.*

Cocúyo, *sm.* Kind of glow-worm peculiar to the Indies.

Códa, *sf.* 1. Tail. V. *Cola.* 2. Burthen of a song or other piece of music.

Codadúra, *sf.* Part of an old vine laid on the ground, from which young buds shoot forth.

Codál, *sm.* 1. Piece of ancient armour which defended the elbow. 2. A short and thick flambeau. 3. Shoot issuing from a vine. 4.

Muscle of the wrist. 5. Frame of a hand-saw. *Codales*, A carpenter's square.
CODÁL, *a.* Cubital, containing only the length of a cubit. *Palo codal*, A stick of the length of a cubit hung round the neck as a penance.
CODÁSTE, *sm.* (Naút.) Stern-post.
CODÁZO, *sm.* Blow given with an elbow.
CODEÁR, *va.* To elbow, to push with the elbows.
CODECILLÁR Y CODICILÁR, *vn.* (Ant.) To make a codicil.
CODÉÑA, *sf.* (Ant.) Body or thickness required in cloth.
CODÉRA, *sf.* Itch or scabbiness on the elbow. *Codera en un cable*, (Naút.) A spring on a cable.
CODÉSO, *sm.* (Bot.) Laburnum, ebony of the Alps. Cytisus laburnum *L.*
CÓDICE, *sm.* Old manuscript, treating on remarkable points of antiquity.
CODÍCIA, *sf.* 1. Covetousness, cupidity, an inordinate desire of riches. 2. (Ant.) Sensual appetite, cupidity. 3. (Met.) Greediness, an ardent desire of good things. *La codicia rompe el saco*, (Prov.) Covet all, lose all.
CODICIÁBLE, *a.* Covetable, that which is or may be wished for or desired.
CODICIADÓR, *sm.* He who covets.
CODICIÁNTE, *a.* Coveting, one who covets.
CODICIÁR, *va.* To covet or desire eagerly.
CODICILÁR, *a.* Pertaining to a codicil.
CODICÍLO, *sm.* Codicil, an appendage to a last will.
CODICIOSAMÉNTE, *ad.* In a greedy or covetous manner.
CODICIOSÍTO, TA, *a.* Somewhat covetous.
CODICIÓSO, SA, *a.* 1. Greedy, covetous, avaricious. 2. (Met.) Diligent, laborious, assiduous.
CÓDIGO, *sm.* Code of laws. *Código Justiniano*, Code of Justinian.
CODILLÉRA, *sf.* Tumor on the knee of horses.
CODÍLLO, *sm.* 1. Knee of horses and other quadrupeds. 2. Angle. 3. Codille, a term at ombre. 4. That part of a branch of a tree which joins the trunk. 5. *Codillo de una curva*, (Naút.) Breech of a knee. 6. Stirrup of a saddle. *Jugarselo á uno de codillo*, (Met.) To trick or outwit a person. *Codillos*, Kind of files used by silversmiths.
CÓDO, *sm.* 1. Elbow, the next joint or curvature of the arm below the shoulder. 2. Cubit, a measure of length equal to the distance from the elbow to the end of the middle finger. *Codo real*, Royal cubit, which is 3 fingers longer than the common. *Dar de codo*, To elbow, to push with the elbow, to treat with contempt. *Hablar con los codos*, To chatter, to prattle. *Apretar ó hincar el codo*, To kick the bucket, to die suddenly. *Levantar de codo, ó levantar el codo*, (Fam.) Applied to tipplers.
CODÓN, *sm.* A leather cover of a horse's tail.
CODORNÍZ, *sf.* (Orn.) Quail, a wild fowl resembling a partridge. Tetrao coturnix *L.*
COEFICIÉNTE, *a.* Coefficient, that which unites its action with the action of another.
COEPÍSCOPO, *sm.* Contemporary bishop.
COEQUÁL, *a.* (Teol.) Coequal; applied to the three Persons of the Trinity.
COERCIÓN, *sf.* Coercion, restraint, check.
COERCITÍVO, VA, *a.* Coercive, that which has the power or authority of restraining.

COETÁNEO, NEA, *a.* Coetaneous, of the same age with another.
COETÉRNO, NA, *a.* Equally eternal with another.
COÉVO, VA, *a.* Coeval, of the same age.
COEXISTÉNCIA, *sf.* Coexistence; existence at the same time with another.
COEXISTÉNTE, *a.* Coexistent.
COEXISTÍR, *vn.* To coexist; to exist at the same time as another.
COEXTENDÉRSE, *vr.* To coextend; to extend to the same space or duration with another.
CÓFA, *sf.* (Naút.) Top or round-house of the lower masts.
CÓFIA, *sf.* 1. A net of silk or thread worn on the head; a kind of cowl. 2. (Bot.) A thin membranaceous substance which covers the parts of fructification. 3. An iron case in which the dye is fastened for coining.
COFIEZUÉLA, *sf.* A small net.
COFÍN, *sm.* A small basket for fruit.
COFÍNA Y COFÍNO, (Ant.) V. *Cofin.*
COFRÁDE, DA, *s.* Member of a confraternity.
COFRADÍA, *sf.* 1. Confraternity, brotherhood, or sisterhood, a body of people united for some religious purpose. 2. Association of persons for any purpose.
COFRÁDRE, *sm.* (Ant.) Member of any society or corporation.
COFRADRÍA, *sf.* Neighbourhood, congregation, confraternity.
CÓFRE, *sm.* 1. Trunk, a chest for clothes, covered with leather and lined. 2. Fish found in the West Indies. 3. (Fort.) Coffer, a hollow lodgment across a dry moat. 4. (Impre.) Coffin of a printing-press. *Pelo de cofre*, Carroty or red hair.
COFRECÍCO, CÍLLO, Y CÍTO, *sm.* A small trunk.
COFRÉRO, *sm.* Trunk-maker, one who makes and sells trunks.
COGÉCHA, *sf.* (Ant.) V. *Cosecha.*
COGEDÉRA, *sf.* (Among bee-keepers) A sort of hive used to gather a swarm which has quitted the stock.
COGEDÉRO, RA, *s.* Collector, gatherer.
COGEDÍZO, ZA, *a.* That which can be easily collected or gathered.
COGEDÓR, *sm.* 1. Collector, gatherer. 2. Dust-box or dust-pan, an instrument in which the dust is carried out of the house. 3. (Ant.) Tax-gatherer. 4. (Among Velvet-weavers) Box in which the woven velvet is put.
COGEDÚRA, *sf.* Act of gathering or collecting.
COGÉR, *va.* 1. To catch, to seize with the hand. 2. To imbibe, to soak. *La tierra no ha cogido bastante agua*, The earth has not drawn in a sufficient quantity of water. 3. To gather fruit or the produce of the ground. 4. To have room to hold. *Esta cámara coge mil fanegas de trigo*, That granary holds a thousand bushels of wheat. 5. To occupy, to take up. *Cogió la alfombra toda la sala*, The carpet covered the whole room. 6. To find, to procure. *Me cogió descuidado*, He took me unawares. *Procuré cogerle de buen humor*, I endeavoured to see him when in good humour. 7. To surprise, to attack unexpectedly. *La tempestad me cogió*, The storm overtook me unexpectedly. *Coger en mentira*, To catch in a lie. 8. To intercept, to obstruct. *Coger las calles*, To stop the

streets. *Coger la calle*, To flee, to escape. *Coger á deseo*, To obtain one's wishes. *Coger un cernícalo, un lobo, ó una mona*, To be intoxicated.

Cogermáno, na, *s.* (Ant.) First cousin.

Cogimiénto, *sm.* The act of gathering, collecting, or catching.

Cogitabúndo, da, *a.* Pensive, thoughtful, musing.

Cogitár, *va.* To reflect, to meditate. *Cogito*, I have caught you; used in arguing.

Cogitatívo, va, *a.* Cogitative, given to meditation.

Cognación, *sf.* Cognation, kindred.

Cognádo, da, *a.* Related by consanguinity, cognate.

Cognición, *sf.* (Ant.) V. *Conocimiento.*

Cognómbre, *sm.* (Ant.) V. *Sobrenombre.*

Cognoménto, *sm.* Cognomination, surname; a name added from any accident or quality.

Cognominár, *va.* To give an additional name; to give a surname.

Cognoscér, *va.* (Ant.) V. *Conocer.*

Cognoscitívo, va, *a.* Cognitive, having the power of knowing.

Cogollíco y Cogollíto, *sm.* A small heart or flower of garden-plants, such as cabbage, lettuce, &c.

Cogóllo, *sm.* 1. Heart of garden-plants, such as lettuce, cabbage, &c. 2. Shoot of a plant. 3. Top, summit. *Cogollos*, Ornaments of the friezes of Corinthian capitals.

Cogolmár, *va.* To fill up a vessel. V. *Colmar.*

Cogombradúra, *sf.* (Ant.) Digging and earthing about plants.

Cogómbro, *sm.* V. *Cohombro.*

Cogóte, *sm.* Occiput, the hind part of the head. *Ser tieso de cogote*, (Met.) To be stiff-necked, headstrong, obstinate.

Cogotéra, *sf.* The hair formerly combed down on the neck.

Cogúcho, *sm.* The most inferior sort of sugar.

Cogujáda, *sf.* (Orn.) Crested lark. Alauda cristata L.

Cogujón, *sm.* Corner of a mattress or bolster.

Cogujonéro, ra, *a.* Pointed as the corners of mattresses or bolsters.

Cogúlla, *sf.* Cowl, monk's hood: habit of a monk.

Cogulláda, *sf.* Neck of a hog or pig.

Cohabitación, *sf.* Cohabitation, the act of living together as married persons.

Cohabitár, *vn.* 1. To dwell with another in the same place. 2. To live together as husband and wife.

Cohechadór, *sm.* 1. Briber, suborner, one that pays for corrupt practices. 2. (Ant.) Bribed judge.

Cohechamiénto, *sm.* (Ant.) V. *Cohecho.*

Cohechár, *va.* 1. To bribe, to gain by bribes, to suborn. 2. To force, to oblige. 3. (Agric.) To plough the ground the last time before it is sown.—*vn.* To accept a bribe, to allow one's self to be bribed.

Cohechazón, *sm.* 1. Act of breaking up the ground for culture. 2. The last ploughing of the ground before it is sown.

Cohécho, *sm.* 1. Bribery, the crime of giving or taking rewards for bad practices. 2. (Agric.) Season for ploughing the ground, and giving it the last preparation for sowing.

Coheredéro, ra, *s.* Coheir or coheiress, one who enjoys an inheritance jointly with another.

Coheréncia, *sf.* Coherence, connexion, dependency.

Coherénte, *a.* Coherent, suitable, consistent.

Cohermáno, *sm.* (Ant.) Cousin. V. *Primo.*

Cohéte, *sm.* (Ant.) Cousin. V. *Primo.*

Cohéte, *sm.* Rocket or sky-rocket, a cylindrical case of paper filled with gunpowder, which mounts in the air to a considerable height, and there bursts. *Cohete corredor*, Rocket which runs along a line. *Cohetes para señales*, Signal rockets.

Coheteria, *sf.* Shop where rockets and other sorts of artificial fire-works are made and sold.

Coheténo, *sm.* Rocket-maker, or dealer in rockets and other artificial fire-works.

Cohibición, *sf.* Prohibition, restraint.

Cohibír, *va.* To prohibit, to hinder, to restrain.

Cohíta de casas, *sf.* (Ant.) Number of contiguous houses or part of a street.

Cohobación, *sf.* Cohobation, the act of distilling the same liquor over again.

Cohól, *sm.* V. *Alcohol.*

Cohombrál, *sm.* Cucumber-bed; a place planted with cucumbers.

Cohombríllo, *sm.* A small kind of cucumber.

Cohómbro, *sm.* Cucumber. Cucumis flexuosus L. *Cohómbro marino*, Sea insect of the shape of a cucumber.

Cohondér, *va.* (Ant.) To corrupt, to vilify.

Cohondimiénto, *sm.* (Ant.) Corruption, reproach, infamy.

Cohonestár, *va.* To give an honest or decent appearance to an action.

Cohorte, *sm.* Cohort, a body of Roman infantry composed of 500 men; ten cohorts made a legion.

Cói, *sm.* Cóyes, *pl.* (Naút.) Hammock, a swinging bed used by sailors on board of ships.

Coidár, *vn.* (Ant.) V. *Cuidar.*

Coiécha, *sf.* (Ant.) Tax. V. *Tributo.*

Coíma, *sf.* Perquisite received by the keeper of a gaming table.

Coincidéncia, *sf.* Coincidence, the state of several things falling to the same point.

Coincidénte, *a.* Coincident, concurrent, consistent.

Coincidír, *vn.* 1. To fall upon or meet in the same point. 2. To concur.

Coinquinárse, *vr.* To be stained. V. *Mancharse.*

Coitárse, *vr.* To accelerate, to hasten.

Coitívo, va, *a.* Relating to the act of generation or coition.

Cóito, *sm.* Coition, carnal copulation.

Cojón, *sm.* Testicle. V. *Testículo.*

Cojúdo, da, *a.* Entire, not gelt, not castrated.

Col, *sf.* Species of cabbage with very large leaves and a short stalk.

Cóla, *sf.* 1. Tail, that which terminates the animal behind. 2. Train, the part of a gown that falls behind, upon the ground. 3. Glue, a viscous substance, commonly made by boiling the skins of animals to a jelly. 4. Word of reproach among students in opposition to that of *victor*. *Cola clara*, A transparent glue used by weavers. *Cola fuerte*, Strong glue made of ox-hides. *Cola de pescado*, Isinglass. *Cola de retazo*, Size with which painters prepare the piece of linen on which they intend to paint. *Cola de boca*, A viscous spittle with which paper may be fastened. 5. (In Music) The prolonged sound of the voice at the end of a song. *Hacer baxar la cola á alguno*, To humble or pull down one's pride. *Cobrirse con la cola*, To make use of frivolous evasions. *Castigado de cola*, Deprived of one's place or office. *Cola de golondrina*, (Fort.) Hornwork. *Á' la cola*, Backwards, behind. *Cola de caballo*, (Bot.) Horsetail. Equisetum *L.*

Colachón, *sm.* Kind of a guitar with a long handle.

Colación, *sf.* 1. Collation, comparing of one thing with another. 2. Collation, act of bestowing an ecclesiastical benefice, or conferring degrees in universities. 3. Conference or conversation between the ancient monks on spiritual affairs. 4. Collation, a slight repast. 5. Potation, the act of drinking. 6. Sweetmeats given to servants on Christmas eve. 7. Precinct or district of a parish. *Traer á colacion*, To produce any proofs or reasons to support a cause.

Colacionár, *va.* 1. To collate one thing of the same kind with another. 2. To collate, to place in an ecclesiastical benefice.

Colactáneo, nea, *s.* (Ant.) Foster brother or sister.

Coláda, *sf.* 1. The bucking of clothes or linen with lye made of ashes. 2. The linen itself thus bucked. 3. Common, an open ground used in common by the inhabitants of a place. 4. Road for cattle leading over a common. 5. One of the swords of the *Cid*: in the jocular style, a good sword. *Todo saldrá en la colada*, The whole fact will be brought to light. *Echar á uno la colada*, (Met.) To scrub or clean one of his filth.

Coladéra, *sf.* 1. Strainer, an instrument used in clearing liquors by filtration. 2. Sieve or searce, used by wax-chandlers.

Coladéro, *sm.* 1. Colander, a sieve through which liquors are poured, and which retains the thicker parts. 2. A narrow passage. 3. (Ant.) Bucking of clothes.

Coladór, *sm.* 1. Colander. V. *Coladero*. 2. Collator, one who confers ecclesiastical benefices. 3. A barrel with holes filled with ashes, on which water is poured, that, passing through the ashes, is converted into lye.

Coladóra, *sf.* (Ant.) Bucking-tub.

Coladúra, *sf.* Collation, the act of filtering or straining liquors through paper. *Coladúras*, Dregs or lees of clarified wax.

Colanílla, *sf.* A small bolt for fastening doors and windows.

Colánte, *a.* Filtering.

Colaña, *sf.* Joist about 20 palms long and 6 inches broad.

Colapéz y Colapíscis, *sf.* Isinglass, glue made of a species of cetaceous fishes. V. *Cola de pescado*.

Colár, *va.* 1. To strain through a colander, to filter. 2. To collate or confer ecclesiastical benefices. 3. To obtain some difficult matter. 4. To spread false news as certain facts; to pass off counterfeit money. *Colar la ropa con la lexía*, To buck linen with lye.—*vn.* 1. To pass through a strait place. 2. To dring wine.—*vr.* 1. To steal into a place, to creep in by stealth. 2. To be displeased with a jest.

Colaterál, *a.* 1. Collateral, situated by the side of another. 2. Standing equal in relation to some ancestor.

Colatívo, va, *a.* 1. Belonging to ecclesiastical benefices which cannot be enjoyed without a canonical collation. 2. That which can be strained or filtered.

Colaudár, *va.* (Ant.) V. *Alabar*.

Colay're, *sm.* (And.) Place through which a current of air passes.

Colcédra, *sf.* Flock or feather bed.

Colcedrón, *sm.* A large feather-bed.

Cólcha, *sf.* 1. Coverlet, an ornamental covering thrown over the rest of the bed-clothes. 2. (Naút.) V. *Colchadura*.

Colchadúra, *sf.* 1. Quilting, act of stitching one cloth over another. 2. (Naút.) Laying or twisting ropes.

Colchár, *va.* 1. To quilt. V. *Acolchar*. 2. *Colchar cabos*, (Naút.) To lay or twist ropes. *Carro de colchar*, A rope-maker's sledge.

Colchéro, *sm.* Quilt-maker, one who makes bed-quilts.

Colchíco, *sm.* (Bot.) Colchicum, meadow saffron. Colchicum montanum *L.*

Colchón, *sm.* Mattress, a kind of quilt made to lie upon. *Colchón de pluma*, Feather-bed.

Colchoncíco, íllo y íto, *sm.* A small mattress.

Colchonéro, ra, *s.* Mattress-maker, one who makes mattresses and feather-beds.

Coleáda, *sf.* Wag or motion of the tail of fishes or other animals.

Coleadúra, *sf.* 1. Wagging of the tail. 2. Wriggling, a ridiculous motion of women in walking.

Coleár, *vn.* 1. To wag or move the tail as dogs do. 2. To wriggle or move in a ridiculous manner in walking.

Colección, *sf.* 1. Collection, an assemblage of things, generally of the same nature. 2. Multitude of people.

Colécta, *sf.* 1. Distribution of a tax levied on a town. 2. Collect, an oration added in the mass. 3. Assemblage of the faithful in churches for the celebration of divine service.

Colectación, *sf.* The act of collecting or gathering rents, taxes, or other dues.

Colectár, *va.* To gather or collect taxes. V. *Recaudar*.

Colectício, cia, *a.* Collectitious; applied to troops assembled together without discipline.

Colectivaménte, *ad.* Collectively, in one body.

Colectívo, va, *a.* 1. Collective, applied to a noun, which expresses a multitude, though itself be singular; as *compañía*, a company. 2. That which may be gathered into one mass.

Colectór, *sm.* 1. Collector, one who collects or gathers scattered things. 2. Tax or rent-gatherer. 3. *Colector de espolios y vacantes*, Collector of church-rents. 4. Collector of the retributions for masses.

Colecturía, *sf.* Office or employ of a tax or rent gatherer.

Colégа, *sm.* Colleague, a partner in office or employment.

Colegiádo, *a.* (Arag.) Collegiate, a member of a college or corporation; applied to physicians, surgeons, lawyers, &c.

COLEGIAL, LA, s. The person who has a burse or place in any college.
COLEGIÁL, a. Collegial, relating to a college. *Iglesia colegial*, A collegiate church, composed of dignitaries and canons, who celebrate divine service as in cathedrals.
COLEGIALMÉNTE, ad. In a collegial manner; in the form of a college.
COLEGIÁTA, sf. A collegiate church.
COLEGIATÚRA, sf. Burse and dress of a collegian.
COLÉGIO, sm. 1. College, a society of men set apart for learning, religion, law, or physic. 2. House in which the collegians reside.
COLEGÍR, va. 1. (Ant.) To collect or gather things which are scattered. 2. To deduce, to infer, to draw consequences from propositions.
COLÉO, sm. (Fam.) V. *Coleadura.*
CÓLERA, sf. 1. Choler, bile; one of the humours of the animal body. 2. Anger, passion. *Montar en colera*, To be angry, to be in a passion. 3. (Ant.) Ornament of the tail of a horse.
COLÉRICO, CA, a. 1. Choleric, abounding with choler. 2. Passionate, hasty, easily provoked.
COLÉTA, sf. 1. Cue, the tail of hair tied with a ribbon. 2. A short addition to a discourse or writing.
COLETÁNEO, NEA, a. (Ant.) V. *Colactáneo.*
COLETÉRO, sm. One who makes buff-doublets and buff-breeches.
COLETÍLLA, sf. A small cue.
COLETÍLLO, sm. A small doublet made of buff or other skins.
COLÉTO, sm. 1. Doublet or jacket without skirts, made of buff or other skins. 2. Body of a man. *Echarse algo al coleto*, To eat or drink it all up.
COLGADÉRO, sm. Hook to hang things upon.
COLGADÉRO, RA, a. Fit to be hung up.
COLGADÍZO, sm. Shed, a slight temporary covering from the inclemencies of the weather.
COLGADÍZO, ZA, a. Pendent, suspended, pensile.
COLGÁDO, DA, a. Suspended. *Dexar á alguno colgado, ó quedarse alguno colgado*, To frustrate one's hopes or desires.
COLGADÓR, sm. (Among printers) Peel, with which printed sheets are hung up to dry.
COLGADÚRA, sf. Tapestry, hanging or drapery, hung or fastened against the walls of a room. *Colgadúra de cama*, Bed-furniture.
COLGÁJO, sm. 1. Tatter or rag hanging from clothes. 2. *Colgajo de uvas*, Bunch of grapes hung up to be preserved for the winter.
COLGÁNTE, a. Hanging, pending.
COLGÁR, va. 1. To hang up, to suspend in the air. 2. To adorn with tapestry or hangings. 3. To hang or kill by suspending by the neck. —vn. 1. To hang from, to be suspended. 2. (Ant.) To be in a state of dependence. *Colgar á uno*, (Met.) To compliment one on his birth-day, or his patron saint's day, by suspending some present at his neck.
CÓLIA ó CÓLIAS, s. A small fish, resembling a pilchard.
COLÍBRE, sm. (Orn.) Colibus, a beautiful small American bird, like the humming bird. Trochilus *L.*
CÓLICA, sf. Colic, a painful spasm in the stomach or bowels.
COLICÁNO, NA, a. Having grey hair in the tail; applied to horses or other animals.

CÓLICO ó DOLOR CÓLICO, sm. Colic, disease of the intestines.
COLIDÍR, va. To collide, to dash or knock together.
COLIFLÓR, sm. (Bot.) Colliflower, or cauliflower; a kind of white-flowered cabbage. Brassica oleracea *L.*
COLIGACIÓN, sf. 1. Colligation, the binding of things close together. 2. Connexion of one thing with another.
COLIGÁDO, DA, pp. United or joined together.—s. Agreed and associated for some purpose.
COLIGADÚRA, sf. Combining or connecting of one thing with another.
COLIGAMIÉNTO, sm. (Ant.) V. *Coligadura.*
COLIGÁNCIA, sf. Connexion, relation, correspondence of one thing with another.
COLIGÁRSE, vr. To be united for some purpose.
COLÍLLA, sf. 1. A small tail. 2. Train of a gown.
COLÍNA, sf. 1. Hill, a small height or eminence. 2. Seed of cabbage. 3. V. *Colino.*
COLÍNO, sm. Small cabbage not transplanted.
COLIQUACIÓN, sf Colliquation, the act of melting or dissolving.
COLIQUÁR, va. To melt, to dissolve.—vr. To become liquid, to be in fusion.
COLIQUECÉR, va. (Ant.) To fuse or melt.
COLÍRIO, sm. Collyrium, a wash for the eyes.
COLISÉO, sm. Opera-house, theatre, playhouse, or stage, upon which dramatic compositions are performed.
COLISIÓN, sf. Collision, the act of striking two bodies together.
COLITÉA, sf. (Bot.) Judas tree.
COLITIGÁNTE, sm. One who carries on a lawsuit against another.
COLITÓRTO, sm. Hypocrite, a dissembler in morality or religion.
CÓLLA, sf. (Ant.) Collet, a piece of ancient armour for the defence of the neck.
COLLACIÓN, sf. V. *Colacion.*
COLLÁDA, sf. (Ant.) V. *Cuello y Collado.*
COLLÁDO, sm. Hill, a small eminence.
COLLÁR, sm. 1. Necklace, an ornamental string of beads or precious stones, worn by women on their neck. 2. (Ant.) *Collar*, a part of the garment worn about the neck. 3. *Collar de un estay*, (Naut.) Collar of a stay.
COLLARÉJO, sm. A small collar or chain.
COLLARÍCO Y COLLARÍTO, sm. A small chain.
COLLARÍN, sm. 1. A black collar, edged with white, worn by the Roman catholic clergy. V. *Alzacuello.* 2. Collar, an ornament put round the neck of a coat.
COLLARÍNO, sm. (Arq.) Ring or list at the top and bottom of the shaft of a column. V. *Astragalo.*
COLLÁZO, sm. 1. Ploughman, who tills the ground for his master, and for which he gets some small tenement or ground to till for himself. 2. Tenant assigned to the lord of the manor with the lands he cultivates, and for which he pays him a certain rent. 3. (Ant.) Fosterbrother. *Collázos*, Poles on which barillaplants are carried to the pit to be burnt.
COLLÉJA, sf. (Bot.) Lamb's-lettuce, or cornsalad. Cucubalus behen *L.* *Collejas*, Little glands which grow on a sheep's neck.
COLLÉR, va. (Ant.) V. *Coger.*
COLLÉRA, sf. 1. Collar, breast-harness made of

leather, and stuffed with hair or straw, for draught cattle. 2. Number of malefactors, chained together, who are going to be transported. 3. Number of breeding mares used to thresh corn. V. *Cobra*.

Colléta, *sf*. (Bot.) A small kind of cabbage.

Colléte, *sm*. (Ant.) An iron ring, through which the pintles of a gun-carriage passes.

Collón, *a*. Dastardly, cowardly, faint-hearted.

Collonería, *sf*. 1. Cowardice, habitual timidity, want of courage. 2. Nonsense, unmeaning language.

Colmadaménte, *ad*. Abundantly, plentifully.

Colmádo, da, *a*. Filled, heaped.

Colmadúra, *sf*. (Ant.) V. *Colmo*.

Colmár, *va*. 1. To heap up, to fill a vessel up to the brim. 2. (Met.) To confer great favours.

Colména, *sf*. Bee-hive, the case or box in which bees are kept. *Tener la casa como una colmena*, To have one's house well stocked or stored with provisions.

Colmenár, *sm*. Apiary, the place where bees are kept, or bee-hives stand.

Colmenéro, *sm*. 1. Bee-keeper, bee-master. 2. (Ant.) Apiary. *Oso colmenero*, A bear who eats bees.

Colmenílla, *sf*. Kind of mushroom.

Colmillázo, *sm*. 1. Grinder or back tooth. 2. Wound made by a grinder.

Colmillejo, *sm*. A small grinder or back tooth.

Colmíllo, *sm*. Grinder or back tooth. *Colmillos de javalí*, Tusks of a wild boar. *Mostrar colmillos*, (Met.) To show spirit and resolution. *Tener colmillos*, (Met.) To be quick-sighted, and not easily imposed upon.

Colmillúdo, da, *a*. 1. Having grinders, fangs or tusks, applied to persons and animals. 2. Sagacious, quick-sighted, not easily imposed upon.

Cólmo, *sm*. 1. Heap, that which exceeds or gets over the brim of a vessel. 2. Complement, completion. *Ella llegó al colmo de sus deseos*, She attained the summit of her wishes. *No llegará á colmo*, It will not come to perfection. *A' cólmo*, Abundantly, plentifully.

Cólmo, ma, *a*. V. *Colmado*.

Cólo, *sm*. (Ict.) Chub, pollard.

Cólo, *sm*. Colon, the largest and widest of all the intestines.

Colacación, *sf*. 1. Employ or employment, place, office. 2. Arrangement of the different parts of a building, speech, &c. or other things, consisting of various parts. 3. Position, situation.

Colocár, *va*. 1. To arrange, to put in due place or order. 2. (Met.) To provide one with a place or employment.

Colocásia, *sf*. (Bot.) The Egyptian bean. Arum colocasia *L*.

Colocutór, *sm*. He who holds a colloquial intercourse with another.

Colódra, *sf*. 1. Milk-pail, a vessel into which cows or goats are milked. 2. A wooden can with which wine is measured and retailed. 3. A wooden can with a handle, used for drinking: horn with a cork bottom, used as a tumbler. *Ser una colodra*, To be a toper, or tippler. 4. (Burg.) Portable grind-stone used by mowers.

Colodrázgo, *sm*. Tax or excise laid on wine which is sold in small quantities.

Colodríllo, *sm*. Occiput, hind part of the head.

Colódro, *sm*. 1. (Ant.) A wooden shoe. 2. (Arag.) Wine-measure.

Colofonía, *sm*. Colophony, a kind of rosin.

Colombróño, *sm*. Namesake, one who has the same name with another.

Colón, *sm*. 1. A point (:) used to mark a pause, greater than that of a comma, and less than that of a period. *Colon imperfecto*, Semicolon (;) 2. *Intestino colon*, Colon, the greatest and widest of the intestines. 3. (Ant.) V. *Cólico y Colono*.

Colónia, *sf*. 1. Colony, a body of people sent from the mother country to inhabit some distant place. 2. The country planted; a plantation. 3. Silk ribbon two fingers wide. *Media colonia*, Silk ribbon one finger wide.

Colónial, *a*. Colonial, relating to a colony.

Colóno, *sm*. 1. Inhabitant of a colony, planter, colonist. 2. Labourer, who cultivates a piece of ground and lives on it.

Colóño, *sm*. (Ast.) Load of wood which a person carries on his back.

Coloquíntida, *sf*. (Bot.) Coloquintida, bitter apple or gourd. Cucumis colocynthis *L*.

Colóquio, *sm*. Colloquy, conversation, talk.

Colór, *sm*. 1. The appearance of bodies to the eye; colour, hue, dye. 2. Rouge, a paint with which ladies colour their cheeks and lips. 3. (Met.) Pretext, pretence; false show or appearance. *Color lleno ó cargado*, A deep colour. *Color vivo*, A bright colour. *Color muerto ó quebrado*, A wan or faded colour. *Color de ayre*, A light delicate colour. *Color de rosa batida*, A mixed rose colour, having the warp of a rose colour and the weft white. *Mudar de colores*, (Met.) To change colour. *Sacarle los colores á una persona*, (Met.) To make a person blush. *Colores*, (Pint.) Mixture of paint. *So colór, ó á color*, On pretence, under pretext.

Cólora, *sf*. (Ant.) V. *Colera*.

Coloración, *sf*. 1. Colouring; the act of laying on colours. 2. Blush; the colour raised on the cheek. 3. Pretence, pretext.

Coloradaménte, *ad*. Speciously, under pretext.

Colorádo, da, *a*. 1. Ruddy, of a blood-red or scarlet colour. 2. Coloured, specious. *Ponerse colorado*, To blush with shame. *Poner á alguno colorado*, To put one to the blush. *A' Dios con la colorada*, Farewell; God be with you; used cheerfully.

Coloramiénto, *sm*. V. *Encendimiento*.

Colorár, *va*. 1. To dye, to colour, or lay on colours. 2. To make plausible.—*vn*. To blush with shame.—*vr*. (Ant.) To be ashamed.

Coloratívo, va, *a*. Colorific, having the power of producing colour.

Coloreár, *va*. To colour, to make plausible, to palliate, to excuse.—*vn*. To redden, to grow red.

Colorído, *sm*. 1. Colouring, the result of the various colours in a painting. 2. Pretext, pretence.

Colorín, *sm*. 1. (Orn.) Linnet, a small singing bird. Fringilla linota *L*. 2. Bright, vivid colour. *Esta muger gusta de colorines*, This woman likes showy colours.

Colorár, *va.* 1. To colour, to mark with some hue or dye. 2. V. *Colorear*.
Colorísta, *sm.* Colourist, a painter who excels in colouring his designs. *Buen ó mal colorista*, A good or bad colourist.
Colosál, *a.* Colossal, colossean, giant-like.
Colóso, *sm.* Colosse or Colossus, a statue of enormous magnitude.
Colóstro, *sm.* Colostrum. V. *Calostro*.
Cólpa, *sf.* A whitish sort of copperas.
Colpár, *va.* V. *Herir*.
Col-péz, *sm.* Isinglass.
Cólpe, *sm.* V. *Golpe*.
Coludír, *va.* 1. To collude. 2. (Ant.) To collide.
Columbíno, na, *a.* Dove-like, innocent, candid.
Columbrár, *va.* 1. To discern at a distance, to see far off. 2. (Met.) To pursue or trace a thing by conjectures.
Columeláres, *sm. pl.* Incisors. V. *Cortadores*.
Colúmna, *sf.* V. *Coluna*.
Columnário, ria, *a.* Columnar; applied to the money coined in South America, with the impressions of 2 columns.
Columnáta, *sf.* Colonnade.
Columpiár, *va.* To swing to and fro a person sitting on a rope or cord, by way of diversion. —*vr.* 1. To fly forward and backward on a rope; to swing. 2. (Met.) To waddle, to shake in walking from side to side.
Colúmpio, *sm.* Swing, a rope suspended or fastened with both ends, on which a person swings himself.
Colúna ó Colúmna, *sf.* 1. Column, a round pillar made to support and adorn a building, and composed of a base, a shaft, and a capital. *Columna ática, compuesta, corintia, dorica, jónica, &c.* Attic, Composite, Corinthian, Doric, Ionic, &c. column. 2. Column of air, a quantity of air at a certain height, and of the thickness of the tube through which it passes. 3. *Coluna fosforica*, Light-house, built on a rock for the safety of navigators. *Coluna hueca*, A hollow column, in which is a spiral staircase, for the purpose of ascending to the top. *Coluna millar ó miliaria*, A mile column, or mile stone. 4. (Met.) Supporter or maintainer. *La justicia, paz, y religion, son la coluna del estado*, Justice, peace, and religion, are the supporters of the state. 5. A long file or row of troops. 6. Half a page, when it is divided into two equal parts, by a line passing down the middle.
Colunica, lla, y ta, *sf.* A small column.
Colurión, *sm.* (Orn.) Lesser butcher-bird, flusher. Lanius collurio *L.*
Colúros, *sm. pl.* Colures; two great circles supposed to pass through the poles of the earth, and to divide the ecliptic into four equal parts.
Colusión, *sf.* 1. Collusion, a deceitful agreement or compact, with a view to defraud. 2. Shock, collision.
Colzál, *sf.* Colewort-seed; the seed of the Brassica arvensis *L.*
Cóma, *sf.* 1. Comma, a point (,) serving to divide the shortest member of a period. 2. Each one of the parts into which a tone is divided. 3. (Ant.) Hair. *Sin faltar una coma, ó sin faltar punto ni coma*, Without a tittle being wanting in the account or narrative.

Comádre, *sf.* 1. Midwife, a woman who assists women in child-birth. 2. Godmother. 3. A gossiping neighbour. *Jueves de comadres*, Gossips' Thursday, the last Thursday before Shrove Tuesday.
Comadréja, *sf.* Weasel. Mustela vulgaris *L.* *Comadreja marina*. Weasel-blenny (Ict.) Blennius mustelaris *L.*
Comadréro, ra, *a.* Running about gossiping from house to house.
Comadrón, *sm.* Man-midwife, a surgeon who assists a woman in child-birth.
Comandamiénto, *sm.* V. *Mando y Mandamiento*.
Comandáncia, *sf.* 1. Command, the office of a commander. 2. The province or district of a commander. *Comandáncia militar*, A military command.
Comandánte, *sm.* Commander, he that has the supreme authority; a chief. *Comandante general*, A commander in chief of a kingdom, province, fleet, &c.
Comandár, *va.* 1. To command, to govern. 2. (Ant.) To commend, to recommend.
Comándo, *sm.* Command. V. *Mando*.
Comárca, *sf.* 1. Territory, district. 2. Border, boundary, limit. *En comarca*, Near.
Comarcáno, na, *a.* Neighbouring, near, bordering upon.
Comarcár, *va.* To plant trees in a straight line, so as to form walks on all sides.—*vn.* To border, to confine upon; to be on the borders.
Comáya, *sf.* 1. A large basket, a pannier. 2. (Orn.) The white owl, or barn-owl. Strix flammea *L.* V. *Zumaya*.
Cómba, *sf.* Curvature or inflexion of timber when warped, or iron when bent. *Hacer combas*, To bend and twist the body from one side to the other.
Combadúra, *sf.* V. *Bóveda*.
Combalachárse, *vr.* To bend one's self into a round ball.
Combár, *va.* To bend, to make crooked.—*vr.* To warp, to become crooked.
Combáte, *sm.* 1. Combat, conflict, engagement. 2. Agitation of the mind.
Combatíble, *a.* Fit to be combated; expugnable.
Combatidór, *sm.* Combatant, champion, antagonist.
Combatiénte, *sm.* Combatant, a fighting soldier of an army.
Combatír, *vn.* To combat, to fight.—*va.* 1. To attack, to invade. 2. To contradict, to impugn another's opinion. 3. (Met.) To agitate the mind, to rouse the passions. *Combatir á la retreta*, (Naút.) To keep up a running fight.
Combeneficiádos, *sm. pl.* Prebendaries of the same church.
Combés, *sm.* (Naút.) Waist of a ship; that is, the part contained between the quarter-deck and forecastle.
Combinázle, *a.* That which may be combined.
Combinación, *sf.* 1. Combination, the act of uniting or combining. 2. Aggregate of several words which begin with the same syllable.
Combinádo, da, *a.* Combined, united.
Combinár, *va.* 1. To combine, to join, to unite. 2. To compare

Combinatório, ria, a. Combining, uniting; applied to the act of combination.
Combléza, sf. (Ant.) A mistress kept by a married man.
Comblezádo, a. Applied to a married man whose wife lives in adultery with another.
Comblézo, sm. (Ant.) He who lives in adultery with another man's wife.
Cómbo, ba, a. Bent, crooked, warped.
Cómbo, sm. Stand or frame for casks.
Combóy, sm. Convoy, escort. V. *Convoy*.
Combustíble, a. y s. Combustible, susceptible of fire, that which may be easily burnt.
Combustión, sf. Combustion, burning; consumption by fire.
Combústo, ta, a. Burnt. V. *Abrasado*.
Comedéro, sm. 1. Dining-room. 2. A feeding trough for fowls and other beasts. 3. V. *Corredor*.
Comedéro, ra, a. Eatable.
Comédia, sf. Comedy, a dramatic composition. *Es una comedia*, It is a complete farce; applied to ridiculous speeches or actions.
Comediánte, ta, s. Player, actor or actress; one whose profession is to act on a stage. *Comediantes de la legua*, Strolling players.
Comediár, va. 1. To divide into equal shares. 2 To regulate, to direct.
Comedición, sf. (Ant.) V. *Pensamiento*.
Comédico, ca, a. Comical. V. *Cómico*.
Comedidaménte, ad. Gently, courteously, civilly.
Comedído, da, a. Civil, polite, gentle, courteous.
Comedimiénto, sm. Civility, politeness, urbanity.
Comédio, sm. 1. Middle of a kingdom or place. 2. Intermediate time between epochs.
Comedír, va. 1. To think, to meditate. 2. (Ant.) To commit, to charge, to intrust.—vr. To govern one's self, to regulate one's conduct, to be civil.
Comedór, ra, s. 1. Eater; commonly applied to persons who devour much meat. 2. Dining-room.
Comején, s. Kind of moth, or winged insect, that eats clothes and hangings; also a sort of wood-louse, which pierces pipe-staves.
Comendáble, a. Commendable. V. *Recomendable*.
Comendadór, sm. 1. Knight of a military order who holds a commandery. 2. Prelate or prefect of some religious houses.
Comendadóra, sf. The superior of a nunnery of a military order, and also of some other nunneries.
Comendamiénto, sm. (Ant.) V. *Encomienda y Mandamiento*.
Comendár, va. V. *Recomendár*.
Comendatário, sm. A secular clergyman of the Roman catholic profession, who enjoys a benefice belonging to some military order.
Comendatícia ó carta comendatícia, sf. Introductory letter, recommendation.
Comendatício, cia, a. Recommendatory letter given by a prelate.
Comendatório, ria, a. Relating or belonging to letters of introduction or recommendation.
Comendéro, sm. He who enjoys a benefice in a place, on condition of his swearing allegiance to the King of Spain.
Comentadór, sm. 1. Commentator, expositor, annotator. 2. (Ant.) Inventor. V. *Inventor*.
Comentár, va. To comment, to write notes or strictures, to explain, to expound.
Comentário, sm. Commentary; a narrative in a familiar manner.
Comento, sm. Comment, exposition or explanation of some writing or circumstance.
Comentuál, a. Relating to a comment.
Comenzadór, sm. One who commences or makes a beginning of any thing.
Comenzamiénto, sm. (Ant.) V. *Principio*.
Comenzánte, pa. Beginning; beginner.
Comenzár, vn. To commence, to begin.
Comér, va. 1. To eat, to chew or swallow any thing. 2. To be in possession of or enjoy an income. *Fulano come tres mil libras esterlinas de renta*, He has or spends three thousand a year. 3. To run through a fortune. 4. To have an itching all over the body. 5. To suppress some letter or syllable in the pronunciation of words. 6. (Met.) To corrode, to consume. *El orin come el hierro*, The rust corrodes the iron. 7. To take a man, in the game of chess. *Comer á dos carillos*, To enjoy two places or benefices at the same time: To trim, to please two persons of opposite principles. *Comer de mogollon*, To live at other people's expense. *Comerse la risa*, To refrain from laughing. *Comerse los codos de hambre*, (Met.) To be starved with hunger. *Comerse unos á otros*, (Met.) To be constantly at drawn daggers. *Tener que comer*, To have a competency or decent fortune to live upon. *Ganar de comer*, To earn a livelihood. *Comer pan con corteza*, (Met.) To be independent; to have a sufficiency without others. *Comer con un sabañon*, To eat excessively.
Comér, sm. (Ant.) V. *Comida*.
Comerciáble, a. 1. Merchantable, marketable. 2. Sociable, social, ready to mix in friendly gaiety.
Comerciál, a. (Ant.) Commercial; sociable.
Comerciánte, sm. Merchant, one who traffics to remote countries.
Comerciár, va. 1. To trade, to carry on trade and commerce. 2. (Met.) To have intercourse; applied to persons and places.
Comércio, sm. 1. Trade, commerce, traffic. 2. Communication, intercourse. 3. An unlawful connexion between the sexes. 4. Body or company of merchants. *El comercio de Indias*, The India company. 5. Exchange, or public place in large towns. 6. A kind of game at cards.
Comestíble, a. Eatable. It is commonly used as a substantive, and in the plural, and implies all sorts of provisions and food.
Cométa, sf. 1. Comet, a heavenly body in the planetary region, appearing suddenly, and again disappearing. 2. Kite, a plaything for boys. 3. Kind of game at cards.
Cometário, sm. A machine, exhibiting the revolutions round the sun, a cometarium.
Cometedór, sm. 1. Offender, a person guilty of a crime. 2. Assaulter, one who violently assaults another. V. *Acometedor*.
Cometér, va. 1. To commit, to charge, to intrust. 2. (Ant.) To undertake, to attempt. 3. (Ant.) To attack, to assault. 4. To commit some criminal act or error. 5. (Gram.) To use

tropes and figures.—vr. 1. To expose one's self. 2. To take something to one's charge.

Comezón, sm. 1. Itching in the body. 2. (Met.) A longing desire. [tor or player-like.

Comicamente, ad. In a comical manner; ac-

Comicios, sm. pl. Roman committees or assemblies for business.

Cómico, ca, a. Comic, relating or pertaining to the stage or theatre.

Cómico, ca, s. 1. Player, actor, or actress. V. *Comediante*. 2. (Ant.) A writer of comedies.

Comida, sf. 1. Eating, food, dressed victuals. 2. Dinner, the chief meal, generally eaten about the middle of the day. *Hacer una buena comida*, To make a good meal.

Comidilla, sf. 1. A slight repast. 2. Peculiar pleasure or delight, afforded by something which strikes our fancy.

Comido, da, a. Satiate, full to satiety. *Comido por servido*, Meat for work; signifying the little value of any employ.

Comienzár, vn. V. *Comenzar*.

Comienzo, sm. (Ant.) Origin, beginning, initiation. *Al ó de comienzo*, From the beginning.

Comilitón, sm. Parasite, sponger, who goes about feasting at other people's expense.

Comilitóna ó Comilóna, sf. A splendid and plentiful repast.

Comilón, na, s. A great eater, a glutton, one who indulges too much in eating.

Cominéro, a. y s. Miserable, niggard, miser.

Comíno, sm. (Bot.) Cumin. Cuminum *L. Cominos*, Cumin seed. *No vale ó no monta un comino*, It is not worth a rush. *Partir el comino*, To split a hair, to be niggardly. *Putas, dados, y cominos de obra matan al hombre*, (Prov.) Whoring, gambling, and drinking, kill men. [to confiscate.

Comisár, va. To declare a thing confiscated,

Comisaría y Comisariáto, s. Office or employment of a commissary.

Comisário, sm. Commissary, delegate, deputy. *Comisario de entradas*, In hospitals, the person charged with taking an account of the patients which enter. *Comisarios de la inquisicion*, Commissaries of the Inquisition, inquisitors delegated to the different towns in the kingdom.

Comisión, sf. 1. Trust, commission, a warrant by which any trust is held. 2. Act of committing a crime. *Pecado de comision*, A sin of commission; a speech or act contrary to divine law. 3. Commission, number of persons appointed to a particular business.

Comisionádo, da, a. Commissioned, deputed, empowered to transact some business.

Comisionár, va. To commission, to depute, to empower, to appoint.

Comisionísta, sm. Commissioner, who has received a commission or power to transact some business.

Comíso, sm. Confiscation of prohibited goods.

Comistión, sf. V. *Conmistion*.

Comistrájo, sm. Hodge-podge, a medley of eatables, jumbled together in a strange or extravagant way.

Comisúra, sf. (Anat.) Commissure, joint; the place whereon one part is joined to another.

Cómite, sm. Count. V. *Conde*.

Comitíva, sf. Suite, retinue. [galley

Cómitre, sm. (Naút.) Boatswain on board

Comíza, sf. (Ict.) A river-fish, a kind of sur mullet.

Commutár, (Ant.) V. *Conmutar*.

Cómo, ad. 1. How, in what manner, to what degree. *¿Como estamos de cosecha?* How is the harvest? 2. As, in a sense of comparison, e. g. *Es fuerte como un leon*, He is as strong as a lion. 3. Why. *¿Como no has venido mas presto?* Why did you not come sooner? 4. In such a manner. *Hago como tu haces*, I do as you do. 5. In what manner. *Diga vd. como hemos llegado*, Please to relate in what condition we arrived. 6. If. *Como ello sea bueno*, If it be good. *Dar como, ó dar un como*, To play a trick, to joke. *Como asi me lo quiero*, As easy as I could wish.

Cómoda, sf. Press, a wooden case for clothes, a chest of drawers in which clothes are kept.

Comodáble, a. That which can be lent or borrowed.

Comodaménte, ad. Conveniently, in a convenient or commodious manner.

Comodatário, sm. 1. Borrower, one who borrows or takes something from another upon credit. 2. Pawnbroker.

Comodáto, sm. Loan, any thing lent to another on condition of returning it at a certain time.

Comodidád, sf. 1. Ease, freedom from want. 2. Convenience. 3. Profit, interest, advantage.

Cómodo, sm. Utility, profit, convenience.

Cómodo, da, a. Convenient, commodious, suitable.

Como quiéra, ad. However, notwithstanding, nevertheless, yet. Used with the negative no.

Como quiéra que, ad. Notwithstanding that, although, yet. [ther.

Comorár, vn. (Ant.) To cohabit, to live together.

Compácto, ta, a. Compact, close, dense.

Compadecérse, vr. 1. To be compassionate, to have a fellow feeling for the afflictions of others. In an active sense; *Compadezco á fulano*, I commiserate his distress; I feel for him. 2. To agree with each other.

Compadrár, vn. To become a godfather, to contract a spiritual affinity.

Compadrázgo, sm. Connexion or affinity contracted by a godfather with the parents of a child for which he stands sponsor.

Compádre, sm. 1. Godfather; a sponsor at the font. 2. Protector, benefactor. 3. Friend; used in Andalusia when casually addressing a person. *Jueves de compadres*, The last Thursday before Shrove Tuesday. [godfathers

Compadrería, sf. Friendly intercourse between

Compáge, sf. Compages, a system of many parts united. [structure

Compaginación, sf. Compagination, union,

Compaginadór, sm. One who joins, unites, or couples.

Compaginár, va. To join, to unite, to couple.

Compágo, sm. (Ant.) Portico of a church door.

Companiéro, ra, s. V. *Compañero*.

Compáña, sf. 1. Out-house, office. 2. (Ant.) Company of soldiers. 3. (Ant.) Family.

Compañería, sf. V. *Mancebía*.

Compañéro, ra, s. 1. Companion, one with whom a person frequently converses. 2. Com-

pañero de quarto, Chamber-fellow; one who sleeps in the same room with another. 3. Comrade, colleague. 4. Partner, associate. 5. One who shares the lot and fortune of another. 6. One thing suited to another. *Buen barco compañero*, (Naút.) A ship that does not part company with the convoy.

Compañía, *sf.* 1. Company or society of persons united for some common design. 2. Company of persons united in a joint trade or partnership. 3. A body of soldiers under the command of a captain. 4. Number of players united to represent pieces on the stage. *Compañía de la legua*, A strolling company of players. 5. Company, conversation of a companion. 6. (Ant.) Family, confederacy. *Compañía de Jesus*, Order of Jesuits founded by Ignatius de Loyola, in 1540, suppressed by Pope Clement 14, 1773, and revived by Pius 7, 1815.

Compaño ó Compañon, (Ant.) V. *Compañero*.

Compañón, *sm.* Testicle. V. *Testículo*

Compañuéla, *sf.* (Ant.) A small family.

Comparáble, *a.* Comparable, worthy to be compared.

Comparación, *sf.* Comparison, the act of comparing one thing with another.

Comparánza, *sf.* (Bax.) V. *Comparacion*.

Comparár, *va.* To compare, to estimate the relative value or quality of things.

Comparativaménte, *ad.* Comparatively.

Comparatívo, **va**, *a.* 1. Comparative, estimated by comparison, or having the power of comparing. 2. The comparative degree, in grammar, expresses more of any quality in one thing than another.

Comparecéncia, *sf.* Appearance before a judge in obedience to a summons.

Comparecér, *vn.* To appear before a judge.

Comparéndo, *sm.* Summons, a call of authority, admonition to appear.

Comparición, *sf.* (For.) Appearance.

Compársa, *sf.* Retinue of great personages represented on the stage.

Compárte, *s.* (For.) Joint party or accomplice in a civil or criminal cause.

Compartímento y Compartimiénto, *sm.* 1. Compartment, the division of a whole into proportionate parts. 2. Inclosure. *Compartimiento interior de un navio*, Accommodations on board a ship.

Compartír, *va.* 1. To divide into equal parts. 2. (Pint.) To arrange or dispose the different parts of a painting.

Compás, *sm.* 1. Pair of compasses, a mathematical instrument having two arms, with which circles are drawn. 2. *Compás de calibre ó de puntas corvas*, Callipers or compasses with bowed or arched limbs, to take the diameter of convex or concave bodies. *Compás de proporcion*, Proportional compasses. V. *Pantómetra*. 3. *Compás de relozero*, Clock-maker's compass. 4. *Compás de azimuth*, Azimuth compass. 5. Power of the voice to express the notes of music. 6. Time in music. *Echar el compás*, To beat time. *A' compás*, In right musical time. 7. (Met.) Rule of life, principle to be governed by, pattern. *Echar el compás*, (Met.) To direct, to regulate, to govern. *Salir de compás*, (Met.) To act without rule or measure. 8. *Compás de muelle*, Spring compass. 9. *Compás de mar*, Mariner's compass. V. *Bruxula y Bitácora*. 10. *Compás mixto*, (Esgr.) Mixed movement partly direct and partly curved; a feint. *Compás trepidante*, (Esgr.) Motion or movement in a right line.

Compasadaménte, *ad.* By rule and measure.

Compasár, *va.* 1. To measure with a rule and compass. 2. (Met.) To regulate things so that there may be neither too much nor too little. 3. (Mús.) To divide a musical composition into equal parts. 4. *Compasar una carta de marear*, (Naút.) To prick the chart; that is, to trace the course of a ship on a chart by the help of a scale and compass.

Compasíble, *a.* 1. Lamentable, deserving pity, worthy of compassion. 2. Compassionate.

Compasíllo, *sm.* Quick musical time.

Compasión, *sf.* Compassion, pity.

Compasívo, **va**, *a.* Compassionate, merciful, tender-hearted.

Compaternidád, *sf.* V. *Compadrazgo*.

Compatía, *sf.* Sympathy, fellow-feeling.

Compatibilidád, *sf.* Compatibility, the power of co-existing with something else.

Compatíble, *a.* Compatible, suitable to, fit for, consistent with.

Compatrióta, *s.* Countryman or woman, one born in the same country.

Compatrióte, *sm.* (Ant.) V. *Compatriota*.

Compatrón, **na**, *s.* Fellow-guardian, fellow-patron or patroness, joint guardian.

Compatronáto, *sm.* Patronage; the right of conferring a benefice.

Compatróno, *sm.* Joint guardian. V. *Compatron*.

Compelér y Compelír, *va.* 1. To compel, to force to some act, to constrain. 2. To extort.

Compendiadór, *sm.* Epitomizer, abridger; one who abridges a work.

Compendiár, *va.* To epitomise, to shorten, to abridge. [briefly.

Compendiariaménte, *ad.* Compendiously,

Compéndio, *sm.* Compendium, epitome, abridgment.

Compendiosaménte, *ad.* Briefly, in a concise manner. [dious.

Compendióso, **sa**, *a.* Brief, abridged, compen-

Compendizár, *va.* V. *Compendiar*.

Compensáble, *a.* Compensable, that which may or ought to be recompensed.

Compensación, *sf.* Compensation, recompense, equivalent.

Compensár, *va.* To compensate, to recompense, to counterbalance, to countervail. *Los malos años se compensan con los buenos*, Good years make amends for bad ones.—*vn.* To enjoy an equivalent for any loss or injury.

Compenzár, *va.* To commence, to begin.

Competéncia, *sf.* 1. Competition, rivalry, contest, claim of more than one to one thing. 2. Competence; the power or competency of a court or judge. *A' competéncia*, Contentiously, with strife and contest.

Competénte, *a.* Competent, sufficient, fit for, consistent with, applicable to; adequate.

Competenteménte, *ad.* In a competent manner. [claim to something. V. *Competir*.

Competér, *vn.* To be one's due, to have a fair

Competición, *sf.* Competition. V. *Competencia*.

Competidór, ra, *s.* Competitor, rival, opponent.
Competír, *vn.* 1. To stand in competition, to rival. 2. To be on a level or upon a par with another.
Compiadárse, *vr.* V. *Compadecerse.*
Compilación, *sf.* Compilation, collection from various authors; mass of things heaped together.
Compilár, *va.* To compile, to draw up from various authors.
Compínche, *s.* Bosom-friend, comrade, confidant.
Complacéncia, *sf.* Pleasure, satisfaction, gratification arising from a thing.
Complacér, *va.* To please another by agreeing to what may be agreeable to him.—*vr.* To be pleased with or take delight in a thing.
Complaciénte, *a.* Pleasing, one who pleases.
Complanár, *va.* (Ant.) V. *Aclarar.*
Complañír, *vn.* To weep; to be compassionate.
Compleménto, *sm.* Complement, perfection, accomplishment. *Complemento de la derrota,* (Naút.) Complement of the course in navigation, that is, the number, of points which the course wants to be equal to 90 degrees, or 8 points, which compose a quarter of the compass.
Completaménte, *ad.* Completely, perfectly.
Completár, *va.* To complete, to render perfect, to finish.
Complétas, *sf. pl.* Compline, the last of the canonical hours or evening prayers; the last act of worship at night.
Completivaménte, *ad.* Absolutely, completely.
Compléto, ta, *a.* Complete, perfect, finished, concluded.
Complexíón, *sf.* Complexion, temperature of the body.
Complexionádo, da, *a.* *Bien ó mal complexionado,* Of a good or bad complexion.
Complexionál, *a.* Complexional.
Compléxô, *sm.* Complex, meeting or union of several things.
Compléxô, *a.* (Anat.) Applied to one of the muscles of the head.
Complicación, *sf.* Complication; the coincidence or meeting of two things contrary to each other.
Complicár, *va.* To complicate, to jumble things together which are contrary to each other.
Cómplice, *s.* Accomplice, co-operator, associate; usually in an ill sense.
Complicidád, *sf.* The condition or state of being an accomplice.
Complidúra, *sf.* (Ant.) Convenient or correspondent quality or measure.
Complimiénto, *sm.* 1. Supply of provisions for a journey. 2. V. *Fin.*
Complir, *va.* (Ant.) V. *Cumplir.*
Complisión, *sf.* V. *Complexion.*
Componedór, ra, *s.* 1. Composer, writer, author. 2. Arbitrator. 3. (Impr.) Compositor.
Componénda, *sf.* Amount of fees paid in the papal chancery at Rome for such bulls and licenses as have no certain tax.
Componér, *va.* 1. To compose, to form a mass by joining different things together. 2. To construct, to give existence to. 3. To sum up. 4. To frame, to devise, to invent. 5. To mend, to repair. 6. To strengthen, to fortify, to restore. *Esa copa de vino me ha compuesto el estómago,* That glass of wine has strengthened my stomach. 7. To furnish, to supply with furniture. 8. To adjust, to settle, to compose differences. 9. To ward off a danger. 10. To compose, to calm, to quiet. 11. To form a tune from the different musical notes. 12. To compose or compile a book. 13. To compose or write verses. *Fulano compone muy bien,* He writes very good verses. 14. (Impr.) To compose types or arrange letters. *Componer el semblante,* To put on a modest or sedate appearance. *Componer tanto de renta,* To have so much a year.—*vr.* To deck out one's self with clothes, to set off one's self with dress.
Componíble, *a.* Compoundable, that which may be compounded.
Componimiénto, *sm.* (Ant.) Disposition, order, distribution. V. *Composicion y Compostura.*
Compórta, *sf.* A large basket in which grapes are carried during the vintage.
Comportáble, *a.* Supportable, tolerable.
Comportár, *va.* 1. (Ant.) To carry or bring together. 2. To suffer, to tolerate.—*vr.* To behave or conduct one's self.
Compórte, *sm.* (Ant.). 1. V. *Sufrimiento.* 2. Proceeding, conduct. 3. Air, manner.
Comportílla, *sf.* A small basket.
Composíble, *a.* V. *Componible.*
Composición, *sf.* 1. Composition, the act of composing something. 2. Adjustment, agreement, compact. 3. A musical composition. 4. A literary composition. 5. (Impr.) Arrangement of types or letters. 6. Modest or sedate appearance.
Compositór, *sm.* 1. Composer, one who produces musical compositions. 2. (Impr.) Compositor, he that arranges and adjusts the types in printing.
Compostúra, *sf.* 1. Composition, the composing of a whole of several parts. 2. Mending or repairing of any thing which is broken. 3. Cleanliness, neatness of dress. 4. Adjustment, agreement, compact. 5. Modesty, circumspection, sedateness. 6. (Ant.) A musical or literary composition.
Compóta, *sf.* Conserve of fruit, boiled or stewed with sugar and water.
Compotéra, *sf.* Vessel in which jams are served up to the table.
Cómpra, *sf.* 1. Purchase. 2. Collection of necessaries bought for the daily use of the house. *Dar compra y vendida.* (Ant.) To permit trade.
Compráble, *a.* That which may be bought or purchased.
Compráda, *sf.* V. *Compra.*
Compradízo, za, *a.* V. *Comprable.*
Comprádo y Compradíllo, *sm.* Kind of play in the game of ombre.
Compradór, ra, *s.* 1. Buyer, purchaser. 2. Caterer, one who buys the daily supply of provisions for a family.
Compránte, *a.* Buying, one who buys.
Comprár, *va.* To buy, to purchase.
Compráda, *sf.* (Ant.) Purchase. V. *Compra.*
Comprehendedór, ra, *s.* One who comprehends or understands.
Comprehendér, *va.* 1. To embrace, to encircle, to comprehend. 2. To comprise, to include, to contain. 3. To understand, to conceive.

COMPREHENSIBILIDÁD, *sf.* Capacity of things, to be understood.

COMPREHENSÍBLE, *a.* Comprehensible, conceivable.

COMPREHENSIÓN, *sf.* 1. Comprehension; the capacity or power of the mind to comprehend or admit ideas. 2. Act of comprising or containing.

COMPREHENSÍVO, VA, *a.* 1. Comprehensive, having the power to comprehend or understand. 2. Comprehensive, having the quality of comprising much.

COMPREHENSÓR, RA, *s.* 1. (Teol.) The blessed; one who enjoys the presence of God in the heavenly mansions. 2. One that understands, attains, or embraces a thing.

COMPREMÍBLE, *a.* Compressible.

COMPREMÍR, *va.* V. *Comprimir.*

COMPRESAMÉNTE, *ad.* (Ant.) Compendiously.

COMPRESBÍTERO, *sm.* A fellow-presbyter or priest.

COMPRESIBILIDÁD, *sf.* Compressibility.

COMPRESIÓN, *sf.* 1. Compression; the act of pressing together. 2. (Gram.) V. *Sinéresis.*

COMPRESIVAMÉNTE, *ad.* Narrowly, contractedly.

COMPRESÍVO, VA, *a.* Compressing or reducing to a smaller compass.

COMPRIMÍR, *va.* 1. To compress, to reduce to a smaller compass. 2. To repress, to restrain, to keep in awe.—*vr.* To subdue one's passion.

COMPRISIÓN, *sf.* (Ant.) V. *Complexion.*

COMPROBACIÓN, *sf.* Comprobation; the act of proving by the joint testimony of several witnesses.

COMPROBÁNTE, *a.* Proving, one who proves.

COMPROBÁR, *va.* 1. To verify, to confirm one thing by comparing it with another. 2. To prove, to give evidence.

COMPROFESÓR, *sm.* Colleague, one who exercises the same profession, and at the same time.

COMPROMETÉR, *va.* 1. To compromise; to leave the decision of a difference or law-suit to a third person. 2. To render one accountable or answerable for a thing.

COMPROMETIMIÉNTO, *sm.* (Ant:) The act of compromising.

COMPROMISÁRIO, *sm.* Arbitrator, umpire; a referee chosen by compromise.

COMPROMISIÓN, *sf.* Act of compromising.

COMPROMÍSO, *sm.* 1. Compromise; a mutual promise of parties at difference to refer their controversies to arbitrators. 2. Arbitration bond. *Poner en compromiso,* To render a matter doubtful which is clear of itself.

COMPROTECTÓR, *sm.* A joint protector, one who protects jointly with another.

COMPROVINCIÁL, *a.* Of the same metropolitan church; applied to a suffragan bishop.

CÓMPTOS, *sm. pl.* (Navar.) Exchequer board.

COMPUÉRTA, *sf.* 1. Hatch or half door. 2. Lock or sluice. 3. Curtain hung before the door of an old fashioned coach. 4. *Compuerta de mareа,* (Naút.) Tide-gate, tide-race. 5. A piece of cloth which formerly bore a knight's badge.

COMPUESTAMÉNTE, *ad.* Regularly, orderly; in a regular manner.

COMPUÉSTO, *sm.* Compound, a mass formed by the union of many ingredients.

COMPUÉSTO, TA, *a.* *Orden compuesto,* The composite order in architecture.

COMPÚLSA, *sf.* An authentic or attested copy of some instrument or other writing.

COMPULSÁR, *va.* 1. (Ant.) To compel, to force. 2. To make an authentic copy or transcript.

COMPULSIÓN, *sf.* 1. Compulsion, the act of compelling to something. 2. The state of being compelled.

COMPULSÓRIO, RIA, *a.* 1. Compulsory, having the power of compelling. 2. Ordering an authentic copy to be made; applied to the decree of a judge or magistrate.

COMPUNCIÓN, *sf.* Compunction, repentance, contrition.

COMPUNGÍRSE, *vr.* To feel compunction; to be pierced with remorse.

COMPUNGÍVO, VA, *a.* Pricking, stinging, stimulating.

COMPURGACIÓN, *sf.* Compurgation, the act or practice of justifying any man's veracity by the testimony of another.

COMPURGADÓR, *sm.* Compurgator, one who bears testimony to the credibility or innocence of another.

COMPURGÁR, *va.* To prove one's veracity or innocence by the oath of another.

COMPUTACIÓN, *sf.* Computation; the manner of counting or calculating time.

COMPUTÁR, *va.* To compute or estimate by the number of years or ages.

COMPUTÍSTA, *sm.* Computist, accomptant; one skilled in computation or calculation.

CÓMPUTO, *sm.* Computation, calculation, accompt.

COMULACIÓN, *sf.* Cumulation; the act of heaping together.

COMULGÁR, *va.* To administer the blessed sacrament.—*vn.* To receive the sacrament.

COMULGATÓRIO, *sm.* Communion-altar, where the blessed sacrament is administered.

COMÚN, *a.* 1. Common, that which belongs to many. *Pastos comunes,* Commons, fields equally used by many persons. 2. Common, generally received. 3. Vulgar, mean, low; of an inferior kind. *Por lo común,* In general, generally.

COMÚN, *sm.* Community, public. *En comun,* Conjointly, collectively.

COMÚNA, *sf.* (Mur.) The principal canal of irrigation.

COMUNÁL, *sm.* Commonalty, common people; the bulk of mankind.

COMUNALÉZA, *sf.* 1. (Ant.) Mediocrity. 2. (Ant.) Communication, intercourse. 3. (Ant.) Common.

COMUNALMÉNTE Y COMUNAMÉNTE, *ad.* V. *Comunmente.*

COMUNÉRO, RA, *a.* 1. Popular, beloved by the multitude, pleasing to the people. 2. Factious, rebellious. 3. Belonging to the sect of levellers, such as existed in Old Castile under the reign of Charles V.

COMUNÉRO, *sm.* 1. A joint holder of a tenure of lands. 2. Leveller; a factious person.

COMUNICABILIDÁD, *sf.* Communicability; the quality of being communicated or imparted.

COMUNICÁBLE, *a.* 1. Communicable, that which may be communicated. 2. Sociable, affable.

COMUNICACIÓN, *sf.* 1. Communication, intercourse. 2. Criminal connexion between persons of a different sex. 3. Junction or union of one thing with another.

Comunicánte, *pa.* Communicating; one who communicates; a communicant.

Comunicár, *va.* 1. To communicate, to impart, to discover or make known. 2. To treat with another either by word of mouth or writing. 3. To consult or confer upon a subject. 4. (Ant.) To take the Lord's Supper.—*vr.* To be joined, united, or contiguous to each other. *Comunicarse entre sí*, To interchange sentiments or ideas.

Comunicatívo, va, *a.* Communicative, inclined to impart, liberal of knowledge, not selfish.

Comunicatório, ria, *a.* That which must be communicated, notified, or published.

Comunidád, *sf.* 1. Commonness; the equal participation among many. 2. Commonalty; the common people; the bulk of mankind. 3. Community, corporation. *De comunidad*, Conjointly, collectively. 4. A rebellious crowd, a factious mob. *Comunidades*, Disturbances, commotions.

Comunión, *sf.* 1. Communion, fellowship, common possession. 2. Familiar intercourse. 3. Communion, the act of receiving the blessed sacrament.

Comunménte, *ad.* 1. Commonly, usually, generally. 2. Frequently, often.

Comúña, *sf.* 1. (Ast.) Dividend or equal share of the produce of lands. 2. Meslin, mixed corn; as wheat and rye. 3. Contracts or agreements between rich proprietors and the poor. *Comuña á armun*, (Astur.) Contract by which a valued herd of cattle is entrusted to another, on condition that he enjoys the milk, butter, and cheese, for his trouble of keeping and taking care of the cattle. *Comuña á la ganancia*, Contract by which a herd of cattle is entrusted to another by a fair appraisement, on condition that, after the capital has been refunded, the profit is to be divided between them. *Comuñas*, Seeds. V. *Camuñas.*

Con, *prep.* 1. With, by. *Con declarar se eximió del tormento*, By confessing, he freed himself from the torture. 2. *Con que*, So that, provided that. *Yo lo haré con que, &c.* I will do it, provided that, &c. 3. *Con que*, then, therefore. *Con que vd. ha hecho esto*, You have then done this.

Con que, *sm.* Condition, stipulation, circumstance.

Con tál que, *ad.* So that, on condition that, provided that. *Con todo ó con todo eso*, Nevertheless, notwithstanding.

Conáto, *sm.* 1. Endeavour, effort, exertion. 2. Crime attempted but not executed. *Conato de hurto*, Attempt at robbery.

Co-naviéro, *sm.* Copartner or part-owner in a ship.

Cónca, *sf.* (Ant.) V. *Cuenca.*

Concadenár, *va.* (Met.) To concatenate; to chain or link together.

Concámbio, *sm.* Exchange. V. *Cambio.*

Concanónigo, *sm.* A fellow canon.

Concaptívo, va, *s.* (Ant.) Companion in captivity; fellow captive.

Concatedralidád, *sf.* Union of two cathedral churches.

Concatenación, *sf.* Concatenation, a series of links.

Concatenár, *va.* To link or connect. V. *Encadenar.*

Concaúsa, *sf.* Exciting cause.

Concáva y Concavidád, *sf.* Concavity, hollowness, the internal surface of a hollow body.

Cóncavo, va, *a.* Hollow, opposed to convex.

Cóncavo, *sm.* Concavity. V. *Concavidad.*

Concebimiénto, *sm.* (Ant.) Conception.

Concebír, *vn.* 1. To conceive, to become pregnant. 2. To think, to have an idea of.—*va.* 1. To form, to conceive. 2. To express. *La claúsula está concebida en estos términos*, The clause is conceived in these terms.

Concedénte, *a.* Conceding; one who concedes.

Concedér, *va.* 1. To give, to grant, to bestow a boon or gift. 2. To allow, to grant, to admit.

Concedído, da, *a.* Conceded, granted. *Dado y no concedido*, Admitted but not agreed.

Concejál, *sm.* Member of a council or board.

Concejál, *a.* Relating to public boards or councils.

Concejeraménte, *ad.* Publicly, without reserve.

Concejíl, *sm.* 1. (Mancha) Foundling, a child exposed before houses; a child found without any parent or owner. 2. Troop or body of armed men, maintained by some council or corporation. 3. (Ant.) The representative of a town, corporation, or village.

Concejíl, *a.* Belonging to a council or corporation.

Concéjo, *sm.* 1. Senate or court of magistrates of a town. 2. Town-house or town-hall, where the magistrates hold their sittings. 3. District or jurisdiction of a council. 4. Foundling. V. *Concejil.*

Concélio y Concéllo, *sm.* (Ant.) V. *Concejo.*

Concenár, *vn.* (Ant.) To sup together.

Concénto, *sm.* Concent, a concert of voices; harmony.

Concentrádo, da, *a.* Concentred, tending towards the centre of a thing.

Concentrárse, *vr.* (Ant.) V. *Reconcentrarse.*

Concéntrico, ca, *a.* Having one common centre.

Concepción, *sf.* 1. Conception, the act of conceiving or quickening with pregnancy. 2. Power of conceiving, and state of being conceived.

Concepteár, *vn.* To give smart repartees, to abound in witty sayings.

Conceptíble, *a.* Conceivable; that may be imagined or thought.

Conceptíllo, *sm.* A witty trifle, an attempt at wit.

Conceptísta, *sm.* One who speaks or writes in an ingenious and witty manner.

Concépto, *sm.* 1. Conceit, thought, idea. 2. Fetus, an animal in embryo, or yet in the womb. V. *Feto.* 3. Sentiment, striking thought. 4. Judgment, opinion. 5. Estimation, favourable opinion.

Conceptuár, *va.* To conceive, judge, think, or be of opinion, *Conceptúo que debe hacerse esto*, He was of opinion that this should be done.

Conceptuosaménte, *ad.* Ingeniously, in a witty manner.

Conceptuóso, sa, *a.* Sharp, witty, abounding in lively thoughts.

Concernéncia, *sf.* Concernment, relation, influence.

Concerniénte, *pa.* Concerning, relating.

Concernír, *v. imp.* To regard, to concern, to belong or appertain to.

Concertadaménte, *ad.* 1. Regularly, orderly, methodically. 2. By agreement.
Concertadór, *sm.* Regulator, adjuster, expediter.
Concertár, *va.* 1. To regulate, to adjust, to set to rights. 2. To settle the price of things, to treat about the price, to cheapen. 3. To bargain, to covenant, to conclude an agreement. 4. To compose or adjust differences. 5. To tune musical instruments. 6. To compare, to estimate the relative goodness and badness of things. 7. To beat about the bushes, to start or rouse the game.—*vn.* To agree, to accord, to suit one another.—*vr.* (Ant.) To dress or deck one's self.
Concesión, *sf.* Concession, the act of granting or yielding.
Concesionário, *sm.* He that makes a concession; he who grants, or yields.
Cóncha, *sf.* 1. Shell, which covers testaceous animals. 2. Oyster. 3. Tortoise-shell. 4. An ancient copper coin, worth about three farthings, or eight maravedis. 5. (Arq.) Volute, any ornament made in the form of a shell. 6. *Concha de cabrestante*, (Naút.) Socket in which the capstern turns. 7. Shell of a dagger or cutlass. 8. The shell-shaped covering of the spike of Indian corn. 9. *Conchas de escobenes*, (Naút.) Navel-woods, or navel-hoods; large pieces of stuff fitted into the hawse-holes, to prevent the cable from being galled, and the hawse-holes from being worn out. *Tener muchas conchas*, (Met.) To be very reserved, artful, and cunning.
Conchabánza, *sf.* 1. The manner of making one's self easy and comfortable, as a fish in its shell. 2. The act of meeting or collecting in unlawful assemblies.
Conchabár, *va.* 1. To mix inferior wool with the superior or middling quality instead of separating it into three kinds, at shearing time. 2. (Ant.) To join, to unite.—*vr.* To be joined or united for some evil purpose, to conspire.
Conchádo, da, *a.* Scaly, covered with scales or shells.
Conchíl, *sm.* Rock-shell. Murex *L.*
Conchílla, ta, *sf.* A small shell.
Conchúdo, da, *a.* 1. Scaly, covered with scales. 2. Cunning, crafty, close, reserved.
Conchuéla, *sf.* V. *Conchilla.*
Concibimiénto, *sm.* 1. Conceit, thought, idea, conception. 2. (Ant.) Act of conceiving.
Conciéncia, *sf.* 1. Conscience; the knowledge or faculty by which we judge of the goodness or wickedness of our own actions. *Ancho de conciencia*, Not scrupulous or delicate with regard to one's morals or feelings. 2. Scrupulosity, tenderness of conscience. *Hacer conciencia de alguna cosa*, To be scrupulous about a thing. *A' conciéncia*, Conscientiously, in a conscientious manner. *Este aderezo está trabajado á conciencia*, This set of jewels is exceedingly well finished. *En conciéncia*, In good earnest.
Concienzúdo, da, *a.* Conscientious, scrupulous, exactly just.
Conciérto, *sm.* 1. The good order and arrangement of things. 2. Bargain, agreement, or contract between two or three persons. 3. Act of beating the wood with hounds to start the game. 4. Concert; many musical performers playing to the same tune. *De conciérto*, According to agreement, by common consent.
Conciliábulo, *sm.* Conventicle, an unlawful assembly; a meeting not convened by lawful authority or for lawful purposes.
Conciliación, *sf.* 1. Conciliation; the act of gaining or reconciling. 2. Resemblance or affinity which different things bear to each other. 3. Act of obtaining esteem, friendship, or favour.
Conciliadór, ra, *s.* Conciliator, one that makes peace between others.
Conciliár, *va.* 1. To conciliate or compose differences. 2. To gain the affection and esteem of others. *Conciliar el sueño*, To induce sleep. 3. To reconcile.
Conciliár, *a.* Belonging or relating to councils.
Conciliár, *sm.* Member of a council.
Conciliatívo, va, *a.* Conciliatory, relating to conciliation.
Concílio, *sm.* 1. Council, meeting, or congress, to treat or deliberate upon public affairs. 2. Collection of decrees of any council. 3. Conventicle, an unlawful meeting. *Hacer ó tener concilio*, To keep or hold clandestine unlawful meetings.
Concinidád, *sf.* Harmony, just proportion of sound.
Concíno, na, *a.* Harmonious, agreeable to number and harmony.
Concíón, *sf.* V. *Sermon.*
Concionadór, ra, *s.* (Ant.) One who preaches or reasons in public.
Concionánte, *sm.* (Ant.) Preacher.
Concisaménte, *ad.* Concisely, briefly, shortly.
Concisión, *sf.* Conciseness, brevity.
Concíso, sa, *a.* Concise, brief, short.
Concitacíon, *sf.* Concitation, the act of stirring up.
Concitadór, *sm.* Instigator, inciter to ill.
Concitár, *va.* To excite, to stir up commotions.
Concitatívo, va, *a.* Inciting, stirring up commotions.
Conciudadáno, *sm.* Fellow-citizen, townsman, one of the same town or city.
Cónclave, *sm.* 1. Room in which the cardinals meet to elect a pope; the meeting held for that purpose by the cardinals; conclave. 2. A private meeting or assembly.
Conclavísta, *sm.* One who waits upon the cardinals in the conclave.
Concloído, da, *a.* (Ant.) Shut up, concealed.
Concluír, *va.* 1. To conclude, to end, to terminate, to finish. 2. To clap up or complete a thing suddenly. 3. To convince with reason, to make evident. 4. To decide, finally to determine. 5. To infer, to deduce. 6. To close judicial proceedings; to submit to a final decision. 7. To disarm an adversary by laying hold of the hilt of his sword.
Conclusión, *sf.* 1. Conclusion, the act of concluding or terminating a thing. 2. The final determination or decision of a thing. 3. Act of laying hold of the hilt of an adversary's sword. 4. The conclusion of the proceedings in a suit at law. 5. Thesis controverted and defended in schools. *En conclusion*, Finally.

Conclúso, sa, *a.* 1. Concluded, closed, terminated. 2. Enclosed, contained.
Concluyénte, *pa.* Concluding, he who concludes.
Concluyentemente, *ad.* In a clear and convincing manner.
Concofrade, *sm.* He who lives with another in confraternity.
Concolega, *sm.* Fellow-collegian, one of the same college.
Concomérse, *vr.* To move the shoulders on account of some itching sensation, or by way of a joke.
Concomimiénto y Concómio, *sm.* Moving of the shoulders on account of some itching sensation.
Concomitáncia, *sf.* Concomitance, or concomitancy; existence together with some other thing.
Concomitánte, *pa.* Concomitant, accompanying; used especially in religious affairs, when our will corresponds with the Divine Grace.
Concomitár, *va.* To concomitate, to attend, to accompany.
Concordáble, *a.* Concordant, conformable, agreeable, consistent with.
Concordación, *sf.* Co-ordination, combination, conformation.
Concordadór, *sm.* Conciliator, peace-maker.
Concordáncia, *sf.* 1. Concordance, concord, agreement between persons and things. 2. Harmony, consent of sounds. 3. A book or table which shows in how many texts of Scripture any word occurs. 4. Grammatical concord.
Concordár, *va.* To accord, to regulate, to make one thing agree with another.—*vn.* To accord, to agree. *La copia concuerda con su original*, The copy agrees with the original.
Concordáta ó Concordáto, *s.* 1. Compact, agreement. 2. Concordate, a covenant made by a prince with the pope, relative to the collation of benefices.
Concórde, *a.* Concordant, agreeable, agreeing, of the same opinion.
Concordeménte, *ad.* With one accord.
Concórdia, *sf.* 1. Concord, conformity, union. 2. Agreement between persons engaged in a lawsuit. *De concórdia*, Jointly, by common consent. [body.
Concorpóreo, rea, *s.* Concorporal, of the same
Concretár, *va.* To combine, to unite.
Concréto, ta, *a.* Concrete, not abstracted.
Concréto, *sm.* A concrete body; or a body formed by concretion.
Concubína, *sf.* 1. Concubine, mistress; a woman who lives with a man as his wife without being married. 2. (Ant.) A lawful wife, yet deprived of civil rights.
Concubinário, *sm.* One who keeps a mistress.
Concubináto, *sm.* Concubinage, the act of living with a woman not married; concubinate.
Concúbio, *sm.* Dead of night, time of rest.
Concúbito, *sm.* Coition.
Conculcár, *va.* To conculcate, to tread or trample under foot.
Concuñádo, da, *s.* Brother or sister-in-law; a term confined to persons who are married to two brothers or sisters.

Concupiscéncia, *sf.* Concupiscence; an irregular desire, a libidinous wish.
Concupiscíble, *a.* Concupiscible; impressing desire, indulging desire.
Concurréncia, *sf.* 1. Convention or assembly of persons. 2. Concurrence, coincidence.
Concurrénte, *a.* Concurrent, coincident. *Concurrénte cantidad*, The quantity necessary to make up the deficiency of a determinate sum.
Concurrír, *vn.* 1. To concur; to meet in one point, time, or place. 2. To concur, to contribute.
Concursár, *va.* To award a commission of bankruptcy against an insolvent debtor.
Concúrso, *sm.* 1. Concourse or confluence of many persons or things. 2. Aid, assistance. 3. Contest between different candidates for a curacy, cathedral, prebend, &c. 4. Proceedings against an insolvent debtor, in consequence of a commission of bankruptcy awarded against him.
Concusión, *sf.* 1. Concussion; the act of shaking. 2. Abuse of power committed by him who holds a public place or station.
Condádo, *sm.* 1. County; the territory belonging to a count or earl. 2. Dignity of a count or earl.
Condál, *a.* Relating to the dignity of an earl or count, or pertaining to him.
Cónde, *sm.* 1. Earl, count. 2. Overseer, who overlooks workmen that they do their work well. 3. Head or chief of gypsies, whom they appoint by election.
Condecábo, *ad.* (Ant.) Another time; again.
Condecénte, *a.* Convenient, fit, proper.
Condecíco, llo, to, *sm. dim.* A little count.
Condecoración, *sf.* Decoration, the act of embellishing or decorating. [bellish.
Condecorár, *va.* To ornament, to adorn, to em-
Condéna, *sf.* The clerk of the court's attestation of the sentence of a condemned criminal.
Condenáble, *a.* Condemnable, blameable, culpable, worthy of punishment.
Condenación, *sf.* 1. Condemnation; the sentence by which any one is condemned to punishment. 2. Punishment inflicted on a malefactor. 3. Mulct, fine, a pecuniary penalty. *Es una condenacion*, It is unbearable, intolerable. 4. (Met.) Eternal damnation.
Condenádo, da, *s.* One condemned to eternal punishment.
Condenádo, da, *pp.* 1. Condemned. *Ser ó salir condenado en costas*, To be sentenced to pay the costs of a suit at law. 2. *Condenada ó tierra condenada*, The earthy, charry, or saline residue, which remains in a vessel after a chemical process or operation has been performed. 3. *Puerta condenada*, A door which is stopped or shut up, and no longer used.
Condenadór, ra, *s.* Condemner, blamer, censurer.
Condenár, *va.* 1. To pronounce judgment against a person found guilty of a crime. 2. To refute or reprove a doctrine or opinion. 3. To dislike, to disapprove. *Condenar una puerta, una ventana ó un pasadizo*, To stop or shut a door, window, or passage, that it may no longer be used.—*vr.* 1. To condemn

or blame one's self, to acknowledge one's fault. 2. To incur eternal punishment in a future state.

Condenatório, ria, *a.* Condemnatory; applied to a sentence pronounced against a malefactor.

Condénsa, *sf.* (Ant.) Place or chamber in which any thing is kept, as pantry, wardrobe.

Condensación, *sf.* Condensation; the act of thickening any body; opposed to rarefaction.

Condensadór, *sm.* Condenser, a pneumatic machine, into which a certain quantity of air is condensed in a given space.

Condensár, *va.* 1. To thicken, to condense, to give a consistence to fluid matters. 2. (Ant.) To hoard or heap up riches.

Condensatívo, va, *a.* Possessing the power or virtue of condensing.

Condésa, *sf.* 1. Countess, the consort of an earl or count, or the heiress to an earldom. 2. (Ant.) A woman whose business was to accompany a lady of rank. 3. (Ant.) Crowd, multitude.

Condesádo, *sm.* Estate from which an earl or count takes his title.

Condesár, *va.* To spare, to save, to preserve. *Quien come y condesa, dos veces pone la mesa,* (Prov.) A penny saved is a penny won.

Condescendéncia, *sf.* Condescendence; voluntary submission. [submit.

Condescendér, *va.* To condescend, to yield, to

Condesíca, lla ó ta, *sf. dim.* A little or young countess. [countess.

Condesíl, *a.* (Ant.) Belonging to a count or

Condestáble, *sm.* 1. Constable, a lord high constable. 2. *Condestable de arsenales,* (Naút.) Gunner of a dock-yard. *Segundo condestable,* Gunner's-mate. 3. (Naút.) Serjeant of marine artillery.

Condestablía, *sf.* The dignity of a constable.

Condexár, *va.* (Ant.) V. *Condesar.*

Condezméro, *sm.* Part-owner of the tithes of a parish.

Condición, *sf.* 1. The natural quality of things. 2. The natural temper or constitution of men. 3. Rank or class of society. 4. Terms on which any thing is promised to be done. *Condicion torpe,* That which is directly opposed by law. *Tener condicion,* To be of a peevish or irritable disposition. *Tener ó poner en condicion,* To hazard, to expose to danger. *De condicion,* So as, on condition that.

Condicionádo, da, *a.* 1. Condition, of a good or bad condition. 2. Condition; by way of stipulation.

Condicionál, *a.* Conditional; by way of stipulation; not absolute.

Condicionalménte, *ad.* Conditionally.

Condicionár, *vn.* To agree, to accord.—*vr.* To be of the same nature or condition.

Condicionáza, *sf.* A strong violent disposition or temper.

Condicioncílla ó Condicioncíta, *sf.* A hasty or passionate disposition or temper.

Condignaménte, *ad.* Condignly, deservedly, according to merit.

Condignidád, *sf.* Condignness, suitableness, or agreeableness to desert.

Condígno, na, *a.* Condign, suitable, deserved, merited. *Castigo condigno,* Condign punishment.

Condimentár, *va.* To condite, to dress or season victuals.

Condiménto, *sm.* Condiment, seasoning sauce.

Condír, *va.* (Ant.) V. *Establecer y Adobar.*

Condiscípulo, *sm.* Condisciple, school-fellow.

Condistinguír, *va.* To distinguish, to make a distinction.

Condolérse ó Condolecérse, *vr.* To condole, to be sorry for, to be in pain for, to sympathise with or feel for another.

Condonación, *sf.* Condonation, pardoning, forgiving.

Condonár, *va.* To pardon, to forgive.

Condór, *sm.* (Orn.) Condur. Vultur gryphus *L.*

Condrila, *sf.* (Bot.) Common gum-succory. Chondrilla juncea *L.*

Conducción, *sf.* 1. Conduct; the act of leading, guiding, or bringing any thing. 2. Reward for conducting.

Conducéncia, *sf.* The conducing to or promoting any end. [tribute.

Conducénte, *a.* Conducive, that may con-

Conducho y Condúcho, *sm.* (Ant.) Such provisions as a lord might demand of his vassals.

Conducidór, *sm.* Conductor, leader.

Conducír, *va.* 1. To convey, carry, or conduct any thing from one place to another. 2. To guide or direct to a place, to show the way. 3. To direct, manage, or adjust any affair or business.—*vn.* To conduce, to promote an end, to contribute.

Condúcta, *sf.* 1. Conduct, management. 2. Number of mules or horses carrying money from one place to another, especially to the court. 3. Money which is carried by mules to the court or a garrison. 4. Government, command, direction. 5. Way or manner of living. 6. Commission for recruiting. 7. V. *Capitulacion ó contrato.* 8. Party of recruits conducted to the regiment. 9. Contract made by a town or village with a physician to attend their sick. In Castile it is called *Partido.* 10. (Naút.) Convoy of money.

Conductéro, *sm.* (Ant.) V. *Conductor.*

Conductívo, va, *a.* Having the power of conveying or transporting.

Condúcto, *sm.* 1. Conduit, sewer, drain, sink. 2. (Met.) Channel through which any business is conducted or managed. *Salvo conducto,* A safe conduct.

Conductór, *sm.* Conductor, leader, usher. *Conductor de embaxadores,* One whose business is to introduce ambassadors.

Condúmio, *sm.* (Ant.) Meat dressed to be eaten with bread.

Condúta, *sf.* (Ant.) V. *Conducta.*

Condutál, *sm.* Spout to carry off the rain-water from the houses.

Condutívo, va, *a.* (Ant.) V. *Conductivo.*

Conejál, *sm.* 1. Rabbit warren. V. *Conejera.* 2. (Met.) Suburb inhabited by the common people.

Conejár, *sm.* Rabbit warren.

Conejéra, *sf.* 1. Warren, a kind of park for breeding rabbits. 2. (Met.) Brothel or bawdy-house. 3. (Met.) Den or cavern inhabited by poor people.

Conejéro, *sm.* Warrener; the keeper of a rabbit warren.
Conejéro, ra, *a.* That which hunts rabbits; commonly applied to the dog for this purpose. [rabbit.
Conejíllo, íto, ó Conejuélo, *sm.* A little
Conéjo, *a.* *Conejo alambre*, Rabbit-wire, copper wire, used in snares or gins for rabbits.
Conéjo, ja, *s.* Rabbit. Lepus cuniculus *L.* *Es una coneja*, (Met.) She breeds like a rabbit.
Conejúna, *sf.* Rabbit down or fur.
Conejúno, na, *a.* Belonging or relating to the rabbit kind. [annexed to the principal.
Conexidádes, *sf. pl.* Rights or other things
Conexión, *sf.* Connexion, conjunction, union.
Conexívo, va, *a.* Having the force or power of connexion.
Conéxo, xa, *a.* Connected, united.
Confabulación, *sf.* Confabulation, easy conversation, chat.
Confabulár, *va.* 1. To confabulate, to talk easily together, to chat. 2. (Ant.) To tell stories.
Confacción, *sf.* (Ant.) V. *Confeccion.*
Confaccionár y Confacionár. (Ant.) V. *Confeccionar.*
Confalón, *sm.* Standard; an ensign in war.
Confaloniér, *sm.* Title of the kings of Aragon.
Confarreación, *sf.* Confarreation, the solemnization of marriage by eating bread together.
Confección, *sf.* Confection, a preparation of fruit with sugar; a compound remedy, an electuary. [trade is to make sweatmeats.
Confeccionadór, *sm.* Confectioner; one whose
Confeccionár, *va.* To confect, to make up into sweetmeats.
Confederación, *sf.* Confederacy, league, union.
Confederádo, da, *a.* y *s.* Confederate, united in a league.
Confederánza, *sf.* V. *Confederacion.*
Confederárse, *vr.* To be confederated or united in a league.
Conferéncia, *sf.* 1. Conference, an appointed meeting for discussing a point. 2. Daily lecture studied by students in universities. 3. (Ant.) Comparison.
Conferenciár, *va.* To confer or treat with another on a subject; to hold a conference.
Conferír, *va.* 1. To compare; to estimate the relative goodness or badness of things. 2. To treat and deliberate upon a subject. 3. To give, to bestow, to confer. *Conferir un beneficio*, To confer or bestow a benefice.
Confesádo, da, *s.* Penitent, one under the spiritual direction of a confessor.
Confesánte, *sm.* (Ant.) Penitent who confesses his sins.
Confesánte, *ps.* Declaratory, that which declares by word or writing before a judge.
Confesár, *va.* 1. To manifest or assert one's opinion. 2. To confess, to acknowledge, to own, to avow. 3. To hear or receive confessions. 4. To disclose the state of the conscience to the priest. *Confesar de plano*, To confess plainly or openly. *Confesar sin tormento*, To be free to confess.
Confesión, *sf.* 1. Confession, avowal. 2. The act of disburdening the conscience to a priest. *Hijo ó hija de confesion*, A person who has a certain constant confessor. 3. Declaration of a criminal either denying or confessing the charges against him. [tive to confession.
Confesionál, *sm.* (Ant.) Doctrinal tract rela-
Confesionário, *sm.* 1. Treatise which teaches or lays down rules for confessing or hearing confessions. 2. Confessionary, the seat where the priest sits to hear confessions. V. *Confesonario.*
Conféso, sa, *s.* 1. Jewish convert or proselyte. 2. Layman or woman that enters a religious order.
Conféso, sa, *a.* (For.) Confessed, answered.
Confesonário, *sm.* Confessional, the seat on which the confessor sits.
Confesór, *sm.* 1. One that hears confessions and prescribes penitence. 2. He who confesses his sins.
Confesório, *sm.* (Ant.) V. *Confesonario.*
Confiáble, *a.* Trusty, fit to be trusted, deserving of confidence.
Confiadaménte, *ad.* Honestly, faithfully.
Confiádo, da, *a.* Presumptuous, confident, arrogant.
Confiadór, *sm.* 1. A joint surety, a fellow bondsman. 2. He who confides or expects.
Confiánza, *sf.* 1. Confidence, trust in the goodness of another. 2. Honest boldness, firmness of opinion. 3. Presumptuousness, vicious boldness. 4. A secret agreement or compact between two or more persons. *En confianza*, Privately, secretly, under the seal of secrecy; in confidence.
Confiár, *vn.* To confide, to trust in, to put trust in.—*va.* 1. To commit to the care of another. 2. To feed with hope, to afford grounds to hope.
Conficiénte, *a.* Conficient, doing any thing jointly with another.
Conficionár, *va.* V. *Confeccionar.*
Confidéncia, *sf.* Confidence. V. *Confianza.*
Confidenciál, *a.* Confidential, in confidence fit to inspire confidence. [manner
Confidencialménte, *ad.* In a confidentia
Confidénte, *sm.* 1. Confident or confidant, a person trusted with secrets or private af fairs. 2. A Moor who is employed as a spy b the Spanish garrisons in Africa.
Confidénte, *a.* True, faithful, trusty.
Confidenteménte, *ad.* 1. Confidently, withou doubt, without fear. 2. Faithfully, withou
Confiéso, sa. (Ant.) V. *Confeso.* [frau
Configuración, *sf.* 1. Configuration, dispositio of the various parts which compose the bod 2. (Ant.) Conformity, resemblance.
Configurádo, da, *a.* Configurated; being the same form.
Configurár, *va.* To configure, to dispose in any form. It is also used reciprocally.
Confín, *sm.* Limit, boundary, confine, borde edge. [conterminou
Confín y Confinánte, *a.* Bordering upo
Confinár, *vn.* To border upon, to touch on oth territories.—*va.* To shut up, to imprison, immure, to confine.
Confirmación, *sf.* 1. Confirmation, or attes tion of a thing done or approved of before. Evidence; an additional proof. 3. Confirn tion, an ecclesiastical rite.
Confirmadaménte, *ad.* Firmly, unalterabl
Confirmádo, da, *pp.* Confirmed.

Confirmadór, *sm.* Confirmator, attester; he that puts a matter past doubt.

Confirmamiénto, *sm.* V. *Confirmacion.*

Confirmánte, *pa.* Confirmer, he who confirms.

Confirmár, *va.* 1. To confirm, to put past doubt by new evidence; to corroborate. 2. To strengthen or support a person or thing. 3. To admit to the full privileges of a Christian by the solemn imposition of hands.

Confirmatório, ria, y Confirmatívo, va, *a.* Confirmatory; applied to a sentence by which a former judgment is confirmed.

Confiscación, *sf.* Confiscation; the act of transferring forfeited goods to public use.

Confiscár, *va.* To confiscate, to transfer private property to the public use.

Confitár, *va.* 1. To confect, to candy with melted sugar. 2. To make up into sweetmeats. 3. (Met.) To dulcify, to sweeten.

Confíte, *sm.* Confit, comfit, confect, paste made up into sweetmeats. *Morder en un confite*, To be hand and glove, to be intimate and familiar. *Confites*, (Joc.) Flogging or whipping given to children by their masters or parents.

Confiténte, *a.* V. *Confeso.*

Confitéra, *sf.* Vessel or pot in which sweetmeats are kept and preserved.

Confitería, *sf.* 1. A confectioner's shop. 2. Street in which confectioners live.

Confitéro, ra, *s.* 1. Confectioner, one whose trade is to make sweetmeats. 2. Tray with two handles in which sweetmeats were formerly served up.

Confitíco y Confitíllo, *sm.* Coverlet which has ornaments wrought on it in the shape of confitures.

Confitón, *sm.* A large sweet-meat.

Confitúra, *sf.* Confiture, Fruit, or any other thing made up into sweetmeats.

Conflación, *sf.* 1. Conflation, the act of blowing many instruments together. 2. Conflation, the act of casting or melting metals.

Conflagración, *sf.* Conflagration, a general fire.

Conflátil, *a.* Fusible, capable of being melted.

Conflícto, *sm.* 1. Conflict, struggle; a violent combat or contest. 2. (Met.) Struggle, agony, pang.

Confluéncia, *sf.* Confluence, the union or junction of two or more rivers or sea currents.

Confluír, *vn.* 1. To join or meet; applied to rivers and sea currents. 2. (Met.) To meet or assemble in one place; applied to a mob.

Confondír, *va.* V. *Confundir.*

Conformación, *sf.* Conformation; the form of things as relating to each other.

Conformár, *va.* To conform, to adjust, to fit; to reduce to the like appearance with something else.—*vn.* 1. To suit, to fit, to conform. 2. To comply with, to agree in opinion.—*vr.* To yield, to submit.

Confórme, *a.* 1. Conformable, correspondent, suitable. 2. Consistent, similar. 3. Compliant, resigned.

Confórme, *ad.* 1. In proportion, or according to proportion. 2. Agreeably, according to.

Conformeménte, *ad.* Conformably, unanimously.

Conformidád, *sf.* 1. Similitude, resemblance, conformity. 2. Union, concord. 3. Symmetry; adaptation of parts to each other. 4. A close attachment of one person to another. 5. Patience and resignation in adversities. *De conformidád*, By common consent; together, in company. *En conformidád*, Agreeably, suitably, according to: on that supposition, under that condition.

Conformísta, *sm.* Conformist, one that complies with the tenets and worship of the church of England.

Confortación, *sf.* Comfort, consolation; the act of comforting or consoling.

Confortadór, ra, *s.* Comforter, one that comforts or administers consolation in misfortune.

Confortár, *va.* 1. To comfort, to strengthen, to enliven, to invigorate. 2. To console, to strengthen the mind under calamities.

Confortatívo, va, *a.* Comfortable, dispensing comfort. It is frequently used as a substantive.

Confórte, *sm.* (Ant.) Comforting, solace.

Confórto, *sm.* V. *Confortacion.*

Confracción, *sf.* Fraction; the act of breaking or separating.

Confradía, *sf.* V. *Cofradía.*

Confragóso, sa, *a.* V. *Fragoso.*

Confraguación, *sf.* The act of mixing, uniting, or incorporating metals with each other.

Confraternidád, *sf.* Confraternity, brotherhood.

Confricación, *sf.* Confrication, friction; the act of rubbing against any thing.

Confricár, *va.* To rub, to produce friction, to rub hard.

Confrontación, *sf.* 1. Confrontation; the act of bringing two evidences or criminals face to face. 2. The act of comparing one thing with another. 3. (Met.) Sympathy, natural conformity.

Confrontánte, *pa.* Confronting, confronter.

Confrontár, *va.* 1. To confront, to bring face to face. 2. To compare one thing with another.—*vn.* 1. To agree in sentiments and opinion. 2. To border or confine upon. 3. (Ant.) To resemble, to be like one another. *Confrontarse*, To assimilate one's self.

Confúgio, *sm.* Refuge, shelter. V. *Refugio.*

Confuír, *vn.* To flee in company with others.

Confundír, *va.* 1. To confound, to mingle things. 2. To throw into confusion and disorder. 3. To confute or refute by dint of argument.—*vr.* 1. To be perplexed or confounded; to be thrown into consternation. 2. To be ashamed and humbled by the knowledge of one's own character.

Confusaménte, *ad.* Confusedly.

Confusión, *sf.* 1. Confusion, irregular mixture, tumultuous medley. 2. Perplexity, perturbation of the mind. 3. Confusedness, want of clearness, indistinct combination. 4. Humiliation, debasement of the mind. 5. Shame, ignominy, reproach. *Echar la confusion á alguno*, (For.) To imprecate or curse any one.

Confúso, sa, *a.* 1. Confused, jumbled together in an irregular or disorderly manner. 2. Obscure, doubtful, indistinct, not clear. 3. Fearful, timorous. *En confúso*, Confusedly; in an irregular or disorderly manner.

Confutación, *sf.* Confutation, disproof.

Confutár, va. To confute, to convince of error, to disprove.
Congelación, sf. Congelation, the act of congealing; the state of being congealed.
Congelamiénto, sm. Congelation.
Congelár, va. To congeal; to turn by cold from a fluid into a solid state.—vr. To concrete by cold, to become congealed. [congelation.
Congelatívo, va, a. Congealable, susceptible of
Congeniál, a. Congenial, partaking of the same genius.
Congeniár, vn. To be congenial, to partake of the same genius, temper, or disposition
Congénito, ta, a. Congenite, connate.
Congérie, sf. Congeries; a mass of bodies heaped up together.
Congestión, sf. Congestion, collection of matter, as in abscesses.
Congiário, sm. Congiary; a gift distributed to the Roman people and soldiery.
Congío, sm. Ancient Roman liquid measure.
Conglobación, sf. 1. Conglobation, a round body, acquired sphericity. 2. (Met.) Mixture and union of immaterial things, viz. affections, passions, &c. 3. (Ret.) Accumulation of a number of proofs and arguments crowded together.
Conglobár, va. To conglobate, to gather into a hard firm ball.
Congloriár, va. To fill or cover with glory.
Conglutinación, sf. Conglutination; the act of gluing or fastening two things together.
Conglutinár, va. To conglutinate, to cement, to reunite.
Conglutinatívo, va, y Conglutinóso, sa, a. Viscous, glutinous. [mind.
Congója, sf. Anguish, dismay, anxiety of
Congojár, va. To oppress, to afflict. V. Acongojar. [with dismay.
Congojosaménte, ad. Anxiously, painfully,
Congojóso, sa, a. 1. Afflictive, painful, tormenting. 2. Afflicted, full of grief and affliction.
Congoréa y Congoría, sf. (Bot.) Black briony, snake-weed. Tamus communis L.
Congósto, sm. Pleasurableness, with pleasure.
Congraciadór, sm. Flatterer, fawner, wheedler. [mean obsequiousness.
Congraciamiénto, sm. Flattery, false praise,
Congraciár, va. To ingratiate, to flatter, to solicit or implore one's benevolence.
Congratulación, sf. Congratulation; the act of expressing joy for the happiness or success of another.
Congratulár, va. To congratulate, to express joy or compliment upon any happy event.
Congratulatório, ria, a. Congratulatory.
Congregación, sf. 1. Congregation, a meeting or assembly to treat on various subjects or affairs. 2. Fraternity, brotherhood. 3. Congregation; an assembly met to worship God in public. *Congregacion de los fieles*, The catholic or universal church.
Congregánte, ta, s. Member of a congregation.
Congregár, va. To assemble, to meet.
Congréso, sm. 1. Congress, a meeting of various persons to deliberate on divers affairs. 2. Congress, a meeting of commissioners to settle terms of peace between powers at war. 3. Carnal union of man and woman.

Cóngrio, sm. (Ict.) Conger-eel, or sea-eel. Muræna conger L.
Cóngrua, sf. A competent sustenance assigned to him who is to be ordained a priest.
Congruaménte, ad. Conveniently, becomingly.
Congruéncia, sf. Convenience, opportunity, congruity, fitness.
Congruénte, a. Congruent, agreeing, corresponding.
Congruenteménte, ad. Conveniently, suitably, in a congruent manner.
Congruidád, sf. V. *Congruencia.*
Cóngruo, ua, a. Congruous, convenient, apt, fit, suitable.
Conhortár, va. (Ant.) To comfort, to console, to animate.
Conhórte, sm. (Ant.) V. *Consuelo.*
Cónico, ca, a. Conical, or conic, having the form of a cone.
Coniécha, sf. (Ant.) V. *Recoleccion ó Recaudacion.*
Coníza, sf. (Bot.) Flea-bane. Conyza L.
Conjetúra, sf. Conjecture, surmise; an inference drawn from uncertain principles.
Conjeturáble, a. Conjecturable, possible to be guessed.
Conjeturadór, ra, s. Conjector, guesser, conjecturer.
Conjeturál, a. Conjectural, depending on conjecture.
Conjeturalménte, ad. Conjecturally, by guess.
Conjeturár, va. To conjecture, to form a guess or conjecture.
Conjuéz, sm. A brother judge; one of two judges appointed to try a cause, or transact any other extraordinary judicial business jointly.
Conjugación, sf. 1. Conjugation, the form of inflecting verbs. 2. The act of comparing one thing with another. 3. Union, connexion; applied to a pair of nerves rising together.
Conjugádo, da, a. 1. Conjugated, inflected; compared. 2. V. *Casado.* [monial.
Conjugál, a. Conjugal, connubial, matri-
Conjugalménte, ad. Conjugally, matrimonially.
Conjugár, va. 1. To conjugate or inflect verbs. 2. To compare.
Conjunción, sf. 1. Conjunction, union, association, league; the act of coupling or joining together. 2. Conjunction, a word used to connect the clauses of a period together. 3. (Astr.) Congress of two planets in the same degree of the Zodiac.
Conjuntaménte, ad. Conjunctly, jointly, together.
Conjuntár, va. (Ant.) V. *Juntar.*
Conjuntívo, va, a. Conjunctive, closely united.
Conjuntívo, sm. The conjunctive mood of a verb. V. *Subjuntivo.*
Conjúnto, ta, a. 1. United, connected, contiguous. 2. Allied by kindred or friendship. 3. Mixed or incorporated with another thing.
Conjúnto, sm. Conjunctness.
Conjuntúra, sf. V. *Coyuntura y Conjuncion.*
Conjúra, sf. (Ant.) V. *Conjuracion.*
Conjuración, sf. 1. Conspiracy; concerted treason. 2. Conjuration; the form or act of summoning another in some sacred name. 3. V. *Conjuro.*

Conjurádo, da, *s.* Conspirator, an accomplice in a conspiracy or traitorous plot.

Conjuradór, *sm.* 1. Conjurer, enchanter, imposter. 2. Exorcist. 3. (Ant.) Conspirator.

Conjuramentár, *va.* 1. To bind by an oath. 2. To take an oath to another.—*vr.* To bind one's self by an oath. V. *Juramentarse.*

Conjuránte, *pa.* Conjuring, conspiring.

Conjurár, *vn.* 1. To conjure, to conspire, to concert treason. 2. To join in a conspiracy formed by others. 3. To swear or take an oath improperly with others.—*va.* 1. To exorcise, to drive away by certain forms of adjuration. 2. To conjure, to summon in a sacred name, to entreat, to implore.

Conjúro, *sm.* 1. Conjuration, the act of expelling an evil spirit by exorcism. 2. Incantation, enchantment.

Conllevadór, *sm.* Helper, assistant, he who aids others in their troubles and fatigues.

Conllevár, *va.* To aid or assist another in his labours; to bear his humours.

Conllorár, *va.* To sympathize, to feel with others, to lament their sufferings.

Conloár, *va.* (Ant.) To praise with others.

Conmemoración, *sf.* 1. Remembrance of a person or thing. 2. Commemoration; public celebration. 3. Anniversary celebrated by the Roman Catholic church in memory of the deceased.

Conmemorár, *va.* To commemorate, to preserve the memory by some public acts.

Conmensál, *s.* One who lives and boards with another at his expense.

Conmensalía, *sf.* Commensality, fellowship of table at another's expense.

Conmensuración, *sf.* Commensuration; the reduction of different things to some common measure.

Conmensurár, *va.* To commensurate, to reduce to some common measure.

Conmensuratívo, va, *a.* Commensurate, reducible to some common measure, proportionable to each other.

Conmígo, *pron. pers.* With me, with myself.

Conmilitón, *sm.* Comrade, a fellow-soldier.

Conminación, *sf.* Commination, a threat, a denunciation of punishment by a judge to induce a criminal to confess the truth.

Conminár, *va.* To threaten; to denounce punishment to a criminal in order to make him declare the truth.

Conminatório, ria, *a.* Comminatory, denunciatory, threatening.

Conmiseración, *sf.* Commiseration, pity, compassion.

Conmistión ó Conmixtión, y Conmistúra, *sf.* Commixtion, a mixture of diverse things.

Conmísto, ta, y Conmixto, ta, *a.* Mixed, mingled, incorporated.

Conmoción, *sf.* 1. Commotion, a violent motion of the mind or body. 2. Tumult, disturbance.

Conmonitório, *sm.* Commonition, advice, warning.

Conmovér, *va.* To disturb, to excite commotions.

Conmovimiénto, *sm.* V. *Conmocion.*

Conmutáble, *a.* Commutable; what may be exchanged for something else.

Conmutación, *sf.* Commutation, change, alteration, exchange.

Conmutár, *va.* To change, to barter, to exchange one thing for another.

Conmutatívo, va, *a.* Commutative, relative to exchange.

Connaturál, *a.* Connatural, suitable to nature; participant of the same nature.

Connaturalizárse, *vr.* To accustom one's self to labour, climate, or food; to inure.

Connaturalménte, *ad.* Connaturally; by the act of nature originally.

Connexidád, *sf.* V. *Conexidad.*

Connivéncia, *sf.* Connivance, the act of conniving or winking at the faults of another.

Connombrár, *va.* V. *Nombrar.*

Connómbre, *sm.* (Ant.) V. *Sobrenombre.*

Connósco, *pron.* (Ant.) With us.

Connotación, *sf.* 1. Connotation, connexion with other things. 2. A distant relation, or remote alliance of kindred and consanguinity.

Connotádo, *sm.* Relationship, kindred.

Connotár, *va.* To connote, to imply, to include.

Connotatívo, va, *a.* (Gram.) Applied to nouns which signify the thing that belongs to the object designated by the primitive noun, or to the office of the subject from which it is derived; as *aquilino, caballar, bacanal, lirico,* &c.

Connovício, cia, *s.* A fellow novice; one who serves or has served the noviciate at the same time with another.

Connubiál, *a.* Connubial, matrimonial, conjugal.

Connúbio, *sm.* (Poét.) Matrimony, marriage, wedlock.

Connumerár, *va.* To enumerate or mention among other things; to include in a number.

Connúsco, *pron.* With us. V. *Con nosotros.*

Cóno, *sm.* Cone, a solid body, of which the base is a circle, and which ends in a point.

Conocedór, ra, *s.* 1. Connoisseur, a person well versed in arts and sciences. 2. Judge or critic in matters of taste. 3. (In Andalusia) The chief or head herd; in Castile he is called *mayoral.*

Conocéncia, *sf.* 1. (Ant.) Knowledge, skill, learning. 2. A criminal's confession of his crime.

Conocér, *va.* 1. To know, to understand; to have a knowledge of a thing. 2. To possess a clear or distinct idea of a person's physiognomy, or the figure of a thing. 3. To perceive, to get a notion of. 4. To experience, to observe. 5. To conjecture, to surmise. 6. To embrace a person of another sex. 7. To acknowledge or confess a crime, guilt, or debt. 8. *Conócer de una causa ó pleyto,* To try a cause; applied to a judge. *Conocer alguno su pecado,* To confess his fault.—*vr.* 1. To know one another. 2. To appreciate one's own good or bad qualities.

Conocíble, *a.* Cognoscible, that may be known.

Conocidaménte, *ad.* Knowingly, evidently.

Conocído, da, *s.* 1. Acquaintance, a person with whom we are acquainted without the intimacy of friendship. 2. Person of family or distinction.

Conocimiénto, *sm.* 1. Acquaintance, friendship. 2. Note of hand, whereby the receipt of any thing, and the obligation to return it, are acknowledged. 3. Cognizance, judicial notice. 4. (Com.) Bill of lading. 5. V. *Agradecimiento.*

Conóide, *sm.* Conoid, a figure partaking of a

cone, having an ellipsis for its base instead of a circle.
Conoscér, *va.* (Ant.) V. *Conocer.*
Conoscimiénto, *sm.* V. *Conocimiento.*
Conoscúdo, Conoseúdo, Conoszúdo, y Conozúdo, *pp. irreg. ant.* of *Conocer.*
Cónque, *sm.* Condition, quality.
Conquerír, *va.* (Ant.) V. *Conquistar.*
Conqueridór, ra, *s.* Conqueror, one who conquers or subdues.
Conquísta, *sf.* 1. Conquest, the act of conquering, subjection. 2. Acquisition by victory; the thing gained. 3. Act of winning or gaining over another man's affections.
Conquistadór, *sm.* Conqueror, he who conquers.
Conquistár, *va.* 1. To conquer, to overcome, to subdue. 2. To acquire, to gain or win another's affections. 3. To seduce a woman.
Conreár, *va.* 1. (In Manufactories) To grease wool by sprinkling oil over it. 2. V. *Binar.*
Conregnánte, *a.* Reigning at the same time with another.
Conréo, *sm.* (Ant.) Benefit, favor.
Conreynár, *vn.* To reign at the same time with another.
Consabér, *vn.* To have the knowledge of a thing jointly with others.
Consabído, da, *a.* Conscious; applied to persons or things already treated of.
Consabidór, ra, *s.* One who possesses the knowledge of a thing jointly with others.
Consacrár, *va.* (Ant.) V. *Consagrar.*
Consagración, *sf.* Consecration, a right of dedicating to the service of God.
Consagradór y Consagránte, *s.* Consecrater; one that performs the rites by which any thing is devoted to sacred purposes.
Consagrár, *va.* 1. To consecrate, to make sacred, to appropriate to sacred uses. 2. To canonize; to deify. 3. To dedicate inviolably to some particular purpose. 4. (Met.) To erect a monument.
Consanguíneo, nea, *a.* Consanguineous, near of kin, related by birth.
Consanguinidád, *sf.* Consanguinity, relation by blood.
Conscernír, (Ant.) V. *Concernir.*
Consciéncia, *sf.* (Ant.) V. *Conciencia.*
Consecración, *sf.* V. *Consagracion.*
Consecrár, *va.* V. *Consagrar.*
Consectário, *sm.* Consectary, corollary, deduction from premises.
Consecución, *sf.* Attainment of a benefice, employ, or other desirable object.
Consecutivaménte, *ad.* Consecutively, one after another without interruption.
Consecutívo, va, *a.* Consecutive; following in train, regularly succeeding.
Conseguienteménte, *ad.* V. *Consiguientemente.*
Conseguimiénto, *sm.* Attainment, obtainment.
Conseguír, *va.* To attain or obtain any desirable or desired object.
Conséja, *sf.* Fable, a feigned story, intended to enforce some moral precept, or amuse.
Consejáble, *a.* Capable of receiving advice.
Consejadór. V. *Aconsejador.*
Consejár, *va.* V. *Aconsejar.*

Consejéra y Consejadríz, *sf.* Counsellor's wife; woman who gives advice.
Consejéro, ra, *s.* 1. Counsellor, one that gives advice. 2. Confident, bosom friend. 3. Magistrate. *Consejero de estado,* A counsellor of state. *Consejero de capa y espada,* A magistrate not bred to the law.
Consejo, *sm.* 1. Counsel, advice, opinion. 2. Council, an assembly of magistrates. 3. Council-house, where the counsellors or magistrates assemble. 4. (Ant.) Way, means.
Consejuéla, *sf.* (Ant.) A little tale or story.
Conséllo. V. *Consejo.*
Consenciénte, *pa.* Consenting, he who connives at any thing bad.
Consentído, *sm.* 1. A spoiled child. 2. Cuckold by his own consent; a wittol.
Consentidór, ra, *s.* One who connives or winks at something.
Consentimiénto, *sm.* Consent, connivance.
Consentír, *va.* 1. To consent, to agree, to be of the same mind. 2. To believe for certain, to rely, to depend.
Consequéncia, *sf.* 1. Consequence, conclusion, inference. *Por consequencia,* Therefore. 2. Result or effect of a cause. 3. Consistence, firmness. *Guardar consequencia,* To be consistent. 4. Importance, moment. *Ser de consequencia,* To be of importance. *En consequencia de,* In consequence of.
Consequénte, *sm.* 1. Consequent, consequence, that which follows from previous propositions. 2. Effect, that which follows an acting cause.
Consequénte, *a.* 1. Consequent, following by rational deduction. 2. Following, as the effect of a cause. 3. Consistent. *Ser consequente en sus operaciones,* To act with consistency.
Consequenteménte, *ad.* 1. Consequently, pursuantly. 2. By consequence, necessarily, inevitably.
Consérge, *sm.* Keeper or warden of a royal palace or castle.
Conserjería, *sf.* Office and employ of the keeper of a royal palace or castle.
Consérva, *sf.* 1. Conserve, fruit preserved in melted sugar or honey. 2. (Ant.) Pickles. 3. Fleet of merchantmen sailing under convoy or escort of a ship of war. *Ir ó navegar de conserva,* To sail under convoy, to navigate in company with other ships.
Conservación, *sf.* Conservation, the act of preserving from corruption.
Conservadór, *sm.* Conservator, preserver.
Conservaduría, *sf.* A place or dignity in the Order of Malta, whose incumbent is obliged to watch over the privileges of the order.
Conservánte, *pa.* Conserving, he who conserves.
Conservár, *va.* 1. To conserve; to preserve without loss or detriment. 2. To guard, to observe, to continue any practice. 3. To candy or pickle fruit.
Conservatívo, va, *a.* Conservative, having the power of preserving.
Conservatívos, *sm. pl.* Spectacles with preservative lenses to preserve the sight.
Conservatoría, *sf.* 1. Place and office of a *Juez conservador,* who is peculiarly charged to preserve and defend the rights and privileges of a

community. 2. Indult, or apostolical letters granted to some communities, by virtue of which they choose their own judges conservators. *Conservatorias*, Letters patent granted by conservatory judges in favour of those who live under their jurisdiction.

CONSERVATÓRIO, RIA, *a.* Conservatory, having a preservative quality.

CONSERVÉRO, RA, *s.* Conserver; a preparer of conserves.

CONSIDERÁBLE, *a.* 1. Considerable, worthy of consideration, attention, and regard. 2. Great, large, plentiful.

CONSIDERABLEMÉNTE, *ad.* Considerably, excessively.

CONSIDERACIÓN, *sf.* 1. Consideration, the act of considering, regard, notice. 2. Contemplation, meditation. 3. Claim to notice, worthiness of regard. *Ser de consideración*, To be of great moment. *En consideración*, In consideration, in proportion.

CONSIDERACIONCÍLLA, *sf.* A slight consideration.

CONSIDERADAMÉNTE, *ad.* Considerately, calmly; with consideration and prudence.

CONSIDERÁDO, *a.* Prudent, considerate.

CONSIDERADÓR, RA, *s.* Considerer, a person of prudence or reflection.

CONSIDERÁNTE, *pa.* Considering, he who considers.

CONSIDERÁR, *va.* To consider, to think or reflect maturely.

CONSIÉRVO, *sm.* A fellow-servant, a fellow-slave.

CONSIGNACIÓN, *sf.* 1. Consignation, the act of consigning. 2. Sum of money destined to serve for a certain time some peculiar purpose. 3. Consignment.

CONSIGNADÓR, *sm.* One who consigns goods or merchandise to a foreign correspondent.

CONSIGNÁR, *va.* 1. To consign, assign, or make over the rent of a house or any other sum for the payment of a debt. 2. To consign, to yield, to intrust. 3. To lay by, to deposit. 4. To deliver. 5. To address goods or merchandise to a foreign correspondent, to be sold for account of the consigners. 6. To give a sentinel his orders or instructions. 7. (Ant.) To sign with the mark of a cross.

CONSIGNATÓRIO, *sm.* 1. Trustee, who receives money in trust for another. 2. Mortgagee, who possesses and enjoys the lands or tenements mortgaged, until the debt be paid out of the proceeds. 3. Consignee, a merchant or factor to whom a ship or cargo, or merely a part of the latter, is consigned.

CONSÍGO, *pro. pers.* With one's self. *Consigo mismo, consigo propio, ó consigo solo*, Alone, by one's self.

CONSIGUIÉNTE, *sm.* (Lóg.) Consequence, result.

CONSIGUIÉNTE, *a.* Consequent, following by a rational deduction, or as the effect of a cause. *Por consiguiente, ó por el consiguiente*, Consequently, by consequence, pursuantly.

CONSIGUIENTEMÉNTE, *ad.* Consequently.

CONSILIÁRO, *sm.* Counsellor or assistant to the heads of colleges, convents, &c. V. *Consejero.*

CONSINTIMIÉNTO. V. *Consentimiento.*

CONSISTÉNCIA, *sf.* 1. Consistence, or consistency; stability, duration; a state in which things continue for some time. 2. Firmness, solidity, intellectual strength.

CONSISTÉNTE, *a.* Consistent, firm, solid.

CONSISTÍR, *vn.* 1. To consist, to subsist, to continue fixed. 2. To be comprised, to be contained. 3. To be composed.

CONSISTORIÁL, *a.* 1. Consistorial, belonging or relating to an ecclesiastical court. 2. *Casa consistorial ó casas consistoriales*, Senate-house, guildhall, town-houses or town-halls, court-house.

CONSISTORIALMÉNTE, *ad.* Consistorially, relating to the consistory of the pope and his cardinals.

CONSISTÓRIO, *sm.* 1. Consistory, a meeting held by the pope and his cardinals on matters concerning the government and discipline of the Roman Catholic church. 2. Meeting held by the magistrates of a city or town to administer justice, or deliberate on the affairs of the community. 3. Town-house or town-hall. *Consistorio divino*, The tribunal of God.

CONSÓCIO, *sm.* Partner, companion.

CONSOLÁBLE, *a.* Consolable, that which admits comfort, or tends to give comfort.

CONSOLABLEMÉNTE, *ad.* Consolably, in manner to give comfort.

CONSOLACIÓN, *sf.* 1. Consolation or comfort; that which lessens grief and alleviates misery. 2. Charity.

CONSOLÁDO, DA, *a.* Consoled, comforted.

CONSOLADÓR, RA, *s.* Consolator, comforter.

CONSOLADÓR, RA, *a.* Consolatory, tending to give comfort.

CONSOLÁNTE, *pa.* Comforting, consoling.

CONSOLÁR, *va.* To console, to comfort, to cheer.

CONSOLATÓRIO, RIA; Y CONSOLATÍVO, VA, *a.* Consolatory, tending to give comfort.

CONSOLDAMIÉNTO, *sm.* V. *Consolidacion.*

CONSÓLIDA, *sf.* (Bot.) V. *Consuelda.*

CONSOLIDACIÓN, *sf.* Consolidation, the act of uniting into one mass.

CONSOLIDÁR, *va.* To consolidate into a compact or solid body, to harden, to strengthen.—*vr.* (For.) To unite the interest with the principal.

CONSOLIDATÍVO, VA, *a.* Consolidant; having the power of uniting and soldering wounds.

CONSONAMIÉNTO, *sm.* (Ant.) Sound of a word.

CONSONÁNCIA, *sf.* 1. Consonance or consonancy, accord of sound. 2. Consistency, congruence. 3. (Met.) Conformity.

CONSONÁNTE, *sm.* 1. A word, the sound of the last syllable of which corresponds with that of another. 2. (Mús.) A consonous or corresponding sound. 3. (Gram.) A consonant.

CONSONÁNTE, *a.* Consonant, agreeable, consistent, conformable. *Letras consonantes*, Consonants, letters which cannot be sounded by themselves.

CONSONANTEMÉNTE, *ad.* Consonantly, agreeably, conformably.

CONSONÁR, *vn.* 1. To make any body sound, to play on musical instruments. 2. To rhyme, to agree in sound. 3. (Met.) To agree, to resemble.

CÓNSONES, *sm. pl.* Concordant sounds.

CÓNSONO, NA, *a.* Consonous, agreeing in sound, harmonious.

CONSÓRCIO, *sm.* 1. Consortion, partnership, society. 2. Friendly intercourse, mutual affection.

CONSÓRTE, *s.* 1. Consort, companion, partner. 2. Consort, a person joined in marriage with another. 3. Accomplice; an associate in the perpetration of a crime. 4. One who enters or defends an action jointly with another.

Consoúno (De), *ad.* V. *De consuno.*

Conspícuo, cua, *a.* 1. Conspicuous, obvious to the sight. 2. Eminent, famous, distinguished.

Conspiración, *sf.* 1. Conspiracy; a concerted treason. 2. An agreement of men to do any thing evil or unlawful.

Conspiradór, *sm.* Conspirator, a man engaged in a traitorous or other criminal plot.

Conspirár, *va.* To implore the assistance or solicit the favour of another.—*vn.* 1. To conspire, to concert a crime, to plot. 2. To agree together, to co-operate. *Fuerzas conspirantes*, Co-operating mechanical powers which concur in producing one and the same effect.

Constáble, *a.* (Ant.) V. *Constante.*

Constáncia, *sf.* Constancy, steadiness, immutability, unalterable continuance.

Constánte, *a.* 1. Constant, firm, unalterable, immutable. 2. Manifest, apparent, clear. 3. Composed of, consisting in. *Constante el matrimonio*, During the marriage.

Constánte, *sm.* A steady man.

Constanteménte, *ad.* 1. Constantly, firmly, unalterably. 2. Evidently, undoubtedly.

Constár, *v. imp.* 1. To be clear, evident, certain. *Consta en autos ó de autos*, It appears from the judicial proceedings. 2. To be composed of, to consist in.

Constelación, *sf.* 1. Cluster of fixed stars. 2. Climate, temperature of the air. 3. Prognostication of the stars. 4. *Corre una constelacion*, An epidemical distemper prevails.

Consternación, *sf.* Consternation, perturbation of the mind, amazement, wonder.

Consternár, *va.* To terrify, to strike with horror or amazement.

Constipación, *sf.* 1. Constipation, a stoppage of the cuticular pores, occasioned by cold; want of perspiration. 2. Costiveness, state of the body in which excretion is obstructed.

Constipár, *va.* To constipate, to obstruct the perspiration of the cuticular pores; to bind the body.

Constipatívo, va, *a.* Constrictive.

Constitución, *sf.* 1. State of being, natural qualities. 2. Established form of government; system of laws and customs. 3. Temper of body with respect to health. 4. Temper of mind. 5. Particular laws, establishment, institution.

Constitucionál, *a.* Constitutional, consistent with the constitution.

Constituír, *va.* 1. To constitute, to give formal existence, to produce. 2. To erect, to establish. 3. To appoint, to depute. 4. *Constituir la dote*, To pay off a woman's portion either by instalments or in one sum. 5. *Constituirse en obligacion de alguna cosa*, To bind one's self to perform any thing.

Constitutívo, va, *a.* Constitutive, essential, productive.

Constituyénte, *sm.* Constituent, the person who constitutes or settles a portion, annuity, &c.

Constreñidaménte, *ad.* Compulsively, by force.

Constreñimiénto, *sm.* Constraint, or compulsion, whereby a person obliges another to perform something.

Constreñír, *va.* 1. To constrain, to compel. 2. (Med.) To bind or make costive; applied to food.

Constricción, *sf.* Constriction, contraction.

Constrictívo, va, *a.* Binding, astringent, or constringent.

Constrictór, *sm.* Constriotor, that which compresses or contracts.

Constriñír, *va.* (Ant.) V. *Constreñir.*

Construcción, *sf.* 1. Construction, the act and form of building. 2. The putting of words together in such a manner as to convey a complete sense. 3. The act of arranging terms in their proper order, the act of interpreting, explanation. 4. The sense, the meaning. 5. Ship-building, naval architecture.

Constructór de navío, *sm.* Ship-builder.

Construír, *va.* 1. To form, to build, to construct. 2. To construe, to range words in their natural order. 3. To translate literally.

Construpadór, *sm.* One who constuprates or debauches a woman, a defiler, a corrupter.

Construpár, *va.* To constuprate, to defile or debauch a woman.

Consubstanciál, *a.* Consubstantial; having the same essence or substance.

Consubstancialidád, *sf.* Consubstantiality; the existence of more than one in the same substance.

Consubstancialménte, *ad.* In a consubstantial manner.

Consuegrár, *vn.* To become a father-in-law, or mother-in-law.

Consuégro, gra, *s.* Father-in-law, mother-in-law.

Consuélda, *sf.* (Bot.) Comfrey. Symphitum officinale *L. Consuelda média*, Common bugle, middle consound. Ajuga reptans *L. Consuelda real*, Larkspur, Lark's-heel. Delphinium consolida *L.*

Consuélo, *sm.* 1. Consolation, comfort, relief. 2. Joy, merriment. 3. Charity, 4. *Sin consuelo*, Out of rule or measure. *Beber sin consuelo*, To drink to excess. *Gastar sin consuelo*, To outrun the constable, to spend in an inconsiderate manner.

Consuéta, *s.* 1. Prompter on the stage. 2. Directory, which contains the order of performing the divine service. *Consuétas*, Short prayers used on certain days in the performance of divine service.

Consuetúd, *sf.* (Ant.) V. *Costumbre.*

Consuetudinário, ria, *a.* 1. Customary, generally practised. 2. Being in the habit of sinning.

Cónsul, *sm.* 1. Consul, the chief magistrate in ancient Rome. 2. Member of the tribunal of commerce. 3. Consul, a civil officer appointed by his sovereign, in foreign parts, to protect the navigation and trade of his country.

Consuládo, *sm.* 1. Consulate, dignity of the chief magistrates of ancient Rome. 2. Tribunal of commerce, appointed to try and decide all causes which concern navigation and trade; the president is called in Spain *prior*, and the members *consules*. 3. Office of consul.

Consulázgo, *sm.* 1. Consulate. V. *Consulado.* 2.

Dues paid to consuls by all merchant vessels.

Consulár, *a.* Consular, relating to a consul. *Varon consular*, One who has been consul.

Consulázgo, *sm.* (Ant.) V. *Consulado.*

Consúlta, *sf.* 1. Consult; a number of persons assembled in deliberation. 2. A question proposed, or a proposal made in writing. 3. Report made and advice given to the king in council. 4. Advice given to the king by the supreme tribunals and officers of state, with regard to persons proposed to fill up some public employments.

Consultáble, *a.* Worthy or necessary to be deliberated upon.

Consultación, *sf.* Consultation, conference, meeting.

Consultánte, *pa.* Consulting, he who consults another. *Ministro consultante*, Minister who lays before the king the opinion of his council.

Consultár, *va.* 1. To ask or take another's advice, to consult. 2. To advise, to give advice. *Consultar con el bolsillo*, To cut the coat according to one's cloth; literally, to consult one's purse. *Consultar con la almohada*, To take into mature consideration; literally, to consult the pillow.

Consultísimo, ma, *a. sup.* Eminently wise or learned.

Consultívo, va, *a.* Advisable; applied to matters which the councils and tribunals are obliged to lay before the king, accompanied with their advice.

Consultór, ra, *s.* Consultor, adviser.

Consumación, *sf.* 1. Consummation, perfection, end. 2. (Rar.) Destruction, suppression.

Consumadaménte, *ad.* Perfectly, completely.

Consumádo, da, *a.* Consummate, complete, perfect.

Consumádo, *sm.* A strong broth or decoction of sheep and calves' feet, stag's horn, &c. which, when cold, concretes into a jelly.

Consumadór, ra, *s.* One who consummates, perfects, or finishes.

Consumár, *va.* To consummate, to finish, to perfect, to complete. *Consumar el matrimonio*, To consummate the marriage.

Consumatívo, va, *a.* Consummate, that which consummates or completes; applied to the sacrament.

Consumición, *sf.* Charge, cost, expense.

Consumído, da, *a.* 1. Lean, meagre, exhausted, spent. 2. Easily afflicted.

Consumidór, ra, *s.* Consumer, one who consumes, spends, or wastes.

Consumiénte, *pa.* Consuming; he who consumes.

Consumimiénto, *sm.* Consumption; the act of consuming, spending, or wasting.

Consumír, *va.* 1. To consume, to destroy, to waste. *Consumir el caudal*, To run out one's fortune. 2. In the sacrifice of the mass, to swallow the elements of bread and wine in the eucharist.—*vr.* 1. To be spent, to be exhausted. 2. To fret, to be uneasy, to be vexed.

Consumitívo, va, *a.* Consumptive, that which has the power of consuming.

Consúmo, *sm.* The consumption of provisions and merchandise. *Consúmos*, (Naút.) The consumption of naval stores and provisions in the course of a voyage.

Consunción, *sf.* (Med.) Consumption; the waste of muscular flesh, attended with a hectic fever.

Consúno (De), *ad.* V. *Juntamente.*

Consuntívo, va, *a.* (Ant.) Consumptive.

Cónta, *sf.* V. *Cuenta.*

Contácto, *sm.* Contact, touch, close union.

Contadéro, ra, *a.* Countable, numerable; that which may be counted or numbered.

Contadéro, *sm.* A narrow passage where sheep or cattle are counted. *Salir ó entrar por contadero*, To go out or enter through a narrow passage.

Contádo, da, *a.* 1. Scarce, rare, not common, not frequent. *De contádo*, Instantly, immediately. *Al contádo*, With ready money. 2. (Ant.) Designed, marked, or pointed out.

Contadór, ra, *s.* 1. Computer, reckoner; one skilled in accounts. 2. Accomptant; one whose business is to keep and make up accounts. 3. Counter; the form or table on which goods are viewed and money told in a shop. 4. Desk. 5. (Ant.) Counting-house. 6. Counter; a false piece of money used for reckoning or marking the game. *Contador de navio de guerra*, Purser of a man of war. *Contador de nuevas*, Prattler, an idle talker.

Contadorcíto, *sm.* A petty clerk or accomptant.

Contaduría y Contadoría, *sf.* 1. Accomptant's office at the exchequer. 2. Office where taxes and other branches of the public revenue are collected and managed. 3. Place and employment of a public accomptant.

Contagiár, *va.* 1. To infect, to communicate a contagious disease, to hurt by contagion. 2. (Met.) To corrupt one's morals by setting him a bad example.

Contágio, *sm.* 1. An infectious or contagious disease. 2. (Met.) Corruption of morals by bad examples and mischievous insinuations.

Contagión, *sf.* 1. V. *Contagio.* 2. The progressive malignity of a distemper which affects one part of the body, but if not timely checked communicates to other parts, as, gangrene. 3. (Met.) Propagation of vice and evil habits.

Contagióso, sa, *a.* 1. Contagious, infectious; caught by contact or approach. 2. (Met.) Infectious; applied to dangerous doctrines, mischievous principles, and bad examples.

Contál de cuentas, *s.* A string of beads for counting or reckoning.

Contaminación, *sf.* Contamination, pollution, defilement.

Contaminár, *va.* 1. To contaminate, to defile, or pollute. 2. To infect by contagion. 3. To corrupt, to vitiate or destroy the integrity of a text or original. 4. (Met.) To profane, to violate any thing sacred.

Contánte, *sm.* 1. Ready money. 2. Narrator, teller. 3. (Ant.) A certain quantity.

Contantéjo, *sm.* A small counter to reckon with.

Contár, *va.* 1. To count, to reckon, to number, to enumerate. 2. To calculate, to compute, to make up accounts. 3. To book, to place to account. 4. To class, to range according to some stated method of distribution. 5. To consider, to look upon. 6. To depend, to rely. *Contar con la amistad de uno*, To rely upon one's friendship. *Mire á quien se lo cuenta*, Expression, signifying that he who hears knows more than he who relates the particulars of an event.

Contemperánte, *pa.* Tempering; moderator.

Contemperár, *va.* To temper, to moderate. V. *Atemperar.*

Contemplación, *sf.* 1. Meditation; studious thought on any subject. 2. Holy meditation; a holy exercise of the soul, employed in attention to sacred things.

Contempladór, *sm.* Contemplator; one employed in study. V. *Contemplativo.*

Contemplár, *va.* 1. To view, to behold, to look upon. 2. To contemplate, to meditate, to muse. 3. To assent, to flatter. 4. To condescend, to do more than mere justice requires.

Contemplativaménte, *ad.* Attentively, thoughtfully, in a contemplative manner.

Contemplatívo, va, *a.* Contemplative, given to thought, studious. *Vida contemplativa,* A life spent in contemplation and study.

Contemplatívo, *sm.* 1. Contemplator; one employed in contemplation and study. 2. Adulator, flatterer; one who endeavours to please by flattery and adulation. 3. A pious devotee.

Contemporáneo, nea, *a.* Contemporary; living in the same age, existing at the same point of time.

Contemporizár, *vn.* To temporize, to comply with the times and occasions, to comply with the will and opinion of another.

Contemptíble, *a.* V. *Contentible.*

Contención, *sf.* 1. Contention, emulation, endeavour to excel. 2. Contest, dispute, strife.

Contencióso, sa, *a.* 1. Being the object of strife or dispute. 2. Quarrelsome, litigious, inclined to lawsuits.

Contendedór, *sm.* V. *Contendor.*

Contendér, *vn.* 1. To contend, to debate, to litigate. 2. (Met.) To argue, to discuss.

Contendiénte, *pa.* Disputant, litigant.

Contendór, *sm.* Contender, or contendent; an antagonist or opponent.

Contendóso, sa, *a.* V. *Contencioso.*

Contenedór, ra, *s.* Holder, one that holds; a tenant.

Conteméncia, *sf.* 1. (Ant.) Contest, dispute. 2. Suspension or short stop in the flight of birds, especially of birds of prey. 3. A peculiar movement in the Spanish dance. 4. (Ant.) Tenor, contents.

Contenénte, *sm.* V. *Continente.*

Contenér, *va.* 1. To contain, to hold as a vessel, to comprise as a writing. 2. To check the motion or progress of any thing. 3. (Met.) To curb, to restrain. *El no puede contenerse,* He has no command of himself.

Contenído, da, *a.* Moderate, prudent, temperate.

Contenído, *sm.* Tenor, contents.

Conteniénte, *pa.* Containing, comprising.

Conténta, *sf.* 1. Endorsement. V. *Endoso.* 2. Reception or present which satisfies any one. 3. Certificate of good conduct given by the magistrate of a place to the commander of troops which have been quartered there for some time.

Contentadízo, za, *a.* *Bien contentadizo,* Easily contented. *Mal contentadizo,* Hard to please.

Contentamiénto, *sm.* Contentment, joy, satisfaction.

Contentár, *va.* 1. To content, to satisfy, to gratify, to please. 2. To endorse. V. *Endosar.*—*vr.* To be contented, pleased, or satisfied. *Ser de buen ó mal contentar,* To be easily pleased, or difficult to be pleased.

Contentíble, *a.* Contemptible, worthy of contempt, deserving scorn.

Contentívo, va, *a.* Containing; that which contains or comprises.

Conténto, ta, *a.* Moderate, temperate, prudent.

Conténto, *sm.* 1. Contentment, joy, satisfaction. 2. Receipt, discharge. *A' conténto,* To one's satisfaction.

Contentór, *sm.* V. *Contendor.*

Contéra, *sf.* 1. A piece of brass, tin, or silver, put at the end of a scabbard, to prevent the point of a sword from piercing through it. 2. Button of the cascabel of a gun. 3. (Poet.) Prelude of a song, or other musical composition. *Por contera,* Ultimately, finally.

Contérmino, na, *a.* Contiguous, bordering upon.

Conterráneo, nea, *s.* Countryman, or country-woman; a person of the same country with another.

Contestación, *sf.* 1. Contestation, the act of contesting; debate, strife. 2. Altercation, disputation.

Contestár, *va.* 1. To confirm the deposition of another. 2. To prove, to attest. 3. To answer, to reply. 4. To plead to an action.—*vn.* To agree, to accord.

Contéste, *a.* Confirming the evidence of another, making the same deposition as another witness.

Contéxto, *sm.* 1. Intertexture; diversification of things mingled or interwoven one among another. 2. Context, the general series of a discourse.

Contextúra, *sf.* 1. The respective union of the parts which compose a whole. 2. Context, the general series of a discourse. 3. (Met.) Frame and structure of the human body.

Contía, *sf.* V. *Cantidad ó Quantia.*

Conticínio, *sm.* Dead of the night, when all is still.

Contiénda, *sf.* Contest, dispute, debate.

Contignación, *sf.* Contignation; a frame of beams or boards joined together.

Contígo, *pron. pers.* With thee, with thy own person.

Contiguaménte, *ad.* Contiguously, without any intervening space.

Contigüidád, *sf.* Contiguity; actual contact.

Contíguo, gua, *a.* Contiguous, meeting so as to touch.

Contína, (A' la), *ad.* V. *A' la continua.*

Continaménte, *ad.* V. *Continuamente.*

Continéncia, *sf.* 1. Continence or continency, restraint or command of one's self. 2. Abstinence from carnal pleasures. 3. Moderation in lawful pleasures. 4. Continuity, uninterrupted course. *Continencia de la causa,* (For.) Unity which should exist in every judgment or sentence. 5. Countenance, air, look.

Continénte, *sm.* 1. That which contains any thing. 2. Countenance, air, mien. 3. Continent, country not disjointed by the sea from other lands.

Continénte, *a.* Continent, chaste, abstinent, moderate in lawful pleasures. *En continente,* Immediately.

Continenteménte, *ad.* Moderately, abstemiously, chastely.

Contingéncia, *sf.* Contingence or contingency, the quality of being fortuitous; accidental possibility.

Contingénte, *a.* Contingent, fortuitous, accidental.

Contingénte, *sm.* Contingent, a proportion that falls to any person upon a division.

Contingenteménte, *ad.* Casually, accidentally.

Contingíble, *a.* (Ant.) V. *Factible.*

Contíno, *sm.* Ancient office in the royal house of Castile.

Contíno, *ad.* Continually.

Continuación, *sf.* 1. Continuation, an uninterrupted succession. 2. Continuity, connexion uninterrupted.

Continuadaménte, *ad.* Continually, without intermission or interruption.

Continuadór, *sm.* Continuer, continuator, one who continues a work begun by another.

Continuaménte, *ad.* Continually.

Continuamiénto y Continuánza, (Ant.) V. *Continuacion.*

Continuár, *vn.* To continue, to remain in the same state, to last, to be durable, to endure.—*va.* To continue, to pursue, to protract.

Continuidád, *sf.* Continuity, connexion uninterrupted, cohesion.

Contínuo, nua, *a.* 1. Continuous, joined together without any intervening space. 2. Constant, lasting, without interruption. 3. Assiduous, persevering; perennial. *A' la continua*, Continually, without interruption.

Contínuo, *sm.* 1. A whole, composed of parts, united among themselves. 2. One of the hundred yeomen formerly appointed in Spain to guard the king's person and palace. *Continuo, ó de continuo, ad.* Continually, constantly.

Contióso, sa. (Ant.) V. *Quantioso.*

Contoneárse, *vr.* To walk with an affected air or manner, to waggle, or waddle.

Contonéo, *sm.* An affected gait or manner of walking.

Contorcérse, *vr.* To distort, twist, or writhe one's body.

Contorción, *sf.* Contortion, twist, wry motion.

Contornádo, *a.* (Blas.) Applied to the heads of animals, turned towards the sinister side of the shield.

Contornár y Contorneár, *va.* 1. To trace the contour or outline of a figure. 2. To form according to a proposed model or design.

Contornéo, *sm.* V. *Rodeo.*

Contórno, *sm.* 1. Environs or vicinity of a place. 2. Contour or outline by which any figure is defined or terminated. *En contórno*, Round about.

Contorsión, *sf.* Contortion, twist, wry motion.

Contra, *prep.* 1. Against, in opposition to, contrary to, opposite to. 2 (Ant.) Towards; by favour of. *En contra*, Against or in opposition to another thing 3. (Ant.) V. *Hácia y en favor.*

Contras, *sf. pl.* The base pipes of a large organ.

Contraalétas, *sf. pl.* (Naút.) Counter-fashion pieces, the outermost timbers of the stern of a ship on both sides.

Contraamantíllas, *sf. pl.* (Naút.) Preventer-braces which serve to succour the main or fore-yard of a ship.

Contraamúras, *sf. pl.* (Naút.) Preventer-tacks, which serve to support the tacks.

Contraapróches, *sm. pl.* Counter-approaches made by the besieged against the besiegers.

Contraarmíños, *sm. pl.* (Blas.) Contrary to ermine, *i. e.* black field and white spots.

Contraatáques, *sm. pl.* Counter-attacks made by the besieged.

Contrabalánza, *sf.* V. *Contrapeso y Contraposicion.*

Contrabalanzeár, *va.* To counterbalance, to act against with an opposite weight.

Contrabandísta, *sm.* Smuggler, one who carries on a contraband trade.

Contrabándo, *sm.* 1. A prohibited commodity. 2. Contraband trade. 3 (Met.) Any unlawful action. *Ir ó venir de contrabando*, To go or come by stealth.

Contrabatería, *sf.* Counter-battery, that which is raised to dismount the enemy's batteries.

Contrabatír, *va.* To fire upon the enemy's batteries.

Contrabáxo, *sm.* 1. Counter-bass, the deepest of all musical sounds. 2. Base or base-viol, a stringed instrument used in concerts.

Contrabítas, *sf. pl.* (Naút.) Standards of the bits, a sort of knees, destined to support or strengthen the bits on board of ships.

Contrabránque, *sm.* (Naút.) Stemson, a strong arching piece of timber destined to reinforce the stem.

Contrabrázas, *sf. pl.* (Naút.) Preventer-braces.

Contracanál, *sm.* Channel or conduit leading from another; counter-channel.

Contracámbio, *sm.* 1. Re-exchange, the loss arising from the necessity of redrawing for the amount of a protested bill of exchange. 2. (Met.) Change, alteration.

Contracción, *sf.* 1. Contraction, the act of contracting, shrinking, or shrivelling. 2. The state of being contracted. 3. Abbreviation.

Contracebadéra, *sf.* (Naút.) Sprit-top-sail.

Contracédula, *sf.* A decree which reverses or annuls another of an anterior date.

Contracífra, *sf.* Countercipher, the key to a secret or occult manner of writing.

Controcodáste interior, *sm.* (Naút.) The inner stern-post. *Contracodáste exterior*, (Naút.) The back of the stern-post.

Contracósta, *sf.* Coast opposite to another.

Contractación, *sf.* V. *Contratacion.*

Contractár, *va.* V. *Contratar.*

Contracuérdas, *sf. pl.* (Naút.) The outward-deck-planks or platforms.

Contracúlto, *sm.* A plain and natural style, in opposition to an affected manner of writing, which is called *culto.*

Contradánza, *sf.* Country-dance, performed by many persons at the same time.

Contradecidór, ra, *s.* V. *Contradictor, ra.*

Contradecír, *va.* To contradict, to oppose verbally, to repugn.

Contradicción, *sf.* 1. Contradiction, verbal opposition. 2. Hostile resistance.

Contradícho, *sm.* (Ant.) V. *Contradiccion.*

Contradictór, ra, *s.* Contradictor, one that contradicts or verbally opposes.

Contradictoriaménte, *ad.* Contradictorily, inconsistently with, oppositely to.

Contradictorio, ria, *a.* Contradictory, inconsistent with, opposite to.

Contradíque, *sm.* Counter-dike, a second dike or mound to prevent inundations.

Contraditór, ra, *s.* V. *Contradictor*.

Contradízo, za, *a.* V. *Encontradizo*.

Contradríza, *sf.* (Naút.) Second-halliard which assists the other and secures the yard.

Contradurménte ó Contradurmiénte, *sm.* (Naút.) Clamp, thick stuff nailed to the inner range of a ship's side, from the stem to the fashion-pieces of the stern.

Contraemboscáda, *sf.* Counter-ambuscade, an ambush made to defeat another contrived by an enemy.

Contraempuñadúra, *sf.* (Naút.) Preventer-ear-ring.

Contraénte, *pa.* (Ant.) V. *Contrayente*.

Contraér, *va.* y *n.* 1. To contract, to join, to unite. 2. To bring two parties together, to make a bargain. 3. To procure, to incur, to get. *Contraer deudas*, To contract debts. 4. To contract or shrink up, as nerves, muscles, cloth, &c. *Contraer enfermedad*, To contract a disease, to be seized with a fit of illness.

Contraescárpa, *sf.* (Fort.) Counterscarp.

Contraescóta, *sf.* (Naút.) Preventer-sheet, which serves to strengthen the sheet.

Contraescotín, *sm.* (Naút.) Preventer-top-sail-sheet.

Contraescritúra, *sf.* Counter-deed, instrument granted to protest against what had been previously given.

Contraestáy del mayor ó del trinquete, (Naút.) Preventer-stay of the main or fore-mast.

Contraestambór, *sm.* (Naút.) A knee which fastens the sternpost to the keel.

Contrafacción, *sf.* V. *Infraccion*.

Contrafallár, *va.* (At cards) To play a wrong card.

Contrafacér, V. *Contrahacer y Contravenir*.

Contrafiánzas, *sf. pl.* Indemnity-bond.

Contrafírma, *sf.* (For.) Inhibition of an anterior decree.

Contrafirmánte, *pa.* The party who obtains an inhibition or countermanding decree.

Contrafirmár, *va.* (For. Arag.) To obtain a countermanding decree or inhibition.

Contrafóque, *sm.* (Naút.) The fore-top-stay-sail; also the flying jib or middle jib of a smack.

Contrafóso ó Antefoso, *sm.* Avant-fosse or outer ditch of a fortress.

Contrafuéro, *sm.* Infringement or violation of a charter or privilege.

Contrafuérte, *sm.* 1. Counter-fort; a fort constructed in opposition to another. 2. Counter-fort; a pillar of masonry serving to prop and support a wall. 3. Strap of leather to secure the girths on a saddle-tree.

Contraguárdia, *sf.* Counter-guard; a work erected to cover a bastion or ravelin.

Contrahacédor, ra, *s.* (Ant.) Imitator, counterfeiter.

Contrahacér, *va.* 1. To counterfeit; to copy with an intention to pass the copy for an original. 2. To imitate, to copy. 3. To pirate the works of an author.

Contraház, *sm.* The wrong side of cloth.

Contrahécho, cha, *a.* 1. Humpbacked, deformed. 2. Counterfeited.

Contrahiléra, *sf.* A second line formed to defend another.

Contrahójas de las ventanas, *pl.* (Naút.) Dead lights of the cabin.

Contraí, *sm.* Sort of fine cotton velvet.

Contraindicánte, *sm.* (Med.) Contra-indication, symptom indicating the impropriety of using an otherwise convenient medium.

Contraindicár, *va.* To contra-indicate, to point out some peculiar symptom contrary to the general tenor of the malady.

Contraír, *va.* V. *Oponer*.

Contralár, *va.* V. *Contrariar*.

Contralladór, ra, *s.* *Contradictor*.

Contrallár, *va.* (Ant.) V. *Contradecir*.

Contrállo, *sm.* V. *Contradiccion*. *Por el contrallo*, On the contrary.

Contralór, *sm.* Comptroller; inspector.

Contraloreár, *va.* To control, to check, to restrain.

Contrálto, *sm.* Middle sound between the treble and tenor.

Contramaéstre, *sm.* 1. (Naút.) Boatswain. 2. Overseer of a manufactory. 3. *Contramaestre de construccion*, The foreman of a dock-yard.

Contramálla ó Contramalladúra, *sf.* A double net for catching fish.

Contramallár, *va.* To make nets with double meshes.

Contramandár, *va.* To countermand; to order the contrary to what was ordered before.

Contramángas, *sf. pl.* Counter-sleeves; a kind of sleeves formerly worn both by men and women.

Contramárca, *sf.* 1. Countermark; a second or third mark on goods, cattle, &c. 2. A duty to be paid on goods which have no Custom-house mark. 3. A mark added to a medal or other piece of coined metal long after it has been struck, by which the curious know the several changes in value. 4. *Cartas ó patentes de contramarca*, Letters of marque, whereby subjects are authorised to cruise against the enemy, and to capture his ships.

Contramarcár, *va.* To countermark; to put a second or additional mark on bale goods, &c.

Contramárcha, *sf.* 1. Counter-march, retrocession, march backward. 2. Part of a weaver's loom. V. *Viadera*. 3. (Mil. y Naút.) Evolution, by means of which a body of troops or division of ships change their front.

Contramarchár, *va.* To counter-march, to march backward.

Contramárco, *sm.* Counter-frame of a glass window.

Contramaréa, *sf.* (Naút.) Counter-tide, or spring-tide.

Contramesána, *sf.* (Naút.) Mizen-mast.

Contramína, *sf.* 1. Countermine; a mine intended to seek out and destroy the enemy's mines. 2. A subterraneous communication between two or more mines of metals or minerals.

Contraminár, *va.* 1. To countermine, to delve a

passage into an enemy's mines. 2. To counter-work, to defeat by secret measures.

CONTRAMURÁLLA y CONTRAMÚRO, *s.* (Fort.) Fausse-braye, an elevation of earth about three feet in height, raised around the foot of the rampart on the outside.

CONTRANATURÁL, *a.* Counternatural; contrary to nature.

CONTRAÓRDEN, *sm.* Countermand, the repeal of some former order.

CONTRAPALANQUÍN, *sm.* (Naút.) Preventer-clew-garnet, fixed to the clews of the courses to aid the clew-garnets.

CONTRAPÁRES, *sf. pl.* Counter-rafters in a building.

CONTRÁPAS, *sm.* (Ant.) Kind of dance, or step in dancing.

CONTRAPASAMIÉNTO, *sm.* The act and effect of passing to the opposite side or party.

CONTRAPASÁR, *vn.* To join the opposite party.

CONTRAPÁSO, *sm.* 1. A back step in dancing. 2. (Ant.) Permutation. 3. (Mús.) Counter-note.

CONTRAPECHÁR, *va.* To strike breast against breast, applied to horses in tilts or tournaments.

CONTRAPELEÁR, *vn.* (Ant.) To defend one's self in an engagement.

CONTRAPÉLO, (A'), *ad.* Against the grain.

CONTRAPESÁR, *va.* 1. To counterpoise, to counter-balance. 2. (Met.) To act with equal power against any person or cause.

CONTRAPÉSO, *sm.* 1. Counterpoise, equiponderance, equivalence of weight. 2. Poy, a rope-dancer's pole. 3. (Met.) Equipollence; equivalence of power. 4. Counterpoise in a velvet-loom.

CONTRAPÉSTE, *sm.* Remedy against the pest.

CONTRAPILÁSTRA, *sf.* 1. (Arq.) Counterpilaster. 2. Moulding laid on the joints of doors or shutters to keep the wind out.

CONTRAPONEDÓR, *sm.* (Ant.) He who compares one thing with another.

CONTRAPONÉR, *va.* To compare, to oppose.

CONTRAPOSICIÓN, *sf.* 1. Contra-position; the placing over against. 2. An act by which the execution of a sentence is barred.

CONTRAPRODUCÉNTEM, (Lat.) Thing alleged contrary to what is designed to prove.

CONTRAPRUÉBA, *sf.* Counterproof; a second impression of a print taken off by printers.

CONTRAPUÉRTA, *sf.* The inner large door of a house after the street door and entrance.

CONTRAPUÉSTO, TA, *pp.* Compared.

CONTRAPUGNÁR, *va.* (Ant.) To combat, to fight.

CONTRAPUNTÁNTE, *sm.* He who sings in counterpoint.

CONTRAPUNTEÁR, *va.* 1. To sing in counterpoint. 2. To compare. 3. To taunt, to revile.—*vr.* To treat one another with abusive language, to wrangle, to dispute.

CONTRAPÚNTO, *sm.* (Mús.) Counterpoint, harmony.

CONTRAPUNZÓN, *sm.* 1. Puncheon for driving in a nail. 2. Counterpunch, an instrument which serves to open others. 3. The gunsmith's counter-mark on guns, to prevent their being exchanged for others, or purloined.

CONTRAQUÍLLA, *sf.* (Naút.) False keel. V. *Zapata de la quilla.*

CONTRARACAMÉNTO, *sm.* (Naút.) Preventer-parrel.

CONTRAREPÁRO, *sm.* (Fort.) Counter-guard, or counter-defence.

CONTRARÉPLICA, *sf.* Rebutter; an answer to the rejoinder.

CONTRARESTÁR, *va.* 1. To strike back a ball, to counter-buff. 2. To resist, to oppose, to check, to countervail.

CONTRARÉSTO, *sm.* 1. A player who is to strike back the ball. 2. Check, opposition, contradiction.

CONTRÁRIA, *sf.* V. *Oposicion. Contrarias,* Contraries, opposite qualities or circumstances.

CONTRARIADÓR. V. *Contradictor.*

CONTRARIAMÉNTE, *ad.* Contrarily, in a contrary manner.

CONTRARIEDÁD, *sf.* Contrariety, repugnance, opposition.

CONTRÁRIO, *sm.* 1. Opponent, antagonist. 2. Competitor, rival. 3. (Ant.) Impediment, obstacle, obstruction. 4. That which causes hurt, damage, or mischief.

CONTRÁRIO, RIA, *a.* Contrary, repugnant. *Tiempo contrario,* (Naút.) Foul weather. *Echar al contrario,* To cross the breed. *Al contrário y por el contrario,* On the contrary. *En contrário,* Against, in opposition to.

CONTRARIOSAMÉNTE, *ad.* V. *Contrariamente.*

CONTRARÓA ó CONTRARÓDA, *sf.* (Naút.) Stemson.

CONTRARÓNDA, *sf.* 1. (Mil.) Counter-round, which follows the first round for greater safety's sake, to visit the different posts. 2. Round made by officers to inspect and examine the posts, guards, and sentinels.

CONTRAROTÚRA, *sf.* (Alb.) Plaster or poultice applied to fractures or wounds by veterinarians.

CONTRASÉÑA, *sf.* 1. Countersign, or countermark. 2. Watchword, by which soldiers of the same body of troops know each other.

CONTRÁSTA, *sf.* V. *Contráste.*

CONTRASTÁNTE, *pa.* Contrasting; he who resists and combats.

CONTRASTÁR, *va.* 1. To contrast, to place in opposition; to oppose. 2. To resist, to contradict.

CONTRÁSTE, *sm.* 1. Assayer of the mint. 2. Assayer's office, where gold and silver are tried and marked. 3. Assayer of weights and measures. 4. A public office where raw silk is weighed. 5. (Met.) Opposition and strife between persons and things. 6. Impediment, check, hindrance. 7. Opposition and dissimilitude of figures, by which one contributes to the visibility or effect of another. 8. (Naút.) Sudden change of the wind, by which it becomes foul or contrary.

CONTRÁSTO, *sm.* V. *Opositor.*

CONTRÁTA, *sf.* 1. Writing in which the terms of a contract or bargain are included. 2. (Ant.) Territory, district.

CONTRATACIÓN, *sf.* 1. Trade, commerce, traffic. 2. (Ant.) Familiar intercourse. 3. (Ant.) Writing which contains the terms of a bargain. 4. (Ant.) Reward, recompense. *Casa de contratacion,* A house or place where agreements and contracts are made for the promotion of trade and commerce.

CONTRATAMIÉNTO, *sm.* (Ant.) The act and effect of trading.

CONTRATÁNTE, *pa.* Trading; a trader.

CONTRATÁR, *va.* 1. To trade, to traffic. 2. To contract or bargain.

CONTRATÉLA, *sf.* Second enclosure of canvas

within which game is enveloped or wild boars are fought.

Contratiémpo, *sm.* Disappointment, misfortune, calamity, trouble.

Contráto, *sm.* 1. Contract, convention or mutual agreement between parties. 2. A public instrument. *Hacer un contrato*, To make a covenant, to strike a bargain. *Contrato nominado, ó innominado*, Definite or indefinite bargain, particular or general agreement.

Contratrancaníles, *sm. pl.* (Naút.) Inner water-ways, long pieces of timber serving to connect the sides of a ship, and to carry off the water by means of scuppers.

Contratréta, *sf.* Stratagem by which another artifice is defeated.

Contratrincheéra, *sf.* (Fort.) Countertrench; an entrenchment made by the besieged against the besiegers.

Contravalación, *sf.* Contravallation; an entrenchment thrown up by the besiegers to prevent the sallies of the besieged.

Contravalár, *va.* To form a line of contravallation.

Contravención, *sf.* Contravention; violation of a law or command.

Contraveneno, *sm.* 1. Antidote, a medicine given to expel poison. 2. (Met.) Precaution taken to avoid some infamy or mischief.

Contravenidór, *sm.* V. *Contraventor.*

Contravenír, *vn.* 1. To contravene, to transgress a command, to violate a law. 2. To oppose, to obstruct, to baffle.

Contravénta, *sf.* V. *Retrovendición.*

Contraventána, *sf.* Window-shutter.

Contraventór, ra, *s.* Offender, transgressor; one who contravenes or acts contrary to any law or command.

Contravidriéra, *sf.* A second glass window to keep off the cold or heat.

Contravolínas, *sf. pl.* (Naút.) Brails, small ropes fastened to the skirts of a sail to haul it up more easily.

Contráy, *sm.* Sort of fine cloth, manufactured at Courtray, in Flanders.

Contrayénte, *pa.* Contracting, he who contracts.

Contrayérba, *sf.* 1. (Bot.) Species of bix-wort; contrayerva. Dorstenia contrayerva *L.* 2. (Met.) Precaution to prevent some damage or mischief.

Contrayúgo, *sm.* (Naút.) Inner transom, which some ship-builders are accustomed to place under the wing-transom, to give it more strength.

Contréchó, *sm.* Spasm in horse's bowels.

Contrécto, *sm.* V. *Contrahecho.*

Contremecér, *vn.* (Ant.) To tremble.

Contribución, *sf.* 1. Contribution; that which is given by many persons for some common purpose. 2. Contribution, tax. *U'nica contribucion*, Income-tax, a tax laid on each person in proportion to his income, rank, &c.

Contribuidór, *sm.* Contributor, one who contributes or bears a part in some common design.

Contribuír, *va.* 1. To contribute, to pay one's share of a tax. 2. To give some common stock, to bear a part in some common design. 3. (Ant.) V. *Atribuir.*

Contribuládo, dá, *a.* Grieved, afflicted.

Contributário, *sm.* Contributor, payer of taxes.

Contribuyénte, *pa.* Contributing; contributor.

Contrición, *sf.* Contrition, penitence, sorrow for sin.

Contrincánte, *sm.* Competitor, rival.

Contristár, *va.* To afflict, to render melancholy, to sadden.

Contríto, ta, *a.* Worn with sorrow, harassed with the sense of guilt, penitent; contrite.

Controvérsia, *sf.* Controversy, a dispute; especially about matters of religion.

Controversísta, *sm.* Controversialist, controvertist, a disputant.

Controvertíble, *a.* Controvertible, disputable.

Controvertír, *va.* To controvert, to debate or dispute any thing in writing.

Contubernál, *sm.* (Ant.) Chamber-fellow, companion who lives in the same apartment.

Contubérnio, *sm.* 1. Cohabitation, the state of inhabiting the same place with another person. 2. The state of living together as married sons, concubinage. [mazmente.

Contumáce y Contumacemente, V. *Contu-*

Contumácia, *sf.* 1. Obstinacy in asserting one's own opinion, perverseness, stubbornness. 2. Contumacy; a wilful contempt and disobedience to any lawful summons or judicial order.

Contumáz, *a.* 1. Obstinate, stubborn, perverse. 2. Disobedient to any lawful summons or judicial order. [nately.

Contumazménte, *ad.* Contumaciously, obsti-

Contumélia, *sf.* Contumely, rudeness or bitterness of language, reproach.

Contumeliosaménte, *ad.* In a contumelious or reproachful manner.

Contumelióso, sa, *a.* Contumelious, reproachful, rude, sarcastic.

Contundénte, *a.* Producing a contusion; applied to weapons which cause a contusion.

Contundír, *va.* To bruise, to cause a contusion.

Conturbación, *sf.* Perturbation, uneasiness of the mind.

Conturbadór, *sm.* Perturber, disturber.

Conturbamiénto, *sm.* (Ant.) Perturbation, disquietude.

Conturbár, *va.* To perturbate, to disquiet, to disturb.

Conturbatívo, va, *a.* That which perturbates or disquiets.

Contusión, *sf.* Contusion; a bruise inflicted by a blow or stroke which causes no wound.

Contúso, sa, *a.* Bruised; afflicted with a contusion.

Contutór, *sm.* Assistant tutor, fellow tutor.

Conúsco, *pron. pers.* (Ant.) With us.

Convalecéncia, *sf.* Convalescence, or convalescency, renewal of health, recovery from disease. *Casa de convalecencia*, An hospital for convalescent patients.

Convalecér, *vn.* 1. To recover from sickness. 2. (Met.) To recover lost prosperity and power.

Convaleciénte, *pa.* Convalescent.

Convalescéncia, *sf.* (Ant.) V *Convalecencia.*

Convalescér, *vn.* (Rar.) To improve, to grow vigorous and robust. [tion.

Convalidación y Convalidád, *sf.* Confirma-

Convecíno, na, *a.* Neighbouring, conterminous.

Convelérse, vr. To shrink, to be contracted; applied to blood vessels. [and convinces.
Convencedór, ra. s. One who demonstrates
Convencér, va. To convince, to force another to acknowledge a contested position.
Convencíble, a. Convincible, capable of conviction, capable of being evidently disproved.
Convencimiénto, sm. Conviction, confutation; the act of convincing or confuting.
Convención, sf. 1. Convention, contract, agreement. 2. Convenience.
Convencionál, a. Conventional, stipulated, agreed upon by compact.
Convencionalménte, ad. According to a convention, in the manner agreed upon.
Convenialménte, ad. By common consent.
Conveníble, a. 1. Docile, tractable, compliant, obsequious. 2. (Ant.) Convenient. 3. (Ant.) Being of a moderate or reasonable price.
Conveniéncia, sf. 1. Utility, profit, advantage. 2. Conformity, congruity. 3. Agreement, convention, adjustment. 4. Service; a servant's place in a house or family. *He hallado conveniencia*, I have got a place. *Busco conveniencia*, I am looking out for a place. 5. Commodiousness, ease, accommodation. *Es amigo de conveniencia*, He loves his ease or convenience. *Conveniéncias*, Emoluments, perquisites: income, property.
Conveniénte, a. 1. Useful, profitable, advantageous. 2. Fit, suitable, agreeable. 3. Commodious, timely. [suitably.
Convenienteménte, ad. Conveniently, fitly,
Convénio, sm. Convention, contract, agreement.
Convenír, vn. 1. To agree, to be of the same opinion. 2. To correspond, to belong to. 3. To assemble, to meet in the same place. 4. (Ant.) To cohabit carnally. 5. To litigate.—v. impers. To suit, to be to the purpose—vr. To compound, to make up matters.
Conventázo, sm. A large convent or monastery.
Conventíco, íllo, y íto, sm. A small convent.
Conventícula y Conventículo, s. Conventicle; a secret assembly for some unlawful purpose.
Conventíllo, sm. Brothel, a bawdy-house.
Convénto, sm. 1. Convent of monks or nuns, monastery, nunnery. 2. (Ant.) Concourse, meeting. 3. Community of religious men or women who live in the same house.
Conventuál, a. Conventual, belonging to a convent, monastic.
Conventuál, sm. 1. Conventual, a monk, one that lives in a convent. 2. Franciscan friar possessing estates or property.
Conventualidád, sf. The state of living together as religious persons in a convent or monastery. [ly.
Conventualménte, ad. Monastically, recluse-
Convergénte, a. Convergent, tending to one point from different places.
Convergér, vn. To converge; to tend to one point from different places.
Converná, fut. imp. (Ant.) Of the verb convenir; now written convendrá.
Convernía, pret. imp. subj. (Ant.) Third person of convenir.
Conversáble, a. Conversable, sociable, qualified for conversation, fit for company.

Conversación, sf. 1. Conversation, familiar intercourse, easy talk. 2. Commerce, intercourse, familiarity. 3. Society, company. 4. Room, bed-room. 5. Criminal intercourse. 6. Club, an assembly. V. *Tertulia*. *Casa de conversacion*, Assembly-house where people meet to converse and play. *La mucha conversacion es causa de menosprecio*, (Prov.) Too much familiarity breeds contempt.
Conversánte, pa. Conversing, he who converses.
Conversár, vn. 1. To converse, to discourse familiarly upon any subject, to convey the thoughts reciprocally in talk. 2. To cohabit, to live together.
Conversión, sf. 1. Change from one religion to another. 2. Change from reprobation to grace 3. Change from one state into another. 4 (Ret.) Apostrophe. 5. (Mil.) Wheel, wheeling. *Quarto de conversion*, Quarter-wheeling.
Conversívo, va, a. Having the power of converting or changing one thing into another.
Convérso, sm. 1. Convert; a person converted from one religion or opinion to another. 2. Lay-brother; a man admitted for the service of a religious house without being ordained.
Convertíble, a. 1. Susceptible of change, transmutable, convertible. 2. Moveable, transferrable.
Convertiénte, pa. Converting, a convert.
Convertír, va. 1. To change into another substance, to convert, to permute. 2. To change from one religion or opinion to another. 3. To apply things to any use for which they were not originally intended. 4. To convert, to direct, to appropriate. *Todo lo convierte en substancia*, (Met.) He minds nothing; nothing makes the least impression upon him.
Convexidád, sf. Convexity, protuberance in a circular form.
Convéxo, xa, a. Convex, rising in a circular form; opposite to concave.
Convicción, sf. V. *Convencimiento*.
Convictór, sm. Boarder, pensioner in a college.
Convictório, sm. (Among the Jesuits,) That part of the college where the pensioners or boarders live and receive their instructions.
Convictorísta, sm. Boarder or pensioner.
Convidadór, ra, s. Inviter, one who invites.
Convidár, va. 1. To invite or ask to dinner. 2. (Met.) To allure, to invite, to persuade.—vr. To offer one's service spontaneously.
Conviénto, sm. (Ant.) Convent. V. *Convento*.
Convincénte, a. Convincing.
Convincenteménte, ad. In a convincing manner; in such a manner as to leave no room for doubt.
Conviniénte, a. (Ant.) V. *Conveniente*.
Convíte, sm. 1. Invitation; the act of inviting. 2. Feast to which persons are invited.
Conviviénte, a. Living together, living with each other. [vening an assembly.
Convocación, sf. Convocation; the act of con-
Convocadéro, ra, a. That is to be convened or convoked. [vokes.
Convocadór, sm. One who convenes or con-
Convocár, va. 1. To convene, to convoke, to call together. 2. To shout in triumph or exultation.

CONVOCATÓRIA, *sf.* Letter of convocation.
CONVOCATÓRIO, RIA, *a.* That which convokes.
CONVÓY, *sm.* 1. Convoy, an escort or guard, to convey something safe from place to place. 2. Retinue, suite.
CONVOYÁNTE, *pa.* Convoying, he who convoys.
CONVOYÁR, *va.* To convoy, to escort or guard from place to place.
CONVULSÁR, *vn.* To feel an involuntary contraction of the nerves.—*vr.* To be convulsed.
CONVULSIÓN, *sf.* Convulsion, an irregular and involuntary contraction of the fibres and nerves.
CONVULSÍVO, VA, *a.* Convulsive; that which gives twitches or spasms. [sions.
CONVÚLSO, SA, *a.* Convulsed, subject to convul-
CONVÚSCO, *pron. pers.* (Ant.) With you.
CONYÚDICE, *sm.* V. *Conjuez.*
CONYUGÁL, *a.* Conjugal, matrimonial, connubial.
CONYUGALMÉNTE, *ad.* Conjugally, matrimonially
CÓNYUGES, *sm. pl.* A married couple, husband and wife.
CONYÚNTO, TA, *a.* (Ant.) *Conjunto.*
COOPERACIÓN, *sf.* Cooperation; the act of contributing and concurring to the same end.
COOPERADÓR, RA, *s.* Cooperator.
COOPERÁNTE, *pa.* Cooperating, cooperator.
COOPERÁR, *va.* To cooperate, to labour jointly with another to the same end, to concur in producing the same effect.
COOPERÁRIO, *sm.* V. *Cooperador.*
COOPERATÍVO, VA, *a.* Cooperative, promoting the same end jointly.
COOPOSITÓR, *sm.* Opponent; one who argues or disputes publicly to obtain a prebend.
COOPTACIÓN, *sf.* Adoption, assumption.
COORDINACIÓN, *sf.* Coordination, collateralness; the state of holding the same rank.
COORDINADAMÉNTE, *ad.* Coordinately.
COORDINAMIÉNTO, *sm.* V. *Coordinacion.*
COORDINÁR, *va.* To arrange, to adjust.
CÓPA, *sf.* 1. Cup, a small vessel to drink in. 2. Meeting of the branches of a tree, a bower. 3. Crown or hollow part of a hat. 4. Brazier, a pan to hold coals. *Copa del horno,* The roof or vault of an oven or furnace. 5. Each one of the cards with a heart.—*pl.* Hearts, one of the four suits at cards. 2. Bosses of a bridle.
COPÁDA, *sf.* V. *Cugujada.*
COPÁDO, DA, *a.* Tufted, coped.
COPALXOCÓL, *sm.* (Bot.) Tree in new Spain resembling a cherry-tree.
COPÁL, *sm.* Copal, a transparent gum. [bark.
COPANÉTE Y CÓPANO, *sm.* (Ant.) A small
COPÁYBA, *sf.* (Bot.) The copaiba-tree, from which the copaiba gum distils. Copaifera officinalis *L.*
COPÁZA, *sf.* (Aum. de *copa.*) A large cup or glass with a foot. [wool. 2. Large flake of snow.
COPÁZO, *sm.* (Aum. de *copo.*) 1. Large fleece of
COPÉLA, *sf.* Coppél, a chemical vessel made of ashes or calcined bones, in which metals are refined.
COPELACIÓN, *sf.* The act of refining metals.
COPELÁR, *va.* To refine or purify metals.
COPÉRA, *sf.* Cupboard, in which cups and other drinking vessels are kept.
COPERÍLLO, *sm.* A little cupbearer, or attendant at a feast to serve wine. [a feast.
COPÉRO, *sm.* Cupbearer, one who serves drink at
COPÉTA, *sf.* A small cup or drinking vessel.
COPÉTE, *sm.* 1. Toupee, a curl of hair worn on the forehead. 2. Crown-work of a looking-glass frame, made in the shape of a shell. 3. Top of a shoe which rises over the buckle. 4. Top, summit. 5. The projecting top of sherbets or ice-creams. *Hombre de copete,* A man of respectability and character. *Tener copete ó mucho copete,* To assume an air of authority, to be lofty and supercilious.
COPETÚDO, DA, *a.* 1. Illustrious, eminent, powerful. 2. High, lofty, supercilious on account of one's noble descent.
COPÉY, *sm.* Indian tree, the leaves of which serve for writing, drawing, or playing cards.
CÓPIA, *sf.* 1. Copiousness, plenty, abundance. 2. Copy, transcript. 3. Portrait taken from original design; copy of a picture. 4. Rate or valuation of tithe. 5. (Gram.) List of nouns and verbs, and the cases which they govern.
COPIADÓR, *sm.* *Libro Copiador,* Among merchants, book in which letters are copied.
COPIÁNTE, *s.* Copyist, a copyer, an imitator.
COPIÁR, *va.* 1 To copy, to transcribe. 2. To imitate, to draw after life. 3. To write on the same subject with another, and nearly in the same manner. 4. (Poét.) To describe, to depict. *Copiar del natural,* To copy from life; among artists, to design from the naked body.
COPÍCA, LLA, Y TA, *sf.* A small cup or drinking vessel.
COPÍCO, LLO, Y TO, *sm.* A small fleece or flake.
COPILACIÓN, *sf.* 1. Compilation, assemblage. V. *Recopilacion.* 2. V. *Resúmen.*
COPILADÓR, *sm.* Compiler, collector; one who frames a composition from various authors.
COPILÁR, *va.* To compile, to draw up from various authors; to collect.
COPÍN, *sm.* (Astur.) A Spanish measure, being equal to half a *celemin,* or the twelfth part of a quintal or *fanega.*
COPIOSAMÉNTE, *ad.* Copiously, abundantly, plentifully.
COPIOSIDÁD, *sf.* (Ant.) Abundance.
COPIÓSO, SA, *a.* Copious, abundant, plentiful.
COPÍSTA, *sm.* 1. Copyist, copyer. 2. A copying machine.
CÓPLA, *sf.* 1. A certain number of consonant verses, a couplet. 2. A sarcastic hint or remark, a lampoon. *Coplas de ciegos,* Ballads. *Echar coplas de repente,* To talk nonsense.
COPLEADÓR, *sm.* (Ant.) Poetaster, rhymer.
COPLEÁR, *vn.* To versify, to make couplets.
COPLÉRO, *sm.* 1. Poetaster; a vile, petty poet. 2. Ballad-seller; one who hawks ballads about the streets.
COPLÍCA ó COPLÍLLA, *sf.* A little ballad.
COPLÍSTA, *sm.* V. *Coplero.*
COPLÓN, *sm.* Low vile poetry; is generally used in the plural number, *Coplones.*
CÓPO, *sm.* 1. A small bundle of cotton, hemp, flax, or silk, put on the distaff to be spun. 2. Flake of snow. 3. Thick part of a fishing-net. 4. (And.) Odour of the flower of the aromatic myrrh-tree.
COPÓN, *sm.* 1. A large cup or drinking vessel. 2. (Naút.) A thick rope or small cable for weighing up the anchor.
COPÓSO, SA, *a.* V. *Copado.*
CÓPRA, *sf.* The pith of the coçoa-nut.

Cópula, sf. 1. The joining or coupling two things together. 2. Carnal union. 3. Key-stone of an arch or vault. 4. (Log.) Verb which unites the predicate with the subject.
Copulár, va. To connect, join, or unite.—vr. To copulate, to come together as different sexes.
Copulativaménte, ad. Jointly.
Copulatívo, va, a. Copulative; joining or uniting together.
Coquéta, sf. (Arag.) Palm or blow with a ruler in the palm of the hand by school-masters.
Coquíllo, sm. 1. A small shell. 2. Cocoa-nut; the fruit of the India palm-tree. 3. An insect which destroys the vines. Curculio Bacchus L.
Coquína, sf. 1. (And.) Shell-fish in general. 2. Cockle. Cardium rusticum L.
Coquinário, ria, a. (Ant.) Culinary. Coquinário del Rey, The king's own cook.
Coquinéro, sm. Fishmonger, one who deals in cockles and other shell fish.
Coquíto, sm. 1. A small cocoa-nut. 2. Grimace made to amuse children and make them laugh.
Cor, sm. (Ant.) 1. V. *Corazon*. 2. V. *Coro*. *De cor*, By heart.
Coracéro, sm. Cuirassier; a trooper or horse-soldier who wears a cuirass.
Corácha, sf. A leather bag, like those in which the cocoa-nuts are exported from India.
Corachín, sm. A little leather bag.
Coracílla, sf. A small coat of mail.
Coracína, sf. A small breast-plate, anciently worn by soldiers.
Corída y Coradéla, sf. V. *Asadura*.
Coráge, sm. 1. Courage, bravery, fortitude. 2. Anger, passion.
Corajóso, sa, a. (Ant.) Animated, courageous.
Corajúdo, da, a. Angry, passionate.
Corál, sm. 1. Coral, a marine calcareous production having an arborescent appearance of various colours, of which the red is the best. *Coráles*, Strings of corals which country-women wear about their necks. 2. (Naút.) A large knee which fastens the sternpost to the keel.
Corál, a. Choral, belonging to the choir.
Coraléro, sm. A worker or dealer in corals.
Coralíllo, sm. The coral-coloured snake.
Coralína, sf. 1. (Zooph.) Sea-coralline, or white worm-seed; a plant-shaped zoophyte, said to be a remedy for gout and inflammation. Sertularia L. 2. (Naút.) A coral fishing-boat. 3. Every sea-animal resembling coral.
Coralíno, na, a. Coralline, belonging to coral.
Corámbre, sf. All hides and skins of animals, dressed or undressed.
Corambréro, sm. Dealer in hides and skins, dressed or undressed.
Coramvóbis, s. A corpulent person, strutting about with affected gravity.
Corascóra, sf. (Naút.) Corascora, a coasting vessel in India.
Coráza, sf. 1. Cuirass, an ancient breast-plate made of iron, which covers the body before and behind, from the neck to the girdle. 2. *Coraza, ó caballo coraza*, Cuirassier, a trooper or horse soldier armed with a cuirass. *Tentar á uno las corazas*, (Met.) To try one's mettle or courage. [casses of the hearts of animals.
Corazináda, sf. 1. Pith of a pine-tree. 2. Fri-

Corazón, sm. 1. Heart, the muscle which by its contraction and dilatation, propels the blood through the body, and is therefore considered the source of vital motion. 2. Spirit, courage. 3. Will, mind. 4. Heart, the middle or centre of any thing. 5. Pith of a tree. 6. *Corazon de un cabo*, (Naút.) Heart-strand. *Llevar ó tener el corazón en las manos*, To be sincere and candid.
Corazón (De), ad. 1. Heartily, sincerely, truly. 2. From memory.
Corazonáda, sf. 1. Courage, an impulse of the heart to encounter dangers. 2. Livers and lights.
Corazonázo, sm. A great heart.
Corazoncíco, llo, y to, sm. A little heart; a pitiful or faint-hearted person.
Corazoncíllo, sm. (Bot.) Perforated St. John's wort. Hypericum perforatum L.
Corbacháda, sf. A stroke or lash given with the gristly part of the penis of a bull or ox.
Corbácho, sm. The gristly part of the penis of a bull or ox.
Corbás, sf. pl. (Cetr.) The 4 largest feathers of a hawk.
Corbáta, sf. Cravat, a neck-cloth worn about the neck, with the two ends hanging down the breast.—sm. Magistrate not brought up to the law; also a layman who has neither studied the civil nor canon law.
Corbatín, sm. Stock; a close neck-cloth, fastened with a buckle or clasps.
Corbáto, sm. Cooler, a vat with water, in which the worm of a still is placed to cool.
Corbatón, sm. (Naút.) A small knee used in different parts of a ship.
Corbéta, sf. A light vessel with 3 masts and square sails.
Corcél, sm. A steady horse, a charger.
Corcésca, sf. Ancient pike or spear.
Córcha, sf. V. *Corcho y Corchera*.
Corchár, va. (Ant.) To entangle or interweave the ends of ropes.
Córche, sm. A sort of sandal or shoe, open at the top, and tied with latchets.
Corchéa, sf. (In Music) Crotchet, a note or character of time, equal to half a minim.
Corcheár, va. (Among Curriers) To grain leather with a cork.
Corchéra, sf. Vessel made of pitched cork or staves, in which a bottle or flask is put with ice or snow, to cool liquor.
Corchéta, sf. Eye of a hook or clasp.
Corchéte, sm. 1. Clasp, a hook and eye. Commonly used in the plural, *Corchetes*, Hooks and eyes. 2. Runner; one whose business is to apprehend offenders, and conduct them to prison. 3. An iron instrument which serves for flattening tin plates. 4. Brace used to connect lines in writing or printing. 5. Bench-hook of a carpenter's bench.
Córcho, sm. 1. Cork; the bark of the cork-tree. 2. Ice-vessel. V. *Corchera*. 3. Bee-hive. V. *Colmena*. 4. Cork; the stopple of a bottle, flask, or jar. 5. Box made of cork, for carrying eatables. 6. Cork-board, put before beds and tables to serve as a shelter. *Nadar sin corcho*, (Met.) Not to need leading strings or other people's advice; literally, to swim with-

out cork. *No tener muelas de corcho,* (Met.) Not to be easily imposed upon; literally, not to have grinders of cork. *Tener cara de corcho,* (Met.) To have a brazen face, to be impudent; literally, to have a cork face.—*pl.* 1. Clogs, a sort of pattens used by women to keep their shoes clean and dry. 2. (Art.) Gun-tompions, plugs to stop the mouths of guns and other pieces of ordnance.

Corcíllo, lla, *s.* A small deer or little fawn.

Corcíno, *s.* A small deer.

Corcóva, *sf.* 1. Hump, a crooked back. 2. Convexity, prominence, protuberance, curvature.

Corcovado, da, *a.* Hump-backed, gibbous.

Corcoveár, *vn.* To curvet; to cut capers.

Corcovéta, *sm.* A crook-backed person.

Corcovílla, ta, *sf. dim.* Little hump or crooked back.

Corcóvo, *sm.* 1. Spring, or curvet, made by a horse on the point of leaping. 2. A wrong step, unfair proceeding.

Córculo, *sm.* Heart-shell; an aquatic insect.

Corcusír, *va.* To darn holes in cloth or stuff, to patch.

Córda, *sf.* *Estar el navío á la corda,* (Naút.) To be close-haled, or lying-to; applied to a ship.

Cordáge, *sm.* (Naút.) Cordage; all sorts of rope used in the rigging of ships.

Cordál, *sm.* Double-tooth. *Cordáles,* Grinders.

Cordáto, ta, *a.* Wise, prudent, discreet, judicious, considerate.

Cordél, *sm.* 1. Rope made of several strands. 2. (Naút.) A thin rope or line used on board a ship; a line. *Cordel alquitranado,* A tarred line. *Cordel blanco,* An untarred line. *Cordel de corredera,* Log-line. *Mozo de cordel,* Porter; one who carries burthens for hire. *Apretar los cordeles,* To oblige one to say or do a thing by violence. *Echar el cordel,* To mark with a line or cord: (Met.) To administer justice impartially: (Met.) To draw lines in order to consider the manner of executing a thing. *Estar á cordel,* To be in a right line.

Cordeládo, da, *a.* Twisted for ribbons or garters, applied to silk.

Cordeláxo, *sm.* Stroke or lash given with a rope. [joke.

Cordeléjo, *sm.* 1. A small rope. 2. Fun, jest,

Cordelería, *sf.* 1. Cordage; all sorts of ropes. 2. Rope-walk, where ropes are made. 3. (Naút.) Rigging.

Cordeléro, *sm.* Rope-maker.

Cordellíco, llo, y to, *sm.* A small rope, cord, or line.

Cordelláte, *sm.* Grogram; a sort of stuff.

Cordéra, *sf.* Ewe lamb.

Cordería, *sf.* 1. Cordage. 2. Place where cordage is kept.

Corderíca, lla, y ta, *sf.* Little ewe lamb.

Corderíco, llo, y to, *sm.* A young or little lamb. [fleece.

Corderíllo, *sm.* Lamb-skin dressed with the

Corderína, *sf.* Lamb-skin. [to lambs.

Corderíno, na, *a.* Of the lamb-kind, belonging

Cordéro, ra, *s.* 1. Lamb. 2. A dressed lamb-skin. 3. Meek, gentle, mild. *Cordero ciclan,* A lamb that never lets down the testicles. *Cordero rencoso,* Lamb with one testicle down, and the other concealed. *Cordero de socesto ó lechal,* House-lamb. *Cordero mueso,* Small-eared lamb. *Cordéro de Escitia,* (Bot.) Polypody of Tartary. Polypodium *L.*

Corderuélo, la, *s.* A small young lamb.

Corderúna, *sf.* Lamb's skin.

Cordéta, *sf.* (Mur.) A small rope made of the platted strands of base-weed.

Cordezuéla, *sf.* A small rope.

Cordíaco, ca, *a.* V. *Cardíaco.*

Cordiál, *a.* 1. Cordial, affectionate, sincere. 2. Cordial, invigorating, reviving.

Cordiál, *sm.* Cordial; a medicine which strengthens and comforts.

Cordialidád, *sf.* Cordiality, sincere friendship. [tionately.

Cordialménte, *ad.* Cordially, sincerely, affec-

Cordíla, *sf.* Spawn of a tunny-fish.

Cordílla, *sf.* Guts of sheep.

Cordilléra, *sf.* 1. Chain or ridge of mountains. 2. A long, elevated, and straight tract of land.

Cordílo, *sm.* An amphibious animal resembling a crocodile.

Cordobán, *sm.* Morocco or Spanish leather, a goat-skin tanned or dressed.

Cordobána, *sf.* Nakedness, nudity. *Andar á la cordobana,* To go stark-naked.

Cordójo, *sm.* Anguish, anxiety, affliction.

Cordón, *sm.* 1. Cord or string made of silk, wool, hemp, &c. 2. Cord or girdle with which monks tie up their habits. 3. A military cordon, formed by a line of troops. 4. (Naút.) Strand of a cable or rope. *Cabo de tres ó quatro cordones,* A three or four stranded rope or cable. 5. (Fort.) A row of stones jutting out between the rampart and the basis of the parapet, where the wall begins to be perpendicular. 6. *Cordon de S. Francisco,* A name given by the Spanish sailors to the Equinox, on account of the storms which prevail about that time, or St. Francis's day, the 4th of October. 7. The milled edge of coined metal. —*pl.* 1. Shoulder-knots, worn by the military. 2. Harness-cords of a velvet-loom.

Cordonázo, *sm.* 1. Stroke or lash with a cord or rope. 2. Large cord. [line.

Cordoncíllo, co, y to, *sm.* A small cord or

Cordoncíllo, *sm.* 1. A twisted cord put on the edge of a coat or great coat. 2. Milling round the edge of coin.

Cordonería, *sf.* 1. All the work of twisters or lace-makers in general. 2. A lace-maker's shop. [woman. 2. Rope-maker.

Cordonéro, ra, *s.* 1. Lace-maker, lace-man or

Cordoyóso, sa, *a.* (Ant.) Languishing, afflicted with anguish.

Cordúla, *sf.* V. *Cordilo.*

Cordúra, *sf.* Prudence, practical wisdom *Hacer cordura,* To act in a prudent manner.

Coréa, *sf.* Dance accompanied with a chorus.

Coreár, *vn.* To sing or play in a chorus. *Música coreada,* Chorus music.

Corechaménte, *ad.* V. *Correctamente.*

Corecíco, *sm.* (dim. of *Cuero*) Small hide or skin.

Co-regéncia, *sf.* Co-regency.

Co-regénte, *sm.* Co-regent, joint regent.

Coréo, *sm.* 1. A foot in Latin verse. 2. Connected harmony of a chorus.

Corezuélo, *sm.* 1. Sucking pig; a small roasted pig. 2. Small hide of leather.

Cori, *sm.* 1. (Bot.) Coris, or Montpelier Coris. Coris monspeliensis *L.* 2. A kind of shells which pass for money in Siam.

Coriámbico, ca, *a.* Choriambic, applied to Latin verse.

Coriándro, *sm.* (Bot.) Coriander, or common coriander. Coriandrum sativum *L.*

Coribánte, *sm.* A priest of Cybele.

Coriféo, *sm.* 1. Corypheus, the principal or leading character in a chorus, play, or tragedy among the Greeks and Romans. 2. Leader of a sect or party.

Coríllo, *sm.* A small choir.

Coríntico, ca, y Corìntio, tia, *a.* Corinthian; applied to one of the orders of architecture.

Corión, *sm.* (Anat.) The exterior membrane that envelopes the fœtus.

Corista, *sm.* Chorist or chorister.

Coríto, *sm.* 1. A nick-name given to the inhabitants of Biscaya, the mountains of Santander, and the Asturias. 2. Timid, pusillanimous man.

Coríza, *sf.* 1. A kind of shoe made of undressed leather, laced from the toe to the instep, worn by the common people in Spain. 2. Mucus of the nose.

Corladúra, *sf.* Gold-varnish.

Corlár ó Corleár, *va.* To put on gold-varnish.

Cormas, *sf. pl.* 1. Fetters, shackles. 2. (Met.) Trouble, uneasiness.

Cormáno, na, *s.* 1. Cousin-german. 2. (Ant.) Uncle. *Cormános*, Children begotten in an anterior marriage.

Cornáda, *sf.* 1. Thrust or stroke with a bull's or cow's horn. 2. Thrust with a foil, in a cunning manner, with the vulgar.

Cornadíllo, *sm.* A small piece of money of little value. *Emplear su cornadillo*, To attain one's end by low means.

Cornádo, *sm.* An old copper coin, mixed with a little silver, and of small value in times of the kings of Castile. *No vale un cornado*, It is not worth a farthing.

Cornadúra, *sf.* Horns; the hard prominent substances which grow on the heads of oxen and other quadrupeds.

Cornál, *sm.* A strap or thong with which oxen are tied to the yoke by the horns.

Cornaménta, *sf.* Horns of any animal.

Cornamúsa, *sf.* 1. Cornemuse, a large musical wind-instrument; a sort of rustic flute. 2. (Naút.) A belaying cleat; a piece of timber nailed to the upper parts of a ship for fastening the ropes. *Cornamusas de los palos*, The belaying cleats of the lower masts. *Cornamusas de ponton*, The notched cleats of a ponton.

Córnas, *sf. pl.* (Naút.) Back-stays. V. *Brandales.*

Cornatíllo, *sm.* A kind of olive.

Cornéa, *sf.* Cornea, the second coat or integument of the eye.

Corneádo, da, *a.* (Ant.) Horned, pointed, having points or horns.

Corneadór, ra, *s.* A horned animal, which butts or plays with the horns.

Corneár, *va.* To butt or play with the horns.

Cornecíco, llo, y to, *sm.* Cornicle, a little or small horn.

Cornéja, *sf.* (Orn.) Crow. Corvus corone *L.*

Cornejílla, *sf.* A small crow.

Cornéjo, *sm.* (Bot.) Cornelian cherry-tree, or cornel-tree, dog-wood. Cornus mascula *L.*

Cornerína y Cornelina, *sf.* Onyx; a cornolian of a pearl-colour.

Cornéro, *sm.* (Ant.) Hollow of the temples. *Cornero de pan*, Crust of bread.

Cornéta, *sf.* 1. Cornet; a musical wind-instrument in the shape of a horn. 2. A French horn. 3. A postilion's horn; hunting horn. 4. Cornet; an ensign of horse who carries the standard. 5. Troop of horse. 6. (Naút.) Broad pendant; a rear admiral's flag. 7. Horn used by swineherds to call their hogs together. 8. Ancient instrument of war.

Cornéte, *sm.* A small musical horn, or bugle-horn.

Cornetíca, lla, y ta, *sf.* A small cornet.

Cornezuélo, *sm.* 1. A small musical horn, or bugle-horn. 2. An instrument for bleeding horses.

Corniál, *a.* Made in the shape of a horn.

Cornicábra, *sf.* 1. (Bot.) Turpentine-tree, of which the *Orihuela* snuff-boxes are made in Spain. 2. A sort of olives.

Corniculáta, *a.* Horned, as the new moon.

Cornifórme, *a.* In the shape of horns.

Cornígero, ra, *a.* (Poét.) Horned.

Corníja, *sf.* Cornice, or corniche.

Cornijál, *sm.* Angle or corner of a building.

Cornijaménto ó Cornijamiénto, *sm.* (Arq.) V. *Cornijon.*

Cornijón, *sm.* (Arq.) The 3d of the three principal pieces on the tops of columns, and which consist of the architrave, frieze, and cornice.

Cornijuéla, *sm.* (Bot.) Alpine mespilus. Mespilus amelanchier *L.*

Corníl, *sf.* V. *Cornal.*

Corniòla, *sf.* V. *Cornerina.*

Cornísa, *sf.* Cornice, or corniche.

Cornisaménto ó Cornisamiénto, *sm.* V. *Cornijon.*

Cornisíca, lla, y ta, *sf.* Small cornice.

Corno, *sm.* (Bot.) Cornelian cherry-tree, or cornet-tree. Cornus mascula *L.*

Cornucópia, *sf.* 1. Horn of plenty. 2. Sconce; a branched candlestick.

Cornudázo, *sm.* A very great cuckold.

Cornudería, *sf.* 1. Cuckold's quarter. Cuckold-street. 2. Cuckoldom, a state of adultery.

Cornudíco, llo, y to, *sm.* A little cuckold.

Cornúdo, *sm.* Cuckold; one whose wife is an adulteress.

Cornúpeta, *sm.* A wild ill-trained ox.

Córo, *sm.* 1. Choir or quire; a part of a church. 2. The people who pray and sing in the choir. 3. Memory. *Decir ó tomar de coro*, To say or get by heart. 4. Verses destined for the choir. 5. Chorus in ancient theatrical pieces. 6. (Ant.) Dance. 7. Summer solstitial wind. 8. Choir of angels. *Hablar á coros*, To speak alternately.

Corócha, *sf.* 1. (Ant.) Coat. 2. Vine-fretter, or vine-grub; an insect destructive to vines.

Corografía, *sf.* Chorography; the art of describing particular regions.

Coróǵrafo, *sm.* Chorographer; one who describes particular regions.

Corolário, *sm.* Corollary, conclusion, inference.
Corólla, *sf.* (Ant.) Small crown.
Coróna, *sf.* 1. Crown; the ornament of the head, which denotes imperial or regal dignity. 2. Crown; the top of the head. 3. Crown; a clerical tonsure. 4. An old Spanish gold and silver coin. 5. An English silver coin. 6. Regal power, royalty. 7. Honour, splendour, ornament, decoration. 8. Laurel with which saints are crowned. 9. Rosary of seven decades offered to the Holy Virgin. 10. Circle or crowd which surrounds a person. 11. Top of the antlers of a stag. 12. Completion, reward. 13. Garland. 14. (Naút.) Pendant; a rope used on board of ships for various purposes. *Coronas de los palos*, Main-tackle pendants. *Coronas de quinales*, Preventer-shroud pendants. 15. (Naút.) Span for launching ships. 16. Glory, triumph. *Eso que se atribuye á mal, es mi corona*, The very thing I am censured for constitutes my glory. 17. (Fort.) Crown-work. 18. (Blas.) Coronet. 19. *Corona de rey*, (Bot.) Common melilot trefoil. Trifolium officinale *L.* 20. *Corona real*, (Bot.) Annual sun-flower. Helianthus annuus *L.* 21. Halo, meteor. *Corona obsidional*, Crown given to the person who compelled an enemy to raise the siege.
Coronación, *sf.* 1. Coronation. 2. The end of any work.
Coronádo, *sm.* A Roman Catholic clergyman who has received the tonsure.
Coronadór, ra, *s.* 1. Crowner. 2. Finisher.
Coronál, *a.* (Anat.) Coronal, belonging to the crown of the head.
Coronaménto y Coronamiénto, *sm.* 1. Ornament placed on the top of a building. 2. (Ant.) Coronation. 3. (Naút.) Taffarel or taffrail; the uppermost part of a ship's stern, generally ornamented with sculpture.
Coronár, *va.* 1. To invest with the crown, or regal and imperial ornament. 2. (Met.) To complete, to perfect, to finish. 3. (Met.) To ornament or decorate the top of a building. 4. To fill a glass up to the brim.
Coronária, *sf.* 1. Vein or artery, fancied to encompass the heart. 2. Crown-wheel of a watch.
Coronário, ria, *a.* 1. Relating to a crown. 2. Extremely refined; applied to gold.
Coronděl, *sm.* 1. (Impr.) Riglet; a ledge of wood by which printers separate their lines or divide their pages into columns. 2. Water-mark, transparent line left in paper by the thicker wires of the mould.
Coronél, *sm.* 1. Colonel; the chief commander of a regiment. 2. (Blas.) Crown.
Coronéla, *sf.* 1. Company of which the colonel is captain. 2. Colonel's lady.
Coronelía, *sf.* A colonel's commission. V. *Regimiento.*
Coronica, lla, y ta, *sf.* A little crown.
Corónica, *sf.* V. *Crónica.*
Corónilla, *sf.* 1. Crown, or top of the head. 2. *Coronilla real.* 3. Among bell-founders, the ear by which a bell is suspended.
Coronista, *sm.* Chronicler. V. *Cronista.*
Coróza, *sf.* Coronet made of strong paper or pasteboard, and worn as a mark of infamy, by those on whom any punishment is inflicted.

Corózo, *sm.* (Bot.) A species of high palm-tree in Africa and America. Elais guineensis *L.*
Corpanchón y Corpázo, *sm.* A very big body or carcass. *Corpanchon de ave*, Carcass of a fowl stripped of its flesh.
Corpecíto, co, llo, y Corpezuélo, *sm.* A little or small body, or carcass.
Corpezuélo, *sm.* An under waistcoat without sleeves or skirts.
Corpíño y Corpiñéjo, *sm.* A little or small body, or carcass.
Córpo, *sm.* V. *Cuerpo.*
Corporál, *a.* Corporal, belonging to the body. *Castigo corporal*, Corporal punishment.
Corporáles, *sm. pl.* Altar linen, on which the communion bread and wine are put to be consecrated.
Corporalidád, *sf.* 1. Corporality, the quality of being embodied. 2. Any corporeal substance.
Corporalménte, *ad.* Corporally, bodily.
Corporeidád, *sf.* Corporeity, corporeality.
Corpóreo, rea, *a.* Corporeal, consisting of matter or body; opposed to spiritual or immaterial.
Corporiénto, ta, *a.* V. *Corpulento.*
Corps, *sm.* (A French term, implying body) Corps, body. *Las guardias de corps*, The life-guards. *Sumiller de corps*, Lord Chamberlain
Corpúdo, da, *a.* Corpulent, bulky.
Corpuléncia, *sf.* Corpulence, or corpulency.
Corpulénto, ta, *a.* Corpulent, bulky, fleshy.
Córpus, *sm.* Corpus Christi day, or the procession held on that day in Roman Catholic countries.
Corpusculár, *a.* Corpuscular, relating to atoms.
Corpusculísta, *sm.* Atomist, one that holds the atomical or corpuscular system.
Corpúsculo, *sm.* Corpuscle, atom.
Corragéro, *sm.* Harness-maker. V. *Guarnicionero.*
Corrál, *sm.* 1. Yard, enclosed ground adjoining to a house. 2. Court, open space before a house. 3. Fish-pond. 4. Pit in play-houses. 5. Blank left in writing. *Corral de ovejas o vacas*, Ruins, fragments of walls, a place devastated. 6. (Ant.) Square formed by a body of foot. 7. *Corral de madera*, Timber-yard. 8. *Corral de ganado*, (Naút.) Place where cattle are kept on board a ship. *Hacer corrales*, (Met.) To loiter about in school or business hours.
Corraléro, *sm.* Keeper of a dung-yard.
Corralíllo y to, *sm.* A small yard.
Corralíza, *sf.* Yard, court.
Corréa, *sf.* 1. Leather strap or thong. 2. (Among Saddlers) Strap which fastens the holsters to the saddle. 3. Flexibility or extension of any thing. *Besar la correa* (Met.) To be obliged to humble one's self to another. *Tener correa*, To bear wit or raillery without irritation; not to be thin-skinned.
Correáge, *sm.* Heap of leather straps or thongs.
Correál, *sm.* Deer skin dressed of a brown colour. *Coser correal, ó labrar de correal*, To sew with small leather thongs instead of thread.
Correár, *va.* To draw out wool, and prepare it for use.
Corrección, *sf.* 1. Correction, reprehension, animadversion. 2. Act of taking away faults,

amendment. 3. (Naút.) Correction made in a ship's reckoning by means of observation.

Correctaménte, *ad.* Correctly.

Correctívo, va, *a.* Corrective; having the power to alter or obviate any bad qualities.

Correctívo, *sm.* Corrective; that which has the power of altering or correcting.

Corrécto, ta, *a.* Exact, conformable to the rules.

Correctór, *sm.* 1. Corrector, amender. 2. Reviser or reader of proof sheets. 3. Superior or abbot in the convents of St. Francis de Paula. 4. Usher, who punishes boys for faults committed in schools.

Corredentór, ra, *s.* One who ransoms or redeems from captivity, jointly with another.

Corredéra, *sf.* 1. Race-ground, on which a horse-race is run. 2. A small wicket or back-door. 3. Runner or upper grinding-stone in a corn-mill. 4. Street. *La corredera de S. Pablo en Madrid*, St. Paul's-street in Madrid. 5. Pimp, procuress. 6. (Naút.) Log; a small triangular bit of board fastened to a line, to make an estimate of the ship's way. *Echar la corredera*, To heave the lead. *Carretel de la corredera*, Log-reel. 7. (In Glass-houses) Roller; a metal cylinder for rolling plate-glass. 8. Wood-louse. V. *Cucaracha*.

Corredéro, ra, *a.* (Ant.) Running much, moving about.

Corredílla, *sf.* A small course.

Corredízo, za, *a.* Easy to be untied, like a running knot.

Corredór, ra, *s.* 1. Runner, one who runs about a great deal. 2. Race-horse. 3. Corridor; a gallery round about a building, which leads to several rooms. 4. (Fort.) Covert-way, lying round a fortress. 5. Broker, one who does business for another with regard to all sorts of purchases and sales. *Corredor de cambios*, Exchange-broker. *Corredor de matrimonios*, Match-maker. *Corredor de oreja*, Exchange-broker. (Met.) Tale-bearer; pimp. 6. Pimp, procurer, procuress. 7. *Corredor de popa*, (Naút.) Balcony, or stern gallery of a ship. 8. (Arag.) Public crier.

Corredorcíllo, *sm.* A small corridor.

Corredóra, *sf.* 1. Liquor which flows over the brim of a vessel with which liquids are measured. 2. Incursion into an enemy's country.

Correduría, *sf.* 1. Trade and business of a broker; brokerage. 2. (Met.) Trade of pimping or pandering. 3. Incursion. 4. Mulct, fine, penalty.

Correería, *sf.* Trade of a strap-maker.

Correéro, *sm.* Strap-maker.

Corregél, *a.* Relating to English sole-leather, or other leather made in imitation of it.

Corregibilidád, *sf.* The quality of being corrigible.

Corregíble, *a.* Corrigible, docile.

Corregidór, *sm.* 1. Corrector, one who punishes and corrects. 2. Lord Mayor; magistrate in Spain, who administers justice in his district in the king's name.

Corregidóra, *sf.* Wife of a *corregidor*.

Corregimiénto, *sm.* The place, office, and district of a *corregidor*.

Corregír, *va.* 1. To correct, to punish. 2. To reprehend, to admonish. 3. To temper, to mitigate. 4. (Ant.) To adorn, to embellish.

Correhuéla, *sf.* 1. A small strap or thong. 2. Play used by boys with a stick and small strap. 3. (Bot.) Bind-weed. Convolvulus arvensis *L.*

Correlación, *sf.* Reciprocal relation, analogy.

Correlativaménte, *ad.* Correlatively.

Correlatívo, va, y Correláto, ta, *a.* Correlative; having a reciprocal relation

Corréncia, *sf.* Looseness, diarrhœa.

Correndílla, *sf.* Incursion. V. *Correría*.

Correntía, *sf.* (Arag.) An artificial irrigation of stubble ground, to make the stalks rot, and convert them into dung.

Correntiár, *va.* (Arag.) To irrigate stubble-ground.

Correntío, tia, *a.* Current, running; applied to fluids.

Correntón, na, *a.* 1. Gay, fond of company, pleasant, cheerful. 2. Taking a great deal of snuff.

Corréo, *sm.* 1. Post-boy, who carries letters from one place to another. *Correo de gabinete*, A king's messenger, state-messenger. 2. Post-office. 3. Mail or bag of letters. *Correo marítimo*, Packet-boat. *Correo mayor*, Post-master. 4. (For.) Accomplice.

Correón, *sm.* A large leather strap.

Corredóso, sa, *a.* Ductile, easily extended without breaking, easily bent.

Corrér, *vn.* 1. To run, to move swiftly, to move at a quick pace. 2. To run, flow, or stream; applied to liquids. 3. To blow; applied to the wind. 4. To run, to pass away; such as time and life. 5. To hasten to put any thing in execution. 6. To solicit one's protection. 7. (Met.) To take the proper course, to pass through the proper channel; applied to business. 8. To snatch away. 9. To persecute. 10. To extend, to expand. 11. To put one to the blush. 12. To arrive, to come to the fixed time for paying any thing. 13. To receive, to admit any thing. 14. To flourish, to prevail for the time. 15. To tend, to guard, or take care of any thing. *Correr los mares*, (Naút.) To frequent the seas, to lead a mariner's life. *Correr á bolina ó á la trinca*, (Naút.) To run close upon a wind. *Correr del otro bordo*, To stand on the other tack. *Correr por bordos, ó bordear*, To ply to windward. *Correr hacia la tierra*, To stand in shore. *Correr norte*, To stand to the northward. *Correr en el mismo rumbo*, To stand onward in the same course. *Correr á dos puños*, To run before the wind. *Correr viento en popa*, To sail before the wind. *Correr sobre un baxel*, To chase a vessel, to fall down upon a vessel. *Correr la cortina*, To draw the curtain; to discover any thing; to conceal or quash. *Correr á rienda suelta*, To ride full speed; (Met.) To give a loose to one's passions. *Corre la voz*, It is reported, the story goes. *Correr monte*, To hunt. *Correr vaquetas*, To run the gantlet. *A' mas correr, á todo correr*, As swiftly as possible. *Correrse*, To be ashamed or confused.

Correría, *sf.* 1. An hostile incursion. 2. Leather strap.

Correspondéncia, *sf.* 1. Correspondence, relation, reciprocal adaptation of one thing to another. 2. Intercourse, reciprocal intelligence. 3. Friendship, interchange of offices or civilities. 4. Proportion, symmetry, congruity.

Corresponder, va. To return a favour, to make a suitable return.—vn. 1. To correspond, to answer, to fit, to suit, to belong to, to regard. 2. To agree, to be congruent.—vr. 1. To communicate with another by letters. 2. To respect or esteem each other.

Correspondiente, a. Correspondent, conformable, agreeable, suitable.

Correspondiente, sm. 1. Correspondent, one with whom intelligence or commerce is kept up by mutual messages or letters. 2. One who deals or traffics with another that resides in a different place.

Correspondientemente, ad. Correspondently.

Corresponsal, sm. V. *Correspondiente.*

Corresponsion, sf. Conformity, proportion, congruity.

Corretage, sm. 1. Brokerage, money paid to a broker for making sales or purchases. 2. Money paid to a pimp or procurer.

Corretear, vn. To walk the streets, to rove, to ramble.

Corretera, sf. A gadding woman, who runs from house to house, without attending to any business.

Corretero, sm. Gadder; one that runs much abroad without business.

Correτora, sf. In convents, the nun who directs the choir.

Correvedile, sm. 1. Tale-bearer, mischief-maker. 2. Procurer, pimp.

Correyuela, sf. V. *Corregüela.*

Corricorriendo, ad. In haste, at full speed.

Corrida, sf. 1. Course, race, career. 2. Incursion. 3. *Corrida de toros,* Bull-baiting. 4. Flow or movement of any liquid. *De corrida,* At full speed, swiftly, in haste.

Corridamente, ad. Currently, easily, plainly.

Corrido, sm. Romance; a merry song, accompanied with a guitar, in the *fandango* style. *Corridos,* Rents due and not paid. V. *Caidos.*

Corrido, da, a. Expert, experienced, artful; abashed.

Corriente, sm. 1. Stream, current, *El giro de los corrientes,* The setting in of currents. 2. Course or despatch of business.

Corriente, a. 1. Current, plain, easy. 2. According to custom. 3. Fluent; applied to the style. 4. Current, running. *Moneda corriente,* Current coin. [ly.

Corrientemente, ad. Currently, easily, plainly.

Corregir, va. V. *Corregir.*

Corrillero, sm. Braggadocio, a puffing, boasting fellow.

Corrillo, sm. Circle or private assembly, where people meet to talk of the news of the day, and censure the conduct of others.

Corrimiento, sm. 1. (Met.) Shame, bashfulness. 2. An acrid humour which affects any part of the body. 3. (Ant.) Concourse, act of assembling. 4. Act of running, course, or flow of waters. 5. (Ant.) V. *Correria.*

Corrincho, sm. Meeting of low vulgar people.

Corro, sm. 1. Circle, or ring, formed by people who meet to talk or see a show. *Escupir en corro,* To drop in the course of conversation. *Hacer corro,* To clear the way, to make room. 2. Sort of dance.

Corroboracion, sf. Corroboration; the act of strengthening or confirming.

Corroborante, a. y s. Corroborative; having the power of increasing strength.

Corroborar, va. 1. To corroborate, to strengthen, to confirm. 2. (Met.) To give new force to an argument or opinion.

Corrobra, sf. Treat or entertainment given at the conclusion of a bargain or contract.

Corroer, va. To corrode, to eat away by degrees. [or vitiates.

Corrompedor, ra, s. Corrupter; one that taints

Corromper, va. 1. To corrupt, to vitiate; to alter the form of a thing. 2. To seduce a woman. 3. To bribe, to suborn; to procure by secret collusion or indirect means.—vn. To stink, to emit an offensive smell.—vr. To rot, to grow putrid.

Corrompible, a. V. *Corruptible.*

Corrompidamente, ad. Corruptly, viciously.

Corrompimiento, sm. 1. Corruption, depravation, depravity. 2. Bribery. V. *Corrupcion.*

Corrosion, sf. Corrosion; the act of corroding.

Corrosivo, va, a. Corrosive; having the power of gnawing or wearing away.

Corroyente, pa. Corroding, that which corrodes. [acutifolius L.

Corruda, sf. (Bot.) Sparrow-grass. Asparagus

Corrugacion, sf. Corrugation; contraction into wrinkles.

Corrugar, va. V. *Arrugar.*

Corrugo, sm. Channel to convey water from a river.

Corrulla, sf. (Naút.) Room under deck in a row-galley.

Corrumper y Corrumpir, va. V. *Corromper.*

Corrupcion, sf. 1. Corruption, putrefaction. 2. A spurious alteration in a book or writing. 3. Looseness or flux of the belly. 4. (Ant.) Destruction. 5. Depravity, depravation or perversion of manners or principles.

Corruptamente, ad. Corruptly, viciously.

Corruptela, sf. 1. Corruption, depravation. 2. Bad habit or practice, contrary to law.

Corruptibilidad, sf. Corruptibility, possibility to be corrupted.

Corruptible, a. Corruptible, susceptible of corruption.

Corruptivo, va, a. Corruptive; having the quality of corrupting, tainting, or vitiating.

Corrupto, ta, a. Corrupted; defiled; perverse.

Corruptor, sm. Corrupter; one who taints or vitiates.

Corrusco, sm. Offal, broken bread.

Corrusion, sf. V. *Corrosion.*

Corsa, sf. (Naút.) A coasting voyage, a cruise.

Corsario, sm. The commander of a cruiser or privateer.

Corsario, ria, a. Cruising; applied to a privateer or letter of marque, authorised to cruise against the enemy.

Corsé, sm. Jumps; limber stays worn by ladies.

Corsear, va. To cruise against the enemy.

Corsia, sf. Passage between the sails in a row-galley.

Córso, *sm.* 1. Cruise; cruising against the enemy. 2. (Ant.) Career. V. *Carrera.*
Córso, sa, *a.* V. *Corzo.*
Córta, *sf.* Felling; the act of cutting down wood. *A' la corta ó á la larga,* Sooner or later, late or early.
Cortabólsas, *sm.* Pick-pocket, or pick-purse, filcher, petty robber.
Cortadéra, *sf.* 1. Chisel for cutting hot iron. 2. Knife or instrument used by bee-keepers to cut out the honey-combs.
Cortadíllo, *sm.* 1. A small drinking-glass, a tumbler. 2. Bombast, fustian.
Cortádo, *sm.* Caper; a leap or jump in dancing.
Cortádo, da, *a.* Adapted, proportioned, accommodated.
Cortadór, ra, *a.* That which cuts.
Cortadór, *sm.* 1. Butcher. V. *Carnicero.* 2. (Ant.) The king's carver. *Cortadóres,* Cutters, incisors, the teeth in the forepart of the mouth which cut the meat.
Cortadoras, *sf. pl.* Cutting-boards in a velvet [loom.
Cortadúra, *sf.* 1. Fissure, or scissure; a cut or notch made in a solid body by a cutting-instrument. 2. (Fort.) Parapet with embrasures and merlons, made in a breach to prevent the enemy from taking possession of it. 3. (Fort.) Work raised in narrow passes to defend them. *Cortadúras,* Shreds of cloth, cuttings of paper, parings: Figures cut out in paper.
Cortafrío, *sm.* A chisel for cutting cold iron.
Cortafuégo, *sm.* A thick wall, in Spain, raised between the roofs of adjoining houses, to prevent a fire from spreading and communicating to neighbouring buildings.
Cortaménte, *ad.* Sparingly, frugally, scantily.
Cortamiénto, *sm.* The act of cutting, or amputating.
Cortán, *sm.* 1. (Catal.) Measure for grain, containing about a peck. 2. Oil-measure, containing 8lbs. 5oz.
Cortánte, *sm.* Cutter, butcher.
Cortánte, *a.* Cutting, that which cuts.
Cortapícos y callares, Hold your prating. V. *Callares.*
Cortapiés, *sm.* Thrust made at the legs in [fencing.
Cortapísa, *sf.* 1. (Ant.) Ornament sewed round the borders of cloths. 2. Elegance and grace with which any thing is said. 3. Condition or restriction with which any thing is given.
Cortaplúmas, *sm.* Pen-knife.
Cortár, *va.* 1. To cut, to divide with the edge of an instrument. 2. To disjoin, to separate. 3. (Mil.) To cut off part of the enemy's army. 4. To interrupt or stop the course of things. 5. To interrupt a conversation. 6. To abridge or abbreviate a speech or discourse. 7. To smother bees. 8. To suspend, to restrain, to keep back. *Cortar el agua,* To cut off the water: (Met.) To navigate or sail through water. 9. To arbitrate, to decide. 10. To cut figures in paper. 11. (Naút.) To cut away a mast or cable. *Cortar la lengua,* To speak a language with propriety and elegance. *Cortar las libranzas,* To stop the payment for goods received. *Cortar de vestir,* To cut and make clothes; (Met.) To murmur or speak evil of any one. *Ayre que corta,* A cutting, piercing, or nipping wind.—*vr.* 1. To be daunted, ashamed, or confounded; not to know what to say. *Cortarse las uñas con alguno,* To pick a quarrel with any one. 2. To open out the folds or wrinkles in cloths. 3. (Ant.) To ransom.
Córte, *sf.* 1. Edge of a sword, knife, or any other cutting instrument. *Ingenio de corte,* A cutting engine. 2. Scissure, cut; the effect of a cutting instrument. 3. Felling of trees. 4. Mediation or reconciliation of persons at variance. 5. Resident town, the place where the sovereign resides. 6. Ministers and other officers of state who compose a court. 7. A subordinate court of chancery in Castile. 8. Retinue, suite. 9. Yard, court. 10. Stable for cattle. 11. Measure or step taken in an affair. 12. Art of pleasing, civility, flattery. *Hacer corte,* To court, to flatter, to endeavour to please. *Hacer la corte,* To attend the levees of the sovereign, or of men in power. 13. (Ant.) District of 5 leagues round the court. *Córtes,* The states of the realm, composed of the clergy, nobility, and solicitors or deputies of cities, or towns; also the assembly of the states.
Cortecíca, Cortecílla, y Cortecíta, *sf.* A small crust.
Cortedád, *sf.* 1. Smallness, littleness, want of bulk. 2. Dulness, stupidity, want of intellect 3. Pusillanimity, timidity; a want of courage and spirit. *Cortedad de medios,* Poverty, indigence, want of means or resources.
Cortéga, *sf.* (Orn.) Hazel-grouse, hazel-hen. Tetrao bonasia *L.*
Cortejadór, *sm.* Wooer; one who courts or makes love to a woman.
Cortejánte, *pa.* Courting; courtier, he who makes love.
Cortejár, *va.* 1. To court, to pay homage. 2. To accompany, to assist another. *Cortejar una dama,* To pay one's addresses to a lady.
Cortéjo, *sm.* 1. Court, homage paid to another. 2. Gift, present, gratification. 3. Gallant, wooer. 4. Lady courted or sued for love.
Cortés, *a.* Courteous, gentle, mild, civil.
Cortesanaménte, *ad.* Courteously, gently, politely.
Cortesanázo, za, *a.* Awkwardly or fulsomely civil.
Cortesanía, *sf.* Courtesy, civility, politeness, complaisance.
Cortesáno, na, *a.* 1. Court-like; belonging or relating to the court. 2. Courteous, gentle, mild. *Dama cortesana,* Courtesan, or courtezan; a woman of the town, a prostitute.
Cortesáno, *sm.* Courtier; one that frequents or attends the courts of kings or princes.
Cortesía, *sf.* 1. Courtesy, an act of civility and respect. 2. Compliment, an expression of civility in the epistolary style. 3. Gift, present gratifications. 4. Days of grace allowed by custom for the payment of a bill of exchange, after the same becomes due. 5. Mercy, favour. 6. Abatement.
Cortesménte, *ad.* Courteously.
Cortéza, *sf.* 1. Bark, the exterior part of a tree. 2. The outside covering of vegetables. 3. A wild fowl of the family of widgeons. 4.

(Met.) Outward appearance of things. 5. (Met.) Rusticity, want of civility and politeness.

Cortezón, *sm.* Thick bark or rind.

Cortezoncíto, *sm.* Thin bark or rind.

Cortezúdo, da, *a.* 1. Having a strong rough bark. 2. Rustic, unmannerly, unpolished.

Cortezuéla, *sf.* Thin bark or rind.

Cortíco, ca, *a.* Somewhat short.

Cortíjo, *sm.* Farm-house.

Cortína, *sf.* 1. Curtain; a cloth hung before doors, windows, beds, &c. 2. (Fort.) Curtain; that part of a wall or rampart which lies between two bastions. 3. Any veil or covering.

Cortináge, *sm.* Sortment or set of curtains for a house.

Cortinál, *sm.* A piece of ground near a village or farm-house, which is generally sown every year.

Cortinón, *sm.* A large curtain to keep out the air.

Cortír, *va.* (Ant.) V. *Curtir.*

Córto, ta, *a.* 1. Short, not long space or extent, scanty. 2. Small, little. 3. Short, not of long duration. 4. (Met.) Dull, stupid, weak of intellect. 5. (Met.) Timid, pusillanimous. 6. (Met.) Short of words, 7. Imperfect, defective. *Corto de vista,* Short-sighted. *Corto de oido,* Hard of hearing. *Corto de manos,* Slow at work, not handy, not dexterous. *A' la corta ó á la larga,* Sooner or later. *Corta pala,* (Vulg.) Unskilful, without knowledge or address. *Corto sastre,* (Met.) Ignorant of any subject discussed.

Cortón, *sm.* 1. Worm, ring-worm which destroys plants in gardens. 2. Field-mouse. Mus sylvaticus *L.*

Corúlla, *sf.* In galleys, place for the stoppers of cables.

Coruscánte y Corúsco, ca, *a.* (Poét.) Coruscant, glittering by flashes, brilliant.

Córva, *sf.* 1. Joint of the knee which bends inside. 2. Curb; a disease in horses.

Corvadúra, *sf.* 1. Curvature, crookedness, inflexion. 2. Bend of an arch or vault.

Corvál, *a.* Of an oblong shape; applied to olives.

Corvár, *va.* To bend. V. *Encorvar.*

Corváto, *sm.* A young crow or rook.

Corváza, *sf.* Curb; a disease in horses' knees.

Corvecíto, *sm.* A young little crow or rook.

Corvedád, *sf.* V. *Corvadura.*

Corvejón, *sm.* 1. Joint of the hind leg of beasts. 2. Spur of a cock. 3. (Orn.) Cormorant or corvorant; a large sea-fowl. Pelecanus carbo *L.*

Corvéta, *sf.* 1. Curvet, leap or bound of a horse in high mettle. 2. (Naút.) Corvette, sloop of war.

Corveteár, *vn.* To curvet, to bound, to leap.

Corvíllo, *sm.* 1. Bill, a kind of hatchet with a hooked point. 2. *Corvillo de podon,* Pruning-knife. 3. *Corvillo de zapatero,* A shoemaker's paring-knife. 4. *Miercoles corvillo,* Ash-Wednesday.

Corvína, *sf.* (Ict.) A kind of conger or sea-eel in the Mediterranean. Sciæna lepisma *L.*

Corvíno, na, *a.* (Ant.) Rook-like, belonging to a rook.

Córvo, va, *a.* Bent, crooked, arched.

Córvo, *sm.* 1. (Ict.) Craw-fish; a kind of sea-fish. 2. Pot-hook.

Córzo, za, *s.* Roe-deer. Cervus capreolus *L.*

Corzuélo, *sm.* Wheat which has been left in the husks by the threshers.

Cósa, *sf.* 1. Thing, substance; that which has being or existence. *Cosa de risa ó cosa ridicula,* Laughing-stock. *Cosa de ver,* A thing worth seeing. *Fuerte cosa,* A hard task. *No es cosa,* It does not matter, it is a trifle. *No hay tal cosa, ó no es asi,* No such thing. *No vale cosa,* It is not worth a rush. 2. Suit, cause.

Cósa de, *ad.* About, little more or less. *Cosa de media legua,* Half a league more or less. *¿Que cosa?* What's the matter? *¿Que es cosa y cosa, ó cosicosa?* What means all this?

Cosário, *sm.* 1. Privateer, corsair, pirate. V. *Corsario.* 2. Carrier; one who carries goods from one place to another. 3. Huntsman by profession. 4. One who is accustomed or in the habit of doing any thing.

Cosário, ria, *a.* 1. Belonging or relating to privateers or corsairs. 2. Beaten, frequented; applied to roads.

Coscaróna, *sf.* Cracknel; a hard crisp cake.

Coscárse, *vr.* V. *Concomerse.*

Coscója, *sf.* 1. (Bot.) Kermes, or scarlet-oak. Quercus coccifera *L.* 2. Dry leaves of the kermes oak. 3. Ring or knob on the cross-bit of a bridle.

Coscojál ó Coscojár, *sm.* Plantation of kermes or scarlet-oaks.

Coscójo, *sm.* Scarlet or kermes grain, after the worm or insect (Coccus ilicis *L.*) has left it. *Coscójos,* Round bits of iron, which compose a chain that is fastened to the mouth-piece of the bridle of a horse.

Coscorrón, *sm.* 1. Contusion; a knock, blow, or bruise, without any effusion of blood. 2. Bruise in a loaf.

Coscorrúdo, *a.* Bruised, contused.

Coscúrro, *sm.* Flat loaf.

Cóse, *sf.* Kind of measure.

Cosécha, *sf.* 1. Crop; the corn gathered off a field. 2. Harvest-time; the season of reaping and gathering the corn and other fruits of the earth. 3. Act of gathering and inning the harvest. 4. (Met.) Collection of immaterial things, as virtues, vices. *De sú cosécha,* Of one's own invention.

Cosechéro, *sm.* Farmer; one who cultivates his own or hired ground.

Cosedéros de los tablónes, *sm. pl.* (Naút.) Plank seams.

Cosedízo, za, *a.* That which can or must be stitched or sewed.

Cosedúra, *sf.* 1. Seam. 2. (Naút.) Seizing, or seising a line, which serves to fasten two ropes or block-straps together.

Coseléte, *sm.* 1. Ancient coat of armour, which covered the whole body. 2. A light corslet. 3. Pikeman, anciently armed with a corslet.

Cosér, *sm.* (Ant.) Draught-horse used in war and tournaments.

Cosér, *va.* 1. To sew, to join by threads drawn with a needle. 2. To join and unite things. *Coser un moton,* (Naút.) To lash or seize a block. *Coserse con la pared,* To stick close to a wall. *Coser á puñaladas*, (Fam.) To strike with the fist.

Coséra, *sf.* Piece of ground which can be irrigated at once.

Cosetáda, *sf.* Race; a violent course or speedy run.

Cosetreár, *va.* V. *Corretear*.

Cosíble, *a.* That which may be sewed.

Cosíca, Cosílla, Cosíta, *sf.* A small thing, a trifle.

Cosicósa, *sf.* V. *Quisicosa*.

Cosído, *sm.* 1. Foul linen stitched together and given to be washed. 2. Horse jaded and grown thin in consequence of hard labour. *Cosido de cama*, Quilt and blankets of a bed stitched together to prevent their separation.

Cosidúras, *sf. pl.* (Naút.) Lashings; ends of ropes used on board of ships to secure moveable things.

Cosigo, *pron.* (Ant.) V. *Consigo*.

Cosmogonía, *sf.* Cosmogony; the science of the formation of the world.

Cosmografía, *sf.* Cosmography, a description of the world.

Cosmográfico, ca, *a.* Cosmographical.

Cosmógrafo, *sm.* Cosmographer, one who writes a description of the world.

Cosmología, *sf.* Cosmology; the science of the laws of nature, or of the natural world.

Cosmopólito, *sm.* Cosmopolite, a citizen of the world.

Cóso, *sm.* 1. Place or square where bulls are fought, or other public entertainments given. 2. Worm which lodges in the trunks of some fruit trees. 3. (Ant.) Course, career.

Cosquíllas, *sf. pl.* 1. Titillation; a pleasing sensation from the gentle touch of some part of the body; tickling. 2. (Ant.) Discord, disagreement, opposition. *Hacer cosquillas alguna cosa*, (Met.) To be tickled by any thing; to excite desire and curiosity. *No consentir cosquillas*, (Met.) To understand or suffer no jokes. *Tener malas cosquillas*, (Met.) To be petulant, impudent, or saucy.

Cosquilloso, sa, *a.* 1. Ticklish, sensible to titillation, easily tickled. 2. Peevish, easily offended.

Cósta, *sf.* 1. Cost, the price paid for any thing. *A' toda costa*, At all hazards, at all events. 2. Expense or charges of a law-suit. *Condenar en costas*, To sentence any party to pay the costs of a suit. 3. (Met.) Labour, expense, fatigue. *A' costa de*, At the expense of. 4. Coast, the land next the sea; the shore. 5. Wedge used by shoemakers to stretch shoes on the last. *Dar á la costa ó en la costa*, To get on shore. *Arrimado á la costa*, Close in shore. *Costa de sotavento*, Lee-shore. *Ir ó navegar costa á costa*, To coast, to sail along the coast.

Costádo, *sm.* 1. Side, the lateral part of animals fortified by the ribs. 2. (Mil.) Flank of a body of troops. 3. Hind or back part. 4. Side of a ship. *Presentar el costado á un enemigo*, To bring the broadside to bear upon an enemy's ship. *Navio de costado derecho*, A wall-sided ship. *Navio de costado falso*, A lap-sided ship. *Dar el costado al navio*, To heave down a ship. *Costádos*, Race, lineage, succession of ancestors. *Arbol de costados*, Genealogical tree.

Costál, *sm.* 1. Sack or large bag. 2. Rammer, or beetle, to beat or press close the earth of a mud-wall or rampart. *No soy costal*, (Fam.) I cannot tell all at once.

Costaláda, *sf.* A fall flat on the ground.

Costalázo, *sm.* 1. Blow or stroke with a sack. 2. A very large sack. *Dar un costalazo*, To fall flat on the ground, like a sack.

Costaléro, *sm.* Porter, who carries goods from one place to another.

Costalíco, íllo, y íto, *sm.* A small sack.

Costanéras, *sf. pl.* (In Building) Rafters, timbers let into the great beam.

Costanéro, ra, *a.* Declivous, inclining downwards.

Costanílla, *sf.* (Dim.) Gentle declivity; little side of a small hill.

Costár, *vn.* 1. To cost, to be bought for, to be had at a price. *Me cuesta tanto*, It stands me in so much. 2. To suffer detriment or loss. *Costar la torta un pan*, (Fam.) The sprat cost a herring.

Cóste, *sm.* V. *Costa*. *A' coste y costas*, At first or prime cost.

Costeadór, *sm.* (Naút.) Coaster; a coasting vessel.

Costeár, *va.* 1. To pay the cost, to bear all charges. 2. To deduct all charges of what is to be sold again. 3. (Naút.) To coast, to sail along the coast.

Costelación, *sf.* V. *Constelación*.

Costéra, *sf.* 1. Side of a bale of goods. 2. A fisherman's basket, wide at the bottom, and narrow at the mouth. 3. (Mil.) Flank of a body of troops. 4. (Ant.) Sea-coast, shore. 5. Outside quire of a ream of paper.

Costéro, *sm.* First plank cut from a pine tree.

Costéro, ra, *a.* 1. Outward. *Papel costero*, Outside quires. 2. Oblique; applied to a cannon-shot or a declivity.

Costezuéla, *sf.* Slight declivity or coast.

Costílla, *sf.* 1. Rib; a side bone of the body, which goes from the spine to the breast. 2. Property, wealth. 3. Stave, the board of a barrel. 4. Furr, a piece of timber which serves to strengthen joists. 5. The triangled part of organ-bellows. 6. (Met.) Property, support. *Hacer costilla*, To bear the brunt. *Costillas de un navio*, (Naút.) Ribs of a ship. *Costillas*, Shoulders, back.

Costilláge y Costillár, *sm.* 1. The whole of the ribs, and their place in the body. 2. The ribs in a flitch of bacon. 3. (Naút.) The timbers or whole frame of a ship.

Costillér, *sm.* Gentleman of the bed chamber.

Costillíca ó Costillíta, *sf.* A small rib.

Costillúdo, da, *a.* 1. Broad-shouldered. 2. Clownish, unmannerly.

Costíno, na, *a.* Belonging to the costus-root, which is stomachic and diuretic.

Cósto, *sm.* 1. Cost, price. 2. Charges, expense. 3. Costus-root. *A' costo y costas*, At prime cost.

Costúmbre, *sf.* V. *Costumbre*.

Costosaménte, *ad.* Costly, at a high price.

Costóso, sa, *a.* 1. Costly, dear, expensive. 2. (Met.) Dear, difficult to be obtained.

Córtra, sf. 1. Crust; the incrusted excrescence which grows on the surface of any thing. 2. Crust of a conserve; the unpolished superficies of glass. 3. Broken biscuit given to the people who serve on board of galleys.
Costráda, sf. Seed-cake, candied with melted sugar, beaten eggs, and grated bread.
Costreñír y Costriñír, va. V. *Constreñir*.
Costribación, sf. V. *Estreñimiento*.
Costribár, va. To indurate, to harden; to make strong.
Costrílla, sf. A little crust.
Costringimiénto, sm. Constraint.
Costringír, va. To constrain, to compel.
Costriñiénte, pa. Constringing.
Costrívo, sm. V. *Apoyo*.
Costróso, sa, a. Crusty, covered with a crust.
Costruír, va. To construct. V. *Construir*.
Costumádo, da, a. (Ant.) Accustomed to any thing.
Costumbrár, va. (Ant.) V. *Acostumbrar*.
Costúmbre, sm. 1. Custom, habit, habitual practice. 2. Custom, a law which has not been written or proclaimed, but which has obtained force by usage. 3. Custom, the common way of acting. 4. Periodical indisposition of women, catamenia. *Costumbres*, Customs, the characteristic manners and habits of a nation.
Costúme, sf. (Ant.) V. *Costumbre*.
Costúra, sf. 1. Seam, the union of two pieces joined together. 2. Needle-work on linen cloth. 3. (Naút.) Splicing of a rope, or uniting the two ends of it. *Costuras de los tablones de un navio*, (Naút.) The seams of the planks of a ship. *Costuras abiertas*, Seams of a ship from which the oakum has been worked or washed out.
Costuréra, sf. Seamstress, a woman who lives by needle-work.
Costuréro, sm. Tailor. V. *Sastre*.
Costurón, sm. 1. Seam, a coarse suture which joins two edges together. 2. A large scar.
Córa, sf. 1. Coat of mail, a kind of armour formerly worn in battle. 2. Coat of arms, formerly worn by the kings at arms in public functions. 3. Jacket. 4. A marginal note, annotation. 5. Quota, a share assigned to each. 6. The back and callous part of a boar's hide. 7. (And.) Mary, a woman's name.
Cotána, sf. Mortise, a hole cut in timber that another piece may be put into it.
Cotánza, sf. Sort of linen made at Coutance, in Britanny.
Cotár, va. V. *Acotar*.
Cotarréra, sf. A gadding woman that runs about without any business.
Cotárro, sm. Charity-hut for the reception of beggars.
Coteár, va. (Ant.) To enclose. V. *Acotar*.
Cotejár, va. To compare one thing with another, to confront.
Cotéjo y Cotejamiénto, sm. Comparison, the act of comparing things.
Cotí, sm. 1. Sort of linen manufactured at Coty. 2. Ticking used for mattresses.
Cotidianaménte, ad. Daily.
Cotidiáno, na, a. Daily, each day.

Cotílla, sf. Stays, a kind of stiff waistcoat worn by ladies.
Cotilléro, sm. Stay-maker.
Cotín, sm. 1. A back stroke given in the a[ir]. 2. Ticking, a strong striped linen for bedding.
Cotíza, sf. (Blas.) Band of a shield only one third the ordinary breadth.
Cotizádo, da, a. Banded, having bands, generally ten of alternate colours, in the field of a shield.
Córo, sm. 1. Enclosure of pasture grounds. 2. Land-mark. 3. Territory, district. 4. Combination among merchants not to sell goods under a certain fixed rate. 5. Measure of a hand-breadth. 6. (Ant.) Fine or mulct. 7. A small fresh-water fish. 8. Rate or fixed price of any thing. 9. A morbid swelling in the throat, very common in Peru.
Cotófre, sm. (Ant.) Drinking-glass.
Cotón, sm. Printed cotton. [flowered
Cotonáda, sf. Sort of cotton cloth, striped and
Cotoncíllo, sm. Button of a mostick or painter's staff, stuffed with hair and covered with leather, on which he rests his left arm when at work.
Cotonía, sf. Dimity, a sort of fine fustian.
Cotonína, sf. Sort of precious stone.
Cotórra, sf. 1. (Orn.) A parrot of the smallest kind. 2. (Orn.) Magpie. Corvus pica *L.* 3. (Met.) A loquacious woman.
Cotorréra, sf. 1. A she or hen parrot. 2. (Met.) A prattling talkative woman.
Cotrái, sm. Sort of linen manufactured at Courtray, in Flanders.
Cotrál, sm. An old ox, worn out with labour, and set to graze.
Cotúfa, sf. 1. (Bot.) Jerusalem artichoke. Helianthus tuberosus *L.* 2. Tid-bits, nice delicate food. *Pedir cotufas en el golfo*, To require things impossible. [food.
Cotuféro, ra, a. Producing tid-bits or delicate
Cotúrno, sm. Buskin, a kind of high shoe worn by the ancient actors of tragedy. *Calzar el coturno*, (Met.) To make use of pompous or high sounding language in poetry.
Couráu, sm. The name of a small vessel in the river Garonne.
Coutelína, sf. A blue or white cotton cloth which is imported from India.
Covácha, sf. A small cave or other hollow place under ground; a grot or grotto.
Covachuéla, sf. 1. A small cave or grot. 2. Office of secretary of state. *Covachuelas*, Shops kept in the vaults of the royal convent of St. Philip, in Madrid.
Covachueléro, sm. Shop-keeper who keeps a shop in the vaults under the royal convent of St. Philip, in Madrid.
Covachuelísta, sm. Clerk in one of the offices of the secretaries of state.
Covanílla y Covanílla, s. Basket with a wide mouth, used for gathering grapes.
Covezuéla y Covanílla, s. A small cave.
A' cox cox ó Á cox coxíta, ad. Lamely.
Cóxa, sf. 1. A lewd woman. 2. V. *Corva*.
Coxeár, va. 1. To limp, to walk lamely. 2. (Met.) To deviate from virtue. *Coxear del mismo pie*, To have the same defect or passion.

Coxeadúra, *sf.* V. *Coxera.*
Coxíndico, *sm.* Hip-bone.
Coxéra y Coxéz, *sf.* Lameness, the act or habit of halting or limping.
Coxíjo, *sm.* 1. Complaint of some slight or trifling injury received. 2. Grub or insect.
Coxijóso, sa, *a.* Peevish, irritable, apt to take fire.
Coxín, *sm.* 1. Cushion, a large pillow stuffed with wool or hair to sit on; formerly used instead of chairs. 2. A soft pad placed on a saddle. *Coxines de bote,* (Naút.) Boat cushions. *Coxines de cámara,* (Naút.) Cabin cushions.
Coxinéte ó Coxinillo, *sm.* A small cushion.
Coxitránco, ca, *a.* Applied by way of a nick-name to lame persons of a wicked disposition.
Coxíto, *sm.* A small grub or insect.
Cóxo, xa, *s.* 1. A lame person or beast. 2. A table or chair which does not stand firm. 3. Variable and unsettled weather.
Coxqueárse, *vr.* To be displeased with any thing.
Coxuélo, la, *a.* Somewhat lame.
Cóy, *sm.* (Naút.) Hammock, cot, a sailor's bed. *Afuera coys,* All hammocks up.
Cóya, *sf.* A very small spider of a venomous kind.
Coyícho, cha, *a.* V. *Cogido.*
Cóyma, *sf.* The price paid to the master of a gaming-house for preserving the gaming tables.
Cóyme y Coyméro, *sm.* Keeper of a gaming table, who also keeps the game and lends the players money; gamester, gambler.
Coytóso, sa, *a.* V. *Apresurado.*
Coyúnda, *sf.* 1. A strap or cord with which oxen are tied to the yoke. 2. (Met.) Dominion, power. 3. Matrimonial union.
Coyundádo, da, *a.* Tied to the yoke with a strap or cord.
Coyundílla, *sf.* A small strap or cord.
Coyuntúra, *sf.* 1. Joint, articulation or juncture of one bone with another. 2. (Met.) A fit or seasonable opportunity for doing any thing.
Coz, *sf.* 1. Kicking with the hind leg; applied to beasts. 2. Kick or blow with the foot. 3. Recoil of a gun. 4. Flowing back of a flood. 5. *Coz de mastelero,* (Naút.) Heel of a mast. *A coces,* By dint of kicking. *Tirar coces contra el aguijon,* To kick against the prick, to spurn at superiority.
Cozcúcho, *sm.* V. *Alcuzcuz.*
Crabrón, *sm.* Hornet. Vespa crabro *L.*
Cralidád, *sf.* (Ant.) V. *Claridad.*
Cralo, la, *a.* V. *Claro.*
Cráneo, *sm.* Skull, the bone which encloses the head and contains the brain.
Crápula, *sf.* Inebriation, intoxication.
Cras, *ad.* V. *Mañana.*
Crasaménte, *ad.* Grossly, rudely.
Crascitár, *vn.* To cackle, to crow, to caw.
Crasedád y Crasézа, *sf.* V. *Crasitud.*
Crasicia ó Crasície, *sf.* Grease, fat.
Crasiénto, ta, *a.* Greasy, smeared with grease.
Crásio, ia, *a.* V. *Craso y Grueso.*
Crasitúd, *sf.* 1. Grease, fat; fatness, corpulency. 2. Ignorance, stupidity, bluntness or dullness of the intellect.
Cráso, sa, *a.* 1. Fat, greasy, oily, unctuous. 2. Thick. *Ignorancia crasa,* Gross ignorance. *Error craso,* Gross error.

Cratícula, *sf.* A small wicket or window, through which nuns receive the communion.
Créa, *sf.* Linen of a middling quality much used in Spain.
Creáble, *a.* Creative, creatable, what can be created.
Creación, *sf.* Creation.
Creadór, *sm.* V. *Criador.*
Creár, *va.* 1. To create, to cause to exist.—V. *Criar.* 2. (Met.) To institute, to establish. 3. (Ant.) To nourish, to support.
Creatívo, va, *a.* Creative, that which has the power to create.
Creatúra, *sf.* (Ant.) V. *Criatura.*
Crebantár y Crebrantár, *va.* V. *Quebrantar.*
Crebíllo, *sm.* (Ant.) Small sieve or riddle.
Creból, *sm.* (Bot.) Holly-tree. V. *Acebo.*
Crecedéro, ra, *a.* Able to grow, that which can grow.
Crecentár, *va.* (Ant.) V. *Acrecentar.*
Crecér, *va.* To augment the extrinsic value of money, to raise its price.—*vn.* 1. To grow, to increase in height or bulk. 2. To swell; applied to rivers.
Créces, *sf. pl.* 1. Augmentation, increase. 2. The additional quantity of corn paid by a farmer to a granary, besides what he borrowed from it.
Crecída, *sf.* Swell of rivers in consequence of heavy falls of rain.
Crecidaménte, *ad.* Plentifully, copiously, abundantly.
Crecidíto, ta, *a.* Somewhat increased or grown.
Crecído, da, *a.* 1. Grown, increased. 2. Grave, important. 3. Large, great.
Crecídos, *sm. pl.* Stitches with the knitting-needle, which enlarge the breadth or width of a stocking.
Creciénte, *sf.* 1. Swell or rise of waters, occasioned by rain or the thaw of snow. 2. (Mur.) Leaven, a ferment mixed with the dough to make it rise. 3. Crescent, the moon in her state of increase. *Creciente de la marea,* (Naút.) Flood tide.
Creciniénto, *sm.* 1. Increase or increment of any thing. *Crecimiento de la marejada,* (Naút.) Swell of the sea. 2. Increase of the price or value of money.
Credéncia, *sf.* 1. Side-board of an altar, on which all the necessaries are placed for celebrating high mass. 2. Credentials.
Credenciál, *sf.* Credential, that which gives a title to credit.
Credenciéro, *sm.* King's butler.
Credér, *va.* V. *Creer.*
Credibilidád, *sf.* Credibility.
Crédito, *sm.* 1. Credit, a sum of money due to any one. 2. Belief, faith. 3. Reputation, character. 4. Credit, trust, confidence, esteem. 5. Note, bill, order for payment.
Crédo, *sm.* Creed, a form of words in which the articles of faith are comprehended. *Cada credo,* Every moment. *En un credo,* In a trice, in a moment.
Credulidád, *sf.* 1. Credulity, easiness of belief. 2. V. *Creencia.*
Crédulo, la, *a.* Credulous, apt to believe.
Creedéro, ra, *a.* Credible, worthy of credit. *Tener buenas creederas,* To be easy of belief, to swallow the bait.

Credór, ra, *a.* Credulous, apt to believe.
Creéncia, *sf.* 1. Credence, belief of the truths of religion. 2. V. *Mensage y Salva.*
Creendéro, ra, *a.* Recommended.
Creér, *va.* 1. To believe, to give faith and credit to a thing. 2. To have a firm persuasion of the revealed truths of religion. 3. To credit, to receive a thing as probable. *Ver y creer,* To see and believe.
Cregüéla, *sf.* Sort of linen.
Creíble, *a.* Credible.
Creiblemente, *ad.* In a credible manner.
Creié, *fut. imp.* (Ant.) Third person sing. indic. of the verb *creer.*
Créligo, *sm.* (Ant.) V. *Clérigo.*
Créma, *sf.* 1. Cream of milk; also a compound of cream, sugar, flour and eggs. 2. The two points which are placed over the ü in the syllables, *güe, güo,* &c.
Cremesín ó Cremesíno, na, *a.* V. *Carmesí.*
Creminál, *a.* V. *Criminal.*
Crémor, *sm.* Cremor, a milky substance, pressed out of grain and other substances. *Cremor de tartaro,* Cream of tartar.
Crencha y Crenche, *sf.* The parting of the hair into two equal parts.
Crepusculíno, na, *a.* Crepusculous, belonging to the dawn or break of day.
Crepúsculo, *sm.* Crepuscule, twilight, dawn.
Crésa, *sf.* 1. Maggot, a small grub, bred in cheese, bacon, &c. Acarus *L.* 2. Eggs of the queen-bee.
Crecemiénto y Crescéncia. V. *Crecimiento.*
Crescentár, *va.* V. *Acrecentar.*
Crescimiénto, *sm.* V. *Crecimiento.*
Crespár, *va.* To curl, to turn the hair into ringlets.—*vr.* To grow angry, to be displeased.
Crespílla, *sf.* An agaric. V. *Cagarria.*
Crespín, *sm.* Ancient ornament worn by women.
Crespína, *sf.* (Ant.) Kind of net used by women for holding up their hair.
Crespíno, *sm.* (Bot.) The barberry-tree.
Créspo, pa, *a.* 1. Crisp, curled. 2. (Bot.) Crisp-leaved. 3. (Met.) Obscure and bombastic; applied to the style. 4. (Met.) Angry, displeased, vexed.
Crespón, *sm.* Crape, a kind of gauze.
Crésta, *sf.* 1. Comb, crest of a cock. 2. Crest on the heads of some birds. 3. Crest of a helmet. 4. Ulcer about the fundament. 5. Cramp-iron which supports the running mill-stone. 6. Crest of the covert-way where the palisades are placed. *Alzar ó levantar la cresta,* (Met.) To be elated or puffed up with pride.
Crestádo, da, *a.* Crested, having a crest.
Crestíca, lla, ta, *sf.* A small crest.
Crestón, *sm.* Crest of a helmet in which the feathers are placed.
Créta, *sf.* Chalk, a white fossil substance of a friable nature.
Crético, ca, *a.* (Med.) V. *Critico.*
Cretóna, *sf.* Sort of linen manufactured in Normandy, in France.
Creyéncia, *sf.* V. *Creencia.*
Creyénte, *pa.* Believing, he who believes.
Creznéja, *sf.* Streak of blanche bass-weed.
Cría, *sf.* 1. Breed or brood of animals. 2. Suckling, a young creature yet fed by the pap. 3. Child reared by a nurse. 4. A concise and pathetic narrative.

Criación, *sf.* V. *Crianza, Cria, y Creacion.*
Criáda, *sf.* 1. Female servant. 2. Wash-ba[t] with which washer-women beat the clothe[s].
Criadéro, *sm.* 1. Plantation of young tre[es] taken out of the nursery. 2. Place destined [to] breed animals.
Criadéro, ra, *a.* Fruitful, prolific.
Criadílla, *sf.* 1. Testicle. 2. A small loaf [in] the form of a testicle. 3. A little worthle[ss] servant maid. 4. (Bot.) Truffle, a kind o[f] mushroom. Lycoperdon tuber *L.*
Criádo, da, *s.* 1. Servant, one who attends a[n]other for stipulated wages. *Criado capitula[]do,* A person who, wishing to go to some co[]lony, and devoid of money to pay for hi[s] passage, engages to serve for it a certai[n] time. 2. Client. 3. Breeding, manners. *Esta[r] criado,* To be independent. *Hablar criad[o],* To speak as a well-bred person.
Criádo, da, *a.* Educated, instructed.
Criadór, ra, *s.* 1. Creator, the Being whic[h] bestows existence. 2. One who rears an[d] trains dogs. 3. Breeder of horses or mule[s]. *Tierra criadora,* A fruitful or fecund soil.
Criaduéla, *sf.* A little servant maid.
Criánza, *sf.* 1. Breeding, manners, education. 2. Act of creating, creation.
Criár, *va.* 1. To create, to produce out of no[]thing, to give existence. 2. To nurse, to suckle. *Criar á sus pechos á alguno,* To inspire an[d] imbue one with his manners and principles, to protect, favour or patronize one. 3. To rea[r] fowls and other animals. 4. To educate, to instruct. 5. (Ant.) To establish, to institute. 6. To commence and pursue any expedient o[r] business. *Criar carnes,* To grow fat an[d] lusty. *Criar molleja,* To grow lazy.
Criatúra, *sf.* 1. Creature, any created being. 2. A human fetus; also a new-born child. *E[s] una criatura,* He is yet an infant. *Tengo lastima de la pobre criatura,* I pity the poor thing.
Criaturíca, Criaturílla, Criaturíta, *sf.* A very young little child.
Criazón, *sf.* Breed or brood of animals; family.
Críba, *sf.* Cribble, sieve.
Cribadúra, *sf.* Cribration, the act of sifting.
Cribár, *va.* To sift, to separate with a sieve.
Críbo, *sm.* Sieve, riddle.
Crída, *sf.* V. *Pregon.*
Cridár, *vn.* (Ant.) To cry, to shout.
Crímen, *sm.* Crime, misdemeanor, offence. *Sala del crimen,* A criminal tribunal.
Criminación, *sf.* V. *Acriminacion.*
Criminál, *a.* 1. Criminal, guilty of a crime. 2. Criminal, not civil. 3. Censorious, addicted to censure.
Criminalidád, *sf.* Criminality.
Criminalísta, *sm.* An author who has written on criminal matters.
Criminalménte, *ad.* In a criminal manner.
Criminár, *va.* To accuse.
Criminóso, sa, *s.* Delinquent, criminal.
Criminóso, sa, *a.* Criminal.
Crímno, *sm.* Sort of coarse flour generally used in making a kind of fritters, called *gachas.*
Crin ó Crínes, *sf.* Mane, the long hair which hangs down on the neck of horses.
Crinádo, da, y Crinito, ta, *a.* Having long hair.

Cometa crinita, A long-bearded comet, surrounded with rays of light.
Criéllo, *sm.* Creole, one born in America or the West Indies of European parents.
Crípta, *sf.* Crypt, a subterraneous vault for the interment of the dead.
Crisálida, *sf.* (Ento.) Chrysalis, caterpillar.
Crisántemo, *sm.* (Bot.) Chrysanthemum, crow-foot.
Crísis, *sf.* 1. Crisis, the point in which a disease kills or changes for the better. 2. Judgment passed after a mature deliberation.
Crísma, *sm.* Chrism, oil mixed with balsam and consecrated by bishops on Holy Thursday, used in baptism, confirmation, and also in the consecration of bishops. *Te quitaré el crisma*, (Fam.) Boasting menace of ruining one.
Crismár, *va.* 1. To perform the ecclesiastic rite of confirmation. 2. To break one's skull.
Crisméra, *sf.* Phial, commonly made of silver, in which the chrism or consecrated oil is preserved.
Crisoberilo, *sm.* Chrysoberyle, a precious stone.
Crisócola, *sf.* Chrysocolla, borax.
Crisól, *sm.* Crucible for melting metals.
Crisoláda, *sf.* Crucible full of metal.
Crisólito, *sm.* Chrysolite, a precious stone.
Crisopásio, *sm.* Chrysoprase, a kind of precious stone.
Crisopéya, *sf.* Alchemy, the pretended art of the transmutation of metals.
Crisopráza, *sf.* Chrysoprase, a stone of a yellowish green colour, and consisting of quartz and oxide of copper.
Crispatúra, *sf.* (Med.) A spasmodic contraction of the nerves.
Cristál, *sm.* 1. Crystal, a pellucid or transparent mineral substance. 2. The best and clearest glass manufactured in glass-houses. 3. Looking-glass. 4. (Poét.) Water. 5. *Cristal tartaro*, Cream of tartar. 6. Fine shining woollen stuff.
Cristalíco, llo, to, *sm. dim.* Little crystal.
Cristalíno, na, *a.* Crystalline, transparent like crystal; one of the humours of the eye.
Cristalización, *sf.* Crystallisation, aggregation of minerals in a geometric form.
Cristalizárse, *vr.* To crystallize, to coagulate or concrete into crystals or regular bodies.
Cristél, *sm.* Clyster. V. *Clister.*
Cristianaménte, *ad.* In a Christian manner.
Cristianár, *va.* To baptize. V. *Bautizar.*
Cristiandád, *sf.* 1. Christianity, the body of the Christians who profess the Christian religion. 2. Observance of the law of Christ.
Cristianésco, ca, *a.* After the Christian manner; applied to Moorish things which imitate the Christian manner.
Cristianíllo, lla, *s.* A little Christian; a nick-name given to the Spaniards by the Moors.
Cristianísmo, *sm.* 1. Christendom, the whole body of Christians. 2. Christening. V. *Bautizo.*
Cristianizár, *va.* To conform to the rites of the Christian religion.
Cristiáno, na, *a.* Christian, of the religion of Christ.
Cristiáno, na, *s.* 1. A professor of the religion of Christ. 2. Brother, friend or neighbour. *A ley de Cristiano*, Upon the word of a Christian.
Cristífero, ra, *a.* Bearing the law and love of Christ in one's heart.
Crísto, *sm.* Christ, our blessed Saviour. *Ni por un Cristo*, By no means, not for the world. *Haber la de dios es cristo*, To have a grand dispute or quarrel. *Ir ó ponerse á lo de dios es Cristo*, To dress one's-self to affect gallantry and spirit.
Crístus, *sm.* Cross printed at the beginning of the alphabet. *No saber el cristus*, To be very ignorant. *Estar en el cristus*, (Met.) To be in the very rudiments of any thing.
Crisuéla, *sf.* The pan of a lamp for holding the oil that drops from the wick.
Crisuélo, *sm.* V. *Candil.*
Crisoléa, *sf.* Aqua regia, nitro-muriatic acid which dissolves gold.
Crít, *sm.* Sort of poniard.
Crítica, *sf.* 1. Criticism, the art and standard of judging well. 2. Judgment formed of the merits or demerits of any writing or publication; a censure.
Criticadór, *sm.* Critic, censurer.
Criticár, *va.* To criticise, to animadvert.
Criticástro, *sm.* Animadverter, would-be critic.
Crítico, *sm.* 1. Critic, a man skilled in the rules of criticism. 2. An affected refiner of style and language.
Crítico, ca, *a.* 1. Critical, decisive. 2. Nicely judicious, relating to criticism.
Criticón, *sm.* A great critic.
Critiquéar, *vn.* To criticise; to play the critic, to censure.
Critiquizár, *va.* (Fam.) V. *Criticar.*
Criznéja, *sf.* Trace or rope made of twisted twigs joined together.
Croazár, *va.* To croak, to make a hoarse noise like a frog.
Crochél, *sm.* (Ant.) Tower of a building.
Crocíno, *sm.* Unguent or oil of saffron.
Crocitár, *vn.* V. *Crascitar.*
Crocodílo, *sm.* Crocodile.
Crocomágma, *sf.* Unguent prepared of saffron, myrrh, red roses, starch, and gum arabic.
Cromático, ca, *a.* Chromatic.
Crónica, *sf.* Chronicle, a register or account of events in order of time.
Crónico, ca, *a.* Chronic; applied to distempers of long duration.
Cronicón, *sm.* Chronicle, a succinct account of events in order of time.
Cronísta, *sm.* Chronicler, one who writes a chronicle.
Cronografía, *sf.* Chronography, the science of time.
Cronógrafo, *sm.* Annalist, one who writes annals.
Cronología, *sf.* Chronology, the science of computing and adjusting the periods of time.
Cronologicaménte, *ad.* Chronologically.
Cronológico, ca, *a.* Chronological.
Cronologísta ó Cronólogo, *sm.* Chronologist, one that studies or explains time.
Crotorár, *va.* To crunk, to cry like a crane or stork.
Cróza, *sf.* (Ant.) Crosier.
Cruaménte y Cruamiéntre, *ad.* (Ant.) Cruelly.
Cruçéra, *sf.* Withers of a horse. *Crucéras*, The two large pins which fasten the body or chest of a cart or wagon to the axle-tree.
Crucería, *sf.* Gothic architecture.
Crucéro, *sm.* 1. Cross-vault or transept of a

church under the dome. 2. Cross-bearer, one who carries the cross before the archbishops in a procession. 3. Piece of timber which lies across the rafters in a building. 4. Crick of a mill. 5. (Impr.) Cross of a chase, which divides the pages. 6. (Naút.) Cruising station. 7. (Astr.) Cross, a southern constellation.

Crúces, *sf. pl.* (Naút.) Preventer leach-lines of the top-sails.

Crucétas, *sf pl.* (Naút.) Cross-trees of the top masts.

Cruciáta, *sf.* (Bot.) Cross-wort. Vallantia muralis *L.*

Cruciferário y Crucífero, *sm.* 1. Cross-bearer. 2. A religious person of the order of the Holy Cross.

Crucífero, ra, *a.* Bearing or carrying a cross.

Crucificádo, da, *a.* Crucified.

Crucificár, *va.* 1. To crucify, to put to death by nailing the hands to a cross set upright. 2. To molest, to vex, to torment.

Crucifixión, *sf.* Crucifixion; the punishment of nailing to a cross.

Crucifíxo, *sm.* Crucifix, the representation in picture or statuary of our Lord's passion.

Crucifixór, *sm.* Crucifier, he who crucifies.

Crucígero, ra, *a.* Carrying or bearing the sign of the cross.

Crucíllo, *sm.* Push-pin; a play.

Crudaménte, *ad.* Rudely, in a rude manner.

Crudéza, *sf.* 1. Crudity, unripeness, want of maturity. 2.(Met.) Rudeness, severity, cruelty. 3. Vapour, vain boasting. *Crudezas del estómago*, The crudities or indigestions of the stomach.

Crudío, día, *a.* (Ant.) 1. V. *Crudo.* 2. Rough, rude.

Crúdo, *sm.* Packing cloth.

Crúdo, da, *a.* 1. Raw; not boiled, roasted, fried, or broiled. 2. Green, unripe; applied to fruit. 3. Rude, cruel, pitiless. 4. Crude, hard of digestion. 5. A blustering, hectoring person. 6. Unripe, not mature; applied to tumours and abscesses. *Lienzo crudo*, Unbleached linen. *Tiempo crudo*, Bleak, raw weather. *Punto crudo*, A critical moment or juncture. *Á punto crudo*, Untimely, unseasonably.

Cruél, *a.* 1. Cruel, delighting in hurting others. 2. (Met.) Intolerable, insufferable, not to be endured. *Un frio cruel*, An intense cold. *Dolores crueles*, Severe pains. 3. (Met.) Bloody, violent. *Batalla cruel*, A bloody battle.

Crueldád, *sf.* Cruelty, a barbarous action.

Cruelézà, Cruentidád, y Cruéza, *sf.* V. *Crueldad.*

Cruelménte, *ad.* In a cruel manner, cruelly.

Cruentaménte, *ad.* Bloodily; with effusion of blood.

Cruentación, *sf.* Bloodiness, the act and effect of imbuing with blood.

Cruentár, *va.* V. *Ensangrentar y Encruelecerse.*

Cruénto, ta, *a.* Bloody, cruel, inhuman.

Cruo, Crua, *a.* V. *Crudo y cruel.*

Cruór, *sm.* (Ant.) Gore, congealed blood.

Crurál, *a.* Crural, belonging to the leg.

Cruréo, *sm.* Muscle of the calf of the leg.

Crustáceo, cea, *a.* Crustaceous, shelly, having jointed shells.

Crústico, ca, *a.* Beating; applied to instruments of pulsation. V. *Pulsatil.*

Crustóso, sa, *a.* V. *Costroso.*

Cruxía, *sf.* 1. (Naút.) The midship-gangway on board a galley. 2. A large open hall or passage in a building. *La cruxia de un hospital*, The great hall of an hospital, with beds on each side. 3. Passage with rails on each side, from the choir to the high altar, in cathedral churches. *Cruxia de piezas*, Flight of rooms one after another. *Pasar cruxia*, To run the gauntlet; (Met.) To suffer great fatigue and misery.

Cruxído, *sm.* Crack, noise made by wood.

Cruxír, *vn.* To crackle, to rustle.

Crúz, *sf.* 1. Cross, an instrument composed of two pieces of timber laid across one another. 2. Cross, the badge of some military order. 3. Toil, trouble, vexation. 4. Withers, the upper juncture of the shoulder-bone in beasts. 5. *Cruz de las bitas*, (Naút.) Cross-tree of the bits. *Cruz y boton*, (Naút.) Frapping; the crossing and drawing together the several parts of a tackle. *Cruz tomada con los cables*, (Naút.) A cross in the hawse. *Bracear en cruz, ó poner las vergas en cruz*, (Naút.) To square the yards. *Quedarse en cruz y en quadro*, To be reduced to poverty and distress. *Cruces*, Wings of a reel. *Estar, andar, ó verse entre la cruz y el agua bendita*, (Fam.) To be in imminent danger of any thing.

Cruzáda, *sf.* 1. Crusade, an expedition against the infidels. 2. Tribunal of the crusade. 3. Indulgences granted to those who support the crusade.

Cruzádo, *sm.* 1. Cruzado; an old Spanish coin of gold, silver, or brass. 2. A Portuguese coin of gold or silver. 3. A soldier enlisted under the banners of the crusade. 4. Knight, who wears the badge of some military order. 5. Manner of playing on the guitar. 6. Figure in dancing.

Cruzadór, ra, *a.* Crossing from one side to another.

Cruzámen de una vela, *sm.* Square or width of a sail.

Cruzár, *va.* 1. To cross, to lay one body across another. 2. To cross a street or road. 3. (Naút.) To cruise. *Cruzar la cara á alguno*, To cut and back one's face.—*vr.* 1. To be knighted, to obtain the cross or badge of any military order. 2. To cross and trip, as horses do which are weak in their pasterns and quarters. *Cruzarse los negocios*, To be overwhelmed with business.

Cuajáda, *sf.* Butter, curd, or coagulated fat part of the milk separated from the serous part.

Cuajadíllo, *sm.* Sort of silk gauze with flowers.

Cuajádo, *sm.* A dish made of meat, herbs, or fruits with eggs and sugar dressed in a pan.

Cuajaléche, *sm.* (Bot.) Lady's bed-straw, yellow goose grass, cheese runnet. Galium verum *L.*

Cuajamiénto, *sm.* Coagulation.

Cuajár, *sm.* Runnet bag or stomach of a calf or sucking animal; the crop of a fowl.

Cuajár, *vn.* 1. To coagulate, to run into concretions. 2. To succeed, to have the desired effect. 3. (Met.) To ornament, to decorate with much ornament. 4. To please. *Pedro no me cuaja*, Peter does not please me.

Cuajaréro, *sm* V. *Cuajar.*

Cuajarón, sm. Grume, clot, gore.
Cuájo, sm. 1. A lacteal substance found in the stomach of animals before they feed. 2. Concretion, coagulation. *Tener buen cuajo*, To be too dull and patient. *Yerbo de cuajo*, (Bot.) Goose-grass. Galium *L. Arrancar de cuajo*, To eradicate, to tear up by the roots.
Cúba, sf. 1. Cask for wine or oil. 2. (Met.) Toper, drunkard. 3. Tub. 4. As much must as may be contained in a cask. *Cada cuba huele al vino que tiene*, (Prov.) Every man is to be judged by his actions; literally, every cask smells of the wine it contains.
Cubáza, sf. A large pipe, a hogshead.
Cubázo, sm. Stroke received from a pipe or hogshead.
Cubéba, sf. (Bot.) Cubeb. Piper cubeba *L.*
Cubéro, sm. Cooper, one who makes coops, or barrels and casks.
Cubertádo, da, a. Covered.
Cubertúra, sf. Cover, covering.
Cubéta, sf. 1. A small barrel or cask. 2. Bucket, a wooden vessel in which water or other liquids are carried. *Cubeta ó bidon donde se come*, (Naút.) Mess bucket. *Cubeta para alquitran*, (Naút.) Tar-bucket.
Cubetílla, sf. A small bucket.
Cubéto, sm. A small barrel.
Cubichéte, sm. (Naút.) Water-boards, or weather-boards; planks put on the upper part of a ship's side to keep off a rough sea.
Cúbico, ca, a. Cubical or cubic; having the form and properties of a cube.
Cubiculário, sm. Groom of the bed-chamber, valet-de-chambre.
Cubiérta, sf. 1. Cover, covering. 2. (Met.) Pretext or pretence. 3. (Naút.) Deck of a ship. *Cubierta primera ó principal*, The lower or gun deck. *Segunda cubierta*, The middle deck. *Tercera cubierta*, The upper deck. *Cubierta entera*, A flush deck. *Cubierta arqueada*, A cambering deck. *Cubierta cortada*, A cut or open deck. 4. Cover of a letter.
Cubiertaménte, ad. Privately, secretly, in a hidden manner.
Cubiérto, sm. 1. Cover, part of a table-service, consisting of a plate, fork, spoon, and knife, for every one who sits down to table. 2. Roof of a house, or any other covering which shelters from the inclemency of the weather. 3. Allowance of a soldier billeted in a house; such as a bed, salt, water, light, and a seat at the fire-place. 4. Course; a number of dishes set at once on a table. 5. (Ant.) Quilt or cover of a bed. *Ponerse á cubierto*, To shelter one's-self from any apprehended danger.
Cubijadéra, sf. V. *Alcahueta.*
Cubijár, va. V. *Cobijar.*
Cubíl, sm. Lair or couch of wild beasts.
Cubilár, vn. To take shelter. V. *Majadear.*
Cubiléte, sm. 1. A copper-pan for baking pies and other pastry. 2. Tumbler, mug; a cup to drink in. 3. Dice-box, from which dice are thrown. 4. A small pie, stuffed with minced meat, or with a batter of cream, eggs, sugar, and flour. [mug.
Cubiletéro, sm. 1. Paste-mould. 2. A large
Cubílla, sf. Spanish fly.
Cubíllo, sm. 1. A small bucket. 2. Spanish fly, blister beetle. Meloe vesicatorius *L.* 3. A small box near the stage. *Cubillos*, The ladles or receptacles of a mill-wheel, into which the water falls and turns it. [cubit.
Cubitál, a. Cubital, containing the length of a
Cúbito, sm. 1. A small bucket. 2. Cubit, a measure from the elbow to the middle-finger. 3. (Anat.) The largest bone of the fore-arm.
Cúbo, sm. 1. Cube; a regular solid body, consisting of six square and equal faces and sides. 2. A wooden pail with an iron handle. 3. Mill-pool, or pond of water to drive a mill-wheel. 4. Barrel of a watch or clock. 5. (Fort.) A small tower, formerly raised on old walls. 6. Product of the multiplication of a square number by its root.
Cubrepán, sm. Sort of fire-shovel, used by pastry-cooks.
Cubríl, sm. V. *Cubil.*
Cubrír, va. 1. To cover, to lay or spread one thing over another. 2. (Met.) To cover, to screen, to consent. 3. (Met.) To dissemble, to cloak, to hide under false appearances. 4. To cover or protect a post, to prevent its being attacked by the enemy. 5. To roof a building. 6. To cover, to copulate with a mare; applied to stone-horses. 7. (Ant.) To dress. *Cubrir la mesa*, To lay the table. *Cubrir la cuenta*, To balance an account.—vr. 1. To deduct part of the rent which has been paid before-hand. 2. To put a place in a state of defence. 3. To be covered, to put on one's hat. 4. To be covered against loss, to be insured. *Cubrirsele á uno el corazon*, To be very melancholy and sorrowful.
Cúca, sf. 1. A kind of fruit. V. *Chufa.* 2. A Peruvian plant. V. *Coca.* 3. Sort of caterpillar. V. *Cuco.* 4. *Cuca y matacán*, Sort of game at cards. *Mala cuca*, A wicked person. *Cuca de aquí*, Be gone, away with you.
Cucáña, sf. 1. A public amusement in many of the cities in Italy. 2. Any thing acquired with little trouble and at other people's expense.
Cucañéro, sm. Parasite, one who lives easy and at other people's expense.
Cucár, va. To mock, to ridicule.
Cucarácha, sf. 1. Wood-louse. Oniscus asellus *L.* 2. Kind of centipede, blatta or short-legged beetle, common aboard of American ships; cock-roach. Blatta americana *L.* 3. Hazel coloured snuff. *Cucaracha martin*, Nick-name given to a brown woman.
Cucarachéra, sf. Luck, good fortune. *Hallarse buena cucarachera*, To be lucky or fortunate.
Cucárda, sf. V. *Escarapela.*
Cucárros, sm. pl. (Naút.) Harpings. V. *Cucharros.* *Cucarro*, Nickname of a boy dressed as a friar.
Cuchár, sm. 1. Tax or duty laid on grain. 2. Spoonful. 3. Ancient corn-measure, the twelfth part of a *celemin* or peck. *Cuchar herrera*, Iron spoon.
Cuchára, sf. 1. Spoon, a concave vessel used in eating liquids. 2. An iron ladle, with a shank and hook, for taking water out of a large earthen jar. *Cuchara para brea*, (Naút.) Pitch-ladle. *Cuchara de cañon*, Gunner's ladle. *Cuchara para sacar el agua de los*

barcos, (Naút.) Scoop for sailing boats. *Cuchara de ponton para limpiar puertos*, (Naút.) Spoon of a pontoon for cleansing harbours. *Cuchàras*, Ladle-boards of a water-wheel in an over-shot mill.

Cucharáda, *sf.* Spoonful; as much as is taken at once in a spoon. *Meter su cucharada*, To meddle or interpose improperly and importunely in other people's conversation.

Cucharál, *sm.* Bag in which shepherds preserve their spoons.

Cucharázo, *sm.* Stroke or blow with a spoon.

Cucharéro, *sm.* 1. He that make or sells spoons. 2. Maker or retailer of wooden spoons.

Cucharéta, *sf.* A small spoon.

Cuchareteár, *vn.* 1. To stir with a spoon. 2. (Met.) To busy one's self with other people's affairs.

Cucharetéro, *sm.* 1. Maker or retailer of wooden spoons. 2. List or linen, nailed to a board, with small interstices to hold spoons. 3. Fringe sewed to under petticoats.

Cucharílla, ca, y ta, *sf. dim.* A small spoon.

Cucharón, *sm.* Ladle for the kitchen, a soup-spoon for the table.

Cuchárros, *sm. pl.* (Naút.) Harpings. *Tablones de cucharros*, (Naút.) Serving planks.

Cucheár, *vn.* (Fam.) To whisper, to speak into the ear of a person.

Cuchicheár, *vn.* To whisper.

Cuchichéo, *sm.* 1. Whisper, whispering. 2. Call of a cock-partridge who wants his hen.

Cuchichéro, ra, *s.* Whisperer; the custom of whispering.

Cuchichiár, *vn.* 1. To call like a partridge. 2. To whisper.

Cuchílla, *sf.* 1. A large kitchen-knife; a chopping-knife. 2. Sort of ancient poniard. 3. (Poet.) Sword. 4. Bookbinder's knife. *Gente de cuchilla*, Nick-name of the military.

Cuchilláda, *sf.* 1. Cut or slash with a knife or other cutting instrument. *Cuchillada de cien reales*. A large cut or wound. 2. Rent in cloth. 3. The surplus of the receipt of one play-house compared with that of another.—*pl.* 1. Wrangles, quarrels. 2. Openings formerly left in clothes to shew the lining.

Cuchilladíca, lla, y ta, *sf.* A small cut or gash.

Cuchillár, *a.* Belonging or relating to a knife.

Cuchillázo, *sm.* A large knife.

Cuchilléja, *sf. dim.* A little knife. V. *Cuchilla*.

Cuchilléjo, *sm.* 1. A small knife. 2. (Bot.) Cockle-weed. Agrostemma *L.*

Cuchillería, *sf.* Cutler's shop.

Cuchilléro, *sm.* Cutler, one who makes or sells knives.

Cuchillíco, Cuchillíto, *sm.* A small knife.

Cuchíllo, *sm.* 1. Knife. *Ser cuchillo de alguno*, To be troublesome at the instigation of another person. 2. Goar, a triangular piece sewed into a garment to make it wider. 3. Piece of ground which cannot be tilled on account of a tree standing too near, or from any other impediment. *Cuchillo de monte*, A hunter's cutlass. *Pasar á cuchillo*, To put to the sword. *Tener horca y cuchillo*, To be invested with the power of pronouncing a sentence of death: (Met.) To command imperiously. 4. (Met.) Right of governing and putting the laws in execution. *Cuchillos*, The six chief feathers in a hawk's wing. *Cuchillos de una vela*, (Naút.) Gorings of a sail.

Cuchillón, *sm.* A large or big knife.

Cuchitríl, *sm.* A narrow hole or corner.

Cuchucheár, *vn.* 1. To whisper, to speak with a low voice. 2. (Met.) To carry tales.

Cuchufléta, *sf.* Joke, jest, fun.

Cucióso, sa, *a.* (Ant.) Diligent. V. *Solícito*.

Cucíta, *sf.* (Ant.) Lap-dog.

Cucleár, *va.* To sing as the cuckoo.

Cuclíllas (En), In a cowering manner. *Sentarse en cuclíllas*, To squat, to sit cowering, to sit close to the ground.

Cuclíllo, *sm* 1. (Orn.) Cuckoo, a bird which appears early in the spring. Cuculus canorus *L.* 2. (Met.) Cuckold, the husband of an adulteress.

Cúco, *sm.* 1. Sort of caterpillar. 2. Person of a swarthy complexion. 3. Sort of game at cards. 4. Sort of sea-shell. Lepas *L.* 5. Tippler. 6. Cuckoo. *Cúcos*, Nick-name given in Castile to the stone-cutters who come from Asturia.

Cucúfa, *sf.* 1. Cap lined with cephalic drugs, and worn against rheumatisms. 2. Sort of wild fowl.

Cucúlla, *sf.* Cowl; a kind of hood formerly worn by men and women.

Cucurúcho, *sm.* Paper rolled up in the form of a cone in which money, tea, spices, or sweetmeats are kept.

Cudiciár, *va.* V. *Codiciar*.

Cúdria, *sf.* A flat woven bass-rope.

Cuébano, *sm.* Basket or hamper for carrying grapes to the vine-press. *Despues de vendimias cuébanos*, (Prov.) After meat, mustard.

Cuéga, *ter. per.* (Ant.) *irreg. sing. pres. subj.* of the verb *cocer*.

Cuégo, *prim. pers.* (Ant.) *irreg. sing. pres. indic.* of *cocer*.

Cueíta, *sf.* (Ant.) V. *Cuita*.

Cuélga, *sf.* 1. Cluster of grapes or other fruit hung up for use. 2. A birth-day's present.

Cuellidegolládo, da, *a.* (Joc.) One who wears cloths cut away about the neck, leaving it bare.

Cuellierguído, da, *a.* Stiff-necked; elated with pride.

Cuéllo, *sm.* 1. Neck; the part between the head and body. 2. (Met.) Neck of a vessel, the narrow part of it near its mouth. 3. Collar of a priest's garment. 4. Small end of a wax candle. 5. A large plaited neck-cloth, formerly worn. 6. Collar-band of a cloak. 7. Collar of a beam in oil-mills. 8. Collar of a shirt. 9. Instep of the foot. *Levantar el cuello*, (Met.) To be in a state of prosperity.

Cuélmo, *sm.* Candle-wood; a piece of pine, or other seasoned wood, which burns like a torch. V. *Tea*.

Cuémbas, *sf.* Sort of silk stuff imported from India.

Cuémo, *ad.* (Ant.) V. *Como*.

Cuénca, *sf.* 1. A wooden bowl. 2. Socket of the eye. 3. V. *Pila*.

Cuénco, *sm.* 1. An earthen bowl. 2. Hod.

Cuénda, *sf.* 1. End of pack-thread, which divides and keeps together a skein of silk or thread. 2. End of a skein of silk or thread.

Madexa sin cuenda, (Met.) An entangled affair, a complicate business.

Cuénde, *sm.* (Ant.) V. *Conde.*

Cuenquecílla, *sf.* A small bowl.

Cuénta, *sf.* 1. Computation, calculation. 2. Account, or reckoning, set down on paper. 3. Account, narrative. 4. (Ant.) Number, proportion. 5. One of the beads which compose a rosary. *Cuentas de ambar*, Amber-beads. 6. Indian-reed. Canna indica *L.* 7. Answerableness; reason, satisfaction. 8. *Cuénta corriente*, (Com.) Account current. *A' buena cuenta*, On account, in part of payment. *A' cuenta*, Upon one's word; relying on any thing. *A' esa cuenta*, At that rate. *Hacer cuentas alegres*, To feed one's self with vain hopes of success. *Pasar cuentas*, To pray without devotion. *Tribunal de cuentas*, Exchequer. *Tener cuenta*, To have carnal connexion with a woman; to take care of any thing. *Tener cuenta alguna cosa*, To answer, to turn out profitable or advantageous. *Estemos á cuentas*, Let us attend to this.

Cuentecíca, lla, y ta, *sf. dim.* A small account.

Cuentecíco, llo, y to, *sm.* A little tale or story.

Cuentéro, ra, *a.* Haggling.

Cuentísta, *sm.* Tale-bearer, informer.

Cuénto, *sm.* 1. Product of one hundred thousand multiplied by ten, a million; a million of millions. 2. But-end of a spear or any other pointed weapon. 3. Variance, disagreement between friends. *Andar en cuentos*, To fall to loggerheads. 4. Prop, support, shore. 5. Fable, fictitious story for children. *Cuento de horno*, Vulgar conversation, fire-side tales. *Cuento de viejas*, Old women's stories. 6. Accompt, number. *Cuento de cuentos*, (Met.) Relation or account difficult to explain; a complex detail. 7. Joint of the wing. *A' cuento*, To the purpose, seasonably, opportunely. *Ese es el cuento*, There is the rub, that is the difficulty. *Dexarse de cuentos*, To come to the point.

Cuér, *sm.* (Ant.) V. *Corazon.*

Cuéra, *sf.* A leather jacket, formerly worn.

Cuérda, *sf.* 1. Rope made of hemp or bass-weed. 2. String for musical instruments, made of gut or wire. 3. Match for firing a gun. 4. Chain of a watch or clock. 5. Cord; a Spanish measure. 6. Fishing-line. 7. Drag-rope for cannon and howitzers. 8. (Ant.) Nerve. 9. *Cuerdas de las cubiertas*, (Naút.) Deck-streaks, or strakes; rows of planks which range from the stem to the stern-post and fashion pieces. 10. (Geom.) Chord, a right line which joins the two ends of an arch. *Aflexar la cuerda*, (Met.) To temper the rigour of the law. *Apretar la cuerda*, (Met.) To treat with severity. *Por debaxo de cuerda*, Under-hand, privately.

Cuerdaménte, *ad.* Prudently, advisedly, deliberately.

Cuerdecíca, lla, ta, y Cuerdezuéla, *sf. dim.* A small cord.

Cuerdecíto, *a.* Somewhat prudent or discreet.

Cuérdo, da, *a.* Prudent, discreet.

Cuerecíco, Cuerecíto, *sm.* A small thin hide or skin.

Cuerezuélo, *sm.* 1. A small and thin skin or hide. 2. A sucking pig. 3. The crackling of a roasted pig.

Cuérna, *sf.* 1. A horn vessel, into which cows or goats are milked. 2. Stag's or deer's horn. 3. Sportsman's horn.

Cuernecíco, llo, y to, *sm.* Cornicle; a small horn.

Cuernezuélo, *sm.* 1. A small horn. 2. A farrier's paring knife.

Cuérno, *sm.* 1. Horn, the hard substance which grows on the heads of some quadrupeds. 2. Feeler; the horn or antenna of insects. 3. An interjection of admiration. V. *Caspita.* 4. Side. 5. (Ant.) Wing of an army. 6. *Obra á cuerno*, (Fort.) Horn-work. 7. Cornet, a musical instrument. *Levantár ó subir á uno sobre lós cuernos de la luna*, To exalt one to the stars. *Cuerno de abundancia*, Horn of plenty; applied to a cuckold whose wife is kept by a rich man. *Verse en los cuernos del toro*, To be in the most imminent danger. *Poner los cuernos*, To cuckold; applied to a wife who wrongs her husband by unchastity. *Cuerno de amon*, (Min.) Cornu ammonis, a fossil shell.

Cuéro, *sm.* 1. Hide or skin of an animal, either raw or dressed. 2. Goat-skin dressed entire, and which serves as a vessel or bag to carry wine or oil. 3. (Met.) Toper, a great drinker. *Estirar el cuero*, To make the most of any thing; literally, to stretch the skin. *En cueros ó en cueros vivos*, Stark-naked. *Entre cuero y carne*, Between skin and flesh. *Cueros*, Hangings or drapery of gilded or painted leather. *Cuero exterior*, Cuticle.

Cuerpecíco, llo; to, y Cuerpezuélo, *sm.* A small body or carcass.

Cuérpo, *sm.* 1. Body, the material substance of an animal. 2. Matter; opposed to spirit. 3. Corporation. 4. Floor or story in a building. 5. Volume, book. *Su librería contiene dos mil cuerpos de libros*, His library contains two thousand volumes. 6. Collection of laws. 7. Degree of thickness of silks, woollens, or cottons. 8. Size, strength. *El vino de mucho cuerpo*, A strong bodied wine. 9. Body; a collective mass. *Cuerpo de exército*, The main body of an army. *Cuerpo de reserva*, A corps of reserve. *Cuerpo de batalla de una esquadra*, The centre division of a fleet. 10. *Cuerpo del cabrestante*, (Naút.) Barrel of a capstern, or capstan, which is considered on board of ships as a perpetual lever. *Cuerpo á cuerpo*, Hand to hand; in single combat. *A' cuerpo descubierto*, Without cover or shelter; (Met.) Manifestly. *En cuerpo de camisa*, Half dressed; having nothing put on but the shirt. *Con el rey en el cuerpo*, Despotically; in a despotic manner. *Cuerpo de guardia*, A guard-room. *Tratar como cuerpo de rey*, To feast like a king. *Hacer del cuerpo*, To ease the body, to go to stool. *Tomar cuerpo*, To increase, to enlarge. *En cuerpo y en alma*, (Fam.) Totally, wholly.

Cuérva, *sf.* (Orn.) Crow. Corvus cornix *L.*

Cuervecíco, llo, to, *sm.* A little rook.

Cuérvo, *sm.* 1. (Orn.) Raven. Corvus corax *L.* 2. *Cuervo marino*, Cormorant. Pelecanus carbo *L.* 3. (Astr.) A southern constellation. *Venir el cuervo*, (Fam.) To receive repeated relief or succour.

Cuésa ó Cuésta, *sf.* (Ant.) Measure of grain.
Cuésco, *sm.* 1. Kernel, an edible substance contained in a shell; the stone or core of pulpy fruit. 2. Millstone of an oil-mill. 3. Wind from behind.
Cuesquíllo, *sm.* A small kernel or stone of fruit.
Cuésta, *sf.* 1. Declivity, gradual descent. 2. (Ant.) Coast. *Ir cuesta abaxo*, To go down hill. *Ir cuesta arriba*, To go up hill. *Cuesta arriba*, Painfully; with great trouble and difficulty. *A' cuestas*, On one's shoulders or back: (Met.) To one's charge or care. *Al pie de la cuesta*, (Met.) At the beginning of any undertaking.
Cuestecíca, lla, ta, y Cuestezuéla, *sf.* A gradual slope or declivity.
Cuetárse, *vr.* V. *Afligirse.*
Cuéva, *sf.* 1. Cave, grot, or grotto; a subterraneous cavity made by art or nature. 2. Cellar. *Cueva de ladrones*, Nest of thieves. *Cueva de fieras*, Den or couch of wild beasts.
Cuevecíca, lla, y ta, *sf.* A little cave.
Cuevéro, *sm.* One who makes caves and grottoes.
Cuétta, *sf.* V. *Cuita.*
Cuéza, *sf.* Ancient measure of grain.
Cuézo, *sm.* 1. Hod; a sort of tray for carrying mortar. 2. (Ant.) A small basket for carrying grapes. 3. Farrago, a medley of things put together without rule or order; applied to literary compositions. 4. Hodge-podge.
Cugujáda, *sf.* (Orn.) Common field-lark, skylark. Alauda arvensis *L.*
Cugúlla, *sf.* Cowl, a monk's hood. V. *Cogulla.*
Cuída, *sf.* In colleges, a woman who takes care of those of tender age.
Cuidadíco, llo, y to, *sm.* A little care, tenderness.
Cuidádo, *sm.* 1. Care, solicitude, attention. 2. Fear, apprehension, anxiety. 3. Charge or trust conferred. 4. Distress, dangerous or critical situation. *Estar de cuidado*, To be in great danger, or very ill. 5. Affectionate regard. 6. Object of care and love; which is generally addressed with the word *Cuidadillo.*
Cuidadór, *sm* 1. (Ant.) One too solicitous and careful. 2. A very thoughtful person.
Cuidadosaménte, *ad.* Carefully, attentively.
Cuidadóso, sa, *a.* Careful, solicitous in the execution of a business; vigilant.
Cuidár, *va.* 1. To heed, to care; to execute any thing with care, diligence, and attention. 2. (Ant.) To discourse, to think.
Cuidóso, sa, *a.* V. *Cuidadoso* y *Angustioso.*
Cuíta, *sf.* 1. Care, grief, affliction, trouble. 2. (Ant.) Earnest desire, craving. *Contar sus cuitas*, To tell one's troubles.
Cuitadaménte, *ad.* Slothfully, afflictedly.
Cuitadéz, *sf.* (Ant.) Propensity to mourn or to be sorrowful.
Cuitadíco, ca, llo, lla, y to, ta, *a.* Having some slight trouble or affliction.
Cuitádo, da, *a.* 1. Anxious, wretched, miserable. 2. Chicken-hearted, pusillanimous, timid.
Cuitamiénto, *sm.* (Ant.) Pusillanimity, timidity.
Cuitár, *va.* V. *Incomodar y Acuitarse.*
Cuitóso, sa, *a.* Urgent, pressing.
Cujára, *sf.* V. *Cuchara.*
Culáda, *sf.* 1. Stroke with the backside or breech of any thing. 2. Fall on one's backside. *Culádas*, (Naút.) Shocks and rollings of a ship.
Culantríllo, *sm.* (Bot.) Maiden's hair.
Culántro, *sm.* (Bot.) Coriander, a plant yielding an aromatic seed.
Culata, *sf.* 1. Breech of a gun, but-end of a musket. 2. Screw-pin, which fastens the breech of a gun to the stock. 3. The back part of any thing. *Dar de culata*, To recoil.
Culatázo, *sm.* 1. A large backside. 2. Recoil of a gun or musket.
Culcusído, *sm.* Botch-work; any thing which is sewed in a bad and clumsy manner.
Culébra, *sf.* 1. Snake. Coluber *L.* 2. Trick, fun, joke. 3. (Met.) A sagacious cunning woman who speaks several languages. *Sabe mas que las culebras*, He is very crafty and cunning.
Culebrázo, *sm.* Whipping given by prisoners in a jail to the new comers who have not paid entrance.
Culebreár, *vn.* To move along like a snake.
Culebríca, lla, y ta, *sf. dim.* A little snake.
Culebrílla, *sf.* 1. A little snake. 2. Tetter, ring-worm; a cutaneous disease. 3. Rocking-staff of a loom. 4. Fissure in the barrel of a gun.
Culebrína, *sf.* (Mil.) Culverin.
Culébro, *sm.* A male snake.
Culebrón, *sm.* 1. A large snake. 2. A cunning, crafty fellow; a double dealer.
Culéra, *sf.* Stain of urine in the swaddling clothes or clouts of children.
Culéro, *sm.* 1. Clout, a cloth for keeping children clean. 2. Disease in birds.
Culéro, ra, *a.* Slothful, lazy.
Culíto, *sm.* A small breech or backside.
Cullidór, *sm.* (Ant.) Receiver, collector.
Culminár, *vn.* To culminate, to be in the meridian.
Cúlo, *sm.* 1. Breech, backside; nates. 2. Bottom, socket, or lowest part of a thing. *Culo de mona*, Very ugly and ridiculous thing. *Culo de pollo*, Rough ill-mended part in stockings or clothes.
Culón, *sm.* A large breech or backside.
Cúlpa, *sf.* Fault, offence, slight crime.
Culpáble, *a.* Culpable; guilty of a fault.
Culpableménte, *ad.* In a culpable manner.
Culpación, *sf.* (Ant.) Crimination, reprehension.
Culpadaménte, *ad.* Culpably, in a culpable manner.
Culpádo, da, *a.* One who has committed a fault.
Culpár, *va.* To blame, to impeach.
Cultaménte, *ad.* 1. Neatly, genteelly; in a polite or genteel manner. 2. Affectedly, politely.
Cultedád, *sf.* An affected elegance and purity of style.
Culteranísmo, *sm.* Sect of purists, who are superstitiously nice in the use of words.
Culteráno, na, *s.* Purist.
Culteráno, na, *a.* Belonging or relating to an affected elegance and purity of style.
Cultería, *sf.* An affected elegance and purity of style.
Cultéro, *sm.* Purist.
Cultiéllo, *sm.* V. *Cuchillo.*
Cultiparlár, *va.* To speak with affected elegance.
Cultiparlísta, *a.* Speaking much with affected elegance and purity of language.

Cultiparlo, ña, *a.* Speaking with affected elegance and in a jeering manner.
Cultivación, *sf.* Cultivation, culture.
Cultivadór, *sm.* 1. Cultivator, one who cultivates lands. 2. Kind of plough.
Cultivár, *va.* 1. To cultivate the soil. 2. *Cultivar á alguno,* To cultivate one's friendship. *Cultivar el conocimiento ó el trato,* To cultivate one's acquaintance. *Cultivar las artes ó las ciencias,* To cultivate the arts and sciences.
Cultívo, *sm.* 1. Cultivation, the art of cultivating and improving the soil. 2. Act of cultivating one's acquaintance or friendship. 3. Culture of the mind, elegance of manners.
Cúlto, *sm.* 1. Respect and veneration paid to a person, as a testimony of his superior excellence and worth. 2. Religious worship.
Cúlto, ta, *a.* 1. Pure, elegant, correct; applied to style and language. 2. Affectedly elegant. 3. Polished, enlightened. *Culto de dulia,* Worship or honour to angels and saints. *Culto de hiperdulia,* Worship of the Virgin Mary. *Culto de latría,* Adoration to God alone. *Culto divino,* Public worship in churches. *Culto externo,* External demonstrations or respect to God and his saints by processions, sacrifices, offerings, &c. *Culto indebido,* Illegal worship, or superstition of appearing to honour God by false miracles, spurious reliques, &c. *Culto sagrado ó religioso,* Honour or worship to God and to the saints. *Culto superfluo,* Worship by means of vain useless things. *Culto supersticioso,* Worship paid either to whom it is not due, or in an improper manner.
Cultór, *sm.* 1. Cultivator. V. *Cultivador.* 2. (Ant.) Worshipper.
Cúltro, *sm.* Plough, with which the first fallow-ploughing is performed.
Cultúra, *sf.* 1. Culture; improvement or melioration of the soil. 2. Culture and improvement of the mind. 3. Elegance of style. 4. (Ant.) Adoration, worship.
Culturár, *va.* (Arag.) To cultivate. V. *Cultivar.*
Cum, *part.* (Ant.) V. *Como.*
Cumbo, *sf.* V. *Comba.*
Cumbé, *sm.* Sort of dance among the Negroes, and also the tune to which it is performed.
Cumbléza, *sf.* (Ant.) Concubine.
Cumbre y Cumbréra, *sf.* 1. Top, summit. 2. (Met.) The greatest height of favour, fortune, and science.
Cumo, *part. comp.* (Ant.) V. *Como.*
Cumpleáños, *sm.* Birth-day.
Cumplidaménte, *ad.* Completely.
Cumplidamiénte ó Cuplidamiéntre, *ad.* (Ant.) completely.
Cumplidéro, ra, *a.* 1. That must be fulfilled or executed. 2. Convenient, fit, suitable.
Cumplído, da, *a.* 1. Large, plentiful. *Una casaca cumplida,* A full coat. *Una comida cumplida,* A plentiful dinner. 2. Gifted with talents, worthy of esteem. 3. Polished, polite, civil, courteous.
Cumplído, *sm.* Compliment, an act or expression of civility.
Cumplidór, *sm.* One who executes or performs any commission or trust.
Cumplimentár, *va.* To compliment or congratulate upon any event or success.
Cumplimentéro, ra, *a.* Full of compliments.
Cumplimiénto, *sm.* 1. Act of complimenting or paying a compliment. 2. Completion, perfection. 3. Compliment, an expression of civility. *No se ande vd. en cumplimientos,* Do not stand upon compliments. 4. Complement, appendage.
Cumplír, *va.* 1. To execute, discharge, or perform one's duty. 2. To provide or supply any one with what he wants. 3. *Cumplir años o dias,* To reach one's birth-day. 4. To fulfil one's promise. *Cumplir de palabra,* To offer to do any thing without performing it. *Cumplir por otro,* to do any thing in the name of another. *Cumpla vm. por mi,* Do it in my name.—*vn.* 1. To be fit or convenient. 2. To suffice, to be sufficient.
Cumuladór, *sm.* V. *Acumulador.*
Cumulár, *va.* To accumulate, to compile or heap together. V. *Acumular.*
Cumulativaménte, *ad.* In heaps.
Cúmulo, *sm.* 1. Heap or pile of many things thrown over one another. 2. (Met.) Throng of business; variety of trouble and difficulties.
Cumunalménte, *ad.* In common, without division.
Cúna, *sf.* 1. Cradle; a small moveable bed, in which children are rocked to sleep. *Cuna de viento,* Cradle suspended between two pillars or upright posts. 2. Foundling-hospital. 3. (Met.) The native soil or country. 4. Family, lineage. *De humilde ó de ilustre cuna,* Of an humble or of an illustrious family. 5. Origin, beginning of any thing.
Cundído, *sm.* 1. The provision of oil, vinegar, and salt, given to shepherds. 2. Honey or cheese given to boys to eat with their bread.
Cundír, *va.* (Ant.) To occupy, to fill.—*vn.* 1. To spread; applied to oil. 2. To yield abundantly. 3. To grow, to increase, to propagate.
Cúneo, *sm.* 1. (Mil.) Triangular formation of troops. 2. Space between the passages in ancient theatres.
Cunéra, *sf.* Rocker; a woman appointed to rock the cradle of the infantas in the royal palace.
Cunéro, ra, *s.* Rocker, one who rocks.
Cunéta, *sf.* (Fort.) A small trench, made in a dry ditch or moat of a fortress, to drain off the rain-water.
Cunica, lla, ta, *sf.* A small cradle.
Cúña, *sf.* Wedge; a sharp-edged tool, made of wood or iron, to cleave wood or other solid bodies, or to tighten them. *Cuñas de mango,* (Naút.) Horsing-irons. *Cuñas de los masteleros,* (Naút.) Fids of the top-masts. *Cuñas de las vasadas ó vasos,* (Naút.) Blocks of a ship's cradle. *Cuñas de puntería,* (Art.) Gunquoins. *Cuñas de rajar,* Splitting wedges.
Cuñadádgo, *sm.* (Ant.) Relationship by affinity.
Cuñadería, *sf.* Gossipred or compaternity, spiritual affinity contracted by being godfather to a child.
Cuñadía ó Cuñadío, *s.* Kindred by affinity.
Cuñadíca, illa, ó ita, *sf.* A little sister-in-law
Cuñadíco, illo, ó ito, *sm.* A little brother-in law.

Cuñádo, da, *s.* A brother or sister-in-law.
Cuñál, *a.* V. *Acuñado.*
Cuñár, *va.* V. *Acuñar.*
Cuñéte, *sm.* Keg, a small barrel or firkin.
Cúño, *sm.* 1. Die for coining money. 2. Impression made by the die. 3. Mark put on silver. 4. A triangular formation of troops.
Cuómo, *ad.* (Ant.) V. *Como.*
Cupé, *sm.* 1. Landau, a four-wheeled carriage with two back seats. 2. Movement in the French dance. 3. Preterper. indic. irreg. of the verb *caber.*
Cupído, *sm.* Bit of steel taken out of the eye of a needle. [arch-ways.
Cupitél. *Tirar de cupitel*, To throw a bow
Cupresíno, na, *a.* (Poet.) Belonging to the cypress-tree, or made of cypress-wood.
Cúpula, *sf.* Cupola, dome, the hemispherical summit of a church or other large building.
Cupulíno, *sm.* Lantern, a small cupola raised upon another, which serves to give light to the vault.
Cuquilléro, *sm.* (Mur.) Baker's boy who fetches the paste of bread, and carries it back when baked.
Cuquíllo, *sm.* 1. (Orn.) Cuckoo. V. *Cuclillo.* 2. (Ent.) Insect which consumes the vines. Coccus vitis *Fabr.*
Cúra, *sm.* 1. Parish priest. 2. Clergyman hired to perform the duty of another.—*sf.* 1. Cure, remedy, restorative. 2. (Ant.) Guardianship, the office and duty of a guardian. 3. Curacy. *Los derechos de cura*, The curate's dues.
Curáble, *a.* Curable, that which admits a remedy.
Curación, *sf.* Cure, the act of healing.
Curádgo, *sm.* (Ant.) Curacy. V. *Curato.*
Curadíllo, *sm.* Cod-fish; ling-fish.
Curádo, da, *a.* 1. Cured, strengthened, restored. 2. Belonging or relating to a curacy. *Beneficio curado*, Curacy, annexed to a benefice.
Curadór, ra, *s.* 1. Overseer, one who has the charge or care of a thing. *Curador de lienzo*, Bleacher of linen cloth. *Curador de bacalao*, Cod-salter. 2. Guardian, one who has the care of minors and orphans. 3. Physician, surgeon; one who cures and heals. 4. Curator, administrator. *Curador ad bona*, (For.) Curator of a minor's estate appointed by a court.
Curaduría y Curadoría, *sf.* Guardianship, the office and duty of a guardian.
Curálle, *sm.* Physic administered to a hawk to make him purge.
Curanderó, *sm.* Quack, an artful and tricking practitioner in physic, who is not an approved physician.
Curár, *vn.* To recover from sickness.—*va.* 1. To administer medicines, and prescribe the regimen of a patient. 2. To salt, to cure meat or fish. 3. To season timber. 4. *Curarse en salud*, To take care of one's self: (Met.) To accuse one's self, to avoid the reproach of any thing. 5. To bleach thread, linen, or clothes. 6. To remedy any evil.
Curatéla, *sf.* (For.) V. *Curaduria.*
Curatívo, va, *a.* Curative, that which serves to cure a disease.
Curáto, *sm.* 1. Curacy, the place and employment of a curate. 2. District of a parish priest, a parish. *Anexo de un curato*, A small cura[cy] annexed to another.
Curázgo, *sm.* V. *Curato.*
Curazón, *sm.* V. *Corazon.* [g
Curcúma, *sf.* Turmeric, a root resembling g[inger].
Curéña, *sf.* 1. Gun-carriage. 2. Stay of a cross-bow. 3. Skin or bag with cocoa-nuts. *A cureña rasa*, (Mil.) Without a parapet or breastwork; applied to a barbet battery: (Met.) Without shelter or defence. *Tirar á cureña rasa*, To fire at random.
Curésca, *sf.* Shear-wool cut off by a cloth[ier] with sheers when the cloth has been combed.
Cúria, *sf.* 1. An ecclesiastic court where church affairs are examined and decided. 2. Care and skill in performing a thing.
Curiál, *a.* 1. Belonging or relating to the Roman *curia*, or tribunal for ecclesiastic affairs. 2. Expert, skilful.
Curiál, *sm.* 1. One who joins in the vote that the Spanish *cortes* or states be assembled. 2. Members of the Roman *curia*. 3. One who employs an agent in Rome to obtain bulls or rescripts. 4. One in a subaltern employ in the tribunals of justice, or who is occupied with others' affairs.
Curialidád, *sf.* (Ant.) Politeness, civility.
Curiána, *sf.* Kind of black fly. *Curiánas*, Chips cut off from wood.
Curiár, *va.* (Ant.) To guard. V. *Cuidar.*
Curiosaménte, *ad.* 1. Curiously. 2. Neatly, cleanly. 3. In a diligent careful manner.
Curiosidád, *sf.* 1. Curiosity, inquisitiveness. 2. Neatness, cleanliness. 3. Curiosity, rarity, an object of curiosity.
Curióso, sa, *a.* 1. Curious, inquisitive, desirous of information. 2. Neat, clean. 3. Handsome, fine, beautiful. 4. Careful, attentive, diligent.
Cúro, *sm.* (Naút.) A small kind of vessel used on the river Garonne in France.
Cúrro, ra, *s.* A familiar proper name, used for Francis and Frances.
Currúca, *sf.* (Orn.) Linnet, babbling warbler. Motacilla curucca *L.*
Cursádo, da, *a.* Accustomed, habituated, inured.
Cursánte, *pa.* Frequenting; assiduous; he who frequents universities or public lectures.
Cursár, *va.* 1. To frequent a place, to repeat or do a thing often. 2. To frequent universities or schools.
Cursário, *sm.* V. *Pirata.*
Cursíllo, *sm.* 1. A short run or walk. 2. A short course of lectures on any science in a university. [printing.
Cursívo, va, *a.* Relating to Italic characters in
Cúrso, *sm.* 1. Course, direction, career. 2. Course of lectures in universites. 3. Laxity or looseness of the body. 4. Series of successive and methodical procedure. 5. (Ant.) V. *Corso.* *Curso de la corriente*, (Naút.) The current's way. *Curso de la marea*, (Naut.) The tide's way.
Cursór, *sm.* 1. (Ant.) V. *Correo.* 2. (Ant.) Messenger of a court of justice.
Curtación, *sf.* (Astro.) Curtation.
Curtído, da, *a.* Accustomed; dexterous, expert. [tan leather.
Curtidór, *sm.* Tanner, one whose trade is to

Curtidós, *sm. pl.* Tanned leather.

Curtidúra, *sf.* (Ant.) Art or trade of tanning.

Curtiduría, *sf.* Tan-yard, a place where leather is tanned.

Curtír, *va.* 1. To tan leather, to impregnate or imbrue with bark. 2. To imbrown by the sun. 3. To inure to hardships.

Curtimiénto, *sm.* The act of tanning leather.

Cúrto, ta, *a.* (Arag.) Short. *Caballo curto*, Short-tailed or docked horse.

Curúca y Curúja, *sf.* (Orn.) Eagle-owl. Strix bubo *L.*

Curuéña, *sf.* V. *Cureña.*

Curúl, *a.* Curule, belonging to a senatorial or triumphal chair in ancient Rome.

Cúrva, *sf.* 1. Curve, flexure. 2. (Naút.) Knee, a timber hewed like a knee, which binds the beams and futtocks together. *Curva quadrada*, Square knee. *Curva capuchina*, Standard of the cut-water. *Curva coral*, Knee of the stern post. *Curvas á la valona*, Lodging knees. *Curvas verticales de las cubiertas*, Hanging knees of the decks. *Curvas bandas*, Checks of the heads. *Curvas de los yugos*, Transom-knee sleepers.

Curvatón, *sm.* 1. Small curve. 2. (Naút.) Little knee.

Curvatúra y Curvidád, *sf.* 1. Curvature, inflexion, bent form. 2. (Naút.) Curvature of any piece of timber employed in ship-building.

Curvilíneo, nea, *a.* Curvilinear, forming a crooked line.

Cúrvo, va, *a.* Curve, crooked, bent, inflected.

Cuscúta, *sf.* The dodder of thyme, a parasitic plant. Cuscuta epithymum *L.*

Cusír, *va.* To sew or stitch clumsily.

Custódia, *sf.* 1. Custody, the act of keeping or preserving any thing. 2. The consecrated vessel in which the sacrament is exhibited in Roman Catholic churches. 3. Guard, escort. 4. Tabernacle. V. *Sagrario.* 5. Number of convents not sufficient to form a province.

Custódio, *sm.* Guard, keeper, watchman.

Custúmbre, *sf.* V. *Costumbre.*

Cutáneo, nea, *a.* Cutaneous, relating to the skin.

Cúte, *sf.* V. *Cutis.*

Cúter, *sm.* (Naút.) Cutter, a small vessel with one mast, and rigged as a sloop.

Cutiáno, na, *a.* V. *Quotidiano.*

Cutícula, *sf.* Cuticle, the first and outermost covering of the body.

Cuticulár, *a.* Cuticular, V. *Cutáneo.*

Cutidéro, *sm.* (Ant.) Shock, blow.

Cutidianaménte, *ad.* V. *Quotidianamente.*

Cútio, *sm.* (Ant.) Labour, work. *Trabajo cutio* (Arag.) Short work.

Cutír, *va.* 1. To knock or dash one thing against another. 2. (Ant.) To oppose, to rival.

Cútis, *s.* Skin, the natural covering of the flesh.

Cúto, *sm.* Hanger or sabre.

Cútre, *sm.* A pitiful miserable fellow.

Cúxa, *sf.* 1. Bag fastened to the saddle, into which a spear or colour-staff is put to carry it more easily. 2. (Ant.) Head of the bed. 3. (Ant.) Thigh, the part between the groin and the knee. V. *Muslo.*

Cúyo, ya, *pron. pos.* Of which, of whom, whose whereof.

Cúyo, *sm.* Gallant, lover, wooer.

Cuz, Cuz, *sm.* A term for calling dogs.

Czár, *sm.* Czar, autocrat or sovereign of all the Russias.

Czarína, *sf.* Consort of the Czar.

D, says the Spanish Academy, is the 5th letter of the alphabet, and the 4th of the consonants. D. is a contraction for *Don*, *Doña*, and Doctor; DD. doctors. As a numeral, *D* is 500.

Dáble, *a.* Easy, possible; that which can be done with ease.

Dabóvis, *sf.* Sort of cotton stuff.

Dáca, *ad.* (Ant.) This here, this side, on this side here. *Daca ó de acá*, From this.

Dáca, *v. def.* Give here. *Daca acá*, Give hither. *En daca las pajas*, In the snap of scissors, in a trice. *Daca, ó da acá, ó dame acá*, Give me here.

Dácio, *sm.* (Ant.) Impost, tax, duty.

Dación, *sf.* (For.) Dedition, yielding or giving up; delivery.

Dáctilo, *sm.* 1. Dactyle, a poetic foot among the Latins of one long syllable and two short. 2. (Con.) Kind of shell. Solon dactylus *L.*

Dáda, *sf.* Possession of any thing given or delivered.

Dadéro, ra, *a.* That which should be given or is to be given.

Dádiva, *sf.* Gift, present, gratification. *Dádivas quebrantan peñas*, (Prov.) Bribes avert the strictest justice.

Dadivádo, da, *a.* Bribed, suborned.

Dadivosaménte, *ad.* Liberally, plentifully.

Dadivosidád, *sf.* Liberality, magnificence, bounty.

Dadivóso, sa, *a.* Bountiful, mágnificent, becoming a gentleman.

Dádo, *sm.* 1. Die, *pl.* Dice, a small cube, marked on its face, with numbers from one to six, which gamesters throw in play. *Dado falso*, Cogged or false dice, filled with quicksilver, with which sharpers play. *A' una vuelta de dado*, At the cast of a die. 2. *Dadó de la roldana*, (Naút.) Coak of a sheave. 3. (Arq.) V. *Neto.* 4. (Ant.) V. *Donacion. Dádos*, Case or grape-shot for large guns. *Dados de las velas*, (Naút.) Tablings of the bowline cringles.

Dadór, ra, *s.* 1. Donor, giver; one who gives or bestows. 2. Drawer of a bill of exchange.

Dága, *sf.* 1. Dagger, a two-edged poniard. 2. Stove of a brick-kiln, the part where the fire is put to bake the bricks.

Dagón, *sm.* A large dagger.

Daguílla, *sf.* 1. Small dagger. 2. V. *Palillo.*

Dála, *sf.* (Naút.) Pump-dale of a ship, a trough in which the water runs overboard, that is fetched up by the pumps.

Dále, *interj.* Hold! Stop, importunate.
Daléra, *sf.* Dollar, a foreign coin.
Dálgo, *Facer mucho dalgo,* To receive any one with great attention and respect.
Dalgún, *a.* (Ant.) V. *Algun y Alguno.*
Dalí, *ad.* (Ant.) V. *De allí.*
Dalínd, *ad.* (Ant.) V. *De allá.*
Dallá, *ad.* (Ant.) V. *De allá.*
Dalladór, *sm.* Mower, one who cuts grass with a scythe.
Dallár, *va.* To mow.
Dálle, *sm.* Scythe, an instrument for mowing, a crooked blade joined to a long pole.
Dallén, *ad.* (Ant.) From the other side there; from the other side.
Dalmática, *sf.* Vestment with open sleeves, worn by the deacons of the Roman Catholic church in the performance of divine service.
Dáma, *sf.* 1. A fine beautiful woman. 2. A young lady of family and fortune. 3. Lady courted by a gentleman. 4. Woman kept in fornication, a mistress or concubine. 5. Queen, in the game of draughts. *Dama de palacio,* Lady of honour at court. *Dama cortesana,* Lady of pleasure, a girl of the town. 6. Affectedly nice. *Es muy dama,* She is excessively nice, difficult, or scrupulous. 7. *Dama,* American fallow deer. Cervus virginianus *L.* *Juego de damas,* Game of draughts. *Soplar la dama,* To huff a queen in the game of draughts. *Soplar la dama,* (Met.) To carry off and marry a lady, who was courted by another man. 8. The principal actress in a comedy. 9. Ancient Spanish dance.
Damacéno, **na**, y **Damascéno**, **na**, *a.* V. *Amaceno.*
Damajuána, *sf.* (Naút.) A large glass bottle used on board of ships.
Damasánio, *sm.* V. *Alisma.*
Damascéna, *sf.* Damson, a small black plum.
Damásco, *sm.* 1. Damask, a silk stuff with flowers and other figures. 2. The Brussels' apricot, of a flavour peculiarly delicious. 3. Damson, a small black plum.
Damasína, *sf.* Light silk stuff resembling damask.
Damasquéta, *sf.* Sort of chintz with gold sprigs, manufactured in Venice.
Damasquíllo, *sm.* 1. Kind of cloth, of silk or wool, resembling damask. 2. (And.) V. *Albaricoque.*
Damasquíno, **na**, *a.* Damaskened, adorned by making incisions, and filling them up with gold or silver wire; applied to iron and steel. *A' la damasquina,* Damascus fashion.
Damáza, *sf.* A fine, handsome, portly woman.
Damería, *sf.* 1. Excessive nicety in conduct, prudery. 2. Affected scrupulosity.
Damiénto, *sm.* V. *Dádiva.*
Damíl, *a.* (Ant.) Female, feminine, belonging to the ladies.
Damiséla, *sf.* 1. A young gentlewoman; applied to all girls that are not of the lower class of people. 2. Lady of pleasure, a girl of the town.
Damnáble, *a.* Damnable.
Damnación, *sf.* Eternal damnation.
Damnár, *va.* V. *Condenar.*
Damnificadór, **ra**, *s.* One who damnifies.
Damnificár, *va.* To hurt, to damage, to injure.
Danchádo, **da**, *a.* (Blas.) Dancette, indented.
Dángo, *sf.* (Orn.) V. *Planga.*

Dánno, *sm.* V. *Daño.*
Dánta, *sf.* Tapir. Tapir americanus *L.*
Dánte, *ad.* (Ant.) Contracted from *de* and *antes;* Anterior; before.
Dánte, *pa.* Giving; he who gives.
Dánza, *sf.* Dance, motions in measure to a tune. *Meter en la danza,* (Met.) To involve another in some business or dispute. *Por donde va la danza?* (Met.) To which side does the multitude incline?
Danzadór, **ra**, *s.* Dancer.
Danzánte, **ta**, *s.* 1. Dancer. 2. A fickle, airy person. *Hablar danzante,* To stammer.
Danzár, *vn.* 1. To dance, to move in measure to an appropriate tune. 2. To turn or whirl a thing round. *Sacar á danzar,* To invite or engage a lady to dance; to cite or to oblige one to take a part in any business. 3. (Fam.) To introduce one's self into any business.
Danzarín, *sm.* 1. A fine neat dancer. 2. (Met.) Giddy, meddling person.
Dañáble, *a.* Prejudicial, condemnable.
Dañadór, **ra**, *s.* Offender, one who hurts, or injures others.
Dañár, *va.* 1. To hurt, to damage, to injure. 2. (Ant.) To condemn.
Dañíno, **na**, *a.* Noxious, hurtful, injurious.
Dáño, *sm.* Damage, hurt, injury, prejudice.
Dañosaménte, *ad.* Hurtfully, mischievously.
Dañóso, **sa**, *a.* Hurtful, noxious, injurious.
Dapnár, *va.* (Ant.) V. *Condenar.*
Daquén, *ad. contr.* From *De aquende,* hither.
Daquí, *ad. contr.* From *De aqui,* hence.
Dar, *va.* 1. To give, to transfer without a price. 2. To strike, to beat, to knock. 3. To administer a remedy. 4. To confer, to bestow. *Dar parte,* To share with. 5. To suppose erroneously. *Dar de ojos,* (Met.) To fall into an error. 6. To consider an affair as concluded. 7. To grant a position, to coincide in opinion. 8. To persist obstinately in doing a thing. 9. To appoint. 10. To sacrifice. 11. To explain, to elucidate. *Dar el texto,* To explain the text. *Dar dado ó de balde,* To give gratis or for nothing. *Dar razon,* To inform, to give an account of any thing. *Dar prestado,* To lend. *Dar á trompon ó á bulto,* To give by the lump or bulk. *Dar á reir,* To set a laughing. *Dar á llorar,* To fall a crying. *Mi ventana da al campo,* My window overlooks the field. *Dar barro á la mano,* To furnish materials. *Dar culadas,* (Naút.) To strike repeatedly. *Dar de traste,* (Naút.) To run aground. *Dar fuego,* (Naút.) To bream a ship. *Dar calda,* To heat the iron. *Dar calle,* To clear the way. *Dar con la entretenida,* To put off with words and excuses. *Dar con uno,* To meet a person one is looking out for. *Dar de comer al diablo,* To wrangle, to quarrel; literally to prepare food for the devil. *Dar de si,* To stretch; applied to clothes. *Dar el nombre ó el santo,* (Mil.) To give the watch-word. *Dar el si,* To consent to marry a person. *Dar en las mataduras,* To touch one to the quick. *Dar en un bazio,* (Naút.) To strike aground, to get on shore. *Dar fiador ó fianza,* To find bail, to give security. *Dar el espiritu,* To expire, to die. *Dar guerra,* To wage war.

Dar higa, To miss fire; applied to fire arms. *Dar la enhorabuena*, To rejoice in another's happiness, to congratulate. *Dar la paz*, To give an embrace, to give an image to be kissed as a token of peace and fraternity. *Dar los dias*, To wish a good day. *Dar madrugon*, To get up early. *Dar mal rato*, To give uneasiness. *Dar pliego*, To conclude a contract or agreement with the king. *Dar puerta y silla*, To invite a person to come in and sit down. *Dar recados*, To greet absent friends; to invite visitors. *Dar señal*, To give earnest, that is, money in token that a bargain is ratified. *Dar tras uno*, To persecute one. *Dar un raspadillo á un baxel*, (Naút.) To scrape the bottom and sides of a ship slightly. *Dar vez*, To give one his turn. *Dar voces*, To call, cry, or scream. *Dar vuelco á un coche*, To overset a coach. *Dar zapatelas*, To leap with joy. *Dar golpe alguna cosa*, To be surprised or struck with the beauty or rarity of any thing. *Dar baya*, To scoff. *Dar diente con diente*, To shiver or gnash the teeth with cold. *Dé donde diere*, Inconsiderately, without reflection. *Dar de mano*, To depreciate or despise. *Dar á luz*, To be delivered of a child; to print, to publish. *Andar en dares y tomares*, To dispute, to contend.

Dárse, *vr.* 1. To conform to the will of another. 2. To give one's self up to virtue or vice. 3. *Darse á la vela*, (Naút.) To set sail. 4. *Darse á merced*, (Mil.) To surrender at discretion. 5. To concern, to interest. *No se me da nada*, It gives me no concern. *Darse de las astas*, To batter one's brains, to screw one's wits: to dispute or argue pertinaciously. *Darse á perros*, To become enraged or furious. *Darse las manos*, To shake hands. *Darse maña*, To manage one's affairs in an able manner. *Darse una panzada*, (Vulg.) To be fed to satiety and sickness. *Darse una panzada de escribir*, (Met.) To get a surfeit of writing. *Darse una vuelta*, To scrutinize one's own conduct, to find out one's own faults. *Darse un repelon*, To gossip, to have a little small talk.

Darága y Dárca, *sf.* V. *Adarga*.

Dardabasí, *sm.* (Orn.) Hawk, kite.

Dardáda, *sf.* Blow given with a dart.

Dárdo, *sm.* 1. Dart, a missile weapon thrown by the hand. 2. Serpent which darts upon its prey.

Dargadandéta, *sf.* Nick-name given to any poor young impudent girl.

Dársena, *sf.* Place in a harbour for preserving and repairing ships.

Dáta, *sf.* 1. Date, the time when a letter is written, or any instrument drawn up. 2. Item or article put down in an account. 3. Condition, quantity. *La cosa está de mala data*, The affair is in a bad state. 4. Written permission to do any thing.

Dataría, *sf.* Datary, an office of the chancery at Rome where the pope's bulls are expedited.

Datário, *sf.* The principal officer of the datary.

Dátil, *sm.* 1. (Bot.) Date, the fruit of the date-tree. 2. Belemnites, arrow-head or finger-stone.

Datiládo, da, *a.* Resembling or like a date.

Datiléra, *sf.* (Ant.) Date-tree.

Datilíllo, *sm.* A small date.

Datívo, *sm.* Dative, the third case in the declension of nouns.

Dáuco, *sm.* (Bot.) Carrot. Daucus carota *L.*

Dávva, *sf.* 1. Mistress, concubine, a kept woman. 2. A female treated with peculiar kindness.

Dáza, *sf.* 1. (Bot.) Lucern. Medicago sativa *L.* 2. (Bot.) Panic-grass. Panicum *L.*

De, *prep.* Which being prefixed to verbs, adverbs, or nouns, alters their sense. *De*, 1. Of; the sign of a genitive or possessive case. *La ley de dios*, The law of God. 2. It serves to point out the matter of which a thing is made. *Vaso de plata*, A silver cup. 3. It is the sign of the ablative case. *Vengo de Flándes*, I come from Flanders. 4. It serves sometimes instead of the preposition *con*. *De intento*, On purpose. 5. It is used in the room of *por*. *De miedo*, From fear. 6. It is of the same import as *desde*. *Vamos de Madrid á Toledo*, We go from Madrid to Toledo. 7. It governs sometimes the infinitive mood. *Hora de comer*, Dinner-time. 8. It is placed before adverbs of time. *De dia*, By day. *De noche*, By night. 9. It sometimes marks an inference. *De aqui se infiere*, Hence it follows. 10. In a familiar style it is used to give more energy to an expression. *El ladron del mozo*, The rogue of a boy. 11. (Ant.) To. *Bueno de comer*, Good to eat.

Déa, *sf.* (Poét.) Goddess. V. *Diosa*.

Deán, *sm.* Dean, a dignitary.

Deanáto y Deanázgo, *sm.* Deanship, the office and dignity of a dean.

Debálde, *ad.* For nothing, gratis. V. *Balde*.

Debandár, *va.* (Ant.) To disband, to disunite.

Debáte, *sm.* Debate, discussion of any point.

Debatír, *va.* 1. To debate, to argue, to discuss 2. To combat, to engage with arms.

Debáxo, *ad.* Under, underneath, below. *De baxo de mano*, Under-hand, privately.—*prep.* Under, subordinate, dependent.

Debda y Debdo, (Ant.) V. *Deuda*.

Debdado y Debdoso, (Ant.) V. *Adeudado*.

Debelación, *sf.* Debellation, the act of conquering in war; conquest.

Debelár, *va.* To debellate, to conquer, to subdue.

Debér, *sm.* 1. Obligation, duty. 2. Debt.

Debér, *va.* 1. To owe, not to pay a debt which is due. 2. It is used as an auxiliary verb. *Debe intenderse asi*, It ought to be understood so.

Debidaménte, *ad.* 1. Justly, with moderation and justice. 2. Duly, exactly, perfectly.

Debidór, *sm.* V. *Deudor*.

Debiénte, *pa.* Owing; he who owes; debtor.

Débil, *a.* 1. Feeble, weak, extenuated. 2. Pusillanimous.

Debilidád, *sf.* 1. Debility, weakness, languor, want of strength. 2. (Met.) Pusillanimity.

Debilitación, *sf.* Debilitation, extenuation, want of vigour and strength.

Debilitár, *va.* To debilitate, to weaken, to extenuate.

Debilménte, *ad.* Weakly, in a feeble manner.

Débito, *sm.* Debt. *Débito conyugal*, Conjugal duty.

Débo, *sm.* Instrument used for scraping skins.

Debrocár, *vn.* To be sick or infirm.

Debuxadúra, *sf.* (Ant.) Design, delineation.

Debuxár, *va.* V. *Dibuxar*.

Década, *sf.* Decade, the number or sum of ten.

Decadéncia, *sf.* Decay, decline; decadency. *Ir en decadencia*, To be on the decline.
Decaeménto y Decaiménto, *sm.* V. *Descaecimiento.*
Decaér, *vn.* 1. To decay, to decline. 2. (Naút.) To fall to leeward.
Decágono, *sm.* Decagon, a polygon of ten sides or angles.
Decálogo, *sm.* Decalogue, the ten commandments given by God to Moses.
Decampaménto, *sm.* Decampment, the act of shifting the camp.
Decampár, *vn.* To decamp, to raise or shift the camp.
Decanáto, *sm.* Dignity of the senior of any community.
Decáno, *sm.* Senior, the most ancient member of a community or corporation.
Decantación, *sf.* Decantation, the act of pouring off liquor gently by inclination.
Decantár, *va.* 1. To cry up, to exaggerate or magnify any thing. 2. To turn any thing from a right line, and to give it an oblique direction. 3. To decant, to draw off liquor gently by inclination.
Decebimiénto, *sm.* (Ant.) Deception, artifice.
Decebír, *va.* (Ant.) To deceive.
Decémbrio, *sm.* *Diciembre.*
Decemviráto, *sm.* Decemvirate.
Decéna, *sf.* 1. Number of ten. 2. (Arag.) Company or party of ten persons. 3. (Mús.) Consonance made of an octave and a third.
Decenál, *a.* Decennial, a space of ten years.
Decenário, ria, *a.* Decennary, making ten in number; the tenth bead of the rosary.
Decéncia, *sf.* 1. Decence or decency, propriety of form or conduct. 2. Reservedness, honesty, modesty.
Decendér, *vn.* V. *Descender.*
Decendimiénto, *sm.* V. *Descendimiento.*
Decénio, *sm.* Space of ten years.
Decéno, na, *a.* Decennial.
Decentár, *va.* 1. To commence the use of things not before used. 2. To begin to lose that which had been preserved.—*vr.* To wound, to gall or injure the skin or body; to be bed-ridden.
Decénte, *a.* 1. Decent, just, honest, becoming. 2. Convenient, reasonable. 3. Decent, modest. 4. Of honest but not noble parents.
Decenteménte, *ad.* 1. Decently, in a decent manner. 2. (Irón.) Abundantly, excessively.
Decepción, *sf.* Deception, illusion.
Decernér, *va.* V. *Discernir.*
Decernumbár, *va.* V. *Derrumbar.*
Decesión, *sm.* (Ant.) Procession; antecedence.
Decéso, *sm.* Decease, a natural death.
Decésor, ra, *s.* V. *Antecesor.*
Dechádo, *sm.* 1. Sample, pattern, design. 2. Linen, on which young girls perform several sorts of needle-work. 3. Example, pattern, or model of virtue and perfection.
Decíble, *a.* Expressible, that which may be expressed or uttered.
Decidéras, *sf. pl.* Eloquence, the power of speaking with fluency and elegance.
Decidéro, ra, *a.* Modest, reserved.
Decidír, *va.* To decide, to determine, to resolve.
Decidór, ra, *s.* 1. One that speaks with fluency and elegance. 2. (Ant.) Versifier, poet.
Deciémbre, *sm.* (Ant.) December. V. *Diciembre.*
Deciénte, *sm.* He who falls or deceases.
Décima, *sf.* 1. (Poét.) A Spanish stanza, consisting of ten verses of eight syllables. 2. Tithe, the tenth part.
Decimál, *a.* 1. Decimal, belonging to the number of ten. 2. Belonging to tithes. *Rentas decimales*, Tithe-rents.
Decimanovéna, *sf.* One of the registers of the pipes of an organ.
Decimár, *va.* (Ant.) V. *Diezmar.*
Décimo, ma, *a.* Tenth, ordinal of ten.
Decimonóno, na, *a.* Nineteenth.
Decimoquínto, ta, *a.* Fifteenth.
Decimoséptimo, ma, *a.* Seventeenth.
Decimotércio, cia, *a.* Thirteenth.
Decinuéve, *sm.* V. *Diez y nueve.*
Deciochéno, na, *a.* 1. Eighteenth. 2. Kind of cloth. 3. V. *Dieziocheno.*
Decír, *va.* 1. To say or utter any thing. *Decir bien*; To speak fluently or gracefully, to explain any thing well. *Decir misa*, To say mass. 2. To assure, to persuade. 3. To name, to give a name to a person or place. 4. To be conformable, to correspond. 5. To declare or depose upon oath. 6. (Ant.) To versify. *Decir de repente*, To make verses off hand. *Decir tixeretas*, To persist in an erroneous opinion. *Digo!* I say; hark; used in calling or speaking to. *Por mejor decir*, More properly speaking. *El decir de las gentes*, The opinion of the people. *Decir de si*, To affirm any thing. *Decir de no*, To deny. *Decir por decir*, To talk for the sake of talking.
Decír, *sm.* A notable saying. *Decires*, Idle talk, false rumours, scandal, slander.
Deciséis, *sm.* (Ant.) Sixteen.
Decisión, *sf.* 1. Decision, determination, resolution. 2. Decision, a sentence pronounced by a court of justice. 3. Disposition, establishment.
Decisivaménte, *ad.* Decisively.
Decisívo, va, *a.* Decisive, that which decides or determines.
Decisório, ria, *a.* Decisive.
Declamación, *sf.* 1. Declamation, a discourse addressed to the passions. 2. Oratorial invective; manner of reciting theatrical compositions. 3. Panegyric on some great achievement.
Declamadór, ra, *s.* Declaimer, one who makes speeches with intent to move the passions.
Declamár, *vn.* To declaim, to harangue, to rhetoricate.
Declamatório, ria, *a.* Declamatory; relating to the practice of declaiming.
Declaración, *sf.* 1. Declaration, explanation of something doubtful. 2. Interpretation, exposition.
Declaradaménte, *ad.* In an explanatory manner.
Declaráno, *a.* Declared; applied to a person who speaks too plainly.
Declaradór, ra, *s.* Declarer, one that makes any thing known.
Declaránte, *sm.* One that declares or explains. *Juan declarante*, A talkative person who speaks his mind too freely.
Declarár, *va.* 1. To declare, to manifest, to make known. 2. To expound, to explain. 3. (In Law) To determine and decide. 4. To witness or depose upon oath.—*vr.* To declare one's opinion, to explain one's mind.

Declaratório, ria, *a.* Declaratory, explanatory.
Decláro, *sm.* V. *Declaracion.*
Declinábile, *a.* (Gram.) Declinable, having variety of terminations.
Declinación, *sf.* 1. Declination, descent, decay; change from better to a worse state. 2. (In Grammar) Declination, the declension or inflection of a noun through its various terminations. 3. (In Astronomy) Distance of a star or planet from the equator.
Declinánte, *a.* Declining, having some declination; bending down.
Declinár, *vn.* 1. To decline, to lean downward. 2. To sink, to be impaired, to decay, to degenerate. 3. To shun, to withdraw out of sight.—*va.* (In Grammar) To decline, to inflect a word by various terminations. 2. To challenge a judge, to transfer a cause to another tribunal.
Declinatória, *sf.* Plea which attacks the competency of a judge.
Declinatório, *sm.* Declinator, or declinatory, an instrument used in dialling.
Declíve ó Declívio, *sm.* Declivity, gradual descent.
Declividád, *sf.* Declivity, inclination, or obliquity.
Decoccion, *sf.* 1. Decoction, the act of boiling any thing. 2. Preparation made by boiling in water.
Decolación, *sf.* V. *Degollacion.*
Decolgár, *vn.* V. *Colgar.*
Decór, *sm.* V. *Adorno.*
Decoración, *sf.* Decoration, ornament.
Decorár, *va.* 1. To decorate, to adorn, to embellish. 2. To illustrate, to ennoble, to honour, to exalt. 3. To learn by heart.
Decóro, ra, *a.* V. *Decoroso.*
Decóro, *sm.* 1. Honour, respect, reverence due to any person. 2. Circumspection, gravity, integrity. 3. Purity, honesty. 4. Decorum, decency, seemliness.
Decorosaménte, *ad.* Decently, in a decorous manner.
Decoróso, sa, *a.* Decorous, decent, suitable to character.
Decorrérse, *vr.* V. *Escurrirse.*
Decorrimiénto, *sm.* (Ant.) Course or flow of water.
Decorticación, *sf.* Decortication, the act of stripping the bark or husk.
Decreménto, *sm.* Decrement, decrease, diminution.
Decrepitár, *va.* To decrepitate, to calcine salt till it has ceased to crackle in the fire.
Decrépito, ta, *a.* Decrepit, worn out with age.
Decrepitúd, *sf.* Decrepitude, the last stage of old age.
Decretación, *sf.* Determination, establishment.
Decretál, *sf.* Letter or rescript of the pope, which decides a question concerning the ecclesiastical law. *Decretáles,* Collection of letters and decrees of the popes.—*a.* Decretal.
Decretalísta, *sm.* Decretist, one that draws up or studies the rescripts, letters, and decrees of the popes.
Decretár, *va.* 1. To decree, to determine, to resolve. 2. To interpret or explain a decree.
Decretéro, *sm.* 1. Catalogue or list of names and offences of criminals. 2. Collection of decrees.
Decretísta, *sm.* Decretist, one who expounds or explains the decretals.
Decréto, *sm.* 1. Decree, decision, resolution. 2. Order or determination issued in the king's name. 3. A judicial decree. 4. Opinion, vote, advice. *Decretos de cazon,* Common decrees, not requiring any peculiar formality of the law.
Decretório, ria, *a.* Decretory; critical; applied to the days when a judgment may be formed on the issue of a fit of illness.
Decúbito, *sm.* 1. (Med.) Particular flow of the humours in diseases. 2. Act of lying down to rest.
Decumána, *sf.* The tenth thing in the numeral order.
Décuplo, pla, *a.* Decuple, tenfold.
Decúria, *sf.* 1. Ten Roman soldiers under a corporal. 2. In universities, the assembly of ten students to take their lessons. 3. (Ant.) The cork of a bee-hive.
Decuriáto, *sm.* A student assigned to the decurion to take his lesson.
Decurión, *sm.* 1. Decurion, the chief or commander of ten soldiers. 2. (In Colleges and Universities) Student who has the care of ten other students, and gives them lessons. *Decurion de decuriones,* A senior decurion, or student who governs the rest.
Decúrsas, *sf. pl.* Arrears of rent.
Decúrso, *sm.* Course, succession of movement or time.
Dedáda, *sf.* 1. That which can be taken up with the finger at once. *Dar á uno una dedada de miel,* (Met.) To put a cheat on one, to deceive; literally, to give one a fingerful of honey. 2. Sort of architectonic ornament of the Doric order.
Dedál, *sm.* 1. Thimble, a metal cover, whereby the fingers are secured from the needle. 2. Thumb-stall of linen or leather used by reapers. 3. A very small drinking glass or cup.
Dedalísimo, *sm.* A very large thimble.
Dedaléra, *sf.* (Bot.) Fox-glove. Digitalis purpurea *L.*
Dedicación, *sf.* Dedication, the act of dedicating to any being or purpose; consecration; inscription.
Dedicánte, *pa.* Dedicating, dedicator.
Dedicár, *va.* 1. To dedicate, to devote, to consecrate. 2. To inscribe a literary work to a patron. *Dedicarse á alguna cosa,* To apply one's self to a thing.
Dedicatória, *sf.* Dedication, an address by which a literary composition is inscribed to a patron.
Dedignár, *va.* To disdain, to despise, to contemn.—*vr.* To scorn doing any thing
Dedíl, *sm.* V. *Dedál.*
Dedíllo, *sm.* A little finger.
Dédo, *sm.* 1. Finger, the flexible member of the hand, by which men catch and hold. 2. Toe, one of the fingers of the feet. 3. The forty-eighth part of a Spanish yard or *vara.* 4. Hand of a clock or watch. 5. A finger's breadth, a small bit. *Ganar á dedos,* To gain by inches. *Meter los dedos,* To pump one. *Señalarle con el dedo,* To point at another with the finger. *Estar á dos dedos de la eternidad,* To be on the brink of eternity. *Dedo meñique*

The little finger. *Dedo pulgar*, Thumb. *Dedo del corazon*, Middle finger.

DEDUCCIÓN, *sf.* 1. Deduction, derivation, origin, consequence. 2. Deduction, that which is deducted. 3. (Mús.) The natural progression of sounds in the rise and fall of music.

DEDUCÍR, *va.* 1. To deduce, to infer. 2. To allege in pleading, to offer as a plea. 3. To subtract, to deduct.

DEDÚR, *ad.* (Ant.) Difficultly.

DEÉSA, *sf.* Goddess. V. *Diosa*.

DEFÁCILE, *ad.* (Ant.) Easily.

DEFÁCTO, *ad.* V. *De hecho*.

DEFALCÁR, *va.* V. *Desfalcar*.

DEFAMÁR, *va.* V. *Infamar*.

DEFECÁDO, DA, *a.* V. *Depurado*.

DEFECCIÓN, *sf.* Defection, apostasy; revolt.

DEFECTÍBLE, *a.* Defectible, imperfect, deficient.

DEFECTÍVO, VA, *a.* Defective, full of defects, imperfect.

DEFÉCTO, *sm.* Defect, a natural or moral imperfection.

DEFECTUOSAMÉNTE, *ad.* In a defective manner.

DEFECTUÓSO, SA, *a.* Defective, imperfect, faulty.

DEFEMINÁDO, DA, *a.* (Ant.) V. *Afeminado*.

DEFENDEDÉRO, RA, *a.* Susceptible of defence.

DEFENDEDÓR, *sm.* 1. Defender, protector. 2. V. *Abogado*.

DEFENDÉR, *va.* 1. To defend, to protect from danger. 2. To assert, to maintain. 3. To defend, to vindicate, to allege in favour of another. 4. To prohibit, to forbid. 5. To resist, to oppose.

DEFENDIMIÉNTO, *sm.* Defence, support, protection.

DEFENECÉR, *va.* (Arag.) To close an account.

DEFÉNSA, *sf.* 1. Defence, safeguard, the means of warding off any danger. 2. Shelter, protection. 3. Prohibition. 4. (In Fortification) The fort which flanks another work. *Linea de la defensa*, Line of defence. *Defensas de los costados*, (Naút.) Skids or skeeds; timbers fastened to the wales with bolts and spike-nails. *Defensas de cabo ó cable viejo*, (Naút.) Fenders, pieces of cable hanging over the sides of a ship, to hinder her from rubbing against the wharf, or any other solid body.

DEFENSÁBLE, *a.* Susceptible of defence.

DEFENSÁR, *va.* V. *Defender*.

DEFENSATRÍZ, *sf.* V. *Defensora*.

DEFENSÍBLE, *a.* DEFENSIBLE. V. *Defensable*.

DEFENSIÓN, *sf.* (Ant.) 1. Defence. V. *Defensa*. 2. (Ant.) Prohibition, obstacle.

DEFENSÍVO, *sm.* 1. Defence, safeguard. 2. Piece of linen steeped in any medical liquor, and applied to some part of the body, to refresh and strengthen it.

DEFENSÍVO, VA, *a.* Defensive, that which serves as a defence or safeguard. *Estar á la defensiva, ó ponerse sobre la defensiva*, To be upon the defensive, to put one's self upon the defensive.

DEFENSÓR, RA, *s.* 1. Defender, one that defends or protects. 2. Lawyer appointed by a court of justice to defend the estate of a bankrupt.

DEFENSORÍA, *sf.* The duty and office of a lawyer appointed to defend the estate of an insolvent person.

DEFENSÓRIO, *sm.* Defence, an apologetic writing in favour of any person or thing; a memoir, a manifesto.

DEFERÉNTE, *a.* Assenting, yielding to the opinion of another without wishing to maintain his own.

DEFERÍR, *vn.* To defer, to pay deference or regard to another's opinion.—*va.* To communicate, to share in the jurisdiction or power.

DEFÉSA, *sf.* V. *Dehesa*.

DEFÉSO, SA, *a.* (Ant.) Prohibited, interdicted.

DEFIÁNZA, *sf.* V. *Desconfianza*.

DEFIÁR, *vn.* V. *Desconfiar*.

DEFICIÉNCIA, *sf.* DEFICIENCY, imperfection.

DEFICIÉNTE, *a.* Defective, faulty, DEFICIENT.

DEFIDACIÓN, *sf.* V. *Fealdad*.

DEFINICIÓN, *sf.* 1. Definition, a short description of a thing by its properties. 2. Decision, determination. *Definiciónes*, Statutes of military orders.

DEFINIDÓR, *sm.* 1. Definer, one who defines, determines, or divides any thing. 2. One who assists the military governor of a province with advice in law matters.

DEFINÍR, *va.* 1. To define, to describe, to explain. 2. To decide, to determine. 3. (Pint.) Concluding any work, finishing all its parts, even the least important, with perfection.

DEFINITIVAMÉNTE, *ad.* Definitively, in a definitive manner.

DEFINITÍVO, VA, *a.* Definitive, determinate, positive.

DEFINITÓRIO, *sm.* 1. Chapter or assembly of the chiefs of religious orders, to deliberate on the affairs and government of the order. 2. House or hall where the above chapters or assemblies are held.

DEFLAQUECIMIÉNTO, *sm.* V. *Enflaquecimiento*

DEFLÚXO, *sm.* 1. Defluxion, the flow of humours downwards. 2. (In Astronomy) The recession of the moon from any planet.

DEFOÍR, *va.* (Ant.) To avoid, to evitate.

DEFONDONÁR, *va.* (Ant.) V. *Desfondar*.

DEFORMACIÓN, *sf.* Deformation, destruction of the exterior form of a thing; defacing. [ures.

DEFORMADÓR, *sm.* One who deforms or disfig-

DEFORMÁR, *va.* To deform, to disfigure.

DEFORMATÓRIO, RIA, *a.* Deforming, disfiguring.

DEFÓRME, *a.* Deformed, disfigured, ugly.

DEFORMEMÉNTE, *ad.* Deformedly.

DEFORMIDÁD, *sf.* 1. Deformity, disfiguration, ugliness. 2. A gross error.

DEFRAUDACIÓN, *sf.* Fraud, deceit, usurpation

DEFRAUDADÓR, *sm.* Defrauder, usurper.

DEFRAUDÁR, *va.* 1. To defraud, to rob or deprive by wile or trick; to usurp what belongs to another. 2. (Met.) To intercept the light of the sun; to spoil the taste; to disturb the sleep.

DEFUÉRA, *ad.* Externally, outwardly, on the outside. *Por defuéra*, Outwardly.

DEFUÍR, *va.* V. *Huir*.

DEFUNCIÓN, *sf.* (Arag.) 1. Death. 2. Funeral, the payment of the last honours to the dead.

DEFÚNTO, *sm.* V. *Difunto*.

DEGÁNA, *sf.* Farm, Farm-house. V. *Granja*.

DEGÁNO, *sm.* (Ant.) Farmer, overseer of a farmery.

DEGASTÁR, *va.* V. *Devastar*.

DEGENERACIÓN, *sf.* Degeneration, a falling from a more excellent state to one of less worth.

DEGENERÁR, *vn.* 1. To degenerate, to fall from its kind, to grow wild or base; applied to plants.

2. To fall from the virtue of our ancestors. 3. (Pint.) To disfigure any thing.

DEGESTÍR, *va.* (Ant.) V. *Digerir.*

DEGLUCÍR, *va.* (Ant.) To swallow, to devour.

DEGOLLACIÓN, *sf.* Decollation, the act of beheading.

DEGOLLADÉRO, *sm.* 1. Throttle, windpipe. 2. Scaffold on which criminals are beheaded. 3. In theatres, seat near the orchestra, and before the pit. *Degolladero de bolsas,* Cut-purse; also a shop where goods are sold at an extravagant price, and bad measure or weight is given. *Llevar al degolladero,* (Met.) To put one in very great danger.

DEGOLLADÓR, *sm.* Executioner, one who beheads.

DEGOLLADÚRA, *sf.* 1. Cut or wound in the throat. 2. Interstice between two bricks filled up with mortar. 3. A slope out of women's jackets. 4. Slender part of balusters.

DEGOLLÁR, *va.* 1. To cut one's throat, to behead. 2. To destroy, to ruin, to annihilate. 3. (Met.) To tease, to importune. *Esta persona me degüella,* This person troubles and harasses me. *Degollar á sangrias,* To debilitate a person by excessive bleeding.

DEGRADACIÓN, *sf.* 1. Degradation, dismission from an office or dignity. 2. Diminution of value.

DEGRADÁR, *va.* To degrade, to deprive one of his place, dignity, or honours.—*vr.* To degrade or demean one's self.

DEGÜÉLLO, *sm.* 1. Decollation, the act of beheading or cutting one's throat. 2. Neck or narrow part of any thing. 3. Destruction, ruin. *Tirar á degüello,* To endeavour to destroy a person; to seek one's ruin.

DEHENDÉR, *va.* To split, to cleave, to divide longitudinally in two.

DEHENDIMIÉNTO, *sm.* The act of splitting, cleaving, or separating in two.

DEHÉSA, *sf.* Pasture-ground. *Dehesa concejil.* Common, a pasture-ground.

DEHESÁR, *va.* To turn arable land into pasture-ground.

DEHESÉRO, *sm.* Keeper of a common.

DEHORTÁR, *va.* (Ant.) To dissuade.

DEICÍDA, *sm.* Deicide; a term applied by some writers to those who concurred in the crucifixion of our Saviour.

DEICÍDIO, *sm.* Murder of Christ.

DEIDÁD, *sf.* 1. Deity, divinity; the nature and essence of God. 2. Deity, goddess; a term of flattery and courtship addressed to women.

DEÍFERO, RA, *s.* One who bears God at heart.

DEIFICACIÓN, *sf.* Deification, the act of deifying or making a god.

DEIFICÁR, *va.* To deify, to praise excessively or in an extravagant manner.

DEÍFICO, DEIFÓRME, *a.* Godlike, divine.

DEÍSMO, *sm.* Deism, acknowledging one God and rejecting revelation.

DEÍSTA, *sm.* Deist, he who acknowledges God, but disbelieves revelation.

DEL, A contraction of the preposition *De* and the article *el,* which is used in the masculine gender of the genitive case. *Del, Della, Dello,* instead of *De el, De ella, De ello,* Of or from him, her, or it. *Dello con dello,* Reciprocally, alternatively, one with the other, good and bad as they come.

DELACIÓN, *sf.* Delation, accusation, impeachment.

DELÁNT, *ad.* (Ant.) V. *Delante.*

DELANTÁL, *sm.* Apron.

DELÁNTE, *ad.* 1. Before, in the presence of. 2. Forward, onward. *Dios delante,* With the help of God. 3. In preference to, with regard to time or place.

DELANTÉRA, *sf.* 1. The fore part of any thing. 2. The front seats, behind the barriers of a place, where bull feasts are held. 3. Fore skirts of clothes. 4. Frontiers, confines. 5. Distance before one on the road. 6. (Ant.) Vanguard of an army. *Coger la delantera,* To get the start of any person. *Ir en la delantera,* To take the lead.

DELANTÉRO, RA, *a.* Foremost, that is or goes first in place.

DELANTÉRO, *sm.* 1. The first, one who takes the lead, or goes before the rest. 2. Postilion, one who guides the first pair of horses put to a coach.

DELATÁBLE, *a.* Accusable, blameable.

DELATÁR, *va.* To inform, to accuse, to denounce, to impeach.

DELÁTE, *sm.* Highwayman, robber on the high roads.

DELATÓR, *sm.* Accuser, informer, denouncer.

DELAXÁR, *va.* V. *Cansar.*

DÉLE, *prep.* (Ant.) Now written *Del,* Of the.

DÉLE, *sm.* (Impr.) A cipher or mark of deletion used by correctors of the press.

DELECTÁBLE, *a.* Delectable, pleasing, delightful. V. *Deleytable.*

DELECTACIÓN, *sf.* Delectation, pleasure, delight. *Delectacion morosa,* The deliberate but unintentional indulgence of some sensual pleasure, that is contrary to good manners.

DELECTÁR, *va.* To delight. V. *Deleytar.*

DELÉCTO, *sm.* (Ant.) Election, choice, deliberation, separation.

DELEGACIÓN, *sf.* Delegation, substitution.

DELEGÁDO, *sm.* Delegate, deputy, commissioner.

DELEGÁNTE, *pa.* One that delegates.

DELEGÁR, *va.* To delegate, to substitute.

DELETREADÓR, *sm.* Speller, one who spells or forms words of letters.

DELETREÁR, *va.* 1. To spell, to learn to read by pronouncing every letter singly. 2. To find out and explain the meaning of what is difficult and obscure, to examine, to scrutinize.

DELEYTÁBLE, *a.* Delectable, pleasing, delightful.

DELEYTABLEMÉNTE, *ad.* Delightfully.

DELEYTACIÓN Y DELEYTABILIDÁD, *sf.* Delectation, pleasure, delight.

DELEYTAMIÉNTO, *sm.* Delight, pleasure.

DELEYTÁR, *va.* To delight, to please, to give pleasure.

DELÉYTE, *sm.* 1. Pleasure, delight. *Deleyte sensual,* The emotion of any lawful pleasure, as music, sweet smells, fine flowers. 2. Lust, carnal appetite.

DELEYTOSAMÉNTE, *ad.* Delightfully, pleasantly, cheerfully.

DELEYTÓSO, SA, *a.* Agreeable, pleasing, delightful.

DELEZNÁBLE, *a.* Slippery, smooth, glib.

DELEZNADÉRO, *sm.* A slippery place.

DELEZNAMIÉNTO, *sm.* Act of slipping.

DELEZNÁR, *vn.* V. *Deslizar.*

DÉLFIN, *sm.* 1. Dolphin, a cetaceous animal. Delphinus delphis *L.* 2. Dolphin of a cannon, one of the two handles placed near the second reinforce-ring of a brass gun, and serving to mount it on the carriage. 3. Dolphin, a northern constellation. 4. Dauphin, eldest son of the king of France.

Delfína, *sf.* Sort of light drugget.

Delfínio, *sm.* (Bot.) Lark-spur. Delphinium consolida *L.*

Delgacéro, ra, *a.* V. *Delgado.*

Delgadaménte, *ad.* 1. Thinly, delicately. 2. (Met.) Acutely, sharply, finely.

Delgadéz, *sf.* 1. Thinness, tenuity, rareness. 2. (Met.) Acuteness, ingenuity.

Delgádo, da, 1. Thin, tenuous, delicate, light. 2. (Met.) Acute, fine, ingenious. 3. Short, little, scanty, poor. *Delgados de un navio,* (Naút.) The narrowing or rising of a ship's floor. *Navio delgado á proa,* (Naút.) A sharp bowed vessel. *Navio delgado para andar,* (Naút.) A sharp built vessel for sailing. *Navio de muchos delgados,* (Naút.) A sharp bottomed ship.

Delgádo, *sm.* A strait place. *Delgados,* Flanks of animals.

Delgazár, *va.* V. *Adelgazar.*

Deliberación, *sf.* 1. Deliberation, consideration, reflection. 2. Resolution, determination. 3. (Ant.) Liberation.

Deliberadaménte, *ad.* Deliberately.

Deliberadór, *sm.* Deliverer, one who rescues another from slavery.

Deliberamiénto, *sm.* Deliverance, the act of freeing from captivity.

Deliberár, *vn.* To consider, to deliberate, to discourse.—*va.* 1. To deliberate, to think in order to choose, to hesitate. 2. To rescue from captivity. 3. To emancipate, to free from paternal power.

Deliberatívo, va, *a.* Deliberative, pertaining to deliberation, apt to consider.

Delibración y Delibránza, *sf.* V. *Rescate.*

Delibrár, *va.* (Ant.) 1. To deliberate, to determine. 2. To liberate. 3. V. *Despachar.*

Delicadaménte, *ad.* Delicately, with delicacy.

Delicadéz, *sf.* 1. Delicacy, weakness of constitution. 2. (Met.) Tenderness, scrupulousness, mercifulness. 3. Gentleness of manners, sweetness of temper. 4. Faintness, idleness, cowardice.

Delicadéza, *sf.* 1. Delicateness, tenderness, softness, effeminacy. 2. Subtlety, dexterity. 3. Exility, fineness, tenuity. 4. (Met.) Acuteness of understanding, refinement of wit; perspicacity.

Delicádo, da, *a.* 1. Delicate, sweet, pleasing, tender. 2. Weak, faint, effeminate. 3. Nice, pleasing to the taste; of an agreeable flavour. 4. Thin, slender, subtile. 5. Nice, scrupulous, fastidious. 6. Beautiful, pleasing to the eye. 7. Arduous, difficult, perplexing.

Delicadúra y Delicamiénto. V. *Delicadez.*

Delícia, *sf.* Delight, comfort, satisfaction.

Deliciárse, *vr.* To delight, to have delight or pleasure in.

Deliciosaménte, *ad.* Deliciously.

Delicióso, sa, *a.* Delicious, delightful, pleasing.

Delineación, *sf.* Delineation, the act of making the first draught or sketch; and the first draught or sketch itself.

Delineaménto ó Delineamiénto, *sm.* V. *Delineacion.*

Delineár, *va.* 1. To delineate, to draw the first draught of a thing; to sketch. 2. (Met.) To describe in prose or verse the beauty or deformity of a thing.

Delinqüénte, *pa.* Delinquent.

Delinquimiénto, *sm.* Delinquency, fault, failure in duty.

Delinquír, *vn.* To transgress the law, to offend.

Delintár ó Delinterár, *va.* V. *Ceder ó traspasar.*

Deliñár, *va.* To dress, to adorn. V. *Aliñar*

Delíquio, *sm.* Swoon, a fainting fit.

Deliraménto, *sm.* Delirium.

Delirár, *vn.* 1. To delirate, to dote, to rave. 2 (Met.) To rant, to talk nonsense, to rave in violent or high-sounding language.

Delírio, *sm.* 1. Delirium, alienation of mind, dotage. 2. (Met.) Rant, nonsense, idle talk.

Delíto, *sm.* Transgression of a law, fault, crime.

Della, dello, Contractions of the words *de ella, de ello.* V. *Del.*

Delongár, *va.* (Ant.) To enlarge, to prolong

Delúbro, *sm.* 1. Temple or altar dedicated to an idol. 2. Idol, an image worshipped as God.

Delusívo, va, *a.* Delusive, fallacious.

Delusór, *sm.* Cheat, impostor.

Delusoriaménte, *ad.* Delusively, deceitfully.

Delusório, ria, *a.* Deceitful, fallacious.

Demáes, *ad.* V. *Demas.*

Demagógo, *sm.* Demagogue, a ringleader of the rabble.

Demánda, *sf.* 1. Demand, claim, pretension, challenge. *Morir en la demanda,* To assert one's right to the last extremity. *Salir á la demanda,* To appear in one's own defence. *Demandas y respuestas,* Haggling between sellers and buyers before they come to a price: chimerical ideas which agitate the mind. 2. Request, petition, the act of asking charity. 3. Charity-box; an image carried about by hermits and other devotees who ask charity. 4. (Naút.) Look-out, the act of looking out for the land or another vessel. 5. Interrogation.

Demandáble, *a.* V. *Apetecible.*

Demandadéro, ra, *s.* A servant man or woman who attends at the door of a nunnery or convent, to go on errands for the nuns.

Demandádo, da, *s.* Defendant, the person accused.

Demandadór, *sm.* 1. One who goes about asking charity for pious uses. 2. Claimant, plaintiff. 3. One who solicits a woman in marriage.

Demandár, *va.* 1. To demand, to ask, to petition. 2. To put in a claim, to enter an action 3. To covet, to have a strong desire. 4. (Joc.) To finger one's money, to steal. 5. (Naút.) To require more water to sail.

Demaniál, *a.* Originating in, proceeding from.

Demarcación, *sf.* Demarcation, the act of marking the limits of a place.

Demarcadór, *sm.* Designator, he who marks or limits.

Demarcár, *va.* To mark out confines or limits. *Demarcar el terreno de un campamento,* To trace or mark out the ground of a camp.

Demarrárse, *vr.* To mislead, to deviate from the right way.

Demás, *ad.* (Ant.) 1. Over and above a certain quantity, measure, or number. 2. It is used with the articles *lo, la, los, las. Asi los demas,*

And so on; so with the rest. *Estar demas*, To be over and above; to be useless or superfluous. *Por demás*, Uselessly, in vain, to no purpose. V. *Ademas*.

DEMÁSES, *sm. pl.* Abundance, excessive copiousness.

DEMASÍA, *sf.* 1. Excess in the price of a thing. 2. An unjust claim or pretension. 3. A superfluous, useless expense. 4. A bold undertaking, an arduous enterprise. 5. Incivility, rudeness, want of respect. 6. Abundance, copiousness, plenty. *En demasía*, Excessively.

DEMASIADAMÉNTE, *ad.* Excessively, extravagantly.

DEMASIÁDO, DA, 1. Excessive, being too much. 2. Bold, daring, enterprising.

DEMASIÁDO, *ad.* Enough, sufficiently.

DEMEDIÁR, *va.* 1. To part asunder, to divide into halves. 2. To wear any thing until it has lost half its value. *Demediar la confesion*, To confess but half one's sins.

DEMÉNCIA, *sf.* Madness, derangement of the mental faculties.

DEMENTÁR, *va.* To render mad or frantic.

DEMÉNTE, *a.* Mad, distracted, frantic.

DEMÉRITO, *sm.* Demerit, the opposite to merit; ill-deserving.

DEMERITÓRIO, RIA, *a.* Without merit.

DEMIÁS, *sf. pl.* In cant language, stockings; trowsers.

DEMIÉNTRA, *ad.* V. *Miéntras*.

DEMIGÁR, *va.* V. *Disipar*.

DEMINUCIÓN, *sf.* V. *Diminucion*.

DEMINUÍR, *va.* V. *Disminuir*.

DEMISIÓN, *sf.* Submission, humility.

DEMITÍR Y DEMETÍR, *va.* *Dimitir*.

DÉMO, *sm.* Demon, a spirit; generally an evil spirit.

DEMOCRACÍA, *sf.* Democracy, a form of government in which the sovereign power is lodged in the people.

DEMOCRÁTICO, CA, *a.* Democratical.

DEMOLÉR, *va.* 1. To demolish, to pull down, to level with the ground. 2. To obliterate, to blot out of the memory.

DEMOLICIÓN, *sf.* Demolition, the act of demolishing or pulling down.

DEMONÍACO, CA, *a.* 1. Demoniacal, tormented by an evil spirit. 2. Belonging to demons.

DEMONIÁDO, DA, *a.* V. *Endemoniado*.

DEMONICHÚCHO, *sm.* An ugly, hideous little devil.

DEMÓNIO, *sm.* 1. Demon. 2. A disease so called.

DEMONSTRACIÓN, *sf.* V. *Demostracion*.

DEMONSTRÁR, *va.* V. *Demostrar*.

DEMOÑUÉLO, *sm.* A little demon or devil.

DEMÓRA Y DEMORÁNZA, *sf.* 1. Delay, procrastination, protraction. 2. Demurrage, an allowance made for the detention of a ship in a port. *Sin demora*, Without delay.

DEMORÁR, *vn.* 1. To remain, to continue long in a place. 2. (Naút.) To bear, to be situated with regard to a ship. *La costa demora Norte*, The coast bears North.

DEMORRÁGE, *sm.* V. *Demora*.

DEMOSTRÁBLE, *a.* Demonstrable, that which can be demonstrated.

DEMOSTRABLEMÉNTE, *ad.* Demonstrably.

DEMOSTRACIÓN, *sf.* Demonstration; manifestation.

DEMOSTRADÓR, RA, Y DEMONSTRADÓR, RA, *s.* Demonstrator, one who demonstrates.

DEMOSTRAMIÉNTO, *sm.* (Ant.) Indication, signification.

DEMOSTRÁNZA, *sf.* (Ant.) Manifestation, exposition.

DEMOSTRÁR, *va.* To prove, to demonstrate.

DEMOSTRATIVAMÉNTE, *a.* Demonstratively.

DEMOSTRATÍVO, VA, *a.* Demonstrative, having the power of demonstration.

DEMUDACIÓN, *sf.* Change, alteration.

DEMUDÁR, *va.* To alter, to change.—*vr.* To be changed.

DENÁNTE Y DENÁNTES, *ad.* (Ant.) V. *Ántes*.

DENÁRIO, *sm.* 1. A small silver coin which was current among the Romans. 2. Decimal or tenth number. 3. Money paid to labourers for one day's labour.

DÉNDE, *ad.* Hence, from. V. *Desde*.

DENDRÍTE, *sf.* Dendrites, a mineral containing the figures of plants.

DENEGACIÓN, *sf.* Denial, refusal, exclusion.

DENEGÁR, *va.* To deny, to refuse.

DENEGRECÉR, *va.* 1. To blacken, to darken. 2. To change the countenance.

DENEGRÍDO, DA, *a.* 1. Blackened, denigrated. 2. Belonging to negroes or black people.

DENEGRÍR, *va.* V. *Denegrecer*.

DENGÓSA, *sf.* Prude, a woman over-nice and scrupulous. V. *Melindrosa*.

DÉNGUE, *sm.* 1. Prudery. 2. A sort of short veil worn by women.

DENGUÉRO, RA, *a.* Prudish, affected. V. *Dengoso*.

DENIGRACIÓN, *sf.* Denigration, stigma, disgrace

DENIGRÁR, *va.* To denigrate or blacken the character of a person, to calumniate, to defame.

DENIGRATIVAMÉNTE, *ad.* Injuriously, infamously.

DENIGRATÍVO, VA, *a.* Blackening, stigmatizing.

DENODADAMÉNTE, *ad.* Boldly, resolutely.

DENODÁDO, DA, *a.* Bold, intrepid, audacious.

DENOMINACIÓN, *sf.* Denomination, distinct appellation.

DENOMINADAMÉNTE, *ad.* Distinctly, definitively.

DENOMINADÓR, *sm.* (Arit.) Denominator.

DENOMINÁR, *va.* To denominate, to give a name or appellation.

DENOSTADAMÉNTE, *ad.* Ignominiously, insultingly.

DENOSTADÓR, *sm.* Vilifier, railer, reviler.

DENOSTÁR, *va.* To insult a person with foul language, to revile.

DENOTACIÓN, *sf.* Designation, denotation.

DENOTÁR, *va.* 1. To denote, to signify. 2. To explain.

DENOTATÍVO, VA, *a.* Denoting.

DENSAMÉNTE, *ad.* Closely, compactly, densely.

DENSÁR, *va.* To condense, to thicken.

DENSIDÁD, *sf.* 1. Density, closeness, compactness. 2. Obscurity, confusion.

DÉNSO, SA, *a.* 1. Dense, thick. 2. Close, compact.

DENSÚNO, *ad.* V. *Juntamente*.

DENT, *pron.* (Ant.) Used for *de él, de ello, de aquello*.

DENTÁDO, DA, *a.* 1. Furnished with teeth. 2. Denticulated, set with small teeth.

DENTADÚRA, *sf.* A set of teeth.

DENTÁL, *sm.* 1. Bed to which the ploughshare is fixed. 2. A wooden fork, with two or more prongs, used by country people to separate the straw from corn. 3. Instrument for drawing or extracting painful teeth. 4. (Conc.) Tooth-shell, a univalve and tubular shell.

Dentár, *va.* To set teeth.
Dentária, *sf.* (Bot.) Tooth-wort. *Dentaria L.*
Denteabrúño, Denteagrúño, ó Dentecíl, *sm.* Royal polypody, great spleen-wort. *Polypodium lonchitis L.*
Dentecér, *vn.* To teeth, to breed teeth.—*va.* To set teeth, to furnish with teeth.
Dentejón, *sm.* Yoke-tree, with which oxen are yoked to the cart.
Dentelária, *sf.* (Bot.) Lead-wort. *Plumbago europea L.*
Dentelláda, *sf.* 1. Gnashing of the teeth. 2. Impression made by a bite of the teeth. *A' dentelladas*, Snappishly, peevishly. *Dar ó sacudir dentelladas*, To speak surlily and uncivilly.
Dentelládo, **da**, *a.* Dental, belonging to the teeth.
Dentellár, *vn.* To gnash, to grind or collide the teeth.
Dentelleár, *va.* To bite, to fix the teeth in any thing.
Dentellón, *sm.* Moulding or ornament of the Corinthian cornice. 2. Piece of a door-lock, which represents a large tooth.
Dentéra, *sf.* 1. An unpleasant sensation or tingling pain in the teeth. 2. (Met.) V. *Envidia.*
Dentezuélo, *sm.* A little tooth.
Dentición, *sf.* Dentition, the act of breeding or cutting the teeth.
Denticulár, *a.* Belonging or relating to the teeth.
Dentísta, *sm.* Dentist, one who professes curing and preserving the teeth.
Dentiváno, **na**, *a.* Having long and large teeth; applied to horses.
Dentón, **na**, *a.* Having large uneven teeth.
Dentón, *sm.* (Ict.) Sea-bream. *Sparus dentex L.*
Dentórno, *ad.* V. *Del rededor.*
Dentrámbos, *pron.* Contraction of *De entrambos.*
Déntro, *ad.* Within. *Dentro del año*, In the course of the year.
Dentúdo, **da**, *a.* Having large uneven teeth.
Denuédo, *sm.* Boldness, audaciousness, courage, intrepidity.
Denuésto, *sm.* Affront, insult.
De nuévo, *ad.* Anew.
Denúncia, *sf.* Accusation; prognostication.
Denunciáble, *a.* Fit to be denounced.
Denunciación, *sf.* 1. Advice, notice. 2. Information laid against another person.
Denunciadór, *sm.* Denunciator, informer.
Denunciár, *va.* 1. To advise, to give notice. 2. To denounce, to lay an information against another. 3. To prognosticate, to foretel. 4. To proclaim, to publish in a solemn manner.
Denunciatório, **ria**, *a.* Belonging or relating to denunciations or informations.
Denúncio, *sm.* V. *Denunciacion.*
Deñár, *va.* (Ant.) To deign, to deem worthy.
Deográcias, *s.* 1. A term used in Spain in saluting, knocking, or calling for entrance in a house. 2. Feigned devotion. *Con su deogracias nos queria engañar*, He tried to deceive us under the cloak of religion. *Deogracias, como va eso!* Bless me, how can that be!
Deparár, *va.* To offer, to furnish, to present.
Departaménto, *sm.* Department, separate allotment, business assigned to a particular person.
Departidaménte, *ad.* Separately, distinctly.
Departidór, *sm.* Distributor, divider.
Departimiénto, *sm.* 1. Division, separation. 2. Distance; difference. 3. Dispute.
Departír, *vn.* To speak, to converse; to contend; to mediate.—*va.* 1. To divide, to separate. 2. To distinguish by notes of diversity. 3. To argue, to contend, to dispute. 4. (Ant.) To teach, to explain; to mark out; to impede, to obstruct.
Depauperár, *va.* 1. To depauperate, to make poor. 2. To debilitate, to weaken, to exhaust.
Dependéncia, *sf.* 1. Dependence, the state of one thing being dependent on another. 2. Subordination to a superior power. 3. Relation by consanguinity or affinity. 4. Business, affair, trust, charge. *Pedro tiene muchas dependencias*, Peter has a deal of business on his hands. 5. Relation or intercourse of business.
Dependér, *vn.* 1. To depend, to rest upon any thing as its cause. 2. To be in a state of dependence or servitude.
Dependiénte y Dependénte, *pa.* A dependent; subject, depending.
Dependienteménte, *ad.* Dependently.
Deploráble, *a.* Deplorable, lamentable, calamitous, hopeless.
Deplorableménte, *ad.* Deplorably.
Deplorár, *va.* To deplore, to lament, to bewail, to bemoan.
Deponénte, *s.* 1. Making a deposition, bearing or giving evidence. 2. (In Grammar) Such verbs as have no active voice are called *deponents*
Deponér, *va.* 1. To depose, to divest. 2. To depose, to declare, to affirm. 3. To depose upon oath before a judge or notary. 4. (Med.) To void by the excretory passages. 5. To displace; to deposit.
Depopulación, *sf.* (Ant.) Desolation, devastation. V. *Despoblacion.*
Depopuladór, *sm.* Depopulator, devastator of a country or city.
Deportación, *sf.* Deportation, transportation or exile to some remote part of the dominions.
Deportár, *va.* To transport to a certain remote part of the dominions.—*vr.* To take a diversion.
Depórte, *sm.* Diversion, amusement, pastime.
Deportóso, **sa**, *a.* V. *Divertido.*
Depós, *ad.* (Ant.) V. *Despues.*
Deposánte, *pa.* Deponent; testifying, asseverating.
Deposár, *va.* V. *Deponer.*
Deposición, *sf.* 1. The act of removing from a place. 2. Deposition, the act of degrading one from dignity or station. 3. Deposition, assertion, affirmation. 4. Deposition upon oath. 5. Alvine evacuation.
Depositadór, *sm.* One who leaves any thing in trust with another.
Depositánte, *pa.* Depositor.
Depositár, *va.* 1. To deposit, to confide or leave any thing in trust or pledge with another. 2. To give, to bestow, to confer without any price or reward. 3. To inclose, to contain. 4. To inter or bury a corpse. 5. To guard, to preserve or liberate.
Depositaría, *sf.* Depository, the place where any thing is lodged or laid up; repository.
Depositário, **ria**, *s.* Depositary, one with whom any thing is lodged in trust.
Depositário, **ria**, *a.* Relating to a depository.
Depósito, *sm.* 1. Deposit, any thing committed

to the trust and care of another. 2. Depository, the place where any thing is safely lodged. 3. Coffin, tomb, or vault, where dead bodies are deposited.

Depóst, *ad.* (Ant.) V. *Despues.*

Depravación, *sf.* Depravation, the act of corrupting any thing or making it bad.

Depravadaménte, *ad.* Depravedly.

Depraváddo, da, *a.* Bad, depraved.

Depravadór, *sm.* Depraver, corrupter.

Depravár, *va.* To deprave, to vitiate, to corrupt.

Deprecación, *sf.* Petition, prayer, deprecation.

Deprecár, *va.* To entreat, to implore, to beg off, to deprecate.

Deprecatívo, va, y Deprecatório, ria, *a.* Deprecative, deprecatory.

Depréces, *sm. pl.* (Ant.) V. *Derechos.*

Deprendér, *va.* To learn. V. *Aprender.*

Depresión, *sf.* 1. Depression, the act of pressing down. 2. Abasement, the act of humbling.

Depresór, *sm.* (Anat.) Depressor, the muscle which brings the head down to the breast.

Depreterición, *sf.* Preterition. V. *Pretericion.*

Deprimír, *va.* To depress, to humble.

Depuración, *sf.* Depuration, purification.

Depurár, *va.* To depurate, to cleanse, to purify.

Depuratório, ria, *a.* That which purifies.

Deputár, *va.* V. *Diputar.*

Déque, *ad.* (Ant.) Since that, immediately that.

Deranchadaménte, *ad.* (Ant.) Disorderly.

Deraygamiénto, *sm.* Extirpation.

Deraygár, *va.* V. *Desarraygar.*

Derecéra, *sf.* Highway, direct road to any place.

Derécha, *sf.* 1. Right hand, right side. 2. (Ant.) Pack of hounds, or the path they pursue in the chase.

Derechaménte, *ad.* 1. Directly, straight; without inclining to one side. 2. Rightly, prudently, justly. 3. Expressly, formally, legally.

Derechéra, *sf.* The direct road, in distinction to that which is circuitous.

Derechéro, *sm.* Clerk appointed to collect the dues of the *Camara*, or privy council of Castile.

Derechéz, *sf.* Rightness, straightness, rectitude.

Derechéza, *sf.* 1. Straightness, the quality of not being crooked. 2. Rectitude, integrity.

Derécho, cha, *a.* 1. Right, even, straight. *Todo derecho*, Straight forward. 2. Just, lawful, well-grounded, reasonable. *Hecho y derecho*, Uprightly, perfectly, in a just and perfect manner. 3. Right, opposite to the left. 4. (Ant.) Certain; directed. *A' derechas*, The right way, rightly, justly. *A' tuertas, ó á derechas*, Right or wrong; inconsiderately. *Derecha la caña*, (Naút.) Right the helm, or midships the helm.

Derécho, *sm.* 1. Right, justice, law. *Derecho divino, canónico, civil, ó municipal*, Divine, canonical, civil, or municipal law. 2. A just claim. 3. The right side of cloth. *Segun derecho*, According to law. 4. (Ant.) Obligation, debt. 5. (Ant.) Road, path. *Derechos*, Taxes, duties, imposts, customs: dues or fees of persons in office.

Derechoreéro, ra, *a.* Just and right or lawful.

Derechuélo ó Derechuelos, *sm.* One of the first seams which mistresses teach little girls.

Derechúra, *sf.* 1. Rectitude; right way. 2. (Ant.) Salary, pay. 3. (Ant.) Right, dexterity. *En derechura*, By the most direct road without delay.

Derechuréro, ra, y Derechuréro, ra, *a.* (Ant.) Right, just, legitimate.

Derechuría, *sf.* (Ant.) Right, justice.

Derezár, *va.* V. *Encaminar.*

Deríva, *sf.* (Naút.) Ship's course.

Derivación, *sf.* 1. Derivation, original. 2. The tracing of a word from its original. 3. The act of separating one thing from another. 4. Descent.

Derivár, *va.* 1. To derive, to separate one thing from another. 2. To deduce any thing from its origin, cause, or source. 3. (Naút.) To conduct, to convoy.—*vn.* To proceed from an original or ancestor.

Derivatívo, va, *a.* Derivative, deriving from a primitive word.

Derogación, *sf.* 1. Derogation or abolition of a law, or of one of its clauses. 2. Deterioration, diminution.

Derogár, *va.* 1. To derogate, to abolish or annul any legal disposition. 2 To reform, to remove.

Derogatório, ria, *a.* Derogatory, that which derogates or lessens the value of any thing.

Deronchár, *va.* (Ant.) To combat, to fight.

Derrabadúra, *sf.* The act of docking, or cutting off the tail of an animal.

Derrabár, *va.* To dock or cut off the tail.

Derráma, *sf.* Assessment of a tax, duty, or impost.

Derramadaménte, *ad.* 1. Profusely, lavishly. 2. Depravedly, corruptly.

Derramadór, *sm.* Prodigal, waster, spendthrift.

Derramamiénto, *sm.* 1. The act of scattering, wasting, or lavishing any thing. 2. Exile, banishment. 3. (Ant.) Flight, escape. *Derramamiento de lágrimas*, Flood of tears.

Derramár, *va.* 1. To drain off water. 2. To publish, to spread. 3. To spill, to scatter, to waste. 4. To assess taxes. *Derramar doctrina*, (Met.) To diffuse a doctrine.—*vr.* 1. To be scattered or spread. 2. To abandon one's self to sensual pleasures and vices. 3. To disembogue itself, as a river. 4. (Ant.) To escape.

Derráme, *sm.* 1. The portion of liquor or seed lost in measuring. 2. Bevel of a wall at a window or door to facilitate the entry of light or other bodies. 3. Declivity.

Derrámo, *sm.* 1. Profusion, prodigality, lavishness. 2. The sloping of a wall in the aperture for a door or window.

Derrancár, *vn.* (Ant.) To assault, to fight impetuously and hastily.

Derrancháddo, da, *a.* Disordered, deranged.

Derranchár, *vn.* To desert, to run away from one's regiment or troop.

Derraspádo, *a.* Beardless; applied to a kind of wheat.

Derraygár, *va.* V. *Desarraygar.*

Derredór, *sm.* Circumference, circuit; round about. It is generally used in the plural, or with the article *al*, or the preposition *en*. *Al derredor, ó en derredor*, Round about.

Derrenegár, *vn.* (Vulg.) To hate, to detest any thing.

Derrengáda, *sf.* (Manch.) Step in dancing.
Derrengádo, da, *a.* Incurvated, bent, crooked.
Derrengadúra, *sf.* Weakness in the hip, dislocation of the hip.
Derrengár, *va.* 1. To hip, to sprain or shoot the hip. 2. To pull down the fruit of a tree. —*vn.* (Vulg.) To abominate, to detest.
Derréngo, *sm.* (Ant.) Stick with which fruits are pulled down.
Derreniégo, *sm.* (Vulg.) Aversion, detestation, abhorrence.
Derrería (A' la), *ad.* At length, in the end.
Derretimiénto, *sm.* 1. Thaw, liquefaction; the melting of any thing congealed. 2. Violent affection.
Derretír, *va.* 1. To liquefy, to melt, to dissolve. 2. To change money. 3. To consume, to expend.—*vr.* 1. To be deeply in love. 2. To grieve, to mourn.
Derribádo, *a.* Applied to horses having the croup rounder and lower than usual.
Derribár, *va.* 1. To demolish, to pull down, to level with the ground. 2. To throw down, to knock down. 3. To depose, to displace, to divest. 4. To ruin, to destroy. 5. (Met.) To incite, to impel.—*vr.* To tumble down, to throw one's self down on the ground.
Derríbo, *sm.* 1. Demolition, the act of pulling down a building. 2. Ruins of a demolished building.
Derrocár, *va.* 1. To precipitate or fling down from a rock. 2. To pull down, to demolish. 3. (Met.) To rob one of his fortune or happiness. 4. To precipitate, to distract any thing spiritual or intellectual.—*vn.* To tumble, to fall down.
Derrochadór, *sm.* A prodigal, he who wastes and spends his fortune.
Derrochár, *va.* 1. To dissipate, to waste or destroy a property. 2. To conquer, to beat down.
Derrompér, *va.* (Ant.) To break, to violate.
Derrostrárse, *vr.* To have one's face disfigured by blows or strokes.
Derróta, *sf.* 1. (Naút.) Ship's course, the tack or line in which a ship sails. *Derrota estimada*, (Naút.) The dead reckoning of a ship. *Seguir en directa derrota*, (Naút.) To steer a direct or straight course. 2. Road, path. 3. Rout or defeat of an army. 4. Opening made in hedges or fences for the cattle which pasture in the stubbles.
Derrotár, *va.* 1. (Naút.) To cause to drive or fall off, applied to the wind or stormy weather. 2. To destroy health or fortune. 3. To rout, to defeat.—*vn.* To arrive in a place in a ruined state, or in the utmost confusion and disorder.
Derróte, *sm.* Defeat, rout, destruction.
Derrotéro, *sm.* 1. (Naút.) Collection of sea-charts, containing the soundings, bearings, and prospective delineations of the sea-coast; the line or track in which ships ought to sail; and the distances of places and other objects. 2. Course, rout. V. *Derrota.*
Derrubiár, *va.* To drain insensibly any river, rivulet, or humid place or thing.
Derrúbio, *sm.* The insensible drain of water from a river, rivulet, or surrounding marsh; or the earth which falls or moulders away by this means.
Derruecár, *va.* To unhorse, to throw off the rider; applied to a horse.
Derruír, *va.* To demolish, to destroy, to ruin. V. *Derribar.*
Derrumbadéro, *sm.* 1. Precipice; a craggy, steep, and broken ground. 2. (Met.) A thorny or arduous affair.
Derrumbamiénto, *sm.* Precipitation, the act of throwing headlong.
Derrumbár, *va.* 1. To precipitate, to throw down headlong. 2. (Met.) To emit or dart rays of light.—*vr.* To precipitate one's self headlong.
Derruviár, *va.* To undermine, to wash away; applied to a river.
Des, 1. A preposition, corresponding with the Latin *dis*, which is never used but in compound words. 2. A contraction of *de ese*, of this, of that.
Des que, *ad.* Contraction of *Desde que*, Since that.
Desabarrancár, *va.* 1. To drag, draw, or pull out of a ditch. 2. (Met.) To disentangle from a state of perplexity, to extricate from difficulties.
Desabastecér, *va.* Not to supply a place with provisions, either through neglect or in consequence of a prohibition.
Desabatír, *va.* (Ant.) To lower, to abate.
Desabejár, *va.* To remove or take away the bees from their hive.
Desabído, da, *a.* 1. Ignorant, illiterate. 2. Excessive, extraordinary.
Desabillé, *sm.* Dishabille, undress; a very common dress for women, consisting of a trimmed petticoat and a half gown or jacket of the same colour and quality, made of silk or other stuff according to the condition of the person. The word is recently adopted from the French, but the costume is very ancient.
Desabitár, *va.* (Naút.) To unbit. *Desabitar el cable*, To unbit a cable; that is, to remove the turns of a cable from the bits.
Desabolladór, *sm.* 1. An instrument used by tin-workers to take bulges out of pewter dishes, plates, or vessels. 2. Tin-worker, who takes bulges out of pewter vessels.
Desabollár, *va.* To take bulges out of pewter dishes, plates, or metal vessels.
Desabóno, *sm.* Prejudice, injury. *Hablar en desabono de alguno*, To speak to the prejudice of another.
Desabór, *sm.* 1. Insipidity, want of taste or flavour. 2. (Met.) Dulness, dejection, want of courage, lowness of spirits.
Desaborár, *va.* 1. To render any thing tasteless, to make it insipid or disgusting. 2. (Met.) To disgust, to vex.
Desabordárse, *vr.* (Naút.) To get clear of a ship which boarded or fell on board of one's vessel.
Desaborrído, da, *a.* Esteemed, not disliked.
Desabotonár, *va.* To unbutton.—*vn.* To blow, to bloom, to blossom.
Desabridaménte, *ad.* Bitterly, rudely, harshly.
Desabrído, da, *a.* 1. Tasteless, insipid. 2. Sour, peevish, severe. 3. Hard, difficult; applied to

guns that rebound much on discharging them. 4. Bleak, sharp; applied to the air and wind.

Desabrigadaménte, *ad.* Nakedly.

Desabrigádo, da, *a.* 1. Uncovered. 2. (Met.) Abandoned, without support.

Desabrigár, *vn.* To be naked, to be unsheltered or unprotected.—*va.* To strip, to make naked; to deprive of covering, shelter, or protection.

Desabrígo, *sm.* 1. Nudity, want of covering or clothes. 2. (Met.) Destitution, want of support or protection.

Desabrimiénto, *sm.* 1. Insipidity, want of taste or flavour. 2. Severity or asperity of temper, rudeness of manners. 3. Despondency, dejection, lowness of spirits. 4. The rebound of guns when discharged.

Desabrír, *vn.* 1. To be insipid or without taste. 2. (Met.) To be dull or heavy, to be peevish.

Desabrochár, *va.* 1. To unclasp, to open or separate what was closed or fastened with clasps. 2. To open, to burst open.—*vr.* To unbosom, to reveal in confidence, to disclose.

Desacabalár, *va.* To pilfer. V. *Descabalar.*

Desacaloràrse, *vr.* 1. To take the fresh air, to cool one's self. 2. (Met.) To grow less warm, with regard to passion or anger.

Desacatadaménte, *ad.* In a disrespectful, saucy, or petulant manner.

Desacatádo, da, *a.* Acting in a disrespectful manner.

Desacatadór, ra, *s.* An irreverent, uncivil, or disrespectful person.

Desacatamiénto, *sm.* Disrespect, want of civility or politeness.

Desacatár, *va.* To treat in a disrespectful manner.

Desacáto, *sm.* Disrespect, incivility, want of reverence, rudeness.

Desacerbár, *va.* To dulcorate, to make less acrimonious, to assuage, to mitigate.

Desacertadaménte, *ad.* Inconsiderately, without reflection.

Desacertádo, da, *a.* Inconsiderate, acting without prudence or reflection.

Desacertár, *va.* To err, to commit a mistake.

Desaceytádo, da, *a.* Destitute of the necessary quantity of oil.

Desaciérto, *sm.* Error, mistake.

Desacobardár, *va.* To remove fear or cowardice, to inspire courage.

Desacollár, *va.* To dig up the ground about vines, to cultivate vines.

Desacomodadaménte, *ad.* Incommodiously, inconveniently, not at ease.

Desacomodádo, da, *a.* 1. Destitute of the conveniences of life. 2. Being out of place or employment. 3. That which causes trouble or inconvenience.

Desacomodamiénto, *sm.* Incommodity, inconvenience, trouble.

Desacomodár, *va.* 1. To incommode, to molest. 2. To deprive of ease or convenience. 3. To turn out of place.—*vr.* To lose one's place, to be out of place; applied to servants.

Desacompañamiénto, *sm.* Want of company or society.

Desacompañár, *va.* To leave the company, to retire.

Desaconsejádo, da, *a.* Acting without prudence or reflection.

Desaconsejár, *va.* To dissuade, to dehort; to divert by reason or importunity from any thing.

Desacordadaménte, *ad.* Inconsiderately, without prudence or reflection, unadvisedly.

Desacordádo, da, *a.* (Pint.) Discordant; applied to colours.

Desacordamiénto, *sm.* V. *Desacuerdo.*

Desacordánza, *sf.* V. *Discordancia.*

Desacordár, *va.* To discord, to disagree, not to suit with. V. *Discordar.*—*vr.* 1. To be forgetful, to be short of memory. 2. To be at variance, to disagree.

Desacórde, *a.* Discordant.

Desacorralár, *va.* 1. To let the flock or cattle out of the penfold. 2. To bring a bull into the open field. 3. (Met.) To inspirit, to animate, to encourage.

Desacostumbradaménte, *ad.* Unusually, contrary to custom.

Desacostumbrádo, da, *a.* Unusual, unaccustomed, contrary to custom and usual order.

Desacostumbrár, *va.* To disuse, to drop or lose the custom.

Desacotádo, *sm.* V. *Desacoto.*

Desacotár, *va.* 1. To raise or withdraw the prohibition of fowling at a certain time. 2. To relinquish a contract, to withdraw from an agreement. 3. To remove the obstacles which prevent boys from playing.

Desacóto, *sm.* The act of raising or withdrawing the prohibition of fowling at a certain time.

Desacreditár, *va.* 1. To discredit, to impair one's credit or reputation, to cry down. 2. To dissemble or conceal the merits of any thing.

Desacuérdo, *sm.* 1. Forgetfulness, oblivion. 2. Derangement of mental faculties. 3. Discordance, disagreement, disunion. 4. Error, mistake; want of accuracy and exactness.

Desaderezár, *va.* To undress, to divest of clothes or ornaments, to disorder, to ruffle.

Desadeudár, *va.* To pay one's debts, to get out of debt.

Desadorár, *va.* To love no more, to cease to love.

Desadormecér, *va.* 1. To wake, to rouse from sleep. 2. To rouse from mental stupor.

Desadornár, *va.* To divest of ornaments or decorations.

Desadórno, *sm.* Want of embellishments and charms.

Desadvertidaménte, *ad.* Inadvertently, inconsiderately.

Desadvertído, da, *a.* Inconsiderate, acting without prudence or reflection.

Desadvertimiénto, *sm.* Want of prudence and reflection.

Desadvertír, *va.* To act inconsiderately, to proceed without judgment or prudence.

Desafamación, *sf.* V. *Disfamacion.*

Desafamár, *va.* V. *Disfamar.*

Desafeár, *va.* To make ugly.

Desafectación, *sf.* Reserve, caution in personal behaviour; unaffectedness.

Desaféeto, ta, *a.* Disaffected, not disposed to zeal or affection.

Desaféeto, *sm.* Disaffection, disaffectedness.

Desaferrár, va. 1. (Naút.) To unfurl the sails. 2. To make loose any thing which was tied or fastened. 3. To make one change an opinion which he strenuously maintained.

Desafeytár, va. 1. To dirty; to make ugly. 2. V. *Desadornar*.

Desafiación y Desafiánza, sf. V. *Desafio*.

Desafiadéro, sm. A private ground on which duels are fought.

Desafiadór, sm. One who sends a challenge.

Desafiamiénto, sm. V. *Desafio*.

Desafiár, va. 1. To challenge, to call one out to fight a duel. 2. To try one's strength against another. 3. To rival, to oppose, to struggle. 4. To decompose, to dissolve; to rescind; to discharge.

Desafición, sf. Disaffection.

Desaficionár, va. To destroy one's desire, wish, or affection for any thing.

Desafijár, va. (Ant.) To deny the filiation of a son.

Desafinadaménte, ad. Dissonantly, discordantly.

Desafinár, vn. To be inharmonious, to be out of tune.

Desafío, sm. 1. Challenge, a summons to combat. 2. Struggle, contest. 3. Dismissal.

Desafiuzár, va. (Ant.) To distrust.

Desafixación, sf. (Ant.) Act of removing.

Desafixár, va. V. *Desfixar*.

Desaforadaménte, ad. Disorderly, excessively, outrageously, impudently.

Desaforádo, da, a. 1. Huge, uncommonly great or large. 2. Disorderly, lawless, impudent.

Desaforár, va. To encroach upon one's rights, to infringe or violate one's privileges.—vr. To relinquish one's rights and privileges.

Desaforrár, va. 1. To take off the lining of any thing. 2. *Desaferrar los cables*, (Naút.) To unserve the cables.

Desafortunádo, da, a. Unfortunate, unhappy, unlucky.

Desafuciamiénto, sm. V. *Desconfianza*.

Desafuéro, sm. Excess, act of injustice, violation of one's rights or privileges.

Desagarrár, va. To release, to set at liberty.

Desagotár, va. V. *Desaguar*.

Desagraciádo, da, a. Ungraceful, inelegant.

Desagraciár, va. To deform, to disfigure, to make ugly.

Desagradáble, a. Disagreeable, unpleasant.

Desagradableménte, ad. Disagreeably.

Desagradár, va. To displease, to cause discontent or displeasure.

Desagradecér, va. To be ungrateful.

Desagradecidaménte, ad. Ungratefully.

Desagradecído, da, a. Ungrateful.

Desagradecimiénto, sm. Ingratitude.

Desagrádo, sm. 1. Asperity, harshness. 2. Discontent, displeasure. *Ser del desagrado del rey*, To have incurred the king's displeasure.

Desagraviár, va. To give satisfaction, or make amends for an injury done.

Desagrávio y Desagraviamiénto, sm. Satisfaction or compensation for an injury done.

Desagregár, va. To disjoin, to separate, to part asunder.

Desaguadéro, sm. 1. Channel, drain for drawing off superfluous water. 2. (Met.) Drain of money. 3. *Desaguaderos de la cebadera*, (Naút.) Eyes of the sprit-sail.

Desaguadór, sm. Water-pipe, channel or conduit for carrying off water.

Desaguár, va. 1. To drain, to draw off water. 2. (Met.) To waste money in extravagant expenses.—vn. To empty into the sea; applied to rivers.—vr. (Met.) To discharge by vomits or stools.

Desaguazár, va. To drain or draw the water from any part.

Deságüe, sm. 1. Channel, drain. 2. Extraordinary expense.

Desaguisadaménte, ad. (Ant.) Injuriously, disproportionately.

Desaguisádo, da, a. (Ant.) 1. Injurious, unjust. 2. Disproportionate, exorbitant. 3. Intrepid, bold.

Desaguisádo, sm. Offence, injury, wrong.

Desahijár, va. To wean, to put from the breast, to separate the young from the dams.—vr. To swarm; applied to bees.

Desahitárse, vr. To relieve indigestion, to unload the stomach.

Desahogadaménte, ad. 1. Freely, without embarrassment or obstruction. 2. In an impudent or brazen-faced manner.

Desahogádo, da, a. 1. Free, unrestrained. 2. Petulant, impudent, brazen-faced, licentious. 3. (Naút.) Having sea-room; applied to a ship.

Desahogár, va. To ease pain, to alleviate distress.—vr. 1. To recover, to grow well from fatigue or disease. 2. To unbosom, to disclose one's grief.

Desahógo y Desahogamiénto, sm. 1. Ease, alleviation from pain, trouble, or affliction. 2. The act of disclosing one's troubles. 3. Freedom of speech, liberty of acting.

Desahuciadaménte, ad. With little or no hope of recovery.

Desahuciádo, da, a. Given over, despaired of.

Desahuciár, va. 1. To despair of, to be without hope, to despond. 2. To drive away cattle from a pasture-ground, at the expiration of the term agreed upon.

Desahúcio, sm. The act of driving away cattle from a pasture-ground at the expiration of the stipulated time.

Desahumádo, da, a. Mild, faded, become vapid; applied to liquor which has lost its strength.

Desahumár, va. To free from smoke, to expel smoke.

Desainadúra, sf. (Alb.) Disease in horses, occasioned by liquefying their fat in overheating them.

Desainár, va. To extenuate the fat of an animal; to lessen or diminish the fatness of any thing.

Desaisláres, vr. To cease to be insulated.

Desajacárse, vr. (Ant.) To excuse, exempt or liberate one's self.

Desajuntár, va. (Ant.) To disunite, to separate.

Desajustár, va. To disproportion, to match unsuitably.—vr. To disagree, to withdraw from an agreement.

Desajúste, sm. The act of disproportioning.

Desalabár, va. To dispraise, to blame, to censure.

DESALABEÁR, *va.* To straighten a plank or board which is warped.

DESALADAMÉNTE, *ad.* Anxiously, swiftly.

DESALÁR, *va.* 1. To cut off the wings. 2. To take the salt out of fish, salt meat, &c. by steeping it in fresh water.—*vr.* (Met.) To run up to one with open arms.

DESALBARDÁR, *va.* To take off the pack-saddle from a beast of burthen.

DESALENTÁR, *va.* 1. To put one out of breath by dint of labour. 2. (Met.) To discourage, to dismay.

DESALFORJÁR, *va.* To take off the saddle-bags from horses or mules.—*vr.* (Met.) To take off one's accoutrements, to make one's self easy.

DESALHAJÁR, *va.* To unfurnish a house or room, to strip it of furniture.

DESALIÉNTO, *sm.* Dismay, fall of courage, dejection of mind.

DESALIÑADAMÉNTE, *ad.* Slovenly, uncleanly.

DESALIÑÁR, *va.* To discompose, to make one slovenly or dirty.

DESALIÑO, *sm.* 1. Slovenliness, indecent negligence of dress. 2. Carelessness, want of care and attention. *Desaliños*, An ornament of diamonds that hangs from women's ears down to their breast.

DESALISTÁR, *va.* To quit the service.

DESALIVÁR, *vn.* To salivate, to discharge saliva.

DESALMADAMÉNTE, *ad.* Cruelly, inhumanly.

DESALMÁDO, DA, *a.* 1. Cruel, inhuman. 2. Impious, profligate. 3. Inanimate, soulless.

DESALMAMIÉNTO, *sm.* Cruelty, impiety, profligacy.

DESALMÁR, *va.* 1. To take away one's life in a violent manner. 2. (Met.) To speak with ingenuity and candour.—*vr.* To desire any thing very anxiously.

DESALMENÁDO, DA, *a.* 1. Without turrets; applied to a castle or fortress. 2. Wanting an ornament or capital.

DESALMIDONÁR, *va.* To take the starch out of linen.

DESALOJAMIÉNTO, *sm.* Expulsion, dislodging.

DESALOJÁR, *va.* To dislodge the enemy's troops, to dispossess them of a place or post.—*vn.* To quit one's house or apartments, to move to other lodgings.

DESALTERÁR, *va.* To allay, to assuage, to settle.

DESALUMBRADAMÉNTE, *ad.* Obscurely, blindly, erroneously.

DESALUMBRÁDO, DA. *a.* 1. Dazzled, overpowered with light. 2. (Met.) Groping in the dark.

DESALUMBRAMIÉNTO, *sm.* Blindness, want of foresight or knowledge, error.

DESAMÁBLE, *a.* Unworthy of being loved, hateful.

DESAMADÓR, *sm.* Hater, he who hates or dislikes.

DESAMÁR, *va.* 1. To love no more, not to love or esteem as formerly. 2. To hate, to detest.

DESAMARRÁR, *va.* 1. (Naút.) To unmoor a ship. 2. To untie. *Desamarrar un cabo*, (Naút.) To unbend a rope.

DESAMASÁDO, DA, *a.* Dissolved, disunited.

DESAMISTÁDO, DA, *a.* Ceased to be a friend, unconnected.

DESAMISTÁD, *sf.* Unfriendliness.

DESAMISTÁRSE, *vr.* To fall out, to quarrel.

DESAMODORRÁR, *va.* To remove lethargy or drowsiness.

DESAMOLDÁR, *va.* 1. To unmould, to change the form or figure of a thing after it has been taken out of the mould. 2. (Met.) To change the proportion or symmetry of any thing.

DESAMÓR, *sm.* Disregard, disaffection, misunderstanding.

DESAMORADAMÉNTE, *ad.* Harshly, rudely.

DESAMORÁDO, DA, *a.* Harsh, rude, disdainful.

DESAMORÁR, *va.* To extinguish love, to cease loving.

DESAMORÓSO, SA, *a.* Unloving, destitute of esteem, friendship, or love.

DESAMORRÁR, *va.* To cheer up, to make one raise one's head and give up his obstinacy.

DESAMOTINÁRSE, *vr.* To withdraw from mutiny and sedition.

DESAMPARADÓR, RA, *s.* Deserter, one who forsakes or abandons.

DESAMPARÁR, *va.* 1. To forsake, to abandon, to relinquish. 2. To quit a place. *Desamparar la apelacion*, To desist from an appeal interposed in a cause. *Desamparar los bienes*, To give up one's property, in order to avoid being molested by one's creditors.

DESAMPÁRO Y DESAMPARAMIÉNTO, *sm.* Abandonment, desertion, want of protection.

DESANCORÁR, *va.* (Naút.) To weigh anchor.

DESANDÁR, *va.* To retrograde, to go back the same road by which one came. *Desandar lo andado*, To undo what has been done.

DESANDRAJÁDO, DA, *a.* Ragged, in tatters.

DESANGRÁR, *va.* 1. To bleed one to excess. 2. To draw off a large quantity of water from a river. 3. (Met.) To exhaust one's means, to make poor.

DESANIDÁR, *vn.* To forsake the nest; applied to birds.—*va.* 1. (Met.) To dislodge from a post. 2. To apprehend fugitives in the haunt or den where they were concealed.

DESANIMADAMÉNTE, *ad.* Inanimately.

DESANIMÁR, *va.* 1. To deprive of life. 2. To dishearten, to dispirit, to discourage; to put a damp upon one's spirits.

DESANUDÁR, *va.* 1. To untie, to loosen a knot. 2. (Met.) To extricate, to disembroil, to disentangle. *Desanudar la voz*, To pronounce clearly and distinctly, to articulate freely.

DESAÑUDADÚRA, *sf.* Explication, disentanglement.

DESAÑUDÁR, *va.* V. *Desanudar*.

DESAOJADÉRA, *sf.* (Ant.) Woman supposed to cure or dispel charms.

DESAPACIBILIDÁD, *sf.* Rudeness, churlishness, peevishness.

DESAPACÍBLE, *a.* Sharp, rough, disagreeable, unpleasant.

DESAPACIBLEMÉNTE, *ad.* Sharply, disagreeably.

DESAPADRINÁR, *va.* (Met.) To disprove, to contradict.

DESAPAÑÁR, *va.* (Ant.) To undress.

DESAPAREÁR, *va.* To unmatch, to disjoin.

DESAPARECÉR, *va.* To remove out of sight, to hide.—*vn.* y *r.* To disappear, to withdraw out of sight.

DESAPARECIMIÉNTO, *sm.* The act of disappearing or vanishing out of sight.

DESAPAREJÁR, *va.* 1. To unharness beasts of draught or burthen. 2. (Naút.) To unrig a ship.

DESAPARROQUIÁRSE, *vr.* 1. To change one's parish, to remove from one parish to another. 2. (Met.) To cease to be a customer of a shop, to deal at another shop.

Desapartár, *va.* 1. To part, to disjoin. V. *Apartar.* 2. (Ant.) To impede, to disturb.
Desapasionadaménte, *ad.* Impartially, without any passion or partiality.
Desapasionár, *va.* To remove or root out a passion, or strong affection for any thing.
Desapegár, *va.* To disjoin, to separate. V. *Despegar.*—*vr.* To be impartial, not to allow one's self to be led away by any passion or affection.
Desapégo, *sm.* 1. Alienation of love or affection. 2. Impartiality, disinterestedness.
Desapercibidaménte, *ad.* Inadvertently, carelessly.
Desapercibído, **da**, *a.* Unguarded, careless.
Desapercibimiénto y Desapercíbo, *sm.* Want of means to attain some certain end.
Desapestár, *va.* To cure persons infected with the plague.
Desapiadadaménte, *ad.* Impiously, cruelly, without compassion.
Desapiadádo, **da**, *a.* Impious, cruel, merciless.
Desapiladór, *sm.* One who takes down the piles of wool in a shearing place.
Desapiolár, *va.* To loose the strings with which game is tied.
Desaplicación, *sf.* Inapplication, carelessness, want of application.
Desaplicadaménte, *ad.* Indolently.
Desaplicádo, **da**, *a.* Indolent, careless, neglectful.
Desapoderadaménte, *ad* Impetuously, precipitately.
Desapoderádo, **da**, *a.* 1. Furious, impetuous, ungovernable. 2. Huge, excessively great and powerful, insurmountable.
Desapoderamiénto, *sm.* 1. Excessive boldness, extreme audacity. 2. (Ant.) The act of depriving or ejecting.
Desapoderár, *va.* 1. To dispossess, to rob one of his property. 2. To repeal or revoke a power of attorney.
Desapolillár, *va.* To free and clear of moths.—*vr.* To take the air when it is cold and sharp.
Desaposentár, *va.* 1. To turn one out of his lodgings, to force him to move. 2. To expel a thing from one's mind.
Desaposesionár, *va.* To dispossess.
Desapostár, *va.* To dislodge the enemy from a post.
Desápostúra, *sf.* (Ant.) Inelegance, deformity, indecency.
Desapoyár, *va.* To remove the foundation of an opinion, or any other thing.
Desapreciár, *va.* To depreciate, to undervalue.
Desaprécio, *sm.* Depreciation; thing of no value.
Desaprendér, *va.* To unlearn, to forget what one has learned by heart.
Desaprensár, *va.* 1. To take away the gloss which clothes or any other things obtain in the press. 2. (Met.) To extricate one's self from a pressing difficulty.
Desapretár, *va.* 1. To slacken, to loosen. 2. (Met.) To ease, to free from anxiety and uneasiness.
Desaprír, *vn.* (Ant.) To separate, to part.
Desaprisionár, *va.* To release from confinement, to set at liberty.—*vr.* (Met.) To extricate one's self from difficulties, to remove an impediment.
Desaprobación, *sf.* Disapprobation, censure, condemnation.
Desaprobár, *va.* To disapprove, to censure, to reprove.
Desapropiamiénto, *sm.* Alienation. V. *Enagenamiento.*
Desapropiárse, *vr.* To alienate, to transfer one's right and property to another.
Desapróprio, *sm.* Alienation, transfer of property.
Desaprovechadaménte, *ad.* Unprofitably, uselessly.
Desaprovechádo, **da**, *a.* 1. Useless, unprofitable. 2. Backward, having made no progress in what is good and valuable.
Desaprovechamiénto, *sm.* Backwardness, want of progress.
Desaprovechár, *va.* To waste, to misspend, to turn to a bad use.—*vn.* To be backward, to make little or no progress.
Desaptéza, *sf.* (Ant.) Ineptitude.
Desápto, **ta**, *a.* (Ant.) Inept.
Desapuésto, **ta**, *a.* (Ant.) Inelegant, unseemly.
Desapuntalár, *va.* To take away the props or supports.
Desapuntár, *va.* 1. To unstitch, to rip up or cut the stitches of a seam. 2. To lose one's aim, to point or level fire arms ill. 3. To efface the days of absence from the choir.
Desarbolár, *va.* 1. (Naút.) To unmast a ship, to take out the masts. 2. (Naút.) To lay up a ship in ordinary.
Desarbólo, *sm.* The act of unmasting a ship or laying her up in ordinary.
Desarenár, *va.* To take away the sand, to clear a place of sand.
Desaréno, *sm.* The act of clearing a place of sand.
Desarmadór, *sm.* He who discharges a gun. V. *Disparador.*
Desarmadúra y Desarmamiénto, *s.* The act and effect of disarming.
Desarmár, *va.* 1. To disarm, to spoil or divest of arms. 2. To prohibit the carrying of arms. 3. To undo a thing, to take it asunder. 4. To disband a body of troops. 5. To dismount a cross-bow, to dismount cannon. 6. To butt, to strike with the horns. 7. (Met.) To pacify, to disarm wrath or vengeance.
Desárme, *sm.* Disarming of ships.
Desarrapádo, **da**, *a.* Ragged, dressed in old torn clothes.
Desarraygár, *va.* 1. To eradicate, to root out, to pull up by the roots. 2. (Met.) To extirpate, to destroy. 3. (Met.) To expel from the country.
Desarray'go, *sm.* Eradication.
Desarrebozár, *va.* 1. To unmuffle, to pull off the covering of the face. 2. (Met.) To lay open, to manifest, to discover.
Desarrebujár, *va.* 1. To unfold, to spread out. 2. To uncover, to take off the covering. 3. To explain, to clear up.
Desarregladaménte, *ad.* Disorderly, irregularly.
Desarregládo, **da**, *a.* Immoderate in eating, drinking, or other things.
Desarreglár, *va.* To disorder, to discompose, to put out of order.
Desarréglo, *sm.* Disorder, confusion.
Desarrevolvér, *va.* V. *Desenvolver.*
Desarrimár, *va.* 1. To remove, to separate, to carry away. 2. To dissuade, to dehort
Desarrímo, *sm.* Want of props or support.

Desarrollár, *va.* To unroll, to open and spread out what was rolled up.
Desarromadizár, *va.* To cure of a cold.
Desarropár, *va.* To uncover, to undress, to take off the clothes.
Desarrugadúra, *sf.* The act of taking out wrinkles.
Desarrugár, *va.* To take out wrinkles.
Desarrumár, *va.* (Naút.) To unload a ship, to discharge the cargo.
Desartillár, *va.* (Naút.) To take the guns out of a ship.
Desasádo, da, *a.* Without handles, or having broken handles.
Desaseadaménte, *ad.* Uncleanly, nastily.
Desaseár, *va.* To make dirty or unclean; to discompose, to disorder.
Desasegurár, *va.* To lose the security of any thing.
Desasentár, *va.* (Met.) To disagree with, to displease, not to suit or sit well.—*vr.* To arise from one's seat, to stand up.
Desaséo, *sm.* Uncleanliness, dirtiness, disorder.
Desasesádo, da, *a.* Senseless, without judgment.
Desasimiénto, *sm.* 1. The act of loosening or letting loose. 2. (Met.) Disinterestedness.
Desasír, *va.* To loosen, to disentangle.—*vr.* To disengage or extricate one's self.
Desasnár, *va.* 1. To deprive one of his asses. 2. (Met.) To polish one's manners, to render more civil, to correct rudeness.
Desasociáble, *a.* Unsociable, averse from company or society.
Desasosegadaménte, *ad.* In a restless manner, without repose.
Desasosegár, *va.* To disquiet, to disturb, to deprive of rest and tranquillity.
Desasosiégo, *sm.* Restlessness, want of tranquillity and repose.
Desastradaménte, *ad.* Wretchedly, in a miserable or disastrous manner.
Desastrádo, da, *a.* 1. Wretched, miserable, unfortunate. 2. Ragged, tattered.
Desástre, *sm.* Disaster, disgrace, misfortune.
Desatacár, *va.* To loosen, to untie. *Desatacar la escopeta*, To draw the charge out of a gun.
Desatadaménte, *ad.* Without order or union.
Desatadór, *sm.* He who unites, absolver.
Desatadúra, Desatamiénto, *s.* The act of untying or loosening a knot.
Desatancár, *va.* To clean or clear the sewers and conduits.
Desatapadúra, *sf.* The act of uncovering.
Desatapár, *va.* To uncover. V. *Destapar.*
Desatár, *va.* 1. To untie, to separate, to detach. 2. To liquefy, to dissolve. 3. To solve, to unravel.—*vr.* 1. To give a loose to one's tongue, to talk much and incoherently. 2. To lose all reserve, fear, or bashfulness.
Desatascár, *va.* 1. To pull or draw out of the mud or mire. 2. (Met.) To extricate one from difficulties.
Desataviár, *va.* To strip of ornaments and decorations.
Desatavío, *sm.* Uncleanliness, the want of cleanliness or neatness in dress.
Desatemplárse, *vr.* V. *Destemplarse.*
Desatención, *sf.* 1. Want of attention, absence of mind. 2. Disrespect, want of respect.
Desatendér, *va.* 1. To pay no attention to what is said or done. 2. To disregard, to slight, to contemn.
Desatentadaménte, *ad.* 1. Disorderly, confusedly. 2. Inconsiderately, unadvisedly.
Desatentádo, da, *a.* 1. Inconsiderate, unadvised. 2. Acting in an absurd and unreasonable manner.
Desatentaménte, *ad.* Disrespectfully, uncivilly.
Desatentamiénto, *sm.* V. *Desatiento.*
Desatentár, *va.* To perturbate the mind, to perplex the understanding.
Desaténto, ta, *a.* 1. Inattentive, careless, heedless. 2. Rude, unmannerly, uncivil.
Desatesádo, da, *a.* Weak, languishing. V. *Floxo.*
Desatesorár, *va.* To remove or spend the treasure.
Desatiénto, *sm.* Inconsiderateness, thoughtlessness, absence of mind.
Desatinadaménte, *ad.* 1. Inconsiderately, indiscreetly. 2. Extravagantly, out of all rule and order.
Desatinádo, da, *a.* Extravagant, beyond all rule and reason.
Desatinádo, *sm.* Idiot, fool, madman.
Desatinár, *va.* 1. To disorder or derange one's mind. 2. To throw into a violent passion. 3. To talk nonsense. 4. To reel, to stagger.
Desatíno, *sm.* 1. Reeling, staggering. 2. Madness, craziness.
Desatollár, *va.* To pull out of the mud or mire. V. *Desatascar.*
Desatolondrádo, da, *a.* Recovered from stupor.
Desatolondrárse, *vr.* To recover one's senses.
Desatontárse, *vr.* To recover one's self from stupefaction.
Desatracár, *va.* (Naút.) To sheer off, to bear away.
Desatraér, *va.* To disjoin, to separate, to remove.
Desatraillár, *va.* To uncouple hounds, to untie the leash with which they are coupled.
Desatrampár, *va.* To clear or clean any conduit, sink, or sewer.
Desatrancár, *va.* To unbar, to take off the bolt or bar of a door.
Desatufárse, *vr.* To grow calm, to allay one's passion.
Desaturdidór, *sm.* He who rouses or animates.
Desaturdír, *va.* To rouse from a state of dizziness or stupor, to animate.
Desautoridád, *sf.* Want of authority.
Desautorizár, *va.* To disauthorize, to deprive of authority or respect.
Desavahádo, da, *a.* Uncovered, free from snow, clouds, or vapours; applied to places.
Desavahár, *va.* To expose to the air, to evaporate.—*vr.* To grow lively or sprightly.
Desavecindádo, da, *a.* Deserted, unpeopled; applied to a place abandoned by its inhabitants.
Desavecindárse, *vr.* To be deserted or abandoned by the inhabitants.
Desavenéncia, *sf.* Discord, disagreement.
Desavenído, da, *a.* Discordant, disagreeing; not coinciding with another's opinion or sentiments.
Desavenír, *va.* To disagree.
Desaventajadaménte, *ad.* Disadvantageously.
Desaventajádo, da, *a.* Disadvantageous, unprofitable.
Desaventúra, *sf.* V. *Desventura.*
Desaventurádo, da, *a.* V. *Desventurado.*
Desavezamiénto, *sm.* Want of use or custom.

Desavezár, *va.* V. *Desacostumbrar.*

Desaviár, *va.* 1. To deviate from the high road, to go astray. 2. To strip of necessaries or conveniencies.

Desaviltádo, da, *a.* V. *Deshonrado.*

Desavío, *sm.* 1. The act of going astray, or losing one's road. 2. Want of the necessary means for attaining some end or purpose.

Desavisádo, da, *a.* Unadvised, inadvertent, indiscreet.

Desavisár, *va.* To give a contrary account, to contradict a former advice.

Desayradaménte, *ad.* Unhandsomely, without grace.

Desayrádo, da, *a.* 1. Unhandsome, graceless; destitute of spirit or grace. 2. (Met.) Disregarded, slighted; not rewarded according to one's merit.

Desayrár, *va.* To disregard, to despise.

Desáyre, *sm.* 1. Scorn, disdain, disrespect. 2. Awkwardness, want of an elegant or graceful deportment. 3. (Met.) Frown of fortune or power.

Desayudár, *va.* Not to assist, but oppose one with regard to his claims or rights.—*vr.* To be negligent or careless in the performance of one's duty.

Desayunárse, *vr.* To breakfast, to eat the first meal in the day. *Desayunar,* To receive the first intelligence of any thing unknown. *Desayunarse, con ó de alguna noticia ó especie,* (Met.) To have the first intelligence of any thing.

Desayúno, *sm.* Breakfast, the first meal in the day.

Desayuntamiénto, *sm.* Dissolution, disjunction.

Desayuntár, *va.* To disunite, to dissolve, to separate.

Desayustár, *va.* (Naút.) To unbend a rope or cable.

Desazogár, *va.* To take off the quicksilver from a looking-glass.

Desazón, *sm.* 1. Insipidity, want of taste or flavour. 2. Disgust, displeasure. 3. (Met.) Disquietness, uneasiness, affliction. 4. (Agric.) Unfitness of a soil.

Desazonádo, da, *a.* 1. Ill-adapted, unfit for some purpose; applied to land. 2. Peevish, impertinent, passionate.

Desazonár, *va.* 1. To render tasteless, to infect with an unpleasant taste. 2. To disgust, to vex.—*vr.* To become indisposed in health, to be sick.

Desbabár, *vn.* To drivel, to slaver.—*vr.* To be in love to extremity, to regard with excessive fondness, to dote upon.

Desbagár, *va.* To extract the flax seed from the capsule.

Desbalijamiénto, *sm.* The act of plundering a portmanteau.

Desbalijár, *va.* To gut one's portmanteau, to rob one of its contents.

Desballestár, *va.* To unbend a cross-bow, to take it asunder.

Desbancár, *va.* 1. To clear a room of the benches, stools, or forms which it contained. 2. To win all the money staked by a gambler, who holds a basset or faro-table. 3. (Met.) To circumvent one in the friendship and affection of another.

Desbandárse, *vr.* To disband, to desert the colours; applied to soldiers.

Desbañádo, *a.* (Volat.) Applied to a hawk that has not taken water when required.

Desbaradaménte, *ad.* Disorderly, without rule or order.

Desbaratádo, da, *a.* Debauched, corrupted with lewdness and intemperance.

Desbaratamiénto, *sm.* Perturbation, commotion; decomposition.

Desbaratadór, ra, *s.* Debaucher, one who debauches or depraves.

Desbaratár, *va.* 1. To destroy or break up any thing. 2. To defeat or rout an army. 3. To waste, to mispend, to dissipate. *Desbaratar la paz,* To break the peace. *Desbaratar la platica,* To interrupt the conversation.—*vn.* To speak foolishly, to talk nonsense.—*vr.* To be confounded, to be disordered in one's mind, to have the mental faculties deranged.

Desbaráte y Desbaráto, *sm.* 1. The act of routing or defeating. 2. Ignorance, folly, madness. *Desbarate de vientre,* Frequent stools, or a looseness.

Desbaraustár, *va.* To discompose, to derange or ruin any thing.

Desbarbádo, da, *a.* Beardless, not yet having a beard.

Desbarbár, *va.* 1. To shave, to cut off the beard with a razor. 2. (Met.) To trim, to cut off the filaments of plants, loose threads of stuff, or other things.

Desbarbillár, *va.* (Agric.) To prune the roots which spring from the stems of young vines.

Desbardár, *va.* To uncover a wall or fence, to remove the brushwood or straw placed on the top of a mud wall to preserve it from injury.

Desbarrár, *vn.* 1. To slip, to rove, to go beyond limits. 2. (Met.) To waver, to fluctuate.

Desbarretár, *va.* To unbar, to unbolt, to take off the bars and bolts.

Desbarrigádo, da, *a.* Little bellied.

Desbarrigár, *va.* To eventerate, to rip up, to open the belly.

Desbárro, *sm.* 1. The act of slipping. 2. Nonsense, madness, extravagance.

Desbastadúra, *sf.* The act of planing, trimming, or polishing.

Desbastár, *va.* 1. To plane, to smooth the surfaces of boards with a plane. 2. To trim, to polish. 3. To waste, to consume, to weaken. 4. To purify one's morals and manners.

Desbáste, *sm.* The act of hewing, polishing, or trimming.

Desbastecído, da, *a.* That which is without sufficient provisions.

Desbautizárse, *vr.* (Met.) To be irritated, to fly into a passion.

Desbazadéro, *sm.* Humid, slippery place.

Desbebér, *vn.* (Joc.) To urine, to make water.

Desbecerrár, *va.* To wean, to deprive young animals of their mother's milk.

Desblanquecído, da, *a.* Blanched. V. *Blanquecino.*

Desbocadaménte, *ad.* Impudently, ungovernedly, without restriction or shame.

Desbocádo, da, *a.* 1. Open-mouthed, wide at the mouth; applied to a piece of ordnance. 2

Broken lipped or mouthed. 3. (Met.) Foul-mouthed, indecent.

Desbocamiénto, *sm.* Impertinence, impudence.

Desbocár, *va.* To break the brim of a mug, jar, or other vessel.—*vn.* To disembogue. V. *Desembocar.*—*vr.* 1. To be hard-mouthed, to be insensible of the bridle. 2. To use injurious or abusive language.

Desbombár, *va.* To pump out water.

Desbonetárse, *vr.* To take off the cap or bonnet, to be uncovered.

Desboquillár, *va.* To break the mouth.

Desbordár, *vn.* To overflow, to inundate, to run over the brim of a vessel.

Desboronár, *va.* V. *Desmoronar.*

Desborrár, *va.* 1. To cut off the loose threads of stuff, when it comes out of the loom. 2. (Murc.) To lop the branches off the trunks of trees, particularly the mulberry.

Desbozár, *va.* To take off the relievos, carvings, or mouldings of a statue.

Desbragádo, da, *a.* Unbreeched, without breeches.

Desbraguetádo, da, *a.* Having the fore-part of the breeches unbuttoned and open.

Desbraváar y Desbravecér, *va.* 1. To tame, to break in; applied to horses. 2. To lessen or diminish the strength or force of any thing, to mollify; to moderate.

Desbrazárse, *vr.* To extend one's arms, to stretch out the arms.

Desbrevárse, *vr.* To evaporate, to lose body and strength; applied to wine and strong liquors.

Desbriznár, *va.* 1. To chop or mince meat, to cut it into small pieces. 2. To cut or divide any thing into small parts.

Desbrozár, *va.* To clear away rubbish.

Desbrózo, *sm.* The act of clearing away rubbish.

Desbruár, *va.* To clean cloth of grease, to put it in the fulling mill.

Desbrujár, *va.* V. *Desmoronar.*

Desbuchár, *va.* 1. To disclose one's secrets, to tell all one knows. 2. To ease the stomach; applied to birds of prey. V. *Desainar.*

Desbúlla, *sf.* The part of an oyster that remains on the shell.

Desbullár, *va.* To extract an oyster from its shell.

Désca, *sf.* (Naút.) Tar-pot.

Descabál, *a.* Imperfect, incomplete.

Descabalár, *va.* 1. To pilfer; to diminish the weight, quantity, or number of things, by petty thefts. 2. To impair the perfection of any thing.

Descabalgadúra, *sf.* The act of dismounting or alighting from a horse.

Descabalgár, *vn.* To dismount, to alight from a horse.—*va.* To dismount. *Descabalgar la artilleria de las cureñas,* To dismount the guns, to take them from their carriages.

Descaballár, *va.* (Among Gardeners.) To take away the leaves and superfluous buds of plants.

Descabelladaménte, *ad.* Without order or regularity.

Descabelládo, da, *a.* 1. Dishevelled; applied to hair which hangs loosely and disorderly. 2. (Met.) Disorderly, out of all rule and order. 3. (Met.) Disproportional, disproportionable. 4. Violent, vehement.

Descabelladúra, *sf.* The act and effect of tossing the hair.

Descabellamiénto, *sm.* V. *Despropósito.*

Descabellár, *va.* To disorder or undress the hair.

Descabeñárse, *vr.* V. *Desgreñarse.*

Descabestrár, *va.* To unhalter. V. *Desencabestrar.*

Descabezádo, da, *a.* 1. Beheaded. 2. Light-headed, injudicious, void of judgment.

Descabezamiénto, *sm.* The act of beheading.

Descabezár, *va.* 1 To behead, to decollate, to cut off the head. 2. To put an end to, to terminate. 3. To surmount, to overcome. 4. To begin, to let the beginning of a thing pass over. *Descabezar el sueño,* To take a nap. *Descabezar la misa,* To let the beginning of the mass be over before one enters church.—*vn.* To terminate, to join another property.—*vr.* 1. To screw one's wits, to batter one's brains. 2. To take the grain from the ears of corn. *Descabezarse una vena,* To burst a blood-vessel.

Descabildadaménte, *ad.* (Ant.) Disorderly.

Descabritár, *va.* To wean goats.

Descabullírse, *vr.* 1. To sneak off, to steal away from a place. 2. (Met.) To elude the strength of an argument, to avoid a difficulty by artifice.

Descacilár, *va.* (And.) To cut the extreme ends of bricks equally.

Descaderár, *va.* To sprain or dislocate the hip.

Descadillár, *va.* (In Woollen Manufactories) To cut off the loose threads or fag-end of the warp.

Descaecér, *vn.* 1. To decline, to droop, to decay. 2. (Naút.) To edge away.

Descaecído, da, *a.* Weak, feeble.

Descaecimiénto y Descaimiénto, *sm.* 1. Weakness, debility, decay. 2. Despondency, lowness of spirits.

Descaér, *vn.* V. *Decaer.*

Descalabazárse, *vr.* To puzzle one's brains, to screw one's wits.

Descalabrádo, da, *a.* Injured. *Salir descalabrado,* Applied to one who has not succeeded in any suit, game, or business.

Descalabradúra, *sf.* Contusion or wound in the head.

Descalabrár, *va.* 1. To break or wound the head with a blow. 2. To attack or impeach one's character. 3. To hurt, to injure. *Descalabrar un navio,* (Naút.) To disable a ship. 4. (In the jocular style) To publish the bans. *Descalábrame con eso,* (Irón.) You overwhelm me with this; you will neither do what you offer, nor give what you promise.

Descalábro, *sm.* A calamitous event, a considerable loss; misfortune.

Descalandrajár, *va.* To rend or tear one's clothes.

Descalcañalár, *va.* To smooth, to take out the flutings or furrows.

Descalcañár, *va.* 1. To cut off the talons or heels. 2. To make tardy in travelling.

Descalcéz, *sf.* 1. Nudity of the feet, want of covering for the feet. 2. Barefootedness of those monks who are not permitted to wear shoes.

Descalladór, *sm.* V. *Herrador.*

Descalorárse, *vr.* V. *Desacalorarse.*

Descalostrádo, da, *a.* Having past the days of the first milk; applied to a child suckled by its mother.

Descalzadéro, *sm.* (And.) Little door of a pigeon-house.

Descalzádo, da, *a.* Barefooted.

Descalzár, *va.* 1. To pull off the shoes and stockings. 2. To remove an impediment, to surmount an obstacle.—*vr.* 1. To be barefooted. 2. *Descalzarse de risa*, To burst out into a fit of laughter. *Descalzarse los guantes*, To pull off one's gloves.

Descálzo, za, *a.* Barefooted. *Descálzos*, Barefooted friars or monks.

Descaminadaménte, *ad.* Absurdly, erratically.

Descamináдo, *sm.* V. *Descamino.*

Descaminár, *va.* 1. To misguide, to mislead, to lead astray. 2. To seduce one from his duty. 3. To seize upon goods, which were run into the country without paying any duty. *Ir descaminado*, To deviate from rectitude, reason, or truth.

Descamíno, *sm.* 1. Seizure of goods for which no duty was paid. 2. The goods thus seized. 3. Deviation from the high road. 4. Error, blindness; deviation from justice, truth, and reason. 5. (Ant.) Duty imposed on things seized.

Descamisádo, da, *a.* Naked, not having a shirt to put on one's back.

Descampádo, da, *a.* Disengaged, free, open, clear. *En descampádo*, In the open air, exposed to wind and weather.

Descampár, *vn.* V. *Escampar.*

Descansadaménte, *ad.* 1. Easily, without any trouble or fatigue. 2. Undoubtedly, surely. *Fulano descansadamente tiene tanto caudal*, He is undoubtedly possessed of so much property.

Descansadéro, *sm.* Place of rest or repose.

Descansádo, da, *a.* Procuring rest or repose, *Vida descansada*, A quiet, easy life.

Descansár, *vn.* 1. To rest from labour and fatigue, to recover strength by repose. 2. To pause in the execution of a thing. 3. To rest, to lean upon, as a joist does upon a beam. 4. To repose, to sleep. *El enfermo ha descansado dos horas*, The patient has slept two hours. *Descansar las tierras*, To lie at rest; applied to lands which lie fallow. 5. *Descansar sobre los remos*, (Naút.) To hold or rest on the oars. 6. To be interred, to repose in the sepulchre.—*va.* To aid or alleviate another in labour or fatigue.

Descánsa, (A') Harriéro, *ad.* Conveniently, handsomely. *Dar á descansa harriero*, To give blows easily to one who does not defend himself.

Descánso, *sm.* 1. Rest, repose, pause from labour and fatigue. 2. Cause of tranquillity and rest. 3. Undress of ladies. 4. Landing-place of stairs; seat, bench, or support of any thing. 5. Day of rest, for which the drivers and muleteers receive payment. 6. Halting-day for soldiers on a march. 7. (Naút.) Partner of the bowsprit. *Descanso exterior del bauprés*, (Naút.) Pillow of the bowsprit. *Descanso interior del bauprés*, (Naút.) The inner partner of the bowsprit. *Descanso de la caña del timon*, (Naút.) Sweep of the tiller. *La caña tiene juego en el descanso*, (Naút.) The tiller shakes.

Descanteár, *va.* To smooth angles or corners.

Descanterár, *va.* To take off the crust of any thing; usually applied to bread.

Descantillár y Descantonár, *va.* 1. To pare off, to break off part of a thing. 2. To tract part from a total. 3. (Met.) To lessen

Descantillón, *sm.* A small line marking the proper scantling to which any thing is to be cut.

Descañár, *va.* To break the arm or leg; to break the stem or branch of any thing.

Descañonár, *va.* 1. To pluck out the feathers of a bird or fowl. 2. To shave close, to shave a second time. 3. (Met.) To trick one out of his money, either by playing or otherwise.

Descapár, *va.* To strip one of his cloak.

Descaperuzárse, *vr.* To take off one's cowl or hood by way of saluting another; to uncover one's head.

Descaperúzo, *sm.* The act of taking off the cowl, hood, or hunting-cap, by way of saluting.

Descapillár, *va.* To take off the hood. V. *Descaperuzarse.*

Descapirotár, *va.* To take off the *capirote* or ancient head-cover, now used by doctors of Universities.

Descaradaménte, *ad.* In an impudent or barefaced manner.

Descarádo, da, *a.* Impudent, barefaced.

Descarárse, *vr.* To behave in an impudent or insolent manner.

Descárga, *sf.* 1. The act of disburthening or alleviating a burthen; mitigating the pressure. 2. Volley, a general discharge of great or small guns. 3. *Descarga de aduana*, (Com.) Clearance at the custom-house. *Descarga general del costado del navio*, (Naút.) Broadside of a man of war. 4. Unloading or discharge of the cargo of a ship.

Descargadéro, *sm.* Wharf, unloading place.

Descargadór, *sm.* Wharfinger, one who keeps a wharf.

Descargadúra, *sf.* The act of taking bones out of meat, to render it more useful.

Descargamiénto, *sm.* (Ant.) The act of discharging, exoneration.

Descargár, *va.* 1. To take off or alleviate a burthen. *Descargar las paredes*, (Arq.) To support walls with buttresses. 2. To take off the flap and bones of meat, to render it more useful. 3. To unload fire-arms, to draw out the charge of powder and ball. 4. To unship a cargo. 5. (Met.) To liberate from a charge or obligation.—*vn.* To disembogue or disgorge waters into the sea. *Descargar ó meter en viento una vela*, (Naút.) To fill a sail again.—*vr.* 1. To assign or allege a cause of non-appearance when summoned. 2. To resign one's place or employment. 3. (In Painting) To lose brightness and lustre; applied to colours.

Descárgo, *sm.* 1. Exoneration, discharge. 2. Acquittance, receipt. 3. Plea or answer to an impeachment or action; acquittal from blame.

Descárgue, *sm.* Alleviation from any burthen.

Descariñárse, *vr.* To lose the love or affection for a thing.

Descaríño, *sm.* Coolness, loss of love or affection.

Descarnadór, *sm.* Instrument with which the flesh is removed from a tooth, that is to be drawn.

Descarnadúra, *sf.* The act of removing the flesh.

Descarnár, va. 1. To separate the flesh from the bone. 2. To take away part of a thing. *Descarnar los pellejos*, (Among Curriers) To scrape hides or skins with the drawing-knife. 3. (Met.) To inquire or examine into any thing minutely.—*vr.* To run through one's fortune to the advantage of another.

Descáro, *sm.* Impudence, barefacedness, effrontery.

Descarriamiénto, *sm.* The act of losing one's way or going astray.

Descarriár, va. 1. To take out of the right road, to lead astray. 2. To separate the cattle one from another.—*vr.* 1. To be disjoined or separated. 2. (Met.) To deviate from justice or reason.

Descarrillár, va. To tear the jaws asunder.

Descarrío, *sm.* The act of losing one's way or going astray.

Descartár, va. 1. To discard, to throw out of the hand such cards as are useless. 2. To dismiss from service; applied to soldiers.—*vr.* To excuse one's self, to plead innocence to a charge or impeachment.

Descárte, *sm.* 1. The cards discarded or thrown out as useless. 2. The act of discarding. 3. (Met.) Evasion, subterfuge. 4. (Met.) Refuse, that which is left or thrown out as useless.

Descasamiénto, *sm.* 1. Act of declaring a marriage null. 2. Divorce, repudiation.

Descasár, va. 1. To divorce or separate a husband and wife from one another; to declare a marriage null. 2. To entertain or amuse. 3. (Met.) To remove or disturb the order of things. 4. To disunite, to separate.

Descascár, va. To decorticate.—*vr.* To break into pieces.

Descascarár, va. 1. To decorticate, to divest of the bark or husk. 2. (Met.) To boast or talk much, to bluster, to bully.—*vr.* To fall or come off; applied to the last superficies of things.

Descaspár, va. 1. (Among Curriers) To scrape off the fleshy parts of a hide which is half dressed. 2. To take the dandruff from the head.

Descásque, *sm.* Decortication, the act of decorticating, particularly the cork-tree.

Descastár, va. To lose the cast, to deteriorate a race or lineage.

Descaudaládo, da, *a.* Applied to those who have lost their fortune.

Descaudilladaménte, *ad.* Disorderly, without a commander or leader.

Descaudillár, va. To be confused, to be disordered or disconcerted for want of a leader.

Descebár, va. To unprime fire-arms, to take away the priming of guns.

Descendéncia, *sf.* Descent, original.

Descendénte, *sm.* 1. Descendant. 2. (Anat.) Descending muscle.

Descendér, vn. 1. To descend, to come from a higher place to a lower. 2. (Met.) To decline in esteem or reputation. 3. To proceed from some other thing. 4. To expatiate on a subject. 5. To let down, to lower any thing.

Descendída, *sf.* 1. Descent, the act of going downwards. 2. (Ant.) Maritime expedition and disembarkment.

Descendiénte, *sf.* Descendant, the offspring of an ancestor. V. *Baxada.*

Descendimiénto, *sm.* 1. The act of descending or growing downwards. 2. Defluxion from the head to the breast.

Descensión, *sf.* 1. Descension. 2. V. *Descendencia.*

Descénso, *sm.* 1. Descent, the act of descending or going downwards. 2. Degradation, dismission or discharge from a public employment or office.

Descénta, *sf.* Descent, invasion; hostile entrance into a country.

Desceñidúra, *sf.* Disjunction, act of untying.

Desceñír, va. To ungird, to loosen or take off the girdle or belt with which clothes are tied.

Descepár, va. 1. To eradicate, to pull up by the root. 2. To demolish the works of a fortress, to level them with the ground.

Descerár, va. To take the empty combs from a bee-hive.

Descercádo, da, *a.* Open, unfortified, undefended.

Descercadór, *sm.* He that forces the enemy to raise a siege.

Descercár, va. 1. To destroy or pull down a wall. 2. To oblige the enemy to raise a siege.

Descérco, *sm.* The act of raising a siege.

Descerrajádo, da, *a.* Corrupt, vicious, wicked, ill-disposed.

Descerrajadúra, *sf.* The act of taking off locks or bolts.

Descerrajár, va. 1. To take off the lock of a door, chest, or trunk. 2. To discharge fire-arms.

Descerrumárse, *vr.* To be wrenched or distorted; applied to the muscles of a beast.

Descervigár, va. To twist the neck.

Descetranár, va. To eat or gnaw wood or timber to its very heart.

Descifradór, *sm.* Decipherer, one who explains writings in cipher.

Descifrár, va. 1. To decipher, to explain writings in cipher. 2. (Met.) To unravel, to unfold.

Descimentár, va. To pull down to the ground.

Descinchár, va. To ungirth a horse.

Descingír, va. V. *Desceñir.*

Desclavadór, *sm.* An instrument for drawing nails.

Desclavár, va. To draw out nails; to unnail.

Descoagulár, va. To liquefy, to dissolve.

Descobajár, va. To pull the stem from a grape.

Descobertúra, *sf.* Discovery, the act of finding any thing which was hidden or concealed.

Descobijár, va. To uncover, to take off one's clothes.

Descobrír, va. V. *Descubrir.*

Descocadaménte, *ad.* Impudently, with effrontery.

Descocádo, da, *a.* Bold, impudent.

Descocár, va. To clean, clear, or free trees from insects.—*vr.* To be impudent, saucy, or petulant.

Descocér, va. 1. To digest, to concoct in the stomach. 2. *Descocer los tablones de un baxel*, (Naút.) To rip off the planks of a ship.

Descócho, cha, *a.* (Ant.) Very much boiled.

Descóco, *sm.* Barefacedness, impudence.

Descodár, va. To rip, to unstitch.

Descogér, *va.* To unfold, to extend and spread what was folded.

Descogollár, *va.* To take out the heart or bud of a plant; to strip the summit.

Descogotádo, da, *a.* Having the neck naked and exposed.

Descogotár, *va.* 1. To kill a beast by one blow on the nape. 2. To knock off with one blow or stroke on the nape. 3. To knock off the horns of a stag at one blow.

Descolár, *va.* 1. To cut off an animal's tail, to dock. 2. To cut off the fag-end of a piece of cloth.

Descolchár, *va.* (Naút.) To untwist a cable.

Descolgár, *va.* 1. To take down what is hung up. 2. To take down hangings or tapestry, hung or fastened against the walls of rooms. —*vr.* 1. To come down gently, by means of a rope or any other thing. 2. (Met.) To glide, flow, or run down; applied to the waters of streams or rivers.

Descoligádo, da, *a.* Withdrawn from a league or coalition.

Descolladaménte, *ad.* Loftily, haughtily; with an air of authority.

Descollamiénto, *sm.* V. *Descuello.*

Descollár, *vn.* To excel, to surpass.—*vr.* To exceed, to outdo, to be superior to others.

Descolmár, *va.* 1. To strike corn in a measure with a strickle. 2. (Met.) To diminish.

Descolmillár, *va.* To draw or pull out the grinders. [growing pale.

Descoloramiénto, *sm.* Paleness, the act of

Descolorár, *va.* To discolour, to change from the natural hue.

Descolorído, da, *a.* Discoloured, pale.

Descolorimiénto, *sm.* Paleness, want of colour.

Descolorír, *va.* To discolour, to change from the natural hue.

Descombrár, *va.* To remove obstacles.

Descomedidaménte, *ad.* Rudely, coarsely, unmannerly; excessively, immoderately.

Descomedído, da, *a.* 1. Haughty, lofty, overbearing. 2. Rude, impudent, insolent.

Descomedimiénto, *sm.* Rudeness, incivility.

Descomedírse, *vr.* To be rude or disrespectful.

Descomér, *vn.* (Joc.) To ease nature, to go to stool.

Descomimiénto, *sm.* An affected disdain of a thing, which in fact is earnestly desired.

Descomodádo ó Descómodo, da, *a.* Incommodious, inconvenient. [nience.

Descomodidád, *sf.* Incommodity, inconve-

Descompadrár, *vn.* To disagree, to fall out.

Descompañár, *va.* V. *Desacompañar.*

Descompás, *sm.* (Ant.) Excess, redundance.

Descompasádo, da, *a.* Excessive, extravagant, beyond all rule and measure.

Descompasárse, *vr.* To exceed all rule and measure, to transgress all bounds and proportion.

Descomponér, *va.* 1. To discompose, to alter the order or composition of a thing. 2. To destroy harmony and friendship among friends. 3. (Quím.) To decompose bodies.—*vr.* 1. To be out of temper, to transgress the rules of modesty and good behaviour. 2. To be indisposed or out of order. 3. To change for the worse; applied to the weather.

Descomposición, *sf.* Disorder, confusion; d[ecomposition].

Descompostúra, *sf.* 1. Discomposure, disord[er], perturbation. 2. Slovenliness, uncleanline[ss]. 3. Forwardness, impudence, want of modest[y], disrespectful conduct.

Descompuestaménte, *ad.* Audaciously, in [an] impudent or insolent manner.

Descompuésto, ta, *a.* Audacious, impuden[t], insolent; immodest. [wicke[d].

Descomulgádo, da, *a.* Perverse, nefario[us],

Descomulgadór, *sm.* He that issues or proclai[ms] an excommunication. V. *Excomulgador.*

Descomulgár, *va.* To excommunicate.

Descomunál, *a.* Uncommon; unproportiona[l], immoderate.

Descomunalménte, *ad.* Uncommonly; imm[o]derately, without measure or proportion.

Descomunión, *sf.* Excommunication. [ed[ly].

Desconcertadaménte, *ad.* Disorderly, conf[us]-

Desconcertádo, da, *a.* Disorderly, slovenly.

Desconcertadór, *sm.* Disturber, disconcert[er].

Desconcertadúra, *sf.* Discomposure, distu[r]bance.

Desconcertár, *va.* To discompose, to distu[rb] the order of things. *Desconcertar medid[as]* To disconcert measures.—*vr.* 1. To disagre[e], not to agree with regard to the price or v[a]lue of any thing, 2. To luxate, to put out [of] joint, to disjoint. 3. To exceed the limits [of] prudence and judgment. 4. To be indispo[s]ed with a looseness of the body.

Desconchár, *va.* To take off the scales [or] shells, to unscale.

Desconciérto, *sm.* 1. Disorder, confusion. [2.] Want of prudence and circumspection. [3.] Indolence, negligence. 4. Flux, or viole[nt] looseness of the body.

Desconcórde, *a.* V. *Desacorde.*

Desconcórdia, *sf.* Discord, disagreement.

Desconejár, *va.* To kill a number of rabbit[s].

Desconfiadaménte, *ad.* Diffidently, in a d[is]trustful manner.

Desconfiádo, da, *a.* Diffident, distrustful.

Desconfiánte, *pa.* Distrusting; he who su[s]pects.

Desconfiánza, *sf.* 1. Diffidence, distrust; wa[nt] of confidence. 2. Jealousy, suspicious fear.

Desconfiár, *vn.* To diffide, to distrust, to ha[ve] no confidence in. *¿ Desconfia vd. de mi in[te]gridad?* Do you doubt my integrity?

Desconformár, *vn.* To dissent, to disagree, [to] differ in opinion.

Desconfórme, *a.* 1. Discordant, disagreein[g], contrary. 2. Unequal, unlike.

Desconformidád, *sf.* 1. Disagreement, opp[o]sition, contrariety of opinion. 2. Inequalit[y], dissimilitude, unlikeness.

Desconhortár, *va.* (Ant.) To dishearten, [to] dishearten. [timidit[y].

Desconhórte, *sm.* (Ant.) Languor, lassitud[e],

Desconocér y Desconoscér, *va.* 1. To disow[n], to disavow. 2. To be totally ignorant of [a] thing, not to know a person. *Desconocer [la] tierra*, To be unacquainted with a county. *Desconocer uno por hijo*, Not to own one [as] a son. *Desconocer el beneficio*, Not to a[c]knowledge a favour received; to be ungrat[e]-

Desconocidaménte, *ad.* Ignorantly. [fu[l].

Desconocído, da, a. 1. Ungrateful, unthankful. 2. Disguised, concealed by an unusual dress.
Desconocimiénto, sm. Ignorance, forgetfulness, ingratitude.
Desconoscéncia, sf. (Ant.) Ingratitude.
Desconsejár, va. V. *Desaconsejar*.
Desconsentír, va. To dissent, to disagree.
Desconsideradaménte, ad. Inconsiderately.
Desconsiderádo, da, a. Inconsiderate, imprudent.
Desconsolación, sf. Disconsolateness, the state of being disconsolate.
Desconsoladaménte, ad. Inconsolably.
Desconsoládo, da, a. 1. Disconsolate, hapless, melancholy. 2. Sick, disordered in the organs of digestion.
Desconsolár, va. To afflict, to put in pain, to treat rudely.
Desconsuélo, sm. 1. Affliction, trouble. 2. Disorder in the organs of digestion.
Descontagiár, va. To purify, to free from contagion.
Descontamiénto, sm. V. *Descuento*.
Descontár, va. To discount, to defalcate, to deduct part of an account.
Descontentadízo, za, a. Discontented, dissatisfied, displeased.
Descontentamiénto, sm. Discontentment, displeasure, grief. [to displease.
Descontentár, va. To discontent, to dissatisfy,
Desconténto, sm. Discontent, disgust.
Descontento, ta, a. 1. Discontent, dissatisfied, displeased. 2. Unpleasant, disgustful.
Descontinuación, sf. Discontinuation, discontinuance, cessation.
Descontinuár, va. To discontinue, to leave off, to break off.
Descontínuo, ua, a. Disjoined, segregated, discontinued.
Desconveníble, a. Discordant, disagreeing, dissimilar.
Desconveniéncia, sf. 1. Incommodity, inconvenience. 2. Discord, disunion, dissimilitude.
Desconveniénte, pa. Discording, inconvenient; incongruous.
Desconvenír, vn. 1. To discord, to disagree. 2. To be unlike or dissimilar; not to suit.
Desconversáble, a. Unsocial, rude in conversation and society.
Desconversár, vn. To be unsocial, to shun all company or society. [scind.
Desconvidár, va. To revoke, to annul, to re-
Descopár, va. To lop off the branches of a tree.
Descorazonadaménte, ad. Inanimately, feebly, imbecilely.
Descorazonár, va. 1. To pull or tear out the heart. 2. (Met.) To dishearten, to discourage. 3. (Met.) To smite with love.
Descorchadór, sm. 1. One who strips off the bark of a cork-tree. 2. *Descorchador de colmena*, One who breaks the hive to steal the honey.
Descorchár, va. 1. To decorticate a cork-tree; to strip off the bark. 2. To break a bee-hive, to steal the honey. 3. To break open a chest or trunk, to get out the contents.
Descordár, va. To uncord an instrument.
Descorderár, va. To wean lambs, to take them from their dams.
Descordójo, sm. (Ant.) Taste, pleasure, joy.

Descornár, va. To dishorn, to knock off the horns of a horned animal. *Descornar la flor*, (Met.) To discover a trick or fraud.
Descorreár, vn. To loosen the skin that covers the tenderlings of a deer.
Descorregído, da, a. Incorrigible, bad beyond correction.
Descorrér, va. 1. To run or flow, as a liquid. 2. To retrograde. *Descorrer la cortina*, To draw the curtain.
Descorrimiénto, sm. The fluxion of any liquid.
Descortés, a. Unpolite, uncivil, unmannerly, ill-bred.
Descortesía, sf. Incivility, want of politeness.
Descortesménte, ad. Incivilly, uncourteously.
Descortezadór, sm. One who strips off the bark.
Descortezadúra y Decortezamiénto, sf. y m. Decortication, the act of stripping off the bark.
Descortezár, va. 1. To decorticate, to strip off the bark of trees. 2. To break in a horse. 3. (Met.) To polish or civilize one.—vr. 1. To be rude and coarse of manners. 2. To pursue an undertaking with steadiness and perseverance. [ing a seam.
Descosedúra, sf. Unseaming, the act of undo-
Descosér, va. 1. To unseam, to rip, to cut open. 2. (Met.) To separate, to disjoin. *No descoser los labios*, To keep a profound silence.—vr. (Met.) To give a loose to one's tongue, to babble incessantly and indiscreetly.
Descosidaménte, ad. Excessively.
Descosído, sm. Ripping. V. *Descosedura*.
Descosído, da, a. Unseamed, unstitched. *Beber ó comer como un descosido*, To eat or drink immoderately.
Descostillár, va. To take out the ribs, to break the ribs.—vr. To fall with great violence on one's back.
Descostrár, va. To take off the crust.
Descostúmbre, sm. Disuse, want of practice or use.
Descotár, va. To remove a restriction from the use of any road, boundary, or property.
Descoyuntamiénto y Descoyúnto, sm. 1. Luxation, the act of disjointing bones. 2. The severe pain which attends the luxation of bones.
Descoyuntár, va. 1. To luxate or disjoint the bones, to put them out of joint. 2. To vex, to molest, to displease.—vr. To experience some violent motion. *Descoyuntarse de risa*, To split one's sides with laughing.
Descrecéncia, sf. Decrement, the act of decreasing.
Descrecér, vn. 1. To decrease, to grow less; to diminish. 2. To fall, to subside; applied to tides and rivers. 3. To grow short; applied to the day.
Descrecimiénto, sm. Decrease, diminution.
Descrédito, sm. Discredit, the loss of fame, reputation, or honour.
Descrepusculár, va. To remove the twilight or dawn.
Descreéncia, sf. (Ant.) Incredulity.
Descreér, va. 1. To disbelieve. 2. To deny due credit to a person; to disown or abjure.
Descreído, da, a. Incredulous, infidel.
Descrestár, va. To take off the crest.

Descriarse, *vr.* To weaken, to extenuate; to pine away with desire or anxiety.
Describir, *va.* 1. To draw, to delineate. 2. To describe, to relate minutely. 3. (Log.) To define imperfectly.
Descrinar, *va.* V. *Desgreñar.*
Descripcion, *sf.* 1. Description, delineation, design. 2. Narration, account, relation. 3. (Log.) Imperfect definition. 4. (For.) V. *Inventario.*
Descriptivo, va, *a.* Descriptive, describing.
Descriptorio, ria, *a.* (Ant.) Descriptive.
Descripto y Descrito, ta, *pp.* Described.
Descrismar, *va.* 1. (Bar.) To excite one's passion or displeasure. 2. To give one a blow on the head. 3. To remove the chrism.
Descristianar, *va.* To enrage. V. *Descrismar.*
Descrucificar, *va.* To take from a crucifix or cross.
Descruzar, *va.* To undo the form or figure of a cross.
Descuajar, *va.* 1. To dissolve, to liquefy. 2. (Agr.) To eradicate, to pluck up weeds. 3. (Met.) To frighten, to terrify.
Descuajo, *sm.* (Agric.) Eradication, act of destroying or eradicating weeds from a soil.
Descubierta, *sf.* 1. Pie, without an upper crust. 2. (Ant.) Discovery, manifestation, revelation. 3. (Mil.) Recognition, inspection made in the morning before opening the gates of a citadel, or the passes of an encampment, to prevent surprises or ambuscades. *A' la descubierta*, Openly, clearly.
Descubiertamente, *ad.* Manifestly, openly.
Descubierto, *sm.* 1. The whole of a discovery, the total of the parts discovered. 2. The uncovered or unroofed part of a house. *Al descubierto*, Openly. 3. The solemn exposition of the sacrament. 4. Balance of accounts.
Descubierto, ta, *a.* Uncovered, defenceless, forsaken, forlorn.
Descubretalles, *sm.* (Ant.) Small fan, so called because it did not hide the figure.
Descubricion, *sf.* (Ant.) The elevation or view which one house has over another.
Descubridero, *sm.* Eminence or rising ground, from which the adjacent country can be overlooked.
Descubridor, ra, *s.* 1. Discoverer, one who discovers or makes discoveries. 2 Investigator, explorer; vessel on a voyage of discovery.
Descubrimiento, *sm.* 1. Discovery; the act of discovering some unknown country, or any other thing. 2. Country or thing discovered.
Descubrir, *va.* 1. To uncover any thing. 2. To discover, to find out. 3. To discover, to reveal. 4. To expose the sacrament to public adoration or worship. 5. (Mil.) To overlook any place in a fortification. *Descubrir una via ó abertura de agua*, (Naút.) To discover a leak. *Descubrir la tierra*, (Naút.) To make the land. *Descubrir el campo*, (Mil.) To reconnoitre. *Descubrir por la popa ó por la proa*, (Naút.) To descry a-stern or a-head. *Descubrir su pecho*, To unbosom, to communicate all one's secrets to another.—*Descubrir el cuerpo*, To expose any part of the body that it might be wounded; (Met.) To favour any perilous undertaking. *Descubrir la hilaza*, (Met.) To manifest the vice or defect which one has unknown to him.—*vr.* To uncover one's self, to take off the hat to any one.
Descuello, *sm.* 1. Excessive stature or height of an animal. 2. (Met.) Pre-eminence, superiority. 3. (Met.) Loftiness, haughtiness.
Descuento, *sm.* 1. Sum paid in part of payment of a debt. 2. Discount. 3. (Met.) Diminution, decrease.
Descuernacabras, *sm.* Cold north wind.
Descuerno y Descuetro, *sm.* V. *Desayre.*
Descuidadamente, *ad.* Carelessly, negligently.
Descuidado, da, *a.* 1. Careless, negligent, neglectful. 2. Unwary, fearless; without dread or apprehension. 3. Slovenly, unclean.
Descuidar, *va.* 1. To relieve from care, to make easy. 2. To render careless or indolent; to want attention or diligence.—*vr.* 1. To be forgetful of one's duty. 2. To make one's self easy. *Descuide vd.* Make yourself easy.
Descuido, *sm.* 1. Indolence, carelessness, neglect of duty. 2. Want of attention, incivility. 3. Improper or disgraceful action. 4. Imprudence, immodesty. *Al descuido*, Affectedly or dissemblingly careless. *Al descuido y con cuidado*, Studiously careless, a carelessness.
Descuitado, da, *a.* Living without trouble or care.
Descular, *va.* (Bar.) To break the bottom or end of a thing.
Desculpa, *sf.* V. *Disculpa.*
Desculpar, *va.* V. *Disculpar.*
Descultizar, *va.* To free the style, or some expressions, from affected elegance and nicety.
Descumbrado, da, *a.* Level, plain.
Descumplir, *va.* Not to fulfil one's duty.
Descura, *sf.* V. *Descuido.*
Desdar, *va.* (Among Rope-makers) To untwist a rope.
Desde, *prep.* Since, after, from. *Desde aqui*, From this place. *Desde luego*, From hence immediately. *Desde entonces*, From this time forward. *Desde niño*, From or since one's childhood. *Desde alli*, Thence; from that period.—*ad.* V. *Despues de.*
Desdecir, *va.* To live the lie to, to charge with falsehood.—*vn.* To degenerate, to fall from its kind. 2. To differ, to disagree. 3. To tumble down, to fall to ruin; applied to buildings.—*vr.* To gainsay, to retract, to recant.
Desdel, *contrac.* of *Desde él*, Since he.
Desden, *sm.* 1. Disdain, scorn, contempt. *Al desden*, Affectedly careless. 2. Affront, insult. *Desdenes de la fortuna*, (Met.) The frowns of fortune.
Desdende, *ad.* (Ant.) V. *Desde entonces.*
Desdentado, da, *a.* Without teeth.
Desdentar, *va.* To draw or pull out teeth.
Desdeñable, *a.* Contemptible, worthy of contempt; despicable.
Desdeñadamente, *ad.* Disdainfully.
Desdeñador, ra, *s.* One who scorns or disdains.
Desdeñar, *va.* 1. To disdain, to scorn. *La tierra le desdeña*, He is universally despised. 2. To vex, to exasperate.—*vr.* To be disdainful; not to condescend.
Desdeño, *sm.* Scorn, contempt, indignation.
Desdeñosamente, *ad.* Disdainfully.
Desdeñoso, sa, *a.* Disdainful, fastidious.
Desdevanar, *va.* To wind or undo a clew.
Desdicha, *sf.* Misfortune, calamity; great poverty.
Desdichadamente, *ad.* Unfortunately, unhappily.

Desdichadíllo, lla; to, ta, *a. dim.* A little unfortunate.

Desdichádo, da, *a.* Unfortunate, wretched, miserable. *Es un desdichado*, He is a sorry, pitiful creature.

Desdinerár, *va.* To rob money.

Desdoblár, *va.* 1. To take out the folds, to unfold, to spread open. 2. To resume the thread of a speech or discourse. 3. To explain, to clear up.

Deslón, *sm.* Silliness. V. *Insulsez*.

Desdonadaménte, *ad.* Rudely, insipidly.

Desdonádo, da, *a.* Graceless, coarse of manners, ungenteel; insipid, foolish.

Desdonár, *va.* To take back what had been given as a present.

Desdorár, *va.* 1. To take off the gilding of any thing. 2. (Met.) To tarnish, to sully.

Desdormído, da, *a.* Alarmed, frightened.

Desdóro, *sm.* Dishonour, blemish, blot of reputation.

Deseáble, *a.* Desirable.

Deseableménte, *ad.* Desirably.

Deseadór, *sm.* He who desires or wishes.

Deseár, *va.* 1. To desire, to wish, to long for. 2. To claim, to demand of right.

Desecación, *sf.* Desiccation, exsiccation.

Desecamiénto, *sm.* Exsiccation.

Desecánte, *pa.* Drying, drier; desiccant.

Desecár, *va.* 1. To dry, to draw the moisture from any thing. 2. To stop, to detain.

Desecatívo, va, *a.* Desiccative.

Desechadaménte, *ad.* Vilely, despicably.

Desechár, *va.* 1. To depreciate, to undervalue. 2. (Naút.) To condemn a vessel. 3. To reject, to reprove. 4. To refuse, not to admit. 5. To expel, to drive away; to exclude, to reprobate.

Desécho, *sm.* 1. Residue, overplus, remainder. 2. Refuse, offal. 3. (Met.) Disregard, contempt.

Desedificación, *sf.* 1. Demolition, destruction. 2. Scandal, bad example.

Desedificár, *va.* 1. To demolish, to destroy. 2. To scandalize, to set a bad example, to offend by some criminal or disgraceful action.

Deseguída, *sf.* A prostitute, a woman who leads an unchaste or licentious life.

Deseguír, *va.* (Ant.) To follow any one's party.

Deselladúra, *sf.* (Ant.) Act of unsealing or taking off the seals.

Desellár, *va.* To unseal, to take off the seals.

Desemballestár, *va.* To dispose to a descent; applied to hawks in the air, when preparing to descend.

Desembanastár, *va.* 1. To take out of a basket what it contains. 2. (Met.) To talk much and at random. 3. (Fam.) To draw the sword.—*vr.* To break out or loose; applied to a person or animal which was confined.

Desembarazadaménte, *ad.* Freely, without embarrassment.

Desembarazádo, da, *a.* Free, unrestrained.

Desembarazár, *va.* 1. To free, to disengage, to remove an impediment or obstruction. 2. To clear a house of useless lumber. 3. To unburthen, to disencumber.—*vr.* To be extricated from difficulties, to be disentangled from embarrassments.

Desembarázo, *sm.* Freedom, or liberty of speech or action.

Desembarcación, *sf.* Disembarkation, landing.

Desembarcadéro, *sm.* Landing-place.

Desembarcár, *va.* To unship, to disembark.—*vn.* 1. To disembark, to land, to go on shore. 2. (Met.) To alight from a coach. *Estar para desembarcar*, To be near one's time; applied to a pregnant woman. 3. To terminate a stair in a landing-place.

Desembárco, *sm.* 1. Disembarcation, landing, unshipment. 2. Landing-place at the top of a flight of stairs. 3. Descent, hostile landing.

Desembargadaménte, *ad.* Freely.

Desembargadór, *sm.* Chief magistrate and privy counsellor in Portugal.

Desembargár, *va.* 1. To remove impediments, or clear away obstructions. 2. (For.) To raise an embargo or sequestration. 3. (Ant.) To perform the usual evacuations.

Desembárgo, *sm.* 1. The act of removing an impediment or obstruction. 2. The act of raising an embargo or sequestration.

Desembárque, *sm.* Disembarkation, landing.

Desembarrár, *va.* To clear any thing of mud or clay.

Desembaúlar, *va.* 1. To empty a trunk, to take out what it contains. 2. (Met.) To speak one's mind freely and without reserve; to disclose one's secret thoughts.

Desembebecérse y Desembebér, *vr.* y *n.* To recover the use of one's senses.

Desembelesárse, *vr.* To recover from amazement or abstraction.

Desemblánza, *sf.* V. *Desemejanza*.

Desembocadéro y Desembocadúra, *s.* The mouth of a river; the point where it empties into the sea.

Desembocár, *va.* 1 To disembogue, to flow out at the mouth of a river. 2. (Met.) To break out into a violent passion. *Desembocar de la calle*, To go from one street to another.

Desembolsár, *va.* 1. To empty a purse, to take out what was in it. 2. To disburse, to expend.

Desembólso, *sm.* Disbursement.

Desemborrachár, *va.* To grow sober.

Desemboscárse, *vr.* To get out of the woods, to get clear of an ambuscade.

Desemboxadéra, *sf.* (Murc.) Woman who takes the pods of silk-worms from the southern wood.

Desemboxár, *va.* To remove the silk-pods from the southern wood.

Desembozár, *va.* 1. To unmuffle or uncover the face. 2. (Met.) To unravel, to decipher.

Desembózo, *sm.* 1. The act of uncovering or unmuffling the face. 2. Freedom or liberty of speech.

Desembravecér, *va.* To tame, to domesticate.

Desembravecimiénto, *sm.* The act of taming or reclaiming from wildness.

Desembrazár, *va.* To dart or throw weapons; to throw from the arms.

Desembriagárse, *vr.* To grow sober, to recover from drunkenness.

Desembridár, *vr.* To unbridle a horse, to take off the bridle.

Desembuchár, *va.* 1. To disgorge, to pour out with violence. 2. (Met.) To unbosom, to disclose all one's sentiments and secrets.

Desembudár, *va.* To draw out any thing as if it were through a funnel.

Desemejáble, *a.* 1. (Ant.) Dissimilar, unlike or unlikely. 2. (Ant.) Strong, large, violent.

Desemejádo, da, *a.* 1. (Ant.) Different, diverse, 2. (Ant.) Horrible, terrible, furious.

Desemejánte, *a.* Dissimilar, unlike, different.

Desemejanteménte, *ad.* Dissimilarly.

Desemejánza, *sf* Dissimilitude, unlikeness, difference.

Desemejár, *vn.* To be dissimilar or unlike.—*va.* To mask, to disguise.

Desempacár, *va.* To unpack, to disembale.—*vr.* To grow calm, to be appeased.

Desempacharse, *vr.* 1. (Met.) To grow bold, to lose all bashfulness. 2. To discharge crudities or indigestions from the stomach. 3. V. *Despachar.*

Desempácho, *sm.* Forwardness, want of bashfulness.

Desempadrár, *va.* To deprive one of his father.

Desempalagár, *va.* 1. To clean one's palate, to remove nauseousness or loathing, to restore the appetite. 2. To clear a mill of stagnant or detained water, and restore its free course.

Desempañár, *va.* 1. To take away the clouts and swaddling clothes of children. 2. To clean a looking-glass which is tarnished.

Desempapelár, *va.* To take any thing out of the paper in which it was wrapped up.

Desempaquetár, *va.* To unpack, to open a packet.

Desemparejár, *va.* To unmatch, to make things unequal which were equal or fellows.—*vn.* To part, to be separated.

Desemparvár, *va.* To heap or store up grain in a granary.

Desempatár, *va.* 1. To make unequal, to do away the equality existing among things. 2. (Met.) To explain, to clear up, to facilitate.

Desempedradór, *sm.* Dilapidator, he who takes down stones.

Desempedrár, *va.* 1. To undo or break up the pavement. 2. To frequent or haunt a place, to beat or ramble about a spot. *Ir desempedrando la calle*, (Met.) To go very rapidly.

Desempegár, *va.* To take off the pitch or glue from any thing.

Desempeñár, *va.* 1. To redeem, to recover what was in another's possession. 2. To extricate one's self from debt. *Sus estados estan desempeñados*, His estates are clear of debt. 3. To perform or fulfil one's duty. *Desempeñar el asunto*, To prove a subject completely. 4. To disengage one's self from a difficult or arduous affair.—*vr.* (In Bull-fighting) To disengage one's self from the attack of a bull. *Desempeñarse de la tierra ó costa*, (Naút.) To claw off, to stand off, to work away from the shore.

Desempéño, *sm.* 1. The act of redeeming a pledge. 2. (Met.) Proof or confirmation of an account or statement. 3. Performance of an obligation or promise. 4. Perfection, completion; utmost height.

Desempeoráse, *vr.* To recover from sickness or disorder, to regain health and vigour.

Desemperezár, *vn.* To relinquish habits of laziness and indolence.

Desempolvoradúra, *sf.* Act of dusting, or clearing of dust.

Desempolvorár, *va.* To dust, to free any thing from dust.

Desemponzoñár, *va.* 1. To heal from the effects of poison, to expel poison. 2. (Met.) To cure any disordinate passion or affection.

Desempotrár, *va.* To remove the stays or props which support any thing.

Desempulgadúra, *sf.* Act of unbending a bow.

Desempulgár, *va.* To unbend a bow.

Desenalbardár, *va.* To take off a pack-saddle.

Desenamorár, *va.* To destroy love or affection.—*vr.* To relinquish or yield up one's opinion.

Desencabalgádo, da, *a.* V. *Desmontado.*

Desencabalgár, *va.* (Art.) To dismount cannon.

Desencabestradúra, *sf.* The act of disentangling a beast from the halter.

Desencabestrár, *va.* To disentangle a beast from the halter, in which the fore feet are entangled.

Desencadenár, *va.* 1. To unchain, to free from chains, to break the chain. 2. (Met.) To dissolve all connexion or obligation.

Desencalabrinár, *va.* To remove dizziness, to free from stupidity.

Desencalcár, *va.* To loosen or dissolve what was caked or close pressed.

Desencallár, *va.* (Naút.) To set a ship afloat which has struck on a rocky ground.

Desencaminár, *va.* 1. To lose one's way, to go astray. 2. To deviate from rectitude.

Desencantár, *va.* To disenchant, to free from the force of an enchantment.

Desencantaración, *sf.* (Ar.) Act and effect of drawing lots or balloting for any thing.

Desencantarár, *va.* 1. To draw from an urn or balloting-box the name or names of any persons for an office or situation. 2. To be withdrawn as incompetent, to take out a name on account of incapacity or privilege.

Desencánto, *sm.* Disenchantment.

Desencapotadúra, *sf.* Act of stripping off a great coat.

Desencapotár, *va.* 1. To strip one of his great coat. 2. (Met.) To uncover, to make manifest. 3. (Met.) To raise and keep up the head of a horse. *Desencapotar las orejas*, To cock up the ears.—*vr.* To lay aside frowns or looks of displeasure, to put on a pleasing countenance. *Desencapotarse el cielo*, To clear up.

Desencaprichár, *va.* To dissuade from error or prejudice.

Desencarcelár, *va.* 1. To release from confinement, to set at liberty. 2. (Met.) To free from oppression, to extricate from difficulties.

Desencarecér, *va.* To lower the price of any thing for sale.

Desencarnár, *va.* 1. To take the fat from dog's meat, lest they should become too corpulent. 2. (Met.) To lose an affection for any thing; to divert the mind from it.

Desencasár, *va.* V. *Desencaxar.*

Desencastár, *va.* To deteriorate a race or breed, to lose the cast.

Desencastillár, *va.* 1. To expel or drive out of a castle. 2. (Met.) To cast or drive out an evil spirit, to exorcise. 3. (Met.) To deprive of employment, power, or favour.

Desencaxamiénto y Desencáxe, *sm.* Act of disuniting or uncasing; luxation.

Desencaxár, *va.* To take a thing out of its place; to disfigure.

Desempaquetár, va. To unpack, to take out of a box what it contained.
Desencentrár, va. (Ant.) To take any thing from its centre.
Desencerrár, va. 1. To free from confinement. 2. To disclose what was hidden or unknown.
Desencintár, va. To untie, to loosen the strings or ribbons with which any thing was tied.
Desenclavár, va. 1. To draw or take out nails. V. *Desclavar*. 2. To put one violently out of his place.
Desenclavijár, va. To take out pins or pegs; *e.g.* of a musical instrument.
Desencogér, va. To unfold what was doubled, to spread.—*vr.* (Met.) To lay aside all bashfulness or reserve, to grow bold.
Desencogimiénto, *sm.* Expediting, removing obstacles.
Desencolár, va. To unglue, to loosen what was fastened with glue.
Desencolerizárse, *vr.* To grow calm, to be appeased.
Desenconár, va. 1. To cure or remove an inflammation. 2. (Met.) To moderate or check one's passion.—*vr.* To make mild, and benign.
Desencóno, *sm.* Settling or mitigating anger or passion.
Desencordár, va. To unstring, to loosen or untie strings.
Desencordelár, va. To loosen or untie ropes.
Desencorvár, va. To straighten, to make straight.
Desencrespár, va. To uncurl, to unfrizzle.
Desénde, *ad.* (Ant.) Contraction of *desde* and *ende*. V. *Desde*.
Desendemoniár y Desendiablár, va. To exorcise, to drive out an evil spirit. *Desendiablárse*, (Met.) To moderate or appease one's fury or passion.
Desendiosár, va. To humble vanity, to pull down presumption and haughtiness.
Desenfadadéras, *sf. pl.* *Tener desenfadaderas*, To take means to extricate one's self from difficulties, or liberate one's self from oppression.
Desenfadádo, dá, *a.* 1. Free, unembarrassed. 2. Wide, spacious, capacious.
Desenfadár, va. To abate anger, to appease passion.—*vr.* To be entertained or amused.
Desenfádo, *sm.* 1. Freedom, ease, facility. 2. Calmness, relaxation.
Desenfaldárse, *vr.* To let fall the train of a gown.
Desenfamár, va. V. *Disfamar*.
Desenfardár y Desenfardelár, va. To unpack, to open bales of goods.
Desenfatuár, va. To undeceive, to free from error.
Desenfraylár, vn. (Joc.) To un-monk.
Desenfrenadaménte, *ad.* Ungovernedly.
Desenfrenamiénto y Desenfréno, *sm.* Unruliness, rashness, headstrongness. *Desenfreno de vientre*, Sudden looseness.
Desenfrenár, va. To unbridle, to take off the bridle.—*vr.* 1. To give a loose to one's passions and desires. 2. To fly into a violent passion.
Desenfundár, va. To take out of a bag, bolster, pillow-case, &c.
Desenfurecérse, *vr.* To grow calm or quiet, to lay aside anger and passion.
Desengañadaménte, *ad.* 1. Clearly, ingenuously. 2. Awkwardly, without care or address, scurvily.
Desengañádo, da, *a.* 1. Undeceived. 2. Despicable, ill executed.
Desengañadór, *sm.* Undeceiver, he who undeceives.
Desengañár, va. To undeceive, to free from error.
Desenganchár, va. To unhook, to take down from a hook.
Desengarifár, va. To free or disengage from the grasp, claws, or fangs of a person or beast.
Desengáño y Desengañamiénto, *sm.* 1. The act of undeceiving or freeing from error. 2. The mere or naked truth. 3. Censure, reproof.
Desengarrafár, va. To unfasten or disengage from claws or clenched fingers.
Desengarzár, va. To unravel, to take off from a string.
Desengastár, va. To take a diamond out of a ring, snuff box, or other thing, where it was set.
Desengoznár, va. To unhinge; to be disjointed. V. *Desgoznar*.
Desengrasár, va. To take out the grease.
Desengrosár, va. To extenuate, to make lean, to debilitate, to make thin or fine.
Desengrudamiénto, *sm.* Act of rubbing off cement or paste.
Desengrudár, va. To scrape or rub off the paste from any thing.
Desenhadár, va. To remove the disgust for any thing.—*vr.* To be rendered pleased.
Desenhebrár, va. 1. To unthread, to take out thread from a needle. 2. (Met.) To explain, to unravel.
Desenhetrábl e, *a.* Extricable, that may be extricated or unravelled.
Desenhetrár, va. To disentangle the hair.
Desenhornár, va. To take out of the oven.
Desenjaezár, va. To unharness mules or horses, to unsaddle.
Desenjaulár, va. To free from a cage, to let loose out of a cage.
Desenlabonár, va. To unchain, to unlink.
Desenláce, *sm.* (Poét.) Developement of the plot of a play or poem.
Desenladrillár, va. To rip or take up floor-tiles.
Desenlazár, va. 1. To unlace, to untie knots. 2. To distinguish, not to confound different things.
Desenlosár, va. To take up a floor made of flags.
Desenlutár, va. 1. To leave off mourning. 2. To banish sorrow.
Desenmarañár, va. 1. To disentangle, to unfold the parts of any thing interwoven. 2. (Met.) To extricate from impediments or difficulties; to explain.
Desenmohecér, va. 1. To rub off rust, to clear from rust. 2. (Met.) To clear up, to make manifest.
Desenmudecér, va. 1. To remove an impediment of speech. 2. To break a long silence.
Desenojár, va. To appease anger, to allay passion.—*vr.* To recreate, to amuse one's self.
Desenójo, *sm.* Abatement or subsidence of anger or wrath.
Desenojóso, sa, *a.* That which can assuage anger.
Deséño, *sm.* V. *Designio*.
Desenquadernár, va. 1. To unbind, to undo the binding of a book. 2. V. *Desquadernar*.
Desenquietár, va. V. *Inquietár*.

Desenrazonádo, da, *a.* Unreasonable, without reason.

Desenredár, *va.* 1. To disentangle, to free from perplexities. 2. To put in order, to set to rights.—*vr.* To extricate one's self from difficulties.

Desenrédo, *sm.* 1. Disentanglement. 2. (Poét.) Developement of the plot of a play.

Desenrollár, *va.* To unrol. V. *Desarrollar.*

Desenronár, *va.* (Ar.) To remove the rubbish from any part.

Desenroñecér, *va.* 1. To take off the rust from metal. 2. (Met.) To polish manners, to cultivate the mind.

Desenroquecér, *va.* To free from hoarseness.

Desensabanár, *va.* 1. To change or take off the sheets. 2. (Met.) To remove an impediment or obstacle.

Desensañár, *va.* To assuage anger, to please, to mitigate irritation.

Desensartár, *va.* To unthread, to take from a string or thread.

Desensebár, *va.* 1. To strip a he-goat of his fat. 2. (Met.) To leave off working for a short time, to draw breath. 3. (Met.) To take away the taste of fat of a thing just eaten.

Desensenár, *vn.* To take out of the breast or bosom.

Desenseñádo, da, *a.* Untaught. [education.

Desenseñamiénto, *sm.* Ignorance, want of

Desenseñár, *va.* To make one forget what he had learned, to unlearn.

Desensillár, *va.* To unsaddle.

Desensoberbecérse, *vr.* To become humble, to moderate one's pride.

Desensortijádo, da, *a.* Luxated, out of joint.

Desentablár, *va.* 1. To rip up or off planks or boards. 2. (Met.) To discompose, to disturb, to throw into confusion. 3. To embroil an affair, to break off a bargain, to interrupt a friendly intercourse.

Desentalingár, *va.* (Naút.) To unbend a cable.

Desentendér ó Desentendérse, *vn. y r.* To feign not to understand a thing. [rant.

Desentendído, da, *a.* Feigned, affected; igno-

Desentendimiénto, *sm.* (Ant.) Ignorance, imprudence, absurdity. [up.

Desenterradór, *sm.* He who disinters, or digs

Desenterramiénto, *sm.* Disinterment.

Desenterrár, *va.* 1. To unbury, to dig up what has been buried under ground. 2. (Met.) To recall to one's memory. *Desenterrar los huesos,* (Met.) To verify the ancestors of any one. *Desenterrar los muertos,* (Met.) To slander or calumniate the dead. [dead.

Desentierramuértos, *sm.* Calumniator of the

Desentoldár, *va.* 1. To take away the awning. 2. (Met.) To strip any thing of its ornaments.

Desentollecér, *va.* 1. (Ant.) To restore the nerves to their usual vigour. 2. (Met.) To liberate, to free from difficulties.

Desentonación, *sf.* Dissonance.

Desentonamiénto, *sm.* Dissonance, excess in the tone of the voice.

Desentonár, *va.* To humble, to wound the pride of any one.—*vn.* To be out of tune, to be inharmonious.—*vr.* To be of a coarse address, to be rude or uncouth; to raise the voice in disrespect

Desentóno, *sm.* 1. Disharmony, want of harmony. 2. A harsh, rude tone of voice. [screw.

Desentornillár, *va.* To unscrew, to loosen a

Desentorpecérse, *vr.* 1. To be freed from torpor, to be restored from numbness. 2. To become lively, smart, or pert.

Desentrañamiénto, *sm.* The act of giving any thing as a proof of love and affection.

Desentrañár, *va.* 1. To eviscerate, to draw out the entrails. 2. (Met.) To penetrate or dive into the most hidden and difficult matters.—*vr.* (Met.) To give away all one's fortune and property out of love and affection for a person.

Desentristecér, *va.* To banish sadness and

Desentronizár, *va.* V. *Destronar.* [grief.

Desentropezár, *va.* V. *Desembarazar.* [ness.

Desentumecérse, *vr.* To be freed from numb-

Desentumír, *va.* To free from torpor.

Desenvaynár, *va.* 1. To unsheath, to draw out of the scabbard. 2. To expose to view any thing which was hidden or covered. 3. To stretch out the claws or fangs; applied to such animals as have talons.—*vn.* To strip, to undress. [of her sails.

Desenvelejár, *va.* (Naút.) To strip a vessel

Desenvendár, *va.* To take off fillets or bands.

Desenvergár, *va.* (Naút.) To unbend a sail.

Desenvergonzadaménte, *ad.* V. *Desvergonzadamente.*

Desenviolár, *va.* To consecrate anew a church which has been profaned.

Desenvoltúra, *sf.* 1. Sprightliness, cheerfulness. 2. A lewd posture or gesture in women. 3. A graceful and easy delivery of one's sentiments and thoughts.

Desenvolvedór, *sm.* Unfolder, investigator.

Desenvolvér, *va.* 1. To unfold, to unroll. 2. (Met.) To decipher, to discover, to unravel. 3. (Ant.) To expedite.—*vr.* To be forward, to behave with too much assurance.

Desenvuélta, *sf.* A forward, impudent woman.

Desenvueltaménte, *ad.* 1. Impudently, licentiously. 2. Expeditiously, with clearness and expedition. [tious.

Desenvuélto, ta, *a.* Forward, impudent, licen-

Desenxalmár, *va.* To unharness mules and horses. [bles.

Desenzarzár, *va.* To disentangle from bram-

Deseñamiénto, *sm.* (Ant.) Want of instruction.

Deseñár, *va.* To make signs to announce any thing. [According to one's wish.

Deséo, *sm.* Desire, wish. *A' medida del deseo,*

Deseóso, sa, *a.* Desirous.

Desequído, da, *a.* Dry. V. *Resequido.*

Deserción, *sf.* Desertion.

Deserrádo, da, *a.* Free from error.

Desertár, *va.* 1. To desert, to forsake or abandon one's colours or post. 2. To separate from a body or company. 3. (For.) To abandon or drop a cause.

Desertór, *sm.* Deserter, a soldier who quits his regiment or colours without leave.

Deservício, *sm.* Disloyalty; a want of loyalty and obedience to the sovereign. [other.

Deservidór, *sm.* He who fails in serving an-

Deservír, *va.* Not to perform one's duty to the sovereign.

Deseslabonár, *va.* To cut the links of a chain.

Desespaldár, *va.* To wound the shoulder.

Desesperación, Desesperáncia, y Desesperánza, *sf.* 1. Despondency, despair, desperation. 2. (Met.) Displeasure, anger, passion. *Es una desesperacion*, (Vulg.) It is unbearable.

Desesperadaménte, *ad.* Desperately, despairingly.

Desesperanzár, *va.* To deprive any one of hope; to despair.

Desesperár, *vn.* To despair, to be without hope. —*va.* To make one despair, to deprive one of all hope.—*vr.* 1. To sink into the utmost despair. 2. To fret, to be grievously vexed.

Desesterár, *va.* 1. To take off the mats. 2. (Met.) To lay aside the winter clothes.

Desestéro, *sm.* The act of taking off the mats.

Desestimación y Desestíma, *sf.* Disrespect, want of esteem or respect.

Desestimadór, ra, *s.* Contemner, one who despises or depreciates.

Desestimár, *va.* To disregard, not to esteem.

Desestivár, *va.* (Naút.) To alter the stowage.

Déset, *ad.* (Ant.) V. *Ademas.*

Desexecutár, *va.* (For.) To liberate one from an execution, to which he was subject.

Desfacedór, *sm.* Destroyer. *Desfacedor de tuertes*, Undoer of injuries.

Desfacér, *va.* (Ant.) V. *Deshacer.*

Desfacimiénto, *sm.* (Ant.) Destruction, ruin, detriment.

Desfalcár, *va.* 1. To defalcate, to cut off, to lop. 2. (Met.) To dissuade from an undertaking or opinion.

Desfalcazár, *va.* (Naút.) To untwist a rope, to make oakum of old ropes.

Desfálco, *sm.* Diminution, the act of diminishing or detracting, defalcation.

Desfalecér el siso, (Ant.) V. *Chochear.*

Desfallecér, *vn.* 1. To pine, to fall away, to lose vigour or strength. 2. To swoon, to faint.

Desfallecimiénto, *sm.* Languor, decline, dejection of mind; extinction.

Desfamár, *va.* To defame.

Desfavorecedór, ra, *s.* One who discountenances; contemner.

Desfavorecér, *va.* 1. To disfavour, to discountenance. 2. To despise, to contemn. 3. To injure, to hurt.

Desfajár, *va.* To ungird, to loosen or take off the girdle.

Desflechár, *va.* (Ant.) To shoot with a bow.

Desfiérra, *sf.* (Ant.) Discord, contention.

Desferrár, *va.* To free from irons.

Desfiguración y Desfiguramiénto, *s.* Deformation, the act of disfiguring.

Desfigurár, *va.* 1. To disfigure, to deform. 2. To disguise, to conceal under false appearances. 3. (Met.) To cloud, to darken.—*vr.* To be disfigured by passion, or some accident.

Desfilachár, *va.* V. *Deshilachar.*

Desfiladéro, *sm.* Defile, a narrow passage.

Desfilár, *va.* To ravel, to unweave.—*vn.* (Mil.) To decrease the front, and change the order of formation for passing a defile; to march off by files.

Desfiuzár, *vn.* (Ant.) To despond, to doubt.

Desfixár, *va.* To unsettle, to remove any thing from the place in which it was fixed.

Desflaquecérse, *vr.* To be emaciated, to grow weak, to pine away.

Desflaquecimiénto, *sm.* Languor, dejection.

Desflecár, *va.* To remove the flakes of wool, or frettings of cloth at the borders.

Desflemación, *sf.* Dephlegmation.

Desflemár, *va.* To dephlegm or dephlegmate; to clear from phlegm or insipid aqueous matter.—*vn.* To brag; to boast of one's achievements, talents, or birth.

Desflocár, *va.* To ravel out the ends of a piece of stuff or ribbon. V. *Desflecar.*

Desfloración, *sf.* Defloration.

Desfloramiénto, *sm.* Violation, the act of deflouring, ravishment.

Desflorár, *va.* 1. To pull out or cut the flowers in a garden or flower-pot. 2. To deflower or take away a woman's virginity. 3. To tarnish; to impair the lustre or beauty of any thing.

Desflorecér, *vn.* To lose the flower.

Desflorecimiénto, *sm.* Falling of the flowers.

Desfogár, *va.* 1. To vent, to make an aperture or opening for the fire. 2. To vent the violence of a passion. 3. To temper or moderate passion or desire.

Desfogonár, *va.* To widen or burst the vent of a cannon.

Desfógue, *sm.* The act of venting or foaming out one's passion.

Desfollonár, *va.* To strip off the useless leaves.

Desfondár, *va.* 1. To break the bottom of any vessel. 2. (Naút.) To penetrate the bottom of a ship.

Desformár, *va.* To disfigure, to deform. V. *Deformar.*

Desfortalecér, *va.* (Fort.) To dismantle, to demolish the works of a fortress.

Desfrenár, *va.* To unbridle. V. *Desinfrenar.*

Desfrutár, *va.* 1. To gather or collect the crops. 2. To enjoy the produce of an estate. 3. To exhaust a soil. 4. To avail one's self of, to profit by. *Desfrutar á alguno*, To profit by or value one's self on another's friendship.

Desfrúte, *sm.* Use, enjoyment.

Desfundár, *va.* *Desenfundar.*

Desgajadúra, *sf.* Disruption, act of tearing off the branch of a tree.

Desgajár, *va.* 1. To lop off the branches of trees. 2. To break or tear in pieces.—*vr.* 1. To be separated or disjoined. 2. To be rent or torn in pieces; applied to clothes. 3. To break off a friendly intercourse and connexion. *Desgajarse el cielo ó las nubes*, (Met.) To rain excessively.

Desgalgadéro, *sm.* A rugged declivous place.

Desgalgádo, da, 1. Precipitated. 2. Light, thin, small-waisted, graceful.

Desgalgár, *va.* To precipitate; to throw headlong from an elevated place.

Desgána, *sf.* 1. Disgust, want of appetite. 2. Aversion, repugnance, reluctance. 3. V. *Congoja.*

Desganár, *va.* To deprive of the idea or desire of doing something.—*vr.* 1. To do with reluctance that which was before done with pleasure. 2. To lose the appetite or desire for food.

Desganchár, *va.* To lop off the branches of trees.

Desgañitárse, Desgañitárse y Desgañírse, *vr.* To shriek, to scream, to bawl.

Desgargamilládo, da, *a.* Cowardly, effeminate.

Desgargantárse, *vr.* To become hoarse by bawling or screaming.

Desgargolár, *va.* To shed the seed; applied to hemp which is ripe and dry.

Desgaritárse, *vr.* 1. (Naút.) To lose the course; applied to a ship. 2. (Met.) To give up a design or undertaking.

Desgarradaménte, *ad.* Impudently, barefacedly.

Desgarrádo, da, *a.* Licentious, dissolute.

Desgarradór, ra, *s.* Tearer, one who tears or rends.

Desgarrár, *va.* To rend, to tear.—*vr.* 1. To withdraw from one's company, to retire. 2. To give a loose to one's passions, to lead a licentious life.

Desgárro, *sm.* 1. Laceration, scissure, breach. 2. Impudence, effrontery. 3. Fanfaronade, idle boast.

Desgarrón, *sm.* 1. A large rent or hole. 2. Piece of cloth torn off.

Desgastadoraménte, *ad.* (Ant.) Injuriously, prejudicially.

Desgastamiénto, *sm.* (Ant.) Prodigality, profusion.

Desgastár, *va.* 1. To consume, to waste by degrees. 2. To corrode, to gnaw, to eat away. 3. (Met.) To pervert, to vitiate.—*vr.* To ruin one's self by extravagant expenses; to debilitate one's self.

Desgatár, *va.* 1. To hunt and destroy cats. 2. To root out the herb called cat-mint.

Desgáyre, *sm.* 1. A graceless mien or deportment; slovenliness, affected carelessness in dress. 2. Gesture, indicating scorn or contempt. *Al desgayre*, Affectedly, careless, without grace; disdainfully, with a gesture of contempt.

Desgaznatárse, *vr.* V. *Desgañitarse.*

Desglosár, *va.* To blot out the note or comment on a thing.

Desglóse, *sm.* Act of blotting or taking away a comment or gloss.

Desgobernádo, da, *a.* Ill governed or regulated, ungovernable; applied to persons.

Desgobernadúra, *sf.* (Albeyt.) Act of confining a vein in animals.

Desgobernár, *va.* 1. To disturb or overset the order of government. 2. To dislocate or disjoint. 3. To bar a vein on a horse's leg. 4. (Naút.) Not to steer steadily the right course.—*vr.* To affect ridiculous motions in dancing.

Desgobiérno, *sm.* 1. Mismanagement, misgovernment; want of conduct and economy. 2. Act of barring a vein on a horse's leg.

Desgolletár, *va.* 1. To break off the neck of a bottle or other vessel. 2. To cut off slopingly the fore part of a woman's gown.

Desgonzár, *va.* 1. V. *Desgoznar.* 2. To unease, to unhinge, to discompose.

Desgorrárse, *vr.* To pull off one's bonnet, hat, or hunting-cap.

Desgotár, *va.* To drain off water. V. *Agotar.*

Desgoznár, *va.* To unhinge, to throw from the hinges.—*vr.* 1. To be dislocated, or disjointed. 2. To be torn in pieces. 3. To distort the body with violent motions.

Desgrácia, *sf.* 1. Misfortune, disgrace, adversity. 2. Enmity, unfriendly disposition. 3. Unpleasantness, rudeness of language and address. *Correr con desgracia*, To be unfortunate in a design or undertaking.

Desgraciadaménte, *ad.* Unfortunately, unhappily.

Desgraciádo, da, *a.* 1. Unfortunate, unhappy. 2. Disagreeable, ungrateful.

Desgraciár, *va.* To displease, to disgust, to offend.—*vr.* 1. To disgrace, to fall out. 2. To be out of order; not to enjoy a good state of health. 3. To lose the perfection formerly possessed.

Desgradár, *va.* (Ant.) To degrade.

Desgrádo, da, *a.* Degraded. *A' desgrado*, Grievously, degradingly, disagreeably.

Desgramár, *va.* To pull up the grass by the root.

Desgranár, *va.* 1. To take out the grain from the ears of corn, or other fruits which contain any. *Desgranar la uva*, To pick a grape. 2. (Met.) To kill, to deprive of life. 3. (Met.) To scatter about.

Desgranzár, *va.* 1. To separate the husks or chaff from the grain. 2. (Pint.) To give colours the first grinding.

Desgreñár, *va.* 1. To dishevel the hair, to pull it out by the root. 2. To discompose, to disturb.

Desguarnecér, *va.* 1. To strip clothes of trimmings and other ornaments. 2. To deprive any thing of its strength, to strip it of all accessaries. 3. To deprive of ornament or lustre. 4. To unharness mules or horses. 5. To disarm. 6. To draw the garrison out of a strong place.

Desguarnír, *va.* 1. (Naút.) To unrig the capstern. 2. To despoil of ornaments.

Desguazár, *va.* (Carp.) To cut asunder any timber or wood.

Desguínce, *sm.* The knife which cuts rags in paper-mills.

Desguindárse, *vr.* To slide down by a rope.

Desguinzár, *va.* To cut cloth or rags in paper-mills.

Desguisádo, da, *a.* 1. Excessive, disproportionate. 2. V. *Desaguisado.*

Desgústo, *sm.* V. *Disgusto.*

Deshabído, da, *a.* Unfortunate, unhappy.

Deshabitádo, da, *a.* Deserted, uninhabited.

Deshabitár, *va.* 1. To quit one's house or habitation. 2. To unpeople, to depopulate, to dispeople.

Deshabituár, *va.* To disaccustom, to disuse.

Deshabituación, *sf.* Disuse.

Deshacedór, *sm.* *Deshacedor de agravios*, Repairer, restorer.

Deshacér, *va.* 1. To undo or destroy the form or figure of a thing. 2. To undo what has been done by another. 3. To consume, to digest. 4. To cancel, to blot or scratch out; to efface. 5. To rout an army. 6. To run through one's fortune, to spend profusely. 7. To melt, to liquefy. 8. To cut up, to divide. 9. To dissolve in a liquid. 10. To violate a treaty or agreement. 11. To lessen, to diminish. 12. To discharge from service.—*vr.* 1. To grieve, to mourn. 2. To excuse or exculpate one's self. 3. To disappear, to get out of one's sight. 4. To do any thing with vehemence. 5. To mollify, to lose the proper consistency; to grow feeble or meagre. *Deshacerse como el humo*, To vanish like smoke. *Deshacerse en lágrimas*, To burst out into a flood of tears.

Deshacer agravios á tuertos, To revenge injuries or wrongs.

DESHACIMIÉNTO, *sm.* 1. Destruction. 2. V. *Desasosiego.*

DESHÁLDO, *sm.* V. *Marzeo.*

DESHARRAPÁDO, DA, *a.* Shabby, ragged, in tatters.

DESHARRAPAMIÉNTO, *sm.* Misery, meanness.

DESHEBILLÁR, *va.* To unbuckle, to loosen or break the buckles.

DESHEBRÁR, *va.* 1. To unthread, to ravel or divide into threads. 2. (Met.) To divide or separate into filaments. 3. (Met.) To shed a flood of tears.

DESHÉCHA, *sf.* 1. Simulation, fiction, evasion. 2. Issue of a road or path. 3. A genteel departure, a polite farewell. 4. Burthen of a song. 5. Step in a Spanish dance.

DESHECHIZÁR, *va.* To disenchant, to defeat the force of an enchantment.

DESHÉCHO, CHA, *a.* 1. Undone. 2. Perfectly mixed; applied to colours. *Borrasca deshecha*, A violent tempest. *Fuga deshecha*, A precipitate flight.

DESHECHÚRA, *sf.* Destruction, destroying.

DESHELÁR, *va.* 1. To thaw. 2 To overcome one's obstinacy. 3. (Met.) To invite, to inspirit.

DESHERBÁR, *va.* To pluck up or extirpate herbs.

DESHEREDACIÓN, *sf.* Disinherison, the act of cutting off from an hereditary succession.

DESHEREDAMIÉNTO, *sm.* Disinheriting.

DESHEREDÁR, *va.* 1. To disinherit, to cut off from an hereditary right. 2. (Met.) To deprive of influence or favour.—*vr.* To degenerate; to fall from the dignity and virtue of one's ancestors.

DESHERMANÁR, *va.* (Met.) To take away the equality and similarity of things which were similar or equal.—*vr.* To violate the love due to a brother.

DESHERRADÚRA, *sf.* (Albeyt.) Surbating, injury done to a horse's foot by being unshod.

DESHERRÁR, *va.* 1. To unchain, to take off chains or fetters. 2. To rip off the shoes of horses.

DESHERRUMBRÁR, *va.* To clear any thing of rust.

DESHILACHÁR, *va.* To ravel, to unweave.

DESHILADÍZ, *sm.* Refuse of silk, cone-silk or pods.

DESHILÁDO, *sm.* Open-work, a kind of embroidery.

DESHILÁDO, DA, *a.* Marching in a file. *A' la deshilada*, In file, one after another; deceitfully, dissemblingly.

DESHILADÚRA, *sf.* Ripping, ravelling out.

DESHILÁR, *va.* 1. To draw out threads from any stuff or cloth, to unweave, to ravel. 2. To reduce, to convert into filaments or lint. 3. To distract bees in order to lead them from one hive to another.

DESHÍLO, *sm.* Act of obstructing the communication of bees, in order to get them into a new hive.

DESHINCADÚRA, *sf.* Act of drawing any thing nailed or fixed.

DESHINCÁR, *va.* To draw a nail, to remove what is fixed.

DESHINCHADÚRA, *sf.* Act of abating a swelling.

DESHINCHÁR, *va.* 1. To reduce a swelling. 2. (Met.) To explain the cause of one's displeasure.—*vr.* 1. To be removed; applied to a swelling. 2. (Met.) To abate presumption.

DESHOJADÓR, *sm.* A stripper of leaves.

DESHOJADÚRA, *sf.* Act of stripping a tree of its leaves.

DESHOJÁR, *va.* 1. To strip off the leaves. 2. (Met.) To display rhetorical elegance in discussing a subject. 3. (Met.) To deprive of all hopes.

DESHOLLEJÁR, *va.* To rip off the bark, to decorticate.

DESHOLLINADÓR, *sm.* 1. Chimney-sweeper. 2. Instrument for sweeping chimneys. 3. (Met.) He who examines and inspects carefully.

DESHOLLINÁR, *va.* 1. To sweep or clean chimneys. 2. To clean what is dirty. 3. (Met.) To shift, to change clothes. 4. (Met.) To view and examine with careful attention.

DESHOMBRECÉRSE, *vr.* To shrug up the shoulders.

DESHONESTAMÉNTE, *ad.* Dishonourably, disgracefully.

DESHONESTÁR, *va.* 1. To dishonour, to disgrace. 2. To disfigure, to deform.

DESHONESTIDÁD, *sf.* 1. Immodest, an affected and lascivious movement of the body. 2. Dishonesty, want of modesty and candour.

DESHONÉSTO, TA, *a.* 1. Immodest, lewd, unchaste. 2. Unreasonable, not conformable to reason; rude, rustic.

DESHONÓR, *sm.* 1. Dishonour, disgrace. 2. Injury, insult.

DESHONORÁR, *va.* 1. To dishonour, to disgrace, to deprive of honour or reputation. 2. To deprive of an office or employ.

DESHÓNRA, *sf.* 1. Dishonour, discredit. 2. Disgrace or infamy arising from some dishonest action. 3. Seduction or defloration of a woman. *Tener á deshonra alguna cosa*, To consider a thing unworthy and beneath the rank of a person.

DESHONRABUÉNOS, *sm.* 1. Calumniator, libeller. 2. He who degenerates from his ancestors.

DESHONRADAMÉNTE, *ad.* Dishonourably, shamefully.

DESHONRADÓR, *sm.* Dishonourer; violator of chastity.

DESHONRÁR, *va.* 1. To affront, to insult, to defame; to dishonour, to disgrace. 2. To scorn, to despise. 3. To seduce, to deflour or violate an honest woman.

DESHONRÓSO, SA, *a.* Dishonourable, indecent.

DESHÓRA, *sf.* An unseasonable or inconvenient time. *A' deshóra*, Untimely, unseasonably; extemporary.

DESHORÁDO, DA, *a.* Untimely, unseasonable.

DESHORNÁR, *va.* To take out of the oven.

DESHOSPEDÁDO, DA, *a.* Destitute of lodging.

DESHOSPEDAMIÉNTO, *sm.* Inhospitality; the act of refusing strangers a lodging.

DESHUESÁR, *va.* To rid of bones.

DESHUMÁNO, NA, *a.* Inhuman.

DESHUMEDECÉR, *va.* To exsiccate, to deprive of humidity.

DESÍ, *ad.* (Ant.) V. *Despues y luego.*

DÉSIDE, *a.* V. *Desidioso.*

DESIRÁBLE, *a.* Desirable.

DESÍDIA, *sf.* Idleness, laziness, indolence.

DESIDIOSAMÉNTE, *ad.* Indolently, idly.

DESIDIÓSO, SA, *a.* Lazy, idle, indolent.

DESIÉRTO, TA, *a.* Deserted, uninhabited.

DESIÉRTO, *sm.* Desert, wilderness.

DESIGNACIÓN, *sf.* Designation.

DESIGNÁR, *va.* 1. To design, to purpose, to intend any thing. 2. To appoint a person for some determined purpose.

Desígnio, *sm.* 1. Design, purpose, intention. 2. Road, course.

Desiguál, *a.* 1. Unequal, dissimilar, unlike. 2. Uneven, unlevelled, broken; applied to the ground. 3. Arduous, difficult. 4. Variable. 5. Excessive, extreme.

Desigualár, *va.* To make unequal or dissimilar.—*vr.* To excel, to surpass.

Desigualdád y Desigualéza, *sf.* 1. Inequality, dissimilitude. 2. Variableness, levity, inconstancy. 3. Wrong, injury, injustice. 4. Unevenness of the ground.

Desigualménte, *ad.* Unequally.

Desimaginár, *va.* To blot out or obliterate in the mind.—*vn.* To be thoughtless or unconcerned about what may happen.

Desimpresionár, *va.* To undeceive.

Desinclinár, *va.* To disincline, to produce a dislike to.

Desincorporárse, *vr.* To separate one's self from a corps or society.

Desindiciár, *va.* To blot out or efface marks.

Desinéncia, *sf.* (Ret.) Termination, end.

Desinficionár, *va.* To free from infection.

Desinflamár, *va.* To cure or remove an inflammation.

Desinsaculación, *sf.* Act of drawing lots.

Desinsaculár y Desinseculár, *va.* To draw lots for some office or place; to draw names from an urn or balloting-box.

Desinterés y Desinteresamiénto, *sm.* Disinterestedness.

Desinteresadaménte, *ad.* Disinterestedly, gratuitously.

Desinteresádo, da, *a.* Disinterested.

Desintestinár, *va.* To eviscerate, to extract the intestines.

Desiñár, *va.* (Ant.) To design, to intend.

Desíño, *sm.* V. *Desígnio.*

Desistimiénto y Desisténcia, *s.* Desistance, the act of desisting.

Desistír, *vn.* To desist, to cease; to abandon.

Desjarretadéra, *sf.* Instrument for houghing cattle, a hooked knife.

Desjarretár, *va.* 1. To hough, to cut the hamstrings of a beast. 2. (Met.) To deprive one of the means of making a fortune. 3. (Met.) To weaken, to debilitate.

Desjarréte, *sm.* Act of houghing.

Desjuntamiénto, *sm.* Separation, disjunction.

Desjuntár, *va.* To divide, to separate, to part.

Desjurár, *va.* To retract an oath.

Deslabonár, *va.* 1. To unlink, to separate one link from another. 2. (Met.) To disjoin, to destroy.—*vr.* To withdraw from a company, to retire.

Desladrillár, *va.* V. *Desenladrillar.*

Deslamár, *va.* To clear of mud.

Deslanguído, da, *a.* Languid, faint, extenuated.

Deslastrár, *va.* To unballast, to take the ballast out of a ship.

Deslatár, *va.* To take the laths or small joists out of a house or other building.

Deslavádo, da, *a.* Impudent, barefaced.

Deslavadúra, *sf.* Washing.

Deslavár y Deslavazár, *va.* 1. To wash or clean any thing. 2. To take away the colour, force, or vigour of a thing. *Cara deslavada,* A pale, puny face.

Desláyo (En), *ad.* V. *A' la deshilada.*

Deslazamiénto, *sm.* Disjunction, dissolution.

Deslazár, *va.* To unlace, to untie a knot.

Desleál, *a.* Disloyal; perfidious.

Deslealménte, *ad.* Perfidiously, disloyally.

Deslealtád, *sf.* Disloyalty, want of fidelity.

Deslechár, *va.* (Mur.) To remove the leaves and dirt from silk-worms.

Desléche, *sm.* (Mur.) Act of cleansing silk-worms.

Deslechugadór, *sm.* Vine-dresser, pruner.

Deslechugár y Deslechuguillár, *va.* (Agr.) To cut and prune the branches of vines.

Desleidúra, *sf.* Dilution, the act of making any thing thin or weak.

Desleír, *va.* To dilute, to make thin or weak.

Deslendrár, *va.* To clear the hair of nits.

Deslenguádo, da, *a.* Loquacious, impudent.

Deslenguamiénto, *sm.* Loquacity, impudence.

Deslenguár, *va.* To cut out the tongue.—*vr.* To talk ill of, to slander.

Desliár, *va.* To untie or loosen a bundle.

Desligadúra, *sf.* Disjunction, untying.

Desligár, *va.* 1. To loosen, to untie. 2. (Met.) To disentangle, to extricate, to unravel. 3. (Met.) To absolve from ecclesiastical censure. *Desligar el maleficio,* To dissolve a spell which prevented a husband from enjoying the marriage rights.

Deslindadór, *sm.* He who marks limits or boundaries.

Deslindár, *va.* 1. To mark the limits and bounds of a place or district. 2. (Met.) To clear up a thing.

Deslínde, Deslindamiénto y Deslindadúra, *s.* Demarcation, act of marking boundaries.

Desliñár, *va.* To clean cloth before it goes to the press.

Deslíz, *sm.* 1. Slip, the act of slipping or sliding. 2. (Met.) Slip, a false step, frailty, weakness. 3. Mercury, which escapes in smelting silver ore.

Deslizáble, *a.* That which can slip or slide.

Deslizadéro, *sm.* A slippery place.

Deslizadízo ó Deslizadéro, ra, *a.* Slippery, lubricous.

Deslizamiénto, *sm.* Act of making slippery.

Deslizár, *vn.* 1. To slip, to slide. 2. (Met.) To do or speak of any thing in a careless manner.

Desloár, *va.* To blame, to censure.

Deslomadúra, *sf.* Act of breaking the back.

Deslomár, *va.* To break the back, to distort or strain the loins. *No se deslomará,* He is sure not to overwork himself.

Deslucidaménte, *ad.* Inelegantly.

Deslucído, da, *a.* 1. Unadorned; applied to persons who speak, preach, or do any thing public without grace, perspicuity, or elegance. 2. Useless, fruitless.

Deslucimiénto, *sm.* Disgrace, dishonour, want of splendour.

Deslucír, *va.* 1. To tarnish or impair the lustre and splendour of any thing. 2. (Met.) To obscure one's merit.

Deslumbramiénto y Deslúmbre, *sm.* Confusion either of the sight or mind; hallucination.

Deslumbrár, *va.* 1. To dazzle or dim the sight. 2. (Met.) To puzzle, to leave in doubt and uncertainty.

Deslustradór, *sm.* Tarnisher

Deslustrár, *va.* 1. To tarnish or sully the brilliancy of a thing. 2. (Met.) To impeach one's character, to obscure his merit.

Deslústre, *sm.* 1. Spot or stain which obscures the lustre or splendor of a thing. 2. Disgrace, ignominy.

Deslustróso, sa, *a.* Unbecoming, ugly.

Desmadejamiénto, *sm.* Languishment, languidness, without spirit or gracefulness.

Desmadejárse, *vr.* To languish, to be enervated and weak.

Desmajolár, *va.* 1. To pull out vines by the roots. 2. To loosen or untie the shoe-strings.

Desmalladór, *sm.* He who breaks a coat of mail.

Desmalladúra, *sf.* Act of ripping up or breaking a coat of mail.

Desmallár, *va.* To cut and destroy a coat of mail.

Desmamár, *va.* V. *Destetar.*

Desmamonár, *va.* To cut off the young shoots of vines or trees.

Desmamperár, *va.* (Ant.) V. *Desamperar.*

Desmán, *sm.* 1. Misbehaviour, misconduct. 2. Misfortune, disaster.

Desmanárse, *vr.* To stray from a flock or herd.

Desmancebár, *va.* (In a jocular style) To part persons who live in a state of fornication.

Desmáncho, *sm.* Dishonour, infamy.

Desmandádo, da, *a.* V. *Desobediente.*

Desmandamiénto, *sm.* Act of countermanding or disbanding.

Desmandár, *va.* To repeal an order, to countermand, to revoke an offer.—*vr.* 1. To transgress the bounds of justice and reason. 2. To disband; applied to a body of troops. 3. To stray from the flock.

Desmaneár, *va.* To unfetter, to take off the fetters or shackles.

Desmangorreár, *va.* To take the handle off any thing.

Desmanotádo, da, *a.* Contracted, cramped.

Desmantecár, *va.* To take off the butter.

Desmanteládo, da, *a.* Dismantled.

Desmantelár, *va.* 1. To dismantle, to destroy the works of a fortress. 2. To abandon, to desert, to forsake. 3. (Naút.) To unmast.

Desmáña, *sf.* 1. Awkwardness, clumsiness, want of handiness or dexterity. 2. Idleness, laziness.

Desmañádo, da, *a.* 1. Unhandy, clumsy. 2. Lazy, idle, indolent.

Desmarañár, *va.* To disentangle. V. *Desenmarañar.*

Desmaridár, *va.* (Ant.) To separate husband and wife.

Desmarojadór, *sm.* He who takes the rind off olives.

Desmarojár, *va.* To take the glutinous rind from olives.

Desmarrído, da, *a.* Sad, languid, exhausted.

Desmatár, *va.* V. *Descuajar.*

Desmayadaménte, *ad.* Weakly, dejectedly.

Desmayádo, da, *a.* Dismayed, appalled.

Desmayár, *vn.* To be dispirited or faint-hearted.—*va.* To dispirit, to frighten.—*vr.* To faint, to sink motionless, to lose the animal functions.

Desmáyo, *sm.* Swoon, a fainting fit; decay of strength and vigour.

Desmazaládo, da, *a.* Weak, dejected, faint hearted, spiritless.

Desmedidaménte, *ad.* Disproportionably.

Desmedído, da, *a.* Unproportionable, out of proportion or measure.

Desmedírse, *vr.* V. *Desmandarse.*

Desmedrár, *vn.* To decrease, to decay.

Desmédro, *sm.* Diminution, decay, detriment.

Desmejorár, *va.* To debase, to make worse.

Desmelancolizár, *va.* To remove melancholy, to cheer.

Desmelár, *va.* To take the honey from a hive.

Desmelenár, *va.* To dishevel, to disorder or discompose the hair.

Desmembración y Desmembradúra, *sf.* Division, the act of dismembering.

Desmembradór, ra, *s.* Divider, one who dismembers or divides.

Desmembramiénto, *sm.* Act of dismembering.

Desmembrár, *va.* To dismember, to divide member from member; to separate.

Desmemoriárse, *vr.* To be forgetful, to forget, to lose memory of.

Desmenguár, *va.* To lessen; to defalcate. V. *Menguar.*

Desmentída, *sf.* The act of giving the lie.

Desmentidór, *sm.* He who convicts or convinces one of a falsehood.

Desmentír, *va.* 1. To give the lie, to convince of a falsehood. 2. To counterfeit, to change with a view to deceive. 3. To lose the right line, to deviate from the right path. 4. To excel, to surpass.

Desmenuzáble, *a.* Friable, easily crumbled, easily reduced to powder.

Desmenuzadór, ra, *s.* A scrutator, investigator, purifier.

Desmenuzár, *va.* 1. To crumble, to comminute, to reduce to powder. 2. (Met.) To sift, to examine minutely.

Desmeollamiénto, *sm.* Act of taking out the marrow.

Desmeollár, *va.* To take out the marrow.

Desmerecedór, *sm.* One who is unworthy or undeserving of a thing.

Desmerecér, *vn.* To be unworthy, or undeserving of a thing.

Desmerecimiénto, *sm.* V. *Demérito.*

Desmesúra, *sf.* 1. Excess, want of moderation and order. 2. Impudence, insolence; rudeness of conduct.

Desmesuradaménte, *ad.* Immensely, uncivilly, too freely.

Desmesurádo, da, *a.* Huge, of a gigantic stature or size.

Desmesurárse, *vr.* To be forward, to act or talk with impudence, to behave with insolence; to disorder, to perturbate.

Desmigajár, *va.* To crumble, to comminute, to break into small bits.

Desmigár, *va.* To crumble bread into small pieces to fry in a pan.

Desminuír, *va.* To diminish. V. *Disminuir.*

Desmirriádo, da, *a.* 1. Lean, extenuated, exhausted. 2. Melancholy.

Desmocár, *vn.* To wipe the nose. V. *Sonarse.*

Desmócha, *sf.* 1. The act of lopping or cutting off. 2. Diminution or destruction of a great part of a thing.

Desmochadúra, *sf.* V. *Desmoche.*

Desmochár, *va.* 1. To lop or cut off, to mutilate. 2. To unhorn; applied to a stag.

Desmóche, *sm.* Truncation, mutilation. V. *Desmocha.* [off.

Desmócho, *sm.* Heap of things lopped or cut

Desmogár, *vn.* To musen, to shake or cast the horns, as deer.

Desmógue, *sm.* Act of casting the head, in deer. [ders.

Desmoládo, da, *a.* Toothless, having no grin-

Desmolér, *va.* To digest. V. *Digerir.*

Desmontár, *va.* 1. To fell or cut down wood. 2. To remove a heap of dirt or rubbish. 3. To uncock fire-arms; to take an instrument to pieces. 4. To dismount a troop of horse, to dismount cannon. 5. *Desmontar el timon,* (Naút.) To unhang the rudder.—*vn.* To dismount, to alight from a horse.

Desmónte, *sm.* That which has been cut down, or taken down; act of dismounting.

Desmoñár, *va.* (Joc.) To undo the toupee of the hair, to loosen the hair.

Desmoronadízo, za, *a.* Easily mouldered.

Desmoronár, *va.* 1. To destroy by little and little, to ruin by insensible degrees. 2. (Met.) To cause to dwindle or moulder off.

Desmostár, *va.* To separate the must from the grapes.

Desmostolár, *va.* To diminish.

Desmotadéra, *sf.* Woman employed to take off knots and coarse naps from cloth.

Desmotadór, ra, *s.* Person employed in taking off knots or naps from cloth or wool.

Desmotár, *va.* To clear cloth of knots and coarse naps.

Desmuélo, *sm.* Want or loss of grinders.

Desmugerár, *va.* To separate from a wife.

Desmugradór, *sm.* Instrument which serves to clean the wool or cloth of grease. [grease.

Desmugrár, *va.* To clean wool or cloth of

Desmullír, *va.* To discompose any thing soft or bland. [mice.

Desmuradór, *sm.* Mouser, a cat that catches

Desmurár, *va.* 1. (Ant.) To exterminate the rats from any place. 2. (Ant.) To ruin walls.

Desmuír, *va.* To pick olives.

Desnarigár, *va.* To cut off the nose.

Desnatár, *va.* 1. To skim milk, to take off the cream. 2. To take the flower or choicest part of a thing. *Desnatar la hacienda,* To live upon the fat of the land.

Desnaturál, *a.* (Ant.) Unnatural, foreign, repugnant.

Desnaturalizár, *va.* To divest of the rights of naturalization, to deprive of the privileges of a citizen. [ous.

Desnecesário, ria, *a.* Unnecessary, superflu-

Desnegár, *va.* To contradict, to retract.

Desnervár, *va.* To enervate.

Desneváde, da, *a.* Without snow; thawed.

Desnevár, *va.* To thaw, to dissolve.

Desnivél, *sm.* Unevenness, inequality of the ground.

Desnivelár, *va.* To make uneven or unequal.

Desnoviár, *va.* (In the Jocular Style) To divorce a new married couple.

Desnucár, *va.* To break the neck, to disjoint the nape.

Desnudadór, *sm.* One that denudes.

Desnudaménte, *ad.* Nakedly; manifestly, with clearness.

Desnudár, *va.* 1. To denudate, to strip off the clothes or coverings. 2. (Met.) To discover, to reveal. 3. (Naút.) To unrig.—*vr.* 1. To undress, to take off one's clothes. 2. (Met.) To deprive one's self of a thing.

Desnudéz, *sf.* Nudity, nakedness.

Desnúdo, da, *a.* 1. Naked, bare, uncovered; ill clothed. 2. (Met.) Plain, evident, apparent. 3. Empty-handed, destitute of merit, interest, &c.

Desnúdo, *sm.* (Met.) A picture or statue without drapery.

Desobedecér, *va.* To disobey, to break commands, to transgress prohibitions. *Desobedecer el timon,* (Naút.) To fall off. *Navio que desobedece la virada,* (Naút.) A ship which misses stays.

Desobediéncia, *sf.* Disobedience.

Desobediénte, *pa.* Disobedient.

Desobedienteménte, *ad.* Disobediently.

Desobligár, *va.* 1. To release from an obligation. 2. To disoblige, to offend; to alienate the affections.

Desocasionádo, da, *a.* Unseasonable, untimely.

Desocupación, *sf.* Leisure, want of business or occupation.

Desocupadaménte, *ad.* Freely, leisurely.

Desocupár, *va.* To evacuate, to quit, to empty.—*vr.* To disengage one's self from a business or occupation.

Desoír, *va.* To pretend not to hear.

Desojárse, *vr.* 1. To strain the sight by looking steadfastly at a thing; to look intently. 2. To break or burst; applied to the eye of a needle, or other instrument with an eye.

Desolación, *sf.* 1. Desolation, destruction. 2. Want of consolation or comfort, affliction.

Desoládo, da, *a.* Desolate, disconsolate.

Desoladór, ra, *s.* V. *Asolador.*

Desolár, *va.* To desolate, to lay waste

Desolladaménte, *ad* Impudently, petulantly.

Desolládo, da, *a.* Forward, impudent, insolent.

Desolladór, *sm.* 1. One who flays or strips off the skin. 2. (Arag.) Slaughter-house, a place where beasts are flayed or skinned. 3. (Met.) Extortioner, one who gains by violence or rapacity.

Desolladúra, *sf.* Excoriation, the act of separating the skin from the flesh.

Desollár, *va.* 1. To flay, to skin, to strip or take off the skin. 2. (Met.) To extort an immoderate price.

Desolución, *sf.* V. *Disolucion.*

Desónce, *sm.* The discount of an ounce or ounces in each pound.

Desoncár, *va.* To discount or deduct an ounce or ounces in the pound.

Desopilár, *va.* To deoppilate, to clear away obstructions.

Desopilatívo, va, *a.* Deoppilative, deobstruent.

Desopinár, *va.* To impeach one's character, to defame.

Desoprimír, *va.* To free from oppression.

Desórden ó Desordenación, *s.* 1. Disorder, confusion. 2 Excess, abuse. [edly.

Desordenadaménte, *ad.* Irregularly, confus-

Desordenádo, da, *a.* Disorderly, irregular.

Desordenamiénto y Desordenánza. V. *Desórden*

Desordenár, *va.* To disturb, to disorder, to confound. V. *Degradar.*—*vr.* To be out of order, to be irregular.

Desorejadór, ra, *s.* One who crops or cuts off the ears.

Desorejamiénto, *sm.* Act of cutting off the ears.

Desorejár, *va.* To crop or cut off the ears.

Desorganización, *sf.* Disorganisation.

Desorganizadór, *sm.* Disorganiser.

Desorganizár, *va.* To disorganise, to destroy the organisation of the body politic.

Desorientár, *va.* To deprive of youth; to cut off a source.

Desorillár, *va.* To cut off the selvage of cloth, or other things.

Desortijádo, da, *a.* Sprained; applied to the muscles or ligaments of mules or horses.

Desortijár, *va.* (Agric.) To hoe or weed plants the first time.

Desosádo, da, *a.* (Ant.) Timorous, not bold.

Desosár, *va.* To deprive of the bones, to take out the bones.

Desoterrár, *va.* V. *Desenterrar.*

Desovár, *va.* To spawn, to produce as fishes do eggs.

Desóve, *sm.* Act of spawning.

Desovillár, *va.* 1. To unclew, to unwind a clew. 2. (Met.) To unravel, to disentangle, to clear up. 3. (Met.) To encourage, to animate.

Despabiladéras, *sf. pl.* Snuffers.

Despabiládo, da, *a.* 1. Snuffed; applied to candles. 2. (Met.) Watchful, vigilant in the time for sleeping. 3. Lively, active, prompt.

Despabiladór, *sm.* He who snuffs; candle-snuffer.

Despabiladúra, *sf.* Snuff of the candle.

Despabilár, *va.* 1. To snuff or crop a candle. 2. (Met.) To cut off any superfluous thing. 3. (Met.) To despatch briefly or expeditiously. 4. (Met.) To rouse, to enliven. 5. (Joc.) To kill. *Despabilar los ojos,* (Met.) To keep a sharp look out.

Despabílo, *sm.* V. *Despabiladura.*

Despachadaménte, *ad.* Swiftly.

Despachadéras, *sf. pl.* Surly words with which some persons answer.

Despachadór, *sm.* Expediter, one who despatches.

Despachár, *va.* 1. To despatch, to transact expeditiously. 2. To decide and expedite suits and causes. 3. To dispose of goods and merchandise, to sell. 4. (Met.) To murder. 5. To expedite, to abridge, to facilitate.

Despácho, *sm.* 1. Expedient, determination. 2. Despatch, the act of despatching. 3. Cabinet, closet, office. 4. Commission, warrant, patent. 5. A smart answer or repartee.

Despachurrádo, da, *a.* Pressed together. *Es un despachurrado,* He is a ridiculous insipid fellow.

Despachurrár, *va.* 1. To press or cake together. 2. (Met.) To mangle a speech, to obscure a subject by a bad explanation. 3. (Met.) To confound one by a smart repartee.

Despácio, *ad.* 1. Insensibly, by little and little. 2. Continually, without interruption.

Despácio, *interj.* Softly, gently.

Despacíto, *ad.* 1. Very gently. 2. Very slowly.

Despacíto, *interj.* Gently, stop a little.

Despagádo, da, *a.* Inimical, adverse, contrary.

Despagamiénto, *sm.* Disgust.

Despagár, *va.* To displease, to disgust.

Despajadúra, *sf.* Winnowing, the act of separating the chaff from the corn.

Despajár, *va.* To winnow, to separate the chaff from the grain.

Despájo, *sm.* Act of winnowing or cleaning grain.

Despaldárse, *vr.* To disjoint or dislocate the shoulder blade.

Despaldillár, *va.* To dislocate or break the shoulder or back of any animal.

Despalmadór, *sm.* Careening-place, where the bottoms of ships are cleaned and payed.

Despalmár, *va.* 1. To clean and pay the bottoms of ships. 2. To pare off a horse's hoof.

Despampanadór, *sm.* Pruner of vines.

Despampanadúra, *sf.* Act of pruning vines.

Despampanár, *va.* 1. To prune or cut off the shoots of vines. 2. (Met.) To unbosom, to give vent to one's feelings.

Despanádo, da, *a.* Breadless, being in want of bread.

Despanár, *va.* To remove the corn from the field after it has been reaped.

Despancijár y Despanzurrár, *va.* To burst the belly.

Despapár, *vn.* To carry the head too high; applied to a horse.

Desparár, *va.* V. *Descomponer y disparar.*

Desparcír, *va.* To scatter, to disseminate.

Desparejár, *va.* (Ant.) To separate.

Desparecér, *vn.* To disappear. V. *Desaparecer.*—*vr.* To be unlike or dissimilar.

Desparejár, *va.* To make unequal or uneven.

Desparpajár, *va.* 1. To undo in a disorderly or irregular manner. 2. To rant, to prattle at random.

Desparpájo, *sm.* Pertness of speech or action.

Desparramádo, da, *a.* Wide, open.

Desparramadór, ra, *s.* Disperser, dilapidator.

Desparramár, *va.* 1. To scatter, to disseminate. 2. To squander, to dissipate.—*vr.* To give one's self up to pleasures with extravagance and excess, to be dissipated.

Despartidór, *sm.* Pacificator.

Despartír, *va.* 1. To part, to divide. 2. To conciliate, to make peace between others.

Desparvár, *va.* To take the sheaves of corn out of the stack or rick to be threshed.

Despasár, *va.* *Despasar un cabo,* (Naút.) To unreeve a cable; to take it out of the block or pulley. *Despasar el virador de combés,* (Naút.) To shift the voyal.

Despasionárse, *vr.* To allay one's passion.

Despasmárse, *vr.* To recover one's self from a stupor or spasm.

Despatarráda, *sf.* Variety in the Spanish dance. *Hacer la despatarrada,* To affect disease or pain.

Despatarrádo, da, *a.* *Quedar uno ó dexarle despatarrado,* To leave one astonished, abashed, or stupified.

Despatarrár, *va.* To silence, to oblige one to be silent.—*vr.* 1. To slip and fall on the ground. 2. To be stupified, to remain motionless.

Despatillár, *va.* To cut grooves or mortices in the wood.

Despavesadúra, *sf.* The act of snuffing the candle.

Despavesár, *va.* To snuff the candle.

DESPAVORIDAMÉNTE, *ad.* Terrifiedly.

DESPAVORÍR Y ÍRSE, *vn. y r.* To be terrified, to be frightened. It has only the infinitive termination and past participle.

DESPEADÚRA, *sf.* The state of one's feet being battered and bruised with travel.

DESPEAMIÉNTO, *sm.* Act of surbating.

DESPEÁRSE, *vr.* To be surbated; to have one's feet bruised or battered with travel.

DESPECHADAMÉNTE, *ad.* Angrily, spitefully.

DESPECHADÓR, *sm.* Extortioner, tormentor, oppressor.

DESPECHAMIÉNTO, *sm.* Act of enraging or overburdening.

DESPECHÁR, *va.* 1. To enrage, to excite indignation. 2. To overwhelm with taxes.—*vr.* 1. To fret, to be peevish. 2. To lose all hopes, to despair.

DESPÉCHO, *sm.* 1. Indignation, displeasure, wrath. 2. Asperity, harshness of temper. 3. Dejection, dismay, despair. 4. Disrespect, insolence. 5. Deceit, infidelity. 6. Derision, scorn. *Á' despecho*, In spite of, contrary to or against one's will.

DESPECHUGADÚRA, *sf.* Act of cutting off or uncovering the breast.

DESPECHUGÁR, *va.* To cut off the breast of a fowl.—*vr.* To uncover the breast, to walk with the breast open.

DESPEDAZADÓR, RA, *s.* Dissector, lacerator, one who cuts to pieces.

DESPEDAZAMIÉNTO Y DESPEDAZADÚRA, *s.* Laceration, dissection, cutting to pieces.

DESPEDAZÁR, *va.* 1. To cut into bits, to tear into pieces. 2. (Met.) To lacerate, to destroy. *Despedazarse de risa*, To burst out into a fit of laughter.

DESPEDÍDA Y DESPEDIMIÉNTO, *s.* 1. The act of taking leave. 2. The act of turning a lodger out of his lodgings.

DESPEDÍR, *va.* 1. To emit, to discharge, to dart. 2. To dismiss from office, to discard. 3. To remove. 4. To deny, to refuse. 5. (Naút.) To pay off a ship's crew. *Despedir la vida*, To die.—*vr.* To take leave.

DESPEDRÁR Y DESPEDREGÁR, *va.* To clear a field or other place of stones.

DESPEGÁBLE, *a.* Dissoluble, dissolvible, capable of dissolution.

DESPEGADAMÉNTE, *ad.* Disgustingly, harshly.

DESPEGÁDO, DA, *a.* Disgusting, unpleasant, harsh; separated.

DESPEGADÚRA, *sf.* Dissolving, separating.

DESPEGAMIÉNTO, *sm.* V. *Desapego.*

DESPEGÁR, *va.* To unglue, to separate, to disjoin. *Despegar los labios ó la boca*, (Met.) To speak.—*vr.* To grow displeased, to withdraw one's affection, to treat with asperity.

DESPÉGO, *sm.* 1. Asperity, moroseness. 2. Displeasure, aversion; want of love or affection.

DESPEJADAMÉNTE, *ad.* Expeditiously, readily, freely.

DESPEJÁDO, DA, *a.* Clear, disengaged; free from imperfection.

DESPEJÁR, *va.* To remove impediments, to surmount obstacles, to clear away obstructions. —*vr.* To cheer up, to amuse one's self. *Despejarse el cielo, el dia, el tiempo,* To become clear, serene weather.

DESPÉJO, *sm.* 1. The act of removing obstacles or clearing away impediments. 2. Sprightliness, liveliness. 3. Forwardness, temerity, audaciousness.

DESPELLEJADÚRA, *sf.* Scratch, a slight wound.

DESPELLEJÁR, *va.* To skin, to strip off the skin. *Despellejar un conejo*, To uncase a rabbit.

DESPELOTÁR, *va.* (Bax.) To dishevel the hair.

DESPELUZAMIÉNTO, *sm.* Act of making the hair stand on end.

DESPELUZÁR Y DESPELUZNÁR, *va.* To make the hair stand on end; applied to fear or terror.

DESPELÚZO, *sm.* Erection of the hair; horror.

DESPENADÓRA, *sf.* A woman who pushes her elbow into the stomach or breast of dying persons to relieve them from agony.

DESPENÁR, *va.* To relieve from pain. *Hincar ó apretar el codo para despenar á alguno*, To suffocate a dying person, in order to relieve him from pain.

DESPENDEDÓR, RA, *s.* Spendthrift, prodigal, lavisher.

DESPENDÉR, *va.* To spend, to expend, to waste.

DESPÉNSA, *sf.* 1. Pantry, larder. 2. Store of provisions for a journey. 3. Market where eatables are sold. 4. Agreement or contract to provide or supply a horse with hay, straw, and barley, all the year round. 5. (Naút.) Steward's room. 6. Any inferior drink. V. *Aguachirle.* 7. Larder of provisions for daily use.

DESPENSÁR, *va.* To be sorry for one's thoughts.

DESPENSERÍA, *sf.* Office of steward.

DESPENSÉRO, RA, *s.* 1. Steward, caterer, provider of provisions. 2. (Naút.) Steward on board of ships. 3. Dispenser, distributer.

DESPEÑADAMÉNTE, *ad.* Precipitately.

DESPEÑADÉRO, *sm.* 1. Precipice, a place where it is not possible to stand firm. 2. (Met.) A bold and dangerous undertaking.

DESPEÑADÉRO, RA, *a.* Fit to be precipitated.

DESPEÑADÍZO, ZA, *a.* Capable of being precipitated, slippery.

DESPEÑÁR, *va.* To precipitate, to fling down a precipice.—*vr.* To precipitate one's self, to throw one's self headlong.

DESPÉÑO Y DESPEÑAMIÉNTO, *sm.* 1. A precipitate fall. 2. Destruction of character or credit. 3. Diarrhœa, looseness or flux of the belly.

DESPEPITÁRSE, *vr.* To give a loose to one's tongue, to vociferate, to speak rashly and inconsiderately; to act imprudently.

DESPERACIÓN Y DESPERÁNZA, *sf.* V. *Desesperacion.*

DESPERÁR, *va.* V. *Desesperar.*

DESPERCUDÍR, *va.* To clean or wash what is greasy.

DESPERDICIADAMÉNTE, *ad.* Profusely.

DESPERDICIÁDO ó DESPERDICIADÓR, RA, *s.* Spendthrift, squanderer, lavisher.

DESPERDICIÁR, *va.* To squander, to mispend.

DESPERDÍCIO, *sm.* 1. Prodigality, profusion. 2. Residuum, reliques, remains.

DESPERDIGÁR, *va.* To separate, to disjoin, to scatter.

DESPERECÉRSE, *va.* To crave, to desire eagerly. *Desperecerse de risa*, To laugh heartily.

DESPEREZÁRSE, *vr.* To stretch out one's limbs on being roused from sleep.

DESPERÉZO, *sm.* V. *Esperezo.*

DESPERFILÁR, *va.* (Pint.) To soften the lines of a painting.—*vr.* To lose the posture of a profile line or contour.

Despernáda, *sf.* A motion in dancing.
Despernádo, da, *a.* Weary, fatigued, tired.
Despernár, *va.* 1. To break or cut off one's legs. 2. To prevent or obstruct the use of the legs.
Desperpentár, *va.* To cut off with one stroke.
Despertadór, ra, *s.* 1. One who awakes or rouses out of sleep. 2. One who wakes lively or sprightly. 3. Alarm bell in clocks to rouse people from sleep.
Despertamiénto, *sm.* The act of awaking or rousing from sleep.
Despertár, *va.* 1. To awake, to rouse from sleep. 2. To enliven, to make lively or sprightly. 3. To call to recollection.—*vn.* 1. To awake, to break from sleep; to cease to sleep. 2. To revive, to grow lively or sprightly.
Despertéza, *sf.* Premeditation, cognition.
Despesár, *sm.* Displeasure, aversion, dislike.
Despestañárse, *vr.* 1. To pluck out the eye-lashes. 2. To look steadfastly at any thing, to inspect it closely. 3. (Met.) To apply one's self to some business with the utmost care and attention.
Despeynár, *vn.* To entangle; applied to the hair.
Despezár, *va.* 1. To dispose and arrange stones at a proper distance. 2. To make thinner at the end; applied to tubes and pipes.
Despézo, *sm.* Diminution of one end of a tube or pipe. *Despezos,* Faces of stones, where they join each other.
Despezonár, *va.* 1. To cut off the end of a thing, to break off the stalk of fruit. 2. To divide, to separate.—*vr.* To break off; applied to the stalk of fruit.
Despicárse, *vr.* To take revenge.
Despicarár, *va.* To clear a place of thieves or robbers.
Despicarazár, *va.* To begin to pick the figs; applied to birds.
Despichár, *va.* 1. (And.) To pick grapes. 2. To expel or discharge moisture or humour.
Despidída, *sf.* Gutter, a passage for water.
Despidiénte, *sm.* V. *Expediente.*
Despído, *sm.* Despatch, dismissal.
Despiertaménte, *ad.* Acutely, livelily.
Despiérto, ta, *a.* 1. Awake, free from slumber or sleep. 2. Vigilant, watchful, diligent. 3. Strong, fierce; applied to the passions. 4. Brisk, sprightly, lively.
Despiézo, *sm.* (Arq.) Juncture or bed of one stone on another.
Despilfarradaménte, *ad.* Unhandsomely, slovenly.
Despilfarrádo, da, *a.* Ragged, in tatters.
Despilfarrár, *va.* To destroy or waste with slovenliness.
Despilfárro, *sm.* 1. Slovenliness, uncleanliness. 2. Waste, mismanagement, misuse.
Despínces y Despínzas, *s. pl.* Tweezers. V. *Pinzas.*
Despintár, *va.* 1. To blot or efface what is painted. 2. (Met.) To frustrate, to disconcert.—*vn.* To degenerate.—*vr.* To be deceived, by mistaking one card for another.
Despinzadéra, *sf.* 1. Woman that plucks the knots off cloth. 2. Tweezers.
Despinzár, *va.* To pick off the knots, hair or straw, from clothes.
Despiojár, *vr.* 1. To louse, to clean of lice. 2. (Met.) To trim or dress, to relieve from misery.
Despíque, *sm.* Vengeance, revenge.
Despiritádo, da, *a.* Languid, spiritless.
Despizcár, *va.* To comminute, to break or cut into small bits.—*vr.* To make the utmost exertions, to use one's best endeavours.
Desplacér, *sm.* Displeasure, disgust.
Desplacér, *va.* To displease, to disgust.
Desplantación, *sf.* Eradication, displantation.
Desplantár, *va.* To eradicate. V. *Desarraygar.* *vr.* (Esgrim.) To lose one's erect posture.
Desplánte, *sm.* An oblique posture.
Desplatár, *va.* To separate silver from other substances with which it is mixed.
Despláte, *sm.* The act of separating silver from other metals or substances.
Desplayár, *vn.* To retire from the shore, as the tide.
Desplegadúra, *sf.* Explication, unfolding, elucidation.
Desplegár, *va.* 1. To unfold, to expand, to spread. 2. (Met.) To explain, to elucidate. 3. (Naút.) To unfurl. *Desplegar las velas,* To unfurl the sails. *Desplegar la bandera,* To hoist the flag.
Despliégo, *sm.* Open declaration, explanation, elucidation.
Despleguetеár, *va.* (Agric.) To remove the folds from the tendrils of vines, that the fruit may be more abundant.
Desplomárse, *vr.* 1. To bulge out; applied to a wall. 2. (Met.) To fall flat to the ground.
Desplómo, *sm.* The bulging or jutting out of a wall.
Desplumadúra, *sf.* Deplumation, act of depluming.
Desplumár, *va.* 1. To deplume, to strip off feathers. 2. (Met.) To despoil or strip one of his property.
Despoblación y Despobláda, *sf.* Depopulation.
Despobládo, *sm.* Desert, an uninhabited place.
Despobládor, *sm.* Depopulator.
Despoblár, *va.* 1. To depopulate, to dispeople. 2. To despoil or desolate any place.—*vn.* To withdraw from a country or place.
Despojadór, ra, *s.* Despoiler, spoiler.
Despojár, *va.* 1. To despoil or strip one of his property. 2. To dismiss, to turn out of a place or employment.—*vr.* 1. To undress, to strip off one's clothes. 2. To relinquish, to forsake. *Despojarse del hombre viejo,* (With Ascetics) To depreciate or despise the evil inclinations of corrupt nature.
Despójo, *sm.* 1. The act of despoiling or depriving one of his property; spoliation. 2. Plunder, spoils. *La hermosura es despojo del tiempo,* Beauty is the spoil of time. 3. Slough, the skin of a serpent. 4. Head, pluck, and feet of animals.—*pl.* 1. Giblets, the wings, neck, heart, and gizzard of fowls. 2. Relics, remains of any thing, broken meat or offals of the table.
Despolvár, *va.* To remove the dust.
Despolvoreár, *va.* 1. To dust, to beat or brush off the dust. 2. (Met.) To separate, to scatter, to dissipate.
Desponérse, *vr.* To cease laying eggs; applied to fowls.
Desportillár, *va.* To break the gullet or neck of a bottle, pot, &c.
Despós, *ad.* (Ant.) V. *Despues.*

Desposájas, *sf. pl.* V. *Esponsales.*

Desposádo, da, *a.* Hand-cuffed.

Desposár, *va.* To marry, to join a man and woman in marriage.—*vr.* 1. To be betrothed or married. 2. (Met.) To be paired or coupled.

Desposeér, *va.* To dispossess, to put out of possession.

Desposeimiénto, *sm.* Act of dispossessing.

Desposório, *sm.* A mutual promise to contract marriage.

Déspota, *sm.* A despot..

Despoticaménte, *ad.* Despotically.

Despótico, ca, *a.* Despotic.

Despotiquéz, *sf.* 1. Despotic power or authority. 2. Pride, haughtiness, loftiness.

Despotísmo, *sm.* Despotism, absolute power

Despóto, *sm.* Despot, an absolute sovereign.

Despotricár, *vn.* To talk inconsiderately.

Despóys, *ad.* (Ant.) V. *Despues.*

Despreciáble, *a.* Contemptible, despicable.

Despreciadór, ra, *s.* Depreciator, asperser.

Despreciár, *va.* To depreciate, to despise.—*vr.* To disdain.

Desprécio, *sm.* Disregard, scorn, contempt.

Desprendér, *va.* To unfasten, to disjoin, to separate.—*vr.* To give way, to fall down.

Desprendimiénto, *sm.* Alienation, disinterestedness.

Desprevención, *sf.* Imprudence, want of forecast, or forethought.

Desprevenciaménte, *ad.* Improvidently.

Desprevenído, da, *a.* 1. Unprovided. 2. Improvident, wanting forecast.

Desprivár, *va.* (Ant.) To deprive; to lose favour.

Desproporción, *sf.* Disproportion. [ately.

Desproporcionadaménte, *ad.* Disproportion-

Desproporcionár, *va.* To disproportion, to mismatch things.

Despropositádo, da, *a.* Absurd, out of reason.

Despropósito, *sm.* Absurdity; an extravagant speech or action.

Desproveér, *va.* To deprive of provisions, to despoil of the necessaries of life.

Desproveidaménte, *ad.* Improvidently; unexpectedly

Desproveído, da, *a.* Unprovided, unprepared.

Desproveimiénto, *sm.* Penury, want of the necessaries of life.

Despuéblo, *sm.* Depopulation.

Despuénte, *sm.* V. *Marzeo.*

Despues, *ad.* After, following in place, posterior in time; afterwards, next. *Despues de Dios,* Under or after God.

Despulsár, *va.* To leave without any vigour or pulse.—*vr.* 1. To be sorely vexed. 2. To be violently affected with any passion.

Despullár, *va.* (Ant.) V. *Desnudar.*

Despumación, *sf.* Despumation, taking off the scum of liquors.

Despumár, *va.* V. *Espumar.*

Despuntadúra, *sf.* The act of blunting or taking off the point.

Despuntár, *va.* 1. To blunt, to break off the point of any thing. 2. To cut away the dry combs in a bee-hive. 3. (Naút.) To double a cape.—*vn.* 1. To advance or make progress in the acquisition of talents and knowledge; to manifest wit and genius. 2. To begin to sprout or bud, as plants. *Al despuntar del dia,* At break of day. 3. V. *Desapuntar.*

Despús y despuxás, *ad.* (Ant.) V. *Despues.*

Desquadernár, *va.* 1. To unbind, to undo the binding of a book. 2. (Met.) To discompose, to disconcert, to disorder.

Desquadrilládo, da, *a.* Separated from the ranks or lines.

Desquadrillárse, *vr.* To be sprained in the haunches; applied to animals.

Desquartizár, *va.* 1. To quarter, to divide or tear the body into four parts. 2. To carve, to cut eatables at the table.

Désque, *ad.* (Ant.) Since, then, presently. V. *Desde que.*

Desquexár, *va.* (Jardin.) To pluck up a shoot near the root of a plant.

Desquéxe, *sm.* Act of pulling up a shoot near the root of a plant lest it should injure the growth of the parent stock.

Desquiciár, *va.* 1. To unhinge, to throw from the hinges. 2. (Met.) To discompose, to disorder. 3. (Met.) To deprive of favour or protection.

Desquiérdo, da, *a.* Left. V. *Izquierdo.*

Desquijerár, *va.* (Carp.) To cut timber on both sides to make a tenon.

Desquiladór, *sm.* V. *Esquilador.*

Desquilatár, *va.* To diminish or reduce the intrinsic value of gold.

Desquitár, *va.* To retrieve or repair a loss.—*vr.* To be avenged, to take revenge.

Desquíte, *sm.* 1. Compensation, recovery of a loss. 2. Revenge, satisfaction. [jaws.

Desquixaramiénto, *sm.* Act of breaking the

Desquixarár, *va.* To break the jaws.

Desrabotár, *va.* To cut off the tails of lambs or sheep.

Desranchárse, *vr.* To withdraw one's self from a mess.

Desraspár, *va.* V. *Raspar.*

Desraygár, *va.* (Ant.) To extirpate. V. *Desarraygar.*

Desrazonáble, *a.* Unreasonable.

Desregladaménte, *ad.* V. *Desarregladamente.*

Desregládo, da, *a.* Disorderly, irregular. V. *Desarreglado.*

Desreglárse, *vr.* To be irregular, to be ungovernable.

Desrelingár, *vn.* (Naút.) To be blown from the bolt-rope by a storm; applied to a sail.

Desreputación, *sf.* Dishonour, ignominy.

Desriscárse, *vr.* To tumble headlong on rocks or craggy places.

Desrizár, *va.* To uncurl, to undo the ringlets of hair.

Desroñár, *va.* (Agric.) To lop decayed branches of trees.

Desrostrár, *va.* To wound or maim the face

Destacaménto, *sm.* Detachment, a body of troops detached on some particular service

Destacár, *va.* To detach a body of troops from the main army on some particular service.

Destajadór, *sm.* A kind of smith's hammer.

Destajamiénto, *sm.* 1. (Met.) Diminution, reduction. 2. Current taking a new course.

Destajár, *va.* 1. To hire or undertake a work by the bulk, to do task-work. 2. To stipulate the terms and conditions on which an undertaking is to be performed. 3. (Ant.) To prevent; to interrupt; to mislead.

Destajéro, *sm.* One who undertakes a work by task.

Destájo, *sm.* 1. Undertaking of a work by task. 2. Undertaking that a work is to be finished within a certain time. 3. Partition of brick, mud, or boards. *A' destájo*, By the bulk, by the lump; earnestly, diligently. *Hablar á destajo*, To talk much, and at random.

Destallár, *va.* (Murc.) V. *Desbervar.*

Destalonár, *va.* 1. To deprive of talons or heels. 2. (Albeyt.) To level horses' hoofs.

Destapáda, *sf.* V. *Descubierta.*

Destapár, *va.* To uncover, to take off the cover. —*vr.* To be uncovered.

Destapiár, *va.* To pull down mud walls.

Destápo, *sm.* Act of uncovering or unstopping.

Destarár, *va.* To diminish the tare allowed in weighing any thing.

Destatár, *va.* (Ant.) To treat, to adjust the price; to relate particularly.

Destazadór, *sm.* He who cuts dead things in pieces.

Destazár, *va.* To cut any thing in pieces.

Deste, ta, to, *pron.* V. *De este, de esta, de esto.*

Destechár, *va.* To unroof, to take off the roof of any building.

Destejár, *va.* 1. To untile, to take off the tiles of the roofs of buildings. 2. To leave a thing defenceless and unprotected.

Destellár, *va.* To pour out drop by drop. V. *Destilar.*—*vr.* To forget.

Destéllo, *sm.* 1. The act of flowing out drop by drop. 2. Sparkle, a small glimmering light; scintillation.

Destempladaménte, *ad.* Intemperately.

Destempládo, da, *a.* (Pint.) Inharmonious, incongruous; applied to paintings.

Destemplánza, *sf.* 1. Unseasonableness, unsteadiness of the weather. 2. Disorder, intemperance, want of moderation in words or actions. 3. Alteration in the pulse, not approaching fever symptoms.

Destemplár, *va.* 1. To distemper, to alter, to disconcert. 2. To dilute, to dissolve. 3. To distort, to destroy the concord or harmony of musical instruments.—*vr.* 1. To be ruffled, to be discomposed. 2. To be out of order, to be ill with a fever. 3. To grow blunt, to lose the temper; applied to instruments.

Destémple, *sm.* 1. Discordance, disharmony. 2. Discomposure, disorder. 3. A slight indisposition.

Destendér, *va.* To fold, to double.

Destentár, *va.* To free from temptation.

Desteñír, *va.* To fade, to lose the colour.

Desternillárse, *vr.* To break one's cartilages or muscles. *Desternillarse de risa*, To laugh violently.

Desterradéro, *sm.* A retired part of the town.

Desterrár, *va.* 1. To banish, to transport. 2. To expel, to drive away. V. *Desenterrar.* *Desterrar del mundo*, To be the outcast of the world.

Desterronár, *va.* To break the clods in the fields with a harrow or spade.

Destetadéra, *sf.* Pointed instrument placed on the teats of cows to prevent the calves from sucking.

Destetár, *va.* To wean, to put from the breast, to ablactate.—*vr.* To wean one's self from an evil habit or custom. [from the breast.

Destéte, *sm.* Ablactation, the act of weaning

Destéto, *sm.* 1. Number of weanlings; applied to cattle. 2. The place where newly-weaned mules are kept.

Destexér, *va.* To unweave, to ravel, to undo a warp prepared for the loom.

Destéz, *sm.* (Ant.) Misfortune, calamity.

Destiémpo, *sm.* An unseasonable time. *A' destiémpo*, Unseasonably, untimely. [mind.

Destiénto, *sm.* Surprise, commotion in the

Destiérro, *sm.* Exile, banishment, transportation.

Destilación, *sf.* 1. Distillation, the act of dropping or falling in drops. 2. The act of extracting by the fire or still. 3. Flow of humours in the body.

Destiladéra, *sf.* 1. Still, alembic; a vessel for distillation. 2. An ingenious device or stratagem for obtaining one's end.

Destiladór, *sm.* 1. Distiller, one whose profession is to distil. 2. Filtering-stone. 3. Alembic.

Destilár, *va.* 1. To drop, to fall in drops. 2. To extract by the fire or still. 3. To filter through a stone.

Destilatório, *sm.* 1. Distillery. 2. Alembic.

Destín, *sm.* (Ant.) Will. V. *Testamento.*

Destinación, *sf.* 1. Destination, the act of appointing for any certain purpose. 2. Destiny, fate.

Destinár, *va.* 1. To destine, to appoint for any use or purpose. 2. (Naút.) To station ships. 3. To lose skill or judgment.

Destíno, *sm.* 1. Destiny, the power that determines fate. 2. Fate, doom. 3. Destination, appointment for any use or purpose. 4. (Naút.) Station.

Destíño, *sm.* Piece of unfinished yellow or green and dry honey-comb in a bee-hive.

Destirár, *va.* To slacken, to unbend.

Destitución, *sf.* Destitution, dereliction, abandonment.

Destituír, *va.* To deprive, to make destitute.

Destocár, *va.* 1. To uncoif, to pull off the cap or head-dress. 2. To uncover the head, to take off the hat.

Destorcér, *va.* 1. To untwist, to undo any thing twisted. 2. To rectify what was not right. 3. (Met.) To regulate, to arrange, to put in order.—*vr.* (Naút.) To deviate from the tract, to lose the way.

Destorgár, *va.* (Extr.) To break the branches of ever-green oaks, taking off their acorns.

Destornilladór, *sm.* Instrument used to unscrew or unbend any thing.

Destornillár, *va.* To unscrew.

Destorpár, *va.* (Ant.) To wound, to injure.

Destosérse, *vr.* To cough without necessity, to feign a cough.

Destótro, tra, *a.* V. *De este otro, de esta otra.*

Destrabár, *va.* 1. To unfetter, to take off fetters or shackles. 2. To untie, to loosen, to separate; to break the barriers.

Destrádos, *sm. pl.* A coarse sort of woollen carpets for floors and tables.

Destrál, *sm.* A small axe or little hatchet.
Destraléja, *sf.* A very small hatchet.
Destraléro, *sm.* One who makes axes and hatchets.
Destramár, *va.* 1. To unweave, to undo the warp. 2. (Mil.) To break or dissolve a conspiracy or intrigue.
Destrejár, *vn.* To wrestle, to combat.
Destrenzár, *va.* To undo a tress of hair.
Destréro, ra, *a.* V. *Diestro.*
Destréza y Destréz, *sf.* 1. Dexterity, address. 2. Skill in fencing.
Destributár, *va.* (Ant.) To exempt from tribute.
Destricía, *sf.* (Ant.) Necessity, scantiness.
Destripár, *va.* 1. To unbowel, to take out the guts. 2. (Met.) To examine into the inside of a thing. *Destripar una botella*, To crack a bottle. 3. To trample, to destroy by trampling.
Destripaterrónes, *sm.* Harrower, day-labourer who harrows the land; clod-beater.
Destriunfár, *va.* To extract all the trumps in some games at cards, leaving the other players without them.
Destrizár, *va.* To mince, to crumble, to comminute into small bits.—*vr.* To break the heart, to wear away with grief.
Destrocár, *va.* To return a thing bartered.
Destroír, *va.* V. *Destruir.*
Destrón, *sm.* A blind man's guide.
Destronár, *va.* To dethrone, to divest of regality, to pull down from the throne.
Destroncamiénto, *sm.* Detruncation, amputation, lopping trees.
Destroncár, *va.* 1. To detruncate, to lop, to cut short. 2. To maim, to cut a body in pieces. 3. (Met.) To ruin, to destroy. 4. (Met.) To cut short a discourse.
Destropár, *va.* To separate or divide troops or flocks into single individuals.
Destrozadór, ra, *s.* Destroyer, one who destroys.
Destrozár, *va.* 1. To destroy, to break into pieces. 2. To rout, to defeat. 3. (Met.) To spend much inconsiderately.
Destrózo, *sm.* 1. The act of destroying or breaking into pieces. 2. Havoc, rout, defeat.
Destrucción, *sf.* Destruction.
Destructivaménte, *ad.* Destructively.
Destructívo, va, *a.* Destructive.
Destructório, ria, *a.* Destroying, that which destroys.
Destruéco y Destruéque, *sm.* The mutual restitution of things bartered or exchanged.
Destruíble, *a.* Destructible, that may be destroyed.
Destruición y Destruício, *s.* V. *Destruccion.*
Destruidór, ra, *s.* Destroyer, devastator.
Destruír, *va.* 1. To destroy, to ruin, to lay waste. 2. To mispend one's fortune. 3. To refute. 4. To deprive one of the means of earning a livelihood.
Destruyénte, *pa.* Destroying; he who destroys.
Desturbár, *va.* To turn out, to drive away. V. *Echar.*
Desubstanciár, *va.* To enervate, to deprive of strength and substance.
Desucación, *sf.* Act of extracting the juice.
Desudár, *va.* To wipe off the sweat.
Desuellacáras, *sm.* 1. Impudence, insolence. 2. An impudent, shameless, wicked person.

Desuéllo, *sm.* 1. The act of flaying, fleecing, or skinning. 2. Forwardness, impudence, insolence. 3. Extortion or an exorbitant price.
De suérte, *ad.* Thus, so that. *De suerte que no debe nada*, So that he owes nothing.
Desuncír, *va.* To unyoke.
Desunidaménte, *ad.* Separately, severally.
Desunión, *sf.* 1. Separation, disunion, disjunction. 2. Discord, dissension.
Desunír, *va.* To separate, to part, to disunite; to occasion discord.
Desúno, *ad.* (Ant.) V. *De Consuno.*
Desuñár, *va.* 1. To tear off the nails. 2. To pull out the roots of trees.—*vr.* To plunge into vice and disorder.
Desurcár, *va.* To remove or undo furrows.
Desurdír, *va.* 1. To unweave cloth. 2. To unravel a plot.
Desús, (Al) *ad.* (Ant.) V. *Por encima.*
Desusadaménte, *ad.* Unusually, out of use.
Desusár, *va.* To disuse, to cease or discontinue the use of.
Desúso, *sm.* Disuse, cessation of use or custom.
De súso, *ad.* From above, from the top. V. *Arriba.*
Desustanciár, *va.* To enervate. V. *Desubstanciar.*
Desvahár, *va.* (Agric.) To take away the dry or withered part of a plant.
Desvaído, da, *a.* Tall, yet weak. V. *Vaciado.*
Desvalído, da, *a.* 1. Helpless, destitute. 2. Eager, ardent.
Desvalimiénto, *sm.* Dereliction, abandonment, want of favour or protection.
Desvalór, *sm.* Cowardice; timidity.
Desván, *sm.* Garret, a room on the highest floor of the house. *Desvan gatéro*, Cock-loft, a room over the garret not habitable.
Desvanecér, *vn.* 1. To divide into imperceptible parts. 2. To cause to vanish or disappear. 3. To undo, to remove. 4. To swell with presumption or pride.—*vr.* 1. To vanish, to evaporate, to exhale. 2. To be affected with giddiness or dizziness.
Desvanecidaménte, *ad.* Vainly, haughtily, proudly.
Desvanecimiénto, *sm.* 1. Pride, haughtiness, loftiness. 2. Giddiness, dizziness, weakness of the head.
Desváño, *sm.* Garret. V. *Desvan.*
Desvaporizadéro, *sm.* Place for evaporating or respiring any thing.
Desvarár, *vn.* 1. V. *Resbalar.* 2. (Naút.) To put a ship in motion that was aground.
Desvariáble, *a.* Variable, inconstant, mutable.
Desvariadaménte, *ad.* 1. Ravingly, foolishly, madly. 2. Differently, diversely, dissimilarly.
Desvariádo, da, *a.* 1. Delirious, raving. 2. Disorder, irregular. 3. Unlike, dissimilar. 4. Long, luxuriant; applied to the branches of trees.
Desvariár, *vn.* 1. To delirate, to dote, to rave. 2. To make extravagant demands. 3. To deviate, to disunite, to vary.
Desvarío, *sm.* 1. Delirium, alienation of mind. 2. An extravagant action or speech. 3. Inequality, inconstancy, caprice. 4. Monstrousness, extravagancy; derangement; disunion.
Desvaynár, *va.* 1. To unsheath. 2. To husk, to strip off the outward integument.

Desvedádo, da, *a.* Unprohibited, free from prohibition.
Desvedár, *va.* To remove or revoke a prohibition against a thing.
Desveladaménte, *ad.* Watchfully, vigilantly.
Desveládo, da, *a.* Watchful, vigilant, careful.
Desvelamiénto, *sm.* Watchfulness. V. *Desvelo.*
Desvelár, *va.* To keep awake.—*vr.* To be watchful or vigilant.
Desvélo, *sm.* 1. Want or privation of sleep. 2. Watchfulness, vigilance.
Desvenár, *va.* 1. To separate or clear the veins of flesh. 2. To extract any thing from the veins, as of mines, and filaments of plants.
Desvencijár, *va.* To disunite, to weaken, to divide.—*vr.* To be ruptured; to be relaxed.
Desvendár, *va.* To take off a bandage.
Desventája, *sf.* Disadvantage, misfortune.
Desventár, *va.* To vent, to let out the air.
Desventúra, *sf.* Misfortune, calamity.
Desventuradaménte, *ad.* Unhappily, unfortunately.
Desventurádo, da, *a.* 1. Unfortunate, calamitous, wretched. 2. Stupid, ignorant. 3. Sordid, niggardly.
Desvergonzadaménte, *ad.* Impudently, shamelessly.
Desvergonzádo, da, *a.* Impudent, immodest.
Desvergonzárse, *vr.* To speak or act in an impudent or insolent manner.
Desvergüénza, *sf.* 1. Impudence, effrontery. 2. Shameless word or action.
Desvezár, *va.* (Agric.) To cut the young shoots of vines near the root.
Desviár, *va.* 1. To divert from the right way, 2. To dissuade, to dehort.
Desviejár, *va.* (Among Shepherds) To separate the old ewes or rams from the flock.
Desvío y Desviamiénto, *sm.* 1. The act of diverting or dehorting. 2. Aversion, displeasure.
Desvirár, *va.* To pare off the fore part of a sole.
Desvirgár, *va.* To deflower a maid.
Desvirtuár, *va.* To take the substance, virtue, or strength from any thing.
Desvivírse, *vr.* To love excessively, to desire anxiously.
Desvolvedór, *sm.* Instrument used by smiths to tighten or slacken a female screw.
Desvolvér, *va.* 1. To unfold, to disentangle. V. *Desenvolver.* 2. To plough, to till the ground.
Desxugár, *va.* To extract the juice from any thing.
Desy, *ad.* (Ant.) Contraction of *Desde y,* Hence. V. *Desde allí.*
Desyérba, *sf.* V. *Escarda.*
Desyuncír y Desyungír, *va.* To unyoke.
Deszocár, *va.* To wound or hurt the foot.
Deszumár, *va.* To extract the juice or substance.
Detál (En), *ad.* (Ant.) In detail. V. *Menudamente.*
Detallár y Detavár, *va.* To detail, to particularize, to enumerate small parts.
Detálle, *sm.* Detail, enumeration.
Detención, *sf.* Detention, delay.
Detenedór, ra, *s.* Detainer, one that detains.
Detenér, *va.* 1. To stop, to detain. 2. To arrest, to imprison. 3. To retain, to reserve, to keep. —*vr.* 1. To be detained, to stop, to be at leisure. 2. To consider a thing maturely.

Detenidaménte, *ad.* Dilatorily, cautiously.
Detenído, da, *a.* 1. Sparing, niggardly, parsimonious. 2. Slow, inactive.
Detentación, *sf.* Embezzlement, retention.
Detentadór, *sm.* Detainer, one who retains possession. [hold.
Detentár, *va.* To detain, to retain, to with-
Detergénte, *a.* Detergent, detersive.
Deterior, *a.* Worse, of an inferior quality.
Deterioración, *sf.* Deterioration, the act of making any thing worse.
Deteriorár, *va.* To deteriorate, to impair, to make any thing worse. [ed.
Deterióro, *sm.* Thing impaired or deteriorat-
Determinación, *sf.* 1. Determination, resolution, decision. 2. Forwardness, audaciousness.
Determinadaménte, *ad.* Definitely, expressly, especially.
Determinádo, da, *a.* Determinate, resolute.
Determinánte, *sm.* 1. (Gram.) The determining verb. 2. Determiner, he who determines.
Determinár, *va.* 1. To determine, to resolve. 2. To distinguish, to discern. 3. To appoint, to assign. 4 To decide. *Determinar pleyto,* To decide a law-suit.
Determinatívo, va, *a.* Determinative.
Detersión, *sf.* Putrefaction, act and effect of cleansing.
Detersório, ria, *a.* Detersive, cleansing.
Detestáble, *a.* Detestable. [bly.
Detestableménte, *ad.* Detestably, abomina-
Detestación, *sf.* Detestation.
Detestár, *va.* To detest, to abhor.
Detienebuéy, *sm.* (Bot.) Rest-harrow, cammock, ground furze. Ononis spinosa *L.*
Detonación, *sf.* Detonation, noise.
Detornár, *va.* (Ant.) To return, to turn a second time. [der.
Detracción, *sf.* Detraction, defamation, slan-
Detractár, *va.* To detract, to defame, to slan-
Detractór, *sm.* Detractor, slanderer. [der.
Detraér, *va.* 1. To detract, to remove. 2. To slander, to vilify.
Detrás, *ad.* 1. Behind. 2. In the absence.
De través, *ad.* Athwart, across.
Detriménto, *sm.* Detriment, damage, loss.
Deturpár, *va.* (Ant.) To pollute, to deform.
Deúda, *sf.* 1. Debt, that which one man owes to another. 2. Fault, offence. 3. That which has relationship or affinity. *Deuda comun,* The last debt; death.
Deudíllas, *sf. pl.* Petty debts.
Deúdo, da, *s.* 1. Parent. 2. Kindred. V. *Parentesco.* 3. (Ant.) Debt.
Deudór, ra, *s.* Debtor.
Deudóso, sa, *a.* V. *Emparentado.*
Devalár, *vn.* (Naút.) To be driven out of the right course by the force of a current; applied to ships.
Deván, *ad.* (Ant.) V. *Antes.*
Devanadéra, *sf.* 1. Reel, a turning frame, upon which yarn or silk is wound into skeins from the spindle. *Devanadera de golpe,* Clock-reel, snap-reel. 2. A moveable picture or decoration on the stage.
Devanadór, ra, *s.* 1. Winder, one who reels yarn off the spindle. 2. Quill, bit of paper, button, or other thing, on which yarn is wound into a clew.

Devanár, *va.* 1. To reel, to gather yarn off the spindle. 2. (Met.) To wrap up one thing in another. *Devanar las tripas*, To importune one with some impertinent affair. *Devanárse los sesos*, To screw one's wits, to fatigue one's self with intense thinking.

Devaneár, *vn.* To rave, to talk nonsense.

Devanéo, *sm.* Delirium, alienation of mind.

Devant, *ad.* (Ant.) Anteriorly. V. *A'ntes.*

Devantál, *sm.* Apron.

Devastación, *sf.* Devastation, destruction.

Devastár, *va.* To desolate, to lay waste.

Devedár, *va.* (Ant.) V. *Vedar.*

Devengár, *va.* To obtain as the reward of labour.

Devenír, *vn.* (Ant.) V. *Sobrevenir.*

Deviédo, *sm.* (Ant.) V. *Prohibicion y deuda.*

Devíno, **na**, *s.* V. *Adivino.*

Devísa, *sf.* 1. V. *Divisa.* 2. Part of the tithes which belong to a plebeian heir. 3. Ancient patrimony in Castile.

Devisár, *va.* (Ant.) To designate, to constitute, to agree, to relate, to divide. V. *Divisar.*

Devoción, *sf.* 1. Devotion, piety; the state of the mind under a strong sense of dependence upon God. 2. Prayer, act of religion. 3. (Met.) Strong affection, ardent love. 4. (Teol.) Devoutness, promptitude in obeying the will of God. *Estar á la devocion de alguno*, To be at one's disposal, to attend his orders.

Devocionário, *sm.* Prayer-book.

Devocionéro, **ra**, *a.* Devotional, relating to devotion.

Devolución, *sf.* Devolution, restitution to a former state or condition.

Devolutívo, *a.* (For.) V. *Efecto.*

Devolvér, *va.* 1. To return a cause to an inferior court to be tried anew. 2. To restore a thing to its former possessor.

Devoradór, **ra**, *s.* Devourer, one who devours.

Devorár, *va.* To devour, to swallow up, to consume ravenously.

Devoráz, *a.* Voracious.

Devotaménte, *ad.* Devoutly.

Devóto, **ta**, *a.* 1. Devout, pious, religious. 2. Exciting devotion. 3. Strongly attached. *Devoto de monjas*, He who very frequently visits and converses with nuns.

Deuteronómio, *sm.* Deuteronomy, the 5th book of the Pentateuch.

Déxa, *sf.* Prominence between two fissures.

Dexación, *sf.* Abdication, resignation. *Dexacion de bienes*, The act of resigning or giving up one's property to one's creditors.

Dexadéz, *sf.* State of being left, abandoned, or reduced; slovenliness.

Dexádo, **da**, *a.* 1. Slovenly, idle, indolent. 2. Dejected, low-spirited.

Dexadór, *sm.* Procreator, he who leaves successors.

Dexamiénto, *sm.* 1. Abdication, resignation. 2. Indolence, idleness, carelessness. 3. Languor, decay of spirits.

Dexár, *va.* 1. To leave, to relinquish, to quit. 2. To omit saying or doing a thing. 3. To permit, to allow, not to obstruct. 4. To forsake, to desert. 5. To yield, to produce. 6. To commit, to give in charge. 7. To nominate, to appoint. *Dexar dicho*, To leave word or orders. *Dexar escrito*, To leave in writing. *Dexalo que venga*, Leave him to be chastised. 8. To leave off, to cease. 9. To leave a legacy to one absent. *Dexar atras*, To excel, to surpass. *Dexar en cueros*, To strip one of his property. *Dexar fresco*, To frustrate, to baffle. *Dexar para mañana*, To delay, to procrastinate.—*vr.* 1. Not to take care of one's self. 2. To allow or suffer one's self to. 3. To become languid. 4. To abandon one's self to. *Dexarse llevar*, To suffer one's self to be led by another. *Dexarse rogar*, To extend the concession required, that the favour may be more estimable. *Dexarse ver*, To appear, to discover itself. *Dexarse vencer*, To yield one's self to the opinion of another. *Dexarse caer abaxo por un rio*, (Naút.) To drop down a river. *Dexarse caer á la popa*, To fall astern. *Dexarse caer á sotavento*, To fall to leeward. *Dexarse alguna cosa en el tintero*, To omit something necessary to the subject.

Dexatívo, **va**, *a.* Lazy, languid, dejected.

Dexemplár, *va.* (Ant.) To defame, to dishonour.

Dexénxo, *sm.* (Ant.) Rheum, cold.

Dexíllo, *sm.* (Dim. of *dexo.*) Slight dereliction, small end.

Dexo, *sm.* 1. Abdication, dereliction. 2. End, termination. 3. Negligence, carelessness. 4. Relish or taste which remains after eating or drinking. 5. Result, effect, or remains of a passion. 6. Particular accentuation on the last syllable of words.

Déxtro, *sm.* The space of 72 to 80 paces, which churches formerly occupied.

Dexugár, *va.* To extract the juice or substance of any thing.

Dezmár, *va.* 1. To pay tithes. 2. To collect or receive tithes. 3. To take the tenth part of any thing.

Dezmatório, *sm.* 1. Place in which tithes are collected. 2. Tithing. 3. Tithe-gatherer.

Dezméño, **ña**; y **Dezméro**, **ra**, *a.* Belonging to tithes.

Dezmería y **Dezmia**, *sf.* Tithe-land.

Dezméro, *sm.* 1. One who pays tithes. 2. One who gathers or collects tithes; a tither.

Dí, *ad.* (Ant.) Contraction of *de y* for *de allí*, Thence.

Dia, *sm.* 1. Day; the time from noon to noon, called the natural day. 2. Day; the time between the rising and the setting of the sun, called the artificial day. 3. (Ant.) Contraction of *Diego* or *Santiago*, James, a proper name. *Dias caniculares*, Dog-days. *Dia de años, ó cumpleaños*, Birth-day. *Dia de ayuno*, Fast-day. *Dia de carne*, Day on which it is permitted to eat meat. *Dia de trabajo*, Working day. *Dia de descanso*, Day of rest on a journey. *Dia diado, ó adiado*, Day appointed for doing any thing. *De dia*, By day. *El dia de hoy, ó hoy en dia*, The present day. *Dia pardo*, A cloudy day. *Dia pesado*, A dull, gloomy day. *En dias de Dios*, Never. *Hombre de dias*, A man in years. *Tener dias*, To vary in one's physiognomy or countenance; to be full of days, to be old. *De hoy en ocho dias*, This day week. *Dias y ollas*, (Fam.) Time and patience attain every thing. *Dias de gracia*, Days of grace allowed for the payment of bills. *De dias*, Some time ago.

Diábla (A' **la**), *ad.* Carelessly, rudely.

Diabláo, vn. To act the part of a devil.
Diablázo, sm. A great devil.
Diablíllo, sm. 1. A little devil. 2. An acute clever man.
Diáblo, sm. 1. Devil, Satan. 2. Person of a perverse temper. 3. An ugly person. 4. A cunning, subtle person. *Hay mucho diablo aquí*, This business is dreadfully entangled or perplexed. *Ser la piel ó de la piel del diablo*, To be a limb of the devil. *Diablo cozuelo*, Artful, deceiving devil. [meat.
Diablotín ó Diabolín, sm. A sort of sweet-
Diablúra, sf. A diabolical undertaking.
Diabolicaménte, ad. Diabolically.
Diabólico, ca, a. Diabolical, excessively bad.
Diacatalicón, sm. An universal medicine or purge.
Diacitrón, sm. Lemon-peel preserved in sugar.
Diaconál, a. Belonging to a deacon.
Diaconáto y Diaconádo, sm. Deaconship.
Diaconía, sf. Deaconry.
Diaconísa, sf. Deaconness. [of the clergy.
Diácono, sm. Deacon, one of the lowest order
Diadéma, sf. 1. Diadem, an ensign of royalty. 2. Crown; circle round the head of images.
Diafanidád, sf. V. *Transparencia*.
Diáfano, na, a. Transparent, pellucid, clear.
Diaforético, ca, a. Diaphoretic.
Diafrágma, sm. 1. Diaphragm, the midriff which divides the upper cavity of the body from the lower. 2. Division or cartilaginous partition of the nostrils.
Diagonál, a. Diagonal, reaching from one angle to another.
Diagonalménte, ad. Diagonally.
Diagráfica, sf. Sketch, design.
Dialéctica, sf. Logic, the art of reasoning.
Dialéctico, sm. Professor of dialectics.
Dialéctico, ca, a. Dialectical, logical.
Dialécto, sm. Dialect, subdivision of language, phraseology, style.
Dialogál, a. Colloquial, in form of a dialogue.
Dialogístico, ca, a. Belonging to a dialogue.
Dialogizár, va. To make or write dialogues.
Diálogo, sm. Dialogue, a conference or conversation between two or more.
Dialtéa, sf. Dialthea, marsh-mallow ointment.
Diamantádo, da, a. Belonging to a diamond.
Diamánte, sm. 1. Diamond, a precious stone; the most valuable and hardest of all the gems. 2. Hardness, resistance.
Diamantíno, na, a. Adamantine, belonging to a diamond.
Diametrál, a. Diametrical.
Diametralménte, ad. Diametrically.
Diámetro, sm. Diameter; the line which, passing through the centre of a circle or other curvilinear figure, divides it into two equal parts.
Diamón, sm. Kind of yellow stone.
Diána, sf. (Mil.) Kind of beat of drum.
Diánche y Diántre, sm. (Vulg.) Devil.
Diapasón, sm. (Mus.) Diapason, an octave.
Diapréa, sf. Sort of round plum.
Diariaménte, ad. Daily. [per. 2. Daily expense.
Diário, sm. 1. Journal, diary; daily newspa-
Diário, ria, a. Daily, happening every day.
Diarísta, sm. Diarist, writer or editor of a diary.
Diarréa, sf. Diarrhœa, a flux of the belly.

Diáspero ó Diáspro, sm. Jasper.
Diástole, sm. (Anat.) Diastole, the dilatation of the heart.
Dibuxadór, ra, s. 1. One who designs figures in painting or sculpture. 2. Graver, a style or tool used in graving.
Dibuxánte, pa. Delineating; designer.
Dibuxár, va. 1. To draw, to design, to delineate. 2. (Met.) To paint any passion of the mind.
Dibúxo, sm. 1. Design, drawing, sketch. 2. Delineation, description. *Es un dibuxo*, It is a picture; applied to a handsome face. *No meterse en dibuxos*, To relate in a plain manner.
Dicacidád, sf. Pertness, sauciness, loquacity.
Dicción, sf. Diction, style, language, expression.
Diccionário, sm. Dictionary, a book containing the words of any language.
Dicér, va. (Ant.) V. *Decir*.
Dícha, sf. Happiness, felicity, fortune. *Dichas*, Honours, riches, dignities, and pleasures. *Por dicha, ó á dicha*, By chance.
Dicharácho, sm. A vulgar, low, or indecent expression. [sion.
Dichído, sm. (Vulg.) A sharp or pert expres-
Dícho, sm. 1. Saying, expression, sentence. 2. Declaration, deposition. 3. Promise of marriage.
Dichosaménte, ad. Happily, fortunately.
Dichóso, sa, a. Happy, fortunate, prosperous.
Diciémbre, sm. December, the last month of the year.
Diciplína, sf. Discipline, education, instruction. V. *Disciplina*.
Dictádo, sm. A title of dignity or honour.
Dictadór, sm. Dictator; an ancient magistrate of Rome, made in times of exigence, and invested with absolute authority.
Dictadúra, sf. Dignity or office of dictator.
Dictámen, sm. 1. Opinion, sentiments. 2. Suggestion, insinuation.
Díctamo, sm. (Bot.) Dittany.
Dictár, va. 1. To deliver one's thoughts to another with authority. 2. To pronounce what another is to say or write, to dictate.
Dictatório, ria, a. Dictatorial.
Dictério, sm. Sarcasm, taunt, keen reproach.
Didáctico ó Didascálico, ca, a. Didactic, preceptive, giving precepts.
Diénte, sm. 1. Tooth, a hard little bone fixed in the socket of the jaws. 2. Prop used by founders to secure the founding-frame. 3. Fang or tusk of wild boars. *Diente molar*, V. *Muela*. *Diente incisivo*, Incisor, fore-tooth. 4. *Diente de lobo*, Burnisher, a burnishing or polishing instrument. 5. *Diente de perro*, Sampler, a piece worked by young girls for improvement. 6. *Diente de leon*, (Bot.) Dandelion, or lion's tooth. Leontodon taxaracum *L.* 7. *Diente de perro*, (Bot.) Dog's tooth violet. Erythronium *L.*—*pl.* 1. The indented edges of different instruments. 2. The prominent parts of wheels. *Dientes de ajo*, Cloves of garlic. *Cruxir de dientes*, To grind the teeth. *Aguzar los dientes*, To whet the appetite. *Tomar á uno entre dientes*, To have an antipathy against a person.
Dientecíco, llo, y to, sm. dim. Little tooth.
Diéresis, sf. Poetical figure which divides a syllable into two.

Diési, *sf.* (Mús.) The smallest and simplest part in which a tone is divided.

Diéstra, *sf.* 1. The right hand. 2. (Met.) Favour, support, protection. *Juntar diestra con diestra*, To shake hands, to make up matters.

Diestraménte, *ad.* Dexterously.

Diéstro, tra, *a.* 1. Right, not left. 2. Dexterous, skilful. 3. Sagacious, prudent. 4. Sly, artful, cunning. 5. Favourable, propitious.

Diéstro, *sm.* 1. A skilful fencer. 2. Halter or bridle for horses.

Diéta, *sf.* 1. Diet, regimen; food regulated by the rules of medicine. 2. Diet, the assembly of the ministers of the states of Germany held at Ratisbon. 3. One day's journey of 10 leagues by land. 4. Daily salary of judges and other officers of the law. *Dietas*, (Naút.) Cattle put on board a fleet to furnish fresh provisions for the sick.

Diéz, *sm.* Ten, twice five. *Diez de bolos*, Pin standing alone in front of the nine pins. *Diez de rosario*, The eleventh bead in a rosary.

Dieziochéno, *sm.* 1. An ancient silver coin in Valencia, worth 18 deniers. 2. Cloth having 1800 threads in the warp.

Diézma, *sf.* V. *Décima y Diezmo.*

Diezmál, *a.* Decimal, tenth.

Diezmár, *va.* 1. To chastise every tenth one of many delinquents. 2. To pay the tithe to the church. 3. To decimate.

Diezméro, *sm.* He who pays or receives the tithe.

Diezmesíno, na, *a.* That which is ten months or belonging to that time.

Diézmo, *sm.* 1. Tithe, the tenth part. 2. Duty of ten per cent. paid to the king. 3. Tithe, the tenth part of the fruits of the earth, assigned to the maintenance of the clergy.

Difamación, *sf.* Defamation.

Difamadór, *sm.* Defamer, he who defames.

Difamár, *va.* To defame, to discredit; to divulge.

Difamatório, ria, *a.* Defamatory, scandalous.

Diferéncia, *sf.* 1. Difference, the quality by which one thing differs from another. 2. State of being distinct from something. 3. The disproportion between one thing and another. *A' diferencia*, With the difference. *Diferéncias*, Differences, controversies, disputes.

Diferenciál, *a.* Differential, different.

Diferenciár, *va.* 1. To differ, to cause a difference. 2. To change or alter the use or destination of things.—*vn.* To dissent, to disagree in opinion.—*vr.* To distinguish one's self, to render one's self conspicuous.

Diferénte, *a.* Different, dissimilar, unlike.

Diferenteménte, *ad.* Differently, diversely.

Diferír, *va.* To defer, to delay, to put off.—*vn.* 1. To differ, to be different. 2. To yield to another's opinion, to refer to another's judgment.

Difícil, *a.* Difficult, arduous.

Dificilménte, *ad.* Difficultly.

Dificultád, *sf.* Difficulty, embarrassment.

Dificultadór, *sm.* One who starts or raises difficulties.

Dificultár, *va.* 1. To start or raise difficulties. 2. To render difficult.

Dificultosaménte, *ad.* Difficultly.

Dificultóso, sa, *a.* Difficult, hard, troublesome; deformed countenance.

Difidación, *sf.* Manifesto, a declaration issued in justification of a war.

Difidéncia, *sf.* Diffidence, distrust, want of confidence.

Difidénte, *a.* Diffident, disloyal, distrustful.

Difinír y Difinecér, *va.* V. *Definir.*

Difinición, *sf.* V. *Definicion.*

Difrácez, *sm.* Dross of melted copper, gathered in the furnace.

Difúgio, *sm.* V. *Efugio.*

Difundír, *va.* 1. To diffuse, to extend. 2. (Met.) To divulge, to publish, to make public.

Difúnto, ta, *a.* 1. Dead, deceased. 2. (Met.) Decayed, withered. *Difunto de taberna*, (In the Jocular Style) A drunken red-faced person.

Difusaménte, *ad.* Diffusely.

Difusión, *sf.* 1. Diffusion, dispersion: the state of being scattered. 2. (Met.) Copiousness or exuberance of style.

Difusívo, va, *a.* Diffusive.

Difúso, sa, *a.* Diffusive, copious; wide, ample.

Digeríble, *a.* Digestible, capable of being digested.

Digerír, *va.* 1. To digest, to concoct in the stomach. 2. (Met.) To bear with patience any loss or affront. 3. (Met.) To examine carefully into a thing. 4. (Met.) To adjust, to arrange. 5. (Quím.) To soften by heat, as in a boiler.

Digestíble, *a.* Digestible.

Digestión, *sf.* 1. Digestion, the act of concocting food. 2. Preparation of matter by a chemical heat. *Hombre de mala digestion*, A man of a peevish fretful temper. *Negocio de mala digestion*, A perplexed affair.

Digestír, *va.* (Ant.) V. *Digerir.*

Digestívo, va, *a.* Digestive, assisting digestion.

Digésto, *sm.* Digest, the pandect of the civil law, usually cited in writing by the cipher *ff.*

Dígito, *sm.* 1. Digit, the twelfth part of the diameter of the sun or moon. 2. Any of the numbers expressed by single figures.

Digladiár, *vn.* To fight with the sword in single combat.

Dignación, *sf.* Condescension, voluntary humiliation, descent from superiority.

Dignaménte, *ad.* Worthily, with dignity.

Dignárse, *vr.* To condescend, to deign.

Dignidád, *sf.* 1. Dignity, rank of elevation. 2. Advancement, preferment, high place. 3. (Astrol.) Dignity, the state of a planet being in any sign.

Dignificánte, *pa.* (Teol.) That which dignifies; applied to grace.

Dignificár, *va.* To dignify, to render or judge worthy of.

Dígno, na, *a.* 1. Meritorious, worthy, deserving. 2. Condign, suitable, correspondent.

Digresión, *sf.* 1. Digression, deviation from the main scope of a speech or treatise. 2. (Astr.) Departure of a planet from the equinoctial line.

Dilaceración, *sf.* Dilaceration.

Dilacerár, *va.* To lacerate. V. *Lacerar.*

Dilación, *sf.* Delay, procrastination; dilatation.

Dilapidación, *sf.* Dilapidation.

Dilapidadór, *sm.* Dilapidator.

Dilapidár, *va.* To dilapidate, to fall to ruin.

Dilatáble, *a.* Dilatable, capable of extension.

Dilatación, *sf.* 1. Dilatation, extension, amplification. 2. The state of being extended. 3. Evenness, greatness of mind.

Dilatadaménte, *ad.* With dilatation.
Dilatádo, *a.* V. *Numeroso.*
Dilatadór, ra, *s.* One who dilates or extends.
Dilatár, *va.* 1. To dilate, to expand, to enlarge. 2. To defer, to retard, to put off. 3. (Met.) To comfort, to cheer up.—*vr.* To expatiate or enlarge on any subject.
Dilatatívo, va, *a.* That which dilates.
Dilatória, *sf.* V. *Dilacion. Andar con dilatorias*, To waste time by deceiving with false promises.
Dilatório, ria, *a.* Dilatory, delaying.
Dilección, *sf.* Dilection, love, affection.
Diлécto, ta, *a.* Loved, beloved.
Diléma, *sm.* Dilemma, an argument equally conclusive by contrary suppositions.
Diligéncia, *sf.* 1. Diligence, assiduity. 2. Activity, briskness in the performance of a thing, or the pursuit of business. *Tengo que ir á una diligencia*, I must go upon some business. 3. Call to ease nature. 4. Return of a writ. 5. Duty, obligation. 6. Love, dilection. *Hacer las diligencias de Christiano*, To perform the duty of a Christian.
Diligenciár, *va.* To exert one's self, to endeavour.
Diligenciéro, *sm.* 1. Agent, attorney. 2. Apparitor, summoner; the lowest officer of an ecclesiastical court.
Diligénte, *a.* 1. Diligent, assiduous, careful. 2. Prompt, swift, ready.
Diligenteménte, *ad.* Diligently.
Dilucidación, *sf.* Explanation, dilucidation, illustration.
Dilucidadór, *sm.* He who dilucidates.
Dilucidár, *va.* To dilucidate, to explain.
Dilucidário, *sm.* Explanatory writing.
Dilúculo, *sm.* The sixth part in which the night is divided.
Diluénte, *pa.* Diluent, that which dilutes.
Diluír, *va.* To dilute any thing.
Dilusión, *sf.* V. *Ilusion.*
Dilusívo, va, *a.* Delusive, apt to deceive.
Diluviár, *vn. impers.* To rain like a deluge.
Dilúvio, *sm.* 1. Deluge, overflow, inundation. 2. (Met.) Vast abundance.
Dimanación, *sf.* Act of springing or issuing from.
Dimanár, *vn.* To spring or proceed from; to originate in.
Dimensión, *sf.* Dimension, extent, capacity, bulk.
Dimensionál, *a.* Belonging to the dimension.
Dimes, *Andar en dimes y diretes*, To use ifs and ands, or quibbles and quirks; to contend, to use altercations.
Dimidiár, *va.* To separate or divide into halves, V. *Demediar.*
Diminución, *sf.* 1. Diminution, the state of growing less. 2. Contraction of the diameter of a column as it ascends. *Ir en diminucion*, To grow tapering to the top. (Met.) To be losing one's character or credit.
Diminuír, *va.* To diminish. V. *Disminuir.*
Diminutaménte, *ad.* 1. Diminutively. 2. Minutely, by retail.
Diminutivaménte, *ad.* (Gram.) Diminutively, by diminishing.
Diminutívo, va, *a.* Diminutive.
Diminúto, ta, *a.* Defective, faulty.
Dimisión, *sf.* Dismission, discharge, from an office. *Hacer dimision de su empleo*, To resign one's place or employment.
Dimisórias, *sf. pl.* Dimissory letters, given by a bishop to a candidate for holy orders, that he may be lawfully ordained.
Dimite, *sm.* Dimity, a fine cotton cloth.
Dimitír, *va.* To give up, to relinquish.
Dimóño, *sm.* (Joc.) Demon. V. *Demonio.*
Dinastía, *sf.* Dynasty, sovereignty, race.
Dineráda, *sf.* (Vulg.) A large sum of money.
Dinerál, *sm.* 1. (Arag.) Measure for wine and oil. 2. Weight used by assayers to fix the purity of the precious metals; a gold *dineral* is divided into 24 *quilates* or carats, each of which is 4 grains; a silver *dineral* is divided into 12 *dineros* of 24 grains each.
Dinerillo, *sm.* 1. (Iron.) A round sum of money. 2. A small copper coin, current in Aragon.
Dinerísta, *sm.* Money-hunter, one who is eagerly employed in the pursuit of money.
Dinéro, *sm.* 1. Coin, money. 2. An ancient Spanish copper coin. 3. Standard of silver. *Dinero llama dinero*, Money gets money. *Tener dinero*, To be rich. *A' dinero, ó al dinero, ó á dinero contante*, In ready money.
Dineróso, sa, *a.* Monied, rich.
Dineruélo, *sm.* Small coin.
Dingolodángos, *sm.* Word without meaning.
Dintél, *sm.* Lintel, that part of a door-frame which lies across the door-frame over head.
Dintelár, *va.* To make lintels.
Dintórno, *sm.* (Pint.) Delineation of the parts of a figure contained within the contour.
Diobre (Par), (Bax.) V. *Par Dios.*
Diocesáno, na, *a.* Belonging to a diocess, diocesan.
Diócesis y Diócesi, *sf.* Diocess, the circuit of a bishop's jurisdiction.
Dionísia, *sf.* A kind of black stone, variegated with red spots.
Dióptrica, *sf.* Dioptrics, a part of optics, treating of the refraction of light.
Diós, *sm.* 1. God, the Supreme Being. 2. A false god, an idol. 3. (Met.) Any person or thing passionately beloved or adored. *A' Dios ó anda con Dios*, Farewell, adieu. *A' Dios, y á ventura*, At all events, at all risks. *Despues de dios*, Under God. *Vaya vd. con Dios*, Farewell, God be with you. *Dios dára*, God will provide; used to stimulate almsgiving. *O' santo Dios*, Oh, gracious God. *Por Dios*, By God, for God's sake. *No lo quiera Dios*, God forbid. *Quiera dios*, God send. *A' Dios*, God's will be done.
Diósa, *sf.* Goddess.
Diosеár, *vn.* To claim divine honours.
Diosecíllo y Diosecíto, *sm.* Cupid; a little god.
Diosecíta, *sf.* A little goddess.
Dióso, sa, *a.* (Ant.) Old, of a long date.
Diplóe, *sm.* Diploe, a medullar substance which separates the two laminas of the skull.
Diplóma, *sm.* Diploma, patent.
Diplomática, *sf.* Diplomacy, the diplomatic art.
Diplomático, ca, *a.* 1. Diplomatic, relating to diplomas. 2. Diplomatical, privileged, authorised; applied to negotiations in politics.
Dipsáca, *sm.* (Bot.) Teasel. V. *Condencha.*
Dípsas, *sf.* Serpent whose bite is said to produce unquenchable thirst.
Díptica, co, *s.* Diptych, a register of bishops and martyrs.
Diptongár, *va.* 1. To unite two vowels. 2. (Met.)

To combine or join two or more things so as to form one whole.

Diptóngo, *sm.* Diphthong, a coalition of two vowels to form one sound.

Diputación, *sf.* 1. Deputation, the act of deputing on a special mission. 2. The body of persons deputed. 3. The object of a deputation.

Diputádo, *sm.* 1. Deputy, commissioner. 2. (Com.) Assignee.

Diputár, *va.* To depute, to send with a special commission.

Díque, *sm.* Dike, a mound to hinder inundations. *Dique de construccion*, (Naút.) A dry dock, where ships are built or careened.

Diquecíllo, *sm.* A small dike.

Dirección, *sf.* 1. Direction, the act of guiding or directing; tendency of motion. 2. Body of persons appointed to superintend the management of some business; order, command.

Directaménte y Diréctè, *ad.* Directly, apparently. *Directè ó indirectè*, (Latin.) Directly or indirectly.

Directívo, va, *a.* Directive, having the power of direction.

Diré́cto, ta, *a.* 1. Direct, in a straight line. 2. Clear, open, apparent, evident.

Directór, *sm.* 1. Director, one that has authority over others. 2. President, director, one who has the management of the concerns of a trading company. 3. Confessor, who guides the conscience of a person. [rect.

Directório, ria, *a.* Directive, able or fit to di-

Directório, *sm.* Directory; a book, containing the rules by which any business ought to be guided.

Dirigír, *va.* 1. To guide, to direct, to conduct. 2. To dedicate a work. 3. To govern, to give rules or laws for the management of any thing.

Dirimír, *va.* 1. To dissolve, to disjoin, to separate. 2. To adjust or accommodate differences. 3. To annul, to declare void.

Diruír, *va.* To ruin, to destroy.

Dis, *prep. neg.* From the Latin, and used in compound words in Spanish.

Disánto, *sm.* (Bax.) Sunday. V. *Domingo.*

Discantár, *va.* 1. To chant, to sing. 2. To compose or recite verses. 3. To descant, to discourse copiously. 4. To quaver upon a note.

Discánte, *sm.* 1. Treble. V. *Tiple.* 2. Concert, especially of stringed instruments. 3. A small guitar.

Disceptación, *sf.* Argument, controversy, dispute.

Disceptár, *va.* To dispute, to argue.

Discernidór, *sm.* He who discerns.

Discernimiénto, *sm.* 1. Discernment, judgment; the power of distinguishing. 2. Appointment of a guardian by the proper magistrates.

Discernír, *va.* 1. To discern, to distinguish, to comprehend. 2. To appoint a guardian.

Disciplína, *sf.* 1. Discipline, education, instruction. 2. Any art or science taught. 3. Rule of conduct, order. 4. Correction or punishment inflicted upon one's self. *Disciplinas*, Instrument for whipping, a cat of nine tails. 5. Flagellation.

Disciplináble, *a.* Disciplinable, capable of instruction.

Disciplinadaménte, *ad.* With discipline.

Disciplinádo, da, *a.* Marbled, variegated.

Disciplinánte, *pa.* Discipliner, flagellator.

Disciplinár, *va.* 1. To discipline, to educate, to instruct, to bring up. 2. To drill, to teach the manual exercise. 3. To chastise, to correct; to scourge one's self as penance.

Discipuládo, *sm.* 1. Number of scholars who frequent the same school. 2. Education, instruction.

Discípulo, la, *s.* Disciple, scholar.

Dísco, *sm.* 1. Disk, a round piece of iron thrown in the ancient sports; a quoit. 2. Face of the sun or moon, such as it appears to the eye. 3. Lens of a telescope. 4. (Bot.) The central part of flowers.

Díscolo, la, *a.* Unteachable, wayward, peevish.

Discolór, *a.* Variegated with different colours.

Disconfórme, *a.* V. *Desconforme.*

Discontinuár, *va.* V. *Descontinuar.*

Discontínuo, a, *a.* Discontinued, separated.

Discordáncia, *sf.* Disagreement, contrariety of opinion, opposition, diversity.

Discordár, *va.* To discord, to disagree, not to suit with.

Discórde, *a.* 1. Discordant, not conformable. 2. (Mús.) Dissonant.

Discórdia, *sf.* 1. Discord, disagreement. 2. Contrariety of opinion, opposition.

Discreción, *sf.* 1. Discretion, prudence, judgment. 2. Acuteness of mind, sharpness of wit, liveliness of fancy. 3. Liberty of acting at pleasure. *Jugar discreciones*, To play for presents, to be chosen or determined by the loser. *Á' discreción*, At the discretion or will of another.

Discrepáncia, *sf.* Discrepance, difference, contrariety.

Discrepánte, (Nemine,) *ad.* (Latin.) Unanimously.

Discrepár, *vn.* To differ, to disagree, not to be conformable.

Discretaménte, *ad.* Discreetly.

Discreteár, *vn.* To be discreet, to talk with discretion.

Discréto, ta, *a.* 1. Discreet, circumspect, prudent. 2. Ingenious, sharp, witty, eloquent. *Es mas delicado que discreto*, He is more nice than wise.

Discréto, *s.* A person elected assistant in the council of some provincial governments.

Discretório, *sm.* Meeting or council of the seniors of religious bodies.

Discrímen, *sm.* Hazard, risk, peril; difference.

Discúlpa y Disculpación, *sf.* 1. Apology, excuse. 2. (In Law) Plea.

Disculpáble, *a.* Excusable.

Disculpadaménte, *ad.* Excusably.

Disculpár, *va.* To exculpate, to excuse.

Discurrimiénto, *sm.* (Bax.) Discourse.

Discurrír, *vn.* 1. To gad, to ramble about without any settled purpose, to run to and fro. 2. To discourse upon a subject. 3. To discuss, to weigh the arguments and reasons which are for and against any thing. *Quien tal discurriera.* Who could imagine such a thing.—*va.* To invent, to discourse; to infer, to deduce.

Discursár, *vn.* To discourse. V. *Discurrir.*

Discursísta, *sm.* One who discusses or handles any subject

Discursívo, va, *a.* Discursive, discussive; reflective.

Discúrso, *sm.* 1. Ramble, irregular excursion. 2. Ratiocination, the act of deducing consequences from premises. 3. Discourse, speech. 4. Dissertation, treatise, tract. 5. Space of time.

Discusión, *sf.* Discussion, argument, dispute.

Discutír, *va.* To discuss, to investigate.

Disecación, *sf.* Dissection. V. *Diseccion.*

Disecadór, *sm.* Dissector, anatomist.

Disecar, *va.* To dissect, to cut in pieces; to separate the parts of animal bodies.

Disección, *sf.* Dissection, anatomy.

Disectór, *sm.* Anatomist, one who dissects.

Diseminár, *va.* To disseminate, to scatter as seed.

Disensión, *sf.* 1. Dissension, contrariety of opinion; contest, strife. 2. The cause or motive of dissension.

Disénso ó Disentimiénto, *sm.* Dissent, disagreement, difference of opinion.

Disentería, *sf.* Dysentery; a bloody flux.

Disentérico, ca, *a.* Belonging to the dysentery.

Disentír, *vn.* To dissent, to disagree or separate.

Diseñadór, *sm.* Designer, delineator.

Diseñár, *va.* To draw, to design.

Diséño, *sm.* 1. Design, sketch, draught, plan. 2. Delineation, description. 3. Picture, image. V. *Designio.*

Disertación, *sf.* Dissertation, discussion.

Disertadór, *sm.* Dissertator, he who discourses or debates on a subject.

Disertár, *va.* To dispute, to debate, to argue.

Disérto, ta, *a.* Eloquent.

Disfamación, *sf.* Defamation, slander, censure.

Disfamadór, *sm.* Defamer.

Disfamár, *va.* To defame, to slander.

Disfámia, *sf.* Defamation, disrepute.

Disfavór, *sm.* 1. Disregard, want of favour. 2. Discountenance, cold treatment.

Disformár, *va.* V. *Deformar.*

Disfórme, *a.* 1. Deform, ugly, horrid. 2. Huge, excessively big.

Disformidád, *sf.* Deformity, excessive bigness.

Disfráz, *sm.* 1. Mask, disguise. 2. (Met.) Dissimulation, the act of dissembling.

Disfrazár, *va.* 1. To disguise, to conceal, to make things appear different from what they are. 2. To cloak, to dissemble.

Disgregación, *sf.* Separation, the act of disjointing or disuniting.

Disgregár, *va.* 1. To separate, to disjoin. 2. To disperse the rays of light.

Disgregatívo, va, *a.* Disjunctive.

Disgustadaménte, *ad.* Disgustingly.

Disgustár, *va.* To disgust, to strike with dislike, to offend.—*vr.* To be displeased, to fall out, to be at variance with another.

Disgustíllo, *sm.* Displeasure, slight disgust.

Disgústo, *sm.* 1. Disgust, aversion of the palate from any thing. 2. Ill-humour, offence conceived. 3. Grief, sorrow. *Á' disgusto,* In spite of, contrary to one's will and pleasure.

Disgustóso, sa, *a.* Disgustful, disagreeable.

Disidénte, *a.* y *s.* Dissident, dissenter, schismatic.

Disílabo, *sm.* A word of two syllables.

Disímil, *a.* Dissimilar.

Disimilár, *a.* Unequal, dissimilar.

Disimilitúd, *sf.* Dissimilitude, want of resemblance.

Disimulación, *sf.* Dissimulation, the act of dissembling; simulation, hypocrisy.

Disimuladaménte, *ad.* Dissemblingly.

Disimuládo, da, *a.* Dissembled, feigned. *Á' lo disimulado,* Dissemblingly.

Disimuladór, ra, *s.* Dissembler.

Disimulár, *va.* 1. To dissemble, to conceal one's real intentions. 2. To cloak, to conceal artfully any bent of the mind. 3. To hide. 4. To tolerate, to allow so as not to hinder. 5. To colour, to misrepresent.

Disimúlo, *sm.* Dissimulation, simulation.

Disipáble, *a.* Easily dissipated.

Disipación, *sf.* 1. Dissipation, the act of spending one's fortune, licentiousness. 2. Separation of the parts which composed a whole. 3. Resolution of any thing into vapour.

Disipádo, da, *a.* Dissipated, devoted to pleasure.

Disipadór, ra, *s.* Spendthrift, a prodigal, a lavisher.

Disipár, *va.* 1. To dissipate, to disperse; to separate one thing from another. 2. To mis-spend, to lavish.

Disípula, *sf.* Erysipelas. V. *Erisipela.*

Disipulárse, *vr.* To be diseased with the erysipelas.

Disláte, *sm.* Nonsense, absurdity. V. *Disparate.*

Dislocación y Dislocadúra, *sf.* 1. Dislocation, the act of shifting or removing things. 2. Luxation, a joint put out.

Dislocárse, *vr.* To be dislocated or put out of joint.

Dismembración, *sf.* V. *Desmembracion.*

Disminución, *sf.* 1. Diminution. 2. Disease in horses' hoofs.

Disminuír, *va.* 1. To diminish, to lessen, to impair. 2. To detract from.

Disociación, *sf.* Disjunction, separation.

Disociár, *va.* To disjoin, to separate one thing from another.

Disolúble, *a.* Dissoluble, capable of separation of one part from another.

Disolución, *sf.* 1. Dissolution, the resolution of a body into its constituent elements. 2. Looseness of manners and morals.

Disolutaménte, *ad.* Dissolutely.

Disolutívo, va, *a.* Dissolvent.

Disolúto, ta, *a.* Dissolute, loose, licentious.

Disolvénte, *sm.* Dissolvent, dissolver.

Disolvér, *va.* 1. To loosen, to untie. 2. To dissolve, to separate, to disunite. 3. To melt, to liquefy. 4. To interrupt.

Disón, *sm.* Harsh dissonant tune.

Disonáncia, *sf.* 1. Dissonance, a mixture of harsh and inharmonious sounds. 2. Disagreement, discord. *Hacer disonancia á la razon,* To be contrary to reason.

Disonánte, *a.* 1. Dissonant, inharmonious; discrepant. 2. (Met.) Discordant, unsuitable.

Disonár, *vn.* 1. To disagree in sound, to be disharmonious. 2. To discord, to disagree. 3. To be contrary or repugnant.

Dísono, na, *a.* Dissonant, inconstant.

Dispár, *a.* Unlike, unequal, different.

Disparadaménte, *ad.* V. *Disparatadamente.*

Disparadór, *sm.* 1. One that discharges a gun. 2. Tumbler of a gun-lock. 3. Ratch or rash, in clock-work; a wheel which serves to lift up the detents every hour, and thereby makes the clock strike.

DISPARÁR, va. 1. To discharge a gun. 2. To cast or throw with violence.—vn. To talk nonsense.—vr. 1. To run headlong. 2. To stoop, to dart down on a prey; applied to a hawk or falcon.

DISPARATADAMÉNTE, ad. Absurdly.

DISPARATÁDO, DA, a. Inconsistent, absurd.

DISPARATÁR, va. To act or talk in an absurd and inconsistent manner.

DISPARÁTE, sm. Nonsense, absurdity.

DISPARATÓN, sm. A great piece of nonsense.

DISPARATÓRIO, sm. Speech or discourse full of nonsense.

DISPARCIALIDÁD, sf. Separation, disunion.

DISPARIDÁD, sf. Disparity, inequality, dissimilitude.

DISPÁRO, sm. 1. Discharge, explosion. 2. Nonsense, absurdity. *Quanto dice es disparo,* All he talks is nonsense.

DISPÉNDIO, sm. 1. Excessive or extravagant expense. 2. (Met.) Voluntary loss of life, honour, or fame.

DISPÉNSA, sf. Dispense, exemption, dispensation; diploma. V. *Expensas.*

DISPENSÁBLE, a. That may be dispensed with.

DISPENSACIÓN, sf. Dispensation, exemption.

DISPENSADÓR, RA, s. 1. One who grants a dispensation. 2. Dispenser, distributer.

DISPENSÁR, va. 1. To dispense, to exempt. 2. To deal out, to distribute.

DISPERSIÓN, sf. Dispersion, the act of scattering or spreading.

DISPÉRSO, SA, a. Dispersed, separated.

DISPERTADÓR, RA, s. V. *Despertador.*

DISPERTÁR, va. V. *Despertar.*

DISPLACÉR, va. V. *Desplacer.*

DISPLICÉNCIA, sf. Displeasure, discontent.

DISPLICÉNTE, a. Displeasing, fretful.

DISPONEDÓR, RA, s. One who disposes or arranges; distributer.

DISPONÉR, va. 1. To arrange, to place things in a due and proper order. 2. To dispose of, to give, to distribute. 3. To deliberate, to resolve, to direct, to command.—vn. To act freely, to dispose of property. *Disponer sus cosas,* To make a last will. *Disponer las velas al viento,* (Naút.) To trim the sails to the wind. *Disponer de bolina ciñendo el viento,* (Naút.) To trim the sails sharp or close to the wind.—vr. To prepare one's self.

DISPONÍBLE, a. Disposable; applied to property.

DISPOSICIÓN, sf. 1. Disposition, arrangement, or distribution of things. 2. Proportion, symmetry, fitness. 3. Resolution, order, command. 4. Power, authority. 5. Tendency, temper of mind. 6. (Naút.) Trim of a ship. 7. Elegance of person. 8. Despatch of business. *A' la disposicion,* At the disposal or will of another.

DISPOSITIVAMÉNTE, ad. Dispositively, distributively.

DISPOSITÍVO, VA, a. Dispositive, that which implies a disposal of any thing.

DISPOSITÍVA, sf. Disposition; expedition, fitness.

DISPUÉSTO, TA, a. 1. Comely, genteel, graceful. *Bien ó mal dispuesto,* Well or ill disposed.

DISPÚTA, sf. 1. Dispute, controversy, argument. 2. Contest, conflict; contention.

DISPUTÁBLE, a. Disputable, controvertible; that which can be defended or maintained.

DISPUTADÓR, sm. Disputant, disputer.

DISPUTÁR, va. 1. To dispute, to controvert. 2. To resist, to oppose with violence and force of arms. *Disputar sobre frioleras,* To pluck a crow with one. *Disputar el barlovento,* (Naút.) To dispute the weather-gage.—vn. To argue, to dispute.

DISPUTATIVAMÉNTE, ad. Disputingly.

DISQUISICIÓN, sf. Disquisition, examination, disputative inquiry.

DISTÁNCIA, sf. 1. Distance, interval; space of time or place. 2. Difference, disparity.

DISTÁNTE, a. 1. Distant, remote, far off. 2. (Naút.) Off, offward.

DISTANTEMÉNTE, ad. Distantly.

DISTÁR, vn. 1. To be distant or remote with regard to time or place. 2. To be different, to vary.

DISTERMINÁR, va. To divide a territory.

DÍSTICO, sm. Distich, couplet.

DISTILÁR, va. *Destilar.*

DISTINCIÓN, sf. 1. Difference, diversity, distinction. 2. Prerogative, privilege. 3. Honourable note of superiority. 4. Order, clarity, precision. *Persona de distincion,* A person of superior rank. *A' distincion,* In contradistinction, with the distinction.

DISTINGUÍBLE, a. Distinguishable.

DISTINGUÍDO, a. Distinguished; applied to a soldier of noble birth, but without fortune to subsist as a cadet, who is allowed a sword, and is exempted from mechanical labour.

DISTINGUÍR, va. 1. To distinguish, to note the difference of things. 2. To see clearly, and at a distance. 3. To discern, to discriminate. 4. To set a peculiar value on things or persons. 5. To clear up, to explain.—vr. To distinguish one's self, especially by warlike exploits.

DISTINTAMÉNTE, ad. Distinctly, diversely.

DISTINTÍVO, VA, a. Distinctive, that which makes distinction or difference.

DISTINTÍVO, sm. 1. A distinctive mark, such as the badge of a military order. 2. A particular attribute.

DISTÍNTO, TA, a. 1. Distinct, different; not the same; diverse. 2. Clear, unconfused; intelligible.

DISTÍNTO, sm. Instinct. V. *Instinto.*

DISTRACCIÓN, sf. 1. Distraction, want of attention; the state in which the attention is called different ways. 2. Licentiousness, boundless liberty as to the way of living; want of constraint.

DISTRÁCTO, sm. Dissolution of a contract.

DISTRAÉR, va. 1. To distract, to fill the mind with contrary considerations; to perplex. 2. To seduce from an honest and virtuous life.

DISTRAIDAMÉNTE, ad. Licentiously.

DISTRAÍDO, DA, a. Dissolute, licentious.

DISTRAIMIÉNTO, sm. 1. Distraction. V. *Distraccion.* 2. A licentious life.

DISTRIBUCIÓN, sf. 1. Distribution, the act of distributing or dealing out to others; division, separation. 2. Proper collocation, arrangement. *Tomar algo por distribúcion,* To do or perform any thing from habit or custom.

Distribuidór, *sm.* Distributer.

Distribuír, *va.* 1. To distribute, to divide among many, to deal out. 2. To dispose, to range. 3. (Impr.) To distribute types.

Distributívo, va, *a.* Distributive.

Distribuyénte, *pa.* Distributer.

Distríto, *sm.* 1. District, circuit of authority, province. 2. Region, country, territory.

Disturbár, *va.* To disturb, to interrupt.

Distúrbio, *sm.* Disturbance, interruption of tranquillity, violation of peace.

Disuadír, *va.* To dissuade, to dehort.

Disuasión, *sf.* Dissuasion, dehortation; the act of counselling to the contrary.

Disuasívo, va, *a.* Dissuasive, dehortative.

Disuría, *sf.* Dysury, a difficulty in making urine.

Disyuncion, *sf.* 1. Disjunction, separation. 2. (In Grammar) A disjunctive particle.

Disyústa, *sf.* (Mus.) Change or mutation of the voice.

Disyuntivaménte, *ad.* Disjunctively, separately.

Disyuntívo, va, *a.* Disjunctive.

Disyúnto, ta, *a.* Separated, disjoined, distant.

Díta, *sf.* Security, surety.

Ditirámbico, ca, *a.* Dithyrambical.

Dito, (Ant.) V. *Dicho.*

Diurético, ca, *a.* 1. Diuretic, having the power to provoke urine. 2. (Met.) Liberal, generous.

Diúrno, na, *a.* 1. Diurnal, relating to the day. 2. Performed in a day, daily.

Diúrno, *sm.* Prayer-book, among Roman Catholics, which contains the canonical hours, except matins.

Diuturnidád, *sf.* Diuturnity, length of duration.

Diutúrno, na, *a.* Being of a long duration.

Divagánte, *sm.* Vagrant, loiterer.

Divagár, *vn.* V. *Vagar.*

Diván, *sm.* Divan, the supreme council among the Turks.

Divergéncia, *sf.* The act or state of diverging or tending to various parts from one point.

Divergénte, *a.* Divergent.

Diversaménte, *ad.* Diversely, with diversity.

Diversidád, *sf.* 1. Diversity, dissimilitude, unlikeness. 2. Variety of things.

Diversificár, *va.* To diversify, to vary.

Diversión, *sf.* 1. Diversion, amusement. 2. Diversion, an attack made upon the enemy to withdraw his attention from the real attack.

Diversívo, va, *a.* Divertive; applied to medicines which draw off humours.

Divérso, sa, *a.* 1. Diverse, different, multiform. 2. Several, sundry.

Diversório, *sm.* Inn, a house of entertainment for travellers.

Divertído, da, *a.* Amused, divertive, diverted, festive. *Andar divertido,* To be engaged in love affairs.

Divertimiénto, *sm.* 1. Diversion, amusement. 2. Avocation, distraction, or alienation.

Divertír, *va.* 1. To divert the attention, to withdraw the mind. 2. To amuse, to entertain. 3. (In War) To draw the enemy off from some design, by threatening or attacking a distant part.

Dividéndo, *sm.* Dividend, a share; the part allotted in division.

Divididéro, ra, *a.* Divisible.

Dividír, *va.* 1. To divide, to disjoin, to disunite. 2. To distribute, to separate.—*vr.* To withdraw one's self from the company and friendship of any one.

Dividúo, dua, *a.* (For.) Divisible.

Diviéso, *sm.* A morbid swelling of the carbuncle kind.

Divinación, *sf.* Divination. V. *Adivinacion.*

Divinaménte, *ad.* Divinely, admirably.

Divinatório, ria, *a.* Belonging to the art of divination.

Divinidád, *sf.* 1. Divinity, participation of the nature and excellence of God; deity, godhead. 2. The Supreme Being. 3. False god. 4. Woman of exquisite beauty. *Decir ó hacer divinidades,* To say or do admirable things.

Divinizár, *va.* 1. To deify, to make a god of, to make divine. 2. (Met.) To sanctify.

Divíno, na, *a.* 1. Divine, partaking of the nature of God, proceeding from God. 2. Excellent in a supreme degree. *Es un ingenio divino,* He is a man of uncommon talents.

Divíno, na, *s.* V. *Adivino.*

Divísa, *sf.* 1. Inheritance, or part of the paternal inheritance. 2. Device, motto.

Divisár, *va.* 1. To descry at a distance, to perceive indistinctly. 2. To make a difference, to vary.

Diviséro, *sm.* Heir who is not of a noble extraction.

Divisibilidád, *sf.* Divisibility.

Divisíble, *a.* Divisible, that can be divided.

División, *sf.* 1. Division, partition, distribution. 2. Diversity of opinion. 3. Hyphen, a note of conjunction. 4. A rule in arithmetic.

Divisionál, *a.* Divisional, relating to division.

Divisívo, va, *a.* Divisible.

Divíso, sa, *a.* Divided.

Divisór, *sm.* 1. Number given, by which the dividend is divided. 2. Any thing which divides another.

Divisório, ria, *a.* Belonging to divisions.

Dívo, va, *a.* Divine, godlike.

Divorciár, *va.* 1. To divorce, to pronounce a sentence of divorce. 2. To separate, to part, to divide.—*vr.* To be divorced.

Divórcio, *sm.* 1. Divorce, the legal separation of husband and wife. 2. Separation, disunion. 3. Rupture among friends.

Divulgáble, *a.* That which may be divulged.

Divulgación, *sf.* Publication, the act of publishing or divulging.

Divulgadór, ra, *s.* Divulger.

Divulgár, *va.* To publish, to divulge.

Dix ó Díxe, *sm.* Relic; corals, fastened to the clothes of children. *Dixes,* Toys, trinkets.

Dixecíllo, to, *sm. dim.* Little trinket.

Do, *ad.* (Ant.) V. *Donde. Do quiera,* In whatever part.

Dóbla, *sf.* An ancient Spanish gold coin.

Dobladaménte, *ad.* 1. Doubly. 2. Deceitfully, artfully.

Dobladílla, *sf.* (Ant.) Ancient game. *A' la dobladilla,* Doubly, repeatedly.

Dobladíllo, lla, *a.* Squat and broad, short and thick.

Dobladíllo, *sm.* Hem, the edge of a garment doubled and sewed, to keep the threads from spreading.

Dobládo, *sm.* Measure of the fold in cloth.

Dobládo, da, *a.* 1. Strong, robust, thick set. 2. (Met.) Deceitful, dissembling. *Tierra doblada*, A broken, mountainous country.

Dobladúra, *sf.* 1. Fold, mark of a fold. 2. Led horse in battle. 3. Dish consisting of fried meat, bread, onions, nuts, &c. 4. Malicious fabrication.

Doblár, *va.* 1. To double, to enlarge any quantity by addition of the same quantity. 2. To double, to fold. 3. To contain twice the quantity. 4. To bend, to make crooked, to crook. 5. To toll or ring the passing bell. *Doblar la servilleta*, To kick the bucket, to die. *Doblar la rodilla*, To kneel. *Doblar un cabo ó promontorio*, (Naút.) To double or weather a cape.—*vn.* To swerve or deviate from justice or reason.—*vr.* 1. To be led away by the opinion of another. 2. To change or alter one's opinion.

Dóble, *a.* 1. Double, twice as much. 2. Thick and short. 3. Strong, robust. 4. Artful, deceitful. *Al doble*, Doubly.

Dóble, *sm.* 1. Fold, crease. V. *Doblez*. 2. Toll or knoll of the passing-bell. 3. Step in a Spanish dance.

Doblegáble, *a.* That which may be doubled or folded.

Doblegadízo, za, *a.* Fit to be doubled.

Doblegár, *va.* 1. To bend, to incurvate, to inflect. 2. To gain by persuasion, to reclaim.

Dobleménte, *ad.* Deceitfully, artfully.

Doblería, *sf.* Double-dealing, deceit.

Dobléro, *sm.* (Arag.) A small loaf of bread.

Dobléte, *a.* That which is between double and single.—*sm.* Factitious gem.

Dobléz, *sm.* 1. Crease, a mark made by doubling or folding any thing. 2. Dissimulation, double-dealing.

Dóblo, *sm.* Double, twice as much.

Doblón, *sm.* 1. Doublon or dobloon, a Spanish gold coin. *Doblon de oro*, Gold coin of the weight and value of two dollars. *Doblon de á quatro ó á ocho*, Pistole or dobloon of 4 or of 8 dollars. *Doblon sencillo*, Nominal money worth 60 reals. 2. *Doblon de vaca*, Tripes or paunch of a bullock or cow.

Doblonáda, *sf.* Heap or large quantity of dobloons or money.

Dóce, *sm.* Twelve, the number of ten and two. *Echarlo á doce*, To carry an affair off with a laugh.

Docéna, *sf.* 1. Dozen, the number of twelve things of the same kind or species. 2. (Navar.) Weight of twelve pounds.

Docenál, *a.* That which is sold by dozens.

Docenário, *sm.* (Arit.) Number consisting of 12 unities.

Docéno, na, *a.* Twelfth, the ordinal number of twelve.

Doceñál, *a.* That which consists of 12 years.

Dociéntos, *a.* V. *Doscientos*.

Dócil, *a.* 1. Docile, mild, tractable. 2. Ductile, pliable, malleable, easily wrought.

Docilidád, *sf.* Docility, aptness to be taught, readiness to learn.

Docilménte, *ad.* Tractably.

Doctaménte, *ad.* Learnedly.

Dócto, ta, *a.* Learned, versed in sciences and literature.

Doctór, ra, *s.* 1. Doctor, physician; divine. 2. Wife of a physician or doctor. 3. Vain, impertinent, assuming woman. 4. One who teaches any art or science.

Doctorál, *a.* Relating to a doctor; applied to canons.

Doctoramiénto, *sm.* The act of graduating as doctor.

Doctorándo, *sm.* One who is on the point of taking out his degrees as doctor.

Doctorár, *va.* To graduate, to dignify with the degrees of a doctor.

Doctorcíllo, *sm.* Quack, a petty physician.

Doctoreár, *vn.* To doctor, to play the doctor.

Doctorísmo, *sm.* (In the Jocular Style) The body of doctors.

Doctrína, *sf.* 1. Doctrine, instruction. 2. Discourse on the tenets of the Christian faith. 3. An Indian village consecrated to the Christian religion. 4. Science, wisdom; opinion. *Niños de la doctrina*, Charity children.

Doctrinadór, ra, *s.* Instructor, teacher.

Doctrinál, *sm.* Catechism, a book which contains an abridgment of the Christian doctrine.—*a.* Doctrinal, relating to doctrine.

Doctrinár, *va.* 1. To teach, to instruct. 2. To break in horses.

Doctrinéro, *sm.* 1. Teacher of the Christian doctrine. 2. Curate or parish priest in India.

Doctríno, *sm.* Orphan educated in a college.

Documénto, *sm.* 1. Instruction, advice to avoid evil. 2. Document; writing.

Dodránte, *sm.* 1. Drink or beverage, prepared from nine different ingredients, viz. herbs, water, juice, wine, salt, oil, bread, honey, and pepper. 2. Weight of nine ounces out of the twelve which made a pound among the Romans. 3. Measure of twelve inches.

Dogál, *sm.* Rope tied round the neck.

Dógma, *sm.* Dogma, established principle, settled notion.

Dogmático, ca, *a.* Dogmatical, or dogmatic, belonging to the dogmas.

Dogmatísta, *sm.* Dogmatist, a teacher of dogmas.

Dogmatizadór y Dogmatizánte, *sm.* Dogmatizer, dogmatist.

Dogmatizár, *va.* To dogmatize, to teach or assert dogmas.

Dógo, *sm.* Terrier; a kind of small dog.

Dóla, *contrac. ant.* of *De ella?* Where is she?

Doladéra, *a.* Applied to a cooper's adze.

Doladór, *sm.* Joiner, one who planes and polishes wood or stone.

Doláje, *sm.* The wine which the staves of pipes imbibe.

Dolamás y Dolamés, *s. pl.* Hidden vices and defects incident to horses.

Dolár, *va.* To plane or smooth wood or stone.

Doléncia, *sf.* 1. Disease, affliction. 2. (Met.) Danger; dishonour.

Dolér, *vn.* 1. To feel pain. 2. To be unwilling to act, to perform with repugnance.—*vr.* 1. To be in pain about any thing, to be sorry; to repent. 2. To feel for the sufferings of others; to lament.

Doliėnte, *a.* Suffering or labouring under a complaint or affliction.
Dolimán, *sm.* Kind of long robe worn by the Turks.
Dolióso, sa, *a.* Sorry, afflicted. V. *Dolorido.*
Dolista, *sm.* Sufferer; deceiver.
Dólo, *sm.* Fraud, deceit, imposition. *Poner dolo,* To judge ill of a person.
Dolór, *sm.* 1. Pain, sensation of uneasiness. 2. Affliction, anguish, grief. 3. Repentance, contrition. 4. Rage, envy. 5. Throes of childbirth. *Estar con dolores,* To be in labour.
Dolorído, da, *a.* Doleful, afflicted. V. *Doliente.*
Dolorído, *sm.* The chief mourner, the nearest relation of a person deceased; one in pain.
Dolorífico, ca, *a.* Causing pain or grief.
Dolorosaménte, *ad.* Painfully, miserably.
Doloróso y Dolorióso, sa, *a.* Sorrowful, afflicted, dolorous, dismal, doleful.
Dolosaménte, *ad.* Deceitfully.
Dolóso, sa, *a.* Deceitful, knavish.
Domáble, *a.* Tameable, susceptive of taming.
Domadór, ra, *s.* Tamer, one who tames.
Domadúra, *sf.* Act of taming or subduing.
Dománio, *sm.* Domain, a prince's private property.
Domár, *va.* 1. To tame, to reduce from wildness, to make gentle. 2. To subdue, to overcome.
Dómbo, *sm.* Dome, cupola.
Domeñár, *va.* To reclaim, to make tractable.
Domesticáble, *a.* Capable of being domesticated.
Domesticaménte, *ad.* Domestically.
Domesticár, *va.* To render gentle, to domesticate.
Domesticidád, *sf.* Domesticity, affability.
Doméstico, ca, *a.* 1. Belonging to the house, domestic. 2. Inhabiting the house, not wild.
Doméstico, *sm.* Servant who lives in the house.
Domestiquéz y Domestiquéza, *sf.* Meekness, tameness.
Domiciliádo, dá, *a.* Received as a denizen or citizen of a place; domiciliated.
Domiciliário, *sm.* Inhabitant, citizen.
Domiciliárse, *vr.* To establish one's self in a residence.
Domicílio, *sm.* Habitation, abode, domicile.
Dominación, *sf.* 1. Dominion, authority, power. 2. (Fort.) Commanding ground.
Dominadór, *sm.* Dominator.
Dominánte, *a.* Dominant, domineering, ascendant; prevailing, excelling.
Dominár, *va.* 1. To domineer, to rule with insolence, to act without control. 2. (Met.) To moderate one's passions, to correct one's evil habits.—*vr.* To rise above others; applied to hills.
Dómine, *sm.* Master or teacher of grammar.
Domíngo, *sm.* Sunday, the first day of the week. *Domingo de quasimodo,* Low Sunday, the next Sunday after Easter. *Domingo de ramos,* Palm Sunday.
Dominguéro, ra, *a.* Belonging to the Sabbath, done or worn on Sunday. *Sayo dominguero,* Sunday-clothes.
Dominguíllo, *sm.* Figure of a boy, made of straw, and used at bull-feasts to frighten the bulls.
Domínica, *sf.* Sunday, in ecclesiastical language.
Dominicál, *a.* Belonging to the Lord's day. *Oracion dominical,* Lord's prayer.
Dominicáno, na, y Domínico, ca, *a.* Belonging to the Dominican friars.
Dominicatúra, *sf.* (Ar.) Certain duty of vassalage paid to the lord of the manor.
Domínio, *sm.* Dominion, command.
Don, *sm.* 1. Don, a title formerly given to the nobility and gentry only, but now common to all classes of people in Spain. 2. Gift, present. 3. Dexterity, ability, gracefulness. 4. It is equivalent to *Mr.* in English, but used only before Christian names, as *Don Juan* or *Don Andrés Perez,* Mr. John or Mr. Andrew Perez. 5. *Don* alone, or with an adjective or epithet, is equivalent to *Señor. Dones sobrenaturales,* Supernatural gifts, as prophecy, &c.
Don de géntes, *sm.* National endowment, the characteristic of a nation.
Don de aciérto, *sm.* Gift of fortune, successful address.
Dóna, *sf.* Lady. V. *Dueña, Monja, y Don.* *Dónas,* Gratification given every year to miners, to work the iron mines in Spain.
Donación, *sf.* Donation, gift, grant.
Donadío, *sm.* 1. V. *Don.* 2. (And.) Property derived from royal donations.
Donádo, da, *s.* Lay-brother or lay-sister, who retires into a convent.
Donadór, ra, *s.* Donor, bestower.
Donár, *va.* To make free gifts, to bestow.
Donatário, *sm.* Donee, a person in whose favour a donation is made.
Donatísta, *a.* Donatist, follower of Donatus.
Donatívo, *sm.* Donative, a free contribution.
Donáyre, *sm.* 1. Grace, elegance. 2. Witty saying. *Hacer donayre de alguna cosa,* To make little of any thing.
Donayrosaménte, *ad.* Facetiously.
Donayróso, sa, *a.* 1. Pleasant. 2. Witty.
Dóncas, *ad.* (Ant.) V. *Pues.*
Doncél, *sm.* 1. An appellation formerly given to the king's pages. 2. A man who has not carnally known a woman. 3. (Mur.) Wormwood. 4. One who having been a royal page enters the army in a particular regiment. *Pino doncel,* Timber of young pines without knots. *Vino doncel,* Wine of a mild pleasant taste.
Doncélla, *sf.* 1. Maid, virgin. 2. Lady's maid, waiting maid. 3. *Doncella de Numidia,* (Orn.) The Numidian heron. Ardea virgo *L.* 4. (Ict.) Snake-fish. Ophidium *L.* 5. (Bot.) The humble plant. Mimosa pudica *L.*
Doncélla jamóna, *sf.* Long-legged old maid who affects learning and prudence; a sibyl.
Doncelléja, *sf.* Little maid.
Doncellería, *sf.* (Joc.) Maidenhead, virginity.
Doncelléz, *sf.* Virginity.
Doncellíca y Doncellíta, *sf.* A young maid.
Doncelliduéña, *sf.* An old maid who marries.
Doncellóna, *sf.* Old maid who affects to be learned and skilful; a sibyl.
Doncelluéca, *sf.* An old maid.
Doncelluéla, *sf.* A young maid.
Dónd, *ad.* (Ant.) V. *De donde.*
Dónde, *ad.* 1. V. *Adonde.* 2. Where, in what place? Whither, to what place? *¿De donde?* From what place? *Donde quiera,* Any where. *Donde no,* On the contrary. *¿Hácia donde?*

Towards what place? ¿ *Por donde?* By what way or road? by what reason or cause?

Dondiégo de noche, *sm.* (Bot.) Jalap; marvel of Peru. Mirabilis jalapa *L.*

Donecíllo, *sm.* A little don, a young master; a small present.

Donillêro, *sm.* Swindler, sharper; a tricking gambler.

Dónna, *sf.* V. *Doña.*

Donosaménte, *ad.* Gracefully, pleasingly.

Donosidád, *sf.* Gracefulness, wittiness, festivity.

Donosílla, *sf.* Piece of plaited muslin, which ladies wear around their necks.

Donóso, sa, *a.* Gay, witty, pleasant.

Donosúra, *sf.* Witty saying, pleasant jest.

Dóña, *sf.* 1. Lady, mistress; an appellation of honour prefixed to the names of ladies, as *Don* is to those of gentlemen. 2. (And.) V. *Dueña.*

Doñeár, *vn.* To pass the time or converse much with women.

Doñegál ó Doñigál, *a.* Applied to a kind of figs very red within.

Doquiér ó Doquiéra, *ad.* V. *Donde quiera.*

Doráda, Doràdo, ó Doradílla, *s.* (Ict.) Gilt-head, gilt-poll. Sparus auratus *L.*

Doradílla, *sf.* (Bot.) Common-spleen-wort. Asplenium *L.*

Doradíllo, *sm.* Fine brass wire.

Doràdo, da, *a.* Gilt. *Sopa dorada*, A high-coloured soup.

Doradór, *sm.* Gilder, one who gilds or lays gold on the surface of any other body.

Doradúra, *sf.* Gilding, gold laid on any surface by way of ornament.

Dorál, *sf.* (Orn.) Fly-catcher. Muscicapa *L.*

Dorár, *va.* 1. To gild, to lay gold on the surface of any thing. 2. (Met.) To palliate, to cover with an excuse. *Dorar á sisa*, To gild with a gold size of linseed oil and pounce. *Dorar á mate*, To lay on a coat of glue size.

Doreás, *sf.* A sort of muslin.

Doremál, *sm.* A sort of flowered muslin, which comes from the East Indies.

Dórico, ca, *a.* Doric.

Dormída, *sf.* Repose, rest, sleep; place where animals repose.

Dormidéras, *sf. pl.* Sleepiness, drowsiness, disposition to sleep.

Dormidéro, ra, *a.* Sleepy, drowsy, disposed to sleep.—*sm.* Place where cattle repose.

Dormidór, *sm.* A great sleeper.

Dormidós, *sm. pl.* (Naút.) Clamps, or thick planks, nailed to the inner range of a ship's side, from the stem to the fashion-pieces of the stern. V. *Durmientes.*

Dormidúra, *sf.* Sleep, the act of sleeping.

Dormiéntes, *sm. pl.* V. *Durmientes.*

Dormilón, na, *s.* A dull sleepy person, one who sleeps much.

Dormír, *vr.* 1. To sleep, to take rest by suspension of the mental powers. *A' duerme y vela*, Between sleeping and waking. 2. To be inattentive, to neglect one's business. 3. (Naút.) To clamp a vessel. *Dormir en Dios, ó en el Señor*, To die; applied to the just. *Dormir como una piedra*, To sleep like a top. *Dormir la siesta*, To take a nap after dinner. *Dormir á cortinas verdes*, To sleep in the open field. *Dormir á pierna suelta ó tendida, ó á sueño suelto*, (Fam.) To sleep carelessly with the legs extended.—*vr.* To be overcome by sleep.

Dormírlas, *sf. pl.* Play, among boys, like hide and seek.

Dormitár, *vn.* To doze, to be half asleep.

Dormitívo, *sm.* A soporiferous potion to induce sleep.

Dormitório, *sm.* 1. (In Convents) Gallery or corridor where the cells of the monks or nuns are. 2. Dormitory, a place to sleep in.

Dornájo, *sm.* Trough, a hollow wooden vessel

Dornás, *sf. pl.* (Gal.) Small fishing boats on the coast of Galicia.

Dorníllo, *sm.* V. *Dornajo y Ortera.*

Dorsál, *a.* Dorsal, belonging to the back.

Dórso, *sm.* The back part of any thing.

Dos, *sm.* 1. Two, a numeral number which follows one. 2. (Ant.) Coin, an *ochavo* or two *maravedis*. *A' dos manos*, With both hands, with open arms. *Dos á dos*, Two by two. *A' dos por tres*, Without fear, audaciously.

Dosañál, *a.* Biennial, relating to or continuing 2 years.

Dosciéntos, tas, *a. pl.* Two hundred.

Dosél, *sm.* Canopy, a covering spread over the head.

Doseléra, *sf.* Valance, the fringes or drapery hanging round a canopy.

Dósis, *sf.* Dose, a quantity of medicine to be taken at once.

Dotación, *sf.* 1. Foundation, a revenue settled and established for any purpose. 2. Dotation, the act of giving a dowry. *Dotacion de navios*, (Naút.) Fund appropriated to the repairing of ships. 3. Munition and garrison of a fortress.

Dotadór, ra, *s.* One who portions or endows; donor, instituter.

Dotál, *a.* Relating to a portion or dowry.

Dotár, *va.* 1. To portion, to endow with a fortune. 2. To endow with powers or talents.

Dóte, *sm.* 1. Portion given with a wife. 2. Stock of counters to play with.—*pl.* 1. The choicest gifts of the blessed. 2. Gifts, blessings, talents received from nature.

Dotór, *sm.* Doctor, physician. V. *Doctor.*

Dotrína, *sf.* V. *Doctrina.*

Dovéla, *sf.* The curved sides of the key-stone of an arch; key-stone.

Doveláge, *sm.* Series of curved stones for an arch.

Dovelár, *va.* To hew a stone in curves for an arch or a key-stone.

Doy, *ad.* (Ant.) V. *De Hoy.*

Dozabádo, da, *a.* Twelve sided.

Dozávo, va, *s.* The twelfth part.

Drába, *sf.* (Bot.) Whitlow. Draba *L.*

Drácma, *sf.* 1. Drachm, the eighth part of an ounce. 2. Greek silver coin.

Dracúnculo, *sm.* (Ento.) Dracunculus, long worm which breeds between the skin and flesh, guinea worm.

Dragánte, *sm.* 1. (Bot.) Goat's thorn. Astragalus tragacantha *L.* 2. Tragacanth, a sort of gum obtained from the goat's thorn. 3. (Naút.) Pillow of the bowsprit.

Drágo, *sm.* (Bot.) Dragon-tree. Pterocarpus draco *L.*

Dragón, *sm* 1. An old serpent; a fabulous monster. 2. *Dragon marino*, (Ict.) Sea-dragon, weather-fish. Trachinus draco L. *Dragónes*, (Mil.) Dragoons, a kind of horse soldiers who serve occasionally on foot. 3. White spot in the pupils of horses' eyes. 4. Kind of exhalation or vapour.

Dragóna, *sf.* 1. Beat of the drum peculiar to dragoons. 2. Shoulder-knot worn by military officers by way of distinction. 3. Female dragon.

Dragoncíllo, *sm.* Kind of ancient gun.

Dragonear, *vn.* (Mil.) To dragoon, to harass with soldiers.

Dragontía ó Dragontía, *sf.* (Bot.) Common dragon. Arum dracunculus *L.*

Dragontíno, na, *a.* Belonging to a dragon.

Dráma, *sm.* Drama, a poem in which the action is not related but represented.

Dramático, ca, *a.* Dramatical.

Dreíto, *sm.* V. *Derecho.*

Dríada ó Dríade, *sf.* Dryad, wood nymph.

Dríno, *sm.* Kind of venomous serpent.

Drízas, *sf. pl.* (Naút.) Haliards, ropes on board of ships, which serve to hoist up the yards.

Drizár, *va.* (Naút.) To hoist or haul up the yards.

Dróga, *sf.* 1. Drug, a general name for all sorts of ingredients used in physic. 2. (Met.) Stratagem, artifice, deceit.

Droguería, *sf.* A druggist's shop; trade in drugs.

Droguéro, *sm.* Druggist, one who deals in drugs.

Droguéte, *sm.* Drugget, a fine and light kind of woollen stuff.

Droguísta, *sm.* Cheat, impostor. V. *Droguéro.*

Dromedário y Dromedário, *sm.* 1. Dromedary, a sort of camel. 2. (Met.) A big unwieldy horse or mule.

Dropacísmo, *sm.* Ointment for taking off hairs.

Drópe, *sm.* (Fam.) Vile, despicable man.

Druída, *sm.* Druid.

Dúa, *sf.* (Mil.) Kind of personal service.

Duál, *a.* (Gram.) Dual, belonging to two. *Duales*, Incisors. V. *Cortadores.*

Duán, *sm.* V. *Divan.*

Dúba, *sf.* Wall or enclosure of earth.

Dubdánza, *sf.* 1. V. *Duda.* 2. Fear, diffidence.

Dubiedád, *sf.* Doubt, the thing that is doubtful.

Dúbio, *sm.* (For.) V. *Dubiedad.*

Dubitáble, *a.* Doubtful, that may be doubted.

Dubitación, *sf.* Dubitation.

Dubitatívo, va, *a.* (Gram.) Doubtful; applied to conjunctions.

Duc, *sm.* V. *Duque.*

Ducádo, *sm.* 1. Duchy, the possessions or estates of a duke. 2. Ducat, an ancient gold and silver coin.

Ducál, *a.* Ducal, pertaining to a duke.

Ducatón, *sm.* An ancient gold coin, which was worth twenty reals vellon.

Dúcha, *sf.* 1. List, a strip of cloth. 2. Straight piece of land reaped by a reaper.

Dúcho, cha, *a.* Dextrous, accustomed.

Ducientos, tas, *a.* Two hundred, twice one hundred. V. *Doscientos.*

Ducír, *sm.* (Ar.) V. *Espitar.*

Ducir, *va.* To guide, to lead, to conduct.

Dúctil, *a.* Ductile; applied to metals which are pliable or malleable.

Ductilidád, *sf.* Ductility.

Ductór, *sm.* 1. Guide. 2. Instrument with which surgeons examine into the depth of wounds.

Ductríz, *sf.* Conductress.

Dúda, *sf.* Doubt, uncertainty, ambiguity; question. *Sin duda*, Doubtless.

Dudáble, *a.* Dubious, doubtful.

Dudánza, *sf.* V. *Dubitacion.*

Dudár, *va.* To doubt, to hesitate.

Dudosamente, *ad.* Doubtfully, dubiously.

Dudóso, sa, *a.* Doubtful, dubious, uncertain.

Duéla, *sf.* 1. Stave, one of the pieces of which casks and barrels are made. 2. Kind of coin of 2 reals and 22 1/2 maravedis.

Duelaje, *sm.* V. *Dolaje.*

Duelísta, *sm.* Duellist, a single combatant; one who professes to live by rules of honour.

Duélo, *sm.* 1. Duel, single combat. 2. Sorrow, pain, grief, affliction. 3. Mourning, funeral. *Duélos*, Troubles, vexations, afflictions. *Sin duelo*, Abundantly.

Duéna, *sf.* (Ant.) Gift, present.

Duénde, *sm.* Elf, fairy, hobgoblin, wizard, phantom. *Tener duende*, To be hypochondriac. *Moneda de duendes*, Small copper coin.

Duendecíllo, *sm.* A little fairy.

Duéndo, da, *a.* Domestic, tame; applied to doves.

Duéña, *sf.* 1. Maiden lady, an unmarried woman. 2. A single woman who has lost her virginity. *Dueñas*, Widows, who, in the royal palace, attend on the maids of honour.

Dueñáza, *sf.* An old widow.

Dueñísima, *sf.* (In the Jocular Style) An old haughty *Dueña.*

Duéño, *sm.* Owner, master, lord.

Duérno, *sm.* Double sheet; two sheets of printed paper, one within another.

Dúla, *sf.* 1. Herd of black cattle belonging to different persons. 2. Horses and mules which graze on the same pasture. *Vete á la dula*, Be gone, get out of my sight.

Dúlce, *a.* 1. Sweet, pleasing to the taste. 2. Tasteless, without flavour. 3. Pleasant, agreeable. 4. Soft, ductile.—*sm.* 1. Confiture, sweetmeat; candied or dried fruits. 2. V. *Dulzura.*

Dulcedúmbre, *sf.* Sweetness. V. *Dulzura.*

Dulcémele, *sm.* Dulcimer, musical instrument.

Dulcemente, *ad.* Sweetly, delightfully.

Dulcificación, *sf.* Dulcification, act of sweetening.

Dulcificánte, *pa.* Dulcifying; sweetener.

Dulcificár, *va.* To sweeten, to render sweet.

Dulcisóno, na, *a.* Sweet-toned.

Dulcír, *va.* To grind plate-glass, to remove the inequalities of the surface, to polish.

Duléro, *sm.* (Arag.) Herd, who takes care of cattle.

Dulía, *sf.* Reverence or worship of the saints.

Dulimán, *sm.* Long robe worn by the Turks.

Dulcamára, *sf.* (Bot.) Woody night-shade, bitter-sweet. Solanum dulcamara *L.*

Dulzáyna, *sf.* 1. A musical wind instrument, resembling a trumpet. 2. (Fam.) Quantity of sweetmeats.

Dulzázo, za, *a.* Nauseously sweet.

Dulzorár, *va.* To sweeten.

Dulzúra y Dulzór, *s.* 1. Sweetness, the quality of being sweet or pleasing to the taste. 2. A grateful and pleasing manner of speaking or writing.

Dulzurár, *va.* 1. To dulcify, to free from acidity. 2. To soften, to mitigate.

Dúnas, *sf. pl.* Downs, banks of sand which the

sea forms on the coasts of England and Flanders.

DUNÉTA, *sf.* (Naút.) The highest part of the poop.

DUNGÁRRAS, *sf.* A sort of white cotton stuff which comes from Persia.

DÚO, *sm.* Duo, a musical composition sung by two persons.

DUODÉCIMO, MA, *a.* Twelfth, the ordinal of twelve.

DUODÉCUPLO, PLA, *a.* Twelve times doubled, or 12 to 1.

DUODÉNO, NA, *a.* Twelfth.

DUOMESÍNO, NA, *a.* Relating to 2 months.

DUÓS, AS, *a.* (Ant.) V. *Dos.*

DÚPLA, *sf.* A double portion or allowance.

DUPLICACIÓN, *sf.* Duplication, the act of enlarging any quantity by addition of the same quantity; the act of multiplying by two.

DUPLICADAMÉNTE, *ad.* Doubly.

DUPLICÁDO, *sm.* Duplicate, a second thing of the same kind, as a transcript of a paper.

DUPLICÁR, *va.* 1. To double, to duplicate. 2. To repeat, to do or say the same thing twice.

DUPLICATÚRA, *sf.* V. *Dobladura.*

DÚPLICE, *a.* Double; applied to ancient monasteries with cells for both friars and nuns.

DUPLICIDÁD, *sf.* DUPLICITY, deceit, doubleness of heart.

DÚPLO, *sm.* Double; twice as much; duple.

DÚQUE, *sm.* 1. Duke, one of the highest order of nobility. 2. Fold made by Spanish women in the veils they wear.

DUQUECÍTO, *sm.* A petty duke.

DUQUÉSA, *sf.* 1. Duchess, the lady of a duke. 2. Species of couch.

DÚRA, *sf.* Duration, continuance.

DURÁBLE, *a.* Durable, that which lasts.

DURACIÓN Y DURÁDA, *sf.* Duration, continuance.

DURADERAMÉNTE, *ad.* Durably.

DURADÉRO, RA, *a.* Lasting, durable.

DURADÓR, RA, *a.* Durable, lasting.

DURAMÁTER, *sf.* (Ant.) Dura mater, membrane enclosing the brain.

DURAMÉNTE, *ad.* Hardly; rigorously.

DURÁNDO, *sm.* Kind of cloth formerly used Spain.

DURÁNTE, *prep.* During.

DURÁR, *vn.* To last, to continue.

DURAZNÍTO, *sm.* A small peach.

DURÁZNO Y DURAZNÉRO, *sm.* 1. (Bot.) Peac tree. Amygdalus persica *L.* 2. Peach, t fruit of a peach-tree.

DURÉZA, *sf.* 1. Hardness, durity, firmness. Steadiness, perseverance, obstinacy. 3. D resse, imprisonment, constraint. 4. Want softness or delicacy in paintings. 5. Tumo or callosity. *Dureza de vientre,* Costivene

DURIÁGRA, *sf.* A sort of cotton striped stu white and blue.

DURÍLLO, LLA, *a.* Rather hard, hardish. *Durillo levante,* Bombast, fustian.—*sm.* (Bot.) Priv

DURINDÁNA Ó DURINDÁYNA, *sf.* (Joc.) A swor

DURMIÉNTE, *sm.* 1. Cruet-stand; piece of wo which rests on another. 2. Sleeper, sleepin

DURMÉNTES Y DURMIÉNTES, *sm. pl.* (Naú Clamps, very thick planks nailed to the i ner range of a ship's side, from the stem the fashion pieces of the stern. *Sota-durm entes,* Thick stuff.

DÚRO, RA, *a.* 1. Hard, solid, firm. 2. Har hearted, unmerciful. 3. Stubborn, obstinat 4. Miserable, avaricious. 5. Rude, ill-nature 6. (Naút.) Carrying a stiff sail; spoken of ship. 7. (Pint.) Harsh and rough, opposit to delicate and soft. *A' duro,* With difficult *A' duras penas,* With difficulty and labour

DÚRO, *sm.* Dollar, a silver coin containing 1 silver reals, or 20 reals vellon. *Pesos duro* Hard dollars, in contradistinction to dolla of exchange.

DURS Ó DUTIDUNGAPÓRTS, *sm.* A kind of co ton stuff.

DUTRÓA, *sf.* (Bot.) Thorn-apple. Datura str monium *L.*

DUUNVIRÁTO, *sm.* Duumvirate.

DUX, *sm.* 1. Duke. 2. Doge, formerly the chie magistrate of Venice and Genoa.

E is called by the Spanish Academy (which considers *ch* as one character) the 6th letter of the alphabet. *E* was formerly used as a copulative conjunction corresponding to *and.* It is now in general replaced by *y,* yet retained when it precedes a word which begins with the vowel *i;* as, *Luis é Ignacio.*

EA, A kind of aspiration used to awaken attention.

EA PUÉS, *interj.* of inference or inquiry, equal to, Well then! Let us see. *Ea Sus,* (Ant.) An aspiration of excitement of the same import.

EAL, *sm.* An amphibious animal of India.

EBANIFICÁR, *va.* To give the colour of ebony; to polish like ebony.

EBANÍSTA, *sm.* Cabinet-maker.

EBANISTERÍA, *sf.* Cabinet-work, shop of a cabinet-maker.

E'BANO, *sm.* Ebony, a hard black valuable wood.

EBRIEDÁD, *sf.* Ebriety. V. *Embriaguez.*

E'BRIO, BRIA, *a.* Inebriated, intoxicated with liquor.

EBRIÓSO, SA, *a.* Intoxicated, drunken.

EBULLICIÓN Ó EBULICIÓN, *sf.* Ebullition, the act of boiling up with heat.

EBÚRNEO, NEA, *a.* (Poét.) Made of ivory, resembling ivory.

EBÚRNO, *sm.* Ivory.

ECCEHÓMO, *sm.* Image of Jesus Christ, as Pilate presented him to the people.

ECETUÁR, *va.* *Exceptuar.*

ECHA, *sf.* Time, turn. V. *Vez.* *De esta echa,* This time.

ECHACÁNTOS, *sm.* (Vulg.) A contemptible rattle-brained fellow.

ECHACORVEÁR, *vn.* To pimp, to procure.

ECHACORVERÍA, *sf.* Act and profession of a pimp or procurer.

ECHACUÉRVOS, *sm.* 1. Pimp, procurer. V. *Alcahuete.* 2. Cheat, impostor; preacher.

ECHÁDA, *sf.* 1. Cast, throw. 2. The act of throwing one's self down on the ground.

Echadéro, sm. Place for resting or reposing.
Echadíllo, sm. Infant exposed.
Echadízo, za, a. 1. Suborned to pry into other people's actions. 2. Supposititious, fictitious. 3. Exposed, as an infant. 4. Versatile, artful.
Echadór, ra, s. One who casts, throws, or darts.
Echadúra, sf. 1. The act of laying one's self down in any place. 2. Squat, the act of cowering, or of lying or sitting close to the ground.
Echamiénto, sm. Projection, elimination; ejection; exposing a child at the church-door.
Echár, va. 1. To cast, to throw, to dart. 2. To turn or drive away. 3. To shoot, to bud. 4. To put, to apply. 5. To lay on or impose as a tax. 6. To raise money at interest. 7. To babble, to prattle. 8. To impute, to ascribe. 9. To incline, to recline. 10. To perform for a wager. 11. To deal out, to distribute. 12. To publish, to give out, to issue. *Echar bando*, To publish a law or edict. 13. To propose. 14. To take a road. *Echar á galeras*, To sentence to the galleys. *Echar á borbotones*, To talk much and at random. *Echar á fondo ó á pique*, (Naút.) To sink a vessel. *Echar agua*, To half-baptize a child. *Echar agua á un niño*, To baptize a child. *Echar á la ó en la piedra*, To throw one's children into the workhouse. *Echar á trompa y talega*, To talk nonsense. *Echar cantos*, To be mad or furious. *Echar carillos*, To grow plump and fat in the cheeks. *Echar coche*, To set up a coach. *Echar de manga*, To make a cat's paw of one. *Echar el compas*, To beat time. *Echar el sello*, To give the finishing stroke. *Echar en sacoroto*, To disregard, to slight, not to mind. *Echar el bofe ó los bofes*, To labour excessively; to solicit anxiously. *Echar la plática*, To cut short the conversation. *Echar las tizeras*, To cut up with scissors. *Echar menos una cosa*, To miss a thing. *Echar piernas*, To strut about. *Echar tierra á alguna cosa*, To bury an affair in oblivion. *Echar al mundo*, To create, to bring forth. *Echar mano*, To give assistance. *Echar un temiendo á la vida*, To take some little refreshment. *Echar el ancla*, (Naút.) To cast anchor. *Echar la corredera*, (Naút.) To heave the log. *Echar en escandallo*, (Naút.) To heave the lead, to take soundings. *Echar en tierra*, (Naút.) To land, to disembark. *Echar raices*, To take root; (Met.) To become fixed or established in a place; to be rooted or confirmed in any passion or thing by inveterate habit or custom.—vr. 1. To lie down on one's bed. 2. To apply one's self to a business. 3. To yield, to desist. *Echarse sobre áncora*, (Naút.) To drag the anchor. *Echarse á pechos*, To gulp or drink immoderately. [board; throwing away.
Echazón, sf. (Ant.) Act of throwing over-
Eclesiástico, sm. Clergyman.—a. Ecclesias-
Eclesiastizár, va. V. Espiritualizar. [tical.
Eclipsáble, a. That may be eclipsed. [ry.
Eclipsár, va. To eclipse, to darken a lumina-
Eclípse, sm. Eclipse, an obscuration of the luminaries of heaven.
Eclípsis, sf. Ellipsis, a figure of rhetoric.
Eclíptica, sf. Ecliptic, a circle supposed to run obliquely through the equator, and making an angle with the equinoctial of 23 degrees and a half. [Egloga.
Ecloga, sf. Eclogue, a pastoral poem. V.
E'co, sm. 1. Echo, the return or repercussion of sound; repetition of the last syllables of verse. 2. A confused remembrance or idea of the past. 3. Hole or hollow in a horse's sole, occasioned by a frush or other humour. *Hacer eco*, To accord, to agree; to do any thing great or notable.
Economía, sf. 1. Economy, prudent management and frugality of expense. 2. (Pint.) Disposition.
Economicaménte, ad. Economically.
Económico, ca, a. 1. Economical, pertaining to the management of a household. 2. Near, avaricious.
Economísta, sm. Economist, professor of rural economy or husbandry in general.
Ecónomo, sm. Curator or guardian, appointed to manage the estates of lunatics or prodigals.
Ecóyco, ca, a. (Poét.) Relating to echoes.
Ectípo, sm. Ectype, copy or model of an ancient medal or inscription.
Ecuménico, ca, a. Œcumenical, universal.
Edád, sf. 1. Age, the duration of a man's life. 2. The space of an hundred years. 3. Any period of time, attributed to something as the whole or part of its duration. *Media ó baxa edad*, Middle or lower ages. *Estar en edad*, Not to have completed the 7th year; applied to animals which cast all their teeth in that time, when their age cannot be known.
Edecán, sm. (Mil.) Aide-de-camp, an officer who attends on a general to convey orders.
Edéma, sf. A white, soft, and insensible tumour.
Edematóso, sa, a. Oedematous.
Edetáno, na, a. Native of *Edetanus*, now Valencia. [or writing.
Edición, sf. Edition, the publication of a book
Edícto, sm. Edict, a proclamation of command or prohibition.
Edificación, sf. 1. Construction, the art of raising any building. 2. Edification, improvement in holiness.
Edificadór, ra, s. One who edifies, constructs, or directs.
Edificánte, a. Edifying; erecting.
Edificár, va. 1. To construct a building. 2. To edify, to instruct, to give a good example.
Edificatívo, va, a. Exemplary, instructive.
Edificatório, ria, a. Relating to edification.
Edifício, sm. Edifice, building, structure.
Edil, sm. Edile, a Roman magistrate.
Edilidád, sf. Evileship.
Editór, sm. Editor, a person engaged in publishing the works of other authors.
Edredón, sm. Eider-down, the feathers of certain birds in Norway, used for filling featherbeds, pillows, and bolsters.
Educación, sf. Education, instruction.
Educadór, ra, s. Instructor.
Educánda, sf. Young person that enters a college or convent to be educated.
Educándo, da, s. y a. Educating, instructing.
Educár, va. To educate, to instruct.
Educción, sf. Eduction, the act of drawing forth or bringing into view.

Educír, va. To educe, to extract.
Efe, sf. Spanish name of the letter *F*.
Efectivaménte, ad. Effectually, powerfully.
Efectívo, va, a. Effective, true, certain.
Efécto, sm. 1. Effect, that which is produced by any operating cause. 2. Purpose, meaning; quality, value.—*pl.* 1. Assets, goods sufficient to discharge the burthen which is cast upon the executor or heir. 2. Goods, moveables. *En efecto*, In fact, in truth, actually.
Efectuál, a. Effectual, real, effective.
Efectualménte, ad. Effectively, effectually.
Efectuár, va. To effectuate, to bring to pass.
Efectuosaménte, ad. Effectually.
Efeméridez, sf. pl. Ephemeris, a journal; an account of daily transactions.
Efeméro, sm. 1. A thing which begins and ends in one day. 2. (Bot.) Iris. Iris sylvestris *L.*
Efeminár, va. To effeminate, to render womanish, to unman. V. *Afeminar*.
Efervescéncia, sf. 1. Effervescence, ebullition. 2. (Met.) Ardour, fervour.
E'feta, ad. Word used to signify the pertinacity with which one maintains a position.
Eficácia, sf. Efficacy, activity, power to act.
Eficáz, a. Efficacious, active, powerful.
Eficazménte, ad. Efficaciously.
Eficiéncia, sf. Efficience or efficiency, the power of producing effects.
Eficiénte, a. Efficient.
Eficienteménte, ad. Efficiently.
Efígie, sf. Effigy, image.
Efímera, sf. 1. Ephemera, a fever that terminates in one day. 2. Any thing of a short duration. 3. An insect that lives but one day.
Efímero, ra, y Efimerál, a. Ephemeral.
Eflorescéncia, sf. Efflorescence, the quality of becoming pulverulent when exposed to the air, by losing the water of crystallization.
Efluéncia, sf. Effluence, effluvium, emanation.
Efluénte, a. Effluent, emanant.
Eflúvio, sm. Effluvium, or effluvia, those small particles which are continually exhaled from all physical bodies.
Efluxíon y Eflúxo, s. Exhalation, evaporation.
Efúgio, sm. Subterfuge, evasion.
Efulgéncia, sf. Effulgence, brightness, lustre.
Efundír, va. To effuse, to pour out, to spill.
Efusión, sf. 1. Effusion, the act of pouring out. 2. Confidential disclosure of sentiments.
Efúso, sa, a. Effused.
Egéno, na, a. (Ant.) Poor, miserable.
Egestád, sf. Necessity, poverty, indigence.
Egestión, sf. Egestion.
Egílope, sf. (Bot.) Wild bastard oat. Ægilops *L.*
Egipcíaco, Egipciáno y Egípcio, a. Egyptian.
Egíra, sf. Hegira, the epocha or account of time used by the Mohammedans.
Eglóga, sf. Eclogue, a pastoral dialogue in verse.
Egoísmo, sm. Egotism, too frequent mention of one's self.
Egoísta, sm. Egotist, one who talks too frequently of himself.
Egregiaménte, ad Illustriously, egregiously.
Egrégio, gia, a. Egregious, eminent, remarkable.
Egresión, sf. Egression, the act of going out.
Egrisadór, sm. A box in which lapidaries preserve the diamond powder for grinding diamonds.
Egrisár, va. To grind and polish diamonds.
Egual, a. V. *Igual. Por egual.* V. *Al igual.*
Egualár, va. V. *Igualar.*
El, An article of the masculine gender.
El, Ella, Ello, pron. He, she, it. *El,* He, is used as a term expressive of displeasure or contempt.
Ela, ad. demon. There she is, behold her there.
Elaboración, sf. Elaboration.
Elaborádo, da, a. Elaborate, finished with labour and care.
Elaborár, va. To elaborate, to finish with care.
Elación, sf. 1. Elation, haughtiness, pride. 2. Magnanimity, generosity. 3. Elevation, sublimity; applied to style and language.
Elamí, sf. The sixth ascending note in the scale of music.
Elasticidád, sf. Elasticity, force in bodies by which they endeavour to restore themselves.
Elástico, ca, a. Elastic, elastical.
Elatério, sm. Elaterium, the inspissated juice of wild cucumbers; a strong and violent purge.
Elatíne, sf. (Bot.) Smooth speedwell. Veronica serpyllifolia *L.*
Eláto, ta, a. Presumptuous, haughty, proud.
Elche, sm. Apostate, renegado.
Ele, ad. demon. See this. V. *Etele.*
Ele, sf. Spanish name of the letter *L.*
Eleborína, sf. (Bot.) Helleborine. Serapias *L.*
Eléboro y Elebór, sm. (Bot.) Hellebore. Helleborus *L.*
Elección, sf. 1. Election, the act of choosing one or more from a greater number. 2. Voluntary preference, liberty of action. 3. The determination of God, by which any were selected for eternal bliss. 4. Choice, discernment.
Electívo, va, a. Elective, exerting the power of choice.
Elécto, ta, a. Elect, chosen.
Elécto, sm. Elect, a person nominated and chosen for some dignity.
Electór, sm. Elector, he who has a voice or vote in the election of an officer.
Electorádo, sm. Electorate, the territory and dignity of an elector of the German empire.
Electorál, a. Electoral.
Electricidád, sf. Electricity, a property in bodies whereby they attract or repel others.
Eléctrico, ca, a. Electric or electrical.
Electríz, sf. Electress, the elector's consort.
Electrizár, va. To electrify, to render or make electric, to communicate or impart electricity.
Eléctro, sm. 1. Electre or amber, which having the quality, when warmed by friction, of attracting bodies, gave to one species of attraction the name of electricity. 2. A mixed metal of four parts gold and one of silver, of much value among the ancients.
Electrómetro, sm. Electrometer, instrument to measure electricity.
Electuário, sm. Electuary, a kind of medicinal conserve in the consistence of honey.
Elefáncia, sf. Elephantiasis, a species of leprosy; so called from incrustations like those on the hide of an elephant.
Elefánte, ta, s. Elephant, the largest and most sagacious of quadrupeds.
Elefantíno, na, a. Elephantine

Elegáncia, *sf.* Elegance, or elegancy; beauty of art; beauty without grandeur. [beauties.

Elegánte, *a.* Elegant, pleasing with minute

Eleganteménte, *ad.* Elegantly, adornedly.

Elegía, *sf.* Elegy, a mournful song, a plaintive kind of poem.

Elegíaco, ca, *a.* Elegiac, mournful.

Elegíble, *a.* Eligible, that which may be chosen; preferable.

Elegídos, *sm. pl.* The elect, the blessed.

Elegír, *va.* To choose, to elect.

Élego, ga, *a.* Mournful, plaintive.

Elementádo, da, *a.* Partaking of the nature of elements, composed of elements.

Elementál y Elementár, *a.* 1. Elemental, partaking of the nature of elements, composed of elements. 2. Essential, fundamental.

Eleménto, *sm.* 1. Element, one of the four elements of which our world consists. 2. The first or constituent principle of any thing. 3. The proper sphere of any thing. 4. Any thing which pleases the fancy. *Elementos*, Elements, rudiments, first principles.

Elemósina y Elimósna, *sf.* V. *Limosna.*

Elénco, *sm.* 1. Table, index. 2. A sort of earrings made of large and oblong pearls.

Eléto, ta, *a.* Astonished, stupified.

Elevación, *sf.* 1. Elevation, the act of raising any thing. 2. Rise, ascent; exaltation. 3. Ecstasy, rapture. 4. Haughtiness, presumption, pride. 5. Altitude, the elevation of the pole above the horizon.

Elevádo, da, *a.* 1. Elevated, great, magnanimous. 2. Sharp-sighted, knowing.

Elevamiénto, *sm.* Elevation, suspension.

Elevár, *va.* 1. To raise, to elevate, to lift up. 2. (Met.) To exalt to a high and honourable station.—*vr.* 1. To be enraptured. 2. To be elated with presumption or pride.

Eley'to, ta, *a.* Elected, chosen.

Elidír, *va.* 1. To weaken, to enervate, to debilitate. 2. (In Grammar) To make an elision.

Eligír, *va.* To choose, to elect. V. *Elegir.*

Elípse, *sf.* (Geom.) Ellipsis.

Elípsis, *sf.* (Gram.) Ellipsis.

Elíptico, ca, *a.* Elliptic or elliptical; relating to or having the form of an ellipsis.

Elíseos Cámpos, *sm. pl.* Elysian fields.

Elixáble, *a.* Capable of being made an elixir.

Elixación, *sf.* Elixation.

Elixár, *va.* To seethe or boil vegetable substances.

Elixír, *sm.* Elixir, a medicine made by strong fusion, where the ingredients are almost dissolved in the menstruum.

Elle, *sf.* Name of the double *ll* in Spanish.

Elo, *ad. demon.* Behold it. V. *Veisle.*

Elocución, *sf.* Elocution, the power of fluent speech, flow of language.

Elogiadór, *sm.* Eulogist, encomiast.

Elogiár, *va.* To praise, to extol.

Elógio, *sm.* Eulogy, praise, panegyric.

Elogísta, *sm.* Encomiast, an eulogist, a praiser.

Eloqüéncia, *sf.* Eloquence, the power of speaking with delicacy and elegance.

Eloqüénte, *a.* Eloquent, having the power of an orator; relating to eloquence.

Eloqüenteménte, *ad.* Eloquently.

Elucidación, *sf.* Elucidation, explanation.

Eludír, *va.* To elude, to avoid any artifice; to escape by stratagem.

Emanación, *sf.* Emanation, the act of issuing or proceeding from any other substance.

Emanadéro, *sm.* Source, origin.

Emanánte, *a.* Emanating.

Emanár, *vn.* To emanate, to issue or proceed from any other substance.

Emancipación, *sf.* Emancipation.

Emancipár, *va.* To emancipate, to set free.

Emanuél, *sm.* Immanuel, the Messiah.

Embabiamiénto, *sm.* Stupidity, foolishness. 2. Distraction, absence of mind.

Embachár, *va.* To pen sheep to be shorn.

Embadurnár, *va.* To besmear, to bedaub.

Embaidór, ra, *s.* Sharper, impostor, swindler.

Embaimiénto, *sm.* 1. Delusion, illusion. 2. Deceit, imposition, imposture.

Embaír, *va.* To impose upon, to deceive.

Embaladór, *s.* Packer. [dles.

Embalár, *va.* To embale, to make up into bun-

Embaláge, *sm.* Packing, act of making bales.

Embaldosádo, *sm.* Tile-floor.

Embaldosár, *va.* To floor with tiles or flags.

Embalijár, *va.* To pack up into a portmanteau.

Emballenadór, *sm.* Stay-maker.

Emballenár, *va.* To stiffen with whalebone.

Emballestádo, *sm.* Contraction of the nerves in the feet of animals.

Emballestárse, *vr.* To be on the point of discharging a cross-bow.

Embalsadéro, *sm.* Pool of stagnant rain-water.

Embalsamadór y Embalsaméro, *sm.* One who professes the art of embalming.

Embalsamár, *va.* To embalm, to impregnate a body with aromatics that it may resist putrefaction.

Embalsár, *va.* To drive cattle into a pool of stagnant water to refresh them.

Embálse, *sm.* Act of driving cattle into stagnant water.

Embalumár, *va.* To load unequally, by putting more on one side of a horse's back than on the other.—*vr.* To embarrass one's self with business.

Embanastár, *va.* To put into a basket.

Embaracíllo, *sm.* A slight embarrassment.

Embarazádo, da, *a.* Embarrassed, perplexed. *Embarazáda*, Big with child.

Embarazadór, ra, *s.* Embarrasser.

Embarazár, *va.* To embarrass, to perplex.

Embarázo, *sm.* 1. Impediment, embarrassment; perplexity. 2. Pregnancy, gestation.

Embarazosaménte, *ad.* Difficultly. [gled.

Embarazóso, sa, *a.* Difficult, intricate, entan-

Embarbascádo, da, *a.* Difficult, intricate.

Embarbascár, *va.* 1. To throw hellebore, mullein, &c. into water, to stupify fish. 2. (Met.) To confound, to embarrass.—*vr.* To be entangled among the roots of plants; applied to a plough.

Embarbecér, *vn.* To have a beard appearing, as at the age of puberty. [gether.

Embarbillár, *va.* To join planks or beams to-

Embarcación, *sf.* 1. Vessel or ship of any size or description. 2. Embarcation. 3. Navigation.

Embarcadéro, *sm.* 1. Quay or key, wharf; a place where persons or goods are shipped or unshipped. 2. Port, harbour.

Embarcadór, *sm.* One who embarks or ships goods.
Embarcár, *va.* 1. To embark, to put on shipboard. 2. (Met.) To engage in any affair or enterprise.—*vr.* 1. To go on shipboard, to embark. *Embarcarse un golpe de mar*, (Naút.) To ship a heavy sea. 2. (Met.) To be deeply engaged in any affair. *Embarcarse con poco bizcocho*, (Met.) To embark in any affair or enterprise without the necessary precaution.
Embárco, *sm.* Embarcation, the act of putting on shipboard.
Embargadór, *sm.* One who sequestrates or lays on an embargo.
Embargánte, *pa.* Arresting, impeding.
Embargánte (No), *ad.* Notwithstanding, nevertheless.
Embargár, *va.* 1. To arrest, to lay on an embargo. 2. (Met.) To impede, to restrain, to suspend.
Embárgo, *sm.* 1. Embargo on shipping, sequestration. 2. (Ant.) Embarrassment, impediment. 3. Indigestion. *Sin embargo*, Notwithstanding. *Sin embargo de embargos*, Notwithstanding all the impediments.
Embarnecér, *vn.* To grow plump, full, or fat.
Embarnizadúra, *sf.* Act of varnishing.
Embarnizár, *va.* 1. To varnish, to cover with varnish. 2. (Met.) To adorn, to embellish, to set off.
Embárque, *sm.* Embarcation.
Embarradór, *sm.* Plasterer, one whose trade is to overlay any thing with plaster or mortar.
Embarradúra, *sf.* The act of overlaying with plaster or mortar.
Embarrár, *va.* 1. To overlay with plaster or mortar. 2. (Met.) To adorn, to embellish, to set off. 3. (Met.) To confound or perplex an affair. 4. To bedaub or besmear with mud.—*vr.* To collect or mount upon trees, as partridges when pursued.
Embarrilár, *va.* To barrel, to put in a barrel.
Embarrotár, *va.* V. *Abarrotar.*
Embasamiénto, *sm.* Basis or foundation of a building.
Embastár, *va.* 1. To put a pack-saddle on a beast of burthen. 2. To baste, to sew slightly.
Embastecér, *vn.* To become corpulent; to become fat or gross.—*vr.* To become gross.
Embáte, *sm.* 1. The dashing of waves against rocks; sudden impetuous attack. 2. A fresh gentle breeze. *Embátes*, Sudden changes or reverses, frowns of fortune.
Embaucadór, *sm.* Sharper, impostor.
Embaucamiénto, *sm.* Deception, illusion.
Embaucár, *va.* To delude, to deceive, to impose upon.
Embaúco, *sm.* Artful delusion, imposture.
Embaulár, *va.* 1. To pack up in a trunk. 2. (Met.) To cram, to fill with food beyond satiety.
Embausamiénto, *sm.* Amazement, astonishment, absence of mind.
Embausonár, *va.* To make one stare with wonder, to strike with amazement.
Embaxáda, *sf.* Embassy, a public or solemn message.
Embaxádor, *sm.* Ambassador.
Embaxadóra y Embaxatríz, *sf.* An ambassador's lady.
Embaxatório, **ria**, *a.* Belonging to an ambassador.

Embáxo, *ad.* (Ant.) V. *Debaxo.*
Embazadór, *sm.* One who shades or darkens a colour.
Embazadúra, *sf.* 1. The act of shading or darkening colours. 2. (Met.) Amazement, astonishment.
Embazár, *va.* 1. To tinge, to shade. 2. (Met.) To astonish, to strike with amazement. 3. (Met.) To impede the execution of any thing.—*vn.* To be amazed or astonished, to remain without action.—*vr.* To fatigue one's self; to be ashamed.
Embebecér, *va.* 1. To astonish, to stupify. 2. To entertain, to amuse.—*vr.* To be struck with amazement.
Embebecidaménte, *ad.* Amazedly, with surprise and astonishment.
Embebecimiénto, *sm.* Amazement, astonishment.
Embebedór, **ra**, *s.* Imbiber, one who imbibes.
Embebér, *va.* 1. To imbibe, to drink in, to draw in. 2. To drench, to soak. 3. To introduce, to case, to include. 4. To squeeze, to press. 5. (Among Curriers) To grease or oil a hide or skin.—*vn.* 1. To shrink, to contract itself. 2. To grow thick and close.—*vr.* 1. To be enraptured or ravished, to be wrapt up in thought. 2. To instruct one's self, to retain firmly in the mind.
Embelecadór, **ra**, *s.* Impostor, sharper.
Embelecár, *va.* To impose upon, to deceive.
Embeléco, *sm.* Fraud, delusion, imposition.
Embeleñádo, **da**, *a.* 1. Enraptured, ravished. 2. Stupified, besotted.
Embeleñár, *va.* To stupify, to besot.
Embelesamiénto, *sm.* Amazement.
Embelesár, *va.* To amaze, to astonish, to arrest the imagination.
Embeléso, *sm.* 1. Amazement, astonishment. 2. Object of amazement.
Embellaquecérse, *vr.* To be low minded, to be mean-spirited; to have wicked or worthless ideas.
Embellecér, *va.* To embellish, to adorn, to decorate.
Embeodár, *va.* To intoxicate.
Emberár, *vn.* To begin to have a ripe colour; applied to grapes.
Embermejár, *va.* To give a red colour.
Embermejecér, *va.* To dye red.—*vn.* To blush, to betray shame or confusion by a red colour in the cheeks; to become red.
Embéro, *sm.* Colour of grapes which are growing ripe.
Emberrinchárse, *vr.* To fly into a violent passion.
Embestída, *sf.* 1. Assault, violent attack. 2. (Met.) Importunate demand by way of charity or loan.
Embestidór, *sm.* One who makes importunate demands.
Embestidúra, *sf.* Act of importuning.
Embestír, *va.* 1. To assail, to attack. 2. To importune with unseasonable demands.
Embetunár, *va.* To cover or coat with gum-resin or bitumen.
Embeudár, *va.* V. *Emborrachar.*
Embicár, *va.* *Embicar las vergas*, (Naút.) To top the yards.
Embijár, *va.* To paint with minium or red lead.
Embión, *sm.* A violent blow or stroke

EMBIZARRÁRSE, *vr.* (In the Jocular Style) To brag, to boast of courage, to bully.

EMBLANDECÉR, *va.* To moisten, to soften with moisture.—*vn.* (Met.) To soften, or move to pity.

EMBLANQUECÉR, *va.* To whiten any thing.—*vr.* To grow white, to be bleaching.

EMBLANQUECIMIÉNTO Y EMBLANQUIMIÉNTO, *sm.* (Ant.) Whitening, bleaching.

EMBLÉMA, *sm.* 1. Emblem, inlay, enamel. 2. An occult representation, an allusive picture.

EMBOBAMIÉNTO, *sm.* Admiration, astonishment, enchantment; stupifying.

EMBOBÁR, *va.* To attract, to elevate the mind. —*vr.* To be in suspense, to stand gaping or gazing.

EMBOBECÉR, *vn.* To become stupified or stultified.

EMBOBECIMIÉNTO, *sm.* Stupefaction, want of understanding.

EMBOCADÉRO Y EMBOCADÓR, *sm.* Mouth of a channel, by which water is conveyed through a mill-dam. *Estar al embocadero*, To be at the point of attaining any thing.

EMBOCÁDO, DA, *a.* Applied to wine which is pleasant to the taste.

EMBOCADÚRA, *sf.* 1. Act of getting in by a narrow passage. 2. Mouth-piece of a bridle. 3. Mouth-piece of a musical instrument.

EMBOCÁR, *va.* 1. To enter any thing by the mouth. 2. To swallow much in a haste. 3. (Met.) To enter by a pass or narrow passage. 4. (Met.) To take hold of, to seize upon. 5. (Met.) To impose upon, to deceive.

EMBODÁRSE, *vr.* To be married.

EMBOLÁR, *va.* To put balls on the ends or tips of bulls' horns.

EMBOLISMADÓR, RA, *s.* Detractor, reviler.

EMBOLISMÁL, *a.* Applied to the intercalary year composed of 13 lunations.

EMBOLISMÁR, *va.* To propagate malicious sarcasms and rumours.

EMBOLÍSMO, *sm.* 1. Embolism, intercalation; insertion of days or years to produce regularity and equation of time. 2. The time inserted, intercalary time. 3. Confusion, mixture of things.

E'MBOLO, *sm.* Embolus, the sucker in a pump.

EMBOLSÁR, *va.* To put money into a purse.

EMBÓLSO, *sm.* The act of putting money into a purse.

EMBONÁR, *va.* 1. To make good or firm. 2. (Naút.) To cover a ship's bottom and sides with planks.

EMBÓNO, *sm.* 1. (Naút.) The act of doubling a ship's bottom and sides with planks. 2. Stiffening, lining.

EMBOÑIGÁR, *va.* To anoint or plaster with cow-dung.

EMBÓQUE, *sm.* Passage of a ball through an arch or strait part.

EMBORNÁLES, *sm. pl.* (Naút.) Scupper-holes.

EMBORRACHADÓR, RA, *a.* Intoxicating, producing drunkenness.—*s.* One who makes drunk.

EMBORRACHÁR, *va.* To intoxicate, to inebriate. —*vr.* To be intoxicated. *Emborracharse de cólera*, To be in a violent passion.

EMBORRÁR, *va.* 1. To stuff with goat's hair. 2. (In Woollen Manufactories) To comb or card the wool a second time. 3. (Vulg.) To swallow victuals without choice, to cram.

EMBORRASCÁR, *va.* To provoke, to enrage.

EMBORRAZAMIÉNTO, *sm.* Act of covering or basting a fowl with pieces of pork while roasting.

EMBORRAZÁR, *va.* To tie pieces of fat pork on the body of a fowl, to serve as basting during the time of roasting.

EMBORRICÁRSE, *vr.* To be stupified, to grow stupid, like an ass.

EMBORRIZÁR, *va.* To give the first combing to wool.

EMBORRULLÁRSE, *vr.* (In the Jocular Style) To be at variance.

EMBOSCÁDA, *sf.* AMBUSCADE, ambush; a post from whence troops fall unexpectedly on the enemy.

EMBOSCADÚRA, *sf.* Act or situation of an ambuscade.

EMBOSCÁR, *va.* 1. (Mil.) To place or post in ambush. 2. (Met.) To hide or conceal in some secret place.—*vr.* To retire into the thickest part of a forest.

EMBOSQUECÉR, *vn.* To become woody, to convert into shrubberies.

EMBOTADÓR, *sm.* He who blunts or renders obtuse the points or edges of swords, &c.

EMBOTADÚRA, *sf.* The act of blunting, or breaking off the edges or points of swords and other edged weapons.

EMBOTAMIÉNTO, *sm.* 1. The act of blunting. V. *Embotadura*. 2. (Met.) Stupefaction, the act of making dull or stupid.

EMBOTÁR, *va.* 1. To blunt, to break off the edges or points of edged tools or weapons. 2. (Met.) To enervate, to debilitate, to render less active or vigorous.

EMBOTELLÁR, *va.* To bottle wine or other liquors.

EMBOTICÁR, *va.* V. *Almacenar*.

EMBOTIJÁR, *va.* To lay a stratum of potsherds, before a tile flooring is put down.—*vr.* 1. To swell, to expand. 2. To be in a passion, to be inflated with arrogance.

EMBOVEDÁDO, DA, *a.* Arched, vaulted.

EMBOXÁR, *va.* To arrange branches for silk-worms, for forming their webs and cods or cones.

EMBÓXO, *sm.* The shed erected for the silk-worms to produce their cods on.

EMBÓZA, *sf.* Inequalities in the bottom of barrels or casks.

EMBOZÁDO, DA, *a.* Covered; involved.

EMBOZÁR, *va.* 1. To muffle the greatest part of the face. 2. (Met.) To cloak, to dissemble.

EMBÓZO, *sm.* 1. Veil or covering for the face. 2. The act of muffling the greatest part of the face. 3. (Met.) An artful way of expressing one's thoughts or sentiments, so as to keep them in part concealed.

EMBÓZO (De), *ad.* Incognito, unknown, private.

EMBRACILÁDO, DA, *a.* Carried about in the arms, as children.

EMBRAGÁR, *va.* (Naút.) To sling.

EMBRAVECÉR Y EMBRAVÁR, *va.* To enrage, to irritate, to make furious.—*vn.* To become strong; applied to plants.—*vr.* 1. To become furious, to be enraged. 2. (Naút.) To be extremely boisterous; applied to the sea.

EMBRAVECIMIÉNTO, *sm.* Fury, rage, passion.

EMBRAZADÚRA, *sf.* 1. Clasping of a shield or buckler. 2. Embracing, clasping.

EMBRAZÁR, *va.* 1. To clasp a shield, as in the posture of fighting. 2. V. *Abrazar*.

Embreadúra, *sf.* (Naút.) The act of paying a ship with pitch.

Embreár, *va.* (Naút.) To pay with pitch the seams, sides, or bottom of a ship.

Embrencárse, *vr.* To quarrel, to wrangle, to dispute.

Embreñárse, *vr.* To hide one's self among brambles or in thickets.

Embriagadaménte, *ad.* Drunkenly.

Embriagár, *va.* To intoxicate, to inebriate.

Embriágo, ga, *a.* Intoxicated, inebriated.

Embriaguéz, *sf.* 1. Intoxication, drunkenness, ebriety. 2. (Met.) Rapture, transport of the mind.

Embriár, *va.* To toss in the air.

Embridár, *va.* 1. To bridle, to guide by a bridle. 2. (Met.) To govern, to restrain.

Embrión, *sm.* 1. Embryo or embryon, the offspring yet unfinished in the womb. 2. (Met.) Assemblage of confused ideas, without method or order.

Embróca y Embrocación, *sf.* (Farm.) Embrocation.

Embrocár, *va.* 1. To pour out of one vessel into another. 2. (With Embroiderers) To wind thread or twist upon quills. 3. (Among Shoe-makers) To fasten with tacks to the last.

Embrochádo, da, *a.* Embroidered with gold or silver.

Embrólla ó Embróllo, *s.* Fraud, snare, deception.

Embrolladór, ra, y Embrollón, *s.* One who entangles, embroils, or confounds.

Embrollár, *va.* 1. To entangle, to twist, to overlace. 2. (Met.) To confound with artful subtleties. 3. *Embrollar la bandera*, (Naút.) To waft the ensign.

Embromádo, da, *a.* Misty, hazy, foggy; applied to the weather.

Embromadór, ra, *s.* One who deceives by artful tricks, frauds, and words.

Embromár, *va.* 1. To excite wrangles or disputes. 2. To deceive with fallacious words.

Embroquelárse, *vr.* V. *Abroquelarse.*

Embrosquilár, *va.* To put cattle into a fold or pen, called, in Spanish, *brosquil.*

Embrujár, *va.* To bewitch. V. *Hechizar.*

Embrutecér, *va.* To stupify, to make stupid. —*vr.* To grow stupid, to become brutal.

Embuchádo, *sm.* A sort of large sausages made of pork, minced very small, with salt and spice.

Embuchár, *va.* 1. To stuff with minced pork or other meat; to make pork sausages. 2. To cram or stuff the maw or stomach of animals. 3. (Met.) To swallow victuals without chewing them.

Embudadór, *sm.* Filler, one who fills vessels with a funnel.

Embudár, *va.* 1. To put a funnel in a wine-bag. 2. (Met.) To scheme, to ensnare.

Embúdo, *sm.* 1. Funnel or pipe, by which liquors are poured into vessels. 2. (Among Wax-chandlers) Tail of a wax-candle mould. 3. (Met.) Fraud, deceit, artifice.

Embudísta, *sm.* Man who makes funnels; an intriguer, deceiver.

Emburujár, *va.* To jumble, to mix a heap confusedly.

Emburriár, *va.* V. *Empujar.*

Emburrión, *sm.* V. *Empujon.*

Embúste, *sm.* 1. Fraud, imposition. 2. (Met.) Pleasing quibble of children. *Embústes*, Gewgaws, baubles, trinkets.

Embusteár, *vn.* To make frequent use of frauds, tricks, and deceits.

Embusterázo, *sm.* A great impostor.

Embustéro, ra, y Embustidór, *s.* 1. Impostor, cheat. 2. Hypocrite, dissembler. 3. Child saying pretty things or quibbles.

Embusterón, na, *s. aum.* Very hypocritical, deceitful or fraudulent.

Embusteruélo, la, *s.* Little impostor.

Embustír, *va.* To cheat, to impose by little fictions.

Embutidéra, *sf.* Instrument for riveting tin-work.

Embutído, *sm.* Inlaid work.

Embutír, *va.* 1. To inlay, to enchase one thing in another. 2. To mix confusedly, to jumble; to insert. 3. (Met.) To cram, to eat much. 4. *Embutir un estay*, (Naút.) To worm a stay. 5. (Ant.) To imbue.

Emélga, *sf.* A large furrow, to serve as a land-mark.

Emelgár, *va.* To make large furrows, which are to serve as land-marks.

Emendáble, *a.* Amendable, corrigible.

Emendación, *sf.* 1. Amendment, correction. 2 Satisfaction, chastisement.

Emendadaménte, *ad.* Correctly, exactly.

Emendadór, *sm.* He who amends or corrects.

Emendadúra y Emendamiénto. V. *Enmienda.*

Emendár, *va.* 1. To amend, to correct. 2. *Emendar un aparejo*, (Naút.) To mend a tackle.

Emergéncia, *sf.* Emergency, accident, incident.

Emergénte, *a.* Emergent, resulting.

Emérito, *a.* Emeritus or emerited, having long served in the army, or rendered long and meritorious services to the church.

Emersión, *sf.* Emersion.

Emético, ca, *a.* Emetic, having the quality of provoking vomits.

Emiénda, *sf.* 1. Amendment, correction. 2. Chastisement. 3. Compensation, satisfaction, reward. 4. Change for the better.

Emigración, *sf.* Emigration.

Emigrádo, da, *a.* y *s.* Emigrated, emigrant.

Emigrár, *vn.* To emigrate, to abandon one country to settle in another.

Emína, *sf.* 1. Measure containing the fourth part of a *fanega*, in Guipuscoa, and other parts of Spain. 2. Ancient tax.

Eminéncia, *sf.* 1. Eminence, height; a commanding ground. 2. (Met.) Eminence, excellence. 3. (Met.) Greatness, power. 4. Title given to cardinals. *Con eminencia*, Virtually, eminently.

Eminenciál, *a.* Eminential.

Eminencialménte, *ad.* Virtually, eminently.

Eminénte, *a.* Eminent, conspicuous.

Eminenteménte, *ad.* Excellently, eminently.

Eminentísimo, *a.* Title of the Romish cardinals.

Emisário, *sm.* Emissary, a secret agent sent on particular messages.

Emisión, *sf.* Emission, the act of sending out; vent.

Emitír, *va.* To emit, to throw or turn out.

Emoliénte, *a.* Emollient, softening.

Emoluménto, *sm.* Emolument, profit, advantage.

Empacár, *va.* To pack up in chests; to wrap up

in habits or shine.—vr. To be sullen, to be displeased.

Empachádo, da, a. Surfeited, glutted, fed to satiety or sickness. *Navio empachado*, (Naút.) A ship which is overloaded.

Empachár, va. 1. To impede, to embarrass, to disturb. 2. To perplex, to confound. 3. To surfeit. 4. To disguise.—vr. To be ashamed.

Empácho, sm. 1. Bashfulness, timidity. 2. Embarrassment, hinderance, obstacle. 3. Surfeit.

Empadronadór, sm. Enroller, one who enrols soldiers or sailors for the army or navy.

Empadronamiénto, sm. List or register of persons liable to pay certain taxes. V. *Padron*.

Empadronár, va. To enter in a register the names of those who are liable to pay certain taxes.

Empalagamiénto, sm. Surfeit.

Empalagár, va. To cloy, to surfeit.—vr. To be cloyed, to be disgusted or displeased.

Empaláeo, sm. Surfeit, sickness arising from over-fulness.

Empalagóso, sa, a. Squeamish, cloying.

Empalár, va. To empale, to put to death by spitting on a stake fixed upright.

Empaliáda, sf. Hangings hung up in cloisters or churches, through which a procession passes.

Empaliár, va. To hang with tapestry a church, cloister, or other place, through which a procession passes.

Empalizáda, sf. (Fort.) Palisade or palisado.

Empalletádo, sm. (Naút.) Netting. [of wood.

Empalmadúra, sf. The junction of two pieces

Empalmár, va. 1. To scarf or join the ends of two pieces of timber. 2. (Naút.) To splice cables.

Empalomár, va. (Naút.) To sew the bolt-rope to the sail. *Empalomar los escarpes*, (Naút.) To shift the scarfs.

Empanáda, sf. Meat-pie, meat covered with a crust, or baked in a crust. *Hacer una empanada*, To conceal part of an affair. *Agua empanada*, Iced water; muddy water.

Empanadílla, sf. 1. A small pie. 2. (And.) Foot-stool put in coaches.

Empanádo, sm. Centre-room, a room surrounded on all sides with other rooms. *Empanados*, (Naút.) Planks laid over the well in a ship.

Empanár, va. 1. To cover with paste, to bake in paste. 2. To sow grain.

Empandár, va. To bend into an arch.

Empandillár, va. To remove by stealth, to hide. [plied to sails.

Empanicár, va. (Naút.) To hand or furl; ap-

Empantanár, va. 1. To submerge, to set under water; to make a pond or lake. 2. To bemire, to fall into the mire. 3. To check or embarrass the course of an affair.

Empañadúra, sf. Swaddling of children.

Empañár, va. 1. To swaddle, to wrap up in swaddling clothes. 2. (Met.) To soil or tarnish a glass with one's breath. 3. (Met.) To denigrate, to impeach one's character or reputation. 4. To cover with clouds or fog; applied to the sky and air.

Empapagayárse, vr. To be bent or incurvated like the beak of a parrot.

Empapár, va. To soak, to drench.—vr. 1. To imbibe, to be soaked; to be surfeited. 2. To be in a trance, to be lost in some one doctrine or opinion.

Empapeladór, sm. Paperer.

Empapelár, va. 1. To wrap up in paper. 2. To waste without any necessity much paper.

Empapiroládo, da, a. Full, satisfied.

Empapirotádo, da, a. Lofty, haughty; puffed up with arrogance or pride.

Empapirotár, va. To adorn, to deck.

Empapujár, va. To fill up and swell to excess.

Empáque, sm. Act of packing.

Empaquetadór, sm. Packer. [into bales.

Empaquetár, va. To pack, to bind up goods

Empára, sf. (For. Ar.) Sequestration.

Emparamentár, va. To adorn, to set off.

Emparamiénto ó Emparamiénto, sm. Sequestration, inhibition.

Emparár, va. To sequestrate, to prohibit.

Emparchár, va. To cover with a plaster.

Emparedádo, da, s. Cloisterer; applied to a devotee who lives in a cloister without the vows.

Emparedamiénto, sm. 1. Confinement, the act of shutting up between walls. 2. Cloister, religious retirement. [up.

Emparedár, va. To confine, to immure, to shut

Emparejadór, sm. He who matches, fits or makes equal.

Emparejadúra, sf. Equalization. [ing equal.

Emparejamiénto, sm. Act of matching or mak-

Emparejár, va. To match, to fit, to equal.—vn. To put abreast, to put on a level; to be equal.

Emparentár, vn. To be related or allied by marriage. *Estar bien emparentado*, To have respectable relations, to be respectably allied.

Emparrádo, sm. Arbour or bower made with the branches and leaves of propped vines.

Emparrár, va. To embower, to form bowers with the branches and leaves of vines.

Emparvár, va. To put grain in order to be thrashed.

Empastár, va. 1. To paste, to form with paste. 2. To cover plentifully with colours.

Empatadéra, sf. Act of checking or impeding, suspension of any thing.

Empatár, va. 1. To equal, to make equal. 2. To check, to suspend. 3. To cut short a speech.

Empáte, sm. 1. Equality, or equal number of votes. 2. Stop, suspension.

Empavesáda, sf. (Naút.) Waist cloths, painted linen or close netting spread on the sides of ships to obstruct the enemy's sight.

Empavesár, va. 1. (Naút.) To spread waist cloths on the sides of a ship. 2. (Naút.) To dress ships.

Empecér, va. To hurt, to offend, to injure.

Empechár, va. V. *Impedir*.

Empecíble, a. Hurtful.

Empedernír, va. To indurate, to make hard.—vr. 1. To be petrified, to grow hard as stone. 2. (Met.) To be obstinate, to be inflexible.

Empedimiénto, sm. V. *Impedimiento*.

Empedrádo, sm. Pavement.

Empedradór, sm. Paver or pavier.

Empedrár, va. 1. To pave, to floor with stones. 2. To fill up any cavity or inequality.

Empéga, sf. Varnish of pitch.

Empegadúra, *sf.* The varnish of pitch which is put on vessels.
Empegár, *va.* To pitch, to cover with pitch.
Empeguntár, *va.* To mark with pitch.
Empelár, *vn.* To get hair, to begin to be hairy.
Empélla, *sf.* 1. The fat of fowls; the lard of swine. 2. Upper leather of a shoe.
Empellár y Empellér, *va.* To push, to impel.
Empellejár, *va.* To cover with skins.
Empellón, *sm.* Push, heavy blow. *A' empellones*, Rudely, with pushes.
Empelotárse, *vr.* 1. To be at variance, to quarrel. 2. To be vexed, to be uneasy.
Empéltre, *sm.* (Ar.) Small olive-tree or sapling springing from an old trunk.
Empenachár, *va.* To adorn with plumes.
Empenár, *va.* To feather an arrow, to dress with feathers.
Empénta, *sf.* Prop, stay, shore.
Empentár, *va.* To push, to impel. V. *Empujar.*
Empéña, *sf.* Upper leather of a shoe. V. *Pella.*
Empeñadaménte, *ad.* Strenuously, in a courageous or spirited manner.
Empeñár, *va.* 1. To pawn, to pledge. 2. To engage, to oblige. *Empeñar la palabra*, To engage one's word.—*vr.* 1. To bind one's self to fulfil a contract, or to pay debts contracted. 2. To persist in a determination or resolution. 3. To encounter dangers with courage and spirit. 4. To intercede, to mediate. 5. (Naút.) To be embayed on a lee-shore.
Empéño, *sm.* 1. Obligation contracted by pledging. 2. Engagement, contract. 3. Earnest desire, ardent love. 4. Boldness; courage and perseverance in overcoming difficulties. 5. Firmness, constancy. 6. Protection, favour; the person who protects or favours. *Con empeño*, With great ardour and diligence.
Empeoramiénto, *sm.* Deterioration, the act of making or growing worse.
Empeorár, *va.* To impair, to make worse.—*vn.* To grow worse.
Empequeñecér, *vn.* To grow smaller, to diminish.
Emperadór, *sm.* Emperor, originally a captain-general, now a monarch, superior to a king.
Emperatríz, *sf.* Empress.
Emperchár, *va.* To suspend on a perch.
Emperdigár, *va.* V. *Perdigar.*
Emperegilárse, *vr.* To be adorned, to be dressed out.
Emperezár, *vn.* 1. To be lazy or indolent. 2. To be dilatory, tardy, slow.
Empericádo, da, *a.* To be dressed in style; to wear false hair.
Emperifollár, *va.* To decorate, to cover with ribbons and bows, to deck with flowers; to ornament a discourse with flowers of rhetoric.
Empernádo, da, *a.* *Bien ó mal empernado*, Well or ill nailed.
Empernár, *va.* 1. (Naút.) To bolt, to fasten with bolts. 2. To fasten or mend stockings.
Empéro, *conj.* Yet, however. V. *Pero.*
Emperráda, *sf.* A sort of game at cards.
Emperrárse, *vr.* To grow mad or furious.
Empesadór, *sm.* Handful of rushes used by weavers for trimming their yarn.
Empestár, *va.* V. *Apestar.*
Empétro, *sm.* (Bot.) Crow-berry. Empetrum nigrum *L.*

Empéyne, *sm.* 1. Groin, the part next the thigh. 2. Instep, the upper part of the foot where it joins the leg. 3. Hoof of a beast. 4. Tetter, ring-worm; a kind of dry scurf on the skin. 5. Flower of the cotton plant.
Empeynóso, sa, *a.* Full of tetters or ring-worms.
Empezár, *va.* To begin, to commence.
Empicár, *va.* To hang, to suspend by the neck.—*vr.* To be too much attached to any thing.
Empicotadúra, *sf.* Act of pilloring.
Empicotár, *va.* To pillory, to put in the pillory; to picket.
Empiédro, *sm.* Paving, the act of making a stone floor.
Empinádo, da, *a.* Elevated, exalted, raised to a high dignity or station.
Empinadúra, *sf.* Exaltation, sublevation.
Empinamiénto, *sm.* Erection, elevation.
Empinár, *va.* 1. To raise, to exalt. 2. To drink much.—*vr.* 1. To stand on tiptoe. 2. To tower, to rise high. *Empinar el puchero*, (Fam.) To have a comfortable subsistence without luxury.
Empingorotár, *va.* (Bax.) To raise any thing and put it upon another.
Empíno, *sm.* Elevation, height.
Empiolár, *va.* 1. To tie the legs of hawks with jesses. 2. (Met.) To bind, to subject, to imprison.
Empíreo, *sm.* Empyrean, the highest heaven.
Empíreo, rea, *a.* Empyreal, celestial.
Empiricaménte, *ad.* Empirically.
Empírico, *sm.* Quack, empiric.
Empirísmo, *sm.* Empiricism, dependence on physical experience without knowledge or art; quackery.
Empizarrádo, *sm.* The whole slates which cover a building.
Empizarrár, *va.* To slate, to roof a building with slates.
Emplastadúra y Emplastamiénto, *s.* Plastering.
Emplastár, *va.* 1. To apply plasters. 2. To paint the face with various glaring colours. 3. To suspend, to obstruct.—*vr.* V. *Embadurnarse.*
Emplastecér, *va.* (Pint.) To level the surface in order to paint any thing.
Emplásto, *sm.* Plaster, a glutinous and adhesive salve. *Estar hecho un emplasto*, To be in a very bad state of health.
Emplastríco, ca, *a.* Glutinous, resembling a plaster.
Emplazadór, *sm.* Summoner, apparitor; messenger of a court who serves summons.
Emplazamiénto y Empláze, *sm.* Summons, citation.
Emplazár, *va.* 1. To summon, to order, to appear before a court or judge. 2. *Emplazar la caza*, To arrange or set the chase.
Empleár, *va.* 1. To purchase, to employ one's money in the purchase of land or other property. 2. To employ, to make use of; to consume.
Emplénta, *sf.* 1. Piece of mud-wall made at once. 2. (Ant.) Impression.
Emplentár, *va.* (Ant.) To print.
Empléo, *sm.* 1. Purchase, the act of employing money in the purchase of land or other property. 2. Employ, public place or station. 3. Employment, calling. 4. Lady courted, sweetheart, mistress.

Empleyta, *sf.* V. *Pleyta.*
Empleytéro, ra, *s.* One who plaits and sells bass-weed.
Emplomádo, *sm.* Roof covered with lead.
Emplomadór, *sm.* He who covers with lead.
Emplomár, *va.* To cover with lead.
Emplumár, *va.* To adorn with feathers or plumes.—*vr.* To mew, to moult, to shed the feathers; to get feathers.
Emplumecér, *vn.* To begin to get feathers.
Empobrecér, *va.* To impoverish, to reduce to poverty.—*vn.* To become poor.
Empobrecimiénto, *sm.* Act of impoverishing.
Empodrecér, *vn.* To corrupt, to reduce to a state of putrefaction.
Empolládo, da, *a.* 1. Hatched. 2. (Met.) Confined, pent up in the house.
Empollár, *va.* To brood, to hatch, to produce young from eggs; to blister.
Empolladúra, *sf.* Brood of bees.
Empoltronecérse, *vr.* V. *Apoltronarse.*
Empolvár, *va.* To powder, to sprinkle powder.
Empolvoramiénto, *sm.* The act of covering with dust.
Empolvorár y Empolvorizár, *va.* To cover with dust or powder.
Emponér, *va.* (Ant.) To instruct, to teach.
Emponzoñadéra, *sf.* (Ant.) Poisoner.
Emponzoñadór, ra, *s.* Poisoner, one who poisons.
Emponzoñamiénto, *sm.* Act and effect of poisoning.
Emponzoñár, *va.* 1. To poison, to infect with poison. 2. (Met.) To taint, to corrupt one's morals.
Emporcár, *va.* To soil, to make dirty.
Empório, *sm.* Emporium, a great mart for the sale of merchandise.
Empós, *ad.* (Ant.) V. *En pos.*
Empotramiénto, *sm.* The act of scarfing two timbers together.
Empotrár, *va.* 1. To mortise, to join with a mortise. 2. To scarf, to splice.
Empozár, *va.* To throw into a well.
Empradizárse, *vr.* To become meadow.
Empremír, *va.* V. *Imprimir.*
Emprendedór, *sm.* One who attempts or directs an undertaking or enterprise.
Emprendér, *va.* 1. To enterprise, to undertake, to engage in an arduous undertaking. 2. To take, to seize.
Emprensár, *va.* To press. V. *Prensar.*
Empreñár, *va.* To impregnate; to beget.
Empresa, *sf.* 1. Symbol, motto. 2. Enterprise, undertaking.
Emprestádo, Empréstido, ó Empréstito, *sm.* 1. Loan, the act of lending money on condition of its being repaid. 2. Tax, duty, impost.
Emprestilladór y Emprestillón, *sm.* Borrower, cheat, impostor.
Emprestillár, *va.* To borrow, to ask the use of any thing.
Emprima, *sf.* V. *Primicia.*
Emprimádo, *sm.* Last combing to wool.
Emprimár, *va.* 1. To print linen or cotton. 2. (In Woollen Manufactories) To comb or card the wool several times, in order to prepare it for spinning. 3. To examine, to probe.
Emprimerár, *va.* To place one in the first rank at a feast, or on any other occasion.
Empringár, *va.* V. *Pringar.*
Emprisionár, *vn.* V. *Aprisionar.*
Empuchár, *va.* To put skeins of thread into a lye, or to buck them before they are bleached.
Empués, *ad.* (Ant.) V. *Despues.*
Empuésta (De), *ad.* V. *Por Detras.*
Empujamiénto, *sm.* 1. The act of pushing away. 2. The force employed for that purpose.
Empujár, *va.* 1. To move or retain with force. 2. To push away, to shove off.
Empúje y Empújo, *sm.* Impulsion, impulse.
Empujón, *sm.* Impulse, push. *A' empujones,* Pushingly, rudely.
Empulgadúra, *sf.* The act of stretching the cord of a cross-bow.
Empulgár, *va.* To stretch the cord of a cross-bow.
Empulguéras, *sf. pl.* 1. Wings of a cross-bow, through which the ends of the cord run. 2. Instrument with which the thumbs are tied together.
Empuñadór, ra, *s.* Grasper, one who seizes by the handle.
Empuñadúra, *sf.* Hilt of a sword. *Empuñaduras,* (Naút.) Ear-rings, thin ropes fastened to the four corners of a sail, in the form of a ring. *Empuñaduras del gratil,* Head-ear-rings. *Empuñaduras de rizos,* Reef-earrings. *Empuñaduras de las consejas,* Beginning of a discourse or narration.
Empuñár, *va.* 1. To seize by the handle. 2. To obtain an employ. *Empuñar el cetro,* To begin to reign, to seize the sceptre. 3. *Empuñar las escotas y amuras,* (Naút.) To bend the tacks and sheets to the clews of the sails.
Empuyárse, *vr.* To prick one's self with nails or prickles.
Emulación, *sm.* Emulation, envy.
Emuladór, ra, *s.* Emulator.
Emulár, *va.* To emulate, to rival.
Emulgénte, *a.* Emulgent.
E'mulo, *sm.* Competitor, rival.
Emulsión, *sf.* Emulsion.
Emunctórios, *sm. pl.* Emunctories.
Emundación, *sf.* Cleansing.
En, *Prep.* of time and place. 1. In. *Estar en Londres,* To be in London. *En un año,* In a year's time. *En adelante,* For the future. 2. On, upon. *Tiene pension en Córdoba,* He has a pension assigned to him upon the bishoprick of Cordova. *En* going before a gerund is equal to *luego que* or *despues que;* as, *En diciendo esto,* In or after saying this. Before adjectives it gives them an adverbial signification; before the infinitive of verbs, it gives them a participial import, as *en decir esto,* In saying this. Formerly it was used for *con* and *entre.*
Enacerár, *va.* To steel, to edge with steel.
Enaceytárse, *vr.* To become oily or rancid.
Enagenáble, *a.* Alienable, that of which the property may be transferred.
Enagenación y Enagenamiénto, *s.* 1. Alienation, the act of transferring property. 2. Change of affection, want of friendly intercourse. 3. Disorder or derangement of the mental faculties.
Enagenár, *va.* 1. To alienate, to transfer property. 2. To transport, to enrapture.—*vr.* 1.

To withdraw one's affection. 2. To be deprived of the use of reason; to be restless or uneasy.
Enaguarchádo, da, a. Loaded with water; applied to the stomach.
Enaguarchár, va. To fill or load with water.
Enáguas, sf. pl. 1. A sort of linen under-petticoat, worn by women over their shifts. 2. Under-waistcoat of black baize, formerly worn by men as mourning.
Enaguazár, va. To irrigate, to cover with water.
Enagüelár, vn. (In the Jocular Style) To have grand-children.
Enagüillas, tas, sf. pl. dim. Of Enaguas.
Enalbár, va. To heat iron to such a degree as to make it appear white.
Enalbardár, va. 1. To lay a pack-saddle on beasts of burthen. 2. To cover meat or any other dish with a batter of eggs, flour, and sugar, and fry it afterwards in oil or butter.
Enalforjár, va. To put into a saddle-bag.
Enalguaciládo, da, a. (In the Jocular Style) Dressed as an alguacil.
Enalienáble, a. Unalienable, that of which the property cannot be transferred.
Enalmagrádo, da, a. 1. Coloured with ochre. 2. Vile, despicable.
Enalmagrár, va. To cover with ochre.
Enalmenár, va. To crown a wall with indented battlements or small turrets.
Enaltecérse, vr. V. Ensalzarse.
Enamarillecérse, vr. To become yellow.
Enamorádo, da, a Lover.
Enamoradaménte, ad. Lovingly, in a loving manner.
Enamoradízo, za, a. Inclined to love, of an amorous disposition.
Enamoradór, sm. Lover, wooer.
Enamoramiénto, sm. Act of enamouring.
Enamorár, va. 1. To excite or inspire love. 2. To make love, to woo, to court.—vr. To be in love.
Enamoricárse, vr. To be slightly in love.
Enamorosaménte, ad. Amorously.
Enanchár, va. To widen, to enlarge.
Enangostár, va. V. Angostar.
Enaníco, ca; llo, lla; to, ta, a. dim. Little, minute.
Enáno, sm. Dwarf.
Enánte ó Enántes, ad. (Ant.) V. Antes.
Enaparejár, vn. V. Emparejar.
Enarbolár, va. To hoist, to raise high. Enarbolar la bandera, (Naút.) To hoist the colours.
Enarcár, va. To hoop barrels.
Enardecér, va. To fire with passion.
Enarenación, sf. Lime and sand, or plaster, used to whiten walls before painting them.
Enarenár, va. To fill with sand, to choak with sand.—vr. (Naút.) To run on shore.
Enarmonár, va. To raise, to rear.—vr. To rise on the hind feet.
Enarración, sf. Narration, relation.
Enarrár, va. To narrate.
Enartár, va. 1. (Ant.) To narrow, to constringe. 2. To deceive.
Enastár, va. To put a handle to any instrument.
Enatiaménte, ad. Rudely, disorderly.
Enatiéza, sf. (Ant.) Unhandsomeness, inelegance, uselessness.
En Ayúnas, ad. Without having taken any food. Quedarse en ayunas, Not to have obtained the least reward for one's labour.
En Bálde, ad. In vain. V. Balde.
Encabalgamiénto, sm. Gun-carriage.
Encabalgár, vn. 1. To parade on horse-back. 2. To have one thing above another.—va. To provide horses.
Encabelladúra, sf. V. Cabellera.
Encabellár, vn. To take to a wig, to begin to wear a wig.
Encabellecér, vn. To have a nice head of hair.
Encabestrár, va. 1. To lead a beast by the halter. 2. (Met.) To force to obedience.—vr. To be entangled in the halter.
Encabezamiénto y Encabezonamiénto, sm. 1. List or register of persons liable to pay a certain tax. 2. To mortise the ends of beams. 3. To raise a head-ridge at the extremities of lands.
Encabezár y Encabezonár, va. To register taxes.—vr. 1. To agree to pay a certain sum of taxes. 2. (Met.) To agree for a certain sum amicably; to be content to suffer a small to avoid a greater evil.
Encabriár, va. To preserve and fashion timber for roofing.
Encabritárse, vr. To rise on the hind feet; applied to horses.
Encabronár, va. To cuckold.
Encachár, va. To thrust or fix any thing in a wall or box.
Encadenadúra y Encadenamiénto, s. 1. Catenation, the act of linking together. 2. State of being linked or connected.
Encadenár, va. 1. To catenate, to chain, to link. 2. (Met.) To connect, to unite.
Encaecér, vn. V. Parir.
Encalabozár, va. To put one into prison.
Encalabriár ó Encalabrinár, va. To affect the head with some unpleasant smell or vapour.
Encaláda, sf. Piece of the trimmings of a saddle.
Encaladór, sm. (In Tan-yards) Pit or vat, into which hides are put to be imbued with lime.
Encaladúra, sf. The act of whitening with lime, or putting in lime.
Encalár, va. 1. To cover with plaster or mortar. 2. To thrust into a pipe or tube. 3. To put hides into the lime vats or pits.
Encalladéro, sm. (Naút.) Shoal, sand-bank.
Encalladúra, sf. (Naút.) Striking on a sand-bank.
Encallár, vn. 1. (Naút.) To get on shore on a sand-bank. 2. To be checked in the progress of some enterprise, not to be able to proceed.
Encallecér, vn. To get corns on the feet.
Encallecído, da, a. 1. Troubled with corns. 2. (Met.) Hardened in wickedness and iniquities.
Encallejonár, va. To enter or put any thing into a narrow street.
Encalletrár, va. To understand or know well.
Encalmadúra, sf. Suffocation of a horse.
Encalmárse, vr. 1. To be worn out with fatigue. 2. (Naút.) To be becalmed; applied to a ship.
Encalostrárse, vr. To make the young sick by sucking the first milk.
Encalvár y Encalvecér, vn. To grow bald.
Encamarádos, sm. pl. Chambers in cannon and mortars.
Encamarár, va. To store up grain in granaries.

Encamárse, *vr.* 1. To go to bed. 2. To couch, to come to the lair; applied to deer.

Encambijár, *va.* To conduct water by means of arched reservoirs.

Encambrár, *va.* To put in a store.

Encambronár, *va.* 1. To enclose with hedges of briers and brambles. 2. To strengthen with iron.—*vr.* To walk stately, with unpleasing formality and constraint.

Encaminadúra ó Encaminamiénto, *s.* The act of putting in the right road.

Encaminár, *va.* 1. To guide, to put in the right road. 2. (Met.) To direct or manage an affair or business.—*vr.* To take a road, to proceed in a road.

Encamisáda, *sf.* (Mil.) Camisado, an attack or surprise made in the dark.

Encamisárse, *vr.* To put a shirt over one's clothes, in order to make a camisado.

Encamorrárse, *vr.* To embroil one's self in disputes.

Encampanádo, **da**, *a.* Bell-shaped; applied to mortars.

Encanalár ó Encanalizár, *va.* To convey through pipes or conduits.

Encanárse, *vr.* To grow senseless with fear or crying; applied to children.

Encanastár, *va.* To pack up in canisters, baskets, or hampers.

Encancerárse, *vr.* V. *Cancerarse.*

Encandecér, *va.* To heat any thing to a white heat.

Encandelár, *vn.* To bud, as trees, instead of flowering.

Encandiladéra ó Encandiladóra, *sf.* Procuress, bawd.

Encandiládo, **da**, *a.* Sharp or high cocked; applied to hats. *Trae el sombrero muy encandilado*, He wears his hat fiercely cocked.

Encandilár, *va.* 1. To dazzle with the light of a candle or lamp. 2. (Met.) To dazzle or deceive with false appearances.—*vr.* To inflame one's eyes, as with drink.

Encanecér, *vn.* 1. To grow grey; to mould. 2. To possess much experience and knowledge.

Encanijamiénto, *sm.* Weakness, meagerness; the act of growing weak and lean; extenuation.

Encanijárse, *vr.* To pine, to be emaciated, to grow weak and thin.

Encanillár, *va.* To ravel or make silk, woollen, or linen thread uneven.

Encantación, *sf.* Enchantment, charm, spell.

Encantadéra, *sf.* Sorceress, enchantress.

Encantádo, **da**, *a.* Haunted, enchanted. *Casa encantada*, A house in which the family lives very retired. *Hombre encantado*, A man who has no kind of intercourse with others.

Encantadór, **ra**, *s.* Enchanter, sorcerer, sorceress.

Encantaménto ó Encantamiénto, *sm.* Enchantment.

Encantár, *va.* To enchant, to charm; to occupy the whole attention.

Encantarár, *va.* To put into a jar.

Encánte ó Encánto, *sm.* (Ant.) Auction, public sale.

Encánto, *sm.* 1. Charm, spell; the effect or result of an enchantment. 2. Absence of mind. *Es un encanto*, It is truly charming, it is bewitching.

Encantório, *sm.* (Joc.) Enchantment.

Encantusár, *va.* To coax, to wheedle, to deceive by flatteries.

Encañádo, *sm.* 1. Conduit of water. 2. Hedge formed with canes or reeds.

Encañadór, **ra**, *s.* One who spools or winds the silk on quills made of cane.

Encañadúra, *sf.* 1. Hedge made of cane or reeds. 2. Strong rye-straw which is not broken. 3. Conduit.

Encañár, *va.* 1. To enclose a plantation with a hedge made of cane. 2. To convey water through conduits or pipes. 3. To wind silk on quills of reed or cane.—*vn.* To form or grow into stalks; applied to corn.

Encañizáda, *sf.* (Mur. y Val.) Enclosure made of cane and reeds for catching mullets.

Encañonádo, *sm.* Wind blowing through a narrow passage.

Encañonár, *vn.* To begin to grow fledged, to get feathers and wings.—*va.* 1. To put into tubes or pipes. 2. To wind silk on quills made of cane.

Encañutár, *va.* To flute, to mould into the form of tubes and pipes.—*vn.* To form straw.

Encapacetádo, **da**, *a.* Covered with a helmet.

Encapachadúra, *sf.* (In Oil-mills) Number of frails for filtering oil.

Encapachár, *va.* To put into a frail or basket.

Encapádo, **da**, *a.* Cloaked, wearing a cloak.

Encapazár, *va.* To collect or put into a basket.

Encaperuzárse, *vr.* To cover one's head with a hood.

Encapilladúra, *sf.* (Naút.) Tie of a shroud or stay.

Encapillár, *va.* 1. (Naút.) To fix the standing rigging to the mast-head. *Encapillárse el agua*, (Naút.) To ship a head-sea. 2. To put on any clothes over the head.

Encapirotádo, **da**, *a.* Wearing a cloak or hood.

Encapirotár, *va.* To hood a hawk.

Encapotadúra y Encapotamiénto. V. *Sobrecejo.*

Encapotár, *va.* 1. To cover with a cloak or great coat. 2. To cover with a veil, to muffle the face.—*vr.* To lower, to be clouded; applied to the sky.

Encaprichárse, *vr.* To indulge in whims and fanciful desires.

Encapuchár, *va.* To cover any thing with a hood.

Encapuzádo, **da**, *a.* Covered with a hood or cowl.

Encapúzar, *va.* To cover with a long gown.

Encára, *ad.* (Ant.) Yet, even, withal. V. *Aun.*

Encarádo, **da**, *a.* Faced. *Bien ó mal encarado*, Well or ill faced.

Encaramadúra, *sf.* 1. Height, eminence. 2. The act of climbing up an eminence.

Encaramár y Encaramillotár, *va.* 1. To raise; to elevate. 2. To extol, to exaggerate.

Encaramiénto, *sm.* The act of facing or aiming.

Encarár, *vn.* To face, to come face to face.—*va.* To aim, to point or level a firelock.

Encaratuládo, **da**, *a.* Masked, disguised.

Encaratulárse, *vr.* To mask or disguise one's self.

Encárbo, *sm.* Pointer, a dog that points out the game to sportsmen.

Encarcavinár, *va.* 1. To infect with a pestilential smell. 2. To put one into a ditch or foss

Encarcaxádo, da, *a.* Armed with a quiver.
Encarcelación, *sf.* Incarceration.
Encarceladíto, ta, *s.* Confined, imprisoned.
Encarcelár y Encarcerár, *va.* 1. To imprison, to confine in a jail. 2. (Carp.) To compress newly glued timbers.
Encarecedór, *sm.* Praiser, extoller; one who exaggerates.
Encarecér, *va.* 1. To raise the price of commodities. 2. (Met.) To enhance, to exaggerate.
Encarecedaménte, *ad.* Exceedingly, highly.
Encarecimiénto, *sm.* 1. Enhancement, augmentation of value. 2. Exaggeration, hyperbolical amplification. *Con encarecimiento*, Ardently. 2. Carefully.
Encargadaménte, *ad.* 1. Greatly, extremely.
Encargár, *va.* To recommend, to charge, to commit, to stimulate, to urge.—*Encargárse de alguna cosa*, To take charge of any thing.
Encárgo, *sm.* 1. Charge, command, trust conferred. 2. Office, place, employ.
Encariñárse, *vr.* To become passionately fond of.
Encárna, *sf.* Act of giving the entrails of the dead game to the dogs.
Encarnación, *sf.* 1. Incarnation, the act of assuming a body. 2. Carnation, the natural flesh colour.
Encarnadíno, na, *a.* Of a reddish colour.
Encarnádo, da, *a.* 1. Dyed flesh colour. 2. Covered with flesh; incarnate.
Encarnadúra, *sf.* 1. The natural state of flesh in living bodies. 2. Wound.
Encarnamiénto, *sm.* Recovering flesh; applied to a wound healing.
Encarnár, *vn.* To incarn, to incarnate, to breed flesh.—*va.* 1. To incarnadine, to give a flesh colour to pieces of sculpture. 2. To make a strong impression upon the mind. 3. To fill a wound with new flesh. 4. To wound, to pierce the flesh with a dart. 5. To embody. 6. To entice or allure dogs; to feed sporting dogs with flesh.—*vr.* To unite or incorporate one thing with another.
Encárne, *sm.* First feed given to dogs of the entrails of game.
Encarnecér, *vn.* To grow fat and fleshy, to increase in bulk.
Encarnizádo, da, *a.* Blood-shot, inflamed; applied to the eyes.
Encarnizamiénto, *sm.* The act of fleshing or satiating with flesh; cruelty.
Encarnizár, *va.* 1. To flesh, to satiate with flesh. 2. To provoke, to irritate.—*vr.* 1. To be glutted with flesh. 2. To become savage and cruel.
Encáro, *sm.* 1. The act of viewing steadfastly. 2. (And.) Blunderbuss, a wide-mouthed short hand-gun. *Encaro de escopeta*, The act of levelling or pointing a musket or firelock.
Encarrillár, *va.* 1. To direct, to guide, to put in the right road. 2. (Met.) To arrange again what had been deranged.—*vr.* (Naút.) To be fouled or entangled on the sheave of a block; applied to a rope.
Encarroñár, *va.* (In the Jocular Style) To infect, to corrupt.
Encarrujádo, *sm.* Ancient kind of silk stuff.
Encarrujárse, *vr.* To be corrugated, curled, or wrinkled.
Encartación, *sf.* 1. Enrolment. V. *Empadronamiento.* 2. Vassalage, the state of a vassal; tenure at will; servitude. 3. The people or place, which enter into a state of vassalage, or acknowledge one as a lord.—*pl.* Places adjoining the province of Biscay, which enjoy the same privileges as that province.
Encartamiénto, *sm.* 1. Outlawry, proscription. 2. Vassalage. V. *Encartacion.*
Encartár, *va.* 1. To outlaw, to proscribe. 2. To involve in an unpleasant affair. 3. To include, to enrol. 4. To enter in the register of taxes.—*vr.* 1. To receive a card which spoils a game. 2. To spoil one another's hand.
Encartuchár, *va.* To fill cartridges with powder.
Encasaménto, *sm.* Niche, a hollow made in a wall, in which a statue may be placed.
Encasamiénto, *sm.* 1. Reparation of ruinous houses. 2. Niche.
Encasár, *va.* To set a dislocated bone.
Encascabeládo, da, *a.* Filled or adorned with bells.
Encascotár, *va.* To cover with a layer of rubbish.
Encasquetár, *va.* 1. To put on one's hat close to the head. 2. (Met.) To induce one to adopt or espouse an opinion.—*vr.* To persist obstinately in maintaining an opinion.
Encastár, *va.* To meliorate or improve a race of animals.
Encastilládo, da, *a.* 1. Fortified with different castles. 2. (Met.) Elated, lofty, haughty.
Encastilladór, ra, *s.* One who shuts himself up in a castle.
Encastillamiénto, *sm.* Act of shutting up in a castle.
Encastillár, *va.* To fortify with castles.—*vn.* To make the cell of the queen-bee in beehives.—*vr.* 1. To shut one's self up in a castle, by way of defence. 2. (Met.) To persevere in maintaining one's opinion.
Encastrár, *va.* (Naút.) To mortise or scarf pieces of timber.
Encatusár, *va.* V. *Engatusar.*
Encáustico, ca, *a.* Encaustic, belonging to enamel-painting.
Encáusto, *sm.* (Pint.) Enamelling.
Encavárse, *vr.* To incave one's self.
Encáxa, *sf.* Shake hands; expression used by the common people at meeting and shaking hands.
Encaxadór, *sm.* 1. He who enchases or inserts. 2. Instrument for enchasing.
Encaxadúra, *sf.* The act of enchasing or enclosing one thing in another.
Encaxár, *va.* 1. To enchase, to enclose one thing in another. 2. To thrust with violence one thing into another. 3. To introduce something with craft and cunning. 4. To impose upon, to deceive. *Encaxar la suya*, To avail one's self of an opportunity. *Encaxar bien*, To be to the purpose, to come to the point, to be opportune. *Encaxar las manos*, To join or shake hands.—*vr.* To thrust one's self into some narrow place.
Encáxe, *sm.* 1. The act of adjusting or fitting one thing to another. 2. The place or cavity in which any thing is inlaid or inserted. 3. The measure of one thing to adjust with another. 4. Lace. 5. Inlaid work. *Ley del encaxe*, An arbitrary law.
Encaxerádo, da, *a.* (Naút.) Fouled or entan-

gled on the sheave of a block or pulley; applied to a rope.
Encajonádo, sm. Mud-wall, supported by pillars of bricks and stones.
Encajonár, va. To put or pack up in a box.
Encebadamiénto, sm. Surfeit, repletion of horses.
Encebadárse, vr. To be surfeited with barley, and water drunk immediately after it.
Encebolládo, sm. Fricassee of beef or mutton and onions, and seasoned with spice.
Encelár, va. To hide, to conceal.—vr. To conceal one's self.
Encélla, sf. A kind of basket, which serves to mould curds and cheese; a cheese-wattle.
Encellár, va. To mould curds or cheese in a wattle.
Encenagádo, da, a. Mixed or filled with mud.
Encenagamiénto, sm. The act of wallowing in dirt or mire.
Encenagárse, vr. 1. To wallow in dirt or mire, to dirty one's self with mud or mire. 2. (Met.) To wallow in crimes and vices.
Encencerrádo, da, a. Carrying a wether-bell.
Encendér, va. 1. To kindle, to light, to make burn. 2. To set fire to, to set on fire. 3. To heat, to produce heat. 4. (Met.) To inflame, to inspirit, to incite. 5. (Met.) To foment a party, to sow discord.
Encendidaménte, ad. Vividly, ardently; efficaciously. [de color, High coloured.
Encendído, da, a. 1. Inflamed. 2. Encendido
Encendimiénto, sm. 1. Incension, the act of kindling; the state of being on fire. 2. (Met.) Inflammation. 3. (Met.) Liveliness and ardour of human passions and affections.
Encenizár, va. To fill or cover with ashes.
Encensár ó Encensuár, va. To give or take at lawful interest; to lease.
Encénsio, sm. V. Incienso.
Encentadór, sm. Beginner.
Encentadúra y Encentamiénto, s. The first attempt of any thing.
Encentár, va. 1. To begin the use of any thing. 2. To cut, to mutilate a member.
Encepadór, sm. Stocker, gun-stocker.
Encepár, va. 1. To put in the stocks. 2. To stock a gun, to stock the anchor.—vn. To take root.
Encerádo, sm. 1. Oil-cloth, oil-skin. 2. Window-blind. 3. (Naút.) Tarpawling, a piece of cloth besmeared with tar, used to cover the hatches. 4. Sticking-plaster.
Encerádo, da, a. 1. Wax-coloured, like wax. 2. Thick, thickened; applied to an egg half boiled. [&c.
Enceramiénto, sm. Act of waxing paper, cloth,
Encerár, va. 1. To fasten or stiffen with wax. 2. To fill or stain with wax.
Encernadár, va. V. Acernadar.
Encerotár, va. To wax thread.
Encerradéro, sm. 1. Place for keeping sheep before or after shearing. 2. V. Encierro.
Encerrádo, da, a. Brief, succinct.
Encerradór, sm. 1. One who shuts or locks up. 2. Driver of black cattle.
Encerradúra, sf. Cloister, enclosure, closure.
Encerramiénto, sm. 1. Cloister, retreat, place of retirement. 2. Prison, jail, dungeon. 3. The locking up of a thing. 4. Enclosure, ground destined for pasture.
Encerrár, va. 1. To lock or shut up. 2. To contain, to conclude.—vr. To retire or withdraw from the world.
Encerróna, sf. A voluntary retreat, a spontaneous retirement.
Encespedár, va. (Mil.) To line or cover the sides of a moat or foss with sods.
Encestár, va. 1. To gather and put in a basket; to toss in a basket. 2. To impose upon, to deceive.
Encha, sf. (Ant.) Satisfaction, compensation.
Enchancletár, va. 1. To put on slippers. 2. To wear shoes in the manner of slippers.
Enchapinádo, da, a. 1. Made in the manner of pattens. 2. Built and raised upon a vault or arch. [be inundated.
Encharcárse, vr. To be covered with water, to
Enchavetár, va. Enchavetar un perno, (Naút.) To forelock a bolt.
Enchicár, va. V. Achicar.
Encías, sf. pl. Gums, the fleshy coverings which contain the teeth.
Encíclico, ca, a. Encyclic, circular; applied to pastoral letters.
Enciclopédia, sf. Encyclopædia, circle of arts and sciences; round of learning.
Enciénte, ad. (Ant.) Lately, shortly before.
Enciérro, sm. 1. Cloister, religious retreat; enclosure. 2. Prison, close confinement. 3. The act of driving bulls into the pen-fold for the bull-feasts.
Encíma, ad. 1. Above, over. 2. At the top. 3. Over and above, besides.
Encimár, va. To place at the top, to raise high.—vr. To raise one's self upon.
Enciméro, ra, a. That which is placed over or upon. [ilex L.
Encína, sf. (Bot.) Ever-green oak. Quercus
Encinál ó Encinár, sm. Wood, consisting of ever-green oak. [bons.
Encintár, va. To garnish or adorn with rib-
Enclarescér, va. V. Esclarecer.
Enclaustrádo, da, a. Shut up in cloisters.
Enclavación, sf. Act of nailing or fixing.
Enclavadúra, sf. The part where two pieces of wood are joined.
Enclavár, va. 1. To nail, to fasten with nails. 2. To prick horses in shoeing. Enclavar la artillería, To spike up guns.
Enclavijár, va. To unite or join closely. Enclavijar un instrumento, To put pegs in a musical instrument.
Enclénque, sm. One who is of a weak or feeble constitution.
Enclocárse y Encloquecérse, vr. To cluck, to manifest a desire to hatch eggs; applied to hens.
Encobár, vn. To cover or hatch eggs.
Encobijár, va. V. Cobijar.
Encobrádo, da, a. Coppery; copper-coloured.
Encobrír, va. (Ant.) V. Encubrir. [to fowls.
Encoclár, vn. To be disposed to cluck; applied
Encogér, va. 1. To contract, to draw together, to shorten. 2. (Met.) To discourage, to dispirit.—vr. 1. To be low spirited, to be dismayed. 2. To humble one's self, to be dejected. Encogerse de hombros, To shrink the

shoulders with fear; to put an end to any debate, to occasion silence.

Encogidaménte, *ad.* Meanly, abjectly.

Encogído, da, *a.* Pusillanimous, narrow-minded.

Encogimiénto, *sm.* 1. Contraction, the act of contracting, drawing together, or shortening. 2. Lowness of spirits; want of courage. 3. Humility, submission, resignation. *Encogimiento de los costados*, (Naút.) The tumbling home or housing in of the sides of a ship.

Encohetádo, da, *a.* Covered or overlaid with squibs.

Encohetár, *va.* To cover with squibs.

Encoladúra ó Encolamiénto, *s.* The act and effect of glueing.

Encolár, *va.* To glue, to join or fasten with a viscous cement.

Encolerizárse, *vr.* To be in a passion, to be vexed or displeased.

Encomendáble, *a.* Recommendable.

Encomendádo, *sm.* Vassal of a chief of a military order.

Encomendaménto, *sm.* V. *Mandamiento.*

Encomendamiénto, *sm.* V. *Encomienda.*

Encomendár, *va.* 1. To recommend, to commit, to charge. 2. To praise, to applaud.—*vn.* To hold a commandery in a military order.—*vr.* 1. To commit one's self to another's protection. 2. To send compliments and messages. *Sin encoméndarse á Dios ni al diablo*, Temerity, inconsiderateness of any word or action.

Encomendéro, *sm.* 1. Agent, who receives and executes commissions and orders in commercial matters. 2. Pensioner or annuitant, he who enjoys a pension or annuity. 3. One who holds a commandery in a military order.

Encomenzár, *va.* V. *Comenzar.*

Encomiástico, ca, *a.* Encomiastic.

Encomiénda, *sm.* 1. Commission, charge. 2. Message, compliment sent to an absent person. 3. Commandery in a military order; land or rent belonging to a commandery. 4. Pension or annuity granted upon a certain place or fund. 5 Patronage, protection, support. *Encomiendas*, Compliments, invitations, respects. 6. *Encomienda de santiago*, (Bot.) Daffodilly, or jacobæa lily. Amaryllis formosissima *L.*

Encómio, *sm.* Praise, encomium, elogy.

Encompadrár, *vn.* To contract affinity by godfather; to be close friends.

Encompasár, *va.* (Ant.) To encompass. V. *Compasar.*

Enconádo, da, *a.* (Ant.) Tainted, stained, spotted.

Enconamiénto, *sm.* 1. Inflammation, a morbid swelling. 2. (Met.) Provocation, the act of exciting passion or anger; venom.

Enconár, *va.* 1. To inflame, to irritate. 2. To rankle, to fester; applied to a wound.

Encóno y Enconía, *s.* Malevolence, rancour.

Enconóso, sa, *a.* 1. Apt to cause or produce an inflammation. 2. Hurtful, prejudicial, malevolent.

Encorreár, *va.* To put the proper quantity of oil on wool to be carded.

Encontinénte, *ad.* V. *Incontinente.*

En Cóntra, *ad.* Against, in opposition to any thing.

Encontráble, *a.* That which is contrary, or may be encountered.

Encontradaménte, *ad.* Contrarily, in a contrary manner.

Encontradízo, za, *a.* Meeting each other by appointment; chiefly applied to love appointments.

Encontrádo, da, *a.* Opposite, in front.

Encontrár, *vn.* To meet, to encounter.—*va.* To find by chance, to light upon.—*vr.* 1. To encounter in a hostile manner. 2. To be of contrary or opposite opinions. 3. To meet at the same place.

Encontrón, *sm.* Push, shock, violent concourse.

Encopetádo, da, *a.* Presumptuous, boastful.

Encopetár, *va.* To raise the hair high, as in a toupee.

Encorachár, *va.* To put in a leather bag.

Encorádo, da, *a.* Wrapped up in leather.

Encorajádo, da, *a.* Excessively haughty, lofty, arrogant; bold, adventurous.

Encorajár, *va.* To animate, to give courage, to inflame.

Encorár, *va.* To cover with leather, to wrap up in leather.—*vn.* To get a skin; applied to wounds nearly healed.

Encorazádo, da, *a.* 1. Covered with a cuirass. 2 Covered with leather in the cuirass fashion.

Encorchár, *va.* To hive bees, to put them into hives made of cork.

Encorchetár, *va.* To hook, to put on hooks or clasps.

Encordár, *va.* 1. To string musical instruments. 2. To lash or bind with cords or ropes.

Encordelár, *va.* To tie or bind with cords. *Encordelar una cáma*, To cord a bed.

Encórdio, *sm.* V. *Incordio.*

Encordonádo, da, *a.* Adorned with cords.

Encordonár, *va.* To put running strings to a purse or other thing; to tie with strings.

Encorecér, *va.* To skin, to heal the skin.

Encoriación, *sf.* Act of skinning over a sore; healing a wound.

Encornijaménto, *sm.* V. *Cornijamento.*

Encornudár, *vn.* To begin to get horns; applied to black cattle.—*va.* To cuckold.

Encorozár, *va.* To cover the head with a *coroza*, or cone-shaped cap, worn by criminals condemned by the Inquisition.

Encorporár, *va.* V. *Incorporar.*

Encorralár, *va.* To enclose and keep in a yard; applied to cattle.

Encorrér, *vn.* V. *Incurrir.*

Encortár, *va.* V. *Acortar.*

Encortinár, *va.* To provide with curtains.

Encorváda, *sf.* 1. The act of bending or doubling the body. 2. A graceless and awkward manner of dancing. 3. (Bot.) Hatchet coronilla or vetch. Coronilla securidaca *L.*

Encorvadúra y Encorvamiénto, *s.* Act of bending or reducing to a crooked shape. *Hacer la encorvadura*, (Met.) To feign disease to avoid something.

Encorvár, *va.* To incurvate, to bend.

Encosadúra, *sf.* The act of sewing or joining fine linen to some of a coarser sort.

Encostárse, *vr.* (Naút.) To stand in shore, to near the coast.

Encostradúra, *sf.* Incrustation, crust.

Encostrár, *va.* To rough-cast with mortar, made of lime and sand; to incrust.

Encovadúra, *sf.* Act of depositing in a cellar.

Encovár, *va.* 1. To put or lay up in a cellar. 2. (Met.) To guard, to conceal, to enclose.

Encoxárse, *vr.* 1. To grow lame. 2. To be seized

with a fit of illness. 3. (Met.) To feign sickness in order to avoid doing some business.

ENCRASÁR, va. To fatten, to grease.

ENCRESPADÓR, sm. Crisping-pin, curling-iron.

ENCRESPADÚRA Y ENCRESPAMIÉNTO, s. Crispation.

ENCRESPÁR, va. To curl, to frizzle.—vr. 1. (Naút.) To become rough and boisterous; applied to the sea. 2. To be rude or unpolite. 3. To be involved in quarrels and disputes.

ENCRÉSPO, sm. The act and effect of curling.

ENCRESTÁDO, DA, a. 1. Adorned with a crest. 2. (Met.) Haughty, lofty.

ENCRESTÁRSE, vr. 1. To get the crest or comb; applied to a young cock. 2. (Met.) To be proud, elated, haughty.

ENCRINÁDO Y ENCRISNEJÁDO, DA, a. Plaited, braided; applied to the hair.

ENCRUCIJÁDA, sf. Crossway, cross-road.

ENCRUDECÉR, va. 1. To make a wound worse or raw. 2. To exasperate, to irritate.—vr. To be enraged, to become furious with passion.

ENCRUELECÉR Y ENCRUDELECÉR, va. To excite to cruelties, to make cruel.

ENCUBÁR, va. 1. To put liquids into casks, barrels, &c. 2. To put a criminal into a butt, by way of punishment.

ENCUBERTÁR, va. To overspread with a covering of cloth or silk.—vr. To dress and arm one's self for defence of the body.

ENCUBIÉRTA, sf. Fraud, deceit, imposition.

ENCUBIERTAMÉNTE, ad. 1. Hiddenly, secretly. 2. Deceitfully, fraudulently.

ENCUBIÉRTO, TA, a. V. *Cubierto*. [hidden.

ENCUBREDÍZO, ZA, a. That can be concealed or

ENCUBRIDÓR, RA, s. Concealer, one who hides or conceals. *Encubridor de hurtos*, Receiver of stolen goods.

ENCUBRIMIÉNTO, sm. Concealment, the act of hiding or concealing.

ENCUBRÍR, va. To hide, to conceal.

ENCUCÁR, va. To gather nuts and filberts, and store them up.

ENCUÉNTRO, sm. 1. Knock, a sudden stroke. 2. The act of going to meet or see any one. 3. Opposition, difficulty. 4. Joint of the wings, in fowls or birds, next to the breast. *Salir al encuentro*, To go to meet a person in a certain place; to encounter; to prevent a person in what he is to say or observe. *Encuentros*, Temples of a loom.

ENCUITÁRSE, vr. To grieve, to afflict one's self.

ENCULATÁR, va. To place in a hive, honey-comb which was formed after it was full.

ENCULPÁR, va. V. *Culpar*. [stately.

ENCUMBRÁDO, DA, a. High, elevated, lofty,

ENCUMBRAMIÉNTO, sm. 1. The act of raising or elevating. 2. Height, eminence.

ENCUMBRÁR, va. 1. To raise, to elevate. 2. To mount or ascend a height. 3. (Met.) To elevate to dignities or honours.—vr. To be raised or elevated.

ENCUNÁR, va. To put a child in the cradle.

ENCUÑÁR, va. To coin. V. *Acuñar*. [stock.

ENCUREÑÁDO, DA, a. Put into the carriage or

ENCURTÍR, va. To souse in pickle or vinegar.

ENDE, ad. (Ant.) V. *Allí, y De allí*. *Facer ende al*, (For.) To do the contrary of what was desired. *Por ende*. V. *Por tanto*.

ENDÉBLE, a. Feeble, weak. [sides.

ENDECÁGONO, sm. Polygon of eleven angles or

ENDECASÍLABO, BA, a. Eleven syllables. [ditty.

ENDÉCHA Y ENDÉCHAS, sf. Dirge, a doleful

ENDECHADÉRA, sf. V. *Planidera*.

ENDECHÁR, va. To sing funeral songs in honour and praise of the dead.—vr. To grieve, to mourn.

ENDECHÓSO, SA, a. Mournful, doleful.

ENDELIÑÁDO, DA, a. (Joc.) Dressed in style.

ENDEMÁS, ad. (Ant.) Particularly, especially.

ENDÉMICO, CA, a. Endemic, peculiar to a climate.

ENDEMONIÁDO, DA, a. 1. Possessed with the devil. 2. Extremely bad, perverse, or hurtful.

ENDEMONIÁR, va. 1. To possess with the devil. 2. (Met.) To irritate, to provoke.

ENDENTÁR, va. To join with a mortise.

ENDENTECÉR, vn. To cut teeth, to breed teeth, to teeth or tooth.

ENDEÑÁDO, DA, a. Damaged, hurt, inflamed.

ENDERECÉRA, sf. Direct way to any place or thing. [ly.

ENDEREZADAMÉNTE, ad. Justly, rightly, direct-

ENDEREZADÓR, sm. Guide, director; governor.

ENDEREZADÚRA, sf. The straight and right road.

ENDEREZAMIÉNTO, sm. Guidance, direction; the act of guiding or setting right.

ENDEREZÁR, va. 1. To guide, to direct. 2. To rectify, to set right. 3. To address, to dedicate. 4. To go and meet a person.—vn. To take the direct road.—vr. 1. To be erect, to stand upright. 2. (Met.) To fix or establish one's self in a place or employment.

ENDERÉZO, sm. The act of directing a letter.

EN DERREDÓR, ad. Round about. V. *Derredor*.

ENDÉRGUE, sm. (Joc.) Guide, governor. [debts.

ENDEUDÁRSE, vr. To get in debt, to contract

ENDIABLÁDA, sf. Masquerade, a diversion in which the company is dressed in masks of a hideous or ridiculous appearance.

ENDIABLADAMÉNTE, ad. Uglily, abominably.

ENDIABLÁDO, DA, a. Ugly, deformed; perverse, wicked. [2. (Met.) To pervert, to corrupt.

ENDIABLÁR, va. 1. To possess with the devil.

ENDÍBIA, sf. (Bot.) Endive, succory. Cichorium endivia *L.*

ENDILGADÓR, RA, s. Pander, inducer, adviser.

ENDILGÁR, va. 1. To pander, to induce, to persuade. 2. To procure, to facilitate, to accommodate.

ENDIOSAMIÉNTO, sm. 1. Haughtiness, loftiness, pride. 2. Ecstasy, abstraction; disregard of worldly concerns.

ENDIOSÁR, va. To deify, to make a god of, to adore as a god.—vr. 1. To be elated, to be puffed up with pride. 2. To be in a state of religious abstraction, or fervent devotion.

ENDOBLÁDO, DA, a. Applied to a lamb that sucks its own mother and another ewe.

ENDONÁR, va. V. *Donar*. [exchange.

ENDOSÁR Y ENDORSÁR, va. To endorse a bill of

ENDOSELÁR, va. To hang, to make hangings or curtains.

ENDÓSO Ó ENDÓRSO, sm. Endorsement of a bill of exchange; a writing on the back of it, to make it payable to another.

ENDRAGONÁRSE, vr. (In the Jocular Style) To grow furious as a dragon.

Endriágo, *sm.* Fabulous monster, said to have sprung from the union of man and woman.
Endrína, *sf.* Sloe, the fruit of the black-thorn.
Endríno, *sm.* (Bot.) Black-thorn, sloe-tree. Prunus spinosa *L.*
Endríno, na, *a.* Of a sloe colour.
Endrómis, *sm.* V. *Bernia.*
Enducír, *va.* V. *Inducir.*
Endulzamiénto, *sm.* Dulcification, act of sweetening.
Endulzár y Endulzorár, *va.* 1. To sweeten, to make sweet. 2. (Met.) To soften, to make mild; to alleviate the toils of life.
Enduradór, *sm.* Miser, a mean avaricious person.
Endurár, *va.* 1. To harden, to indurate, to make hard. 2. To live in a parsimonious manner. 3. To endure, to bear, to suffer. 4. To delay, to put off.
Endurecér, *va.* 1. To make hard, to harden. 2. (Met.) To accustom the body to labour and hardships; to inure. 3. (Met.) To render one steady in his sentiments and opinions; to exasperate, to irritate.—*vr.* To become rigorous or cruel.
Endurecidaménte, *ad.* Pertinaciously.
Endurecído, da, *a.* 1. Indurated, hardened. 2. Tutored by experience, inured.
Endurecimiénto, *sm.* Hardness; obstinacy, tenacity.
E'ne, *sf.* Spanish name of the letter *N. Ene de palo*, (Joc.) Gallows.
Enéa, *sf.* (Bot.) Cat's-tail, reed-mace. Typha *L.*
Eneático, ca, *a.* Belonging to the number nine.
Enebrál, *sm.* Plantation of juniper-trees.
Enebrína, *sf.* Fruit of the juniper-tree.
Enébro, *sm.* (Bot.) Juniper-tree. Juniperus *L.*
Enechádo, da, *a.* Exposed, as children.
Enéldo, *sm.* 1. (Bot.) Dill. Anethum graveolens *L.* 2. (Ant.) Difficult respiration.
Enemíga, *sf.* 1. Enmity; depravity. 2. An unkind mistress who meets not the affections of a lover.
Enemigáble, *a.* Inimical.
Enemigableménte, *ad.* Inimically.
Enemigaménte, *ad.* In an hostile manner.
Enemigárse, *vr.* To be in a state of enmity.
Enemígo, ga, *a.* Inimical, hostile, contrary.
Enemígo, *sm.* 1. Enemy, antagonist, foe. 2. Fiend; the devil.
Enemistád, *sf.* Enmity, hatred.
Enemistár, *va.* To make an enemy.—*vr.* To become an enemy.
E'neo, ea, *a.* (Poét.) Brazen, belonging to brass.
Energía, *sf.* Energy, power, vigour; strength of expression, force of signification.
Energicaménte, *ad.* Energetically.
Enérgico, ca, *a.* Energetic, forcible, active, vigorous.
Energúmeno, na, *s.* Person possessed with a devil.
Enerizár, *va.* V. *Erizar.*
Enéro, *sm.* January, the first month in the year.
Enertárse, *vr.* (Ant.) To become inert.
Enervár, *va.* To enervate, to deprive of force.
Enesár, *va.* To white-wash.
Enexár, *va.* To put an axle-tree to a cart or carriage.
Enfadadízo, za, *a.* Irritable, irascible.
Enfadár, *va.* To vex, to molest, to trouble.
Enfádo, *sm.* Trouble, vexation, molestation.
Enfadosaménte, *ad.* Vexatiously.
Enfadóso, sa, *a.* Vexatious, troublesome.
Enfaldár, *va.* To lop off the lower branches of trees.—*vr.* To tuck or truss up the skirts of one's clothes.
Enfáldo, *sm.* Act of tucking up one's clothes.
Enfangárse, *vr.* (Naút.) To touch ground in a miry or muddy place.
Enfardadór, *sm.* Packer, he who embales or packs up bales and packages.
Enfardár, *va.* To pack, to embale, to make packages.
Enfardeladór, *sm.* Packer, one who makes up bales.
Enfardeladúra, *sf.* Act of packing merchandise.
Enfardelár, *va.* To bale, to make up into bales.
E'nfasis, *sm.* Emphasis, a remarkable stress laid on a word or sentence.
Enfastiár, *va.* (Ant.) To loathe, to disgust.
Enfaticaménte, *ad.* Emphatically.
Enfático, ca, *a.* Emphatical, impressive.
Enfermaménte, *ad.* Weakly, feebly.
Enfermár, *vn.* To be seized with a fit of illness, to fall ill.—*va.* 1. To make sick. 2. To cause damage or loss. 3. To weaken, to enervate.
Enfermedád, *sf.* 1. Infirmity, indisposition, illness. 2. Damage, disorder, risk.
Enfermería, *sf.* Infirmary, lodgings for the sick. *Enfermería del sollado*, (Naút.) Cock-pit, on board of ships of war, where the surgeons attend the wounded. *Estar en enfermería*, To be in the artisan's shop to be mended.
Enferméro, ra, *s.* Overseer or nurse, who has the care of the sick.
Enfermizár, *va.* To make sick or infirm.
Enfermízo, za, *a.* 1. Infirm, sickly. 2. Not conducive to health.
Enférmo, ma, *a.* 1. Infirm, indisposed, unhealthy. 2. Weak, feeble. 3. Of little importance or consideration. 4. Corrupted, tainted.
Enfermoseár, *va.* V. *Hermosear.*
Enferozár, *va.* To irritate, to infuriate.
Enfervorecér y Enfervorizár, *va.* To heat, to inflame, to incite.
Enfestár, *va.* V. *Enhestar.*—*vr.* To rebel.
Enfeudación, *sf.* Infeudation, the act of putting one in possession of a fee or estate.
Enfeudár, *va.* To feoff, to invest with a right or estate.
Enfiár, *va.* To trust in another.
Enfielár, *va.* To put in a balance.
Enfierecído, da, *a.* Furious, fierce.
Enfilár, *va.* 1. To continue as if united in a file or line. 2. To enfilade, to pierce in a right line; to carry off by a cannot-shot a whole file of the enemy's troops.
En Fin, *ad.* In fine, lastly.
Enfintóso, sa, *a.* (Ant.) Fraudulent, deceitful.
Enfíta, *sf.* Fraud, deceit.
Enfitéusis ó Enfitheósis, *s.* A species of alienation, by which the use and usufruct are transferred, but not the whole right of property.
Enfitéuta, *sm.* Emphyteuta, or emphyteutes.
Enfiteuticário, ria, y Enfitéutico, ca, *a.* Emphyteutic.
Enflaquecér, *va.* To weaken, to diminish, to make thin and lean.
Enflaquecidaménte, *ad.* Effeminately.

Enflaquecimiénto, *sm.* Attenuation, debilitation.

Enflautádo, da, *a.* Turgid, inflated.

Enflautadór, ra, *s.* Inciter, pander.

Enflautár, *va.* To inflate, to stimulate or excite to evil; to procure.

Enflechádo, da, *a.* Applied to a bent bow or arrow ready to discharge.

Enflechástes, *sm. pl.* (Naút.) Ropes which lie across the shrouds, and serve to get up to the mast-head.

Enflorecér, *va.* To adorn or deck with flowers.

Enfogár, *va.* (Ant.) To inflame, to set fire to.

Enfonsádo, da, *a.* Free and exempt from all charges and taxes.

Enfórcia, *sf.* Violence done to any person.

Enfornár, *va.* V. *Enhornar.*

Enfortalecér, *va.* V. *Fortalecer.*

Enfoscádo, da, *a.* Brow-beaten. 2. Confused, entangled.

Enfoscárse, *vr.* To be uneasy, to be troubled or perplexed; to be immersed in business; to be cloudy.

Enfranquecér, *va.* To frank, to make free.

Enfraquecér, *va.* V. *Enflaquecer.*

Enfrascamiénto, *sm.* The act of being entangled between brambles and briers.

Enfrascárse, *vr.* 1. To be entangled between brambles and briers. 2. (Met.) To be involved in difficulties and troubles.

Enfraylár, *va.* To make one a monk or a friar, to induce him to take the vows of a religious order.

Enfrenadór, *sm.* Bridler, one who puts on a bridle.

Enfrenamiénto, *sm.* The act of bridling a horse or putting on the bridle.

Enfrenár, *va.* 1. To bridle, to put on the bridle, to govern by the bridle. 2. To curb, to restrain.

Enfrénte, *ad.* Over against, opposite, in front, front to front.

Enfriadéra, *sf.* Back or cooler, the vessel for cooling any liquid; refrigeratory.

Enfriadéro y Enfriadór, *sm.* Cooling place; refrigeratory.

Enfriamiénto, *sm.* Refrigeration, the act of cooling, the state of being cooled.

Enfriár, *va.* 1. To cool, to refrigerate. 2. (Met.) To allay the heat of passion, to calm the mind.—*vr.* (Met.) To cool, to grow less warm with regard to passion.

Enfroscárse, *vr.* V. *Enfrascarse.*

Enfuciár, *va.* V. *Confiar.*

Enfundadúra, *sf.* The act of casing or putting into cases.

Enfundár, *va.* 1. To case, to put into a case. 2. To fill up to the brim, to cram to stuff. 3. To include, to contain.

Enfurción, *sf.* V. *Infurcion.*

Enfurecér, *va.* To irritate, to enrage; to make proud.—*vr.* To rage, to grow boisterous or furious: applied to the wind and sea.

Enfurruñárse, *vr.* To grow angry, to tiff, to be in a pet.

Enfurtír, *va.* 1. To full or mill clothes. 2. (Among Hatters) To felt.

Engabanádo, da, *sm.* Covered with a *gaban*, or a great coat, with a hood and close sleeves.

Engáce, *sm.* Catenation, connexion. V. *Engarce.*

Engafár, *va.* 1. To bend a cross-bow with a hook or lever. 2. (And.) To carry in a hook a gun charged, when travelling in the fields.

Engalanár, *va.* 1. To adorn, to deck. 2. (Naút.) To dress a ship, to display a variety of colours, ensigns, or pendants.

Engalgár, *va.* To pursue closely, not to lose sight of; applied to greyhounds which are in pursuit of a hare. *Engalgar el ancla,* (Naút.) To back an anchor.

Engalládo, da, *a.* 1. Erect, upright. 2. Haughty, elated.

Enganchádor, *sm.* Crimp, one who decoys into the service of the king.

Enganchamiénto y Engánche, *sm.* Act of entrapping, alluring.

Enganchár, *va.* 1. To hook, to catch with a hook. 2. To entrap, to ensnare. 3. To crimp, to decoy into the service.

Engandújo, *sm.* Twisted thread hanging from fringe.

Engañabóbos, *sm.* Impostor. V. *Engaytador.*

Engañadízo, za, *a.* Deceptible, easily deceived.

Engañadór, *sm.* Cheat, impostor, deceiver.

Engañamiénto y Engañánza. V. *Engaño.*

Engañapastór, *sm.* (Orn.) Kind of owl. V. *Autillo.*

Engañár, *va.* To cheat, to deceive.—*vr.* To be deceived, to mistake. *Ser malo de engañar,* (Fam.) To be not easily deceived, to be sagacious.

Engañífa, *sf.* Deceit, trick, fraudulent action.

Engáño, *sm.* Deceit, fraud, imposition.

Engañosaménte, *ad.* Deceitfully.

Engañóso, sa, *a.* Deceitful, artful, fallacious.

Engarabatár, *va.* To hook, to seize with violence.—*vr.* To grow crooked.

Engarabitárse, *vr.* To climb, to mount, to ascend.

Engarbárse, *vr.* To perch on the highest branch of a tree; applied to birds.

Engarbullár, *va.* To entangle, to involve.

Engárce, *sm.* 1. Catenation, link. 2. Close union or connexión.

Engargantár, *va.* To put any thing into the throat; to thrust the foot into the stirrup, quite to the instep.

Engargolár, *va.* To fit the end of one water-pipe into that of another.

Engaritádo, da, *a.* 1. Cheated, deceived. 2. Surrounded with sentry-boxes.

Engaritár, *va.* 1. To fortify, to adorn with sentry-boxes. 2. To impose upon or deceive in an artful or dexterous manner.

Engarrafadór, *sm.* Grappler.

Engarrafár, *va.* 1. To claw, to seize with the claws or talons. 2. To grapple with hooks.

Engarrotár, *va.* To squeeze and press hard. V. *Agarrotar.*

Engarzadór, *sm.* 1. One who links or enchains, stringer of beads. 2. (Met.) Pimp.

Engarzár, *va.* To enchain, to link; to curl.

Engasajár, *va.* V. *Agasajar.*

Engastadór, *sm.* Enchaser, encloser.

Engastár, *va.* To enclose one thing in another without being screened, such as a diamond in gold; to enchase.

Engáste y Engastadúra, *s.* 1. The act of enchasing or infixing. 2. The hoop or envelope. 3. A pearl flat on one side.

Engatádo, *sm.* A petty robber, a sharper, a thief guilty of petty larceny.

Engatár, *va.* To cheat in a dexterous manner.
Engatilládo, da, *a.* Thick, high-necked; applied to horses and bulls. [iron.
Engatillár, *va.* (Arq.) To bind with a cramp-
Engatusamiénto, *sm.* Deception, cheat.
Engatusár, *va.* To trick without intention to rob or hurt.
Engavillár, *va.* V. *Agavillar.*
Engaytadór, *sm.* Deceiver, seducer, swindler.
Engaytár, *va.* To cheat, to deceive, to swindle one out of something.
Engarzadór, ra, *s.* V. *Engarzador.*
Engarzamiénto, *sm.* V. *Engarce.*
Engazár, *va.* 1. To enchain, to link. 2. (Naút.) To stop or splice an end of a rope in a circular form about a block. 3. To dye in the cloth.
Engendráble, *a.* That may be engendered.
Engendradór, ra, *s.* One who engenders or produces.
Engendrár, *va.* 1. To beget, to engender. 2. To produce, to bear fruit; to create.
Engéndro, *sm.* Fœtus, a shapeless embryo. *Mal engendro,* A low breed; a perverse youth.
Engénio, *sm.* (Ant.) V. *Ingenio.*
Engéño, *sm.* V. *Ingenio* y *Máquina.*
Engibár, *va.* To crook, to make gibbous.
Engilmár, *va.* (Naút.) To pick up a mast which is floating in the sea. [mend a spar.
Engimelgár, *va.* (Naút.) To fish a mast, to
Engína, *sf.* Quinsy. V. *Angina.*
Englandádo, da; y **Englantádo, da**, *a.* (Blas.) Covered with acorns; applied to the oak.
Engoládo, da, *a.* Collared, wearing a collar.
Engolfár, *vn.* (Naút.) To enter a gulf or deep bay.—*vr.* 1. To be engaged in arduous undertakings or difficult affairs. 2. To be lost in thought, to be absorbed in meditation.
Engolilládo, da, *a.* Wearing always the ruff or collar which is worn by lawyers in Spain.
Engollár, *va.* To make a horse carry his head and neck by means of the bridle.
Engolletádo, da, *a.* (Joc.) Elated, puffed up, presumptuous, haughty. [ty.
Engolletárse, *vr.* To elate, to become haugh-
Engolondrinárse, *vr.* 1. (Joc.) To be elated, to be puffed up with pride. 2. (Bax.) To fall in love, to be smitten with love. [thing.
Engolosinár, *va.* To inspire a longing for any
Engomadéro, ra, *a.* That may be stiffened with starch or gum.
Engomadúra, *sf.* 1. Act of gumming. 2. Coat which bees lay over their hives before making the wax.
Engomár, *va.* To gum, to stiffen with gum.
Engorár, *va.* To addle. V. *Enhuerar.*
Engordadéro, *sm.* Stall or sty to fatten hogs.
Engordadór, *sm.* One who makes it his sole business to pamper himself.
Engordár, *va.* To pamper, to fatten.—*vn.* 1. To grow fat. 2. To grow rich, to amass a fortune.
Engorgetádo, da, *a.* Palisaded breast-high.
Engorrár, *va.* (Ant.) To obstruct, to detain.
Engórro, *sm.* Impediment, embarrassment.
Engorróso, sa, *a.* Troublesome, tiresome.
Engoznár, *va.* To hinge, to put hinges on doors and windows.
Engrandár, *va.* V. *Agrandar.*
Engrandecér, *va.* 1. To augment, to aggrandize. 2. To promote to a higher station, to exalt. 3. (Met.) To exaggerate, to magnify.
Engrandecimiénto, *sm.* 1. Increase, aggrandisement. 2. Exaggeration, hyperbolical amplification.
Engranerár, *va.* To enclose in a granary.
Engranujár, *vn.* To be filled with grain.
Engrapár, *va.* To secure, to unite or bind with cramp-irons.
Engrasár, *va.* 1. To grease, to oil. 2. To stain with grease. 3. To dress cloth. 4. (Met.) To pickle. [to affect gravity
Engravedár, *va.* To assume an air of dignity
Engredár, *va.* To bedaub with marl or fuller's earth. [pomp in dress
Engreimiénto, *sm.* Presumption, vanity, vain
Engreír, *va.* To encourage any one's pride and petulance, to make him pert and saucy.—*r.* To deck or attire one's self in style, to be extravagant in dress.
Engrifárse, *vr.* To tiff, to be in a pet, to be displeased.
Engrosár, *va.* 1. To make any thing fat and corpulent, to increase its bulk. 2. To make strong or vigorous.—*vn.* To grow strong, to increase in vigour and bulk.
Engrudadór, *sm.* Paster, one who pastes.
Engrudamiénto, *sm.* Act of pasting.
Engrudár, *va.* To fasten with paste.
Engrúdo, *sm.* 1. Paste, flour and water boiled together so as to make a cement. 2. (Naút.) Cement, made chiefly of pounded glass and cow-hair, used to stanch the planks of a ship
Engrumecérse, *vr.* To clot.
Engualdrapár, *va.* To caparison a horse with rich trappings.
Enguantádo, da, *a.* Wearing gloves.
Enguantárse, *vr.* To make too much use of gloves. [dressed
Enguedejádo, da, *a.* Dressed in style, ful
Enguijarrár, *va.* To pave with pebbles.
Enguillár, *va.* (Naút.) To wind a thin rope around a thicker one.
Enguirnaládo, da, *a.* Adorned with garlands
Enguizgár, *va.* To excite, to incite, to set on
Engullidór, ra, *s.* Devourer, one who swallows without mastication.
Engullír, *va.* To devour and swallow meat without chewing it.
Engurruñárse, *vr.* To be melancholy; applied to birds.
Enhacinár, *va.* V. *Hacinar.*
Enhadár, *va.* V. *Enfadar.*
Enhambrecér, *vn.* To be hungry.
Enharinár, *va.* To cover or besprinkle with flour. [to cloy.
Enhastiár, *va.* To disgust, to excite disgust,
Enhastillár, *va.* To put arrows in a quiver.
Enhatijár, *va.* To cover the mouths of hives with bass weed in order to move them from one place to another.
Enhebrár, *va.* 1. To thread a needle. 2. (Met.) To link, to unite or connect closely.
Enhenár, *va.* To cover with hay, to wrap up in hay. [herbs.
Enherbolár, *va.* To poison with venomous
Enhestadór, *sm.* He who erects.
Enhestadúra y **Enhestamiénto**, *s.* Erection.

Enhestár, va. To erect, to set upright; to raise an army. [gling, entanglement.
Enhestradúra y Enhestramiénto, s. Entan-
Enhielár, va. To mix with gall or bile.
Enhiládo, da, a. Well arranged, disposed in good order.
Enhilár, va. 1. To thread, to pass through with a thread. 2. To direct, to tend; to take the way or road to any thing or place; to arrange.
Enhorabuéna, sf. Congratulation, the act of expressing joy for the happiness or success of another.
En hora buéna, ad. Term of congratulation.
En hora mála, ad. Word of scorn, displeasure, or contempt; in an evil hour.
Enhornár, va. To put into an oven to be baked.
Enhotádo, a. (Ant.) V. *Confiado.*
Enhotár, va. V. *Azuzar.*
Enhuecár, va. V. *Ahuecar.*
Enhuerár, va. To lay addle eggs, to addle.
Enibír, va. V. *Inhibir.*
Enigma, sm. Enigma, a riddle; an obscure question; a position expressed in obscure or ambiguous terms.
Enigmático, ca, a. Enigmatical.
Enigmatísta, sm. Enigmatist.
Enjaezár, va. To caparison a horse with rich trappings.
Enjaguadiéntes, sm. V. *Enjuagadientes.*
Enjaguár, va. To rinse the mouth and teeth. V. *Enjuagar.*
Enjalbegadór, ra, s. White-washer, a plasterer who white-washes walls. [walls.
Enjalbegadúra, sf. Act of white-washing
Enjalbegár, va. 1. To white-wash the walls of a building. 2. (Met.) To paint, to lay white paint on the face.
Enjardinár, va. To put a bird of prey into a meadow or green field.
Enjaretádo, sm. (Naút.) Gratings, a kind of lattice-work between the main and fore-mast, which serves for a defence when the enemy attempts to board. *Enjaretádo de proa,* The beak or head gratings.
Enjaulár, va. 1. To cage, to shut up in a cage. 2. (Met.) To imprison, to confine.
Enjorguinárse, vr. To be stained or blackened with soot.
Enjoyár, va. 1. To adorn with jewels. 2. To set a ring with diamonds or other precious stones. 3. (Met.) To heighten the lustre and brilliancy of any thing, to give additional splendour. [used in jewellery.
Enjoyeládo, da, a. Applied to gold or silver
Enjoyeladór, sm. Enchaser, he who enchases.
Enjuagadiéntes, sm. Mouthful of water or wine for rinsing or cleansing the mouth and teeth after a meal.
Enjuagadúra, sf. Act of rinsing the mouth.
Enjuagár, va. 1. To rinse or cleanse the mouth and teeth. 2. To rinse clothes, to wash the soap out.
Enjuágue, sm. 1. Water, wine, or other liquid, used to rinse or cleanse the mouth and teeth. 2. (Met.) Change or alteration made without sufficient reflection and consideration. 3. (Met.) Self-complacency, vain-gloriousness on account of noble descent, riches, or talents; ostentation.

Enjuanetádo, da, a. Troubled with corns.
Enjuiciár, va. To prepare a cause or law-suit for judgment.
Enjúllo, sm. The cloth-beam of a loom.
Enjuncár, va. To tie with ropes made of rush.
Enjúnque, sm. (Naút.) The heaviest or most weighty part of a cargo, which serves as ballast, such as iron, &c.
Enjuramiénto, sm. A legal oath.
Enjurár, va. (Ant.) To yield, to transfer.
Enlabiadór, ra, s. Wheedler, cajoler, seducer.
Enlabiár, va. To wheedle, to cajole, to entice or persuade by kind and soft words.
Enlábio, sm. Suspension, persuasion, enchantment by eloquence or words.
Enláce, sm. 1. Connexion or coherence of one thing with another. 2. (Met.) Kindred, affinity. 3. Flourish, figures formed by lines curiously drawn with a pen.
Enlaciár, vn. To be lax, or languid.—vr. To wither, to become dry, to decay; applied to plants and fruit.
Enladrilládo, sm. Pavement made of tiles.
Enladrilladór, sm. Tiler, one who paves with flags or tiles. [or tiles.
Enladrillár, va. To floor or pave with flags
Enlamár, va. To cover land with slime; applied to inundations. [wool.
Enlanádo, da, a. Covered or supplied with
Enlardár, va. To rub with grease, to baste. V. *Lardar.*
Enlárgues, sm. pl. (Naút.) Rope-ends fastened to the head of a sail, with which it is tied to the yard.
Enlazadór, ra, s. Binder, uniter.
Enlazamiénto y Enlazadúra, s. Connexion, binding, uniting.
Enlazár, va. To bind, to join, to unite; to connect.
Enlechuguilládo, da, a. Applied to one who wears a ruff round the neck.
Enlevár, va. V. *Elevar.*
Enlexiár, va. To make into lye.
Enligárse, vr. To be united or joined by means of a viscous or glutinous substance; to stick, to adhere. [to soil.
Enlizár, va. To vitiate, to corrupt; to stain,
Enlizár, va. To provide a loom with leashes.
Enllenár, va. V. *Llenar.*
Enllentecér, vn. To soften, to blandish.
Enlodadúra, sf. Act of daubing and filling up with mud.
Enlodár, va. 1. To bemire, to bedaub with mud. 2. To stop or shut up a vessel with loam or clay. 3. (Met.) To tarnish one's character or reputation.
Enloquecér, va. To enrage, to make mad.—vn. To become enraged, to grow mad; to grow barren; applied to trees. [ing.
Enloquecimiénto, sm. Enraging, immadden-
Enlosár, va. To flag or lay a floor with flags.
Enlozanárse, vr. To boast of one's dexterity or strength.
Enlucernár, va. V. *Deslumbrar.*
Enlucidór, sm. Whitener.
Enlucimiénto, sm. 1. The white-washing of a wall. 2. The scouring of plate.
Enlucír, va. 1. To white-wash a wall. 2. To scour or clean plate with whiting or chalk.

ENLUSTRECÉR, va. To clean, to brighten, to render bright.
ENLUTÁR, va. 1. To put in mourning. 2. To veil, to cover with a veil.
ENMACHAMBRÁR, va. To scarf pieces of timber together. [or cover of wood.
ENMADERAMIÉNTO ó ENMADERACIÓN, s. Work
ENMADERÁR, va. To roof or cover a house with timber.
ENMAGRECÉR, vn. To grow lean or meagre; to lose fat.
ENMALECÉR, vn. To fall sick.
ENMALLETÁDO, DA, a. (Naút.) Fouled; applied to cables and ropes. V. *Enredado.*
ENMANTÁR, va. To cover with a blanket.—vr. To be melancholy; applied to birds.
ENNÁR, va. (Naút.) To wet the sails.
ENMARAÑÁR, va. 1. To entangle, to perplex, to involve in difficulties. 2. (Met.) To puzzle, to confound.
ENMARÁRSE, vr. (Naút.) To get or take sea-room.
ENMARIDÁR, vn. To marry.
ENMARILLECÉRSE, vr. To become pale or yellow.
ENMAROMÁR, va. To tie with a rope.
ENMASCARÁR, va. 1. To mask, to cover the face with a mask. 2. (Met.) To cloak, to give a false appearance.
ENMECHÁR, va. (Naút.) To rabbet, to fit and join two pieces of timber.
ENMELÁR, va. 1. To bedaub or besmear with honey. 2. (Met.) To sweeten, to give a pleasing taste.
ENMENDACIÓN, sf. Emendation.
ENMENDADAMÉNTE, ad. Accurately, exactly.
ENMENDADÓR, sm. Corrector, emendator.
ENMENDADÚRA Y ENMENDAMIÉNTO. V. *Enmienda.*
ENMENDÁR, va. 1. To correct, to reform. 2. To repair, to compensate. 3. (For.) To revoke, to abrogate. *Enmendar la plana,* (Met.) To excel, to surpass others.
ENMERDÁR, va. To dirty, to make dirty.
ENMIÉNDA, sf. 1. Emendation, correction. 2. Reward, premium 3. (For.) Satisfaction, compensation.
ENMIÉNTE, sf. V. *Memoria.*
ENMIENZÁR, va. (Ant.) V. *Empezar.*
ENMOCECÉR, vn. To recover the vigour of youth.
ENMOCHIGUÁR, va. V. *Multiplicar.*
ENMOHECÉRSE, vr. To mould, to grow mouldy or musty.
ENMOLLECÉR, va. To soften, to make soft or tender.
ENMONDÁR, va. To clear off the knots from cloth in woollen manufactories.
ENMONTADÚRA, sf. Elevation, erection.
ENMORDAZÁR, va. To gag.
ENMUDECÉR, vn. 1. To grow dumb, to be deprived of speech. 2. To be silent, to be still. —va. To impose silence, to hush.
ENNEGRECÉR, va. 1. To blacken, to make black. 2. (Met.) To darken, to obscure.
ENNOBLECÉR, va. 1. To ennoble, to illustrate. 2. (Met.) To adorn, to embellish.
ENNOBLECIMIÉNTO, sm. Act of ennobling.
ENNOVIÁR, va. (Joc.) To contract marriage.
ENNUDECÉR, vn. V. *Anudarse.*
ENODACIÓN, sf. Illustration, explanation.

ENÓDIO, sm. Fawn, a young deer.
ENODRÍDA, a. Barren; applied to a hen which is past laying eggs.
ENOJADAMÉNTE, ad. Fretfully.
ENOJADÍZO, ZA, a. Fretful, peevish.
ENOJÁNTE, pa. He who vexes.
ENOJÁR, va. 1. To vex, to irritate. 2. To molest, to trouble. 3. To offend, to injure.—vr. To be fretful, or peevish.
ENÓJO, sm. 1. Fretfulness, peevishness. 2. Offence, injury.
ENOJOSAMÉNTE, ad. Vexatiously.
ENOJÓSO, SA, a. Offensive, vexatious.
ENOJUÉLO, sm. Slight peevishness.
ENORFANECÍDO, DA, a. V. *Huérfano.*
ENÓRME, a. 1. Enormous, vast, huge. 2. Wicked beyond common measure.
ENORMEMÉNTE, ad. Immoderately, enormously.
ENORMIDÁD, sf. 1. Enormity, deviation from all rule and measure. 2. An enormous deed, an atrocious crime. [L.
ENÓTERA, sf. (Bot.) Primrose. Primula veris
ENOYÁR, va. V. *Enojar.*
EN POS, ad. After, in pursuit of.
ENQUADERNACIÓN, sf. The act of binding books, the cover or binding of books.
ENQUADERNADÓR, sm. 1. Book-binder. 2. (Met.) Uniter.
ENQUADERNÁR, va. 1. To bind books. 2. (Met.) To join again what was disjoined; to reconcile. [cion.
ENQUÉSTA, sf. (Ant.) INQUEST. V. *Averigua-*
ENQUICIÁDO, DA, a. 1. Hung upon hinges. 2. (Met.) Built upon a strong and solid foundation.
ENQUICIÁR, va. To hinge, to put on hinges.
ENQUILLOTRÁRSE, vr. 1. To be jumbled together 2. (Fam.) To fall in love, to be enamoured.
ENQUIRIDIÓN, sm. Compendium, summary, abridgment.
ENRAMÁDA, sf. 1. Hut covered with the branches of trees. 2. Shed, pent-house.
ENRAMÁR, va. To cover with the branches of trees or boughs.
ENRANCIÁRSE, vr. 1. To grow rancid, to be stale. 2. (Met.) To keep, to preserve itself from corruption.
ENRARECÉR, va. To thin, to rarefy.
ENRASÁDO, DA, a. Smoothed. *Puertas enrasadas,* Plain doors, without any carved work or ornaments.
ENRASÁR, va. To smooth, to plane, to make even.—vn. To be bald, or without hair.
ENRASTRÁR, va. (Murc.) To string the silk-cods in order to extract the seed and wind the silk.
ENRAYÁR, va. To fix spokes in a wheel.
ENRAYGONÁR, va. To fix bass-weed in the walls of silk-worm sheds for the worms to begin to spin.
ENREDADÉRA, sf. Small bind-weed, bell-bind. Convolvulus arvensis *L.* It is also a general name for all twining plants.
ENREDÁDO, DA, a. 1. Entangled, matted. 2. (Naút.) Foul; applied to cables and ropes which are entangled.
ENREDADÓR, RA, s. 1. One who entangles, insnares, or involves in difficulties. 2. Tattler, tale-bearer; one who scatters seeds of discord.

Enredamiento, *sm.* Intertillation, turning into a circle.

Enredár, *va.* 1. To entangle, to insnare. 2. To involve in difficulties or perplexities. 3. To play tricks, as boys are wont to do. 4. To sow discord. 5. To lay snares or nets for birds.

Enrédo, *sm.* 1. The act of involving or insnaring. 2. Perplexity, embarrassment. 3. Imposition, falsehood. 4. Plot of a play.

Enredóso, sa, *a.* Full of snares and difficulties.

Enrehojár, *va.* (Among Wax-chandlers) To remove the bleached leaves and thin cakes of wax.

Enrejádo, *sm.* 1. Trellis, a structure of iron, wood, or osier, the parts crossing each other like a lattice. 2. Kind of open embroidery or lace worn by ladies.

Enrejár, *va.* 1. To fix a grating to a window. 2. To fix the ploughshare to the plough. 3. To make a trellis. 4. To wound cattle's feet with a ploughshare.

Enrevesádo, da, *a.* V. *Revesado.*

Enriadór, *sm.* One who steeps or submerges.

Enriár, *va.* To steep or put hemp and flax in water, in order to macerate the stalky parts of the plant.

Enridár, *va.* V. *Enredar y Azuzar.*

Enrielár, *va.* To make ingots of gold or silver.

Enripiár, *va.* To fill up the cavities of any thing.

Enriquecedór, ra, *s.* One who enriches.

Enriquecér, *va.* 1. To enrich, to aggrandise. 2. To adorn.—*vn.* To grow rich.

Enriquéño, ña, *a.* Belonging to Henry.

Enriquez, *sm.* Fitz-Henry; a family name.

Enriscádo, da, *a.* Mountainous, craggy; full of rocks and cliffs.

Enriscár, *va.* To place on the top of mountains or rocks.—*vr.* To take refuge among rocks.

Enristrár, *va.* 1. To fix the but-end of a lance in the rest or support; to range or file. 2. (Met.) To go direct to any place, to meet any difficulty.

Enristre, *sm.* Act of fixing a lance.

Enrizamiénto, *sm.* Act of curling; irritating.

Enrizár, *va.* To curl, to turn into ringlets; to irritate. [oak.

Enroblescído, da, *a.* Hard and strong, like an

Enrobustecér, *va.* To make robust.

Enrocár, *va.* (At Chess) To castle the king.

Enrodár, *va.* To break or execute on the wheel.

Enrodeládo, da, *a.* Armed with a shield.

Enrodrigonár, *va.* To prop vines with stakes.

Enromár, *va.* To blunt, to dull an edge or point.

Enróna, *sf.* (Ar.) Rubbish or refuse of works.

Enronár, *va.* To throw rubbish in any place.

Enronquecér, *va.* To make hoarse.—*vn.* To grow hoarse.

Enronquecimiénto, *sm.* V. *Ronquera.*

Enroñár, *va.* To fill with scabs or scurf.

Enrosár, *va.* To tinge, dye, or give a rose-colour.

Enroscadaménte, *ad.* Intricately.

Enroscadúra, *sf.* Act of twisting; sinuosity.

Enroscár, *va.* To twine, twist, or lay any thing round.

Enrozár ó Enroxecér, *va.* 1. To make iron red-hot. 2. To tinge, dye, or give a red colour. 3. To put to the blush

Enrubescér, *va.* To make red. [making red.

Enrubiadór, ra, *s.* That which has the power of

Enrubiár, *va.* To tinge, dye, or give a bright reddish colour.

Enrubío, *sm.* Rubefaction.

Enrudecér, *va.* To weaken the intellect, to make dull.

Enruinecér ó Enruinescér, *vn.* To become vile. [ed.

Enruinecído, da, *a.* Ruined, reduced, corrupt-

Enrunár, *va.* V. *Enronar.*

Ensabanár, *va.* To wrap up in sheets.

Ensacár, *va.* To enclose or put in a sack.

Ensaláda, *sf.* 1. Salad, a food of raw herbs, seasoned with salt, oil, vinegar, &c. 2. Hodge-podge, medley.

Ensaladéra, *sf.* Salad-dish or bowl.

Ensaladílla, *sf.* 1. Dry sweetmeats of different sorts and sizes. 2. Jewel made up of different precious stones.

Ensaladísta, *sm.* Green grocer, or purveyor of vegetables to the king.

Ensálma, *sf.* Pack-saddle. V. *Enzalma.*

Ensalmadéra, *sf.* 1. Sorceress, enchantress. 2. A beautiful woman.

Ensalmadór, ra, *s.* 1. Bone-setter, one who adjusts dislocated bones. 2. One who pretends to cure by charms.

Ensalmár, *va.* 1. To set dislocated bones. 2. To enchant, to charm, to bewitch; to lure by spells. 3. To make pack-saddles. V. *Enxalmar. Ensalmar á alguno*, To break the head.

Ensálmo, *sm.* Enchantment, spell, charm.

Ensalobrárse, *vr.* To become putrid and corrupt, as stagnant water.

Ensalvajár, *va.* To brutalize, to brutify.

Ensalzadór, *sm.* Exalter, praiser.

Ensalzamiénto, *sm.* Exaltation.

Ensalzár, *va.* 1. To extol, to exalt, to aggrandise. 2. To magnify, to exaggerate.—*vr.* To boast, to display one's own worth or actions.

Ensambenitár, *va.* To put on the *sambenito*, a gown marked with a yellow cross before and behind, and worn by penitent convicts of the Inquisition.

Ensambladór, *sm.* Joiner, one whose trade is to make utensils of wood joined.

Ensambladúra y Ensambláge ó Ensámble, *s.* 1. Joinery, the trade of a joiner. 2. Art of joining boards, planks, and timbers together. *Ensambladura de miláno*, (Naút.) A swallow-tail-scarf.

Ensamblár, *va.* To join or unite pieces of wood.

Ensáncha, *sf.* Extension, ampliation, enlargement. *Ensánchas*, Gores put in clothes. V. *Ensanche. Dar ensánchas*, To give too much license or liberty for any actions.

Ensanchár, *va.* To widen, to extend, to enlarge. *Ensanchar el corazon*, To cheer up, to raise one's spirit, to unburthen the mind. —*vr.* To assume an air of importance, to affect grandeur and dignity.

Ensanchamiénto y Ensánche, *sm.* 1. Dilatation, augmentation. 2. Outlet of clothes.

Ensandecér, *vn.* To grow crazy, to turn mad.

Ensangostár, *va.* To narrow, to contract.

Ensangrentamiénto, *sm.* Stain of blood.

Ensangrentár, *va.* 1. To imbrue, to stain with

blood. 2. To impeach one of a crime in terms of aggravation, to aggravate a criminal action.—vr. 1. To be over-zealous in the pursuit of a thing; to be obstinate. 2. (Met.) To proceed in a cruel and barbarous manner.

Ensáñwo, sm. V. *Denuesto.*

Ensañár, va. To irritate, to enrage.

Ensarbyár ó Ensarillár, va. (Gal. y Ast.) To reel yarn in order to form it into skeins.

Ensarnecér, vn. To get the itch.

Ensartár, va. 1. To string, to file on a string. 2. (Met.) To make or propose a string of observations.

Ensayadór, sm. 1. Assayer, an officer of the mint appointed to try precious metals. 2. Rehearser, prompter on the stage.

Ensayár, va. 1. To assay precious metals. 2. To instruct, to teach, to make dexterous. 3. To rehearse a play. 4. To examine, to prove.

Ensáy ó Ensáye, sm. Assay, trial, proof.

Ensáyo, sm. 1. Assay, trial, proof. 2. Rehearsal of a play. 3. Essay.

Ensebár, va. To grease, to anoint with grease.

Enselvár, va. V. *Emboscar.*

Ensémbla, Ensemble, Ensembra, ad. (Ant.) V. *Juntamente.*

Ensenáda, sf. Creek, cove; a small bay between two points of land.

Ensenádo, a. Having the form of a bay, creek, or gulf.

Ensenár, va. To imbosom, to put in one's bosom. *El navio se enseno,* (Naút.) The ship is entered the bay.

Enséña, sf. Standard, colours.

Enseñáble, a. That may be taught.

Enseñadéro, ra, a. Susceptible of instruction.

Enseñádo, da, a. 1. Taught, learned. 2. Accustomed. *Enseñado á trabajos,* Inured to hardships.

Enseñádor, ra, s. Teacher, instructor.

Enseñánza ó Enseñamiénto, s. Teaching, instruction.

Enseñár, va. 1. To teach, to instruct. 2. To show the way, to point out the road.—vr. To accustom or habituate one's self; to be inured.

Enséño, sm. V. *Enseñanza.*

Enseñoreadór, sm. He who domineers.

Enseñoreár, va. To lord, to domineer.

Enserár, va. To cover with bass-weed.

Enséres, sm. pl. Chattels, marketable effects.

Enserpentádo, da, a. Enraged, furious.

Enserrinár, va. To varnish.

Ensilár, va. 1. To preserve grain in a place under ground. 2. (Met.) To gobble, to eat much.

Ensilládo, da, a. Hollow-backed; applied to horses.

Ensilladúra, sf. The part on which a saddle is placed on a horse or mule.

Ensillár, va. 1. To saddle. 2. To raise, to exalt.

Ensoberbecér, va. To make proud, to puff up with haughtiness and pride.—vr. 1. To become proud and haughty, to be arrogant. 2. (Naút.) To become boisterous; applied to the sea.

Ensogár, va. To tie or fasten with a rope.

Ensolerár, va. To fix stools to bee-hives.

Ensolvedór, ra, s. Resolver, declarer.

Ensolvér, va. 1. To jumble, to mix confusedly together. 2. (Med.) To resolve, to discuss, to dissipate.—vr. To be included or contained, to be reduced.

Ensoñár, va. V. *Soñar.*

Ensopár, va. To make soup by steeping bread in wine.

Ensordadéra, sf. V. *Enes.*

Ensordamiénto, sm. Deafness.

Ensordecér, va. To make deaf, to cause deafness.—vn. 1. To grow deaf, to be deprived of the sense of hearing. 2. To become silent, to observe silence.

Ensordecimiénto, sm. Act of making deaf, surdity.

Ensortijamiénto, sm. Act of curling the hair, or ringing animals.

Ensortijár, va. 1. To ring, to form into a ring. 2. To ring hogs, buffaloes, or other beasts; to restrain them by iron rings in their noses. *Ensortijar las manos,* To wring the hands in grief.

Ensotárse, vr. To conceal one's self in a thicket.

Ensuciadór, ra, s. Stainer, defiler.

Ensuciamiénto, sm. Act of dirtying, staining, or polluting.

Ensuciár, va. 1. To stain, to dirty. 2. (Met.) To defile, to pollute with vicious habits.—vr. 1. To dirty one's bed, clothes, &c. 2. To allow one's self to be bribed by presents.

Ensuéño, sm. Sleep, the act of sleeping. V. *Sueño.*

En Súma, ad. In short, in fine.

Ensuyár, va. V. *Emprender.*

Enta, ad. V. *Desde y Hácia.*

Entablación, sf. Register, note, memorandum.

Entabládo, sm. 1. Floor made of boards. 2. *Entablado de la cofa,* (Naút.) Flooring or platform of the top.

Entabladúra, sf. Act of flooring.

Entablamiénto, sm. 1. Roof of boards. 2. Shed, pent-house.

Entablár, va. 1. To cover with boards, to floor with boards. *Entablar un navio,* (Naút.) To plank a ship. *Entablar con solapadura,* (Naút.) To plank with clincher-work. 2. To bring an affair on the tapis, to take the necessary preparatory steps for attaining one's end. 3. To write a memorial on tablets in churches.

Entablillár, va. To secure with small boards, to bind up a broken leg.

Entalamádo, da, a. Hung with tapestry.

Entalamadúra, sf. Awning of a boat, carriage, &c.

Entalamár, va. To cover with cloth or tapestry.

Entalegár, va. To put in a bag or sack.

Entalingadúra, sf. (Naút.) The act of fastening the cable to the anchor, or of clinching the cable.

Entalingár, va. (Naút.) To clinch the cable, to fasten it to the anchor.

Entalláble, a. Capable of being sculptured.

Entalladór, sm. 1. Sculptor, a cutter in wood or stone. 2. Engraver.

Entalladúra y Entallamiénto, s. Sculpture, act of sculpturing.

Entallár, va. 1. To sculpture, to carve; to cut figures in wood or stone. 2. To engrave, to picture by incisions in copper.—vn. To cut or shape a thing so as to fit it to the body.

Entálle, *sm.* The work of a sculptor or engraver.

Entallecér, *vn.* To shoot, to sprout; applied to plants.

En tánto, *ad.* In the mean time.

Entapizár, *va.* To hang or adorn with tapestry.

Entarascár, *va.* (Fam.) To cover with too many ornaments.

Entarimádo, *sm.* Boarded floor.

Entarimár, *va.* To cover a floor with boards.

Entarquinár, *va.* To bemire, to cover with mud or mire; to manure land with mud.

Ente, *sm.* 1. Entity, being. 2. Ridiculous man.

Entecádo, **da**, *a.* 1. Stiff, unable to move. 2. (Met.) Pusillanimous, timid.

Entéco, **ca**, *a.* Infirm, weak, languid.

Entejádo, **da**, *a.* Made in the form or shape of tiles.

Entelarañárse, *vr.* To be clouded or overcast; applied to the sky.

Entelerído, **da**, *a.* Fearful, timid.

Enténa, *sf.* (Naút.) Lateen yard.

Entenádo, **da**, *s.* Child of a former marriage.

Entenállas, *sf. pl.* A small hand-vice.

Entendéras, *sf. pl.* Understanding, judgment.

Entendedór, **ra**, *s.* One who understands.

Entendér, *va.* 1. To understand, to comprehend, to conceive, to believe, to hear. 2. To remark, to take notice of. 3. To reason, to think, to judge.—*vn.* 1. To be employed about or engaged in any thing. *Dar en que entender*, To molest, to disturb; to put one in care or make anxious, to distress. 2. To intend, to have an intention of doing any thing. 3. To make one understand. *A' mi entender*, In my opinion. *No lo entenderá galvez*, It is an intricate difficult thing.—*vr.* 1. To have some motive for doing any thing. *El se entiende*, He knows what he is about. 2. To be agreed.

Entendidaménte, *ad.* Knowingly, prudently.

Entendído, **da**, *a.* Wise, learned, prudent. *Darse por entendido*, To manifest by signs or words that the thing is understood; to answer any attention or compliment in the customary manner.

Entendimiénto, *sm.* 1. Understanding, knowledge, judgment. 2. Explanation, illustration.

Entenebrecér, *va.* To obscure, to darken.

Enteraménte, *ad.* Entirely, fully, completely.

Enterár, *va.* 1. (Ant.) To complete, to make entire. 2. To reimburse, to pay. 3. To inform, to acquaint, to instruct.

Enteréza, *sf.* 1. Entireness, integrity. 2. Rectitude, uprightness; perfection. 3. Fortitude, firmness of mind. 4. Severe and rigid observance of discipline. 5. Haughtiness, presumption. *Entereza virginal*, Virginity.

Enterízo, **za**, *a.* Entire, complete.

Enternecér, *va.* 1. To soften, to make tender or soft. 2. (Met.) To move to compassion.—*vr.* To be moved to compassion, to pity, to commiserate.

Enternecidaménte, *ad.* Compassionately.

Enternecimiénto, *sm.* Compassion, pity.

Entéro, **ra**, *a.* 1. Entire or intire, undiminished. 2. Perfect, complete. 3. Sound, without a flaw. 4. Just, right. 5. Honest, upright; pure, uncorrupted. 6. Strong, robust, vigorous. 7. Informed, instructed. 8. Uncastrated. *Caballo entero*, Stone-horse. 9. Strong, coarse; applied to linen. 10. (Ant.) Whole. *Numeros enteros*, Whole numbers, numbers without fractions. 11. Constant, firm. *Por entéro*, Entirely, fully, completely.

Enterradór, *sm.* Grave-digger, burier.

Enterramiénto, *sm.* 1. Interment, burial, funeral; the act of burying or interring. 2. Tomb, burying place.

Enterrár, *va.* To inter, to bury, to put into the grave. *Enterrar las vasijas en el lastre*, (Naút.) To stow the casks in ballast.

Entesadaménte, *ad.* Intensely.

Entesamiénto, *sm.* The act of stretching, the effect of being stretched; fulness.

Entesár, *va.* To extend, to stretch out, to make any thing tense and stiff.

Entestádo, **da**, *a.* (Ant.) Fixed or enclosed in the head.

Entibadór, *sm.* One who shores up mines.

Entibár, *vn.* To rest, to lean upón.—*va.* To prop, to shore up mines.

Entibiadéro, *sm.* Cooler, a bath in which any thing is cooled.

Entibiár, *va.* To cool, to make cool.—*vr.* (Met.) To become cool, to slacken, to relax.

Entíbo, *sm.* Stay, prop, shore.

Entidád, *sf.* 1. Entity, a real being. 2. (Met.) Consideration, estimation, value.

Entiérro, *sm.* 1. Burial, funeral; the act of burying or interring. 2 Tomb, grave.

Entigrecérse, *vr.* To be as enraged or furious as a tiger.

Entinár, *va.* To tinge, to colour.

Entintár, *va.* 1. To stain with ink. 2. To tinge or give a different colour.

Entirár, *va.* (Ant.) V. *Estirar*.

Entitulár, *va.* V. *Intitular*.

Entiznár, *va.* To revile, to defame. V. *Tiznar*.

Entoldamiénto, *sm.* Act of covering with an awning.

Entoldár, *va.* 1. To cover with an awning. 2. To hang the walls with clothes or silks.—*vr.* 1. To dress or clothe pompously. 2. To grow cloudy or overcast; applied to the sky.

Entomecér, *vn.* To swell. V. *Entumecer*.

Entomizár, *va.* To tie bass cords around posts, or laths, that the plaster may stick to them.

Entomología, *sf.* Entomology, the science of insects.

Entonación, *sf.* 1. Modulation, the act of tuning the voice to a certain key. 2. The act of blowing the bellows of an organ. 3. (Met.) Haughtiness, presumption.

Entonadór, *sm.* 1. Organ-blower, one who blows the bellows of an organ. 2. One who tunes the first verse of a psalm.

Entonár, *va.* 1. To tune, to modulate, to intone. 2. To commence a tune. 3. (Pint.) To harmonise colours. 4. To blow the bellows of an organ.—*vr.* (Met.) To grow haughty, to be puffed up with pride.

Entónces y Entónce, *ad.* Then, at that time, on that occasion.

Entonelár, *va.* To barrel.

Entóno, *sm.* 1. The act of intoning. 2. (Met.) Arrogance, haughtiness, pride.

Entontecérse, *vr.* To grow foolish, to be stupid.

Entontecimiénto, *sm.* Act of growing foolish or stupid.

Entorchádo, *sm.* A twisted cord, which serves

for embroideries. *Entorchádos,* Cords for a musical instrument covered with silver wire.
ENTORCHÁR, *va.* 1. To twist a cord. 2. To cover cords for musical instruments with wire.
ENTORMECIMIÉNTO, *sm.* Torpor. V *Adormecimiento.*
ENTORNÁR, *va.* To turn.
ENTORNILLÁR, *va.* To make any thing in the form of a screw or ring. 2. To stupefy.
ENTORPECÉR, *va.* 1. To benumb, to make torpid.
ENTORPECIMIÉNTO, *sm.* 1. Torpor, dulness. 2. Stupidity, bluntness of intellect.
ENTORTADÚRA, *sf.* Crookedness, curvity.
ENTORTÁR, *va.* 1. To bend, to make crooked. 2. To pull out an eye.
ENTORTIJÁR, *va.* V. *Ensortijar.*
ENTOSIGÁR Y ENTOSICÁR, *va.* V. *Atosigar.*
ENTRÁDA, *sf.* 1. Entrance, the passage by which a place is entered; avenue. 2. Beginning of a musical clause. 3. Entry, the act of entering publicly into a city. 4. The act of a person being admitted into a community or society. 5. Concourse or conflux of people. *Hubo una grande entrada tal dia á la comedia,* The play-house was crowded on that day. 6. Commencement or beginning of any work. 7. Familiar access, intimacy. 8. (Naút.) Leak. 9. A good hand at cards. 10. Second-sized dishes of a course of meat. 11. Receipts, property vested in any concern. *Derechos de entrada,* Import duty. *Entrádas,* Temples, the upper parts of the sides of the head.
ENTRADÉRO, *sm.* A narrow entrance into a place.
ENTRÁMBOS, BAS, *pron. pl.* Both. V. *Ambos.*
ENTRAMIÉNTO DE BIENES, *sm.* (For.) Sequestration.
ENTRÁMOS, MAS, *pron.* (Ant.) Both. V. *Entrambos.*
ENTRAMPÁR, *va.* 1. To entrap, to ensnare, to catch in a trap. 2. (Met.) To involve in difficulties, to perplex; to deceive. 3. (Met.) To encumber an estate with debts, to contract debts.—*vr.* To borrow money, to become indebted.
ENTRÁNTE, *sm.* 1. Angle. 2. One who enters.
ENTRAÑÁBLE, *a.* Intimate, affectionate.
ENTRAÑABLEMÉNTE, *ad.* Affectionately.
ENTRAÑÁR, *va.* To receive in a friendly and affectionate manner.—*vn.* To penetrate to the core, to know profoundly.—*vr.* To contract intimacy and familiarity.
ENTRÁÑAS, *sf. pl.* 1. Entrails, bowels. 2. (Met.) centre of a city, heart of a country. 3. (Met.) Mind, affection; disposition; idiosyncracy. *Entrañas mias,* My dear, my love. *Dar las entrañas, ó dar hasta las entrañas,* To give one's very heart-blood away. *Esto me llega á las entrañas,* That goes to my heart.
ENTRAÑIZÁR, *va.* To love, to be passionately fond of.
ENTRAÑO, ÑA, *a.* (Ant.) Internal, interior.
ENTRAPÁDA, *sf.* A coarse scarlet cloth.
ENTRAPAJÁR, *va.* To tie with rags.
ENTRAPÁR, *va.* 1. To powder the hair to clean it. 2. (Agr.) To put woollen rags to the roots of plants as manure.—*vr.* To be covered with dust.
ENTRÁR, *vn.* 1. To enter, to go in. 2. To commence, to begin. 3. To win a trick at cards. 4. To be classed or ranked.—*va.* 1. To thrust or put one thing upon another. 2. To set down or place to account. *Entrar en una partida de trigo, lana, &c.* To purchase a quantity of wheat, wool, &c. 3. To invade and overrun an enemy's country. 4. To take possession of a place by force of arms. 5. (Naút.) To gain upon a vessel steering the same course. 6. Followed by the prepositions *a, en,* it signifies to begin or commence, as *Entrar á cantar,* To begin to sing in concert. *Entrar en rezelo,* To begin to suspect. *Ahora entre yo,* Now I begin; said to one who has engrossed all the conversation or argument. *Entrar á uno,* To prevail upon one. *Entrar de por medio,* To settle a scuffle or fray, to adjust, to agree disputants. *Entrarse,* To apply one's self
ENTRÁTICO, *sm.* Entrance of a friar or nun.
ENTRE, *prep.* 1. Between. *Entre año, semana, dia,* In the course of the year, week, day. *Entre dos aguas,* Wavering, irresolute. *Traer á uno entre dientes,* To take a dislike to some body. 2. In, or in the number of things. *Entre tanto,* In the interim.
ENTREABRÍR, *va.* To half open a door, to leave it a-jar.
ENTREÁNCHO, CHA, *a.* Neither wide nor strait.
ENTRECANÁL, *sf.* (Arq.) Space between the striæ or flutings of a column.
ENTRECÁNO, NA, *a.* Between black and grey; applied to the hair or beard.
ENTRECAVÁR, *va.* To dig shallow, not to dig deep.
ENTRECÉJO, *sm.* 1. The space between the two eye-brows. 2. A frowning supercilious look.
ENTRECÍRCA, *sf.* Space between one enclosure and another.
ENTRECIÉLO, *sm.* Awning. V. *Toldo.*
ENTRECLÁRO, RA, *a.* Slightly clear.
ENTRECOGEDÚRA, *sf.* Act of catching.
ENTRECOGÉR, *va.* To catch, to intercept.
ENTRECÓRO, *sm.* Distance or space between the choir and the chief altar; chancel.
ENTRECORTADÚRA, *sf.* Cut made in the middle of any thing without dividing it.
ENTRECORTÁR, *va.* To cut in the middle, to divide into two.
ENTRECRIÁR, *va.* To rear plants among others.
ENTRECUBIÉRTAS ó ENTREPUÉNTES, *s. pl.* (Naút.) Between decks.
ENTRECUÉSTO, *sm.* Back-bone.
ENTREDECÍR, *va.* To interdict, to prohibit.
ENTREDÍCHO, *sm.* 1. Interdiction, prohibition. 2. Ecclesiastical censure or interdict. 3. V. *Contradiccion.*
ENTREDÓBLE, *a.* Neither double nor single.
ENTREFÍNO, NA, *a.* Between coarse and fine.
ENTRÉGA, *sf.* Delivery, the act of delivering.
ENTREGADAMÉNTE, *ad.* Really, perfectly.
ENTREGADÓR, *sm.* 1. Deliverer. 2. Executor.
ENTREGAMÉNTE Y ENTREGAMIÉNTRE, *ad.* V. *Enteramente.*
ENTREGAMIÉNTO, *sm.* Delivery.
ENTREGÁR, *va.* 1. To deliver, to put into the hands of another. 2. To consign to prison. 3. To restore.—*vr.* 1. To deliver one's self up into the hands of another. *Entregarse á vicios,* To abandon one's self to vices. 2. To take possession of lands and goods on one's own account.
ENTRÉGO, *sm.* Delivery.—*a.* V. *Integro.*
ENTREJUNTÁR, *va.* To nail or join the pannels of a door to the cross-bars or ledges.
ENTRELAZÁR, *va.* To interlace, to intermix, to put one thing into another.

Entreliño, *sm.* Space of ground between the rows of vines or olives.
Entrelistádo, da, *a.* That which is striped or variegated.
Entrelucír, *vn.* To glimmer, to shine faintly in the midst of other things.
Entre mános, *ad.* In hand. *Tomar entre manos,* To take in hand.
Entremédias, *ad.* In the mean time.
Entremés, *sm.* 1. An interlude, a farce. 2. Interval.
Entremesár, *va.* (In the Jocular Style) To entertain with feasts and banquets.
Entremeseár, *va.* To act a part in a farce or interlude.
Entremesísta, *sm.* Player of farces or interludes.
Entremetér, *va.* 1. To put one thing between others. 2. To put on a clean cloth without undressing children, or taking off the swaddling clothes.—*vr.* 1. To thrust one's self into a place without being called or invited. 2. To take charge of. 3. To intermeddle.
Entremetído, *sm.* One who intermeddles in other people's business; a busy-body.
Entremetimiénto, *sm.* Interposition, interjection; intermeddling.
Entremezcladúra, *sf.* Intermixture.
Entremezclár, *va.* To interweave, to intermix.
Entremiénte, *ad.* V. *Entre tanto.*
Entremíso y Entremíjo, *sm.* A long bench on which cheeses are formed.
Entremorír, *vn.* To die away by degrees, to be nearly extinguished; applied to a flame.
Entrencár, *va.* To put rods in a bee-hive.
Entrenzár, *va.* To plait hair.
Entreoír, *va.* To hear without perfectly understanding what is said.
Entreordinário, ria *a.* Middling, between good and bad.
Entrepalmadúra, *sf.* (Albeyt.) Disease in horses' hoofs.
Entrepánes, *sm. pl.* Pieces of unsown ground between others that are sown.
Entrepañádo, da, *a.* Composed of several panels; applied to doors.
Entrepáño, *sm.* 1. Panel. 2. Space between pilasters.
Entreparecérse, *vr.* To be transparent.
Entrepechúga, *sf.* Small piece of flesh on the breast of birds.
Entrepelár, *va.* To variegate hair or mix it of different colours.
Entreperniár, *vn.* To put the legs between those of others for the ease of sitting.
Entrepeynes, *sm. pl.* The wool which remains in the comb after combing.
Entrepiérnas, *sf. pl.* 1. Opening between the legs. 2. Pieces put into the fork of a pair of breeches.
Entreponér, *va.* To interpose.
Entrepretádo, da, *a.* (Albeyt.) Applied to a mule or horse with a weak breast or shoulder.
Entrepuéntes, *sm. pl.* (Naút.) Between decks.
Entrepunzadúra, *sf.* Pricking pain of an unripe tumor.
Entrepunzár, *va.* To prick slightly.
Entrerenglón, *sm.* Interline, space between lines.
Entrerenglonadúra, *sf.* Inscribed or written within lines; interlineal note.
Entrerenglonár, *va.* To interline, to write between the lines.

Entresáca y Entresacadúra, *sf.* The act of cutting down trees, in order to thin a wood.
Entresacár, *va.* To pick or choose out of a number or parcel of things.
Entrescúro, ra, *a.* Somewhat obscure.
Entresíjo, *sm.* 1. Mesentery, that round which the guts are convolved. 2. (Met.) Any thing occult, hidden.
Entresuélo, *sm.* A small room between two stories; floor between the ground and first floor, or principal apartment.
Entresúrco, *sm.* Space between furrows.
Entretálla y Entretalladúra, *sf.* Sculpture in bass-relief.
Entretallár, *va.* 1. To sculpture in basso-relievo. 2. To cut, slash, or mangle. 3. (Met.) To intercept or obstruct the passage.
Entretéla, *sf.* Buckram, a sort of thin linen stiffened with glue, and put between the linings of clothes.
Entretelár, *va.* To put buckram or strong linen between the lining and cloth.
Entretenedór, *sm.* He who entertains.
Entretenér, *va.* 1. To delay or protract an operation. 2. To dally, to put off, to amuse. 3. To allay pain, to make less troublesome. 4. To amuse, to entertain the mind.—*vr.* 1. To amuse one's self with playing at cards. 2. To joke, to jest. 3. To be a busy-body, to be full of bustle.
Entretenído, da, 1. Entertaining, pleasant, amusing. 2. Doing business in an office, in hopes of obtaining a place.
Entretenimiénto, *sm.* 1. Amusement, entertainment. 2. Pay, allowance, appointment. 3. Delay, procrastination. 4. Fun, jest, joke.
Entretexedúra, *sf.* Intertexture, a work interwoven with another.
Entretexér, *va.* 1. To tissue, to variegate. 2. To interweave, to intermix. 3. To insert in a book or writing.
Entretexímiénto, *sm.* Intertexture; variegation.
Entretiémpo, *sm.* The middle season between the beginning and end of Spring or Autumn.
Entreuntár, *va.* To anoint slightly.
Entrevenárse, *vr.* To diffuse or run through the veins.
Entrevenír, *va.* V. *Intervenir.*
Entreventána, *sf.* Space between windows.
Entrevér, *va.* To have a glimpse of, to see imperfectly.
Entreverádo, da, *a.* Interlined with fat and lean; applied to meat.
Entreverár, *va.* To intermix, to insert one thing in another.
Entrevísta, *sf.* Interview; concurrence.
Entrexerír, *va.* To insert, to intermix.
Entreyacér, *vn.* (Ant.) To be in the middle.
Entricádo, da, *a.* Perplexed, double; deceitful.
Entricár, *va.* To entangle.
Entrincádo, da, *a.* Intricate. V. *Intrincado.*
Entripádo, da, *a.* Contained in the entrails or intestines.
Entripádos, *sm. pl.* Dissembled anger or displeasure.
Entristecér, *va.* To sadden, to make sad or melancholy.—*vr.* 1. To grow sad or melancholy. 2. To wither, to decay; applied to plants.
Entristecimiénto, *sm.* Becoming melancholy.
E'ntrò, *ad.* (Ant.) V. *Hasta.*

Entrometér, va. V. *Entremeter.*
Entronár, va. To enthrone. V. *Entronizar.*
Entroncár, vn. To be descended from the same stock, to belong to the same family.
Entronerár, va. To drive the ball into the hole of a truck or billiard-table.
Entronización, sf. Elevation to a throne.
Entronizár, va. 1. To enthrone, to place on the throne. 2. To exalt, to raise to a distinguished rank or station.—*vr.* To be elated or puffed up with pride.
Entrónque, sm. Cognation, relationship with the root or chief of a family. [barns.
Entrojár, va. To gather or put up grain in
Entrucháda, sf. A clandestine operation, an underhand business.
Entruchár, va. To decoy, to lure into a snare.
Entruchón, sm. Decoyer, schemer.
Entruéjo, sm. V. *Antruejo.*
Entuértos, sm. pl. After-pains.
Entullecér, vn. To be crippled or maimed.—*va.* To stop, to check, to obstruct.
Entumecér, va. 1. To swell, to make tumid. 2. To benumb, to make torpid.—*vr.* To swell, to surge, to rise high.
Entumecimiénto, sm. 1. Swelling. 2. Torpor, deadness, numbness.
Entumírse, vr. To become torpid.
Entupír, va. To make torpid; to obstruct.
Enturbiár, va. 1. To muddle, to make muddy or turbid. 2. To obscure, to confound.—*vr.* To disorder or derange any thing.
Entusiasmár, va. To transport, to enrapture.—*vr.* To become enthusiastic, to be enraptured.
Entusiásmo, sm. Enthusiasm, heat of imagination, elevation of fancy.
Entusiásta, sm. Enthusiast, visionary, fanatic.
Entusiástico, ca, a. Enthusiastic, fanatic.
Enúla, sf. (Bot.) Starwort.
Enumeración, sf. Enumeration, the act of numbering or counting over.
Enumerár, va. To enumerate.
Enunciación, sf. Enunciation, declaration.
Enunciár, va. To declare, to proclaim.
Enunciatívo, va, a. Enunciative.
Envalentonár, va. To encourage, to inspirit, to render bold.—*vr.* To become courageous.
Envanecér, va. To make vain.
Envarádo, da, a. Deadened, benumbed.
Envaramiénto, sm. 1. Deadness, stiffness, numbness. 2. A number of bailiffs or petty officers of justice. [stupify.
Envarár, va. To benumb, to make torpid, to
Envaronár, vn. (In the Jocular Style) To grow up to manhood, to become robust and strong.
Envasadór, sm. Filler, funnel; he who fills.
Envasár, va. 1. To tun, to put liquor into casks, to barrel. 2. To drink to excess any kind of liquor. 3. (Mur.) To put corn into bags. *Envasar á uno,* To run one through the body. 4. To fill guts with minced meat.
Envaynár, va. To sheath, to put the sword into the scabbard. *Envayne vd.* Be quiet, sir; put up your sword. [wrangle.
Envedijárse, vr. 1. To get entangled. 2. To
Envejecér, va. To make old, to make a person or thing look old.—*vn.* To grow old.—*vr.* 1. To be of an old date or fashion. 2. To hold out a long time, to be of long duration.

Envejecído, da, a. 1. Grown old. 2. Accustomed, habituated.
Envejecimiénto, sm. Oldness. [so
Envenenadór, ra, s. Poisoner; one who p
Envenenár, va. 1. To envenom, to poison; infect with poison. 2. To reproach, to jud ill of one.
Envenenamiénto, sm. Act of poisoning.
Enverdecér, vn. To grow green.
Enverdír, va. To tinge green.
Envergár, va. (Naút.) To bend the sails, fasten them to the yards.
Envergonzár, va. V. *Avergonzar.*
Envérgues, sm. pl. (Naút.) Rope-bands, whic are used to bend or fasten the sails to the yard
Envés, sm. 1. The wrong side of any thing, cloth, &c. V. *Reves.* 2. Back, shoulders.
Envesádo, sm. (Among Tanners and Leathe dressers) The fleshy part of hides.
Envesár, va. To overset. [office or plac
Envestidúra, sf. Act of investing one with
Envestír, va. 1. To invest, to put in possessio of a place or office. 2. To adorn, to set off. To illuminate, to enlighten. 4. To cover.—*vr.* To accustom or habituate one's self, contract a habit; to introduce one's self to interfere in any thing.
Enviáda, sf. Message, errand.
Enviadízo, za, a. Missive.
Enviádo, sm. Messenger.
Enviáado, da, a. (Arq.) Oblique, sloped.
Enviár, va. 1. To send, to transmit. 2. T send, to give, to bestow. 3. To exile.
Enviciár, va. To vitiate, to corrupt, to mak vicious.—*vn.* To have luxurious foliage an little fruit; applied to plants.—*vr.* To be im moderately addicted to, to be excessivel fond of.
Enviciosárse, vr. To vitiate, to corrupt.
Envidadór, sm. Gambler who induces other to gamble.
Envidár, va. (Among Gamesters) To invite to induce another to play a card; to open th game by staking a certain sum. *Envidar d falso,* To induce to play for small sums, hop ing to make them larger; (Met.) To trea one with any thing, desiring that he may no accept it.
Envídia, sf. Envy, pain felt at the sight of ex cellence or happiness; emulation.
Envidiáble, a. Enviable.
Envidiadór, ra, s. An envious person.
Envidiár, va. To envy, to feel envy, to feel pain at the sight of excellence or felicity.
Envidióso, sa, a. Envious; invidious.
Envilecér, va. To vilify, to debase, to make contemptible.—*vr.* To degrade one's self, to be disgraced. [of wine.
Envinádo, da, a. Having the taste or flavour
Envinagrár, va. To put vinegar in any thing.
Envinár, va. To mix wine with water.
Enviperádo, da, a. (In the Jocular Style) Viper-like, enraged, furious.
Envirár, va. To clasp or unite together corkwood to form a bee-hive.
Enviscamiénto, sm. Act of glueing.
Enviscár, va. 1. To glue, to fasten with glue. 2. To irritate, to anger.—*vr.* To be glued with bird-lime, applied to birds and insects.

Envíte, *sm.* 1. The act of inviting at cards, or opening the game by staking a certain sum. 2. Invitation, the act of bidding or calling to any thing with civility; any kind of polite offer.
Enviudár, *vn.* To become a widower or widow.
Envolcárse, *vr.* V. *Envolcarse.*
Envoltório, *sm.* 1. Bundle of clothes. 2. Fault in cloth, arising from the inequality of the yarn.
Envoltúras, *sf. pl.* Swaddling-clothes, clothes wrapped round new-born children. [cover.
Envolvedéro ó Envolvedór, *sm.* Wrapper,
Envolvér, *va.* 1. To inwrap, to cover by involution. 2. (Met.) To convince by force of reasoning or argument.—*vr.* 1. To be implicated in an affair; to be unlawfully connected with women. 2. To be mixed with a crowd.
Envolvimiénto, *sm.* The act of inwrapping or enveloping.
Envuélto, ta, *pp. irreg.* Involved.
Enxabonadúra, *sf.* V. *Xabonadura.*
Enxabonár, *va.* 1. To soap, to wash with soap. 2. (Met.) To insult with foul language and blows. [creditors of a ship.
Enxágue, *sm.* Adjudication required by the
Enxálma, *sf.* Kind of pack-saddle used by the Moors.
Enxalméro, *sm.* Pack-saddle-maker.
Enxálmo, *sm.* V. *Ensalmo.*
Enxaltár, *va.* V. *Exáltar.*
Enxambradéra, *sf.* 1. King or master-bee of a hive. 2. V. *Casquilla.*
Enxambradéro, *sm.* Place where bees collect or swarm to form their hives.
Enxambrár, *va.* 1. To gather a scattered swarm of bees. 2. To form a new hive of bees, which left another hive.—*vn.* To breed a new hive of bees; to produce abundantly. [bees.
Enxambrazón, *sf.* Generation or swarming of
Enxámbre, *sm.* 1. Swarm of bees. 2. Crowd, multitude of people.
Enxáno, *ad.* (Ant.) V. *Cada año.*
Enxarciár, *va.* To put the tackle aboard ship.
Enxármo, *sm.* V. *Ensalmo.*
Enxebrár, *va.* To steep in lie, to buck.
Enxébe, *sm.* Lie in which cloth is put to be cleansed or scoured; act of bucking.
Enxémplo, *sm.* (Ant.) V. *Exemplo.*
Enxénzos, *sm. pl.* V. *Axenjos.*
Enxéño, *sm.* Kind of jack for turning a spit.
Enxergár, *va.* To set about a business, to bring a thing on the tapis. [Budded.
Enxerído, da, *a.* 1. Benumbed with cold. 2.
Enxeridór, *sm.* 1. One who buds or propagates trees by insertion and inoculation. 2. A grafting knife
Enxeridúra y Enxerimiénto, *s.* Act of budding, inserting, or inoculating trees.
Enxerír, *va.* 1. To bud, to insert a scion or branch of one tree into the stock of another. 2. (Met.) To insert, to include.
Enxéro, *sm.* (And.) Beam of a plough. [ding.
Enxertación, *sf.* Insertion, inoculation, bud-
Enxertál, *sm.* Nursery of inoculated fruit trees.
Enxertár, *va.* V. *Inxertar.*
Enxérto, *sm.* 1. V. *Inxerto.* 2. (Met.) Mixture of divers things.
Enxugadór, ra, *s.* 1. Drier, one who dries. 2. Round horse for drying and warming linen.

Enxugár, *va.* 1. To dry in the air or at the fire, to make dry. 2. To wipe off moisture.—*vr.* To dry up, to grow lean.
Enxúllo, *sm.* A weaver's beam.
Enxúndia, *sf.* 1. Fat in the inside of fowls. 2. (Met.) A soft endearing word, a caress.
Enxundióso, sa, *a.* Fat, fatty.
Enxúta, *sf.* (Arq.) Small triangle made by describing a circle on a square. [thing.
Enxutár, *va.* To dry with lime, or any other
Enxutéz, *sf.* Siccity, dryness.
Enxúto, ta, *a.* 1. Dried. 2. Sparing, parsimonious. *A' pie enxuto,* Without pain or labour.
Enxútos, *sm. pl.* 1. Small dry brush-wood for lighting a fire. 2. Dry crust of bread. [sum.
Enyesadúra, *sf.* Act of plastering with gyp-
Enyesár, *va.* To plaster, to cover with plaster; to parget, to white-wash.
Enyescárse, *vr.* To become inflamed.
Enyugár, *va.* To yoke cattle.—*vr.* (Met.) To marry.
Enzamarrádo, da, *a.* Dressed in a shepherd's great coat made of sheep-skins, with the wool on. [hair.
Enzarzádo, da, *a.* Curled, matted; applied to
Enzarzár, *va.* 1. To throw among brambles and briers. 2. (Met.) To sow discord, to excite dissensions. 3. To put hurdles for silkworms.—*vr.* 1. To be entangled among brambles and briers. 2. (Met.) To be involved in difficulties.
Enzaynárse, *vr.* To look side-ways, to become insidious, to be treacherous and ostentatious.
Enzurdecér, *vn.* (In the Jocular Style) To grow left-handed.
Enzurronár, *va.* 1. To put in a bag or sack. 2. (Met.) To enclose one thing in another.
Epácta, *sf.* 1. Epact. 2. V. *Añalejo.*
Epactílla, *sf.* A small calendar for the performance of divine service, which is published every year.
Epéntesis, *sf.* (Gram.) Figure interposing a letter or syllable in the middle of a word.
Epián, *sm.* Sort of venereal disease in America, said to be contagious.
E'picaménte, *ad.* In an epic or heroic manner.
Epicédio, *sm.* Epicedium, or elegy formerly recited before burying a dead body; now, any poetical eulogy of the dead. [sexes.
Epicéno, na, *a.* Epicene, belonging to both
Epicíclo, *sm.* Epicycle, a small circle, whose centre is in the circumference of a greater.
E'pico, ca, *a.* Epic; narrative, containing narrations; it is usually supposed to be heroic.
Epicúreo, rea, *a.* Epicurean.
Epidémia, *sf.* An epidemic disease, which falls at once upon a great number of people.
Epidemiál, *a.* Epidemic or epidemical.
Epidémico, ca, *a.* Epidemical.
Epidérmis, *sf.* Epidermis, the scarf-skin of the human body.
Epifanía, *sf.* Epiphany.
Epigástrico, ca, *a.* Epigastric, belonging to the upper region of the belly.
Epiglótis, *sf.* Cartilage of the larynx, which covers the opening of the wind-pipe.
Epígrafe, *sf.* Title, inscription; motto.
Epigráma, *sf.* Epigram, short poem ending in a point of wit, or some lively idea.

Epigramatário, ria, *a.* y *s.* Epigrammatic; epigrammatist.

Epigramático, Epigramatísta, y Epigramísta, *sm.* Epigrammatist, one who writes epigrams.

Epilépsia, *sf.* Epilepsy, a convulsive contraction of the muscles, with the loss of sense.

Epiléptico, ca; **Epiléctico**, ca, *a.* Epileptic.

Epilogál, *a.* Compendious, summary.

Epilogár, *va.* To recapitulate, to sum up.

Epilogísmo, *sm.* Calculation, computation.

Epílogo, *sm.* 1. Epilogue, poem or speech at the end of a play. 2. Recapitulation, a brief or compendious statement.

Epipáctide, *sf.* (Bot.) Sort of bastard black hellebore.

Epiquéya, *sf.* A mild and prudent interpretation of the law, according to the circumstances of time, place, and persons.

Episcopádo, *sm.* Episcopate, bishopric; the dignity of a bishop.

Episcopál, *a.* Episcopal, relating to bishops.

Episcopizár, *va.* (In the Jocular Style) To pant after bishoprics.

Episcopológio, *sm.* A chronological list of bishops.

Episódico, ca, *a.* Episodic, episodical.

Episódio, *sm.* Episode, an incidental narrative or digression in a poem.

Epístola, *sf.* 1. Epistle. 2. Part of the mass which is read or sung. *O'rden de epistola*, Subdeaconship; the office of reading or singing the epistle at the mass.

Epistolár, *a.* Epistolary, belonging to letters, suitable to letters.

Epistolár, *va.* (Joc.) To write epistles.

Epistolário, *sm.* 1. Collection of epistles which are read or sung at the mass. 2. Volume of letters.

Epistoléro, *sm.* Priest who sings the epistles; subdeacon.

Epistólico, ca, *a.* Epistolary.

Epitáfio, *sm.* Epitaph, inscription on a tomb.

Epitalámio, *sm.* Epithalamium, a nuptial song; a compliment upon marriage.

Epítasis, *sf.* Epitasis, the most complex part of the plot of a play.

Epíteto, *sm.* Epithet, an adjective denoting any quality, good or bad.

Epítima, *sf.* Epithem, a liquid medicament, externally applied.

Epitimár, *va.* To apply an epithem.

Epítimo, *sm.* Flower of thyme.

Epitomadaménte, *ad.* Summarily, briefly.

Epitomár, *va.* To epitomise, to abstract, to contract into a narrow space.

Epítome, *sm.* Epitome, abridgment.

E'poca, *sf.* Epoch or epocha, the time at which a new computation of years is begun.

E'podo ó E'poda, *s.* Epode, the stanza following the strophe or antistrophe.

Epopéya, *sf.* Epopee, an epic or heroic poem.

Epóto, ta, *a.* Intoxicated. V. *Bebido.*

Epulón, *sm.* 1. An epicure or great eater. 2. Applied to persons gospel-greedy.

Equáble, *a.* Equable, equal to itself; chiefly applied to moveable bodies, moving with the same continued velocity in an equal space of time.

Equación, *sf.* 1. Equation, the difference between the time marked by the sun's apparent motion, and that measured by its real motion. 2. Equation, expression of the same quantity in two dissimilar terms, but of equal value.

Equadór ó Equatór, *sm.* Equator, a great circle, whose poles are the poles of the world. It divides the globe into two equal parts, the northern and southern hemispheres.

Equanimidád, *sf.* Equanimity; evenness of mind, neither elated nor depressed.

Equánte, *a.* Equal. V. *Igual.*

Eqüéstre, *a.* Equestrian, belonging to horses or horsemanship.

Equiángulo, la, *a.* (Geom.) Equiangular.

Equidád, *sf.* 1. Equity, right, honesty; justice. 2. (Vulg.) Moderation in the execution of laws, or price of things which are bought or sold.

Equidistáncia, *sf.* An equal distance.

Equidistár, *vn.* To be equidistant.

Equilátero, ra, *a.* Equilateral, having all sides equal.

Equilibrár, *va.* 1. To equipoise, to balance in a scale. 2. (Met.) To balance the power and forces of states.

Equilíbre, *a.* Balanced.

Equilíbrio, *sm.* Equilibrium, equipoise, equality of weight.

Equíno, na, *a.* (Poét.) Belonging to a horse.

Equíno, *sm.* 1. Echinus, a hedge-hog. 2. (Ict.) A shell fish, set with prickles. 3. (Arq.) Convex moulding, the quadrant of a circle.

Equinocciál, *a.* Equinoctial.

Equinóccio, *sm.* Equinox, the time when the sun enters one of the equinoctial points.

Equipáge, *sm.* 1. Provision or supply of every thing necessary for a voyage or journey. 2. (Naút.) Ship's company, crew of a ship; also the effects which every one of the crew takes with him on a voyage.

Equipár, *va.* To fit out, to supply with every necessary article, to equip.

Equiparación, *sf.* Comparison; collation.

Equiparár, *va.* To compare, to match.

Equipoléncia, *sf.* Equipollence, equality of force or power.

Equipolénte, *a.* Equivalent, equipollent.

Equiponderár, *vn.* To equiponderate, to weigh equal to another thing.

E'quis, *sf.* Ecs, the Spanish name of the letter X. *Estar hecho una équis*, To be intoxicated and staggering.

Equitación, *sf.* Horsemanship.

Equitatívo, va, *a.* 1. Equitable; applied to a judge who administers justice with impartiality and mercy. 2. Conformable to reason and justice.

Equivaléncia, *sf.* Compensation, equivalency.

Equivalénte, *a.* Equivalent.

Equivalér, *vn.* To be of equal value and price.

Equivocación, *sf.* 1. Equivocation, ambiguity of speech, double meaning. 2. Mistake, error.

Equivocadaménte, *ad.* Equivocatingly.

Equivocaménte, *ad.* Ambiguously.

Equivocár, *va.* 1. To use ambiguous language. 2. To mistake, to take one thing for another; to conceive wrong.

Equívoco, ca, *a.* Ambiguous.

Equívoco, *sm.* An ambiguous expression, a word having a double meaning; equivocation.

E'quo, a, *a.* (Ant.) Right, just.

Equóreo, rea, *a.* (Poét.) Belonging to the sea.

E'ra, *sf.* 1. Era, a certain computation of years from any particular date or epoch. 2. Age, or long space of time. 3. Spot of ground paved and raised above the level for threshing or treading out corn. 4. Bed or plot in a garden, sown with salad-seeds, &c. &c.

Eráge, *sm.* (Ar.) Virgin honey.

Erál, *sm.* A two-year old ox.

Erár, *va.* To lay out garden ground for sowing and growing garden-stuff.

Erário, *sm.* Exchequer, public treasury.

Erário, ria, *a.* Liable to pay taxes.

Ercér, *va.* V. *Levantar.*

Erección, *sf.* Foundation and erection of a building.

Erectór, *sm.* Erecter, founder.

Erécha, *sf.* Satisfaction, compensation.

Eremíta, *sm.* Hermit, anchoret, recluse.

Eremítico, ca, *a.* Solitary, relating to a hermit.

Eremitório, *sm.* Hermitage, place for hermits.

Ergoteár y Ergotizár, *vn.* (Burl.) To argue, to debate without reason.

Ergotéo, *sm.* (Burl.) Sophistry, debate on trifling things.

Ergotísta y Ergotizánte, *sm.* (Fam.) Debater, arguer about frivolous things, a sophist.

Erguír, *va.* To erect, to raise up straight.—*vr.* To be elated or puffed up with pride.

Eriál y Eriázo, za, *a.* Unploughed, untilled, uncultivated; applied to the ground.

Ericéra, *sf.* Kind of hut without a roof.

Erigír, *va.* To erect, to raise from the ground.

Erínge, *sf.* (Bot.) Eryngo. Eryngium pusillum *L.*

Eríno, *sm.* (Med.) Errhine, head-purge, medicine snuffed up the nose.

Erío, ría, *a.* Unploughed, untilled.

Erísimo, *sm.* (Bot.) Hedge-mustard. Sinapis arvensis *L.*

Erisipéla y Erisípula, *sf.* Erysipelas, a pustulous inflammation under the scarf-skin.

Erisipelár, *va.* To cause erysipelas.

Erisipelóso, sa, *a.* (Med.) Erysipelatous, belonging to erysipelas.

Erítreo, trea, *a.* (Poét.) Reddish, ruddy; erythrean.

Erizádo, da, *a.* That which is covered with bristles.

Erizamiénto, *sm.* Act of setting on end, as the hair.

Erizár, *va.* To set on end.—*vr.* To stand on end; applied to the hair.

Erízo, *sm.* 1. Hedge-hog, an animal set with prickles, like thorns in a hedge. Erinaceus europæus *L.* 2. Sea hedge-hog, or urchin. 3. The prickly husk or coat of a chesnut. 4. (Bot.) Rough water-thistle. Anthyllis erinacea *L.*

Ermadór, *sm.* Destroyer, devastator.

Ermár, *va.* To destroy, to lay waste. V. *Asolar.*

Ermíta, *sf.* 1. Hermitage, habitation of an hermit. 2. Tavern, where wine is sold by retail.

Ermitáño, *sm.* Hermit, one who takes care of an hermitage.

Ermitório, *sm.* V. *Eremitorio.*

Ermúnio, *sm.* Ancient immunity, exempting noblemen from every kind of tribute and service.

Erogár, *va.* To distribute, to divide.

Erogatório, *sm.* Pipe, through which liquor is drawn out of a vessel.

Erosión, *sf.* Erosion, corrosion.

Erótico, ca, *a.* Belonging to the passion of love.

Erótima, *sf.* (Ret.) Interrogation.

Erotísmo, *sm.* A violent love.

Erotomanía, *sf.* Erotomania, love-madness.

Errabúndo, da, *a.* Wandering, strolling about.

Erradaménte, *ad.* Erroneously, falsely.

Erradicación, *sf.* Eradication, extirpation.

Erradicár, *va.* To eradicate.

Erradízo, za, *a.* Wandering to and fro.

Errádo, *a.* Erring, wandering.

Erránte, *pa.* Errant, roving.

Erránza, *sf.* (Ant.) V. *Error.*

Errár, *va.* 1. To err, to commit errors. 2. Not to perform one's engagements. 3. To offend any one.—*vn.* To wander about without knowing one's way. *Errar el camino,* To miss the right way. *Errar el golpe,* To miss a blow.

Erráta, *sf.* Error in writing or printing.

Errático, ca, *a.* Wandering, vagabond, vagrant.

Errátil, *a.* Wavering, not firm or steady.

Erráz, *sm.* Coal made of the stones of olives.

E'rre, *sm.* The Spanish name of the letter R.

Erre que Erre, *ad.* Pertinaciously, obstinately.

Erroneaménte, *ad.* Erroneously.

Erróneo, nea, *a.* Erroneous.

Erronía, *sf.* (Bar.) Opposition, hatred.

Errór, *sm.* 1. Deceit, falsity, illusion. 2. Deficiency, fault, defect. 3. Error of the press.

Erubescéncia, *sf.* Shame, the act of blushing with shame.

Eructación, *sf.* Eructation, belch; the act of belching.

Eructár, *vn.* To belch.

Erúcto, *sm.* V. *Regüeldo.*

Erudición, *sf.* Erudition, learning.

Eruditaménte, *ad.* Learnedly.

Erudíto, ta, *a.* Erudite, learned.

Eruginóso, sa, *a.* That which is thick, coarse, and knotty.

Erumnóso, sa, *a.* Laborious, painful, miserable.

Erupción, *sf.* Eruption, the act of bursting forth.

Eruptívo, va, *a.* Eruptive.

Erutación, *sf.* Eructation, belching.

Erutár, *vn.* To eruct, to belch.

Erúto, *sm.* Belch, eructation.

Erváto, *sm.* (Bot.) Sea sulphur-wort, Hog's fennel. Peucedanum officinale *L.*

Ervelláda, *sf.* (Bot.) Bean-trefoil. Cytisus hirsutus *L.*

Ervílla, *sf.* Seed of the bitter vetch.

Esbatimentár, *va.* (Pint.) To delineate a shadow.—*vn.* To cast the shadow of one body on another.

Esbatimiénto, *sm.* Shade in a picture.

Esbeltéza, *sf.* A tall and elegant stature.

Esbélto, ta, *a.* Tall, genteel, and well shaped.

Esbírro, *sm.* Bailiff, apparitor; a petty officer of courts of justice.

Esblandecér y Esblandír, *va.* V. *Blandir.*

Esbózo, *sm.* Sketch, outline; a rough draught.

E'sca, *sf.* Food, nourishment.

Escabechár, *va.* To souse, to steep in pickle.

Escabéche, *sm.* 1. Souse, pickle made of salt, vinegar, &c. 2. Pickled fish.

Escabél, *sm.* Foot-stool; small seat.

Escabelíllo, *sm.* A small foot-stool.

Escabiósa, *sf.* (Bot.) Field-scabious. Scabiosa arvensis *L.*

Escábro, *sm.* 1. A kind of scab, itch, or mange, in sheep. 2. The large amphibious crab.

Escabrosaménte, *ad.* Roughly.

Escabroseárse, *vr.* To be offended or irritated, to take offence.

Escabrosidád, *sf.* 1. Inequality, unevenness, roughness. 2. Hardness, asperity.

Escabróso, **sa**, *a.* 1. Rough, uneven. 2. Rude, unpolished.

Escabullimiénto, *sm.* Evasion, act of escaping.

Escabullírse, *vr.* To escape, to evade; to slip through one's hands.

Escacádo, **da**, *a.* Checkered, variegated in the manner of a chess-board with alternate colours.

Escácho, *sm.* (Ict.) Thornback. Raia clavata *L.*

Escála, *sf.* 1. Stair-case. V. *Escalera.* 2. Ladder made of ropes. *Escala del alcázar,* (Naút.) Quarter-deck ladder. *Escala real,* (Naút.) Accommodation ladder. *Escala de la toldilla,* (Naút.) Poop-ladder. 3. Passage or inlet into a country. 4. Port. *Escala de comercio,* A sea-port. *Escala franca,* Free port. 5. Scale, a line divided into a number of equal parts. *A' escala visa,* A day-light scalade.

Escaláda, *sf.* Scalade or scalado, the act of scaling or storming a place by the help of ladders.

Escaládo, **da**, *a.* Applied to fish cut open to be salted or cured.

Escaladór, *sm.* He who scales walls.

Escalamiénto, *sm.* Act of scaling walls.

Escálamo, *sm.* (Naút.) Thole or thoal, an iron or wooden pin with a ring or strop, through which the rowers put the oars, when they row.

Escalánte, *pa.* Scaling, climbing.

Escalár, *va.* To scale, to climb by the help of ladders.

Escaldáda, *sf.* Prostitute.

Escaldádo, **da**, *a.* Fearful, cautious, suspicious.

Escaldár, *va.* 1. To burn, to scald; to bathe with very hot water. 2. To make iron red-hot.

Escaldrántes, *sm. pl.* (Naút.) Kevels, wooden pin on which tackle and sails are put to dry.

Escaldrído, **da**, *a.* Cunning, sagacious.

Escaldufár, *va.* To take broth out of the pot when it is too full.

Escaléno, *a.* (Geom.) Scalene.

Escalentamiénto, *sm.* Inflammation, disease in the feet of animals, occasioned by want of care in keeping them clean.

Escalentár, *vn.* To foment and preserve the natural heat.

Escaléra, *sf.* 1. Stairs, steps by which we ascend from the lower part of a building to the upper. *Escalera de caracol,* A winding stair. 2. Ladder. 3. Sloats of a cart.

Escalerílla, **ta**, *sf.* 1. A small ladder. 2. Drenching instrument. *En escalerilla,* In degrees, scalary.

Escaléta, *sf.* Engine for raising cannon and mortars on their carriages.

Escalfádo, **da** *a.* Applied to white-washed walls full of blisters.

Escalfadór, *sm.* 1. A barber's pan for keeping water warm. 2. Chafing-dish, a vessel for keeping victuals warm.

Escalfár, *va.* 1. To warm, to keep warm. 2. To put bread into an oven which is too hot, and scorches it.

Escalfarótes, *sm. pl.* A kind of wide boots lined with hay.

Escalféta, *sf.* 1. Chafing-dish. V. *Escalfador.* 2. Water-dish, or water-plate, for keeping meat hot.

Escálio, *sm.* Land abandoned for tillage.

Escalimárse, *vr.* (Naút.) To be spit or worked out of the seams of a ship; applied to oakum.

Escálmo, *sm.* V. *Escálamo.*

Escalofriádo, **da**, *a.* Shivering.

Escalofrío, *sm.* Indisposition attended with shivering.

Escalón, *sm.* 1. Step of a stair. 2. (Met.) Degree of dignity. *Escalónes de los portalones,* (Naút.) Steps of the entering gang-way.

Escalóña, *sf.* (Bot.) Eschalot, shalot, scallion. Allium ascalonicum *L.*

Escalpélo, *sm.* (Cir.) Scalpel, a surgeon's instrument.

Escálplo, *sm.* Currier's knife.

Escáma, *sf.* 1. Scale, a small horny plate, many of which lying one over another, form the coat of some fishes. 2. A small scaly piece, many of which lapping one over another form a coat of mail.

Escamáda, *sf.* Embroidery in figure of scales.

Escamádo, *sm.* Work wrought with the figure of scales.

Escamadúra, *sf.* Act of embroidering like scales.

Escamár, *va.* 1. To scale fish, to take off the scales. 2. (Met.) To offend, to irritate, to molest.—*vn.* To embroider scale or shell fashion. —*vr.* To be offended, to be exasperated.

Escambronál, *sm.* Plantation of buck thorns.

Escamél, *sm.* Instrument used by sword-makers.

Escamíta, *sf.* A light cotton stuff.

Escamocheár, *vn.* (Ar.) V. *Pavordear.*

Escamóchos, *sm. pl.* Broken victuals, leavings.

Escamónda, *sf.* Pruning trees.

Escamondadúra, *sf.* Useless branches of trees.

Escamondár, *va.* 1. To prune or clear trees of noxious excrescences. 2. To clean, to cleanse.

Escamóndo, *sm.* Clearing trees of their useless branches.

Escamonéa, *sf.* (Bot.) Scammony. Convolvulus scammonia *L.*

Escamoneádo, **da**, *a.* Relating to scammony.

Escamoneárse, *vr.* To be timorous, to fear or dread any thing.

Escamóso, **sa**, *a.* Scaly, having scales.

Escamotár, *va.* (In Jugglery) To make a thing disappear from among the hands.

Escampádo, *a.* V. *Descampado.*

Escampár, *vn.* 1. To cease raining. 2. To leave off working.—*va.* To clean or clear out a place. *Ya escampa,* (Fam.) It is importunate babbling.

Escámpo, *sm.* 1. Cessation. 2. V. *Escape.*

Escamujár, *va.* To prune olive-trees, to lop off the superfluous branches.

Escamújo, *sm.* A lopped-off branch of an olive-tree.

Escanciadór, **ra**; y **Escanciáno**, *s.* The person that serves with wine at feasts.

Escanciár, *va.* To pour wine from one vessel into another to drink.—*vn.* To drink wine.

Escánda, *sf.* (Bot.) Spelt-wheat. Triticum spelta *L.*

Escandalár, *sm.* Apartment for the compass.

Escandalizadór, *sm.* Scandalizer, calumniator.

Escandalizár, *va.* To scandalize, to offend by a scandalous action.—*vr.* To irritate.

Escandalizatívo, va, *a.* Scandalous.

Escandallár, *va.* (Naút.) To sound.

Escandállo, *sm.* 1. (Naút.) Deep sea-lead, a plummet fixed to the end of a line to sound the bottom of the sea. 2. (Met.) Proof, trial.

Escándalo, *sm.* 1. Scandal, offence given by the faults of others. *Escandalo farisayco*, Pharisaical scandal. 2. Admiration, astonishment. 3. Tumult, commotion.

Escandalósa, *sf.* (Naút.) Gaff-sail.

Escandalosaménte, *ad.* Scandalously.

Escandalóso, sa, *a.* Scandalous; turbulent.

Escandecéncia, *sf.* Anger, passion.

Escandecér, *va.* To irritate, to provoke.

Escandelár, *sm.* (Naút.) The second cabin in a row-galley. [a row-galley.

Escandelaréte, *sm.* (Naút.) A small cabin in

Escándia y Escáña, *sf.* V. *Escanda.*

Escandír, *va.* (Poét.) To scan verses.

Escanílla, *sf.* (Burg.) V. *Cuna.*

Escantár, *va.* V. *Encantar.*

Escantillár, *va.* To trace lines on walls to make them of different colours.

Escañéro, *sm.* Seat-keeper, one who takes care of seats and benches in council-chambers or courts.

Escáño, *sm.* 1. Bench or form with a back. 2. (Naút.) Sheer-rail, which divides the quick works from the dead works. 3. V. *Escanda.*

Escañuélo, *sm.* Small bench placed at the feet.

Escapáda y Escapamiénto, *s.* Escape, flight.

Escapár, *vn.* To escape, to get out of danger; to evade.—*va.* To liberate from danger; to slip from the memory. *Escapar en una tabla*, To have a happy escape.

Escaparáte, *sm.* Cupboard, a kind of frame with shelves, in which china, earthenware, and glasses are kept.

Escaparatíco, *sm.* A little cupboard.

Escapatória, *sf.* Escape; excuse, evasion, subterfuge.

Escápe, *sm.* 1. Escape, flight; the act of running away. 2. Subterfuge, evasion. 3. Escapement, part of a watch or other machine.

Escápo, *sm.* Shaft of a column without base or capital.

Escapulár, *va.* (Naút.) To double or clear a cape.

Escapulário, *sm.* Scapulary, part of the habit of various religious orders, consisting of a piece of cloth 3 yards long, in the middle of which an incision is made to admit the head to pass through, while the ends hang down before and behind.

Escáques, *sm. pl.* 1. Checker-work of a draught or chess-board. 2. Any work done so as to resemble the checkers of a draught or chess-board.

Escaqueádo, da, *a.* Checkered, variegated with alternate colours, like a draught or chess-board.

Escaqueár, *va.* To play at chess or draughts.

Escára, *sf.* The scurf which forms round healing wounds.

Escarabajeár, *vn.* 1. To crawl to and fro like insects. 2. To scrawl, to scribble. 3. To sting, to give pain.

Escarabájo, *sm.* 1. (Ento.) The common black-beetle. Scarabæus *L.* 2. Nickname given to a thick, short, ill-shaped person. 3. Twisted threads in the warp of cloth. 4. (Art.) Sand-hole or cavity in the inside of cannons. *Escarabajos*, Ill-formed and irregular letters in writing.

Escarafullár, *va.* To deceive, to gloss over.

Escaramújo, *sm.* (Bot.) Dog-rose, hep-tree; hep. Rosa canina *L.*

Escaramuceár, *vn.* To skirmish.

Escaramúza, *sf.* 1. Skirmish, slight engagement. 2. (Met.) Contest, dispute.

Escaramuzadór, *sm.* 1. Skirmisher. 2. (Met.) Disputer.

Escaramuzár, *va.* To skirmish.

Escarapéla y Escarapúlla, *sf.* 1. Dispute which terminates in blows. 2. Cockade worn in the hat.

Escarapelárse, *vr.* To dispute, to wrangle, to quarrel; generally used of women.

Escárba, *sf.* (Naút.) Scarf, whereby the keel, wales, stem, and stern-post are joined.

Escarbadéro, *sm.* Place where boars, wolves, and other animals scrape or scratch the ground.

Escarbadiéntes, *sm.* V. *Mondadientes.*

Escarbadór, *sm.* Scratcher, scraper.

Escarbadúra, *sf.* Act and effect of scratching.

Escarbajuélo, *sm.* (Ento.) Vine-fretter. Curculio bacchus *L.*

Escarbaoréjas, *sm.* Ear-pick, an instrument for taking out the wax of the ear.

Escarbár, *va.* 1. To scrape or scratch the earth, as fowls. 2. (Met.) To inquire minutely, to investigate. [scratching.

Escárbo, *sm.* Act and effect of scraping or

Escarcéla, *sf.* 1. A large pouch fastened to the girdle; sportsman's net for catching the game. 2. Armour which covers the thigh. 3. Kind of head-dress for women.

Escarcéo, *sm.* Small broken waves occasioned by currents. *Escarceos*, Bounds and windings of spirited horses.

Escárcha, *sf.* 1. White frost. 2. The frozen watery vapours which, on a cold morning, are observable on windows, and other articles of glass.

Escarchádo, *sm.* A kind of gold or silver twist. *Escarchádos*, Ice creams.

Escarchár, *vn.* To be frozen or congealed; applied in particular to dew and watery vapours.—*va.* 1. To curl, to turn the hair into ringlets. 2. To dilute potter's clay with water. [barbatus *L.*

Escárcho, *sm.* (Ict.) Red surmullet. Mullus

Escarchósa, *sf.* (Bot.) Ice-plant, fig-marigold. Mesembryanthemum crystallinum *L.*

Escarcína, *sf.* A kind of cutlass.

Escarcinázo, *sm.* Blow with a cutlass.

Escarcuñár, *va.* (Murc.) V. *Escudriñar.*

Escárda, *sf.* 1. Weed-hook, a hook with which thistles and other weeds are cut away. 2. The act of weeding corn-fields, and clearing them of thistles and other weeds.

Escardadéra, *sf.* 1. Woman employed to clear corn-fields of weeds or noxious herbs. 2. Hoe.

Escardadór, *sm.* Weeder, a man who weeds corn-fields.
Escardadúra, *sf.* Hoe. V. *Escarda.*
Escardár, *va.* 1. To weed corn-fields, to clear them of noxious herbs. 2. (Met.) To part good from bad; to root out vice. *Enviár á escardár*, (Fam.) To refuse harshly.
Escardíllo, lla, *s.* 1. Small weed-hook. 2. Thistle-down. [per-smiths.
Escariadór, *sm.* Kind of punch used by cop-
Escarizár, *va.* To clear from a scab.
Escarladór, *sm.* Iron instrument for polishing combs.
Escarláta, *sf.* 1. Scarlet, cloth dyed with a scarlet colour. 2. (Ento.) Kermes. Coccus ilicis *L.*
Escarlatín, *sm.* A coarse kind of scarlet.
Escarmenadór, *sm.* V. *Escarpidor.*
Escarmenár, *va.* 1. To pick wool. 2. To fine, to mulct.
Escarmentár, *vn.* To be tutored by experience.—*va.* 1. To correct severely, to inflict an exemplary punishment. 2. (Met.) To warn of danger.
Escarmiénto, *sm.* 1. Warning, caution. 2. Fine, mulct, chastisement.
Escarnecedór, ra, *s.* Scoffer, saucy scorner.
Escarnecér, *va.* To scoff, to mock, to ridicule.
Escarnecidaménte, *ad.* Scornfully.
Escarnecimiénto, *sm.* Scoffing; derision.
Escarnído, da, *a.* V. *Descarnado.*
Escárnio, *sm.* Scoff, contemptuous ridicule. *A' escarnio ó en escarnio*, Scoffingly.
Escáro, *sm.* 1. (Ict.) A kind of mutton fish. Labrus scarus *L.* 2. One who has crooked feet.
Escaróla, *sf.* 1. (Bot.) Endive, garden-succory. Cichorium endivia *L.* 2. (Met.) Plaited frill round the neck, ruff.
Escarolár, *va.* V. *Alechugar.*
Escarótico, ca, *a.* Escharotic, caustic.
Escárpa, *sf.* Scarp, the talus or slope on the inside of a ditch towards the rampart.
Escarpádo, da, *a.* Sloped.
Escarpár, *va.* 1. (Naút.) To scarf or join timbers. 2. To rasp or cleanse works of sculpture. [keel.
Escárpe de la quilla, *s.* (Naút.) Scarf of the
Escarpélo, *sm.* Rasp, a coarse file; scalpel.
Escárpia, *sf.* Tenter, a large nail with a hooked head. [nails.
Escarpiár, *va.* To fasten with hook-headed
Escarpidór, *sm.* Comb with large wide teeth.
Escarpín, *sm.* 1. Sock, something put between the foot and shoe. 2. Shoe with a thin sole and low heel, a pump.
Escarpión (En), *ad.* In the form of a tenter or hook.
Escarramanchónes (A'), *ad.* (Ar.) V. *A' horcajadas.*
Escárza, *sf.* A sore in the hoofs of horses or mules.
Escarzáno, na, *a.* Applied to an arch whose curve is less than a semicircle. [ary.
Escarzár, *va.* To castrate bee-hives in Febru-
Escárzo, *sm.* 1. Blackish green honey comb found in the hive without honey. 2. Operation and time of castrating bee-hives. 3. Fungi on the trunks of trees

Escárzo, za, *a.* Lame on account of sores in the hoof; applied to mules and horses.
Escasaménte, *ad.* 1. Scantily, sparingly. 2. Hardly, scarcely, difficultly.
Escaseár, *va.* 1. To give sparingly and with repugnance. 2. To spare, to live in a frugal and saving manner.—*vn.* 1. To grow less, to decrease. 2. (Naút.) To grow scanty; applied to the wind.
Escaséz y Escaséza, *sf.* Scantiness, niggardliness.
Escáso, sa, *a.* 1. Small, short, limited. 2. Sparing, parsimonious, niggardly. 3. Scanty, defective, narrow.
Escatimádo, da, *a.* Little, scanty.
Escatimár, *va.* 1. To curtail, to lessen. 2. To haggle, to be tedious in a bargain. 3. To vitiate or corrupt the sense and meaning of words. 4. To examine closely.
Escatimosaménte, *ad.* Maliciously, viciously.
Escatimóso, sa, *a.* Cunning, malicious.
Escaupíl, *sm.* Armour of quilted cotton, stuffed with cotton wool, to keep off the arrows.
Escáva, *sf.* A pit made round the root of a tree to preserve the water.
Escayóla, *sf.* Paste or composition which resembles marble in colour and appearance.
Escéna, *sf.* 1. Stage, the place where dramatic compositions are performed. 2. Scene, part of a play. 3. (Met.) Revolution, vicissitude. 4. Bed and shepherd's hut made of branches.
Escénico, ca, *a.* Scenic, belonging to the stage.
Esceníta, *sm.* One who lives in a tent.
Escenografía, *sf.* Scenography, the art of perspective.
Escenógrafo, *sm.* An instrument for representing perspective views.
Escepticísmo, *sm.* Scepticism.
Escéptico, ca, *a.* Sceptic, sceptical.
Esciatério, *sm.* An instrument for making sun-dials.
Esciéna, *sf.* (Ict.) A species of craw-fish. Sciæna *L.*
Escientífico, ca, *a.* (Ant.) Scientific. V. *Científico.*
Escíolo, *sm.* Sciolist, one who knows things superficially. [thia.
Escítico, ca, *a.* Native or belonging to Scy-
Esclarecér, *va.* 1. To lighten, to produce light; to illuminate. 2. (Met.) To illustrate, to ennoble.—*vn.* To dawn.
Esclarecidaménte, *ad.* Illustriously.
Esclarecído, da, *a.* Illustrious, noble.
Esclarecimiénto, *sm.* Dawn, the time between the first appearance of light and the sun's rise.
Esclavíllo, lla; to, ta, *s.* A little slave.
Esclavína, *sf.* 1. A long robe worn by pilgrims. 2. Pilgrim's pall, to which shells are fixed. 3. Collar worn by priests in Spain. 4. Kind of cloth worn over women's shoulders in winter.
Esclavitúd, *sf.* 1. Slavery, bondage, servitude. 2. (Met.) Brotherhood, congregation. 3. (Met.) Servile subjection of passions and sentiments. 4. Ornament of jewels, worn by women on the breast.
Esclavizár, *va.* 1. To make one a slave, to reduce to slavery. 2. (Met.) To enclose.
Esclávo, va, *s.* 1. Slave, captive. 2. Member of

a brotherhood or confraternity. 3. (Met.) Slave of one's own desires and passions.

Esclúsa, *sf.* Lock, sluice, flood-gate.

Escóas, *sf. pl.* (Naút.) Rung-heads, floor-heads, floor-timbers of the head.

Escóba, *sf.* 1. Broom; a besom so called from the matter of which it is made. *La primera muger escoba, la segunda señora,* (Prov.) The first wife is a slave, the second a lady. 2. (Bot.) Knapeweed. Centaurea scabiosa *L.* 3. (Naút.) North and north-west wind.

Escobáda, *sf.* The act of sweeping slightly.

Escobájo, *sm.* 1. The remains of an old broom. 2. Rape, whole grapes plucked from the cluster.

Escobár, *sm.* A place where broom grows.

Escobár, *va.* 1. To pick grapes from the rape. 2. To sweep.

Escobazár, *va.* To sprinkle water in drops with a broom. [broom.

Escobázo, *sm.* Stroke or blow given with a

Escobéra, *sf.* Broom. V. *Retama.*

Escobéres, *sm. pl.* Hawses, or hawse-holes, two round holes through which the cable passes when the ship lies at anchor.

Escobéta y Escobílla, *sf.* 1. Brush. 2. A small broom or besom. 3. *Escobilla de ambar,* (Bot.) Flower of amber. Centaurea moschata *L.* 4. Sweepings of gold or silver in the work-shop of a gold or silver-smith.

Escobillón, *sm.* (Art.) Sponge of a cannon.

Escobína, *sf.* Chips or dust made in boring any thing.

Escobón, *sm.* 1. An old hair-broom. 2. Brush, with which a smith sprinkles water on the fire in his forge, to slacken its fierceness.

Escóbos, *sm. pl.* Brushwood, briers, brambles.

Escocér, *va.* 1. To cause a sharp lively pain, as if the painful part had been burnt. 2. (Met.) To make one smart or feel a poignant pain. 3. (Met.) To irritate, to provoke.

Escocés, sa, *a.* Scot, Scotch, belonging to Scotland.

Escócia, *sf.* (Arq.) Scotia, a semicircular concave moulding around the base of a column.

Escocimiénto, *sm.* V. *Escozor.*

Escóda, *sf.* An edged hammer, used by stone-cutters. [horns.

Escodadéro, *sm.* Place where cattle rub their

Escodár, *va.* To hew stones with an edged hammer.

Escodriñár, *va.* V. *Escudriñar.*

Escófia, *sf.* V. *Cofia.*

Escofiár, *va.* To adorn or dress the head with a net. [&c.

Escofiéta, *sf.* Women's head-dress of gauze,

Escofietéro, ra, *s.* Milliner, one who makes head-dresses for women.

Escofína, *sf.* 1. Rasp, a large coarse file used by carpenters. 2. Wire-brush, a brush with which silver-smiths clean their work.

Escofinár, *va.* To rasp, to mould wood with a large file.

Escofión, *sm.* V. *Garbin.*

Escogedór, ra, *s.* Selecter.

Escogér, *va.* To choose, to select, to pick out.

Escogidaménte, *ad.* 1. Choicely, selectly. 2. Elegantly, nicely.

Escogimiénto, *sm.* Choice, selection.

Escolár, *sm.* Scholar, student.—*a.* Scholastic.

Escolár, *va.* V. *Colár.*

Escolasticaménte, *ad.* Scholastically.

Escolástico, ca, *a.* Scholastic, pertaining to schools.

Escolástico, *sm.* A professor of theology.

Escoliadór, *sm.* Annotator.

Escoliár, *va.* To gloss, to explain, to comment.

Escoliarnóso, sa, *a.* Harsh, untractable.

Escolimádo, da, *a.* Weak, delicate. [please.

Escolimóso, sa, *a.* Difficult, severe, hard to

Escólio, *sm.* 1. Scholion or scholium, a brief explanatory observation. 2. (Geom.) Note which refers to a preceding proposition.

Escollár, *va.* (Naút.) To strike upon a rock, to get on shore upon a rock; applied to a ship.

Escolléra, *sf.* (Naút.) Rocky place or cliff.

Escóllo, *sm.* 1. A hidden rock. 2. (Met.) Embarrassment, difficulty, danger.

Escolopéndra, *sf.* 1. (Ento.) Scolopendra, centipede, an insect of the order *Aptera.* Scolopendra forficata *L.* 2. A fish. 3. (Bot.) Spleenwort, hart's tongue. Asplenium scolopendrium *L.* [to place.

Escólta, *sf.* Escort, convoy, guard from place

Escoltár, *va.* To escort, to convoy, to guard from place to place.

Escómbra, *sf.* Purgation, removal of obstacles.

Escombrár, *va.* To remove obstacles, to free from obstructions; to purify.

Escómbro, *sm.* 1. Rubbish, fragments of materials used in building. 2. (Ict.) Mackerel. Scomber scombrus *L.*

Escomenzár, *va.* V. *Comenzar.* [use or time.

Escomérse, *vr.* To be wasted or worn out with

Escónce, *sm.* Corner, angle. [seek.

Escondecúcas, *sm.* Boys' play of hide and

Escondedéro, *sm.* A hiding or lurking place.

Escondedíjo y Escondedríjo, *sm.* Concealment, hiding place.

Escondér, *va.* 1. To hide, to conceal. 2. (Met.) To disguise, to dissemble. 3. To include, to contain.

Escondidaménte, *ad.* Privately, secretly.

Escondídas (A') y A' Escondadillas, *ad.* Privately, in a secret manner.

Escondidíjo, *sm.* V. *Escondrijo.*

Escondído (En), *ad.* Privately, secretly.

Escondimiénto, *sm.* Concealment, the act of hiding or concealing any thing.

Escondíte, *sm.* Concealment, a hiding-place. *Juego de escondite,* Hide and seek.

Escondríjo, *sm.* Concealment, a hiding-place.

Escóntra, *ad.* (Ant.) V. *Hácia.*

Escontréte, *sm.* (Naút.) Prop, stay, shore.

Esconzádo, da, *a.* Angular, oblique.

Escoperadúras, *sf. pl.* (Naút.) Planks nailed to the sides of the ship.

Escopéros, *sm. pl.* (Naút.) Pitch-brushes for paying the seams of ships with pitch and tar.

Escopéta, *sf.* Firelock, fire-arm. *Escopeta de viento,* An air-gun. *A' tiro de escopeta,* Within gun-shot: (Met.) At first view, easily.

Escopetár, *va.* To dig or hollow out gold mines.

Escopetázo, *sm.* 1. Gun or musket-shot. 2. Wound made by a gun-shot.

Escopeteárse, *vr.* 1. To discharge firelocks at each other. 2. (Met.) To insult each other with foul language.

Escopetéo, *sm.* Act of discharging firelocks.
Escopetería, *sf.* 1. Infantry armed with muskets. 2. Multitude of gun-shot wounds.
Escopetéro, *sm.* 1. Musketeer, a foot-soldier armed with a firelock. 2. Gunsmith, armourer.
Escopír, *va.* V. *Escupir.*
Escopleadúra, *sf.* Mortise-hole made in timber, into which a tenon is put.
Escopleár, *va.* To chisel, to cut with a chisel.
Escóplo, *sm.* Chisel, an instrument with which a mortise is cut.
Escópo, *sm.* Scope, aim, purpose.
Escóra, *sf.* (Naút.) That part of a ship's side which makes the most resistance. *Navio de escora baxa,* A ship which carries a stiff sail. *Escóras,* (Naút.) Shores, out-riggers.
Escorár, *va.* 1. (Naút.) To prop, to shore up. 2. (Naút.) To wedge a chest, &c. in order to prevent it from moving about.
Escorbútico, ca, *s.* Person affected with scurvy.
Escorbútico, ca, *a.* Scorbutic, scorbutical.
Escorbúto, *sm.* Scurvy.
Escorchapín, *sm.* Passage-boat, ferry.
Escorchár, *va.* V. *Desollar.*
Escórche, *sm.* Decrease of a tuberous body.
Escórdio, *sm.* (Bot.) Water germander. Teucrium scordium *L.*
Escória, *sf.* 1. Dross, the recrement or despumation of metals. 2. (Met.) Any mean or worthless thing.
Escoriación, *sf.* Incrustation, scurf formed on a sore.
Escoriál, *sm.* An exhausted mine of gold, silver, &c.
Escoriárse, *vr.* To excoriate one's self.
Escorpína y Escorpéra, *sf.* Grooper, a small sea fish. Scorpœna *L.*
Escorpión, *sm.* 1. Scorpion. Scorpio *L.* 2. An ancient warlike machine, used chiefly in the defence of walls. 3. Kind of fish. 4. Sign in the zodiac. 5. Instrument of torture, a cat-o'-nine-tails armed with metal points. 6. (Bot.) Scorpion hypnum. Hypnum scorpioides *L.*
Escorrózo, *sm.* (Vulg.) Pleasure, enjoyment.
Escorzár, *va.* 1. To contract the size of a figure. 2. To form a depressed arch.
Escorzádo ó Escórzo, *sm.* (Pint.) Contraction, or decrease of a figure in perspective.
Escorzón, *sm.* V. *Escuerzo.*
Escorzonéra, *sf.* (Bot.) Viper-root, or viper-grass. Scorzonera hispanica *L.*
Escoscárse, *vr.* To scratch one's self.
Escóta, *sf.* 1. (Naút.) Sheet, a rope fastened to one or both the lower corners of a sail, for the purpose of extending or retaining it in a particular situation. 2. (Arq.) Scotia, a semicircular concave moulding around the base of a column.
Escotádo, *sm.* A sort of dress formerly worn by women, and sloped so much about the neck that the shoulders were exposed to view.
Escotadúra, *sf.* 1. Sloping of a jacket or pair of stays. 2. The large trap-door of a theatre or stage.
Escotár, *va.* 1. To cut out clothes so as to make them fit the body. 2. To pay one's share of scot and taxes. 3. (Naút.) To free a ship by means of the pumps; to extract water.
Escóte, *sm.* 1. Sloping of a jacket or other garment. 2. Tucker, a small piece of linen that shades the breast of women. 3. One's share of a reckoning at a club, feast, &c.
Escotéras, *sf. pl.* (Naút.) Sheet-holes, through which the main and fore-sheets are reeved.
Escotéro, ra, *a.* Free, disengaged.
Escotíllas, *sf. pl.* Hatches, a kind of trap-doors through which bulky goods are let down into the hold. *Escotilla mayor,* The main hatchway.
Escotillón, *sm.* Scuttle, trap-door.
Escotínes, *sm. pl.* (Naút.) Top-sail-sheets, fastened to the lower corners of top-sails and top-gallant-sails.
Escotísta, *sm.* A follower of Duns Scotus.
Escotomía, *sf.* Dizziness or swimming in the head.
Escoznéte, *sm.* (Ar.) Instrument for taking the core or kernel out of a nut.
Escozór, *sm.* 1. A smart pungent pain. 2. (Met.) A lively sensation or perception of the mind.
Escrebidór y Escribidór, *sm.* (Ant.) V. *Escritor.*
Escríba, *sm.* Scribe, among the Hebrews.
Escribanía, *sf.* 1. Office or employment of a notary or scrivener. 2. Office or place where contracts and other notarial deeds and instruments are drawn up. 3. Scrutoire, a case of drawers for writings, with a desk.
Escribáno, *sm.* 1. Notary or scrivener, who keeps an office for drawing instruments, deeds, &c. or attesting writings. 2. Clerk at a public office. 3. Penman. *Es un grande escribano,* He writes a very neat hand, he writes like copperplate. *Escribano ó escribanillo del agua,* Water spider.
Escribiénte, *sm.* 1. Amanuensis, one who writes what another dictates. 2. Author, writer.
Escribír, *va.* 1. To write, to draw or form letters. 2. To write, to compose literary works as an author. 3. To keep up an epistolary correspondence. 4. To enrol, to enter in a register or roll. *Escribir en la arena,* To bury in oblivion.
Escriño, *sm.* Sort of hamper made of straw, and matted together with osier.
Escrípto, ta, *pp. irreg.* of *Escribir.*
Escríta, *sf.* A kind of fish.
Escritíllas, *sf. pl.* Lambs' stones.
Escríto, *sm.* 1. Book, or other literary composition. 2. Libel or petition exhibited in a court of justice. 3. A signed receipt.
Escritór, *sm.* 1. Writer, author. 2. Copist, one who transcribes or copies.
Escritório, *sm.* 1. Scrutoire, a chest of drawers with a desk for writing. 2. Press, a large chest of drawers, or sort of cupboard, adorned with inlaid ivory, ebony, &c. 3. (Tol.) A warehouse where goods are sold by wholesale. 4. Office, study.
Escritúra, *sf.* 1. Writing, the act of putting any thing on paper. 2. Deed, instrument, bond. 3. Writing, a work or treatise written. 4. *Escritura de seguro,* Policy of insurance.
Escriturár, *va.* To bind one's self by a public instrument.
Escriturário, *sm.* One who professes to explain the holy Scripture, a professor of divinity.
Escriturário, ria, *a.* (For.) Scriptory, scriptorian.
Escrófula, *sf.* Scrofula.
Escrofulária, *sf.* (Bot.) Figwort. Scropularia *L.*
Escrofulóso, sa, *a.* Scrofulous.
Escróto, *sm.* Scrotum.

Escrudriñár, *va.* To inquire, to examine into. V. *Escudriñar.*

Escrupuléte, *sm.* A slight doubt or scruple.

Escrupulíllo, *sm.* 1. Slight hesitation. 2. Small piece of metal put into a hollow brass globe to ring as a bell for animals.

Escrupulizár ó **Escrupuleár**, *vn.* To scruple, to doubt, to hesitate.

Escrúpulo, *sm.* 1. Doubt, scruple, hesitation. 2. Scrupulosity, a great nicety or tenderness of conscience. 3. Scruple, a small weight of 24 grains Spanish, and 20 English, being the third part of a drachm. 4. (Astr.) Minute on a graduated sphere. [scrupulous manner.

Escrupulosaménte, *ad.* Scrupulously, in a

Escrupulosidád, *sf.* Scrupulosity, minute and nice doubtfulness ; tenderness of conscience.

Escrupulóso, sa, *a.* Scrupulous ; exact.

Escrutadór, *sm.* Scrutator, examiner.

Escrutínio, *sm.* Scrutiny, inquiry, close exami-

Escrutiñadór, *sm.* Scrutator, censor. [nation.

Escúcha, *sf.* 1. Sentinel, sentry. 2. A listening place. 3. A nun who is sent with another to the grate, to listen to what is said. 4. Scout, one who is sent privily to observe the motions of the enemy. 5. A small window, made for the purpose of hearkening or listening. 6. Servant who sleeps near her mistress, in order to wait on her. [hearkens.

Escuchadór, ra, *s.* Hearer, one who listens of

Escucháte, *pa.* Listener ; hearkening.

Escuchár, *va.* To listen, to hearken.—*vr.* To hear one's self with complacency, to be highly gratified with one's eloquence.

Escudár, *va.* 1. To shield, to defend with a shield. 2. To guard or protect from danger. —*vr.* (Met.) To depend on some means of evading danger.

Escuderáge, *sm.* Escuage, or service of the shield ; a certain tenure or manner whereby tenements are holden.

Escudereár, *va.* To hold tenements by escuage : to perform shield-service ; to perform the functions of a squire or attendant on a noble warrior. [bearer.

Escudería, *sf.* Service of a squire or shield-

Escuderíl, *a.* Belonging to the office of a shield-bearer.

Escuderilménte, *ad.* In the style and manner of a squire or shield-bearer.

Escudéro, *sm.* 1. Shield-bearer, a squire or attendant on a noble warrior. 2. Gentleman descended from some illustrious family. 3. Page who attends a lady. 4. A young boar that follows an old one. *Escudero de á pie*, A servant kept to carry messages or errands.

Escuderón, *sm.* Squire puffed with vanity and pride.

Escudéte, *sm.* 1. Gusset, a piece of lace sewed on a surplice, under the arm-pit, in order to strengthen it. 2. (Arag.) Damage sustained by olives in consequence of falls of rain before the month of September. *Enxerir de escudete*, To graft or insert the branch of one tree into the stock of another. 3. (Bot.) White water-lily. V. *Nenufar.*

Escudílla, *sf.* Porringer, a vessel in which broth is eaten.

Escudillár, *va.* 1. To pour out broth into porringers, to distribute broth. 2. (Met.) To lord, to domineer.

Escudíllo, to, *sm.* A small shield.

Escudíto, *sm.* A gold coin formerly worth 20 reals vellon, now worth 21 reals and a quarter.

Escúdo, *sm.* 1. Shield, buckler ; a piece of defensive armour. 2. Plate on which arms are engraved. 3. Scutcheon of a lock. 4. Patronage, protection. 5. Back of a wild boar. 6. Gusset, a piece of linen sewed on the sides of a shirt, to strengthen it. 7. *Escudo de bote*, (Naút.) The back-board of a boat. *Escudo de popa*, (Naút.) Stern-scutcheon. 8. Crown, a coin of a different value in different countries. In Spain there are gold coins or *escudos* worth 2 dollars or 40 reals, and silver pieces or *escudos* of 8 and of 10 reals.

Escudriñáble, *a.* Investigable.

Escudriñadór, ra, *s.* Prier, scrutator ; a person who with sedulous curiosity inquires into the secrets of others.

Escudriñamiénto, *sm.* Investigation, scrutiny.

Escudriñár, *va.* To search, to pry into ; to inquire after.

Escudríño, *sm.* V. *Escudriñamiento.*

Escuéla, *sf.* 1. School, a house where children are taught and instructed ; a house of discipline and instruction. 2. Instruction given in schools. 3. System of doctrine as delivered by particular teachers ; style of a teacher. 4. University, a place of literary education. *Escuelas*, School-house or edifice for public instruction.

Escuérzo, *sm.* Toad. Rana bufo *L.* [brances.

Escuéto, ta, *a.* Disengaged, free from encum-

Escueznár, *va.* (Ar.) To extract the kernel of nuts. [nut fit for eating.

Escuézno, *sm.* (Ar.) Pulp or soft kernel of a

Esculcár, *va.* (Ant.) To spy, to explore.

Esculladór, *sm* In oil-mills, a vessel for carrying off the oil. [firm.

Escullírse, *vr.* To slip, to slide, not to tread

Esculpidór, *sm.* V. *Escultor.* [or stone.

Esculpír, *va.* To sculpture, to engrave in wood

Escúlto, ta, *pp. irreg.* of *esculpir.*

Escultór, *sm.* Sculptor, carver ; one who cuts wood or stone into images.

Escultóra, *sf.* Female sculptor, wife or daughter of a sculptor.

Escultúra, *sf.* 1. Sculpture, the art of cutting wood or stone into images. 2. Carved work, the work made by a sculptor. *Escultura de navios*, (Naút.) Carved work on board of ships.

Escupidéra, *sf.* Spitting-box.

Escupidéro, *sm.* 1. Spitting-place. 2. (Met.) Despicable or abject situation.

Escupído, *sm.* V. *Esputo.*

Escupidór, ra, *s.* A great spitter.

Escupidúra, *sf.* 1. The act of spitting or ejecting moisture from the mouth. 2. Spittle, the moisture ejected from the mouth. 3. Efflorescence, the breaking out of some humours in the skin.

Escupír, *va.* 1. To spit, to eject moisture from the mouth. 2. To break out in the skin ; applied to morbid humours. 3. (Met.) To discharge balls from fire-arms. 4. (Met.) To dart, to flash. 5. (Met.) To depreciate, to underrate the value of a thing. *Escupir en la cara*, To deride to the face, to ridicule. *Escupir al cielo*, (Met.) To act rashly, to act contrary to prudence and reason. *Escupir doblones*, (Met.) To boast of one's riches. *Escupir sangre en bacín de oro*, (Met.) To enjoy little happiness in the midst of plenty and wealth; literally, to spit blood in a basin of gold. *Escupir las estopas*, (Naút.) To work out the oakum from the seams; spoken of a ship. *No escupir alguna cosa*, (Fam.) To be attached to any thing.

Escupíta y Escupitína, *sf.* V. *Saliva*.

Escurár, *va.* To scour cloth, to cleanse or free it from grease before it is milled.

Escúras (A'), *ad.* 1. Obscurely, darkly. 2. (Met.) Blindly, ignorantly.

Escurecér, *vn.* (Ant.) V. *Obscurecer*.

Escuréza y Escuridád, *sf.* V. *Obscuridad*.

Escurína, *sf.* (Murc.) Obscurity, darkness.

Escúrra, *sf.* Buffoon. V. *Truhan*.

Escurribánda, *sf.* 1. (Joc.) Evasion, subterfuge. 2. Diarrhœa, bowel-complaint. 3. Scuffle, bustle.

Escurrída, *a.* Applied to a woman who wears her petticoats well-fitted.

Escurridízo, za, *a.* 1. Slippery, not affording firm footing. 2. Hard to hold, hard to keep, easily escaping. *Lazo escurridizo*, A running knot.

Escurridúras y Escurrímbres, *sf. pl.* Dregs, the sediment of liquors; the lees, the grounds.

Escurrimiénto, *sm.* V. *Desliz*.

Escurrípa, *sf.* (Bot.) Cardinal's flower. Lobelia cardinalis *L.*

Escurrír, *va.* To drain off liquor to the dregs. —*vn.* 1. To drop, to fall in drops; applied to liquor. 2. To slip, to slide. 3. To escape from danger.

Escusalí, *sm.* A small apron.

Escútas ó Escutíllas, *sf. pl.* (Naút.) Scuttles.

Escuyír, *sm.* Purveyor of meat to the palace.

Esdrúxulo, *sm.* A Spanish word of more than two syllables, the last two of which are short.

E'se, *sf.* 1. Spanish name of the letter S. 2. Link of a chain of the figure of this letter. *Eses*, Reeling and staggering of a drunken man.

E'se, E'sa, E'so, *pron. dem.* This. *E'so mesmo*, *ad.* (Ant.) The very same thing. V. *Asimismo*.

Esecílla, *sf.* Small link of a chain.

Esecutár, *va.* (Ant.) V. *Executar*.

Eséncia, *sf.* Essence, formal existence. *Quinta esencia*, Quintessence, an extract from any thing, containing all its virtues in a small quantity. *Ser de esencia*, To be indispensably necessary.

Esenciál, *a.* Essential, necessary to the constitution or existence of any thing; principal.

Esencialménte, *ad.* Essentially, principally, naturally.

Esenciárse, *vr.* To be intimately united, to grow essential.

Esér, *vn.* (Ant.) To be. V. *Ser*.

Eseyénte, *a.* (Ant.) Being, that which is.

Esféra, *sf.* 1. Sphere, a globe or orbicular body. 2. Globe, representing the earth or sky. 3. Quantity, state, condition, compass. 4. (Poét.) Heaven. *Está fuera de mi esfera*, That is out of my reach or power.

Esfericidád, *sf.* Sphericity, rotundity.

Esférico, ca, *a.* Spherical, globular, globous.

Esferísta, *sm.* Astronomer.

Esferóyde, *sf.* Spheroid. *Bóveda esferoyde*, Elliptical arch.

Esfínge, *sm.* Sphinx, a fabulous monster, having the face of a virgin and the body of a lion.

Esfintér, *sm.* Sphincter, muscle which contracts any part.

Esflorecér ó Eflorecér, *vn.* (Quim.) To effloresce, to fall into powder when exposed to the air.

Esforrocíno, *sm.* Sprig shooting out of the trunk of the vine.

Esforzadaménte, *ad.* Strenuously, vigorously.

Esforzádo, *sm.* One of the books of the civil law which treats of testaments and last wills.

Esforzádo, da, *a.* Strong, vigorous, valiant. *Caldo esforzado*, Strong broth; invigorating.

Esforzadór, ra, *s.* Exciter, animater.

Esforzár, *va.* 1. To strengthen, to invigorate, to enforce. 2. (Met.) To aid, to corroborate. —*vr.* 1. To exert one's self, to make efforts. 2. To be confident, to assure one's self.

Esfuérzo, *sm.* 1. Courage, spirit, vigour. 2. Effort, strong endeavour. 3. Confidence, faith.

Esfumádo, *sm.* The first sketch of a painting, drawn with a pencil or charcoal.

Esfumár, *va.* (Pint.) To shade over the penciled outlines of a picture.

Esgambéte, *sm.* V. *Gambeta*.

Esgárro, *sm.* (Indias) V. *Gargajo*

Església, *sf.* V. *Iglesia*.

Esgoardár, *va.* V. *Atender*

Esgríma, *sf.* Fencing, the art of manual defence. *Maestro de esgrima*, Fencing-master.

Esgrimidór, *sm.* Fencer, one who teaches or professes the use of weapons. *Casa de esgrimidor*, (Met.) House without furniture.

Esgrimír, *va.* 1. To practise the use of weapons. 2. To fight according to art.

Esguardár, *va.* V. *Tocar y Mirar*.

Esguazáble, *a.* Fordable, that may be forded.

Esguazár, *va.* To ford, to cross a river without swimming.

Esguázo, *sm.* The act of fording or passing a river without swimming. V. *Vado*.

Esgúcio, *sm.* (Arq.) Concave moulding, the profile of which is a quarter-circle.

Esguín, *sm.* Young salmon before entering the sea.

Esguínce, *sm.* 1. Movement of the body to avoid a blow or stroke. 2. Frown.

Esguízaro, *sm.* A poor miserable fellow, a ragamuffin. V. *Suizo*.

Eslabón, *sm.* 1. Link of a chain. 2. Steel for striking fire out of a flint-stone. 3. Steel for sharpening knives. 4. A very poisonous scorpion. 5. *Eslabones de guimbalete*, (Naút.) Swivels, rings made to turn round in staples.

Eslabonadór, *sm.* Chair-maker.

Eslabonár, *va.* 1. To link, to join one ring to another. 2. (Met.) To add, to unite.

Esledór, *sm.* (Vitoria) Elector.

Esleér, *va.* (Ant.) V. *Elegir*.

Esleidór, *sm.* (Ant.) V. *Elector*.

Eslínga, *sf.* (Naút.) Sling, a rope with which bales or casks are hoisted out of a ship. *Eslinga de boya*, (Naút.) Buoy-sling.

Eslingár, *va.* To sling, to throw with a sling.

Eslóra ó Eslória, *sf.* Length of a ship from the stem to the stern-post. *Esloras*, Beams running from stem to stern.

Esmalequén, *sm.* Sort of linen made in Flanders.

Esmaltadór, *sm.* Enameller.
Esmaltár, *va.* 1. To enamel, to variegate with colours inlaid. 2. (Met.) To adorn, to embellish.
Esmálte, *sm.* 1. Enamel, any thing enamelled or variegated with colours inlaid in other things. 2. An azure colour, made of paste. V. *Lustre.*
Esmarcházo, *sm.* Bully; a bragging, puffing fellow. [bling a pilchard. Smaris *L.*
Esmarído, *sm.* (Ict.) A small sea-fish, resem-
Esmeráado, da, *a.* High-finished, executed with care. [stone.
Esmeralda, *sf.* Emerald; a green precious
Esmerár, *va.* To polish, to brighten by attrition.—*vr.* To endeavour to attain eminence or superior excellence.
Esmerejón, *sm.* 1. (Orn.) Merlin, the yellow-legged falcon. Falco æsalon *L.* 2. Small piece of artillery.
Esmeríl, *sm.* 1. Emery, a very hard mineral used in cleaning and polishing steel. 2. Small piece of ordnance.
Esmerilár, *va.* To burnish, to polish.
Esmerilázo, *sm.* Shot of a gun called *esmeril.*
Esméro, *sm.* Careful attention, elaborate effort.
Esmoladéra, *sf.* Whetstone, instrument used for sharpening edged tools. [the hands.
Esmuciárse, *vr.* (Burg.) To slip or fall from
Esófago, *sm.* Œsophagus, gullet; the throat.
Esótro, tra, *pron. dem.* This or that other; pointing out not the first, but the second, third, &c. person or thing.
Espabiladéras, *sf. pl.* Snuffers. [*lar.*
Espabilár, *va.* To snuff a candle. V. *Despabi-*
Espaciár, *va.* 1. To extend, to dilate, to spread. 2. (Impr.) To separate the lines with a blank space in printing.—*vr.* 1. To walk to and fro, to amuse one's self. 2. (Met.) To cheer up, to grow gay or gladsome.
Espacíco, ca, *a.* V. *Aciago.*
Espácio, *sm.* 1. Space, capacity; distance between objects. 2. Space, interval of time. 3. Slowness, delay, procrastination. 4. Recreation, diversion. 5. Musical interval. 6. (Impr.) Space, type which separates words. 7. (Ast.) V. *Descampado.*
Espaciosaménte, *ad.* Deliberately, spaciously.
Espaciosidád, *sf.* Spaciousness, capacity.
Espacióso, sa, *a.* 1. Spacious, capacious, wide, roomy. 2. Slow, deliberate.
Espáda, *sf.* 1. Sword, a weapon used either in cutting or thrusting. 2. Ace of spades at cards. 3. (Ict.) Sword-fish. Xiphias gladius *L.* *Espada negra ó de esgrima*, Foil, a blunt sword used in fencing. *Es una buena espada*, He is a good or dexterous swordsman. *Hombre de capa y espada*, Secular who does not expressly profess any faculty or follow any profession. *Espada ancha, ó espada de á caballo*, Broad-sword, which serves rather for cutting than stabbing; dragoon's sabre. *Espádas*, Spades, one of the suits at cards.
Espadachín, *sm.* Bully, one who affects courage and valour.
Espadáda, *sf.* (Ant.) Blow with a sword.
Espadádo, da, *a.* Armed with a sword.
Espadadór, *sm.* One who breaks flax or hemp with a swing-staff.
Espadáña, *sf.* 1. (Bot.) Reed-mace, cat's-tail. Typha latifolia *L.* 2. Spire.
Espadañáda, *sf.* Flow of liquor out of a vessel.
Espadañár, *va.* To divide into long thin slips, resembling flags. [swing-staff.
Espadár, *va.* To break hemp or flax with a
Espadárte, *sm.* (Ict.) Sword-fish. V. *Espada.*
Espadería, *sf.* Sword-cutler's shop, where swords are sold and furbished.
Espadéro, *sm.* Sword-cutler.
Espadílla, *sf.* 1. A small sword. 2. Red insignia of the order of Santiago in the shape of a sword. 3. Swing-staff used in breaking hemp and flax, a scotching handle. 4. (Naút.) A small oar, or helm for boats. 5. Ace of spades at *Ombre.* 6. Hair-bodkin, with which country women tie up their hair.
Espadillár, *va.* To break or scotch hemp or flax with a swing-staff. V. *Espadar.*
Espadillázo, *sm.* Adverse fortune at cards, where the ace is lost for want of other suitable cards.
Espadín, *sm.* A small short sword.
Espadón, *sm.* 1. A large sword, a broad sword 2. Eunuch, one that is castrated. [issues.
Espadrápo, *sm.* Kind of cerecloth, applied to
Espagírico, ca, *a.* Belonging to the art of chemistry. *Espagírica*, Chemistry.
Espaladinár, *va.* (Ant.) To explain.
Espaís, *sm. pl.* Spahis, Turkish horse soldiers.
Espálda, *sf.* 1. Shoulder, the joint which connects the arm with the body; the upper part of the back. 2. (Fort.) Shoulder of a bastion. *Espáldas*, Back or back part: (Met.) Aid, protection. *A' las espaldas de la iglesia*, At the back part of the church. *A' espaldas*, At one's back, in one's absence. *A' espaldas vueltas*, Treacherously, behind one's back. *Echar á las espaldas*, To forget designedly, to abandon. *Sobre mis espaldas*, At my expense.
Espaldár, *sm.* 1. Back-piece of an armour, shoulder-piece of a coat of mail. 2. Place where one puts his back to rest against. 3. Espalier in gardens. *Espaldáres*, Pieces of tapestry against which the chairs lean.
Espaldarázo, *sm.* Blow with a flat side of a sword on the shoulders.
Espaldarcéte, *sm.* Piece of ancient armour.
Espaldarón, *sm.* Ancient armour for the shoulders.
Espaldeár, *va.* (Naút.) To break the waves with too much impetuosity against the poop of a vessel. [ley.
Espaldér, *sm.* The first or stern rower in a gal-
Espaldéra, *sf.* Espalier, trees planted and cut so as to join; wall-trees.
Espaldílla, *sf.* 1. Shoulder-blade, the part of the shoulder next to the arm. 2. Hind quarter of a waistcoat or jacket. [back.
Espalditendído, dá, *a.* Stretched on one's
Espaldón, *sm.* 1. (Albañ.) V. *Rastro.* 2. Entrenchment or barrier to defend one from any attack.
Espaldudaménte, *ad.* Rudely, unmannerly.
Espaldúdo, da, *a.* Broad-shouldered.
Espaléra, *sf.* Espalier.
Espalmadúra, *sf.* Hoofs of quadrupeds.
Espalmár, *va.* (Naút.) To clean and pay a ship's bottom. V. *Despalmar.*
Espálto, *sm.* 1. Dark-coloured paint, which

gives the mummy colour. 2. (Fort.) Esplanade. 3. Talk, a scaly transparent stone.
Espantáble, *a.* 1. Frightful, horrid, terrible. 2. Excellent, admirable, marvellous.
Espantablemente, *ad.* Horribly, terribly.
Espantadízo, za, *a.* Timid, easily frightened.
Espantadór, ra, *s.* Bug-bear, one that frightens or terrifies.
Espantájo, *sm.* 1. Scarecrow, an image or clapper set up to frighten birds. 2. One who cuts grimaces for the purpose of frightening.
Espantalóbos, *sm.* (Bot.) Bladder or bastard senna. Colutea arborescens *L.*
Espantamóscas, *sm.* Net put on horses to scare away flies.
Espantanubládos, *sm.* Rake, vagabond going begging in long robes, who the vulgar think has power over the clouds.
Espantár, *va.* To frighten, to terrify; to chase away.—*vr.* To be surprised or astonished, to marvel.
Espantavillános, *sm.* Sort of shining or glittering gaudy stuff.
Espánto, *sm.* 1. Fright, consternation. 2. Menace, threat. 3. Admiration, wonder, surprise.
Espantosaménte, *ad.* Dreadfully, marvellously
Espantóso, sa, *a.* 1. Frightful, dreadful, horrid. 2. Marvellous, wonderful.
Españól, *sm.* Spanish language.
Españól, la, *a.* Spanish, born in Spain. *A' la Española,* In the Spanish manner.
Españoládo, da, *a.* Talking the language and following the customs and manners of Spain.
Españolár, *va.* V. *Españolizar.*
Españolerías, *sf. pl.* Spanish taste, manners, and customs.
Españoléta, *sf.* Ancient Spanish dance.
Españolizár, *va.* 1. To talk the Spanish language, to translate into the Spanish idiom. 2. To adopt and follow the customs and manners of Spain.
Espár, *sm.* Spar, a kind of aromatic drug.
Esparagón, *sm.* Grogram, a sort of coarse stuff.
Esparamarín, *sm.* Serpent which mounts trees to dart on its prey.
Esparaván, *sm.* 1. (Albeyt.) Tumour in the legs of horses which stiffens them, jardes. 2. (Orn.) Sparrow-hawk. Falco nisus *L.*
Esparavél, *sm.* Kind of fishing-net.
Esparcidaménte, *ad.* Distinctly, separately; gaily.
Esparcído, da, *a.* 1. Scattered. 2. (Met.) Serene, cool; festive, gay.
Esparcílla, *sf.* (Bot.) Spurrey. Spergula *L.*
Esparcimiénto, *sm.* 1. Scattering, dissemination. 2. (Met.) Frankness, openness. 3. (Met.) Liberality of sentiments, generosity of mind.
Esparcír, *va.* 1. To scatter, to disseminate. 2. (Met.) To divulge, to spread abroad.—*vr.* To amuse one's self, to make merry.
Espargánio, *sm.* (Bot.) Burr-reed. Sparganium *L.*
Espáro, *sm.* (Ict.) Gilt-head, a sea-fish. Sparus *L.*
Esparragádo, *sm.* A dish of asparagus.
Esparragadór, *sm.* He who collects and takes care of asparagus.
Esparragár, *va.* To guard or collect asparagus. *Anda ó vete á esparragar,* Expression, to despatch or dismiss one contemptuously or angrily.

Espárrago, *sm.* 1. (Bot.) Sprout of asparagus. Asparagus *L.* *Solo como el espárrago,* As lonely as asparagus; every stalk growing by itself. 2. Pole to support an awning.
Esparragón, *sm.* Silk stuff that forms a cord thicker and stronger than taffety.
Esparraguéra, *sf.* 1. Asparagus plant; stem of this plant. 2. An asparagus-bed, a place where much asparagus grows.
Esparraguéro, ra, *s.* One who gathers and sells asparagus.
Esparrancádo, da, *a.* Wide-legged, divaricated.
Esparrancárse, *vr.* To stride, to open one's legs immoderately.
Esparsón, *sf.* Dissemination, dispersion, the act of scattering.
Espartál, *sf.* Field of bass-weed. V. *Espartizal.*
Espartenéro, ra, *a.* (Ant.) *Ag*[a] *espartenera,* Bass-weed needle.
Espartéña, *sf.* A sort of sandal made of bass-weed.
Espartería, *sf.* Place where bass-mats are made.
Espartéro, ra, *s.* One who makes and sells articles of bass-weed.
Espartílla, *sf.* Handful of bass-weed which serves as a brush for cleaning animals.
Espartizál, *sm.* Field or tract on which bass-weed is growing.
Espárto, *sm.* (Bot.) Sedge, bass-weed. Stipa tenacissima *L.*
Espásmo, *sm.* V. *Pasmo.*
Espáto, *sm.* Spar, a calcareous mineral.
Espátula, *sf.* Spatula or slice used by apothecaries and surgeons in spreading plasters, or stirring medicines.
Espaviénto, *sm.* V. *Aspaviento.*
Espavorído y Espavorecído, da, *a.* Frightened.
Especería, *sf.* 1. Shop where spices are sold. 2. Spices, and all sorts of aromatic drugs.
Especéro, *sm.* One who deals in spices and aromatic drugs.
Especia, *sf.* Spice. *Especias,* Medicinal drugs; desert.
Especiál, *a.* Special, particular. *En especial,* Specially.
Especialidád, *sf.* Speciality or specialty, particularity.
Especialménte, *ad.* Especially, in particular.
Especiár, *va.* To spice broth or food.
Espécie, *sf.* 1. Species: a kind, a sort; a subdivision of a general term. 2. Image or idea of any object in the mind. 3. Event, incident; any thing which has happened. 4. Subject of discussion or dispute. 5. Cause, motive. 6. Feint in fencing. 7. Specie. *Especies sacramentales,* The accidents of colour, taste, and smell, which remain in the sacrament, after the conversion of the bread and wine into the body and blood of Christ.
Especiería, *sf.* V. *Especeria.*
Especiéro, *sm.* Dealer in spices. V. *Boticario.*
Especificación, *sf.* Specification, a minute enumeration of things.
Especificadaménte, *ad.* Specifically, distinctly, expressly.
Especificár, *va.* To specify, to state minutely; to show by some particular mark of distinction.
Especificatívo, va, *a.* That which has the power of specifying or distinguishing.

Específico, *sm.* Specific, a remedy appropriated to the cure of some particular distemper.
Específico, ca, *a.* Specific, specifical.
Espécimen, *sm.* Specimen, sample; a part of any thing exhibited that the rest may be known.
Especióso, sa, *a.* 1. Neat, beautiful; finished with care. 2. Superficial, apparent, specious.
Espectáble, *a.* Conspicuous, eminent, worthy of admiration.
Espectáculo, *sm.* 1. Spectacle, show; public diversion. 2. An object eminently remarkable.
Espectadór, *sm.* Spectator, one who views or beholds with attention.
Espéctro, *sm.* Spectre, a dreadful vision, a frightful or ridiculous phantom.
Especulación, *sf.* Speculation, contemplation, intellectual examination, mental view; commercial adventure.
Especuladór, ra, *s.* Speculator.
Especulár, *va.* To view, to examine by the eye, to meditate, to contemplate.
Especulário, ria, *a.* Specular. [culating.
Especulatíva, *sf.* Faculty of viewing or spe-
Especulativaménte, *ad.* Speculatively.
Especulatívo, va, *a.* Speculative; thoughtful.
Espedazár, *va.* V. *Despedazar.*
Espedírse, *vr.* V. *Despedirse.*
Espejádo, da, *a.* Mirror-like, resembling or consisting of looking-glasses.
Espejár, *va.* To clean, to polish. V. *Despejar*; which is the common term.—*vr.* 1. To view one's self in a looking-glass. 2. (Met.) To regard with complacency the actions of others, to be pleased with them.
Espejeár, *vn.* To shine, to reflect as a mirror.
Espejería, *sf.* 1. Glass-shop, a place where looking-glasses are sold. 2. Glass-house, where plate-glass is made.
Espejéro, *sm.* One whose trade is to make looking-glasses.
Espejíco, llo, to, *sm. dim.* Little mirror.
Espéjo, *sm.* 1. Looking-glass, mirror; a glass which shows forms reflected. *Limpio como un espejo*, As clean as a penny. *Espejo ustorio*, A burning glass. 2. *Espejo de popa*, (Naút.) Stern frame.
Espejuéla, *sf.* Arch with two openings in the interior.
Espejuélo, *sm.* 1. A small looking-glass. 2. Lapis specularis, a kind of transparent lamellated gypsum. 3. Transparent leaf of talc. 4. Instrument used by bird-catchers in catching larks. 5. A kind of transparent sweetmeat. 6. Dirt collected round the combs of bee-hives in winter. *Espejuélos*, Crystal lenses, of which spectacles are made.
Espélta, *sf.* (Bot.) Spelt, or spelt-corn. Triticum spelta *L.*
Espélteo, ea, *a.* Belonging to spelt.
Espelúnca, *sf.* V. *Cueva.*
Espeluzár, *va.* V. *Despeluzar.*
Espeluznárse, *vr.* To have the hair set on end with fear; to have the hair dishevelled.
Espéques, *sm. pl.* (Naút.) Handspikes, wooden levers.
Espéra, *sf.* 1. Stay, the act of waiting; expectation. 2. Respite. 3. A kind of heavy ordnance. 4. Pause, stop. *Estar en espera*, To be in expectation of. *Hombre de espera*, A cool composed man. [hoped.
Esperáble, *a.* That which may be expected or
Esperadór, *sm.* Expectant, he who expects or hopes.
Esperánza, *sf.* 1. Hope. 2. Anchor of hope.
Esperanzár, *va.* To give hope.
Esperár, *va.* 1. To hope, to live in expectation of some good. 2. To stay, to wait for, to expect. 3. To fear. *Espero la calentura*, I am afraid of the fever.—*vr.* V. *Desperezarse.*
Esperézo, *sm.* The act of stretching one's arms and legs after being roused from sleep.
Esperiégo, ga, *a.* V. *Asperiega.* *Esperiego*, Tart apple-tree. *Esperiega*, Tart apple.
Esperlán, *sm.* V. *Eperlano.*
Espérma, *sf.* Sperm. V. *Sémen.* *Esperma de ballena*, Spermaceti.
Espermático, ca, *a.* Spermaceti, a kind of unctuous substance found in one species of whale.
Espermático, *sm.* Spermatic, seminal; belonging to the sperm.
Espernáda, *sf.* End of a chain.
Esperón, *sm.* (Naút.) The forecastle-head.
Esperónte, *sm.* Kind of ancient fortification, being a salient angle in the middle of the curtain.
Esperriáca, *sf.* (And.) The last must or juice which is drawn from grapes, and usually consumed by the workmen.
Esperriár, *va.* (Ant.) V. *Espurriar.*
Espesár, *va.* 1. To thicken, to inspissate, to condense what is liquid or fluid. 2. To close, to join, as silk or stuff does.—*vr.* To grow thick. [of thickening.
Espesatívo, va, *a.* That which has the power
Espéso, sa, *a.* 1. Thick, condensed. 2. Bulky, corpulent. 3. Close, contiguous. 4. Frequent, often repeated. 5. Slovenly, dirty.
Espesór, *sm.* Thickness, grossness.
Espesúra, *sf.* 1. Thickness, density. 2. (Fort.) Thickness, solidity of the works of a fortress. 3. Thicket, a close knot of trees, a close wood. 4. Slovenliness, indecent negligence of dress.
Espetamiénto, *sm.* Stiffness, formality, stateliness of mien or deportment.
Espetár, *va.* 1. To spit, to run through with a spit. 2. To run through with a sword. 3. To tell, to relate. *Le espetó fuertes razones*, He gave strong reasons.—*vr.* 1. To be stiff and stately, to be puffed up with pride. 2. (Met.) To sidle or thrust one's self into some narrow place.
Espetéra, *sf.* 1. Rack, a board with hooks, on which kitchen utensils are hung. 2. Kitchen furniture.
Espéto, *sm.* V. *Asador.*
Espetón, *sm.* 1. Spit, a long iron prong. 2. A large pin. 3. (Ict.) Sea-pike, spit-fish. Esox sphyræna *L.* 4. Blow given with a spit.
Espía, *s.* 1. Spy, one sent to watch the conduct and motions of others. *Espía doble*, Person who betrays the secrets of both parties. *Espía del purgatorio*, Nickname of persons very feeble and languid. 2. (Naút.) Warp, a rope used in moving a ship along by means of the stream-anchor.

Espiadór, *sm.* Spy.
Espiár, *va.* 1. To spy, to watch closely. 2. (Naút.) To warp, to move a ship along by means of a warp and stream-anchor.
Espírio ó Espirión, *sm.* (Albeyt.) Dislocation or contraction in the nape of the neck of animals.
Espicacéltica, *sf.* (Bot.) Yellow or Roman valerian. Valeriana celtica *L.*
Espicanárdi, *sf.* (Bot.) Spikenard. Andropogon nardus *L.*
Espichár, *va.* To prick. V. *Pinchar.*
Espíche, *sm.* A sharp-pointed weapon. *Espiches*, (Naút.) Pegs, small pointed pieces of wood driven into the holes of the planks of ships.
Espichón, *sm.* Wound with a pointed weapon.
Espíga, *sf.* 1. Ear, the spike of corn; that part which contains the seed; bud for inoculating. 2. Tenon, the end of a piece of timber fitted into another. 3. Brad, a nail without a head to floor rooms with. 4. Fusee of a bomb or shell. 5. (Naút.) Spile, a small wooden pin driven into the nail-holes of ships when the sheathing is taken off; sail of a galley. 6. *Espiga de agua*, (Bot.) Pond-weed. Potamogeton *L.* *Quedarse á la espiga*, (Fam.) to remain to the last, to collect the fragments or refuse.
Espigadéra ó Espigadóra, *sf.* Gleaner, a woman who gathers ears of corn after the reapers.
Espigádo, da, *a.* Tall, grown; applied to growing persons.
Espigár, *vn.* 1. To ear, to shoot into ears. 2. (Met.) To grow, to increase in bulk and stature.—*va.* 1. To glean, to gather ears of corn left by the reapers. 2. To make presents, or regale a bride. 3. To make a tenon.
Espigón, *sm.* 1. Ear of corn. 2. Sting, a sharp point with which bees, wasps, and other animals are armed. 3. Point of a dart or javelin. 4. Sharp point of a hill without trees. *Ir con ó llevar espigon*, (Met.) To retire indignant or irritated.
Espiguílla, *sf.* 1. Small edging or lace, tape, inkle. 2. Flower of some trees.
Espilócho, *sm.* Poor, destitute person.
Espilorchería, *sf.* Sordid avarice.
Espilladór, *sm.* (In cant) Player, gambler.
Espín, *sm.* Porcupine.
Espína, *sf.* 1. Thorn, a prickle growing on a thorn bush or brier. 2. *Espina blanca*, (Bot.) White-thorn. Cratægus oxyacantha *L.* 3. Spine. 4. (Met.) Doubt, suspicion. *Espinas*, Bones of fishes.
Espináca, *sf.* (Bot.) Spinage. Spinacia oleracea *L.*
Espinadúra, *sf.* Act of pricking with a thorn.
Espinál ó Espinár, *sm.* 1. Place full of thorn-bushes, brambles, and briers. 2. (Met.) A dangerous undertaking, an arduous enterprise.
Espinál, *a.* Spinal, dorsal.
Espinár, *va.* 1. To prick with thorns. 2. To surround trees with briers and thorn-bushes. 3. (Met.) To nettle, to make uneasy.
Espinázo, *sm.* Spine, the back-bone.
Espinél, *sm.* A fishing-line with many hooks, to catch conger-eels, and other large fishes.
Espinéla, *sf.* 1. A piece of Spanish poetry, consisting of ten verses of 8 syllables. 2. Spinel-ruby, a precious stone.

Espíneo, ea, *a.* Made of thorns.
Espinéta, *sf.* Spinet, a small harpsichord.
Espingárda, *sf.* 1. A small piece of ordnance 2. A large hand-gun or musket.
Espingardáda, *sf.* Wound of a ball from an *espingarda*.
Espingardéro, *sm.* Gunner, musketeer.
Espinílla, *sf.* Shin or shin-bone, the fore part of the leg.
Espiníta, *sf.* A little thorn.
Espíno, *sm.* 1. (Bot.) Thorn; buckthorn Rhamnus catharticus *L.* 2. *Espino amarillo* (Bot.) Christ's thorn. Rhamnus vel Zizyphus paliurus *L.* 3. (Orn.) Siskin. Fringilla spinus *L.*
Espinóso, sa, *a.* 1. Spiny, thorny, full of thorns 2. (Met.) Arduous, dangerous.
Espinóso, *sm.* (Ict.) Three-spined stickleback Gasterosteus aculeatus *L.*
Espinzár, *va.* To burl; to dress cloth, as fullers do, after it has been milled.
Espión, *sm.* Spy. V. *Espía.*
Espióte, *sm.* A sharp pointed weapon. V. *Espiche.*
Espíque, *sm.* V. *Espicanardi.*
Espíra, *sf.* Spire, a kind of winding staircase
Espiración, *sf.* Respiration; transpiration
Espiradéro, *sm.* V. *Respiradero.*
Espiradór, *sm.* He who expires or breathes.
Espirál, *a.* Spiral, winding.
Espiránte, *pa.* Expiring, respiring.
Espirár, *vn.* 1. To expire, to breathe the last. 2. To make an emission of the breath, to expire. 3. To finish, to come to an end. 4. To fly out with a blast.—*va.* 1. To exhale, to send out in exhalations. 2. To infuse a divine spirit. 3. To inspire. 4. To take the spigot out of a faucet. [breathe or respire
Espiratívo, va, *a.* (Teol.) That which can
Espiréa, *sf.* (Bot.) Dropwort, meadow-sweet. Spiræa filipendula *L.*
Espirénque, *sm.* (Ict.) Smelt. Salmo eperlanus *L.*
Espiritár, *va.* To irritate or agitate. V. *Endemoniar.*—*vr.* To be possessed with an evil spirit.
Espiritíllo, *sm.* A little spirit.
Espiritosaménte, *ad.* Spiritedly, ardently.
Espiritóso, sa, *a.* 1. Spirituous, having the quality of spirit; defecated. 2. (Met.) Spirited lively, active, ardent.
Espíritu, *sm.* 1. Spirit, an immaterial substance. 2. Soul of man. 3. Genius, vigour of mind; power of mind, moral or intellectual 4. Spirit, ardour, courage. 5. That which gives vigour or cheerfulness to the mind or body. 6. Inclination, turn of mind. 7. Spirit, inflammable liquor, raised by distillation. 8 True sense or meaning. *Espíritus*, Spirits, demons; spirits, subtile vapours, ether.
Espirituál, *a.* Spiritual.
Espiritualidád, *sf.* 1. Spirituality, incorporality, intellectual nature. 2. Principle and effect of what is spiritual. *Espiritualidades de un obispo*, Revenue of a bishop arising from his jurisdiction.
Espiritualísta, *sm.* He who treats of the vital spirits.
Espiritualizár, *va.* 1. To spiritualize, to purify from the feculencies of the world. 2. To refine the intellect.

Espiritualménte, *ad.* Spiritually.
Espiritudóso, sa, *a.* Spirituous. V. *Espirituoso.*
Espíta, *sf.* 1. Faucet, a pipe inserted into a vessel to give vent or draw out the liquor. 2. Tippler, a sottish drunkard. 3. Span, the space from the end of the thumb to the end of the little finger extended.
Espitár, *va.* To put a faucet in a tub or other vessel.
Espíto, *sm.* Peel, a piece of wood used to hang up paper to dry.
Esplanáda, *sf.* (Fort.) Esplanade, the declivity extending from the parapet of the covert-way into the country.
Esplendénte, *pa.* (Poét.) Shining, resplendent.
Esplendér, *vn.* (Poét.) To shine, to glitter, to be resplendent.
Esplendidaménte, *ad.* Splendidly, magnificently.
Esplendidéz, *sf.* Splendour, magnificence; ostentation.
Espléndido, da, *a.* 1. Splendid, magnificent. 2. (Poét.) Resplendent.
Esplendór, *sm.* 1. Splendour, eclat, brilliancy, lustre. 2. Excellence, eminence. 3. White paint made of pounded egg-shells.
Esplénico, ca, *a.* Splenic, belonging to the spleen or milt.
Esplénico ó Esplénio, *sm.* One of the fourteen muscles by which the head is moved.
Espliégo, *sm.* (Bot.) Lavender. Lavandula spica *L.* In Andalusia it is called *Alhucema.*
Esplíque, *sm.* Machine for catching sparrows.
Espódio, *sm.* 1. Calx found in copper furnaces. 2. Ashes of burnt ivory or reeds.
Espoláda, *sf.* 1. Prick with a spur. 2. A large draught of wine.
Espolázo, *sm.* A violent prick or puncture with a spur.
Espoleadúra, *sf.* Wound made with a spur.
Espoleár, *va.* 1. To spur, to prick with a spur. 2. To instigate, to incite, to urge forward.
Espoléta, *sf.* 1. Fusee of a bomb, a wooden pipe filled with a composition of gun-powder and other combustibles, by which the fire is communicated to the charge. *Espoletas de cubierta*, (Naút.) Fusees of a fire-ship. 2. Small bone between the wings of birds.
Espolín, *sm.* 1. A small spool for raising flowers on stuff. 2. Silk stuff, on which flowers are raised.
Espolinádo, da, *a.* Flowered; applied to silk stuffs.
Espolinár, *va.* To weave silk in flowers.
Espólio, *sm.* The property which a prelate leaves at his death.
Espolíque, *sm.* Property of a deceased prelate.
Espolísta, *sm.* One who farms the fruits of an ecclesiastical benefice of a deceased bishop.
Espolón, *sm.* 1. Spur, the sharp point on the legs of a cock. 2. The acute angle of the pier of a stone-bridge, to break the force of the current. 3. (Naút.) Beakhead of a galley. 4. (Fort.) Kind of salient angle. 5. Chilblain, sore made by cold. 6. Angular point of a rock, by which people descend.
Espolvoreár, *va.* 1. To powder. 2. V. *Despolvorear.*
Espolvorizár, *va.* To scatter powder.
Espondéo, *sm.* Spondee, a foot of verse consisting of two long syllables.
Espondil, *sm.* V. *Vértebra.*
Esponjiosidád, *sf.* Sponginess.
Espónja, *sf.* 1. Spunge or sponge, a soft porous substance. 2. Pumice-stone. 3. (Met.) One who by mean arts deprives others of their property, or lives on them.
Esponjádo, *sm.* (And.) A sponge made of sugar, which instantly dissolves.
Esponjadúra, *sf.* 1. Act of sponging. 2. Cavity or defect in cast metal.
Esponjár, *va.* To sponge, to soak or imbibe.—*vr.* To be puffed up with pride.
Esponjóso, sa, *a.* Spongy, soft and porous.
Esponsáles, *sm. pl.* Espousals, the act of affiancing a man and woman to each other; a mutual promise of marriage.
Esponsalício, cia, *a.* Belonging to espousals.
Espontaneaménte, *ad.* Spontaneously.
Espontáneo, nea, *a.* Spontaneous, voluntary.
Espontón, *sm.* Spontoon, a half pike, formerly used by officers of infantry when on duty.
Espontonáda, *sf.* Salute to royal personages or generals with a spontoon.
Esportáda, *sf.* That which ends in a basket.
Esporteár, *va.* To carry in panniers or baskets.
Esportílla, *sf.* A small pannier or wicker vessel.
Esportilléro, *sm.* Porter, one who carries burthens for hire.
Esportíllo, *sm.* Pannier, a wicker vessel.
Esportón, *sm.* A large pannier.
Espórtulas, *sf. pl.* Judicial fees.
Espósas, *sf. pl.* Manacles, fetters or chains for the hand.
Esposáyas, *sf. pl.* Espousals.
Espóso, sa, *s.* Spouse, husband, wife.
Espotático, ca, *a.* (Ant.) V. *Espontaneo.*
Espringa-Bálas, *sf.* (Naút.) Pump-handle.
Espuéla, *sf.* 1. Spur, a sharp point fixed on the rider's heel. 2. (Met.) Spur, stimulus, incitement. *Mozo de espuelas*, Groom, stable-boy. *Poner espuelas*, (Met.) To incite, to urge on. 3. *Espuela de caballero*, (Bot.) Lark's spur, or lark's heel. Delphinium consolida *L.*
Espuénda, *sf.* (Nav.) Margin or border of a river.
Espuérta, *sf.* Pannier, basket.
Espulgadéro, *sm.* Place where beggars use to clean themselves from lice.
Espulgadór, ra, *s.* One who cleans off lice or fleas.
Espulgár, *va.* 1. To louse, to clean from lice or fleas. 2. To examine closely.
Espúlgo, *sm.* The act of cleaning from lice or fleas.
Espúma, *sf.* 1. Froth, spume, foam; the bubbles caused in liquors by agitation. *Espuma de plata*, Litharge of silver. 2. Spittle.
Espumadéra, *sf.* 1. Skimmer, a sort of ladle with holes, for taking off the scum of liquids. 2. Vessel used by confectioners to clarify sugar. 3. (Naút.) Pitch-skimmer.
Espumajeár, *vn.* To froth at the mouth.
Espumájo, *sm.* Froth, spume, saliva.
Espumajóso, sa, *a.* Full of froth or spume.
Espumánte, *pa.* Foaming at the mouth, like enraged animals.
Espumár, *va.* To skim, to take off the scum;

to clear the upper part by passing a vessel a little below the surface.—*vn.* To throw out spittle or spume.

ESPUMARÁJO, *sm.* Foam, the frothy substance thrown from the mouth.

ESPUMÉRO, *sm.* Place where salt-water is collected to crystallize.

ESPUMÍLLA, *sf.* Thread-crape, a sort of thin cloth loosely woven.

ESPUMILLÓN, *sm.* Silk crape or gauze.

ESPUMÓSO, SA, *a.* Spumy, frothy.

ESPÚNDIA, *sf.* (Albeyt.) Tumour in horses.

ESPÚRIO, RIA, *a.* 1. Spurious, not legitimate. 2. (Met.) Adulterated, corrupted.

ESPURRIÁR, *va.* To spurt, or to moisten any thing with water.

ESPURRÍR, *vn.* To stretch out the legs.

ESPÚTO, *sm.* Spittle, saliva.

ESQUÁDRA, *sm.* 1. Square, an instrument for describing and measuring right angles. 2. Socket, in which the pivot or spindle of a door turns. 3. Division or small body of horse-soldiers; squadron, troop. 4. Squadron of ships. *A' esquadra,* In a square manner. *Xefe de esquadra,* (Naút.) Rear-admiral.

ESQUADRÁR, *va.* 1. To square, to form with right angles; to reduce to a square. 2. To fix the trunnions horizontally in a piece of ordnance.

ESQUADRÉO, *sm.* Dimension, valuation of the square contents of a piece of ground.

ESQUADRÍA, *sf.* Square, a measure having or forming right angles. [Quadro.

ESQUÁDRO, *sm.* 1. Species of dog-fish. 2. V.

ESQUADRÓN, *sm.* 1. Squadron, troop; a small body of horse. 2. (Mil.) *Esquadron quadrado,* A hollow square. *Esquadran volante,* A flying camp.

ESQUADRONÁR, *va.* To draw up troops in rank and file, to form troops in squadrons.

ESQUADRONCÍTO, ÍLLO, *sm.* A small party of troops. [squadrons.

ESQUADRONÍSTA, *sm.* (Mil.) He who forms

ESQUÁLO, *sm.* Dog-fish.

ESQUEBRAJÁRSE, *vr.* To become open, to be split or full of chinks, as wood.

ESQUÉLA, *sf.* Billet, a small paper, a note. *Esquéla amatoria,* Billet-doux, a love-letter.

ESQUELÉTO, *sm.* 1. Skeleton, the bones of the body preserved together in their natural situation. 2. Person who is very thin and meagre. 3. Watch, the work and movement of which are exposed to view. 4. (Naút.) Carcass of a ship, without cover or sheathing.

ESQUELÍN, *sm.* Skilling, a foreign silver coin.

ESQUÉNA, *sf.* Spine of fishes.

ESQUÉRO, *sm.* A leather bag or pouch.

ESQUÉRRO, RA, *a.* (Ant.) V. *Izquierdo.*

ESQUÉXE, *sm.* (Jardin.) Root, sprout, shoot of plants. [ated.

ESQUICIÁDO, DA, *a.* Sketched, traced, deline-

ESQUICIÁR, *va.* To sketch, to draw the outlines of a painting; to trace, to delineate.

ESQUÍCIO, *sm.* Sketch, outline. [of a cistern.

ESQUIFÁDA, *sf.* 1. A skiff or boat load. 2. Vault

ESQUIFÁR, *va.* 1. (Naút.) To arm a boat with oars. 2. To fit out a ship.

ESQUÍFE, *sm.* 1. A skiff, a small boat. 2. (Arq.) Cylindrical vault.

ESQUÍLA, *sf.* 1. A small bell; also a bell carried by cattle. 2. The act and time of sheep-shearing. V. *Esquileo.* 3. (Ict.) Shrimp. Cancer squilla *L.* 4. (Ento.) Water-spider. 5. (Bot.) Squill.

ESQUILÁDA, *sf.* (Ar.) V. *Cencerrada.*

ESQUILADÓR, *sm.* Sheep-shearer.

ESQUILÁR, *va.* 1. To shear sheep, to cut off the wool or hair of animals. 2. (Burg.) To climb a tree with the hands and feet only. *A' dios que esquilan,* An expression used by persons who are in a great haste and cannot stop.

ESQUILÉO, *sm.* Sheep-shearing-time; also the act and place of shearing.

ESQUILÉTA, *sf.* Small bell.

ESQUILFÁDA, *sf.* V. *Esquifada.*

ESQUILIMÓSO, SA, *a.* Fastidious, over nice.

ESQUILMÁR, *va.* To gather and inn the harvest. *Esquilmar la tierra,* To impoverish the earth too much; applied to trees.

ESQUÍLMO, *sm.* 1. Harvest, the corn inned. 2. Produce of vines.

ESQUÍLO, *sm.* 1. Shearing-time; also the act of shearing. 2. Kind of squirrel.

ESQUILÓN, *sm.* 1. A small bell. 2. Large bell worn by cattle.

ESQUÍNA, *sf.* Corner, the outward angle formed by two lines. *Estar de esquina,* (Fam.) To be opposed to each other.

ESQUINÁDO, DA, *a.* Cornered, angled.

ESQUÍNCO, *sm.* Kind of serpent or crocodile.

ESQUINÉLA, *sf.* Armour for the legs.

ESQUINÉNCIA ó ESQUINÁNCIA, *sf.* Quinsy, a tumid inflammation in the throat.

ESQUINÁNTE ó ESQUINÁNTO, *sm.* Kind of aromatic or medicinal rush.

ESQUINÁR, *va.* To make a corner, to form into an angle.

ESQUINÁZO, *sm.* 1. Corner, a very acute outward angle. 2. (Vulg.) Quinsy.

ESQUINZADÓR, *sm.* Large apartment in paper-mills for putting the rags in after cutting them. [paper-mills.

ESQUINZÁR, *va.* To cut rags in small pieces in

ESQUIPÁDO, DA, *a.* Made boat-fashion.

ESQUIPÁR, *va.* (Naút.) To equip, to fit out a ship. V. *Esquifar.*

ESQUIRÁZA, *sf.* Kind of ancient ship.

ESQUÍRLA, *sf.* Splinter of a bone.

ESQUIRÓL, *sm.* (Ar.) V. *Ardilla.*

ESQUISÁR, *va.* (Ant.) To search, to investigate.

ESQUITÁR, *va.* To pardon, to remit a debt. V. *Desquitar.*

ESQUIVÁR, *va.* To shun, to avoid, to evade, to escape.—*vr.* To disdain, to scorn; to view with contempt.

ESQUIVÉZ, *sf.* Disdain, scorn, asperity.

ESQUIVÉZA Y ESQUIVIDÁD, *sf.* (Ant.) Disdain.

ESQUÍVO, VA, *a.* 1. Scornful, severe, stubborn, fastidious. 2. Shy, reserved, difficult. 3. Large, strong, terrible.

ESQUIZÁDO, DA, *a.* Applied to spotted marble.

E'ST, *sm.* (Naút.) East. V. *Este.* [nence.

ESTABILIDÁD, *sf.* Stability, duration, perma-

ESTÁBLE, *a.* Stable, permanent, durable, steady.

ESTABLEÁR, *va.* To tame, to domesticate, to accustom to the stable.

ESTABLECEDÓR, *sm.* Founder, he that establishes an institution or law.

ESTABLECÉR, *va.* 1. To establish, to enact a law.

2. To found; to render a thing durable and permanent.—*vr.* To establish or fix one's self in a place.

Establecienté, *pa.* Establisher; establishing.

Establecimiénto, *sm.* Establishment, law, ordinance; foundation.

Estableménte, *ad.* Stably, firmly.

Establéro ó Establerízo, *sm.* Hostler, one who has the care of horses at an inn.

Establíllo, *sm.* A small stable.

Estáblo, *sm.* 1. Stable for horses and mules. 2. Cow-house, sheep-cot, stall for oxen.

Estáca, *sf.* 1. Stake, a pole with one end pointed. *Estar á estaca,* To be reduced or confined to a small space. *A' estaca,* Copiously, abundantly. 2. Slip of a tree put into the ground to grow. 3. Stick, cudgel.—*pl.* 1. (Naút.) Tholes, or thoals. V. *Toletes.* 2. Divisions or partitions made in mines. 3. Clamp-nails, large nails used by carpenters.

Estacáda, *sf.* 1. (Mil.) Palisades or palisadoes. 2. Any enclosure surrounded with paling. 3. Place for a duel. 4. New plantation of olives.

Estacádo, *sm.* Field of battle.

Estacár, *va.* 1. To put stakes into the ground; to enclose a spot with stakes. 2. To tie to a stake.—*vr.* To be enclosed or surrounded with stakes.

Estacázo, *sm.* Blow given with a stake.

Estácha, *sf.* Rope or cord fastened to a harpoon, to give the whale room to dive.

Estación, *sf.* 1. State, situation, position. 2. Season of the year. 3. Hour, moment. 4. Station, a place assigned for some certain end. 5. Visit paid to a church in order to pray. *Andar estaciones,* To perform stationary prayers in order to gain indulgences. 6. Business. *Ir ó andar las estaciones,* To go and mind one's business, to perform the duty of one's place or station. *Tornar á andar las estaciones,* (Met.) To return to one's former evil habits.

Estacionál, *a.* Belonging to the seasons.

Estacionário, ria, *a.* Stationary, fixed, not progressive. *Estacionario,* Stationer, paper-seller.

Estacionéro, ra, *a.* 1. One who frequently performs the stations, or visits the fixed places for prayers. 2. (Ant.) Bookseller.

Estacón, *sm.* A large stake. [fresh myrrh.

Estácte, *sm.* Odoriferous liquor extracted from

Estáda, *sf.* Stay, sojourn, residence.

Estadál, *sm.* 1. Land-measure, containing about three square yards and two thirds, or eleven feet. 2. Kind of ornament or holy ribbon worn at the neck. 3. (And.) Fathom of wax taper.

Estádio, *sm.* 1. Race-course. 2. Distance or extent of a course which made 125 geometrical paces.

Estadísta, *sm.* Statist, statesman, politician.

Estadízo, za, *a.* Stagnant, corrupted; applied to water.

Estádo, *sm.* 1. State, the actual condition of a thing. 2. Rank, station in life. 3. Stature or height of a person. 4. State, commonwealth. 5. Statement, account. 6. Suite, attendants. *Estado general ó llano,* Community or peasantry of any district, not including the nobles. *Materias de estado,* State affairs. *Poner á uno en estado,* To set one up in life. *Estado mayor,* (Mil.) Staff; generals and commanders of an army. *Hombre de estado,* Statesman. *Poner á uno en estado,* To marry one. *Estádos,* States of a country; the clergy, nobility, and cities, which compose the legislative assembly in Germany, and several other countries.

Estadójo ó Estadóño, *sm.* Stake. V. *Estaca.*

Estáfa, *sf.* Trick, deceit, imposition.

Estafadór, ra, *s.* Impostor, swindler.

Estafár, *va.* 1. To deceive, to defraud. 2. (Among Sculptors) To size a statue with a white coat, in order to gild it.

Estaférmo, *sm.* 1. A wooden moveable figure of an armed man. 2. (Met.) An idle fellow, who affects dignity and importance.

Estaféro, *sm.* Foot-boy, errand-boy, stable-boy. [post-office for letters.

Estaféta, *sf.* 1. Courier, express. 2. General

Estafetéro, *sm.* Post-master, director of the post-office for letters. [letters.

Estafetífero, ra, *a.* Carrying or conveying

Estafetíl, *a.* Belonging to a courier or post.

Estafiléa, *sf.* (Bot.) Bladdernut. Staphylea pinnata *L.*

Estafiságra, *sf.* (Bot.) Stavesacre, lousewort. Delphinium staphisagria *L.* [ed.

Estaimbóuc, *sf.* A kind of shamois skin dress-

Estála, *sf.* 1. Stable. 2. Sea-port.

Estalación, *sf.* Class, rank, order.

Estaláge, *sm.* Stay, sojourn. V. *Estancia.*

Estalingadúra, *sm.* (Naút.) The bending of a cable, or act of fastening it to the ring of the anchor.

Estalingár, *va.* (Naút.) To bend a cable, to make it fast to the ring of the anchor.

Estallár, *vn.* 1. To crack, to burst into chinks with a loud sound. 2. (Met.) To break out into fury or rage.

Estallído y Estállo, *sm.* Sound of any body bursting or falling. *Dar un estallido,* To publish, to expose; to make a noise or confusion.

Estamátes, *sm.* A sort of cloth manufactured in Flanders.

Estambór, *sm.* (Naút.) Stern-post.

Estambrádo, *sm.* (Manch.) Kind of cloth made of worsted.

Estambrár, *va.* To twist wool into yarn, to spin worsted.

Estámbre, *sm.* 1. Fine worsted or woollen yarn. 2. Fine wool. 3. (Bot.) Stamen of flowers. *Estambre de la vida,* (Poét.) The thread of life. 4. Warp. V. *Urdimbre.*

Estaménto, *sm.* 1. Assembly of the *Cortes,* or states of Aragon and Valencia. 2. State, degree, sphere of life.

Estaméña, *sf.* Serge, a kind of woollen stuff.

Estameñéte, *sm.* Kind of serge.

Estámpa, *sf.* 1. Print, a figure or image printed. 2. The first sketch or design of a drawing or painting. 3. Press, or printing machine for printing books. 4. Track, an impression left by the foot. 5. Pattern, model.

Estampádo, *sm.* Impression, act and effect of stamping.

Estampádo, da, *a.* Stamped linen, cotton, &c.

Estampadór, *sm.* 1. One who makes or sells prints. 2. Printer.

Estampár, *va.* 1. To print, to mark by pressing any thing upon another. 2. To leave in the ground an impression of the foot. 3. (Met.) To fix in one's mind or memory.

Estampería, *sf.* Office for printing or selling prints.

Estampéro, *sm.* He who makes or sells stamps.

Estampída, *sf.* Report of a gun. *Dar estampida*, To publish, to propagate, to make a noise.

Estampído, *sm.* Report of a piece of ordnance.

Estampílla, *sf.* 1. A small print. 2. A small press. 3. Signet, a seal manual, used instead of a signature.

Estancár, *va.* 1. To stop, to check, to stem a current. 2. (Naút.) To fother a leak. 3. To interdict, to prohibit, to suspend.

Estáncia, *sf.* 1. Mansion, habitation; stay, sojourn. 2. A sitting-room, a bed-room. 3. (Poét.) Stanza, a division of a song or poem. 4. (America) Landed property. *Estáncias*, (Mil.) Camp, quarters.

Estanciéro, *sm.* Bailiff of a farm, overseer of a mansion or domain.

Estánco, *sm.* 1. Forestalling, monopoly. 2. Place where patent goods are sold exclusively by the patentee. 3. Stop, stay, detention. 4. Repository, archives. 5. Tank.

Estánco, ca, *a.* (Naút.) Water-fast, applied to a ship.

Estandárte, *sm.* 1. Banner, standard, colours. 2. *Estandarte real*, (Naút.) Royal standard, used only by the commanding admiral of a fleet.

Estangúrria, *sf.* 1. Strangury, a difficulty in evacuating urine, attended with pain. 2. Catheter, a hollow instrument, to assist in bringing away the urine when the passage is obstructed. 3. Spring, from which the water proceeds only in drops.

Estánque, *sm.* Pond, basin; dam of water.

Estanquéro, *sm.* 1. Keeper of reservoirs. 2. Retailer of privileged goods, such as tobacco and snuff in Spain.

Estanquilléro, *sm.* Wholesale tobacconist.

Estanquíllo, *sm.* (Madrid) Shop where tobacco and snuff are sold, by virtue of an exclusive privilege.

Estantál, *sm.* Buttress. V. *Estribo.*

Estánte, *sm.* 1. Shelf, a frame of boards without doors for receiving books. 2. (Murc.) He who carries in company with others, images in processions. *Estántes*, (Naút.) Props of the crossbeams.—*a.* 1. Being, existing in a place. 2. Fixed, permanent; applied to sheep which are not driven to the mountains in summer.

Estanteról, *sm.* Centre of a galley, where the captain stands in an engagement.

Estantígua, *sf.* 1. Phantom, vision, hobgoblin. 2. A deformed person dressed in a ridiculous garb.

Estantío, tia, *a.* 1. Standing still and immoveable on a spot. 2. (Met.) Dull, hebetated; without life or spirit.

Estañádo, *sm.* Vessel or bath with melted pewter, in which copper or iron plates are immersed to be tinned. [or iron tinned over.

Estañadór, *sm.* Tinman, a manufacturer of tin,

Estañadúra, *sf.* Act of tinning.

Estañár, *va.* To tin, to cover with tin.

Estañéro, *sm.* He who works and sells tin-ware.

Estáño, *sm.* 1. Tin, a primitive metal. 2. Iron plates covered with tin. 3. Pond, pool of stagnant water.

Estaquíno, *sm.* Buck or doe of a year old.

Estaquílla, *sf.* 1. (In Shoe-making) Peg, a wooden nail driven into the heel of a shoe. 2. (Carp.) Any wooden pin or nail which fastens one piece of timber to another. 3. Beam of a velvet-loom.

Estaquilladór, *sm.* An awl to bore for pegs.

Estaquillár, *va.* To peg, to fasten with pegs.

Estár, *vn.* 1. To be in a place. 2. To understand or comprehend. *Estoy en lo que vd. me dice*, I understand what you tell me. 3. To be security, to answer for. *Estoy por fulano*, I will answer for him. 4. To be of opinion. *Estoy en que*, I am of opinion that. 5. To be; an auxiliary verb, derived from the Latin *stare*, to stand, and used always with reference to existing or being in a place. *Estar escribiendo*, To be writing. 6. To undertake, to oblige or subject one's self to. *Donde estámos!* Expression of admiration or disgust at what we see or hear. *Estar á exámen*, To subject one's self to an examen. *Estar sobre sí*, To be tranquil or serene; to be greatly elated. 7. To cost. *Este vestido me está en veinte doblones*, These clothes cost me 20 doubloons. *Estar á erre*, To be doing any thing with the utmost care. 8. With the preposition *en*, it signifies cause, motive; *En eso está*, In this it consists, on this it depends. *Estar por ó para partir*, To be ready to set out. *Estar algo por suceder*, To expect something to happen.—Estárse, *vr.* To be detained.

Estarcído, *sm.* Outline of a drawing.

Estarcír, *va.* To chalk the outlines of a drawing.

Estárna, *sf.* (Orn.) Kind of small partridge.

Estatéra, *sf.* 1. Balance, steel-yard. 2. An ancient Grecian coin.

Estática, *sf.* Statics, the science which treats on the weight of bodies.

Estátua, *sf.* 1. Statue, a solid representation of living bodies. 2. A dull stupid fellow.

Estatuária, *sf.* Statuary, the art of carving images or representations of life.

Estatuário, *sm.* Statuary, one who professes the art of carving images.

Estatuír, *va.* To establish, to ordain, to enact.

Estatúra, *sf.* Stature, the height of a person from the feet to the head.

Estatutário, ria, *a.* Belonging to a statute or law.

Estatúto, *sm.* 1. Statute, law, ordinance. 2. Form of government established by laws and customs.

Estáy, *sm.* (Naút.) Stay, a strong rope which serves to support the masts and topmasts on the fore part.

E'ste, *sm.* East, one of the four cardinal winds or points of the compass.

E'ste, E'sta, E'sto, *pron. dem.* This.

En Estas y en Estótras, *ad.* In the mean while. *En esto*, At this time. *Para éstas, ó por estas*, Expression of anger and menace used by fathers to their children.

Estéba, *sf.* (Bot.) Snake-weed, red-shanks. Polygonum persicaria *L.*

Estebár, *va.* With dyers, to put the cloth into the caldron to dye it.

Estéla, *sf.* (Naút.) Wake, the track of a ship on the surface of the water.

Estelária, *sf.* (Poét. y Bot.) V. *Alquimila.*

Estellífero, ra, *a.* (Poét.) Starry, containing stars.
Estelión, *sm.* 1. Stellion, a small spotted lizard. Lacerta stellio *L.* 2. Toad-stone.
Estelionáto, *sm.* Stellionate, a crime consisting in defrauding, wilfully and maliciously, unwary persons.
Estelón, *sm.* Toad-stone.
Estemenáras, *sf. pl.* (Naút.) Futtock-timbers. V. *Ligazones.*
Estépa, *sf.* (Bot.) Rock-rose. Cistus laurifolius *L.*
Estepár, *sm.* Place filled with rock-roses.
Estepenóles, *sm. pl.* (Naút.) Scupper-nails, short and small headed nails used to fasten leather or canvass to wood.
Estéra, *sf.* Mat; a texture of sedge, flags, or rushes.
Esterár, *va.* To cover with mats.—*vn.* (Met.) To keep one's self warm with clothes.
Estercár, *va.* To dung. V. *Estercolar.*
Estercoladúra y Estercolamiénto, *s.* 1. The act of ejecting excrements; applied to beasts. 2. The act of dunging, or fattening land with dung.
Estercolár, *va.* To dung, to fatten with dung. —*vn.* To void the excrements; applied to animals.
Estercoléro, *sm.* 1. Boy or servant who drives the muck cart, or carries dung into the fields. 2. Dunghill, the place where dung is heaped up and preserved.
Estercolízo, za, *a.* Stercoraceous.
Estercúlio, *sm.* Stercoration.
Estereografía, *sf.* Stereography, art of drawing forms of solids upon a plane.
Estereográfico, ca, *a.* Stereographic, delineated on a plane.
Estereometría, *sf.* Stereometry, art of measuring solids.
Estereotípia, *sf.* The art of printing in stereotype, or with fixed plates.
Estereotípico, ca, *a.* Belonging to stereotype.
Estereotipár, *va.* To stereotype or print with solid plates.
Esteréro, *sm.* Mat-maker, one who makes or sells mats.
Estéril, *a.* Barren, unfruitful.
Esterilidád, *sf.* 1. Sterility, barrenness. 2. A narrow lace made of thread or silver.
Esterilizár, *va.* To sterilize, to make sterile.
Esterílla, *sf.* 1. Small mat. 2. Ferret lace, made of gold, silver, or thread.
Esterlín, *sm.* V. *Bocací.*
Esterlíno, na, *a.* Sterling, an epithet by which genuine, lawful English money is designated.
Esternón, *sm.* Breast-bone, which forms the fore part of the breast.
Estéro, *sm.* 1. A large lake. V. *Albufera.* 2. Matting, the act of covering with mats. 3. (Naút.) A small creek, into which the tide flows at flood tides.
Esterquéro, *sm.* V. *Estercolero.*
Esterquilínio, *sm.* Dunghill, a heap of dung.
Estertór, *sm.* Rattle in the throat of agonized persons.
Estéva, *sf.* 1. Plough-handle, with which the ploughman guides the plough. 2. (Naút.) Stowage. 3. Carved bar of wood on the bottom of coaches, which is connected with the shafts.
Estevádo, da, *a.* Bow-legged, one who has bent or crooked legs.
Estevón, *sm.* V. *Esteva.*
Estezádo, *sm.* V. *Correa.*
Estiár, *vn.* To stop. V. *Pararse.*
Estíbia, *sf.* Luxation. V. *Espibio.*
Estíbio, *sm.* Antimony.
Estiércol, *sm.* 1. Dung, the excrement of animals. 2. Filth, uncleanliness. 3. Any thing unclean or rotten.
Estígio, gia, *a.* Stygian, belonging to the fabulous river Styx.
Estilár, *vn.* 1. To use, to be accustomed. 2. To draw up in writing according to the usual style or practice. 3. (Vulg.) To distil. V. *Destilar.*
Estilicídio, *sm.* 1. Stillicide, a succession of drops. 2. Gutter, a passage for water.
Estílo, *sm.* 1. Style, a pointed iron formerly used to write on tables of wax. 2. Gnomon or style of a dial. 3. Style, the manner of talking or writing. 4. Form or manner of proceeding in suits at law. 5. Use, custom. *Estilo castizo,* A correct style.
Estíma, *sf.* 1. Esteem, respect. 2. (Naút.) Dead reckoning, the estimation of a ship's way by the log, with allowance made for drift and lee-way. *Propasar la estima,* (Naút.) To outrun the reckoning.
Estimabilidád, *sf.* Estimableness.
Estimáble, *a.* Estimable, valuable; worthy of honour and esteem.
Estimación, *sf.* 1. Estimation, esteem; valuation. *Estimacion propria,* Self-love. 2. Instinct, natural desire or aversion.
Estimadór, *sm.* Esteemer.
Estimár, *va.* 1. To estimate, to value; to set a value on a thing. 2. To esteem, to respect. 3. To judge, to form an opinion. 4. To thank, to acknowledge.
Estimatíva, *sf.* 1. Power of judging and forming an opinion. 2. Instinct, natural propensity or aversion.
Estimulación, *sf.* (Ant.) Stimulation.
Estimulánte, *pa.* Stimulating, exciting; stimulator.
Estimulár, *va.* 1. To sting, to stimulate. 2. To incite, to encourage.
Estímulo, *sm.* Sting, stimulus; incitement.
Estínco, *sm.* Scink, a kind of lizard. Lacerta scincus *L.*
Estío, *sm.* The hottest season of the year.
Estiomenádo, da, *a.* Mortified, corrupted.
Estiomenár, *va.* To corrode, to mortify.
Estioméno, *sm.* Mortification, gangrene.
Estipendiár, *va.* To give stipend.
Estipendiário, *sm.* Stipendiary, one who performs any service for a settled payment.
Estipéndio, *sm.* Stipend, salary, pay, wages.
Estípite y Estípe, *sm.* (Arq.) Pilaster in form of a reversed pyramid.
Estipticár, *va.* To use or apply a styptic.
Estipticidád, *sf.* 1. Stypticity, the power of stanching blood. 2. Costiveness.
Estíptico, ca, *a.* 1. Styptic, astringent; having the power of binding. 2. Costive, bound in the body. 3. (Met.) Miserly, avaricious. 4. (Met.) Difficult to be obtained.

Estiptiquéz, *sf.* Costiveness, the state of the body in which excretion is obstructed.
Estipulación, *sf.* Stipulation, promise.
Estipulánte, *pa.* Stipulator; stipulating.
Estipulár, *va.* To stipulate, to contract.
Estíra, *sf.* Kind of knife used by tanners, to render the skin more soft and pliable.
Estiradaménte, *ad.* 1. Scarcely, difficultly. 2. Violently, forcibly.
Estirádo, da, *a.* 1. Extended, dilated; excellent. 2. (Met.) Grave, stiff, lofty; full of affected dignity and starchness.
Estirajár y Estirazár, *va.* (Bax.) V. *Estirar.*
Estirajón y Estirijón, *sm.* (Vulg.) V. *Estiron.*
Estirár, *va.* 1. To dilate, to stretch out. 2. To fit, to adjust. 3. To extend a discourse, to enlarge upon a subject. *Estirar la barra,* (Met.) To make every possible effort to attain any thing. *Estirar la pierna,* (Fam.) To die.—*vr.* 1. To be stretched out; applied to the body or a single member. 2. To hold up one's head with affected gravity.
Estirón, *sm.* Pull, the act of pulling; pluck. *Dar un estiron,* (Fam.) To grow rapidly.
Estírpe, *sf.* Race, origin, stock.
Estítico, ca, *a.* V. *Estíptico.*
Estitiquéz, *sf.* Costiveness. V. *Estiptiquez.*
Estíva, *sf.* 1. Rammer. V. *Atacador.* 2. Stowage, the disposition of the several goods and articles contained in a ship's hold. *Mudar la estiva,* To shift the cargo.
Estivación, *sf.* The barrelling of herrings or pilchards.
Estivadór, *sm.* Packer of wool at shearing.
Estivál, *a.* Estival, pertaining to the summer.
Estivár, *va.* 1. To stow, to lay up the cargo in the hold. 2. To compress wool, to straiten.
Estívo, va, *a.* V. *Estival.*
Estocáda, *sf.* Stab, a thrust given with a pointed weapon. *Estocada de vino,* Breath of a person intoxicated. *Estocada por cornada,* (Fam.) Injury which one receives in striking another. [tard.
Estocafrís, *sm.* Stock-fish dressed with mustard.
Estocár, *va.* V. *Estoquear.*
Estófa, *sf.* 1. Quilted stuff. 2. (Met.) Quality, condition.
Estofádo, da, *a.* Quilted.
Estofádo, *sm.* Stewed meat.
Estofadór, *sm.* Quilter.
Estofár, *va.* 1. To quilt, to stitch one cloth upon another with something soft between them. 2. To paint relievos on a gilt ground. 3. To stew meat with wine, spice, or vinegar.
Estóla, *sf.* Stole, a sacerdotal garment worn by priests who officiate in church service.
Estolidéz, *sf.* Stupidity, incapacity.
Estólido, da, *a.* Stupid, foolish.
Estolón, *sm.* A large stole.
Estomacál, *a.* Stomachic, belonging to the stomach.
Estomagár, *va.* 1. To disorder the stomach, to cause the stomach to be out of order. 2. (Met.) To enrage, to make angry.
Estomagázo, *sm.* Large stomach.
Estómago, *sm.* 1. Stomach, the ventricle in which food is digested. *Estómago aventurero,* Sponger, one who hangs for a maintenance on others. 2. Valour, resolution; patience. *Tener buen estómago,* To bear insults patiently. [applied to the stomach of children.
Estomaguéro, *sm.* Stomacher, a piece of baize
Estomaticál, *a.* Stomachic.
Estomaticón, *sm.* Stomach plaster.
Estónce ó Estónces, *ad.* V. *Entonces.*
Estópa, *sf.* 1. Tow, the coarsest filamentous substance of hemp and flax. 2. Coarse cloth made of tow. 3. (Naút.) Oakum, ropes untwisted and reduced to a filamentous substance.
Estopáda, *sf.* Quantity of tow for spinning.
Estopéño, ña, *a.* Belonging to tow.
Estoperól, *sm.* 1. (Naút.) Short round-headed tarpawling nails. 2. Match or wick made of tow. [pump round which tow is wound.
Estopéro, *sm.* That part of the piston of a
Estopílla, *sf.* 1. The finest filamentous substance of hemp or flax. 2. Long-lawn, a sort of cambric. [off a gun.
Estopín, *sm.* Quick-match, which serves to fire
Estopón, *sm.* Coarse tow.
Estopóso, sa, *a.* Belonging to tow.
Estóque, *sm.* 1. Tuck, a long narrow sword. 2. (Bot.) Corn flag. Gladiolus communis *L.*
Estoqueadór, *sm.* Thruster; applied to bull-fighters, who use a long narrow sword.
Estoqueár, *va.* To thrust with a tuck.
Estoquéo, *sm.* Act of thrusting or stabbing.
Estoráque, *sm.* 1. (Bot.) Storax. Styrax officinale *L.* 2. Gum of the storax-tree.
Estorbadór, ra, *s.* Hinderer, obstructer.
Estorbár, *va.* To hinder, to impede, to obstruct. [struction.
Estórbo, *sm.* Hinderance, impediment, ob-
Estorcér, *va.* (Ant.) To liberate, to evade.
Estorménte, to, *sm.* (Ant.) V. *Instrumento.*
Estorníja, *sf.* 1. An iron ring or hoop, which goes round the end and arms of an axle-tree, and secures the linch-pin holes. 2. (Ar.) Boys' play.
Estorníno, *sm.* (Orn.) Starling. Sturnus *L.*
Estornudár, *vn.* To sneeze, to emit wind audibly by the nose.
Estornúdo, *sm.* Sternutation, sneeze, an emission of wind audibly by the nose.
Estornutatório, *sm.* Sternutatory, medicine that provokes to sneeze.
Estótro, tra, A compound pronoun of *esto* and *otro,* This other.
Estovár, *va.* V. *Ahogar.*
Estoicismo, *sm.* Stoicism.
Estóyco, ca, *a.* Stoic, stoical.—*sm.* Stoic.
Estrábo ó Estrabón, *sm.* V. *Bizco.*
Estracílla, *sf.* Kind of fine blotting paper.
Estráda, *sf.* Causeway, paved road; turnpike road. *Estrada encubierta,* (Fort.) Covert-way.
Estradióta, *sf.* 1. Ancient mode of riding with long stirrups and stiff legs. 2. Kind of lance.
Estradióte, ta, *a.* Relating to riding with long stirrups. *Estradiote,* Soldier mounted with long stirrups.
Estrádo, *sm.* 1. Drawing-room, where company is received. 2. Carpets and other embellishments of a drawing-room. *Estrádos,* Halls where courts of justice hold their sittings. 3. Baker's table for holding the loaves to be put into the oven.

Estrafalariamente, *ad.* Carelessly, slovenly.
Estrafalário, ria, *a.* Slovenly, uncleanly dressed; indecently neglectful of dress; extravagant.
Estragadamente, *ad.* Depravedly.
Estragádo, da, *a.* Exhausted or emaciated by criminal excesses.
Estragadór, ra, *s.* Corrupter, destroyer.
Estragamiénto, *sm.* 1. Ravage, waste, ruin. 2. (Met.) Disorder, corruption of morals.
Estragár, *va.* 1. To destroy, to vitiate, to ruin, to waste. 2. To spoil, to disfigure. *Estragar la cortesía*, To make fulsome compliments.
Estrágo, *sm.* 1. Ravage, waste, ruin. 2. Wickedness, corruption of morals, depravity.
Estragón, *sm.* (Bot.) Mugwort. Artemisia vulgaris *L.*
Estrambosidád, *sf.* Distortion of the eyes.
Estrambóte, *sm.* Burthen or last verse of a song repeated. [irregular.
Estrambótico, ca, *a.* Strange, extravagant,
Estramónio, *sm.* (Bot.) Thorn-apple. Datura stramonium *L.* [tongue.
Estrangól, *sm.* Inflammation in a horse's
Estrangúl, *sm.* Mouth-piece of reed for a hautboy, or any other wind-instrument.
Estrapontína, *sf.* Kind of hammock.
Estratagéma, *sf.* 1. Stratagem, an artifice in war. 2. Trick, artful deception.
Estratificación, *sf.* Stratification, state of the strata of minerals in the earth, arrangement of layers. [strata.
Estratificár, *va.* To stratify, to dispose in
Estratióte, *sm.* (Bot.) Water soldier. Stratiotes *L.* [ship's head.
Estráve, *sm.* (Naút.) Kind of wheel at the
Estráza, *sf.* Rag, fragment of cloth. *Papel de estraza*, Brown paper.
Estrazár, *va.* To tear or break into pieces.
Estrechadúra, *sf.* Act of narrowing.
Estrechaménte, *ad.* 1. Narrowly, tightly, closely. 2. (Met.) Exactly, punctually. 3. (Met.) Strongly, forcibly. 4. (Met.) Strictly, rigorously. 5. (Met.) Scantily, penuriously.
Estrechamiénto, *sm.* Act of tightening, tightness.
Estrechár, *va.* 1. To tighten, to make narrow. 2. (Met.) To confine, to pin up. 3. (Met.) To constrain, to compel. 4. (Met.) To restrain, to obstruct.—*vr.* 1. To bind one's self strictly. 2. (Met.) To reduce one's expenses. 3. (Met.) To act in concert with another. 4. (Met.) To relate or communicate in confidence. 5. (Met.) To be dejected. 6. To be intimate with.
Estrechéz, *sf.* 1. Straitness, narrowness. 2. (Met.) Intimate union. 3. (Met.) Intimacy, friendship. 4. (Met.) Arduous or dangerous undertaking. 5. (Met.) Austerity, abstraction from worldly objects. 6. (Met.) Poverty.
Estrécho, *sm.* 1. Strait or frith, a narrow arm of the sea. 2. Pass, a narrow passage between two mountains. 3. (Met.) Peril, danger, risk.
Estrécho, cha, *a.* 1. Narrow, close. 2. Strait, tight. 3. (Met.) Intimate, familiar. 4. (Met.) Rigid, austere. 5. (Met.) Exact, punctual. 6. (Met.) Narrow-minded, illiberal, mean-spirited. 7. (Met.) Poor, indigent, penurious, needy, necessitous. *Al estrecho*, Necessarily, forcedly.
Estrechón, *sm.* Strait, pass, peril. V. *Estrechez.*
Estrechúra, *sf.* 1. Narrowness, straitness. 2. (Met.) Austerity, abstraction from the world. 3. (Met.) Distress, danger. 4. Intimate familiarity. [bing off dirt.
Estregadéra, *sf.* Brush, an instrument for rub-
Estregadéro, *sm.* 1. Place where beasts are accustomed to rub themselves against a tree, stone, &c. 2. Place for washing clothes.
Estregadúra, *sf.* Friction, act of rubbing.
Estregamiénto, *sm.* Frication, friction.
Estregár, *va.* 1. To rub one thing against another, to scour. 2. To scratch.
Estrélla, *sf.* 1. Star, one of the luminous bodies which appear in the sky. 2. (Met.) A white mark on a horse's face. 3. Asterisk, a mark in printing. 4. (Met.) Fate, lot, destiny. *Tener estrella*, To be fortunate. 5. (Fort.) Starfort, a work with five or more faces, having salient and re-entering angles. *Tomar la estrella*, (Naút.) To take the altitude of a star. *Estrellas errantes ó erráticas*, Planets, satellites. *Con estrellas*, After night or before sun-rise.
Estrelladéro, *sm.* Kind of frying-pan for dressing eggs, without breaking the yolks.
Estrelládo, da, *a.* Starry, full of stars. *Caballo estrellado*, Horse with a white mark on the face. *Huevos estrellados*, Eggs fried in oil or butter; poached eggs.
Estrellamár, *sm.* (Bot.) Buckthorn plantain. Plantago coronopus *L.*
Estrellár, *a.* Stellated, starry.
Estrellár, *va.* 1. To dash to pieces, to break by collision. 2. To confound, to make ashamed. *Estrellar huevos*, To fry eggs in a pan with oil or butter, without breaking the yolks. *Estrellarse con uno*, To fall out with one, to knock one's self against another.
Estrelléra, *sf.* (Naút.) Plain rigging without runners.
Estrelléro, *sm.* Star-gazer; one who wastes his time in looking up to the windows.
Estrellíca, ta, y Estrelluéla, *sf. dim.* Little star. [stars.
Estrellizár, *va.* To embellish or beautify with
Estrellón, *sm.* 1. Large star. 2. Star-ball, used in artificial fire-works. 3. (Met.) Uncommon good luck. *Estrellones*, Caltrops, crow-feet; irons with spikes, thrown into breaches and narrow passages to annoy the enemy's horse.
Estremecér, *va.* 1. To shake, to make tremble. 2. (Naút.) To work or labour hard; applied to a ship.—*vr.* To shake or shudder with fear.
Estremecimiénto, *sm.* Trembling, quaking.
Estremézo, *sm.* (Arag.) Trembling.
Estremíche, *sm.* (Naút.) A piece of timber which is notched into the knees of a ship.
Estréna ó Estrénas, *sf.* 1. A new year's gift. 2. Handsel, the first act of using any thing; the first act of sale. 3. Treat on wearing a new suit of clothes.
Estrenár, *va.* To commence, to begin; to regale.—*vr.* To begin to put any thing in execution.
Estréno, *sm.* Commencement, the first beginning of bringing any thing into execution.
Estrénque, *sm.* (Naút.) Rope made of bass or sedge, much used in America.

Estrenuidád, *sf.* (Ant.) Strength, valour, strenuousness.

Estreñído, da, *a.* 1. Close bound. 2. Miserable, niggardly.

Estreñimiénto, *sm.* Obstruction; the act of binding or restraining; costiveness.

Estreñír, *va.* To bind, to tie close, to restrain. —*vr.* To restrain one's self.

Estrépito, *sm.* Noise, clamour, bustle.

Estrepitóso, sa, *a.* Noisy, boisterous.

Estriár, *va.* To flute, to cut columns into channels and grooves.—*vr.* To be grooved.

Estrías, *sf. pl.* Flutings, channels cut along half the length of shafts or pilasters.

Estribadéro, *sm.* Prop, stay.

Estribadór, ra, *s.* (Ant.) That which supports itself on another.

Estribár, *vn.* 1. To prop, to support with props. 2. (Met.) To found, to build upon; to be supported.

Estribéra, *sf.* 1. Buttress, arch, pillar. 2. Joiner's bench.

Estribería, *sf.* Place where stirrups are kept.

Estriberón, *sm.* Prominences made on earth or wood by cross bars, to serve as steps.

Estribíllo, *sm.* 1. Introduction or beginning of a song. 2. Tautology, a needless and superfluous repetition of the same words.

Estríbo, *sm.* 1. Buttress, arch, pillar. 2. Stirrup, an iron hoop, suspended by a strap, in which the horseman sets his foot when he mounts or rides. 3. Step on the side of a coach. 4. Staple fixed at the end of a cross-bow. 5. Bone of the ear resembling a stirrup. 6. V. *Estribillo*. 7. (Art.) Clasp on the felloes of gun-carriage wheels. *Estribos*, (Naút.) Stirrups of a ship, pieces of timber fastened to the keel with iron plates. *Estribos de guardamancebos de las vergas*, Stirrups of the horses. *Estribos de los pelones de las vergas*, Stirrups of the yard arms. *Estribos de las cadenas*, Stirrups of the chain plates.

Estribórd, *sm.* (Naút.) Starboard, the right hand side of a ship or boat looking to the head.

Estribordários, *sm. pl.* People on the starboard hand.

Estrícia, *sf.* (Ant.) Extremity, straitness.

Estricóte (Al), *ad.* Without rule or order. *Tener á uno al estricote*, To amuse one with vain promises.

Estrictaménte, *ad.* Strictly.

Estridénte, *a.* (Poét.) That which causes noise, or cracking.

Estridór, *sm.* (Ant.) Noise, crack.

Estríge, *sf.* Night-bird, said to be of an unlucky omen; screech-owl, vampire.

Estrillár, *va.* (Ant.) To rub, scour, or wash [horses.

Estrínga, *sf.* V. *Agujeta*.

Estrínque, *sm.* (Naút.) V. *Estrenque*.

Estripár, *va.* (Ext.) V. *Destripar*.

Estrófa, *sf.* (Poét.) Strophe.

Estropajeár, *va.* To clean a wall with a dry brush or rubber.

Estropajéo, *sm.* Act of rubbing a wall.

Estropájo, *sm.* 1. Dishclout, with which dishes and plates are cleaned. 2. Brush, made of bass or sedge, to clean culinary vessels. 3. (Met.) A worthless trifling thing.

Estropajosaménte, *ad.* Stammeringly.

Estropajóso, sa, *a.* 1. Ragged, despicable, lo[w] mean. 2. (Met.) Troublesome, useless. 3 (Met.) Stuttering, stammering.

Estropalína, *sf.* Refuse of wool.

Estropeamiénto, *sm.* Act of maiming, wounding or taming.

Estropeár, *va.* To maim, to cripple, to muti-late. 2. To mix lime and sand.

Estropecíllo, *sm.* A slight stumble or impe[dimen]t

Estropéo, *sm.* Maim, hurt, injury.

Estropezadúra, *sf.* V. *Tropiezo*.

Estropiézo, *sm.* Stumble, hinderance, impedi[ment]

Estrovíto, *sm.* (Naút.) A small strap.

Estróvo, *sm.* (Naút.) Strap, a piece of rop[e] spliced in a circular manner, and used fo[r] strapping blocks.

Estructúra, *sf.* 1. Structure, manner of build-ing or constructing an edifice. 2. Order method.

Estruéndo, *sm.* 1. Clamour, noise, outcry. 2 Confusion, bustle. 3. Pomp, ostentation show. 4. Fame, renown, celebrity.

Estruendosaménte, *ad.* Clamorously.

Estruendóso, sa, *a.* 1. Noisy, clamorous. 2 Pompous, full of ostentation.

Estruír, *va.* V. *Destruir*.

Estruménto, *sm.* V. *Instrumento*.

Estrupadór, *sm.* V. *Estuprador*.

Estrupár, *va.* V. *Estuprar*.

Estrúpo ó Estúpro, *sm.* V. *Estupro*.

Estruxadúra, *sf.* Pressing, squeezing.

Estruxamiénto, *sm.* Compressing, pressure.

Estruxár, *va.* To press, to squeeze. *Estruxa[r] el dinero*, To be avaricious or extremely co-vetous.—*vr.* To be hard pressed.

Estruxón, *sm.* The last pressing of grape[s] which gives a poor miserable wine; compre[s-sion]

Estuación, *sf.* Flow of the tide.

Estuánte, *a.* Very hot, boiling, scorching.

Estuário, *sm.* A low ground, overflowed b[y] the sea at high tides; an estuary.

Estucadór, *sm.* A stucco-plasterer.

Estucár, *va.* To stucco or white-wash an[y] [thing]

Estúche, *sm.* 1. Case for scissors or other in-struments. 2. Scissors or instruments con-tained in a case. 3. (Fam.) The two rows o[f] teeth shown when a person laughs. 4. Sma[ll] comb. 5. (Met.) One who knows a little o[f] every thing, or is capable of any thing. *E[s] un estuche*, (Met.) He is a very clever ma[n] *Estuche del rey*, Surgeon to the king.

Estúco, *sm.* Stucco, a kind of fine plaste[r] made of lime, sand, gypsum, and pounde[d] marble.

Estudiadór, *sm.* Student, one who applie[s] himself to the study of the sciences.

Estudiantázo, *sm.* He who is reputed a grea[t] scholar.

Estudiánte, *sm.* 1. Student, a man given t[o] the study of books. 2. Prompter to player[s]

Estudiantíl, *a.* (Joc.) Scholastic, belongin[g] to a student.

Estudiantíno, na, *a.* Belonging to a studen[t] *A' la estudiantina*, In the manner of student[s]

Estudiantón, *sm.* An old big student.

Estudiár, *va.* 1. To study, to employ the under-standing in the acquisition of knowledge. [2] To muse, to ponder; to commit to memor[y] 3. To draw or make a drawing after a mod[el] or mature. 4. To attend the classes in a university.

Estúdio, *sm.* 1. Study, application. 2. Room where languages or sciences are taught. 3. Study, apartment appropriated to literary employment; a lawyer's study. 4. Hall where models, prints, and plans are kept, to be copied or studied. *Hacer estudio de alguna cosa,* (Met.) To act with art, cunning, or crafty reflection. *Juez de estudio,* Chancellor of a university.—*pl.* 1. Time, trouble, and care applied to the study of the sciences. 2. Sciences, letters. *Studios Mayores,* The higher sciences. *Dar estudios á uno,* To maintain one at his studies.

Estudiosaménte, *ad.* Studiously, with care and reflection. [study.

Estudiosidád, *sf.* Studiousness, addiction to

Estudióso, sa, *a.* 1. Studious, given to study and reflection. 2. (Met.) Studious, careful, solicitous.

Estúfa, *sf.* 1. A stove; a warm close room. 2. Bath or bathing-room. 3. Sulphuring for bleaching wool and cotton. 4. Brasier for coals. 5. (Naút.) Stove or room where pitch and tar are heated for use. 6. V. *Carroza.*

Estufadór, *sm.* (Cocin.) Vessel in which meat is stewed. [tofar.

Estufár, *va.* 1. To warm any thing. 2. V. *Es-*

Estuféro, *sm.* He who makes stoves.

Estufílla, *sf.* 1. Muff, a cover made of fur, to keep the hands warm. 2. A small brasier, used by women to warm the feet on.

Estultaménte, *ad.* Foolishly, sillily.

Estultícia, *sf.* Folly, silliness.

Estúlto, ta, *a.* Foolish, silly.

Estuosidád, *sf.* Burning, excessive hotness.

Estuóso, sa, *a.* Very hot, ardent, burnt with the heat of the sun.

Estupefacción, *sf.* Stupefaction, numbness.

Estupefactívo, va, *a.* Stupifying. [dously.

Estupendaménte, *ad.* Wonderfully, stupen-

Estupéndo, da, *a.* Stupendous, wonderful.

Estupidaménte, *ad.* Stupidly.

Estupidéz, *sf.* Stupidity, insensibility.

Estúpido, da, *a.* Stupid, insensible.

Estupór, *sm.* 1. Stupor, suspension of sensibility. 2. Amazement, admiration, astonishment.

Estupradór, *sm.* Ravisher, he that embraces a woman by violation.

Estuprár, *va.* 1. To ravish, to commit a rape. 2. (Met.) To violate, to oppress.

Estúpro, *sm.* Ravishment, rape, constupration.

Estúque, *sm.* V. *Estuco.*

Estuquísta, *sm.* Plasterer.

Esturár, *va.* 1. To dry by the force of fire. 2. To overdo meat by the force of fire.

Esturgár, *va.* To polish delft ware.

Esturión, *sm.* (Ict.) Sturgeon. Acipenser *L.*

E'sula, *sf.* (Bot.) Spurge. Euphorbia esula *L.*

Et, *conj.* (Ant.) V. *y* or *é.* [troops in the field.

Etápa, *sf.* (Mil.) The ration of necessaries to

Et cétera, *ad.* And so on.

E'tela, le, lo, *conj.* See, behold.

E'ter, *sm.* 1. Ether or æther, an element more fine and subtile than air. 2. The matter of the highest regions above. 3. (Quim.) Ether.

Etéreo, rea, *a.* Ethereal.

Eternál, *a.* Eternal.

Eternalménte, *ad.* Eternally.

Eternaménte, *ad.* 1. Eternally, for ever. 2. (Met.) For a long time. 3. Never.

Eternidád, *sf.* 1. Eternity, duration without beginning or end. 2. Duration or length of continuance, which comprehends many ages.

Eternizár, *va.* 1. To eternize, to perpetuate. 2. To prolong for a great length of time.

Etérno, na, *a.* 1. Eternal, endless, without beginning or end. 2. Durable, lasting.

Eterománcia, *sf.* Divination by the flight or song of birds.

Etésio, *a.* Applied to wind which begins to blow in April, and continues to September on the eastern coast of Spain.

E'tica, *sf.* 1. Ethics, morals; the doctrine of morality. 2. Hectic fever, consumption.

E'tico, ca, *a.* 1. Hectic, labouring under a consumption. 2. Ethical.

Etimología y E'timo, *s.* Etymology, origin, source, and derivation of words.

Etimológico, ca, *a.* Etymological.

Etimologísta, *sm.* Etymologist.

Etimologizár, *va.* To etymologize.

Etiópico, ca, *a.* Ethiopian.

Etiópide, *sf.* (Bot.) Clary, Ethiopian mullein. Salvia sclarea *L.*

Etiquéta, *sf.* Etiquette, ceremonious customs.

Etiquetéro, ra, *a.* y *s.* Relating to etiquette, ceremonious; an observer of etiquette.

Etítes, *sf.* Eagle-stone.

E'tnico, ca, *a.* Ethnic. V. *Gentil.*

Eubólia, *sf.* The act of expressing one's thoughts with propriety.

Eucaristía, *sf.* Eucharist.

Eucarístico, ca, *a.* Eucharistical; belonging to works in prose or verse on the subject of grace.

Eucológio y Eucólogo, *sm.* Euchology, book containing the service for all the sundays and festivals in the year.

Eucrático, ca, *a.* Euchratical.

Eufonía, *sf.* Euphony.

Eufórbio, *sm.* (Bot.) Officinal spurge. Euphorbia officinarum *L.* [officinalis *L.*

Eufrásia, *sf.* (Bot.) Eye-bright. Euphrasia

Eunúco, *sm.* Eunuch, one that is castrated.

Eupatório, *sm.* (Bot.) V. *Agrimonia. Eupatorio vulgar,* Hemp agrimony. Eupatorium cannabinum *L.*

Eurípo, *sm.* Strait of the sea.

Eurítmia, *sf.* (Arq.) Proportion and harmony in an edifice.

E'uro, *sm.* Eurus, the east wind; one of the four cardinal winds. *Euro austro, ó Euro noto,* South-east wind. *Euro zefirio,* Motion of the sea from east to west.

Européo, a, *a.* European. [Eutyches

Eutiquiáno, na, *a.* Belonging to the sect of

Eutrapélia y Eutropélia, *sf.* 1. Moderation in jests, jokes, and pleasures. 2. Pastime, sport.

Eutropélico, ca, *a.* Moderate, temperate.

Evacuación, *sf.* Evacuation, the act of emptying any vessel or other thing.

Evacuár, *va.* 1. To evacuate, to empty. 2. To weaken, to enervate, to debilitate. 3. To finish or complete a business. [of evacuating.

Evacuatívo, va, *a.* That which has the power

Evacuatório, ria, a. That which evacuates.

Evad, evas, evat, v. def. (Ant.) Look here, see; know, understand.

Evadír, va. To evade, to escape, to fly, or properly to flee from danger.

Evagación, sf. Evagation, the act of wandering; excursion.

Evanescér, vn. To vanish, to disappear.

Evangelicaménte, ad. Evangelically.

Evangélico, ca, a. Evangelical.

Evangélio, sm. Gospel. *Evangelios*, Small book, containing the first chapters of St. John and the other evangelists, placed between relics, and worn at children's necks.

Evangelísta, sm. 1. Evangelist. 2. One who chants the Gospels in churches.

Evangelistério, sm. 1. Priest or deacon who chants the books of the evangelists at solemn masses. 2. Gospel book-stand, on which the Gospel book is laid to sing the Gospel at high mass.

Evangelizár, va. To evangelise, to preach the Gospel.

Evaporáble, a. That may be evaporated.

Evaporación, sf. 1. Evaporation, exhalation of vapour. 2. Act of damping cloth, or placing it over steam, to render the wool softer.

Evaporár, vn. To evaporate, to fly away in vapours or fumes.—va. To evaporate, to drive away in fumes.—vr. To vanish, to pass away.

Evaporatório, a. Having the power of evaporating.

Evaporizár, vn. a. y r. To evaporate.

Evasión, sf. Evasion, escape, subterfuge.

Eváta, sf. Kind of black wood resembling ebony.

Evenír, v. impers. V. *Acontecer*.

Evénto, sm. Event, accident.

Eventuál, a. Eventual, fortuitous.

Eversión, sf. Destruction, ruin, desolation.

Evicción, sf. Eviction, security.

Evidéncia, sf. Evidence, manifestation, proof.

Evidenciár, va. To prove, to render evident.

Evidénte, a. Evident, clear, manifest.

Evidenteménte, ad. Evidently.

Eviláša, sf. Kind of ebony which grows in the island of Madagascar.

Evitáble, a. Avoidable, that may be avoided.

Evitación, sf. Evitation, act of avoiding.

Evitádo, da, a. V. *Excomulgado*.

Evitár, va. To avoid, to escape.—vr. To free one's self from vassalage.

Evitérno, na, a. Durable, lasting, without end.

E'vo, sm. 1. (Poét.) Age, a long period of time. 2. (Teol.) Eternity, endless duration.

Evocación, sf. Evocation, pagan invocation.

Evocár, va. 1. To call out. 2. To invoke, to solicit a favour, to implore assistance.

Evolución, sf. (Mil.) Evolution, the act of changing the position of troops. *Evoluciones navales*, Naval evolutions.

Ex, prep. Lat. Used in the Spanish only in composition, where it either amplifies the signification, as *exponer*; or serves as a negative, as *exánime*. *Ex-provincial*, Former or late provincial.

Ex, sm. (Poét.) V. *Exe*.

Ex abrúpto, ad. Abruptly, violently.

Exâcción, sf. 1. Exaction, the act of levying taxes. 2. Impost, tax, contribution. 3. Exactness, punctuality.

Exâcerbár, va. To irritate, to exasperate.

Exâctaménte, ad. Exactly.

Exâctitúd, sf. Exactness, punctuality.

Exâcto, ta, a. Exact, punctual, assiduous.

Exâctór, sm. Tax-gatherer, collector of taxes.

Exâgeración, sf. Exaggeration, hyperbolical amplification.

Exâgeradór, ra, s. Exaggerator.

Exâgeránte, pa. (Poét.) Amplifier; exaggerating.

Exâgerár, va. To exaggerate, to heighten by misrepresentation.

Exâgerativaménte, ad. With exaggeration.

Exâgeratívo, va, a. Exaggerating.

Exâgóno, na, a. Hexagonal.

Exâltación, sf. Exaltation, elevation.

Exâltár, va. 1. To exalt, to elevate. 2. To praise, to extol; to cry up.—vr. To irritate one's self.

Exâmen, sm. 1. Examen, examination, disquisition; trial, inquiry. 2. Care and diligence exerted in searching out any thing.

Exâmetro, sm. Hexameter verse.

Exâminación, sf. Examination.

Exâminadór, sm. Examiner.

Exâminándo, sm. He who has to be examined.

Exâminante, sm. He who examines, or is to be examined.

Exâminár, va. 1. To examine, to investigate. 2. To inquire into books or writings.

Exângüe, a. 1. Bloodless, without blood; pale from the loss of blood. 2. (Met.) Weak, without strength.

Exângulo, la, a. Having six angles.

Exânimación, sf. Exanimation.

Exâ'nime, a. Spiritless, without force or vigour.

Exârcádo, sm. Exarchate or vice-royalty.

Exâ'rco, sm. Exarch, viceroy.

Exâsperación, sf. Exasperation.

Exâsperár, va. To exasperate, to irritate, to offend.

Exâudíble, a. Grateful, acceptable, of a nature to be favourably heard.

Exâudír, va. To hear favourably.

Excáva y Excavación, sf. Excavation, the act of digging a cavity in the ground for a foundation, &c.

Excavár, va. To excavate, to dig out, to cut into hollows.

Excavíllo, sm. (Mancha.) A little spade used in making excavations.

Excedénte, a. Excessive.

Excedér, va. To exceed, to surpass, to excel. *Excederse á si mismo*, To praise or extol one's own merits.

Exceléncia, sf. 1. Excellence, eminence; superior worth or merit. *Por excelencia*, Excellently. 2. Excellency, a title of honour which is applied in Spain to the grandees, peers, and to persons either for their rank or office.

Exceléntе, a. Excellent. *Excelente de la granada*, Ancient gold coin worth 11 reals and a maravedi, or 375 maravedis.

Excelenteménte, ad. Excellently.

Excelentísimo, ma, a. superl. Most excellent; applied in courtesy to persons receiving the title of excellency.

Excelsaménte, ad. Sublimely.

Excelsitúd, sf. Excelsitude, loftiness.

Excélso, sa, a. Elevated, sublime, lofty.

Excentricaménte, ad. Eccentrically.

Excentricidád, sf. Deviation from the centre, excursion from the proper orb.

Excéntrico, ca, a. Eccentric.

Excepción, *sf.* 1. Exception, exclusion of any thing from a general position or law. 2. Plea.

Excepcionár, *va.* To except, to object.

Exceptación y Exceptuación, *sf.* V. *Excepcion.*

Exceptár, *va.* V. *Exceptuar.*

Exceptívo, va, *a.* (Lóg.) Exceptive.

Excépto, *ad.* Except that, besides that. [clude.

Exceptuár, *va.* To except, to exempt, to ex-

Excesivaménte, *ad.* Excessively.

Excesívo, va, *a.* Excessive, immoderate.

Excéso, *sm.* 1. Excess, more than enough; superfluity. 2. Intemperance, unreasonable indulgence. 3. Great wickedness, enormity of crime. 4. Violence of passion. 5. Transport, rapture. *En exceso,* Excessively.

Excídio, *sm.* Destruction, ruin. [dities.

Excísa, *sf.* Excise, a tax levied upon commo-

Excitár, *va.* To excite, to move, to stimulate.

Excitatívo, va, *a.* Exciting, stimulative.

Exclamación, *sf.* 1. Exclamation, vehement outcry, clamour. *Exclamaciones de regocijo,* Shouts of joy. 2. An emphatical utterance.

Exclamár, *vn.* To exclaim, to cry out.

Exclamatívo, va, *a.* Exclaiming.

Exclamatório, ria, *a.* Exclamatory.

Excluír, *va.* To exclude, to shut out, to debar.

Exclusión, *sf.* 1. The act of shutting out or denying admission. 2. Exception.

Exclusíva, *sf.* Refusal of place or employment; rejection of an application to become member of a community.

Exclusivaménte y Exclusíve, *ad.* Exclusively.

Exclusívo, va, *a.* Exclusive.

Excogitáble, *a.* Imaginable, possible to be conceived. [strike out by thinking.

Excogitár, *va.* To excogitate, to meditate; to

Excomulgación y Excomunicación. V. *Excomunion.*

Excomulgádo, da, *a.* Excommunicated. *Excomulgado vitando,* An excommunicated person with whom no intercourse can be held.

Excomulgadór, *sm.* Excommunicator.

Excomulgár, *va.* 1. To excommunicate, to eject from the communion of the church, and from the use of the sacraments. 2. (Met.) To treat with foul language, to use ill.

Excomunión, *sf.* Excommunication, exclusion from the fellowship of the church.

Excoriación, *sf.* Excoriation, privation of skin, the act of flaying.

Excrecéncia y Excrescéncia, *sf.* Excrescence or excrescency; something growing out of another without use, or contrary to the common order of production.

Excreción, *sf.* Excretion.

Excrementál, *a.* Excremental.

Excrementício, cia, *a.* Excrementitious.

Excrementár, *va.* To purge, to void by stool.

Excreménto, *sm.* 1. Excrement, that which is thrown out as useless from the natural passages of the body. 2. Particles separated from plants by putrefaction.

Excrementóso, sa, *a.* Excremental, that which is voided as excrement.

Excretár, *vn.* To eject the excrements.

Excréto, ta, *a.* That which is ejected.

Excretório, ria, *a.* Excretory, having the quality of separating and ejecting superfluous parts.

Excréx, *sm.* (For. Ar.) Increase of portion. In the plural it is written *excreex.*

Excursión, *sf.* 1. Excursion; expedition into some part of the enemy's country. 2. (For.) Liquidation of the estate of a debtor for paying off his debts. [from the main tenor.

Excúrso, *sm.* Digression, a passage deviating

Excúsa y Excusación, *sf.* Excuse, plea offered in extenuation. *Excusas,* Exemptions, immunities or emoluments granted to certain persons. *Á' excusa ó excusas,* Dissemblingly.

Excusabaraja, *sf.* Basket or pannier with a cover or lid of osiers.

Excusáble, *a.* Excusable, pardonable.

Excusadaménte, *ad.* Uselessly, voluntarily, without necessity; not to the purpose.

Excusádo, da, *a.* 1. Superfluous, useless. 2. Preserved, laid up as useless. 3. Exempted, privileged.

Excusádo, *sm.* A subsidy levied on the clergy of Spain by the Spanish monarch, to assist him in carrying on the war against infidels; commonly called *Casa excusada.*

Excusadór, ra, *s.* 1. One who performs another's functions in his stead. 2. Vicar or curate, the substitute of the rector of a parish church. 3. (For.) One who excuses the nonappearance of a defendant in court.

Excusalí, *sm.* Small apron.

Excusáña, *sf.* (Ant.) Peasant who watches the enemy in a pass. *Á' excusañas,* Hiddenly, secretly.

Excusár, *va.* 1. To excuse, to extenuate by apology. 2. To exempt from taxes. 3. To obstruct, to hinder, to prevent. 4. To shun, to avoid.—*vr.* To decline or reject a request.

Excusión, *sf.* (For.) Liquidation of debts.

Ex Diámetro, *ad. Lat.* Diametrically.

E'xe, *sm.* 1. Axis, one of the most principal parts of machinery. 2. Axle-tree, a piece of wood fixed under a cart or coach. 3. Centre. 4. A word used to frighten dogs.

Execráble, *a.* Execrable, detestable, hateful.

Execración, *sf.* Execration, detestation.

Execradór, *sm.* Execrater.

Execraménto, *sm.* (Ant.) 1. Execration. 2. Superstitious imitation of the sacrament.

Execrándo, da, *a.* Execrable.

Execrár, *va.* To execrate, to detest, to curse.

Execución, *sf.* 1. Execution, the act of carrying into effect. 2. Execution, the last act of the law, in civil cases, by which possession is given of body or goods.

Executáble, *a.* Performable, that may be performed or carried into effect.

Executadéro, ra, *a.* That may be required. [ly.

Executánte, *ps.* Executer of any thing judicial-

Executár, *va.* 1. To execute, to carry into effect, to perform. 2. (Met.) To impel, to urge, to importune, to incite. 3. To oblige one to pay what he owes to others. 4. To put to death according to the form of justice. 5. To attack with foul language or other ill usage.

Executivaménte, *ad.* 1. Promptly, swiftly. 2. In an executive manner.

Executívo, va, *a.* Executive, active; having the power of executing or performing.

Executór, ra, *s.* 1. Executor or executrix. 2. Officer of justice who serves executions.

Executória, *sf.* 1. Warrant of attorney, decree of execution. 2. Decree or letters patent of nobility. 3. Executorship.
Executoriál, *a.* Applied to the execution of the sentence of an ecclesiastical tribunal.
Executoriár, *va.* 1. To obtain a verdict or judgment in one's favour. 2. To establish or render evident the truth or certainty of a thing.
Executório, ria, *a.* Belonging or relating to the apprehension of a debtor.
Exegético, ca, *a.* Exegetical, explanatory.
Exemplár, *sm.* 1. Exemplar, a pattern to be imitated. 2. Comparison, example. 3. Copy of a work.
Exemplár, *a.* Exemplary, such as may deserve to be proposed to imitation. *Sin exemplar*, Not to be a precedent; used in conceding special grants. [strument.
Exemplár, *va.* To transcribe, to copy any in-
Exemplarménte, *ad.* 1. Exemplarily, so as deserves imitation. 2. Exemplarily, so as may warn others.
Exemplificación, *sf.* Declaration by examples.
Exemplificár, *va.* To exemplify.
Exémplo, *sm.* 1. Example, precedent, instance; comparison. 2. Pattern, copy; exemplar, that which is proposed to be resembled. *Por exemplo*, For instance.
Exêncion, *sf.* Exemption, immunity, privilege.
Exêntaménte, *ad.* Freely, clearly; simply, sincerely.
Exêntár, *va.* To exempt, to grant immunity, to excuse, to disengage from any obligation. —*vr.* To except one's self.
Exênto, ta, *a.* 1. Exempt, freed, disengaged. 2. Clear, open, free from impediment.
Exênto, *sm.* Officer in the Spanish life-guards, who holds the rank and brevet of a colonel in the army.
Exêquiál, *a.* Exequial, relating to funerals.
Exêquias, *sf. pl.* Exequies, funeral rites. [ed.
Exêquíble, *a.* Attainable, that may be attain-
Exercér, *va.* To exercise, to practise.
Exercício, *sm.* 1. Exercise, the act of practising or using in order to attain habitual skill. 2. Employment, office, task. 3. Military evolutions. *Hacer exercicio*, To exercise troops, to train to military operations; to use exercise, to take a walk, to labour for health.
Exercitación, *sf.* Exercitation, practice.
Exercitadór, ra, *s.* Exerciser, practiser.
Exercitánte, *sm.* Exerciser, he who performs spiritual exercises.
Exercitár, *va.* 1. To exercise, to put into practice. 2. To exercise troops, to learn by practice. *Exercitar á alguno*, To molest, to incommode.—*vr.* To apply one's self to the functions of an office or place. [ercised.
Exercitatívo, va, *a.* That which may be ex-
Exército, *sm.* Army, a body of armed men.
Exérgo, *sm.* Exergue, for the inscription in medals.
Exfoliácion, *sf.* Exfoliation, the process of separating lamina or pieces from a carious bone.
Exfoliár, *va.* To exfoliate, to shell off part of a bone.—*vr.* To become exfoliated. [foliation.
Exfoliatívo, va, *a.* Exfoliative, producing ex-
Exguardiáno, na, *s.* Ex-guardian.
Exhalación, *sf.* 1. Exhalation, the act of exhaling or sending out in vapours. 2. (Met.) Great celerity or velocity.
Exhaladór, ra, *s.* Exhaler, one who exhales.
Exhalár, *va.* To exhale, to send or draw out vapours or fumes.—*vr.* 1. To exhale, to evaporate. 2. To be consumed or wasted gradually. 3. To be exhausted by violent exercise of the body. *Exhalarse por alguna cosa*, To covet or desire any thing with anxious eagerness. [or drawn out.
Exhaústo, ta, *a.* Exhausted, totally drained
Exheredación, *sf.* Disinherison, privation of an inheritance.
Exheredár, *va.* To disinherit. [ing.
Exhibición, *sf.* Exhibition, the act of exhibit-
Exhibír, *va.* To exhibit, to prevent, to make manifest.
Exhíbita, *sf.* (For. Arag.) Exhibition.
Exhortación, *sf.* Exhortation, admonition.
Exhortadór, ra, *s.* Exhorter, monitor.
Exhortár, *va.* To exhort, to excite by words to any good action.
Exhortatório, ria, *a.* Exhortatory.
Exhórto, *sm.* Letters requisitorial sent by one judge to another.
Exhumación, *sf.* Exhumation.
Exhumár, *va.* To disinter, to unbury; to take out of the grave.
Exiciál, *a.* Mortal, fatal. [peculiar to dogs.
Exîda, *sf.* (Ant.) V. *Salida*. *Exîdas*, A disease
Exîdo, *sm.* A small level spot, adjacent to a barn or other place commonly intended for threshing corn.
Exigéncia, *sf.* Exigence, want, pressing necessity, exaction. [quired.
Exigíble, *a.* Capable of being demanded or re-
Exigidéro, ra, *a.* That which may be demanded or exacted.
Exigír, *va.* 1. To exact, to demand, to recover 2. To wish for, to desire.
Exigüidád, *sf.* Exiguity, smallness.
Exí'guo, gua, *a.* Exiguous, small.
Eximición, *sf.* Exemption.
Exí'mio, mia, *a.* Eximious, famous, eminent.
Eximír, *va.* To exempt, to free from an obligation, to clear from a charge.
Exinanición, *sf.* Want of vigour and strength; debility.
Exinanído, da, *a.* Debilitated, without strength.
Exír, *vn.* (Ant.) V. *Salir*.
Existéncia, *sf.* Existence, state of being; actual possession of being.
Existénte, *pa.* Existing.
Existimación, *sf.* Existimation, opinion, esteem. [judge.
Existimár, *va.* To hold, to form an opinion, to
Existír, *vr.* To exist, to be; to have a being.
E'xito, *sm.* 1. Departure, act of leaving a place. 2. End or termination of any thing.
E'xodo, *sm.* Exodus, the second book of Moses.
Exôneración, *sf.* Exoneration, the act of disburthening.
Exônerár, *va.* To exonerate, to unload; to disburthen.
Exôpilatívo, va, *a.* Deobstruent. [treaty.
Exôráble, *a.* Exorable, to be moved by en-
Exôrbitáncia, *sf.* Exorbitance. [sive.
Exôrbitánte, *a.* Exorbitant, enormous, exces-
Exôrbitanteménte, *ad.* Exorbitantly.

Exôrcísmo, *sm.* Exorcism, adjuration by which evil spirits are driven away.
Exôrcísta, *sm.* Exorciser.
Exôrcizánte, *pa.* Exorcising; exorciser.
Exôrcizár, *va.* To exorcise, to adjure by some holy name, to drive away by adjuration.
Exôrdio, *sm.* Exordium, the proëmial part of a composition; origin, beginning.
Exôrnación, *sf.* 1. Exornation, ornament, embellishment. 2. Elegance of style.
Exôrnár, *va.* To adorn, to embellish.
Exôrtación, *sf.* Exhortation, familiar admonition to piety.
Exotérico, ca, *a.* Exoteric, public, common.
Exótico, ca, *a.* 1. Exotic, foreign. 2. Extravagant, odd.
Expalmádo, da, *a.* Worn out by use; applied to the blade of a razor.
Expansibilidád, *sf.* Expansibility.
Expansión, *sf.* Expansion, extension.
Expansívo, va, *a.* Expansive, capable of extension.
Expánso, *sm.* 1. Expanse, a body widely expanded without inequalities. 2. Space between the superior sphere of the air and the empyrean or highest heaven.
Expatriación, *sf.* Expatriation.
Expatriár, *va.* To expatriate.—*vr.* To be exiled.
Expavecérse, *vr.* To alarm or frighten one's self.
Expectáble, *a.* Illustrious, conspicuous.
Expectación, *sf.* Expectation, anxious desire, hope. *Joven de expectacion*, A hopeful youth. *Hombre de expectacion*, A celebrated man.
Expectatíva, *sf.* 1. Right or claim respecting some future thing. 2. Hope of obtaining a reward, employment, or other thing.
Expectoración, *sf.* Expectoration.
Expectoránte, *a.* Expectorating.
Expectorár, *va.* To expectorate, to eject from the mouth and fauces.
Expedición, *sf.* 1. Expedition, a warlike enterprise. 2. Haste, speed, activity. 3. Readiness, velocity of saying or doing. 4. Brevet or bull despatched by the see of Rome.
Expedicionério, *sm.* He who superintends expeditions or despatches.
Expedído, da, *a.* Expedite, quick, prompt, nimble.
Expediénte, *sm.* 1. Affair or matter of easy discussion and despatch. 2. Shift, means to an end contrived in an exigency. 3. Despatch, a writing issued from public boards or offices. 4. Facility or dexterity in the management of affairs. 5. Title, reason, motive, pretext. 6. Preparation, provision.
Expediénte, *a.* Convenient, fit, suitable.
Expedír, *va.* 1. To expedite, to facilitate, to free from impediment. 2. To despatch, to issue from a public office.—*vr.* To retire from the military profession.
Expeditaménte, *ad.* Expeditiously, easily.
Expeditívo, va, *a.* Apt in expedients.
Expedíto, ta, *a.* Prompt, expeditious.
Expelér, *va.* To expel, to eject, to throw with violence.
Expeliénte, *pa.* Expelling.
Expendedór, ra, *s.* 1. Spendthrift, lavisher. 2. One who passes counterfeit money, knowing it to be so. 3. Receiver of stolen goods.
Expendér, *va.* To expend, to spend, to lay out.
Expénsas, *sf. pl.* Expenses, charges, costs.
Experiéncia, *sf.* 1. Experience, knowledge gained by practice. 2. V. *Experimento.*
Experimentádo, da, *a.* Experienced.
Experimentadór, ra, *s.* Experimenter.
Experimentál, *a.* Experimental.
Experimentalménte, *ad.* Experimentally.
Experimentár, *va.* 1. To experience, to learn or know by practice. 2. To experiment, to search out by trial.
Experiménto, *sm.* Experiment, trial of any thing; something done in order to discover an uncertain or unknown effect.
Expertaménte, *ad.* Expertly.
Expérto, ta, *a.* Expert, able, experienced.
Expiación, *sf.* 1. Expiation, the act of atoning for any crime. 2. Atonement, purification.
Expiár, *va.* 1. To expiate, to atone for any crime. 2. To cleanse from guilt, to purify.
Expiatívo, va, *a.* That which serves for an expiation.
Expiatório, ria, *a.* Expiatory.
Expíllo, *sm.* V. *Matricaria.*
Explanación, *sf.* Explanation, elucidation.
Explanáda, *sf.* (Fort.) Esplanade.
Explanár, *va.* 1. To level. V. *Allanar.* 2. (Met.) To explain, to elucidate, to clear up.
Explayár, *va.* To extend, to dilate, to enlarge. —*vr.* To enlarge or dwell upon a subject.
Expletívo, va, *a.* Expletive.
Explicáble, *a.* Explicable, explainable.
Explicación, *sf.* Explanation, elucidation.
Explicadaménte, *ad.* Explicitly.
Explicadéras, *sf. pl.* Manner in which any thing is explained; facility of explaining.
Explicár, *va.* To explain, to elucidate, to clear up.—*vr.* To explain or speak one's mind with propriety and freedom.
Explicatívo, va, *a.* Explicative.
Explicitaménte, *ad.* Explicitly, manifestly.
Explícito, ta, *a.* Explicit, clear, distinct.
Exploración, *sf.* Exploration.
Exploradór, ra, *s.* Explorator.
Explorár, *va.* To explore, to search into, to examine by trial.
Exploratório, *sm.* Probe, catheter.
Explosión, *sf.* Explosion.
Expolición, *sf.* Illustration of any saying.
Exponenciál, *a.* (Algeb.) Exponential.
Exponénte, *pa.* y *s.* 1. Expositor. 2. (Algeb.) Exponent.
Exponér, *va.* 1. To expose, to lay before the public. 2. To expound, to explain. 3. To lay open to danger, to make liable to, to hazard.
Exportación, *sf.* Exportation, the act of sending or carrying out commodities to other countries.
Exposición, *sf.* Exposition, explanation.
Expositívo, va, *a.* Explanatory.
Expósito, ta, *a.* Exposed; applied to infants abandoned.
Expositór, *sm.* Expounder, interpreter.
Expremíjo, *sm.* Cheese-vat, a wooden case in which cheeses are formed and pressed.
Expresaménte, *ad.* Expressly.
Expresár, *va.* 1. To express, to declare one's sentiments clearly and distinctly. 2. To delineate, to sketch, to design.
Expresión, *sf.* 1. Expression, a clear and distinct declaration of one's sentiments and opinions. 2. Form or cast of language in which thoughts are uttered. 3. The act of squeezing or forcing

out the juice from succulent fruit. 4. Present, gift. *Envió esa expresion*, He sent this present.

Expresívo, va, *a.* Expressive; affecting.

Expréso, sa, *a.* Clear, manifest.

Expréso, *sm.* 1. Express, extraordinary messenger. 2. (Naút.) Packet-boat, advice-boat.

Exprimidéra, *sf.* A small press used by apothecaries to squeeze out the juice of herbs.

Exprimidéro, *sm.* Press, an instrument by which any thing is crushed or squeezed.

Exprimído, da, *a.* Dry, extenuated.

Exprimír, *va.* 1. To squeeze or press out. 2. To express, to declare clearly and distinctly.

Exprobración, *sf.* Exprobration, reproachful accusation or censure.

Ex Proféso, *ad. Lat.* Avowedly, designedly, on purpose. [vincial.

Exprovinciál, *sm.* Ex-provincial, a late provincial.

Expugnación, *sf.* Expugnation.

Expugnadór, *sm.* He who takes by assault.

Expugnár, *va.* To conquer, to reduce a place by force of arms.

Expulsár, *va.* To expel, to eject. [out.

Expulsión, *sf.* Expulsion, the act of driving out.

Expulsívo, va, *a.* Expulsive.

Expultríz, *a.* That which expels or has the power of expelling.

Expungír, *va.* To expunge, to rub out.

Expurgación, *sf.* Expurgation.

Expurgár, *va.* To cleanse, to purify.

Expurgatório, *sm.* Index of the books prohibited by the Inquisition.—*a.* Expurgatory.

Exquisitaménte, *ad.* Exquisitely.

Exquisíto, ta, *a.* Exquisite, excellent, curious.

E'xtasi ó E'xtasis, *sm.* Enthusiasm, excessive elevation of the mind; ecstasy.

Extático, ca, *a.* Ecstatical.

Extemporál, *a.* Extemporal, done or uttered without premeditation.

Extemporaneaménte, *ad.* Extemporaneously.

Extemporáneo, nea, *a.* Extemporaneous, sudden.

Extendér, *va.* To extend, to enlarge, to widen.—*vr.* 1. To be extended or enlarged; to increase in bulk; to propagate. 2. To swell, to look big, to be elated with pride. 3. To commit to writing at length.

Extendidaménte, *ad.* Extensively.

Extendído, da, *a.* Extensive, spacious, roomy.

Extendimiénto, *sm.* Extension, dilatation.

Extensaménte, *ad.* Extensively.

Extensibilidád, *sf.* Extensibility, quality of being extensible.

Extensión, *sf.* Extension, ampliation.

Extensivaménte, *ad.* Amply, extensively.

Extensívo, va, *a.* Extensive, ample.

Exténso, sa, *a.* Extensive. *Por extenso*, At large; clearly and distinctly.

Extenuación, *sf.* Extenuation.

Extenuár, *va.* To extenuate, to diminish, to debilitate.

Extenuatívo, va, *a.* That which extenuates.

Exterión, *a.* Exterior, external.

Exterión, *sm.* Outward appearance, composure, modest deportment.

Exterioridád, *sf.* 1. Mark, outward appearance. 2. Pomp, ostentation, pageantry.

Exteriorménte, *ad.* Externally.

Exterminadór, ra, *s.* Exterminator.

Exterminár, *va.* 1. To banish, to drive away. 2. To root out, to tear up, to destroy.

Extermínio, *sm.* 1. Expulsion, banishment. 2. Extermination, desolation. [reign.

Extérno, na, *a.* 1. External, visible. 2. Foreign.

Ex Testaménto, *ad. Lat.* By will or testament.

Extinción, *sf.* Extinction, the act of quenching.

Extinguíble, *a.* Extinguishable.

Extinguír, *va.* 1. To quench, to extinguish, to put out. 2. To suppress, to destroy.

Extínto, ta, *pp.* Extinguished, extinct. [out.

Extirpación, *sf.* Extirpation, act of rooting out.

Extirpadór, *sm.* Extirpator.

Extirpár, *va.* 1. To extirpate, to root out. 2. To destroy.

Extorsión, *sf.* Extortion, the act or practice of gaining by violence or rapacity.

E'xtra, *prep.* Out, without, besides.

Extracción, *sf.* 1. Exportation, the act or practice of sending money or merchandise to other countries. 2. (Quím.) Extraction, the act of drawing one part out of a compound. 3. Drawing numbers in the lottery.

Extrácta, *sf.* (For. Ar.) True extract from a writing or public instrument.

Extractadór, *sm.* Extracter.

Extractár, *va.* To extract, to abridge.

Extracción, *sf.* *Extracvion de fondos*, (Com.) The secreting of effects.

Extractívo, va, *a.* Extractive.

Extrácto, *sm.* 1. Extract, a short abridgment of a large work or book. 2. Substance extracted; the chief parts of a compound drawn out.

Extractór, *sm.* Extracter.

Extraénte, *pa.* Extracting, he who extracts.

Extraér, *va.* 1. To extract, to remove, to export. 2. To draw out the chief parts of a compound. 3. (For.) To extract from any document.

Extrajudiciál, *a.* Extrajudicial, out of the regular course of judicial proceedings.

Extrajudicialménte, *ad.* Extrajudicially.

Extra Múros, *ad. Lat.* Out of the walls of a town or place.

Extrangería, *sf.* 1. The quality of being a stranger or foreigner. 2. The manner, use, and customs of a foreigner.

Extrangéro, ra, *s.* Stranger, foreigner, alien.

Extrañaménte, *ad.* Wonderfully, extraordinarily. [aversion.

Extrañamiénte, *sm.* Alienation, rejection,

Extrañár, *va.* 1. To alienate, to banish from one's sight and intercourse. 2. To admire, to wonder. 3. To censure, to chide, to reprimand.—*vr.* To refuse, to decline; to break off any engagement.

Extrañéza y Extrañéz, *sf.* 1. Alienation or change of affection, aversion. 2. Singularity, irregularity. 3. Admiration, wonder.

Extráño, ña, *a.* 1. Foreign, extraneous. 2. Rare, singular, uncommon. 3. Extravagant, irregular, wild. 4. Unwelcome, not well received.

Extraordinariaménte, *ad.* Extraordinarily.

Extraordinário, ria, *a.* Extraordinary, casual.

Extraordinário, *sm.* Extraordinariness, extraordinary expenses for a dinner or household affairs. *Correo extraordinario*, Extraordinary courier.

Extratémpora, *sf.* Dispensation for receiving orders out of the time specified by the church.

Extravagáncia, *sf.* Extravagancy, irregularity, disorder.

Extravagánte, *a.* Extravagant.

Extravasación, *sf.* Extravasation, the act of forcing or state of being forced out of the proper containing vessels.

Extravasárse, *vr.* To extravasate, to spring or force out of a vessel.

Extravenádo, da, *a.* Forced out of the veins.

Extravenárse, *vr.* To let out of the veins.

Extraviár, *va.* To mislead, to lead out of the way.—*vr.* To deviate from rectitude.

Extravío, *sm.* 1. Deviation, the act of wandering out of the right road. 2. Irregularity, disorder.

Extremadaménte, *ad.* Extremely.

Extremadáno, na, *a.* Belonging to Extremadura.

Extremadás, *sf. pl.* The time of making cheese.

Extremádo, da, *a.* 1. Extreme, absolute, consummate either in good or bad. 2. Facetious, cheerful, gay.

Extremaménte, *ad.* Extremely.

Extremár, *va.* 1. To reduce to an extreme; generally used in a bad sense. 2. To finish, to complete; to give the finishing stroke. 3. To separate.—*vr.* 1. To be punctual or exact in the execution or performance of any thing. 2. To persist obstinately in an enterprise or undertaking.—*vn.* To winter in Extremadura; applied to sheep.

Extremaunción, *sf.* Unction, the rite of anointing in the last hours, extreme unction.

Extreméño, ña, *a.* Belonging or relating to Extremadura.

Extremidád, *sf.* Extremity. *Extremidades*, Extremities, head, feet, hands, &c. of animals.

Extrémo, ma, *a.* 1. Extreme, last. 2. Excessive, utmost. *Con extremo, en extremo, por extremo*, Extremely, in the utmost degree.

Extrémo, *sm.* 1. Extreme, utmost point, highest degree. 2. (Met.) Extreme care or application. *Hacer extremos*, To caress, to fondle; to manifest grief and displeasure. 3. The winter or summer of migrating flocks.

Extremóso, sa, *a.* Extremadurian.

Extrinsecaménte, *ad.* Exteriorly.

Extrínseco, ca, *a.* Extrinsic, outward.

Exturbár, *va.* To expel, to eject.

Exûberáncia, *sf.* Exuberance, utmost plenty.

Exûberánte, *a.* Exuberant, overabundant, superfluous.

Exûberár, *vn.* To be exuberant, to exuberate.

Exûlceración, *sf.* Ulceration.

Exûlcerár, *va.* To ulcerate, to disease with sores.

Exûltación, *sf.* Exultation.

Exvóto, *sm.* Offering to God in consequence of a vow; such offerings consist of relics, pictures, images of almost every thing, &c. which are hung up in churches.

Ezquerdeár, *va.* (Ant.) To carry any thing on the left side.—*vn.* To deviate from right.

Ezquiérda, *sf.* (Ant.) V. *Izquierda.*

E'zula, *sf.* (Bot.) Spurge. V. *Esula.*

F was formerly used instead of the aspirated *H*, as *fablar* for *hablar*; and even now they are occasionally used promiscuously in some words, as *funega* or *hanega*, but the former is the more general orthography. In law works *ff* signify digest or pandect of the civil law.

Fa, *sm.* (Mús.) Fourth note in the gamut.

Fába, *sf.* (Ant.) V. *Haba.*

Fabaráz, *sm.* (Bot.) Lousewort, stavesacre. Delphinium staphisagria *L.*

Fabeár, *va.* (Arag.) To vote with black and white beans.

Fábla, *sf.* 1. V. *Fábula.* 2. (Ant.) Confabulation.

Fabladór, ra, *s.* (Ant.) V. *Hablador.*

Fablílla, *sf. dim.* Slight rumour.

Fabót, *sm.* A kind of wind instrument serving as a double base to the hautboy.

Fábrica, *sf.* 1. Fabrication, the act and manner of building. 2. Structure, building, edifice. 3. Manufactory, the place where any thing is manufactured. 4. Manufacture. 5. A fantastic or chimerical idea. 6. Money or lands applied to the maintenance and repairs of churches. *Hombre de fábrica*, An artful, crafty fellow. *Pared de fábrica*, Brick wall.

Fabricadaménte, *ad.* Beautifully, according to beauty and art.

Fabricadór, ra, *s.* 1. Manufacturer, artisan. 2. Inventor, contriver, deviser. 3. *Fabricador de dinero*, Coiner, minter.

Fabricánte, *sm.* 1. Builder, architect. 2. Maker, manufacturer, master-workman, artificer.

Fabricár, *va.* 1. To build, to construct. 2. To manufacture, to make by art and labour. 3. To contrive, to devise. *Fabricar á piedra perdida*, To build upon a false foundation.

Fabríl, *a.* Belonging to manufacturers, artisans, or workmen.

Fabriquéro, *sm.* 1. Manufacturer, artisan, artificer. 2. Person charged with taking care of cathedrals and church buildings.

Fábro, *sm.* 1. (Ict.) John Doree, St. Peter's fish. Zeus faber *L.* 2. (Ant.) V. *Artífice.*

Fabúco y Fabúca, *s.* Beech-mast, the fruit of the beech-tree.

Fabuéno, *sm.* Westerly wind.

Fábula, *sf.* 1. Rumour, report, common talk of the people. 2. Fiction, falsehood. 3. Fable, a feigned story intended to enforce some moral precept. 4. Laughing-stock. *Está hecho fábula del mundo*, He is become the laughing-stock of the whole world.

Fabulación, *sf.* Conversation.

Fabuladór, *sm.* Author of fables, dealer in fictions.

Fabulár, *va.* To fable, to invent or deal in fictions.

Fabulílla, ta, *sf. dim.* A little fable.

Fabulísta, *sm.* Fabulist, a writer of fables.
Fabulosaménte, *ad.* Fabulously.
Fabulosidád, *sf.* Fabulousness.
Fabulóso, sa, *a.* Fabulous, feigned, full of fables.
Fáca, *sf.* V. *Haca.*
Faccénda, *sm.* Busy-body, one who is constantly employed without doing any thing useful.
Facción, *sf.* 1. Military exploit, engagement, action. 2. Faction, a turbulent party in a state. 3. People of the same trade or profession. 4. Face, visage, aspect. *Faccion de testamento,* Faculty of testating. *Facciones,* Features; the lineaments, cast, or form of the face.
Faccionár, *va.* (Ant.) To fashion, to form.
Faccionário, ria, *a.* Belonging to a party or faction.
Faccióso, sa, *a.* Factious, turbulent, unruly.
Facécia, *sf.* Facetiousness, gaiety, mirth.
Facecióso, sa, *a.* Facetious, cheerful, witty.
Facedór, ra, *s.* V. *Hacedor* y *Factor.*
Facér, *va.* (Ant.) V. *Hacer.*
Facería, *sf.* (Nav.) Society or community of pastors, who feed each other's flocks.
Facéro, ra, *a.* (Nav.) Relating to pastors. V. *Fronterizo.*
Fáces, *sf. pl.* V. *Mexillas.*
Facéta, *sf.* (Among Diamond Cutters) Face or side of a precious stone cut into a number of angles.
Facéto, ta, *a.* Merry, witty, gay, lively.
Fácha, *sf.* Face. V. *Cara* y *Traza.*
Fácha á Fácha, *ad.* Face to Face. *En Fácha,* (Naút.) Backed. *Véla en facha,* Sail backed, or laid back. *Ponerse en facha,* (Naút.) To take the sails aback; to bring to.
Facháda, *sf.* 1. Facade, front or fore part of a building. 2. (Met.) Broad or plump face. 3. Frontispiece of a book. 4. *Fachada de proa,* (Naút.) Fore front of a ship.
Fachénda, *a.* Vain, ostentatious; applied to persons who affect great business.
Fachendeár, *va.* To affect having much important business; to make an ostentatious parade of business.
Fachendísta, *a.* y *s.* One vain and ostentatious.
Fachendón, na, *a.* Very vain and ostentatious.
Fachín, *sm.* Porter, he who carries loads for hire.
Fácia, *ad.* (Ant.) V. *Hácia.*
Faciál, *a.* Intuitive, obvious at first sight.
Fácies, *sf. pl.* Faces of crystals.
Fácil, *a.* 1. Facile, easy; performable with little trouble. 2. Pliant, flexible, easily persuaded. 3. Easy of access; applied to lewd women. 4. Frail, weak of resolution.
Facilidád, *sf.* 1. Facility, easy to be performed; free from difficulty. 2. Inconstancy, levity. 3. Easiness of access, licentiousness.
Facilíllo, lla; to, ta, *a.* Rather easy. *Facilillo es eso,* (Iron.) That is easy enough; meaning that it is extremely difficult.
Facilitación, *sf.* Facility, expedition.
Facilitár, *va.* To facilitate, to make easy, to free from difficulties.
Facilménte, *ad.* Easily.
Facineróso ó Facinoróso, *a.* Facinorous, wicked, atrocious, detestably bad.

Facón, *sf.* (Ant.) Military exploit. V. *Hechura.* *A' facion,* (Ant.) In the fashion or manner.
Facistól, *sm.* Chorister's desk or stand on which choir-books are placed; bishop's seat.
Fáco, *sm.* 1. Pony, a little nag. 2. (Fam.) Francis.
Factíble, *a.* Feasible, practicable.
Factício, cia, *a.* Factitious, made by art in opposition to what is made by nature.
Factór, *sm.* 1. Performer, one who does any thing. 2. Factor, an agent for another.
Factoráge, *sm.* Factorage.
Factoría, *sf.* 1. Factory, foreign traders embodied in a distant country; also the district where they reside. 2. Factorage, the commission of a factor.
Factorizár, *va.* To establish commerce by factors.
Factúra, *sf.* 1. Facture, the act and manner of doing any thing. 2. (Among Organ-builders) The quality, length, breadth, and thickness of the tubes or pipes. 4. Invoice, an account of the quality and price of merchandise, including duty and other charges.
Facturár, *va.* To note on merchandise the amount of the prime cost.
Fácula, *sf.* Bright spot on the sun's disk.
Facultád, *sf.* 1. Faculty, power of doing any thing. 2. Force, resistance. 3. Art, science. 4. Authority, right, privilege. 5. License, permission.
Facultativaménte, *ad.* According to the faculty.
Facultatívo, va, *a.* 1. Belonging to some faculty, art, or science. 2. Granting power, faculty, leave, or permission. 3. That may be done or omitted at pleasure.
Facultóso, sa, *a.* Rich, powerful.
Facúndia, *sf.* Eloquence, the power of speaking with fluency and elegance.
Facúndo, da, *a.* Facund, eloquent.
Fáda, *sf.* A small apple of the pippin kind.
Fadár, *va.* (Ant.) V. *Hadar.*
Fadíga, *sf.* (Arag.) Leave granted to sell a fief or feudal estate.
Fadrín, *sm.* (Catal.) Comrade, fellow-workman.
Faéna, *sf.* 1. Work, labour, fatigue. 2. (Naút.) Duty on board of ships.
Faetón, *sm.* Phaeton, a kind of open carriage.
Fagína, *sf.* 1. Fascine, a small bundle of branches or bavins bound up. 2. Fagot, a bundle of sticks or brush-wood for fuel. 3. V. *Facna.* *Meter fagina,* To talk much at random.
Faginàda, *sf.* Collection of fascines or fagots.
Fájo, *sm.* V. *Haz.*
Falácia, *sf.* Fallacy, fraud, sophism.
Falagár, *va.* To soften, to enliven. V. *Halagar.*
Falagüéño, ña, *a.* Lovely, endearing.
Falánge, *sf.* 1. Phalanx. 2. (Ant.) Phalanges.
Falángia ó Falángio, *s.* A venomous spider with a red head and a black body.
Falaríde, *sf.* (Bot.) Canary-grass. Phalaris *L.*
Fálaris ó Fáleris, *s.* Kind of small duck.
Faláz y Faláce, *a.* Deceitful, fraudulent.
Falbalá, *sf.* 1. Flounce, an ornament sewed to a garment, and hanging loose. V. *Farfalá.* 2. Skirt of a gown or coat plaited.
Fálca, *sf.* A small wedge of wood used by carpenters.
Falcádo, da, *a.* Hooked, curvated.

Falcár, *va.* 1. To reap, to cut down corn with a sickle or reaping-hook. 2. To cut with a hook or sithe.

Falcário, *sm.* Roman soldier armed with a falchion.

Falcás, *sf. pl.* (Naút.) Waist-boards, or wash-boards.

Falcazár, *va.* (Naút.) To whip a rope's end with pack-thread or spun-yarn, to prevent its being untwisted.

Fálce, *sf.* 1. Sickle, reaping-hook, sithe, bill-hook. 2. Falchion, a short crooked sword.

Falcídia, *sf.* 1. Fourth part of an inheritance. 2. The part curtailed from a student's pittance in a university.

Falcinélo, *sm.* (Orn.) Gray ibis, sithe bill. Tantalus falcinellus *L.*

Falcón, *sm.* Ancient piece of artillery.

Falconéte, *sm.* Falconet, a small piece of ordnance.

Fálda, *sf.* 1. Skirt, the loose edge of a garment; that part which hangs loose below the waist; lap. 2. Train, that part of a gown which trails upon the ground. 3. Brow of a hill, that part of an eminence which slopes into the plain. 4. Leaf of a hat. 5. That part of the belly which covers the guts of animals. *Cortar faldas*, To backbite. *Perrillo de falda, ó perrillo faldero*, Lap-dog. *Cortar faldas*, To give a kind of ignominious punishment to abandoned women. 6. *Faldas*, Petticoats.

Faldaménto, *sm.* Fold, flap, skirt. V. *Falda.*

Faldár, *sm.* Tasses, armour for the thighs.

Faldellín, *sm.* 1. A short under-petticoat used by women. 2. An ornamental covering for beasts of burthen, much used by the carriers of Catalonia. [dog-

Falderíllo, lla, *a.* 1. Small lap. 2. Little lap-

Faldéro, ra, *a.* 1. Belonging to the lap. *Perrillo faldero*, Lap-dog. 2. Fond of being constantly among women, and of busying himself with women's affairs.

Faldétas, *sf. pl.* 1. Tassels. 2. Fringes, trimmings.

Faldicórto, ta, *a.* Having short skirts.

Faldíllas, *sf. pl.* Small skirts of a jacket.

Faldistório, *sm.* Stool on which bishops sit during the performance of church functions.

Faldón, *sm.* 1. A long flowing skirt. 2. Band or bandelet; any flat low moulding round a building. 3. A worn out mill-stone of a horse-mill.

Faldriquéra, *sf.* Pocket. V. *Faltriquera.* [men.

Faldulário, *sm.* An old tattered garment of wo-

Faléncia, *sf.* Want of security, uncertainty.

Falibilidád, *sf.* Fallibility, liableness to be deceived.

Falíble, *a.* Fallible, liable to be deceived.

Falidaménte, *ad.* Vainly, without foundation.

Falimiénto, *sm.* Deception, deceit, falsehood.

Falír, *vn.* To fail in the performance of one's promise.

Fálla, *sf.* 1. Defect, deficiency. V. *Falta.* 2. A sort of light loose cover, worn by women over their head-dress at night.

Falladór, ra, *s.* V. *Hallador.*

Fallár, *va.* To trump, to win a trick with trumps.—*v. impers.* To be deficient, to be wanting. V. *Hallar*

Falléba, *sf.* An iron instrument for fastening doors and windows.

Fallecedór, ra, *a.* Perishable, liable to perish or die.

Fallecér, *vn.* 1. To fail, to decay. 2. To die.

Fallecimiénto, *sm.* 1. Fault, defect. V. *Falta.* 2. Decease, death.

Fallído, da, *a.* Deceived, disappointed, frustrated.

Fállo, *sm.* 1. Sentence, decree. 2. (In the Game of Ombre) Not to play a card of the same suit, but to trump.

Falordía, *sf.* (Arag.) Deception, imposition, deceit; fable.

Fálsa, *sf.* 1. (Ar.) Garret. 2. (Mús.) Dissonance.

Falsa-Amárra, *sf.* (Naút.) Preventer-rope, employed at times to support another which suffers an unusual strain.

Falsabrága, *sf.* (Fort.) Fausse-braye, an elevation of earth about three feet above the level, which runs round the foot of the rampart on the outside.

Falsáda, *sf.* V. *Calada.*

Falsaménte, *ad.* Falsely, deceitfully.

Falsário, ria, *a.* 1. Falsifying, forging, counterfeiting. 2. Accustomed to tell falsehoods.

Falseadór y Falsadór, *sm.* Forger, one who falsifies or counterfeits any thing.

Falseár, 1. *va.* To falsify, to adulterate, to counterfeit. 2. To pierce, to penetrate. *Falsear el cuerpo*, To draw back the body in order to avoid a blow. *Falsear la llave*, To counterfeit a key. *Falsear las guardas ó centinelas*, To bribe the guards or sentries.—*vn.* 1. To slacken, to lose strength and firmness. 2. Not to agree in sound; applied to the strings of musical instruments. 3. Hollow left in seats to make them easy.

Falsedád, *sf.* Falsehood, deceit; a malicious dissimulation of the truth.

Falséte, *sm.* 1. Faint treble in music. 2. (And.) Spigot, cord or pin for a faucet. *Venir de falsete*, To act in a treacherous manner.

Falsificación, *sf.* Falsification, the act of falsifying or counterfeiting.

Falsificadór, ra, *s.* Falsifier, one who falsifies or counterfeits.

Falsificár, *va.* To falsify. V. *Falsear.*

Falsío, *sm.* (Mur.) Kind of sausage.

Fálso, sa, *a.* 1. False, deceitful; counterfeiting. 2. Untrue, uncertain. 3. Vicious; applied to horses or mules. 4. Producing no fruit; applied to blossoms. 5. Defective, false; applied to weights or honey-combs. *De falso*, Falsely, deceitfully. *En falso*, Without due security.

Fálta, *sf.* 1. Fault, defect. 2. Want or stoppage of the catamenia in women. *Tiene quatro faltas*, She is in the fifth month of her pregnancy. 3. Deficiency in the weight of coin. 4. Default, non-appearance in court at a day assigned. *Sin falta*, Without fail. *A' falta de*, In want or for want of. *Hacer falta*, To be absolutely necessary to any thing; not to be punctual to the fixed time.

Faltár, *vn.* 1. To be deficient, to be wanting. 2. To be consumed, to fall short. 3. Not to fulfil one's promise, not to perform one's en-

gagement. 4. To need, to be in want of. 5. To die.
Faltílla, *sf.* A slight fault.
Fálto, ta, *a.* 1. Wanting, deficient. 2. Miserable, wretched. 3. Mad, insane.
Faltréro, ra, *s.* Pickpocket, petty thief.
Faltriquéra, *sf.* Pocket, a small bag inserted into clothes.
Falúa y Falúca, *sf.* (Naút.) Boat, barge.
Fáma, *sf.* 1. Report, rumour. 2. Fame, reputation, repute.
Fáme, *sf.* (Gal.) Hunger. V. *Hambre.*
Famélico, ca, *a.* Hungry. V. *Hambriento.*
Família, *sf.* 1. Family, the people who live in the same house together. 2. Family, those that descend from one common progenitor; a race, a generation. 3. Religious order. 4. Number of servants or retainers.
Familiár, *a.* 1. Familiar, domestic, belonging to the family. 2. Well known, well acquainted with. 3. Agreeable, conformable, useful.
Familiár, *sm.* 1. Servant, especially of the clergy. 2. Officer of the Inquisition. 3. College-servant, who waits upon all the collegians collectively, not upon one of them in particular. 4. Demon, a familiar spirit. 5. Familiar or intimate friend.
Familiarcíto, *sm.* 1. Servant-boy, a little servant. 2. One who affects great familiarity or intimacy.
Familiaridád, *sf.* 1. Familiarity, easiness of conversation or intercourse. 2. Familiar. V. *Familiatura.*
Familiarizár, *va.* To familiarize, to render familiar, to make easy by habitude.—*vr.* To become familiar, to descend from a state of distant superiority.
Familiarménte, *ad.* Familiarly.
Familiatúra, *sf.* Place and employment of an officer of the Inquisition, or college familiar.
Famílio ó Famíllo, *sm.* (Ant.) College familiar or servant.
Fámis, *sf.* A kind of gold cloth or brocade which comes from Smyrna.
Famosaménte, *ad.* Famously, excellently.
Famóso, sa, *a.* 1. Famous, celebrated, renowned. 2. Noted; applied to robbers and other offenders.
Fámula, *sf.* (Joc.) Maid-servant.
Famuláto y Famulício, *sm.* Servitude, the state and employment of a servant.
Fámulo, *sm.* Servant of a college.
Fanál, *sm.* 1. (Naút.) Poop-lantern of a commodore's ship. 2. Lantern of crystal, made in the form of a conoid. 3. (Met.) Guide, friend, adviser in difficulties and dangers.
Fanático, ca, *a.* Fanatic, obstinate, enthusiastic, superstitious.
Fanatísmo, *sm.* Fanaticism, religious phrensy.
Fandángo, *sm.* 1. A lively Spanish dance; the music to this dance. 2. Festive entertainment; dance with castanets or balls in the hands.
Fandanguéro, *sm.* 1. Fandango-dancer. 2. One who is fond of festive entertainments.
Fanéca ó Fanéga, *sf.* (Ict.) Pout, whiting pout. Gadus barbatus *L.*
Fanéga, *sf.* 1. Measure of grain and other seed of about a hundred weight. 2. Extent of tilled ground, which requires a *fanega* of grain to be properly sown. *Media fanega,* A measure equal to an *almud* or 6 *celemines.*
Fanegáda, *sf.* Extent of arable land, which takes a *fanega* of seed. *Á' fanegadas,* In great plenty or abundance.
Fanfarreár, *vn.* To bully, to brag.
Fanfarría, *sf.* Empty arrogance of a bragger.
Fanfarrón, *sm.* Fanfaron, a bully, a hector.
Fanfarrón, na, *a.* Boasting, vaunting; inflated.
Fanfarronáda, *sf.* Fanfaronade, boast, brag.
Fanfarronázo, za, *a.* Great boasting, vaunting.
Fanfarroneár, *vn.* To bully, to brag.
Fanforronería, *sf.* Fanfaronade, braggartism.
Fanforronésca, *sf.* Manner of a fanfaron.
Fanfurriña, *sf.* Passion or displeasure, arising from a slight motive.
Fangár, *sm.* Mire, fen.
Fángo, *sm.* (Naút.) Oozy bottom of the sea.
Fáno, *sm.* (Ant.) Fane, temple.
Fantaseár, *vn.* To fancy, to imagine.
Fantasía, *sf.* 1. Fancy, imagination; the power by which the mind forms to itself images and representations. 2. Fiction, conception, image. 3. Presumption, vanity. *Fantasías,* Pearls joined or stringed together.
Fantasióso, sa, *a.* Fantastic.
Fantásma, *sf.* Phantom, a fancied vision; apparition, spectre.—*sm.* A vain presumptuous man.
Fantasmón, *sm.* A presumptuous coxcomb, a vain pretender.
Fantasmonázo, *sm.* Huge phantom; large rude person assuming importance.
Fantasticaménte, *ad.* Fantastically, fallaciously, pompously.
Fantasticár, *vn.* V. *Fantasear.*
Fantástico, ca, *a.* Fantastic, whimsical; fanciful; vain, presumptuous.
Fañár, *va.* (Ant.) To cut off the tip of an animal's ears.
Faquír, *sm* Porter, one who carries loads for hire.
Far, *va.* (Ant.) V. *Hacer.*
Fára, *sf.* A kind of serpent.
Farachár, *va.* To beat or clean hemp.
Farallón, *sm.* (Naút.) Small pointed island in the sea.
Faramálla, *sf.* 1. Imposition, artful trick. 2. Tale or story calculated to excite wrangling or discord. 3. Prattling, babbling.—*sm.* Tale-bearer, deceitful treacherous man.
Faramalleár, *va.* To tattle; to babble.
Faramalléro y Faramallón, *sm.* Tattling, deceitful man.
Farándula, *sf.* 1. Profession of a low comedian or player. 2. A low mean trade or calling. 3. Artful trick, stratagem.
Farandoléro, *sm.* 1. Actor, player. 2. Idle tattler, deceitful talker.
Farandúlico, ca, *a.* Relating to a low comedian.
Faraón, *sm.* Game at cards.
Faráute, *sm.* 1. Messenger, he who carries messages from one party to another. 2. Interpreter, translator. 3. Principal manager or director. 4. A noisy meddling fellow. 5. Player who recites or delivers the prologue of a play. 6. (Cant.) Prostitute's bully.

Farcinadór, *sm.* One who stuffs or fills any thing.
Fárda, *sf.* 1. Irrigation duty. 2. Tax, tribute.
Fardácho, *sm.* (Arag.) V. *Lagarto.*
Fardáge, *sm.* Collection of cargoes, equipage.
Fardár, *va.* To furnish or supply with clothes.
Fardél, *sm.* Fardel, bag, knapsack.
Fardelería, *sf.* Baggage; place for luggage.
Fardelíllo y ézo, *sm. dim.* A small bag.
Fardíllo, *sm.* A small bundle.
Fárdo, *sm.* Bale of goods, parcel, bundle.
Farellón, *sm.* 1. Point, cape, headland. 2. Rock, cliff in the sea.
Fáres, *sm. pl.* Church service sung in the holy week.
Farfalá, *sf.* Flounce, ornament of a gown or curtain.
Farfallóso, sa, *a.* Stammering.
Farfán, *sm.* Christian dragoon serving a Mohammedan king. [bler.
Farfánte y Farfantón, *sm.* A boasting babbler.
Farfantonáda y Farfantonería, *sf.* Idle boast
Fárfara, *sf.* 1. (Bot.) Colt's foot. Tussilago farfara *L.* 2. Membrane which covers the white of an egg. *En fárfara*, Immature; applied to an egg without a shell; (Met.) Unfinished, half done.
Farfúlla, *sm.* A stammering talkative person.
Farfulladaménte, *ad.* Stammeringly.
Farfulladór, *sm.* Stammerer.
Farfullár, *va.* 1. To talk quick and stammeringly. 2. (Met.) To do in a hurry and confusion.
Fargallón, na, *a. y s.* Applied to those careless, unpolished, or dirty in their dress.
Farillón, *sm.* (Naút.) V. *Farallon.*
Farína, *sf.* (Ant.) Farina. V. *Harina.*
Farináceo, ea, *a.* Farinaceous, mealy.
Farinétas, *sf. pl.* Fritters made of flour, honey, and water.
Faringe, *sm.* Gullet, opening of the wind-pipe.
Farisaísmo, *sm.* The sect of Pharisees.
Farisaíco, ca, *a.* Pharisaical.
Fariséo, *sm.* 1. Pharisee, a member of the sect of Pharisees. 2. (Met.) Cruel, hard-hearted person.
Farmacéutico, ca, *a.* Pharmaceutical.
Farmácia, *sf.* Pharmacy.
Fármaco, *sm.* V. *Medicamento.*
Farmacopéa, *sf.* Pharmacopœia. [list.
Farmacópola, *sm.* Apothecary, pharmacopolist.
Farnéro, *sm.* (Ast.) Receiver of rents.
Fáro, *sm.* Pharos or phare, a light-house; a high building on a coast, at the top of which lights are put to guide ships.
Faról, *sm.* Lantern, a transparent case for a candle. *Faroles de señales*, (Naút.) Signal lanterns.
Faroléro, *sm.* 1. One who makes lanterns. 2. Lamp-lighter.
Farolíllo, to, co, *sm.* 1. Small lantern. 2. (Bot.) Indian heartseed, smooth-leaved heart pea. Cardiospermum halicacabum *L.*
Farón, *sm.* Lantern. V. *Fanal.*
Faróta, *sf.* (Mur.) A brazen-faced woman, without sense or judgment.
Farotón, *sm.* (Mur.) A brazen-faced stupid fellow.
Farotóna, *sf.* Tall slovenly woman.
Farpádo, da, *a.* Scalloped.

Fárpas, *sf. pl.* Notches, scollops, hollows cut in any thing.
Fárra, *sf.* Kind of fish.
Fárrago, *sm.* Farrago, a mass formed confusedly of several ingredients; a medley.
Farraguísta, *sm.* One who disorders things or amasses them together.
Fárro, *sm.* 1. Peeled barley, barley freed from the husk by the operation of a mill. 2. A sort of wheat. V. *Escanda.*
Farropéa, *sf.* (Ast.) V. *Arropea.*
Fársa, *sf.* 1. Farce, a kind of dramatic representation, merely intended to raise the broad laugh. 2. Company of players.
Farsálico, ca, *a.* Belonging to Pharsalia.
Farsánte, ta, *s.* Low comic actor, or actress.
Farsár, *vn.* (Ant.) To play farces or comedies.
Farséto, *sm.* Quilted jacket with cotton sewed between the cloth and lining.
Fartár, *va.* V. *Hartar.*
Fárte y Fartál, *sm.* Fruit-tart or pie.
Fartriquéra, *sf.* Pocket. V. *Faltriquera.*
Fas (Por) ó por Néfas, *ad.* Justly or unjustly.
Fascál, *sm.* Shock, a pile of sheaves of corn.
Fáscas, *ad.* V. *Hasta* and *Casi.*
Fásces, *sf. pl.* Fasces, bundle of reeds.
Fascinación, *sf.* 1. Fascination, the power or act of bewitching; enchantment. 2. Imposition, deceit.
Fascinadór, ra, *s.* Fascinater; charmer.
Fascinánte, *pa.* Fascinater, fascinating.
Fascinár, *va.* 1. To fascinate, to bewitch, to enchant. 2. To deceive, to impose upon.
Fáse, *sf.* (Ast.) Phases of the moon or planet.
Fasóles, *sm. pl.* French-beans. V. *Judihuelos.*
Fasquía, *sf.* 1. (Ant.) Loathing, distaste, squeamishness, arising from weakness of the stomach, or stench and bad smell. 2. (Naút.) Ledge of boards four or five inches wide and one inch thick.
Fasquiár, *va.* To loathe, to consider with the disgust of satiety.
Fásta y Fáta, *prep.* V. *Hasta.*
Fastiál, *sm.* Pyramid placed on the top of an edifice. V. *Hastial.*
Fastidiár, *va.* 1. To excite disgust. 2. To loathe, to look on with dislike or abhorrence.
Fastídio, *sm.* 1. Squeamishness, arising from a weak or disordered stomach, or from a bad smell. 2. Distaste, disgust.
Fastidiosaménte, *ad.* Fastidiously.
Fastidióso, sa, *a.* 1. Fastidious, squeamish, delicate to a vice. 2. Disdainful, disgusted.
Fastígio, *sm.* 1. Pinnacle, the top of any thing which ends in a point. 2. Frontispiece of a building.
Fásto, *sm.* 1. Haughtiness, pride. 2. Splendour, pomp, grandeur. *Fastos*, Feasts or anniversaries among the Romans.
Fastosaménte, *ad.* Fastuously, pompously.
Fastóso y Fastuóso, sa, *a.* Fastuous, proud, haughty.
Fatál, *a.* 1. Fatal, proceeding by destiny, inevitable. 2. Unfortunate, destructive, deadly.
Fatalidád, *sf.* Fatality, tendency to danger, unfortunate.
Fatalísmo, *sm.* Fatalism.
Fatalísta, *sm.* Fatalist, one who maintains that all things happen by invincible necessity.

Fatalménte, *ad.* Fatally.
Fatídico, ca, *a.* Fatidical, prophetic; having the power to foretel.
Fatíga y Fatigación, *sf.* 1. Toil, hard labour, fatigue. 2. Anguish, grief; importunity.
Fatigadaménte, *ad.* Difficultly.
Fatigadór, ra, *s.* Molester, one who molests.
Fatigár, *va.* 1. To fatigue, to tire, to molest. 2. To desolate or lay waste by warlike incursion or invasion.—*vr.* To be in a hurry, to do things in great haste. *Fatigar la selva,* (Poét.) To employ one's self in hunting or sporting.
Fatigosaménte, *ad.* Painfully.
Fatigóso, sa, *a.* 1. Tiresome, troublesome. 2. Anxious, painful.
Fáto, *sm.* (Ant.) V. *Hado y Hato.*
Fatór, *sm.* Performer. V. *Factor.*
Fatoría, *sf.* Factory. V. *Factoría.*
Fátua, *sf.* Silly, hypocritical female.
Fatuidád, *sf.* 1. Fatuity, weakness of mind. 2. A stupid speech, a foolish action.
Fátuo, tua, *a.* Fatuous, stupid, foolish.
Fatúra, *sf.* Invoice. V. *Factura.*
Fáuces, *sf. pl.* Fauces, gullet.
Faufáu, *sm.* Stateliness of deportment, affected dignity and importance.
Fáusto, ta, *a.* Happy, fortunate, prosperous.
Fáusto, *sm.* Splendour, pomp, pageantry.
Faustóso, sa, *a.* Fastuous, haughty, proud.
Fautór, ra, *s.* Fautor, fautress, countenancer.
Fautoría, *sf.* Aid, favour, auxiliary.
Fávila, *sf.* (Poét.) Ashes of an extinguished fire.
Fávo, *sm.* Cake of yellow wax.
Favónio, *sm.* Westerly wind.
Favór, *sm.* 1. Favour, protection, support. 2. Favour granted, honour. 3. Compliment, an expression of civility and kindness. 4. Something given by a lady to be worn. *Favor al rey,* Military assistance given in the king's name. *A' favór,* By favour of.
Favorábles, *a.* Favourable, advantageous, propitious.
Favorablemente, *ad.* Favourably.
Favorcíllo, *sm.* A small favour.
Favorecedór, ra, *s.* Fautor, fautress, favourer.
Favorecér, *va.* 1. To favour, to protect. 2. To grant favours.—*vr.* To enjoy favour or protection, to avail one's self of a favour.
Favoríto, ta, *a.* Favoured, esteemed.
Fáxa, *sf.* 1. Bandage, roller. 2. Border, a line which divides any superficies.
Faxadúra, *sf.* (Naút.) Patched clothes rolled round a rope to preserve it.
Faxamiénto, *sm.* Act of rolling or swathing.
Fáxas, *sf. pl.* 1. Stuff-rollers around the legs, serving for stockings. 2. Girdles. *Faxas de rizos,* (Naút.) Reef-bands.
Faxár, *va.* To swathe, to bind as a child with bands and rollers.
Faxárdo, *sm.* Kind of meat pie.
Faxeádo, da, *a.* That which has girdles or rollers.
Faxéro, *sm.* A knitted swaddling band for children.
Fáxo, *sm.* Bundle. V. *Haz. Fáxos,* Swaddling clothes.
Faxuéla, *sf.* Small bandage or roller.
Fayádo, *sm.* A small garret or lumber room.

Fayánca, *sf.* Position of the body, in which it does not stand firm and steady.
Fayánco, *sm.* A flat basket made of osier.
Fáysa, *sf.* Band, roller. V. *Faxa.*
Faysán, na, *s.* Pheasant, a bird.
Faysár, *va.* To bind with a roller. V. *Faxar.*
Fáz, *sf.* 1. Face. V. *Rostro.* 2. Front, the fore part of a building or any other thing. V. *Haz.*
Faz á Faz, *ad.* Face to face. *A' prima faz,* At first sight. *En faz y en paz,* Publickly and peacefully.
Fáza, *sf.* y *ad.* (Ant.) V. *Haza y Hácia.*
Fazáña, *sf.* V. *Hazaña.*
Fazoléto, *sm.* Handkerchief. V. *Pañuelo.*
Fé, *sf.* 1. Faith, belief of the revealed truths of religion. 2. Confidence, trust. 3. Promise given. 4. Assertion, asseveration. 5. Certificate, testimony. *Fe de erratas,* List of the errors of the press. 6. Honour, social confidence. *Dar fe,* To attest, to certify. *Poseedor de buena fe,* A bona fide possessor; one who thinks he is the right owner, although he is not. *En fe,* Consequently. *De buena fe,* With truth and sincerity.
Fe (A') *ad.* In truth, in good earnest. *A' fe mia, ó por mi fe,* Upon my honour. *A' la buena fe,* With candour and sincerity, without malice. *En fe,* Consequently.
Fealdád, *sf.* 1. Ugliness, deformity; disproportion of the different parts which compose a whole. 2. (Met.) Turpitude, dishonesty; moral depravity.
Feaménte, *ad.* 1. In an ugly or deformed manner. 2. (Met.) Brutally, inordinately.
Feázo, za, *a.* Very ugly or deformed.
Febéo, bea, *a.* (Poét.) Relating to Phœbus.
Féble, *a.* 1. Weak, faint, feeble. 2. (Among Silversmiths) Deficient in point of weight or quality; applied to silver.
Féble, *sm.* 1. Frailty, foible; the weak or blind side. *Le dió por el feble,* He attacked or gained his weak side. 2. Light money or coin.
Febledád, *sf.* Debility, feebleness; weakness.
Febleménte, *ad.* Feebly.
Fébo, *sm.* (Poét.) Phœbus, the sun.
Febréra, *sf.* V. *Cacera.*
Febréro, *sm.* February, 2d month of the year.
Febricitánte, y Febrático, ca, *a.* V. *Calenturiento.*
Febrído, da, *a.* (Ant.) Shining, resplendent. V. *Bruñido.*
Febrifúgo, ga, *a.* Febrifuge.
Febríl, *a.* Febrile, constituting a fever; caused by a fever.
Fecál, *a.* Feculent, excrementitious.
Fécha, *sf.* Date of a letter or other writing. *Larga fecha,* Old date; great age. *De la cruz á la fecha,* From the beginning to the end.
Fechár, *va.* 1. To shut up, to lock up. V. *Cerrar.* 2. To date, to put the date to a letter or other writing.
Fécho, *sm.* 1. Action, fact, exploit. V. *Hecho y Hazaña.* 2. *Fecho de azúcar,* Chest of sugar, not containing more than twelve *arrobas,* or about three hundred weight. *Fiel de fechos,* Clerk who performs the functions of a notary in small villages.
Fécho, cha, *pp. irreg. ant.* of *Facer.* Used in legislative writings.

Fechoría ó Fechuría, *sf.* Action, fact, deed, exploit; commonly used in a bad sense.
Fechúra, *sf.* Form, structure. V. *Hechura.*
Feculénto, ta, *a.* Feculent, foul, dreggy.
Fecundaménte, *ad.* Fertilely, fruitfully.
Fecundár, *va.* To fertilize, to make fruitful.
Fecundidád, *sf.* Fecundity, fertility.
Fecundizár, *va.* To fecundate, to fertilize.
Fecúndo, da, *a.* Fecund, fruitful, fertile.
Federatívo, va, *a.* Federative.
Feéza, *sf.* Ugliness, deformity.
Feiúgo, ga, (Ar.) V. *Aspero.*
Feiugéz, *sf.* (Ar.) V. *Pesadez.*
Feléndrio, *sm.* (Bot.) Water-hemlock. Cicuta aquatica *L.*
Felibóte, *sm.* (Naút.) Fly-boat, a large flat bottomed Dutch vessel with a high stern and broad end.
Felicidád, *sf.* Felicity, happiness, success.
Felicitár, *va.* 1. To make happy. 2. To congratulate, to compliment upon any happy event.
Felicitación, *sf.* Congratulation, the act of professing joy for the happiness or success of another.
Feligrés, sa, *s.* 1. Parishioner, one who belongs to a certain determinate parish. 2. (Met.) A constant visitant at a house.
Feligresía, *sf.* District of a parish, and the body of inhabitants belonging to the same.
Felíz, *a.* Happy, fortunate, lucky, prosperous.
Felizménte, *ad.* Happily, fortunately.
Felódrio, *sf.* (Bot.) Evergreen-oak. Quercus ilex *L.*
Felonía, *sf.* Treachery, disloyalty, deceit, felony.
Félpa, *sf.* 1. Plush, a strong silk stuff. 2. (In the Jocular Style) A good drubbing.
Felpádo, da, y Felpúdo, da, *a.* V. *Afelpado.*
Felpílla, *sf.* Corded silk for embroidering.
Femenil, *a.* Feminine, effeminate.
Femenilménte, *ad.* Effeminately.
Femeníno, na, *a.* Feminine.
Fementidaménte, *ad.* Falsely, fallaciously.
Fementído, da, *a.* False, unfaithful, deficient in the performance of one's promise.—*s.* Liar.
Feméneo, nea, *a.* Feminine.
Feminál y Femeníl, *a.* (Ant.) Feminine.
Fendér, *va.* (Ant.) V. *Hender.*
Fendiénte, *sm.* Gash, a deep cut or wound.
Fenecér, *vn.* 1. To terminate, to be at an end. 2. To degenerate, to decline. 3. To die.—*va.* To finish, to conclude, to close.
Fenecimiénto, *sm.* 1. Close, finish, termination, end. 2. Settling of an account.
Fenedál, *sm.* Hay-loft, where hay is kept for fodder.
Fengír, *va.* (Ant.) V. *Fingir.*
Feniégno, na, *a.* Having the nature of hay.
Fenix, *sm.* 1. Phœnix, a fabulous bird. 2. (Met.) Exquisite, unique.
Fenogréco, *sm.* (Bot.) Fenugreek. Trigonella fœnum græcum *L.*
Fenómeno, *sm.* Phenomenon, an appellation given to any thing in nature which strikes by a new appearance.
Féo, ea, *a.* 1. Ugly, deformed, disproportionate. 2. Immodest, dishonest.
Fer, *va.* (Ant.) V. *Hacer.*
Feracidád, *sf.* Feracity, fecundity, fruitfulness, fertility.
Ferál, *a.* 1. Gloomy, sad, mournful. 2. Cruel, blood-thirsty.
Feráz, *a.* 1. Fertile, fruitful. 2. Abundant, copious, plentiful.
Féretro, *sm.* Bier, coffin.
Féria, *sf.* 1. Any day of the week, excepting Saturday and Sunday. *Féria segunda, ó lunes,* Monday. 2. Fair, an annual or stated meeting of sellers and buyers. 3. Rest, repose. *Revolver la feria,* To disturb the course of business. *Ferias,* Fairings, presents given at a fair.
Feriádo, da, *a.* (For.) Applied to the day in which the tribunals are shut.
Feriál, *a.* 1. Belonging to fairs. 2. Relating to the days of the week.—*s.* (Ant.) Market, fair.
Feriánte, *sm.* One who trades at fairs.
Feriár, *va.* 1. To sell, to buy; to exchange one thing for another. 2. To give fairings, to make presents at a fair. 3. V. *Suspender.*
Feríno, na, *a.* Wild, savage, ferocious.
Ferír, *va.* (Ant.) V. *Herir y Aferir.*
Ferlín, *sm.* An ancient coin, now out of use.
Ferlingótos, *sm. pl.* Kind of paste so called.
Fermentacion, *sf.* Fermentation, motion of the intestine particles of mixed bodies.
Fermentár, *va.* 1. To ferment, to introduce leaven into bread or paste to make it rise. 2. To exalt or rarify by intestine motion of the parts.—*vn.* To ferment, to have the intestine parts put into motion.
Fermentatívo, va, *a.* Fermentative.
Ferménto, *sm.* 1. Ferment, that which causes intestine motion. 2. Intestine motion, tumult.
Fermosúra, *sf.* (Ant.) V. *Hermosura.*
Fernandína, *sf.* 1. Kind of linen. 2. Stuff made of silk and wool.
Ferocidád y Ferócia, *sf.* Ferocity, wildness.
Feróz, *a.* Ferocious, cruel, savage.
Ferozménte, *ad.* Ferociously.
Férra, *sf.* V. *Farra.*
Ferráda, *sf.* Iron club, used formerly as an offensive and defensive weapon.
Ferrádo, *sm.* 1. (Gal.) Measure for corn, which makes about the 4th part of a bushel. 2. (Gal.) Measure for land of twelve yards square.
Ferrár, *va.* To garnish with points of iron, to strengthen with iron-plates. V. *Herrár.*
Férreo, rea, *a.* 1. Ferreous, made of iron, containing iron. 2. (Met.) Hard; iron, applied to an age.
Ferrería, *sf.* Iron work. V. *Herrería.*
Ferreruélo, *sm.* A long cloak with a collar, but without a hood or cape.
Ferréte, *sm.* 1. Burnt copper or brass used to colour or stain glass. 2. Marking iron.
Ferreteádo, da, *a.* Garnished, fastened or marked with iron.
Ferreteár, *va.* To bind, fasten, or work with iron.
Ferrificárse, *vr.* To be converted into iron.
Ferrión ó Ferrióna, *s.* Expression or gesture indicative of anger or displeasure.
Férro, *sm.* (Naút.) Anchor.
Ferrón, *sm.* 1. Iron-manufacturer. 2. Ironmonger, one who deals in iron.
Ferropéa, *sf.* (Gal.) V. *Arropea.*
Ferrugíneo, nea, *a.* Ferruginous.
Ferrugiénto, ta, *a.* Belonging to or containing iron.
Ferruginóso, sa, *a.* Ferruginous, irony.
Fértil, *a.* Fertile, fruitful, copious, plentiful.
Fertilidád, *sf.* Fertility, copiousness, plenty.

Fertilizár, *va.* To fertilize, to make the land or soil fruitful by cultivation.
Férula, *sf.* 1. Ferula, an instrument with which boys are beaten on the hand in schools. 2. (Met.) A severe reprimand. 3. V. *Cañaheja.*
Feruláceo, ea, *a.* Like a ferula.
Ferventísimo, ma, y Ferviëntísimo, ma, *a. sup.* of *Ferviente.*
Fervído, da, *a.* Fervid, ardent.
Ferviénte, *a.* Fervent, ardent. V. *Fervoroso.*
Fervór, *sm.* 1. Fervour, violent heat; warmth. V. *Hervor.* 2. (Met.) Heat of mind, zeal.
Fervorcíllo, *sm.* A slight fervour or zeal of short duration.
Fervorizár, *va.* To heat, to inflame, to incite.
Fervorosaménte, *ad.* Fervently.
Fervoróso, sa, *a.* Fervent, ardent; active, officious.
Fescenínos, *sm. pl.* Obscene nuptial verses sung by the Romans.
Festejadór, ra, *s.* Feaster, courtier, entertainer.
Festejár y Festeár, *va.* 1. To entertain, to make much of. 2. To court, to woo, to make love.
Festéjo y Festéo, *sm.* 1. A civil or polite expression of joy for the happiness or success of another. 2. Courtship, solicitation of a woman to marriage.
Festéro, *sm.* Director of church music on festive occasions.
Festín, *sm.* Feast, festival.
Festinación, *sf.* Festination, haste, hurry.
Festivál, *a.* (Ant.) V. *Festivo.*
Festivaménte, *ad.* Festively.
Festividád, *sf.* 1. Festivity, rejoicing, gaiety, merry-making. 2. Solemn manner of celebrating some event or occurrence.
Festívo, va, *a.* 1. Festive, gay, merry. 2. Festival, pertaining to feasts. *Dia festivo*, Holiday.
Festón, *sm.* Garland, wreath of flowers; festoon.
Fétido, da, *a.* Fetid, stinking; having a small strong and offensive.
Féto, *sm.* Fœtus, child in the womb after it is perfectly formed.
Feudál, *a.* Feudal, belonging to a fief.
Feudalidád, *sf.* Quality and nature of a fief or feudal estate.
Feudár, *va.* V. *Enfudar.*
Feudatário, *sm.* Feudatory, one who holds not in chief but by some conditional tenure.
Feudísta, *sm.* Author who has written on fees or tenures by which lands are held of a superior lord.
Feúdo, *sm.* 1. Fief or fee, all lands or tenements held by any acknowledgment of a superior lord. 2. Tribute or rent paid to a feudal lord.
Fez, *sf.* (Ant.) V. *Hez.*
Fi, *sm.* (Ant.) V. *Hijo.*
Fiable, *a.* (Ant.) Trust-worthy.
Fiádo, *sm.* Security given for another; bail. *Al fiado*, Upon trust. *En fiado*, Upon bail.
Fiadór, ra, *s.* 1. One who trusts another and places confidence in him. 2. Surety, one who becomes security for another. 3. Kind of small lace. 4. Bolt or instrument with which any thing is bound or made fast. 5. Backside, where boys are chastised. 6. Dog of a musket-lock. 7. Crank or staple which supports a gutter. *Dar fiador*, To give a pledge for security.
Fiambrár, *va.* To fry meat, and leave it to cool for eating.

Fiámbre, *sm.* Dressed meat set to cool, that it may not be eaten hot.—*a.* 1. Cold; applied to meat. 2. Of a long standing. 3. Taken upon trust.
Fiambréra, *sf.* 1. Cold meat, roasted or boiled, which is kept in a larder. 2. Pannier or basket in which cold meat is carried into the country. 3. Stupid or foolish speech.
Fiambréro, *sm.* One who takes care of the larder, and cold meat preserved for use.
Fiánza, *sf.* 1. Caution; security given for the performance of one's promises and engagements. 2. Reversion. 3. Bond, security. *Fianza bancaria*, Bank-security given in Rome, to insure pensions charged on ecclesiastical works. *Dar fianza*, To give a pledge.
Fiár, *va.* 1. To bail, to give bail or security. 2. To trust, to sell upon trust. 3. To place confidence in another, to commit to another.—*vn.* To confide, to be sure of a thing. *Fiar el pecho*, (Met.) To unbosom.
Fíat, *sm.* 1. Consent, that something may be done. 2. Brief order or warrant of a judge or magistrate; fiat.
Fíbra, *sf.* Fibre, filament.
Fibróso, sa, *a.* Fibrous.
Fíbula, *sf.* Buckle, a link of metal with a tongue or catch to fasten one thing to another.
Ficción, *sf.* 1. Fiction, the act of feigning or inventing. 2. The thing feigned or invented. 3. Falsehood, lie. 4. Grimace, gesture. 5. Stratagem, artifice.
Fíco, *sm.* (Ict.) Whiting. Gadus merlangus *L.*
Fícha, *sf.* Small piece of ivory or bone for mounting a cane.
Ficticio, cia, *a.* Fictitious, fabulous.
Fícto, ta, *a.* Feigned, counterfeited. 2. Vain, useless, of no value.
Fidálgo, ga, *s.* V. *Hidalgo.*
Fidedígno, gna, *a.* Worthy of credit, deserving of belief.
Fideicomisário, *sm.* Trustee, one who holds any thing in trust for another.
Fideicomíso, *sm.* Trust, feoffment of any executor.
Fidelidád, *sf.* 1. Fidelity, honesty, veracity. 2. Fidelity, faithful adherence. 3. Punctuality in the execution or performance of any thing.
Fidelísimaménte, *ad. sup.* of *Fielmente.*
Fidelísimo, ma, *a. super.* of *Fiel.*
Fidéos, *sm. pl.* Paste composed like vermicelli, but made flat and curled in the form of narrow shavings of wood.
Fiébre, *sf.* Fever. V. *Calentura.*
Fiél, *a.* 1. Faithful, honest, loyal. 2. True, right.
Fiél, *sm.* 1. Clerk of the market, a person appointed in towns and cities to inspect weights and measures. *Fiel de romana*, Magistrate, who has the inspection of slaughter-houses and public shambles. 2. Needle of a balance. 3. Pivot of a steelyard. 4. Pin which keeps the two blades of scissors together. *Fiel de muelle*, Wharfinger, who has the direction or inspection of a wharf. 5. Catholic Christian who lives in obedience to the Romish church. 6. (And.) V. *Tercero.* *En fiel*, Equal weight, even balance.
Fielázgo, *sm.* The office of town-clerk, or clerk of the market.

Fieldád, *sf.* 1. Place and employment of the inspector of weights and measures, or of the clerk of the market. 2. Security, bail. 3. Fidelity, faithfulness. 4. Warrant expedited by the court of Exchequer for those who farm the public revenue.

Fielménte, *ad.* Faithfully.

Fieltrár, *va.* 1. To felt, to unite without weaving. 2. To stuff a saddle with short hair.

Fiéltro, *sm.* 1. Felt, cloth made of wool united without weaving. 2. Surtout, a large great [coat.

Fiémo, *sm.* Dung, manure.

Fiéra, *sf.* A wild beast.

Fierabrás, *sm.* Bully, bragger, blusterer.

Fieraménte, *ad.* Fiercely, savagely.

Fieréza, *sf.* 1. Fierceness, cruelty. 2. Deformity, ugliness.

Fiéro, ra, *a.* 1. Fierce, cruel, blood-thirsty. 2. Ugly, deformed. 3. Rough, rude. 4. Great, huge, enormous. 5. Furious, terrible; wild, savage.

Fiéros, *sm. pl.* Fierce threats and bravadoes.

Fiérra, *sf.* (Ant.) V. *Herradura.*

Fiérro, *sm.* Iron. V. *Hierro.* *Fiérros,* Irons with which prisoners are chained; imprisonment.

Fiésta, *sf.* 1. Feast, entertainment, rejoicing. 2. Church-feast, holiday; the day of some ecclesiastical festival. *Fiesta de consejo,* Working day of vacation in the tribunals. *Fiesta de guardar,* Day of obligation to hear mass. *Fiesta doble,* A double feast in the church; a ball and entertainment.—*pl.* 1. Holidays, vacations. *No estar para fiestas,* To be out of humour. *Fiestas reales,* Royal festivals. 2. *Fiestas de pólvora,* Artificial fire-works; (Met.) Any thing very quick, rapid, and of short duration. 3. (Met.) Money wasted or mispent in a very short time.

Figménto, *sm.* Image, utensil, or other thing, made of potter's clay.

Fígo, *sm.* Fig. V. *Higo.*

Figón, *sm.* Eating-house, chop-house.

Figonéro, *sm.* One who keeps an eating house.

Figuéra, *sf.* Fig-tree. V. *Higuera.*

Figuerál, *sm.* Plantation of fig-trees.

Figulíno, na, *a.* Made of potter's clay.

Figúra, *sf.* 1. Figure, the form of any thing as terminated by the outline. 2. Face, mien, countenance. 3. Statue, image; something formed in resemblance of something else. 4. (For.) Form, mode. 5. (Geom.) Figure, a space included in certain lines. *Figura de proa,* (Naút.) Head of a ship. *Hacer figura,* To make a distinguished appearance. *Hacer figuras,* To make grimaces. *Levantar figura,* To assume an air of importance.—*sm.* A foolish person assuming an air of importance and dignity.—*s. com.* Person of a mean or ridiculous appearance.—*sf. pl.* 1. Characters represented on the stage. 2. Modes of speaking in which words are distorted from their literal and primitive sense. 3. Musical notes. 4. (In Games at Cards) King, queen, and knave.

Figurábl, *a.* That which may be figured.

Figuradaménte, *ad.* Figuratively.

Figuráda, *sf.* An antic posture, a gesture of affected gravity or importance.

Figurádo, da, *a.* Figurative, typical; not literal; rhetorical.

Figurál, *a.* Belonging to figures; represented by delineation.

Figuránza, *sf.* Resemblance.

Figurár, *va.* 1. To figure, to form into any determinate shape. 2. To adorn with figures. —*vr.* To image in the mind, to conceive.

Figurativaménte, *ad.* Figuratively.

Figuratívo, va, *a.* Figurative, typical; not literal.

Figurería, *sf.* V. *Mueca.*

Figuréro, *sm.* Mimic, a ludicrous imitator; a buffoon who copies another's actions.

Figurílla, *s. com.* A ridiculous little figure.

Figurón, *sm.* 1. A huge or enormous figure of a ridiculous appearance. 2. A low-bred person assuming an air of dignity and importance

Fijodálgo, *sm.* V. *Hijodalgo.*

Fíl, *sm.* 1. Needle of a balance, beam of a steelyard. 2. Equipoise, equality of weight, equilibration. 3. *Fil de roda,* (Naút.) Right ahead. *Estar en fil ó en un fil,* To be in line, to be equal.

Fíla, *sf.* 1. A long row or series of persons or things. 2. A line of soldiers ranged one behind another. *En fila,* In a line, in a row.

Filácica, *sf.* (Naút.) Rope-yarn. V. *Filástica,*

Filactéria, *sf.* Phylactery.

Filadién, *sm.* (Naút.) A small boat used on the river Garonne in France.

Filadíz ó Filáro, *s.* 1. Ferret-silk, spun from the cone. 2. Filament, fibre.

Filaménto, *sm.* Filament.

Filamentóso, sa, *a.* Filamentous, consisting of filaments. [tory.

Filamiénto, *sm.* Spinning part of a manufac-

Filándrias, *sf. pl.* Worms bred in the intestines of birds and fowls.

Filantropía, *sf.* Philanthropy, love of mankind; good-nature.

Filántropos, *sm.* (Bot.) Cleavers, common goose-grass. Galium aparine *L.*

Filár, *a.* Threaden, made of thread. *Triangulo filar,* A mathematical instrument serving as a sector, for various uses.—*va.* V. *Hilar.*

Filaréte, *sm.* (Naút.) Netting, put on the waist or sides of a ship.

Filástica, *sf.* (Naút.) Rope-yarn, yarn made of ropes untwisted. *Filástica fina para maniobras,* Fine rope-yarn for running rigging.

Filatería, *sf.* Verbosity, exuberance or superfluity of words to express an idea.

Filatéro, *sm.* A verbose speaker.

Filáucia, *sf.* Self-love, vicious fondness for one's self.

Filderretór, *sm.* Sort of superfine camblet.

Filelí, *sm.* A very thin woollen stuff; superfine flannel.

Filéno, na, *a.* Delicate, effeminate, soft.

Filéra, *sf.* Row, line. V. *Hilera.*

Filéte, *sm.* 1. (Arq.) Fillet, a small member which appears in ornaments and mouldings, otherwise called *listel.* 2. Hem, the edge of a garment doubled and sewed to keep the threads from spreading. 3. A thin and small spit for roasting. 4. Welt of a shoe. 5. A twist-like ornament raised on plate. *Gastar muchos filetes,* To talk very sprucely.

Fileteár, *va.* To adorn with fillets.

Filetón, *sm.* 1. (In Architecture) A large fillet or listel. 2. Kind of embroidery.

Filiación, *sf.* 1. Filiation, the relation of a son to a father. 2. Relation of a community to a superior lord. 3. (Mil.) Regimental register of a soldier's height and physiognomy.

Filiál, *a.* Filial, pertaining to a son, befitting a son.

Filiár, *vn.* To prove one's descent.—*va.* To enrol a soldier.

Filibóte, *sm.* Fly-boat, a light vessel of 100 tons burthen.

Filicída, *sm.* Murderer of one's own son.

Filigrána, *sf.* 1. Filigree, a kind of fine work made of gold and silver threads. 2. (Met.) Any thing neatly wrought.

Fililí, *sm.* Fineness, neatness, delicacy.

Filipéndula, *sf.* (Bot.) Water dropwort. Œnanthe fistulosa *L.*

Filipichín, *sm.* Kind of stamped woollen cloth.

Filiréa, *sf.* (Bot.) Mock-privet. Phillyrea *L.*

Fílis, *sf.* 1. Grace, a graceful manner of doing or saying any thing. 2. Gewgaw made of clay.

Filistéo, tea, *a.* Gigantic, bulky, enormous.

Fíllo, *sm.* (Gal.) Son. V. *Hijo. Filloa*, Sort of fritters.

Fílo, *sm.* 1. Thread. V. *Hilo.* 2. Equipoise, equilibration. 3. Edge of a sword, or any other cutting or thrusting instrument. *Filo rabioso*, Wire edge. *Darse un filo á la lengua*, To murmur, to detract. *Embotar los filos*, (Met.) To abate one's ardour or energy.

Filodóxo, *sm.* Person wedded to his own opinion.

Filología y Filológica, *sf.* Philology.

Filológico, ca, *a.* Philological.

Filólogo, *sm.* Philologer, one whose chief study is language; one who is akilful in languages, a linguist.

Filoména, *sf.* Nightingale. Motacilla luscina *L.*

Filomostérra, *sf.* (Bot.) Fumitory. Fumaria *L.*

Filónio, *sm.* Kind of opiate.

Filópos, *sm. pl.* Pieces of linen made use of to drive game into a place assigned for that purpose.

Filoséda, *sf.* Silk and worsted cloth.

Filosofadór, ra, *s.* Philosopher.

Filosofánte, *sm.* (Satir.) Philosophaster.

Filosofár, *va.* 1. To philosophise, to examine into any thing as a philosopher. 2. To play the philosopher, to assume the critic.

Filosofástro, *sm.* A pretended philosopher, a smatterer in philosophy, philosophaster.

Filosofía, *sf.* 1. Philosophy, a science which treats of the essence, properties, and affections of natural things and beings. 2. System of opinions on the nature and qualities of natural substances.

Filosoficaménte, *ad.* Philosophically.

Filosófico, ca, Filósofo, fa, *a.* Philosophical.

Filosofísmo, *sm.* (Satir.) Philosophism, sophistry.

Filosofísta, *sm.* (Sat.) Philosophist, sophist.

Filósofo, *sm.* Philosopher.

Filotímia, *sf.* A moderate desire of honour.

Filtración, *sf.* Filtration, the act of separating the terrestrious parts from liquors.

Filtrár, *va.* To filter, to filtrate, to defecate, to separate the terrestrious parts from liquors.

Fíltro, *sm.* 1. Filter, a piece of cloth, linen, or paper, through which liquors are filtered or strained. 2. Philter, a potion to cause love.

Fímbria, *sf.* Edge or lower part of any garment doubled in.

Fímo, *sm.* Human excrement.

Fín, *sm.* 1. End, close, termination. 2. Limit, boundary. 3. End, object, purpose. *Al fin*, At last, at length. *En fin ó por fin*, Finally, lastly.

Finádo, da, *a.* Dead, deceased. *Dia de los finados*, All Souls' day.—*s.* Person dead.

Finál, *a.* Final, ultimate, conclusive.

Finál, *sm.* End, termination, conclusion. *Por finál*, In fine, ultimately, lastly.

Finalizár, *va.* To finish, to conclude.—*vn.* To be finished or brought to a conclusion.

Finalménte, *ad.* Finally.

Finaménte, *ad.* Finely, nicely, delicately.

Finamiénto, *sm.* Death, decease.

Finár, *vn.* To die.—*vr.* To long for, to wish for with anxious eagerness.

Fínca, *sf.* 1. Security, mortgage. 2. A threatening or menacing attitude.

Fincáble, *a.* Existing, having actual existence.

Fincár, *vn.* y *a.* V. *Quedar* y *Hincar.*

Finéza, *sf.* 1. Fineness, goodness, purity, perfection. 2. Expression of friendship or love. 3. Delicacy, beauty. 4. Friendly activity and zeal. 5. A small, friendly gift.

Fingidaménte, *ad.* Feignedly.

Fingído, da, *a.* Feigned, dissembled.

Fingidór, *sm.* Dissembler, simulator.

Fingimiénto, *sm.* Simulation, deceit, false appearance.

Fingír, *va.* 1. To feign, to dissemble. 2. To fancy, to imagine what does not really exist.

Finíble, *a.* Capable of being finished.

Finiéstra, *sf.* (Ant.) Window. V. *Ventana.*

Finiquíto, *sm.* 1. Close of an account. 2. Final receipt or discharge.

Finír, *vn.* V. *Acabar.*

Finísimo, ma, *a. sup.* Very fine, extremely neat.

Finítimo, ma, *a.* Bordering, contiguous, near.

Finíto, ta, *a.* Finite, limited, bounded.

Fíno, na, *a.* 1. Fine, perfect, pure. 2. Delicate, nice. 3. Excellent, eminent in any good quality. 4. Affectionate, true. 5. Acute, sagacious, cunning.

Fínta, *sf.* Tax paid to government; deception.

Finúra, *sf.* Fineness, purity, delicacy.

Fío, *sm.* Son. V. *Hijo.*

Fíque, *sm.* A filaceous substance, resembling hemp, made of the leaves of the *Maguey-tree.* Agave americana *L.*

Fírma, *sf.* 1. Sign-manual, signature, subscription. 2. Exemption from attending the school, signed by the master. 3. Collar or neckband of a shirt. 4. (For.) Order or rescript of a tribunal for keeping possession.

Firmamiénto, *sm.* 1. Firmament, sky. 2. Prop, support.

Firmánte, *pa.* Supporter, subscriber.

Firmár, *va.* 1. To sign, to subscribe. 2. To affirm, to attest.—*vr.* To style one's self, to assume an appellation or title.

Fírme, *a.* Firm, stable, strong, secure.

Firmedúmbre, *sf.* (Ant.) Firmness.
Firmeménte, *ad.* Firmly.
Firméza, *sf.* 1. Firmness, stability. 2. Gold or silver clasp; ornament made of a precious stone in a triangular form.
Fiscál, *sm.* 1. Attorney-general, an officer of state who defends the king's civil rights, and prosecutes criminals in his name. *Fiscal civil ó de lo civil,* Chancellor of the exchequer. 2. (Met.) Informer, one who denounces offenders to the magistrates.
Fiscál, *a.* Belonging to the exchequer or public revenue of the state.
Fiscalía, *sf.* Office and business of a fiscal.
Fiscalidád, *sf.* State of the exchequer.
Fiscalizár y Fiscaleár, *va.* To accuse of a criminal offence. *Fiscalear,* (Joc.) To become public accuser.
Fisco, *sm.* Fisc, fiscal, exchequer.
Fisétre, *sm.* (Ict.) The small blunt-headed whale, or cachalot. Physeter catodon *L.*
Fisga, *sf.* 1. Harpoon with three hooks for catching fish. 2. (Met.) Raillery, jest, scoff. 3. (Ant.) Wheat of the finest quality; bread of spelt-wheat.
Fisgadór, ra, *s.* Harpooner; one who burlesques.
Fisgár, *va.* 1. To mock, to scoff, to jeer. 2. To fish with a harpoon.
Fisgón, na, *sm.* y *f.* Punster, buffoon.
Física, *sf.* Physics, the science of the natural constitution of things.
Fisicaménte, *ad.* Physically, corporally, really.
Físico, ca, *a.* 1. Physical, relating to nature or natural philosophy. 2. Natural, really existing.
Físico, *sm.* Naturalist, a student of physics; professor of physics or of medicine.
Fisil, *a.* Brittle, easily broken.
Fisonomía, *sf.* 1. Physiognomy, lineaments, features; cast of the look. 2. Physiognomy, the art of discovering the temper and talents by the features of the face.
Fisonómico, ca, *a.* Physiognomical.
Fisonomista y Fisónomo, *sm.* Physiognomist, one who judges of the temper and talents by the features of the face.
Fistigo, *sm.* (Bot.) Fistic-nut or pistachio-tree. Pistacia vera *L.*
Fistól, *sm.* A crafty cunning person; applied especially to gamblers.
Fístola, *sf.* 1. Fistula, a sinuous ulcer callous within. 2. Pipe kept in a fistula, while it runs.
Fístula, *sf.* 1. Pipe or conduit through which water runs. 2. Musical wind-instrument, resembling a flute or flagelet, commonly made of reed. 3. (Cir.) Fistula.
Fistulóso, sa, *a.* Fistulous, having the nature and properties of a fistula.
Fisúra, *sf.* Fissure, a longitudinal fracture of a bone.
Fitéte, *sm.* A sort of cake.
Fito, *sm.* V. *Hito ó Mojon.*
Fitonisa, *sf.* V. *Pitonisa.*
Fiúcia, *sf.* (Ant.) V. *Confianza.*
Fixa, *sf.* Kind of hinge, bat-hinge.
Fixación, *sf.* 1. Fixation, stability, firmness. 2. The act of posting up printed bills, edicts, &c. 3. Fixation, the act of fixing mercury or any other volatile spirit.
Fixaménte, *ad.* 1. Firmly, assuredly. 2. Intensely, attentively.
Fixár, *va.* 1. To fix, to fasten. 2. To establish, to settle. 3. To fix volatile spirits or salts; to deprive of volatility.—*vr.* To fix or settle itself in a place, as a pain; to determine, to resolve. *Fixar las plantas,* (Met.) To confirm one's self in an opinion or idea.
Fixénes, *sm. pl.* Cheeks of a press.
Fixéza, *sf.* Firmness, stability.
Fixo, xa, *a.* 1. Fixed, firm, secure. 2. Settled, permanent.
Flacaménte, *ad.* Languidly, weakly.
Fláco, ca, *a.* 1. Lank, lean, meagre. 2. Dejected, low-spirited. 3. Frail, weak of resolution, liable to error or seduction. *Flaco de memoria,* Weak or short of memory. *Hacer un flaco servicio,* To do or serve an ill turn.
Flacúra, *sf.* Meagreness, leanness, weakness.
Flagelación, *sf.* Flagellation, the act of inflicting a chastisement or correction.
Flagelánte, *sm.* Flagellant.
Flagélo, *sm.* Lash, scourge, chastisement.
Flagício, *sm.* Flagitiousness, wickedness; an enormous crime.
Flagicióso, sa, *a.* Flagitious, wicked.
Flagránte, *pa.* Flagrant, resplendent.
Flagrár, *vn.* To burn, to glow, to flame.
Fláma, *sf.* Flame, excessive ardour. V. *Llama.*
Flamánte, *a.* 1. Flaming, bright, resplendent. 2. Quite new, spick and span.
Flameár, *vn.* (Naút.) To shiver; applied to the sails.
Flaménco, *sm.* (Orn.) Flamant or flamingo. Phœnicopterus ruber *L.*
Flamenquílla, *sf.* Dish of a middling size.
Flámeo, *sm.* A kind of yellow veil, with which formerly the face of a bride was covered during the ceremony of marriage.
Flamígero, ra, *a.* (Poét.) Flammiferous, emitting flames.
Flámula, *sf.* (Bot.) Sweet-scented virgin's bower. Clematis flammula *L.* *Flámulas,* (Naút.) Streamers hoisted at the top-mast-head.
Flánco, *sm.* 1. (Fort.) Flank, the part of a bastion which reaches from the curtain to the face. 2. (Mil.) Flank of an army. 3. (Naút.) Side of a ship.
Flándes, *sm.* *Es un flandes,* It is a most valuable thing.
Flanéla, *sf.* Flannel, a fine woollen stuff.
Flanqueár, *va.* (Fort.) To flank or flanker; to defend by lateral or parallel fortifications.
Flaón, *sm.* 1. Custard, a kind of sweetmeat, made by boiling milk with eggs and sugar. 2. Piece of gold or silver ready to be coined.
Flaqueár, *vn.* 1. To flag, to grow feeble, to lose vigour. 2. To grow spiritless or dejected, to be disheartened. 3. To slacken in the zeal and ardour with which an enterprise was commenced.
Flaquecér, *vn.* V. *Enflaquecer.*
Flaquéza, *sf.* 1. Leanness, extenuation of the body, want of flesh, meagreness. 2. Weakness, frailty. 3. Importunity, molestation.
Flaquíllo, lla; to, ta, *a. dim.* of *Flaco.*
Flásco, *sm.* Flask. V. *Frasco.*
Fláto, *sm.* 1. Blast or gust of wind. 2. Flatus, wind gathered in any cavity of the body.
Flatóso ó Flatuóso, sa, *a.* Flatuous, windy; full of wind.

Flatulénto, ta, *a.* Flatulent, turgid with air, windy.

Fláuta, *sf.* 1. (Naút.) A Dutch flight, a kind of three-masted ship. 2. Flute, a musical wind instrument. 3. Pipe of an organ.

Flautádo, da, *a.* Resembling a flute.

Flautádo, *sm.* Stop in an organ, which produces the sound of a flute.

Flautéro, *sm.* 1. One who makes flutes. 2. Player on the flute.

Flautíllo, *sm.* V. *Caramillo.*

Flautísta, *sm.* Player of the flute.

Fláutos, *sm. pl.* (Joc.) Pastimes, idle diversions.

Flávo, va, *a.* Of a fallow or honey colour.

Flébil, *a.* Mournful, deplorable, lamentable.

Flebotomía, *sf.* Phlebotomy, the act or practice of blood-letting, or opening a vein for medical purposes

Flebotomiáno, *sm.* One whose profession is to bleed or let blood for medical purposes.

Flebotomizár, *va.* To bleed, to let blood.

Flécha, *sf.* 1. Arrow, a pointed weapon shot from a bow; dart. 2. Any thing which stings or causes an unpleasant sensation.

Flechadór, *sm.* Archer, he who shoots with a bow and arrow. [*chastes.*

Flechadúras, *sf. pl.* (Naút.) Ratlings. V. *Fle-*

Flechár, *va.* 1. To dart, to threw or dart an arrow or dart. 2. To wound or kill with a bow and arrow. 3. (Met.) To insult with foul language, to impeach one's character and honour. —*vn.* To have a bow drawn ready to shoot.

Flechástes, *sm. pl.* (Naút.) Ratlings, or ratlines, small lines which traverse horizontally the shrouds of a ship.

Flecházo, *sm.* Blow or stroke given with a dart or arrow.

Flechería, *sf.* Body or party of archers and bowmen.

Flechéro, *sm.* Archer, bow-man; bow-maker.

Fléco, *sm.* Flock, small locks of wool, cotton, &c.

Flégma, *sf.* Phlegm. V. *Flema.*

Flegmático, ca, *a.* Phlegmatic.

Flegmón, *sm.* Phlegmon, a hot tumour.

Fléma, *sf.* 1. Phlegm, watery humour of the body. 2. Dulness, sluggishness.

Flemático, ca, *a.* 1. Phlegmatic, generating phlegm; abounding in phlegm. 2. Dull, cold, sluggish. [cattle.

Fléme, *sf.* Fleam, an instrument used to bleed

Flemón, *sm.* 1. Phlegm, thick spittle or humour ejected from the mouth. 2. Phlegmon, a hard tumid inflammation in the mouth or gums. 3. Great sluggishness.

Flemóso, sa, *a.* Pituitous, consisting of phlegm.

Flemúdo, da, *a.* (Mur.) Dull, sluggish, cold, frigid.

Flequezuélo y Flequíllo, to, *sm.* A little fringe, a small ornamental appendage of dress or furniture; a little flock.

Flet ó Fles, *sm.* (Ict.) Halibut. Pleuronectes hippoglossus *L.*

Fletadór, *sm.* Freighter of a ship.

Fletaménto y Fletamiénto, *sm.* Freightment, the act of freighting a ship.

Fletár, *va.* 1. To freight a ship, to load her with goods to be carried from one port to another. 2. To foliate a looking-glass; to put on a foil of tin and mercury.

Fléte, *sm.* Freight, money paid to the owner of a ship for the transportation of goods.

Flexibilidád, *sf.* 1. Flexibility, pliableness, ductility. 2. Obsequiousness, mildness of temper.

Flexíble, *a.* 1. Flexible, ductile. 2. Docile.

Flexión, *sf.* Flexion, flexure.

Fléxo, *sm.* Movement of the lips in the pronunciation of words. [vessel.

Flibóte, *sm.* Fly-boat, a small fast-sailing

Flín, *sm.* Stone used for edging and polishing steel; a kind of emery.

Flinflón, *sm.* A fresh-coloured corpulent man.

Flocadúra, *sf.* Fringe, an ornament of dress.

Flóña, *sf.* (Mur.) Futility, triflingness.

Floqueádo, da, *a.* Fringed.

Floquecíllo, *sm.* A small fringe.

Flór, *sf.* 1. Flower, that part of a plant which contains the seeds. 2. The most excellent or valuable part of any thing. 3. Cuticle or thin skin formed on the surface of liquors. 4. The most supple part of minerals. 5. Virginity; catamenia. 6. Grain, the outside of tanned leather. 7. Trick or artifice among gamesters or gamblers. 8. Flowers or beauties of polite literature. *Flor de la harina,* Superfine flour. *A' flor de agua,* (Naút.) Between wind and water. *A' la flor del agua,* Even with the surface of the water. *Flor de viento,* (Naút.) Direction of a gale of wind; point of the compass. 9. *Flores de mano,* Artificial flowers. *En flor,* In a state of infancy, imperfect. *Andarse en flores,* To decline entering into a debate. *Tener por flor,* To acquire a habit or custom, generally of a bad kind.

Floráda, *sf.* (Ar.) The season of flowers, with bee-masters. [Flora.

Floráles, *a. pl.* Floral; feasts in honour of

Flordelisádo, da, *a.* Adorned with flower-de-luce.

Floreádo, da, *a.* 1. Flowered. 2. The finest flour or meal. *Pan floreado,* Bread made of the finest flour.

Floreár, *va.* 1. To adorn or garnish with flowers. 2. To bolt, to sift; to separate the finest flour by means of a sieve. *Florear el naype,* Not to play fair, to cheat at play.

Florecér, *vn.* 1. To bloom, to blossom. 2. To thrive, to prosper. 3. To flourish in any age. —*vr.* To mould, to become mouldy.

Floreciénte, *pa.* Flourishing.

Florecílla ó Florecíta, *sf.* A small flower.

Florentína, *sf.* A silk stuff, first manufactured at Florence.

Floréo, *sm.* 1. Flourish made by fencers before they engage, or on the guitar. 2. A luxuriant redundancy of useless words. 3. Cross caper, a movement made in dancing. 4. Idle pastime.

Floréro, *sm.* 1. Flower-pot. 2. One who makes or deals in artificial flowers. 3. Painting representing flowers. 4. Case destined for artificial flowers. 5. One who makes use of florid empty language.

Florescéncia, *sf.* (Bot.) Inflorescence, the time and manner of plants flowering.

Floresta, *sf.* 1. Forest, shrubbery, thicket. 2. A fine delightful place. 3. Collection of fine things pleasing to the taste; beauties.

Florestéro, *sm.* Forester, keeper of a forest.

FLORÉTA, *sf.* 1. Border or selvage of Morocco leather put on the edge of a girt. 2. A peculiar movement or flourish in dancing. 3. A small or little flower.

FLORETÁDA, *sf.* Slap on the face.

FLORÉTE, *sm.* Foil, a blunt sword used to learn to fence.

FLORÉTE, *a.* Very white and fine; applied to paper.

FLORETEÁR, *va.* To garnish or adorn with flowers.

FLORIDAMÉNTE, *ad.* Elegantly.

FLORÍDO, DA, *a.* 1. Florid, flowery; full of flowers. 2. Choice, elegant, select, excellent. 3. Clear, cheerful; applied to the weather. *Dia florido*, A clear cheerful day. *Dinero florido*, Money which has been easily earned.

FLORÍFERO, RA, *a.* Floriferous, bearing flowers.

FLORILÉGIO, *sm.* Florilegium, anthology, select writings.

FLORÍN, *sm.* Florin, a silver coin current in several parts of Germany, and other countries.

FLORIPÓNDIO, *sm.* 1. (Bot.) Floripondium, a fragrant plant of the West Indies. 2. Large flowers on cloth of a bad taste.

FLORÍSTA, *sm.* Florist, a cultivator of flowers.

FLORLISÁDO, DA, *a.* V. *Flordelisado.*

FLORÓN, *sm.* Ornament resembling a large flower.

FLORÓNCOS, *sm. pl.* (In the Jocular Style) Horns.

FLÓTA, *sf.* 1. (Naút.) Fleet of merchant ships which sail in company. 2. (Met.) Multitude, great number.

FLOTADÚRA Y FLÓTE, *s.* The act of stroking or rubbing gently with the hand.

FLOTAMIÉNTO, *sm.* Stroking, gentle friction.

FLOTÁR, *vn.* To float, to swim on the surface of the water.—*va.* To stroke, to rub gently.

FLOTÍLLA, *sf. dim.* Small fleet.

FLOXAMÉNTE, *ad.* Slowly, carelessly.

FLOXEÁR, *vn.* To slacken, to grow weak. V. *Flaquear.*

FLOXEDÁD, *sf.* 1. Weakness, feebleness, laxity. 2. (Met.) Sloth, laziness, negligence.

FLOXÉL, *sm.* 1. Wool shorn from cloth by the shearer. 2. Down, soft feathers.

FLOXÉRA, *sf.* Weakness. V. *Floxedad.*

FLÓXO, XA, *a.* 1. Feeble, lax, weak, flaccid; soft; slack. *Vino floxo*, Flaggy insipid wine. *Seda floxa*, Soft untwisted silk. 2. Lazy, slothful, negligent.

FLUCTUACIÓN, *sf.* 1. Fluctuation, the alternate motion of the waves. 2. Uncertainty, indetermination, irresolution.

FLUCTUÁNTE, *pa.* Fluctuating.

FLUCTUÁR, *vn.* 1. To fluctuate, to float backwards and forwards. 2. To be in danger of being lost or destroyed. 3. To hesitate, to be irresolute, to vacillate. 4. To be in an uncertain state.

FLUCTUÓSO, SA, *a.* Fluctuant, wavering.

FLUÉCO, *sm.* Fringe, an ornamental appendage added to dress or furniture; flock. V. *Fleco.* *Fluecos*, Kind of net-work put over horses to drive away the flies; flocks.

FLUÉNTE, *pa.* Fluent, flowing.

FLUEQUECÍLLO, *sm.* A small fringe.

FLUIDÉZ, *sf.* Fluidity, the quality of being liquid.

FLÚIDO, DA, *a.* 1. Fluid, not solid. 2. (Met.) Fluent; applied to style.

FLUÍR, *vn.* 1. To flow, to run or spread as water. 2. To be in constant motion; applied to other things not liquid.

FLUSLÉRA, *sf.* Latten. V. *Fruslera.*

FLUVIÁL, *a.* Fluviatic.

FLUX, *sm.* 1. Flush, a run of cards of the same suit. *Hacer flux*, To spend one's whole fortune without paying any debt. 2. (Quim.) Flux, any matter mixed with ores or minerals to facilitate their fusion.

FLUXIBILIDÁD, *sf.* Fluidity, fluency, liquidity.

FLUXÍBLE, *a.* Fluid, liquid.

FLUXIÓN, *sf.* 1. Fluxion, the act of flowing. 2. The matter which flows.

FLÚXO, *sm.* Flux, the course or motion of liquid things. *Fluxo de palabras*, Flow of words. *Fluxo de risa*, Fit of laughter. *Fluxo de reir*, Habit of laughing.

FÓCA, *sf.* Sea-calf.

FOCÍNO, *sm.* Kind of goad used by keepers of elephants.

FÓCO, *sm.* 1. Focus, the point of convergence and concourse in a glass. 2. (Naút.) Foresail, jib. 3. Flash of fire-arms. 4. Hole bored in a piece of timber, to drive another into it.

FÓFO, FA, *a.* Spongy, soft, bland.

FOGÁDA, *sf.* Fougade, a small mine dug under some work, especially of field-fortification.

FOGÁGE, *sm.* Hearth-money, a tax formerly laid on houses in Spain.

FOGÁR, *sm.* V. *Hogar.*

FOGÁTA, *sf.* 1. Blaze, the light of a flame. 2. Heat occasioned by the fumes of wine.

FOGÓN, *sm.* 1. Hearth, the place on or in which fire is made. 2. Vent or touch-hole of a gun. 3. (Naút.) Caboose, a portable kitchen on board of ships, made of timber, lined with iron or tin-plates. 4. (Naút.) Galley, cook-room; the kitchen on board of ships of war.

FOGONADÚRAS, *sf. pl.* (Naút.) Partners, strong pieces of timber nailed round the scuttles or holes, into which the masts are put.

FOGONÁZO, *sm.* Flame of the priming of a gun.

FOGOSIDÁD, *sf.* Excessive vivacity or liveliness.

FOGÓSO, SA, *a.* 1. Fiery, ardent, burning. 2. Impetuous, lively, choleric.

FOGÓTE, *sm.* A live coal, fagot, match.

FOGUEACIÓN, *sf.* Enumeration of hearths or fires.

FOGUEÁR, *va.* 1. To foment, to inflame. 2. To fire or discharge a gun.

FOGUÉRA, *sf.* V. *Hoguera.*

FÓJA, *sf.* 1. Leaf. V. *Hoja.* 2. (Orn.) Coot, or common coot. Fulica atra *L.*

FÓLGA, *sf.* (Bax.) Amusement, pastime. V. *Huelga.*

FOLGÁNZA, *sf.* V. *Holgura.*

FÓLGO, *sm.* Bag made of skin to cover and protect the feet and legs when sitting.

FOLÍA, *sf.* (Ant.) Folly, madness. *Folías*, Kind of merry Portuguese and Spanish dance with castanets.

FOLIATÚRA, *sf.* State of being in leaves.

FOLIÁR, *va.* To number the leaves of a book.

FOLÍCULO, *sm.* 1. Follicle or seed-vessel of plants. 2. (Ant.) Membranous sac from which an excretory duct originates.

FOLIJÓNES, *sm. pl.* Castilian dance to the guitar and castanets.

FÓLIO, *sm.* 1. Folio, leaf of a book or manuscript. 2. (Bot.) Phyllon, knot-grass. Malabathrum

L. De à folio, Jocularly applied to any thing too bulky. *Al primer folio*, At first sight.
Fólla, *sf.* 1. An irregular conflict in a tournament. 2. Medley of a variety of things confusedly jumbled together.
Folládas, *sm. pl.* Sort of hollow paste.
Folládos, *sm. pl.* Ancient kind of trousers.
Folláge, *sm.* 1. Foliage, tuft of leaves. 2. Gaudy ornament of trifling value.
Follár, *va.* 1. To blow with bellows. V. *Afollar*. 2. To mould or form in leaves.—*vr.* To discharge wind without noise.
Folléro ó Folletéro, *sm.* One who makes or sells bellows.
Folléta, *sf.* Wine measure nearly equal to an English pint.
Folléto, *sm.* 1. (Mur.) Pack of cards wrapped up in a sheet of paper. 2. A small manuscript newspaper.
Follón, na, *a.* Feeble, inert, lazy, negligent.
Follón, *sm.* 1. Rogue, villain, an idle fellow. 2. Rocket which discharges without noise. 3. Bud or branch springing from the root or trunk of a tree. 4. Breaking wind without noise.
Follonería, *sf.* Idleness, laziness, carelessness.
Follonía, *sf.* (Ant.) Vanity, presumption.
Folúz, *sm.* The third part of a *blanca*, a small coin.
Fomentación, *sf.* Fomentation or steeping for producing heat or warmth in the body.
Fomentadór, *sm.* Fomenter.
Fomentár, *va.* 1. To foment, to produce warmth or heat in the body by fomentation or warm baths. 2. (Met.) To protect, to favour, to patronise.
Foménto, *sm.* 1. Fomentation. 2. Fuel, 3. Patronage, protection, support.
Fómes, *sm.* Incentive, that which excites or invites to action.
Fómite, *sm.* Motive, stimulus to an action.
Fónas, *sf. pl.* Pieces sewed to a cloak.
Fónda, *sf.* 1. Inn, tavern, coffee-house. 2. V. *Honda*.
Fondáble, *a.* That may be sounded with a plummet.
Fondádo, da, *a.* Applied to pipes or barrels, the bottoms of which are secured with cords or nails.
Fondeadéro, *sm.* (Naút.) Anchoring ground.
Fondeár, *va.* 1. To sound, to explore the depth of water. 2. (Naút.) To search a ship, whether she has prohibited goods on board. 3. To examine closely. 4. To bring up any thing from the bottom of water.
Fondéo, *sm.* The act of searching a ship.
Fondéza, *sf.* (Ant.) Profundity.
Fondillón, *sm.* 1. The dregs and lees at the bottom of a cask of liquor. 2. Rancid Alicant wine.
Fondírse, *vr.* V. *Hundirse*.
Fondísta, *sm.* Victualler, master of a lodging-house.
Fóndo, *sm.* 1. Bottom of any hollow vessel. 2. Bottom of the sea; bottom of a hill or valley. 3. Ground of silks and other stuffs. 4. Plain or cut velvet. 5. Foil of a diamond. 6. Any thing principal or essential. *Hombre de fondo*, A man of great talents and abilities. 7. V. *Profundo*. 8. (Mil.) Space occupied by files of soldiers. *Dar fondo*, (Naút.) To cast anchor. *Dar fondo con codera sobre el ancla*, (Naút.) To anchor with a spring on the cable. *Dar fondo con reguera*, (Naút.) To anchor by the stem. *Irse á fondo*, To go to the bottom, to founder. *A' fondo*, Perfectly, completely. *Fondos*, The intrinsic brilliancy of diamonds; effects, funds. *Fondos vitalicios*, Life-annuities. *Fondos de un navío*, (Naút.) The floor or flat of a ship.
Fondón, *sm.* 1. V. *Fondillon*. 2. Ground of silk or velvet. *De fondon*, Razed to the foundation; deeply.
Fondúra, *sf.* V. *Hondura*.
Fónge, *a.* Bland, soft, spongy.
Foníl, *sm.* Funnel, an instrument through which liquors are poured into vessels.
Fonsadéra, *sf.* Ancient tax, formerly paid for the repairs of moats of castles.
Fonsádo, *sm.* 1. V. *Fonsadera*. 2. Work of a foss or ditch.
Fonsário, *sm.* (Ant.) Moat or ditch around a walled town.
Fontál, *a.* Main, chief, principal.
Fontána, *sf.* (Poét.) Fountain.
Fontanál, *sm.* 1. Source or spring of water 2. Place abounding in springs.—*a.* Belonging to a fountain.
Fontánche, *sm.* Ornament worn in the front of the head.
Fontanéla, *sf.* Surgeon's instrument for opening issues.
Fontanería, *sf.* 1. The art and profession of making wells, and conducting water through pipes. 2. Pipes, conduits.
Fontanéro, *sm.* Well-maker, conduit-maker.
Fontaníl, *a.* Fontalis, relating to a fountain.
Fontáno, na, *a.* Belonging to fountains.
Fontanóso, sa, *a.* Containing springs or fountains.
Fónte, *sf.* V. *Fuente*.
Fontecíca y Fontezuéla, *sf.* A small fountain.
Fóque, *sm.* (Naút.) Jib, a triangular sail extended from the outer end of the bowsprit towards the fore-top-mast head, by means of the jib-boom. *Botalon del foque*, Jib-boom. *Contra foque*, Standing-jib.
Fóra y Fóras, *ad.* (Ant.) V. *Fuera*.
Foradár y Foracár, *va.* V. *Horadar*.
Foragído, da, *a.* Robbing in forests and woods.
Forál, *a.* Belonging to courts of justice. *Bienes forales*, Lands and tenements held by any acknowledgment of superiority to a higher lord.
Foralménte, *ad.* In the manner of the courts.
Forámen, *sm.* Hole in the under stone of a mill.
Foráneo, nea, *a.* Foreign, alien, not of this country.
Foráno, na, *a.* (Ant.) 1. Rustic, rude. 2. Exterior, extrinsic; foreign.
Foráño, ña, *a.* (Ant.) V. *Exterior*.
Forastería, *sf.* Place for strangers, inn for foreigners.
Forastéro, ra, *a.* 1. Strange, foreign, not domestic. 2. Exotic, not produced in this country.
Forastéro, *sm.* Stranger, foreigner.
Fórca, *sf.* Fork. V. *Horca*.
Forcadór, *sm.* Silversmith, who forms his work with a hammer.
Forcejár, *vn.* 1. To endeavour, to make a stre-

nooss effort. 2. To oppose, to make a vigorous resistance.—*va.* V. *Forzar.*

Forcéjo, *sm.* Act of forcing or opposing.

Forcejón, *sm.* Struggle, effort made to disengage one's self from another.

Forcejúdo, da, *a.* Strong, robust; possessed of great strength.

Forchína, *sf.* Warlike instrument in the shape of a fork.

Fórcia, *sf.* V. *Fuerza.*

Forciblemente, *ad.* (Ant.) Forcibly.

Forcína, *sf.* Trident.

Forénse, *a.* 1. Belonging to the bar. 2. V. *Forastero.*

Foréro, ra, *a.* Conformable to law.

Fórfolas, *sf. pl.* Scurf, dandruff or scabs in the head.

Forisséco, ca, *a.* Abroad, from without.

Forísta, *sm.* (Ant.) Lawyer, jurist.

Fórja, *sf.* 1. Forge, the place where silver is beaten into form. 2. Forging, fabricating, manufacturing. 3. Mortar, a cement of sand, lime, and water, used in building.

Forjádo, *sm.* (Among Gold-beaters) Piece of gold or silver beaten into a leaf.

Forjadór, *sm.* Smith, gold-beater.

Forjadúra, *sf.* 1. The act of beating any metal into form or shape. 2. Trap, snare, imposition. V. *Trampa.*

Forjár, *va.* 1. To forge, to beat any metal into form or shape; to form by the hammer. 2. To fill the vacant spaces between the beams with rubbish, plaster, and loam. 3. To counterfeit, to falsify.

Forlón, *sm.* Kind of chaise with four seats.

Fórma, *sf.* 1. Form, the external appearance of any thing; shape, figure. 2. Being, as modified by a particular shape. 3. Regularity, method, order. 4. Particular model or modification, mould, matrix. 5. Method, established practice. 6. (Impr.) Form, a frame containing the pages arranged for press, as they appear on one side of a printed sheet. 7. A small stand or desk on which nuns put their breviaries in the choir. 8. Host to be consecrated by a priest. *Forma de zapatero,* Shoemaker's last. *Forma para los quesos,* Cheese-vat, a wooden case in which curds are pressed into cheese. *De forma que,* In such a manner that. *En forma ó toda forma,* Perfectly, completely; certainly, truly; formally, according to law. *Hombre de forma,* A man of merit and distinction. *Dar forma,* To regulate or arrange that which was disordered.

Formáble, *a.* That which may be formed.

Formación, *sf.* 1. Formation, the act of forming or generating. 2. Manner of fashioning or manufacturing. 3. Twisted cord of silk, gold, silver, &c. used by embroiderers.

Formadór, ra, *s.* One that forms, fashions, or shapes.

Formadúra, *sf.* Form, shape, figure.

Formáge, *sm.* Cheese-vat; cheese.

Formál, *a.* 1. Regular, methodical. 2. Proper, genuine. 3. Serious, grave.

Formalidád, *sf.* 1. Formality, the quality by which any thing is what it is. 2. Exactness, punctuality. 3. Formality, ceremony; established mode of behaviour. 4. Gravity, seriousness, solemnity. 5. Established form of judicial proceedings, or legal precedent.

Formalizár, *va.* To formalize, to model, to modify.—*vr.* To grow formal, to affect gravity.

Formalménte, *ad.* Formally, expressly.

Formár, *va.* 1. To form, to shape, to fashion. 2. To form, to make out of materials; to put in order. 3. To form or draw up troops.—*vn.* To adjust the edges of embroidery work. *Formar concepto,* To form a judgment. *Formar queja,* To complain.

Formatívo, va, *a.* Formative.

Formatríz, *a.* Forming.

Formejár, *va.* (Naút.) To arrange every thing in due order on board of ships; to trim the hold.

Forméros, *sm. pl.* Side arches of a vault.

Formicánte, *a.* Applied to a low, weak, and frequent pulse

Formidáble, *a.* Formidable, dreadful, tremendous.

Formidoloso, sa, *a.* Timorous, timid, fearful; frightful, horrible.

Formón, *sm.* 1. Paring chisel, used by carpenters and joiners. 2. Punch, an instrument used to cut wafers for consecration.

Fórmula, *sf.* Formule, rule.

Formulário, *sm.* Formulary, a book containing stated and prescribed models.

Formulísta, *sm.* One who punctually observes or follows the prescribed models.

Fornálla, *sf.* V. *Horno.*

Fornáz, *sm.* (Poét.) V *Fragua.*

Fornáza, *sf.* V. *Hornaza.*

Fornecér, *va.* (Ant.) To furnish, to provide.

Fornecimiénto, *sm.* Provisions and munition of a place.

Fornecíno, na, *a.* Bastard, illegitimate; applied to children.

Fornélo, *sm.* A portable little oven or furnace.

Fornicación, *sf.* 1. Fornication, a criminal connexion with an unmarried woman. 2. In Scripture, sometimes idolatry.

Fornicadór, *sm.* Fornicator, one that has carnal commerce with unmarried women.

Fornicár, *va.* To fornicate, to commit lewdness.

Fornicário, ria, *a.* Relating to fornication.

Fornício, *sm.* (Ant.) Fornication.

Fornído, da, *a.* 1. Furnished. 2. Robust, corpulent; possessed of great strength.

Fornimiénto, *sm.* The act of furnishing or providing necessary things. V. *Arreo.*

Fornír, *va.* To furnish, to provide, to supply.

Fornitúra, *sf.* 1. Leather straps worn by soldiers. 2. (Impr.) Types cast to complete sorts.

Fóro, *sm.* 1 Court of justice, the hall where tribunals hold their sittings. 2. Bar. 3. Lordship, the right of a superior lord, of whom lands or tenements are held. 4. Back ground of the stage or theatre. *Por tal foro,* On such conditions.

Forquílla, *sf.* A small fork.

Forrageteár, *va.* To scribble, to scraw.

Forráge, *sm.* 1. Forage; grain, hay or grass, which horse-soldiers collect for their horses; foraging. 2. Abundance of things of little value; plentiful medley of things of no moment.

Forrageadór y Forragéro, *sm.* Forager, a soldier detached in search of forage or provender.

Forrageár, *va.* To forage, to collect forage.

Forrár, *va.* V. *Aforrar.*

Fórro, *sm.* 1. Lining, the inner covering of a thing. 2. (Naút.) Furring of a ship, double planks laid on the sides. 3. (Naút.) Sheathing. 4. *Forro de cabos*, (Naút.) Service, the act of serving ropes, or covering them with spun-yarn or canvas, to preserve them from fretting or galling. *Forro sobrepuesto de cable*, (Naút.) Keckling, rounding. 5. *Forro interior de un navio*, Ceiling or foot-waling of a ship.

Fortachón, na, *a.* possessed of uncommon strength.

Fortalecedór, ra, *s.* Fortifier.

Fortalecér, *va.* 1. To fortify, to strengthen. 2. To fortify a place. 3. To aid, to encourage, to support; to corroborate.

Fortalecimiénto, *sm.* 1. Act of fortifying. 2. That which fortifies any place or people, as towers, walls, &c.

Fortaléza, *sf.* 1. Fortitude, firmness. 2. Valour, courage. 3. Strength, vigour. 4. Strong hold, fortress, fortified place.

Fórte, (Naút.) Avast! A term used on board of ships, signifying stop, stay, hold.

Fortepiáno, *sm.* Piano-forte, a musical instrument.

Fortezuélo, la, *a. dim.* of *Fuerte.*

Fortezuélo, *sm.* A small fort.

Fortificación, *sf.* 1. Fortification, the science of military architecture. 2. Works raised for the defence of a place; fortification. *Fortificacion de campaña*, Field-fortification.

Fortificánte, *pa.* Fortifying.

Fortificár, *va.* 1. To strengthen, to fortify. 2. To erect works for the defence of a place.

Fortín, *sm.* 1. A small fort. 2. Field or temporary fortifications for the defence of a corps or army.

Fortitúd, *sf.* V. *Fortaleza.*

Fortuitaménte, *ad.* Fortuitously.

Fortúito, ta, *a.* Fortuitous, accidental, unexpected.

Fortúna, *sf.* 1. Fortune, chance, fate. 2. Good luck, success. 3. Storm, tempest. 4. Chance, unforeseen event. *Fortuna de la Mancha*, Omelet made of eggs and chopped bacon. *Moza de fortuna*, A girl of the town. *Probar fortuna*, To try one's fortune.

Fortunádo, da, *a.* (Ant.) Fortunate.

Fortunál, *a.* (Ant.) Perilous, dangerous.

Fortunár, *va.* To enrich.

Fortúno, na; y óso, sa, *a.* (Ant.) Tempestuous.

Forzadaménte, *ad.* Forcibly, violently.

Forzádo, da, *a.* 1. Forced, necessitated. 2. Indispensable, necessary. 3. Stormy, boisterous. *Tiempo forzado*, (Naút.) Stress of weather. *Correr un viento forzado*, (Naút.) To sail in a storm.

Forzádo, *sm.* Criminal sentenced to the galleys.

Forzadór, *sm.* 1. Ravisher. 2. One who forces or commits acts of violence to attain some purpose.

Forzál, *sm.* The middle part of a comb between the two rows of teeth.

Forzár, *va.* 1. To force, to compel, to constrain. 2. To enforce, to urge. 3. To subdue by force of arms. 4. To ravish, to commit a rape. 5. To oblige or enforce.

Forzósa, *sf.* 1. A decisive move at the game of chess. 2. Necessity of acting against one's will.

Forzosaménte, *ad.* Forcibly, necessarily, violently.

Forzóso, sa, *a.* Indispensable, necessary, violent.

Forzúdo, da, *a.* Strong, vigorous, potent.

Fósa, *sf.* 1. Pit, hole dug in the ground. 2. Grave.

Fosádo, *sm.* 1. A large pit or hole dug in the ground, fosse or ditch. 2. Ancient tribute paid to the king on his commencing a campaign.

Fosadúra, *sf.* V. *Zanja.*

Fosál, *sm.* Church-yard, burying-ground.

Fosár, *va.* To make a pit, ditch or fosse round any thing.

Fósca, *sf.* A thick wood or grove.

Fósco, ca, *a.* Brow-beaten, frowning.

Fósforo, *sm.* Phosphorus, a substance which, exposed to the air, takes fire.

Fosfórico, ca, *a.* Phosphoric.

Fosíco, *sm.* A small moat or ditch.

Fosíl, *sm.* Fossil, any metallic or mineral substance dug out of the ground.

Fosíno, *sm.* (Ict.) Pink, minow; a sort of roach. Cyprinus phoxinus *L.*

Fóso, *sm.* 1. Pit, hole dug in the ground. V. *Hoyo.* 2. Bog, a marshy ground covered with water. 3. Moat, ditch, fosse.

Fóxa, *sf.* Kind of duck.

Fóya, *sf.* An oven full of charcoal.

Foyo, *sm.* V. *Hoyo.*

Foz, *sf.* V. *Alfoz y Hoz.*

Fracasár, *vn.* 1. To crumble, to break into pieces. 2. To be lost or destroyed.

Fracáso, *sm.* 1. Downfal, ruin, destruction. 2. Calamity, an unfortunate event.

Fracción, *sf.* 1. Fraction, the act of breaking or dividing into parts. 2. (Arith.) A broken part of an integral.

Fraccionário, ria, *a.* Fractional.

Fractúra, *sf.* 1. Fracture, breach, separation of contiguous parts. 2. (Ant.) Weakness.

Fracturár, *va.* To fracture, to break a bone.

Fracúra, *sf.* V. *Flaqueza.*

Fradeár, *vn.* To become a friar.

Frága y Fragária, *sf.* Species of raspberry.

Fragáncia, *sf.* 1. V. *Fragrancia.* 2. Actual commission of a crime.

Fragánte, *a.* 1. Fragrant, odoriferous. V. *Fragrante.* 2. Present, actual, notorious. *En fragante*, In the act itself.

Fragáta, *sf.* Ship, vessel. *Fragata de guerra*, Frigate. *Fragata de aviso*, Packet-boat. *Fragata ligera*, A light fast-sailing vessel.

Frágil, *a.* 1. Brittle, easily broken. 2. Frail, liable to seduction. 3. Decaying, perishable.

Fragilidád, *sf.* 1. Fragility, brittleness, easiness to be broken. 2. Liableness to a fault. 3. Sin of infirmity, sensual pleasure.

Fragilménte, *ad.* Frailly.

Fragménto, *sm.* Fragment, a small part broken or separated from the whole.

Fragolíno, *sm.* Sea fish, less than bream.

Fragosidád, *sf.* Unevenness or roughness of the road, imperviousness of a forest.

Fragóso, sa, *a.* Craggy, rough, uneven; full of brambles and briers; noisy.

Fragráncia, *sf.* 1. Fragrance, or fragrancy; sweetness of smell, pleasing scent. 2. (Met.) Fame, reputation of virtues.

Fragránte, *a.* Fragrant, odoriferous; sweet-scented.

Frágua, *sf.* 1. Forge, the place where iron is

hammered into form and shape. 2. Place where intrigues are plotted or planned.

Fraguadór, *sm.* Schemer, one who plots or plans an intrigue; one who counterfeits or forges.

Fraguánte (En), V. *En Fragante.*

Fraguár, *va.* 1. To forge, to reduce iron or other metal by the hammer into shape. 2. (Met.) To plan, to plot.—*vn.* To unite in a mass; applied to clay and mortar.

Fragúra, *sf.* Roughness of the road; imperviousness of a forest.

Framasón, *sm.* Freemason.

Frambuésa, *sf.* Raspberry.

Frambuéso, *sm.* (Bot.) Raspberry-tree. Rubus idæus *L.*

Framéa, *sf.* Javelin, dart.

Francachéla, *sf.* Dissoluteness, drinking and intemperance, licentious merriment.

Francaléte, *sm.* Strap, or narrow long slip of leather with a buckle.

Francaménte, *ad.* Frankly, openly, freely.

Francatúra, *sf.* Frank, or act of franking letters or packets by the post.

Francés, sa, *a.* 1. Gallic, French, belonging to France. 2. French man or woman.

Francesílla, *sf.* (Bot.) V. *Anémone.*

Franchipán, *sm.* A perfume used for the dress, and in confectionary.

Franciscáno, na, *a.* 1. Franciscan, belonging to the religious order of St. Francis. 2. Gray-coloured, like the dress of the Franciscans.

Fránco, *sm.* 1. Franc; a French coin, divided into centimes or hundredths, and worth about 10*d.* sterl. 2. Fair-time, when merchandise is sold free from duty.

Fránco, ca, *a.* 1. Frank, open, generous, liberal, bountiful. 2. Free, disengaged. 3. Exempt, privileged. 4. Ingenuous, plain, sincere. 5. Free, exempt from duty. *Lengua franca,* The trading jargon of the Levant. *Puerto franco,* A free port, frequented by the ships of all nations without paying any duty.

Francolín, *sm.* (Orn.) Francolin, the African or Indian partridge. Tetrao francolinus *L.*

Franéla, *sf.* Kind of fine woollen cloth.

Frangeár, *va.* To fringe, to adorn with fringes; to decorate with ornamental appendages.

Fránge, *sm.* (Blas.) Division of the field of a shield.

Frangénte, *sm.* Accident, disaster.

Frangíble, *a.* Brittle, easily broken or parted.

Frangír, *va.* To break or divide a thing into several pieces.

Frangíta, *sf.* A small fringe.

Frangollár, *va.* To shell or grind corn coarse.

Frangóllo, *sm.* Pottage made of wheat boiled in milk.

Frangóte, *sm.* Bale of goods.

Frángula, *sf.* (Bot.) Berry-bearing alder, alder buckthorn. Rhamnus frangula *L.*

Fránja, *sf.* Fringe, an ornamental appendage, made of silk, gold, or silver.

Franjár y Franjeár, *va.* To fringe, to trim with fringe.

Franjón, *sm.* A large fringe.

Franjuéla, *sf.* A small fringe.

Franqueamiénto, *sm.* (Ant.) Manumission, act of giving liberty.

Franqueár, *va.* 1. To exempt, to grant immunity from. 2. To gratify, to make liberal grants or gifts. 3. To disengage, to extricate; to clear from obstacles or impediments. 4. *Franquearse por encima de un bazo,* (Naút.) To forge over a shoal under a press of sail.—*vr.* To give one's self up easily to the desire of others; to become liberal.

Franquéza, *sf.* 1. Freedom, liberty, exemption. 2. Frankness, generosity, liberality of sentiment; sincerity.

Franquía, *sf.* (Naút.) Offing, the main.

Franquícia, *sf.* 1. Immunity or exemption from paying taxes. 2. A privileged place, which enjoys an exemption from taxes and imposts.

Frañér, *va.* (Ant.) V. *Quebrantar.*

Fráo, *sm.* (Ar.) V. *Fraude.*

Frásca, *sf.* Dry leaves or small branches of trees.

Frásco, *sm.* 1. Flask, a square bottle. 2. Powder-horn.

Fráse y Frásis, *sf.* 1. Phrase, a mode of speech. 2. Idiomatic expression.

Frasía, *sf.* Dish made of tripes and other ingredients.

Frasísta, *sm.* One who is extremely nice in the use of words.

Frasquéra, *sf.* Bottle-case. *Frasquéra de fuego,* (Naút.) Fire-case or fire-chest.

Frasquerílla, ta, *sf.* Small bottle-case.

Frasquéta, *sf.* Frisket of a printing-press.

Frasquíto, llo, *sm.* A small flask.

Fratacár, *va.* To lay a mortar casing on a wall with a square wooden trowel.

Fratérna, *sf.* A severe reprimand.

Fraternál, *a.* Fraternal, brotherly.

Fraternalménte, *ad.* Fraternally.

Fraternidád, *sf.* Fraternity, the state or quality of a brother.

Fratérno, na, *a.* Fraternal, brotherly.

Fratricída, *s. com.* Murderer of a brother.

Frátres, *sm. pl.* (Ant.) Brothers, appellation among ecclesiastics; hence the words *Freyle* and *Frayle,* which see.

Fratricídio, *sm.* Fratricide, murder of a brother.

Fraudadór, *sm.* V. *Defraudador.*

Fráude, *sm.* Fraud, deceit.

Fraudulência, *sf.* Fraudulence, deceitfulness; proneness to deceive.

Fraudulentaménte, *ad.* Fraudulently.

Fraudulénto, ta, *a.* Fraudulent, deceitful.

Fraudulosaménte, *ad.* Fraudulently, deceitfully.

Fraustína, *sf.* A wooden head for fashioning ladies' head-dresses.

Fraxinéla, *sf.* (Bot.) White dittany. Fraxinella dictamnus albus *L.*

Fráy, *pron. app.* A contracted appellation of respect addressed to religious men; brother. V. *Frayle.*

Frayláda, *sf.* A monkish trick; rude action.

Fráyle, *sm.* 1. Friar, brother; appellation of the members of some religious orders. *Frayle de misa y olla,* Friar destined to serve in the choir and at the altar, but not in the pulpit or chair. V. *Religioso.* 2. Fold or plait in petticoats. 3. (Impr.) That part of a printed page which is white or pale for want of ink. 4. The upright post of a floodgate in water-mills. 5. (In Sugar Mills) Refuse of the sugar-cane after it is pressed. 6. Kind of sea-fish.—*pl.* 1.

A sort of pulse resembling kidney-beans. 2. (In Powder-mills) Frames which support the bolter. 3. (Fort.) Fraises, stakes six or seven feet in length, put under the cordon to prevent a scalade.

Fraylecíco, llo, ó ito, *sm.* 1. A little friar. 2. Wild pigeon. 3. Wedge securing the spindle of a silk reel. 4. Boyish sport with the husks of beans.

Frayllecíllo, *sm.* 1. Child which wears a friar's habit. 2. (Orn.) Lapwing. Tringa vanellus *L.*

Fraylengo, ga, y **Frayleño**, ña, *a.* V. *Fraylesco.*

Frayleria, *sf.* Number of friars assembled together.

Frayléro, ra, *a.* Friar-like.

Frayllésco, ca, *a.* Monkish, belonging to friars.

Frayllezuélo, *sm. dim.* A little friar.

Fraylía, *sf.* 1. State of monks, monastic life. 2. Regular clergy.

Fraylíllos, *sm. pl.* (Bot.) V. *Arisaro.*

Fraylón, *sm.* A big friar.

Fraylóte, *sm.* Licentious friar. V. *Bigardo.*

Frayluco, *sm.* A despicable or contemptible friar.

Frazáda, *sf.* Blanket, a woollen cover of a bed, soft and loosely woven.

Frazadílla, *sf.* A small or light blanket.

Frechár, *va.* V. *Flechar.*

Fredór, *sm.* (Ant.) V. *Frio.*

Fregación, *sf.* Friction, the act of rubbing two bodies together.

Fregadéro, *sm.* Scullery, the place where kitchen-utensils are scoured and cleaned.

Fregádo, *sm.* The act of scouring or cleaning kitchen utensils. *Muger de buen fregado,* A buxom girl, a nice woman; a prostitute.

Fregadór, *sm.* 1. Scullery. V. *Fregadero.* 2. Dishclout.

Fregadúra, *sf.* The act of rubbing or scouring.

Fregájo, *sm.* V. *Estropajo.*

Fregamiénto, *sm.* V. *Fricacion.*

Fregár, *va.* 1. To rub one thing against another. 2. To scour or wash kitchen-utensils.

Fregatríz, *sf.* Kitchen-maid.

Fregáta y **Fregóna**, *sf.* Kitchen-maid.

Fregoncílla, *sf.* A little kitchen-maid.

Fregonil, *a.* Belonging to or becoming a kitchen-wench.

Fregonzuéla, *sf.* A little kitchen-girl.

Freidúra, *sf.* Act of frying or dressing in a pan.

Freír, *va.* To fry or dress in a frying-pan. *Freirse de calor,* To be excessively hot. *Al freir de los huevos,* (Met.) In a short time, in a minute. *Freirsela á alguno,* To deceive one premeditatedly.

Frémito, *sm.* A loud noise. V. *Bramido.*

Frenár, *va.* To curb, to check, to restrain.

Frendiénte, *a.* Enraged, furious; gnashing or colliding the teeth with fury and passion.

Frenería, *sf.* 1. Business of bridle-making. 2. Place or shop in which bridles are made or sold.

Frenéro, *sm.* One who makes the bits of a bridle, a bridle-maker.

Frenesí, *sm.* 1. Frenzy, madness, distraction of mind. 2. (Met.) Folly, extravagant caprice.

Frenético, ca, *a.* Mad, distracted.

Frenillár, *va.* (Naút.) To bridle the oars.

Freníllo, *sm.* 1. Impediment of the tongue, with which some children are born, said to be tongue-tied. 2. (Naút.) Bridle of the oars, a rope with which the oars are tied.

Fréno, *sm.* 1. Bridle or bit of the bridle. 2. (Met.) Curb, restraint, check. *Morder el freno,* To bite the bridle.

Frentál, *a.* Frontal; applied to the forehead.

Frentáza, *sf.* A broad forehead.

Frénte, *sf.* 1. Forehead, front; the part of the face which reaches from the eye-brows to the hair. *Frente á frente,* Face to face. 2. The blank space left at the beginning of a letter. 3. Forepart of a building, or any other thing, which meets the eye. *Frente ó en frente,* Opposite. 4. (Mil.) Front rank of a body of troops. *Navigar de frente,* (Naút.) To sail a-breast. 5. (Poét.) V. *Semblante.* *A' frente,* In front; in a right line. 6. Obverse of coins.

Frentecílla, ta, ca, *sf.* A small front.

Frentéro, *sm.* Band worn on the forehead of children to save their face in case of falling.

Freo, *sm.* (Naút.) Narrow channel of the passage of boats; it is used in the Levant.

Frequéncia, *sf.* Frequency, the condition of being often seen or done.

Frequentación, *sf.* Condition of visiting often, or being much in a place.

Frequentadór, ra, *s.* Frequenter.

Frequentár, *va.* To frequent.

Frequentatívo, *a.* (Gram.) Frequentative; applied to verbs.

Frequénte, *a.* Frequent, often done or seen.

Frequénte y **Frequenteménte**, *ad.* Frequently

Frére, *sm.* (Ant.) V. *Freyle.*

Frés, *sm.* (Ar.) Gold or silver lace.

Frésa, *sf.* Strawberry.

Fresál, *sm.* 1. (Bot.) Strawberry-plant. Fragaria *L.* 2. Ground bearing strawberry-plants.

Frésca, *sf.* 1. V. *Fresco.* *Tomar la fresca,* To take the air. *Salir con la fresca,* To go out during the fresh air in the evening. 2. (Fam.) Declaring one's sentiments freely.

Frescachón, na, *a.* Very fresh.

Frescál, *a.* Not very fresh, rather stale; applied to fish.

Frescaménte, *ad.* 1. Freshly, recently, lately. 2. Coolly, without passion; peacefully.

Frésco, ca, *a.* 1. Fresh, coolish; rather cool. 2. Plump, ruddy. 3. Brisk, gay, lively, cheerful. 4. Serene, calm, unruffled. *Dinero fresco,* Ready money, cash paid off hand. *Viento fresco,* (Naút.) A fresh freeze. *Pintura al fresco,* Painting in fresco, done on fresh plaster not yet dry and with water colours. *Dexar fresco á alguno,* To leave one scoffed at.

Frésco, *sm.* Cool refreshing air. V. *Frescura.*

Frescón, na, *a.* (*aum.* of *Fresco.*) Very fresh; blooming.

Frescón, *sm.* Bloomy, of a healthy ruddy countenance.

Frescór, *sm.* Freshness; ruddiness. V. *Frescura.*

Frescúra, *sf.* 1. Freshness, coolness. 2. Amenity, agreeableness of situation. 3. Frankness, openness. 4. An untimely jest, smart repartee. 5. Carelessness. 6. Serenity, tranquillity.

Fresnéda, *sf.* Grove or plantation of ash-trees.

Frésno, *sm.* 1. (Bot.) Ash-tree. Fraxinus *L.* 2. (Poét.) Staff of a lance, a spear. *Fresno de flor,* (Bot.) Flowering ash-tree. Fraxinus ornus *L.*

Fresón ó Fresón de Chili, *sm.* (Bot.) Chili-strawberry. Fragaria chiloensis *L.* [*Fresco.*

Fresquecíto, ta, Fresquíllo, lla, *a dim.* of

Fresquísta, *sm.* A painter particularly employed in painting in fresco.

Fretádo, *a.* Banded. V. *Cotizado.*

Fretár, *va.* V. *Fletar.*

Frétes, *sf. pl.* Frets, the narrow bands which form the body of a shield.

Fréie, *sm.* V. *Lio.* In Sevilla, arch or member which unites the three divisions of any thing.

Frexól, *sm.* V. *Judihuelo.*

Frey, *pron. app.* Friar or brother, an appellation of respect given to religious persons belonging to a military order.

Fréyla, *sf.* 1. A religious woman of a military order. 2. Lay sister of religious orders. [order.

Freylár, *va.* To receive or admit in a military

Fréyle, *sm.* 1. Knight of a religious military order. 2. Priest belonging to the regular clergy.

Freyría, *sf.* (Ant.) Friary, assemblage of friars.

Fréz y Fréza, *sf.* 1. Dung, the excrement of animals. 2. Ground turned up by the snout of a hog or other animal. 3. Track, trace of fish in spawning. 4. Rustling of silk worms when they are feeding on mulberry leaves.

Frezadór, *sm.* (Ant.) Eater, dissipator.

Frezár, *vn.* 1. To eject excrements; applied to animals. 2. To nibble the leaves of mulberry trees; applied to silk-worms. 3. To rub in order to spawn; applied to fishes. 4. To turn up the ground, as hogs. 5. To eject the larvæ of young bees from hives. 6. To approach.

Fría, *a.* (Gal.) Applied to dead fowls paid as tribute. *A' frias*, Heavily, coldly.

Friabilidád, *sf.* Friability, brittleness.

Friáble, *a.* Friable, fragile, brittle.

Frialdád, *sf.* 1. Frigidity, coldness; insipidity; dulness. 2. Cold, a disease caused by cold; the obstruction of perspiration. 3. Negligence, lassitude, folly. *Impedimento de frialdad*, Impediment of coldness, incapacity of enjoying the nuptial rights.

Friaménte, *ad.* In a heavy, stupid, and graceless manner; coldly, frigidly.

Friático, ca, 1. Foolish, graceless. 2. Chilly.

Fricación, *sf.* Friction.

Fricándo, *sm.* Scotch collop; veal cut into small pieces and stewed.

Fricár, *va.* To rub, to scour.

Fricasé, *sm.* Fricassee, a dish made by cutting chickens, fowls, veal, &c. into small pieces, and dressing them with strong sauce.

Fricción, *sf.* Friction. V. *Fricacion.*

Friecíllo, to, *sm. dim.* A slight cold.

Friéga, *sf.* The act of rubbing with flannel for medical purposes.

Friéra, *sf.* 1. Chilblain. 2. An aquatic plant.

Frigidéz y Friéza, *sf.* V. *Frialdad.*

Frígido, da, *a.* (Poet.) Cold. V. *Frio.*

Frigón, *sm.* (Ict.) Fire-flaire, sting-ray. Raia pastinaca *L.*

Frigoriénto, ta, *a.* V. *Friolento.*

Friísimo, ma, *a. sup.* of *Frio.*

Fringilágo, *sm.* V. *Monge.*

Frío, ia, *a.* 1. Cold, frigid, tepid. 2. Cold, impotent, unfit, graceless; insipid; inefficacious.

Frío, *sm.* 1. Cold, the effect of coldness or frigidity. 2. Cool, fresh air. 3. Concreted beverage, congealed sugar. 4. Dulness, want of intellectual fire. *Dios da el frio conforme á la ropa*, (Prov.) God tempers the wind to the shorn lamb.

Frioléntо, ta, *a.* Chilly; very sensible of cold.

Frioléra, *sf.* An insignificant speech or action.

Frioléro, ra, *a.* Chilly.

Frión, na, *a. aum.* of *Frio*, Very insipid or awkward

Frísa, *sf.* Frieze, a sort of coarse woollen stuff.

Frisádo, *sm.* Silk plush or shag.

Frisadór, *sm.* Frizzler, one who frizzles or raises the nap on frieze or cloth.

Frisadúra, *sf.* Act of frizzling or shagging.

Frisár, *va.* To frizzle, to raise the nap on frieze or other woollen stuff; to rub against the grain.—*vn.* To resemble, to be like, to have likeness to; to assimilate; to approach.

Friso, *sm.* (Arq.) Frieze, the part of a column between the architrave and cornice.

Frisól, *sm.* (Bot.) French or kidney bean. Phaseolus vulgaris *L.*

Frisón, *sm.* 1. A large draught-horse, a cart or dray-horse. 2. An animal of a large size.

Frisuélos, *sm. pl.* Dry French-beans; fritters

Fríta, *sf.* Frit, the matter or ingredients of which glass is made.

Fritáda, *sf.* Dish of fried meat or fish.

Fritilária, *sf.* (Bot.) Fritillary, checkered lily. Fritillaria meleagris *L.*

Fritíllas, *sf. pl.* Fritters, pancakes.

Fríto y Fritúra, *s.* V. *Fritada.*

Friúra, *sf.* Frigidity, cold.

Frixión, *sf.* (Farm.) Frixion, frying, operation of drying plants.

Frivolaménte, *ad.* Frivolously.

Frivolidád, *sf.* Frivolity.

Frívolo, la, *a.* Frivolous, slight, trifling, of no moment.

Fróga, *sf.* Brickwork.

Frogár, *va.* To make a wall of brick and mortar.—*vn.* To lay a coat of mortar over the joints of bricks.

Frondosidád, *sf.* 1. Foliage, tuft of leaves. 2. Redundancy of words or phrases.

Frondóso, sa, *a.* Frondiferous, full of leaves.

Frontál, *sm.* Front-ornament of an altar.

Frontaléra, *sf.* Ornament for the front; place where such ornaments are kept.

Frónte, *sf.* Front. V. *Frente.*

Frontéra, *sf.* 1. Frontier, limit, confine. 2. Fillet of a bridle; binder of a frail-basket.

Fronterízo, za, *a.* 1. Bounding or bordering upon. 2. Fronting, opposite, over-against.

Frontéro, *sm.* 1. Governor or magistrate of a frontier town. 2. Frontlet or brow-band worn by children to prevent their heads or faces from being hurt by a fall.—*ad.* In front.

Frontéro, ra, *a.* Frontier.

Frontíl, *sm.* Bassweed matting placed on the foreheads of draught-oxen to preserve them from injury.

Frontíno, na, *a.* Applied to animals marked in the face.

Fróntis, *sm.* Frontispiece.

Frontispício, *sm.* 1. Frontispiece, the fore part of a building or any other thing which meets the eye. 2. (Joc.) Face, visage.

Frontón, *sm.* 1. Wall from which the bowl rebounds at fives. 2. Frontispiece.
Frontúdo, da, *a.* Broad-faced.
Frontúra, *sf.* Front of a stocking-frame.
Frotación y Frotadúra, *sf.* Friction, the act of rubbing two bodies together.
Frotár, *va.* To rub or stroke gently with the hand. V. *Flotar.*
Fructéro, ra, *a.* V. *Frutal.*
Fructiferaménte, *ad.* Fruitfully.
Fructífero, ra, *a.* Fructiferous, bearing fruit.
Fructificación, *sf.* Fructification.
Fructificadór, ra, *s:* Fertilizer.
Fructificár, *va.* 1. To fructify, to fertilize, to make fruitful. 2. (Met.) To edify; to promote piety and morality, or the exercise of religious and social duties.
Fructuosaménte, *ad.* Fruitfully.
Fructuóso, sa, *a.* Fruitful, useful.
Frugál, *a.* Frugal, parsimonious.
Frugalidád, *sf.* Frugality, parsimony, husbandry.
Fruición, *sf.* 1. Fruition, enjoyment. 2. Satisfaction, gratification, taste.
Fruír, *vn.* To live in happiness, to enjoy.
Fruitívo, va, *a.* Fruitive, enjoying.
Frumentáceo, ea, *a.* (Bot.) Frumentacious.
Frumentício, cia, *a.* Belonging to wheat.
Fruncído, da, *a.* Frizzled, corrugated. *Fruncido de boca*, Hare-lipped.
Fruncidór, *sm.* Plaiter, folder.
Fruncimiénto, *sm.* 1. The act of pursing up into corrugations. 2. Fiction, deceit, imposture.
Fruncír, *va.* 1. To gather the edge of stuff or cloth into plaits. 2. (Met.) To reduce to a smaller compass. 3. (Met.) To conceal the truth. 4. To affect modesty and composure.
Frusléra, *sf.* Metal made of latten filings.
Fruslería, *sf.* Trifle, a thing of no value, frivolity.
Fruseléro, ra, *a.* Trifling, frivolous, insignificant.
Frustráneo, nea, *a.* Frustraneous, vain, useless.
Frustrár, *va.* To frustrate, to disappoint, to balk.—*vr.* To be disappointed, to be balked.
Frustratório, ria, *a.* V. *Frustráneo.*
Frúta, *sf.* Fruitage, eatable fruit borne by trees and plants. *Fruta de sarten*, Pancake, fritter. *Fruta nueva*, (Met.) Any thing new. *Fruta del tiempo*, (Met.) Distempers incident to the season.
Frutáge, *sm.* Fruitage, ornament of fruit.
Frutál, *a.* Fruitful; applied to trees.
Frutár, *va.* To fructify, to fertilize.
Frutéra, *sf.* Fruit-woman, she who sells fruit.
Frutería, *sf.* Place where fruit is kept or preserved.
Frutéro, *sm.* 1. Fruiterer, one who deals in fruit. 2. Fruit-basket served up at table. 3. Piece of painting representing various sorts of fruit.
Frútice, *sm.* Any perennial shrub.
Fruticóso, sa, *a.* Applied to a plant with many branches from its root.
Frutiér, *sm.* Purveyor of fruit for the royal family, who is an officer of the king's household.
Frutificár, *va.* V. *Fructificar.*
Frutílla, *sf.* 1. Small fruit. 2. (In Peru) Strawberry. 3. Round shell or nut of which rosaries are made.
Frutillár, *sm.* Strawberry-bed.
Frúto, *sm.* 1. Fruit, the quantity of fruit annually produced by a tree or plant. 2. Benefit, profit. *Fruto de bendicion*, Children lawfully begotten.—*pl.* 1. Seeds, grain. 2. Produce of an estate, place, or employment.
Fú, *interj.* Of disgust.
Fucár, *sm.* A rich opulent man.
Fúcia, *sf.* (Ant.) V. *Confianza. A' fucia*, In confidence.
Fuégo, *sm.* 1. Fire, the igneous element. 2. Any thing burning. 3. Conflagration. 4. (Met.) Family, the number of persons who live in the same house. 5. Eruption or breaking out of humours in the skin. 6. Firing of soldiers. 7. Hearth, fire-place. *Un lugar tiene tantos fuegos*, A place contains so many hearths or inhabitants. 8. Ardour, heat of any action. *Fuego de San Elmo*, (Naút.) Castor or Pollux, a shining vapour without heat, sometimes observed adhering to ships after a storm. *Dar fuego á un navio*, (Naút.) To breem a ship. *Dar fuego á los tablones*, (Naút.) To heat planks for the purpose of bending them. *Estar hecho un fuego*, (Met.) To burn with heat. *Fuego greguisco ó guirguesco*, (Ant.) Greek fire. *Fuégos*, (Naút.) Lights; lighthouse for directing ships which are sailing off the coast. *Fuego granado*, (Mil.) Successive or incessant firing, effected by small divisions firing together. *Fuego de San Anton*, Erysipelas.
Fuego! Fuego de dios! *interj.* Bless me, what is this!
Fueguecíllo y Fueguezuélo, *sm.* A small fire.
Fuelán, *sm.* (Ant.) V. *Fulano.*
Fuellár, *sm.* Paper ornament around wax-tapers.
Fuélle, *sm.* 1. Bellows, an instrument used to blow the fire. 2. (Joc.) Tale-bearer. 3. Leather curtain of an open chaise, to shelter from the inclemency of the weather. 4. Puff for powdering hair. *Fuelles*, Puckers or corrugations in clothes.
Fuén, *sm.* Fountain, spring. V. *Fuente.*
Fuénte, *sm.* 1. Fountain, a spring of water. 2. Jet, a spout of water. 3. (Met.) Original, first principle, first cause. 4. Dish, a broad wide vessel in which food is served up at table. 2. Issue, fontanel; an incision made in the skin for the discharge of humours.
Fuentecílla, ca, ta, *sf.* A small fountain.
Fuéra, *ad.* 1. Without, out of the place where one is. V. *Afuera.* 2. Over and above. *Fuera de si*, Absent of mind; deranged. *Estar fuera*, To be abroad. *De fuera*, Exteriorly.
Fuéra, *interj.* Out of the way, clear the way.
Fuéras, *ad.* (Ant.) V. *Fuera.*
Fuercecílla, ta, *sf. dim.* Little strength.
Fuéro, *sm.* 1. Statute-law of a country. 2. Jurisdiction, judicial power. *Fuero exterior ó externo*, Canon and civil laws. *Fuéros*, Charters or privileges granted to a province, town, or person. *A' fuero*, According to law. *Fuero de la conciencia*, The tribunal of conscience. *De fuero*, Of right, by right or law.
Fuérte, *sm.* 1. Fortification, entrenchment. 2. Coin over weight.
Fuérte, *a.* 1. Strong, possessed of strength and vigour. 2. Hard, not easily wrought; not malleable. 3. Enormous, dreadful. *Lance fuerte*, A hard case. 4. Rough, rude, harsh. 5. Strong, intoxicating. 6. Efficacious, cogent. 7. Firm, manly.

Fuérte, *ad.* Strongly.

Fuertecíllo, to, co, *sm.* Small fortress; a blockhouse.

Fuerteménte, *ad.* Strongly, vehemently.

Fuérza, *sf.* 1. Force, strength, might. 2. Fortitude, valour, courage. 3. Proneness, strong propensity. 4. Violence, outrage. 5. Rape, violent defloration, or violation of a woman. 6. Mental power. 7. Fortress, strong place. 8. Grievance or injury done by a judge. 9. Strong part of a sword near the hilt. 10. Buckram, strong linen put on the inside of clothes to keep them stiff. 11. Power, efficacy. *Á fuerza de*, By the dint of, by the force of. *Por fuérza*, By force, in a violent manner, forcibly; necessarily; without excuse. *Hacer fuerza de velas*, (Naút.) To crowd sail, to carry a press of sail. *Hacer fuerza de remos*, (Naút.) To pull hard with the oars. *Á viva fuerza*, With great resolution, by main force.

Fúga, *sf.* 1. Flight, escape, elopement. 2. State of the utmost perfection of a thing. 3. Prop, support. 4. Fugue, a piece of musical composition. *Fuga de risa*, Fit of laughter.

Fugacidád, *sf.* Fugacity, volatility, brevity.

Fugáda de viénto, *sf.* (Naút.) Squall or gust of wind.

Fugáz, *a.* 1. Shy, apt to fly away. 2. Fugitive, running away. 3. (Met.) Perishable, decaying.

Fugído, da, *a.* (Poét.) V. *Fugaz.*

Fugitívo, va, *a.* Fugitive.

Fuída, *sf.* V. *Huida.*

Fuimiénto, *sm.* Farmer of sheep walks.

Fuína, *sf.* V. *Garduña.*

Fulán, *sm.* (Ant.) V. *Fulano.*

Fulaníto, ta, *s.* Little master, little miss.

Fuláno, na, *s.* Such a one.

Fulgecér, *vn.* (Poét.) To shine, to be resplendent.

Fulgénte, *a.* (Poét.) Refulgent, brilliant.

Fulgído, da, *a.* (Poét.) Resplendent.

Fulgór, *sm.* Resplendence, brilliancy.

Fulgúra, *sf.* V. *Holgura.*

Fulguránte, *pa.* (Poét.) Resplendent, shining.

Fulgurár, *vn.* (Poét.) To yield splendour and brilliancy.

Fuliginóso, sa, *a.* Fuliginous, dark, obscure.

Fulleràzo, *sm. aum.* Great cheat or sharper.

Fulleresco, ca, *a.* Belonging to sharpers.

Fullería, *sf.* 1. Cheating, sharping at play. 2. Cunning, arts used to deceive.

Fullerito, *sm.* A little sharper.

Fulléro, *sm.* Sharper, cheater at play.

Fullét, *sm.* A very small saw.

Fullóna, *sf.* (Bax.) Dispute, quarrel.

Fulminación, *sf.* Fulmination, the act of thundering.

Fulminádo, *a.* Wounded with lightning.

Fulminadór, *sm.* Thunderer.

Fulminánte, *pa.* Fulminating; fulminator.

Fulminár, *va.* 1. To fulminate, to emit lightning. 2. To throw out as an object of terror, to express wrath. 3. To issue ecclesiastical censures.

Fulmíneo, nea, *a.* (Poét.) Belonging to thunder and lightning.

Fulminóso, sa, *a.* (Poét.) Fulminatory, thundering, striking horror.

Fumáda, *sf.* The act of smoking tobacco.

Fumánte, *pa.* Fuming, smoking.

Fumár, *va.* To smoke tobacco.

Fumaráda, *sf.* 1. Blast of smoke. 2. A pipeful of tobacco.

Fumária, *sf.* (Bot.) Fumitory, earthsmoke. Fumaria officinalis *L.*

Fumentación, *sf.* V. *Fomentacion.*

Fumentár, *va.* V. *Fomentar.*

Fumífero, ra, *a.* (Poét.) Smoking, emitting smoke.

Fumigación, *sf.* 1. Fumigation, fumes raised by fire. 2. Fumigation, application of medicines to the body in fumes.

Fumigadór, *sm.* Fumigator, an instrument used for injecting clysters of the smoke of tobacco.

Fumigár, *vn.* V. *Humear.*

Fumoróla, *sf. pl.* Cavities in the earth which emit a sulphureous smoke.

Fumosidád, *sf.* Fumidity, smokiness.

Fumóso, sa, *a.* Full of smoke or fume.

Funámbulo, *sm.* Rope-dancer. V. *Volatin.*

Función, *sf.* 1. Employment, office. 2. Solemnity, festival. 3. Festive concourse of people. 4. Compliment, act of civility or respect. 5. Flight, engagement, battle.

Fúnda, *sf.* 1. Pillow-case; also a case for other things. 2. Foundation, groundwork. 3. Mould of a button. 4. Carpet or covering of a table.

Fundación, *sf.* 1. Foundation, groundwork. 2. Beginning or origin of a thing. 3. Revenue settled and established for any purpose, particularly charity.

Fundadaménte, *ad.* Fundamentally.

Fundadór, ra, *s.* Founder, builder; one who raises an edifice.

Fundágo, *sm.* Magazine, warehouse, storehouse.

Fundamentál, *a.* 1. Fundamental, serving for the foundation. 2. Essential, principal.

Fundamentalménte, *ad.* Fundamentally.

Fundamentár, *va.* 1. To lay the foundation of a building. 2. (Met.) To found, to establish.

Fundaménto, *sm.* 1. Foundation, ground-work. 2. Source, origin, root.

Fundár, *va.* 1. To found, to lay the foundation or basis of a building. 2. To found, to establish. 3. To raise upon, as on a maxim.

Fundénte, *sm.* Flux. V. *Flux.*

Fundería, *sf.* Foundery, a place where melted metal is cast into forms; a casting-house.

Fundíble, *a.* Fusible, capable of being melted.

Fundíbulo, *sm.* An ancient warlike machine for throwing stones; a sling.

Fundición, *sf.* 1. Fusion, the act of melting metals. 2. Foundery. 3. (Impr.) A complete set of types, or printing letters.

Fundidór, *sm.* 1. Founder, one who melts and casts metals. 2. A level and smooth place for casting metals.

Fundilário, *sm.* Slinger, Roman soldier who used a sling.

Fundír, *va.* 1. To found or melt metals. 2. To cast fused metals into moulds.

Fúndo, *sm.* A piece of arable land, set apart for the use of the owner of a farm.

Fúnebre, *a.* Mournful, sad, lamentable; expressive of grief.

Funepéndulo, *sm.* Pendulum, any weight hung so that it may easily swing backward and forward, the oscillations whereof are always in equal time.

Funerál, *a.* Funeral, used at the ceremony of interment of the dead.

Funeráles, *sm. pl.* Funeral solemnities. *Á la funerala*, Mode of carrying arms, used by soldiers during the holy week, and at funerals with their muskets inverted.

FUNERÁLIAS ó FUNERÁRIAS, *sf. pl.* V. *Funerales.*

FUNERÁRIO, RIA, *a.* Funeral, funereal.

FUNÉREO, REA, *a.* (Poét.) Mournful, sad. V. *Fúnebre.*

FUNESTÁR, *va.* To sadden, to make sad.

FUNESTAMÉNTE, *ad.* Mournfully.

FUNÉSTO, TA, *a.* Mournful, sad, dismal.

FUNESTÓSO, SA, *a.* Melancholy, direful.

FÚNGO, *sm.* (Cir.) Fungus, fleshy excrescence.

FUNGÓN, *sm.* (Joc.) A great snuff-taker.

FUNGÓSO, SA, *a.* Fungous, excrescent, spongy.

FUNICULÁR, *a.* Funicular, consisting of cords or fibres.

FURACÁR, *va.* (Ant.) To bore.

FURÉNTE, *a.* (Poét.) Furious, raving, transported by passion.

FÚRIA, *sf.* 1. Fury, rage; a violent agitation of the mind. 2. Hurry, velocity, and vigour, used in the performance of a thing.

FURIÁL, *a.* (Poét.) Belonging to the Furies.

FURIBÚNDO, DA, *a.* Furious, enraged.

FURIOSAMÉNTE, *ad.* Furiously.

FURIÓSO, SA, *a.* 1. Furious, mad, frantic. 2. Raging, violent, transported by passion beyond reason. 3. Very great, excessive.

FURLÓN ó FORLÓN, *sm.* A coach with four seats, hung with leather curtains.

FÚRO, RA, *a.* (Ar.) Ferocious, fierce; severe. *Hacer furo,* To conceal a thing artfully with the design of keeping it.

FURÓR, *sm.* 1. Fury, madness; derangement of the mental faculties. 2. Rage, passion of anger, tumult of mind approaching to madness. 3. Enthusiasm, exaltation of fancy.

FURRIÉLA, *sf.* V. *Furriera.*

FURRIÉR, *sm.* 1. Quarter-master, a non-commissioned officer of foot. 2. Clerk of the king's mews.

FURRIÉRA, *sf.* Place of keeper of the keys of the king's palace.

FURRIÉTA, *sf.* Bravado, boast, brag.

FURTADAMÉNTE Y FURTIBLEMÉNTE, *ad.* Furtively.

FURTÁR, *va.* V. *Hurtar.*

FURTÍBLE, *a.* Liable to be stolen.

FURTIVAMÉNTE Y FURTIVOLMÉNTE, *ad.* By stealth, in a clandestine manner.

FURTÍVO, VA, *a.* Furtive, gotten by theft, done in a clandestine manner.

FÚSA, *sf.* Note in music.

FÚSCA, *sf.* A kind of dark-coloured duck.

FUSCÁR, *va.* Ant.) To obscure.

FÚSCO, CA, *a.* Dark; brown inclining to black.

FUSELÁDO, DA; FUSADO, DA, *a.* (Blas.) Charged with fusils or spindles.

FUSIBILIDÁD, *sf.* Fusibility, quality of being fusible.

FUSÍBLE Y FUSÍL, *a.* Fusible.

FUSÍL, *sm.* Fusil, firelock; a small musket. *Fusil de boca negra,* (Naút.) Sea-musket. *Fusil rayado,* Rifle gun.

FUSILÁZO, *sm.* Musket-shot; blow given with a musket.

FUSILERÍA, *sf.* Body of fusileers or musketeers.

FUSILÉRO, *sm.* Fusileer, musketeer.

FUSIÓN, *sf.* Fusion, liquation.

FUSÍQUE, *sm.* Kind of snuff-box in the shape of a small apple, with two holes in its neck from which the snuff is taken into the nostrils.

FÚSTA, *sf.* 1. Small vessel with lateen sails. 2. Thin boards of wood. 3. Kind of woollen cloth.

FUSTÁGA, *sf.* (Naút.) A large rope, serving to hoist and lower the mainsail.

FUSTÁN, *sf.* Fustian, a kind of cotton stuff.

FUSTANÉRO, *sm.* Fustian manufacturer.

FÚSTE, *sm.* 1. Tree and bows of a saddle; (Poét.) a saddle. 2. Shaft of a lance. 3. Foundation of any thing; groundwork made of wood. 4. (Ant.) Wood, timber. 5. Substance of any thing. *Hombre de fuste,* Man of weight and importance. 6. (Arq.) Fust or body of a column. 7. (Naút.) A vessel of burthen with a flush deck, navigated by sails and oars.

FUSTÉRO, RA, *a.* Belonging to a fust, foundation, &c.

FUSTÉRO, *sm.* Turner or carpenter.

FUSTÉTE, *sm.* (Bot.) Red or Venice sumac-tree. Rhus cotinus *L.* Its wood dyes yellow, and its bark tans.

FUSTIGÁR, *va.* (Ant.) To whip.

FUSTÍNA, *sf.* Place destined to fusing metals.

FÚSTOC, *sm.* Fustic, a yellow die-wood, Venice sumac.

FÚTIL, *a.* Futile, trifling, worthless.

FUTILIDÁD, *sf.* Futility, weakness, want of solidity.

FUTÚRA, *sf.* Survivorship.

FUTURÁRIO, RIA, *a.* Future.

FUTURICIÓN, *sf.* Futurition, the state of being to be.

FUTÚRO, A, *a.* Future, that which will be hereafter.

FUTÚRO, *sm.* 1. Future, time to come. 2. (Gram.) Future tense, which denotes time to come. *En lo futuro,* For the future.

FUYR, *vn.* V. *Huir.*

G, before the vowels, *a, o,* and *u,* has nearly the same sound in Spanish and English; but before *e* and *i,* it is the same as the Spanish *x,* or the English *h* strongly aspirated, as *genio* is pronounced *henio; gemido, jemido,* or *xemido,* have all the same sound, *hemido;* before the diphthong *ue,* as in *guerra, guion,* the *u* becomes liquid, and the *g* has the hard sound as in the English words *gelding, girl;* with a diæresis over the *ü,* both letters have their proper sound, as in *agüero.* The Latin *c* is often changed into *g* in Spanish, and vice versá, as *catus* makes *gato; gangrena, cangrena,* &c. In like manner, the Latin aspirated *hi* are changed into *g,* in Spanish, as *hieroglyphicus, Hieronymus,* &c. make *geroglífico, Gerónimo,* &c.

GABÁCHA, *sf.* Kind of loose garment.

GABÁCHO, *sm.* Sloven, a dirty miserable fellow.

GABÁCHO, CHA, *a.* Applied to persons, or their property, residing at the foot of the Pyrenees; used also in derision to the French.

GABÁN, *sm.* Great coat with a hood and close sleeves.

GABÁNZO, *sm.* (Bot.) Dog's rose. Rosa canina *L.*

GABÁRDA, *sf.* (Ar.) Wild white rose.

GABARDÍNA, *sf.* Kind of cassock with close buttoned sleeves.

GABÁRRA, *sf.* (Naút.) Lighter, a large boat used to load and unload ships.

GABARRÉRO, *sm.* 1. Dealer in wood and timber. 2. (Naút.) Lighterman.

GABÁRRO, *sm.* 1. A morbid swelling on the pastern of horses. 2. Pip, a horny pellicle which grows on the tongues of fowls. 3. Flaw or defect in cloth. 4. Defect discovered in goods after they have been bought. 5. (Met.) Obligation, burthensome charge; error in accounts.

GABÁTA, *sf.* Bowl, a small basin made of wood.

GABÁZO, *sm.* (In Sugar-mills) Bruised sugar-cane.

GABÉLA, *sf.* 1. Tax or duty paid to government. 2. An open public place, where wrestling, fencing, and other similar exercises are performed.

GABESÍNA, *sf.* Ancient kind of arms.

GABINÉTE ó GABINÉTO, *sm.* 1. Cabinet, a meeting of ministers of state and privy counsellors for the discussion of state matters. 2. Cabinet, a private room in which consultations are held. 3. Dressing-room.

GABIÓN, *sm.* 1. Sort of clouded stuff made of silk, mixed with wool. 2. (Mil.) Gabion, a large cylindric basket, filled with earth. V. *Gavion.*

GABISÓN, *sm.* A conic heap of the herb *kali,* to dry and prepare it for burning.

GABÓTE, *sm.* Shuttlecock.

GÁCHAS, *sf. pl.* 1. Sort of fritters, made of flour, honey, and water. 2. Any sort of soft pap. *Á gachas,* On all fours. *Hacerse unas gachas,* To manifest extraordinary emotion in the presence or at the recollection of any thing. *Ánimo á las gachas,* Expression of incitement to the execution of any thing difficult or laborious.

GACHÉTA, *sf.* Spring in large locks.

GÁCHO, CHA, *a.* 1. Curvated, bent downwards. 2. Having horns curvated downwards; applied to black cattle. 3. Slouching; applied to hats.

GACHÓN, ÓNA, *a.* y *s.* 1. Pampered, spoiled; applied to children. 2. Graceful, sweet, attractive.

GACHONERÍA, *sf.* Caress, endearment, fondness.

GACHUPÍN, *sm.* Name given in New Spain to a European, who in Lima is called *Chapeton,* and in Buenos Ayres *Maturrango.*

GADITÁNO, NA, *a.* Belonging to Cadiz.

GÁFA, *sf.* A kind of hook, used to bend a cross-bow.—*pl.* 1. (Naút.) Can-hooks, used to raise or lower casks. 2. Spectacles; mounting of spectacle-glasses.

GAFÁR, *va.* To hook, to catch with a hook.

GAFEDÁD, *sf.* 1. Kind of leprosy. 2. Contraction of the nerves.

GAFÉRI ó GAFÉTI, *sm.* (Bot.) Agrimony. Agrimonia *L.*

GAFÉTE, *sm.* Clasp, a hook and eye. V. *Corchete.*

GÁFO, FA, *a.* 1. Infected with a leprosy. 2. Indisposed with a contraction of the nerves.

GAFÓN, *sm.* (Orn.) Green-finch. Loxia chloris *L.*

GAGÁTE ó GAGÁTES, *sm.* V. *Azabache.*

GÁGE, *sm.* 1. Challenge, a summons to fight. 2. Salary, pay, wages.—*pl.* Perquisites, emolument gained by a place or office over and above the settled wages.

GÁGO, GA, *a.* V. *Tartamudo.*

GÁJAS, *sf. pl.* Wages, salary.

GÁJO, *sm.* 1. Branch of a tree torn or broken off. 2. Part of a bunch of grapes torn off.

GAJÓSO, SA, *a.* Branchy; spreading.

GÁLA, *sf.* 1. GALA or court-dress. *Dia de gala,* Holiday or court-day. 2. Graceful pleasing address. 3. Choicest part of a thing. 4. (America) Present or premium given to any one as a reward of merit. *Hacer gala,* To glory in having done any thing. *Hacer gala del sambenito,* To boast in one's wickedness.

GALACTÍTE, *sf.* Fuller's earth, alumina.

GALAFÁTE, *sm.* 1. An artful thief, a cunning rogue. 2. Hangman, public executioner. 3. Porter who carries burthens for hire.

GALAMÉRO, RA, *a.* Dainty, fond of nice and exquisite food. V. *Goloso.*

GALÁN, *sm.* 1. A spruce, fine, and well-made man. 2. Gentleman in full dress. 3. Gallant, courtier; wooer, one who courts a woman. 4. Actors who perform serious characters in plays are distinguished in order as first, second, &c. *Galan. Galan de noche,* (Bot.) Bastard jasmine. Cestrum nocturnum *L.*

GALÁNA, *sf.* 1. (Bot.) A kind of chick-pea. Lathyrus cicera *L.* 2. Gay dressing woman.

GALANAMÉNTE, *ad.* Gallantly, in a gallant manner; elegantly.

GALANCÉTE, *sm.* A spruce little man, a buck, a spark, a little gallant.

GALÁNGA, *sf.* (Bot.) Galangal. Alpinia galanga *L.*

GALÁNO, NA; ó GALÁN, NA, *a.* 1. Splendidly dressed. 2. Elegant, ingenious, spacious.

GALÁNTE, *a.* 1. Brave, generous, liberal. 2. Elegant, handsome; witty, facetious.

GALANTEADÓR, *sm.* Wooer, lover.

GALANTEÁR, *va.* 1. To court, to woo; to solicit favour. 2. To ornament or deck.

GALANTEAMÉNTE, *ad.* Gallantly, civilly.

GALANTÉO, *sm.* 1. The act of soliciting favour. 2. Courtship, the solicitation of a woman to marriage.

GALANTERÍA, *sf.* 1. Gallantry, courtship, a refined address to women. 2. Splendour of appearance, show, magnificence; a graceful manner. 3. Liberality, munificence, generosity.

GALANÚRA, *sf.* A showy splendid dress.

GALÁPAGO, *sm.* 1. Fresh-water tortoise. Testudo lutaria *L* 2. Bed of a plough-share. 3. A convex frame, on which vaults are formed. 4. Cleft in a horse's foot. 5. Frame for boring guns. 6. Ancient military machine. 7. An artful cunning fellow.—*pl.* 1. (Naút.) Cleats, pieces of wood of different forms and use, chiefly employed to fasten ropes on the decks and sides of ships. 2. Spring-hooks of a weaver's bench.

GALÁPO, *sm.* Frame for twisting ropes.

GALARDÓN, *sm.* Reward or recompense for useful services.

GALARDONADÓR, RA, *s.* Remunerator.

GALARDONÁR, *va.* To reward, to recompense, to requite.

GALARÍN ó GALLARÍN, *sm.* A mode of counting by doubling the numbers.

GALÁTA, *a.* Native of Galatia.

Galatíte, *sf.* V. *Galactite.*
Galavárdo, *sm.* A tall, lean, and weak man.
Galaxía, *sf.* 1. (Astron.) Galaxy, the milky way. 2. Gray clay, fuller's earth.
Galbána, *sf.* 1. (Bot.) A small sort of pease. Lathyrus cicera *L.* 2. Sloth, laziness.
Galbanádo, da, *a.* Of the colour of galbanum.
Galbanéro, ra, *a.* Lazy, indolent.
Gálbano, *sm.* (Farm.) Galbanum, a sort of white gum, issuing from the Bubon galbanum *L.*
Gálbulo, *sm.* The nut of the cypress-tree.
Galdrés, *sm.* (Ant.) A kind of loose great coat.
Galdrecíllo, *sm.* A kind of tight great coat.
Galdrópe, *sm.* (Naút.) Wheel-rope, the rope of the steering wheel.
Galdrúpa, *sf.* Top, an inverted conoid, which children set to turn on the point.
Galeáto, ta, *a.* Applied to the prologue or preface of any work, in which a reply or defence is made to the objections against it.
Galeáza, *sf.* (Naút.) Galleass, a kind of vessel.
GALE'NA, *sf.* Galena, sulphuret of lead.
Galénico, ca, *a.* Galenic, galenical.
Galenísmo, *sm.* Doctrine of Galen.
Galéno, *a.* (Naút.) V. *Galerno.*
Galéo, *sm.* (Ict.) Sword-fish. Xiphias gladius [L.
Galeónes, *sm. pl.* (Naút.) Armed ships of burthen used in Spain for trade in time of war.
Galeóta, *sf.* 1. (Naút.) Galliot, a kind of vessel. 2. (Naút.) A small galley. 3. Gutter-ledge. —*pl.* (Naút.) Carlings of the hatch-ways.
Galeóte, *sm.* Galley-slave.
Galéra, *sf.* 1. Galley, a vessel with oars, in use in the Mediterranean. 2. Vessel with a net, used for washing wool. 3. Wagon, a heavy covered carriage for burthens. 4. House of correction for lewd women. 5. (In Hospitals) Row of beds in the middle of a room for the reception of the sick. 6. (Impr.) Galley, an oblong square frame with ledges to preserve together a column of types as they are composed. 7. Ancient female dress. 8. (Arit.) Line cutting off the quotient in division.—*pl.* Punishment of rowing on board of galleys. *Estar en galeras*, (Met.) To be in distress or affliction. *Azotes y galeras*, (Met.) Applied to ordinary food never varied.
Galeráda, *sf.* (Impr.) Galley of types composed, or the proof of a galley for correction.
Galeréro, *sm.* Wagoner, one who drives a wagon.
Galería, *sf.* 1. Gallery, a kind of walk along the floor of a house into which the doors of the apartments open. 2. (Fort.) A narrow covered passage across a moat. 3. *Galeria de popa*, (Naút.) Stern-gallery or balcony, into which there is a passage out of the great cabin.
Galeríla, *sf.* A small galley.
Galerísta, *sm.* Soldier who does duty on board of galleys. [tata *L.*
Galeríta, *sf.* (Orn.) Crested lark. Alauda cris-
Galérno, *a.* (Naút.) Applied to a soft, mild wind. [liffs.
Galfárro, *sm.* Rogue, swindler.—*pl.* Bumbai-
Gálga, *sf.* 1. Greyhound bitch; the female of the *Canis grajus L.* 2. Stone rolling down a steep hill; wheel of the stone of an oil-mill. 3. Kind of itch. 4. Bier with which poor people are buried. 5. (Naút.) Back of an anchor.

Galgána, *sf.* V. *Galbana.*
Gálgo, *sm.* Greyhound. Canis grajus *L.* *El que nos vendió el galgo*, The very man we spoke of. [a greyhound.
Galgueño, ña, *a.* Resembling or concerning
Gálgulo, *sm.* (Orn.) Roller. Coracias garrula *L.* [bele.
Galiámbo, *sm.* Song of the Gallic priest of Cy-
Galíbos, *sm. pl.* (Naút.) Models of ships.
Galicádo, da, *a.* Infected with the venereal disease.
Galicár, *va.* To infect with the French disease.
Galicínio, *sm.* Cock-crowing time. [gy.
Galicísmo, *sm.* Gallicism, French phraseolo-
Gálico, *sm.* Venereal disease.
Galína, *sf.* Pilfering.
Galimár, *va.* To pilfer, to rob. [verum *L.*
Gálio, *sm.* (Bot.) Lady's bedstraw. Galium
Galiópsis, *sf.* (Bot.) Hemp or dead nettle. Galeopsis tetrahit *L.*
Galipót, *sm.* White frankincense, or the white resin which distils from the pine-tree.
Galívos, *sm. pl.* Compassings; bevelings; pieces of timber incurvated in the form of an arch. [in the Levant trade.
Galizábra, *sf.* Kind of vessel with lateen sails
Galladúra, *sf.* Tread, the cock's part or sperm in the egg.
Gallárda, *sf.* A kind of airy Spanish dance.
Gallardaménte, *ad.* Elegantly, gracefully.
Gallardeár, *vn.* To play wild pranks, to be merry.
Gallardéte, *sm.* (Naút.) Pendant, streamer.
Gallardetón, *sm.* (Naút.) Broad pendant.
Gallardía, *sf.* 1. A graceful air and deportment. 2. Activity, briskness in the execution or performance of a thing. 3. Liberality of sentiments, disinterestedness. 4. Magnanimity, greatness of mind.
Gallárdo, da, *a.* 1. Gay, graceful, elegant. 2. Magnanimous, great of mind, exalted in sentiments. 3. Generous, disinterested, pleasant. 4. Brave, daring, bold.
Gallaréta, *sf.* (Orn.) Widgeon. Anas ferina *L.*
Gallarín, *sm.* Excessive gain or loss. *Salir al gallarin*, To experience a loss or disgrace.
Gallarón, *sm.* (Orn.) A kind of bustard. [L.
Gallaríto, *sm.* (Bot.) Lousewort. Pedicularis
Gallarúza, *sf.* A coarse garment worn by country people.
Galleár, *va.* 1. To tread, to copulate as birds. 2. (Met.) To assume an air of importance.—*vn.* To raise the voice with a menace or call; to become irritated.
Galléga, *sf.* (Bot.) Goat's rue.
Gallegáda, *sf.* 1. Number of natives of Galicia assembled together. 2. Manners or behaviour of the natives of Galicia. [people of Galicia.
Gallégo, ga, *a.* Belonging or peculiar to the
Gallégo, *sm.* (Castil.) North-west wind.
Galléta, *sf.* 1. A small copper pan. 2. (Naút.) Biscuit. 3. (Naút.) Mess-bowl.
Gallicínio, *sm.* Cock-crowing, the time when the cocks crow at midnight.
Gallíllo, *sm.* (Anat.) Uvula, a soft spongeous body suspended from the palate over the glottis.
Gallína, *sf.* 1. Hen, a domestic fowl. 2. (Met.) Coward, a chicken-hearted fellow. 3. In universities, second orator or student destined to

deliver the eulogium at graduating. *Gallina ciega*, Blind man's buff; a play among boys. *Hijo de la gallina blanca*, A lucky fortunate man. *Gallina de rio*, V. *Gallineta*.

Gallinaza, *sf.* 1. Hen-dung. 2. (Orn.) Carrion vulture, kite. Falco brasiliensis *L.* In Vera Cruz it is called *Sopilote*.

Gallinería, *sf.* 1. Poulterer's shop. 2. Hen-coop, or hen-house. 3. (Met.) Cowardice, pusillanimity.

Gallinéro, ra, *a.* Preying or feeding upon fowls.

Gallinéro, *sm.* 1. Poulterer, one who deals in poultry. 2. Hen-yard, hen-coop. 3. Basket in which fowls are carried to market. 4. (Met.) Place where many women meet.

Gallinéta, *sf.* (Orn.) Sand piper. Tringa hypoleucus *L.*

Gallinóso, sa, *a.* Timorous, cowardly.

Gallipávo, *sm.* (Orn.) Turkey. Meleagris gallopavo *L.*

Gallipuénte, *sm.* Bridge without rails.

Gallíto, *sm.* Beau, coxcomb.

Gállo, *sm.* 1. (Orn.) Cock, the male to the hen. Gallus *L.* 2. (Ict.) Doree, a sea-fish. Zeus faber *L.* 3. Kind of small windmill for children to play with. 4. (Met.) Chief of a village or parish. 5. In universities he who makes the eulogium of the person graduating. 6. (Carp.) Wall-board in the roofing of a house. *Pata de gallo*, An artful device. *Tener mucho gallo*, To be very arrogant and proud.

Gallo-bósque, *sm.* (Orn.) Wood-grouse. Tetrao urogallus *L.*

Gallo-crésta, *sf.* (Bot.) Clary, wild sage. Salvia verbenaca *L.*

Gallófa, *sf.* 1. Morsel of bread given to pilgrims. 2. Pulse, garden-stuff. 3. A lazy indolent life. 4. An idle tale. 5. Directory of divine service.

Gallofeár y Gallofár, *vn.* To saunter about and live upon alms.

Gallofero, ra, *s.* Beggar, an idle, lazy person.

Gallófo, fa, *a.* Idle, lazy, poor, mendicant.

Gallón, *sm.* (Arag.) Green sod, turf; a clod covered with grass. *Gallónes*, Festoons, an ornament or carved work.

Gallonáda, *sf.* (Arag.) Wall made of sods.

Gallúda, *sf.* (Ict.) Tope, sweet William. Squalus galeus *L.*

Gallundéro, ra, *a.* Applied to fishing-nets.

Gálo, *sm.* (Bot.) Gale or sweet gale, Louisiana cherry-tree. Myrica gale *L.*

Galócha, *sf.* 1. Clog, a sort of wooden shoe. 2. Patten, a shoe of wood with an iron ring, worn under the common shoe by women. 3. Calotte, a cap or coif worn by the Roman catholic clergy.

Galón, *sm.* 1. Galloon; a texture of silk, thread, gold or silver. 2. (Naút.) Wooden ornament on the sides of ships. *Galónes*, (Naút.) Rails, narrow laths nailed around the quarter-deck.

Galonázo, *sm.* Large galloon; excessive ornament.

Galoneadúra, *sf.* The act of garnishing with lace.

Galoneár, *va.* To lace, to adorn with lace.

Galonéro, *sm.* Lace or galloon maker.

Galopár y Galopeár, *vn.* To gallop, to go at a gallop.

Galópe, *sm.* 1. Gallop, a motion of a horse performed by leaps. 2. Hasty execution of a thing. *A' galope, ó de galope*, Gallopingly.

Galopeádo, da, *a.* Done in a hurry.—*sm.* Whipping, flogging.

Galopín, *sm.* 1. (Naút.) Swabber, a boy who swabs the deck; a cabin-boy. 2. Scullion, a kitchen-boy, employed in cleaning plates, dishes, and other culinary vessels; a contemptible rogue. 3. Boy meanly dressed. 4. An experienced and clever knave.

Galopináda, *sf.* (Murc.) Action of a cunning crafty person.

Galóta, *sf.* V. *Galocha.*

Galpíto, *sm.* A weak, sickly chicken.

Galvanísmo, *sm.* Galvanism, electricity of metals.

Gáma, *sf.* 1. Gamut, the scale of musical notes. 2. Doe, a she-deer; the female to a buck.

Gamalogía, *sf.* Discourse on marriage.

Gamárra, *sf.* Martingal, a broad strap made fast to the girths under the belly of a horse, the other end being fastened under the nose-band of the bridle.

Gamárza, *sf.* (Bot.) Wild Syrian rue. Peganum harmala *L.*

Gámba, *sf.* Leg.

Gámbalo, *sm.* (Ant.) Kind of linen.

Gambalúa, *sf.* A tall, lank, ill-shaped man without life or spirit.

Gámbaro, *sm.* A kind of small craw-fish.

Gambéta, *sf.* 1. Cross-caper in dancing; ancient dance. 2. Affected language or tone of voice. 3. *Gambeta de mar*, Scaled centre shell. Lepas pollicipes *L.*

Gambeteár, *vn.* To caper like a horse.

Gambéto, *sm.* A kind of quilted great coat.

Gámbo y Gambúx, *sm.* Cap for a new-born child.

Gambótes, *sm. pl.* (Naút.) Counter-timbers, arched timbers.

Gambóx, *sm.* A small bonnet or cap for children.

Gaméla, *sf.* Kind of basket.

Gamélla, *sf.* 1. Yoke for oxen and mules. 2. A large wooden trough. 3. V. *Camellon.*

Gamellón, *sm. aum.* Trough in which grapes are trodden.

Gamézno, *sm.* Little young buck.

Gámma, *sf.* Gamut. V. *Gáma.*

Gámo, *sm.* Buck of the fallow deer. Cervus dama *L.*

Gamón, *sm.* (Bot.) White and yellow asphodel

Gamonál, *sm.* Place in which asphodels flourish.

Gamoníto, *sm.* 1. Young shoots springing round trees or shrubs. 2. Young asphodel.

Gamonóso, sa, *a.* Abounding in asphodels.

Gamúno, na, *a.* Applied to the skins of deer.

Gamúza, *sf.* 1. Chamois. Antelope rupicapra *L.* 2. Chamois, or Chamois leather.

Gamuzádo, da, *a.* Chamois colour.

Gána, *sf.* 1. Appetite, keenness of stomach; hunger. 2. A healthy disposition of the body. 3. Inclination, desire. *De gana*, Designedly. *De su gana*, Voluntarily. *De buena ó mala gana*, With pleasure, or with reluctance.

Ganáda, *sf.* Act of gaining or winning.

Ganadería, *sf.* Stock of cattle.

Ganadéro, ra, *a.* Belonging to cattle.

Ganadéro, ra, *s.* Grazier, owner of cattle; dealer in cattle.

Ganádo, *sm.* 1. Head of cattle of the same kind. 2. Cattle, word of contempt applied to men and women. 3. Vermin. 4. Collection of bees of a bee-hive. *Ganado mayor*, Black cattle. *Ganado menor ó menudo*, Sheep and goats. *Ganado de cerda*, Hogs, pigs, swine.

Ganadór, *sm.* One who gains or acquires.

Ganáncia, *sf.* Gain, profit. *Hijo de ganancia*, Bastard. *Andar de ganancia*, To pursue any thing successfully.
Ganancíal, *a.* Lucrative. *Bienes gananciales*, Acquest during marriage.
Gananciόso, sa, *a.* Lucrative, gainful.
Ganapán, *sm.* Porter, one who carries burthens for hire.
Ganapiérde, *sm.* A mode of playing drafts, where he who loses all his men wins the game.
Ganár, *va.* 1. To gain, to obtain as profit or advantage. 2. To attain, to acquire. 3. To conquer. 4. To surpass. *Ganar el barlovento*, (Naút.) To get to windward. *Ganar el viento*, To gain the weather-gage. *Ganar sobre un bazel*, To gain upon a ship. *Ganar la vida*, To gain a living. *Ganar las albricias*, To get the start in bringing favourable news.
Ganchéro, *sm.* Conductor of a raft of timber.
Gáncho, *sm.* 1. Hook, which remains after a branch of a tree has been broken off. 2. Hook, an incurvated piece of iron; a crotch. 3. Crook a sheep-hook. 4. An allurer, one who artfully insinuates himself into the favour of another to attain some purpose. 5. Pimp, procurer, pander. 6. (Naút.) An iron hook with an eye. *Gancho de bichero*, Boat-hook. *Gancho de botalon*, Gooseneck of a boom. *Gancho de aparejo*, Tackle-hook. *Gancho de las estrelleras del trinquete*, Hook of the fore-tackle. *Gancho de la gata*, Cat-hook. *Gancho de guimbalete de las estagas*, Swivel-hook of the top-sail-ties. *Ganchos de pescantes de anclas*, Fish-hooks of an anchor. *Ganchos de las arraigadas*, Foot-hooks or futtocks. *Ganchos de revirar maderas*, Cant-hooks.
Ganchóso, sa, *a.* Hooked, curved.
Gandáya, *sf.* 1. Laziness, idleness. 2. V. *Cofia.*
Gandído, da, *a.* Seduced or led astray for some evil purpose.
Gandír, *va.* To eat. V. *Comer.*
Gandujádo, *sm.* Ornament or ruffle of a woman's dress.
Gandujár, *va.* To bend. V. *Encoger ó Encorvar.*
Ganfalonéro, *sm.* Ganfalonier, Pope's standard-bearer.
Ganfanón, *sm.* Ganfalon, ensign of the Romish church, and some Italian states.
Ganfórro, ra, *s.* Vagrant, vagabond.
Gánga, *sf.* 1. (Orn.) The little pin-tailed grouse. Tetras alchata *L.* 2. (Met.) A worthless or useless trifle. *Andar á caza de gangas*, To be engaged in idle useless pursuits. 3. (Min.) Gangue, bed or matrix of minerals.
Gangarílla, *sf.* Ancient company of strolling players.
Gánglios, *sm. pl.* (Anat.) Ganglions; tumours.
Gangóso, sa, *a.* Snuffling or speaking through the nose.
Gangréna, *sf.* Gangrene, mortification.
Gangrenárse, *vr.* To become gangrenous.
Gangrenóso, sa, *a.* Gangrenous.
Ganguear, *vn.* To snuffle, to speak through the nose.
Ganguíl, *sm.* A sort of large barge, used for fishing or in the coasting trade; lighter.
Ganóso, sa, *a.* Desirous, full of desire; longing after.
Gansarón, *sm.* 1. Gosling, a young goose. 2. A tall, thin man.
Gánso, sa, *s.* 1. (Orn.) Gander, goose. Anas anser *L.* 2. Tall slender person; rustic.—*pl* Giblets, the parts of a goose which are cu off before it is roasted.
Gánte, *sm.* A kind of linen manufactured in Ghent.
Ganzúa, *sf.* 1. Picklock, an instrument with which locks are opened. 2. Thief who picks locks. 3. One who wheedles out a secret. 4. Executioner, hangman.
Ganzuár, *va.* To pick a lock, to open it with a picklock.
Gañán, *sm.* 1. Servant of a shepherd, herdsman. 2. Day-labourer; ploughman.
Gañanía, *sf.* Number of day-labourers.
Gañído, *sm.* Yelping or howling of a dog.
Gañíles, *sm. pl.* Fauces, organs of the voice.
Gañír, *va.* 1. To yelp or howl like a dog. 2. To croak, to cackle, to crow.
Gañivéte, *sm.* Penknife. V. *Cañavete.*
Gañón y Gañóte, *sm.* 1. Pipe or organs in the interior of the throat. 2. Kind of fritters.
Gápa, *sf.* (Bot.) Honey flower. Melianthus major *L.*
Garabatáda, *sf.* Act of throwing a hook.
Garabateár, *va.* 1. To hook, to catch with a hook. 2. To scrawl, to scribble. 3. To use tergiversations.
Garabatéo, *sm.* Act of hooking.
Garabatíllo, *sm.* 1. A small hook. 2. Difficulty of evacuating any peccant matter from the lungs.
Garabáto, *sm.* 1. Pot-hook, a hook to fasten pots or kettles with. 2. Hook to hang meat on. 3. An attractive graceful gait and deportment. *Mozo de garabato*, A thief.—*pl.* 1. Ill-formed or scrawling letters or characters. 2. Improper gestures or movements of the hands and fingers.
Garabatóso, sa, *a.* Elegant, charming, attractive.
Garabíto, *sm.* A linen cover spread over fruit-stalls in a market-place.
Garambáyna, *sf.* Extravagant finery in dress. —*pl.* 1. Grimaces, wry faces, ridiculous gestures. 2. Pot-hooks, ill formed letters.
Garánte, *sm.* Guarantee, warranter, one who gives security.
Garantía, *sf.* Warrantry, security; an undertaking to see stipulations performed.
Garañón, *sm.* 1. Jack-ass. 2. Lecher, whoremaster.
Garapácho, *sm.* Kind of dressed meat.
Garapíña, *sf.* 1. The congealed particles of any liquid. 2. A kind of black lace. *Bizcochos de garapiña*, Biscuits covered with concreted sugar.
Garapiñár, *va.* To ice, to turn to ice, to cover with ice
Garipiñéra, *sf.* Vessels in which liquids are congealed.
Garapíta, *sf.* Fishing-net with small meshes.
Garapíto, *sm.* Small insect, like a tick.
Garapúllo, *sm.* Dart made of paper.
Garatúsa, *sf.* 1. A sort of game at cards. 2. Caress, act of endearment.
Garavíto, *sm.* Stall, a small wooden shed, in which greens, fruit, and other things are sold at market.
Gárba, *sf.* Sheaf, a bundle of stalks of corn bound together that the ears may dry.
Garbanzál, *sm.* A piece of ground sown with chick-peas.
Garbánzo, *sm.* (Bot.) Chick-pea. Cicer arieti-

zum *L.* A sort of pulse much esteemed in Spain. *Cuenta garbanzos*, A covetous or avaricious person.

Garbanzuélo, *sm. dim.* 1. Small chick-pea. 2. (Albeyt.) Disease in horses' feet.

Garbár ó Garbeár, *va.* 1. To form sheaves, to tie stalks of corn into bundles. 2. To seize, to lay hold of any thing eagerly.—*vn.* To affect an air of dignity and grandeur.

Garbéña, *sf.* (Bot.) Common heath. Erica vulgaris *L.*

Gárbias, *sm. pl.* A sort of ragout, made of herbs, cheese, flour, eggs, sugar, and butter.

Garbilladór, *sm.* Sifter, riddler.

Garbillár, *va.* To garble, to sift; to separate the bad from the good. [bass or sedge.

Garbíllo, *sm.* Riddle, a coarse sieve made of

Garbín, *sm.* Coif made of net work.

Garbíno, *sm.* South-west wind.

Gárbo, *sm.* 1. A clever and genteel way of doing things. 2. A gentlemanlike air and deportment. 3. Frankness, disinterestedness; liberality of sentiments.

Garbóso, sa, *a.* Genteel, sprightly, gay.

Garbúllo, *sm.* Crowd, a multitude confusedly pressed together.

Garcéro, *sm.* (Orn.) Heron-hawk. Falco *L.*

Garcés, *sm.* (Naút.) Main-top-sail. V. *Gavia.*

Garcéta, *sf.* 1. A young heron. 2. Hair which falls in locks on the cheeks and temples. 3. (Naút.) Point or reef-band, a small rope which serves to furl the sails. *Garcétas*, Tenderlings, the first horns of a deer.

Gardúja, *sf.* Barren stone thrown away in quicksilver mines.

Gardúña, *sf.* Martin. Mustela foina *L.*

Gardúño, *sm.* 1. He or male martin. 2. Filcher, a petty thief or robber.

Gárfa, *sf.* Claw, the foot of a beast or bird armed with sharp nails; a hand, in contempt; an ancient tax.

Garfáda ó Garfiáda, *sf.* The act of clawing or seizing any thing with the nails.

Garfeár, *vn.* To use a drag-hook for getting any thing out of a well or river.

Gárfio, *sm.* Hook, drag-hook; gaff.

Gargageáda, *sf.* Spitting, ejecting phlegm from the mouth.

Gargageár, *vn.* To spawl, to throw moisture out of the mouth.

Gargagéo, *sm.* Spitting, the act of ejecting moisture from the mouth.

Gargajál, *sm.* Place full of spittle.

Gargajiénto, ta, *a.* Spitting, ejecting moisture from the mouth.

Gargájo, *sm.* 1. Spittle, saliva which collects in the mouth. 2. An ill-formed child.

Gargajóso, sa, *a.* Spitting.

Garganchón, *sm.* V. *Gargüero.*

Gargánta, *sf.* 1. Throat, gullet, meat-pipe. 2. Instep, the upper part of the foot where it joins to the leg. 3. Mountain-flood, torrent. 4. A narrow pass between mountains or rivers. 5. A sweet and easy modulation of the voice.

Gargantáda, *sf.* Quantity of water, wine, or blood, ejected at once from the throat.

Garganteadúras, *sf. pl.* (Naút.) Throat-seizings of the blocks; cords or lines with which blocks are fastened.

Garganteár, *vn.* To quaver, to shake the voice, to warble. [lation of the voice.

Gargantéo, *sm.* Quavering, a tremulous modu-

Gargantéza y Garganteria, *sf.* V. *Glotonería.*

Gargantílla, *sf.* 1. Necklace worn by women. 2. The upper part of the beam of a potter's wheel.

Gargantón, na, *a.* Greedy, ravenous.

Gárgara, *sf.* Noise made by gargling or washing the throat with a liquid not suffered immediately to descend.

Gargarísmo, *sm.* 1. Gargarism, a medicated liquor to wash the mouth with. 2. The act of washing the throat with medicated liquor.

Gargarizár, *va.* To gargle, to gargalize, to wash the mouth or throat with medicated liquor.

Gárgol, *sm.* Groove. V. *Ranura.* *Gárgoles*, Grooves or notches of casks, where the head and bottom pieces come in.

Gargól, *a.* Empty, addle; applied to eggs.

Gárgola, *sf.* 1. Spout of a gutter in the form of a lion or other animal. 2. Linseed, the seed of flax. [part of the throat. 2. Windpipe.

Gargüéro ó Garguéro, *sm.* 1. Gullet, the inner

Garifálte, *sm.* V. *Gerifalte.*

Garífo, fa, *a.* V. *Xarifo.*

Gariofiléa, *sf.* (Bot.) Common avens or herb bennet. Geum urbanum *L.*

Garióřilo, *sm.* (Bot.) Clove-tree. Eugenia caryophyllata *L.*

Garíta, *sf.* Sentry-box; seat in a public walk.

Garitéro, *sm.* 1. Master of a gaming-house. 2. Gamester, gambler.

Garíto, *sm.* Gaming-house; profits of gaming.

Garladór, ra, *s.* Babbler, prattler.

Garlánte, *pa.* (Fam.) Babbling; prater.

Garlár, *va.* To babble, to prattle, to chatter.

Garlíto, *sm.* 1. Weel, a twiggen snare or trap for fish. 2. Snare or trap in general.

Garlócha, *sf.* Goad, a pointed instrument with which oxen are driven forwards. V. *Garrocha.*

Garlópa, *sf.* Jack-plane, a long plane; an instrument for smoothing the surface of a board.

Garnácha, *sf.* 1. Robe, a dress of office worn by counsellors. 2. Dignity or employment of a counsellor. 3. A liquor made of honey and wine. 4. A large red grape. 5. Company of strolling players.

Garnáto, *sm.* Garnet. V. *Granate.*

Gáro, *sm.* 1. A kind of lobster. 2. Brine or pickle for fish or meat. 3. V. *Gira.*

Gárra, *sf.* 1. Claw of a wild beast, talon of a bird of prey. 2. Hand, in contempt. *Gente de la garra*, Filchers, petty thieves. 3. *Navio de media garra*, (Naút.) Vessel which carries no top-sails.

Garráfa, *sf.* Vessel for cooling liquors.

Garrafál, *a.* Great, vast, huge.

Garrafiñár, *va.* To grapple, to snatch away.

Garráma, *sf.* 1. Tax or duty anciently paid by the Moors. 2. Imposition, fraud, robbery.

Garramár, *va.* 1. To rob, to plunder and pillage. 2. To collect an ancient tax.

Garráncha, *sf.* 1. (Vulg.) Sword. 2. V. *Gancho.* [splinter.

Garráncho, *sm.* Branch of a tree broken off;

Garrapáta, *sf.* 1. Tick, the louse of dogs and

sheep. Acarus ricinus; Acarus reduvius L. 2. A short little person. 3. Bumbailiff, catchpole.
Garrapateár, vn. To scribble, to scrawl.
Garrapáto, sm. A kind of moths.—pl. Pothooks, ill-formed characters or letters.
Garrár, vn. (Naút.) To drag, to be driven from the moorings; applied to a ship. *El ancla garra*, The anchor drags.
Garridaménte, ad. Gracefully, neatly.
Garridéza, sf. Elegance.
Garrído, da, a. Handsome, neat, graceful.
Garrobál, sm. Plantation of carob-trees.
Garrobílla, sf. Chips of carob-trees used to tan and dye leather a reddish yellow.
Garróbo, sm. (Bot.) Carob-tree, or St. John's bread. Ceratonia siliqua L. V. *Algarrobo*.
Garrócha, sf. Goad, a pointed instrument for driving oxen forwards.
Garrocháda, sf. Prick with a goad or spear.
Garrocheadór, sm. Goader, pricker.
Garrocheár, va. V. *Agarrochar*.
Garrochón, sm. Spear, with which bull-fighters fight bulls on horseback.
Garrófa ó Garróba, sf. 1. (Bot.) Smooth-tare; little smooth tare. Ervum tetraspermum L. 2. Fruit of the carob-tree. V. *Algarroba*.
Garrón, sm. 1. Spur of cocks and other birds. 2. Talon of a bird of prey. 3. V. *Calcañar*. *Tener garrones*, (Fam.) To be experienced, not to be easily deceived.
Garrotázo, sm. Blow with a stick.
Garrotál, sm. (Agri.) A large hazel basket.
Garróte, sm. 1. Cudgel, a strong stick. 2. Strangulation, the act of strangling. 3. The act of tying a rope or cord very tight. 4. Hazel basket or pannier. *Vino de garrote*, The last wine pressed out of grapes.
Garroteár, va. (Ant.) To cudgel.
Garrotíllo, sm. Quinsy, a tumid inflammation in the throat.
Garrúbia, sf. V. *Algarroba*.
Garrúcha, sf. 1. Pulley, one of the principal mechanical powers. 2. Horse or board on which the card is fixed for combing wool.
Garruchón, sm. Body of a coach without straps and buckles.
Garrúchos, sm. pl. (Naút.) Cringles, a sort of rings for a variety of uses on board of ships.
Garrúdo, da, a. Nervous, brawny, strong.
Garrulación, sf. Garrulity, loquacity.
Garruladór, ra, s. A garrulous person.
Garrulár, vn. To chatter, to babble, to talk much and idly.
Gárrulo, la, a. 1. Chirping; making a cheerful noise, as birds. 2. Chattering, prattling; garrulous.
Garúlla, sf. 1. Ripe grapes which remain in the basket. 2. Rabble, assembly of low people.
Gárza, sf. (Orn.) Heron. Ardea L.
Gárzo, sm. Agaric. Agaricus L.
Gárzo, za, a. Blue-eyed.
Garzón, sm. 1. Lad, boy; stripling, in familiar language. 2. Adjutant in the life-guards of the king of Spain. 3. (Ant.) Wooer, lover.
Garzoneár, vn. To make a parade of boyish actions; to solicit, to court.
Garzonía, sf. A juvenile, boyish action.
Garzóta, sf. 1. (Orn.) Night-heron. Ardea nycticorax L. 2. Plumage worn as an ornament.

Garbúl, a. (And.) Applied to a certain kind of meat.
Gas, sm. (Quím.) Gas, air.
Gása, sf. Gauze, a very thin transparent cloth.
Gasajádo y Gasájo, sm. (Ant.) V. *Agasajo*.
Gasajár, va. (Ant.) To divert, to rejoice.
Gasconáda, sf. Gasconade, boast.
Gasón, sm. 1. V. *Yeson*. 2. Large clods of earth unbroken. 3. (Ar.) V. *Cesped*.
Gastáble, a. That may be wasted or spent.
Gastadéro, sm. Waster, spender.
Gastadór, ra, s. 1. Spendthrift, prodigal, lavisher. 2. Pioneer, artificer; a labourer employed in an army, without being obliged to fight. 3. Person sentenced to public labour. 4. (Met.) Corrupter, destroyer.
Gastamiénto, sm. 1. V. *Gasto*. 2. Consumption of any thing.
Gastár, va. 1. To expend, to spend or lay out money. 2. To wear out gradually. 3. To apply to some purpose. 4. To plunder, to pillage, to sack. 5. To digest, to concoct in the stomach.—vr. 1. To be sold or disposed of. 2. To grow old, to become useless. 3. To become rotten or corrupted.
Gásto, sm. Act of spending or consuming. *Gástos*, Expenses, charges.
Gáta, sf. 1. She-cat. 2. (Bot.) Dragon-wort. 3. (Naút.) Kind of ship; a cat. 4. Cloud covering the top of a mountain. 5. *Gata de ancla*, (Naút.) Cat-tackle. *Tiro del aparejo de la gata*, Cat-fall. *Quadernal de la gata*, Cat-block. *Enganchar la gata en el ancla*, To cat the anchor. *Gátas*, (Fort.) Props or stays, with thick boards at top, by which miners shore up the earth. *A' gatas*, On all fours.
Gatáda, sf. 1. Clawing, the act of wounding with claws. 2. Turn of a hare which is closely pursued. 3. Theft or robbery effected in an artful manner.
Gatafúra, sf. Cake made of herbs and sour milk.
Gatatúmba, sf. Affected civility or submission.
Gatázo, sm. 1. A large cat. 2. A clumsy joke. 3. An artful trick.
Gateádo, da, a. Feline, cat-like.
Gateamiénto y Gateádo, sm. Scratching, the act of tearing with the nails.
Gateár, vn. 1. To climb up, to clamber with hands and feet. 2. To scratch or claw. 3. To steal, to rob.
Gatéra, sf. 1. A cat's hole, through which cats go in and out. 2. (Bot.) Cat-mint. Nepeta cataria L.
Gatería, sf. 1. Number of cats brought together in a place. 2. Cringing submission, mean servility.
Gatésco, ca, a. Belonging to cats, feline.
Gaticída, sm. (In the Jocular Style) Cat-killer.
Gatilllázo, sm. Grasp of pincers, catch of a pelican, clawing of a cat.
Gatíllo, sm. 1. A little cat. 2. Pelican, an instrument for drawing teeth. 3. Cock of a gun. 4. Nape of a bull or ox. 5. Cramp-iron. 6. Filcher, a petty thief or robber.
Gatíta, sf. A small cat.
Gáto, sm. 1. Cat. Felis catus L. 2. Skin of a cat. 3. A petty thief, filcher. 4. Tongs used for hooping casks. 5. Cramp-iron. 6. Instrument used for searching and examining into

the bore of a cannon. 7 Jack, an engine for raising ponderous bodies. *Gato cornaqui*, Jack-screw used on board of ships for raising great weights. *Gato de algalia*, Civet-cat. Viverra zibetha *L.* *Gato montes ó de clavo*, Mountain cat. Felis catus agrestis *L.*

Gatúna ó Gatúña, *sf.* (Bot.) Rest-harrow, cammock. Ononis arvensis *L.*

Gatúno, na, *a.* Cat-like, belonging to a cat.

Gatunéro, *sm.* (And.) He who sells smuggled meat.

Gatupério, *sm.* Mixture of liquors without art and proportion.

Gaúcho, cha, *a.* (Arq.) Applied to unlevel superficies. [ment.

Gaudeámus ó Gaudéte, *sm.* Feast, entertainment.

Gáudio, *sm.* V. *Gozo.*

Gaudívis, *sf.* A white cotton stuff.

Gavánza, *sf.* Flower of the dog-rose.

Gavánzo, *sm.* Dog-rose. V. *Escaramujo.*

Gavása, *sf.* Harlot, strumpet.

Gavéta, *sf.* 1. Drawer of a desk. 2. Ring in silk-worm sheds.

Gávia, *sf.* 1. (Naút.) Main-top-sail. 2. Place where madmen are confined. 3. Pit or hole into which a tree is transplanted with its roots. 4. V. *Gaviota.* *Gávias*, (Naút.) Top-sails of the main and fore-mast.

Gaviéro, *sm.* (Naút.) Seaman who works at the top-masts. *Gaviero mayor de la cofa de trinquete*, Captain of the fore-top.

Gaviéta, *sf.* (Naút.) Scuttle.

Gaviéte de las lanchas, *sm.* (Naút.) Davit in a long boat. *Gaviéte del bauprés*, (Naút.) Saddle of the bowsprit.

Gavilán, *sm.* 1. (Orn.) Sparrow-hawk. Falco nisus *L.* 2. Fine hair-stroke in letters; either side of the nib of a pen.—*pl.* 1. Cross bars of the guard of a sword. 2. (Naút.) Tholes. V. *Toletes.* 3. Dry flowers of artichokes or thistles.

Gavilancíllo, *sm.* 1. A young hawk. 2. The incurvated point of an artichoke leaf.

Gavílla, *sf.* 1. Sheaf of corn; a bundle of vine-shoots. 2. Gang of suspicious persons.

Gavilléro, *sm.* Place where suspicious persons assemble; a nest of thieves.

Gavína, *sf.* Gull. V. *Gaviota.*

Gavión, *sm.* 1. (Mil.) Gabion, a large cylindrical basket, open at both ends, which serves to cover the besiegers in their approaches. 2. A large hat. [nus *L.*

Gavióta, *sf.* (Orn.) Gull, sea-gull. Larus canus *L.*

Gáya, *sf.* 1. Stripe of different colours on stuffs, silks, ribbons, &c. 2. Trophies, emblems of victory. 3. V. *Picaza.* *Gaya ciencia ó gaya doctrina*, Poesy or the art of poetry.

Gayadúra, *sf.* Garniture, an ornamental trimming of various colours.

Gayár, *va.* To garnish or adorn with trimming of a different colour from the stuff.

Gayáta, *sf.* Crook, sheep-hook.

Gaycáno, *sm.* Sea-fish used for catching others.

Gáyo, *sm.* (Orn.) Jay. Corvus glandarius *L.*

Gayóla, *sf.* 1. (Nav.) V. *Jaula.* 2. (And.) Kind of hut raised for watching vineyards.

Gayómba, *sf.* (Bot.) Sweet-scented broom. Spartium monospermum *L.*

Gaýta, *sf.* 1. Bag-pipe. 2. Flagelet, a small flute. 3. Hand-organ. 4. Pipe or syringe with which a clyster is administered. 5. Neck, the part between the head and body.

Gayterá, *sf.* A gay or gaudy dress.

Gaytéro, ra, *a.* Gay, gaudy, showy.

Gaytéro, *sm.* 1. Piper, one who plays on a bag-pipe. 2. Fop, buck; a person ridiculously ostentatious in dress.

Gayúba, *sf.* (Bot.) Bear-berry, red-berried trailing arbutus. Arbutus uva ursi *L.*

Gáza, *sf.* (Naút.) Strap, spliced in a circular form, and used to fasten blocks to the masts, yards, and rigging. *Gaza de esta*, (Naút.) Collar of a stay. *Gaza de un moton*, (Naút.) Stay of a block.

Gazapatón ó Gazapatón, *sm.* Nonsense, foolish talk.

Gazápa, *sf.* (Fam.) Lie, falsehood.

Gazapéla, *sf.* Clamorous wrangling or quarrelling.

Gazapéra, *sf.* Warren, a place where rabbits burrow in the ground.

Gazapíllo, to, co, *sm.* A small rabbit.

Gazapína, *sf.* Assembly of vulgar vile people.

Gazápo, *sm.* 1. A young rabbit. 2. A dissembling artful knave; a great liar.

Gazél, *sm.* V. *Gamo.*

Gazéla, *sf.* Gazelle, antelope.

Gazéta, *sf.* Gazette, newspaper; a paper of news or public intelligence.

Gazetéro, *sm.* Conductor or vender of a newspaper.

Gazetéra, *sf.* She who sells gazettes.

Gazetísta, *sm.* 1. One who delights in reading newspapers. 2. News-monger, one whose employment is to collect and tell news.

Gazíes, *sm. pl.* Converted Moors in Spain.

Gazmiár, *va.* To steal and eat tid-bits.—*vn.* To complain, to resent.

Gazmól, *sm.* Kind of cancer on the tongue of hawks.

Gazmoñáda y Gazmoñería, *sf.* Prudery, hypocrisy.

Gazmoñéro, ra; y Gazmóño, ña, *a.* Hypocritical, dissembling; hypocrite.

Gaznár, *vn.* V. *Graznar.*

Gaznatáda, *sf.* Blow or stroke on the throttle.

Gaznáte, *sm.* Throttle, windpipe.

Gaznatíco, llo, to, *sm.* Small windpipe.

Gaznatón, *sm.* 1. Blow on the throat. 2. Pancake, fritter.

Gazón, *sm.* (Bot.) Common thrift, sea gilly-flower. Statice armeria *L.*

Gazofilácio, *sm.* Place in which the riches of the temple of Jerusalem were collected.

Gazpachéro, *sm.* He who carries the dinner to the labourers and workmen; maker of the soup called *Gazpacho.*

Gazpácho, *sm.* Dish made of bread, oil, vinegar, onions, salt, and red pepper, mixed together in water. [hunger.

Gazúza, *sf.* Keenness of stomach, violent hunger.

Ge, *sf.* Name of *g* pronounced *h* or *ay*, in Spanish.—*pron.* (Ant.) V. *Se.*

Géfe, *sm.* Chief. V. *Xéfe.*

Gefimbriél, *sm.* A kind of sealing-wax which comes from Smyrna.

Gelasíno, na, *s.* Applied to the teeth seen in laughing.

GELATÍNA, *sf.* Jelly, any thing brought to a state of glutinousness and viscosity. V. *Jaletina.*
GELATINÓSO, SA, *a.* Gelatinous, glutinous.
GELÉA, *sf.* V. *Jalea.*
GÉLIDO, DA, *a.* (Poét.) Gelid, frigid.
GELÍZ, *sm.* Overseer who weighs and sells silk.
GELOSÍA, *sf.* Jealousy. V. *Celosia.*
GÉMA, *sf.* Beam having some bark owing to its being ill squared. [a span.
GEMÁL, *a.* Being of the length or breadth of
GÉME, *sm.* 1. A span. 2. (Joc.) Woman's face.
GEMÉLA, *sf.* Flower exhaling the odour of orange and jessamine.
GEMECÁR, *vn.* To sob, to sigh with convulsion.
GEMÉLOS, *sm. pl.* 1. Twins, two children born at a birth. 2. (Naút.) Cheeks or side-beams of the masts, employed to strengthen them.
GEMÍDO, *sm.* 1. Groan, breath expired with noise and difficulty. 2. Howl, the cry of a wolf or dog.
GEMIDÓR, *sm.* Lamenter, mourner.
GEMINACIÓN, *sf.* Repetition, reiteration.
GEMINÁR, *va.* To double, to repeat.
GÉMINIS, *sm.* 1. Gemini, a sign of the Zodiac. 2. A kind of resolving and healing plaster.
GÉMINO, NA, *a.* Doubled, repeated.
GEMÍR, *vn.* 1. To groan, to moan, to grieve. 2. To howl, to cry as a wolf or dog. 3. To roar, to whistle; to sound as the sea or wind.
GEMÓSO, SA, *a.* Barky; applied to wrought timber with pieces of the bark on it.
GENCIÁNA, *sf.* (Bot.) Gentian. Gentiana *L.*
GENEALOGÍA, *sf.* Genealogy, the history of the succession of families.
GENEALÓGICO, CA, *a.* Genealogical.
GENEALOGÍSTA, *sm.* Genealogist, he who traces descents. [race.
GENEÁRCO, *sm.* Head or chief of a family or
GENEÁTICO, CA, *a.* Genethliacal, relating to divination by nativities. [duced or begotten.
GENERÁBLE, *a.* Generable, that may be pro-
GENERACIÓN Y GENERÁCIO, *sf.* 1. Generation, the act of begetting or producing. 2. Progeny, race. 3. A single succession. 4. Nation; age.
GENERÁL, *sm.* 1. Hall or room in a public school where the sciences are taught. 2. A general officer. 3. (Arag.) Custom-house. 4. Superior of a religious order. 5. V. *Generala.*
GENERÁL, *a.* General, comprehending many species or individuals; not special; common. *En generál,* Generally, in general.
GENERÁLA, *sf.* 1. Beat of the drum which calls troops to arms. 2. (Naút.) Signal to join convoy.
GENERALÁTO, *sm.* Generalship, commission or dignity of a general either of soldiers or religious.
GENERALÉRO, *sm.* (Arag.) V. *Aduanero.*
GENERALIDÁD, *sf.* 1. Generality, the whole, totality. 2. (Arag.) Community, corporation. 3. Custom-duties on goods. *Generalidádes,* (Arag.) Custom-house fees; discourse consisting of only general principles.
GENERALÍF Ó GENERALÍFE, *sm.* Country-house.
GENERALÍSIMO, *sm.* 1. Generalissimo, the commander in chief of an army or fleet of ships of war. 2. Superior of a religious order.
GENERALIZÁR, *va.* To generalize.
GENERALMÉNTE, *ad.* Generally.
GENERÁNTE, *pa.* Generator; engendering.
GENERATÍVO, VA, *a.* Generative, having the power of propagation.
GENERICAMÉNTE, *ad.* Generically.
GENÉRICO, CA, *a.* Generic, that which comprehends a genus or many species.
GÉNERO, *sm.* 1. Genus, a kind; a sort. *Género humano,* Mankind. 2. Sex, gender. 3. (Grammar) Gender, denomination given to nouns, from their requiring adjectives with terminations applicable to the male or female sex. *Generos,* Goods, merchandise.
GENEROSÍA, *sf.* (Vulg.) V. *Generosidad.*
GENEROSIDÁD, *sf.* 1. Hereditary nobility. 2. Generosity, the quality of being generous; magnanimity, liberality. 3. Valour and fortitude in arduous undertakings.
GENERÓSO, SA, *a.* Noble, generous, magnanimous, liberal, frank; excellent.
GÉNESIS, *sm.* Genesis, the first book of the Old Testament.
GENETÍVO, *sm.* V. *Compañon.*
GENETLÍACA, *sf.* Genethliacs, science of casting nativities. [cating by nativities.
GENETLÍACO, CA, *a.* Genethliacal, prognosti-
GENGÍBRE, *sm.* (Bot.) Ginger, an aromatic root of a hot and pungent taste.
GENIÁL, *a.* Conformable to the genius or natural disposition. *Dias geniales,* Festivals, festive days. [bits.
GENIALIDÁD, *sf.* Genialness, disposition, ha-
GENIALMÉNTE, *ad.* Genially.
GÉNIO, *sm.* 1. Genius, the disposition of nature, by which any one is qualified for some peculiar employment. 2. Genius, attending spirit. 3. (Pint.) Little angel.
GÉNIPI, *sm.* (Bot.) Silky mugwort or wormwood. Artemisia glacialis *L.*
GENÍSTA, *sf.* (Bot.) Broom.
GENITÁL, *a.* Genital.—*sm.* V. *Testiculo.*
GENITÍVO, VA, *a.* 1. Having the power of generation. 2. (In Grammar) The genitive or possessive case.
GENITÓR, *sm.* Begetter, one who begets or engenders.
GENITÚRA, *sf.* 1. Generation, procreation. 2. Seed or matter of generation. 3. Horoscope, the configuration of the planets at the hour of birth.
GENÍZARO, RA, *a.* 1. Begotten by parents of different nations. 2. Composed of different species.
GENÍZAROS, *sm. pl.* 1. Correctors and revisers of the Pope's bulls. 2. Janizaries, the foot guards of the Grand Signior.
GÉNOLES, *sm. pl.* (Naút.) Futtocks, the timbers raised over the keel, which make the breadth of a ship.
GÉNOLI Ó GÉNULI, *sm.* A light yellow paste made of sandarac, used by painters.
GENT, *ad.* (Ant.) V. *Presto.*
GENTÁLLA, *sf.* Rabble, mob. V. *Gentualla.*
GÉNTE, *sf.* 1. People, men or persons in general. 2. Nation, those who compose a community; a family. 3. Army, troops. 4. Quality or character; as *gente de paz,* A friend; in reply to a sentinel. *Gente bahuna ó del gordillo,* Rabble, mob. *Gente de bien ó de buen pro-*

ceder, Honest people. *Gente de la hampa*, A debauched set of people. *Gente de modo ó de traza*, People of fashion. *Gente de pelo ó de pelusa*, People of property. *Gente de trato*, Tradesmen, dealers. *Hacer gente*, To raise recruits, to make a party. *Gentes*, Gentiles. *De gente en gente*, From one to another, from generation to generation.

Gentecílla, *sf.* Mob, rabble.

Gentíl, *sm.* Gentile, pagan, heathen.

Gentíl, *a.* 1. Genteel, elegant, graceful. 2. Spirited, daring, bold. 3. Excellent, exquisite. *Gentil necedad*, (Iron.) A pretty piece of folly.

Gentil hómbre, *sm.* 1. Nobleman, gentleman. 2. Person sent to the king with important despatches. *Gentil hombre de cámara*, Lord of the bed-chamber. *Gentil hombre de manga*, Nobleman who attends the infants of Spain, when they go abroad. *Gentil hombre de placer*, Buffoon.

Gentiléza, *sf.* 1. Genteel deportment and address. 2. Easiness, freedom from constraint in the execution of a thing. 3. Ostentation, pageantry. 4. Civility, politeness, genteelness.

Gentilício, ia, *a.* Gentile, heathen; gentilitious.

Gentílico, ca, *a.* Heathen, gentile, pagan.

Gentilidád, *sf.* 1. Religion of the heathens. 2. Body of the heathens or gentiles.

Gentilísmo, *sm.* Gentilism.

Gentilizár, *vn.* To observe the rites of the gentiles or heathens.

Gentilménte, *ad.* Genteelly; heathenishly.

Gentío, *sm.* Crowd, multitude.

Gentuálla, *sf.* Rabble, mob. [ing the knee.

Genuflexión, *sf.* Genuflexion, the act of bend-

Genuíno, na, *a.* Genuine, pure.

Geodesía, *sf.* Geodæsia, the doctrine or art of measuring surfaces; land surveying.

Geografía, *sf.* Geography.

Geograficaménte, *ad.* Geographically.

Geográfico, ca, *a.* Geographical.

Geógrafo, *sm.* Geographer, one who describes the earth according to the position of its different parts. [ing by figures.

Geománcia, *sf.* Geomancy, the act of foretell-

Geomántico, *sm.* Geomancer.—*a.* Geomantic.

Geómetra, *sm.* Geometer, a geometrician.

Geometría, *sf.* Geometry, the science of quantity, extension, or magnitude, abstractedly considered.

Geometricaménte, *ad.* Geometrically.

Geométrico, ca, *a.* Geometrical, geometric.

Geometrizár, *vn.* To geometrize.

Geopónico, ca, *a.* Geoponic, agricultural.

Geoscópia, *sf.* Geoscopy, knowledge of the soil.

Geótico, ca, *a.* Geotic, belonging to the earth.

Geránio, *sm.* (Bot.) Crane's bill. Geranium *L.*

Geraplièga, *sf.* (Farm.) Hierapicra, a bitter purgative medicine. [order.

Gerárca, *sm.* Hierarch, the chief of a sacred

Gerarquía, *sf.* Hierarchy, sacred government, ecclesiastical government.

Gerárquico, ca, *a.* Hierarchical.

Gerifálte, *sm.* 1. (Orn.) Gerfalcon. Falco gyrfalco *L.* 2. A kind of ordnance of a small bore or caliber. [stuff. V. *Xerga.*

Gérga *sf.* Coarse frieze, a kind of woollen

Gerigónza, *sf.* 1. Jargon, unintelligible gibberish; especially of the gipsies. *Andar en gerigonzas*, To quibble, to shift, to evade, to cavil. 2. Ridiculous and extraordinary wit. 3. (Met.) Any thing obscure and difficult.

Gerigonzár, *va.* To speak a jargon.

Germanésco, ca, *a.* Belonging to the jargon of the gipsies.

Germanía, *sf.* 1. Jargon or gibberish of the gipsies. 2. Concubinage, the act of living with a woman not married. 3. Faction in Valentia during the days of Charles V. [many.

Germánico, ca, *a.* Germanic, relating to Ger-

Germáno, na, *a.* Pure, genuine, not spurious.

Gérmen, *sm.* Germ, bud, shoot.

Germinación, *sf.* Germination.

Germinár, *vn.* To germinate, to bud.

Geroglífico, *sm.* Hieroglyph or hieroglyphic, an emblem, a figure by which a word is implied.

Geroglífico, ca, *a.* Hieroglyphical. [the root.

Gérpa, *sf.* Small sterile shoot of a vine near

Gerricótе, *sm.* Dish made of blanched almonds, boiled in mutton broth, and seasoned with sugar, sage, and ginger.

Gerviguílla, *sf.* Kind of short boot.

Gerúndio, *sm.* (In Grammar) Gerund, a kind of verbal noun. *Fray Gerundio*, Friar Gerund, the title of an excellent work by father Isla.

Gésta, *sf.* (Bot.) Common broom. V. *Retama.* *Géstas*, (Ant.) Actions, feats, achievements.

Gesteár, *va.* To gesticulate, to play antic tricks; to make grimaces. [grimaces.

Gestéro, ra, *a.* Playing antic tricks, making

Gesticulación, *sf.* Gesticulation, gesture.

Gesticulár, *a.* Relating to gesture.

Gestión, *sf.* Conduct, administration, exertion; the word is French.

Gésto, *sm.* 1. Face, visage. 2. Gesticulation, grimace. 3. Aspect, appearance. 4. Likeness, resemblance. *Estar de buen gesto*, To be in good humour. *Ponerse á gesto*, To set one's self off for the purpose of pleasing. *Gestos*, (Mil.) Feats, achievements.

Géta, *sf.* 1. Blobber-lip. 2. Mushroom. 3. (Ar.) V. *Espita.* 4. Native of Dacia, now Moldavia. [lips.

Gético, ca, *a.* Thick-lipped, relating to thick

Getúdo, da, *a.* Having thick lips.

Gialomína, *sf.* Sort of yellow ochre.

Gíba, *sf.* 1. Hump, crooked back. 2. Importunity, tiresomeness.

Gibádo, da, *a.* Crooked, hump-backed.

Gibár, *va.* 1. To oppress, to make one double with a load. 2. To trouble, to vex, to molest.

Gibóso, sa, *a.* Gibbous, crook-backed.

Giferáda, *sf.* Cut with a butcher's knife. V. *Xiferada.*

Gíga, *sf.* Jig, lively tune.

Gigánta ó Gigantéa, *sf.* V. *Girasol.*

Gigantázo, za, *s.* A huge giant.

Gigánte, ta, *s.* 1. Giant, one unnaturally large. 2. One superior in courage, talents, or virtues.—*a.* Gigantic.

Gigantéo, tea; Gigantésco, ca; y Gigántico, ca; Gigantíno, na, *a.* Gigantic, giant-

Gigantéz, *sf.* Gigantieness. [like.

Giganticaménte, *ad.* Gigantically

GIGANTÍLLA, *sf.* 1. A figure made of paste or pasteboard, with a very large head. 2. A very short and lusty woman.
GIGANTIZÁR, *vn.* To grow as big as a giant.
GIGANTÓN, NA, *s.* Giant of an enormous size. *Gigantones*, Gigantic figures made of pasteboard. *Echar á alguno los gigantones*, To reprehend severely.
GIGÓTE, *sm.* Minced meat, meat chopped small and stewed.
GÍJAS, *sf. pl.* Strength, force, vigour. V. *Carnes.*
GÍLBO, BA, *a.* Applied to a colour between white and red.
GILECUÉLCO, *sm.* A kind of short coat worn by African convicts.
GILGUÉRO, *sm.* (Orn.) Linnet. V. *Xilguero.*
GILMAÉSTRE, *sm.* Officer of artillery who takes charge of the horses which draw the cannons.
GIMÉLGA, *sf.* (Naút.) Fish, a piece of timber, convex on one side and concave on the other, used to strengthen masts and yards.
GIMNASIÁRCA, *sm.* Gymnasiarcha, head of a college or school.
GIMNÁSIO, *sm.* School, academy ; gymnasium.
GIMNÁSTA, *sm.* Master of athletic exercises.
GIMNÁSTICO, CA, *a.* Gymnastic.
GÍMNICA, *sf.* Science of gymnastics.
GÍMNICO, CA, *a.* Gymnastical.
GIMNOSOFÍSTA, *sm.* Gymnosophist.
GINÉBRA, *sf.* 1. Rattle, an instrument used to make a noise ; much in use among the Moors. 2. A confused clamorous noise. 3. Game at cards.
GINEBRÁDA, *sf.* Sort of puff paste.
GINECOCRACÍA, *sf.* Gynecocracy, female government.
GINÉSTA, *sf.* (Bot.) Common broom. V. *Retama.*
GINESTÁDA, *sf.* Kind of sauce made of milk, rice, flour, spices, figs, and raisins, boiled together.
GINÉTA, *sf.* 1. Office of a serjeant. 2. Ancient kind of lance borne by captains. 3. Genet, a kind of weasel. 4. Ancient tribute paid for cattle. 5. Art of horsemanship. *Andar á la gineta*, To pace or go at a short trot. *Tener los cascos á la gineta*, To have little judgment, to be a tumultuous, turbulent person.
GINÉTE, *sm.* 1. Trooper, a horse soldier. 2. Any person who goes on horseback. 3. A good horseman. 4. Small fine horse.
GINGLÁR, *vn.* To vibrate, to swing to and fro like the pendulum of a clock.
GÍNJA Y GINJÓL. V. *Azufayfa.*
GINJOLÉRO Y GINJO, *sm.* (Ar.) V. *Azufayfo.*
GIPSÓSO, SA, *a.* Gypseous, containing gypsum.
GÍRA, *sf.* 1. Sample of stuff or cloth. 2. Feast, a splendid banquet among friends ; public rejoicing.
GIRÁDA, *sf.* Gyration ; circumvolution on one foot in dancing.
GIRÁFA, *sf.* Camelopard. Camelopardalis *L.*
GIRÁLDA, *sf.* 1. Vane or weathercock in the form of a statue ; derived from the statue of a woman put on the spire of the cathedral church of Seville. 2. (Bot.) Corn marigold. Chrysanthemum segetum *L.*
GIRALDÉTE, *sm.* Rochet or surplice without sleeves.
GIRÁNDULA, *sf.* 1. (In Artificial Fireworks) Box of rockets, which turns swiftly and emits a quantity of rockets. 2. Girandole, a large kind of branched candlestick.

GIRÁNTE, *sm.* V. *Novilunio.*
GIRAPLIÉGA, *sf.* A sort of medical confection, which serves to purge and purify the blood.
GIRÁR, *vn.* 1. To turn round, to make a gyre. 2. To remit by bills of exchange from one place to another.
GIRASÁL, *sm.* Fruit of the lac-tree.
GIRASÓL, *sm.* (Bot.) Sun-flower. Helianthus annuus *L.*
GIRÉL, *sm.* Caparison, trappings for a horse.
GIRIFÁLTE, *sm.* V. *Gerifalte.*
GIRÍNO, *sm.* Embryo of a frog.
GÍRO, RA, *a.* Handsome, perfect.
GÍRO, *sm.* 1. Gyre, a circular motion. 2. Circulation of specie or bills of exchange. 3. Circumference. 4. Gash or cut in the face. 5. Menace, bravado.
GIROFÍNA, *sf.* Ragout, made of the livers and lights of sheep.
GIRÓFLE, *sm.* (Bot.) Clove-tree. Caryophyllus aromaticus *L.*
GIROMÁNCIA, *sf.* Gyromancy.
GIRÓN, *sm.* 1. Facing of a garment. 2. A triangular piece of cloth sewed in between clothes, to make them wider. 3. Piece torn off from a gown or other cloth. 4. Standard, the ensign of a regiment of horse.
GIRONÁDO, DA, *a.* 1. Garnished with triangular pieces of cloth. 2. Torn into rags.
GIROVÁGO, GA, *a.* V. *Vagabundo.*—*sm.* Wandering monk.
GIRPEÁR, *va.* To dig about a vine.
GIS, *sm.* (Pint.) Crayon.
GÍSMA, *sf.* V. *Chisme.*
GÍSTE, *sm.* Barm, yest ; used as a leaven or ferment.
GITANÁDA, *sf.* Blandishment, wheedling like gipsies.
GITANAMÉNTE, *ad.* In a sly, winning manner.
GITANEÁR, *va.* To flatter, to wheedle, to entice by soft words.
GITANERÍA, *sf.* Wheedling, flattery.
GITANÉSCO, CA, *a.* (Joc.) Gipsey-like.
GITANÍLLO, LLA, *s. dim.* Little gipsey.
GITÁNO, NA, *s.* 1. Gipsey, a vagabond who pretends to foretel futurity. 2. A sly artful fellow. 3. A person of a genteel pleasing address.
GITÓN, *sm.* Ancient copper coin used only as the title of unity. V. *Guiton.*
GLACIÁL, *a.* Glacial, icy, frozen. V. *Helado.*
GLACIS, *sm.* (Fort.) V. *Explanada.*
GLADIATÓR Ó GLADIADÓR, *sm.* Gladiator, a sword player ; a prize fighter.
GLADIATÓRIO, IA, *a.* Relating to gladiators.
GLADIÓLO, *sm.* (Bot.) Corn-flag.
GLAGLÁR, *va.* To gaggle, to talk in a voice resembling the cry of a goose.
GLANDÍFERO, RA, *a.* Glandiferous, bearing acorns.
GLÁNDULA, *sf.* Gland, a soft spongy substance, serving to separate some particular humour from the mass of the blood.
GLÁNDULAS, *sf. pl.* (Bot.) Glandules, kernels.
GLANDULÓSO, SA, *a.* Glandulous, pertaining to the glands ; subsisting in the glands.
GLARÉA, *sf.* Coarse gravel mixed with sand.
GLASE, *sm.* A sort of bright shining silk, the warp whereof is of a different colour from the woof.
GLASEÁDO, DA, *a.* Variegated, embroidered,

Glásto, *sm.* (Bot.) Woad, dyers' woad. Isatis tinctoria *L.*
Gláucio, *sm.* A sea-green plant.
Gláuco, *sm.* (Ict.) A kind of blueish mackerel.
Glèba, *sf.* Sod of earth turned up by the plough.
Gléra, *sf.* V. *Cascajal.*
Glicónico, *sm.* A kind of Latin verse.
Glífo, *sm.* (Arq.) Glyph, a concave ornament.
Glóbo, *sm.* 1. Globe, a spherical body, of which every part of the surface is at the same distance from the centre. 2. Sphere, a terrestrial or celestial globe on which the various regions of the earth are geographically delineated, or the constellations and stars depicted.
Globóso, sa, *a.* Globular, spherical.
Globúlo, *sm.* Globule.
Globulíllo, *sm. dim.* Little globule.
Globulóso, sa, *a.* Globulous.
Glória, *sf.* 1. Glory, honour, fame; majesty, splendour. 2. Pleasure, delight in any thing. 3. A sort of light thin taffety, of which veils are made. 4. Glory, blessedness; that which ennobles or illustrates. 5. A sort of tart or pie. 6. A kind of oven or stove, in which straw is burnt instead of wood.
Gloriárse, *vr.* 1. To glory, to boast in, to be proud of. 2. To take a delight in any thing.
Glorieta, *sf.* Summer-house, bower, arbour.
Glorificación, *sf.* Glorification, the act of giving glory.
Glorificadór, *sm.* Glorifier, he that glorifies; an appellation given to God.
Glorificánte, *pa.* Glorifying; glorifier.
Glorificár, *va.* 1. To glorify, to pay honour in worship. 2. To exalt to glory or dignity.
Gloriosaménte, *ad.* Gloriously.
Glorióso, sa, *a.* 1. Glorious, excellent; elate. 2. Enjoying the bliss of heaven, blessed.
Glósa, *sf.* 1. Gloss, a scholium; a comment. 2. Note added to a document, or inserted in a book of accompts, to explain its contents. 3. (Poét.) Amplification of a verse. 4. (Mús.) Variation in a tune.
Glosadór, *sm.* Commentator.
Glosár, *va.* 1. To gloss, to explain by comment. 2. To palliate by specious exposition or representation. 3. (Poét.) To amplify the sense of a verse. 4. (Mús.) To vary notes.
Glosário, *sm.* Glossary, a dictionary explaining obscure or antiquated words.
Glóse, *sm.* Act of glossing or commentating.
Glosílla, *sf. dim.* (Impr.) Small printing type.
Glosografía, *sf.* Description of the tongue.
Glótis, *sf.* (Anat.) Glottis, opening of the larynx.
Glotón, na, *s.* Glutton, one who indulges too much in eating.
Glotonázo, za, *s.* Great glutton.
Glotoncíllo, lla, *s.* Little glutton.
Glotoneár, *vn.* To indulge one's self too much in eating, to devour, to gluttonise.
Glotonería y Glotonía, *sf.* Gluttony.
Glúten, *sm.* Gluten, a viscous substance.
Glutinosidád, *sf.* Glutinousness.
Glutinóso, sa, *a.* Glutinous, viscous.
Gnafálio, *sm.* (Bot.) Gnaphalium, cudweed; used for dysentery.
Gnómico, ca, *a.* Gnomologic, sententious.
Gnómo, *sm.* Gnome, fabulous, being supposed to inhabit the interior of the earth.
Gnomón, *sm.* 1. Gnomon, the hand or pin of a dial. 2. Bevel square, composed of two moveable rules.
Gnomónica, *sf.* Gnomonics, the science which teaches the art of making sun-dials.
Gnomónico, ca, *a.* Relating to dialling.
Gobernación, *sf.* Government. V. *Gobierno.*
Gobernádo, da, *a.* Governed.
Gobernadór, ra, *s.* Governor, ruler.
Gobernálle y Gobernáculo, *sm.* (Naút.) Rudder, a piece of timber which serves to direct the course of a ship.
Gobernánte, *sm.* (Fam.) Governor.
Gobernár, *va.* 1. To govern, to command; to direct. 2. To entertain, to maintain. 3. *Gobernar el timon,* (Naút.) To steer the ship.
Gobernatívo, va, *a.* V. *Gubernativo.*
Gobiérno, *sm.* 1. Government, administration of public affairs; establishment of legal authority. 2. District or province under the command of a governor. 3. The act of entertaining or maintaining. *Muger de gobierno,* House-keeper, a woman servant that has care of a house or family, and superintends the servants.
Góbio, *sm.* (Ict.) Gudgeon.
Góce, *sm.* Enjoyment, fruition; possession.
Gocéte, *sm.* Piece of ancient armour for the head.
Gociáno, na, *a.* Gothic.
Gócha, *sf.* Sow.
Gócho, *sm.* Pig, hog. V. *Cochino ó Puerco.*
Góden, *sm.* (Extrem.) A kind of large black fig.
Godíble, *a.* (Ant.) Jovial, jolly, merry.
Gódo, da, *a.* Gothic; a Goth.
Gófo, fa, *a.* Stupid, ignorant, rude: gofish. *Gofo,* (Pint.) A little figure or image.
Gója, *sf.* Basket in which gleaners put their corn.
Góla, *sf.* 1. Gullet, throat, œsophagus. 2. Ancient armour used to cover the throat and neck. 3. Gorget, a piece of silver or brass worn by officers of foot when on duty. 4. Collar, a part of the dress of the clergy. 5. (Fort.) Gorge, the entrance of a bastion, ravelin, or other work. *Media gola,* (Fort.) Demi-gorge, the line which passes from the angle of the bastion to the capital. 6. (Arq.) Moulding, the profile of which represents an *S.*
Góldre, *sm.* Quiver, a case for arrows.
Goléta, *sf.* A kind of small vessel.
Golfán, *sm.* V. *Nenufar.*
Golfíllo, *sm.* A small gulf.
Golfín, *sm.* V. *Delfin.*
Gólfo, *sm.* 1. Gulf, a bay; an opening into land. 2. Chaos, abyss. 3. Multitude.
Golílla, *sf.* 1. Collar, forming part of the dress of lawyers in Spain. 2. Counsellor, lawyer.
Golilléro, ra, *s.* Collar-maker.
Gollería y Golloría, *sf.* V. *Gulloria.*
Golléte, *sm.* 1. Throttle, the superior part of the throat. 2. The narrow part or neck of a bottle.
Gollízo, *sm.* Narrow passage of mountains or rivers.
Golmageár, *vn.* (Rioj.) V. *Golosinear.*
Golmájo, ja, *a.* (Rioj.) V. *Goloso.*
Golondrína, *sf.* 1. (Orn.) Swallow. Hirundo *L.* 2. (Ict.) Sapphire gurnard, tub-fish. Trigla hirundo *L.*
Golondrinéra, *sf.* (Bot.) Swallow-wort.

Golondrino, *sm.* 1. A male swallow. 2. Vagrant, deserter. 3. Tub-fish. 4. A large tumour in the arm-pit.
Golóndro, *sm.* Desire, longing. *Campar de golondro*, To encamp at another's expense. *Andar en golondros*, To feed on vain hopes.
Golosamente, *ad.* Gluttonously.
Golosázo, *sm.* Glutton, a greedy guttler.
Golosear, *va.* To guttle or guzzle dainties.
Golosína, *sf.* 1. Gluttony, excess of eating. 2. Cupidity, desire. 3. Dainty, something nice or delicate.
Golosinár, Golosinear y Golosmear, *vn.* To guttle or guzzle dainties.
Golóso, sa, *a.* Gluttonous, given to excessive feeding.
Golpázo, *sm.* A great blow.
Gólpe, *sm.* 1. Blow, stroke. 2. Wound, contusion. 3. Crowd, throng of people; abundance. 4. An unfortunate accident. 5. Spring bolt of a lock. 6. V. *Latido*. 7. With gardeners, holes for planting seeds. *Golpe de mar*, (Naút.) Surge, a heavy sea. *Golpe de música*, Band of music. *Golpe de remo*, Stroke in rowing. *Golpe de fortuna*, Fortunate event. *De golpe*, Plump, all at once. *De golpe y zumbido*, Unexpectedly, unaware. *De un golpe*, Once, all at once. *Golpes*, Flaps, the pieces of cloth which cover the pockets.
Golpeadéro, *sm.* Place much beaten.
Golpeadór, ra, *s.* Beater; pulsator.
Golpeadúra, *sf.* Percussion, the act of beating or hammering.
Golpeár, *va.* To beat, to strike, to hammer, to give blows.
Golpecíllo, co, to, *sm.* A slight blow.
Golpéo, *sm.* V. *Golpeadura*.
Goltschút, *sm.* Ingot of gold which comes from China.
Golusmiéro, ra, *a.* Gluttonous. V. *Goloso*.
Góma, *sf.* 1. Gum, a vegetable substance differing from resin, in its being more viscid, less friable, and dissolving in aqueous menstruums. 2. A morbid swelling.
Gomár, *va.* V. *Engomar*.
Gomecíllos, *sm. pl.* (Naút.) Watermen, lighter-men.
Gomía, *sf.* 1. Bugbear to frighten children. 2. Glutton, a voracious eater. *Gomia del caudal*, Spendthrift.
Gomitár, *va.* (Ant.) V. *Vomitar*.
Gomosidád, *sf.* Gumminess, viscosity.
Gomóso, sa, *a.* 1. Gummy, gummous; productive of gum. 2. Full of viscous humours.
Gónce, *sm.* Kind of hinge. V. *Gozne*.
Góndola, *sf.* Gondola, a Venetian flat boat.
Goniometría, *sf.* Goniometry, art of measuring angles.
Goniómetro, *sm.* Goniometer, instrument for measuring angles.
Gonorréa, *sf.* Gonorrhœa, venereal disease.
Gorbión, *sm.* 1. A kind of flowered taffety. 2. Gum euphorbium.
Gordál, *a.* Fat, big, fleshy.
Gordána, *sf.* Oil extracted in India from the testicles of oxen, and used for wool.
Gordázo, za, *a.* Very fat and big.
Gordiflón, na, *s.* A very corpulent, flabby person.
Górdo, da, *a.* 1. Fat, corpulent. 2. Fat, rich, greasy, oily. *Tocino gordo*, Fat pork. 3. Coarse, thick. *Lienzo gordo*, Coarse linen. 4. Great, large, big. 5. (Ant.) Torpid, stupid. *Mentira gorda*, A gross falsehood. *Hablar gordo*, To speak thick.
Górdo, *sm.* Fat, suet, lard.
Gordolóbo, *sm.* (Bot.) Great-mullein. Verbascum thapsus *L.*
Gordón, na, *a.* Very fat and corpulent.
Gordór, *sm.* Corpulence, bigness.
Gordúra, *sf.* 1. Grease, fat; the oily substance in the animal body. 2. Fatness, corpulence.
Górga, *sf.* 1. Food of hawks. 2. (Arag.) Whirlpool, a place where the water moves with a circular motion.
Gorgeadór, ra, *s.* Warbler, modulator.
Gorgeár, *vn.* To warble, to quaver, to shake the voice in a melodious manner.—*vr.* To gabble, applied to a child which begins to speak.
Gorgéo, *sm.* Trilling, quaver; a melodious shake of the voice; imperfect articulation.
Gorgería, *sf.* Chatter of a child which begins to talk.
Gorgojárse, *vr.* V. *Agorgojarse*.
Gorgójo, *sm.* 1. Grub, weevil. 2. A dwarfish little boy.
Gorgojóso, sa, *a.* Full of grubs or weevils.
Gorgorán, *sm.* Sort of silk grogram.
Gorgorear, *vn.* To cry like a Turkey cock.
Gorgorita, *sf.* Bubble formed on water by the fall of rain. *Gorgoritas*, Quavers, trilling.
Gorgoritear, *vn.* To warble, to quiver the voice.
Gorgoritos, *sm. pl.* Quivers of the voice.
Gorgorotáda, *sf.* The quantity of liquid swallowed at once.
Gorgotéro, *sm.* Pedler, hawker.
Gorguéra, *sf.* 1. A kind of neckcloth, formerly worn by ladies of fashion. 2. Armour of the neck.
Gorguerín, *sf.* Small kind of ruff or frill formerly worn round the neck.
Gorgúz, *sm.* Javelin, a kind of missive weapon.
Goriegóri, *sm.* Song with which children mimic the clerk's chant at processions.
Górja, *sf.* 1. Throat, throttle. 2. Rejoicing, merry-making. 3. (Naút.) Head of the keel.
Gorjál, *sm.* 1. Collar of a coat. 2. Piece of armour to defend the neck or throat.
Gormár, *va.* 1. To vomit, to throw up from the stomach. 2. To return what belongs to another.
Górra, *sf.* 1. Cap, a covering of the head. 2. Hunting cap. 3. Intrusion at feasts without invitation. 4. Parasite, sponger.
Gorráda, *sf.* V. *Gorretada*.
Gorréro, *sm.* 1. Cap-maker. 2. Parasite, sponger.
Gorretáda, *sf.* 1. Salute with a cap. 2. Stroke or blow given with a cap.
Gorréte, *sm.* Cap.
Gorrílla, *sf.* A small cap.
Gorrín ó Gorríno, *sm.* A small pig, a sucking pig.
Gorrión, *sm.* (Orn.) Sparrow. Fringilla domestica *L.*
Gorrionéra, *sf.* Rendezvous or hiding-place of rogues.
Gorrísta, *sm.* Parasite, sponger.
Górrito, ta, *s. dim* of *gorro, ra*.
Górro, *sm.* A round cap.
Gorrón, *sm.* 1. A poor student, who goes from house to house to get his dinner; parasite. 2. Spindle, pivot, or gudgeon of a gate or door.

glossy. 3. Lazy unhealthy silkworm. 4. A round smooth pebble. 5. Man given to debauchery and lewdness. 6. A large cap. 7. Dried morsel of lard fried.

Gorróna, sf. Strumpet, prostitute. V. *Pasa.*

Gorronál, sm. Place full of pebbles or coarse gravel.

Gorronázo, sm. A great lecher or rake.

Gorúllo, sm. A small button or ball of wool or other matter which sticks together.

Gorúpo, sm. (Naút.) Granny's bend, a kind of seaman's knot.

Gostár, va. V. *Gustar.*

Góta, sf. 1. Drop, a globule of moisture which falls at once. 2. A small quantity of any liquor. 3. Gout, a disease which affects the joints or extremities of the human body. *Gota á gota,* Drop by drop. *Gotas,* (Arq.) Ornaments of the Doric order. *Gotar coral ó caduca,* Epilepsy.

Goteádo, da, a. Spotted, speckled.

Goteár, vn. 1. To drop, to fall drop by drop. 2. To give by driblets.

Gotéra, sf. 1. Gutter, the water which drops or runs through a gutter. 2. Mark left by the dropping of rain. 3. Fringe of bed-hangings.

Goterón, sm. A large gutter or spout.

Goteroncíllo, sm. A small gutter or spout.

Gotíca, Gotílla, ó Gotíta, sf. Droplet, a small drop.

Gótico, ca, a. 1. Gothic; chiefly applied to the pointed style of building. 2. Illustrious, noble.

Gotóso, sa, a. Gouty, diseased with the gout.

Góyo, sm. (Ant.) V. *Gozo.*

Gozánte, pa. Enjoyer; enjoying.

Gozár, va. To enjoy, to have possession or fruition of.—*vr.* To rejoice.

Gózne, sm. 1. Kind of hinge. 2. The first vertebre or joint of the neck.

Gózo, sm. 1. Joy, pleasure, satisfaction. 2. Sprout, branch, shoot. *Gozos,* Verses in which certain words are repeated at the end of every couplet.

Gozosaménte, ad. Joyfully, cheerfully.

Gozóso, sa, a. Joyful, cheerful, content.

Gózque y Gozquéjo, sm. A small kind of dog.

Grabádo, sm. Art of engraving.

Grabadór, sm. Engraver; a cutter in stone, metal, or wood.

Grabadúra, sf. Act of engraving; sculpture.

Grabár, va. To engrave, to picture by incisions in stone, wood, or metal. *Grabar al agua fuerte ó de agua fuerte,* To etch.

Grabazón, sm. Engraving, sculpture.

Gracejánte, pa. Jester, joker; burlesquing.

Gracejár, vn. To joke, to jest.

Gracéjo, sm. 1. Joke, jest. 2. A graceful or pleasing deliverance, or manner of speaking.

Grácia, sf. 1. Grace, a genteel air or carriage; a pleasing address. 2. Elegance, beauty. 3. Gift, benefaction. 4. Remission of a debt. 5. Benevolence, friendship. 6. A witty saying or expression. 7. Name, the discriminative appellation of an individual. *Como es la gracia de vd?* Pray, what is your name? 8. Gratitude for favours received. *Dar gracias,* To give thanks. 9. Grace, effect of God's influence. *De grácia,* Gratis, for nothing; without a recompense. *Grácias,* Pontifical grants or concessions. *Decir dos gracias,* To tell one some home truths.

Graciáble, a. 1. Good-natured, affable. 2. Easily obtained; applied to favours.

Gracieccíta, sm. dim. A little grace or favour.

Grácil, a. Gracile, slender, small.

Graciola y Graciadéi, sf. (Bot.) Water-hyssop. Gratiola officinalis *L.*

Graciosaménte, ad. Graciously; gratuitously.

Graciosidád, sf. 1. Gracefulness, beauty, perfection, elegance and dignity of manners. 2. Facetiousness, cheerful wit.

Gracióso, sa, a. 1. Graceful, beautiful, accomplished. 2. Facetious, witty. 3. Benevolent, inclined to grant favours. 4. Gratuitous, granted without claim. 5. Ridiculous, extravagant.

Gracióso, sa, s. 1. Merry-andrew, buffoon, harlequin. 2. Comic actor or actress, generally in the character of servants in Spanish plays.

Gráda, sf. 1. Step of a staircase. 2. (In Nunneries) Room where the nuns are allowed to hold conversation with their friends through a grate; a parlour. 3. Steps round an altar. 4. Harrow, a frame of timbers, crossing each other, and set with teeth, to break the clods after ploughing. 5. *Grada de construccion,* (Naút.) Stocks for ship-building. *Navio en la grada,* Ship on the stocks.—*pl.* 1. Bar, the place where causes of law are tried. 2. Seats of an amphitheatre. [scale of music.

Gradación, sf. A harmonious gradation or

Gradádo, da, a. Graduated.

Gradár, va. To harrow, to break with the harrow.

Gradátim, ad. (Latin) Gradually, by degrees.

Gradería, sf. Series of seats or steps. V. *Gradas.*

Gradílla, sf. Small step or seat; tile-mould.

Gradinár, va. To cut off with a chisel.

Gradíno, sm. 1. Chisel, an edged tool used by stone-cutters to pare off the superfluous parts of stones. 2. Graver, the tool used in graving.

Grádo, sm. 1. Step of a staircase. 2. Value or quality of a thing. 3. Degree of kindred, order of lineage. 4. Will, pleasure. 5. Degree, an academical title of honour conferred by universities. 6. (In Geometry) The three hundred and sixtieth part of the circumference of a circle. *Grados,* Minor orders in religious communities. 7. (In Music) The intervals of sounds. 8. Measure of quality of state.

Gradóso, sa, a. (Ant.) Agreeable.

Graduación, sf. Graduation; qualification.

Graduádo, da, a. Graduated; applied to officers enjoying higher rank than they possess.

Graduál, a. Gradual, proceeding by degrees; advancing by steps.

Graduál, sm. A verse read between the epistle and gospel at the celebration of the mass.

Gradualménte, ad. Gradually.

Graduándo, sm. Candidate for academical degrees.

Graduár, va. 1. To measure or compare different things. 2. To graduate, to dignify with an academical degree; to give military rank. 3. To divide the circumference of a circle into degrees.

Gráf, sm. Graver, a stile or tool used in graving.

Grafíla, sf. The little border on the edge of coin.

Gráfio, sm. A stone-cutter's chisel.

Gráfico, ca, a. Graphic, graphical, relating to engraving; well delineated.

Graficaménte, ad. Graphically; in a picturesque manner.

Grafiôles, *sm. pl.* Kind of biscuits made in the form of an S.
Grafómetro, *sm.* Graphometer, a semi-circle divided into 180 degrees.
Gragéa, *sf.* A kind of very small sugar-plum.
Grája, *sf.* (Orn.) Jay. Corvus glandarius *L.*
Grajádo, *sm.* (Naút.) Top of the rudder.
Grajál, *a.* Belonging to crows, ravens, or magpies.
Grajéro, ra, *a.* Applied to rookeries. [L.
Grájo, *sm.* (Orn.) Jack-daw. Corvus monedula
Grajúno, na, *a.* Belonging to jack-daws.
Gráma, *sf.* 1. Brake, a wooden instrument for dressing hemp or flax. 2. (Bot.) Panic-grass. Panicum dactylon *L.*
Gramálla, *sf.* (Arag.) A long scarlet gown anciently worn by the magistrates of Aragon; it is at present the dress of a mace-bearer of a corporation.
Gramalléra, *sf.* Pot-hanger. [bread.
Gramár, *va.* (Gal.) To knead the dough of
Gramática, *sf.* 1. Grammar, the science of speaking correctly; the art which teaches the relations of words to each other. 2. Study of the Latin language. *Gramatica parda*, Soundness of faculties; strength of natural reason.
Gramaticál, *a.* Grammatical.
Gramaticalménte, *ad.* Grammatically.
Gramático, *sm.* Grammarian.
Gramaticón, *sm.* Grammerian. [grammar.
Gramatiquería, *sf.* Any thing belonging to
Gramátista, *sf.* Professor of grammar.
Gramílla, *sf.* A wooden instrument for drawing lines.
Gramíneo, ea, *a.* (Poét.) Gramineous, grassy.
Gramóso, sa, *a.* Grassy, belonging to Gramina.
Gran, *a.* Great. V. *Grande.* It is used only before substantives singular, as *Gran Maestre*, Grand Master.
Grána, *sf.* 1. Grain, the seed of plants. 2. The time when corn, flax, &c. form their seed. 3. Fine scarlet cloth. 4. Cochineal. Coccus cacti *L.* 5. Fresh red colour of the lips and cheeks. *Grána del Paraiso*, (Bot.) Cardamomum. Amomum cardamomum *L.*
Granáda, *sf.* 1. Pomegranate. 2. (Mil.) Hand-grenade, a small hollow globe or ball, filled with fine powder, which, when kindled, is thrown into a fortress or work, or among troops, where it bursts and does much mischief.
Granadéra, *sf.* (Mil.) A grenadier's pouch, in which grenades and other warlike stores are carried.
Granadéro, *sm.* (Mil.) Grenadier; a kind of foot-soldier, frequently employed to throw grenades.
Granadílla, *sf.* (Bot.) Passion-flower. Passiflora granadilla vel capsularis *L.*
Granádo, da, *a.* 1. Large, remarkable. 2. Principal, chief, illustrious; select.
Granádo, *sm.* (Bot.) Pomegranate-tree. Punica granatum *L.*
Granálla, *sf.* Granulation; grains of metal.
Granár, *vn.* To grow to maturity, to be full of seed. [ruby; garnet.
Granáte, *sm.* A precious stone, resembling a
Granatín, *sm.* Kind of ancient cloth.

Granazón, *sf.* Granulation, the act of forming or breaking into small grains or parts.
Granbéstia, *sf.* Elk.
Grandánime, *a.* (Ant.) Magnanimous.
Grandária, *sf.* Magnitude, size of things.
Grandázo, za, *a.* Very great.
Gránde, *a.* Great, grand, large.
Gránde, *sm.* **Grandee**, a Spanish nobleman of the first rank, who enjoys the privilege of being covered in the presence of the king.
Grandecíllo, lla; co, ca; to, ta, *a.* Growing rather big; pretty large or big. [ly.
Grandeménte, *ad.* Greatly, very well, extreme-
Grandéza, *sf.* 1. Greatness, bigness. 2. Grandeur, power. 3. Pre-eminence, and dignity of a grandee of Spain. 4. Meeting of grandees.
Grandificéncia, *sf.* (Ant.) Magnificence.
Grandillón, na, *a.* Excessively large and big.
Grandilóquo, qua, *a.* Making use of a lofty or pompous style.
Grandiosaménte, *ad.* Magnificently.
Grandiosidád, *sf.* Greatness, grandeur; magnificence; abundance. [did.
Grandióso, sa, *a.* Grand, magnificent, splen-
Grandór, *sm.* Size and bigness of things.
Grandúra, *sf.* (Ant.) Magnitude, greatness.
Graneádo, da, *a.* Reduced to grains; spotted.
Graneadór, *sm.* A kind of graver, or tool for engraving.
Granéar, *va.* 1. To sow grain in the earth. 2. To engrave. 3. (In Tan-yards) To grain leather. [heap; (Naút.) In bulk.
Granél, *sm.* Heap of corn. *A' Granél*, In a
Granéro, *sm.* 1. Granary, a storehouse for grain. 2. A fruitful country.
Granevíno, *sm.* (Bot.) Goat's-thorn. Astragalus tragacantha *L.*
Grangeár, *va.* 1. To till, to cultivate the ground, to husband, to farm. 2. To obtain one thing by means of another. 3. To gain the good-will of another by caresses and flatteries. *Grangear á barlovento*, (Naút.) To gain to windward; applied to a ship.
Grangéo, *sm.* 1. Cultivation of the ground. 2. Emolument, flattery. [the soil.
Grangería, *sf.* Gain, profit; improvement of
Grangéro, ra, *s.* 1. Farmer, husbandman. 2. Dealer in profitable commodities. 3. Broker.
Granguárdia, *sf.* (Mil.) Grand-guard, an advanced guard in front of an army.
Graníco, *sm.* Small grain.
Granílla, *sf.* 1. The small seed of herbs and other plants. 2. Rough nap on cloth.
Granilléro, ra, *a.* Applied to hogs that feed on what they find in the fields.
Granillo, *sm.* 1. Small grain. 2. Gain or profit frequently obtained. 3. Pimple growing at the extremity of the rump of canary birds and linnets.
Granillóso, sa, *a.* Granulous.
Graníto, *sm.* 1. Granite, a hard stone used in building. 2. Small egg of a silk-worm.
Granizáda, *sf.* 1. Copious fall of hail. 2. (Met.) Multitude of things which fall in abundance.
Granizár, *vn.* 1. To hail, to pour down hail. 2. To pour down any thing with violence.
Graníso, *sm.* 1. Hail, drop of rain frozen in falling. 2. Cloud or web in the eyes.

Gránja, *sf.* 1. Grange, farm, farm-house. 2. Recreation in the country.
Gráno, *sm.* 1. Grain, the seed of corn. 2. Any minute particle, any thing proverbially small or round. 3. Direction of the fibres of wood or other fibrous matter. 4. Grain, a small weight of gold, silver, or precious stones. 5. Pimple, a pustule on the skin.
Granóso, sa, *a.* Granulous.
Granugiénto, ta, *a.* Full of grain.
Granúja, *sf.* 1. Ripe grapes separated from the branches. 2. Stones of grapes and other fruit.
Granujádo, da, *a.* 1. Full of pimples. 2. Full of stones, full of seeds.
Granújo, *sm.* Pimple or tumour in the flesh.
Granujóso, sa, *a.* Granulous.
Granulación, *sf.* Granulation, the act of reducing metal into grains by pouring it, when melted, into cold water.
Granulár, *va.* To granulate, to reduce to small pieces like grains.
Granulóso, sa, *a.* Granulous.
Granúza, *sf.* Coal made of the stalks of hemp.
Granzas, *sf. pl.* 1. Siftings, the refuse of corn which has been winnowed and sifted. 2. Dross of metals.
Granzónes, *sm. pl.* Refuse of straw, not eaten, but left by the cattle.
Granzóso, sa, *a.* Applied to grain having much refuse.
Grañón, *sm.* 1. Pap made of boiled wheat. 2. V. *Grano.*
Gráo, *sm.* Strand, shore.
Grápa, *sf.* 1. Cramp-iron. 2. Kind of mangy ulcers in the articulations or joints of horses.
Grapón, *sm.* A large cramp-iron.
Grása, *sf.* 1. Suet, fat; grease. *Grasa de ballena*, Blubber. 2. Gum of juniper-trees. 3. Ink paste for writing. 4. Grease of clothes.
Grasèra, *sf.* 1. Vessel for holding ink-paste. 2. Vessel for fat or grease.
Grasería, *sf.* Tallow-chandler's shop.
Graséza, *sf.* Quality of fat or grease.
Grasiénto, ta, *a.* Greasy; rusty, filthy.
Grasílla, *sf.* 1. Pounce, a kind of powder made of gum sandarac, which, when rubbed on paper, makes it less apt to imbibe the ink. 2. (Bot.) Sanicle, butterwort. Pinguicula vulgaris *L.*
Gráso, sa, *a.* Fat, unctuous, oily.
Gráso, *sm.* Fat, grease.
Grasónes, *sm. pl.* Fast-dish, made of flour, milk of almonds, sugar, and cinnamon.
Grasúra, *sf.* V. *Grosura.*
Gratamènte, *ad.* Graciously, in a kind and benevolent manner.
Grátas y Gratagújas, *sf.* Instrument for burnishing silver or silver gilt.
Gratár, *va.* To burnish.
Gratificación, *sf.* Gratification, reward, recompense; allowance to officers for expenses.
Gratificadór, *sm.* Gratifier.
Gratificár, *va.* To reward, to requite, to recompense, to please.
Gratíl, *sm.* (Naút.) Head of a sail.
Grátis, *ad.* Gratis.
Gratisdáto, ta, *a.* Gratuitous.
Gratitúd, *sf.* Gratitude, acknowledgment of favours received, desire to return benefits.

Gráto, ta, *a.* 1. Graceful, pleasing, pleasant. 2. Grateful, having a due sense of benefits.
Gratonáca, *sf.* Kind of ragout or fricassee, made of chickens half roasted, bacon, almonds, rich broth, fresh eggs, spice, and greens.
Gratuitamènte, *ad.* Gratuitously.
Gratúito, ta, *a.* Gratuitous, gratis.
Gratulación, *sf.* 1. Cheerful readiness to oblige another. 2. Congratulation.
Gratulár, *va.* To congratulate.—*vr.* To rejoice.
Gratulatório, ria, *a.* Congratulatory.
Gravámen, *sm.* Obligation to perform or execute any thing. [to molest.
Gravár, *va.* To burthen, to oppress, to fatigue,
Gravatívo, va, *a.* Grievous, injurious.
Gráve, *a.* 1. Weighty, ponderous, heavy. 2. Great, huge, vast. 3. Grave, circumspect, causing veneration and respect. 4. Haughty, lofty. 5. Important, momentous, of great consequence. 6. Troublesome, vexatious. *Ponerse grave*, To assume an air of importance. 7. (Mús.) Grave tone.
Graveár, *vn.* To weigh, to gravitate, to sink with weight.
Gravedád, *sf.* 1. Gravity, weight, heaviness; tendency to the centre. 2. Gravity, modesty, composure, circumspection. 3. Atrociousness, weight of guilt. 4. Vanity, pride.
Gravedóso, sa, *a.* Haughty, vain, elevated, full of pride.
Gravedúmbre ó Gravidúmbre, *sf.* (Ant.) V. *Dificultad.*
Gravemènte, *ad.* Gravely, seriously.
Gravéza, *sf.* (Ant.) Gravity. V. *Gravámen y Dificultad.*
Gravidád, *sf.* (Ant.) V. *Gravedad.*
Gravitación, *sf.* Gravitation.
Gravitár, *va.* To gravitate, to weigh down, to tend to some part slightly.
Gravóso, sa, *a.* Grievous, weighty, offensive.
Graznadór, ra, *s.* Croaker; cawing, cackling.
Graznár, *vn.* To croak, to caw, to cackle.
Graznído, *sm.* A croak, caw, or cackle.
Gréba, *sf.* Ancient armour for the leg.
Gréca, *sf.* Grecian fret, ornament consisting of a line forming many right angles. *A' la Gréca*, In the Grecian style.
Greciáno, na; **Gréco, ca**; y **Grecáno, na**, *a.* Grecian.
Grecísco, *a.* Greek, applied to the fire that burns in water.
Grecísmo, *sm.* Grecism.
Grecizár, *vn.* To affect to speak Greek.
Gréda, *sf.* 1. Chalk, marl. 2. Fuller's earth.
Gredál, *sm.* Pit where chalk, marl, or fuller's earth is found.
Gredóso, sa, *a.* Chalky, marly.
Greffiér, *sm.* Keeper of the rolls; an officer of distinction in the king's palace.
Gregál, *sm.* North-east wind in the Mediterranean.
Gregál, *a.* Gregarious, going in flocks or herds.
Gregalizár, *vn.* (Naút.) To be north-easting, to drive or decline to north-east.
Gregário, ria, *a.* Gregarious.
Gregoriáno, na, *a.* Gregorian.
Gregorillo *sm.* Neckcloth worn by women.
Gregüería, *sf.* Outcry, confused clamour.

Gregüéscos, *sm. pl.* A wide sort of breeches made in the Grecian fashion.

Gregorizár, *va.* To talk Greek, to convert into Greek.

Gremiál, *sm.* Lapcloth, used by bishops when they officiate at divine service.

Grémio, *sm.* 1. Lap, the part from the waist to the knees. 2. Body, society, company. *Gremio de artesanos*, Corporation of tradesmen.

Gréña, *sf.* 1. Entangled or clotted hair. 2. Any thing entangled. *Andar á la greña*, To pull one another by the hair. 3. (And.) Heap of grain laid to be thrashed. 4. (And.) First leaves of a vine-shoot.

Greñúdo, da, *a.* Dishevelled, having clotty or entangled hair.

Greñuéla, *sf.* The first shoots of a vine.

Grésca, *sf.* 1. Clatter, tumult, outcry, confusion. 2. Wrangle, quarrel.

Gresíble, *a.* Moveable.

Grévas, *sf. pl.* Greaves, a sort of boots or armour for the legs.

Gréuge, *sm.* Grievance, complaints usually made in the courts of Aragon.

Grey, *sf.* 1. Flock, a number of sheep or goats. 2. (Met.) Congregation of the faithful. 3. V. *República.*

Gribár, *vn.* (Naút.) To fall to leeward, or be carried out of her course by the currents; applied to a ship.

Grida, *sf.* Signal to call soldiers to arms. V. *Grita.*

Gridár, *va.* V. *Gritar.*

Griégo, ga, *a.* Greek, belonging to Greece.

Griésco ó Griésgo, *sm.* (Ant.) Encounter, conflict, battle.

Griéta, *sf.* 1. Crevice, a crack, a cleft. 2. Scratch or fissure in the skin. 3. A sore breast, an infirmity in women who suckle children.

Grietóso, sa, *a.* Full of cracks or crevices.

Grifádo, da, *a.* Applied to a certain kind of letters or characters.

Grifálto, *sm.* Small kind of culverin.

Grífo, fa, *a.* Applied to the letters invented by Haldus Pius Manutius, that superseded the Gothic characters.

Grífo, *sm.* Griffin or griffon, a fabled animal. *Grifos*, Frizzled hair.

Grifón, *sm.* A cock for water.

Grílla; *esa es grilla*, Vulgar expression of doubt respecting the truth or accuracy of any thing heard.

Grillár, *vn.* To chirp or squeak; applied to crickets.—*vr.* To shoot, to sprout.

Grilléra, *sf.* Cricket-cage, a place where crickets are kept.

Grilléro, *sm.* He who takes the irons off prisoners.

Grillétes, *sm. pl.* Shackles, fetters.

Grillo, *sm.* 1. Cricket, an insect that chirps about fire-places, and in fields. Gryllus domesticus, gryllus campestris *L.* 2. Shoot issuing from seed in the earth. *Andar á grillos*, To waste one's time in useless pursuits. *Grillos*, Irons, shackles, fetters, impediment.

Grillotálpa, *sm.* Mole-cricket, fen-cricket, church-worm. Gryllus gryllotalpa *L.*

Grima, *sf.* Fright, horror, astonishment.

Grimázo, *sm.* A grotesque posture or contortion of the face.

Grímpola, *sf.* (Naút.) Vane, a sort of weather-cock on the top-mast head, which turns round with the wind. *Huso de la grimpola*, Spindle of a vane.

Grinálde, *sm.* Machine of artificial fire-work.

Griñón, *sm.* 1. A sort of cowl worn by religious women. 2. Apricot ingrafted in a peach-tree.

Grípo, *sf.* (Naút.) A kind of vessel formerly used for trade.

Grís, *sm.* 1. Mixture of white and black, grizzle, gray. 2. A grizzle-coloured squirrel or weasel. Sciurus *L.* 3. (And.) Cold sharp air or weather.

Grís, *a.* Gray, grizzled.

Griséta, *sf.* Kind of flowered silk.

Gríta, *sf.* 1. Clamour, outcry, vociferation. 2. Halloo; a word of encouragement when dogs are let loose on their game. 3. Exclamations of applause or censure. *Grita foral*, (Arag.) Summons, citation.

Gritadór, ra, *s.* Crier, vociferator.

Gritár, *vn.* To shout, to hoot.

Gritería, *sf.* Confused cry of many voices.

Gríto, *sm.* Clamour, outcry, shout. *Estar en un grito*, To be in continual pain. *A grito herido*, Loud outcry.

Gritón, na, *a.* Vociferous, clamorous.

Gróya, *sf.* Vile prostitute.

Grómo, *sm.* The heart of plants or trees.

Grópos, *sm. pl.* Cotton put in inkstands or inkhorns.

Grós, *sm.* Ancient money. *En gros*, By whole-sale.

Grósca, *sf.* Kind of venomous serpent.

Grosedád, *sf.* V. *Grosura y Grosería.*

Groséllа, *sf.* (Bot.) Currant, a tartish berry. Ribes *L.*

Groseraménte, *ad.* In a rude unmannerly way.

Grosería, *sf.* Rudeness, ill-breeding.

Groséro, ra, *a.* 1. Gross, coarse, rough; opposite to delicate. 2. Rude, unpolished.

Groséza, *sf.* Corpulence, bulkiness of body.

Gróso, *a.* Coarse snuff, badly powdered.

Grosór, *sm.* Crassitude. V. *Grosura.*

Grosúra, *sf.* 1. Suet, tallow, fat of animals. 2. Extremities, heart, liver, and lungs of an animal. *Dia de grosura*, Saturday, so called in Castile, because on that day the entrails and members of animals are eaten, but not their flesh, nor fish as on Fridays.

Grotésco, *sm.* V. *Grutesco.*

Grúa, *sf.* 1. Crane, a machine for raising stones and other ponderous or weighty things. 2. (Orn.) Crane. 3. (Naút.) Bend of an incurvated piece of timber. *Grua de la quaderna maestra*, (Naút.) Midship-bend. *A la grua*, In and out.

Gruéras, *sf. pl.* (Naút.) Rope-holes, round holes through which the ropes work on board of ships. *Grueras de barbiquejo*, (Naút.) Bowstay-holes.

Gruéro, ra, *a.* Belonging to birds of prey, trained to pursue cranes.

Gruésa, *sf.* 1. Gross, the number of twelve dozen. 2. Chief part of a prebend.

Gruesaménte, *ad.* Grossly, coarsely; by wholesale.

Gruéso, sa, *a.* 1. Bulky, corpulent, thick. 2. Large, great. 3. (Met.) Dull, stupid. 4. Coarse, rude, ordinary; dense.

Gruéso, *sm.* 1. Corpulence, bulkiness of body. 2. Chief or main part of a whole. *El grueso de un exercito*, The main body of an army. *Tratar en grueso, ó vender por mayor*, To deal by wholesale; to sell in the lump, not in separate parcels.

Gruesidón, *sm.* Steel instrument used by glaziers for rounding glass.

Gruír, *vn.* To crank or crankle; to cry like a crane.

Grúlla, *sf.* 1. (Orn.) Crane. Ardea grus *L.* 2. Crane, the name of a southern constellation.

Grullláda, *sf.* Mob, crowd of constables. V. *Garullada.*

Grulléro, **ra**, *a.* Applied to falcons or birds of prey in chase of cranes.

Gruméte, *sm.* (Naút.) Younker, ship's boy.

Grúmo, *sm.* 1. Grume, a thick viscid consistence in a fluid; a clot. *Grumo de leche*, Curds. 2. Cluster, bunch. 3. Heart or pith of trees. *Grumos*, Pinions, the joints of the wings remotest from the body.

Grumóso, **sa**, *a.* Grumy, clotty; full of grumes.

Gruñído, *sm.* Grunt, the noise made by a hog or pig.

Gruñidór, **ra**, *s.* Grunter.

Gruñimiénto, *sm.* Grunting.

Gruñír, *vn.* 1. To grunt, to murmur like a hog. 2. To creak or creek, to make a harsh noise; applied to doors, hinges, carts, &c. 3. (Met.) To grumble, to growl, to snarl. *Mamar y gruñir*, (Vulg.) To suck and murmur; to be discontented with every thing.

Grúpa, *sf.* 1. Croup, the buttocks of a horse. 2. Portmantle or portmanteau, any bag carried on the croup of a horse.

Grupáda, *sf.* 1. Squall or gust of wind. 2. Croupade, a kind of leap of a horse.

Grupéra, *sf.* Crupper, that part of the horse's furniture which reaches from the saddle to the tail.

Grúpo, *sm.* 1. Group, assemblage. 2. Clump of sprigs growing out of the same root.

Grúta, *sf.* Cavern, cavity between rocks. *Grutas*, Crypts, vaults, subterranean edifices.

Grutésco, *sm.* Grotesk or grotesque, a kind of ornament in painting, composed of leaves, shells, &c.

Gruyére, *sm.* A kind of rich cheese, made at Gruyere in France.

Guacamáyo, *sm.* (Orn.) Macao or macaw. Psittacus macao *L.*

Guachapeár, *va.* To paddle, to play with the feet in stagnant water.—*vn.* To clap as horses' shoes when loose.

Guachapéli, *sm.* Solid strong wood, which grows in Guayaquil, and used for ships.

Guácharo, **ra**, *a.* 1. Whining, one who is continually moaning and crying. 2. Sickly, not in health. 3. Dropsical, diseased with a dropsy.

Guacharráda, *sf.* A sudden fall or plunge of a thing into mud or water.

Guachichíles, *sf. pl.* Kind of sea-fowl resembling a duck.

Guachinángos, *sm. pl.* A name of contempt given by the inhabitants of the Havannah to the inhabitants of Mexico or New Spain.

Guácia, *sf.* The tree or gum called acacia.

Guadafiónes, *sm. pl.* Fetters, with which the legs of horses are shackled.

Guadamacíl, *sm.* Printed leather, gilt and adorned with figures. [printed leather.

Guadamacilería, *sf.* Manufactory of gilt or

Guadamaciléro, *sm.* Manufacturer of printed leather. [men.

Guadaméco, *sm.* (Ant.) Kind of dress of wo-

Guadáña, *sf.* 1. Sithe, an instrument for mowing. 2. A knife used by manufacturers of leather wine-bags. [sithe.

Guadañár, *va.* To mow, to cut grass with a

Guadañéro, **Guadañeadór y Guadañíl**, *sm.* Mower, one who cuts down grass or corn with a sithe.

Guadañón, *sm.* Mower. V. *Guadañero.*

Guadapéro, *sm.* 1. (Bot.) Wildpear-tree. Pyrus sylvestris *L.* 2. A boy who carries victuals to reapers or mowers.

Guadarnés, *sm.* 1. Harness-room, a place where harness is kept. 2. Harness-keeper, an officer of the king's mews.

Guadixéño, *sm.* Poniard, stiletto; knife.

Guadramáña, *sf.* Trick, deceit, imposition.

Guadúa, *sf.* Kind of large cane or reed in Peru.

Guaduál, *sm.* Plantation of large reeds.

Guajáca, *sf.* Kind of cocoa.

Gualardonár, *va.* (Ant.) V. *Galardonar.*

Gualatína, *sf.* Dish made of boiled apples, milk of almonds, and broth, and beaten up with spice and rose water.

Guálda, *sf.* (Bot.) Wild woad, dyer's weed, weld, a plant which dyes yellow. Reseda luteola *L.* *Cara de gualda*, Pale face.

Gualdádo, **da**, *a.* Weld coloured, yellowish.

Gualdéras, *sf. pl.* The sides, cheeks, or brackets of a gun-carriage. *Gualdéras de las carlingas*, (Naút.) Cheeks of the mast-steps.

Guáldo, **da**, *a.* Weld, yellow or gold colour.

Gualdón, *sm.* (Bot.) Base-rocket. Reseda lutea *L.*

Gualdrápa, *sf.* 1. Horse-cloth, housing. 2. Tatter, rag hanging down from clothes.

Gualdrapázos, *sm. pl.* (Naút.) Slaps of the sails against the masts.

Gualdrapeár, *va.* To put one thing upon another.—*vn.* (Naút.) To slap against the masts; applied to sails. [low.

Gualdrapéro, *sm.* Ragamuffin, a ragged fel-

Gualdrínes, *sm. pl.* Lists of cloth, with which the edges or fissures of windows are stuffed up, to keep out the wind and rain.

Guáno, *sm.* Kind of American palm-tree.

Guañín, *a.* Applied to gold under the legal standard.

Guantáda, *sf.* Slap or blow given with the palm or inner part of the hand.

Guánte, *sm.* 1. Glove, a cover of the hands 2. Gauntlet, an iron glove used for defence, and thrown down in challenges. 3. Familiarly, the hand. *Echar el guante á otro*, To challenge, to send a challenge. *Poner á uno como un guante*, To render one as pliable as a glove. *Guántes*, Drink-money given to workmen above their wages. *Adobar los guantes*, To regale and remunerate any person.

Guanteléte, *sm.* Gauntlet.

Guantería, *sf.* A glover's shop.

Guantéro, *sm.* Glover, one who makes gloves.

Guañir, *vn.* (Extrem.) To grunt or make a noise like pigs.
Guapaménte, *ad.* Bravely, courageously.
Guapázo, za, *s.* Brave, courageous, valiant.
Guapeár, *vn.* 1. To boast or brag of courage. 2. To take a pride in fine dress.
Guapetón, *sm.* Boaster, bragger. [dress.
Guapéza, *sf.* Bravery, courage, ostentation in
Guápo, pa, *a.* 1. Stout, courageous, valiant, bold, enterprising. 2. Spruce, neat, elegant, ostentatious, vain. 3. Gay, sprightly; fond of courting women.
Guár (En), *ad.* (Ant.) V. *En Lugar.*
Guarácha, *sf.* An epithet of contempt given to poor French adventurers in Spain.
Guarápo, *sm.* Sub-acid drink made in sugar-mills with the cane-liquor fermented.
Guárda, *s. com.* Guard, keeper; any thing that preserves others from injury.—*sf.* 1. Custody, care manifested in the preservation of a thing. 2. Observance of a law or ordinance. 3. Nun who accompanies men through convents. 4. Each of the outside ribs or guards of a fan. 5. Sheet of paper placed at the beginning and end of volumes to guard the printed sheets in binding. 6. Place where any thing is preserved. *Guarda almacen*, Store-keeper. *Guarda bosques*, Keeper of a forest. *Guarda bauprés*, (Naút.) Knight-heads, bollard-timbers. *Guardabrázo*, Armour of the arm. *Guardacabras*, Goat-herd. *Guardacalláda*, Window in the roof, whence the street may be seen. *Guardabaco*, (Naút.) Thimble or bull's eye, to prevent ropes from being galled by the tackle-hooks. *Guardacadenas*, (Naút.) Laths of the chain-wales. *Guardacartuchos*, (Naút.) Cartridge-cases. *Guardacosta*, (Naút.) Custom-house cutter, a vessel employed to keep the coast clear of smugglers. *Guardacoymas*, (In Cant) Servant to the father of a prostitute. *Guardacuños*, Keeper of the dies in the mint. *Guardadamas*, Officer appointed to keep the apartments of the Queen clear of obstruction during a public festival. *Guardafuego*. 1. Screen for keeping off the heat of a chimney-fire: 2. Fender: 3. (Naút.) Breaming-board. *Guardainfantes*, (Naút.) Capstern whelps. *Guardajoyas*, Officer of the king's palace, who keeps the jewels, and other precious things belonging to the royal family; also a room where the jewels or other precious things are kept. *Guardalado*, Battlement of a bridge. *Guardalobo*, (Bot.) Poet's cassia. Osyris alba L. *Guardamancebos*, (Naút.) Man-rope, entering rope. *Guardamancebos de una escala*, (Naút.) Ladder-rope. *Guardamancebos de sondear*, (Naút.) Breast-ropes for sounding. *Guardamancebos de las vergas*, (Naút.) Foot-ropes or horses. *Guardamangier*, Pantry, a room in which provisions or viands are kept; groom of the pantry. *Guardamayor*, Chief-guard. *Guardamáno*, Guard of a sword. *Guardaméa*, Porter of a palace; person appointed to prevent the commission of any nuisance near the porches of palaces. *Guardamecha*, (Naút.) Match-tub. *Guardamontes*, Forester, keeper of a forest. *Guardapuerta*, Screen or curtain before a door. *Guarderopa*, Wardrobe; keeper of the wardrobe. *Guardasellos*, Keeper of the privy seal. *Guardasol*, Parasol. V. *Quitasol*. *Guardatimones*, (Naút.) Stern-chases. *Guardavela*, (Naút.) A small rope with which the top-sails are furled. *Guardazacia*, (Naút.) Cross-pieces or racks of the shrouds. *Guardas*, Wards of a lock; sides of a pocket-knife haft.
Guárda, *interj.* Take care! beware.
Guardadaménte, *ad.* Guardedly.
Guardadór, ra, *s.* 1. Keeper, guardian. 2. One who observes a law. 3. Miser, a wretch covetous to extremity.
Guardainfánte, *sm.* Farthingale, ladies' hoop.
Guardája, *sf.* V. *Guedeja.*
Guardamangél, *sm.* Pantry, buttery.
Guardamateriáles, *sm.* Person appointed to purchase bullion and other necessaries for a mint.
Guardamiénto, *sm.* Custody, act of guarding.
Guardamónte, *sm.* Guard of a gun lock, sword, &c. [to the ladies of honour.
Guardamugér, *sf.* Servant of the queen, next
Guardapápo, *sm.* Ancient piece of armour to protect the face.
Guardapiés, *sm.* Silk petticoat. V. *Brial.*
Guardapólvo, *sm.* 1. Any piece of cloth or leather to guard against the dust. 2. Piece of leather attached to the instep of spatterdashes.
Guardár, *va.* 1. To keep, to take care of. 2. To guard, to watch, to preserve from damage; to observe, to respect. 3. To fulfil one's duty. 4. To protect, to defend. 5. To impede, to avoid.—*vr.* To be upon one's guard, to avoid, to abstain from. *Guarda pablo*, Avoiding any thing supposed to be dangerous. *Guardar batideros*, To anticipate and avoid difficulties. [ispida L.
Guardário, *sm.* (Orn.) King's fisher. Alcedo
Guardería, *sf.* The occupation of a guard.
Guárdia, *sf.* 1. Guard, a body of soldiers or armed men. 2. (Naút.) Watch. *Guardia de babor*, Larboard-watch. *Guardia de estribor*, Starboard-watch. *Guardia de la madrugada*, Morning-watch. *Guardia del tope*, Mast-head look-out. *Guardias marinas*, Midshipmen.—*sm.* Soldier belonging to the guards.
Guardián, na, *s.* 1. Keeper, one who has the care or charge of any thing. 2. The local superior of convents of the order of St. Francis. 3. (Naút.) Keeper of the arms and store-room. 4. *Guardian del contra-maestre*, (Naút.) Boatswain's mate.
Guardianía, *sf.* 1. Guardianship, the dignity and employment of a guardian. 2. The district assigned to every convent to beg in.
Guardílla, *sf.* 1. Garret, a room on the highest floor of the house; skylight. 2. With seamstresses, ornament and guard of a seam.
Guardín de la caña, *sm.* (Naút.) Tiller-rope: an untarred rope which acts upon the rudder with the power of a crane or windlass.
Guardóso, sa, *a.* 1. Frugal, parsimonious. 2. Niggardly, stingy.
Guarecér, *vn.* To grow well, to recover.—*va.* 1. To aid, to succour, to assist. 2. To guard, to preserve; to cure.—*vr.* To take refuge, to escape from danger.
Guarentício y Guarentígio, gia, *a.* (For.)

Applied to a contract, writing, or clause, which empowered the justices to cause it to be executed.

Guarecimiénto, *sm.* Healing, curing.

Guarída, *sf.* 1. Den, the cave or couch of a wild beast. 2. Haunt, a place where one is frequently found. 3. Protection, aid, shelter.

Guarín, *sm.* Young pig.

Guarír, *va.* y *n.* To subsist. V. *Curar* y *Sanar*.

Guarísmo, *sm.* Figure, cipher; an arithmetical character by which some number is noted.

Guarísmo, ma, *a.* Arithmetical.

Guarnecedór, *sm.* 1. Hatter who cocks hats. 2. One who garnishes or surrounds a thing with ornamental appendages.

Guarnecér y Guarnescér, *va.* 1. To corroborate, to authorize. 2. To garnish, to surround with ornamental appendages, to set in gold. 3. To trim, to adorn. 4. To harness horses or mules. 5. To garrison a town or other place.

Guarnés, *sm.* (Naút.) Parts or turns of a tackle-fall.

Guarnición, *sf.* 1. Flounce, furbelow, trimming. 2. Setting of any thing in gold or silver. 3. Guard of a sword. 4. Garrison, a body of soldiers placed in a fortified town to defend it. 5. Garniture, ornament. 6. *Guarnicion de la bomba,* (Naút.) The upper or spear-box of a pump.—*pl.* 1. Ancient steel armour of defence. 2. Gears or traces of mules and horses; harness.

Guarnicionería, *sf.* Shop of a harness-maker.

Guarnicionéro, *sm.* Harness-maker.

Guarniél, *sm.* Leather purse used by carriers with divisions for paper, money, and other things.

Guarnír, *va.* To reeve, to pass a rope through the eyes of different blocks in order to form a tackle. *Guarnir el cabrestante,* To rig the capstern.

Guárra, *sf.* Sow.

Guarríllo, *sm.* A small pig.

Guárro, *sm.* Hog, pig, whether large or small.

Guastár, *va.* V. *Consumir.*

Guáy, *interj.* Oh! an exclamation of pain or grief. V. *Ay. Tener muchos guayes,* To labour under many afflictions.

Guáya, *sf.* Grief, sorrow, affliction.

Guayába, *sf.* Fruit of the guava tree.

Guayáco, *sm.* (Bot.) Lignum vitæ, guaiacum. Guaiacum officinale *L.*

Guayadéro, *sm.* Place of mourning.

Guayapíl ó Guaypín, *sm.* A loose Indian dress for women.

Guayár, *vn.* To mourn, to grieve, to lament.

Guayás, *interj.* (Ant.) V. *Guay.*

Guáyco, *sm.* Rugged, hollow between ridges of mountains.

Gubernatívo, va, *a.* Administrative, relating to government.

Gúbia, *sf.* Gouge, a round hollow chisel.

Gubiadúra, *sf.* (Naút.) Notch, channel. *Gubiadura del tamborete,* (Naút.) Channel of a cap. *Gubiadura de un moton,* (Naút.) Notch of a block.

Gubiléte, *sm.* (Ant.) Kind of vase.

Guedéja, *sf.* 1. Lock of hair falling on the temple, forelock. 2. Lion's mane.

Guedejár, *va.* To dress the hair, to adorn the head with locks of hair.

Guedejílla, *sf.* A small lock of hair.

Guedejón, na; y Guedejóso, sa, *a.* Bushy.

Guedejúdo, da, *a.* Bushy, clotted; applied to hair.

Guélde, *sm.* (Bot.) Water-elder, guelder-rose. Viburnum opulus *L.*

Guéltre, *sm.* (In Cant) Money, cash. V. *Dinero.*

Guerméces, *sm.* A morbid swelling in the throat of hawks, and other birds of prey.

Guérra, *sf.* 1. War, a state of hostility between sovereign powers. 2. Art of war, military science. 3. Profession of arms. 4. Opposition, quarrel; conflict of passions. *Guerra galana,* Cannonading, distant fighting. *Guerra guerreada,* Experienced war. *En buena guerra,* By fair and lawful means.

Guerreadór, ra, *s.* Warrior; one passionately fond of military fame.

Guerreánte, *pa.* Warrior, warring.

Guerreár, *va.* To war, to wage war.

Guerreramente, *ad.* Warlikely.

Guerréro, *sm.* 1. Warrior. V. *Guerreador.* 2. A soldier, a military man.

Guerréro, ra, *a.* Martial, warlike.

Guerrílla, *sf. dim.* 1. War of partisans; predatory warfare. 2. Skirmish, a slight engagement. 3. Game at cards between two persons, each with twenty cards.

Guéta, *sf.* (Mil.) A white gaiter.

Guía, *sm.* 1. Guide, conductor, leader. 2. Permit, cocket, docket; a writing, proving that the customs and duty are paid at the custom-house. 3. A young shoot or sucker of a vine. 4. A person who leads down a country dance. *En guia ó en la guia,* (Ant.) Guiding. 5. (Mús.) Fugue. 6. (Naút.) Guy, a small rope, used on board of ships to keep weighty things in their places. 7. Directory, book of public roads. 8. A little fish that guides the whale. 9. Earth which indicates the vein of a mine. 10. Guard of a fan.—*pl.* 1. Trains of powder in rockets or fire-works. 2. Horses or mules, which go before the wheel horses or mules. *A' guias,* Driving four in hand; applied to a coachman driving four horses. 3. The two stiff bones of stays.

Guiadéra, *sf.* Guide or conductor in mills. · *Guiaderas,* Two upright pieces of wood in oil-mills.

Guiádo, da, *a.* Guided.

Guiadór, ra, *s.* Guide, guider, director.

Guiamiénto, *sm.* Guidance, the act of guiding or conducting; security.

Guiár, *va.* 1. To guide, to conduct, to show the way. 2. To teach, to direct. 3. To lead a dance. *Guiar el agua á su molino,* To bring grist to one's mill.

Guíja, *sf.* 1. Pebble, pebble-stone; coarse gravel. 2. (Ar.) Kidney bean. Phaseolus *L.*

Guijarrál, *sm.* Heap of pebble-stones, a place abounding in pebbles.

Guijarrázo, *sm.* Blow with a pebble-stone.

Guijarréño, ña, *a.* 1. Pebbly, gravelly. 2. Hardy, strong and rude.

Guijárro, *sm.* Pebble, or smooth stone.

Guijarróso, sa, *a.* Pebbly.

Guijéño, ña, *a.* 1. Full of pebbles, or coarse gravel. 2. Hard, sour, difficult.

Guíjo, *sm.* Small pebbles, or gravel for roads.

Guijón, *sm.* A worm that corrodes the teeth.

Guijóso, sa, *a.* 1. Gravelly. 2. V. *Guijéño.*

Guílla, *sf.* A plentiful harvest.

Guilláme, *sm.* Rabbet-plane, a tool used by carpenters.

Guilledín, *sm.* Gelding.
Guillóte, *sm.* 1. Husbandman who enjoys the produce of a farm. 2. Tree-nail or iron pin. 3. Vagrant, sponger; an idle fellow who strolls about without any business or employment.
Guimbalète, *sm.* (Naút.) Brake or handle of a pump.
Guinchár, *va.* To prick; to stimulate.
Guíncho, *sm.* 1. (Orn.) Gull, sea-gull. Larus canus *L.* 2. Goad, pike.
Guínda, *sf.* Cherry, a reddish stony fruit. *Mucha guinda*, (Naút.) Taunt or high masted.
Guindádo, **da**, *a.* Hoisted, set up. *Los masteleros estan guindados*, (Naút.) The top-masts are an end.
Guindál, *sm.* (Bot.) Cherry-tree. V. *Guindo.*
Guindaléra, *sf.* Cherry-garden, a plantation of cherry-trees.
Guindaléta, *sf.* 1. Crank-rope, a rope used to raise materials to the top of a building. 2. Fulcrum of a balance.
Guindaléza, *sf.* (Naút.) Hawser, a rope used for warping or other purposes on board of ships.
Guindamáyna, *sf.* (Naút.) Salute between ships or squadrons.
Guindár, *va.* 1. To lift, to elevate, to raise. 2. To snatch, to seize any thing hastily. 3. (Naut.) To make fast with hawsers. 4. (Naút.) To hoist, to raise aloft. 5. To hang.—*vr.* To be suspended, to hang by or on any thing.
Guindástes, *sm. pl.* (Naút.) Gears or jeers, an assemblage of tackles.
Guindílla, *sf.* Small kind of red pepper.
Guindíllo, *sm.* Indian cherry-tree.
Guíndo, *sm.* (Bot.) Cherry-tree. Prunus cerasus *L.* *Guindo griego*, Large cherry-tree. *Don Guindo*, (Joc.) Coxcomb.
Guíndola, *sf.* (Naút.) A triangular hanging stage.
Guinéa, *sf.* Guinea, an English gold coin.
Guinéo, *sm.* Dance used among the negroes.
Guingáns, *sf.* A kind of cotton stuff.
Guiñáda ó Guiñadúra, *sf.* 1. Wink, a hint given by a motion of the eye. 2. (Naút.) Yaw, the deviation of a ship from her right course.
Guiñadór, **ra**, *s.* Winker.
Guiñápo, *sm.* 1. Tatter, rag. 2. Ragamuffin, tatterdemalion; a ragged fellow.
Guiñár, *va.* 1. To wink, to hint or direct by a motion of the eye-lids. 2. (Naút.) To yaw or make yaws; not to steer in a steady manner.
Guíño, *sm.* V. *Guiñada.*
Guión, *sm.* 1. Cross, the standard carried before prelates and corporations or communities. 2. Royal standard. 3. Master of ceremonies; chief conductor. 4. (Mús.) Sign or mark, indicating that a piece played is to be repeated. 5. *Guion de un remo*, (Naút.) Loom of an oar. 6. Hyphen or division in writing.
Guionáge, *sm.* (Ant.) Guide or conductor.
Guirigáy, *sm.* Gibberish, obscure or confused language; unmeaning words.
Guirindóla, *sf.* Bosom of a shirt.
Guirnálda, *sf.* 1. Garland, a wreath or open crown interwoven with flowers. 2. (Mil.) Light-ball. 3. (Naút.) Puddening, a wreath of cordage put around a variety of things on board of ships. *Guirnalda del ancla*, Puddening of the anchor-ring. *Guirnalda de un palo*, Puddening of a mast. *Guirnalda de las vergas*, Puddening of the yards.

Guirnaldár, *va.* To surround a thrashing-place with trees.
Guísa, *sf.* (Ant.) Guise, mode, manner, class, species.
Guisadíllo, *sm.* A small dish of ragout or fricassee.
Guisádo, **da**, *a.* (Ant.) Useful, convenient, prepared, seasonable.
Guisádo, *sm.* 1. Ragout, fricassee; a dish of stewed meat, with broth, spice, &c. 2. (Met.) Action or deed performed under very remarkable circumstances. *Estar uno mal guisado*, To be disgusted and discontented.
Guisadór, **ra**; y **Guisandéro**, **ra**, *s.* Cook, one who dresses victuals.
Guisánte, *sm.* (Bot.) Pea. Pisum sativum *L.*
Guisár, *va.* 1. To cook or dress victuals; to cure meat. 2. (Met.) To arrange, to adjust.
Guíso, *sm.* The seasoning of a dish; sauce of meat, and other victuals.
Guisopíllo, *sm.* V. *Hisopillo.*
Guisóte, *sm.* Dish of meat dressed country-fashion.
Guíta, *sf.* A small hempen cord.
Guitár, *va.* To sew with a hempen cord.
Guitárra, *sf.* 1. Guitar, a small stringed instrument. 2. Pounder, a sort of pestle or mallet for pounding gypsum or whiting. *Ser buena guitarra*, (Fam.) To be artful and cunning.
Guitarréro, **ra**, *s.* 1. Guitar-maker. 2. Player on the guitar.
Guitarrésco, **ca**, *a.* (Joc.) Belonging to the guitar.
Guitarríllo y Guitárro, *sm.* Very small guitar.
Guitarrísta, *sm.* Player on the guitar.
Guitarrón, *sm.* 1. A large guitar. 2. An acute knave.
Guíto, **ta**, *a.* Treacherous, vicious; applied to mules.
Guitón, **na**, *s.* Mendicant, vagrant, vagabond.
Guitoneár, *vn.* To loiter or idle about, to lead a vagabond life.
Guitonería, *sf.* Idleness; a vagrant or vagabond life.
Guizcár, *va.* To excite, to invite. V. *Enguizgar.*
Guízque, *sm.* 1. (Mancha.) Hook of a hanging lamp. 2. (Arag.) Sting of a wasp.
Gúja, *sm.* Arm used by archers.
Gúla, *sf.* 1. Gullet. 2. Gluttony, inordinate desire of eating and drinking. 3. (And.) A low eating-house.
Gulóso, **sa**, *a.* Gluttonous, greedy.
Gullería, *sf.* 1. Dainty, something nice and delicate, a delicacy. 2. Excess in eating and drinking. 3. (Met.) Cupidity, excessive desire of any thing. 4. (Orn.) Kind of lark.
Gúmena, *sf.* Cable.
Gumenéta, *sf. dim.* A small cable.
Gúmia, *sf.* Kind of dagger or poniard.
Gurbión, *sm.* 1. Twisted silk, of a coarse quality. 2. Silk stuff, resembling grogram. 3. (Bot.) Officinal spurge. Euphorbia officinarum *L.* 4. Gum of euphorbium.
Gurbionádo, **da**, *a.* Made of twisted coarse silk.
Gúrdo, **da**, *a.* (Ant.) Silly, simple.
Gurrár, *vn.* 1. (Naút.) To get clear of another ship. 2. To retrograde, to fall back.
Gurrufálla, *sf.* A worthless trifle, a thing of no value.
Gurruféro, *sm.* A deformed nag or horse.

Gurrumína, *sf.* Uxoriousness, an unbecoming submission to one's wife.
Gurrumíno, *sm.* A husband who is unbecomingly obedient and submissive to his wife.
Gurulláda, *sf.* 1. Club, a society of friends. 2. Crowd, multitude.
Gurúllo, *sm.* Lump or knot. V. *Burujo.*
Gurumête, *sm.* Ship's boy. V. *Grumete.*
Gurúpa, *sf.* Croup of a horse. V. *Grupa.*
Gurupéra, *sf.* Crupper. V. *Grupera.*
Gurupetín, *sm.* A small crupper.
Gúrvio, a, *a.* Curved, arched, incurvated.
Gusaneár, *vn.* To itch. V. *Hormiguear.*
Gusanéra, *sf.* 1. Place or spot where maggots or vermin are bred. 2. (Met.) Remorse, a sting which pricks one's conscience.
Gusaniénto, ta, *a.* Troubled with maggots or vermin; full of worms; worm-eaten.
Gusanillo, *sm.* 1. A small worm or maggot. 2. A kind of embroidery. 3. Bit of a gimlet or augur.
Gusáno, *sm.* 1. Maggot, worm. 2. An humble meek person. 3. Distemper among sheep. *Gusano de seda,* Silk-worm. *Gusano marino,* Sea-worm. *Gusano de santanton,* Gray grub.
Gusarapiénto, ta, *a.* Wormy, full of worms; corrupted.
Gusarápo, *sm.* Water-worm, an aquatic insect.
Guséppe, *sm.* Kind of polypus.
Gustáble, *a.* Tastable, gustable, capable of being tasted or relished. V. *Gustoso.*

Gustación, *sf.* Gustation.
Gustadúra, *sf.* Gustation, the act of tasting.
Gustár, *va.* 1. To taste, to discern and perceive the relish and flavour of things. 2. To enjoy a thing with pleasure. 3. To experience, to examine. 4. To take a pleasure or delight in a thing.
Gustatívo, *a.* Lingual; applied to a branch of the inferior maxillary nerve.
Gustázo, *sm.* A great pleasure.
Gustíllo, *sm. dim.* Agreeable, delicate taste.
Gústo, *sm.* 1. Taste, the sense by which any thing on the palate is perceived. 2. The sensation which all things taken into the mouth give, particularly to the tongue. 3. Pleasure, delight. 4. One's own will and determination. 5. Election, choice. 6. Taste, intellectual relish or discernment. 7. Caprice, fancy, diversion. *Gustos,* Sensual pleasures; evil habits; vices.
Gustosaménte, *ad.* Tastefully.
Gustóso, sa, *a.* 1. Tasty, savoury. 2. Cheerful, merry, content. 3. Pleasing, pleasant, entertaining.
Gutagámba y Gutiambár, *sm.* Gamboge.
Guturál, *a.* Guttural, pronounced in the throat, belonging to the throat.
Gutturalménte, *ad.* Gutturally.
Guzmánes, *sm. pl.* Noblemen who serve as midshipmen in the navy.
Guzpatárra, *sf.* Ancient play of boys.

H Is not properly considered as a letter, but as a mere aspiration. The syllables *cha, che, chi,* are pronounced as in English. Formerly *ch* had sometimes the sound of *k,* as in *chímico, chimera, chamelote:* but the Spanish Academy has very properly fixed the pronunciation of all words in which they had the hard sound, by writing them as in *químico, quimera, camelote.* The moderns use *h* to soften the pronunciation of many words, as *facer, fijo,* are now written *hacer, hijo.* For the same purpose it is placed before *u,* followed by *e,* in many words derived from the Latin, as *huevo,* from *ovum,* an egg, *hueso* from *os.* The *h* is never sounded in the Spanish language, except by the common people in *Andalusia;* and those words in which it was preceded by a *p,* and took the sound of *f,* are now written as pronounced, thus, *fenómeno,* phenomenon. After *r* and *t* the *h* is entirely omitted, as in *reuma,* rheum, *teatro,* theatre; but it is retained and aspirated in all words which originally began with *h,* or between two vowels, as *honor, almohaza.*
Ha! *interj.* 1. Ah! alas! 2. (Naut.) Haul away!
Hába, *sf.* 1. (Bot.) Bean, a kind of pulse. Vicia faba *L. Haba de perro,* (Bot.) Dog's bane. Apocynum *L.* 2. A kind of mange in horses and oxen. *Habas,* Little white and black balls used in giving votes. *Esas son habas contadas,* A thing clear and manifest.

Habanéro, ra, *a.* Native of Havannah. [nah.
Habáno, na, *a.* Applied to tobacco of Havan-
Habár, *sm.* Beanfield, a field sown with beans.
Habér, *va.* 1. To possess, to have in one's power or custody. 2. To have; an auxiliary verb. 3. To take, to recover. 4. To happen, to fall out, to befal. 5. To exist.—*v. Impers.* V. *Acaecer. Haberlas ó habérselas con alguno,* To dispute, to contend with any one.—*vr.* To behave, to act, to conduct one's self.
Habér, *sm.* Property, income, fortune. *Mas vale saber que haber,* (Prov.) Knowledge is preferable to wealth.
Habichuéla, *sf.* (Bot.) Common white kidney-bean. Phaseolus vulgaris *L.*
Hábil, *a.* 1. Capable, intelligent; able to understand. 2. Agile, active, ready. 3. Apt, fit, qualified for.
Habilidád, *sf.* 1. Hability, dexterity in performing. 2. Nimbleness, quickness, speed. 3. Instinct.
Habilitación, *sf.* Habilitation, qualification.
Habilitádo, *sm.* Paymaster or commissary of a regiment.
Habilitadór, ra, *s.* Qualifier, one who makes fit or able.
Habilitár, *va.* 1. To qualify, to enable, to habilitate. 2. To provide, to supply.
Habillamiénto, *sm.* (Ant.) Habiliment, dress.
Habilménte, *ad.* Dexterously, ably.
Habitáble, *a.* Habitable.

Habitación, *sf.* 1. Habitation, abode; the place or house in which a person resides. 2. Set of rooms, that part of a house which is destined to be inhabited.
Habitáculo, *sm.* V. *Habitacion.*
Habitadór, ra, *s.* Inhabitant, resident.
Habitánte, *pa.* Inhabitant; inhabiting.
Habitár, *va.* To inhabit, to live or reside in a place.
Habitíllo, co, to, *sm.* A small dress or habit.
Hábito, *sm.* 1. Dress, habit, habiliment, garment. *Habitos*, Dress of ecclesiastics and students. 2. Habit, a power in man of doing any thing acquired by frequent doing. 3. Badge or insignia of military orders.
Habituación, *sf.* Habitude, custom.
Habituál, *a.* Habitual, accustomed, inveterate.
Habitualidád, *sf.* Custom, use.
Habitualménte, *ad.* Habitually.
Habituárse, *vr.* To be accustomed, to accustom one's self.
Habitúd, *sf.* Habitude; the respect or relation which one thing bears to another; custom.
Hábla, *sf.* 1. Speech, idiom, language. 2. Discourse, argument. 3. Talk, conversation. *Estar en habla*, To talk about a matter. *Estar sin habla, ó perder el habla*, To be speechless. *Negar ó quitar el habla*, To refuse speaking to a person.
Habladór, ra, *s.* An impudent prattler; a trifling talker.
Habladorcíllo, lla, *s.* A babbling dandiprat.
Habladuría, *sf.* An impertinent speech.
Hablantín ó Hablanchín, na, *s.* A talkative person.
Hablár, *va.* 1. To speak, to utter articulate sounds; to express thoughts by words. 2. To reason, to converse. 3. To harangue, to make a speech. 4. To advise, to admonish. *Hablar Dios á alguno*, To be inspired. *Hablar á bulto ó á tiento*, To talk at random. *Hablar disparates ó necedades*, To talk nonsense. *Hablar al ayre*, To talk to the air, to speak vaguely. *Hablar el alma*, To speak one's mind. *Hablar al caso*, To speak to the purpose. *Hablar alto*, To talk loud. *Hablar de burlas ó de chanza*, To jeer, to mock. *Hablar de la mar*, To talk on an endless subject. *Hablar de memoria*, To talk without reflection. *No dexar que hablar*, To convince any one, to impose silence. *Hablar de veras*, To speak seriously. *Hablar paso, quedo, ó baxo*, To talk low. *Hablar con los ojos*, To indicate one's sentiments by looks. *Hablar de hilvan*, To speak too rapidly and confusedly. *Hablar de vicio*, To be loquacious. *No hablarse*, Not to speak to each other from enmity or aversion. *Hablar de ó en boveda*, To speak pompously or arrogantly.
Hablatísta, *sm.* (Joc.) A trifling prattler, an idle talker.
Hablílla, *sf.* Rumour, report, little tale.
Habón, *sm.* Large kind of bean.
Háca, *sf.* Pony, a small horse. *¿ Que haca ? ó que haca morena ?* For what good ? to what purpose ?
Hacanéa, *sf.* Nag, a small horse somewhat bigger than a pony.
Háce, *sm.* V. *Haz.*
Hacecíto, *sm.* A small sheaf.

Hacedéro, ra, *a.* Feasible, practicable; easily effected.
Hacedór, ra, *s.* 1. Maker, author; factor. 2. Steward, one who manages the estate of another. 3. A good workman, an able performer.
Hacendádo, da, *a.* Applied to persons of property.
Hacendár, *va.* To transfer or make over the property of an estate.—*vr.* To make a purchase of land in order to settle in a place.
Hacendéra, *sf.* Public work, at which all the neighbourhood assists.
Hacendéro, ra, *a.* Industrious, laborious, sedulous.
Hacendílla y Hacenduéla, *sf.* 1. A small farm. 2. A trifling work.
Hacendóso, sa, *a.* Assiduous, diligent.
Hacér, *va.* 1. To make, to form of materials, to produce; to conceive. 2. To put in execution, to carry into effect; to effect. *Hacer por alguno*, To do for any one. 3. To make up a number, to complete. 4. To agree, to suit, to answer. 5. To give, to grant. 6. To include, to contain. 7. To cause, to occasion. 8. To resolve, to determine, to judge, to consider. 9. To dispose, to compose, to prepare. *Hacer á todo*, Disposed or ready to admit. 10. To assemble, to convoke; to correspond. 11. To habituate, to accustom one's self. 12. To oblige, to compel; in this sense it is followed by an infinitive verb. *Hacer venir*, To oblige to come. 13. To dress, applied to hawks or cocks for fighting. 14. To grow, to increase or receive any thing. 15. Joined with *de, se, el, la, lo*, it signifies to represent or become, as *hacer del bobo*, To become an idiot; *hacer el rey*, to personate the king; with *por* or *para* to an infinitive verb, it signifies taking pains and care in executing the import of such verb, as *hacer por llegár*, to endeavour to arrive; *hacer para salvarse*, to strive to save one's self; followed by substantives it gives them a verbal signification, as *hacer estimacion*, to esteem. *Hacer de escribano*, To act as a scrivener or notary. *Hacerlo changa*, To turn into ridicule. *Hacer agua*, (Naút.) To water, to make water; applied to a ship which is leaky. V. *Orinar.* *Hacer alarde*, (Mil.) To review troops. *Hacer ayre*, (Met.) To chastise, to give a drubbing. *Hacer carne*, To wound, to maltreat; to kill. *Hacer correrias*, To make incursions. *Hacer del cuerpo*, To go to stool. *Hacer de tripas corazon*, To pluck up a heart, to inspirit. *Hacer el bastardo*, (Naút.) To veer or tack so as to bring the ship before the wind. *Hacer estrados*, To give a hearing; applied to judges and magistrates. *Hacer fanal*, (Naút.) To carry the poop-lantern lighted; applied to the headmost ship which leads the van. *Hacer fiestas*, To flatter, to cajole. *Hacer honras*, To honour, to pay honours; to hold in esteem. *Hacer humo*, (Met.) To continue long in a place. *Hacer juego*, To be well matched. *Hacer la barba*, To shave, to get shaved. *Hacer la mamona*, To pull one's nose, to scoff or ridicule. *Hacer razon*, To join in a toast. *Hacer merced ó mercedes*, To confer honours or employments. *Hacer milagros*,

To do wonders. *Hacer morisquetas*, To play pranks. *Hacer papel ó el papel*, To act a part, to cut a figure; to acquit one's self well. *Hacer penitencia con alguno*, To take pot-luck or a family dinner; to dine with one on whatever he chances to have. *Hacer plato*, to carve. *Hacer prenda*, To take a pledge or security for a debt. *Hacer pucheros*, To make wry faces, as children are used to do before they begin to cry. *Hacer pie*, To find the bottom of water without swimming; to be firm and secure in any thing; to stop, to reside in a place. *Hacer que hacemos*, To act officially, to affect doing some business. *No hay que hacer, ó eso no tiene que hacer*, It is only to act, it is easily done. *Hacerse á la vela, ó hacer vela*, (Naút.) To set sail. *Hacerse de algo*, To purchase what is wanting. *Hacerse antesala*, To attend in a hall, in order to speak to any person of consequence in passing. *Hacerse de miel*, To treat one gently. *Hacerse lugar*, (Met.) To get a name or reputation. *Hacerse tortilla*, To fall down as flat as a cake. *Hacer sombra*, (Met.) To impede, to obscure; to protect, to support. *Hacer fuerza de vela*, (Naút.) To crowd sail, to carry a press of sail. *Hacer poca vela*, (Naút.) To carry an easy sail. *Hacer derrota*, (Naút.) To stand on the course. *Hacer agua*, (Naút.) To spring a leak. *Hacer buen bordo*, (Naút.) To make a good tack. *Hacer camino para avante*, (Naút.) To have headway. *Hacer camino para popa*, (Naút.) To make sternway. *Hacer cabeza*, (Naút.) To head.—*vn.* 1. To import, to matter. 2. To be, to exist. *Hacer frio*, to be cold.—*vr.* To separate, to recede; to become. *Hacerse memorable*, To become memorable.

Hacerír, *va.* (Ant.) V. *Zaherir*.

Hacezuélo, *sm. dim.* of *Haz*.

Hácha, *sf.* 1. A large taper with four wicks. *Hacha de viento*, Flambeau, torch, link. *Page de hacha*, Link-boy. 2. Hatchet, a small axe. *Hacha de armas*, Battle-axe. 3. Ancient Spanish dance.

Hachazo, *sm.* Blow or stroke with a hatchet.

Hachear, *va.* To cut with a hatchet.—*vn.* To strike with a hatchet.

Hachéro, *sm.* 1. Torch-stand, a large candlestick for tapers or torches. 2. Person appointed for making signals in a watch-tower or light-house. 3. Wood-cleaver or wood-cutter; a labourer employed to fell wood and cut timber. 4. Carpenter.

Hachéta, *sf.* 1. A small hatchet. 2. A small torch or link.

Hácho, *sm.* Faget, or bundle of bass-wood covered with pitch or resin.

Hachón, *sm.* 1. A large torch made of bass and pitch. 2. Kind of altar, on which bonfires are lighted for illuminations.

Hachuéla, *sf.* A small hatchet or axe. *Hachuela de abordar*, (Naút.) Boarding-axe.

Hácia, *ad.* Towards, in direction to, near to. *Hácia donde*, Whither, towards which, to what place, to where.

Haciénda, *sf.* 1. Landed property, lands, tenements. 2. Estate, fortune, wealth. 3. Domestic work done by the servants of the house. *Hacer hacienda*, To mind one's business, to do what is to be done. *Haciendas apalabradas*, Goods already bespoken.

Haciénte, *pa.* Agent, doer. *Fe haciente*, (For.) Applied to such testimonies and instruments as constitute evidence in a court of justice.

Hacimiénto, *sm.* Acting, doing, the act or action. *Hacimiento de gracias*, Thanksgiving. *Hacimiento de rentas*, The act of disposing of a farm, lease, &c. by public auction.

Hacína, *sf.* Stack or rick of corn piled up in sheaves.

Hacinadór, ra, *s.* Stack-maker, one who piles up the sheaves of corn. *Hacinador de riquezas*, Hoarder of riches.

Hacinamiénto, *sm.* Accumulation, act of heaping or hoarding up.

Hacinár, *va.* 1. To stack or pile up sheaves of corn. 2. To hoard, to make hoards.

Hacíno, na, *a.* V. *Avaro* y *Triste*.

Hádas ó Hadádas, *sf. pl.* Witches; enchanted nymphs; fortune-tellers; the fates.

Hadádo, da, *a.* Fortunate, lucky.

Hadadór, ra, *s.* Sorcerer, fortune-teller.

Hadár, *va.* To divine, to foretel future events.

Hádo, *sm.* Fate, destiny, inevitable doom.

Hadróbla, *sf.* Fraud, deceit or imposition in selling and buying.

Hae, *interj.* (Ant.) V. *He*.

Hála, *interj.* Holla! a word used in calling to any one at a distance. *Hala el bote á bordo*, (Naút.) Haul the boat aboard.

Halacabúllas y Halacuérdas, *sm.* Fresh-water sailors.

Halagadór, ra, *s.* Cajoler, flatterer.

Halagár, *va.* To cajole, to flatter; to caress.

Halágo, *sm.* Cajolery, flattery, caress, adulation.

Halagüeñaménte, *ad.* Endearingly, flatteringly.

Halagüéño, ña, *a.* Endearing, attractive, fawning, flattering.

Halár, *va.* (Naút.) To haul, to pull by a rope. *Halar al viento*, (Naút.) To haul the wind.

Halcón, *sm.* (Orn.) Falcon, a hawk trained for sport. Falco *L.*

Halconádo, da, *a.* Falcon or hawk-like.

Halconeár, *va.* 1. To look and inveigle; applied to women of the town. 2. (Met.) To look about as haughty as a falcon; to view with contempt.

Halconéra, *sf.* Place where falcons are kept.

Halconería, *sf.* Falconry, the act of rearing and training hawks.

Halconéro, *sm.* Falconer, one who rears or trains hawks for sport.

Hálda, *sf.* 1. Bag or sack made of sack-cloth. 2. Skirt of a garment. V. *Falda*. *Haldas en cinta*, (Fam.) Disposed and ready for any thing.

Haldáda, *sf.* Skirt full of any thing.

Haldeár, *vn.* To run along with the skirts flying loose.

Haldúdo, da, *a.* Having flying skirts.

Haléche, *sm.* Kind of mackerel. V. *Escombro*.

Haliéto, *sm.* Sea eagle.

Hálito, *sm.* 1. Breath, the air drawn in and ejected out of the body; vapour. 2. (Poét.) Soft air.

Halládo, da, *a.* Found. *Bien hallado*, Very familiar, welcome.

Halladór, ra, *s.* Finder, discoverer, inventer.

HALLÁR, va. 1. To find, to meet with, to fall upon. 2. To find out, to discover. 3. To observe, to note; to compare, to verify; to understand, to comprehend. 4. To manifest, to show any thing unexpected.—vr. 1. To meet occasionally in any place. 2. To be content or pleased in any place. 3. To be somewhere.

HALLÁZGO Y HALLAMIÉNTO, sm. 1. The act of finding or recovering any thing lost. 2. Reward given for finding any thing lost. 3. Thing found. [feed fowls.

HALLÚLLA, sf. A kind of paste made and used to

HALLÚLLO, sm. Cake baked on or under cinders.

HÁLO ó HALÓN, sm. Halo, a red circle round the sun or moon.

HALOTÉCNIA, sf. (Quim.) The science which treats of salts.

HALÓZA, sf. Wooden shoe. V. *Galocha*.

HAMÁCA, sf. Hammock, a kind of bed suspended between two trees or posts.

HAMAQUÉRO, sm. Person who conducts a hammock.

HAMÁNO, sm. A kind of pink cotton stuff which comes from the Levant.

HÁMBRE, sf. 1. Hunger, the natural desire of food; appetite; the pain felt from fasting. *Tener hambre*, To be hungry, to have an appetite. 2. Scarcity and dearth of provisions. 3. A violent desire of any thing.

HAMBREÁR, vn. To be hungry, to crave victuals.—va. To cause hunger. To starve, to kill with hunger, to subdue by famine.

HAMBRIÉNTO, TA, a. Hungry, starved; incessant desire.

HAMBRÓN, NA, s. A hungry person, starved for want of victuals.

HAMÉDIS, sf. A sort of muslin.

HAMÉZ, sf. A distemper in hawks or falcons which makes them lose their feathers.

HÁMPA, sf. Bully, bragger, boaster; life of a company of rogues and vagabonds formerly in Andalusia, who used a jargon, like gypsies, called *Gerigonza* or *Germanía*.

HAMPÉSCO, CA, a. Vagabond, villainous, vainglorious.

HÁMPO ó HAMPÓN, a. Bold, valiant, licentious.

HANÉGA, sf. A dry measure. V. *Fanega*.

HANEGÁDA, sf. Quantity of land sown with a *fanega* of corn.

HANQUÍLLA, sf. A kind of boat.

HÁNZO, sm. (Ant.) Hilarity, fecundity.

HÁO, interj. Holla, a vulgar word used in calling to any one at a distance.

HAQUÍLLA, sf. dim. Very little pony.

HARAGÁN, NA, s. Idler, an idle lazy person.

HARAGANAMÉNTE, ad. Idly, lazily.

HARAGÁNZO, ZA, a. Very idle.

HARAGANEÁR, vn. To lead an idle life, to be lazy, to act the truant.

HARAGANERÍA, sf. Idleness, laziness.

HARÁLDO Y HARAÚTE, sm. (Ant.) Herald, king at arms. [clothes, fringe.

HARÁPO, sm. Rag hanging down from torn

HARBÁR, va. To huddle, to perform in a hurry.

HARÉM, sm. Harem, Turkish seraglio.

HARÍJA, sf. Mill-dust, the flour which flies about in a corn-mill.

HARÍNA, sf. 1. Flour, the edible part of corn and meal. 2. (Met.) Powder, dust.

HARINÁDO, sm. Flour dissolved in water.

HARINÉRO, sm. 1. Mealman, one who deals in flour. 2. Place where meal or flour is kept.

HARINÉRO, RA, a. Made of flour, belonging to flour. [meal.

HARINÓSO, SA, a. Mealy, that which contains

HARMÁGA, sf. (Bot.) Wild rue. *Ruta montana* L.

HARMONÍA, sf. Harmony. V. *Armonia* and its adjuncts.

HARMONÍSTA, sm. Musician.

HARNÉRO, sm. Sieve. V. *Criba*. *Estar hecho un harnero*, To be covered with wounds.

HARÓN, NA, a. Slow, inactive, sluggish.

HARPAGÓN, sm. Harrow.

HARPÉO, sm. (Naút.) Grappling-iron or grapple.

HARPÓN, sm. V. *Arpon*.

HARRIÉRO, sm. Carrier.

HARTÁR, va. 1. To stuff with eating and drinking; to glut. 2. To satiate, to saturate. 3. To fill beyond natural desire; followed by *de*, it signifies to give or cause in abundance or excess. [filling beyond natural desire.

HARTÁZGO, sm. Satiety, the act of glutting or

HÁRTO, ad. Enough.

HÁRTO, TA, a. Sufficient, full, complete.

HARTÚRA, sf. 1. Satiety. 2. Plenty, abundance.

HASÍZ, sm. Guard or keeper of silk.

HÁSTA, ad. Until, as far as; also, even. *Hasta no mas*, To the highest pitch.

HASTIÁL, sm. (Ant.) V. *Fachada ó Frontispicio*.

HASTIÁR, va. To loathe, to create disgust.

HASTÍO, s. Loathing, want of appetite, disgust.

HATÁCA, sf. 1. A large kind of wooden ladle. 2. Rolling-pin, with which paste is moulded.

HATAJÁR, va. To divide cattle into flocks or herds. [semblage, collection; abundance.

HATÁJO, sm. 1. A small herd of cattle. 2. As-

HATEÁR, vn. To collect one's clothes necessary for travelling, when on a journey.

HATERÍA, sf. Allowance of provisions, and clothes for shepherds when travelling with their flocks.

HATÉRO, sm. Shepherd or other person who carries provisions to those who attend a flock of sheep. [carry the shepherd's baggage.

HATÉRO, RA, a. Applied to the animals that

HATÍJO, sm. Covering of straw or bass-weed over bee-hives.

HATÍLLO, sm. A few clothes. *Echar el hatillo al mar*, To irritate, to vex one's self.

HÁTO, sm. 1. Clothes, wearing apparel. 2. A large herd of cattle. *Un hato de carneros*, A flock of sheep. 3. Provisions for shepherds, for some days' consumption. 4. Crowd, multitude, meeting of suspicious people. 5. Place chosen by shepherds to eat and sleep near their flocks.

HAUBÍTZ, sm. (Art.) Howitzer, a kind of ordnance.

HÁYA, sf. (Bot.) 1. Beech-tree. *Fagus* L. 2. Presents formerly given to dancing-masters by their pupils. [trees.

HAYÁL Y HAYÉDO, sm. Plantation of beech-

HAYÉNO, NA, a. (Ant.) Beechen.

HÁYO, sm. Indian shrub.

HAYUCÁL, sm. (Leon.) Grove of beech-trees.

HAYÚCO, sm. Beech mast, fruit of the beech.

HÁZ, sm. Fagot, fascine, a bundle of brushwood; a bundle of hay or grass; a sheaf of corn.—sf. 1. Bundle, sheaf, fasces, fasciculus, collection of any vegetable. 2. Outside or right

side of cloth. 3. Surface of the ground, face of the country. 4. Face or front of a wall; facade of a building. *Sobre la haz de la tierra*, Upon the face of the earth. *A' sobre haz*, Apparently, exteriorly, at first view. *En haz y en paz*, With common consent and approbation. *Ser de dos haces*, To be double-faced, to say one thing and think another. 5. (Ant.) Rank and file of soldiers.

Háza, *sf.* 1. Piece of cultivated land. 2. (Ant.) Bundle of thongs.

Hazábra, *sf.* A small kind of coasting vessels.

Hazáda, *sf.* Spade. V. *Azada*.

Hazadón, *sm.* A large spade. V. *Azadon*.

Hazaléja, *sf.* A towel.

Hazáña, *sf.* 1. Exploit, achievement, a heroic feat. 2. Ignoble action.

Hazañería, *sf.* Show or affectation of scrupulosity.

Hazañéro, **ra**, *a.* Prudish, affectedly grave and scrupulous.

Hazañéro, **ra**, *s.* Affected prudish person.

Hazañosaménte, *ad.* Valorously.

Hazañóso, **sa**, *a.* Valiant, courageous, heroic.

Hazcóna, *sf.* Dart. V. *Dardo*.

Hazmerreír, *sm.* Ridiculous person, laughing-stock.

Hazteálla, *sf.* (Fam.) Roughness or austerity in behaviour or disposition.

He, *ad.* Behold, look here. It is used with pronouns, as *te*, *le*, *los*, &c. and *aqui* or *alli*.

He, *interj.* 1. Ho, a sudden exclamation to give notice of any thing. 2. What?

Hebdómada, *sf.* Week. V. *Semana*. 2. Seven years.

Hebdomadário, **ria**, *s.* Person who officiates a whole week in a choir.

Hebén, *a.* 1. Applied to white grapes, like moscatels. 2. Empty, futile; applied to persons.

Hebetár, *va.* To hebetate, to stupify.

Hebílla, *sf.* Buckle, a link of metal with a tongue or catch, made to fasten one thing to another.

Hebilláge, *sm.* Collection of buckles, or mounting of horses, accoutrements.

Hebilléta, **íca**, **íta**, **uéla**, *sf. dim.* Small buckle.

Hebillár, *va.* To buckle, to fasten with a buckle.

Hébra, *sf.* 1. Thread of linen yarn, worsted, or silk. 2. Capillament of the flower or blossom of saffron and other plants. 3. Vein of minerals or metals. 4. Fibre, filament; hair. *Cortar la hebra*, To cut the thread of life. *Ser ó estar de buena hebra*, To be strong and robust. 5. Toughness, flexibility, pliability. *Hebras*, Filaments, small fibres of the roots of trees; hairs.

Hebráico, **ca**, *a.* Belonging to the Hebrews.

Hebraizánte, *sm.* Hebrician, hebraist.

Hebraísmo, *sm.* Hebraism.

Hebréo, **ea**, *s.* A Hebrew; name given to Abraham the son of Heber, and his descendants.

Hebréo, **ea**, *a.* Hebraic, Judaical. *A' la Hebrea*, In the Hebrew manner. *Hebreo*, Hebrew language.

Hebréro, *sm.* (Ant.) February. V. *Febrero*.

Hebróso, **sa**, *a.* Fibrous, flaceous; consisting of many fibres and threads.

Hecatómba ó Hecatómbe, *sm.* Hecatomb, a sacrifice of an hundred cattle.

Hécha, *sf.* (Ant.) 1. V. *Hecho*. 2. (Ar.) Land-tax. *De esta hecha*, From this time.

Hechiceresco, **ca**, *a.* Relating to witchcraft.

Hechicería, *sf.* 1. Witchcraft, the practices of witches. 2. Charmingness, the power of pleasing.

Hechicéro, **ra**, *a. y s.* 1. Witch; bewitching, performing witchcraft. 2. Charmer, attractive, pleasing.

Hechizár, *va.* 1. To bewitch, to injure by witchcraft. 2. To charm, to please irresistibly.

Hechízo, *sm.* 1. Bewitchment, fascination. 2. Enchantment, irresistible power of pleasing; enchanter, charmer. 3. Entertainment, amusement.

Hechízo, **za**, *a.* Made or done on purpose; artificial, fictitious, imitated, well-adapted.

Hécho, **cha**, *a.* 1. Made, done. 2. Accustomed, used. *Hecho al trabajo*, Inured to labour and hardship. *Hecho un leon*, Like a lion. *Hombre hecho*, A man of experience. *Tiempo hecho*, (Naút.) Settled weather. *Viento hecho*, (Naút.) Steady wind.

Hécho, *sm.* 1. Action, well or ill performed. 2. Event, incident. 3. Subject or matter discussed. 4. (For.) Point litigated. *De hecho*, In fact, actually, effectually. *En hecho de verdad*, In truth. *Hombre de hecho*, A man of his word. *Hecho y derecho*, Perfect, absolute, complete. *A' hecho*, Incessantly, indiscriminately.

Hechór, **ra**, *s.* Factor.

Hechúra, *sf.* 1. Act of performing or doing any thing. 2. The work done or made. 3. Form or figure of a thing. 4. Effigy, statue. 5. Workmanship. 6. Creature, a person who owes his rise or fortune to another.

Heciénto, **ta**, *a.* Full of lees.

Hectóreo, **ea**, *a.* Belonging to Hector.

Hedentína, *sf.* Stench, stink.

Hedér, *vn.* 1. To stink, to emit an offensive smell. 2. (Met.) To vex, to fatigue, to be intolerable.

Hediondaménte, *ad.* Stinkingly.

Hediondéz, *sf.* A strong stench or stink; thing stinking.

Hedióndo, **da**, *a.* 1. Fetid, emitting an offensive smell. 2. Irascible, pettish, unpleasant. *Este es un hediondo*, He is a stinkard.

Hedór, *sm.* Stench, stink, fetor.

Hedrár, *va.* To dig a second time about the vines.

Hegíra, *sf.* Hegira, epocha of the flight of Mohammed from Mecca, from which the Arabians begin to compute time.

Helábe, *a.* Congealable.

Heláda, *sf.* Frost.

Heladína, *sf.* Jelly.

Heladízo, **za**, *a.* Easily congealed.

Heládo, **da**, *a.* Gelid, frigid; astonished; languid.

Heládo, *sm.* Ice-cream, concreted sugar.

Helamiénto, *sm.* Congelation.

Helár, *vn.* 1. To freeze, to be congealed with cold. 2. To be stupified; to be dispirited.—*vr.* 1. To be congealed or frozen, to be coagulated. 2. To grow motionless, to remain without action.

Héle, **Hételе aquí**, *ad.* Behold it, look here. V. *He*.

Helear, *va.* To point with the finger.

Helécho, *sm.* (Bot.) Male and female fern. Polypodium et Pteris *L.*

Heléna, *sf.* (Naút.) Castor and Pollux, a meteor, which in violent tempests sometimes appears on the masts of ships.

Helenísmo, *sm.* Hellenism, Greek idiom.

Helenísta, *sm.* Name given to the Jews of Alex-

andria, who spoke Greek, or the Greeks who embraced Judaism.
HELÉRA, *sf.* Pip, disease in fowls.
HELGÁDO, DA, *a.* Jag-toothed.
HELGADÚRA, *sf.* Irregularity of the teeth.
HELÍACO, CA, *a.* Heliacal, rising or setting of a star.
HELÍCE, *sf.* (Astr.) Northern constellation of ursa major. V. *Voluta* y *Espira.*
HELIÓMETRO, *sm.* Heliometer.
HELIOSCÓPIO, *sm.* 1. (Bot.) Wart-wort, sun-spurge. Euphorbia helioscopia *L.* 2. Telescope peculiarly fitted for viewing the sun.
HELIOTRÓPIO, *sm.* 1. (Bot.) Turnsol. Heliotropium *L.* 2. Precious stone.
HELXÍNE, *sf.* Pellitory. V. *Parietaria.*
HEMATÍTES, *sm.* Hæmatites, ore of iron.
HÉMBRA, *sf.* 1. Female, one of the sex which brings forth young. 2. Head of hair of women. 3. Nut of a screw. 4. Eye of a hook. 5. *Hembras del timon,* (Naút.) Googings of the rudder. 6. (Ant.) V. *Muger.*
HEMBREÁR, *vn.* 1. To be inclined to females; applied to males. 2. To generate or produce females only.
HEMBRÍCA, LLA, TA, *sf. dim.* of *Hembra.*
HEMBRÍLA, *sm.* 1. A sort of wheat of very fine grain. 2. Spool of a loom. 3. (And.) Leather trace of horses for ploughing.
HEMBRÚNO, NA, *a.* Belonging to the female sex.
HEMENCIÁR, *va.* (Ant.) To work or execute with the greatest care and pains.
HEMICÍCLO, *sm.* V. *Semicirculo.*
HEMICRÁNEA, *sf.* Hemicranium. V. *Xaqueca.*
HEMÍNA, *sf.* (Cast.) A measure containing the third part of a fanega; Greek liquid measure.
HEMIONÍTE, *sf.* (Bot.) Spleen wort, male fern.
HEMISFÉRIO, *sm.* Hemisphere, the half of a globe, where it is supposed to be cut through its centre.
HEMISTÍQUIO, *sm.* Hemistic, half a verse.
HEMORRAGÍA, *sf.* Hemorrhage, flux of blood.
HEMORRÓIDAS Y HEMORRÓIDES, *sf. pl.* Hemorrhoids, piles. V. *Almorranas.*
HEMORROIDÁL, *a.* Hemorrhoidal.
HEMORRÓO Y HEMORROÍDA, *s.* Kind of serpent.
HENÁR, *sm.* Meadow of hay.
HENCHIDÓR, RA, *s.* Filler, satiater, one who fills.
HENCHIDÚRA, *sf.* Repletion, act of filling.
HENCHIMIÉNTO, *sm.* Abundance, repletion. *Henchimientos,* (Naút.) Filling timbers, used to fill up the vacant part of the ship's frame.
HENCHÍR, *va.* 1. To fill up. 2. To sow discord, to produce mischief.—*vr.* To fill one's self. *Henchirse de lepra,* To be covered with the leprosy.
HENDEDÓR, RA, *s.* Divider, one who divides or splits any thing.
HENDEDÚRA, *sf.* Fissure, crack, rent; an opening in any matter which is separated.
HENDÉR, *va.* 1. To split, to divide; to open a passage. 2. To break into pieces.
HENDÍBLE, *a.* Fissile, capable of being split.
HENDIDÚRA, *sf.* V. *Hendedura.*
HENDIÉNTE, *sm.* Down-stroke of a sword or edged tool.
HENDRIJA, *sf.* A small fissure.
HENÍL, *sm.* Hay-loft, a place where hay is preserved.
HÉNO, *sm.* Hay, grass dried to fodder cattle in winter.

HEÑÍR, *va.* 1. To knead dough or the paste of bread. *Hay mucho que heñir,* There is much to do.
HEPÁTICA, *sf.* (Bot.) Liverwort.
HEPÁTICO, CA, *a.* Hepatic, belonging to the liver.
HEPTÁGONO, *sm.* Heptagon, a figure consisting of seven sides and angles.
HERÁLDICO, CA, *a.* Heraldic, that which relates or belongs to a herald.
HERÁLDO, *sm.* Herald, an officer whose business it is to register genealogies and adjust ensigns armorial. V. *Rey de Armas.*
HERAPRÍCA, *sf.* (Farm.) Hierapicra, a bitter purgative medicine.
HERBÁCEO, CEA, *a.* Herbaceous.
HERBÁGE, *sm.* 1. Herbage, grass, pasture. 2. Payment for pasturage. 3. (Ar.) Tribute to a new king for cattle. 4. Kind of ancient coarse cloth made of herbs.
HERBAGÉRO, *sm.* One who rents meadows or pastures; one who lets pasturage.
HERBAJÁR, *vn.* To pasture, to graze cattle.—*va.* To inclose a field for pasture.
HERBÁR, *va.* To dress skins with herbs.
HERBÁRIO, *sm.* 1. Herbal, a book which treats of plants. 2. Herbarium, collection of dried plants.—*a.* Herbarious.
HERBÁTU Ó HERBÁTUM, *sm.* (Bot.) Sulphurwort, hog's fennel. Peucedanum *L.*
HERBAZÁL, *sm.* Pasture-ground for cattle.
HERBECÉR, *vn.* To prevent the growth of herbs.
HERBOLÁDO, DA, *a.* Applied to things poisoned with the juice of plants, as daggers, darts.
HERBOLÁRIO, *sm.* 1. Herbalist, a person skilled in herbs. 2. Herbman, he who sells herbs. 3. A ridiculous extravagant man.
HERBORIZACIÓN, *sf.* Herborization, botanizing.
HERBORIZADÓR Ó HERBORIZÁNTE, *sm.* Herbalist, herbarist, one who herborises.
HERBORIZÁR, *va.* To herborise, to go in search of different herbs and plants.
HERBÓSO, SA, *a.* Herbous, abounding in herbs.
HERCÚLEO, EA, *a.* 1. Herculean. 2. Epileptic.
HÉRCULES, *sm.* 1. Epilepsy, a convulsive motion of the whole body, or of its parts, with loss of sense. 2. (Astr.) Northern constellation.
HEREDÁD, *sf.* 1. Piece of ground which is cultivated and bears fruit. 2. Hereditament.
HEREDADÉSA, *sf. dim.* of *Heredad.*
HEREDÁDO, DA, *a.* V. *Hacendado. Estar heredádo,* To be in possession of his house.
HEREDAMIÉNTO, *sm.* V. *Herencia.*
HEREDÁR, *va.* 1. To inherit. 2. To make over any kind of property to another, to be possessed by himself and his heirs or successors. 3. To possess the disposition and temperament of their fathers; applied to children.
HEREDÉRO, RA, *s.* 1. Heir, one that is inheritor to any thing left by a deceased person, one possessing the same propensities as the predecessors. 2. Vintager, one who gathers the vintage. *Heredero forzoso,* Heir apparent.
HEREDITÁRIO, RIA, *a.* Hereditary, belonging to or claiming by right of inheritance.
HERÉGE, *s. com.* Heretic, one who propagates opinions in opposition to the catholic church *Cara de herege,* Hideous or deformed aspect of any one.
HEREGÍA, *sf.* 1. Heresy, an opinion of private men different from that of the orthodox church.

2. Literary error, contrary to the principles of a science. 3. Injurious expression against any one.

Heréja, sf. (Ant.) Female heretic.

Herejóte, ta, s. aum. A pertinacious heretic.

Herén, sm. (Bot.) Vetch. V. *Yervo*.

Heréncia, sf. Inheritance, hereditament.

Heresiárca, sm. Heresiarch, a leader in heresy.

Heresiólogo, sm. Writer on heresies.

Hereticál, a. Heretical, containing heresy.

Hereticár, vn. To believe and defend pertinaciously any heresy.

Herético, ca, a. Heretical, concerning heresy, or belonging to it.

Héria, sf. Strolling vagrant. V. *Hampa*.

Herída, sf. 1. Wound. 2. Affliction, any thing which afflicts the mind. 3. Place where the game perches when pursued by the hawk.

Heridéro, sm. Place where a wound is inflicted.

Herído, da, a. 1. Wounded. 2. Cruel. *A' grito herido*, With loud cries. *A' pendon herido*, Ardently, contentiously. *Bienes heridos*, Estates burthened with some encumbrance by their former possessors.

Heridór, ra, s. Wounder, striker.

Herimiénto, sm. 1. Act of wounding. 2. Conjunction of vowels in a syllable; elision.

Herír, va. 1. To wound, to break the continuity of the animal body. 2. To knock or strike, to hurt, to affect, to move; to fall on. 3. To infest, to contaminate. *Herir el casco de un navio*, (Naút.) To hull a ship, to wound her hull.—*vn.* To tremble, to be troubled with convulsions; to be afflicted with convulsive fits.

Hermafrodíta, to, sm. An animal or plant uniting two sexes.

Hermanáble, a. Fraternal, brotherly.

Hermanableménte, ad. Fraternally.

Hermanál, a. Brotherly, belonging to a brother.

Hermanár, va. 1. To match, to suit, to proportion. 2. To own for a brother.—*vn.* To fraternize, to join, to unite.—*vr.* To love one another as brothers.

Hermanástro, sm. Half-brother.

Hermanázgo, sm. Fraternity, brotherhood.

Hermandád, sf. 1. Fraternity, the state or quality of a brother. 2. Conformity, resemblance. 3. Amity, friendship. 4. Brotherhood, an association of men under certain rules for some determinate purpose; fraternity. *La santa hermandad*, A kind of court of justice, which has the right of trying and punishing without appeal such persons as have committed any offences or misdemeanors in fields and roads.

Hermanear, va. To treat as a brother.

Hermáno, na, a. Matched, suitable, having resemblance.

Hermáno, na, s. 1. Brother, sister; one born of the same parents with another. 2. Brother-in-law. 3. Similarity; as among the members of a religious community. *Hermano carnal*, Brother by the same father and mother. *Hermano de leche*, Foster-brother. *Hermano de trabajo*, Fellow-labourer or workman. *Medio hermano*, Half-brother.—*pl.* 1. Members of the same religious confraternity. 2. Lay-brothers or sisters of a religious order. *Hermanos del ave maria*, (Madrid) Poor belonging to public charities.

Hermanúco, sm. A great brother.

Hermeticaménte, ad. Hermetically.

Herméticо, ca, a. Hermetical, chemical.

Hermosaménte, ad. Beautifully, handsomely; perfectly, properly.

Hermoseadór, ra, s. Beautifier.

Hermoseár, va. To beautify, to embellish.

Hermosílla, sf. 1. (Bot.) Blue throat-wort. Trachelium cœruleum *L.* 2. Kind of silk stuff.

Hermóso, sa, a. 1. Beautiful, handsome. 2. Rare, uncommon.

Hermosúra, sf. 1. Beauty, that assemblage of graces which pleases the eye. 2. Symmetry, agreement of one part to another.

Hérnia, sf. Hernia, rupture.

Herníста, sm. Surgeon who applies himself in particular to the cure of ruptures.

Herodiáno, na, a. Herodian, belonging to Herod.

Héroe, sm. Hero, a man eminent for bravery and valour.

Heroicaménte, ad. Heroically.

Heroicidád, sf. Quality or character which constitutes an heroic action.

Heróico, ca, a. 1. Heroic, eminent for bravery. 2. Heroical, befitting a hero. 3. Reciting the acts of heroes. *A' la heroica*, Fashion of heroic times.

Heroína, sf. Heroine, a female hero.

Heroísmo, sm. Heroism, the qualities or character of a hero.

Hérpes, sm. pl. Herpes, a cutaneous disease.

Herpético, ca, a. Herpetic.

Herráda, sf. Pail, a wooden vessel in which liquids are carried.

Herráda, a. Applied to water in which red-hot iron has been cooled.

Herradéro, sm. 1. Place destined for marking cattle with a hot iron. 2. The act of marking cattle with a hot iron.

Herradór, sm. Farrier, a shoer of horses.

Herradúra, sf. 1. Horse-shoe. 2. Collar or necklace in the form of a horse-shoe, which ladies wear about their neck.

Herráge, sm. 1. Ironwork, pieces of iron used for ornament and strength. *Herrage de un navio*, (Naút.) Ironwork of a ship. 2. Horse-shoe, an iron plate nailed to the feet of horses.

Herramentál, sm. Bag or pouch with instruments for shoeing horses.

Herramiénta, sf. 1. Set of tools or instruments for workmen. 2. Ironwork. 3. Horns of a beast. 4. (Joc.) Teeth, grinders.

Herrár, va. 1. To garnish any thing with iron. 2. To shoe horses, to nail a piece of iron-plate to their feet. 3. To mark cattle with a hot iron. 4. To mark a slave in the face.

Herrén, sm. Mixed corn for feeding horses; meslin.

Herrenál ó Herreñál, sm. Piece of ground in which meslin is sown.

Herrería, sf. 1. Ironworks, where iron is manufactured and moulded into pigs or bars. 2. Forge, the place where iron is beaten into form. 3. Clamour, a loud confused noise.

Herreríllo, sm. Small bird with blue back and red breast.

Herréro, sm. Smith, one who forges with the hammer, or beats iron into form.

Herrerón, sm. A bad smith.

Herreruélo, *sm.* 1. (Orn.) Stone-chatter. Motacilla provincialis *L.* 2. V. *Ferreruelo.*
Herréte, *sm.* Tag, the point of tin or other metal put at the end of a lace, cord, or string.
Herreteár, *va.* To tag a lace, to put a point of metal to a cord, string, or ribbon.
Herretéro, ra, *s.* Tag-maker, a person who puts tags to cords or strings.
Herrezuélo, *sm.* Light piece of iron.
Herriál, *a.* Applied to a kind of large black grapes, and to the vines which bear them.
Herrín, *sm.* Rust of iron. V. *Herrumbre.*
Herrón, *sm.* Staple with a ring, in the middle of which is a hole, at which boys pitch quoits; a quoit.
Herronáda, *sf.* 1. A violent blow or stroke. 2. (Met.) Blow with a bird's beak.
Herrugiénto, ta, *a.* Rusty.
Herrúmbre, *sf.* Rust of iron; irony taste.
Herrumbróso, sa, *a.* 1. Rusty, drossy, scaly. 2. Participating of the qualities of iron.
Herventár, *va.* To boil any thing.
Hervidéro, *sm.* 1. Ebullition, the noise and agitation of a fluid which boils in bubbles. 2. Kind of water-clock or small spring, whence water bubbles out. 3. Rattling in the throat. 4. Multitude, great quantity or number.
Hervír, *vn.* 1. To boil, to be agitated by heat. 2. (Met.) To swarm with vermin; to be crowded with people. 3. To be fervent, to be vehement. *Hervir el garbanzuelo*, To be too solicitous and clamorous.
Hervór, *sm.* 1. Ebullition, the agitation of boiling fluids. 2. Fervour, heat, vigour. 3. (Met.) Noise and movement of waters.
Hervoróso, sa, *a.* Fervent, fervid.
Hesitación, *sf.* Hesitation, doubt, perplexity, want of resolution.
Hesitár, *vn.* To hesitate, to doubt.
Hespérides, *sf. pl.* V. *Pleyades.*
Hespéride y Hespérido, da, *a.* 1. Relating to the Pleiades. 2. (Poét.) The West.
Héspero, *sm.* The planet Venus.
Heterodóxo, xa, *a.* Heterodox, deviating from the established opinion; not orthodox.
Heterogeneidád, *sf.* Heterogeneousness.
Heterogéneo, nea, *a.* Heterogeneous, not kindred; opposite or dissimilar in nature.
Hética y Hetiquéz, *sf.* Phthisis, consumption.
Hético, ca, *a.* Hectic, affected with a slow hectic fever; languid.
Hexáedro, *sm.* Hexaedron, a cube.
Hexágono, *sm.* Hexagon, a plain figure consisting of six sides.
Hexámetro, *sm.* Hexameter, a verse of six [feet.
Hexápeda, *sf.* V. *Toesa.*
Hez, *sf.* 1. Lees, the dregs of liquors. 2. Dross of metals. 3. Grains of malt. 4. *La hez del pueblo*, The scum of the people. *Heces*, Fæces, excrements.
Hi, Hi, Hi, *interj.* Expression of merriment or laughter.
Hi, *ád.* (Ant.) V. *Allí.*
Hi, *sm.* Used for *hijo*, son. *Hi de puta*, (Fam.) A by-word, expressive of astonishment or wonder.
Hiádas ó Hiádes, *sf. pl.* V. *Pleyades.*
Hiánte, *a.* Applied to a verse with a hiatus.
Hiáto, *sm.* Hiatus, pause or cacophony of two vowels together in a word.

Hibernál ó Hibernízo, za, *a.* Hibernal, wintry.
Hibiernár, *vn.* To be the winter season.
Hibiérno, *sm.* Winter. V. *Invierno.*
Hibléo, blea, *a.* (Poét.) Abundant; pleasant; belonging to mount Hybla.
Hibísco, *sm.* (Bot.) Syrian mallow, althæa frutex. Hibiscus syriacus *L.*
Híbrida, *sf.* Hybridous animal, as a mule; hybridous words.
Hicocérvo, *sm.* Fabulous animal; chimera, a vain and wild fancy.
Hidalgaménte, *ad.* Nobly, in a gentlemanlike manner.
Hidalgárse, *vr.* (Joc.) To assume the nobleman, to affect the gentleman.
Hidálgo, ga, *a.* Noble, illustrious, excellent.
Hidálgo, ga, *s.* Noble man or woman, a person of noble descent. *Hidalgo de bragueta*, One who enjoys the privileges of nobility on account of his being father of seven sons without one intervening female child. *Hidalgo de gotera*, He who enjoys the rights of nobility in one place or town only.
Hidalgón, na; y **Hidalgóte, ta**, *s. aum.* An old noble man or woman, proud of the rights and privileges.
Hidalguéjo, ja; **Hidalguéte ó Hidalguíllo, lla**, *s. dim.* A petty country squire, poor gentleman or lady.
Hidalguía, *sf.* 1. Nobility, the rights and privileges of noblemen. 2. Nobleness of mind, liberality of sentiments.
Hidiondéz, *sf.* V. *Hediondez.*
Hídra, *sf.* 1. Hydra, a fabulous monster with many heads, related to have been killed by Hercules. 2. Poisonous serpent. 3. (Met.) Seditions, plots.
Hidráulica, *sf.* The science of hydraulics.
Hidráulico, ca, *a.* Hydraulical, relating to the conveyance of water through pipes.
Hidráulico, *sm.* Professor of hydraulics.
Hídria, *sf.* Jar or pitcher for water.
Hidrocéfalo, *sm.* Dropsy in the head.
Hidrodinámica, *sf.* Science of hydrodinamics.
Hidrofilácio, *sm.* Great cavern full of water.
Hidrofóbia, *sf.* Hydrophobia, dread of water.
Hidrófobo, *sm.* Person suffering hydrophobia.
Hidrogógia, *sf.* The art or science of taking the level of the water.
Hidrografía, *sf.* Hydrography, the description of the watery part of the terraqueous [globe.
Hidrográfico, ca, *a.* Hydrographical.
Hidrógrafo, *sm.* Hydrographer. [water.
Hidromántica, *sf.* Superstitious divination by
Hidrómetra, *sm.* Professor of hydrometry.
Hidrometría, *sf.* Hydrometry.
Hidrómetro, *sm.* Hydrometer, instrument for measuring the weight of fluids.
Hidropesía, *sf.* 1. Dropsy. 2. (Met.) Insatiable desire of riches or honours.
Hidrópico, ca, *a.* Diseased with the dropsy.
Hidroscópo, *sm.* Hydroscope, water-clock.
Hidrostática, *sf.* Hydrostatics, the science of weighing fluids, or weighing bodies in fluids.
Hidrostático, ca, *a.* Hydrostatical.
Hidrotécnia, *sf.* The art of making engines for moving and raising water.
Hiél, *sf.* 1. Gall, bile; an animal juice of a yellow colour and bitter taste. 2. (Met.) Bitter-

nem, asperity. *Echar la hiel*, To labour excessively. *No tener hiel*, To be simple and gentle. *Estar hecho de hieles*, To be as bitter as gall. *Hieles*, Calamities, misfortunes, toils.
HIÉL DE LA TIERRA, *sm.* (Bot.) Common fumitory or earth smoke. Fumaria officinalis *L.*
HIÉLO, *sm.* 1. Frost, ice, crystallized water. 2. Congelation. 3. (Met.) Coolness, indifference. 4. Astonishment, stupefaction. *Hielos*, Ice-creams.
HIÉLTRO, *sm.* Kind of measure.
HIEMÁL, *a.* Hyemal, hibernal.
HIÉNA, *sf.* 1. Hyen or Hyena, a fierce animal, belonging to the family of dogs. Canis hyena *L.* 2. Fish in the Indian sea.
HIÉRDA, *sf.* Dung. V. *Estiércol.*
HIERÁCIO, *sm.* (Bot.) Hawk-weed.
HIEROGLÍFICO, CA, *a.* Hieroglyphic. V. *Geroglífico.*
HIEROSCÓPIA, *sf.* V. *Aruspicina.*
HIEROSOLIMITÁNO, NA, *a.* Native or belonging to Jerusalem.
HIERRECÍCO, LLO, TO, *sm.* Small piece of wrought iron.
HIÉRRO, *sm.* 1. Iron, a malleable metal. 2. Brand, a mark made by burning with a hot iron. 3. An iron instrument to wound with. 4. *Hierro de la grimpola*, (Naút.) Spindle of the vane. *Hierro colado*, Cast iron. *Hierro forjado*, Forged iron. *El es de hierro*, He is indefatigable, or as hardy as steel. *Machucar ó majar en hierro frio*, To labour in vain. *Tienda de hierro*, An ironmonger's shop. *Hierros*, Irons, fetters; jail. *Le echaron en hierros*, They put him in irons.
HÍGA, *sf.* 1. Amulet, charm, an appendant remedy; a thing hung about the neck for preventing or curing disease. 2. Method of shutting the hand. 3. Ridicule, derision.
HIGADÍLLO, *sm.* A small liver.
HÍGADO, *sm.* 1. Liver, one of the entrails. 2. (Met.) Courage, valour, bravery. *Tener malos higados*, To be white livered, to be ill-disposed; (Met.) to hate. *Echar los higados*, To be fatigued or vexed; to desire anxiously. *Higado de azufre*, (Quím.) Liver of sulphur. *Hasta los higados*, To the heart.
HIGÁTE, *sm.* Potage, formerly made of figs, pork, and fowl, boiled together, and seasoned with sugar, ginger, cinnamon, pimento, and other spices.
HÍGO, *sm.* 1. Fig, the fruit of the fig-tree. *Higo chumbo ó de pala*, Fruit of the nopal or Indian fig-tree. *Pan de higos*, Cake made of figs. 2. A kind of piles. *Higo maduro*, (Orn.) Green wood-pecker.
HIGROMETRÍA, *sm.* Hygrometry.
HIGRÓMETRO, *sm.* Hygrometry, an instrument to measure the degrees of moisture.
HIGUÉRA, *sf.* (Bot.) Fig-tree. Ficus *L.*
HIGUERÁL, *sm.* Plantation of fig-trees.
HIGUÉRO, *sm.* Large tree in America.
HIJÁR ó IJAR, *sm.* Ilia, the flank.
HIJÁSTRO, TRA, *s.* Step-child.
HIJÉZNA, *sm.* The young of any bird.
HIJÍCO, CA; LLO, LLA; TO, TA, *s.* Little child, little dear.
HÍJO, JA, *s.* 1. Child. 2. Young of all living animals. 3. Native of a place. 4. A happy or fortunate man. 5. Bud or root of the horns of animals. *Hijo del agua*, A good sailor, a good swimmer. *Hijo de la piedra*, Foundling. *Hijo de leche*, Foster-child. 6. Any product of the mind. *Hijo de su madre*, (Fam.) Bastard.
HIJODÁLGO, HIJADÁLGO, *s.* V. *Hidalgo.*
HIJUÉLA, *sf.* 1. Piece of cloth or linen joined to another which is too short or narrow. 2. A small mattress, put between others, to make the bed even. 3. Pall, a square bit of linen or paste-board put over the chalice. 4. A small drain for drawing off water from an estate. 5. Inventory, a catalogue of the articles which belong to the estate of a deceased person. 6. Cross-road. 7. Post-man who delivers the letters from the office. 8. Palm-seed. 9. Fascine of wood. 10. Corn made of the gut of silk-worms.
HIJUÉLO, LA, *s. dim.* A young child.
HÍLA, *sf.* 1. Row, line. V. *Hilera.* 2. Thin gut. 3. Act of spinning. 4. Lint scraped into a soft woolly substance, to lay on sores. 5. Small trench for dividing the water which is destined for the irrigation of different pieces of ground. *Á la hila*, In a row or line, one after another.
HILÁCHA, *sf.* Filament or threads ravelled out of cloth.
HILACHÓSO, SA, *a.* Filamentous.
HILÁDA, *sf.* Row or line of bricks or stones in a building. V. *Hilera.*
HILADÍLLO, *sm.* 1. Ferret silk. 2. Narrow ribbon or tape.
HILÁDO, *sm.* Spun flax, hemp, wool, silk, or cotton.
HILADÓR, RA, *s.* Spinner, spinster.
HILANDÉRA, *sf.* Spinster, woman who spins.
HILANDERÍA, *sf.* Place where hemp is spun.
HILANDÉRO, *sm.* Spinner; spinning room, a rope-walk.
HILÁNZA, *sf.* Thread, line, mode of spinning.
HILÁR, *va.* 1. To spin, to draw silk, cotton, wool, &c. into thread. 2. To argue, to discuss. *Hilar delgado*, To handle a subject in too subtle and nice a manner. 3. To form the pod; applied to silk worms.
HILARÁCHA, *sf.* Filament. V. *Hilacha.*
HILÁZA, *sf.* 1. Any thing spun or drawn out into thread. V. *Hilado.* 2. Yarn. *Hilazas*, Filaments or slender threads of plants.
HILÉRA, *sf.* 1. Row or line of several things following one after another; file. 2. The hollow part of a spindle. 3. An iron plate with holes, for drawing gold or silver into wire. 4. Beam which forms the top of the roof.
HILÉRO, *sm.* 1. Sign of currents in the sea. 2. Thread-seller.
HILÍLLO, CO, TO, *sm. dim.* Small thread, filament.
HÍLO, *sm.* 1. Thread, a small line or twist, formed of wool, cotton, silk, &c. 2. Wire metal drawn into slender threads. 3. A slender thread, formed by liquids falling down in drops. 4. (Met.) Thread or connexion of a discourse. 5. Fine thread of spiders or silk-worms. 6. V. *Filo. Hilo á hilo*, Drop by drop. *Hilo de palomar, ó hilo bramante*, Packthread. *Hilo de perlas*, String of pearls. *Hilo de una corriente*, (Naút.) Direction of a current. *Á hilo*, Successively, one after another. *Ir al hilo del mundo*, To follow the opinion of the rest of the world. *De hilo*, Directly, instantly.
HILVÁN, *sm.* Basting, long stitches set in clothes to keep them in order for sewing.
HILVANÁR, *va.* 1. To baste, to sew slightly. 2. To act or perform in a hurry.

Himenéo, *sm.* 1. (Poét.) Marriage, matrimony. 2. Epithalamium.
Himnísta, *sm.* Composer of hymns.
Himno, *sm.* Hymn, an encomiastic song, or song of adoration to the Supreme Being.
Himplár, *vn.* To roar or bellow; applied to the panther and ounce.
Hin, *sm.* Sound emitted by mules or horses.
Hincadúra, *sf.* Act of fixing any thing.
Hincapié, *sm.* An effort made with the foot by fixing it firmly on the ground. *Hacer hincapie*, To make a strenuous attempt.
Hincár, *va.* 1. To thrust in, to drive into, to nail one thing to another. *Hincar la rodilla*, To kneel down. 2. To plant. *Hicar el diente*, To appropriate property to one's self; to censure, to calumniate.
Hínca, *sf.* Hatred, displeasure, enmity.
Hinchadaménte, *ad.* Haughtily, loftily.
Hinchádo, da, *a.* 1. Vain, arrogant, presumptuous. 2. Inflated, applied to a pompous style.
Hinchár, *va.* 1. To fill a musical instrument with air. 2. To swell, to raise to arrogance. —*vr.* 1. To swell, to grow turgid. 2. To be elated with arrogance or anger.
Hinchazón, *sm.* 1. Swelling, a tumid inflammation. 2. Ostentation, vanity, pride; inflation.
Hinchír, *va.* To fill, to inflate. V. *Henchir*.
Hincón, *sm.* Post to which cables are fastened on the banks of rivers.
Hiniésta, *sf.* (Bot.) Spanish broom. Spartium junceum *L.*
Hiniéstra, *sf.* (Ant.) Window. V. *Ventana*.
Hiniéstro, *sm.* V. *Retama*.
Hinníble, *a.* Capable of neighing; applied to a horse.
Hinójos Fitos, (Ant.) On bended knees.
Hinojál, *sm.* Bed or place full of fennel.
Hinojár, *vn.* To kneel. V. *Arrodillar*.
Hinójo, *sm.* 1. Knee. V. *Rodilla*. 2. (Bot.) Fennel. Anethum fœniculum *L.* 3. *Hinojo marino*, (Bot.) Samphire. Crithmum maritimum *L.* [their dough.
Hintéro, *sm.* Table on which bakers knead
Hiñír, *va.* V. *Heñir*.
Hipár, *vn.* 1. To hiccough, to sob with frequent convulsions of the stomach. 2. To be harassed with anxiety and grief. 3. To pant, to desire eagerly, to be anxious. 4. To follow the chase by the smell; spoken of pointers.
Hipeár, *vn.* To hiccough. V. *Hipar*.
Hipecóo, *sm.* (Bot.) Horned cumin.
Hipérbola, *sf.* (Geom.) Section of a cone made by a plane, so that the axis of the section inclines to the opposite leg of the cone.
Hipérbole, *sf.* Hyperbole, a figure in rhetoric, by which any thing is increased or decreased beyond the exact truth.
Hiperbolicaménte, *ad.* Hyperbolically.
Hiperbólico, ca, *a.* Hyperbolical.
Hiperbolizár, *vn.* To use hyperboles.
Hiperbóreo, rea, *a.* Hyperborean.
Hiperdulía, *sf.* Worship of the Virgin Mary.
Hipérico y Hipéricon, *sm.* (Bot.) St. John's wort. Hypericum *L.*
Hipnál, *sm.* Kind of serpent said to occasion sleep.
Hípo, *sm.* 1. Hiccough, a convulsive motion of the stomach. 2. Wish, desire, anxiety. 3. Anger, displeasure, fury.
Hipocámpo, *sm.* Hippopotamus.
Hipocentáuro, *sm.* V. *Centauro*.
Hipocístide y Hipocísto, *s.* Shoot from the foot of a kind of cistus.
Hipocondría, *sf.* Hypochondriac affection.
Hipocondríaco, ca; y **Hipocóndrico, ca**, *a.* Hypochondriac, hypochondriacal.
Hipocóndrios, *sm. pl.* Hypochondres, the two regions, which contain one the liver, and the other the spleen.
Hipocrás, *sm.* Hippocras, a medicated wine, composed of wine, sugar, cinnamon, clove, and other ingredients.
Hipocrénides, *sf. pl.* (Poét.) Epithet, applied to the muses of Parnassus.
Hipocresía, *sf.* Hypocrisy, dissimulation with regard to the moral or religious character.
Hipócrita, *a.* Hypocritical, dissembling, insincere.—*s.* Hypocrite.
Hipocritaménte, *ad.* Hypocritically. [critical.
Hipócrito, ta, *a.* Feigned, dissembled, hypo-
Hipocritón, na, *a.* Extremely hypocritical or dissembling.
Hipódromo, *sm.* Hippodrome, circus.
Hipogástrico, ca, *a.* Hypogastric.
Hipogástro, *sm.* Hypogastrium.
Hipoglósa, so, *s.* (Bot.) Horse-tongue.
Hipógrifo, *sm.* Hippogriff, a winged horse.
Hipolibónoto, *sm.* South-east wind. [cients
Hipománes, *sm.* Kind of poison with the an-
Hipomarátro, *sm.* (Bot.) Wild fennel.
Hipomóclio ó Hipomoclion, *sm.* Fulcrum of a lever, part on which the beam of a balance revolves.
Hipopótamo, *sm.* Hippopotamus, a river-horse.
Hipóstasis, *sf.* (Teol.) Hypostasis.
Hipostático, ca, *a.* Hypostatical.
Hipotéca, *sf.* 1. Mortgage, pledge; security given for the performance of an engagement. 2. (Iron.) A trifling worthless thing, not to be relied upon.
Hipotecáble, *a.* Capable of being pledged.
Hipotecár, *va.* To pledge, to mortgage.
Hipotecário, ria, *a.* Belonging to a mortgage.
Hipotenúsa, *sf.* Hypothenuse, the line that subtends the right angle of a right-angled triangle; the subtense.
Hipótesis, *sf.* Hypothesis, a supposition; a system formed upon some principles not proved.
Hipotético, ca, *a.* Hypothetic; conditional.
Hiriásco, *sm.* A castrated he-goat.
Hirmár, *va.* V. *Afirmar*.
Hirme, *a.* V. *Firme*.
Hirsúto, ta, *a.* Hirsute, rough, rugged
Hirundinário, *sf.* V. *Celidonia*.
Hísca, *sf.* Birdlime, a glutinous substance spread upon twigs, by which the birds that light upon them are entangled.
Hiscál, *sm.* A bass rope of three strands.
Hisopáda, *sf.* Water sprinkled about with a water-sprinkler.
Hisopeár, *va.* To sprinkle or scatter water about with a water-sprinkler.
Hisopíllo, *sm.* 1. A small water-sprinkler. 2. Bit of soft linen put at the end of a stick, and used to wash and refresh the mouth of a sick person.

Hisópo, *sm.* 1. (Bot.) Hyssop. Hyssopus *L.* 2. Water-sprinkler, with which holy water is scattered or sprinkled, made of a lock of horse-hair fastened to the end of a stick. *Hisopo húmedo*, Grease collected in washing fleeces of wool. [la.

Hispalénse, *a.* Native of or belonging to Sevil-

Hispánico, ca, *a.* Spanish.

Hispanísmo y Hispanidád, *s.* Hispanism, Spanish idiom peculiar to the Spanish language.

Hispanizár, *va.* V. *Españolizar.*

Hispáno, na, *s.* (Poét.) A Spaniard.

Híspido, da, *a.* Bristly, having bristles like hogs.

Hispír, *va.* To beat as eggs, to make spongy, to rarefy. [fits.

Histérica, *sf.* Woman troubled with hysteric

Histérico, *sm.* Hysterics.

Histérico, ca, *a.* Hysteric; disordered in the regions of the womb; troubled with fits.

Histerotómia, *sm.* An anatomical dissection of the womb.

Histiodromía, *sf.* Art of navigating by means of sails.

História, *sf.* 1. Narration of events and facts delivered with dignity. 2 Tale, story; fable. 3. An historical painting, representing some remarkable event. *Meterse en historias*, To meddle in things without possessing sufficient knowledge thereof, or being concerned in them.

Historiádo, *a.* Applied to a painting consisting of various parts harmoniously united. *Libro historiado*, Book illustrated with plates.

Historiadór, ra, y Historiál, *s.* Historian, a writer of facts and events.

Historiál, *a.* Historical.

Historialménte, *ad.* Historically.

Historiár, *va.* 1. To historify, to record in history. 2. To represent events in painting or tapestry.

Historicaménte, *ad.* Historically.

Histórico, ca, *a.* Historical, belonging to history.—*sm.* (Ant.) Historian.

Historiéta, *sf.* A short novel, love tale, an anecdote mixed with fact and fable.

Historiógrafo, *sm.* Historiographer; historian, a writer of history.

Historión, *sm.* A tedious long-winded story.

Histrión, *sm.* 1. Actor, player; a person engaged in performing plays. 2. Buffoon, juggler, puppetman.

Histriónico, ca, *a.* Histrionic, befitting the stage; suitable to players.

Histrionísa, *sf.* Actress, a woman that plays on the stage.

Híta, *sf.* Brad, a sort of nails to floor rooms with. [tunate.

Híto, ta, *a.* 1. Black. 2. Fixed, firm; impor-

Híto, *sm.* 1. Landmark, any thing set up to mark boundaries. 2. Pin or mark at which quoits are cast by way of amusement; mark to shoot at. *A' hito*, Fixedly, firmly. *Mirar de hito en hito*, To view with close attention, to fix the eyes on any object.

Hiúlco, ca, *a.* Harsh, unharmonious; applied to poetry.

Hobachón, na, *a.* Slothful, sluggish, lazy.

Hobéchos, *sm. pl.* Soldiers armed with pikes; pikemen.

Hombrecíllo, *sm.* (Bot.) Hops. Humulus lupulus *L.*

Hoblonéra, *sf.* Hop-ground, where hops are cultivated.

Hobús, *sm.* (Art.) Howitzer, a sort of mortar, or short cannon with a wide mouth, for throwing shells.

Hocicáda, *sf.* 1. Fall upon the face, or headlong on the ground. 2. A smart reprimand.

Hocicár, *va.* To break up the ground with the snout.—*vn.* 1. To fall headlong with the face to the ground. 2. To stumble or slide into errors.

Hocíco, *sm.* 1. Snout, the nose of a beast. 2. Mouth of a man who has very prominent lips. 3. Any thing disproportionably big or prominent. 4. Gestures of thrusting out the lips, pouting. 5. (Met.) The face. *Meter el hocico en todo*, To meddle in every thing. *De hocicos*, By the nose.

Hocicúdo, da, *a.* 1. Long snouted. 2. Looking sullen by thrusting out the lips.

Hocíno, *sm.* 1. Bill, a sort of hatchet with a hooked point. 2. Skirt of an eminence or mountain stretching towards a river; bottom or garden. 3. Arch made of brick and mortar which supports the flights of a staircase. *Hocinos*, The narrow beds of rivers which flow between mountains.

Hociquíllo, *sm.* A little snout.

Hogáño, *ad.* This present year.

Hogár, *sm.* 1. Hearth, the place on which fire is made; the pavement of a room where fire is kindled. 2. (Met.) House, residence.

Hogáza, *sf.* A large loaf of household bread.

Hoguéra, *sf.* A quick and transitory blaze.

Hója, *sf.* 1. Leaf, the green deciduous part of trees, plants, and flowers. 2. Any thing foliated or thinly beaten; scales of metal. 3. Leaf, one side of a double door, shutter, &c. 4. Blade of a sword. 5. Half of each of the principal parts of a coat, &c. 6. Each part of which armour was composed. *Hoja de lata*, Tin. *Hoja de lata negra*, Iron plate. *Hoja de papel*, Leaf of paper. *Hoja de un libro*, Leaf of a book, containing two pages. *Hoja de tocino*, Flitch of bacon. *Hoja de estaño*, Sheet of bismuth, tin, and quicksilver laid on the backside of a looking-glass. *Doblemos la hoja*, No more of that. *Volver la hoja*, To turn a new leaf, to alter one's sentiments and proceedings.—*pl.* 1. Thin cakes of wax; lamina. 2. (And.) Pieces of ground destined for seed-sowing. *Vino de dos, tres, ó mas hojas*, Wine two, three, or more, years old. 3. *Hojas de las puertas*, (Naút.) Port-lids.

Hojalatéro, *sm.* Tin-man, a manufacturer of tin, or iron tinned over.

Hojaldrádo, *a.* Laminated, foliated, resembling thin cakes.

Hojaldrár, *va.* To make any thing of puff paste.

Hojáldre, *sf.* A sort of pancake or paste. *Quitar la hojaldre al pastel*, To detect any fraud, to discover a plot.

Hojaldrísta, *sm.* Maker of buttered cakes.

Hojarásca, *sf.* 1. Withered leaves; redundancy of leaves; foliage. 2. Useless trifles.

Hojeár, *va.* To turn the leaves of a book.—*vn.* To form metal into sheets; to foliate.

Hojecér, *vn.* To leaf, to shoot forth leaves.
Hojóso, sa; y **Hojúdo, da**, *a.* Leafy, full of leaves; covered with leaves.
Hojuéla, *f.* 1. A small leaf. 2. Puff paste, composed of thin flakes lying on one another. 3. Gold or silver leaf which surrounds the thread whereof lace is made. 4. Skins of olives after pressing.
Hóla, *interj.* 1. Holla, a word used in calling to any one at a distance. 2. Ho, ho, a sudden exclamation of wonder or astonishment.
Holán, *sm.* (And.) Cambric.
Holánda, *sf.* Holland, fine Dutch linen.
Holandílla y **Holandéta**, *sf.* A lead coloured glazed linen, used for lining.
Holgadaménte, *ad.* Widely, disproportionately.
Holgádo, da, *a.* 1. Disproportionally wide or broad. 2. V. *Desocupado.* *Estar holgado*, (Met.) To be at ease.
Holgánza, *sf.* 1. Width, breadth. 2. Repose, ease, tranquillity of mind. 3. Amusement, entertainment.
Holgár, *vn.* 1. To rest from labour, to be at ease. 2. To be glad of, to be pleased with. 3. To be well entertained at a feast or walk. 4. To be laid up as useless; applied to inanimate things.
Holgazán, na, *s.* Idler, loiterer, vagabond.
Holgazaneár, *vn.* To be idle, to loiter, to be lazy.
Holgazanería, *sf.* Idleness, laziness; aversion from work.
Holgín, na, *a.* V. *Hechicero.*
Holgón, *sm.* An egregious loiterer who wastes his whole life in idleness and amusements.
Holgório, *sm.* (Joc.) Mirth, jollity, merriment.
Holguéta ó **Holgúra**, *sf.* 1. Country-feast, an entertainment in the country. 2. Width, breadth. 3. Ease, repose.
Holladúra, *sf.* 1. Act of trampling. 2. Duty paid for the run of cattle.
Hollár, *va.* 1. To tread upon, to trample under foot. 2. To pull down, to humble, to depress.
Holléca, *sf.* (Orn.) V. *Herrerillo.*
Holléjo, *sm.* Pellicle, peel, the thin skin which covers grapes and other fruit.
Hollí, *sm.* Balsam or resinous liquor which is imported from New Spain.
Hollín, *sm.* Soot, the condensed, gross, and oily parts of smoke.
Holliniénto, ta, *a.* Fuliginous, sooty.
Holocáusto, *sm.* Holocaust, a burnt sacrifice.
Homarráche, *sm.* Buffoon, jack-pudding, a merry-andrew.
Hombrácho, *sm.* A squat and square thick man.
Hombráda, *sf.* V. *Herrerillo.*
Hómbre, *sm.* 1. Man, a rational animal. *Hombre bueno*, Any one of the community, not an ecclesiastic. 2. Subject, vassal. 3. A word of familiarity bordering on contempt. 4. Husband, when mentioned by the wife. 5. Horse, a frame on which clothes are brushed and cleaned. 6. Game at cards. 7. One possessing the qualities necessary for an undertaking. *Hombre hecho*, A grown man. *Hombre de bien ú honrado*, An honest worthy man. *Hombre de negocios*, Man of business. *Hombre de calzas atacadas*, A poor hearted or mean spirited man. *Es hombre*, He is a great man in his way. *No tener hombre*, To be without protection. *Hombre sin dolo*, A plain dealing man. *Hombre de su palabra*, A man of his word. *Ser muy hombre*, To be a man of spirit and courage.
Hombreár, *vn.* 1. To vie with another; to put himself upon a level with another, in point of rank, merit, or abilities. 2. To assume the man before the time.
Hombrecíllo y **Hombrezuélo**, *sm.* Mannikin, a pitiful little fellow. *Hombrecillos*, (Bot.) Hops. Humulus lupulus *L.*
Hombrecíto, *sm.* Youth, a young man.
Hombredád, *sf.* Masculineness.
Hombréra, *sf.* Piece of ancient armour for the shoulders.
Hombría de bien, *sf.* 1. Probity, honest dealing. 2. *Rica-hombria de España*, The ancient nobility of Spain.
Hombríllo, *sm.* Gusset, a piece sewed to cloth in order to strengthen it.
Hómbro, *sm.* Shoulder, the joint which connects the arm to the body. *Hombro con hombro*, Cheek by jole. *Encogerse de hombros*, To shrug up the shoulders. *A' hombro*, On the shoulders. *Llevar en hombros*, To support, to protect.
Hombrón, *sm.* 1. A big lusty man. 2. A man distinguished for talents, knowledge, and valour.
Hombronázo, *sm.* A huge vulgar man.
Hombrúno, na, *a.* 1. Manlike, civil; belonging to man. 2. Relating to the shoulders.
Hómbu, *s.* (Bot.) Poke-weed, red night-shade Phytolacca *L.*
Home, *sm.* (Ant.) V. *Hombre.*
Homecío y **Homecíllo**, *sm.* (Ant.) V. *Homicidio.*
Homenáge, *sm.* Homage, service paid and fealty professed to a superior lord; obeisance. *Rendir homenage*, To pay homage, to profess fealty. *Torre de homenage*, Tower in a castle where the governor took the oath of fidelity.
Homicída, *s. com.* Murderer, one who commits homicide.
Homicídio, *sm.* 1. Murder, homicide. 2. Ancient tribute.
Homicíllo, *sm.* 1. Fine for wounding or killing any one. 2. V. *Homicidio.*
Homilía, *sf.* Homily, a discourse read in a congregation.
Homiliadór, *sm.* Homilist, preacher.
Homiliário, *sm.* Collection of homilies.
Homilísta, *sm.* Author or writer of homilies.
Hominicáco, *sm.* A paltry, cowardly fellow.
Homogeneidád, *sf.* Homogeneity, or homogenoousness; participation of the same principles of nature, similitude of kind.
Homogéneo, nea, *a.* Homogeneous, having the same nature or principles.
Homologación, *sf.* Homologation, publication, or confirmation of a judicial act to render it more valid.
Homólogo, ga, *a.* Homologous, having the same manner or proportions; synonymous.
Homónima, *sf.* Homonymy.
Homónimo, ma, *a.* Homonymous, equivocal.
Hónda, *sf.* 1. Sling, a stringed instrument for casting stones with great violence. 2. (Naut.) Parbuckle, a rope used on board of ships, and on keys, wharfs, &c. to ship and unship casks, pieces of ordnance, and other heavy articles

Hondaménte, *ad.* In a deep or sagacious manner; profoundly.

Hondárras, *sf. pl.* (Rioja) Dregs or lees of any liquor remaining in the vessel which contained it.

Hondázo, *sm.* Cast or throw with a sling.

Hondeár, *va.* To unload a vessel.

Hondéro, *sm.* Slinger, a soldier anciently armed with a sling.

Hondíjo, *sm.* V. *Honda.*

Hondíllos, *sm. pl.* Pieces of cloth or linen which form the seats of breeches or drawers.

Hóndo, da, *a.* 1. Profound, low. 2. Deep, sagacious, ingenious.

Hondón, *sm.* 1. Bottom of a vessel or jar where the dregs of liquor settle. 2. Any deep or broken ground. 3. A deep hole. 4. Eye of a needle.

Hondonáda, *sf.* Dale, bottom of a steep place.

Hondrár, *va.* (Ant.) V. *Honrar.*

Hondúra, *sf.* Depth, profundity.

Honestád, *sf.* (Ant.) Honesty. V. *Honestidad.*

Honestaménte, *ad.* Honestly; modestly.

Honestár, *va.* 1. To honour, to dignify. 2. To excuse, to palliate.

Honestidád, *sf.* 1. Composure, modesty, moderation. 2. Honesty, purity of sentiments and principles; urbanity.

Honésto, ta, *a.* 1. Honest, decent, honourable. 2. Pure, chaste, virtuous. 3. Reasonable, just. *Muger de estado honesto*, A spinster.

Hóngo, *sm.* 1. (Bot.) Mushroom. Fungus *L.* 2. Fungus, an excrescence which grows upon the bark of trees, and serves for tinder. 3. A fleshy excrescence growing on the lips of wounds.

Hongóso, sa, *a.* Fungous, spongy.

Honór, *sm.* 1. Honour, a public mark of respect to virtue or merit. 2. Dignity, rank. 3. Reputation, fame, celebrity. 4. Chastity in women. *Palabra de honor*, Word of honour. *Hombre de honor*, Man of honour. *Señoras de honor*, Maids of honour. *Honores*, Privileges of rank or birth; civilities paid.

Honoráble, *a.* Honourable, illustrious, noble.

Honorableménte, *ad.* Honourably.

Honorár, *va.* (Ant.) V. *Honrar.*

Honorário, ria, *a.* 1. Giving or conferring honour. 2. Bestowing honour without gain. *Consejero honorario*, Honorary counsellor, one who has the rank and title of a counsellor without receiving any pay.

Honorário, *sm.* Salary or stipend given to any one for his labour.

Honorificaménte, *ad.* Honourably.

Honorificéncia, *sf.* The act of honouring or doing honour.

Honorífico, ca, *a.* That which gives honour.

Hónra, *sf.* 1. Honour, reverence, respect. 2. Reputation, celebrity, fame. 3. Chastity in women. 4. Favour conferred or received. *Honras*, Funeral honours.

Honradaménte, *ad.* Honourably, reputably, with integrity and exemption from reproach.

Honradéz, *sf.* Honesty, probity, integrity, exactness in the performance of engagements.

Honrádo, da, *a.* 1. Honest, honourable, reputation. 2. Exact in the performance of engagements. 3. (Iron.) Refined in point of roguery and fraud.

Honradór, ra, *s.* Honourer, one that honours.

Honramiénto, *sm.* Act of honouring.

Honrár, *va.* 1. To honour, to reverence, to respect. 2. To cajole, to caress, to fondle. 3. To dignify, to illustrate, to exalt. 4. To praise, to applaud.

Honrílla, *sf.* A false point of honour. *Por la negra honrilla he omitido hacerlo*, I have left it undone from some little point of honour or bashfulness.

Honrosaménte, *ad.* Honourably, honestly.

Honróso, sa, *a.* 1. Honourable, decent, decorous. 2. Just, equitable, honest. 3. Jealous of one's honour.

Honrúdo, da, *a.* Firm in maintaining one's honour, and acting conformably to it.

Hontanál, *sm.* Fountain, spring. *Hontanales*, Feasts which the ancients held at fountains.

Hontanár, *sm.* Place in which water rises, source of springs and rivers.

Hópa, *sf.* A long cassock with sleeves.

Hopalánda, *sf.* Tail or train of a gown worn by students.

Hopeár, *vn.* To wag the tail; applied to animals.

Hopéo, *sm.* (Joc.) Volatile coxcomb.

Hópo, *sm.* Tail with a tuft of hair, similar to that of a fox or squirrel. *Seguir el hopo*, To dog; to pursue closely. *Volver el hopo*, To escape, to run away.

Hóque, *sm.* Treat given at the conclusion of a bargain or contract, to celebrate its completion. V. *Alboroque.*

Hóra, *sf.* 1. Hour, a measure of time, which makes the twenty-fourth part of a natural day. 2. Way made in an hour, a league. 3. Time between twelve and one o'clock on the day of the ascension, during which that mystery is celebrated in Catholic churches. *Hora horada*, Hour passed over. *A' buena hora*, At a seasonable time. *A' la hora*, At the nick of time; then. *En hora buena*, It is well. *Por hora*, Each hour. *Por horas*, By instants. —*pl.* 1. Book of devotion, which contains the office of the blessed Virgin, and other devotions. 2. Canonical hours, the first, third, sixth, and ninth.

Hóra, *ad.* Now, at this time, at present.

Horacár, *va.* (Ant.) V. *Horadar.*

Horadáble, *a.* Capable of being pierced.

Horadación, *sf.* Act of boring or piercing.

Horadádo, *sm.* Silkworm's pod bored through.

Horadár, *va.* To bore or pierce from side to side.

Horádo, *sm.* 1. Hole bored from side to side. 2. Cavern, a hollow place in the ground; a grotto; niche or cavity in a wall.

Horámbre, *sm.* Hole in the cheeks of mills.

Horáño, ña, *a.* V. *Huraño.*

Horário, ria, *a.* Horary; relating to an hour, continuing for an hour.

Hórca, *sf.* 1. Gallows; a beam laid over two posts, on which malefactors are hanged. *Señor de horca y cuchillo*, Lord of the manor, who is invested both with the civil and criminal jurisdiction within the circuit of his estate. 2. Sort of yoke put on the neck of dogs or hogs, to prevent them from doing mischief; also used in Galicia and Asturias to disgrace servants. 3. Fork with two wooden prongs, used

by husbandmen for lifting up straw, corn, hay, &c. 4. Rope of onions.
Horcádo, da, a. Forked into different branches.
Horcadúra, sf. Fork of a tree, part where it divides into two main branches.
Horcajádas (A') ó á horcajadíllas, ad. Astride on horseback.
Horcajadúra, sf. Fork formed by the two thighs.
Horcájo, sm. Yoke or collar put on the neck of mules, when employed in drawing.
Horcáte, sm. 1. A yoke or collar of a horse. 2. Hame, that part to which the draft is attached.
Horchàta, sf. A refreshing drink made of the seeds of melons or pumpkins; an emulsion of melon seeds.
Hórco, sm. Rope of onions.
Horcón, sm. A forked pole, set upright, to support the branches of fruit trees.
Hórda, sf. Horde, clan, tribe.
Hordiáte, sm. 1. Beverage of barley water. 2. Barley without awns or beard.
Horfandád, sf. Orphanage, state of an orphan.
Horizontál, a. Horizontal, parallel to the horizon; on a level.
Horizontalménte, ad. Horizontally.
Horizónte, sm. Horizon, the line which terminates the view; the largest circle of the sphere, which divides it into two equal parts.
Hórma, sf. 1. Mould, model, in which any thing is cast, formed, or modelled. *Horma de zapatero*, Shoemaker's last. *Hallar la horma de su zapato*, (Fam.) To meet one's wishes, to accommodate or satisfy any one: (Irón.) To meet with any one who understands his artifices, and can oppose his designs. 2. A dry wall, built without lime or mortar.
Hormázo, sm. 1. (Cord.) House and garden. 2. V. *Tapia.*
Horméro, sm. Last-maker.
Hormíga, sf. 1. Ant, pismire, or emmet. 2. Disease of the skin.
Hormígo, sm. 1. A sort of ragout, made of pounded filberts, grated bread, and honey. 2. Coarse parts of flour, or ill-ground wheat.
Hormigón, sm. A fine sort of plaster.
Hormigóso, sa, a. Relating to ants.
Hormigueamiénto y Hormiguéo, sm. Act of itching or moving like ants.
Hormigueár, vn. 1. To itch, to feel that uneasiness in the skin which is in some measure removed by rubbing. 2. To run about like ants.
Hormiguéro, sm. 1. Ant-hill. 2. (Met.) Mob, moving multitude.—a. Relating to the itch.
Hormiguílla, sf. 1. A small ant. 2. V. *Hormiguillo.*
Hormiguillár, va. To mix grains of silver with salt.
Hormiguíllo, sm. 1. Distemper which affects the hoof of horses. 2. File of soldiers who pass from hand to hand the materials for a work to be raised. 3. (Mexico) Beverage made of pounded biscuit, sugar, and spice, boiled together. 4. Mixture of salts with silver.
Hormílla, sf. 1. A small last. 2. Bit of wood, bone, or ivory, of which buttons are formed, by covering it with gold or silver twist, silk, &c.
Hornabéque, sm. (Fort.) Hornwork, an outwork, composed of a front and two demi-bastions, joined by a curtain.
Hornacéro, sm. Person who watches crucibles with silver and gold in the furnace.

Hornácho, sm. 1. Shaft of a mine. 2. Furnace in which metal is melted for casting statues.
Hornachuéla, sf. Hole made in a wall.
Hornáda, sf. Batch, the quantity of bread baked at one time.
Hornáge, sm. (Rioja) Money paid to a baker for the baking of bread.
Hornaguear, va. To open the ground in search of pit-coals.
Hornaguéra, sf. Pit-coal. V. *Turba.*
Hornaguéro, ra, a. 1. Wide, spacious. 2. Coally; applied to ground containing coals.
Hornáza, sf. 1. A small furnace, used by gold and silversmiths, and other founders, to melt and cast metal. 2. A yellow glass, made of red calcined antimony and tin, used by potters to varnish their earthenware.
Hornázo, sm. 1. Cake made up with a batter of eggs and butter. 2. Present given on Easter Sunday by the inhabitants of a village to the clergyman who has preached the Lent-sermons.
Horneár, va. To carry on the trade of a baker.
Hornería, sf. Trade of a baker.
Hornéro, ra, s. Baker, one whose business is to bake bread.
Horníja, sf. Brushwood burnt in an oven to heat it for baking bread.
Hornijéro, sm. Person who supplies the oven with fuel.
Hornílla, sf. 1. Stew-hole, a small stove in a kitchen-hearth on which any thing is put to boil or stew. 2. Pigeon-hole, a hole made for pigeons to make their nests and breed in.
Horníllo, sm. 1. A small stove. 2. (Mil.) Chamber of a mine. 3. (Mil.) Fougade, a small mine dug under some work or fortification, in order to blow it up, if the enemy should make himself master of the work.
Hórno, sm. 1. Oven, an arched cavity for baking bread, pastry, and meat. *Horno de ladrillo.* Brick-kiln. 2. Lime-kiln. 3. Cavity, in which bees lodge. *Calentarse el horno*, (Met.) To grow warm in conversation or argument.
Horometría, sf. Horometry, art of measuring hours.
Horón, sm. (And.) Large round hamper or frail.
Horóscopo, sm. Horoscope, the configuration of the planets at the hour of birth.
Horquéta, sf. dim. of *Horcon;* a little fork.
Horquílla, sf. 1. Forked stick, for hanging up and taking down things from an elevated place. 2. Disease which causes the hair of the head to split. 3. Plant with which cloth is dyed. *Horquillas*, (Naút.) Crotches, the crooked timbers which are placed upon the keel in the fore and hind part of a ship. *Horquillas del fondo*, Fore crotches. *Horquillas de sobre-pluro*, Crotches of the riders. *Horquillas de dar fuego*, Breaming forks.
Hórra, a. Among graziers, applied to females not with young; also to the head of cattle given to herds to keep at the expense of their owners.
Horrendaménte, ad. Dreadfully.
Horréndo, da, a. 1. Vast, enormous, dreadful. 2. Extraordinary, uncommon.
Horréo, sm. A kind of granary built upon

pilastes, to prevent rats and mice from injuring the grain.

Horréro, *sm.* One who has the care of a granary; store-keeper.

Horribilidád, *sf.* Horribleness, dreadfulness.

Horríble, *a.* Horrid, dreadful, hideous.

Horriblemén te, *ad.* Horribly.

Hórrido y Horrífico, ca, *a.* Horrid, vast, enormous.

Horripilácion, *sf.* Horripilation, raising the hair with fear.

Horripilatívo, va, *a.* Causing the hair to stand an end with fear.

Horrísono, na, *a.* (Poét.) Horrisonous, sounding dreadfully.

Hórro, ra, *a.* 1. Enfranchised, set at liberty from slavery. 2. Free, disengaged. *Ovejas horras*, Barren ewes.

Horrór, *sm.* 1. Horror, consternation, fright. 2. The cause of fright or astonishment.

Horrorizar, *va.* To cause horror, to terrify. —*vr.* To be terrified.

Horrorosaménte, *ad.* Horribly.

Horroróso, sa, *a.* Very ugly; horrid.

Horrúra, *sf.* 1. Scoria, dross, recrement. 2. Dreariness of a thicket or close wood. 3. Filth, dirt, obscenity. 4. (Ant.) Terror, horror.

Hortál, *sm.* Kitchen garden, a garden in which esculent plants are produced. V. *Huerto.*

Hortalíza, *sf.* Garden stuff, all sorts of esculent plants produced in a garden.

Hortatório, ria, V. *Exhortatorio.*

Hortelanear, *vn.* To cultivate an orchard.

Horteláno, na, *s.* Gardener, one who cultivates garden-ground; gardener's wife. *Hortelano*, (Orn.) Ortolan. Emberiza hortulana *L.*

Horténse, *a.* Hortensial, hortulan.

Hortéra, *sf.* 1. A wooden bowl. 2. Nick-name of shop-boys in Madrid.

Hósco, ca, *a.* 1. Dark brown, but little different from black. 2. Sullen, gloomy. 3. Boastful, ostentatious, vain-glorious, arrogant.

Hoscóso, sa, *a.* Crisp, rough.

Hospedáble, *a.* Hospitable, kind to strangers.

Hospedádo, da, *a.* Applied to a house receiving guests.

Hospedadór, ra, *s.* One who kindly receives and entertains guests and strangers.

Hospedáge, *sm.* 1. Kind reception of guests and strangers. 2. Inn, a house of entertainment for travellers.

Hospedamiénto, *sm.* Reception of guests.

Hospedár, *va.* To receive and entertain strangers and travellers.—*vn.* To complete the college courses.

Hospedería, *sf.* A house kept at the expense of communities and convents, for the reception and accommodation of travellers and strangers. V. *Hospedage.*

Hospedéro, *sm.* 1. One who kindly receives guests and strangers. 2. Hospitaller, he whose trade is to receive and accommodate travellers and strangers. [house of charity.

Hospiciáno, na, *s.* Poor person who lives in a

Hospício, *sm.* Hospitium, charitable institution, house of charity. V. *Hospedage* y *Hospederia.*

Hospitál, *a.* Hospitable, affable.

Hospitál, *sm.* Hospital, infirmary, a place built for the reception of the sick or poor.

Hospitalário, ria, *a.* Applied to the religious communities which keep hospitals.

Hospitaléro, ra, *s.* Person intrusted with the care and direction of an hospital.

Hospitalidád, *sf.* Hospitality, the practice of kindly entertaining travellers and strangers.

Hospitalménte, *ad.* Hospitably.

Hosquíllo, lla, *a.* Darkish, somewhat gloomy.

Hostál, *sm.* V. *Hosteria.*

Hostaléro, *sm.* Inn or tavern-keeper; one who keeps an inn or tavern for the reception and accommodation of travellers and strangers.

Hóste, *sm.* 1. Enemy. 2. Host, army. *Hoste puto*, Expression of repugnance, or aversion from any thing disagreeable.

Hosteláge, *sm.* 1. V. *Meson.* 2. (Ant.) Pay at an inn.

Hostería, *sf.* Inn, tavern.

Hóstia, *sf.* 1. Victim, sacrifice. 2. Host, the sacrifice of the mass in the Romish church.

Hostiário, *sm.* Box, in which the bread is kept that is to be consecrated.

Hostiéro, *sm.* Person who prepares the host.

Hostigamiénto, *sm.* Chastisement, vexation.

Hostigár, *va.* 1. To chastise, to punish. 2. To vex, to trouble, to molest.

Hostígo, *sm.* 1. That part of a wall which looks towards the south. 2. The injurious dashing of water against a wall.

Hostíl, *a.* Hostile, adverse.

Hostilidád, *sf.* Hostility, opposition in war.

Hostilizár, *vn.* To commence hostilities.

Hostilménte, *ad.* Hostilely.

Hoto, *sm.* (Ant.) V. *Confianza.*

Hóy, *ad.* 1. To-day, this present day. 2. The present time, the time we live in. *Hoy dia, hoy en el dia, ó hoy en dia*, Now-a-days. *Hoy por hoy*, This very day. *De hoy en adelante, ó de hoy mas*, Henceforward, in future. *Antes hoy que mañana*, Rather to-day than to-morrow.

Hóya, *sf.* 1. Hole, cavity, pit. V. *Sepultura.* 2. Excavation made for the purpose of preparing charcoal. 3. (Naút.) A kind of scrubbing broom for cleaning a ship's bottom. 4. Socket of the eye, dimple in the cheek.

Hoyáda, *sf.* The lowest part of a field.

Hoyánco, *sm.* Great cavity or hollow.

Hóyo, *sm.* 1. Hole, pit, excavation. 2. V. *Sepultura.* 3. Inequality of a superficies, unevenness of a surface.

Hoyóso, sa, *a.* Pitted, full of holes.

Hoyuélo, *sm.* 1. A little hole; boy's play. 2. Dimple in the chin or cheek.

Hóz, *sf.* 1. Sickle, a reaping-hook, with which corn is cut down. 2. Defile, ravin; a narrow pass.

Hoz, *ad.* *De hoz y de coz*, Headlong.

Hozadéro, *sm.* Place where hogs turn up the ground.

Hozadúra, *sf.* Grubbing, the act of turning up the ground as hogs do with their snouts.

Hozár, *va.* To grub, to turn up the ground as hogs do with their snouts.

Hu, *ad.* V. *Donde.* [built vessel.

Hucár, *sm.* (Naút.) Hooker, a kind of Dutch-

Húcia, *sf.* (Ant.) V. *Confianza.*

Húcha, *sf.* 1. A large chest in which labouring people are accustomed to keep their clothes,

money, and other valuable articles. 2. Money-box. 3. Money kept and saved in a money-box.
Hucheár, va. To hoot, to shout at in derision.
Huchóho, sm. Word used to call birds.
Huébra, sf. 1. Extent of ground which a yoke of oxen can plough every day. 2. Pair of mules with a boy hired or let out for a day's work. 3. (Ar.) V. *Barbecho.*
Huebréro, sm. Boy who attends a pair of mules labouring by the day.
Huéca, sf. Notch at the small end of a spindle.
Huéco, ca, a. 1. Hollow, empty, concave at the inside. 2. Empty, vain, ostentatious. 3. Tumid, resonant, inflated. *Voz hueca*, Sonorous and hollow voice. 4. Soft, spongy; applied to ground, or to short wool fit only for carding.
Huéco, sm. 1. Notch or nick of a wheel, into which the leaves of a pinion or the teeth of a wheel hitch, and set it in motion. 2. Interval, space of time between the ceasing and recommencement of any thing. 3. Any vacant space or aperture in a house or other building. V. *Muesca.* 4. (Met.) Office or post vacant. 5. Fill, the place between the shafts of a carriage. *Huecos des las olas*, (Naút.) Trough of the sea; the hollow space between two waves or billows which follow each other in rapid succession.
Huégo, sm. (Ant.) V. *Fuego.*
Huélfago ó Huérfago, sm. Difficulty of breathing in beasts and hawks or other birds.
Huélga, sf. 1. Rest, repose; relaxation from work. 2. Recreation, merry-making. 3. *Huelga de la bala*, (Art.) Windage of a piece of ordnance, being the difference between the diameter of the bore and that of the ball.
Huélgo, sm. 1. Breath, respiration. *Tomar huelgo*, To breathe, to respire. 2. V. *Holgura.*
Huélla, sf. 1. Track, footstep; the print of the foot of a man or beast. 2. The horizontal width of the steps of a staircase. 3. Act and effect of treading or trampling. 4. Impression of a plate or other thing on paper.
Huéllo, sm. 1. Ground, the floor or level of a place. 2. Step, pace. 3. Lower part of an animal's hoof. [hueco.
Huequecíco, ca; llo, lla; to, ta, a. dim of
Huequecíto, sm. A small cavity or space.
Huérco, sm. (Ant.) Bier. V. *Muerte.*
Huérfano, na, s. Orphan, a child who has lost a father or mother, or both. *Huerfano de padre*, Fatherless.
Huérgano, sm. V. *Organo.* [sickly.
Huéro, ra, a. 1. Empty, addle. 2. Languid,
Huérta, sf. 1. Kitchen-garden where esculent plants are produced. 2. (Mur. y Val.) Land which can be irrigated.
Huérto, sm. Orchard or fruit-garden.
Huésa, sf. Grave, sepulture.
Huesarrón, sm. Large grave, sepulchre.
Huesecíllo, co, to, sm. A little bone.
Huéso, sm. 1. Bone, the solid part of the body of an animal. 2. Stone, the case which contains the seeds and kernels of some fruit. 3. The part of a lime-stone which remains unburnt in the kiln. 4. Piece of ground of little value and bad quality; a useless thing. 5. Labour, toil. *Huesos*, Teeth.
Huesóso, sa, a. Bony, osseous.

Huésped, da, s. 1. Guest, one entertained in the house of another. 2. Host, he who entertains others in his house. 3. Inn-keeper, tavern-keeper. 4. Stranger. [Hosts, armies.
Huéste, sf. Host, army in campaign. *Huestes*,
Huesúdo, da, a. Bony, having large bones.
Huéva, sf. Egg or spawn of fishes.
Huevár, vn. To lay eggs. [egg.
Huevecíco, llo, y zuélo, sf. dim. A small
Huevéra, sf. 1. Ovarium of birds. 2. Egg-stand.
Huevéro, ra, s. Dealer in eggs.
Huévo, sm. 1. Egg, laid by feathered animals, from which their young is produced. 2. Spawn, sperm. 3. Hollow piece of wood used by shoe-makers for shaping shoes. 4. Small waxen vessel filled with scented drops. *Huevo de juanelo*, Applied to any thing which appears the most difficult to make, but when tasted and known seems easy. *A' huevo*, For a trifle, at a low price.
Hugonóte, ta, s. Hugonot, a French protestant.
Huída, sf. 1. Flight, escape. V. *Fuga. Huidas*, Evasions, subterfuges. 2. Hole made to put in or draw out any thing with facility.
Huidéro, sm. 1. (Caza) Place of retreat, whither game retires. 2. Labourer in quicksilver mines, who opens the holes in which the beams or supporters of the mine are introduc-
Huidízo, za, a. Fugitive, flying. [ed and fixed.
Huír, vn. 1. To fly, to escape. 2. To slip away, to pass. 3. To shun, to avoid doing a bad thing.—vr. To run away, to escape. *Huir el cuerpo*, To avoid or decline.
Huláno, na, s. (Ant.) V. *Fulano.* [gum.
Húle, sm. 1. Oil-cloth, oil-skin. 2. Elastic
Húlla, sf. Pit-coal.
Humáda, sf. V. *Ahumada.*
Humanaménte, ad. Humanely, kindly. It is also used to denote the impossibility of doing any thing, as, *Eso humanamente no se puede hacer*, That cannot possibly be done.
Humanár, va. (Poét.) To transform or convert into man.—vr. 1. To become man; applied to the Son of God. 2. To become humane, to be humbled, to grow familiar.
Humanidád, sf. 1. Humanity, the nature of man. 2. Corpulence, bulkiness of body, fleshiness. 3. Propensity for carnal pleasures. 4. Human weakness. 5. Benevolence, tenderness. 6. Philology, grammatical studies.
Humanísta, sm. Humanist, philologer, grammarian.
Humanizárse, vr. V. *Humanarse.*
Humáno, na, a. 1. Human, belonging or peculiar to man. 2. Humane, kind, benevolent.
Humarázo, sm. V. *Humazo.*
Humaréda, sf. 1. A great deal of smoke. 2. Confusion, perplexity.
Humázga, sf. Hearth-money, tax paid on fire-places.
Humázo, sm. 1. Smoke; fume proceeding from burning paper which is doubled and twisted. 2. *Humazo de narices*, (Met.) Displeasure, disdain, vexation.
Humeár, vn. 1. To smoke, to emit smoke; to exhale. 2. To inflame; applied to the passions. 3. To be kindled or stirred up; applied to disturbances or quarrels.
Humectación, sf. Humectation.

Humectánte, pa. Moistening.
Humectár, va. To moisten, to humectate.
Humectatívo, va, a. Causing moisture.
Humedád, sf. Humidity, moisture.
Humedál, sm. Humid soil, a marsh.
Humedecér, va. To moisten, to wet, to soak, to steep. [damp.
Húmedo, da; y Húmido, da, a. Moist, wet,
Huméro, sm. Tunnel, funnel, the shaft of a chimney; the passage for the smoke.
Humildád, sf. 1. Humility, freedom from pride. 2. Meanness, lowness of mind or birth; submission. *Humildad de garabato*, Feigned humility.
Humílde, a. 1. Humble, modest, submissive. 2. Low, not tall. 3. Ignobly born, meanly extracted.
Humildeménte, ad. Humbly.
Humillación, sf. 1. Humiliation, submission, obsequiousness. 2. Self-contempt.
Humilladéro, sm. Oratory, a private place devoted and allotted for prayers.
Humilladór, ra, s. Humiliator.
Humillár, va. 1. To humble, to lower. 2. To bring down from loftiness and pride.—vr. To become humble, to resign one's authority.
Humíllo, sm. 1. A little pride. 2. A little vapour. 3. Disease of sucking pigs.
Húmo, sm. 1. Smoke, the visible effluvium or sooty exhalation from any thing burning. 2. Vapour, steam. 3. Thin, clear, black silk stuff.—pl. 1. Families or houses in a town or village. 2. (Met.) Vanity, haughtiness, presumption.
Humór, sm. 1. Humour, moisture. 2. Effect, occasioned by some predominant humour. 3. General turn or temper of mind. 4. Good nature, pleasant disposition. 5. Grotesque imagery, jocularity.
Humoráda, sf. 1. Graceful sprightliness. 2. A witty saying.
Humorádo, da, a. 1. Full of humours. 2. Well or ill-disposed.
Humorál, a. Humoral.
Humorázo, sm. aum. of *Humor*.
Humorosidád, sf. Copiousness of humours.
Humoróso, sa, a. Humorous.
Humóso, sa, a. Smoky; vapoury.
Hundíble, a. Fusible, capable of submersion or destruction.
Hundimiénto, sm. Submersion, immersion, the act of sinking.
Hundír, va. 1. To submerge, to immerge. 2. To crush, to overwhelm, to beat down. 3. To refute, to confound; to destroy, to ruin.—vr. To sink; to hide, to abscond; to have dissensions and quarrels.
Húra, sf. 1. Furuncle, any angry pustule. 2. A wild boar's head.
Huracán, sm. Hurricane, a violent storm.
Huráco, sm. Hole. V. *Agujero*.
Hurañaménte, ad. 1. Wildly, in a savage and intractable manner. 2. Diffidently, disdainfully.
Hurañería, sf. 1. Shiness, diffidence, mistrust. 2. Disdain, contempt.
Hurañía, sf. Stubbornness, aversion to deal with the world.
Huráño, ña, a. 1. Shy, diffident; intractable. 2 Disdainful.
Hurción, sf. V. *Infurcion*.
Hurgamandéra, sf. (Cant.) Prostitute.
Hurgár, va. 1. To stir, to move with a stick or iron. 2. To stir up disturbances, to excite quarrels.
Hurgón, sm. 1. Poker, an iron bar for stirring the fire. 2. Thrust in fencing.
Hurgonáda, sf. V. *Estocada*.
Hurgonázo, sm. A violent thrust.
Hurgoneár, va. 1. To stir the fire with a poker. 2. To make a thrust in fencing.
Hurgonéro, sm. Poker. V. *Hurgon*.
Hurón, na, s. 1. Ferret. Mustela furo *L.* 2. One who pries into others' secrets. 3. V. *Huraño*.
Huroneár, va. 1. To ferret, to hunt with a ferret. 2. To hunt another in his privacies.
Huronéra, sf. 1. Ferret-hole. 2. Lurking-place where a person conceals himself.
Huronéro, sm. Ferret-keeper.
Hurráca, sf. (Orn.) Magpie. Corvus pica *L.*
Húrta agua, sf. V. *Regadera*. *A' Hurta cordel*, Spinning a top in the palm of the hand: (Met.) Suddenly, insidiously, unexpectedly. *A' Hurtas*. V. *A' Hurtadillas*. *Hurta-ropa*, A boy's play.
Hurtáble, a. Capable of being stolen.
Hurtadíllas (A') y A Hurtádas, ad. By stealth, privately, in a hidden manner.
Hurtadinéros, sm. (Ar.) V. *Alcancia*.
Hurtadór, ra, s. Robber, thief.
Hurtár, va. 1. To steal, to rob. 2. To cheat in weight or measure. 3. To wrest a piece of ground from the sea or rivers. 4. To separate, to part. *Hurtar el cuerpo*, To flee, to avoid any difficulty. 5. To commit plagiary.—vr. To remove or withdraw; to abscond.
Hurtarópa, sf. Boy's play.
Húrto, sm. 1. Theft, robbery. 2. The thing stolen. 3. In mines, passage between the principal apartments. *A' hurto*, By stealth.
Husáda, sf. A spindleful of thread or worsted.
Husáno, sm. A large spindle.
Husár, sm. Hussar, Hungarian soldier.
Husilléro, sm. One who attends the spindle in oil-mills.
Husíllo, sm. Spindle, a hollow cylinder running round in a spiral nut; a screwpin. *Husillos*, Drains, small channels for draining fens.
Husíta, sm. A follower of John Huss.
Husmeadór, ra, s. Scenter, smeller.
Husmeadorcíllo, lla, s. dim. Little smeller.
Husmeár, va. 1. To scent, to find out by smelling. 2. To guess, to suspect.—vn. To stink; applied to flesh.
Húsmo, sm. Smell of meat which is somewhat tainted. *Estar al husmo*, To be upon the scent; to watch a favourable opportunity for obtaining one's end. *Andar á la husma*, To search and conjecture.
Húso, sm. Spindle, the pin by which the thread is formed, and on which it is wound.
Húta, sf. Hut, kind of shed in which huntsmen hide, in order to start their dogs at the chase.
Husón, sm. (Ict.) Sturgeon. Acipenser huso *L.*
Hutía, sm. Indian rat.
Hy, ad. (Ant.) V. *Hi*.

THE Latin vowel *i* greatly differs from the consonant *j*, in point of pronunciation, the latter being a guttural letter, pronounced in the throat, like the English *h* strongly aspirated, as in *help*. Formerly much confusion prevailed with regard to the use of the Latin *i* and *y*. This has been removed by the rules laid down in the Orthography of the Spanish Academy. In all cases where the *i* served as a conjunction, it is now superseded by *y*, and where the latter is a vowel, as in *lyra*, it must yield to *i*, notwithstanding the etymon of the word, and be written *lira*, *pira*, &c. *I* in Spanish is sounded like the English long *e* in *even*.

Ibérico, Ibério, Ibéro, a, *a.* Native of Iberia.
I'bice, *sm.* Ibex, kind of goat. Capra ibex *L.*
I'bis, *sf.* (Orn.) Ibis, a kind of bird. Tantalus *L.*
Icáco, *sm.* (Bot.) Kind of small plum which grows in the Antillas.
Ichneumón, *sm.* Ichneumon, a small animal.
Ichnografía, *sf.* Ichnography, ground plan, a delineation of the length, breadth, angles, and lines, of a fortification or building.
Ichnográfico, ca, *a.* Ichnographical.
Iconología, *sf.* Iconology, representation by figures.
Iconoclásta y Iconomáco, *sm.* Iconoclast, Image-breaker, heretic who denies the worship due to the holy images.
I'cor y Icoróide, *s.* Gleet, ichor, a thin watery humour from a sore.
Icoróso, sa, *a.* Ichorous; serous.
Ictericia, *sf.* Jaundice, a disease of the liver, which makes the patient look yellow.
Ictericiádo, da; Ictérico, ca, *a.* Icterical, belonging to the jaundice.
Ictiófago, ga, *a.* Fish-eating, relating to the ichthyophagists.
Ictiología, *sf.* Ichthyology, the science of the nature of fish.
I'da, *sf.* 1. Departure, act of going from one place to another. 2. (Met.) Impetuosity; rash, inconsiderate or violent proceeding; sally. 3. Act of driving a ball out of the truck-table. 4. Mark or impression of the feet of game on the ground. *Ida del humo*, Departure never to return. *I'das*, Frequent visits. *Darse dos idas y venidas*, To talk a matter over very briefly, to transact business expeditiously. *En dos idas y venidas*, Briefly, promptly.
Ide, *sm.* (Ict.) Kind of Carp, a fresh-water fish. Cyprinus idus *L.*
Idéa, *sf.* 1. Idea, a mental image. 2. Thread of a discourse. 3. Design, intention; model, example. 4. Genius, talent; extravagant notion, conceit. 5. (Bot.) Butcher's broom.
Ideál, *a.* Ideal, mental, intellectual; not physical.
Idealménte, *ad.* Ideally, intellectually.
Ideár, *va.* 1. To form or conceive an idea. 2. To discuss a subject on vain futile grounds; to indulge in vain or airy conceptions.
I'dem, *pron.* (Lat.) Item, the same.
Idénticaménte, *ad.* Identically.
Idéntico, ca, *a.* Identic, the same, implying the same thing.
Identidád, *sf.* Identity, sameness; opposite to diversity.
Identificár, *va.* To identify; to ascertain the sameness of two objects.
I'deo, ea, *a.* (Poét.) Belonging to mount Ida.
Idióma, *sm.* 1. Idiom, the language peculiar to a nation or country. 2. Mode of speaking peculiar to a dialect or language. 3. Sounds with which brutes express their wants or sensations.
Idiopatía, *sf.* Idiopathy, a disease peculiar to some particular part of the body.
Idióta, *sm.* Idiot, fool, an ignorant person.
Idiotéz, *sf.* Idiotism, silliness, ignorance.
Idiotísmo, *sm.* 1. Idiotism, peculiarity of expression. 2. Folly, natural imbecility of mind.
Idólatra, *sm.* 1. Idolater, a worshipper of idols. 2. One who idolizes a woman, or loves her with excessive fondness.
Idolatrár, *va.* 1. To worship idols. 2. To idolize, to love with excessive fondness.
Idolatría, *sf.* 1. Idolatry, the worship of images or idols. 2. Inordinate love, excessive fondness.
Idolátrico, ca, *a.* Idolatrous.
Idolíllo, co, to, *sm.* 1. A little idol. 2. Darling, favourite, the object of fondness.
Idolísmo, *sm.* Idolatry. V. *Idolatría.*
I'dolo, *sm.* 1. Idol, an image worshipped as God. 2. One loved or honoured to adoration.
Idoneidád, *sf.* Aptitude, fitness, capacity.
Idóneo, nea, *a.* Idoneous, fit, convenient.
I'dus, *sm.* Ides, one of the three parts into which the Romans divided the month.
Idy'lio, *sm.* (Poét.) Idyl, a short poem.
Iglésia, *sf.* 1. Church, the collective body of Christians. 2. Body of Christians adhering to some particular form of worship. 3. Place which Christians consecrate to the worship of God. 4. Temple, place either of Christian or Heathen worship. 5. Ecclesiastical state; chapter; diocese. *Hombre de iglesia*, An ecclesiastic. 6. Right of impunity enjoyed in churches. *Iglesia fria*, Church where a malefactor does not enjoy protection against the laws of his country. *Iglesia me llamo*, The church calls me, expression of delinquents when they do not wish to tell their name, but seek the immunity of the church.
Ignáro, ra, *a.* Ignorant, unlearned, uninstructed.
Ignávia, *sf.* Idleness, laziness, carelessness.
Igneo, ea, *a.* Igneous, fiery.
Ignición, *sf.* Ignition, the act of kindling or setting on fire.
Ignífero, ra, *a.* Igniferous, containing or emitting fire.
Ignícola, *s.* Fire-worshipper.
Ignipoténte, *a.* (Poét.) Ignipotent, powerful over fire.
Ignito, ta, *a.* Ignited, inflamed, red-hot.
Ignívomo, ma, *a.* Ignivomous, vomiting fire.
Ignóble, *a.* V. *Innoble.*
Ignomínia, *sf.* Ignominy, infamy, public disgrace.
Ignominiosaménte, *ad.* Ignominiously.
Ignominióso, sa, *a.* Ignominious.
Ignoráncia é Ignoración, *sf.* Ignorance, want of knowledge, illiterateness.

Ignoránte, *a.* Ignorant, unlearned, stupid.
Ignoranteménte, *ad.* Ignorantly.
Ignorantón, **na**, *a. aum.* Grossly ignorant.
Ignorár, *va.* To be ignorant of, not to know.
Ignóto, **ta**, *a.* Unknown.
Igual, *a.* 1. Equal, similar. 2. Level, even, flat. 3. Like, resembling. 4. Constant, firm, determined, consistent. *En igual de*, Instead of, in lieu of. *Al igual*, Equally. *Por un igual*, Equally, with equality.
Iguála, *sf.* 1. Agreement, convention, stipulation, contract. 2. Level, an instrument whereby masons adjust their work. 3. Gratification given by farmers to their day-labourers, over and above their usual wages. *A' la iguala*, Equally.
Igualación, *sf.* 1. Equalization, the act of equalizing or making equal. 2. Counter-gage, scarf. 3. (Algebra) Equation, an expression of the same quantity in two dissimilar terms, but of equal value.
Igualádo, **da**, *pp.* Equalled. *Dexar á uno igualado*, (Vulg.) To give one a severe drubbing.
Igualadór, **ra**, *s.* 1. Equalizer, leveller. 2. Harrower, one who makes ploughed ground even and level with a harrow.
Igualamiénto, *sm.* Equalizing, act of equalling.
Igualár, *va.* 1. To equalize, to make equal. 2. To judge without any partiality, to hold in equal estimation. 3. To level the ground, to make even. *Igualar las mercaderías*, To put a fair price upon merchandise.—*vr.* 1. To place one's self upon a level with others. 2. To agree, to adjust differences. 3. To settle by mutual agreement the amount of wages or any other kind of pay. *Igualar la sangre*, To bleed a second time; (Met.) To give a second blow to one.
Igualdád, *sf.* 1. Equality, similitude. 2. Evenness of mind; constancy, uniformity.
Igualménte, *ad.* Equally.
Iguána, *sf.* Guana, a kind of lizard, a native of America. Lacerta iguana *L.*
Iguárias, *sf. pl.* Viands dressed and served up.
Ijáda, *sf.* 1. Flank, that part of the side of a quadruped near the hinder thigh. 2. The fleshy part of the side of a pig, without bones. 3. Pain in the side, cholic. *Tener su ijada*, (Met.) To have a weak side.
Ijadeár, *vn.* To pant, to palpitate.
Ijár, *sm.* Flank of an animal. *Caballo de pocos ijares*, A light flanked horse.
Ilación, *sf.* Inference; conclusion drawn from previous arguments.
Ilápso, *sm.* 1. A gradual gentle fall. 2. Heavenly influence.
Ilécebra, *sf.* Allurement, enticement, temptation.
Ilegál, *a.* Illegal, unlawful, contrary to law.
Ilegalidád, *sf.* Illegality, contrariety to law.
Ilegalménte, *ad.* Illegally.
Ilegíble, *a.* Illegible, what cannot be read.
Ilegitimaménte, *ad* Illegitimately.
Ilegitimár, *va.* To deprive of legitimacy.
Ilegitimidád, *sf.* Illegitimacy.
Ilegítimo, **ma**, *a.* 1. Illegal, contrary to law. 2. Illegitimate, unlawfully begotten.
Ileón ó **Ilión**, *sm.* Colon, the largest and widest of all the intestines.
Iléso, **sa**, *a.* Unhurt, free from damage.

ILIBA'TO, TA, *a.* Sound, entire, safe, untouched.
Iliberál, *a.* (Ant.) Illiberal.
Ilicitaménte, *ad.* Illicitly.
Ilícito, **ta**, *a.* Illicit, unlawful.
Ilimitádo, **da**, *a.* Unlimited, boundless.
Ilíquido, **da**, *a.* Unliquidated; applied to accounts or debts.
Iliteráto, *a.* Illiterate, unlearned.
Iludír, *va.* V. *Burlar.*
Iluminación, *sf.* 1. Illumination, the act of supplying with light. 2. Festive lights, hung out as a token of joy. 3. Infusion of intellectual light, knowledge, or grace.
Iluminadór, *sm.* Illuminator, one who illumines; one who adorns with colours.
Iluminár, *va.* 1. To illumine or illuminate, to supply with light. 2. To adorn with festive lamps. 3. To enlighten intellectually, to infuse knowledge or grace. 4. To give light and shade to a piece of painting; to colour, to illumine books. 5. To render transparent
Iluminatívo, **va**, *a.* Illuminative.
Ilusión, *sf.* 1. Illusion, false show, counterfeit appearance. 2. A sort of smart and lively irony
Ilusívo, **va**, *a.* Delusive, false, deceitful.
Ilúso, **sa**, *a.* Deluded, deceived, ridiculed.
Ilusório, **ria**, *a.* 1. Delusive, deceitful, having a counterfeit appearance. 2. (For.) Null, void of effect; of no value.
Ilustración, *sf.* 1. Illustration, brightness, splendour. 2. Revelation, divine inspiration 3. Explanation, elucidation.
Ilustradór, **ra**, *s.* Illustrator.
Ilustrár, *va.* 1. To illustrate, to clear up. 2 To inspire, to infuse supernatural light. 3. To aggrandize, to ennoble, to illustrate.
Ilústre, *a.* Illustrious, magnificent, noble, celebrated.
Ilustreménte, *ad.* Illustriously.
Ilustrísimo, **ma**, *a.* Appellation of honour given to prelates, &c. in Spain, when they are addressed either in writing or conversation.
Imádas, *sf. pl.* (Naút.) Sliding planks used in the launching of ships.
Imágen, *sf.* 1. Image, figure, representation, statue, effigy. 2. (Ret.) Picture or lively description.
Imagencíca, **lla**, **ta**, *sf. dim.* A little image.
Imagináble, *a.* Imaginable.
Imaginación, *sf.* 1. Imagination, fancy; the power of forming ideal pictures. 2. Conception, image of the mind. 3. False or erroneous idea.
Imaginár, *va.* 1. To imagine, to fancy, to paint in the mind. 2. To form erroneous suppositions. 3. To adorn with images.
Imaginária, *sf.* (Mil.) Reserve guard, corps ready to assist the actual guards.
Imaginariaménte, *ad.* In a visionary manner.
Imaginário, **ria**, *a.* **Imaginary**, that which may be conceived. 2. Fancied, visionary, existing only in the imagination.—*sm.* Painter or sculptor of images.
Imaginatíva, *sf.* Imagination, fancy.
Imaginatívo, **va**, *a.* Imaginative, fantastic, full of imagination.
Imaginería, *sf.* Imagery, an embroidery representing flowers, birds, or fishes.
Imán, *sm.* 1. Loadstone, a hard and solid stone which attracts iron. 2. Charm, attraction.

Imantár, *va.* To touch the mariner's compass-needle with a loadstone, to give it a direction north and south.
Imbeáto, ta, *a.* Unfortunate, unhappy.
Imbécil, *a.* Weak, feeble. [ty, want of strength.
Imbecilidád, *sf.* Imbecility, weakness, debili-
Imbéle, *a.* Feeble, weak.
Imbibición, *sf.* Imbibition.
Imbiérno, *sm.* Winter. V. *Invierno.*
Imbornál, *sm.* (Naút.) Scupper-hole. *Imbornal de bomba*, Pump scupper-hole. *Imbornales de varengas*, Limber-holes. *Imbornales de la caza de agua*, Scuppers of the manger.
Imbricádo, da, *a.* Applied to shells that are waved.
Imbuír, *va.* To imbue, to admit into the mind; to infuse into the mind, to instruct. [sack.
Imbursación, *sf.* (Ar.) Act of putting into a
Imbursár, *va.* (Ar.) To put into a sack or bag.
Imitáble, *a.* Imitable.
Imitación, *sf.* Imitation, the act of copying; attempt to resemble. *A' imitacion*, After the example, in imitation of.
Imitadór, ra, *s.* Imitator. [to resemble.
Imitár, *va.* To imitate, to copy, to endeavour,
Imitatório, ria, *a.* Imitative.
Impaciéncia, *sf.* 1. Impatience, inability to suffer pain; rage under suffering. 2. Vehemence of temper, heat of passion.
Impacientár, *va.* To vex, to irritate, to make one lose all patience.—*vr.* To become impatient, to lose all patience.
Impaciénte, *a.* Impatient.
Impacienteménte, *ad.* Impatiently.
Impácto, ta, *a.* Impacted, thrust into, packed tight. [ed by the touch.
Impalpáble, *a.* Impalpable, not to be perceiv-
Impar, *a.* 1. Unequal, dissimilar. 2. Uneven, not divisible into equal numbers.
Imparciál, *a.* 1. Impartial, equitable, free from regard of party. 2. Retired or withdrawn from all society and intercourse with others.
Imparcialidád, *sf.* Impartiality.
Impartíble, *a.* 1. Indivisible, what cannot be divided or separated. 2. Communicable, what can be bestowed or conferred.
Impartír, *va.* 1. To demand or require assistance; chiefly applied to courts of judicature, which demand one another's assistance for the effectual administration of justice. 2. To grant, to impart.
Impasibilidád, *sf.* Impassibility, exemption from the agency of external causes; exemption from sensibility of pain.
Impasíble, *a.* 1. Impassible, incapable of suffering. 2. Exempt from external impression, insensible of pain.
Impavidaménte, *ad.* Intrepidly, undauntedly.
Impavidéz, *sf.* Intrepidity, courage, boldness.
Impávido, da, *a.* Dauntless, intrepid.
Impecabilidád, *sf.* Impeccability.
Impecáble, *a.* Impeccable, exempt from possibility of sin.
Impedído, da, *a.* Incapable of making use of one's limbs; having lost the use of the limbs.
Impedidór, ra, *s.* Obstructor, what impedes.
Impediménto, *sm.* Impediment, obstacle.
Impedír, *va.* To impede, to hinder, to obstruct, to prevent, to suspend.

Impeditívo, va, *a.* Impeding, hindering.
Impelér, *va.* 1. To impel, to give an impulse. 2. To incite, to stimulate.
Impenetrabilidád, *sf.* Impenetrability.
Impenetráble, *a.* 1. Impenetrable, what cannot be pierced or penetrated. 2. Incomprehensible, not to be conceived by the mind.
Impeniténcia, *sf.* Impenitence, want of penitence.
Impeniténte, *a.* Impenitent, obdurate.
Impensadaménte, *ad.* Unexpectedly.
Impensádo, da, *a.* Unexpected, unforeseen, not thought of. [star.
Imperánte, *a.* (Astrol.) Ruling; applied to a
Imperár, *vn.* To command, to reign.—*va.* To command a person, to direct his actions.
Imperativaménte, *ad.* Imperatively.
Imperatívo, va, *a.* Imperative, commanding, expressive of command; a mode in grammar.
Imperatória, *sf.* (Bot.) Masterwort. Imperatoria ostruthium *L.*
Imperatório, ria, *a.* 1. Imperial, royal; belonging to an emperor or monarch. 2. Eminent, possessed of superior qualities.
Imperceptíble, *a.* Imperceptible.
Imperceptibleménte, *ad.* Imperceptibly.
Imperdíble, *a.* Imperdible, not to be lost or destroyed. [failure.
Imperfección, *sf.* Imperfection, fault, slight
Imperfectaménte, *ad.* Imperfectly.
Imperfécto, ta, *a.* Imperfect, not complete.
Imperiál, *sm.* 1. Roof of a coach or carriage. 2 (Naút.) Poop-royal, a platform which serves as a covering of the poop-gallery of a ship.
Imperiál, *a.* Imperial. *Polvos imperiales*, Powder of peculiar efficacy.
Imperícia, *sf.* Unskilfulness, want of knowledge or experience.
Império, *sm.* 1. Empire, dominion, command 2. Dignity of an emperor. 3. Empire, the dominions or possessions of an emperor. 4. Kind of linen made in Germany. *Alto ó baxo imperio*, Upper or lower empire.
Imperiosaménte, *ad.* Imperiously.
Imperióso, sa, *a.* 1. Imperious, commanding, arrogant, haughty. 2. Powerful, overbearing.
Imperitaménte, *ad.* Unskilfully, ignorantly.
Imperíto, ta, *a.* Unlearned, unskilled; deficient in the practical knowledge of arts and sciences.
Impermeabilidád, *sf.* Impermeability.
Impermeáble, *a.* Impermeable, that which is not permeable, or cannot be passed through.
Impermutáble, *a.* Immutable. [*table*
Imperscrutáble, *a.* Inscrutable. V. *Inescru-*
Impersonál, *a.* 1. Impersonal, not varied according to the persons; applied to verbs. 2. Mode of speaking impersonally. *En ó por impersonal*, Impersonally.
Impersonalménte, *ad.* Impersonally, according to the manner of an impersonal verb.
Impersuasíble, *a.* Impersuasible, not to be moved by persuasion. [dauntless.
Imperterríto, ta, *a.* Intrepid; unterrified.
Impertinéncia, *sf.* 1. Impertinence or impertinency, folly, rambling thought, foolish action. 2. Peevishness, fretful disposition. 3 Troublesomeness, intrusion. 4. Minute accuracy in the performance of a thing.

Impertinénte, *a.* 1. Impertinent, intrusive, importunate. 2. Of no relation to the matter in hand, of no weight. 3. Peevish, fretful.
Impertinenteménte, *ad.* Impertinently.
Imperturbáble, *a.* Imperturbable, free from perturbation, not to be disturbed.
Impérvio, via, *a.* Impervious, impassable, impenetrable.
Impétra, *sf.* 1. Diploma, license, permission. 2. Bull by which dubious benefices are granted, with a proviso of the incumbent removing or clearing up the doubts at his own expense.
Impetración, *sf.* Impetration, the act of obtaining by prayer or entreaty. [treaty.
Impetradór, ra, *s.* One who obtains by en-
Impetrár, *va.* To obtain by entreaty.
Ímpetu ó Ímpeto, *sm.* 1. Impetus, a violent tendency to any point; a violent effort. 2. Impetuosity, violence or vehemence of passion.
Impetuosaménte, *ad.* Impetuously.
Impetuosidád, *sf.* Impetuosity, vehemence.
Impetuóso, sa, *a.* 1. Impetuous, violent, forcible, fierce. 2. Vehement, passionate.
Impía, *sf.* (Bot.) A kind of rosemary.
Impiaménte, *ad.* Impiously.
Impiedád, *sf.* 1. Impiety, irreverence to the Supreme Being; contempt of the duties of religion. 2. Wickedness, cruelty.
Impígero, ra, *a.* Active, prompt, lively.
Impío, pia, *a.* Impious, irreligious, wicked.
Impiréo, rea, *a.* Empyreal. V. *Empíreo.*
Impla, *sf.* (Ant.) Woman's veil.
Implacáble, *a.* Implacable, not to be pacified; inexorable; constant in enmity.
Implacableménte, *ad.* Implacably.
Implaticáble, *a.* 1. Impracticable, not to be performed; unfeasible. 2. Intractable, unmanageable. [contradiction.
Implicación ó Implicáncia, *sf.* Implication;
Implicár, *vn.* To oppose, to contradict one another; applied to terms and propositions.—*va.* To implicate, to involve.
Implícitaménte, *ad.* Implicitly.
Implícito, ta, *a.* Implicit, inferred; tacitly comprised, not expressed. [ing.
Imploración, *sf.* Entreaty, the act of implor-
Implorár, *va.* 1. To implore, to call upon in supplication, to solicit. 2. To ask, to beg.
Implúme, *a.* Unfeathered, naked of feathers.
Impolítico, ca, *a.* Impolitic, rude, uncivil.
Impolúto, ta, *a.* Unpolluted, pure, free from stain, clean.
Imponderáble, *a.* Inexpressible, unutterable.
Imponedór, *sm.* He who imposes or charges.
Imponér, *va.* 1. To impose, to lay on as a burthen or penalty. 2. To charge upon or impute falsely. 3. To advise, to give notice. 4. To obtrude fallaciously, to impose upon. 5. (Impr.) To arrange pages of types for the press. [ed.
Importáble, *a.* Unsupportable, not to be endur-
Importáncia, *sf.* 1. Importance, consequence, moment. 2. Respectable character, worthiness of regard, claim to respect.
Importánte, *a.* Important, momentous, of great consequence.
Importanteménte, *ad.* Importantly, usefully.
Importár, *v imp.* 1. To be important or convenient. 2. To import, to imply, to infer. 3. To amount to. 4. (Ant.) To occasion, to cause.
Impórte, *sm.* Import, value. [licitation
Importunación, *sf.* Importunity, incessant so-
Importunadaménte, *ad.* Importunately.
Importunádo, da, *a.* Importunate.
Importunaménte, *ad.* 1. Importunely, with importunity. 2. Unseasonably, out of time.
Importunár, *va.* 1. To importune, to disturb by reiteration of the same request. 2. To vex, to molest, to harass.
Importunidád, *sf.* Importunity.
Importúno, na, *a.* 1. Importunate, unseasonable. 2. Importune, troublesome, vexatious.
Imposibilidád, *sf.* 1. Impossibility, impracticability; the state of not being feasible. 2. That which cannot be done. [sible.
Imposibilitár, *va.* To disable, to render impos-
Imposíble, *a.* Impossible, impracticable, unfeasible. *Los imposibles*, A kind of Spanish dance. *Imposible de toda imposibilidad*, (Fam.) Altogether impossible.
Imposibleménte, *ad.* Impossibly.
Imposición, *sf.* 1. Imposition, the act of laying any thing on another. 2. Injunction of any thing as a law or duty. 3. Charge or duty imposed. 4. (Impr.) Arrangement of pages for the press.
Impósta, *sf.* (Arq.) Imposts, that part of a pillar in vaults and arches on which the weight of the whole building lies.
Impostór, ra, *s.* Impostor, one who cheats by a fictitious character.
Impostúra, *sf.* 1. A false imputation or charge. 2. Imposture, fiction, deceit.
Impoténcia, *sf.* 1. Impotence or impotency; want of power, inability, weakness. 2. Impotence, incapacity of propagation.
Impoténte, *a.* 1. Impotent, disabled from performing a thing. 2. Without power of propagation.
Impracticáble, *a.* 1. Impracticable, impossible, unfeasible. 2. Impassable; applied to roads. [by which any evil is wished.
Imprecación, *sf.* Imprecation, curse; prayer
Imprecár, *va.* To imprecate, to curse.
Imprecatório, ria, *a.* Imprecatory, containing wishes of evil.
Impregnación, *sf.* Impregnation.
Impregnárse, *vr.* To be impregnated.
Impremír, *va.* (Ant.) V. *Imprimir.*
Imprénta, *sf.* 1. Art of printing. 2. Printing-office, where books are printed. 3. Form in which books are printed; impression.
Imprescindíble, *a.* Inseparable, that which cannot be separated.
Imprescriptíble, *a.* That cannot be prescribed.
Impresión, *sf.* 1. Impression, the act of pressing one body upon another. 2. Mark made by pressure, stamp; quality or form of the letter. 3. Image fixed in the mind. 4. Edition, number printed at once; one course of printing. 5. (Astrol.) Influence of the stars; impression or effect.
Impresionár, *va.* To imprint, to fix on the mind or memory.
Impréso, *sm.* Pamphlet, a small book; a short treatise.
Impresór, *sm.* Printer, one that prints books.
Impresóra, *sf.* Wife of a printer or proprietor of a printing-office.

Imperdtáble, *a.* That cannot be lost.
Imprevísto, ta, *a.* Unforeseen, unexpected.
Imprimación, *sf.* Priming, the act of laying on the first colours on canvass or boards, to be painted; stuff for priming.
Imprimadéra, *sf.* Brush, pencil; the instrument used in printing or painting.
Imprimadór, *sm.* One who lays the first colours on a piece of linen or board to be painted.
Imprimár, *va.* To prime, to lay the first colours on in painting.
Imprimír, *va.* 1. To impress, to print by pressure or stamps. 2. To imprint, to fix an idea on the mind or memory. 3. To put a work to press, to get it printed.
Improbabilidád, *sf.* Improbability, unlikelihood, difficulty to be believed.
Improbáble, *a.* Improbable, unlikely, difficult to be proved.
Improbablemente, *ad.* Improbably.
Improbár, *va.* To disapprove, to dislike, to censure.
Ímprobo, ba, *a.* 1. Corrupt, wicked. 2. Laborious, yet useless.
Improperár, *va.* To upbraid, to charge contemptuously with any thing disgraceful.
Impropério, *sm.* Contemptuous reproach, an injurious censure.
Impropiamente, *ad.* Improperly.
Impropiár, *vr.* To twist or distort the true sense of a law, injunction, or word.
Impropiedád, *sf.* Impropriety, unfitness, want of justness.
Impropio, pia, *a.* Improper, unfit; not conducive to the right end; unqualified.
Improporción, *sf.* Disproportion, want of proportion.
Improporcionádo, da, *a.* Disproportionate, unsymmetrical; unsuitable in point of quality or quantity.
Impropriamente, *ad.* Improperly.
Impropriár, *va.* To impropriate.
Impropriedád, *sf.* Impropriety.
Imprópric, ria, *a.* Improper, unfit. [rogued.
Improrogáble, *a.* That which cannot be pro-
Impróspero, ra, *a.* Unfortunate, unprosperous, unhappy.
Improvidamente, *ad.* Improvidently.
Improvidéncia, *sf.* Improvidence.
Impróvido, da, *a.* Improvident, wanting forecast, wanting care to provide.
Improvisamente, *ad.* Unexpectedly, improvidently.
Improviso, sa; ó Imprevísto, ta, *a.* Unexpected, unforeseen, not provided against. *De improviso ó á la imprevista,* Unexpectedly, on a sudden. [dence, indiscretion.
Imprudéncia, *sf.* Imprudence, want of pru-
Imprudénte, *a.* Imprudent, indiscreet.
Imprudentemente, *ad.* Imprudently.
Impudicamente, *ad.* Lewdly, impudently.
Impudicícia, *sf.* Unchastity, lewdness, incontinence.
Impúdico, ca, *a.* 1. Unchaste, lewd. 2. Impudent, shameless.
Impuésto, *sm.* Tax, impost, duty.—*p.* Imposed.
Impugnáble, *a.* That which may be impugned.
Impugnación, *sf.* Opposition, contradiction, refutation.

Impugnadór, ra, *s.* One who refutes, or contradicts; impugner. [
Impugnár, *va.* To impugn, to contradict,
Impugnatívo, va, *a.* Impugning.
Impulsár, *va.* To impel, to give an impulse, urge on.
Impulsión, *sf.* 1. Impulsion, impulse, communicated force; effect of one body acting upon another. 2. Influence acting upon mind, motive.
Impulsívo, va, *a.* Impulsive.
Impúlso, *sm.* Impulse.
Impulsór, ra, *s.* Impeller. [nished.
Impúne, *a.* Exempt from punishment, unpu-
Impunemente, *ad.* With impunity.
Impunidád, *sf.* Impunity, freedom from punishment.
Impuréza, *sf.* 1. Impurity, want of purity; dishonesty. 2. Infection of the blood, arising from the admixture of bad humours.
Impuridád, *sf.* Impurity. V. *Impureza.*
Impúro, ra, *a.* Impure, foul.
Imposición, *sf.* (Ant.) V. *Imposicion.*
Imputáble, *a.* Imputable, chargeable.
Imputabilidád, *sf.* Imputableness.
Imputación, *sf.* Imputation, attribution of any thing; generally of ill.
Imputadór, ra, *s.* Imputer.
Imputár, *va.* To impute, to charge upon, to attribute; generally ill.
In, *prep. lat.* Used only in composition, where it has generally a negative signification, as *incapaz,* incapable.
Inacabáble, *a.* Interminable, that cannot be brought to an end.
Inaccesibilidád, *sf.* The state or quality of being inaccessible.
Inaccesíble, *a.* Inaccessible, not to be reached, not to be approached.
Inaccesiblemente, *ad.* Inaccessibly.
Inaccéso, sa, *a.* Inaccessible.
Inacción, *sf.* Inaction, cessation from labour, forbearance of labour.
Inadaptáble, *a.* Not capable of adoption.
Inadequádo, da, *a.* Inadequate.
Inadmisíble, *a.* Inadmissible.
Inadverténcia, *sf.* Inadvertence, carelessness, inattention.
Inadvertidamente, *ad.* Inadvertently.
Inadvertído, da, *a.* 1. Inadvertent, inconsiderate, careless. 2. Unseen, unnoticed.
Inafectádo, da, *a.* Natural, free from affectation. [alienated.
Inagenáble, *a.* Inalienable, that cannot be
Inagotáble, *a.* 1. Inexhaustible, not possible to be emptied. 2. Unexhausted; applied to the powers of the mind. [be borne.
Inaguantáble, *a.* Insupportable, that cannot
Inalienáble, *a.* Inalienable.
Inalteráble, *a.* That cannot be altered.
Inalterablemente, *ad.* Unalterably.
Inalterabilidád, *sf.* Immutability, stability.
Inalterádo, da, *a.* Unchanged, stable.
Inamisíble, *a.* Inamissible, not to be lost.
Ináne, *a.* Empty, void, inane.
Inanición, *sf.* Inanition, emptiness of a body; want of fulness in the vessels of an animal.
Inanimádo, da, *a.* Inanimate, void of life; without animation.

Inapagáble, a. Inextinguishable, unquenchable.

Inaperáble, a. 1. That cannot be lowered or levelled. 2. Incomprehensible, inconceivable. 3. Obstinate, stubborn, fixed in opinion or resolution.

Inapelábel, a. Without appeal, not admitting appeal.

Inapetáncia, sf. Want of appetite or desire of food.

Inapeténte, a. 1. Having no appetite or desire of food. 2. Disgusted.

Inaplicáble, a. Inapplicable.

Inaplicación, sf. Indolence, want of application.

Inaplicádo, da, a. Indolent, careless, inactive.

Inapreciáble, a. Inestimable, invaluable, too valuable to be rated, transcending all price.

Inarticuládo, da, a. Inarticulate, not uttered with distinctness, like that of the syllables of human speech.

Inasequíble, a. That which cannot be followed.

Inaudíto, ta, a. Unheard of, strange.

Inauguración, sf. 1. Inauguration, investiture by solemnities. 2. Auguration, the practice of augury.

Inaugurál, a. Inaugural.

Inaugurár, va. 1. To divine by the flight of birds. 2. To inaugurate, to invest with a new office by solemnities.

Inaveriguáble, a. That cannot be ascertained, that cannot be easily proved.

Inbár, sf. A sort of stuff which comes from Cairo.

Incalár, va. (Ant.) V. *Pertenecer.*

Incansáble, a. Indefatigable, unwearied, not exhaustible by labour.

Incansablemente, ad. Indefatigably.

Incantáble, a. That cannot be sung.

Incantación, sf. (Ant.) V. *Encanto.*

Incapacidád, sf. 1. Incapacity, inability, want of power or strength of body, want of comprehensiveness of mind. 2. Want of legal qualifications.

Incapáz, a. Incapable, wanting power, wanting understanding, unable to comprehend, learn, or understand; want of talent. *Incapaz de sacramentos,* (Fam.) Applied to a very weak silly person.

Incardinación, sf. Administration without property.

Incasáble, a. Unfit for marriage.

Incásto, ta, a. Unchaste, dishonest, impure.

Incatólico, ca, a. Uncatholic; one who does not profess the Roman catholic religion.

Incautaménte, ad. Unwarily.

Incáuto, ta, a. Incautious, unwary, heedless.

Incendiár, va. To kindle, to set on fire, to inflame.

Incendiário, ria, s. Incendiary, one who sets houses or towns on fire in malice or for robbery.

Incéndio, sm. 1. Fire, conflagration. 2. Inflammation, the act of setting on flame; the state of being in flame.

Incendióso, sa, a. Fiery, igneous.

Incensación, sf. The act of perfuming with incense.

Incensár, va. 1. To perfume, to offer incense on the altar. 2. To bestow fulsome praise or adulation. 3. To run up and down, to go here and there.

Incensário, sm. Incensory, the vessel in which incense is burnt and offered.

Incensór, ra, a. (Ant.) V. *Incendiario.*

Incensuráble, a. Unblamable, not culpable.

Incentívo, sm. 1. Incentive, that which kindles. 2. Incitement, that which provokes; spur; that which encourages.

Incepción, sf. V. *Principio.*

Inceptór, sm. Beginner, he that commences any thing.

Incertidúmbre, sf. Incertitude, uncertainty.

Incertitúd ó Incertéza, sf. (Ant.) V. *Incertidumbre.*

Incesáble ó Incesánte, a. Incessant, without intermission.

Incesableménte, ad. Incessantly.

Incesanteménte, ad. Incessantly, continually.

Incestár, va. To commit incest.

Incésto, sm. Incest, an unnatural and criminal connexion of persons of a different sex within degrees prohibited.

Incestuosaménte, ad. Incestuously.

Incestuóso, sa, a. Incestuous, that which belongs to incest.

Incidéncia, sf. 1. Incidence, or incidency; an accident, hap, casualty. 2. The direction with which one body strikes upon another.

Incidénte ó Incidentál, a. Incident, casual, incidental.

Incidénte, sm. 1. Incident, hap, accident. 2. Something happening besides the main design.

Incidenteménte, ad. Incidentally.

Incidír, vn. To happen, to befal.

Inciénso, sm. 1. Incense, an aromatic gum used in religious functions to perfume the altar. 2. Peculiar reverence and veneration paid to a person. 3. Court paid to a person out of flattery or interested views. *Incienso hembra,* Impure frankincense, that which is obtained by incision. *Incienso macho,* Pure frankincense, that which flows from the trees spontaneously.

Inciénte, a. (Ant.) Ignorant.

Inciertaménte, ad. Uncertainly.

Inciérto, ta, a. 1. Uncertain, doubtful. 2. Unstable, inconstant; unknown.

Incindénte, a. Cutting, that which cuts.

Incineración, sf. Incineration, the act of burning any thing to ashes.

Incinerár, va. To burn to ashes.

Incipiénte, a. Beginning, that which commences.

Incircuncíso, sa, a. Uncircumcised, not circumcised.

Incircunscrípto, ta, a. Uncircumscribed.

Incisión, sf. 1. Incision, a cut; a wound made with a sharp instrument. 2. V. *Cesura.*

Incisívo, va, a. Incisive.

Incíso, sm. Comma. V. *Coma.*

Incíso, sa, a. Cut. V. *Cortado.*

Incisóres, sm. pl. Incisors, cutters, teeth in the forepart of the mouth.

Incisório, ria, a. Incisory, that which cuts.

Incitación, sf. Incitation, incitement.

Incitadór, ra, s. Instigator, one who incites.

Incitaménto ó Incitamiénto, sm. Incitement, impulse, inciting power.

Incitár, va. To incite, to excite, to spur, to stimulate.

Incitatíva, sf. (For.) Writ from a superior tribunal to the common judges that justice may be administered.

Incitatívo, va, a. Incentive.

Incivíl, *a.* Uncivil, unpolished.
Incivilidád, *sf.* Incivility, rudeness.
Incivilménte, *ad.* Uncivilly, rudely.
Incleméncia, *sf.* 1. Harshness, rigour, unmercifulness. 2. Inclemency of the weather. *A' la inclemencia*, Openly, without shelter.
Incleménte, *a.* Inclement.
Inclinación, *sf.* 1. Inclination, the act of inclining and the state of being inclined. 2. Love, affection. 3. Disposition of the mind. 4. Tendency towards any point. 5. (In Pharmacy) Inclination, the operation by which a clear liquor is poured out by gently sloping the vessel.
Inclinadór, ra, *s.* One who inclines.
Inclinánte, *a.* Inclinatory, inclining.
Inclinár, *va.* 1. To incline, to bend; to give a tendency or direction. 2. To turn the desire towards any thing.—*vn.* To resemble.—*vr.* 1. To be favourably disposed to. 2. To bend the body, to bow. 3. To have a particular reason to follow some opinion or do something.
Inclinatívo, va, *a.* Inclinatory.
I'nclito, ta, *a.* Famous, renowned, conspicuous, illustrious.
Incluír, *va.* 1. To include, to comprise; to comprehend. 2. To allow one a share in a business.
Inclúsa, *sf.* Foundling-hospital.
Incluséro, ra, *s.* y *a.* Foundling; enclosed.
Inclusión, *sf.* 1. Inclusion, the act of enclosing or containing a thing. 2. Easy access, familiar intercourse.
Inclusivaménte é Inclusíve, *ad.* Inclusively.
Inclusívo, va, *a.* Inclusive.
Inclúso, sa, *a.* Enclosed.
Incluyénte, *pa.* Including.
Incoádo, da, *a.* Begun, commenced.
Incoár, *va.* To commence, to begin.
Incoatívo, va, *a.* Inchoative, inceptive; noting inchoation or beginning.
Incobrábl, *a.* Irrecoverable, irretrievable.
Incógnito, ta, *a.* Unknown. *De incógnito*, Incog.
Incognoscíble, *a.* Imperceptible, which cannot be perceived or known.
Incoherénte, *a.* Incoherent, inconsistent.
Incoheréncia, *sf.* Incoherence, want of connexion.
Incóla, *sm.* Inhabitant.
Incolumidád, *sf.* Incolumity, safety.
Incombustíble, *a.* Incombustible, not to be consumed by fire.
Incombústo, ta, *a.* Unburnt, not consumed by fire.
Incomerciáble, *a.* 1. Contraband, unlawful, prohibited; applied to objects or articles of trade. 2. Intractable, rude, harsh. 3. (Met.) Unpassable; applied to roads.
Incomodaménte, *ad.* Incommodiously.
Incomodár, *va.* To incommode.
Incomodidád, *sf.* 1. Incommodity, inconvenience, trouble. 2. (Naút.) Distress.
Incómodo, da, *a.* Incommodious, inconvenient.
Incomparáble, *a.* 1. Not to be acquired or purchased. 2. Incomparable.
Incomparableménte, *ad.* Incomparably.
Incomparádo, da, *a.* V. *Incomparable.*
Incompartíble, *a.* Indivisible, not to be divided into equal parts.
Incompasíble é Incompasívo, va, *a.* Incompassionate, void of pity.
Incompatibilidád, *sf.* Incompatibility, inconsistency.
Incompatíble, *a.* Incompatible.
Incompeténcia, *sf.* Incompetency, inability, want of adequate ability or qualification
Incompeténte, *a.* Incompetent; inconvenient.
Incompletaménte, *ad.* Incompletely.
Incompléto, ta, *a.* Incomplete.
Incompléxo, xa, *a.* Incomplex, simple.
Incomponíble, *a.* Incompoundable, not to be compounded together.
Incomportáble, *a.* Intolerable, unbearable.
Incomposibilidád, *sf.* Incompossibility.
Incomposíble, *a.* Incompossible.
Incomposición, *sf.* 1. Want of proportion, or defective composition. 2. V. *Descompostura.*
Incomprehensibilidád, *sf.* Incomprehensibility.
Incomprehensíble, *a.* 1. Incomprehensible, that cannot be comprehended or conceived. 2. Expressing thoughts in an obscure or confused manner.
Incompresíble, *a.* Incompressible.
Incompuestaménte, *ad.* (Ant.) Disorderly.
Incompuésto, ta, *a.* Simple, uncomposed; unadorned.
Incomunicabilidád, *sf.* Incommunicability.
Incomunicáble, *a.* Incommunicable, that cannot be communicated.
Inconceptíble, *a.* Inconceptible.
Inconcerniénte, *a.* Improper, unfit, unsuitable.
Inconcíno, na, *a.* Disordered, unhandsome.
Inconcusaménte, *ad.* Certainly, indubitably.
Inconcúso, sa, *a.* Incontrovertible, incontestable, not to be disputed, not admitting debate.
Inconducénte, *a.* Incongruous.
Inconnexión, *sf.* Want of connexion.
Inconéxo, xa, *a.* 1. Unconnected, incoherent. 2. Independent, not supported by any other.
Inconféso, sa, *a.* Unconfessed; applied to a criminal who does not confess his guilt.
Inconfidéncia, *sf.* 1. Distrust, mistrust, want of confidence. 2. Disloyalty, want of fidelity to the sovereign.
Incongruaménte, *ad.* Incongruously.
Incongruéncia, *sf.* Incongruence, want of symmetry or proportion.
Incongruénte, *a.* Incongruous.
Incongruenteménte, *ad.* Incongruously.
Incongruidád, *sf.* (Ant.) Incongruity.
Incóngruo, grua, *a.* Incongruous, disproportionate, unsuitable.
Inconmensuráble, *a.* Incommensurable, not to be reduced to any measure common to both.
Inconmutabilidád, *sf.* V. *Inmutabilidad.*
Inconmutáble, *a.* Incommutable; that cannot be exchanged, commuted, or bartered.
Inconquistáble, *a.* Unconquerable, impregnable, inexpugnable; invincible.
Inconseqüéncia, *sf.* Inconsequence, inconclusiveness, want of just inference.
Inconseqüénte, *a.* Inconsequent.
Inconsideración, *sf.* Inconsideration, want of thought, inattention, inadvertency.
Inconsideradaménte, *ad.* Inconsiderately.
Inconsiderádo, da, *a.* Inconsiderate, thoughtless, inattentive, inadvertent.
Inconsiguiénte, *a.* Inconsequent, without just conclusion, without regular inference.
Inconsisténcia, *sf.* Inconsistency, inconstancy.
Inconsoláble, *a.* Inconsolable, not to be comforted.

Inconsolableménte, ad. Inconsolably.
Inconstáncia, sf. Inconstancy, fickleness, want of constancy and firmness.
Inconstánte, a. Inconstant, changeable.
Inconstanteménte, ad. Inconstantly.
Inconstruíble, a. 1. Whimsical, fantastical, fanciful, variable, fickle. 2. Obscure, unintelligible; difficult to be construed.
Inconsúlto, ta, a. Unadvised, indeliberate.
Inconsútil, a. Seamless, having no seam.
Incontáble, a. Innumerable.
Incontaminádo, da, a. Undefiled, unpolluted, not contaminated.
Incontestáble, a. 1. Incontestable, indisputable. 2. False, unjust, unlawful.
Incontinéncia, sf. Incontinence or incontinency, inability to restrain the appetites; unchastity. [ing unlawful pleasure.
Incontinénte, a. Incontinent, unchaste, indulg-
Incontinénte ó Incontinénti, ad. Instantly, immediately. [continently.
Incontinenteménte, ad. (Ant.) Instantly; in-
Incontrastáble, a. Insurmountable, irresistible, insuperable.
Incontratáble, a. V. *Intratable.* [putable.
Incontrovertíble, a. Incontrovertible, indis-
Inconvencíble, a. Inconvincible.
Inconvencíble, a. (Ant.) Inconvenient.
Inconveniéncia, sf. Inconvenience, incommodity, unfitness; incongruence.
Inconveniénte, a. Inconvenient, incommodious, troublesome.
Inconveniénte, sm. Difficulty, obstacle, obstruction, impediment. [tive.
Inconversáble, a. Unsociable, incommunica-
Inconvertíble, a. Inconvertible, that cannot be converted or changed.
Incórdio, sm. Bubo, a tumour in the groin.
Incorporáble, a. That cannot be incorporated.
Incorporación, sf. Incorporation, the act of uniting or being united in one mass.
Incorporál, a. Incorporeal.
Incorporalménte, ad. Incorporeally.
Incorporár, va. To incorporate, to unite in one mass.—vr. 1. To be incorporated or united in one mass or body; to be embodied. 2. *Incorporarse en la cama,* To sit up in bed. 3. (Naút.) To sail in company, to join the convoy. [ality.
Incorporeidád, sf. Incorporeity, immateri-
Incorpóreo, rea, a. Incorporeal, immaterial,
Incorpóro, sm. V. *Incorporacion.* [unembodied.
Incorrección, sf. Incorrectness, inaccuracy, want of correctness.
Incorregibilidád, sf. Incorrigibleness, hopeless depravity; badness beyond all means of
Incorregíble, a. Incorrigible. [amendment.
Incorrupción, sf. 1. Incorruption, incapacity of corruption. 2. Incorruptness, purity of manners, integrity, honesty.
Incorruptaménte, ad. Incorruptly.
Incorruptibilidád, sf. Incorruptibility, insusceptibility of corruption, incapacity of decay.
Incorruptíble, a. Incorruptible, not to be perverted.
Incorrúpto, ta, a. 1. Incorrupt or uncorrupted; free from foulness or depravation. 2. Pure of manners, honest, good, incorruptible. *Incorrupta,* A virgin.

Incrasár, va. To inspissate, to thicken, to incrassate; applied to humours.
Increádo, da, a. Uncreated, not created; an attribute peculiar to God.
Incredibilidád, sf. Incredibility, the quality of exceeding or surpassing belief.
Incredulidád, sf. Incredulity, hardness of belief; want of faith.
Incrédulo, la, a. Incredulous, hard of belief, refusing credit.
Increíble, a. Incredible, surpassing belief, not to be credited.
Increibleménte, ad. Incredibly.
Increménto, sm. Increment, increase; act of growing greater, cause of growing more.
Increpación, sf. Increpation, reprehension, chiding.
Increpadór, ra, s. Chider, rebuker; scold.
Increpár, va. To increpate, to chide, to reprehend, to scold.
Incruénto, ta, a. Unstained with blood.
Incrustación, sf. Incrustation.
Incrustár, va. To incrust or incrustate, to cover with an additional coat.
Íncubo, sm. Incubus, the night-mare: a morbid oppression in the night, resembling the pressure of a weight upon the breast.
Inculcación, sf. (Impr.) Act of binding or wedging in a form.
Inculcár, va. 1. To inculcate, to impress by frequent admonitions. 2. To make one thing tight against another. 3. (Impr.) To lock up types.—vr. To be obstinate, to conform one's self in an opinion or sentiment.
Inculpáble, a. Inculpable, unblameable
Inculpableménte, ad. Inculpably.
Inculpadaménte, ad. Faultlessly.
Inculpádo, da, a. Faultless.
Inculpár, va. To accuse, to blame.
Incultaménte, ad. Rudely, without culture.
Incultiváble, a. Incapable of cultivation.
Incúlto, ta, a. 1. Incult, uncultivated, untilled. 2. Uncivilized, unpolished, unrefined.
Incultúra, sf. Want of culture.
Incumbéncia, sf. Duty imposed upon a person: incumbency.
Incumbír, vn. To be incumbent upon any one, to have any thing imposed as a duty.
Incuráble, a. Incurable, not admitting remedy; irremediable, hopeless.
Incúria, sf. Negligence, indolence.
Incurióso, sa, a. Negligent, indolent.
Incurrimiénto, sm. Act of incurring.
Incurrír, vn. To incur, to become liable to punishment or reprehension; to deserve.
Incursión, sf. 1. Incursion, the act of incurring. 2. Incursion without conquest, the act of overrunning an enemy's country.
Incúrso, sm. Attack, incursion.
Incusár, va. To accuse. V. *Acusar.*
Indáble, a. That cannot be given or granted.
Indagación, sf. Indagation, search, inquiry, examination. [gator.
Indagadór, ra, s. Investigater, inquirer, inda-
Indagár, va. To search, to inquire, to examine into; to investigate.
Indebidaménte, ad. Unjustly, illegally.
Indebído, da, a. Undue, illegal, unlawful, void of equity and moderation.

INDECÉNCIA, *sf.* Indecency, any thing unbecoming, any thing contrary to good manners.
INDECÉNTE, *a.* Indecent, dishonest, unbecoming.
INDECENTEMÉNTE, *ad.* Indecently.
INDECÍBLE, *a.* Inexpressible, unutterable.
INDECIBLEMÉNTE, *ad.* Inexpressibly.
INDECISIÓN, *sf.* Irresolution, want of firmness of mind.
INDECÍSO, SA, *a.* Irresolute, not constant in purpose, not determined, undecided.
INDECLINÁBLE, *a.* 1. Incapable of a decline or decay, firm, unshaken. 2. (In Grammar) Indeclinable, not varied by terminations.
INDECÓRO, *sm.* Indecorum, indecency.
INDECOROSAMÉNTE, *ad.* Indecorously.
INDECORÓSO, SA, *a.* Indecorous, indecent, unbecoming.
INDEFECTIBILIDÁD, *sf.* Indefectibility, quality of suffering no decay or defect.
INDEFECTÍBLE, *a.* INDEFECTIBLE.
INDEFECTIBLEMÉNTE, *ad.* Indefectibly.
INDEFENSÁBLE, *a.* Indefensible.
INDEFÉNSO, SA, *a.* Defenceless, destitute of defence.
INDEFICIÉNTE, *a.* Indefectible, unfailing; that which cannot fail.
INDEFINÍBLE, *a.* Indefinable, that cannot be defined.
INDEFINÍDO, DA, *a.* 1. Indefinite, that which is not defined. 2. Not determined, not settled. 3. Large beyond the comprehension of man.
INDEFÍNITO, TA, *a.* INDEFINITE.
INDELÉBLE, *a.* Indelible, not to be blotted out.
INDELEBLEMÉNTE, *ad.* Indelibly.
INDELIBERACIÓN, *sf.* 1. Indetermination, irresolution. 2. Inadvertency, want of attention.
INDELIBERADAMÉNTE, *ad.* Inadvertently.
INDELIBERÁDO, DA, *a.* Indeliberate, unpremeditated; done without sufficient consideration.
INDÉMNE, *a.* Undamaged, unhurt.
INDEMNIDÁD, *sf.* Indemnity, exemption from damage or hurt.
INDEMNIZACIÓN, *sf.* Indemnification, reimbursement of loss or penalty.
INDEMNIZÁR, *va.* To indemnify, to secure against loss; to maintain unhurt.
INDEPENDÉNCIA, *sf.* Independence or independency, freedom from reliance or control.
INDEPENDÉNTE ó INDEPENDIÉNTE, *a.* Independent, not supported by any other, not relying on another, uncontrolled. *Independiente de eso*, Independent of that, besides that.
INDEPENDENTEMÉNTE ó INDEPENDIENTEMÉNTE, *ad.* Independently.
INDESCRIBÍBLE, *a.* Indescribable.
INDESIGNÁBLE, *a.* That which cannot be designed.
INDESTRUCTÍBLE, *a.* Indestructible, that cannot be destroyed.
INDESTRUCTIBILIDÁD, *sf.* Indestructibility, impossibility of being annihilated.
INDETERMINÁBLE, *a.* INDETERMINABLE, that cannot be determined or fixed; doubtful.
INDETERMINACIÓN, *sf.* Indetermination, irresolution; want of determination or resolution.
INDETERMINADAMÉNTE, *ad.* Indeterminately.
INDETERMINÁDO, DA, *a.* 1. Indeterminate, unfixed, not defined. 2. Irresolute, doubtful. 3. Pusillanimous, chicken-hearted. 4. Indefinite.
INDEVOCIÓN, *sf.* Indevotion, want of devotion.
INDEVÓTO, TA, *a.* Indevout, irreligious.
I'NDEX, *s.* Index. V. *Indice. Conservacion del index*, Commission appointed at Rome, under the papal government, to examine into the contents of books.
I'NDIA, *sf.* (Met.) Great wealth, abundance of money and other precious things.
INDIÁNA, *sf.* Chints, printed cotton.
INDIANIZÁR, *va.* To speak like Indians.
INDIÁNO, *sm.* 1. One who has resided in India. 2. Nabob, one who has acquired great wealth in India.
INDICACIÓN, *sf.* Indication, mark, token sign, symptom.
INDICÁNTE, *sm.* Symptom, mark, sign.
INDICÁR, *va.* 1. To indicate, to show. 2. (In Physic) To point out a remedy.
INDICATÍVO, VA, *a.* 1. Indicative, pointing. 2. (Gram.) Mode used in affirming.
INDICCIÓN, *sf.* Indiction, the convening of a synod, council, or in general a public assembly. *Indiccion Romana*, Roman indiction; a manner of computing time, introduced by Constantine the Great, which extends to a cycle of 15 years, and when finished they begin again.
I'NDICE, *s.* 1. Mark, sign. 2. Hand of a watch or clock. 3. Pin that casts the shade on a sun-dial. 4. Table of contents to a book, index. 5. Forefinger.
I'NDICE EXPURGATÓRIO, *sm.* Catalogue of books prohibited or ordered to be corrected by the Inquisition.
INDICIÁDO, DO, *a.* Suspicious, liable to suspicion; giving reason to imagine ill.
INDICIADÓR, RA, *s.* 1. One who entertains suspicions. 2. Informer, one who discovers offenders to the magistrates.
INDICIÁR, *va.* 1. To give reasons to suspect or surmise. 2. To discover offenders to the magistrates. V. *Indicar.*
INDÍCIO, *sm.* Indication, mark, sign, token: any thing from which inferences are drawn.
I'NDICO, *sm.* INDIGO. V. *Añil.*
I'NDICO, CA, *a.* Indian.
INDÍCULO, *sm.* A short index.
INDIÉSTRO, TRA, *a.* Awkward, unhandy, clumsy; unskilful.
INDIFERÉNCIA, *sf.* 1. Indifference, a state of the mind in which no moral or physical reason preponderates. 2. Neglect, unconcern, want of affection, coolness. 3. Neutrality, suspension; equipoise or freedom from motives on either side.
INDIFERÉNTE, *a.* 1. Indifferent, neutral; not determined to either side. 2. Unconcerned, inattentive, regardless.
INDIFERENTEMÉNTE, *ad.* Indifferently.
INDIGÉNA, *a.* Indigenous, native.
INDIGÉNCIA, *sf.* Indigence, want, penury, poverty.
INDIGÉNTE, *a.* Indigent, necessitous, poor
INDIGESTÍBLE, *a.* Indigestible, not soluble in the stomach.
INDIGESTIÓN, *sf.* 1. Indigestion, the state of meats or other viands inconcocted. 2. Rudeness of temper, ill-nature.
INDIGÉSTO, TA, *a.* 1. Indigest, or indigested, not concocted in the stomach. 2. Confused, not separated into distinct parts. 3. Rude, ill-natured.
INDIGÉTE, *sm.* Indigite, native demi-god or hero of antiquity.
INDIGNACIÓN, *sf.* Indignation, anger mingled with contempt or disgust.

Indignaménte, *ad.* Unworthily.

Indignánte, *pa.* Indignant, irritating.

Indignár, *va.* To irritate, to provoke, to tease. —*vr.* 1. To be inflamed with anger and disdain, to become angry or indignant. 2. To be inflamed; applied to a wound.

Indignidád, *sf.* 1. Indignity, want of merit, want of the necessary qualities for obtaining some end. 2. Meanness. 3. Indignation, passion.

Indígno, na, *a.* 1. Unworthy, undeserving. 2. Incongruous, unsuitable. 3. Vile, mean, despicable.

Indiligéncia, *sf.* Want of diligence, carelessness.

I'ndio, dia, *s.* A native of India.

I'ndio, ia, *a.* Of a blue colour, azure. ¿ *Sómos indios ?* (Fam.) A retort to any one who wishes to deceive or delude.

Indirécta, *sf.* Innuendo, an oblique hint. *Indirecta del P. Cobos,* A broad hint.

Indirectaménte ó Indirécte, *ad.* Indirectly.

Indirécto, ta, *a.* Indirect, not tending otherwise than collaterally and consequentially to a point.

Indiscerníble, *a.* Indiscernible, inconspicuous.

Indisciplína, *sf.* Want of discipline or subordination.

Indisciplináble, *a.* Incapable of instruction, subordination, or discipline.

Indisciplinádo, da, *a.* Untaught, undisciplined.

Indiscreción, *sf.* Indiscretion, imprudence, rashness, inconsideration.

Indiscretaménte, *ad.* Indiscreetly.

Indiscréto, ta, *a.* Indiscreet, imprudent, incautious; inordinate.

Indisculpáble, *a.* Inexcusable, not to be excused.

Indisolubilidád, *sf.* Indissolubility.

Indisolúble, *a.* Indissoluble, not separable as to its parts.

Indisolubleménte, *ad.* Indissolubly.

Indispensáble, *a.* Indispensable, that cannot be dispensed with.

Indispensableménte, *ad.* Indispensably.

Indisponér, *va.* To disable, to indispose, to render unfit.—*vr.* 1. To be indisposed, to grow ill, to be out of order. 2. To be peevish or fretful.

Indisposición, *sf.* Indisposition; slight disorder.

Indisposicioncílla, *sf.* Slight indisposition.

Indispuésto, ta, *a.* Indisposed, disordered with regard to health.

Indisputáble, *a.* Indisputable, incontrovertible; that admits no doubt.

Indisputableménte, *ad.* Indisputably.

Indistinción, *sf.* Indistinction, confusion.

Indistinguíble, *a.* Undistinguishable.

Indistintaménte, *ad.* Indistinctly.

Indistínto, ta, *a.* Indistinct, indiscriminate, that cannot be discerned from other things.

Individuación, *sf.* Individuation, that which makes an individual.

Individuál, *a.* Individual, separate from others of the same species, numerically one.

Individualidád ó Individuidád, *sf.* Individuality.

Individualizár, *va.* To specify individually, to individuate.

Individualménte, *ad.* Individually.

Individuaménte, *ad.* Individually, distinctly.

Individuidád, *sf.* Individuality.

Individuár, *va.* To individuate, to distinguish from others of the same species; to particularise, to detail.

Indivíduo, *sm.* Individual, a single particular person or thing.

Indivíduo, dua, *a.* Individual, single particular; indivisible, inseparable.

Indivisaménte, *ad.* Indivisibly.

Indivisibilidád, *sf.* Indivisibility, a state in which no more division can be made.

Indivisíble, *a.* Indivisible, that cannot be broken or separated into parts.

Indivisibleménte, *ad.* Inseparably.

Indivíso, sa, *a.* Undivided, not broken or separated into parts. *Pro indiviso,* (For.) Applied to an inheritance without partitions.

Indiyudicáble, *a.* Not to be judged.

I'ndo, *sm.* (Bot.) A kind of myrobalan.

Indócil, *a.* 1. Indocile, unteachable. 2. Inflexible, not to be prevailed upon.

Indocilidád, *sf.* 1. Indocility, refusal of instruction. 2. Inflexibility, stubbornness of mind.

Indócto, ta, *a.* Ignorant, uninstructed, unlearned.

Indoctrinádo, da, *a.* (Ant.) Uninstructed, ignorant.

I'ndole, *sf.* Disposition, temper, inclination, peculiar genius, idiosyncrasy.

Indoléncia, *sf.* Indolence, indifference, laziness; a state of insensibility of grief or pain.

Indolénte, *a.* Indolent, indifferent.

Indomáble ó Indomenáble, *a.* 1. Untameable, unmanageable; applied to wild animals. 2. Inflexible, unconquerable; applied to the passions.

Indomádo, da, *a.* Untamed.

Indomesticáble, *a.* Untameable, not to be tamed, not to be subdued or domesticated.

Indoméstico, ca, *a.* Untamed, fierce, intractable.

Indómito, ta, *a.* Untamed, ungoverned.

Indotación, *sf.* Loss of a wife's portion.

Indotádo, da, *a.* 1. Unendowed, wanting endowments or talents. 2. Having lost her portion, portionless; applied to a married woman.

Indubitáble, *a.* Indubitable, unquestioned, certain.

Indubitableménte, *ad.* Undoubtedly.

Indubitádo, da, *a.* (Ant.) Undoubted.

Inducción, *sf.* 1. Induction, inducement, persuasion. 2. Induction, the act of inferring a general proposition from several particular ones.

Inducidór, ra, *s.* Inducer, persuader.

Inducimiénto, *sm.* Inducement, motive to any thing, that which allures or persuades to any thing.

Inducír, *va.* To induce, to persuade, to influence; (Ant.) To cause, to occasion.

Inductívo, va, *a.* Inductive.

Indulgéncia, *sf.* 1. Indulgence, forbearance, tenderness; opposite to rigour. 2. Fond kindness. 3. Favour or indulgence granted by the pope, as head of the Roman catholic church.

Indulgénte, *a.* Indulgent, kind, mild, gentle.

Indultár, *va.* 1. To pardon, to forgive. 2. To free, to exempt.

Indultário, *sm.* He who in virtue of a pontifical privilege can dispense ecclesiastical benefices.

Indúlto, *sm.* 1. Pardon, forgiveness, amnesty. 2. Indult, privilege, exemption. 3. Impost, tax, or duty imposed on merchandise imported into Spain.

Induménto, *sm.* Wearing apparel.

Induración, *sf.* (Med.) Induration, hardening; applied to wounds. V. *Endurecimiento.*

INDÚSTRIA, *sf.* 1. Industry, diligence, assiduity. 2. Ingenuity, subtilty, acuteness. *De Indústria*, Designedly, purposely, intentionally.

INDUSTRIÁL, *a.* Belonging to industry.

INDUSTRIÁR, *va.* To teach, to instruct.

INDUSTRIOSAMÉNTE, *ad.* 1. Industriously. 2. Designedly.

INDUSTRIÓSO, SA, *a.* 1. Industrious, skilful, dexterous. 2. Subtle, crafty, cunning.

INEBRIÁR, *va.* 1. (Ant.) To inebriate, to make drunk. 2. (Met.) To intoxicate; applied to violent commotions of the mind.

INEBRIATÍVO, VA, *a.* Inebriating.

INÉDIA, *sf.* Fast, abstinence from food.

INÉDITO, TA, *a.* Not published, unedited.

INEFABILIDÁD, *sf.* Ineffability, unspeakableness; impossibility of being explained.

INEFÁBLE, *a.* Ineffable, unspeakable.

INEFABLEMÉNTE, *ad.* Ineffably.

INEFICÁCIA, *sf.* Inefficacy, want of power, want of effort.

INEFICÁZ, *a.* Inefficacious, unable to produce effects; weak.

INEFICAZMÉNTE, *ad.* Inefficaciously.

INEGUÁL, *a.* (Ant.) V. *Desigual.*

INELEGÁNTE, *a.* Inelegant.

INENARRÁBLE, *a.* Inexplicable, incapable of being explained.

INÉPCIA, *sf.* Ineptitude, unfitness, imbecility.

INEPTAMÉNTE, *ad.* Unfitly, ineptly.

INEPTITÚD, *sf.* Ineptitude, inability.

INÉPTO, TA, *a.* Inept, unfit, useless.

INÉRCIA, *sf.* Dullness, inactivity, indolence.

INÉRME, *a.* Disarmed, without arms.

INERRÁBLE, *a.* Inerrable, exempt from error.

INERRÁNCIA, *sf.* Unerrableness, infallibility.

INERRÁNTE, *a.* Fixed; applied to the stars.

INÉRTE, *a.* 1. Inert, dull, sluggish. 2. Unskilful, wanting art, wanting knowledge.

INESCRUTÁBLE, *a.* Inscrutable, unsearchable; not to be traced out by inquiry or study.

INESCUDRIÑÁBLE, *a.* Inscrutable.

INESPERADAMÉNTE, *ad.* Unexpectedly.

INESPERÁDO, DA, *a.* Unexpectedly, unforeseen.

INESTIMABILIDÁD, *sf.* Inestimableness.

INESTIMÁBLE, *a.* Inestimable, too valuable to be rated, exceeding all price.

INESTIMÁDO, DA, *a.* That which is without price.

INEVITÁBLE, *a.* Inevitable, unavoidable.

INEVITABLEMÉNTE, *ad.* Inevitably.

INEXCUSÁBLE, *a.* 1. Inexcusable, not to be palliated by apology. 2. Inevitable, indispensable, not to be dispensed with.

INEXCUSABLEMÉNTE, *ad.* Inexcusably.

INEXHÁUSTO, TA, *a.* 1. Unexhausted, unemptied, unspent. 2. Full, abundant, plentiful.

INEXISTÉNCIA, *sf.* Existence of one thing in another.

INEXISTÉNTE, *a.* Existent.

INEXORÁBLE, *a.* Inexorable, not to be moved by entreaty.

INEXPERIÉNCIA, *sf.* Inexperience, want of experimental knowledge.

INEXPÉRTO, TA, *a.* Inexpert, unskilful.

INEXPIÁBLE, *a.* Inexpiable, not to be atoned; not to be mollified by atonement.

INEXPLICÁBLE, *a.* Inexplicable, not to be explained.

INEXPUGNÁBLE, *a.* 1. Inexpugnable, impregnable; not to be subdued. 2. Firm, constant.

INEXTINGUÍBLE, *a.* Inextinguishable, unquenchable; perpetual.

INEXTRICÁBLE, *a.* Inextricable, not to be disentangled, not to be cleared.

INFACÉTO, TA, *a.* Dull, unpleasant, graceless.

INFACTÍBLE, *a.* Infeasible, impracticable; that cannot be done.

INFACÚNDO, DA, *a.* Ineloquent, not persuasive, not oratorical.

INFALIBILIDÁD, *sf.* Infallibility.

INFALÍBLE, *a.* Infallible, privileged from error, incapable of mistake.

INFALIBLEMÉNTE, *ad.* Infallibly.

INFAMACIÓN, *sf.* Slander, calumny; the defaming or injuring the reputation of another.

INFAMADÓR, RA, *s.* Defamer, one that injures the reputation of another.

INFAMÁR, *va.* To defame, to make infamous, to deprive of honour, to dishonour by reports.

INFAMATÍVO, VA, *a.* That which defames.

INFAMATÓRIO, RIA, *a.* Defamatory.

INFÁME, *a.* Infamous, vile, despicable.

INFAMEMÉNTE, *ad.* Infamously, vilely.

INFÁMIA, *sf.* Infamy, dishonour, public reproach, notoriety of bad character.

INFÁNCIA, *sf.* 1. Infancy, the first part of life. 2. First age of any thing, beginning, original.

INFANCÍNO, *sm.* Oil made of green olives.

INFÁNDO, DA, *a.* Infamous, wicked, too bad to be mentioned.

INFÁNT, *sm.* V. *Infante.*

INFÁNTA, *sf.* 1. Infanta, a princess of the royal blood of Spain. 2. Child under seven years old

INFANTÁDO, *sm.* Territory or revenue assigned to a prince of the royal blood of Spain.

INFÁNTE, *s.* 1. Infant, a child under seven years of age. 2. Infante, a title given to all the sons of the king of Spain, except the heir apparent to the crown. 3. Mute letter.—*pl.* 1. Choristers, boys brought up to sing in some cathedral churches. 2. Foot-soldiers.

INFANTERÍA, *sf.* Infantry, a body of foot-soldiers.

INFANTICÍDA, *sm.* Murderer of an infant.

INFANTICÍDIO, *sm.* Infanticide, the murder of a child or infant.

INFANTÍCO, CA; LLO, LLA; TO, TA, *s. dim.* of *Infante, ta.*

INFANTÍL, *a.* Infantile.

INFANZÓN, *sm.* (Arag.) Nobleman.

INFANZONÁDO, DA, *a.* Pertaining to a noble.

INFANZONÁZGO, *sm.* Territory of a nobleman.

INFANZONÍA, *sf.* (Arag.) Nobility.

INFATIGÁBLE, *a.* Indefatigable, unwearied, untired, unexhausted by labour.

INFATIGABLEMÉNTE, *ad.* Indefatigably.

INFATUÁR, *va.* To infatuate, to strike with folly, to deprive of understanding.

INFAUSTAMÉNTE, *ad.* Unluckily.

INFÁUSTO, TA, *a.* Unlucky, unhappy, unfortunate.

INFECCIÓN, *sf.* Infection, contagion; mischief by communication.

INFECÍR, *va.* V. *Inficionar.*

INFECTÁR, *va.* To infect, to hurt by contagion.

INFECTÍVO, VA, *a.* Infective.

INFÉCTO, TA, *a.* Infected, tainted.

INFECUNDÁRSE, *vr.* To become sterile.

INFECUNDIDÁD, *sf.* Infecundity, sterility.

INFECÚNDO, DA, *a.* Barren, unfruitful.

INFELICIDÁD, *sf.* Misfortune, calamity, disgrace.

INFELÍZ, a. Unhappy, unfortunate; weak, inert.
INFELIZMÉNTE, ad. Unhappily.
INFERÉNCIA, sf. Inference, illation.
INFERIÓR, a. Inferior, subordinate, subject.
INFERIORIDÁD, sf. Inferiority, subjection.
INFERÍR, va. To infer, to deduce by ratiocination.
INFERNÁCULO, sm. A kind of boyish play.
INFERNÁL, a. 1. Infernal, hellish, tartarean. 2. Extremely hurtful or prejudicial.
INFERNÁR, va. 1. To damn, to doom to eternal torments. 2. To tease, to vex, to provoke.
INFÉRNO, NA; ó I'NFERO, RA, a. (Poét.) Infernal.
INFESTACIÓN, sf. Act of harassing, annoyance.
INFESTÁR, va. To infest, to harass, to plague; to annoy the enemy.
INFÉSTO, TA, a. Prejudicial, dangerous.
INFEUDÁR, va. V. *Enfeudar*.
INFICIÓN, sf. Infection. V. *Infeccion*.
INFICIONÁR, va. 1. To infect, to hurt by contagion. 2. To defile the honours of a noble descent, to taint the purity of noble blood; to vitiate.
INFIDELIDÁD, sf. 1. Infidelity, treachery, deceit. 2. Want of faith, disbelief of Christianity. 3. The whole body of infidels.
INFIDÉNCIA, sf. Unfaithfulness.
INFIDÉNTE, a. Unfaithful.
INFIDÉL ó INFÍDO, DA, a. V. *Infiel*.
INFIÉL, a. Unfaithful, infidel, disloyal; pagan.
INFIELMÉNTE, ad. Unfaithfully.
INFIÉRNO, sm. 1. Hell, the place of the devil and wicked souls; torment of the wicked, limbo. 2. Any thing which causes confusion, pain, or trouble; discord, dispute. 3. Refectory or eating room in a convent, where the sick, strangers, or servants, take their meals. 4. A large retort or other chemical vessel. 5. Place under ground where the machinery and movement of a horse-mill are seen and felt.
INFIGURÁBLE, a. That which cannot be represented by any figure.
INFILTRACIÓN, sf. Infiltration.
INFILTRÁRSE, vr. To infiltrate, to insinuate into by filtration.
I'NFIMO, MA, a. 1. Lowest, most inferior; the least. 2. Abject, vile, low bred.
INFINGIDÓR, RA, s. (Ant.) Dissembler.
INFINIDÁD, sf. 1. Infinity, immensity, boundlessness. 2. Endless number.
INFINITAMÉNTE, ad. Infinitely.
INFINITESIMÁL, a. (Mat.) Infinitesimal; applied to fluxions.
INFINITÍSIMO, MA, a. sup. (Fam.) Most infinite.
INFINITÍVO, sm. (Gram.) Infinitive, one of the moods in the conjugation of verbs, which does not denote any determinate time.
INFINÍTO, TA, a. Infinite, unbounded, unlimited, immense; very numerous, excessive.
INFINÍTO, ad. Infinitely, immensely.
INFINTÓSO, SA, a. (Ant.) Feigned, simulated.
INFIRMÁR, va. To infirm, to weaken, to shake.
INFLACIÓN, sf. 1. Inflation, the state of being swelled with wind; flatulence. 2. Vanity, haughtiness, vain-gloriousness.
INFLAMÁBLE, a. Inflammable, easy to be set on flame.
INFLAMACIÓN, sf. 1. Inflammation, the act of setting on flame; the state of being in flame. 2. (Cir.) Inflammation, a tumour attended with preternatural heat arising from the blood.
INFLAMÁR, va. 1. To inflame, to kindle, to set on fire. 2. To inflame, to kindle desire.—vr. To become red, to be inflamed or heated.
INFLAMATÓRIO, RIA, a. Inflammatory.
INFLÁR, va. 1. To inflate, to swell with wind. 2. (Met.) To elate, to puff up with pride.
INFLATÍVO, VA, a. That which inflates.
INFLEXIBILIDÁD, sf. Inflexibility, stiffness; quality of resisting flexure; constancy.
INFLEXÍBLE, a. 1. Inflexible, not to be bent. 2. Not to be prevailed upon, immoveable.
INFLEXIBLEMÉNTE, ad. Inflexibly.
INFLEXIÓN, sf. 1. Inflection, the act of bending or turning. 2. Variation of a noun or verb. 3. Modulation of the voice.
INFLICTÍVO, VA, a. Inflictive, used as punishment.
INFLIGÍR, va (Ant.) To inflict, to condemn.
INFLUÉNCIA, sf. 1. Influence, the power of the celestial bodies upon terrestrial bodies and affairs. 2. (Met.) Ascendant power, power of directing or satisfying. 3. (Met.) Inspiration of divine grace.
INFLUÍR, va. 1. To influence, to act upon with directive or impulsive power; to modify to any purpose; to prevail upon. 2. To interfere; to inspire with grace.
INFLÚXO, sm. Influx, influence, power.
INFORCIÁDO, sm. Second part of the digest or pandects of Justinian.
INFORMACIÓN, sf. 1. Information, intelligence given; instruction. 2. Information, charge, or accusation exhibited. 3. Judicial inquiry and process. 4. Brief, the writing given to the pleaders, containing the case.
INFORMADÓR, RA, s. (Ant.) Informer.
INFORMÁNTE, sm. One who is peculiarly charged to collect information respecting the descent and character of a person; instructor.
INFORMÁR, va. 1. To form, to model to a particular shape. 2. To inform, to instruct, to supply with intelligence or knowledge. 3. To state a case to a counsellor or judge.—vr. To take cognizance, to make an inquiry.
INFORMATÍVO, VA, a. Instructive, that which informs.
INFÓRME, sm. 1. Information, the act of communicating intelligence or imparting knowledge. 2. Brief. V. *Informacion*.
INFÓRME, a. 1. Informous, shapeless; of no regular figure. 2. Not performed in a proper and regular manner.
INFORMIDÁD, sf. Informity, shapelessness.
INFORTIFICÁBLE, a. That which cannot be fortified.
INFORTÚNA, sf. Sinistrous influence of the stars.
INFORTUNÁDO, DA, a. Unfortunate, unlucky, unhappy.
INFORTÚNIO, sm. Misfortune, ill luck, calamity.
INFOSÚRA, sf. Surfeit in cattle and other animals.
INFRACCIÓN, sf. 1. Infraction, the act of breaking. 2. Breach, violation of a compact; misdemeanor, trespass.
INFRÁCTO, TA, a. Steady, not easily moved.
INFRACTÓR, RA, s. One who violates a compact or law.
INFRAESCRÍTO, TA, a. Underwritten, undersigned; applied to names.
IN FRAGÁNTE, ad. V. *En fragante*.
INFRANGÍBLE, a. Infrangible, inviolable.
INFRAOCTÁVA, sf. Six days comprehended in any church festival of eight days, not counting the first and the last.

Infraoctávo, va, *a.* Applied to any of the six days within the eight day festival.
Infrucción, *sf.* V. *Infurcion.*
Infructiféro, ra, ó Infrugívero, ra, *a.* Unfruitful, not bearing or producing fruit; useless.
Infructuosaménte, *ad.* Unfruitfully.
Infructuóso, sa, *a.* Fruitless, unproductive, unprofitable.
Infrunito, ta, *a.* Torvous, sour of aspect; stern, severe of countenance.
I'nfulas, *sf. pl.* 1. Ornaments or marks of sacerdotal or pontifical dignity. 2. Expectation; presumption, ostentation.
Infundíble, *a.* Infusible, incapable of fusion.
Infundír, *va.* 1. To infuse, to pour liquor into a vessel. 2. To pour into the mind, to instil. 3. To introduce. 4. To steep in liquor, to soak.
Infurción ó Infulción, *sf.* Tribute paid in Spain to the lord of the manor for the ground of houses.
Infurcioniégo, ga, *a.* Subject to pay the ground-rent of a house.
Infuscár, *va.* (Ant.) To obscure.
Infusión, *sf.* 1. Infusion, the act of pouring in; instillation. 2. Liquor made by infusion. 3. Inspiration, the act of pouring into the mind; act of sprinkling water on the person baptized. *Estar en infusion para alguna cosa,* (Fam.) To be ready and disposed for any thing.
Infúso, sa, *a.* Infused, introduced; applied solely to the grace of God in the soul.
Ingenerável, *a.* Ingenerable, not to be produced or brought into being.
Ingeniár, *va.* To conceive, to contrive, to strike out.—*vr.* To work in the mind, to endeavour to find out.
Ingeniatúra, *sf.* Industry, diligence, assiduity.
Ingeniería, *sf.* Enginery, art of an engineer.
Ingeniéro, *sm.* 1. Contriver, inventor. 2. Engineer, he that plans and directs all works of military architecture. *Ingeniero hydraulico,* (Naút.) Shipwright, shipbuilder.
Ingénio, *sm.* 1. Genius, mental power or faculties. 2. A man endowed with superior faculties. 3. Engine, any mechanical complication in which various movements and parts concur to one effect. 4. Means, expedient, address, industry. 5. Plough, a tool used by bookbinders. *Ingenio de azúcar,* Sugar-work, sugar-mill. *Ingenio de pólvora,* Powder-mill.
Ingeniosaménte, *ad.* Ingeniously.
Ingeniosidád, *sf.* Ingenuity, invention.
Ingenióso, sa, *a.* Ingenious, inventive.
Ingénito, ta, *a.* 1. Unbegotten, not generated. 2. Innate, inborn, ingenerate.
Ingénte, *a.* Very large, huge, prodigious.
Ingenuaménte, *ad.* Ingenuously.
Ingenuidád, *sf.* Ingenuousness, candour.
Ingénuo, nua, *a.* 1. Ingenuous, open, candid. 2. Free-born, not of servile extraction.
Ingerír, *va.* To insert, to graft. V. *Enxerir.*
Ingína, *sf.* V. *Quixada.*
I'ngle, *sf.* Groin, the part next the thigh.
Inglés, sa, *a.* English, native of England. *A' la Inglesa,* In the English fashion.
Inglés, *sm.* English language.
Inglete, *sm.* Oblique line which divides a square into two triangles.
Inglosáble, *a.* That admits no gloss or comment.

Ingobernáble, *a.* Ungovernable, that cannot be governed.
Ingraduáble, *a.* That cannot be graduated.
Ingrataménte, *ad.* Ungratefully.
Ingratitúd, *sf.* Ingratitude, ungratefulness; retribution of evil for good.
Ingráto, ta, *a.* 1. Ungrateful, unthankful. 2. Harsh, disagreeable, unpleasing.
Ingrediénte, *sm.* Ingredient, a component part of a body, consisting of different materials.
Ingréso, *sm.* 1. Ingress, entrance, the power of entering. 2. Duty on imports, toll, customs. 3. Price of admittance. 4. Entry, a sum charged in accounts. 5. Foot of the altar.
Inguinário, ria, *a.* Inguinal, belonging to the groin.
Ingurgitación, *sf.* Ingurgitation.
Ingurgitár, *va.* To ingurgitate, to swallow.
Ingustáble, *a.* 1. Ingustable, not perceptible by the taste. 2. Tasteless, having no taste.
Inhábil, *a.* 1. Unable, incapable, unqualified; disqualified. 2. Unskilful, clumsy, awkward.
Inhabilidád, *sf.* Inability, incapacity, unfitness.
Inhabilitación, *sf.* Act of disabling or disqualifying.
Inhabilitár, *va.* To disable, to render unable or unfit: to make impossible.
Inhabitáble, *a.* Uninhabitable; incapable of being inhabited.
Inhabitádo, da, *a.* Uninhabited.
Inhalláble, *a.* Not to be found.
Inherencia, *sf.* Adherence, adhesion, union of things inseparable.
Inherénte, *a.* Inherent, existing in something else.
Inhestár, *va.* V. *Enhestar.*
Inhibición, *sf.* Inhibition, prohibition. *O'rden de inhibicion,* Writ to forbid a judge from farther proceeding in the cause depending before him.
Inhibír, *va.* 1. To inhibit, to prohibit; to prevent from doing any thing. 2. (For.) To prohibit an inferior court to proceed any farther in a cause depending before them.
Inhibitório, ria, *a.* Prohibitory.
Inhiésto, ta, *a.* Entangled, perplexed. V. *Enhiesto.*
Inhonestaménte, *ad.* Dishonestly.
Inhonestidád, *sf.* Dishonesty.
Inhonésto, ta, *a.* 1 Dishonest, void of honesty or probity. 2. Indecent, immodest.
Inhonorár, *va.* V. *Deshonorar.*
Inhospitáble ó Inhospedáble, *a.* Inhospitable, affording no kindness or entertainment to strangers.
Inhospitál, *a.* Uninhabitable.
Inhospitalidád, *sf.* Inhospitality, want of hospitality; want of courtesy to strangers.
Inhumanaménte, *ad.* Inhumanly.
Inhumanidád, *sf.* Inhumanity, want of humanity.
Inhumáno, na, *a.* Inhuman, savage, cruel, incompassionate.
Iniciación, *sf.* Initiation, introduction.
Iniciál, *a.* Initial, placed at the beginning.
Iniciárse, *vr.* To be initiated, to receive the first orders.
Iniciatívo, va, *a.* Initiating or producing initiation.
Iníco, ca, *a.* (Ant.) V. *Inique.*
Iniésta, *sf.* V. *Retama.*
Iniguál, *a.* V. *Desigual.*
Inimagináble, *a.* That cannot be imagined.
Inimicícia, *sf.* Enmity. V. *Enemistad.*

Inimitáble, *a.* Inimitable, above imitation; not to be copied. [be understood.
Ininteligíble, *a.* Unintelligible, that cannot
Iniquaménte, *ad.* Iniquitously.
Iniquidád, *sf.* Iniquity, wickedness, crime.
Inícuo, cua, *a.* Iniquitous, wicked, unjust.
Injúria, *sf.* 1. An unreasonable action, an absurd speech. 2. Hurt without justice. 3. Mischief, annoyance. 4. Contumelious language.
Injuriadór, ra, *s.* Aggressor, injurer.
Injuriánte, *pa.* Injuring, injurer.
Injuriár, *va.* To injure, to wrong, to annoy.
Injuriosaménte, *ad.* Injuriously.
Injurióso, sa, *a.* Injurious, contumelious, reproachful.
Injustaménte, *ad.* Unjustly.
Injustícia, *sf.* Injustice, iniquity, wrong.
Injústo, ta, *a.* Unjust, contrary to justice.
Inlegíble, *a.* Illegible, that cannot be read.
Inlícito, ta, *a.* V. *Ilícito.*
Inllevable, *a.* Insupportable.
Inmaculadaménte, *ad.* Immaculately. [less.
Inmaculádo, da, *a.* Immaculate, pure, spot-
Inmadúro, ra, *a.* Immature, unripened, unmellowed.
Inmanejáble, *a.* Unmanageable, incapable of being managed; intractable.
Inmanénte, *a.* Immanent, inherent.
Inmarcesíble, *a.* Immarcessible, unfading.
Inmateriál, *a.* Immaterial, incorporeal; distinct from matter, void of matter.
Inmaterialidád, *sf.* Immateriality.
Inmatúro, ra, *a.* Immature.
Inmediación, *sf.* Contiguity, actual contact.
Inmediataménte, *ad.* Contiguously; immediately.
Inmediáte, *ad.* Immediately: contiguously.
Inmediáto, ta, *a.* Contiguous, meeting so as to touch. *Llegar á las inmediatas,* To arrive at the critical moment of a dispute or contest.
Inmedicáble, *a.* Incurable.
Inmemoráble, *a.* Immemorable.
Inmemorableménte, *ad.* Immemorably.
Inmemoriál, *a.* Immemorial, past time, out of memory; so ancient that the beginning cannot be traced.
Inmensaménte, *ad.* Immensely. [ness; infinity.
Inmensidád, *sf.* Immensity, unbounded great-
Inménso, sa, *a.* Immense, unlimited, unbounded.
Inmensuráble, *a.* Immensurable, not to be measured: not to be counted.
Inmeritaménte, *ad.* Unmeritedly.
Inmérito, ta, *a.* Undeserved, undeserving.
Inmérito, *ad.* Undeservedly, without reason or desert.
Inmeritório, ria, *a.* Without merit.
Inmersión, *sf.* Immersion, the act of putting any person or thing into a fluid below the surface.
Inminénte, *a.* Imminent, impending, at hand.
Inmiscíble, *a.* Immiscible, incapable of being mixed. [ed; constant.
Inmóble, *a.* Unmoveable, unshaken, unaffect-
Inmoderación, *sf.* Immoderation, want of moderation; excess.
Inmoderadaménte, *ad.* Immoderately.
Inmoderádo, da, *a.* Immoderate, excessive, exceeding the due mean.
Inmodestaménte, *ad.* Immodestly.

Inmodéstia, *sf.* Immodesty, want of chastity or delicacy.
Inmodésto, ta, *a.* Immodest, wanting shame, wanting delicacy or chastity.
Inmódico, ca, *a.* Superfluous, excessive.
Inmolación, *sf.* Immolation, the act of sacrificing; a sacrifice offered.
Inmoladór, ra, *s.* Immolator.
Inmolár, *va.* To immolate, to sacrifice. [less.
Inmortál, *a.* Immortal, exempt from death; end-
Inmortalidád, *sf.* Immortality, exemption from death. [mortal; to perpetuate.
Inmortalizár, *va.* To immortalize, to make im-
Inmortalménte, *ad.* Immortally.
Inmortificación, *sf.* Licentiousness, want of spiritual mortification.
Inmortificádo, da, *a.* Unmortified, free from mortification.
Inmóto, ta, *a.* Unmoved. [moble.
Inmovíble ó Inmóvil, *a.* Immoveable. V. *In-*
Inmovilidád, *sf.* Immobility, want of motion; resistance to motion; firmness, constancy.
Inmudáble, *a.* Immutable. V. *Inmutable.*
Inmuéble, *a.* Fixed; applied to landed, opposed to chattel, property.
Inmundícia, *sf.* Uncleanliness, nastiness, dirtiness; impurity.
Inmúndo, da, *a.* 1. Unclean, filthy, dirty. 2. Obscene, unchaste.
Inmúne, *a.* 1. Free, exempt. 2. Enjoying immunity.
Inmunidád, *sf.* Immunity, privilege, exemption, freedom, discharge from any obligation.
Inmutabilidád, *sf.* Immutability.
Inmutáble, *a.* Immutable, not liable to a change; invariable, unalterable.
Inmutación, *sf.* Change, alteration.
Inmutár, *va.* To change, to alter.—*vr.* To change one's appearance.
Inmutatívo, va, *a.* That which changes or causes alterations. [ed.
Innacíble, *a.* Unborn, unbegotten, ungenerat-
Innaciénte, *a.* That which is not born of another. [natural.
Innáto, ta, *a.* Innate, inborn, ingenerate,
Innavegáble, *a.* Innavigable, not to be passed by sailing; incapable of sailing, applied to
Innecesário, ria, *a.* Unnecessary. [ships.
Innegáble, *a.* Incontestable, incontrovertible.
Innóble, *a.* Ignoble, not nobly born; mean of birth; not of noble descent.
Innocentáda, *sf.* State of innocence.
Innócuo, ua, *a.* Innoxious.
Innominádo, da, *a.* Nameless, having no name.
Innóto, ta, *a.* Unknown. V. *Ignoto.*
Innovación, *sf.* Innovation, change by the introduction of novelty.
Innovadór, ra, *s.* Innovator, one who makes changes; introducer of novelties.
Innovár, *va.* 1. To innovate, to bring in something not known before; to introduce novelties. 2. To pursue a cause while an appeal or decree of inhibition is yet pending.
Innumerabilidád, *sf.* Innumerability.
Innumeráble, *a.* Innumerable, not to be counted for multitude; innumerous.
Innumerableménte, *ad.* Innumerably. [men.
Innúpta, *a.* Unmarried, single; applied to wo-
Inobedecér, *va.* V. *Desobedecer.*

Inobediéncia, sf. Disobedience, want of obedience; violation of lawful commands or prohibition.
Inobediénte, a. 1. Disobedient, not observant of lawful authority. 2. Inflexible; applied to inanimate things.
Inobservable, a. Unobservable.
Inobserváncia, sf. Inadvertency, neglect.
Inobservánte, a. Deficient in observing.
Inocéncia, sf. 1. Innocence, purity from injurious actions; untainted integrity. 2. Freedom from guilt imputed. 3. Harmlessness, sincerity; simplicity in words and actions.
Inocénte, a. 1. Innocent, pure, void of mischief; free from any particular guilt; candid; innoxious. 2. Simple, easily imposed upon. 3. Innocent; applied to children.
Inocenteménte, ad. Innocently.
Inoculación, sf. Inoculation, the practice of transplanting the small or cow-pox, by infusing the matter of ripened pustules into the cutis of the uninfected by means of slight incisions.
Inoculadór, sm. Inoculater.
Inoculár, va. To inoculate, to propagate by means of incisions or insertions.
Inofénso, sa, a. V. Ileso.
Inoficióso, sa, a. Done at an improper time, and not in the manner prescribed by law.
Inojeta, sf. Top of a boot; that part which covers the knee.
I'nope, a. Poor, indigent.
Inópia, sf. Indigence, poverty, penury, want of the necessaries of life.
Inopinable, a. 1. Unthought of, not to be foreseen or expected. 2. Indisputable, incontrovertible; not admitting any diversity of opinion.
Inopinadaménte, ad. Unexpectedly.
Inopinádo, da, a. Inopinate, unexpected.
Inordenadaménte, ad. Inordinately.
Inordenádo, da; ó Inordinádo, da, a. Inordinate, irregular, disorderly.
Inórme, a. Enormous. V. Enorme.
In Próntu, ad. Promptly; readily.
Inquietación, sf. Uneasiness, inquietude, restlessness, want of quiet.
Inquietadór, ra, s. Disturber.
Inquietaménte, ad. Inquietly.
Inquietár, va. 1. To disquiet, to perturb the rest or quiet. 2. To molest, to vex. 3. To stir up or excite disturbances.
Inquiéto, ta, a. 1. Restless, turbulent. 2. Noisy, troublesome, clamorous. 3. Anxious, solicitous, uneasy.
Inquietúd, sf. Inquietude, restlessness.
Inquilináto, sm. Right acquired by the tenant of a house.
Inquilíno, na, s. 1. Tenant, the inhabitant of a house that is hired from another. 2. One that on certain conditions has temporary possession and use of the property of another.
Inquína, sf. (Fam.) Aversion, hatred.
Inquiridór, ra, s. Inquirer, inquisitor.
Inquirír, va. 1. To inquire, to look for carefully or anxiously. 2. To ascertain by research and inquiry.
Inquisición, sf. 1. Inquisition, examination, judicial inquiry. 2. A court established in Spain, and other countries subject to the Pope, for the detection of heresy. 3. Building, where the tribunal of Inquisition holds its sittings. Hacer inquisicion, To examine papers or books in order to burn the useless ones.
Inquisidór, ra, s. 1. Inquirer, examiner. 2. Inquisitor, a member of the tribunal of Inquisition.
Inquisitívo, va, a. Inquisitive, curious; busy in search; active to pry into any thing.
Inráno, sm. A kind of spun cotton, which comes from the Levant.
Inrazonáble, a. V. Irracional.
Inreparáble, a. V. Irreparable.
Insabíble, a. (Ant.) Inscrutable, inexplicable.
Insaciabilidád, sf. Insatiableness, greediness not to be appeased.
Insaciáble, a. Insatiable, greedy beyond measure.
Insaciableménte, ad. Insatiably.
Insaculación, sf. (For.) Act of casting lots or balloting for names.
Insaculadór, sm. (For.) Balloter.
Insaculár, va. To ballot, to put the name of any person destined for an office into a bag or box.
Insalúbre, a. Insalubrious, unhealthy.
Insalubridád, sf. Insalubrity, unhealthfulness.
Insignificación, sf. Insignificance.
Insanáble, a. Incurable, irremediable.
Insánia, sf. Insanity. V. Locura.
Insáno, na, a. Insane, mad.
Inscribír, va. To inscribe, to write on any thing; to draw a figure within another.
Inscripción, sf. Inscription, something written or engraved.
Inscrutáble, a. V. Inescrutable.
Insculpír, va. To insculp, to engrave, to cut.
Insecáble, a. Not to be dried, that cannot be dried.
Insección, sf. Incision, cut; a wound made with an edged instrument.
Insectíl, a. Insectile.
Insécto, sm. Insect.
Inseculación, sf. Balloting. V. Insaculacion.
Insecular, va. To ballot. V. Insacular.
Insenescéncia, sf. Quality of not becoming old.
Insensatéz, sf. Insensateness, stupidity, folly.
Insensáto, ta, a. Insensate, stupid.
Insensibilidád, sf. Insensibility, inability to perceive, dulness of mind; hard-heartedness.
Insensíble, a. 1. Insensible, void of feeling either mental or corporeal; callous, stupid. 2. Imperceptible, not discoverable by the senses. 3. Hard, stupid, unfeeling.
Insensibleménte, ad. Insensibly.
Inseparabilidád, sf. Inseparableness.
Inseparáble, a. Inseparable, not to be disjointed.
Inseparableménte, ad. Inseparably.
Insepúlto, ta, a. Unburied, not interred.
Inserción, sf. Insertion, the act of placing any thing in or among other matter.
Inserír, va. To insert, to place in or among other things; to plant.
Insertár, va. To insert, to introduce.
Insérto, ta, a. V. Enxerto.
Inservíble, a. Unserviceable, useless.
Insídia, sf. Ambush, snare, contrivance.
Insidiadór, ra, s. Plotter, or way-layer.
Insidiár, va. To plot, to way-lay.
Insidiosaménte, ad. Insidiously.
Insidióso, sa, a. Insidious, sly, circumventive.
Insígne, a. Notable, remarkable.
Insigneménte, ad. Notably, signally.
Insígnia, sf. 1. A distinctive mark of honour. 2. Mark of infamy. Insignias, Badges.

Insignificativo, va, a. Insignificant.

Insimulár, va. To accuse, to charge with a crime.

Insinuación, sf. 1. Insinuation, gentle introduction of one thing into another. 2. Power of pleasing or stealing upon the affections. 3. (For.) Exhibition of a public instrument before a judge. 4. (Ret.) Kind of exordium.

Insinuár, va. 1. To insinuate, to introduce any thing gently. 2. To hint, to impart indirectly. 3. To touch slightly on a subject.—vr. To gain another's favour and benevolence by artful means; to insinuate any virtue or vice into the mind.

Insipidéz, sf. Insipidity, insipidness.

Insípido, da, a. Insipid, tasteless, unpleasant; spiritless.

Insipiéncia, sf. Insipience, ignorance, want of knowledge or taste.

Insipiénte, a. Ignorant, tasteless, uninformed, wanting knowledge or instruction.

Insisténcia, sf. Persistence, steadiness, constancy, obstinacy.

Insistír, vn. 1. To rest, to lean upon. 2. To persist in, not to recede from terms or assertions. 3. To dwell upon in discourse.

Ínsito, ta, a. Ingrafted, natural.

Insociabilidád, sf. Insociability, unsociableness.

Insociáble, a. Insociable, averse from conversation and society.

Insolación, sf. Insolation, the exposing to the sun.

Insolár, va. To insolate, to dry in the sun; to expose to the action of the sun.—vr. To disease one's self by the heat of the sun.

Insoldáble, a. 1. That cannot be soldered, or will not admit of any metallic cement. 2. Irreparable, irretrievable; that cannot be remedied or replaced.

Insoléncia, sf. 1. Insolence, impudence, effrontery. 2. Unusual or uncommon act.

Insolentár, va. To make bold; to become insolent.

Insolénte, a. 1. Insolent, impudent. 2. Performing uncommon things. 3. Unusual, uncommon; unaccustomed.

Insolenteménte, ad. Insolently.

Insólidum, ad. Jointly, so as to be answerable for the whole.

Insólito, ta, a. Unusual, unaccustomed.

Insolúble, a. 1. Indissoluble, not to be dissolved. 2. Insolvable, that cannot be paid.

Insolutundación, sf. Assignment of goods or effects in payment of a debt.

Insolvéncia, sf. Insolvency.

Insolvénte, a. Insolvent, unable to pay.

Insómne, a. Sleepless, wanting sleep.

Insómnio, sm. Insomnolency, watchfulness.

Insondáble, a. 1. Unfathomable, not to be sounded by a line. 2. Inscrutable, unsearchable; not to be traced out by inquiry or study.

Insoportáble, a. Insupportable, intolerable.

Insostenible, a. Indefensible.

Inspección, sf. Inspection, survey; superintendence.

Inspeccionár, va. To inspect, to examine.

Inspectór, ra, s. Inspector, a careful examiner; superintendent.

Inspiración, sf. 1. Inspiration, the act of drawing in the breath. 2. The act of breathing into any thing. 3. (Met.) Inspiration, infusion of ideas into the mind by a superior power.

Inspiradór, ra, s. One who inspires.

Inspirár, va. 1. To inspire, to breathe into, to infuse into the mind. 2. To animate by supernatural infusion, to inspire. 3. To draw in with the breath.—vn. (Poét.) To blow.

Inspiratívo, va, a. That which has the power of inspiring.

Instabilidád, sf. Instability.

Instáble, a. Instable, inconstant, changing.

Instalación, sf. Installation, the act of giving possession of a rank or office.

Instalár, va. (For.) To install.

Instáncia, sf. 1. Instance or instancy, persistency, urgency. 2. Prosecution or process of a suit. 3. Instance, pressing argument. *De primera instancia*, Instantly, on the first impulse; first, in the first place.

Instantaneaménte, ad. Instantly, instantaneously.

Instantaneidád, sf. Instantaneity, unpremeditated production or instantaneous existence.

Instantáneo, nea, a. Instantaneous, done in an instant.

Instánte, sm. Instant, so short a part of duration that we perceive no succession. *Al instante*, Immediately. *Cada instante*, Every moment, frequently. *Por instantes*, Incessantly, continually.

Instánte, a. Instant, pressing, urgent.

Instanteménte, ad. Instantly, urgently.

Instár, va. 1. To press or urge a request or argument. 2. In schools, to impugn the solution of a question.—vn. To urge the prompt execution of any thing.

Instauración, sf. Instauration, restoration.

Instaurár, va. To renew, to re-establish, to rebuild.

Instauratívo, va, a. Restorative.

Instigación, sf. Instigation, incitement, impulse.

Instigadór, ra, s. Instigator.

Instigár, va. To instigate, to incite.

Instilación, sf. Instillation, the act of pouring in by drops.

Instilár, va. 1. To instil, to infuse by drops. 2. To insinuate any thing imperceptibly into the mind; to infuse.

Instínto, sm. 1. Instinct, natural desire or aversion; natural tendency. 2. Divine inspiration. 3. Encouragement, incitement, impulse.

Institór, sm. (For.) Factor, agent.

Institución, sf. 1. Institution, establishment, settlement. 2. Education, instruction. 3. Collation or bestowing of a benefice. *Instituciones*, Institutes of any science.

Instituénte, pa. Instituting; founder.

Instituidór, ra, s. Institutor, founder.

Instituír, va. 1. To institute, to establish, to found. 2. To teach, to instruct. 3. To nominate, to appoint; to determine or resolve.

Institúta, sf. Institute, a part or section of the Roman law, which contains its principles.

Institúto, sm. Institute, established law; settled order; design, object, end.

Institutór, ra, s. V. *Instituidor*.

Instituyénte, pa. Institutor: founding.

Instridénte, a. Pressing, compressing.

Instrucción, sf. 1. Instruction, the art of teaching. 2. Precepts conveying knowledge. *Instrucciones*, Instructions, authoritative information.

INSTRUCTIVAMÉNTE, *ad.* Instructively.

INSTRUCTÍVO, VA, *a.* Instructive, conveying knowledge.

INSTRUCTÓR, RA, *s.* Instructor, teacher.

INSTRUÍR, *va.* 1. To instruct, to teach, to form by precept. 2. To inform authoritatively.

INSTRUMENTÁL, *a.* Instrumental, conducive as means to some end.

INSTRUMENTALMÉNTE, *ad.* Instrumentally.

INSTRUMENTÍSTA, *sm.* Player on an instrument of music.

INSTRUMÉNTO, *sm.* 1. Instrument, a tool used for any purpose; an engine or machine. 2. The agent or means of any thing. 3. A writing containing a contract, or serving as a proof or evidence of any thing. 4. Any machine or instrument made to yield harmonious sounds.

INSUÁVE, *a.* Unpleasant, disagreeable.

INSUBSISTÉNCIA, *sf.* Instability, inconstancy.

INSUBSISTÉNTE, *a.* Unable to subsist, incapable of duration; baseless.

INSUBSTANCIÁL, *a.* Unsubstantial, futile.

INSUDÁR, *vn.* To toil, to work hard.

INSUFICIÉNCIA, *sf.* INSUFFICIENCY, inadequateness to any end or purpose.

INSUFICIÉNTE, *a.* INSUFFICIENT, inadequate to any need, use, or purpose; wanting abilities.

INSUFLÁR, *va.* To blow. V. *Soplar.*

INSUFRÍBLE, *a.* Intolerable, insufferable.

INSUFRIBLEMÉNTE, *ad.* Insufferably.

I'NSULA, *sf.* 1. Isle. V. *Isla.* 2. (Joc.) A petty state or government.

INSULÁR ó INSULÁNO, NA, *a.* Insular. V. *Isleño.*

INSULSAMÉNTE, *ad.* Insipidly.

INSULSÉZ, *sf.* Insipidity.

INSÚLSO, SA, *a.* 1. Insipid, tasteless. 2. (Met.) Dull, heavy.

INSULTADÓR, RA, *s.* Insulter.

INSULTÁNTE, *pa.* Insulting, insulter.

INSULTÁR, *va.* To insult, to attack unexpectedly and violently; to treat with contempt.—*vr.* To meet with an accident, to be suddenly attacked with disease.

INSÚLTO, *sm.* 1. Insult, act of insolence or contempt. 2. A sudden and violent attack. 3. Damage done by an attack or contemptuous treatment.

INSUPERÁBLE, *a.* Insuperable, insurmountable; not to be overcome.

INSUPURÁBLE, *a.* Endless, not to be consumed.

INSURGÉNTE, *sm.* Insurgent.

INSURGÍR, *vn.* V. *Alzarse.*

INSURRECCIÓN, *sf.* Insurrection, rebellion.

INTÁCTO, TA, *a.* Untouched; entire, unmixed.

INTANGÍBLE, *a.* INTANGIBLE.

INTEGÉRRIMO, MA, *a. super.* Very sincere.

INTEGRACIÓN, *sf.* Integration.

INTEGRÁL, *a.* Integral, whole; applied to a thing as comprising all its constituent parts.

INTEGRALMÉNTE, *ad.* Integrally.

I'NTEGRAMENTE ó I'NTEGRAMENT, *ad.* V. *Enteramente.*

INTEGRÁNTE, *a.* Integral, integrant.

INTEGRÁR, *va.* 1. To give integrity, to compose a whole of its integral parts. 2. V. *Reintegrar.*

INTEGRIDÁD, *sf.* 1. Integrity, honesty, purity of manners. 2. Entireness; unbroken, whole. 3. Virginity, maidenhood.

I'NTEGRO, GRA, *a.* 1. Entire, complete. 2. Candid, upright, honest, disinterested.

INTEGUMÉNTO, *sm.* 1. Integument, envelope, covering. 2. Fable, fiction.

INTELECCIÓN, *sf.* Intellection, the act of understanding.

INTELECTÍVO, VA, *a.* Intellective, having power to understand.

INTELÉCTO, *sm.* (Ant.) Intellect, understanding

INTELÉCTO, *sm.* V. *Inteligencia.*

INTELECTUÁL, *a.* Intellectual, relating to the understanding; belonging to the mind.

INTELECTUALMÉNTE, *ad.* Intellectually.

INTELIGÉNCIA, *sf.* 1. Intelligence, commerce of information; mutual communication. 2. Understanding, skill, ability, experience. 3. Commerce of acquaintance, friendly intercourse. 4. Sense, signification of a passage. 5. Spirit, unbodied mind. *En inteligencia*, Intellectually, in the understanding, suppositively.

INTELIGENCIÁDO, DA, *a.* Instructed, informed.

INTELIGÉNTE, *a.* Intelligent, skilful.

INTELIGÍBLE, *a.* Intelligible, perspicuous, to be conceived by the understanding; to be perceived by the senses.

INTELIGIBLEMÉNTE, *ad.* Intelligibly.

INTEMPERÁNCIA, *sf.* Intemperance, want of moderation; excess in eating, drinking, or any other gratification.

INTEMPERÁNTE, *a.* Intemperate. V. *Destemplado.*

INTEMPÉRIE ó INTEMPERATÚRA, *sf.* Intemperateness, want of proportion or harmony.

INTEMPÉSTA, *a.* (Poét.) Excessively dark and dreary; applied to the dead of the night.

INTEMPESTIVAMÉNTE, *ad.* Unseasonably.

INTEMPESTÍVO, VA, *a.* Unseasonable, not suitable to the time of the year or occasion.

INTENCIÓN, *sf.* 1. Intention, design. 2. Instinct of brutes. *Hombre de intencion*, A dissembler.

INTENCIONADAMÉNTE, *ad.* Designedly.

INTENCIONÁDO, DA, *a.* Inclined, disposed.

INTENCIONÁL, *a.* Intentional, designed; done by design.

INTENCIONALMÉNTE, *ad.* Intentionally.

INTENDÉNCIA, *sf.* 1. Administration, management. 2. Place, employment, or district of an intendant.

INTENDÉNTA, *sf.* Lady of an intendant.

INTENDÉNTE, *sm.* Intendant, an officer of high rank who oversees any particular allotment of the public business. *Intendente de matriculas*, Intendant or commissary general of the impress service.

INTENSAMÉNTE, *ad.* Intensely.

INTENSIÓN, *sf.* Intension; vehemence.

INTENSÍVO, VA, ó INTÉNSO, SA, *a.* Intense, vehement, ardent.

INTENTÁR, *va.* 1. To try, to attempt, to endeavour. 2. To enter an action, to commence a law-suit.

INTÉNTO, *sm.* INTENT, purpose, design. *De Inténto*, Purposely, designedly.

INTENTÓNA, *sf.* (Fam.) An extravagant design, a chimerical attempt.

I'NTER, *ad.* In the mean while. V. *Interin.* A prepositive particle used in composition.

INTERCADÉNCIA, *sf.* 1. Interruption, interposition. 2. Inconstancy. 3. (Med.) Intermission or inequality of the pulse.

INTERCADÉNTE, *a.* Changeable, variable.

INTERCADENTEMÉNTE, *ad.* Changeably.

INTERCALACIÓN, *sf.* Intercalation, the act of inserting or placing in or amongst other things.

INTERCALÁR, *va.* To intercalate, to insert or place in or among other things.

INTERCALAR, *a.* Intercalary, inserted.

INTERCEDÉR, *vn.* To intercede, to mediate.—*vr.* To act between two parties, to entreat for another. [in the way.

INTERCEPTÁR, *va.* To intercept, to stop and seize

INTERCESIÓN, *sf.* Intercession, mediation, interposition; entreaty for another.

INTERCESÓR, RA, *s.* Intercessor, solicitor.

INTERCESORIAMÉNTE, *ad.* Entreatingly.

INTERCESÓRIO, RIA, *a.* Interceding, intervening between two parties; entreating for another.

INTERCÍSO, SA, *a.* Applied to a day the morning of which is a festival and the afternoon for

INTERCLUSIÓN, *sf.* Interclusion. [labour.

INTERCOLÚNIO, *sm.* Intercolumniation, the space between pillars or columns. [ribs.

INTERCOSTÁL, *a.* Intercostal, placed between the

INTERCURRÉNTE, *a.* Intercurrent, intervening.

INTERCUTÁNEO, NEA, *a.* Placed between the skin and flesh.

INTERDECIR, *va.* To interdict, to prohibit.

INTERDICCIÓN, *sf.* Interdiction, prohibition.

INTERÉS, *sm.* 1. Interest, concern, advantage. 2. Gain, pecuniary advantage. 3. (Poét.) Pathos or interest of dramatic incidents. 4. Money paid for the use of money; usury. *Interés de interés*, Compound interest.

INTERESÁBLE, *a.* Lucrative, profitable; bringing money.

INTERESÁDO, DA, *a.* Interested, paying too much regard to private profit; moved merely by pecuniary views; selfish.

INTERESÁNTE, *a.* Interesting, useful, convenient.

INTERESÁR, *vn.* y *r.* To be concerned or interested in, to have a share in.—*va.* 1. To interest, to concern, to give a share in. 2. (Poét.) To move the passions.

INTERESÉNCIA, *sf.* Personal assistance at any thing. *Interesencias*, (Mexico) Residence of the prebendaries, and their presence at the

INTERESÉNTE, *a.* Present, concurring. [choir.

INTERÉSO, *sm.* Interest. V. *Interés.*

INTERIN, *sm.* V. *Interinidad.*—*ad.* Interim, mean while.

INTERINAMÉNTE, *ad.* In the intervening time, in the interim, in the mean while.

INTERINÁR, *va.* (For.) To ratify, to confirm.

INTERINIDÁD, *sf.* Quality of holding a temporary charge or office.

INTERÍNO, NA; *ó* INTERINÁRIO, RIA, *a.* Appointed provisionally, having the temporary charge of an employ.

INTERIÓR, *a.* Interior, internal, inward.

INTERIÓR, *sm.* 1. The interior, inside. 2. Any thing hidden. *Interiores*, Entrails, intestines.

INTERIORIDÁD, *sf.* 1. Inside, interior part; the part within. 2. The act of concealing any thing.

INTERIORMÉNTE, *ad.* In the interior, internally.

INTERJECCIÓN, *sf.* Interjection, a part of speech that discovers the mind to be seized or affected with some passion.

[illegible], *sf.* Interlineation.

INTERLINEÁL, *a.* Interlineal.

INTERLINEÁR, *va.* V. *Entrerenglonar.*

INTERLOCUCIÓN, *sf.* 1. Interlocution, dialogue; interchange of speech. 2. Intervention, mediation.

INTERLOCUTÓR, RA, *s.* Interlocutor, one who speaks in the name of another; person in a dialogue.

INTERLOCUTORIAMÉNTE, *ad.* In an interlocutory manner.

INTERLOCUTÓRIO, RIA, *a.* Interlocutory, preparatory to a definitive decision.

INTERLÚNIO, *sm.* Time when the moon, about to change, is invisible. [dle.

INTERMEDIÁR, *vn.* To interpose, to be in the mid-

INTERMÉDIO, DIA, *a.* Intermediate, intervening, interposed.

INTERMÉDIO, *sm.* Interlude, an entertainment between the acts of a play; farce; interval.

INTERMINÁBLE, *a.* Interminable, endless.

INTÉRMINO, NA, *a.* Interminable, immense.

INTERMISIÓN, *sf.* Intermission, interruption.

INTERMITÉNCIA, *sf.* Discontinuance of an intermittent fever, the interval between the different fits.

INTERMITÉNTE, *a.* Intermittent, coming by fits.

INTERMITÍR, *va.* To intermit, to discontinue.

INTERNACIÓN, *sf.* Importation. *Derechos de internacion*, Importation duties. [mente.

INTERNAMÉNTE, *ad.* Internally. V. *Interior-*

INTERNÁR, *va.* To pierce, to penetrate beyond the surface; to penetrate into the interior of a country.—*vr.* To insinuate, to gain upon the affections by gentle degrees; to wheedle.

INTERNECIÓN, *sf.* Internecion, massacre, slaugh-

INTÉRNO, NA, *a.* Interior, internal. [ter.

INTERNÓDIO, *sm.* Space between two knots or joints of the stalk of a plant.

INTERNÚNCIO, *sm.* Internuncio, an agent of the court of Rome; interlocutor.

INTERPELACIÓN, *sf.* Interpellation, summons; a call upon.

INTERPELÁR, *va.* 1. To appeal to, to implore the aid of. 2. (For.) To summon, to cite.

INTERPOLACIÓN, *sf.* 1. Interpolation, something added or put into the original matter. 2. Act of adding or putting something into the original matter. [manner.

INTERPOLADAMÉNTE, *ad.* In an interpolating

INTERPOLÁR, *va.* 1. To interpolate, to foist in. 2. To interpose, to intermix; to intermit.

INTERPONÉR, *va.* 1. To interpose, to place between. 2. To refer. 3. To thrust in as an interruption or obstruction.

INTERPOSICIÓN, *sf.* Interposition, intervenient agency, mediation; interval.

INTERPÓSITA PERSONA, *sm.* (Lat. For.) Person who acts for another in law proceedings.

INTERPRENDÉR, *va.* To carry a place by assault; to seize by main force.

INTERPRÉSA, *sf.* Enterprise, an undertaking of hazard; an arduous attempt.

INTERPRETACIÓN, *sf.* Interpretation, elucidation, explanation.

INTERPRETADÓR, RA, *s.* Interpreter; translator.

INTERPRETÁNTE, *pa.* Interpreting, translator.

INTERPRETÁR, *va.* To interpret, to explain, to translate; to attribute; to understand.

Interpretativaménte, *ad.* Interpretatively.
Interpretatívo, va, *a.* Interpretative.
Intérprete, *s. com.* Interpreter, expounder, translator; indication, sign.
Interréyno, *sm.* Interreign, the time in which a throne is vacant; vacancy of the throne.
Interrogación, *sf.* Interrogation, a question put; an inquiry; the mark ?.
Interrogánte, *a.* Interrogative, applied to marks of interrogation.
Interrogár, *va.* V. *Preguntar.*
Interrogativaménte, *ad.* Interrogatively.
Interrogatívo, va, *a.* Interrogative.
Interrogatório, *sm.* Interrogatory, a series of questions put to a person in a law-suit.
Interrumpidaménte, *ad.* Interruptedly.
Interrumpír, *va.* To interrupt, to hinder or obstruct the continuance of a thing.
Interrupción, *sf.* Interruption, discontinuance.
Intersecárse, *vr.* To intersect each other.
Intersección, *sf.* Intersection, the point where lines cross each other.
Interserír, *va.* (Ant.) To intersert.
Intersticio, *sm.* Interstice; interval.
Interusúrio, *sm.* Interest for a certain time. *Interusurio dotal,* Interest allowed to a woman for the delay in repaying or returning her marriage portion.
Intervalo, *sm.* 1. Interval, space between places; time passing between two assignable points. 2. Remission of delirium or madness.
Intervención, *sf.* Intervention, assistance.
Intervenír, *vn.* 1. To intervene, to come between things or persons; to mediate. 2. To assist, to attend.—*v. impers.* V. *Acontecer.*
Interventór, ra; ó Intervenidór, ra, *s.* One who intervenes.
Intervacénte, *a.* Adjacent.
Intestádo, da, *a.* Intestate, dying without a will.
Intestinál, *a.* Intestinal, belonging to the intestines.
Intestíno, na, *a.* Intestine, internal; civil, domestic.
Intestíno, *sm.* Intestine, the gut; the bowels.
Intimación ó Intíma, *sf.* Intimation, hint.
I'ntimaménte, *ad.* Intimately.
Intimár, *va.* To intimate, to hint, to make known.—*vr.* To gain on the affections, to insinuate.
Intimatório, ria, *a.* (For.) Applied to writs, letters, or despatches, in which a decree or order is intimated.
Intimidád, *sf.* Intimacy, familiarity.
Intimidár, *va.* To intimidate, to make fearful; to make cowardly.
I'ntimo, ma, *a.* 1. Internal, innermost. 2. Intimate, familiar; closely acquainted.
Intitulár, *va.* 1. To entitle, to prefix a title to a book or writing. 2. To grace or dignify with a title or honourable appellation.
Intituláta, *sf.* Title prefixed to a book or writing.
Intolerabilidád, *sf.* Intolerableness.
Intoleráble, *a.* Intolerable, insufferable.
Intolerância, *sf.* Intolerance.
Intoleránte, *a.* Intolerant, not enduring.
Intolerantísmo, *sm.* Intoleration, opinion of those who will not admit any religion but that which they profess.
Intónso, sa, *a.* (Poét.) 1. Unshorn, having the hair uncut. 2. Ignorant, unpolished.

Intra Múros, *ad.* Within the walls.
Intransitáble, *a.* Impassable, impenetrable.
Intransitívo, va, *a.* (Gram.) Intransitive.
Intransmutáble, *a.* Intransmutable.
Intransmutabilidád, *sf.* Immutability.
Intratáble, *a.* Intractable, rude; impassable; unsociable.
Intrepidéz, *sf.* 1. Intrepidity, courage, boldness. 2. Temerity.
Intrépido, da, *a.* Intrepid, daring, temerarious.
Intricár, *va.* (Ant.) To involve, to perplex.
Intrincáble, *a.* Intricate, perplexed, easily entangled.
Intrincación, *sf.* Intricacy.
Intrincadaménte, *ad.* Intricately.
Intrincádo, da, *a.* Perplexed, intricate.
Intrincamiénto, *sm.* Intricateness.
Intrincár, *va.* To perplex, to entangle, to involve; to confound, to obscure.
Intrinsecaménte, *ad.* Intrinsically, essentially.
Intrínseco, ca, *a.* 1. Intrinsic, internal, hidden. 2. Close, habitually silent. V. *Intimo.*
Introducción, *sf.* 1. Introduction, the act of conducting or ushering to any place or person. 2. Preparation, previous disposition. 3. Access, intercourse.
Introducír, *va.* 1. To introduce, to conduct or usher into a place. 2. To bring into notice or practice. 3. To induce, to facilitate, to conciliate.—*vr.* To insinuate, to gain on the affections; to interfere.
Introductór, ra; ó Introducidór, ra, *s.* One who introduces.
Introductório, ria, *a.* Introductory.
Intróito, *sm.* 1. Entrance, entry. 2. Introit, the beginning of the mass; the commencement of public devotions.
Intrusaménte, *ad.* Intrusively.
Intrusión, *sf.* Intrusion, the act of forcing or thrusting any thing or person into any place or state.
Intrúso, *sm.* Intruder, one who forces into company or affairs without right.—*a.* Intruded.
Intuición, *sf.* Intuition, knowledge not obtained by deduction of reason.
Intuitivaménte, *ad.* Intuitively.
Intuitívo, va, *a.* Intuitive, evident; perceived by the mind immediately and without ratiocination.
Intuito (Por), *ad.* On account of, in consideration.
Intuitu, *sm.* View. V. *Vista ú ojeada.* *Por Intuitu,* In consideration of.
Intumescéncia, *sf.* V. *Hinchazon.*
Intususcepción, *sf.* (Med.) Intrasusception, union of one part of a cavity in another.
Inulto, ta, *a.* (Poét.) Unrevenged, unpunished.
Inumeridád, *sf.* V. *Innumerabilidad.*
Inundación, *sf.* 1. Inundation, overflow of waters; deluge. 2. Confluence of any kind.
Inundánte, *pa.* Inundating; what inundates.
Inundár, *va.* 1. To inundate, to overflow, to deluge. 2. To spread, to diffuse.
Inurbanaménte, *ad.* Incivilly, uncivilly.
Inurbanidád, *sf.* Incivility, want of education.
Inurbáno, na, *a.* Incivil, rude, unpolished.
Inusitadaménte, *ad.* Unusually.
Inusitáda, do, *a.* Unusual, not in use, not accustomed.

Inútil á Inútile, a. Useless, unprofitable.
Inutilidád, sf. Inutility.
Inutilizár, va. To render useless.
Inutilménte, ad. Uselessly.
Invadeáble, a. Not fordable, impassable without swimming.
Invadír, va. To invade, to attack a country; to make a hostile entrance.
Invalidación, sf. The act of invalidating or rendering void and invalid.
Invalidád, sf. V. Nulidad.
Invalidaménte, ad. Invalidly.
Invalidár, va. To invalidate, to deprive of force or efficacy; to render null.
Inválido, da, a. Invalid, without force; of no weight or cogency; feeble, weak, null.
Inválido, sm. (Mil.) Invalid, retired soldier. Dar ó conceder inválidos, To give pensions to veteran soldiers, to invalide soldiers.
Invariabilidád, sf. Invariability.
Invariáble, a. Invariable, that cannot be altered or changed.
Invariableménte, ad. Invariably.
Invariación, sf. Immutability, invariableness, constancy.
Invariadaménte, ad. Unvariedly.
Invariádo, da, a. Unvaried, constant.
Invasión, sf. Invasion, hostile entrance, attack.
Invasór, ra, s. Invader.
Invectíva, sf. Invective, a severe censure in speech or writing.
Invehír, va. To inveigh, to censure.
Invencíble, a. Invincible, insuperable, unconquerable.
Invencibleménte, ad. Invincibly.
Invención, sf. Invention, contrivance, discovery; fiction, artifice. Hacer invenciones, To make wry faces. Vivir de invenciones, To live by tricks and cunning.
Invencionéro, ra, s. 1. Inventor. 2. Boaster, decider. 3. (Vulg.) Gesticulator, mimic.
Invendíble, a. Unmerchantable; not marketable, not saleable.
Inveníble, a. That may be found.
Invenír, va. (Ant.) V. Hallar.
Inventár, va. To invent, to discover; to feign.
Inventariár, va. To make an inventory, to register, to place in a catalogue; to commemorate. [logue of chattels and estates.
Inventário, sm. Inventory, account or cata-
Inventíva, sf. The faculty of invention.
Inventívo, va, a. Inventive, quick at contrivance, ready at expedients.
Invénto, sm. Invention, discovery.
Inventór, ra, s. Inventor, contriver; forger.
Inverecúndo, da, a. Shameless, impudent.
Inverisímil, a. Unlike, improbable.
Inverisimilitúd, sf. Improbability, unlikelihood. [plants in winter.
Invernáculo, sm. Green-house for preserving
Invernáda, sf. Winter-season.
Invernadéro, sm. Winter-quarters.
Invernál, a. (Ant.) Hyemal.
Invernár, vn. To winter, to pass the winter; to be the winter season.
Invernízo, za, a. 1. Winterly, suitable to the winter; of a wintry kind. 2. Winter-beaten, harassed by frost and severe weather.
Inverosímil, a. V. Inverisimil.

Inversión, sf. Inversion; change of order, time, or place; change of property.
Invérso, sa, a. Inverse, inverted, reciprocal.
Invertír, va. To invert, to turn upside down; to change the order of time or place; to change property.
Investidúra, sf. Investiture, the act of giving possession of a manor, office, or benefice.
Investigáble, a. Uninvestigable, not to be searched out.
Investigación, sf. Investigation, research.
Investigadór, ra, s. Investigator.
Investigár, va. To investigate, to search out; to find out by rational disquisition.
Investír, va. To invest. V. Envestir.
Inveteradaménte, ad. Inveterately.
Inveterárse, vr. To be antiquated, to grow old.
Inviár, va. V. Enviar.
Invictaménte, ad. Unconquerably, valiantly.
Invícto, ta, a. Unconquerable, not subdued.
Invídia, sf. Envy. V. Envidia.
Invidiár, va. V. Envidiar.
Invidióso, sa; á Ínvido, da, a. V. Envidioso.
Inviérno, sm. Winter, the cold season of the year. [servant, to be attentive.
Invigilár, vn. To watch, to be cautiously ob-
Invincíble, a. Invincible. V. Invencible.
Inviolabilidád, sf. Inviolability.
Invioláble, a. Inviolable, not to be violated.
Inviolableménte, ad. Inviolably; infallibly.
Invioládo, da, a. Inviolate, unhurt, uninjured.
Invirtúd, sf. Vice, want of virtue.
Invirtuosaménte, ad. Not virtuously. [ous.
Invirtuóso, sa, a. Contrary to virtue, not virtu-
Invisibilidád, sf. Invisibility.
Invisíble, a. Invisible, not perceptible to the sight; not to be seen. En un invisible, In an instant.
Invisibleménte, ad. Invisibly.
Invitár, va. To invite.
Invitatório, sm. Psalm or anthem sung at the beginning of the matins or morning worship.
Invocación, sf. Invocation, the act of calling upon in prayer.
Invocadór, ra, s. One who invokes.
Invocár, va. To invoke, to call upon in prayer, to implore.
Invocatório, ria, a. That which invocates.
Involuntariaménte, a. Involuntarily.
Involuntariedád, sf. The quality of being involuntary.
Involuntário, ria, a. Involuntary. [wounded.
Invulneráble, a. Invulnerable, not to be
Inxeridúra, sf. The place where a tree is grafted.
Inxerír, va. 1. To insert, to introduce; to enclose within another. 2. To ingraft, to inoculate.—vr. To interfere. [culate.
Inxertár, va. To ingraft a tree, to graft, to ino-
Inxérto, sm. Graft, the tree ingrafted.
Inyección, sf. Injection, the act of casting in; the introduction of liquids by means of a syringe or other instrument.
Inyectár, va. To inject.
Inyungír, va. (Ant.) V. Prevenir.
Ipecacuána, sf. Ipecacuanha, a medicinal root.
Ipso Jure, sm. (For.) Used in courts of law to denote that a thing does not require the declaration of the judge, as it constitutes the

law itself. *Ipso facto*, (Lat.) By this fact, without delay. [Constantinople.

I'psola, *sf.* A kind of wool which comes from

Ir, *vn.* 1. To go, to walk, to move step by step. 2. To be, to exist. 3. To bet, to lay a wager. *Van cien doblones que es cierto*, I would lay a hundred pistoles that it is true. 4. To consist, to depend on. 5. To import, to concern. 6. To differ, to be different, to be distant. 7. To lead; applied to a road. 8. To devote one's self to a calling, to follow a profession. 9. To proceed, to act. 10. To decline a noun or conjugate a verb for another. *Ir en demanda de*, (Naút.) To be on the look out for. *Ir á la mano á alguno*, To restrain or moderate one. *Ir al amor del agua*, To temporize. *Ir* joined to present participles implies the existence or actual execution of the action designated; joined with past participles it signifies to suffer their action, as *ir vendido*, to be betrayed; with the preposition *á* and infinitive mode, it implies disposition towards, as *ir á oir la misa*, To go to hear mass; *ir á los halcones*, to pursue as closely as a hawk; followed by *con*, it gives the noun an adverbial import, as *ir con tiento*, to go on softly; and accompanied by the preposition *contra* or *fuera de*, it signifies to persevere or to act contrary to.—*vr.* 1. To be gone, to be dying. 2. To leak, to ooze. 3. To exhale, to evaporate; to discharge wind. 4. *Irse á pique*, (Naút.) To founder, to go to the bottom. 5. To break; to grow old. *Irse á la mano*, To become moderate or restrain one's self. *Irse á leva y monte*, To escape, to retire. *Irse con Dios ó irse con su madre de Dios*, To absent one's self; to despatch with disgust or disapprobation. *Irsele á alguno la cabeza*, To perturb the mind, to confuse the reason. *¿ Quien va? ó quien va allá?* Who is there, or who goes there? *Vaya vd. ó vete con Dios*, Farewell; God be with you. *Vaya vd. al cielo, al rollo, á pasear, &c.* expressions of contempt for what another says.

I'ra, *sf.* 1. Anger, passion, indignation, wrath, fury. 2. Ire, desire of vengeance, chastisement threatened or executed. 3. (Met.) Violence of the elements or weather.

Iracúndia, *sf.* Violent anger, excessive rage.

Iracúndo, da, *a.* 1. Passionate, easily moved to anger. 2. (Poét.) Enraged, furious; applied to the winds.

Irádo, *a.* V. *Bandido.*

Irascéncia, *sf.* Passionateness, irascibleness.

Irárse, *vr.* V. *Airarse.*

Irascíble, *a.* Irascible, partaking of the nature of anger; impetuous, determined.

I'ride salvága, *sf.* (Bot.) V. *Efémero.*

I'ris, *sf.* 1. Iris, the rainbow; a semicircle of various colours, which appears in showery weather; circle round the pupil of the eye. 2. Mediator, peace-maker. 3. (Bot.) Flower de luce. Iris pseudacorus *L.* 4. Prism.

Irlánda, *sf.* 1. Cloth made of cotton and woollen yarn. 2. Fine Irish linen.

Ironía, *sf.* Irony, a mode of speech in which the meaning is contrary to the words.

Ironicaménte, *ad.* Ironically.

Irónico, ca, *a.* Ironical.

Irracionál, *a.* Irrational, void of reason.

Irracionalidád, *sf.* Irrationality.

Irracionalménte, *ad.* Irrationally.

Irradiación, *sf.* 1. Irradiation, the act of emitting beams of light. 2. Illumination, intellectual light. [light.

Irradiár, *va.* To irradiate, to emit beams of

Irrazonáble, *a.* Unreasonable.

Irreconciliáble, *a.* Irreconcileable, not to be reconciled, not to be appeased.

Irrecuperáble, *a.* Irrecoverable, not to be regained.

Irrecusáble, *a.* Not to be refused or declined; inevitable. [ed.

Irredimíble, *a.* That which cannot be redeemed.

Irreducíble, *a.* 1. Irreducible, not to be reduced. 2. Stubborn, obstinate. [claimed.

Irreformáble, *a.* Not to be reformed or re-

Irrefragáble, *a.* Irrefragable, not to be confuted; superior to argumental opposition.

Irrefragableménte, *ad.* Irrefragably.

Irregulár, *a.* Irregular, disorderly.

Irregularidád, *sf.* Irregularity, impropriety.

Irregularménte, *ad.* Irregularly.

Irreligión, *sf.* Irreligion, contempt of religion; impiety.

Irreligiosaménte, *ad.* Irreligiously.

Irreligiosidád, *sf.* Irreligiousness, impiety.

Irreligióso, sa, *a.* Irreligious, impious.

Irremediáble, *a.* Irremediable, incurable; admitting no cure.

Irremediableménte, *ad.* Irremediably.

Irremisíble, *a.* Irremissible, unpardonable.

Irremisibleménte, *ad.* Unpardonably.

Irremunerádo, da, *a.* Unremunerated.

Irreparáble, *a.* Irreparable, not to be repaired.

Irreparableménte, *ad.* Irreparably.

Irreprehensíble, *a.* Irreprehensible, exempt from blame.

Irreprehensibleménte, *ad.* Irreprehensibly.

Irreprocháble, *a.* Irreproachable, free from reproach.

Irresistibilidád, *sf.* Irresistibility.

Irresistíble, *a.* Irresistible.

Irresistibleménte, *ad.* Irresistibly.

Irresolúble, *a.* 1. Indeterminable, not to be defined; not to be resolved. 2. Irresolute, not constant in purpose.

Irresolución, *sf.* Irresolution, want of firmness of mind.

Irresolúto, ta; Irresuélto, ta, *a.* Irresolute, unsteady.

Irreveréncia, *sf.* Irreverence, want of reverence, respect, or veneration.

Irreverénte, *a.* Irreverent, not paying due homage or reverence.

Irreverenteménte, *ad.* Irreverently.

Irrevocabilidád, *sf.* The state of being irrevocable. [brought back, irrevocable.

Irrevocáble, *a.* Not to be recalled, not to be

Irrevocableménte, *ad.* Irrevocably.

Irrisíble, *a.* Risible, laughable.

Irrisión, *sf.* Irrision, the act of laughing at another.

Irrisoriaménte, *ad* Laughingly, derisively.

Irrisório, ria, *a.* Derisive, risible.

Irritabilidád, *sf.* Irritability.

Irritáble, *a.* That can be rendered void or annulled.

Irritación, *sf.* 1. Irritation, commotion, agitation. 2. Invalidation, abrogation.
Irritadór, ra, *s.* Irritator, stimulator.
Irritaménte, *ad.* Invalidly, vainly.
Irritamiénto, *sm.* Irritation; abrogation.
Irritánte, *a.* Annulling or making void. *Irritantes*, (Med.) Stimulants.
Irritár, *va.* 1. To annul, to render void. 2. To irritate, to exasperate, to agitate violently. 3. To alter, to produce a material change.
Irrito, ta, *a.* Null, void.
Irrupción, *sf.* Irruption, the act of forcing an entrance; inroad, burst of invaders into a country or place.
Isagóge, *sf.* Introduction.
Isagógico, ca, *a.* Introductive, introductory.
Ischión, *sm.* Hip-bone.
Isidoriáno, na, *a.* Belonging to St. Isidore.
Isípula é Irisípula, *sf.* (Ant.) V. *Erisipela.*
Isla, *sf.* 1. Isle, island; a tract of land surrounded by water. 2. A remote or retired spot. *En isla*, Insulated. 3. Square, an area of four sides, with houses on each side. *Islas de barlovento*, Windward islands. *Islas de sotavento*, Leeward islands.
Islán, *sm.* A kind of veil worn by women.
Isléño, ña, *s.* Islander, an inhabitant of a country surrounded by water.
Isléo, *sm.* Island formed by rocks.
Isléta, *sf.* A small isle.
Islilla, *sf.* Flank, that part of the animal body which goes from the hip to the armpit.
Islóte, *sm.* A small barren island.
Ismaelíta, *a.* Mahommedan, Ishmaelite.
Isógono, na, *a.* Having two equal angles.
I'spida, *sf.* (Orn.) Kingfisher. Alcedo ispida *L.*
Ispír, *vn.* (Burg.) To puff up, to render spungy.
Israelíta, *sm.* Israelite, Jew.
Israelítico, ca, *a.* Israelitish, Jewish.
I'stmo, *sm.* Isthmus, a narrow neck of land between two arms of the sea, joining the peninsula to the continent.
Istriár, *va.* To flute. V. *Estriar.*
Istrúto, ta, *a.* (Ant.) V. *Instruido.*
Italianizár, *va.* To do after the Italian manner.
Italiáno, na; Itálico, ca, *a.* Italian, Italic.
I'tem, *s.* Item, another or new article.—*ad.* Also.
Iteráble, *a.* Repeated or reiterated, capable of repetition.
Iteración, *sf.* Iteration, repetition.
Iterár, *va.* To iterate, to repeat. V. *Repetir.*
Iterativo, va, *a.* Iterative, repeating, redoubling.
Itinerário, *sm.* Itinerary, book of roads; march, route
I'va, *sf.* (Bot.) Ground-pine. Iva *L.*
Ixído, *sm.* (Ant.) V. *Exido.*
Iza, *sf.* (Cant.) Woman of the town.
Izága, *sf.* Place abounding in rushes and reeds.
Izár, *va.* (Naút.) To hoist, to raise up on high.
Izquierdeár, *vn.* To degenerate, to fall from its kind; to grow wild.
Izquiérdo, da, *a.* 1. Left-handed; left; sinister. *A' la izquierda*, To the left. 2. Crooked, not right or straight. 3. Applied to horses which turn out their toes in travelling.
Izquiérdo, da, *s.* A left-handed person.

JAC JAL

THE *j* serves in the Spanish language always as a consonant, and its pronunciation is guttural, or like the sound of *h* strongly aspirated. According to the rules of the Spanish Academy, the *j* precedes *a*, *o*, and *u*, as in *jactancia*, *joven*, *justicia*, except a few words, which from their origin and use are written with *x*; the vowels *e* and *i* are preceded by *g*, except in some names; but *j* is used in all diminutives, as *paja*, *pajita*; *viejo*, *viejecito*.
Jabalí, *sm.* Wild boar. Sus *L.*
Jabalína, *sf.* 1. Sow of a wild boar. 2. Javelin, a kind of spear, chiefly used for hunting of wild boars.
Jabalúno, na, *a.* Resembling or belonging to a wild boar.
Jabardeár, *va.* To swarm, to rise as bees in a body.
Jabardíllo, *sm.* Company of strolling players.
Jabárdo, *sm.* 1. A small swarm of bees. 2. Crowd, multitude.
Jabáto, *sm.* A young wild boar.
Jabí, *sf.* 1. Small wild apple or crab. 2. Small kind of grapes.
Jabíno, *sm.* V. *Chaparro.*
Jáca, *sf.* Nag, pony. V. *Haca.*
Jacerína, *sf.* Mail, a coat of steel net-work for defence.—*a.* Hard, steely.
Jácht, *sf.* Yacht, a small vessel.
Jacínto, *sm.* 1. (Bot.) Hyacinth; hairbel. Hyacinthus *L.* 2. Precious stone.
Jáco, *sm.* Nag, pony.
Jactáncia, *sf.* Jactitation, act of boasting, arrogance.
Jactanciosaménte, *ad.* Boastingly.
Jactancióso, sa, *a.* Boastful, vain-glorious; arrogant.
Jactár, *va.* To bestow fulsome praise, to grant boundless applause.—*vr.* To vaunt, to boast, to display with ostentation.
Jaculatória, *sf.* Ejaculation, a short prayer darted out occasionally.
Jáde, *sm.* Jade, a mineral.
Jadeár, *vn.* To pant, to palpitate, to have the breast heaving as for want of breath; to jade.
Jadéo, *sm.* Pant, palpitation.
Jaecéro, ra, *s.* Harness-maker.
Jaén, *sm.* A kind of large grapes, with thick rinds.
Jaéz, *sm.* 1. Harness, the traces of draught horses. 2. Manner or quality in which several things resemble each other. *Jaeces*, Ornaments or harness of horses in processions.
Jagüéy, *sm.* (Perú) Large pool or lake.
Jaharrár, *va.* To plaster, to overlay or make even with plaster.
Jaharro, *sm.* Plaster, the act of plastering.
Jalbegár, *va.* 1. To whiten, to whitewash. 2. To

paint excessively, to lay too much white on the face.

Jalbégue, *sm.* Whitewash, paint.

Jalbegueádo, **da**, *a.* Whitewashed, painted.

Jalbégue, *sm.* 1. Whitewashing, the act of whitening a wall with lime. 2. Whitewash, a wash to make the skin seem fair.

Jaldádo, **da**; **Jáldo**, **da**, *a.* Of a bright yellow colour.

Jálde, *a.* Bright yellow, crocus-coloured.

Jáldre, *sm.* A bright yellow colour, peculiar to birds.

Jaléa, *sf.* Jelly, the inspissated juice of fruit, boiled with sugar. *Hacerse una jalea*, (Met.) To love with excessive fondness. *Jalea del agro*, Conserve of citron.

Jaleár, *va.* To encourage hounds to follow the chase.

Jaletína, *sf.* Compound jelly, made of animal substances, with a mixture of fruit and sugar.

Jalméro, *sm.* One whose trade is to make pack saddles, and harness for mules.

Jamás, *ad.* 1. Never, at no time. 2. (Met.) Once. *Para siempre jamas*, For ever. *Jamas por jamas*, Never.

Jamavás, *sf.* A kind of flowered silk.

Jámba, *sf.* (Arq.) Door-jamb, window-post, which supports the lintel or head-piece.

Jambáge, *sm.* (Arq.) Collection of jambs.

Jámbo, *sm.* V. *Yambo.*

Jamerdána, *sf.* Sewer which runs from a slaughter-house, and into which the filth is thrown.

Jamerdár, *va.* To clean the guts of animals; to wash hastily.

Jametería, *sf.* (Mur.) V. *Zalameria.*

Jamíla, *sf.* V. *Alpechin.*

Jamís, *sm.* A kind of cotton stuff which comes from the Levant.

Jamón, *sm.* Ham, the thigh of a hog salted.

Jamóna, *a.* Belonging to the thigh.

Jamoncíllo, **co**, **to**, *sm. dim.* Little ham.

Jangáda, *sf.* Raft, a frame or float made by laying pieces of timber across each other. *Jangada de perchas para arboladura*, (Naút.) Raft of spars for masting.

Jángua, *sf.* A small armed vessel, like a raft.

Jannequín, *sm.* A sort of cotton which comes from the Levant.

Japonés, **sa**, *a.* Native of Japan.

Jaqueládo, **da**, *a.* Applied to cut diamonds or precious stones.

Jaqués, **sa**, *a.* Of Jaca in Aragon; applied to an ancient Spanish coin, struck at Jaca.

Jaquír, *va.* (Ant.) V. *Dexar.*

Jardín, *sm.* 1. Garden, a piece of ground inclosed and cultivated, planted with herbs, flowers, or fruits. 2. Privy, necessary on board of ships. 3. Spot which disfigures an emerald. *Jardines de popa*, (Naút.) Quarter-galleries.

Jardinería, *sf.* Gardening, the art of cultivating or laying out gardens.

Jardinéro, **ra**, *s.* Gardener, one that attends or cultivates gardens.

Jardincíco, **Jardiníco**, **llo**, **to**, *sm. dim.* Little garden.

Jaréta, *sf.* Seam made by doubling the edge of cloth. *Jaretas*, (Naút.) Harpings. *Jaretas del pie de las arraigadas*, (Naút.) Cat harpings.

Jaretéra, *sf.* V. *Jarretera.*

Járo, **ra**, *a.* Resembling a wild boar; applied to hogs.

Járra, *sf.* 1. Jug or jar, an earthen vessel with a swelling and a narrow neck. 2. (Ar.) Ancient equestrian order. *En jarra, ó de jarras*, With the arms crossed; with the hands fixed in the girdle.

Jarreár, *vn.* To fetch or take out water or wine with a jug.

Jarréro, *sm.* Vender of jugs or jars.

Jarretár, *va.* 1. To hough, to hamstring. V. *Desjarretar.* 2. To enervate, to deprive of strength or courage.

Jarréte, *sm.* Ham, the upper part of the leg. *Tener bravos jarretes*, To have strong hams.

Jarretéra, *sf.* 1. Garter. 2. Order of knighthood.

Jarretéro, *sm.* Hamstring, a muscle of the ham.

Jarríllo, *sm.* 1. A small jug. 2. Chamber-pot. 3. (Bot.) Dragon. V. *Dragontea.*

Járro, *sm.* Jug with one handle only.

Jarrón, *sm.* A large jug, an urn.

Jasár, *va.* (Ant.) V. *Sajar.*

Jáspe, *sm.* Jasper, a hard stone of a beautiful green colour, sometimes clouded with white.

Jaspeádo, **da**, *a.* Spotted, like jasper; marbled.

Jaspeadúra, *sf.* Act of marbling.

Jaspeár, *va.* To marble, to paint with variegated colours in imitation of the jasper.

Jastiál, *sf.* Facade of an edifice.

Játo, **ta**, *s.* V. *Becerro.*

Jáula, *sf.* 1. Cage, an enclosure of twigs or wire, in which birds are kept. 2. Cell for mad or insane persons.

Jaúto, **ta**, *a.* (Ar.) V. *Soso.*

Javalína, *sf.* Javelin.

Javéque, *sm.* Kind of small vessel used in the Mediterranean, with three masts, like a frigate, but using oars.

Jayán, **na**, *s.* A tall, strong, and robust person.

Jayanázo, *sm.* A huge big fellow.

Jazaríno, **na**, *a.* Native of Argel, Algerine.

Jay'me, *sm.* James. V. *Santiago.*

Jasmín, *sm.* (Bot.) Jessamine, a fragrant flower. Jasminum *L. Jasmin real ó de España*, Royal or Spanish jasmine. Jasminum odoratissimum *L.*

Jazminórro, *sm.* (Bot.) Bastard jessamine or box-horn. Jasminum fructicans *L.*

Jébe, *sm.* Roche-alum.

Jerosolimitáno, **na**, *a.* A native of Jerusalem.

Jesucrísto, *sm.* Jesus Christ.

Jesuíta, *sm.* Jesuit.

Jesuítico, **ca**, *a.* Jesuitical, relating to the Jesuits.

Jesús, *sm.* Jesus, the name of the second person of the Holy Trinity. *Decir los Jesuses*, To assist dying persons. *En un decir Jesus*, In an instant. *Jesus mil veces!* Good God!

Jesuseár, *vn.* To repeat often the name of Jesus.

Jijóna, *sf.* Species of large wheat which grows in the Mancha.

Jo, *interj.* Used to stop horses.

Jocosaménte, *ad.* Jocosely, jocularly.

Jocosério, **ria**, *a.* Half jocose, and half serious.

Jocosidád, *sf.* Jocularity, jocoseness.

Jocóso, **sa**, *a.* Jocose, jocular.

Jocúndo, **da**, *a.* (Ant.) Jocund, merry; gay.

Jofáyna, *sf.* A china jug. V. *Aljafayna.*

Joliéz, *sf.* Jollity, juvenile merriment.

Jolíto, *sm.* Rest, leisure, calm. *Haber jolito*

(Naút.) To be becalmed; applied to a ship.
Jónico, ca; Jónio, nia, a. 1. Native of Ionia. 2. (Arq.) Ionic, applied to an order of architecture.—sm. A foot in poetry.
Jonjolí, sm. V. *Ajonjolí*.
Jorcár, va. (Extr.) V. *Ahechar*.
Jórco, sm. A feast, and licentious dance among the vulgar.
Jordán, sm. Any thing which revives or gives a fresh bloom.
Jórfe ó Jorfe, sm. A wall made of dry stones only.
Jorfeár, va. To construct dry walls.
Jorgína y Jorguína, sf. Witch, sorceress whose charms consist in soporiferous drafts.
Jorguín, sm. Soot, condensed smoke.
Jornáda, sf. 1. March or journey performed in one day. 2. Opportunity, occasion, circumstance. 3. Journey, travel; military expedition. 4. Road, way. 5. Passage through life. 6. Act, one of the parts into which Spanish plays are divided. 7. Number of sheets printed off in one day, which in Spain is regularly 1500. *Á' grandes ó á largas jornadas*, With celerity and promptness.
Jornál, sm. Wages paid to day-labourers for one day's work. *Muger que trabaja á jornal*, Char-woman. *Á' jornal*, By the day.
Jornalár, va. To work by the day.
Jornaléro, sm. Day-labourer, one that works by the day.
Joróba, sf. 1. Hump, a prominence on the back. 2. Importunity, incessant troublesome solicitation.
Jorobádo, da, a. Crooked, gibbous.
Jorobár, va. To importune, to tease or harass by the frequent repetition of the same request.
Jórro (Á'), ad. (Naút.) V. *Remolque*.
Joselasár, sm. A sort of spun cotton which comes from Smyrna.
Jostrádo, da, a. Round-headed; applied to a foil, shaft, or dart.
Jóta, sf. 1. Name of the letter *J*. 2. Jot, tittle. 3. V. *Ojota*. 4. Spanish dance. 5. Kind of pottage or broth made with parsley and other herbs, spices, and bacon. *No saber una jota*, To be a very ignorant of any thing.
Jóven, a. Young, youthful, juvenile.—sm. Youth, a stripling; one in the state of adolescence.
Jovenádo, sm. The time or place in which young persons, after taking the vows, are under the direction of a master in convents.
Jovencíllo, lla, to, ta, s. dim. Youngster.
Jovenéte, sm. Youth, a young man.
Joventúd, sf. V. *Juventud*.
Joviál, a. 1. Jovial, under the influence of Jupiter. 2. Jovial, gay, airy, merry.
Jovialidád, sf. Joviality, jollity, mirth, merriment.
Jóya, sf. 1. Jewel, a precious stone set in gold or silver. 2. Any thing well polished and finished. 3. Present, gift. 4. Astragal, an ornament on pieces of ordnance. *Joyas*, Jewels, trinkets; all the wearing apparel and ornament of women, especially of brides.
Joyánte, a. Extremely glossy; applied to silks. *Polvora joyante*, Refined gunpowder.
Joyál, sm. Jewel of little value.
Joyéra, sm. Woman who keeps a jeweller's shop.
Joyería, sf. Jeweller's shop, where jewels and trinkets are sold.
Joyéro, sm. Jeweller, one who traffics in jewels, trinkets, and toys.
Jóyo, sm. (Bot.) Bearded darnel, darnel-grass. Lolium temulentum *L.*
Joyuéla, sf. Jewel of small value.
Juan, sm. John. *Es un buen Juan*, He is a poor silly fellow. *Hacer san Juan*, To leave a place before the expiration of the time agreed upon; applied to servants. *Juan rana*, (Burles.) A simpleton.
Juanéte, sm. 1. Joint-bone of the great toe. 2. (Naút.) Top-gallant sail, carried above the main and fore-top sails. *Juanete de sobremesana*, Mizen-top-gallant sail.
Juanetúdo, da, a. Bony, having large joint bones.
Juárda, sf. Stain in cloth, occasioned by the wool having imbibed too much oil before it was carded and spun.
Juardóso, sa, a. Stained, spotted; applied to woollen cloth.
Jubertár, va. (Naút.) To hoist the boat on board.
Jubetería, sf. (Ant.) Shop where jackets and doublets are sold; a slop shop.
Jubetéro, sm. One who makes and sells jackets and doublets.
Jubilación, sf. 1. Rejoicing, festivity, merriment. 2. Exemption from fatigue and labour.
Jubilár, vn. 1. To rejoice, to make merry. 2. To enjoy an exemption from fatigue and labour.—va. 1. To exempt from toil and labour. 2. To lay aside as useless.
Jubiléo, sm. Jubilee, a public festivity; concession of plenary indulgence; an ecclesiastic solemnity, celebrated by the Jews every fifty years. *Por jubileo*, Rarely, happening seldom.
Júbilo, sm. Glee, joy, merriment.
Jubón, sm. 1. Doublet, jacket. 2. (Joc.) A public whipping.
Juboncíllo, sm. A small jacket, a doublet of little value.
Jubonéro, sm. Maker of jackets or doublets.
Judaísmo, sm. Judaism, religion of the Jews.
Judaizánte, pa. Judaizing, one who judaizes.
Judaizár, va. To follow or observe the rites of the Jews.
Judas, sm. 1. One that treacherously deceives his friend, an impostor, traitor. 2. Silkworm that does not spin. 3. Effigy of Judas burnt in the streets in the Spanish towns during lent.
Juday'co, ca, a. Judaical, relating to the Jews.
Judería, sf. Quarter or part of the town where the Jews live; tax on Jews.
Judía, sf. (Bot.) French bean. Phaseolus vulgaris *L. Judia de careta*, Kind of small spotted French beans.
Judicación, sf. Judgment, the power and act of passing judgment.
Judicánte, sm. Judge appointed to inquire into the conduct and proceedings of officers of justice.
Judicár, va. (Ant.) V. *Juzgar*.
Judicatúra, sf. 1. Judicature, the power and act of administering justice. 2. Dignity of a judge.
Judiciál, a. Judicial, practised in the distribution of justice.
Judicialménte, ad. Judicially.
Judiciário, ria, a. Professing the art of foretelling future events by means of the stars.
Judicióso, sa, a. Judicious. V. *Juicioso*.

Judías, sf. Kind of olives good for making oil, but not eating.
Judiégo, ga, a. Jewish.
Judihuélo, sm. 1. A young Jew. 2. French bean.
Judío, día, a. Judaical, Jewish.
Judío, día, s. 1. Jew, Jewess. 2. Appellation given by boys to the trumpeters who attended the processions in the holy week. 3. Word of contempt, used by angry persons. *Judío de señal*, Converted Jew, who living among Christians wears a mark on his shoulders.
Judíos, sm. pl. A large sort of French beans; Dutch kidney beans. Phaseolus multiflorus *L.*
Juégo, sm. 1. Play, amusement, diversion. *Por juego, ó por modo de juego*, By way of diversion. 2. Disposition for doing any thing. 3. Sneer, ludicrous scorn, sportive insult. 4. Game, sport. *Juego de suerte y ventura*, Game of hazard or chance. 5. A single match at play. 6. Method, convenient order. 7. A fixed or complete number of things. *Juego de libros*, Set of books. *Juego de velas*, Set of sails. 8. Pun, quibble, equivocation. 9. *Tener juego*, (Naút.) To have fetched way; not to be firm or steady. *El palo mayor tiene juego en su fogonadura*, The main-mast has fetched way in its partners. *Juegos*, Public feasts, exhibitions, or rejoicings. *Juego trasero*, Hind part of a four-wheeled carriage. *Por juego ó por modo de juego*, In jest. *Conocer el juego*, (Met.) To discover any one's designs.
Juegueciíllo, sm. A little game, a bit of play.
Juéra, sf. (Extr.) Kind of sieve made of bass-weed.
Juéves, sm. Thursday. *Cosa del otro Jueves*, Something that is seldom seen. *Jueves de comadres*, The penultimate Thursday before carnival. *Jueves de compadres*, The antepenultimate Thursday before lent.
Juéz, sm. 1. Judge, one invested with power and authority to decide and determine causes and lawsuits. 2. Judge, one who has sufficient skill to form a correct opinion or judgment of the merit of any thing. *Juez arbitro*, Arbitrator, umpire. *Juez de enquesta*, (Ar.) Judge whose duty is to investigate the conduct and decisions of judges, ministers of justice, notaries, solicitors, &c. and to punish them if guilty by virtue of his office, and not at the instance of others.
Jugáda, sf. 1. Play, the act of playing. 2. Ill turn, wicked trick.
Jugadéra, sf. Shuttle used to make net-work. V. *Lanzadera*.
Jugadór, ra, s. 1. Player, one who plays. 2. Gamester, gambler. *Jugador de manos*, Juggler, one who practises sleight of hand, or plays tricks by legerdemain.
Jugár, vn. 1. To play, to sport, to frolic; to lose at play; to venture. 2. To match, to suit, to fit. 3. To move on joints or hinges. 4. To intervene; to take an active part in an affair; to exercise. 5. To mock, to wanton.
Jugarréta, sf. Bad play, unskilful manner of playing.
Júgez, sm. (Ant.) V. *Juez*.
Juglár, sm. Buffoon, mimic.
Juglarésa, sf. A female buffoon or mimic.
Juglería, sf. Buffoonery, mimicry.

Juguéte, sm. 1. Toy, play-thing, gewgaw. 2. Jest, joke. *Por juguete*, Jestingly. 3. Carol, a song of joy and exultation.
Juguetéar, vn. 1. To act the buffoon, to play childish tricks. 2. To play loosely, to wave, to float; applied to flags, pendants, or streamers.
Juguetón, na, a. Playish, acting the buffoon, wanton.
Juício, sm. 1. Judgment, the power of discerning the relation between one term or proposition and another; act of the understanding. 2. Opinion, advice. 3. Prudence, wisdom; applied to practice. 4. Judgment, sentence, verdict. 5. Judges assembled in court, tribunal, court of judicature. *Poder en juicio*, To sue at law. *Ser un juicio*, (Fam.) To be a confused multitude of persons or things.
Juiciosaménte, ad. Judiciously.
Juicióso, sa, a. Judicious, prudent.
Julépe, sm. Julap, a medical potion.
Julgár, va. (Ant.) V. *Juzgar*.
Júlio, sm. July, the seventh month of the year.
Julo, sm. Bell-mule, that takes the lead of a sumpter's or carrier's mules. [with partners.
Jumelár, va. (Naút.) To strengthen masts
Juméllas, sf. pl. Cheeks; a general name among mechanics for almost all those pieces of machines which are double.
Jumélos, sm. pl. (Naút.) Partners, strong pieces of timber, bolted to the beams which surround the masts on the deck, to keep them steady in their steps.
Juménta, sf. Female ass.
Jumentál y Jumentíl, a. Belonging to the ass.
Jumentíllo, lla, s. A little ass or beast of burthen. [A stupid person.
Juménto, sm. 1. Beast of burthen. 2. Ass. 3.
Juncáda, sf. 1. Kind of fritters. 2. A horse medicine against the glanders.
Juncál ó Juncár, sm. Marshy ground full of rushes.
Júncia, sf. (Bot.) Sweet cypress. English galangal. Cyperus *L.*
Junciána, sf. Brag, boast.
Junciéra, sf. An earthen vessel with a perforated lid, in which aromatics are kept.
Juncíno, na, a. Rushy, consisting of rushes.
Juncír, va. (Ant.) V. *Uncir*.
Júnco, sm. 1. (Bot.) Rush. Juncus *L.* 2. Junk, small Chinese ship. [es.
Juncóso, sa, a. Full of rushes, resembling rush-
Junoláda, sf. Stewed hare. V. *Lebrada*.
Júnio, sm. June, the sixth month of the year.
JunióR, sm. In convents, one still subject to instruction.
Junípero, sm. V. *Enebro*.
Junquéra, sf. (Bot.) Rush.
Junquerál, sm. V. *Juncal*.
Junquíllo, sm. 1. (Bot.) Jonquille. Narcissus junquilla *L.* 2. A small round moulding.
Júnta, sf. 1. Junta, board, council, court of jurisdiction, tribunal. 2. Meeting, assembly; union, conjunction. 3. Joint of a horse. 4. Each of the lateral superficies of a square stone which has to be joined to others.
Juntadór, ra, s. Joiner, one who joins.
Juntaménte, ad. Jointly; at the same time.
Juntamiénto, sm. Congregation, act of assembling.

Juntár, *va.* To join, to unite, to congregate; to amass or collect.—*vr.* 1. To join, to meet, to assemble. 2. To be closely united. 3. To copulate; applied to beings of different sexes. *Juntar meriendas*, (Fam.) To unite interests.
Juntéra, *sf.* Carpenter's plane.
Junterílla, *sf.* Small plane.
Júnto, ta, *a.* United, conjoined.
Júnto, *ad.* Near, close to; at the same time. *Por junto, ó de por junto*, In the bulk, by the lump, wholesale.
Juntório, *sm.* Kind of tribute.
Juntúra y Juntadúra, *sf.* 1. Joint, articulation of limbs; juncture of moveable bones in animal bodies. 2. (Naút.) Scarf. 3. V. *Junta*.
Júpiter, *sm.* 1. Jupiter, a planet. 2. (Among Chemists) Tin. 3. Sky, heaven.
Jur, *sm.* (Ant.) V. *Derecho*.
Júra, *sf.* 1. Oath, an affirmation, negation or promise, corroborated by the attestation of the Divine Being. 2. Oath of allegiance.
Jurádo, *sm.* Jurat, juror, juryman.
Juradór, ra, *s.* Swearer, one who is in the habit of obtesting the great name wantonly and profanely.
Juraduría, *sf.* Office of a jurat.
Juramentár, *va.* To swear, to put to an oath.—*vr.* To bind one's self by an oath, to obtest by an oath.
Juraménto, *sm.* Oath, an affirmation, negation or promise, corroborated by the attestation of the Divine Being. *Juramento asertorio*, Declaratory oath.
Jurár, *va.* To obtest some superior power; to attest the great name; to promise upon oath; to swear, to make oath.
Juratória, *sf.* Plate of silver containing the holy evangelists, on which magistrates lay their hands in taking an oath.
Juratório, *sm.* Instrument setting forth the oaths taken by Aragonese magistrates.
Jurdía, *sf.* Kind of fishing instrument.
Jurél, *sm.* A sea fish.
Jurgína, *sf.* Witch, sorceress.
Jurídicaménte, *ad.* Lawfully, legally.
Jurídico, ca, *a.* Lawful, legal; done according to law.
Jurisconsúlto, *sm.* Jurisconsult, one who gives his opinion in law. V. *Jurisperito*.
Jurisdicción, *sf.* 1. Legal authority, extent of judicial power; power, authority, jurisdiction. 2. District to which any judicial authority extends.
Jurisdiccionál, *a.* Relating to jurisdiction.
Jurispericía, *sf.* Jurisprudence.
Jurisperíto, *sm.* Civilian, a professor of jurisprudence or the science of law. [law.
Jurisprudéncia, *sf.* Jurisprudence, science of
Jurisprudénte, *sm.* Civilian. V. *Jurisperito*.
Jurísta, *sm.* 1. Jurist, a student in law. 2. Pensioner, one who has an annuity assigned to him upon the revenue of the crown.
Júro, *sm.* 1. Right of perpetual property. 2. Annuity assigned upon the revenue of the crown. *De juro*, Certainly.
Jusbárba, *sf.* (Bot.) Field myrtle. V. *Brusco*.
Jusíllo, *sm.* Pottage made of broth, parsley, grated cheese, eggs, and spice.

Jusgár, *va.* (Ant.) To condemn any one by justice.
Jústa, *sf.* 1. A mock encounter on horse-back. 2. Literary contest in poetry or prose.
Justacór, *sm.* (Ant.) Waistcoat, doublet.
Justadór, *sm.* Tilter, one who plays at jousts.
Justaménte, *ad.* Justly, exactly; precisely.
Justár, *vn.* To joust, to tilt.
Justícia, *sf.* 1. Justice, the virtue by which we give to every man what is his due. 2. Retribution, punishment. 3. Reason, equity; right. 4. Justice, magistrate or tribunal. 5. Public punishment. *Justicia de Aragon*, The chief magistrate of Aragon. *Justicia mayor*, The lord chief justice of Spain. *De justicia*, According to justice, duly, meritedly.
Justiciár, *va.* To execute a malefactor.
Justiciázgo, *sm.* The place and office of a justice.
Justiciéro, ra, *s.* Justicer; one who rigorously observes justice; one who chastises all crimes with rigid justice.
Justificación, *sf.* 1. Justification, defence, maintenance, support. 2. Production of the documents or instruments tending to establish a claim or right. 3. Equity, conformity with justice. 4. Sanctification by grace. 5. (Impr.) Adjustment of lines in a page of types.
Justificadaménte, *ad.* Justly, correctly.
Justificádo, da, *a.* Equal, justified; conformable to justice.
Justificadór, *sm.* Sanctifier. V. *Santificador*.
Justificánte, *pa.* Justifying; justifier.
Justificár, *va.* 1. To justify, to clear from imputed guilt; to absolve from an accusation. 2. To prove or establish a claim in a court of judicature. 3. To render just by the infusion of grace. 4. To rectify, to adjust, to arrange, to regulate exactly. 5. (Impr.) To justify or equalize a line of types.—*vr.* To vindicate one's character, to clear one's self from imputed guilt.
Justificatívo, va, *a.* Justificative, justifying.
Justíllo, *sm.* An under garment, or jacket without sleeves.
Justipreciár, *va.* To estimate any thing.
Justipreciadór, *sm.* Appraiser, a person appointed to set a price upon things.
Jústo, ta, *a.* 1. Just, conformable to justice. 2. Exact, strict, punctual. 3. Tight, close. 4. Good, pious.
Jústo, *sm.* A just and pious man. *En justos y en verenjustos*, Right or wrong, with reason or without.
Jústo, *ad.* Tightly, straitly. *Al justo*, Fitly, duly; completely, punctually.
Juvénco, ca, *s.* V. *Novillo*.
Juveníl, *a.* Juvenile, young, youthful.
Juventúd, *sf.* Youthfulness, youth.
Juzgádo, *sm.* Tribunal, court of justice; judicature.
Juzgadór, ra, *s.* Judge, one who judges.
Juzgamúndos, *s. com.* One who censures the actions of every one but himself.
Juzgánte, *pa.* Judging; judge.
Juzgár, *va.* To pass judgment, to award, to adjudge.—*vn.* To apprehend, to form an opinion.

THE letter *k* is not now used in the Spanish language; and even in the few words in which it was, its place has been supplied by *c* before *a*, *o*, and *u*, and *qu*, before *e* and *i*. Its pronunciation is similar to that of the *c* before *a*, *o*, and *u*; but its figure is retained in Spanish only for the intelligence of other languages.

KÁLI, *sm.* KALI, sea-weed. V. *Alcali.*

KARÁJO ó CARÁJO, A vulgar exclamation very common in Spain; its original import was the same as the Greek φαλλος.

KÁRMES, *sm.* KERMES, scarlet grain. V. *Carmesí.*

KERATOFÍTA, *sm.* (Bot.) A marine plant.

KYSTO, *sm.* (Ant.) Cyst, A kind of bag.

KY'RIES, *sm.* Responses in the liturgy.

THE *l* is in the Spanish language a semi-vowel, and sometimes becomes a liquid when a mute letter precedes it; *e. g.* in the words *claustro*, *gloria*, *flueco*. Joined to another *l* it has the sound of the Italian *gl*, of the Portuguese *lh*, and of the *i* and *ll* in the English words, *million*, *postillion*.

LA, is an article denoting the feminine gender in the singular number. It is also the accusative case of the personal pronoun feminine.

LÁBARO, *sm.* Standard of Constantine with the cipher of Christ on it.

LÁBE, *sf.* Stain, spot. V. *Mancha.*

LABERÍNTO, *sm.* 1. Labyrinth, maze; a place formed with inextricable windings. 2. An intricate and obscure matter, hard to be understood. 3. (Anat.) Labyrinth of the ear.

LÁBIA, *sf.* Sweet, winning eloquence.

LABIA'DO, DA, *a.* Labiated.

LABIÁL, *a.* Labial, uttered by the lips; applied to letters.

LÁBIO, *sm.* 1. Lip, the outer part of the mouth; the muscles which cover the teeth. 2. The edge of any thing. *Labio hendido*, Hare-lip.

LABIODENTÁL, *a.* Labiodental.

LABÓR, *sf.* 1. Labour, work, task. V. *Labranza*. 2. Symmetry, adaptation of parts to each other; design. 3. Needle-work, embroidery. *Labor blanca*, White work. *Sacar la niña de la labor*, To take a child from her needle. 4. A thousand tiles or bricks. 5. Cultivation, husbandry. 6. (Arag.) Egg of a silk-worm. *Labóres*, Figures raised upon a ground; variegated needle-work; diaper.

LABORÁBLE, *a.* LABORABLE.

LABORADÓR, *sm.* V. *Trabajador ó Labrador.*

LABORÁNTE, *sm.* 1. Labourer, workman. 2. Laborant, chemist.

LABORATÓRIO, *sm.* Laboratory, a chemist's work-room.

LABOREÁR, *va.* 1. To culture, to till the ground. 2. (Naút.) To work a ship, to direct her movements. V. *Maniobrar.*

LABORÉO, *sm.* Culture, labour.

LABORÉRA, *sf.* Clever, skilful; applied to a good workwoman.

LABORÍO, *sm.* V. *Labor.*

LABORIOSIDÁD, *sf.* Laboriousness.

LABORIÓSO, SA, *a.* 1. Laborious, assiduous. 2. Requiring much toil and labour, tiresome, not easy.

LABRÁDA, *sf.* Land ploughed and fallowed to be sown the ensuing season.

LABRADÉRO, RA, *a.* Labourable, capable of labour.

LABRADÍO, DÍA, *a.* V. *Labrantío.*

LABRÁDO, DA, *a.* Worked; applied to figured cloth in opposition to that which is plain.

LABRADÓR, RA, *s.* 1. Labourer who works at the plough or spade. 2. Cultivator, farmer, husbandman or woman. 3. Rustic, peasant.

LABRADÓR, RA, 1. Born or residing in a small village. 2. Laborious.

LABRADORCÍCO, CA; LLO, LLA; TO, TA, *s. dim.* of *labrador* y *labradora.*

LABRADORÉSCO, CA, *a.* Laborious, rustic, belonging to labour.

LABRANDÉRA, *sf.* Seamstress, she who supports herself by needle-work.

LABRÁNTE, *sm.* Stone-cutter, sculptor.

LABRANTÍN, *sm.* A petty farmer, who cultivates a small farm.

LABRANTÍO, TÍA, *a.* Producing grain; applied to arable land fit for the culture of grain.

LABRÁNZA, *sf.* 1. Tillage, the cultivation of the ground. 2. Husbandry, the employment of a cultivator or farmer. 3. Farm, land let to a tenant; an estate applied to the purposes and pursuits of agriculture. 4. Labour, work.

LABRÁR, *va.* 1. To work, to labour. 2. To till, to cultivate the ground. 3. To build, to construct buildings. 4. To do needle-work, to embroider. 5. To inform, to instruct. 6. To finish, to polish to the degree of excellence intended or required. 7. To harass, to mortify. 8. *Labrar un madero*, (Naút.) To fashion a piece of timber.—*vn.* To make a strong impression on the mind.

LABRÉRO, RA, *a.* Applied to a kind of fishing-net.

LABRIÉGO, *sm.* Peasant.

LÁBRIO Y LÁBRO, *sm.* (Ant.) V. *Labio.*

LABRÚSCA, *sf.* Rural life.

LÁCA, *sf.* 1. Lac, a red brittle resinous substance brought from India and used for dying and making sealing-wax. 2. Red colour.

LACÁRGAMA, *sf.* (Bot.) Alkanet, red-rooted bugloss. Anchusa tinctoria *L.*

LACÁYO, *sm.* 1. Lackey, footman, servant; foot soldier. 2. Knot of ribbons worn by women.

LACAYUÉLO, *sm.* Footboy.

LACAYÚNO, NA, *a.* Belonging to a lackey.
LACEÁR, *va.* 1. To adorn with ribbons tied in bows. 2. To pin up the game or drive it into an appointed place.
LACERACIÓN, *sf.* Laceration.
LACERÁDO, DA, *a.* 1. Unfortunate, unhappy. 2. Leprous.
LACERÁR, *va.* 1. To mangle, to tear in pieces. 2. To suffer, to labour under pains or fatigue. 3. To lead the life of a miser.
LACÉRIA, *sf.* 1. Misery, poverty, wretchedness. 2. Labour, fatigue. 3. Leprosy, scrofula. 4. A set of nets laid out together for some particular purpose.
LACERIÓSO, SA, *a.* Miserable; scrofulous.
LÁCHA, *sf.* Shad. V. *Alacha.* [guid.
LÁCIO, CIA, *a.* Faded, withered, dried up, lan-
LACIVIÓSO, SA, *a.* V. *Lascivo.*
LACONICAMÉNTE, *ad.* Laconically.
LACÓNICO, CA, *a.* Laconic, brief, concise.
LACONÍSMO, *sm.* Laconism, concise expression or style.
LÁCRA, *sf.* 1. Mark left by some wound or disorder. 2. Fault, vice, wickedness.
LACRÁR, *va.* 1. To injure or impair the state of health. 2. To hurt or injure in point of property or money.
LÁCRE, *sm.* Sealing-wax.
LACREÁR, *va.* To seal with sealing-wax.
LÁCRIMA, *sf.* V. *Lágrima.*
LACRIMACIÓN, *sf.* Effusion of tears.
LACRIMÁL, *a.* Lachrymal.
LACRIMATÓRIO, RIA, *a.* Lachrymatory.
LACRIMÓSO, SA, *a.* Weeping, shedding tears.
LÁCRIS, *sm.* Fruit of rosemary.
LACTÁNCIA, *sf.* Lactation, the time of giving suck, or during which a child sucks.
LACTÁNTE, *sm.* Sucker, one who sucks milk.
LACTÁRIO, RIA, *a.* Lactary, lacteous.
LÁCTEO, TEA, *a.* Lacteous, milky; resembling milk. *Via lactea,* (Astr.) Galaxy, the milky way.
LACTICÍNIO, *sm.* Milk-pottage, and, in general, all sorts of food prepared with milk.
LACTÍFERO, RA, *a.* Lactiferous, lacteal.
LACTÚMEN, *sm.* Scab breaking out on the head of sucking children. [ing.
LACÚNA, *sf.* Blank, a vacant space left in writ-
LACÚSTRE, *a.* Marshy, belonging to lakes. V. *Palustre.*
LÁDA, *sf.* V. *Xara.*
LÁDANO, *sm.* Labdanum, gum or resinous juice obtained by boiling from the *Cistus ladaniferus L.* a kind of rock-rose, very common in Portugal and Spain.
LADEÁR, *va.* To move or turn to one side; to go side by side; to go along rails.—*vn.* 1. (Naút.) To incline; applied to the needle of a mariner's compass. 2. To go by the side, to incline to one side.—*vr.* To incline to an opinion or party.
LADÉO, *sm.* Inclination or motion to one side.
LADÉRA, *sf.* Declivity, gradual descent.—*pl.* 1. Rails or staves of a common cart. 2. Cheeks of a gun-carriage. [ternus L.
LADIÉRNA, *sf.* (Bot.) Buckthorn. Rhamnus ala-
LADÍLLA, *sf.* 1. Crablouse. Pediculus pubis *L.* 2. Kind of barley with two rows of grain in the ear.
LADÍLLOS, *sm. pl.* Shifting panels in the sides of coaches, which in Spain are generally taken out in spring. [ciously.
LADINAMÉNTE, *ad.* Sideways, artfully, saga-
LADÍNO, NA, *a.* 1. Versed in an idiom, speaking different languages fluently. 2. Sagacious, cunning, crafty.
LÁDO, *sm.* 1. Side, that part of the human body which extends from the armpit to the hipbone; side or half of an animal. 2. (Met.) Companion, comrade. 3. (Met.) Faction, party. 4. Mat used to cover carts, &c. 5. (Met.) Patron, protector. 6. Course, manner; mode of proceeding. *Al lado,* Just by, near at hand. *De lado,* Incidentally. *A un lado,* Clear the way.
LADÓN, *sm.* V. *Xara.*
LÁDRA, *sf.* Cry of hounds after the game.
LADRADÓR, RA, *s.* 1. Barker, one who barks or clamours. 2. Talker, one who talks much and to no purpose.
LADRÁNTE, *pa.* Barking; barker.
LADRÁR, *vn.* 1. To bark, howl, or cry like a dog. 2. To use empty threats. 3. To clamour, to vociferate, to make outcries. *Ladrar el estomago,* To be hungry.
LADRÍDO, *sm.* 1. Barking or howling of a dog. 2. Vociferation, outcry; calumny; incitement.
LADRILLÁDO, *sm.* Floor made with bricks.
LADRILLADÓR, *sm.* V. *Enladrillador.*
LADRILLÁL Y LADRILLÁR, *sm.* Brickfield, a place where bricks are made and baked.
LADRILLÁZO, *sm.* Blow with a brick-bat.
LADRILLÉJO, *sm.* 1. Little brick. 2. Boy's amusement of knocking at doors with a piece
LADRILLÉRA, *sf.* Brick-kiln. [of brick.
LADRILLÉRO, *sm.* Brick-maker.
LADRÍLLO, *sm.* 1. Brick, a mass of clay burnt for building. 2. Cake of chocolate.
LADRILLÓSO, SA, *a.* Made of brick.
LADRÓN, NA, *s.* 1. Thief, robber. 2. Lock, sluice-gate. 3. Snuff of a candle that makes it melt.
LADRONAMÉNTE, *ad.* Thievishly, dissemblingly.
LADRONCÍLLO, *sm.* Filcher, a petty thief.
LADRONÉRA, *sf.* 1. Nest of rogues, den of robbers. 2. Filching, stealing; defrauding, extortion. 3. Sluice-gate in a mill. 4. Box. V. *Hucha.*
LADRONERÍA, *sf.* V. *Ladronicio.* [ish.
LADRONÉSCO, CA, *a.* Belonging to thieves, thiev-
LADRONÍCIO, *sm.* Larceny, theft, robbery.
LAGÁÑA, *sf.* A slimy humour running from the eyes.
LAGAÑÓSO, SA, *a.* Blear-eyed, being troubled with a slimy matter running from the eyes.
LAGÁR, *sm.* Wine-press, an engine for squeezing the juice out of grapes.
LAGARÉJO, *sf.* A small wine-press.
LAGARÉRO, *sm.* Wine-presser, one employed in squeezing the juice out of grapes, or olives.
LAGARÉTA, *sf.* Small wine-press.
LAGÁRTA, *sf.* Female lizard.
LAGARTÁDO, DA, *a.* V. *Alagartado.*
LAGARTÉRA, *sf.* Lizard-hole, a hollow place under ground where lizards breed.
LAGARTÉRO, RA, *a.* Catching lizards; applied to such animals as are fond of devouring lizards.

Lagartíja, *sf.* A small lizard.

Lagartijéro, ra, *a.* Catching lizards; applied to animals.

Lagartíllo, *sm.* A small lizard.

Lagárto, *sm.* 1. Lizard. Lacerta agilis *L.* 2. Insignia of the order of Santiago. 3. Gusset, a piece of lace put into the side of a surplice. 4. A large muscle of the arm. 5. A sly artful person.

Lágo, *sm.* Lake, a large diffusion of inland water; a large quantity of any liquid. *Lago de leones*, A den of lions.

Lagostin, *sm.* V. *Langostin.*

Lagoteár, *vn.* To flatter, to wheedle, to cajole.

Lagotería, *sf.* Flattery, adulation.

Lagotéro, ra, *a.* Flattering, soothing.

Lágrima, *sf.* 1. Tear, the water which any emotion forces from the eyes. 2. Any moisture trickling in drops; a drop or small quantity. 3. (Bot.) Gray-mill, gromwell. Lithospermum *L. Lagrima de Moyses, ó de Job*, (Bot.) Job's tears. Coix lacryma Jobi *L.* 4. Wine extracted from the grape by very slight pressure, in order to have the purest juice. *Lagrimas de S. Pedro*, Pebbles, stones with which persons were put to death. *Lagrima de Holanda*, Prince Rupert's drops, glass globules.

Lagrimáble, *a.* Worthy of tears.

Lagrimál, *sm.* Corner of the eye near the nose.

Lagrimár y Lagrimeár, *vn.* To weep, to shed tears.

Lagrimílla, ta, *sf.* A little tear.

Lagrimóso, sa, *a.* 1. Weeping, shedding tears. 2. Watery; applied to humours running from the eye; lachrymary.

Lagúna, *sf.* 1. Lake, a large diffusion of stagnant water. 2. An uneven country full of marshes. 3. Blanks in a book or writing.

Lagunájo, *sm.* Small pool of water in a field after rain.

Lagunár, *sm.* Timber-roof.

Lagunéro, ra, *a.* Belonging to marshes or lakes.

Lagunóso, sa, *a.* Marshy, fenny, abounding in lakes.

Láma, *sf.* 1. Mud, slime, ooze. 2. Cloth of gold or silver. 3. A flat even country. 4. Fine sand used for mortar. 5. Foam on the surface of water. 6. Dust of ores in mines.

Lamár, *va.* V. *Llamar.*

Lambér, *va.* V. *Lamer.*

Lambrequínes, *sm. pl.* (Blas.) Ornaments which hang from helmets.

Lambríja, *sf.* 1. Worm bred in the human body. V. *Lombriz.* 2. Meager, slender person.

Lamedál, *sm.* A musty miry place.

Lamedór, ra, *s.* 1. Licker, one that laps and licks. 2. Wheedler. *Dar lamedor*, To feign losing at play in order to insure greater success.

Lamedúra, *sf.* Act of licking.

Lamelár, *va.* To roll copper into sheets.

Lamentáble, *a.* Lamentable, deplorable.

Lamentableménte, *ad.* Lamentably.

Lamentación, *sf.* Lamentation, expression of sorrow.

Lamentadór, ra, *s.* Lamenter, weeper.

Lamentár, *vn.* y *r.* To lament, to express sorrow.

Laménto, *sm.* Lamentation, expression of sorrow.

Lamentóso, sa, *a.* Lamentable, to be lamented.

Lameplátos, *sm.* Lick-plate, nickname given to the servants who attend at table.

Lamér, *va.* To lick, to pass over with the tongue; to lap, to take in by the tongue.

Lametáda, *sf.* Thing licked or polished.

Lámia, *sf.* 1. Fabulous monster. 2. Kind of shark. 3. (Met.) Harlot, a woman of the town.

Lamído, da, *a.* Deformed, worn out with use.

Lamiénte, *pa.* Licking, licker.

Lamín, *sm.* (Ar.) V. *Golosina.*

Lámina, *sf.* 1. Plate, sheet of metal, any thin plate. 2. Copper-plate. 3. Painting or print put on fans.

Lamináda, da, *a.* Covered with plates or laminas.

Laminár, *va.* (Ar.) 1. To lick, to guzzle dainties. 2. To roll or beat metal into sheets.

Laminéra, *sf.* (Ar.) Bee advanced before its companions.

Laminéro, ra, *s.* Manufacturer of metal plates; one who makes shrines for relics.

Laminéro, ra, *a.* (Ar. y Murc.) Gluttonous.

Laminíca, lla, ta, *sf.* A small plate.

Lamiscár, *va.* To lick with haste and great eagerness.

Lamiznéro, ra, *a.* Lickerish, lickerous.

Lamóso, sa, *a.* (Naút.) Oozy, slimy; applied to the anchoring ground.

Lampaceár, *va.* (Naút.) To swab, to clean the decks with a swab.

Lampadáforo, *sm.* The victor in ancient races with torches at religious festivals.

Lámpara, *sf.* 1. Light, a luminous body. 2. Glass-lamp. 3. Spot or stain of oil or grease. 4. Branch of a tree placed at the door on festivals or rejoicings. *Lampara de bitácora*, (Naút.) Binacle-lamp.

Lamparéro, ra, *s.* Lamp-lighter.

Lamparílla, *sf.* 1. A small lamp. 2. A small bit of paper, twisted at the end, which when put in oil and lighted serves for a lamp. 3. A sort of coarse camblet.

Lamparín, *sm.* Case into which a glass lamp is put.

Lamparísta, *s. com.* Lamp-lighter.

Lamparón, *sm.* King's evil, a scirrhous tumour in the neck.

Lampatón, *sm.* A Chinese plant.

Lampázo, *sm.* 1. (Bot.) Burdock. V. *Bardana.* 2. (Naút.) Swab, a mop made of old ropes or rope-yarn, and used to clean the decks and cabin of a ship. *Paños de lampazo*, Tapestry, on which landscapes are represented. *Lampázos*, Pimples breaking out on the face.

Lampiño, ña, *a.* Beardless; having little hair.

Lampión, *sm.* A large lantern.

Lámpo, *sm.* (Poét.) Light, splendour, blaze.

Lampóte, *sm.* Cotton cloth made in the Philippine isles.

Lampréa, *sf.* (Ict.) Lamprey. Petromyzon *L.*

Lampreár, *va.* To dress a lamprey.

Lamprehuéla ó Lampreílla, *sf.* Kind of small lamprey.

Lampsána, *sf.* Kind of wild cabbage.

Lampúga, *sf.* (Ict.) Kind of crab.

Lána, *sf.* 1. Wool, the fleece of sheep. 2. Short curled hair of some animals. 3. Woollen manufacture in general. 4. (Joc.) Cash, money. *A' costa de lanas*, At another man's expense. *Lana burda*, Coarse wool.

Lanáda, *sf.* Sponge for cleaning cannons.

Lanádo, da, a. V. *Lanuginoso*. [wool.
Lanár, a. Woollen; belonging to wool, made of
Lanária, sf. (Bot.) Cud-weed.
Lánce, sm. 1. Cast, throw. 2. Casting of a net into the water to catch fish. 3. A favourable opportunity, critical moment. 4. Chance; fortuitous event. 5. Sudden quarrel or dispute. 6. Skill and industry of a player. *De lance*, Cheap.—*pl.* 1. Missile weapons. 2. Plot or intrigues of a play. *A' pocos lances*, In a short time and with little labour.
Lanceár, va. To wound with a lance.
Lancéola, sf. (Bot.) Plantain.
Lancéra, sf. Hooks in an armoury, on which arms are placed.
Lancéro, sm. 1. Pikeman, lancier, one armed with a pike or lance. 2. Maker of pikes.
Lancéta, sf. 1. Lancet, a small pointed chirurgical instrument. 2. Potter's knife.
Lancetáda y Lancetázo, s. Act of opening or wounding with a lancet.
Láncha, sf. 1. A thin and flat piece of stone. 2. (Naút.) Barge, lighter; longboat of a ship of war. *Lancha cañonera*, Gun-boat. 3. Snare for partridges.
Lancháda, sf. A lighter full of goods; as much as a lighter carries at once.
Lancházo, sm. Blow with a flat stone.
Lanchón, sm. (Naút.) Lighter. *Lanchon de lastrar*, Ballast-lighter.
Lanchonéro, sm. Lighterman.
Lancílla, sf. A small lance. [India.
Lanción, sm. (Naút.) A kind of guardship in
Lancúrdia, sf. Small trout.
Lánda, sf. An extensive tract of heath-land.
Lánde, sf. (Ast.) Acorn, the fruit of the oak-
Landéla. V. *Padre*. [tree.
Landgráve, sm. Landgrave, a German title.
Lándre, sf. 1. A morbid swelling of the glands. 2. A purse concealed in the clothes. 3. Acorn. V. *Bellota*. [glands.
Landrecílla, sf. Round lump among the
Landréro, ra, a. Applied to one who hoards money in a bag or purse concealed in his clothes. [under the tongues of hogs.
Landrécillas, sf. pl. Small grains which grow
Lanería, sf. Shop where washed wool is sold.
Lanéro, sm. 1. Dealer in wool. 2. Warehouse for wool.
Langarúto, ta, a. Tall, lank, ill-shaped.
Langór, sm. Languor, faintness; a decay of spirits.
Langósta, sf. 1. Locust, a devouring insect. Gryllus *L.* 2. Lobster, a crustaceous sea-fish. Cancer homarus *L.* 3. One who extorts money.
Langostín, sm. A small locust. [sus *L.*
Langostíno, sm. Grass-hopper. Gryllus gros-
Langostón, sm. The large green locust.
Languénte, a. Infirm, weak.
Languidaménte, ad. Languidly.
Languidéz ó Languidéza, sf. 1. Weariness, faintness. 2. Decay of spirits, melancholy.
Lánguido, da, a. 1. Languid, faint, weak. 2. Dull, heartless.
Languór, sm. Languor. V. *Languidez*.
Lanífero, ra, a. (Poét.) Laniferous.
Lanifício y Lanificación, s. Woollen manufacture, the art of manufacturing wool.

Lanílla, sf. 1. Nap of cloth, down, villous substance. 2. Swanskin, a kind of very fine flannel. 3. (Naút.) Buntine, a thin woollen stuff, of which flags and colours are made.
Lanío, a, a. Woollen. V. *Lanar*.
Lanosidád, sf. Down of the leaves of plants.
Lanóso, sa, a. V. *Lanudo*.
Lantéja, sf. Lentil. V. *Lenteja*.
Lantejuéla, sf. 1. Spangle, a small plate of shining metal. 2. Scurf left on the skin after any sore. [terna.
Lantérna, sf. Lantern or Lanthorn. V. *Lin-*
Lantía de Bitácora, sf. (Naút.) Binnacle-lamp. [clothed with wool.
Lanúdo, da, a. Woolly, consisting of wool,
Lanuginóso, sa, a. Lanuginous, downy; covered with soft hair.
Lánza, sf. 1. Lance, spear, javelin. 2. Pole of a coach or wagon. 3. Pikeman, soldier armed with a pike or lance. *Lánza en ristre*, Ready for action. *A' punta de lanza*, Strenuously, with all might. *Lánzas*, Duty paid to the Spanish government by the grandees and nobility of the realm, in lieu of military services.
Lanzáda, sf. Blow or stroke with a lance.
Lanzadéra, sf. Shuttle, the instrument with which the weaver shoots the cross threads.
Lanzadór, ra, s. Thrower, ejecter.
Lanzamiénto, sm. 1. The act of launching, casting, or throwing; dispossessing, ejectment. 2. (Naút.) Flaring of the bows and knuckle-timbers; rake of the stem and sternpost. *Lanzamientos*, Length of a ship from stem to sternpost.
Lanzár, va. 1. To elance, to throw, to dart. 2. To cast up, to vomit. 3. (For.) To eject, to dispossess. 4. To let loose.—*vr.* To rush or dart upon.
Lanzón, sm. A short and thick lance.
Láña, sf. 1. Cramp-iron. 2. Green cocoa nut.
Lañár, va. 1. To fasten two things together with a cramp-iron. 2. To open and gut fish. 3. To lament.
Lápa, sf. 1. Scum or pellicle raised on the surface of some liquors. 2. (Ict.) A kind of shell-fish. Lepas *L.* 3. (Bot.) Common burdock. Arctium lappa *L.*
Lapachár, sm. Hole full of mud and mire.
Lapáde, sf. (Ict.) Acorn shell-fish. Lepas *L.*
Lapicéro, sm. A metal pencil-case.
Lápida, sf. A flat stone, on which inscriptions are engraved.
Lapidária, sf. The art or profession of a lapidary, who deals in stones and gems.
Lapidário, sm. Lapidary, one who deals in stones and gems.
Lapidário, ria, a. Lapidary.
Lapídeo, dea, a. Lapideous, stony; of the nature of stone.
Lapidificación, sf. Petrification. [trify.
Lapidificár, va. To convert into stone, to pe-
Lapidífico, ca, a. Lapidescent, growing or turning to stone.
Lapidóso, sa, a. Lapideous, stony.
Lapílla, sf. (Bot.) Hound's tongue.
Lapislázuli, sf. An azure stone of which the ultramarine colour is prepared by calcination.
Lápiz, sm. Black chalk used in drawing; black lead. *Lapiz encarnado*, Red ochre

Lapizár, *sm.* Black lead mine.
Lapizár, *va.* To draw or delineate with black chalk or black lead.
Lápo, *sm.* Blow with the flat side of a sword.
Lápso, *sm.* Lapse or course of time.
Laqué, *sm.* Running footman.
Lar, *sm.* An amphibious bird.
Láres, *sm. pl.* 1. House-gods of the ancient Romans. 2. Pot-hooks, hooks on which pots are hung over the fire.
Larário, *sm.* Place where the pagans worshipped their house-gods.
Lardár ó Lardeár, *va.* 1. To baste, to drip oil or butter upon meat on the spit. 2. To beat with a stick.
Lardéro, (Juéves), *sm.* Thursday before lent.
Lárdo, *sm.* Lard, the fat or grease of swine.
Lardón, *sm.* A marginal note of a book.
Lardosíllo, lla; to, ta, *a.* Greasy, dirty with grease.
Lardóso, sa, *a.* Greasy, fatty.
Lárga, *sf.* Delay, procrastination.
Largaménte, *ad.* Largely, copiously, completely, liberally, frankly, for a long time.
Largár, *va.* 1. To loosen, to slacken, to ease a rope. *Larga las brazas de la gavia*, (Naút.) Let go the main top-sail braces. *Larga el lof*, (Naút.) Up tack sheets. *Toda vela larga*, (Naút.) All sails out. *Largar el cable por el chicote ó por ojo*, To pay out the cable end for end. 2. *Largar las velas*, (Met.) To enlarge upon a subject. *Largarse*, To set sail.
Lárgo, ga, *a.* 1. Large, wide. 2. Long, extensive. V. *Longitud*. 3. Generous, free, liberal. 4. Copious. 5. Prompt, expeditious. *Largo de lengua*, Too free and unguarded in the use of expressions. *Largo de uñas*, Light-fingered. *De largo á largo*, Lengthwise. *Navegar a lo largo de la costa*, (Naút.) To navigate along the coast. *Pasar de largo*, To pass by without stopping. *A' la larga*, At length, extensively, gently.—*ad.* Largely, profusely.
Largomíra, *sf.* Telescope.
Largór, *sm.* Length, the extent of any thing material from end to end. V. *Longitud*.
Largueádo, da, *a.* Striped. V. *Listado*.
Larguéro, *sm.* Jamb-post of a door or window. V. *Cabezal*.
Larguéza, *sf.* 1. Length, extent, largeness, width. 2. Liberality, generosity, frankness.
Larguíco, ca; llo, lla; to, ta, *a.* Not very large.
Largúra, *sf.* Length, longitude.
Laríce, *sm.* (Bot.) Larch-tree. Pinus larix *L.*
Laricíno, na, *a.* Belonging to the larch-tree.
Laríge, *a.* Applied to a kind of very red grapes.
Larínga, *sf.* Turpentine extracted from the larch-tree; Venice turpentine.
Larínge, *sm.* (Anat.) Larynx, the upper part of the trachea, through which the voice passes.
Láro, *sm.* (Orn.) Gull, sea-gull. Larus *L.*
Lárva, *sf.* 1. Mask. V. *Mascara y Fantasma*. 2. (Ent.) Larva, grub-state of an insect. *Larvas*, Hobgoblins.
Larvál, *a.* Frightful, ghastly; like a mask.
Lasaménto, *sm.* Lassitude, weariness. V. *Lasitud*.
Lasáña, *sf.* A sort of paste fried in a pan.
Lasárse, *vr.* (Ant.) To fatigue one's self.
Lascár, *va.* (Naút.) To ease off, to slacken. *Lascar el virador de combes*, (Naút.) To surge the capstern.
Lascivaménte, *ad.* Lasciviously.
Lascívia, *sf.* 1. Luxuriance, luxury; excess in delicious fare. 2. Lasciviousness, lewdness.
Lascívo, va, *a.* 1. Lascivious, lewd, lustful. 2. Luxuriant, exuberant.
Láser, *sm.* (Bot.) Benzoin.
Laserpício, *sm.* (Bot.) Laserwort. Laserpitium *L.*
Lasíllo, *sm.* A small knot.
Lasitúd, *sf.* Lassitude, weariness, faintness.
Láso, sa, *a.* Weary, tired with labour, subdued by fatigue.
Lastár, *va.* To pay, answer, or suffer for another.
Lástima, *sf.* 1. Grief, compassion, pity. 2. Object of compassion or pity. *Lastima es*, It is a pity.
Lastimár, *va.* 1. To hurt, to wound, to offend. 2. To move to compassion, to excite pity, to pity.—*vr.* To be moved to compassion, to grieve, to be sorry, to complain.
Lastiméro, ra, *a.* Sad, doleful, mournful, miserable.
Lastimosaménte, *ad.* Miserably, pitifully; in a doleful manner.
Lastimóso, sa, *a.* Doleful, sad. V. *Lastimero*.
Lásto, *sm.* Receipt given or belonging to him who has paid for another.
Lástra, *sf.* (Naút.) Boat, lighter. V. *Lancha*.
Lastrár, *va.* 1. (Naút.) To ballast a ship; to put stones, iron, or other weighty articles at the bottom of a ship. 2. To keep any thing steady by means of a weight. *Vela de lastrar*, (Naút.) Port-sail. *Lancha de lastrar*, (Naút.) Ballast-lighter.
Lástre, *sm.* 1. Rough stones which are merely used to ballast ships or build walls. 2. Ballast, a weight put at the bottom of ships, to keep them steady. *Lastre grueso*, Heavy ballast. *Lastre lavado*, Washed ballast. *Ir en lastre*, To go in ballast. *El lastre se corre*, The ballast shifts. 3. Weight, motive, judgment.
Láta ó Hoja de Lata, *sf.* Tin-plate, or tinned iron-plate. *Latas*, Laths, ledges.
Lataménte, *ad.* Largely, amply.
Latástro, *sm.* (Arq.) V. *Plinto*.
Latebróso, sa, *a.* Hiding, concealing from view.
Laterál, *a.* Lateral, belonging to the side.
Lateralménte, *ad.* Laterally.
Lateranénse, *a.* Belonging to the church of St. John of Lateran.
Latído, *sm.* 1. Pant, palpitation; motion of the heart. 2. Howling or barking of a dog after game.
Latigadéra, *sf.* (And.) Shock received by any thing in a cart from the motion.
Latigázo, *sm.* 1. Lash, crack of a whip. 2. Unexpected offence.
Látigo, *sm.* 1. Thong or point of a whip. 2. Rope with which any thing to be weighed is fastened to the steelyard. 3. Plume with which a hat is adorned.
Latigueár, *vn.* To smack or crack with the lash of a whip.
Latiguéra, *sf.* Cord for fastening to a weight or balance.
Latiguéro, *sm.* Maker or seller of whip thongs or lashes.

Latín, sm. Latin, the Latin tongue. *Saber mucho latin*, To be full of wit and cunning.

Latinájo, sm. Latin jargon.

Latinaménte, ad. In pure Latin.

Latinár y Latinizár, vn. To speak or write Latin.

Latinidád, sf. Latinity, the Latin tongue.

Latinísmo, sm. Latinism, a mode of speech peculiar to the Latin idiom.

Latinizár, va. To latinize, to give names a Latin termination; to make them Latin.—vn. To use words borrowed from the Latin.

Latíno, na, a. 1. Native of Latium; one who knows the Latin language. 2. Applied to the Western church, opposed to the Greek. *A' la latina*, In a lateen or triangular fashion. *Vela latina*, Lateen sail, of a triangular shape, and used chiefly in the Mediterranean.

Latír, vn. 1. To palpitate, to beat at the heart; to flutter. 2. To yelp, to bark as a hound in pursuit of game.

Latitár, vn. To lie concealed, to hide one's self.

Latitúd, sf. 1. Breadth, width, latitude, extent. 2. Distance of any point or object from the equator. *Latidud corregida*, (Naút.) Corrected latitude. *Latitud por estima*, (Naút.) Latitude by dead reckoning. *Latitud arribada*, (Naút.) Latitude come to.

Latitudinál, a. Relating to the latitude.

Láto, ta, a. Large, diffuse, extensive.

Latón, sm. Brass, latten.

Latonéro, sm. 1. Brazier, a manufacturer who works in brass. 2. (Bot.) V. *Almez*. 3. (Murc.) Little drain.

Latónes, sm. pl. (Naút.) Laths or ledges of different thickness, used on board of ships.

Latría, sf. Worship, adoration due to God only.

Latrína, sf. Privy-house. V. *Letrina*.

Latrocínio, sm. V. *Ladronicio*.

Laúd, sf. 1. Lute, a stringed musical instrument. 2. Merchant vessel.

Lauda, sf. Tombstone. V. *Laude*.

Laudáble, a. Laudable, praiseworthy.

Laudableménte, ad. Laudably.

Láudano, sm. Laudanum, a soporific tincture extracted from opium.

Laudár, va. To praise.

Laudatório, ria, a. Laudative.

Laúde, sf. 1. A tombstone with an epitaph engraved on it. 2. Prayers read in the Arabic language at Toledo, and in other places in Spain. *Laudes*, Lauds, that part of the divine service which is said after matins, and consists in praise of the Almighty. *Ad laudes*, At all hours, frequently. *Tocar á laudes*, To praise one's self.

Laudémio, sm. Dues paid to the lord of the manor on all transfers of landed property, within the precinct of the manor.

Laúsa, sf. 1. Lamina, a thin plate of metal. 2. Schistous clay used for covering houses.

Láura, sf. Solitary situation where the ancient monks had their detached cells.

Laúrea, sf. A laurel leaf or crown.

Laureándo, sm. He who is to receive a degree in a university.

Laureár, va. 1. To crown with laurel. 2. To graduate, to dignify with a degree in the universities.

Lauredál, sm. Plantation of laurel trees.

Laurél, sm. 1. (Bot.) Laurel. Laurus L. 2. A crown of bays as a reward.

Lauréntе, sm. Workman who takes the mould from the vat-man in paper-mills.

Laureóla, sf. 1. A crown of laurel. 2. (Bot.) Bay-tree. Daphne laureola L.

Laúrino, na, a. Belonging to laurel.

Laúro, sm. (Bot.) Laurel. Laurus L.

Laúto, ta, a. Rich, wealthy.

Láva, sf. 1. Washing of metals in mines. 2. Lava, a volcanic production.

Lavacáras, sm. 1. Water which washed the face. 2. Flatteries or caresses.

Lavácias, sf. pl. Foul water which runs from a washing place.

Lavación, sf. Lotion, wash.

Lavácro, sm. 1. Washing place, a lavatory. 2. Place where the baptism is administered; baptistery.

Lavadéro, sm. 1. Washing place, where wool and other things are washed. 2. Vat or pit in which tanners or skinners clean their skins.

Lavadór, ra, s. 1. Washer, one who washes wool. 2. Burnisher, an instrument which serves to clean and brighten fire-arms.

Lavadúra, sf. 1. Wash, the act of washing any thing. 2. Composition of water, oil, and eggs beat together, in which glove-leather is prepared. 3. V. *Lavazas*.

Lavájos, sm. pl. Pool, a small lake of standing water where cattle go to drink and clean themselves.

Lavamános, sm. A washing stand in a sacristy.

Lavánco, sm. A kind of wild duck.

Lavandéra, sf. Laundress, a woman whose employment is to wash clothes.

Lavandéro, sm. 1. Washer, he who washes. 2. One who carries and brings the foul linen to the washing place, to be washed.

Lavándula, sf. Lavender. V. *Espliego*.

Lavár, va. 1. To wash, to cleanse by ablution. 2. To clear from an imputation or charge of guilt. 3. To white-wash a wall with lime or chalk. *Lavar de lana á alguno*, To dive into the truth of any thing.

Lavatíva, sf. Clyster, a medicinal injection.

Lavatório, sm. 1. Lavation, the act of washing. 2. Medicinal lotion with which diseased parts are washed. 3. Ceremony of washing the feet on Holy Thursday. 4. V. *Lavamanos*.

Lavázas, sf. pl. Foul water running from a washing place.

Láve, sm. Washing of metals in mines.

Láxa, sf. Thin flat stone.

Laxación, sf. Loosening, laxation.

Laxamiénto, Laxitúd y Laxidád, s. Laxation, laxity.

Laxár, va. To loosen, to soften.

Laxatívo, va, a. Laxative.

Láxo, xa, a. Feeble, lax; loose opinions or morals.

Láya, sf. 1. Quality, nature. 2. A two-pronged instrument, with which the ground is turned up.

Layadór, sm. He who labours the soil with a two-pronged instrument.

Layár, va. To turn up the ground with a *laya*, or two-pronged instrument.

Laycál, a. Laical, belonging to the laity or people as distinct from the clergy.

Lat'do, da, a. V. *Ignominioso* y *Feo*.
Lazáda, sf. Knot formed with a ribbon or cord.
Lazaréto, sm. Lazaretto, a public building destined for the reception of persons coming from places which are suspected of being infected with the plague, to perform quarantine.
Lazarillo, sm. Boy who guides a blind man; a blind person's guide.
Lazaríno, na, a. Leprous.
Lázaro, sm. 1. Beggar covered with rags. 2. A cunning artful fellow.
Lázo, sm. 1. Bow, a slip-knot. 2. Snare, trick, scheme. 3. Tye, bond, chain. 4. The act of decoying, or driving the game to a certain spot.—*pl.* 1. Figures in dancing. 2. Flourishes made with the pen.
Le, *pronom.* Him or her, dat. and accus. sing. of the personal pronoun *el*, he or it; and dative of the feminine, *ella*, she.
Leál, a. Loyal, true to government; faithful.
Lealménte, ad. Loyally, faithfully.
Lealtád, sf. 1. Loyalty, fidelity, faithful attachment to the laws and government. 2. Gentleness towards a master; applied to beasts.
Lebéche, sm. South-west wind.
Lebráda, sf. Fricassee made of hare.
Lebrastón, sm. 1. An old hare. 2. A cunning crafty fellow.
Lebratíllo, sm. A young hare, a leveret.
Lebráto y Lebroncíllo, sm. Young hare.
Lebrél, sm. Greyhound. Canis variegatus *L.*
Lebréla, sf. Greyhound bitch.
Lebréro, ra, a. Applied to dogs for hunting hares.
Lebríllo, sm. A glazed earthen-ware tub or pan.
Lebrón, sm. 1. A large hare. 2. Coward, poltroon.
Lebrúno, na, a. Of the hare kind.
Lección, sf. 1. Art of reading; reading. 2. Lesson, any thing read or repeated to a teacher. 3. Lecture, a discourse upon any subject.
Leccionário, sm. Lesson-book of the matins.
Lecháda, sf. Lime slaked or dissolved in water.
Lechál ó Lechár, a. 1. Suckling; applied to all animals which live upon milk. 2. Lactiferous.
Léche, sf. 1. Milk, the liquor with which animals feed their young from the breast; milk or white fluid in plants. *Cochinillo de leche*, Sucking pig. *Vaca de leche*, Milk cow. *Leche de canela*, Oil of cinnamon. *Leche de gallina*, (Bot.) Star of Bethlehem. Ornithogalum *L.* 2. First principle of a science or art. 3. Blanching of coined silver in Mexico. *Hermano de leche*, Foster-brother. *Leche de los viejos*, Old wine. *Estar alguna cosa en leche*, Not to have attained a state of maturity. *Echar la mar en leche*, The sea being calm and smooth. *Mamarlo en la leche*, To imbibe in one's infancy. 4. *Leche de tierra*, Magnesia. *Como una leche*, (Fam.) Any thing very soft and tender.
Lechecíllas, sf. pl. 1. Sweetbread of calves, lambs, and kids. 2. Livers and lights.
Lechéra, sf. (Ant.) 1. Milk-pail. 2. V. *Litera*. 3. Bier. 4. (Mil.) Esplanade.
Lechería, sf. Cow-house, dairy.
Lechéro, ra, a. Milky, containing milk or having the property of it.
Lechéro, ra, s. 1. Milkman or woman, one who sells milk. 2. Tan-pit, where the ooze of bark is prepared.
Lecherón, sm. 1. Milk-pail, milk-vessel. 2. (Ar.) Flannel in which new-born infants are rolled.
Lechetrézna, sf. (Bot.) Spurge. Euphorbia *L.*
Lechigáda, sf. 1. Litter, a number of pigs farrowed at once. 2. Crowd of people; band of ruffians.
Lechín, sm. 1. Tent, pledget. 2. Olives rich in oil.
Lechíno, sm. 1. Tent, a roll of lint put into a sore. 2. Small tumour in horses.
Lécho, sm. 1. Bed, a place of repose. 2. Litter, straw laid under animals. *Lecho de lobo*, Haunt of a wolf. *Lecho de respeto*, Bed of state. 3. Bed of a river; horizontal surface of a seat. *Lechos*, Layers, strata.
Lechón, sm. 1. A sucking pig; pig of any size. 2. A dirty fellow in point of dress or manner of living.
Lechóna, sf. Sucking female pig.
Lechoncíllo, co, to, sm. A very young pig.
Lechóso, sa, a. Milky; applied to plants or fruits full of juice.
Lechúga, sf. 1. (Bot.) Lettuce. Lactuca *L.* 2. V. *Lechuguilla*.
Lechugádo, da, a. Having leaves like lettuce.
Lechuguéro, ra, s. Retailer of lettuce.
Lechuguílla, sf. 1. Small lettuce. 2. Frill, formerly worn around the neck.
Lechuguíno, sm. Plot of small lettuce.
Lechúza, sf. 1. (Orn.) Owl. Strix passerina *L.* 2. Filly one year old.
Lechúzo, za, a. 1. Suckling; applied to colts and fillies. 2. Collecting debts in trust for another.—*sm.* Nickname of an agent, collector, or commissioner who collects money or debts.
Lecíto, sm. Ancient vase like a bottle.
Lecticário, sm. 1. With the Romans, maker of sedan-chairs. 2. Sedan-chairman.
Lectistérnio, sm. Banquet of the heathen gods.
Lectívo, va, a. Applied to the time of lecture in universities.
Léctor, ra, s. 1. Reader, one that peruses any thing written. 2. Lecturer, a teacher or instructor by means of lectures; professor. 3. (In the Roman Catholic Church) A clergyman of the four minor orders.
Lectorádo, sm. Institution of lecturer.
Lectorál, sm. 1. Office of lecturer. 2. Reading canon.
Lectoría, sf. Lectureship, the place and office of a lecturer.
Lectúra, sf. 1. Lecturer, a discourse pronounced by way of instruction; public lesson. V. *Lectoria*. 2. (Among Printers) Small pica.
Ledaménte, ad. Merrily, cheerfully.
Ledóna, sf. (Ant.) Daily flow of the sea.
Leér, va. 1. To read or peruse any thing written. 2. To lecture, to instruct formally or publicly. 3. To penetrate into one's inmost thoughts.
Léga, sf. Laical nun exempt from the choir, but obliged to serve the community.
Legacía y Legación, sf. 1. Embassy, legation, deputation. 2. Message sent by an ambassador or deputy. 3. Province of the ecclesiastical state governed by a cardinal. 4. Duration of a legate's embassy.
Legádo, sm. 1. Deputy, ambassador, legate. 2

Legacy, a particular thing given by last will and testament. *Legado á latere*, A cardinal plenipotentiary of his holiness the Pope to a sovereign prince.

Legadór, *sm.* Day-labourer, who ties the feet of sheep.

Legadúra, *sf.* Ligature, cord or strap for tying or binding.

Legájo, *sm.* Bundle of loose papers tied together.

Legál, *a.* 1. Legal, lawful. 2. True, penitent, faithful in the performance of duty.

Legalidád, *sf.* Legality, fidelity, punctuality.

Legalización, *sf.* Attestation of a signature or subscription by which an instrument or writing is legalized.

Legalizár, *va.* To legalize, to authorise, to make lawful.

Legalménte, *ad.* Legally; faithfully.

Legaménte, *ad.* Ignorantly, in an illiterate manner.

Légamo, *sm.* Slime, mud, or clay left by water.

Legamóso, sa, *a.* Slimy, greasy.

Legáña, *sf.* V. *Lagaña.*

Legár, *va.* 1. To depute, to send on an embassy. 2. To bequeath, to leave any particular thing by a last will or testament. V. *Ligar y Llegar.*

Legatário, *sm.* Legatee, a person to whom a legacy is left.

Legatína, *sf.* A kind of stuff made of silk and wool.

Legénda, *sf.* (Ant.) Legend, traditionary history of saints, &c.

Legendário, *sm.* 1. Legend, a chronicle or register of the lives of saints. 2. Author of a legend.

Legíble, *a.* Legible, such as may be read.

Legicón, *sm.* Dictionary. V. *Lexicon.*

Legión, *sf.* Legion, a Roman corps; an indefinite number.

Legionário, ria, *a.* Legionary, belonging to a legion.

Legionénse, *a.* V. *Leonés.*

Legislación, *sf.* Legislation.

Legisladór, ra, *s.* Legislator, law-giver; censor.

Legislár, *va.* 1. To legislate, to enact laws. 2. To censure, to criticise.

Legislatívo, va, *a.* Legislative.

Legislatúra, *sf.* Legislature, the power that makes laws.

Legisperíto, *sm.* V. *Jurisperito.*

Legísta, *sm.* Professor of laws; student of jurisprudence.

Legítima, *sf.* Portion or share of the paternal or maternal estate, which belongs to the children, according to law.

Legitimación, *sf.* Legitimation, the act of investing with the privileges of lawful birth.

Legitimaménte, *ad.* Legitimately.

Legitimár, *va.* 1. To prove, to establish in evidence. 2. To procure to any the rights of legitimate birth; to make legitimate or adequate; to legalize.

Legitimidád, *sf.* Legitimacy.

Legítimo, ma, *a.* 1. Legitimate, born in marriage; lawfully begotten. 2. True, certain.

Légo, *sm.* 1. Layman, one of the people distinct from the clergy. 2. Lay-brother or lay-friar, a pious person admitted for the service of a religious body. 3. Ignorant, illiterate. *Carta de legos*, Decree which excludes an ecclesiastic judge from the cognizance of civil causes. —*a.* Laical.

Legón, *sm.* Spade.

Legoncíllo, *sm.* A small spade.

Légra, *sf.* Trepan, surgeon's instrument.

Legración ó Legradúra, *sf.* Act of trepanning.

Legrár, *va.* To trepan, to perforate the skull with a trepan.

Légua, *sf.* League, a linear measure; 17 1-2 Spanish leagues make a geographical degree: 8000 Spanish yards make a Spanish league or nearly 4 English miles. *A' legua, á la legua, á leguas, de cien leguas, ó desde media legua*, Very far, at a great distance.

Leguílla, *sf.* V. *Liguilla.*

Legúmbre, *sm.* 1. Pulse, leguminous plants. 2. (Joc.) The people distinct from the clergy.

Leguminóso, sa, *a.* (Bot.) Leguminous, having legumes or pods.

Leíble, *a.* Legible, readable.

Leido, da, *a.* Having read much, book-learned.

Leijár y Lejár, *va.* (Ant.) *Dexar.*

Léimma, *sm.* Interval of music.

Lejanía, *sf.* Distance, remoteness in place

Lejáno, na, *a.* Distant, remote.

Léjos, *ad.* At a great distance, far off. *Buen lejos*, Looking best at a distance.

Léjos, *sm.* 1. Perspective, distant prospect. 2. (Met.) Similarity, appearance, resemblance. *A' lo lejos, de lejos, de muy lejos, ó desde lejos*, At a great distance.

Léjos, jas, *a.* Distant, very remote; generally used in the feminine.

Lejuélos, *ad.* At a little distance.

Lelilí ó Lililí, *sm.* War-whoop of the Moors.

Lélo, la, *a.* Stupid, ignorant.

Léma, *sm.* 1. Argument of a poem explained in the title; motto. 2. Lemma, a proposition previously assumed.

Léme, *sf.* (Naút.) Tiller.

Leméra, *sf.* (Naút.) V. *Limera.*

Lemosín, na, *a.* 1. Native of Limoges. 2. Relating to the Lemosin language or that of the Troubadours.

Lén, *a.* Applied to soft untwisted silk.

Lencería, *sf.* 1. Sortment of linen of different sorts; plenty of linen. 2. Linen-draper's shop; linen-hall, where linen is sold.

Lencéro, ra, *s.* Linen-draper, dealer in linen.

Lendél, *sm.* Circle described by a horse turning a wheel to raise water out of a well.

Lendréra, *sf.* A close comb for taking out nits.

Lendréro, *sm.* Place full of nits.

Lendróso, sa, *a.* Nitty, full of nits on hair.

Léne, *a.* (Ant.) Mild, soft, bland.

Léngua, *sf.* 1. Tongue, the organ of speech in human beings; the part by which animals lick. 2. Language, idiom, speech; discourse. 3. Information, advice; interpreter. 4. Clapper of a bell. 5. Needle of a balance. *Lenguas*, (In the Order of Malta) Provinces into which the possessions of the order are divided. *Lengua del agua*, At the edge of the water. *Lengua de tierra*, Neck of land running out into the sea. *Con la lengua de un palmo*, With great anxiety or eagerness. *Tener algo en el pico de la lengua*, To have any thing at the tongue's end. *Lengua sábia*, Learned language. *Lengua canina ó de perro*, (Bot.) Hound's tongue. Cynoglossum *L.* *Lengua de buey*, (Bot.) Viper's bugloss. Echium fruticosum *L.*

Lenguádo, *sm.* (Ict.) Sole. Pleuronectes solea et linguatula *L.*

Lengúage, *sm.* Language, idiom; style, manner of speaking or writing.

Lenguaráda, *sf.* V. *Lengüetada*.

Lenguaráz, *a.* 1. Fluent, voluble; applied to one who expresses himself with ease and propriety. 2. Forward, petulant. 3. Talkative.

Lengúáz, *a.* Loquacious, garrulous.

Lengüeár, *va.* (Ant.) To spy, to watch and observe.

Lengüéta, *sf.* 1. A small tongue. 2. Epiglottis, windpipe. 3. Needle of a balance. 4. Bookbinder's cutting knife. 5. (Arq.) Buttress; moulding. 6. Borer used by saddlers and chairmakers. *Lengüetas*, Moveable plates or valves in musical wind instruments.

Lengüetáda, *sf.* The act of licking.

Lengüetería, *sf.* Collection of tubes with valves in an organ.

Lenidád, *sf.* Lenity, mildness.

Lenificár, *va.* To lenify, to soften. V. *Suavizar*.

Lenificatívo, va, *a.* Mollifying, softening.

Lenír, *va.* (Ant.) To mollify, to assuage.

Lenitívo, va, *a.* Lenitive, assuasive.

Lenitívo, *sm.* Emollient, mitigator.

Lenizár, *va.* To soften, to mollify.

Lenocínio, *sm.* Pimping, pandering. V. *Alcahuetería*.

Lenón, *sm.* V. *Alcahuete*.

Lentaménte, *ad.* Slowly.

Lénte, *sf.* Lens, a glass spherically convex on both sides.

Lentéja, *sf.* (Bot.) Lentil. Cicer lens *L.*

Lentejuéla, *sf.* Spangle, a small plate of gold or silver used in embroideries.

Lentéza, *sf.* Slowness.

Lenticulár, *a.* Lenticular, in the form of a lens.

Lentísco, *sm.* (Bot.) Mastich-tree. Pistacea lentiscus *L.*

Lentitúd, *sf.* Slowness, sluggishness.

Lénto, ta, *a.* Slow, sluggish, tardy; glutinous.

Lentór, *sm.* Lentor, a viscous humour.

Lenzuélo, *sm.* Handkerchief.

Léña, *sf.* Wood, timber.

Leñadór, ra, *s.* Woodman, wood-cutter, dealer in wood.

Leñár, *va.* To cut wood.

Leñéra, *sf.* Place for fire-wood.

Leñázgo, *sm.* Pile of wood or timber.

Leñéro, *sm.* 1. Timber-merchant. 2. Timber-yard, where timber is sold.

Léño, *sm.* 1. Block, a heavy piece of timber; the trunk of a tree cut down. 2. (Naút.) Ship, vessel. 3. (Met.) Person of little talent or ability.

Leñóso, sa, *a.* Woody, ligneous.

León, *sm.* 1. Lion. Felis leo *L.* *Leon pardo.* V. *Leopardo.* 2. (Met.) An irritable and cruel person.

Leóna, *sf.* Lioness, the female of the lion.

Leonádo, da, *a.* Lion-coloured, reddish yellow.

Leoncíllo, co, to, *sm.* Whelp of a lion.

Leonéra, *sf.* Cage or place where lions are shut up.

Leonéro, *sm.* 1. Keeper of lions. 2. Master of a gambling house.

Leonés, sa, *a.* Natural or belonging to the kingdom or city of Leon.

Leónica, *sf.* Vein or gland under the tongue; chiefly used of horses.

Leoníno, na, *a.* 1. Leonine, belonging to lions. 2. Leonine verses are those of which the end rhymes to the middle.

Leonína, *sf.* Elephantiasis, kind of leprosy.

Leontepetalón, *sm.* (Bot.) A plant, the root of which is an antidote for the poison of a snake.

Leopárdo, *sm.* Leopard, a spotted beast of prey. Felis pardus *L.*

Lepídio, *sm.* (Bot.) Pepper-wort. Lepidium *L.*

Lépra, *sf.* Leprosy, a loathsome distemper which covers the body with a kind of white scale.

Lepróso, sa, *a.* Leprous.

Lérda, *sf.* (Albey.) V. *Lerdon*.

Lerdaménte, *ad.* Slowly, heavily.

Lerdéz, *sf.* Slowness, tardiness, heaviness.

Lérdo, da, *a.* Slow, heavy; dull of comprehension.

Lerdón, *sm.* (Albey.) Tumour in a horse's pastern.

Lesión, *sf.* Hurt, damage, wound; injury.

Lesívo, va, *a.* Prejudicial, injurious.

Lésna, *sf.* Awl, a pointed instrument to bore holes.

Lesnordéste, *sm.* (Naút.) East-north-east wind.

Léso, sa, *a.* Wounded, hurt, damaged; perverted. *Lesa magestad*, Leze majesty.

Lest, *sm.* 1. Last, a certain weight or measure. 2. (Met.) East, Levant.

Léste, *sm.* East wind; east.

Lesuéste, *sm.* (Naút.) East-south-east wind.

Letál, *a.* Mortal, deadly, destructive.

Letáme, *sm.* (Ant.) Mud, mire to manure the soil.

Letanía, *sf.* 1. Litany, a form of supplicatory prayer. *Letanias*, Supplicatory processions. 2. (Fam.) List or enumeration of many things.

Letárgico, ca, *a.* Lethargic.

Letárgo, *sm.* Lethargy, a morbid drowsiness.

Letéo, a, *a.* (Poét.) Lethean.

Letícia, *sf.* Joy, mirth.

Letífero, ra, *a.* Lethiferous, deadly, that which is the cause or sign of death.

Letificánte, *pa.* Exhilarating.

Letificár, *va.* To rejoice, to make merry.

Letíjo, *sm.* (Ant.) V. *Litigio*.

Létra, *sf.* 1. Letter, one of the elements of syllables. 2. Writing composed of letters. 3. Type, a printing letter. 4. Motto, inscription. 5. Order, decree, despatch. 6. Words of a song. 7. Grammatical sense of a phrase. *Letra de cambio*, Bill of exchange. *Á la letra*, Literally, punctually, entirely. *Saber mucha letra*, To be very artful and cunning. *Letras*, The learned professions; rescript; certification, testimony. *Tener las letras gordas*, To be dull or ignorant in point of sciences and learning.

Letráda, *sf.* Lawyer's wife.

Letradería y Letraduría, *sf.* 1. (Baxo.) Body or society of lawyers, inn. 2. A foolish speech uttered with an air of dignity and importance.

Letrádo, da, *a.* 1. Learned, erudite. 2. Vain, presumptuous.—*sm.* 1. Literato, a learned man. 2. Lawyer, professor of law; advocate.

Letradúra, *sf.* V. *Literatura*.

Letréro, *sm.* Inscription, legend on medals or coins

Letrílla, *sf.* 1. A small letter. 2. Song, a poem modulated by the voice.
Letrína, *sf.* Privy, necessary house.
Letrónes, *sm. pl.* Capital letters or large characters.
Letuário, *sm.* Electuary, a medicine in the consistence of honey.
Leudár, *va.* To ferment the mass of dough with leaven.
Leúdo, da, *a.* Fermented, leavened; applied to bread.
Léva, *sf.* 1. (Naút.) Act of weighing anchor. *Pieza de leva*, Shot fired as a signal for weighing anchor. 2. Press, a commission to force men into military service. 3. (Naút.) Swell of the sea. *Hay mar de leva*, There is a swell in the offing.—*pl.* 1. Tricks, artful devices. 2. (In Powder-mills) Lifters, which raise the pounding pestles.
Leváda, *sf.* 1. Silkworm which moves from one place to another. 2. Salute or flourish made with the foil by fencers before they set to. V. *Llevada.*
Levadéro, ra, *a.* That which is to be demanded.
Levadízo, za, *a.* That can be lifted or raised.
Levadúra, *sf.* 1. Ferment, leaven, yeast. 2. Board cut off from a piece of timber, to give it the proper dimension.
Levantáda, *sf.* Rise, the act of rising.
Levantadaménte, *ad.* In an elevated or exalted manner.
Levantadór, ra, *s.* 1. One who raises or lifts up. 2. Disturber, he that excites disturbances.
Levantamiénto, *sm.* 1. Elevation, the act of raising; sublimity. 2. Insurrection, revolt, rebellion. 3. Balance of accounts.
Levantár, *va.* 1. To raise, to lift up. 2. To build, to erect a building. 3. To impute or attribute falsely. 4. To elevate, to aggrandize, to promote. 5. To cut the cards. *Levantar la casa*, To break up house, to move to another place. *Levantar velas*, (Met.) To abandon one's residence. *Levantar la cerviz*, (Met.) To exalt, to extol one's self. *Levantar polvareda*, To raise a dust, to excite disturbances. *Levantar el caballo*, To drive a horse at the gallop.—*vr.* 1. To stand up, to rise from bed. 2. To recover from sickness. 3. To raise one's self on a high place.
Leválnte, *sm.* 1. Levant, particularly the coasts of the Mediterranean east of Italy. 2. Rise, the act of getting up. 3. East, east-wind. *Estar de levante*, To be ready to set sail. *Comercio de Levante*, The Levant trade.
Levantíno, na, y Levantísco, ca, *a.* Relating or belonging to the Levant.
Levár, *va.* 1. (Ant.) To carry, to transport. 2. (Naút.) To weigh anchor.
Léve, *a.* Light, of little weight; trifling.
Levedád, *sf.* Lightness, levity, inconstancy.
Leveménte, *ad.* Lightly, gently, venially.
Levigár, *va.* To levigate.
Levita, *sm.* Levite, one of the tribe of Levi.
Levítico, *sm.* 1. Book of Leviticus. 2. Ceremonial.
Lexía, *sf.* 1. Lye, water boiled with ashes, and thus impregnated with an alkaline salt. 2. (Met.) Severe reprehension.
Lexicógrafo, *sm.* Lexicographer, author or writer of a dictionary.
Lexicón, *sm.* Dictionary, lexicon.
Lexío, *sm.* (Among Dyers) Lye.
Léy, *sf.* 1. Law, a rule of action. 2. Loyalty, faithful attachment to a superior or master. 3. Religion. 4. Alloy, base metal mixed in coinage with gold or silver, to render it harder. *Ley de encaxe*, (Fam.) Dictamen of a judge without regard to the laws. *Ley de la trampa*, Fraud, deceit. *A' la ley*, With propriety and neatness. *A' toda ley*, Perfectly, according to rule.—*pl.* 1. Body or collection of laws. 2. Study and profession of the law.
Leyénda, *sf.* 1. Lecture, the act of reading. 2. Legend.
Léyla, *sf.* A Moorish dance.
Lézda, *sf.* Ancient tax on merchandise.
Lía, *sf.* A thin bass-rope. *Lias*, Husks of pressed grapes.
Liár, *va.* To tie, to bind.—*vr.* To contract an alliance. *Liarlas*, (Fam.) To elope, to die.
Liára, *sf.* (And.) V. *Aliara ó Cuerna.*
Liáza, *sf.* Collection of hoops used by coopers.
Libación, *sf.* Libation, pouring out wine for a sacrifice.
Libamiénto, *sm.* The offering in ancient sacrifices.
Libár, *va.* 1. To suck, to sip, to extract the juice; to taste. 2. To perform a libation.
Libelár, *va.* To petition, to sue at law.
Libelático, ca, *a.* Applied to the Christians who renounced the Christian religion in a written declaration, for which the Roman emperors exempted them from persecution.
Libelísta, *sm.* Libeller, author of libels.
Libélo, *sm.* 1. Petition, libel; a declaration of charge in writing against a person, in court. 2. A defamatory writing, lampoon, libel.
Liberál, *a.* 1. Liberal, generous, free, open. 2. Quick in the performance of a thing; brisk, active. 3. Liberal; applied to the arts as opposed to mechanics.
Liberalidád, *sf.* Liberality, generosity.
Liberalménte, *ad.* Liberally, expeditiously.
Liberamént y Liberaménte, *ad.* V. *Libremente.*
Libérrimo, ma, *a. sup.* Most free.
Libertád, *sf.* 1. Liberty, freedom, as opposed to slavery. 2. Exemption, privilege, immunity. 3. License, permission. 4. Freedom, agility, address, alacrity, independence.
Libertadaménte, *ad.* Freely.
Libertádo, da, *a.* 1. Libertine, impudent. 2. Free, ungoverned. 3. Idle, disengaged.
Libertadór, ra, *s.* Deliverer, liberator.
Libertár, *va.* 1. To free, to set at liberty; to preserve. 2. To clear from an obligation or debt.
Libertináge, *sm.* Libertinism, licentiousness of opinion or practice; irreligion, libertinage.
Libertíno, na, *s.* Child of a freed man.—*a.* Libertine, irreligious, dissolute, impudent.
Libérto, *sm.* A freed man, an emancipated slave.
Líbi, *sm.* (Buenos Ayres) Instrument with which the Indians catch ostriches.
Libicoáfrico, *sm.* Westerly wind.
Libiconóto, *sm.* South-west wind.
Libidinosaménte, *ad.* Libidinously.
Libidinóso, sa, *a.* Libidinous, lewd, lustful.
Líbitum (Ad), *ad.* (Lat.) At will.
Líbra, *sf.* 1. A pound weight. *Libra carnicera,*

Flesh-pound of thirty-six ounces. 2. *Libra esterlina*, A pound sterling. *Libra Tornesa*, A French livre. 3. (In Oil-mills) Weight with which the husks of olives are pressed. 4. (Astr.) Libra, sign of the zodiac.

Libracho, *sm.* An old worm-eaten book or paper.

Libración, *sf.* Libration, the state of being balanced.

Librador, *sm.* 1. Deliverer, one who sets at liberty. 2. (Corn-mills) Shoe with a hole and feeder, through which the corn falls into the eye of the mill-stone. 3. Store-keeper of the king's mews. 4. Copper-shovel, used by grocers and confectioners to take out dry sweetmeats, brown sugar, &c.

Libramiénto, *sm.* 1. Delivery, the act of delivering. 2. Deliverance, the act of freeing from captivity. 3. Warrant, order of payment.

Librancísta, *sm.* 1. One who holds a warrant or order of payment. 2. Clerk who draws up warrants.

Librante, *sm.* Solicitor, procurator.

Libranza, *sf.* V. *Libramiento.*

Librár, *va.* 1. To free, to deliver, to rid from danger. 2. To give a warrant or order for paying a certain sum. 3. To despatch, to expedite. 4. To give leave to converse in the parlour; applied to nuns. 5. To commit, to entrust. 6. To decide, to sentence. 7. To draw a bill or money. *Librar bien ó mal*, To get over a thing well or ill. *A' bien ó á buen librar*, The best that could possibly happen.

Libratório, *sm.* V. *Locutorio.*

Librázo, *sm.* 1. A large book. 2. Blow with a book.

Líbre, *a.* 1. Free, uncumbered, unrestrained; independent; unembarrassed. 2. Exempt, privileged. 3. Innocent, guiltless. 4. Single, unmarried. 5. Licentious, impudent. 6. Rash, forward, thoughtless.

Libréa, *sf.* Livery, clothes given to servants.

Librear, *va.* To weigh, to sell or distribute by pounds.

Libréjo, *sm. dim.* A little book.

Libremente, *ad.* Freely, boldly, audaciously, impudently.

Librería, *sf.* 1. Bookseller's shop, stationer's shop. 2. Profession and trade of a bookseller. 3. Library, a large collection of books; the apartment which contains a collection of books properly arranged.

Librero, *sm.* Bookseller, one who deals in books.

Libréta, *sf.* 1. Small pound of twelve ounces; the troy-weight pound. 2. Loaf of bread which weighs sixteen ounces. 3. Small memorandum book.

Librete, *sm.* 1. A small book. 2. Small vessel with coals used by women for warming their feet.

Librílla, *sf.* A small book. V. *Libreta.*

Libríllo, to, *sm.* 1. A small book. 2. Wax-taper rolled up in the form of a book.

Líbro, *sm.* 1. Book, a volume in which we read or write. 2. Division or part of a work. 3. (Met.) Contribution, impost, tax. *Libro becerro*, Doomsday-book. *Libro del diario*, (Naút.) Journal. *Libro mayor*, Ledger. *Libro de memoria*, Memorandum-book. *Libro de quarenta*, Pack of cards. *Libro verde*, Book for topographical and genealogical remarks; also, the compiler of such writings.

Librote, *sm. aum.* Large book; applied to persons in contempt.

Libúrnica, *sf.* Light vessel used at Leghorn.

Licantrópia, *sf.* Lycanthropy, violent insanity

Licéncia, *sf.* 1. License, permission, leave. *Primero en licencias*, (Alcala) The first candidate to be admitted to the degree of a doctor; degree of licentiate. 2. Excessive liberty.

Licenciadíllo, *sm.* Nick-name given to a little ridiculous person, dressed in clerical habits.

Licenciádo, *sm.* 1. Licentiate, a graduate in Spanish and German universities. 2. Appellation of jurisconsults, although doctors. 3 (Fam.) Scholastic, wearing robes.

Licenciádo, da, *a.* Licensed, vainglorious.

Licenciamiénto, *sm.* Act of graduating.

Licenciár, *va.* To license, to permit by a legal grant; to graduate.—*vr.* To become dissolute.

Licenciosaménte, *ad.* Licentiously.

Licencióso, sa, *a.* Licentious, dissolute.

Licéo, *sm.* Lyceum, a public school.

Licéra, *sf.* (Murc.) V. *Lisera.*

Lichén, *sm.* (Bot.) Lichen, liverwort. Lichen L.

Lichéra, *sf.* Woollen cover of a bed.

Lício, *sm.* (Bot.) Box thorn. Lycium *L.*

Lición, *sf.* Lesson. V. *Leccion.*

Lícitamente, *ad.* Lawfully, justly.

Lícito, ta, *a.* Licit, lawful; just.

Licór, *sm.* Liquor, any thing liquid; spirits.

Licoróso, sa, *a.* Applied to generous wine, which is spirituous and aromatic.

Lictór, *sm.* Minister of justice in ancient Rome.

Líd, *sm.* Conflict, contest; dispute, argument

Lidiadór, *sm.* Combatant, one who publicly disputes or argues.

Lidiár, *vn.* To fight, to oppose, to contend.—*va.* To run or fight bulls.

Liebrastón, *sm.* Leveret, a small or young hare.

Liebrático, *sm.* Young hare.

Liébre, *sf.* 1. Hare. Lepus *L.* 2. Coward, poltron. *Coger una liebre*, To fall into mud or mire.—*pl.* 1. (Naút.) Racks or ribs. 2 (Naút.) Dead eyes.

Liencecíco, llo, to, *sm.* Little linen cloth.

Liéndre, *sf.* Knit, the egg of a louse.

Lientéra y Lientéria, *sf.* Lientery, diarrhœa which carries off the food undigested.

Lientérico, ca, *a.* Lienteric.

Liénto, ta, *a.* Damp, moist.

Liénzo, *sf.* 1. Linen, cloth made of flax or hemp. *Lienzo encerrado*, Glazed linen. 2. Handkerchief. 3. Painting on linen. 4 (Fort.) Curtain, the part of a rampart which runs between two bastions, or joins the flanks thereof. 5. Face or front of a building.

Lievár, *va.* (Ant.) V. *Llevar.*

Lifára, *sf.* (Ar.) V. *Alifara.*

Líga, *sf.* 1. Garter, a string or riband by which the stocking is held upon the leg. 2. (Bot.) Misletoe. Viscum album *L.* 3. Bird-lime. 4. League, coalition. 5. Alloy. V. *Ley.*

Ligación, *sf.* Act of tying, union, mixture.

Ligádas, *sf. pl.* (Impr.) Ligatures.

Ligadúra, *sf.* 1. Ligature, truss. 2. League, mutual correspondence. 3. (Naút.) Seizing, the fastening of two ropes with a thin line; lashing. *Dar una ligadura*, (Naút.) To seize.

Ligagámba, *sf.* Garter. V. *Liga.*
Ligállo, *sm.* (Ar.) V. *Mesta.*
Ligamáza, *sf.* Viscous or glutinous matter around some fruits.
Ligaménto, *sm.* 1. Bandage. V. *Ligatura.* 2. Ligament, a nervous cord which connects the junctures of the body.
Ligamentóso, sa, *a.* Ligamentous.
Ligamiénto, *sm.* 1. Union, act of tying or uniting. 2. Ligament.
Ligár, *va.* 1. To tie, to bind. 2. To allay or alloy; to mix base metals with gold or silver, to render them fitter for coinage. 3. To league, to coalesce, to confederate. 4. To render impotent by charms or spells. 5. To exorcise, to purify from the influence of malignant spirits.—*vr.* 1. To be leagued, to be allied. 2. To bind one's self to the performance of a contract.
Ligazón, *sf.* 1. Union, contexture. 2. (Naút.) Futtock-timbers, the compass-timbers which form the breadth of a ship. *Navio que carece de ligazones,* A ship slightly built.
Ligeraménte, *ad.* Swiftly, lightly, easily, without reflection.
Ligeréza, *sf.* 1. Lightness, want of weight. 2. Agility, nimbleness. 3. Levity, unsteadiness, inconstancy. 4. Unchastity, want of conduct in women.
Ligéro, ra, *a.* 1. Light, of little weight. 2. Light, thin; applied to stuff or cloth. 3. Swift. 4. Unsteady. 5. Easy. *Ligero de dedos,* Light fingered. *A' la ligera,* Lightly, expeditiously. *De ligero,* Rashly, easily.
Ligeruéla, *sf.* Early grape.
Lígio, a, *a.* Feudal, bound to one lord only.
Lignumcrúcis, *sm.* Relique of the cross of [Christ.
Ligóna, *sf.* (Ar.) V. *Azada.*
Ligomélas (**Uvas**), *a.* Early grapes.
Liguílla, *sf.* Kind of narrow riband.
Lígula, *sf.* An opening in the larynx.
Ligústico, *sm.* (Bot.) Lovage. Ligusticum *L.*
Ligústico, ca, *a.* Belonging to Liguria.
Ligústro, *sm.* (Bot.) Privet. V. *Alheña.*
Lila, *sf.* 1. (Bot.) Lilac tree. Syringa vulgaris *L.* 2. Lilac flower. 3. A kind of light woollen stuff of various colours.
Lilac, *sm.* (Bot.) Lilac. V. *Lila.*
Liláo, *sm.* Ostentation, ambitious display, outward show.
Liláyla, *sf.* 1. Thin woollen stuff. 2. Ridiculous impertinence. 3. Prank, trick.
Lililíes, *sm. pl.* War-hoop of the Moors.
Líma, *sf.* 1. (Bot.) Lime, the fruit. 2. (Bot.) Lime-tree, which produces limes. 3. File, an instrument to cut or smooth metals. 4. (Met.) Correction, finish, polish. 5. Channel in the roof of a house for the water to pass to the eaves. *Lima sorda,* (Met.) That which imperceptibly consumes any thing.
Limadúra, *sf.* 1. Act of filing. 2. Filings, metallic fragments rubbed off by the file.
Limálla, *sf.* Filings.
Limár, *va.* 1. To file, to cut with a file. 2. To gnaw, to corrode. 3. To file, to polish; to give the finishing stroke to literary produc-[tions.
Limatón, *sm.* Coarse round file.
Limáza, *sf.* Snail. Limax *L.*
Limázo, *sm.* Viscosity, sliminess.

Limazón, *sm.* Slug, a snail or slimy animal without a shell.
Límbo, *sm.* 1. Limbo, a region assigned to the departed souls of children. 2. Limb; edge, border, extremity.
Límen, *sm.* (Poét.) V. *Umbral.*
Liméño, ña, *a.* Native of Lima.
Liméra, *sf.* 1. Shop-woman who sells files. 2. (Naút.) Helmport, where the tiller is fastened to the rudder of the ship.
Liméro, ra, *s.* 1. Shopkeeper who sells files or limes. 2. (Bot.) Lime-tree. Citrus *L.*
Liméta, *sf.* Phial, a small bottle.
Limíste, *sm.* Cloth made of Segovia wool; cloth of the first quality.
Limitación, *sf.* Limitation, restriction, modification; limit, district.
Limitadaménte, *ad.* Limitedly.
Limitádo, da, *a.* Limited, possessed of little talent.
Limitáneo, nea, *a.* Limitary, placed on the boundaries; belonging to limits.
Limitár, *va.* 1. To limit, to confine within certain bounds. 2. To form boundaries, to establish limits. 3. To restrain, to circumscribe; to reduce expense.
Límite, *sm.* Limit, boundary.
Limítrofe, *a.* Limiting; applied to frontier provinces.
Límo, *sm.* Slime, mud.
Limón, *sm.* 1. Lemon, the fruit of the lemon-tree. 2. (Bot.) Lemon-tree. Citrus medica *L.* *Limones,* Shafts of a cart.
Limonáda, *sf.* Lemonade, a liquor made of water, sugar, and the juice of lemons. *Limonada de vino,* A cool tankard.
Limonádo, da, *a.* Lemon-coloured.
Limonáge, *sm.* (Naút.) The act of boats and pilot-barges going out of a harbour, to work or pilot a vessel into port.
Limonár, *sm.* Plantation of lime-trees.
Limoncíllo, *sm.* A small lemon.
Limonéro, ra, *s.* Dealer in lemons; lemon-tree.—*a.* Applied to the shaft horses in carriages, &c. [teeth.
Limosidád, *sf.* Sliminess; matter between
Limósna, *sf.* Alms, charity.
Limosnéro, *sm.* Almoner, the officer employed in the distribution of charity.—*a.* Charitable.
Limóso, sa, *a.* Slimy, muddy.
Límpia, *sf.* The act of cleaning or cleansing.
Limpiadéra, *sf.* Instrument used for washing.
Limpiadiéntes, *sm.* Toothpick.
Limpiadór, ra, *s.* Cleanser, scourer.
Limpiadúra, *sf.* Act of cleansing; dirt.
Limpiaménte, *ad.* Cleanly, neatly, purely, sincerely, faithfully. [ing.
Limpiamiénto, *sm.* Act of cleaning or cleans-
Limpiár, *va.* 1. To clean, to scour. 2. To purify, to clear from guilt. 3. To pursue, to persecute. 4. (Joc.) To steal. *Limpiar las faltriqueras á uno,* To pick one's pockets.—*vr.* To clear one's self from imputed guilt.
Limpiéza, *sf.* 1. Cleanness, cleanliness. 2. Chastity, purity of morals. 3. Integrity, rectitude; disinterestedness. *Limpieza de bolsa,* Emptiness of the purse.
Límpio, pia, *a.* 1. Clean, free from stain. 2. Neat, elegant. 3. Pure; applied to families

unconnected with Moors or Jews. *Limpio de polvo y paja*, Clear or free from all charges. *Jugar limpio*, To deal fair, to act in an upright manner. *Poner en limpio*, To make a fair copy. *Tierra limpia*, Even flat country. *Costa limpia*, (Naút.) Clear coast, that which has no shoals, sand-banks, or shallows. *En limpio*, In substance; neat price; clearly.

Limpión, *sm.* 1. The act of cleaning. 2. One who sweeps the streets.

Linága, *sm.* 1. Lineage, race, progeny. 2. Class, condition. *Linages*, Nobles, nobility.

Linagísta, *sm.* Genealogist, a writer of pedigrees or family. 2. Genealogist.

Linajúdo, *sm.* 1. One who boasts of his origin

Linálos, *sm.* Aloes. V. *Aloe*.

Linámen, *sm.* V. *Ramage*.

Linár, *sm.* Flax-field, land on which flax is grown.

Linária, *sf.* (Bot.) Wild flax.

Lináza, *sf.* Linseed, the seed of flax. *Aceyte de linaza*, Linseed oil.

Líncs, *sm.* 1. Lynx. Felis lynx *L.* 2. Person of great acuteness and perspicaciousness.

Lindaménte, *ad.* Neatly, elegantly.

Lindáño, *sm.* Landmark, limit.

Lindár, *vn.* To be contiguous.

Línde y Lindázo, *sm.* Landmark, boundary.

Línde, *a.* Contiguous, bordering upon.

Lindéro, ra, *a.* Contiguous. V. *Linde*.

Lindéro, *sm.* V. *Linde*.

Lindéza, *sf.* Neatness, elegance, proportion.

Líndo, da, *a.* 1. Neat, handsome, pretty. 2. Complete, perfect.

Líndo, *sm.* Beau, coxcomb.

Lindón, *sm.* Ridge, ground thrown up between asparagus-beds.

Lindúra, *sf.* Elegance, proportion, neatness.

Línea, *sf.* 1. Line, longitudinal extension. V. *Raya*. 2. Lineage, progeny. 3. Boundary, limit. V. *Renglon*. 4. Class, order. 5. Military entrenchments or order of troops. *Linea de agua de mayor carga ó del fuerte*, (Naút.) Load-water line. *Linea ó arrufo de la astilla muerta*, (Naút.) The cutting-down line. *Linea de los reveses del costado*, (Naút.) The top timber lines. 6. Equinoctial line.

Lineál, *a.* Lineal, composed of lines.

Lineaménto, *sm.* Lineament, feature; discriminating mark in the form.

Lineár, *va.* To draw lines, to form any thing with lines.

Linéro, ra, *s.* Dealer in flax or linen.

Línfa, *sf.* 1. Lymph, watery humour. 2. (Poét.) Water.

Linfático, ca, *a.* Lymphatic, containing lymph.

Lingóte, *sm.* Ingot, a mass of unwrought gold or silver.

Linguéte, *sm.* (Naút.) Paul or parol, a short bar of wood or iron put into the capstern to prevent its rolling back.

Linimento y Leniménto, *sm.* (Med.) Liniment.

Linio, *sm.* V. *Liño*.

Líno, *sm.* 1. (Bot.) Flax. Linum *L.* 2. Linen. 3. Sailcloth, canvass. (Poét.) Sails of a ship.

Linón, *sm.* Lawn, the finest kind of light linen.

Lintél, *sm.* Lintel of a door. V. *Dintel*.

Lintérna, *sf.* 1. Lantern or lanthorn, a transparent case for a candle. 2. An iron cage in which the heads of decapitated criminals are exposed to public view. 3. Small wheel in mills. *Linterna magica*, Magic lantern. *Linterna secreta*, Dark lantern. 4. (Arq.) Lantern of church-towers over the cupola.

Linternéro, *sm.* Lantern-maker.

Linuésa, *sm.* V. *Linaza*.

Líño, *sm.* 1. Row of vines in a vineyard. 2. Ridge between two furrows in ploughed land.

Lío, *sm.* Bundle, a parcel tied together.

Liquáble, *a.* Liquable, that may be melted.

Liquación, *sf.* Liquation, the act of melting.

Liquár, *va.* To liquefy, to dissolve, to melt.

Liquefación, *sf.* Liquefaction.

Liquefactíble, *a.* Liquable.

Liquidáble, *a.* Liquefiable, liquidable.

Liquidación, *sf.* Liquidation, the act of liquidating.

Liquidámbar, *sm.* Liquidambar, a yellow resinous substance, obtained by incision from the *Liquidambar styraciflua L.*

Liquidaménte, *ad.* In a liquid manner.

Liquidár, *va.* 1. To melt. 2. To clear. 3. To liquidate.—*vr.* To become liquid, used of letters.

Liquidéz, *sf.* Liquidness, quality of being liquid.

Líquido, da, *a.* 1. Liquid, fluid. 2. Evident.

Liquór, *sm.* Liquor. V. *Licor*.

Líra, *sf.* Lyre, a harp; a lyric poem.

Líria, *sf.* V. *Liga*.

Lírico, ca, *a.* Lyric.

Lírio, *sm.* (Bot.) Lily. Lilium *L.*

Lirón, *sm.* Dormouse. Myoxus glis *L.*

Liróndo, da, *a.* Pure, clean, neat. *Mondo y lirondo*, Nice and cleanly.

Lis, *sf.* (Bot.) Flower-de-luce.

Lisaménte, *ad.* Smoothly, plainly.

Liséra, *sf.* Large cane used in silk-worm sheds.

Lisiádo, da, *a.* (Arag.) Anxiously desirous.

Lisiár, *va.* To lame; to hurt a limb.

Lisimáquia, *sf.* (Bot.) Loose strife. Lysimachia *L.*

Líso, sa, *a.* 1. Plain, even. 2. Clear, evident. *Hombre liso*, A plain-dealing man.

Lisongeraménte, *ad.* Flatteringly.

Lisongéro, ra, *a.* Flattering, pleasing, agreeable.

Lisónja, *sf.* 1. Adulation, fulsome flattery. 2. (Blas.) Lozenge, or losenge. 3. (Geom.) Rhomb or rhombus.

Lisonjádo, a, *a.* (Blas.) Lozenge; rhombic.

Lisonjeadór, ra, *s.* Flatterer.

Lisonjeár, *va.* To flatter, to praise in a deceitful manner; to delight, to please.

Lisonjéro, ra, *s.* A mean flatterer, a deceitful praiser.

Lísta, *sf.* 1. Slip of paper, shred of linen. 2. Selvage, the edge of cloth 3. List, catalogue. *Lista del equipage*, (Naút.) Muster-book of the ship's company. *Pasar lista*, To muster, to review troops. *Lista de gastos*, Bill of expense and charges.

Listádo, da, y Listeádo, da, *a.* Striped.

Listár, *va.* V. *Alistar*.

Listél ó Listélo, *sm.* (Arq.) V. *Filéte*.

Lísto, ta, *a.* Ready, diligent, prompt.

Listón, *sm.* 1. A large shred. 2. Ferret, a narrow silk riband. 3. Lath, a thin narrow board. *Listones*, (Naút.) Battens. *Listones de las escotillas*, (Naút.) Battens of the hatchways.

Listonería, *sf.* Parcel of ribands, tapes, and inkles.

Listonéro, ra, s. Riband-maker.
Lisúra, sf. 1. Smoothness, evenness. 2. Sincerity, ingenuousness, candour.
Litación, sf. Sacrificing.
Litár, va. To sacrifice to the divinity.
Litárge y Litargírio, sm. Litharge. V. *Almártaga.*
Líte, sf. Lawsuit, process. V. *Pleyto.*
Litéra, sf. Litter, a kind of vehiculary bed.
Literál, a. Literal, following the letter.
Literalísta, sm. He who professes to understand words and expressions in their literal sense.
Literalménte, ad. Literally.
Literário, ria, a. Literary.
Literáto, ta, a. Learned, versed in sciences and letters.
Literatúra, sf. Literature, learning ; skill in sciences and letters.
Literéro, sm. Director of literature.
Litigánte, pa. Litigater, litigating.
Litigár, va. To litigate, to manage a suit, to carry on a cause.
Litígio, sm. Litigation, suit at law ; process.
Litigióso, sa, a. Litigious, inclined to lawsuits.
Litis, sf. V. *Pleyto.*
Litiscontestación, sf. (For.) Answer to a juridical demand.
Litisconsórte, s. com. Associate in a lawsuit.
Litispendéncia, sf. Under judgment, pending.
Litócola, sf. Lithocolla, lapidary's cement.
Litófito, sm. Lythophyte, zoophyte having a hard calcareous stem.
Litografía, sf. A description of stones.
Litógrafo ó Litólogo, sm. Author who describes stones.
Litología, sf. Natural history of stones.
Lituo, sm. 1. Ancient military instrument of music. 2. Lituus, augur's staff.
Liturgía, sf. Form of prayers, manner of celebrating the mass.
Litúrgico, ca, a. Belonging to the liturgy.
Liúdo, da, a. V. *Leudo.*
Livianaménte, ad. Licentiously ; with levity.
Livian dád, sf. 1. Lightness, want of weight. 2. Levity, imprudence. 3. Incontinence.
Liviáno, na, a. 1. Light, of little weight. 2. Imprudent. 3. Incontinent, unchaste.
Liviános, sm. pl. Lungs. V. *Bofes.*
Lívido, da, a. V. *Amoratado.*
Líxa, sf. 1. (Ict.) Dog-fish. 2. Skin of the dog-fish.
Lixár, va. To smooth, to polish.
Líza, sf. 1. Skate, a sea-fish. 2. List for tilts and jousts.
Lízo, sm. Skein of silk.
Lizón, sm. V. *Alisma.*
LL. are considered by the Spanish Academy as a single character, double in figure but single in value. It also places them after all other words beginning with *l*; here they are retained according to the English custom.
Llága, sf. 1. Wound, hurt, damage ; infirmity. 2. Crack or opening between the bricks of a wall.
Llagadór, ra, s. Wounder, one that wounds.
Llagár, va. To wound, to hurt, to injure.
Llaguíca, lla, ta, sf. dim. of *Llaga.*
Lláma, sf. 1. Flame, light emitted from fire. 2. Force and violence of passion.
Llamáda, sf. 1. Call, the act of calling. 2. Marginal note. 3. Parley, oral treaty ; discussion by word of mouth ; military signal.
Llamadór, ra, s. 1. Servant of a salesman who calls people into his shop ; vulgarly called barker or clicker. 2. Beadle, messenger. 3. Knocker or rapper of a door.
Llamamiénto, sm. 1. Convocation, the act of convening the members of an assembly or corporation. 2. Inspiration, divine vocation. 3. Attraction of humours to one part of the body.
Llamár, va. 1. To call, to summon, to invite, to invoke. 2. To name, to denominate. 3. To incline, to attract ; to excite thirst.—vn. To refer to a book or writing ; to quote. *Llamar á la puerta,* To knock or rap at the door. *El viento llama á popa,* (Naút.) The wind veers aft. *El viento llama á proa,* (Naút.) The wind hauls forward. *Llamarse andana ó antana,* (Fam.) To deny obstinately that which one has said or offered.
Llamaráda, sf. 1. A sudden blaze of fire, a flash. 2. Forcible emotion of the mind.
Llamatívo, va, a. Exciting thirst.
Lláña, sf. 1. Trowel, a tool for taking up and spreading mortar. 2. Page of a book or writing. 3. Plain.
Llanáda, sf. A wide tract of level ground ; a plain.
Llanaménte, ad. Ingenuously, simply, sincerely ; plainly.
Llanéza, sf. 1. Evenness, equality. 2. Plainness, sincerity, simplicity. 3. Want of attention and respect, familiarity. 4. Uncultivated style.
Lláno, na, a. 1. Plain, even, level. 2. Meek, affable. 3. Unmannerly, uncivil. 4. Clear, evident. 5. Frank, liberal ; simple ; easy. *Carnero llano,* A castrated ram. *A' la llana,* Simply, sincerely, candidly.
Lláno, sm. A level field, an even ground.
Llánta, sf. 1. (Bot.) A kind of cabbage. Brassica *L.* 2. Iron hoop which covers the felloes of coach and cart wheels.
Llantén, sm. (Bot.) Plantain. Plantago *L.*
Llánto, sm. Flood of tears.
Llapár, va. To add an additional portion of quicksilver in extracting metals.
Llanúra, sf. 1. Evenness, equality. 2. A vast tract of level ground.
Lláres, sm. pl. Pot hanger, an iron chain, on which pots are hung over the fire by means of a hook.
Lláve, sf. 1. Key, instrument for locking and unlocking doors, chests, &c. 2. Winch of a stocking-frame. 3. Lock, the part of a gun by which fire is struck. 4. Key, explanation of any thing difficult ; introduction to knowledge. 5. (Naút.) Knee. V. *Curvas.* 6. Cock for fountains, barrels, &c. *Llave maestra,* Master-key, which opens many doors. *Debaxo de llave,* Under lock and key. *Llave de la mano,* Breadth of the palm of a man's hand. *Llave capona,* Honorary key worn on the flap of the coat-pocket by royal chamberlains in Spain.
Llavéro, ra, s. 1. Keeper of the keys of a place. 2. Ring in which keys are put.
Lle, pron. ant. V. *Le.*

Lléco, ca, *a.* Uncultivated; applied to land not broken up.
Lléga *sf.* (Ar.) Juncture, act of joining or uniting.
Llegáda, *sf.* Arrival, the act of coming to a place.
Llegár, *vn.* 1. To arrive, to come to any place. 2. To last, to continue. 3. To attain a purpose. 4. To suffice, to be enough. 5. To ascend; to amount to.—*va.* To approach, to join.—*vr.* To proceed to some neighbouring place; to unite. *Llegar á las manos*, To come to blows, to fight. *Llegar á oir*, To hear.
Lleíra, *sf.* (Ant.) Place full of pebbles or coarse gravel.
Lléna, *sf.* Alluvion, overflow of rivers.
Llenaménte, *ad.* Fully, copiously.
Llenár, *va.* 1. To fill, to put into any place till no more can be admitted. 2. To occupy a public place. 3. To make up a number. 4. To beget young.—*vr.* 1. To feed gluttonously. 2. To be irritated after having suffered long. *Llenar la luna*, To be full moon.
Llenéro, ra, *a.* (For.) Full, complete, absolute.
Lléno, *sm.* 1. Glut, plenty, abundance. 2. Perfection, completeness. 3. Full-moon.
Lléno, na, *a.* Full; complete. *Lleno de bote en bote*, Brimful, or full to the brim. *Hombre lleno*, A learned man. *De lleno*, Entirely, totally.
Lléta, *sf.* Stalk of plants bearing fruit.
Lleudár, *va.* To ferment bread, to make it rise by means of leaven.
Lléva, *sf.* Act of carrying.
Lleváda, *sf.* Carriage, transport.
Lleva déro, ra, *a.* Tolerable.
Llevadór, ra, *s.* Carrier, conductor.
Llevár, *va.* 1. To carry, to convey, to transport; to cut off. 2. To recover. 3. To bear, to wear, to produce. 4. To excel, to exceed. 5. To suffer, to endure. 6. To lead, to guide. 7. To manage a horse. 8. To gain, to obtain, to induce. 9. To obtain possession. 10. To carry in accounts. 11. With the preposition *por*, it signifies to exercise whatever may be the import of the following noun. *Llevar por cortesanía*, To be polite, courteous, or complaisant.—*vn.* To be reprimanded, to suffer chastisement. *Llevar la proa al norueste*, (Naút.) To stand to the north-west. *Llevar las velas á buen viento*, (Naút.) To fill the sails. *Llevar las velas llenas*, (Naút.) To keep the sails full. *Llevar los juanetes viados*, (Naút.) To have the top-gallant sails set. *Llevar á cuestas*, (Fam.) To burthen one's self with other's affairs.—*vr.* 1. To suffer one's self to be led away by passion. 2. *Llevarse el dia*, To carry the day.
Lloradéra, *sf.* Mourner, a woman hired to weep and mourn at funerals.
Lloradór, ra, *s.* Weeper, one who sheds tears.
Lloraduélos, *sm.* Weeper, mourner over misfortunes.
Llorár, *va.* 1. To weep, to shed tears. 2. To mourn, to lament, to bewail. 3. To affect poverty and distress. 4. (Met.) To fall drop by drop. *Llorar la aurora*, (Poét.) To fall dew at sunsetting.
Llóro, *sm.* Act of weeping.
Llorón, *sm.* Weeper, one who is apt to cry or shed tears.
Lloróñas, *sf. pl.* Weepers, mourners.
Llorosaménte, *ad.* Weepingly.
Lloróso, sa, *a.* Mournful, sorrowful, full of tears.
Llósa, *sf.* (Ant.) Enclosed estate.
Llovedíza (agua), *a.* Rain-water.
Llovér, *vn.* 1. To rain, to fall in drops from the clouds. 2. To pour down as rain. 3. To shower, to abound, to come in abundance, as troubles.—*vr.* To penetrate the roof with rain.
Llovído, *sm.* Man who secretly steals on board a ship for the Indies, and does not discover himself till on the high seas.
Llovióso, sa, *a.* V. *Lluvioso.*
Lloviżna, *sf.* Mist, a small rain not perceived in drops.
Lloviznár, *vn.* To drizzle, to fall in short slow drops.
Llóyca, *sf.* (Orn.) V. *Pechicolorado.*
Lluéco, ca, *a.* V. *Clueco.*
Lluvecíta, lla, *sf. dim.* Small rain.
Llúvia, *sf.* 1. Rain, water dropping from the clouds. 2. Shower, abundance, copiousness.
Lluvióso, sa, *a.* Rainy, wet, showery.
Lo, *pron. neutr.* It; placed before or after verbs.
Lo, *art. neutr.* Used only with adjectives, as *lo bueno*, the good.
Lóa, *sf.* 1. (Ant.) Praise. 2. (Naút.) Lee. V. *Lua.* 3. Prologue of a play.
Loáble, *a.* Laudable, praiseworthy.
Loableménte, *ad.* Laudably.
Loadór, ra, *s.* Praiser, one who bestows praise.
Loám, *sm.* Loam, a fat unctuous earth.
Loánda, *sf.* Kind of scurvy.
Loár, *va.* To praise; to approve. V. *Alabar.*
Lóba, *sf.* 1. She-wolf. 2. Long gown worn by clergymen and students. 3. Ridge between two furrows.
Lobádo, *sm.* Morbid swelling incident to horses.
Lobagánte, *sm.* Sea-locust. Cancer cæruleus *L.*
Lobanillo, *sm.* Wen, a callous excrescence.
Lobáto, *sm.* Young wolf.
Lobéra, *sf.* Strait door or passage.
Lobéro, ra, *a.* Relating to wolves.
Lobéro, *sm.* V. *Espantanublados.*
Lobézno, *sm.* A young wolf.
Lóbo, *sm.* 1. Wolf. Canis lupus *L.* 2. Lobe, a distinct part; usually applied to the lungs. 3. (Joc.) Intoxication, inebriation. *Fulano cogió un lobo*, He was tipsy. 4. Iron instrument for defending or scaling walls.
Lóbo Marino, *sm.* (Ict.) Sea-wolf. Anarhichas lupus *L.*
Lobóso, sa, *a.* Full of wolves; applied to countries or forests.
Lóbrego, ga, *a.* Murky, obscure, sad.
Lobreguecér, *vn.* To grow dark, to be dark.—*va.* To make dark.
Lobreguéz, *sf.* Obscurity, darkness.
Lóbulo, *sm.* A small lobe of the lungs.
Lobúno, na, *a.* Wolfish, resembling a wolf in qualities and form.
Locación y Conducción, *sf.* (For.) Contract of letting on lease.
Locál, *a.* Local, relating to a particular place.
Localidád, *sf.* Locality, existence in place, relation of place.

Locaménte, *ad.* Madly; immoderately.
Locárias, *sm.* Fool. V. *Loco.*
Lóche ó Lója, *sf.* (Ict.) Loach, a small fish.
Lción, *sf.* Lotion, wash; act of washing.
Lóco, ca, *a.* 1. Mad, crack-brained. 2. Fool. 3. Abundant, luxuriant. *A' tontas y á locas*, Inconsiderately, without reflection.
Locucíon, *sf.* Locution, manner of speech.
Locúra, *sf.* Madness, folly, absurdity. *Hacer locuras*, To act in an absurd foolish manner.
Locutório, *sm.* Parlour, place in monasteries for receiving visits.
Lodazál, Lodachár, y Lodazár, *sm.* A muddy place, a place full of mud and mire.
Lódo, *sm.* Mud, mire.
Lodóño, *sm.* (Bot.) Nettle-tree. Celtis orientalis *L.*
Lodóso, sa, *a.* Muddy, miry.
Lóf ó Ló, *sm.* (Naút.) The weather-side of a ship. *Amura del lof*, (Naút.) Weather tack. *No mas de lof*, (Naút.) Not nearer, *e. g.* to the wind.
Logár, *sm.* V. *Lugar, Sitio, y Motivo.*—*va.* V. *Alquilar.*
Logarítmo, *sm.* Logarithm.
Lógica, *sf.* Logic.
Logicál, *a.* Logical.
Logicaménte, *ad.* Logically.
Lógico, ca, *a.* Logical, relating to logic.
Logística, *sf.* Logistics, algebra.
Logogrífo, *sm.* Enigma in which the different parts of a word are taken in divers meanings.
Logomáquia, *sf.* Logomachy, dispute about words.
Lográr, *va.* 1. To gain, to obtain. 2. To possess, to enjoy. 3. To avail one's self of. 4. To hit upon.—*vr.* To reap the benefit of one's labour and exertions.
Logreár, *vn.* To borrow or lend on interest.
Logrería, *sf.* Dealing in interest, usury.
Logréro, ra, *s.* Lender at interest, usurer.
Lógro, *sm.* 1. Gain, benefit. 2. Attainment of some purpose. 3. Interest; usury. *Dar á logro*, To put out money at usurious interest.
Lóma, *sf.* Top of a hill.
Lombárda, *sf.* 1. Kind of gun, first brought from Lombardy. 2. (Bot.) Red cabbage. Brassica capitata rubra *L.*
Lombardáda, *sf.* Shot from a Lombardy gun.
Lombardeár, *va.* To discharge Lombardy guns.
Lombardería, *sf.* Park of Lombardy guns.
Lombardéro, *sm.* Soldier appointed to Lombardy guns.
Lombriguéra, *sf.* Hole made by worms.
Lombríz, *sf.* Worm bred in the human body, or in the earth.
Lombrizál, *a.* (Anat.) Vermiform.
Lomeár, *vn.* To yerk or move the loins of horses in a circular manner.
Loméra, *sf.* 1. Strap of harness which crosses the loins. 2. (Mur.) Ridge of a house.
Lomiáncho, a, *a.* Strong or broad backed.
Lomíllo, *sm.* 1. A small lion. 2. A kind of needle-work.
Lominhiésto, ta, *a.* 1. High-crooped. 2. Presumptuous, arrogant.
Lómo, *sm.* 1. Loin. 2. Back of a book or cutting tool; double of any cloth, crease. 3. Ridge between two furrows. *Llevar ó traer á lomo*, To carry on the back. *Jugar de lomo*, To be idle and lascivious. *Lomos*, Ribs.
Lomóso, sa, *a.* Belonging to the loins.
Lóna, *sf.* Canvass, sail-cloth.
Lóncha, *sf.* 1. Thin flat stone. 2. Lunch, long slice of meat.
Lóndiga, *sf.* V. *Alóndiga.*
Londrína, *sf.* A sort of woollen cloth.
Londríno, na, *a.* Belonging to or in the fashion of London manufactures.
Lóndro, *sm.* Low vessel like a galley.
Lónga, *sf.* Long, musical note.
Longanimidád, *sf.* Longanimity, forbearance; patience of offences.
Longánimo, ma, *a.* Forbearing, generous.
Longaníza, *sf.* A kind of long sausage.
Longár, *a.* Applied to a long piece of honeycomb in the hive.
Longázo, za, *a. aum.* of *Luengo.* [length.
Longimetría, *sf.* (Geo.) Measurement of
Longínquo, qua, *a.* Distant, remote.
Longitúd, *sf.* 1. Length. 2. Longitude, the distance of any place from the first meridian to the east or west.
Longitudinál, *a.* Longitudinal.
Longitudinalménte, *ad.* Longitudinally.
Longobárdo, da, *a.* Native of Lombardy.
Longuéra, *sf.* Long and narrow strip of land.
Lónja, *sf.* 1. Exchange, a public place where merchants meet to treat on matters of trade. 2. Store room for washed wool. 3. Grocer's shop; warehouse, saleroom. *Lonja cerrada ó abierta*, Shut or open shop, or exchange. 4 Slice of ham. 5. Portico, raised space round the entrance of an edifice. 6. Leather strap.
Lonjéro, *sm.* Grocer; one who keeps a grocer's shop.
Lonjéta, *sf.* V. *Cenador.*
Lonjísta, *s. com.* Shopkeeper who deals in cocoa-nuts, spices, and other articles of grocery.
Lopícia, *sf.* Disease which makes the hair fall off. V. *Alopecia.*
Loquacidád, *sf.* Loquacity, talkativeness.
Loquáz, *a.* Talkative, garrulous.
Loqueár, *vn.* 1. To act the fool, to talk nonsense. 2. To rejoice, to exult, to revel.
Loquéla, *sf.* Each one's particular mode of speaking.
Loquéro, ra, *s.* 1. Keeper of a mad-house. 2. Physician to a mad-house.
Loquésca, *sf.* The frantic demeanour of mad people.
Lóquios, *sm. pl.* Lochia, the evacuations attending childbirth.
Lorenzána, *sf.* A sort of linen.
Loríga, *sf.* 1. Coat of mail, cuirass. 2. Nave-band, the hoop which surrounds the nave of a coach-wheel.
Lorigádo, da, *a.* Armed with a coat of mail.
Loriguíllo, *sm.* Shrub used by dyers.
Lóro, ra, *a.* Tawny, brown colour.
Lóro, *sm.* 1. Parrot. Psittacus *L.* 2. (Bot.) Tree with variegated leaves.—*a.* Mulatto or negro-coloured.
Lósa, *sf.* 1. Flag, a square stone used for pavements. 2. Painter's block of marble on which colours are ground. 3. Trap made for catching birds or rats.
Losádo, *sm.* V. *Enlosado.*

Losánje, *sm.* (Blas.) Losange; rhomb.
Losár, *va.* V. *Enlosar*.
Losílla ó íta, *sf.* A small trap or snare. *Coger en la losilla*, To deceive one cunningly.
Lóta, *sf.* (Ict.) Lote, eelpout, a kind of river lamprey.
Lóte, *sm.* Lot, fortune, chance.
Lotería, *sf.* Lottery.
Lóto, *sm.* (Bot.) Lote, lotus, or lotos.
Loxôdromía, *sf.* (Naút.) Loxodromy, rhombs which a ship describes.
Lóza, *sf.* Delft, a fine sort of earthen-ware. *Andola loza*, (Fam.) Noisy mirth and jollity of many persons together.
Lozanaménte, *ad.* Luxuriantly.
Lozaneár, *vn.* To affect pomp and ostentation in words and actions.
Lozanía, *sf.* 1. Luxuriance of verdure, exuberant growth of plants. 2. Elegance.
Lozáno, na, *a.* 1. Luxuriant. 2. Sprightly.
Lúa, *sf.* 1. (Ant.) Glove. 2. (Toledo) A sort of crane for raising weights. 3. (Naút.) Lee. 4. (Manch.) Saffron bag. *Tomar por la lua*, (Naút.) To bring to the lee.
Lubricár y Lubrificár, *va.* (Ant.) To make smooth or slippery.
Lubricidád y Lubricación, *sf.* 1. Lubricity, slipperiness. 2. Lewdness.
Lúbrico, ca, *a.* Slippery; lubric; lewd.
Lucencía, *sf.* V. *Claridad*.
Lucérna, *sf.* 1. Glow-worm. 2. Lamp.
Lucérnula, *sf.* (Bot.) Lucerne, saintfoin.
Lucéro, *sm.* 1. Morning-star, Venus. 2. Splendour. 3. Part of a window where light enters.
Lúcha, *sf.* 1. Struggle, strife, contest, wrestle. 2. Dispute, argument.
Luchadór, ra, *s.* Wrestler, one who wrestles.
Luchár, *vn.* 1. To wrestle, to contend, to struggle. 2. To discuss, to debate.
Lucharniégo, ga, *a.* Applied to dogs used for catching hares at night.
Lucidaménte, *ad.* Lucidly, brightly.
Lucidár, *va.* To copy a picture on transparent paper, which was laid upon it.
Lúcido, da, *a.* Lucid, shining; graceful, splendid.
Lucidúra, *sf.* (Fam.) Whiteness of white-washed walls.
Luciénte, *pa.* Shining.
Luciérnaga, go, *s.* Glow-worm. Lampyris *L.*
Lucifér, *sm.* Lucifer, Satan; morning star.
Lucífero, ra, *a.* (Poét.) Resplendent, shining. —*sm.* V. *Lucero*.
Lucífugo, ga, *a.* That which shuns the light.
Luciferíno, nà, *a.* Belonging to Lucifer, devilish.
Lucíllo, *sm.* Tomb; sarcophagus.
Lucimiénto, *sm.* 1. Lucidity, brightness. 2. Splendour, lustre, applause.
Lucína, *sf.* V. *Ruiseñor*.
Lúcio, cia, *a.* Lucid, bright.—*sm.* (Ict.) Common pike. Esox lucius *L.*
Lucír, *va.* 1. To emit light, to glitter, to gleam. 2. To illuminate, to enlighten. 3. To outshine, to exceed.—*vn.* y *r.* 1. To shine, to be brilliant. *Le luce el trabajo*, He enjoys the fruits of his labour. 2. To dress to advantage.
Lucratívo, va, *a.* Lucrative, productive of gain.
Lúcro, *sm.* Gain, profit, lucre.
Lucróso, sa, *a.* Lucrific, gainful.
Luctuósa, *sf.* Ancient tax paid to lords and bishops for the dead.

Luctuosaménte, *ad.* Mournfully, sorrowfully.
Luctuóso, sa, *a.* Sad, mournful.
Lucubración, *sf.* Lucubration, study by candle-light; nocturnal study.
Lucubrár, *va.* To lucubrate, to study by night.
Lúdia, *sf.* (Extr.) Ferment, yeast.
Ludiár, *va.* To ferment.
Ludíbrio, *sm.* Mockery, derision, scorn.
Lúdio, a, *a.* V. *Fermentado*.
Ludír, *va.* To rub, to waste by friction.
Lúdria, *sf.* V. *Nutria*.
Luégo, *ad.* 1. Presently, immediately. 2. Soon afterwards.—*conj.* Then, therefore.
Luéllo, *sm.* (Ar.) Bad seed which grows among grain, like barley.
Luéngo, ga, *a.* (Ant.) V. *Largo*.
Luént y Luéñe, *ad.* (Ant.) V. *Lejos*.
Lugáno, *sm.* Small singing bird.
Lugár, *sm.* 1. Place, spot, situation, position. 2. City, town, village. 3. Employment, office, dignity. 4. Time, opportunity, occasion. 5. Cause, motive, reason. 6. Text, authority or sentiment of an author. *Lugar comun*, Privy-house, water-closet. *Lugares de un combate*, (Naút.) Quarters in a sea-fight. *En lugar de*, Instead of.
Lugarcíllo, co, to; y **Lugaríllo y íjo**, *sm.* A small place, a little hamlet.
Lugarón, *sm.* A large place.
Lugarteniénte, *sm.* Deputy, substitute, lieutenant.
Lúgo, *sm.* Kind of linen.
Lúgubre, *a.* Sad, mournful, gloomy, melancholy.
Luición, *sf.* Collection of rent.
Luír, *vn.* (Naút.) To be galled or fretted, to wear away by friction.—*va.* To gather rent.
Luísmo, *sm.* (Ar.) V. *Laudemio*.
Lumbál, *a.* Lumbar, lumbary.
Lumbráda y Lumbraráda, *sf.* Excessive fire, a fierce conflagration.
Lúmbre, *sf.* 1. Fire, the igneous element. 2. (Ant.) Light. 3. Spark, a small particle of fire struck out of a flint. 4. Splendour, lucidity, clearness. *Ni por lumbre*, By no means. —*pl.* 1. Tinder-box, in which a flint, steel, and tinder, are kept for striking fire. 2. Hammer, that part of a gun or pistol lock which strikes fire out of the flint. 3. Fore-part of horse-shoes.
Lumbréra, *sf.* 1. Luminary, any body which gives or emits light. 2. Sky-light. 3. Luminary, he who from his transcendent abilities is fit to instruct mankind.
Luminár, *sm.* 1. Luminary, any body which emits light. 2. (Among Painters) Light, as opposed to shade. 3. Luminary, a man eminent in science.
Luminária, *sf.* 1. Illumination, festival lights hung out as a token of joy. 2. Lamp which is kept burning in Roman catholic churches before the sacrament. *Luminarias*, Money paid for the expenses of illuminations.
Luminóso, sa, *a.* Luminous; emitting light.
Lúna, *sf.* 1. Moon, the changing luminary of the night. 2. Glass plate for mirrors, glass for optical instruments. 3. Effect of the moon upon lunatic people. 4. *Media luna*, (Fort.) Half-moon, a ravelin built before the angle or

curtain of a bastion. 5. (Ar.) Open, uncovered court or hall. *Luna llena ó menguante*, Full or waning moon.

Lunación, *sf.* Lunation, the revolution of the moon.

Lunáda, *sf.* Ham, a gammon of salt pork.

Lunádo, da, *a.* Lunated.

Lunánco, ca, *a.* Applied to animals with one quarter higher than another.

Lunár, *sm.* 1. Mole, a natural spot or discoloration of the body. *Lunar postizo*, Patch, a spot of black silk which ladies wear on their faces as an ornament. 2. Note or stain of infamy.—*a.* Lunar, relating to the moon.

Lunário, *sm.* V. *Calendario.*

Lunático, ca, *a.* Lunatic, having the imagination influenced by the moon.

Lunecíllo, *sm.* Crescent worn by females.

Lúnes, *sm.* Monday, the second day of the week.

Lunéta, *sf.* 1. Opening left in an arch in form of a half-moon. 2. Pit, the middle part of the playhouse behind the orchestra. 3. Opera-glass; eye-glass. 4. Crescent worn in the hair or shoes of females.

Lunísta, *sm.* Lunatic, a mad person, whose imagination is influenced by the moon.

Lupanár, *sm.* Brothel, a bawdy house.

Lupanário, ia, *a.* Belonging to a brothel.

Lupía, *sf.* Encysted tumour.

Lupicía, *sf.* V. *Alopecia.*

Lúpulo, *sm.* (Bot.) Hops. Humulus lupulus *L.*

Luqués, sa, *a.* Belonging to, or native of Lucca.

Luquéte, *sm.* 1. Zest, a slice of an orange with the peel thrown into wine. 2 Match, combustible matter.

Lustración, *sf.* Lustration, purification by water.

Lustradór, *sm.* 1. Hot-press, a machine which gives a gloss to clothes. 2. Hot-presser, one whose trade is to give a gloss to clothes.

Lustrál, *a.* Applied to water used in purifications.

Lustrár, *va.* 1. To expiate, to purify. 2 To illustrate, to make brilliant. 3. To wander.

Lústre, *sm.* Gloss, lustre; splendour, glory.

Lústrico, ca, *a.* (Poét.) Belonging to a lustre.

Lustrína, *sf.* A kind of glossy silk stuff.

Lústro, *sm.* Lustre, five years.

Lustrosaménte, *ad.* Brilliantly, splendidly.

Lustróso, sa, *a.* Bright, brilliant.

Lúten, *sm.* (Quim.) Lute, a kind of paste to make vessels air-tight.

Luteranísmo, *sm.* Lutheranism, relating to the opinions of Luther.

Lúto, *sm.* Mourning, the dress of sorrow.

Lútria, *sf.* V. *Nútria.*

Luxación, *sf.* Luxation.

Luxárse, *vr.* To luxate, to put out of joint.

Lúxo, *sm.* Luxury, pomp.

Luxúria, *sf.* Luxury, carnal pleasure; excess.

Luxuriánte, *pa.* Luxuriant; abounding to excess.

Luxuriár, *vn.* To be luxurious; to be libidinous.

Luxuriosaménte, *ad.* Luxuriously.

Luxurióso, sa, *a.* Luxurious, voluptuous.

Lúz, *sf.* 1. Light, clearness. *Luces*, Windows, lanterns. 2. Any thing that gives light; a candle, taper, &c. 3. Day. 4. Notice, information; inspiration; a learned and enlightened man. 5. Lustre, splendour. 6. Light-house. 7. (Pint.) Light and shade. *A' buena luz*, Carefully, after a due examination. *A' dos luces*, Ambiguously. *Sacar á luz, ó dar á luz*, To publish a literary production. *Luz de luz*, Reflected or borrowed light.

THE letter *m* has in the Spanish language the same sound as in English. M is never doubled in Spanish, notwithstanding the rule that it and not *n* should precede *b*, *m*, and *p*; to obviate this, *n* is introduced before *m*, and is sometimes substituted for *mp* to soften the sound, as *inmemorial* for immemorial, *asuncion* for asumpcion, &c.

Máca, *sf.* 1. Bruise in fruit, occasioned by a fall from the tree. 2. Spot, stain. 3. Deceit, fraud, trick.

Macáco, ca, *s.* Parrot. Psittacus macao *L.*

Macána, *sf.* A wooden weapon in the form of a cimeter, in use among the Indians.

Macaréno, *sm.* Braggadocio, bully.

Macarrón, *sm.* Macaroon, a kind of paste formed into small cylindrical tubes. *Macarrones*, (Naút.) Awning stanchions. V. *Candeleros.*

Macarrónea, *sf.* A kind of burlesque poetry, made up of words of different languages, mixed confusedly together.

Macarrónico, ca, *a.* Macaronic.

Macarronísmo, *sm.* The macaronic style of poetry.

Macárse, *vr.* To rot, to be spoiled in consequence of a bruise or hurt; applied to fruit.

Maceadór, *sm.* Beater, hammerer.

Maceár, *va.* To beat or drive with a mallet, to hammer down.—*vn.* To repeat frequently the same demand, to insist upon it.

Maceración, *sf.* 1. Maceration, an infusion with or without heat, wherein the ingredients are intended to be nearly dissolved. 2. Mortification, corporal severity.

Macerár, *va.* 1. To macerate, to soften any hard substance by steeping it nearly to solution, either with or without heat. 2. To mortify, to harass with corporal hardships. 3. (Quim.) To bruise plants, to extract their juice.

Macerína, *sf.* A kind of waiter with a round cavity in the middle to hold the chocolate-cup, when served.

Macéro, *sm.* Mace-bearer, one who carries the mace before sovereigns, corporations, &c.

Macéta, *sf.* 1. Flower-pot, in which flowers are reared. 2. Handle of a stick used at Spanish truck-tables. 3. Haunch of mutton. 4. Two-clawed hammer. 5. (Naút.) Maul, mallet. *Maceta de aforrar*, A serving mallet. *Maceta de calafate*, A calking mallet. *Maceta de ajustar*, A driving mallet. *Macetas*, Mallets or beetles, with which rope-ends are beaten to make oakum.

MACHÁCA, *s. com.* An ignorant tiresome person.

MACHACADÉRA, *sf.* Instrument for pounding or breaking.

MACHACADÓR, RA, *s.* Pounder, beetler, bruiser.

MACHACÁR, *va.* To pound or break any thing into small pieces.—*vn.* To importune, to harass, to molest. *Machacar en hierro frio*, To hammer cold iron; phrase indicating inutility.

MACHACÓN, NA, *a.* Heavy, monotonous, importunate, tediously diffuse. [dad.

MACHÁDA, *sf.* 1. Flock of he-goats. 2. V. *Necedad.*

MACHÁDO, *sm.* Hatchet, a small axe for cutting and hewing timber.

MACHÁR, *va.* To pound. V. *Machacar. Á' macha martillo*, Firmly, strongly; in a solid manner. *Creer en Dios á macha martillo*, To believe in God firmly and sincerely. [males.

MACHEÁR, *vn.* To beget more males than females.

MACHETÁZO, *sm.* Blow or stroke with a hatchet.

MACHÉTE, *sm.* Chopping-knife.

MACHETÉRO, *sm.* One who clears away bushes with a bill-hook.

MACHIÉGA, *a.* V. *Abeja machiega.*

MACHIHEMBRÁR, *va.* (Carp.) To join or dovetail pieces of wood in a box with grooves

MACHINÉTE, *sm.* (Mur.) Chopping-knife.

MÁCHO, *sm.* 1. Male animal. 2. He-mule, got by a stone-horse and a she-ass, or by a jack-ass and a mare. 3. Flesh of a he-goat, eaten in Valencia and other parts of Spain instead of mutton. 4. Mould in which bells are cast. 5. An uncouth ignorant fellow. 6. Pillar of masonry to support a building. 7. Hook to catch hold in an eye. 8. Screw-pin. 9. Sledge or large hammer, used to forge iron. 10. Block on which a smith's anvil is fixed. 11. *Machos del timon*, (Naút.) Rudder-pintles, hooks by which the rudder is fastened to the sternpost.

MÁCHO, *a.* Masculine, vigorous, robust.

MACHÓN, *sm.* Buttress, an arched pillar to support a wall or building.

MACHÓRRA, *sf.* A barren ewe. [mallet.

MACHÓTA Y MACHÓTE, *s.* A kind of beetle or

MACHUCADÚRA, *sf.* The act of pounding or bruising.

MACHUCAMIÉNTO, *sm.* V. *Machucadura.*

MACHUCÁR, *va.* To pound, to bruise. V. *Machacar.*

MACHÚCHO, CHA, *a.* Mature, ripe of age and understanding; judicious.

MACHUÉLO, *sm.* (Agr.) Heart of an onion.

MACICÉZ, *sf.* Solidity, compactness.

MACILÉNTO, TA, *a.* Lean, extenuated; withered, decayed.

MACÍS Y MACIÁS, *sf.* Mace, a kind of spice; the second of the three coverings of the nutmeg.

MACIZAMÉNTE, *ad.* In a firm and solid manner.

MACIZÁR, *va.* 1. To close or stop any opening or passage, to form into a compact body. 2. To support a proposition by solid arguments and convincing reasons.

MACÍZO, ZA, *a.* 1. Compact, close, solid. 2. Firm, certain.

MÁCLA, *sf.* 1. (Bot.) Water-caltrops. Trapa natans *L.* 2. Wooden instrument to scotch flax or hemp.

MACÓCA, *sf.* A large sort of early figs.

MACÓLLA, *sf.* Bunch of flowers, &c. growing on one stalk.

MACÓNA, *sf.* (Burg.) Basket without handles.

MACÚCA, *sf.* (Bot.) Kind of wild pear, or pear-tree.

MÁCULA, *sf.* Stain, spot, blemish.

MACULÁR, *va.* 1. To maculate, to stain, to spot; to make a double impression in printing with types or copper-plates. 2. To mark with infamy.

MACULATÚRA, *sf.* (Impr.) Sheet which has received a double impression in printing.

MACULÓSO, SA, *a.* Full of spots, stains, and blemishes.

MACUQUÍNO, NA, *a.* Applied to coin with the milled edges cut away.

MADÁMA, *sf.* Madam; an appellation of honour given to ladies when they are addressed in conversation. V. *Señora.*

MADAMISÉLA, *sf.* An appellation given in Spain to young women who are over nice in point of dress, and affect the lady.

MADÉRA, *sf.* 1. Timber, wood. *Madera de construccion*, Timber for ship-building. *Madera de vuelta*, Compass-timber. *Madera derecha*, Straight timber. 2. Green or unripe fruit. 3. *Madera del ayre*, Horn of animals. *Á' media madera*, Scarfed timbers.

MADERÁDA, *sf.* Raft, a frame or float, made by laying pieces of timber across each other.

MADERÁGE Y MADERÁMEN, *sm.* The whole of the timber necessary for a building; a house in frame.

MADERÁR, *va.* To plank. V. *Enmaderar.*

MADERERÍA, *sf.* Timber-yard.

MADERÉRO, *sm.* Timber-merchant; carpenter

MADERÍLLO, TO, CO, *sm.* Small timber.

MADERÍSTA, *sm.* Conductor of a raft or float of timber.

MADÉRO, *sm.* Trunk, the body of a tree felled for use.

MADÉXA, *sf.* 1. Hank or skein of thread, worsted, silk, or cotton. 2. Lock of hair. 3. A weak, lazy person. *Madeza sin cuenda*, Confused, disordered, irregular person or thing. *Hacer madeza*, To be ropy; applied to liquors.

MADEXUÉLA, *sf.* A small skein.

MADÍOS, (Ant.) V. *Par dios.*

MADÓNA, *sf.* Lady. V. *Señora.*

MADRÁZA, *sf.* aum. of *madre.*

MADRÁSTRA, *sf.* 1. Step-mother, a woman married to a man who has children by a former wife. 2. (Met.) Any thing disagreeable.

MÁDRE, *sf.* 1. Mother, a woman who has borne a child; correlative to son or daughter. 2. Hen, a bird hatching young from eggs. 3. Mother, a title of respect given to religious women. *Madre de leche*, A wet-nurse. 4. Matron in an hospital. 5. Basis, foundation, origin. 6. Matrix, womb. 7. Bed of a river. 8. Sewer, sink. 9. Mother of vinegar. *Madre del timon*, (Naút.) Main piece of the rudder. *Madre de la rueda del timon*, (Naút.) Barrel of the steering-wheel. *Madres*, (Naút.) Gallows-beams.

MADREÁR, *vn.* To resemble the mother; to copy the manners of the mother; to call mother

MADRECÍLLA, *sf.* Ovarium of birds.

Madreclávo, sm. Clove, a spice which has remained on the tree two years.

Madréña, sf. V. *Almadreña.*

Madreperla, sf. Mother of pearl; pearl-oyster. Mytilus margaritiferus *L.*

Madrepóra, sf. Madrepore, white coral.

Madréro, ra, a. Fondling, caressing a mother.

Madreselva, sf. (Bot.) Honey-suckle. Lonicera caprifolium *L.*

Madrigado, da, a. 1. Cunning, crafty. 2. Applied to the bull that has been with cows. 3. Applied to a woman twice married.

Madrigál, sm. Madrigal, a pastoral song.

Madriguéra, sf. 1. Burrow, the holes made in the ground by rabbits or conies. 2. Den, lurking place.

Madrileño, ña, a. Native of Madrid.

Madrílla, sf. (Ar.) A small river fish.

Madrilléra, sf. (Ar.) Instrument for catching small fish.

Madrína, sf. 1. Godmother, a woman who has become a sponsor in baptism. 2. Protectress. 3. Prop, stanchion. 4. Straps or cords which yoke two horses.

Madríz, sf. 1. Matrix, womb. V. *Matriz.* 2. Place where quails nestle. 3. (Orn.) Daker hen. Rallus crex *L.*

Madróna, sf. Mother over fond of her children, who spoils them by excessive tenderness.

Madroncíllo, sm. Strawberry.

Madroñál, sm. Plantation of strawberry-trees.

Madroñéro, sm. (Bot.) Strawberry-tree.

Madróño, sm. 1. Strawberry-tree. Arbutus unedo *L.* 2. Fruit of the strawberry-tree. 3. Silk tassel.

Madrugáda, sf. 1. Dawn, the time between the first appearance of light and the sun's rise. 2. Habit of rising early in the morning. *De madrugada,* At break of day.

Madrugadór, ra, s. Early riser.

Madrugár, vn. 1. To rise early in the morning. 2. To contrive, to premeditate. 3. To anticipate, to be beforehand.

Madrugón, sm. 1. Act of rising early in the morning. 2. Early riser.

Maduración, sf. Ripeness, maturity.

Maduradéro, sm. Place for ripening fruits.

Maduradór, ra, s. One who matures or ripens.

Maduraménte, ad. Maturely, prudently.

Maduránte, pa. Maturing, ripening.

Madurár, va. To ripen, to make ripe.—vn. To ripen, to grow ripe; to attain the age of maturity.

Madurativo, va, a. That which matures.—sm. Means employed to soften any person to yield to a request.

Maduréz, sf. 1. Maturity, ripeness. 2. Prudence, wisdom.

Madúro, ra, a. 1. Ripe, mature, perfect. 2. Prudent, judicious.

Maése, sm. (Ant.) Master. V. *Maestro. Maese coral,* A kind of game played with balls.

Maesíl, sm. V. *Maestril.*

Maéstra, sf. 1. Mistress, school-mistress. 2. Master's wife in all trades and professions. 3. Queen bee. 4. Whatever instructs. *La historia es maestra de la vida,* History is the instructress of life.

Maestrádgo, sm. 1. Territory of the master of a military order. 2. Office of master.

Maestrál, a. 1. Magisterial, suiting a master. 2. North-west; applied to the wind. *Mesa maestral,* The sheep-walk board.—sm. Cell of the queen or principal bee.

Maestralizár, vn. (Naút.) To have variation or declination to west or north-west; applied to the compass-needle.

Maestraménte, ad. Masterly, dexterously, skilfully.

Maestránte, sm. Equestrian, rider.

Maestránza, sf. 1. Cavalcade, exercise on horseback. 2. Dock-yard; naval storehouse. 3. Riding-school.

Maestrázgo, sm. Dignity of a grand-master of a military order, or his jurisdiction.

Maéstre, sm. 1. (Naút.) Master of a merchant-ship, ship-master; in the Mediterranean he is called *patron.* 2. (Naút.) Master on board of a ship of war. 3. *Maestre de plata,* (Naút.) Supercargo on board the royal Spanish galleons. 4. *Maestre de raciones,* (Naút.) Purser. 5. (Ant.) Master, doctor.

Maestreár, vn. 1. To domineer, to act the master. 2. To lop vines. 3. To adulterate, to falsify. 4. To level the surface of a wall.

Maestresála, sm. The chief waiter at the king's table in Spain.

Maestrescolía, sf. Office of a schoolmaster.

Maestrescuéla, sm. 1. Schoolmaster in cathedral churches. 2. Chancellor in some universities.

Maestría, sf. 1. Instruction of a master. 2 Masterly execution or performance; address; stratagem. 3. Gravity, seriousness, solemnity. 4. Degree of master. 5. Mastership of a vessel.

Maestríl, sm. Cells in which the king or queen bees are bred.

Maéstro, sm. 1. Master one who teaches any art or science; professor; governor or director. 2. Master of arts, a graduate in universities.

Maéstro, tra, a. Masterly, principal.

Magacén, sm. Magazine. V. *Almacen.*

Magánto, ta, a. Spiritless, dull, faint, languid.

Magáña, sf. Honey-comb, a flaw in the bore of a gun.

Magárza, sf. (Bot.) Ox-eye, greater daisy. Chrysanthemum *L.*

Magdaleón, sm. Sticks of plaster, made up in small cylindrical rolls for use.

Magénca, sf. Hollow round vines.

Magencár, va. (Mur.) To dig the earth up about vines, and to clear them of weeds.

Magestád, sf. 1. Majesty, dignity; grandeur of appearance. 2. The title of emperors, kings, empresses, and queens. 3. Power, sovereignty, elevation.

Magestuosaménte, ad. Majestically.

Magestuosidád, sf. Majesty, dignity.

Magestuóso, sa, a. 1. Majestic, august, grand. 2. Stately, pompous. 3. Grave, solemn.

Mágia, sf. 1. Magic, the art of producing surprising effects by the secret agency of natural powers. 2. The pretended science of putting in action the power of spirits.

Mágico, ca, a. Magic, incantating; necromantic.

Mágico, ca, s. Magician, one who professes magic.

Magisterial, *a.* Magisterial.

Magistério, *sm.* 1. Mastery, rule of a master. 2. Mastership, the title and rank of a master in the universities. 3. Gravity, seriousness; affected solemnity. 4. Magistery, a chemical preparation of mixed bodies.

Magistrádo, *sm.* 1. Magistrate, a chief officer of justice. 2. Magistracy, the office or dignity of a magistrate. 3. Court, tribunal.

Magistrál, *a.* Magisterial, such as suits a master.—*sf.* Title of a prebendary, in the Roman catholic church, whose functions consist in teaching and preaching.—*sm.* 1. A prebend. 2. (Farm.) Anti-venereal potion.

Magistralménte, *ad.* Magisterially.

Magistratúra, *sf.* Magistracy.

Magnanimaménte, *ad.* Magnanimously.

Magnanimidád, *sf.* Magnanimity, elevation of mind; elevation of soul.

Magnánimo, ma, *a.* Magnanimous.

Magnáte, *sm.* Peer, a nobleman of the first distinction in a country or province.

Magnésia, *sf.* Magnesia, a medicinal powder, a radical earth.

Magnético, ca, *a.* Magnetic, relating to the magnet; attractive.

Magnetísmo, *sm.* Magnetism, power of the loadstone; power of attraction.

Magnetizár, *va.* To touch with the loadstone or magnet, to render magnetic.

Magnificaménte, *ad.* Magnificently.

Magnificár, *va.* To magnify, to extol, to exalt, to raise in estimation.

Magníficat, *s. com.* The song of the blessed virgin. *Criticar ó corregir el magníficat*, To criticise without reason or judgment.

Magnificéncia, *sf.* Magnificence, grandeur of appearance; splendour.

Magnífico, ca, *a.* 1. Magnificent, splendid. 2. Title of honour.

Magnitúd, *sf.* 1. Magnitude, greatness, grandeur. 2. Comparative bulk.

Mágno, na, *a.* Great; used as an epithet in the Spanish language; *e. g. Alexandro el magno*, Alexander the Great.

Mágo, ga, *s.* 1. A title formerly given in the east to philosophers, kings, or wise men, called magi. 2. Magician, one skilled in magic; a necromancer.

Mágra, *sf.* Rasher, slice of pork.

Mágro, gra, *a.* Meager, lean; wanting flesh.

Mágro, *sm.* Rasher, a thin slice of bacon or ham.

Magrújo, ja, *a.* Meager. V. *Magro.*

Magrúra, *sf.* Leanness, thinness.

Magüér y Magüéra, *ad.* (Ant.) Although. V. *Aunque.*

Magüéto, ta, *s.* V. *Novillo.*

Maguéy, *sm.* (Bot.) American aloes. Agave Americana *L.*

Maguíllo, *sm.* Species of crab-tree.

Magújo, *sm.* (Naút.) Rave-hook; an instrument with a crooked point, which serves to pick old oakum out of the seams of the ship's sides and decks.

Magúlla, *sf.* V. *Magulladura.*

Magulládo, da, *a.* Bruised, worn out.

Magulladúra, *sf.* Bruise, contusion; a hurt with something blunt and heavy.

Magullamiénto, *sm.* Act of bruising.

Magullár, *va.* To bruise, to mangle.

Maharón, na, *a.* Unhappy, unfortunate.

Mahernír, *va.* To convene, to antisipate.

Mahometísmo, *sm.* Mohammedanism, a system of religion introduced by Mohammed, and adhered to by his sect.

Mahometísta, *sm.* Follower of Mohammed.

Mahometizár, *vn.* To profess Mohammedanism.

Mahón, *sm.* Strong broad cotton cloth.

Mahóna, *sf.* Turkish transport vessel.

Maído, *sm.* Mew. V. *Maullido.*

Maionequín, *sm.* Inequality in cloth. [mays *L.*

Maíz, *sm.* (Bot.) Maize, Indian corn. Zea

Maizál, *sm.* Field sown with Indian corn.

MA'JA, *sf.* Mallet, batlet, maul, beetle.

Majáda, *sf.* 1. Sheep-cot, sheep-fold. 2. Inn.

Majadál, *sm.* Land used for a sheep-fold.

Majadeár, *vn.* To take shelter in the night; applied to a flock of sheep.

Majadería, *sf.* Absurd speech, nonsense.

Majaderíllo, *sm.* Bobbin for lace.

Majadéro, *sm.* 1. Pestle, an instrument with which any thing is broken in a mortar. 2. Pounder, one that pounds or breaks any thing in a mortar. 3. Place where hemp or bass is beaten. 4. Gawk, a foolish troublesome fellow *Majaderos*, Bobbins for making bone-lace.

Majadór, ra, *s.* Pounder, bruiser.

Majadúra, *sf.* The act of pounding or bruising.

Majagránzas, *sm.* A stupid brute; nickname for an ignorant troublesome fellow.

Majamiénto, *sm.* Whipping, chastisement.

Majáno, *sm.* A small heap of stones serving as a landmark.

Majár, *va.* 1. To pound, to break in a mortar 2. To importune, to vex, to molest.

Majarrána, *sf.* Fresh pork.

Majéncia, *sf.* Boast, vaunt.

Májo, ja, *s.* Boaster, bragger.

Majolár, *va.* To put straps to the shoes, to tie them tight.

Majórca, *sf.* V. *Mazorca.*

Majuéla, *sf.* 1. Fruit of the white hawthorn. 2. Strap with which shoes are tied.

Majuélo, *sm.* Vine newly planted.

Mál, *sm.* 1. Imperfection, evil, hurt. 2. Illness, disease. 3. Fault, trespass.—*a.* V. *Malo;* it is used only before masculine substantives.—*ad.* Badly, injuriously. *Anda mal*, He is a bad walker. *Mal caduco*, Epilepsy. *Mal hecho*, Ill-shaped; applied to persons who are hump-backed, or have some other remarkable defect. *Mal que bien*, With good or ill will. *Mal por mal*, For want of something better. *Del mal el menos*, The least of two evils. *De mal en peor*, Worse and worse. *Mal frances*, Venereal disease. *Mal de ojo*, Evil eye.

Mála, *sf.* 1. Mail, a postman's bundle. 2. Deuce of spades.

Maláche, *sm.* A sickly person.

Malacostumbrádo, da, *a.* Having bad habits or customs.

Malacotón, *sm.* V. *Melocoton.*

Malacuénda, *sf.* Coarse cloth made of tow. V. *Razago.*

Malagáña, *sf.* Pole set up with dry furze to catch bees swarming.

Malagueño, ña, *a.* Belonging to Malaga.

MALAMÉNTE, ad. Badly, wickedly.
MALANDÁNZA, sf. Misfortune, calamity.
MALANDÁR, sm. (Extr.) Wild hog.
MALANDRÍN, sm. Highwayman, one who robs on the highway.—a. Malign, perverse.
MALATÍA, sf. Malady, disease, distemper.
MALÁTO, TA, s. A person indisposed with some disease.
MALAVENÍDO, DA, a. Quarrelsome person, one who applies himself to sow discord.
MALAVENTÚRA, sf. Calamity, misfortune.
MALAVENTURÁDO, DA, a. Unfortunate, ill-fated.
MALAVÉS ó MALAVÉZ, ad. (Ant.) V. *Apénas*.
MALBARATADÓR, RA, s. Spendthrift, one who wastes his fortune and other people's money in extravagance, and useless things.
MALBARATÁR, va. 1. To mispend, to lavish. 2. To disorder, to put into disorder.
MALCASÁDO, DA, a. Not well married.
MALCASÁRSE, vr. To contract an improper or unfortunate marriage.
MALCÁSO, sm. Treason, turpitude, crime.
MALCOCINÁDO, sm. Tripes, liver and lights of a quadruped or four-footed animal.
MALCOMÍDO, DA, a. Hungry, destitute of wholesome food.
MALCONTÉNTO, sm. 1. MALECONTENT, a peevish person dissatisfied with every thing. 2. Kind of game at cards.
MALCONTÉNTO, TA, a. Discontented.
MALCÓRTE, sm. Transgression of the mountain laws in cutting wood or making charcoal.
MALCRIÁDO, DA, a. Ill-bred, unmannerly.
MALDÁD, sf. Wickedness, iniquity.
MADADÓSO, SA, a. Wicked, ill-disposed.
MALDECIDÓR, RA, s. Detracter.
MALDECIMIÉNTO, sm. Backbiting, privy calumny; censure of the absent.
MALDECÍR, va. To curse, to accurse; to detract.
MALDÍCHO, CHA, pp. irr. of *maldecir*, Accursed; calumniated.
MALDICIÓN, sf. 1. Malediction, curse, imprecation. 2. Divine chastisement.
MALDÍTA, sf. (Fam.) The tongue.
MALDÍTO, TA, a. 1. Perverse, wicked. 2. Chastised by divine justice; damned. 3. (Fam.) None, not one. *Soltar la maldita*, To give a loose to one's tongue.—pp. irr. of *maldecir*, Accursed.
MALEABILIDÁD, sf. Malleability, quality of being extended by the hammer.
MALEÁBLE, a. Malleable.
MALEADÓR, RA, s. Rogue, villain, corrupter.
MALEÁNTE, sm. Corrupter, injurer.
MALEÁR, va. To pervert, to corrupt, to injure.
MALECÓN, sm. Dike, a mound to prevent inundations.
MALEDICÉNCIA, sf. Slander, calumny.
MALEFICÉNCIA, sf. Malefaction.
MALEFICIÁR, va. 1. To adulterate, to corrupt, to vitiate. 2. To bewitch, to injure by witchcraft.
MALEFÍCIO, sm. 1. Hurt, damage, injury. 2. Witchcraft, charm, enchantment.
MALÉFICO, CA, a. Mischievous, injurious to others, especially by witchcraft.
MALENCONÍA, sf. V. *Rabia*.
MALÉTA, sf. 1. Portmanteau, a bag in which clothes are carried. *Hacer la maleta*, To make the necessary preparations for a journey. 2. Prostitute kept by any one for interest.

MALETÉRO, sm. Harness-maker, saddler; portmanteau maker.
MALETÍA, sf. Malice; injury to the health.
MALETÍLLA, TA, CA, sf. A small portmanteau.
MALETÓN, sm. A large leather bag, in which bags are carried on a journey.
MALEVOLÉNCIA, sf. Malevolence, ill-nature, ill-will.
MALÉVOLO, LA, a. Malevolent, malignant.
MALÉZA, sf. 1. Wickedness, malice. 2. Piece of ground, rendered unfruitful by brambles and briers with which it is covered.
MALFECHÓR, sm. (Ant.) V. *Malhechor*.
MALGÁMA, sm. V. *Amalgama*.
MALGASTÁR, va. To mispend, to waste, to lavish.
MALGRÁDO, ad. Maugre, in spite of; notwithstanding.
MALHABLÁDO, DA, a. Bold, impudent in speaking.
MALHADÁDO, DA, a. Wretched, unfortunate.
MALHÉCHO, sm. Flagitious action.
MALHÉCHO, CHA, a. 1. Badly done, ill finished. 2. Unjust, contrary to equity and justice.
MALHECHÓR, RA, s. Malefactor, offender.
MALHERÍDO, DA, a. Badly wounded.
MALHERÍR, va. To wound badly.
MALHÓJO, sm. Refuse, that which is thrown away or disregarded when the rest is taken.
MALHUMORÁDO, DA, a. Ill-humoured, peevish; having gross humours.
MALÍCIA, sf. 1. Malice, perversity, wickedness, malignity. 2. Suspicion, apprehension. 3. Cunning, artifice. 4. Dissimulation, hypocrisy; evil disposition; injurious quality.
MALICIÁR, va. To corrupt, to adulterate.—vn. To put a malicious construction on a thing, to discourse in a malicious manner; to suspect.
MALICIOSAMÉNTE, ad. Maliciously.
MALICIOSÍCO, CA; LLO, LLA; TO, TA, a. dim A little malicious.
MALICIÓSO, SA, a. Malicious, suspicious, wicked.
MALIGNAMÉNTE, ad. Malignantly.
MALIGNÁR, va. To vitiate, to corrupt, to deprave.—vr. To become sore.
MALIGNIDÁD, sf. Malignity, malice, perverseness; noxiousness.
MALÍGNO, NA, a. Malignant, perverse, malign.
MALÍLLA, sf. 1. Manille, the deuce of spades or clubs, or the seven of hearts or diamonds, in the game of Ombre. 2. Person full of wickedness and malice.
MÁLLA, sf. 1. Mesh, the space between the threads of a net. 2. (Naút.) Network of a ship. 3. Coat of mail.
MALLÁR, va. To mail, to arm with a coat of mail.
MALLÉRO, sm. Armourer, maker of coats of mail.
MALLÉTES, s. pl. (Naút.) Partners, strong pieces of timber bolted to the beams, encircling the masts, to keep them steady in their steps, and prevent them from rolling or pitching by the board.
MÁLLO, sm. 1. Game of bowls, skittles or ninepins. 2. Bowling-green, skittle-ground. 3. Mallet.
MALLORQUÍN, NA, a. Native of Majorca.
MALMANDÁDO, DA, a. Disobedient, obstinate.
MALMETÉR, va. To incline, to induce to evil; to make one differ with another.
MALMIRÁDO, DA, a. Unpolite, indiscreet.
MÁLO, LA, a. 1. Imperfect, defective. 2. Bad wicked, perverse. *El malo*, The devil. 3

Artful, cunning, crafty. 4. Sickly, disordered. 5. Difficult, inquiet. *De mala*, Deceitfully, in an insidious manner. *Andar á malas*, To go in enmity.

Málo, *interj.* Bad, disgusting, injurious.

Malogramiénto, *sm.* Disappointment.

Malográr, *va.* 1. To disappoint, to disconcert. 2. (Com.) To waste or spoil goods.—*vr.* To be disappointed, to fail of success.

Malógro, *sm.* Disappointment, miscarriage.

Malordenádo, da, *a.* Badly contrived, ill arranged.

Malparádo, da, *a.* Languid, ill conditioned.

Malparár, *va.* To ill-treat, to destroy one's glory.

Malparída, *sf.* Woman who has miscarried.

Malparír, *vn.* To miscarry, to have an abortion.

Malpárto, *sm.* Abortion.

Malqueréncia, *sf.* Ill-will, hatred. [will.

Malquerér, *va.* To abhor, to hate, to bear ill-

Malquistár, *va.* To excite disputes and quarrels among friends and other persons.—*vr.* To incur hatred and displeasure.

Malquísto, ta, *a.* Odious, detested.

Malrotár, *va.* To mispend, to lavish, to run through one's fortune.

Malsáno, na, *a.* Unhealthy, sickly, infirm.

Malsín, *sm.* Tale-bearer, one who endeavours to sow discord and breed disturbances.

Malsinár, *va.* To inform against one from malice and spite. [nant information.

Malsindád y Malsinería, *sf.* (Ant.) Malig-

Malsonánte, *a.* Applied to doctrines offensive to pious ears.

Maltraér, *va.* (Ant.) To treat ill. V. *Maltratar.*

Maltratamiénto, *sm.* Ill treatment, bad usage; affliction. [spoil, to destroy.

Maltratár, *va.* 1. To treat ill, to abuse. 2. To

Maltráto, *sm.* Ill treatment.

Málva, *sf.* (Bot.) Mallows. Malva *L.*

Malvadaménte, *ad.* Wickedly.

Malvádo, da, *a.* Malicious, wicked, insolent, vicious, nefarious, very perverse.

Malvár, *sm.* Place covered with mallows.—*va.* (Ant.) To vitiate, to corrupt.

Malvasía, *sf.* Malmsey grape; malmsey wine.

Malvavísco, *sm.* (Bot.) Marsh-mallows. Althæa officinalis *L.*

Malversación, *sf.* Malversation.

Malversadór, ra, *s.* Evil-doer, trickster.

Malversár, *va.* To waste, to misapply property.

Malvís ó Malvíz, *sm.* Bird resembling a thrush.

Mamá, *sf.* 1. Mam, mamma; a fond word for mother. 2. (Anat.) Teat, nipple.

Mamacállos, *sm.* Dolt, simpleton. [ing.

Mamáda, *sf.* Time which a child takes in suck-

Mamadéra, *sf.* Sucking-glass used to draw milk out of a woman's breast.

Mamadór, ra, *s.* Sucker, one who sucks.

Mamalúco, *sm.* Dolt, simpleton, fool.

Mamáncia, *sf.* (Joc.) Childishness, silliness.

Mamánte, *a.* Sucking. *Piante ni mamante*, Not one, none, accompanied with the verb leave, &c. [mals.

Mamantón, na, *a.* Sucking; applied to ani-

Mamár, *va.* 1. To suck, to draw milk out of the breast of a female. 2. To cram and devour victuals. *Mamarse el dedo*, To bite the nails.

Mamário, ria, *a.* Belonging to teats and nipples.

Mamarrachada, *sf.* Collection of rude figures.

Mamarrachísta, *sm.* Dauber, bad painter.

Mamarrácho, *sm.* An ill-drawn figure of a man.

Mamelládo, da, *a.* (Ant.) Mammellated; applied to animals having loose projecting skins on their necks.

Mamelúco, *sm.* 1. Mameluke, Egyptian soldier. 2. Epithet of contempt to a rude, uncivilized, and ignorant person.

Mamíla, *sf.* The chief part of a woman's breast round the nipple.

Mamilár, *a.* Mammillary. [mouth.

Mamílas, *sf. pl.* Papillæ in the roof of the

Mamóla, *sf.* Chuck under the chin.

Mamón, na, *s.* 1. A sucking animal. 2. Milksop, a soft effeminate fellow who acts like a child. —*pl.* 1. Tender quills, which begin to be formed on birds. 2. Soup-meagre made with oil. 3. Suckers, young twigs shooting from the stock.

Mamóna, *sf.* Chuck. V. *Mamola.*

Mamóso, sa, *a.* 1. Sucking. 2. Applied to panic grass.

Mamotréto, *sm.* Memorandum-book. [place

Mampára, *sf.* Screen before a door or any other

Mamparár, *va.* To shelter, to protect.

Mampáros, *sm. pl.* (Naút.) Bulkheads, partitions in a ship to keep powder, stores, provisions, &c, separate. *Mamparos de quita y pon*, (Naút.) Ship and unship bulkheads.

Mampirlán, *sm.* A wooden ladder or step.

Mampórro, *sm.* Thump.

Mampostrár, *va.* To raise mason work, to cement with mortar.

Mampostería, *sf.* 1. Work made of stone and mortar without regularity and order. 2. A covered battery. 3. The employment of collecting alms for the hospitals of St. Lazarus and St. Anthony.

Mampostéro, *sm.* 1. Mason, who builds with stone and mortar. 2. Collector of alms for the hospitals of St. Lazarus and St. Anthony.

Mamprebár, *va.* (Mancha) To begin to break horses.

Mampuésta, *sf.* Row or line of bricks.

Mampuésto, *sm.* Materials for raising work of masonry. *De mampuesto*, Provisionally.

Mamujár, *va.* To play with the breast, not to have an inclination to suck; applied to children. [to mutter; to mumble.

Mamullár, *va.* To eat or chew as if sucking;

Mán, *sf.* (Ant.) Hand. V. *Mano.*

Maná, *sm.* 1. Manna, food of the Israelites. 2. Manna, a gum obtained from ash-trees. 3. Tart made of blanched almonds, sugar, spice, and other ingredients. 4. Kind of small sugarplums.

Manáda, *sf.* 1. Flock, herd; drove of cattle. 2. Handful of corn, &c. or any other things which can be held in the hand. 3. Crowd, multitude. *A' manadas*, In troops or crowds.

Manadéra, *sf.* Strainer, an instrument for filtration.

Manadéro, *sm.* 1. Source, spring. 2. Shepherd; one who has the care of a herd or flock.

Manadéro, ra, *a.* Springing, that which issues.

Manánte, *pa.* Proceeding, issuing.

Manantiál, *sm.* 1. Source, spring. 2. Source, origin, principle.

Manár, *vn.* 1. To spring from; to distil from, as a liquor. 2. To proceed, to issue, to arise. 3. To abound, to be in great plenty.
Manatí ó Manáto, *sm.* (Ict.) Sea-cow.
Mánca, *sf.* The left hand.
Mancamiénto, *sm.* Want, defect, privation, deficiency.
Mancár, *va.* 1. To maim, to disable an arm or hand from being used. 2. To fail, not to produce the desired effect. 3. To disable a man from doing any business.
Mancéba, *sf.* Mistress, concubine.
Mancebía, *sf.* 1. (Ant.) Youth. V. *Juventud.* 2. Brothel, bawdy-house.
Mancébo, ba, *s.* 1. Young person, not yet forty years of age. *Mancebo de mercader*, Shopman, shop-boy. 2. Journeyman, one who works under a master for weekly or daily wages.
Mancél, *sm.* Place of rendezvous for travellers and caravans.
Mancellár y Mancillár, *va.* V. *Amancillar.*
Mancellóso, sa, *a.* (Ant.) V. *Malicioso.*
Mancér, *sm.* Son of a prostitute.
Mancéra, *sf.* Plough-tail, handle of a plough.
Mancerína, *sf.* Saucer. V. *Macerina.*
Máncha, *sf.* 1. Stain, spot, discoloration. 2. Stigma, mark of infamy, a disgraceful taint of guilt. 3. Piece of ground covered with copse and weeds. 4. (Met.) Dishonour either from mean birth or an ignominious act. *No es mancha de judío*, It is but a trifling thing.
Manchádo, da, *a.* Spotted, speckled.
Manchár, *va.* 1. To stain, to make any thing lose its natural colour; to corrupt, to soil. 2. To defile one's character, to tarnish one's name and reputation. *Manchar papel*, To scribble, to write much and nothing to the purpose. 3. (Pint.) To lay in spots of light colour before defining the figure.
Manchéga, *sf.* Garter of different colours, made of worsted, especially in *Mancha.*
Manchégo, ga, *a.* Native of La Mancha.
Manchón, *sm.* Spot where grain grows rank or thick.
Mancílla, *sf.* 1. Wound, sore. 2. Spot, blemish. 3. Commiseration.
Mancipár, *va.* To subject, to enslave.
Mánco, ca, *a.* Maimed, defective, faulty, imperfect.
Mancomún, *sm.* Concurrence of two or more persons in the execution of a thing. *De mancomun*, Jointly, by common consent.
Mancomunadaménte, *ad.* Conjointly.
Mancomunárse, *vr.* To associate, to join in the execution of a thing; to unite.
Mancomunidád, *sf.* Union, conjunction or fellowship.
Mancuérda, *sf.* One of the implements of torture.
Mánda, *sf.* 1. Offer, proposal. 2. Legacy or donation, left by virtue of a last will.
Mandadéra, *sf.* V. *Demandadera.*
Mandadéro, ra, *s.* 1. Porter, messenger; one who is engaged to go on errands. 2. V. *Demandadero.*
Mandádo, *sm.* 1. Mandate, precept, command. 2. Errand, message; advertisement, notice.
Mandamiénto, *sm.* 1. Mandate, precept, order, command. 2. Peremptory order issued by a judge, respecting the execution of his sentence. *Mandamientos*, Commandments, the ten precepts of the decalogue; the five fingers of the hand.
Mandár, *va.* 1. To command, to give orders. 2. To leave or bequeath in a last will or testament. 3. To send, to transmit. 4. To offer, to promise.—*vr.* 1. To communicate with. 2. To have the free use of one's limbs, to manage one's self without the aid of others; applied to the infirm. *Mandar á alguno á puntapies, á puntillazos, ó á zapatazos*, To have complete ascendency over any one. *Mandar á coces*, To command harshly.
Mandárria, *sf.* (Naút.) Iron maul, a large iron hammer or sledge.
Mandatário, *sm.* Attorney, agent.
Mandáto, *sm.* 1. Mandate, precept, injunction. 2. Charge, trust, commission. 3. Ecclesiastical ceremony of washing twelve persons' feet on Maundy Thursday.
Mánde, *interj.* (Naút.) Holla! a word of command on board of ships, enjoining silence and attention.
Mandíbula, *sf.* Jaw-bone. V. *Quixada.*
Mandíl, *sm.* 1. Coarse apron used by men or women. 2. Servant to a pimp, or prostitute.
Mandilár, *va.* To wipe a horse with a coarse apron or cloth.
Mandiléjo, *sm.* 1. Ragged apron. 2. Servant of a rogue or prostitute; pimp, pander.
Mandiléte, *sm.* (Art.) Door of the port-hole of a battery.
Mandilón, *sm.* Coward, a mean dastardly fellow
Mandióca, *sf.* Kind of Indian corn.
Mándo, *sm.* Command, authority, power.
Mandoble, *sm.* 1. A two-handed blow. 2. A severe reprimand.
Mandón, na, *a.* Imperious, domineering.
Mándra, *sf.* A shepherd's cot.
Mandrachéro, *sm.* Proprietor of a gaming-table
Mandrácho, *sm.* Gambling-house.
Mandrágora, *sf.* (Bot.) Mandrake. Atropa mandragora *L.*
Mándria, *sm.* Coward, poltron.
Mandriéz, *sf.* Debility, weakness.
Mandrón, *sm.* First stroke of a ball or stone thrown from the hand.
Manducación, *sf.* Act of eating or chewing.
Manducár, *va.* To eat, to chew.
Manducatória, *sf.* Dining-room, refectory.
Manéa, *sf.* Shackles, fetters. V. *Maniota.*
Manear, *va.* To chain, to tie with fetters or shackles.
Manecílla, *sf.* 1. A small hand; mark ☞ or index, in grammar. 2. Handle of a plough. 3. Book-clasp. 4. Hand of a clock or watch. 5. Tendril of vines.
Manejáble, *a.* Manageable, tractable.
Manejádo, *a.* (Pint.) Handled.
Manejár, *va.* 1. To manage, to wield, to move with the hand. 2. To train a horse to graceful action. 3. To conduct, to govern.
Manéjo, *sm.* 1. Employment of the hands to any purpose. 2. Government of a horse. 3. Management, administration. 4. Intrigue, device. *Manejos de cortes*, Court intrigues.
Manezóta, *sf.* Shackles, fetters. V. *Maniota.*

MANÉRA, *sf.* 1. Manner, form, figure; method; manner of style, deportment. 2. Pocket, a small bag inserted into clothes, pocket-hole. 3. Opening, forepart or fall of breeches. 4. Quality, condition; kind, species. *De manera ó por manera*, So as, in such a manner. *Maneras*, MANNERS. V. *Costumbres*.

MANÉRO, RA, *a.* Manageable, tractable.

MÁNES, *sm.* Manes, ghost of the dead.

MANEZUÉLA, *sf.* A small hand. V. *Manecilla*.

MÁNFLA, *sf.* 1. Concubine, a woman kept in fornication. 2. Old sow.

MÁNGA, *sf.* 1. Sleeve, the part of a garment which covers the arms. 2. Arm of an axle-tree, on which turns the nave of a coach or other carriage. 3. Kind of cloak-bag or portmanteau, which can be fastened with a running string; strip of cloth hanging from the shoulder of clerical cloaks. 4. Body of troops formed in a line. 5. Fishing-net. 6. Bag made of woollen, linen, or paper, in the form of a sleeve, but narrow below and wide at the top, which is used to strain and clarify liquors. 7. Hurricane, whirlwind, water-spout. *Manga del navio*, (Naút.) Extreme breadth of a ship. *Mangas*, Conveniencies. *Ir de manga*, To join in the execution of some wicked or malicious design. *Manga de angel*, Women's wide sleeves.

MANGAJÁRRO, *sm.* A long ill-shaped sleeve.

MANGANÉSA, *sf.* Manganese, a semi-metal.

MANGANÍLLA, *sf.* 1. Slight of hand, a juggling trick. 2. Pole for gathering acorns.

MÁNGLA, *sf.* Gum which exudes from the rock-rose or dwarf sun-flower. Cistus ladaniferus *L.*

MANGLÁR, *sm.* Plantation of mangrove trees.

MÁNGLE, *sm.* (Bot.) Mangle or mangrove tree.

MÁNGO, *sm.* Handle, haft; that part of an instrument or tool which is held in the hand.

MANGÓN, *sm.* V. *Grandillon y Recaton*.

MANGONÁDA, *sf.* Push with the arm.

MANGONEÁR, *vn.* To wander about; to rove or ramble idly; to intermeddle.

MANGORRÉRO, RA, *a.* 1. Wandering, roving, rambling. 2. Hafted; applied to a knife.

MANGÓTE, *sm.* A large and wide sleeve.

MANGUÁL, *sm.* Weapon consisting of a pole with iron chains terminated by balls attached to it. [for various uses.

MANGUÉRA, *sf.* (Naút.) Piece of canvass tarred

MANGUÉRO, *sm.* Commander of a body of troops.

MANGUÉTA, *sf.* 1. Bladder and pipe for administering clysters. 2. Jamb of a glass-door. V. *Palanca*.

MANGUITÉRO, *sm.* 1. Muff maker, one whose trade is to make and sell muffs. 2. Leather-dresser, one who dresses fine skins or white leather.

MANGUÍTO, *sm.* 1. Muff, a cover for the hands to keep them warm. 2. Sleeve which is tight from the elbow to the waist.

MANÍA, *sf.* 1. Mania, phrensy, madness; perturbation of the faculties or mental powers. 2. Extravagance, whimsical obstinacy. 3. Inordinate desires.

MANIACÁL, *a.* Mad, frantic.

MANIÁLBO, *a.* White-footed; applied to a horse.

MANIATÁR, *va.* To manacle, to chain the hands; to handcuff.

MANIÁTICO, CA; y MANIACO, CA, *a.* Mad, frantic.

MANICÓRDIO, *sm.* V. *Monacordio*.

MANICÓRTO, TA, *a.* Illiberal, parsimonious.

MANÍDA, *sf.* Mansion, dwelling-house. *Manida de picaros*, Nest of thieves.

MANÍDO, DA, *a.* Hidden, concealed.

MANIFACÉRO, RA, *a.* Intriguing, meddlesome, intrusive.

MANIFACTÚRA, *sf.* 1. Manufacture, the art of working any thing by hand. 2. Manufacture, workmanship.

MANIFESTÁBLE, *a.* Manifestable, easy to be discovered.

MANIFESTACIÓN, *sf.* 1. Manifestation, declaration. 2. (For.) Decree of manifestation or emancipation.

MANIFESTADÓR, RA, *s.* Discoverer, publisher.

MANIFESTÁR, *va.* To discover, to manifest, to declare; to set at liberty. *Manifestar la herida*, (Cir.) To probe a wound.

MANIFIESTAMÉNTE, *ad.* Manifestly.

MANIFIÉSTO, TA, *a.* Manifest, plain, open.

MANIFIÉSTO, *sm.* 1. Act of exposing the Holy Sacrament to the public adoration. 2. Manifest, written instrument.

MANIGUÉTAS, *sf. pl.* (Naút.) Kevels on the quarter-deck, to which the rope-ends are fastened.

MANIGUETÓNES, *sm. pl.* (Naút.) Snatch-cleats, pieces of wood of different shapes and size, to which ropes are fastened.

MANÍJA, *sf.* 1. Handle of an instrument or working tool. 2. Shackles, handcuffs. 3. Ring, brace.

MANIJÉRO, *sm.* Manager, foreman of a number of workmen, who has the direction of the rest.

MANILÁRGO, GA, *a.* Large-handed.

MANÍLLA, *sf.* 1. Bracelet, an ornament worn by women around their arm or wrist. 2. Book-clasp. 3. Manacle, handcuff.

MANIÓBRA, *sf.* 1. Work performed and finished with the hand. 2. (Mil.) Manœuvre, movement of troops. 3. (Naút.) Working of a ship. *Navio que maniobra bien*, Ship that works freely. *Maniobras altas*, Upper running rigging. *Maniobras baxas*, Lower running rigging. *Maniobras de carena*, Careening jeers. *Maniobras de combate*, Preventer rigging.

MANIOBRÁR, *va.* 1. To work with the hands. 2. (Naút.) To work a ship. 3. (Met.) To seek the means of effecting any thing. 4. (Mil.) To manœuvre troops.

MANIOBRÍSTA, *sm.* (Naút.) A skilful naval tactician.

MANIÓTA, *sf.* Manacles, shackles, handcuffs.

MANIPÓDIO, *sm.* Bawdry, pollution.

MANIPULÁNTE, *sm.* Administrator, negotiator.

MANIPULÁR, *va.* To handle, to manage business in a peculiar manner, to meddle with every thing.

MANÍPULO, *sm.* 1. Part of the garments worn by the priests of the Roman catholic church when they officiate. 2. Division of the Roman army. [cheism.

MANIQUÉO, *a.* Manichean, belonging to Mani-

MANIQUÍ, *sm.* An artificial moveable figure, which can be put in different postures according to the will of the mover.

MANÍR, *va.* 1. To keep meat until it grows tender; to mellow. 2. To use, to waste, to consume.

Manirróto, ta, *a.* Liberal, generous, bountiful.

Manirrotúra, *sf.* Liberality, generosity, frankness.

Manivacío, cia, *a.* Empty-handed; idle, lazy.

Manjár, *sm.* 1. Food, victuals; provision for the mouth. 2. (Met.) Refection or entertainment which recruits the spirits. *Manjar blanco*, Dish made of the breast of fowl boiled and mixed with sugar, milk, and rice flour. *Manjar de angeles*, Dish composed of milk and sugar. *Manjar imperial*, Dish made of milk, yolks of eggs, and rice flour. *Manjáres*, The four suits of a pack of cards.

Manjelín, *sm.* Weight used for diamonds.

Manjolár, *va.* To carry a hawk in the hand lest it should be hurt in a basket or cage.

Manjorradá, *sf.* Excessive eating, too much victuals.

Manlevár, *va.* To contract.

Manlieva, *sf.* Tax levied in haste, and collected by going from house to house.

Manliéve, *sm.* A fraudulent deposit of a chest or trunk, said to contain valuable things, but which in fact contains nothing but earth or stone.

Máno, *sf.* 1. Hand, the palm with the fingers. 2. (Naút.) Snatch-cleat. 3. Proboscis, the snout or trunk of an elephant. 4. Maniple, handful. 5. Pestle. 6. Hand of a clock or watch. 7. A long cylindrical stone, with which cocoa is ground, to make chocolate. 8. First hand at play. 9. Command. 10. Reprimand, censure. 11. Last hand or finishing stroke. 12. Quire of paper. 13. (In Silk-mills) Hand of silk, composed of six or eight skeins. 14. Troop of reapers or harvest-men. 15. Workmanship, power or act of manufacturing or making. 16. Side, right or left. 17. Paw or forefoot of animals. 18. (Mús.) V. *Escala.* *A' mano*, At hand, with the hand; studiously. *A' la mano*, Near. *Mano de gato*, Ladies' paint; correction of any writing made by a superior hand.—*pl.* 1. (Among Butchers) Feet of cattle. *Manos de carnero*, Sheep's trotters. *Manos de vaca*, Cow-heels. 2. Handicraft, handiwork, workmanship. 3. *Manos á la obra*, (Naút.) Bear a hand! *Manos libres*, Emoluments annexed to an office or place. *Manos muertas*, Mortmain, such a state of possession as prevents all future alienation. *A' dos manos*, Willingly, readily; with the aid of both hands. *A' manos llenas*, Liberally, abundantly, copiously. *Ser sus pies y sus manos*, To be one's chief support and consolation in distress. *Venir con sus manos lavadas*, To enjoy the fruit of another's labour. *Mano á mano*, In company, familiarly; alone.

Manóbra, *sf.* Raw material.

Manóbre, *sm.* (Mur.) Hodman, a labourer that carries mortar.

Manobréro, *sm.* He who cleans and preserves fountains or aqueducts.

Manójo, *sm.* Handful, as much as the hand can grasp or contain. *Manojo de llaves*, Bunch of keys. *A' manojos*, Abundantly.

Manóla, *sf.* A common girl, a low wench.

Manópla, *sf.* 1. Gauntlet, a strong glove used for defence. 2. Coachman's whip. *Tela de manoplas*, A sort of silk with large flowers.

Manoseár, *va.* 1. To handle, to touch, to feel. 2. To rumple clothes.

Manoséo, *sm.* Handling, or touching with the hand.

Manotáda y Manotázo, *s.* Blow with the hand.

Manoteár, *va.* To strike with the hand.—*vn.* To move the hands indicating strong emotion.

Manoteádo y Manotéo, *sm.* 1. Blow with the hand. 2. Manual gesticulation.

Manqueár, *vn.* To affect the cripple, to pretend to be maimed.

Manquedád, *sf.* Lameness, a hurt which prevents the use of the hands; defect.

Manquéra, *sf.* Lameness, fault, defect; imperfection.

Manquíllo, lla; to, ta, *a. dim.* of *Manco.*

Mansaménte, *ad.* Meekly, slowly, quietly.

Mansedúmbre, *sf.* Meekness, gentleness of behaviour and deportment; peacefulness.

Mansejón, na, *a.* Tame; applied to animals.

Mansér, *sm.* Son of a prostitute.

Mansión, *sf.* 1. Stay, sojourn, residence. 2. Habitation, mansion.

Mansionário, *a.* Applied to ecclesiastics who live in a cloister.

Mansíco, ca; to, ta, *a. dim.* Genteel, mild.

Mansíto, *ad.* V. *Quedito.*

Mánso, sa, *a.* 1. Tame; applied to horses and other animals. 2. Meek, gentle, tractable; soft, quiet, mild. *A' lumbre mansa*, By a mild light.

Mánso, *sm.* 1. Male which guides the flocks of goats, sheep, or black cattle. 2. Manor, district inherited, manor house.

Mánta, *sf.* 1. Blanket, a woollen cover, soft and loosely woven. 2. Tapestry, paper-hanging. 3. Mantelet, a kind of moveable parapet made of thick planks, for covering troops. 4. Thrashing, drubbing. 5. Tossing in a blanket. 6. Any of the quill-feathers in birds of prey. *A' manta ó á manta de Dios*, Copiously, plentifully; in great abundance. *Tomar la manta*, To undergo a course of salivation. *Dar una manta*, V. *Mantear.*

Mantaterílla, *sf.* Coarse hempen cloth used for blankets.

Manteadór, ra, *s.* Tosser, one who tosses in a blanket.

Manteamiénto, *sm.* Tossing in a blanket.

Manteár, *va.* To toss in a blanket.—*vn.* To gad frequently abroad in a mantle; spoken of women.

Mantéca, *sf.* 1. Lard, the grease of swine; pomatum. 2. Butter, the unctuous part of milk. 3. Pulpy and oily part of fruits. 4. (Joc.) Money.

Mantecáda, *sf.* Toast, a piece of bread dried before the fire and buttered.

Mantecádo, *sm* Butter-cake.

Mantecón, *sm.* Milksop, sweet-tooth; a person dainty and fond of nice fare.

Mantecóso, sa, *a.* Buttery, consisting of butter.

Manteísta, *sm.* Student in universities, who wears a priest's gown.

Mantéles, *sm. pl.* 1. Diaper, linen cloth woven in flowers and figures. *Juego de manteles adamascados*, Damask service; a table-cloth

with a dozen of napkins. 2. Altar-cloth. *Levantar los manteles*, To clear the table.
Mantelería, *sf*. Table-linen.
Manteléta, *sf*. Scarf worn by ladies.
Manteléte, *sm*. 1. Mantlet, a short mantle worn by bishops. 2. A moveable parapet, made of thick planks, to cover troops.
Mantellína, *sf*. A short cloak worn by women.
Mantenéncia, *sf*. (Ant.) Maintenance, aliment, support.
Mantenér, *va*. 1. To support, to keep up with the hand; to prevent from falling. 2. To keep, to feed, to supply with food. 3. To be the first challenger at a tournament. 4. To persevere, to persist in the execution of a design. 5. To support a weight. 6. To pursue, to continue. 7. To defend or sustain an opinion. *Mantener correspondencia*, To keep up a correspondence.—*vr*. 1. To continue residing in a place. 2. To continue in the same condition without alteration, to maintain one's self. *Mantenerse á la mar*, To keep the sea.
Manteniénte, *sm*. A violent blow given with both hands. *A' manteniente*, With all one's might.
Mantenimiénto, *sm*. 1. Maintenance, sustenance, subsistence; a supply of the necessaries of life. 2. Ration, allowance.
Mantéo, *sm*. 1. A long cloak or mantle, worn by priests and students. 2. Sort of woollen petticoat worn by women.
Mantequéra, *sf*. Churn, a vessel in which butter is made.
Mantequéro, ra, *s*. Butterman, butterwoman; one who sells butter.
Mantequílla, *sf*. A kind of buttercake.
Mantéra, ro, *s*. Mantua-maker, one who makes or sells mantles.
Mantílla, *sf*. 1. Head-cover for women, made of baize or other stuff. 2. Mixture of dung, short and well rotten. 3. Housing, horsecloth. *Mantillas*, Swaddling-clothes, clothes wrapped round new-born children. *Estar en mantillas*, To be in a state of infancy.
Mantíllo, *sm*. Short dung, rotten and well mixed.
Mantillón, na, *a*. Dirty, slovenly.
Mánto, *sm*. 1. Silken veil for ladies. 2. Cloak, robe, a mantle of state. 3. Mantle-piece of a chimney. 4. In mines, a vein. 5. Veil, cover.
Mantón, *sm*. 1. A large cloak or mantle. 2. Quill. V. *Manta*. 3. Trimming on women's jackets.—*a*. V. *Mantudo*.
Mantúdo, da, *a*. Applied to fowls with their wings falling down.
Manuáble, *a*. Tractable, manageable.
Manuál, *a*. 1. Manual, performed by the hand. 2. Easily handled or performed with the hand. 3. Tractable, pliant; light, prompt.
Manuál, *sm*. 1. Manual, a portable book, such as may be carried in the hand. 2. Book in which the heads of matters are set down. 3. Journal, a book of trade, in which the business of every day is entered from the waste-book, under proper heads and in due order. *Manuales*, Presents to choristers given in the choir.
Manualménte, *ad*. Manually, with the hand.
Manúbrio, *sm*. Hand of an instrument or tool.
Manucodiáta, *sf*. Bird of paradise.
Manuélla, *sf*. Handspike.
Manufactúra, *sf*. V. *Manifactura*.

Manumisión, *sf*. Manumission, the act of setting a slave at liberty.
Manumisór, *sm*. (For.) Liberator.
Manumitír, *va*. (For.) To emancipate, to release from slavery.
Manus Crísti, *sm*. A sort of electuary, a kind of plaster.
Manuscríto, *sm*. Manuscript, a book written and not printed.
Manutención, *sf*. Conservation, prohibition, maintaining.
Manutenér, *va*. To maintain. V. *Mantener*.
Manutísa, *sf*. (Bot.) Kind of pink.
Manzána, *sf*. 1. Apple, the fruit of the apple tree. 2. Pommel, the round ball or knob at the end of the guard of a sword. 3. Square, area of four sides, surrounded with houses. 4. Cypress nut.
Manzanál ó Manzanár, *sm*. Orchard, a garden of apple-trees.
Manzaníl, *a*. Like an apple.
Manzanílla, *sf*. 1. (Bot.) Chamomile, feverfew. Matricaria chamomilla *L*. 2. Small ball or knob put by way of ornament at the top of coaches, bedsteads, &c. 3. Kind of small olive. 4. Lower part of the chin. 5. Claws of animals.
Manzaníllo, *sm*. (Bot.) 1. Little apple-tree. 2. Kind of olive-tree. 3. Indian apple-tree.
Manzaníta de Dama, *sf*. V. *Acerola*.
Manzáno, *sm*. (Bot.) Apple-tree. Pyrus malus *L*.
Máña, *sf*. 1. Hardiness, dexterity. 2. Artifice, craft. 3. An evil habit or custom. 4. Bundle of hemp or flax when reaped.
Mañána, *sf*. Morning, the part of the day from the first appearance of light to twelve o'clock at noon. *De mañana*, In the morning.—*ad*. 1. To-morrow, on the day after this current day. 2. Soon, erelong, immediately. 3. Expression of negation.
Mañanár, *vn*. (Joc.) To arrive to-morrow.
Mañaneár, *vn*. To rise early. V. *Madrugar*.
Mañaníca, ta, *sf*. Break of day.
Mañear, *va*. To act with craft and address in order to attain one's end.
Mañería, *sf*. 1. (Ant.) Sterility; cunning. 2. Right of succeeding to the possessions of those who die without legitimate succession.
Mañéro, ra, *a*. 1. Dexterous, skilful, artful. 2. Meek, tractable. 3. Charged to pay for another. 4. Similar, like, neighbouring.
Mañosaménte, *ad*. Dexterously; subtlely; maliciously.
Mañóso, sa, *a*. Dexterous, skilful, artificial.
Mañuéla, *sf*. Low cunning, mean tricks. *Mañuelas*, An artful cunning person.
Mápa, *sf*. 1. Map, a geographical picture, on which lands and seas are delineated according to the longitude and latitude. 2. Any thing excellent and prominent in its line.
Mapália, *sf*. Sheep-cot, sheep-fold.
Maquí, *sm*. Kind of ginger.
Maquiavélico, ca, *a*. Machiavelian, resembling the principles of Machiavelli.
Maquiavelísmo, *sm*. Machiavelism.
Maquíla, *sf*. 1. Toll-corn, that part of the corn which the miller takes for grinding. 2. Toll or tollage in general. 3. Corn-measure in Galicia, the 24th part of a *fanega*.

Maquilandéro, *sm.* Measure or instrument with which corn is tolled.
Maquilár, *va.* 1. To measure and take the miller's dues for grinding corn. 2. To clip, to retrench, to cut off.
Maquiléro ó Maquilón, *sm.* One who measures or takes the miller's dues for grinding corn.
Máquina, *sf.* 1. Machine, engine. 2. Great number, abundance, crowd. *Hubo una gran máquina de gente*, There was a great concourse of people. 3. A vast sumptuous structure. 4. Intrigue, machination, contrivance. *Máquina de arbolar*, (Naút.) Sheers, sheer-hulk.
Maquinación, *sf.* Machination, artifice, contrivance.
Maquinadór, ra, *s.* Contriver, schemer; an artful person.
Maquinál, *a.* Machinal.
Maquinalménte, *ad.* Mechanically.
Maquinár, *va.* To machinate, to plan, to contrive.
Maquinária, *sf.* Mechanics, the geometry of motion; the art of contriving and building machines.
Maquinéte, *sm.* (Mur.) Chopping-knife.
Maquínica, *sf.* Mechanics. V. *Maquinaria.*
Maquinísta, *sm.* Machinist, a constructor of engines.
Már, *s. com.* 1. Sea, a large collection of salt-water; the water opposed to the land; tide. 2. A large lake. 3. (Met.) Abundance. *De mar á mar*, Copiously, excessively; in the extreme of fashion. *Baxa mar*, (Naút.) Low-water, ebb-tide. *Mar llena ó plena*, (Naút.) High-water. *Correr con la mar en popa*, (Naút.) To scud before the sea. *Mantener dos señales de mar enfilados*, (Naút.) To keep two seamarks in one. *Hay mar gruesa afuera*, There is a great sea in the offing. *Ir con la proa á la mar*, (Naút.) To head the sea. *Mar de través*, (Naút.) A sea on the beam. *La mar arde*, The sea sparkles.
Maragáto, *sm.* Ornament on women's tuckers.
Maragúto, *sm.* (Naút.) Jib. V. *Foque.*
Maráña, *sf.* 1. Place covered with brambles or briers, which render it impassable. 2. Entanglement of a skein of silk, thread, cotton, yarn, or worsted. 3. Refuse of silk. 4. Perplexity, puzzle. 5. Plot of a play. 6. Prostitute.
Marañádo, da, *a.* Enfangled, perplexed.
Marañéro, ra; y Marañóso, sa, *a.* Entangling, ensnaring, perplexing.
Marásmo, *sm.* (Med.) Tabes, consumption.
Marátro, *sm.* V. *Hinojo.*
Maravedí, *sm.* Maravedi, a Spanish coin, now disused.
Maravílla, *sf.* 1. Wonder, an uncommon event; admiration. 2. (Bot.) Turnsol, heliotrope. Heliotropium indicum *L.* 3. Flower of the garden smilax. 4. (Bot.) Common marigold. Calendula officinalis *L. A' las maravillas*, Uncommonly well; exquisitely. *A' maravilla*, Marvellously. *Es una maravilla*, He is a prodigy. *Por maravilla*, Very seldom.
Maravillárse, *vr.* To wonder, to be struck with admiration.—*va.* To admire.
Maravillosaménte, *ad.* Wonderfully.
Maravillóso, sa, *a.* Wonderful, marvellous.
Marbéte, *sm.* 1. Stamp, the manufacturer's mark on cloth. 2. Label.
Márca, *sf.* 1. Landmark; a frontier province. 2. The due measure or weight of any thing. 3. Mark in paper. 4. Landmark, light-house. 5. Brand, a mark made by burning with a hot iron; act of marking. 6. Prostitute. *De marca*, Excellent of its kind.
Marcadór, *sm.* Marker, assay-master.
Marcár, *va.* 1. To mark, to brand. *Marcar el campo*, To mark or trace the ground for a camp. 2. To observe, to note; to designate.
Marceár, *va.* To shear, to cut off the wool, hair, or fur of animals, with a pair of shears.
Márcha, *sf.* 1. March, a solemn movement of troops; a journey of soldiers. *A' marchas forzadas*, Forced marches. 2. Signal to move, given with a drum or trumpet. 3. Tune beat on a drum or sounded with the trumpet. 4. Bonfire, made as a signal of rejoicings. 5. (Naút.) Headway, the forward motion of a ship. *Sobre la marcha*, Off hand, on the spot.
Marchamár, *va.* To put a mark on goods at the custom-house.
Marchaméro, *sm.* Custom-house officer who marks the goods which are reported at the custom-house.
Marchámo, *sm.* Mark put on goods at the custom-house.
Marchánte, *sm.* y *a.* V. *Traficante y mercantil.*
Marchár, *vn.* 1. To march, to begin to move. 2. (Naút.) To have much head-way, to sail fast.
Marcházo, *sm.* Braggadocio, boaster, bragger.
Marchitáble, *a.* Perishable.
Marchitár, *vn.* 1. To wither, to fade; to dry up. 2. To pine away, to grow lean.
Marchitéz, *sf.* Languor, lassitude.
Marchíto, ta, *a.* Languid, feeble, decayed.
Marchitúra, *sf.* Decay, decline.
Marciál, *sm.* Aromatic powder.
Marciál, *a.* Martial, warlike.
Márco, *sm.* 1. Door-case, window-case. 2. Picture-frame. 3. Mark, a weight of eight ounces. 4. Branding iron. 5. The necessary size of timber for being felled. 6. Model, archetype. 7. Measure of ground which should have a fanega of grain.
Marcóla, *sf.* Pruning-hook.
Maréa, *sf.* 1. Tide, the periodical motion of the waters of the sea. 2. Sea, shore. 3. Soft wind. 4. Collection of street-dirt. *Marea creciente*, Flood-tide. *Marea menguante*, Ebb-tide. *Direccion de las mareas*, Setting of the tide. *Establecimiento de marea*, Time of high-water. *Ir contra marea*, To sail against the tide. *Navegar con la marea*, To tide it up or down. *Marea parada*, Slack-tide. *Mareas vivas*, Spring-tides.
Mareáje, *sm.* Art of navigating a ship.
Mareamiénto, *sm.* Sea-sickness.
Mareánte, *a.* Skilled in navigating a ship.
Mareár, *va.* 1. To work a ship. 2. To molest and harass by impertinent questions. 3. To sell goods by public auction. 4. *Marear las velas*, (Naút.) To trim the sails.—*vr.* 1. To be sea-sick. 2. To be damaged at sea; to be averaged; applied to goods or merchandise.
Marejáda, *sf.* Swell of the sea. *Tuvimos una marejada del N. O.* We had a great sea from N. W.
Mare magnum, *sm.* (Lat.) Expressing the abundance or magnitude of any thing.

Maréo, *sm.* 1. Sea-sickness. 2. Molestation, vexation.

Maréro, *a.* Sea-breeze, wind coming from the sea.

Maréta, *sf.* (Naút.) A slight commotion of the sea.

Maretázo, *sm.* Surge of the sea.

Marfága, *sf.* Rug, a coverlet of a bed.

Márfega, *sf.* Sack of straw, coarse mattress.

Marfíl, *sm.* Ivory, the tusk of the elephant.

Marfileño, **ña**, *a.* (Poét.) Belonging to ivory.

Márga ó Margéga, *sf.* 1. Mourning; coarse cloth. 2. Clay, marl. 3. Sackcloth.

Margallón, *sm.* V. *Palmito.*

Marganésa, *sf.* Manganese. V. *Manganesa.*

Margár, *va.* To marle, to manure with marl.

Margaríta, *sf.* 1. Pearl. 2. (Bot.) Common daisy. Bellis perennis *L.* 3. (Naút.) Messenger, a rope sometimes used in weighing anchor. *Margaritas*, Periwinkles.

Margaxíta, *sf.* V. *Marquesita.*

Márgen, *sm.* 1. Border, edge, verge. 2. Margin, the edge left blank in a book or writing. *Dar margen*, To give an opportunity. 3. Marginal note.

Margenár, *va.* 1. V. *Marginar.* 2. To make or leave a margin in paper.

Marginál, *a.* Marginal, belonging to the margin.

Marginár, *va.* To make annotations on the margin.

Margóso, **sa**, *a.* Marly, partaking of marl.

Marguéra, *sf.* Marl-pit, a place where marl is dug.

Marhójo, *sm.* Moss, a vegetable growing on the bark of trees. V. *Malhojo.*

María, *sf.* 1. A white wax-taper, placed in the middle of eight shorter yellow wax-candles in Roman catholic churches. 2. Silver coin worth 12 reals vellon. 3. Mary, a proper name. *Arbol de maria*, Balsam of tolu-tree. Toluifera balsamum *L.*

Mariál, *a.* Applied to books containing praises of the Holy Virgin.

Marica, *sf.* 1. Magpie. V. *Urraca.* 2. An effeminate mean-spirited person. 3. Thin tasteless asparagus.

Maricón, *sm.* Coward, poltroon.

Maridáble, *a.* Marriageable, fit for marriage.

Maridablemènte, *ad.* Conjugally.

Maridáge, *sm.* Marriage, conjugal union. 2. Intimate connexion or union.

Maridánza, *sf.* (Extr.) Treatment given to a wife.

Maridár, *vn.* To marry.—*va.* To unite, to join.

Maridázo, *sm.* V. *Gurrumino.*

Maridíllo, *sm.* 1. A sorry pitiful husband. 2. A small brasier, covered with a lid, which women make use of to warm their feet.

Marído, *sm.* Husband, the correlative to wife; a man married to a woman.

Marimácho, *sm.* Virago, a robust masculine woman.

Marimánta, *sf.* Bugbear, phantom with which children are frightened.

Marimoréna, *sf.* Dispute, difference, quarrel.

Marína, *sf.* 1. Marine, sea-affairs; nautical art. 2. (Among Painters) Sea-piece. 3. Sea-coast.

Marináge, *sm.* 1. Seamanship, the art of working a ship. 2. Profession of mariners.

Marinár, *va.* To man a ship.

Marineár, *vn.* To be a mariner.

Marineràdo, **da**, *a.* V. *Tripulado.*

Marinería, *sf.* 1. Seamanship, the art of working a ship. 2. Profession of sea-faring men, with every thing relating to it. 3. Speculation. *Me ha salido mal esta marinería*, That speculation has turned out very unfortunate.

Marinéro, *sm.* Mariner, seafaring man. *A' lo marinero*, In a seamanlike manner.

Marinésco, **ca**, *a.* Nautical. *A' la marinesca*, In a seamanlike manner.

Maríno, **na**, *a.* Marine, belonging to the sea.—*sm.* Marine, seaman.

Marión y Maron, *sm.* (Ict.) V. *Sollo.*

Marióna, *sf.* Spanish dance.

Mariperéz, *sf.* Hand at cards in which the gain or loss is double.

Maripósa, *sf.* 1. Butterfly. Papilio *L.* 2. Rush-light.

Mariquétas, *sf. pl.* Armbands, with which women tie up their mittens.

Mariquíta, *sf.* 1. Insect found among grapes. 2. Courtesan, woman of easy virtue.

Mariscál, *sm.* 1. Marshal, a general officer of high rank in armies. 2. Farrier, blacksmith. *Mariscal de campo*, Camp-marshal, a rank inferior to lieutenant-general.

Mariscaláto y Mariscalía, *s.* Dignity of marshal.

Mariscár, *va.* To gather shell-fish on the strand.

Marísco, *sm.* Cockles and other small shell-fish sticking to the rocks in the sea.

Marísma, *sf.* Lake formed by the overflow of the tide.

Marísmo, *sm.* V. *Salgada.*

Maritál, *a.* Marital, pertaining to a husband.

Maritimár, *vn.* To lead a maritime life.

Marítimo, **ma**, *a.* Maritime, marine.

Marjál, *sm.* Fen, marshy ground. In Murcia it is called *armajal.*

Marjoléta y Marjoléto. V. *Majuela y Majuelo.*

Marlóta, *sf.* A kind of Moorish dress.

Marméla, *sf.* Flock of wool hanging from the necks of sheep.

Marmelládo, **da**, *a.* Having matted locks of wool under the throat.

Marmíta, *sf.* Kettle, a small copper.

Marmitón, *sm.* Scullion, one who is engaged to wash the dishes and plates in the kitchen.

Mármol, *sm.* 1. Marble. Marmor *L.* *Marmol pintado*, Spotted marble. *Marmol rayado*, Streaked marble. 2. Pillar, column.

Marmoléjo, *sm.* A small pillar or column of marble.

Marmoléño, **ña**, *a.* Made of marble, resembling marble.

Marmolería, *sf.* Any work made of marble.

Marmolísta, *sm.* Worker in marble, sculptor.

Marmoración, *sf.* V. *Estuco.*

Marmóreo, **ea**, **Marmoróso**, **sa**, *a.* Made of marble, marbled.

Marmóta, *sf.* Marmot. Arctomys marmota *L.*

Maro, *sm.* (Bot.) Germander, common marum. Teucrium marum *L.*

Marójo, *sm.* (And.) V. *Almuerdago.*

Maróma, *sf.* Rope, a thick cord made of bass or hemp. *Andar en la maroma*, To dance on a rope; (Met.) To engage in a perilous undertaking.

Marqués, *sm.* Marquis.

Marquésa, *sf.* 1. Marchioness, the lady of a marquis. 2. V. *Marquesina.*

Marquesádo, *sm.* Marquisate.

Marquesína, *sf.* Marquee, tilt over an officer's tent, serving more effectually to keep out the rain.

Marquesíta, *sf.* Marcasite, mundic, a metallic fossil.

Marquetería, *sf.* 1. Cabinet-manufactory. 2. Marquetry, chequered or inlaid work.

Marquída ó Marquísa, *sf.* Prostitute.

Marquíta, *sf.* Crude cake of wax.

Márra, *sf.* 1. Want, deficiency, defect. 2. A kind of pick-axe. 3. Opening in a row of vines, some of them being missing.

Márraga y Márrega, *sf.* 1. (Ant.) Coarse grogram worn by shepherds. 2. Mourning. V. *Marga.*

Marrájo, *sm.* 1. (Ict.) White shark. Squalus carcharias *L.* 2. V. *Martagon.*

Marrána, *sf.* Sow; fresh pork.

Marranálla, *sf.* V. *Canalla.*

Marráncho, Marranchón, na, *s.* V. *Marrano.*

Marranéta, *sf.* A young sow.

Marráno, *sm.* 1. Hog. V. *Cochino.* 2. Rafter or wood-work which supports a floor or a cistern.

Marráno, na, *a.* Cursed, excommunicated.

Marrár, *vn.* To deviate from truth or justice.

Márras, *ad.* Long ago, long since.

Marregón, *sm.* Straw-sack. V. *Xergon.*

Marrído, da, *a.* Melancholy. V. *Amarrido.*

Marríllo, *sm.* Thick short stick.

Márro, *sm.* 1. Kind of game, quoits. 2. Slip given by a deer or hare in the course of the chase. 3. Disappointment, failure. 4. Crooked bat for striking a ball.

Marrojár, *va.* To lop off the useless branches of trees.

Marrón, *sm.* Quoit, pitcher.

Marroquín, na, *a.* Belonging to Morocco.

Marrotár, *va.* To waste, to mispend. V. *Malrotar.*

Marrúbio, *sm.* (Bot.) Common white hoarhound. Marrubium vulgare *L.*

Marrullería, *sf.* Cunning, craft; artful tricks.

Marrulléro, ra, *a.* Crafty, cunning.

Marsellés, *sm.* A sailor's short jacket.

Marsópa, *sf.* Blunt-headed cachalot, spermaceti-whale. Physeter macrocephalus *L.*

Márta, *sf.* Pine marten. Mustela martes *L.* *Martas,* Martens, dressed marten skins.

Martagón, na, *s.* 1. Cunning, artful person. 2. (Bot.) Wild lily.

Márte, *sm.* Mars; iron.

Martélo, *sm.* Fondness, love; tender affection.

Mártes, *sm.* Tuesday, the third day of the week. *Martes carnestolendas,* Shrove-Tuesday.

Martilláda, *sf.* Stroke with the hammer.

Martilladór, ra, *s.* Hammerer.

Martillár, *va.* To hammer, to beat with a hammer. *Martillar al caballo,* To spur a horse.

Martilléjo, *sm.* Smith's hammer.

Martíllo, *sm.* 1. Hammer, an instrument composed of a handle and iron head, with which any thing is driven. 2. Person who perseveres in any thing. 3. Tuning hammer. *A' martillo,* With strokes of a hammer. *De martillo,* Wrought metal.

Martín Pescador, *sm.* (Orn.) King fisher. Alcedo ispida *L.*

Martinéte, *sm.* 1. (Orn.) Bird of the family of herons. 2. Jack in a harpsichord. 3. Hammer in copper-works. 4. Copper-mill.

Martingála, *sf.* 1. Martingal, a leather strap fastened to the girth and noseband of a horse. 2. Ancient kind of breeches.

Martiniéga, *sf.* Tax payable on St. Martin's day.

Mártir, *sm.* Martyr, one who by his death bears witness to the truth; one who suffers great hardships and calamities.

Martírio, *sm.* Martyrdom, the death of a martyr; great sufferings and hardships.

Martirizadór, ra, *s.* One who commits martyrdom.

Martirizár, *va.* To martyr, to make one suffer the death of a martyr; to inflict great sufferings and hardships.

Martirológio, *sm.* Martyrology, book of martyrs.

Marúja, *sf.* Prostitute, wench.

Marzádga, *sf.* Tax payable in March.

Marzál, *a.* Belonging to the month of March.

Marzeár, *va.* To cut the hair of cattle in spring.

Marzéo, *sm.* Cutting of dry honey-combs in a hive in spring.

Márzo, *sm.* March, the third month of the year.

Más, *ad.* 1. More, to a greater degree. 2. But, yet. V. *Pero.* 3. Besides, moreover. V. *Sino.* *A' mas correr,* With the utmost speed. *A' mas tardar,* At latest. *A' mas y mejor,* Greatly, excellently. *De mas á mas,* Still more and more. *Mas si,* Perhaps, if. *Mas que,* Although, even. *N. se ha ido, mas que nunca vuelva,* N. is gone, even or should he never return.—*sm.* Farm-house and stock.

Mása, *sf.* 1. Dough, paste made of water and flour. 2. Mortar. 3. Mass of gold, silver, or other metal. 4. League, coalition. 5. (Arag.) Farm-house, with all the necessary tools and utensils. 6. (Mil.) Arrears of pay. 7. Nature, condition, disposition.

Masáda, *sf.* (Ar.) Country-house, farm-house.

Masadéro, *sm.* (Ar.) Neighbour.

Masár, *va.* To heap, to pile up. V. *Amasar.*

Mascabádo, da, *a.* Applied to inferior sugar.

Mascadór, ra, *s.* Chewer, masticator.

Mascadúra, *sf.* Act of chewing, mastication.

Mascár, *va.* 1. To chew, to grind with the teeth; to masticate. 2. To pronounce or talk with difficulty.

Máscara, *sf.* y *com.* 1. Person whose face is covered with a mask. 2. Mask with which the face is covered; pretext. 3. Masquerade. 4. (Cir.) Bandage; applied to a burn on the face. 5. Exercise of horsemanship in which the gentlemen are dressed alike, and wear masks.

Mascaráda, *sf.* Masquerade.

Mascaréro, *sm.* Dealer in masks.

Mascarílla, *sf.* 1. A small mask. *Quitarse la mascarilla,* To take off the mask, to declare one's sentiments boldly. 2. Mould taken from the face of a dead person.

Mascarón, *sm.* 1. A large hideous mask. 2. Hideous or grotesque forms; *e. g.* satyrs' faces, used to adorn fountains and buildings. 3. Person ridiculously grave and solemn.

Mascujár, *vn.* 1. To masticate difficultly. 2. To pronounce with difficulty.

Masculinidád, *sf.* Masculinity.

Masculíno, na, *a.* Masculine, male, virile.

MASCULLÁR, *vn.* To falter in speaking.
MASECORÁL Y MASECICOMAR, *sm.* A kind of game. [formed.
MASÉRA, *sf.* Any thing in which a mess is
MASERÍA Y MASÍA, *sf.* (Ar.) Farmhouse.
MASÍLLA, TA, *sf.* 1. (Mil.) Pittance kept to purchase shoes for soldiers. 2. Sinapism, mustard poultice. [rupeds.
MÁSLO, *sm.* Trunk or root of the tail of quad-
MASÓN, *sm.* Mess of dough given to fowls.
MASÓRA, *sf.* Massorah or tradition, criticism on the Hebrew Bible.
MASORÉTICO, *a.* Massoretic, belonging to the Massorites or Jewish doctors.
MASILIÉNSE, *a.* Native of Marseilles.
MASTELÉRO, *sm.* (Naút.) Topmast. *Masteleros de respeto*, Spare topmasts. *Masteleros de juanete*, Top-gallant masts.
MASTICACIÓN, *sf.* Mastication.
MASTICÁR, *va.* To masticate, to chew. V. *Mascar y Rumiar.*
MASTICATÓRIO, RIA, *a.* Masticatory.
MASTIGADÓR, *sm.* Instrument put into horses' mouths to prevent their chewing.
MASTÍL, *sm.* 1. Mast. V. *Mastelero.* 2. Upright post of a bed or loom. *Mástil de barrena*, Shank of an auger. 3. Trunk or stem of a tree. 4. Wide breeches worn by Indians.
MASTÍN, *sm.* 1. Mastiff, a dog of the largest size; bull-dog. 2. A clumsy-fellow; clown.
MASTÍNA, *sf.* Mastiff bitch.
MÁSTO, *sm.* (Arag.) Trunk or stock in which a sprig is planted or ingrafted.
MASTRÁNTO Y MASTRÁNZO, *sm.* (Bot.) Watermint. Mentha viridis *L.*
MASTUÉRZO, *sm.* (Bot.) Water-cresses. Sisymbrium nasturtium *L.*
MÁTA, *sf.* 1. Small bush, shrub. 2. Sprig, blade. 3. Copse or coppice. 4. Lock of matted hair. 5. Young evergreen oak. 6. Game at cards.
MATACÁN, *sm.* 1. Old hare. 2. (Bot.) Dog-bane. Apocynum *L.* 3. Stone with which a dog is killed. 4. Any troublesome or painful work.
MATACANDÉLAS, *sf.* Extinguisher.
MATACANDÍL, *sm.* (Mur.) Lobster.
MATACHÍN, *sm.* 1. Merry-andrew, jack pudding. 2. Dance performed by grotesque figures.
MATACÍA, *sf.* (Ar.) Slaughter, havoc.
MATADÉRO, *sm.* Slaughter-house, a place where cattle are slaughtered; severe labour.
MATADÓR, RA, *s.* 1. Murderer, one who takes away another's life. 2. One of the three chief cards in the game of Ombre.—*a.* Mortal.
MATADÚRA, *sf.* 1. Wound on a horse's back made by the harness. 2. A foolish troublesome person.
MATAFUÉGO, *sm.* Fire-engine. *Matafuegos*, Fireman.
MATAJUDÍO, *sm.* (Ict.) V. *Cabezudo.*
MATALAHÚGA Ó VA, *sf.* (Bot.) Anise. V. *Anis.*
MATALÓBOS, *sm.* (Bot.) Wolf's bane. Aconitum lycoctonum *L.*
MATALÓN Ó MATALÓTE, *sm.* An old horse worn out with age and fatigue.
MATALOTÁGE, *sm.* 1. (Naút.) Stores or provisions on board of ships. 2. Heap of divers things jumbled together.
MATÁNZA, *sf.* 1. The action of slaughtering, cattle to be slaughtered. 2. Slaughter or havoc in the field of battle. 3. Obstinacy, eagerness of pursuit.
MATÁR, *va.* 1. To kill, to put to death, to murder. 2. To put out a light; to extinguish; to slake lime. 3. To worry, to vex, to molest. 4. To make a horse's back sore by the rubbing of the harness. *Á mata caballo*, In the utmost hurry. *Vender á mata candelas*, To sell at public auction by inch of candle.—*vr.* 1. To make the utmost exertions to obtain a thing. 2. To be extremely concerned at a failure or disappointment. *Matarse con otro*, To be at daggers drawn.
MATARRÁTA, *sf.* Game at cards.
MATARÍFE, *sm.* Slaughterman, butcher; one employed in killing cattle in a slaughter-house.
MATASÁNOS, *sm.* Quack, charlatan; empiric.
MATASIÉTE, *sm.* Bully, braggadocio.
MÁTE, *sm.* 1. Check-mate, the last move in the game of chess. *Dar mate*, To scoff, or laugh at any one. 2. Size, glue-water boiled with lime, much used by painters and gilders; gold or silver sizing.—*a.* Unpolished, rough; faded.
MATEÁRSE, *vr.* To grow up into large stalks; applied to wheat and barley.
MATEMÁTICA, *sf.* Mathematics, the science which contemplates whatever is capable of being numbered or measured.
MATEMATICAMÉNTE, *ad.* Mathematically.
MATEMÁTICO, CA, *a.* Mathematical.
MATEMÁTICO, *sm.* Mathematician.
MATÉRIA, *sf.* 1. Matter, substance extended. 2. Materials of which any thing is composed. *Prima ó primera materia*, Raw material. 3. Subject, thing treated; cause, occasion. 4. Question considered, point discussed. 5. Matter, purulent running. 6. Copy at a writing-school.
MATERIÁL, *a.* 1. Material, consisting of matter, not spiritual. 2. Rude, uncouth, ungenteel.—*sm.* Ingredient, materials of which any thing is made.
MATERIALIDÁD, *sf.* 1. Materiality, corporeity; not spirituality. 2. Rudeness, coarseness of manners, incivility.
MATERIALÍSMO, *sm.* Materialism.
MATERIALÍSTA, *s. com.* Materialist.
MATERIALMÉNTE, *ad.* Materially.
MATERNÁL, *a.* Maternal. V. *Materno.*
MATERNALMÉNTE, *ad.* Maternally.
MATERNIDÁD, *sf.* Maternity, the character or relation of a mother.
MATÉRNO, NA, *a.* Maternal, motherly; befitting or pertaining to a mother.
MATIGUÉLO Ó MATINUÉLO, *sm.* Figure of a shabby boy, made of straw, and used as a play-thing at bull-feasts. V. *Dominguillo.*
MATÍZ, *sm.* Shade of colours; mixture of a variety of colours.
MATIZÁR, *va.* 1. To mix different colours in a beautiful manner and proportion. 2. To embellish, to adorn, to beautify.
MÁTO, *sm.* V. *Matorral.*
MATÓN, *sm.* Bully, a noisy, quarrelling fellow
MATORRÁL, *sm.* Field full of brambles and briers.
MATORRÓSO, SA, *a.* Full of brambles
MATRÁCA, *sf.* 1. A wooden rattle. 2. Jest, contemptuous joke; contumelious ridicule. 3 Coxcomb, a silly presumptuous fellow

Matraqueár, va. To jest, to scoff; to ridicule.
Matraquísta, sm. Wag, jester, punster; one who delights in ridiculing others.
Matráz, sf. Matrass, vessel used by apothecaries.
Matréro, ra, a. Cunning, sagacious, knowing. —sm. Artful knave; cunning knavish soldier.
Matricária, sf. (Bot.) Feverfew. Matricaria parthenium L.
Matricída, s. com. Murderer of one's mother.
Matricídio, sm. Matricide.
Matrícula, sf. Register, list.
Matriculádor, sm. He who matriculates.
Matriculár, va. To matriculate, to register, to enrol, to enter in a list.
Matrimoniál, a. Matrimonial.
Matrimonialménte, ad. Matrimonially.
Matrimónio, sm. 1. Marriage, matrimony. 2. (Joc.) Husband or wife. *Matrimonio rato*, Legal marriage not consummated.
Matriténse, a. Native of Madrid.
Matríz, sf. 1. Mother church, metropolitan church. 2. Matrix, womb; the place of the fœtus in the mother. 3. Mould, form. 4. The original draft of any writing. 5. The channelled and concave or female part of a screw. *Lengua matriz*, Native language.—a. First, principal, chief.
Matróna, sf. 1. Matron, a virtuous and accomplished woman, who is mother of a family. 2. Midwife, a woman who assists women in child-birth. *Matronaza*, Corpulent respectable woman.
Matronál, a. Matronal.
Maturángo, ga, s. Appellation given to a European in Buenos Ayres.
Matúte, sm. Smuggling, act of running or goods run into a country without paying duty.
Matuteár, va. To smuggle, to import goods without paying the duty laid on them.
Matutéro, sm. Smuggler.
Matutinál, a. Belonging to the morning mass.
Matutíno, na, a. Belonging to the morning.
Maúla, sf. 1. Any thing found in the street, or which may be purchased for little money. 2. Cunning, craft; deceitful tricks, imposition. 3. Drink-money given to servants.—s. com. Cheat, bad payer.
Maulería, sf. 1. Frippery; place where old clothes are sold; a piece-broker's shop. 2. Craft, cunning; art or skill applied to deceive.
Mauléro, sm. 1. Piece-broker, seller of old clothes. 2. Impostor, cheat, swindler.
Maulládor, ra, a. Applied to a cat which mews or cries much.
Maullár, vn. To mew, to cry as a cat.
Maullído, Maúllo, sm. Mew, cry of a cat.
Mausoléo y Mauseólo, sm. Mausoleum, a pompous funeral monument.
Maxílla, sf. Cheek. V. *Mexilla*.
Maxilár, a. Maxillary, maxillar.
Máxima, sf. 1. Rule, principle. 2. Idea, thought. 3. Maxim, axiom, aphorism. 4. Musical point.
Maximaménte, ad. Chiefly.
Máxime, ad. Principally.
Máximo, ma, a. sup. Chief, principal; very great.
Maxmordón, sm. 1. A rude unmannerly fellow, a dolt. 2. A sharp cunning fellow.
Máya, sf. 1. (Bot.) Common daisy. Bellis perennis L. 2. May-queen, a little girl dressed and adorned with flowers, and placed in the street to collect money.
Mayadór, ra, s. Mewer.
Mayál, sm. 1. Flail, an instrument with which corn is thrashed. 2. Lever in oil-mills.
Mayár, va. To mew. V. *Maullar*.
Mayéto, sm. Mallet for beating paper in mills.
Maymóna, sf. Beam of a horse-mill in which the spindle runs.
Maymonétes, sm. pl. (Naút.) Pegs or pins, placed on deck near the main and foremost, to which rope-ends are fastened.
Mávo, sm. 1. May, the fifth month of the year. 2. May-pole, a long straight pole erected on the first of May in some public place.
Mayór, a. Greater, larger, more extensive. *Hombre mayor*, An elderly man, also a man of great age.—sm. 1. Superior, mayor or chief of a community; commander of a corps; serjeant-major. 2. Person who is of age. 3. Larger sort of beasts of burthen, such as mules and horses. 4. A square stone, used in building. 5. Major, a field officer of horse or foot, next in rank to the lieutenant-colonel. 6. (Naút.) Mainsail. *Por mayor*, By wholesale, by the bulk or lump; summarily.—sf. (Lóg.) First proposition in a syllogism.—pl. 1. Ancestors, forefathers. 2. Superiors. 3. (Naút.) Three principal sails of a ship.
Mayóra, sf. Mayoress.
Mayorál, sm. 1. Chief or principal person of a corps or society. 2. Head shepherd; leader.
Mayorána, sf. V. *Mejorana*.
Mayorázga, sf. She who enjoys the right of primogeniture.
Mayorázgo, sm. 1. Right of succession in family estates, vested in the first-born son. 2. First-born son possessing the right of primogeniture. 3. Family estate which devolves to the first-born son by right of inheritance.
Mayorazguísta, sm. Author who treats on the succession in family estates.
Mayordóma, sf. Steward's wife.
Mayordomeár, va. To administer or manage an estate.
Mayordomía, sf. Administration, stewardship.
Mayordómo, sm. Major domo, steward, the principal servant of a nobleman or gentleman, to whom the others are subordinate; superintendent. *Mayordomo de propios*, City steward.
Mayoría, sf. 1. Advantage, excellence, superiority. 2. Major's commission. *Mayoría de plaza*, A town-major's place. 3. Majority, full age; end of minority.
Mayoridád, sf. Superiority.
Mayorísta, sm. Student of the highest classes in grammar-schools.
Mayorménte, ad. Principally, chiefly.
Mays, ad. (Ant.) V. *Mas*.
Maytinánte, sm. One who attends matins.
Maytinário, sm. Book containing the matins.
Maytínes, sm. pl. Matins, the morning worship in the Roman catholic church.
Mayúscula, a. Capital; applied to large letters.
Máza, sf. 1. Club, a stick shod with iron. 2. Mace, an ensign of authority borne before kings and magistrates. 3. Engine, or pile engine. 4. Clog, a piece of wood fastened to

the waist of a monkey, to prevent him from running away. 5. Rag pinned to men or women's clothes, to make a laughing-stock of them. 6. Beetle for flax or hemp. *Mázas*, Pestles in powder-mills, with which the ingredients of gunpowder are pounded. *Maza de fraya*, Hammer. *Maza sorda*, V. *Espadaña*. *La maza y la mona*, (Fám.) Applied to two persons who constantly walk together.

Mazacóte, *sm*. 1. Kali, barilla. 2. Mortar, cement. 3. Dry tough mass. 4. Injurious nickname for a peevish person.

Mazáda, *sf*. Blow with a mallet; offensive expression.

Mazagátos, *sm*. Noise, dispute, contention.

Mazamórra, *sf*. 1. Bread-dust; biscuit or any other thing spoiled and broken in pieces. 2. Any thing broken and reduced to small bits. 3. Sort of pap made of the flour of Indian corn, honey, and sugar, much used in Peru.

Mazanéta, *sf*. Apple-shaped ornament in jewels.

Mazapán, *sm*. Marchpane, a kind of sweet paste, made up of almonds, sugar, and other ingredients.

Mazár, *va*. To churn milk.

Mazarí, *sf*. Brick. V. *Ladrillo*.

Mazmórra, *sf*. Moorish dungeon.

Maznár, *va*. To squeeze and handle any thing gently to soften or disjoin it.

Mázo, *sm*. 1. Mallet, a large hammer made of wood. 2. Bundle, a quantity of ribands or other things tied together. *Mazo de llaves*, Bunch of keys. 3. Clown, clumsy fellow.

Mazonería, *sf*. Masonry, brick-work; relief.

Mazórca, *sf*. 1. Spindle full of thread, spun from the distaff into the shape of a cone. 2. Ear of corn.

Mazorrál, *a*. Rude, uncouth, clownish.

Mazorralménte, *ad*. Rudely.

Mazóte, *sm*. 1. A kind of cement or mortar. 2. Blockhead, a dull heavy fellow.

Me, *pro*. Me, the oblique case of the pronoun *yo*, which serves as a dative or accusative, and is placed either before or after a verb.

Méa, *sf*. Term used by children to express their want of making water.

Meáda, *sf*. Quantity or mark of urine made at once.

Meadéro, *sm*. Place to which people generally repair to make water.

Meádos, *sm. pl.* V. *Orines*.

Meája, *sf*. 1. A small coin, formerly current in Castile. 2. Duty required by judges on executions. 3. The small embryo in the white of an egg, called the tread.

Meajuéla, *sf*. Small pieces attached to the bits of a bridle.

Meár, *vn*. To urine, to make water. V. *Orinar*.

Meáto, *sm*. Passage, conduit, or pore of the body.

Méauca, *sf*. (Orn.) A sea fowl so called from its cry.

Méca, *sf*. *Casa de meca*, House of noise and confusion.

Mecánica, *sf*. 1. Mechanics. V. *Maquinaria*. 2. A mean despicable action or thing. 3. (Mil.) Management of soldiers' affairs.

Mecanicaménte, *ad*. Meanly, sordidly.

Mecánico, ca, *a*. 1. Mechanical or mechanic, done by hand. 2. Mean, servile; of mean occupation. *Potencias mecanicas*, Mechanical powers.

Mecánico, *sm*. Mechanic, manufacturer; a low workman, a petty tradesman.

Mecaniquéz, *sf*. Meanness, lowness of occupation or employment.

Mecanísmo, *sm*. Mechanism, action performed according to mechanical laws.

Mecedéro ó Mecedór, ra, *s*. Agitator, mover.

Mecedúra, *sf*. Act of stirring.

Mecér, *va*. 1. To stir, to agitate, to jumble, to mix. 2. To rock, to shake; to move forwards and backwards.

Mecereón, *sm*. (Bot.) Mezereon. Daphne mezereum *L*.

Mécha, *sf*. 1. Wick, twist of cotton, round which wax or tallow is applied, to make candles, tapers, and torches. 2. Roll of lint put into a sore or wound. 3. Match, a rope slightly twisted and used to fire pieces of ordnance. 4. Bacon, with which fowls and meat are larded. *Alargar la mecha*, To augment a salary, to protract a business; to allow a needy debtor sufficient time to discharge his debt.

Mechár, *va*. To lard fowls, game, or meat, with bacon.

Mechéra, *sf*. Larding-pin.

Mechéro, *sm*. Nosle of a lamp, in which the wick is put; socket of candlesticks.

Mechinál, *sm*. Square stones left projecting in a wall to be continued.

Mechoacán, *sm*. (Bot.) Species of scammony, native of New Spain. Convolvulus *L*.

Mechón, *sm*. 1. Large lock of hair; large match. 2. Bundle of threads or fibres separated from the rest.

Mechóso, *sa*. Full of matches or wicks.

Mecónio, *sm*. 1. Meconium of children. 2. Poppy juice.

Méda, *sf*. (Gal.) V. *Hacina*.

Medálla, *sf*. 1. Medal, a piece of metal stamped in honour of some remarkable event or performance. 2. Gold coin weighing an ounce.

Medallón, *sm. aum.* Medallion.

Médano y Médaño, *sm*. Sand-bank on the sea-shore.

Medár, *va*. (Gal.) V. *Hacinar*.

Medéro, *sm*. (Gal.) Collection of vine-shoots.

Média, *sf*. 1. Stocking, a covering for the leg. 2. Measure of capacity, which makes about half a hundred weight. 3. Liquid measure making two pints.

Mediación, *sf*. 1. The nearest distance of one thing from another, a third being placed in the middle. 2. Mediation, intervention.

Mediadór, ra, *s*. Mediator, intercessor.

Mediána, *sf*. 1. Flesh of the shoulder near the neck of animals. 2. Household bread. 3. Top of a fishing-rod. 4. V. *Barzon*.

Medianaménte, *ad*. Middlingly.

Medianería, *sf*. 1. Bounds or limits of contiguous things. 2. Moiety of land or rent equally divided and enjoyed by halves. 3 Partition-wall.

Medianéro, ra, *a*. 1. Mediating, interceding. 2. Intermediate; having the moiety. *Pared medianera*, Partition-wall.

Mediaña y Medianidád, *sf.* Moderation in the execution of a thing.
Medianíl, *sm.* (Agr.) Middle-piece of ground.
Medianísta, *sm.* Student of the fourth class in grammar.
Mediáno, na, *a.* Moderate, middling; neither great nor small.
Mediánte, *ad.* By means of, by virtue of.
Mediár, *vn.* 1. To come to the middle of a thing, to be at the middle 2. To intercede for another.
Mediataménte, *ad.* Mediately.
Mediáto, ta, *a.* Mediate.
Medicáble, *a* Curable, that may be cured by means of medicines.
Medicaménto, *sm.* Medicament, any thing used in healing; generally an external application.
Medicár, *va.* To administer medicines; to apply medicaments.
Medicástro, *sm.* Quack, an empirical practitioner in physic.
Medícea, *a.* Satellite.
Medicína, *sf.* 1. Physic, the art of healing. 2. Medicine, any remedy administered by a physician.
Medicinál, *a.* Medicinal, belonging to physic, having the power of healing.
Medicinár, *va.* To administer medicines, to apply medicaments.
Medición, *sf.* Measurement, mensuration.
Médico, *sm.* Physician, one who professes the art of healing.—**Médico, ca**, *a.* Medical.
Medída, *sf.* 1. Measure, any instrument for finding out the length, breadth, or quantity of a thing. 2. Mensuration, the act of measuring. 3. Height, length, breadth, or quantity measured. 4. Proportion, relation, correspondence. 5. Moderation, prudence. *A' medida de sus deseos*, According to one's wishes. 6. Girdle on the statues of saints bearing their names.
Medidaménte, *ad.* Moderately.
Medidór, *sm.* Measurer.
Mediéro, *sm.* 1. Hosier, one who deals in stockings. 2. Copartner, one who goes halves with another in the cultivation of lands or rearing of cattle.
Médio, dia, *a.* Half, in part. *Medio dia*, Noon, the middle hour of the day. *Medio borracho*, Half-seas over. *Media Naranja*, V. *Cúpula*. *A' medio-nao*, (Naút.) Midships.
Médio, *sm.* 1. Middle, the part equally distant from the extremities. 2. Way, means, method, medium, moderation. 3. Work half done and not finished. 4. Twin, one of two children born at a birth. 5. *Medios*, Rents, income, revenue, fortune. *En medio*, In the middle, midway; nevertheless, notwithstanding, however. 6. Logical reason.
Medíocre, *a.* Middling.
Mediocridád, *sf.* Mediocrity, small degree, middle rate, middle state.
Mediodía, *sf.* Noon, mid-day; south.
Mediopáño, *sm.* Thin woollen cloth.
Mediopartír, *va.* To divide in the middle.
Medír, *va.* 1. To measure, to ascertain the length, magnitude, or quantity of a thing. 2. To extend the body or to fall flat on the ground. 3. To compare, to estimate the relative badness or goodness of things.—*vr.* To be moderate, to act with prudence.
Meditación, *sf.* Meditation, deep thought, close attention, contemplation.
Meditár, *va.* To meditate, to revolve in the mind, to contemplate.
Mediterráneo, nea, *a.* Mediterranean, encircled with land.
Médra, *sf.* Proficiency, progress.
Medrár, *vn.* To thrive, to prosper, to improve.
Medrosaménte, *ad.* Timorously.
Medrosía, *sf.* Timorousness.
Medróso, sa, *a.* 1. Fearful, timorous. 2. Terrible, inspiring fear.
Medúla, *sf.* Marrow, an oleaginous substance contained in bones; principal substance.
Medulár, *a.* Medullar, medullary.
Meduló*s*o, sa, *a.* Full of marrow.
Mefítico, *a.* Mephitic; applied to noxious air.
Megído, da, *a.* Beaten up with sugar and water; applied to the yolk of eggs.
Még*o*, ga, *a.* Gentle, mild, meek, peaceful.
Mejór, *a.* Better.—*ad.* Better, more exactly.
Mejóra, *sf.* 1. Improvement, melioration. 2. Appeal to a superior court.
Mejoramiénto, *sm.* Improvement, melioration.
Mejorána, *sf.* (Bot.) Sweet marjoram. Origanum majorana *L.*
Mejorár, *va.* To improve, to meliorate.—*vn.* To recover, to grow well from a disease or calamity.—*vr.* To improve, to grow better.
Mejoría, *sf.* 1. Improvement, melioration, mending. 2. Repairs. 3. The state of growing better in point of health.
Meláda, *sf.* 1. A slice of toasted bread steeped in honey. 2. A slice of dry marmalade.
Meládo, da, *a.* Of the colour of honey; generally applied to horses.
Meladúcha, *sf.* Any coarse mealy apple.
Melancolía, *sf.* Melancholy, a kind of gloomy madness, in which the mind is constantly fixed on one sad and painful object.
Melancólico, ca, *a.* Melancholy, sad.
Melancolizár, *va.* To affect with melancholy, to render gloomy and dejected.
Melánia, *sf.* A kind of silk stuff.
Melantería, *sf.* Kind of black mineral containing vitriol.
Melápia, *sf.* Kind of apple.
Melár, *vn.* 1. (In Sugar-works) To boil down the juice of the sugar-cane a second time, until it obtains the consistency of honey. 2. To deposit honey as bees.
Meláza, *sf.* (Mur.) Dregs of honey.
Melcócha, *sf.* Cake made of honey, flour, and spice; ginger-bread.
Melcochéro, *sm.* Ginger-bread baker.
Melecína, *sf.* V. *Clister*.
Meléna, *sf.* 1. Dishevelled hair hanging loose over the eyes. 2. Fore-top hair or mane that falls on a horse's face. 3. A soft fleecy skin put on the forehead of working oxen to prevent their being hurt by the yoke. *Traer á la melena*, To compel one to execute a thing against his will.
Melenúdo, da, *a.* Hairy, having bushy hair.
Meléra, *sf.* State of melons spoiled by rain.
Meléro, *sm.* 1. Dealer in honey. 2. Place destined to preserve honey.
Melésa, *sf.* 1. Candle-wood. V. *Tea*. 2. (Bot.) Larch-tree. Pinus larix *L.*

Melgácho, *sm.* (Ict.) Dog-fish. Squalus catulus *L.*
Melífero, **ra**, *a.* Melliferous, productive of honey.
Melificádo, **da**, *a.* Mellifluous.
Melificár, *va.* To make honey as bees.
Melifluaménte, *ad.* Mellifluently.
Melifluidád, *sf.* Mellifluence, suavity, delicacy. [flowing with honey.
Melífluo, **flua**, *a.* Mellifluous, mellifluent;
Melilóto, *sm.* 1. (Bot.) Bird's foot trefoil; melilot. Trifolium officinale *L.* 2. Silly stupid person.
Melíndre, *sf.* 1. A sort of fritters made of honey and flour. 2. Prudery, overmuch nicety in conduct.
Melindreár, *vn.* To act the prude.
Melindréro, **ra**; y **Melindróso**, **sa**, *a.* Prudish, affectedly grave.
Melindríllo, *sm.* Ferret, narrow tape.
Melindrizár, *vn.* (Joc.) To act the prude. V. *Melindrear.*
Mélla, *sf.* 1. Notch in edged tools. 2. Gap, empty space. *Hacer mella*, To make an impression upon the mind by reproach or advice.
Melládo, **da**, *a.* 1. Notched. 2. Toothless, wanting one or more teeth.
Mellár, *va.* 1. To notch, to cut in small hollows. 2. To deprive of lustre and splendour. *Mellar la honra*, To wound one's character and honour.
Mellíza, *sf.* Kind of sausage made of lean pork, almonds, pine-apple kernels, and honey. In Extremadura they are called *mellicas.*
Mellízo, **za**, *a.* V. *Gemelo.*
Mellón, *sm.* A handful of straw.
Melocotón, *sm.* 1. (Bot.) Peach-tree ingrafted in a quince-tree. Amygdalus persica *L.* 2. Fruit of that tree. [vity.
Melodía, *sf.* Melody, harmony of sound; suavity.
Melodióso, **sa**, *a.* Melodious, musical.
Melója, *sf.* Metheglin, honey boiled with water and fermented.
Melón, *sm.* (Bot.) Melon. Cucumis melo *L.* *Catar el melon*, To sound or pump one.
Melonár, *sm.* Field or bed of melons.
Meloncéte, *sm.* A small melon.
Melonéro, *sm.* One who rears melons or deals in them.
Melosidád, *sf.* 1. Sweetness arising from honey. 2. Meekness, gentleness of behaviour.
Melóso, **sa**, *a.* 1. Having the taste or qualities of honey. 2. Gentle, mild, pleasing.
Melóte, *sm.* 1. Conserve made up with honey. 2. Molasses.
Mélsa, *sf.* 1. V. *Baza.* 2. Phlegm, lentor, slowness.
Membrána, *sf.* Membrane, a thin skin.
Membranóso, **sa**, *a.* Membranous.
Membréte, *sm.* 1. Pocket-book, memorandum-book. 2. Card of invitation, address.
Membrílla, *sf.* (Mur.) The tender bud of a quince-tree.
Membrillár, *sm.* Plantation of quince-trees.
Membrilléro y **Membríllo**, *sm.* 1. (Bot.) Quince-tree. Pyrus cydonia *L.* 2. The fruit of the quince-tree.
Membrudaménte, *ad.* Robustly, strongly.
Membrúdo, **da**, *a.* Strong, robust, corpulent.
Meméntos, *sm. pl.* The two parts of the mass, in which the sacrifice is offered for the quick and the dead.
Mémo, **ma**, *a.* Silly, foolish.
Memoráble y **Memorándo**, **da**, *a.* Memorable, worthy of memory.
Memorár, *va.* To remember, to record, to mention.
Memoratísimo, **ma**, *a. sup.* Worthy of eternal memory.
Memória, *sf.* 1. Memory, the power of retaining or recollecting things past; reminiscence, recollection. 2. Fame, glory. 3. Monumental record; anniversary. 4. Bill, account. 5. Codicil. *Hacer memoria*, To remember, to put in mind. *De memoria*, By heart. *Hablar de memoria*, To talk at random.—*pl.* 1. Compliments, expressions of kindness and civility. 2. Memorandum-book. 3. Two or more rings put on the finger as a memorandum.
Memoriál, *sm.* 1. Memorandum-book. 2. Memorial, brief.
Memorión, *sm.* A strong memory.
Memorióso, **sa**, *a.* Mindful, retentive; applied to the memory.
Ména, *sf.* 1. (Naút.) Girt or size of cordage. 2. (Ict.) Small sea-fish, kind of anchovy.
Menadór, **ra**, *s.* Winder, one who turns a wheel to wind silk.
Menáge, *sm.* Furniture, moveables; goods put in a house for use or ornament.
Menár, *va.* To wind, to conglomerate.
Mención, *sf.* Mention, oral or written recital of any thing.
Mencionár, *va.* To mention, to write or express in words or writing.
Mendicación, *sf.* The act of begging or asking charity.
Mendicánte, *a.* Mendicant, begging. *Mendicantes*, Religious order of mendicants.
Mendicidád, *sf.* Mendicity.
Mendigánte, **ta**, *s.* Mendicant, beggar.
Mendigár, *va.* To ask charity, to live upon alms, to crave, to entreat, to beg.
Mendígo, *sm.* Beggar, a person who asks charity in the streets and lives upon alms.
Mendiguéz, *sf.* Beggary, indigence.
Mendosaménte, *ad.* Falsely, erroneously, equivocally.
Mendóso, **sa**, *a.* False, fictitious, erroneous.
Mendrúgo, *sm.* Broken bread given to beggars.
Mendruguíllo, *sm.* A small bit or crumb of bread.
Meneadór, **ra**, *s.* Mover, manager, director.
Meneár, *va.* 1. To move from place to place. 2. To manage, to direct.—*vr.* 1. To be brisk and active, to stir about. 2. To wriggle, to waddle; to move from side to side. *Menear las manos*, To fight; to work expertly.
Menéo, *sm.* A wriggling or waddling motion of the body; trade, business.
Menestér, *sm.* 1. Necessity, need, want. *Ser menester*, To be necessary. 2. Employment, office; place under government. *Menesteres*, Corporal necessaries, necessary implements.
Menesteróso, **sa**, *a.* Needy, necessitous; wanting something.
Menéstra, *sf.* Pottage made of different pulse and roots.

Menestrál, sm. Mechanic, tradesman.
Mengáje, sm. Rag, tatter.
Méngua, sf. 1. Decay, decline. 2. Poverty, indigence. 3. Disgrace arising from a cowardly conduct.
Menguadaménte, ad. Ignominiously.
Menguádo, sm. 1. Coward; a silly, mean-spirited fellow. 2. An avaricious miserable wretch. 3. Decrease, narrowing of stockings, &c.
Menguádo, da, a. 1. Diminished, impaired. 2. Coward, pusillanimous; foolish. *Hora menguada*, Fatal moment.
Menguánte, sm. 1. Ebb-tide, low-water. 2. Decline, decay; decrease of the moon.
Menguár, vn. 1. To decay, to decline. 2. To fail, to be deficient. 3. To diminish the size of stockings by taking in two stitches instead of one with the knitting needles.
Meniánta, sf. (Bot.) Marsh-trefoil, buck-bean.
Menína, sf. A young lady who from her childhood entered into the service of the royal family of Spain, by waiting upon the queen.
Menino, sm. 1. Page of the queen and *infantas* of Spain. 2. (Mur.) An affected spruce little fellow.
Menipéa, sf. Kind of satire containing prose and verse.
Meníque ó Meñíque, sm. The little finger, the [small toe.
Menísco, sm. Meniscus, glass, concave on one side and convex on the other.
Menjuí, sm. (Bot.) Benzoin. V. *Benjuí*.
Menjúnge ó Menjúrge, sm. Beverage composed of different ingredients, and of an unpleasant taste.
Menológio, sm. The martyrology of the Greeks divided into the months of the year.
Menónia, sf. Black kind of bird.
Menór, sm. 1. A minor. 2. Second or minor proposition. 3. Franciscan friar or nun.—a. 1. Less, smaller. 2. Minor, under age. *Menores*, sf. pl. Being of the third class of a grammar-school; applied to scholars. *Por menor*, By retail, in small parts, minutely.
Menoréte, a. dim. of *Menor*. *Al menorete, ó por el menorete*, At least.
Menoría, sf. Inferiority, subordination.
Menorísta, sm. Student of grammar in the third class.
Ménos, ad. 1. Less, in a smaller or lower degree. *Menos valer*, Less worthy. 2. Except, with exception of. *A' lo menos, ó por lo menos*, At least. *Mucho menos*, Much less. *Poco mas ó menos*, A little more or less. *Venir á menos*, To decay, to grow worse.
Menoscabadór, ra, s. Detracter, lessener.
Menoscabár, va. 1. To impair, to lessen, to make worse. 2. To reduce, to deteriorate.
Menoscábo, sm. Diminution, deterioration.
Menospreciadaménte, ad. Contemptuously.
Menospreciadór, ra, s. Contemner, despiser.
Menospreciár, va. To underrate, to undervalue; to despise, to contemn.
Menospréçio, sm. Contempt, scorn; the act of undervaluing or underrating a thing.
Menotísa, sf. V. *Minutisa*.
Menságe, y Mensagería, s. Message, errand.
Mensagéro, ra, s. 1. Messenger, one who carries or brings a message. 2. (Naút.) Bull's eye traveller, a wooden thimble.

Menstruación, sf. Catamenia, menstruation.
Menstruál, a. Menstrual.
Menstrualménte, ad. Monthly, menstrually.
Menstruánte, a. Menstruating.
Menstruár, vn. To menstruate.
Ménstruo, a, a. Menstruous, monthly.
Menstruósa, a. Female menstruating.
Ménstruo, sm. Menstruum, any liquor used as a dissolvent, or to extract the virtues of ingredients by infusion or decoction.
Mensuál, a. Monthly.
Mensualménte, ad. Monthly.
Ménsula, sf. (Arq.) Member which projects over any thing and serves to support others.
Mensúra, sf. Measure.
Mensurabilidád, sf. Mensurability.
Mensuráb le, a. Mensurable, that may be measured.
Mensuradór, ra, s. Measurer, meter.
Mensurár, va. V. *Medir y Juzgar*.
Ménta, sf. (Bot.) Mint. Mentha officinalis *L.*
Mentádo, da, a. Famous, celebrated, renowned.
Mentál, a. Mental, intellectual.
Mentalménte, ad. Mentally, intellectually.
Mentár, va. To mention, to record.
Ménte, sf. 1. Mind, understanding; intellectual power. 2. Sense, meaning; will, disposition.
Mentecatería, sf. Folly, absurdity, nonsense.
Mentecáto, ta, a. Silly, foolish, stupid.
Mentidéro, sm. Talking corner, where idlers meet to converse on trifling and futile subjects.
Mentír, va. 1. To lie, to utter falsehoods. 2. To disappoint, to frustrate, to deceive, to feign. 3. To gainsay, to retract; to equivocate, to falsify.
Mentíra, sf. 1. Lie, falsehood; mentition. 2. Error, mistake in writing.
Mentirilla, ca, ta, sf. Falsehood told by way of a jest. *De mentirillas*, Jesting lies.
Mentirón, sm. aum. Great lie.
Mentirosaménte, ad. Falsely, deceitfully.
Mentirosíto, ta, a. dim. A little false, deceitful.
Mentiróso, sa, a. 1. Lying, telling falsehoods; deceptious. 2. Erroneous, equivocal, incorrect.
Méntis, You lie, or thou liest.
Menucéles, sm. pl. V. *Minucias*.
Menudaménte, ad. Minutely, particularly.
Menudeár, va. To repeat, to detail minutely. —vn. To relate or describe little things.
Menudéncia, sf. Trifle, littleness, minuteness, exility, minute accuracy. *Menudencias*, Small matters; offal of young pigs.
Menudéo, sm. Act of repeating minutely.
Menudéro, ra, s. Dealer in tripes, giblets, sausages, &c.
Menudillo, sm. Extremities of animals. *Menudillos*, Giblets of fowls.
Menudíto, ta; co, ca, a. Somewhat small.
Menúdo, da, a. 1. Small, slender of body: minute. 2. Of no moment or value, worthless. 3. Common, vulgar. 4. Examining minutely into things. 5. Small money, change. *Hombre menudo*, A mean miserable fellow. *A' menudo*, Repeatedly, frequently, continually. *Por menudo*, Minutely; by retail.
Menúdo, sm. 1. Intestines, viscera. 2. Tithe of fruits. *Menudos*, Copper coin.

Meñique, *a.* Very small.—*sm.* Little finger.
Meollada, *sf.* (And.) Fry of brain.
Meollar, *sm.* (Naút.) Thin line or spun-yarn made of oakum or untwisted ropes.
Meóllo, *sm.* 1. Marrow. V. *Medula.* 2. Judgment, understanding. 3. Soft part of bread, crumb.
Meón, na, *a.* Continually making water.
Meóna, *sf.* Newborn female infant in distinction from the male.
Mequetréfe, *sm.* Insignificant noisy fellow.
Meraménte, *ad.* Merely, solely.
Merár, *va.* To mix one liquor with another.
Mérca, *sf.* V. *Compra.*
Mercachífle, *sm.* Pedler, hawker.
Mercadánte, *sm.* V. *Mercader.*
Mercadeár, *vn.* To trade, to traffic; to buy and sell.
Mercadér, *sm.* Dealer, trader, shopkeeper.
Mercadéra, *sf.* Shopkeeper's wife, tradeswoman.
Mercadería, *sf.* 1. Commodity, merchandise. 2. Trade, the business of a trader or dealer.
Mercádo, *sm.* 1. Market, the concourse of people to sell and buy. 2. Market-place where goods are sold. 3. Fair, an annual or stated meeting of buyers and sellers.
Mercaduría, *sf.* Merchandise, trade.
Mercál, *sm.* Ancient Spanish coin.
Mercancía, *sf.* 1. Trade, traffic. 2. Merchandise, saleable goods.
Mercánte, *sm.* y *a.* Dealer, trader; mercantile, commercial.
Mercantíl, *a.* Commercial, mercantile.
Mercantilménte, *ad.* Merchantly, in a commercial or mercantile manner.
Mercár, *va.* V. *Comprar.*
Mercéd, *sf.* 1. Wages, pay given for service, especially to day-labourers. 2. Gift, favour. 3. Will, pleasure. 4. Appellation of civility and respect, with which persons are addressed who cannot claim the title of *señoria. Vuestra ó vuesa merced ó usted,* Your honour, your will, sir. 5. A royal military order, whose chief object is to redeem captives. *Estar á merced,* To live at another's expense. *Muchas mercedes,* Many thanks for the favours received.
Mercenário, *sm.* 1. Day-labourer, one who works for daily wages. 2. Friar or nun of the religious order *De la Merced.*
Mercenário, ria, *a.* Mercenary, hired.
Mercería, *sf.* Trade of a haberdasher, who deals in small wares.
Mercéro, *sm.* Mercer, haberdasher.
Merchánte, *sm.* Merchant, who buys and sells goods without keeping an open shop.—*a.* Merchant, applied to a trading-vessel.
Merculíno, na, *a.* Belonging to Wednesday.
Mercuriál, *sm.* y *a.* 1. (Bot.) All good, mercury. 2. Mercurial.
Mercuríno, na, *a.* Relating to Wednesday.
Mercúrio, *sm.* 1. Mercury, quicksilver. 2. Planet Mercury. 3. Newspaper, periodical publication.
Merdellón, na, *a.* Slovenly, unclean, dirty.
Merdóso, sa. *a.* Nasty, filthy.
Mére, *ad.* Merely. V. *Meramente.*
Merecedór, ra, *s.* One who deserves reward or punishment.
Merecér, *va.* 1. To deserve, to merit. V. *Lograr.* 2. To owe, to be indebted for. *He merecido á mi fratello aquella honra,* I am indebted to my brother for that honour.—*vn.* To do any thing deserving reward or censure.
Merecidaménte, *ad.* Worthily.
Merecído, da, *a.* Meritorious.
Merecído, *sm.* Condign punishment.
Merecimiénto, *sm.* V. *Mérito.*
Merendár, *vn.* 1. To take a collation between dinner and supper. 2. (Mur.) To eat the principal meal at noon.—*va.* 1. To pry into another's writings or actions. 2. To anticipate, to take something sooner than another so as to prevent him.
Merendéro, ra, *a.* Picking up the seeds in corn-fields; applied to crows.
Merendóna, *sf.* A plentiful or splendid collation.
Meréngue, *sm.* Sweetmeat made of sugar and whites of eggs.
Meretrício, cia, *a.* Meretricious.
Meretrício, *sm.* Carnal sin.
Meretríz, *sf.* V. *Ramera.*
Meréy, *sf.* (Bot.) Cashew-tree. Anacardium occidentale *L.*
Mergánsar, *sm.* (Orn.) Goosander. Mergus merganser *L.*
Mérgo, *sm.* (Orn.) Diver. Margus *L.*
Meridiána, *sf.* Meridional line. *A' la meridiana,* At mid-day, noon.
Meridiáno, *sm.* Meridian, a large circle of the celestial sphere, passing through the poles, zenith, and nadir, and crossing the equator at right angles. *Meridianos,* Gladiators who fought naked.—*a.* Meridional.
Meridionál, *a.* Southern.
Meriénda, *sf.* 1. (Mur.) Principal meal eaten at noon. 2. Nunchion, a piece of victuals eaten between meals; collation. 3. (Joc.) Humpback. *Merienda de negros,* Confusion made in order to gain some advantage.
Meridád, *sf.* District of the jurisdiction of a *merino,* or judge of the sheep-walks.
Meríno, *sm.* 1. Royal judge and superintendent or inspector of sheep-walks. 2. Shepherd of merino sheep.
Meríno, na, *a.* 1. Moving from pasture to pasture; applied to sheep. 2. Applied to thick curled hair.
Meritaménte, *ad.* V. *Merecidamente.*
Meritár, *va.* To merit, to deserve.
Mérito, *sm.* Merit, desert.
Meritoriaménte, *ad.* Meritoriously.
Meritório, ria, *a.* Meritorious, worthy of reward.
Mérla, *sf.* (Orn.) Black-bird. Turdus merula *L.*
Merlí, *sm.* Crape, a sort of stuff resembling gauze.
Merlín, *sm.* 1. (Naút.) Marline, a small loosely twisted hempen line. 2. Magician. V. *Magico.*
Mérlo, *sm.* (Ict.) A sea fish very frequent in the Mediterranean. Labrus merula *L.*
Merlón, *sm.* (Fort.) The part of the parapet of a battery which lies between two embrasures
Merlúza, (Ict.) Cod, hake. Gadus merluccius *L.*
Mérma, *sf.* Waste, leakage, soakage.
Mermár, *vn.* To waste, to diminish, to dwindle.
Mermeláda, *sf.* Marmalade, a conserve made of quinces or oranges and sugar. *Bruta* *mermi*-

lada, A fine hodge podge; in contempt.
Méro, *sm.* (Ict.) Pollack. Gadus pollachius *L.*
Méro, ra, *a.* Mere, pure, simple.
Meróde, *sm.* V. *Pillage.*
Merodeadór, *sm.* Marauder, pillager.
Merodeár, *vn.* To pillage, to go marauding.
Merodísta, *sm.* (Mil.) Pillager, marauder.
Més, *sm.* 1. Month, one of the twelve calendar divisions of the year. 2. Catamenia, courses. 3. Monthly wages. *Meses mayores*, Last months of pregnancy; months immediately preceding the harvest. *Al mes*, In a month's time, by the month.
Mésa, *sf.* 1. Table, a horizontal surface raised above the ground for meals and other purposes. 2. Meat or viands put on the table. 3. Landing-place, the upper part of a stair-case. 4. Any flat or level surface. 5. Spanish truck-table, or the hire of it. 6. Mess, business, situation. 7. Communion table of the altar. *Mesa de cambios*, Bank. *Mesa franca*, Open table. *Sentarse á mesa puesta*, To live at other people's expense. *Mesas de guarnicion*, (Naút.) Channels or chain-wales; strong timbers projecting horizontally from the ship's side, to which the shrouds are fastened. *Mesas de guarnicion del palo mayor*, Main chain-wales. *Mesas de guarnicion del trinquete*, Fore chain-wales. *Mesa de milanos*, Scanty table.
Mesáda, *sf.* Monthly pay or wages.
Mesána, *sf.* (Naút.) Mizen-mast or sail.
Mesár, *va.* To pluck off the hair with the hands.
Mése, *sf.* V. *Mies.*
Meseguería, *sf.* 1. Guard or watch of fruits. 2. Collection among labourers to pay for the guard of grain or fruits.
Meseguéro, *sm.* Keeper of the fruits of the harvest; guard of the vineyard.
Meseguéro, ra, *a.* Relating to the harvest fruits.
Mesentérico, ca, *a.* Mesenteric.
Mesentério, *sm.* Mesentery.
Meséro, *sm.* Journeyman who works for monthly wages.
Meséta, *sf.* Landing-place of a staircase. *Meseta de guarnicion*, (Naút.) Back-stay stool.
Mesías, *sm.* Messiah, Jesus Christ.
Mesiázgo, *sm.* Dignity of Messiah.
Mesílla, *sm.* 1. Small table; side-board. 2. Screw. 3. Board-wages. 4. Censure by way of a jest.
Mesíllo, *sm.* First menses after parturition.
Mésmo, ma, *pron. pers.* (Ant.) V. *Mismo. Eso mesmo.* V. *Tambien.*
Mesnadéro, *sm.* (Ant.) Commander of a body of armed men.
Mesón, *sm.* Inn, a house of entertainment for travellers.
Mesonáge, *sm.* Street or place which contains numerous inns and public-houses.
Mesonéro, ra, *s.* Inn-keeper, publican.
Mesonéro, ra, *a.* Waiting, serving in an inn.
Mesonísta, *s. com.* Waiter in an inn or public-house.
Mésta, *sf.* 1. Meeting of the principal proprietors of black cattle and sheep, to take into consideration the best means of rearing, feeding, and improving them. 2. Pasture-land. 3. Annual meeting of shepherds and owners of flocks to consider of the best and most economical management of sheep, which bears the title *El honrado concejo de la Mesta*, the honourable board of *Mesta;* because the members of the king's privy council preside in it by rotation, according to seniority, under the title of *President of the Mesta.*
Mestál, *sm.* A piece of barren uncultivated ground.
Mestéño, ña, *a.* 1. Belonging to the *mesta* or graziers. 2. V. *Mostrenco.*
Mestér, *sm.* (Ant.) V. *Menester.*
Mestízo, za, *a.* Of a mongrel breed.
Mésto, *sm.* (Bot.) Large prickly oak. Quercus ægylops *L.*
Mestúra, *sf.* Meslin, mixed corn, as wheat and rye.
Mesturár, *va.* To mix. V. *Mixturar.*
Mesúra, *sf.* 1. A grave deportment, a serious countenance. 2. Civility, politeness. 3. Moderation; measure.
Mesuradaménte, *ad.* Gently, prudently.
Mesuráno, da, *a.* Moderate, circumspect, modest; regular, temperate, regulated.
Mesurár, *va.* To assume a serious countenance, to act with solemn reserve.—*vr.* To behave with modesty and prudence.
Méta, *sf.* Boundary, limit. V. *Limite.*
Metacárpo, *sm.* (Anat.) Metacarpus, palm of the hand.
Metacronísmo, *sm.* Metachronism, anachronism.
Metafísica, *sf.* 1. Science of metaphysics. 2. Excessive subtilty.
Metafisicaménte, *ad.* Metaphysically.
Metafísico, ca, *a.* Metaphysical; difficult to be believed.—*sm.* Metaphysician.
Metáfora, *sf.* Metaphor, a rhetorical figure, not improperly defined to be "a simile comprised in a word."
Metafóricaménte, *ad.* Metaphorically.
Metafórico, ca, *a.* Metaphorical.
Metaforizár, *va.* To use metaphors.
Metál, *sm.* 1. Metal. 2. Brass, latten. 3. Compass or strength of the voice. 4. Quality, nature, or condition of a thing.
Metalário, Metálico, y Metalísta, *sm.* Workman or dealer in metal.
Metálica, *sf.* V. *Metalurgia.*
Metálico, ca, *a.* Metallic; medallic.
Metalífero, ra, *a.* (Poét.) Metalliferous.
Metalografía, *sf.* Metallography, a description of metals.
Metalurgía, *sf.* Metallurgy.
Metalúrgico, *sm.* Metallurgist.
Metálla, *sf.* Small pieces of gold leaf used to cover parts imperfectly gilt.
Metamorfósis ó Metamorfóseos, *sf.* Metamorphosis, transformation.
Metánea, *sf.* Correction, reproof.
Metedór, ra, *s.* 1. Smuggler, one who runs goods into a country without paying any duty. 2. He who puts one thing into another. 3. Clout, a linen cloth put under the swaddling clothes of new-born children.
Metedurís, *sf.* Smuggling, the act of importing goods without paying the duty or customs.
Metemuértos, *sm.* 1. Attendant in a play-house. 2. Busy-body, a vain meddling person.
Metempsícosis, *sf.* Metempsychosis.

Meteórico, ca, *a.* Meteoric.
Meteorísta, *sm.* Meteorologist.
Metéoro, *sm.* Meteor, a luminous body of a transitory nature, which appears in the skies.
Meteorología, *sf.* Meteorology.
Meteorológico, ca, *a.* Meteorological.
Metér, *va.* 1. To put in, to include. 2. To run goods into the country without paying the customs. 3. To make, to occasion. 4. To engage, to prevail upon. 5. To stake, to put to hazard. 6. To cram down victuals. 7. To induce, to deceive. 8. To compress, to straiten, to reduce. 9. To eat. V. *Comer*. *Meter en calor*, To excite, to incite. *Meter zizaña*, To sow discord, to breed disturbances. *Meter el cuezo*, To introduce one's self to any thing with little ceremony. *Meter paz*, To accommodate matters between contending parties.—*vr.* 1. To intermeddle, to interfere. 2. To be on terms of familiarity with a person. 3. To choose a profession or trade. 4. To be led astray, to plunge into vice. 5. To empty into the sea; applied to rivers. 6. To attack or assail with sword in hand. *Meterse con alguno*, To pick a quarrel. *Meterse en si mismo*, To revolve in the mind; to follow one's own opinion. *Meterse soldado*, To become a soldier. *Meterse á sabio*, To affect learning and knowledge.
Meticulóso, sa, *a.* V. *Medroso*.
Metído, *sm.* Strong ley used by washer-women.
Metimiénto, *sm.* Introduction, insertion.
Metódicamente, *ad.* Methodically.
Metódico, ca, *a.* Methodical, arranged or proceeding in due and just order.
Método, *sm.* Method, manner, mode, custom.
Metonímia, *sf.* Metonymy, a rhetorical figure by which one word is used for another, or the cause for the effect.
Metoposcópia, *sf.* Art of discovering men's character by the features of the face.
Metrálla, *sf.* Grape-shot, case-shot.
Metrésa, *sf.* Mistress of a house; a woman courted.
Metréta, *sf.* Greek and Roman measure.
Métrica, *sf.* Metrical art, poesy.
Metricadór, *sm.* Versifier, a maker of verses.
Metricaménte, *ad.* Metrically.
Metricár, *va.* To versify, to make verses.
Métrico, ca, *a.* Metrical, composed in verse.
Metrísta, *s. com.* Versifier. V. *Versificador*.
Métro, *sm.* Metre, verse, a certain number and harmonic disposition of syllables.
Metromanía, *sf.* Metromania, rhyming-madness.
Metrópoli, *sf.* 1. Metropolis, the chief or principal city of a country. 2. Archiepiscopal church.
Metropolitáno, *sm.* Metropolitan, archbishop.
Metropolitáno, na, *a.* Metropolitan.
Mexicána, *sf.* (Bot.) V. *Maravilla*.
Mexicáno, *sm.* Mexican language.
Mexílla, *sf.* Cheek, the side of the face below the eye.
Mexillón y Mixillón, *sm.* Kind of cockle.
Méya, *sf.* Kind of large crab.
Meyór, *a.* (Ant.) V. *Mejor*.
Meytád, *sf.* V. *Mitad*.
Mézcla, *sf.* 1. Mixture, composition. 2. Mortar. 3. Mixed cloth.

Mezcladaménte, *ad.* In a mixed or promiscuous manner.
Mezcladíllos, *sm. pl.* A kind of paste made by confectioners.
Mezcladór, ra, *s.* 1. One who mixes or mingles. 2. Tattler, one who spreads false reports.
Mezcladúra y Mezclamiénto. V. *Mezcla*.
Mezclár, *va.* 1. To mix, to mingle, to unite. 2. To spread false reports, to sow discord, to excite disturbances.—*vr.* 1. To marry a person of inferior rank. 2. To introduce one's self into any thing.
Mezclílla, *sf.* Mixed cloth.
Mezcolánza, *sf.* Bad mixture of colours.
Mezquinaménte, *ad.* Miserably, avariciously.
Mezquindád, *sf.* 1. Penury, poverty, indigence. 2. Avarice, covetousness.
Mezquíno, na, *a.* 1. Poor, indigent, penurious, diminutive. 2. Avaricious, covetous; sordidly parsimonious; mean. 3. Petty, minute.
Mezquíta, *sf.* Mosque, a Mohammedan temple or place of worship.
Mí, *pro.* The oblique case of the pronoun *yo*, which serves for the genitive, dative, accusative, and ablative, as follows—*de mi*, of me; *para mi*, for me; *contra mi*, against me; *por mi*, by me.
Mí, *pro. pos.* My; placed before substantives, as *mio* is placed after them; thus *Mi amor*, *ó amor mio*, My love. V. *Mio*.
Miagár, *vn.* (Burgos.) V. *Maullar*.
Miája, *sf.* 1. Crumb. 2. Small copper coin.
Miár, *vn.* To mew, as a cat.
Miáu, *sm.* Mew or voice of a cat.
Mícho y Mícha, *s.* Puss, fondling name of a cat.
Micér, *sm.* Ancient title of respect.
Míco, *sm.* Monkey, an ape with a long tail.
Microcósmos, *sm.* Microcosm, the little world; man is so called.
Micrófono, *sm.* Instrument to augment sound.
Micrografía, *sf.* Micrography, description of microscopic objects.
Micrómetro, *sm.* Micrometer.
Microscópio, *sm.* Microscope, an optic instrument, contrived to give to the eye a larger appearance of objects which could not otherwise be seen.
Mída, *sf.* Worm that breeds in vegetables.
Miédo, *sm.* Fear, dread, apprehension. *Morirse de miedo*, To die for fear. *No haya miedo*, There is nothing to be apprehended.
Miél, *sm.* 1. Honey, a viscous substance of a whitish or yellowish colour, and sweet to the taste. 2. Sweet liquor distilled from the sugar-cane.
Miélga, *sf.* 1. (Bot.) Lucern. Medicago sativa *L.* 2. (Ict.) A kind of dog-fish. Squalus centrina *L.* 3. Rake, an instrument with teeth for dividing the mould or raking hay and straw together. 4. Strip of ground.
Miélgo, *sm.* A four-pronged pitchfork.
Miémbro, *sm.* 1. Member, a limb appendant to the body. 2. One of a community or corporation. 3. Branch, any part of an integral.
Miénta, *sf.* (Bot.) Mint. Mentha *L.*
Miénte, *sf.* Mind, inclination, will. *Mientes*, Thoughts, ideas. *Parar mientes*, To reflect, to consider.
Miéntra y Miéntre, (Ant.) V. *Mientras*.

Miéntras, *ad.* In the mean time, in the mean while; when. *Mientras que*, Whilst, during the time that.

Miéra, *sf.* 1. Juniper oil. 2. Resin.

Miércoles, *sm.* Wednesday, the fourth day of the week. *Miercoles corvillo*, (Fam.) Ash-Wednesday.

Miérda, *sf.* 1. Excrement, fæces, ordure. 2. Dirt, grease.

Mierdacrúz, *sf.* (Bot.) Daphne, a shrub.

Miérla, *sf.* (Orn.) Blackbird. V. *Merla.*

Miés, *sf.* 1. Wheat and other grain which grows in ears, and of which bread is made. 2. Harvest, the time of reaping and housing the grain. 3. (Met.) Multitude converted or ready for conversion.

Míga, *sf.* 1. Crumb or crum, the soft part of bread, not the crust. 2. A small particle or fragment of any thing. 3. Marrow, substance or principal part. *Migas*, Crumbs of bread fried in a pan, with oil, salt, and pepper. *Hacer, ó no buenas migas*, (Fam.) To agree or disagree readily with one.

Migája, *sf.* 1. The smallest particle of bread or any other thing. 2. Nothing, little or nothing. *No tiene migaja de juicio*, He has not a grain of sense. *Migájas*, Offals, leavings; broken victuals.

Migajáda, *sf.* A small particle.

Migajón, *sm.* Crumb or crum, without crust; marrow, core.

Migár, *va.* To crumble, to break into small bits.

Migratório, ria, *a.* Migrating, migratory.

Migueléte, *sm.* V. *Miquelete.*

Miguelíto, *sm.* Boy who goes on a pilgrimage to mount St. Michael.

Miguéro, ra, *a.* Crumby, relating to crumbs fried in a pan. *Lucero Miguero*, The Morning Star, so called by pastors, because on seeing it they prepare their dish of fried crumbs.

Mijediéga, *sf.* (Bot.) Shrubby trefoil. Lotus dorycnium *L.* Dorycnium monspeliense *Will.*

Míjo, *sm.* 1. (Bot.) Millet. Panicum miliaceum *L.* 2. (Bot.) Turkey-millet. Holcus sorghum *L.*

Míl, *sm.* One thousand, or ten hundred. *Sala de mil y quinientas*, The supreme court of appeals in Spain. *Perdió muchos miles pesos*, He lost several thousand dollars. *Mil y quinientas*, (Fam.) Lentils. *Mil en rama*, Milfoil, yarrow. Achillea microphylla *L.*

Milagréro, ra, *s.* Person fond of considering natural events as miracles, and publishing them as such.

Milágro, *sm.* 1. Miracle, wonder; something above human power. 2. Offering of wax or any other substance, hung up in churches in commemoration of a miracle. *Vida y milagros*, (Fam.) Life, character, and behaviour.

Milagrón, *sm.* (Fam.) Dread, astonishment; extreme.

Milagrosaménte, *ad.* Miraculously, marvellously.

Milagróso, sa, *a.* Miraculous, done by miracle; marvellous, admirable.

Miláno, *sm.* 1. (Orn.) Glead, kite. Falco milvus *L.* *Mesa de milanos*, Keen hunger and little to eat. 2. Bur or down of the thistle.

Milenário, ria, *a.* Millenary.—*sm.* Millenium.

Milengrána, *sf.* (Bot.) Rupture-wort. Herniaria glabra *L.*

Miléno, na, *a.* Applied to cloth, the warp of which contains a thousand threads.

Milenrána, *sf.* (Bot.) Common milfoil or yarrow. Achillea millefolium *L.* V. *Mil en rama.*

Milénta, *sf.* (Vulg.) V. *Mil.*

Milésimo, ma, *a.* 1. Thousandth, the ordinal of a thousand. 2. The thousandth part of any thing.

Milésio, ia, *a.* Applied to ridiculous tales for pastime.

Milhójas, *sf.* (Bot.) *Milenrama.*

Miliár, *a.* Miliary; applied to a cutaneous disease.

Milícia, *sf.* 1. Art and science of war. 2. Military men in general. *Milicias*, Militia, the trained bands of the inhabitants of a country.

Miliciáno, na, *a.* Military.

Militánte, *a.* Militant, military; soldier.

Militár, *sm.* Soldier, a military man.—*a.* Military, martial.—*vn.* 1. To serve in the army, to follow the profession of arms. 2. To hold, to stand good, to go against; applied to argument and reasons.

Militarménte, *ad.* In a military style.

Mílite, *sm.* Soldier, military man.

Mílla, *sf.* 1. Mile, a linear measure; 8 stadia or 1000 geometric steps. 2. (Ant.) Quarter of a league.

Millár, *sm.* 1. Number of thousand; an indefinite number. 2. A certain quantity of cocoa, which in some parts is three pounds and a half, and in others more. 3. Character used to denote a thousand, thus Ɑ.

Millaráda, *sf.* Several thousands. *Echar millaradas*, To brag of wealth and riches. *A' millaradas*, Innumerable times.

Millón, *sm.* Million, the number of ten hundred thousand; an indefinite number. *Millones*, Excise or duty levied in Spain on wine, vinegar, oil, meat, soap, and tallow candles, to defray the expenses of the army. *Sala de millones*, Board of excise, (composed of lords of the exchequer, and deputies of the *Cortes* or states,) which regulates and manages the duty or tax called *Millones*.

Milócha, *sf.* V. *Cometa.*

Milór, *sm.* My lord.

Mimár, *va.* To coax, to wheedle, to flatter.

Mimbrál, *sm.* Plantation of osiers.

Mímbre, *sm.* (Bot.) Osier. Salix viminalis *L.*

Mimbreár, *vn.* V. *Cimbrar.*

Mimbréño, ña, *a.* Of the nature of osiers.

Mimbréra y Mimbrerál, *s.* Plantation of osiers.

Mimbróso, sa, *a.* Made of osiers.

Mímico, ca, *a.* Mimic.

Mímo, *sm.* 1. Buffoon, Merry-Andrew. 2. Prudery, delicacy; fondness, endearingness. 3. Ancient mimes, or farcical representations.

Mimología, *sf.* Mimology, art of imitating the voice and actions of others.

Mimóso, sa, *a.* Delicate, prudish, fond.

Mína, *sf.* 1. Conduit, mine; a subterraneous canal or cavity in the ground. 2. Mine, a place which contains metals or minerals. 3. Spring, source of water. 4. Business which produces or yields great profit, and demands but little exertion. 5. A large quantity of money. 6. (Fort.) Mine under a fortress.

Minadór, ra, *s*. Miner, one who works in mines; one who makes military mines; engineer.
Minál, *a*. Belonging to a mine.
Minár, *va*. 1. To dig mines and burrows. 2. To make uncommon exertions to attain some end or collect information.
Minéra, *sf*. Mine which contains metals.
Minerage, *sm*. Labour of mining.
Minerál, *a*. Mineral, consisting of fossil bodies.
Minerál, *sm*. Mineral, a fossil body; matter dug out of the earth.
Mineralogía, *sf*. Mineralogy, that part of natural history which treats of minerals.
Minéro, *sm*. 1. Mineral, a fossil body. 2. Miner, one who digs for metals; one who makes military mines. 3. Source, origin.
Mineón, *sm*. (Joc.) Great want; pusillanimity.
Míngos, *sm. pl*. Small stockings.
Miniár, *va*. To shade a painting.
Miniatúra, *sf*. Miniature, a painting on vellum, ivory, or paper, with points or dots, and fine water-colours.
Miniaturísta, *s. com*. Miniature painter.
Minimísta, *sm*. Student of the second class in grammar.
Mínimo, ma, *a*. Least, smallest.—*s*. Religious of the order of St. Francis de Paula. *Minimos*, Second class in grammar-schools kept by the order of Minims.
Mínio, *sm*. Minium, red-lead; an oxide of lead of a bright reddish colour.
Ministeriál, *a*. Ministerial.
Ministerialménte, *ad*. Ministerially.
Ministério, *sm*. 1. Office, public place, or employment. 2. Manual labour. 3. Ministry, administration; the members or principal officers of the executive government; time in office.
Minístra, *sf*. Ministréss, she who serves.
Ministradór, ra, *s*. One who ministers.
Ministránte, *a*. Serving, ministrating.
Ministrár, *va*. 1. To serve an office or employment, to perform the functions of a public place. 2. To supply, to furnish.
Ministríl, *sm*. 1. Apparitor, tipstaff; a petty officer of justice. 2. Minstrel, one who plays the flute and other musical wind-instruments. *Ministriles*, Musical wind-instruments.
Minístro, *sm*. 1. Minister, agent; officer of the law. 2. Minister employed in the administration of justice. 3. Minister of state. 4. One of the heads of a religious community.
Minoracíon, *sf*. Minoration.
Minorár, *va*. To lessen, to reduce to a smaller compass.
Minoratívo, va, *a*. Lessening, that decreases or lessens.
Minoridád, *sf*. Minority, nonage; the state of being under age.
Minotáuro, *sm*. Minotaur, fabulous monster.
Minúcia, *sf*. 1. Small tithes paid of wool, lambs, &c. 2. Mite, atom; any thing proverbially small; minutia.
Minuéta, *sf*. (Naút.) Shipwright's boat or punt.
Minué y Minuéte, *sm*. Minuet, a kind of grave and stately dance..
Minúscula, *a*. Small; applied to small letters in opposition to capitals or mayúscula.
Minúta, *sf*. 1. Minute, first draught of an agreement in writing; an enumeration of the principal heads of a contract. 2. Paper containing brief notes or memorandums. *Libro de minutas*, Minute-book, memorandum-book.
Minutár, *va*. To take down the principal heads of an agreement; to make the first draught of a contract.
Minutéro, *sm*. Minute-hand of a watch or clock.
Minutía, *sf*. (Bot.) Carnation, a kind of pink. Dianthus pungens *L*.
Minutísa, *sf*. (Bot.) Kind of small Jamaica pepper.
Minúto, *sm*. Minute, the sixtieth part of an hour, one of the sixty parts into which the degrees of a circle is divided.
Miñósa, *sf*. Worm. V. *Lombriz*.
Mío, Mía, *pron. poss*. My, mine. *Es muy mio*, He is much my friend. *Soy mio*, I am my own master.
Mío, *sm*. Puss, the common appellation of a cat.
Miología, *sf*. Myology, part of anatomy which treats of the muscles; a treatise on muscles.
Míope, *sm*. Miope or myope, one near-sighted.
Miopia, *sf*. Myopy, short-sightedness.
Miqueléte, *sm*. 1. Miquelet, mountain soldier belonging to the militia of Catalonia and the Pyrenees. 2. Robber, highwayman.
Míra, *sf*. 1. A mathematical instrument to direct the sight in the levelling of a gun. 2. Care, vigilance. *Estar á la mira*, To be on the look out, to be on the watch. 3. *Miras de proa*, (Naút.) Bow-chases, guns mounted on the ship's head, on each side of the bowsprit. 4. (Astr.) Fixed star in the swan's neck.
Mirabél, *sm*. 1. (Bot.) Cypress-spurge. Euphorbia cyparissias *L*. 2. *Mirabel de jardín*, (Bot.) A kind of goose-foot. Chenopodium scoparia *L*. 3. (Bot.) Kind of white plum.
Mirabolános, *sm. pl*. Myrobalans, a kind of dried fruit of five different kinds, being all the productions of different trees in the East Indies.
Miráda, *sf*. 1. Glance, a transient view. 2. The act of looking steadfastly at an object.
Miradéro, *sm*. Place exposed to view on all sides; watch-tower, an elevated spot which commands an extensive prospect.
Mirádo, da, *a*. Considerate, circumspect, prudent.
Miradór, ra, *s*. 1. Spectator, looker-on. 2. Gallery which commands an extensive view. 3. Balcony.
Miradúra, *sf*. Act of looking.
Miráglo, *sm*. (Ant.) Miracle. V. *Milagro*.
Miramamolín, *sm*. Appellation given to the sovereign of the Moors.
Miramiénto, *sm*. 1. The act of taking any thing into consideration; reflection. 2. Circumspection, prudence.
Mirár, *va*. 1. To behold, to look steadfastly at an object. 2. To respect, to have regard for, to esteem, to appreciate. 3. To aim at, to have in view. 4. To observe, to watch, to spy. 5. To inquire, to collect information; to consider, to reflect.—*vn*. To be placed or situated in front. *Mirarse á los pies*, To examine into one's own failings and imperfections. *Mirar por encima*, To examine slightly. *Mirar sobre el hombro*, To cast a contemptuous look or frown. *Mirarse las uñas*, (Met.) To be idle; to play at cards.

Mı́ra, *interj.* Look! behold! take care!
Mirasól, *sm.* (Bot.) Turnsol. V. *Girasol.*
Mirifíco, ca, *a.* Marvellous, admirable.
Miriñáque, *sm.* Bauble, gewgaw.
Mírla, *sf.* (Orn.) Blackbird. V. *Merla.*
Mirlamiénto, *sm.* Air of importance, affected gravity.
Mirlárse, *vr.* To assume an air of importance, to affect gravity.
Mírlo, *sm.* 1. (Orn.) Blackbird. V. *Merla.* 2. Air of importance, affected gravity.
Mirón, na, *s.* 1. Spectator, looker-on, by-stander. 2. Prier, one who inquires with too much cupidity and officiousness.
Mírra, *sf.* Myrrh, a resinous gum.
Mirrádo, da, *a.* Composed of myrrh, perfumed with myrrh.
Mirráuste, *sm.* Pigeon-sauce, made of bread, almonds, and other ingredients.
Mirríno, na, *a.* Belonging to myrrh.
Mirtidáno, *sm.* Sprout which springs at the foot of a myrtle.
Mirtíno, na, *a.* Resembling myrtle.
Mírto, *sm.* (Bot.) Myrtle. Myrtus *L.*
Mísa, *sf.* Mass, the service of the Roman church. *Misa del gallo,* Midnight mass.
Misacántano, *sm.* Priest who says the mass.
Misál, *sm.* Missal, the mass-book.
Misantropía, *sf.* Misanthropy.
Misantrópo, *sm.* Misanthropist.
Misário, *sm.* Acolite, one who attends on the priest while he is celebrating the mass.
Miscelánea, *sf.* Miscellany, mixture, a mass composed of various ingredients.
Miserable, *a.* 1. Miserable, wretched. 2. Exhausted, dejected. 3. Covetous, avaricious.
Miserablemente, *ad.* Miserably, sordidly.
Miseración, *sf.* V. *Misericordia.*
Miseramente, *ad.* Meanly. V. *Miserablemente.*
Miseráyca ó Meseráyca, *a.* Mesenteric.
Miserear, *vn.* To act penuriously.
Miserére, *sm.* 1. The Psalm *miserere.* 2. Violent colic or iliac passion.
Miséria, *sf.* 1. Misery, calamity, wretchedness. 2. Covetousness, avariciousness; meanness. 3. Trifle, a very small matter.
Misericórdia, *sf.* Mercy.
Misericordiosamente, *ad.* Piously, clemently.
Misericordióso, sa, *a.* Pious, humane, compassionate.
Míséro, ra, *a.* 1. Mass-loving. 2. V. *Miserable.*
Misérrimo, ma, *a. sup.* Very miserable.
Misión, *sf.* 1. Mission, the act of sending. 2. Travels undertaken by priests and other religious persons to propagate religion. 3. Country or province where missionaries preach the gospel among infidels. 4. Missionary discourse or sermon. 5. Charges, costs, expense. 6. Money and victuals allowed to reapers during the harvest.
Misionéro y Misionário, *sm.* Missionary, one who is sent to propagate religion.
Misívo, va, *a.* Missive; applied to a letter or small packet.
Mismísimo, ma, *a. sup.* Very same.
Mísmo, ma, *a.* Same, similar, equal, self-same.
Mísquio, *sm.* A sort of marble intermixed with a variety of stones.
Mistár, *va.* To speak or make a noise with the mouth; used generally with a negative.
Mistéla, *sf.* Drink made of wine, water, sugar, and cinnamon.
Mistério, *sm.* 1. Mystery. 2. Secret, any thing artfully made difficult.
Misteriosamente, *ad.* Mysteriously, secretly.
Misterióso, sa, *a.* Mysterious, dark, obscure.
Místíca, *sf.* Mysticalness.
Misticamente, *ad.* Mystically; spiritually.
Místico, ca, *a.* Mystic; sacredly obscure.
Misticón, *sm.* A mystic, sanctimonious person.
Míta, *sf.* Division made for drawing lots among the Indians for any public service.
Mitád, *sf.* Moiety, half. *Por mitadas,* By halves. *Mitad y mitad,* By equal parts.
Mitán, *sm.* A kind of glazed linen for lining.
Mitáyo, *sm.* Indian drawn for any public labour.
Mitigación, *sf.* Mitigation, moderation.
Mitigadór, *sm.* Mitigator.
Mitigár, *va.* 1. To mitigate, to soften, to mollify. 2. To quench, to assuage.
Mitigatívo, va; y Mitagatório, ria, *a.* Lenitive, mitigant.
Mitología, *sf.* Mythology, the history of the fabulous gods of antiquity.
Mitológico, ca, *a.* Mythological.
Mitónes, *sm. pl.* Mittens, a sort of ladies' gloves without fingers.
Mitóte, *sm.* Indian dance.
Mítra, *sf.* Mitre, an ornament for the head, worn by bishops; the dignity of a bishop.
Mitrádo, *a.* Mitred; applied to persons bearing a mitre at festivals.
Mitrár, *vn.* To be mitred or wear a mitre.
Mitridáto, *sm.* Mithridate, antidote.
Mítulo, *sm.* Mytulus or sea muscle.
Mixtamente, *ad.* Belonging to both ecclesiastical and civil courts.
Mixtífori, *sm.* (Lat.) Crime that may be tried either in ecclesiastical or secular courts.
Mixtión, *sf.* Mixtion, mixture.
Míxto, ta, *a.* Mixed, mingled; of a cross breed.
Mixtúra, *sf.* 1. Mixture, a mass formed by mingled ingredients. 2. Meslin, mixed corn, as rye and wheat.
Mixturár, *va.* To mix, to mingle.
Mízo, za, *s.* V. *Micho, cha.*
Miz, *sm.* Puss, the common appellation of cats.
Mó, *sm.* *Anvir* or juice of fermented tobacco leaves evaporated to a syrup. *Mo dulce,* Mo combined with *urao.*
Moblár, *va.* To plenish, to fill with furniture.
Móble, *a.* V. *Movil.*
Mocadéro ó Mocadór, *sm.* Pocket handkerchief.
Mocárro, *sm.* 1. Snot, the mucus of the nose. 2. Money or treat given by a journeyman to his companions the first day he works at a shop.
Moceár, *va.* To act as a boy; to revel, to rake.
Mocedád, *sf.* 1. Boyhood. 2. Debauchery.
Mocéro, *a.* Lascivious, mulierose.
Mocetón, na, *s.* A young robust person.
Mocháda, *sf.* Butt, a stroke by the head of a horned animal.
Mochár, *va.* To cut, to lop off. V. *Desmochar.*
Mocházo, *sm.* Blow with the but-end of a musket.
Mochéta, *sf.* End of a column and cornice whence an arch is sprung.

Mochíl, *sm.* Farmer's boy.

Mochíla, *sf.* 1. A kind of caparison or cover for a horse. 2. Knapsack, a bag in which soldiers carry their linen and provisions. *Hacer mochila*, To provide provisions for a journey.

Mochiléro ó Mochilér, *sm.* One who carries the luggage or baggage of soldiers.

Mochín, *sm.* Young shoot of a tree. V. *Verdugo.*

Mócho, cha, *a.* 1. Dishorned, having the horns cut off. 2. Cropped, shorn. 3. Lopped, having the branches cut off; applied to trees. 4. Maimed, mutilated.

Mochuélo, *sm.* (Orn.) Red owl. Strix asio *L.* *Tocar el mochuelo*, To take always the worst side of a thing.

Moción, *sf.* Motion, movement.—*sm.* V. *Monzon.*

Mocíto, ta, *a.* Juvenile, youthful.

Móco, *sm.* 1. Snot, the mucus of the nose. 2. Any mucous matter engendered on the surface of liquor. 3. Snuff of a lamp or candle. 4. Gutter of a candle. *Moco de pavo*, Crest which hangs over the forehead of a turkey; a thing in contempt. *El niño tiene mocos*, The youth is not to be despised. *A' moco de candil*, By candle light; applied to things hastily or inconsiderately done.

Mocosidád, *sf.* Mucosity, mucousness.

Mocóso, sa, *a.* Snotty, snivelly; ignorant, thoughtless; worthless, despicable.

Móda, *sf.* Fashion, form, mode, custom; especially that which operates upon dress.

Modál, *a.* Fashionable. *Modales*, Manners, customs.

Modelár, *va.* To model, to form.

Modélo, *sm.* Model, pattern, copy, example.

Moderación, *sf.* Moderation, temperance, frugality.

Moderadaménte, *ad.* Moderately, reasonably.

Moderádo, da, *a.* Moderate, temperate.

Moderadór, ra, *s.* Moderator, one who moderates or regulates.

Moderár, *va.* To moderate, to regulate, to adjust.—*vr.* To become moderate, to refrain from excesses.

Moderatívo, va, *a.* Moderating.

Moderatório, ria, *a.* That which moderates.

Modernaménte, *ad.* Recently, lately.

Modérno, na, *a.* Late, recent, modern.

Modestaménte, *ad.* Modestly.

Modéstia, *sf.* Modesty, decency, chastity.

Modésto, ta, *a.* Modest, decent, pure, chaste.

Modificación, *sf.* Modification, the act of modifying any thing and giving it a new accidental form.

Modificadór, ra, *s.* Modifier.

Modificár, *va.* To modify, to reduce to a certain state.

Modificatívo, va, *a.* That which modifies.

Modíllo, *sm.* Manner, mien; the diminutive of *Modo.*

Modillón, *sm.* (Arq.) Modillion.

Modío, *sm.* Roman dry measure.

Modísmo, *sm.* Peculiar phraseology in a language deviating from the rules of grammar.

Modísta, *s. com.* A person fond of dress, fashionable; prone to catch and follow the fashions as they rise; maker or seller of fashionable dresses.

Módo, *sm.* 1. Mode, method, manner. 2. Moderation, temperance, civility. 3. Mood, the change which the verb undergoes to signify the various intentions of the mind. 4. (Mús.) Tone. *A' modo*, After a similar manner. *De modo*, So that. *Sobre modo*, Extremely.

Modórra, *sf.* 1. Drowsiness. 2. Dawn or approach of day. 3. Flabby softness of the pulp of fruit.

Modorrár, *va.* To drowse, to render heavy with sleep.—*vr.* To become flabby; applied to the pulp of fruit.

Modorrílla, *sf.* The third night-watch.

Modórro, ra, *a.* Drowsy, sleepy, heavy, stupid.

Modrégo, *sm.* Dunce, dolt, thickskull.

Modulación, *sf.* Modulation, agreeable harmony.

Moduladór, ra, *s.* Modulator.

Modulár, *vn.* To modulate, to sing with harmony and variety of sound.

Módulo, *sm.* (Arq.) Module, measure of columns. 2. Modulation.

Modúrria, *sf.* Folly. V. *Bobería.*

Moéda, *sf.* 1. Thicket of old oak intermixed with bushes and brambles. 2. Moidore, a Portuguese gold coin.

Mófa, *sf.* Mockery, jeer, scoff.

Mofadór, ra, *s.* Scoffer, scorner.

Mofadúra, *sf.* Jeer, scoff, scorn.

Mofár, *va.* To deride, to jeer, to scoff.

Moféta, *sf.* Mephites; it is used by the Spanish chemists to denote a mixture of hydrogen, carbonic and azotic gases.

Mofetizádo, da, *a.* Mephitic, mephitical.

Moflétes, *sm. pl.* Chub-cheeks or blub-cheeks.

Mofletúdo, da, *a.* Chub-cheeked.

Moflón, *sm.* Siberian sheep. Ovis ammon *L.*

Móga, *sf.* (Vulg.) Cash.

Mogáte, *sm.* Varnish, a glazed cover put on earthenware by potters. *A' medio mogate*, Carelessly, heedlessly.

Mogéles, *sm. pl.* (Naút.) Nippers, braided cordage made of spun-yarn.

Mogér, *sf.* (Ant.) V. *Muger.*

Mogicón, *sm.* 1. Blow given on the face with the fist clenched. 2. Kind of sweetmeat.

Mogigánga, *sf.* A public diversion in which the company appear in ridiculous masks, and particularly in the attitude of animals; ridiculous action.

Mogigatéz, *sf.* Hypocrisy.

Mogigáto y Mogáto, *sm.* Hypocrite, one who affects humility and servile submission to obtain his end.—*a.* Deceitful, hypocritical.

Mogollón, *sm.* 1. Parasite. 2. The arrival of a parasite at a feast to which he was not invited.

Mogóte, *sm.* 1. (Naút.) An insulated rock or cliff with a flat crown, appearing at sea. 2. Pointed stack of corn. *Mogotes*, Tendrils, the soft tops of the horns of deer when they begin to shoot.

Mogróllo, *sm.* 1. Parasite, spunger. 2. Clown.

Moháda, *sf.* Humectation. V. *Mojada.*

Mohárra, *sf.* The point in which an ensign or flag-staff terminates.

Moharráche ó Moharrácho, *sm.* Jack-pudding, Merry-Andrew; a low jester.

Mohátra, *sf.* The act of selling for high prices and buying on the lowest terms, in order to cheat and overreach the buyer or seller.

Mohatreár, *va.* To sell any thing too dear.
Mohatréro, ra, *s.* Extortioner.
Mohatrón, *sm.* Extorter.
Mohecér, *va.* To cover with moss.
Mohína, *sf.* Animosity, desire of revenge.
Mohíno, na, *a.* 1. Fretful, peevish. 2. Begotten by a stone-horse and she-ass; applied to mules. 3. Black; applied to horses.
Mohíno, *sm.* One who plays alone against several others. *Tres al mohino*, Three against one.
Móho, *sm.* 1. (Bot.) Moss. 2. Mould, a concretion on the top or outside of things, kept motionless and damp. 3. Bluntness occasioned for want of application.
Mohóso, sa, *a.* Mouldy, musty.
Mojábana, *sf.* V. *Almojabana.*
Mojáda, *sf.* 1. Humectation, the act of wetting or moistening. 2. Sop, a piece of bread soaked or steeped in liquor. 3. (Vulg.) Stab, a wound given with a pointed weapon.
Mojadór, ra, *s.* Wetter, moistener.
Mojadúra, *sf.* Act of moistening or wetting.
Mojáma, *sf.* Salt tunny-fish, dried or smoked.
Mojár, *va.* 1. To wet, to moisten. 2. To meddle, to interfere.—*vn.* To be immersed in any business.
Mojarrílla, *sm.* Punster, jester.
Móje, *sm.* Sauce of fricassee, ragout, or any other dressed meat.
Mojón, *sm.* 1. Landmark, a stone or mound erected to mark the limits and boundaries of land. 2. Heap, pile. 3. Kind of play, like pitching.
Mojóna, *sf.* 1. Duty on wine sold by retail. 2. Survey of land; the setting up of landmarks.
Mojonación, *sf.* V. *Amojonamiento.*
Mojonár, *va.* V. *Amojonar.*
Mojonéra, *sf.* Place in which landmarks are fixed.
Mojonéro, *sm.* Gauger, a person appointed by government to measure wine.
Mola ó Mola-Matriz, *sf.* 1. Mole, a formless concretion of extravasated blood which grows into a kind of flesh in the uterus. *Mola*, Barley, flour mixed with salt and used in sacrifices.
Moláda, *sf.* Quantity of colours ground at once.
Molár, *a.* Belonging to a millstone, or any other thing fit for grinding, as the teeth.
Moldár, *va.* To mould. V. *Amoldar.*
Mólde, *sm.* Mould, the matrix in which any thing is cast or receives its form; pattern, model. *De molde*, In print, printed, or published; fitting, to the purpose.
Moldeár, *va.* To mould, to make moulds.
Moldúra, *sf.* Moulding, an ornamental cavity in wood or stone. *Molduras de proa de un navio*, (Naút.) The carved work of a ship's head.
Moldurár, *va.* To make a moulding or ornament of any thing.
Móle, *a.* Soft, mild.—*sf.* Vast size or quantity.
Molécula, *sf.* Molecule, particle of bodies.
Moledéro, ra, *a.* That which is to be ground.
Moledór, ra, *s.* 1. Grinder, one who grinds and prepares colours. 2. Iron-pot or copper in which printer's ink is prepared. 3. Coxcomb, a tiresome fellow.
Moledúra, *sf.* The act of grinding. V. *Molienda.*
Molendéro, *sm.* 1. Miller, grinder. 2. Chocolate manufacturer, one who grinds the cocoa, and beats it up with sugar and cinnemon.
Molér, *va.* 1. To grind, to pound, to pulverise. 2. To vex, to molest; to fatigue. 3. To waste, to consume by use. 4. To masticate, to chew. *Moler á azotes*, To lash, to whip.
Moléro, *sm.* Maker or seller of mill-stones.
Molestadór, ra, *s.* Disturber, vexer.
Molestaménte, *ad.* Troublesomely, vexatiously.
Molestár, *va.* To vex, to disturb, to molest.
Molestía, *sf.* Injury, molestation.
Molésto, ta, *a.* Grievous, vexatious.
Moléta, *sf.* Muller, a stone flat at the bottom and round at the top, used by painters to grind colours on marble.
Molibdéna, *sf.* Molybdena, a semi-metal.
Molície, *sf.* 1. Tenderness, softness, effeminacy. 2. An unnatural crime.
Molído, da, *pp.* Ground; fatigued; flogged.
Moliénda, *sf.* 1. The act of grinding or pounding. 2. Quantity pounded or ground at once. 3. Mill in which any thing is ground. 4. Weariness or fatigue caused by grinding or pounding.
Moliénte, *pa.* Grinder, grinding.
Molificación, *sf.* Mollification.
Molificár, *va.* To mollify, to soften, to mitigate.
Molificatívo, va, *a.* That which mollifies.
Molimiénto, *sm.* 1. The act of grinding or pounding. 2. Fatigue, weariness.
Molinéra, *sf.* Miller's wife.
Molinería, *sf.* Collection of mills.
Molinéro, *sm.* Miller.
Molinéro, ra, *a.* Any thing which is to be ground or pounded; any thing belonging to a mill.
Molinéte, *sm.* 1. (Naút.) Windlass, a cylindrical piece of wood with holes, into which levers or handspikes are thrust to heave up the anchor. 2. Turnstile.
Moliníllo, *sm.* 1. A little mill. 2. Churn-staff, a stick with which chocolate is beat up in a chocolate pot. 3. Ancient trimming of clothes.
Molinísmo, *sm.* Molinism or quietism, principles of a sect.
Molíno, *sm.* 1. Mill, an engine in which corn is ground into meal, or any other body comminuted. *Molino de viento*, Windmill. *Molino de sangre*, Mill turned by men or animals, in contradistinction to such as are turned by wind, water, or steam. 2. A restless noisy fellow. 3. (Fam.) Mouth.
Molitívo, va, *a.* Mollient.
Mólla, *sf.* Crum or crum of bread.
Mollár, *a.* Soft, tender, flexible, credulous; useful, rich.
Molleár, *vn.* To soften, to grow less hard.
Mollédo, *sm.* 1. The fleshy part of a limb. 2. Crum of bread.
Molléja, *sf.* 1. Gland, particularly that which is seated at the roof of the tongue. 2. Gizzard, the strong musculous stomach of a fowl.
Mollejón, *sm.* 1. A large gland. 2. A big corpulent person.
Mollejuéla, *sf.* A small gland.
Mollentár, *va.* To mollify. V. *Amollentar.*
Molléra, *sf.* Crown or top of the head. *Ser duro de mollera*, To be obstinate.

Molléro, *sm.* Fleshy part of the arm.

Molléta, *sf.* 1. Snuffers. 2. Bread made of the finest flour.

Molléte, *sm.* A small loaf made of the finest flour. *Molletes*, Plump or round cheeks.

Mollína y Mollízna, *sf.* Mist, small rain.

Molliznár ó Mollisnear, *vn.* To drizzle, to fall in small slow drops.

Molóndro ó Molondrón, *sm.* A sluggish, mean-spirited, and ignorant fellow, poltron.

Molóso, *sm.* Foot of Latin verse, consisting of three long syllables.

Moltúra, *sf.* (Ar.) V. *Maquila.*

Momentaneaménte, *ad.* Momentally.

Momentáneo, nea, *a.* Momentaneous, of short duration.

Moménto, *sm.* 1. Moment, a small space of time. 2. Moment, consequence; momentum, weight, importance. *Al momento*, In a moment. *Por momentos*, Successively, continually.

Momería, *sf.* Mommery, a farcical entertainment, in which masked persons play frolics and antic tricks.

Mómio, mia, *a.* Meager, lean.

Mómia, *sf.* Mummy, a dead body preserved by embalming.

Mómo, *sm.* Buffoonery, low jests, scurrile mirth, wry faces, grimaces.

Monperáda, *sf.* A kind of glazed woollen stuff.

Móna, *sf.* 1. Female monkey or ape. 2. (Fam.) Mimic. 3. (Joc.) Drunkenness. 4. (Val. y Mur.) Cake made of flour, eggs, and milk. 5. Instrument for copying pictures and prints in any size or proportion.

Monacál, *a.* Monkish, belonging to monks.

Monacáto, *sm.* Monkhood.

Monacíllo, *sm.* Boy who serves in a monastery or convent of monks.

Monacórdio, *sm.* Monochord, a stringed musical instrument.

Monáda, *sf.* Grimace, a ludicrous or ridiculous distortion of the countenance.

Mónago ó Monaguíllo, *sm.* V. *Monacillo.*

Monaquísmo, *sm.* Monachism, monasticness.

Monárca, *sm.* Monarch, king, sovereign.

Monarquía, *sf.* Monarchy, the government of a single person, kingdom, empire.

Monárquico, ca, *a.* Monarchical.

Monasteriál, *a.* Monastic.

Monastério, *sm.* Monastery, a house of religious retirement; convent.

Monásticamente, *ad.* Monastically.

Monástico, ca, *a.* Monastic, recluse.

Monázo, za, *s.* Large monkey or ape.

Mónda, *sf.* Pruning of trees, the pruning season. *Mondas*, Feasts of the Virgin del Prado.

Mondadiéntes, *sm.* Toothpick.

Mondadór, ra, *s.* Cleaner, purifier.

Mondadúra, *sf.* Cleaning, cleansing; the act of freeing from filth. *Mondaduras*, Parings, peelings; any thing which comes off by cleaning.

Mondaoréjas, *sm.* Ear-pick.

Mondár, *va.* 1. To clean, to cleanse; to free from filth. 2. To strip off the husks of fruit, to peel, to decorticate; to deprive of money. 3. To cut the hair. *Mondar los huesos*, To pick bones quite clean.

Mondéjo, *sm.* Paunch or belly of a pig or sheep stuffed with minced meat.

Móndo, da, *a.* Neat, clean, pure, unadulterated. *Mondo y lirondo*, Pure, without any admixture.

Mondónga, *sf.* (Contempt.) Kitchen-wench.

Mondóngo, *sm.* Paunch, tripes, black pudding.

Mondongonizár, *va.* To dress tripe, to make black puddings.

Mondonguéro, ra, *s.* One who makes black puddings or deals in them.

Mondonguíl, *a.* (Joc.) Relating to tripes or puddings.

Monéda, *sf.* Money, pieces of gold, silver, or copper, coined for the purpose of commerce and trade. *Moneda de vellon*, Copper-coin.

Monedáge, *sm.* Duty paid to the king for coining.

Monedár y Monedeár, *va.* To coin.

Monedería, *sf.* Mint, factory of money.

Monedéro, *sm.* Officer of the mint who coins money, coiner.

Monería, *sf.* 1. Grimace, a ludicrous or ridiculous distortion of the countenance; mimicry. 2. Trifle, gewgaw, bauble.

Monésco, ca, *a.* Apish, having the qualities of a monkey.

Monetário, *sm.* Cabinet of ancient coins and models.

Monfí, *sm.* Name given to Moorish highwaymen.

Monfórte, *sm.* Everlasting, strong cloth.

Mónge, *sm.* 1. Monk. 2. (Orn.) Brown peacock. Pavo bicalcaratus *L.*

Mongía, *sf.* 1. Monkhood. 2. Prebend enjoyed by a monk in his convent.

Mongíl, *sm.* 1. Habit or dress of a nun. 2. Mourning-dress or weeds of a widow.

Mongío, *sm.* State of a nun.

Moniáco, *sm.* (In contempt) Myrmidon, partisan.

Monicángo, *sm.* (In contempt) Conceited person.

Monición, *sf.* Admonition, publication of the bans of marriage.

Monigóte, *sm.* Lay-brother of religious orders.

Monillo, *sm.* Corset, a jacket without sleeves, worn by women.

Monipódio, *sm.* Monopoly, exclusive privilege of dealing in certain goods and merchandise.

Mónis, *sf.* 1. (Arag.) A kind of fritters. 2. Any small and neat thing.

Monitór, *sm.* V. *Admonitor.*

Monitória, *sf.* Summons issued by an ecclesiastical judge to command the personal appearance of a witness.

Monitório, ria, *a.* Monitory, admonitory.

Mónja, *sf.* Nun, a religious woman, secluded from the world, and confined in a cloister. *Monjas*, Appellation given to sparks in burned papers.

Monjíta, *sf.* (Joc.) A little nun.

Móno, na, *a.* Neat, pretty, nice.

Móno, *sm.* Monkey, ape.

Monocerónte y Monocerónte, *sm.* Unicorn.

Monóculo, la, *a.* Monoculous, one-eyed.—*sm.* Bandage after operating for the lachrymal fistula.

Monocromáta, *sf.* Monochromaton, one-coloured painting.

Monogamía, *sf.* Monogamy, marriage of one wife.
Monógamo, *sm.* He who marries only once.
Monólogo, *sm.* Monologue, soliloquy.
Monográma, *sm.* Monogram, a cipher or character compounded of several letters, and containing some name.
Monomáquia, *sf.* Monomachy, a duel.
Monopástos, *sm.* Pulley with one wheel.
Monopétala, *a.* Monopetalous, having only one flower leaf.
Monopólio, *sm.* Monopoly. V. *Monipodio.*
Monopolísta, *sm.* Monopolist, forestaller.
Monoptério, *sm.* Monopteron, circular open temple.
Monosílabo, **ba**, **y Monosilábico**, **ca**, *a.* Monosyllabled.
Monospérmo, **ma**, *a.* (Bot.) Monospermous.
Monotónia, *sf.* Monotony, uniformity of sound.
Monotóno, **na**, *a.* Monotonous.
Monseñór, *sm.* Title of honour applied to Italian prelates, and the Dauphin of France.
Monsiúr, *sm.* Mr., sir; applied to Frenchmen.
Mónstruo, *sm.* 1. Monster, a fœtus or production contrary to the order of nature. 2. Any thing excessively large or very ugly.
Monstruosaménte, *ad.* Monstrously.
Monstruosidád, *sf.* Monstruosity, excessive ugliness.
Monstruóso, **sa**, *a.* Monstrous, contrary to the order of nature.
Mónta, *sf.* 1. Amount, sum total. 2. Value, worth, price. 3. Signal given with a trumpet for the cavalry to mount their horses.
Montadéro, *sm.* One who mounts; mounting-stone.
Montádo, *sm.* 1. A substitute sent by a knight to serve in a campaign. 2. Trooper, horseman. 3. Horse ready for being mounted.
Montadór, *sm.* He who mounts; mounting-block.
Montadúra, *sf.* The whole of the accoutrements of a trooper.
Montáge, *sm.* Act of mounting artillery. *Montages,* Mounting or bed of a piece of ordnance.
Montanéra, *sf.* The feeding of hogs with acorns, driven for that purpose into groves of oak.
Montanéro, *sm.* Forester, keeper of a forest.
Montáno, **na**, *a.* Mountainous.
Montantáda, *sf.* 1. Ostentation. 2. Multitude.
Montánte, *sm.* 1. A broad sword used by fencing-masters. 2. The upright post of a machine.
Montanteár, *vn.* 1. To wield the broad sword in a fencing-school. 2. To vaunt, to brag.
Montantéro, *sm.* He who fights with a broad sword.
Montáña, *sf.* Mountain, a ridge of mountains.
Montañés, **sa**, *a.* Belonging to mountains; mountaineer
Montañóso, **sa**, *a.* Mountainous.
Montár, *vn.* 1. To mount or go on horseback. 2. To amount to, to be worth. 3. To cock a gun. 4. (Naut.) To double a cape. *Montar un navio,* To take the command of a ship. *Montar en cuidado,* To be on one's guard, to be careful.—*va.* To impose a penalty for cattle entering a mountain. *Montar la brecha,* (Mil.) To mount the breach.
Montaráz, *a.* y *sm.* Mountaineer; guard of mountains.
Montás, *ad.* (Vulg.) Indeed.
Montazgár, *va.* To levy or collect the toll for cattle passing from one province into another.
Montázgo, *sm.* 1. Toll to be paid for cattle passing from one province into another. 2. Place through which the cattle pass.
Mónte, *sm.* 1. Mountain, hill, elevated ground. 2. Wood, forest. *Monte de malezas,* Thicket, a close copse or coppice. 3. Difficulty, obstruction. 4. Stock of cards which remain after each player has received his share. 5. Thick head of hair. *Andar á monte,* To skulk, to lurk in hiding places. *Monte de piedad,* Pawnbroker's shop. V. *Monte pio.*
Montéa, *sf.* 1. Art or trade of cutting or hewing stone. 2. Plan or profile of a building. 3. Sweep of an arch on the convex side.
Monteár, *va.* 1. To beat a wood in pursuit of game. 2. To draw the plan or profile of a building. 3. To vault, to form arches.
Montecíllo, *sm.* A small wood.
Mónte Pio, *sm.* House for lending money on pledges without interest; depository of money for annuities to survivors.
Montéra, *sf.* Hunting-cap.
Monteréro, *sm.* One who makes hunting-caps.
Monteréy, *sm.* A kind of thin paste rolled up into spiral tubes.
Montería, *sf.* 1. Hunting, hunt, chase. 2. Place where hunting-caps are made or sold.
Montéro, *sm.* Huntsman.
Montés, **sa**, *a.* Bred or found in a forest or mountain.
Montésa, *sf.* The military order of Our Lady.
Montéscos, *s. Haber montescos y capeletes,* To have great disputes and contentions.
Montesíno, **na**, *a.* Bred or found in a forest or mountain.
Mónto, *sm.* V. *Monta.*
Montón, *sm.* 1. Heap, pile. *Monton de gente,* Crowd, multitude. 2. A dirty lazy fellow. *Monton de tierra,* Very old infirm person. *A' montones,* Abundantly.
Montuóso, **sa**, *a.* Full of woods and thickets.
Montúra, *sf.* 1. Horses and mules intended for the saddle. 2. Saddle, trappings, and accoutrements of horses.
Monuménto, *sm.* 1. Monument, tomb, cenotaph. 2. Altar raised in churches on Holy Thursday to resemble a sepulchre. *Monumentos,* Monuments or remains of antiquity.
Monzón, *sm.* Monsoon, a periodical wind in the East Indian ocean.
Móña, *sf.* 1. Doll dressed to display the prevailing fashion. 2. Peevishness, fretfulness. 3. Drunkenness.
Móño, *sm.* 1. Hair on the crown of the head tied together. 2. Tuft of feathers on the heads of some birds.
Moñúdo, **da**, *a.* Crested, topped.
Moqueár, *vn.* To snivel, to run at the nose; to blow the nose.
Moquéro, *sm.* Pocket handkerchief.
Moquéte, *sm.* Blow on the face or nose.
Moqueteár, *vn.* To discharge much mucus from the nose.—*va.* To give blows in the face.
Moquíreo, **ra**, *a.* Snotty, mucous.

Moquíllo, *sm.* 1. A little mucus. 2. Pip, a disease in fowls.
Moquíta, *sf.* Snivel, running from the nose in cold weather.
Móra, *sf.* 1. Delay, procrastination. 2. Mulberry, the fruit of the mulberry-tree.
Morabíto, *sm.* Appellation given by the Mohammedans to their religious sages.
Moráсho, cha, *a.* Dark purple.
Moráda, *sf.* Habitation, abóde, residence.
Morádo, da, *a.* Violet, mulberry-coloured.
Moradór, *sm.* Inhabitant.
Morága, *sf.* Handful or bundle formed by female gleaners.
Morál, *sm.* 1. (Bot.) Mulberry-tree. Morus nigra *L.* *sf.* 2. Ethics, treatise on morality. 3. Morality, practice of the duties of life.—*a.* Moral, relating to the duties of life.
Moraléja, *sf.* A brief moral observation.
Moralidád, *sf.* 1. Morality, the doctrine of the duties of life. 2. Form of an action, which makes it the subject of reward or punishment.
Moralísta, *sm.* Moralist, one who teaches the duties of life.
Moralizadór, *sm.* Commentator, critic.
Moralizár, *va.* To moralize, to apply to moral purposes; to explain in a moral sense.
Moralménte, *ad.* Morally; by common sense.
Morár, *vn.* To inhabit, to dwell, to reside.
Moráto, ta, *a.* (Poét.) Relating to manners and morals.
Moratória, *sf.* Letter of license granted to a debtor.
Morbidéz, *sf.* (Among Painters) Softness or mellowness of tint.
Mórbido, da, *a.* Morbid, diseased, soft.
Morbífico, ca, *a.* Morbific, causing disease.
Mórbo, *sm.* Disease, distemper, infirmity.
Morbóso, sa, *a.* Diseased, not healthy.
Morcájo, *a.* Blackish; applied to wheat.
Morcélla, *sf.* Spark flying from a lamp.
Morcílla, *sf.* Black pudding.
Morcilléro, ra, *s.* One who makes black puddings or deals in them.
Morcíllo, lla, *a.* Entirely black; applied to horses.
Morcíllo, *sm.* The fleshy part of the arm from the shoulder to the elbow.
Morcón, *sm.* 1. A large black pudding made of the blind gut; a large sausage. 2. A short dirty fellow.
Mordacidád, *sf.* 1. Mordacity, biting quality. 2. Roughness, asperity; sarcastic language.
Mordacílla, *sf.* Small gag with which the loquacity of novices is chastized in convents.
Mordánte, *sm.* (Impr.) Instrument made of wood or iron for adjusting or composing types.
Mordáz, *a.* Corrosive, biting, nipping; sarcastic; acrimonious, satirical.
Mordáza, *sf.* 1. Gag, something put into the mouth to prevent speaking or crying. 2. Sort of nippers or pincers.
Mordazménte, *ad.* Acrimoniously.
Mordedór, ra, *s.* Biter, one who bites.
Mordedúra, *sf.* Bite, wound made by biting.
Mordér, *va.* 1. To bite, to seize with the teeth. 2. To make the mouth smart with an acrid taste. 3. (Naút.) To bite, to hold fast in the ground; applied to an anchor. 4. To press one thing against another; to waste away insensibly, as with a file. 5. (Met.) To taunt, to satirize. *No morderse los labios*, (Fam.) To speak one's opinion frankly and openly. *Morderse los dedos*, To bite the thumbs, to be irritated and vexed from desire of revenge.
Mordicación, *sf.* Mordication, smarting.
Mordicánte, *pa.* Biting, pungent.
Mordicár, *va.* To gnaw, to nibble.
Mordicatívo, va, *a.* Biting, gnawing, mordicant.
Mordído, *sm.* Bit, as much meat as is put into the mouth at once.—*a.* Diminished, too small.
Mordiénte, *sm.* Gold size, used by painters.
Mordihúi, *sm.* Weevil, a grub bred in wheat which is laid up in granaries.
Mordimiénto, *sm.* Bite, mordication.
Mordiscár, *va.* To gnaw, to nibble. V. *Morder.*
Mordísco y Mordiscón, *sm.* Bite, the act of seizing with the teeth; the piece bitten off.
Morel de sál, *sm.* (Pint.) Purple red used for painting in fresco.
Moréna, *sf.* Brown bread.
Morenílla ó Morenítа, *sf.* Brunette, a woman with a brown complexion.
Morenílo, *sm.* A kind of black powder, used by sheep-shearers when they wound the sheep with the shears.
Morenílo, lla; to, ta, *a. dim.* of *Moreno;* used always as endearing.
Moréno, na, *a.* 1. Brown, a dark colour, inclining to black. 2. Swarthy; applied to the complexion. *Sobre ello morena*, If you do not, you will be punished; a menace.
Moréra, *sf.* (Bot.) White mulberry-tree. Morus alba *L.*
Morerál, *sm.* Plantation of white mulberry-trees.
Morería, *sf.* Suburb or quarter of the town where Moors reside.
Moréta, *sf.* A kind of sauce.
Morféx, *sf.* Cormorant, a water-fowl.
Mórga, *sf.* Lees or dregs of oil.
Moribúndo, da, *a.* Dying.
Moriégo, ga, *a.* Moorish, belonging to Moors.
Morigeración, *sf.* Complaisance; temperance.
Morigerár, *va.* To endeavour to curb or restrain one's affections and passions; to moderate.
Moríllo, *sm.* 1. A little Moor. 2. Andiron; a dog.
Morír, *vn.* 1. To die, to expire, to perish, to cease to exist; to become extinct. *Morir vestido*, To die a violent death, not to die in bed. 2. To desire excessively; to experience any violent emotion or effect, as cold, hunger, &c.—*vr.* To be benumbed; applied to a limb; to be extinguished; applied to fire or light. *Morirse por alguno*, To be excessively fond of.
Morísco, ca, *a.* Moorish, belonging to the Moors.—*s.* Moor who revolted from Christianity to Mohammedanism, and was expelled Spain by Philip III.
Morísma, *sf.* Mohammedan sect, multitude of Moors.
Morisquéta, *sf.* Moorish trick, deception, fraud.
Moriáco, ca, *a.* Affecting ignorance and stupidity.
Morlés, *sm.* A sort of linen loosely woven, made at Morlaix; lawn. *Morles de morles* All of a piece; the finest linen.

Morlón, na, *a.* V. *Morlaco.*

Mormúllo ó Mormurío, *sm.* Mutter, murmur; a low shrill noise.

Mormuradór, *sm.* Murmurer, detractor.

Mormurár, *va.* To murmur. V. *Murmurar.*

Móro, ra, *s.* Moor, a native of Africa. *Haber moros y cristianos*, To have a great scuffle or dispute. *Moro*, Pure wine, not mixed with water or christened.

Morocáda, *sf.* Blow given by a ram with its horn.

Morón, *sm.* Hill, hillock.

Moróncho, cha, *a.* Bald, leafless, naked of leaves.

Morondánga, *sf.* Hodge-podge, a medley of useless things heaped together.

Moróndo, da, *a.* Bald; leafless, naked of leaves.

Moronía, *sf.* A dish made of a variety of vegetables.

Morosaménte, *ad.* Slowly, tardily.

Morosidád, *sf.* Slowness, tardiness, detention.

Moróso, sa, *a.* Slow, tardy, heavy. *Juro moroso*, Law giving the king any property till a just claim is made of it.

Morquéra, *sf.* (Bot.) Kind of thyme or savory.

Mórra, *sf.* 1. Upper part of the head, top, crown. 2. Vulgar play with the fingers.

Morráda, *sf.* Butt with the heads given by two persons against each other.

Morrál, *sm.* A little bag hung to the mouths of mules or horses, out of which they eat their corn when an army is encamped.

Morrálla, *sf.* 1. Heap or medley of useless things. 2. Jack. V. *Boliche.*

Morríllo, *sm.* 1. Pebble. 2. Fat of the nape of a sheep.

Morrína, *sf.* 1. Disease among cattle. 2. Sadness, melancholy.

Morrión, *sm.* 1. Murrion, steel helmet. 2. Vertigo, a disease in hawks.

Mórro, *sm.* 1. Any thing that is round. 2. A prominent overhanging lip.

Mórro, ra, *a.* Purring; applied to a cat.

Morróncho, cha, *a.* Mild, meek.

Morrúdo, da, *a.* Having large prominent lips.

Morsána, *sf.* (Bot.) Bean caper. Zygophylum fabago *L.*

Mortája, *sf.* 1. Shroud, winding-sheet; the dress of the dead. 2. Mortise, a hole cut into wood that another piece may be put into it.

Mortál, *a.* 1. Mortal, subject to death. 2. Deadly, destructive; bringing death. 3. One who has the appearance or symptoms of death.

Mortalidád, *sf.* Mortality, subjection to death; state of a being subject to death.

Mortalménte, *ad.* Mortally.

Mortandád, *sf.* Mortality, frequency of death.

Mortecíno, na, *a.* 1. Dying a natural death. 2. Being on the point of dying. 3. Weak, exhausted. *Hacer la mortecina*, To feign being dead.

Morteráda, *sf.* 1. Sauce made at once in a mortar. 2. Quantity of stones thrown out at once by a stone mortar.

Morteréte, *sm.* 1. A small mortar. 2. Piece of wax formed in the shape of a mortar, with a wick in it, to serve as a lamp; it is placed in a glass with water. 3. (Met.) Hollow piece of iron used for firing gunpowder at rejoicings.

Mortéro, *sm.* 1. Mortar, a short but wide piece of ordnance, out of which bombs and shells are thrown. 2. Mortar, a vessel in which materials are broken by being pounded with a pestle. 3. A short thick taper, made of yellow wax; a short thick person. 4. Mortar, a cement made of lime and sand with water, and used for building. *Mortero de una bomba de agua*, (Naút.) Pump-box of a ship's pump. *Mortero de brúxula*, Compass-box.

Morteruélo, *sm.* 1. A kind of play-thing for boys. 2. Fricassee made of hog's liver.

Morticínio, *sm.* Carrion, carcass of animals not fit for food.

Mortífero, ra, *a.* Mortiferous, fatal.

Mortificación, *sf.* 1. Mortification, gangrene; humiliation. 2. Vexation, trouble.

Mortificár, *va.* To mortify, to afflict, to disgust.—*vr.* To conquer one's passions.

Mortuório, *sm.* 1. Burial, funeral. 2. Legacy left to a parish church, as a compensation for tithes and offerings not discharged in due time. *Casa mortuoria*, House of the deceased.

Moruéca, *sf.* Heap of loose stones.

Moruéco, *sm.* Ram, a male sheep.

Mórula, *sf.* A short stay, slight stoppage.

Morúno, na, *a.* 1. Belonging to the mulberry. 2. Moorish, belonging to the Moors.

Morúsa, *sf.* Cash, specie; money in hand.

Mosáyco, ca, *a.* Mosaic. *Obra mosáyca*, Mosaic work, composed of small pieces of stone, or of glass, and shells, of various colours.

Mósca, *sf.* 1. Fly, a small-winged insect. 2. (Joc.) Cash, specie; money in hand. *Tener mucha mosca*, To be very rich. 3. An impertinent intruder. 4. Vexation, trouble. *Moscas*, Sparks from a light. *Mosca de burro*, Horse-fly. Oestrus equi *L.* *Mosca en leche*, Brown or black woman dressed in white. *Mosca muerta*, A mean spiritless fellow. *Andar con mosca*, To fly into a passion.

Móscas, *interj.* Exclamation of complaint or surprise.

Moscárda, *sf.* 1. Gad-fly. Oestrus *L.* 2. Eggs of bees.

Moscardeár, *vn.* To lay eggs as bees in the cells of their combs.

Moscardón, *sm.* 1. Large gad-fly. 2. An importuning sly-fellow, a cheat.

Moscaréta, *sf.* (Orn.) Fly-catcher. Muscicapa *L.*

Moscatél, *a.* 1. Muscadine: applied to a kind of grapes. 2. A tiresome ignorant fellow.

Moscélla, *sf.* V. *Morcella.*

Moscón, *sm.* 1. A large fly. 2. A crafty deceitful fellow. 3. (Bot.) The great maple or bastard sycamore. Acer pseudoplatanus *L.* 4. Maple-sugar, made of a sweet liquid which is obtained by incision from the maple-tree.

Mosíllos, *sm. pl.* (Naút.) A kind of shell-fish which sticks to the bottom of ships.

Mosqueádo, da, *a.* Spotted, painted.

Mosqueadór, *sm.* 1. Flap for killing flies. 2. (Met.) Tail of animals.

Mosqueár, *va.* 1. To drive or frighten flies away with a flap; to catch flies. 2. To retort a joke, to make a smart repartee. *Mosquear las espaldas*, (Fam.) To whip or flog the shoulders.—*vr.* To reject or repel embarrassments with violence.

Mosqueo, *sm.* The act of catching flies or driving them away with a flap.
Mosquéro, *sm.* Fly-trap.
Mosqueruéla, *sf.* Muscadine pear of a reddish colour.
Mosquéta, *sf.* White musk-rose.
Mosquetázo, *sm.* Musket-shot.
Mosquéte, *sm.* Musket, a large fire-lock.
Mosquetería, *sf.* 1. Body of infantry or musketeers; musketry. 2. The persons sitting in the pit of a play-house or theatre.
Mosqueteríl, *a.* Relating to the pit of a theatre.
Mosquetéro, *sm.* 1. Musketeer, a foot soldier. 2. Person who frequents the pit in a play-house.
Mosquíl y Mosquíno, na, *a.* Belonging to flies.
Mosquitéro, ra, *s.* A gauze cover hung over a bed, as a shelter against gnats and mosquitoes.
Mosquíto, *sm.* 1. Gnat, mosqueto. 2. Tippler, one who frequents tippling houses.
Mósssen, *sm.* Ancient title in Aragon; Sir.
Mostácho, *sm.* 1. Whisker. V. *Bigote.* 2. Spot in the face, gloom in the countenance. *Mostachos* (Naút.) Standing lifts *Mostachos del baupres*, (Naut.) Bowsprit-shrouds.
Mostachón, *sm.* A kind of ginger-bread.
Mostachóso, sa, *a.* Wearing whiskers.
Mostacílla, *sf.* Sparrow-shot, the smallest of all kinds of hail-shot.
Mostájo, *sm.* (Bot.) White beam-tree; Cumberland hawthorn. Cratægus aria *L.*
Mostáza, *sf.* 1. (Bot.) Mustard. Sinapis *L.* 2. Mustard-seed. 3. Hail-shot. *Hacer la mostaza*, To make the nose bleed with a blow.
Mostázo, *sm.* 1. (Bot.) Mustard; a plant. 2. Strong thick must.
Mosteár, *vn.* 1. To yield must; applied to grapes. 2. To put must into vats or large earthen jars to ferment. 3. To mix must with old wine in order to revive it. V. *Remostar.*
Mostéla, *sf.* Sprig or twig of vines.
Mosteléra, *sf.* Place where the sprigs or twigs of vines are laid up.
Mostíllo, *sm.* 1. Cake made of must and other ingredients. 2. Sauce made of must and mustard.
Mósto, *sm.* 1. Stem, the pressed juice of the grape not yet fermented. 2. Must, new wine.
Mostráble, *a.* That which may be shewn.
Mostrádo, da, *a.* Accustomed, habituated.
Mostradór, *sm.* 1. One who shows or demonstrates; professor, demonstrator. 2. Hand of a clock or watch. 3. Counter, the place in a shop where goods are shown and viewed.
Mostrár, *va.* 1. To show, to exhibit to view, to point out. 2. To establish, to prove. 3. To explain, to elucidate. *Mostrar las suelas de los zapatos*, To run away.—*vr.* To appear, to show one's self.
Mostrénco, ca, *a.* 1. Strayed, having no owner. 2. Vagabond, vagrant. 3. Dull, ignorant, stupid. 4. Fat, bulky.
Móta, *sf.* 1. A small knot on cloth, which is taken off with burling irons or scissors. 2. A bit of thread or any similar thing sticking to cloths. 3. A slight defect or fault. 4. Bank or mound of earth.
Motacén, *sm.* Clerk of the market. V. *Almotacen.*
Motacílla y Motolíta, *sf.* V. *Aguzanieves.*
Móte, *sm.* 1. Motto, a sentence added to a device, or prefixed to any thing written. 2. Nick-name, a name given in scoff or contempt.
Moteár, *vn.* To speckle, to mark with spots.
Motejadór, ra, *s.* Mocker, scoffer, censurer.
Motejár, *va.* To censure, to ridicule.
Motéte, *sm.* A short musical composition to be sung in church.
Motilár, *va.* To cut off the hair, to crop.
Motilón, *sm.* Lay-brother of a religious order.
Motín, *sm.* Mutiny, insurrection, riot.
Motíta, *sf.* Brief motto; short song.
Motivár, *va.* To give reason or cause for any thing, to assign a motive.
Motívo, *sm.* Motive, cause, reason. *De su motivo*, Of one's own accord.—*a.* Moving.
Motolíto, ta; y **Motolótico**, ca, *a.* Easily deceived, ignorant.
Motón, *sm.* (Naút.) Block, a piece of wood, in which the sheaves of pullies are placed for the ropes to run in. *Moton ciego*, Dead-block. *Moton sencillo*, Single-block. *Moton de gancho*, Hook-block. *Moton de aparejo*, Tackle-block. *Moton de amantillo*, Lift-block. *Moton de la gata*, Cat-block. *Moton del virador del tamborete*, Top-block. *Motónes*, (Naút.) Pullies with sheaves through which the ropes run. *Motones herrados*, Iron-bound blocks. *Motones de retorno*, Leading-blocks. *Motones de aparejo de combés*, Winding-tackle-blocks. *Motones de las cañas de la cebadera*, Sprit-sail sheet-blocks. *Motones de la driza mayor*, Main geer-blocks. *Motones de los palanquines de las velas mayores*, Clue-garnet blocks.
Motonería, *sf.* Blocks and pullies, in which the ropes run on board of ships.
Motonéro, *sm.* Block-maker.
Motór, *sm.* V. *Movedor.*
Motríl, *sm.* V. *Mochil.*
Motríz, *a.* Motory, motive; moving cause.
Mótu proprio, (Lat.) By his own will.
Movedízo, za, *a.* 1. Moveable, easily moved. 2. Variable, unsteady, inconstant.
Movedór, ra, *s.* Mover, motor.
Movér, *va.* 1. To move, to put out of one place into another. 2. To prevail upon, to persuade, to induce, to excite. 3. To inspire.—*vn.* 1. (Arq.) To spring an arch. 2. To bud, to begin to sprout. 3. To miscarry, to have an abortion.
Movíble, *a.* Moveable, that can be moved.
Moviénte, *pa.* Moving, mover.
Móvil, *a.* Moveable. *Primer móvil*, Primum mobile.
Movilidád, *sf.* 1. Mobility, aptitude to be moved. 2. Inconstancy, unsteadiness, levity.
Movimiénto, *sm.* 1. Movement, motion. 2. Commotion, disturbance, sedition, revolt. 3. (Arq.) V. *Arranque.*
Moxi ó Moxil. V. *Cazuela.*
Moxána, *sf.* 1. A small calverin, now of little or no use. 2. Lie, falsehood. 3. Bread made of bran for the feed of dogs.
Móyo, *sm.* 1. Liquid measure of Galicia, about sixteen quarts. 2. Number of tiles fixed at one hundred and two.
Moyuélo, *sm.* Grits, pollard.

Móza, *sf.* 1. Girl, a young woman. 2. Wench, girl of the town. *Moza de cámara*, Chambermaid. *Moza de cántaro*, Girl to carry water. *Moza de fortuna*, Prostitute. 3. Stick to beat linen with when it is washing. 4. Last or conquering game.

Mazalbéte ó Mozalbíllo, *sm.* A beardless lad.

Mozallón, *sm.* A young robust labourer.

Mozárabe, *s.* Applied to a Christian who formerly lived among the Moors in Spain, and also to the church service, used in Toledo.

Mozcórra, *sf.* (Vulg.) A common prostitute.

Mózo, za, *a.* Young, youthful.

Mózo, *sm.* 1. Man-servant engaged to do all kind of work in the house. 2. Bachelor, a man unmarried. 3. Cat, commonly called *miz* in Spanish. 4. (Naút.) An ordinary seaman. *Mozo de caballos*, Groom. *Mozo de paja y cebada*, Hostler, one who has the care of horses at an inn. 5. Dumb-waiter. *Mozo de cordel*, Porter in the street. *Mozo de mulas ó de espuelas*, Muleteer who walks at the head of his mules; feeder of mules.

Mozón, *sm.* A robust young man.

Mozuélo, la, *s. dim.* Young, youthful.

Mú, *sf.* 1. Term imposing silence to children. 2. Sleep, repose.—*sm.* Bellowing of a bull.

Mucéta, *sf.* Part of the dress worn by bishops when they are officiating.

Muchacháda, *sf.* A boyish trick.

Muchacheár, *va.* To act in a boyish or childish manner.

Muchachería, *sf.* 1. Boyish trick. 2. Clamorous noise made by a crowd of boys.

Muchachéz, *sf.* Childhood; puerility.

Muchácho, cha, *s.* Boyish, girlish; youthlike.

Muchedúmbre, *sf.* Multitude, abundance, plenty.

Múcho, cha, *a.* Much, many, abundant, plentiful. *No ha mucho*, Not long since. *No es mucho*, It is no wonder.—*ad.* Much, in a great degree; excessively.

Mucilaginóso, sa, *a.* Mucilaginous, slimy.

Mucilágo, *sm.* Mucilage, a slimy body.

Múda, *sf.* 1. Change, alteration. 2. Change of linen. 3. Paint used by women. 4. Mute letter. 5. Time of moulting or shedding feathers. 6. Roost of a hawk and other birds of prey. *Estar en muda*, To keep a profound silence in company.

Mudáble, *a.* Changeable, variable.

Mudaménte, *ad.* Silently, tacitly.

Mudánza, *sf.* 1. Alteration, change; mutation. 2. Removal from one place to another. 3. Inconstancy, levity. 4. Certain number of motions in a dance.

Mudár, *va.* 1. To change, to vary, to deviate, to remove. 2. To moult.—*vr.* 1. To change sentiments and manners. 2. To shift, to dress in fresh linen or clothes. 3. To move into another house. 4. (Fam.) To wander from the topic of conversation.

Mudéz, *sf.* Dumbness, incapacity to speak; impediment of speech.

Múdo, da, *a.* Dumb, incapable of speech; silent, still, mute.

Mué ó Muér, *sm.* Tabby, a kind of thin wove silk.

Muébles, *sm. pl.* Moveable goods, chattels.

Muéca, *sf.* Grimace, wry face.

Muéla, *sf.* 1. (In Corn-mills) Runner, the upper mill-stone. 2. Grind-stone, whet-stone. 3. Mill-dam, as much water as is sufficient to set a mill in motion. 4. Hill, hillock; a mound erected by man. 5. A kind of coarse tabby. 6. Track or circle made with any thing. *Muélas*, Grinders, the back teeth. *Muelas de gallo*, As toothless as a cock.

Muélle, *a.* 1. Tender, delicate, soft. 2. Licentious, luxurious.—*sm.* 1. Spring, an elastic body, which, when compressed, has the power of restoring itself. 2. Regulator, a small spring which regulates the movements of a watch. 3. (Naut.) Mole, pier; quay, key, wharf; a space of ground in a port or on a river for shipping and unshipping goods. 4. Gewgaw, trinket, toy.

Muelleménte, *ad.* Tenderly, gently, softly.

Muérdágo, *sm.* (Bot.) Misseltoe. Viscum album *L.*

Muermera, *sf.* (Bot.) Common virgin's bower; traveller's joy. Clematis vitalba *L.*

Muérmo, *sm.* 1. Cold and coughing, with which animals are affected. 2. Glanders, a distemper in horses, which consists in the running of a corrupt matter from the nose.

Muermóso, sa, *a.* Snoring, breathing difficultly.

Muérte, *sf.* 1. Death, the extinction of life. 2. Murder, assassination. 3. Image of mortality, represented by a skeleton. 4. Violent fatigue, severe affliction. 5. Loss of liberty and civil rights. *Bazo pena de muerte*, On pain of death. *Hasta la muerte*, Until death. *A' muerte ó á vida*, Killing or curing; blow high blow low, at all risks.

Muérto, *sm.* 1. Corpse, a dead body. 2. (Naút.) The standing part of a running rope.—*pl.* 1. Stripes, strokes, blows. 2. (Naút.) Groundways.

Muérto, ta, *a.* 1. Dead, extinguished. 2. Languid, faded; applied to spirits or colours; slaked; applied to lime.

Muésca, *sf.* 1. Notch or groove cut into the staves of casks and baskets, in which the bottoms and head-pieces are fixed. 2. An empty or void space. V. *Mella.* 3. Dove-tail scarf.

Muéso, sa, *a.* (Vulg.) V. *Nuestro.*

Muéstra, *sf.* 1. Pattern, a small piece of cloth, a specimen shown as a sample of the rest. 2. Design, model. 3. (Mil.) Muster-roll. 4. Circle on a dial containing the hours; dial, clock which does not strike. *Muestra de faltriquera*, Watch.

Múfla, *sf.* Muffle, an earthen cover placed over tests and coppels in the assaying of metals. *Muflas*, Thick winter gloves, which serve instead of a muff.

Múga, *sf.* V. *Mojon ó Termino.*

Mugér, *sf.* 1. Woman, the female of the human race. *Ser muger*, To be a woman, to have attained the age of puberty. 2. Wife. 3. An effeminate fellow, without spirit or strength. *Muger pública*, Street-walker. 4. *Muger de bigotes*, Clever commanding woman.

Mugerácha, *sf.* Large coarse woman.

Mugercílla, *sf.* A worthless woman, a prostitute.

Mugeriégo, ga, *a.* 1. Feminine, belonging to women. 2. Womanish, given to women.

Mugerniégo, *sm.* Woman-kind; the female sex of a town or place.
Mugeríl, *a.* Belonging to woman.
Mugerilménte, *ad.* Effeminately.
Mugerióna, *sf.* A lusty woman.
Mugído, *sm.* The lowing of an ox, cow, or bull.
Mugíl, *sm.* (Ict.) Mullet. Mugil cephalus *L.*
Mugír, *vn.* To low, to bellow like an ox.
Múgre, *sm.* Dirt, filth, nastiness.
Mugriénto, ta, *a.* Greasy, dirty, filthy.
Mugrón, *sm.* Sprig or shoot of a vine.
Muhárra, *sf.* The steel or iron point at the top of the pole or staff of a pair of colours.
Muíd, *sm.* A French liquid measure, equal to a hogshead.
Muír, *va.* (Arag.) To ordain.
Mujól, *sm.* V. *Mugil.*
Múla, *sf.* She-mule, a hybrid animal from the ass and mare, which is the most common kind; that from the horse and she-ass the English call hinny, the *equus asinus hinnus L.*
Muladár, *sm.* Place where the dirt and sweepings of houses are put; any thing dirty.
Mulár, *a.* Belonging to mules.
Mulatéro ó Muletéro, *sm.* Muleteer, a mule-driver; a mule-boy.
Muláto, ta, *a.* Mulatto, begotten between a white and a black; tawny.
Muléro, *sm.* Mule-boy, who takes care of mules employed for the purpose of agriculture.—*a.* Applied to a horse fond of mules.
Muléta, *sf.* 1. A young she-mule not yet trained to work. 2. Crutch, prop, support. 3. Lunch or luncheon. *Muleta de filar filastica*, (Naút.) Winch for making spun-yarn. 4. Mullar. V. *Moleta.*
Muletáda, *sf.* Herd of mules.
Muléto, *sm.* A young he-mule not yet broken in.
Mulílla, *sf.* Sort of thick-soled shoes.
Múlla, *sf.* The act of digging around vines.
Mullidór, ra, *s.* Bruiser, mollifier. V. *Muñidor.*
Mullír, *va.* 1. To beat up any thing in order to make it soft and spongy. *Mullir la cama*, To beat up the bed. 2. To call, to convene. V. *Muñir.* 3. To adopt the most proper measures for attaining one's purpose. 4. To dig around the roots of vines and trees.
Múlo, *sm.* Mule. Equus asinus mulus *L.*
Múlta, *sf.* Mulct, fine; a pecuniary penalty.
Multár, *va.* To mulct, to impose a fine or pecuniary penalty.
Multifórme, *a.* Multiform, having various shapes and appearances.
Multilátero, ra, *a.* Multilateral.
Multiplicáble, *a.* Multiplicable.
Multiplicación, *sf.* 1. Multiplication, the act of increasing any number by addition or production of more of the same kind. 2. (Aritm.) Multiplication, the increasing of any number by another, so often as there are units in that number by which the first is increased.
Multiplicadór, ra, *s.* Multiplier; multiplicator.
Multiplicár, *va.* To increase, to multiply.
Multíplice, *a.* Multiple.
Multiplicidád, *sf.* Multiplicity, a great number of the same kind; the state of being many.
Multiplíco, *sm.* Multiplication.
Multitúd, *sf.* Multitude, a great number.
Mundanalidád, *sf.* Worldliness.
Mundáno, na, *a.* Mundane, worldly; belonging to the world. *Muger mundana*, Common prostitute.
Mundificár, *va.* To mundify, to cleanse, to make clean.
Mundificatívo, va, *a.* Mundificative, cleansing.
Mundíllo, *sm.* 1. An arched frame put over braziers to dry or air linen. 2. Cushion on which bone-lace is made. 3. Warming pan.
Mundinóvi ó Mundinuévo, *sm.* Rareeshow, magic lantern.
Múndo, *sm.* 1. World, the collective idea of all bodies whatever; terrestrial sphere, globe. 2. Great multitude. 3. The manners of men; worldly desires and practices. 4. (Cant.) The face. *El nuevo mundo*, North and South America.
Munición, *sf.* Munition or ammunition, materials for war; warlike stores; charge of fire-arms. *De municion*, Done in a hurry, and consequently badly.
Municionár, *va.* To supply with ammunition or warlike stores.
Municipál, *a.* Municipal, belonging to a corporation.
Munícipe, *sm.* Citizen, denizen; member of a corporation.
Município, *sm.* Place which enjoys the rights and privileges of a city.
Munificéncia, *sf.* Munificence.
Munífico, ca, *a.* Munificent, liberal.
Munitória, *sf.* The art which teaches the fortification of places.
Muñéca, *sf.* 1. Wrist, the joint which connects the hand with the arm. 2. Doll, a little girl's puppet or baby. 3. Medicine taken in food. *Menear las muñecas*, (Met.) To work rapidly at any thing.
Muñéco, *sm.* 1. Puppet representing a male figure. 2. A soft effeminate fellow.
Muñequeár, *va.* To play with the wrist in fencing.
Muñequéra, *sf.* Bracelet, an ornament for the wrist of dolls.
Muñequería, *sf.* Excessive fondness of dress.
Muñidór, *sm.* Beadle of a corporation or confraternity; apparitor, messenger.
Muñír, *va.* To summon, to call to a meeting.
Muñón, *sm.* 1. Brawn, the musculous or fleshy part of the body. 2. Stump of an arm or leg which is cut off.
Mur, *sm.* (Ant.) V. *Raton.*
Muradál, *sm.* V. *Muladar.*
Murál, *a.* Mural, belonging to walls.
Murálla, *sf.* Rampart which surrounds a place; wall.
Murár, *va.* To wall, to surround with a rampart.
Murciégalo, Murciélago, ó Murceguíllo, *sm.* Bat, an animal with wings, but hair instead of feathers. Vespertilio *L.*
Murecíllo, *sm.* V. *Músculo.*
Muréna, *sf.* (Ict.) A kind of eel.
Muréte, *sm.* A slight wall for an aqueduct.
Múrice, *sm.* (Con.) Porcelain shell-fish.
Murmuceár, *va.* To murmur, to mutter, to utter in a low voice.
Murmúllo, *sm.* V. *Mormullo.*
Murmuración, *sf.* Backbiting, privy calumny, slander.
Murmuradór, ra, *s.* Murmurer, detractor.
Murmurár, *va.* 1. To murmur, to flow with a considerable noise; applied to streams. 2.

To grumble, to mutter. 3. To backbite, to censure an absent person.

Murmúrio, *sm.* The purling or murmuring of a stream.

Múro, *sm.* V. *Pared ó Muralla.*

Múrria, *sf.* Heaviness of the head, lowness of spirits, melancholy.

Murrína, *sf.* Ancient drink made of wine and aromatics.

Múrrio, ria, *a.* Sad, melancholy.

Múrta, *sf.* V. *Arrayan y Murton.* [Chili.

Murtílla y Murtína, *sf.* Fruit of a tree in

Murtón, *sm.* Myrtle-berry.

Murucúya, *sf.* (Bot.) Species of passion flower.

Músa, *sf.* Muse, the goddess of poetry.

Musaráña, *sf.* 1. Fetid shrew-mouse. Sorex araneus *L.* 2. Spirit, ghost, hobgoblin. 3. Any insect or small animal.

Muscicária, *sf.* (Orn.) Muscovy duck.

Muscicápa, *sf.* (Orn.) Fly-catcher. Muscicapa *L.*

Músco, *sm.* 1. Moss. 2. Musk.

Músco, ca, *a.* Chesnut colour.

Muscosidád, *sf.* Mossiness.

Musculár, *a.* Muscular, belonging to the muscles.

Músculo, *sm.* 1. Muscle, a small part of the animal body, composed of fibres and tendons. 2. Whale of a prodigious size. 3. Muscle, a small shell-fish. Mytilus edulis *L.*

Musculóso, sa, *a.* Musculous, full of muscles.

Muselína, *sf.* Muslin, fine cotton cloth.

Muséo, *sm.* 1. Museum, a place set apart for the study of the sciences and arts. 2. Repository of learned curiosities.

Museróla, *sf.* Nose-band of a bridle.

Musgáño, *sm.* 1. Shrew-mouse. V. *Musaraña.* 2. Large field spider.

Músgo, *sm.* 1. Motion of a horse when about to kick. 2. Coral, a sea-plant. 3. Moss, lichen.

Música, *sf.* 1. Music, the science of harmonical sounds. 2. Instrumental or vocal harmony. *Música de campanas,* Chimes. *Música ratonera,* Harsh music, produced by bad voices or instruments.

Musicál, *a.* Musical, belonging to music.

Músico, ca, *s.* Musician, one skilled in harmony; one who performs upon instruments of music.—*a.* Musical.

Musiquíllo, lla; to, ta, *s. dim.* of *Músico, ca.*

Musitár, *vn.* To mumble, to mutter.

Muslíllo, *sm.* A small thigh.

Múslo, *sm.* Thigh, which includes all between the buttocks and the knee. *Múslos,* Breeches. V. *Calzones.*

Musmón, *sm.* Musmon, an animal generated between a ram and a she-goat.

Musquerola, *sf.* V. *Almizcleña.*

Mustéla, *sf.* 1. (Ict.) Sea-loach, whistle-fish, five-bearded cod. Gadus mustela *L.* 2. Weasel. Mustela vulgaris *L.*

Mustiaménte, *ad.* In a sad and melancholy manner. [rica.

Mústico, *sm.* (Ent.) Long-legged insect of Af-

Mústio, tia, *a.* Parched, withered; sad, sorrowful.

Musulmán, *sm.* Mussulman.

Múta, *sf.* Pack of hounds.

Mutabilidád, *sf.* Mutability, inconstancy.

Mutación, *sf.* Mutation, changes. V. *Mudanza.*

Mutilación, *sf.* Mutilation.

Mutilár, *va.* To mutilate, to maim, to cripple.

Mutuál, *a.* Mutual, reciprocal. V. *Mutuo.*

Mutuaménte, *ad.* Mutually.

Mutuatário, *sm.* One who borrows money.

Mútuo, tua, *a.* Mutual, reciprocal; each acting in return or correspondence to the other.

Mútuo, *sm.* Loan.

Múy, *ad.* Very, a particle which, being joined to a positive adjective, converts it into a superlative one. *Muy ilustre,* Most illustrious. *Muy mucho,* Very much. *Es muy mucho de mi gusto,* It is very much to my taste. *Soy muy de vd.,* I am entirely yours. In political phraseology or connected with a negative, it is somewhat less than a superlative; as *muy ilustre* is less than *ilustrisimo,* and *no estoy muy bueno,* I am not very well.

Muyér, *sf.* (Ant.) V. *Muger.*

Múyto, ta, *a.* (Ant.) V. *Mucho.*

Múz, *sm.* (Naút.) Floor-timber.

Muzárabe *a.* V. *Mozárabe.*

N

NAB

The pronunciation of the letter *n* is the same in the Spanish as in the English language, except when it is marked with a dash, waved line, or Greek circumflex, thus ñ, which softens and converts its pronunciation into the sound of the French *ign* in *ignorant,* or of the English *nn* in *biennial.* In this case, however, the ñ is considered by the Spanish academy as a distinct character, and placed after all the other words beginning with an *n.* As it is foreign to the English alphabet, the example of the academy is necessarily followed here. *N* in Spanish stands for some proper name unknown, or not wished to be expressed; as, *N tal ó fulano,* N such a one.

Na, *art. fem.* (Ant.) V. *La.*

Nába, *sf.* (Bot.) Round-rooted turnip. Brassica rapa *L.*

Nabál ó Nabár, *sm.* Turnip-field, a piece of ground sown with turnips.—*a.* Belonging to turnips, made of turnips, pottage made of turnips.

Nabería, *sf.* Turnip pottage, or heap of turnips.

Nabíllo, *sm.* A small turnip.

Nabína, *sf.* Turnip-seed.

Nabíza, *sf.* (Bot.) Turnip-rooted cabbage Brassica napo-brassica *L.*

Nábla, *sf.* Ancient instrument of music.

Nábo, *sm.* 1. (Bot.) Rape, navew, colewort.

Brassica napus *L.* 2. Any round root. 3. Solid part of animals' tails, whence the hairs grow. 3. Mast; cylindrical timber.

Nacár, *sm.* 1. Mother of pearl. 2. Pearl-colour.

Nácara, *sf.* Button-shell, a kind of sea-cockle. Trochus *L.*

Nacarádo, da, *a.* Set with mother of pearl; of a pearl colour.

Nacarón, *sm.* Large pearl shell of inferior quality.

Nacéla, *sf.* (Arq.) Scotia, a concave moulding at the base of a column.

Nacér, *vn.* 1. To be born, to come into life. 2. To flower, to blossom. 3. To bud, to shoot. 4. To rise, to appear on the horizon. 5. To spring, to take its rise. 6. Followed by a preposition, it signifies natural propensity or destiny; as, *Nació para ser gran general,* He was born to be a great general. *Nacer de cabeza,* To be born to wretchedness. *Nacer de pies,* To be born to happiness and good luck. *No le pesa de haber nacido,* He is very proud of his merits and talents.—*vr.* To be propagated by nature, not sown, as grass.

Nacído, da, *a.* Proper, apt, fit, connate.

Nacído, *sm.* Pimple, pustule, tumour, abscess.

Nacimiénto, *sm.* 1. Birth, the act of coming into life: beginning. 2. Nativity, the coming of our Lord into the world. 3. Origin, descent; lineage. *De nacimiento,* From its birth.

Nación, *sf.* 1. Birth, issue into life. 2. Nation, a people distinguished from another people. 3. (Vulg.) Stranger. *De nacion,* Native of.

Nacionál, *a.* National, that which is peculiar to a nation.

Nacionalidád, *sf.* National manners and customs.

Nacionalménte, *ad.* Nationally.

Nácho, cha, *a.* V. *Romo ó Chato.*

Náda, *sf.* Nothing, non-existence, nothingness; nihility; little or very little. *En menos de nada ó en una nada,* In an instant.

Náda, *ad.* In no degree, by no means. *Nada menos,* Nothing less; a particular negation.

Nadadéras, *sf. pl.* Corks or bladders used to learn to swim.

Nadadéro, *sm.* Swimming-place.

Nadadór, ra, *s.* Swimmer.

Nadadóra, *sf.* Dragon-fly. Libellula *L.*

NADADU'RA, *sf.* Natation; the art of swimming.

Nadánte, *pa.* (Poét.) Natant, swimming.

Nadár, *vn.* 1. To swim, to move progressively in the water by the motion of the limbs. 2. To float on the water, not to sink. 3. To be wide or loose. *Se me nadan los pies en los zapatos,* The shoes are quite loose about my feet. 4. (Met.) To abound, to be plentiful.

Nadería, *sf.* Nothing, a trifle.

Nadi, *pron. indef.* (Ant.) V. *Nadie.*

Nádie, *sm.* Nobody, no one.

Nadír, *sm.* Nadir, the point under foot, diametrically opposite to the zenith.

Nádo, *sm.* Á *nado,* Afloat. *Poner un baxel á nado,* To set a ship afloat. *Pasó el rio á nado,* He swam across the river. *Salir á nado,* To save one's self by swimming; to effect with great difficulty and labour.

Nadrénas, *sf. pl.* Clogs, wooden shoes, worn by the common people in several countries.

Náfa, *sf.* Orange-flower water.

Náfta, *sf.* Naphtha, fluid bitumen.

Náguas, *sf. pl.* Under petticoat. V. *Enaguas.*

Nálga, *sf.* Buttock, hip, rump.

Nalgáda, *sf.* 1. Ham, the thigh of a hog salted. 2. Blow with the rump.

Nalgádo, da, *a.* Having round and fleshy posteriors.

Nalgatório, *sm.* Seat, posteriors, nates.

Nalgúdo, da, *a.* Large breech.

Nalguzár, *vn.* To shake or rock the posteriors in walking.

Namóre, *sm.* (Bot.) Tree in the kingdom of New Granada.

Nána, *sf.* (Ant.) Married woman, mother.

Nánsa, *sf.* Fish-pond.

Náo, *sf.* Ship, vessel. V. *Nave.*

Napéa, *sf.* Wood nymph.

Napélo, *sm.* (Bot.) Wolf's bane. Aconitum napellus *L.*

Narangéro, *a.* Applied to a blunderbuss with a mouth the size of an orange.

Naránja, *sf.* Orange, the fruit of the orange-tree. *Media naranja,* (Arq.) Cupola.

Naranjáda, *sf.* Conserve of oranges.

Naranjádo, da, *a.* Orange-coloured.

Naranjál, *sm.* Grove or plantation of orange-trees.

Naranjázo, *sm.* Blow with an orange.

Naranjéro, ra, *s.* 1. One who sells oranges. 2. Orange-tree.

Naranjéro, ra, *a.* Applied to pieces of artillery, which carry balls of the size of oranges.

Naránjo, *sm.* (Bot.) 1. Orange-tree. Citrus aurantium *L.* 2. Rude ignorant man.

Narcíso, *sm.* 1. (Bot.) Daffodil. Narcissus *L.* 2. Narcissus flower. 3. A precious stone of the colour of daffodil. 4. Fop, coxcomb.

Narcótico, ca, *a.* Narcotic, producing stupor or stupefaction.

Nardíno, *a.* Made of spikenard.

Nárdo, *sm.* (Bot.) Spikenard. Nardus *L.*

Naricíca, lla, ta, *sf. dim.* of *Nariz.*

Narigál, *sm.* (Joc.) Nose, the prominence on the face, containing the organ of smell.

Narigón, *sm.* A large nose, a person who has a large nose.

Narigón, na; y Narigúdo, da, *a.* Having a large and long nose.

Nariguéta ó Nariguílla, *sf.* A small nose.

Naríz, *sf.* 1. Nose; nostril. V. *Narigal. Nariz de tomate,* Copper-nose. *Caballete de la nariz,* Bridge of the nose. *Ventanas de la nariz,* Nostrils. 2. Sense of smelling. 3. The projecting point of a bridge or pier, which breaks the violence of the current. 4. (Naút.) Cut-water, break of a ship's head. *Hinchar las narices,* To be excessively irritated.

Narizádo, da, *a.* Having a large nose.

Narración, *sf.* Narration, account, relation.

Narrár, *va.* To narrate, to relate; to recite.

Narratíva, *sf.* 1. Narrative, relation, history. 2. Art or talent of relating things past.

Narratívo, va; ó Narratório, ria, *a.* Narrative.

Nárria, *sf.* 1. Sledge, a carriage without wheels. 2. Ronion, a fat, heavy, bulky woman.

Narvál, *sm.* (Ict.) Narval, sea unicorn.
Nása, *sf.* 1. A wicker or osier basket, narrow at the top and wide in the middle, for catching fish. 2. Round narrow-mouthed net.
Nasál, *a.* Nasal, relating to the nose.
Nasárdo, *sm.* One of the registers of an organ.
Náta, *sf.* 1. Cream, the unctuous or oily part of milk. 2. The main or principal part of a thing. *Nátas.* V. *Natillas.*
Natál, *a.* Natal, native.—*sm.* Birth, birth-day.
Natalício, cia, *a.* y *s.* Natal; natilitious; nativity, birth-day.
Natátil, *a.* Swimming, natatile.
Natatório, a, *a.* Relating to swimming.
Natarón, *sm.* Second curds after the first cheese is made. V. *Requeson.*
Natíllas, *sf. pl.* Composition of flour, milk, eggs, and sugar boiled together.
Natío, *sm.* Birth; sprouting; used of plants.
Natividád, *sf.* Nativity.
Nativitáte (A') (Lat.) V. *De nacimiento.*
Natívo, va, *a.* 1. Native, produced by nature; not artificial. 2. Fit, proper, apt.
Natrón, *sm.* Natron, carbonated soda, a salt used in glass-houses and founderies.
Natúra, *sf.* Nature, the native state or properties of any thing.
Naturál, *sm.* 1. Temper, genius, natural disposition. 2. Instinct, the natural disposition and propensity of brutes. 3. Native of a place or country.—*a.* 1. Natural, consonant to natural notions. 2. Produced by nature, not artificial. 3. Common, usual, regular, resembling nature. *Al natural*, Without art or affectation.
Naturaléza, *sf.* 1. Nature, the native state or property of things. 2. Aggregate, order, and disposition of all created beings. 3. Constitution of an animated body. 4. Compass of natural existence. 5. State or operation of the material world. 6. Virtue, quality of things; instinct, disposition, propensity; source; sex; privileges; complexion.
Naturalidád, *sf.* 1. State of being born in a certain place or country; birth-right. 2. Naturalness, conformity to nature and truth. 3. Ingenuity, candour.
Naturalísta, *sm.* Naturalist, one who studies and investigates the properties of created beings.
Naturalización, *sf.* Naturalization, the act of investing aliens with the rights of native subjects.
Naturalizár, *va.* To naturalize, to invest with the rights of native subjects.—*vr.* To be accustomed, to grow fit for any purpose.
Naturalménte, *ad.* Naturally; humanly.
Naucléro, *sm.* Ship-master, pilot of a ship, master of a merchantman. [to be cast away.
Naufragár, *vn.* To be stranded or shipwrecked,
Naufrágio, *sm.* 1. Shipwreck, the loss of a ship at sea. 2. Miscarriage, disappointment, calamity, heavy loss.
Náufrago, ga, *a.* Relating to shipwreck.
Naumáquia, *sf.* Naumachy, a mock sea-fight.
Náusea, *sf.* Nauseousness, squeamishness, propensity to vomit.
Nauseabundo, *a.* Producing nausea; sea-sick.
Nauseár, *vn.* To nauseate, to loathe, to reject with disgust.
Nauseatívo, va, *a.* Nauseous.
Naúta, *sm.* Mariner, a sea-faring man.
Náutica, *sf.* Navigation, the art of navigating or conducting a ship from one place to another.
Náutico, ca, *a.* Nautical.
Nautílo, *sm.* (Ict.) Nautilus, shell-fish.
Náva, *sf.* A plain or level piece of ground.
Navája, *sf.* 1. Clasp-knife, folding-knife. 2. Razor, an instrument for shaving. 3. Tusk of a wild boar. 4. Tongue of backbiters.
Navajáda ó **Navajázo**, *s.* Cut with a razor.
Navajéro, *sm.* 1. Razor-case. 2. A piece of linen on which a barber cleans his razor.
Navajíllo, *sm.* A small clasp knife.
Navájo, *sm.* 1. Pool, a small lake of standing water. 2. A level piece of ground. 3. Red circle round the sun or moon.
Navajón, *sm.* A kind of poniard in the form of a knife.
Navajonázo, *sm.* Cut with a razor-shaped knife.
Navál, *a.* Naval, consisting of ships; belonging to ships. *Armada naval*, Royal navy, royal fleet.
Navázo, *sm.* Pool. V. *Navajo.*
Náve, *sf.* 1. Ship, a vessel with decks and sails. 2. Nave, the principal part of the body of a church.
Navecílla, ca, y ta, *sf.* A small vessel. V. *Naveta.* [by ships or boats.
Navegáble, *a.* Navigable, that can be passed
Navegación, *sf.* 1. Navigation, the act or practice of passing by water. 2. Passage, time which a ship takes in going from one place to another. 3. Art of navigating.
Navegánte, *pa.* Navigator; navigating.
Navegár, *vn.* 1. To navigate, to sail, to pass by water. 2. To go from place to place for the purpose of trade and commerce. 3. (Met.) To travel.—*va.* To conduct merchandise by sea from one port to another.
Navéta, *sf.* 1. Incensory, vessel for the incense in the church. 2. Small drawer.
Navichuélo, *sm.* (Naút.) A small vessel.
Naviculár, *a.* Applied to the middle bone of the foot before the heel.
Navidád, *sf.* Nativity. V. *Nacimiento y Año. Tiene muchas navidades*, He is aged.
Navidéño, ña, *a.* Belonging to the time of nativity.
Naviéro, *sm.* Proprietor of a ship or vessel capable of navigating the high seas.
Navigación, *sf.* (Ant.) V. *Navegacion.*
Navío, *sm.* A large ship, a ship of war. *Navio guarda costa*, Guard-ship. *Navio de carga*, Ship of burthen. *Navio pesado*, A bad sailer. *Navio de tres puentes*, Three-decked ship.
Nayáde, *sf.* Naiad, water-nymph.
Nay'pe, *sm.* A rough diamond, unwrought and unpolished.
Nay'pe, *sm.* Playing-card, a piece of pasted paper painted with figures, and used for gaming.
Nay're, *sm.* Elephant-keeper.
Nazaréno, na, *a.* 1. Nazarean, native of Nazareth. 2. Nazarite, one who neither shaved the beard, cut the hair, nor drank strong drinks.—*sm.* He who goes in processions in Passion Week, dressed in a long brown robe.

Nazaréo, *a.* Nazarite; among the Jews.
Názula, *sf.* (Tol.) Second curds, after the first cheese has been made.
Ne, *conj.* (Ant.) V. *Ni.*
Nebéda, *sf.* (Bot.) Cat-mint. Nepeta cataria *L.*
Neblí, *sm.* (Orn.) Falcon gentle.
Neblína, *sf.* 1. Mist, a small rain, not perceived in drops. 2. Confusion, obscurity.
Nebrína, *sf.* Juniper-berry.
Nebulóso, sa, *a.* Misty, cloudy.
Neceár, *vn.* To talk nonsense, to play the fool.
Necedád, *sf.* Gross ignorance, stupidity; imprudence.
Necesária, *sf.* Privy, necessary, water-closet.
Necesariaménte, *ad.* Necessarily.
Necesário, ria, *a.* Necessary, indispensably requisite.
Necesidád, *sf.* Necessity, need, neediness, cogency. *La necesidad carece de ley*, Necessity has no law. *Necesidad mayor ó menor*, Evacuation of the body by stool or water.
Necesitádo, da, *a.* 1. Compelled, constrained, necessitated. 2. Necessitous, pressed with poverty.
Necesitár, *va.* To necessitate, to constrain, to compel.—*vn.* To want, to need, to stand in need of.
Neciaménte, *ad.* Ignorantly, stupidly.
Nécio, cia, *a.* 1. Ignorant, stupid. 2. Imprudent, injudicious.
Necrológio, *sm.* Necrology, mortuary, register of bishops.
Nectár, *sm.* Nectar, liquor said to be drank by the heathen deities; any drink uncommonly pleasing to the taste.
Nefandaménte, *ad.* Basely, nefariously.
Nefándo, da, *a.* Base, nefarious. *Pecado nefando*, An unnatural crime.
Nefário, ria, *a.* Nefarious, extremely wicked.
Néfas, *ad. Por fas ó por nefas*, Right or wrong.
Nefásto, *a.* Applied to days of rest among the Romans.
Nefrítico, ca, *a.* 1. Nephritic, troubled with the gravel. 2. Applied to a kind of jasper. 3. Indian wood.
Negación, *sf.* 1. Negation, the act of denying, denial. 2. Want or total privation of any thing. 3. Negative particle.
Negádo, *a.* Incapable, inapt, unfit.
Negadór, *sm.* Denier, disclaimer.
Negár, *va.* 1. To deny, to refuse. 2. To disturb, to forbid, to prohibit. 3. To forget, to disown, to disclaim. 4 To hide, to conceal. 5. To dissemble. 6. Not to perform one's duty.—*vr.* 1. To decline doing any thing. 2. To desire to be denied to persons who call to see one. *Negarse á si mismo*, To govern one's passions and appetites by law.
Negatíva, *sf.* Negation; repulse.
Negativaménte, *ad.* Negatively.
Negatívo, va, *a.* Negative, implying negation or denial.
Negligéncia, *sf.* Negligence, habit of acting carelessly.
Negligénte, *a.* Negligent, careless, heedless.
Negligenteménte, *ad.* Negligently.
Negociación, *sf.* Negotiation, treaty of business.
Negociádo, *sm.* V. *Negocio.*
Negociadór, *sm.* 1. A man of business. 2. One employed to treat with others, negotiator.
Negociánte, *sm.* Trader, dealer.
Negociár, *vn.* 1. To trade, to carry on commerce by buying and selling goods. 2. To negotiate bills of exchange; to negotiate political affairs. 3. To bribe, to suborn.
Negócio, *sm.* 1. Occupation, employment, business. 2. Affair, pretension, treaty, agency. 3. Negotiation, trade, commerce. *Fingir negocios*, To affect the man of business. 4. Utility or interest in trading.
Negocióso, sa, *a.* Diligent, prompt, careful.
Negozuélo, *sm. dim.* of *negocio.*
Négra, *sf.* Unpolished sword with a knob on the end for fencing. 2. Negress, black woman.
Negrál, *a.* Blackish.
Negreár y Negregueár, *vn.* To grow black, to appear black.
Negrecér, *vn.* To blacken, to become black.
Negreguénte, *pa.* Blackening.
Negregúra, *sf.* Blackness.
Negréta, *sf.* (Orn.) A kind of duck of a blackish colour. Anas fusca *L.*
Negrílla, *sf.* (Ict.) Kind of black fish.
Negrilléra, *sf.* Plantation of black poplar.
Negríllo, *sm.* 1. A young negro. 2. (Bot.) Black poplar. Populus nigra *L.*
Négro, gra, *a.* 1. Black. 2. Brown or grey; not well bleached. 3. Blackish; of a dark brown colour. 4. Gloomy, dismal, melancholy. 5 Unfortunate, wretched.
Négro, *sm.* Negro, a blackmoor. *Negro de la uña*, Black of the nail; (Met.) the least of any thing. *Boda de negros*, (Fam.) Any noisy rout and confusion.
Negrúra y Negrór, *s.* Blackness. V. *Negregura.*
Negrúzco, ca, *a.* Blackish, of a dark brown colour.
Neguijón, *sm.* Caries, rottenness of the teeth.
Neguílla, *sf.* 1. (Bot.) Fennel-flower. Nigella arvensis *L.* 2. (Vulg.) Obstinate denial.
Neguillón, *sm.* (Bot.) Corn-rose, campion Agrostemma githago *L.*
Néma, *sf.* Seal.
Némine discrepánte, (Lat.) Unanimously.
Nemoróso, sa, *a.* Woody, consisting of wood; relating to wood.
Néna, *sf.* A female infant, a babe.
Néne, *sm.* A male infant, a baby.
Nenufár, *sm.* (Bot.) White water-lily. Nympha alba *L.*
Neófito, *sm.* Neophyte, one regenerated, a convert.
Neografísmo, *sm.* New method of writing; contrary to the received custom.
Neoménia, *sf.* First day of new moon.
Nepóte, *sm.* Nephew. V. *Sobrino.*
Nequáquam, *ad.* (Lat.) By no means.
Nerei'da, *sf.* Nereid, fabulous nymph.
Nervíno, na, *a.* Nervous; applied to ointments for strengthening the nerves.
Nérvio, *sm.* 1. Nerve, one of the organs of sensation, passing from the brain to all parts of the body. 2. The main and most powerful part of any thing. 3. String of a musical instrument. 4. (Naút.) A small rope, the middle of which is fixed to a stay. 5. Energy, vigour.

NERVIOSIDÁD, *sf.* Nervousness.
NERVIÓSO, SA, *a.* Nervous; applied to a discourse, or the leaves of plants.
NERVOSAMÉNTE, *ad.* Nervously.
NERVOSIDÁD, *sf.* Strength, nervousness; efficacy, vigour; flexibility, tenacity.
NERVÓSO, SA, *a.* 1. Nervous, having strong or weak nerves. 2. Strong, vigorous, robust.
NERVÚDO, DA, *a.* Having strong nerves.
NESCIÉNCIA, *sf.* Ignorance, want of knowledge.
NESCIÉNTE, *a.* Ignorant, foolish.
NÉSGA, *sf.* Goar, a triangular piece of linen or other stuff sewed upon cloth.
NÉSPERA, *sf.* (Bot.) Medlar, a fruit.
NETEZUÉLO, *sm.* A little grand-child.
NÉTO, TA, *a.* Neat, pure, clean, unadulterated; without any foreign mixture. *Producto neto,* Neat produce. *En neto,* Purely. *Peso neto,* Net weight.
NÉTO, *sm.* (Arq.) Naked pedestal of a column.
NEURÍSMA, *sf.* V. *Aneurisma.*
NEURÍTICO, CA, *a.* Strengthening the nerves; applied to herbs.
NEUROLOGÍA, *sf.* Neurology, a description of the nerves.
NEUTRÁL, *a.* Neutral, indifferent; not engaged on either side.
NEUTRALIDÁD, *sf.* 1. Neutrality, a state of indifference. 2. Neutrality, state of peace with belligerent nations.
NEUTRALIZÁR, *va.* (Quim.) To neutralize.
NÉUTRO, TRA, *a.* 1. Neutral, neuter; not engaged on either side. 2. (Gram.) A noun that implies no sex; a verb that is neither active nor passive.
NEVÁDA, *sf.* A heavy fall of snow.
NEVADÍLLA, *sf.* (Bot.) Whitlow-wort. Illecebrum paronychia *L.*
NEVÁDO, *a.* White as snow.
NEVÁR, *vn.* To snow; to fall in snow.—*va.* To make white as snow.
NEVÁSCA ó NEVÍSCA, *sf.* Fall of snow.
NEVATÍLLA, *sf.* (Orn.) Wag-tail. V. *Aguzanieve.*
NEVÁZO, *sm.* Great fall of snow.
NEVÉRA, *sf.* Ice-house; cold cellar.
NEVERÍTA, *sf.* V. *Aguzanieve.*
NEVERÍA, *sf.* Ice-house, a place where ice is sold.
NEVÉRO, RA, *s.* One who sells ice.
NEVISCÁR, *vn.* To ice, to congeal a beverage; to snow.
NEVÓSO, SA, *a.* Snowy, abounding with snow.
NÉXO, *sm.* Knot, string, union.
NI, *conj.* Neither, nor.
NIÁRA, *sf.* Rick or pile of straw.
NICERÓSINO, *a.* Applied to a precious ointment used by the ancients.
NÍCHO, *sm.* 1. NICHE, a hollow in a wall in which a statue is or may be placed. 2. Employ, station.
NÍCLE, *sf.* Species of agate.
NICOCIÁNA, *sf.* Tobacco, so called from Nicot, French ambassador in Portugal in 1560.
NICTALÓPE, *sm.* Nyctalope, one who sees best at night.
NIDÁDA, *sf.* Nest full of eggs, on which a hen sits; brood, covey, nide.
NIDÁL, *sm.* 1. Nest, a place where a hen or other bird lays her eggs. 2. Nest-egg, an egg left in the nest. 3. Basis, foundation, motive. 4. Haunt, a place much frequented by a person.
NIDIFICÁR, *vn.* To nest, to build nests.
NÍDO, *sm.* 1. Nest, the bed formed by the bird for incubation. 2. Any place where animals are produced. 3. Habitation, abode, place of residence. *Nido de ladrones,* Nest of thieves.
NIÉBLA, *sf.* 1. Fog, mist. 2. Disease of the eyes, which dims the sight. 3. Mildew which blasts corn and fruit. 4. Cloud formed on the surface of urine. 5. Mental obscurity, confusion of ideas.
NIÉGO, *a.* V. *Halcon.*
NIÉL, *sm.* Embossment, relief; rising work.
NIELÁR, *va.* To form with protuberance, to carve in relief or rising work on plate; to engrave, to enamel.
NIERVECÍCO, TO, LLO, *sm.* A small nerve.
NIÉSPERA, *sf.* (Bot.) Medlar, a fruit.
NIETECÍTO, TA; LLO, LLA; CO, CA, *s.* A little grandson or daughter.
NIÉTO, TA, *s.* 1. Grandson, grand-daughter. 2. Descendant.
NIÉTRO, *sm.* (Arag.) A wine-measure, containing sixteen *cantaras.*
NIÉVE, *sf.* 1. Snow, small particles of water frozen before they unite into drops. 2. Fall of snow. 3. Extreme whiteness.
NIGROMÁNCIA, *sf.* Necromancy.
NIGROMÁNTE, *sm.* Necromancer, conjurer.
NÍGUA, *sf.* Chigoe, an insect found at Vera Cruz and other parts of America, which lodges between the skin and flesh. Pulex penetrans *L.*
NIMIAMÉNTE, *ad.* Excessively.
NIMIEDÁD, *sf.* 1. Superfluity, excess; extravagant nicety. 2. Penury, poverty, indigence.
NÍMIO, MIA, *a.* Excessive.
NÍN, *conj.* (Ant.) V. *Ni.*
NÍNFA, *sf.* Nymph; a young lady.
NINFÉA, *sf.* (Bot.) Water-lily. Nymphæa *L.*
NÍNFO, *sm.* A beau, a young effeminate fop.
NINGÚN, *a.* None, not one; used before nouns. *De ningun modo,* In no manner.
NINGÚNO, NA, *a.* None, not one.
NINI NANA, Words without meaning for humming a tune.
NÍÑA, *sf.* Pupil, apple of the eye. *Niña de los ojos,* Darling.
NIÑÁDA, *sf.* Puerility, a childish speech or action.
NIÑÁTO, *sm.* Calf found in the belly of a cow which has been killed.
NIÑEÁR, *vn.* To act like a child, to behave in a childish manner.
NIÑÉRA, *sf.* Servant-maid employed to take care of children.
NIÑERÍA, *sf.* 1. Puerility, childish action. 2. Bauble, gewgaw, plaything. 3. Trifle, a thing of no moment.
NIÑÉRO, RA, *s.* One who is fond of children, or who delights in childish tricks.
NIÑÉTA, *sf.* The small pupil of the eye.
NIÑÉZ, *sf.* 1. Childhood, infancy. 2. Beginning, commencement.
NIÑÍLLA ó NIÑÍTA, *sf.* Babe, infant.
NÍÑO, ÑA, *a.* Childish, not yet seven years old; puerile.—*s.* 1. Child, infant. 2. Person of little experience or prudence. *Desde niño,* From infancy, from a child.

Niñuélos, *sm. pl.* Plaited ropes made of sedge, to join mats of bass.
Nióto, *sm.* (Ict.) V. *Cazon.*
Niquiscócio, *sm.* Trifle, a thing of little moment.
Níspero, *sm.* (Bot.) Medlar tree. Mespilus germanica *L.*
Nispóla, *sf.* Fruit of the medlar.
Nítido, da, *a.* (Poét.) Bright, shining, lustrous.
Níto, *sm.* A jet black horse. *Nitos,* Insignificant word, meaning nothing in reply to an impertinent question, or to conceal any thing.
Nitrál, *sm.* Place where nitre is formed.
Nitrería, *sf.* Saltpetre work, where saltpetre is prepared and refined.
Nítrico, *a.* Nitric, applied to acid; consisting of nitre.
Nítro, *sm.* Nitre, saltpetre; a crystalline, pellucid, and whitish salt, of a cold, acrid, and bitterish taste; nitrate of potash.
Nitróso, sa, *a.* Nitrous, impregnated with nitre.
Nivél, *sm.* 1. Level, instrument for ascertaining the level of a surface. 2. Level, a plane or surface without protuberances or inequalities. *A' nivel,* Perfectly level, in a line or row.
Nivelár, *va.* 1. To ascertain the level of a surface. 2. To make even, to level. 3. To observe equity and justice.
No, *ad.* No, or not. *No importa nada,* It signifies nothing. *Decir de no,* To give a flat denial. *No sino,* Not only so. *No sino no,* It cannot be otherwise. *Pues no,* But no, not so. *No se que,* I know not what, an inexplicable something.
Nobiliário, *sm.* A genealogical account of the peerage of a country.
Nóble, *a.* 1. Noble, of noble extraction. 2. Illustrious, eminent, conspicuous. 3. Honourable, respectable. *Estado noble,* Nobility.
Noblemente, *ad.* Nobly, generously.
Noblézá, *sf.* 1. Nobleness, splendour of descent. 2. Nobility; excellency. 3. Fine damask silk.
Nóche, *sf.* 1. Night, the time of darkness; the time from sun-set to sun-rise. 2. Obscurity, confusion. 3. (Poét.) Death. *Noche buena,* Christmas eve. *Noche toledana,* A restless night. *A' noche ó ayer noche,* Last night. *Noche y dia,* Night and day, always.
Nochebuéno, *sm.* 1. A large cake. 2. A large log of wood put into the fire on Christmas eve.
Nochiélo, la, *a.* Darkish, of a dark colour.
Nochízo, *sm.* (Bot.) Hazel-nut tree. Corylus avillana *L.*
Nocimiénto, *sm.* (Ant.) Injury, arrogance.
Noción, *sf.* 1. Notion, idea. 2. Acceptation, meaning of a word.
Nocionál, *a.* Notional.
Nocír, *va.* To hurt, to do mischief.
Nocívo, va, *a.* Noxious, hurtful, mischievous.
Noctámbulo, *sm.* Noctambulo, noctambulist, one who walks in his sleep.
Noctíluca, *sf.* Glow-worm. V. *Luciérnaga.*
Noctívago, ga, *a.* Running about at night.
Nocturnál, *a.* Nocturnal, nightly; done or doing by night.
Nocturnáncia, *sf.* The dead time of the night.
Noctúrno, na, *a.* 1. Nocturnal, nightly. 2. Lonely, melancholy, mournful. *Ave nocturna,* Night-bird, such as owls.—*sm.* 1. Vesper, the evening star. 2. Part of the matin service.

Nodación, *sf.* Nodation, the action of making knots, or obstructions in the nerves.
Nódo, *sm.* 1. Node, a morbid swelling on the bone. 2. Knot. 3. (Astr.) Node.
Nodríza, *sf.* Nurse, a woman that has the care of another's child.
Nogáda, *sf.* Sauce made of pounded walnuts and spice.
Nogál, *sm.* (Bot.) Wood of the walnut-tree.
Nogueña, *sf.* Flower or blossom of a walnut-tree.
Noguéra, *sf.* (Bot.) Walnut-tree. Juglans regia *L.*
Nogueráda, da, *a.* Of a walnut colour.
Noguerál, *sm.* Plantation of walnut-trees.
Nolición, *sf.* Nolition, unwillingness.
Nolimetángere, *sm.* A malignant ulcer growing on the face or nose.
Nombradaménte, *ad.* Namely, expressly.
Nombradía, *sf.* V. *Nombre.*
Nombradór, *sm.* Nominator, appointer.
Nombramiénto, *sm.* 1. Nomination, the act of naming or mentioning by name. 2. Appointment, commission.
Nombrár, *va.* 1. To name, to mention by name. 2. To nominate, to appoint.
Nómbre, *sm.* 1. Name, the discriminative appellation of an individual; title. *Nombre de bautismo,* Christian name. 2. Fame, reputation, credit. 3. Nick-name, a name given in scoff or contempt. *Poner nombres á uno,* To call one names. 4. Watch-word. 5. (Gram.) Noun, one of the parts of speech. 6. Power by which any one acts for another.
Nomenclatór, *sm.* Nomenclator.
Nomenclatúra, *sf.* Nomenclature, dictionary.
Nómina, *sf.* 1. Catalogue, an alphabetical list of things or persons. 2. Ancient relic of saints.
Nominación, *sf.* 1. Nomination, the act of mentioning by name. 2. Power of presenting to a benefice.
Nominadór, ra, *s.* Nominator.
Nominál, *a.* Nominal, belonging to a name; relating to names rather than things.
Nominár, *va.* To name. V. *Nombrar.*
Nominatívo, *sm.* (Gram.) Nominative, the case that primarily designates the name of any thing. *Nominativos,* Elements, rudiments.
Nómino, *sm.* Individual, possessing the necessary qualities for being appointed to a public office.
Nomocánon, *sm.* Collection of imperial constitutions and of canons.
Nón, *ad.* (Ant.) V. *No.*—*a.* Odd, uneven.
Nón, *sm.* An odd or uneven number. *Quedar de non,* To be or remain quite alone. *Andar de nones,* To be idle, to have nothing to do. *Estar de non,* To serve for nothing.
Nóna, *sf.* None, last of the minor canonical hours, answering to 3 o'clock P. M.
Nonáda, *sf.* Trifle, little or nothing.
Nonadílla, *sf. Dim.* of *Nonada.*
Nonagenário, ria, *a.* Ninety years old.
Nonagésimo, ma, *a.* Ninetieth.
Nonagonál, *a.* Enneagonal, nine-sided.
Nonagón, *sm.* Nonagon.
Nóno, na, *a.* Ninth. V. *Noveno.*
Non plus ultra, (Lat.) 1. Nonpareil. 2. (Impr.) Pearl; name of a kind of small printing type.
Noña, *sf.* Hypocritical nun. V. *Beata.*

Nosteria, *sf.* V. *Bosteria.*
No obstánte, *ad.* Nevertheless, notwithstanding.
Nopál, *sm.* (Bot.) Nopal, cochineal fig-tree, prickly Indian pear-tree. Cactus opuntia *L.* It is vulgarly called in Castile *higuera chumba.*
Nóque, *sm.* 1. A tanning pit or vat in which the ooze is kept for tanning hides. 2. Heap or basket with bruised olives.
Noquéro, *sm.* Currier, leather-dresser.
Norabuéna, *sf.* Congratulation. V. *Enhorabuena.*
Noramála, *sf.* A term of contempt or displeasure. V. *Enhoramala.*
Nórd, *sm.* (Naút.) North wind.
Nordést ó Nordéste, *sm.* North-east. *Nordéste quarto al Norte*, North-east by North. *Nordéste quarto al Este*, North-east by East.
Nordesteár, *vn.* To be North-easting.
Nordóvest ó Noruéste, *sm.* North-west.
Nordovesteár, *vn.* To decline to North-west.
Nória, *sf.* 1. Engine or wheel for drawing water out of a well. 2. Draw-well, a deep well out of which water is drawn by a long rope. 3. Affair or business in which, with a great deal of trouble, but little progress is made.
Noriál, *a.* Belonging or relating to wells.
Nórma, *sf.* 1. Square, a rule or instrument by which workmen form or measure their angles. 2. Model, standard; that by which any thing is measured.
Nornordéste, *sm.* (Naút.) North-north-east.
Noroesteár, *vn.* V. *Nordestear.*
Nórte, *sm.* 1. North, the arctic pole. 2. North, the northern part of the sphere. 3. Rule, law, guide.
Norteár, *va.* (Naút.) To steer or stand to the Northward.
Noruéste, *sm.* North-west.
Noruesteár, *vn.* To decline to the North-west; applied to the magnetic needle.
Nós, *pron.* We; chiefly used in the regal style.
Nosología, *sf.* Nosology, doctrine of diseases.
Nosótros, **tras**, *pron.* We ourselves.
Nostalgía, *sf.* Nostalgia, inordinate desire to return to one's native country.
Nóta, *sf.* 1. Note, mark, token, memorandum. *Notas*, Minutes of proceedings taken by a notary. 2. Explanatory annotation; something added to the text. 3. Censure, critique; reproach, stigma. 4. Style, manner of writing. *Autor de nota*, Author of repute. 5. Musical character.
Notáble, *a.* Notable, remarkable; very great.
Notáble, *sm.* Introductory observation.
Notableménte, *ad.* Notably.
Notár, *va.* 1. To note, to mark. 2. To remark, to observe. 3. To take short notes on a subject. 4. To comment, to expound; to criticise; to reprehend. 5. To dictate what another may write.
Notaría, *sf.* 1. Employment or profession of a notary. 2. A notary's office, the place where business is transacted by a notary.
Notariáto, *sm.* Title of a notary.
Notário, *sm.* 1. Notary, an officer whose business is to take notes of protests and other transactions, to draw and pass public instruments, and to attest and legalize private dealings and writings. 2. Amanuensis.
Notícia, *sf.* 1. Notice, knowledge, information. 2. News. *Noticias alegres*, Glad tidings.
Noticiár, *va.* To give notice, to communicate intelligence.
Noticióso, **sa**, *a.* Informed, learned, instructed.
Notificación, *sf.* Notification, judicial intimation.
Notificádo, **da**, *a.* Notified, intimated to a person.
Notificár, *va.* To notify, to make known, to intimate; to inform.
Nóto, **ta**, *a.* 1. Known, notorious. *En noto*, Knowingly. 2. Illegitimate, unlawfully begotten; not born in wedlock. *Terciana nota*, An irregular ague.
Nóto, *sm.* South wind.
Notoriaménte, *ad.* Notoriously, manifestly.
Notoriedád, *sf.* Notoriety, public knowledge.
Notório, **ria**, *a.* Notorious, publicly known.
Novación, *sf.* Renovation.
Novál, *a.* Newly broken up and converted into arable ground; applied to land.
Novár, *va.* To renew an obligation formerly contracted.
Nováto, **ta**, *a.* (Joc.) New, commencing in any thing.
Novatór, *sm.* Innovator, an introducer of novelties.
Novecién tos, **tas**, *a.* Nine hundred.
Novedád, *sf.* 1. Novelty, a new state of things. 2. Admiration excited by novelties.
Novél, *a.* New, unexperienced.
Novéla, *sf.* 1. Novel, a fictitious story. 2. Falsehood, fiction. 3. (For.) Any new law added to the Justinian codes.
Noveladór, *sm.* Novelist, a writer of novels.
Novelár, *vn.* To compose, write, or publish novels.
Novelería, *sf.* 1. Narration of fictitious stories. 2. Taste for novels and novelties.
Noveléro, **ra**, *a.* 1. Fond of novels and fictitious tales. 2. Inconstant, wavering, unsteady.
Novéna, *sf.* 1. Term of nine days appropriated to some special worship. 2. Offering for the dead.
Novenário, *sm.* Novenary, or nine days' condolence for the deceased, or in the worship of some saint.
Novendiál, *a.* Applied to any day of the novenary, or worship offered for the souls of the faithful.
Novéno, **na**, *a.* Ninth, the ordinal number of nine.
Novéno, *sm.* One of the nine parts into which tithes are divided.
Novénta, *sm.* Ninety.
Nóvia, *sf.* 1. Bride, a woman newly married. 2. Woman betrothed or bound by a promise of marriage.
Noviciádo, *sm.* 1. Novitiate, the time spent in a religious house by way of trial before the vow is taken. 2. House or apartment in which novices live. 3. Novitiate, the time in which the rudiments of a science or art are learned.
Novício, *sm.* 1. Novice, one who has entered a religious house but not yet taken the vow. 2. Novice, a fresh man.
Novício, **cia**, *a.* Probationary, novitiate.
Novicióte, *sm.* (Joc.) An overgrown novice, old and big in size.
Noviémbre, *sm.* November.

Novílla, *sf.* Cow between three and six years of age.
Novilláda, *sf.* 1. Drove of young bulls or bullocks. 2. Fight of young bulls or bullocks.
Novillejo, ja, *s.* A young bull, a heifer.
Novilléro, *sm.* 1. Stable in which young cattle are kept. 2. Herd, who attends young cattle. 3. Piece of pasture-ground where calves are put, separate from other cattle, to be weaned. 4. Truant, idler.
Novíllo, *sm.* 1. A young bull or ox. 2. (Joc.) Cuckold. *Hacer novillos*, To play truant.
Novilúnio, *sm.* New moon.
Nóvio, *sm.* 1. Bridegroom. 2. A man betrothed to a woman.
Novísimo, ma, *a.* Newest, most recent; last in the order of things.—*sm.* Each one of the 4 last incidents of mankind, death, judgment, heaven, and hell.
Nóxa, *sf.* Damage, hurt. V. *Daño.*
Nubáda y Nubarráda, *sf.* 1. Shower of rain. 2. Plenty, abundance.
Nubarrádo, da; y Nubádo, da, *a.* Clouded, figured like clouds; applied to cloth.
Nubarrón, *sm.* A heavy shower of rain, a large cloud.
Núbe, *sf.* 1. Cloud, a dense collection of vapours in the air. 2. Any thing that spreads wide so as to interrupt the view. 3. Film, a thin pellicle which obstructs the sight; a disease. 4. Cloud or shade in precious stones.
Nubecílla, ca, ta, *sf.* A small cloud.
Nubládo, *sm.* 1. A large cloud. 2. Perturbation of the mind; dread or fear of an impending danger.—*a.* Cloudy.
Nublár ó Nublárse, *va.* y *r.* V. *Anublar.*
Núblo, bla, *a.* Cloudy. V. *Nublado.*
Nublóso, sa, ó Nubiloso, sa, *a.* 1. Cloudy, dark, overcast. 2. Gloomy, ill-fated.
Núca, *sf.* Nape, the joint of the neck behind.
Núcleo, *sm.* Kernel of a nut.
Nudaménte, *ad.* V. *Desnudamente.*
Nudíllo, *sm.* 1. Knuckle, the joint of the fingers protuberant when the fingers close. 2. Note or billet folded up as a knot. 3. (Arq.) Wooden butment to roofing timbers.
Núdo, da, *a.* Naked. V. *Desnudo.*
Núdo, *sm.* 1. Knot, a complication of a cord or string not easily to be disentangled. 2. Knot or joint of plants. 3. Joint in animal bodies. 4. Tie, union, bond of association. 5. Impotence produced by charm or witchcraft. 6. Intricacy, difficulty. 7. (Naút.) Seaman's knot. 8. *Nudos del cordel de la corredera*, (Naút.) Knots of the log-line. *Echamos doce nudos por hora*, We run twelve knots an hour. *Nudo gordiano*, Insuperable difficulty.
Nudóso, sa, *a.* Knotty, full of knots.
Nuégados, *sm. pl.* A sort of paste.
Nuéra, *sf.* Daughter-in-law.
Nuéso, sa, *a.* (Vulg.) V. *Nuestro.*
Nuestrámo, *sf.* (Vulg.) Our master, contracted for *nuestro amo.*
Nuéstro, tra, *a.* Our, pertaining, belonging to us. *Nuestros*, Being of the same party or profession as the speaker.
Nuéva, *sf.* News, fresh account of any thing.
Nuevaménte, *ad.* Newly, recently.
Nuéve, *sm.* Nine, card with nine marks.—*a.* Nine.
Nuévo, va, *a.* 1. New, not old; recently made. *Nuevo flamante*, Spick and span, quite new. 2. Recently arrived in a country or place. 3. Renovated, repaired. 4. Unexperienced, not habituated. 5. Beginning. *De nuévo*, Anew, recently, of late. *¿ Que hay de nuevo ?* Are there any news?
Nuéz, *sf.* 1. Walnut, the fruit of the walnut-tree. 2. Fruit of some trees of the shape of a nut. 3. Adam's apple, the prominent part of the throat. *Apretar á uno la nuez*, (Vulg.) To strangle one. 4. Plummet. 5. *Nuez moscada ó de especia*, (Bot.) Nutmeg. Myristica aromatica *L.* *Nuez metela*, (Bot.) Thorn-apple. Datura metel *L.* *Nuez vomica*, (Bot.) Nux vomica. Strychnos nux vomica *L.*
Nuéza, *sf.* (Bot.) Briony. Bryonia *L.*
Nugatório, ria, *a.* Nugatory, futile, deceitful.
Nulaménte, *ad.* Invalidly, ineffectually.
Nulidád, *sf.* 1. Nullity, defect. 2. Defeasance, a condition annexed to an act or deed, which when performed by the obligee, renders the act or deed void.
Núlo, la, *a.* Null, void of effect.
Númen, *sm.* 1. Divinity, deity. 2. Genius, talent.
Numerábla, *a.* Numerable.
Numeración, *sf.* Numeration, the act or art of numbering; first part of arithmetic.
Numeradór, *sm.* 1. Numerator, he who numbers. 2. Numerator, the number which serves as a common measure to others.
Numerál, *a.* Numeral, relating to numbers.
Numerár, *va.* 1. To number, to enumerate. 2. To page, to mark the pages of a book. 3. To number, to reckon as one of the same kind.
Numerário, ria, *a.* Numerary, belonging to a certain number.—*sm.* Hard cash, coin.
Numericaménte, *ad.* Individually, numerically.
Numérico, ca, *a.* Numerical, individual, numeral; denoting number.
Número, *sm.* 1. Number, an aggregate of units. 2. Character, cipher or figure, which denotes the number. 3. Multitude. 4. Harmony, proportions calculated by numbers. 5. (Gram.) Variation or change of termination in words to signify any number more than one. *Sin número*, Numberless, without number; innumerable. 6. Determinate number of persons of any company or society. *Académico del número*, One of the appointed number of Spanish academicians. *Números*, Numbers, one of the books of the Pentateuch. 7. Verse, consisting of a certain number of syllables.
Numerosaménte, *ad.* Numerously.
Numerosidád, *sf.* Numerosity, numerousness.
Numeróso, sa, *a.* 1. Numerous, containing many. 2. Harmonious, melodious; consisting of parts rightly numbered.
Numísma, *sf.* Coin, money. V. *Moneda.*
Numismática, *sf.* Science of medals.
Numismático, ca, *a.* Numismatical.
Numismatografía, *sf.* Description of ancient medals.
Númo, *sm.* Money, coin, formerly worth ten maravedies.
Numulária, *sf.* (Bot.) Money-wort. Lysimachia numularia *L.*
Numulário, *sm.* Commerce or trade in money.
Núnca, *ad.* Never, at no time. *Nunca jamas*, Never, never.

Nunciatúra, *sf.* Nunciature, the office or house of a nuncio.

Núncio, *sm.* 1. Messenger. 2. Envoy or ambassador from the pope to the Roman catholic princes. 3. Madhouse in Toledo.

Nuncupatívo, va, *a.* Nuncupative, nominal; verbally pronounced.

Nuncupatório, ria, *a.* Nuncupatory.

Nupciál, *a.* Nuptial, pertaining to marriage.

Núpcias, *sf. pl.* Nuptials, wedding. V. *Boda.*

Núsco, *pron.* (Ant.) We, ourselves. V. *Nosotros.*

Nutación, *sf.* 1. Direction of plants towards the sun. 2. (Astr.) Nutation, movement of the earth's axis, by which it inclines more or less to the plane of the ecliptic.

Nútria y Nútra, *sf.* Otter. Mustela lutra *L.*

Nutrício, cia, *a.* Nutritious, nourishing.

Nutrición, *sf.* 1. Nutrition, the act or quality of nourishing. 2. Preparation of medicines.

Nutrimentál, *a.* Nutrimental, having the quality of food.

Nutriménto, *sm.* Nutriment, food, aliment.

Nutrír, *va.* 1. To nourish, to increase or support by food. 2. To support, to encourage.

Nutritívo, va, *a.* Nutritive, nourishing.

Nutríz, *sf.* Nurse.

Ñ is the 17th letter in the Spanish alphabet. The ancient Spanish writers used nn in words derived from the Latin having *gn*, as from *lignum* was written *lenno*, and now *leño*, the *n* with a *tilde*, or circumflex, being substituted in their place.

Ñagáza, *sf.* Bird-call, a decoy. V. *Añagaza.*

Ñáque, *sm.* Heap of useless trifles.

Ñiquiñáque, An expression, used by the vulgar, of no precise meaning but to depreciate any thing.

Ñóclos, *sm. pl.* A kind of macaroons, or round sweetmeat, made of flour, butter, sugar, eggs, and aniseed.

Ñóño, ña, *a.* Decrepit, having the intellect impaired by age.

Ñóra, *sf.* (Mur.) V. *Noria.*

Ñubládo, *sm.* V. *Nublado.*

Ñublár, *va.* V. *Nublar.*

Ñúblo, *sm.* V. *Nublo.*

Ñudíllo, *sm.* V. *Nudillo.*

Ñúdo, *sm.* V. *Nudo.*

Ñudóso, sa, *a.* V. *Nudoso.*

OBE OBI

O IS the eighteenth letter in the Spanish alphabet, *ch*, *ll*, and *ñ*, being considered distinct characters. *O*, in arithmetic, serves for nought or cipher; it is also used as a circle, of which there is no end, and therefore emblematic of eternity. *O*, in sea-charts, signifies West. The seven anthems sung in the church, the seven days before the nativity of our Lord, are called *OO*, because they all commence with this letter. Likewise, *nuestra Señora de la O*, our lady of the O, is so called from the exclamations of the holy men expecting the advent of the Messiah.

O' *conj.* Or, either. *O'rico ó pobre*, Either rich or poor. When followed by another *o* the conjunction *ú* is used to avoid cacophony, as *siete ú ocho*, seven or eight.

O. *ad.* (Ant.) V. *De.*

O' *interj.* *O' quiera Dios*, God grant. *¡O' que hermosa casa!* Oh! what a fine house. *¡O' ruin hombre!* Oh, you wretch! *O'* (Naút.) Ho! *O', el navio*, (Naút.) Ho, the ship!

Obcecádo, da, *a.* Blind.

Obcecár, *va.* To blind, to make blind, to darken or obscure.

Obduración, *sf.* Hardness of heart, obstinacy.

Obedecedór, ra, *s.* One who obeys or submits.

Obedecér, *va.* To obey, to pay submission to, to yield to.

Obedeciniénto, *sm.* Obedience, obsequiousness.

Obediéncia, *sf.* 1. Obedience, submission to authority. 2. Precept of a superior. 3. Pliancy, flexibility. 4. Docility in animals. 5. Permission or license to a monk or friar from his superior to preach or travel. *A' la obediencia*, At your service, your most obedient.

Obedienciál, *a.* Obediential, according to the rules of obedience.

Obediénte, *a.* Obedient. *Navio obediente al timon*, (Naút.) Ship which answers the helm readily.

Obedienteménte, *ad.* Obediently.

Obelísco, *sm.* 1. Obelisk, a high piece of marble or stone, having usually four faces and lessening upwards by degrees. 2. A mark or reference in the margin of a book in the form of a dagger †.

Obélo, *sm.* Obelisk. V. *Obelisco.*

Obencadúra, *sf.* (Naút.) A complete set of shrouds; shrouds in general.

Obénques, *sm. pl.* Shrouds, thick ropes which extend from the mast-heads down to the deck, where they are fastened by chains to the ship's sides, both on the larboard and starboard side, and serve to support the masts, and enable them to carry the sails.

Obertúra, *sf.* (Mús.) Overture.

Obesidád, *sf.* Obesity, morbid fatness.

Obéso, sa, *a.* Obese, fat; loaden with flesh.

O'bice, *sm.* Obstacle, impediment.

Obispádo, *sm.* Bishoprick; prelacy.

Obispál, *a.* Episcopal, belonging to a bishop.

Obispalía, *sf.* Palace of a bishop; bishoprick.

Obispár, *vn.* 1. To be made a bishop, to obtain a bishoprick. 2. To die, to expire. 3. To be disappointed.

Obispíllo, *sm.* 1. Boy-bishop; a chorister boy dressed like a bishop on the feast of St. Nicholas of Bari or of Myra, and allowed to imitate a bishop during that festival. This custom still exists in Coruña and other cities in Spain, and formerly prevailed in Salisbury. 2. A little bishop, a title which the students in universities by way of ridicule give to new comers. 3. A large black pudding; a pork or beef sausage. 4. Rump of a fowl.

Obíspo, *sm.* Bishop. *Obispo de anillo ó titulo,* Bishop in *partibus*, suffragan bishop.

Objeción, *sf.* Objection, opposition.

Objetár, *va.* To object, to oppose, to present in opposition.

Objetivaménte, *ad.* Objectively.

Objetívo, va, *a.* Belonging to the object, presented as an object.

Objéto, *sm.* 1. Object, that which any power or faculty is employed to attain. 2. Something presented to the senses to occasion any emotion in the mind. 3. End, object, design.

Oblación, *sf.* Oblation, offering.

Obláda, *sf.* Funeral offering of bread for the souls of the deceased.

Oblapié, *sf.* The act of hauling a ship or barge along with ropes.

Obláta, *sf.* 1. Sum of money given to the church to defray the expense of bread, wine, candles, &c. for celebrating mass. 2. Host and chalice offered before being consecrated in the celebration of the mass. *Incensar la oblata,* To give incense to the offering.

OBLA'TO, *sm.* Invalided soldier maintained in a royal religious establishment.

Obléa, *sf.* Wafer, paste made to close letters.

Oblería, *sf.* Art of making wafers.

Obléro, *sm.* One who sells or cries wafers about the streets.

Obliér, *sm.* Confectioner, who provides wafers or thin cakes, rolled up in tubes, for the royal family of Spain.

Obligación, *sf.* 1. Obligation, the binding power of any contract or agreement. 2. Notarial instrument or deed. 3. Favour by which one is bound to gratitude. 4. Contract, to provide a city or other place with provisions. 5. Provision-office, the place where provisions are sold, pursuant to a previous contract.—*pl.* 1. Talents and other accomplishments which render a man respectable and worthy of universal esteem. *Es hombre de obligaciones,* He is a man of strict integrity and honour. 2. Family which one is obliged to maintain. *Está cargado de obligaciones,* He has a large family to support.

Obligádo, *sm.* Contractor who engages to supply a city with provisions.

Obligánte, *pa.* Obligating, imposing.

Obligár, *va.* 1. To oblige, to impose obligation. 2. To confer favours, to lay obligations of gratitude.

Obligatório, ria, *a.* Obligatory, imposing an obligation; binding, coercive.

Obliquaménte, *ad.* Obliquely.

Obliqüidád, *sf.* Obliquity, deviation from physical rectitude.

Oblíqüo, qüa, *a.* Oblique, not direct, not perpendicular, not parallel.

Oblóngo, ga, *a.* Oblong, longer than broad.

Obnóxio, xia, *a.* Obnoxious, hurtful.

Oboé, *sm.* 1. Hautboy or oboe, a musical wind instrument. 2. Player on the hautboy.

O'bolo, *sm.* 1. Obolus, Athenian money. 2. Obole, a weight of 12 grains.

O'bra, *sf.* 1. Work, any thing made. 2. Writings of an author. 3. Means, virtue, power. 4. Toil, labour, employment. 5. Action, feat, deed. *Obra de arte mayor,* Masterly piece of work. *Poner por obra,* To set on work. 6. Works, acts, with regard to their religious character. *Obras,* Works. *Obras de marea,* (Naút.) Graving, calking, and paying a ship's bottom. *Obras muertas,* (Naút.) Upperworks, the part of a ship which is above the surface of the water. *Obras vivas,* (Naút.) Quick or lower works, the part of a ship which is under the surface of the water when loaded. *Obra de ó á obra de,* Nearly, about, more or less.

Obráda, *sf.* As much ground as two mules or oxen can plough in a day.

Obradór, ra, *s.* 1. Work man or woman, artificer, mechanic. 2. Work-shop. *Obradores,* (Naút.) Work-shop or working places in a dock-yard.

Obradúra, *sf.* That which is expressed at every press-full in oilmills.

Obráge, *sm.* 1. Manufacture, any thing made by art. 2. Manufactory, work-shop.

Obragéro, *sm.* 1. Foreman, overseer, who overlooks the other workmen. 2. Quarter-man in a dock-yard.

Obrár, *va.* 1. To work, to manufacture. 2. To operate, to produce the desired effect; applied to medicines. 3. To put into practice, to execute; to construct, to edify. 4. To ease nature.

Obrepción, *sf.* Obreption, false narration to obtain some end.

Obrepticiaménte, *ad.* Falsely, deceitfully.

Obreptício, cia, *a.* Obreptitious, obtained by a false statement of matters of fact, deceit, or surprise.

Obrería, *sf.* 1. Task of a workman. 2. Money destined for the repairs of a church.

Obréro, ra, *s.* 1. Worker, day-labourer. 2. Missionary. 3. Prebendary who superintends the repairs of church buildings. 4. Person who collects money for the building of churches.

Obrílla, *sf.* Small or little work.

Obrízo, za, *a.* Pure, refined; applied to gold.

Obscenaménte, *ad.* Obscenely.

Obscenidád, *sf.* Obscenity, impurity of thought or language, unchastity, lewdness.

Obscéno, na, *a.* Obscene, impure, lewd.

Obscuraménte, *ad.* Obscurely, confusedly, indecently.

Obscúras (A'), *ad.* Obscurely, darkly.

Obscurecér, *va.* 1. To obscure, to darken, to deprive of light. 2. To impair the splendour and lustre of things. 3. To denigrate. 4. To render a subject less intelligible by extravagant ideas and pedantic language. 5. (Pint.) To use deep shades.—*v. impers.* To grow dark.—*vr.* To disappear, to be lost.

Obscurecimiénto, *sm.* The act of darkening or rendering obscure.

Obscuridád, *sf.* 1. Obscurity, darkness; opacity, density. 2. Meanness of extraction. 3. Want of knowledge or understanding, confusedness, difficulty of comprehension.

Obscúro, ra, *a.* 1. Obscure, dark, unintelligible, gloomy, indistinct, confused. 2. (Pint.) Dark, deep, heavy. *Andar á obscuras ó á escuras,* (Met.) To grope in the dark, to proceed in a business without knowing its nature or first principles.

Obsecración, *sf.* Obsecration, entreaty, supplication.

Obseqüénte, *a.* Obsequious, obedient.

OBSEQUIÁNTE, *pa.* Obsequious; courtier, gallant.
OBSEQUIÁR, *a.* To court, to wait upon, to serve, to obey.
OBSÉQUIAS, *sf. pl.* OBSEQUIES. V. *Exequias.*
OBSÉQUIO, *sm.* Obsequiousness.
OBSEQUIOSAMÉNTE, *ad.* Obsequiously.
OBSEQUIÓSO, SA, *a.* Obsequious, obedient, compliant.
OBSERVACIÓN, *sf.* 1. Observation, the act of observing; remark or thing observed. 2. Observance, careful obedience.
OBSERVADÓR, RA, *s.* 1. Observer, observator, close remarker; astronomer. 2. Observer, one who keeps any law, custom, or practice.
OBSERVÁNCIA, *sf.* 1. Observance, respect, ceremonial reverence, obedient regard. 2. Attentive practice, careful obedience. 3. The original or primitive state of some religious orders in contradistinction to their reformed condition. *Poner en observancia,* To execute punctually whatever is ordered.
OBSERVÁNTE, *sm.* 1. Monk of certain branches of the order of St. Francis.—*pa.* OBSERVANT, exact.
OBSERVANTEMÉNTE, *ad.* Observingly.
OBSERVÁR, *va.* 1. To observe, to regard attentively. 2. To obey, to execute an order with punctuality and exactness. *Observar la altura,* (Naút.) To take the meridian altitude. 3. (Astr.) To observe the stars.
OBSERVATÓRIO, *sm.* Observatory, a place built for astronomical observations.
OBSESIÓN, *sf.* Obsession, the first attack of Satan previous to possession.
OBSÉSO, SA, *a.* Beset, tempted; applied to persons with evil spirits.
OBSIDIÁNA, *sf.* Obsidian stone.
OBSIDIONÁL, *a.* Obsidional, belonging to a siege.
OBSISTÉNTE, *a.* Resonant, resounding; applied to a wall or building.
OBSOLÉTO, TA, *a.* Obsolete, out of use, disused.
OBSTÁCULO, *sm.* Obstacle, impediment, obstruction.
OBSTÁNCIA, *sf.* V. *Objecion.*
OBSTÁNTE, *pa.* Withstanding. V. *No obstante.*
OBSTÁR, *vn.* To oppose, to obstruct, to hinder, to impede, to withstand.
OBSTINACIÓN, *sf.* Obstinacy, stubbornness, obduracy.
OBSTINADAMÉNTE, *ad.* Obstinately.
OBSTINÁDO, DA, *a.* Obstinate, obdurate, hard of heart.
OBSTINÁRSE, *vr.* To be obstinate, to persist in an opinion with stubborn perseverance.
OBSTRUCCIÓN, *sf.* (Med.) Obstruction, stoppage in the vessels of the animal body.
OBSTRUÍR, *va.* To obstruct or block up the natural passages of the animal body.—*vr.* To be blocked up; applied to an opening or aperture.
OBTENCIÓN, *sf.* Attainment, the act of attaining or obtaining any thing.
OBTENÉR, *va.* 1. To attain, to obtain. 2. To preserve, to maintain.
OBTÉNTO, *sm.* Benefice, prebend, living.
OBTENTÓR, *sm.* One who obtains a living on being ordained priest.
OBTESTACIÓN, *sf.* Obtestation, supplication, entreaty, menace.
OBTUSÁNGULO, *a.* Obtuse angled.
OBTÚSO, SA, *a.* Obtuse, blunt, not pointed; not shrill.
OBUÉ, *sm.* Hautboy; player on the hautboy.
OBÚS, *sm.* Howitzer, a kind of mortar mounted on a field-carriage, and used for firing shells and grape-shot at a small degree of elevation.
OBVENCIÓN, *sf.* A casual profit.
OBVENTÍCIO, CIA, *a.* Casual, accidental, happening by chance.
OBVIÁR, *va.* To obviate, to prevent.—*vn.* To oppose.
O'BVIO, VIA, *a.* Obvious, evident, easily discovered.
OBYÉCTO, TA, *a.* (Met.) Interposed.
OBYÉCTO, *sm.* V. *Objecion ó Réplica.*
O'CA, *sf.* 1. (Orn.) Goose. (Anas anser *L.*) 2. (Bot.) A sweet edible root of Peru. 3. Kind of game called royal goose.
OCÁL, *sm.* 1. Pod or cone of silk formed by two silk-worms together. 2. A coarse sort of silk. —*a.* Applied to very delicate sweet pears and other fruits.
OCALZÁR, *vn.* To make pods; applied to silk-worms.
OCASIÓN, *sf.* 1. Occasion, opportunity; season, juncture. 2. Cause, motive. 3. Danger, risk. *Ponerse en ocasion,* To expose one's self to danger; to put or lead one into jeopardy. *Asir la ocasion por la melena ó por los cabellos,* (Fam.) To take time by the firelock.
OCASIONÁDO, DA, *a.* Provoking, vexatious, insolent; perilous.
OCASIONÁL, *a.* Occasional.
OCASIONALMÉNTE, *ad.* Occasionally.
OCASIONÁR, *va.* 1. To cause, to occasion; to move, to excite. 2. To endanger, to expose to risk or hazard.
OCÁSO, *sm.* 1. Occident, the west. 2. Death.
OCCIDENTÁL, *a.* Occidental, western.
OCCIDÉNTE, *sm.* Occident, the west.
OCCIPITÁL, *a.* Occipital, placed in the hinder part of the head.
OCCIPÚCIO, *sm.* Occiput.
OCCISIÓN, *sf.* Occision, murder, act of killing.
OCCÍSO, SA, *a.* Murdered, killed. *Tañer de occiso,* To blow the bugle horn indicating the death of the game.
OCEÁNO, *sm.* 1. Ocean, the main, the great sea. 2. Any vast expanse.
OCHÁVA, *sf.* The eighth part of any thing.
OCHAVÁDO, DA, *a.* Octagonal, eight-sided.
OCHAVÁR, *va.* To form an octagon, or a figure consisting of eight sides and angles.
OCHAVEÁR, *vn.* To be divided into eighths.
OCHÁVO, *sm.* 1. A small Spanish brass coin, value two maravedies or half a quarto. 2. Any thing octagonal.
OCHÉNTA, *a.* Eighty.
OCHENTAÑÁL, *a.* Having 80 years.
OCHENTÓN, NA, *a.* Eighty years old.
O'CHO, *sm.* y *a.* 1. Eight, the number of four multiplied by two; eight, the figure. 2. (Sevilla) The fourth part of a pint of wine.
OCHOCIÉNTOS, *a.* Eight hundred.
OCHOSÉN, *sm.* The smallest coin among the ancient Spaniards.
OCIÁR, *va.* To disturb one in the performance of a business in which he is engaged.—*vn.* To loiter, to spend time carelessly.
O'CIO, *sm.* 1. Leisure, freedom from business; vacancy of mind. 2. Pastime, diversion, amusement.

Ociosaménte, ad. Idly, uselessly.
Ociosidád, sf. Idleness, the act of wasting time in a useless manner; state of being idle.
Ocióso, sa, a. Idle, vacant; fruitless, unprofitable.
Oclocracía, sf. Ochlocracy, plebeian government.
Ocozoál, sm. Mexican serpent.
Ocozól, sm. (Bot.) American tree which produces the liquid amber.
O'cre, sm. Ochre, a brown or yellow ferruginous earth.
Ocróto, sm. V. Onocrótalo.
Octaédro, sm. Octahedron.
Octagonál, a. Octagonal.
Octágono, na, a. Having eight sides and angles.—sm. Octagon, a figure consisting of eight sides and angles.
Octánte, sm. Octant, an instrument containing the eighth part of a circle, or 45 degrees.
Octáva, sf. 1. Octave, a space of eight days after a festival celebrated by the Roman Catholic church in honour of some saint. 2. (Mús.) Octave, interval of eight sounds.
Octavár, vn. To form octaves on stringed instruments; to deduct the eighth part.
Octavário, sm. Festival continued eight days.
Octavílla, sf. 1. Half pint for excise taken on the retail of vinegar, oil, and wine. 2. (Mús.) Octave.
Octávo, sm. 1. Eighth, each of the eighth parts into which a whole is divided. 2. Octavo volume, a book the sheets whereof are folded into eight leaves.
Octocentésimo, a. Eight hundredth.
Octogenário, ria, a. Octagenary, eighty years old.
Octogésimo, a. Eightieth.
Octosilábico, ca; y Octosílabo, ba, a. Consisting of eight syllables.
Octúbre, sm. October, the eighth month of the year.
Oculár, a. Ocular, depending on the eye; known by the eye. *Testigo ocular*, Eye-witness. *Dientes oculares*, Eye-teeth.—sm. Eye-glass.
Ocularménte, ad. Ocularly, to the observation of the eye.
Oculísta, sm. Oculist, one who professes to cure distempers of the eyes.
Ocultación, sf. The act of hiding or concealing.
Ocultaménte, ad. Secretly, hiddenly.
Ocultár, va. To hide, to conceal, to disguise, to remove out of sight; to keep secret.
Ocúlto, ta, a. Hidden, concealed. *De oculto*, Incog, incognito. *En oculto*, Secretly, in secret.
Ocupación, sf. Occupation; business; employment, office.
Ocupáda, sf. V. Preñada.
Ocupadór, sm. Occupier, possessor; one who takes into his possession.
Ocupánte, sm. An actual possessor of lands.
Ocupár, va. 1. To occupy, to take possession of. 2. To hold an employ, to fill a public station. 3. To employ, to give employment. 4. To disturb, to interrupt, to obstruct. 5. To inhabit a house. 6. (Met.) To occupy or gain the attention.
Ocurréncia, sf. 1. Occurrence, accident, incident. *Ocurrencia de acreedores*, Meeting of creditors to divide the debtor's effects. 2. Idea which occurs to the mind.
Ocurrénte, pa. Occurring; obvious.
Ocurrír, vn. 1. To meet, to go to meet, to anticipate. 2. To occur, to happen on the same day. 3. To obviate, to make opposition to. 4. To repair, to proceed.—v. impers. To occur, to be present to the memory.
Ocúrso, sm. Concourse or meeting of different persons or things in the same place.
O'da, sf. Ode, a poem written to be set to music; a lyric poem.
Odiár, va. To hate, to abhor, to detest.—vr. To render one's self odious and hateful.
O'dio, sm. Hatred, abhorrence, detestation.
Odióso, sa, a. Odious, hateful, detestable.
Odómetro, sm. Instrument for measuring the road passed over.
Odontálgico, sm. Remedy for the tooth-ache.
Odorábile, a. Odorous, odorate.
Odoratísimo, ma, a. Very fragrant or odoriferous.
Odoráto, sm. Smell, odour. V. *Olfato*.
Odorífero, ra, a. Odoriferous, fragrant, perfumed.
O'dre, sm. 1. Bag very generally used for wine, oil, and other liquids; it is commonly made of an entire dressed hog-skin, the body uncut, the legs sewed up, the neck forming a mouth, the hairs turned inside and covered with pitch; a leather bottle lined with pitch. 2. (Joc.) Drunkard.
Odrecíllo, sm. A small leathern or hog-skin bag for wine and other liquors.
Odrería, sf. Shop where leather bottles are made or sold.
Odréro, sm. One who makes or deals in leather bottles.
Odrezuélo, sm. A little leathern bottle or flask.
Odrína, sf. 1. (Met.) Drunkard. 2. Ox-skin bag.
Oedicnémo, sm. (Orn.) Stone-curlew.
Oénas, sf. Stock-dove, wood-pigeon.
Oenánte, sf. (Orn.) Fallow finch, stone-chatter.
Oesnoruéste, sm. West-north-west.
Oéste, sm. 1. West wind. 2. Point where the sun sets at the equinoxes. *Oeste quarta á Norte*, West by north. *Oeste quarta al Sur*, West by south. *Oeste Sudeste*, y *Oesudueste*, West-south-west.
Ofendedór, ra, s. V. *Ofensor*.
Ofendér, va. To offend, to injure, to make angry.—vr. To be vexed or displeased; to take offence. *Offenderse del ayre*, To be of an irritable disposition.
Ofénsa, sf. Offence, injury, transgression, crime.
Ofensión, sf. Offence, grievance; injury.
Ofensivaménte, ad. Offensively, injuriously.
Ofensívo, va, a. 1. Offensive, displeasing, disgusting. 2. Assailant, not defensive. 3. Offensive; applied to arms.
Ofensívo, sm. Any thing which serves as a defence or remedy.
Ofensór, ra; y Ofensadór, ra, s. Offender, one who injures or offends another.
Oferénte, sm. Offerer, one who offers.
Oférta, sf. Offer, promise; gift, offering.
Ofertório, sm. Offertory, the act of offering; the thing offered; the part of the mass where

the priest, before the consecration, offers up the host and wine.

Oficiál, *sm.* 1. Workman, artificer, tradesman, clever journeyman. 2. Officer who holds a commission in the army or navy. 3. Clerk in a public office. 4. Hangman, executioner. 5. Butcher, one who cuts up and retails meat. 6. Magistrate. *Oficial de la sala,* Actuary in criminal causes. *Oficial general de mar,* (Naút.) Flag-officer. *Oficiales de la mayoría,* Adjutants. *Oficiales del ministerio de la marina,* Civil officers of the navy. *Es buen oficial,* He is a clever workman.

Oficiála, *sf.* She who is occupied at work or business, workwoman.

Oficialázo, *sm.* A skilful workman.

Oficialéjo, *sm.* A petty workman.

Oficialiá, *sf.* 1. Clerk's place in a public office. 2. Artist's working-room.

Oficialidád, *sf.* Body of officers of an army.

Oficiár, *va.* To officiate, to assist in the celebration of the mass.

Oficina, *sf.* 1. Work-shop. 2. Office, counting-house, business-room. *Oficinas,* Offices, the lower apartments in houses, such as cellars.

Oficinál, *a.* Officinal, applied to the drugs prepared by apothecaries.

Oficinísta, *sm.* Shop-keeper, druggist.

Oficio, *sm.* 1. Office, employ, work. 2. Function, operation; official letter. 3. Trade, business. 4. Notary's office. 5. Benefit, service. *Correr bien el oficio,* To make the most of a place or office. *De oficio,* Officially, by duty, not in consequence of any application or request. *Mozo de oficio,* An under-servant in the king's palace. *Tener oficio,* To be rotten; spoken of spoiled olives. *Tomarlo por oficio,* To do a thing frequently. *Oficio de boca ó de la boca,* Purveyor to the king. *Oficios,* Solemn church offices.

Oficionário, *sm.* Book containing the canonical offices.

Oficiosidád, *sf.* 1. Diligence, application to business. 2. Officiousness.

Oficióso, sa, *a.* Officious, diligent, attentive to business. *Mentira oficiosa,* Falsehood, useful to some, and injurious to none.

Ofrecedór, *sm.* Offerer.

Ofrecér, *va.* 1. To offer, to make an offer. 2. To present, 3. To exhibit, to manifest. 4. To dedicate. to consecrate. 5. To go to drink in a tavern.—*vr.* To offer, to occur, to present itself.

Ofrecimiénto, *sm.* 1. Offer, promise, offering. 2. Occurrence, incident. 3. Extemporary discourse.

Ofrénda, *sf.* Offering, oblation.

Ofrendár, *va.* 1. To present offerings to God. 2. To contribute towards some end or purpose.

Oftálmia y Oftálmia, *sf.* Ophthalmy, a disease of the eyes.

Oftálmico, *a.* Ophthalmic.

Ofuscamiénto y Ofuscación, *s.* Offuscation, dimness of the sight; confused reason.

Ofuscár, *va.* To offuscate, to darken, to render obscure. *Ofuscarse la razon ó el entendimiénto,* To disturb the mind, to confuse the judgment.

Oído, da, *pp.* Heard. *De oidas ó por oidas,* By hearsay.

Oído, *sm.* 1. Hearing, the sense by which sounds are perceived. 2. Ear, organ of hearing. 3. Ear, power of judging of harmony. 4. Vent of a piece of ordnance. *Está sordo de un oido,* He is deaf of one ear. *Dos dedos del oido,* Clearly, distinctly, freely. *Lisonjear el oido,* To tickle the ear. *Negar los oidos,* To refuse a hearing. *Hablar al oido,* To whisper into one's ear.

Oidór, *sm.* 1. Hearer, one who hears. 2. Judge.

Oidoría, *sf.* Office or dignity of a judge.

Oír, *va.* 1. To hear, to perceive by the ear. *Oir campanadas y no saber donde,* To hear without understanding. 2. To understand, to comprehend. 3. To assist at the lectures on some science or art, in order to study it. *Oir misa,* To assist at or hear mass. *Oyes, ú oye vd.* I say, do you hear? *Oyga se, ú oygámosnos,* Silence, attention. *Oyga, ú oygan,* Exclamation of surprise. *Oye, Oye,* Hear! Hear!

Ojál, *sm.* 1. Buttonhole, the loop in which the button of clothes is caught. 2. Hole through any thing.

Ojaladéra, *sf.* A woman whose profession is to work buttonholes.

Ojaladúra, *sf.* The whole of the buttonholes in a suit of clothes.

Ojalár, *va.* To make buttonholes.

Ojánco, *sm.* V. *Ciclope.*

Ojeáda, *sf.* Glance, glimpse, sudden cast of the eye; transitory view.

Ojeadór, *sm.* One who rouses or starts the game for the chase.

Ojeadúra, *sf.* Act of glazing clothes.

Ojeár, *va.* 1. To eye, to view, to look with attention. 2. To rouse or start the game.

Ojéra, *sf.* Blueish circle under the lower eyelid, indicative of indisposition.

Ojeríza, *sf.* Spite, grudge, ill-will.

Ojerúdo, da; y Ojeróso, sa, *a.* Applied to persons with blackish circles under the eyes.

Ojéto, *sm.* 1. Eyelet hole in clothes. 2. Anus.

Ojeteádo, da, *a.* Perforated by eyelet holes.

Ojeteár, *va.* To make round eyelet holes in clothes.

Ojetéra, *sf.* Piece of whalebone sewed near the eyelet holes in clothes.

Ojialégre, *a.* Having lively sparkling eyes.

Ojienxúto, ta, *a.* Dry-eyed; applied to those who do not shed tears.

Ojimoréno, na, *a.* Brown-eyed.

Ojinégro, gra, *a.* Black-eyed.

Ojizárco, ca, *a.* Blue or grey-eyed.

Ojizáyno, na, *a.* Squint-eyed, having the sight directed oblique.

O'jo, *sm.* 1. Eye, the organ of vision. 2. Sight, ocular knowledge. 3. Eye of a needle. 4. Any small perforation formed like an eye. 5. Head formed on liquors; drop of oil or grease which swims on liquors. *Ojo de gallo,* Red sparkling wine. 6. Arch of a bridge. 7. Channel of a mill, through which the water falls on the wheel. 8. Care, attention, observation, notice. 9. Lather, froth made by beating soap with water. 10. Marginal note, formed of two oo with a stroke across them. 11. Anus, the orifice of the fundament. 12.

Mesh, the space between the threads of a net. 13. Eye or hollow in bread or cheese. 14. Expression of ardent affection or endearment. *Abrir tanto ojo*, To stare with joy. *A' cierra ojos, ó á ojos cerrados*, Without hesitation; at all events. *Al ojo*, At sight, at hand; by the bulk or lump. *A' sus ojos*, In his presence, before his eyes. *A' ojos vistos*, Apparently, publicly; barefacedly. *Ojos de bitoque*, Goggle eyes. *Avivar el ojo* To be on one's guard. *Ojo alerta*, Look sharp. *Costar un ojo*, To be excessively dear. *Escalera de ojo*, A circular or winding staircase. *Tener sangre en el ojo*, To be prompt and honourable in fulfilling engagements. *Hacer ojo*, To overbalance, to outweigh. *Mal de ojo*, Fascination, enchantment. *De medio ojo*, Lurkingly, concealedly. *Ojo de buey*, (Bot.) Ox-eye; (Fam.) Doubloon of 8 dollars.

Ojóta, *sf.* A kind of shoe worn by Indian women.

Ojuélo, *sm.* A small eye.—*pl.* 1. Sparkling eyes, smiling eyes. 2. Spectacles.

O'la, *sf.* 1. Wave, water raised above the level of the surface. 2. A sudden violent commotion.

O'la, *interj.* Holla!

Olágе, *sm.* Succession of waves.

Oleáda, *sf.* 1. Surge, swell of the sea. 2. A plentiful produce of oil. 3. Violent emotion.

Oleaginosidád, *sf.* Oleaginousness, oiliness.

Oleaginóso, sa, *a.* Oleaginous, oily.

Oleár, *va.* To administer the last unction; to anoint a dying person with oil.

Oleário, ria, *a.* Oily.

Oleástro, *sm.* V. *Acebuche.*

Oleáza, *sf.* (Arag.) The watery dregs which remain in the mill after the oil has been extracted.

Olecránon, *sm.* Eminence behind the elbow to prevent the arm from bending backwards.

Oledéro, ra, *a.* Odorous, emitting a fragrant odour.

Oledór, ra, *s.* 1. Smeller, he who smells. 2. Smelling bottle.

O'leo, *sm.* 1. Oil. V. *Aceyte. Al oleo*, In oil colours. 2. Extreme unction; the holy oil; act of anointing.

Oleomiél, *sm.* Oil of the consistence of honey.

Oleóso, sa, *a.* Oily. V. *Aceytoso.*

Olér, *vn.* 1. To smell, to emit a fragrant odour. *Huele á herege*, He smells of heresy, he appears or has traits of a heretic. *Olió á petardo*, It savoured of imposition or fraud. *Huelele el pescuezo á cañamo*, The neck savours of the halter, to be at the point of being hanged. *No oler bien alguna cosa*, (Met.) To be a suspicious thing.—*va.* 1. To perceive a smell or odour. 2. To investigate, to scent or search out, to discover.

Olfateár, *va.* To smell, to scent; to perceive colours.

Olfáto, *sm.* 1. Smell, the sense, the organ of which is the nose; odour. 2. Scent, chase followed by the smell.

Olfatório, ria, *a.* Olfactory.

Oliénte, *pa.* Smelling, odorous, emitting a smell.

Oliéra, *sf.* Vessel in which the holy oil is kept.

Oligarquía, *sf.* Oligarchy, a form of government which consigns the supreme power into the hands of a few persons.

Oligárquico, ca, *a.* Oligarchical.

Olimpiáda, *sf.* Olympiad, period of four years.

Olímpico, ca, *a.* Olympic.

Olímpo, *sm.* Height, eminence.

O'lio, *sm.* Oil. V. *Oleo. Al olio*, In oil.

Oliscár, *va.* 1. To smell, to scent; to perceive by the nose. 2. To investigate, to ascertain.—*vn.* To stink.

Olíva, *sf.* Olive, the fruit of the olive-tree. 2. Owl. V. *Lechuza.* 3. Olive-tree. V. *Olivo.*

Olivár, *sm.* Plantation of olive-trees.

Olivárda, *sf.* (Bot.) Flea bane. Erigeron glutinosum *L.*

Olivardílla, *sf.* (Bot.) Groundsel. Senecio solidaginoides *L.*

Olivárse, *vr.* To form bubbles; applied to bread, the dough of which had cooled too much before it was put into the oven.

Olivástro de Rodas, *sm.* (Bot.) Rosewood, a kind of wood full of yellow and black veins.

Olivéra, *sf.* Olive-tree. V. *Olivo.*

Olivífero, ra, *a.* (Poét.) Producing olives.

Olivílla, *sf.* (Bot.) Widow-wail. Cneorum tricoccon *L.*

Olívo, *sm.* (Bot.) Olive-tree. Olea *L.*

O'lla, *sf.* 1. A round earthen pot. 2. Dish of boiled or stewed meat. 3. (Met.) Stomach. 4. Any gulf of seas or rivers in which are whirlpools; a whirlpool. *Olla ciega.* V. *Alcancia. Olla carnicera*, Boiler, a kettle in which large pieces of meat may be boiled. *Olla fetida*, (Art.) Stink-pot, an earthen shell charged with combustible materials, emitting a suffocating smell. *Olla podrida*, Dish composed of different sorts of meat boiled together. *Olla de campaña*, Copper vessel with a cover for carrying dressed meat.

Olláos, *sm. pl.* (Naut.) Eyelet holes, round holes made in the sails. *Ollaos de los rizes*, Reef-eyelet holes.

Olláza, *sf.* A large pot or boiler.

Ollázo, *sm.* Blow with a pitcher.

Olléjo, *sm.* Peel, rind. V. *Hollejo.*

Ollería, *sf.* Pottery, a shop where earthenware is sold.

Olléro, *sm.* 1. Potter, one who makes pots and other earthen-ware. 2. Dealer in earthenware.

Ollíca, Ollílla, ó Olluéla, *sf.* Pipkin, a small pot.

Olluéla, *sf.* Pit or hollow under the Adam's apple.

Olnéda y Olnído, *s.* Elm-grove, a plantation of elm-trees.

Olmedáno, na, *a.* Native of Olmedo.

O'lmo, *sf.* (Bot.) Elm-tree. Ulmus *L.*

Olór, *sm.* 1. Odour, fragrant smell, sweet scent. 2. Stink, stench, an offensive smell. 3. Hope, promise, offer. 4. Cause or motive of suspicion. 5. (Met.) Fame, reputation. *Agua de olor*, Sweet-scented water.

Olorcíllo, ca, to, *sm.* A slight smell.

Oloróso, sa, *a.* Odoriferous, fragrant.

Olvidadízo, za, *a.* Short of memory, forgetful.

Olvidádo, da, *a.* Forgotten.

Olvidár, *va.* To forget, to neglect, to omit.

Olvído, *sm.* Forgetfulness, carelessness, heedlessness; oblivion. *Echar al olvido ó en olvido*, To forget designedly; to cast in oblivion.

O'MBLA, *sf.* (Ict.) Crow-fish. Sciæna umbra *L.*

OMBLIGÁDA, *sf.* Part corresponding to the navel, in skins.

OMBLÍGO, *sm.* 1. Centre or middle of a thing. 2. Navel-string. 3. Navel, the point in the middle of the belly by which embryos communicate with the parent. *Ombligo de Venus*, Venus navel-wort. Cynoglossum lusitanicum *L.*

OMBLIGUÉRO, *sm.* Bandage put upon the navel of new-born children.

OMBRÍA, *sf.* Shade, place secluded from the sun.

OMÉGA, *sf.* Last letter in the Greek alphabet.

OMENTÁL, *a.* Belonging to the omentum.

OMÉNTO, *sm.* Omentum, the caul or reticular covering of the bowels.

O'MICRON, *sm.* Name of the Greek short O.

OMINÁR, *va.* To ominate, to foretoken; to show prognostics.

OMINÓSO, SA, *a.* Ominous, exhibiting bad tokens of futurity; forboding ill.

OMISIÓN, *sf.* Omission, carelessness, neglect.

OMÍSO, SA, *a.* Neglectful, amiss.

OMITÍR, *va.* To omit, to pass over in silence, to neglect.

OMNIMODAMÉNTE, *ad.* Entirely, by all means.

OMNÍMODO, DA, *a.* Entire, total.

OMNIPOTÉNCIA, *sf.* Omnipotence.

OMNIPOTÉNTE, *a.* Omnipotent, almighty.

OMNIPOTENTEMÉNTE, *ad.* Omnipotently.

OMNISCÍO, IA, *a.* Omniscient.

OMOPLÁTOS, *sm. pl.* The two shoulder plates.

O'NAGRA, *sf.* A warlike engine, used by the ancients to throw stones.

ONÁGRO, *sm.* Wild ass, the skin of which is made into shagreen.

O'NCE, *sm.* y *a.* Eleven; figure eleven. *Estar á las once*, (Vulg.) To be on one side; applied to clothes.

ONCEÁR, *va.* To weigh out by ounces.

ONCEJÉRA Y ONCIJÉRA, *sf.* A kind of small snare or net for catching birds.

ONCÉJO, *sm.* (Arag.) String, band.

ONCÉNO, NA, *a.* Eleventh, the ordinal number of eleven. *El onceno no estorbar*, Obstruct not industrious persons at their business.

O'NDA, *sf.* 1. Wave, a quantity of water raised above the level of the rest. 2. Reverberation of light. 3. Fluctuation, agitation, danger. 4. Sling. V. *Honda.*

O'NDE, *conj.* (Ant.) Wherefore.—*ad.* (Ant.) V. *Donde.*

ONDEÁDO, *a.* Undulated.—*sm.* Any thing in waves.

ONDEÁR, *va.* 1. To undulate, to play as waves in curls; to form waves. 2. To fluctuate.—*vr.* To float backwards and forwards, to move with a reciprocating motion; to seesaw.

ONERÓSO, SA, *a.* Burthensome, troublesome.

ONFACÍNO, NA, *a.* Extracted from green olives; applied to oil.

ONFACOMÉLI, *sm.* Oxymel made of honey and the juice of unripe grapes.

ONIROCRÁCIA, *sf.* Pretended art of explaining dreams.

ONÍQUE Y ONÍX, *sf.* Onyx, a precious stone.

ONOBRÍQUE, *sf.* (Bot.) Sainfoin.

ONOCRÓTALO, *sm.* (Orn.) White pelican. Pelecanus onocrotalus *L.*

ONOMANCÍA, *sf.* Onomancy.

ONOQUÍLES, *sf.* (Bot.) Yellow alkanet.

ONÓSMA, *sf.* (Bot.) Stone bugloss.

ONOTÁURO, *sm.* Jumart, an animal produced between a bull and a mare.

ONTOLOGÍA, *sf.* Ontology, science of being.

O'NZA, *sf.* 1. Weight, the twelfth part of a pound, troy weight, or 16th of a Castilian pound. 2. Ounce, one of the parts into which a pound is divided. 3. Twelfth part of a Roman foot. 4. Ounce. Felis uncia *L.* *Por onzas*, With a sparing hand.

ONZÁVO, VA, *a.* Eleventh.—*sm.* Eleventh part.

OPACAMÉNTE, *ad.* Obscurely, darkly.

OPACIDÁD, *sf.* Opacity, cloudiness, want of transparency.

OPÁCO, CA, *a.* 1. Opacous, opaque; not transparent. 2. Melancholy, gloomy.

O'PALO, *sm.* Opal, precious stone.

OPCIÓN, *sf.* Option, choice; power of choosing.

O'PERA, *sf.* 1. Any tedious and intricate work. 2. Opera, a drama represented by vocal and instrumental music.

OPERÁBLE, *a.* Capable of operating.

OPERACIÓN, *sf.* 1. The act of exerting or exercising some power or faculty; operation; cutting or opening the body. 2. Result or effect of medicines. 3. A chemical process. *Operaciones*, Works, deeds, actions.

OPERADÓR, *sm.* Surgical operator.

OPERÁNTE, TA, *s.* Operator.

OPERÁR, *vn.* 1. To operate, to act, to have agency; to produce effects.

OPERÁRIO, *sm.* 1. Operator, labourer. 2. Friar who assists sick or dying persons.

OPERATÍVO, VA, *a.* Operative.

OPERÍSTA, *s. com.* Operator, performer, executor.

OPERÓSO, SA, *a.* Laborious, requiring labour; not easy.

OPIÁDO, DA, *a.* Opiate, narcotic.

OPIÁTA, *sf.* Opiate, a medicine that causes sleep.

OPIÁTO, TA, *a.* y *s.* Opiate, narcotic.

OPÍFICE, *sm.* Workman, artificer, artist.

OPILACIÓN, *sf.* Oppilation, obstruction of the vessels of the body.

OPILÁR, *va.* To oppilate, to obstruct.

OPILATÍVO, VA, *a.* Obstructive.

OPÍMACO, *sm.* Ophymachus, kind of lizard supposed to fight with serpents.

O'PIMO, MA, *a.* Rich, fruitful, abundant.

OPINÁBLE, *a.* Disputable, problematical.

OPINÁNTE, *pa.* Arguer; opinionated.

OPINÁR, *vn.* To argue, to judge, to form an opinion.

OPINATÍVO, VA, *a.* Opinionative.

OPINIÓN, *sf.* 1. Opinion, persuasion of the mind, judgment. 2. Reputation, character. *Andar en opiniones*, To render any one's credit doubtful. *Hacer opinion*, To form an opinion, to be a man whose opinion is an authority.

OPINIONCÍTA, LLA, *sf.* Opinion founded on very slight grounds.

O'PIO, *sm.* Opium, the juice of poppies.

OPÍPARO, RA, *a.* Applied to a splendid entertainment.

OPITULACIÓN, *sf.* Aid, help, assistance.

OPOBÁLSAMO, *sm.* Opobalsam, or balm of Gilead

Oponér, *va.* 1. To oppose, to contradict. 2. To object.—*vr.* 1. To oppose, to be adverse. 2. To front, to be opposite to. 3. To stand in competition with another.
Opopónaco, *sm.* Opoponax, a gum-resin.
Oportunaménte, *ad.* Opportunely.
Oportunidád, *sf.* Opportunity, convenience.
Oportúno, na, *a.* Convenient, seasonable.
Oposición, *sf.* Opposition, competition.
Opósito, *sm.* 1. Impediment, obstacle. 2. Part or place opposite to another. *Al oposito*, To the contrary, by contraposition.
Opositór, ra, *s.* Opposer, opponent.
Opresión, *sf.* 1. Oppression, pressure. 2. Hardship, calamity.
Opresivaménte, *ad.* Oppressively.
Opresívo, va, *a.* Oppressive, cruel.
Opresór, *sm.* Oppressor, one who harasses others with unjust severity.
Oprimír, *va.* 1. To oppress, to crush; to afflict severely. 2. To overpower, to overwhelm.
Opróbio, *sm.* Opprobrium, ignominy, shame, injury.
Oprobióso, sa, *a.* Opprobrious, reproachful.
Opróbrio, *sm.* (Ant.) V. *Oprobio.*
Optár, *va.* To choose, to elect, to obtain.
Optatívo, *sm.* (In Grammar) One of the moods of verbs expressive of desire.
O'ptica, *sf.* Optics, the science of the nature and laws of vision.
O'ptico, ca, *a.* Optic, visual; relating to the science of vision.—*sm.* Optician.
O'ptimamente, *ad.* Eminently, excellently.
O'ptimo, ma, *a.* Best, eminently good.
O'puestaménte, *ad.* Oppositely.
Opuésto, ta, *a.* Opposite, contrary, adverse.
Opugnacíon, *sf.* Oppugnancy, opposition.
Opugnadór, *sm.* Oppugner, opposer.
Opugnár, *va.* To oppugn, to impugn, to attack, to resist, to contradict.
Opuléncia, *sf.* Opulence, wealth, riches.
Opulentaménte, *ad.* Opulently.
Opulénto, ta, *a.* Opulent, wealthy, rich.
Opúsculo, *sm.* A short compendious treatise.
Oquedál, *sm.* Plantation of lofty trees.
Oqueruéla, *sf.* Entangled knotted thread.
O'ra, *ad.* At present. V. *Ahora.*—*sf.* Kisser.
Oración, *sf.* 1. Prayer, supplication, petition. 2. Position, a proposition which denies or affirms a thing. 3. Part of the mass. *Las oraciones*, Sun-setting, when the Angel's salutation to the Virgin is repeated by all the people, also the bell which calls to this prayer.
Oracionál, *sm.* Prayer-book.
Oracionéro, *sm.* He who goes praying from door to door.
Oráculo, *sm.* 1. Oracle, something delivered by supernatural wisdom. 2. The place where, or person of whom, the determinations of heaven are inquired. 3. Person listened to with great attention.
Oráda, *sf.* V. *Doráda.*
Oradór, *sm.* 1. Orator, a public speaker. 2. Panagyrist, encomiast.
Oráge, *sm.* Storm, tempest.
Orár, *vn.* 1. To harangue, to deliver a speech. 2. To pray, to make petition to heaven. 3. To ask, to demand.
Oráte, *s. com.* Lunatic, a deranged or silly person.
Oratória, *sf.* Oratory, eloquence; rhetorical skill.
Oratoriaménte, *ad.* Oratorically.
Oratório, *sm.* 1. Oratory, a private place allotted for prayer alone. 2. Oratorio, a spiritual composition sung particularly in churches. 3. Congregation of presbyters.
Orbayár, *vn.* To dew, to fall in mist, to drizzle.
Orbáyo, *sm.* Mist, small rain.
O'rbe, *sm.* 1. Orb, sphere, orbicular body; circular body. 2. Terrestrial sphere, celestial body. 3. Circle described by any of the mundane spheres.
Orbiculár, *a.* Orbicular, round, circular.
Orbicularménte, *ad.* Orbicularly.
O'rbita, *sf.* 1. Orbit, the line described by the revolution of a planet. 2. Cavity or socket wherein the eye is placed.
O'rca, *sm.* (Ict.) Grampus. Delphinus orca *L.*
Orchílla, *sf.* (Bot.) Archil or argil. Lichen roccella *L.*
O'rco, *sm.* 1. (Ict.) Grampus. V. *Orca.* 2. Hell.
Ordália, *sf.* Ordeal, a trial by fire or water.
Ordeáta, *sf.* 1. Peeled barley. 2. Ptisan, a medical drink made of barley decocted with raisins.
O'rden, *s. com.* 1. Order, regular disposition, method, series, rule. 2. A religious fraternity. 3. The sixth sacrament of the Roman catholic church. 4. Arrangement or disposition of chords in a musical instrument. 5. Mandate, precept, command. 6. Relation of one thing to another. 7. Order of architecture, a system of the several members, ornaments, and proportions of columns and pilasters. *En orden*, In an orderly manner; with regard to. *Por su orden*, In its turn; successively.
Ordenación, *sf.* 1. Methodical disposition or arrangement; ordination. 2. Edict, ordinance. 3. Clerical ordination.
Ordenadaménte, *ad.* Orderly.
Ordenádo, da, *a.* Ordained, ordinate.
Ordenadór, *sm.* One who orders or ordains.
Ordenamiénto, *sm.* Law, edict, ordinance.
Ordenándo y Ordenánte, *sm.* He who is ready to receive holy orders.
Ordenánte, *pa.* Ordering, disposing.
Ordenánza, *sf.* 1. Method, order. 2. Orderly man, a corporal of soldiers who attends a commanding officer. 3. Law, statute, ordinance; command; ordination. *Estar de ordenanza*, To be on duty, to be in waiting.
Ordenár, *va.* 1. To arrange, to put in order. 2. To order, to command. 3. To ordain, to regulate; to direct. 4. To confer holy orders.—*vr.* To be ordained, to receive holy orders.
Ordeñadéro, *sm.* Milk-pail, vessel for receiving milk drawn from the cow.
Ordeñadór, *sm.* Milker, one who milks or draws milk from animals.
Ordeñár, *va.* 1. To suck, to draw the teat of a female. 2. To milk, to draw milk with the hand from animals. 3. To pick or gather olives with the hand. 4. To obtain gradually the fruits of a thing.
Ordinación, *sf.* 1. (Arag.) Ordinance. V. *Ordenanza.* 2. Disposition, order.
Ordinál, *a.* Ordinal, noting order.—*sm.* Ordinal, ritual; a book containing orders.

Ordinariaménte, *ad.* Frequently; ordinarily, rudely.

Ordinário, ria, *a.* Ordinary, common, usual; coarse, mean, of low rank, vulgar.

Ordinário, *sm.* 1. Settled establishment of daily expense. 2. Judge who takes cognizance of causes in the first instance. 3. Decree given by a judge at the instance of one of the contending parties. 4. Mail, post, carrier, messenger or courier, who goes and arrives at stated times. 5. Catamenia, courses. 6. Ambassador, envoy. *De ordinario*, Regularly, commonly.

Ordinatívo, va, *a.* Ordering, regulating.

Oréade y Oréa, *a.* Belonging to the oreades or nymphs.—*sf.* Wood nymph.

Oreár, *va.* 1. To cool, to refresh; applied to the wind. 2. To dry, to air, to expose to the wind or air.—*vr.* To take the air, to take an airing.

Orecér, *va.* (Joc.) To convert into gold.

Orégano, *sm.* (Bot.) Wild marjoram. Origanum vulgare *L.*

Oréja, *sf.* 1. Auricle, the external ear. 2. Ear, the organ of hearing. 3. Tale-bearer. 4. Shoe-strap. *Orejas de un ancla*, (Naút.) Palms of an anchor. *Orejas de mercader*, Deaf ear. *Con las orejas caidas*, Down in the mouth; dejected. *Pan de orejas*, (Madrid) Small indented bread. *Majar la oreja*, (Met.) To conquer or excel another. *Vino de dos orejas*, (Vulg.) A strong-bodied wine. *Oreja de abad ó monge*, (Bot.) Venus navel-wort. *Oreja de raton*, (Bot.) Mouse-ear. Myosotis *L.*

Orejeádo, da, *a.* Informed, advised, instructed.

Orejeár, *vn.* 1. To move the ears forwards and backwards, to shake the ears; applied to horses and mules. 2. To act with reluctance. 3. To whisper in the ear.

Orejéra, *sf.* 1. Covering for the ears to defend them from cold. 2. Pot-ear, kettle-ear, to which hooks are fastened to handle the pots or kettles more easily. 3. A sort of ear-rings worn by the Indians.

Orejón, *sm.* 1. Preserved peach. 2. Pull by the ear. 3. Hind part of the plough. *Orejones*, The young nobility of Peru, educated for public employments.

Orejúdo, da, *a.* Having long ears.

Orellána, *sf.* (Bot.) Anotta, or arnotto; an orange drug or dye-stuff prepared from the seeds of the Bixa orellana *L.*

Orénga, *sf.* (Naút.) V. *Quaderna.*

Oréo, *sm.* Breeze, fresh air.

Oreoselíno, *sm.* (Bot.) Mountain parsley.

Orfandád y Orfanidád, *sf.* State of orphans; want of friends or support.

Orfebrería, *sf.* Gold or silver twist.

O'rfo, *sm.* (Ict.) Rud, finscale. Cyprinus orfus *L.*

Organéro, *sm.* Organ-maker.

Organicaménte, *ad.* Organically.

Orgánico, ca, *a.* 1. Consisting of various parts, co-operating with each other; organical. 2. Harmonious.

Organíllo, to, co, *sm.* Chamber-organ.

Organísta, *s. com.* Organist, one who plays on the organ.

Organización, *sf.* Organization.

Organizár, *va.* 1. To tune an organ. 2. To organize, to form.

O'rgano, *sm.* 1. Organ, a musical instrument, consisting of pipes filled with wind, and of stops touched by the hand. 2. Natural instrument, as the tongue is the organ of speech. 3. Machine for cooling liquors. 4. (Met.) Organ or medium by which a thing is communicated.

Orgúllo, *sm.* 1. Pride, haughtiness. 2. Activity, briskness.

Orgullóso, sa, *a.* 1. Proud, haughty. 2. Brisk, active.

Oricálco, *sm.* Orichalch, brass.

Orientál, *a.* Oriental, eastern.

Orientár, *va.* To turn any thing to eastward. *Orientar una vela*, (Naút.) To trim a sail, *Navio bien orientado á la bolina ó á la trinca*, (Naút.) A sharp-trimmed or close-hauled ship.—*vr.* To consider and ascertain the course to be taken.

Oriénte, *sm.* 1. Orient, the east; the part where the sun first appears. 2. Source, origin. 3. Youth, juvenile age. 4. East wind. 5. Orient or brilliant whiteness of pearls.

Orífice, *sm.* Goldsmith.

Orifícia, *sm.* Art, trade, and profession of a goldsmith.

Orifício, *sm.* Orifice, mouth, aperture.

Orígen, *sm.* 1. Origin, source, beginning, motive. 2. Natal country; family, lineage.

Originál, *a.* Original, primitive.

Originál, *sm.* 1. Original, first copy, archetype. 2. Source, fountain.

Originalménte, *ad.* Originally, radically.

Originár, *va.* To originate, to bring into existence.—*vr.* To descend, to derive existence from.

Originariaménte, *ad.* Radically, originally.

Originário, ria, *a.* Originary.

Originário, *sm.* Native, descendant.

Origíneo, nea, *a.* (Ant.) Original.

Orílla, *sf.* 1. Limit, extent, border. 2. Edge of stuff or cloth. 3. Bank of a river, shore of the sea. 4. Footpath in a street. 5. A sharp piercing wind. *A' la orilla*, Near a place, on the brink. *Salir á la orilla*, To overcome difficulties.

Orillár, *vn.* 1. To approach or make the shore. 2. To leave a selvage or border on cloth. 3. To abandon, to forsake, to relinquish.—*va.* To arrange, to conclude, to order, to expedite.

Orílo, *sm.* Selvage, the edge of cloth.

Orín, *sm.* 1. Rust, the red oxide of iron. 2. Stain, taint of guilt; defect. 3. Urine. V. *Orina. Orines*, Urine of animals.

Orína, *sf.* Urine, animal water separated from the blood.

Orinál, *sm.* Chamber-pot. *Orinal del cielo*, Country where it rains much.

Orinár, *vn.* To emit urine, to make water.

Oriniénto, ta, *a.* Rusty, mouldy.

Orínque, *sm.* (Naút.) Buoy-rope.

Oriól, *sm.* (Orn.) Golden oriole or thrush. Oriolus galbula *L.*

Orión, *sm.* (Astr.) Orion, a southern constellation.

Oriúndo, da, *a.* Originated, derived from.

O'rla, *sf.* List, selvage, border.

Orladór, *sm.* Borderer, he who makes borders.

Orladúra, *sf.* Border, edging, list.

Orlár, *va.* To border, to garnish with an edging.

Orlánda, *sm.* A sort of linen.

O'ELO, *sm.* A kind of musical wind instrument.
ORMESÍ, *sm.* A kind of silk stuff.
ORNABÉQUE, *sm.* (Fort.) Hornwork.
ORNADAMÉNTE, *ad.* Ornamentally.
ORNAMENTÁR, *va.* To adorn, to embellish.
ORNAMÉNTO, *sm.* Ornament, embellishment. *Ornamentos*, Sacred vestments; frets, mouldings, &c. in architectural work; moral qualities of any person.
ORNÁR, *va.* To adorn, to embellish.
ORNÁTO, *sm.* Dress, apparel, ornament, decoration.
ORNITÓLITA, *sf.* Part of a bird petrified.
ORNITOLÓGIA, *sf.* Ornithology, the science of [birds.
ORNITÓLOGO, *sm.* Ornithologist.
O'RO, *sm.* 1. Gold, the most valuable of all metals. 2. Gold colour; applied to the hair. 3. Toys, trinkets. 4. Wealth, riches. *Oro batido*, Leaf-gold. *Oro mate*, Gold size. *De oro y azul*, Neatly dressed. *Es otro tanto oro*, So much the better. *O'ros*, Diamonds, one of the suits at cards.
ORÓBIAS, *sm.* One of the finest sorts of incense.
ORÓNDO, DA, *a.* Pompous, showy; hollow.
OROPÉL, *sm.* 1. A thin plate of brass. 2. Tinsel, any thing showy and of little value.
OROPELÉRO, *sm.* Brass-worker.
OROPÉNDOLA, *sf.* (Orn.) Witwall, loriot.
OROPIMÉNTE, *sm.* Orpiment, a foliaceous fossil, of a fine texture, remarkably heavy, and of a bright yellow; a sulphuret of arsenic.
OROZÚZ, *sm.* (Bot.) Liquorice or licorice. Glycyrrhiza *L.*
ORQUÉSTA, *sf.* Orchestra, the place in a playhouse where the musicians sit.
ORRÁCA, *sf.* A kind of spirit distilled from the cocoa-nut.
ORTÉGA, *sf.* (Orn.) Hazel-grouse. Tetrao bonasia *L.*
ORTÍGA, *sf.* (Bot.) Nettle. Urtica *L.*
ORTÍVO, VA, *a.* (Astr.) Oriental, eastern.
O'RTO, *sm.* Rising of a star.
ORTODOXÍA, *sf.* Orthodoxy.
ORTÓDOXO, XA, *a.* Orthodox, sound in opinion and doctrine; not heretical.
ORTOGÓNIO, *a.* Right-angled.
ORTOGRAFÍA, *sf.* Orthography, the art or practice of writing or spelling according to the rules of grammar.
ORTÓGRAFO, *sm.* Orthographer, one skilled in orthography.
ORTOLÓGIA, *sf.* Orthoepy, art of pronunciation.
ORTOPÉDIA, *sf.* Art of correcting deformities in children.
ORÚGA, *sf.* 1. (Bot.) Rocket. Brassica eruca *L.* 2. Caterpillar. 3. Sauce made of rocket and sugar.
ORÚJO, *sm.* Skin or peel of pressed grapes.
O'RZA, *sf.* 1. Gallipot. 2. (Naút.) Luff. *Orza á la banda*, (Naút.) Hard a-lee. *A' orza*, (Naút.) Luff, luff.
ORZADÉRAS, *sf. pl.* (Naút.) Lee-boards.
ORZÁGA, *sf.* (Bot.) Orach. Atriplex halimus *L.*
ORZÁR, *vn.* (Naút.) To luff, to bear away.
ORZUÉLO, *sm.* 1. A small morbid tumour on the eye-lid. 2. Snare to catch birds; a trap for catching wild beasts.
O's, *pron.* You or ye. It is placed before and after verbs, and used instead of *vos*, to denote the authority of a superior to an inferior, or the greater respect of an inferior to his superior.
O'SA, *sf.* She-bear. *Osa mayor*, Ursa major.
OSADAMÉNTE, *ad.* Boldly, daringly.
OSADÍA, *sf.* 1. Courage, boldness, intrepidity. 2. Zeal, fervour, ardour.
OSÁDO, DA, *a.* Daring, bold, high-spirited.
OSAMÉNTE Y OSÁMBRE, *s.* Skeleton, the bones of the body preserved together in their natural situation.
OSÁR, *vn.* 1. To dare, to venture. 2. To imagine, to fancy.
OSÁRIO Y OSÁR, *sm.* Charnel-house, the place where the bones of the dead are deposited.
OSCILACIÓN, *sf.* Oscillation, vibration of a pendulum.
OSCILÁNTE, *pa.* Oscillating, vibrating.
OSCILÁR, *vn.* To oscillate, to vibrate, as a pendulum.
OSCILATÓRIO, RIA, *a.* Oscillatory, vibratory.
OSCITÁNCIA, *sf.* Oscitancy, carelessness, heedlessness.
O'SCULO, *sm.* Kiss. V. *Beso.*
OSECÍCO, LLO, Y OSEZUÉLO, *sm.* Small bone.
OSÉO, A, *a.* Osseous, bony.
OSÉRA, *sf.* Den of bears.
OSÉRO, *sm.* Charnel-house.
OSÉZNO, *sm.* Whelp or cub of a bear.
OSIFICACIÓN, *sf.* Ossification.
OSIFICÁRSE, *vr.* To ossify, to become bone.
OSIFRÁGA Y OSIFRÁGO, *s.* Osprey, a ravenous eagle. Falco ossifragus *L.*
O'SO, *sm.* Bear. Ursus *L.* *O'so hormiguero*, Ant eater. Myrmecophaga *L.* *Oso colmenero*, Bear that robs bee-hives.
OSÓSO, SA, *a.* Osseous, bony.
O'STA DE ENTÉNA, *sf.* (Naút.) Brace of a lateen yard.
OSTÁGA, *sf.* (Naút.) Tie, runner.
OSTENSÍBLE, *a.* Ostensible, apparent.
OSTENSIÓN, *sf.* Show, exhibition to view.
OSTENSÍVO, VA, *a.* Ostensive, showing, betokening.
OSTENTACIÓN, *sf.* 1. Outward show, appearance. 2. Ambitious display, vain show.
OSTENTADÓR, RA, *s.* Boaster, ostentator.
OSTENTÁR, *va.* To show, to demonstrate.—*vn.* To boast, to brag, to make an ambitious display; to be fond of vain shows.
OSTENTATÍVO, VA, *a.* Ostentatious.
OSTÉNTO, *sm.* Show, spectacle, ostent, prodigy.
OSTENTOSAMÉNTE, *ad.* Ostentatiously.
OSTENTÓSO, SA, *a.* Sumptuous, ostentatious.
OSTEOLÓGIA, *sf.* Osteology, that part of anatomy which explains the nature and structure of the bones of the animal body.
OSTIÁRIO, *sm.* Door-keeper, one of the minor orders of the Roman catholic church.
OSTIÁTIM, *ad.* From door to door.
O'STRA, *sf.* Oyster. Ostrea *L.*
OSTRACÍSMO, *sm.* Ostracism, banishment or exile of ten years, used by the Athenians.
OSTRÉRA Y OSTRÁL, *s.* Oyster-bed, a place where oysters are reared.
OSTRÉRO, *sm.* Dealer in oysters, one who keeps an oyster-shop.
OSTRÍFERO, RA, *a.* Producing oysters; ostriferous.
O'STRO, *sm.* 1. Oyster; large oysters are denominated in the masculine gender, they are also called *Ostrones.* 2. South-wind.

Ostrogódo, da, a. Ostrogothic, eastern Goths.
Ostúgo, sm. 1. Vestige, mark left in passing. 2. Private entrance.
Osúdo, da, a. Bony, full of bones.
Osúno, na, a. Bear-like, of the nature of a bear.
Ostacústa, sm. Spy, eaves-dropper, tale-bearer.
Otacústico, a. That which improves the sense of hearing.—sm. Otacousticon, Instrument to assist hearing.
Otáñez, sm. (Joc.) An old squire who courts or attends a lady; an old beau. *Iba con su Don otáñez*, She went with her old beau.
Otár, va. To spy, to examine. V. *Otear*.
Oteadór, sm. Spy, sly observer; one who searches or discovers by artifice.
Oteár, va. To observe, to examine, to pry into, to discover by artifice; to inspect.
Otéro, sm. Hill, eminence, height.
Oteruélo, sm. dim. A little height or elevation.
O'to, sm. (Orn.) Bustard. V. *Abutarda*.
Otománo, na, a. Ottoman, relating to the Turkish empire, so called from Othomanus.
Otóna, sf. (Bot.) Ragwort.
Otoñáda, sf. Autumn-season, harvest-time.
Otoñál, a. Autumnal.
Otoñár, vn. 1. To spend the autumn-season. 2. To grow in autumn; applied to plants.—vr. To be seasoned, to be tempered; applied to earth after rain.
Otóño, sm. Autumn; second crop of grass.
Otorgadór, ra, s. Consenter, granter, stipulator.
Otorgamiénto, sm. 1. Grant, license. 2. The act of making an instrument in writing.
Otorgáncia, sf. Authorization. *Auto de otorgancia*, Act of impowering or authorizing.
Otorgánte, pa. Granter; authorizing.
Otorgár, va. 1. To consent, to agree to, to condescend. *Otorgar de cabeza*, To nod assent. 2. To covenant, to stipulate.
Otórgo, sm. Matrimonial contract.
Otraménte, ad. (Ant.) Otherwise.
Otre, Otri, Otrie, a. (Ant.) V. *Otro*.
O'tro, tra, a. Another, other. *Otro que tal*, (Fam.) Another such.
O'tro, interj. Again! exclamation of disgust.
Otrosí, ad. Besides, moreover.—sm. (For.) Every petition made after the principal.
O'va, sf. (Bot.) Sea-wreck, laver. Ulva *L*. *Ovas*, Eggs. V. *Huevas*.
Ovación, sf. 1. Ovation, a lesser triumph among the Romans. 2. Spawning season of fish.
Ováde, da, a. Rounded, ovated; fecundated; applied to hens after being with cocks.
Ovál, a. Oval, oblong.
Ovaládo, da, a. Egg-shaped, oval-formed.
O'valo, sm. Oval, that which has the shape of an egg.
Ovánte, a. Victorious, triumphant.
Ovár, va. To lay eggs.
Ovário, sm. 1. Ornament in architecture in the form of an egg. 2. Ovary, the part of the female body in which impregnation is performed. 3. Seed-vessel of plants.
Ovecíco, sm. A small egg.
Ovéja, sf. Ewe, a female sheep.—pl. 1. A kind of South American sheep or camels, called Glamas. 2. White spume or froth of waves which break against rocks. 3. Flock of the faithful
Ovejéro, sm. Shepherd.
Ovejuéla y Ovejíta, sf. A young sheep.
Ovejúno, na, a. Relating to ewes.
Ovéra, sf. Ovary, womb of animals.
Ovéro, ra, a. Egg-coloured, speckled or trout-coloured; applied to a horse.
Ovéro, sm. Pigeon. *Overos*, (Joc.) Eyes which look quite white, and appearing as if without any pupil.
Ovést, sm. West.
Ovíl, sm. V. *Redil*.
Ovillár, vn. To wind up into a clew.—vr. To shrug or contract one's self into a ball or clew.
Ovilléjo, sm. 1. A small clew or ball. 2. A kind of metrical composition. *Decir de ovillejo*, To make verses extempore.
Ovíllo, sm. 1. Clew, thread wound upon a bottom. 2. Heap, confused multitude of things.
Ovíparo, ra, a. Oviparous, bringing forth eggs.
Ovispíllo, sm. 1. Rump of a fowl. 2. Anus.
O'volo, sm. (Arq.) Ovolo, egg-like moulding. V. *Equino*.
Ovóso, sa, a. Full of sea-weeds.
O'x, A word used to frighten fowls, birds, and other animals away.
Oxalá, interj. Would to God, God grant.
Oxaláte, sm. (Quím.) Oxalate, salt formed of Oxalic acid.
Oxálico, a. Oxalic, applied to acid made from sorrel.
Oxalís, sf. (Bot.) Sorrel. Rumex acetosa *L*.
Oxálme, sf. Oxalme, a mixture of salt, water, and vinegar.
Oxeadór, sm. Rouser, starter of game.
Oxeár, va. 1. To rouse game by hallooing. 2. To startle and frighten any thing.
Oxéo, sm. The act of rousing game by hallooing.
Oxiacánta, sf. (Bot.) White-thorn, hawthorn. Cratægus oxyacantha *L*.
Oxicráto, sm. Beverage of vinegar and water.
Oxidación, sf. (Quím.) Oxidation, process by which bodies or metals imbibe oxygen, and are converted into oxyds.
O'xido, sf. Oxide, a body formed by the union of a certain basis, with a smaller proportion of oxygen than is necessary for its conversion into an acid.
Oxigenádo, da, a. Oxygenated, that which can be formed into an acid.
Oxigenárse, vr. To oxygenate, to be oxygenated, to saturate with oxygen.
Oxígeno, sm. Oxygen, the acidifying principle.—a. Applied to oxygen gas.
Oxígono, sm. V. *Acutángulo*.
Oximáco, sm. (Orn.) Bird of prey.
Oximél ó Oximiél, sm. Oxymel, a mixture of honey and vinegar boiled to the consistence of a sirup. *Oximiel escilítico*, Oxymel of squills.
Oxizácre, sm. Sauce made of milk, honey, and sugar.
O'xte, interj. Keep off, begone. *Sin decir oxte ni moxte*, (Vulg.) Without asking leave or saying a word. *Oxte puto*, Exclamation on touching or taking into the hand any thing very hot or burning.
Oyénte, pa. Hearing; auditor, hearer.

THE letter *p* is pronounced in the Spanish as in the English language; joined with an *h* it has the pronunciation of *f*, with which character it is now written, as *fenomeno*, instead of *phenomeno*, as formerly used. *P* is retained in several words in order to indicate their origin, as in *precepto*, *aptitud*, in which case its pronunciation is softer; but it is most generally omitted before *s* and *t*, as *psalmo* is now written *salmo*, &c.

P. is a contraction for father; in the complimentary style, for feet; in petitions, for powerful. *PP*. fathers. *P*. in the Italian music signifies soft. *PP*. softer; and *PPP*. softest.

Pabellón, *sm*. 1. Pavilion, a kind of tent. 2, Curtain hanging in the form of a tent. 3. *Pabellon de armas*, (Mil.) Bell tent. 4. (Naút.) National colours. 5. Summer-house, or arbour in a garden made in the shape of a pavilion.

Pábilo, *sm*. 1. Wick, the substance around which is applied the wax or tallow, to make a torch or candle. 2. Snuff of a candle.

Pablár, *va*. (Vulg. Joc.) Word used for consonance, as *ni hablar*, *ni pablar*, Not to speak.

Pábulo, *sm*. 1. Nourishment, food, provender. 2. Aliment, support, nutriment.

Páca, *sf*. 1. The spotted cavy. Cavia paca *L*. 2. Bale of goods, bundle, package.

Pacádo, da, *a*. V. *Apaciguado*.

Pacáto, ta, *a*. Pacific, quiet, tranquil.

Pacción, *sf*. V. *Pacto*.

Paccionár, *va*. V. *Pactar*.

Pacedéro, ra, *a*. Pasturable, fit for pasture; applied to the ground.

Pacedúra, *sf*. Pasture ground.

Pacér, *va*. 1. To pasture, to graze. 2. To gnaw, to corrode, to feed.

Pachón, *sm*. 1. A peaceful phlegmatic man. 2. Pointer, a dog that points out the game to sportsmen.

Pachóna, *sf*. Pointer bitch.

Pachoncíco, ca; llo, lla; to, ta, *sm*. y *f*. *dim*. [of *Pachon*.

Pachórra, *sf*. Sluggishness, a slow and phlegmatic disposition.

Pachorrúdo, da, *a*. Sluggish, tardy, phlegma- [tic.

Paciéncia, *sf*. 1. Patience, endurance. 2. Sufferance. 3. Tranquil hope of things much desired. 4. Slowness, tardiness in executing things which should be done promptly. 5. Exhortatory exclamation to conform one's self with patience.

Paciénte, *a*. Suffering, forbearing. V. *Sufrido*.

Paciénte, *sm*. 1. Patient. 2. (Fil.) V. *Paso*.

Pacienteménte, *ad*. Patiently, tolerantly.

Pacienzúdo, da, *a*. Patient, tolerant.

Pacificación, *sf*. Pacification, quietness, peace of mind.

Pacificadór, ra, *s*. Pacificator, pacifier.

Pacificaménte, *ad*. Pacifically.

Pacificár, *va*. To pacify, to appease.—*vn*. To treat for peace.

Pacífico, ca, *a*. Pacific, peaceful; desirous of peace; tranquil, undisturbed; peace-offering.

Páco, *sm*. A kind of Indian camel. Camelus paco *L*.

Páco, ca, *s*. Proper name. Francis or Frances.

Pacotílla, *sf*. (Naút.) Venture goods permitted to be embarked in a ship on the private account of an individual.

Pactár, *va*. To covenant, to contract, to stipu- [late.

Pácto, *sm*. Compact, contract.

Padecér, *va*. 1. To suffer any physical or corporal affliction. 2. To experience or sustain an injury. 3. To be liable to.

Padecimiénto, *sm*. Suffering, sufferance.

Padílla, *sf*. 1. A small frying-pan. 2. A small kind of oven.

Padrástro, *sm*. 1. Step-father, a man married to a woman who had children by a former husband. 2. Obstacle, impediment. 3. Height. eminence which commands a tower or other place. 4. Hang-nail or agnail on the finger.

Pádre, *sm*. 1. Father, he by whom a son or daughter is begotten. 2. Male of all sorts of animals. 3. Ancestor, the first ancestor. 4. Source, origin, principal author. 5. One who acts with paternal care. 6. An ecclesiastical writer of the first centuries. 7. The title of a confessor. *Padre Santo*, The Pope. *Padre nuestro*, The Lord's prayer; the large bead in the rosary over which the Lord's prayer is to be said.

PADRE Landóla, *sm*. A clèver man, he who knows to rule and exhibit authority.

Padreár, *vn*. 1. To resemble the father; to call often father. 2. To be kept for procreation; applied to cattle. 3. (Joc.) To fornicate.

Padrejón, *sm*. Chief patron or ancestor.

Padrína, *sf*. God-mother. V. *Madrina*.

Padrinázgo, *sm*. Compaternity, act of assisting at baptism; title or charge of a god-father.

Padríno, *sm*. 1. God-father, the sponsor at the font. 2. Second, one who accompanies another in a duel. 3. Protector, assistant.

Padrón, *sm*. 1. Poll, a register or list of persons in a town or other place who pay taxes. 2. A kind of public monument among the Romans. 3. Mark or note of infamy. 4. An indulgent parent. 5. V. *Patron*.

Padronéro, *sm*. (Ant.) V. *Patron*.

Pága, *sf*. 1. Payment, the act of paying. 2. Satisfaction for a fault or error committed. 3. Sum or fine paid. 4. Monthly pay of a soldier. 5. Friendly intercourse, mutual friendship. *En tres pagas*, Bad payment, badly or never paid.

Pagadéro, ra, *a*. Payable.

Pagadéro, *sm*. Time and place when and where payment is to be made.

Pagádo, da, *a*. Peaceful, agreeable, pleased.

Pagadór, *sm*. 1. One who pays. 2. Paymaster of the army or navy.

Pagaduría, *sf*. Paymaster's office.

Pagaménto, *sm*. Payment.

Paganía, *sf*. Paganism.

Paganísmo, *sm*. Paganism, the state and prin- [ciples of heathens.

Pagáno, *sm*. 1. Heathen, a person unacquainted with the covenant of grace. 2. Peasant, rustic. 3. (Joc.) One who pays or contributes his share.

Pagáno, na, *a*. Heathenish, belonging to the [Gentiles, unchristian

Pagár, *va*. 1. To pay, to discharge a debt. 2. To

atone, to make amends. 3. To please, to give pleasure. 4. To reward, to requite. *Pagar la visita*, To return a visit. *Pagar con el pellejo*, (Fam.) To die. *Pagar el pato*, (Fam.) To receive an unmerited punishment, or that which one has occasioned to another. *Esta muy pagado de sí mismo*, He entertains a high opinion of himself. *Pagarse*, To be pleased with one's self.

PÁGE, *sm.* 1. PAGE, a young boy attending on a great personage. 2. (Naút.) Cabin-boy. *Page de guion*, The oldest page of the Spanish monarch, who carries the king's arms in the absence of the arms-bearer. *Pages*, (Fam.) Whippings or floggings inflicted at school.

PAGECÍCO, LLO, TO, *sm.* 1. A small page. 2. Stand for a candlestick. [thinus *L.*

PAGÉL, *sm.* (Ict.) Red sea-bream. Sparus ery-

PAGERÍA, *sf.* (Burl.) Whipping-place.

PÁGINA, *sf.* Page of a book. V. *Plana.*

PÁGO, *sm.* 1. Payment, discharge of a debt. 2. Lot of land, especially of vineyards. *Pronto pago*, Prompt payment. *Dar cuenta con pago*, To close or balance an account. *En pago*, In payment.—*a.* (Vulg.) Paid.

PAGÓDE, *sm.* Pagod or pagoda, Indian temple.

PAGÓTE, *sm.* 1. One who is charged with the faults of others, and pays or suffers for them all. 2. Servant of a bawd or procuress.

PÁGRE, *sm.* (Ict.) Sea-bream. Sparus pagrus *L.*

PAGÚRO, *sm.* Small crab.

PAIRÁR, *vn.* (Naút.) To try; to lie to. V. *Capear.* [sails set.

PAÍRO, *sm.* (Naút.) Act of lying to with all the

PAÍS, *sm.* 1. Country, land, region. 2. (In Painting) Landscape. 3. (Met.) Field, subject; applied to scientific researches.

PAISÁGE, *sm.* Landscape.

PAISÁNA, *sf.* Country-dance.

PAISANÁGE, *sm.* 1. Peasantry, lay inhabitants of a country. 2. Quality of being of the same country.

PAISÁNO, NA, *a.* Being of the same country.

PAISÁNO, *sm.* Countryman; used by soldiers.

PÁJA, *sf.* 1. Straw, the stalk on which corn grows. 2. Beard of grain, blade of grass. 3. Any thing proverbially worthless. *A' lumbre de pajas*, In a trice, speedily. *Paja pelaza*, Barley-straw cut small. *Paja trigaza*, Wheat-straw. *Echar pajas*, To draw lots with straw. *Todo eso es paja*, That is all stuff and nonsense.

PAJÁDA, *sf.* Straw boiled with bran.

PAJÁDO, DA, *a.* Pale, straw-coloured.

PAJÁR, *sm.* Place where straw is kept.

PAJÁS, *interj.* Of equality or comparison. *Pedro es valiénte, pues Juan pajas*, Peter is valiant, but John is not less so.

PAJÁZA, *sf.* Refuse of straw which horses leave in the manger.

PAJÁZO, *sm.* Prick of stubbles received in a horse's face when feeding among them.

PAJEÁR, *vn.* (Fam.) To make a litter.

PAJÉRA, *sf.* A small place where straw is kept.

PAJÉRO, *sm.* One who deals in straw, and carries it from one place to another for sale.

PAJÍCA, LLA, TA, *sf.* Short light straw. *Pajica*, Cigar made of a maize leaf.

PAJÍZO, ZA, *a.* Made of straw, thatched or covered with straw; being of the colour of straw.

PAJÓN, *sm.* Coarse straw.

PAJÓSO, SA, *a.* Straw, made of straw.

PAJÓTE, *sm.* Straw interwoven with bulrush, with which gardeners cover fruit trees and plants.

PAJUÉLA, *sf.* 1. Short light straw. 2. Match, a piece of rope or wood dipped in sulphur in order to catch fire.

PAJUGÉRO, *sm.* (Arag.) Place where straw is deposited to rot and become manure.

PAJÚNCIO, *sm.* (Contempt.) Rush, any thing worthless. [the manger or stable.

PAJÚZ, *sm.* Refuse of straw which remains in

PAJÚZO, *sm.* Bad straw designed for manure.

PÁLA, *sf.* 1. A wooden shovel for throwing or heaping the grain; fire-shovel. 2. Peel used by bakers to put bread in and out of the oven. 3. Battledoor. 4. Blade of an oar. 5. Upper-leather of a shoe. 6. Upper row of teeth. 7. Craft, cunning, artifice. 8. Dexterity, cleverness. 9. (Lapid.) Metal in which stones are set. *Corta pala*, (Fam.) He who is ignorant of a thing. *Meter su media pala*, To have a share in the business. *Higuera de pala*, (Bot.) V. *Nopal.*

PALÁBRA, *sf.* 1. Word, a single part of speech. 2. Affirmation, confirmation. 3. Promise, offer. 4. (Teol.) The Word or only begotten Son. *Palabra de matrimonio*, Promise of marriage. *Palabra preñada*, A word which means more than it expresses. *A' media palabra*, At the least hint. *De palabra*, By word of mouth. *Mi palabra es prenda de oro*, My word is as good as a bond. *Tomar la palabra*, To take a man at his word. *A' la primera palabra*, At a word. *Remojar la palabra*, (Vulg.) To drink. *Palabras*, Superstitious words used by sorcerers; sentence extracted from any work; formula of the sacraments, table on which the words of consecration are written.

PALABRÁDA, *sf.* Low, scurrilous language.

PALÁBRAS, *interj.* I say, a word with you.

PALABRÉRO, RA, *a.* Talkative, full of prate, loquacious.

PALABRIMUGÉR, *sm.* Man who has an effeminate voice.

PALABRÍSTA, *s. com.* One who is full of prate, a loquacious person.

PALABRÍTA, *sf.* 1. An endearing short expression. 2. A word full of meaning. *Palabritas mansas*, Soft winning expressions.

PALACIÉGO, GA, *a.* Pertaining or relating to the palace.

PALACIÉGO, *sm.* Courtier.

PALÁCIO, *sm.* 1. Palace, a royal residence; a house eminently splendid. 2. Castle, the mansion of the ancient nobility. 3. (Mur.) A little hut of mud walls and only one room. 4. (Toledo) A hall or antechamber without furniture, where people meet and converse. *Hacer palacio*, To develope, to discover what was concealed.

PALÁCRA ó PALACRÁNA, *sf.* A piece of native gold; ingot of pure gold.

PALÁDA, *sf.* 1. A shovel-full, as much as a shovel can take up at once. 2. (Naút.) Every pull or stroke with the blade or wash of an oar in the water.

PALADÁR, *sm.* 1. Roof of the palate of an animal. 2. Taste, relish; longing desire. *A' medida ó á sabor de su paladar*, According to the taste or desire of any one.

PALADEÁR, *va.* 1. To rub the palate of a new-born child with honey or any other sweet substance. 2. To amuse, to divert. 3. To clean the mouth or palate of animals.—*vn.* To manifest a desire of sucking; applied to a new-born child.—*vr.* To get the taste of a thing by little and little; to relish.

PALADÉO, *sm.* The act of tasting or relishing.

PALADÍN, *sm.* A stout valiant knight.

PALADINAMÉNTE, *ad.* Publicly, clearly.

PALADÍNO, NA, *a.* Manifest, clear, apparent, public. *A' paladinas*, (Ant.) Publicly.

PALADIÓN, *sm.* Palladium.

PALAFRÉN, *sm.* Palfrey, a small horse for ladies; a servant's horse.

PALAFRENÉRO, *sm.* Groom. *Palafrenero mayor*, First equerry to the king.

PALAMÁLLO, *sm.* Pall-mall, a play in which the ball is struck with a mallet.

PALAMÉNTA, *sf.* The oars of a row-galley. *Estar debaxo de la palamenta*, To be at the beck of any one, to be subject to any one's pleasure.

PALÁNCA, *sf.* 1. Lever, one of the principal mechanical powers used to raise or elevate a great weight. 2. Cowl staff, a staff or pole in which a vessel is supported between two men. 3. Exterior fortification with stakes. 4. (Naút.) Strong rope at the stays of a sail.

PALANCÁDA, *sf.* Stroke or blow with a lever.

PALANCÁNA ó PALANGÁNA. *sf.* Basin, a vessel for various uses.

PALANQUÉRA, *sf.* Enclosure made with stakes or poles.

PALANQUÉRO, *sm.* Driver of stakes, pile-driver.

PALANQUÉTA, *sf.* 1. (Art.) Bar-shot, two balls joined by a bar, and used chiefly at sea to wound the masts and cut the rigging of the enemy's ships. 2. A small lever.

PALANQUÍN, *sm.* 1. Porter who carries burthens for hire. 2. (Naút.) Double or twofold tackle. 3. (In Cant) Thief.

PALANQUÍTA, *sf.* A small lever. V. *Palanqueta*.

PALÁSTRO, *sm.* Iron plate, sheet of hammered iron.

PALATÍNA, *sf.* Tippet, a sort of neckcloth worn by women.

PALATINÁDO, *sm.* Palatinate; dignity of a palatine.

PALATÍNO, NA, *a.* Belonging to the palace or courtiers.

PALÁZO, *sm.* Blow given with a shovel or stick.

PALAZÓN, *sm.* (Naút.) Masting, the masts of ships and vessels in general.

PÁLCO, *sm.* Scaffold or stage raised for spectators to see any remarkable transaction.

PALEADÓR, *sm.* Man who works with the shovel.

PALEÁGE, *sm.* The act of unshipping grain with a shovel.

PALEÁR, *va.* V. *Apalear*.

PALEOGRAFÍA, *sf.* Paleography, art of reading ancient MSS. containing contractions.

PALÉNQUE, *sm.* 1. Palisade, enclosure made with piles; paling. 2. Passage from the pit to the stage in a play-house, made of boards.

PALÉRA, *sf.* Enclosure made with fig-trees.

PALERÍA, *sf.* Art and business of draining low wet lands.

PALÉRO, *sm.* 1. One who makes or sells shovels. 2. Ditcher, drainer; pioneer.

PALÉSTRA, *sf.* 1. Place for wrestling, tilting; debating, and disputing. 2. (Poét.) Art of wrestling.

PALÉSTRICO, CA, *a.* Relating to wrestling or debating.

PALESTRÍTA, *sm.* One versed in athletic or logical exercises.

PALÉTA, *sf.* 1. Fire-shovel. 2. Palette, a thin oval board, on which painters put and hold their colours. 3. Iron ladle, used in public kitchens to distribute viands. 4. A small shovel. 5. Blade-bone of the shoulder. 6. Trowel, a tool to take up mortar and spread it on a wall. 7. *Paleta de azotar*, (Naút.) Cobbing-board, used to punish mariners on board of ships. *De paleta*, Opportunely. *En dos paletas*, Shortly, briefly.

PALETÁDA, *sf.* Trowel-full of mortar or plaster.

PALETÍLLA, *sf.* 1. A little shoulder-blade. V. *Palmatoria*. 2. A cartilage under the pit of the stomach.

PALÉTO, *sm.* 1. Fallow deer. V. *Gamo*. 2. Clown, rustic.

PALETÓN, *sm.* Bit, the part of a key in which the wards are formed.

PALETÓQUE, *sm.* Kind of dress like a scapulary which hangs to the knees.

PÁLIA, *sf.* 1. Altar-cloth. 2. Veil or curtain which hangs before the tabernacle; square piece of linen put over the chalice.

PALIACIÓN, *sf.* Palliation, the act of palliating or extenuating; extenuation.

PALIADAMÉNTE, *ad.* Dissemblingly, in a palliative manner.

PALIÁR, *va.* To palliate, to extenuate, to cover, to excuse; to cloak.

PALIATÍVO, VA, Y PALIATÓRIO, RIA, *a.* Palliative, that may be palliated.

PALIDÉZ, *sf.* Paleness, wanness, want of colour.

PÁLIDO, DA, *a.* Pallid, pale, yellowish.

PALILLÉRO, *sm.* 1. One who makes or sells tooth-picks. 2. Tooth-pick case.

PALÍLLO, *sm.* 1. A small stick. 2. Knitting-needle case. 3. Rolling-pin. 4. Tooth-pick. 5. Table-talk. 6. Trigger of a gun.—*pl.* 1. Bobbins, small pins of wood for making bone-lace. 2. Drum-sticks. 3. First rudiments of arts and sciences. 4. Trifles, things of no moment.

PALINDRÓMO, *sm.* Writing which read either from left to right or vice versâ has the same meaning.

PALINGENÉSIA, *sf.* Regeneration.

PALINÓDIA, *sf.* Palinody, recantation.

PÁLIO, *sm.* 1. Cloak, short mantle. 2. Pall, a pontifical ornament worn by patriarchs and archbishops of the Roman catholic church. 3. Any thing of the form or shape of a canopy. 4. Premium or plate given as a reward in racing. *Recibir con palio*, To receive under a pall, as kings, &c.

PALÍQUE, *sm.* Trifling conversation.

PALÍTO, *sm.* A little stick.

PALITRÓQUE Y PALITÓQUE, *sm.* A rough ill-shaped stick.

PALÍZA, *sf.* Cudgelling or drubbing with a stick.

PALIZÁDA, *sf.* 1. Palisade or palisado. 2. Paling, fence made with pales. V. *Estacada*.

Pallár, va. To extract or select the richest metallic part of minerals.

Palléta y Pallète, s. (Naút.) Mat, a thick clout, woven of spun-yarn or of the strands of untwisted ropes, and used to preserve yards or masts from galling. *Palleta afelpada*, Chafe-mat or panch, a mat interwoven with twists of rope-yarn to increase its strength.

Pallón, sm. 1. The quantity of gold or silver resulting from an assay. 2. Assay of gold when incorporated in the cupellation before separation with aquafortis.

Pálma, sf. 1. (Bot.) Date palm-tree. Phœnix dactylifera L. 2. Bud shooting out of a palm-tree. V. *Palmito*. 3. Palm of the hand. 4. Quick sole of a horse's hoof. 5. Palm leaf, with which baskets are made. *Llevarse la palma*, To carry the day, to conquer. *Andar en palmas*, To be universally esteemed and applauded.

Palmachristi, sf. (Bot.) Common palma christi. Ricinus communis L.

Palmáda, sf. Slap given with the palm of the hand.—*Palmadas*, Clapping of hands.

Palmadílla, ca, ta, sf. 1. A slight clap with the palm of the hand. 2. A kind of dance.

Palmár, a. 1. Measuring a palm or three inches. 2. Belonging or relating to palms. 3. Clear, obvious, evident.

Palmár, sm. 1. Plantation or grove of palm-trees. 2. Fuller's thistle, which serves to raise the nap or bur on cloth. 3. Basket made of reeds, in which the washed wool is pressed after it has been taken out of the washing-tub.

Palmár, vn. (Fam.) To die.

Palmário, ria, a. Clear, obvious, evident.

Palmatória, sf. 1. A kind of rod with which boys at school are beaten on the hand. 2. A small candlestick with a handle.

Palmeádo, da, a. 1. Palmipede, web-footed; applied to fowls. 2. (Bot.) Palmate; applied to the leaves and roots of plants.

Palmeár, va. To slap with the open hand; to clap.

Palmejáres, sm. pl. (Naút.) Thick-stuff, large thick planks nailed to the inner sides of ships from stem to stern. *Palmejares del plan*, Floor thick-stuff. *Palmejares de los escarpes*, Scarf thick-stuff. *Palmejares de los dormientos*, Clamp thick-stuff.

Palméra, sf. Palm-tree. V. *Palma*.

Palméro, sm. Palmer, an appellation formerly given to pilgrims who returned from the holy land, carrying a palm in their hand; keeper of palms.

Palméta, sf. 1. A kind of rod. V. *Palmatoria*. 2. Slap in the palm of the hand.

Palmífero, ra, a. (Poét.) Palmiferous.

Palmílla, sf. 1. A sort of blue woollen cloth manufactured chiefly in Cuenca. 2. Sole of a shoe.

Palmitiéso, a. Hard-hoofed horse.

Palmíto, sm. 1. Bud shooting out from a palm-tree. 2. (Bot.) Palmetto, species of palm-tree. Chamærops humilis L. *Como un palmito*, Neat, clean, genteel. 3. Little face; applied to women and damsel-like youths. *Buen palmito*, A pretty face.

Pálmo, sm. 1. Palm, a measure of length from the thumb to the end of the little finger stretched out. *En un palmo de tierra*, In a short space of ground. 2. Game, commonly called span-farthing. *Palmo á palmo*, Inch by inch. *Medir á palmos*, (Met.) To have a complete knowledge of any thing.

Palmoteár, va. To slap with the open hand. V. *Palmear*.

Palmotéo, sm. Clapping of hands.

Pálo, sm. 1. Stick, a piece of wood of any length or size. 2. Timber. 3. Blow given with a stick. 4. Execution on the gallows. 5. Suit at cards. 6. Stalk of fruit. 7. (Met.) Indecent expression. *Alcalde de palo*, Ignorant, useless *alcalde*. *Tener el mando y el palo*, To have absolute power over any thing. 8. (Naút.) Mast. *Palo de una sola pieza*, Pole-mast. *Palo reforzado*, Fished mast. *Palo en bruto*, Rough mast. *A' palo seco*, Under bare-poles. *Palo mayor*, Main-mast. *Palo de trinquete*, Fore-mast. *Palo de mesana*, Mizen-mast. *Palos principales*, Lower or standing masts.

Pálo santo, sm. (Bot.) Lignum vitæ. Guaiacum officinale L.

Pálo dulce, sm. (Bot.) Liquorice. V. *Orozuz*.

Palóma, sf. 1. (Orn.) Pigeon. Columba L. 2. (Naút.) Sling of a yard. 3. A meek mild person.

Palomadúras, sf. pl. (Naút.) Seams of the sails, where the bolt-rope is sewed to them.

Palomár, a. Applied to hard twisted linen or thread.—sm. Pigeon-house.

Palomariégo, ga, a. Applied to domestic pigeons in the fields.

Palomeár, vn. To shoot pigeons.

Paloméra, sf. 1. A bleak place, much exposed to the wind. 2. Small dove-cot.

Palomería, sf. Pigeon-shooting.

Paloméro, a. Applied to arrows with long iron points.

Palomílla, sf. 1. A young pigeon. 2. (Bot.) Common fumitory. Fumaria officinalis L. 3. Back-bone of a horse. 4. Chrysalis or aurelia, the first apparent change of a maggot, of butterflies, or any other species of insect. 5. Horse of a milk-white colour. 6. A sort of white nymph or fly reared in barley. 7. Peak of a pack-saddle. 8. Brass box of the axis of a wheel. 9. Sort of light stuff.

Palomína, sf. 1. Pigeon-dung. 2. (Bot.) Fumitory. 3. A kind of black grape.

Palomíno, sm. 1. A young pigeon. 2. (Joc.) Stain in a shirt from dirt.

Palómo, sm. Cock-pigeon. *Juan palomo*, An idle useless fellow.

Palór, sm. Paleness. V. *Palidez*.

Palotáda, sf. Stroke or blow with a battledoor. *No dar palotada*, Not to have hit on the right thing in all that is said or done; not to have begun a line or tittle of what was undertaken or ordered.

Palóte, sm. 1. Stick of a middling size; drum-stick. 2. Rule or line used by scholars in writing.

Paloteádo, sm. 1. Rustic dance performed with sticks. 2. Noisy scuffle or dispute.

Paloteár, vn. To scuffle, to clash, to strike sticks against one another; to contend, to dispute.

PALOTÍO, *sm.* Fight with sticks.
PALPÁBLE, *a.* 1. Palpable, perceptible to the touch. 2. Plain, evident.
PALPABLEMÉNTE, *ad.* Palpably, evidently.
PALPADÚRA, *sf.* Feeling, touching.
PALPAMIÉNTO, *sm.* The act of feeling or perceiving by the touch.
PALPÁR, *va.* 1. To feel, to touch. 2. To grope, to search by feeling in the dark; to know positively. *Palpar la ropa,* To be near death; to be confused and irresolute.
PALPÉBRA, *sf.* Eye-lid. V. *Párpado.*
PALPITACIÓN, *sf.* Palpitation, beating of the heart; panting.
PALPITÁNTE, *pa.* Vibrating, palpitating.
PALPITÁR, *vn.* To palpitate, to pant, to flutter.
PÁLTA, *sf.* (Bot.) Aligator-pear.
PÁLTO, *sm.* (Bot.) Aligator pear-tree. Laurus persea *L.*
PALUDAMÉNTO, *sm.* Purple mantle trimmed with gold and worn by the Roman emperors in war.
PALÚDE, *sf.* Lake, pool. V. *Laguna.*
PALUDÓSO, SA, *a.* Marshy, swampy, full of fens and bogs.
PALUMBÁRIO, *a.* Applied to the gose-hawk which pursues pigeons.
PALÚRDO, DA, *a.* Rustic, clownish, rude.
PALÚSTRE, *a.* Marshy, fenny, boggy.—*sm.* Trowel.
PÁMPANA, *sf.* Vine-leaf. *Tocar ó zurrar la pampana,* To threaten to chastise.
PAMPANÁDA, *sf.* Juice of tendrils or vine-shoots.
PAMPANÁGE, *sm.* 1. Abundance of vine-shoots. 2. Vain parade or show.
PAMPANÍLLA, *sf.* Covering of leaves.
PÁMPANO, *sm.* 1. Young vine branch or tendril. 2. (Ict.) V. *Salpa.*
PAMPANÓSO, SA, *a.* Covered with foliage or leaves, leafy.
PAMPIROLÁDA, *sf.* 1. Sauce made of garlic, bread, and water, pounded in a mortar. 2. Any silly thing without substance.
PAMPLÍNA, *sf.* 1. (Bot.) Duck weed. Lemna arhiza *L.* 2. (Bot.) Mouse-ear. 3. Trifle, a futile worthless thing.
PAMPOSÁDO, DA, *a.* Lazy, idle, cowardly.
PAMPRINGÁDA, *sf.* 1. V. *Pringada.* 2. (Met.) Frivolous futile thing.
PÁN, *sm.* 1. Bread, food made of corn ground. 2. Paste made of seeds in the shape of bread. 3. Food in general, as the support of life. *Pan perdido,* (Met.) He who leaves his house and becomes a vagrant. 4. All seeds, except wheat, of which bread is made. 5. Host, the consecrated bread. 6. Wafer. 7. Leaf of gold or silver. *Pan de la boda,* Honey-moon. *Pan de municion,* Ammunition-bread. *A' pan y cuchillo,* Familiarly, assiduously, frequently. *A' pan y manteles,* At bed and board. *Pan de perro,* Very bad bread; chastisement or injury to any one.
PANÁCE, *sf.* (Bot.) All heal.
PANACÉA, *sf.* Panacea, universal medicine.
PANÁDA, *sf.* Panado.
PANADEÁR, *va.* To make bread for sale.
PANADÉO, *sm.* Baking bread.
PANADERÍA, *sf.* 1. Trade or profession of a baker. 2. Baker's shop, bakehouse.
PANADÉRO, RA, *s.* Baker, maker or seller of bread.
PANADÍZO Y PANARÍZO, *sm.* 1. Whitlow, a swelling in the finger. 2. Pale-faced sickly person.
PANÁDO, DA, *a.* Applied to bread macerated in water for sick persons.—*sm.* PANADO.
PANÁL, *sm.* 1. Honey-comb, the spongious cells of wax in which the bees store their honey. 2. Any thing pleasing to the taste.
PANÁRRA, *sm.* Dolt, simpleton.
PÁNAS IMBORNALERAS DE LAS VARENGAS, *sf. pl* (Naút.) Limber-boards, short pieces of plank which form part of the lining of the ship's floor close to the kelson, and immediately above the timbers. *Pánas de bote ó lancha,* (Naút.) Boat timber-boards.
PANATÉLA, *sf.* Panado. V. *Panatela.*
PANÁTICA, *sf.* Provision of bread.
PANCÁDA, *sf.* 1. (Gal.) Kick with the foot. 2. Contract for disposing of goods by wholesale.
PANCÁRPIA, *sf.* Garland made of a variety of flowers.
PANCÉRA, *sf.* The part of the armour which covers the belly.
PÁNCHO, *sm.* (Joc.) Paunch, belly. V. *Panza.*
PANCRÉAS, *sm.* (Anat.) Pancreas, sweetbread.
PANCREÁTICO, CA, *a.* Pancreatic.
PANDEÁR, *vn.* To bend, to be inclined, to belly, to bulge out.
PANDÉCTA, *sf.* (Among Merchants) Account-book which serves as an alphabetical index to the ledger. *Pandéctas,* Pandects, a collection of the various works of the Roman civil law, made by order of the emperor Justinian.
PANDÉO, *sm.* Bulge, any thing that juts or bulges out in the middle.
PANDERÁDA, *sf.* 1. Number of timbrels joined in concert. 2. Stroke or blow with a timbrel. 3. A silly, untimely, or unreasonable proposition.
PANDERÁZO, *sm.* Blow with a timbrel.
PANDERETEÁR, *vn.* To play on the timbrel.
PANDERETÉO, *sm.* The act of beating the timbrel.
PANDERETÉRO, *sm.* One who beats the timbrel.
PANDERÍLLO Y PANDERÍTE, *sm.* A small timbrel.
PANDÉRO, *sm.* 1. Timbrel, a musical instrument of high antiquity. 2. Silly person who talks at random. 3. V. *Cometa.*
PANDÍLLA, *sf.* Plot, league, party, faction.
PANDILLADÓR, PANDILLÉRO, Y PANDILLÍSTA, *sm.* Author and fomenter of plots and factions.
PÁNDO, DA, *a.* 1. Bulged, jutting out in the middle. 2. Slow, not quick of motion; applied to deep waters that run slow. 3. Tardy, grave.
PANDÓRGA, *sf.* 1. Concert of various musical instruments. 2. (Joc.) Fat bulky woman. 3. Comet. V. *Cometa.*
PANDORGÓNA, *sf.* aum. of *Pandorga.*
PANECÍLLO, CO, Y TO, *sm.* A small loaf of bread.
PANEGÍRICO, CA, *a.* Panegyrical.
PANEGÍRICO, *sm.* Panegyric, eulogy; an encomiastic piece of composition.
PANEGIRÍSTA, *sm.* Panegyrist, encomiast, eulogist.
PANÉLA, *sf.* 1. A kind of cake made of Indian corn. 2. Brown unpurified sugar. 3. (Bla.) Pannel.
PANÉRA, *sf.* 1. Granary, a store-house for threshed corn. 2. Pannier, a bread-basket.
PÁNES, *sm. pl.* 1. Corn or grain in the field. 2. Fauns, satyrs.

Panetéla, *sf.* Panado, soup made by boiling bread in water.

Paneteria, *sf.* Room or office in the palace of the Spanish monarch, where bread and linen are kept for use; PANTRY.

Pánfilo, *sm.* 1. A slow, sluggish, heavy person. 2. A jesting game, extinguishing a small candle in pronouncing this word.

Paniaguádo, *sm.* 1. Table-fellow, one who receives board and lodging from a friend. 2. Comrade, an intimate friend.

Pánico, ca, *a.* Panic, struck with groundless fear.

Panículo, *sm.* Panniele, pellicle, a membrane.

Paniégo, ga, *a.* Eating or yielding much bread.

Paniégo, *sm.* Bag made of coarse cloth, in which charcoal is generally carried and sold.

Panificádo, da, *a.* Tilled, cultivated.

Panificár, *va.* To break up pasture-land and convert it into arable ground or corn-fields.

Panílla, *sf.* A small measure of oil.

Panízo, *sm.* (Bot.) Panic-grass; panic. Panicum *L.*

Panója, *sf.* Ear of panic and millet.

Pantálla, *sf.* 1. Screen for the light of a candle or lamp. 2. Any screen or shelter. *Pantallas*, Coverings made of straw and bulrush, to preserve garden plants.

Pantáno, *sm.* 1. Pool of stagnant water; reservoir or lake for the purpose of irrigation. 2. Hinderance, obstacle, difficulty.

Pantanóso, sa, *a.* 1. Marshy, fenny, boggy. 2. Full of difficulties, obstacles, and obstructions.

Panteón, *sm.* Pantheon, a temple of ancient Rome, dedicated to all her gods, but now consecrated to the Holy Virgin, under the title of Our Blessed Lady of the Rotunda. *Panteon del Escurial*, A vault in the Escurial where the remains of the Spanish monarchs are interred.

Pantéra, *sf.* Panther. Felis pardus *L.*

Pantómetra, *sf.* Pantometer; proportional compasses for measuring heights and angles.

Pantomímo, *sm.* Pantomime, one who has the power of universal mimicry; one who expresses his meaning by mute action.

Pantóque, *sm.* (Naút.) Floor or flat of the ship.

Pantorrílla, *sf.* Calf; the thick, plump, bulbous part of the leg.

Pantorrilléra, *sf.* A sort of stocking used to make the calf look big.

Pantorrillúdo, da, *a.* Having very large or thick calves.

Pantufláso, *sm.* Blow or stroke given with a slipper.

Pantúflo, *sm.* Slipper, a kind of shoe without hind leather.

Pánza, *sf.* Belly, paunch. *Panza en gloria*, (Fam.) One who is too placid and feels nothing.

Panzáda, *sf.* 1. Belly full of eating and drinking. 2. Push with the belly.

Panzón, *sm.* Large-bellied person.

Panzúdo, da, *a.* Big-bellied.

Pañál, *sm.* 1. Swaddling-clout or cloth. 2. Cloth in which any thing is wrapped up. 3. Tail of a shirt.—*pl.* 1. The first elements of education and instruction. *Estar en pañales*, To have little knowledge of any thing. 2. Childhood, infancy.

Pañalón, *sm. aum.* One who has part of his clothes always falling off.

Pañéro, *sm.* Woollen-draper, one who deals in cloth.

Pañétes, *sm. pl.* 1. A kind of trowsers worn by fishermen and tanners, when they are at work. 2. Linen attached to the crucifix below the waist.

Pañíto y **Pañizuélo**, *sm.* A small cloth.

Paño, *sm.* 1. Cloth, woollen stuff of various sorts. 2. Any woven stuff, whether of silk, flax, hemp, wool, or cotton. 3. Piece of tapestry. 4. The red colour of a blood-shot eye; livid spot on the face. 5. Spot in looking-glasses, crystals, or precious stones. 6. (Naút.) Canvass, sail-cloth. *El barco va con poco paño*, The vessel carries but little sail. *Paños*, Clothes, garments. *Paños menores*, Small clothes. *Paños calientes*, (Met.) Exertions to stimulate one to do what is desired; efforts to moderate any one's rigour. *Al paño*, Peeping; applied to a person looking through the drop-curtain of a theatre, or listening.

Pañól, *sm.* (Naút.) Room in a ship where stores are kept. *Pañol de polvora*, (Naút.) Magazine. *Pañol de proa*, (Naút.) Boatswain's store-room. *Pañol de las velas*, (Naút.) Sail-room. *Pañol del condestable*, (Naút.) Gunner's-room.

Pañoléro de santa Barbara, *sm.* (Naút.) The gunner's yeoman. *Pañolero del pañol de proa*, (Naút.) The boatswain's yeoman.

Pañóso, sa, *a.* Ragged, dressed in rags.

Pañuélo, *sm.* Handkerchief.

Pápa, *sm.* 1. Pope, the head of the Roman catholic church. *Papá*, Papa, a fond name for father. 2. Pap, a soup for infants; any sort of pap; any kind of food. V. *Puches*. *Pápas*, (Bot.) Potatoes. Solanum tuberosum *L.*

Papacóte, *sm.* V. *Cometa*.

Papáda, *sf.* Double-chin; much flesh hanging under the chin of a man or woman. *Papada de buey ó toro*, Dewlap, the flesh that hangs down from the throat of oxen.

Papadílla, *sf.* The fleshy part under the chin.

Papádo, *sm.* Popedom, pontificate.

Papafígo, *sm.* (Orn.) Epicurean warbler. Motacilla ficedula *L.*

Papagáya, *sf.* Female parrot.

Papagáyo, *sm.* 1. (Orn.) Parrot. Psittacus *L.* 2. (Bot.) Flower like a tulip. 3. Red fish full of venomous prickles, with a blue neck.

Papahígos, *sm. pl.* (Naút.) Courses, the lower sails, viz. The main-sail, fore-sail, and mizen.

Papahuévos, *sm.* Simpleton, clodpoll. V. *Zapato*.

Papál, *a.* Papal, belonging to the pope.

Papalína, *sf.* Cap with flaps, which cover the ears.

Papalménte, *ad.* In a papal manner.

Papamóscas, *sm.* (Orn.) V. *Doral*.

Papanátas, *sm.* Oaf, simpleton, ninny.

Papandújo, ja, *a.* (Vulg.) Too soft; applied to over-ripe fruit.

Papár, *va.* 1. To swallow soft food without chewing. 2. To pay little attention to things which claim much notice. *Papenle duelos*, (Joc.) Expression censuring the indolence of any one in respect to the vices of others, which he ought to excuse or remedy. *Papar moscas ó viento*, To go with the mouth open like a fool.

Paparísmo, *sm.* Clownishness, awkward manners.
Páparo, *sm.* Clown, a coarse ill-bred person.
Paparrábias, *sf.* (Fam.) A testy, fretful person. [children.
Paparrasólla, *sf.* Hobgoblin, a bugbear for
Paparrúcha, *sf.* Dainty; riches. *Contar grandes paparruchas,* To reckon great riches.
Papasál, *sm.* Play among boys; any trifling amusement. [paya *L.*
Papáyo, *sm.* (Bot.) Papaw-tree. Carica pa-
Papáz, *sm.* Christian priest so called in Africa.
Papázgo, *sm.* Popedom, pontificate.
Papél, *sm.* 1. Paper, a substance on which men write and print, chiefly made by macerating linen rags in water. 2. Writing, treatise, discourse. 3. Part acted in a play; actor, actress. 4. Delegate or deputy of a body politic. *Papel de estraza,* Brown paper. *Papel sellado,* Stamped paper, stamp. *Papel que se cala,* Paper which sinks. *Papel pintado,* Stained paper. *Papel volante,* A small pamphlet.—*pl.* 1. Manuscripts. 2. Wry faces, gesticulations.
Papeleár, *vn.* To run over papers.
Papeleadór, *sm.* Searcher of papers; scribbler.
Papeléra, *sf.* 1. A number of writings or written papers placed together. 2. Writing-desk, scrutoire, paper-case. [without order.
Papelería, *sf.* Heap or large bundle of papers
Papeléro, *sm.* Paper-manufacturer.
Papeléta, *sf.* 1. Slip of paper on which any thing is written or noted. 2. Case of paper in which money or sweet-meats are kept.
Papelína, *sf.* 1. A small wine-glass with a foot. 2. A very thin sort of stuff or cloth, poplin.
Papelísta, *sm.* One who is always employed about papers and writings. [curl.
Papelíto, *sm.* A small paper, paper for a hair-
Papelón, *sm.* 1. A large piece of paper posted up, such as edicts and proclamations; prolix writing. 2. Pamphlet. 3. Boaster, ostentator. *Escritor de papelones sueltos,* Pamphleteer, a writer of pamphlets.
Papéra, *sf.* Tumour under the jaws.
Papéro, *sm.* Pot in which a child's pap is made.
Papialbíllo, *sm.* Weasel. Mustela *L.*
Papigordíllo, lla; to, ta, *a.* Plump-cheeked.
Papilár, *a.* Papillary, very small eminences on the skin.
Papílla, *sf.* 1. Pap, food given to sucking children. 2. Guile, deceit, artifice. *Dar papilla,* To deceive by false and insidious caresses.
Papilonáceo, a, *a.* Papilionaceous, butterfly-like.
Papión, *sm.* A kind of large monkey. V. *Cefo.*
Papíro, *sm.* (Bot.) Egyptian papyrus or paper-tree. Cyperus papyrus *L.*
Papiroláda, *sf.* Sauce made of garlic and bread. V. *Pampirolada.*
Papirotáda, *sf.* Fillip on the neck or face.
Papiróte, *sm.* (Vulg.) Fillip.
Papísta, *s. com.* Papist, one who adheres to the doctrines of the Roman catholic church.
Pápo, *sm.* 1. The fleshy part which hangs down from the chin. 2. Quantity of food given to a bird of prey at once. 3. Down of thistles. *Papo de viento,* (Naút.) A small sail. *Hablar de papo,* To speak big. *Pápos,* Furbelow, an ornament sewed on the lower part of a woman's garment.
Papúdo, da, *a.* Double-chinned.
Papújado, da, *a.* 1. Full gorged; applied to birds and fowls. 2. Swoln, thick, elevated
Pápula, *sf.* Pimple or scrofulous tumour on the throat.
Paquebót, *sm.* Packet, a vessel appointed to carry the mail or bag of letters.
Paquéte, *sm.* 1. A small packet, a little bale 2. Bundle of letters tied up together.
Par, *a.* Equal, alike, on a par; even. *Sin par,* Matchless.—*ad.* Near. V. *Cerca ó Junto.* *Par Dios ó par diez,* A minced oath instead of *Por Dios,* By God.
Pár, *sm.* 1. Pair, two of the same sort. 2. Peer, a nobleman or baron of the realm. 3. Handle of a bell. *Pares y nones,* Odd or even; a play. *A' la par,* Jointly, equally; at par, without any charge or discount. *A' pares,* By pairs, two and two. *De par en par,* A-jar; applied to the door; openly, clearly, without obstruction. *Ir á la par,* To go halves, to have an equal share in the business.
Páres, *sf. pl. Las pares,* The placenta or afterbirth, so called from its dividing into two equal parts. V. *Placenta.*
Pára, *prep.* For, to, in order to, towards, wherefore, fit. *Para evitar,* To avoid. *Dar para nieve ó fruta,* To buy snow or fruit, or to give money for snow or fruit. *N. es para nada,* N. is fit for nothing. *¿ Para que?* Why? *Leer para si,* To read to one's self *Para conmigo,* Compared with me. *Para siempre,* For ever. *Para eso,* For that, for so much; in derision. *Para en uno,* To one and the same end. *Para esta,* You will pay me for this; uttered as a menace, placing the fore-finger on the nose. *Sin que ni para que,* Without any motive, without rhyme or reason. *Para con él no vale nada,* According to him it is worth nothing. [the step of an altar
Parabás, *sm.* Thick border of a palm-mat on
Parabién, *sm.* Compliment of congratulation. *Dar el parabien,* To congratulate, to compliment upon any happy event.
Parabienéro, *sm.* One who congratulates; a person full of compliments. [bola
Parábola, *sf.* 1. Parable. 2. (Geom.) Para-
Paraboláno, *sm.* He who uses parables or fictions. [rables or parabolas
Parabólico, ca, *a.* Parabolical, relating to pa-
Paráclето ó Paraclito, *sm.* Name given to the Holy Ghost, sent as an advocate or comforter. [chronology
Paracronísmo, *sm.* Parachronism, error in
Paráda, *sf.* 1. Halt, the act of halting or stopping in a place. 2. End of a course. 3. Stop, suspension, pause. 4. Fold where cattle are kept. 5. Relay, a set of mules or horses on the road to relieve others. 6. Dam, bank. 7 Stake, bet; any thing staked or wagered. 8 Parade, a place where troops are assembled to exercise.
Paradéra, *sf.* Sluice, flood-gate.
Paradéro, *sm.* 1. Halting-place, a place where one stops or intends to stop. 2. Term or end of any thing. *Paradero de los carros,* An inn where carts or wagons put up.

Paradíta, illa, *sf.* A short stop. *Paradetas*, A kind of Spanish dance.
Paradígma, *sm.* Example, instance.
Paradisléro, *sm.* 1. Sportsman waiting for his game. 2. Newsmonger, one whose employment is to hear and tell news.
Parádo, da, *a.* 1. Remiss, careless, indolent. 2. Being without any business or employment. *Coche parado*, Balcony. *Al lo bien parado*, To reject old things, however good, for new ones.
Paradór, *sm.* 1. One who stops or halts. 2. Inn, a house of entertainment for travellers.
Paradóxa, *sf.* Paradox.
Paradóxico, ca, *a.* Paradoxical.
Paradóxo, xa, *a.* Paradoxical, strange, extravagant.
Parafernáles (Bienes), *s. pl.* Paraphernalia, goods which a wife brings independent of her portion, and which are at her disposal.
Parafrasear, *va.* To paraphrase, to interpret with laxity of expression; to translate loosely.
Paráfrasi, *sf.* Paraphrase.
Parafráste, *sm.* Paraphrast.
Parafrasticaménte, *ad.* Paraphrastically.
Parafrástico, ca, *a.* Paraphrastic.
Paráge, *sm.* 1. Place, residence. 2. Condition, disposition.
Paragóge, *sf.* (Gram.) Addition of a letter or syllable at the end of a word.
Paragón, *sm.* Paragon, model, example.
Paragonár, *va.* To paragon, to compare, to equal.
Parágrafo, *sm.* V. *Párrafo.*
Paraíso, *sm.* 1. Paradise, any pleasant or delightful place. 2. Paradise, heaven. *Paraiso de bobos*, Imaginary pleasures, fancied enjoyments.
Parál, *sm.* Wooden trough in which the keel of a ship runs in launching.
Paraláctico, ca, *a.* Parallactic.
Paraláxe ó Paraláxis, *sf.* (Astron.) Parallax.
Paralelipípedo, *sm.* (Geom.) Parallelopiped.
Paralelísmo, *sm.* Parallelism.
Paralelizár, *va.* To parallel, to compare.
Paralélo, la, *a.* Parallel, similar, correspondent.
Paralélo, *sm.* Parallel, resemblance, comparison.
Paralelógramo, *sm.* Parallelogram.
Parálio, *sm.* (Bot.) Kind of sea-spurge.
Paralipómenos, *sm.* One of the books of the Holy Bible, as a supplement.
Parálisis, *sf.* V. *Parlesia.*
Paraliticádo, da, *a.* Paralytic, palsied.
Paralítico, ca, *a.* V. *Perlático.*
Paralogísmo, *sm.* Paralogism, false reasoning.
Paralogizár, *va.* To use false arguments.
Paramentár, *va.* To adorn, to embellish.
Paraménto, *sm.* 1. Ornament, embellishment. 2. Cloth with which any thing is covered.
Páramo, *sm.* Desert, wilderness, a bleak cold place.
Parancéro, *sm.* Bird-catcher, one who catches birds by means of nets, lime-sticks, and other contrivances.
Parangón, *sm.* Paragon, model, comparison.
Parangóna, *sf.* (Imp.) Large type.
Parangonár y Parangonizár, *va.* To paragon, to match, to compare.
Paraninfico, *a.* (Arq.) Applied to a style of building having statues of nymphs instead of columns.
Paraninfo, *sm.* 1. Paranymph, he who conducts the bride to the marriage solemnity; a harbinger of felicity. 2. He who announces the commencement of a course in a university.
Paránza, *sf.* Hut made with sods of earth and branches of trees, where fowlers and other sportsmen lie in ambush for their game.
Paráo, *sm.* Small vessel without a keel, and moved by oars in the East Indies.
Parapéto, *sm.* 1. (Fort.) Parapet, breast-work. 2. Rails or battlements on bridges and quays. *Parapetos de combate*, (Naút.) Netting, parapets made in the waist of the ship.
Parár, *sm.* Lansquenet, a game at cards.
Parár, *vn.* To stop, to halt. *Ir á parar*, To be the object or end of any thing.—*va.* 1. To stop, to detain. 2. To prevent, to prepare. 3. To end, to bring to a close. 4. To treat or use ill. 5. To stake at cards. 6. To point out the game; applied to pointers. 7. To devolve, to come to the possession of. 8. To happen, to fall out. 9. To come to an end, to finish. 10. To change one thing into another. *Parar la consideracion*, To take into consideration. *Sin parar*, Instantly, without delay.—*vr.* To stop, to halt; to be prompt, to be ready; to assume another character.
Parascéve, *sm.* Preparations for Good Friday.
Paraséléne, *sf.* (Meteor.) Mock-moon.
Parasísmo, *sm.* Paroxysm, a fit; a periodical exacerbation of a disease.
Parásito, *sm.* Parasite, sponger; one that frequents rich tables and earns his welcome by flattery.
Parasól, *sm.* Parasol. V. *Quitasol.*
Paratítla, *sf.* Summary of a treatise; half-title.
Paraúso, *sm.* Drill for boring holes in metal.
Parazónio, *sm.* Broad sword without a point.
Párca, *sf.* Fate, death.
Parcaménte, *ad.* Sparingly, parsimoniously.
Párce, *sm.* Schedule of pardon given to grammar scholars.
Parcemíqui, *sm.* (Fest.) *Parce mihi*, the first section of the service or office of the dead.
Parcería, *sf.* Partnership or co-partnership in trade. V. *Aparceria.*
Parcéro, *sm.* Partner, co-partner.
Parchaménto, *sm.* (Naút.) Trim of the ship when the sails are backed.
Parcházo, *sm.* (Met. y Fam.) Deception, jest.
Párche, *sm.* 1. Piece of linen covered with ointment or plaster, to be applied to a wound or sore. 2. Parchment, skins dressed for the writer. 3. Patch, a small spot of black silk put on the face.
Parciál, *a.* 1. Partial, affecting only one part; subsisting only in a part. 2. Partial, friendly, familiar. 3. Sociable, communicable.
Parcialidád, *sf.* 1. Partiality, prejudice against or in favour of a person. 2. Friendship, familiar intercourse, sociability. 3. Party, faction.
Parcializár, *va.* To partialize, to render partial.
Parcialménte, *ad.* Partially, inclined to one part only; familiarly, friendly.
Parcidád, *sf.* Parsimony, frugality.
Parcionéro, *sm.* Partner, one that has a share in a business.
Párco, ca, *a.* 1. Sparing, scanty. 2. Sober, moderate.—*sm.* V. *Parce*
Pardál, *a.* Clownish, rustic; cunning.—*sm.* 1. (Orn.) Grey sand piper. Tringa squatarola L. 2. A kind of leopard. 3. A crafty cunning fellow. 4. V. *Gorrion.*

Pardeár, vn. To grow grey or brownish; to become dusky. [V. *Par Dios.*

Par Diéz, Kind of jocular affirmation or oath.

Pardíllo, sm. (Orn.) Greater redpole. Fringilla cannabina *L.*—a. Greyish, brown; applied to coarse cloth.

Párdo, da, a. Grey, a mixture of black and white. *Pardo blanquizco*, Silver-grey.—sm.

Pardúsco, ca, a. Dark grey. [Tigre.

Pareár, va. To match, to pair, to couple.

Parecér, sm. 1. Opinion, advice. 2. Countenance, air, mien.—vn. 1. To appear, to become visible; to seem. 2. To re-appear; applied to a thing which was lost. 3. To judge, to approve or disapprove. *Al parecer*, Seemingly, to all appearance. *Por el bien parecer*, To save appearances.—vr. To show or present one's self to view; to assimilate or con-

Pareciénte, a. Similar, apparent. [form to.

Parecído, da, a. 1. Resembling, like. 2. Well or ill-featured, with the adverbs *bien* or *mal*.

Paréd, sf. 1. Wall, a series of bricks or stones carried upwards, commonly cemented with mortar. 2. Surface of a field of barley which is close and even. *Pared medianera*, Party-wall. *Paredes*, House or home. *Entre quatro paredes*, Confined, retired; imprisoned.

Paredáño, ña, a. Having a wall between.

Paredílla, sf. A slight wall.

Paredón, sm. A thick wall.

Paregórico, a. Paregoric, assuasive.

Paréja, sf. Pair, couple, brace.

Paréjo, ja, a. Equal, similar. *Por parejo ó por un parejo*, On equal terms, upon a par.

Parejúra, sf. Equality, similitude, uniformity.

Parélia ó Parélio, s. Meteor or mock sun.

Parénesis, sf. Admonition, precept, instruction.

Parenético, ca, a. Admonitory.

Parentación, sf. Funeral service.

Parentál, a. Parental, pertaining to parents and relations.

Parentár, va. To perform the funeral rites for deceased parents or relations.

Parentéla, sf. Parentage; relations in general.

Parentésco, sm. 1. Cognation, kindred. 2. Union, chain, link.

Paréntesis, sm. 1. Parenthesis, a short digression included in a sentence. 2. Interruption or suspension of other things unconnected with language. *Entre ó por paréntesis*, Parenthetically, by parenthesis. 3. (Imp.) Character ( ). [matching.

Paréo, sm. The act of pairing, coupling, or

Parergón, sm. Additional ornament.

Pargamíno, sm. Parchment. V. *Pergamino.*

Párias, sf. 1. Tribute paid by one prince to another as an acknowledgment of superiority. 2. The lowest cast of the Indians. 3. Placenta.

Parición, sf. Child-bearing, parturition; season of bringing forth young.

Parída, sf. Woman lately delivered.

Paridád, sf. Parity, the act of comparing; equality.

Paridéra, a. Fruitful, prolific; applied to females.—sf. 1. Place where cattle bring forth their young. 2. Act of bringing forth young.

Parído, da, a. Delivered.

Pariénte, ta, a. 1. Parentage; relations in general. 2. Resembling, like; having resemblance. 3. Appellation given by husband and wife to each other. 4. Parental.

Parietária, sf. (Bot.) Pellitory. Parietaria *L.*

Parificár, va. To exemplify, to prove by example. [of a balance.

Parigüéla, sf. Fork which supports the arms

Paríllas, sf. pl. Gridiron, a kitchen utensil.

Pário (Marmol), sm. Marble of Paros, Parian marble.

Parír, va. 1. To bring forth a fœtus, to produce. 2. To lay eggs, to spawn. 3. To explain, to clear up; to publish. *Poner á parir*, To oblige one to perform a thing.

Parisiénse, a. Parisian.

Párla, sf. Easy delivery, expeditious way of talking; loquacity.

Parladíllo, sm. An affected style.

Parladór, ra, s. A chattering prating person.

Parlamentál, a. Parliamentary.

Parlamentár y Parlamenteár, vn. 1. To talk, to converse. 2. To parley, to treat of the surrender of a place or post.

Parlaméntário, sm. Member of parliament. —rio, ria, a. Parliamentary.

Parlaménto, sm. 1. Speech or harangue delivered in a public assembly. 2. Parliament, the legislative assembly of Great Britain. composed of the king, the lords spiritual and temporal, and the commons.

Parlánte, pa. Speaking; a talker.

Parlár, va. 1. To chatter, to talk much or fast. 2. To disclose or discover what ought to be kept secret. *Parlar en balde*, To talk nonsense.

Parlatório, sm. 1. Converse, parley. 2. Parlour, the place in convents where nuns are allowed to see and converse with their friends.

Parléra, Parlantína, y Parlerüéla, sf. A talkative little woman.

Parlería, sf. 1. Loquacity, garrulity; prating. talking, tale, jest. 2. Singing or chirping of birds; purling or gentle murmuring of brooks and rivers. [lous.

Parleríto, ta, a. dim. (Joc.) Talkative, garru-

Parléro, ra, a. Loquacious, talkative.

Parléro, sm. 1. Tale-bearer, tattler. 2. Bird that chirps and chatters. 3. Purling brook or rill. 4. Interesting conversation.

Parléta, sf. Conversation on the weather, or the like trifling subjects.

Parlón, na, a. Loquacious, garrulous.

Parloteár, vn. To prattle, to prate, to chatter, to talk much.

Parlotéo, sm. Prattle, talk.

Parnáso, sm. (Poét.) Parnassus.

Páro, sm. (Orn.) Titmouse. Parus *L.*

Paróla, sf. 1. Eloquence, fluency of speech, volubility of tongue. 2. Chat, idle talk.

Parolí, sm. Double of what was laid in stakes at the game of bank.

Parolína, sf. V. *Parola.*

Paroníquia, sf. (Bot.) Whitlow-grass.

Paronomásia, sf. Paronomasia, rhetorical figure.

Parótida, sf. Tumour of the parotid glands.

Paroxismál, a. Relating to a paroxysm.

Paroxísmo, sm. Paroxysm. V. *Parasismo.*

Parpadeár, vn. To twinkle, to open and shut the eyes by turns.

Párpado, *sm.* Eye-lid, the membrane that shuts over the eye.

Parpálla, Parpallóta, y Parparála, *sf.* A milled copper piece, value two quartos, or one half-penny English. [a duck.

Parpár, *sm.* The act of quacking or crying like

Párque, *sm.* 1. Park, a small enclosed wood. 2. Park of artillery, park of provisions.

Parquedád, *sf.* Parsimony.

Párra, *sf.* 1. Vine raised on stakes and nailed to a wall. 2. Earthen jar or pot for honey and other substances.

Párrafo, *sm.* Paragraph, a distinct part of a discourse; a mark (¶) in printing.

Parrál, *sm.* 1. Vine abounding with shoots for want of dressing; place where there are such vines. 2. A large earthen jar with two handles.

Parrár, *vn.* To extend, to spread out in branches and bowers.

Parricída, *s. com.* Parricide, one who destroys his father or mother.

Parricídio, *sm.* Parricide.

Parrílla, *sf.* An earthen jar with two handles, a broad bottom, and narrow mouth. *Parrillas*, Gridiron, an instrument for broiling meat.

Parríza, *sf.* Wild vine.

Párro, *sm.* V. *Ganso*.

Párroco, *sm.* Curate, rector of a parish.

Parrón, *sm.* V. *Parriza*.

Parróquia, *sf.* Parish, the precinct or territory of a parochial church; curate's jurisdiction.

Parroquiál, *a.* Parochial.—*sf.* V. *Parroquia*.

Parroquialidád, *sf.* Parochial right, the right of a parishioner.

Parroquiáno, na, *a.* 1. Belonging to a parish, a parishioner. 2. Being in the habit of buying at a particular shop; a customer.

Parsimónia, *sf.* Parsimony, frugality; temperance, moderation in eating and drinking.

Párte, *sf.* y *m.* 1. Part, portion, share. *Parte aliquanta ó aliquota*, Aliquant or aliquot part. 2. District, territory; situation, place. 3. Party, a person concerned in a business with others; part, connexion. 4. King's messenger; despatch sent by a messenger. 5. Receiving-house for the post-office. 6. Part, character appropriated in a play. 7. Present time. *De ocho dias á esta parte*, Eight days ago. *De parte*, By orders, by command. *En parte*, In part.—*pl.* 1. Parts, talents, endowments. 2. Privy parts. 3. Party, faction. *Por todas partes*, On all hands, on all sides.—*ad.* In part, partly.

Parteár, *va.* To assist women in child-birth.

Parténcia, *sf.* Departure, the act of going away from a place.

Partéra, *sf.* Midwife.

Partería, *sf.* Midwifery.

Partéro, *sm.* Man-midwife.

Partesána, *sf.* Partisan; an offensive weapon.

Partesanéro, *sm.* Pikeman.

Partíble, *a.* Divisible, separable.

Partición, *sf.* Partition, division, distribution.

Participonéro, ra, *a.* Participant, having a share or part in a business. [tion, conversation.

Participación, *sf.* Participation, communica-

Participánte, *pa.* Sharing; participant.

Participár, *va.* To participate, to give part or advice.—*vn.* To partake, to share, to receive.

Partícipe, *a.* Participant, sharing. [ciple.

Participiál, *a.* Participial, relating to a parti-

Participio, *sm.* Participle, a word partaking at once the qualities of a noun and a verb; participation.

Partícula, *sf.* 1. Particle, small part. 2. (Gram.) Particle.

Particulár, *a.* Particular, peculiar, special, singular.—*sm.* 1. Private gentleman, a person without any title or profession. 2. Play represented on a private theatre. 3. A peculiar matter or subject treated upon. *En particular*, Particularly, in particular.

Particularidád, *sf.* 1. Particularity, peculiarity. 2. Friendship, intimacy.

Particularizár, *va.* To particularize, to mention distinctly; to make particular mention of a person or thing.—*vr.* To singularize.

Particularménte, *ad.* Particularly, especially.

Partída, *sf.* 1. Departure, the act of going away from a place. 2. Death, decease. 3. Party of soldiers. 4. Item in an account. 5. Parcel, a determinate quantity. *Partida de azúcar*, A parcel of sugar. 6. Game at play. 7. (Naút.) Crew of a ship. *Buena partida*, Excellent conduct!—*pl.* 1. Parts, talents, accomplishments. 2. The laws of Castile, compiled by the order of King Ferdinand.

Partidaménte, *ad.* Separately, distinctly.

Partidário, *sm.* 1. Partisan, the commander of a party of troops, generally of light troops. 2. Adherent to a faction, follower, abettor.—*a.* Having the care of a certain district; applied to physicians and surgeons.

Partído, da, *a.* Free, liberal, munificent.

Partído, *sm.* 1. Partiality, party. 2. Favour, protection, interest. 3. Party engaged to play any game. 4. Treaty, agreement; terms proposed for adjusting or accommodating a difference. 5. District of the jurisdiction of one of the principal towns in Spain. 6. District intrusted to the care of a physician or surgeon. 7. Party, a number of persons who follow and maintain the same opinion. 8. Interest, convenience; advantage. 9. Proper or fit means, medium. *Muger del partido*, Woman of the town, common strumpet. *Tomar partido*, To embrace a resolution; to resolve.

Partidór, *sm.* 1. One who parts or divides. *Partidor de leña*, Cleaver, the instrument and workman employed in cleaving wood. 2. Bodkin, an instrument used by country-women to divide the hair. 3. (Ant.) V. *Divisor*.

Partíja, *sf.* V. *Partícion*.

Partíl, *a.* Applied to the astrological aspects.

Partiménto ó Partimiénto, *sm.* V. *Particion*.

Partír, *va.* 1. To part, to divide, to sever. 2. To divide, to distribute. 3. To crack the stones of fruit. 4. To depart, to set out on a journey. 5. To attack, to engage in combat or battle. 6. To resolve, to come to a determination. 7. (Ant.) To divide. *Partir la diferencia*, To split the difference. *Partir al puño*, (Naút.) To gripe, to carry a weatherly helm. *Partir las amarras*, (Naút.) To part the cable. *Partir por entero*, To carry off the whole; to divide a number. *Partir mano*, To desist, to abandon.—*vr.* 1. To set out on a journey. 2. To be divided in opinion. *Partirse el alma*, To die; to die broken-hearted. *Partir*, To divide a bee-hive into two, at the proper season. V. *Peon*. *Partir abierto*, To uncover a bee-hive that it may swarm. *Partir cerrado*, To divide a bee-hive when it is full.

PARTITÍVO, VA, *a.* (Gram.) Partitive.

PÁRTO, *sm.* 1. Child-birth, parturition; the act of bringing forth a child. 2. New-born child. 3. Any natural production. 4. Any literary composition.

PARTURIÉNTE, *a.* Parturient, about to bring forth.

PARÚLIS, *sm.* Gum-bile, a morbid swelling of the gums; tumour in the fauces.

PÁRVA, *sf.* 1. Unthrashed corn laid in heaps to be thrashed. 2. Multitude, large quantity.

PARVÁDA, *sf.* Place for unthrashed corn.

PARVEDÁD ó PARVIDÁD, *sf.* Littleness, minuteness.

PARVIFICÉNCIA, *sf.* Parsimony, sordid avarice.

PARVÍFICO, CA, *a.* Parsimonious, miserable.

PÁRVO, VA, *a.* Small, little.

PARVULÉZ, *sf.* Smallness, small size.

PARVULÍLLO, LLA; TO, TA, *a. dim.* Very little.

PÁRVULO, LA, *a.* Very small; innocent; humble, low.

PÁSA, *sf.* 1. Raisin, grapes dried by the heat of the sun or in an oven. 2. Passage of birds which pass from one region to another. 3. Paint used by women, made of raisins. *Pásas*, The curled hair of blacks and negroes.

PASÁBLE, *a.* Tolerable, passable.

PASACÁLLE, *sm.* Kind of music played on the guitar in the streets.

PASÁDA, *sf.* 1. Passage, the act of passing from one place to another. 2. Pace, step; measure of 5 feet. 3. Competency, a decent livelihood. 4. Manner, behaviour. *Jugar una mala pasada*, To play an uncivil or unbecoming trick. *Dar pasada*, To tolerate, to permit. *De pasada*, On the way, in passing, hastily, cursorily.

PASADÉRA, *sf.* 1. Stepping-stone, a stone put in a ford to facilitate the passage. 2. (Naút.) Spun-yarn.

PASADERAMÉNTE, *ad.* Passably.

PASADÉRO, RA, *a.* 1. Supportable, sufferable. 2. Passable, tolerably good.—*sm.* V. *Pasadera.*

PASADÍA, *sf.* Competency, a decent livelihood.

PASADÍLLO, *sm.* A small embroidery wrought on both sides of a piece of stuff.

PASADÍZO, *sm.* A narrow passage or covered way which leads from one place to another. *Pasadizo continuado de quartos*, A flight of rooms contiguous to each other.

PASÁDO, DA, *a.* Passed, past. *Lo pasado pasado*, What is past is forgotten and forgiven. *Pasados*, Ancestors. V. *Ascendientes ó antepasados.*

PASADÓR, *sm.* 1. Smuggler, one who deals in contraband goods, or runs merchandise into a country without paying the duty laid on them. 2. A sharp-pointed arrow, from a cross-bow. 3. Bolt of a lock; woman's brooch. 4. (Naút.) Marling-fid, an iron pin tapered with a round head, used in splicing ropes.

PÁSA-GAZNÁTE, *sm.* Eatables, any thing that can be eaten.

PASÁGE, *sm.* 1. Passage, the act of passing from one place to another; the place of passing, straits. 2. Reception given to travellers or other persons. 3. State of health. *¿ Está vd. de buen pasage ?* Are you in good health ? 4. Passage-money, duty paid for passing bridges or rivers in boats. *Pagar el pasage*, (Naút.) To pay for one's passage. 5. (Mús.) Transition or change of voice. 6. Passage, clause, short portion of a book or writing.

PASAGÉRO, RA, *a.* Transient, transitory.—*s.* Traveller, passenger; bird of passage.

PASAGONZÁLO, *sm.* A slight blow briskly given.

PASAMANERÍA, *sf.* The trade of a laceman; the profession of a fancy-trimming maker, twister, or ribbon-weaver.

PASAMANÉRO, *sm.* Lace-maker, a fancy-trimming maker, a twister, a ribbon-maker.

PASAMANÍLLO, *sm.* A narrow lace, a small twist for the edge of a coat.

PASAMÁNO, *sm.* 1. Balustrade, a row of little turned pillars, called balusters. 2. Kind of lace or edging for clothes. *Pasamanos*, Gangways, the passages or ways round about a ship.

PASAMIÉNTO, *sm.* Passage, transit.

PASÁNTE, *sm.* 1. Assistant of a physician or lawyer, to acquire a practical knowledge of medicine or jurisprudence. 2. Student who delivers lectures to beginners. 3. Game at cards. *Pasante de pluma*, An attorney's clerk.

PASANTÍA, *sf.* Profession of a student of the law who practises under the direction of another.

PASAPÁN, *sm.* (Fam.) V. *Garguero.*

PASAPÁSA, *sm.* Legerdemain, slight of hand performed by a juggler.

PASAPÓRTE, *sm.* Passport, permission of leaving a country; license; furlough.

PASÁR, *vn.* 1. To pass, to move from one place to another. 2. To go to any determinate place. 3. To ascend, to be promoted to a higher post. 4. To travel through a place or country. 5. To be executed before a notary. 6. To die.—*va.* 1. To bring or convey from one place to another. 2. To pierce, to penetrate, to run through. 3. To pass beyond the limit of the place of destination. 4. To change for better or worse. 5. To exceed in number, quantity, quality, or abilities. 6. To depart, to decease. 7. To suffer, to bear, to undergo. *Pasar á cuchillo*, To put to the sword, to kill. 8. To strain liquor. 9. To present an act, charter, or privilege, to be confirmed. 10. To pass over in silence, to omit. 11. To dissemble, to overlook. 12. To have currency; applied to coin or money. 13. To stop, to terminate. 14. To run over one's lesson; to rehearse; to run over a book or treatise. 15. To reprimand, to censure. 16. To draw up an instrument. 17. To dry by the heat of the sun or in an oven. *Pasar muestra ó revista*, To muster. *Pasar un cabo.* (Naút.) To reeve a rope, to pass it through a block or hole.—*v. impers.* To pass, to happen, to turn out.—*vr.* 1. To go over to another party. 2. To cease, to finish; to exceed. 3. To forget, to consign to oblivion. 4. To be out of season, to be spoiled; applied to fruit. 5. To pass unimproved; applied to a favourable opportunity of attaining one's end. 6. To leak, to ooze through the pores of a vessel: applied to liquors. 7. To kindle or light with; applied to lamps or candles. 8. To surpass. *Pasarse con poco*, To be satisfied with a little. *Un buen pasar*, A competency.

Pasatiempo, *sm.* Pastime, diversion, amusement.
Pasatúro, *sm.* A student with whom another repeats lectures on any art or science.
Pasavolánte, *sm.* 1. An inconsiderate speech or action. 2. A culverin of a small caliber. 3. (Naút.) Fagot, a seaman entered in the muster-book but not actually existing; false muster.
Pasavoléo, *sm.* Ball which passes the line in bowling.
Pascásio, *sm.* Student who goes to pass the holidays at home.
Páscua, *sf.* 1. Passover, a feast instituted and celebrated among the Jews. 2. Easter, the day on which the Christian church commemorates our Saviour's resurrection. 3. (Met.) Christmas, the day on which the nativity of our blessed Saviour is celebrated. 4. Any festival of the church which lasts three days. *Decir los nombres de las pascuas,* To use injurious language. *Estar como una pascua,* To be as merry as a cricket. *Hacer la pascua,* To begin to eat meat after Lent. *Santas pascuas,* Be it so.
Pascuál, *a.* Paschal, relating to Easter.
Páse, *sm.* 1. An act of a court of justice which orders a decree to be expedited and carried into effect. 2. Passport; license for goods.
Paseadéro, *sm.* Walk, avenue.
Paseadór, *sm.* 1. One who walks or takes a walk. 2. Walk, the place where people walk for air or exercise.
Paseánte, *pa.* Walker. *Paseante en corte,* One who has neither office nor employ.
Paseár, *vn.* 1. To walk, to move for air or exercise. 2. To move the slowest pace; applied to a horse.—*va.* 1. To take out on a walk; to take the air or exercise on horseback or in a coach. 2. To argue in a desultory manner. *Pasear la calle,* To court a lady in the street. *Pasearse,* To muse; to wander about idle. *Pasear las calles,* To be whipped through the streets by order of a judge or justice. *Anda ó vayase vd. á pasear,* Go along; an expression of displeasure.
Paseáta, *sf.* A walk, airing, drive.
Paséo, *sm.* 1. The act of taking a walk for air or amusement. 2. Walk, a public place destined for walking. 3. Gait, manner of walking. 4. Cavalcade, procession.
Paséra, *sf.* (Extrem.) Place where raisins are dried; act of drying them.
Pasibilidád, *sf.* Passibleness, the quality of receiving impressions from external agents.
Pasíble, *a.* Passible, capable of suffering.
Pasicórto, ta, *a.* Short-stepped; applied to horses, which take short steps.
Pasilárgo, ga, *a.* Long-stepped; applied to horses.
Pasíllo, *sm.* 1. A short step. 2. A small narrow passage. 3. Basting stitch.
Pásio, *sm.* (Ar.) Passion, suffering of our Saviour. V. *Pasion.*
Pasión, *sf.* 1. The act of suffering torments. 2. Passion, the last suffering of the Redeemer of the world. 3. Passion, affection, or violent emotion of the mind; ardent inclination. 4. Sermon on the sufferings and death of our Saviour. 5. Violent pain felt in any part of the body.
Pasionária, *sf.* (Bot.) Passion-flower.
Pasionários, *sm. pl.* Passion-books, from which the passion is sung in the holy week.
Pasioncíllo, lla, *s.* Slight emotion.
Pasionéro, *sm.* One who sings the passion. *Pasioneros,* Priests who attend the patients in the hospital of Zaragoza.
Pasionísta, *sm.* V. *Pasionero.*
Pasíto, *sm.* A short step.
Pasíto y Pasitaménte, *ad.* Gently, softly. *Pasito á pasito,* Very leisurely or gently.
Pasitróte, *sm.* Short trot of horses alone.
Pasivaménte, *ad.* Passively.
Pasívo, va, *a.* 1. Passive, receiving impression from some external agent. 2. (Gram.) Passive; applied to voices. *Voz pasiva,* Capable of being elected.
Pasmár, *va.* 1. To benumb, to make torpid; to stupify. 2. To chill, to deaden.—*vn.* To be enraptured with admiration.—*vr.* To be spasmodic, to suffer spasms.
Pasmaróta, *sf.* 1. A feigned spasm, often used by beggars to excite compassion and obtain charity. 2. Admiration or astonishment without cause or motive.
Pásmo, *sm.* 1. Spasm, convulsion; violent and involuntary contraction. *Pasmo de la quixada inferior,* A locked jaw. 2. Astonishment, amazement, admiration. 3. Object of admiration.
Pasmosaménte, *ad.* Wonderfully, astonishingly.
Pasmóso, sa, *a.* Marvellous, wonderful.
Páso, sa, *pp. irreg.* Dried; applied to fruit.
Páso, *sm.* 1. Pace, step; quantity of space measured by one removal of the foot. 2. Gait, manner of walking. 3. Flight of steps. 4. Passage, the place through which persons pass from one part to another. 5. Step, measure; instance of conduct, mode of life. 6. Footstep, print of the foot. 7. Passport, license, permission. 8. Explanation given by a master or usher. 9. Passage, part of a book; single place in writing. 10. Progress, advance, improvement. 11. Death, decease. 12. Image carried about in the holy week. *Paso de garganta,* Trill, quaver; a harmonious tremulousness of the voice.—*pl.* 1. Running stitches with which clothes are basted. 2. Conduct, proceedings.
Páso, *ad.* Softly, gently. *Paso á paso,* Step by step; slowly. *A' buen paso,* At a good rate or step. *A' ese paso,* At that rate. *Al paso,* Without delay, instantly; going along; in the manner of, like. *A' pocos pasos,* At a short distance; with little care. *Dar paso,* To clear the way; to promote, to facilitate. *De paso,* Passing by; lightly, briefly, by the way; at the same time, at once. *Vista de paso,* A cursory view. *Mas que de paso,* Hastily, in a hurry.
Paspié, *sm.* A kind of dance.
Pasqüílla, *sf.* The first Sunday after Easter.
Pasquín, *sm.* Pasquinade, pasquil, lampoon.
Pasquináda, *sf.* Pasquinade.
Pasquinár, *va.* To ridicule, to lampoon, to satirize.
Pásta, *sf.* 1. Paste, flour and water boiled together so as to make a cement. 2. Bullion,

mass of gold or silver for coining. 3. Pasteboard, cartoon. 4. Excessive meekness or mildness. 5. Artificial mixture in imitation of precious stones.

Pastár, *vn.* To pasture, to graze.—*va.* To lead cattle to graze.

Pastéca, *sf.* (Naút.) Snatch-block, a single block with one sheave.

Pastél, *sm.* 1. Pie, a composition of flour, milk, butter, and minced meat. 2. (Bot.) Woad. Isatis tinctoria *L.* 3. Trick in the dealing of cards. 4. Meeting, assembly for some secret design. 5. (Imp.) Mass of types to be recast; words too black, having too much ink. *Pastel de glasto*, Crayon for drawing. *Pastel embote*, Short fat person; dish of spiced meat.

Pasteléra, *sf.* Pastrycook's wife, she who makes and sells pastry.

Pastelería, *sf.* 1. Pastrycook's shop. 2. Pastry, pies or baked paste.

Pasteléro, *sm.* Pastrycook.

Pastelíllo, *sm.* 1. A little pie. 2. Tart; a kind of sweetmeat.

Pastelón, *sm.* A large pie.

Pastéro, *sm.* One who procures pasture for cattle.

Pastílla, *sf.* Any small piece of paste baked hard. *Pastilla de olor*, Lozenge, a small cake made up with aromatics.

Pastináca, *sf.* 1. (Bot.) Carrot. Daucus carota *L.* 2. (Ict.) Fire-flaire, sting-ray. Raia pastinaca *L.*

Pásto, *sm.* 1. Pasture, the act of grazing. 2. Pasture, the grass which serves for the feed of cattle; pasture-ground. 3. Food, aliment, nourishment. 4. Pabulum, support; doctrine preached to the faithful. *A' pasto*, Abundantly, plentifully. *A' todo pasto*, Limited to certain food or drink exclusively.

Pastofório, *sm.* Habitation for priests in gentile temples.

Pastór, *sm.* 1. Shepherd, one who tends sheep in a pasture. 2. Pastor, a clergyman who has the care of a flock. 3. Blur or blot of ink in the copy of a school-boy.

Pastóra, *sf.* Shepherdess, pastor's wife.

Pastorágo, *sm.* Pasturage, the business of feeding cattle.

Pastorál, *a.* Pastoral, rural, rustic.

Pastoralménte, *ad.* Pastorally, rustically.

Pastorcíco, ca, *s.* A little shepherd or shepherdess.

Pastoreár, *va.* 1. To graze, to pasture; to bring cattle to pasture. 2. To feed souls with sound doctrine.

Pastoréla, *sf.* Pastoral, a poem in which the speakers assume the character of shepherds; an idyl.

Pastoréo, *sm.* Pasturing, act of tending flocks.

Pastoría, *sf.* A pastoral or rural life, pastors.

Pastoríl y Pastorício, cia, *a.* Pastoral.

Pastorilménte, *ad.* V. *Pastoralmente.*

Pastóso, sa, *a.* 1. Plump, full. 2. Painted or drawn with a coloured crayon or pencil.

Pastúra, *sf.* 1. Pasture, the grass on which animals feed. 2. (Mancha) Refuse of straw eaten by cattle. 3. Fodder, dry food for cattle.

Pasturáge, *sm.* 1. Pasturage, a common field or ground on which cattle graze. 2. Duty paid for the right of grazing cattle on a certain ground or field.

Páta, *sf.* 1. Foot and leg of beasts. 2. Duck, the female of the drake. 3. Flap, that part of a coat which hangs over the pocket. *Pata de cabra*, An unforeseen impediment. *Pata de pobre*, An ulcerated leg. *A' la pata coja*, Hoppers, or Scotch hoppers; a kind of play. *A' pata*, On foot. *A' pata llana*, Plainly, without ornament or affectation. *Patas arriba*, Reversed, overturned.

Patáca, *sm.* 1. Dollar, patacoon, a silver coin, worth about four shillings and eightpence sterling. 2. (Bot.) Sun-flower. V. *Girasol* 3. Copper coin worth *two quartos.*

Patáche, *sm.* (Naút.) Tender, a vessel attending a squadron, and employed in carrying men and orders from one ship or place to another.

Patacón, *sm.* Dollar or patacoon, a silver coin, weighing an ounce.

Patáda, *sf.* 1. Kick, a blow with the foot. 2. Step, pace. 3. Track, mark left by the foot of an animal. *No dar pie ni patada*, Not to take the least trouble to obtain some end.

Patagalána, *sf.* (Fam.) Limping; having a short leg.

Patagón, *sm.* A large clumsy foot.

Patagorríllo, lla, *s.* Fricassee made of the livers and lights of animals.

Pataleár, *vn.* 1. To kick about violently. 2. To stamp the foot suddenly downward; to stamp.

Pataléo, *sm.* The act of stamping or striking the foot suddenly downwards.

Pataléta, *sf.* 1. A fainting fit which takes away the use of the senses. 2. A ridiculous speech or action; an absurd enterprise.

Pataletílla, *sf.* A kind of dance.

Patán, *sm.* Clown, a rude illiterate person.—*a.* Large-footed.

Patanería, *sf.* Clownishness, rusticity, rudeness.

Pataráta, *sf.* 1. Fiction, a false idle story. 2. An affected demonstration of concern or affection.

Pataratéro, ra, *a.* Using fictitious or artificial appearances.

Patarráez, *sm.* (Naút.) Preventer-shroud, a thick rope employed occasionally to strengthen the shrouds and support the masts. *Patarraez de una máquina de arbolar*, (Naút.) The shroud of a sheer-hulk for masting ships.

Patáta, *sf.* (Bot.) Potato. V. *Batata.* *Patata gallega*, Goat's rue. Galega officinalis *L.*

Patatál, *sm.* Potato-field.

Patatús, *sm.* Swoon, a fainting fit.

Patax ó Patáxe, *sm.* V. *Patache.*

Pateadúra, *sf.* The act of kicking or stamping.

Pateamiénto, *sm.* Act of kicking.

Pateár, *va.* 1. To kick, to strike with the foot. 2. To drive about to obtain some end. 3. To be extremely irritated.

Paténa, *sf.* 1. A large medal worn by countrywomen. 2. Patine, the lid or cover of a chalice. 3. V. *Pátera.*

Paténte, *a.* Patent, manifest, evident; easily conceived.—*sf.* 1. Patent, a writ conferring some exclusive right or privilege; warrant, commission. 2. Letters of marque. 3. Letter of obedience expedited by prelates, and addressed to their religious subjects. 4. Money paid by new comers to the elder members of a company or office.

Patentemente, *ad.* Openly, clearly, visibly.

Pátera, *sf.* Goblet; a wide-mouthed vessel.

Paternál, *a.* Paternal, fatherly; having the relation of a father.

Paternalménte, *ad.* Paternally.

Paternidád, *sf.* 1. Paternity, fathership; the relation of a father. 2. A title of respect given to religious men.

Patérno, na, *a.* Paternal, fatherly.

Paternóster, *sm.* 1. The Lord's prayer; paternoster. 2. A big tight knot.

Patésca, *sf.* (Naút.) A large block.

Patéta, *sm.* 1. A nick-name given to a lame person. 2. (Joc.) Devil, Old Nick.

Patético, ca, *a.* 1. Pathetic, passionate, moving. 2. Plaintive, expressive of sorrow.

Patiabiérto, ta, *a.* Straddling, having the legs far removed from each other in an irregular manner.

Patialbíllo, *sm.* Weasel. V. *Papialbillo.*

Patíbulo, *sm.* Gibbet, gallows.

Patíca, *sf.* (Iron.) A small foot.

Patíco, *sm.* A young goose, a gosling.

Paticójo, ja, *a.* (Joc.) Lame, crippled.

Patiesteváдо, da, *a.* Bow-legged.

Patihendído, da, *a.* Cloven-footed.

Patílla, *sf.* 1. A small foot. 2. Manner of playing on the guitar. 3. (Naút.) Spike nailed to the stern-post, on which the helm hangs and moves. 4. Trigger. 5. Portion of hair left between the temple and posterior part of the ear. *Patillas*, (Vulg.) Demon.

Patimacízo, za, *a.* Solid-footed; applied to animals which do not divide the hoof.

Patimuléño, ña, *a.* Mulefooted; applied to horses with narrow hoofs.

Patína, *sm.* 1. A small court or yard. 2. (Orn.) Goosander. Mergus *L.* *Patines*, Skates, a sort of shoes armed with iron for sliding on the ice.

Patinéjo ó Patinillo, *sm.* A small court or [yard.

Patíno, *sm.* Gosling, a young goose.

Pátio, *sm.* 1. Court, an open space in front of a house or behind it. 2. Pit in play-houses. 3. Hall in universities, academies, or colleges. *Estar á patio*, To live at one's own expense, not to be on the foundation; applied to students in universities and colleges.

Patitiéso, sa, *a.* 1. Deprived by some sudden accident of sense and feeling. 2. Stiff, stately, starchy; applied to a proud presumptuous person of an affected gait. 3. Benumbed, stupefied, surprised.

Patituérto, ta, *a.* 1. Crook-legged, having crooked legs or feet. 2. Ill-disposed, perverse; without rectitude of mind.

Patizámbo, ba, *a.* Bandy-legged.

Páto, ta, *a.* Equal, similar.

Páto, *sm.* (Orn.) Goose. V. *Ansar.*

Patocháda, *sf.* Blunder, nonsense.

Patognómica, *a.* Pathognomic, symptomatic.

Patójo, ja, *a.* Waddling, walking like a goose.

Patología, *sf.* Pathology, that part of medicine which relates to the distempers incident to the body, with their differences, causes, and effects.

Patón, *sm.* Clumsy foot.—na, *a.* Large footed.

Patráña, *sf.* A fabulous story, a fictitious account. [Fit or proper place for any thing.

Pátria, *sf.* 1. Native country, place of birth. 2.

Patriárca, *sm.* 1. Patriarch, a father and head of a numerous progeny in primitive ages. 2. Founder of any religious order. 3. Bishop, who possesses, or pretends to possess, an absolute power and authority in the provinces of his jurisdiction. 4. Honorary title conferred by the pope on certain persons.

Patriarcádo, *sm.* Patriarchate, the dignity and jurisdiction of a patriarch.

Patriarcál, *a.* Patriarchal.

Patriciádo, *sm.* Dignity of a patrician.

Patrício, cia, *a.* Native, national; patrician.

Patrício, *sm.* Patrician, noble.

Patriedád, *sf.* V. *Patrimonialidád.*

Patrimoniál, *a.* Patrimonial, possessed by right of inheritance.

Patrimonialidád, *sf.* The quality of being a native of a certain place or country.

Património, *sm.* 1. Patrimony, an estate possessed by right of inheritance. 2. Property acquired on any title whatever.

Pátrio, tria, *a.* 1. Belonging to a native place or country. 2. Paternal, belonging to a father.

Patrióta, *s. com.* 1. Countryman, born in the same country. 2. Patriot.

Patriótico, ca, *a.* Patriotic, beneficent.

Patriotísmo, *sm.* Patriotism. [tect.

Patrocinár, *va.* To favour, to patronise, to pro-

Patrocínio, *sm.* Protection, patronage.

Patrón, na, *s.* 1. Patron, protector; one who countenances, supports, or protects. 2. Master or commander of a trading vessel. 3. Landlord or landlady of a house or inn. 4. Guardian saint of a country. 5. One who has the donation of ecclesiastical preferment. 6. Pattern, sample, copy. *Patron de bote ó de lancha*, (Naút.) The cockswain of a boat.

Patróna, *sf.* 1. Mistress of a house, hostess; patroness; tutelar saint of a church, protectress of a province, &c. 2. Galley which follows immediately that of the commodore, and the captain whereof is the next in command.

Patronádo, da, *a.* Having a patron; applied to churches and prebends.—*sm.* V. *Patronato.*

Patronáto y Patronázgo, *sm.* 1. Patronage, the right of presenting to an ecclesiastical benefice. 2. Foundation of some charitable or pious establishment.

Patronía, *sf.* Mastership of a vessel.

Patronímico, *sm.* Patronymic, surname formed from the proper name of the father, as Johnson from John.

Patróno, *sm.* 1. Lord of the manor, one of whom lands or tenements are held. 2. V. *Patron.*

Patrúlla, *sf.* Patrol, a small detachment of soldiers to secure the peace and safety of a street, place, or camp.

Patrullár, *vn.* To patrol, to go the rounds in a camp or garrison. [feet.

Patúdo, da, *a.* Club-footed, having clumsy

Patué, *sm.* Corrupt language used in some provinces; provincialism.

Patullár, *vn.* 1. To beat or dash through muddy places, to run through thick and thin. 2. To labour hard in the pursuit of any thing.

Paulatinamente, *ad.* Gently, slowly, by little and little.
Paulatino, na, *a.* Slowly, by degrees.
Paulina, *sf.* 1. Decree of excommunication, interdict. 2. Foul injurious language.
Pauperrimo, ma, *a. sup.* Very poor.
Pausa, *sf.* 1. Pause, stop; a time of intermission. 2. Rest, repose. 3. Suspense, delay. *A' pausas*, At leisure, by pauses or intervals.
Pausadamente, *ad.* Slowly, deliberately.
Pausado, da, *a.* 1. Slow, deliberate. 2. Calm, quiet.
Pausan, na, *s.* V. *Bausan.*
Pausar, *vn.* To pause, to cease.
Pauta, *sf.* 1. Ruler, an instrument, by the direction of which lines are drawn on paper. 2. Rule, guide, pattern, example.
Pautador, *sm.* One who makes rulers, or draws lines by the direction of a ruler.
Pautar, *va.* 1. To draw lines on paper by the direction of a ruler. 2. To give rules, to prescribe the manner of performing an action.
Pautkas, *sf.* A sort of cotton stuff which comes from India.
Pava, *sf.* 1. (Orn.) Turkey-hen, the female of the turkey. 2. Pea-hen, the female of the pea-cock.
Pavada, *sf.* A large fat hen.
Pavana, *sf.* 1. A kind of Spanish dance. *Pasos de pavana*, A grave solemn step; a stately gait. 2. Kind of neckcloth, formerly worn by women.
Pavería, *sf.* Place for rearing turkeys.
Pavero, ra, *a.* Rearing or feeding turkeys.—*s.* One who feeds or sells turkeys.
Paves, *sm.* Kind of large shield.
Pavesa, *sf.* 1. Embers, hot cinders; ashes not yet extinguished; snuff of the candle. 2. Remains, relic; that which is left of any thing. 3. Mildness, meekness; gentleness of manners. 4. A weak extenuated or debilitated person.
Pavesadas, *sf. pl.* (Naút.) Waistclothes; long pieces of painted canvas or baize, extended on the outside of the quarter-netting for shelter or ornament. *Pavesadas de las cosas*, (Naút.) Top armour of the lower masts.
Pavía, *sf.* Kind of quince or peach.
Pávido, da, *a.* Timid, timorous, fearful.
Pavimento, *sm.* Pavement, the floor of a house or other building made of stone, tiles, or other materials.
Paviota, *sf.* (Orn.) Mew, sea-gull. Larus *L.*
Pavipollo, *sm.* A young turkey.
Pavito Real, *sm.* Pea-chicken.
Pavo, *sm.* 1. (Orn.) Turkey. Meleagris gallipavo *L.* 2. (Ict.) Peacock fish. Labrus pavo *L.* *Pavo silvestre*, (Orn.) Wood grouse. Tetras urogallus *L.* *Pavo real*, (Orn.) Peacock. V. *Pavon.* *Pavo carbonero*, (Orn.) Lapland finch. Fringilla lapponica *L.*
Pavo, va, *a.* (Burl.) Peacock-like; applied to fops.
Pavón, *sm.* 1. (Orn.) Peacock. Pavo *L.* 2. A piece of wood with which gunpowder is glazed. 3. (Astr.) Northern constellation.
Pavonada, *sf.* 1. Short walk. 2. Strut, an affectation of stateliness in the walk.
Pavonar, *va.* To give iron or steel a bluelsh colour.
Pavonazo, *sm.* (Pint.) Crimson or purple colour.
Pavonear, *vn.* To strut, to walk with affected dignity; to flaunt about the streets.
Pavón, *sm.* Fear, dread, terror.
Pavorde, *sm.* 1. Provost of a cathedral, chapter, or other community. 2. Professor of divinity in the university of Valencia.
Pavordear, *va.* To swarm; applied to bees.
Pavordía, *sf.* Place and dignity of a provost.
Pavorido, da, *a.* Intimidated, struck with terror; full of fear and dread.
Pavorosamente, *ad.* Awfully, fearfully.
Pavoroso, sa, *a.* Awful, that which strikes with awe or fear.
Pavura, *sf.* Fear, dread, terror. V. *Pavor.*
Pázara, *sf.* 1. Hen, the female of any bird. 2. Paper kite.
Pazarear, *vn.* 1. To go a bird-catching. 2. To idle or loiter about.
Pazarel, *sm.* V. *Xilguero.*
Pazarera, *sf.* 1. Aviary, a place enclosed to keep birds. 2. Collection of jests and jokes.
Pazarería, *sf.* Abundance of sparrows or little birds.
Pazarero, *sm.* 1. Bird-catcher. 2. One who idles or loiters about.
Pazarero, ra, *a.* 1. Merry, cheerful, gay. 2. Shy; applied to horses.
Pazaril, *sm.* (Naút.) Passaree or passarado, a rope fastened to the corner of a sail.
Pazarilla, *sf.* 1. A small hen or female of a bird. 2. Milt of a hog or pig. 3. Bashfulness, shame. 4. (Met.) Stuttering from diffidence. *Caerse las pazarillas*, To be intolerably hot.
Pazarillo, lla; co, ca; to, ta, *s. dim.* A small bird.
Pázaro, *sm.* (Orn.) 1. Bird, a general term for all sorts of wild fowl. 2. Sparrow. Fringilla domestica *L.* *Adiestrar pázaros*, To teach birds to sing. 3. (Met.) A conspicuous person; a sly acute fellow. *Pázaro solitario*, Man who shuns the company of others.
Pazarota ó Pazarotada, *sf.* A false idle report.
Pazarraco ó Pazaruco, *sm.* A large bird.
Paya, *sf.* Hoiden, an ill-taught awkward country girl.
Payla, *sf.* A large pan of copper, brass, or iron.
Paylón, *sm.* A large copper.
Payo, *sm.* Clown, a rude unmannerly fellow.
Payrar, *vn.* (Naút.) To bring-to, to lie-to. *Al payro*, Lying-to.
Paz, *sf.* 1. Peace, tranquillity, ease. 2. A pleasant peaceful disposition. 3. Equality of luck among card-players, when there are neither considerable winners nor losers. 4. Balance of accounts. 5. Recrimination, return of foul or injurious language. *A' la paz de Dios*, God be with you. *Bandera de paz*, A flag of truce. *Paz y pan*, Peace and bread, the source of public tranquillity.
Paz! *interj.* Peace! *Paz sea en esta casa*, Peace be in this house, a salute on entering.
Pazán, *sm.* Egyptian antelope. Antilope oryx *L.*
Pazguato, ta, *s.* Dolt, a simple, stupid person.
Pazpuerco, ca, *a.* Dirty, slovenly.
Pe, *ad.* *De pe á pa*, Entirely, from beginning to end.
Peage ó Pedage, *sm.* Bridge-toll, ferryage.
Peagero, *sm.* Toll-gatherer.
Peal, *sm.* 1. Sock, a covering of the foot, worn between the stocking and the shoe; foot of a stocking. 2. Worthless person.
Peal, *a.* Heavy, dull, stupid, sickly.

Peána, *sf.* 1. Pedestal, the basis of a statue. 2. Frame put at the foot of an altar to tread upon. *Peana de las muniquetas*, (Naút.) Step of the kevels.

Peáña, *sf.* 1. A morbid swelling on a horse's tongue. 2. V. *Peana.*

Peázgo, *sm.* Bridge-toll. V. *Peage.*

Pebéte, *sf.* 1. An aromatic composition made up into small sticks and used as a perfume. 2. Stench, an unpleasant smell. 3. Tube filled with gunpowder and other ingredients, and used to convey fire to rockets, and other artificial fireworks.

Pebetéro, *sm.* Censer, a vessel in which perfumes are burnt.

Pébre y Pebráda, *s.* 1. A kind of sauce made of garlic, cloves, and other spice. 2. Pepper. V. *Pimienta.*

Péca, *sf.* Freckle, a spot raised in the skin by the sun.

Pecáble, *a.* Peccable, liable to sin.

Pecadíllo, *sm.* A slight fault.

Pecádo, *sm.* 1. Sin, an act against the laws of God; a violation of the laws of religion. *Pecado mortal*, Deadly sin. 2. Extravagance, excess. 3. (Fam.) Devil, the instigator or inciter to sin.

Pecadór, *sm.* 1. One who violates the laws of God and religion; a sinner, offender. 2. (Met.) Delinquent; one who neglects totally that which he ought to do. *Pecador de mi!* Poor me, sinner as I am. 3. An ignorant stupid person.

Pecadóra, *sf.* Prostitute, a woman of the town.

Pecadorázo, *sm.* A great sinner.

Pecadorcíllo, lla; to, ta, *s. dim.* Little sinner.

Pecaminóso, sa, *a.* Sinful, belonging to sin.

Pecánte, *a.* Peccant, vicious, abundant.

Pecár, *vn.* 1. To violate the laws of God; to transgress the precepts of religion; to be wanting in what is right and just, or in the rules of art. 2. To commit excesses of any kind and description. 3. To boast, to brag. 4. To predominate; applied to peccant humours of the body. 5. To have a strong propensity. 6. To occasion or to merit punishment. *Darle por donde peca*, To retort, or reproach any one with a fault which he cannot deny.

Pecatríz, *a.* V. *Pecadora.*

Péce, *sf.* 1. Fish. V. *Pez.* 2. Clay wetted for the purpose of making mud walls. 3. Pitch. 4. Ridge of land to be laboured.

Pececíllo, *sm.* A small fish.

Pecéño, ña, *a.* Of the colour of pitch; applied to the hair of horses; to have a pitchy taste.

Pecezuéla, *sf. dim.* A small piece.

Pecezuélo, *sm. dim.* 1. Small foot. 2. Small fish.

Pécha, *sf.* Tax, impost, tribute.

Pechár, *vn.* To pay taxes.

Pecházo, *sm.* A brave generous man.

Péche, *sm.* V. *Pechina.*

Pechéra, *sf.* 1. Stomacher, a piece of silk or linen worn by women on the breast. 2. The exterior part of a woman's breast. 3. Tax, impost, duty.

Pechería, *sf.* The act of paying tax, toll, or duty.

Pechéro, ra, *a.* Liable to pay duty or taxes.

Pecheréro, *sm.* Bib, a small piece of linen put on the breast of children over their clothes.

Pechiblánco, ca, *a.* White-breasted.

Pechicoloráddo, *sm.* (Orn.) Kind of goldfinch.

Pechigónga, *sf.* A kind of game at cards.

Pechína, *sf.* 1. A kind of shell which pilgrims carry on their hats and shoulders. 2. Curvilineal triangle, formed by the arches, where they meet, to receive the annulet of the cupola.

Pécho, *sm.* 1. Breast, the forepart of the animal body, from the throat to the pit of the stomach. *Pecho de carne carnilla*, Brisket. 2. The internal part of the breast, especially in men; chest. 3. Teat, nipple of a woman's breast. 4. Regard, esteem, confidence. 5. Courage, valour, fortitude. 6. Quality and strength of the voice. 7. Faithful observance of a secret. 8. Tax paid to the Spanish government by those who do not belong to the nobility. 9. Duty paid by all the inhabitants of the Spanish dominions, excepting the king. 10. Bosom, heart, soul. 11. Power of voice to sing or preach. *Dar el pecho*, To suckle. *Hombre de pecho*, A firm spirited man. *Tener pecho*, To have patience, to endure with firmness. *Tomar á pechos*, To take to heart. *A' pecho descubierto*, Unarmed, without defence. *Echarse á pechos*, To drink greedily and copiously; to undertake any thing with ardour, to be active in any thing without considering the difficulties.

Pechuélo, *sm.* A small or little breast.

Pechúga, *sf.* Breast of a fowl; bosom.

Pechugón, *sm.* Blow on the breast.

Pechuguéra, *sf.* Cough, hoarseness.

Peciénto, ta, *a.* Of a pitchy colour.

Pecilgár, *va.* (Arag.) To pinch. V. *Pellizcar.*

Pecílgo, *sm.* (Arag.) Pinch, the act of pinching.

Peciluéngo, ga, *a.* Long-stalked; applied to fruit with stalks on trees.

Pecína, *sf.* Fish-pond.

Pecinál, *sm.* Pool of standing or muddy water.

Pécora, *sf.* 1. A sheep. 2. A cunning fellow, knave; a gay merry person.

Pecoréa, *sf.* 1. Robbery committed by straggling soldiers. 2. Idle strolling, and loitering about the streets.

Pecóso, sa, *a.* Freckly, full of freckles.

Pectorál, *a.* Pectoral, belonging to the breast. —*sm.* Cross worn by bishops on the breast; a breast-plate.

Peculádo, *sm.* Peculation, theft, or embezzlement of public money.

Peculiár, *a.* Peculiar, appropriate; belonging to any one with exclusion of others.

Peculiarménte, *ad.* Peculiarly.

Pecúlio, *sm.* Stock or capital which the father permits a son to hold for his own use and benefit.

Pecúnia, *sf.* Hard cash, specie.

Pecuniário, ria, *a.* Pecuniary, relating to money.

Pedacíco, llo, y to, *sm.* A small piece or bit.

Pedáge, *sm.* Bridge-toll. V. *Peage.*

Pedagógo, *sm.* Pedagogue, schoolmaster, prompter.

Pedáneo, *a.* Puny or puisne, petty, inferior; applied to the members of inferior courts of justice.

Pedánte, *sm.* Pedant, a schoolmaster; a man vain of low knowledge.
Pedanteár, *vn.* 1. To teach, to profess, to act the master. 2. To be or to act the pedant.
Pedantería, *sf.* Pedantry, awkward ostentation of needless learning.
Pedantésco, ca, *a.* Pedantic, awkwardly ostentatious of learning.
Pedantísmo, *sm.* Pedantry.
Pedantón, *sm. aum.* A great pedant.
Pedázo, *sm.* Piece, bit; a part of a whole. *Pedazo del alma*, My dear, my love. *A' pedazos, ó en pedazos*, In bits, in fragments. *Estar hecho pedazos*, To be broken in pieces. (Met.) To be very fatigued. *Morirse por sus pedazos*, To languish with amorous desire.
Pedernál, *sm.* Flint; any thing proverbially hard. V. *Pedreñal.*
Pedestál, *sm.* 1. Pedestal, the basis of a column or statue. V. *Peana.* 2. Foundation, the fundamental part of a thing.
Pedéstre, *a.* Pedestrious, going on foot.
Pedicón, *sm.* Jump on one foot.
Pediculár, *a.* Pedicular, lousy.
Pedículo, *sm.* 1. Louse. V. *Piojo.* 2. (Bot.) Pedicle, or peduncle of a flower.
Pedído, *sm.* A voluntary contribution, which is called for by government in urgent necessities of the state; petition.
Pedidór, ra, *s.* Petitioner, one who asks.
Pedidúra, *sf.* Begging, petitioning.
Pedigón, *sm.* (Joc.) V. *Pedidor y Pedigüeño.*
Pedigüéño, ña, *a.* Craving, demanding frequently and importunely.
Pedilúvio, *sm.* Pediluvium, a bath for the feet.
Pediménto, *sm.* Petition. V. *Peticion.*
Pedír, *va.* 1. To petition, to beg; to ask, to demand; to require; to wish, to desire. 2. To fix a price on merchandise; to demand one's right before a judge. *A' pedir de boca*, According to desire; with much propriety, exactly, adequately.
Pédo, *sm.* Wind from the bowels. *Pedo de lobo*, (Bot.) Puff balls.
Pedorreár, *va.* To discharge wind.
Pedorréras, *sf. pl.* 1. A kind of very tight breeches. 2. Flatulencies.
Pedorréro, ra; y **Pedórro, rra**, *a.* Discharging much wind, flatulent. [the mouth.
Pedorréta, *sf.* Noise made by children with
Pedráda, *sf.* 1. Throw or cast of a stone; lapidation. 2. Cockade, bow of ribbons. 3. A smart repartee, taunt, sneer. *Pedrada, ó pedradas*, An exclamation of denouncing a crime, you should be stoned! (Joc.) A sneer at one who shows his teeth.
Pedréa, *sf.* Conflict of boys belonging to different wards or districts fighting with stones; lapidation.
Pedregál, *sm.* Place full of stones.
Pedregóso, sa, *a.* 1. Stony, abounding with stones. 2. Afflicted with the gravel.
Pedrejón, *sm.* Large loose stone.
Pedreñál, *sm.* Kind of small firelock.
Pedréra, *sf.* Quarry, a stone-pit.
Pedrería, *sf.* A collection of precious stones of various sorts.
Pedréro, *sm.* 1. Stone-cutter, one whose trade is to hew stones. 2. Pedrero, a swivel-gun. 3. Slinger, one who slings or throws with a sling. 4. Lapidary, who who deals in precious stones or gems. 5. (Toledo) Foundling, a child exposed to chance; a child found without any known parent.
Pedrezuéla, *sf.* A small stone.
Pedrisco, *sm.* Hail-stone, a large quantity of drops of rain frozen in their falling.
Pedríza, *sf.* 1. Quarry. V. *Pedrera.* 2. Heap of loose stones.
Pédro, *sm.* (In Cant.) Dress used by thieves. *Pedro entre ollas*, Cotquean.
Peér, *vn.* To break wind.
Péga, *sf.* 1. The art of joining one thing to another by means of some tenacious matter. 2. Varnish of pitch put on earthen vessels. 3. Tanning or currying of leather. 4. (Orn.) Magpie. Corvus pica *L.* *Ser de la pega*, To belong to the gang.
Pegadíllo, *sm.* 1. A little patch; a sticking plaster. 2. Man who is introduced into a house or conversation, and who continues so to the general annoyance.
Pegadízo, za, *a.* 1. Clammy, glutinous, viscous. 2. Catching, contagious. 3. Adhering selfishly; applied to one who sticks to another for base motives.
Pegádo, *sm.* Patch, sticking plaster, cataplasm.
Pegadúra, *sf.* 1. Pitching, the act of daubing with pitch. 2. The sticking of one thing to another.
Pegajóso, sa, *a.* 1. Sticky, viscous, glutinous. 2. Catching, contagious. 3. Attractive, alluring; adhesive.
Pegamiénto, *sm.* The act of conglutinating or cementing, and the effect thereof.
Pegánte, *a.* Viscous, glutinous, uniting.
Pegár, *va.* 1. To join one thing to another by means of some cement or viscous matter. 2. To join, to unite. *Pegar mangas*, To introduce one's self, to participate in any thing. 3. To dash or knock one thing violently against another. 4. To chastise, to punish, to beat 5. To communicate, to catch a distemper.—*vn.* 1. To take root. 2. To make an impression on the mind; to communicate vices, manners, &c. 3. To assault, to attack. 4. To join, to be contiguous. 5. To begin to take effect. 6. To fall asleep. 7. To say or do something disagreeable or displeasing. *Pegarla*, To betray one's confidence. *Pegarla de puño*, To violate entirely the confidence reposed in one.—*vr.* 1. To intrude, to enter without invitation or permission. 2. To stick, to adhere; to unite itself by its tenacity or penetrating power. 3. To insinuate itself, to steal upon the mind. 4. To be taken with, to be strongly affected with a passion. 5. To spend one's fortune on things which belong to others. *Pegar un petardo*, To borrow money and not return it.
Pegáseo, sea, *a.* (Poét.) Belonging to Pegasus.
Pégaso, *sm.* Pegasus, a winged horse.
Pegáta, *sf.* Trick, fraud, imposition.
Pegatísta, *sm.* An indigent wretch who lives upon the offals of other men's tables; a sponger.
Pegóte, *sm.* 1. Kind of sticking plaster. 2. Fricassee with a thick clammy sauce. 3. An im-

pertinent intruder who sticks close to a person.

Pegunéra, *sf.* 1. Pile of pine-wood, burnt for the purpose of making pitch. 2. Place where sheep are marked with pitch or tar.

Peguéro, *sm.* One who makes pitch or deals in it.

Pegujál y Pegujár, *sm.* 1. Stock or capital which a son holds by permission of his father for his own use and benefit. 2. A small dead or live stock on a farm.

Pegujaléro y Pegujaréro, *sm.* A small farmer, grazier who keeps but a small flock of sheep.

Pegujón, *sm.* Pile of wool or hair well packed and pressed together.

Pegúnta, *sf.* Mark on wool, cattle, &c.

Peguntár, *va.* To mark cattle, &c.

Pel, *s.* Skin, hide. V. *Piel.*

Péla, *sm.* (Gal.) Boy richly dressed on the shoulders of a man in processions.

Peláda, *sf.* Pelt, the skin of a dead sheep stripped of the wool.

Peladéra, *sf.* Shedding of the hair.

Peladíllas, *sf. pl.* 1. Confected almonds covered with melted sugar. 2. Small pebbles, round whitish stones.

Peládo, da, *a.* 1. Decorticated. 2. Treeless; applied to mountains without shrubs or plants. *Letra pelada*, Clear neat formed letter. *Muerte pelada*, Baldhead; a nickname.

Peladór, *sm.* Plucker, one who plucks or decorticates.

Peladúra, *sf.* Plucking, decortication.

Pelafustán, *sm.* Ragamuffin, a ragged idle vagabond or vagrant.

Pelagátos, *sm.* Cutpurse, pickpocket, ruffian.

Peláge, *sm.* 1. Colour of the hair. 2. Quality and external appearance, especially of clothes.

Pelámbre, *sm.* 1. Hair of the animal body in general. 2. Want of hair.

Pelambréra, *sf.* 1. Quantity of hair in one place. 2. Want or shedding of hair.

Pelámen, *sm.* V. *Pelambre.*

Pelamésa, *sf.* 1. Scuffle in which the hair is pulled or torn off. 2. A bushy head of hair.

Pelamíde y Pelamída, *sm.* Young brood of tunny-fish.

Pelandúsca, *sf.* Strumpet, a girl of the town.

Pelantrín, *sm.* (Sevilla) A petty farmer.

Pelár, *va.* 1. To pull out the hair; to strip off the feathers. 2. To decorticate, to divest of the bark or husk. 3. To trick, to cheat, to rob. 4. To boil, to scald. *Esta agua esta pelando*, This water is boiling.—*vr.* To cast the hair. *Pelarselas*, To execute any thing with vigour and efficacy.

Peláyre, *sm.* Wool-dresser, one whose trade is to comb wool, and lay it smooth for spinning.

Pelayría, *sf.* Trade of a wool-comber.

Peláza, *sf.* Quarrel, affray, scuffle.—*a.* Applied to the straw or haum of onions.

Peldefébre, *sm.* Camblet, baracan; a stuff made of wool and goat's hair mixed.

Peléa, *sf.* 1. Battle, action, engagement. 2. Quarrel, dispute. 3. Struggle, toil, fatigue. *Peleas de gallos*, Cock-fight.

Peleadór, *sm.* Fighter, combatant.

Peleánte, *pa.* Combating, fighter.

Peleár, *va.* 1. To fight, to combat. 2. To quarrel, to contend, to dispute. 3. To toil, to labour hard.—*vr.* To scuffle, to come to blows.

Pelechár, *va.* 1. To get hair. 2. To change the coat, applied to horses. 3. To improve one's fortune, to recover health.

Pelendéngue, *sm.* Frivolous foppery, extreme nicety in dress.

Peleóna, *sf.* Scuffle, quarrel, dispute.

Peléte, *sm.* One who punts at certain games at cards. *En pelete*, Nakedly.

Peletería, *sf.* 1. Trade or profession of a furrier or skinner. 2. Fellmonger's shop where skins and furs are sold.

Peletéro, *sm.* Furrier, one who dresses fine skins or deals in furs.

Peliagúdo, da, *a.* 1. Downy, furry; having long fine hair or fur. 2. Arduous, difficult. 3. Ingenious, skilful, dexterous.

Pelibláno, da, *a.* Having fine soft hair.

Pelicábra, *sf.* Satyr, fabulous animal, like a goat.

Pelícano, *sm.* (Orn.) Pelican. Pelecanus onocrotalus *L.*

Pelicáno, na, *a.* Having grey hair; hoary.

Pelicórto, ta, *a.* Having short hair.

Película, *sf.* Pellicle, a thin membrane or skin.

Pelifórra, *sf.* Whore, a common prostitute.

Peligrár, *vn.* To be in danger; to be in peril.

Pelígro, *sm.* Danger, risk, hazard.

Peligrosaménte, *ad.* Perilously.

Peligróso, sa, *a.* Dangerous, perilous; venturous.

Pelilárgo, ga, *a.* Having long hair.

Pelíllo, *sm.* 1. Short tender hair. 2. Trifle, a slight cause of disgust or displeasure. *Reparar en pelillos*, To take offence at trifles.

Pelillóso, sa, *a.* Downy, full of soft tender hair.

Pelinégro, gra, *a.* Having black hair.

Pelirúbio, bia, *a.* Having fair or flaxen hair.

Pelitiéso, sa, *a.* Having strong bushy hair.

Pelíto, *sm.* Short tender hair. *Pelitos á la mar*, All animosities done away; the act of friends making up a quarrel.

Pelítre, *sm.* (Bot.) Pellitory of Spain. Anthemis pyrethrum *L.*

Pelitríque, *sm.* Fiddle-faddle, trifle.

Pélla, *sf.* 1. Ball, any thing made in a round form. 2. Parcel of things packed close together. 3. Mass of metal in its crude state. 4. Lard in the state in which it is taken from hogs. 5. Large quantity of things. 6. Fleece, a quantity of shorn wool. 7. Great sum of money. 8. (Orn.) Heron. Ardea major *L.*

Pelláda, *sf.* 1. Gentle blow, dab. 2. A trowel full of mortar or slaked lime.

Pelléja, *sf.* 1. Skin or hide stripped off from the animal. 2. Strumpet, a woman of the town.

Pellejería, *sf.* Shop where skins are dressed and sold.

Pellejéro, *sm.* Fellmonger, he whose trade is to dress and sell skins.

Pellejína, *sf.* A small skin.

Pelléjo, *sm.* 1. Skin, hide. 2. A skin dressed and pitched, in which liquors are carried. 3. (Joc.) Tippler, drunkard. *Mudar el pellejo*, To change customs and manners.

Pellíca, *sf.* Coverlet of fine furs.

Pellíco, *sm.* 1. Dress made of skins or furs. 2. Offensive language.

Pellíza, *sf.* Pelisse, dress formed of skins.

Pellizcár, *va.* 1. To pinch, to squeeze between

the fingers and thumb; to pinch or wound artfully. 2. To pilfer, to commit petty thefts. 3. To take but little food; to take only a bit or pinch.—*vr.* 1. To prick one's self. 2. To long for any thing.

Pellízco, *sm.* 1. Pinch, the act of pinching. 2. A small bit or portion. 3. (Met.) Remorse, disquietude. *Pellizco de monja*, A lozenge or sugar drop.

Pellón y Pellóte, *sm.* A long robe made of skins or furs. *Pellónes*, (Among Bakers) Large pieces of dough formed for the oven.

Pelluzgón, *sm.* Lock of hair, wool, or tow.

Pelmacéria, *sf.* Heaviness, slowness.

Pelmázo y Pélma, *sm.* 1. Heavy paste or cake. 2. Food which lies heavy on the stomach. 3. A slow heavy person.

Pélo, *sm.* 1. Hair, a slender filament which grows through the pores of the animal body. 2. Down, the soft tender feathers which grow on birds under the large ones. 3. Soft fibres of plants. 4. Thread of silk or worsted. 5. Pile, the hair or bur on the right side of cloth. 6. Colour of the coat of animals. 7. Flaw, defect in precious stones or crystals; split in metals, horses' hoofs, &c. 8. Abscess in a woman's breast. 9. Trifle, any thing of little value. 10. Skin on the barrel of a quill. 11. Colour of animals' skins. V. *Pelage*. *Ser de buen pelo*, (Irón.) To be ill-disposed. *Pelo arriba*, Against the grain. *A' pelo*, For the purpose, to the purpose, timely. *Al pelo ó á pelo*, Along the grain. *Gente de pelo*, Rich people. *Tener pelos*, To be intricate; applied to some affair or business. *En pelo*, Barebacked, naked.

Pelón, na, *a.* 1. Poor, indigent. 2. Second son of a knight in Cordova. 3. (Joc.) Bald.

Pelóna y Pelonía, *sf.* V. *Peladera*.

Pelonería, *sf.* Poverty, want, indigence.

Pelosílla, *sf.* (Bot.) Crapeny, mouse-ear, hawk-weed. Hieracium pilosella *L.*

Pelóso, sa, *a.* Hairy, covered with hair.

Pelóta, *sf.* 1. Ball, a round thing to play with. 2. Any thing made in a round form. 3. Cannon or musket ball. 4. Diversion or play performed with balls. 5. Strumpet, prostitute. *En pelota*, Entirely naked. *Pelotas*, (Extrem.) A kind of round sausage.

Pelotázo, *sm.* Blow or stroke with a ball.

Pelóte, *sm.* Goat's hair.

Pelotéar, *vn.* 1. To play at ball. 2. To argue, to dispute; to contend. 3. To throw from one part to another.—*va.* To examine the items of an account, and compare them with the parcels received.—*vr.* To throw snowballs at each other; to quarrel, to dispute.

Pelotéra, *sf.* Battle or quarrel among women.

Pelotería, *sf.* Heap of balls.

Pelotéro, *sm.* 1. Ball-maker. 2. Scuffle, affray, quarrel. 3. A malicious mean person. V. *Escarabajo*.

Pelotílla, *sf.* 1. A small ball. 2. Small ball made of wax, stuck with small pieces of glass, and fastened to a cat o'nine tails, with which penitent persons lash themselves. *Hacer pelotillas*, To pick the nose rudely.

Pelóto, *a.* V. *Derraspado ó Chamorro*.

Pelotón, *sm.* 1. A large ball. 2. Bundle or ball of hair closely pressed together. 3. (Mil.) Platoon, a small body of foot soldiers; one of the sections into which a battalion is divided when under arms.

Pélta, *sf.* Pelta, ancient kind of light buckler.

Péltre, *sm.* Pewter, a metal made of tin and lead.

Peltréro, *sm.* Pewterer, pewter-worker.

Pelúca, *sf.* Wig; the person who wears a wig. *Peluca redonda*, Bob-wig. [bushy wig.

Pelucón, *sm.* One who struts about in a large

Pelúdo, da, *a.* Hairy, covered with hair.

Pelúdo, *sm.* A bass-mat of an oval shape.

Peluquería, *sf.* Shop where wigs are made and sold.

Peluquéro, *sm.* Peruke-maker.

Peluquín, *sm.* A small bag-wig.

Pelúsa, *sf.* 1. Down which covers some plants or fruit. 2. Villous substance falling off from clothes during the wear of them. 3. (Joc.) Cash, riches.

Péna, *sf.* 1. Punishment, pain, penalty; chastisement inflicted for crimes and offences. 2. Care, concern; a violent emotion of the mind. 3. Difficulty, toil, labour. 4. Necklace, an ornament which women wear around the neck. *Pena de la mesana*, (Naút.) Peak of the mizen. *A' malas penas*, Immediately that, instantly. *A' duras penas*, With a great deal of difficulty or trouble.

Penachéra, *sf.* V. *Penacho*.

Penácho, *sm.* 1. Tuft or crest of feathers on the heads of some birds. 2. Plumes, feathers worn as an ornament. 3. Loftiness, haughtiness, presumption.

Penadaménte, *ad.* V. *Penosamente*.

Penadíllo, lla, *a.* Having a very small opening; applied to vessels.

Penádo, da, *a.* 1. Punished, chastised. 2. Painful. 3. Narrow-mouthed; applied to vessels.

Penál, *a.* Concerning or including punishment.

Penalidád, *sf.* 1. Act of suffering punishment. 2. Suffering, calamity, trouble; penalty.

Penánte, *a.* Suffering pain or affliction; lovelorn, love-sick.—*s.* Lover, gallant.

Penár, *vn.* 1. To suffer pain, to agonize; to be tormented in a future life. 2. To crave, to desire anxiously.—*va.* To chastise, to inflict punishment.—*vr.* To grieve, to mourn, to sorrow.

Penátes, *sm. pl.* The house gods of the ancient heathens.

Penatígero, *sm.* He who carried the household gods, or penates.

Pénca, *sf.* 1. Pricking leaf of a chard or other similar plant. 2. A leather strap with which convicts are whipped by the hangman.

Pencázo, *sm.* Lash with the hangman's strap.

Pencúdo, da, *a.* Acuminated.

Pencúria, *sf.* Prostitute.

Pendánga, *sf.* 1. A common prostitute. 2. Knave of diamonds in a game at cards, called *Quinolas* or *Reversis*.

Pendéjo, *sm.* 1. Short tender hair. 2. Coward, poltron.

Pendéncia, *sf.* Quarrel, affray, dispute.

Pendenciár, *vn.* To wrangle, to quarrel.

Pendenciéro, ra, *a.* Quarrelsome.

Pendér, *vn.* 1. To impend, to hang over. 2. To

depend. 3. To be irresolute, to leave a thing undecided.

PENDIÉNTE, *a.* Pendent, hanging.

PENDIÉNTE, *sm.* 1. Slope, declivity. 2. Ear-ring, an ornament suspended from the ears of women.

PENDÍL, *sm.* A kind of mantle worn by women. *Tomar el pendil*, To elope unexpectedly.

PÉNDOLA, *sf.* 1. A writing pen. V. *Pluma*. 2. Pendulum, the piece of a clock which regulates its motion. *Dar pendolas á un navio*, (Naút.) To boot-top a ship, to give her a parliament heel.

PENDOLÉRO, RA, *a.* Hanging, pendent.

PENDOLÍSTA, *sm.* 1. Penman, one who professes the art of writing. 2. Cheat, swindler, impostor.

PENDÓN, *sm.* 1. Standard, the colours of a country. 2. Banner carried about in processions. 3. Remnants, pieces of stuff cabbaged by tailors. 4. A young tree left for growth at the felling of woods. 5. Nickname of a tall, awkward woman. 6. Rein of the leading mule. *Pendon real*, (Naút.) Parliament heel, boot-topping.

PÉNDULO, LA, *a.* Pendent, hanging.

PENÉQUE, *sm.* Drunkard.

PENETRABILIDÁD, *sf.* Penetrability.

PENETRÁBLE, *a.* Penetrable, that can be pierced.

PENETRACIÓN, *sf.* 1. Penetration, the act of piercing or penetrating; discernment, complete intelligence. 2. Acuteness, sagacity.

PENETRADÓR, *sm.* Discerner, he who penetrates or distinguishes.

PENETRÁL, *sm.* (Poét.) The interior or most retired part.

PENETRÁNTE, *pa.* 1. Penetrating. 2. A deep wound.

PENETRÁR, *va.* 1. To penetrate, to pierce; to pass through the body. 2. To affect the mind. 3. To reach the meaning with acuteness and sagacity. 4. To permeate; to pervade.—*vr.* To co-exist as two bodies in the same place.

PENETRATÍVO, VA, *a.* Penetrative.

PENÍNSULA, *sf.* Peninsula, a piece of land almost surrounded by the sea.

PENÍQUE ó PENÉQUE, *sm.* Penny, an English coin.

PENITÉNCIA, *sf.* Penitence, penance; grief or sorrow for crimes; penalty, mulct, fine. *Hacer penitencia*, Familiar invitation to a family repast; to take pot-luck.

PENITENCIÁL, *a.* Penitential.

PENITENCIÁR, *va.* To impose a penance for a fault committed.

PENITENCIARÍA, *sf.* Charge or office of a penitentiary or a priest invested with the power of absolving in certain reserved cases; ecclesiastical court at Rome.

PENITENCIÁRIO, *sm.* Penitentiary; canon who assists the confessor in cathedrals.

PENITÉNTA, *sf.* A female penitent.

PENITÉNTE, *a.* Penitent, repentant.

PENITÉNTE, *sm.* 1. Penitent, one who does penance. 2. Associate in some party of pleasure or debauchery.

PENOSAMÉNTE, *ad.* Painfully.

PENÓSO, SA, *a.* Painful, that which gives pain.

PENÓSO, *sm.* An affected fop, a buck or beau.

PENSÁDO, DA, *a.* Deliberate, premeditated. *De pensado*, On purpose, designedly.

PENSAMIÉNTO, *sm.* 1. Thought, idea; meditation, contemplation. 2. Resolution, design. 3. Great swiftness or promptitude. *En un pensamiento*, In a trice.

PENSÁR, *vn.* 1. To think, to consider, to reflect; to take into serious consideration; to weigh maturely. 2. To feed cattle. *Sin pensar*, Unexpectedly, thoughtlessly. *Pensèque*, (Vulg.) I thought so or as much.

PENSATÍVO, VA, *a.* 1. Pensive, thoughtful. 2. (Joc.) Applied to cattle when they stop eating, as if to think.

PENSIÉR, *sm.* (Bot.) Sneezewort.

PENSÍL, *sm.* A pensile or hanging garden; a beautiful or delightful garden.

PENSIÓN, *sf.* 1. Pension, an annual charge laid upon any thing. 2. Pension, a fixed sum paid annually by government. 3. Toil, labour naturally attending an enterprise or office.

PENSIONÁDO, DA, *s.* Pensioner, one who receives a pension.

PENSIONÁR, *va.* To impose annual charges, pensions, or other burthens.

PENSIONÁRIO, *sm.* 1. One who pays a pension. 2. Pensionary, the recorder of a city.

PENSIONÍSTA, *s. com.* 1. One who gives a pension. 2. Pensioner, one who receives a pension. 3. Boarder, in a boarding house.

PENTACÓRDIO, *sm.* Five-stringed harp.

PENTADÁCTILO Y PENTÁFILON, *sm.* V. *Quinquefolio*.

PENTAGLÓTTO, *a.* Written in five languages.

PENTÁGONO, *sm.* Pentagon, a figure of five sides.

PENTÁMETRO, *sm.* Pentameter, a Latin verse.

PENTATÉUCO, *sm.* Pentateuch, the five books of Moses.

PENTECÓSTES, *sm.* Pentecost, Whitsuntide.

PENÚLTIMO, MA, *a.* Penult, last but one.

PENÚMBRA, *sf.* Penumbra, partial shade.

PENÚRIA, *sf.* Penury, poverty, indigence.

PÉÑA, *sf.* Rock, large stone. *Por peñas*, A long time.

PEÑÁDO, *sm.* V. *Peñasco*.

PEÑASCÁL, *sm.* Rocky hill or mountain.

PEÑÁSCO Y PEÑÉDO, *sm.* 1. Ridge of rocks. 2. A light silk stuff.

PEÑASCÓSO, SA, *a.* Rocky, mountainous.

PEÑÍSCOLA, *sf.* Peninsula, rocky point of land.

PEÑÓL, *sm.* 1. A large rock. 2. (Naút.) Yard-arm, the extremity of the yard on either side of a mast.

PEÑÓN, *sm.* A large rock, rocky mountain.

PEÓN, *sm.* 1. Pedestrian, one who travels on foot. *A' peon*, (Fam.) A-foot. 2. Day-labourer, one who works for his daily hire. *Peon de albañil*, Hodman. 3. Foot-soldier. 4. Spinning-top, humming-top. 5. (Pros.) A foot of verse. *Peones*, Men of chess or draughts. 6. Hive of bees, working-bee.

PEONÁDA, *sf.* Day-work of a labourer.

PEONÁGE, *sm.* Multitude of people on foot.

PEONERÍA, *sf.* As much land as can be ploughed in one day.

PEONÍA, *sf.* 1. (Bot.) Piony. 2. Piece of ground that may be laboured in a day; quantity of land given to a soldier in a conquered country. V. *Peonada*.

PEÓNTA, *sf.* Rate of tithes and price of labour.

Peónza, *sf.* 1. Whipping-top. 2. A noisy little fellow. *A' peonza*, On foot.

Peór, *a.* Worse.—*ad.* Worse. *Peor que peor*, Worse and worse.

Peoría, *sf.* Deterioration, detriment.

Pépe, pa, *s.* Proper name, Joseph, Josephine.

Pepián, *sm.* V. *Pipian.*

Pepinár, *sm.* Cucumber-field, a piece of ground sown or planted with cucumbers.

Pepinázo, *sm.* Blow with a cucumber.

Pepíno, *sm.* (Bot.) Cucumber. Cucumis sativus *L.* *No darsele un pepino*, Not to give a fig or rush for a thing.

Pepión, *sm.* An ancient Spanish gold coin of the reign of Alphonsus the Wise.

Pepíta, *sf.* 1. Seed of some fruits. 2. Pip, a distemper in fowls. *No tener pepita*, To speak out, not to mince the matter. *Pepitas*, (Peru) Grains of pure native gold found in the mines.

Pepitória, *sf.* Fricassee made of giblets, livers, and lights. 2. Joining of hands and feet. 3. Medley of things jumbled confusedly together.

Pepitóso, sa, *a.* 1. Abounding in grains or seeds. 2. Applied to fowls with the pip.

Péplide, *sf.* (Bot.) Purslain. Portulaca *L.*

Péplo, *sm.* (Bot.) Water-purslain. Peplis *L.*

Pepón, *sm.* (Bot.) Water-melon. Cucurbita citrullus *L.*

Pequeñéz, *sf.* 1. Parvity, smallness of size; littleness. 2. Youth, tender age. 3. Lowness of mind, pusillanimity.

Pequéño, ña, *a.* 1. Little or small of size; narrow. 2. Young, of a tender age. 3. Low-spirited, humble, abject.

Pequeñíto, ta; y **Pequeñuélo, la**, *a. dim.* Somewhat little.

Pequín, *sm.* Silk stuff manufactured in Pekin.

Per, *prep.* Latin, used in Spanish, in composition only, as *perdonable*, pardonable.

Péra, *sf.* 1. Pear, the fruit of the pear-tree. 2. A small tuft or lock of hair which some clergymen let grow on the chin. 3. Plum, a large sum of money. *Poner las peras á quatro ó á ocho*, To constrain one to do or concede what he does not wish.

Peráda, *sf.* Conserve made of the juice of pears.

Perál, *sm.* (Bot.) Pear-tree. Pyrus communis [*L.*

Peraléda, *sf.* Orchard of pear-trees.

Peraltár, *va.* To raise the arch of a vault or dome above a semicircle to the figure of a parabola.

Perantón, *sm.* 1. (Bot.) Marvel-plant. Euphorbia cyparissias *L.* 2. Large fan. 3. A very tall person.

Peráyle, *sm.* Wool comber. V. *Pelayre.*

Peráza, *sf.* Fruit of an ingrafted pear-tree.

Pérca, *sf.* (Ict.) Perch. Perca Fluviatilis *L.*

Percalál y **Percalín**, *sm.* A sort of linen.

Percánce, *sm.* Perquisite, something gained by a place or office over and above the settled salary, pay, or wages.

Percatár, *va.* 1. To think, to consider maturely. 2. To take care, to be on one's guard.

Percebimiénto, *sm.* Prevention, warning.

Percebír, *va.* To perceive.

Percepción, *sf.* Perception, notion, idea.

Perceptíble, *a.* Perceptible.

Perceptívo, va, *a.* Perceptive

Pércha, *sf.* 1. Perch, a long piece of timber to sustain or support any thing. 2. Cloth-rack. 3. Snare for catching partridges. 4. String or strap on which fowlers hang their game. 5. Sign-post of a barber's shop. 6. (Ict.) Perch. *Perchas*, (Naút.) Floor-timbers. *Estar en percha*, To be safe and secure.

Perchadór, *sm.* Napper, one who raises the nap on cloth with a teasel.

Perchár, *va.* To raise the nap on cloth.

Perchón, *sm.* A long or principal shoot of vines.

Perchonár, *vn.* 1. To leave on a vine-stock several long shoots. 2. To lay snares for catching game. [comprehend.

Percibír, *va.* 1. To receive. 2. To perceive, to

Percíbo, *sm.* Act of receiving or perceiving any thing.

Percnoptéro, Percnotéro ó Percoptéro, *sm.* (Orn.) Bald buzzard. Falco haliaetos *L.*

Percocería, *sf.* Small work of silver or spangles, filagree, &c.

Percuciénte, *a.* Percutient, striking.

Percudír, *va.* To tarnish the lustre of things.

Percusión, *sf.* Percussion, impression of one body in striking another.

Percusór, *sm.* One who strikes.

Perdedéro, *sm.* Occasion or motive of losing.

Perdedór, ra, *s.* Loser.

Perdér, *va.* 1. To lose, to be deprived of any thing; to miss. 2. To lavish, to mispend. 3. To sustain a loss, to receive damage. 4. To bet, to lay a wager. *¿ Que quiere vd. perder ?* What will you lay ? *La marea pierde*, (Naút.) The tide falls.—*vr.* 1. To go astray, to miss one's way. 2. To be lost, to be confounded. 3. To be erased from the memory. 4. To be spoiled; to be given up to vice. 5. To be out of fashion. 6. (Naút.) To be cast away, to be shipwrecked. 7. To sustain a loss. 8. To conceal itself; applied to rivers which disappear under the earth and rise again. *Perderse de vista*, To excel in an eminent degree. *Tener que perder*, To be a person of credit, to have much to lose.

Perdición, *sf.* 1. The act of losing any thing. 2. Perdition, destruction, ruin; eternal damnation. 3. Excessive love. 4. Prodigality, extravagance.

Pérdida, *sf.* 1. Loss, detriment, damage. 2. Quantity or thing lost. *De perdida*, In a hazardous perilous manner. [uselessly.

Perdidaménte, *ad.* Desperately, furiously;

Perdidízo, za, *a.* Lost designedly or on purpose. *Hacerse perdidizo*, To lose designedly at cards, as gamesters do at times.

Perdído, da, *a.* Lost, strayed, misguided. *Gente perdida*, Vagrants, vagabonds. *Muger perdida*, Prostitute.

Perdidóso, sa, *a.* Sustaining loss.

Perdigána, *sf.* (Arag.) A young partridge.

Perdigár, *va.* 1. To boil partridges slightly before they are roasted. 2. To stew larded meat in an earthen pan. 3. To dispose, to prepare.

Perdigón, *sm.* 1. A young partridge. 2. Partridge trained to decoy others. 3. Squanderer, lavisher of money at the gaming table. 4. (Fam.) Spark of saliva from the mouth in speaking. *Perdigones*, Hail-shot, small shot.

Perdiguéra, *sf.* (Bot.) Sun flower. Helianthus *L.*

Perdiguéro, ra, *a.* Setting, pointing; applied to a dog used by fowlers who pursue partridges.

Perdiguéro, *sm.* Poulterer, dealer in partridges.

Perdimiénto, *sm.* V. *Perdicion* y *Perdida.*

Perdíz, *sf.* (Orn.) Partridge. Tetrao perdix *L.* *Perdiz real,* Common partridge. *Patas de perdiz,* Nickname to a person who wears coloured stockings, particularly women. *O' perdiz ó no comerla,* Neck or nothing.

Perdón, *sm.* 1. Pardon, forgiveness of an injury; remission of a debt. 2. Drop of oil, wax, &c. which falls burning. *Con perdon,* Under favour; with your leave.

Perdonáble, *a.* Pardonable.

Perdonadór, *sm.* Pardoner.

Perdonánza, *sf.* V. *Disimulo* y *Perdon.*

Perdonár, *va.* 1. To pardon, to forgive an injury; to remit a debt. 2. To beg leave or permission; an expression of courtesy. 3. To clear one from an obligation, to exempt; used as an excuse for not giving a charity.—*vr.* To decline doing any thing.

Perdonavídas, *sm.* Bully, hector.

Perduláro, ria, *a.* Extremely careless or heedless with regard to one's own interest.

Perduráble, *a.* Perpetual, everlasting, continual.

Perdurableménte, *ad.* Eternally, perpetually.

Peréales, *sm.* A sort of linen which comes from India.

Pereceár, *va.* To protract, to delay, to put off.

Perecedéro, ra, *a.* Perishable, decaying, fading.

Perecedéro, *sm.* Misery, extreme want.

Perecér, *vn.* 1. To perish, to be destroyed; to perish spiritually. 2. To undergo uncommon toil and fatigue. 3. To crave, to desire anxiously. 4. To be extremely poor, to perish for want of the necessaries of life.—*vr.* To be violently agitated, to die with love.

Perecído, da, *a.* Lost, undone.

Pereciniénto, *sm.* Loss, decay, decline.

Peregrinación, *sf.* 1. Peregrination, travelling in foreign countries. 2. Pilgrimage.

Peregrinaménte, *ad.* Rarely, curiously.

Peregrinánte, *pa.* Sojourner; travelling.

Peregrinár, *va.* 1. To peregrinate, to travel in foreign countries. 2. To go on a pilgrimage; to exist in this mortal life.

Peregrinidád, *sf.* Strangeness, wonderfulness.

Peregríno, na, *a.* 1. Peregrine, foreign. 2. Travelling or sojourning in foreign countries. 3. Going on a pilgrimage. 4. Strange, wonderful.

Perendéca, *sf.* Trull, a low dirty wench.

Perendéngues, *sm. pl.* Pendants of the ears, embellishments; gaudy dress of women.

Perennál, *a.* 1. V. *Perenne.* 2. Continually mad without lucid intervals.

Perennalménte, *ad.* V. *Perennemente.*

Perénne, *a.* Perennial, perpetual. *Loco perenne,* Madman who has no lucid intervals.

Perenneménte, *ad.* Continually, perpetually.

Perennidád, *sf.* Perennity, continuity.

Perentoriaménte, *ad.* Peremptorily.

Perentório, ria, *a.* Peremptory, absolute, decisive.

Peréro, *sm.* Instrument formerly used to pare fruit.

Perexíl, *sm.* 1. (Bot.) Parsley. Apium petroselinum *L.* 2. Showy dress or apparel. *Perexiles,* Honorary titles attached to offices.

Peréza, *sf.* Laziness, tardiness, negligence, carelessness, sloth; reluctance to rise up.

Perezosaménte, *ad.* Lazily, slothfully.

Perezóso, sa, *a.* Lazy, careless, indolent, slothful, tardy; bed-loving.

Perfección, *sf.* Perfection, superior excellence; beauty, grace; high degree of virtue.

Perfeccionár, *va.* To perfect, to complete.

Perfectaménte, *ad.* Perfectly, completely.

Perfectísimo, ma, *a. sup.* Most perfect; a pleonasm best applied to the divine attributes.

Perfectívo, va, *a.* Perfective, conducing to bring to perfection.

Perfécto, ta, *a.* Perfect, complete, accomplished; beautiful, able, excellent.

Perfécto, *sm.* Improvements made in an inheritance.

Perficiénte, *a.* That which perfects.

Perficionár, *va.* V. *Perfeccionar.*

Perfidaménte, *ad.* Perfidiously.

Perfídia, *sf.* Perfidy, treachery.

Pérfido, da, *a.* Perfidious, treacherous, disloyal.

Perfíl, *sm.* 1. Profile, contour, outline: *Tomar perfiles,* To place oiled paper over a painting, in order to draw the outlines of it with a pencil. 2. Light architectural ornament; hair; stroke of certain letters; position of the body, side-view.

Perfiládo, *a.* Applied to a well-formed arched nostril.

Perfiladúra, *sf.* Art of drawing profiles; the sketching of outlines.

Perfilár, *va.* To draw profiles, to sketch outlines.—*vr.* To incline, to be bent to one side.

Perfoliáda ó Perfoliáta, *sf.* (Bot.) Common thorough wax. Bupleurum rotundifolium *L.*

Perforación, *sf.* Perforation.

Perforár, *va.* To perforate.

Perfruidór, *sm.* Enjoyer.

Perfumadór y Perfumadéro, *sm.* 1. Perfumer. 2. Vessel in which perfumes are kept.

Perfumár, *va.* To perfume; to diffuse odour.

Perfúme, *sm.* Perfume; sweet odour, fragrance; good or bad smell.

Perfumería, *sf.* A perfumer's shop.

Perfuméro, ra, *s.* Perfumer, one who makes or sells perfumes.

Perfumísta, *sm.* Perfumer, dealer in perfumes.

Perfunctório, ria, *a.* Perfunctory, passing slightly without making any impression on the mind.

Perfunctoriaménte, *ad.* Superficially.

Pergaminería, *sf.* Place where parchment is made or sold.

Pergaminéro, *sm.* Parchment-maker.

Pergamíno, *sm.* Skin dressed for writing.

Pergénio, *sm.* V. *Pergeño.*

Pergeñár, *va.* To dispose and perform in a dexterous and skilful manner.

Pergéño, *sm.* Skill, dexterity.

Pericárdio, *sm.* Pericardium, covering of the heart.

Pericárpio, *sm.* Pericarpium, covering of any fruit.

Pericia, *sf.* Skill, knowledge.

Perico, *sm.* 1. Curls formerly worn by women.

2. A kind of small parrot. *Perico entre ellas,* A cot or cotquean.

Pericón, *sm.* 1. Knave of clubs in the game of *Quinolas.* 2. A large fan.

Pericóno, na, *a.* Fit for all things; generally applied to horses fit for draught or saddle.

Pericóna, *sf.* Shaft mule; a mule fit for the coach as well as the saddle.

Pericráneo, *sm.* Pericranium, the membrane which covers the skull.

Periécos, *sm. pl.* Perœci, people on the opposite side of the globe, in the same latitude.

Periféria, *sf.* Periphery. V. *Circunferencia.*

Perifóllo, *sm.* (Bot.) Common chervil. Scandix cerefolium *L.* *Perifóllos,* Ribbons and other showy ornaments of women.

Perifraseár, *va.* To periphrase, to make use of circumlocutions.

Perífrasis ó Perífrasi, *sf.* (Ret.) Periphrasis.

Perigállo, *sm.* 1. Skin hanging down from the chin of lean persons. 2. Kind of glossy ribbon worn by women. 3. A tall lean man. 4. Kind of slender sling. 5. (Naút.) Line, a thin rope; navel-line; topping-lift.

Perigéo, *sm.* Perigee, point at which a planet comes nearest the earth, and opposed to its apogee.

Períglo, *sm.* V. *Peligro.*

Perihélio, *sm.* Perihelium, the point of a planet's orbit which is nearest the sun.

Perílla, *sf.* 1. A small pear. 2. Ornament in the form of a pear. 3. Pommel, a piece of brass or other metal at the top of a saddle-bow. *De perilla,* To the purpose, at a proper time.

Perillán, na, *a.* Artful, knavish, vagrant.

Perillán, *sm.* A sly crafty fellow.

Perillos, *sm. pl.* Gingerbread nuts.

Perilústre, *a.* Very illustrious.

Perímetro, *sm.* V. *Ámbito.*

Períncllito, ta, *a.* Famous, renowned.

Perinéo, *sm.* (Anat.) Perinæum.

Perineumónia, *sf.* Peripneumony, disease of the lungs.

Perinóla, *sf.* 1. A kind of die with four faces. 2. A neat little woman.

Periodeceár, *vn.* To make or form periods.

Periódicamente, *ad.* Periodically.

Periódico, ca, *a.* Periodical, done at certain periods; applied to literary works, or intermitting diseases.

Período, *sm.* 1. Period, a determinate number of years or space of time. 2. Period, a complete sentence from one full stop to another.

Peripatético, ca, *a.* 1. Peripatetic or Aristotelian philosophy. 2. Ridiculous or extravagant opinions.

Peripáto, *sm.* System of Aristotle.

Peripécia, *sf.* Sudden change from one condition to another in the persons of the drama, or in fortune.

Períplo, *sm.* Periplus, voyage round a coast.

Peripuésta, *a.* Placed around.

Periquíllo, *sm.* A kind of small sweetmeat made of sugar alone.

Periquíto, *sm.* 1. (Naút.) Stay-sail. *Periquito de juanete mayor,* (Naút.) Flying stay-sail. *Periquito de sobremesnna,* (Naút.) Mizen top-gallant stay-sail. 2. (Orn.) Parroquet, small kind of parrot.

Periscios, *sm. pl.* Periscii, inhabitants of the polar circles.

Perisología, *sf.* Superfluous repetition in a discourse.

Peristáltico, ca, *a.* Peristaltic; applied to the spiral motion of the intestines.

Peristilo, *sm.* (Arq.) Peristyle.

Períta, *sf.* A small pear.

Períto, *sm.* Skilful man in any art or trade.

Períto, ta, *a.* Skilful, able, experienced.

Peritóneo, *sm.* (Anat.) Peritoneum.

Perjudicadór, ra, *s.* One who prejudges or prejudicates.

Perjudicár, *va.* To prejudicate, to prejudge, to injure, to hurt.

Perjudiciál, *a.* Prejudicial, hurtful.

Perjudicialménte, *ad.* Prejudicially.

Perjudício, *sm.* 1. Prejudice, mischief, hurt, injury. 2. Prejudice, prepossession; judgment rashly formed before-hand without examination.

Perjurádor, ra, *s.* Perjurer, forswearer.

Perjurár, *vn.* 1. To forswear, to swear falsely; to commit perjury. 2. To swear, to obtest the great name profanely.—*vr.* To perjure one's self.

Perjúrio, *sm.* Perjury, false oath.

Perjúro, ra, *a.* Perjured, forsworn.—*sm.* Perjury.

Pérla, *sf.* Pearl, a hard, white, smooth, and transparent substance, found in a testaceous fish; any thing precious, clear, or bright. *Perlas,* Fine teeth. *De perlas,* Much to the purpose; excellently, eminently fine.

Perlacía, *sf.* (Ant.) V. *Prelacía.*

Perlático, ca, *a.* Paralytic, palsied.

Perlería, *sf.* Collection of pearls.

Perlesía, *sf.* Paralysis, palsy.

Perlezuéla, *sf.* Small pearl.

Perliquiténcia, *sf.* A mock title of honour.

Perlongár, *vn.* (Naút.) To coast, to sail along the coast.

Permanecér, *vn.* To persist, to remain firmly in the same state, to endure.

Permaneciénte, *pa.* Permanent.

Permanéncia, *sf.* Duration, permanency, perseverance.

Permanénte, *a.* Permanent, durable.

Permansión, *sf.* V. *Permanencia.*

Permisíble, *a.* Permissible.

Permisión, *sf.* 1. Permission, leave. 2. Confession, grant; the thing yielded.

Permisivaménte, *ad.* Permissively.

Permisívo, va, *a.* Permissive, containing the power of permitting or granting.

Permíso, *sm.* Permission, leave, license.

Permisór, *sm.* Granter. V. *Permitidor.*

Permiténte, *pa.* He that grants or permits.

Permitidéro, ra, *a.* What may be permitted.

Permitidór, *sm.* Permitter, granter.

Permitír, *va.* 1. To permit, to consent, to agree to. 2. To grant, to admit what is not yet proved.—*vr.* To show one's self to appear benign, generous, and liberal.

Permixtión, *sf.* Mixture of various things.

Permúta y Permutación, *sf.* Permutation, the exchange of one thing for another.

Permutár, *va.* To exchange, to barter.

Pérna, *sf.* Flat shell fish.

Pernáda, *sf.* Kick with the foot, a violent motion with the foot.
Pernáza, *sf.* A thick or big leg.
Pernadór, *a.* Strong-legged.
Pernеár, *vn.* 1. To kick, to shake the legs; to put them in a violent motion. 2. To drive about in pursuit of an affair. 3. To be vexed, to fret.—*va.* To drive pigs to market and sell them by retail.
Pernéo, *sm.* Public sale of hogs.
Pernería, *sf.* Collection of pins or bolts.
Pernétas (En), *ad.* Bare-legged.
Pernéte, *sm.* (Naút.) Small pin, peg, or bolt.
Perniabiérto, ta, *a.* Open or wide-legged.
Pernigóaba, *sf.* (Joc.) Using false calves for the legs.
Perniciosaménte, *ad.* Perniciously.
Pernicióso, sa, *a.* Pernicious, mischievous, destructive.
Pernigón, *sm.* Genoese plum.
Pernil, *sm.* 1. Ham, the thigh of a hog salted. 2. Thigh of breeches. [windows.
Pérnio, *sm.* A kind of hinges for doors and
Perniquebrár, *va.* To break the legs.
Pernituérto, ta, *a.* Crooked-legged.
Pérno, *sm.* 1. A round-headed pin; a large nail, a spike. 2. Hook of a hinge for doors and windows. 3. (Naút.) Bolt, a large pin for various uses on board of ships. *Perno de gancho*, (Naút.) Hook-bolt. *Perno de ojo*, (Naút.) Eye-bolt: *Perno de argolla*, (Naút.) Ring-bolt. *Perno de cadena*, (Naút.) Chain-bolt. [the whole night.
Pernoctár, *vn.* To pass the night; to be awake
Péro, *sm.* 1. A kind of apple; apple-tree. Pyrus malus *L.* 2. Fault, defect.
Péro, *conj.* But, except, yet.
Perogrulláda ó verdad de perogrullo, *sf.* Truth of no moment and universally known.
Peról, *sm.* Boiler, kettle, copper.
Peróne, *sm.* The lesser bone of the leg.
Peroración, *sf.* Peroration, the conclusion of an oration.
Perorár, *va.* 1. To conclude, to put an end to a speech or oration. 2. To solicit effectually.
Perpejána, *sf.* V. *Parpalla.*
Perpendiculár, *a.* Perpendicular, crossing the horizon at right angles.
Perpendicularménte, *ad.* Perpendicularly.
Perpendículo, *sm.* 1. Perpendicular, something crossing the horizon at right angles. 2. Plumb, plummet; a weight of lead hung at a string, by which perpendicularity is discerned. 3. Pendulum. [mitting a crime.
Perpetración, *sf.* Perpetration, the act of com-
Perpetradór, *sm.* Perpetrator, aggressor.
Perpetrár, *va.* To perpetrate, to commit a crime.
Perpétua, *sf.* (Bot.) Eternal flower, everlasting, the blossom of goldilocks, the plant. Gnaphalium stœchas *L.* *Perpétua Encarnada*, (Bot.) Globe Amaranth. Gomphrena globosa *L.*
Perpetuación, *sf.* Perpetuation.
Perpetuál, *a.* (Ant.) V. *Perpetuo.*
Perpetuaménte, *ad.* Perpetually.
Perpetuán, *sm.* Everlasting, a kind of woollen stuff. [petual.
Perpetuár, *va.* To perpetuate, to make per-
Perpetuidád, *sf.* Perpetuity.
Perpétuo, tua, *a.* Perpetual.
Perpiaño, *sm.* A front binding-stone in a wall.
Perplexaménte, *ad.* Perplexedly, confusedly.
Perplexidád, *sf.* Perplexity, irresolution, embarrassment.
Perpléxo, xa, *a.* Doubtful, uncertain.
Perpúnte, *sm.* A quilted under-waistcoat.
Pérque, *sm.* Lampoon, libel.
Pérra, *sf.* 1. Bitch, the female of the canine kind. *Perra salida*, A proud bitch. *Saltar la perra*, (Arag.) To run through one's fortune; to boast of any thing beforehand. 2. Drunkenness, intoxication.
Perráda, *sf.* 1. Pack of dogs. 2. A false compliment. 3. Hasty morning repast of grapes.
Perraménte, *ad.* Very ill; badly.
Perrázo, *sm.* A large dog. [ness.
Perréngue, *sm.* Surliness, peevishness, fretful-
Perréra, *sf.* 1. Kennel, a cot for dogs. 2. Employment attended with much fatigue and little profit. 3. A bad paymaster. 4. Mule or horse spent with age, and cast off.
Perrería, *sf.* 1. Pack of dogs. 2. Set or nest of rogues. 3. Any thing vexatious or teasing.
Perréro, *sm.* 1. Beadle who drives dogs out of the church. 2. Boy or servant whose business is to take care of hounds or dogs used in the chase. 3. One who is very fond of hounds and dogs. 4. Impostor, cheat.
Perrézno, na, *s.* Whelp, puppy.
Perríllo, *sm.* 1. A little dog. *Perrillo raposero*, Harrier, a dog for hunting hares. *Perrillo de falda*, Lap-dog. 2. Tricker or trigger, the catch that, being pulled, loosens the cock of a gun.
Perríto, ta; y co, ca, *s.* A little dog.
Pérro, *sm.* 1. Dog. Canis *L.* *Perro de aguas*, Water dog. *Perro de muestra*, Pointer. *Perro de presa*, Bull-dog. *Perro de ayuda*, Newfoundland-dog, a large dog kept to defend his master. *Perro de ageo*, Setting dog used for partridges. 2. One who obstinately asserts an opinion or perseveres in an undertaking. 3. Damage, loss, deception. 4. (Met.) Name of contempt or ignominy given to a person. *Perro carcador*, Shepherd's dog.
Perroquéte, *sm.* (Naút.) Top-mast.
Perrúna, *sf.* Dog-bread, coarse bread made for dogs.
Perrúno, na, *a.* Doggish, canine.
Persecución, *sf.* 1. Persecution; act of persecuting. 2. Toils, troubles, fatigue.
Perseguidór, *sm.* Persecutor, one who persecutes, harasses, or molests.
Perseguimiénto, *sm.* Persecution.
Perseguír, *va.* 1. To pursue a fugitive. 2. To dun, to harass, to molest, to persecute.
Perséo, *sm.* (Astr.) Perseus, a northern constel-
Persevánte, *sm.* Pursuivant at arms. [lation.
Perseveráncia, *sf.* Perseverance, constancy, permanency, duration.
Perseveranteménte, *ad.* Constantly.
Perseverár, *vn.* To persevere, to persist in an attempt, not to give over, to be permanent.
Persiána, *sf.* A silk stuff with large flowers. *Persianas*, Venetian blinds.
Persicária, *sf.* (Bot.) Spotted snakeweed. Polygonum persicaria *L.*

PÉRSICO, *sm.* (Ict.) Perch. Perca fluviatilis *L.*

PERSIGNÁRSE, *vr.* 1. To make the sign of the cross. 2. To admire, to be surprised at a thing. 3. To handsel, to begin to sell; to make the first act of sale.

PERSIGNUMCRÚCIS, *sm.* (Fam.) By the sign of the cross; wound or mark in the face. [ca *L.*

PÉRSIGO, *sm.* (Bot.) Peach. Amygdalus persi-

PERSÍLLA, *sf.* A sort of linen.

PERSISTÉNCIA, *sf.* Persistence, steadiness, perseverance, obstinacy.

PERSISTÉNTE, *pa.* Permanent, firm, persisting.

PERSISTÍR, *vn.* To persist, to continue firm, to persevere; to endure a long time.

PERSÓNA, *sf.* 1. Person, individual or particular man or woman. 2. Exterior appearance. 3. Personage, a distinguished character; a man of merit or talents. 4. (Gram.) The quality of the noun, that modifies the verb. 5. Man or woman represented in a fictitious dialogue. *De persona á persona,* Personally. *En persona, ó por su persona,* In person, one's self; not a representative.

PERSONÁDO, *sm.* Benefice which confers a prerogative on the incumbent, yet without any jurisdiction.

PERSONÁGE, *sm.* 1. A considerable person, a man or woman of eminence. 2. Character assumed, a disguised person, a stranger, a person not known. 3 An ecclesiastical benefice.

PERSONÁL, *a.* Personal, affecting individuals or peculiar people; particular, proper to him or her.—*sm.* 1. Personal tax. 2. Good or bad qualities of any one.

PERSONALIDÁD, *sf.* Personality, the personal existence or individuality of any one; personal satire.

PERSONALMÉNTE, *ad.* Personally, in person.

PERSONALIZÁR, *va.* To personify, to change from a thing to a person.

PERSONÁZA, *sf.* Huge personage.

PERSONERÍA, *sf.* Charge or employment of an agent, deputy, or attorney.

PERSONÉRO, RA, *s.* Deputy, agent, attorney.

PERSONIFICÁR, *va.* To personify. [fellow.

PERSONÍLLA, *sf.* Mannikin, a ridiculous little

PERSPECTÍVA, *sf.* 1. Perspective, the science by which things are ranged and delineated in a picture, according to their appearance in the real situation. 2 Work executed according to the rules of perspective. 3. View, vista. 4. A false or deceitful appearance.

PERSPECTÍVO, *sm.* Professor of perspective.

PERSPICÁCIA Y PERSPICACIDÁD, *sf.* 1. Perspicaciousness, quickness of sight. 2. Perspicacity, clearness of the mind or understanding.

PERSPICÁZ, *a.* 1. Perspicacious, quick-sighted; sharp of sight. 2. Acute, sagacious.

PERSPICUIDÁD, *sf.* 1. Perspicuity, clearness, transparency. 2. Clearness of the mind, neatness of style. [rent.

PERSPÍCUO, CUA, *a.* Perspicuous, clear, transpa-

PERSPIRACIÓN, *sf.* Perspiration, excretion by the cuticular pores.

PERSUADIDÓR, RA, *s.* Persuader, one who persuades.

PERSUADÍR, *va.* To persuade, to influence by argument or expostulation; to induce, to bring to any particular opinion or act.—*vr.* To be persuaded, to form a judgment or opinion; to believe in virtue of argument and [reason.

PERSUASÍBLE, *a.* Persuasible.

PERSUASIÓN, *sf.* Persuasion, the act or state of being persuaded; opinion, judgment.

PERSUASÓR, RA, *s.* (Raro.) Persuader.

PERSUASÍVA, *sf.* Persuasiveness.

PERSUASÍVO, VA, *a.* Persuasive, having the power of persuading.

PERTENECÉR, *vn.* 1. To belong to, to appertain. 2. To behove, to become, to pertain; to re- [late to.

PERTENECÍDO, *sm.* V. *Pertenencia.*

PERTENECIÉNTE, *pa.* 1. Belonging, appertaining. 2. Apt, fit, ready.

PERTENÉNCIA, *sf.* 1. Right of property; place or territory belonging to any one. 2. Appurtenance, dependence; that which belongs to any thing; an accessory or appendage.

PÉRTICA, *sf.* Perch, a measure consisting of 10 geometric feet.

PÉRTIGA, *sf.* 1. A long pole or rod. 2. A tall slender woman. 3. Hook on which a door or window is hung.

PÉRTIGO, *sm.* Pole of a wagon or cart.

PERTIGÁL, *sm.* Pole. V. *Pertiga.*

PERTIGUEÁR, *va.* To beat a tree with a pole to gather the fruit. [ger.

PERTIGUERÍA, *sf.* Office or employment of a ver-

PERTIGUÉRO, *sm.* Verger, he that carries the mace before the dean. [ness

PERTINÁCIA, *sf.* Pertinacy, obstinacy, stubborn-

PERTINÁZ, *a.* Pertinacious, obstinate.

PERTINAZMÉNTE, *ad.* Pertinaciously.

PERTINÉNTE, *a.* Pertinent, relating, regarding, related to the matter in hand, just to the purpose. [ly

PERTINENTEMÉNTE, *ad.* Pertinently, opportune-

PERTRECHÁR, *va.* 1. To supply a place with ammunition and other warlike stores. 2. To dispose, to arrange, to prepare.—*vr.* To be furnished or provided with the necessary stores and tools for defence.

PERTRÉCHOS, *sm. pl.* 1. Ammunition, arms, and other warlike stores. 2. Tools, instruments

PERTUGÁDA, *sf.* Shock, concussion.

PERTUGUEÁR, *vn.* To be agitated, to be in a violent motion.

PERTURBÁBLE, *a.* Capable of being perturbed.

PERTURBACIÓN, *sf.* Perturbation, disquiet of mind; restlessness of passions.

PERTURBADAMÉNTE, *ad.* Confusedly.

PERTURBADÓR, RA, *s.* Perturbator, disturber; one who excites commotions. [terrupt.

PERTURBÁR, *va.* To PERTURB, to disturb; to in-

PERUÁNO, NA, *a.* V. *Perulero.*

PERÚCHO, *sm.* Proper name, Peter.

PERUÉTANO, *sm.* 1. (Bot.) Wild or choak pear-tree. Pyrus *L.* 2. Any thing that overtops or rises above the rest.

PERULÉRO, RA, *a.* 1. Made or manufactured in Peru. 2. Native of Peru. 3. Nabob, a rich moneyed man.

PERULÉRO, *sm.* (And.) A narrow-bottomed pitcher, wide in the middle and strait-mouthed.

PERVERSAMÉNTE, *ad.* Perversely. [ness.

PERVERSIDÁD, *sf.* Perversity, obstinate wicked-

PERVERSIÓN, *sf.* Perversion; depravation.

PERVÉRSO, SA, *a.* Perverse, extremely wicked.

PERVERTIDÓR, RA, *s.* Perverter, corrupter.

Pervertimiénto, *sm.* Act of perverting.
Pervertír, *va.* 1. To pervert, to disturb. 2. To seduce from the true doctrine and faith.
Pervigílio, *sm.* Restlessness, want of sleep.
Pésa, *sf.* Weight, a piece of a determined weight; piece of metal suspended from clocks. *Pesa de una romana*, Weight or drop-ball of a steel-yard.
Pesáda, *sf.* 1. Quantity weighed at once. 2. Night-mare. V. *Pesadilla*.
Pesadaménte, *ad.* 1. Heavily, weightily, ponderously. 2. Sorrowfully, with trouble and vexation; grievously. 3. Slowly, tardily.
Pesadéz, *sf.* 1. Heaviness, the quality of being heavy or ponderous. 2. Slowness, sluggishness, drowsiness. 3. Peevishness, fretfulness. 4. Obesity, excessive corpulence. 5. Trouble, pain, fatigue.
Pesadílla, *sf.* Night-mare, a morbid oppression on the chest while sleeping, generally accompanied with ideas of spectres and suffocation.
Pesádo, da, *a.* 1. Peevish, fretful, troublesome, violent. 2. Offensive, causing pain, injurious. 3. Heavy, weighty, ponderous. 4. Slow, tardy, sluggish. 5. Fat, gross, corpulent.
Pesadór, *sm.* Weigher, he who weighs.
Pesadúmbre, *sf.* 1. Heaviness, weightiness. 2. Quarrel, dispute, contest, cause of unhappiness. 3. Grief, trouble, displeasure, affliction, disgust; injury.
Pésame, *sm.* Compliment of condolence.
Pesánte, *sm.* Weigher; weight of half a drachm.
Pesantéz, *sf.* V. *Pesadez*.
Pesár, *sm.* Sorrow, grief; repentance.
Pesár (A'), *ad.* In spite of, notwithstanding.
Pesár, *vn.* 1. To weigh, to be of weight. 2. To be valuable, to deserve esteem. 3. To repent, to be concerned or sorry for. 4. To prevail, to preponderate.—*va.* 1. To weigh, to ascertain by the balance the weight of a thing. 2. To examine, to balance in the mind.
Pesaróso, sa, *a.* 1. Sorrowful, full of repentance. 2. Restless, uneasy, disquiet.
Pésca, *sf.* Fishing, fishery, fish.
Pescáda, *sf.* Fish salted, dried, or smoked.
Pescadázo, *sm. aum.* Great fish.
Pescadéra, *sf.* Fish-woman.
Pescadería, *sf.* Fish-market, the place where fish is sold.
Pescadéro, *sm.* Fishmonger.
Pescadíllo, *sm.* A little fish.
Pescádo, *sm.* (Ict.) 1. Fish, a general name for all sorts of fish. *Dia ó comida de pescado*, Friday, day of abstinence with Catholics. 2. Codfish. V. *Abadejo y Bacallao*.
Pescadór, ra, *s.* 1. Fisher-man or woman, fish-monger. *Pescador*, Sovereign pontiff. 2. Fish having a kind of pouch under the jaws to catch others.
Pescánte, *sm.* 1. Crane, an instrument made with ropes, pullies, and hooks, by which great weights are raised. 2. Coach-box. 3. Machine used in shifting of the decorations on the stage. 4. (Naut.) Davit, a piece of timber used to haul up the flukes of an anchor.
Pescár, *va.* 1. To fish, to catch fish. 2. To pick up any thing. 3. To take one by his word, to catch in an act. 4. To obtain one's end.
Péscola, *sf.* The beginning of a furrow in a ploughed field.

Pescóso, sa, *a.* Abounding in fish.
Pescozáda ó Pescozón, *sf.* y *m.* Slap on the neck with an open hand.
Pescozúdo, da, *a.* Having a thick neck.
Pescuézo, *sm.* 1. Neck, the part of the animal body between the head and shoulders; in women, front part of the neck surrounded with a tucker or frill. 2. Haughtiness, loftiness. *Sacar el pescuezo*, To be haughty, to be elated. *Andar al pescuezo*, To take one another by the throat.
Pescúño, *sm.* Large wedge for fastening the colter of a plough.
Pése, *interj.* Kind of imprecatory exclamation.
Pesébre, *sm.* 1. Crib, the rack or manger in a stable. 2. (Fam.) Eating-room.
Pesebréjo, *sm.* Cavity in which horses' teeth are fixed.
Pesebréra, *sf.* Range of mangers in a stable.
Pesebrón, *sm.* Boot of a coach.
Peséta, *sf.* Piece of two reals *de plata*, or silver reals, equal to 4 reals vellon, worth about 11d. sterling. *Peséta Columnaria*, Piece of two reals and a half of *plate*, or five reals *vellon*, value about 13 1-2d. sterling.
Pésete, *sm.* A sort of oath, curse, or imprecation; a word of execration.
Pésga, *sf.* Weight. V. *Pesa* y *Peso*.
Pesía ó Pesiatál, *sm.* Curse, imprecation. V *Pesete*.
Pesíllo, *sm.* Small scales for weighing gold or silver coin.
Pésimamente, *ad. super.* Very badly.
Pésimo, ma, *a. super.* Very bad.
Pesíta, *sf. dim.* A small weight.
Péso, *sm.* 1. Weight, gravity, heaviness; tendency to the centre. 2. Weight, the determined quantity of. 3 Importance, consequence, moment. 4. Balance, scales. 5. Weight or power of reason. 6. Spanish coin, dollar, weighing one ounce; piaster; piece of eight. 7. (Met.) Charge, burthen of an undertaking. *De peso*, Of due weight. *De su peso*, Naturally *En peso*, Suspended in the air; totally, entirely; doubting. *Llevar en peso*, To carry in the air.
Pésoles, *sm. pl.* French beans. V. *Frisoles*.
Pespuntadór, ra, *s.* Back-stitcher.
Pespuntár, *va.* To back-stick, to sew with a back seam.
Pespúnto, *sm.* Back-stitching, back seam.
Pesquéra, *sf.* Fishery, a place frequented by fishermen for catching fish.
Pesquería, *sf.* 1. Trade or profession of a fisherman. 2. Act of fishing. 3. Fishery.
Pesquísa, *sf.* Inquiry, indagation, examination.
Pesquisánte, *pa.* Investigating; inquirer.
Pesquisár, *va.* To inquire, to examine, to indagate.
Pesquisidór, ra, *s.* Examiner, searcher, inquirer. *Juez pesquisidor*, Coroner, a magistrate appointed to inquire into the causes and circumstances of a violent death.
Pestáña, *sf.* 1. Eye-lash, the hair with which the eye-lids are fringed. 2. Fag-end of a piece of linen. 3. Fringe, edging.
Pestañeár, *va.* To move the eye-lashes or eye-lids. *No ó sin pestañear*, Fixed look, attention.

Pestañéo, *sm.* Moving of the eye-lids or eye-lashes.
Péste, *sf.* 1. Pest, plague, pestilence. 2. Any thing troublesome, vexatious, or mischievous; corruption of manners. 3. Great plenty or abundance of any thing. *Pestes*, Words of menace, aversion, or wrath.
Pestiferaménte, *ad.* Pestiferously.
Pestífero, ra, *a.* Pestiferous, causing much damage.
Pestiléncia, *sf.* Pest, plague, pestilence.
Pestilenciál, *a.* Pestiferous, pestilential.
Pestilencialménte, *ad.* V. *Pestiferamente.*
Pestilencióso, sa, *a.* Pestilential.
Pestilénte, *a.* Pestilent, pernicious.
Pestíllo, *sm.* Bolt, a small iron bar for fastening a door.
Pestorejázo, *sm.* V. *Pescozon.*
Pestoréjo, *sm.* Poll, the posterior fleshy part of the neck.
Pestorejón, *sm.* Blow on the back of the neck.
Pesúña, *sf.* Solid hoof, the horny substance on the foot of graminivorous animals.
Pesúño, *sm.* Hoof of cloven-footed animals.
Petáca, *sf.* A kind of trunk or chest covered with hides or leather.
Petalísmo, *sm.* Exile or banishment in Syracuse, so named from writing the names of the persons on a leaf.
Pétalo, *sm.* (Bot.) Petal, flower-leaf.
Petaquílla, *sf.* Hamper covered with hides or leather; a small trunk.
Petár, *vn.* To seek, to search.
Petardeár, *va.* To beat down a gate or door with petards.—*vn.* To cheat, to deceive.
Petardéro, *sm.* 1. Gunner, whose duty consists in landing, fixing, and firing petards. 2. Impostor, cheat, swindler.
Petardísta, *s. com.* Deceiver, defrauder.
Petárdo, *sm.* 1. Petard, a warlike engine made of metal, almost in the shape of a hat, which is loaded with fine powder, and applied to gates and barriers, to blow them up. 2. Cheat, fraud, imposition.
Petáte, *sm.* 1. Fine sort of mat made of palm. 2. Impostor, swindler; despicable person.
Petéquias, *sf. pl.* Spots on the skin, which break out in some malignant fevers.
Petequiál, *a.* Petechial, spotted in consequence of a malignant fever.
Peticáno ó Peticánon, *sm.* Petty canon, name of a size of types.
Petición, *sf.* 1. Demand, claim. 2. Request, petition; prayer annexed to a libel or other judicial declaration produced in court.
Petíllo, *sm.* A small stomacher; a breast jewel.
Petimétre, ra, *s.* Fop, coxcomb; belle.
Petirójo, *sm.* (Orn.) Robin-redbreast.
Petís, *sm.* A fondling name of a little dog.
Petitória, *sf.* V. *Peticion.*
Petitório, ria, *a.* Petitory, petitionary. [tion.
Petitório, *sm.* Impertinent and repeated petition.
Péto, *sm.* 1. Breast-plate, an armour for the breast. 2. Plastron, a piece of leather stuffed, which fencers use to receive the partees made at them. 3. Stomacher, an ornamental covering worn by women on the breast.
Petrál, *sm.* Breast-leather of a horse, breast-plate. V. *Pretal.*

Petraría, *sf.* Ancient machine for throwing stones.
Petraquísta, *a. y s.* Follower of Petrarch.
Petréra, *sf.* Battle fought with stones.
Petrificación, *sf.* Petrification.
Petrificánte, *a.* Petrifying.
Petrificár, *va.* To petrify, to change to stone.
Petrífico, ca, *a.* That which petrifies.
Petríl, *sm.* Battlement, breastwork. V. *Pretil.*
Petrína, *sf.* Girdle. V. *Pretina.*
Petrísca, *sf.* Battle fought with stones. [men.
Petróleo, *sm.* Petroleum, a black liquid bitumen.
Petrus in cunctis, (Lat.) One who affects to know all things. [ness.
Petulância, *sf.* Petulance, insolence, scurviness.
Petulánte, *a.* Petulant, insolent.
Petúnsa, *sf.* Stone of which the Chinese make porcelain. [danum *L.*
Peucedáno, *sm.* (Bot.) Sulphur-wort. Peucedanum *L.*
Peujaléro, *sm.* A petty drover, one who keeps but few cattle.
Péxe, *sm.* 1. Fish. 2. Cunning crafty fellow.
Pexemullér, *sm.* Mermaid, a sea-woman.
Pexiguéra, *sf.* Difficulty, embarrassment; disgust. [dressing hair.
Peynáda, *sf.* Combing, the act of combing and dressing hair.
Peynádo, *sm.* 1. Combing or dressing of the hair. 2. An effeminate man in point of dress.
Peynadór, *sm.* 1. Hair-dresser, one whose profession is to dress hair. 2. Cloth put about the neck while the hair is combed or dressed.
Peynadúra, *sf.* 1. The act of combing or dressing the hair. 2. Hair pulled out with a comb.
Peynár, *va.* 1. To comb or dress the hair. 2. To comb wool. 3. To touch or rub slightly. 4. To excavate or cut away part of a rock, or earth. 5. (Poét.) To move or divide a thing gently. *Las aves peynan las olas*, The birds skim the waves. *Peynar el estilo*, To tower, to soar; applied to the style. *No peynarse para alguno*, To reject a proposal of marriage. *No peynar canas*, (Fam.) To be young.
Peynázo, *sm.* Cross-piece of a door or window frame.
Péyne, *sm.* 1. Comb, an instrument to separate and adjust the hair. 2. Card, an instrument to card wool. 3. Rack, an engine of torture. 4. Weaver's reed. 5. Instep of the foot; hoof. *A' sobre peyne*, Lightly, slightly; imperfectly.
Peynería, *sf.* Shop where combs are made and sold.
Peynéro, *sm.* Comb-maker, one who makes or sells combs.
Peynéta, *sf.* Small comb.
Pez, *sm.* 1. Fish, an animal that swims and inhabits the water; chiefly applied to fresh-water fish having no name. 2. Heap of thrashed corn. 3. *sf.* Rosin, pitch. 4. Meconium, the first excrement of children. 5. Any useful thing gained or obtained. *Peces*, (Met.) Men, in the gospel. *Pez griega*, Colophony. *Pez de palo*, Stock-fish. *Pez con pez*, Quite empty, or unoccupied. *Dar la pez*, To be at the last extremity.
Pezoláda, *sf.* Threads at the fag end of cloth.
Pezón, *sm.* 1. Stalk of fruit, leaves, or flowers. 2. Nipple, the teat of women or dug of animals.

3. Arm of an axle-tree; end of a vertical beam in paper-mills. 4. Cape or point of land.

Pezonéra, *sf.* 1. Linch-pin, a pin which passes through the arms of an axle-tree. 2. A round piece of lead and pewter used by suckling women, to form the nipples.

Pezpíta y Pezpítalo, *s.* (Orn.) Wagtail. Motacilla *L.*

Pezuélo, *sm.* The beginning of cloth where the warp is knotted in order to commence the weaving.

Pezúña, *sf.* Nose-worm; a disease incident to sheep. V. *Pesuña.*

PH, words formerly beginning with these letters will now be found under *F.*

Phalánge, *sf.* V. *Falange.*

Pharmacía, *sf.* V. *Farmacia.*

Pháse, *sm.* Jewish passover previous to leaving Egypt. V. *Fase.*

Pía, *sf.* A pied horse, one whose skin is mottled with various colours.

Piáche, *ó Tarde piache,* Too late, act of coming or being late.

Piáda, *sf.* 1. Chirping of birds, puling of chickens. 2. Mimicking of another's voice.

Piadór, ra, *s.* One who pules like a chicken or chirps like a bird.

Piadosaménte, *ad.* Piously; mercifully, faithfully, credibly.

Piadóso, sa, *a.* 1. Pious, mild, merciful; exciting compassion. 2. Reasonable, moderate.

Piamáter, *sm.* Pia mater, membrane covering the brain.

Piaménte, *ad.* In a mild manner, piously.

Pian Piáno, *ad.* Gently, softly.

Piáno ó Piano-forte, *sm.* Piano-forte, musical instrument.

Piánte, *pa.* Puling. *No dexar piante ni mamante,* To leave neither chick nor child, to root out entirely.

Piár, *vn.* To pule, to cry, to chirp; to whine.

Piára, *sf.* Herd of swine; flock of ewes, mares, or mules.

Piariégo, ga, *a.* Applied to a person who has a herd of mares, mules, or swine.

Píca, *sf.* 1. Pike, a kind of long lance. 2. A measure equal in length to the handle of a spear. 3. Pikeman, a soldier armed with a pike. *A' pica seca,* With great labour without utility.

Picácho, *sm.* Top, summit; sharp point of any thing.

Picacéro, ra, *a.* Applied to birds of prey that chase magpies.

Picacuréba, *sf.* Brazilian pigeon.

Picáda, *sf.* Puncture, incision made by pricking.

Picadéro, *sm.* 1. Riding-house, riding-school. 2. Place where a buck troats and scrapes at rutting time. *Picadéros,* (Naút.) Blocks or pieces of wood put under the keel of a ship, while she is building.

Picadíllo, *sm.* Minced meat. *Estar ó venir de picadillo,* To be piqued and desirous of showing it.

Picádo, *sm.* Pattern pricked on paper.

Picádo, da, *a.* 1. Pricked. 2. Pitted with the small pox. *Estar picado del alacran,* (Fam.) To be smitten with love; to have the venereal disease. *Estar picada la piedra,* To eat much and rapidly.

Picadór, *sm.* 1. Riding-master, one whose employment is to tame and break in horses. 2. Block on which meat is chopped.

Picadúra, *sf.* 1. The act of pricking. 2. Puncture, a wound made by pricking. 3. Ornamental gusset in clothes. 4. Bite of an animal or bird.

Picaféo, *sm.* (Orn.) V. *Pico verde.*

Picaflóres, *sm.* (Orn.) Humming bird. Trochilus *L.*

Picagallína, *sf.* (Bot.) V. *Alsine.*

Picamadéros, *sm.* Wood-pecker.

Picánte, *pa.* Piquant.

Picánte, *sm.* Piquancy, pungency, acrimony; keen satire.

Picanteménte, *ad.* Piquantly.

Picáño, *sm.* Patch on a shoe.

Picáño, na, *a.* Deceitful, roguish, shameless.

Picapedréro, *sm.* Stone-cutter.

Picapléytos, *sm.* A litigious person; a petty-fogging lawyer.

Picaporte, *sm.* Clicket, picklock for opening doors.

Picapuérco, *sm.* (Orn.) Bird less than a pigeon.

Picár, *va.* 1. To prick, to make punctures. *Picar el dibuxo,* To prick out a design. 2. To sting like an insect, or bite like an animal. 3. To pound, to break into small pieces. 4. To peck like birds. 5. To nibble. 6. To fret, to get angry. 7. To pursue or harass an enemy. 8. To itch. 9. To taste a little; to eat a bunch of grapes. 10. To spur a horse; to stimulate. 11. To discover the utility of a thing; to be dear. 12. To begin to operate; to be superficially informed. 13. To finish a painting by some happy touches. *Picar en poeta,* To be a poet.—*vr.* 1. To be offended or vexed. 2. To be moth-eaten. 3. To begin to rot. 4. To be elated with pride. 5. (Met.) To be deceived. 6. To be proud; applied to animals. *Picar el pez,* (Fam.) To ensnare.

Picaraménte, *ad.* In a base roguish manner.

Picaráżo, za, *a.* Great rogue.

Picardeár, *vn.* To play the knave.

Picardía, *sm.* 1. Knavery, roguery; deceit. 2. Lewdness. 3. Meeting of rogues.

Picarésca, *sf.* A nest of rogues, meeting of knaves.

Picarésco, ca, y Picaríl, *a.* Roguish, knavish.

Picaríllo, *sm.* A little rogue.

Pícaro, ra, *a.* 1. Knavish, roguish, vile, low. 2. Mischievous, malicious, crafty, sly. 3. Merry, gay.—*s.* Rogue, knave.

Pícaros, *sm. pl.* Scullions, kitchen-boys.

Picarón, na, *a.* y *s.* Great rogue, villain.

Picaronázo, za, *a.* Very roguish, villanous.

Picaróte, *a.* Subtle, crafty; notorious villain.

Picarrelíncho, *sm.* (Orn.) V. *Andario.*

Picatóste, *sm.* Toast of bread fried with slices of ham.

Picáza, *sf.* 1. (Orn.) Magpie. Corvus pica *L.* 2. (Mur.) Hoe for clearing the ground of weeds. *Picaza marina,* (Orn.) Flamingo. Phœnicopteros *L.*

Picázo, *sm.* 1. Blow given with a pike. 2. Sting of an insect; stroke with the beak of a bird. 3. Young magpie.

Picazón, *sm.* 1. Itching, prurience. 2. Peevishness, fretfulness, displeasure.
Pícea, *sf.* (Bot.) Pine. Pinus abies *L.*
Pichél, *sm.* Pewter-tankard; a mug.
Pichelería, *sf.* Factory of tankards or tin pots.
Picheléro, *sm.* Maker of pewter pots or tankards. [or mug.
Pichelète ó Pichelíllo, *sm.* A small tankard
Pichichuélas, *sm.* (Joc.) Nickname, tankard-face. [containing about a pint.
Pichóla, *sf.* A wine-measure used in Galicia,
Pichón, *sm.* A young pigeon. [columns.
Pichostílo, *sm.* (Arq.) Too little space between
Píco, *sm.* 1. Beak, the extreme part of a bird's head. 2. A sharp point of any kind. 3. A kind of spade with a long crooked bill. 4. Spout of a jar. 5. Peak, top or summit of a hill. 6. Balance of an account. 7. Mouth. *De pico,* By the mouth, without works or deeds. 8. Loquacity, garrulity. 9. (Orn.) Woodpecker. Picus *L.* *Pico verde,* Green woodpecker. *Pico de oro,* A man of great eloquence. *Pico de un ancla,* (Naút.) Bill of an anchor. *Picos de un sombrero,* Cocks of a hat. *Perder por el pico,* To lose by too much chattering. *Pico à viento,* With the wind in the face. *Andarse á picos pardos,* To loiter or follow idle pursuits instead of profitable ones.
Picolète, *sm.* Staple, an iron hoop through which the bolt of a lock runs.
Picón, na, *a.* Applied to animals with the upper teeth projecting over the under ones; or to cattle nipping the grass the contrary way for want of teeth.
Picón, *sm.* 1. Lampoon or nipping jest employed to induce another to do or perform any thing. 2. A sort of very small charcoal used in braziers. 3. Small fresh-water fish. 4. (Mur. y Val.) Rice flour. [braziers.
Piconéro, *sm.* Maker of small charcoal for
Picór, *sm.* The pungent taste left by any thing which is hot or piquant.
Picóso, sa, *a.* Pitted with the small pox.
Picóta, *sf.* 1. Pillory. 2. (Naút.) Cheek of a pump. 3. Top of a mountain, point of a turret or steeple.
Picotázo y Picotáda, *s.* Stroke with the bill or beak of a bird.
Picóte, *sm.* 1. Coarse stuff made of goat's hair. 2. A glossy silk stuff.
Picoteádo, da, *a.* Peaked, having many points or angles.
Picoteár, *va.* 1. To strike with the beak or bill. 2. To speak much, to prattle, to tattle. 3. To toss the head about; applied to a horse.—*vr.* To wrangle or quarrel; applied to women.
Picotería, *sf.* Loquacity, volubility of speech.
Picotéro, ra, *a.* Wrangling, chattering, prattling.
Picotíllo, *sm.* Inferior cloth of goats' hair.
Píctima, *sf.* V. *Apósito y Epítima.*
Pictórico, ca, *a.* Pictorial.
Picudílla, *sf.* Kind of olive.
Picúdo, da, *a.* 1. Beaked; acuminated, sharp pointed. 2. Prattling, babbling, chattering.
Pidientéro, *sm.* Beggar. V. *Pordiosero.*
Pído, *sm.* (Joc.) Demand, request, petition.
Pidón, na, *a.* (Joc.) V. *Pedidor.*

Pie, *sm.* 1. Foot, the part on which we tread; the part opposed to the head. 2. Basis, foundation, groundwork. 3. Trunk of trees and plants. 4. Lees, sediment. 5. Last hand or player in a game at cards. 6. The last word pronounced by an actor on the stage. 7. Foot, a measure of length; in Castile it is to the old Roman foot as 923 to 1000. 8. Motive, occasion. 9. Footing, rule, use, custom. 10. End or conclusion of a writing. 11. Heap of tread grapes ready to be squeezed in the press. 12. Woollen yarn warped. 13. First colour given in dying, that the next may be more permanent. 14. Foot of a stocking. *Pie de carnero,* (Naút.) Samson's post. *Pie derecho,* (Naút.) Stanchion. *Pie de roda,* (Naút.) Forefoot, a piece of timber which terminates the forepart of the keel. *Pie ante pie,* Step by step. *A' pie,* On foot. *Al pie,* Near, at the foot of. *A' pie enxuto,* Without labour or pain. *A' pie llano,* On even ground; easily, commodiously. *En pie,* Constantly, firmly. *En un pie de tierra,* Shortly, in a little time. *Tener ó traer debaxo de los pies,* To trample under foot. *Tener pies de mar,* (Naút.) To be a swift sailer, to be a good sea boat; applied to a ship. *Pie de amigo,* Prop, shore: iron instrument used to keep up the head of persons when they are publicly whipped. *Pie de cabra,* A kind of pronged lever.
Piececíca, lla, ta; Piecezuéla, *sf.* Little piece; diminutive of *Pieza.*
Piececíllo, to; Piecezuélo y Piecíco, llo, to, *sm.* A little foot.
Piedád, *sf.* 1. Piety, mercy, pity, commiseration. 2. Charity.
Piédra, *sf.* 1. Stone, a body insipid, hard, not ductile or malleable, and not soluble in water. 2. Gravel, a sandy matter concreted in the kidneys. 3. Hail, drops of rain frozen in their falling. 4. Place where foundlings are exposed. 5. Gun-flint. 6. Hardness of things. *Piedra de amolar ó afilar,* Whet-stone, grinding-stone. *Piedra de toque,* Touch-stone. *Piedra pomez,* Pumice-stone. *No dexar piedra por mover,* Not to leave a stone unturned. *Piedras,* Counters used at play to mark the game. *Tirar piedras,* To be insane.
Piedrecílla, ta, ca, *sf.* A little stone.
Piél, *sf.* 1. Skin, the natural covering of the flesh. 2. Hide of an animal cured and dressed. 3. Life. *Alargó la piel,* He gave up the ghost. *Ser de la piel del diablo,* To be a limb of the devil.
Piélago, *sm.* 1. Main or high sea. 2. Great plenty or abundance. V. *Tarquin.*
Piéleo, *sm.* V. *Piezgo.*
Piénso, *sm.* The common daily allowance of barley given to horses or mules in Spain.
Piério, ria, *a.* (Poét.) Pierian, relating to the muses.
Piérna, *sf.* 1. Leg, the limb by which we walk: particularly the part between the knee and the foot. 2. Leg of butcher's meat or of fowls. 3. Stripe or oblong part which, joined to another, forms a whole. 4. A long jar with a narrow mouth in which honey is kept or carried. 5. Inequality in the selvage of cloth. 6. Down-stroke of letters. 7. Cheek of a printing press.

A' modo de pierna de nuez, Not done with rectitude, carelessly, obliquely. *En piernas,* Bare legged.

PIERNITENDÍDO, DA, *a.* With extended legs.

PIÉZA, *sf.* 1. Piece, a part of a broken whole; a fragment. 2. Coin, piece of money. *Pieza de á ocho,* A dollar, an ounce of silver or 8 silver reals. 3. Piece of furniture. 4. Room, any apartment in a house. 5. Piece of ordnance. 6. Buffoon, wag, jester. *Buena ó gentil pieza!* (Iron.) An artful blade, cunning designing fellow. 7. Space or interval of time. 8. Piece of cloth woven at once. 9. Ball used in various games. *Pieza de autos,* Records or pleadings of a lawsuit sewed or stitched together. *Tocar la pieza,* To touch upon a subject.

PIÉZGO, *sm.* 1. Neck of a leather bottle; the hind or fore foot of an animal. 2. A dressed skin for carrying wine or other liquors.

PÍFANO ó PÍFARO, *sm.* 1. Fife, a military musical instrument. 2. Fifer, he who plays on a fife.

PIFÍA, *sf.* Sound of a rebounding billiard ball.

PIFIÁR, *va.* 1. To suffer the breath to be too audible in playing the flute. 2. To sound like a billiard ball.

PIGÁRGO, *sm.* 1. White-faced antelope. Antilope pygarga *L.* 2. Cinereous eagle. Falco albicilla *L.* 3. Ring-tail hawk. Falco pygargus *L.*

PIGMÉO, MEA, *a.* Dwarfish, below the natural bulk.

PIGNÓTICOS, *sm. pl.* Pycnotics.

PÍGRE, *a.* Slothful, lazy, indolent.

PIGRÍCIA, *sf.* 1. Laziness, idleness. 2. Place in schools destined for lazy boys.

PÍGRO, RA, *a.* Negligent, careless, lazy.

PÍHUA, *sf.* V. *Coriza.*

PIHUÉLA, *sf.* 1. A short leather strap tied to a hawk's leg. 2. Obstruction, hindrance, impediment. *Pihuélas,* Fetters, shackles.

PIÍSIMO, MA, *a. sup.* Most pious.

PIJÓTA, *sf.* (Ict.) Hake, poor jack. V. *Merluza.*

PIJÓTE, *sm.* (Naút.) Swivel-gun loaded with small grape shot.

PÍLA, *sf.* 1. A large stone basin or trough for water, in which beasts or cattle drink. 2. Font, a stone vessel in which the water is kept in the church for baptism. 3. Heap of any things thrown together. 4. Pile of shorn wool. 5. Parish church, parish. 6. Stone basin in which the holy water is kept. *Nombre de pila,* Christian name. *Sacar de pila,* To stand godfather or godmother.

PILÁDA, *sf.* Quantity of mortar beaten up or made at once; pile, heap.

PILÁR, *sm.* 1. The large water basin of a fountain. 2. Pillar, a column of stone; post. 3. Pillar, a person who supports or maintains any thing. 4. Stone or mound for a landmark on roads. *Pilar de una cama,* Bed-post.

PILARÉJO ó PILARÍTO, *sm.* A small pillar.

PILÁSTRA, *sf.* Pilaster, a square column.

PILASTRÍLLA, *sf. dim.* A small pilaster.

PILASTRÓN, *sm. aum.* A large pilaster.

PILASTRONCÍLLO, *sm. dim.* of *Pilastron.*

PILATÉRO, *sm.* In woollen factories, fuller who assists at fulling the cloth.

PÍLDORA, *sf.* 1. Pill, a medicine made in a small ball. 2. Lint, a roll of lint steeped in some medicine to be put into wounds. 3. Affliction, bad news.

PÍLEO, *sm.* 1. A kind of hat or cap worn by the ancient Romans. 2. Red hat worn by cardinals.

PILÉTA ó PILÍCA, *sf. dim.* of *Pila.*

PÍLLA, *sf.* Pillage, plunder.

PILLÁDA, *sf.* Act of a plunderer or villain.

PILLADÓR, *sm.* Pillager, plunderer, swindler.

PILLÁGE, *sm.* Pillage, plunder.

PILLÁR, *va.* 1. To pillage, to plunder. 2. To seize, to lay hold of. *No pillar fastidio,* Not to be easily vexed. *Pillar un cernícalo, una mona, un lobo, una zorra, &c.* To become intoxicated.

PILLÁSTRO, *sm.* (Fam.) Tall slender person.

PILLASTRÓN, *sm.* (Fam.) A long thin man.

PILLERÍA, *sf.* Pillaging, marauding, swindling.

PÍLLO, LLA, *a.* Applied to a rogue without education and example.—*s.* Swindler, robber.

PILÓN, *sm.* 1. A large water basin or trough in which beasts or cattle drink. 2. Sugar-loaf. 3. Drop, ball, or weight of a steelyard. 4. Heap of grapes ready to be pressed. 5. Heap of mortar.

PILONÉRO, RA, *s.* Newsmonger.

PILÓNGO, GA, *a.* 1. Peeled and dried; applied to a chesnut. 2. Thin, lean, meager.

PILÓRO, *sm.* 1. Musk-rat. Mus pilorides *L.* 2. (Anat.) Pylorus, inferior part of the stomach.

PILÓSO, SA, *a.* V. *Peludo.*

PILOTÁGE, *sm.* 1. Pilotage, the art of piloting a ship. 2. Rate of pilotage, a pilot's hire. 3. Foundation of piers or dikes to resist water.

PILOTÍNES, *sm. pl.* 1. Foundation stones. 2. Pilot's mate, or second pilot.

PILÓTO, *sm.* 1. Pilot, he whose office is to steer the ship. 2. Bibber, tippler; one who drinks a great deal of wine, and pretends to be a connoisseur with regard to its quality. 3. A skilful careful guide in any affair or business. *Piloto de altura,* Pilot of the high sea, who steers by observation of the stars. *Piloto práctico,* Practical pilot, who steers vessels by his practical knowledge of the coast and harbour.

PILTRÁCA ó PILTRÁFA, *sf.* Piece of flesh or meat which is almost nothing but skin.

PIMENTÁDA, *sf.* Sauce, the principal ingredient of which is Cayenne pepper.

PIMENTÁL, *sm.* Ground bearing pepper.

PIMENTÉRO, *sm.* 1. Pepper-box. 2. (Bot.) Indian or Cayenne pepper plant.

PIMENTÓN, *sm.* Ground Cayenne pepper.

PIMIÉNTA, *sf.* (Bot.) Pepper, an aromatic spice. Piper nigrum *L. Pimienta larga,* Long pepper. Piper longum *L. Es una pimienta,* He is all life and spirits. *Tener mucha pimienta,* To be very dear.

PIMIÉNTO, *sm.* 1. (Bot.) Red Cayenne or Indian pepper plant. Capsicum baccatum *L.* 2. Garden capsicum. Capsicum annuum *L.* 3. Mildew, blight in plants, as wheat, barley, &c. 4. V. *Agnocasto.*

PÍMPIDO, *sm.* (Ict.) Cat-fish

PIMPÍN, *sm.* Children's play.

PIMPINÉLA, *sf.* (Bot.) Burnet, pimpernel. Poterium sanguisorba *L.*

PIMPOLLÁR, *sm.* Nursery of young plants and trees.

Pimpollecér, *vn.* To sprout, to bud.

Pimpóllo, *sm.* 1. Sucker, sprout, shoot. 2. Rose-button not yet opened. 3. A spruce lively lad. 4. Any thing perfect in its kind.

Pimpollúdo, da, *a.* Full of buds or sprouts.

Pína, *sf.* 1. A round mound of earth raised in the form of a cone. 2. Plug which boys put in a squirt or syringe.—*pl.* 1. Small turrets raised on a wall. 2. Felloes, the pieces of wood which form the circumference of a coach or cart wheel.

Pinabéte, *sm.* (Bot.) Spruce fir-tree. Pinus abies *L.*

Pináculo, *sm.* Pinnacle, the highest part of a magnificent building.

Pinál ó Pinár, *sm.* Grove of pines.

Pinariégo, ga, *a.* Belonging to pines.

Pinástro, *sm.* Wild pine.

Pináza, *sf.* (Naút.) Pinnace, a small vessel. *Pinázas,* A sort of Indian stuffs made of the bark of trees.

Pincarrascál, *sm.* Grove of small branchy pines.

Pincarrásco, *sm.* Species of branchy pine.

Pincél, *sm.* 1. (Naút.) Instrument for tarring a vessel. 2. Pencil, a small brush used by painters. 3. Painter. *Es un gran pincel,* He is a great painter. 4. Second feather in a martin's wing.

Pinceláda, *sf.* Stroke with a pencil. *Dar la ultima pincelada,* To give the finishing stroke.

Pinceléro, *sm.* Pencilmaker, one who makes and sells hair pencils or small brushes.

Pincelóte, *sm.* Large pencil.

Pincérna, *s. com.* One who serves drink at feasts.

Pinchadúra, *sf.* (Vulg.) Puncture, act of pricking.

Pinchár, *va.* (Vulg.) To prick, to wound.

Pinchaúvas, *sm.* Nick-name for a despicable person.

Pínche, *sm.* Scullion, kitchen boy.

Píncho, *sm.* Thorn, prickle of plants.

Pindonguear, *vn.* To gad about; applied to women.

Pinéda, *sf.* Kind of garters.

Pingájo, *sm.* Rag hanging down from clothes.

Pinganéllo, *sm.* V. *Calamoco.*

Pinganítos, *sm.* *En pinganitos,* In a prosperous or elevated state.

Pingorotúdo, da, *a.* High, lofty, elevated.

Píngue, *sm.* (Naút.) Pink, a vessel with a very narrow stern.

Píngüe, *a.* 1. Fat, greasy, oily. 2. Rich, plentiful, abundant.

Pingüedinóso, sa, *a.* Fatty, oleaginous, pinguid.

Pingüédo, *sf.* V. *Gordura.*

Pingüísimo, ma, *a. sup.* Excessively fat.

Pingüosidád, *sf.* Fatness.

Piníco, *sm.* Small step.

Piníllo, *sm.* (Bot.) Ground-pine, germander. Teucrium chamæpitys *L.*

Pinjádo, *sm.* *Rico ó pinjado,* Determined, resolute in any purpose.

Pinjánte, *sm.* (Arq.) Moulding at the eaves of buildings.

Píno, na, *a.* Very perpendicular or direct, as the sides of a mountain.

Píno, *sm.* 1. (Bot.) Pine. Pinus *L.* 2. Ship built or constructed of pine. *Pinos,* The first steps of a child when it begins to walk. *A' pino,* Erect, upright; applied to bells turned half-round in ringing.

Pinócha, *sf.* Pine leaf.

Pínola, *sf.* 1. Detent of a repeating watch. 2. Spindle. *Pinola de cabrestante,* (Naút.) Capstern-spindle. *Pinola de quadrante,* (Naút.) Vane of a quadrant.

Pínole, *sm.* An aromatic powder used in making chocolate.

Pinóso, sa, *a.* Producing pines or belonging to them.

Pínta, *sf.* 1. Spot, blemish, scar. 2. Mark on playing cards. 3. Drop. 4. Pint, a liquid measure.—*pl.* 1. Spots which appear on the skin in some malignant fevers. V. *Tabardillo.* 2. Basset, a game at cards. *No quitar pinta,* The greatest similarity in every part of two persons or things.

Pintacílgo ó Pintadíllo, *sm.* (Orn.) Goldfinch. Fringilla carduelis *L.*

Pintadéra, *sf.* Instrument used for ornamenting bread.

Pintádo, da, *a.* Painted, mottled. *Venir pintado,* To fit exactly. *Al mas pintado,* To the wisest, most able.

Pintár, *va.* 1. To paint, to represent by delineation and colours. 2. To describe, to delineate, to define; to write. 3. To fancy, to imagine. 4. To exaggerate, to heighten by representation. 5. To pay, to discharge, to satisfy.—*vn.* 1. To begin to ripen; applied to fruit. 2. To show, to give signs of.—*vr.* To paint one's face.

Pintamónas, *sm.* Nickname for a bad painter.

Pintaróxo, *sm.* (Orn.) V. *Pardillo.*

Pintarrajár, *va.* (Fam.) V. *Pintorrear.*

Pintarrajeár, *va.* To daub.

Pintarrájo, *sm.* A coarse bungling piece of painting.

Pintarróxa, *sf.* V. *Lixa.*

Pintílla, ca, ta, *sf.* A little spot or dot.

Pintiparádo, da, *a.* Perfectly like, closely resembling; apposite, fit.

Pintiparár, *va.* (Joc.) To compare, to estimate relative goodness and badness.

Pintójo, ja, *a.* Spotted, stained, mottled.

Pintór, ra, *s.* Painter, one who professes or exercises the art of painting; painter's wife.

Pintorésco, ca, *a.* Picturesque, belonging to paintings and painters.

Pintorreadór, *sm.* Dauber, a coarse miserable painter.

Pintorreár, *va.* To daub, to paint without skill.

Pintúra, *sf.* 1. Painting, the art of representing objects by delineation and colours. 2. Picture, a painted resemblance. *Pintura figulina,* Painting in divers colours on earthenware. *Pintura al temple,* Size painting. 3. Forming letters with the pen. 4. (Met.) Picture, written description of any thing. *Pintura cerífica ó encaustica,* Encaustic painting, enamelling with coloured wax burnt in. *Pintura embutida,* Painting in mosaic, &c.

Pínula, *sf.* 1. Detent of a repeating watch. 2. Sight of an optical instrument.

Pínzas, *sf. pl.* Nippers, small pincers; an iron instrument for drawing nails.

Pinzón, *sm.* (Orn.) Chaffinch. Fringilla cœlebs *L.*

Pinzóte, *sm.* (Naút.) Whipstaff, formerly fastened to the rudder, but now disused.

PIÑA, *sf.* 1. Cone or nut of the pine tree, which contains the seed. 2. Pine-apple. Bromelia ananas *L.* 3. Mass of silver in the shape of a pine-apple. 4. (Naút.) Wall-knot, a particular kind of knot at the end of a rope.

PIÑÁTA, *sf.* Pitcher, pot.

PIÑÓN, *sm.* 1. Cone or seed of the pine-tree. 2. Pinion, the joint of the wing remotest from the body. 3. Pinion, the tooth of a small wheel answering to that of a larger. 4. Spring-nut of a gun. *Comer los piñones*, To celebrate Christmas eve.

PIÑONÁTA, *sf.* Conserve of pine-nut kernels.

PIÑONÁTE, *sm.* Paste made of the kernels of pine-nuts and sugar.

PIÑONCÍLLO, CO, TO, *sm.* A small pine-nut kernel.

PIÑUÉLA, *sf.* 1. Figured silk. 2. Nut or fruit of cypress.

PÍO, IA, *a.* 1. Pious, devout, religious. 2. Mild, merciful. 3. Pied, of various colours, piebald; applied to a horse. *Pia madre*, Pia mater, membrane which covers the brain.

PÍO, *sm.* 1. Puling or cry of chickens. 2. Anxious desire.

PIÓCHA, *sf.* Trinket for women's head-dresses.

PIOJÉNTO, TA, *a.* Lousy, full of lice.

PIOJERÍA, *sf.* 1. Lousiness, the state of abounding with lice. 2. Misery, poverty.

PIOJICÍDA, *s. com.* (Joc.) Killer of lice.

PIOJÍLLO, *sm.* 1. A small louse; a plant covered with noxious insects. 2. A white spot in leather which is not well dressed or stained.

PIÓJO, *sm.* 1. Louse, a small insect, living on animal bodies. Pediculus *L.* 2. Disease in hawks and other birds of prey. *Piojo pegadizo*, Crab-louse; a troublesome hanger-on.

PIOJÓSO, SA, *a.* Lousy, swarming with lice; miserable.

PIOJUÉLO, *sm.* A small louse.

PIÓLA, *sf.* (Naút.) Housing, house-line; a line made of three fine strands.

PIÓRNO, *sm.* (Bot.) Spanish-broom. Spartium scorpius *L.*

PÍPA, *sf.* 1. Pipe, a wine or brandy vessel containing two hogsheads. 2. Tobacco pipe. 3. Pipe which children make of the stalks of corn; reed of a clarion. 4. Fusee of a bomb.

PIPÁR, *vn.* To smoke, to draw the fume of tobacco into the mouth with a pipe.

PIPERÍA, *sf.* Collection of pipes.

PIPÉRO, *sm.* Cooper, pipe or butt maker.

PIPI, *sm.* (Orn.) A small African bird said to follow travellers till they kill some animal, when it sucks the blood.

PIPIÁN, *sm.* A kind of Indian fricassee.

PIPIÁR, *vn.* To pule, to chirp.

PIPIRIGÁLLO, *sm.* (Bot.) Saintfoin. Hedysarum onobrychis *L.*

PIPIRIPÁO, *sm.* (Vulg.) A splendid feast.

PIPITÁÑA, *sf.* Flute made by boys of green cane.

PÍPO, *sm.* Small bird that eats flies.

PIPÓRRO, *sm.* A round earthen jug with a spout.

PIPÓTE, *sm.* Keg, a small barrel.

PIPOTÍLLO, *sm.* A small keg.

PÍQUE, *sm.* 1. Pique, displeasure. 2. Courtship, gallantry. V. *Chichisveo.* 3. Term in a game. 4. Bottom, ground. *Irse á pique*, (Naút.) To founder. *Echar á pique un bazel*, (Naút.) To sink a ship. *A' pique*, In danger, on the point of. *Piques*, (Naút.) Crotches. V. *Horquillas.*

PIQUÉRA, *sf.* 1. A small hole in a bee-hive, through which bees fly out and in. 2. Cock-hole in a barrel.

PIQUERÍA, *sf.* Body of pikemen.

PIQUÉRO, *sm.* Pikeman, a soldier armed with a pike.

PIQUÉTA, *sf.* Pick-axe, mattock.

PIQUÉTE, *sm.* 1. Sore or wound of little importance. 2. Small hole made in clothes with a pinking iron. 3. A sharp-pointed stake shod with iron. 4. Piquet or picket, a small detachment of soldiers stationed in the front or rear of a larger body.

PIQUETÉRO, *sm.* In mines, boy who carries the picks or mattock to the workmen.

PIQUETÍLLA, *sf.* A small pick-axe.

PIQUÍLLO ó PIQUÍTO, *sm.* A small beak or bill.

PIQUITUÉRTO, *sm.* (Orn.) Cross-bill. Loxia curvirostra *L.*

PÍRA, *sf.* A funeral pile on which the bodies of the dead are burnt.

PIRAGÓN Y PIRÁL, *sm.* V. *Pirausta.*

PIRÁGUA, *sf.* (Naút.) A kind of small vessel.

PIRAMIDÁL, *a.* Pyramidal, having the form of a pyramid.

PIRAMIDALMÉNTE, *ad.* Pyramidally.

PIRÁMIDE, *sf.* Pyramid, a solid figure whose base is a polygon.

PIRAMÍSTA, *sf.* A kind of butterfly.

PIRÁTA, *sm.* 1. Pirate, corsair. 2. A cruel wretch.

PIRATEÁR, *vn.* To pirate, to rob by sea.

PIRATERÍA, *sf.* Piracy.

PIRÁTICO, CA, *a.* Piratical.

PIRÁUSTA, *sf.* Large fire-fly. Pyralis *L.*

PIRÍTES, *sf.* 1. Pyrites, an obsolescent name for the sulphurets of iron, copper, and other metals. 2. Marcasite, a fossil. V. *Marcasita.*

PIROFILÁCIO, *sm.* Subterraneous fire.

PIROMÁNCIA, *sf.* Pyromancy, divination by fire.

PIRÓMETRO, *sm.* Pyrometer, an instrument for measuring the different degrees of heat.

PIRONÓMIA, *sf.* Pyronomy, the art of regulating the fire, and making it subservient to all descriptions of chemical processes.

PIRÓPO, *sm.* 1. Precious stone. V. *Carbunclo.* 2. Sound of pompous high-flowing words.

PIROTÉCNIA, *sf.* Pyrotechny, the art of managing fire.

PIRRÍQUIO, *sm.* Foot of Latin verse.

PIRRONÍSMO, *sm.* Pyrrhonism. V. *Escepticismo.*

PIRUÉTA, *sf.* Pyroet or piroet, circumvolution, spring round in dancing, gyration.

PIRUETÁNO, *sm.* V. *Perutano.*

PÍSA, *sf.* 1. Tread, the act of treading. 2. Kick, a violent blow given with the foot. 3. Portion of olives or grapes pressed out at once.

PISÁDA, *sf.* 1. Footstep, the impression left by the foot. *Seguir las pisadas*, To follow one's step or example. 2. Kick, a blow with the foot.

PISADÓR, *sm.* 1. Treader, he who treads out the juice of grapes. 2. Horse that prances in walking.

PISADÚRA, *sf.* Act of treading.

PISAFÁLTO ó PISASFÁLTO, *sm.* Mixture of bitumen and pitch.

PISÁNTE, *sm.* (Cant.) Foot; shoe.

PISÁR, *va.* 1. To tread, to trample; to stamp on

the ground. 2. To beat down stones and earth with a mallet. 3. To touch upon, to be close to. 4. To despise, to abandon.—*vn.* To be the ground floor or basement story of a building. *Pisar el sapo,* To have a ridiculous dread of bad success.

Pisaúvas, *sm.* Treader of grapes.

Pisavérde, *sm.* Fop, coxcomb, popinjay.

Piscatór, *sm.* A universal almanack.

Piscatória, *sf.* Eclogue, in which fishermen are the interlocutors.

Piscatório, ria, *a.* Piscatory.

Piscína, *sf.* 1. Fish-pond. 2. Bath used by the Turks. 3. Piscina, place in churches where the remains of water and other articles used in the sacred offices are thrown.

Píscis, *sm.* (Astr.) Pisces, a zodaical sign.

Píso, *sm.* 1. Tread, trampling. 2. Toll, a duty paid for passing through a place or country. 3. Floor, pavement, surface; foundation of a house. 4. Story or floor, as first floor, second floor, &c. *Piso baxo,* Ground floor. *A' un piso,* On the same floor.

Pisón, *sm.* Rammer, an instrument for driving down earth, stones, or piles. *A' pison,* By blows of a rammer.

Pisoneár, *va.* To ram, to drive down earth, stones, or piles.

Pisoteár, *va.* To trample, to tread under foot.

Pisotéo, *sm.* The act of treading or trampling under foot.

Písta, *sf.* 1. Trace, the foot-print of a wild beast. 2. Piste, the tread of a horse when he is marching.

Pistácho, *sm.* V. *Alfónsigo.*

Pistadéro, *sm.* Pestle, instrument for pounding.

Pistár, *va.* To pound, to grind with a pestle; to extract the juice of a thing.

Pistílo, *sm.* (Bot.) Pistil, the central part of a flower consisting of the germen, style, and summit; it is the female organ, and is surrounded by the stamens.

Písto, *sm.* 1. Substance, juice. 2. Dish of tomates and red pepper fried together with oil. *A' pistos,* By little and little, by driblets; in a miserable or penurious manner.

Pistóla, *sf.* Pistol, a small hand-gun.

Pistoletázo, *sm.* Shot or wound of a pistol.

Pistoléte, *sm.* Pocket-pistol.

Pistón, *sm.* Piston, embolus, such as the sucker of a pump.

Pistorésa, *sf.* Short dagger.

Pistráge ó Pistráque, *sm.* Broth or sauce of an unpleasant taste.

Pistúra, *sf.* Act of pounding.

Píta, *sf.* 1. (Bot.) Agave, American aloe. Agave Americana *L.* 2. Kind of thread made of the agave. 3. Term used to call hens. 4. Play among boys.

Pitáco, *sm.* Stem or stalk of the aloe-plant.

Pitancería, *sf.* 1. Place where allowances of meat and other things are distributed. 2. Distribution or office of distributor of allowances.

Pitancéro, *sm.* 1. Person appointed to distribute allowances of meat or other things. 2. Friar who is not ordained, but lives upon the charity which he is able to collect. 3. Steward or purveyor to a convent. 4. Superintendent of a choir in cathedrals.

Pitancíca, lla, ta, *sf. dim.* Small pittance.

Pitáno, *sm.* (Bot.) Cress-rocket. Vella pseudocytisus *L.*

Pitánza, *sf.* Pittance, daily allowance; alms.

Pitáña, *sf.* V. *Lagaña.*

Pitañóso, sa, *a.* V. *Lagañoso.*

Pitár, *vn.* To pipe, to play on a pipe.—*va.* 1. To discharge a debt. 2. To distribute allowances of meat or other things.

Pitárra, *sf.* Distemper of the eyes. V. *Lagaña.*

Pitarróso, sa, *a.* Blear-eyed. V. *Lagañoso.*

Pitézna, *sf.* Bolt which fastens stocks or pieces of wood for holding animals.

Pitíllo, *sm.* Flagelet, a small pipe or flute.

Pitipié, *sm.* V. *Escala.*

Pitirróxo, *sm.* (Orn.) Robin red-breast. Motacilla rubecola *L.*

Pífo, *sm.* 1. Pipe, a small flute. 2. (Orn.) Magpie. Picus *L.* 3. A species of bug in India. 4. Play among boys. 5. (Mur.) Pod of a silkworm open at one end.

Pitóféro, *sm.* Piper, whistler, fluter.

Pitométrica, *sf.* Gage or gauge, the art of measuring or gauging vessels.

Pitón, *sm.* 1. Tenderling, the top of an animal's horn when it begins to shoot forth. 2. Protuberance, prominence. 3. Sprig or young shoot of a tree; sprout of the agave.

Pitonísa, *sf.* Witch, sorceress, enchantress.

Pitórra, *sf.* (Orn.) Woodcock. V. *Chochaperdiz.*

Pitúita, *sf.* A kind of phlegm.

Pituitóso, sa, *a.* Pituitous.

Píxide, *sf.* 1. A small box of wood or metal. 2. Pyx, box in which the consecrated host is kept.

Pizárra, *sf.* Slate, a grey fossil, in thin plates, used to cover buildings or write upon.

Pizarrál, *sm.* Slate quarry.

Pizarréño, ña, *a.* Slate-coloured, resembling slate.

Pizarréro, *sm.* Slater, one who polishes slates, and covers buildings with them.

Pízca, *sf.* Mite, any thing proverbially small.

Pizcár, *va.* (Fam.) To pinch. V. *Pellizcar.*

Pízco, *sm.* V. *Pellizco.*

Pizcolábis, *sm.* (Joc.) Lip-biter, nickname for affected persons.

Pizmiénto, ta, *a.* Resembling pitch.

Pizpiréta, *af.* Sharp, brisk, lively; applied to women.

Pizpirigáña, *sf.* Play among boys, in which they pinch one another's hands.

Pizpíta, *sf.* (Orn.) Wag-tail. V. *Pezpita.*

Pláca, *sf.* 1. Ancient Spanish coin worth 10 maravedis. 2. Clasp with which a broadsword belt is fastened. 3. Insignia of an order of knighthood.

Placabilidád, *sf.* Placability or willingness to be appeased.

Placáble, *a.* Placable, willing or possible to be appeased.

Placación, *sf.* V. *Aplacacion.*

Placárte, *sm.* Placard, manifesto.

Placatívo, va, *a.* Peaceable.

Placeár, *va.* To publish, to proclaim, to post up.

Placél, *sm.* (Naut.) Banks of sand or rocks in the sea.

Pláceme, *sm.* Compliment of congratulation.

Placénta, *sf.* (Anat.) Placenta, after birth.

Placenteraménte, *ad.* Joyfully.

PLACENTÉRO, RA, *a.* Joyful, merry, pleasant, full of mirth.

PLACENTÍNO, NA, *a.* Belonging to Plasencia.

PLACÉR, *sm.* 1. Pleasure, content, merriment, rejoicing, amusement. 2. Will, consent. 3. V. *Placel. Á' placer,* With the greatest pleasure; gently, commodiously. *Que me place,* It pleases me; I approve of it.

PLACÉR, *v. impers.* To please, to be grateful. V. *Agradar.*

PLACERAMÉNTE, *ad.* Publicly, without a cover.

PLACÉRO, RA, *a.* 1. Belonging to a market or other public place. 2. Roving or walking idly about.

PLACÉTA, *sf.* A small square or public place.

PLACÍBLE, *a.* Placid, agreeable.

PLÁCIDO, DA, *a.* Placid, easy, quiet.

PLACIÉNTE, *a.* Pleasing, mild; acceptable.

PLAFÓN, *sm.* (Arq.) Soffit of an architrave.

PLÁGA, *sf.* 1. Wound. V. *Llaga.* 2. Plague, a disease extremely contagious. 3. A great calamity or disaster. 4. Plenty, abundance. 5. Climate, country; zone. *Plagas,* (Naút.) The four cardinal points in which the mariner's compass is divided.

PLAGÁR, *va.* To plague, to torment.

PLAGIÁR, *va.* To commit literary thefts; to steal the thoughts or writings of another.

PLAGIÁRIO, RIA, *a.* y *s.* Plagiary, plagiarist.

PLÁGIO, *sm.* Plagiarism, a literary theft.

PLAGÓSO, SA, *a.* Wounding, making wounds.

PLÁN, *sm.* 1. Plan, design, draught; ichnography. 2. The first surface or plane of any thing. 3. Extract, epitome. *Plan de combate,* (Naút.) Quarter-bill. *Plan de las varengas,* (Naút.) Flat of floor-timbers. *Navio de mucho plan,* (Naút.) A very flat floored ship.

PLÁNA, *sf.* 1. Trowel, a tool to spread mortar with. 2. Page, a side of a printed book or writing. 3. A level fruitful piece of ground. 4. Copy or page written by scholars during the school hours. *Á' plana renglon,* Copied exactly, or word for word; arriving or happening at the nick of time. *Navegacion plana,* (Naút.) Plane navigation.

PLANÁDA, *sf.* Plain, extent of level ground.

PLÁNCHA, *sf.* 1. Plate, a thin piece of metal. 2. Iron for ironing or smoothing clothes. 3. Cramp-iron. 4. (In Paper-mills) Moulds, a square frame on which the paper is laid and formed. *Plancha de agua,* (Naút.) Punt, floating stage. *Plancha de desembargar,* (Naút.) Gang-board. *Plancha de viento,* (Naút.) Hanging stage.

PLANCHÁDA, *sf.* (Naút.) Framing or apron of a gun.

PLANCHÁR, *va.* To iron linen, to smooth it with a hot iron. V. *Aplanchar.*

PLANCHEÁR, *va.* To plate, to sheath, to cover or case with metal.

PLANCHÉTA, *sf.* Instrument used to measure distances, and take heights, plans, &c.

PLANCHUÉLA, *sf.* A small plate. *Planchuelas de las arraigadas,* (Naút.) Foothooks, the ground or upper-futtocks of a ship.

PLÁNCO, *sm.* V. *Planga.*

PLÁNES, *sm. pl.* (Naút.) Flat floor-timbers.

PLANÉTA, *sm.* 1. Planet, one of the heavenly bodies which revolves around the sun. 2. Kind of cope shorter before than behind.

PLANETÁRIO, *sm.* 1. Planetarium, instrument showing the planetary movement. 2. Astronomer.

PLANETÁRIO, RIA, *a.* Planetary.

PLANETOLÁBIO, *sm.* Orrery, an astronomical instrument which represents the revolution of the planets and other heavenly bodies.

PLÁNGA, *sf.* Kind of eagle, with black and white feathers.

PLANÍCIE, *sf.* V. *Llano ó Llanura.*

PLANIPÉDIA, *sf.* A mean play acted by strollers without proper dresses or decorations.

PLANISFÉRIO, *sm.* Planisphere, a sphere projected on a plane.

PLÁNO, NA, *a.* Plain, level, smooth.

PLÁNO, *sm.* 1. Plan, design, draft. 2. Plane. *De plano,* Openly, clearly.

PLANOMETRÍA Y **PLANIMETRÍA**, *sf.* Planometry, the mensuration of plane surfaces.

PLANOPLÁNO, *sm.* Biquadrate, the fourth power arising from the multiplication of a square by itself.

PLÁNTA, *sf.* 1. Sole of the foot. 2. Plant, any thing produced from seed; any vegetable production. 3. Nursery of young plants; plantation. 4. Plan of a building. 5. Position of the feet in dancing or fencing. 6. Project; disposition; point of view. 7. (Pint.) Plant or site of a building, &c. *Plantas,* Brags, boasts. *De planta,* Anew; from the foundation.

PLANTACIÓN, *sf.* Plantation, act of planting.

PLANTADÓR, *sm.* One who plants; an instrument used for planting.

PLANTÁGE, *sm.* 1. (Mur.) Plantain. V. *Llanten.* 2. Collection of plants.

PLANTANÁL, *sm.* Grove of plantains.

PLÁNTANO, *sm.* (Bot.) Plantain-tree, Adam's fig, a shrub having leaves nine feet long and two broad. *Musa L.*

PLANTÁR, *va.* 1. To plant, to put or set into the ground in order to grow. 2. To set up, to fix upright. 3. To strike or hit a blow. 4. To thrust or put into any place. *Plantar en la carcel,* To throw into jail. 5. To found, to establish. 6. To leave in the lurch, to disappoint.—*vr.* 1. To stand upright, to stop. 2. To arrive soon.

PLANTÁRIA, *sf.* V. *Esparganio.*

PLANTÁRIO, *sm.* Plot of ground where young plants are reared.

PLANTEÁR, *va.* To plan, to trace, to try, to attempt.—*vn.* (Ant.) To weep.

PLANTÉL, *sm.* Nursery, a plantation of young trees.

PLANTIFICACIÓN, *sf.* V. *Plantacion.*

PLANTIFICÁR, *va.* 1. To plant. V. *Plantar.* 2. (Joc.) To beat, box, or kick.

PLANTÍLLA, *sf.* 1. A young plant. 2. The first sole of a shoe. 3. Vamp, a sole of linen put to the feet of stockings. 4. Mould, model; plate of a gun-lock. 5. (Naút.) Mould, a piece of timber which serves as a pattern for the curve of a ship's frame. 6. (Astrol.) Celestial configuration.

PLANTILLÁR, *va.* To vamp or sole shoes or stockings.

PLANTÍO, ÍA, *a.* Planted; applied to ground.

PLANTÍO, *sm.* 1. Plantation, the act of planting. 2. Nursery, a plantation of young trees.
PLANTISTA, *sm.* Bully, hector, bravado; planter.
PLÁNTO, *sm.* Weeping, crying, whining.
PLANTÓN, *sm.* 1. Cion, or scion, a sprout or shoot from a plant; a shoot engrafted on a stock. 2. (Mil.) Sentry who performs that duty by way of punishment. *Estar de planton,* To be fixed in a place for a long time.
PLANÚDO, DA, *a.* (Naút.) Applied to a vessel which draws little water as being too flat.
PLAÑIDÉRA, *sf.* Mourner, woman who is paid for attending funerals to express grief.
PLAÑÍDO, *sm.* Moan, lamentation.
PLAÑÍR, *vn.* To lament, to grieve, to bemoan.
PLAQUÍN, *sm.* Kind of coat of arms.
PLÁSMA, *sf.* Prase, a precious stone.
PLASMADÓR, RA, *s.* Moulder, former.
PLASMÁNTE, *pa.* Moulding; moulder.
PLASMÁR, *va.* To mould, to form of clay.
PLÁSTA, *sf.* Paste, soft clay; any thing soft. 2. (Met.) Done without order or rule.
PLÁSTE, *sm.* Size.
PLASTECÉR, *va.* To size, to cover with size.
PLASTECÍDO, *sm.* Act of sizing.
PLÁSTICA, *sf.* Art of moulding.
PLÁSTICO, CA, *a.* Plastic.
PLÁTA, *sf.* 1. Silver, a precious white metal. 2. Plate in horse-racing; plate, jewels. 3. (America) Money. *Plata quebrada,* That which retains its value although disfigured. *En plata,* Briefly, without turnings or windings. *Como una plata,* Shining like silver, very clean and pretty.
PLATAFÓRMA, *sf.* 1. (Fort.) Platform, an elevation of earth raised on ramparts; temporary platform made of cross ground-timbers or sleepers. 2. (Naút.) Orlop, a platform of planks laid over the beams in the hold of a ship of war, on which the cables are usually coiled.
PLATANÁL ó PLATANÁR, *sm.* Plantation of plane trees.
PLÁTANO, *sm.* 1. (Bot.) Plane-tree. Platanus *L.* 2. Plantain-tree. V. *Plantano.*
PLATÁZO, *sm.* Platter, a large dish.
PLATÉA, *sf.* V. *Patio.*
PLATEÁDO, DA, *a.* 1. Silvered, having the colour of silver. 2. Plated.
PLATEÁR, *va.* To silver, to plate, to cover with silver.
PLATÉL, *sm.* A small dish.
PLATERÉSCO, CA, *a.* Applied to fanciful ornaments in architecture.
PLATERÍA, *sf.* 1. Silversmith's shop. 2. Trade of a silversmith.
PLATÉRO, *sm.* Silversmith, plate-worker.
PLÁTICA, *sf.* 1. Discourse, conversation; mutual intercourse of language. 2. Speech delivered on some public occasion; discourse pronounced by preachers. 3. Pratic or pratique, a license or permission given to the crew of a ship to come on shore, to buy and traffic. V. *Práctica. Tomar plática,* To obtain pratic.
PLATICÁBLE, *a.* V. *Practicable.*
PLATICÁNTE, *sm.* Practitioner. V. *Practicante.*
PLATICÁR, *va.* 1. To converse, to convey ideas reciprocally in talk. 2. To practise, to exercise any profession.

PLÁTICO, CA, *a.* Skilful, dexterous, expert.
PLATIFICÁR, *va.* To turn or convert into silver.
PLATÍJA, *sf.* (Ict.) Plaice. Pleuronectes platessa *L.*
PLATÍLLA, *sf.* A sort of Silesia linen.
PLATÍLLO, *sm.* 1. A small dish or plate. 2. An extraordinary dish allowed in convents on festive days. 3. Backbiting.
PLATÍNA, *sf.* 1. Platina, the heaviest metal hitherto discovered; it is found in the mines of Choco in Peru, and was entirely unknown in Europe before the year 1748. 2. A metallic composition consisting of silver and copper, imported from China. 3. Twisted silver wire. 4. An iron plate for glazing stuff.
PLÁTO, *sm.* 1. Dish, a vessel either broad and wide or deep and hollow, in which solid or liquid food is served up at the table. 2. Food served up in a dish. 3. Daily fare. *Poner el plato,* To afford one an opportunity of saying or doing what he did not think of.
PLATONICAMÉNTE, *ad.* Platonically.
PLATÓNICO, CA, *a.* Platonic, relating to the philosophy of Plato.
PLATÚCHA, *sf.* (Gal.) V. *Platija.*
PLAUSIBILIDÁD, *sf.* Plausibility, speciousness: superficial appearance of right.
PLAUSÍBLE, *a.* Plausible, specious; superficially pleasing.
PLAUSIBLEMÉNTE, *ad.* Plausibly.
PLAÚSO, *sm.* Applause or approbation bestowed by the clapping of hands.
PLAÚSTRO, *sm.* Cart, wagon, carriage. V. *Carro.*
PLÁYA, *sf.* Shore, strand, sea-coast, beach.
PLAYÁDO, DA, *a.* Applied to a river or sea with a shore.
PLAYÁZO, *sm.* Wide or extended shore.
PLAYÉRO, *sm.* Fisherman who brings fish to market.
PLAYÓN, *sm.* A large shore or beach.
PLÁZA, *sf.* 1. Square; market-place, an open place where eatables are sold. 2. Place, a fortified town. 3. Room, space; stall. 4. Place, office, public employment. 5. Enlisting or enrolling of soldiers in the king's service. 6. Reputation, character, fame. *Pasa plaza de valiente,* He passes for a man of courage. *Plaza fuerte,* A strong place. *Plaza viva,* An effective soldier. *Plaza muerta,* False muster. *Hombre de plaza,* One who holds or might occupy an honourable place. *Sacar á plaza,* To publish, to render public. *Plaza, plaza,* Clear the way, make room.
PLÁZO, *sm.* 1. The fixed time for making payment or answering a demand. 2. Ground appointed for a duel. 3. Writ or summons.
PLAZUÉLA, *sf.* A small square or place.
PLEAMÁR, *sf.* High water.
PLEBÁNO, *sm.* Curate of a parish.
PLÉBE, *sf.* Common people, populace.
PLEBÉYO, YA, *a.* Plebeian.
PLÉCA, *sf.* (Impr.) Type which forms a straight line, a rule.
PLÉCTRO, *sm.* (Poét.) Plectrum; poesy.
PLEGÁBLE, *a.* Pliable, capable of being folded.
PLEGADAMÉNTE, *ad.* Confusedly.
PLEGADÉRA, *sf.* Folding-stick used by bookbinders.
PLEGADÍZO, ZA, *a.* Pliable.

Plegadór, *sm.* 1. A folding instrument, with which any thing is folded or plaited. 2. Collector of alms for religious communities. 3. Beam of a silk-loom.
Plegadúra, *sf.* Fold, double, complication; the act of folding or doubling.
Plegár, *va.* To fold, to double; to fold sheets to be bound.—*v. impers.* To please. *Plega ó plegue á Dios*, Please God.
Plegária, *sf.* 1. Public prayer, supplication. 2. Bell rung at noon for prayer. 3. (Toledo) Canon's servant.
Plenamár, *sf.* V. *Pleamar*.
Plenaménte, *ad.* Fully, completely.
Plenariaménte, *ad.* Completely, fully, entirely.
Plenário, ria, *a.* Complete, full; plenary.
Plenilúnio, *sm.* Full moon.
Plenipoténcia, *sf.* Full powers.
Plenipotenciário, *sm.* Plenipotentiary, a negotiator invested with full power.
Plenitúd, *sf.* Plenitude, fulness, abundance.
Pléno, na, *a.* Full. V. *Lleno*.
Pleonásmo, *sm.* Pleonasm, a figure of speech, by which more words are used than are necessary.
Plétora, *sf.* Plethora, fulness of blood.
Pletórico, ca, *a.* Plethoric.
Pleuresía, *sf.* Pleurisy, an inflammation of the pleura, or membrane which covers the inside of the breast.
Pleurético, ca, *a.* Pleuritical, pleuritic.
Pléyada ó Pleyade, *sf.* Each one of the Pleiades or seven stars.
Pléyta, *sf.* A plaited strand of bass.
Pleyteadór, ra, *s.* Pleader, a litigious person.
Pleyteánte, *a.* Litigating; pleader.
Pleyteár, *va.* To plead, to litigate.
Pley'tes, *sm.* Mediator, conciliator.
Pleytesía, *sf.* Agreement, covenant.
Pleytísta, *sm.* Barrator, an encourager of law-suits.
Pléyto, *sm.* 1. Covenant, contract, bargain. 2. Dispute, contest. 3. Debate, contention. 4. Law-suit, process. *Pleyto de acreedores*, Proceedings under a commission of bankruptcy.
Plíca, *sf.* Parcel closed and sealed, containing a will or some document to be opened at a proper time.
Pliégo, *sm.* 1. Fold, double, complication. 2. Sheet of paper. 3. Parcel of letters enclosed in one cover. 4. Memorial or proposal presented by rent-holders for the collection of rent.
Pliégue, *sm.* 1. Fold or double in clothes. 2. Ruff, anciently worn.
Plínto, *sm.* (Arq.) Plinth of a pillar.
Plomáda, *sf.* 1. Blacklead pencil. 2. Plumb, plummet. 3. (Naút.) Lead used by fishermen for sounding the depth of water, in order to stream the buoy accordingly. 4. (Art.) Apron, a piece of lead covering the vent or touch-hole of a cannon to keep out moisture. 5. Whip armed with lead.
Plomár, *va.* 1. To mark or draw lines with a blacklead pencil. 2. To fill the cavities of carious teeth with lead.
Plomazón, *sm.* Gilding cushion.
Ploméro, *sm.* Plumber, one who works upon lead.
Plomízo, za, *a.* Leaden, made of lead; having the qualities of lead.
Plómo, *sm.* 1. Lead, a whitish metal, very heavy and ductile. 2. Ball of lead. *Andar con pies de plomo*, To proceed with the utmost circumspection. *Arrendador del plomo*, A heavy unpleasant person. *A' plomo*, Perpendicularly, flat down. 3. Plumb, perpendicular; a plummet.
Plomóso, sa, *a.* Leaden. V. *Plomizo*.
Plúma, *sf.* 1. Feather, the plume of birds. 2. Pen, an instrument for writing. 3. Art of writing, penmanship. 4. Writer, author. *Buena pluma*, A good penman, a skilful writer. *Golpe de pluma*, Dash with the pen. 5. Wealth, opulence. 6. (Fam.) Portion of air expelled from the bowels. *Tiene pluma*, He has feathered his nest well. *Plumas*, (Naút.) Relieving tackles, two strong tackles which prevent a ship from being upset while she is careening.
Plumáda, *sf.* Dash with a pen, a line drawn with a crayon.
Plumádo, da, *a.* Feathered.
Plumáge, *sm.* 1. Plumage, all the feathers which adorn a fowl or bird. 2. Plume, an ornament of feathers.
Plumageár, *va.* To shove, to move from one side to another.
Plumagería, *sf.* Heap of feathers.
Plumagéro, *sm.* One who dresses feathers and makes plumes.
Plumário, *sm.* 1. One who lives by writing, a petty scrivener or notary. 2. Painter of fowls or birds.
Plumázo, *sm.* Down, soft short feathers of fowls or birds.
Plumazón, *sm.* Collection of feathers.
Plúmbeo, bea, *a.* Leaden, made of lead; having the qualities of lead. V. *Plomado*.
Plumeádo, *sm.* (Pint.) Series of lines similar to those made with a pen in a miniature.
Plumeár, *va.* (Pint.) To draw lines with a pen or pencil, to darken a design.
Plúmeo, mea, *a.* Plumigerous, having feathers.
Plumería, *sf.* V. *Plumagería*.
Pluméro, *sm.* 1. Bunch of feathers. 2. Box or chest in which feathers or plumes are preserved.
Pluméta, *sf.* A sort of cloth manufactured at Lisle.
Plumífero, ra, *a.* (Poét.) Plumigerous.
Plumísta, *sm.* One who lives by writing, a petty scrivener or notary.
Plumón ó Plumión, *sm.* 1. Soft downy feathers. 2. Feather-bed, flock-bed.
Plumóso, sa, *a.* Covered with feathers.
Plurál, *a.* (In Grammar) Plural, denoting many, or more than one.
Pluralidád, *sf.* Plurality, multitude; a great number. *A' pluralidad de votos*, By the majority of voices.
Pluspriés, *sm.* (Naút.) Lying close to the wind.
Plus ultra, *Ser el non plus ultra*, To be transcendent.
Plutéo, *sm.* Each compartment of book-shelves in a library.
Plúvia, *sf.* Rain. V. *Lluvia*.
Pluviál, *sm.* 1. (Orn.) Golden plover. Charadrius pluvialis *L.* 2. Pluvial, a priest's cope, worn at the celebration of the mass.

PLUVIÁL Y PLUVIÓSO, SA, *a.* Rainy, relating to rain.

PNEUMÁTICO, CA, *a.* Pneumatic, moved by wind; relating to wind, or the doctrine of pneumatics. *Instrumentos pneumaticos*, Musical wind instruments.

PO, *interj.* V. *Pu.*

POÁS, *sf. pl.* (Naút.) Bow-line bridles, ropes by which the bow-line is fastened to the leech of the sail.

POBÉDA, *sf.* Plantation of poplars.

POBLÁCHO, *sm.* Populace, rabble, mob.

POBLACHÓN, *sm.* Great rabble, populace.

POBLACIÓN Y POBLAZÓN, *sf.* 1. Population, the act of populating. 2. Population, the state of a country with regard to the number of its inhabitants. 3. V. *Poblado.*

POBLÁDO, *sm.* Town, village or place inhabited.

POBLADÓR, RA, *s.* Populator, founder.

POBLÁR, *va.* 1. To found a town, to populate a district. 2. To fill, to occupy. 3. To breed, to procreate fast. 4. To bud, to get leaves; applied to trees.

POBLÁZO, *sm.* V. *Populacho.*

POBLAZÓN, *sm.* A large town; a population.

PÓBO, *sm.* (Bot.) White poplar. V. *A'lamo blanco.*

PÓBRA, *sf.* Female mendicant.

POBRÁR, *va.* (Ant.) V. *Poblar.*

PÓBRE, *a.* 1. Poor, necessitous, indigent; begging. 2. Humble, modest. 3. Unhappy, wretched. 4. Pacific, quiet. *Pobre y soberbio*, Proud pauper.

PÓBRE, *sm.* A poor person, a beggar.

POBRECÍLLO, LLA; TO, TA; CO, CA, *a.* Somewhat poor, penurious.

POBREMÉNTE, *ad.* Poorly, miserably.

POBRERÍA, *sf.* Poor people, beggars.

POBRÉRO, *sm.* One who is appointed by a religious community to distribute charities.

POBRÉTA, *sf.* Strumpet, a prostitute.

POBRÉTE Y POBRÉTO, *sm.* 1. A poor unfortunate man. 2. An useless person, of mean abilities and sentiments.

POBRETERÍA, *sf.* 1. Poor people, beggars. 2. Poverty, indigence.

POBRETÓN, NA, *a.* Very poor.

POBRÉZA, *sf.* 1. Poverty, indigence, necessity, want; poorness, littleness of spirit. 2. Heap of worthless trifles. 3. Voluntary vow of poverty, taken on professing a religious order.

POBRÍSMO, *sm.* Poor people, beggars.

POCÉRO, *sm.* 1. One who digs pits and wells. 2. Nightman, one who cleanses wells, pits, or common sewers.

PÓCHO, CHA; Ó PONCHO, CHA, *s.* Proper name Alphonsus, Alphonsa.

POCÍLGA, *sf.* 1. Hog-sty, a place where swine are kept to be fed. 2. Any nasty, dirty place.

POCÍLLO, *sm.* 1. Small well. 2. Vessel for collecting any liquor or fluid. 3. (And.) Chocolate cup.

PÓCIMA, *sf.* Potion, a physical draught.

POCIÓN, *sf.* Drink, liquor; potion. V. *Bebida.*

PÓCO, CA, *a.* Little, small in quantity; few. *Poco antes ó despues*, A little before or after. *Poco ha que*, Lately, a short time since.

PÓCO, *ad.* Little, in a scanty manner, shortly, briefly, in a short time. *Poco á poco*, Gently, softly, stop! *Hombe para poco*, A cowardly pusillanimous man. *A' poco*, Immediately, in a short time. *Tener en poco*, To set little value on a thing. *A' pocas, por poco, ó en poco*, To be very near a thing. *Que poco*, How little; indicating the difficulty or impossibility of any thing. *Darsele poco*, To make nothing of a thing, to despise it entirely.

PÓCO, *sm.* Scarcity, small quantity.

PÓCULO, *sm.* Drink, liquor. V. *Bebida.*

PÓDA, *sf.* Pruning of trees, pruning season.

PODADÉRA, *sf.* Pruning-knife, pruning-hook.

PODADÓR, RA, *s.* Pruner of trees or vines.

PODÁGRA, *sf.* Gout in the feet.

PODÁR, *va.* To prune, to lop off the superfluous branches of trees.

PODATÁRIO, *sm.* Steward; attorney.

PODAZÓN, *sm.* The pruning season.

PODÉNCO, *sm.* Hound. Canis familiaris sagax L. *Vuelta de podenco*, A severe beating with a stick.

PODENQUÍLLO, *sm.* A young or small hound.

PODÉR, *sm.* 1. Power, faculty, authority, dominion. 2. Military strength of a state. 3. Power or letter of attorney. 4. Power, possession. 5. Force, vigour, capacity, possibility. *A' mas no poder*, Able to resist no longer. *A' poder de*, By force. *Poder de Dios*, Exclamation exaggerating the greatness of any thing as representing the power of God. *Poder esmerado*, Supreme power. *No poder menos*, To be unavoidable; to be necessary.

PODÉR, *va.* 1. To be able, may or can; to possess the power of doing or performing any thing. 2. To be invested with authority or power. 3. To have force or energy to act or resist. 4. (In Geometry) To value, to produce.—*v. impers.* To be possible or contingent.

PODERHABIÉNTE, *sm.* Attorney, one who is authorised or impowered to transact another person's business.

PODERÍO, *sm.* 1. Power, authority, dominion, jurisdiction. 2. Wealth, riches.

PODEROSAMÉNTE, *ad.* Powerfully, mightily.

PODERÓSO, SA, *a.* 1. Powerful, mighty, potent. 2. Rich, wealthy. 3. Eminent, excellent; efficacious.

PODÓMETRO, *sm.* Pedometer, instrument for measuring a man's steps or the circumvolutions of a wheel.

PODÓN, *sm.* Mattock, hoe, an instrument for pulling up weeds.

PÓDRE, *sf.* Pus, corrupted blood or humour.

PODRECÉRSE, *vr.* To be putrid, rotten, or corrupt. V. *Pudrir.*

PODRECIMIÉNTO, *sm.* 1. Rottenness, putrefaction. 2. Pain, grief.

PODREDÚMBRE, *sf.* 1. Pus, putrid matter, putrescence. 2. Grief, internal pain.

PODRICIÓN, *sf.* V. *Pudricion.*

PODRIDÉRO, *sm.* V. *Pudridero.*

PODRIMIÉNTO, *sm.* V. *Pudrimiento.*

PODRÍR, *va.* V. *Pudrir.*

POÉMA, *sm.* Poem, the work of a poet; metrical composition.

POESÍA, *sf.* 1. Poetry; poesy, the art or practice of writing poems. *Poesias*, Poetical works. 2. Poetical piece, metrical composition.

Poéta, *sm.* Poet, a writer of poems.
Poetástro, *sm.* Poetaster.
Poética, *sf.* Poetry. V. *Poesía.*
Poeticaménte, *ad.* Poetically.
Poético, ca, *a.* Poetic, expressed in poetry; suitable to poetry.
Poetíllo, *sm.* Poetaster.
Poetísa, *sf.* Poetess, a female poet.
Poetizár, *vn.* To write verses, to write like a poet.
Poetón, *sm.* Poetaster, a vile poet.
Poíno, *sm.* A wooden frame, on which barrels of wine or beer are laid.
Poláca, *sf.* Top of the shoe which covers the instep.
Polácra, *sf.* (Naút.) Polacre, a vessel with three pole-masts, used in the Mediterranean.
Polár, *a.* Polar, relating to the poles; issuing from the poles.
Polaína, *sf.* Spatterdashes, a kind of covering for the legs.
Poléa, *sf.* 1. Pulley, a small wheel, turning on a pivot, with a furrow on its outside, in which a rope runs. 2. (Naút.) Tackle-block.
Poleádas, *sf. pl.* V. *Gachas ó Puchas.*
Poleáme, *sm.* Collection of masts for vessels.
Poleíta, *sf.* (Naút.) A small block.
Polémica, *sf.* Polemics, dogmatical divinity.
Polémico, ca, *a.* Polemical.
Polemónio, *sm.* (Bot.) Jacob's ladder, Greek valerian. Polemonium cœruleum *L.*
Polemoscópio, *sm.* (Opt.) Spy-glass or telescope used by military commanders.
Polénta, *sf.* A kind of batter or hasty pudding.
Poléo, *sm.* 1. (Bot.) Penny-royal. Mentha pulegium *L.* 2. A strutting gait; a pompous style. 3. Stiff cold wind.
Polevî ó Ponleví, *sm.* A high wooden heel formerly worn by women.
Polex, *sm.* V. *Police.*
Poliántea, *sf.* Polyanthea, a collection of various literary extracts and observations.
Poliánto Tuberóso, *sm.* (Bot.) Polyanthes.
Poliarquía, *sf.* Polygarchy, government of many persons.
Policán ó Pelicán, *sm.* Pelican, instrument for drawing teeth.
Pólice, *sf.* Thumb, a short strong finger.
Policía, *sf.* 1. Police, that branch of the executive government of a country, which watches over the preservation of public order and tranquillity, and provides for the safety and convenience of the inhabitants of a state. 2. Politeness, good breeding. 3. Cleanliness, neatness.
Policitación, *sf.* Vow, a promise made to God or the state.
Polidéro, *sm.* V. *Pulidero.*
Poligámia, *sf.* Polygamy, state of having two or more wives or husbands at once.
Polígamo, *sm.* 1. Polygamist. 2. He who has had several wives successively.
Polígloto, ta, *a.* Polyglott, written in various languages.
Polígono, *sm.* 1. Polygon, a multilateral figure, the perimeter of which consists of more than four sides or angles. 2. (Bot.) A prickly plant.
Poligrafía, *sf.* Polygraphy, the art of writing in several unusual manners or ciphers.
Polihédro, *sm.* (Geom.) Polyhedron, a solid figure with many planes.
Polílla, *sf.* 1. Moth, a small insect which eats clothes and hangings. 2. Consumer, waster. *Comerse de polilla,* (Fam.) To be insensibly wasting property; to be wasting away internally.
Polilléra, *sf.* (Bot.) Mullein, or moth mullein. Verbascum blattaria *L.*
Polímato, *sm.* One who is versed in several branches of useful knowledge.
Polímita, *a.* Applied to stuffs of variegated colours.
Polínes, *sm. pl.* (Naút.) Wooden rollers, for moving great guns from one place to another.
Pólipo, *sm.* 1. Polypus, a callous swelling in the nostrils. 2. V. *Pulpo.*
Polipódio, *sm.* (Bot.) Polypody. Polypodium *L.*
Polír, *va.* To polish, to adorn. V. *Pulir.*
Polisílabo, *sm.* Polysyllable, a word of many syllables.
Polisindetón, *sm.* Polysyndeton, a figure of rhetoric by which the copulative is often repeated.
Polisinódia, *sf.* Multiplicity of councils.
Polispástos, *sf.* Machine or engine composed of several pullies and small wheels, for raising heavy bodies.
Politeísmo, *sm.* Polytheism, plurality of gods.
Polítíca, *sf.* 1. Policy, politics: the art or science of government. 2. Politeness, civility.
Politicaménte, *ad.* Politically, civilly.
Político, ca, *a.* 1. Political, relating to policy or politics. 2. Polite, courteous.—*sm.* Politician.
Póliza, *sf.* 1. A written order to receive or recover a sum of money. 2. Meeting to discuss or treat upon a subject. *Poliza de seguro,* Policy of insurance.
Polizón, *sm.* 1. Vagrant, lazy vagabond. 2. (America) Spaniard who passes by stealth to the Spanish possessions in America, without having obtained leave or a passport from the king and government of Spain. 3. Parasite, sponger, abandoned profligate who commits lewdness in the streets.
Polizoncíto, *sm. dim.* of *polizon,* An European Spanish youth; many of them acquire fame and fortune in Spanish America.
Pólla, *sf.* 1. Pullet, a young hen, a chicken. 2. A comely young lass. 3. Money staked in some games at cards by all the players.
Polláda, *sf.* Flock of young fowls.
Pollagallína, *sf.* Hen-chicken. *Muger jamona ó pollagallina que va á villavieja,* (Met.) Woman affecting youth, yet thin and old maidish.
Pollástro, ra, *s.* A large pullet.
Pollastrón, *sm.* Fine stout lad; a knowing person.
Pollazón, *sm.* Hatching and rearing of fowls.
Polléra, *sf.* 1. A narrow-mouthed basket or net, wide at the bottom, in which pullets are kept; a hencoop. 2. A kind of go-cart, in which children learn to walk. 3. A short hooped petticoat.
Pollería, *sf.* Shop or market where poultry is sold.
Polléro, *sm.* 1. One who keeps or rears fowls. 2. Place or yard where fowls are kept. 3. One who keeps or feeds fowls for sale; a poulterer.
Pollíco, ca; llo, lla; to, ta, *s.* A small chicken.
Pollína, *sf.* Young she ass.
Pollinarménte, *ad.* V. *Asnalmente.*
Pollinéjo, a, *s.* A little young ass.
Pollíno, *sm.* A young untamed ass, simpleton.

Pollíto, ta, *a.* Of a tender age; applied to boys and girls.—*s.* Little pullets.
Póllo, *sm.* 1. Chicken just hatched. 2. Young bee. 3. (Fam.) Artful clever man. 4. (Ar.) Trench for water in vineyards. *Pollo con espolones,* (Fam.) Man growing oldish.
Polluélo, la, *s.* A small chicken.
Pólo, *sm.* 1. Pole, the extremity of the axis of the earth; either of the points on which the world turns. 2. Pole of the magnetic needle. 3. Support, foundation.
Poltrón, na, *a.* 1. Idle, lazy. 2. Commodious, easy. *Silla poltrona,* Elbow-chair.
Poltronería, *sf.* Idleness, laziness, indolence.
Poltronizárse, *vr.* To become lazy, to abandon one's self to laziness.
Polución, *sf.* 1. Pollution, stain; defect of the body which causes deformity. 2. An involuntary effusion of semen.
Polúto, ta, *a.* Polluted, contaminated, defiled; unclean.
Polvaréda, *sf.* 1. Cloud of dust. 2. Altercation, dispute, debate.
Polvificár, *va.* (Joc.) To pulverize, to reduce to powder; to reduce to dust.
Polvíllo, to, *sm.* Fine dust. *Gente del polvillo,* Day-labourers at buildings, hard working people.
Pólvo, *sm.* Dust, powder. *Un polvo,* Pinch of snuff.—*pl.* 1. Powders, solid bodies comminuted and reduced to small particles; hair-powder. 2. Very small comfits. *Polvos de cartas,* Sand for drying up the ink of letters or other writings. *Polvos de juánes,* Red precipitate, red nitrate of mercury. *Polvos de la madre celestina,* (Fam.) Secret and miraculous mode in which any thing is done.
Pólvora, *sf.* 1. Gun-powder, a composition of sulphur, saltpetre, and charcoal. 2. Artificial fireworks. 3. Provocation, an act or cause by which anger is raised. 4. Vivacity, liveliness, briskness. 5. Powder, dust. *Es una polvora,* He is as hot as pepper. *Mojar la polvora,* To appease, to allay the rage of an angry person.
Polvoreamiénto, *sm.* Pulverization, the act of reducing to powder or dust.
Polvoreár, *va.* To powder, to sprinkle as with dust.
Polvoriénto, ta, *a.* Dusty, full of dust; clouded or covered with dust.
Polvorín, *sm.* 1. Powder reduced to the finest dust. 2. Powder-flask, a priming horn.
Polvorísta, *sm.* 1. Manufacturer of gun-powder. 2. Maker of fire-works.
Polvorizáble, *a.* Pulverizable.
Polvorización, *sf.* Pulverization.
Polvorizár, *va.* 1. To pulverize. 2. V. *Polvorear.*
Polvorόso, sa, *a.* Dusty, covered with dust.
Póma, *sf.* 1. Apple, the fruit of the apple-tree. V. *Manzana.* 2. Perfume-box, a bottle containing perfumes. 3. Metallic vessel with different perfumes, having small apertures to admit their escape when set on a fire to perfume rooms.
Pomáda, *sf.* Pomatum, a perfumed ointment.
Pomár, *sm.* Orchard, a garden or plantation of fruit-trees, particularly of apple-trees.
Pomez, *sf.* Pumice-stone.
Pomífero, ra, *a.* (Poet.) Pomiferous, having apples.
Pómo, *sm.* 1. Fruit in general, but in particular the fruit of the apple-tree. 2. Glass-ball in the shape of an apple, used to hold perfumes. 3. Pommel, the knob which balances the blade of a sword. 4. Nosegay, a bunch of flowers.
Pómpa, *sf.* 1. Pomp, pageantry, splendour; a procession of splendour and ostentation. 2. Bubble, a small globule of water; fold in clothes raised by the wind. 3. The expanded tail of a turkey or peacock. 4. (Naút.) Pump. V. *Bomba.*
Pompeárse y Pomponeárse, *vr.* To appear with pomp and ostentation.
Pomposaménte, *ad.* Pompously, magnificently.
Pompόso, sa, *a.* Pompous, ostentatious, magnificent; inflated, swelled.
Poncéla, *sf.* Maid, virgin. V. *Doncella.*
Pónche, *sm.* Punch, a liquor made by mixing spirits with water, sugar, and the juice of lemons.
Póncho, cha, *a.* Soft, mild, careless, heedless.—*s.* V. *Pocho.*
Ponchón, na, *a.* Extremely careless, excessively lazy.
Poncíl, Ponci, y Poncídre, *a.* Applied to a shrivelled or bitter orange or lemon.
Ponderáble, *a.* 1. Ponderable, capable to be weighed; measurable by scales. 2. Wonderful, important.
Ponderación, *sf.* 1. The act of weighing mentally, pondering or considering. 2. Exaggeration.
Ponderádo, da, *a.* Presumptuous, arrogant, insolent.
Ponderadór, ra, *s.* Ponderer, one who ponders; he who exaggerates.
Ponderál, *a.* Ponderal.
Ponderár, *va.* 1. To weigh, to examine by the balance. 2. To ponder, to consider. 3. To exaggerate.
Ponderatívo, va, *a.* Exaggerating, hyperbolical.
Ponderosaménte, *ad.* Attentively, carefully with great attention.
Ponderosidád, *sf.* Ponderousness, weightiness.
Ponderόso, sa, *a.* 1. Heavy, ponderous, weighty. 2. Grave, circumspect, cautious.
Ponedéro, ra, *a.* 1. Laying eggs. 2. Capable to be laid or placed.
Ponedéro, *sm.* 1. Nest, the place where hens lay their eggs. 2. Nest-egg, an egg left in the nest for hens to lay in.
Ponedór, ra, *s.* Bettor, one who lays bets or wagers.—*a.* Applied to horses trained to rear on their hind legs, and to fowls laying eggs.
Ponénte, *a.* Applied to the cardinal, who brings any matter before the assembly of cardinals.
Ponentíno, na, *a.* Occidental, western.
Ponentísco, ca, *a.* Western, westerly; belonging to the West.
Ponér, *va.* 1. To put, to place; to set, to lay. *Al poner del sol,* At sun-setting. 2. To dispose, to arrange; to determine. 3. To suppose, to believe. 4. To impose, to enjoin, to oblige. 5. To bet, to stake at a wager. 6. To appoint, to invest with an office. 7. To leave, to permit without interposition. *Yo lo pongo en vd.,* I leave it to you. 8. To write, to set down. 9. To lay eggs; to bring forth. 10. To employ; to apply, to cite an example. *Poner toda su fuerza,* To act with all one's might.

11. To labour in order to attain some end. 12. To add, to join something to that which was before. 13. To contribute, to bear a part; to contribute to some common stock. 14. To enforce; to adduce; to concert; to agree. *Poner al sol*, To sun. *Eso no quita ni pone*, That neither adds nor diminishes. *Poner por escrito*, To put down in writing. *Poner en duda*, To question, to doubt, to be uncertain of. *Poner pies en polvorosa*, To fly, to escape. *Poner pies en pared*, To maintain one's opinion with obstinacy. *Poner nombre*, To rate or appraise goods. *Poner por tierra*, To take down a building.—*vr.* 1. To apply one's self to, to set about. 2. To object, to oppose. 3. To undergo a change. *Ponerse pálido*, To grow pale. 4. To set; applied to the luminous heavenly bodies. 5. To arrive in a short time. *Ponerse bien*, To get on in the world; to obtain full information of an affair. *Ponerse en la calle*, To appear in a splendid manner, to make a showy appearance. *Ponerse en gracia*, To expiate a crime by confession, to put one's self in a state of grace.

PONIÉNTE, *sm.* 1. West, the part of the horizon where the sun sets. 2. (Naút.) West wind.

PONLEVÍ, *sm.* High wooden heel worn by women.

PONTÁZGO Y PONTÁGE, *sm.* Bridge-toll, pontage; a duty paid for the reparation of bridges by those who pass over them.

PONTEÁR, *va.* To erect bridges over rivers or arms of the sea.

PONTEZUÉLO, LA, *s. dim.* Small bridge.

PONTIFICÁDO, *sm.* Pontificate, the dignity of the sovereign pontiff; the reign or government of the pope.

PONTIFICÁL, *a.* Pontifical, papal; belonging to the pope.

PONTIFICÁL, *sm.* 1. A pontifical robe worn by bishops when they officiate at the mass. 2. Pontifical, a book containing the rites and ceremonies of the Roman catholic church. 3. Parochial tithes.

PONTIFICALMÉNTE, *ad.* Pontifically.

PONTIFICÁR, *vn.* To reign or govern as high pontiff.

PONTÍFICE, *sm.* 1. Pope, pontiff; the supreme head of the Roman catholic church. 2. Archbishop or bishop of a diocess.

PONTIFÍCIO, CIA, *a.* Pontificial.

PONTÓN, *sm.* 1. Ponton or pontoon, a floating bridge to cross a river. 2. (Naút.) A kind of flat-bottomed boat, furnished with pullies, tackles, &c. to clean harbours. 3. Timber above 19 feet long.

PONZÓÑA, *sf.* 1. Poison, venom; that which injures or destroys life in a manner not obvious to the senses. 2. Any thing infectious or malignant.

PONZOÑÁR, *va.* To poison. V. *Emponzoñar.*

PONZOÑOSAMÉNTE, *ad.* Poisonously.

PONZOÑÓSO, SA, *a.* Poisonous, venomous.

PÓPA, *sf.* (Naút.) Poop, stern; the hindermost part of a ship. *Navio de popa llana*, (Naút.) A square-sterned vessel. *Bazel de popa de cucharro*, (Naút.) A lutesterned vessel. *Pasar por la popa*, (Naút.) To pass under a ship's stern. *Quedarse por la popa*, (Naút.) To drop astern. *Velas de popa*, (Naút.) Aftersails. *De popa á proa*, (Naút.) From stem to stern. *A' popa, en popa, de pópa*, (Naút.) Aft, abaft. *Viento en popa*, (Naút.) Before the wind: (Met.) Prosperity.

POPAMIÉNTO, *sm.* Act of despising or cajoling.

POPÁR, *va.* 1. To depreciate, to make little of; to contemn. 2. To cajole, to flatter, to caress.

POPELÍNA Ó POPULÍNA, *s.* Poplin, a stuff made of silk and worsted.

POPÉSES, *sm. pl.* (Naút.) Stays of the mizenmast; aftermost, sternmost.

POPÓTE, *sm.* A kind of Indian straw, of which brooms are made.

POPULÁCHO, *sm.* Populace, mob, rabble.

POPULACIÓN, *sf.* Population. V. *Poblacion.*

POPULÁR, *a.* Popular, relating or pleasing to the people; prevailing among the people.

POPULARIZÁRSE, *vr.* To make one's self popular, to conciliate the esteem of the people.

POPULARIDÁD, *sf.* Popularity, graciousness among the people; the state of being favoured by the people.

POPULARMÉNTE, *ad.* Popularly.

POPULÁZO, *sm.* Populace, mob, rabble.

POPULEÓN, *sm.* White poplar ointment.

POPULÓSO, SA, *a.* Populous, numerous.

POQUEDÁD, *sf.* 1. Parvity, paucity, littleness. 2. Cowardice, pusillanimity. 3. Trifle, thing of no value. *Poquedad de ánimo*, Imbecility.

POQUEDÚMBRE Y POQUÉZA, (Ant.) V. *Poquedad.*

POQUÍLLO, LLA; Y POQUÍTO, TA, *a.* 1. Small, little, exiguous. 2. Trifling.

POQUÍLLO, *ad. dim.* Very little time.

POQUÍSIMO, MA, *a.* Very little, excessively small.

POQUITÍCO, CA; LLO, LLA; TO, TA, *a. dim.* of *Poquito.*

POQUÍTO, TA, *a.* Very little; weak of body and mind, diminutive. *Poquita cosa*, A trifling thing. *A' poquitos*, In minute portions. *De poquito*, Pusillanimous. *Poquito á poco*, Gently.

PÓR, *prep.* 1. For, by, about. *Por ahí, por ahí*, About that, a little more or less. *Por tanto ó ende*, For so much, for that. *Ir por leña*, To go for fire-wood. 2. Through; between; to. 3. As, by, on account. *Recibir por esposo*, To take as a husband. 4. By means of, indicating the future action of the verb. *Está por venir, por ver, por saber*, That is to come, to be seen, to be known. 5. It is sometimes redundant, as *Fernando está por corregidor*, Ferdinand is mayor. *Uno vale por muchos*, One is worth many. *La casa está por acabar*, The house is not yet finished. *Por ahora*, For the present. *Por ce ó por be*, Some way or other.—*Por encima, ad.* Slightly, superficially; over, upon. *Por acá ó por allá*, Here or there. *Por mas que ó por mucho que*, Ever so much. *Por si acaso*, If by chance. *Sin que ni por que*, Without rhyme or reason. *Si por cierto!* Yes, indeed! yes, forsooth! *De por si*, By itself.

PÓRA, *prep.* (Ant.) V. *Para.*

PORIÁL, *a.* Applied to a kind of large plums.

PORCÉL, *sm.* (Mur.) A young pig.

PORCELÁNA, *sf.* 1. Porcelain, China ware. 2. Enamel, used by goldsmiths and jewellers. 3. Porcelain-colour, a mixture of white and blue. 4. Kind of wide China cup.

PÓRCHE, *sm.* Covered walk.

PORCÍNO, *sm.* 1. A young pig. *Pan Porcino,*

(Bot.) Sow bread. 2. Bruise, a swelling caused by a knock or blow on the head.

Porcíno, na, *a.* Hoggish, relating to a hog.

Porción, *sf.* 1. Part, portion; a small quantity taken from a larger. 2. Lot, parcel of goods. 3. Pittance, the daily allowance of meat or other food.

Porcioncíca, lla, ta, *sf.* A small portion.

Porcionéro, ra, *a.* Apportioning; participant.

Porcionísta, *s. com.* 1. Holder of a share or portion. 2. Pensioner in a college.

Porcipélo, *sm.* Bristle, the stiff hair of swine.

Porciúncula, *sf.* 1. A small portion or allowance. 2. Indulgence in a Franciscan convent.

Pórco, *sm.* (Gal.) V. *Puerco.* [of a hog.

Porcúno, na, *a.* Hoggish, having the qualities

Pordiosear, *vn.* To beg alms, to ask charity.

Pordiosería, *sf.* Beggary, the habit of asking charity. [charity and alms.

Pordioséro, ra, *s.* Beggar, one who lives upon

Porfía, *sf.* 1. An obstinate dispute or quarrel. 2. Frequent repetition; importunity. *A' porfia*, In an obstinate manner; emulously.

Porfiadaménte, *ad.* Obstinately, pertinaciously.

Porfiádo, da, *a.* Obstinate, stubborn.

Porfiadór, ra, *s.* Contender, disputer, emulator.

Porfiár, *va.* 1. To contend, to dispute obstinately. 2. To importune by the frequent repetition of a demand. 3. To persist in a pursuit.

Pórfido y Pórfiro, *sm.* Porphyry, a kind of marble of a red or purple colour.

Porfijár y Porhijár, *va.* (Ant.) V. *Prohijar.*

Porfirión, *sm.* (Orn.) V. *Calamon.*

Porgadéro, *sm.* (Ar.) Sieve or riddle for cleaning corn.

Póro, *sm.* Pore, spiracle of the skin; passage of perspiration.

Porosidád, *sf.* 1. Porosity, the quality of having pores. 2. That which is exhaled through the pores. [sages.

Poróso, sa, *a.* Porous, having pores or pas-

Pórque, *conjunc.* Because, for the reason that, on this account that.

Porqué, *sm.* 1. (Fam.) Cause, reason, motive. 2. Allowance, pittance, pension.

Porquecílla, *sf. dim.* of *Puerca.*

Porquéra, *sf.* Lair, the couch of a wild boar.

Porquería, *sf.* 1. Nastiness, uncleanliness, filth. 2. Hoggishness, brutishness, rudeness. 3. Trifle, any thing of little or no value. 4. A dirty ungenteel action. *Porquerias*, (Fam.) Small dishes made of the entrails of swine.

Porqueríza, *sf.* Hog-sty, the place where hogs are kept and fed.

Porquerízo ó Porquéro, *sm.* Swineherd, one who attends or keeps swine.

Porquerón, *sm.* Catchpoll, bumbailiff.

Porquezuélo, la, *s.* 1. A young pig. 2. A nasty dirty person, a slut.

Pórra, *sf.* 1. Stick with a large head or thick knob at the end. 2. The last player in certain games played by boys. 3. Vanity, boast, presumption. 4. A stupid, heavy, ignorant person. *Hacer porra*, To boggle, to stop without being able to proceed or pass forward.

Porráceo, a, *a.* Of a dark or leek green colour.

Porráda, *sf.* 1. Knock or blow given with a club-headed stick. 2. Foolishness, nonsense.

Porrázo, *sm.* Blow with a club-headed stick.

Porreár, *vn.* To persist importunely, to dwell long upon. [ness.

Porrería, *sf.* Stupidity, folly, silliness, tedious-

Porréta, *sf.* The green leaf of leeks, garlic, or onions. *En porreta*, Stark naked.

Porrílla, *sf.* 1. A small hammer used by smiths. 2. A small club-headed stick. 3. (Albey.) Osseous tumour in horses' joints.

Porrillo (A'), *ad.* Copiously, abundantly.

Porrína, *sf.* Field of green corn; the state of grain standing green in the field. V. *Porreta.*

Porríno, *sm.* The tender plant of a leek.

Porrízo, *sm.* Bed or plot of leeks.

Pórro, rra, *a.* Dull, stupid, ignorant.

Porrón, *sm.* 1. An earthen pitcher for water. 2. A thick club-headed stick. *Porrónes*, Kind of casks or hogsheads.

Porrúdo, *sm.* (Mur.) Shepherd's crook.

Pórta, *sf.* 1. (Ant.) Door, gate. V. *Puerta.* 2. The Turkish government; the hall or room in the Grand Signor's palace where the Divan meets. *Pórtas*, (Naút.) Gun-ports, the holes through which the cannon play. *Portas del acastillage*, (Naút.) Gun-ports of the quarter-deck and fore-castle. *Portas de las miras de proa*, (Naút.) Head chace-ports. *Portas de lastrar*, (Naút.) Ballast-ports. *Portas de embarcar madera*, (Naút.) Raft-ports. *Portas de guardatimon*, (Naút.) Stern-ports.

Portabandéra, *sf.* Pocket in the girdle which supports the staff of the colours.

Portacártas, *sm.* Mail, the post-boy's bag, in which the letters are contained; postman.

Portacarabína, *sf.* Leather bag in which the muzzle of a horseman's carabine rests.

Portáda, *sf.* 1. Portal, porch. 2. Frontispiece, the principal front of a building. 3. Title-page of a book. *Portadas*, Warp, that order of threads in any thing woven, which crosses the woof or weft.

Portadéras, *sf. pl.* Covered chests for provisions carried on sumpter horses. V. *Aportaderas.*

Portadór, ra, *s.* 1. Bearer, carrier, porter. 2. Tray, a board or wooden vessel on which bread or meat is carried. [corne

Portaestandárte, *sm.* (Mil.) Standard-beare

Portafusíl, *sm.* (Mil.) Sling of a musket.

Portázgo, *sm.* V. *Puerto* y *Portazgo.*

Portaguión, *sm.* Standard-bearer of cavalry.

Portál, *sm.* 1. Porch, entry, entrance in a house. 2. Portico, piazza; a covered walk, supported by columns. 3. (Arag. y Val.) Gate of a town.

Portalázo, *sm.* A large door or porch.

Portaléjo, *sm.* Little porch or portico.

Portaléña, *sf.* 1. Embrasure, the aperture in a battery or rampart through which a cannon is pointed. V. *Cañonera.* 2. Planks of which doors are made.

Portaléro, *sm.* Porter, one that has the charge of a gate; one who waits at the door to receive messages. [porch.

Portalíco, llo, to, *sm.* A small vestibule or

Portálo, *sm.* (Naút.) Gangway, that part of the side of a ship where people go on board or disembark.

Portamantéo, *sm.* Portmanteau or portmantle, a chest or bag in which clothes are carried

Portanário, *sm.* Pylorus, organ which receives the food from the stomach.

Portánte, *sm.* A kind of quick pace of a horse.

Portantíllo, *sm.* A gentle amble, an easy pace.

Portanvóces, *sm.* (Arag.) Coadjutor, assistant.

Portañólas, *sf. pl.* (Naút.) Port-holes. *Portañolas de la luz de los camarotes,* (Naút.) Light-ports. *Portañolas de los remos,* (Naút.) Row-ports, holes left in vessels for rowing them.

Portañuéla, *sf.* Lining of the fall of breeches.

Portapáz, *s. com.* The plate or salver on which the pax or image is presented to be kissed by the pious at mass.

Portár, *va.* (Gal. y Ast.) To carry, to bring. —*vr.* To behave; to conduct one's self decently. *Un baxel que se porta bien,* (Naút.) A fine sailer, a good sea boat.

Portátil, *a.* Portable, that may be easily carried or removed from one place to another.

Portaventanéro, *sm.* Carpenter who makes windows and doors.

Portázgo, *sm.* Toll, turnpike-duty.

Portazguéro, *sm.* Toll-gatherer, collector of turnpike-duty.

Portázo, *sm.* 1. A loud slap given with a door. 2. Act of slapping a door in one's face.

Pórte, *sm.* 1. Porterage, money paid for carrying a thing from one place to another. 2. Deportment, demeanour, conduct, good or bad. 3. Nobility; illustrious descent. 4. Size or capacity of a thing. 5. Carriage. 6. Postage. *Porte franco,* Frank, free of postage. 7. (Naút.) Burthen or tonnage of a ship. *Navio de mil toneladas de porte,* (Naút.) A ship of one thousand tons burthen.

Porteár, *va.* To carry or convey from one place to another.—*vn.* To slap or shut a door or window with violence and noise.—*vr.* To pass from one place to another.

Porténto, *sm.* Prodigy, wonder.

Portentosaménte, *ad.* Prodigiously.

Portentóso, sa, *a.* Prodigious, marvellous, strange.

Porteréjo, *sm.* A little porter.

Portería, *sf.* 1. The principal port of a convent or other large building. 2. Employment or office of a porter. 3. (Naút.) All the ports in a ship.

Portéro, ra, *s.* Porter, one who attends the door and takes messages. *Portero de cadena,* Person appointed to prevent people from committing any nuisance near a palace. *Portero de vara,* Petty constable.

Portezuéla, *sf.* 1. A little door. 2. Flap which covers a pocket-hole.

Pórtico, *sm.* Portico, piazza; porch supported by columns.

Portíllo, *sm.* 1. Aperture or opening in a wall. 2. Opening, passage, gap, breach. 3. Means to obtain some end. 4. Cavity in any thing broken. *Portillos,* Small gates of a town, through which nothing is allowed to pass that is liable to pay duty.

Portón, *sm.* The inner or second door of a house.

Portugués, sa, *a.* Native of Portugal. *A' la Portuguesa,* In the Portuguese fashion.

Porvída, *sf.* By the living God; an oath much in use among the common people in Spain.

Pós (En), *ad.* After, behind.

Pósa, *sf.* 1. Passing bell; the ringing of bells for persons deceased. 2. Stops made by the clergy who conduct a funeral, to sing a responsary. *Posas,* Breech, seat, the lower parts of the human body; buttocks.

Posáda, *sf.* 1. Home, dwelling-house. 2. Lodging-house, inn, tavern. 3. Pocket-case, containing a knife, spoon, and fork. *Mas acá hay posada,* How he swells or exaggerates. *Posadas,* Apartments for the ladies in waiting in the royal palace.

Posadéras, *sf. pl.* Buttocks. V. *Asentaderas.*

Posadería, *sf.* Inn, tavern, lodging house for travellers.

Posadéro, *sm.* 1. Inn-keeper, the keeper of a lodging house or tavern. 2. Seat made of flags or bass-ropes. 3. V. *Posaderas.*

Posádo, *a.* Defunct; formerly used.

Posánte, *pa.* Reposing; used at sea for smooth sailing.

Posár, *vn.* 1. To lodge, to board. 2. To sit down, to repose, to rest. 3. To perch, to light or sit upon.—*va.* To lay down a burthen.

Posavérgas, *sf. pl.* (Naút.) Booms or sails formerly used to support the yards, but now disused.

Pósca, *sf.* Mixture of vinegar and water formerly given by way of refreshment.

Posdáta, *sf.* Postscript, an additament to a letter already written.

Poseedór, ra, *s.* Possessor, one who holds or possesses any thing.

Poseér, *va.* 1. To hold, to possess. 2. To be perfectly master of a language or other thing.

Poseído, *sm.* 1. He who executes desperate actions; possessed. 2. Enclosed arable land as distinguished from commons.

Posesión, *sf.* 1. Possession, the act of possessing or holding any corporal thing. 2. Possession, the thing possessed. 3. Possession of the human body by evil spirits. 4. (Met.) Reputation, good or bad.

Posesionál, *a.* Including possession or relating to it.

Posesionéro, *sm.* Cattle-keeper, who has acquired possession of pasturage.

Posesívo, va, *a.* (Gram.) Possessive, an epithet given to nouns or pronouns which denote possession.

Poséso, sa, *a.* Possessed, possessed by evil spirits. *Pagar el poseso,* To give an entertainment on entering upon a public office or employment.

Posesór, ra, *sm.* y *f.* V. *Poseedor.*

Posesoriaménte, *ad.* In a possessory manner.

Posesório, ria, *a.* Possessory.

Poseyénte, *pa.* Possessor; possessing.

Posibilidád, *sf.* 1. Possibility, capability to exist. 2. Wealth, riches.

Posibilitár, *va.* To render possible, to facilitate.

Posíble, *a.* Possible, that can be or may happen. *Posibles,* Wealth, income, capital, means. *Mis posibles no alcanzan á eso,* My means do not extend so far. *Serviré á vd. con mis posibles,* I will serve you with all my might. *Es posible?* Is it possible?

Posibleménte, *ad.* Possibly.

Posición, *sf.* 1. Position, the art of placing. 2.

Posture. V. *Postura*. 3. Questions and answers of an interrogatory. 4. Position, rule in arithmetic.

Positivaménte, *ad.* Positively.

Positívo, va, *a.* 1. Positive, sure, certain. 2. (In Grammar,) Positive, without comparison in adjectives. *De positivo*, Certainly, without doubt.

Pósito, *sm.* A public granary. *Pósito pio*, Granary for charity, which lends grain to widows or poor labourers without charging interest.

Positúra, *sf.* Posture; disposition. V. *Postura*.

Pósma, *sm.* Drone, dull sluggish humdrum; astonishment; spasm.

Póso, *sm.* 1. Sediment, dregs, lees. 2. Rest, repose.

Posón, *sm.* Seat made of bass. V. *Posadero*.

Pospárto, *sm.* V. *Postparto*.

Pospélo (A'), *ad.* Against the grain, reluctantly.

Pospiérna, *sf.* Thigh, the part of an animal which extends from the buttock to the knee.

Posponér, *va.* To place one thing after or behind another; to postpone.

Pósta, *sf.* 1. Post-horses, horses placed on the roads at the distance of ten or more miles from one relay to another. 2. Post-house, the house or place where the post-horses are stationed. 3. Post, distance from one relay or post-house to another. 4. Military post; a sentinel. 5. Chop, a piece of meat or fish cut off to be dressed. 6. Slug, a piece of lead cut off from a larger piece, but not round. 7. Night-sentry. 8. Stake, money staked at a game of cards.—*sm.* Person who rides or travels post. *Correr la posta*, To travel post. *A' posta*, Designedly. *Por la posta*, With all speed, in haste.

Postár, *va.* To bet, to wager, to stake.

Póste, *sm.* 1. Post, pillar; a piece of timber or a stone set upright to support a building. 2. Kind of punishment inflicted in colleges. *Oler el poste*, To smell a rat, to have some presentiment of an impending danger.

Posteár, *vn.* To travel post.

Posteléros, *sm. pl.* (Naút.) Skids or skeeds, long pieces of timber, intended to preserve the flanks of the ship's sides when heavy bodies are hoisted on board. *Posteleros de las amuras*, (Naút.) Chess-trees.

Postéma, *sm.* 1. Sore, bile, imposthume. 2. Dull troublesome person.

Postemèro, *sm.* Large lancet.

Postergación, *sf.* Act of leaving behind.

Postergár, *va.* To leave behind.

Posteridád, *sf.* Posterity, succeeding generations.

Posteriór, *a.* Posterior, placed or happening after.

Posterioridád, *sf.* Posteriority, opposed to priority.

Posteriorménte, *ad.* Lastly.

Postéta, *sf.* Number of printed sheets stitched together; gathering, a quantity of sheets put together for the purpose of packing up books.

Postígo, *sm.* 1. By-door, or small door in a house. 2. (Fort.) Sally-port. *Postigos*, Parts of which a door or window is composed.

Postiguíllo, *sm.* A small wicket or back door

Postíla, *sf.* Marginal note.

Postilación, *sf.* Act of making marginal notes.

Postiladór, *sm.* Annotator.

Postilár, *va.* To explain or illustrate with notes.

Postílla, *sf.* Scab which grows on wounds or pustules when they begin to dry.

Postillón, *sm.* 1. Postillion, driver. 2. Hack.

Postillóso, sa, *a.* Scabby, pustulous.

Postíza, *sf.* 1. (Naút.) Dead work on galleys for guiding the oar. 2. V. *Castañuela*.

Postízo, za, *a.* Artificial, not natural.

Postízo, *sm.* With wig-makers, hair to supply the front or back of the head.

Postliminio, *sm.* Postliminy, among the Romans, reinstatement of one taken by the enemy to his possessions.

Postmeridiáno, na, *a.* Postmeridian.

Postór, *sm.* Bidder at a public sale; better.

Postpárto, *sm.* The latest young of animals in the season, applied chiefly to ewes.

Postración, *sf.* Prostration, the act of kneeling down or prostrating one's self.

Postradór, ra, *s.* 1. One who prostrates or humbles himself. 2. Footstool placed at the foot of the stall or seat in the choir, on which the chorister kneels.

Postrár, *va.* 1. To prostrate, to humble, to humiliate. 2. To debilitate, to weaken, to exhaust.—*vr.* To prostrate one's self, to kneel down to the ground.

Póstre, *a.* Last in order. *A' la postre*, At the long run, at last. *Por fin y postre*, (Vulg.) Finally.

Póstres, *sm. pl.* Dessert, the fruit and sweetmeats served up at table in the last course.

Postrémas (A'), *ad.* (Ant.) Ultimately.

Postreraménte, *ad.* Ultimately, lastly.

Postréro, ra; Postrér y Postrémo, ma, *a.* Last in order. *Postrero*, V. *Trasero*.

Postrimeraménte, *ad.* Finally, at last.

Postrimería, *sf.* 1. Death. V. *Novisimo*. 2. The last period or last years of life.

Postriméro, ra, *a.* V. *Postrero y Trasero*.

Postulación, *sf.* Postulation; petition.

Postuládos, *sm. pl.* Postulates, principles so clear and evident that they need no proof; positions assumed without proof.

Postuladór, *sm.* 1. Member of a chapter who votes for an unqualified prelate. 2. One who solicits the canonization of a saint.

Postulár, *va.* To elect a prelate disqualified by the canon law, or labouring under a canonical impediment.

Póstumo, ma, *a.* Posthumous, published after the death of the author.

Postúra, *sf.* 1. Posture, position. 2. Act of planting trees or plants. 3. Assize of eatables or of all sorts of provisions. 4. Price fixed by a bidder or buyer. 5. Bet, wager. 6. Paint which women put on their faces. 7. Egg of a fowl or bird. 8. Agreement, convention. *A' postura de regidor*, Not to fix the price of goods all at one time, but take an average. *Posturas*, Young plants transplanted from one place to another.

Potáble, *a.* Potable, drinkable; that can be drunk.

Potadór, *sm.* He who examines and marks weights and measures.

Potáge, *sm.* 1. Broth of boiled meat. 2. Vegetables dressed for food in days of abstinence. 3. Drink made up of several ingredients. 4. Medley of various useless things. 5. (Joc.) Water not cold.

Potagería, *sf.* 1. Quantity of dry pulse heaped up together. 2. Place where dry pulse or vegetables are kept, and preserved for the use of the kitchen.

Potagiér, *sm.* Officer of the king's palace who has the care of dry pulse and vegetables.

Potála, *sf.* Stone fixed in any point which serves to moor boats.

Potár, *va.* To equalize and mark weights and measures.

Potása, *sf.* Pot-ash, vegetable alkali, the ashes of wood and other vegetables.

Póte, *sm.* 1. Pot, jar, flower-pot. 2. Standard measure or weight by which others are regulated. *A' pote*, Abundantly.

Poténcia, *sf.* 1. Power, the faculty of performing or executing any thing. 2. Possibility. 3. Power of generation; productive virtue. 4. Potentate; power, dominion; kingdom, state. *Potencias beligerantes*, Powers at war. *Potencias*, The nine rays of light which encircle the head of the infant Jesus.

Potenciál, *a.* 1. Potential, possessing or including a power. 2. (Gram.) Potential mode.

Potencialidád, *sf.* Potentiality; equivalence.

Potencialménte, *ad.* Potentially; equivalently.

Potentádo, *sm.* Potentate, sovereign.

Poténte, *a.* Potent, powerful, great, strong.

Potenteménte, *ad.* Powerfully.

Potérna, *sf.* (Fort.) Postern, sally-port.

Potéro, *sm.* V. *Potador*.

Potestád, *sf.* 1. Power, dominion, command, jurisdiction. V. *Potentado*. 2. (Arit.) Power, any product arising from the multiplication of a number by itself. *Potestades*, Angelic powers.

Potestatívo, va, *a.* (For.) That which is in the faculty or power of any thing.

Potísimo, ma, *a.* Most special, peculiar, particular.

Potísta, *s. com.* (Fam.) Tippler, drunkard.

Pótra, *sf.* Rupture, a kind of scrotal hernia.

Potráda, *sf.* Troop of young mares at pasture.

Potránca, *sf.* Filly, young mare.

Potreár, *va.* (Fam.) 1. To rupture; to get buboes. 2. To herd mares.

Potréra, *a.* Applied to a hempen head-stall for horses.

Potréro, *sm.* 1. Surgeon who cures ruptures. 2. Horse-herd.

Potríl, *s.* Pasture in which young horses are reared when separated from their mothers.

Potrílla, *sf.* Nickname given to old persons affecting rakish youth.

Pótro, ra, *s.* 1. Colt, a young horse; a filly. 2. A wooden horse; rack, a kind of torture. 3. A wooden frame for shoeing unruly horses. 4. Any thing which molests or torments. 5. An earthen chamber-pot. 6. (Joc.) Bubo, a venereal tumour in the groin. 7. Pit in the ground, about 1 foot wide and 2 deep, in which bee-keepers divide a bee-hive into two portions, giving a king to each, and thus forming two distinct hives.

Potróso, sa, *a.* 1. Afflicted with a rupture. 2. (Fam.) Fortunate.

Póya, *sf.* Duty or money paid for baking bread in a public oven.

Poyál, *sm.* 1. A sort of striped stuff with which benches or seats are covered. 2. V. *Poyo*.

Poyáta, *sf.* Shelf, board, cupboard.

Poyatílla, *sf.* A little shelf.

Poyátos, *sm. pl.* Terraces, supported by mud-walls, in order to derive greater advantages from a sloping ground by cultivation.

Póyo, *sm.* 1. Bench, a seat made of stone and mortar against a wall near the street, door, or in a court or yard. 2. Fee given to judges.

Póza, *sf.* 1. Puddle, a small lake of stagnant water. 2. Hole made in children's bread, and filled with boiled must, honey, or treacle. *Lamer la poza*, To lick the honey or butter off bread; to drain one's pocket of money.

Pozál, *sm.* 1. Bucket, a vessel in which water is drawn out of a well. 2. Coping of a well. 3. Vessel sunk in the earth to catch any fluid.

Pozánco, *sm.* Pond of stagnant water.

Pozéro, *sm.* Well-digger, he who makes or cleans wells.

Pózo, *sm.* 1. Well. 2. A deep hole in a river; a whirlpool. 3. Any thing deep and full. *Es un pozo de ciencia*, He is deeply learned; a man of profound erudition. *Navio de pozo*, (Naút.) A deep-waisted ship. *Pozo de cable*, (Naút.) Cable-stage, cable-tier. *Pozo de nieve*, Ice-house, snow-pit.

Pozuéla, *sf.* A small puddle or pond.

Pozuélo, *sm.* 1. A small well or pit. 2. Vessel sunk in the ground to collect oil, &c. in mills.

Práctica, *sf.* 1. Practice, constant habit of doing any thing; custom. 2. Manner, mode, method. 3. Apprenticeship.

Practicáble, *a.* Practicable, feasible.

Practicadór, ra, *s.* Practiser, practitioner.

Practicaménte, *ad.* Practically.

Practicánte, *sm.* Practitioner in surgery and medicine under a distinguished master.

Practicár, *va.* To practise, to perform; to exercise under a master.

Práctico, ca, *a.* 1. Practical, belonging to practise. 2. Skilful, experienced.

Practicón, na, *s.* One of great practical knowledge and experience.

Pradál, *sm.* Extent of country abounding in meadows and pasture-lands.

Pradéño, ña, *a.* Relating to meadows or fields.

Pradería y Pradéra, *sf.* 1. Country abounding in meadows and pasture-grounds. 2. Mead, piece of fruitful or rich pasture-ground.

Praderóso, sa, *a.* Relating to meadows.

Pradíco, íllo y Pradecíllo, *sm.* A small meadow.

Prádo, *sm.* 1. Lawn, field, meadow; a piece of pasture-ground. 2. Prado, walk surrounded with trees and fountains in Madrid. *Prado de guadáña*, Meadow mowed annually.

Pragmática, *sf.* Royal ordinance or edict. 2. Rescript or answer of a sovereign to an application made to him in a particular case.

Práma, *sf.* Pram or prame, a kind of lighter used in northern countries.

Prásio, *sm.* Prase, a green precious stone.

Práta, *sf.* V. *Plata*.

Prática, *sf.* V. *Práctica*.

PRAVEDÁD, *sf.* Perversity, iniquity; corruption of manners.
PRÁVO, VA, *a.* Depraved, perverse.
PRÁXIS, *sf.* Practice. V. *Práctica.*
PRE, *sm.* Daily pay allowed to soldiers.
PRE, *prep. lat.* Before, fore. *Pre manibus,* Between the hands.
PREA, *sf.* (Ant.) V. *Presa.*
PREÁMBULO, *sm.* 1. Preamble, exordium, preface. 2. (Fam.) Evasion, circumlocution.
PREBÉNDA, *sf.* 1. Prebend; benefice. 2. Portion, money from motives of piety given to a girl to get her married. 3. Sinecure. 4. (Met.) Office or employ by means of which a living is gained. *Prebenda de oficio,* Any of the four prebends doctoral, magisterial, lectural, or penitentiary.
PREBENDÁDO, *sm.* Prebendary, a dignitary who enjoys a prebend in a cathedral or collegiate church.
PREBESTÁDGO Y PREBESTÁD, *s.* Provostship, the place or dignity of a provost.
PREBOSTÁL, *a.* Provostal, belonging to a provost.
PREBÓSTE, *sm.* 1. Provost, one who governs a college or community. 2. (Mil.) Provost of an army, an officer appointed to secure deserters and other criminals, and to superintend the infliction of punishments.
PRECARIAMÉNTE, *ad.* Precariously.
PRECÁRIO, RIA, *a.* Precarious, uncertain.
PRECAUCIÓN, *sf.* Precaution.
PRECAUCIONÁRSE, *vr.* To be cautious, to be on one's guard.
PRECAUTELÁR, *va.* To caution, to warn.
PRECAVÉR, *va.* To prevent or obviate.—*vr.* To guard against, to be on one's guard.
PRECEDÉNCIA, *sf.* Precedence, act of preceding or going before; preference; superiority.
PRECEDÉNTE, *pa.* Precedent, preceding.
PRECEDÉR, *va.* To precede, to go before; to be superior in rank or order; to excel.
PRECELÉNTE, *a.* (Ant.) Very excellent.
PRECEPTÍSTA, *sf.* One who enjoins or gives precepts and injunctions.
PRECEPTIVAMÉNTE, *ad.* Preceptively.
PRECEPTÍVO, VA, *a.* Preceptive, containing or including precepts.
PRECÉPTO, *sm.* Precept, order, injunction, mandate; rule. *Precéptos,* The commandments, the ten precepts of the decalogue.
PRECEPTÓR, *sm.* Master, teacher, preceptor.
PRECEPTÓRA, *sf.* School-mistress.
PRÉCES, *sf. pl.* Prayers; public devotion.
PRECESION, *sf.* V. *Reticencia.*
PRECIÁDO, DA, *a.* 1. Valued, appraised; esteemed. 2. Valuable, precious, excellent.
PRECIADÓR, RA, *s.* Appraiser.
PRECIÁR, *va.* To value, to appraise.—*vr.* To boast, to brag; to take a pride in.
PRECÍNTAS, *sf. pl.* (Naút.) Parcelling, narrow pieces of tarred canvass, with which the seams of ships are covered by the calkers, and which are also put around cables and ropes to prevent their being galled.
PRECINTÁR, *va.* 1. To strap the corners of boxes with leather to prevent their opening. 2. To cross boxes of goods as a mark that they are not to be opened at any intermediate custom-house before arriving at their final destination.
PRÉCIO, *sm.* 1. Price, value; premium. 2. Esteem, consideration; character, credit. *Tener en precio,* To esteem.
PRECIOSAMÉNTE, *ad.* Preciously, richly.
PRECIOSIDÁD, *sf.* Worth, excellence.
PRECIÓSO, SA, *a.* 1. Precious, valuable, excellent. 2. Pleasant, gay, merry.
PRECIÓSA, *sf.* Allowance in the choir to prebendaries for assisting at prayers for a benefactor.
PRECIPÍCIO, *sm.* 1. Precipice, a steep height. 2. A violent sudden fall. 3. Ruin, destruction.
PRECIPITACIÓN, *sf.* 1. Precipitation, inconsiderate haste; abruptness. 2. Precipitation, a chemical process, by which particles, dissolved in any liquid, are made to fall down to the bottom; contrary to sublimation.
PRECIPITADAMÉNTE, *ad.* Precipitately.
PRECIPITADÉRO, *sm.* V. *Precipicio.*
PRECIPITÁDO, *sm.* (Quím.) Precipitate.
PRECIPITÁNTE, *sm.* (Quím.) Precipitater, that which precipitates.
PRECIPITÁR, *va.* 1. To precipitate, to throw down a precipice; to throw headlong. 2. To expose to ruin. 3. To perform the chemical process of precipitation.—*vr.* To act in a rash and precipitate manner; to run headlong into ruin and destruction.
PRECÍPITE, *a.* In danger or on the point of falling.
PRECIPITOSAMÉNTE, *ad.* V. *Precipitadamente.*
PRECIPITÓSO, SA, *a.* 1. Steep, slippery. 2. Precipitous, rash, inconsiderate.
PRECIPUAMÉNTE, *ad.* Principally.
PRECÍPUO, PUA, *a.* Chief, principal.
PRECISÁDO, DA, *a.* Necessitated, obliged.
PRECISAMÉNTE, *ad.* 1. Precisely, exactly, nicely. 2. Inevitably, indispensably, necessarily.
PRECISÁR, *va.* To compel, to oblige, to necessitate.
PRECISIÓN, *sf.* 1. Necessity, obligation. 2. Preciseness, exactness, accuracy; precision.
PRECISÍVO, VA, *a.* That which prescinds or abstracts.
PRECÍSO, SA, *a.* 1. Necessary, requisite. 2. Precise, exact, punctual. 3. Distinct, clear. 4. Severed, cut off; abstracted.
PRECÍTO, TA; Y PRESCÍTO, TA, *a.* Damned, condemned to the pains of hell.
PRECLARAMÉNTE, *ad.* Illustriously, distinctly.
PRECLÁRO, RA, *a.* Illustrious, famous, eminent.
PRECOCIDÁD, *sf.* Precocity, ripeness of fruit before the usual time.
PRECOGNICIÓN, *sf.* Precognition.
PRECONIZACIÓN, *sf.* Preconization.
PRECONIZÁR, *va.* To preconize, to proclaim, to publish in the Román consistory.
PRECONOCEDÓR, RA, *s.* One who foresees or anticipates some future event.
PRECONOCÉR, *va.* To foreknow, to foretel; to anticipate the result of a thing.
PRECÓZ, *a.* Precocious, ripe before the usual time.
PRECURSÓR, RA, *a.* Preceding, going before.—*s.* Precursor, harbinger, fore-runner.
PREDECESÓR, RA, *s.* Predecessor, antecessor.
PREDECÍR, *va.* To foretel, to anticipate, to predict.
PREDEFINICIÓN, *sf.* Predetermination of the Divine Providence that things are to exist and events to happen at a certain time.
PREDEFINÍR, *va.* To predetermine, to determine

the time at which things are to exist or events to happen.
Predestinación, *sf.* Predestination.
Predestinadór, *sm.* He who predestines or destines.
Predestinánte, *pa.* Predestinating; he who predestines.
Predestinár, *va.* To predestine, to predestinate.
Predeterminación, *sf.* Predetermination.
Predeterminár, *va.* To predetermine, to resolve beforehand; to anticipate a resolution, to doom by previous decree.
Prediál, *a.* Consisting in landed property, or relating to it; consisting of farms.
Prédica, *sf.* Sermon, a discourse delivered by a sectarian preacher.
Predicáble, *a.* 1. Fit to be preached. 2. Commendable, worthy of praise. 3. (Lóg.) Predicable.
Predicación, *sf.* Act of preaching; sermon.
Predicadéra, *sf.* (Arag.) Pulpit. *Predicaderas*, Style of the pulpit, facility of preaching or praying.
Predicádo, *sm.* (Lóg.) Predicate.
Predicadór, ra, *s.* Preacher, orator, eulogist.
Predicamentál, *a.* Predicamental.
Predicaménto, *sm.* Predicament, degree of estimation in which a person is held; predicament.
Predicánte, *sm.* Sectarian or heretical preacher.
Predicár, *va.* 1. To render clear and evident, to publish. 2. To preach, to deliver a sermon. 3. To praise to excess. 4. To reprehend or inveigh against any vice.—*vr.* To predicate. *Subirse á predicar*, (Fam.) To mount to the head; applied to good wine.
Predicatório, *sm.* V. *Púlpito.*
Predicción, *sf.* Prediction, the act of foretelling future events.
Predícho, cha, *pp. irreg.* of *Predecir.*
Predilección, *sf.* Predilection.
Predilécto, ta, *a.* Beloved in preference to others; darling, favourite.
Prédio, *sm.* Landed property, land whether cultivated or waste; farm. *Prédio rústico*, Piece of arable ground cultivated either in the fields or as a garden near dwellings. *Predio urbano*, Dwelling-house either in town or country.
Predíolo, *sm.* A small farm.
Predisponér, *va.* To predispose.
Predominación, *sf.* V. *Predominio.*
Predominánte, *pa.* Predominant.
Predominár, *va.* 1. To predominate, to have a power over. 2. To exceed in height, to overlook, to command; to prevail.
Predomínio, *sm.* Predominance, predominant power, superiority; prevalence of humours.
Preeminéncia, *sf.* Pre-eminence.
Preeminénte, *a.* Pre-eminent, superior.
Preexcélso, sa, *a.* Illustrious, great, or eminent in an uncommon degree.
Preexisténcia, *sf.* Pre-existence.
Preexisténte, *pa.* Pre-existent.
Preexistír, *vn.* To pre-exist, to exist before.
Prefácio, *sm.* 1. Part of the mass which immediately precedes the canon. 2. Preface, an introductory discourse.
Prefación, *sf.* Preface, introduction.
Prefacioncílla, *sf.* A short preface.
Prefécto, *sm.* 1. Prefect, a magistrate in ancient Rome. 2. President, chairman. 3. Master or principal of a college.
Prefectúra, *sf.* Place or dignity of a prefect.
Preferéncia, *sf.* Preference.
Preferénte, *pa.* Pre-eminent; preferring.
Preferíble, *a.* Preferable, more valuable or eligible; worthy of being preferred, eligible before something else.
Preferír, *va.* To prefer, to regard more than another.—*vr.* To offer spontaneously to do any thing.
Prefiguración, *sf.* Prefiguration.
Prefigurár, *va.* To prefigurate, to show by an antecedent representation; to model a statue, to sketch a painting.
Prefinición, *sf.* Act of prefining or fixing a term.
Prefinír, *va.* To prefine, to determine.
Prefixár, *va.* To determine, to fix before-hand.
Prefíxo, xa, *pp. irreg.* of *Prefixar*, Prefixed.
Prefulgénte, *a.* Resplendent, lucid, shining.
Pregária, *sf.* V. *Plegaria.*
Pregón, *sm.* Publication made in public places by the common crier.
Pregonár, *va.* 1. To cry or proclaim in public places. 2. To cry goods or provisions about the streets. 3. To render public, to make known; to applaud publicly.
Pregonería, *sf.* 1. Office of common crier. 2. Tax or tribute.
Pregonéro, *sm.* 1. Common crier, an officer whose business is to proclaim or give notice in a loud voice in public places. 2. One who renders public or divulges a secret. 3. One who proclaims the biddings at public sales.—*a.* Publishing, praising, proclaiming.
Pregúnta, *sf.* Question, query, inquiry.
Preguntadór, ra, *s.* Questioner, examiner, interrogator.
Preguntánte, *pa.* Inquirer.
Preguntár, *va.* To question, to demand, to make inquiries.
Preguntón, na, *s.* An inquisitive person, a busy inquirer.
Preinsérto, ta, *a.* That which is previously inserted.
Prejudiciál, *a.* Requiring a previous judicial decision before the final sentence. V. *Perjudicial.*
Prejuício, *sm.* V. *Perjuicio.*
Prelacía, *sf.* Prelacy, dignity of a prelate.
Prelación, *sf.* Preference, prelation, setting of one above the other.
Preláda, *sf.* A female prelate, the abbess or superior of a convent or nunnery.
Preládo, *sm.* Prelate, a dignity of the church, superior of a convent or religious house.
Prelatúra, *sf.* 1. Prelacy, the dignity of a prelate. 2. The whole body of prelates.
Preliminár, *a.* Preliminary, proëmial.
Preliminares, *sm. pl.* Preliminaries, previous terms and arrangements of a treaty of peace.
Prelucír, *vn.* To sparkle or shine forth.
Prelúdio, *sm.* Prelude, something introductory.
Prelusión, *sf.* Prelude, prelusion, preface.
Premática, *sf.* V. *Pragmática.*
Prematuraménte, *ad.* Prematurely.
Prematúro, ra, *a.* Premature, precocious, ripe before the proper time; unseasonable.
Premeditación, *sf.* Premeditation, the act of meditating beforehand.

Premeditár, *va.* To consider carefully, to weigh maturely, to conceive beforehand.

Premiadór, ra, *s.* Rewarder, one who rewards.

Premiár, *va.* To reward, to remunerate.

Premícia. V. *Primicia.*

Prémio, *sm.* 1. Reward, recompense, remuneration. 2. Premium, interest. *Premio de seguro*, Rate or premium of insurance.

Premiosaménte, *ad.* Tightly, compressedly; by force.

Premióso, sa, *a.* 1. Tight, close, pinching. 2. Troublesome, tiresome, burthensome.

Premísa, *sf.* 1. Premise, any of the first two propositions of a syllogism; an antecedent proposition. 2. Mark, indication.

Premíso, sa, *a.* Premised. V. *Prevenido.*

Premitír, *va.* V. *Anticipar.*

Premoción, *sf.* Previous movement or motion.

Premonstraténse y Premostraténse, *a.* Premonstratensian; applied to an order of regular canons founded by S. Norbert.

Premoriéncia, *sf.* Prior death.

Premorír, *vn.* (For.) To die before another.

Premúra, *sf.* Narrowness, pressure. V. *Aprieto.*

Prénda, *sf.* 1. Pledge, security given for the fulfilment of an obligation. 2. Piece of furniture put up at sale. *Casa de prendas*, Broker's shop, where old furniture is sold. 3. Present made as a pledge of love or friendship. 4. Any object dearly loved. *Préndas*, Endowments, accomplishments, talents. *Meter prendas*, To take a part in any business.

Prendadór, *sm.* Pledger, pawner; one who takes out of pawn or redeems a pledge.

Prendamiénto, *sm.* Act of pledging or pawning.

Prendár, *va.* To take pledges, to lend on pledges.—*vn.* To please, to ingratiate one's self.

Prendedéro, *sm.* 1. Hook, any instrument which serves to catch and hold. 2. Fillet, a band tied round the head, which serves to keep up the hair.

Prendedór, *sm.* Catcher, one who catches.

Prendér, *va.* 1. To seize, to grasp, to catch. 2. To detain for the purpose of entertaining in a friendly manner. 3. To adorn, to embellish, to set off. 4. To take, to accept.—*vn.* 1. To take root. 2. To begin to show some quality or virtue. 3. To cover; applied to the act of brutish procreation.

Prendería, *sf.* Shop or place in which old clothes and pieces of furniture are sold; pawnbroker's shop; frippery.

Prendéro, ra, *s.* 1. Broker, one who sells old furniture and clothes; fripperer. 2. Pawnbroker. [Pattern for bone-lace.

Prendído, *sm.* 1. Dress or attire of women. 2.

Prendimiénto, *sm.* Seizure, act of seizing, grasping, or taking; capture.

Prenoción, *sf.* Prenotion or first knowledge of things. [that of the family.

Prenómbre, *sm.* Prenomen, name prefixed to

Prenosticár, *va.* (Ant.) V. *Pronosticar.*

Prenotár, *va.* To note by anticipation.

Prénsa, *sf.* 1. Press, an instrument with which any thing is squeezed or pressed down. 2. Press, a machine for printing. 3. Impression. V. *Imprenta. Prensa recargada*, A hot-press, to give a gloss or lustre to stuff. *Dar á la prensa*, To publish.

Prensádo, *sm.* Lustre, gloss which remains on stuff.

Prensadór, ra, *s.* Presser, one who presses clothes and stuff.

Prensadúra, *sf.* The act of pressing, pressure.

Prensár, *va.* To press, to put any thing into press. V. *Aprensar.*

Prensísta, *sm.* Pressman in a printing-office.

Prenunciár, *va.* To foretel, to prognosticate.

Prenúncio, *sm.* Prediction, prognostication.

Preñádo, da, *a.* 1. Full, pregnant. 2. Big with child, pregnant. 3. Paunched, bulging out. *Pared preñada*, Wall which bulges out and is near giving way.—*sm.* Pregnancy, the state of being with child, period of gestation.

Preñéz, *sf.* 1. Pregnancy; conception. 2 State of hanging over, impendence. 3. Confusion, difficulty, obscurity.

Preocupación, *sf.* 1. Preoccupation, anticipation in acquiring or taking possession of a thing. 2. Prepossession, bias, prejudice.

Preocupadaménte, *ad.* Prejudicedly.

Preocupár, *va.* 1. To occupy or take possession before another. 2. To prejudice, to prepossess the mind.

Preordinación, *sf.* (Teol.) Preordination.

Preordinadaménte, *ad.* In a manner preordained. [ordain

Preordinár, *va.* (Teol.) To preordain, to fore-

Preparación, *sf.* Preparation, the act of preparing or disposing any thing. [ration.

Preparamiénto ó Preparaménto, *sm.* Prepa-

Preparár, *va.* To prepare, to fit, to get ready. —*vr.* To be prepared, to be in readiness, to be disposed.

Preparatívo, va, *a.* Preparative, qualifying, having the power of preparing.—*sm.* Thing prepared, preparative.

Preparatoriaménte, *ad.* Preparatorily.

Preparatório, ria, *a.* Preparatory, previous, introductory.

Preponderáncia, *sf.* Preponderance.

Preponderánte, *a.* Preponderant, that which preponderates or turns the scale.

Preponderár, *vn.* 1. To preponderate, to outweigh, to overbalance. 2. To prevail.

Preponér, *va.* To put before, to prefer.

Preposición, *sf.* (Gram.) Preposition, an indeclinable part of speech which precedes the word it governs, or unites with it.

Prepósito, *sm.* 1. President, chairman. 2. Provost.

Prepositúra, *sf.* Dignity of a provost.

Preposteración, *sf.* Inversion of the regular order of things, the act of turning things topsyturvy.

Preposteraménte, *ad.* Preposterously.

Preposterár, *va.* To render preposterous, to transpose.

Prepóstero, ra, *a.* Preposterous, absurd.

Prepoténcia, *sf.* Preponderance, superiority

Prepoténte, *a.* Very powerful.

Prepúcio, *sm.* Prepuce.

Prepuésto, ta, *pp.* Preferred.

Prerogatíva, *sf.* Prerogative, privilege.

Présa, *sf.* 1. Capture, seizure; the act of grasping or seizing. 2. Prize, spoils or booty taken from an enemy. 3. Carcass of a fowl or bird killed by a hawk or other bird of prey. 4.

Dike, dam, mole, bank; drain, trench, conduit. 5. Slice of meat; a bit of any other kind of eatables. 6. Broth or diet of a sick person; small bit of food. *Presa de caldo*, Pulp, juice. V. *Pisto*. *Hacer presa*, To catch and tie any thing so that it cannot escape. *Présas*, Tusks, fangs, claws; the long sharp teeth of some animals.

PRESÁDA, *sf.* Colour of a leek, a pale green colour.

PRESAGÍR, *va.* To presage, to forebode.

PRESÁGIO, *sm.* Presage, foretoken.

PRESAGIÓSO, SA; Y PRÉSAGO, GA, *a.* Ominous, containing foretokens or relating to them.

PRESBÍTERA, *sf.* Wife of a presbyter.

PRESBITERÁDO Ó PRESBITERÁTO, *sm.* Priesthood, the dignity or order of a priest.

PRESBITERÁL, *a.* Sacerdotal, relating to a presbyter.

PRESBITERIÁNO, NA, *a.* Presbyterian.

PRESBITERIÁTO, *sm.* Dignity of a presbyter or elder among the presbyterians.

PRESBITÉRIO, *sm.* Presbyterium, chancel; the part in a church where the high altar stands.

PRESBÍTERO, *sm.* Presbyter.

PRÉSBITO, *sm.* He who sees only distant objects.

PRESCIÉNCIA, *sf.* Prescience, a foreknowledge of future events.

PRESCINDÍBLE, *a.* Capable of being prescinded or abstracted.

PRESCINDÍR, *va.* To prescind, to cut off; to abstract. *Prescindiendo de eso*, Laying that aside.

PRESCÍTO, TA, *a.* V. *Precito*.

PRESCRIBÍR, *va.* 1. To prescribe, to mark, to determine. 2. To acquire a right by means of an uninterrupted possession. 3. To despair of success; to stand in need of.

PRESCRIPCIÓN, *sf.* 1. Prescription, the act of prescribing. 2. Introduction, any thing proëmial. 3. (For.) Right or title acquired by a peaceful possession for a number of years.

PRESCRIPTÍBLE, *a.* Prescriptible, that may be prescribed.

PRESCRÍPTO, TA, *pp. irreg.* of *Prescribir*, Prescribed.

PRESÉA, *sf.* Jewel, any ornament of great value.

PRESÉNCIA, *sf.* 1. Presence, state of being present; co-existence, contrary to absence. 2. Figure, port, air, mien, demeanour. 3. (Met.) Memory or representation of a thing.

PRESENCIÁL, *a.* Presential, relating to actual presence.

PRESENCIALMÉNTE, *ad.* Presentially.

PRESENCIÁR, *vn.* To assist, to be present.

PRESENTACIÓN, *sf.* 1. Presentation, the act of presenting; exhibition; church festival in memory of the Virgin's presentation in the temple. 2. The act of offering or presenting an ecclesiastical benefice.

PRESENTÁDO, *sm.* 1. Teacher of divinity who expects soon to be ranked as master. 2. Presentee, person presented.

PRESENTADÓR, RA, *s.* Presenter, one that presents; one who offers a benefice.

PRESENTÁLLA, *sf.* Gift offered by the faithful to the saints.

PRESENTANEAMÉNTE, *ad.* Quickly, readily.

PRESENTÁNEO, NEA, *a.* Presentaneous, quick, ready, immediate.

PRESENTÁNTE, *pa.* Presenter.

PRESENTÁR, *va.* 1. To present, to place in the presence of another. 2. To favour with a gift, to give formally and ceremoniously. 3. To prefer to ecclesiastical benefices. *Presentar la batalla*, To offer battle. *Presentar la bolina mayor*, (Naút.) To snatch the main bow-line *Presentar el costado*, (Naút.) To bring the broadside to bear. *Presentar la proa al viento*, (Naút.) To head the wind. *Presentar la proa á las olas*, (Naút.) To head the sea.—*vr.* To appear in a court of justice.

PRESÉNTE, *sm.* Present, gift.—*a.* Present. *Al presente ó de presente*, At present, in the present time; now. *Tener presente*, To bear in mind. *Hacer presente*, To consider one as present; to put one's self before another for some end.

PRESENTEMÉNTE, *ad.* Presently, at present.

PRESENTÉRO, *sm.* Presenter; one who offers a benefice.

PRESENTÍLLO, *sm.* A small gift, a little present.

PRESENTIMIÉNTO, *sm.* Presentiment, presension, perception beforehand.

PRESENTÍR, *va.* To have a presentiment or perception beforehand of a future event, to foresee.

PRESÉRA, *sf.* (Bot.) Goose grass, cleavers.

PRESÉRO, *sm.* Prize-master, person who guards prizes.

PRESERVACIÓN, *sf.* Preservation, the act of preserving.

PRESERVADÓR, RA, *s.* Preserver.

PRESERVÁR, *va.* To preserve, to defend from evil; to keep.

PRESERVATIVAMÉNTE, *ad.* Preservatively.

PRESERVATÍVO, VA, *a.* Preservative, that which has the power of preserving.

PRESIDÉNCIA, *sf.* 1. Presidency, the place or dignity of a president. 2. Act of presiding, superintendence.

PRESIDÉNTA, *sf.* President's wife.

PRESIDÉNTE, *sm.* 1. President, one placed with authority over others, one at the head of others; speaker, judge. 2. Substitute of a prelate in some religious communities. 3. Professor in universities.

PRESIDÁR, *va.* To garrison, to place soldiers in a place to defend it.

PRESIDIÁRIO Y PRESIDÁRIO, *sm.* A criminal condemned to hard labour in a garrison.

PRESÍDIO, *sm.* 1. Garrison of soldiers, placed in it for its defence. 2. Fortress, a fortified place garrisoned by soldiers. 3. Assistance, aid, help, protection. 4. Place destined for chastising criminals; bridewell, house of correction.

PRESIDÍR, *va.* 1. To preside, to hold the first place in an assembly or community. 2. To occupy the chair of a professor in an university.

PRESÍLLA, *sf.* 1. A small string with which any thing is tied or fastened. 2. Loop in clothes which serves as a button-hole. 3. Sort of linen. *Presilla de un sombrero*, Loop for a hat.

PRESIÓN, *sf.* Pressure, the act of pressing or crushing any thing. V. *Presa* y *Prision*.

PRÉSO, SA, *s.* 1. Prisoner. 2. (Fam.) V *Pedo*.—*pp. irreg.* of *Prender*, Taken.

PRESÓNA, *sf.* (Ant.) V. *Persona*.

PREST, *sm.* V. *Pre*.

PRÉSTA, *sf.* (Ext.) (Bot.) Spearmint. Mentha viridis *L.*

PRESTACIÓN, *sf.* Act of lending or granting.

PRESTADÍZO, ZA, *a.* That may be lent or borrowed.

Prestádo, da, *a.* Lent. *Tomar prestado*, To borrow. *Dar prestado*, To lend. *De prestado*, For a short time; improperly.

Prestadór, ra, *s.* Lender; one who lends money at an usurious interest.

Prestaménte, *ad.* Speedily, promptly, quickly.

Prestaméra, *sf.* A kind of ecclesiastical benefice or sinecure which does not require personal attendance.

Prestamería, *sf.* Dignity of an ecclesiastical sinecure.

Prestaméro y Prestamísta, *sm.* Incumbent of a *prestamera*, or ecclesiastical sinecure; he who holds a benefice which does not require personal attendance.

Préstamo, *sm.* 1. Loan. V. *Empréstito.* 2. Portion or part of a dismembered ecclesiastical benefice. 3. Concession of the use of any thing for a certain time, on condition of its being restored.

Prestáncia, *sf.* Excellence. V. *Excelencia.*

Prestánte, *a.* V. *Excelente.*

Prestár, *va.* 1. To lend, to grant the use of any thing for a certain time. It is also used in the sense of to *borrow.* 2. To aid, to assist. 3. To give, to communicate. 4. (Arag.) To extend, to expand. 5. (For.) To pay the interest, duty, &c. which is ordered. *Prestar paciencia*, To bear with patience the frowns of fortune.—*vn.* 1. To be useful, to contribute to the attainment of any object. 2. To guard, to preserve; applied to God who lends all things.—*vr.* To offer one's self, to agree to any thing.

Préste, *sm.* Priest who celebrates the high mass. *Preste Juan*, Prester John, Abyssinian king.

Prestér, *sm.* 1. Hurricane, a violent storm. 2. Meteor like lightning.

Prestéza, *sf.* Quickness, promptitude.

Préstido, *sm.* V. *Empréstito.*

Prestigiadór, *sm.* Cheat, juggler, impostor.

Prestigiár, *va.* (Ant.) To cheat, to juggle.

Prestígio, *sm.* Prestigation, deceiving, juggling, playing legerdemain, illusion, imposture.

Prestigióso, sa, *a.* Deceitful, illusory.

Prestinónio, *sm.* Prebend for the maintenance of poor clergymen on condition of their saying five pater-nosters and five ave-marias; prestimony.

Prestíños, *sm. pl.* A sort of fritters baked in a pan.

Présto, ta, *a.* Quick, prompt, ready.

Présto, *ad.* Soon, quickly, speedily. *De presto*, Promptly, swiftly.

Presumíble, *a.* Presumable.

Presumidíco, ca; llo, lla; to, ta, *a. dim.* Confident, a little presumptuous.

Presumído, da, *a.* Presumptuous, arrogant, insolent.

Presumír, *va.* To presume, to suppose, to suspect.—*vn.* To boast, to arrogate.

Presunción, *sf.* 1. Presumption, supposition, conjecture. 2. Presumptuousness, blind and arrogant confidence; vanity. 3. Suspicion, imagining something ill without proof.

Presúnta, *sf.* V. *Presuncion.*

Presuntaménte, *ad.* Presumptively.

Presuntivaménte, *ad.* Conjecturally.

Presuntívo, va, *a.* Presumptive, taken by previous supposition.

Presúnto, ta, *pp. irreg.* of *Presumir*, Presumed.

Presuntuosaménte, *ad.* Presumptuously, arrogantly.

Presuntuóso, sa, *a.* Presumptuous, vain, arrogant.

Presuponér, *va.* To presuppose, to suppose as previous; to take for granted.

Presuposición, *sf.* Presupposition, supposition previously formed; pretext.

Presupuésto, *sm.* Motive, pretext, pretence. presupposed or presumed cost. V. *Supuesto*

Presúra, *sf.* 1. Pressure, oppression; anxiety. 2. Hurry, promptitude, nimbleness.

Presurosaménte, *ad.* Hastily, promptly.

Presuróso, sa, *a.* Hasty, prompt; light, nimble.

Pretál, *sm.* Poitrel, breast-plate or breast leather of a horse.

Pretendéncia, *sf.* V. *Pretension.*

Pretendér, *va.* 1. To pretend, to claim, to solicit. 2. To try, to attempt.

Pretendiénte, a, *s. y pa.* Pretender, one who pretends, candidate, solicitor.

Pretensión, *sf.* Pretension; claim.

Preténso, *sm.* V. *Pretension.*

Pretensór, *sm.* Pretender, claimant.

Preterición, *sf.* 1. Preterition, the act of going past; the state of being past. 2. (For.) Preterition, the act of omitting or not mentioning lawful children in a last will.

Preterír, *va.* To omit or not mention lawful children in a last will.

Pretérito, ta, *a.* 1. Preterit, past. 2. (Gram.) Applied to past tenses of verbs.

Pretermitír, *va.* To omit.

Preternaturál, *a.* Preternatural, different from the common order of nature.

Preternaturalizár, *va.* To pervert, to render preternatural.

Preternaturalménte, *ad.* Preternaturally.

Pretéxta, *sf.* A long gown with a purple border, worn by the magistrates of ancient Rome.

Pretextár y Pretextuár, *va.* To make use of a pretext or pretence.

Pretéxto, *sm.* Pretext, pretence, false allegation.

Pretíl, *sm.* Battlement, breast-work.

Pretína, *sf.* 1. Girdle, waistband; belt. 2. Waist; every thing which girds or surrounds.

Pretinázo, *sm.* Blow given with a girdle or belt.

Pretinéro, *sm.* One who makes girdles or belts.

Pretinílla, *sf.* A small belt or girdle.

Pretór, *sm.* Pretor, a magistrate in ancient Rome, and in Germany; black spot on tunny fish.

Pretória, *sf.* Dignity of a pretor. V. *Preturn*.

Pretoriál y Pretoriáno, na, *a.* Pretorian.

Pretoriénse, *a.* Belonging to the pretor's palace

Pretório, *sm.* Place in ancient Rome where the pretor resided and administered justice

Pretúra, *sf.* Pretorship, office of a pretor.

Prevalecér, *vn.* 1. To prevail, to outshine; to possess some superiority or advantage over others. 2. To take root; applied to plants.

Prevaleciénte, *pa.* Prevalent.

Prevalér, *vn.* To use any thing, or to avail one's self of it; to prevail.

Prevaricación, *sf.* Prevarication.

Prevaricadór, ra, *s.* Prevaricator.

Prevaricár, *va.* To prevaricate, to quibble, to shuffle, to cavil.—*vn.* To fail in one's word, duty, or judgment.

Prevaricáto, *sm.* (For.) Prevarication in a solicitor or advocate.

Prevencion, *sf.* 1. Disposition, preparation; previous arrangement. 2. Supply of provisions; sustenance, subsistence. 3. Foresight, forecast. 4. Advice, intimation, warning. 5. (Mil.) Police guard. *A' prevencion ó de prevencion*, By way of precaution.

Prevenidamente, *ad.* Beforehand, previously.

Prevenido, da, *a.* 1. Prepared, provided; plentiful, abundant. 2. Provident, careful, cautious.

Preveniente, *pa.* Predisposing.

Prevenir, *va.* 1. To prepare, to arrange or dispose beforehand. 2. To foresee, to foreknow. 3. To prevent, to anticipate. 4. To advise, to caution, to give notice. 5. To prevent, to impede. 6. To ingratiate one's-self. 7. To supervene.—*vr.* To be prepared; to be predisposed.

Preventivamente, *ad.* Preventively.

Preventivo, va, *a.* Preventive, tending to hinder; previously prepared or arranged.

Prever, *va.* To foresee, to foreknow.

Prevertir, *va.* To pervert. V. *Pervertir.*

Previlegiar, *va.* To privilege. V. *Privilegiar.*

Prévio, via, *a.* Previous, antecedent, going before, prior.

Prevision, *sf.* Foresight, foreknowledge, prescience.

Previsor, ra, *s.* One who foresees.

Prevendar, *va.* (Ant.) V. *Prendar.*

Prez, *sm.* 1. Honour or glory gained by some meritorious action. 2. Notoriety.

Priapísmo, *sm.* (Med.) Priapism, a disease.

Priésa, *sf.* 1. Haste, speed, expedition. V. *Prisa.* 2. Hurry, tumult, confusion. *Andar de priesa*, To be in a hurry. *Darse priesa*, To make haste. *De priesa*, Hastily, in a hurry.

Prietamente, *ad.* V. *Apretadamente.*

Prieto, ta, *a.* 1. Blackish, of a very dark colour. 2. Narrow-minded, miserable, illiberal. 3. (Arag.) Indigent, penurious.

Príma, *sf.* 1. Morning, the first three hours of the day. 2. Prime, one of the seven canonical hours. 3. (Mil.) The first quarter of the night from eight to eleven o'clock. 4. Treble, the first and most slender string of stringed instruments, and the acutest in sound. 5. (Com.) Premium, sum given for insurance.

Primacía, *sf.* 1. Priority, precedence in time; precedence in place. 2. Primateship, the dignity and office of a primate.

Primacial, *a.* Relating to primacy.

Primado, *sm.* 1. Primeness, the state of being first. 2. Primate, the chief ecclesiastic, superior to all bishops and archbishops of a country. 3. V. *Primazgo.*

Primado, da, *a.* Primary, first in intention; first in dignity. *Primada iglesia*, Primacial church.

Primal, la, *a.* Yearling, being a year old; applied to an ewe or goat.

Primal, *sm.* Lace, a plaited cord of silk.

Primamente, *ad.* Finely, handsomely.

Primariamente, *ad.* Principally, chiefly.

Primario, ria, *a.* Principal, chief of the first rate.—*sm.* Professor who lectures at the hour of prime.

Primavera, *sf.* 1. Spring, the season in which plants spring and vegetate. 2. Kind of flowered silk. 3. (Bot.) Primrose. Primula veris L. 4. (Met.) Season of beauty, health, and vigour.

Primaz, *sm.* Primate.

Primazgo, *sm.* Cousinship, relation of consanguinity which subsists among cousins.

Primearse, *vr.* To treat each other as cousins.

Primer, *a.* First. V. *Primero.*

Primera, *sf.* 1. Kind of game at cards. 2. Fruit season.

Primeramente, *ad.* First, in the first place.

Primería, *sf.* V. *Primacía.*

Primerizo, za, *a.* First, that antecedes or is preferred to other persons or things.

Primeriza, *sf.* Woman who has borne her first child.

Primero, ra, *a.* 1. First, the ordinal number of one. 2. Chief, principal. 3. Superior, most excellent. 4. Prior, former. *De buenas á primeras*, All at once, rashly, without reflection.

Primero, *ad.* First, rather, sooner. *Primero pediria limosna que prestado*, He would rather beg than borrow. *De primero*, At the beginning, before.

Primévo, va, *a.* Primeval, primevous; such as was first; original.

Primicério, ria, *a.* Principal, first in rank; first in one's line.

Primicério y Primiclério, *sm.* 1. Precentor, chanter, a dignitary in a cathedral church. 2. Chief of the university of *Salamanca.*

Primichon, *sm.* Skein of fine soft silk used for embroidering.

Primicial, *a.* Primitial, relating to first fruits.

Primícia, *sf.* 1. First fruits of any thing. 2. Offering of the first fruits. *Primicias*, First fruits; first production of the imagination or mind.

Primigénio, nia, *a.* Primogenial, first-born.

Primilla, *sf.* 1. Pardon of the first fault committed. 2. A little female cousin.

Primísimo, ma, *a. sup.* Uncommonly neat, extremely spruce.

Primitívo, va, *a.* Primitive, original.

Prímo, ma, *a.* 1. First, the ordinal number of one. *Primo hermano*, First cousin; (Met.) Similar, very like, resembling. 2. Great, excellent. 3. Skilful, dexterous. 4. Highly finished; applied to works of art. *Hilo primo*, Fine waxed thread used by shoemakers for closing.

Prímo, *sm.* 1. Cousin-german. 2. (Joc.) Black, negro. *Primos*, Cousins, an appellation given by the kings of Spain to the peers of the realm.

Primogénito, ta, *a.* y *s.* Primogenial, first-born.

Primogenitúra, *sf.* Primogeniture, seniority; the state of being first-born.

Primoprímus, *sm.* The first impulse or emotion of the mind.

Primór, *sm.* 1. Beauty; dexterity, ability; excellence. 2. Nicety, neatness of workmanship. 3. V. *Primacía.*

Primordial, *a.* Primordial, original; existing from the beginning.

Primorear, *vn.* To perform with elegance and neatness.

Primorosamente, *ad.* Finely, nicely, neatly.

Primoróso, sa, *a.* Neat, elegant, excellent, perfect; dexterous. *Artesano de manos primorosas*, A neat able workman.

Prímula, *sf.* (Bot.) Primrose, cowslip. Primula vulgaris et veris *L.*
Princésa, *sf.* 1. Princess, the consort or daughter of a prince. 2. In Spain, the apparent heiress to the crown.
Principáda, *sf.* Act of authority or superiority performed by him who has no right to execute it.
Principádo, *sm.* 1. Principality, the territory of a prince. 2. Dignity of a prince. 3. Pre-eminence, superior excellence.
Principál, *a.* 1. Principal, chief, of the first rate. 2. Illustrious, renowned, celebrated. *Casa principal*, Capital house, hotel. *Quarto principal*, Apartments in the first floor or story.
Principál, *sm.* 1. In a garrison, the main guard. 2. Principal, capital, stock.
Principalidád, *sf.* Principalness, the state of being principal; nobility.
Principalménte, *ad.* Principally, chiefly, above all.
Príncipe, *sm.* 1. Prince, a sovereign or chief ruler. 2. Son of a king, kinsman of a sovereign. 3. Appellation of honour granted by kings. *Príncipe de la sangre*, Prince of the blood. 4. With beemasters, the young or king bees not yet in a state to breed.
Principéla, *sf.* A sort of light camlet.
Principiadór, ra, *s.* Beginner, one who commences or begins.
Principiánte, *sm.* Beginner, an inexperienced attempter.
Principiár, *va.* To commence, to begin; to enter upon.
Principiéra, *sf.* A small metal saucepan in which broth is warmed.
Principíllo y Principíto, *sm.* A petty prince.
Princípio, *sm.* 1. Beginning, commencement. 2. Principle, original cause; ground of action, motive. 3. First position, fundamental truth. *Principios*, First course at table; preliminaries to a volume, as license, approbation, dedication, &c. 4. Element, constituent part. *Al principio, ó á los principios*, At the beginning. *Del principio al fin*, From beginning to end.
Principóte, *sm.* He who assumes a lofty air and importance.
Pringáda, *sf.* A slice of toasted bread steeped in gravy.
Pringár, *va.* 1. To baste, to drip lard or butter on meat which is roasting. 2. To stain with grease, to begrease; to scald with boiling fat; this is the punishment of slaves. 3. To wound; to ill-treat. 4. To meddle, to interfere; to take a share in. 5. (Fam.) To stain the reputation.—*vr.* To draw unlawful advantage from a thing entrusted to one's care.
Pringón, na, *a.* Nasty, dirty, greasy.
Pringón, *sm.* 1. The act of begreasing one's self. 2. Stain of grease.
Pringóso, sa, *a.* Greasy, fat.
Príngue, *s. com.* 1. Grease, lard. 2. Greasiness, oiliness, fatness. 3. The act of begreasing or staining with grease.
Pringuéra, *sf.* Dripping-pan.
Prióm, *sm.* 1. Prior, the superior of some convents or religious houses. 2. Rector, curate; prior in some cathedrals. 3. President of the *Consulado* in Andalusia, a court appointed to try and decide causes concerning trade and navigation.—*a.* Prior, preceding.
Prióra y Prioresa, *sf.* Prioress, the female superior of a convent of nuns.
Priorál, *a.* Belonging to a prior or prioress.
Prioráto, *sm.* 1. Priorship, dignity of a prior or prioress. 2. District of the jurisdiction of a prior. 3. Priory of Benedictines.
Prioráxgo y Prioradgo, *sm.* Priorship. V. *Priora.*
Prioridád, *sf.* Priority, the state of being first; precedence in time or place.
Prióste, *sm.* Steward of a brotherhood or confraternity.
Prísa, *sf.* Celerity, promptness with which any thing is executed. *A' toda prisa*, With the greatest promptitude. *Darse prisa*, To hurry one's self. *Estar de prisa*, To be much occupied.
Priscilianísmo, *sm.* The heresy of Priscillian.
Prísco, *sm.* A kind of peach.
Prisión, *sf.* 1. Seizure, capture, caption, apprehension. 2. Prisoner. 3. Prison, jail. 4. Commitment, imprisonment. 5. Darting or stooping of a hawk on its prey. 6. Bond, union; cement or cause of union. *Prisiones*, Chains, shackles, fetters.
Prisionéro, *sm.* 1. Prisoner, a soldier taken by an enemy. 2. Captivated by affection or passion.
Prísma, *sm.* (Geom.) Prism.
Prismático, ca, *a.* Prismatic, belonging to a prism.
Príste, *sm.* (Ict.) Saw-fish. Pristis *L.*
Prístino, na, *a.* Pristine, first, ancient, original.
Pristíños, *sm. pl.* Sort of fritters baked in a pan.
Prisuélo, *sm.* Muzzle, which serves to keep the mouths of ferrets shut.
Pritanéo, *sm.* Prytaneum, senate house in Athens.
Privación, *sf.* 1. Privation, want, the removal or destruction of any thing or quality. 2. The act of degrading from rank or office. 3. (Met.) Deprivation of any thing desired.
Priváda, *sf.* 1. Privy, place of retirement, necessary-house, water-closet. 2. Filth or dirt thrown into the street.
Privadaménte, *ad.* Privately, privily; separately.
Privadéro, *sm.* He who deprives or deposes.
Privádo, da, *a.* 1. Deprived, despoiled, destitute. 2. Privy, private; performed in the presence of a few.—*sm.* Favourite. V. *Valido.*
Privánza, *sf.* Favour, protection; familiar intercourse between a prince or great personage and a person of inferior rank.
Privár, *va.* 1. To deprive, to despoil; to dispossess of a public place or employment. 2. To prohibit, to interdict. 3. To suspend sensation.—*vn.* To enjoy the peculiar protection of a prince or great personage.—*vr.* To deprive one's self.
Privativaménte, *ad.* Singularly, privatively.
Privatívo, va, *a.* 1. Privative, causing privation. 2. Singular, particular, peculiar.
Privilegiadaménte, *ad.* In a privileged manner.
Privilegiár, *va.* To privilege, to grant a privilege.
Privilegiatívo, va, *a.* Containing a privilege.

Privilégio, *sm.* Privilege, immunity, peculiar advantage; grant. *Privilegio del fuero*, Exemption from secular jurisdiction, enjoyed by ecclesiastics.
Pro, *s. com.* Profit, benefit, advantage. V. *Provecho.* *Buena pro*, Much good may it do you. *En pro*, In favour of, for the benefit of. *Hombre de pro*, A worthy man.
Pro, *prep. lat.* Placed before verbs or nouns, as *promediar*, *prorata*, which see.
Próa, *sf.* (Naút.) Prow, head of the ship. *Por nuestra proa*, (Naút.) A-head of us. *Llevar la proa hácia la mar*, (Naút.) To stand off, to stand out to sea. *Poner la proa al rumbo*, (Naút.) To stand on the course.
Probabilidád, *sf.* Probability, likelihood; appearance of truth.
Probabilísimo, ma, *a. sup.* Most probable.
Probabilísmo, *sm.* Probability, doctrine of probable opinions.
Probabilísta, *sm.* One who acts upon probabilities.
Probáble, *a.* Probable, likely; capable of proof.
Probablemènte, *ad.* Probably.
Probación, *sf.* Proof, evidence. *Año de probacion*, The year of probation, the novitiate.
Probádo, da, *a.* Proved, tried.
Probadór, ra, *s.* Taster, one who tries or proves any thing; defender, advocate.
Probadúra y Probatúra, *sf.* Trial, the act of tasting or trying any thing.
Probánza, *sf.* Proof, evidence.
Probár, *va.* 1. To try, to examine into the quality of a thing. 2. To prove, to give evidence, to justify, to evince. 3. To taste, to try by the mouth. 4. With the preposition *á* and an infinitive mood, it signifies to attempt, to endeavour. *Probó á levantarse y no pudo*, He attempted or tried to rise and could not. —*vn.* To suit, to fit, to agree. *Me probó bien el pais*, The country agreed well with me.
Probática, *a.* Applied to a pool near Solomon's temple.
Probatívo, va; **y Probatório, ria**, *a.* Probatory, serving for trial.
Próbe, *a.* (Ant.) V. *Pobre.*
Probidád, *sf.* Probity, honesty, sincerity, veracity.
Probléma, *sm.* 1. Problem, a doubtful question proposed. 2. (Geom.) Practical proposition.
Problematicamènte, *ad.* Problematically.
Problemático, ca, *a.* Problematical, disputable, unsettled, uncertain.
Procacidád, *sf.* Procacity, petulance, insolence, forwardness.
Procáz, *a.* Procacious, petulant, forward, insolent, loose.
Procedènte, *a.* (Naút.) Having sailed.
Procedér, *sm.* Manner of proceeding, conduct, demeanour, management.—*vn.* 1. To proceed, to go on. 2. To issue, to be produced from. 3. To behave, to act, to conduct one's self. 4. To prosecute any design. 5. To carry on a judicial process. 6. To proceed by generation.
Procedído, *sm.* V. *Producto.*
Procedimiènto, *sm.* Procedure, manner of proceeding, conduct.
Proceloso, sa, *a.* Procellous, tempestuous, stormy.
Prócer, *a.* Tall, lofty, elevated.—*sm.* Person of the first distinction; one who occupies an exalted station, or is high in office.
Proceridád, *sf.* 1. Procerity, tallness, height of stature. 2. Elevation, eminence.
Procéro, *a.* V. *Procer.*
Procesádo, *a.* Applied to the writings in a process.
Procesál, *a.* Belonging to a process or lawsuit.
Procesár, *va.* To inform against, to pursue by law, to sue criminally.
Procesión, *sf.* 1. Procession, the act or state of one thing proceeding from another. 2. Train marching in ceremonious solemnity.
Procesionál, *a.* Processional or processionary; relating to processions.
Procesionalmènte, *ad.* Processionally.
Procesionário, *sm.* Book carried about in processions.
Procéso, *sm.* 1. Process, suit at law. 2. Judicial records concerning a lawsuit. *Error de proceso*, One who by ability, although convicted, evades the fine. 3. Progress. V. *Progreso.* *Proceso en infinito*, Procession of an endless series of things.
Procínto, *sm.* Procinct, complete preparation, preparation brought to the point of action.
Proción, *sm.* (Astr.) Procyon, a star.
Procláma, *sf.* Proclamation, publication, public notice, ban of marriage.
Proclamación, *sf.* 1. Proclamation, the publication of a decree by superior order. 2. Acclamation, public applause.
Proclamár, *va.* 1. To proclaim, to give public notice. 2. To bestow public praise, to shout.
Proclíve, *a.* Proclivous, inclining; disposed.
Proclividád, *sf.* Proclivity; propensity to evil.
Próco, *sm.* Wooer, suiter, lover.
Procónsul, *sm.* Proconsul, a magistrate in ancient Rome.
Proconsuládo, *sm.* Office of proconsul or viceconsul.
Proconsulár, *a.* Proconsular, viceconsular.
Procreación, *sf.* Procreation, generation.
Procreadór, ra, *s.* Procreator, generator.
Procreánte, *pa.* Procreating.
Procreár, *va.* To procreate, to generate, to produce.
Procronísmo, *sm.* Anachronism, anticipating an event.
Procúra, *sf.* (Arag.) Power of attorney.
Procuración, *sf.* 1. Care, diligence, careful management. 2. Power of attorney. 3. Place and office of an attorney or administrator. V. *Procuraduría.* 4. Fees exacted by prelates from such churches as are visited by them.
Procuradór, ra, *s.* 1. Procurer. 2. Attorney, one who takes upon himself the charge of other people's business. 3. Proctor, attorney at law, solicitor. 4. She who manages the affairs of a nunnery.
Procuraduría, *sf.* Attorney's office; the employment of an attorney.
Procuránte, *pa.* Solicitor, intendant.
Procurár, *va.* 1. To solicit, to adopt the necessary measures for attaining some end. 2. To act as an attorney.
Procurrènte, *sm.* Cape, headland; high land jutting out into the sea.
Prodición, *sf.* Prodition, treason, treachery.

Prodigalidád, *sf.* 1. Prodigality, profusion, extravagance, waste. 2. Plenty, abundance.

Prodigaménte, *ad.* Prodigally.

Prodigár, *va.* To waste, to lavish, to mispend.

Prodigiadór, *sm.* Prognosticator, foreknower, foreteller.

Prodígio, *sm.* Prodigy, portent, monster; any thing excellent or out of the ordinary course of nature; a marvel.

Prodigiosaménte, *ad.* Prodigiously, miraculously; beautifully. *Ella cantó prodigiosamente*, She sung charmingly.

Prodigiosidád, *sf.* Prodigiousness.

Prodigióso, sa, *a.* 1. Prodigious, marvellous, extraordinary. 2. Fine, exquisite, excellent.

Pródigo, ga, *a.* Prodigal, wasteful, lavish; liberal, generous, munificent.

Proditório, ria, *a.* Traitorous, treacherous, insidious.

Producción, *sf.* Production, the act of producing.

Producénte, *pa.* Generating, producing.

Producibilidád, *sf.* Producibleness.

Producíble, *a.* Producible, such as may be exhibited.

Producidór, ra, *s.* Producer, one that generates or produces.

Producír, *va.* 1. To produce, to bring forth, to engender. 2. (For.) To allege, to maintain, to exhibit. 3. To produce, as countries.

Productívo, va, *a.* Productive, having the power to produce.

Prodúcto, *sm.* 1. Product, something produced; such as grain, fruit, metals. 2. Proceed, produce. 3. (Arit.) Quantity arising from, or produced by, the multiplication of two or more numbers.—*pp. irreg.* of *producir*.

Proejár, *vn.* 1. To row against the wind or current. 2. To resist, to bear up under misfortunes.

Proél, *sm.* 1. (Naút.) The fore or headmost part of a ship. 2. (Naút.) Seaman stationed at the prow.

Proemiál, *a.* Proemial, preliminary, introductory.

Proémio, *sm.* Proem, preface, introduction.

Proéza, *sf.* Prowess, valour, bravery.

Profanación, *sf.* Profanation, the act of violating any thing sacred; irreverence to holy things or persons.

Profanadór, ra, *s.* Profaner, polluter, violator.

Profanaménte, *ad.* Profanely.

Profanamiénto, *sm.* V. *Profanacion.*

Profanár, *va.* 1. To profane, to violate; to treat sacred things or persons with irreverence. 2. To defile, to disgrace, to dishonour.

Profanidád, *sf.* 1. Profaneness, irreverence of what is sacred. 2. Extravagance in dress and outward show.

Profáno, na, *a.* 1. Profane, irreverent to sacred names or things. 2. Extravagant in dress and outward show. *Aquel vestido es muy profano*, That is a very extravagant dress.

Profazár, *va.* (Ant.) To calumniate, to libel.

Profecía, *sf.* 1. Prophecy, a supernatural knowledge of future events. 2. Prophecy, prediction; the declaration of something to come. 3. Conjecture, surmise.

Proferénte, *pa.* Pronouncer, profferer.

Proferír, *va.* To pronounce, to utter.—*vr.* To make an offer of doing something, to proffer.

Profesánte, *pa.* Professor.

Profesár, *va.* 1. To profess, to declare openly, to teach publicly an art or science. 2. To be admitted into any religious order by making the solemn vows; to profess, to exercise.

Profesión, *sf.* 1. Profession, calling, vocation, known employment. 2. Declaration, strong assurance. 3. Custom, habit.

Proféso, sa, *a.* Professed; applied to religious persons who have taken the solemn vows.

Profesór, *sm.* Professor, one who publicly teaches any art or science.

Proféta, *sm.* Prophet, one who tells future events.

Profetál, *a.* Relating to prophecy.

Profetár, *va.* To prophesy, to give predictions.

Profeticaménte, *ad.* Prophetically.

Profético, ca, *a.* Prophetic, prophetical; foreseeing or foretelling future events.

Profetísa, *sf.* Prophetess, a woman who foretels future events or prophecies.

Profetizánte, *pa.* Prophetizing, foretelling.

Profetizár, *va.* 1. To prophetize, to prophesy; to foretel future events, to predict. 2. To conjecture, to surmise.

Proficiénte, *a.* Proficient, making progress or advancement in any business.

Profícuo, cua, *a.* Proficuous, useful, advantageous.

Profijár, *va.* (Ant.) V. *Prohijar.*

Profiláctica, *sf.* Prophylactic, medicine which prevents diseases.

Profligár, *va.* To overcome, to destroy, to undo.

Prófugo, ga, *a.* Fugitive, vagabond.

Profundaménte, *ad.* Profoundly, deeply; highly, acutely.

Profundár, *va.* 1. To dig any thing deep, to make deep; to go far below the surface. 2. To discourse profoundly, to examine thoroughly.—*vn.* To profound, to dive, to penetrate deeply.

Profundidád, *sf.* 1. Profundity, profoundness, depth. 2. Height, excellence, grandeur; impenetrability; intensity.

Profundizár, *va.* To profound. V. *Profundar.*

Profúndo, da, *a.* 1. Profound, deep; descending far below the surface; low with respect to the neighbouring places. 2. Intense, dense; at full extent. 3. High, great. 4. Most humble, most submissive.

Profúndo, *sm.* 1. The sea, the deep. 2. (Poét.) Hell.

Profusaménte, *ad.* Profusely, lavishly, prodigally.

Profusión, *sf.* Profusion, lavishness.

Profúso, sa, *a.* 1. Profuse, over-abounding, plentiful. 2. Lavish, prodigal; extravagant in point of expense.

Progénie, *sf.* Progeny, race, generation, offspring.

Progenitór, *sm.* Progenitor, ancestor, forefather.

Progenitúra, *sf.* Primogeniture; progeny. V. *Progenie.*

Progimnásma, *sm.* Essay, attempt; a preparatory exercise.

Prográma, *sm.* 1. Anagram. V. *Anagrama.* 2. Program, a printed bill, inviting to an academical exercise, oration, or argument.

Progresión, *sf.* Progression, process; a regular and gradual advance.
Progresivamente, *ad.* Progressively, by gradual steps, by regular course. [advancing.
Progresivo, va, *a.* Progressive, going forward,
Progreso, *sm.* Progress, advancement.
Prohibente, *pa.* Prohibiter.
Prohibición, *sf.* Prohibition, forbiddance, interdict; the act of forbidding. [bid.
Prohibir, *va.* To prohibit, to interdict, to for-
Prohibitivo, va, *a.* Prohibitory, forbidding.
Prohibitorio, ria, *a.* Prohibitory.
Prohidiar, *va.* (Ant.) V. *Porfiar.*
Prohijación, *sf.* V. *Prohijamiento.*
Prohijador, *sm.* Adopter, he that gives some one by choice the rights of a son.
Prohijamiento, *sm.* Adoption, the act of adopting; the state of being adopted.
Prohijar, *va.* 1. To adopt, to take a son by choice; to make him a son who is not so by birth. 2. To ascribe, to attribute, to impute.
Próis, *sm.* (Naút.) Breast-fast, a rope with which a ship is fastened to the shore.
Proiza, *sf.* (Naút.) Cable at the head of a ship attached to the anchor.
Prolación, *sf.* Prolation, pronunciation, utterance.
Próle, *sf.* Issue, offspring, progeny.
Prolegómeno, *sm.* Prolegomena, previous discourse; introductory observations.
Proletário, ria, *a.* Miserable, wretched; applied to authors.
Prolífero, ra, *a.* Prolific.
Prolífico, ca, *a.* Prolific, fruitful, generative, productive.
Prolixamente, *ad.* Prolixly, tediously.
Prolixidád, *sf.* 1. Prolixity, tediousness; excessive delay in the performance of a thing. 2. Minute attention to trifles; trifling nicety.
Prolíxo, xa, *a.* 1. Prolix, tedious. 2. Excessively careful, triflingly nice. 3. Troublesome, impertinent, importune.
Prólogo, *sm.* 1. Prologue, preface; introduction to any discourse or performance. 2. Prologue, something spoken before the entrance of the actors of a play.
Prologuísta, *sm.* Writer of prologues.
Prolónga, *sf.* (Artil.) Rope which ties the carriage of a cannon when passing difficult places.
Prolongación, *sf.* Prolongation, the act of lengthening; delay to a longer time.
Prolongadamente, *ad.* Tardily, in a dilatory manner.
Prolongádo, da, *a.* Prolonged, extended.
Prolongador, ra, *s.* One who prolongs or delays any thing.
Prolongamiento, *sm.* Delay. V. *Prolongacion.*
Prolongár, *va.* To prolong, to protract, to lengthen, to stretch out; to make endure.—*vr.* (Naút.) To go along-side. *Prolongarse á la costa,* (Naút.) To range along the shore.
Prolóquio, *sm.* Maxim, axiom. [*sion.*
Prolusión, *sf.* Prolusion, prelude. V. *Prelu-*
Promediár, *va.* To divide into equal parts, to share equally.—*vn.* To mediate, to form by mediation; to interpose in a friendly manner.
Promédio, *sm.* Middle, the part equally distant from the two extremities.

Proméza, *sf.* Promise, declaration of some benefit to be conferred; pious offering. [mises.
Prometedór, ra, *s.* Promiser, one who pro-
Prometér, *va.* 1. To promise, to make declaration of some benefit to be conferred. 2. To asever, to assure, to insure; used menacing. —*vr.* To flatter one's self, to expect with some degree of confidence. 2. To devote one's self to the service or worship of God. 3. To give a promise of marriage.
Prometído, *sm.* 1. Promise. 2. Outbidding, over-bidding.
Prometiénte, *pa.* Promising; assurer.
Prometimiénto, *sm.* Promise.
Prominéncia, *sf.* Prominence, protuberance.
Prominénte, *a.* Prominent, protuberant; jutting out.
Promiscuamente, *ad.* Promiscuously.
Promíscuo, cua, *a.* Promiscuous, confusedly mingled; ambiguous.
Promisión, *sf.* Promise, the act of promising. *Tierra de promision,* Land of promise.
Promisório, ria, *a.* Promissory, containing a promise.
Promoción, *sf.* Promotion, advancement, encouragement, preferment.
Promontório, *sm.* 1. Promontory, head-land, cape. 2. Any thing bulky and unwieldy; an impediment, obstruction.
Promotór, *sm.* Promoter, advancer, forwarder.
Promovedór, ra, *s.* Promoter, one who promotes or advances. [tion.
Promovéndo, *sm.* He who aspires to promo-
Promovér, *va.* 1. To promote, to advance. 2. To raise to a higher dignity or employment.
Promulgación, *sf.* Promulgation, the act of publishing or promulging.
Promulgadór, ra, *s.* Promulger, publisher, promulgator.
Promulgár, *va.* To promulge, to promulgate, to publish.
Proneidád, *sf.* Proneness, inclination, disposition, propensity.
Próno, na, *a.* 1. Prone, bending downward; too much inclined. 2. Propense, inclined, disposed.
Pronómbre, *sm.* (Gram.) Pronoun, a word used instead of names or nouns.
Pronosticación, *sf.* Prognostication, the prediction of future events.
Pronosticadór, ra, *s.* Foreteller, prognosticator. [future events.
Pronosticár, *va.* To prognosticate, to predict
Pronóstico, *sm.* 1. Prognostic, prediction, divination. 2. Almanac or calendar, published by astrologers. 3. (Med.) Signs indicating the duration and termination of a disease.—ca, *a.* Prognostic.
Prontaménte, *ad.* Promptly.
Prontéza, *sf.* Promptitude, promptness.
Prontitúd, *sf.* 1. Promptitude, promptness. 2. Readiness or liveliness of wit, quickness of fancy.
Prónto, ta, *a.* Prompt, quick, ready.—*Prónto,* *sm.* A sudden emotion of the mind, a quick motion. *De prónto,* *ad.* Suddenly, hastily. *Por el pronto,* Provisionally, temporarily. *Primer pronto,* First movement.
Prontuário, *sm.* Memorandum-book; a book

containing various remarks, observations, or annotations.

Prónuba, *sf.* (Poét.) Bridemaid, goddess of wedlock.

Pronunciación y Pronúncia, *sf.* Pronunciation, the act of uttering or pronouncing; publication.

Pronunciadór, ra, *s.* Publisher, pronouncer.

Pronunciamiénto, *sm.* (For.) Publication.

Pronunciár, *va.* To pronounce, to utter, to announce, to publish judgment; to articulate letters or words.

Propagación, *sf.* Propagation, continuance or diffusion by generation or successive production; extension.

Propagadór, ra, *s.* Propagator, one who propagates.

Propagánda, *sf.* College or public board at Rome, consisting of cardinals, peculiarly charged with maintaining and propagating the Roman catholic faith.

Propagár, *va.* 1. To propagate, to multiply by way of generation. 2. To diffuse, to extend. 3. To dilate, to increase.

Propagatívo, va, *a.* That which propagates.

Propaládia, *sf.* Title of a play.

Propalár, *va.* To publish, to divulge.

Propáo, *sm.* (Naút.) Breast-work. [parting.

Propartída, *sf.* Time approaching that of de-

Propasár, *va.* To go beyond, to transgress. *Propasar la estima*, (Naút.) To outrun the reckoning.—*vr.* To be deficient in politeness or good breeding.

Propensaménte, *ad.* In a propense manner, with inclination or propension.

Propensión, *sf.* Propension, propensity, inclination.

Propénso, sa, *a.* Propense, inclined, disposed.

Propiaménte, *ad.* Properly, with propriety.

Propiciación, *sf.* 1. Propitiation, atonement; the offering by which propitiousness is obtained. 2. Act of making propitious.

Propiciadór, ra, *s.* Propitiator, one that propitiates.

Propiciaménte, *ad.* Propitiously.

Propiciár, *va.* To propitiate, to induce to favour, to conciliate.

Propiciatório, ria, *a.* Propitiatory, having the power of making propitious.—*sm.* Propitiatory, mercy-seat; the covering of the ark of the covenant in which the tables of the law were deposited.

Propício, cia, *a.* Propitious, benign, kind, favourable.

Propiedád, *sf.* 1. Dominion, possession. V. *Dominio.* 2. Right of property, in contradistinction to the use or usufruct. 3. Landed estate or property. 4. Propriety, property, particular quality. 5. Habit, custom. 6. Propensity, inclination. 7. Close imitation. 8. Property, or wealth, viciously enjoyed by those who took vows of religious poverty. 9. Musical propriety. 10. (Fil.) V. *Propio.*

Propiénda, *sf.* List nailed to the sides of a quilting or embroidering frame.

Proprietariaménte, *ad.* With the right of property.

Proprietário, ria, *a.* Proprietary, invested with the right of property; belonging with full right of property.—*s.* 1. Proprietary, religious who sins against the vow of poverty. 2. Proprietor.

Propína, *sf.* Present, entertainment, salary, pay; perquisite, fees of office.

Propinár, *va.* To invite to drink, to present a glass of wine or liquor.

Propinquidád, *sf.* Propinquity, proximity.

Propínquo, qua, *a.* Near, contiguous.

Própio, pia, *a.* 1. Proper, peculiar, belonging to any one; fit, convenient. 2. V. *Consegüente y Mismo.* 3. Resembling, like, similar.—*Própio*, *sm.* 1. (Fil.) Proper, peculiar or distinctive quality; characteristic property of a class, genus, or species. 2. Express, messenger, postman. *Própio marte ó ingenio*, Of one's own efforts. *Al propio*, Properly. *Propios*, Lands, estates, &c. belonging to a city or other corporation, the proceeds whereof are applied to defray the public expense.

Propóleos, *sm.* Glutinous substance with which bees cover their hives before they begin to work.

Proponedór, ra, *s.* Proposer, offerer.

Proponénte, *pa.* Proposer, representing.

Proponér, *va.* 1. To propose, to represent. 2. To resolve, to determine. 3. To present; to propose the means.

Proponíble, *a.* Proposable, capable of being proposed.

Proporción, *sf.* 1. Proportion, comparative relation of one thing to another. 2. Symmetry, adaptation of one thing to another; aptitude, fulness. 3. Similarity of arguments and reasons. *A' proporcion*, Conformably, proportionally.

Proporcionáble, *a.* Proportionable. V. *Proporcionado.*

Proporcionadaménte y Proporcionableménte, *ad.* Proportionably, in a stated degree.

Proporcionádo, da, *a.* Proportionate, regular, competent, fit for the purpose.

Proporcionál, *a.* Proportional.

Proporcionalidád, *sf.* V. *Proporcion.*

Proporcionalménte, *ad.* Proportionally.

Proporcionár, *va.* 1. To proportion, to form symmetrically. 2. To adjust, to adapt.—*vr.* To prepare one's self for any design.

Proposición, *sf.* 1. Proposition, the act of proposing. 2. Proposal, scheme or design offered to consideration for acceptance. 3. Opinion, judgment.

Propósito, *sm.* 1. Purpose, design, intention. 2. Purport, tendency of a writing or discourse. *A' proposito*, For the purpose. *De propósito*, On purpose, purposely. *Fuera de propósito*, Untimely, not to the purpose, foreign to the subject. *Volvamos al proposito*, Let us return to the point in question.

Propretór, *sm.* Roman magistrate.

Próprio, a, *a.* Proper; similar. V. *Propio.*—*sm.* V. *Propiedad. Al proprio*, Properly, with propriety.

Propuésta, *sf.* 1. Proposal, proposition. 2. Representation, declaration. 3. Application for employment. [ed.

Propuésto, ta, *pp. irreg.* of *proponer*, Propos-

Propugnáculo, *sm.* 1. Fortress, a strong or fortified place. 2. (Met.) Bulwark, defence, support.

Propúlsa y Propulsión, *sf.* The act of repelling the enemy.

Propulsíva, *sf.* V. *Propulsa.*

Próra, *sf.* (Naút.) Prow of a ship. V. *Proa.*

Proráta, *sf.* Quota, a share or portion assigned to each contribuent.

Prorateár, *va.* To divide a quantity into certain shares.

Proratéo, *sm.* Division into certain shares, distribution.

Prórroga y Prorogación, *sf.* Prorogation, the state of lengthening out to a distant time; prolongation.

Prorogáble, *a.* Capable of being prorogued.

Prorogár, *va.* To prorogue, to put off, to adjourn.

Prorrumpír, *vn.* To burst forth, to burst out into cries and lamentations.

Prósa, *sf.* 1. Prose, language not restrained to harmonic sounds or set number of syllables. 2. Tedious conversation, dull absurd speech. 3. Prose chanted after mass.

Prosadór, *sm.* A sarcastic speaker, a malicious babbler.

Prosápia, *sf.* Race, a generation of people.

Prosáyco, ca, *a.* Prosaic, written in prose; belonging to prose.

Proscénio, *sm.* Proscenium, place on the stage between the scene and the orchestra.

Proscribír, *va.* To proscribe, to censure capitally; to doom to destruction.

Proscripción, *sf.* Proscription, banishment, outlawry.

Proscrípto, ta, *pp. irreg.* Proscribed.

Prosecución, *sf.* Prosecution, pursuit, endeavour to carry on any thing.

Proseguíble, *a.* Pursuable.

Proseguimiénto, *sm.* V. *Prosecucion.*

Proseguír, *va.* To pursue, to follow, to continue any thing begun.

Prosélito, *sm.* Proselyte, convert.

Proseyánte, *sm.* Pursuivant, king's messenger. V. *Persevante.*

Prosísta, *sm.* 1. Author who writes in prose. 2. Prattler, babbler, idle talker.

Prósit, (Lat.) Much good may it do you.

Prosíta, *sf.* Short discourse and in prose.

Prosódia, *sf.* 1. Prosody, the part of grammar which teaches the sound and quantity of syllables, and the measures of verse. 2. Loquacity, idle talk. 3. Poetry.

Prosopografía, *sf.* Description of a person's physiognomy.

Prosopopéya, *sf.* 1. Prosopopœia, personification; a figure by which things are made persons. 2. Splendour, pageantry.

Prospécto, *sm.* Prospectus, proposals and conditions for any work.

Prosperaménte, *ad.* Prosperously, luckily.

Prosperár, *va.* To prosper, to make happy; to favour.—*vn.* To be prosperous.

Prosperidád, *sf.* Prosperity, good fortune.

Próspero, ra, *a.* Prosperous, successful, fortunate.

Prosternación, *sf.* Prosternation, profound reverence and humiliation.

Prostílo, *a.* (Arq.) Prostyle, having only pillars in front.

Prostitución, *sf.* Prostitution, the act of setting or being set to sale for vile purposes; the life of a strumpet.

Prostituír, *va.* To prostitute, to expose to crimes for a reward; to expose on vile terms.

Prostitúta, *sf.* Prostitute, woman of the town.

Prostitúto, ta, *pp. irreg.* of *prostituir*, Prostituted.

Prostrár, *va.* (Ant.) V. *Postrar.*

Prótasis, *sf.* First piece of a dramatic poem.

Protección, *sf.* Protection, support, favour, shelter.

Protectór, ra, *s.* 1. Protector, protectress, defender. 2. Steward of a community, charged with maintaining its interest.

Protectoría, *sf.* Protectorship, protectorate; office of a protector.

Protectório, ria, *a.* Relating to a protector.

Protectríz y Protectóra, *sf.* Protectress, a woman that protects.

Protegér, *va.* To protect, to defend, to favour.

Proterbaménte, *ad.* Forwardly, insolently, arrogantly.

Protérvia y Protervidád, *sf.* Insolence, arrogance; peevishness, frowardness, stubbornness.

Protérvo, va, *a.* Stubborn, peevish, arrogant, insolent.

Protésta, *sf.* 1. (For.) Protest, a solemn declaration made for the purpose of preserving one's right. 2. A solemn promise, asseveration, or assurance.

Protestación, *sf.* 1. Protestation, a solemn declaration of resolution, fact, or opinion. 2. Threat, menace. 3. (For.) V. *Protesta.*

Protestánte, *sm.* Protestant, a general name for all persons who believe Christianity, but oppose the Roman catholic church.

Protestár, *va.* 1. To give a solemn declaration of opinion or resolution. 2. To assure, to assever. 3. To threaten, to menace. 4. To make a public declaration of faith and belief. 5. (For.) To make a solemn declaration for the purpose of preserving one's right. *Protestar una letra*, To protest a bill of exchange.

Protestatívo, va, *a.* That which protests.

Protésto, *sm.* 1. Protest of a bill. 2. V. *Protesta. Protesto la fuerza*, I yield to your persuasiveness.

Proto, A Greek word used in composition, signifying first; often applied jocularly as *protopobre*, *protodiablo*, &c.

Protoalbéytar, *sm.* First or chief veterinary surgeon, head of the veterinary college who attends the royal horses and examines students in the veterinary art.

Protoalbeyteráto, *sm.* Tribunal or college for examining veterinary surgeons previously to licensing them to practise.

Protocolár y Protocolizár, *va.* To place in the protocole.

Protocólo, *sm.* A judicial record; a book in which notaries enter their minutes or rough drafts.

Protomártir, *sm.* Protomartyr, St. Stephen.

Protomedicáto, *sm.* 1. Tribunal or college of king's physicians, where students of medicine are examined and licensed. 2. Office of a first or royal physician.

Protomédico, *sm.* First physician, one of the three physicians to the king.

Protonotário, *sm.* Prothonotary.

Prototípo, *sm.* Prototype, original.

Protuberáncia, *sf.* Protuberance, prominence.

Provécho, *sm.* 1. Profit, benefit, advantage, utility. 2. Proficiency, progress; advancement in arts, sciences, or virtues. *Hombre de provecho*, An useful man. *Ser de provecho*, To be useful or profitable. *Buen provecho*, Much good may it do you; used at eating or drink-[ing.

Provechosaménte, *ad.* Profitably.

Provechóso, sa, *a.* Profitable, beneficial.

Provécto, ta, *a.* Advanced in years, learning, or other things; experienced.

Proveedór, ra, *s.* Purveyor, contractor.

Proveeduría, *sf.* 1. Storehouse where provisions are kept and distributed. 2. Employment and office of a purveyor.

Proveér, *va.* 1. To supply with provisions, to provide provisions for an army. 2. To dispose, to adjust. 3. To confer a dignity or employment. 4. To decree, to doom by a decree. 5. To minister, to supply any one with the necessaries of life, to maintain.—*vr.* To ease the body.

Proveído, *sm.* Judgment, sentence, decree.

Proveimiénto, *sm.* Supply, the act of providing or supplying with provisions.

Provéna, *sf.* Provine, a branch of vine laid in the ground to take root.

Proveniénte, *pa.* Proceeding, originating in.

Provenír, *vn.* To arise, to proceed; to take rise or origin from, to originate in.

Provénto, *sm.* Product, rent.

Proverbiadór, *sm.* Collector of proverbs.

Proverbiál, *a.* Proverbial, mentioned in a proverb, resembling or suitable to a proverb.

Proverbialménte, *ad.* Proverbially.

Proverbiár, *vn.* To use proverbs.

Provérbio, *sm.* 1. Proverb, a short sentence frequently repeated by the people. 2. Prophecy, prediction from certain words. *Proverbios*, Book of proverbs, a canonical book of the Old Testament. [proverbs.

Proverbísta, *s.* One attached to the use of

Providaménte, *ad.* Providently, carefully.

Providéncia, *s.* 1. Providence, foresight, timely care, forecast. 2. Divine Providence, the care of God over created beings; divine superintendence. 3. State or order of things. *Auto de providencia*, Interlocutory decree; provisional judgment.

Providenciál, *a.* Providential, effected by providence; referrible to providence.

Providencialménte, *ad.* Providentially, provisionally.

Providenciár, *va.* To ordain, to command.

Providénte, *a.* Provident, prudent, careful.

Próvido, da, *a.* Provident, careful, diligent.

Província, *sf.* 1. Province, part of a country. 2. A certain number of convents under the direction of a provincial. 3. Provincial court appointed to try and decide civil causes. 4. The province, proper office or business of any one. [vince.

Provinciál, *a.* Provincial, relating to a pro-

Provinciál, *sm.* 1. Provincial, a dignitary of the Roman catholic church who superintends and governs a certain number of convents. 2. Pasquinade, a libel.

Provincialáto, *sm.* Place, dignity, or office of a provincial, duration of this office.

Provinciáno, na, *a.* y *s.* Native of Guipuzcoa.

Provisión, *sf.* 1. Store of provisions collected for use. 2. Decree or sentence issued by some Spanish tribunals in the king's name. 3. Title or instrument, by virtue whereof an incumbent holds his benefice. 4. Act of conferring some employment or office.

Provisionál, *a.* Provisional.

Provisionalménte, *ad.* Provisionally.

Províso ó al Províso, *ad.* Upon the spot, immediately, instantly.

Provisór, ra, *s.* 1. Provisor, provider, one who provides or procures. V. *Proveedor*. 2. Vicar-general, an ecclesiastical judge, who decides all ecclesiastical matters by virtue of the power vested in him by the bishop. [dore.

Provisoráto, *sm.* Office of provider or provo-

Provisoría, *sf.* 1. Store-room, where provisions are kept; pantry. 2. Place or office of a *provisor* or vicar-general.

Provisório, ria, *a.* Provisional, temporarily established; provided for present need.

Provísto, ta, *a.* Provided with a benefice.

Provocación, *sf.* 1. Provocation, the act of provoking or raising anger or displeasure. 2. Cause, or motive of anger.

Provocadór, ra, *s.* Provoker, one that raises anger; causer, promoter.

Provocár, *va.* 1. To provoke, to rouse, to excite. 2. To anger, to enrage. 3. To vomit, to throw up from the stomach. 4. To facilitate, to promote. 5. To move, to excite.

Provocatívo, va, *a.* 1. Provocative, exciting, inducing. 2. Quarrelsome, provoking.

Proximaménte, *ad.* Nearly, immediately, without intervention.

Proximidád, *sf.* 1. Proximity, nearness, vicinity. 2. Relation, kindred by birth.

Próximo, ma, *a.* Next, nearest.

Próximo, *sm.* 1. Fellow-creature; neighbour. 2. (Joc.) An ass. *No tener próximo*, To be unfeeling or cruel.

Proyección, *sf.* Projection, the appearance of one or more objects on a perspective plane.

Proyectár, *va.* To project, to scheme, to form in the mind, to contrive.

Proyectísta, *sm.* Projector, schemer.

Proyécto, *sm.* Project, scheme, plan, design.

Proyécto, ta, *a.* Projected, expanded, dilated.

Proyectúra, *sf.* Part of a building which projects or juts out beyond the wall. V. *Vuelo*.

Prudéncia, *sf.* 1. Prudence, wisdom; applied to practice. 2. Temperance, moderation.

Prudenciál, *a.* Prudential, eligible on the principles of prudence.

Prudencialménte, *ad.* Prudentially.

Prudénte, *a.* Prudent, practically wise.

Prudenteménte, *ad.* Prudently.

Pruéba, *sf.* 1. Proof, reason, argument, evidence. 2. Sign, token, indication. 3. Experiment, essay, attempt. 4. Relish, taste; a small quantity of any eatable. 5. (Imp.) Proof, rough impression of a sheet on which corrections are to be made. 6. With tailors, fitting on of basted clothes. *A prueba de bomba*, Bomb-proof; satisfactorily. *Tomar un criado á prueba*, To take a servant on liking or trial. *A' prueba y estése*, (Met.) Stopped or delayed without being despatched. *De prueba*, Firm, solid. *Pruebas*, Proof, evidence,

Pruína, *sf.* White frost.

Prúna, *sf.* (Bot.) Plum.

Prurito, *sm.* 1. Prurience, pruriency, itching. 2. Great desire or appetite.

Prusiáte, *sm.* (Quím.) Prussiate, salt formed of Prussic acid with a base.

Pú, *sf.* Excrements of children.—*interj.* An exclamation of disgust at a bad smell.

Púa, *sf.* 1. Sharp point, prickle. 2. Shoot of a tree engrafted in another. 3. Painful sensation. 4. (Fam.) V. *Pú.* 5. Weaver's reed. 6. Subtlety, acuteness. *Es buena pua*, He is a keen blade.

Pubertád y Pubescéncia, *sf.* Puberty, age of maturity.

Pubescér, *vn.* To attain the age of puberty.

Pública, *sf.* In universities, a lecture before the examination for the degree of Doctor.

Publicación, *sf.* Publication, the act of publishing or proclaiming.

Publicadór, ra, *s.* Publisher, one who publishes or proclaims.

Publicaménte, *ad.* Publicly.

Publicáno, *sm.* Roman toll-gatherer.

Publicár, *va.* 1. To publish, to render public, to proclaim; to manifest before the public; to print a book. 2. To reveal, to lay open, to disclose.

Publicáta, *sf.* Certificate of publication.

Publicidád, *sf.* 1. Publicity, the state of being public. 2. Place of general resort, a public place. *En publicidad*, Publicly.

Público, ca, *a.* 1. Public, notorious. 2. Vulgar, common.

Público, *sm.* Public, the general body of a nation. *En público*, Publicly.

Pucéla, *sf.* V. *Doncella.*

Puceláña, *sf.* Potter's earth, a kind of argillaceous earth, very adhesive.

Puchád/a, *sf.* A kind of cataplasm, chiefly consisting of flour.

Púches, *sf. pl.* Sort of fritters. V. *Gachas.*

Puchecílla, *sf.* A thin batter made of flour and water.

Puchéra, *sf.* Pitcher. V. *Olla.*

Pucherico, llo, y to, *sm. dim.* Pipkin. *Pucherito*, Crying grimaces of children.

Puchéro, *sm.* 1. A glazed earthen pot. 2. Meat boiled in an earthen pot. 3. Daily food, regular aliment. 4. Grimace or distortion of the face which precedes crying. *Meter la cabeza en el puchero*, To equivocate and maintain an opinion obstinately.

Pudéndo, da, *a.* Bashful, shy.

Pudéndo, *sm.* Pudendum.

Pudibúndo, da, *a.* (Joc.) Shamefaced, modest.

Pudicícia, *sf.* Pudicity, chastity.

Púdico, ca, *a.* Chaste, modest.

Pudiénte, *a.* Powerful, rich, opulent.

Pudín, *sm.* Pudding.

Pudór, *sm.* Bashfulness, modesty, shyness.

Pudrición, *sf.* Rottenness, the act of rotting or turning into corruption.

Pudridéro, *sm.* 1. Rotting-place, where any thing is put to rot; fermenting pit. 2. Royal vault or cemetery in the monastery at Escurial. [for making paper.

Pudridór, *sm.* Vessel in which rags are steeped

Pudrigório, *sm.* A sickly infirm man.

Pudrimiénto, *sm.* Rottenness. V. *Pudricion.*

Pudrír, *va.* To rot, to make putrid, to bring to corruption.—*vn.* To rot, to be rotten.—*vr.* To be broken-hearted, to die with grief; to become rotten, to decay.

Puébla, *sf.* 1. Seed which a gardener sows of every kind of vegetable. 2. V. *Poblacion.*

Puéblo, *sm.* 1. Town, village; any place that is peopled or inhabited. 2. Population, the inhabitants of a place. 3. Common people.

Puéca, *sf.* Slut; term of slight contempt for a woman.

Puénte, *s.* 1. Bridge, a building raised over water for the convenience of passage. *Puente volante*, Flying-bridge. *Puente levadiza*, Drawbridge. 2. (Naút.) Deck of a ship. *Puente á la oreja*, (Naút.) Flush-deck. *Puente de enjaretada*, (Naút.) Grating deck. *Puente de redes*, (Naút.) Netting deck. 3. (Mús.) Bridge, the supporter of the strings in stringed instruments. 4. Transom, lintel, any cross-beam.

Puentecílla y Puentezuéla, *sf.* A little bridge

Puérca, *sf.* 1. Sow, a female pig. 2. Nut of a screw. 3. Millepede, an insect. *Puércas*, Scrofulous swellings, glandulous tumours.

Puercaménte, *ad.* Dirtily, rudely.

Puérco, ca, *a.* Nasty, filthy, dirty; rude.

Puérco, *sm.* 1. Hog, a domestic animal. 2. Wild boar. V. *Jabali.* *Puerco espin*, Porcupine; chevaux-de-frise. 3. A brutish ill-bred person. [tween infancy and manhood.

Puerícia, *sf.* Boyhood, the middle state be-

Pueríl, *a.* Boyish, childish, puerile.

Puerilidád, *sf.* Puerility, boyishness; trifle.

Puerilménte, *ad.* Puerilely, childishly.

Puerpério, *sm.* Child-birth, travail, labour.

Puerquezuéla, *sf.* Slut, dirty wench.

Puerquezuélo, *sm. dim.* Little pig.

Puérro, *sm.* (Bot.) Leek. Allium porum *L.*

Puérta, *sf.* 1. Door, or doorway, gateway, an opening in a wall to give entrance. 2. Beginning or commencement of an undertaking. 3. Door, gate, that which serves to stop any passage. 4. Duty paid at the entrance of the gates in towns. 5. Narrow pass between mountains. *Puerta de dos hojas*, Folding-door. *Puerta trasera*, Back door; (Joc.) Anus. *Llamar á la puerta*, To knock at the door. *Estar por puertas*, To be reduced to beggary. *A' esotra puerta*, That wont do, no objections can persuade me to the contrary.

Puertaventána, *sf.* Door with a window in it.

Puertecíca, lla, *sf.* A small door.

Puertecíllo, *sm.* A small port.

Puérto, *sm.* 1. Port, harbour; a safe station for ships. 2. Pass, a narrow road through mountains. 3. Orifice of the womb. 4. Asylum, shelter, refuge. 5. Dam in a river. *Puerto Otomano*, Ottoman Porte.

Púes, *particul.* 1. Then, therefore. 2. In as much as; since. 3. Sure, surely; certainly; aye, yes. 4. (Ant.) V. *Despues.*

Púes, *interj.* Well then. *¿ Y pues?* Well, and what of that? *Pues sí* (Irón.) Yes, indeed!

Puésta, *sf.* 1. V. *Posta.* 2. Resigning a hand of cards. *Puesta de sol*, Sunsetting. *A' puesta ó puestas del sol*, At sunsetting.

Puésto, *sm.* 1. Place or space occupied; particular spot. 2. Shop or place where any thing is sold by retail. 3. Post, employment, dignity, office. 4. State, condition. 5. House in which stallions are kept and let to mares. 6. (Mil.) Barrack for soldiers. 7. Apartment or bed for child-birth. 8. Place covered with bushes to conceal sportsmen.

Puésto, ta, *pp. irreg.* of *poner*, Put.

Puésto, *ad.* Because, for this reason that, on this account that. *Puesto que*, Although. V. *Aunque.*

Púf, *interj.* A word expressive of the unpleasant sensation of a bad smell.

Púga, *sf.* (Gal.) V. *Pua.*

Púgil, *sm.* Prize-fighter, boxer, bruiser, pugilist.

Pugilár, *sm.* Hebrew manual of the scriptures used in synagogues.

Púgna, *sf.* Combat, conflict, battle.

Pugnacidád, *sf.* Pugnacity, quarrelsomeness; inclination to fight.

Pugnánte, *pa.* Fighting, opposing.

Pugnár, *vn.* To fight, to combat, to contend; to solicit earnestly; to rival.

Pugnáz, *a.* Pugnacious, quarrelsome, inclined to fight.

Púja, *sf.* 1. Outbidding at a public sale, offer of a higher price. 2. Superiority in prowess or address. *Sacar de la puja*, To outwit, to conquer by stratagem or address.

Pujadéro, ra, *a.* That which might be outbid, or enhanced.

Pujadór, ra, *s.* Outbidder, one who bids or offers a higher price than another.

Pujáme y Pujámen, *sm.* (Naút.) Under part of the sails.

Pujamiénto, *sm.* Flow or violent agitation of the blood or humours.

Pujánte, *a.* Powerful, strong, predominant.

Pujánza, *sf.* Power, might, strength.

Pujár, *vn.* 1. To rise, to exceed in height. 2. To endeavour, to be eager in the pursuit of a thing.—*va.* 1. To outbid, to bid more than another. 2. To labour under an impediment of speech, to falter.

Pujavánte, *sm.* Butteris, an instrument used in paring the sole of a horse's foot.

Pujés, *sm.* Pointing the thumb in contempt. V. *Higa.*

Pújo, *sm.* 1. Tenesmus, a continual urgent need to go to stool. 2. Violent desire, great eagerness, longing; anxiety. *A' pujos*, Slowly, with some difficulty.

Pulcritúd, *sf.* Pulchritude, beauty, grace, genteel appearance.

Púlcro, cra, *a.* 1. Beautiful, graceful. 2. Affectedly nice in dress.

Púlga, *sf.* Flea, a small insect, remarkable for its agility in leaping. *Púlgas*, Playing tops for children.

Pulgáda, *sf.* Inch, the twelfth part of a foot.

Pulgár, *sm.* 1. Thumb, the first short and thick finger of the hand. *Dedo pulgar del pie*, The great toe. 2. Shoots left on vines. *Menear los pulgares*, To hasten the execution of any thing; to turn over a hand of cards.

Pulgaráda, *sf.* 1. Fillip, a jerk of the middle finger let go from the thumb. 2. Pinch, any small quantity taken between the thumb and fore finger. V. *Pulgada.*

Pulgón, *sm.* Vine-fretter, vine-grub. Curculio Bacchus *L.*

Pulgóso, sa, *a.* Full of fleas.

Pulguéra, *sf.* 1. Place abounding with fleas. 2. (Bot.) Pulic, flea-wort. Plantago psyllium *L.* *Pulguéras*, Wings of the cross-bow. V. *Empulgueras.*

Pulguílla, ca, ta, *sf.* A little flea. *Pulguillas*, A restless, fretful person.

Pulicán, *sm.* Pelican, instrument for drawing teeth.

Pulicária, *sf.* Flea-wort. V. *Zaragatona.*

Pulicía, *sf.* Police. V. *Policia.*

Pulidaménte, *ad.* Neatly, sprucely, cleanly.

Pulidéro, *sm.* 1. Polisher, one who polishes. 2. Polisher, an instrument for polishing or burnishing.

Pulidéz y Pulidéza, *sf.* Neatness, cleanliness.

Pulído, da, *a.* Neat, cleanly.

Pulidór, *sm.* 1. Polisher, one who polishes. 2. Instrument used for polishing and burnishing.

Pulimentár, *va.* To gloss, to polish very bright.

Puliménto, *sm.* Polish, artificial gloss; brightness given by attrition.

Pulír, *va.* 1. To polish, to burnish; to finish a work of art. 2. To adorn, to beautify.—*vr.* To be polished, to be elegant in point of dress and manners.

Púlla, *sf.* 1. Loose obscene expression. 2. Smart repartee, a witty saying. 3. Kind of eagle that dwells in the trunks of trees.

Pulmón, *sm.* 1. Lungs. V. *Bofes.* 2. (Albeyt.) Fleshy tumour on the joint of horses.

Pulmonária, *sf.* (Bot.) Lungwort, hazel-rag. Lichen pulmonarius *L.*

Pulmonía, *sf.* Pulmonary consumption; phthisis, inflammation of the lungs.

Pulmoníaco, ca; y Pulmonário, ria, *a.* Affected with an inflammation of the lungs; pulmonary.

Púlpa, *sf.* 1. Pulp, the fullest and most solid part of the flesh. 2. Pulp, the soft and succulent part of fruit.

Pulpéjo, *sm.* The fleshy prominence of the fingers opposite to the nails.

Pulpería, *sf.* (In New Spain) Chandler's shop, where all sorts of provisions are retailed.

Pulpéro, *sm.* (In New Spain) One who keeps a chandler's shop or retails provisions.

Pulpéta, *sf.* Slice of stuffed meat.

Pulpetón, *sm.* Large slice of stuffed meat.

Púlpito, *sm.* Pulpit, desk placed in the church, where sermons are pronounced; preacher.

Púlpo, *sm.* 1. (Ict.) Cuttle-fish, polypus. Sepia octopus *L.* 2. Prostitute. *Poner como un pulpo*, To make like pulp; to beat severely.

Pulpóso, sa, *a.* Pulpous, fleshy.

Púlque, *sm.* Liquor prepared in America of a species of aloes, the Agave Americana *L.*

Pulquería, *sf.* Shop or place where the above liquor is sold.

Pulsación y Pulsáda, *sf.* Pulse, pulsation, the act of beating or moving with quick strokes against any thing opposing.

Pulsadór, ra, *s.* One who examines the pulse.

Pulsár, *va.* 1. To touch. V. *Tocar.* 2. To feel the pulse.—*vn.* To pulse, to beat as the pulse.

Pulsátil, *a.* Sounding when struck or touched; such as bells.
Pulsatívo, va, *a.* Pulsing, beating.
Pulsatório, ria, *a.* Relating to the pulse.
Pulséra, *sf.* Bandage applied to the vein or artery of a sick person, steeped in some strengthening liquid.—*pl.* 1. Locks of hair which fall over the temples. 2. Bracelets or other ornaments worn by women about the wrists.
Pulsísta, *sm.* A person well acquainted with the different movements of the pulse.
Púlso, *sm.* 1. Pulse, the motion or beating of the heart and arteries as far as it is perceived by the touch. 2. That part of the wrist where the pulse is felt. 3. Firmness or steadiness of the hand. *A' pulso*, With the strength of the hand. 4. Attention, care, circumspection. *Obra con gran pulso*, He proceeds or acts with a deal of circumspection.
Pululár, *vn.* To pullulate, to germ, to bud.
Pulverizáble, *a.* Reducible to powder; pulverable, possible to be reduced to dust.
Pulverización, *sf.* Pulverization.
Pulverizár, *va.* To pulverize.
Pulzól, Puzól, ó Punzó, *sm.* A bright scarlet colour.
Punár, *va.* V. *Pugnar.*
Púncha, *sf.* Thorn, prick or point of any thing that pricks the flesh.
Punchár, *va.* (Ant.) To prick. V. *Punzar.*
Pundonór, *sm.* Point of honour, a subject in which the honour or character of a person is concerned.
Pundonorcíllo, *sm.* Punctilio.
Pundonorcilaménte, *ad.* Punctiliously.
Pundonoróso, sa, *a.* Having a nice sense of honour. [cockles, oysters, &c.
Punganés, *sm. pl.* Instruments used to open
Pungénte, *pa.* Pungent. [ing.
Pungimiénto, *sm.* Act of punching or prick-
Pungír, *va.* 1. To punch, to prick. 2. To invite, to stimulate.
Pungitívo, va, *a.* Punching, pricking.
Puníble, *a.* (For.) Punishable.
Punición, *sf.* Punishment, chastisement.
Púnico, ca, *a.* Punic, relating to the Carthaginians.
Punír, *va.* To punish. V. *Castigar.*
Púnta, *sf.* 1. Point, the sharp end of an instrument. 2. Extremity of any thing which terminates in an angle. 3. Point, headland, promontory. 4. Colter, the sharp iron of the plough which cuts the earth. 5. A small part of any thing. 6. Act of a dog in marking out the game. 7. Tartness, a sourish taste. *Hacer punta*, To excel, to surpass; to oppose, to contradict; to take the road to. 8. Sharp bodkin.—*pl.* 1. Bone-lace. 2. Horns of a bull. *De puntas*, On tiptoe, softly.
Puntación, *sf.* Punctuation, the act of marking letters with dots or points.
Puntáda, *sf.* 1. Stitch made with a needle and thread. 2. Word carelessly dropped in the course of conversation.
Puntadór, *sm.* V. *Apuntador.*
Puntál, *sm.* 1. Prop, an upright post fixed in the ground to support a wall or building; shore. 2. (Naút.) Stanchion. *Puntal de la bodega*, (Naút.) Depth of the hold.
Puntapié, *sm.* Kick, a blow with the foot.
Puntár, *va.* To mark with small dots or points.
Punteadúra, *sf.* Teeth of a wheel.
Punteár, *va.* 1. To play upon the guitar, by pinching the strings according to the rules of art. 2. To mark, to point out. 3. To sew, to stitch.—*vn.* (Naút.) To go obliquely, catching the wind when it is slack.
Puntél, *sm.* Iron tube for blowing glass.
Puntéra, *sf.* (Bot.) A kind of evergreen. Sedum *L.*
Puntería, *sf.* 1. The act of levelling or pointing fire-arms. 2. Aim, the direction of a massive weapon. 3. Teeth of a wheel.
Puntéro, *sm.* 1. Fescue, a small wire or stick, by which those who teach or learn to read, point out the letters. 2. A pointed instrument for marking any thing. 3. Punch or puncheon of a farrier. 4. Chisel used by stone-cutters.
Puntéro, ra, *a.* Taking a good aim with fire-arms. [or closing hempen sandals.
Punteról, *sm.* A large needle, used in sewing
Puntiagúdo, da, *a.* Sharp-pointed.
Puntílla, *sf.* 1. A small point. 2. A narrow lace edging. *De puntillas*, Softly, gently; on tiptoe. *Ponerse de puntillas*, To persist obstinately in one's opinion. 3. Burine, graver.
Puntilláso, *sm.* Kick, a blow with the foot.
Puntíllo, *sm.* Trifling, despicable thing in which a punctilious person places honour.
Puntillón, *sm.* Kick. V. *Puntillazo.*
Puntillóso, sa, *a.* Ticklish, difficult, litigious.
Púntivi, *sm.* Sort of Silesia linen.
Púnto, *sm.* 1. Point, an indivisible point of time or space. 2. Point, subject or matter under consideration. 3. End or design. 4. Degree, state. 5. Point of honour; punctilio. 6. Opportunity, fit place or time. *A' buen punto*, Opportunely. *Al punto*, Instantly. 7. Point, stop; a note of distinction in writing. 8. Aim, sight. 9. Stitch, a pass of the needle and thread through any thing. 10. Tumbler of a gun-lock. 11. Hole in stockings; mesh of a net; vacancy in lace. 12. Right, just sound of musical instruments. 13. Close of a course of lectures.—*pl.* 1. Stitches serving to unite the lips of a wound. 2. Points or dots marked on dice or cards. *Poner los puntos muy altos*, To soar very high; to make extravagant claims or pretensions. *Por puntos*, From one moment to another. *Punto de malla*, Mesh of a net.
Puntóso, sa, *a.* 1. Acuminated, having many points. 2. Spirited, full of fire, lively, courageous. 3. Too punctilious in etiquette. *Hombre ó muger de punto*, Principal person of distinction.
Puntuación, *sf.* Punctuation, the art or mode of pointing.
Puntuál, *a.* Punctual, exact. 2. Certain, sure. 3. Convenient, adequate.
Puntualidád, *sf.* 1. Punctuality, exactness. 2. Certitude, preciseness.
Puntualizár, *va.* 1. To imprint, to fix on the mind or memory. 2. To finish, to accomplish, to complete.
Puntualménte, *ad.* Punctually, exactly.
Puntuár, *va.* To punctuate, to point.
Puntuóso, sa, *a.* V. *Puntoso* y *Pundonoroso.*

Puntúra, *sf.* 1. Puncture, a small prick; a hole made with a very sharp point. 2. Point which holds the sheet in a printing press.
Punzáda, *sf.* 1. Prick, a small hole made with a sharp point. 2. Sting, pain; compunction.
Punzadór, ra, *s.* Pricker, one who pricks or wounds.
Punzadúra, *sf.* Puncture, prick.
Punzánte, *pa.* Pointed, pricking.
Punzár, *va.* 1. To prick, to wound with a sharp point. 2. To sting, to cause pain.
Punzón, *sm.* 1. Punch, a pointed instrument used by many artists and workmen; type-founder's punch. 2. Figure of a key worn on the flap of the coat-pocket by gentlemen of the bed-chamber to his Spanish majesty. 3. Young horn of a deer.
Punzoncíco y Punzoncíllo, *sm.* A small punch.
Punzonería, *sf.* Collection of moulds for making a fount of types.
Puñáda, *sf.* Blow given with the fist. *Venir á las puñadas*, To come to blows.
Puñádo, *sm.* Handful, as much as can be seized or grasped by the hand at once; a few. *Á' puñados*, Plentifully, abundantly. *Gran ó que puñado!* (Fam.) Expression of contempt for the small quantity or the quality of a thing offered.
Puñál, *sm.* Poniard, dagger; a short stabbing weapon.
Puñaláda, *sf.* 1. Stab, a wound given with a poniard. 2. A sudden shock of grief or pain.
Puñaléjo, *sm.* Small poniard.
Puñaléro, *sm.* Maker or seller of poniards.
Puñetázo, *sm.* Blow with the shut fist.
Puñéte, *sm.* Blow given with the fist. *Puñetes*, Bracelets, ornaments wore round the wrists.
Púño, *sm.* 1. Fist, the hand clenched, with the fingers doubled down. 2. Handful, as much as can be grasped by the hand at once. 3. Scantiness, narrowness. *Un puño de casa*, A small house. 4 Wristband, the fastening of the shirt at the hand. 5. Hand-ruffle, plaited cambric, muslin, or lace, fastened to the wristband by way of ornament. 6. Hilt, guard of a sword; handle; head of a staff. 7. (Naút.) Each of the lower points of a sail in which the tacks are fastened. *Apretar los puños*, To exert the utmost efforts. *Á' puño cerrado*, With might and main. *Hombre de puños*, A strong valiant man. *Ser como un puño*, To be miserable; close-fisted.
Puónes, *sm. pl.* The large uneven teeth of combing cards.
Púpa, *sf.* 1. Pustule, pimple. 2. The plaintive sound whereby children express uneasiness.
Pupíla, *sf.* 1. Eye-ball, pupil. 2. Orphan girl.
Pupiláge, *sm.* 1. Pupilage, the state of being a pupil. 2. Board, the state of a boarder who diets with another at a certain rate. 3. Boarding-house.
Pupilár, *a.* 1. Pupilary, belonging to a pupil or ward. 2. Relating or pertaining to the eye-ball.
Pupiléro, ra, *s.* Master or mistress of a boarding-house or boarding-school.
Pupílo, *sm.* 1. Pupil, ward; one under the care of his guardian. 2. Pupil, scholar, student; one under the care of a tutor.
Pupóso, sa, *a.* Pustulous, full of pustules.

Puraménte, *ad.* Purely, chastely; entirely.
Puréza, *sf.* Purity, innocence, integrity, chastity; purity of diction.
Púrga, *sf.* Purge, purging-draft, a cathartic medicine which evacuates by stool.
Purgáble, *a.* That may be purged.
Purgación, *sf.* 1. Purgation, the act of cleansing or expelling bad humours. 2. Catamenia. 3. Act of clearing from imputation of guilt.
Purgadór, ra, *s.* One who purges, purger.
Purgánte, *pa.* Purgative.
Purgár, *va.* 1. To purge, to purify, to cleanse. 2. To atone, to expiate. 3. To purge, to cleanse or evacuate the body by stool. 4. To clear from guilt or imputation of guilt. 5. To correct and moderate the passions.—*vr.* To rid one's self of, to free or clear one's self from guilt.
Purgatívo, va, *a.* Purgative, cathartic.
Purgatório, *sm.* 1. Purgatory, a place where souls suffer for a time on account of their sins. 2. Any place where life is imbittered by painful drudgery and troubles.
Puridád, *sf.* 1. Purity, freedom from foulness or dirt. 2. Secret, secrecy. *En puridad*, Clearly, openly, without tergiversation; in secret.
Purificación, *sf.* 1. Purification, the act of making pure. 2. Purification, a festival of the Christian church, observed on the second day of February. 3. The act of churching a woman after her lying-in. 4. Cleansing the chalice after the wine is drank at the mass.
Purificadéro, ra, *a.* Cleansing, purifying.
Purificadór, ra, *s.* 1. Purifier, one who cleanses or purifies. 2. Purificatory, the cloth with which the priest wipes and cleans the chalice.
Purificár, *va.* To purify, to clean, to cleanse. —*vr.* 1. To be purified, to be cleansed. 2. To be churched after a lying-in.
Purificatório, ria, *a.* Purificatory, having the power or tendency to make pure.
Purísmo, *sm.* Affecting too much purity of diction.
Purísta, *sm.* Purist, one who aims at an affected purity of diction.
Puritáno, na, *s.* Puritan, a sectary pretending to eminent purity of religion.
Púrna, *sf.* (Arag.) Spark, sparkle.
Púro, ra, *a.* 1. Pure, free, unmingled, absolute; simple, disinterested; chaste. 2. Vast, excessive. *De puro*, Extremely.
Púrpura, *sf.* 1. Rock-shell, purple-shell. Murex *L.* 2. Cloth died with cochineal. 3. Dignity of a king or cardinal. 4. (Poét.) Blood.
Purpurádo, *a.* V. *Cardenal.*
Purpuránte, *pa.* Giving a purple colour.
Purpurár, *va.* 1. To make red, to colour with purple. 2. To dress in purple.—*vn.* To take or show a purple colour.
Purpúreo, rea, *a.* Of a purple colour.
Purréla, *sf.* Wine of the most inferior quality.
Purriéla, *sf.* Any thing despicable or of little value.
Purulénto, ta, *a.* Purulent.
Pus, *sm.* Pus, the matter of wounds.
Pusilánime, *a.* Pusillanimous, mean-spirited, narrow-minded.
Pusilanimidád, *sf.* Pusillanimity, want of courage; meanness of spirit.
Pústula, *sf.* Pustule, pimple.
Púta, *sf.* Whore, prostitute.

Putaísmo y Putanísmo, *sm.* Putanism, the manner of living or trade of a prostitute.

Putañeár, *vn.* To whore.

Putañéro, *sm.* Whoremaster, whoremonger.

Putatívo, va, *a.* Putative, supposed, reputed.

Puteál, *sm.* Stone used as the cover of a well, on which soothsayers prophesied.

Puteár, *vn.* (Fam.) To whore.

Putería, *sf.* 1. The manner of living and trade of a prostitute. 2. Brothel, a bawdy-house. 3. Arts used by lewd women to attract the attention of men.

Putéro, *sm.* Whoremaster, whoremonger.

Putésco, ca, *a.* Relating or belonging to whores.

Putíca, lla, ta, *sf. dim.* Young prostitute.

Púto, *sm.* Catamite, sodomite. *A' puto el postre,* (Fam.) The devil take the hindmost.

Putpút, *sm.* (Orn.) Hoop. V. *Abubilla.*

Putredinál, *a.* Putrefying, corrupting.

Putrefacción, *sf.* Putrefaction, the state of growing rotten.

Putrefactívo, va, *a.* Putrefactive.

Pútrido, da, *a.* Putrid, rotten.

Putuéla, *sf. dim.* A little prostitute.

Púya, *sf.* V. *Pua.*

Puyár, *vn.* (Ant.) To mount, to ascend.

Puzól y Puzoléna, *s.* Puzzolana, a volcanic production, being a kind of martial argillaceous marl, of a gray colour, and containing a great portion of silex.

Q Is always followed by the letter *u*; in *querer* it has the sound of *k*, in *quando,* &c. that of the English *q*. The *u* is never doubled in Spanish after *q*; and when it has its proper sound is marked with a diæresis, thus, *qüestion* is pronounced the same in Spanish and English.

Quadérna, *sf.* 1. The fourth part of any thing. 2. (Naút.) Frame, the timber-work which forms the ribs of a ship. *Quaderna muestra,* (Naút.) Midship-frame. *Quaderna del cuerpo popés,* (Naút.) Stern-frame. *Quadernas de henchimiento,* (Naút.) Filling-timbers. *Quadernas de la amura,* (Naút.) Loof-frames. *Quadernas reviradas,* (Naút.) Cant-timbers. *Quadernas á esquadra,* (Naút.) Square-timbers.

Quadernál, *sm.* (Naút.) Block, a piece of wood with sheaves and pullies, on which the running rigging is reeved. *Quadernales de carenar,* (Naút.) Careening gears.

Quadernaléte, *sm.* (Naút.) Short and double block.

Quadernário, ria, *a.* Quaternary, consisting of four.

Quadernillo, *sm.* 1. Five sheets of paper sewed together like a book. 2. Clerical directory, containing the daily order of divine service.

Quadérno, *sm.* 1. Parcel of paper stitched together. 2. Small memorandum book. 3. Book composed of four printed sheets placed within each other. 4. Chastisement of collegians, depriving them of their pittance. 5. (Fam.) Pack of cards.

Quádra, *sf.* 1. Hall, saloon; drawing-room. 2. Stable, a house for beasts. 3. (Peru) Length of a street. 4. (Naút.) Quarter of a ship. *Por la quadra,* (Naút.) On the quarter.

Quadradaménte, *ad.* Exactly, completely.

Quadrádo, da, *a.* 1. Square, squared. 2. Perfect, without any defect or imperfection.

Quadrádo, *sm.* 1. Square, a figure of four equal sides and four right angles. 2. Clock, the flowers or inverted work in stockings about the ancle. 3. Gusset of a shirt sleeve. 4. Die. V. *Troquel.* 5. (Impr.) Quadrate, the square of a letter. *De quadrado,* In front, opposite, face to face; squared.

Quadragenário, ria, *a.* Forty years old; of forty years.

Quadragesimál, *a.* Quadragesimal, belonging to Lent.

Quadragésimo, ma, *a.* Fortieth, the fourth tenth.

Quadrál, *sm.* (Arq.) Piece of timber which crosses two others diagonally.

Quadrangulár, *a.* Quadrangular, having four right angles.

Quadrángulo, *sm.* Quadrangle, a surface with four right angles.

Quadrantál, *a.* Quadrantal.

Quadránte, *sm.* 1. Quadrant, the fourth part of a circle. 2. A mathematical instrument with which latitudes are taken. 3. Dial-plate of a sun-dial. 4. A square board put up in churches, pointing out the order of masses to be celebrated. 5. The fourth part of an inheritance. 6. The smallest coin current in a country. *Hasta el ultimo quadrante,* To the last farthing.

Quadrár, *va.* 1. To square, to form into a square. 2. To adjust, to regulate, to fit, to quadrate. 3. To please, to accommodate. 4. To square timbers. 5. (Arit.) To multiply a number by itself. 6. (Pint.) V. *Quadricular.*

Quadratín, *sm.* (Impr.) Quotation, piece of type-metal used to fill up blanks in pages.

Quadratúra, *sf.* 1. Quadrature, the act of squaring or reducing to a square. 2. First and last quarter of the moon. 3. Pentagraph, an instrument whereby drawings and pictures may be copied in any proportion.

Quadréte, *sm.* A small square.

Quadricenál, *a.* That which is done every forty years.

Quadrícula, *sf.* Reduction of a drawing to a smaller size by means of the pentagraph, or chequered lines.

Quadriculár, *va.* To copy a drawing by means of the pentagraph; to copy by means of squares.

Quadrienál, *a.* Quadrennial, comprising four years; happening once in four years.

Quadriénio, *sm.* Time and space of four years.

Quadrifórme, *a.* Fourfaced.

Quadríga, *sf.* Carriage drawn by four horses.

Quadríl, *sm.* Haunch-bone in beasts.

Quadrilátero, ra, *a.* Quadrilateral, having four sides and four angles.
Quadriliterál, *a.* Consisting of four letters.
Quadrílla, *sf.* 1. Meeting of four or more persons, assembled for some particular purpose. 2. Any one of the four divisions of sheep-masters which form the board of *Mesta.* 3. Band of armed men, sent in pursuit of robbers and highwaymen by the court of *La Santa Hermandad. Alcalde de quadrilla,* Director of one of the four sections of the council of *Mesta.*
Quadrilléro, *sm.* Member of the court of *La Santa Hermandad;* the commander of an armed band employed by that court.
Quadríllo, *sm.* 1. A small square. 2. Dart, or any other missive weapon of that kind.
Quadrilóngo, *sm.* 1. Oblong square. 2. Formation of a corps of infantry into an oblong form.
Quadrilóngo, ga, *a.* Having the shape or form of a long square.
Quadriméstre, *sm.* Space of four months.
QUADRINO'MIO, *sm.* (Algeb.) Quadrinomial.
Quádriple, *a.* Quadruple, fourfold.
Quadriplicádo, da, *a.* Quadrupled.
Quadrisílabo, ba, *s.* Word of four syllables.
Quadrívio, *sm.* 1. Place where four paths or roads meet. 2. Any thing which may be undertaken four different ways.
Quadrivísta, *sm.* One who attempts four different ways to attain some end. V. *Matemático.*
Quadriyúgo, *sm.* Cart with four horses.
Quádro, dra, *a.* V. *Quadrado.*
Quádro, *sm.* 1. Figure having for equal sides and four angles. *En quadro,* Squared, in a square form. 2. Picture, painting. 3. A square bed of earth in a garden. 4. Picture frame, frame of a window. 5. (Mil.) Square body of troops. 6. (Impr.) Platen, part of a printing-press which makes the impression.
Quadrupedál, *a.* Four-footed; applied to beasts. [going on four feet.
Quadrupedánte, *a.* (Poet.) Quadrupedant,
Quadrúpedo, da; y Quadrúpede, *a.* Quadruped, having four feet.
Quadruplicación, *sf.* Quadruplication, the taking of a thing four times.
Quadruplicár, *va.* To quadruplicate, to multiply by four.
Quádruplo, pla, *a.* Quadruple, fourfold.
Qual, *a.* 1. Which; he who. V. *El que. ¿ Qual de los dos quiere vd. ?* Which of the two will you have? 2. Same, like, such. V. *Qualquiera.* 3. One, other, partly. *Tengo muchos libros quales de Latin, quales de Romance,* I have many books, some Latin, others Spanish. *Qual ó qual,* V. *Tal qual. Cada qual,* Each one.—*ad.* As. V. *Como.* —*interj.* How then.
Qualidád, *sf.* Quality. V. *Calidad.*
Qualificár, *va.* (Ant.) V. *Calificar.*
Quálque, *a.* (Ant.) V. *Alguno.*
Qualquiér, *a.* Any one; used only before a substantive, with which it is joined.
Qualquiéra, *a.* Any one, some one, either one or the other, whichsoever, whoever.
Quamáño, ña, *a.* (Ant.) How great, so big.
Quán, *ad.* How, as; used only before nouns. V. *Quanto.*
Quándo, *ad.* 1. When, pointing out a certain time. 2. In case that; if. 3. Though, although; even. *Quando no hubiera mas razon,* Were there even no other ground. 4. Sometimes, at times. *Quando con los criados, quando con los hijos,* Sometimes with the servants, sometimes with the children. *De quando en quando,* From time to time. *Quando mas ó quando mucho,* At most, at best. *Quando menos,* At least. *Quando quiera,* When you please, whensoever. *Hasta quando,* Until when. *¿ De quando acá ?* Since when? in what time? expression intimating that a thing is extraordinary.—*sm.* A determinate space or period of time.
Quantía, *sf.* 1. Quantity. V. *Cantidad.* 2. Rank, distinction. *Hombre de gran quantía,* A man of high rank.
Quantiár, *va.* To estimate or regulate the possessions of neighbours in villages.
Quantidád, *sf.* Quantity. V. *Cantidad.*
Quantimás, V. *Quanto mas.*
Quantiosaménte, *ad.* Copiously.
Quantióso, sa, *a.* Numerous, copious.
Quantitatívo, va, *a.* Quantitive, estimable, according to quantity.
Quánto, ta, *a.* 1. Containing quantity or relating to it, susceptible of quantity. 2. As many as, as much as, the more. *Quanto uno es mas pobre se le debe socorrer mas,* The poorer a person is the more should he be supported. *Quanto vd. quiera,* As much as you like. 3. All, whatever. 4. Excessive, great in some way.—*ad.* Respecting, whilst. *Quanto ántes,* Immediately, as soon as possible. *Quanto mas,* Moreover, the more as. *En quanto,* With regard to; in the mean time. *Quanto quier,* Although. *Por quanto,* In as much as.
Quarángo, *sm.* The vulgar name of the *Cinchona* or Peruvian bark-tree.
Quarénta, *a.* Forty, four times ten. *El año de quarenta,* The days of yore; an expression used for antiquated things long out of fashion.
Quarenténa, *sf.* 1. Space of forty days, months, or years; the fortieth part. 2. Lent, the forty days of fast prescribed by the Roman catholic church. 3. (Met.) Suspension of assent to any thing. 4. The number 40 in general. 5. (Naút.) Quarantine, the time which a ship, suspected of infection, is obliged to abstain from intercourse with the inhabitants of a country. *Hacer quarentena,* (Naút.) To perform quarantine.
Quarentón, na, *a.* y *s.* Person 40 years old.
Quarésma, *sf.* 1. Lent, the quadragesimal fast prescribed by the Roman catholic church. 2. Collection of Lent sermons.
Quaresmál, *a.* Belonging to Lent.
Quaresmár, *vn.* To keep Lent.
Quárta, *sf.* 1. Fourth, one of the four parts into which a whole is divided; a quarter. 2. Sequence of four cards in the game of piquet. 3. Quadrant, fourth part of a circle. 4. (Naút.) Point of the compass. 5. Part of the masses which belong to the parish where the deceased person was a member. *Quártas,* Body mules of a carriage.

Quartágo, *sm.* Nag, pony.
Quartagoíllo, *sm. dim.* Little nag.
Quartál, *sm.* 1. Kind of bread weighing the fourth part of a loaf. 2. Quarter, dry measure, fourth part of a fanega.
Quartaménte, *ad.* (Ant.) Fourthly.
Quartána, *sf.* Quartan, an ague which returns every four days.
Quartanál, *a.* Intermittent. [tan.
Quartanário, ria, *a.* Labouring under a quar-
Quartár, *va.* To plough the ground the fourth time.
Quartázo, *sm.* A large room, a large quarter. *Quartázos*, A coarse corpulent person.
Quarteár, *va.* 1. To quarter, to divide into four parts. 2. To bid a fourth more at public sales. 3. To make a fourth person at a game.—*vr.* To split into pieces.
Quartél, *sm.* 1. Quarter, the fourth part of a garden or other thing. 2. Quarter, district, ward of a city. 3. Lodging for soldiers. 4. Duty imposed on villages for the quartering of soldiers. This, however, is at present generally called *utensilios*. 5. Dwelling, habitation, home. 6. Quarter, remission of life granted by hostile troops. 7. V. *Quarteto*. 8. (Naút.) Hatch, the lid of a hatchway. *Quartel de la salud*, A safe place free from hazard and danger. *Quartel maestre general*, (Mil.) General officer appointed to regulate encampments and furnish maps, plans, and descriptions of the country which is the theatre of war.
Quarteléro, *sm.* (Mil.) Soldier in each company who keeps their apartment clean.
Quartéra, *sf.* A dry measure in Catalonia, containing about 15 pecks.
Quartéro, ra, *a.* Applied to those who collect the rents of the grain of farms, which pay the fourth part to the landlords. [fluids.
Quarteróla, *sf.* Quarter cask of liquors or
Quarterón, na, *s.* y *a.* 1. Quartern, Quarter, the fourth part of a whole; quarter of a pound. 2. (America) Child begotten between a creole and a native of Spain. 3. Upper part of windows which may be opened and shut. *Quarterones*, Squares of wainscot in a door or window-shutter.
Quartéta, Quartéte, y **Quartéto**, *s.* Quatrain of a sonnet.
Quartílla, *sf.* 1. Fourth part of an *arroba*, or sixteenth part of a quintal. 2. Fourth part of a sheet of paper. 3. Pastern of horses.
Quartíllo, *sm.* 1. Pint, the fourth part of a pottle in liquids, and of a peck in grain. 2. Fourth part of a real. *Ir de quartillo*, To share the profits or losses in any business. *Tumba quartillos*, Tippler.
Quartillúdo, da, *a.* Applied to a horse with long pasterns.
Quárto, *sm.* 1. Fourth part, quarter of an hour. 2. Habitation, dwelling, room, apartment. V. *Aposento*. *Quarto bazo*, Room on the ground floor. 3. Copper coin worth four *maravedis*. 4. Series of paternal or maternal ancestors. 5. Crack in horses' hoofs. 6. Quarter of clothes, quarter of animals, or of criminals whose body is quartered and exposed in public places. *Quarto á quarto*, In a mean, miserable manner. *De tres al quarto*, Of little moment. *Poner quarto*, To take lodgings; to furnish apartments. *Quarto principal*, (Madrid) First floor. *No tener un quarto*, Not to be worth a farthing. *Quartos*, Cash, money; well-proportioned members of an animal's body. *Quarto de culebrina*, (Art.) Culverin which carries a 5lb. ball.
Quárto, ta, *a.* Fourth, the ordinal of four.
Quartodecimáno, na, *a.* Applied to the heretics who fixed the passover on the 14th of March, although it were not Sunday.
Quartogénito, ta, *a.* The fourth born child.
Quartón, *sm.* 1. Large joist or girder, a beam 16 feet long. 2. (Barcelona) Measure of wine and vinegar.
Quártzo, *sm.* Quartz, a crystallized stone of a siliceous nature. *Quartzo zitrino*, Occidental topaz.
Quarzóso, sa, *a.* Quartzose, resembling or containing quartz.
Quasi, *ad.* V. *Casi ó Como*. *Quasi contrato*, A contract, though not formal, yet effectual.
Quasimódo, *sm.* First Sunday after Easter.
Quaternário, ria, *a.* Containing or making up the number of four.
Quaternidád, *sf.* Quaternity, collection of four units.
Quaternión, *sm.* Union of four things, or four sheets in printing.
Quatórce, *a.* (Ant.) V. *Catorce*.
Quatrálbo, ba, *a.* Having four white feet; applied to a horse or other quadruped.
Quatrálbo, *sm.* Commander of a galley of four oars.
Quatrátuo, a, *a.* V. *Quarteron*.
Quatréro, *sm.* Thief who steals horses, sheep, or other beasts.
Quatriduáno, na; **Quatridiál** y **Quatridiáno, na**, *a.* Lasting four days.
Quatriénnio, *sm.* V. *Quadrienio*.
Quatríllo, *sm.* Quadrille, a fashionable game at cards; otherwise called *Cascalera* in Spain.
Quatrín, *sm.* 1. A small coin, formerly current in Spain. 2. (Fam.) Cash in general.
Quatrínca, *sf.* 1. Union of four persons or things. 2. Four cards of the same print in the game of *Basset*.
Quatrisílabo, ba, *ad.* V. *Quadrisilabo*.
Quátro, *a.* 1. Four, twice two. 2. V. *Quarto*.
Quátro, *sm.* 1. Character or figure 4. 2. One who votes for four absent persons. 3. Musical composition sung by four voices. 4. Card with four marks. *Mas de quatro*, A great number or multitude of persons.
Quatrociéntos, tas, *a.* Four hundred.
Quatrodiál, *a.* (Ant.) That which is of 4 days.
Quatrodoblár, *va.* To quadruple.
Quatropéa, *sf.* Horse-tax, duty laid on horses which are sold at market; quadruped.
Quatropeádo, *sm.* Step in dancing.
Quatropeár, *vn.* To run on all fours.
Quatrotánto, *sm.* Fine amounting to four times the value of the object of a defraud, or other misdemeanour.
Qué, *pron. rel.* 1. Which, that; a relative particle. *El ó la que*, He or she that. *Lo que*, that which. *¿ Que cosa es esa ?* What is that? 2. What! a particle expressive of ad-

miration. *Que desgracia!* What a misfortune! 3. A comparative particle; *mas que*, more than; *tanto que*, as much as. *Algo que*, More than. 4. Whether. *Que llueva, que no llueva*, Whether it rains or not. *Tarde que temprano*, Late or early. 5. Because, why. 6. Used after a verb it is a particle which governs and determines another verb. *Le mandó que viniese*, He ordered him to come. 7. Where, in what place. *¿ Que es del libro?* Where is the book?

Qué, *sm.* Something, somewhat.

Quebráda, *sf.* Broken, uneven ground.

Quebradéro, *sm.* 1. Breaker, he that breaks. *Quebradero de cabeza*, Object of amorous care; that which molests and importunes.

Quebradíllo, *sm.* 1. Wooden shoe-heel. 2. Flexure of the body in dancing.

Quebradízo, za, *a.* 1. Brittle, fragile, apt to break. 2. Infirm, sickly. 3. Flexible; applied to the voice. 4. (Met.) V. *Fragil.*

Quebrádo, da, *a.* Broken; debilitated, enervated. *Andar de pie quebrado*, To be on the decline. *Plata quebrada*, Payment made in articles equivalent to money.

Quebrádo, *sm.* 1. (Arit.) Fraction, broken number. 2. (Poét.) Verse consisting of four syllables. 3. Bankrupt.

Quebradór, ra, *s.* 1. Breaker, one who breaks. 2. One who violates or transgresses a law or statute.

Quebradúra, *sf.* 1. The act of breaking or splitting; fracture. 2. Rupture, hernia.

Quebrajár, *va.* V. *Resquebrajar.*

Quebrajóso, sa, *a.* Brittle, fragile.

Quebramiénto, *sm.* V. *Quebrantamiento.*

Quebrantáble, *a.* That which may be broken, frangible.

Quebrantadór, ra, *s.* 1. Breaker; debilitator. 2. (Met.) Violator, transgressor of any law.

Quebrantadúra, *sf.* Fracture, rupture.

Quebrantahuésos, *sm.* 1. (Orn.) Osprey. Falco ossifragus *L.* 2. A troublesome importunate person. 3. Play among boys.

Quebrantamiénto, *sm.* 1. Fracture, rupture; breaking a prison. 2. Weariness, fatigue. 3. Violation or transgression of the law. 4. (For.) Act of breaking a will.

Quebrantanuéces, *sm.* (Orn.) Nutcracker. Corvus caryocatactes *L.*

Quebrantár, *va.* 1. To break, to crack, to burst or open by force. 2. To pound, to grind. 3. To persuade, to induce. 4. To move to pity. 5. To transgress a law, to violate a contract. 6. To vex, to molest, to fatigue. 7. To weaken, to debilitate. 8. To annul, to revoke; to break a will. *Quebrantar la cabeza*, To humble one's pride.

Quebránto, *sm.* 1. The act of breaking. 2. Weakness, want of strength, debility, lassitude. 3. Commiseration, pity, compassion. 4. Object worthy of pity. 5. Great loss, severe damage. 6. (Naút.) Cambering of a ship's deck or keel.

Quebrár, *va.* 1. To break, to disunite, to burst or open by force. 2. To double, to twist. 3. To interrupt, to intercept. 4. To transgress a law, to violate a contract. 5. To temper, to moderate. 6. To fade, to spoil the bloom of the countenance. 7. To overcome, to conquer. 8. To diminish friendship, to dissolve a connexion or abandon a correspondence.—*vn.* To be insolvent, to become a bankrupt.—*vr.* 1. To be ruptured, to labour under a rupture. 2. To interrupt the continuity of hills or banks. *Quebrar el ojo al diablo*, (Fam.) To do that which is the best, most just and reasonable. *Al quebrar del alba*, At dawn of day.

Quéche, *sf.* (Naút.) Smack, a kind of Dutch-built vessel.

Quéda, *sf.* Tattoo, the signal of retirement into quarters; time of retirement marked by the sound of bell.

Quedáda, *sf.* Stay, residence, sojourn.

Quedár, *vn.* 1. To stay, to delay, or to stop in a place. 2. To continue, to tarry, to remain; to last. *Quedar por andar*, To have to walk farther. *Quedar por cobarde*, To shrink back as a coward. 3. To behave, to conduct one's self; to be reputed. *Quedar por valiente*, To enjoy the reputation of a brave man. *Quedar limpio*, (Fam.) To remain with an empty purse. *Quedar con uno*, To agree, to arrange or compound with any one. *Quedar por uno*, To leave another's business to be executed by himself. *Quedar por alguno*, To become surety. 4. Followed by an adjective it signifies To be, as *Quedar armado*, To be armed.—*va.* (Vulg.) To leave.—*vr.* 1. To remain, to continue; to retain, to possess. 2. To falter, to lose the thread and order of a speech or argument; to stop short. *Quedarse helado*, To be astonished, to be thunderstruck. *Quedarse pie*, To be disappointed; to be surprised. *Quedarse sin pulsos*, To be dispirited, to lose all courage. *Quedarse para tia ó para vestir imágenes*, (Fam.) To become an old maid.

Quedíto, ta, *a. dim.* Soft, gentle; easy. This diminutive is more energetic than its primitive *quedo.*

Quédo, *ad.* Softly, gently; in a low voice.

Quédo, da, *a.* Quiet, still, easy, gentle. *A pie quedo*, Fair and easy, without trouble or fatigue. *Quedo que quedo*, Obstinate, pertinacious.

Quehacér, *sm.* Ocupation, business. *Cada uno tiene sus quehaceres*, Every one has his own affairs.

Quéja, *sf.* 1. Complaint, representation of pains or injuries. 2. Resentment of an injury or insult; quarrel, dispute.

Quejárse, *vr.* To complain of, to mention with sorrow, to lament. *Quejarse de vicio*, To complain without cause. V. *Querellarse.*

Quejicóso, sa, *a.* Plaintful, complaining.

Quejidíco, llo, to, *sm. dim.* Slight complaint.

Quejído, *sm.* Complaint.

Quejílla, ta, *sf. dim.* Murmur; resenting.

Quejosaménte, *ad.* Querulously.

Quejóso, sa, *a.* Plaintful, querulous.

Quejumbróso, sa, *a.* Complaining, plaintive.

Quéma, *sf.* 1. Burn, hurt by fire. 2. Fire, conflagration. 3. (Met.) Oven, furnace.

Quemadéro, *sm.* Place where convicts are burnt.

Quemadór, ra, *s.* Incendiary.

Quemadúra, *sf.* Mark or hurt made by fire.

Quemajóso, sa, *a.* Pricking, burning.
Quemánte, *pa.* Burning, consuming.
Quemár, *va.* 1. To burn, to consume by fire. 2. To destroy, to waste; to parch.—*vn.* To be too hot.—*vr.* 1. To be very hot, to be parched with heat; to heat one's self. 2. To fret, to be impatient, to be offended. 3. To be near, to almost attain or touch a thing desired. *Quemarse las cejas,* To study much. *A' quema ropa,* Immediate, very near, (Met.) unexpectedly; applied to an unanswerable and convincing argument, or to an action unobjectionable either from its promptitude or justice.
Quemazón, *sm.* 1. Burn, hurt by fire; combustion, conflagration. 2. The act of burning. 3. Excessive heat. 4. Eagerness, covetousness. 5. Pert language, smart repartee.
Quéncho, *sm.* (Orn.) Gull. Larus *L.*
Quequiér, *a.* (Ant.) V. *Qualquiera.*
Querélla, *sf.* 1. Complaint, expression of pain or grief. 2. Petition or libel exhibited to a court of justice by children, praying that the last will of their parents be set aside.
Querellánte, *pa.* Murmuring.
Querellárse, *vr.* To complain, to prefer a complaint in a court of justice; to be querulous.
Querellosaménte, *ad.* Plaintively, querulously
Querellóso, sa, *a.* Painful, one who complains of every thing; querulous.
Queréncia, *sf.* 1. Haunt of wild beasts. 2. Place which we often frequent; benevolence.
Querencióso, sa, *a.* Applied to a place frequented by wild beasts.
Querér, *va.* 1. To wish, to desire. *Quiero comer,* I have an appetite. 2. To love, to cherish. 3. To will, to resolve, to determine. 4. To attempt, to procure; to require. 5. To conform, to agree. 6. To accept a challenge at a game of hazard. 7. To suit, to fit. 8. To cause, to occasion.—*vn.* To be near being, to verify any thing. *Sin querer,* Unwillingly, undesignedly, without intention or design. *¿ Que quiere decir eso ?* What does that mean? *¿ Que quiere ser esto ?* What is all this? *¿ Que mas quiere ?* What more does he wish? what more is necessary? *Como vd. ó usted quisiere,* As you will it, let it be so. *Como asi me lo quiero,* (Joc.) Conformable to my will and pleasure.—*sm.* Will, desire, study.
Querído, da, *a.* Dear, beloved; my dear, minion.
Querócha, *sf.* V. *Cresa.*
Querochár, *vn.* To emit the semen of bees.
Querubín, *sm.* Cherub, a celestial spirit, which, in the hierarchy, is placed next in order to the seraphim.
Quesadílla, *sf.* A sort of cheesecake, made of cheese and paste; a kind of sweetmeat.
Queseár, *vn.* To make cheese.
Queséra, *sf.* 1. Dairy, the place where cheese and butter are made. 2. Cheese-board, cheese-mould, cheese-vat.
Queseríá, *sf.* Season for making cheese.
Queséro, *sm.* Cheesemonger, one who deals in or sells cheese.—**ra,** *a.* Caseous, cheesy.
Quesíllo, to, *sm. dim.* A small cheese.
Quéso, *sm.* Cheese, a kind of food made by pressing the curd of milk. *Dos de queso.* A trifle.

Qüésta, *sf.* Quest, charity; money collected by begging. [rity.
Qüestéro, *sm.* One who collects alms or charity.
Qüestión, *sf.* 1. Question, inquiry into the truth of any thing. 2. Dispute, quarrel, riot. 3. Problem. *Qüestion de tormento,* (For.) Torture of criminals to discover their crimes.
Qüestionáble, *a.* Questionable, problematical.
Qüestionár, *va.* To question, to dispute.
Qüestionário, *sm.* Collection of questions; a book that treats on questions.
Qüestór, *sm.* 1. Questor, a magistrate of ancient Rome. 2. Mendicant, one who collects alms.
Qüestuóso, sa; y **Questuário, ria,** *a.* Lucrative, productive of profit.
Qüestúra, *sf.* Questorship, the place or dignity of a questor.
Qüetzále, *sm.* (Orn.) A large Indian bird.
Quexigál, *sm.* Plantation of oaks.
Quexíso, *sm.* (Bot.) A kind of evergreen oak.
Quí, *a.* (Ant.) V. *Quien.*
Quíbey, *sm.* (Bot.) Dog's bane, a plant in *Puerto Rico* which kills dogs.
Quiciál y **Quicialéra,** *s.* Sidepost or cheek or jamb of a door or window.
Quício, *sm.* 1. Hook-hinge of the jamb of a door, on which the eye-hinge turns. 2. Prop, support. *Fuera de quicio,* Violently, unnaturally. *Sacar una cosa de quicio,* To unhinge, to overturn, to violate, to pervert.
Quídam, *sm.* A certain person.
Quididád, *sf.* Quiddity, essence.
Quiditatívo, va, *a.* Belonging to the essence of any thing.
Quid pro quo, (Lat.) Quid pro quo, an equivalent.
Quiébra, *sf.* 1. Crack, fracture. 2. Gaping or opening of the ground. 3. Loss, damage. 4. Failure, bankruptcy.
Quiébro, *sm.* 1. Trill, a musical shaking of the voice. 2. Movement or inclination of the body.
Quién, *pron. rel.* 1. Who, which. 2. One or the other. V. *Qual y Que.*
Quienquiéra, *a.* Whosoever, whatever.
Quiér, *conj.* (Ant.) Or. V. *Ya, ó ya sea.* [ing.
Quietación, *sf.* The act of quieting or appeasing.
Quietadór, ra, *sm.* y *f.* Quieter.
Quietaménte, *ad.* Quietly, calmly.
Quietár, *va.* To appease. V. *Aquietar.*
Quiéte, *sf.* Rest, repose, quiet.
Quietísmo, *sm.* Quietism, sect of mystics.
Quietísta, *a.* y *sm.* Quietist.
Quiéto, ta, *a.* 1. Quiet, still, pacific, undisturbed. 2. Orderly, virtuous; not given to vices.
Quietúd, *sf.* Quietness, want of motion, rest, repose.
Quijáda, *sf.* Jaw-bone. V. *Quixada.*
Quijéra, *sf.* Cheeks of a cross-bow.
Quilatadór, *sm.* Assayer, an officer appointed for the trial of gold and silver.
Quilatár, *va.* To assay, to try gold or silver.
Quiláte, *sm.* 1. Degree of purity of gold or silver; carat, the 24th part in weight and value of gold. 2. The 140th part of an ounce of precious stones. 3. Ancient coin. 4. Degree of perfection.
Quilatéra, *sf.* Instrument for ascertaining the carats of pearls.

Quilificación, *sf.* (Med.) Chylification.
Quilificár, *va.* To chylify, to make chyle.
Quílma, *sf.* V. *Costal.*
Quílla, *sf.* (Naút.) Keel, the principal timber first laid down in the construction of ships. *Descubrir la quilla*, To heave down a ship.
Quillótro, **tra**, *a.* (Fam.) This or that other.
Quílo, *sm.* Chyle, the white juice formed in the stomach by the digestion of aliments.
Quilóso, **sa**, *a.* Chylous, belonging to chyle.
Quiméra, *sf.* 1. Dispute, quarrel, scuffle. 2. Vain imagination, wild fancy, chimera.
Quimérico, **ca**; y **Quimerino**, **na**, *a.* Chimerical.
Quimerísta, *sm.* 1. Wrangler, brawler; fond of quarrels. 2. One who indulges in chimeras.
Quimerizár, *vn.* To fill the head with fantastic ideas.
Química y **Químia**, *sf.* Chemistry, art of examining mineral bodies.
Quimicaménte, *ad.* Chemically.
Químico, *sm.* Chemist.—**ca**, *a.* Chemical.
Quimísta, *sm.* Chemist. V. *Alquimista.*
Quimón, *sm.* Fine printed cotton.
Quína ó **Quinaquína**, *sf.* Peruvian bark.
Quinàles, *sm. pl.* (Naút.) Preventer-shrouds.
Quinário, **ria**, *a.* Consisting of five; a Roman coin.
Quinás, *sf. pl.* 1. Arms of Portugal consisting of five scutcheons in memory of the five wounds of Christ. 2. Fives on dice.
Quincálla, *sf.* Hardware, utensils of tin, copper, &c.
Quincallería, *sf.* Ironmongery, hardware trade.
Quínce, *a.* 1. Fifteen. 2. Fifteenth.
Quincéna, *sf.* One of the registers in the tubes of an organ.
Quincéna, **Quincenário**, *s.* Fifteen.
Quincéno, **na**, *a.* Fifteenth, the ordinal number of fifteen.
Quincúnce, *sm.* (Jard.) Quincunx.
Quincurión, *sm.* A chief or corporal of five soldiers.
Quindécima, *sf.* The fifteenth part.
Quindéjas, *s.* (Mancha) Rope of three strands, made of bass or *Sparto.*
Quindénio, *sm.* Space or period of five years.
Quinéte, *sm.* Kind of camblet.
Quingentésimo, **ma**, *a.* The five hundredth.
Quiniéntos, **tas**, *a.* Five hundred.
Quínolas y **Quinolíllas**, *sf. pl.* *Reversis*, a game at cards, in which the knave is the leading card. *Estar en Quinolas*, To wear clothes of various glaring colours.
Quinoleár, *va.* To prepare the cards for the game of reversis.
Quinquagenário, **ria**, *a.* Fiftieth.
Quinquagésima, *sf.* Quinquagesima, the Sunday which precedes the beginning of Lent.
Quinquagésimo, **ma**, *a.* Fiftieth.
Quinquátro, *sm.* Roman festival in honour of Minerva, which lasted five days.
Quinquefólio, *sm.* (Bot.) Cinquefoil. V. *Cinco en rama.*
Quinquenérvia, *sf.* (Bot.) V. *Lanceola.*
Quinquénio, *sm.* Space or period of five years.
Quinquércio, *sm.* Five Grecian games of wrestling, jumping, running, quoits, &c.
Quinquenál, *a.* Quinquennial.
Quinquillería, *sf.* Hardware. V. *Buhoneria.*
Quinquilléro, *sm.* Hawker, pedler. V. *Buhonero.*

Quínta, *sf.* 1. Country seat, so called because the stewards only give a fifth part of its products to the proprietor. 2. The act of choosing one out of five to serve in the army: drawing lots for soldiers. 3. Quint, the sequence of five cards in the game of piquet. 4. Musical interval.
Quintadór, **ra**, *s.* One who draws lots in fives.
Quintaesséncia, *sf.* Quintessence.
Quintál, *sm.* 1. Quintal, one hundred weight. 2. Fifth part of one hundred weight.
Quintaláda, *sf.* The sum of 2 1/2 per cent. on the freights paid to masters of vessels.
Quintaléño, **na**; y **Quintaléro**, **ra**, *a.* Capable to contain a quintal.
Quintána, *sf.* Fever occurring every fifth day.
Quintanár, *sm.* Quintain, ancient tilting post.
Quintañón, **na**, *a.* A hundred years old; being much advanced in years.
Quintár, *va.* 1. To draw out five. 2. To come to the number of five. 3. To pay to government the duty of twenty per cent. on gold or silver. 4. To plough a piece of ground the fifth time.—*vn.* To attain the fifth, applied to the moon on the fifth day.
Quintería, *sf.* Farm; grange.
Quintérno, *sm.* Number of five sheets of paper.
Quintéro, *sm.* 1. Farmer, one who rents a farm. 2. Overseer of a farm; servant who takes care of a farm.
Quintíl, *sm.* The month of July, according to the ancient Roman calendar.
Quintílla, *sf.* A metrical composition of five feet.
Quintíllo, *sm.* 1. The fifth story in the houses of the great square in Madrid. 2. Game of ombre with five persons.
Quintín, *sm.* Sort of fine cloth of a loose texture.
Quínto, *sm.* 1. Fifth, one of the five parts into which a whole is divided. 2. Fifth, a duty of twenty per cent. on prizes, &c. paid to the Spanish government. 3. Share of a pasture-ground. 4. He on whom the lot falls to serve in the army.
Quínto, **ta**, *a.* Fifth, the ordinal number of five.
Quíntuplo, **pla**, *a.* Quintuple, five-fold.
Quiñón, *sm.* Share of profit arising from an enterprise undertaken in common with another person.
Quiñonéro, *sm.* Part-owner, one who has a share of the profit arising from an enterprise undertaken in common with other persons.
Quípos, *sm. pl.* Ropes of various colours, and with different knots, used by the ancient inhabitants of Peru to record memorable events, and keep accounts.
Quirágra, *sf.* Gout in the hand.
Quirieleysón, *sm.* Lord have mercy upon us; the responses chanted in the funeral service.
Quíries, *sm. pl.* Responses used in the liturgy, or that part of it which contains the *quirieleyson.*
Quirinál, *a.* Relating to the feast of Romulus.
Quiríte, *sm.* Roman citizen or knight.
Quirománcia, *sf.* Chiromancy, palmistry.
Quiromántico, *sm.* Professor of palmistry.
Quirotéca, *sm.* (Fam.) Glove.
Quirúrgico, **ca**, *a.* Chirurgic or chirurgical, belonging or relating to surgery.

Quirúrgo, sm. Chirurgeon.
Quisicósa, sf. Enigma, riddle; obscure question.
Quisquemíl, sm. A small cloak worn by American women.
Quisquílla y Quisquilería, sf. A ridiculous nicety; bickering, trifling dispute.
Quisquillóso, sa, a. Fastidious, precise, morose.
Quistión, sf. (Ant.) Question. V. *Question*.
Quísto, ta, pp. *irreg*. Dear, beloved; well or ill esteemed.
Quíta, sf. Receipt, acquittance, discharge.
Quíta, *interj*. God forbid! *Quita de ahi!* Away with you! out of my sight!
Quitación, sf. Salary, wages, pay, income.
Quitadór, ra, s. One who takes away, remover.
Quitaménte, ad. Totally, entirely.
Quitameriéndas, sf. (Bot.) Meadow saffron. Colchicum pratense *L*.
Quitamiénto, sm. V. *Quita*.
Quitánza, sf. (Ant.) Receipt, discharge.
Quitapelíllos, s. com. Flatterer, fawner, wheedler.
Quitapesáres, s. com. Comfort, consolation.
Quitár, va. 1. To take away, to remove; to separate. *Quitar la paja*, (Fam.) To be the first that tasted the wine in a vessel. 2. To redeem a pledge. 3. To hinder, to disturb. 4. To forbid, to prohibit. 5. To abrogate, to annul. 6. To free from any obligation. 7. To usurp, to rob. 8. To suppress an office.—*vr*. 1. To abstain, to refrain. 2. To retire, to withdraw. 3. To get rid of. *De quitar*, Of short duration. *Quitado esto*, Excepting this, besides this. *Quitarse el embozo*, (Fam.) To unmask.
Quitasól, sm. Parasol.
Quitapón ó Quitaypón, sm. Ornament of the headstall of draught horses and mules, consisting in fringes and tassels.
Quíte, sm. Obstacle, impediment.
Quíto, ta, a. Free from an obligation, clear or exempt from a charge.
Quixáda, sf. Jaw, the bone of the mouth in which the teeth are fixed.
Quixál ó Quixár, s. Grinder, a back tooth; jaw.
Quixarúdo, da, a. Large-jawed.
Quixéro, sm. Sloping bank of a canal; gradual descent.
Quíxo, sm. A hard fossil found in several mines, as the matrix of ore.
Quixónes, sm. pl. Legs of a fowl.
Quixotáda, sf. A Quixotic enterprise, an action ridiculously extravagant.
Quixóte, sm. 1. Armour which covers and defends the thigh. 2. A man ridiculously extravagant, one who engages in Quixotic enterprises. 3. Fleshy part over the hoofs of horses or asses.
Quixotería, sf. Conduct or enterprise ridiculously extravagant, quixotism.
Quixotésco, ca, a. Quixotic.
Quizá ó Quizás, ad. Perhaps. V. *Acaso*.
Quizáves, ad. (Vulg.) V. *Quizás*.
Quociénte, sm. Quotient, the number resulting from the division of one number by another.
Quodlibetál y Quodlibético, ca, a. Quodlibetical.
Quodlibéto, sm. Quodlibet, a nice paradoxical point or question.
Quóndam, (Lat. Arag.) Former, late.
Quóque, sf. (Bot.) Tree in New Granada bearing fruit the size of a goose-egg.
Quóta, sf. A share or portion assigned to each.
Quotidianaménte, ad. Daily.
Quotidiáno, na, a. Quotidian, daily; happening every day.
Quotídie, ad. y sm. Daily, every day.

R Is pronounced nearly as in English. It sometimes becomes liquid, when preceded by a mute letter, as in *frio*, and its pronunciation is stronger when two *r's* are to be pronounced, as in *tierra*. This letter is never doubled after *b, l, n, s*, or at the beginning of a word, nor even in compound words, but when it is between vowels and requires its strongest sound, as in *barra, carro*. *R* is used as a contraction of *reprobar*, like *A* for *aprobar*, in voting for degrees in universities; it also signifies *refina* on wool-packs.
Rába, sf. Bait used in the pilchard fishery.
Rabadán, sm. The principal shepherd of a sheep-walk.
Rabadílla, sf. Rump, the extremity of the backbone.
Rabadoquín, sm. (Ant.) A small piece of ordnance.
Rabanál, sm. Field or piece of ground, sown with radishes.
Rabanéro, ra, a. Very short; applied to the garments of women.—*s*. Seller of radishes.
Rabanillo, sm. 1. Small radish. 2. The tart sharp taste of wine which is on the turn. 3. Ardent desire, longing; acrimony, asperity, rudeness.
Rabaníza, sf. Radish seed.
Rábano, sm. 1. (Bot.) Radish. Raphanus sativus *L*. 2. Sourness, tartness.
Rabazúz, sm. Inspissated juice of licorice.
Rabeár, vn. To wag the tail.
Rabél, sm. 1. An ancient musical instrument with three strings, played with a bow. 2. Breech, backside.
Rabeléjo, íco, íllo, íto, sm. *dim*. of *Rabel*.
Rabéra, sf. 1. Tail, the hind or back part of any thing. 2. Handle of a cross-bow. 3. Remains of uncleaned grain or seeds.
Rabí, sm. Rabbi, a doctor or interpreter of the law among the Jews.
Rábia, sf. 1. Phrensy, madness; a disease. 2. Rage, fury, violent passion.—*interj*. Fury!
Rabiár, vn. To rage, to be mad or delirious, to be in a violent passion or furious, to suffer severe pain. *Rabiar de hambre*, To be very hungry. *Rabiar por algo*, To long for a thing.
Rabiatár, va. To tie by the tail.
Rabiazórras, sm. Among shepherds, the East wind.
Rabicaliénte, s. y a. Rut; rutting, hot.

Rabicán ó Rabicáno, *a.* Having some white hair in the tail; applied to horses.
Rabicórto, ta, *a.* Short-tailed.
Rábido, da, *a.* (Poét.) V. *Rabioso.*
Rabiéta, *sf. dim.* Violent fretting, impatience.
Rabihorcádo, *sm.* (Orn.) Frigate pelican. Pelecanus aquilus *L.*
Rabilárgo, ga, *a.* Long-tailed; having a long train.
Rabilárgo, *sm.* (Orn.) Blue crow. Corvus cyanus *L.*
Rabíllo, *sm.* 1. Mildew or black spot on the stalk or straw of corn. 2. Little tail.
Rabínico, ca, *a.* Rabbinical.
Rabinísmo, *sm.* Rabbinism, the doctrine of the rabbis.
Rabinísta, *s. com.* Follower of the doctrine of the rabbis.
Rabíno, *sm.* Rabbi, a doctor or interpreter of the law among the Jews.
Rabiosaménte, *ad.* Furiously, outrageously.
Rabióso, sa, *a.* 1. Rabid, mad; applied to dogs and other brutes. 2. Furious, outrageous, choleric, violent. *Filo rabioso*, Wire edge.
Rabisalséra, *a.* Sprightly, petulant, forward, saucy, impudent; applied to women.
Rabiséco, ca, *a.* 1. Dry-tailed, poor, lean, starving. 2. (Met.) Snappish, peevish, giving short answers.
Rabíza, *sf.* 1. Point of a fishing-rod, to which the line is fastened. 2. (Naút.) Point, the tapering end of a rope. *Moton de Rabiza*, (Naút.) Tail-block. 3. Trull, low prostitute.
Rabizár, *va.* To point the end of a rope.
Rábo, *sm.* 1. Tail, that which terminates the animal behind; applied particularly to certain animals, as pigs, &c. instead of *cola.* 2. The lower, back, or hind part of any thing; train. *Rábo de Gallo*, (Naút.) Stern-timbers. *Rábo de Puerco*, (Bot.) Hog's fennel, sulphur-wort. Peucedanum officinale *L.* *Rábo de junco*, (Orn.) Tropic bird. Phæton *L.* *Rábos*, Tatters, fluttering rags hanging down from clothes. V. *Rabera.*
Rabón, na, *a.* Docked, short-tailed.
Rabóna, *sf.* With gamblers, a trifling game.
Raboseáda y Raboseadúra, *sf.* Spattering or bespattering.
Raboseár, *va.* To spatter, to sprinkle with dirt.
Rabóso, sa, *a.* Ragged, full of tatters.
Rabotáda, *sf.* Docked or cropped tail.
Raboteár, *va.* To cut or crop the tail.
Rabotéo, *sm.* Act of cutting sheep's tails in spring.
Rabúdo, da, *a.* Long-tailed.
Ráca, *sf.* (Naút.) Traveller, a large iron ring or thimble which moves up and down the jib-boom. *Raca de la amura*, (Naút.) Jib-iron.
Racaménto, *sm.* (Naút.) Parrel, a wooden frame which surrounds the mast, and serves to hoist and lower the yards.
Racéles, *sm. pl.* (Naút.) Run of a ship.
Racimádo, da, *a.* V. *Arracimado.*
Racimár, *va.* (Arag.) V. *Rebuscar.*
Racímo, *sm.* 1. Bunch of grapes, the fruit of the vine. 2. (Fam.) Criminal hanging on the gallows. 3. Cluster of small things disposed in order.
Racimóso, sa, *a.* Full of grapes, racemose.

Raciocinación, *sf.* Ratiocination, the art of reasoning; the art of deducing consequences from premises.
Raciocinár, *vn.* To reason, to argue.
Raciocínio, *sm.* Reasoning, argument.
Ración, *sf.* 1. Ration, the quantity of food destined for one meal. 2. Daily allowance for servants, board-wages; allowance for soldiers or sailors. *Racion de hombre*, Scanty allowance. 3. Prebend.
Racionabilidád, *sf.* Rationality, the power of reasoning.
Racionál, *a.* Rational, having the power of reason; reasonable.—*sm.* 1. Power of reason. 2. Treasurer, an officer on the *Aragon* establishment of the king's household. 3. One of the sacred vestments of the chief priests among the Jews.
Racionalidád, *sf.* 1. Rationality, conformity with reason. 2. Reason, power of reasoning.
Racionalménte, *ad.* Rationally.
Racioncíca, lla, ta, *sf. dim.* Small pittance.
Racionéro, *sm.* Prebendary, the incumbent of a prebend; he who distributes the rations in a convent.
Racionísta, *s. com.* One who enjoys a certain daily allowance or pay.
Ráda, *sf.* Road, anchoring ground for ships at some distance from shore.
Radéro, *sm.* (Naút.) Ship riding at anchor in the road. *Buen radero*, (Naút.) A good roader, a ship which rides well at anchor.
Radiación, *sf.* Radiation, emission of rays.
Radiánte, *a.* Radiant, emitting or diffusing rays of light.
Radiár, *vn.* (Poét.) To radiate.
Radicación, *sf.* Radication, act of taking root; act of fixing deeply and firmly any custom.
Radicál, *a.* 1. Belonging or relating to the root. 2. Radical, original, primitive.
Radicalménte, *ad.* Radically, fundamentally, originally.
Radicárse, *vr.* To radicate, to take root, to plant deeply and firmly.
Radicóso, sa, *a.* Radical, pertaining to the root
Rádio, *sm.* 1. Radius, the semi-diameter of a circle. 2. Ray, a beam of light. 3. (Anat.) Lesser bone of the arm.
Radiómetro, *sm.* Forestaff, instrument for measuring heights.
Radióso, sa, *a.* Radiant, that emits or diffuses rays of light.
Raedéra, *sf.* 1. Scraper, an instrument with which any thing is scraped. 2. Roller or cylinder for reducing lead into sheets.
Raedízo, za, *a.* Easily scraped.
Raedór, ra, *a.* Scraper, eraser. V. *Rasero.*
Raedúra, *sf.* Scrapings, filings, parings.
Raér, *va.* To scrape, to grate; to erase. *Raer de la memoria*, To erase from memory.
Ráfa, *sf.* 1. Buttress to support mud walls. 2. A small cut or opening in a canal.
Ráfaga, *sf.* 1. A violent squall or gust of wind. 2. A small cloud.
Ráfe, *sm.* (Ar.) Eaves of a house.
Rafeár, *va.* To support or secure with buttresses.
Raféz y Rahéz, *a.* (Ant.) Vile, despicable, cheap. V. *Facil.*
Ragádia, *sf.* V. *Resquebrajadura.*

Raíble, *a.* That which may be scraped, rasped, or scratched.

Raicílla, Raizuéla y Raicéja, *sf.* A small root.

Raído, da, *a.* 1. Scraped. 2. Impudent, shameless; free, undisguised.

Raigál, *a.* Belonging or relating to the root.

Raigámbre, *sf.* Collection of roots of different trees united.

Raigár, *vn.* V. *Arraygar.*

Raigón, *sm.* 1. A large strong root. 2. Stump of a back tooth or grinder.

Raimiénto, *sm.* 1. Act of scraping, rasure. 2. (Met.) Impudence, boldness.

Raíz, *sf.* 1. Root, that part of a plant which grows in the ground. 2. Foot, base; bottom, basis, foundation. 3. Origin, original. 4. V. *E'poca.* 5. (Gram.) Root of a noun or verb from which its inflexions are derived. *A' raiz*, Close to the root. *De raiz*, From the root; entirely. *Tener raices*, To be well grounded. *Bienes raices*, Landed property.

Rája, *sf.* 1. Splinter, chip of wood. 2. Chink, crack, fissure, opening. 3. Part, portion, share. 4. Sort of coarse cloth formerly worn. *Salir de capa de raja*, To cast off old clothes; to better one's fortune. *A' raja tabla*, Courageously, vigorously. *Raja broqueles*, Braggart, boasting fellow.

Rajadíllo, *sm.* Comfit of sliced almonds incrustated with sugar.

Rajadízo, za, *a.* That which is easily split.

Rajánte, *pa.* Splitter, boaster.

Rajár, *va.* 1. To split, to divide a log of wood into chips. 2. (Fam.) To crack, to boast, to tell falsehoods.

Rajéta, *sf.* Sort of coarse cloth of mixed colours.

Rajuéla, *sf.* A small splinter or chip of wood.

Raléa, *sf.* 1. Race, breed; genus, species, quality. 2. Any bird or game which the hawk pursues in preference to others.

Raleár, *vn.* To thin, to make thin, to make rare; to manifest or discover the bad inclination or breed of any thing.

Raleón, na, *a.* Applied to a bird of prey which takes the game pursued by another.

Raléza, *sf.* Thinness, want of compactness or closeness; rarity.

Ralladéra, *sf.* Grater, an instrument for grating.

Ralladór, ra, *s.* V. *Hablador.*

Ralladúra, *sf.* Mark left by the grater; the small particles taken off by grating.

Rallár, *va.* 1. To grate, to reduce a hard body to powder. 2. To vex, to molest. *Rallar las tripas á alguno*, To importune any one.

Rállo, *sm.* Grater, an instrument used for grating.

Rallón, *sm.* Arrow or dart.

Rálo, la, *a.* Thin, rare, not close, not compact. V. *Raro.*

Ráma, *sf.* 1. Shoot or sprig of a plant, branch of a tree. 2. Branch of a family. 3. Rack, used in manufactories, to bring cloth to its proper length and breadth. 4. (Impr.) Chase for enclosing types. *En rama*, Raw material, crude stuff. *Andarse por las ramas*, To go about the bush, not to come to the point. *Asirse á las ramas*, To seek or make frivolous pretexts.

Ramadán, *sm.* Mohammedan Lent kept thirty days, during which time they fast strictly while the sun is above the horizon, and at night eat, dance, and rejoice as much as they can.

RAMA'GE, *sm.* Flowering, branches designed in cloth.

Ramáje, *sm.* Collection of branches.

Ramál, *sm.* 1. End of a rope which remains hanging. 2. Any thing springing from another, as a stair-case. 3. Halter, a rope fastened to the headstall of a horse or mule. 4. Principal passage in mines; branch, division.

Ramalázo, *sm.* 1. Lash, a stroke with a cord or rope. 2. Marks left by lashes. 3. A sudden and acute pain or grief. 4. Spot in the face. 5. Result, consequence of injuring another.

Rámbla, *sf.* 1. A sandy place, a sandy beach. 2. Cavern in a rock.

Ramblázo y Ramblézo, *sm.* Gravelly bed of a current or rivulet.

Raméra, *sf.* Licensed whore, common prostitute.

Ramería, *sf.* Brothel, bawdy-house; street formerly destined for the residence of licensed prostitutes in Spanish towns.

Rameríta y Rameruéla, *sf.* (Joc.) A little wench.

Raméro, *sm.* Young hawk hopping from branch to branch.

Ramificación, *sf.* Ramification, the production of branches; the division into branches.

Ramificárse, *vr.* To ramify, to de divided into branches.

Ramílla, ta, *sf. dim.* 1. Small shoot or sprig. 2. (Met.) Any light trifling thing.

Ramilléte, *sm.* 1. Nosegay, bunch of flowers. *Ramillete de Constantinopla.* V. *Minutisa.* 2. Pyramid of sweetmeats and fruits served on table. 3. Collection of flowers or beauties of literature.

Ramilletéro, ra, *s.* One who makes and sells nosegays.—*sm.* Vase with artificial flowers, put on altars by way of ornament.

Ramíllo, *sm.* 1. A small branch. 2. V. *Dinerillo.*

Ramíza, *sf.* Collection of lopt branches.

Rámo, *sm.* 1. Branch of a tree which is cut off; branch, germ. 2. Any part separated from a whole. 3. Disease or distemper not sufficiently known. 4. Antler of a deer's horn. *Ramo de comercio*, Branch of trade. *Vender al ramo*, To retail wine. *Domingo de ramos*, Palm Sunday. 5. Rope of onions. 6. Threads of silk with which figures are made.—*pl.* 1. Engraved flowers or other figures placed at the beginning or end of books; vignettes. 2. Arteries, veins, and nerves of the animal body.

Ramójo, *sm.* Small branch lopt from a tree.

Ramón, *sm.* Top of branches cut off for the feed of sheep in snowy weather.

Ramoneár, *vn.* To cut off the branches of trees, to nipple the tops of branches; applied to cattle.

Ramonéo, *sm.* Act of cutting or lopping branches.

Ramóso, sa, *a.* Branchy, full of branches.

Rámpa, *sf.* 1. Spasm, convulsion. 2. (Mil.) Slope of a glacis.

Rampánte, *a.* (Blas.) Rampant.

Rampiñéte, *sm.* Bar of iron with a curved point used by artillerymen.

Ramplón, na, *a.* Applied to a large coarse shoe; rude, unpolished.

Ramplón, *sm.* Calkin of horses' shoes. *A' ramplon*, Having the shoes made with calkins.

Rampójo, *sm.* 1. Rape, the stalk of a cluster of grapes when freed from the fruit. 2. (Mil.) Caltrop, an iron with three spikes thrown into the road, to annoy the enemy's horse.
Rampóllo, *sm.* Branch cut from a tree to be planted.
Ramúja, *sf.* Top of branches cut off. V. *Ramon.*
Rána, *sf.* Frog, an amphibious animal. *Ranas,* V. *Alevosa. Rana marina ó pescadora.* (Ict.) Frog-fish, fishing-frog or angler. Lophius piscatorius *L. No ser rana,* (Fam.) To be able and expert.
Ranacuájo, *sm.* Spawn of frogs. V. *Renacuajo.*
Rancajáda, *sf.* Wound in plants, or sprouts.
Rancajádo, da, *a.* Wounded with a splinter of wood.
Rancájo, *sm.* Splinter sticking in the flesh.
Rancheadéro, *sm.* Place containing huts.
Rancheár, *va.* To build huts, to form a mess.
Ranchería, *sf.* Hut or cottage where several labourers meet to mess together.
Ranchéro, *sm.* Steward of a mess.
Rãncho, *sm.* 1. Mess, a set of persons who eat and drink together. 2. A free clear passage. *Hacer rancho,* To make room. 3. A friendly meeting of persons assembled to discuss some question or other. 4. (Naút.) Mess-room; mess. *Rancho de enfermería,* Mess-room for the sick. *Rancho de Santa Bárbara,* (Naút.) Gun-room; chamber of the rudder.
Ranciárse, *vr.* V. *Enranciarse.*
Ráncio, cia; y Ranciόso, sa, *a.* Rank, rancid; old; strong scented; having the taste of oil.
Ráncio, *sm.* Rancidity, rankness.
Rancór, *sm.* Rancour. V. *Rencor.*
Ránda, *sf.* Lace, trimming.
Randádo, da, *a.* Laced, adorned with lace.
Randál, *sm.* Sort of stuff made lace or net fashion.
Randéra, *sf.* Lace-worker.
Raneár, *vn.* To croak as frogs.
Ranéta, *sf.* Rennet, a kind of apple.
Rangífero, *sm.* Rein-deer. Cervus tarandus *L.*
Rángua, *sf.* An iron box in which the spindles of machines move and play.
Raníla, *sf.* 1. A small frog. 2. Frog of the hoof of a horse or mule. 3. Cracks in hoofs of horses. 4. Disease in the bowels of cattle.
Ranínas, *sf. pl.* Ranulary veins, two veins under the tongue.
Raníz, *s.* A kind of linen.
Ranquár, *vn.* V. *Renquear.*
Ránula, *sf.* Tumour under the tongue of a horse.
Ranúnculo, *sm.* (Bot.) Crow-foot. Ranunculus *L.*
Ranúra, *sf.* Groove.
Ranzón, *sm.* Ransom, money paid for the redemption of captives.
Rápa, *sf.* (Bot.) Flower of the olive-tree.
Rapacéjo, *sm.* Border, edging.
Rapacería, *sf.* Puerility; a childish, boyish speech or action; rapacity.
Rapacidád, *sf.* Rapacity, rapaciousness; robbery.
Rapacíllo, lla, *s.* A little boy or girl.
Rapacíllo, lla, *a. dim.* of *rapaz,* Greedy.
Rapadór, ra, *s.* 1. One who scrapes, or plunders. 2. Barber.
Rapadúra, *sf.* Shaving, the act of shaving; the state of being shaved; rasure; plundering.
Rapagón, *sm.* A beardless young man.

Rapamiénto, *sm.* Act of shaving or erasing.
Rapánte, *a.* 1. Snatching, robbing or tearing off. 2. Rampant. V. *Rampante.*
Rapapiés, *sm.* Squib that runs along the ground.
Rapár, *va.* 1. To shave, to take hair off with a razor. V. *Afeytar.* 2. To plunder, to snatch away; to carry off with violence; to skin, to peel. *A' rapa terron,* Entirely, from the root.
Rapáz, *a.* Rapacious; seizing by violence.
Rapáz, za, *s.* A young boy or girl.
Rapazáda, *sf.* Childish action or speech.
Rapazuélo, la, *a. dim.* Rapacious, greedy.
Rápe, *sm.* (Fam.) Shaving, cutting off the hair or beard carelessly.
Rapidaménte, *ad.* Rapidly.
Rapidéz, *sf.* Rapidity, velocity, celerity.
Rápido, da, *a.* Rapid, quick, swift.
Rapiégo, ga, *a.* Ravenous; applied to birds of prey.
Rapíña, *sf.* Rapine, robbery; theft committed with violence. *Ave de rapiña,* Bird of prey.
Rapiñadór, ra, *s.* Plunderer, robber.
Rapiñár, *va.* To plunder, to commit robbery.
Rapísta, *sm.* Barber, shaver.
Rápo, *sm.* A round-rooted turnip.
Rapónchigo, *sm.* (Bot.) Esculent bellflower, rampion. Campanula rapunculus *L.*
Rapósa, *sf.* 1. Female fox. Canis vulpes *L.* 2. (Met.) Cunning deceitful person.
Raposeár, *vn.* To use artifices like a fox.
Raposéra, *sf.* Fox-hole, fox den.
Raposería, *sf.* Cunning of a fox; artful kindness.
Raposílla, ta, *sf. dim.* Artful wench.
Raposíno, na, *a.* Vulpine. V. *Raposuno.*
Rapóso, *sm.* Male fox. *Raposo ferrero,* Iron coloured fox, whose skin is used for furs.
Raposúno, na, *a.* Vulpine, belonging to a fox.
Rapsódia, *sf.* Rhapsody, any number of parts joined together without mutual dependence or natural order.
Rapsodísta, *sm.* Rhapsodist, poet who recites his extemporary verses.
Rápta, *a.* Applied to a woman who snatches men by force or artifice.
Rápto, *sm.* 1. Rapine, robbery. 2. Ecstasy, rapture. 3. Rape, ravishment. 4. Vapours or humours in the head impairing the senses. 5. (Astr.) V. *Movimiento.*
Raptór, *s.* Ravisher, he who commits a rape.
Raptór, ra, *s.* (Ant.) Robber, thief.
Ráque, *sm.* Arrack, a spirituous liquor.
Raquéta, *sf.* 1. Racket, battledoor. 2. Game played with battledoors or rackets.
Raquetéro, *sm.* Racket-maker, one who makes or sells rackets.
Raquítico, ca, *a.* Rickety, diseased with the rickets.
Raquítis, *sf.* Rickets, a disease incident to children.
Raraménte, *ad.* Rarely, seldom; ridiculously.
Rarefacción, *sf.* Rarefaction, extension of the parts of a body that augments its volume; especially applied to the air.
Rarefacérse, *vr.* To rarefy, to become thin and extended. V. *Rarificar.*
Rarefaciénte, *a.* Rarefying.
Rarefactívo, va, *a.* Rarefactive.
Raréza y Raridád, *sf.* 1. Rarity, uncommonness, infrequency. 2. A thing valued for its scarcity; singularity, strangeness, oddity

Rarificár, *va.* To rarefy, to make thin, to dilate.

Rarificatívo, va, *a.* That which has the power of rarefying.

Ráro, ra, *a.* 1. Rare, porous; having little density and compactness. 2. Rare, scarce, extraordinary, uncommon. 3. Renowned, famous, excellent; extravagant. *Es raro de genio*, He is an odd genius. *Rara vez*, Seldom.—*ad.* Rarely.

Rás, *sm.* Level, an even surface. *Ras en ras ó ras con ras*, On an equal footing, upon a par.

Rasadór, *sm.* 1. One who strikes corn and other dry materials with a strickle to level them with the bushel. *Rasador de la sal*, An officer appointed by the king to measure the salt with a strickle. 2. Strickle, the instrument with which salt is measured.

Rasadúra, *sf.* The act of measuring salt, and other dry articles, with a strickle. *Rasadúras*, The grain of salt taken off with the strickle.

Rasaménte, *ad.* Publicly, openly, clearly.

Rasár, *va.* 1. To measure corn with a strickle. 2. To touch another lightly. *Rasarse los ojos de agua*, To have tears standing in the eyes.

Rascadéra, *sf.* V. *Rascador y Almohaza.*

Rascadór, *sm.* 1. Scraper, an instrument used to scrape and clean bones, metals, &c.; scratcher; rasp. 2. Headpin, bodkin.

Rascadúra, *sf.* 1. The act of scratching, scraping or rasping. 2. Scratch, the mark made by scraping.

Rascalíño, *sm.* V. *Tiñuela.*

Rascamiénto, *sm.* Act of scraping or scratching.

Rascamóño, *sm.* Women's headpin, bodkin.

Rascár, *va.* 1. To scratch, to scrape. 2. To seize an opportunity, not to miss a favourable occasion. *Un asno rasca á otro*, One fool praises another.

Rascazón, *sf.* Pricking, tickling, or itching sensation which excites to scratch.

Rásco, *sm.* V. *Rascadura. Tener gana de rasco*, (Vulg.) To be desirous of romping or playing.

Rascón, na, *a.* Sour, sharp, acrid.

Rascón, *sm.* (Orn.) Land-rail. Rallus crex *L.*

Rascuñár, *va.* 1. To scar, to scratch, to scrape. 2. (Pint.) To delineate, to design a figure to be painted.

Rascúño, *sm.* 1. V. *Rasguño.* 2. First sketch of a painting.

Rasél, *sm.* (Naút.) Narrow part of a ship towards the head and stern.

Raséro, *sm.* 1. Strickle. V. *Rasador.* 2. Strict equality observed in things where a proportionate inequality should be attended to. *Ir por un rasero*, To act or proceed without making a proper distinction.

Rasgádo, da, *a.* 1. Rent, open. 2. Applied to a wide balcony or large window shutter. *Ojos rasgados*, Large or full eyes. *Boca rasgada*, Wide mouth.—*sm.* V. *Rasgon.*

Rasgadór, ra, *s.* Tearer, cleaver, one who scratches, tears, or lacerates.

Rasgár, *va.* To tear asunder, to rend, to claw, to lacerate. V. *Rasgueár.*

Rásgo, *sm.* 1. Dash, stroke; line drawn in a nice and elegant manner. *Rasgo de pluma*, Dash of a pen. 2. A grand, fine, or magnanimous action. 3. Generosity, liberality of sentiments.

Rasgón, *sm.* Rent, rag, tatter.

Rasgueádo y Rasguéo, *sm.* Act of making flourishes.

Rasgueár, *vn.* To flourish, to form figures by lines variously drawn.—*va.* To flourish the whole hand over the guitar.

Rasguñár, *va.* 1. To scratch, to scrape. 2. To sketch, to form the outlines of a drawing or picture with dots.

Rasgúño, *sm.* 1. Scratch, scar. 2. Sketch, the dotted outlines of a drawing or picture.

Rasguñuélo y ñíto, *sm. dim.* Slight scratch or sketch.

Rasílla, *sf.* 1. Serge, a kind of woollen stuff. 2. A fine tile used for flooring.

Rasión, *sf.* 1. The act of shaving or taking off hair with a razor. 2. Reduction of any hard body to powder.

Ráso, *sm.* Satin, a shining silk.

Ráso, sa, *a.* 1. Clear of obstructions, disengaged from impediments; plain. 2. Having no title or other mark of distinction. *Tabla rasa*, (Met.) Applied to the infant mind without ideas; canvass framed for painting. *Tiempo raso*, Fine weather. *Cielo raso*, Clear sky. *Caballero raso*, A private gentleman. *Al raso*, In the open air.

Ráspa, *sf.* 1. Beard of an ear of corn. 2. Backbone of fish. 3. Stalk of grapes. 4. Rasp, a coarse file. 5. Film on the barrels of quills. *Ir á la raspa*, (Fam.) To go in search of plunder. *Tender la raspa*, To lay one's self down to rest. 6. Spark struck out of a stone.

Raspadíllo, *sm.* Fraud or imposition practised by gamblers.

Raspadór, *sm.* Rasp, coarse file.

Raspadúra, *sf.* 1. The act of filing, rasping or scraping. 2. Filings, raspings, scrapings.

Raspamiénto, *sm.* Act of rasping or filing.

Raspánte, *pa.* Rasping, rough; applied to wine which grates the palate.

Raspár, *va.* 1. To scrape, to rasp, to pare off. 2. To prick, to have a sourish taste; applied to wine. 3. To steal, to carry off.

Raspeár, *vn.* To have a hair in the pen, which occasions blots.

Raspinégro, gra, *a.* (And.) V. *Arisprieto.*

Rasgón (De), *ad.* Scrapingly, thievishly.

Rasquéta, *sf.* (Naút.) Scraper, an instrument with which the dirt or filth is scraped off the planks of a ship.

Rastél, *sm.* Bar or lattice of wood or iron.

Rastilladór, ra, *s.* V. *Rastrillador.*

Rastillár, *va.* To hackle flax. V. *Rastrillar.*

Rastilléro, *sm.* Shoplifter, robber who steals and flies.

Rastíllo, *sm.* V. *Rastrillo.*

Rástra, *sf.* 1. Sled, or sledge, a carriage without wheels. 2. The act of dragging along. 3. Any thing hanging and dragging about a person. 4. A track or mark left on the ground. 5. Person constantly walking in company with another. 6. String of dried fruit. 7. Final decision, verdict, judgment. 8. (Naút.) Creeper, an instrument in the form of an anchor, used to drag for an anchor lost. 9. Rake.

Rastrallár, *vn.* To crack with a whip.
Rastrár, *va.* To drag. V. *Arrastrar.*
Rastreadór, ra, *s.* Tracer, smeller, follower.
Rastreár, *va.* 1. To trace, to follow by the footsteps or remaining marks. 2. To inquire into, to investigate. 3. To skim the ground, to fly very low. 4. *Rastrear por un ancla,* (Naút.) To drag for an anchor. 5. To sell carcasses by wholesale in a slaughterhouse.—*vn.* To float in the air, yet almost touching the ground.
Rastréo, *sm.* (Ar.) Fringe or small pieces of stuff hanging round.
Rastréro, ra, *a.* 1. Creeping, dragging, that which hangs. 2. Applied to a dog that runs by a trail. 3. Low, humble, cringing.
Rastréro, *sm.* Inspector of a slaughterhouse, a workman employed there.
Rastrilladór, ra, *s.* Hackler; cleaner.
Rastrillár, *va.* 1. To hackle, to dress flax. 2. To separate the straw from the corn with the rake.
Rastríllo, *sm.* 1. Hackle, an instrument used to clean and dress flax and hemp. 2. (Fort.) Portcullis, a machine in the shape of a harrow, suspended over the gates of a city, in order to be let down in case of a surprise. 3. Hammer of a gun-lock. 4. Rake, an instrument for separating the straw from the corn. 5. Muzzle, a fastening for the mouth, which hinders biting. 6. Ward of a key. *Rastrillo de pesebre,* Rack of a manger.
Rástro, *sm.* 1. Track, a mark left on the ground. 2. Sled, or sledge. V. *Rastra.* 3. Slaughter-house, the place where cattle are killed; place where meat is sold by the carcass. 4. Sign, token, vestige, relic. 5. V. *Mugron.*
Rastrojéra, *sf.* Stubble ground, land on which stubbles remain, or the time which they last.
Rastrójo, *sm.* Stubble, the stalks of corn left in the field by the reapers.
Rasúra, *sf.* 1. Shaving, the act of taking off the beard with a razor. 2. Scraping, filing. *Rasuras,* Boiled lees of wine, which serve to clean plate, and several other uses.
Rasuración, *sf.* V. *Rasion.*
Rasurár, *va.* To shave, to take off the beard or hair with a razor.
Ráta, *sf.* 1. She-mouse. 2. Rat. Mus rattus *L.* 3. Share, portion. *Rata parte,* Quota, assigned portion. 4. Cue of hair. *Rata por cantidad ó pro rata,* In proportion, ratably. V. *Prorata.*
Ratafía, *sf.* Ratafia, a fine spirituous liquor, chiefly made of cherries, and the kernels of apricots and peaches. V. *Rosoli.*
Rateár, *va.* 1. To lessen or abate in proportion. 2. To distribute or divide proportionally. 3. To filch, to commit petty thefts.—*vn.* To trail along the ground.
Ratéo, *sm.* Distribution made at a certain rate, or in a certain proportion.
Ratería, *sf.* 1. Larceny, petty theft. 2. Vile mean conduct in things of little value.
Ratéro, ra, *a.* 1. Creeping or crawling on the ground. 2. Skimming the ground, flying low; spoken of birds. 3. Committing petty thefts; thievish. 4. Mean, vile.
Ratetuélo, la, *s.* Little pilferer.

Ratíco, llo, to, *sm. dim.* A little while, short time.
Ratificación, *sf.* Ratification, the act of ratifying; confirmation.
Ratificár, *va.* To ratify, to approve of, to confirm.
Ratigár, *va.* To tie or secure with a rope any load on carts.
Rátigo, *sm.* Articles or goods carried in carts.
Ratihabición, *sf.* (For.) Ratification, making valid.
Ratína, *sf.* 1. Ratteen, a kind of woollen cloth, woven like serge. 2. Musk-rat. Mus zibethicus *L.*
Ráto, *sm.* 1. He-mouse. V. *Raton.* 2. Short space of time. *Al cabo de rato,* It turned out ill after thinking so long about it. *Rato ha, ó ya ha rato,* Some time ago. *Buen rato,* A pretty time, a good while; many or a great quantity. *A' ratos perdidos,* In leisure hours. *De rato en rato, ó á ratos,* From time to time, occasionally.
Ráto, ta, *a.* Firm, valid, conclusive.
Ratón, *sm.* 1. He-mouse. Mus musculus *L.* 2. (Naút.) Hidden rock. 3. (Cant.) Cowardly thief.
Ratóna, *sf.* Female mouse or rat.
Ratonár, *va.* To gnaw like mice or rats.—*vr.* To become sick as cats with eating rats.
Ratoncíllo, lla; to, ta; co, ca, *s. dim.* A little mouse.
Ratonéra, *sf.* 1. Mouse-trap. *Caer en la ratonera,* To fall into a snare. *Ratonera ó gata de agua,* Rat-trap, placed on water. 2. Hole where rats breed.
Raudál, *sm.* 1. Torrent, a rapid stream. 2. Plenty, abundance.
Raudaménte, *ad.* Rapidly.
Ráudo, da, *a.* Rapid, precipitate.
Ráuta, *sf.* Road, way, route. *Coger ó tomar la rauta,* To take one's course.
Ráya, *sf.* 1. Stroke or line drawn with a pen. 2. Limit, bounds, termination. 3. (Ict.) Ray. Raia *L. Tener á raya,* To keep within bounds. *Tener á uno á raya,* To keep one at bay. 4. Line or wrinkle in the palm of the hand. 5. Narrow piece of ground cleared of combustible matter to prevent conflagration. *Tres en raya,* A boyish play. *A' raya,* Correctly, within just limits.
Rayáno, na, *a.* Neighbouring, contiguous.
Rayár, *va.* 1. To form strokes, to draw lines. 2. To mark with lines or strokes. 3. To rifle or striate the interior of fire-arms.—*vn.* 1. To excel, to surpass. *Raya muy alto,* He stands very high in his profession. 2. (Met.) To approximate, to approach; to radiate, to emit rays.
Rayéta, *sf.* A striped cloth of various colours.
Ráyo, *sm.* 1. Ray, a beam of light; a right line. 2. Radius, the semi-diameter of a circle; spoke of a wheel. 3. Thunderbolt; fire-arms. 4. Radius, a small bone of the arm. 5. Severe pain, unforeseen misfortune. 6. (Met.) Sudden havoc, misfortune, or chastisement. 7. A lively ready genius; great power or efficacy of action. *Rayo directo, incidente, reflexo, refracto, y visual.* Direct, incidental, reflected, refracted, and visual ray. *Rayo textorio,*

Weaver's shuttle. *Rayo de leche*, Stream of milk from a nurse's nipple. *Rayos*, Rays made by artists to represent a crown of glory. *Echar rayos*, To show great wrath.

RÁYO, *interj.* Fury!

RAYÓSO, SA, *a.* Full of rays.

RAYONÁNTE, *a.* (Blas.) Radiated.

RAYUÉLA, *sf.* 1. A small line or ray. 2. Game of drawing lines.

RAYUÉLO, *sm.* (Orn.) Small kind of snipe.

RÁZA, *sf.* 1. Race, generation, lineage; branch of a family; usually taken in a bad sense. 2. Quality of cloth and other things. 3. Ray, a beam of light. 4. Cleft in a horse's hoof.

RAZÁDO, *a.* Applied to coarse woollen cloth of unequal colour.

RÁZAGO, *sm.* Coarse cloth made of tow.

RAZÓN, *sf.* 1. Reason, the power by which man deduces one proposition from another; ratiocination. 2. Reasonableness, justice, equity, moderation. *Pongase vd. en la razon*, Be moderate in your demand. 3. Account, calculation. 4. Order, mode, method. 5. Argument, proof. 6. Motive, cause; relation, account. 7. Firm, partnership, name of a commercial establishment. *Razon de pie de banco*, (Fam.) Futile silly allegation. *A' razon de*, At the rate of. *A' razon de catorce*, A term denoting a want of punctuality in accounts. *En razon*, With regard to. *Hacer la razon*, To pledge in drinking. *Por razon*, Consequently.

RAZONÁBLE, *a.* Reasonable; moderate.

RAZONABLÉJO, JA, *a.* (Joc.) Moderate, rational.

RAZONABLEMÉNTE, *ad.* Reasonably; moderately.

RAZONÁDO, DA, *a.* Rational, prudent, judicious.

RAZONADÓR, RA, *s.* Reasoner. (Ant.) Advocate.

RAZONAMIÉNTO, *sm.* Reasoning, argument, discourse.

RAZONÁNTE, *pa.* Reasoning, reasoner.

RAZONÁR, *vn.* 1. To reason, to discourse. 2. To talk, to converse.—*va.* (Ant.) 1. To name, to call. 2. To advocate, to allege. 3. To take a memorandum of things, to place to account. 4. (Ant.) To compute, to regulate.

RE, *prep.* Always used in composition, signifying repetition.

RE, *sm.* (Mús.) The second note of music.

RÉA, *sf.* Criminal, she who has committed a crime.

REACCIÓN, *sf.* Re-action.

REÁCIO, CIA, *a.* Obstinate, stubborn.

REACRIMINACIÓN, *sf.* Recrimination.

REACRIMINÁR, *va.* To recriminate.

REAGRADECÉR, *va.* To estimate any thing highly.

REAGRADECIMIÉNTO, *sm.* Act of esteeming, estimation.

REAGRAVACIÓN, *sf.* Re-aggravation.

REAGRAVÁR, *va.* To aggravate anew.

REAGÚDO, DA, *a.* Very acute.

REÁL, *a.* 1. Real, actual. 2. Royal, kingly; belonging or relating to kings. 3. Grand, magnificent, splendid. 4. True, certain. 5. Open, fair, ingenuous, candid; generous, noble. 6. Royal, an attribute of the principal galley of some foreign states. 7. (Ant.) Very good.—*sm.* 1. Camp, the king's tent. 2. Main body of an army. 3. Real, a Spanish coin, containing thirty-four *maravedis* in a real vellon. *Sentar el real*, To settle, to form an establishment. *Real de á ocho*, A dollar, or piece of eight, consisting originally of eight reals of plate, now of twenty reals vellon, and weighing an ounce in silver, equal to the 16th part of an ounce in gold. *Real de plata*, Real of plate, or two reals vellon. *Real de agua*, The portion of water which can pass an aperture the size of a real. *Real de minas*, (New Spain) Town having silver mines in its vicinity. *Tirar como á real de enemigo*, To ruin or destroy any person or thing.

REÁLCE, *sm.* 1. Raised work, embossment; any work raised on the superficies of plate or other things. 2. Brightness of colours, reflexion of light. 3. Lustre, splendour.

REÁL-HACIÉNDA, *sf.* Exchequer, or royal treasury.

REALÉJO, *sm.* 1. A chamber organ. 2. *Dim.* of *Real.*

REALÉNGO, GA, *a.* Royal, kingly.

REALÉRA, *sf.* V. *Maestril.*

REALÉTE, *sm.* V. *Dieziocheno.*

REALÉZA, *sf.* Regal dignity, royal magnificence.

REALIDÁD, *sf.* Reality, what is and not merely seems; truth and sincerity in things.

REALÍLLO, TO, *sm.* Little real, or real vellon, containing 8 1-2 quartos vellon; about 2 1-2d. sterling.

REALÍSTA, *sm.* Royalist, one who adheres to the king, and asserts the prerogatives of the crown.

REALIZÁR, *va.* To realize, to bring into being or action.

REÁLME, *sm.* (Ant.) REALM. V. *Reyno.*

REALMÉNTE, *ad.* Really, effectually; royally.

REALZÁR, *va.* 1. To raise, to elevate; to emboss. 2. To heighten the brightness of the colours in a painting. 3. To illustrate, to aggrandize.

REAMÁR, *va.* To love again; to love much.

REANIMÁR, *va.* To cheer, to encourage.

REAÑÉJO, JA, *a.* Oldish, growing old.

REAPRETÁR, *va.* To press again, to squeeze.

REAQUISTÁR, *va.* (Ant.) To reacquire any thing.

REARÁR, *va.* To replough, to plough again.

REASUMÍR, *va.* To retake, to resume.

REASUNCIÓN, *sf.* The act of resuming or reassumption.

REÁTA, *sf.* 1. Rope which ties one horse or mule to another, to make them go in a straight line. 2. The leading mule of three that draw a cart. 3. (Met.) Submission to the opinion of others. *Reatas*, (Naút.) Woolding, ropes tied round a mast in order to strengthen it.

REATADÚRA, *sf.* The act of tying one beast after another with a rope.

REATÁR, *va.* 1. To tie one beast to another with a rope; to retie or tie tightly. 2. To follow blindly the opinion of others. 3. (Naút.) To woold, to tie ropes round masts or yards in order to strengthen them.

REÁTE ó RIÁTE, *sm.* Border of flowers around the beds and walks in a garden.

REÁTO, *sm.* The state of a criminal.

REAVENTÁR, *va.* To winnow corn a second time in order to separate it from the chaff.

REBÁBA, *sf.* Reslavering, drivelling.

REBALÁGE, *sm.* Crooks or windings in a river.

REBÁLSA, *sf.* 1. Stagnant water, a pool or puddle.

2. Stagnation of humours in some part of the body.

Rebalsár, va. 1. To stop the course of water that it may form a pool. 2. To stop, to detain.

Rebanáda, sf. Slice of bread, meat, or other things.

Rebanadílla, sf. A small slice.

Rebanár, va. To cut into slices, to divide.

Rebánco, sm. (Arq.) The second bench or seat.

Rebañadéra, sf. Drag, a hooked instrument for taking things out of a well.

Rebañár, va. To pick up, to gather. [flocks.

Rebañégo, ga, a. Gregarious, belonging to

Rebáño, sm. 1. Flock of sheep, herd of cattle. 2. Crowd, heap; assembly of the faithful.

Rebañuélo, sm. Small flock or heap.

Rebaptizándo, da, a. He who is to be rebaptized. [pass.

Rebasadéro, sm. (Naút.) Difficult place to

Rebasár, va. (Naút.) To sail past any point or difficult place.

Rebastár, vn. To be more than enough.

Rebatár, va. V. *Arrebatar*.

Rebáte, sm. Dispute, disagreement.

Rebatimiénto, sm. Repulsion.

Rebatíña, sf. (Ant.) V. *Arrebatiña*. *Andar á la rebatiña*, (Fam.) To run zealously, clapping the hands, to stop any thing.

Rebatír, va. 1. To rebate, to curb, to resist; to repel. 2. To parry, to ward off. 3. To object, to refute; to repress. 4. To settle accounts.

Rebáto, sm. 1. An unexpected attack, a surprise; any unexpected event; alarm. 2. A sudden fit of passion; rapid change of humours. *De rebato*, Suddenly.

Rebautización, sf. Act of rebaptizing.

Rebautizár, va. To rebaptize.

Rebáxa, sf. 1. Abatement, deduction, diminution. 2. Drawback, the return of a part of the duty paid on foreign commodities at the exportation thereof.

Rebaxár, va. 1. To abate, to lessen, to diminish. 2. To lower the price, to dock a bill or account; to curtail the quantity. 3. To weaken the light and give a deeper shade to the tints of a piece of painting. *Rebaxar un baxel*, (Naút.) To cut down the upper works of a ship.—vr. To become sick as an assistant in some hospitals.

Rebáxo, sm. Groove made in timber or stone.

Rebebér, va. To drink often. V. *Embeber*.

Rebéco, ca, a. Cross-grained, intractable, harsh.

Rebelárse, vr. 1. To revolt; to rebel, to rise in rebellion. 2. To get at variance, to break off all friendly intercourse. 3. To resist, to oppose; to excite the passions irrationally.

Rebélde, sm. Rebel, one who revolts.

Rebélde, a. 1. Stubborn, intractable, perverse. 2. Not attending the summons of a competent judge; non-appearance in court on the day appointed. 3. Rebellious; contumacious.

Rebeldía, sf. 1. Rebelliousness, contumacious disobedience. 2. Obstinacy, stubbornness. 3. Default, non-appearance in court to plead to an action. *En rebeldía*, By default.

Rebéle y Rebélle, a. (Ant.) V. *Rebelde*.

Rebelión, sf. Rebellion, revolt, insurrection against lawful authority.

Rebellín, sm. (Fort.) Ravelin, a detached work raised before the curtain on the counterscarp of a fortress.

Rebelón, na, a. Restive, applied to a horse which will not obey his rider, and neither go forwards nor turn to either side. [rope.

Rebencázo, sm. Blow or stroke with a port-

Rebendecír, va. To bless or consecrate anew.

Rebénque, sm. Rope with which seamen are whipped on board of galleys. *Rebenque de portas*, (Naút.) Port-rope.

Rebésa, sf. (Naút.) Change in the course of tides or currents on a coast.

Rebézo, sm. Thick lip, pouting lip.

Rebién, ad. Very well.

Rebinadúra, sf. (Agr.) Ploughing a third time.

Rebinár, va. (Agric.) V. *Terciar*.

Rebisabuélo, la, s. The great, great grandfather or mother.

Rebisniéto, ta; Rebisnièto, ta, s. The great, great grandson or daughter.

Reblandecér, va. To make bland or tender.

Rebocíño, sm. A short cloak or mantle worn by women.

Rebollár, sm. Thicket of oak saplings.

Rebollidúra, sf. (Art.) Honey-comb, a flaw in the bore of a piece of ordnance.

Rebóllo, sm. 1. (Bot.) The Turkey oak. Quercus cerris *L.* 2. Boll or trunk of a tree.

Rebollúdo, da, a. 1. V. *Rehecho y doble*. 2. Applied to a rude hard diamond.

Rebosár, vn. To stop on account of too much water; applied to a water-mill.

Rebosadéro, sm. Place where any thing overflows.

Rebosadúra, sf. Overflow, the act of any liquor running over the verges of a vessel.

Rebosár, va. 1. To run over, to overflow. 2. To abound, to be in great plenty. 3. To show, to evince, to display.

Rebotadéra, sf. Iron plate which raises the nap on cloth to be shorn.

Rebotadór, ra, s. One who rebounds; clincher.

Rebotár, vn. 1. To rebound; applied to a ball. 2. To change the colour, to turn; applied to wine and other liquors. 3. To grow dull.—va. 1. To clinch the point of a spike or nail. 2. To raise the nap of cloth to be shorn. 3. To repel.—vr. To change one's opinion, to retract.

Rebóte, sm. Rebound, act of flying back, resilience. *De rebote*, On a second mission.

Rebotíca, sf. Back-room behind the shop.

Rebotíga, sf. (Ar.) Back-room adjoining a shop. [mulberry leaves.

Rebotín, sm. The second growth or shoot of

Rebozadíto, ta, a. dim. Slightly muffled or basted.

Rebozár, va. To overlay or baste meat. V. *Embozár*.—vr. To be muffled up in a cloak.

Rebózo, sm. 1. The act of muffling one's self up. V. *Embozo*. 2. Muffler, a cover for the face. V. *Rebociño*. *Rebozo de calafate*, (Naút.) Drive-bolt, used by calkers to drive out another. *De rebozo*, Secretly, hiddenly.

Rebramár, va. To low and bellow repeatedly; to answer one noise by another.

Rebrámo, sm. Noise with which the deer respond to each other.

Rebrotín, *sm.* The second growth of clover, which has been once cut.
Rebudiár, *va.* To snuffle and grunt; applied to a wild boar.
Rebuéno, na, *a.* Very good, excellent.
Rebufár, *vn.* To blow or snort repeatedly, like animals.
Rebúfo, *sm.* Act of snorting, blowing, or sniffling.
Rebujál, *sm.* Number of cattle in a flock below even fifties.
Rebujaléro, *sm.* A petty farmer.
Rebujár, *va.* To take up linen and other cloth in an awkward manner.
Rebújo, *sm.* 1. Muffler, a part of the dress of women, with which they muffle up their face. 2. Portion of tithe paid in money. 3. Wrapper for any common article.
Rebullício, *sm.* Great clamour or tumult.
Rebullír, *vn.* To stir, to begin to move.
Reburujár, *va.* To wrap up, to pack up in bundles.
Reburujón, *sm.* Bundle wrapped up carelessly, and without order.
Rebúsca, *sf.* 1. Research, the act of searching. 2. The act of gleaning fruit and grain. 3. Refuse, remains, relics. *Que hermosura de rebusca ó rebusco*, Fine gleaning; applied to those who expect much fruit with little labour.
Rebuscadór, ra, *s.* Gleaner; researcher.
Rebuscár, *va.* 1. To glean the remains of grapes left by the vintagers. 2. To search, to inquire with great curiosity and attention.
Rebúsco, *sm.* Research; gleaning. V. *Rebusca.*
Rebutír, *va.* To stuff, to fill up.
Rebuznadór, ra, *s.* One who brays like an ass.
Rebuznár, *va.* 1. To bray, to cry or make a noise like an ass. 2. (Joc.) To be a bad singer.
Rebúzno, *sm.* Braying of an ass.
Recabár, *va.* To obtain by entreaty.
Recabdár y Recadár, (Ant.) V. *Recaudar.*
Recádo, *sm.* 1. Message, errand; compliment. 2. Present, gift. *Con recado*, With compliments. 3. Provision of things necessary for some purpose. 4. Daily supply of provisions. 5. Tool, implement. 6. Plenty, abundance. 7. Instrument, record. *Recado de escribir*, Escritoir, writing-desk. *A' recado ó á buen recado*, With great care and attention. *Llevar recado*, To be reprimanded. *Sacar los recados*, To take out a matrimonial license. *Ser mozo de buen recado*, To be a youth of good conduct; (Irón.) To mismanage an affair.
Recaér, *vn.* 1. To fall back, to relapse. 2. To devolve. 3. To fall under another's power.
Recaída, *sf.* 1. Relapse, regression from a state of recovery to sickness. 2. A second fall, the act of falling again; second offence.
Recaláda, *sf.* (Naút.) The act of making or descrying the land.
Recalár, *va.* 1. To soak, to impregnate with liquor. 2. (Naút.) To stand in shore.
Recalcadaménte, *ad.* Closely, contiguously; vehemently.
Recalcár, *va.* 1. To squeeze, to press closely. 2. To stuff, to fill up.—*vr.* 1. To inculcate, to utter repeatedly and decidedly. 2. To lean back in a chair. *Recalcarse el pie*, To strain one's foot.
Recalcitrár, *vn.* 1. To wince, to kick as unwilling of the rider; spoken of a horse. 2. To oppose, to make resistance where obedience is due.
Recalentamiénto, *sm.* Excandescence.
Recalentár, *va.* To heat again; to rekindle; to excite; applied to the sexual appetite.
Recalzár, *va.* 1. To prick the outlines of a design on paper. 2. To mould up plants; to prepare mortar or cement.
Recálzo, *sm.* 1. The act of repairing a decayed wall. 2. Outside felloe of a cart-wheel.
Recalzón, *sm.* Outer felloe or felly of a wheel.
Recamadór, ra, *s.* Embroiderer.
Recamár, *va.* To embroider with raised work.
Recámara, *sf.* 1. Wardrobe, a room where clothes are kept. 2. Household furniture; equipage for travelling or domestic purposes *Recámara de cañon*, (Art.) Chamber of a gun.
Recambiár, *va.* 1. To rechange, to change a second time. 2. To add the re-exchange on a protested bill. 3. To recompense, to reward one for favours received.
Recámbio, *sm.* 1. A new exchange or barter. 2. Re-exchange. 3. Reward, retribution.
Recámo, *sm.* 1. Embroidery of raised work. 2. Button-hole, bordered with lace, and garnished at the end with a tassel.
Recanación, *sf.* Act of measuring by *canas*, a measure of about two ells.
Recancanílla, *sf.* 1. Affectation of limping, done by boys for play and amusement. 2. Tergiversation, an affected tone of talking.
Recantación, *sf.* Recantation, public retractation.
Recantón, *sm.* Corner-stone, set upright at the corners of houses and streets.
Recapacitár, *va.* To call to recollection, to recall to mind.
Recapitulación, *sf.* Recapitulation, summary,
Recapitulár, *va.* To recapitulate, to sum up the heads of a charge or discourse.
Recárga, *sf.* 1. Additional tax or duty. 2. Second charge of fire-arms.
Recargár, *va.* 1. To recharge, to charge again. 2. To remand to prison on a new charge. 3. To renew the attack, to attack again.
Recárgo, *sm.* 1. A new charge or accusation. 2. Increase of a fever.
Recáta, *sf.* The act of tasting or trying again.
Recatadaménte, *ad.* Cautiously; prudently.
Recatádo, da, *a.* 1. Prudent, circumspect, shy. 2. Honest, candid, modest.
Recatár, *va.* 1. To secrete or conceal carefully. 2. To try or taste again.—*vr.* 1. To take care, to proceed with prudence and circumspection; to be cautious. 2. To doubt, to apprehend.
Recateár, *vn.* To haggle, to proceed slowly. V. *Regatear.*
Recatería, *sf.* V. *Regatonería.*
Recáto, *sm.* 1. Prudence, circumspection. 2. Secrecy, privacy. 3. Bashfulness, modesty.
Recatón, *sm.* Metal socket of a lance or pike.
Recatón, na, *a.* y *s.* V. *Regaton.*
Recatonázo, *sm.* Stroke or blow with a pike or lance.
Recatoneár, *va.* To buy by wholesale, in order to retail again.
Recatonería y Recatonía, *sf.* V. *Regatonería.*
Recaudación, *sf.* 1. The act of collecting or gathering rents or taxes; recovery of debts. 2. Collector's office.

Recaudadór, *sm.* Tax-gatherer, collector of rents.

Recaudamiénto, *sm.* 1. Collection of rents or taxes. 2. Office or district of a collector.

Recaudár, *va.* 1. To gather, to collect rents or taxes. 2. (Met.) To obtain, to attain.

Recáudo, *sm.* 1. Collection of rents or taxes. 2. Provision, supply. V. *Recado.*

Recavár, *va.* To dig the ground a second time.

Recazár, *va.* To seize prey in the air or on the ground like a hawk.

Recázo, *sm.* 1. Guard, a part of the hilt of a sword. 2. Back part of the blade of a knife.

Recebír, (Ant.) V. *Recibir.*

Recél, *sm.* A sort of striped tapestry.

Recentadúra, *sf.* Leaven preserved for the kneading and raising of bread.

Recentál, *a.* Applied to a sucking lamb.

Recentár, *va.* To put sufficient leaven into the dough to raise it. V. *Renovarse.*

Receñír, *va.* To regird, to gird tight.

Recepción, *sf.* Reception, the act of receiving.

Recépta, *sf.* Book in which fines are entered. V. *Receta.*

Receptación, *sf.* Reception of stolen goods.

Receptáculo, *sm.* 1. Receptacle, the hollow vessel which receives any liquid. 2. Refuge, asylum. 3. Gutter which conveys the water from the eaves of buildings.

Receptadór, *sm.* Receiver of stolen goods; abetter or abettor of crimes.

Receptár, *va.* To receive stolen goods; to abet any crime.—*vr.* To take refuge. V. *Recetar.*

Receptívo, **va**, *a.* Receptive.

Recépto, *sm.* Asylum, a place of refuge.

Receptór, **ra**, *s.* 1. Receiver, treasurer. 2. Secretary or actuary who attends a delegate judge.

Receptoría, *sf.* 1. Receiver's or treasurer's office. 2. Place of a receiver or treasurer. 3. Power of a delegate judge.

Recercár. V. *Cercar.*

Recésit, *sm.* Vacation. V. *Recle.* [cession.

Recéso, *sm.* Recess, remote apartment; re-

Recéta, *sf.* 1. Recipe, a prescription in writing by a physician or surgeon. 2. Memorandum of orders received, or articles demanded; order for goods. 3. Account of parcels sent from one office to another. [medicines.

Recetadór, *sm.* Prescriber, he who prescribes

Recetár, *va.* 1. To prescribe medicines. 2. (Met.) To make extravagant charges. *Recetar en buena botica,* (Fam.) To have rich friends to support extravagance.

Recetário, *sm.* 1. Memorandum or register of the prescriptions made by a physician. 2. Apothecary's file, containing the prescriptions which are not yet paid for by his customers.

Recetéro, *sm.* One who preserves or collects some particular prescriptions of physicians. *Recetéros,* Pedlers, hawkers.

Recetór, *sm.* Receiver, treasurer. V. *Receptor.*

Recetoría, *sf.* Treasury, place for keeping money.

Rechazadór, **ra**, *s.* Repeller, contradicter.

Rechazamiénto, *sm.* Repulsion.

Rechazár, *va.* 1. To repel, to repulse, to drive back. 2. To contradict, to impugn.

Recházo, *sm.* Rebound, resilition, re-action.

Rechífla, *sf.* Whistle, whistling of the winds.

Rechinadór, **ra**, *s.* Creaker. [gnashing of teeth.

Rechinamiénto, *sm.* Creaking of a machine,

Rechinár, *vn.* 1. To creak, to make a harsh noise. 2. To engage in any thing with reluctance.

Rechíno, *sm.* Creaking, clang, any harsh noise.

Rechóncho, **cha**, *a.* Chubby; applied to a short thick person. [on a descent.

Reciál, *sm.* Rapid, impetuous current of rivers

Reciaménte, *ad.* Strongly, forcibly, stoutly.

Recibidéro, **ra**, *a.* Receivable, that can be received.

Recibidór, *sm.* Receiver, he that receives.

Recibiénte, *pa.* Recipient, receiving.

Recibimiénto, *sm.* 1. Reception, the act of receiving. 2. Entertainment given to one who comes from abroad. 3. Antechamber, the room that leads to the principal apartment; general reception of company. 4. (Toledo) An altar erected in the streets for the reception of the sacrament on procession days.

Recibír, *va.* 1. To accept, to receive. 2. To take charge of. 3. To imbibe, to drink in, to draw in. 4. To suffer, to admit; to receive company or visits as a lady. 5. To go and meet any person. 6. To fasten, to secure with mortar. 7. To experience any injury; to receive an attack determined to resist it. *Recibir á cuenta,* To receive on account. *Recibirse de abogado,* To be admitted as a counsellor; to be called to the bar.

Recíbo, *sm.* 1. Reception, the act of receiving. 2. Receipt, discharge, acquittance. *Estar de recibo,* To be disposed for receiving visits. *Madera de recibo,* (Naút.) Timber fit for service. *Pieza de recibo,* Drawing-room. 3. Visit, entertainment, or reception of friends.

Récien, *ad.* Recently, lately; used always before participles instead of *reciente.*

Reciénte, *a.* Recent, new, fresh; just made.

Recienteménte, *ad.* Recently, newly.

Recinchár, *va.* To bind round one thing to another with a girdle.

Recínto, *sm.* Precinct, district.

Récio, **cia**, *a.* Stout, strong, robust, vigorous. 2. Coarse, thick, clumsy. 3. Rude, uncouth, intractable. 4. Arduous, rigid, rapid, impetuous. *Recio de complexion,* Of a strong constitution.

Récio, *ad.* Strongly, stoutly, rapidly, vehemently, vigorously. *Hablar recio,* To talk loud. *De recio,* Strongly, violently, precipitately, rapidly.

Récipe, *sm.* 1. (Lat.) Prescription of a physician. 2. Displeasure, disgust; ungenteel or bad usage. [—*a.* Receiving.

Recipiénte, *sm.* (Quím.) Recipient, receiver.

Reciprocación, *sf.* Reciprocation, reciprocalness.

Reciprocaménte, *ad.* Reciprocally, mutually.

Reciprocár, *va.* To reciprocate, to act interchangeably.—*vr.* To correspond mutually.

Recíproco, **ca**, *a.* Reciprocal, mutual. *Verbo recíproco,* Reciprocal verb, the action of which is reflected on the agent which governs it, and is always used with the pronouns *me, te,* or *se,* as *reciprocarse.* [of annulling.

Recisión, *sf.* Rescission, abrogation; the act

Recísimo, **ma**, *a. sup.* Most vehement.

Recitación, *sf.* Recitation, the act of reciting.
Recitádo, *sm.* Recitative, a kind of tuneful pronunciation, more musical than common speech, and less than song.
Recitadór, ra, *s.* Reciter.
Recitánte, ta, *s.* V. *Comediante y Farsante.*
Recitár, *va.* To recite, to rehearse.
Recitatívo, va, *a.* Recitative.
Reciúra, *sf.* Strength, force; rigour of the season.
Recizálla, *sf.* Second filings or fragments.
Reclamación, *sf.* 1. Reclamation, the act of reclaiming. 2. Objection, remonstrance.
Reclamár, *va.* 1. To decoy birds with a call or whistle. 2. To reclaim, to demand. 3. (Naút.) To hoist or lower a yard by means of a block. *vn.* To contradict, to oppose.
Reclámes, *sm. pl.* (Naút.) Sheave-holes in a top-mast-head.
Reclámo, *sm.* 1. Decoy-bird, a bird trained to decoy others. 2. Call, an instrument to call birds. 3. Allurement, inducement, enticement. 4. (Naút.) Tye-block. 5. Reclamation. 6. (Impr.) Catch-word. 7. (Cant.) Prostitute's bully. *Acudir al reclamo,* (Fam.) To answer, to go where there is a thing suitable to one's purpose.
Recle, *sm.* Vacation, rest from choir-duties.
Reclinación, *sf.* Reclining.
Reclinár, *va.* To recline, to lean back. *Reclinarse en ó sobre,* To lean on or upon.
Reclinatório, *sm.* Couch, any thing fit to lean on.
Recluír, *va.* To shut up, to seclude.
Reclusión, *sf.* 1. Reclusion, the act of shutting up. 2. Place in which one is secluded.
Reclúso, *a.* y *s.* Recluse.
Reclusório, *sm.* Recess, place of retirement.
Reclúta, *sf.* Recruiting, the act of raising men for the army; supply.—*sm.* Recruit, a new soldier; a man enlisted for the service.
Reclutár, *va.* 1. To recruit, to supply an army with new men. 2. To repair any thing wasted by new supplies.
Recobrár, *va.* 1. To recover, to get back what was lost. 2. (Naút.) To rouse in, to take up the end of a rope which hangs loose.—*vr.* To recover from sickness, to regain vigour of body or mind.
Recóbro, *sm.* Recovery, the restoration of what had been lost.
Recocér, *va.* To boil again, to boil too much. —*vr.* To consume one's-self with rage and indignation.
Recócho, cha, *a.* Boiled too much, over-done.
Recocído, da, *a.* 1. Over-boiled. 2. Skilful, clever. 3. Over-ripe, dried up.
Recodadéro, *sm.* Place for leaning on one's elbow.
Recodárse, *vr.* To lean with the elbow upon any thing.
Recodír, *vn.* V. *Recudir.*
Recódo, *sm.* A corner or angle jutting out.
Recogedéro, *sm.* 1. Place where things are gathered or collected. 2. Instrument with which things are gathered.
Recogedór, *sm.* 1. One who shelters or harbours. 2. Gatherer, gleaner.
Recogér, *va.* 1. To retake, to take back. 2. To gather, to collect; to contract. 3. To receive, to protect, to shelter. 4. To lock up in a mad-house. 5. To suspend the use, or stop the course, of any thing. 6. To extract intelligence from books. *Recoger una proposicion,* To retract a proposal. *Recoger un vale,* To take up and pay a note. *Recoger velas,* To conclude or finish a discourse; to become continent, or moderate.—*vr.* 1. To take shelter or refuge, to withdraw into retirement. 2. To reform or retrench one's expenses. 3. To go home, to retire to rest. 4. To abstract one's self from worldly thoughts.
Recogídas, *sf. pl.* Women shut up in a house of correction.
Recogidaménte, *ad.* Retiredly.
Recogído, da, *a.* Retired, secluded; contracted.
Recogimiénto, *sm.* 1. Collection, assemblage. 2. Retreat, shelter. V. *Reclusion.* 3. House where women are confined, or live in retirement. 4. Abstraction from all worldly concerns; preparation for spiritual exercises.
Recolár, *va.* To strain a second time.
Recolección, *sf.* 1. Summary, abridgment. 2. Convent, where a stricter observance of the rules of religious orders prevails. 3. Retirement, abstraction from worldly concerns and affairs. 4. Crop of grain or fruits.
Recolegír, *va.* V. *Colegir.*
Recoléto, ta, *a.* Belonging to a convent where a stricter observance of the rules of religious orders is maintained.—*s.* Devotee who lives retired from all worldly pomp, a recollect.
Recoloráde, da, *a.* Copper-nosed, having a very red face or nose.
Recombinár, *va.* To recombine.
Recomendáble, *a.* Commendable, laudable; worthy of praise.
Recomendableménte, *ad.* Laudably.
Recomendación, *sf.* 1. Recommendation, the act of commending. 2. Injunction, application. 3. Praise, eulogy. 4. Dignity, authority. *Carta de recomendacion,* Letter of introduction.
Recomendár, *va.* 1. To charge, to enjoin. 2. To recommend, to commend.
Recomendatório, ria, *a.* Recommendatory.
Recompénsa, *sf.* 1. Compensation, satisfaction. 2. Recompense, reward, remuneration. *En recompensa,* In return.
Recompensáble, *a.* Capable of being rewarded.
Recompensación, *sf.* Compensation, reward.
Recompensár, *va.* To recompense, to reward.
Reconcentramiénto, *sm.* Act of introducing or establishing in the centre.
Reconcentrár, *va.* 1. To introduce, to enter into something else. 2. To dissemble, to hide or conceal sentiments or affections.—*vr.* To root, to take root; applied to sentiments and affections.
Reconciliación, *sf.* 1. Reconciliation, renewal of friendship; agreement of things seemingly opposite. 2. Short confession, detailing things previously omitted.
Reconciliadór, ra, *s.* Reconciliator, reconciler.
Reconciliár, *va.* 1. To reconcile, to make to like and be liked again. 2. To hear a short confession. 3. To consecrate anew any sacred place which has been polluted or defiled.—*vr.* To confess some slight offences.
Reconcomérse, *vr.* To scratch frequently in consequence of a continual itching.
Reconcómio, *sm.* 1. Prurience, itching. 2. Fear, apprehension. 3. Craving, violent desire. 4.

Raising or shrugging the shoulders with satisfaction or resignation.

Recóndito, ta, *a.* Recondite, secret, concealed.

Reconducción, *sf.* Renewal of a lease. [again.

Reconducír, *va.* To renew a lease or contract

Reconfesár, *va.* To confess again.

Reconocedór, ra, *s.* Examiner, one who tries or examines; one who recognises.

Reconocér, *va.* 1. To try, to examine closely. 2. To submit to the command or jurisdiction of others. 3. To acknowledge favours received. 4. To consider, to contemplate. 5. To comprehend, to conceive. 6. To acknowledge the right of property of others; to recognise. 7. To reconnoitre.

Reconocidaménte, *ad.* Gratefully, confessedly.

Reconocído, da, *a.* y *s.* 1. Acknowledged, confessed. 2. Grateful, obliged. 3. Recognisee, one in whose favour a bond is given.

Reconociénte, *pa.* Recognising.

Reconocimiénto, *sm.* 1. Recognition, the act of recognising. 2. Acknowledgment, mark of gratitude. 3. Recognisance; subjection, submission. 4. Examination, inquiry. 5. Recognisance, acknowledgment of a bond or other writing in court.

Reconquísta, *sf.* Reconquest, a place reconquered. [again.

Reconquistár, *va.* To reconquer, to conquer

Recontánte, *pa.* Repeater; reporting.

Recontár, *va.* To recount, to relate distinctly.

Reconténto, *sm.* Content, perfect content.

Reconténto, ta, *a.* Very content.

Reconvalecér, *vn.* To recover from sickness.

Reconvención, *sf.* Charge, accusation; recrimination.

Reconvenír, *va.* 1. To charge, to accuse. 2. To retort, to recriminate, to accuse the prosecutor; to convert the plaintiff into the defendant.

Recopilación, *sf.* 1. Summary, abridgment. 2. Collection of a variety of things taken out of books. *Recopilacion de las leyes,* Abridgment or collection of the statutes.

Recopiladór, *sm.* Compiler, collector, abridger.

Recopilár, *va.* To abridge, to collect.

Recoquín, *sm.* A chubbed little fellow, short and thick.

Recordáble, *a.* Worthy of being recorded.

Recordación, *sf.* Remembrance, the act of calling or bringing any thing to recollection.

Recordadór, ra, *s.* Recorder, one who records.

Recordánte, *pa.* Recording; register.

Recordár, *va.* To remind, to put in mind; to call to recollection.—*vn.* To awaken from sleep, to cease sleeping. [may be recorded.

Recordatívo, va, *a.* That which records or

Recorrér, *va.* 1. To run over, to examine, to survey. 2. To read over, to peruse. 3. To mend, to repair.—*vn.* To recur, to have recourse to. *Recorrer la memoria,* To call to recollection. *Recorrer un bazel,* (Naút.) To repair a ship. *Recorrer los cables,* (Naút.) To underrun the cables. *Navio en recorrida,* A ship under repairs. *Recorrer los cañaverales,* To run from house to house asking for something.

Recortádo, *sm.* 1. Figure cut out of paper. 2. Piece of painting which is not well finished.

Recortár, *va.* 1. To cut away, to shorten, to pare off. 2. To cut out figures of paper; to delineate a figure in profile.

Recorvár, *va.* V. *Encorvar.*

Recórvo, va, *a.* V. *Corvo.*

Recosér, *va.* To sew again what had been ripped up or rent.

Recostadéro, *sm.* Reclining or resting-place.

Recostár, *va.* To lean against, to recline.—*vr.* To go to rest; to repose or recline.

Recóva, *sf.* 1. Act of purchasing in the country, eggs, butter, or poultry, in order to retail them in town. 2. Pack of hounds. 3. (And.) Shed, stall.

Recovéco, *sm.* 1. Turning, winding. 2. Simulation, artifice.

Recovéro, *sm.* Huckster, one who buys eggs, butter, or poultry, to retail them.

Récre, *sm.* Vacation of choristers. V. *Recle.*

Recreación, *sf.* Recreation, diversion, amusement.

Recreár, *va.* To amuse, to delight, to gratify.—*vr.* To divert one's self.

Recreatívo, va, *a.* Recreative, diverting.

Recrecér, *vn.* 1. To grow again. 2. To grow to excess, to be overgrown. 3. To occur, to happen.

Recrecimiénto, *sm.* Growth, increase, augmentation. [hawk

Recreído, da, *a.* Intractable; applied to a

Recreméntos, *sm. pl.* Recrements, spume, dregs, dross, scoria; residuum.

Recréo, *sm.* 1. Recreation, relief after toil or pain; amusement. 2. Place of amusement.

Rectaménte, *ad.* Rightly, justly.

Rectángulo, la, *a.* Rectangular, right angled; having angles of ninety degrees.

Rectángulo, *sm.* Rectangle, a right angle.

Rectificación, *sf.* Rectification, the act of rectifying. [til.

Rectificár, *va.* To rectify, to clarify; to redis-

Rectificatívo, va, *a.* That which rectifies or corrects.

Rectilíneo, nea, *a.* Rectilinear or rectilineous, consisting of right lines.

Rectitúd, *sf.* 1. Straightness, the shortest distance between two points. 2. Rectitude, justness, uprightness; exactitude.

Récto, ta, *a.* 1. Straight, erect; right. 2. Just, upright.

Rectór, ra, *s.* 1. Superior of a community or establishment. *Rector de una universidad,* Rector of a university. 2. Curate, rector.

Rectorádo, *sm.* Rectorship, the dignity or office of a rector, and the time of its duration.

Rectorál, *a.* Rectorial, belonging to a rector.

Rectorár, *vn.* To attain the office of rector.

Rectoría, *sf.* 1. Rectory, curacy; an ecclesiastical living. 2. Office and dignity of a rector.

Récua, *sf.* 1. Drove of beasts of burthen. 2. Multitude of things following one after another.

Recuáge, *sm.* Custom or duty for the passage of cattle.

Recudimiénto y Recudimiénto, *sm.* Power vested in a person to gather rents or taxes.

Recudír, *va.* 1. To pay some money in part of wages or other dues. 2. V. *Acudir.*—*vn.* 1. To rebound, to set out again, to revert to the original place or state. 2. To meet, to concur.

Recuénto, *sm.* 1. (Gal.) Inventory. V. *Inventario.* 2. Recension.

Recuérdo, *sm.* Remembrance, hint given of what has passed.

Recuéro, *sm.* Muleteer, mule-driver.

Recuésto, *sm.* Declivity, a gradual descent.

Recúla, *sf.* Recoil, retrocession.

Reculáda, *sf.* (Naút.) The falling of a ship astern; falling behind.

Reculár, *vn.* 1. To fall back, to retrograde. 2. To give up, to yield.

Recúlo, la, *a.* Having no tail; applied to hens or pullets.—*sm.* V. *Reculada.*

Reculónes (A'), *ad.* Retrogradely.

Recuperáble, *a.* Recoverable, that may be recovered.

Recuperación, *sf.* Recovery, the act of recovering or rescuing.

Recuperadór, ra, *s.* Rescuer, redeemer.

Recuperár, *va.* To recover, to rescue, to regain.—*vr.* To recover from sickness.

Recuperatívo, va, *a.* That which recovers or has the power of recovering.

Recúra, *sf.* Comb-saw, an instrument used by comb-makers for making combs.

Recurár, *va.* To make or open the teeth of combs.

Recurrír, *va.* To recur, to have recourse to.—*vn.* To revert.

Recúrso, *sm.* 1. Recourse, application for help or protection. 2. Recourse, return to the same place. 3. Appeal, recourse to a higher court of justice. *Sin recurso*, Definitively, without appeal.

Recusáble, *a.* That may be refused, or rejected.

Recusación, *sf.* Refusal; recusation.

Recusánte, *pa.* Refuser, refusing.

Recusár, *va.* 1. To refuse to admit, to decline admission. 2. To recuse or challenge a judge. *Recusar los testigos*, To object to witnesses, not to admit them.

Red, *sf.* 1. Net, a texture woven with interstices or meshes; in particular that which is used for fishing and fowling. 2. Grate of the parlour in nunneries. 3. Grate through which fish or bread is sold. 4. Prison with a strong grate, used in the villages in Spain to secure criminals. 5. Snare, wile, fraud. 6. Silk coif or head-dress. *Red barredera*, Drag-net. *Red de araña*, Cobweb. *Red de combate*, (Naút.) Netting. *Red de pazaros*, A thin clear stuff. *Caer en la red*, To fall into the snare. *A' red barredera*, In a destructive manner.

Redactór, *sm.* Compiler, editor.

Redáda, *sf.* 1. Casting of a net, a netful of fish. 2. Multitude, crowd.

Redáño, *sm.* Caul, the integument in which the bowels are enclosed.

Redár, *va.* To cast a net.

Redargución, *sf.* Retort, refutation.

Redargüír, *va.* To retort, to reply.

Redecílla, ca, ta, *sf.* A small net. V. *Punto de malla.*

Redecír, *va.* (Ant.) To repeat.

Rededór, *sm.* Environs. V. *Contorno. Al rededor*, Round about, thereabout, a little more or less.

Redél, *sm.* (Naút.) Loof-frame.

Redemír, *va.* To rescue, to redeem. V. *Redimir.*

Redención, *sf.* 1. Redemption, the act of redeeming. 2. Recovery of lost liberty, ransom. 3. Aid, assistance, support; redemption.

Redentór, ra, *s.* Redeemer, one who rescues, redeems, or ransoms; Jesus Christ.

Redéro, *sm.* 1. Net-maker; one who catches birds or fish with nets. 2. Hawk caught in a net.

Redéro, ra, *a.* Reticular, retiform; reticulated.

Redición, *sf.* Repetition of what had been said before.

Rediezmár, *va.* To decimate again, to tithe a second time.

Rediézmo, *sm.* The ninth part of crops which have already been tithed.

Redíl, *sm.* Sheepfold, sheepcot.

Redimíble, *a.* Redeemable, that may be redeemed.

Redimír, *va.* 1. To redeem, to rescue, to ransom; to pay off a mortgage or redeem a pledge. 2. To succour, to relieve; to extricate or liberate. *Redimirse de algun trabajo*, To extricate one's self from some trouble and difficulties.

Redingót, *sm.* Riding-coat, a kind of great coat.

Redistribución, *sf.* A new or second distribution.

Rédito, *sm.* Revenue, rent, proceeds.

Redituáble ó Reditual, *a.* Producing rent, benefit, or profit; rentable.

Reditüár, *va.* To yield or produce any benefit or profit; to rent.

Redobládo, da, *a.* 1. Redoubled. 2. Stout and thick.

Redoblamiénto, *sm.* Reduplication.

Redoblár, *va.* 1. To redouble, to increase by a half. 2. To clinch, to rivet. 3. To touch twice the same chord.

Redóble, *sm.* 1. A repeated touching of the same chord; double beat on the drum. 2. Ampliation of a discourse by alleging new arguments.

Redoblegár, *va.* V. *Redoblar y Doblegar.*

Redolíno, *sm.* (Ar.) Wheel in which lots are to be drawn.

Redóma, *sf.* 1. Phial, broad-bottomed bottle. 2. (Vulg.) Present given to a new married couple.

Redomadázo, za, *a.* Very artful, or sly.

Redomádo, da, *a.* Artful, sly, crafty, cunning.

Redomázo, *sm.* Stroke or blow in the face with a bottle of ink.

Redomílla, ca, ta, *sf.* A small phial.

Redónda, *a.* Applied to a round ball or capsule of silk.—*sf.* 1. Circle, neighbourhood. V. *Comarca.* 2. Pasture-ground.

Redondaménte, *ad.* 1. In circumference, in a circle, around. 2. Roundly, clearly, plainly.

Redondeár, *va.* To round, to make round. *Redondear la hacienda*, To manage one's income or property in such a manner as to be free from debt.—*vr.* To extricate one's self from difficulties, to exonerate one's self of debts.

Redondél, *sm.* A round cloak; a circle.

Redondéte, *a. dim.* Roundish, circular.

Redondéz, *sf.* Roundness, circular form.

Redondílla, *sf.* Roundel or roundelay, a stanza of four verses of eight syllables each.

Redóndo, da, *a.* 1. Round, of a circular or spherical form; round or Roman; applied to letters. 2. Free from debts, unencumbered, in easy circumstances. 3. Defenceless, without arms. 4. Applied to land turned to pasture. 5. Applied to persons whose grandfathers and grandmothers were of equal rank by birth. 6. Common, not distinguishable from the community. 7. Clear, manifest, straight. *A' la redonda*, Round about.
Redóndo, *sm.* 1. Specie, hard cash. 2. Globe, orb. *De redondo*, In round clothes; applied to children beginning to walk. *En redondo*, All around; in round characters.
Redondón, *sm.* A large circle or orbicular figure.
Redopélo, *sm.* 1. The act of rubbing cloth against the grain. 2. Scuffle, affray. *Al redopelo*, Preposterously, against all rule and reason. *Traer al redopelo*, To vex, to drag about contemptuously.
Redór, *sm.* A round mat.
Rédro, *ad.* (Fam.) Behind, backwards.—*sm.* Rough circles which form every year on the horns of black cattle, and serve to indicate their age.
Redrójo y Redruéjo, *sm.* 1. A small bunch of grapes remaining after the vintage. 2. After-fruit or blossom. 3. A puny weak child, slow in its growth. [not thrive.
Redrojuélo, *sm.* (Fam.) Languid boy who does
Redrúña, *sf.* Left hand or side. V. *Vuelta*.
Reducción, *sf.* 1. Reduction, the act of reducing. 2. Mutation, alteration. 3. Dissolution, liquefaction. 4. Exchange of one coin for another, reduction of one kind of money into another. *Reduccion de guineas á shelines*, A reduction of guineas into shillings. 5. Powerful persuasion. 6. Reduction of a place or country. 7. Conversion of infidels to the true religion; Indian people converted. 8. (Quím.) Resolution of compounds.
Reducíble, *a.* Reducible, convertible.
Reducimiénto, *sm.* Reduction.
Reducír, *va.* 1. To reduce any thing to its former state. 2. To exchange one thing for another, to barter; to convert, to commute; to resolve. 3. To diminish, to lessen; to contract, to abridge. 4. To comprehend, to contain, to include. 5. To reclaim, to bring back to obedience. 6. To persuade, to convert. 7. (Pint.) To reduce a figure or picture to smaller dimensions retaining its original character.—*vr.* To confine one's self to a moderate way of life; to resolve on punctuality.
Redúcto, *sm.* (Fort.) Redoubt.
Redundáncia, *sf.* Superfluity, redundance; excess.
Redundánte, *pa.* Redundant, superfluous.
Redundanteménte, *ad.* Redundantly.
Redundár, *vn.* 1. To exundate, to overflow, to be redundant. 2. To redound, to conduce, to contribute.
Reduplicación, *sf.* Reduplication.
Reduplicár, *va.* To reduplicate, to double; to repeat the same thing over again.
Reedificación, *sf.* Rebuilding.
Reedificadór, ra, *s.* Rebuilder, re-edifier.
Reedificár, *va.* To rebuild, to build again that which is ruined or fallen; to restore.

Reelección, *sf.* Re-election.
Reelegír, *va.* To re-elect, to elect again.
Reembarcár, *va.* To reship, to re-embark.—*vr.* To re-embark, to take shipping again.
Reembárco, *sm.* Re-embarkation, reshipment.
Reembargár, *va.* To seize or embargo a second time.
Reembolsáble, *a.* Capable of re-imbursing.
Reembolsár, *va.* To recover any money advanced; to reimburse.
Reembólso, *sm.* Recovery of money advanced.
Reemplázar, *va.* To replace.
Reemplázo, *sm.* 1. Replacing, the act of placing any thing in its former place. 2. Substitute in the militia.
Reempleár, *va.* To re-employ, to repurchase.
Reencargár, *va.* To recommend again, to recharge. [commend eagerly.
Reencomendár, *va.* To commend again, to re-
Reencuéntro, *sm.* 1. Rencounter, collision; a slight combat, a skirmish. 2. Scuffle, affray.
Reenganchár, *va.* (Mil.) To re-enlist.—*vr.* To enlist one's self again, or to be crimped.
Reenganchamiénto y Reengánche, *sm.* (Mil.) Act of re-enlisting or being crimped again into the army; money given to a soldier who enlists again.
Reengendradór, *sm.* One who regenerates or restores, regenerator.
Reengendramiénto, *sm.* Regeneration.
Reengendrár, *va.* 1. To regenerate, to reproduce, to produce anew. 2. To renew, to revive.
Reensayár, *va.* To re-examine, to prove again.
Reensáye, *sm.* Re-examination; second assay.
Reesperár, *va.* To have great hope.
Reexâminación, *sf.* Re-examination.
Reexâminár, *va.* To re-examine.
Refacción, *sf.* 1. Refection, refreshment. 2. Restitution, reparation.
Refacér, *va.* V. *Rehacer*.
Refalsádo, da, *a.* False, deceitful.
Refáxo, *sm.* A kind of short petticoat used by mountaineers or highlanders; kilt.
Refección, *sf.* Refection, refreshment; reparation.
Refectório, *sm.* Refectory, the eating-room in convents.
Referéncia, *sf.* Reference, relation to; narration.
Referendário, *sm.* 1. (Ant.) Reporter. 2. Officer appointed to countersign ordinances, and other public acts. V. *Refrendario*.
Referénte, *a.* Referring, referrible.
Referíble, *a.* Referrible.
Referír, *va.* 1. To refer, to relate, to report. 2. To direct, to mark out a certain course. 3. To mark weights and measures.—*vr.* 1. To refer, to have a relation to; to respect. 2. To refer to some former remark. *Referirse al parecer de otro*, To refer to another's opinion.
Refertéro, ra, *a.* Quarrelsome, wrangling.
Reféz, *a.* *De refez*, (Ant.) V. *Fácilmente*.
Refiérta, *sf.* (Ant.) Opposition, contradiction.
Refigurár, *va.* To retrace any image formerly seen or conceived. [librium.
Refilón (De), *ad.* Sharply, cuttingly; in equi-
Refína, *sf.* A kind of superfine wool.
Refinación, *sf.* Purification, defecation.

Refinadéra, *sf.* Refiner, a long stone in the form of a cylinder, smaller than that with which the cocoa nut is ground, called *mano*, which serves to work the chocolate, after the cocoa has been mixed with sugar and cinnamon.
**Refiná
do, da**, *a.* Refined, subtle, artful.
Refinadór, *sm.* Refiner, one who refines or purifies.
Refinadúra, *sf.* Refining, the act of purifying liquors or metals.
Refinár, *va.* 1. To refine, to purify. 2. To render more dexterous or useful.
Refíno, na, *a.* Double refined, extremely clarified. *Lana refina*, Very fine white wool.
Refíno, *sm.* (Sevilla) A grocer's shop, where sugar, cocoa, chocolate, and spices are sold. V. *Refinacion*. [tify.
Refirmár, *va.* To strengthen, to secure, to ra-
Refitoléro, ra, *s.* One who has the care of the refectory.
Refitór, *sm.* In some bishoprics, the portion of tithe received by the chapter of the cathedral.
Refitório, *sm.* Refectory. V. *Refectorio*.
Reflectír ó Reflectár, *vn.* (Opt.) To reflect, to cast back.
Refléxa, *sf.* 1. Craft, cunning, artifice. 2. Reflection, observation, remark.
Reflexár, *vn.* To reflect the rays of light; to meditate. V. *Reflexionar*.
Reflexíble, *a.* Reflexible, that is capable of reflexion.
Reflexión, *sf.* (Catop.) 1. Reflection, the act of throwing back; reflection of light; when rays of light falling on any surface are bent outwards, they are *reflected;* when they pass through transparent bodies, as glass, water, &c. and are bent inwards, they are *refracted*. The angle of reflection is always equal to the angle of incidence; and it is by reflected light that all objects are visible, and colours produced. 2. Meditation, attentive consideration, reflection. [consider.
Reflexionár, *vn.* To reflect, to meditate, to
Reflexivaménte, *ad.* Reflexively.
Reflexívo, va, *a.* Reflective, that which reflects; considerate. *Verbo reflexivo*. V. *Reciproco*.
Refléxo, *sm.* Reflex, light reflected.
Refléxo, xa, *a.* Reflected, mediated.
Reflorecér, *vn.* 1. To blossom or flourish again. 2. To return to former splendour.
Refluénte, *pa.* Refluent.
Refluír, *vn.* To flow back, to reflow.
Reflúxo, *sm.* Reflux, a backward course of water. *Refluxo de la marea*, (Naút.) Ebb or ebb-tide.
Refocilación, *sf.* Refocillation, restoration of strength by refreshment.
Refocilár, *va.* To strengthen, to revive.—*vr.* To be strengthened or revived.
Refocílo, *sm.* Refocillacion.
Refollár, *va.* (Ant.) V. *Rehollar*.
Reforjár, *va.* To reforge, to execute again.
Refórma, *sf.* 1. Reform, correction, amendment. 2. Dismission from an office or employment. 3. Reformation, the act of reforming. 4. Renovated discipline in religious houses.
Reformáble, *a.* Reformable, capable of reform.
Reformación, *sf.* Reformation, reform. V. *Reforma*.

Reformádo, *sm.* A reformed officer, an officer on half-pay.
Reformadór, ra, *s.* Reformer.
Reformár, *va.* 1. To reform, to restore any thing to its primitive form. 2. To reform, to correct, to mend. 3. To lessen, to reduce, to diminish. 4. To dispossess of a place or employment, to discharge, to dismiss. 5. To clear up, to explain.—*vr.* 1. To have one's manners reformed or corrected. 2. To use prudence and moderation in speech and conduct.
Reformatívo, va, *a.* That which reforms.
Reformatório, ria, *a.* Corrective.
Refórme, *sm.* Correction. V. *Reforma*.
Reforzáda, *sf.* 1. Sort of narrow tape. 2. A small kind of sausage. 2. The base chord of a stringed musical instrument.
Reforzádo, *sm.* 1. A reinforced gun, which has more metal than usual at the breech, to make it stronger. 2. List, fillet, tape.
Reforzár, *va.* To strengthen, to fortify; to animate.—*vr.* To be strengthened and recovered.
Refoséto, *sm.* (Fort.) Cuvette in a fosse.
Refracción, *sf.* (Diop.) Refraction; rays of light passing obliquely from one medium to another are bent or *refracted*, but still incline to a perpendicular according as the medium is rarer or denser. [one's promise.
Refractário, ria, *a.* Refractory, not fulfilling
Refrácto, ta, *a.* Refracted, broken by refraction; applied to rays of light.
Refrán, *sm.* Proverb, a short sentence frequently repeated by the people. *Tener refranes*, To be versed in tricks and villanies of every colour and description.
Refrancíllo, co, to, *sm.* A very short proverb.
Refrangibilidád, *sf.* Refrangibility, capacity of being directed from a right line. [tion.
Refrangíble, *a.* Refrangible, capable of refrac-
Refregadúra, *sf.* V. *Refregon*.
Refragamiénto, *sm.* Frication, friction, the act of rubbing one thing against another.
Refregár, *va.* 1. To perfricate, to rub one thing against another. 2. To upbraid, to censure, to reprove.—*vr.* To be stained all over.
Refregón, *sm.* 1. Frication, friction, the act of rubbing one thing against another. 2. Mark made or left by rubbing. 3. A brief conversation on a subject. *Darse un refregon*, (Fam.) To speak briefly on any subject.
Refreír, *va.* To fry well or excessively.
Refrenamiénto y Refrenación, *s.* Curb, the act of curbing or refraining.
Refrenár, *va.* To curb, to check; to refrain.
Refrendación, *sf.* Legalizing by subscription.
Refrendár, *va.* To legalize any public act, to countersign; to return to again; to mark weights, &c.
Refrendário, *sm.* Officer appointed to countersign edicts, ordinances, or other public acts.
Refrendáta, *sf.* 1. Counter-signature, the act of counter-signing. 2. (Vulg.) Reprimand, reproof, censure, reprehension.
Refrescadór, *sm.* Refresher, refrigerator.
Refrescadúra, *sf.* Refreshing.
Refrescár, *va.* 1. To refresh, to correct or moderate the heat of any thing. 2. To drink iced liquors. 3. To renew, to refresh; to awaken

any feeling. 4. To recover strength and vigour, to rest after fatigue. *Refrescar los cables*, (Naút.) To freshen the hause. *Refrescar los víveres*, (Naút.) To take in fresh provisions.—*vn.* To cool, to attemperate; to take the air.

Refrescatívo, va, *a.* Refrigerative, refreshing.

Refrésco, *sm.* 1. Refreshment; ice-cream; entertainment given on a visit of a cool beverage, sweetmeats, and chocolate. 2. (Naút.) Fresh provisions. *De refresco*, Anew, once more.

Refriár, *va.* (Ant.) V. *Enfriar*.

Refriéga, *sf.* Affray, skirmish, encounter.

Refriegufila, *sf.* A short variable gale of wind.

Refrigeración, *sf.* Refrigeration, the act of cooling, privation of heat.

Refrigeránte, *a.* Refrigerant, cooling.—*sm.* (Quim.) Refrigeratory.

Refrigerár, *va.* To cool, to refresh, to comfort.

Refrigeratívo, va, *a.* Refrigerative.

Refrigeratório, *sm.* Refrigeratory, that part of a still employed to cool the condensing vapours.

Refrigério, *sm.* Refrigeration, refreshment; consolation; comfort; refection.

Refringénte, *pa.* Refracting.

Refringír, *va.* To refract, break, or intercept the rays of light.

Refrotár, *va.* To rub.

Refuélle, *sm.* A kind of net for catching fish.

Refuérzo, *sm.* Reinforcement, succour; strengthener.

Refugiár, *va.* To shelter, to afford protection.—*vr.* To take refuge, to fly to for shelter.

Refúgio, *sm.* 1. Refuge, retreat, asylum. 2. (Madrid) Confraternity, whose employment is to succour or relieve the poor.

Refulgéncia, *sf.* Refulgence, splendour.

Refulgénte, *a.* Refulgent.

Refundición, *sf.* The act of casting metals anew.

Refundír, *va.* 1. To melt or cast metals anew. 2. To contain, to include.—*vn.* To convert to any thing. *Refundir infamia*, To defame, to dishonour.

Refunfuñadúra, *sf.* Growling, grumbling.

Refunfuñár, *vn.* To snarl, to growl.

Refunfúño, *sm.* Grumbling, murmuring.

Refusár, *va.* V. *Rehusar*.

Refutación, *sf.* Refutation.

Refutár, *va.* To refute, to prove false or erroneous. V. *Rehusar*.

Refutatório, ria, *a.* That which refutes.

Regadéra, *sf.* 1. Sprinkling pot, a vessel for sprinkling water. 2. Canal for irrigation.

Regadéro, *sm.* V. *Reguera*.

Regadío, *sm.* Irrigated land.

Regadío, ía, *a.* Irrigated, watered; applied to land.

Regadízo, za, *a.* That can be irrigated or watered; applied to land.

Regadór, *sm.* 1. Instrument used by comb-makers to determine the length of the teeth of combs. 2. (Mur.) One who has a right to a certain share of water for irrigating his grounds.

Regadúra, *sf.* Irrigation.

Regajál ó Regájo, *sm.* Puddle or pool, a collection of stagnant water and dirt.

Regála, *sf.* (Naút.) Gunnel or gunwale.

Regaláda, *sf.* King's stables.

Regaladaménte, *ad.* Delicately, pleasantly.

Regaládo, da, *a.* Convenient, pleasant, delicate.

Regaladór, ra, *s.* 1. One who is fond of entertaining his friends; a person of a generous and liberal disposition. 2. Sort of stick used by wine-bag makers for cleaning the skins.

Regalamiénto, *sm.* Regalement.

Regalár, *va.* 1. To regale, to refresh, to entertain. 2. To caress, to cajole; to delight, to cherish.—*vr.* 1. To entertain one's self, to take pleasure. 2. To be dissolved, to melt.

Regaléro, *sm.* Purveyor of fruit and flowers for the royal family.

Regalía, *sf.* 1. Regalia, the ensigns of royalty; the rights or prerogatives of the crown. 2. Privilege, exemption. 3. Pipe of an organ which imitates the human voice. *Regalías*, Perquisites.

Regalícia, Regalíz, ó Regalíza, *s.* (Bot.) Licorice. Glycyrrhiza *L.* V. *Orozuz*.

Regalíllo, *sm.* 1. A small present. 2. Muff, a soft cover for the hands.

Regalíolo, *sm.* (Orn.) Golden crested wren. Motacilla regulus *L.*

Regálo, *sm.* 1. Present, gift. 2. Pleasure, gratification. 3. Dainty, something nice and delicate. 4. Convenience, repose. 5. Affliction dispensed by Providence. *Caballo de regalo*, A fine saddle-horse.

Regalón, na, *a.* 1. Delicate, fond of convenience and ease. 2. Spoiled, pampered; applied to children.

Regamiénto, *sm.* Irrigation.

Reganár, *va.* To regain.

Regantío, ía, *a.* Applied to the land or its fruits, that are usually watered. V. *Regadio*.

Regañáda, *sf.* A kind of cake.

Regañádo, da, *a.* 1. Given reluctantly, or with repugnance. 2. Applied to a kind of plum or bread which splits. 3. Frowning.

Regañamiénto, *sm.* Grumbling, snarling.

Regañár, *vn.* 1. To snarl, to growl, to murmur. 2. To be peevish, to quarrel. 3. To crack or open like ripe fruit. 4. To dispute familiarly at home, to have domestic broils. *A' regaña dientes*, Reluctantly, with reluctance.

Regañír, *vn.* To yelp, to howl repeatedly.

Regáño, *sm.* 1. Torvity, sourness of countenance; sternness of look. 2. Bread which is scorched.

Regañón, na, *a.* 1. Snarling, growling; a grumbler, murmurer, snarler. 2. Troublesome; generally applied to the North-east wind.

Regár, *va.* 1. To water, to irrigate. 2. To sprinkle with water; to rain heavily. 3. To wash or water countries; applied to rivers. 4. To moisten as bees do the vessels containing their young.

Regáta, *sf.* A small channel or conduit, through which water is conveyed to gardens.

Regatár, *vn.* (Naút.) V. *Regatear*.

Regáte, *sm.* 1. A quick motion of the body to avoid a blow. 2. Escape, evasion.

Regateár, *vn.* 1. To wriggle, to move sideways; to use evasions. 2. (Naút.) To rival in sailing.—*va.* 1. To haggle, to be tedious in a bargain; to retail provisions bought by whole-

sale. 2. To refuse or decline the execution of any thing; to avoid.
REGATÉO, *sm.* The act of haggling or bartering.
REGATERÍA, *sf.* Huckster's shop.
REGATÉRO, RA, *a.* Haggling. V. *Regaton.*
REGÁTO, *sm.* A small rivulet.
REGATÓN, NA, *s.* 1. Huckster, regrater. 2. Haggler, one that haggles much. 3. Socket, ferrule.—*a.* Retailing.
REGATONEÁR, *vn.* To huckster, to buy by wholesale and sell by retail.
REGATONERÍA, *sf.* 1. Huckster's shop. 2. Sale by retail. 3. Huckster.
REGAZÁR, *va.* To tuck up. V. *Arregazar.*
REGÁZO, *sm.* 1. Lap of a woman, the part of the dress from the waist to the knees. 2. Reception in a fond and endearing manner.
REGÉNCIA, *sf.* 1. Regency, the act of ruling or governing. 2. Regency, government. 3. Administration of a regent during the minority or inability of the lawful sovereign.
REGENERACIÓN, *sf.* 1. Regeneration. 2. (Cir.) Granulation in a wound.
REGENERÁR, *va.* To regenerate, to reproduce; to produce anew.
REGENERATÍVO, VA, *a.* That which regenerates.
REGENTÁR, *va.* To rule; to govern; to exercise any business affecting superiority.
REGÉNTA, *sf.* Wife of a regent.
REGÉNTE, *sm.* 1. Regent, ruler. 2. President of a court of justice. 3. Master of a school, which belongs to religious orders; manager, director.
REGENTEÁR, *vn.* 1. To domineer, to rule as master. 2. To be a pedant.
REGÉRA, *sf.* (Naút.) Stern-fast, stern-moorings.
REGIAMÉNTE, *ad.* Royally, in a kingly manner.
REGIBÁDO, DA, *a.* Hump-backed, crook-backed, gibbous.
REGICÍDA, *sm.* Regicide, murderer of a king.
REGICÍDIO, *sm.* Murder of a king, a regicide.
REGIDÓR, RA, *s.* 1. Governor, director, prefect; governor's wife. 2. Magistrate of a city, a municipal officer.—*a.* Ruling, governing. V. *Regitivo.*
REGIDORÍA Y REGIDURÍA, *sf.* Governorship.
REGILÉRA, *sf.* Windmill made of paper, as a plaything for children.
RÉGIMEN, *sm.* 1. Regimen, management, rule, conduct. 2. (Gram.) Government of verbs.
REGIMIÉNTO, *sm.* 1. Administration, government. 2. Regimen, diet. 3. Magistracy of a city; office or employment of a city magistrate; municipality. 4. Regiment, a certain number of soldiers under the command of a colonel.
RÉGIO, GIA, *a.* 1. Royal, regal, kingly. 2. Stately, sumptuous, magnificent. *Aqua regia,* Aqua regis, nitro-muriatic acid, a liquid which dissolves gold.
REGIÓN, *sf.* 1. Region, tract of country. 2. Space occupied by an element; one of the cavities of the human body.
REGIONÁL, *a.* Belonging to any region or district.
REGÍR, *va.* 1. To rule, to govern, to direct; to govern as verbs or prepositions. 2. To conduct, to manage. 3. To have the bowels in good order.—*vn.* (Naút.) To obey the helm.
REGISTRÁDO, DA, *a.* Registered, entered in a register.
REGISTRADÓR, *sm.* 1. Register or registrer; recorder, master, or clerk of records. 2. Searcher. 3. Toll-gatherer, who takes the toll at the gates of a town, and enters all goods in the toll-register which are imported.
REGISTRÁR, *va.* 1. To survey, to inspect; to view in a careful manner. 2. To investigate, to examine. 3. To record, to enter in a register. 4. To put slips of paper between the leaves of a book. *No registrar,* (Met.) To do any thing precipitately.—*vr.* To be registered or matriculated.
REGÍSTRO, *sm.* 1. The act of searching or examining. 2. Place or spot from whence any thing can be surveyed. 3. Entry of goods or merchandise. 4. Enrolling office, the office where registers or records are kept; census. V. *Protocolo.* 5. Register, in which the entries of goods or other things are made; a certificate of entry. 6. Register of a stove or grate. 7. (Impr.) Catchword, a word placed at the bottom of a page for the direction of the bookbinder; register or correspondence of the pages. 8. Priér, one who inquires too narrowly or closely. 9. Regulator of a watch or clock. 10. Mark put in breviaries or missals at certain places. 11. Register in an organ or harpsichord. 12. (Com.) Register ship, a single vessel from India with goods registered in port. 13. Direction to bookbinders at the end of a volume.
REGITÁR, *va.* V. *Vomitar.*
REGITÍVO, VA, *a.* Ruling, governing.
REGIZGÁR, *vn.* To shake or shudder with cold.
RÉGLA, *sf.* 1. Rule, ruler; an instrument for drawing a straight line; rule in arithmetic. 2. Rule of religious orders. 3. Law, statute, precept; canon, fundamental principle. 4. Instrument by which paper is ruled for musical compositions. 5. Manner of making or casting up accounts. 6. Moderation, measure, rule. 7. Order of nature. 8. Catamenia. *Á regla,* Regularly, prudently. *Regla lesbia,* Flexible rule which may be adjusted to any body to be measured.
REGLADAMÉNTE, *ad.* Regularly, orderly.
REGLÁDO, DA, *a.* Regulated, temperate.
REGLAMÉNTO, *sm.* Regulation, order.
REGLÁR, *a.* Regular. *Puerta reglar,* The regular door by which people enter nunneries.
REGLÁR, *va.* 1. To regulate, to direct. 2. To rule paper; to conform to rule.—*vr.* To mend, to reform. *Reglarse á lo justo,* To be right.
REGLÉRO, *sm.* Ruler, an instrument for drawing lines.
REGLÉTA, *sf.* (Impr.) Lead or piece of metal put between the lines of types.
REGLÓN, *sm.* Level used by masons.
REGNÁR, *vn.* (Ant.) V. *Reynar.*
REGNÍCOLO, LA, *a.* y *s.* Native of a kingdom or country.
REGOCIJADAMÉNTE, *ad.* Merrily, joyfully.
REGOCIJÁDO, DA, *a.* Merry, joyful, rejoicing.
REGOCIJADÓR, RA, *s.* Rejoicer, cheerer.
REGOCIJÁR, *va.* To gladden, to cheer, to delight, to exhilirate.—*vr.* To rejoice, to be merry.
REGOCÍJO, *sm.* 1. Joy, pleasure, satisfaction. 2.

Rejoicing, demonstration of joy. 3. Bull-feast in the morning.
REGODEÁRSE, *vr.* 1. To be merry, to rejoice; to be delighted. 2. To assume an air of reluctance to cloak some ardent desire. 3. To joke, to jest.
REGODÉO, *sm.* 1. Joy, mirth, merriment. 2. A feigned refusal of a thing earnestly desired. 3. Joke, jest, diversion.
REGÓJO, *sm.* 1. Crum or piece of bread left on the table after meals. 2. A little boy.
REGOJUÉLO, *sm.* A very small morsel of bread.
REGOLÁR, *sm.* Scholar, student.
REGOLDADÓR, *sm.* (Vulg.) He who belches.
REGOLDÁNO, NA, *a.* Applied to the wild chesnut.
REGOLDÁR, *vn.* 1. To belch, to eject wind from the stomach. 2. To boast, to brag.
REGOLFÁR, *vn.* To flow back.
REGÓLFO, *sm.* 1. Reflux, the act of flowing back against the current; whirlpool. 2. Gulf, bay; an arm of the sea between two points of land.
REGOMÉLLO, *sm.* Remorse, sting of conscience.
REGÓNA, *sf.* Large canal for irrigating lands.
REGORDÉTE, TA, *a.* Chubbed, plump.
REGORDÍDO, DA, *a.* Fat, plump.
REGOSTÁRSE, *vr.* To delight, to take pleasure.
REGÓSTO, *sm.* Delight, pleasure.
REGRACIACIÓN, *sf.* Act of grace, gracefulness, gratitude.
REGRACIÁR, *va.* To testify gratitude, to thank.
REGRESÁR, *vn.* To retain or recover possession of an ecclesiastical benefice; to return.—*va.* 1. To resign a benefice in favour of another. 2. To submit or yield to the opinion of others.
REGRESIÓN, *sf.* Regression, return; regress.
REGRÉSO, *sm.* 1. Return, regression. 2. Reversion, devolution. 3. The act of resigning a benefice. 4. The act of retaking possession of a benefice or property resigned or ceded.
REGRUÑÍR, *vn.* To snarl, to growl.
REGUARDÁRSE, *vr.* To take care of one's self.
REGÜÉLDO, *sm.* 1. Eructation, belch; the act of ejecting wind from the stomach. 2. Boast, brag.
REGUÉRA, *sf.* 1. Canal for watering lands or plants. 2. Stern of a ship or tail of a greyhound.
REGUÉRO, *sm.* 1. A small rivulet. 2. Line arising from any liquid being spilt. V. *Reguera.*
REGUERÓN, *sm.* The principal canal of irrigation.
REGUIZÁR, *va.* To patch a suit of clothes.
REGULACIÓN, *sf.* Regulation, adjustment; comparison, computation.
REGULÁDO, DA, *a.* V. *Regular.*
REGULADÓR, RA, *s.* 1. Regulator, that part of a machine which regulates its movements. 2. Prebendary, who acts as teller at a scrutiny.
REGULÁR, *va.* To regulate, to adjust; to put in order, to compare.—*a.* 1. Regular, orderly. 2. Moderate, sober. 3. Common, ordinary, frequent.—*s.* A regular; applied or belonging to a religious order. *Por lo regular,* Commonly.
REGULARIDÁD, *sf.* 1. Regularity, order. 2. Common usage, custom. 3. Exact discipline.
REGULARMÉNTE, *ad.* Regularly, in an orderly manner; generally, naturally.
RÉGULO, *sm.* 1. Chief of a petty state. 2. Basilisk. 3. (Quím.) Regulus, the purest part of the metal, which sinks to the bottom of the crucible or furnace in smelting the ore. 4. (Astr.) Regulus, a star of the first magnitude. 5. (Orn.) Wagtail.
REGURGITÁR, *vn.* To regurgitate, to overflow.
REHABILITACIÓN, *sf.* The act of restoring an offender to the rank and condition which he held before he committed the offence.
REHABILITÁR, *va.* To restore an offender to his former rank in life; to reinstate one in his former rights and privileges.
REHABITUÁRSE, *vr.* To return to vicious habits.
REHACÉR, *va.* 1. To mend, to repair. 2. To add new strength and vigour. 3. To increase the weight or quantity of any thing.—*vr.* 1. To regain strength and vigour. 2. (Mil.) To rally; to form anew; to resume the former position.
REHACIMIÉNTO, *sm.* Renovation, renewal.
REHÁCIO, CIA, *a.* Obstinate, stubborn.
REHÁRTO, TA, *pp. irreg.* Supersaturated.
REHARTÁR, *va.* To satiate again.
REHÉCHO, CHA, *a.* 1. Renewed, renovated; done over again. 2. Squat, broad shouldered.
REHÉN, *sm.* Hostage, one given in pledge for security of the performance of conditions.
REHENCHIDÚRA, *sf.* Act of stuffing or refilling.
REHENCHÍR, *va.* To fill again, to stuff anew.
REHENDÍJA Y REHENDRÍJA, *sf.* Crevice, cleft.
REHERIMIÉNTO, *sm.* Repulsion; inspection of weights.
REHERÍR, *va.* 1. To repel. 2. To inspect and mark anew measures and weights.
REHERRÁR, *va.* To reshoe a horse.
REHERVÍR, *vn.* 1. To boil again. 2. To be inflamed with love, to be blinded by passion.—*vr.* To ferment, to grow sour.
REHÉZ, *a.* V. *Rahez.*
REHÍJO, *sm.* Shout, sprout.
REHILADÍLLO, *sm.* Ribbon. V. *Hiladillo.*
REHILANDÉRA, *sf.* Windmill made of paper. V. *Regilera.*
REHILÁR, *va.* To twist or contract too much. —*vn.* To stagger, to reel.
REHILÉTE Y REHILÉRO, *sm.* 1. A kind of shuttlecock played with battledoors. 2. A small arrow bearded with paper or feathers.
REHÍLO, *sm.* (Val.) Shaking, shivering.
REHINCHIMIÉNTO, *sm.* The act of filling or stuffing again.
REHIRMÁR, *va.* (Ant.) V. *Reafirmar.*
REHOGÁR, *va.* To dress meat with a slow fire, basting it with butter or oil.
REHOLLÁR, *va.* To trample under foot, to tread upon. V. *Pisotear.*
REHÓYA, *sf.* V. *Rehoyo.*
REHOYÁR, *va.* To dig holes again for planting trees.
REHÓYO, *sm.* A deep hole or pit.
REHUÍDA, *sf.* A second flight, the act of running away again; rapid turn of hunted game.
REHUÍR, *vn.* 1. To withdraw, to retire. 2. To return or fly back to the place from whence it was roused; applied to game. 3. To reject, to condemn.—*va.* To deny, or refuse.
REHUNDÍR, *va.* 1. To sink, or immerse to the

bottom. 2. To melt any metal. 3. To waste, to dissipate, to lavish.—vn. To increase perceptibly, or in such a manner as may be observed.

Rehurtádo, da, a. 1. Making a variety of windings to make the dogs lose the scent; applied to game. 2. Artfully evasive, delusive, furtive.

Rehurtárse, vr. To take a different route whence it rose; applied to game.

Rehúrto, sm. A movement of the body to avoid some impending danger; a shrug.

Rehusár, va. To refuse, to decline.

Reíble, a. Laughable. V. *Risible.*

Reidéro, sm. Immoderate laugher.

Reidór, ra, s. Laugher.

Reimpresión, sf. Reimpression; an edition.

Reimprimír, va. To reprint.

Reincidéncia, sf. Reiteration, falling in again.

Reincidénte, pa. Reiterating.

Reincidír, vn. To reiterate, to fall into any error or fault again.

Reincorporación, sf. Re-incorporation, renewing.

Reincorporár, va. To incorporate a second time.

Reintegración, sf. Reintegration, or redintegration; the act of restoring.

Reintegrár, va. To reintegrate, to restore.—vr. To be reinstated or restored.

Reintégro, sm. Redintegration, the act of integrating or restoring.

Reír, vn. 1. To laugh, to make that noise which sudden merriment excites; to smile. *Reir á carcajadas,* To laugh excessively and loudly. 2. To laugh at, or sneer. 3. (Med.) To laugh, to have convulsions which resemble laughter. 4. To smile; applied to agreeable landscapes, arbours, lakes, and meads.—vr. 1. To begin to tear or rend; applied to cloth. 2. To scoff, to make jest of. *Reirse por nada,* To giggle or titter idly.

Reiteración, sf. Repetition, reiteration.

Reiteradaménte, ad. Repeatedly.

Reiterár, va. To reiterate, to repeat.

Reivindicación, sf. (For.) Recovery.

Reivindicár, va. To recover.

Réja, sf. 1. Ploughshare, the iron part of the plough, which serves to break the ground. 2. Aration. 3. Iron grate of a window.

Rejacár, va. V. *Arrejacar.*

Rejáda, sf. V. *Arrejada.*

Rejádo, sm. Grate of a door or window.

Rejalcár, va. To plough.

Rejalgár, sm. Realgar, red sulphuret of arsenic.

Rejázo, sm. Stroke or blow given with a ploughshare.

Rejería, sf. Manufactory of the iron work of grates, doors, or windows.

Rejéro, sm. Maker of bars, lattices, and grates.

Rejílla, sf. 1. A small lattice in confessionals, to bear women's confessions. 2. *Dim.* of *Reja.*

Réjo, sm. 1. A pointed iron bar or spike. 2. Sting of a bee or other insect. 3. Nail or round iron with which quoits are played. 4. Rim of iron put around the frame of a door to strengthen it. 5. Strength, vigour.

Rejón, sm. 1. Dagger, poniard. 2. A kind of lance or spear used by bull-fighters. 3. A short broad knife with a sharp point.

Rejonázo, sm. Thrust given with a dagger.

Rejoneadór, sm. Bull-fighter who throws the spear, which is called *rejon.*

Rejoneár, va. To wound bulls with the spear used by bull-fighters.

Rejonéo, sm. The act of fighting bulls with a spear.

Rejuéla, sf. A small grate, a small brazier of wood covered with brass.

Rejurár, vn. To swear again.

Rejuvenecér, vn. To grow young again.

Relación, sf. 1. Relation, report, narration. 2. A brief report or narrative made to a judge of the state and merits of a cause. 3. Prologue, prelude. 4. Romance; ballad. 5. Relation, correspondence, analogy. *Relacion jurada,* Deposition upon oath. 6. A distant relation. *Relacion de ciego,* Applied to any thing read all in the same tone.

Relacionár, va. To relate, to report.

Relacionéro, sm. Reporter, narrator; ballad-singer.

Relamér, va. To relick, to lick again.—vr. 1. To lick one's lips; to relish. 2. To be extravagantly fond of dress; to paint. 3. To boast, to brag.

Relamído, da, a. Affected, too fine or nice in dress.

Relámpago, sm. 1. Flash of lightning, meteor. 2. Any thing passing as suddenly as a flash of lightning. 3. Thought or idea flashing upon the mind; ingenious witticism. 4. Cloud and blemish in the eyes of horses. 5. Opening or closing rapidly the mantle worn by women.

Relampagueánte pa. Lightening.

Relampagueár, vn. 1. To lighten, to emit flashes of lightning. 2. To flash, to sparkle.

Relampaguéo, sm. The act of flashing or darting light.

Relampaguzár, vn. (Bax.) V. *Relampaguear.*

Relánce, sm. 1. A repeated casting of a net; a second chance or lot. 2. A fortuitous event. 3. A repeated attempt. 4. Series of lucky or unlucky chances. *De relance,* Fortuitously, by chance.

Relanzár, va. 1. To repel, to repulse. 2. To cast in again the tickets or lots to be drawn.

Relápso, sa, a. Relapsed, falling back into the former criminal conduct.

Relatadór, ra, s. Relater, narrator.

Relatánte, pa. Reporter, narrating.

Relatár, va. To relate, to report, to narrate.

Relativaménte, ad. Relatively.

Relatívo, va, a. 1. Relative, bearing relation to another thing. 2. (Gram.) Relative, relating to an antecedent.

Relatór, ra, s. Narrator; reporter or his wife. V. *Refrendario.*

Relatoría, sf. Office of a reporter of judicial causes in a court of justice.

Relavíge, sm. Washing place for stuffs or clothes.

Relavár, va. To wash over again.

Reláve, sm. Second washing of metals. *Relaves,* Washings or sweepings in a silversmith's or gold-worker's shop.

Relavíllo, sm. dim. Slight rewashing.

Relaxación, sf. 1. Relaxation, extension, dilatation. 2. Relaxation, remission; abatement of mental vigour; laxity of manners. 3. Commutation of a vow, release from an oath. 4. Intermission, discontinuance. 5. Delivery of an offender by the ecclesiastical judge to a criminal court of justice, in cases of murder. V. *Quebradura.*

RELAXADAMÉNTE, *ad.* Dissolutely, licentiously.

RELAXADÓR, RA, *a.* Relaxing, remitting.

RELAXAMIÉNTO, *sm.* Relaxation. V. *Relaxacion.*

RELAXÁR, *va.* 1. To relax, to slacken, to make less tense. 2. To render less rigorous or severe. 3. To annul a vow, to release from an oath or obligation. 4. To deliver a capital offender from an ecclesiastical to the criminal tribunal. 5. To ease, to amuse, to divert.—*vr.* 1. To be relaxed, loosened, or dilated; applied to a member of the animal body. 2. To grow vicious; to be corrupted by evil customs. 3. V. *Quebrarse.*

RELEÉR, *va.* To read over again, to revise.

RELEGACIÓN, *sf.* Relegation, judicial banishment; exile.

RELEGÁR, *va.* To relegate, to banish; to exile.

RELÉNTE, *sf.* Softness, occasioned by the falling of the dew.

RELENTECÉR, *vn.* y *r.* To be softened, to relent.

RELEVACIÓN, *sf.* 1. Relevation, the act of raising or lifting up; liberation. 2. Alleviation, relief. 3. Remission, forgiveness, pardon.

RELEVÁNTE, *a.* Excellent, great, eminent.

RELEVÁR, *va.* 1. To emboss, to make relief or rising work. 2. To exonerate, to disburthen; to relieve from a burthen or charge. 3. To assist, to succour. 4. To forgive, to pardon. 5. To exalt, to aggrandise. 6. (Pint.) To paint an object to appear as if rising. 7. To substitute one soldier for another.

RELÉVO, *sm.* (Mil.) V. *Relevacion.*

RELÉX, *sm.* 1. A gradual diminution of a wall. 2. A clammy moisture sticking to the lips or mouth.

RELEXÁR, *vn.* To diminish in thickness in proportion to the height; applied to a wall.

RELÉXE, *sm.* (Art.) Raised work in the chamber of a piece of ordnance where the powder is placed, in order to economise it; used in a kind of *pedreros.*

RELICÁRIO, *sm.* 1. Reliquary, a shrine or casket in which the relics of saints are kept. 2. Decoration of a relic. 3. Convent distinguished for some particular devotion.

RELIÉF, *sm.* (Mil.) Warrant for an officer to receive either rank or pay that fell to him during his absence.

RELIÉVE, *sm.* 1. Relief, relievo, rising work, embossment. *Alto relieve,* Alto relievo, that in which figures are raised more than half their thickness above the plane. *Baxo relieve,* Bas-relief. *Medio relieve,* Demi-relief. 2. Offals, scraps, or remnants which remain on the table after meals; broken victuals.

RELIÉVO, *sm.* (Ant.) V. *Relieve.*

RELÍGA, *sf.* The second portion of alloy put to a metal to make it fit for working.

RELIGACIÓN, *sf.* Binding, tying.

RELIGÁR, *va.* To bind, to tie strongly; to solder.

RELIGIÓN, *sf.* Religion; piety, worship.

RELIGIONÁRIO Y RELIGIONÍSTA, *s. com.* Religionist, sectary; protestant.

RELIGIOSAMÉNTE, *ad.* Religiously, punctually, moderately.

RELIGIOSIDÁD, *sf.* Religiousness; piety, sanctity; punctuality.

RELIGIÓSO, SA, *a.* 1. Religious, pious. 2. Teaching or professing religion. 3. Exact, strict, moderate.

RELIMÁR, *va.* To file again.

RELIMPIÁR, *va.* To clean, to purify a second time.

RELÍMPIO, IA, *a.* Very neat, clean.

RELINCHADÓR, RA, *a.* Neighing, crying.

RELINCHÁNTE, *pa.* Neigher.

RELINCHÁR, *vn.* 1. To neigh, to utter the voice of a horse. 2. To shout, to cry in triumph or exultation.

RELÍNCHO Y RELINCHÍDO, *sm.* Neigh, the voice of a horse. *Relinchos,* Shouts, cries of triumph or exultation.

RELÍNDO, DA, *a.* Very neat and fine.

RELÍNGA, *sf.* (Naút.) Bolt-rope, sewed to the skirts of the sails, to prevent them from rending. *Relinga del gratil,* Head-bolt-rope. *Relinga del pujamen,* Foot-bolt-rope. *Relinga de las caidas,* Leech-bolt-rope.

RELINGÁR, *va.* (Naút.) To sew bolt-ropes to the extremities of the sails.—*vn.* To rustle or move the bolt-ropes and sails with the wind.

RELÍQUIA, *sf.* 1. Relic, residue, remains. 2. Relics of saints. 3. Footstep, track, vestige. 4. Habitual complaint. *Reliquia insigne,* The head, arm, or leg of a saint.

RELLANÁR, *va.* To relevel or make even again.—*vr.* To stretch one's-self out at full length.

RELLÁNO, *sm.* Landing place of a stair.

RELLENÁR, *va.* 1. To fill again. 2. To stuff with victuals, to feed plentifully. 3. To stuff a fowl or gut with forced meat.—*vr.* To resate one's-self.

RELLÉNO, *sm.* 1. Forced meat. 2. Repletion, act of refilling.

RELLÉNTE, *sm.* Softness. V. *Relente.*

RELLENTECÉR, *vn.* To be softened. V. *Relentecer.*

RELÓCO, CA, *a.* Raving mad, furiously insane.

RELÓX, *sm.* Clock, watch. *Relox de agua,* Clepsydra. *Relox de arena,* Sand-glass. *Relox de faltriquera,* Watch. *Relox de sol* ó *relox solar,* Sun-dial. *Relox de repeticion,* A repeater or repeating-watch. *Relox lunar,* Lunar dial. *Estar como un relox,* (Fam.) To be regular and well-disposed.

RELOXÉRA, *sf.* Clock-case.

RELOXERÍA, *sf.* 1. The art of making clocks and watches. 2. Watchmaker's shop.

RELOXÉRO, *sm.* Watchmaker, one that makes clocks and watches.

RELUCHÁR, *vn.* To struggle, to wrestle, to strive, to labour, to debate.

RELUCIÉNTE, *a.* Relucent.

RELUCÍR, *vn.* To shine, to emit light; to excel, to be brilliant. *Relucir la espalda,* To have a large portion; applied to women.

RELUMBRÁNTE, *pa.* Resplendent.

RELUMBRÁR, *vn.* To sparkle, to shine.

RELÚMBRE, *sm.* Coppery or irony taste; applied to meat dressed in vessels of copper or iron.

RELUMBRÉRA, *sf.* V. *Lumbrera.*

RELUMBRÓN, *sm.* Lustre, dazzling brightness; fleeting idea or sound.

Remachádo, da, a. 1. Clinched, riveted. 2. Flat-nosed.

Remachár, va. To flatten; to clinch, to rivet; to secure; to affirm.

Remáche, sm. Flattening, ill-inclining, securing.

Remachón, sm. Buttress. V. *Machon.*

Remadór, sm. Rower. V. *Remero.*

Remaldecír, va. To curse the cursers.

Remallár, va. To mend portmanteaus or trunks.

Remamiénto, sm. Rowing.

Remandár, va. To order several times.

Remanecér, vn. 1. To appear, to occur. 2. To remain, to be left out of a greater quantity or number.

Remanecié nte, pa. Remaining, remainder.

Remanénte, sm. Remainder, residue; remanent, or remnant.

Remangár, va. To tuck up. V. *Arremangar.*

Remángo, sm. Plaits of the petticoat at the waist.

Remansárse, vr. To obstruct or suspend the course or current of any fluid.

Remánso, sm. 1. Smooth stagnant water. 2. Tardiness, lentitude.

Remánte, sm. Rower.

Remár, vn. 1. To row, to impel a vessel with oars. 2. To toil, to struggle.

Remarcár, va. To mark again.

Rematáda, sf. A decayed strumpet.

Rematadaménte, ad. Entirely, totally.

Rematádo, da, a. 1. Ended, terminated. 2. Totally lost, utterly ruined. *Es loco rematado,* He is stark mad. *Rematado á galeras ó presidio,* Condemned to the galleys or house of correction.

Rematamiénto, sm. V. *Remate.*

Rematár, va. To close, to terminate, to finish.—vn. 1. To terminate, to be at an end. 2. To adjudge to the best bidder. 3. To kill the game at one shot. 4. To finish a seam.—vr. To be utterly ruined or irremediably destroyed.

Remáte, sm. 1. End, conclusion. 2. The last or best bidding. 3. Artificial flowers put at the corners of altars. 4. Vignette, a flower or other printed ornament placed at the end of a book. 5. (Arq.) Finial, an ornament terminating any part of a building. *De remáte,* Utterly, irremediably, without hope. *Por remate,* Finally.

Remecedór, sm. He who manages olives to increase their oil.

Remecér, va. To rock; to swing, to move to and fro.

Remedáble, a. Imitable, that which may be imitated or mimicked.

Remedadór, ra, s. Imitator, mimic, a ludicrous imitator, who takes off or copies another's action and manner.

Remedamiénto, sm. V. *Remedo.*

Remedár, va. 1. To copy, to imitate, to mimic. 2. To follow the track and footstep of others; to adopt the dress and manners of another.

Remediáble, a. Remediable.

Remediadór, ra, s. Protector, comforter; curer.

Remediár, va. 1. To remedy, to mend, to repair. 2. To assist, to support. 3. To free from danger, to liberate, to evitate. 4. To establish or marry a young woman.

Remedición, sf. Act of measuring a second time.

Remédio, sm. 1. Remedy, reparation; means of repairing. *No tener remedio,* Irremediable, unavoidable. 2. Amendment, correction. 3. Resource, refuge. 4. Remedy, medicine by which any illness is cured. 5. Action at law. *No tener un remedio,* To be destitute of all aid or assistance.

Remedír, va. To re-measure, to measure again.

Remédo, sm. Imitation, copy.

Remembración, sf. V. *Recordacion.*

Remembrár, va. (Ant.) To remember.

Rememorár, va. To remember, to record.

Rememoratívo, va, a. That which remembers or records.

Remendádo, da, a. 1. Patched; mended. 2. Spotted, tabby, applied to horses, dogs, and other animals.

Remendár, va. 1. To patch, to mend; to correct. 2. To adjust one thing to another.

Remendón, sm. Botcher, patcher; one who mends old clothes.

Rementír, vn. To lie frequently.

Reméro, sm. Rower, one who rows or works with an oar.

Reméssa, sf. Sending of goods; remittance of money. V. *Cochera.*

Remesár, va. To pull or pluck out the hair.

Remesón, sm. 1. Handful of hair; act of plucking it out. 2. The action of stopping a horse in full gallop. 3. A kind of skilful thrust in fencing.

Remetér, va. To put back, to put in; to put a clean cloth on children.

Remíche, sm. Space in galleys between the benches in which the convicts are.

Remiél, sm. The second extract of soft sugar taken from the cane.

Remiéndo, sm. 1. Patch, clout. 2. Amendment, addition. 3. Reparation, repair. 4. Brindle, the state of being spotted or tabby. 5. Badge of military orders worn by the knights. 6. (Impr.) Short work of which few copies are printed. *A' remiendos,* By patchwork, by piecemeal.

Remilgadaménte, ad. Affectedly forming the mouth.

Remilgádo, da, a. Affected nicety, delicacy or grace.

Remilgárse, vr. To be affectedly nice or grave.

Remílgo, sm. Affected nicety or gravity; prudery.

Reminiscéncia, sf. Reminiscence, recollection.

Remirádo, da, a. Prudent, cautious, wary.

Remirár, va. To revise, to inspect or examine a second time; to review.—vr. 1. To do or finish any thing with great care. 2. To inspect or consider with pleasure. 3. To reflect on or examine one's-self.

Remisaménte, ad. Remissly, without due attention.

Remisíble, a. Remissible, admitting forgiveness.

Remisión, sf. 1. Remission, forgiveness. 2. Remissness, indolence. 3. Abatement, cessation of intenseness. 4. The act referring to another book or work.

Remisivaménte, ad. With remission.

Remisívo, va, a. Remitting, that which serves to remit.

Remíso, sa, a. Remiss, careless, indolent.

Remisório, ria, *a.* Having the power of forgiving or pardoning. *Letras remisorias,* Judge's orders transferring a cause to another court.
Remisória, *sf.* Order of a superior judge to refer a cause to another tribunal.
Remitír, *va.* 1. To remit, to transmit, to send from one place to another. 2. To pardon, to forgive. 3. To suspend, to defer, to put off. 4. To return a cause to an inferior court. 5. To relax, to make less tense.—*vr.* 1. To refer or submit to the judgment and opinion of another. 2. To quote, to cite.
Rémo, *sm.* 1. (Naút.) Oar, a long pole with a broad end, by which vessels are driven along in the water. *Pala de un remo,* (Naút.) Wash of an oar. *Manual de un remo,* (Naút.) Handle of an oar. 2. Long and hard labour or toil. *Á remo y sin sueldo,* Labour in vain.
Remoción, *sf.* Removal.
Remojadéro, *sm.* Steeping-tub.
Remojár, *va.* To steep, to soak again. *Remojar la palabra,* (Vulg.) To go to drink in a dram-shop.
Remójo, *sm.* The act of steeping or soaking.
Remolácha, *sf.* (Bot.) Beet-root. V. *Betarraga.*
Remolár, *sm.* The master carpenter or the shop where oars are made.
Remolcár, *va.* (Naút.) To tow, take in tow; to draw a ship through the water by means of a tow-rope.
Remolér, *va.* To regrind, to grind excessively.
Remolimiénto, *sm.* Act of regrinding.
Remolinár, *vn.* To make gyrations.—*vr.* 1. To whirl or turn one's-self round. 2. To be surrounded by a multitude of people; to be confounded with the crowd.
Remolineár, *va.* To whirl any thing round about.—*vn.* V. *Remolinar.*
Remolíno, *sm.* 1. Whirlwind, a stormy wind moving circularly. 2. Whirlpool. 3. Lock of hair hanging over the forehead. 4. Crowd, throng. 5. Disturbance, commotion.
Remolliér ó Remollléro, *sm.* (Ant.) V. *Remolar.*
Remolón, na, *a.* Soft, indolent. V. *Posma.*
Remolón, *sm.* The upper tusk of a wild boar; sharp tooth in horses.
Remolonneárse, *vr.* To be idle, to refuse stirring from sloth and indolence.
Remólque, *sm.* 1. (Naút.) The act of towing or drawing a vessel along in the water by means of a tow-rope. *Dar remolque,* V. *Remolcar. Á remolque,* (Naút.) Towing. 2. (Naút.) Tow-rope.
Remondár, *va.* To clean a second time; to take away what is useless.
Remónta, *sf.* The act of supplying the cavalry with fresh horses; collection of cavalry horses; remounting cavalry.
Remontamiénto, *sm.* Act of soaring or towering.
Remontár, *va.* 1. To frighten away, to oblige one to withdraw. 2. To remount the cavalry; to supply them with fresh horses. 3. To repair the saddles of mules and horses.—*vr.* 1. To tower, to soar; applied to birds. 2. To conceive great and sublime ideas; to form sublime conceptions.
Remónte, *sm.* Soar, a towering flight; elevation or sublimity of ideas.
Remontísta, *sm.* Commissioner for the purchase of cavalry horses.
Remóque, *sm.* Poignant or sarcastic word.
Remoquéte, *sm.* 1. Thump with the fist. 2. A witty expression. 3. Gallantry, courtship.
Remór, *sm.* (Ant.) V. *Rumor.*
Rémora, *sf.* 1. (Ict.) Sucking fish. Echineis remora L. 2. Let, obstacle; cause of delay.
Remordedór, ra, *a.* Causing remorse.
Remordér, *va.* 1. To bite repeatedly. 2. To cause remorse, to sting, to make uneasy.—*vr.* To manifest or express concern.
Remordimiénto, *sm.* Remorse, sting of conscience, uneasiness.
Remostár, *va.* To put must into old wine.—*vr.* 1. To jumble grapes together so that they lose part of their juice. 2. To grow sweet and assume the flavour of must; applied to wine.
Remostecérse, *vr.* V. *Remostarse.*
Remósto, *sm.* The act of putting must into old wine.
Remotaménte, *ad.* Remotely, confusedly; dissimilarly.
Remóto, ta, *a.* Remote, distant; unlike.
Removér, *va.* 1. To remove, to shift from one place to another. 2. To remove an obstacle. 3. To alter, to change the animal humours.
Removimiénto, *sm.* 1. Removal, remotion. 2. Revulsion, internal fermentation of the humours of an animal body.
Remozadúra, Remozamiénto, *s.* Act of appearing or becoming young.
Remozár, *va.* To endeavour to appear young; to make one appear younger than he really is.
Rempujár, *va.* 1. To push or shove a person out of his place. 2. To impel, to carry away. 3. To approach game.
Rempújo, *sm.* 1. Impulse, push, thrust. 2. Pressure of an arch upon its pillars and supporters. V. *Empuje.*
Rempujón, *sm.* Impulse, push, thrust.
Remúda, *sf.* Exchange, re-exchange.
Remudamiénto, *sm.* Removal, exchange.
Remudár, *va.* 1. To move or change again. 2. To exchange one thing for another, to permute.
Remugár, *va.* (Ar.) *Rumiar.*
Remullír, *va.* To beat up again, to mollify.
Remuneración, *sf.* Remuneration, recompense, reward.
Remuneradór, ra, *s.* Remunerator.
Remunerár, *va.* To reward, to remunerate.
Remuneratório, ria, *a.* Remunerative, given by way of a reward.
Remusgár, *vn.* (Vulg.) To suspect, to presume.
Remúsgo, *sm.* Too cool an atmosphere or situation.
Remusguíllo, *sm. dim.* Coolish place, chilly situation.
Rén, *s.* Kidney. V. *Riñon.*
Renacér, *vn.* 1. To be born again, to be new born. 2. To acquire grace by baptism.
Renacimiénto, *sm.* Regeneration; new birth.
Renacuájo, *sm.* 1. Spawn of frogs. 2. Little shapeless man.
Renál, *a.* Belonging to the kidneys. V. *Reynal.*
Rencílla, *sf.* A slight grudge remaining after a quarrel.
Rencillóso, sa, *a.* Peevish, quarrelsome.
Rencionár, *va.* (Ant.) To occasion grudges or heart-burnings.

Rénco, ca, a. Hipshot, having the hip dislocated; lame.
Rencór, sm. Rancour, animosity, grudge.
Rencorosaménte, ad. Rancorously.
Rencoróso, sa; y Rencorióso, sa, a. Rancorous, spiteful.
Rencóso, a. Applied to a ram with one testicle concealed.
Rénda, sf. (Gal.) the second dressing of vines.
Rendáge, sm. Reins of the bridle of horses or mules.
Rendájo, sm. Mimic. V. *Arrendajo.*
Rendár, va. (Gal.) To dress vines a second time.
Rendición, sf. Rendition, surrendering, act of yielding; product, profit accruing; price of redemption.
Rendidaménte, ad. Humbly, submissively.
Rendíja, sf. Crevice, crack, cleft.
Rendimiénto, sm. 1. Rendition, the delivery of a thing into the hands of another. 2. Weariness, faintness. 3. Humiliation, submission; obsequiousness. 4. Rent, income; the yearly produce.
Rendír, va. 1. To subject, to subdue, to reduce to submission. 2. To yield, to deliver up. *Rendir el alma á Dios,* To expire, to die. *Rendir el puesto ó la posta,* (Mil.) To give up a post, to commit it to another. 3. To return, to restore; to produce. 4. To vomit, to throw up from the stomach.—*vr.* 1. To be tired, to be worn out with fatigue. 2. To yield, to submit to the will and command of another. 3. (Naút.) To spring; applied to a mast.
Rendón (De), ad. V. *De Rondon.*
Renegádo, sm. 1. Renegado, apostate. 2. A malicious wicked person. 3. Ombre, a sort of game at cards.
Renegadór, ra, s. Swearer, blasphemer; apostate.
Renegár, va. 1. To deny, to disown. 2. To detest, to abhor.—*vn.* 1. To apostatize, to forsake one's religion. 2. To blaspheme, to curse.
Renglón, sm. 1. Line written from one margin to another. 2. Part of one's revenue or income. *Renglónes,* Writings.
Renglonadúra, sf. Ruling of paper with a pencil.
Réngo, ga, a. Hurt in the reins, back, or hip.
Réngue, sm. A sort of gauze which counsellors wear in Spain on their collars and sleeves.
Reniégo, sm. Execration, blasphemy.
Reniténcia, sf. Resistance, opposition.
Reniténte, a. Renitent, repugnant.
Réno, sm. Rein-deer. Cervus tarandus *L.*
Renombrádo, da, a. Renowned, celebrated.
Renombrár, va. (Ant.) To name, to give a name.
Renómbre, sm. 1. Surname, family name. 2. Renown, glory, fame.
Renovación, sf. 1. Renovation, renewal. 2. Change, reform. 3. Act of consuming old bread designed for the host, and of consecrating new.
Renovadór, ra, s. Renovator, reformer, renewer.
Renovánte, pa. Renovating, renewer.
Renovár, va. 1. To renew, to renovate; to begin anew. 2. To change, to reform. 3. To polish, to give lustre. 4. To barter. 5. To reiterate, to republish. 6. To consume old wafers designed for the host, and consecrate new bread. *Renovar la memoria,* To bring to recollection.—*vr.* To recollect one's self, to reform.
Renovéro, sm. 1. Usurer, one who lends money on excessive interest. 2. One who deals in old clothes, fripperer.
Renqueár, vn. To limp, to halt, to claudicate.
Rénta, sf. Rent, profit, income. *A' renta,* Let at a rent.
Rentár, va. To produce, to yield.
Renteria, sf. Productive land or property.
Rentéro, ra, s. Renter, farmer; farmer's wife. 2. One who farms out land.
Rentílla, sf. 1. A small rent. 2. A sort of game at cards. 3. A sort of game at dice.
Rénto, sm. Country residence with farm-yard. 2. Annual rent paid by a labourer or colonist.
Rentóy, sm. A kind of game at cards.
Renuéncia, sf. Contradiction, reluctance.
Renuévo, sm. 1. Sprout, shoot; a young plant which is to be transplanted. 2. Nursery of young trees and plants. 3. Renovation, renewal. V. *Remuda.*
Renúncia, sf. Renunciation, resignation.
Renunciáble, a. That can be renounced or resigned; transferable.
Renunciación, sf. Renunciation.
Renunciamiénto, sm. Renouncement.
Renunciánte, pa. Renouncer, renouncing.
Renunciár, va. 1. To renounce, to resign. 2. To refuse, to reject; to depreciate, to abandon. *Renunciarse á si mismo,* To deprive one'self entirely of doing or following one's own will or taste.
Renunciatário, sm. He to whom any thing is resigned.
Renúncio, sm. 1. Fault committed on playing at cards, by not furnishing a card of the same suit which was played by another. 2. (Met.) Error, mistake.
Reñído, da, a. Being at variance with another.
Reñidór, ra, s. Quarreller, wrangler.
Reñír, vn. 1. To wrangle, to quarrel, to dispute. 2. To scold, to reprimand, to chide, to reproach.—*va.* To argue, to discuss.
Reñón, sm. Kidney. V. *Riñon.*
Réo, sm. 1. Offender, criminal. 2. Defendant in a suit at law. 3. Series, continuity. 4. (Ict.) Ray trout. Salmo hucho *L.*
Réo, ea, a. (Ant.) Criminal, culpable.
Reoctáva, sf. V. *Octavilla.*
Reoctavár, va. To extract the eighth part of an eighth, as an excise or king's duty.
Reojár, va. To bleach wax.
Reójo, sm. *Mirar de reojo,* To look obliquely, to dissemble the looks by directing the view above a person; to look contemptuously or angrily.
Repacér, va. To consume the entire grass of pasture ground.
Repadecér, va. y n. To suffer extremely.
Repagár, va. To repay.
Repájo, sm. Enclosure, ground enclosed for the pasture of cattle.
Repantigárse, vr. To lean back in a chair with the legs stretched out.
Repapilárse, vr. To eat to excess, to overload one's stomach with dainties.
Reparáble, a. Reparable, remediable.
Reparación, sf. 1. Reparation, the act of repairing. 2. Repeating a lesson among scholars.
Reparáda, sf. Sudden bound of a horse.
Reparadór, ra, s. 1. Repairer, one who repairs.

2. Observer, one who makes observations and remarks.

Reparamiénto, *sm.* V. *Repara y Reparacion.*

Reparár, *va.* 1. To repair. 2. To observe with careful attention. 3. To consider, to reflect. 4. To mend, to correct. 5. To suspend, to detain. 6. To guard, to defend, to protect. 7. To give the final touch to moulds. *Reparar en pelillos*, (Fam.) To notice trifles; to take offence at nothing.—*vn.* 1. To regain strength and vigour; to recover from a fit of illness. 2. To stop or halt in any part. *Reparar el timon*, (Naút.) To right the helm.—*vr.* To refrain, to forbear.

Reparatívo, va, *a.* Reparative.

Repáro, *sm.* 1. Restoration, recovery; repair. 2. Careful inspection and investigation. 3. Consideration, reflection, circumspection. 4. Inconveniency, difficulty, doubt. 5. Strengthening cataplasm put on the stomach. 6. Any thing to support, assist, or defend.

Reparón, *sm.* Great doubt, difficulty, caution or reparation.—*a.* Cautious, circumspect.

Repartíble, *a.* Distributable, that which may be divided.

Repartición, *sf.* Partition, distribution; the act of dividing into parts.

Repartidaménte, *ad.* In divers portions or partitions.

Repartidéro, ra, *a.* Distributing, parting.

Repartidór, ra, *s.* 1. Distributer, one who distributes or divides into parts. 2. Assessor of taxes.

Repartimiénto, *sm.* 1. Partition, division, distribution. 2. Instrument stating the amount of a dividend. 3. Assessment of taxes.

Repartír, *va.* 1. To divide, to distribute; to dispart. 2. To grant or bestow favours. 3. To assess taxes.

Repasadéra, *sf.* Plane, an instrument or tool used by carpenters.

Repasadóra, *sf.* Woman occupied in carding wool.

Repasár, *va.* 1. To repass, to pursue the same course. 2. To re-examine, to revise. 3. To explain again, to run over the results of one's former studies. 4. To air clothes at the fire. 5. To clean dyed wool for carding. 6. To sow again. 7. To remix mercury with metal to purify it.

Repasáta, *sf.* Reprehension, censure.

Repasión, *sf.* Reaction of the agent on the patient.

Repáso, *sm.* 1. To repass or remix quicksilver with metal. 2. To run over a thing studied before. 3. Revision, the act of re-examining and revising. 4. Reprimand, chastisement.

Repastár, *va.* To feed or give food a second time.

Repásto, *sm.* Increase of food; an additional meal.

Repatriár, *vn.* To return to one's country.

Repechár, *va.* y *n.* To mount any declivity or slope.

Repécho, *sm.* Declivity, slope.

Repedír, *va.* To repeat, to supplicate again.

Repeládo, *sm.* Salad of herbs.

Repelár, *va.* 1. To pull out the hair of the head. 2. To put a horse to his speed. 3. To take by small parts and portions. 4. To nip the tops of grass; applied to grazing cattle.

Repeléntе, *sm.* Repellent.

Repelér, *va.* To repel, to refute, to reject.

Repellár, *va.* To take trowelfuls of plaster or lime from a new built or repaired wall.

Repélo, *sm.* 1. A small part or share. 2. Any thing which goes against the grain, crooked grain. 3. A slight scuffle or dispute. 4. Repugnance, aversion.

Repelón, *sm.* 1. The action of pulling out the hair. 2. A small part torn from any thing; a thread loose in stockings. 3. A short gallop. 4. A slight fall. *A' repelones*, By degrees, by little and little. *De repelon*, By the way; in haste.

Repelóso, sa, *a.* 1. Being of a bad grain, having transverse fibres; applied to wood. 2. Touchy, possessed of a lively sense of honour; rigid.

Repensár, *va.* To consider, to reflect, to contemplate; to think deeply.

Repénte, *sm.* A sudden movement, an unexpected event. *De repente*, Suddenly, on a sudden.

Repentinaménte, *ad.* Suddenly.

Repentíno, na, *a.* Sudden, unforeseen, unexpected.

Repentírse, *vr.* V. *Arrepentirse.*

Repentísta, *sm.* Maker of extemporary verses.

Repentón, *sm.* 1. An unexpected event or incident. 2. A sudden movement.

Repeór, *a.* Much worse.

Repercudída, *sf.* Repercussion, rebound.

Repercudír, *vn.* To rebound. V. *Repercutir.*

Repercusión, *sf.* Repercussion, reverberation.

Repercusívo, va, *a.* Repercussive; repellent.

Repercutír, *vn.* To cause a repercussion or rebound; to retrograde, to reverberate.—*va.* To repel.

Repertório, *sm.* Repertory, index.

Repesár, *va.* To re-weigh, to weigh again.

Repéso, *sm.* 1. The act of weighing a second time. 2. Weigh-office, whither provisions and other articles may be carried to be weighed a second time. 3. Charge of re-weighing. *De repeso*, With the whole weight of a body; with the whole force of authority and persuasion.

Repeténcia, *sf.* Repetition.

Repetición, *sf.* 1. Repetition, reiteration. 2. Repeater, a repeating clock or watch. 3. Collegial dissertation or discourse; a thesis.

Repetidaménte, *ad.* Repeatedly.

Repetidór, ra, *s.* Repeater, a teacher or student who repeats with another his lessons and explains them.

Repetír, *va.* 1. To demand or claim repeatedly and urgently. 2. To repeat, to reiterate.—*vn.* 1. To have the taste of what was ate or drank in the mouth. 2. To deliver a public discourse previous to the examination for the higher degrees in universities.—*vr.* To repeat one's self; applied to artists.

Repetitívo, va, *a.* That which contains a repetition.

Repicádo, da, *a.* 1. Chopped, cut into small bits. 2. Starched, stiff; affectedly nice.

Repicapúnto, *ad.* *De repicapunto*, Nicely, delicately, excellently.

Repicár, *va.* 1. To chop or cut into small bits.

2. To chime, to ring a merry peal. 3. To reprick. 4. In the game of piquet, to count ninety before the adverse party counts one.—*vr.* To glory, to boast, to pique one's self on.

Repilogár, *va.* To recapitulate, to epitomize.

Repinárse, *vr.* To soar, to elevate.

Repintár, *va.* 1. To repaint, to paint over that which has already been painted. 2. To paint one's self. 3. (Impr.) A double or false impression of letters.

Repíque, *sm.* 1. Act of chopping or cutting. 2. Chime, a merry peal rung on festive occasions. 3. Dispute, altercation; a slight scuffle. 4. In the game of piquet, the act of counting ninety before the other player can count one.

Repiquéte, *sm.* 1. A merry and joyful peal rung on festive occasions. 2. Chance, opportunity.

Repiqueteár, *va.* To ring a merry peal on festive occasions.—*vr.* To bicker, to wrangle, to quarrel.

Repísa, *sf.* Pedestal or abutment for a bust or vase.

Repíso, *sm.* Weak vapid wine.

Repitiénte, *pa.* Repeating, he who repeats and defends a thesis.

Repizcár, *va.* To pinch. V. *Pellizcar.*

Repízco, *sm.* The act of pinching. V. *Pellizco.*

Replantár, *va.* To replant any ground.

Replanteár, *va.* To mark out the ground plan of an edifice again.

Replantéo, *sm.* Second description of the ground plan of a building.

Repleción, *sf.* Repletion arising from an abundance of humours in the animal body.

Replegár, *va.* To redouble, to fold often.

Replléto, ta, *a.* Replete, very full.

Réplica, *sf.* Reply, answer; repartee.

Replicación, *sf.* (Ant.) Repetition, replication. V. *Réplica.*

Replicadór, ra, *s.* Respondent.

Replicánte, *pa.* Replier, disputant.

Replicár, *vn.* To reply, to impugn the arguments of the adverse party; to contradict.—*va.* (For.) To respond; to repeat.

Replicón, na, *a.* Replier, frequent disputer.

Repoblación, *sf.* Repopulation, act of repeopling.

Repoblár, *va.* To repeople.

Repodrír, *va.* To rot excessively.—*vr.* To become rotten, to consume or pine away in silence under any calamity.

Repollár, *vn.* To form round heads of leaves, like cabbage.

Repóllo, *sm.* 1. (Bot.) Sort of round cabbage. 2. Round head formed by the leaves of plants.

Repollúdo, da, *a.* Having the shape of a head of cabbage; cabbage-headed; round-head.

Repónche, *sm.* V. *Ruiponce.*

Reponér, *va.* 1. To replace, to put any thing in its former place; to collocate. 2. To restore a suit at law to its primitive state. 3. To oppose anew; to reply.—*vr.* To recover health or property lost.

Reportación, *sf.* Moderation, forbearance.

Reportádo, da, *a.* Moderate, temperate, forbearing.

Reportamiénto, *sm.* Forbearance.

Reportár, *va.* 1. To moderate or repress one's passions, to refrain, to forbear. 2. To obtain, to reach; to attain. 3. To carry or bring. 4. To return an instrument with the certificate of its execution.

Reportório, *sm.* 1. Repertory, memorandum-book. V. *Repertorio.* 2. Almanac, calendar.

Reposadaménte, *ad.* Peaceably, quietly.

Reposádo, da, *a.* Quiet, peaceful.

Reposár, *vn.* To rest, to repose; to take a sleep; to repose in the grave; to rest in peace.—*vr.* To settle; applied to liquors.

Reposición, *sf.* 1. The act of restoring a suit at law to its primitive state. 2. (Quím.) Preservation of liquids in proper vessels.

Repositório, *sm.* (Ant.) Repository.

Repóso, *sm.* Rest; repose; tranquillity.

Repóste, *sm.* (Ar.) V. *Despensa.*

Reposteríá, *sf.* Office in the royal palaces of Spain where the plate is kept, and all sorts of comfits and sweetmeats are prepared; place of king's butler or keeper of the royal plate.

Repostéro, *sm.* The principal officer of the *reposteria;* king's butler. 2. Covering ornamented with a coat of arms. *Repostero de camas,* Queen's chamberlain. *Repostero de estrados,* Keeper of the king's drawing-room.

Repregúnta, *sf.* A second demand or question on the same subject.

Repreguntár, *va.* To question repeatedly about the same subject.

Reprehendér, *va.* To reprehend, to reprimand, to blame, to censure.

Reprehendiénte, *pa.* Censurer.

Reprehensíble, *a.* Reprehensible.

Reprehensión, *sf.* Reprehension, blame, censure, reprimand. *Sugeto sin reprehension,* An irreprehensible person.

Reprehensór, ra, *s.* Reprehender, censurer.

Repréndа, *sf.* Pledge taken a second time.

Represа, *sf.* 1. Water collected for the purpose of working a mill. 2. The act of stopping or retaining; restriction. 3. The act of resenting an injury or insult. 4. (Naút.) Vessel retaken after being captured by the enemy.

Represália y Represária, *sf.* Reprisal.

Represár, *va.* 1. To recapture or retake from the enemy. 2. To stop, to detain, to retain. 3. To repress, to moderate one's passions.

Representáble, *a.* That which may be represented.

Representación, *sf.* 1. Representation, the act of representing. 2. Power, authority. 3. Dramatic poem. 4. Figure, image, idea. 5. Remonstrance, memorial, address. 6. (For.) Right of succession to an inheritance in the person of another.

Representadór, ra, *s.* 1. Representative, one who represents. 2. Player, actor.

Representánte, ta, *s.* Player. V. *Cómico.*

Representár, *va.* 1. To represent, to make appear, to set forth; to manifest; to refer. 2. To play on the stage. 3. To represent another, as his agent, deputy, or attorney. 4. To be the symbol or image of any thing.—*vr.* To offer, to occur; to present itself.

Representatívo, va, *a.* Representing another thing or person.

Represión, *sf.* Repression.

Repriménda, *sf.* Reprimand.

Reprimír, *va.* To repress, to refrain, to contain.

Reprobáble, *a.* Reprehensible.

Reprobación, *sf.* Reprobation, reproof; the act of reproving.
Reprobadór, ra, *s.* Reprover, condemner.
Reprobár, *va.* To reject, to condemn, to contradict, to exclude; to reprobate; to damn.
Reprobatório, ria, *a.* That which reprobates or reproves.
Réprobo, ba, *s.* y *a.* Reprobate; wicked.
Reprochár, *va.* To reproach; to challenge the witnesses produced by the adverse party.
Repróche, *sm.* Reproach, reproof.
Reproducción, *sf.* 1. Reproduction, the second production of the same. 2. Reproduction of a summons, or any other judicial precept or decree, with the certificate of service.
Reproducír, *va.* To reproduce, to produce again.
Repromisión, *sf.* Repeated promise.
RepróPio, *a.* Restive, or restiff; applied to a horse.
Repruéba, *sf.* New proof in addition to a preceding one.
Reptár, *va.* V. *Retar.*
Reptíl, *a.* y *s.* Reptile; applied to animals which creep on the ground.
República, *sf.* 1. Republic, commonwealth; democracy. 2. Public welfare; political government. *República literaria*, The republic of letters.
Republicáno, na; y **Repúblico, ca**, *s.* y *a.* Republican, inhabitant or subject of a republic; statesman or politician; democrat; democratic.
Repudiación, *sf.* Repudiation, divorce.
Repudiár, *va.* 1. To repudiate, to divorce a wife. 2. To renounce, to relinquish.
Repúdio, *sm.* Repudiation, divorce.
Repudrírse, *vr.* To decay or become rotten internally.
Repuésta, *sf.* Money staked in the game of Ombre.
Repuésto, *sm.* Store or stock laid up to meet some future events; depository. V. *Repuesta.* *De repuésto*, By way of precaution.
Repugnáncia, *sf.* 1. Reluctance, repugnance. 2. Opposition, contradiction. *Con repugnancia*, In a reluctant manner.
Repugnánte, *pa.* Incompatible.
Repugnár, *va.* 1. To oppose, to contradict. 2. To act with reluctance, to proceed reluctantly; to implicate, to imply.
Repulgádo, *a.* V. *Afectado.*
Repulgár, *va.* To hem, to double in the border of cloth with a seam; to border, to double the edge.
Repúlgo, *sm.* 1. Hem, the border of cloth doubled in with a seam. 2. The external ornament of a pie.
Repulído, da, *a.* Prim, neat, spruce.
Repúllo, *sm.* 1. Jerk, leap; a sudden violent motion of the body. 2. A small arrow or dart. 3. A demonstration or external mark of pain or grief.
Repúlsa, *sf.* Refusal.
Repulsár, *va.* To reject, to decline, to refuse.
Repúnta, *sf.* 1. Point, headland. 2. Sign of displeasure; disagreement, dispute, scuffle. 3. Very short thing, very small portion.
Repuntár, *vn.* (Naút.) To begin to ebb.—*vr.* 1. To be pricked, to be on the turn; applied to wine. 2. To be soured, to be displeased with one another.
Repúrga, *sf.* A second purge or purging draught.
Repurgár, *va.* 1. To clean or purify again. 2. To administer a second purging draught.
Reputación, *sf.* Reputation, character, credit, fame, renown.
Reputánte, *pa.* One who estimates.
Reputár, *va.* To repute, to estimate, to judge; to appreciate.
Requadrár, *va.* (Pint.) V. *Quadricular.*
Requádro, *sm.* (Arq.) Square compartment.
Requánta, *sf.* One of the chords of a guitar.
Requebrádo, da, *a.* Enamoured, using tender expressions.—*s.* Lover, loving expression.
Requebradór, *sm.* Wooer, one who courts a woman.
Requebrár, *va.* To woo, to court, to make love to a lady.
Requemádo, da, *a.* 1. Brown-coloured, sunburnt. 2. Thin silk used for veils.
Requemamiénto, *sm.* V. *Resquemo.*
Requemár, *va.* 1. To burn a second time. 2. To roast to excess. 3. To extract the juice of plants. 4. To inflame the blood or humours. V. *Resquemar.*—*vr.* To burn with a passion, to be deeply in love.
Requemazón, *sf.* V. *Resquemo.*
Requerér, *va.* To wish again, to desire anxiously.
Requeridór, *sm.* He who requests, advises, or intimates.
Requerimiénto, *sm.* 1. Request, requisition. 2. Intimation, injunction.
Requerír, *va.* 1. To intimate, to notify. 2. To investigate, to examine into. 3. To request, to require, to need. 4. To take care, to be on one's guard. 5. To court, to make love to a woman. 6. To research with care. 7. To induce, to persuade.
Requesón, *sm.* Second curds made after the cheese.
Requesonárse, *vr.* To become curds a second time; applied to whey or milk.
Requésta, *sf.* Request, petition. V. *Requerimiénto.* *A' toda requesta*, At all events.
Requestár, *va.* 1. (Ant.) To solicit, to entreat, to demand. 2. To endear, to engage with all the fondness of a lover. 3. V. *Desafiar.*
Requíbe, *sm.* V. *Arrequive.*
Requiébro, *sm.* 1. Endearing expressions, the engaging language of love. 2. Quiver, trill of the voice.
Requintadór, ra, *s.* Outbidder, in the letting of lands or tenements.
Requintár, *va.* 1. To outbid a fifth part, in tenements after an agreement is made. 2. To exceed, to surpass, to superadd. 3. (Mús.) To raise or lower the tone.
Requínto, *sm.* 1. The second-fifth taken from any quantity from which one-fifth had before been taken. 2. An advance of a fifth part in rent. 3. Extraordinary impost levied on the Peruvians.
Requirír, *va.* V. *Requerir.*
Requísa, *sf.* Night and morning visit of a gaoler to his prisoners.
Requisíto, *sm.* Requisite, a necessary circumstance or condition.
Requisitório, ria, *a.* *Requisitoria*, Warrant

from one judge to another requiring compliance to his orders.
Res, *sf.* Head of cattle.
Resabér, *va.* To know very well; to affect too much the learned man.
Resabiár, *vn.* To become vicious, to contract evil habits.—*vr.* To be discontent. V. *Saborearse.*
Resabído, *a.* Very learned; affecting learning.
Resábio, *sm.* 1. An unpleasant taste left on the palate. 2. Vicious habit, bad custom.—*a.* Very learned; affecting much knowledge.
Resáca, *sf.* (Naút.) Surge, surf.
Resalír, *vn.* To jut out, to project.
Resaltár, *vn.* 1. To rebound, to fly back. 2. To crack, to burst into pieces. 3. To jut out, to project. 4. To appear, to be evident.
Resálte, *sm.* Prominence, protuberance; any striking point.
Resálto, *sm.* Rebound, resilience; prominence; act of shooting boars when rising from their bed.
Resaludár, *vn.* To return a salute, to salute again.
Resalutación, *sf.* Return of a salute, the act of resaluting.
Resangría, *sf.* Bleeding again.
Resarcimiénto, *sm.* Compensation.
Resarcír, *va.* To compensate, to recompense, to reward, to indemnify. *Resarcirse de lo perdido,* To make up one's loss.
Resbaladéro, *sm.* A slippery place or road; any thing dangerous.—*a.* V. *Resbaladizo.*
Resbaladízo, za, *a.* Slippery, exposed to temptation. *Memoria resbaladiza,* A treacherous memory.
Resbaladór, ra, *s.* Slider, backslider.
Resbaladúra, *sf.* Slippery track; backsliding.
Resbalánte, *pa.* Slider; slipping.
Resbalár, *vn.* 1. To slip, to slide; not to tread firm. 2. To fail in the performance of one's engagements.
Resbalón, *sm.* 1. Slip, the act of slipping or sliding. 2. Slip, fault, error, offence. *De resbalon,* Erroneously, unsteadily.
Resbalóso, sa, *a.* Slippery. V. *Resbaladizo.*
Rescaldár, *va.* To heat, to scorch.
Rescatadór, ra, *s.* Redeemer, ransomer.
Rescatár, *va.* 1. To ransom, to redeem, to extricate. 2. To exchange, to barter.
Rescáte, *sm.* 1. Ransom, redemption by purchase. 2. Ransom-money, money paid for the redemption of slaves. 3. Exchange, permutation, barter.
Rescáza, *sf.* (Ict.) V. *Escorpina.*
Rescóldo, *sm.* 1. Embers, hot ashes, cinders. 2. (Met.) Scruple, doubt, apprehension.
Rescibír, *va.* (Ant.) V. *Recibir.*
Rescindír, *va.* To rescind, to annul.
Rescisión, *sf.* Rescission.
Rescisório, ria, *a.* Rescissory.
Rescontrár, *va.* To balance in accounts, to compensate.
Rescribír, *va.* To write an answer to a letter.
Rescrípto, *sm.* Rescript, order, mandate.
Rescriptório, ria, *a.* Belonging to a rescript.
Rescuéntro, *sm.* Balance of accounts, compensation.
Resecación, *sf.* Exsiccation.
Resecár, *va.* To dry again.
Reséco, ca, *a.* Too dry; very lean.
Reséco, *sm.* Exsiccation of trees or shrubs; dry part of a honey-comb.
Resegár, *va.* To reap again, to cut or mow a second time.
Resellánte, *pa.* Recoiner; restamping.
Resellár, *va.* To recoin, to coin again.
Reséllo, *sm.* Recoinage, the act of coining again.
Resemblár, *va.* (Ant.) To resemble.
Resembrár, *va.* To resow, to sow anew.
Resentído, da, *a.* Angry, displeased.
Resentimiénto, *sm.* 1. Flaw, crack, cleft. 2. Resentment, displeasure.
Resentírse, *vr.* 1. To begin to give way, to fail; to be out of order. 2. To resent, to express displeasure.
Reséña, *sf.* 1. Review of soldiers. 2. Signal. *Reseñas,* Signs, tokens, marks.
Reseñár, *va.* To notice the marks or characters by which a thing is known.
Resequído, da, *a.* V. *Reseco.*
Resérva, *sf.* 1. Reserve, any thing kept in store; secret. 2. Reservation; exception. 3. Reservedness, closeness, want of openness; circumspection, prudence. 4. V. *Reservado. Andar con reserva,* To proceed cautiously.
Reservación, *sf.* Reservation, the act of reserving.
Reservadaménte, *ad.* Secretly, reservedly.
Reservádo, da, *a.* Reserved, cautious, circumspect. *Caso reservado,* A great crime, which none but the superior can absolve.
Reservádo, *sm.* The eucharist kept in the ciborium.
Reservár, *va.* 1. To reserve, to keep in store. 2. To defer, to postpone. 3. To privilege, to exempt. 4. To separate, to set aside. 5. To restrain, to limit, to confine. 6. To conceal, to hide; to shut up. 7. V. *Jubilar.*—*vr.* 1. To preserve one's self. 2. To act with circumspection, to be cautious.
Reservatório, *sm.* 1. Reservoir, a place where water is collected. 2. Green-house, hothouse.
Resfriádo, *sm.* Cold, a disease caused by cold; the obstruction of perspiration.
Resfriadór, *sm.* Refrigerator.
Resfriadúra, *sf.* Cold in horses.
Resfriamiénto, *sm.* Refrigeration. V. *Enfriamiento.*
Resfriánte, *pa.* Cooler, refrigerating.
Resfriár, *va.* 1. To cool, to make cold. 2. To moderate ardour or fervour.—*vn.* To begin to be cold.—*vr.* 1. To catch cold, to have the perspiration obstructed. 2. To proceed with coolness, not to pursue a business with the activity it requires.
Resfriecér, *vn.* (Vulg.) To begin to grow cold; applied to the weather.
Resfrío, *sm.* (Vulg.) Cold. V. *Resfriado.*
Resguardár, *va.* To preserve, to defend; to protect.—*vr.* To be guarded against, to be on one's guard.
Resguárdo, *sm.* 1. Guard, preservation, security, safety. 2. Defence, shelter, protection. 3. Security for the performance of a contract or agreement. 4. Watchfulness to pre-

vent smuggling. 5. Body of custom-house officers.

Residéncia, *sf.* 1. Residence, place of abode, mansion. 2. Residence, the time appointed for clergymen to reside at a benefice. 3. Account demanded of a person who holds a public station; instrument or account rendered. 4. Place and function of a resident at foreign courts. 5. (Among the Jesuits) A house of residence not yet formed into a college.

Residenciál, *a.* Residentiary.

Residenciár, *va.* To call a public officer to account for his administration.

Residenciádo, da, *pp.* Resident, residentiary.

Residénte, *a.* Residing or resident in a place. —*sm.* Resident, a public agent or minister residing at foreign courts.

Residenteménte, *ad.* Constantly, assiduously.

Residír, *vn.* 1. To reside, to dwell, to live in a place. 2. To be at one's disposal; to assist personally.

Resíduo, *sm.* Residue, remainder. *Resíduos de una mesa,* Leavings, offals, fragments.

Resiémbro, *sm.* Seed thrown on ground without letting it remain.

Resígna, *sf.* Resignation of a benefice.

Resignación, *sf.* 1. Resignation, voluntary submission to the will or command of another. 2. Resignation, the act of resigning a public place or employment.

Resignadaménte, *ad.* Resignedly.

Resignánte, *pa.* Resigner; resigning.

Resignár, *va.* To resign, to give up, to yield up.—*vr.* To submit to the will of another.

Resína, *sf.* Resin, a viscous substance oozing from trees; rosin. [consisting of resin.

Resinóso, sa, *a.* Resinous, containing resin;

Resísa, *sf.* The eighth part taken as duty on wine, vinegar, or oil.

Resisár, *vr.* To diminish any measures or things which have already been taxed.

Resisténcia, *sf.* Resistance, opposition, defence.

Resisténte, *pa.* Resister, repeller.

Resistéro, *sm.* 1. The hottest part of the day, from twelve to two o'clock in the summer season. 2. Heat produced by the reflection or reverberation of the sun's rays.

Resistidéro, *sm.* The hottest part of the day. V. *Resistero.*

Resistidór, ra, *s.* Resister, opponent.

Resistír, *vn.* 1. To resist, to oppose. 2. To contradict, to repel.—*va.* 1. To endure, to tolerate. 2. To reject, to oppugn.

Résma, *sf.* 1. Ream, a bundle of paper, containing twenty quires. 2. Isinglass, a fine fish-glue, used to clarify wine and other liquors.

Resobrár, *vn.* To be much over and above.

Resobríno, na, *s.* Son or daughter of a nephew or niece.

Resól, *sm.* Reverberation of the rays of the sun.

Resoláno, na, *s.* Place covered from the wind to take the sun.

Resolár, *va.* To re-pave; to re-sole, as shoes.

Resolladéro, *sm.* Vent, air-hole; a breathing hole.

Resollár, *vn.* 1. To respire, to breathe audibly. 2. To talk; it is commonly used with a negative. *No resolló,* He did not utter a word. 3. To rest, to take breath. *Resollar por la herida,* To expel air from the body, through a wound; (Met.) To explain some latent sentiment.

Resolución, *sf.* 1. Resolution, deliberation. 2. Determination, courage, boldness. 3. Decision, solution of a doubt; determination of a difference. 4. Easiness of address, freedom from constraint. *En resolucion,* In short, in a word. 5. Dissolution; analysis or resolution. 6. Activity, promptitude. 7. (Med.) Ordinary termination of an inflammation.

Resolúble, *a.* Resoluble.

Resolutaménte, *ad.* Resolutely, determinately.

Resolutívo, va, *a.* Resolutive, having the power to dissolve; analytical.

Resolutívo, *sm.* Ultimate reason, fundamental principle.

Resolúto, ta, *a.* Resolute, bold, audacious; compendious, brief; prompt, dexterous.

Resolutoriaménte, *ad.* Resolutely.

Resolutório, ria, *a.* Resolute, prompt, swift.

Resolvénte, *pa.* Resolvent.

Resolvér, *va.* 1. To resolve, to determine, to decide. 2. To summon up, to reduce to a small compass. 3. To decide, to decree. 4. To solve a difficulty, to unriddle. 5. To dissolve, to divide into parts, to analyze; to dissipate. —*vr.* 1. To resolve, to determine. 2. To be included or comprised.

Resón, *sm.* (Naút.) A kind of small anchor for boats. [cussion.

Resonación, *sf.* Resounding, noise of reper-

Resonáncia, *sf.* 1. Resonance, repercussion of sound. 2. (Poét.) Consonance, harmony.

Resonánte, *pa.* Resonant.

Resonár, *vn.* To resound, to be echoed back.

Resoplár, *vn.* 1. To breathe audibly and with force. 2. To snort, to blow through the nose as a high mettled horse. 3. To huff, to storm with passion.

Resoplído y Resóplo, *sm.* A continued audible breathing; a continual blowing through the nose.

Resorbér, *va.* To sip again, to reabsorb.

Resórte, *sm.* 1. Spring, an elastic body; an elastic piece of tempered steel. 2. Cause, medium, means. V. *Muelle.*

Respaldár, *sm.* Leaning-stock. V. *Respaldo.*—*va.* To endorse, to note on the back of a writing.—*vr.* 1. To lean, to recline against a chair or bench. 2. To dislocate the backbone; applied to a horse.

Respáldo, *sm.* 1. Back or fore part of any thing. 2. Endorsement. 3. Leaning-stock, back of a seat.

Respectár, *v. impers.* V. *Respetar.*

Respectivaménte y Respectíve, *ad.* Respectively, proportionally.

Respectívo, va, *a.* Respective, relative.

Respécto, *sm.* Relation, proportion; relativeness; respect. *Respecto ó á respecto de,* In consideration of.—*ad.* With respect to, with regard to. *Al respecto,* Relatively, respectively.

Respeluzár, *va.* V. *Despeluzar.*

Respetáble, *a.* Respectable, worthy of respect.

Respetadór, ra, *s.* Respecter, venerator.

Respetár, *va.* To respect, to venerate, to revere. *v. impers.* To pertain, to relate, to respect.

Respéto, *sm.* Respect, regard, consideration, veneration; attention. *Respeto de*, In respect to. *Respeto á ó respeto de*, With regard to. *De respeto*, Preventively; for ceremony's sake. *Mastelero de respeto*, (Naút.) A spare top-mast. *Pertrechos de respeto del contramaestre*, (Naút.) The boatswain's spare stores.

Respetosaménte, *ad.* Respectfully.

Respetóso, sa, *a.* 1. Respectable, worthy of respect. 2. Respectful, ceremonious.

Respetuosaménte, *ad.* Respectfully.

Respetuóso, sa, *a.* Respectful. V. *Respetoso.*

Réspice, *sm.* Mass-offering; short reply.

Respigadéra, *sf.* Gleaner, a woman employed in gleaning.

Respigadór, *sm.* Gleaner, he that gleans.

Respigár, *va.* To glean, to gather what the reapers have left in the field.

Respigón, *sm.* Hag-nail; sty on the eyelid.

Respingár, *vn.* 1. To kick, to wince. 2. To obey reluctantly, to perform with grumbling.

Respíngo, *sm.* 1. Kick, yerk. 2. Reluctance, unwillingness, peevishness.

Respiráble, *a.* Respirable, capable of being respired or of respiration.

Respiración, *sf.* Respiration, breathing; vent.

Respiradéro, *sm.* Vent, breathing hole; rest, repose. *Respiraderos*, Nostrils.

Respirár, *vn.* 1. To respire, to breathe; to emit breath. 2. To rest, to respire, to take rest from toil. 3. To spread scents or odours. 4. To speak. In this sense it is frequently used with a negative. *No respiró*, He did not open his lips. 5. To exhale, to animate.

Resplandecéncia, *sf.* Resplendency, splendour, lustre; fame, glory.

Resplandecér, *vn.* 1. To glitter, to emit rays of light; to glisten, to gleam. 2. To shine, to be eminent or conspicuous; to be brilliant.

Resplandeciénte, *a.* Resplendent.

Resplandecimiénto, *sm.* V. *Resplandor.*

Resplandór, *sm.* 1. Splendour, brightness, brilliancy. 2. A kind of shining paint for women.

Respondedór, ra, *s.* Answerer.

Respondér, *va.* y *n.* 1. To answer; to resolve a doubt. 2. To re-echo. 3. To acknowledge, to own as a benefit received; to be grateful. 4. To yield, to produce. 5. To answer, to have the desired effect. 6. To correspond; to be situated; to be responsible for.

Respondidaménte, *ad.* Suitably, answerably.

Respondiénte, *pa.* Respondent.

Respondón, na, *a.* Giving constantly answers; ever ready to reply.

Responsáble, *a.* Responsible.

Responsabilidád, *sf.* Responsibility.

Responsár y **Responseár**, *vn.* To say or repeat the responses.

Responsión, *sf.* Sum which the members of the Order of St. John, who enjoy an income, contribute to the treasury of the Order.

Respónso, *sm.* Responsary separate from the divine office for the dead.

Responsório, *sm.* Response.

Respuésta, *sf.* 1. Answer, reply. 2. Report, the sound produced by the discharge of fire-arms. 3. Sound echoed back.

Resquebradúra y **Resquebrajadúra**, *sf.* Crack, cleft.

Resquebrajár, *vn.* To crack, to split.

Resquebrájo, *sm.* Crack, cleft.

Resquebrajóso, sa, *a.* Brittle, easily cracked or cleft.

Resquebrár, *vn.* To crack, to split, to begin to open; to burst.

Resquemár, *va.* To burn or sting the tongue; applied to pungent aliments.

Resquémo y **Resquemazón**, *s.* Pungency of any aliment.

Resquício, *sm.* 1. Chink, the aperture between the jamb and leaf of a door; crack, cleft. 2. Subterfuge, evasion.

Résta, *sf.* Rest, residue, remainder. V. *Resto.*

Restablecér, *va.* To restore, to re-establish, to establish anew; to reinstate.—*vr.* To recover from a disease.

Restablecimiénto, *sm.* Re-establishment, restoration.

Restadór, *sm.* (Ant.) Remainder, number subtracted.

Restallár, *vn.* To smack, to click.

Restánte, *pa.* Remainder, residue.

Restañár, *va.* To stanch, to stop blood, to hinder from running.

Restañasángre, *sf.* Stone. V. *Alaqueca.*

Restáño, *sm.* 1. Kind of glazed silk, interwoven with gold or silver. 2. Monopoly, forestalling. V. *Estanco.*

Restár, *va.* To subtract, to find the residue of any thing.—*vn.* To be left, to remain due.

Restauración, *sf.* Restoration, redintegration.

Restauradór, ra, *s.* Restorer.

Restauránte, *sm.* Restorer, re-establisher.

Restaurár, *va.* To restore, to retrieve; to repair, to renew.

Restaurativo, va, *a.* Restorative, that has the power of restoring.

Restínga, *sf.* Ridge of rocks in the sea; sand-bank.

Restingár, *sm.* Place containing ridges of rocks or sand banks.

Restitución, *sf.* Restitution.

Restituíble, *a.* That which may be restored.

Restituidór, ra, *s.* Restorer, re-establisher.

Restituír, *va.* 1. To restore, to return to the right owner. 2. To re-establish, to put on the former footing. 3. To reanimate.—*vr.* To return, to go back to the place of departure.

Restitutório, ria, *a.* Relating to restitution.

Résto, *sm.* 1. Remainder, residue, balance. 2. Sum staked at play. 3. Rebound of the ball in the game of tennis. *A' resto abierto*, Unlimitedly. 4. Arrest, attachment.

Restregár, *va.* To scrub.

Restreñír, *va.* (Ant.) V. *Restriñír.*

Restricción, *sf.* Restriction, limitation, modification.

Restrictivaménte, *ad.* Restrictively.

Restrictívo, va, *a.* Restrictive; restringent.

Restrícto, ta, *a.* Limited, confined; kept within bounds.

Restrínga, *sf.* V. *Restinga.*

Restringénte, *sm.* Restrainer; restringent.

Restringíble, *a.* Capable of being restrained or limited.

Restringír, *va.* To restrain, to confine.

Restriñénte, *pa.* Restringent.

Restriñidór, ra, *s.* Restrainer, binder.

Restriñimiénto, *sm.* Restriction, making costive.

Restriñír, *va.* To bind, to make costive.

Restrojéra, *sf.* Female servant taken to attend reapers in the time of harvest.

Restróјo, *sm.* V. *Rastrojo.*

Resucitádo, *a.* *Paxaro resucitado.* Little humming bird; it is but 1 1-2 inch long, and is dormant in winter, hence its name. Trochilus exilis *L.*

Resucitadór, ra, *s.* Restorer, reviver.

Resucitár, *va.* 1. To resuscitate, to revive, to restore to life. 2. To renew, to renovate.—*vn.* 1. To revive, to return to life. 2. To recover from a dangerous disease.

Resúcha, *sf.* Worthless, despicable thing.

Resudación, *sf.* Perspiration, transudation.

Resudár, *vn.* To transude, to perspire, to transpire.

Resudór, *sm.* Slight perspiration.

Resuéllo, *sm.* 1. Breath, breathing, respiration. 2. Pursiness, shortness of breath.

Resueltaménte, *ad.* Resolutely.

Resuélto, ta, *a.* Resolute, audacious, bold; prompt, quick.

Resúlta, *sf.* 1. Rebound, resilience. 2. Result, effect, consequence. 3. Vacancy, a post or employment unoccupied.

Resultádo, *sm.* Result, issue, consequence.

Resultáncia, *sf.* Result.

Resultánte, *pa.* Resulting.

Resultár, *vn.* 1. To rebound, to fly back. 2. To result, to rise as a consequence or effect, to proceed from. 3. To remain to be done or provided for.

Resumbrúno, na, *a.* Brown, of the colour of a hawk's feathers, between red and black.

Resúmen, *sm.* 1. Abridgment, summary. 2. Recapitulation, detail repeated. 3. Brief, the writing given to the counsellor, containing the case. *En resúmen,* Briefly, in short; lastly.

Resumidaménte, *ad.* Briefly, compendiously, summarily.

Resumído, da, *a.* Abridged. *En resumidas cuentas,* In short, briefly.

Resumír, *va.* 1 To abridge, to reduce to a smaller compass. 2. To bring to a close, to conclude. 3. To reassume, to resume. *Resumir corona,* (For.) To resume the clerical tonsure and habit. V. *Reasumir.* 4. To resolve, to determine.—*vr.* To include; to convert.

Resunción, *sf.* 1. Summary, abridgment. 2. Repetition of several words inserted in a speech.

Resuntívo, va, *a.* That which restores or resumes.

Resurgír, *vn.* (Ant.) V. *Resucitar.*

Resurrección, *sf.* Resurrection, revival; restitution.

Resurtída, *sf.* Rebound, repercussion, resilience.

Resurtír, *vn.* To rebound, to fly back; to set out again from the same place.

Resuscitár, *va.* (Ant.) V. *Resucitar.*

Retáblo, *sm.* 1. Picture or painting drawn on a board. 2. Splendid ornament of altars. 3. Sight, spectacle of human miseries.

Retacár, *va.* To hit the ball twice on a truck-table.

Retacería, *sf.* Collection of remnants.

Retáco, *sm.* 1. A short light fowling-piece. 2. A short tack or stick of a truck-table. 3. A short thick person.

Retadór, *sm.* Challenger, one who challenges.

Retaguárdia y Retaguárda, *sf.* Rear-guard.

Retahíla, *sf.* File, range or series of many things following one another.

Retajár, *va.* 1. To cut round. 2. To cut again and again the nib of a pen. 3. To circumcise.

Retál, *sm.* Remnant, a small piece remaining of cloth or of lace.

Retallár, *vn.* To shoot or sprout anew.—*va.* To regrave, to retouch a graving.

Retallecér, *vn.* To re-sprout, to put forth new shoots.

Retállo, *sm.* A new sprout or shoot of a plant.

Retáma, *sf.* (Bot.) 1. Broom. Spartium scorpius *L.* 2. Furze, green-weed. Genista florida *L.* *Estar mascando retama,* (Met.) To be vexed and irritated at not pursuing a thing which is in the hands of another.

Retamál, Retamár y Retaméra, *sm.* Place where furze or broom grows, and is gathered.

Retaméro, ra, *a.* Belonging to broom or furze.

Retamílla, *sf.* (Bot.) Jointed furze. Genista sagittalis *L.*

Retapár, *va.* To cover again.

Retár, *va.* 1. To impeach or charge one with a criminal offence before the king. 2. To challenge, to call out to combat; to reprehend.

Retardación, *sf.* Retardation, delay, detention.

Retardár, *va.* To retard, to defer, to delay.

Retardílla, *sf.* A slight difference or dispute.

Retása, *sf.* Second duty or impost.

Retasación, *sf.* New valuation or assessment.

Retasár, *va.* To tax a second time.

Retazár, *va.* To tear in pieces.

Retázo, *sm.* Remaining piece, remnant.

Retejár, *va.* 1. To repair the roof of a house or other building; to tile anew. 2. To mend, to patch; to risk.

Retéjo, *sm.* Repairing of a roof, retiling.

Retemblár, *vn.* To tremble or shake repeatedly; to vibrate.

Retén, *sm.* Store, stock, reserve.

Retención, *sf.* Retention; the act of keeping back; suspension; stagnation.

Retenedór, ra, *s.* One who retains or keeps back.

Retenér, *va.* 1. To retain, to keep back, to withhold. 2. To guard, to preserve; to maintain; to suspend. 3. To retain the acts of an inferior judge in a superior tribunal.

Retenída, *sf.* (Naút.) Guy. *Retenida de proa,* (Naút.) Head-fast, a rope which serves to fasten the head of the ship.

Retenidaménte, *ad.* Retentively.

Retentár, *va.* To threaten with a relapse of a former disorder.

Retentíva, *sf.* 1. Power of retaining. 2. Consideration, circumspection, prudence, retention.

Retentívo, va, *a.* Retentive, retaining.

Retentríz, *a.* (Med.) Retentive.

Reteñír, *va.* To dye over again, to tinge a second time.—*vn.* To tingle, to sound, to resound. V. *Retiñir.* *Reteñir las orejas,* To grate the ear with unpleasant sounds or speeches.

Retesamiénto, *sm.* Coagulation, hardness.

Retesárse, *vr.* To become hard, to be stiff, as teats with milk.

Retéso, *sm.* Stiffness or distension of teats with milk. V. *Teso.*
Retexér, *va.* To re-weave, to weave closely.
Reticéncia, *sf.* Reticence.
Reticulár, *a.* Reticular, having the form of a net.
Retína, *sf.* Retina, one of the tunics of the eye.
Retínte, *sm.* 1. Second dye given to any thing. 2. A tingling sound.
Retintín, *sm.* 1. A tingling sound. 2. An affected tone of voice.
Retínto, *a.* Dark, obscure, almost black.
Retiñír, *vn.* To tingle, to resound.
Retiración, *sf.* (Impr.) Reiteration, second impression on a sheet.
Retiráda, *sf.* 1. (Mil.) Retreat, the retrograde movement of a body of troops. *Tocar la retirada,* To sound a retreat. 2. Retreat, retirement. 3. Place of retirement. 4. Resource, any thing laid by or preserved as a resource in case of necessity. 5. Step in a Spanish dance.
Retiradaménte, *ad.* Secretly, retiredly.
Retirádo, da, *a.* Retired, solitary; remote, distant. *Hombre retirado,* A man fond of retirement.
Retiramiénto, *sm.* Retirement. V. *Retiro.*
Retirár, *va.* 1. To withdraw, to separate; to refuse, to decline. 2. To repel, to force the enemy to retire or retreat. 3. (Impr.) To print the back of a sheet. 4. To revoke; to retreat.—*vr.* 1. To retreat; to cease to pursue; to recede. 2. To withdraw from an intercourse with the world; to retire from trade. 3. To take refuge; to retire to one's house or department. 4. (Mil.) To raise a siege or blockade; to abandon a post.
Retíro, *sm.* 1. Retreat, the act of retiring; recess; act of declining any business. 2. A sequestered spot, a place of retirement. 3. Rupture, breach of friendship; difference among friends.
Retiróna, *sf.* (Fam.) V. *Retirada.*
Réto, *sm.* 1. Impeachment or charge preferred before the king. 2. Challenge, a summons to combat. 3. Threat, menace.
Retocár, *va.* 1. To retouch a painting, to paint again. 2. To finish any work completely.
Retoñár y Retoñecér, *vn.* 1. To sprout or shoot again; applied to a plant which has been cut. 2. To appear again; applied to cutaneous distempers.
Retóño, *sm.* Sprout or shoot sprung up from a plant which has been cut.
Retóque, *sm.* Finishing stroke, the last hand applied to a work to render it perfect; stroke of the palsy, &c.
Retór, *sm.* (Ant.) Rhetorician.
Retóra, *sf.* Governness of any community.
Retorcedúra, *sf.* Twisting, wreathing.
Retorcér, *va.* 1. To twist, to contort, to convolve. 2. To retort, to convince by returning an argument. 3. (Met.) To interpret perversely.
Retorcído, *sm.* A kind of twisted sweetmeat.
Retorcíjo y Retorcimiénto, *sm.* Twisting, wreathing, contorsion.
Retórica, *sf.* Rhetoric, the art of speaking with correctness and elegance.
Retoricaménte, *ad.* Rhetorically.
Retoricár, *vn.* To speak or write rhetorically.
Retórico, ca, *a.* Rhetorical.—*sm.* Rhetorician, one who speaks with elegance; one who teaches rhetoric.
Retornamiénto, *sm.* Return.
Retornánte, *pa.* Restorer; returning.
Retornár, *vn.* To return, to come back; to retrocede or retrograde.—*va.* 1. To return, to restore, to give back. 2. To turn, to twist, to contort.
Retornélo, *sm.* Ritornello, the burthen of a song.
Retórno, *sm.* 1. Return, the act of coming back; return chaise or horse. 2. Repayment, return of a favour received. 3. Barter, exchange, traffic.
Retorsión, *sf.* Retortion, the act of retorting.
Retorsívo, va, *a.* That which retorts.
Retórta, *sf.* 1. Retort, a round-bellied vessel, used in chemical operations. 2. A sort of linen. 3. Retort, smart reply.
Retortéro, *sm.* Twirl, rotation, circular motion. *Andar al retortero,* To hover about.
Retortijár, *va.* To twist, to form into a ring. V. *Ensortijar.*
Retortijón, *sm.* The act of twisting, contorsion.
Retostádo, da, *a.* Brown-coloured.
Retostár, *va.* To toast again, to toast brown.
Retozadór, ra, *s.* Frisker, one not constant, a wanton.
Retozadúra, *sf.* V. *Retozo.*
Retozár, *vn.* 1. To frisk and skip about, to hoiden. 2. To tickle, to invite to laughter and merriment; to titillate amorously. *Retozar con el verde,* To revel, to feast merrily. *Retozar la risa,* To suppress the emotion to laughter.
Retózo, *sm.* Friskiness, wantonness, lascivious gaiety. *Retozo de la risa,* Suppressed laugh.
Retozón, na, *a.* Wanton, frolicsome, playful.
Retozóna, *sf.* Romp, a rude noisy girl.
Retrabár, *va.* To revive a quarrel.
Retracción, *sf.* Retraction, the act of drawing back.
Retractación, *sf.* Retractation, recantation.
Retractár, *va.* To retract, to undo or unsay.
Retrácto, *sm.* (For.) Retraction, the act or right of retracting.
Retraér, *va.* 1. To retract, to draw back. 2. To reclaim, to dissuade. 3. To reproach, to upbraid. 4. To mock, to ridicule. 5. To retrieve, to recover a thing sold to another. 6. To assimilate; to refer.—*vr.* To take refuge; to flee.
Retraído, *sm.* Fugitive, one who has taken sanctuary in a sacred place.
Retraimiénto, *sm.* Retreat, refuge, asylum.
Retránca, *sf.* A kind of large crupper for mules and other beasts of burden.
Retrasár, *va.* To defer, to put off.—*vn.* To retrograde, to fall off, to decline.
Retratáble, *a.* Retractable, that which may be retracted.
Retratación, *sf.* Retractation, recantation.
Retratadór, ra, *s.* Limner, portrait-painter.
Retratár, *va.* 1. To portray, to draw portraits. 2. To imitate, to copy. 3. To retract, to gainsay, to disavow. 4. To paint, to describe.—*vr.* To unsay, to retract, to recant.
Retratísta, *sm.* Portrait-painter.

Retráto, *sm.* 1. Portrait, effigy. 2. Copy, resemblance, close imitation. 3. Metrical description, poetical portrait. V. *Retracto.*
Retrayénte, *pa.* Retracter, recanter.
Retrechería, *sf.* (Fam.) Flattery, sycophancy.
Retrechéro, ra, *a.* y *s.* Flattering; a flatterer.
Retréta, *sf.* (Mil.) Retreat or tattoo, the beat of a drum which calls the soldiers to their quarters.
Retréte, *sm.* Water-closet, necessary-house.
Retretíco, llo, to, *sm. dim.* of *retrete*, Little water-closet, close-stool, night-table.
Retribución, *sf.* Retribution, recompense, reward.
Retribuír, *va.* To retribute, to pay back, to recompense.
Retribuyénte, *pa.* Retributive.
Retroacción, *sf.* Retroaction.
Retroactívo, va, *a.* Retroactive; spoken of a law which is applied to past transactions.
Retrocedér, *vn.* To retrocede, to fall back; to grow worse; to recede from.
Retrocesión, *sf.* Retrocession, the act of returning or receding.
Retrocéso, *sm.* Retrocession.
Retrogradación, *sf.* Retrogradation, the act of retrograding.
Retrogradár, *vn.* To retrograde.
Retrógrado, da, *a.* Retrograde, moving backwards.
Retronár, *vn.* To thunder again, to continue thundering after a thunder-storm is nearly over.
Retropilástra, *sf.* Pilaster behind a column.
Retrotracción, *sf.* (For.) Antedating any thing.
Retrotraér, *va.* To apply to the present time what happened before.
Retrovendéndo, *sm.* (For.) Reselling to the original vender.
Retrovendér, *va.* To sell back to the first vender.
Retrovendición, *sf.* The act of selling back to the first vender.
Retrucár, *vn.* To hit again, like a ball rebounding.
Retrúco, *sm.* Repercussion of a ball.
Retruécano, *sm.* Rhetorical figure which turns words into divers meanings.
Retrúque, *sm.* Betting a higher wager on a card.
Retuérto, ta, *pp.* Retwisted.
Retulár, *va.* (Ant.) V. *Rotular.*
Retumbánte, *pa.* Resonant, pompous, sonorous, bombastic.
Retumbár, *vn.* To resound, to make a great noise.
Retúmbo, *sm.* Resonance, echo.
Retundír, *va.* 1. To equal or hew stones in a building. 2. (Med.) To repel, to discuss.
Reúma, *sf.* Rheum, defluxion.
Reumático, ca, *a.* Rheumatic.
Reumatísmo, *sm.* Rheumatism.
Reunión, *sf.* Reunion, union.
Reunír, *va.* To reunite, to unite.
Revalidación, *sf.* Confirmation, ratification.
Revalidár, *va.* To ratify, to confirm.—*vr.* To be admitted into some company or society.
Revecéro, ra, *a.* Changeable, mutable; applied to labouring cattle.
Reveedór, *sm.* V. *Revisor.*
Revejecér, *vn.* To grow prematurely old.
Revejecído, da, *pp.* Prematurely old, antiquated.
Revejído, da, *a.* That is become old prematurely.
Revelación, *sf.* Revelation, the communication of sacred and mysterious truths by a teacher from heaven.
Reveladór, ra, *s.* Revealer.
Revelamiénto, *sm.* V. *Revelacion.*
Revelánte, *pa.* Revealing; discoverer.
Revelár, *va.* 1. To reveal, to manifest, to discover a secret. 2. To impart from heaven.
Revelér, *va.* (Med.) To make the humours flow in an opposite direction.
Revellín, *sm.* (Fort.) Ravelin. V. *Rebellin.*
Revendedór, ra, *s.* Retailer, hawker, huckster, pedler, re-seller.
Revendér, *va.* To retail, to sell by small parcels; to sell by proclaiming in the streets.
Revenído, da, *pp.* Dried, consumed, soured, abandoned.
Revenírse, *vr.* 1. To be consumed by little and little, to be spent by degrees. 2. To be pricked, to grow sour; applied to wine and conserves. 3. To relinquish a preconceived opinion, to give up a point obstinately contested. 4. To discharge moisture.
Revénta, *sf.* Retail, sale by small parcels; second sale.
Reventadéro, *sm.* 1. A rough uneven ground, and of difficult access. 2. Any painful and laborious work.
Reventár, *vn.* 1. To burst, to break into pieces. 2. To toil, to drudge. 3. To burst forth, to break loose; applied to a violent passion. 4. To sprout, to shoot; to grow. 5. To long for, to crave.—*va.* To molest, to harass; to violate. *Reventar de risa*, To burst into laughter; to suppress laughter. *Á todo reventar*, At most, at the extreme. *Reventar la mina*, (Met.) To discover any thing hidden or concealed.
Reventazón, *sm.* Disruption; rupture; vanishing in spray.
Reventón, *sm.* 1. The act of bursting or cracking. 2. Great difficulties and distress; arduous or steep declivity. 3. Toil, drudgery; severe labour and fatigue.
Revér, *va.* To review, to revise.
Reverberación, *sf.* 1. Reverberation, the reflexion of light. 2. Calcination performed in a reverberatory furnace.
Reverberár, *va.* To reverberate, to reflect.
Reverbéro, *sm.* V. *Reverberacion.*
Reverdecér, *vn.* 1. To grow green again; applied to fields and plants. 2. To sprout again, to acquire new vigour and strength.
Reveréncia, *sf.* 1. Reverence, respect, veneration. 2. Bow, an act of reverence and submission. 3. Reverence, title of honour given in Spain to the clergy.
Reverenciáble, *a.* Reverend.
Reverenciadór, ra, *s.* One who reveres, reverences, and respects.
Reverenciál, *a.* Reverential.
Reverenciár, *va.* To venerate, to respect.
Reveréndo, da, *a.* 1. Reverend, the honorary epithet of the clergy; worthy of reverence. 2. Extremely circumspect and cautious. *Reverendas*, Prelate's dimissory letters; qualities and titles which are worthy of reverence.

Reverénte, *a.* Respectful, reverent.
Reversár, (Ant.) V. *Revesar.*
Reversión, *sf.* Reversion, return.
Revérso, *sm.* 1. Reverse, the side of the coin on which the head is not impressed. 2. Back part of any thing.
Revertér, *vn.* To overflow. V. *Rebosar.*
Revés, *sm.* 1. Back part or back side. 2. Stroke with the back of the hand. 3. Disappointment, frowns of fortune. 4. Change of temper and disposition. 5. *Reves del tajamar,* (Naút.) Hollow or flaring of the cutwater. *Reveses de la estela,* (Naút.) Eddy of the dead water. *De reves,* Diagonally, from left to right. *Al reves ó del reves,* On the contrary. *Reves de la medalla,* (Met.) Diametrically opposite in character, genius, and disposition.
Revesádo, da, *a.* 1. Intractable, stubborn, obstinate. 2. Difficult, entangled, perplexed.
Revesár, *va.* To vomit, to throw up from the stomach.
Revesíno, *sm.* Reversis, a game at cards. *Cortar el revesino,* To interrupt, to impede.
Revestimiénto, *sm.* 1. Dress. 2. Act of strengthening the wall of a parapet.
Revestír, *va.* 1. To dress, to put on clerical robes, to revest. 2. To repair or fortify a wall.—*vr.* 1. To be swayed or carried along by some power or other; to be invested with. 2. To be haughty, lofty, or elated with pride.
Revezár, *vn.* To alternate, to come in by turn, to relieve one after another, to work in rotation.
Revezéro, *sm.* One who alternates.
Revézo, *sm.* Alternacy, the act of relieving one another; reciprocal succession.
Revidár, *va.* To reinvite.
Reviéjo, *sm.* Withered branch of a tree.
Reviéjo, ja, *a.* Very old.
Reviérnes, *sm.* Each of the first seven Fridays after Easter.
Révino, *sm.* (Naút.) Canting or flaring, the curvature given to any piece of timber in the construction of a ship.
Revisár, *va.* To revise, to review, to examine. *Revisar las cuentas,* To audit accounts.
Revisión, *sf.* Revision, the act of revising or reviewing.
Revisíta, *sf.* Revision, second examination.
Revisór, *sm.* Reviser, censor.
Revisoría, *sf.* Office of censor or reviser.
Revísta, *sf.* Review, a second careful examination; revision, a new trial. *Revista de inspeccion,* Inspection of troops.
Revistár, *va.* To revise a suit at law, to try a cause a second time; to review troops.
Revividéro, *sm.* Place for rearing silk-worms.
Revivificár, *va.* To revivificate, to vivify.
Revíte, *sm.* Invitation to play in some games.
Revivír, *vn.* To revive, to return to the primitive state of life; to acquire new life; to resuscitate.
Revocáble, *a.* Revocable, that may be recalled or repealed.
Revocación, *sf.* Revocation, the act of repealing or annulling; the act of rendering void any contract or agreement; act of recalling.
Revocadór, ra, *s.* 1. One who revokes, abrogates or recalls. 2. Plasterer, one who plasters or whitewashes houses or walls.
Revocadúra, *sf.* Painted borders of canvass. V. *Revoque.*
Revocánte, *pa.* Revoker, recalling, abrogating.
Revocár, *va.* 1. To revoke, to repeal, to annul. 2. To dissuade from, to reconcile one to desist. 3. To plaster, to whitewash. 4. To yield to an impulse, to retrocede. 5. To recall, to call one from one place to another.
Revocatório, ria, *a.* That which revokes or annuls.
Revóco, *sm.* 1. Plaster, whitewash. V. *Revoque.* 2. Cover of broom or furze laid on coal baskets.
Revolár, *vn.* To fly again, to take a second flight. V. *Revolotear.*
Revolcadéro, *sm.* A weltering place, whither wild boars and other beasts resort to wallow in the mire.
Revolcárse, *vr.* 1. To wallow, to roll one's self in mire or any thing filthy. 2. To be obstinately bent upon any idea or design.
Revolear, *vn.* To flutter, to take short flights with turnings and windings; to fly precipitately.
Revoloteár, *vn.* To flutter, to fly round about.
Revolotéo y Revoltíjo, *sm.* Fluttering; a short flight; a quick motion with the wings.
Revoltíllo, *sm.* 1. Parcel of things jumbled together without rule or order. 2. Tripes of a sheep. 3. Medley, confusion, disorder.
Revoltón, *sm.* Vine-fretter, vine-grub. Cuculio bacchus *L.*
Revoltóso, sa, *a.* Turbulent, seditious.
Revolución, *sf.* 1. The act of revolving or being revolved; revolution of a planet. 2. Disturbance, sedition, commotion; revolution, a new system of government.
Revolvedéro, *sm.* Coursing place.
Revolvedór, ra, *s.* Revolter, disturber; a turbulent, seditious, or rebellious person.
Revolvér, *va.* 1. To move a thing up and down; to return; to revert; to retrace or go back again. 2. To revolve; to wrap up. 3. To stir up disturbances, to excite commotions. *Revolver caldos,* (Fam.) To excite disturbances and disputes anew. 4. To revolve in the mind, to hesitate. 5. To evolve, to separate. 6. To turn short swiftly; applied to horses.—*vr.* 1. To move to and fro. 2. To change as the weather. 3. To copulate. 4. (Astr.) To perform a revolution.
Revolvimiénto, *sm.* Commotion, perturbation, revolution.
Revóque, *sm.* 1. Act of whitewashing. 2. Plaster, whitewash, rough-cast laid on houses or walls.
Revuélco, *sm.* Wallowing, rolling.
Revuélo, *sm.* 1. Flying to and fro of a bird. 2. Irregular motion; disturbance. *De revuelo,* By the way, speedily, promptly.
Revuélta, *sf.* 1. Second turn, return. 2. Revolution, sedition; contention, dissension. 3. Delay, tardiness. 4. Meditation, reflection. 5. Commutation, change. 6. Point from which any thing commences a tortuous or oblique direction. *A' revuelta,* Conjointly.
Revuélto, ta, *a.* 1. Easily turned; applied to

horses. 2. Perverse, dissatisfied. 3. Intricate, difficult.

Revulsión, *sf.* Revulsion, contrary course of humours.

Revulsívo, va; Revulsório, ria, *a.* Revulsory, having the power of causing revulsion.

Réy, *sm.* 1. King, the sovereign of a kingdom. 2. Swineherd. *Rey en el nombre*, Nominal king. *Rey de bastos*, A wooden king, a king without authority. *Los reyes*, Epiphany; twelfth-night. *Dios guarde al rey*, God save the king. 3. Spanish dance. 4. King or chief bee; chief among animals. 5. King of a feast. 6. King in cards or chess. *Rey de banda*, Partridge which leads the covey. *Rey de codornices*, Large quail which guides others in their flight. 7. (Met.) One magnanimous and liberal in his conduct.

Reyérta, *sf.* Dispute, difference.

Reyertár, *va.* To dispute, to contend.

Reyezuélo, *sm.* 1. A petty king. 2. (Orn.) Golden-crested wren, a small bird. Motacilla regulus *L.*

Rey'na, *sf.* 1. Queen, the consort of a king; queen bee. 2. Any woman we admire and love. 3. Queen at cards or chess. *Reyna mora.* V. *Infernáculo.*

Reynádo, *sm.* Reign, the space of time in which a sovereign rules or governs.

Reynánte, *a.* Reigning, prevailing, excelling.

Reynár, *va.* To reign, to govern, to command; to prevail, to predominate.

Réyno, *sm.* Kingdom, all the vessels subject to a king; a state; kingdom of nature; kingdom of heaven.

Rezadéro, ra, *a.* Praying often.

Rezádo, *sm.* Prayer, divine service. V. *Rezo.*

Rezadór, ra, *s.* One who prays often.

Rezága, *sf.* Rear-guard. V. *Retaguardia.*

Rezagánte, *pa.* Delayer; leaving behind.

Rezagár, *va.* To leave behind; to defer.

Rezágo, *sm.* Remainder, residue.

Rezár, *va.* 1. To pray, to say or read prayers. 2. To quote, to recite. 3. (Vulg.) To announce, to foretel. *El calendario reza agua*, The almanac announces rain or rainy weather. 4. To grunt, to grumble.

Rezeladór, *sm.* Stone-horse.

Rezelamiénto, *sm.* V. *Rezelo.*

Rezelár, *va.* 1. To apprehend, to fear, to suspect. 2. To bring a stone-horse to a mare. 3. To guard, to defend.—*vr.* To startle, to fear, to be afraid.

Rezélo, *sm.* Dread, suspicion, mistrust.

Rezelóso, sa, *a.* Fearful, apprehensive, shy.

Rézno, *sm.* Tick, sheep-tick, dog-tick. Acarus ricinus et reduvius *L.*

Rézo, *sm.* 1. Prayer, the act of praying. 2. Divine office, formulary of devotion.

Rezón, *sm.* (Naút.) Grappling.

Rezongadór, ra, *s.* Grumbler, growler.

Rezongár, *vn.* To grumble, to mutter, to murmur.

Rezonglón, na; y Rezongón, na, *s.* y *a.* Grumbler.

Rezumadéro, *sm.* Dripping place; dripping.

Rezumárse, *vr.* 1. To ooze, to flow by stealth; to run gently. 2. To transpire, to escape from secrecy to notice.

Rezúra, *sf.* Fastness, strong hold. V. *Reciura.*

Ría, *sf.* Mouth of a river where it empties itself into the sea.

Riachuélo y Riatíllo, *sm.* Rivulet, streamlet; a small river.

Ríba, *sf.* (Ar.) Bank between a higher and lower field.

Ribadoquín, *sm.* Small gun now disused.

Ribaldería, *sf.* Ribaldry; wickedness.

Ribáldo, da, *a.* y *s.* Ribaldous; ribald; wicked, obscene. V. *Rufian.*

Ribázo, *sm.* A sloping bank or ditch.

Ribéra, *sf.* Sea-shore, bank of a river. *Ser de monte y ribera*, To be fit for every thing.

Riberéño, ña, *a.* Belonging to the sea-shore or bank of a river.

Riberiégo, ga, *a.* Grazing on the banks of rivers; applied to such flocks as are not removed to other sheep-walks, or are not *trashumantes*, as opposed to *estantes*.—*sm.* Grazier of sheep on the banks of rivers.

Ribéro, *sm.* Bank or parapet of a dam of water.

Ríbes, *sf.* (Bot.) Currant-tree. Ribes *L.*

Ribéte, *sm.* 1. Ribbon or tape sewed to the edge of cloth; seam, border. 2. Cantle, the small part or quantity given over and above the precise measure or weight. 3. Additions to a tale or story by way of ornament or embellishment.

Ribeteár, *va.* To hem, to border, to embellish.

Ricácho, cha, *a.* (Vulg.) Very rich.

Ricaduéña, *sf.* Lady, daughter, or wife of a noble.

Ricafémbra y Ricahémbra, *sf.* Lady, daughter or wife of a noble.

Ricahombría, *sf.* Dignity of the *ricos hombres*, ancient nobility of Castile.

Ricaménte, *ad.* 1. Richly, opulently. 2. Excellently, splendidly.

Ricázo, za, *a.* Very rich, most opulent.

Riciál, *a.* Growing again; applied to the after crop of corn, cut down green for the feed of cattle.

Ricíno, *sm.* (Bot.) Palma christi. Ricinus communis *L.*

Ríco, ca, *a.* 1. Noble, of an ancient and illustrious family. 2. Rich, wealthy, opulent. 3. Pleasing to the taste, delicious. 4. Choice, select.

Ricohómbre ó Ricohóme, *sm.* Grandee, a peer of the first rank in Spain; a nobleman belonging to the ancient nobility of Castile.

Ridiculaménte, *ad.* Ridiculously, in a manner worthy of contempt.

Ridiculéz, *sf.* 1. A ridiculous speech or action. 2. Extreme nicety or sensibility.

Ridiculizár, *va.* To ridicule, to burlesque.

Ridículo, la, *a.* 1. Ridiculous, exciting laughter. 2. Strange, contemptible; despicable. 3. Excessively nice and sentimental.

Ridiculóso, sa, *a.* Ridiculous, extravagant.

Riégo, *sm.* Irrigation.

Riél, *sm.* A small ingot of gold or silver unrefined and unwrought.

Rieládo, da, *a.* Reduced to ingots; applied to gold or silver.

Rieléra, *sf.* Mould in which ingots of gold or silver are cast.

Riénda, *sf.* 1. Rein or reins of a bridle. 2. Moderation in speech and action. *Riendas*, Government, direction; reins of the leading horse. *A' rienda suelta*, Loose reined, violently, swiftly.

Riénte, *pa.* Smiling, smiler.
Riésgo, *sm.* Danger, risk, hazard.
Riéto, *sm.* V. *Reto.*
Rífa, *sf.* 1. Scuffle, dispute, contest. 2. Raffle, a species of game, in which many stake a small part of the value of some thing, in consideration of a chance to win it.
Rifadór, *sm.* Raffler; disputer.
Rifadúra, *sf.* (Naút.) Act of splitting a sail.
Rifár, *va.* 1. To raffle, to cast dice for a prize. 2. (Naút.) To split a sail, owing to a violent storm.—*vn.* To quarrel, to dispute.
Riféo, **ea**, *a.* Applied to the mountains of Scythia, always covered with snow.
Rifirráfe, *sm.* (Fam.) A short quarrel, hasty words.
Rigidaménte, *ad.* Rigidly.
Rigidéz, *sf.* Rigidity, asperity.
Rígido, **da**, *a.* Rigid, rigorous, severe.
Rigodón, *sm.* Rigadoon, a country-dance.
Rigór, *sm.* 1. Rigour, a convulsive shuddering with a sense of cold; rigidity of the nerves. 2. Sternness, severity, want of condescension. 3. Strictness, rigid exactness; power, intensity. 4. Cruelty or excess of chastisement. 5. The last push or extremity. *A' todo rigor,* If the worst comes to the worst. *En rigor,* At most.
Rigorísmo, *sm.* Rigorousness, severity.
Rigorísta, *s. com.* Rigorist, one very rigorous.
Rigorosaménte y Rigurosaménte, *ad.* Rigorously.
Riguridád, *sf.* Rigour, severity. V. *Rigor.*
Riguróso, **sa**, *a.* Rigorous, strict, exact, austere.
Ríja, *sf.* A lachrymal fistula.
Rijénte, *a.* Rough, cruel, horrid.
Ríma, *sf.* 1. Rhyme, the consonance of verses. 2. Arrangement, the act of placing a variety of things in a regular series or order.
Rimádo, **da**, *a.* Versified.
Rimár, *va.* 1. To inquire after, to investigate. 2. To rhyme, to make verses.
Rimbombánte, *pa.* Resonant.
Rimbombár, *vn.* To resound, to echo.
Rimbómbe ó Rimbómbo, *sm.* Repercussion of sound.
Riméro, *sm.* Collection of things placed regularly one over another.
Rincón, *sm.* 1. Inside corner, an angle formed by the meeting of two walls. 2. Place of privacy or retirement. 3. House, dwelling. 4. Small district or country.
Rinconáda, *sf.* Corner, the angle formed by two houses, streets, or roads.
Rinconcíllo, *sm.* A small corner.
Rinconéra, *sf.* Small triangular table placed in a corner.
Rinconéro, **ra**, *a.* Transverse, athwart; applied to honey-combs.
Rîngle, **Rîngla**. V. *Ringléra.*
Ringléra, *sf.* Row, file.
Ringléro, *sm.* Line drawn with a pencil for the purpose of writing straight.
Ringorángo, *sm.* 1. Flourish formed with a pen. 2. Extravagant nicety in point of dress.
Rinoceróntе, *sm.* Rhinoceros, a large wild beast with one horn in front.
Ríña, *sf.* Quarrel, scuffle, dispute.
Riñón, *sm.* 1. Kidney, one of the two glands, called reins, which separate the urine from the blood. *Tener cubierto el riñon,* To be rich. 2. Central point of a country.
Riñonáda, *sf.* 1. Coat of fat about the kidneys, 2. Dish made of kidneys.
Río, *sm.* River, stream; any large quantity of fluids. *A' rio revuelto,* In confusion or disorder. *Rio de lágrimas,* Flood of tears.
Rioláda, *sf.* River-side.
Rióstra, *sf.* Post placed obliquely to strengthen an upright post.
Riostrár, *va.* To strengthen by means of oblique posts.
Rípa, *sf.* Shingle, a small thin board which serves to roof houses or other buildings.
Ripiár, *va.* To fill up the chinks of a wall with small stones and mortar.
Rípio, *sm.* 1. Remainder, residue. 2. Word used to fill up a verse. *No perder ripio,* Not to miss the least occasion.
Ripónce, *sm.* (Bot.) Rampion. Phyteuma spicatum *L.* V. *Ruiponce.*
Riquéza, *sf.* 1. Riches, wealth. 2. Fertility, fruitfulness. 3. Ornament, embellishment.
Rísa, *sf.* 1. Laugh, laughter, the convulsion caused by merriment. 2. Cause or object of laughter; pleasing emotion. 3. Derisory smile or laugh.
Risáda, *sf.* Horse-laugh, a loud laugh.
Rísco, *sm.* A steep rock.
Riscóso, **sa**, *a.* Steep and rocky.
Risibilidád, *sf.* Risibility, the faculty of laughing.
Risíble, *a.* Risible, laughable.
Risíca, **ta**, *sf. dim.* Feigned laugh.
Risosardónico, *a.* (Med.) Sardonic laugh; (Met.) sneer.
Risotáda, *sf.* Loud laugh, horse laugh.
Ríspido, **da**, *a.* V. *A'spero.*
Rístra, *sf.* 1. String of onions or garlic. 2. Row, file; a series of things following one after another.
Rístre, *sm.* Rest or socket for a lance.
Risuéño, **ña**, *a.* Smiling; pleasing, agreeable.
Ríta, *sf.* Word used by shepherds speaking to one of their flocks.
Rítmico, **ca**, *a.* Rythmical.
Rítmo, *sm.* Rhyme, rhythm. V. *Rima.*
Ríto, *sm.* Rite, use, custom, ceremony.
Rituál, *sm.* Ritual, a book in which the rites and observances of religion are set down; ceremonial.
Rivál, *sm.* Rival, competitor.
Rivalidád, *sf.* Rivality, competition.
Rivéra, *sf.* (Extrem.) River, stream.
Ríxa, *sf.* Scuffle, dispute, disturbance.
Rixadór, **ra**, *a.* Quarrelsome, litigious.
Ríxo, *sm.* Concupiscence, a propensity to sensual pleasures.
Rixóso, **sa**, *a.* Quarrelsome, lascivious.
Ríza, *sf.* 1. Green stubble of grain cut down for food. 2. Desolation, ravage, destruction.
Rizadór, *sm.* 1. Curling iron, with which the hair is frizzled. 2. Hair-dresser.
Rizál, *a.* V. *Ricial.*
Rizár, *va.* 1. To curl or frizzle hair. 2. To crimple crape with a crimpling-iron; to plait.
Rízo, **za**, *a.* Naturally curled or frizzled.
Rízo, *sm.* 1. Curling or frizzling of the hair, crimpling of cloth. 2. Cut velvet. *Rizos,* (Naút.) Points, short pieces of braided cordage, used to reef the courses and top-sails of a ship. *Coger rizos,* (Naút.) To take in reefs.

Ró, *interj.* Word used to lull children.
Róa, *sf.* (Naút.) Stem. V. *Roda.*
Roán, *sm.* A sort of linen manufactured in Rouen.
Roáno, na, *a.* Sorrel; applied to a horse which is nearly of the colour of a fox.
Rób, *sm.* Rob, the inspissated juice of ripe fruit, mixed with honey or sugar to the consistency of a conserve.
Roba, *sf.* (Arag.) V. *Arroba.*
Robáda, *sf.* Space of ground of 400 square yards in extent.
Robádo, da, *a.* Robbed; naked without ornament.
Robadór, ra, *s.* Robber.
Robadorcíllo, lla, *s. dim.* Little robber.
Robalíza, *sf.* Kind of fish, perch.
Róbalo, *sm.* A fish like bream.
Robamiénto, *sm.* Robbery.
Robár, *va.* 1. To rob, to plunder, to steal. 2. To carry off or run away with a woman. 3. To sweep away part of its banks; applied to a river. 4. To overcharge, to over-reach in the sale of goods. 5. To gain another's affections, to ingratiate one's self. 6. To diminish the colour, to weaken or lower the colouring. 7. With beemasters, to take all the bees from a divided hive and put them into an empty one, by removing the honey-comb, placing the hive over a pit, and agitating it till the bees retire into the empty hive.
Róbda, *sf.* Kind of ancient tribute.
Robézo, *sm.* A wild goat. V. *Bicerra.*
Robín ó Ruín, *sm.* Rust, the corroded surface of metal.
Róbla, *sf.* Cocket, permit, bill of sale.
Robladéro, ra, *a.* Clenched; recurvated.
Robladúra, *sf.* Recurvation, recurvity.
Roblár, *va.* 1. To authorise, to permit. 2. To clench, to bend the point of a nail on the opposite side.
Róble, *sm.* 1. (Bot.) Oak-tree. Quercus robur *L.* 2. Any thing very strong and hard.
Robledál y Robledo, *sm.* Plantation of oak-trees.
Roblízo, za, *a.* Oaken, strong, hard.
Roblón, *sm.* Rivet, a nail headed at both ends.
Róbo, *sm.* 1. Robbery, theft; the thing robbed or stolen. 2. (Navar.) Measure of grain about half a bushel.
Roboración, *sf.* Corroboration, strengthening.
Roboránte, *pa.* Corroborant; applied to strengthening medicines.
Roborár, *va.* To confirm, to corroborate, to give strength.
Roborativo, va, *a.* Corroborative.
Róbra, *sf.* 1. Cocket, docket, permit. 2. V. *Alboroque.*
Robradúra, *sf.* Clenching, riveting.
Robramiénto, *sm.* Permission. V. *Robra.*
Robrár, *va.* To authorise, to permit. V. *Roblar.*
Róbre, *sm.* V. *Roble.*
Robrédo, *sm.* V. *Robledal.*
Robustaménte, *ad.* Robustly.
Robustéz ó Robusticidád, *sf.* Robustness, strength.
Robústo, ta, *a.* Strong, robust, vigorous.
Róca, *sf.* 1. Rock, cliff. *Rocas,* Precipices. 2. Any thing very firm and hard.
Rocadéro, *sm.* 1. Knob or head of a distaff. 2. Piece of paper formed like a cone, and put round the flax or wool on a distaff. 3. Rock of a distaff or spinning-wheel.
Rocadór, *sm.* Head of a rock or distaff.
Rocálla, *sf.* 1. Heap of pebbles washed together by floods or torrents. 2. Pieces of rock crystal, of which beads and rosaries are made.
Róce, *sm.* Familiarity, frequent conversation.
Rociáda, *sf.* 1. The act of sprinkling or irrigating gently. 2. (Naút.) Spray, the foam of the waves. 3. Drops of dew found in the mornings and evenings on the grass and plants; herbs with dew on them, given to animals as medicine. 4. Shower of stones or balls; scattering, strewment. 5. Slander, malicious censure.
Rociadór, *sm.* Instrument with which cloth is sprinkled.
Rociamiénto, *sm.* Sprinkling or bedewing.
Rociár, *vn.* To be bedewed or sprinkled with drops of dew; to fall in dew.—*va.* 1. To sprinkle with wine, water, or other fluids. 2. To strew or scatter about. 3. To slander or calumniate several persons at the same time.
Rocín, *sm.* 1. Hack, working horse; a horse of little value. *Rocin y manzanas,* Resolution of performing any thing even at peril and loss. 2. A heavy ignorant clown. *Ir de rocin á ruin,* To go from bad to worse.
Rocinál, *a.* Belonging to a hack horse.
Rocinánte, *sm.* 1. Very ignorant clown. 2. A miserable hack.
Rocío, *sm.* 1. Dew, the moisture collected on the grass and plants in the morning and evening. 2. Slight shower of rain; sprinkling. 3. Divine inspiration; holy thoughts. *Rocio de la mar,* (Naút.) Spoon-drift, the foam of the sea in a storm.
Rocló, *sm.* An upper coat fitted tight to the body.
Róda, *sf.* 1. (Naút.) Stem. 2. Duty or impost on sheep-flocks.
Rodabállo, *sm.* (Ict.) Turbot. Pleuronectes maximus *L.*
Rodáda, *sf.* Rut, the track of a wheel.
Rodadéro, ra, *a.* Rolling or wheeling easily.
Rodadízo, za, *a.* Easily rolled round.
Rodádo, da, *a.* 1. Dapple or dappled; applied to horses. 2. V. *Privilegio.* 3. Round, fluent; applied to sentences. *Venir rodado,* To attain any object accidentally.
Rodádo, *sm.* (Min.) V. *Suelto.*
Rodadór, *sm.* 1. Roller, any thing that rolls or falls rolling down. 2. Vagabond, vagrant.
Rodadúra, *sf.* 1. Rolling, the act of rolling. 2. Rut, the track of a wheel.
Rodája, *sf.* 1. A small wheel. 2. Rowel of a spur. 3. Jagging iron used by pastry-cooks; bookbinder's tool.
Rodáje, *sm.* Wheelworks, collection of wheels as in a watch.
Rodál, *sm.* Place, spot, seat.
Rodánte, *pa.* Roller, rolling.
Rodapélo, *sm.* The act of rubbing against the grain. V. *Redopelo.*
Rodapié, *sm.* 1. Fringe or ornament of silk or other stuff which hangs round the feet of a bedstead, table, or balcony to hide the feet. 2. The stained or painted lower part of white-

washed walls, about a foot from the ground; coarse cloth put round the feet of tables, &c.

RODAPLÁNCHA, *sf.* The main ward of a key.

RODÁR, *vn.* 1. To roll, to move along on the surface of the ground; to roll down a hill. 2. To run on wheels. V. *Rodear.* 3. To abound, to be in great plenty. 4. To wander about in vain in quest of business; to be tossed about. 5. To lose an employ, station, dignity, or esteem. 6. To happen accidentally.—*va.* To drive, to impel, to give an impulse.

RODEABRÁZO, (A'), *ad.* Drawing the arm to throw any thing with it.

RODEÁDO, DA, *pp.* Surrounded. *Rodeado de negocios,* Overwhelmed with business.

RODEADÓR, RA, *s.* Roller, wrapper.

RODEÁR, *vn.* 1. To go round a place or other object; to encompass. 2. To go a round-about way. 3. To make use of circumlocutions; to use circuitous language or indirect expressions.—*va.* 1. To wrap up, to put one thing around another. 2. To turn or whirl about. 3. To dispose, to arrange.

RODÉLA, *sf.* 1. Shield, a kind of round buckler or target. 2. A kind of drop-earrings.

RODELÉRO, *sm.* 1. Soldier armed with a shield or target. 2. A wild extravagant young man; a rake.

RODÉNO, *sm.* A kind of porous stone.

RODÉO, *sm.* 1. Circumition, the act of going round; a circuitous way or road; turn to elude another. 2. Place in a fair or market where horned cattle are exposed to sale. 3. Delay, protraction, tedious method. 4. Evasion, subterfuge.

RODEÓN, *sm.* A complete rolling or winding round.

RODÉRO, RA, *a.* Belonging or relating to wheels.

RODÉRO, *sm.* Collector of the duty on sheep.

RODÉTE, *sm.* 1. A large wheel, formed of many pieces. 2. Bolster, a kind of horizontal circle at the fore axle-tree of a carriage for turning it. 3. A kind of ward in a key. 4. A kind of pad or bolster put on the head of women, to carry vessels or buckets with greater ease, or for ornament. 5. Border round the sleeves of gowns.

RODÉZNO, *sm.* A large wheel, consisting of many pieces.

RODÍLLA, *sf.* 1. Knee, the joint where the leg is joined to the thigh: In quadrupeds, V. *Codillo.* 2. Rubber, clout. 3. Knot for carrying burthens. *De rodillas,* On one's knees. *Doblar las rodillas,* To bend the knees; to kneel down. *Rodíllas,* (Naút.) Knees of ship-timber.

RODILLÁDA, *sf.* Push with the knee; a kneeling position.

RODILLÁZO, *sm.* Push with the knee.

RODILLÉRAS, *sf. pl.* Ancient ornament on stockings around the knees.

RODILLÉRO, RA, *a.* Belonging to the knees.

RODÍLLO, *sm.* 1. Roller, a plain cylinder of wood for moving beams, stones, and other heavy things. 2. A heavy cylinder of stone to level walks or roads. 3. A brass roller, used to form plate glass. In the glass-house of *St. Ildefonso* it is called *Rulo.* *De rodillo ó á rodillo,* Striking another ball in play. 4. Rolling-pin used by pastry-cooks.

RODILLÚDO, DA, *a.* Having large knees.

RODOMÉL, *s.* The juice of roses mixed with honey.

RODRIGÁR, *va.* To stay or prop up vines.

RODRIGAZÓN, *sm.* Time for putting props to vines.

RODRIGÓN, *sm.* 1. Stay or prop for vines. 2. Page or servant who waits upon women.

ROEDÉRO, *sm.* Place frequently gnawed.

ROEDÓR, RA, *s.* Gnawer, one that gnaws; detractor. *Gusano roedor,* A gnawing worm; remorse.

ROEDÚRA, *sf.* Gnawing, the act of gnawing or corroding.

ROÉLA, *sf.* Round piece of crude silver or gold.

ROÉR, *vn.* 1. To gnaw, to corrode; to consume by degrees; to destroy gradually. 2. To calumniate, to detract, to backbite. 3. To molest, to harass. *Roer el anzuelo,* To free one's-self from peril. 4. To gnaw the cells after they are closed; applied to bees. 5. To gnaw bones. 6. (Met.) To corrode, to introduce or effect insensibly.

ROÉTE, *sm.* Rob, a liquor distilled from pomegranates.

ROFIANEÁR, *vn.* V. *Rufianear.*

ROGACIÓN, *sf.* Request, petition, supplication.

ROGADÓR, RA, *s.* Supplicant, petitioner.

ROGÁNTE, *pa.* Petitioner, asking.

ROGÁR, *va.* 1. To implore, to entreat; to ask 2. To pray, to say prayers.

ROGATÍVA Y ROGÁRIA, *sf.* Supplication, prayer.

ROGATÍVO, VA, *a.* Supplicatory.

ROÍDO, *a.* 1. Gnawed, corroded. 2. Penurious, despicable.—*sm.* V. *Ruido.*

RÓL, *sm.* List, roll, catalogue.

ROLDÁNA, *sf.* (Naút.) Sheave, a solid cylindrical wheel, moveable about an axis.

RÓLDE, *sm.* Circle formed by persons or things.

ROLÉO, *sm.* Volute. V. *Voluta.*

RÓLLA, *sf.* Collar of a draught horse.

ROLLÁR, *va.* V. *Arrollar.*

ROLLÍZO, ZA, *a.* Plump, round, robust.

RÓLLO, *sm.* Any thing round and long, or of a cylindrical form; roll of cloth. V. *Rolla.* 2. Gallows erected in a cylindrical form. 3. Acts or records rolled up, that they may be carried with greater ease. 4. Long round stone. *Enviár ó irse al rollo,* To pack one off.

ROLLÓN, *sm.* V. *Acemite.*

ROLLÓNA, *a.* (Joc.) Fat, plump, and robust; applied to a short lusty woman.

ROMADIZÁRSE, *vr.* V. *Aromadizarse.*

ROMADÍZO, *sm.* Catarrh, cold or defluxion in the head or nose.

ROMÁNA, *sf.* Steelyard, a kind of balance or lever. *La barra de la romana,* Beam of the steelyard. *El pilon de la romana,* Dropball or weight of the steelyard. *Hacer romana,* To balance, to equipoise.

ROMANADÓR, *sm.* Weighmaster in a slaughter-house.

ROMANEÁR, *va.* To weigh with a steelyard.

ROMÁNCE, *sm.* 1. The common or vernacular Spanish language, as derived from the Roman or Latin. 2. Romance, a species of poetry; a tale of wild adventures in war or love. *Hablar en romance,* To speak out, to speak plainly. *Románces*, Wiles, stratagems, deceitful tricks.

ROMANCEÁR, *va.* 1. To translate into Spanish. 2. (Gram.) To translate into another language; to express the same meaning in different words.

ROMANCÉRO, RA, *a.* 1. Singing or composing romances or ballads. 2. Using evasions and subterfuges.—*sm.* Collection of romances or ballads; legendary tales.

ROMANCÍSTA, *sm.* 1. Author who writes in the vulgar or native language, on subjects which are generally discussed in the Latin tongue. 2. One who understands no other language but his native tongue.

ROMANEÁR, *va.* To weigh with a steelyard.—*vn.* To outweigh, to preponderate.

ROMANÉRO, *sm.* V. *Romanador.*

ROMANIZÁR, *va.* To romanise, to follow or adopt the manners, customs, and fashions of Rome.

ROMÁNO, NA, *a.* 1. Roman, belonging or relating to Rome. 2. Tabby, variegated with grey and black; applied to a cat. 3. Large flesh-coloured peach. *Á la Romana*, In the Roman fashion.

ROMANZÁDO, DA, *a.* Turned or translated into Spanish.

ROMANZADÓR, *sm.* (Ant.) Translator into Spanish.

ROMANZÁR, *va.* To translate into Spanish. V. *Romancear.*

ROMANZÓN, *sm.* A long and tedious romance.

ROMÁZA, *sf.* (Bot.) Dock, sharp pointed dock. Rumex acutus *L.*

RÓMBO, *sm.* 1. Rhomb, a parallelogram; a quadrangular figure, having its four sides equal with unequal angles. 2. Pentagraph, an instrument for copying drawings in a larger or smaller size. 3. (Ict.) Rhomb.

ROMERÁGE, *sm.* V. *Romería.*

ROMERÁL, *sm.* Place abounding with rosemary.

ROMERÍA, *sf.* Pilgrimage, a journey on account of devotion.

ROMÉRO, *sm.* 1. (Bot.) Rosemary. Rosmarinus *L.* 2. (Ict.) Little fish which precedes the shark. 3. Pilgrim. [count.

ROMÉRO, RA, *a.* Travelling on a religious account.

ROMÍ ó ROMÍN, *sm.* Bastard saffron. V. *Azafran romin.*

RÓMO, MA, *a.* Flat-nosed; blunt, obtuse.—*s.* Hinny, mule begotten by a horse and she-ass.

ROMPECÓCHES, *sm.* Everlasting, a strong cloth.

ROMPEDÉRA, *sf.* Chisel for cutting hot iron.

ROMPEDÉRO, RA, *a.* Brittle, fit to be broken.

ROMPEDÓR, RA, *s.* Breaker, destroyer; one who wears out his clothes very soon.

ROMPEDÚRA, *sf.* V. *Rotura.*

ROMPÉR, *va.* 1. To break, to force asunder; to break into pieces. 2. To destroy or wear out clothes very soon. 3. To defeat, to rout. 4. To break up land, to plough it for the first time. 5. To pierce, to penetrate. 6. To break off; to fall out, to quarrel. 7. To dawn, to begin. 8. To interrupt a speech or conversation. 9. To deliberate, to resolve. 10. To break out, to spring up; to dissipate clouds. 11. To violate, to infringe; to transgress. 12. To exceed, to go beyond the bounds or limits. *De rompe y rasga*, Undaunted; plain, open, free. 13. To prune vine-stalks of their useless green branches. *Rompe esquinas*, Nickname for a street bully. *Rompe galas*, Ironical nickname for one who goes carefully dressed.—*vr.* To become free and easy in one's deportment and action.

ROMPÍDO, DA, *a.* Throwing forward the foot in a Spanish dance.

ROMPIMIÉNTO, *sm.* 1. Rupture, the act of breaking. 2. Aperture in any solid body; crack, cleft, fracture. 3. Funeral dues paid by such as have their own tomb. 4. An apparent depth of a piece of painting which seems to break its superficies. 5. First ploughing of land. 6. (Met.) Rupture, dispute among persons.

RON, *sm.* Rum, spirit made of sugar.

RÓNCA, *sf.* 1. Threat, menace; boast, brag. 2. Cry of a buck in rutting time. *Echar roncas*, To threaten, to menace; to be hoarse. 3. Kind of halberd.

RONCADÓR, RA, *s.* Snorer, one who snores.—*sm.* 1. Snoring fish. 2. V. *Sobrestante.*

RONCAMÉNTE, *ad.* Hoarsely, with a rough harsh voice; in a coarse vulgar manner.

RONCÁR, *vn.* 1. To snore, to breathe hard and audibly through the nose; to make a harsh noise; to roar. 2. To threaten, to boast, to brag. 3. To cry like a buck in rutting time.

RÓNCE, *sm.* Blandiloquence. V. *Roncería.*

RONCEÁR, *vn.* 1. To defer, to protract, to use evasions. 2. To wheedle, to entice by soft words. 3. (Naút.) To sail badly or slowly.

RONCERÍA, *sf.* 1. Sloth, laziness, tardiness. 2. Flattery, soft soothing expressions. 3. (Naút.) Bad sailing.

RONCÉRO, RA, *a.* 1. Slothful, tardy. 2. Snarling, growling. 3. Flattering, wheedling, melliloquent. 4. Slow, tardy; applied to the sailing of a ship.

RÓNCHA, *sf.* 1. Wheal, pustule; a small swelling filled with matter. 2. Loss of money, arising from a fraud or imposition. 3. Slice of any thing cut round.

RONCHÁR, *va.* To chew any thing crisp or hard. V. *Ronzar.*—*vn.* To make wheals.

RONCHÓN, *sm.* A large swelling.

RÓNCO, CA, *a.* Hoarse, having a rough coarse voice.—*sm.* (Joc.) Snore. V. *Ronquido.*

RONCÓN, *sm.* Drone of a bag-pipe.

RÓNDA, *sf.* 1. Rounds, the act of going about at night. 2. Night-patrole; rounds performed by the night-watch or guards. *Coger la ronda*, To catch one in the act of committing a crime or offence. 3. Space between the houses and the inside of the wall of a fortress. 4. Three first cards in a hand to play.

RONDADÓR, *sm.* Watchman, night-guard.

RONDÁLLA, *sf.* Fable, story.

RONDÁR, *vn.* 1. To go rounds by night in order to prevent disorders. 2. To take walks by night about the streets.—*va.* 1. To go round, to follow any thing continually. 2. To move round a thing. 3. To threaten to relapse, to impend.

RONDÉL, *sm.* Roundelay, kind of poetry.

RONDÍN, *sm.* 1. Rounds of a corporal on the walls to visit the sentinels. 2. Watchmen in naval arsenals.

Rondís ó Rondíz, *sm.* Base or face of a precious stone.
Rondó, *sm.* (Mús.) Music repeated several times.
Rondón, A word merely used adverbially. *De rondon*, Rashly, abruptly; intrepidly.
Ronfía, *sf.* A long broad sword.
Ronfiáta, *sf.* V. *Rehilete.*
Ronquear, *vn.* To be hoarse with cold.
Ronquedád, *sf.* Hoarseness, roughness of voice.
Ronquéra y Ronquéz, *sf.* Hoarseness, a disorder occasioned by catching cold.
Ronquído, *sm.* 1. Snore, an audible respiration of sleepers through the nose. 2. Any rough harsh sound.
Ronquíllo, lla; to, ta, *a. dim.* of *Ronco*, Slightly hoarse.
Rónza, *sf.* (Naút.) The state of a vessel which is adrift, and carried along by the wind, tide, or current.
Ronzál, *sm.* Halter, a rope with which a beast is tied to a manger or post. V. *Palanca.*
Ronzár, *va.* 1. (Naút.) To rouse, to haul without the aid of a tackle. 2. To chew hard things.
Roña, *sf.* 1. Scab, a cutaneous disorder in sheep. 2. (Fam.) Craft, fraud, cunning. 3. (Met.) Nastiness, dirt, filth. 4. (Met.) Moral infection or hurt. 5. (Naút.) Garland. *Roñada de rancho*, (Naút.) Mess-garland; a bag or hanging locker for sailors' provisions. *Roñada de la guirnalda de un palo*, (Naút.) Dolphin of a mast.
Roñería, *sf.* 1. Craft, cunning, deceitfulness. 2. Niggardliness, sordid parsimony.
Roñóso, sa, *a.* 1. Scabby, diseased with a scab; leprous. 2. Dirty, nasty, filthy. 3. Wily, sly, crafty. 4. Mean, niggardly, sordidly parsimonious.
Rópa, *sf.* 1. Cloth; all kinds of stuff, whether silk, woollen, or linen, used in domestic purposes. 2. Wearing apparel; all sorts of clothes. 3. Robe, loose garment worn over the rest of the clothes; gown. *Ropa blanca*, Linen. *Ropa de camara*, Mourning gown. *Poca ropa*, Ill clothed; poor. 4. (Met.) Judge, advocate, minister robbed; dress of particular authority for the bar, senate, &c. 5. Any thing put between or under others for a seat. *Ropa vieja*, Boiled meat, afterwards fried in a pan. *Ropa buena*, Person or thing of good quality.
Ropáge, *sm.* 1. Wearing apparel, all sorts of clothes. 2. Drapery, representation of the clothing of human figures in pictures and statues.
Ropálico, ca, *a.* Applied to verses with the first word a monosyllable, and all the others increasing progressively.
Ropavejería, *sf.* Frippery, a place where old clothes are sold.
Ropavejéro, *sm.* Fripperer, one who deals in old clothes.
Ropería, *sf.* 1. Trade or profession of dealers in old clothes. 2. Salesman's shop, where clothes are sold ready made. 3. Wardrobe of a community. 4. Office or keeper of a wardrobe. *Ropería de viejo.* V. *Ropavejería.*
Ropéro, *sm.* 1. Salesman who deals in clothes. 2. Keeper of the wardrobe or vestiary in a religious community. 3. Head shepherd, who superintends the making of cheese, and has the care of them. 4. Boy who guards the clothes of herdsmen.
Ropéta y Ropíta, *sf.* A short garment.
Ropetílla, *sf.* 1. A wretched short garment. 2. Jacket with loose hanging sleeves.
Ropílla, *sf.* Kind of short jacket with double sleeves, the outer ones hanging loose.
Ropón, *sm.* A wide loose gown worn over the rest of the clothes.
Róque, *sm.* Rook, a man at chess. *Ni rey ni roque*, No living soul.
Roquéda, *sf.* Rocky place.
Roquédo, *sm.* Rock, stony precipice.
Roquéño, ña, *a.* Rocky, full of rocks.
Roquéro, ra, *a* Rocky, abounding with rocks; situated on rocks.
Roquéta, *sf.* 1. Ancient kind of tower in a fortress. 2. (Bot.) Yellow flower.
Roquéte, *sm.* 1. A kind of garment worn by bishops and abbots. 2. Rocket. V. *Atacador.*
Rórro, *sm.* A sucking child.
Rósa, *sf.* 1. (Bot.) Rose, a sweet-scented flower. Rosa *L.* 2. Red spot appearing in any part of the body. 3. Rose diamond. 4. Kind of comet. 5. Rosy or florid aspect; rose colour. 6. Flower of saffron; artificial rose. *Rosas*, Flowers, delights, pleasures; amenity. *Rosa náutica*, (Naút.) Card of a mariner's compass. *Rosa seca*, Pale red or flesh colour, dried rose colour.
Rosáda, *sf.* V. *Escarcha.*
Rosádo, da, *a.* 1. Rosy, belonging or relating to roses. 2. Made up with roses. *Agua rosada*, Rose-water.
Rosál, *sm.* (Bot.) Rose-bush. Rosa rubiginosa et gallica *L. Rosal silvestre*, Dog-rose. Rosa canina *L.*
Rosariéro, *sm.* Maker and seller of rosaries.
Rosário, *sm.* 1. Rosary, a string of beads for praying, consisting of 150, divided into tens and fifties, with a crucifix. 2. Collection of *Ave Marias* and *Pater nosters* said at once; number of persons reciting it in public. *Parte de rosario*, The third part of the rosary, or five tens. 3. A kind of pigeon with variegated colours. 4. Chain-pump. 5. Backbone.
Rosárse, *vr.* V. *Sonrosearse.*
Rósca, *sf.* 1. Screw, one of the principal mechanical powers. 2. Any thing round and spiral; spiral motion. 3. A distinctive badge of the scholars in some colleges in Spain. *Rosca de cable*, (Naút.) Flake of a cable. *Rosca de mar*, (Naút.) Sea-rusks, a kind of biscuit.
Roscón, *sm.* A large screw.
Roséga, *sf.* (Naút.) Creeper, a grapnel with a shank and four hooks or claws, to recover anchors and other things fallen into the water.
Róseo, sea, *a.* Rosy, of a rose colour.
Roséro, ra, *s.* Collector of saffron flowers.
Roséta, *sf.* 1. A small rose. 2. Tassel, worn instead of shoe-buckles. 3. The blooming colour of the cheeks.
Rosetón, *sm.* A large rose on pieces of architecture and sculpture.
Rosiclér, *sm.* 1. A bright rose colour. 2. Rich silver ore.

Rosíllo, lla, *a.* Clear red.

Rosmáro, *sm.* Morse, waltron, sea-horse. Trichechus rosmarus *L.*

Róso, sa, *a.* Red, rosy. V. *Rozo.* *A' roso y velloso*, Without distinction; totally.

Rosoléa, *sf.* A sort of stuff made of wool and silk.

Rosóli, *sm.* Rosolio, sundew; a pleasant sweet spirituous liquor, composed of brandy, sugar, cinnamon, anise, &c.

Rosónes, *sm.* Worms, troubled with worms in the body.

Rosquéte, *sm.* Middle-sized screw.

Rosquílla, *sf.* 1. A small screw. 2. Paste made in a spiral shape. 3. Vine-fretter. *No saber á rosquillas*, (Fam.) To have occasioned great pain or uneasiness.

Rostrádo, da, *a.* Formed in the shape of a beak.

Rostríllo y Rostríco, *sm.* 1. Veil or head-dress put on the heads of images. 2. Small seed pearl.

Rostrituérto, ta, *a.* Showing anger or displeasure in the countenance.

Róstro, *sm.* 1. Bill or beak of a bird. 2. Human face. 3. Aspect of affairs. *A' rostro firme*, Resolutely, in front of. *Hacer rostro*, To bear up under adversities. *Rostro á rostro*, Face to face.

Róta, *sf.* 1. Rout, defeat. 2. (Naút.) Course. 3. Court of judicature in Rome. V. *Nunciatura.* 4. Ratan, a kind of Indian cane. Calamus rotang *L.* *De rota ó de rota batida*, On a sudden, in a careless manner; with total ruin.

Rotación, *sf.* 1. Rotation, circular motion; the act of turning round like a wheel. 2. Revolution of planets.

Rotaménte, *ad.* Impudently, in a bare-faced manner.

Rotánte, *pa.* Rolling, vagrant.

Rotár, *vn.* V. *Rodar.*

Roteño, ña, *a.* Belonging to the town of Rota.

Róto, ta, *a.* y *pp. ir.* of *Romper.* 1. Broken, destroyed. 2. Debauched, lewd, intemperate; ragged.

Rótula, *sf.* Whirlbone of the knee-pan. V. *Trocisco.*

Rotulár, *va.* To inscribe, to put inscriptions or titles on books and papers.

Rótulo, *sm.* 1. Inscription put on books and papers. 2. Printed bill posted up in public places. 3. Certificate of the virtues of one for beatification. 4. List of bachelors who are to become masters or doctors in the university of Alcala.

Rotúnda, *sf.* Rotunda, a round building.

Rotundidád, *sf.* Roundness. V. *Redondez.*

Rotúndo, da, *a.* Round, circular. V. *Redondo.*

Rotúra, *sf.* 1. Rupture, fracture. V. *Rompimiento.* 2. Dissoluteness, libertinism. V. *Contrarotura.*

Roxeánte, *pa.* Rubific, rubifying.

Roxeár, *vn.* To redden, to blush; to rubify.

Roxéte, *sm.* Rouge, red paint for the face.

Roxéz y Roxéza, *sf.* Redness, red colour.

Roxízo, za, *a.* Reddish, inclining to red.

Róxo, xa, *a.* Red, reddish, ruddy; ruby.

Roxúra, *sf.* Redness.

Roy ó Ruy, *sm* Proper name, Rodrigo.

Róya, *sf.* Mildew.

Royál, *sm.* Kind of French linen.

Róyo, ya, *a.* Red. V. *Rezo.*

Róza, *sf.* 1. Stubbing, the act of clearing the ground of brambles and bushes. 2. Ground cleared of brambles and bushes.

Rozadéro, *sm.* Stubbing-place; ground cleared of trees.

Rozádo, da, *a.* 1. Stubbed, cleared of brambles and bushes. 2. (Naút.) Fretted, galled.

Rozadór, ra, *s.* Stubber, weeder.

Rozadúra, *sf.* Interfering; clashing, act of cutting.

Rozagánte, *a.* 1. Pompous, showy, trailing on the ground; applied to robes and gowns. 2. Haughty, lofty, arrogant.

Rozár, *va.* 1. To stub up, to clear the ground of brambles and bushes. 2. To nibble the grass; applied to cattle. 3. To scrape or pare off. 4. To graze, to touch slightly.—*vn.* To touch slightly against each other.—*vr.* 1. To strike or cut each other; applied to the feet. 2. To treat or discourse familiarly; to be similar. 3. To falter, to stammer. 4. (Naút.) To fret, to gall; applied to cables or other things which rub against one another.

Rozavillón, *sm.* (Cant.) Toad-eater, sponger.

Roznár, *vn.* 1. To crack hard things and grind them with the teeth. 2. To bray, as an ass.

Roznído, *sm.* 1. Noise made by the teeth on eating things hard. 2. Braying of an ass.

Rózno, *sm.* A little ass.

Rózo, *sm.* 1. Chip of wood. 2. Stubbing, weeding; rubbing.

Rú ó Rús, *sm.* Sumac. V. *Zumaque.*

Rúa, *sf.* 1. Street, formed by rows of houses built on both sides. 2. High road.

Ruán, *sm.* Sort of linen manufactured in Rouen.

Ruánes, *sm. pl.* Linens or cloth made at Rouen.

Ruanéte, *sm.* Kind of foreign linen.

Ruáno, na, *a.* 1. Prancing about the streets; applied to horses. 2. Sorrel coloured; spoken of horses. 3. Round, of a circular form.

Ruánte, *a.* 1. Prancing or strutting through the streets. 2. Spreading the tail; applied to peacocks.

Ruár, *vn.* 1. To roll through the streets; applied to carriages. 2. To strut about the streets, to court the ladies.

Rúbeo, ea, *a.* Ruby, reddish.

Rubéta, *sf.* Toad. Rana bufo *L.*

Rubí, *sm.* 1. Ruby, a precious stone of a red colour. 2. Red colour; redness of the lips.

Rúbia, *sf.* 1. (Bot.) Madder; a root used by dyers and in medicine. Rubia tinctorium *L.* 2. (Ict.) Small red coloured river fish.

Rubiál, *sm.* 1. Field planted with madder. 2. District or soil having a red colour.

Rubicán, *a.* Of a bay or sorrel colour with white hairs; applied to a horse.

Rubicúndo, da, *a.* Reddish, rubicund.

Rubificár, *va.* To rubify, to make red.

Rubín, *sm.* Ruby. V. *Rubí.*

Rúbio, bia, *a.* Red, reddish, fair.

Rúbio, *sm.* (Ict.) Red gurnard. Trigla cuculus *L.*

Rubión, *a.* Of a bright reddish colour; applied to a kind of wheat.

Rúbo, *sm.* (Bot.) Common bramble, blackberry-bush. Rubus fruticosus *L.*

Rubór, *sm.* 1. Blush, the red colour of the cheeks. 2. Shame, bashfulness.
Ruboróso, sa, *a.* Shameful. V. *Vergonzoso.*
Rúbrica, *sf.* 1. Red mark. 2. Flourish or dash with the pen annexed to the signature. 3. Rubric, inscription or title of law and prayer books, formerly printed with red-ink. 4. Red ochre, with which carpenters mark the timber. 5. (Met.) Blood used to attest any truth. *Rúbrica sinópica.* V. *Minio.*
Rubricánte, *pa.* Rubifying, rubific.—*sm.* Junior counsellor appointed to mark the divisions of the acts or proceedings of the council.
Rubricár, *vr.* 1. To mark with a red colour. 2. To annex a flourish with red ink to a writing. 3. To subscribe, sign, and seal a writing. 4. (Met.) To sign any thing with one's blood.
Rubriquísta, *sm.* A person versed in the ceremonies of the church.
Rubro, bra, *a.* Red, reddish; rubric.
Rúc, *sf.* Very large fabulous bird.
Rucio, cia, *a.* 1. Bright silver gray; applied to a horse. 2. Light gray; applied to the hair; gray-haired.—*sm.* V. *Recio.*
Rúda, *sf.* (Bot.) Rue. Ruta *L.*
Rudaménte, *ad.* Rudely, roughly.
Rudéra, *sf.* Rubbish, ruins of demolished buildings.
Rudéza, *sf.* 1. Roughness, asperity or unevenness of surface. 2. Stupidity, dulness.
Rudiméntos, *sm. pl.* Rudiments, the first principles of a science or art.
Rúdo, da, *a.* 1. Rude, rough, unpolished, coarse. 2. Hard, rigorous, severe. 3. Stupid, dull of understanding.
Ruéca, *sf.* 1. Distaff, the staff from which the flax is drawn in spinning. 2. Winding, twisting. 3. (Naút.) Fish of a mast or yard. *Armar una rueca*, (Naút.) To fish a mast or yard; to strengthen it with pieces of timber.
Ruéda, *sf.* 1. Wheel, a circular body turning round upon an axis; roll. 2. (Ict.) Short sunfish, molebut. Tetrodon mola *L.* *Rueda de un salmon ú otro pescado*, A round slice of salmon or other fish. 3. Circle or ring formed by a number of persons; crown. 4. Wool put into the fold of men's coats to make them stiff. 5. Turn, time, succession. *Rueda del timon*, (Naút.) Steering wheel. *Rueda del pavo real*, Peacock's tail.
Ruedecíca, cílla, y zuéla, *sf.* A small wheel.
Ruédo, *sm.* 1. Rotation, the act of turning or going round; circuit. 2. Border, selvage. *A' todo ruedo*, At all events. *Ruédos*, Plats made of bass, and formed into round or square mats.
Ruégo, *sm.* Request, prayer, petition. *A' ruego ó á su ruego*, At the petition or request of any one.
Ruéso de molíno, *sm.* (Arag.) Mill-wheel.
Ruéllo, *sm.* A roller, which is rolled over the ground where corn is to be thrashed.
Ruequecílla, *sf.* A small distaff.
Rufalandário, ria, *a.* Slovenly, negligent of dress; not cleanly.
Rufalandáyna, *sf.* Noisy mirth.
Rufián, *sm.* Ruffian, pimp, pander; the bully of a brothel.
Rufiána, *sf.* Bawd, procuress.
Rufianár, *va.* To pimp, to pander.
Rufianejéte, cíllo, y ízo, *sm. dim.* Little ruffian or pimp.
Rufianería, *sf.* Pimping. V. *Alcahuetería.*
Rufianésco, ca, *a.* Pimplike, belonging or relating to bawds and pimps.
Rúfo, fa, *a.* 1. Carroty, red-haired. 2. Frizzed, curled. 3. (Cant.) Pimp, procurer.
Rúga, *sf.* 1. Wrinkle, corrugation. V. *Arruga.* 2. A slight fault.
Rugár, *va.* To wrinkle, to corrugate. V. *Arrugar.*
Rugíble, *a.* Capable of bellowing or roaring.
Rugído y Rugimiénto, *sm.* 1. Bellowing or roaring of a lion. 2. Sound made by the bowels from flatulency.
Rugiénte, *a.* Bellowing, roaring.
Ruginóso, sa, *a.* Covered with rust, rusty.
Rugír, *vn.* 1. To roar, to bellow. 2. To make a noise, to crack.—*vr.* To be whispered about.
Rugosidád, *sf.* The state of being wrinkled or corrugated.
Rugóso, sa, *a.* Rugose, full of wrinkles.
Ruibárbo, *sm.* (Bot.) Rhubarb. Rheum palmatum *L.*
Ruído, *sm.* 1. Noise, clamour, din; loud sound; murmur. 2. Dispute, difference, lawsuit. 3. Rumour, report; empty sound or show.
Ruidosaménte, *ad.* Noisily.
Ruidóso, sa, *a.* Noisy, clamorous.
Ruín, *a.* 1. Mean, vile, low, despicable; little. 2. Humble; decayed; wicked, malicious. 3. Covetous, avaricious; insidious, treacherous.—*sf.* 1. Small nerve in the tail of cats. *Ruines*, (Joc.) Beard. 2. Vicious animal. *Un ruin ido, otro venido*, When one evil is gone another comes.
Ruína, *sf.* 1. Ruin, decline, downfall, destruction. *Ruinas*, Ruins of an edifice. *Ir en ruina*, To be destroyed, to go to destruction or ruin. 2. Cause of ruin, decadence. *Batir en ruina*, (Mil.) To batter in breach.
Ruinár, *va.* To ruin, to destroy. V. *Arruinar.*
Ruindád, *sf.* 1. Meanness, baseness. 2. Humility, poverty. 3. Covetousness, avariciousness.
Ruinménte, *ad.* Basely, meanly.
Ruinóso, sa, *a.* Worthless, little, ruinous.
Ruipónce, *sm.* (Bot.) Rampion. Phyteuma spicatum *L.*
Ruipóntico, *sm.* (Bot.) Rhapontic, knapweed. Centaurea rhaponticum *L.*
Ruiseñór, *sm.* (Orn.) Nightingale. Motacilla luscinia *L.*
Ruíz, *sm.* Proper name, Son of *Ruy* or *Rodrigo.*
Rulár, *va.* (Vulg.) To roll. V. *Rodar.*
Rúlo, *sm.* Ball, bowl; any globular thing which easily rolls.
Rumbádas, *sf. pl.* V. *Arrumbadas.*
Rúmbo, *sm.* 1. Point of the compass; an intersection of the plane of the horizon, represented by the card of the compass. 2. Road, way; course, the point on which a ship steers. *Rumbo compuesto*, (Naút.) Traverse, a compound course. *Hurtar el rumbo*, (Naút.) To alter the course. 3. Pomp, ostentation, pageantry. *Rúmbos*, Tufts or tassels of coarse silk, fastened to the headstalls of mules.
Rumbosaménte, *ad.* Pompously, magnificently.
Rumbóso, sa, *a.* Pompous, magnificent, splendid.
Rúmia, *sf.* Rumination, the act of chewing the cud.

Rumiadór, ra, *s.* Ruminator; meditator.
Rumiadúra, *sf.* Rumination.
Rumiánte, *pa.* Ruminant; musing.
Rumiár, *va.* 1. To ruminate, to chew the cud. 2. To muse, to meditate over and over again.
Rumión, na, *a.* Ruminating much.
Rúmo, *sm.* The first hoop of the head of a cask.
Rumór, *sm.* 1. Rumour, report. 2. A gentle noise or sound.
Rumorcíllo, co, to, *sm.* A flying report.
Rúnfla, *sf.* Series, multitude, number of things.
Runrún, *sm.* (Fam.) Rumour, report. V. *Rumor.*
Ruñár, *va.* To groove the ends of staves for the heads and bottoms of barrels, to fit.
Rupicápra, *sf.* Chamois-goat.
Ruptório, *sm.* (Med.) Escharotic, caustic.
Ruptúra, *sf.* Rupture. V. *Rotura.*
Ruquéta, *sf.* (Bot.) Rocket. Brassica eruca *L.*
Rurál, *a.* Rural.
Ruralménte, *ad.* Rurally.
Rús, *sm.* V. *Zumaque.*
Rúsco, ca, *a.* Rude, peevish, froward. V. *Brusco.*
Ruseñól, *sm.* (Orn.) Nightingale. V. *Ruiseñor.*
Rusiénte, *a.* Ruby, reddish, rubicund.
Rusticál, *a.* Rustical, rural, wild.
Rusticaménte, *ad.* Rustically, rudely, boisterously.
Rusticidád, *sf.* Rusticity, simplicity; asperity, rudeness.
Rústico, ca, *a.* Rustic, unmannerly, clownish, unpolished.
Rústico, *sm.* Rustic, peasant, country clown.
Rustiquéz ó Rustiquéza, *sf.* Rusticity.
Rustrír, *va.* (Ast.) To toast and eat bread when it is toasted.
Rústro, *sm.* V. *Rumbo.*
Rúta, *sf.* Route, itinerary.
Rutilánte, *a.* Brilliant, flashing, rutilant.
Rutilár, *vn.* (Poét.) To radiate, to shine, to be splendid, to rutilate.
Rútilo, la, *a.* Of a bright yellow or orange colour.
Rutína, *sf.* Custom, habit acquired by practice more than theory; routine.
Ruxáda, *sf.* Heavy shower of rain.
Ruxár, *va.* (Arag.) To irrigate, to bathe.
Rúy, *sm.* (Ant.) Proper name. V. *Rodrigo.*
Ruypóncе, *sm.* (Bot.) Rampion. V. *Ruipónce.*

S IS the 22d letter in the order of the Spanish alphabet; it does not become a liquid letter at the beginning of Spanish words, but is nearly pronounced as in English, in consequence of which, in all words derived from other languages, the *s* is either omitted or preceded by an *e*, as in *ciencia*, science; or *escolastico*, scholastic.

S is a contraction for *Señor*, saint, semi, sanctity or holiness; *su*, his or her; and *sur*, south. S. O. South West. S. E. South East. *SS* stands for § section. *S. S. S. su seguro servidor*, His faithful servant.
Sá, *sf.* (Fam.) Contraction of *Señora.*
Sába, *sf.* Sap, the vital juice of plants.
Sábado, *sm.* Saturday, the last day of the week.
Sabaléra, *sf.* Kind of grate in furnaces, for holding the fire.
Sabaléro, *sm.* Shad-fisher.
Sábalo, *sm.* (Ict.) Shad. Clupea alosa *L.*
Sábana, *sf.* 1. Sheet, a piece of cloth sufficiently long and wide to cover a bed. 2. A large plain covered with snow. 3. Altar-cloth.
Sabandíja, *sf.* 1. A grub, beetle, or insect. 2. Little, deformed or despicable person.
Sabanílla, *sf.* 1. A small sheet; short piece of linen. 2. Altar-cloth; napkin. 3. (Navar.) Handkerchief or piece of white muslin, which married women wear round their head-dress. In Aragon it is called *pañuelo blanco.*
Sabañón, *sm.* Chilblain, a sore or swelling occasioned by cold. *Comer como un sabañon*, To eat greedily, to devour.
Sabatário, *a.* Applied to the Jews who keep Saturday for their sabbath.
Sabático, ca, *a.* Belonging to Saturday or the sabbath of the Jews.
Sabatína, *sf.* Divine service performed on Saturday; literary exercise performed by students on Saturday evening.
Sabatíno, na, *a.* Performed on Saturday.
Sabatísmo, *sm.* Rest or repose after labour.
Sabedór, ra, *sm.* y *f.* V. *Sabidor.*
Sabeísmo, *sm.* Ancient fire-worship.
Sabeliáno, na, *a.* y *s.* Sabellian, belonging to Sabellius.
Sabér, *sm.* 1. Learning, knowledge. V. *Sabiduria.* 2. (Ant.) Science, faculty.—*va.* 1. To know, to have a knowledge of. 2. To experience, to know by experience. 3. To be able, to be possessed of talents or abilities; to be learned or knowing. *Saber mucho latin*, To be very sagacious and prudent. 4. To subject, to submit. 5. To fit, to suit. 6. To relish, to savour, to taste. 7. To use, to practise customarily; to be in the habit. *No saber lo que se pesca*, Not to know what one is about. 8. To resemble, to appear like. 9. V. *Podér.*—*v. impers.* To have a taste of. *Saber á la pez*, To taste of pitch. *Es á saber, ó conviene á saber*, Viz. to wit, that is. *Hacer saber*, To make known, to communicate. *Sabérselo todo*, (Irón.) To know every thing; applied to assuming intolerant persons. *No se sabe*, It is not known.
Sabiaménte, *ad.* Wisely, knowingly.
Sabído, da, *a.* Learned, well informed.
Sabidór, ra, *s.* 1. A learned well-informed person. 2. Literato, sage; a wise man.
Sabiduría, *sf.* Learning, knowledge, wisdom. V. *Noticia.*
Sabiéndas (A'), *ad.* Knowingly and prudently.
Sabiénte, *pa.* Sapient, knowing.

Sabiéza, *sf.* (Ant.) Knowledge, wisdom.
Sabína, *sf.* (Bot.) Savin. Juniperus sabina *L.*
Sabíno, na, *a.* Applied to horses or mules of a mixed white and chesnut colour.
Sábio, bia, *a.* Sage, wise, learned.
Sábio, bia, *sm. y f.* A sage, a wise person.
Sabiónda, *sf.* Female pedant, woman who affects learning and wisdom.
Sabiondéz, *sf.* Malicious sagacity, a profound knowledge of wicked tricks.
Sabióndo, da, *a.* Presuming to decide difficult questions without being possessed of sufficient knowledge for that purpose.
Sabláso, *sm.* Stroke or cut with a sabre.
Sáble, *sm.* 1. Sabre, cutlass. 2. (Blas.) Sable, black. 3. (Ast.) Sand.
Sablón, *sm.* Coarse sand.
Sabóga y Sabóca, *sf.* (Ict.) Shad. Clupea alosa *L.* [shads.
Sabogál, *a.* Applied to the net for catching
Sabór, *sm.* Relish, taste; desire. *A' sabor*, At pleasure; to the taste; according to one's wish. *Sabores*, Pieces attached to the bits of a bridle to guard the horse's mouth.
Saborcíco, llo, to, y Saboréte, *sm. dim.* of *sabor.* [a relish or taste.
Saboreadór, ra, *s.* Seasoner, that which gives
Saboreár, *va.* 1. To give a taste or relish; to give a zest. 2. To engage one's affections; to make one embrace our opinion.—*vr.* 1. To enjoy eating and drinking with peculiar pleasure and delight. 2. To be pleased or delighted.
Saboyána, *sf.* 1. A kind of wide petticoat. 2. A sort of delicious paste of a particular composition. [ard; belonging to Savoy.
Saboyáno, na, Saboyárdo, da, *a. y s.* Savoy-
Sábre, *sm.* (Ant.) V. *Arena.*
Sabrosaménte, *ad.* Pleasantly, tastefully.
Sabrosíco, ca; llo, lla; to, ta, *a. dim.* A little savoury. [salted.
Sabróso, sa, *a.* Savoury, pleasing to the taste;
Sabuésa, *sf.* Bitch of a hound or beagle.
Sabuéso, *sm.* Hound, bloodhound, beagle.
Sábulo, *sm.* Gravel, coarse sand. [velly.
Sabulóso, sa, *a.* Sabulous, gritty, sandy, gra-
Sáca, *sf.* 1. Exportation, extraction; the act of extracting or exporting. 2. Sack, a large bag made of coarse stuff. *Estar de saca*, To be on sale; to be marriageable. 3. First authorised register of a sale. 4. (Arag.) Valuation, computation; agreement. *No parecer saca de paja*, To have a genteel appearance. *Renta de sacas*, Duty on exports.
Sacabála, *sf.* Crow's bill; worm.
Sacabocádo ó Sacabocádos, *sm.* 1. A hollow punch used by sieve-makers and other artisans. 2. Any thing that cuts out a round piece or effects one's purpose.
Sacabótas, *sf.* Boot-jack.
Sacabrócas, *sf.* Pincers used by shoe-makers to draw out the tacks.
Sacabúche, *sf.* 1. (Naút.) A tube or pipe which serves as a pump. 2. Sackbut, a kind of musical wind instrument resembling a trumpet. 3. Player on the sackbut. 4. Nickname of a despicable person.
Sacacórchos, *sm.* Corkscrew.
Sacáda, *sf.* District separated from a province.

Sacadinéro ó Sacadinéros, *sm.* (Fam.) Catch-penny; expensive toys or baubles.
Sacadílla, *sf.* Noise made to rouse game.
Sacadór, ra, *s.* Extracter, exporter.
Sacadúra, *sf.* A sloping cut, by which tailors make clothes fit better.
Sacafilásticas, *sf.* A kind of iron used by artillery-men to take the spikes out of guns.
Sacalíña, *sf.* 1. An ancient kind of dart. 2. Means of extorting. [off clothes.
Sacamánchas, *sm.* He who cuts the sleeves
Sacamiénto, *sm.* The act of taking any thing from the place where it is.
Sacamuélas, *sm.* 1. Tooth-drawer, dentist, one whose profession is to draw teeth. 2. Any thing which causes a shedding of teeth.
Sacanábo, *sm.* (Naút.) Pump-hook.
Sacanéte, *sm.* Game at cards.
Sacapelótas, *sm.* 1. Nickname given to common people. 2. Ancient instrument for extracting balls.
Sacapótras, *sm.* Nickname of a bad surgeon.
Sacár, *va.* 1. To extract, to draw out, to remove, to put out of place. 2. To dispossess of an employment or office; to except or exclude. 3. To manufacture, to produce. 4. To imitate, to copy. 5. To clear, to free; to place in safety. 6. To find out, to resolve, to know; to dissolve; to discover, to invent. 7. To pull out, to eradicate, to take, to extort, to sack. 8. To compel to bring forth what was hidden; to show, to manifest. 9. To excite passion or anger; to lose the judgment. *Esa pasion te saca de ti*, This passion carries you beside yourself. 10. To deduce, to infer; to deride. 11. To ballot, to draw lots. 12. To procure, to obtain; to gain at play. 13. To colour, to cover with paint. 14. To wash and rinse linen after it has been bucked. 15. To extend, to enlarge. 16. To buy in a shop. 17. To transcribe, to copy. 18. To appear or go out with any thing new. 19. To carry corn to be thrashed. 20. To draw a sword, bayonet, &c. 21. It is used in preference to *salir con*, as *hemos sacado buen tiempo*, We set out with fine weather. V. *Traer.* 22. To cite, to name, to quote. *Sacar á baylar*, (Fam.) To name or cite unnecessarily any person or thing not alluded to in conversation. 23. To injure, to impair; applied to things which affect the beauty, health, &c. *Sacar á baylar una señora*, To invite a lady to dance. *Sacar al campo*, To challenge, to call out. *Sacar de pila*, To become sponsor at baptism. *Sacar el baxel á tierra*, (Naút.) To haul a vessel on shore. *Sacar en limpio*, To clear up all doubts. *Sacar fruto*, To reap the fruit of one's labour. *Sacar raja*, To obtain part of a demand. *Sacar á luz*, To print, to publish; to develope, to exhibit. *Sacar apodos*, To call nicknames. *Sacar una letra*, To draw a bill of exchange.
Saca síllas y mete muértos, (Fam.) Persons employed for the menial works of the stage; servants; in general, persons holding mean offices.
Sacatrápos, *sm.* 1. Worm, an iron screw fastened to the end of a ramrod for drawing out the wad of a firelock. 2. One who ob-

tains from another what he wants by cunning and artifice.
Sacerdócio, *sm.* Priesthood.
Sacerdotál, *a.* Sacerdotal.
Sacerdóte, *sm.* Priest.
Sacerdotísa, *sf.* Priestess.
Sachadúra, *sf.* The act of hoeing or turning up the ground with a hoe or dibble.
Sachár, *va.* To turn the ground with a hoe or dibble.
Sácho, *sm.* Hoe, an iron instrument for turning up the ground.
Saciáble, *a.* That may be satiated or satisfied.
Saciár, *va.* 1. To satiate, to sate, to satisfy the appetite; to fill. 2. To gratify desire.
Saciedád, *sf.* Satiety, fulness beyond desire or pleasure.
Sáco, *sm.* 1. Sack, a bag for carrying or transporting any thing. 2. A coarse stuff worn by country people; coarse cloth worn as penance. 3. The act of playing a ball. V. *Saque.* 4. Short round jacket worn by the Roman soldiers, a sagum. 5. Imaginary place for immaterial beings. 6. Pillage, plunder; heap. V. *Saqueo. A' saco,* Sacking, plundering. *Saco del mar,* (Naút.) Bay, port, harbour. *Saco de una vela,* (Naút.) Drop of a sail.
Sacománo, *sm.* V. *Saqueo y Forrageador.*
Sácra, *sf.* Each of the three tablets on the altar, which the priest in saying mass may read without opening the missal.
Sacramentál, *a.* Sacramental, belonging to the sacraments.—*s.* Individual or confraternity destined to the worship of the sacrament of the altar.
Sacramentalménte, *ad.* Sacramentally; with or in confession.
Sacramentár, *va.* To administer the sacraments.—*vn.* V. *Juramentar.*—*vr.* To transubstantiate Christ into the eucharist.
Sacramentário, *a.* Applied to the heretics who deny the real presence of Christ in the eucharist.
Sacraménte, *ad.* V. *Sagradamente.*
Sacraménto, *sm.* 1. Sacrament. 2. V. *Misterio y Juramento. Sacramento del altar,* The eucharist.
Sácre, *sm.* 1. (Orn.) Sacre. Falco sacer *L.* 2. A sly artful pilferer. 3. Small cannon.
Sacrificadéro, *sm.* Place where a sacrifice is performed.
Sacrificadór, *sm.* Sacrificer.
Sacrificánte, *a.* Sacrificing, hazarding.
Sacrificár, *va.* 1. To sacrifice, to offer or perform a sacrifice. 2. To pay homage. 3. To expose to great hazard and danger.—*vr.* 1. To devote one's self to God. 2. To submit, to conform one's self to.
Sacrifício, *sm.* 1. Sacrifice, submission, obsequiousness; obedience, compliance. *Sacrificio del altar,* Sacrifice of the mass. 2. Surgical operation. *Sacrificio propiciatorio,* Peace-offering, propitiatory sacrifice.
Sacrilegaménte, *ad.* Sacrilegiously.
Sacrilégio, *sm.* Sacrilege, the violation of any thing sacred; pecuniary punishment for sacrilege.
Sacrílego, ga, *a.* Sacrilegious, committing sacrilege.
Sacrilléjo, *sm.* Breaking of any thing sacred.
Sacristimóche, cho, *sm.* (Joc.) A man dressed in a ragged black coat.
Sacristán, *sm.* 1. Sacristan, sexton. 2. Hoop formerly worn by women.
Sacristána, *sf.* 1. Sacristan or sexton's wife. 2. Nun or lay woman who provides every thing necessary for church service.
Sacristanear, *va.* (Joc.) To gormandise.
Sacristanía, *sf.* Office of a sexton; vestry.
Sacristía, *sf.* 1. Sacristy, vestry; a room appendant to the church, in which the sacerdotal garments and consecrated vessels are deposited. 2. Office and employment of a sacristan or sexton. 3. (Joc.) Stomach. *Llenar la sacristia,* To guzzle, to gormandise.
Sácro, cra, *a.* Holy, sacred. V. *Sagrado. Fuego sacro,* St. Anthony's fire, erysipelas.
Sacrosánto, ta, *a.* Sacred, consecrated; very holy.
Sacudída, *sf.* The act of shaking off or rejecting any thing. *De sacudida,* Resulting from.
Sacudidaménte, *ad.* Rejectingly.
Sacudído, da, *a.* Harsh, indocile, intractable.
Sacudído, *sm.* Spanish step in dancing.
Sacudidór, *sm.* 1. Shaker, one who shakes off. 2. Instrument for beating or cleansing.
Sacudidúra, *sf.* Dusting, act of cleaning.
Sacudimiénto, *sm.* Act of shaking off or rejecting.
Sacudír, *va.* 1. To shake, to move violently from one side to another. 2. To dart, to throw, to discharge; to beat, to chastise with blows. 3. To remove, to separate. 4. (Naút.) To flap in the wind; applied to the sails. *Sacudir el polvo,* To give blows; to chastise severely; to reprehend; to refute. *Sacudir el yugo,* To shake off the yoke.—*vr.* To reject with disdain, to turn away in a harsh and violent manner.
Saducísmo, *sm.* Sadducism, doctrine of the Sadducees.
Saducéo, *sm.* Sadducee.
Saducéo, ea, *a.* Belonging to the Sadducees.
Saéta, *sf.* 1. Arrow, dart. 2. Cock of a sundial, gnomon; hand of a watch or clock. 3. Magnetic needle. 4. Bud of a vine. 5. Object or dart, which makes an impression on the mind. 6. Moral sentence or couplet of missionaries. 7. (Astr.) A northern constellation. *Echar saetas,* To evince agitation by words or gestures. *Saétas,* Pious ejaculations.
Saetáda y Saetázo, *s.* Arrow-wound, wound received from an arrow or dart.
Saetear, *va.* V. *Asaetear.*
Saetéra, *sf.* 1. Loop-hole in turrets and old walls, through which fire-arms are discharged. 2. A small grated window in prisons.
Saetéro, ra, *a.* 1. Relating to arrows. 2. Applied to a honey-comb made in a right line.
Saetéro, *sm.* Archer, bowman.
Saetía, *sf.* 1. (Naút.) Settee, a vessel with lateen sails, used in the Mediterranean. 2. Loop-hole. V. *Saetera.*
Saetílla, *sf. dim.* 1. Small arrow or dart. 2. Small magnetic needle. 3. Hand of a watch 4. Moral sentence.
Saetín, *sm.* 1. Mill-trough, a narrow channel through which the water runs from the dam to

the wheel of a mill. 2. Peg, pin, tack. 3. Sort of drag-net. 4. Tenter-hook.
SAETÓN, *sm.* Dart, a sharp-pointed weapon from a cross-bow.
SÁFICO, CA, *a.* Sapphic; applied to verse.
SAFÍNA, *sf.* Vein, containing the blood of the foot.
SAFÍO, *sm.* (And.) V. *Congrio.*
SÁFRA, *sm.* (Min.) Zafre, blue oxide of cobalt.
SAFUMÁR, *va.* V. *Sahumar.*
SÁGA, *sf.* Witch.
SAGACIDÁD, *sf.* 1. Sagacity, the quickness of scent in dogs. 2. Sagaciousness, penetration.
SAGAPÉNO, *sm.* Gum sagapen, a resinous juice.
SAGÁTI, *sm.* Kind of woollen cloth like serge.
SAGÁZ, *a.* 1. Sagacious, quick of scent; applied to a dog. 2. A sly, crafty, and cunning person.
SAGAZMÉNTE, *ad.* Sagaciously.
SÁGE, *a.* (Ant.) V. *Sabio.*
SAGÍTA, *sf.* Segment of a diameter, contained between the vertex and the plane.
SAGITÁL, *a.* 1. Sagittal; belonging to an arrow. 2. (Anat.) Sagittal, applied to a suture of the skull.
SAGITÁRIO, *sm.* 1. Archer. 2. Sagittarius, sign in the Zodiac.
SÁGMA, *sf.* (Arq.) Measure taken of many members, as of a cornice.
SÁGO, *sm.* A loose wide great coat. V. *Sayo.*
SAGRADAMÉNTE, *ad.* In a sacred manner.
SAGRÁDO, DA, *a.* 1. Sacred, consecrated; venerable. 2. Cursed, execrable.
SAGRÁDO, *sm.* Asylum, a sacred place where debtors or malefactors take refuge.
SAGRARIÉRO, *sm.* Keeper of reliques.
SAGRÁRIO, *sm.* 1. Place in a church wherein consecrated things are deposited. 2. Cibary, the place where the consecrated host is kept. 3. The inmost recesses of the human breast.
SÁGULA, *sf.* A small or little frock. V. *Sayuelo.*
SAHORNÁRSE, *vr.* To be excoriated.
SAHÓRNO, *sm.* Excoriation, the loss of skin by rubbing.
SAHUMÁDO, DA, *a.* Select, apposite, proper.
SAHUMADÓR, *sm.* 1. Perfumer, one who prepares or sells perfumes. 2. A perfuming pot, used to impregnate any thing with a sweet scent.
SAHUMADÚRA, *sf.* 1. The act of perfuming or impregnating with a sweet scent. 2. (Naút.) Fumigation on board of ships.
SAHUMÁR, *va.* 1. To perfume. 2. To fumigate, to smoke.
SAHUMÉRIO, *sm.* 1. Smoke, vapour, steam. 2. The medical application of fumes to particular parts of the body; aromatics burnt for perfumes.
SAHÚMO, *sm.* Smoke, steam, vapour. V. *Sahumerio.*
SAÍN, *sm.* Grease or fat of an animal; dirt on clothes.
SAÍNA, *sf.* V. *Alcandia.*
SAINÁR, *va.* To fatten animals.
SAINÉTE, *sm. dim.* Slight grease on clothes.
SÁJA Y SAJADÚRA, *sf.* Scarification, an incision in the flesh.
SAJÁR, *va.* To scarify, to make incisions in the flesh.
SÁL, *sf.* 1. Salt, a substance of a pungent taste and soluble in water. 2. Wisdom, prudence. 3. Wit, vivacity of expression. *Sales,* Salts, a general term for all chemical bodies susceptible of dissolution and crystallization. *Echar en sal,* To reserve for another occasion. *Sal gema, piedra ó de compas,* Salt rock, culinary salt. *Con su sal y pimienta,* With great labour and difficulty. *Ser un terron de sal,* (Fam.) To be very witty and facetious.
SÁLA, *sf.* 1. Hall, the first large room in a house. 2. Hall where judges meet to try and decide causes. 3. Board of commissioners. 4. A public meeting, a public entertainment. *Sala de galibos,* (Naút.) The mould-loft of a ship. *Sala de secretos,* A whispering-gallery. *Hacer sala,* To form a court or quorum; (Ant.) To give splendid entertainments.
SALACIDÁD, *sf.* Salacity, lechery.
SALADAMÉNTE, *ad.* Wittily, facetiously.
SALADÁR, *sm.* Piece of ground rendered barren by the overflowing of salt-water.
SALADÉRO, *sm.* Salting-place.
SALADÍLLO, *sm.* A small sea; witticism.
SALÁDO, DA, *a.* 1. Salted, salty. 2. Witty, facetious.
SALÁDO, *sm.* 1. Sea. 2. (Bot.) Salt-wort. Salsola *L.* 3. Land rendered barren by too large a portion of saline particles.
SALADÓR, RA, *s.* Salter; salting-place where meat is salted.
SALADÚRA, *sf.* 1. Salting, the act of seasoning with salt. 2 Fish or meat salted for use. 3. Hung-beef, smoked or dried by smoke. 4. Saltness.
SALAMÁNDRA Y SALAMÁNDRIA, *sf.* 1. Salamander, a kind of lizard. Lacerta salamandra *L.* 2. (Met.) That which exists in the ardour of love or affection.
SALAMANQUÉS, SA; Y QUÍNO, NA, *a.* V. *Salmantino.*
SALAMANQUÉSA, *sf.* Star-lizard. Lacerta stellio *L.*
SALÁR, *va.* To salt, to season with salt; to preserve by impregnating with salt.
SALARIÁR, *va.* To give a salary or wages.
SALÁRIO, *sm.* Wages, salary; a temporary stipend; military pay.
SALÁZ, *a.* 1. Salty. 2. Salacious, lustful.
SALAZÓN, *sf.* Seasoning, salting.
SÁLCE, *sm.* (Bot.) Willow. Salix *L.* V. *Sauce.*
SALCÉDA, *sf.* Plantation of willows.
SALCERÉTA, *sf.* Dice-box.
SALCHÍCHA, *sf.* 1. Kind of small sausage. 2. (Mil.) Saucisse, a long narrow bag of pitched cloth, filled with powder, serving to set fire to mines.
SALCHICHERÍA, *sf.* Shop in which sausages are sold.
SALCHICHÉRO, RA, *s.* Maker or seller of sausages.
SALCHICÓN, *sm.* A large saucisse filled with powder.
SALCOCHÁR, *va.* To dress meat, leaving it half raw and without salt.
SALDÁR, *va.* To liquidate a debt.
SÁLDO, *sm.* Finish or conclusion of a count.
SALEBROSIDÁD, *sf.* Saltness.
SALEDÍZO, ZA, *a.* Jutting out, prominent.
SALÉRA, *sf.* Place where salt is given to animals to eat.
SALÉRO, *sm.* 1. Salt-cellar, a vessel with salt for the use of the table. 2. Salt-mine, from which rock-salt is obtained. 3. Salt-pan; magazine of salt.
SALÉTA, *sf.* A small hall.
SÁLGA LO QUE SALIERE. V. *Salir.*
SALGÁDA Y SALGADÉRA, *sf.* (Bot.) Sea purslain. Atriplex halimus *L.*

Salíca, *sf.* A small ball.—*a.* Salique; applied to a law.
Salicór, *sf.* (Bot.) Glasswort. Salicornia *L.*
Salída, *sf.* 1. The act of going out of a place. 2. Outlet, passage outwards. 3. Environs of a town. 4. Issue, result; conclusion. 5. Projection, prominence, any thing jutting out. 6. Saleableness, the quality of being saleable. 7. Expenditure, outlayings. 8. (Mil.) Sally, sortie. *Puerta de salida*, Sally-port. 9. (Naút.) Departure. 10. (Naút.) Headway; progressive motion of a vessel. *Estar de salida*, To be ready for sailing. *Llevar salida*, To be under weigh or way. *Llevar buena salida*, To have fresh head-way.
Salidízo, za, *a.* Jutting out. V. *Saledizo.*
Salído, *a.* Projecting, prominent. *Salida*, Proud, eager for the male; applied to a bitch.
Saliénte, *a.* Salient, projecting.
Salín, *sm.* Salt magazine. V. *Salero.*
Salína, *sf.* Salt-pit, salt-works.
Salinéro, *sm.* Salter, one who deals in salt.
Salíno, na, *a.* Saline, containing salt; consisting of salt.
Salír, *vn. irr.* 1. To go out of a place. 2. To depart, to set out. 3. To get out of a narrow place or crowd. 4. To appear, to show itself. 5. To shoot, to spring; to grow. 6. To proceed, to issue from. 7. To get over difficulties, to escape from danger; to extricate one's self from errors or doubts. 8. To exceed, to excel; (Naút.) To pass another vessel in sailing. 9. To happen, to occur. *Salga lo que saliere*, (Fam.) Happen what will, it does not concern me. 10. To cost. *El caballo me salió en sesenta guineas*, The horse stood me in sixty guineas. *Salen caros en Madrid los generos Ingleses*, English goods are dear in Madrid. 11. To finish well or ill; to correspond or imply; to complete a calculation. 12. (Mil.) To sally, to issue out. 13. To acquire; to become; to grow common or vulgar. 14. To dismiss, to dispose of. 15. To say or do any thing unexpectedly or unseasonably. 16. To resemble, to appear like. 17. To separate, to retire, to desist, to be chosen or elected. *Salir á luz*, To leave the press, to be published or printed; to be produced; to be developed. *Salir con algo*, To obtain any thing. *Salir de sí*, To be enraptured. *Salir de sus casillas*, To step out of one's line or usual way of acting. *Salir de mantillas*, Not to want leading strings. *Salir los colores al rostro*, To blush. *Salir por la bentana*, To be turned out.—*vr.* 1. To violate a contract, not to fulfil one's engagements. 2. To drop, to leak. 3. To support or maintain an opinion. *Salirse de la religion*, To quit a religious order.
Salitrádo, da, *a.* Impregnated with saltpetre; composed of it.
Salitrál, *a.* Nitrous.—*sm.* Saltpetre bed or [works.
Salítre, *sm.* Saltpetre, nitrate of potash.
Salitrería, *sf.* Saltpetre-work.
Salitréro, ra, *a.* Saltpetre-refiner, dealer in saltpetre.
Salitróso, sa, *a.* Nitrous.
Salíva, *sf.* Saliva, humour formed in the mouth.
Salivación, *sf.* Salivation.
Salivál, *a.* Salivous.
Salivár, *vn.* To spit, to salivate.
Salivéra, *sf.* Round knob on the bits of a bridle.
Salivóso, sa, *a.* Salivous.
Salladór, *sm.* Weeder, a weeding-hook, hoe.
Sallár, *va.* To weed.
Sálma, *sf.* Ton, a measure of weight of twenty hundred.
Salmantíno, na; **Salmanticénse y Salmaticénse**, *a.* Belonging to or native of Salamanca.
Salmeár ó Salmodiár, *va.* To sing psalms.
Salmér, *sm.* (Arq.) Plane or impost from which an arch springs.
Salmísta, *sm.* Psalmist, a writer or composer of psalms; chanter of psalms.
Sálmo, *sm.* Psalm.
Salmodía, *sf.* Psalmody.
Salmógrafo, *sm.* Writer of psalms.
Salmón, *sm.* (Ict.) Salmon. Salmo salar *L.*
Salmonádo, da, *a.* Tasting like salmon.
Salmonéte, *sm.* (Ict.) Red-mullet, or sur-mullet. Mullus barbatus *L.*
Salmoréjo, *sm.* 1. Sauce for rabbits. 2. Reprimand, offensive language.
Salmuéra, *sf.* 1. Brine, water impregnated with salt. 2. Pickle made of salt and water.
Salmuerárse, *vr.* To be diseased by eating too much salt; applied to cattle.
Salobrál, *a.* Salty, briny.—*sm.* Brine.
Salóbre, *a.* Brackish, saltish.
Salobréño, ña, *a.* Saltish, containing salt; applied to earth.
Salóma, *sf.* 1. (Naút.) Singing out of sailors. 2. (Ict.) Goldline, gilt-head.
Salomár, *vn.* (Naút.) To sing out.
Salón, *sm.* 1. Saloon, a large hall. 2. Meat salted and smoked.
Saloncéte, cíllo, cíto, *sm. dim.* Small saloon.
Sálpa, *sf.* (Ict.) Goldline. Sparus salpa *L.*
Salpicadúra, *sf.* The act of spattering, and the stain made by it.
Salpicár, *va.* 1. To bespatter, to sprinkle with dirt. 2. To work without continuity or order; to fly from one subject to another.
Salpicón, *sm.* 1. Salmagundi, cold meat chopped small and dressed with oil, vinegar, salt, and pepper. 2. Bespattering.
Salpimentár, *va.* 1. To season with pepper and salt. 2. To treat with smart or abusive language; to dissimulate.
Salpimentón, *sm.* Salmagundi. V. *Salpicon.*
Salpimiénta, *sf.* Mixture of salt and pepper.
Salpínga, *sf.* African serpent.
Salpresár, *va.* To season with salt.
Salpúga, *sf.* Biting kind of ant.
Salpullído, *sm.* Collection of pustules on the skin.
Salpullír, *va.* To break out in pustules or pimples on the skin.
Sálsa, *sf.* 1. Sauce, any liquid composition that promotes the flavour of victuals. 2. Ornaments, decorations. *Salsa de San Bernardo*, (Joc.) Hunger.
Salsafrás, *sm.* (Bot.) Saxifrage. V. *Saxífraga.*
Salsedúmbre, *sf.* Salineness, saltness.
Salséra, *sf.* Saucer, a small pan, in which sauce is served on table. V. *Salserilla.*
Salseréta, *sf.* A small saucer; a dice-box.

Salserílla, *sf.* A small saucer, in which ingredients or colours are mixed.
Salséro, *sm.* (Bot.) Thyme. Thymus zygis *L.*
Salserón, *sm.* 1. (Burg.) Measure of grain, containing about a peck. 2. V. *Salsa.*
Salseruélo, *sm.* V. *Salserilla.*
Salsifrágia ó Salsifráx, *sf.* (Bot.) Saxifrage.
Salsílla, *sf.* Sauce of little flavour or taste.
Saltabáncos, Saltabánco ó Sálta en Bancos, *sm.* Mountebank, quack.
Saltabardáles, *sm.* Romp, a wild youth.
Saltabarráncos, *sm.* A noisy turbulent fellow.
Saltacábras, *sf.* Kind of Spanish serpent which attracts the eyes of goats.
Saltacharquíllos, *sm.* Boy who walks in play on tiptoes.
Saltación, *sf.* The act of leaping, hopping, or dancing.
Saltadéro, *sm.* 1. Leaping-place, a high ground from which leaps can be conveniently taken. 2. An artificial fountain, jet, a contrivance by which water is violently spouted up. *Estar al saltadero*, (Fam.) To be near promotion.
Saltádo, da, *a.* Prominent, jutting out.
Saltadór, ra, *s.* One that hops, jumps, or leaps.
Saltadúra, *sf.* Hollow or hole made in the surface of a stone when hewing it.
Saltambárca, *sf.* A rustic dress, open behind.
Saltánte, *pa.* Salient, leaping.
Saltaparédes, *sm.* V. *Saltabardales.*
Saltár, *vn.* 1. To leap, to jump; to skip, to rebound. *Saltar en tierra*, To disembark. 2. To burst, to break into pieces; to fly asunder. 3. To be clear and obvious, to occur to the memory; to excel, to surpass. 4. To be irritated, to be agitated, to betray emotion; to speak incoherently and irrelevantly. 5. (Naút.) To chop about, to change suddenly; applied to the wind. *Salte gente á la banda*, (Naút.) Man the ship's side; a word of command. *Saltar de gozo*, To be highly delighted. *Andar á lo que salta*, To give one's self up to a vagrant or vagabond life without labour.—*va.* 1. To cover the female; applied to male animals. 2. To pass from one to another.
Saltarégla, *sf.* A sliding rule.
Saltaréo, *sm.* Ancient Spanish dance.
Saltarén, *sm.* 1. Certain tune on the guitar. 2. Grashopper.
Saltarín, na, *s.* 1. Dancer, one who professes the art of dancing. 2. A restless young rake.
Saltaterandáte, *sm.* A kind of embroidery.
Saltatríz, *sf.* An immodest female dancer.
Salteadór, *sm.* Highwayman, footpad; one who extorts or takes away by violent means.
Salteamiénto, *sm.* Assault.
Salteár, *va.* 1. To assault, to attack, to invade; to rob on the highway. 2. To fly from one work to another without continuity. 3. To anticipate maliciously in the purchase of any thing; to surprise, to take by surprise. 4. To circumvent, or gain ascendency over another's feelings.
Saltéo, *sm.* Assault, the act of attacking travellers on the high road.
Saltério, *sm.* 1. Psalter, a collection of psalms; a psalm book. 2. Psaltery, a kind of harp. 3. Rosary.
Saltéro, ra, *a.* Living on mountains, highlander.
Saltimbáncos, *sm.* Mountebank, quack.
Saltíllo, *sm.* 1. A little hop or leap. *A' saltillos*, Leaping, hopping. 2. (Naút.) Beak, bulkhead. *Saltillos de los pasamanos*, (Naút.) Steps of the gangway.
Saltimbánco y Saltimbanqui, *sm.* Mountebank.
Sálto, *sm.* 1. Leap, the act of leaping; distance leaped. 2. Leaping-place, a high ground from which leaps can conveniently be taken. 3. Irregular transition from one thing to another. 4. Assault, plunder, robbery. 5. Heel-piece of a shoe. V. *Tacon. Salto de corazon*, Palpitation. *A' salto de mata*, By flight for fear of punishment. *Salto de trucha*, Tumbling; tricks played by various vibrations of the body. *Salto mortal*, Somersault, or somerset; a leap by which a jumper throws himself from a beam and turns over his head. *Salto de viento*, (Naút.) The sudden shifting of the wind. *Dar un salto á bolina*, (Naút.) To check the bowline. *A' saltos*, Leaping by hops. *De sálto*, On a sudden. *De un sálto*, At one jump. *Por sálto*, Irregularly, by turns.
Saltón, *sm.* Grashopper, an insect of the family of locusts.
Saltón, na, *a.* Hopping, or leaping much. *Saltones ojos*, Goggle-eyes.
Salubérrimo, ma, *a. sup.* Most salubrious.
Salúbre, *a.* Healthful. V. *Saludable.*
Salubridád, *sf.* Healthfulness, a sound state of things, salubrity.
Salúd, *sf.* 1. Health, sound state of the body. 2. Welfare, prosperity. 3. Salvation, preservation from eternal death. *En sana salud*, In good health. *Salúdes*, Compliments, greetings; courteous actions and expressions.
Saludáble, *a.* Salutary, healthful, salubrious; good for the soul.
Saludableménte, *ad.* Salubriously, healthfully.
Saludadór, *sm.* 1. One who greets or salutes. 2. Quack, who pretends to cure distempers by prayers and religious ceremonies.
Saludár, *va.* 1. To greet, to salute. 2. To express content or joy by words or actions. 3. To proclaim one king; to fire a salute. 4. To apply some delusive remedies to cure diseases, like quacks. 5. To punish with stripes. *Saludar á la voz*, (Naút.) To give cheers, to huzza.
Salúdo, *sm.* Salute with a volley of fire-arms.
Salúmbre, *sf.* Flower of salt, red spume which forms on salt.
Salutación, *sf.* 1. Salutation, the act of saluting. 2. Exordium or introductory part of a sermon.
Salúte, *sm.* Ancient Castilian gold coin.
Salutiferaménte, *ad.* Salubriously.
Salutífero, ra, *a.* Salutiferous, healthful.
Sálva, *sf.* 1. Pregustation, the previous tasting of viands before they are served up. 2. Salute, discharge of fire-arms. 3. Chirping and warbling of birds at break of day. 4. Salver, a plate on which any thing is presented. *Hacer la salva*, To drink to one's health; to beg leave to speak. 5. Rash proof which any one makes of his innocence, by running a great risk. 6. Oath, solemn promise, assurance. *Señor de salva*, Person of great distinction.

Salvachía, *sf.* (Naút.) Salvage, a kind of strap formed of three or more braided cords, serving chiefly to fasten shrouds and stays.
Salvación, *sf.* Salvation.
Salvadéra, *sf.* Sand-box for writing.
Salvádo, *sm.* Bran, the husk of wheat ground.
Salvadór, ra, *s.* Saviour, rescuer, Redeemer.
Salváge, *a.* Savage, wild, barbarous, rude, uncivilized, uncultivated; ignorant, foolish; undomesticated.—*sm.* 1. A savage, one born and brought up in forests and wildernesses. 2. Mountainous country.
Salvagemènte, *ad.* Savagely, wildly.
Salvagería, *sf.* Rusticity; clownish, rude, or uncouth conduct.
Salvagéz, *sf.* Savageness, rustic indocility.
Salvagína, *sf.* 1. Collection of the skins of wild beasts. 2. Having the taste of game; applied to meat.
Salvagíno, na, *a.* Savage, wild, untamed.
Salvaguárdia, *sm.* Safeguard, security, protection; shield of friendship.—*sf.* Passport.
Salvajáda, *sf.* Rude, unmannerly behaviour.
Salvaménte, *ad.* Securely, safely.
Salvaménto y Salvamiénto, *sm.* Safety, the act of saving; place of safety; salvation. *Derechos de salvamento*, Salvage-money.
Salvánte, *pa.* Saver; excepting.—*ad.* Save.
Salvár, *va.* 1. To save, to free from risk or danger; to receive into eternal happiness. 2. To remove impediments or difficulties. 3. To mention and correct errors of the pen in a notarial instrument, at the foot thereof. 4. To pass over or near any thing. 5. To taste, to prove the food or drink of nobles.—*vr.* To escape from danger, to get over difficulties; to attain salvation.
Salvatiquéz, *sf.* Rudeness, rusticity.
Sálve, *v. defect.* God bless you.—*sf.* Salutation, or prayer to the Virgin Mary.
Sálvia, *sf.* (Bot.) Sage. Salvia hispanica *L.*
Salviádo, da, *a.* Containing sage.
Salvílla, *sf.* Salver, a plate on which any thing is presented.
Sálvo, va, *pp. irreg.* of *Salvar*. Saved, proved, corrected.
Sálvo, *ad.* Saving, excepting. *Salvo el guante*, Excuse the glove; used in shaking hands with a glove on. *A' salvo*, Without injury or diminution. *A' su salvo*, To one's satisfaction, safely, leisurely, easily. *En salvo*, In security, at liberty.
Salvocondúto y Salvocondúcto, *sm.* Safe conduct, passport; license or permission.
Salyohonór, *sm.* Breech, posteriors.
Sálz, *sm.* V. *Sauce.*
Sáma, *sf.* (Ict.) A kind of sea-bream.
Sambeníto, *sm.* 1. Garment worn by penitent convicts of the Inquisition, having a yellow cross before and behind. 2. An inscription in churches, containing the name, punishment, and signs of the chastisement of those doing penance; note of infamy.
Sambláge, *sm.* Joinery. V. *Ensambladura.*
Sambúca, *sf.* Triangular musical instrument; ancient warlike machine.
Sámio, a, *a.* Belonging to the island of Samos.
Samnítico, ca, *a.* Belonging to the Samnites, or to the ancient gladiators.

Sampsúco, *sm.* (Bot.) Marjoram. V. *Almoradux.*
Sampsuquíno, *sm.* Unguent, the principal ingredient of which is marjoram and thyme.
Samúga, *sf.* A kind of side-saddle used by women. V. *Xamuga.*
Sán, *a.* Holy; used always in the masculine gender and before the name. V. *Santo.*
Sanáble, *a.* Curable, that may be cured.
Sanadór, ra, *s.* Curer, one who cures or heals.
Sanalotódo, *sm.* Panacea, remedy or plaster for all distempers and sores; a general remedy.
Sanaménte, *ad.* Naturally; agreeably.
Sanár, *va.* 1. To heal, to cure. 2. To reclaim from vice, to recal to virtue.—*vn.* To recover from sickness.
Sanatívo, va, *a.* Sanative, curative.
Sanchéte, *sm.* Ancient silver coin.
Sáncho, *sm.* (Arag.) Word used to call tame rabbits.
Sanción, *sf.* Sanction.
Sancionár, *va.* To sanction, to authorize.
Sancochár, *va.* To parboil, to half boil.
Sanct, ta, *a.* (Ant.) V. *Santo.*
Sanctasanctórum, *sm.* Sanctuary.
Sanctidád, *sf.* V. *Santidad.*
Sanctiguár, *va.* V. *Santiguar.*
Sanctimónia, *sf.* V. *Santimonia.*
Sánctus, *sm.* Mass. *Tocan á sanctus ó santus*, They ring the bell at mass before the canon.
Sandália, *sf.* Sandal, a kind of slippers.
Sandalína, *sf.* A kind of stuff manufactured in Venice.
Sandalíno, na, *a.* Tinctured with saunders.
Sándalo, *sm.* 1. (Bot.) Red mint. Mentha gentilis *L.* 2. (Bot.) Saunders, sandal-wood. Santalum *L.*
Sandaráca, *sf.* 1. Sandarach, a red sulphuret of arsenic. 2. Sandarac, a white gum exuded by the juniper-tree.
Sandéz, *sf.* Folly, simplicity; want of understanding.
Sandía, *sf.* (Bot.) Water-melon. Cucurbita citrullus *L.*
Sándio, dia, *a.* Foolish, nonsensical.
Sandíx, *sm.* Minium, red lead.
Saneamiénto, *sm.* Surety, bail, guarantee; indemnification, reparation.
Saneár, *va.* 1. To give security, to give bail. 2. To indemnify, to repair.
Sanedrín, *sm.* Sanhedrim, supreme Jewish council.
Sangléy, *sm.* Chinese who trade to the Philippine islands.
Sangradéra, *sf.* 1. Lancet, a chirurgical instrument for letting blood. 2. Lock, sluice, drain.
Sangradór, *sm.* 1. Phlebotomist, a blood-letter. *Es gran sangrador*, He is a great blood-letter; applied to a physician who orders to bleed much. 2. Fissure, opening.
Sangradúra, *sf.* 1. Bleeding, an incision made in a vein to let blood; part of the arm usually bled. 2. Draining of a canal or river.
Sangrár, *va.* 1. To bleed, to let blood; to open a vein. 2. To drain, to draw off any quantity of water from a canal or river. 3. (Impr.) To indent the first line of a paragraph. *Me sangró bien la bolsa*, He drained my purse well.—*vn.* To bleed.—*vr.* To be bled.

Sanguáza, *sf.* Serous blood, thin blood abounding with water.

Sángre, *sf.* 1. Blood, the red humour or fluid contained in the veins and arteries of the animal body. 2. Race, family, kindred. 3. Substance, fortune. 4. Wound, incision where blood issues. 5. Entertainment given to one who bleeds. 6. Inside of the arm where a vein is usually opened. 7. Drink made of lemon and red wine. 8. (Impr.) Indention of a line. *A' sangre fria*, In cool blood. *A' sangre y fuégo*, By violent means, with the utmost rigour.

Sangría, *sf.* 1. Bleeding, an incision made in a vein to let blood; any wound or incision which emits blood. 2. Present made to a person who is blooded. 3. Taking away or drawing out any thing in small quantities or parts. 4. (Impr.) Act of indenting a line. 5. Inside of the arm. V. *Sangradura*. 6. **Sangrée**, a beverage made of red wine, lemon, and water.

Sangrientaménte, *ad.* Bloodily, cruelly.

Sangriénto, ta, *a.* 1. Bloody, stained with blood, blood-coloured. 2. Sanguinary, bloodthirsty.

Sanguál, *sm.* (Orn.) Osprey. Falco ossifragus L.

Sanguázo, za, *a.* y *s.* Serous blood; reddish fluid.

Sangueño, *sm.* (Bot.) Dogberry-tree, cornelian cherry-tree. Cornus sanguinea *L.*

Sangüeso, *sm.* (Bot.) Raspberry-bush. Rubus idæus *L.*

Sanguífero, ra, *a.* Containing blood.

Sanguificár, *va.* To produce blood, to sanguify.

Sanguificatívo, va, *a.* That which produces blood.

Sanguijuéla, *sf.* 1. Leech. Hirudo *L.* 2. Sharper, one who by artful tricks cheats unwary persons out of their money.

Sanguinária, *sf.* 1. (Bot.) Knot-grass. Illecebrum paronychia *L.* 2. Stone resembling an agate, of the colour of blood.

Sanguinariaménte, *ad.* Sanguinarily.

Sanguinário, ria, *a.* Sanguinary, cruel, bloody.

Sanguíneo, nea; y **Sanguíno, na**, *a.* Having the colour of blood, sanguine; sanguineous, abounding in blood.

Sanguinolénto, ta, *a.* (Poét.) Sanguinary, bloody.

Sanguinóso, sa, *a.* Sanguineous; cruel.

Sánguis, *sm.* (Lat.) Blood of Christ.

Sanguisórva, *sf.* (Bot.) Burnet.

Sanguisuéla y **Sangüja**, *sf.* Leech. V. *Sanguijuela.*

Sanícula, *sf.* (Bot.) Sanicle. Sanicula *L.*

Sanidád, *sf.* 1. Soundness, health, vigour, sanity. *En sanidad*, In health. *Carta de sanidad*, Bill of health. *Casa de sanidad*, Office of health. *Juez de sanidad*, Commissioner of the board of health. 2. Candour, ingenuousness.

Sanie ó **Sanies**, *sf.* (Med.) V. *Icor.*

Sanióso, sa, *a.* V. *Icoroso.*

Sanjacádo ó **Sanjacáto**, *sm.* Government of a Turkish province.

Sanjáco, *sm.* Turkish governor of a province.

Sanjuanáda, *sf.* Vigil of St. John.

Sanjuanéro, ra, *a.* Applied to fruits ripe at St. John's day.

Sanjuanísta, *a.* Religious of the Order of St. John of Jerusalem.

Sanluqueño, ña, *a.* Belonging to St. Lucar.

Sanmigueláda, *sf.* Michaelmas.

Sanmigueléño, ña, *a.* Applied to fruits ripe at Michaelmas.

Sáno, na, *a.* 1. Sound, healthy, wholesome; salutary; secure. 2. Sincere, well disposed; discreet, wise, steady. 3. Safe, free from fault. 4. Entire, complete. *Sano y salvo*, Safe and sound.

Sánt, *a.* (Ant.) V. *San.*

Sánta, *sf.* Female saint.—*sm.* V. *Santuario.*

Santa Bárbara, *sf.* 1. (Naút.) Magazine, powder room of a ship. 2. St. Barbara.

Santaménte, *ad.* 1. Reverently, holily, saintly; religiously, simply. 2. Briskly, freely. *Me entré santamente en la casa*, I stept into the house without ceremony.

Santasantórum, *sm.* Sanctuary.

Santélmo, *sm.* (Naút.) A fiery meteor which at times appears on the masts of ships in stormy weather.

Santéro, ra, *s.* Hermit, who begs charity for keeping the hermitage in repair.

Santiágo, *sm.* 1. St. James, the war-hoop of the Spaniards on engaging Moors and other infidels. 2. A middling sort of linen manufactured in *Compostella.*

Santiagueño, ña, *a.* Applied to fruits ripe at St. James's-day.

Santiaguísta, *a.* Belonging to the order of Santiago.

Santiámen, *sm.* Moment, twinkling of an eye.

Santíco, ca, *s.* Little image of a saint; in familiar language, a good child.

Santidád, *sf.* 1. Sanctity, moral perfection. 2. Holiness, a title of honour given to the pope.

Santificación, *sf.* Sanctification, the act of making holy.

Santificadór, *sm.* Sanctifier.

Santificánte, *pa.* Blessing, sanctifying.

Santificár, *va.* 1. To sanctify, to render holy. 2. To devote or dedicate any thing to God. 3. To bless, to praise. 4. (Met.) To justify, to exculpate.—*vr.* 1. To employ one's self in pious works. 2. To justify, to clear from guilt.

Santiguáda, *sf.* Blessing, the act of making the sign of the cross.

Santiguadéra, *sf.* Act of making the sign of the cross over a sick person. V. *Santiguadora.*

Santiguadéro, *sm.* He who makes the sign of the cross over sick persons, saying certain prayers.

Santiguadór, ra, *s.* One who cures by the sign of the cross.

Santiguamiénto, *sm.* Act of crossing or curing with the sign of the cross.

Santiguár, *va.* 1. To bless, to make the sign of the cross over a sick person. 2. To chastise, to punish.—*vr.* To make the sign of the cross over one's self, to cross one's self.

Santíguo, *sm.* The act of making the cross over one's self.

Santimónia, *sf.* 1. Sanctity. V. *Santidad.* 2. (Bot.) Corn marigold. Chrysanthemum coronarium *L.*

Santiscário, *sm.* (Vulg.) Caprice, whim. V. *Capricho.*

Santísimo, ma, *a.* Most holy. *El santísimo*, The holy sacrament.

Sánto, ta, *a.* 1. Saint, holy, virtuous. 2. Simple, plain, artless. 3. Sacred, dedicated to God; inviolable. 4. Grateful, delightful, pleasant. 5. Just, upright, pious. 6. Holy, applied to the Roman catholic and apostolic church. *Santa bárbara,* (Naút.) Gun-room. *Santo dia,* The whole day. *Pasó el santo dia en ociosidad,* He spent the whole day in idleness. *Santo de pajares,* Hypocrite. *Todos Santos,* All Saints' day. *Santo varon,* A holy man; a harmless idiot or simpleton; a great hypocrite. *A' santo tapado,* Clandestinely, cautiously and secretly. *Santo mocarro,* Vulgar play in which one besmears the face of another, calling him by this name, on condition of not laughing; if he laughs, he loses, and takes the saint's place.

Sánto, *sm.* 1. Saint, the image of a saint. 2. (Mil.) Watch-word. *Anda con mil santos,* Leave me, away with you.

Santolína, *sf.* (Bot.) Lavender-cotton. Santolina *L.*

Santón, *sm.* A pretended saint, a hypocrite.

Santorál, *sm.* A collection of sermons or lives of the saints; church-choir book.

Santuário, *sm.* Sanctuary; temples and sacred things. [crite.

Santúcho, cha; y Santurrón, na, *s.* Hypo-

Santulário, ria, *a.* (Joc.) Applied to those who keep things as holy relics. [ness.

Santurrón, *s.* Hypocrite; pretending holi-

Santurronería, *sf.* Hypocrisy, feigned piety. V. *Beatería.*

Sántus, *sm.* Mass. V. *Sanctus.*

Sáña, *sf.* Anger, passion, rage and its effects.

Sañosaménte, *ad.* Furiously.

Sañóso, sa, *a.* Furious.

Sañudaménte, *ad.* Furiously.

Sañúdo, da, *a.* Furious, enraged.

Sapán, *sm.* (Bot.) Narrow-leaved prickly brasiletto; sappan-tree. Cæsalpinia sappan *L.*

Sapéra, *sf.* (Bot.) Sea-heath. Frankenia lævis *L.* [site taste.

Sapído, da, *a.* High-flavoured, of an exqui-

Sapiéncia, *sf.* Wisdom.

Sapienciáles, *sm. pl.* Books of wisdom, works on morals.

Sapiénte, *a.* Wise. V. *Sabio.*

Sapíllo, *sm.* 1. A little toad. 2. A small tumour under the tongue.

Sapíno, *sm.* (Bot.) Kind of pine.

Sápo, *sm.* 1. A large toad. V. *Escuerzo.* 2. A bloated swelled person. 3. Dolt, a dull stupid person. *Pisar el sapo,* To sleep much. V. *Pisar.* [officinalis *L.*

Saponária, *sf.* (Bot.) Soap-wort. Saponaria

Saporífero, ra, *a.* Saporific, having the power to produce taste.

Sáque, *sm.* 1. The act of playing out the ball. 2. He that plays out the ball.

Saqueadór, ra, *s.* Depopulator, ransacker.

Saqueár, *va.* 1. To ransack, to plunder. 2. To take away any thing in an unlawful manner.

Saquéo y Saqueamiénto, *sm.* Pillage, the act of plundering a place.

Saquéra, *sf.* Needle for sewing sacks, a packing needle.

Saquería, *sf.* Place for, or collection of, sacks.

Saquéte ó Saquéto, *sm.* Little sack.

Saquiláda, *sf.* A small quantity of grain put into a sack to be ground.

Saquíllo, *sm.* A small bag.

Saraguéte, *sm.* Hop, a private family dance.

Sarampión, *sm.* Measles, a kind of eruptive and infectious fever.

Sarangósti, *sm.* (Naút.) Saragosti, a gum used in the East Indies, instead of pitch and tar, to calk ships.

Saráo, *sm.* Ball, an entertainment of dancing.

Sarcásmo, *sm.* Sarcasm, a keen and bitter irony, intended to insult an adversary or opponent.

Sárcia, *sf.* Load, burthen. V. *Carga.*

Sarcíllo, *sm.* (Burg.) Hoe, an instrument to cut up the earth. [Persia.

Sarcócola, *sf.* A resinous gum imported from

Sarcófago, ga, *a.* Escharotic.

Sarcófago, *sm.* 1. Tomb, grave. 2. Sarcophagus, a sort of pumice-stone, of which, anciently, coffins were made to consume the flesh.

Sarcótico, ca, *a.* Sarcotic, serving to fill up ulcers with new flesh; applied to medicine.

Sárda, *sf.* (Ict.) A kind of mackerel. Scomber colias *L.* [2. Rude, stubborn.

Sardésco, ca, *a.* 1. Belonging to a small ass.

Sardésco, *sm.* A small ass.

Sardína, *sf.* (Ict.) Anchovy. Clupea encrasicolus *L.* *La ultima sardina de la banasta,* The last shift. [chards.

Sardinéro, ra, *s.* Dealer in anchovies or pil-

Sardinéro, ra, *a.* Belonging to anchovies.

Sardinéta, *sf.* 1. A small anchovy or pilchard. 2. Part of cheese which overtops the cheese vat. 3. (Naút.) Knittle, a small line either plaited or twisted, for various purposes on board of ships. *Sardinetas,* Fillips with wet fingers.

Sárdio ó Sárdo, *sm.* Sardine, a semi-pellucid stone of a blood colour.

Sardónia, *sf.* (Bot.) Crow-foot, spearwort. *Risa sardonia ó Sardonica,* Sardonic laughter; consisting in a violent contraction of the muscles of the face.

Sardónix, *sf.* Sardonyx, a precious stone.

Sárga, *sf.* 1. Serge, a silk stuff; also a kind of woollens. *Sarga de una vara,* Serge de Rome. *Sarga de dos varas,* Serge de Nismes. 2. A kind of osier or willow.

Sargádo, da, *a.* Serge-like. V. *Asargado.*

Sargázo, *sm.* (Bot.) Sea-lentils, gulf-weed. Fucus natans *L.*

Sargénta, *sf.* 1. Lay nun of the religious order of Santiago. 2. Serjeant's halbert.

Sargenteár, *va.* 1. To perform the duty of a serjeant. 2. To take the command. 3. To act in an imperious and overbearing manner.

Sargentería, *sf.* Place or duty of a serjeant.

Sargentía, *sf.* Office of a serjeant.

Sargénto, *sm.* Serjeant, an under or non-commissioned officer.

Sargentón, *sm.* A strong masculine woman.

Sárgo, *sm.* (Ict.) A kind of sea-roach or sea-bream. Sparus sargus *L.*

Sarguéro, *sm.* Painter of serge.

Sarguéta, *sf.* A thin light serge.

Saríllа, *sf.* (Bot.) Mountain-hyssop. Teucrium montanum *L.*

Sarjár, *va.* To scarify. V. *Sajar.*
Sarjía, *sf.* Scarification. V. *Saja.*
Sarmentadór, ra, *s.* One who gathers pruned vine shoots.
Sarmentár, *va.* To gather vine shoots.
Sarmentéra, *sf.* Place where vine shoots are kept; collecting of vine shoots.
Sarmentício, cia, *a.* Applied to Christians in derision, because they suffered themselves to be burned with the slow fire of vine shoots.
Sarmentóso, sa, *a.* Full of vine shoots.
Sarmiénto, *sm.* Vine shoot, the branch on which the grapes grow.
Sárna, *sf.* 1. Itch, a very contagious cutaneous disease. *No le falta sino sarna que rascar*, He has every thing which his heart can wish for. 2. Violent desire.
Sarnázo, *sm.* Contagion of the itch.
Sarnóso, sa, *a.* Itchy, affected with the itch, rough, scaly.
Sarpullído, *sm.* 1. Flea-bite. 2. Efflorescence, the breaking out of some humours in the skin.
Sarpullír, *vn.* To be flea-bitten.—*vr.* To be full of flea-bites.
Sarracína, *sf.* A tumultuous contest between a number of persons.
Sárria, *sf.* 1. A kind of wide net made of ropes, in which straw is carried. In Toledo it is called *Sarrieta*. 2. (Ar.) Large basket.
Sarríllo, *sm.* 1. A kind of rattling sound in the throat of a dying person. 2. V. *Yaro.*
Sárrio, *sm.* A kind of wild goat, with the horns bent forward.
Sárro, *sm.* Incrustation of the tongue in violent fevers; foulness of the teeth; sediment which adheres to vessels.
Sarróso, sa, *a.* Incrusted, covered with sediment.
Sárta, *sf.* String of beads or pearls, any set of things filed on a line; series.
Sartál, *a.* Stringed.—*sm.* String of beads, &c.
Sartaléjo, *sm.* A small string of pearls, or precious stones.
Sartén, *sf.* Frying-pan, a vessel in which meat is fried.
Sartenáda, *sf.* As much meat or fish as a frying-pan can hold at once.
Sartenázo, *sm.* 1. Blow with a frying-pan. 2. Trick played off; jest, joke.
Sartenílla, ca, ta, *sf.* A small frying-pan.
Sárzo, *sm.* V. *Zarzo.*
Sasafrás, *sm.* (Bot.) Sassafras. Laurus sassafras *L.*
Sástra, *sf.* Wife of a tailor.
Sástre, *sm.* Tailor, one who cuts or makes clothes. *Sastre remendon*, Botching tailor. *Es un cazon de sastre*, He is a superficial scribbler.
Sastrecíllo, *sm.* A petty tailor.
Sastrería, *sf.* 1. Profession or trade of a tailor. 2. A tailor's shop.
Satanás y Satán, *sm.* Satan.
Satanicaménte, *ad.* Satanically.
Satánico, ca, *a.* Satanic, devilish.
Satélite, *sm.* 1. Bailiff, constable, petty officer of justice. 2. (Astr.) Satellite.
Saterión, *sm.* V. *Satirion.*
Sátira, *sf.* 1. Satire, a poem, in which wickedness or folly is censured. 2. A lively, bitter, and witty woman.
Satiricaménte, *ad.* Satirically.
Satírico, *sm.* Satirist, one who writes satires.—**ca**, *a.* Satirical, censorious; full of invectives.
Satiríllа, *sf.* A sharp sneering insinuation.
Satiríllo, *sm.* A little satyr.
Satírio, *sm.* Kind of water rat.
Satirión, *sm.* (Bot.) Lizard flower, white satyrion. Satyrium albidum *L.*
Satirizár, *va.* To satirize, to write satires.
Sátiro, *sm.* Satyr, a fabulous kind of demigod.
Satisdación, *sf.* (For.) V. *Fianza.*
Satisfacción, *sf.* 1. Satisfaction, amends, atonement, recompense, apology, excuse. 2. Gratification, the act of pleasing. 3. Presumption; confidence, security.
Satisfacér, *va.* 1. To satisfy, to pay fully what is due. 2. To expiate, to atone; to reward. 3. To allay the passions, to content desire; to sate or satiate. 4. To free from doubt, perplexity, or suspense.—*vr.* 1. To satisfy one's self; to be satisfied, to vindicate one's self. 2. To be convinced, to be undeceived. 3. To content hunger, thirst, or sleep.
Satisfactoriaménte, *ad.* Satisfactorily.
Satisfactório, ria, *a.* Satisfactory, that which can satisfy or give content.
Satisfécho, cha, *a.* Arrogant, confident.
Satívo, va, *a.* Sative, that which is sown, planted, or cultivated, as opposed to what grows wild.
Sáto, *sm.* Corn-field. V. *Sembrado.*
Sátrapa, *sm.* 1. Governor of a province among the ancient Persians. 2. A sly crafty fellow.
Satrapía, *sf.* Dignity of a Persian governor.
Saturación, *sf.* 1. Saturity, the act of filling one thing with another. 2. Saturation, the impregnation of an acid with alkali.
Saturár, *va.* 1. To saturate, to imbibe, to imgregnate. 2. To fill, to glut.
Saturnál, *a.* Saturnian. *Saturnales*, Saturnalia.
Saturníno, na, *a.* Saturnine, melancholy, grave, gloomy.
Satúrno, *sm.* 1. (Astr.) Saturn. 2. Lead; a great mishap.
Sáuce ó Sáuz, *sm.* (Bot.) Willow. Salix *L.*
Saucedál ó Saucéra, *s.* Plantation of willows.
Saúco, *sf.* 1. (Bot.) Elder or alder-tree. Sambucus *L.* 2. Second hoof of horses.
Saudáda, *sf.* An ardent desire of any thing absent.
Sauquíllo, *sm.* (Bot.) Dwarf elder. Sambucus ebulus *L.*
Sausería, *sf.* Larder in a palace.
Sausiér, *sm.* Chief of the larder in a palace.
Sauzál, *sm.* V. *Saucedal* y *Salceda.*
Sauzgatíllo, *sm.* (Bot.) Agnus castus tree, chaste tree. Vitex agnus castus *L.*
Saxâfrax, *sf.* V. *Saxifraga.*
Saxâtil, *a.* Applied to fish breeding among stones.
Sáxêo, êa, *a.* Stony.
Saxîfrága ó Saxîfrágua, *sf.* (Bot.) The saxifrage plant; mountain saxifrage.
Saxôso, sa, *a.* Containing stones, stony.
Sáya, *sf.* 1. Upper petticoat of a woman. 2. A certain sum of money which the queen of Spain gives her maids when they marry. 3. Ancient tunic or gown worn by men. *Saya saya*, Chinese silk. *Saya entera*, A gown with a train.
Sayál, *sm.* A coarse stuff, sackcloth.
Sayalería, *sf.* Shop for weaving coarse cloth.
Sayaléro, *sm.* Weaver of coarse stuff.

Sayaléсo, ca, *a.* Made of sackcloth or other coarse stuff.

Sayaléte, *sm.* A thin or light stuff.

Sayáza, *sf.* An outward coarse petticoat.

Sayéte, *sm.* A thin or light stuff.

Saynéte, *sm.* 1. Bit of marrow given to a hawk. 2. Any delicate bit of a fine taste or relish. 3. Any thing pleasing or engaging. 4. A high-flavoured sauce. 5. Taste or elegance in dress. 6. Entertainment, farce.

Saynetíllo, *sm.* A slight relish.

Sáyno, *sm.* Kind of Indian pig.

Sáyo, *sm.* A large wide coat without buttons; any loose coat or dress. *Sayo bobo*, Tight dress worn by clowns in plays. *Sayo vaquero*, A loose jacket worn by cowherds. *Á' su sayo*, Of one's own accord, in one's own mind.

Sayón, *sm.* 1. Bailiff; executioner. 2. A corpulent ill-looking fellow.

Sayonázo, *sm.* Bailiff; executioner.

Sayuéla, *sf.* 1. Woollen shift worn by some religious. 2. Kind of fig.

Sayuélo, *sm.* Little frock, small kind of jacket.

Sáz, *sm.* V. *Sauce.*

Sazgatíllo, *sm.* V. *Agnocasto.*

Sazón, *sf.* 1. Maturity, state of perfection. 2. Taste, relish, flavour. 3. Occasion, opportunity, season. *Á' la sazon*, Then, at that time. *En sazon*, Seasonably, opportunely.

Sazonadaménte, *ad.* Maturely, seasonably.

Sazonádo, *sm.* A witty saying, a word to the purpose.—**da**, *a.* Having a relish.

Sazonadór, **ra**, *s.* Seasoner.

Sazonár, *va.* To season, to give a taste or relish; to bring to maturity.—*vr.* To ripen, to attain maturity.

Se, A pronoun, possessive to the person or thing that governs the verb; used before the pronouns *me, te, le*, it reflects the action of the verb on the object which they represent.

Se, *prep.* Used in composition, as *separar*, To separate.

Sea, *ad.* Whether. *Sea que*, Whether that.

Sébe, *sf.* Place enclosed with high pales.

Sebastián y Sebastiáno, *sm.* Sebesten-fruit.

Sebestén, *sm.* (Bot.) Sebesten-tree. Cordia sebestena *L.*

Sebíllo, *sm.* Paste made up with a kind of suet, to soften the hands; kind of soap.

Sébo, *sm.* 1. Suet, a hard and solid grease or fat taken from the kidneys of animals; any sort of grease or fat. 2. A large capital, a great fortune. 3. (Naút.) Animal grease, with which the bottoms of ships, the masts, &c. are rubbed or besmeared.

Sebóso, **sa**, *a.* Fat, greasy, unctuous; greased.

Séca, *sf.* 1. Drought, dry weather. 2. Mint, the building where money is coined. 3. Sand-bank not covered by the sea. 4. Inflammation and swelling in the glands. *Secas*, Sands, rocks. *Á' secas*, Alone, singly.

Secacúl, *sm.* (Bot.) V. *Eringe.*

Secadál, *sm.* A dry barren ground.

Secadéro, *sm.* Place where fruit is dried.—**ra**, *a.* Capable of being dried; applied to fruit.

Secadíllos, *sm. pl.* A sort of dry round biscuits.

Secaménte, *ad.* 1. Drily, morosely; without attention or politeness. 2. Coldly, frigidly.

Secáno, *sm.* 1. Dry arable land which is not irrigated. 2. Siccity, dryness. 3. Dry sand-bank.

Secánsa, *sf.* Kind of game at cards.

Secánte, *sm.* Dryer, a drying oil used for painting, and composed of linseed-oil boiled with garlic, ground-glass, and litharge.—*sf.* (Geom.) Secant, a line that cuts another or divides a superficies into two parts.

Secár, *va.* To dry, to extract moisture, humour, or juice.—*vr.* 1. To dry, to be dried up, to grow dry. 2. To become lank, lean, or meager; to decay. 3. To grow cool in the intercourse with a friend. 4. To be extremely thirsty. 5. To feel repugnance to do any thing however necessary.

Secarál, *sm.* Dryness, drought. V. *Sequeral.*

Secatúra, *sf.* A scarcity of news.

Sección, *sf.* 1. Act of cutting. 2. Section, the division of a work composed of books, chapters, and paragraphs. 3. (Geom.) Section, the cutting of lines, figures, and solid bodies. 4. (Arq.) Section of a building; delineation of its height and depth. 5. Width and depth of the bed of a river. 6. Superficies which cuts the visual rays.

Secéno, **na**, *a.* Sixteenth. V. *Decimosexto.*

Secesión, *sf.* Secession.

Secéso, *sm.* Excrement, stool.

Seclúso, **sa**, *a.* (Ant.) Secluded, separated.

Séco, **ca**, *a.* 1. Dry, wanting moisture. 2. Barren, arid, sapless; withered. 3. Lean, lank, meager. 4. Bare, only, mere. *Á' secas*, Solely. *Tres shelines secos*, Only three shillings. 5. Barren, without ornament or embellishment. 6. Rude, ill-mannered. 7. Lukewarm, cold, without affection. *Pan seco*, Dry bread. *Á' secas y sin llover*, Without preparation or advice, unexpectedly. *En seco*, Without cause or motive. *Navio á palo seco*, (Naút.) Ship under bare poles. *Correr á palo seco*, (Naút.) To scud under bare poles.

Secreción, *sf.* (Med.) Secretion, act of separating the various fluids of the body.

Secrestación, *sf.* Sequestration. V. *Sequestro.*

Secrestár, *va.* (Ant.) 1. To sequester, to sequestrate. 2. To pick out, to set apart.

Secréta, *sf.* 1. The private examen which, in the Spanish universities, precedes the graduation of licentiates in the common law. 2. Privy, a necessary house, water-closet. 3. Secret or private orisons said in a low voice at the beginning of the mass.

Secretaménte, *ad.* Secretly, clandestinely.

Secretária, *sf.* 1. Confident, a woman entrusted with a secret; wife of a secretary. 2. Woman who writes a lady's letters; secretary of a nunnery. *Secretaría.* 1. Secretary's office, the place where a secretary transacts business. 2. Place or employment of a secretary.

Secretariár, *vn.* To fill the office, or discharge the duties, of secretary.

Secretário, *sm.* 1. Confident, the person entrusted with secrets. 2. Secretary, one entrusted with the management of business; one who writes for another. 3. Clerk; amanuensis.

Secreteár, *vn.* To secrete, to separate.

Secretíllo, *sm.* A trifling secret. *Secretillos*, Private conversation between friends.

SECRETÍSTA, *sm.* 1. Author who writes on the secrets of nature, naturalist. 2. Secretist, a dealer in secrets.
SECRÉTO, TA, *a.* Secret; hidden, obscure.—*sm.* 1. Secrecy, careful silence. 2. Secret, the thing hidden or concealed; arcanum. 3. Caution, silence, dissimulation. 4. Fob, a small pocket in the waistband of breeches. 5. Scrutoire, a case or hidden drawer for papers. *Secreto de anchuela*, A stage-secret. *De secreto*, Secretly, privately, without ceremony. *En secreto*, Without formality, in secret, in private, secretly.
SECRETÓN, *sm.* Fine dimity.
SÉCTA, *sf.* 1. Sect, a body of men following some particular master, or united in some tenets. 2. Doctrine or opinion followed by a body of men.
SECTADÓR, RA, *s.* Sectarist.
SECTÁRIO, RIA, *a.* Sectarian, sectary.
SECTÓR, *sm.* (Geom.) Sector.
SECUESTRACIÓN, *sf.* Sequestration. V. *Seqües-tro.*
SECUESTRÁR, *va.* To sequestrate. V. *Seqüestrar.*
SECUÉSTRO, *sm.* V. *Seqüestro.*
SECULÁR, *a.* 1. Secular, happening or coming once in a century. 2. Not spiritual, relating to the affairs of the present world. 3. Not bound by monastic rules.
SECULARIDÁD, *sf.* Secularity, the state or quality of being secular.
SECULARIZACIÓN, *sf.* Secularization.
SECULARIZÁR, *va.* To secularize, to convert from spiritual appropriations to common use.
SECUNDARIAMÉNTE, *ad.* Secondarily.
SECUNDÁRIO, RIA, *a.* Secondary, accessory.
SECUNDÍNA, *sf.* Afterbirth; beam of beasts.
SECÚRA, *sf.* Dryness, siccity, droughtiness; want of humidity or moisture.
SECUTÁR, *va.* (Ant.) V. *Executar.*
SÉD, *sf.* 1. Thirst, the pain suffered for want of drink. 2. Eagerness, anxiety; violent desire. *No dar ni aun una sed de agua*, Not to give as much as a draught of water.
SÉDA, *sf.* 1. Silk, the thread of the silk-worm. 2. Work or stuff formed of silken threads. 3. Hog's bristle; strong hair. *Texedor de seda*, Silk-weaver. *Seda cruda*, Raw silk. *Seda floza*, Flock silk. *Ser una seda*, To be of a sweet temper.
SEDADÉRA, *sf.* Hackle, an instrument for dressing flax.
SEDÁL, *sm.* 1. Angling-line fixed to a fishing-hook. 2. Seton, horse-hair or threads drawn through the skin to produce a salutary discharge of pus; by farriers it is called a rowel.
SEDATÍVO, VA, *a.* (Med.) Sedative.
SÉDE, *sf.* 1. Chair, a seat made of wood or any other matter on which one can sit. *Sedeplena*, Actual occupation of a chair or dignity. *Sedevacante*, Vacant bishoprick. 2. See, seat of episcopal power.
SEDEÁR, *va.* To clean jewels, gold, or silver, with a brush.
SEDENTÁRIO, RIA, *a.* Sedentary, passive in sitting still; wanting motion or action.
SEDÉÑA, *sf.* Fine tow of flax, produced by the second hackling; cloth made of such tow.
SEDÉÑO, ÑA, *a.* 1. Silky, silken; silk-like. 2. Made or consisting of hair.
SEDÉRA, *sf.* Weaver's seat, the bench on which weavers sit to work.
SEDERÍA, *sf.* 1. Silks, silk stuff. 2. Shop of a silk-mercer or silk-man.
SEDÉRO, *sm.* Silk-mercer, silk-man.
SEDICIÓN, *sf.* Sedition, popular commotion.
SEDICIOSAMÉNTE, *ad.* Seditiously.
SEDICIÓSO, SA, *a.* Seditious.
SEDIÉNTO, TA, *a.* 1. Thirsty, dry; droughty. 2. Eagerly desirous, anxious.
SEDIMÉNTO, *sm.* Sediment.
SEDUCCIÓN, *sf.* Seduction, the act of seducing or deceiving.
SEDUCÍR, *va.* To seduce, to corrupt, to deprave.
SEDUCTÓR, RA, *s.* Seducer, deceiver; misleader.
SEE, *sf.* (Ant.) SEE. V. *Sede.*
SEER, *v.* y *s.* (Ant.) V. *Ser* y *Sentarse.*
SEGÁBLE, *a.* Fit to be reaped.
SEGÁDA, *sf.* V. *Siega.*
SEGADÉRA, *sf.* Reaping-hook.
SEGADÉRO, RA, *a.* Fit to be reaped.
SEGADÓR, RA, *s.* Reaper, harvester.
SEGÁR, *va.* 1. To reap, to cut down with a reaping-hook. 2. To cut off; to abscind any thing grown higher than the rest.
SEGAZÓN, *sf.* Harvest season, reaping.
SEGLÁR, *a.* Worldly; secular, laical.
SEGLARMÉNTE, *ad.* Secularly.
SEGMÉNTO, *sm.* Segment, any part cut off.
SEGREGACIÓN, *sf.* Segregation, separation.
SEGREGÁR, *va.* To segregate, to separate.
SEGREGATÍVO, VA, *a.* That which separates.
SÉGRI, *sm.* A sort of silk stuff resembling double taffety.
SEGUDÁR, *va.* To persecute, to pursue or persevere.
SEGUÍDA, *sf.* The act of following, or state of being followed; succession. *De seguida*, Successively, without interruption.
SEGUIDÍLLA, *sf.* A merry Spanish tune and dance.—*Seguidillas*, Diarrhœa, a looseness.
SEGUIDILLÉRA, *sf.* Person fond of singing and dancing *seguidillas.*
SEGUÍDO, DA, *a.* Continued, successive, followed, direct.—*sm.* 1. Narrowing the stitches of a stocking at the foot. 2. (Art.) A kind of pedrero having the powder chamber smaller than the other part of a cannon.
SEGUIDÓR, RA, *s.* 1. Follower, one who follows another person or thing. 2. A leaf of ruled paper which serves to direct boys to write straight.
SEGUIMIÉNTO, *sm.* Pursuit, the act of following another; continuation of a law-suit.
SEGUÍR, *va.* 1. To follow, to pursue. 2. To prosecute, to be in pursuit of one. 3. To accompany, to attend. 4. To follow, profess, or exercise any science or art. 5. To conduct or manage a suit at law or any other business. 6. To agree or conform to. 7. To copy, to imitate. 8. To direct to the proper road or method. *Seguir en compañia*, (Naút.) To sail in company with other ships.—*vr.* 1. To ensue, to follow as a consequence. 2. To succeed, to follow in order. 3. To issue, to spring from.
SEGÚLLO, *sm.* The first stratum or layer of a gold mine.
SEGÚN, *prep.* According to. *Segun vd. me dice,*

According to what you tell me. *Segun y como*, Just as. *Vuelvo la caxa segun y como la recibí*, I return the box just as I received it.

Segundaménte y Segundariaménte. V. *Secundariamente.*

Segundár, *vn.* 1. To repeat over again. 2. To be second, to follow next to the first in saying and doing.

Segundário, ria, *a.* Secondary, second in order. V. *Secundario.*

Segundílla, *sf.* 1. Snow-water again frozen after congealing other water. 2. Small bell used for certain acts of devotion.

Segundíllo, *sm.* 1. The second portion of bread distributed at table in convents. 2. (Mús.) Semi-tone, one of those which are called accidentals.

Segúnda, *sf.* 1. Second in music. 2. Double wards of a lock or key.

Segúndo, da, *a.* Second, immediately following the first; favourable.—*sm.* Second of time, or of a degree of the earth's circumference; 60th part of a minute.

Segundogénito, ta, *a.* Second born; applied to children.

Segundón, *sm.* The second son of a family; a younger brother.

Segúnt, *prep.* (Ant.) V. *Segun.*

Segúr, *sf.* 1. Axe, a large hatchet with a long handle or helve. 2. Axe or emblem of the law. 3. Sickle, a reaping-hook.

Seguradór, *sm.* Securer, asserter.

Seguraménte, *ad.* Securely, certainly.

Segurár, *va.* V. *Asegurar.*

Seguréja, *sf.* A small hatchet, a hollow draw-knife for clearing the inside of staves.

Seguridád, *sf.* Security, surety, certainty.

Segúro, ra, *a.* 1. Secure, free from danger. 2. Certain, not doubtful. 3. Firm, constant.—*sm.* 1. Tumbler of a gun-lock. 2. Permission, leave, license. 3. Insurance of ships, or goods on board of ships. *Compañía de seguros*, Insurance company. *Camara ú oficina de seguros*, Insurance office. *Poliza de seguro*, Policy of insurance. *Premio de seguro*, Premium of insurance. *A' buen seguro*, Certainly, indubitably. *Al seguro*, Securely. *De seguro*, Assuredly. *En seguro*, In security or safety. *Sobre seguro*, Confidently.

Seído, da, *pp.* of *seer*, Been.

Séis, *a.* Six, sixth. V. *Sexto.*—*sm.* 1. Six, character which represents 6. 2. In cathedrals, any one of the boys which sing in the choir; any one of those members of corporations or chiefs of villages who aspires to the principal power.

Seisavádo, da, *a.* That which has six sides and six angles.

Seisávo, *sm.* 1. V. *Exágono.* 2. The sixth part of a number.

Seiscientos, tas, *a.* Six hundred.

Seisén, *sm.* Silver coin worth half a real or six *dineros* of Aragon.

Seiséno, na, *a.* Sixth. V. *Sexto.*

Seisíllo, *sm.* (Mús.) Union of six equal notes.

Selección, *sf.* Selection, choice.

Seléctо, ta, *a.* Select, chosen.

Selenítes, *sf.* Selenites, crystallized gypsum.

Selenografía, *sf.* Selenography, description of the moon.

Seléucide, *sf.* (Orn.) A bird which devours locusts.

Selladór, *sm.* Sealer, one who seals.

Selladúra, *sf.* Act of sealing.

Sellár, *va.* 1. To seal, to put on a seal. 2. To stamp, to mark with a stamp. 3. To conclude, to finish any thing. 4. To cover, to close up. 5. To obligate, to constrain by benefits. *Sellar los labios*, To silence.

Selléнca, *sf.* Prostitute who carries on her trade privately, not a street-walker.

Séllo, *sm.* 1. Seal, impression with a seal; thing stamped. 2. Stamp office. *Sello de aduana*, Cocket. 3. Perfection, completion. *Sello del estómago*, Any solid food taken to settle others. *Sello de Salomon*, (Bot.) Solomon's seal. Convallaria polygonatum *L.*

Sélva, *sf.* Forest. *Selva espesa*, Thicket.

Selvático, ca, *a.* Forest-born, reared in a forest.

Selvatiquéz, *sf.* Rusticity, savageness, wildness.

Selvóso, sa, *a.* Belonging to forests.

Semána, *sf.* 1. Week, the space of seven natural days. *Mala semana*, Menstruation. *Semana santa*, Passion-week; book containing the offices of this week. *Dia entre semana*, Working-day. 2. Any septenary period of time.

Semanál, *a.* Hebdomadal, belonging to a week.

Semanalménte, *ad.* Weekly.

Semanário, ria, *a.* y *s.* Weekly publication.

Semanería, *sf.* Functions performed, or work done in the course of a week.

Semanéro, *sm.* One who enters upon some weekly functions in his turn.

Semanéro, ra, *a.* Applied to persons engaged by the week.

Semáxio, *sm.* Nickname applied to the Christian martyrs, who were bound to the middle of the axle-tree of a car when burnt.

Semblánte, *sm.* Face; aspect; countenance.

Semblár, *vn.* (Ant.) V. *Semejar.*

Sémble y En sémbra, *ad.* (Ant.) Similarly; jointly.

Sembradéra, *sf.* Any thing or instrument used for sowing seed.

Sembradío, día, *a.* Fit or prepared for sowing of seed; applied to land.

Sembrádo, *sm.* Cornfield, a piece of ground sown with grain.

Sembradór, *sm.* Sower, he that sows or scatters seed in order to a harvest.

Sembradúra, *sf.* Insemination, the act of sowing or scattering seed on ground.

Sembrár, *va.* 1. To sow, to scatter seed in the ground in order to growth. 2. To scatter, to spread, to propagate, to divulge. 3. To give a cause or beginning. 4. To perform any useful undertaking. 5. To collect without order. *Sembrar de sal*, To chastise those proprietors who have been guilty of treason or disloyalty.

Seméja, *sf.* 1. Resemblance, likeness. 2. Mark, sign. *No es el, ni su semeja*, It is not he, nor any thing like him.

Semejáble, *a.* Like, resembling, similar.

Semejableménte, *ad.* Likely.

Semejádo, da, *a.* Like. V. *Parecido.*

Semejánte, *a.* Similar, like.—*sm.* V. *Semejanza.*

Semejantemente, *ad.* Likewise, in the same manner.
Semejánza, *sf.* Resemblance, conformity, similitude. V. *Simil.*
Semejár, *vn.* To be like, to resemble; to liken.
Sémen, *sm.* Semen, or seed by which animals are propagated.
Semencéra, *sf.* Sowing, the act of scattering seed for growth.
Sementál, *a.* Seminal, belonging to seed, contained in the seed.
Sementár, *va.* To sow, to scatter seed.
Sementéra, *sf.* 1. Sowing, the act of scattering seed in the ground in order to growth. 2 Land sown with seed; the seed sown. 3. Seed-time, the season proper for sowing. 4. Origin, cause, beginning.
Sementéro, *sm.* 1. Seedlip or Seedlop, the vessel or bag in which the sower carries his seed. 2. Sowing, the act of scattering seed.
Sementílla, *sf. dim.* of *Simiente.*
Sementíno, na, *a.* Belonging to seed or seed-time.
Seméstre, *a.* Lasting six months.—*sm.* Space of six months, leave of absence for six months.
Sémi, *s.* Semi, a word which, in composition, signifies *half*; sometimes it is equivalent to *casi.*
Semibréve, *sf.* (Mús.) Semibrief, a note or measure of time comprehending the space of two minims.
Semicápro y Semicabrón, *sm.* Satyr.
Semicirculár, *a.* Semicircular.
Semicírculo, *sm.* Semicircle.
Semicorchéa, *sf.* (Mús.) Semiquaver.
Semicromático, ca, *a.* (Mús.) Semichromatic.
Semidéo, a, *s.* Demi-god, demi-goddess.
Semidiámetro, *sm.* Semidiameter, radius.
Semidiapasón, *sm.* (Mús.) Semidiapason, defective octave.
Semidiapénte, *sm.* (Mús.) Semidiapente, defective fifth.
Semidiatesarón, *sm.* (Mús.) Semidiatessaron, defective fourth.
Semidifúnto, ta, *a.* Half dead, almost dead.
Semidiós, ósa, *s.* Demi-god, demi-goddess.
Semiditóno, *sm.* (Mús.) Semiditone, imperfect third.
Semidóble, *a.* Applied to a feast celebrated with little ceremony; almost double.
Semidócto, *sm.* Sciolist, one who knows a thing superficially; a half-learned man.
Semidormído, da, *a.* Half asleep, sleepy.
Semidragón, *sm.* Semidragon.
Semiénte, *sf.* V. *Linage y Simiente.*
Semigóla, *sf.* (Fort.) Demigorge, the right line that passes from the angle of a flank of a bastion to the capital.
Semihómbre, *sm.* Half-man.
Semílla, *sf.* 1. Seed, the organized particles from which plants and animals are produced. 2. Origin, cause. *Semillas*, All sorts of seed and grain, wheat and barley excepted; quantity of seed sown.
Semilléro y Semilladéro, *sm.* Seed-plot, the ground on which plants are sown to be afterwards transplanted.
Semilúnio, *sm.* Half the space of time in which the moon performs her course.
Seminál, *a.* Seminal, belonging to seed, contained in the seed; radical.
Seminário, *sm.* 1. Seminary, the ground where plants are sown to be afterwards transplanted. 2. Seminary, a school, place of education. 3. Musical school, for the instruction of children. 4. Beginning, root, origin, source.
Seminarísta, *s* A scholar, who boards and is instructed in a seminary.
Semínima, *sf.* 1. (Mús.) Crotchet. 2. Trifle, a thing of no moment.
Semioctáva, *sf.* Poetical composition of four verses in alternate rhymes.
Semipedál, *a.* Belonging to half a foot.
Semipelagiáno, na, *s.* One who adopts part of the errors of Pelagius.
Semipléna, *sf.* Imperfect proof, half-proof.
Semiplenaménte, *ad.* Half-proved.
Semipléno, na, *a.* Half full, half finished.
Semipoéta, *sm.* Poetaster.
Semiprobánza, *sf.* A half proof, imperfect evidence.
Semipútrido, da, *a.* Half rotten, half putrid.
Semiracionál, *a.* Stupid, ignorant.
Semiréćto, *a.* Being of forty-five degrees; applied to an angle.
Semís, *sm.* Half a pound. V. *Semi.*
Semitóno, *sm.* (Mús.) Semitone.
Semivibración, *sf.* Vibration of the pendulum that ascends or descends.
Semivívo, va, *a.* Half alive.
Semivocál, *s.* Semivowel, as *f, l, m, n, r, s.*
Semivúlpa, *sf.* Animal like a wolf.
Sémola, *sf.* Groats or grits, made of decorticated wheat, wheat ground coarse.
Semoviénte, *a.* Moving of itself, without the assistance of any other thing.
Sempitérna, *sf.* Sort of serge, everlasting.
Sempiternaménte, *ad.* Eternally.
Sempitérno, na, *a.* Eternal, everlasting.
Sén ó Séna, *sf.* 1. (Bot.) Sena or senna, a purgative shrub. Cassia senna *L.* 2. Six marks on dice.
Senádo, *sm.* 1. Senate, a council of senators. 2. Senate-house, town-hall.
Senadoconsúlto, *sm.* Senatus-consultum, decree of a senate.
Senadór, *sm.* Senator, one of the chief magistrates of a city or republic.
Senára, *sf.* A piece of sown ground, assigned to servants as part of their wages.
Senaréro, *sm.* Servant, who enjoys a piece of sown ground as part of his wages.
Senário, *sm.* A number consisting of six units; a verse consisting of six iambic feet.
Sénas, *sf. pl.* Sixes, in the game of backgammon.
Senatório, ria, *a.* Senatorial, belonging to the senate or senators.
Senciénte, *pa.* Sentient, perceiving.
Sencillaménte, *ad.* Ingenuously, plainly.
Sencilléz, *sf.* 1. Slightness, slenderness. 2. Simplicity, plainness, artlessness. 3. Silliness, weakness, ignorance.
Sencíllo, lla, *a.* 1. Simple, unmixed, uncompounded. 2. Light, slight, slender. 3. Silly, weak, easily imposed upon. 4. Ingenuous, plain, artless. 5. Applied to cannons of a due thickness of metal for their caliber. 6.

Single; applied to coin of the same name, but of more value than the single.

Sénda, *sf.* Path, footpath; means.

Senderár, *va.* To make a path, to walk on a path or footpath.

Sendereár, *va.* 1. To guide or conduct on a footpath. 2. To adopt extraordinary means to obtain some end. 3. To make a path.

Sendéro, *sm.* Path, footpath.

Sendíca, lla, ta, *sf. dim.* Little pathway.

Séndos, das, *a.* Each of two, either.

Séne, *sm.* An old man. V. *Viejo.*

Senectúd, *sf.* (Ant.) Old age.

Senescál, *sm.* 1. Seneschal, lord high chamberlain or high steward. 2. Chief commander of a town, especially in time of war. 3. Lord chief justice. [of a seneschal.

Senescalía, *sf.* Place, dignity, or employment

Seníl, *a.* Senile, belonging to old age.

Senión, ra, *s.* (Ant.) V. *Señor.*

Senitês, *sf.* Selenites, crystallized gypsum.

Séno, *sm.* 1. Breast, bosom. V *Pecho.* 2. Lap of a woman. 3. Womb, place of the fœtus in the mother. 4. Circular space formed by moving round. 5. Hole, cavity, sinus. 6. Gulf or gulph, bay. 7. Deceit, craft, dissimulation. 8. Sinus. 9. Security, support; asylum, refuge. 10. (Met.) Divinity of the father; used of spiritual things. 11. Cavity of a wound. 12. Hell, purgatory; pit. 13. (Naút.) Curvature of a sail. *Seno todo ó total,* Total sine or radius.

Senogíl, *sm.* V. *Cenogil.*

Sensación, *sf.* Sensation.

Sensáto, ta, *a.* Sensible, judicious, prudent.

Sensibilidád, *sf.* Sensibility, quickness of perception; sensibleness.

Sensíble, *a.* 1. Sensible, perceptible by the senses. 2. Sensible, having the power of perceiving by the senses. 3. Perceived by the mind. 4. Causing grief, anguish, or pain. 5. Easily moved or affected.

Sensibleménte, *ad.* Sensibly, perceptible by the senses, with grief or pain.

Sensitíva, *sf.* (Bot.) Sensitive plant; so denominated from its remarkable property of receding from the touch. Mimosa sensitiva *L.*

Sensitívo, va, *a.* Sensitive, having sense or perception; sensual; sensible.

Sensório, *sm.* Sensorium or sensory, the part where the senses transmit their perceptions to the mind; organ of sensation.

Sensório, ria, *a.* Belonging to the sensorium.

Sensuál, *a.* 1. Sensitive, having sense or perception. 2. Sensual, devoted to sense; lewd; luxurious. 3. Belonging to the carnal appetites.

Sensualidád, *sf.* Sensuality, addiction to corporeal pleasures.

Sensualménte, *ad.* Sensually.

Sentáda, *sf.* Stone put in its proper place. V. *Asentada.*

Sentadíllas (A'), *ad.* With the legs on one side, in contradistinction to astride; applied to persons riding on horseback with both legs on one side.

Sentádo, da, *a.* Sedate, judicious, grave, prudent. *Pulso sentado,* A steady pulse.

Sentamiénto, *sm.* (Arq.) V. *Asiento.*

Sentár, *va.* 1. To fit, to set up, to establish. *Sentar el real,* To establish one's self in any place. V. *Asentar.* To smooth or press down the seams of clothes, as tailors, with an iron, called *a goose.* *Sentar las costuras,* (Met.) To chastize with blows, to reprehend or accuse. 3. To please, to be agreeable. *No le sentó bien la conversacion,* The conversation did not please him.—*vr.* 1. To sink, to subside. V. *Asentarse.* 2. To sit down, to squat on one's hams; (Joc.) To fall plump upon one's breech. 3. To occupy the seat which belongs to one's place or employment; to seat one's self in any office or dignity. *Sentarse los paxaros sobre una rama,* To perch upon a branch; applied to birds.

Senténcia, *sf.* 1. Sentence, the judicial decision or determination of a suit at law. 2. Opinion, persuasion of the mind. 3. A maxim, an opinion generally moral. *Decir sentencias á alguno,* To scold, to abuse one.

Sentenciár, *va.* 1. To sentence, to pass judgment; to condemn. 2. To give or express one's opinion. 3. To determine, to decide. *Estar á juzgado y sentenciado,* (For.) To be obliged to hear and submit to the sentence pronounced.

Sentenciário, *sm.* Collection of sentences.

Sentención, *sf.* A severe rigorous sentence.

Sentenciosaménte, *ad.* Sententiously.

Sentencióso, sa, *a.* Sententious, abounding with short sentences, axioms, and maxims.

Sentenzuéla, *sf. dim.* Slight sentence. [bles.

Senticár, *sm.* A place full of briers and bram-

Sentidaménte, *ad.* Feelingly, in a painful manner.

Sentído, da, *a.* Sensible, feeling, expressive of sensibility or sentiment; putrifying; split, cloven, relaxed. *Darse por sentido,* To show resentment.

Sentído, *sm.* 1. Sense, the power or faculty of perceiving objects; any one of the five senses. 2. Sense, understanding, reason. 3. Acceptation, signification, import. 4. Wrinkles of persons, represented in painting or sculpture. *Sentido comun,* Common sense.

Sentimentál, *a.* Sentimental, affecting, pathetic.

Sentimiénto, *sm.* 1. Perception, the act of perceiving objects by the senses. 2. Feeling, sensation. 3. Grief, pain. 4. Chink or opening in a wall. 5. Resentment, deep sense of injury. 6. Judgment, opinion, sentiment.

Sentína, *sf.* 1. (Naút.) Well, a place in the ship's hold, close to the keel, which encloses the pumps. 2. Sink, drain, any place where corruption is gathered; place of iniquity.

Sentír, *va.* 1. To feel, to perceive by the senses. 2. To hear, to perceive by the sense of hearing. *Sin sentir,* Without being seen, felt, or known. 3. To endure, to suffer. 4. To grieve, to regret. 5. To judge, to form an opinion. 6. To foresee, to foreknow. 7. To taste. 8. To accommodate the action to the expression, to exhibit a suitable feeling.—*vr.* 1. To be moved, to be affected, to complain. 2. To get a crack or flaw; applied to a glass, bell, or other similar thing. 3. To be in a ruinous state. 4. To be sensible of, to feel pain in any part of the body; to acknowledge the obligation or necessity. 5. To resent. 6. (Naút.) To spring; applied to a yard or mast. *Se sentio nuestro palo mayor*, (Naút.) Our main-mast sprung.—*sm.* Feeling, opinion, judgment. V. *Sentimiento.*

Séña, *sf.* 1. Sign, mark, token. V. *Señal.* 2. (Mil.) Password, watchword. 3. (Ant.) Standard, banner, colours. *Por mas señas*, As a stronger proof of it.

Señál, *sm.* 1. Sign, mark, token. 2. Landmark, a stone or post set up to mark a boundary. 3. Sign, indication, symptom. 4. Vestige, stump, impression; scar. 5. Representation, image. 6. Earnest, handsel, pledge. 7. (Mil.) Standard, banner. 8. Prodigy, any thing extraordinary prognosticating some event. 9. Signal. *Señales de incomodidad*, (Naút.) Signals of distress. *En señal*, In proof of.

Señaladaménte, *ad.* Especially; remarkably.

Señaladamiénte y Señaladamiéntre, *ad.* (Ant.) Signally.

Señaládo, da, *a.* Famous, celebrated, noble.

Señalamiénto, *sm.* Assignation, the act of determining or appointing a certain time or place.

Señalár, *va.* 1. To stamp, to mark. 2. To sign decrees or despatches. 3. To point out, to make known. 4. To speak positively, to say expressly; to name; to determine. 5. To mark with a wound, especially in the face. 6. To make signals; to indicate. *Señalar con el dedo*, To point with the finger.—*vr.* 1. To distinguish one's self, to excel. 2. To mark the game at piquet.

Señaléja, *sf.* A little sign or mark.

Señaléro, *sm.* He who formerly bore the royal ensign; king's ensign.

Señár, *va.* (Arag.) To make signs.

Señéra, *sf.* Ancient signal or pendant.

Señeraménte, *ad.* Singularly, particularly.

Señéro, ra, *a.* Making signs or signals; solitary.

Señolear, *vn.* To catch birds with a lure.

Señór, ra, *s.* 1. Lord, master or owner of a thing; lady, mistress. 2. Sir, a title given to an equal or inferior; madam, an equivalent title to women. 3. God, the lord and master of all things, sacrament of the Eucharist. 4. Master; governor; father-in-law, mother-in-law. *Señor ó Señora mayor*, Aged man or woman. *Señora*, The Virgin Mary, mistress of a house or school.

Señoráge, *sm.* Seigniorage. V. *Señoreage.*

Señorázo, za, *s. aum.* One of feigned nobility; used ironically.

Señorcíco, ca; llo, lla; to, ta, *s. dim.* of *Señor, ra*, Little lord or lady.

Señoreáge, *sm.* 1. Seigniorage, acknowledgment of power. 2. Duty belonging to the king for the coining of money.

Señoreánte, *pa.* Domineerer.

Señoreár, *va.* 1. To master, to domineer, to lord, to rule despotically. 2. To excel, to occupy a higher station. 3. To treat another repeatedly with the title of lord. 4. To govern one's passions.—*vr.* To affect a peculiar gravity in one's deportment; to assume an air of importance.

Señoría, *sf.* 1. Lordship, a title given to persons of rank and distinction. V. *Señorío.* 2. Person to whom this title is given. 3. Government of any particular state; senate; prince.

Señoríl, *a.* Lordly, belonging to a lord.

Señorilménte, *ad.* Nobly, grandly, majestically.

Señorío, *sm.* 1. Seigniory, dominion, command. 2. Imperiousness, arrogance of command. 3. Manor or territory belonging to a lord. 4. Gravity or stateliness of deportment. 5. Freedom and self-control in action.

Señoríssimo, ma, *a. sup.* Most noble lord or lady; often used ironically. *Señorísima*, Mistress, a woman of easy virtue.

Señoríto, ta; co, ca, *s.* Master, miss; a title of honour given to young gentlemen or ladies. *Señorito*, Lordling, one who assumes an air of dignity and importance.

Señorón, na, *s.* Great seignior or lady.

Señuélo, *sm.* Lure, enticement; attraction.

Séo, *sf.* (Arag.) Cathedral church.

Seór, *sm.* Lord, sir. V. *Señor.*

Sepanquántos, *sm.* Box on the ear, slap on the face.

Separación, *sf.* Separation, the act of separating or disjoining.

Separáble, *a.* Separable.

Separadaménte, *ad.* Separately, severally.

Separadór, ra, *s.* Separater, divider.

Separánte, *pa.* Separating.

Separár, *va.* 1. To separate, to part, to divide; to divorce. 2. To anatomize, to dissect in order to show or study the structure of animal bodies.—*vr.* To withdraw, to drop all communication and intercourse.

Separatívo, va; y Separatório, ria, *a.* That which separates.

Sepedón, *sm.* A kind of serpent.

Sepelír, *va.* To bury, to inter. V. *Sepultar.*

Sépia, *sf.* (Ict.) Cuttle-fish. V. *Xibia.*

Septenário, *sm.* Septenary, a number composed of seven units; space of seven days.

Septénio, *sm.* Space of seven years.

Septentrión, *sm.* Septentrion, the north, that part of the sphere which extends from the equator to the arctic pole; north-wind.

Septentrionál, *a.* Septentrional, northern.

Séptico, ca, *a.* Septic, putrefying.

Septiémbre, *sm.* September.

Séptima, *sf.* Sequence of seven cards, in the game of piquet.

Séptimo, ma, *a.* Seventh, the ordinal number of seven, one of the seven parts into which a whole is divided.

Septuagenário, ria, *a.* Septuagenary, seventy years old.

Septuagésima, *sf.* The third Sunday before the first Sunday in Lent.

Septuagésimo, ma, *a.* Seventieth, the ordinal number of seventy.

Septúnx, *sm.* 1. Coin weighing seven ounces. 2. Measure of nine inches and one-third.

Séptuplo, pla, *a.* Septuple, seven times as much.

Sepulcrál, *a.* Sepulchral, belonging to a grave.

Sepúlcro, *sm.* 1. Sepulchre, grave, tomb. 2. A small chest in which the sacred host is preserved in Roman Catholic churches. 3. (Met.) An unhealthy country.

Sepultación, *sf.* Sepulture; interment.

Sepultadór, *sm.* Burier, grave-digger.
Sepultár, *va.* 1. To bury, to inter. 2. To hide, to conceal
Sepultúra, *sf.* 1. Sepulture, interment. 2. Tomb, grave.
Sepulturéro, *sm.* Grave-digger.
Sequáz, *a.* Sequacious, ductile, pliant; following the opinions of others.
Sequedád, *sf.* 1. Aridity, dryness, want of moisture. 2. Barrenness, sterility, scarcity of provisions in a country. 3. Asperity of intercourse, sourness of temper; dryness of style. 4. Want of devotion and fervour in spiritual matters.
Sequedál ó Sequerál, *sm.* A dry barren soil.
Seqüéla, *sf.* 1. Sequel, continuation. 2. Sequence, the act of following a party or doctrine. 3. Consequence, induction.
Seqüéncia, *sf.* A sequence in prose or verse said in mass after the epistles.
Sequéro, *sm.* Dry arable ground irrigated. *De sequero*, Adry, arid.
Sequeróso, sa, *a.* Dry, wanting moisture.
Seqüestración, *sf.* Sequestration.
Seqüestradór, *sm.* Sequestrator, he who sequesters.
Seqüestrár, *va.* To sequester, to sequestrate.
Seqüestrário, ria, *a.* Belonging to sequestration.
Seqüéstro, *sm.* 1. Sequestration; deprivation of the use and profits of a possession; the person or property sequestered. 2. Arbitrator, umpire. *Depositario de un seqüestro*, Garnishee, he in whose hands money is attached.
Sequéte, *sm.* 1. Piece of hard, dry bread. 2. Harshness and asperity of address or intercourse. 3. A violent shock.
Sequía, *sf.* Dryness; thirst; drought.
Sequíllo, *sm.* Biscuit made of flour and sugar.
Sequío, *sm.* Dry arable ground not irrigated.
Séquito, *sm.* 1. Retinue, suite. 2. Popularity, public applause.
Sequízo, za, *a.* Dry; applied to fruits and other eatables, that are not juicy.
Ser, *vn.* 1. To be; an auxiliary verb, by which the passive is formed. 2. To be in some place or situation; to be in existence. 3. To be worth. *A' como es ese caballo?* What is the price of that horse? 4. To be born in a place; to originate in. *Cervantes es de Alcala*, Cervantes is a native of Alcala. 5. To affirm or deny. *Sea lo que fuere*, Be that as it may. *Soy con vd.* I will attend you presently. *En ser*, In being, in existence. 6. To belong to, to pertain. 7. To serve, to contribute to any thing. 8. To occur, to happen.—*sm.* Being, essence, nature; value; point or burthen of a piece.
Séra, *sf.* A large pannier or basket.
Serádo, *sm.* A parcel of panniers or baskets.
Seráfico, ca, *a.* Seraphic, angelic; applied to St. Francis and his religionists. *Hacer la seráfica*, (Fam.) To play the angel to effect some purpose.
Serafín, *sm.* 1. Seraph, angel. 2. An extreme beauty. 3. St. Francis of Assis.
Serafína, *sf.* A sort of swanskin, resembling a fine baize.
Serágos, *sm.* Panniers or baskets of charcoal.
Seráo, *sm.* (Ant.) V. *Sarao*.
Serancolín, *sm.* A sort of marble, found in the Pyrenees.
Serapíno, *sm.* A sort of gum, obtained by incision from the fennel-giant.
Serása, *sf.* Chints, a fine cotton cloth.
Serasquiér, *sm.* A Turkish general.
Sérba, *sf.* A kind of wild pear, the fruit of the service-tree.
Serbál y Sérbo, *sm.* (Bot.) Service-tree. Sorbus L.
Serenár, *va.* 1. To put water into the night air, to cool. 2. To quiet, to pacify, to quell disturbances.
Serenaménte, *ad.* Serenely.
Serenár, *vn.* 1. To clear up, to grow fair; to become serene; applied to the weather. 2. To settle, to grow clear; applied to liquors. 3. To pacify, to tranquillize, to moderate; to be serene.
Serenáta, *sf.* Serenade, concert, night-music.
Serenéro, *sm.* Nightrail, a loose cover which ladies throw over the head at night.
Serení, *sm.* Small boat used for greater despatch.
Serenidád, *sf.* 1. Serenity, the clearness of mild and temperate weather. 2. Serene highness, a title of honour given to princes. 3. Meekness, mildness, easiness of temper.
Serenísimo, ma, *a. sup.* Most serene, honorary titles of princes or kings' children.
Seréno, *sm.* 1. Evening dew, dew that wets the ground in the night. 2. Night-watch, watchman.—**na**, *a.* 1. Serene, clear, free from clouds. 2. Calm, quiet, unruffled. *Al sereno*, In the night-air, in the open air, exposed to the evening dew.
Sérgas, *sf. pl.* Exploits, achievements, adventures.
Seriaménte, *ad.* Seriously.
Sérico, ca, *a.* Silken, made of silk.
Série, *sf.* Series, a regular succession of things.
Seriedád, *sf.* 1. Seriousness, gravity. 2. Sternness of mien, truculence of aspect, rudeness of address. 3. Simplicity, plainness, sincerity.
Seríjo ó Seríllo, *sm.* A small basket made of palm-leaves.
Sério, ria, *a.* 1. Serious, grave, dignified. 2. Grand, majestic; solemn; important. 3. Uncouth, rude, severe. 4. Plain, true, sincere.
Sermocinál, *a.* Oratorical, relating to a public speech or harangue.
Sermón, *sm.* (Ant.) 1. Language, tongue, idiom. 2. Sermon, a discourse of instruction pronounced by a divine for the edification of the people. 3. Censure, reprehension.
Sermonário, ria, *a.* Relating to a sermon.
Sermonário, *sm.* 1. Collection of sermons. 2. Author, who has published sermons, or a divine who preaches or pronounces sermons.
Sermoncíco, llo, to, *sm. dim.* Short address, brief advice.
Sermoneár, *va.* To lecture, to censure, to reprimand, to reprehend frequently; to sermonize.
Sermonización, *sf.* The act of speaking in public; colloquy, conversation.
Sérna, *sf.* (Ant.) Cultivated field.
Serója y Serójo, *s.* A withered leaf, fallen from a tree. *Serójas*, Small trees which are left on a

piece of woodland, after the large trees have been cut down.

Serón, *sm.* Frail, pannier, seron. *Seron de almendras*, A seron of almonds. *Seron caminero*, Horse pannier.

Seronéro, *sm.* Basket or pannier-maker.

Serosidád, *sf.* Serosity, state of thin or watery blood, having much serum.

Seróso, sa, *a.* Serous, thin, watery.

Sérpa, *sf.* Provine, a long shoot of vine planted in the ground in order to raise another stock.

Serpeár, *vn.* To wind and turn like a serpent, to move in undulations, to crawl, to creep.

Serpentária, *sf.* (Bot.) Snake-root. Aristolochia serpentaria *L.*

Serpentário, *sm.* A northern constellation.

Serpenteár, *vn.* To advance or move like a serpent.

Serpenticída, *s. com.* Serpent-killer.

Serpentígero, ra, *a.* (Poét.) Bearing serpents.

Serpentín, *sm.* 1. (Min.) Serpentine, a curiously speckled green stone resembling the serpent's skin. 2. Cock of a gun or musket-lock. 3. Worm used for distilling liquors. 4. Serpent, a musical instrument, serving as a bass to the cornet. 5. Ancient piece of ordnance.

Serpentína, *sf.* 1. Cock of a gun-lock. 2. Culverin; missile weapon. 3. Green marble.

Serpentinaménte, *ad.* In a serpentine manner.

Serpentíno, na, *a.* Serpentine, winding like a serpent; resembling a serpent; belonging to the oil of serpents; a slanderous tongue.

Serpentón, *sm.* 1. A large serpent. 2. Serpent, a musical instrument. V. *Serpentin.*

Serpezuéla, *sf. dim.* of *sierpe*, Little spiteful ugly woman. [vine-stock.

Serpía, *sf.* Gummy, or viscous matter of a

Serpiénte, *s.* 1. Serpent. *Serpiente de campanilla ó de cascabel*, Rattle-snake. 2. Serpent, devil, Satan.

Serpígo, *sm.* (Cir.) Tetter, ring-worm.

Sérpol, *sm.* (Bot.) Thyme. Thymus serpyllum *L.* [Biserrula *L.*

Serradílla, *sf.* (Bot.) Bastard hatchet vetch.

Serradízo, za, *a.* Fit to be sawed; applied to timber.

Serrádo, da, *a.* Dentated, toothed like a saw.

Serradór, *sm.* Sawer or sawyer. V. *Aserrador.*

Serradúras, *sf. pl.* Sawdust. V. *Aserraduras.*

Serrállo, *sm.* Seraglio, the palace of the Grand Signior; place of obscenity.

Serranía, *sf.* Ridge of mountains, a mountainous country.

Serraniégo, ga, *a.* V. *Serrano.*

Serraníl, *sm.* Kind of knife.

Serráno, na, *a.* Mountaineer, highlander, inhabiting mountains.

Serrár, *va.* To saw. V. *Aserrar.*

Serráto, ta, *a.* (Anat.) Denticulated, serrated.

Serretas, *sf. pl.* (Naút.) Pieces of tarred canvass for various uses on board of ships.

Serrezuéla, *sf.* A small saw.

Serrijón, *sm.* Short chain of mountains.

Serrín, *sm.* Sawdust. V. *Aserraduras.*

Serríno, na, *a.* 1. Belonging to chains of mountains. 2. Applied to a quick, irregular pulse.

Serrúcho, *sm.* Hand-saw with a small handle. *Serrucho braguero*, Pit-saw, a large two-handed saw.

Servadór, *sm.* Preserver, he that guards or defends; applied by poets to Jupiter.

Serváto, *sm.* (Bot.) Sulphur-wort or hog's fennel. Peucedanum alpestre *L.*

Serventésio, *sm.* (Poét.) Quartetto, like the first four verses of an octave.

Servíble, *a.* Fit for service. [dues.

Serviciadór, *sm.* Collector of the sheep-walk

Serviciál, *a.* Obsequious, diligent.—*sm.* Clyster. [bly.

Servicialménte, *ad.* Obsequiously, serviceably.

Serviciár, *va.* To collect the sheep-walk dues, donations to the state, &c.

Servício, *sm.* 1. Service, the act of serving; the state of a servant. 2. Favour, kind office; divine service. 3. Sum of money voluntarily offered to the king. 4. Utility, benefit, advantage. 5. Close-stool, privy-chair. 6. Cover, course. *Servicio de mesa*, Service for the table. 7. Personal service or residence of beneficed clergy. 8. Service to kings in war.

Servidéro, ra, *a.* 1. Fit for service. 2. Requiring personal attendance.

Servído, da, *a.* 1. Served, pleased. *Donde Dios es servido*, Wherever God pleases. *Ser servido*, To please, to deign to grant. *Siendo Dios servido*, Please God. 2. Second-hand, used.

Servidór, ra, *s.* 1. Servant, waiter. 2. One who pays courtship to a lady; one who politely tenders his services to another. *Servidor de vd.* Your servant. 3. Pan of a close-stool. *Servidóra*, Maid, female servant; term of courtesy used by women.

Servidúmbre, *sf.* 1. Attendance, servitude; whole establishment of servants. 2. Slavery, state of a slave. 3. Dressing-chest, travelling-case; domestic utensils. 4. Privy, common-sewer. 5. Mighty or inevitable obligation to do any thing. 6. (For.) Right which one has over another person or thing, as the liberty of passing through a house or garden. 7. Subjection of the passions.

Serviénte, *pa.* y *s.* Servant, domestic.

Servíl, *a.* 1. Servile, relative or peculiar to servants. 2. Low, mean, abject. [maids.

Servílla, *sf.* A kind of pumps worn by servant

Servilléta, *sf.* Napkin, cloths used at table to wipe the hands and mouth. *Doblar la servilleta*, (Fam.) To die.

Servilletéro, ra, *a.* Relating to table linen.

Servilménte, *ad.* In a mean and slavish manner; basely; indecently.

Serviòla, *sf.* (Naút.) Catheads, two short beams which project over the ship's bow on both sides of the bowsprit.

Servír, *va.* 1. To serve, to perform menial services. *Servir de mayordomo*, To serve as butler. 2. To do a favour or kind office. 3. To hold an employment, to occupy a public station. 4. To court a lady. 5. To worship the Supreme Being. 6. To perform another's functions; to act as a substitute. 7. To pay voluntarily some money to the king or government. 8. To wait at table. 9. To heat the oven. 10. To dress victuals for the table. *Para servir á vd.* At your service.—*vn.* 1. To be in the service of another, to be subject to another. 2. To correspond, to agree. 3. To serve, to answer the purpose; to be useful; to be a soldier. 4. To be employed at any thing by another's orders.—*vr.* 1. To deign, to vouchsafe, to condescend, to please. *Sírvase vd. venir*, Please to come. 2. To make use of; to employ for some purpose.

Servítas ó Siérvos de María, *s.* Religious order dedicated to the service of the blessed Virgin.

Servitór, *sm.* (Fam.) Servant. V. *Servidor.*

Sesáda, *sf.* Fried brains. [*c* and *i* at *ss.*

Seseár, *vn.* To lisp, to pronounce the *c* before

Seséli, *sm.* (Bot.) Wild spignel. Seseli *L.*

Sesén, *sf.* A copper coin in *Arragon* of six maravedis.

Seséntа, *sm.* Sixty, figure of 60.—*a.* Sixtieth.

Sesentón, na, *s.* One turned of sixty.

Seséra, *sf.* Brain-pan, the part of the skull which contains the brain.

Sésga, *sf.* Goar or goaring. V. *Nesga.*

Sesgadaménte, *ad.* V. *Sesgamente.*

Sesgadúra, *sf.* Slope, the act of sloping.

Sesgaménte, *ad.* Obliquely, slopingly; mildly.

Sesgár, *va.* To slope, to cut slantwise, to take or give an oblique direction.

Sésgo, *sm.* 1. Slope, obliqueness, oblique direction. 2. Mean, medium.

Sésgo, ga, *a.* 1. Sloped, oblique, turned or twisted obliquely. 2. Serene, tranquil, unruffled. 3. Severe of aspect, grave, uncouth. *Al sesgo*, Slopingly, obliquely.

Sesíllos, *sm. pl. dim.* of *seso*, Little brains.

Sesión, *sf.* 1. Session, sitting, meeting of a council or congress. 2. Conference, consultation.

Sésma, *sm.* The sixth part of a yard or any other thing; division of territory.

Sesméro, *sm.* Manager or steward of the affairs of a district or province.

Sésmo, *sm.* 1. District or tract of country under the government of a steward. 2. Division. V. *Linde.* 3. (Ant.) Six.

Séso, *sm.* 1. Brain, the soft whitish substance which is enclosed in the skull; generally used in the plural. 2. Understanding, prudence, wisdom. 3. Stone put under a pot to keep it steady on the fire. 4. (Ant.) Sense, meaning, judgment.

Sésqui, *sm.* (Lat.) Used in composition, and implying the whole and one half, or whatever part it is joined with, more.

Sesquiáltero, ra, *a.* One and a half.

Sesquimódio, *sm.* A bucket and a half.

Sesquipedál, *a.* A foot and a half in length.

Sesquitércio, cia, *a.* Sesquitertian, having one and a third, having the ratio of 4 to 3.

Sesteadéro Sestéro y Sestíl, *sm.* A proper place for taking a nap after dinner; resting place for cattle.

Sesteár, *vn.* To take a nap or rest after dinner; to sleep from 1 to 3 o'clock P. M.

Sesudaménte, *ad.* Maturely, wisely, prudently.

Sesúdo, da, *a.* Judicious, discreet, prudent.

Séta, *sf.* 1. Bristle, the stiff hair of swine. 2. (Bot.) Mushroom. Fungus *L.* 3. Blubberlip. V. *Geta.* 4. Snuff of a candle. 5. Sect. V. *Secta.*

Séte, *sm.* Mint or office where money is struck with a die.

Setecièntos, tas, *a.* Seven hundred.

Seténa, *sf.* Seventh, the ordinal number, sevenfold. *Setenas*, Sevenfold.

Setenário, ria, *a.* Septenary.

Seténo, na, *a.* Seventh. V. *Séptimo.*

Seténta, *a.* Seventy, seven times ten.

Setentón, na, *a.* Turned of seventy.

Setéro, ra, *a.* Bristly, hairy.

Sétimo, ma, *a.* Seventh.

Séto, *sm.* Fence, defence, enclosure.

Séudo, *sm.* Pseudo, false.

Seudónimo, *a.* Fictitious; assumed name under which one publishes any work.

Severaménte, *ad.* Severely.

Severidád, *sf.* 1. Severity, rigour, harshness, austerity; gravity. 2. Punctuality, exactness.

Severizárse, *vr.* To become serious or grave.

Sevéro, ra, *a.* 1. Severe, rigorous. 2. Grave, serious. 3. Punctual, exact.

Sevícia, *sf.* Fierceness, cruelty.

Sexagenário, ria, *a.* Sixty years old.

Sexagésima, *sf.* Second Sunday before Lent.

Sexagésimo, ma, *a.* Sixtieth.

Sexagonál, *a.* Hexagonal.

Sexángulo, la, *a.* Sexangular.—*sm.* Sexangle.

Sexcúns ó Sexcúncia, *sf.* Coin weighing an ounce and a half.

Sexénio, *sm.* Space of six years.

Séxma, *sf.* Coin, worth a real and 5 maravedis.

Sexméro, *sm.* V. *Sesmero.*

Séxô, *sm.* 1. Sex, the property by which any animal is either male or female. 2. Womankind, by way of emphasis.

Séxta, *sf.* 1. One of the hours in which the Hebrews and Romans divided the artificial day, and including three of the hours now used. 2. A sequence of six cards at the game of piquet. 3. Sixth, one of the minor canonical hours after tierce.

Sextánte, *sm.* Coin weighing two ounces.

Sextário, *sm.* Ancient measure.

Sextíl, *a.* (Astro.) Sextile.—*sm.* (Ant.) August.

Sextílla, *sf.* A Spanish metrical composition of six feet.

Sextína, *sf.* A kind of Spanish poetry in which every 6th verse rhymes.

Séxto, ta, *a.* Sixth, the ordinal number of six.

Séxto, *sm.* Book containing canonical decrees.

Sextúla, *sf.* Coin worth one real and five maravedis.

Sevér, *va.* (Ant.) V. *Ser.*

Sezéno, sa, *a.* Seventeenth.

Sí, *ad.* 1. Yes, yea, without doubt; indeed. 2. It is often used ironically, and is then a negation or nay.—*conj.* If, although; in case that, provided that, unless, when. *Si bien*, Although. V. *Aunque. Si acaso ó por si acaso*, If by chance. *Un sí es no es*, An expression indicating the paucity, littleness, or nihility of any thing, which can scarcely be distinguished or perceived by the senses; ever so little.—*pron.* Himself. *De por sí*, Apart, separately. *De sí*, Spontaneously.—*sm.* 1. Assent or consent to any thing. 2. Note in the gamut.

Siampán, *sm.* Dye-stuff produced in the province of this name.

Sibíl, *sm.* A small cellar under ground, where wine, water, or other things are kept fresh.

Sibíla, *sf.* 1. Prophetess; sibyl. 2. (Fam.) A tall, portly, good looking woman. *Sibila, doctora ó doncella jamona,* (Joc.) Old maid who pretends to be very learned and discreet.
Sibilánte, *a.* (Poét.) Sibilant, hissing.
Sibilíno, na, *a.* Sibyline.
Sicamór, *sm.* (Bot.) V. *Arbol de amor.*
Síclo, *sm.* Shekel, an ancient Jewish coin, in value about two shillings and sixpence.
Sicofánta, *sm.* Sycophant, a flatterer, a parasite.
Sicología, *sf.* Psychology, discourse of the soul.
Sicómoro, *sm.* (Bot.) Sycamore, the mulberry-leaved fig-tree. Ficus sycomorus *L.*
Sideritis, *sf.* Siderites, a mineral. *Sederitis ó Sideritide,* (Bot.) Iron-wort. Sideritis *L.*
Sidéreo, rea, *a.* Sidereal, siderean, starry.
Sídra, *sf.* Cider, a liquor made of apple juice.
Siéga, *sf.* Harvest, reaping-time; fruits gathered.
Siémbra, *sf.* 1. Seed-time, the proper season for sowing. 2. Corn-field, a piece of ground sown with corn.
Siémpre, *ad.* Always, at all times. *Siémpre jamás,* For ever and ever. *Siempre enxúta,* Blue daisy. Globularia vulgaris *L.*
Siempreviva, *sf.* (Bot.) House-leek. Sempervivum *L.*
Sién, *sf.* Temple, the upper part of the side of the head.
Siérpe, *sf.* 1. Serpent. V. *Serpiente.* 2. Very ugly woman. 3. Any thing which moves by undulation in a serpentine shape. 4. A peevish, fretful person.
Sierpecílla, *sf.* A small serpent.
Siérra, *sf.* 1. Saw, a dentated instrument with which wood, stone, and metals are cut. 2. Ridge of mountains and craggy rocks. 3. Waves rising mountain-high in a storm. 4. (Ict.) Sawfish. Pristis *L.* *Sierra de agua,* Saw-mill.
Sierrecilla, *sf.* A small saw.
Siérvo, va, *s.* 1. Serf, slave, servant. 2. Servant by courtesy.
Siéso, *sm.* Fundament, anus.
Siésta, *sf.* 1. The hottest part of the day; the time for taking a nap after dinner; generally from 1 to 3 o'clock. 2. Sleep taken after dinner. 3. Afternoon-music in churches.
Siéte, *a.* 1. Seven. 2. V. *Septimo.*—*sm.* 1. Seven, the character or cipher 7. 2. Card with seven figures.
Sietedurmiéntes, *sm. pl.* Seven sleepers, great sleepers.
Siéte en Ráma, *sf.* (Bot.) V. *Tormentilla.*
Sietelevár, *sm.* In the game of bank, the third chance by which seven times the stake is won.
Sietemesíno, na, *a.* Born seven months after the conception.
Sieteñál, *a.* Seven years old, septennial.
Sifác, *sm.* (Anat.) V. *Peritoneo.*
Sifón, *sm.* Syphon, a bent tube.
Sigilación, *sf.* Impression, mark.
Sigiládo, da, *a.* Branded, marked with a crime.
Sigilár, *va.* 1. To keep any thing secret. 2. To seal.
Sigílo, *sm.* 1. Seal. V. *Sello.* 2. Secret. *Sigilo sacramental,* Inviolable secrecy which confessors should keep respecting what is told them in confession.
Sigilosaménte, *ad.* Silently, secretly.
Sigilóso, sa, *a.* Silent, reserved; keeping a secret.
Síglo, *sm.* 1. Century, the space of a hundred years. 2. Age, duration of any thing. 3. A very long time. *Un siglo ha que no te veo,* I have not seen you this age. 4. Worldly intercourse, the concerns of this life; the world. *Buen siglo,* Eternal bliss, eternal life. *Por el siglo de mi madre ó de todos mis pasados,* By the life of my fathers; a familiar oath generally accompanied with a menace. *Por ó en los siglos de los siglos,* For ever and ever.
Signáculo, *sm.* Seal, signet.
Signár, *va.* To sign, to mark with a signet.—*vr.* To make the sign of the cross.
Signatúra, *sf.* Sign, mark; signature in printing; a Roman tribunal.
Signífero, ra, *a.* Carrying a mark or sign.
Signífero, *sm.* Standard-bearer.
Significación, *sf.* Signification, meaning.
Significádo, *sm.* Object signified by means or words.
Significadór, ra, *s.* One who signifies.
Significánte, *a.* Significant, expressive.
Significanteménte, *ad.* V. *Significativaménte.*
Significár, *va.* 1. To signify, to denote. 2. To declare, to make known. 3. To import, to be worth.
Significativaménte, *ad.* Significatively.
Significatívo, va, *a.* Significative.
Sígno, *sm.* 1. Sign, mark. 2. Fate, destiny. 3. Benediction with the sign of the cross. 4 Notarial signet or flourish, which the notaries in Spain add to their signatures. 5. (Astr.) Sign of the zodiac. 6. Type, emblem, that which represents any thing distinct from itself. *Signo por costumbre,* Sign established by usage, as a branch, at the door of a liquor-seller.
Siguidór, ra, *s.* V. *Seguidor.*
Siguiénte, *a.* Following, successive.
Síl, *sm.* A kind of red ochre used by painters.
Sílaba, *sf.* 1. Syllable. 2. (Mús.) Two or three sounds which correspond with every letter of the gamut. 3. Metrical composition.
Silabár, *va.* To syllable, to form syllables.
Silabário, *sm.* A book which contains and explains syllables.
Silábico, ca, *a.* Syllabical.
Silbadór, ra, *s.* Whistler, one that whistles.
Silbár, *vn.* 1. To whistle. 2. To whiz, to make a hissing noise as a musket-ball.—*va.* To hiss, to express disapprobation.
Silbáto, *sm.* Whistle, a small wind instrument.
Silbído, *sm.* Whistle. *Silbido de oidos,* Whizzing or humming in the ear.
Sílbo y Silbído, *sm.* Whistle, hiss.
Silbóso, sa, *a.* (Poét.) Whistling, hissing.
Silenciário, *sm.* Officer appointed to take care that silence be observed in a place or assembly; silent place.
Silenciário, ria; y Silenciéro, ra, *a.* Observing a profound silence.
Siléncio, *sm.* 1. Silence, a voluntary restraint of speech; habitual taciturnity; secrecy. 2. State of holding peace. 3. Reservedness, prudence. 4. Stillness, repose.—*interj.* Silence! an authoritative restraint of speech.

Silenciosaménte, *ad.* Silently, softly, gently.
Silencióso, sa, *a.* Silent; lonely, solitary.
Siléno, *sm.* Silenus, a demigod.
Siléр Montáno, *sm.* (Bot.) Lovage.
Silería, *sf.* Place where subterraneous granaries are made.
Siléro, *sm.* A subterraneous granary where wheat is kept.
Sílfo, *sm.* Sylph.
Silguerillo, *sm.* (Orn.) A little linnet.
Silguéro, *sm.* (Orn.) Linnet. V. *Xilguero.*
Silíbo, *sm.* (Bot.) Broad-leaved thistle.
Silício, *sm.* A shirt or girdle made of hair; hair-cloth; wire-net made with projecting points and worn as a penance. V. *Cilicio.*
Silígo, *sm.* V. *Neguilla.*
Síliqua, *sf.* 1. Siliqua, a carat, of which six make a scruple. 2. Seed-vessel, husk, pod or shell of such plants as are of the pulse kind.
Sílla, *sf.* 1. Chair, moveable seat. 2. See, the seat of episcopal power; the diocese of a bishop. 3. Saddle, the seat which is put upon the horse for the accommodation of the rider. 4. Seat, any thing on which one may sit. 5. Seat, anus. *Silla de manos*, Sedan-chair. *Silla poltrona*, Arm or elbow-chair; a lazy chair. *Silla de posta*, Post-chaise. *Silla volante*, Gig. *De silla á silla*, Face to face. *Hombre de ámbas ó de todas sillas*, A man of general information; a clever fellow.
Sillár, *sm.* 1. A square hewn stone. 2. Back of a horse where the saddle is placed.
Sillaréjo, *sm.* A small hewn stone.
Silléra, *sf.* Place where sedan-chairs are shut up.
Sillería, *sf.* 1. Seat, set or parcel of chairs. 2. Shop where chairs are made or sold. 3. Stalls about the choir or quire of a church. 4. Building of hewn stone.
Silléro, *sm.* Saddler; chair-maker.
Silléta, *sf.* 1. A small chair. 2. Hollow stone on which chocolate is ground. 3. Close-stool, privy-chair. 4. Side-saddle. V. *Xamugas.*
Silletéro, *sm.* 1. Chairman, one employed in carrying sedan-chairs. 2. Chair-maker, one who makes or sells chairs.
Sillíco, *sm.* Basin of a close-stool.
Sillón, *sm.* 1. (And.) A large arm or elbow-chair. 2. Side-saddle for ladies.
Síro, *sm.* 1. A subterraneous granary where wheat is kept. 2. Any cavern or dark place. 3. A constant drinker of water.
Silogísmo, *sm.* Syllogism.
Silogístico, ca, *a.* Syllogistic.
Silogizár, *va.* To syllogize, to reason, to argue.
Silúro, *sm.* (Ict.) Sheat-fish. Silurus glanis *L.*
Sílva, *sf.* 1. Forest, wood. 2. A kind of Spanish metrical or poetical composition. 3. A miscellany.
Silvános, *sm. pl.* Sylvans.
Silvático, ca, *a.* V. *Selvático.*
Silvéstre, *a.* Wild, uncultivated; rustic, savage.
Silvóso, sa, *a.* V. *Selvoso.*
Síma, *sf.* 1. Deep and dark cavern or cave. 2. Whirlwind, hurricane.
Simádo, da, *a.* (And.) Deep; applied to land.
Simaróuba ó Simarúba, *sf.* (Bot.) Guiana-bark Quassia simaruba *L.*
Simbólico, ca; y Símbolo, la, *a.* 1. Symbolical, representative; expressing by signs. 2. Analogous, having analogy or resemblance.
Simbolización, *sf.* Symbolization.
Simbolizár, *vn.* To symbolize; to resemble.
Símbolo, *sm.* 1. Symbol, mark, sign, device. 2. (Mil.) Watchword. 3. Type, that which comprehends in its figure a representation of something else. 4. Creed, belief, articles of faith.
Simbología, *sf.* (Med.) Treatise on the symptoms of diseases.
Simetría, *sf.* Symmetry, adaptation of parts to each other; proportion; harmony.
Simetricaménte, *ad.* Symmetrically.
Symétrico, ca, *a.* Symmetrical, proportionate.
Símia, *sf.* A female ape. V. *Mona.*
Simiénte, *sf.* Seed; source, origin. V. *Semen.*
Simiénza, *sf.* Seed-time. V. *Sementera.*
Símil, *sm.* 1. Resemblance, similarity. V. *Semejanza.* 2. Simile, comparison, parallel.—*a.* Similar, like. V. *Semejante.*
Similár, *a.* 1. Similar, homogeneous. 2. Resembling, bearing a resemblance.
Similicadéncia, *sf.* V. *Simulcadencia.*
Similidesidéncia, *sf.* (Poét.) Rhetorical figure, in which the verses have only assonants.
Similitúd, *sf.* Similitude, resemblance.
Similitudinariaménte, *ad.* Similarly.
Similitudinário, ria, *a.* Similar, similitudinary.
Similór, *sm.* Pinchbeck, a composition of 5 parts copper to 1 of zinc.
Símio, *sm.* Male ape. V. *Mono.*
Simón, na, *a.* y *s.* Applied to hackney coaches or coachmen in Madrid. *Alquilé un simon para ir á paseo*, I let or hired a coach to go to the public walk.
Simonía, *sf.* Simony, the crime of buying or selling church preferments.
Simoníaco, ca; y Simoniático, ca, *a.* Simoniac or simoniacal, guilty of simony.
Simpár, *a.* Matchless, unequalled.
Simpatía, *sf.* Sympathy, fellow-feeling, mutual sensibility; similarity, congeniality. *Tener simpatia*, To sympathize, to feel with another.
Simpaticaménte, *ad.* Sympathetically. V. *Conformemente.*
Simpático, ca, *a.* Sympathetic, analogous.
Simplázo, za, *s.* A great simpleton; a stupid person.
Símple, *a.* 1. Single, simple, pure; uncompounded; unsigned; unconditional. 2. Silly, foolish. 3. Undesigning, artless. 4. Plain, mild, gentle; ingenuous. 5. Insipid, tasteless. 6. Single, brief; applied to the church services in which there is no repetition whatever. *Simple sacerdote*, Clergyman without dignity, degree, benefice, or ecclesiastical jurisdiction.—*sm.* Simple, an herb or plant which alone serves for medicine.
Simplecíllo, lla; to, ta, *s.* A little simpleton.
Simpleménte, *ad.* Simply, with simplicity and plainness; absolutely.
Simpléza, *sf.* 1. Simpleness, silliness. 2. Rusticity, rudeness. 3. (Ant.) Simplicity, sincerity.
Simplicidád, *sf.* 1. Simplicity, plainness, artlessness. 2. Simpleness, silliness.
Simplicísta, *sm.* Simplist; herbalist.
Simplificár, *va.* To simplify, to make simple

SIMPLÍSIMO, MA, *a.* Extremely silly or foolish.
SIMPLÍSTA, *sm.* Simplist, herbalist.
SIMPLÓN, NA; Y SIMPLONÁZO, ZA, *s.* Great simpleton.
SIMULACIÓN, *sf.* 1. Simulation, the part of hypocrisy, which pretends that to be what it is not. 2. Subterfuge, evasion.
SIMULÁCRO, *sm.* 1. Image representing something venerable; idol. 2. Ghost, phantom.
SIMULADAMÉNTE, *ad.* In a dissembling or hypocritical manner.
SIMULADÓR, RA, *s.* Simulator, dissembler.
SIMULÁR, *va.* To practise simulation; to pretend to be that which it is not.
SIMULCADÉNCIA, *sf.* (Ret.) Figure of rhetoric repeating a consonant in a word forming a cadence.
SIMULCADÉNTE, *a.* Applied to words or sentences having a cadence. [tion.
SIMULTÁD ó SIMULTANEIDÁD, *sf.* Union, junc-
SIMULTANEAMÉNTE, *ad.* Simultaneously.
SIMULTÁNEO, NEA, *a.* Simultaneous, acting together, existing at the same time.
SIN, *prep.* Without, besides. Joined to a verb it is a negative or privative. *Sin embargo*, Notwithstanding, nevertheless. *Sin pies ni cabeza*, Without head or tail, without order.
SINABÁFA, *sf.* Cloth or stuff of the natural colour of wool.
SINAGÓGA, *sf.* Synagogue, an assembly of Jews to worship; the place where the Jews meet to worship.
SINAPÍSMO, *sm.* Sinapism, mustard-poultice.
SINCATEGOREMÁTICO, CA, *a.* Word without signification till joined with another.
SINCÉL, *sm.* Chisel. V. *Cincel.*
SINCELADÓR, RA, *s.* Graver, engraver.
SINCELÁR, *va.* V. *Cincelar.*
SINCERADÓR, RA, *s.* Exculpator, excuser.
SINCERAMÉNTE, *ad.* Sincerely, freely, frankly.
SINCERÁR, *va.* To exculpate, to clear from guilt.
SINCERIDÁD, *sf.* Sincerity; purity of mind.
SINCÉRO, RA, *a.* Sincere, ingenuous, honest; pure.
SINCIPÚCIO, *sm.* Sinciput, front top of the head.
SINCONDRÓSIS, *sf.* (Anat.) Union of two bones by means of a cartilage.
SÍNCOPA, *sf.* 1. Syncope, a contraction of words, by cutting off a part. 2. Division of a note.
SINCOPADAMÉNTE, *ad.* With syncope. [cope.
SINCOPÁL, *sm.* Fever commencing with syn-
SINCOPÁR, *va.* 1. To contract words by cutting off letters or syllables. 2. To abridge.
SÍNCOPE, *sf.* (Med.) Syncope, a fainting fit.
SINCOPIZÁR, ÁRSE, *va.* y *r.* To swoon, to suffer a suspension of thought and sensation, to
SINCRONÍSTA, *s. com.* A contemporary. [faint.
SÍNCRONO, NA, *a.* Synchronous, contemporaneous. [of a guilty conscience.
SINDÉRESIS, *sf.* Remorse, pain of guilt, anguish
SINDICÁDO, *sm.* 1. Tribunal or court appointed to try and punish such crimes as are denounced. 2. Judgment or sentence of the court.
SINDICADÓR, RA, *s.* Informer, prosecutor.
SINDICÁR, *va.* To inform; to lodge an information; to accuse. [dic.
SINDICADÚRA, *sf.* Office and dignity of a syn-
SÍNDICO, *sm.* 1. Syndic; recorder. 2. One whose office is to collect the fines imposed by a court. 3. Depositary of the alms of some religious houses.
SINÉCDOQUE ó SINÉDOQUE, *sf.* (Ret.) Synecdoche, a part for the whole. [hall.
SINÉDRA, *sf.* Seats for the audience in a public
SINÉDRIO, *sm.* V. *Sanedrin.*
SINÉRESIS, *sf.* Synaeresis; a figure, whereby two syllables are united into one.
SINERETÍSMO, *sm.* Conciliation of various religious sects.
SINFÍSIS, *sf.* (Anat.) Union of the bones.
SÍNFITO, *sm.* V. *Consuelda.*
SINFONÍA, *sf.* Symphony, the consonance or concert of several concordant sounds, agreeable to the ear; composition of instrumental music.
SINGLADÚRA, *sf.* (Naút.) A day's run.
SINGLÁR, *va.* (Naút.) To sail daily with a favourable wind on a direct course.
SINGLÓNES, *sm. pl.* (Naút.) Timbers placed over the keel.
SINGULÁR, *a.* 1. Singular, extraordinary; excellent; individual. 2. (Gram.) Singular number. *Cosas singulares*, Strange things.
SINGULARIDÁD, *sf.* Singularity.
SINGULARIZÁR, *va.* To distinguish, to particularise.—*vr.* To distinguish one's self; to be singular.
SINGULARMÉNTE, *ad.* Singularly, in a peculiar manner. [tion.
SINGÚLTO, *sm.* Hiccough, a spasmodic affec-
SINIÉSTRA, *sf.* The left hand. V. *Izquierda.*
SINIESTRAMÉNTE, *ad.* Sinistrously, perversely.
SINIÉSTRO, TRA, *a.* 1. Placed on the left side. 2. Sinistrous, vicious, cross, froward. 3. Unhappy, unlucky, inauspicious. [habit.
SINIÉSTRO, *sm.* Perverseness, depravity, evil
SINIGUÁL, *a.* Unequalled, unparalleled, unrivalled in excellence.
SINJUSTÍCIA, *sf.* Injustice. V. *Injusticia.*
SINNÚMERO, *sm.* A numberless quantity; that which cannot be reduced to a fixed number.
SÍNO, *part. conj.* 1. If not; a conditional particle. *Sino vinieres*, If you do not come. 2. But. *No es blanco, sino negro*, It is not white, but black. 3. Except; besides. 4. Solely, only; in this sense it is preceded by a negative proposition. 5. Otherwise; followed by an interrogation.—*sm.* 1. (Fam.) Fate, destiny. 2. (Met.) V. *Signo.*
SINÓCA, *sf.* Putrid fever.
SINOCÁL, *a.* Applied to a putrid fever.
SINODÁL, *a.* Synodic, synodal; relating to a synod.—*sm.* Examiner of curates and confessors.
SINODÁTICO, *sm.* Pecuniary contribution, paid by the clergy to the bishops.
SINÓDICO, CA, *a.* 1. Synodal, synodical. 2. Synodic, reckoned from one conjunction of the moon with the sun until another.
SÍNODO, *sm.* 1. Synod, an assembly of bishops, and other ecclesiastics to treat on matters of religion. 2. Conjunction of the heavenly bodies. 3. Stipend or charity allowed to missionaries employed in America.
SINÓN, *conj. cond.* (Ant.) V. *Sino.*
SINONÍMIA, *sf.* Synonymy, the repetition of words of the same signification.
SINÓNIMO ó SINÓNOMO, MA, *a.* Synonymous, ex-

pressing the same thing by different words.
SINÓPLE, *s.* (Blas.) Green.
SINÓPSIS, *sf.* Synopsis, compendium, epitome.
SINÓVIA, *sf.* Synovia, the liquor of the joints.
SINRAZÓN, *sf.* Injustice, the act of doing any thing against justice.
SINSABÓR, *sm.* Displeasure, disgust, pain, uneasiness.
SINTÁXIS, *sf.* 1. Syntax, the manner of co-ordinating the parts of a discourse. 2. Co-ordination or arrangement of things among themselves.
SÍNTESIS, *sf.* (Alg.) Synthesis, the act of arranging and joining; opposed to *Analysis*.
SINTÉTICO, CA, *a.* Synthetical.
SÍNTOMA, *sm.* Symptom or preternatural sign or token of a disease.
SINTOMÁTICO, CA, *a.* Symptomatic or symptomatical, relating to symptoms.
SINTOMATOLOGÍA, *sf.* (Med.) Part of pathology treating of the symptoms of diseases.
SINTONÍA, *sf.* Brief account, concise exposition.
SINUOSIDÁD, *sf.* Sinuosity.
SINUÓSO, SA, *a.* Sinuous, bending in and out.
SIÑÁR, *va.* (Ant.) V. *Signar.*
SIÑO, *sm.* (Ant.) V. *Signo ó señal.*
SÍO ó SÍON, *sm.* (Bot.) Water-parsnep. Sium *L.*
SÍPEDON ó SÍPIDON, *sm.* Serpent.
SÍPIA, *sf.* Refuse of olives, which remains in oil-mills, and serves as food for swine.
SIQUIÉRA, SIQUIÉR, Y SIQUIÉRE, *conj.* At least; though, although; or, scarcely; otherwise.
SIRASCÓSIS, *sm.* (Anat.) Syssarcosis, union of bones by means of muscles.
SÍRE, *sm.* Sire, a title given to kings chiefly in England and France.
SIRÉNA, *sf.* 1. Siren, a sea-nymph. 2. A woman who sings charmingly.
SÍRGA, *sf.* 1. (Naút.) Tow-rope, tow-line; a rope for drawing a barge on a canal. 2. Line used in dragging nets. *A' la sirga,* Sailing with a dragging line.
SIRGADÚRA, *sf.* (Naút.) The act of towing or hauling a barge or vessel along on a canal or by the banks of a river.
SIRGÁR, *va.* (Naút.) To tow or haul a vessel along with a rope or line.
SÍRGO, *sm.* Twisted silk; stuff made of silk.
SIRGUÉRO, *sm.* (Orn.) Linnet. V. *Xilguero.*
SIRINGÁR, *va.* V. *Xeringar.*
SÍRIO, *sm.* Sirius or dog-star.
SÍRLE ó SÍRRIA, *s.* Sheep-dung.
SIRÓCO ó XALÓQUE, *sm.* Sirocco, a south-east wind.
SÍRTE, *sf.* 1. Syrtes, hidden rock, quicksand, moving sandbank. 2. Peril, danger.
SIRVIÉNTA, *sf.* Female servant.
SIRVIÉNTE, *s. com.* Serving, being a servant.
SÍSA, *sf.* 1. Petty theft committed by servants. 2. Clippings, which tailors cabbage or steal in cutting clothes. 3. Size, linseed-oil boiled with ochre, and used by gilders. 4. Assize. *Sisa de pan,* Assize of bread. 5. Excise, a tax or duty laid on eatables or liquors.
SISADÓR, RA, *s.* Filcher, a petty thief; one that exacts more than is due; sizer; cutter.
SISÁR, *va.* 1. To pilfer, to filch; to steal small quantities of what one buys for another; to curtail, to lessen. 2. To cut clothes. 3. To size, to prepare with size what is to be gilded.
SÍSCA, *sf.* (Mur.) V. *Cisca.*
SISÉLIS, *sm.* (Bot.) Wild spignel. Seseli *L.*
SISÉRO, *sm.* Excise collector.
SISÍMBRIO, *sm.* (Bot.) Water-radish, radish water-cress. Sisymbrium amphibium *L.*
SISÓN, *sm.* 1. Filcher, pilferer, petty thief. 2. (Orn.) Godart or moorcock.
SISTÉMA, *sm.* 1. System, any complexure or combination of many things acting together. 2. A scheme which reduces many things to a regular dependence or corporation. 3. Hypothesis, supposition. 4. Gold or silver lace of one pattern.
SISTEMATICAMÉNTE, *ad.* Systematically.
SISTEMÁTICO, CA, *a.* Systematic.
SISTÍLO, *sm.* (Arq.) Systyle, an order of building having the columns two diameters distant.
SÍSTOLE, *sf.* 1. Systole, the contraction of the heart. 2. (Ret.) Shortening of a long syllable.
SÍSTRO, *sm.* An ancient musical wind-instrument, resembling a trumpet.
SITÁRCIA, *sf.* A kind of knapsack, in which travellers carry their provisions.
SITIÁDA, *sf.* (Ar.) Assembly or committee for the particular government of a house or community.
SITIÁDO, *sm.* V. *Situado.*
SITIADÓR, *sm.* Besieger, one who lays siege to a place.
SITIÁL, *sm.* 1. Seat of honour for princes and prelates at a public assembly. 2. Stool, form, seat without a back.
SITIÁR, *va.* 1. To besiege, to lay siege to a place. 2. To surround, to hem in. 3. To deprive of the means of effecting any thing. *Sitiar por hambre,* (Met.) To compel one by necessity to submit.
SITIBÚNDO, DA, *a.* V. *Sediento.*
SÍTIO, *sm.* 1. Place, a space taken up by a body or substance. 2. Situation of a town or other place. 3. Siege, blockade. 4. Country-house, country-seat. 5. (Arag.) Anniversary, festival.
SÍTO, TA, *a.* Situated, assigned. V. *Situado.*
SITUACIÓN, *sf.* Situation, position; state of affairs; assignation, appointment, assignment.
SITUÁDO, *sm.* Allowance, pay or salary assigned upon certain goods or effects.
SITUÁR, *va.* 1. To put any thing in a certain place, to situate. 2. To assign a fund, out of which any salary, rent, or interest, is to be paid.—*vr.* To be established in any place or business; to station one's self.
SIZÍGIA, *sf.* (Astro.) Syzygia, period from the conjunction to the opposition of the moon.
SÓ, *prep.* Under; below. Used in composition, it sometimes retains its signification; as it occasionally diminishes the import of the verb, as in *soasar,* to underdo meat; and in other cases it augments it, as *sojuzgar,* to subjugate. *Soterrar,* To put under ground, to inter. *So color,* Under colour; on pretence. *De so uno,* Conjointly, at one time.—*pron. pos.* (Ant.) V. *Su.*—*interj.* Used as, *cho* and *ze,* to stop horses or cattle.
SOASÁR, *va.* To half roast, to parboil.
SÓBA, *sf.* The act of making any thing soft and limber; rumpling; contusion, beating.

Sobáco, *sm.* Armpit, the cavity under the shoulder.
Sobadéro, ra, *a.* That may be handled.
Sobádo, *sm.* The repeated and violent working, and handling of any thing. V. *Sobadura. Sobados*, Loaves of bread made in La Mancha.
Sobadúra, *sf.* Kneading, rubbing.
Sobajadúra, *sf.* Scrubbing, frication.
Sobajamiénto, *sm.* Friction, rubbing, scrubbing.
Sobajanéro, *sm.* (Vulg.) Errand boy.
Sobajár, *va.* To scrub, to rub hard.
Sobánda, *sf.* Bottom or end of a rush.
Sobaquéra, *sf.* Opening left in clothes under the armpit.
Sobaquído, *sm.* (Cant.) Thief who carries stolen goods under his arm.
Sobaquína, *sf.* Smell of the armpit.
Sobár, *va.* 1. To handle, to soften. 2. To pummel, to chastise with blows. 3. To scrub, to rub hard. 4. To rumple clothes.
Sobárba, *sf.* Noseband. *Sobarbas*, Levers or prominent bars, which raise the pestles in a fulling-mill.
Sobarbáda, *sf.* Check under the chin; reprimand.
Sobarcár, *va.* 1. To carry any thing heavy under the arm. 2. To draw the clothes up to the arm-holes.
Sobéo, *sm.* (And.) Leather draughts or traces.
Soberanaménte, *ad.* Sovereignly, supremely.
Soberanía, *sf.* 1. Sovereignty, supreme power over others. 2. Pride, haughtiness, arrogance, loftiness.
Soberáno, na, *a.* Sovereign, holding supreme power.—*sm.* Sovereign; lord paramount.
Sobérbia, *sf.* 1. Pride, haughtiness; an inordinate desire of being preferred to others; presumption; arrogance. 2. Pomp, pageantry. 3. Anger, passion. 4. Insulting word or action. [proudly.
Soberbiaménte, *ad.* Haughtily, arrogantly,
Sobérbio, bia, *a.* 1. Proud, arrogant, elated. 2. Lofty, sublime, eminent. 3. Fiery, mettlesome; applied to horses.
Soberbiosaménte, *ad.* Haughtily.
Soberbióso, sa, *a.* V. *Soberbio.*
Sobína, *sf.* A wooden pin or peg.
Sóbo, *sm.* Frequent working of any thing to make it soft and limber.
Sobón ó Soboncázo, *sm.* A sly lazy fellow.
Sobornación, *sf.* V. *Soborno.*
Sobornádo, *sm.* Misshaped loaf of bread in the oven.
Sobornadór, ra, *s.* Suborner, one that suborns or bribes; one who procures a bad action to be done.
Sobornál, *a.* Added to the load or burthen which a beast carries.
Sobornár, *va.* To suborn, to procure by secret collusion; to procure by indirect means.
Sobórno, *sm.* 1. Subornation, the act of suborning. 2. Bribe or money offered for doing a bad action. 3. Incitement, inducement.
Sóbra, *sf.* 1. Overplus, surplus, excess. *Sobras de la comida*, Offals, leavings, broken victuals. 2. Grievous offence, injury. *De sobra*, Over and above; superfluously.

Sobradaménte, *ad.* Abundantly; superabundantly; excessively.
Sobradár, *va.* To erect edifices with lofts or granaries.
Sobradíllo, *sm.* 1. A small granary. 2. A small part or remain. 3. Penthouse; a shelter over a balcony or window.
Sobrádo, *sm.* Granary, loft; a story or floor. —*ad.* V. *Sobradamente.*
Sobrádo, da, *a.* Bold, audacious, licentious; rich, wealthy.
Sobrája y Sobramiénto. V. *Sobra.*
Sobrancéro, ra, *a.* 1. Disengaged, unemployed. 2. A supernumerary ploughman, who supplies the place of another.
Sobránte, *pa.* y *sm.* 1. Residue, superfluity. 2. Rich, wealthy.
Sobrár, *va.* To exceed, to surpass.—*vn.* 1. To have more than is necessary or required. 2. To be over and above; to be more than enough; to be intrusive. 3. To remain, to be left. [it boil.
Sobrasár, *va.* To put fire under a pot to make
Sóbre, *prep.* 1. Above, over. V. *Encima.* 2. Super, over; used in composition, as *sobrecargar*, To overcharge or overload. *Tiene mucha ventaja sobre todos los demas*, He possesses great advantages over the rest. 3. Moreover, besides. 4. A little more; a few more. *Tendré sobre cien reales*, I will or shall have about a hundred reals; a little more than a hundred reals. 5. Above, higher; with power or superiority. 6. (Naút.) Off. *El baxel está sobre el cabo de San Vicente*, The vessel is off Cape St. Vincent. *Sobre sí*, Selfishly; carefully, separately; elated by real or supposed acquirements. 7. To, towards; near. 8. On, upon. 9. After, since. *Sobre comida*, After dinner. *Sobre manera*, Excessively, irregularly. *Ir sobre alguno*, To go in pursuit of a person. 10. Before or around. *Estar sobre una plaza*, To besiege a place.—*sm.* Direction and cover of a letter.
Sobreabundáncia, *sf.* Superabundance.
Sobreabundánte, *a.* Superabundant.
Sobreabundanteménte, *ad.* Superabundantly.
Sobreabundár, *vn.* To superabound; to be exuberant.
Sobreaguár, *vn.* To be on the surface of water, to float or swim on water.
Sobreagúda, *sf.* One of the seven small letters in music.
Sobreagúdo, *sm.* (Mus.) Highest treble in music.
Sobrealiénto, *sm.* Difficult respiration.
Sobrealzár, *va.* To praise, to extol.
Sobreañadír, *va.* To superadd, to add over and above.
Sobreañál, *a.* Applied to animals more than a year old.
Sobreasádo, *sm.* (Mallorca) Sausage half roasted, and done over again when it is to be eaten. [roasted before.
Sobreasár, *va.* To roast again what was half
Sobrebebér, *va.* (Joc.) To guzzle liquor; to quaff one bottle after another.
Sobreبóya, *sf.* (Naút.) Break-water, a small booy fastened to a large one in the water, to show its position.

Sobrecáma, *sf.* Coverlet, quilt.
Sobrecáña, *sf.* (Alb.) Tumour in a horse's leg.
Sobrecañál, *sm.* Frame of a weaver's comb.
Sobrecárga, *sf.* 1. An additional bundle thrown over a load. 2. Additional trouble or vexation. 3. Rope thrown over a load to make it fast.
Sobrecargár, *va.* 1. To overload, to load to excess. 2. To make one seam over another.
Sobrecárgo, *sm.* Supercargo of a vessel.
Sobrecárta, *sf.* 1. Cover of a letter. 2. The second injunction; decree or warrant, repeating a former order.
Sobrecartár, *va.* To repeat a former injunction.
Sobrecebadéra, *sf.* (Naút.) Sprit top-sail.
Sobrecédula, *sf.* Second royal order or despatch.
Sobrecéja, *sf.* The part of the forehead over the eye-brows.
Sobrecéjo, *sm.* Frown; supercilious aspect.
Sobrecelestiál, *a.* Supercelestial.
Sobrecéño, *sm.* Frown. V. *Sobrecejo.*
Sobrecérco, *sm.* Ornament or fringe placed round another to strengthen it.
Sobrecíncha, *sf.* One of the girths of a saddle.
Sobrecíncho, *sm.* Surcingle, an additional girth, put over the common girth.
Sobrecláustro, *sm.* Apartment over a cloister.
Sobrecogér, *va.* To surprise, to take by surprise.
Sobrecomída, *sf.* Dessert. V. *Postre.*
Sobrecópa, *sf.* Cover or lid of a cup.
Sobrecrecér, *vn.* To out-grow, to over-grow.
Sobrecrúces, *sm. pl.* Cross-joints to strengthen a wheel.
Sobrecubiérta, *sf.* Double cover put on any thing; coverlet, quilt.
Sobrecuéllo, *sm.* Collar. V. *Collarin.*
Sobrecútis, *sf.* V. *Epidermis.*
Sobredezméro, *sm.* Assistant in collecting duties.
Sobredícho, cha, *a.* Above-mentioned.
Sobrediénte, *sm.* Gag-tooth which grows over another.
Sobredorár, *va.* 1. To gild anew. 2. To palliate, to extenuate, to exculpate.
Sobreedificár, *va.* To build over any thing.
Sobreempéyne, *sm.* That part of spatterdashes or gaiters which covers the instep of the foot.
Sobreescribír, *va.* To superscribe, to inscribe; to direct a letter. V. *Sobrescribir.*
Sobreescríto, ta, *a.* Written on the outside.
Sobreescríto, *sm.* 1. Superscription, inscription, direction, address. 2. Mien, aspect; pretext. V. *Sobrescrito.*
Sobreesenciál, *a.* That which is more than essential.
Sobreexcedér, *va.* (Ant.) To surpass, to exceed.
Sobreexceléntе, *a.* Superexcellent.
Sobrefáz, *sf.* 1. Superficies, surface, outside. 2. (Fort.) Face prolonged, the distance between the angle of the shoulder of a bastion and the curtain.
Sobrefíno, na, *a.* Superfine.
Sobreguárda, *sm.* Second guard placed for greater security.
Sobreguardílla, *sf.* Penthouse, shelter, shed.
Sobreház, *sf.* 1. Surface, outside. 2. Outside cover of any thing.
Sobrehuéso, *sm.* 1. Morbid swelling on the bones or joints. 2. Trouble, encumbrance, burthen.
Sobrehumáno, na, *a.* Beyond the power of man.
Sobrejuéz, *sm.* Superior judge.

Sobrelécho, *sm.* The side of a stone which lies on a bed of mortar.
Sobrelláve, *sf.* 1. Double key; a large key. 2. In the royal palaces, an officer who keeps a second or reserved key of every door.
Sobrelléno, na, *a.* Overfull, superabundant.
Sobrellevár, *va.* 1. To ease or alleviate another's burthen; to carry. 2. To inure to hardships by degrees, to undergo. 3. To overlook the defects or failings of inferiors or subjects.
Sobremanéra, *ad.* Beyond measure; excessively.
Sobremáno, *sm.* (Albeyt.) Osseous tumour on the hoofs of horses' fore feet.
Sobreméssa, *sf.* 1. Table-carpet, a cover over a table; table-cloth. 2. Dessert. V. *Postre. De sobremesa*, Immediately after dinner.
Sobremesána, *sf.* (Naút.) Mizen-top-sail.
Sobremuñonéra, *sf.* (Naút.) Clamp or cap-square, a piece of iron which covers the trunions of a cannon.
Sobrenadár, *va.* To swim on the surface of any fluid.
Sobrenaturál, *a.* Supernatural, preternatural.
Sobrenaturalménte, *ad.* Supernaturally.
Sobrenómbre, *sm.* 1. Surname; the name of the family, the name which one has over and above the Christian name. 2. Nickname; a name given in scoff or contempt.
Sobreójo, *sm.* A supercilious aspect; a look of envy, hatred, or contempt. *Llevar sobreojo á uno*, To keep a watchful eye over one.
Sobrepága, *sf.* Increase or augmentation of pay.
Sobrepáño, *sm.* Upper cloth, put over others.
Sobrepárto, *sm.* Time of lying in, which follows the delivery.
Sobrepellíz, *sf.* Surplice.
Sobrepéso, *sm.* Overweight.
Sobrepéyne, *sm.* The act of cutting the hair but very slightly.
Sobrepíe, *sm.* (Albeyt.) Osseous tumour at the top of horses' hoofs.
Sobreplánes, *sm. pl.* (Naút.) Riders.
Sobreponér, *va.* To add one thing to another; to put one over another.—*vr.* To exalt or put one's self over or above other things.
Sobreprécio, *sm.* Extra-price.
Sobrepuésto, ta, *a.* Counterfeit, fictitious.
Sobrepuésto, *sm.* 1. A third person. 2. Honey-comb formed by the bees after the hive is full. 3. Earthen vessel added to bee-hives when they are too full.
Sobrepúja, *sf.* Outbidding, the act of bidding more than another.
Sobrepujánte, *pa.* Surpassing, excelling.
Sobrepujánza, *sf.* Great strength and vigour.
Sobrepujár, *va.* To exceed, to surpass, to excel.
Sobrequílla, *sf.* (Naút.) Keelson or kelson, a piece of timber next to the keel, lying right over it on the inside.
Sobrerónda, *sf.* (Mil.) Counter-round.
Sobrerópa, *sf.* A sort of long robes worn over other clothes.
Sobresalído, da, *pp.* Elated, inflated, haughty.
Sobresaliénte, *a.* Excelling, surpassing the rest.—*sm.* 1. (Mil.) Officer who commands a picket, and the troops who compose it. 2. Substitute.
Sobresalír, *va.* To exceed in height; to excel, to surpass.

Sobresaltadaménte, *ad.* Suddenly, unexpectedly.
Sobresaltár, *va.* 1. To surprise; to make an unexpected attack. 2. To frighten, to terrify. —*vn.* To fly in one's face; to be striking; applied to paintings.—*vr.* To be startled at.
Sobresálto, *sm.* Surprise; sudden dread or fear. *De sobresalto*, Unexpectedly.
Sobresanár, *va.* 1. To heal superficially. 2. To screen, to palliate. [ly; feignedly.
Sobresáno, *ad.* Cured superficially; affected-
Sobresános, *sm. pl.* (Naút.) Tabling, a broad hem on sails, to strengthen that part which is fastened to the bolt-rope.
Sobrescribír, *va.* To superscribe, to inscribe, to address or direct a letter.
Sobrescríto, *sm.* Superscription, address or direction of a letter.
Sobreseér, *vn.* To desist from a design; to relinquish a claim or pretension. [risk.
Sobreseguro, *ad.* In a safe manner; without
Sobreseimiénto, *sm.* Omission, suspension.
Sobreséllo, *sm.* A double seal.
Sobresembrár, *va.* 1. To sow over again what has been sown before. 2. To diffuse erroneous doctrines; to sow discord.
Sobreseñál, *sf.* Ensign or standard arbitrarily adopted by the ancient knights.
Sobresolár, *va.* 1. To pave anew. 2. To newsole a pair of boots or shoes.
Sobrestánte, *sm.* Overseer; foreman.
Sobrestánte, *a.* Immediate, near.
Sobresuéldo, *sm.* Addition to one's pay or allowance. [laid over another.
Sobresuélo, *sm.* A second floor or pavement
Sobretárde, *sm.* Close of the evening.
Sobretercéro, *sm.* One more than three to collect duties.
Sobretódo, *sm.* Surtout, a wide or great coat.
Sobretódo, *ad.* Above all; before all things.
Sobretrancaniles, *sm. pl.* (Naút.) Spirketing, the range of planks which lies between the water-ways and the lower edge of a ship's gun-ports.
Sobreveedór, *sm.* Supervisor, overseer.
Sobrevéla, *sf.* (Ant.) Second sentinel.
Sobrevénda, *sf.* (Cir.) Surband, bandage placed over others.
Sobrevenída, *sf.* Supervention.
Sobrevenír, *vn.* To happen, to fall out; to come unexpectedly; to supervene. V. *Venír.*
Sobreventár, *va.* (Naút.) To gain the weather-gage of another ship.
Sobreverterése, *vr.* To run over, to overflow.
Sobrevésta y Sobrevéste, *sf.* Surtout, great coat.
Sobrevestír, *va.* To put on a great coat.
Sobrevidriéra, *sf.* Wire net before a glass window. [ous fury, surprise.
Sobreviénta, *sf.* (Ant.) Gust of wind; impetu-
Sobreviénto, *sm.* (Naút.) Weather-gage.
Sobrevísta, *sf.* Beaver of a helmet.
Sobreviviénte, *pa.* y *s.* Survivor; surviving.
Sobrevivír, *vn.* To survive. *Sobrevivir á alguno*, To outlive or survive a person.
Sobrezálma, *sf.* Woollen cover for a pack-
Sobriaménte, *ad.* Soberly. [saddle.
Sobriedád, *sf.* Sobriety.
Sobrinito, *ta*, *s.* Little nephew or niece.
Sobríno, *na*, *s.* Nephew, niece.
Sóbrio, *ria*, *a.* Sober, temperate.
Sobronádo, *a.* V. *Sobornado.*
Socalíña, *sf.* Cunning, artifice to gain a thing from one who is not obliged to give it. [gem.
Socaliñár, *va.* To extort by cunning or strata-
Socaliñéro, *ra*, *s.* Artful exacter.
Socápa, *sf.* Pretext, pretence, ostensible cause. *A' socapa*, On pretence, under colour.
Socapiscól, *sm.* V. *Sochantre.*
Socár, *va.* (Naút.) To set taught a rope, shroud, or stay, which is slack or loose.
Socárra, *sf.* 1. The act of half roasting meat or leaving it half rear. 2. Craft, cunning.
Socarrár, *va.* To half roast or dress meat.
Socarrén, *sm.* Eave, the edge of the roof, which juts out over the wall of a house.
Socarréna, *sf.* Hollow, cavity, interval.
Socarrína, *sf.* (Fam.) Scorching, singeing.
Socarrón, *na*, *a.* Cunning, sly, crafty.
Socarronaménte, *ad.* Slyly, artfully.
Socarronería, *sf.* Craft, cunning, artfulness.
Socáva, *sf.* 1. The act of mining or undermining. 2. The act of opening the ground around trees.
Socavár, *va.* To excavate, to undermine. *Socavár la tierra*, To turn up the ground; applied to wild boars.
Socavón, *sm.* Cave, cavern; a passage under ground. *Socavónes*, Pits or shafts in mines.
Socáyre, *sm.* 1. (Naút.) Slatch, the part of a rope or cable, which hangs slack. 2. Shelter.
Socayréro, *sm.* Sculker, lurker, one who hides himself from his business or duty.
Sochántre, *sm.* Sub-chanter, the deputy of the precenter in a cathedral.
Sociabilidád, *sf.* Sociableness, inclination to company and converse, sociability.
Sociáble, *a.* 1. Sociable, ready to unite in a general interest; inclined to company. 2. Familiar, friendly, amiable.
Sociableménte, *ad.* Sociably, friendly.
Sociál, *a.* Relating to company, and friendly intercourse, social.
Sociedád, *sf.* 1. Society, the company and converse of persons of sense and information. 2. Friendship, familiar intercourse. 3. Union of many in one general interest.
Sócio, *sm.* 1. Comrade, partner, associate. V. *Compañero.* 2. Member of a literary society.
Socolláda, *sf.* (Naút.) Jerk, the violent straining and slackening of the ropes, cables, and shrouds, caused by the rolling and pitching of
Socolór, *sm.* Pretext, pretence, colour. [a ship.
Socóno, *sm.* (Cant.) Thing sent by a prostitute to her bully.
Socóro, *sm.* (Ant.) Place under the choir.
Socorredór, *ra*, *s.* Succourer, assister; administering relief.
Socorrér, *va.* 1. To succour, to aid, to administer relief. 2. To pay a part of what is due.
Socorrído, *da*, *a.* Furnished, supplied. *La plaza de Madrid es muy socorrida*, The market of Madrid is well supplied.
Socórro, *sm.* 1. Succour, support, assistance. 2. Part of a salary or allowance, advanced or paid beforehand. 3. Succour, a fresh supply of men or provisions thrown into a besieged place. *El socorro de españa*, (Fam.) Tardy arrival of the necessary succour.

Socrócio, *sm.* 1. Poultice, or cataplasm of a saffron colour. 2. Pleasure, delight, satisfaction. [*Sosa.* 2. Headache.
Sóda, *sf.* 1. (Bot.) Glasswort. Salsola *L.* V.
Sodomía, *sf.* Sodomy, an unnatural crime.
Sodomíta, *sm.* Sodomite, one who is guilty of sodomy.
Soéz, *a.* Mean, vile, base, worthless.
Sofá, *sf.* Sofa.
Sofaldár, *va.* To truss up; to raise; to tuck up; to lift up, to discover any thing.
Sofáldo, *sm.* The act of trussing or tucking up clothes.
Sofión, *sm.* Hoot, shout in scorn or contempt; reprimand, censure.
Sofísma, *sm.* Sophism, a fallacious argument.
Sofísta, *sm.* Sophister, a disputant fallaciously subtle; an artful but insidious logician; a caviller; anciently a sophist.
Sofistería, *sf.* Sophistry.
Sofisticación, *sf.* Sophistication, adulteration.
Sofisticaménte, *ad.* Sophistically, with fallacious subtilty.
Sofisticár, *va.* To cavil, to use fallacious arguments; to falsify; to sophisticate.
Sofístico, ca, *a.* Sophistical, fallaciously subtle, logically deceitful.
Sofíto, *sm.* (Arq.) Underside of the cornice ornamented with panels, &c.
Sofláma, *sf.* 1. A subtle flame; the reverberation of fire. 2. Glow, blush. 3. Deceitful language.
Soflamár, *va.* 1. To use deceitful language, to impose upon, to deceive. 2. To raise a blush.
Soflaméro, *sm.* Sophister, one that makes use of captious or deceitful language.
Sofocánte, *sm.* 1. Ribbon with a tassel, worn by ladies round the neck. 2. A large pin used by women to scratch their heads.
Sofocár, *va.* V. *Sufocar.*
Sofreír, *va.* To fry slightly.
Sofrenáda, *sf.* 1. A sudden check given to a horse with the bridle. 2. A rude reprehension; a severe reprimand. 3. Fit of sickness.
Sofrenár, *va.* 1. To check a horse by a violent pull of the bridle. 2. To reprehend rudely; to reprimand severely.
Sofrenázo, *sm.* A violent pull of the bridle.
Sofríto, ta, *pp. irreg.* of *sofreir.*
Sóga, *sf.* 1. Rope made of bass-weed. 2. A sly, cunning fellow. 3. Measure of land which varies in different provinces; measure of rope. *Soga de un pozo,* Bucket-rope for a well. *Hacer soga,* To make a rope; to remain behind one's company; to introduce improper things in the course of conversation.—*interj.* A term expressive of astonishment and aversion.
Soguear, *va.* To measure with a rope.
Soguería, *sf.* Rope-walk or rope-yard, where bass-ropes are made and sold; collection of ropes.
Soguéro, *sm.* Bass-rope maker.
Soguíllo, lla; to, ta, *s.* A small rope; plaited hair.
Soéz, *a.* Vile, base. V. *Soez.*
Sojuzgadór, *sm.* Conqueror, subduer.
Sojuzgár, *va.* To conquer, to subjugate, to subdue.

Sol, *sm.* 1. Sun, the principal luminary of the world. 2. Any thing that affords either moral or physical light. 3. Day. 4. (Quim.) Gold. 5. (Mus.) Fifth note in the gamut. *El sol sale,* The sun rises. *El sol se pone,* The sun sets. *Al sol puesto,* At the fall of night. *El sol pica ó abrasa,* The sun scorches. *No dexar á sol ni á sombra,* Not to let a man rest, but molest him constantly. *Tomar el sol,* To walk in the sun. *Sóles,* Sparkling, dazzling eyes.—*ad.* (Ant.) V. *Solamente.*
Solacear, *va.* To solace, to administer consolation. V. *Solazar.*
Solácio, *sm.* V. *Consuelo.*
Soláda, *sf.* Floor, site; seat.
Soládo, *sm.* Floor, covered with tiles or flags; pavement.
Soladór, *sm.* Tiler, he who paves with flags or tiles.
Soladúra, *sf.* Act of paving; materials used for paving or flooring.
Solaménte, *ad.* Only, solely.
Solána, *sf.* 1. Place struck or beaten by the sun. 2. V. *Solanar.*
Solanár, *sm.* (Arag.) An open gallery for taking the sun.
Solanázo, *sm.* A violent, hot, and troublesome easterly wind.
Soláno, *sm.* 1. Easterly wind. 2. (Bot.) Nightshade. Solanum nigrum *L.*
Solápa, *sf.* 1. Lappel, a double breast on clothes 2. Colour, pretence, pretext. 3. (Albeyt.) Cavity of a small wound in animals.
Solapadaménte, *ad.* In a dissembling manner; deceitfully.
Solapádo, da, *a.* Cunning, crafty, artful.
Solapadúra (Obra de), *sf.* (Naút.) Clincher-work.
Solapamiénto, *sm.* Cavity of a wound in animals.
Solapár, *va.* 1. To button one breast-part of clothes over another. 2. To cloak, to hide under a false pretence.
Solápo y Solápe, *sm.* Lappel; pretence. V. *Solapa.* *A' solapo,* In a hidden or furtive manner.
Solár, *sm.* 1. Ground on which a house is built. 2. Spot on which stands the original mansion of a noble family.—*a.* Solar, belonging to the sun.—*va.* 1. To floor a room; to pave a stable or coach-yard. 2. To sole shoes or boots.
Solariégo, ga, *a.* 1. Belonging to the ancient mansion of a noble family. 2. Relating to freehold and other estates, which appertain with full and unlimited right of property to the owner. 3. Descending from an ancient noble family.
Soláz, *sm.* Solace, consolation, comfort. *A' solaz,* Pleasantly, agreeably.
Solazárse, *vr.* To be comforted; to be joyful; to solace.
Solázo, *sm.* (Fam.) A scorching sun.
Solazóso, sa, *a.* Comfortable, delectable.
Soldáda, *sf.* 1. Wages, pay given for service. 2. (Naút.) Sailors' pay or wages. V. *Pré.*
Soldadádo, *sm.* A soldier who has lost his pay.
Soldadéro, ra, *a.* Stipendiary, receiving wages or hire.
Soldadésca, *sf.* 1. Soldiery, the profession of a

soldier; military art or science. 2. Sham-fight, a diversion performed in imitation of military evolutions. *A' la soldadesca,* In a soldierly manner, for the use of soldiers.

SOLDADÉSCO, CA, *a.* Soldierly, soldier-like.

SOLDADÍCO, LLO, *sm.* A little soldier.

SOLDÁDO, *sm.* 1. Soldier, a military man. *Soldado raso,* A common soldier, a private. *Soldado de infantería,* A foot-soldier. *Soldado de á caballo,* Trooper, horse-soldier. 2. A Christian.

SOLDADÓR, *sm.* 1. Solderer, one who solders or mends metal utensils. 2. Soldering-iron. 3. Gold-beater.

SOLDADÚRA, *sf.* 1. The act of soldering or joining by means of a metallic cement. 2. Solder, the metallic cement used for soldering. 3. Correction or mending of any thing. *Este desacierto no tiene soldadura,* That error or mistake cannot be redressed.

SOLDÁN, *sm.* Sultan, Mohammedan title.

SOLDÁR, *va.* 1. To soder or solder; to unite by means of a metallic cement. 2. To mend, to correct.

SOLDEMÉNTE, *ad.* (Vulg.) V. *Solamente.*

SOLEÁR, *va.* V. *Asolear.* [word to another.

SOLECÍSMO, *sm.* Solecism, unfitness of one

SOLECÍTO, *sm.* A scorching sun. This word is a diminutive in terminology and an augmentive in sense.

SOLEDÁD, *sf.* 1. Solitude, want of company. 2. A lonely place; a desert. 3. Want of comfort, consolation or relief. 4. A work or poem on solitude.

SOLEJÁR, *sm.* A place exposed to the sun.

SOLÉMNE, *a.* 1. Anniversary, performed once a year at the revolution of the sun. 2. Celebrated, famous. 3. Grand, solemn. 4. Festive, joyous, gay, cheerful.

SOLEMNEMÉNTE, *ad.* Solemnly, in a festive manner.

SOLEMNIDÁD, *sf.* 1. Solemnity, the state and manner of being solemn. 2. Pomp or magnificence of a feast or festival. 3. Formalities prescribed by law. *Pobre de solemnidad,* A poor man in real distress.

SOLEMNIZADÓR, RA, *s.* One who solemnizes; a panegyrist.

SOLEMNIZÁR, *va.* 1. To solemnize, to praise, to applaud. 2. To perform in a festive manner; to celebrate joyously.

SOLÉR, *vn. irr. y defect.* To be accustomed; to wont, to be went.

SOLÉR, *sm.* (Naút.) Under-flooring of a ship.

SOLÉRA, *sf.* 1. Entablature, the uppermost row of stones of a wall, on which the beams or joists rest. 2. A flat stone, which serves as a foundation to the base of a pillar; a plinth. 3. The fixed millstone, on which the runner turns and grinds the grain. 4. (And.) Lees of wine. *Solera de balaustres de balcones,* (Naút.) Foot-rails of the gallery of a ship. 5. Plank on which earthenware is dried.

SOLÉRCIA, *sf.* Industry; abilities, talents; artfulness.

SOLERÍA, *sf.* 1. Floor or pavement made of flags. 2. Parcel of skins used for soles. V. *Solado.*

SOLÉRO, *sm.* (And.) Lower millstone. [ous.

SOLÉRTE, *a.* Cunning, sagacious; able, industri-

SOLÉTA, *sf.* A linen sole put into stockings. *Apretar ó picar de soleta,* To run away; to sheer off.

SOLETÁR ó SOLETEÁR, *va.* To vamp a pair of stockings with a linen sole.

SOLETÉRO, RA, *s.* Vamper, one who soles and pieces old things with something new.

SOLEVANTÁDO, DA, *a.* Inquiet, agitated, perturbed. [rebellion. V. *Sublevacion.*

SOLEVANTAMIÉNTO, *sm.* The act of rising in

SOLEVANTÁR, *va.* 1. To raise any thing and put another under it. 2. To induce one to leave his habitation, home, or employment. 3. To agitate, to excite commotion.

SOLEVÁR, *va.* To raise, to lift up. V. *Solevantar.*

SÓLFA, *sf.* 1. The art of uniting the various sounds of music. 2. Accordance, harmony; concord. 3. (Joc.) A sound beating or flogging.

SOLFEADÓR, *sm.* 1. Songster, one who sings according to the rules of melody and measure. 2. Music-master. 3. One who deals out blows.

SOLFEÁR, *vn.* 1. To sing according to the rules of melody and measure. 2. To cudgel, to flog.

SOLFÉO, *sm.* 1. Melodious song. 2. Beating, flogging, drubbing. [music.

SOLFÍSTA, *s. com.* Musician, a person skilled in

SOLICITACIÓN, *sf.* Solicitation, importunity, temptation, inducement.

SOLICITADÓR, RA, *s.* Solicitor, agent.

SOLICITAMÉNTE, *ad.* Solicitously, diligently.

SOLICITÁNTE, *pa.* Solicitor; applied to persons who solicit criminal favours in confession. *Confesor solicitante,* Priest who seeks to seduce women at confession.

SOLICITÁR, *va.* To solicit, to importune, to entreat; to require; to urge.

SOLÍCITO, TA, *a.* Solicitous, anxious, careful.

SOLICITÚD, *sf.* Solicitude, anxiety, importunity.

SOLIDAMÉNTE, *ad.* Firmly; in a firm and solid manner, with true reasons.

SOLIDÁR, *va.* 1. To harden, to render firm and solid. 2. To consolidate, to establish.

SOLIDÉO, *sm.* Calotte, a small cap worn by clergymen under the hat.

SOLIDÉZ, *sf.* 1. Solidity, firmness, strength. 2. Integrity, firmness of mind.

SÓLIDO, DA, *a.* 1. Solid, firm, compact. 2. Built on strong, sound, and solid reasons.

SÓLIDO, *sm.* A solid compact body.

SOLILOQUIÁR, *vn.* To discourse or reason with one's self; to talk to one's self.

SOLILÓQUIO, *sm.* Soliloquy; a discourse made by one to himself.

SOLIMÁN, *sm.* (Quím.) Corrosive sublimate.

SÓLIO, *sm.* Throne, a royal seat with a canopy over it.

SOLÍPEDO, DA, *a.* Solipede, having the feet solid and undivided, whole hoofed.

SOLÍSA, *sf.* (Mur.) V. *Descarada.*

SOLITARIAMÉNTE, *ad.* Solitarily.

SOLITÁRIO, RIA, *a.* 1. Solitary, lonely, lonesome. 2. Cloistered, retired.

SOLITÁRIO, *sm.* 1. A sort of game, played by one person alone. 2. Post-chaise, with one seat only; berlin. *Pazaro solitario,* (Orn.) Solitary thrush, erroneously called the solitary sparrow. Turdus solitarius *L.* [ly.

SÓLITO, TA, *a.* Wont, accustomed. *Sólito,* Lone-

Soliviadúra, *sf.* The act of rising a little.
Soliviár, *va.* 1. To raise or lift up in order to take any thing from underneath. 2. To rob, to steal.—*vr.* To rise, to get up a little.
Solívio, *sm.* The act of rising or raising a little.
Solivión, *sm.* A sudden and violent lifting up.
Sólla, *sf.* (Gal.) V. *Suela.*
Solládo, *sm.* (Naút.) Orlop; a platform of planks, laid over the beams of a ship of war, where the cables are coiled. *Sollado de los pañoles de la despensa,* (Naút.) Cock-pit, a place abaft the capstern for the purser, surgeon, and surgeon's mate.
Solladór, *sm.* (Ant.) Blower, one who blows.
Sollamár, *va.* To scorch, to singe; to burn slightly.
Sollár, *va.* (Met.) To blow, to blow with bellows.
Sollástre, *sm.* Scullion, kitchen boy; skilful rogue.
Sollastría, *sf.* Scullery; the business of a scullion.
Sollastrón, *sm. aum.* A crafty juggler.
Sóllo, *sm.* (Ict.) Common pike. Esox lucius *L.*
Sollozár, *vn.* To sob, to sigh with convulsion.
Sollózo, *sm.* Sob, a convulsive sigh.
Sólo, *sm.* Musical composition for one voice.
Sólo, **la**, *a.* 1. Alone, single. 2. Lonely, without company; bereft of favour and protection. *A' solas,* Alone, unaided. *A' sus solas,* Quite alone, in solitude.
Sólo, *ad.* Only. V. *Solamente.*
Solomíllo ó Solómo, *sm.* Loin, the fleshy and boneless part on the spine.
Solsticiál, *a.* Solstitial, belonging to the solstice.
Solstício, *sm.* Solstice, the tropical point, the point at which the day is longest in summer, or shortest in winter.
Soltadízo, **za**, *a.* Easily untied, cleverly loosened.
Soltadór, **ra**, *s.* One that unties, loosens, lets go or dismisses.
Soltár, *va.* 1. To untie, to loosen. 2. To set at liberty, to discharge. 3. To burst or break out into laughter or crying. 4. To explain, to decipher, to solve. 5. (Ant.) To pardon, remit, absolve, or annul. *Soltar la capa,* To pull off the cloak; (Met.) To make a slight sacrifice to avoid danger. *Soltar la carga,* To throw down a burthen. *Soltar la deuda,* To forgive a debt. *Soltar la taravilla,* To give a loose to one's tongue. *Soltar la palabra,* To absolve one from an obligation or promise; to pledge one's word for any thing. *Soltar la presa,* (Met.) To shed tears copiously, to be dissolved in tears. *Soltar una especie,* To throw out a suggestion by way of sounding the opinions of others. *Soltar el trapo ó la rienda,* (Met.) To give one's self entirely up to vices, passions, or bad habits. *Soltar el preso,* (Joc.) To break wind. *Soltar el relox,* To raise the spring that a clock may run down, in token of public rejoicing. *El tablon ha soltado su cabeza,* (Naút.) The butt-end of the plank has started. *El ancla ha soltado el fondo,* (Naút.) The anchor is aweigh.—*vr.* 1. To get loose. 2. To grow expeditious and handy in the performance of a thing. 3. To forego all decency and modesty.
Soltería, *sf.* Celibacy; the state of a single life.
Soltéro, **ra**, *s.* Bachelor, a man unmarried; spinster, an unmarried woman.—*a.* V. *Suelto.*
Solterón, *sm.* An old bachelor.
Soltúra, *sf.* 1. The act of discharging or setting at liberty; freedom. 2. Agility, activity. 3. Licentiousness. 4. (Ant.) Remission.
Solúble, *a.* 1. Soluble, that can be loosened or untied. 2. Resoluble, that may be resolved.
Solución, *sf.* 1. Solution, the act of loosening or untying. 2. Resolution of a doubt, removal of an intellectual difficulty. 3. Solution, the reduction of a solid body into a fluid state. 4. Reduction of a natural body into its chemical principles.
Solutívo, **va**, *a.* Solutive, having the power of loosening, untying, or dissolving.
Solvénte y Solviénte, *a.* Solvent, unbinding, dissolvent.
Solvér, *va.* To loosen, to untie; to solve.
Solvíto, *sm.* Coral, or any other play-thing put into the hands of children.
Sóma, *sf.* 1. The coarse sort of flour, which by farmers, especially in Spain, is generally destined for servants' bread. 2. Load, burthensomeness. *Bestia de soma,* A beast of burthen.
Sománta, *sf.* Beating, severe chastisement.
Somatén, *sm.* Armed corps destined for the defence of a city or province; one who serves in such a corps.
Sómbra, *sf.* 1. Shade, darkness occasioned by the interception of light. 2. Spirit, ghost, manes. 3. (Met.) Protection. 4. Resemblance, appearance. 5. Sign, vestige. 6 Parts of a picture not brightly coloured. 7 (Ict.) Grayling. Salmo thymallus *L.* 8. Umber, a brown colour. *Andar á sombra de tejado,* To abscond. *Andar sin sombra,* To crave, to desire anxiously. *Ni por sombra,* By no means. *Sombras, ó sombras invisibles,* Dance behind a curtain where the shadows only are seen. *Poner á la sombra,* (Joc.) To imprison.
Sombráge, *sm.* Hut covered with branches.
Sombrájo, *sm.* Shade or figure corresponding to the body, by which the light is intercepted; shed or hut in vineyards.
Sombrár, *va.* To frighten, to astonish. V. *Asombrar.*
Sombreár, *va.* 1. To shade, to mark with different gradations of colour; to paint in obscure colours. 2. To shade gold or silver by adding a little silk, to diminish the glaring lustre.
Sombrerázo, *sm.* 1. A large hat. 2. A flap or blow with a hat.
Sombreréra, *sf.* 1. (Bot.) Butter-bur. Tussilago petasites *L.* 2. Hat-box, hat-case.
Sombrerería, *sf.* 1. Manufactory of hats. 2 Shop where hats are sold.
Sombreréro, *sm.* Hatter, hat-maker.
Sombrerillo, **y to**, *sm.* 1. A small or little hat. *Sombrerillo de Señora,* Lady's hat. 2. (Bot.) Navel-wort. Cotyledon umbilicus *L.*
Sombréro, *sm.* 1. Hat, a cover and ornament for the head. *Sombrero de tres picos,* Three-cocked hat. 2. Sounding-board; canopy of a pulpit. 3. Rights and privileges of a Spanish grandee. 4. Chief or head of a house or family. *Sombrero de cabrestante,* (Naút.) Drum of the capstan. 5. *Sombrero del patron,* (Naút.) Hat-money, allowance per ton to captains on their cargo.

Sombría, *sf.* Shady place.
Sombrílla, *sf.* 1. Parasol. 2. Slight shade.
Sombrío, **bría**, *a.* Shady, full of shade.
Sombrío, *sm.* 1. Part of a piece of painting, which is to be shaded or painted in darker colours than the rest. 2. A dull, heavy colour.
Sombróso, **sa**, *a.* Shady.
Someraménte, *ad.* Superficially.
Soméro, **ra**, *a.* Superficial, shallow; making but a slight impression on the mind.
Sometér, *va.* To subject, to subdue.—*vr.* To subject or humble one's self; to submit.
Sometimiénto, *sm.* Submission, subjection.
Somír, *va.* (Ant.) V. *Sumir.*
Somnambulísmo, *sm.* Somnambulism, state of walking in sleep.
Somnámbulo, *sm.* Somnambulo, somnambulist, he who walks in his sleep. V. *Sonambulo.*
Somnífero, **ra**, *a.* Somniferous, soporiferous.
Somnoléncia, *sf.* Heaviness, drowsiness.
Sómo, *sm.* (Ant.) Top, summit.
Somónte, *sm.* 1. Pile or shaggy part of cloth or stuff. 2. Rudeness; unartfulness.
Somorgujadór, *sm.* Diver, one that sinks voluntarily under water; one that goes under water to search for any thing.
Somorgujár, *va.* To dive, to sink voluntarily under water.
Somorgújo, **Somorgujón**, y **Somormújo**, *sm.* (Orn.) Dun-diver. Mergus castor *L.* *A' lo somorgujo, á lo somormujo, ó á somormujo,* Under water; privately, secretly.
Sompesár, *va.* To take up any thing in order to form a guess at its weight; to weigh.
Són, *sm.* Sound, noise, report, tale; reason, mode. *En son,* In such a manner; apparently. *Sin ton y sin son,* Without rhyme or reason. *A' que son, ó á son de que,* With what motive, for what reason. *A' son,* At or to the sound of.
Sonáble, *a.* Sonorous; famous.
Sonáda, *sf.* V. *Sonata.*
Sonadéra, *sf.* The act of blowing the nose.
Sonadéro, *sm.* 1. Handkerchief. 2. V. *Sonadera.*
Sonádo, **da**, *a.* 1. Blown, wiped; applied to the nose. 2. Celebrated, famous. 3. Generally reported.
Sonadór, **ra**, *s.* 1. One who makes a noise. 2. Handkerchief.
Sonája, *sf.* Timbrel, a musical instrument.
Sonajéro, *sm.* A small timbrel.
Sonajíca, **lla**, **ta**, *sf. dim.* Small tabour or timbrel. [in his sleep.
Sonámbulo, *sm.* Somnambulo, one who walks
Sonánte, *a.* Sounding, sonorous.
Sonár, *va.* 1. To sound, to play upon a musical instrument. 2. To like or dislike. *Mal me suena la cantada,* I do not like the song. *Bien me sonó lo que dixo,* I was much pleased with what he said. 3. To sound, to pronounce. 4. To allude, to refer to a thing without any direct mention.—*vn.* To sound or make a noise.—*v. imp.* To raise or propagate rumours, to report.—*vr.* To blow one's nose.
Sonáta, *sf.* Sonata, a kind of musical composition.
Sónco, *sm.* (Bot.) V. *Cerrajas.*
Sónda, *sf.* 1. (Naút.) Sounding, any place in the sea, where the ground may be reached with a lead and line. 2. Borer, an instrument for examining into the bowels and different layers or strata of the earth. 3. (Cir.) Cathéter. *Sonda del escandallo,* (Naút.) Lead soundings. *Navegar en sonda por la sondaleza,* To sail by the log.
Sondáble, *a.* That may be sounded.
Sondaléza, *sf.* (Naút.) Lead-line, the log. *Sondaleza de mano,* (Naút.) Hand-lead. *Sondaleza de la bomba,* (Naút.) Gage-rod of the pump.
Sondár ó **Sondeár**, *va.* 1. (Naút.) To sound, to heave the lead; to try the depth of water. *Sondar la bomba,* (Naút.) To sound the pump. 2. To try, to sift, to sound another's intentions.
Sonecíllo, *sm.* 1. A slight sound, scarce perceptible. 2. A short little tune.
Sonetázo, *sm.* A loud sound.
Sonetíco, *sm.* Merry little song; slight sound.
Sonetín, *sm.* An insignificant sonnet.
Sonéto, *sm.* Sonnet, a poetical composition.
Sonído, *sm.* 1. Sound, noise, motion of the air. 2. Fame, report, rumour. 3. Sound, pronunciation. 4. Literal signification. *Sonido agudo,* Acute sound.
Sonlocádo, **da**, *a.* V. *Alocado.*
Sonóra, *sf.* Cithern, a musical instrument.
Sonoraménte, *ad.* Sonorously; harmoniously.
Sonoridád, *sf.* Sonorousness, the quality of giving sound.
Sonóro, **ra**; y **Sonoróso**, **sa**, *a.* 1. Sonorous, sounding. 2. Pleasing, agreeable, harmoni- [ous.
Sonreírse, *vr.* To smile.
Sonrísa y **Sonríso**, *sf.* y *m.* Smile. [mud.
Sonrodadúra, *sf.* The act of sticking in the
Sonrodárse, *vr.* To stick in the mire or mud; applied to the wheels of a cart or carriage.
Sonrosár y **Sonroseár**, *va.* To dye a rose colour. *Sonrosearse, vr.* To blush.
Sonroséo, *sm.* Blush.
Sonroxár, *va.* To make one blush with shame.
Sonróxo, *sm.* 1. Blush, the act of blushing. 2. Offensive word which causes a blush.
Sonrugírse, *vr.* V. *Susurrarse.*
Sonsáca, *sf.* Wheedling; petty theft.
Sonsacadór, **ra**, *s.* Wheedler; petty thief.
Sonsacamiénto, *sm.* Wheedling, extortion, petty theft.
Sonsacár, *va.* 1. To steal privately out of a bag. 2. To obtain by cunning and craft. 3. To pump a secret out of a person.
Sonsáque, *sm.* Wheedling; petty theft.
Sonsonéte, *sm.* 1. Noise arising from repeated gentle beats. 2. Sneer, a tone of scorn and derision.
Soñadór, **ra**, *s.* Dreamer; one who relates dreams and idle stories.
Soñár, *va.* 1. To dream, to be troubled with dreams. 2. To entertain fantastical ideas and opinions. *Ni soñarlo,* Not even dreamt of.
Soñarréra, *sf.* (Vulg.) Practia or act of dreaming, heavy sleep; visions.
Soñoléncia, *sf.* Sleepiness, heaviness, drowsiness. V. *Somnolencia.*
Soñolientaménte, *ad.* Sleepily, heavily.
Soñoliénto, **ta**, *a.* Heavy, sleepy, drowsy; causing sleep.
Sópa, *sf.* 1. Sop, a piece of bread steeped in

broth or other liquors. 2. Soup, a decoction of meat for the table. 3. The whole dinner or series of dishes, served up at table. 4. Broken victuals given to the poor. *Sopa de gato*, Meagre soup, made of bread, oil, salt, garlick, and water. *Sopa de leche*, Milk porridge. *Sopa borracha*, Soup made with wine, biscuit, sugar, and cinnamon. *Andar á la sopa*, To go begging from door to door. *Hecho una sopa de agua*, Wet through to the skin. *Sopa de vino*, (Bot.) Flower of the crowfoot. *¿ Porquería son sopas ?* Familiar retort to one who depreciates any thing worthy of respect.

Sopalancár, *va.* To put a lever under any thing to lift it.

Sopalánda, *sf.* Ragged clothes worn by poor students.

Sopándas, *sf. pl.* Braces, the thick leather thongs which support the body of a coach; lintels, cross-beams over gate-ways.

Sopápo, *sm.* 1. Box, a blow or slap given with the hand. 2. Sucker, a moveable valve used in hydraulic vessels or pumps.

Sopár ó Sopeár, *va.* 1. To sop, to steep bread in broth or other liquors. V. *Ensopar*. 2. To tread, to trample; to domineer.

Sopáypa, *sf.* A sort of fritter steeped in honey.

Sopéna, *ad.* On pain. *Sopena de muerte*, On pain of death.

Sopéña, *sf.* Cavity or pit formed by a rock.

Sopéra, *sf.* Soup-dish, a vessel in which soup is served up at table.

Sopéro, *sm.* Soup-plate; lover of soups.

Sopesár, *va.* To try the weight. V. *Sompesar*.

Sopeteár, *va.* 1. To sop; to steep bread in sauce, broth, or other liquors. 2. To abuse with foul language.

Sopetón, *sm.* 1. Plentiful soup. *Sopeton de molino*, Bread toasted and steeped in oil. 2. A heavy box or slap with the hand. *De sopeton*, Suddenly.

Sopílla ó Sopíta, *sf.* Sippet, a light soup.

Sopilóte. V. *Gallinaza*.

Sopísta, *sm.* Person living upon charity.

Sópla, *interj.* O strange! expressing admiration.

Sopladéro, *sm.* Draught or air-hole to subterraneous passages.

Sopládo, da, *a.* Blown; overnice and spruce.

Sopladór, ra, *s.* 1. Blower, that which blows. 2. That which excites or inflames.

Soplamócos, *sm.* Box or slap on the face or nose.

Sopiánte, *pa.* Blowing, exciting.

Soplár, *vn.* 1. To blow, to emit wind at the mouth. 2. To blow with bellows. 3. To be blown away by the wind.—*va.* 1. To separate with wind. 2. To rob or steal in an artful manner. 3. To suggest notions or ideas, to inspire. *Soplar la musa*, To get a strain or vein of poetry, to inspire the muse. 6. (In the Game of Draughts) To huff a man. 7. To tipple, to drink much. 8. To charge with a fault. *Soplar la dama*, (Met.) To marry a woman supposed to be engaged or offered to another.—*vr.* To dress in style; to be overnice in dress. *Soplarse las manos ó las uñas*, (Met.) To be disappointed and burlesqued.

Sopléte, *sm.* (In Glass-houses) Blowing-pipe, a hollow iron tube with which bottles and all glasswares are blown or formed.

Soplíllo, *sm.* 1. Crape, a thin crisp stuff. 2. Any thing extremely thin and light.

Sóplo, *sm.* 1. Puff, blast; the act of blowing. 2. Advice given secretly, and with great caution. 3. Denunciation, accusation, information. 4. Interest, favour, protection. 5. Instant, moment; very short space of time. 6. (Naút.) A sudden gust of wind, which soon dies away.

Soplón, na, *s.* Tale-bearer, informer.

Soploncíllo, lla, *s.* Little tattler.

Sopón, *sm.* Person living upon charity soup.

Sopóncio, *sm.* Grief arising from disappointment.

Sopór, *sm.* Heaviness, drowsiness, sleepiness.

Soporífero, ra, *a.* Soporific, soporiferous.

Soporóso, sa, *a.* Soporific.

Soportáble, *a.* Tolerable, supportable.

Soportadór, ra, *s.* Supporter.

Soportál, *sm.* Portico, a large porch at the entrance of a house.

Soportár, *va.* To suffer, to tolerate; to support.

Soprión, *sm.* V. *Subprior*.

So protésta, *ad.* (Com.) Under protest.

Sopuntár, *va.* To place marks under a wrong word.

Sór ó Séor, *sm.* Sir, master. V. *Señor*.

Sor, *sf.* Sister. V. *Hermana*. *Sor María*, Sister Mary; used only to nuns.

Sóro, *sf.* Peruvian drink made of a decoction of maize.

Sórba, *sf.* Sorb-apple. V. *Serba*.

Sorbedór, *sm.* Sipper, one who sips.

Sorbér, *va.* 1. To sip, to suck, to take a small quantity of liquors in at the mouth. 2. To absorb, to swallow; to consume. 3. To imbibe, to soak as a sponge. *Sorbérsele á alguno*, To conquer or to surpass any one.

Sorbéte, *sm.* Sherbet, a liquor made of sugar and preserved fruit.

Sorbetón, *sm.* A large draught of liquor.

Sorbíble, *a.* That may be sipped up.

Sorbición, *sf.* (Med.) Absorption.

Sorbíto y llo, *sm.* Sup, a small draught.

Sórbo, *sm.* 1. The act of drinking or sipping; absorption. 2. Sup, draught, the quantity of liquor drank at once. 3. Any thing comparatively small. 4. (Bot.) Service-tree. Sorbus [L.

Sórce, *sm.* Field-mouse.

Sordaménte, *ad.* Secretly, silently.

Sordástro, tra, *a.* Deaf, hard of hearing.

Sordéra y Sordéz, *sf.* Deafness, surdity.

Sordidaménte, *ad.* Sordidly, dirtily.

Sordidéz, *sf.* Sordidness, nastiness.

Sórdido, da, *a.* Sordid, nasty, dirty, filthy; licentious.

Sordíllo, lla; to, ta, *a. dim.* Slightly deaf.

Sordína, *sf.* 1. Kit, a small fiddle. 2. Mute, a piece put on the bridge of a fiddle, to weaken the sound. *A' la sordina*, Secretly, privately, without noise.

Sórdo, da, *a.* 1. Deaf, deprived of the sense of hearing; insensible of reason. 2. Silent, still, quiet. 3. Deafening, producing deafness. 4. Surd; incapable of hearing; insensible. *A' la sorda, á lo sordo, ó á sordas*, Silently, quietly. *Dar música á un sordo*, To labour in vain.

Sóri, *sm.* Sory, a vitriolic mineral.

Sórico, *a.* Belonging to the itch.

Sorítes, *sm.* (Log.) Sorites, proposition or argument accumulated on another.
Sormigrár, *va.* (Ant.) V. *Sumergir.*
Sórna, *sf.* Sluggishness, laziness, slowness of performance; feigned sloth.
Sornavirón, *sm.* Sudden stroke with the back of the open hand.
Sóro, *sm.* Year-old hawk.
Soroftálmia, *sf.* Disease in the eyelids.
Sorór, *sf.* Sister. V. *Sor.*
Sorprehendér, *va.* To execute any thing silently: to surprise, to take by surprise, to deceive.
Sorprésa, *sf.* 1. Surprise; the act of taking by surprise, deceit, imposition. 2. Amazement, astonishment. *Sorpresa de una carta*, The act of intercepting a letter.
Sórra, *sf.* 1. (Naút.) Ballast of stones or coarse gravel. 2. Jole or side of a tunny fish.
Sorregár, *va.* To water in another course; applied to rivulets which casually change their channels.
Sorréro, ra, *a.* V. *Zorrero.*
Sorriégo, *sm.* Water which passes occasionally from one channel to another.
Sorrostráda, *sf.* Great face or beak.
Sorteadór, *sm.* 1. One who casts lots. 2. Bull-fighter, who fights with great skill.
Sorteamiénto, *sm.* V. *Sorteo.*
Sorteár, *va.* 1. To draw or cast lots. 2. To fight bulls with skill and dexterity.
Sortéo, *sm.* Act of casting or drawing lots.
Sortéro, *sm.* Fortune-teller. V. *Agorero.*
Sortíja, *sf.* 1. Ring worn on the hand. 2. Ring, a circle of metal used for a variety of purposes; hoop. 3. Buckle, the state of the hair crisped and curled. *Sortijas*, Hoops of vessels. [ringlet.
Sortijíta y Sortijuéla, *sf. dim.* Little ring,
Sortijón, *sm.* A large ring.
Sortilégio, *sm.* Sortilege, sorcery.
Sortílego, ga, *s.* Sorcerer, conjurer, fortune-teller.
Sortú, *sm.* 1. Great coat. 2. Piece of plate.
Sósa, *sf.* 1. (Bot.) Saltwort. Salsola *L.* 2. Soda, barilla. 3. Dross of silver used in some glass manufactories.
Sosacár, *va.* (Ant.) V. *Sonsacar.*
Sosaménte, *ad.* Insipidly, tastelessly.
Sosáño, *sm.* Derision, mockery.
Sosegadaménte, *ad.* Quietly, calmly.
Sosegádo, da, *a.* Quiet, peaceful.
Sosegadór, ra, *s.* Pacifier, appeaser.
Sosegár, *va.* 1. To appease, to calm, to pacify. 2. To lull, to put to sleep.—*vn.* 1. To rest, to repose. 2. To be calm or composed. *Sosegarse el ayre*, To grow calm. *Sosiéguese vd.* Compose yourself. [pid expression.
Sosería, *sf.* Insipidity, dull tastelessness; insi-
Sosés, *sf.* Insipidness, silliness. *Decir soseces*, To use silly jokes.
Sosiégo, *sm.* Tranquillity, calmness. [ly.
Soslayár, *va.* To do or place a thing oblique-
Sosláyo, *ad.* Obliquely. *Al soslayo ó de soslayo*, Askew, sideways.
Sóso, sa, *a.* Insipid, unsalted; silly, senseless.
Sospécha, *sf.* Suspicion, surmise.
Sospechár, *va.* To suspect; to imagine guilt without proof.
Sospechílla, *sf.* Slight suspicion. [fully.
Sospechosaménte, *ad.* Suspiciously, doubt-
Sospechóso, sa, *a.* Suspicious, liable to suspicion; inclined to suspect; suspected.
Sospesár, *va.* To suspend, to raise above the ground.
Sospíro, *sm.* V. *Suspiro.*
Sosquín, *sm.* Slap or blow treacherously given.
Sostén, *sm.* 1. Support, the act of sustaining or supporting. 2. (Naút.) Firmness or steadiness of a ship in pursuing her course.
Sostenedór, ra, *s.* Supporter; one who sustains or supports.
Sostenér, *va.* 1. To sustain, to support, to maintain. 2. To supply with the necessaries of life. *Sostener la caza*, (Naút.) To pursue the chase. 3. To suffer, to tolerate.—*vr.* 1. To support or maintain one's self. 2. (Naút.) To bear up.
Sosteniénte, *pa.* Sustainer, supporting.
Sostenimiénto, *sm.* Sustenance, the act of sustaining or bearing up.
Sostituír, *va.* To substitute. V. *Substituir.*
Sostitúto, *sm.* Substitute. V. *Substituto.*
Sóta, *sf.* 1. Knave, at cards. 2. Deputy, substitute.
Sóta, *prep.* (Ant.) Under, below. V. *De Baxo.*
Sotabánco, *sm.* (Arq.) Pediment of an arch over a cornice.
Sotacaballerízo, *sm.* Deputy-equerry.
Sotacochéro, *sm.* Postillion.
Sotacóla, *sf.* Crupper. V. *Ataharre.*
Sotacómitre, *sm.* (Naút.) Boatswain's mate.
Sotacóro, *sm.* Place under the upper choir.
Sotalúgo, *sm.* The second hoop of a cask.
Sotamaéstro, *sm.* Usher at a school.
Sotaminístro, *sm.* Under-secretary of state.
Sotamontéro, *sm.* Under-huntsman, deputy-forester.
Sotána, *sf.* 1. Cassock, the long under-gown of a priest. 2. Flogging, drubbing.
Sotanádo, da, *a.* Vaulted, arched.
Sotaneár, *va.* To beat, to chastise or reprehend severely.
Sotaní, *sm.* Short round under petticoat without plaits.
Sotanílla, *sf.* A small cassock; dress of some collegians.
Sótano, *sm.* Cellar under ground. [ward.
Sotaventádo, da, *a.* (Naút.) Driven to lee-
Sotaventár, *va.* (Naút.) To fall to leeward, to lose the weather-gage.
Sotavénto, *sm.* Leeward; the side opposite to windward. *Tener buen sotavento*, (Naút.) To have sea-room. *Banda de sotavento*, (Naút.) Lee-side of a ship. *Costa de sotavento*, (Naút.) Lee-shore. *A' sotavento*, Under the lee.
Sotayúda, *sm.* Under assistant to officers at court.
Sotechádo, *sm.* A roofed or covered place.
Sotéño, ña, *a.* Produced in groves or forests.
Soterráneo, ea, *a.* Subterraneous.
Soterráño, *sm.* V. *Subterraneo.*
Soterrár, *va.* 1. To bury, to put under ground. 2. To hide, to conceal.
Sotíl, *a.* Subtle, subtile. V. *Sutil.*
Sotíllo, *sm.* Little grove.
Sóto, *sm.* Grove, thicket, forest.
Sóto, *prep.* Under, beneath, below. V. *Debaxo*
Sotominístro, *sm.* Assistant clerk of the kitchen or steward in convents of the Jesuits.

Sotrózos, *sm. pl.* Linch-pins.
Sozprión, *sm.* (Ant.) V. *Suprior.*
Spát, *sm.* (Min.) Spar. V. *Espato.*
Sú, *pron. poss.* His, her; in the plural, *Sus,* theirs.
Suadír, *va.* (Ant.) V. *Persuadir.*
Suasívo, **va**, *a.* V. *Persuasivo.*
Suasório, **ria**, *a.* Suasory, suasive.
Suáve, *a.* 1. Smooth, soft, delicate. 2. Easy, tranquil, quiet. 3. Gentle, tractable, docile.
Suavemênte, *ad.* Gently, sweetly, softly.
Suavidád, *sf.* 1. Softness, delicacy, sweetness. 2. Suavity, meekness; tranquillity.
Suavizadór, *sm.* Razor-strap.
Suavizár, *va.* 1. To soften, to mitigate. 2. To render metals more pliable or ductile.
Subalcáyde, *sm.* Deputy or sub-governor or jailer.
Subalternánte, *pa.* That to which another thing is subject.
Subalternár, *va.* To subject, to subdue.
Subaltérno, **na**, *a.* Subaltern, inferior, subject.
Subarrendadór, **ra**, *s.* Under-tenant, sub-renter. [under another renter.
Subarrendamiénto, *sm.* Farming or renting
Subarrendár, *va.* To rent a farm from another farmer or tenant.
Subarriéndo, *sm.* Renting or farming under another farmer.
Subásta y Subastación, *sf.* Juridical sale of goods by public auction.
Subastár, *va.* To sell by auction.
Subcantór, *sm.* Subchanter, he who officiates in the absence of the precentor.
Subcinerício, **cia**, *a.* Baked under ashes.
Subclavéro, *sm.* Under-treasurer or cashier; deputy key-bearer.
Subclávio, **via**, *a.* Subclavian, under the arm-pit or shoulder.
Subcolectór, *sm.* Sub-collector.
Subcomendadór, *sm.* Deputy-governor.
Subconservadór, *sm.* Judge deputed by a conservator. [legated.
Subdelegáble, *a.* That which may be subde-
Subdelegación, *sf.* Subdelegation, substitution.
Subdelegádo, *sm.* Subdelegate, one to whom the delegate has committed his jurisdiction or power.
Subdelegánte, *pa.* He who subdelegates.
Subdelegár, *va.* To subdelegate, to commit to another one's jurisdiction or power.
Subdiaconádo ó áto, *sm.* Subdeaconship.
Subdiácono, *sm.* Subdeacon, clergyman who is ordained to assist the deacon at divine service.
Subdistinción, *sf.* Subdistinction.
Subdistinguír, *va.* To distinguish that which has already been distinguished.
Súbdito, **ta**, *a.* Subject, inferior to another.
Subdividír, *va.* To subdivide, to divide a part already divided, into more parts.
Subdivisión, *sf.* Subdivision.
Subdúplo, **pla**, *a.* Subduple, containing one part of two. [ly meant.
Subentendér, *va.* To understand what is tacit-
Subexecutór, *sm.* Deputy executor.
Subfletár, *va.* (Naút.) To hire a ship of another freighter.

Subída, *sf.* 1. Ascension, the act of going up. 2. Ascent, acclivity, rise. 3. Accession of a disease. 4. Enhancement, augmentation of value or price, melioration of things.
Subidéro, **ra**, *a.* Mounting, rising.
Subidéro, *sm.* Ladder, mounting-block.
Subído, **da**, *a.* Finest, most excellent.
Subidór, *sm.* Porter, one who carries goods or other effects from lower to higher places.
Subiénte, *sm.* (Arq.) Ornaments of foliage ascending on columns or pilasters.
Subílla, *sf.* Awl. V. *Alesna.*
Subinquilíno, *sm.* Subtenant, one who rents a house of another tenant.
Subintración, *sf.* Immediate succession of one thing after another.
Subintránte, *pa.* Applied to fevers, one paroxysm of which has not subsided when another begins. [another.
Subintrár, *va.* To enter successively one after
Subír, *vn.* 1. To mount, to ascend. 2. To increase, to swell as rivers, &c. 3. To enter leaves, as silk-worms on commencing their cods. 4. To rise in dignity, fortune, &c. 5. (Mús.) To raise the voice gradually.—*va.* 1. To climb, to ascend. 2. To raise, to lift up: to go up. 3. To set up, to erect. 4. To amount to. 5. To enhance, to raise or increase the value. *Subir el color,* To raise a colour, to render it brighter. *Subír á caballo,* To mount a horse. *Subir la consulta al rey,* To lay an affair before the king. *Subirse á talones,* To grow proud and haughty. *Subirse á las bobedillas,* (Fam.) To be violently irritated.
Subitaneaménte y Subitanamênte, *ad.* Suddenly, on a sudden.
Subitáneo, **nea**; **y Subitáño**, **ña**, *a.* Sudden, unexpected, happening of a sudden.
Súbito, **ta**, *a.* Sudden, hasty, unforeseen, unexpected. *Súbito ó de súbito, ad.* Suddenly, unexpectedly.
Subjectár y Subjetár. V. *Sujetar.*
Subjeción, *sf.* (Ret.) A figure used in debating and answering within ourselves. [jeto.
Subjécto, *sm.* (Ant.) Subject, matter. V. *Su-*
Subjetívo, **va**, *a.* Subjective.
Subjugár, *va.* To subdue, to subject. V. *Sojuzgar.*
Subjuntívo, *sm.* Subjunctive, one of the modes of conjugating verbs.
Sublevación y Sublevamiénto, *s.* Insurrection, sedition, revolt.
Sublevár, *va.* To excite a rebellion; to rise in rebellion. [ing.
Sublimación, *sf.* Sublimation, act of sublimat-
Sublimádo, *sm.* Sublimate, the subtle substance raised by fire in the retort.
Sublimár, *va.* 1. To heighten, to elevate, to exalt. 2. To sublimate, to raise by the force of chemical fire.
Sublimatório, **ria**, *a.* (Farm.) Sublimatory.
Sublíme, *a.* Sublime, exalted, eminent.
Sublimeménte, *ad.* Sublimely, loftily.
Sublimidád, *sf.* Sublimity, loftiness, grandeur.
Sublunár, *a.* Sublunar or sublunary, situated beneath the moon; terrestrial, earthly. [joint.
Subluxación, *sf.* An imperfect luxation of a
Subministrár, *va.* (Ant.) V. *Suministrar.*

Subordinación, *sf.* Subordination, subjection to the command of another.
Subordinadaménte, *ad.* Subordinately.
Subordinár, *va.* To subordinate, to subject to the command of another.
Subpolár, *a.* Situated or falling under the pole.
Subrepción, *sf.* 1. A hidden action, an underhand business. 2. Subreption, the act of obtaining a favour by false representation, surreption.
Subrepticiaménte, *ad.* Surreptitiously.
Subrepticio, cia, y Subreticio, cia, *a.* 1. Subreptitious, obtained by unfair representation, fraudulently obtained. 2. Done in a hidden or clandestine manner, surreptitious.
Subrigadiér, *sm.* Sub-brigadier, an officer under the brigadier.
Subrogación, *sf.* The act of surrogating or substituting.
Subrogár, *va.* To surrogate, to substitute, to appoint another person in one's stead or place.
Subsacristán, *sm.* Deputy sacristan or sexton.
Subsacristanía, *sf.* Office of deputy sacristan.
Subsanár, *va.* 1. To exculpate, to excuse. 2. To mend, to repair.
Subscribír, *va.* To subscribe. V. *Suscribir.*
Subscripción, *sf.* 1. Subscription, signature. V. *Subscripcion.* 2. Subscription, the act or state of contributing to any undertaking.
Subseguírse, *vr.* To follow next, to come immediately after.
Subseqüénte, *a.* Next following, subsequent.
Subsidiariaménte, *ad.* In a subsidiary manner.
Subsidiário, ria, *a.* Brought or given in aid, subsidiary.
Subsídio, *sm.* 1. Subsidy, aid; such as is commonly given in money. 2. Subsidy, war-tax.
Subsiguiénte, *a.* Subsequent, next following.
Subsisténcia, *sf.* 1. Subsistence, permanence, stability. 2. Subsistence, competence, means of supporting life..
Subsisténte, *pa.* Subsistent.
Subsistír, *vn.* To subsist, to last, to be firm in, to retain the present state.
Subsoláno, *sm.* North-east wind.
Substáncia, *sf.* V. *Sustancia.*
Substanciál, *a.* Substantial.
Substancialménte, *ad.* Substantially.
Substanciár, *va.* 1. To extract the substance, to abridge. 2. To substantiate, to prove fully, to establish the truth of a fact or event. 3. To pursue the proceedings in a cause until its final determination.
Substancióso, sa, *a.* Substantial, responsible; moderately wealthy.
Substantífico, ca, *a.* V. *Sustantifico.*
Substantivár, *va.* To use adjectives as substantives. V. *Sustantivar.*
Substantívo, *sm.* (Gram.) Substantive.
Substitución, *sf.* Substitution. V. *Sustitucion.*
Substituír, *va.* To substitute. V. *Sustituir.*
Substituyénte, *pa.* Substituting.
Substitúto, *sm.* Substitute. V. *Sustituto.*
Substracción, *sf.* 1. Subtraction, division, separation. 2. Privation, concealment.
Substraér, *va.* To subtract. V. *Sustraer.* *Substraerse*, To withdraw one's self.
Subtendér, *va.* To subtend.
Subteniénte, *sm.* V. *Alferez.*
Subténsa, *sf.* (Matem.) Subtense.
Subténso, sa, *pp. irreg.* of *Subtender.*
Subterraneaménte, *ad.* Subterraneously.
Subterráneo, nea, *a.* Subterraneous, lying under the earth.—*sm.* Cave, vault under ground.
Subtiléza, *sf.* V. *Sutileza.*
Subtilménte, *ad.* Subtlely, subtilly, subtly.
Subtilización, *sf.* Subtiliation, subtleness.
Subtraér, *va.* (Ant.) V. *Sustraer.*
Suburbáno, na, *a.* Inhabiting a suburb.
Subúrbio, *sm.* Suburb, an inhabited place without the walls of a city.
Subvención, *sf.* Help, assistance, aid.
Subvenír, *va.* 1. To aid, to assist, to succour. 2. To provide, to supply, to furnish.
Subversión, *sf.* Subversion. V. *Suversion.*
Subversór, *sm.* Subverter, overturner.
Subvertír, *va.* To subvert, to destroy, to ruin.
Subyugár, *va.* To subdue, to subjugate, to overcome.
Succíno, *sm.* Amber. V. *Ambar.*
Succión, *sf.* Suction, the act of drawing in with the breath.
Sucedér, *vn.* 1. To succeed, to follow. 2. To inherit, to succeed by inheritance.—*v. impers.* To happen, to come to pass. *Sucedió asi*, It happened so.
Sucediénte, *pa.* Successor.
Sucesíble, *a.* Capable of success.
Sucesión, *sf.* 1. Succession, series. 2. Issue, offspring, children.
Sucesivaménte, *ad.* Successively.
Sucesívo, va, *a.* Successive, following in order one after another.
Sucéso, *sm.* Event, incident. V. *Transcurso.*
Sucesór, ra, *s.* Successor.
Suciaménte, *ad.* Nastily, filthily, dirtily.
Suciedád, *sf.* Nastiness, filthiness.
Sucintaménte, *ad.* Succinctly, briefly.
Sucintárse, *vr.* V. *Ceñirse.*
Sucínto, ta, *a.* 1. Girded, tucked up. 2. Brief, succinct, compendious, concise.
Súcio, cia, *a.* 1. Dirty, nasty, filthy. 2. Stained with sin, tainted with guilt. 3. Obscure; applied to language. 4. Uncivil, unpolished. 5. Soiled, ill-coloured. 6. Unhealthy, unwholesome. 7. (Naút.) Foul; applied to the bottom of a ship.
Súco, *sm.* Juice; sap.
Sucóso, sa, *a.* Juicy, succulent. V. *Xugoso.*
Sucotríno, *a.* Succotrine; applied to fine aloes.
Súcubo, *sm.* Succuba, incubus, night-mare.
Sucúcho, *sm.* Store-room on board of a ship. *Sucucho del condestable*, (Naút.) Gunner's room. *Sucucho del contramaestre*, Boatswain's store-room.
Súcula, *sf.* Cylinder. V. *Cábria.*
Suculénto, ta, *a.* Succulent. V. *Xugoso.*
Sucumbír, *vn.* (For.) To lose a process.
Súd, *sm.* South, the southern part of the sphere. *Sud-oeste*, South-west. *Sud-oeste quarto al oeste*, South-west by west. *Sud-oeste quarto al sur*, South-west by south.
Sudadéro, *sm.* 1. Handkerchief for wiping off the sweat. 2. Bath, sweating-room. 3. Moist ground, a place where water oozes out by drops. 4. Sweating-place for sheep previous to their being shorn. V. *Bacho.*
Sudánte, *pa.* Sweater, one that perspires much.
Sudár, *va.* 1. To sweat, to emit sweat, to per-

spire. 2. To give with repugnance. 3. To toil, to labour. 4. To ooze, to distil. *Sudar la prensa*, To print much.

Sudário, *sm.* 1. Handkerchief or cloth for wiping off the sweat. 2. Cloth put on the face of the dead.

Sudatório, ria, *a.* Sudorific, causing or producing sweat.

Sudéste, *sm.* South-east.

Sudór, *sm.* 1. Sweat, the matter evacuated at the pores by heat or labour. *Sudores*, Perspirations; salivation for venereal diseases. 2. Labour, toil, drudgery. 3. Viscous matter or gum, that distils from trees.

Sudoriénto, ta, *a.* Sweated, moistened with sweat.

Sudorífero, ra, *a.* Sudorific, causing sweat.

Sudorífico, ca, *a.* (Med.) Sudorific, promoting sweat.

Sudóso, sa, *a.* Sweaty, moist with sweat.

Sudouéste, *sm.* South-west.

Sudsudéste, *sm.* South south-east.

Sudsudouéste, *sm.* South south-west.

Sudueste, *sm.* South-west. V. *Africo.*

Suegrecíta, *sf.* (Joc.) Little mother-in-law.

Suégro, gra, *s.* 1. Father-in-law, mother-in-law. 2. Hard crust of bread.

Suéla, *sf.* 1. Sole, the bottom of the shoe. 2. Sole-leather, hides tanned for soles. 3. (Ict.) Sole. Pleuronectes solea *L.* 4. A horizontal joist or rafter, laid as the foundation for partition-walls. *Suelas*, A kind of sandals, worn by some religious orders. *De tres ó quatro suelas*, Firm, solid. *Tonto de quatro suelas*, A downright fool.

Suélda, *sf.* V. *Consuelda.*

Sueldacostílla, *sf.* (Bot.) A bulbous plant.

Suéldo, *sm.* 1. (Arag.) Coin or money worth half a real of plate; ancient Roman coin. 2. Pay, given or assigned to soldiers. 3. Wages, salary, stipend. *Sueldo á libra ó sueldo por libra*, Rated at so much a pound or per pound.

Suélo, *sm.* 1. Ground, soil, surface; superficies. 2. Bottom of a vessel. 3. Dregs, lees. 4. Groundplot, the piece of ground on which a building stands. 5. Pavement, ground-floor. 6. Bottom of a jar of wine which is usually stronger. 7. Region, district, province. 8. Hoof of a horse. 9. Limit, bounds, end. 10. Ignoble origin or condition of any one. 11. (Met.) Earth, world. *Suelo del estribo*, Rest of a stirrup. *N. lleva de suelo el ser necio*, N. was always an ignorant dunce. *Sin suelo*, To excess; without bounds.—*pl.* 1. Grain, scattered by cleaning in the field, where it is afterwards gathered together. 2. The under shafts of a carriage. 3. Straw and grain remaining in barns from one year to another.

Suélta, *sf.* 1. Act of loosening or letting loose; solution. 2. Fetters, with which the feet of a beast are tied, when grazing. 3. Relay of oxen, which travel loose to relieve those that are put to the carts. 4. Place where yoked oxen halt and receive refreshments. *Dar suelta*, To liberate for a short time.

Sueltaménte, *ad.* Loosely, lightly, expeditiously; licentiously; spontaneously.

Suélto, ta, *a.* 1. Loose, light, expeditious, swift, able. 2. Free, bold, daring. 3. Easy, disengaged. 4. Voluble, fluent of words. 5. Blank; applied to verse without rhyme. 6. V. *Soltero. Suelto de lengua*, Audacious, shameless, ill-tongued.

Suélto, *sm.* Loose piece of metal or mineral found near mines.

Suéno, *sm.* (Ant.) V. *Sonido.*

Suéño, *sm.* 1. Sleep, the act of sleeping. 2. Vision, dream, phantasm of sleep, the thoughts and fancies of a sleeping person. 3. Drowsiness, heaviness, inclination to sleep. *Tengo sueño*, I am sleepy. 4. Any fantastical idea without foundation. 5. Shortness, lightness, or swiftness with which any thing appears or passes. *A' sueño suelto*, Without any care. *En sueños, ó entre sueños*, Dreaming, sleeping. *A' sueño pesado*, In a profound sleep; deep heavy sleep, and difficult to dispel. *Ni por sueño*, By no means; it was never dreamt of. *No dormir sueño*, To be watchful, to be unable to sleep.

Suéro, *sm.* 1. Whey, the thin or serous part of the milk. 2. Serum, aqueous humour of the blood.

Suerósо, sa, *a.* V. *Seroso.*

Suérte, *sf.* 1. Chance, fortuitous event: lot, fortune. 2. Kind, sort; species. 3. Manner, mode, way. *De la misma suerte*, The same way. 4. Skilful movements of a bull-fighter. 5. Piece of ground, separated from the rest by bounds or land-marks. 6. Lottery-ticket. *La suerte está echada*, The die is cast. *Suerte y verdad*, Arbitration, or appeal from players to the spectators for the justness of their case. 7. Original stock, lineage. 8. (Ant.) Capital, stock in trade. *De suerte*, So as, so that. *De suerte que no debe nada*, So that he owes nothing. *Echar suertes*, To cast or draw lots. *Este me cupo en suerte*, It fell to my lot.

Suéste, *sm.* South-east. *Sueste quarto al este*, (Naút.) South-east by east. *Sueste quarto al sur*, (Naút.) South-east by south.

Suficiéncia, *sf.* Sufficience, sufficiency. *A suficiencia*, Sufficiently, enough.

Suficiénte, *a.* Sufficient, enough; qualified, apt, fit, capable.

Suficienteménte, *ad.* Sufficiently.

Sufocación, *sf.* Suffocation, the act of suffocating; the act of being suffocated or choked.

Sufocadór, ra, *s.* Suffocater, choker.

Sufocánte, *pa.* Suffocater, suffocating.

Sufocár, *va.* 1. To suffocate, to choke, to smother. 2. To quench or put out the fire. 3. To molest, to harass, to oppress.

Sufóco, *sm.* Suffocating; fumigation.

Sufragáneo y Sufragáno, *sm.* Suffragan, a bishop subject to a metropolitan.

Sufragáneo, ea, *a.* Belonging to a suffragan.

Sufragár, *va.* 1. To favour, to aid, to assist. 2. To suffice, to be sufficient.

Sufrágio, *sm.* 1. Vote, suffrage, voice. 2. Favour, support, aid, assistance. 3. Any work appropriated to the souls of the deceased in purgatory.

Sufríble, *a.* Tolerable, that may be endured.

Sufridéra, *sf.* Smith's tool for punching holes on an anvil.

Sufridéro, ra, *a.* Supportable, tolerable.

Sufrído, da, *a.* 1. Bearing up under adversities

and misfortunes. 2. Consenting, accommodating; spoken of a contented cuckold. *Mal sufrido*, Impatient, rude, severe.
Sufridór, ra, *s.* Sufferer, one who suffers or endures with patience.
Sufriénte, *pa.* Tolerating, bearing.
Sufrimiénto, *sm.* Sufferance, patience, tolerance.
Sufrír, *va.* 1. To suffer, to bear or endure with patience. 2. To bear or carry any load; to sustain an attack. 3. To clinch a nail on the other side of a board. 4. To permit, to tolerate. 5. To pay and suffer.
Sufumigación, *sf.* Suffumigation, operation of fumes, administered as a remedy or cure.
Sufusión, *sf.* Suffusion, kind of cataract in the eyes.
Sugeriénte, *pa.* Suggesting.
Sugerír, *va.* 1. To hint, to suggest, to intimate. 2. To prompt, to instigate to an evil action.
Sugestión, *sf.* Suggestion, intimation, hint.
Sugésto, *sm.* 1. Pulpit, a high desk for preaching. 2. Stage, scaffold.
Sugéto, *sm.* 1. Any undefined person or individual; distinguished person. 2. Activity, vigour, strength. 3. Matter, subject, topic, theme. 4. That in which any thing inheres or subsists. 5. Subject, that of which any thing is announced. 6. Disposal, intention, disposition.
Súgo, *sm.* Juice; sap. V. *Xugo.*
Suíza, *sf.* Company of persons dressed in the Swiss fashion at a public festival.
Sujeción, *sf.* 1. Subjection, the act of subduing; the act of submitting or surrendering; connexion. 2. Objection, argument.
Sujetár, *va.* 1. To subdue, to reduce to submission. 2. To overcome, to conquer.—*vr.* To be inherent; to adhere.
Sujéto, ta, *a.* 1. Subject, liable, exposed. 2. Amenable before a court of justice.—*sm.* Subject, topic.
Sulcár, *va.* To furrow, to plough. V. *Surcar.*
Súlco, *sm.* Furrow. V. *Surco.*
Sulfonéte, *sm.* Match. V. *Alguáquida.*
Súlfur, *sm.* Brimstone, sulphur. V. *Azufre.*
Sulfúreo, rea, *a.* Sulphureous, sulphurous.
Sulfúrico, *a.* Sulphuric; applied to acid; consisting of sulphur.
Súlla, *sf.* (Bot.) French honey-suckle. Hedysarum coronarium *L.*
Sultán, *sm.* Sultan; an appellation which the Turks give to their emperor.
Sultána, *sf.* 1. Sultana or sultaness, the queen of a Turkish emperor. 2. (Naút.) Admiral's ship, among the Turks.
Súma, *sf.* 1. Sum, the whole of any thing, many particulars aggregated to a total; substance, heads of any thing. 2. Amount or result of reasoning or computation; act of summing up, conclusion. 3. Compendium, abridgment. *En suma*, In short; finally.
Sumaménte, *ad.* Chiefly; extremely.
Sumár, *va.* 1. To sum, to collect particulars into a total; to add. 2. To collect into a narrow compass; to sum up, to recapitulate. —*vn.* To cast up accounts; to result.
Sumária, *sf.* The first or preparatory proceeding in a suit at law; verbal process.
Sumariaménte, *ad.* Summarily; in a plain manner.
Sumário, ria, *a.* Summary, compendious; plain, without formalities.
Sumário, *sm.* Compendium, abridgment, summary; result of computation.
Sumergimiénto, *sm.* V. *Sumersion.*
Sumergír, *va.* 1. To submerge, to sink, to put under water, to drown. 2. To embarrass, to involve in difficulties.
Sumersión, *sf.* Submersion, immersion.
Sumidád, *sf.* Top, summit, utmost height.
Sumidéro, *sm.* Sewer, drain, sink.
Sumído, da, *a.* Drowned; overflowed; plunged into vice.
Sumillér, *sm.* Chief of several offices in the king's household. *Sumiller de corps*, Lord chamberlain. *Sumiller de cortina*, Groom of the bed-chamber. *Sumiller de la cava y panateria*, Lord high steward.
Sumillería, *sf.* Lord chamberlain's office.
Suministración, *sf.* Supply, the act of furnishing or supplying.
Suministradór, ra, *s.* Provider, one who subministers.
Suministrár, *va.* To subminister, to supply, to furnish.
Sumír, *va.* To take, to receive. This term is confined to the receiving of the chalice in the celebration of the mass.—*vr.* 1. To sink under ground, to be swallowed up. 2. To be sunk; applied to the features of the face.
Sumisaménte, *ad.* Submissively.
Sumísa vóce, *ad.* (Lat.) In a low voice.
Sumisión, *sf.* 1. Submission, obsequiousness, compliance. 2. (For.) Renunciation.
Sumíso, sa, *a.* Submissive, humble, resigned.
Sumísta, *sm.* Abridger, writer of compendiums or summaries; computer; young student in morality.
Súmo, ma, *a.* Highest, loftiest, greatest; most elevated. *A lo sumo*, At most; to the highest pitch.
Sumónte, *sm.* Pile on cloth. V. *Somonte.*
Sumoscápo, *sm.* (Arq.) Curved termination of a scapus or first moulding on the top of a column.
Súmulas, *sf. pl.* Compendium, containing the first elements of logic.
Sumulísta, *sm.* Scholar who studies the first rudiments of logic.
Sumulístico, ca, *a.* Belonging to summaries of logic.
Súncho, *sm.* Clamp, a piece of timber joined to another to strengthen it; also an iron plate used for the same purpose. *Sunchos de la bomba*, (Naút.) Pump-clamps. *Sunchos de botalones de las alas*, Studding-sail-boom irons. *Sunchos de cabrestante*, Capstern-hoops. *Sunchos del cepo del ancla*, Anchor-stock-hoops. *Sunchos de fogonaduras*, (Naút.) Partners. *Sunchos de los palos*, Mast-hoops.
Suntuário, ria, *a.* Sumptuary, relating to expense; regulating the costs of life.
Suntuosaménte, *ad.* Sumptuously.
Suntuosidád, *sf.* Sumptuosity, expensive magnificence.
Suntuóso, sa, *a.* Sumptuous, costly, expensive; splendid.
Supedáneo, *sm.* Species of pedestal to a crucifix.

Supeditación, *sf*. The act of subduing or trampling under foot.
Supeditádo, da, *pp*. Trampled under foot. *Supeditado de los contrarios*, Suppressed by enemies.
Supeditár, *va*. To subdue, to trample under foot.
Superáble, *a*. Superable, conquerable; that may be overcome.
Superabundáncia, *sf*. Superabundance, excessive abundance, great plenty.
Superabundánte, *pa*. Superabundant.
Superabundanteménte, *ad*. Superabundantly.
Superabundár, *vn*. To superabound, to be exuberant, to abound to excess.
Superádito, ta, *a*. Superadded, added over and above.
Superáno, *sm*. Treble, the highest musical sound. V. *Tiple*.
Superánte, *pa*. Surpassing, surmounting.
Superár, *va*. To overcome; to surpass, to excel.
Superávit, *sm*. Overplus, residue.
Superbaménte, *ad*. V. *Soberbiamente*.
Supérbo, ba, *a*. Proud, arrogant, haughty. V. *Soberbio*.
Superchería, *sf*. 1. Artful fallacy, fraud, or deceit. 2. Incivility, want of civility and politeness; impudence, irreverence.
Superchéro, ra, *a*. 1. Wily, deceitful, insidious. 2. Uncivil, unpolite, impudent.
Supereminéncia, *sf*. Supereminence.
Supereminénte, *a*. Supereminent.
Supererogación, *sf*. Supererogation, performance of more than duty requires.
Superfetación, *sf*. Superfetation, one conception following another, so that both are in the womb together.
Superficiál, *a*. 1. Superficial, that remains on the surface, or belongs to it. 2. Shallow, not profound.
Superficialidád, *sf*. Superficiality, the state or quality of being superficial.
Superficialménte, *ad*. Superficially.
Superfície, *sf*. Superficies, outside, surface.
Superficionário, ria; ó **Superficiário, ria**, *a*. (For.) Applied to those who occupy or use the property of others by paying hire or rent.
Superfíno, na, *a*. Superfine.
Superfluaménte, *ad*. Superfluously, in a superfluous manner.
Superfluidád, *sf*. Superfluity, plenty beyond use or necessity; the superfluous thing.
Supérfluo, ua, *a*. Superfluous, exuberant; more than enough.
Superhumerál, *sm*. Ephod, scapulary; band for the cover of a reliquary.
Superintendéncia, *sf*. Superintendence, direction; office and duty of superintendent.
Superintendénte, *s. com*. Superintendent, intendant; an officer of high rank, who oversees any particular allotment of public business. *Superintendente de la casa de moneda*, Lord warden of the mint.
Superiór, *a*. Superior, higher; greater. *Alemania superior*, Upper Germany.
Superiór, ra, *s*. Superior, one who has the command of another.
Superiorázto, *sm*. Office of a superior.
Superioridád, *sf*. Superiority, pre-eminence, superior excellence.

Superioreménte, *ad*. Masterly, in a superior manner.
Superlativaménte, *ad*. Superlatively.
Superlatívo, va, *a*. Superlative, implying or expressing the highest degree.
Supérno, na, *a*. Supreme, highest.
Supernumerário, ria, *a*. Supernumerary; being above a stated, usual, or round number.
Superparciénte, *a*. (Arit.) Superpartient, containing a number and some aliquot part more.
Supersólido, da, *a*. (Arit.) The fifth power.
Superstición, *sf*. 1. Superstition, religion without morality; worship unduly given to what ought not to be worshipped; a consecrated selfishness. 2. Over-nicety, too scrupulous exactness.
Supersticiosaménte, *ad*. Superstitiously.
Supersticióso, sa, *a*. Superstitious; scrupulous beyond need.
Supersubstanciál, *a*. Supersubstantial; applied to the Eucharistical bread.
Supervacáneo, nea, *a*. V. *Superfluo*.
Supervalénte, *a*. Prevalent, exceeding in value.
Supervalér, *vn*. To exceed in value; to be worth more.
Supervención y **Superveniéncia**, *sf*. Supervention, the act of supervening.
Superveniénte, *a*. Supervenient; supervening.
Supervenír, *vn*. To supervene; to come as an extraneous addition. V. *Sobrevenir*.
Supervivéncia, *sf*. 1. Survivorship, the state of surviving another. 2. Money or annuity, stipulated in marriage-settlements in favour of the surviving consort.
Supinación, *sf*. Supination, lying on the back with the arms turned up and the head resting on the palms of the hands as a pillow: act of turning up the hands behind the head.
Supíno, na, *a*. Supine, indolent, lying with the face upwards; ignorant from negligence.
Supíno, *sm*. Supine, a verbal noun in grammar
Supír, *va*. (Ant.) V. *Saber*.
Súpito, ta, *a*. (Ant. Fam.) V. *Súbito*.
Suplantación, *sf*. The act of supplanting.
Suplantadór, ra, *s*. Supplanter, one that supplants or displaces another.
Suplantár, *va*. 1. To falsify a writing by blotting out words, and putting others in their place. 2. To supplant, to displace by stratagem.
Suplección, *sf*. (Ant.) Act and effect of supplying.
Suplefáltas, *sm*. (Fam.) Substitute, one who supplies the absence or wants of another.
Supleménto, *sm*. Supply, the act of supplying; supplement, auxiliary.
Supléncia, *sf*. Substitution, the act of supplying the place of another.
Supletório, ria, *a*. Suppletory, that which is to fill up deficiencies.
Súplica, *sf*. Petition, request; memorial.
Suplicación, *sf*. Request, petition. *Suplicaciones*, Conical tubes of thin and light paste thrust into one another, a kind of pastry. *A suplicacion*, By petition, memorializing.
Suplicacionéro, *sm*. Dealer in conical tubes of thin or light paste, pastry-seller.
Suplicánte, *pa*. Supplicant, petitioning
Suplicár, *va*. 1. To entreat, to implore, to supplicate. 2. To make an humble reply to a

superior. *Suplicar en revista,* To apply for a new trial. *Suplicar de la sentencia,* To petition against the sentence.

Suplicatoría, *sf.* Office existing among tribunals or judges of equal authority, that they may attend to what is solicited in the king's name.

Suplício, *sm.* 1. Capital punishment, pain of death. 2. Place of execution.

Suplidór, ra, *s.* Substitute, deputy.

Supliénte, *pa.* Substitute; supplying.

Suplimiénto, *sm.* V. *Suplemento.*

Suplír, *va.* 1. To supply deficiencies; to perform another's functions. 2. To excuse, to overlook, to disguise.

Suponedór, ra, *s.* Supposer, one who supposes.

Suponér, *va.* 1. To suppose, to surmise. *Supongase esto,* Let us suppose. 2. To fancy, to imagine.—*vn.* To possess weight or authority.

Suportár, *va.* V. *Sobrellevar.*

Suposición, *sf.* 1. Supposition, surmise. 2. Authority, distinction, eminence in point of talents. 3. Imposition, falsehood.

Supositár, *va.* (Teolog.) To exist under both divine and human nature in one person.

Supositício, cia, *a.* Supposititious. V. *Fingido.*

Supósito, *sm.* V. *Supuesto.*

Supositório, *sm.* (Med.) Probe. V. *Cala.*

Supraespína, *sf.* (Anat.) Cavity at the top of the shoulder, the supra-spinal fossa of the scapula.

Supraespinàto, *sm.* (Anat.) Supra-spinatus, muscle which serves to raise the arm.

Supréma, *sf.* The supreme council of the Inquisition.

Supremacía, *sf.* Supremacy.

Supremaménte, *ad.* Ultimately.

Supremidád, *sf.* (Ant.) V. *Supremacia.*

Supremo, ma, *a.* Supreme; highest, most exalted.

Supresión, *sf.* Suppression; obstruction.

Suprimír, *va.* 1. To suppress, to impede, to obstruct. 2. To abolish a place or employment. 3. To omit, to conceal.

Suprióр, ra, *s.* Sub-prior, sub-prioress.

Supriorato, *sm.* Office of sub-prior or prioress.

Supuésto, *sm.* 1. Supposition, the object or matter which is not expressed but implied in a proposition. 2. (Fil.) Individuality of a complete and incommunicable substance.

Supuésto, ta, *a.* Supposed. *Supuesto que,* Allowing that, granting that.

Supuración, *sf.* Suppuration, the ripening or change of the matter of a tumour into pus:

Supurár, *va.* 1. To waste or consume moisture by means of heat or fire. 2. (Cir.) To suppurate, to form pus. 3. (Met.) To dissipate, to evaporate; to lavish.

Supuratívo, va, *a.* Suppurative, promoting suppuration.

Supuratório, ria, *a.* Digestive, that which suppurates.

Suputación, *sf.* Computation, calculation.

Suputár, *va.* To compute, to calculate.

Sur, *sm.* South; south wind. *Navegar al sur,* (Naút.) To steer a southerly course; to stand to the southward.

Súra, *sf.* One of the bones in the leg.

Suráles, *a. pl.* Sural, belonging to the ball of the leg.

Surcadór, ra, *s.* Ploughman, plougher, one who makes furrows.

Surcár, *va.* 1. To furrow, to cut the ground into furrows with a plough. 2. (Met.) To furrow, to flute. 3. To run or pass through any liquid. *Surcar los mares,* (Naút.) To plough the seas.

Surcír, *va.* To darn or dearn. V. *Zurcir.*

Súrco, *sm.* 1. Furrow, hollow part of ploughed land; hollow track. 2. Line, wrinkle. *A surco,* Applied to pieces of ground furrowed in the middle.

Surculádo, da, *a.* Applied to plants of one stem without any branches.

Súrculo, *sm.* Single stem of a tree or plant without branches.

Surculóso, sa, *a.* Applied to a plant which has only one stem.

Surgénte, *pa.* Surging, salient.

Surgidéro, *sm.* Road, port, anchoring-place.

Surgidór, *sm.* He who anchors.

Surgír, *va.* 1. (Naút.) To anchor. 2. To surge. V. *Surtir.*

Suría, *sf.* Ancient kind of Syrian cloth.

Surtída, *sf.* 1. (Fort.) Sallyport, a small gate or passage under ground, leading from the body of the out-works, to facilitate a sally. 2. Sally, sortie. 3. Back-door.

Surtidéro, *sm.* Country abounding in grain. *Surtidero de trigo,* Public granary. *Surtidero de agua,* Reservoir, basin.

Surtído, *sm.* Assortment, supply. *De surtido,* In common use.

Surtidór, ra, *s.* 1. Purveyor, caterer. 2. Mouth whence water rises forcibly.

Surtimiénto, *sm.* Supply, the act of supplying; assortment.

Surtír, *vn.* To rebound, to fly back.—*va.* To supply, to furnish, to provide. *Surtir efecto,* To have the desired effect.

Súrto, ta, *pp.* Anchored; it is the old irregular participle of *surgir.*

Surtú, *sm.* V. *Sortú.*

Sus, *prep.* (Ant.) V. *Arriba.* *Sus de gayta,* Blast, whiff; any light airy thing without substance; wind of a syringe.—*interj.* Holla!

Susamiél, *sm.* Paste, made of almonds, sugar, and spice.

Susáno, na, *a.* (Ant.) Superior, above.

Suscepción, *sf.* Susception, the act of taking.

Susceptíble, *a.* Susceptible.

Susceptibilidád, *sf.* Susceptibility, quality of admitting, tendency to admit.

Susceptívo, va, *a.* Susceptible, susceptive.

Suscitación, *sf.* (Ant.) Suscitation.

Suscitár, *va.* 1. To excite, to stir up. *Suscitar una pendencia,* To stir up a quarrel. 2. To rouse, to promote vigour.

Suscribír, *va.* 1. To subscribe. 2. To accede to the opinion of another. 3. To contribute.

Suscriptór, ra, *s.* Subscriber.

Suséro, ra, *a.* (Ant.) Superior, above.

Susléro, *sm.* Rolling-pin.

Súso, *ad.* Above. V. *Arriba.*

Susodícho, cha, *a.* Forementioned, aforesaid

Suspección, *sf.* (Ant.) V. *Sospecha.*

Suspendedór, ra, *s.* Suspender.

Suspendér, *va.* 1. To suspend, to keep suspended in the air; to hang. 2. To suspend, to stop, to delay. *Suspenderse el caballo*, To rear, to stand on the hind legs, as a horse.

Suspensión, *sf.* 1. Suspension, detention, pause. 2. Hesitation, suspense. 3. Admiration, amazement. 4. Suspension, privation, an ecclesiastical censure. *Suspension de armas*, Cessation of hostilities.

Suspensívo, **va**, *a.* That which has the power of suspending.

Suspénso, **sa**, *pp. irreg.* of *suspender*, Hung; suspended.

Suspensório, **ria**, *a.* Suspensory, belonging to that by which any thing hangs.—*sm.* Brace, truss, suspensory.

Suspicácio, *sf.* Suspiciousness.

Suspicáz, *a.* Suspicious.

Suspicazménte, *ad.* Suspiciously.

Suspición, *sf.* (Ant.) V. *Sospecha.*

Suspiradór, *sm.* One who continually sighs or suspires; one who breathes with difficulty.

Suspirár, *va.* 1. To sigh, to suspire. 2. To crave, to desire anxiously. *Suspirar por el favor de la corte*, To gape for court favour. *Suspirar por el mando*, To aspire after command.

Suspíro, *sm.* 1. Sigh, suspiration; breath. 2. Hissing of the wind; sharp sound of a piece of glass. 3. Fine, delicate comfit made of sugar. 4. (Bot.) V. *Trinitaria.*

Suspiróso, **sa**, *a.* Suspiring with difficulty.

Sustáncia, *sf.* 1. Substance; essence; being; nature of things; something existing. 2. Support, nutriment, means of life. 3. Estate, fortune. 4. Value, estimation. *En substancia*, Briefly; (Med.) In substance.

Sustanciál, *a.* V. *Substancioso.*

Sustantífico, **ca**, *a.* Giving substance.

Sustantivadaménte, *ad.* Substantively.

Sustantivár, *va.* To use adjectives as substantives.

Sustantívo, *sm.* V. *Substantivo.*

Sustén, *sm.* Support. V. *Sosten.*

Sustenedór, **ra**, *s.* V. *Sostenedor.*

Sustenér, *va.* To support. V. *Sostener.*

Sustenído, *sm.* Spanish step in dancing.

Sustenído, **da**, *a.* (Mús.) Applied to a chord a semitone higher.

Sustentáble, *a.* Defensible, sustainable.

Sustentación, *sf.* Sustentation, support; the act of sustaining.

Sustentáculo, *sm.* Prop, stay, support.

Sustentadór, **ra**, *s.* One who sustains.

Sustentamiénto, *sm.* Sustenance, necessaries of life.

Sustentánte, *sm.* Defender, supporter; he who sustains conclusions in any faculty.

Sustentár, *va.* 1. To sustain, to bear up; to feed or support. 2. To assert, to maintain. *Sustentarse del ayre*, To live on vain hopes; to live upon the air; to be extravagant.

Susténto, *sm.* 1. Food, sustenance. 2. Support, the act of supporting, sustaining, or maintaining.

Susțíllo, *sm.* A slight fright.

Sustitución, *sf.* Substitution, surrogation.

Sustituidór, *sm.* He that substitutes.

Sustituír, *va.* To substitute, to surrogate, to appoint in one's place; to put one thing in the stead of another.

Sustitúto, **ta**, *s.* Substitute, surrogate, delegate.

Súsfo, *sm.* Fright, sudden terror.

Sustraér, *va.* To subtract, to take a part from a whole.—*vr.* To retire, to withdraw.

Susurración, *sf.* Susurration.

Susurradór, **ra**, *s.* Whisperer, he that whispers or mutters in a low voice.

Susurránte, *pa.* Whispering; tattler.

Susurrár, *vn.* 1. To whisper, to speak with a low voice; to divulge a secret. 2. To purl, as a stream; to whiz gently as the air.

Susúrro, *sm.* Whisper, humming.

Susurrón, **na**, *a.* Murmuring or whispering secretly.—*s.* Grumbler, malecontent.

Sutíl, *a.* Subtile, thin, slender. 2. Subtle, acute, cunning. 3. (Naut.) Light swift galley.

Sutiléza, *sf.* 1. Subtilty, thinness, slenderness. 2. Subtlety, artfulness, sagacity; acumen, perspicacity. 3. One of the four qualities of celestial bodies. *Sutileza de manos*, Address in handling or operating; sleight of hand; light-fingeredness or nimbleness of a thief.

Sutilidád, *sf.* Subtilty, subtlety.

Sutilización, *sf.* Subtilization, the act of subtilizing.

Sutilizadór, **ra**, *s.* One who subtilizes or attenuates.

Sutilizár, *va.* 1. To subtilize, to make thin and subtile. 2. To file, to polish. 3. To discuss in a profound and ingenious manner.

Sutilménte, *ad.* Subtly, pointedly; subtilely.

Sutíro, *sm.* (And.) Noise made by applying the hand to the ear.

Sutório, **ria**, *a.* Belonging to the shoe-maker's trade.

Sutúra, *sf.* Seam, suture. V. *Costura.*

Suversión, *sf.* Subversion, ruin, destruction.

Súyo, **ya**, *pron. poss.* His, hers. *De suyo*, Spontaneously, of one's own accord.

Súya, *sf.* View, intention, design. *Llevar la suya adelante*, To carry one's point.

Súyos, *sm. pl.* Near friends, relations, acquaintances, servants.

FORMERLY the *t* was sometimes used instead of *d*, as *turar* for *durar*; but this practice is now exploded. Children and stammerers substitute *t* for *s*, and say *tenor* in lieu of *señor.*

Ta! *interj.* Take care. *Ta, ta*, Sure, is it so? V. *Tate.*

Tába, *sf.* 1. Bone of the knee-pan; a small bone in the leg or heel. 2. Vulgar game with sheep's shanks. *Menear las tabas*, To stir about nimbly. *Tomar la taba*, To give a loose to one's tongue.

Tabáco, *sm.* 1. (Bot.) Tobacco. Nicotiana *L.* *Tabaco de polvo*, Snuff. *Tabaco de hoja*, Leaf-tobacco. *Tabaco somonte, sumonte*, *ó hubano*, Tobacco in a natural state. *Tabaco* *de palillos*, Snuff made of the stalks of tobacco-plants. *Tabaco rapé*, Rappee. 2. Mildew on plants, as wheat, barley, &c. V. *Roya*. *A' mal dar tomar tabaco*, What cannot be cured, must be endured.

Tabacóso, sa, *a*. Using much tobacco, snuffy.

Tabaláda, *sf*. A heavy fall upon one's breech. V. *Tabanázo*.

Tabalário, *sm*. (Joc.) The breech, seat, posteriors.

Tabaleár, *va*. To rock to and fro.—*vn*. To beat with the fingers on the table as a drum.

Tabaléo, *sm*. (Joc.) Beating on the breech.

Tabaléte, *sm*. A kind of woollen stuff finer than drugget.

Tabanázo, *sm*. Blow or buffet with the hand.

Tabánco, *sm*. Stall for selling eatables to the poor.

Tabáno, *sm*. (Ento.) Hornet. Vespa crabro *L*.

Tabánque, *sm*. Treadle, which serves for putting a potter's wheel in motion.

Tabaóla, *sf*. Confused noise of a crowd.

Tabáque, *sm*. 1. A small work basket. 2. A kind of nails somewhat larger than tacks. *Como pera en tabaque*, Carefully kept.

Tabaquéra, *sf*. 1. A kind of round snuff-box, with a neck and holes at the end, used by common people. The Galicians call it *funqueyra*. 2. Case for a tobacco-pipe. *Tabaquera de humo*, Tobacco-pipe for smoking. 3. Tobacco-plantation.

Tabaquería, *sf*. Tobacco and snuff shop.

Tabaquéro, *sm*. Tobacconist, one who prepares and sells snuff and tobacco.

Tabaquíllo, *sm*. 1. A weak sort of tobacco. 2. A small work basket.

Tabaquísta, *s. com*. One who takes much snuff, or professes to be a judge of tobacco.

Tabardéte y Tabardíllo, *sm*. A burning fever. *Tabardillo pintado*, A spotted fever.

Tabárdo, *sm*. Wide loose coat of coarse cloth with hanging sleeves, worn by labourers in bad weather.

Tabelión, *sm*. V. *Escribano*.

Tabellár, *va*. (Ant.) To fold or double cloth in woollen manufactories.

Tabérna, *sf*. A liquor-shop, where wine and other liquors are retailed.

Tabernáculo, *sm*. Tabernacle; a temporary habitation; place where the host is kept. *Fiesta de los tabernáculos*, Feast of the tabernacles; a feast kept by the Jews.

Tabernéra, *sf*. Tavern-keeper's wife, woman who keeps a tavern.

Tabernería, *sf*. Business of a tavern-keeper.

Tabernéro, *sm*. 1. Tavern-keeper, one who keeps a liquor-shop. 2. A frequenter of dram-shops.

Tabescéncia, *sf*. Corruption, putrefaction.

Tabí, *sm*. Tabby, a kind of silken stuff.

Tabíca, *sf*. (Arq.) Lintel or cross-board put over any vacancy in a wall.

Tabicár, *va*. 1. To shut up with a wall; to wall up. 2. To close, to shut up.

Tabicón, *sm*. A thick wall.

Tábido, da, *a*. (Med.) Putrid; corrupted; very meagre and dry.

Tabíllas, *sf. pl*. Husks of clover-seed; husks of radish-seed.

Tabíque, *sm*. A thin wall; a partition-wall.

Tabitéña, *sf*. (Burg.) A kind of pipe or small flute, made of a stalk of wheat.

Tábla, *sf*. 1. Board, a piece of wood of more length and breadth than thickness. 2. Board, a table at which a council or court is held. 3. Table, a horizontal surface raised above the ground, for eating and other purposes. 4. Place where meat is weighed and sold; butcher's block. 5. Map or description of a country. 6. Table, an index or repertory of the subjects treated upon, prefixed to a book. 7. A piece of painting on boards or stones. 8. Bed or plot of earth in a garden. 9. Plain space on cloths. 10. V. *Arancel*. 11. The broadest and most fleshy part of any of the members of the body. 12. Plank or board of a ship to escape drowning in shipwreck. 13. Chest, seat or bench. 14. House where merchandise is registered as sold at market, in order to collect the duty. 15. List, catalogue. *Tabla de sembrado*, A fine field of corn. *Tabla de juego*, Gambling-house. *Tabla de chilla*, Thin board of slit deal. *Tabla de rio*, Bed of a river. *Dinero en tabla*, Ready-money. *Tabla de manteles*, Table-cloth.—*pl*. 1. Stages on which actors perform. 2. An equal or drawn game at chess or drafts. 3. Astronomical tables. 4. Tables containing the decalogue. *Tablas reales*, Backgammon-tables.

Tablachína, *sf*. Kind of wooden shield or buckler.

Tablácho, *sm*. Sluice or floodgate. *Echar el tablacho*, To interrupt one that is speaking with some reason.

Tabladíllo, *sm*. A small stage.

Tabládo, *sm*. 1. Scaffold, stage. 2. Boards or bottom of a bedstead. 3. (Naút.) Platform. *Tablado de la cirugia*, (Naút.) Cockpit. *Tablado de la coca*, (Naút.) Flooring of the cap.

Tabláge, *sm*. 1. Pile of boards. 2. Gambling or gaming-house; perquisites of the keeper of a gaming-table.

Tablageár, *vn*. To gamble; to be a gambler or gamester by profession.

Tablagería, *sf*. Gaming, gambling; hire of the gaming-table.

Tablagéro, *sm*. 1. Scaffold-maker; a carpenter, who builds scaffolds and stages. 2. Collector or gatherer of the king's-taxes. 3. Keeper of a gaming-house; gambler. 4. Butcher. V. *Cortador*. 5. (Ar.) Young surgeon walking the hospital.

Tablár, *sm*. Division of gardens into plots or beds.

Tablázo, *sm*. 1. Blow or stroke with a board. 2. Arm of the sea or of a river.

Tablazón, *sm*. 1. Boards or planks put together, so as to form a platform, or other piece of construction. 2. Decks and sheathing of a ship. *Tablazon de la cubierta*, (Naút.) Deck-planks. *Tablazon exterior*, (Naút.) Outside planks or planking. *Tablazon de los fondos*, (Naút.) Floor-planking. *Tablazon inferior ó forro*, (Naút.) Inside planking; ceiling, foot-railing.

Tableár, *va*. 1. To divide a garden into beds or plots. 2. To make the ground even with a thick board. 3. To hammer bars of iron into plates.

Tabléro, *sm*. 1. Board, planed and fashioned for some purpose or other. 2. Dog-nail, a sort of nails used in the flooring of houses. 3. Chess-board, draft-board. 4. Gambling-house, gaming-table. 5. Shop-counter; money-table. 6. Stock of a cross-bow. 7. (Arq.) Any plane level part of a building surrounded with a moulding. V. *Abaco*. 8. Kneading-board. 9. Skirts of a coat. 10. Tailor's shop-board. 11. Public, populace. *Estar en el tablero*, To be exposed to public view. *Tablero de cocina*, Dresser; kitchen table; chopping-block for meat.

TABLÉTA, *sf.* 1. Tablet, a small piece of board; a board containing the letters of the alphabet for children; a tablet or memorandum. 2. Cracknel, a kind of paste hard baked. *Estar en tabletas*, To be in suspense.

TABLETEÁDO, *sm.* The crackling sound of boards trod upon. [making a noise with them.

TABLETEÁR, *vn.* To move tables or boards,

TABLETÍLLA, CA, *sf. dim.* 1. A small tablet. 2. Kind of hard pastry cakes. *Trueno de tabletilla*, Thundering or hollow sound made on a table.

TABLÍCA, LLA, ó TA, *sf.* 1. A small board. 2. Board on which indulgences to a condemned criminal are written and exposed in the streets while the convict is in the chapel. 3. Table or lists of persons excommunicated exhibited in churches. 4. Kind of sweet-cakes. 5. Bands on a billiard or truck-table. 6. V. *Tableta* y *Tabletilla*. *Tablilla de meson*, Sign of an inn. *Tablilla de santero*, Poor-box of an hermit. *Tablillas de san Lázaro*, Three pieces of wood united with a cord and made to sound together; they are used in begging for the hospitals of St. Lazarus. *Por tablilla*, Indirectly.

TABLÓN, *sm.* Plank, a thick board.

TABLÓZA, *sf.* (Pint.) V. *Paleta*.

TABÚCO, *sm.* Hut, small apartment.

TABUQUÍLLO ó TABUQUÍTO, *sm.* A small miserable hut or cottage.

TABURACÚRA, *sf.* A kind of yellow rosin.

TABURÉTE, *sm.* Chair without arms. *Taburetes*, Forms with backs in the pit of a play-house.

TABURETÍLLO, *sm.* Drawing-room chair for ladies.

TÁCA, *sf.* (Ar. y Ast.) V. *Mancha*. [resin.

TACAMÁCA Y TACAMAHÁCA, *sf.* Kind of gum

TACAÑAMÉNTE, *ad.* Sordidly, meanly.

TACAÑEÁR, *va.* To act the miser; to behave in a wicked or malicious manner.

TACAÑERÍA, *sf.* 1. Malicious cunning; low craft. 2. Narrowness of mind; sordid parsimony.

TACÁÑO, ÑA, *a.* 1. Malicious, artful, knavish. 2. Stingy, sordid.

TACÁR, *va.* To mark; to stain. [oil-mills.

TACÉTA, *sf.* A copper basin or bowl, used in

TÁCHA, *sf.* 1. Fault, defect, imperfection. 2. Crack, fissure. 3. A sort of small nails, somewhat larger than tacks. *Miren que tacha*, (Fam.) An exclamation indicating the particular goodness or quality of a thing which enhances its merit.

TACHÁR, *va.* 1. To censure, to find fault with; to charge with a fault; to reprehend. *Tachar á alguno de ligero*, To accuse one of levity. 2. To blot, to efface, to scratch out.

TACHÓN, *sm.* 1. Stroke or line drawn through a writing, to blot it out. 2. Tacks used as an ornament for chairs; lace trimming. 3. A sort of large nails with gilt or plated heads.

TACHONÁR, *va.* To adorn with lace trimming; to garnish with tacks or nails with gilt heads.

TACHONERÍA, *sf.* Ornamental work with gilt-headed nails.

TACHÓSO, SA, *a.* Faulty, having some defect or blemish. [head.

TACHUÉLA, *sf.* Tack, a small nail with a round

TACITAMÉNTE, *ad.* Silently, secretly; tacitly.

TÁCITO, TA, *a.* Tacit, silent; implied, inferred.

TACITURNIDÁD, *sf.* Taciturnity, profound silence, melancholy.

TACITÚRNO, NA, *a.* Tacit, silent, reserved; melancholy.

TÁCO, *sm.* 1. Stopper, stopple. 2. Wad, wadding forced into a gun to keep the powder close in the chamber. 3. Rammer. 4. Pop-gun. 5. (Fam.) Draught of wine or other liquor. 6. (Fam.) Volley of oaths. 7. Mace of a billiard-table. *Tacos de los escobenes*, (Naút.) Hawse-plugs. *Ayre de taco*, Genteel, lively motion; applied to women. *Echar tacos*, To swear or speak in a great rage.

TACÓN, *sm.* Heel-piece, the hind part of the sole of a shoe.

TACONÁZO, *sm.* Blow with a shoe-heel.

TACONEÁR, *vn.* (Fam.) To make a noise with the heel-piece; to walk or strut loftily on the heels.

TACONÉO, *sm.* Noise made with the heels in some dancing steps.

TACONÉRO, *sm.* Heel-maker, one who makes wooden heels.

TÁCTICA, *sf.* (Mil.) Tactics, the art of forming troops and directing their evolutions. *Táctica naval*, Naval tactics.

TÁCTO, *sm.* Touch, the sense of feeling; the act of touching or feeling. [na *L.*

TADÓRNO, *sm.* (Orn.) Shell-drake. Anas tador-

TAFÁLLO, *sm.* V. *Chafallo*.

TAFANÁRIO, *sm.* (Joc.) Breech, nates.

TAFETÁN, *sm.* Taffety, a thin silk. *Tafetanes*, Flags, colours, standard, ensign.

TAFILÉTE, *sm.* Morocco-leather. [ther.

TAFILETEÁR, *va.* To adorn with Morocco lea-

TAFILETERÍA, *sf.* Art of dressing Morocco leather, and the place where it is dressed. [boat.

TAFURÉA, *sf.* (Naút.) A kind of flat-bottomed

TAGARÍNO, *sm.* Moor who lived among the Christians, and by speaking their language well could scarcely be known.

TAGARNILLÉRA, *sf.* An artful deceitful person.

TAGARNÍNA, *sf.* V. *Cardillo*.

TAGARÓTE, *sm.* 1. (Orn.) Hobby. Falco subbuteo *L.* 2. Quill-driver, a writer in any office. 3. A decayed gentleman, who earns a dinner by flattery and adulation. 4. A tall ill-shaped person.

TAGAROTEÁR, *va.* To write a bold, free and running hand.

TÁHA, *sf.* District, region.

TAHALÍ, *sm.* Shoulder-belt.

TAHARÁL, *sm.* Plantation of tamarisk-trees.

TAHÉÑO, *a.* Having a red beard.

TAHÓNA, *sf.* Horse-mill, a corn-mill worked by mules or horses.

TAHONÉRO, *sm.* Miller, who directs or manages a horse-mill.

TAHÚLLA, *sf.* (Mur.) A piece of ground, near 40

square yards, sown with about two pecks of grain.

TAHÚR, RA, *s.* Gambler, gamester.

TAHURERÍA, *sf.* Gambling; gaming-house; fraudulent gambling.

TÁJA, *sf.* 1. A kind of saddle-tree put over pack-saddles for carrying loads or burthens. 2. Cut, incision; dissection; operation of cutting for the stone. 3. Tally, a stick cut or notched in conformity to another stick.

TAJÁDA, *sf.* 1. Slice, a portion or part cut from another. 2. Hoarseness. *Hacer tajadas*, To threaten, to menace.

TAJADÉRA, *sf.* 1. Chopping-knife, chopping-block. 2. Sluice of a mill-dam. 3. V. *Cortafrio.*

TAJADÉRO, *sm.* Chopping-block for meat; trencher.

TAJADÍLLA, *sf.* 1. A small slice of liver, &c. in low chop-houses. 2. (And.) Bit of confected orange sold as a relish by the retailers of brandy.

TAJÁDO, DA, *pp.* 1. Cut, notched. 2. (Blas.) Applied to a diagonal bar of a shield.

TAJADÓR, RA, *s.* One who cuts or chops. V. *Tajadero.*

TAJADÚRA, *sf.* Cut, notch; section.

TAJAMÁR, *sm.* (Naút.) Cutwater, the fore part of a ship's head, which cuts the water. *Escoras del tajamar*, Props of the cut-water.

TAJAMÓCO, *sm.* (Ent.) Goatchafer. Cerambyx *L.*

TAJÁNTE, *sm.* Butcher.

TAJAPLÚMAS, *sm.* Pen-knife. [To cut a pen.

TAJÁR, *va.* 1. To cut, to divide into parts. 2.

TAJARÍNA, *sf.* A thin Italian paste.

TAJÉRO, *sm.* V. *Tarjero.*

TÁJO, *sm.* 1. Cut, incision. 2. Cutting of a quill with a pen-knife. 3. Chopping-block or board. 4. V. *Filo.* 5. Cutting, reaping, or digging of labourers in a line; cut or opening in a mountain.

TAJÓN, *sm.* 1. A large block; chopping-block. 2. A vein of earth or soft stone in a lime-stone quarry.

TAJONCÍLLO, *sm.* A small block. [feet.

TAJUÉLO ó TAJUÉLA, *s.* A low stool with four

TAL, *a.* 1. Such, so, as. 2. Equal, similar, of the same form or figure. 3. As much, so great. *Tal qual*, Middling, so so. *La tal ó el tal*, A certain person. *Tal qual vez*, Sometimes, from time to time. *Tal qual carga de pan*, A few loads of bread. *Tal por qual*, Worthless, of no importance; good and bad. *No hay tal*, There is no such thing. *A' tal*, With such a condition, under the circumstances. *Con tal*, Provided that. *Otro que tal*, Similar, very like, equally worthless.

TÁLA, *sf.* 1. Felling of trees. 2. Destruction, ruin, desolation.

TALABÁRTE, *sm.* Sword-belt.

TALADÓR, RA, *s.* Destroyer, one that desolates or lays waste.

TALADRADÓR, RA, *s.* Borer, piercer, penetrater.

TALADRÁR, *va.* 1. To bore, to perforate. 2. To pierce, to penetrate the ear. 3. To penetrate into or comprehend a difficult point.

TALADRÍLLO, *sm.* A small borer, little bore.

TALÁDRO, *sm.* 1. Borer, gimlet, auger. 2. Bore, hole made with a borer or auger. 3. (Ent.) Weevil. Curculio granarius *L.*

TALAMÉRA, *sf.* 1. (Bot.) Capsule which contains the seed. 2. Tree used for ensnaring birds.

TÁLAMO, *sm.* 1. Bride-chamber, bride-bed. 2. Virginal womb of the blessed Mary.

TALANQUÉRA, *sf.* Parapet, breast-work of pales raised round the circle for bull-feasts; defence.

TALÁNTE, *sm.* 1. Mode or manner of performing any thing. 2. Appearance, aspect. 3. Will, pleasure, disposition.

TALANTÓSO, SA, *a.* Good-humoured, of a pleasant disposition.

TALÁR, *va.* 1. To fell trees. 2. To desolate, to lay waste a country. 3. To steal flour out of the meal bags.—*sm.* 1. A long robe hanging down to the heels. 2. Each one of the wings on the heels of Mercury.

TALASOMÉLI, *sm.* Purgative medicine made of honey, rain, and salt water, placed before the sun. [town of Talavera.

TALAVÉRA, *sf.* Earthenware manufactured in the

TÁLCO, *sm.* Talc, a transparent fossil, which easily separates into scales or leaves; it is distinguished from mica by the want of elasticity.

TALÉGA, *sf.* 1. Bag, a wide short sack. 2. Sack of hard dollars, containing 20,000 reals vellon, or 1000 dollars. 3. A bagful. 4. (Fam.) Sins, which a penitent sinner is going to confess. 5. Bag for the hair. 6. Knowledge which one has acquired previous to attending any public school. 7. (Ant.) Store of provisions.

TALEGÁZO, *sm.* Stroke or blow with a full bag.

TALÉGO, *sm.* 1. Bag or sack made of coarse sackcloth. *Tener talego*, To have money. 2. A clumsy awkward fellow.

TALEGÓN, *sm. aum.* of *talega* or *talego.*

TALEGUÍLLA, TA, CA, *sf.* A small bag. *Taleguilla de la sal*, (Fam.) Daily expenditure, money spent each day.

TALENTÁDA, *sf.* Will, propensity, inclination.

TALÉNTE, *sm.* (Ant.) Talent, will, mind. V. *Talante.*

TALÉNTO, *sm.* 1. Talent, ancient weight or money of different value. 2. Talents, abilities, endowments, or gifts of nature which are carried into practice; ingenuity; genius.

TALENTÓSO, SA, *a.* Able, ingenious.

TALIDÁD, *sf.* (Escol.) That which determines a thing to be included generically or specifically in another. [trum *L.*

TALIÉSTRO, *sm.* (Bot.) Meadow-rue. Thalic-

TALIÓN, *sf.* Retaliation, requital.

TALIONÁR, *va.* To retaliate, to requite.

TALISMÁN, *sm.* 1. Talisman, a magical character. 2. Doctor of the Mohammedan law.

TÁLLA, *sf.* 1. Raised work, cut in wood or stone; sculpture. 2. Dues paid by the vassals to the lord of the manor. 3. Ransom. 4. (And.) Jug with water put into the air to cool, or suspended in a draught. 5. (Arag.) Tare. 6. Stature, size. *A' media talla*, Carelessly, perfunctorily. *Media talla*, Half-relief, in sculpture. 7. Mark or measure of any thing. 8. Hand, in the game of basset. 9. (Cir.) Operation of cutting for the stone. *Poner talla*, To offer a reward for the apprehension of a criminal.

TALLÁDO, DA, *a.* Cut, carved, engraved. *Bien ó mal tallado*, Of a good or bad figure.

TALLADÓR, *sm.* Engraver.

TALLADÚRA, *sf.* Engraving.

TALLÁR, *sm.* Mount or forest of fire-wood which

is fit for cutting; wood fit for cutting.—a. Fellable; applied to wood for fuel.—va. 1. To cut, to chop. 2. To carve in wood; to engrave on copper-plate. 3. To charge with dues or imposts. 4. To show all the cards in one's hand at basset.

TALLARÍN, *sm.* A thin paste which comes from Italy. [silk in velvet-looms.

TALLARÓLA, *sf.* Iron-plate used for cutting the

TALLÁZO, *sm.* (Joc.) A tall lofty stature.

TÁLLE, *sm.* 1. Shape, size, proportion. 2. Waist, the middle of the body. 3. Mode or manner of performing any thing, fashion of clothes. 4. Form, figure, position, attitude. 5. Genus, species, class. 6. Manners, disposition.

TALLECÉR, *vn.* To shoot, to sprout.

TALLECÍLLO, *sm.* (Iron.) A small slender waist.

TALLÉR, *sm.* 1. Workshop, office; laboratory. 2. School, academy; a seminary of arts and sciences. 3. Ancient coin. *Taller de Mesa*, Cruet-stand for salt, pepper, oil, and vinegar.

TALLÍSTA, *sm.* Carver in wood, engraver.

TÁLLO, *sm.* Shoot, sprout.

TALLÚDO, DA, *a.* 1. Grown into long stalks. 2. Tall, slender. 3. Callous, hardened in vicious habits. 4. Overgrown; grown to seed.

TALMÚD, *sm.* Talmud, a book which contains the doctrines and ceremonies of the law of Moses.

TALMUDÍSTA, *sm.* Professor or interpreter of the Talmud.

TALÓN, *sm.* 1. Heel, the hind part of the foot. 2. Heel-piece of a shoe. 3. Follower, hanger-on. 4. (Arq.) Cymatium, ogee fluting. *Ir á talon*, To go on foot. *Apretar los talones*, To take to one's heels. *Dar con el talon en el fondo*, (Naút.) To touch ground with the stern-post.

TALONEÁR, *vn.* To be nimble, to walk fast.

TALONÉSCO, *a.* (Joc.) Relating to the heels.

TÁLPA ó TALPÁRIA, *sf.* (Cir.) Abscess in the pericranium; tumour in the head.

TÁLQUE, *sm.* A kind of argillaceous earth, of which crucibles are made.

TALÚS ó TALUD, *sm.* Talus, a slope on the outside part of a wall or rampart.

TALVÍNA, *sf.* A kind of milk, extracted from several seeds, of which porridge and dumplings are made.

TAMANDÓA, *sf.* Ant-eater of Peru. Myrmecophaga *L.*

TAMAÑAMÉNTE, *ad.* As great as; tantamount.

TAMAÑÍTO, TA; LLO, LLA; CO, CA, *a.* Very small. *Tamañito*, Fearful, intimidated.

TAMÁÑO, *sm.* Size, shape, bulk, stature. *Hombre de tamaño*, A man of great respectability and endowments; one who holds a high employment.

TAMÁÑO, ÑA, *a.* Showing the size, shape, or bulk of any thing; very little.

TAMAÑUÉLO, LA, *a. dim.* Small, slender, little.

TÁMARAS, *sf. pl.* 1. Clusters of dates. 2. Chips, fagots of brushwood.

TAMARÍNDO, *sm.* (Bot.) Tamarind-tree and fruit. Tamarindus *L.*

TAMARÍSCO Y TAMÁRIZ, *sm.* (Bot.) Tamarisk-shrub. Tamarix *L.*

TAMARRIZQUÍTO ó TAMORRUSQUÍTO, TA, *a.* (Fam.) Very small.

TÁMBA, *sf.* (Cant.) Blanket of a bed.

TAMBALEÁR ó TAMBALEÁRSE, *vn.* y *r.* To stagger, to waver.

TAMBALÉO, *sm.* A waddling motion; reeling, staggering.

TAMBANÍLLO, *sm.* A raised ornament on the angles of buildings.

TAMBARÍLLO, *sm.* Chest or trunk with an arched cover.

TAMBÉSCO, *sm.* (Burg.) Swing, in which boys rock themselves.

TAMBIÉN, *conj.* y *ad.* Also, likewise; as well.

TÁMBO, *sm.* (Peru.) Inn.

TAMBÓR, *sm.* 1. Drum, a cylindric instrument of military music. 2. Drummer, he who plays on the drum. *Baquetas del tambor*, Drum-sticks. *Tambor mayor*, Drum-major. 3. A small room, made in another room by means of partition-walls; tambour or wooden screen at the doors of churches. 4. Barrel of a watch or clock; any cylindrical part of machinery. 5. Tambour-frame for embroidering silk, muslin or linen. *Á tambor ó con tambor batiente*, Beating the drum. *Tambor del oido*, Drum of the ear. 6. Iron cylinder, with holes for roasting chesnuts. 7. (For.) Small enclosure as a screen to the gates of a fortress. 8. Sieve used in refining sugar. 9. (Arq.) Tholus, keystone of a vaulted roof or cupola.

TAMBORÉTA, *sf.* Timbrel.

TAMBORÉTE, *sm.* (Naút.) Cap of the mast-head.

TAMBORÍL, *sm.* 1. Tabour, a kind of drum beaten in villages on festive occasions. 2. (Joc.) Breech.

TAMBORILÁDA, *sf.* Fall on one's breech; a slap on the face or shoulders.

TAMBORILÁZO, *sm.* Blow or fall.

TAMBORILEÁR ó TAMBORITEÁR, *va.* 1. To beat the tabour with one stick, accompanied by a pipe. 2. To cry up, to be loud in one's praise. 3. (Imp.) To plain or level types.

TAMBORILÉRO Y TAMBORITÉRO, *sm.* One that beats the tabour, tabouret, or tambourine.

TAMBORILÉTE, *sm.* (Impr.) Plainer, flat piece of wood to level the face of types.

TAMBORITÍLLO, *sm.* A small drum for children.

TAMBORÍN, *sm.* V. *Tamboril.*

TAMÍZ, *sm.* A fine sieve, made of silk or hair. *Pasar por tamiz*, To sift.

TÁMO, *sm.* 1. Down which falls from woollen or linen in weaving. 2. Dust in corn. 3. Mould under beds on dusty floors.

TAMORLÁN, *sm.* Emperor of the Tartars.

TAMPÓCO, *ad.* Neither, not either.

TAMÚJO, *sm.* (Bot.) A kind of furze. Rhamnus lycioides *L.*

TAN, *sm.* 1. Pulverized bark of oak. 2. Sound of the tabour or tambourine.—*ad. comp.* So much, as much. *Tan grande*, So great, very great. V. *Tanto.*

TANACÉTO, *sm.* (Bot.) Tansy. Tanacetum *L.*

TÁNCA, *sf.* A viscous matter with which bees daub their hives before they begin to work at the honey-comb.

TÁNDA, *sf.* 1. Turn, rotation. 2. Task, something to be done imposed by another. 3. Cloak. V. *Capa.* 4. Certain number of persons or cattle employed in any work. 5. Number of stripes or lashes.

Tanganillas (En), *ad.* Waveringly, in a vacillating manner.
Tanganíllo, *sm.* A small prop or stay.
Tángano, *sm.* Hob, a play among boys; bone used in this play.
Tangénte, *a.* (Geom.) Tangent.
TANGIBILIDA'D, *sf.* Tangibility, quality or condition of being tangible.
Tangíble, *a.* That may be touched.
Tangidéra, *sf.* (Naút.) Cable.
Tangír, *va.* (Ant.) V. *Tocar y Tañer.*
Tángo, *sm.* Bone to pitch at. V. *Tángano.*
Táni, *sf.* A sort of raw silk which comes from Bengal.
Tantarantán, *sm.* Tantarara, redoubled beat of a drum; a sounding blow.
Tanteadór, *sm.* Measurer, calculator.
Tanteár, *va.* 1. To measure, to proportion. 2. To mark the game with counters. 3. To consider, to examine. 4. (For.) To sell at the price offered by others. 5. (Pint.) To sketch or trace the outlines of a design.—*vr.* 1. To agree to pay the same sum for a thing which was bid for it at a public sale. 2. To redeem a barony or lordship.
Tantéo, *sm.* 1. Computation, calculation. 2. Number of counters for marking a game. 3. Agreement to take any thing at a fair appraisement. 4. Outlines of a picture. 5. Valuation. 6. Prudent judgment in any affair.
Tantíco y Tantíllo, *sm.* Small sum or quantity.
Tánto, *sm.* 1. A certain sum or quantity. 2. Copy of a writing. 3. Blow, stroke. 4. Counter, mark of a game.
Tánto, ta, *a.* 1. So much, as much; very great. 2. Odd, something over a determined number. *Veinte y tantos*, Twenty and upwards.
Tánto, ta, *a.* 1. So, in such a manner. 2. A long time. *Tanto mas ó menos*, So much more or less. *Tanto que*, As soon as. *Tanto mejor ó peor*, So much the better or the worse. *En tanto, ó entre tanto*, In the mean time. *Tanto por tanto*, At the same price; upon a par. *Tantos á tantos*, Equal numbers. *Al tanto*, For the same price; used to express one's desire of an article at the same price paid by others. *Por el tanto*, On that ground. *Per tanto*, Therefore, for the reasons expressed. *Tanto de ello*, Enough, abundantly. *En su tanto*, Proportionably. *Algun tanto*, A few.
Tañedór, ra, *s.* Player on a musical instrument.
Tañér, *v. impers.* To concern, to be of consequence or importance. V. *Tocar.*—*sm.* (Ant.) Act of playing on any musical instrument.
Tañído, da, *pp.* Played; touched.
Tañído, *sm.* Tune; sound.
Táo, *sm.* Badge worn by officers of the orders of St. Anthony and St. John.
Tápa, *sf.* 1. Lid, cover. 2. Horny part of a hoof. 3. Heel-piece of a shoe. *Tapa de los sesos*, Top of the skull.
Tapabalázos, *sm. pl.* (Naút.) Shot-plugs.
Tapabóca, *sf.* 1. Slap given on the mouth. 2. Any action or observation which interrupts the conversation, and cuts one short.
Tapabón, *sm.* Cap, worn by English sailors.
Tapacúlo, *sm.* Fruit of the dog-rose.
Tapáda, *sf.* Woman disguised with her mantle over her face.
Tapadéra, *sf.* A loose lid or moveable cover of a pot or other vessel.
Tapadéro, *sm.* A large stopper or stopple.
Tapadíllo, *sm.* 1. The act of a woman's covering herself with her veil or mantle, that she may not be seen. 2. V. *Cobertizo.* 3. One of the registers in the tube of an organ. *De tapadillo*, Without ceremony or show, secretly.
Tapadízo, *sm.* 1. Action of women hiding the face with a mantle. 2. V. *Cobertizo.*
Tapadór, ra, *s.* 1. One who stops or shuts up, coverer. 2. Plug, stopper, stopple. 3. (Cant.) Father of a prostitute, keeper of a brothel.
Tapadúra, *sf.* Act of stopping, covering or hiding.
Tapafogón, *sm.* Cap of a gun, which covers the vent-hole.
Tapafúnda, *sf.* Holster-cover or holster-housings of pistols.
Tapamiénto, *sm.* Act of stopping or covering.
Tápana y Tápara, *sf.* (Mur.) V. *Alcaparra.*
Tapapiés, *sm.* V. *Brial.*
Tapár, *va.* 1. To stop up, to cover, to put under cover. *Tapa agujeros*, A bad mason. 2. To conceal, to hide; to dissemble. *Tapar la boca*, To stop one's mouth. *Tapar una abertura de agua*, (Naút.) To stop or fother a leak. *Taparse de medio ojo*, To cover the face to the eyes with a mantle, as women do to conceal themselves. *Taparse el caballo*, To cover the piste of the fore feet with those of the hind ones.
Tapatán ó Taparapatán, *sm.* Word indicating the sound of a drum.
Taperujárse, *vr.* To cover one's face with a mantle or veil; applied to women.
Taperújo, *sm.* (Joc.) 1. An ill-shaped plug or stopple. 2. The awkward manner in which a woman covers her face with a veil.
Tapetádo, da, *a.* Being of a dark brown or blackish colour.
Tapéte, *sm.* A small floor-carpet.
Tapía, *sf.* 1. Mud-wall. 2. Measure of a mud-wall containing fifty square feet. *Tapia real*, Wall made of earth and lime.
Tapiadór, *sm.* Builder of mud-walls.
Tapiál, *sm.* Mould for making mud-walls. *Tener el tapial*, To have patience, to rest.
Tapiár, *va.* 1. To stop up with a mud-wall. 2. To stop a passage, to obstruct a view.
Tapicería, *sf.* 1. Tapestry. 2. Office in the royal palace where the tapestry and carpets are kept.
Tapicéro, *sm.* One who makes or weaves tapestry. *Tapicero mayor*, Tapestry-keeper in a palace.
Tapiería, *sf.* Series of mud-walls.
Tapínes ó Tapínos, *sm. pl.* (Naút.) Stoppers for vent-holes.
Tapinósis, *sf.* (Ret.) Figure where, with words and low phrases, any thing great is explained.
Tapirujárse, *vr.* V. *Taperujarse.*
Tapisóte, *sm.* (Bot.) Yellow-flowered pea. Pisum ochrus *L.*
Tapíz, *sm.* 1. Tapestry. 2. Grass-plot adorned with flowers. *Arrancado de un tapiz*, Nickname for a ridiculous looking ill-dressed person.
Tapizár, *va.* To hang with tapestry.

Tapón, *sm.* Cork, plug, bung.
Tapsía, *sf.* (Bot.) Kind of giant fennel.
Tapujárse, *vr.* To muffle one's self up in a cloak or veil.
Tapújo, *sm.* Muffle, a cover for the face.
Táque, *sm.* Noise made by a door which slaps.
Taquétes, *sm. pl.* (Naút.) Cleats, pieces of wood used in repairing the seams of ships which are careened.
Taquigrafía, *sf.* Tachygraphy, the art of writing short-hand.
Taquígrafo, *sm.* Short-hand writer.
Taquín, *sm.* V. *Carnicol.*
Taquinéro, *sm.* Player with a bone.
Tára, *sf.* 1. Tare, an allowance made for the weight of sacks, bags, or casks which contain merchandise. 2. Tally, on which the weight, number, or quality of things is noted. *Ménos de tara*, Making an allowance for.
Taracéa, *sf.* Marquetry, checkered work, work inlaid with variegation.
Taraceár, *va.* To make inlaid work.
Taragállo, *sm.* Clog, a piece of wood suspended from the necks of beasts, to prevent them from running away.
Taragontía, *sf.* V. *Dragontea.*
Tarambána, *s. com.* Giddy person of little stability or judgment.
Tarándo, *sm.* Rein-deer. Cervus tarandus *L.*
Tarángana, *sf.* (Vulg.) V. *Morcilla.*
Tarantéla, *sf.* A powerful impressive tune, such as is played for the bite of the *Tarantula*. *Dar la tarantela*, (Fam.) To excite or agitate one inordinately.
Taránțula, *sf.* Tarantula, a kind of venomous spider, most frequent in the city and neighbourhood of Tarento, in Apulia. Aranea tarantula *L.* *Picado de la tarántula*, (Met.) Infected with some malady, vulgarly the venereal disease.
Tarantuládo, da, *a.* V. *Atarantado.*
Tarará, *sf.* Sound of a trumpet, as a signal to prepare for action.
Tarareár, *va. y n.* 1. To sound the trumpet. 2. To chuck under the chin.
Tararíra, *sf.* Noisy mirth.—*s. com.* Noisy person.
Tarásca, *sf.* 1. Figure of a serpent borne in processions, indicating the triumph of Christ over the devil. 2. Crooked, ugly, ill-natured, licentious and impudent woman.
Tarascáda, *sf.* 1. Bite, a wound made with the teeth. 2. A pert harsh answer.
Tarascár, *va.* To bite, to wound with the teeth.
Tarascón, *sm. aum.* V. *Tarasca.*
Taravílla, *sf.* 1. Clack or clapper of a mill. 2. A kind of wooden latch for shutting doors or windows. 3. A person who prattles much and fast.
Taráy, *sm.* V. *Tamarisco.*
Tarazána, *sf.* V. *Atarazana.*
Tarazanál, *sm.* Shed. V. *Atarazana.*
Tarazár, *va.* 1. To bite, to wound with the teeth. 2. To molest, to harass, to mortify.
Tarazón, *sm.* A large slice, especially of fish.
Tarazoncíllo, *sm.* A small slice.
Tarbéa, *sf.* A large hall.
Tardadór, ra, *s.* Delayer, deferrer.
Tardaménte, *ad.* Slowly, softly.
Tardanaós, *sf.* Fish. V. *Rémora.*
Tardánza, *sf.* Slowness, delay, detention; demurrage.
Tardár, *vn.* To delay, to put off.
Tárde, *sf.* 1. Afternoon; the time from noon till night. 2. Evening, the close of the day. 3. (Arag.) The first hours of the night.—*ad.* Late; past the time. *De tarde en tarde*, Now and then, occasionally. *Hacerse tarde*, To grow late. *Mas vale tarde que nunca*, Better late than never.
Tardecíllo, *ad.* A little late; slowly.
Tardecíta y ca, *sf.* The close of the evening.
Tardiaménte, *ad.* Too late, out of time.
Tardío, dia, *a.* 1. Late, too late, after the proper time. 2. Slow, tardy, dilatory.
Tárdo, da, *a.* 1. Slow, sluggish, tardy. 2. Dull, inactive.
Tardón, na, *a.* Very tardy, phlegmatic.
Taréa, *sf.* 1. Task, work to be done, imposed by another. 2. Care, toil, drudgery. *Ahora disfruta sus tareas*, He now enjoys the fruit of his labour.
Targúm, *sm.* Targum, Chaldaic version of the Bible.
Tári, *sm.* Tari, a liquor extracted in India from the cocoa-nut.
Tarída, *sf.* Ancient vessel used in the Mediterranean for carrying implements of war.
Tarífa, *sf.* Tariff, a list of the prices of goods or merchandise; book of rates or duties.
Tarína, *sf.* 1. A moveable platform or boarded frame on a floor or pavement; low bench, table, foot-stool. 2. Bedstead.
Tarimílla, *sf.* A small bedstead.
Tarimón, *sm.* A large bedstead.
Tarín, *sm.* Silver real of 8 1/2 quartos.
Tarína, *sf.* Middle-sized dish for meat.
Tárja, *sf.* 1. An ancient Spanish copper coin worth about the fourth part of a real. 2. Tally. 3. Target, shield, buckler. 4. Sign-board. 5. (Fam.) Blow.
Tarjadór, ra, *s.* One who keeps or marks a tally.
Tarjár, *va.* To score on a tally, to mark on a tally what has been sold on credit.
Tarjéro, *sm.* Tally-keeper. V. *Tarjador.*
Tarjéta, *sf.* 1. A small target or shield with a coat of arms. 2. Board with an inscription giving notice of things to be sold, or any other thing. 3. Card, ticket. *Tarjeta de visita*, A visiting card. *Tarjeta de despedida*, A farewell card.
Tarjetón, *sm.* A large buckler.
Tarlatána, *sf.* A sort of thin linen or thread-crape.
Tárma, *sf.* Wood-tick. Termes pulsatorium *L.*
Tarquín, *sm.* Mire, mud.
Tarquináda, *sf.* (Fam.) Rape.
Tarrája, *sf.* (Arq.) Metal instrument for cutting ornamental mouldings in gypsum.
Tarréña, *sf.* Cup, dish. *Tarreñas*, Two pieces of slate or earthenware placed between the fingers by boys to rattle.
Tárro, *sm.* 1. A glazed earthen pan, in which conserves and pickles are preserved. 2. An earthen milk-pan, into which shepherds milk the sheep. *Cabeza de tarro*, Big-headed fool.
Társo, *sm.* Instep, the upper part of the foot.
Tárta, *sf.* 1. Tart, a delicate kind of pastry. 2. Pan for baking tarts.

Tártago, *sm.* 1. (Bot.) Spurge. Euphorbia lathyris *L.* 2. Incident, unfortunate event. 3. A severe jest, galling satire or lash.
Tartajeár, *vn.* To stut, to stutter, to stammer.
Tartajóso, sa, *a.* Stammering, stuttering.
Tartaleár, *vn.* 1. To reel, to stagger. 2. (Fam.) To be perplexed; not to be able to talk.
Tartaléta, *sf.* A kind of light paste for covering tarts. *Tartaletas*, Fruit-pies.
Tartamudeár, *vn.* To stutter, to stammer.
Tartamúdo, da, *a.* y *s.* Stuttering, stammering; stutter or stutterer.
Tartána, *sf.* 1. (Naút.) Tartan, a small coasting vessel in the Mediterranean. 2. Long covered carriage for passengers with two wheels.
Tartáreo, rea, *a.* (Poét.) Tartarean.
Tartári, *sm.* (Ant.) Tartarus. V. *Tartaro.*
Tartarizár, *va.* To tartarize, to impregnate with tartar, to refine by means of the salt of tartar.
Tártaro, *sm.* 1. Argol, tartar, the lees of wine. 2. (Poét.) Tartarus, hell.
Tartéra ó Tortéra, *sf.* 1. Pan for baking tarts and other pastry. 2. Dripping-pan.
Tarúga, *sf.* A swift animal like a sheep in America.
Tarúgo, *sm.* A wooden peg or pin; stopper, plug, bung.
Tas, *sm.* 1. Kind of anvil used by silversmiths. 2. Clapping of hands.
Tása, *sf.* 1. Assize, price of provisions fixed by magistrates. 2. Measure, rule. 3. Rate, settled price or value; duty, tax.
Tasación, *sf.* Valuation, appraisement; taxation.
Tasadaménte, *ad.* Barely, scantily, scarcely.
Tasadór, *sm.* Appraiser.
Tasájo, *sm.* Hung-beef, beef salted and hung in the air.
Tasár, *va.* 1. To appraise, to value, to estimate. 2. To observe method and rule; to fix a regimen. 3. To tax, to rate at.
Tascadór, *sm.* Brake, an instrument for breaking or dressing flax or hemp.
Tascár, *va.* 1. To break or dress flax or hemp. 2. To nibble the grass; applied to beasts. *Tascar al freno*, To bite the bridle; to resist or complain.
Tásco, *sm.* 1. Refuse of flax or hemp. 2. (Naút.) Toppings of hemp.
Tascónio, *sm.* V. *Talque.*
Tasquéra, *sf.* Dispute, scuffle, contest.
Tasquíl, *sm.* Fragment of a stone.
Tástana, *sf.* The partition which divides the kernel of a walnut.
Tástara, *sf.* (Arag.) Coarse bran.
Tastáz, *sm.* Polishing powder made of old crucibles.
Tásto, *sm.* Bad taste of any food.
Tasúgo, *sm.* V. *Texon.*
Tatarabuélo, la, *s.* The great great grandfather or mother.
Tataradéudo, da, *s.* Very old and distant relation.
Tataraniéto, ta, *s.* A great great grandson or daughter.
Tátas, *ad.* (Astur.) *Andar á tatas*, To walk timidly; to go on all fours.
Táte, *interj.* Take care, beware; stay, I recollect. V. *Ta.*
Táto, *sm.* 1. (Fam. Ar.) A younger brother. 2. Hog-headed armadillo.
Táto, ta, *a.* y *s.* Stammering; stutterer who converts *c* and *s* into *t*.
Táu, *sm.* V. *Tao.*
Taumalín, *sm.* A viscous matter found in the bodies of crabs, and other shell-fish.
Taumatúrgo, *sm.* The author of great and stupendous things, miracle-worker.
Tauréte, *sm.* V. *Taburete.*
Tauríno, na, *a.* Relating to a bull.
Táuro, *sm.* (Astr.) Taurus, a sign of the zodiac.
Tautología, *sf.* Tautology, a needless repetition of the same words in a sentence.
Tautológico, ca, *a.* Tautological.
Táuxia, *sf.* V. *Atauria.*
Tavelládo, da, *a.* Marked with the stamp of the manufactory; applied to cloths.
Taxativaménte, *ad.* Limitedly.
Taxatívo, va, *a.* (For.) Limited to circumstances.
Taxéa, *sf.* Furrow or small channel opened for the irrigation of land. V. *Atarzea.*
Taybíque, *sm.* Partition-wall. V. *Tabique.*
Táyfa, *sf.* V. *Taha.*
Taymádo, da, *a.* Sly, cunning, crafty.
Taymonía, *sf.* Malicious cunning, impudent craft.
Táyta, *sf.* A fondling name, with which a child calls its father. *Ajo tayta*, (Fam.) Said to one who acts like a child.
Taz á Taz, ó Taz por Taz, *ad.* This for that; tit for tat.
Táza, *sf.* 1. Cup, small bowl, dish; jug, or drinking vessel. *Taza de te*, Cup of tea. 2. Basin of a fountain. 3. A large wooden bowl. 4. (Joc.) Buttocks, breech. 5. (Mil.) Bucket, a pouch in which a dragoon rests the muzzle of his carbine, while he is on horseback. *Amigo de taza de vino*, A selfish friend, a sponger.
Tazáña, *sf.* Serpent. V. *Tarasca.*
Tazmía, *sf.* Share of tithes.
Tazón, *sm.* A large bowl or basin; pitcher.
Te, *sm.* 1. (Bot.) Tea; a plant. Thea *L.* 2. Tea, water or decoction of tea leaves.—*pron.* Thee, the oblique case of Thou.
Téa, *sf.* Candlewood, a piece of pine or other resinous wood, which burns like a torch. *Teas maritales*, Hymeneal torches.
Teáme ó Teamíde, *sf.* A stone repelling iron.
Teatíno, *sm.* 1. A delicate sort of paste. 2. Theatin, one of a religious order founded by Pope Paul IV.
Teatrál, *a.* Theatral, belonging to the theatre.
Teatrísta, *sm.* Dramatist; performer in public; exhibiter.
Teátro, *sm.* 1. Theatre, playhouse; the concourse of people attending at a playhouse; collection of plays belonging to one nation 2. Lecture-hall in a university; the room where lectures are delivered. 3. Stage. 4. Place where any thing is exposed to the censure of the world. *Teatro literario*, The literary world.
Techár, *va.* To roof; to cover with a roof.
Técho ó Techádo, *sm.* 1. Roof, ceiling, the inner roof of a building. 2. (Met.) Dwelling-house, habitation, place of abode; native soil.
Techúmbre, *sm.* Upper roof, ceiling.
Técla, *sf.* 1. Key of a harpsichord or piano-

forte. 2. A delicate point, which is to be handled with great prudence. *Dar en la tecla*, To touch the right chord, to hit the mark.

Tecládo, *sm.* The whole series of the keys of an organ, harpsichord, or other similar musical instrument.

Tecleár, *va.* To strike or touch the keys of a musical instrument; to move the fingers as if touching the keys of an instrument.—*va.* To try a variety of ways and means for obtaining some end.

Técnico, ca, *a.* Technical.

Tecnología, *sf.* Technology.

Tedéro, *sm.* Iron candlestick for holding burning fir or torch.

Tediár, *va.* To loathe, to hate, to abhor.

Tédio, *sm.* Disgust, dislike, abhorrence.

Tedióso, sa, *a.* Loathful, fastidious, nauseous to the taste or mind.

Teguál, *sm.* Tax or duty paid to the king.

Teguménto, *sm.* Tegument, covering.

Teísta, *sm.* Theist, a deist.

Téja, *sf.* 1. Roof-tile, a piece of baked clay for covering buildings. *Teja concava*, Gutter or pan-tile. 2. (Mur.) Cavity at the bottom of a tree. *Teja de gimelga*, (Naút.) The hollow part of a fish. *A' teja vana*, With a shed cover. *Caerse las tejas*, (Fam.) To be growing dark. *De tejas abajo*, In a natural order.

Tejadíllo, *sm.* 1. Roof of a coach. 2. Veil, which covers every part of a woman's head, but leaves the face exposed to view. 3. Braces of a coach harness. 4. A small shed. 5. Mode of cheating at cards.

Tejádo, *sm.* Roof covered with tiles. *Andar á sombra de tejado*, To lurk, to skulk; to be at hide and seek.

Tejár, *sm.* Tile-works, place where tiles are made and burnt.—*va.* To tile, to cover with tiles.

Tejaróz, *sm.* Penthouse, a shed covered with tiles.

Tejázo, *sm.* Blow given with a tile.

Tejéra y Tejería, *sf.* Tile-kiln. V. *Tejar*.

Tejéro, *sm.* Tile-maker, one whose profession is to make tiles.

Tejíllo, *sm.* A small tile.

Téjo, *sm.* 1. Quoit, round tile with which boys play, also the game. 2. (Bot.) Yew-tree. Taxus *L.* 3. A round metal plate; piece of gold.

Tejoléta, *sf.* Piece of burnt clay; tile.

Tejuéla, *sf.* 1. A small tile. 2. Saddle-tree.

Tejuélo, *sm.* 1. Sole, a square piece of iron, stone, or timber, on which the point of a gate or large door turns. 2. Space between the bands on the back of a book. V. *Tejo*.

Téla, *sf.* 1. Cloth, any stuff woven in a loom; gold or silver lace. 2. Chain or warp of cloth. 3. Circus, a place enclosed and fitted up for public shows. 4. Examen, argument; matter; thread of a discourse. 5. Pellicle, the thin interior skin of the animal body, or of fruits; membrane; speck in the eye. 6. Film or pellicle collected on the surface of liquors. 7. Quibble, quirk. 8. Place enclosed with linen to catch game. *Tela encerada ó engomada*, Buckram. *Tela de araña*, Trifling discourse; cobweb.

Telamón, *sm.* (Arq.) V. *Atlante*.

Telár, *sm.* Loom, a frame in which cloth is woven; a frame, in which other things are made.

Telaráña, *sf.* 1. Cobweb. 2. A small cloud. 3. Any thing trifling and of little weight. *Mirar las telarañas*, (Fam.) To blunder in consequence of inattention to what one is doing or saying.

Teléa, *sf.* (Bot.) Shrub-trefoil. Ptelea *L.*

Teléfio, *sm.* (Bot.) Orpine stonecrop, livelong. Sedum telephium *L.*

Telégrafo, *sm.* Telegraph, a machine invented to communicate intelligence from one distant point to another.

Teléra, *sf.* 1. A small iron pin, with which the plough-share is fastened to the plough. 2. (And.) A kind of brown bread. *Telera de araña*, (Naút.) Dead-eye of a crow-foot. 3. Railing to enclose sheep, kind of hurdle. 4. Screw or keeper on a carpenter's bench for holding the wood fast. 5. Transom, each of the pieces which cross a gun carriage. 6. Sloat of a car or cart.—*a.* Applied to a woman fond of making cloth.

Teléro, *sm.* (Ar.) Rail in the sides of carts or wagons.

Telescópio, *sm.* Telescope, an instrument for viewing distant objects.

Teléta, *sf.* 1. Blotting paper. 2. Sieve used in paper-mills.

Teletón, *sm.* A strong silken stuff.

Televoéto, ta, *a.* (Ant.) Loved in preference.

Telílla, *sf.* 1. A light woollen stuff. Rind of fruit. V. *Camisa*.

Telína, *sf.* V. *Almeja*.

Telíno, *sm.* A precious unguent, composed of oil, honey, melilot, and other ingredients.

Tellína, *sf.* Bivalve shell-fish.

Tellíz, *sm.* Cloth thrown over the saddle of a horse by way of ornament.

Tellíza, *sf.* Coverlet of a bed.

Telón, *sm.* 1. Linsey woolsey, a sort of coarse stuff. 2. Curtain in a playhouse.

Telónio, *sm.* Custom-house.

Téma, *sm.* Text, proposition, theme, subject, matter of argument.—*sf.* 1. Topic of madmen's discourse. 2. Dispute, contention; obstinacy in asserting a controverted point. 3. Animosity, passionate malignity; capricious opposition. *A' tema*, Emulously, obstinately. *Tema celeste*, (Astr.) Map or delineation of the heavens.

Temático, ca, *a.* Relating to a theme or subject. V. *Temoso*.

Tembladál, *sm.* V. *Tremedal*.

Tembladéra, *sf.* 1. Tankard, a wide-mouthed vessel with two handles. 2. Diamond-pin, or other similar ornament of the head-dress of ladies. 3. (Ict.) Cramp-fish, elastic ray. Raia torpedo *L.*

Tembladór, ra, *s.* Quaker, shaker, trembler.

Temblánte, *sm.* Kind of loose bracelet worn by women.—*pa.* Trembling, quavering.

Temblár, *vn.* To tremble, to shake with fear, to move with violent agitation; to quake. *Temblar la barba*, To enter with caution and dread on any arduous undertaking. *Temblar la contera*, (Met. y Fam.) To be greatly afraid of any thing. *Temblar las carnes*, (Fam.) To have a horror of any thing.

Temblèque, *sm.* Diamond pin or plume, or

other similar ornament of the head-dress of ladies.

Tembleuquear ó Tembletear, vn. To tremble, to shake with fear; to move with violent agitation. [na, To affect timidity.

Temblón, na, a. Tremulous. *Hacer la temblo-*

Temblón, sm. (Bot.) Aspen or asp-tree. Populus tremula *L.*

Temblór, sm. Trembling, an involuntary motion, which proceeds from fear or weakness. *Temblor de tierra,* Earthquake.

Temblorcíllo, sm. A slight shivering.

Temblóso, sa, a. Tremulous.

Temedór, ra, a. Awful, dreadful.

Temedór, ra, s. Trembler.—a. Dreadful.

Temér, va. To apprehend, to fear, to dread; to reverence, to respect; to suspect.

Temerariaménte, ad. Rashly.

Temerário, ria, a. Rash, inconsiderate, imprudent, temerarious.

Temeridád, sf. Temerity, rashness, imprudence; excess. *Ser una temeridad,* To be excessive. [bullying.

Temerón, na, a. Affecting noise, authority, or

Temerosaménte, ad. Timorously.

Temeróso, sa, a. Timid, timorous, fearful; cowardly.

Temíble, a. Dreadful, terrible.

Temído, da, a. Feared.

Temiénte, pa. One who dreads or apprehends.

Temór, sm. Dread, fear, apprehension, suspicion.

Temorizár, va. (Ant.) V. *Atemorizar.*

Temóso, sa, a. Obstinate, stubborn.

Tempanadór, sm. Instrument for cutting the tops off beehives, resembling a small bill-hook.

Tempanár, va. To furnish staves; to cover the tops of beehives.

Témpano, sm. 1. Flitch of bacon. 2. V. *Tímpano.* 3. Tympan, stretched skin or other thing; open, plain space. 4. Large cork put in the top of beehives. 5. (Arq.) Tympan of an arch. *Tempano de cuba,* Side staves of a barrel or cask.

Temperación, sf. V. *Temperamento.*

Temperadaménte, ad. V. *Templadamente.*

Temperaménto, sm. Temperament, temperature, constitution.

Temperáncia y Temperánza, V. *Templanza.*

Temperánte, pa. (Med.) That which tempers.

Temperár, va. V. *Atemperar.*

Temperatúra, sf. V. *Temperamento.*

Tempérie, sf. Temperature of the air.

Tempéro, sm. Seasonableness, fitness for the growth of seeds.

Tempestád, sf. 1. Tempest, the utmost violence of the wind. 2. Violent commotion or perturbation of the mind. 3. Appointed or seasonable time. *Tempestades,* Violent, abusive language.

Tempestár, vn. To be a tempest. [tunely.

Tempestivaménte, ad. Seasonably, opportunely.

Tempestividád, sf. Tempestivity, seasonableness, opportunity.

Tempestívo, va, a. Seasonable, opportune.

Tempestuosaménte, ad. Tempestuously.

Tempestuóso, sa, a. Tempestuous, stormy.

Témpla, sf. (Pint.) Distemper, size for painting.

Templación, (Ant.) V. *Templanza y Temple.*

Templadaménte, ad. Temperately, moderately.

Templadéra, sf. (Naút.) Sluice put into a channel to let a certain quantity of water pass.

Templadíco, ca, a. dim. Somewhat temperate.

Templádo, da, a. Temperate, moderate.

Templadór, ra, s. 1. Tuner; one who tempers. 2. Key for tuning musical instruments.

Templadúra, sf. Temperature; the act of tempering.

Templánza, sf. 1. Temperance, moderation. 2. Disposition of the air or climate of a country. 3. Degree of heat or cold. 4. Temperament, temperature. 5. V. *Temple.* 6. (Pint.) Mixture of colours.

Templár, va. 1. To temper, to soften, to moderate. 2. To temper steel, to anneal glass. 3. To tune musical instruments. 4. To observe due proportion of parts in a piece of painting. 5. (Naút.) To trim the sails to the wind. 6. To mix, to assuage, to soften. 7. To prepare, to dispose. 8. To train a hawk.—vr. To be moderate; to refrain from excess. *Templar la gayta,* (Fam.) To pacify, to please.

Templário, sm. Templar, one of the order of Templars.

Témple, sm. 1. Temperature, the degree of heat and cold of the season or climate. 2. Temper, the proper degree of hardness or softness given to metals. 3. Frame or disposition of the mind. 4. The harmonical concordance of musical instruments. 5. Religion of the Templars; a temple or church. *Al temple,* Painted in distemper.

Templéte, sm. dim. Architectural ornament in form of a temple.

Templísta, sm. Painter in distemper.

Témplo, sm. 1. Temple, a building erected for the worship of God. 2. Blessed soul. 3. Temple dedicated to the false gods of the Gentiles.

Témpora, sf. Days of fast prescribed by the Roman Catholic church.

Temporáda, sf. A certain space of time.

Temporál, a. Temporary; secular.—sm. 1. Season whether good or bad. 2. Tempest, storm. 3. (And.) Temporary labourer.

Temporalidád, sf. Temporality, the secular revenues of the clergy; temporal concerns.

Temporalizár, va. To make temporary, what might or should be everlasting. [time.

Temporalménte, ad. Temporally, for some

Temporáneo, nea, a. Temporary, instable.

Temporário, ria, a. Temporary.

Temporéro ó Temporíl, sm. Temporary labourer, one who works only for a season.

Temporizár, vn. 1. To pass the time in any place or thing. 2. V. *Contemporizar.*

Tempranál, a. Producing early fruits; applied to land.

Tempranaménte, ad. Early, prematurely.

Tempranéro, ra, a. V. *Temprano.*

Tempraníllas, sf. pl. A sort of early grapes.

Tempráno, na, a. Early, soon, anticipated.

Tempráno, ad. Very early, prematurely.

Temulénto, ta, a. Intoxicated, inebriated, temulent.

Téna, sf. V. *Tinada.*

Tenacear, va. To tear with pincers.—vn. To insist in an obstinate and pertinacious manner.

Tenacíco, sm. He who makes or uses pincers.

Tenacícas y llas, sf. pl. Pincers; snuffers.

Tenacidád, *sf.* Tenacity, tenaciousness; pertinacity.
Tenáda, *sf.* Sheepfold, sheepcot.
Tenallón, *sm.* (Fort.) Outwork on the flanks of a fortification.
Tenánte, *sm.* (Blas.) Supporter; figure of a man, angel, &c. which supports a shield.
Tenáz, *a.* 1. Tenacious, sticking. 2. Firm, stubborn, obstinate. 3. Avaricious, niggardly, covetous.
Tenáza, *sf.* 1. (Fort.) Tenaille, a kind of outwork of a fortress. 2. Claws or talons of animals. 3. Beam-ends of oil-mills. 4. Tongs. 5. Two leading cards at a game. *Tenazas*, Pincers, an instrument by which any thing is griped and held fast.
Tenazáda, *sf.* 1. The act of griping with pincers. 2. The act of biting strongly.
Tenazménte, *ad.* Tenaciously.
Tenazón, *sm.* (Cetr.) Act of a falcon trussing without binding. *Parar de tenazon*, To stop a horse short in his course.
Tenazuélas, *sf. pl.* Tweezers, small nippers or pincers.
Ténca, *sf.* (Ict.) Tench. Cyprinus tinca *L.*
Tención, *sf.* Tension, the act of stretching.
Tencón, *sm.* (Ict.) A large tench.
Tencontén, *sm.* Moderation, temperance. *Tén con tén*, *ad.* Equally, making both ends meet. *Andar con un tén con tén*, To act guardedly, to proceed with moderation and equity.
Tendál, *sm.* (Naút.) Tilt of a row-galley. V. *Limon* y *Tendedero*.
Tendaléra, *sf.* (Fam.) Confusion and disorder of things lying about on the floor.
Tendedéro y **Tendaléro**, *sm.* Place where washed wool is dried; stretcher.
Tendedór, *sm.* Stretcher, one who extends or stretches.
Tendedúra, *sf.* Act of stretching or extending.
Tendejón, *sm.* Sutler's tent in a camp.
Tendél, *sm.* Line by which masons raise a wall.
Tendéncia, *sf.* Tendence, tendency, inclination.
Tendénte, *a.* Tending, leading, directing.
Tendér, *va.* To stretch, to extend, to spread out; to distend.—*vn.* To direct, to tend, to refer.—*vr.* 1. To stretch one's self at full length. 2. To give up an intention; to relinquish a claim. *Tenderla*, To challenge, to provoke a dispute. *Tender el paño de púlpito*, (Fam.) To speak largely and diffusively. *Tender la raspa*, To lay one's-self down to sleep or rest. *Tender las redes*, To cast the nets; (Met.) To use the proper means of attaining an object.
Tenderéte, *sm.* 1. Kind of game at cards. 2. V. *Tendalera*.
Tendería, *sf.* Place full of shops.
Tendéro, ra, *s.* Shopkeeper; tent-maker.
Tendezuéla, *sf. dim.* of *tienda*.
Tendidaménte, *ad.* Diffusely, diffusively.
Tendído, *sm.* 1. A row of seats for the accommodation of the spectators at a bull-feast. 2. Floor-carpet. 3. Portion of lace wrought on one pattern. 4. Quantity of clothes dried by a laundress at once. 5. Batch of bread baked at one time. 6. Roof of a house from the ridge to the eaves.
Tendiénte, *pa.* Tending, expanding.

Tendinóso, sa, *a.* Tendinous, relating to or consisting of tendons.
Tendón, *sm.* Tendon, a ligature by which the joints are moved.
Tenebrário, *sm.* A large candlestick or girandole, with a triangular branch, holding fifteen candles, used in Roman Catholic churches.
Tenebrosidád, *sf.* Darkness, obscurity. [style.
Tenebróso, sa, *a.* Dark, gloomy; obscure in
Tenedéro, *sm.* (Naút.) Gripe or hold of an anchor. *Fondo de buen tenedero*, Good anchoring ground.
Tenedór, *sm.* 1. Holder, keeper, tenant; guardian. *Tenedor del gran sello*, Keeper of the great seal. *Tenedor de libros*, Book-keeper. *Tenedor de bastimentos*, (Naút.) Store-keeper of the navy. 2. Fork, an instrument with a haft and prongs to eat with. *Tenedor de caldero*, Flesh-hook. 3. He who detains balls at play.
Tenedurìa, *sf.* (Naút.) Store-house, a magazine of naval stores.
Tenéncia, *sf.* 1. Possession, the act of holding or possessing. 2. Lieutenancy, the commission and charge of a lieutenant.
Tenér, *va.* 1. To take, to gripe, to hold fast. 2. To hold, to possess, to enjoy; to subject. Sometimes it is used as an auxiliary verb. V *Haber*. 3. To maintain, to support. 4. To contain, to comprise, to comprehend. 5. To hold an opinion, to keep, to retain. *Tener miedo*, To be afraid. 6. To be rich, and opulent. 7. To hold, to estimate, to judge, to take. In this sense it is followed by the preposition *en* and the adjectives *poco*, *mucho*, &c. 8. To lodge, to receive in one's house. 9. To be obliged, to have to do; to be at the expense of any thing. 10. To be adorned or favoured with any thing. 11. To detain, to stop. 12. To keep or fulfil. With nouns of time, it signifies duration or age; when united with *que* and followed by an infinitive verb, it implies necessity or obligation. *Tener zelos de uno*, To be jealous of one. *Tener brazos*, To have interest or powerful friends. *Tener mucho de miserable*, To have much of the miser. *Tener para sí*, To maintain a particular or singular opinion, liable to objections. *Tener de ahí*, Hold! stop! to be clever in some thing.—*vr.* 1. To take care not to fall. 2. To stop, to halt. 3. To resist, to oppose. 4. To adhere, to stand to. *Tenerse en pie*, To keep on foot; to stand. *Tener y tengamos*, (Fam.) To take and give; a mutual security.
Tenería, *sf.* Tan-yard, a place where leather is dressed or tanned.
Tenésmo, *sm.* Tenesmus, a continual wanting to go to stool.
Ténia, *sf.* Tape-worm.
Teniénta, *sf.* Wife of a deputy or lieutenant.
Tenientázgo, *sm.* Office of deputy.
Teniénte, *a.* 1. Immature, unripe. 2. Possessing. 3. Deaf. 4. Miserly.
Teniénte, *sm.* 1. Deputy, substitute. 2. Person who is hard of hearing. 3. Miser, a person sordidly parsimonious. 4. Lieutenant. *Teniente de una compañia*, Lieutenant of a company. *Teniente general*, Lieutenant-general.

Tenór, *sm.* 1. Permanent establishment or order of any thing; continuity of state. 2. Tenor, contents, sense contained. 3. Tenor, one of the four voices in music; tenorist, who sings the tenor.

Tensión, *sf.* Tension, the act of extending; the state of being extended.

Ténso, sa, *a.* Tense, tight, extended.

Tentación, *sf.* Temptation, instigation.

Tentacioncílla, *sf.* A slight temptation.

Tentadór, ra, *s.* Tempter, one who tempts or instigates to evil.

Tentaleár, *va.* To try, to feel, to examine.

Tentár, *va.* 1. To touch; to try, to examine or prove by touching. 2. To tempt, to instigate, to incite, to stimulate. 3. To attempt, to procure. 4. To hesitate, to be doubtful. 5. To probe a wound. 6. To experiment; to try; to prove. *Andar tentando*, To make essays or trials. *Tentar el vado*, To sound one's abilities or sentiments: to try the depth either physical or moral. *Tentar la ropa*, (Met.) To tergiversate, to use evasions.

Tentatíva, *sf.* Attempt, trial; first examination.

Tentatívo, va, *a.* Tentative.

Ténte Bonéte, *ad.* Abundantly, excessively. *Á ó hasta tente bonete*, Excessively, extremely.

Tentemózo, *sm.* Prop put to a house, to prevent its falling down.

Tentón, *sm.* Caution, prudence; seeking or groping for support.

Tenuaménte, *ad.* Slightly.

Tenúdo, da, *pp. irreg.* of *tener*, Held. It is generally joined with the verb *ser*, when it signifies, To be obliged, to be necessitated.

Ténue y Ténuo, *a.* 1. Thin, slender, delicate. 2. Worthless, of little value or importance. 3. Applied to soft consonants.

Tenuidád, *sf.* 1. Tenuity, weakness. 2. Trifle, any thing of little value or importance.

Tenúta, *sf.* Provisional possession of an estate during the course of a law-suit.

Tenutário, ria, *a.* Provisional tenant.

Teñidúra, *sf.* Art of dying or tingeing.

Teñír, *va.* 1. To tinge, to dye; to impregnate cloth with colour; to stain; to paint the face. *Teñir en rama*, To dye in grain. 2. (Met.) To give another colour to things, to dissemble or misrepresent. 3. To instil into the mind some opinion, idea, or affection. 4. (Pint.) To darken, to sadden a colour.

Teocracía, *sf.* Theocracy.

Teodolíta, *sf.* Theodolite, an instrument much used in surveying, to take angles.

Teogonía, *sf.* Theogony, generation of the gods.

Teologál, *a.* Theological. *Vertud teologal*, Theological virtue, faith, hope, and charity. —*sf.* Theological prebendary. V. *Lectoral.*

Teología, *sf.* Theology, divinity. *No meterse en teologias*, (Fam.) Not to involve one's self in subtleties.

Teologicaménte, *ad.* Theologically.

Teológico, ca, *a.* V. *Teologal.*

Teologizár, *vn.* To treat or discourse upon the principles of theology, to theologize.

Teólogo, *sm.* A divine; a clergyman.

Teólogo, ga, *a.* Theological.

Teoréma, *sf.* Theorem.

Teorético, ca, *a.* Theoretic.

Teórica y Teoría, *sf.* Theory, speculation, not practice.

Teoricaménte, *ad.* Theoretically.

Teórico, ca, *a.* Theoretic, theoretical, speculative.

Teóso, sa, *a.* Resinous.

Teosofía, *sf.* V. *Teologia.*

Tépe, *sm.* Green sod.

Tepeizquínte, *sm.* South American animal, resembling a sucking pig.

Tequío, *sm.* Custom, duty, in South America.

Terapéutas, *sm. pl.* Therapeutæ, persons wholly devoted to religious offices.

Terapéutica, *sf.* Practical physic, therapeutics.

Tercéna, *sf.* Wholesale tobacco warehouse.

Tercenál, *sm.* (Ar.) Heap containing thirty sheaves of corn.

Tercenísta, *sm.* Keeper of a wholesale tobacco warehouse.

Tercér, *sm.* Third.—*a.* Third; used before a substantive.

Tercéra, *sf.* 1. Procuress, bawd. 2. (Múa.) Consonance comprehending an interval of 2 1/2 tones; one of the 5 strings of a guitar. 3. Series of three cards in order at play.

Terceraménte, *ad.* Thirdly.

Tercería, *sf.* 1. Mediation, arbitration. 2. Arbitration-dues or fees. 3. Depositary. 4. Temporary occupation of a castle, fortress, &c.

Tercerílla, *sf.* A kind of metrical composition.

Tercéro, ra, *a.* Third.

Tercéro, *sm.* 1. Mediator, arbitrator; a third person. 2. Collector of tithes. 3. Religious of the third order. *Tercero en discordia*, Umpire between two disputants.

Terceról, *sm.* (Naút.) Main-sail; third pair of oars.

Terceróla, *sf.* 1. A short kind of carbine. 2. Tierce, a kind of barrel or small cask.

Tercéto, *sm.* Triplet, three verses.

Tércia, *sf.* 1. Third, the third part. 2. Storehouse or barn, where tithes are deposited. 3. Canonical hour which follows immediately the first, so called from falling at three o'clock. 4. At cards. V. *Tercera. Tercias*, Two-ninths of the ecclesiastical tithes, which in Spain are deducted for the king.

Terciación, *sf.* Act of ploughing a third time.

Terciádo, *sm.* 1. Cutlass, a short and broad sword. 2. Kind of ribbon somewhat broader than tape. *Pan terciado*, Rent of ground paid in grain, two-thirds wheat, and one-third barley.

Terciána, *sf.* Tertian, an ague intermitting but one day, so that there are two fits in three days.

Tercianário, ria, *s.* A person affected with a tertian.

Terciané la, *sf.* A sort of silk, resembling taffety.

Terciáno, na, *a.* Tertian.

Terciár, *va.* 1. To sling any thing diagonally. 2. To divide a thing into three parts. 3. To plough the third time.—*vn.* 1. To make up the number of three. 2. To mediate, to arbitrate. 3. To join, to share, to make one of a party. *Terciar el baston ó el palo*, To strike one directly with a stick. *Terciar la cara*, To cut one's face across. *Terciar la carga*, To divide a load or burthen into three equal parts. *Terciar una pieza*, (Art.) To prove a gun.

Terciário, *sm.* (Arq.) Rib in the vaulting of Gothic arches.

Terciazón, *sm.* Third ploughing.

Tércio, cia, *a.* Third.

Tércio, *sm.* 1. The third part. 2. Half a load. 3. Regiment of infantry. 4. Third part of a horse course. 5. Third part of the Rosary; third part of a sword. *En tercio y quinto*, Great advantage which one does to another. *Hacer buen tercio*, To mediate, to intercede.—*pl.* 1. Height of horses, measured by hands. 2. Robust or strong limbs of a man.

Terciodécuplo, pla, *a.* Product of any quantity multiplied by 13.

Terciopeládo, *sf.* Stuff resembling velvet.

Terciopeládo, da, *a.* Velvet-like.

Terciopeléro, *sm.* Velvet-weaver.

Terciopélo, *sm.* Velvet, a kind of silk with a short fur or pile upon it.

Térco, ca, *a.* 1. Pertinacious, obstinate. 2. Firm or hard as marble.

Terebintína, *sf.* Turpentine, a resinous juice extracted from pine trees. V. *Trementina.*

Terebínto, *sm.* (Bot.) Turpentine or mastich-tree. Pistacia terebinthinus *L.*

Tereniabín, *sm.* White sweetish purgative matter, resembling mastich, which adheres to the leaves of plants; liquid manna. [flesh.

Teréte, *a.* Round, plump, robust, having firm

Tergiversación, *sf.* Tergiversation, evasion, subterfuge.

Tergiversár, *va.* To tergiversate, to shuffle, to use subterfuges. Originally it signified, to shrug the shoulders.

Teriáca, *sf.* Treacle. V. *Triaca.*

Teriacál, *a.* Theriacal, like treacle.

Terícia, *sf.* V. *Ictericia.*

Terístro, *sm.* Light veil.

Terlíz, *sm.* Tick, ticking, twilled stuff for beds.

Termál, *a.* Relating to hot baths.

Térmas, *sf. pl.* Hot baths.

Terminable, *a.* Terminable, that may be finished or brought to a close.

Terminácho, *sm.* Rude word or phrase.

Terminación, *sf.* 1. Termination, the act of bounding, limiting, or closing. 2. (Gram.) Termination, the ending or last syllable of a word. 3. (Med.) Termination of a disease.

Termináдо, *sm.* Story, a floor or flight of rooms.

Terminadór, ra, *s.* One who terminates.

Terminájo, *sm.* (Fam.) A low, vulgar, or barbarous expression.

Terminál, *a.* Final, ultimate.

Terminánte, *a.* Conclusive or decisive with regard to a point in question; definite. *En terminos terminantes*, In definite terms, with propriety or punctuality.

Terminár, *va.* To end, to close, to terminate.—*vn.* 1. (Med.) To come to a crisis. 2. (Gram.) To end a word. [term.

Terminatívo, va, *a.* Respective, relative to a

Término, *sm.* 1. The end of any thing. 2. Boundary, land-mark; limit. 3. Manner, behaviour, conduct. 4. District of a town or city. 5. Aim, object. 6. Term, word, diction; conception. 7. Term, the appointed time or determined place for doing any thing. 8. State, condition. 9. Crisis of a disease. 10. Determinate object of any operation. 11. Period including the beginning and end of any thing. 12. The precise moment to do any thing. 13. Term or word of any language, a technical word. 14. (Arq.) Stay, resembling the support which the ancients gave the head of their god Terminus. 15. (Pint.) Compartment in a painting. *En terminos habiles*, On reasonable terms, so as not to prejudice another. *Terminos*, Terms of an argument, syllogism, or arithmetical question. *Medios terminos*, Evasions by which any one avoids a disagreeable subject.

Terminóte, *sm. aum.* of *termino*, A vulgar or affected expression.

Termómetro, *sm.* Thermometer, an instrument for measuring the degrees of heat and cold.

Térna, *sf.* 1. A ternary number. 2. A kind of stuff of a fine appearance after the fur or pile is fallen off. 3. Game at dice.

Ternário, ria, *a.* Ternary, containing three unities.

Ternário, *sm.* Three days' devotion or religious offices.

Ternecíco, ca; to, ta, *a.* Very tender. [calf

Terneríllo, lla; to, ta; co, ca, *s.* A young

Ternéro, ra, *s.* Calf; veal.

Ternejón, na; rón, róna, *a.* Easily moved, weeping at will.

Ternerúela, *sf.* A sucking calf.

Ternéza, *sf.* 1. Softness, delicacy, pliantness. 2. Tenderness, affection, endearment. 3. Suavity, softness or smoothness of words. 4. Readiness to shed tears.

Ternílla, *sf.* Gristle, the cartilaginous part of the animal body.

Ternillóso, sa, *a.* Gristly, cartilaginous; webbed, fin-footed.

Térno, *sf.* 1. Ternary number. 2. Wearing apparel, dress; rich clothes. 3. Ornaments for celebrating high mass. 4. Oath. V. *Voto. Echar ternos ó tacos*, To swear excessively, to speak in a great rage. 5. (Impr.) Union of three sheets one within another. *Terno seco*, Happy and unexpected fortune.

Ternúra, *sf.* Tenderness, delicacy. V. *Terneza.*

Terquedád, *sf.* Stubbornness, obstinacy, pertinacity.

Terquería y Terquéza, *sf.* Perseverance, pertinacity, obstinacy.

Terráda, *sf.* Kind of bitumen made with ochre and glue.

Terrádgo, *sm.* V. *Terrazgo.*

Terrádo, *sm.* Terrace, platform; a flat roof of a building, for taking the air.

Terrázge, *sm.* Rent paid to the owner of land.

Terrajéro, *sm.* V. *Terrazguero.*

Terrája, *sf.* Instrument for making screws, a screw-plate. V. *Tarraja.*

Terrál, *sm.* A land breeze.

Terraplén y Terrapléno, *sm.* (Fort.) The horizontal surface of a rampart, terrace.

Terraplenár, *va.* To raise a rampart; to make a platform or terrace.

Terraplenadór, *sm.* One who makes a terrace or platform.

Terráqueo, quea, *a.* Terraqueous, composed of land and water.

Terrása, *sf.* Terrace.

Terrateniénte, *sm.* Master or possessor of land or property.

Terrázza, *sf.* A glazed jar with two handles.

Terrázgo, *sm.* 1. Arable land, ground fit for tillage. 2. Land-tax or rent of arable land paid to the landlord.

Terrazguéro, *sm.* Labourer who pays rent to the lord of the manor for the arable land which he occupies.

Terrázo, *sm.* (Pint.) Ground or field of a painting.

Terreár, *vn.* To show the ground; speaking of crops which stand very thin.

Terrecér, *va.* (Ant.) To terrify.

Terregóso, sa, *a.* Cloddy, full of clods.

Terremóto, *sm.* Earthquake.

Terrenál, *a.* Terrestrial, terrene.

Terrenidád, *sf.* Quality of the soil or ground.

Terréno, na, *a.* 1. Terrene, terreous, earthy, earthen. 2. Worldly, perishable.

Terréno, *sm.* 1. Place or space of ground. 2. Quality or properties of the soil.

Térreo, rea, *a.* Terreous, consisting of earth.

Terréra, *sf.* 1. A declivous or slanting piece of ground. 2. (Orn.) Kind of lark.

Terréro, *sm.* 1. Terrace, platform. 2. Heap of earth. 3. Mark, aim to shoot at. 4. Terrace, or other part of the palace, where court is paid to the ladies. *Hacer terrero*, To court a lady. 5. Horse that does not lift his feet high.

Terréro, ra, *a.* 1. Earthy, terreous. 2. Abject, low, humble.

Terréstre, *a.* Terrestrious, terreous.

Terrestridád, *sf.* Earthiness, the quality and properties of the earth.

Terretrémo, *sm.* (Mur.) Earthquake.

Terrezuéla, *sf.* 1. A small piece of ground. 2. Light and poor soil.

Terribilidád y Terribléza, *sf.* Terribleness, roughness, asperity, ferocity.

Terríble, *a.* Terrible, dreadful, ferocious, rude, unmannerly; immense, very large.

Terribleménte, *ad.* Terribly.

Terrícola, *sm.* Inhabitant of the earth.

Terrífico, ca, *a.* Terrific.

Terrígeno, na, *a.* Earth-born, engendered from the earth.

Terrín, *sm.* Peasant, countryman.

Terríno, na, Terrene, earthy.

Territoriál, *a.* Territorial, belonging to a territory.

Território, *sm.* Territory; district.

Terrízo, za, *a.* Earthy, earthen.

Terrójo, *sm.* Red earth.

Terromontéro, *sm.* Hill, hillock, mount of earth.

Terrón, *sm.* 1. A flat clod of earth. 2. Lump of any thing; heap, collection of things. *Terron de azúcar*, Lump of sugar. 3. Dregs of olives which remain in the mill. *Terrónes*, Landed property. *Terron de sal*, (Met.) A great wit.

Terronázo, *sm.* Blow with a clod.

Terroncíllo, *sm.* A small clod.

Terrontéra, *sf.* Break in a mountain.

Terrór, *sm.* Terror, dread, fear.

Terrosidád, *sf.* V. *Terrestridad.*

Terróso, sa, *a.* Terreous, earthy.

Terrúño, *sm.* The good or bad quality of the soil or ground.

Tersár, *va.* To smooth, to make smooth.

Tersidád, *sf.* Smoothness, terseness.

Térso, sa, *a.* Smooth, polished, clean, pure, elegant; correct, terse; applied to style.

Tersúra, *sf.* Smoothness, cleanliness, purity.

Tertíl, *sm.* Tax on silk, paid in the kingdom of Granada.

Tertúlia, *sf.* 1. Club, assembly, circle, meeting, conversation of friends and acquaintances; evening party. 2. Part of the pit in the play-house.

Tertuliáno, na, *a.* Member of a club.

Tertúlio, a, *a.* Relating or belonging to a meeting of friends or a tea-party.

Teruélo, *sm.* Bowl or box in which lots are put to be cast.

Terzón, na, *a.* y *s.* Heifer or ox of three years old.

Terzuéla, *sf.* Distribution gained for attending mass at the hour of tierce.

Terzuélo, la, *a.* Applied to the third bird which leaves the nest.

Terzuélo, *sm.* Third part of any thing.

Tesár, *va.* *Tesar un cabo*, (Naút.) To haul taught a rope, to stretch it tight.

Tesáuro, *sm.* Dictionary, vocabulary, index.

Tésera, *sf.* Sign or countersign; a cubical piece of wood or bone used by the Romans.

Tésis, *sf.* Thesis. V. *Conclusion.*

Téso, sa, *a.* V. *Tieso.*

Téso, *sm.* 1. Hardness, tenaciousness. 2. Brow or crown of a hill.

Tesón, *sm.* Tenacity, firmness, inflexibility.

Tesorár, *va.* To treasure, to hoard up.

Tesorería, *sf.* Treasury; treasurer's place.

Tesoréro, ra, *s.* 1. Treasurer. 2. Canon who keeps the reliques.

Tesóro, *sm.* 1. Treasure, wealth, riches. 2. Abridgment or short account of news. 3. Treasure, any thing valuable and precious.

Tésta, *sf.* 1. Forehead, forepart of the head; front, face. 2. Understanding, prudence. *Testa ferrea ó de ferro*, He who lends his name to any business which in reality belongs to another.

Testáceo, cea, *a.* Testaceous, covered with a shell.

Testación, *sf.* 1. Leaving by will. 2. Obliteration.

Testáda, *sf.* V. *Testerada.*

Testádo, da, *a.* Dying testate.

Testadór, ra, *s.* Testator.

Testadúra, *sf.* Obliteration.

Testamentaría, *sf.* Testamentary execution.

Testamentário, *sm.* Executor.

Testamentário, ria, *a.* Relating to a last will or testament, testamentary.

Testaménto, *sm.* 1. Last will, testament. 2. Part of the Holy Scriptures.

Testár, *va.* 1. To will, to make a last will or testament, to leave, to bequeath. 2. To blot, to scratch out.

Testarúdo, da, *a.* Obstinate, stubborn.

Testéra, *sf.* 1. Front or fore part of any thing; forehead of an animal. 2. Head-stall of the bridle of a horse. *Testera de un coche*, Back seat of a coach.

Testeráda, *sf.* 1. Stroke or blow with the head. 2. Stubbornness, obstinacy.

Testéro, *sm.* V. *Testera.*

Testículo, *sm.* Testicle.

Testificación, *sf.* Attestation, the act of attesting or certifying.

Testificánte, *pa.* Witness; attesting.

Testificár, *va.* To attest, to witness, to certify, to testify.
Testificáta, *sf.* (For.) Legal testimony.
Testificatívo, **va**, *a.* That which testifies.
Testígo, *sm.* Witness. *Testigo de oidos*, Auricular witness. *Testigo de vistá*, Ocular witness. [*sf. pl.* Testimonials.
Testimoniál, *a.* Testimonial. *Testimoniales*,
Testimoniár, *va.* To testify, to attest.
Testimoniéro, **ra**, *a.* Bearing false witness or testimony.
Testimónio, *sm.* 1. Testimony, deposition of a witness, attestation, proof. 2. Instrument legalized by a notary. 3. False accusation. V. *Testigo*. [mony.
Testimoñéro, **ra**, *a.* Hypocritical, false testi-
Testín, *sm.* A coin having a head.
Testúdo, *sm.* Machine for covering soldiers in an attack on a fortification.
Testúz y Testúzo, *sm.* Hind part of the head, poll.
Tesú, *sm.* Tissue of gold and silver. V. *Tisú*.
Tesúra, *sf.* 1. Stiffness, firmness. 2. Starched and affected gravity.
Téta, *sf.* Dug, teat. *Teta de vaca*, Teat or dug of a cow; kind of large grapes. *Dar la teta*, To give suck, to suckle. *Niño de teta*, Sucking child; (Met.) one who is greatly inferior to another.
Tétano, *sm.* Spasm, contraction or rigidity of the muscles; tetanus, locked jaw.
Tetár, *va.* To suckle, to give suck. V. *Atetar*.
Tetáza, *sf.* Flabby, ugly dugs. *Tetazas*, Person possessed of talents and genius.
Tetéra, *sf.* Tea-pot.
Tetílla, *sf.* 1. A small dug or teat. 2. Kind of paste in the figure of a teat. *Dar por la tetilla*, To touch a person to the quick.
Této, *sm.* (Ast.) V. *Teta*.
Tetóna, *a.* Having large teats.
Tetracórdio, *sm.* (Mus.) Tetrachord, fourth.
Tetraédro, *sm.* (Geom.) Tetraedron.
Tetragramáton, *sm.* Word composed of four letters, particularly the name of *Dios*.
Tetrárca, *sm.* Tetrarch; absolute governor.
Tetrástilo, *sm.* Building sustained by four columns or pilasters.
Tetrasílabo, **ba**, *a.* V. *Quatrisílabo*.
Tétrico, **ca**, *a.* Froward, serious, grave, gloomy.
Tétro, **tra**, *a.* Black, spotted.
Tetúda, *a.* 1. Having large teats or nipples. 2. Applied to a kind of oblong olives.
Téucrio, *sm.* (Bot.) Germander. Teucrium *L.*
Téucro, **ra**, *a.* Trojan. V. *Troyano*.
Téxa, *sf.* (Bot.) V. *Texo*.
Texedéra, *sf.* 1. Female weaver. 2. Water-spider.
Texedór, **ra**, *s.* Weaver; cloth-manufacturer.
Texedúra, *sf.* 1. Texture, the act of weaving. 2. Any thing woven.
Texér, *va.* 1. To weave, to form cloth in a loom with the woof and warp. 2. To regulate, to adjust. 3. To discuss, to devise, to entangle. 4. To cross and mix according to rule, as in dancing. 5. To make webs, although not woven, like spiders, &c.
Texído, *sm.* V. *Tela*.
Texíllo, *sm.* Kind of band used by women as a girdle.

Téxo, *sm.* (Bot.) Yew-tree. Taxus *L.*
Texón, *sm.* 1. Badger. 2. Yew.
Téxto, *sm.* 1. Text, the original words of an author; sentence or text of Scripture. 2. (Impr.) Name of a size of types. [ing.
Textório, **ria**, *a.* Textrine, belonging to weav-
Textuál, *a.* Agreeing with the text.
Textualísta, *sm.* Textuarist, he who adheres to the text.
Textualménte, *ad.* According to the text.
Textúra, *sf.* 1. Texture, the disposition and order of threads in a stuff or cloth. 2. Succession and order of things.
Teynáda, *sf.* V. *Tinada*. [head.
Teyträl, *sm.* (Ant.) Ornament on a horse's
Tez, *sf.* 1. Grain; shining surface. 2. Bloom of the human face, complexion.
Tezádo, **da**, *a.* Very black. V. *Atezado*.
Tí, The termination of the oblique case of *tu*, *thou*. When preceded by the preposition *con*, it always takes the termination *go*, as *contigo*, With *thee*: the pronouns *mí* and *sí* do the same.
Tialísm, *sm.* Ptyalism, discharge of saliva.
Tiára, *sf.* 1. Tiara, mitre, a diadem worn by the pope. 2. Pontificate, papal dignity.
Tíbia, *sf.* 1. Shin-bone. 2. A flute.
Tibiéza, *sf.* 1. Tepidity, lukewarmness. 2. Carelessness, negligence; want of zeal and fervour.
Tibiaménte, *ad.* Tepidly, carelessly. [miss.
Tíbio, **bia**, *a.* Tepid, lukewarm, careless, re-
Tibír, *sm.* Name of gold-dust on the African coast.
Tibór, *sm.* A large china jar.
Tibórna, *sf.* V. *Toston*. [rias *L.*
Tiburón, *sm.* (Ict.) Shark. Squalus carcha-
Tiempecíllo y Tiempecíto, *sm.* A little time.
Tiémpo, *sm.* 1. Time, successive duration. 2 Term, a limited space of time. 3. Any of the four seasons of the year. 4. Occasion, opportunity; leisure. 5. Temperature of the air, climate. 6. State, condition. 7. Draft, portion. 8. (Gram.) Time, tense. 9. Age, number of years one has lived. 10. Time, part, space, duration of an action. 11. Measure of music. *Tiempo cargado*, (Naút.) Thick hazy weather. *Tiempo borrascoso*, Stormy weather. *Tiempo grueso*, Hazy weather. *El tiempo va á meterse en agua*, The weather sets in for rain. *Tiempo variable*, Unsettled weather. *Tiempo hecho*, Settled weather. *Tiempo contrario*, Foul weather. *Tiempo apacible*, Moderate weather. *Tiempo de juanetes*, (Naút.) Top-gallant gale. *A tiempo*, Timely, in time. *A un tiempo*, At once; at the same time. *De tiempo en tiempo*, From time to time. *En tiempo*, Occasionally. *Por tiempo*, For some time, undetermined time. *Un tiempo*, Formerly, in other times.
Tiénda, *sf.* 1. Tent, a soldier's moveable lodging-place, made of canvass. 2. (Naút.) Awning, a linen or woollen cover spread over vessels. 3. Tilt, a linen cover for carts or waggons. 4. Shop or stall, a place where any thing is sold. *La tienda de los cozos*, The next shop. *Poner tienda*, To open a shop.
Tiénta, *sf.* 1. Probe, an instrument with which surgeons search the depth of wounds. 2.

Craft, cunning, artful industry. *A' tientas,* Doubtfully, uncertainly. *Andar á tientas,* To grope in the dark.

TIÉNTO, *sm.* 1. Touch, the act of feeling. 2. A blind man's stick, which serves to guide him. 3. Circumspection, prudent consideration. 4. Poy, a rope-dancer's pole. 5. Mostic, a stick which a painter holds in his left hand, and on which the right rests when at work. 6. (Mús.) Prelude. 7. Stroke. V. *Golpe.* 8. Pole used to fasten fowling nets to the ground. *Dar un tiento,* To make a trial. *Por el tiento,* By the touch. *A' tiento,* Obscurely, doubtfully.

TIERNAMÉNTE, *ad.* Tenderly, in a tender manner.

TIERNECÍCO, CA; LLO, LLA; TO, TA, *a. dim.* of [tierno.

TIÉRNO, NA, *a.* 1. Tender, soft, docile; delicate; young; easily moved to tears. 2. Affectionate, fond, amiable. 3. Recent, modern; tender; applied to age. *Tierno de ojos,* Tender-eyed.

TIÉRRA, *sf.* 1. Earth; landed property; province; arable land. 2. (Met.) Mankind, mortals. 3. Earth, globe, world. 4. (Quim.) Prepared antimony. *Tierra de los duendes,* Fairy land. *Tierra de batan ó de manchas,* Fuller's earth. *Sin sentirlo la tierra,* Without any one's knowledge. *Tierra á tierra,* (Naút.) Coasting, sailing along the coast; cautiously, securely. *Tierra dentro,* (Naút.) Inland. *Correr hacia la tierra,* (Naút.) To stand in shore. *Buscar tierra,* (Naút.) To make for the land. *Tomar tierra,* (Naút.) To anchor in a port. *Tierra de Sevilla.* V. *Aceche.* *Tierra firme,* Continent. *Besar la tierra,* (Fam.) To fall on one's mouth against the ground.

TESAMÉNTE, *ad.* Firmly, stiffly.

TIÉSO, SA, *a.* 1. Stiff, hard, firm, solid. 2. Robust, strong in point of health; valiant, animated. 3. Stubborn, obstinate, inflexible. 4. Tight, rigid; too grave or circumspect. *Tieso de cogote,* (Fam.) Stiff-necked, vain, obstinate, elated, indocile. *Tenerse tieso, ó tenerse las tiesas,* (Fam.) To be firm in one's opinion or resolution; to insist on or oppose another firmly.—*ad.* Firmly, strongly.

TIÉSO, *sm.* Firmness, inflexibility; hardness. *Tieso que tieso,* (Fam.) Pertinacity, obstinacy in maintaining an opinion.

TIÉSTO, *sm.* 1. Potsherd, part of a broken pot. 2. A large earthen pot.—*a.* V. *Tieso.*

TÍFO, *sm.* (Med.) Typhus, a malignant fever. *Tifo icterodes,* Yellow fever.

TIFÓN, *sm.* Whirlwind. V. *Torbellino.*

TIGNÁRIA, *sf.* Knowledge of the fittest timber for building.

TÍGRE, *sm.* Tiger. Felis tigris *L.*

TÍLA ó TÍLIA, *sf.* (Bot.) Lime-tree. Tilia *L.*

TILÁR, *sm.* Grove or plantation of lime or linden trees.

TILDÁR, *va.* 1. To blot, to scratch out. 2. To brand, to stigmatise. 3. To mark letters with a dot or dash, as the ñ.

TÍLDE, *sf.* Dot or dash over a letter; point, [very small thing.

TILDÓN, *sm.* A long dash or stroke.

TILÍNO, *sm.* A kind of perfume.

TÍLLA, *sf.* (Naút.) Midship, gangway.

TÍLO, *sm.* (Bot.) Linden-tree. Tilia *L.*

TILÓSIS, *sf.* Falling out of the eyelashes.

TÍMALO, *sm.* (Ict.) Grayling. Salmo thymal- [lus *L.*

TIMBÁL, *sm.* Kettle-drum. V. *Atabal.*

TIMBALEÁR, *vn.* To beat the kettle-drum.

TIMBALÉO, *sm.* Beat of the kettle-drum.

TIMBALÉRO, *sm.* Kettle-drummer, one who beats a kettle-drum.

TÍMBRA, *sf.* (Bot.) Mountain hyssop. Thymbra *L.*

TIMBRÁR, *va.* To put the crest to the shield in a coat of arms.

TÍMBRE, *sm.* 1. Crest of a coat of arms. 2. Any glorious deed or achievement. *Es el mejor timbre de su escudo,* That is the best gem in his crown.

TIMIÁMA, *sf.* Sweet perfume. V. *Almea.*

TIMIDAMÉNTE, *ad.* Timidly, fearfully.

TIMIDÉZ, *sf.* Timidity, fear, dread.

TÍMIDO, DA, *a.* Timid, fearful, cowardly.

TÍMO, *sm.* V. *Timalo.*

TIMÓN, *sm.* 1. Beam of a plough; pole of a coach; part which governs any machine. 2. (Naút.) Helm, rudder. *La madre del timon,* The main piece of the rudder. *El azafran del timon,* The afterpiece of the rudder. *La cabeza del timon,* The rudder-head. *La mortaja del timon,* The mortise of the rudder. *Forro ó espalda del timon,* The back of the rudder. *Sacar ó apear el timon,* To unship the rudder. *Calar el timon,* To hang the rudder. 3. (Met.) Person or office in which the chief power exists.

TIMONEÁR, *va.* (Naút.) To govern the helm; to steer.

TIMONÉL, *sm.* (Naút.) Timoneer, helmsman.

TIMONÉRA, *sf.* (Naút.) The timoneer's post before the bittacle.

TIMONÉRO, *sm.* Timoneer, helmsman.

TIMORÁTO, TA, *a.* Full of the fear of God.

TIMPANÍLLO, *sm. dim.* (Impr.) Smaller or inner tympan of a printing-press.

TIMPANÍTICO, CA, *a.* Affected with a tympanites or dropsy.

TIMPANÍTIS, *sf.* (Med.) Tympanites, kind of dropsy.

TÍMPANO, *sm.* 1. Kettle-drum. 2. Tympanum, the drum of the ear. 3. Part of a printing-press. 4. Cylinder. 5. (Arq.) Tympan, pediment.

TÍNA, *sf.* 1. A large jar. 2. Vat, copper. 3. Back, a tub for cooling wort. 4. Building, in which sheep are shorn.

TINÁCO, *sm.* Wooden trough, tub or vat.

TINÁDA, *sf.* 1. Pile of wood or timber. 2. Shed for cattle.

TINÁDO ó TINADÓR, *sm.* Shed for keeping cattle from the inclemency of the weather.

TINAHÓN, *sm.* (And.) Cow-house, sheepfold, sheepcot.

TINÁJA, *sf.* A large jar.

TINAJERÍA, *sf.* (And.) Shop where water-jars are kept or sold.

TINAJÉRO, *sm.* One who makes water-jars.

TINAJÓN, *sm.* 1. A large wide-mouthed jar for catching rain. 2. A very fat and lusty person.

TINÁO Y TINAÓN, *sm.* (And.) Stable for oxen or bullocks.

TINÉA, *sf.* Worm in wood rotten in the earth.

TINELÉRO, RA, *s.* Keeper of the servants' room.

TINÉLO, *sm.* Dining-room of servants in great houses.

Tiñéro, *sm.* Dyer who takes care of the copper in woollen manufactories.
Tiñéta, *sf.* (Ict.) Ox-eyed cockerel. Sparus boops *L.*
Tíngr, *sm.* (Orn.) Kind of a black owl.
Tingládo, *sm.* Workshop, shed. *Tinglado de la toneleria*, Cooper's shed, cooperage.
Tíngle, *sf.* Instrument used by glaziers for opening the lead and flatting it on the glass.
Tinícla, *sf.* Kind of large coat of arms.
Tiniébla, *sf.* Darkness, obscurity, privation of light. *Tiniéblas*, Utter darkness, hell; gross ignorance; matins sung the three last days of the holy week.
Tíno, *sm.* 1. Habit or skill in finding or discovering things by the act of feeling. 2. A firm hand to hit the mark. 3. Judgment, prudence, circumspection. *Salir de tino*, To be out of one's senses. *Sacar de tino*, To astound, to confound.
Tínta, *sf.* 1. Tint, hue, colour. 2. Ink, a liquor used for writing. *Tinta incarnada*, Red Ink. 3. Art of dying. *De buena tinta*, Efficaciously, ably, lively.
Tintár, *va.* To tinge, to dye. V. *Teñir.*
Tínte, *sm.* 1. Tint, paint, colour; dye. 2. A dyer's shop. 3. Palliation, cloak, colour.
Tintéro, *sm.* Inkhorn, inkstand. *Dexarse en el tintero*, To forget or omit designedly. *Quedárse á uno en el tintero*, (Fam.) To entirely forget a thing.
Tintíllo, *sm.* 1. A light-coloured wine. *Tintillo de rota*, A deep-coloured sweetish wine. 2. A despicable dolt.
Tintirintín, *sm.* Echo or sound of a trumpet or other sharp sounding musical instrument.
Tínto, ta, *a.* Deep-coloured; applied to wine. V. *Teñido. Vino tinto*, Red wine.
Tintorería, *sf.* A dyer's shop.
Tintoréro, ra, *s.* Dyer.
Tintúra, *sf.* 1. The act of dying. 2. Paint for ladies. 3. A superficial knowledge of any art or science. 4. Tincture, extract of the colour or substance of drugs.
Tinturár, *va.* 1. To tinge, to die. 2. To instruct, to teach superficially.
Tiña, *sf.* 1. Scab, a kind of leprosy. 2. Poverty, indigence, misery. 3. Small spider which injures beehives.
Tiñería, *sf.* Poverty, indigence, misery.
Tiñóso, sa, *a.* 1. Scabby, scurvy. 2. Penurious, niggardly, miserable; sordid. 3. Old-nick.
Tiñuéla, *sf.* Plant which grows round the stems of flax.
Tío, ía, *s.* 1. Uncle, aunt. 2. Good old man or woman; among the peasants, old people so called, who do not merit the title of *Don. Á tu tia que te dé para libros*, I am neither willing nor obliged to give you any thing; or, ask not me but your aunt.
Tiórba, *sf.* Theorbo, a large lute for playing a thorough bass.
Típle, *sm.* 1. Treble, the third and highest sound. 2. One who sings the treble. 3. A kind of small guitar.
Tiplisonánte, *a.* (Joc.) Treble-toned, acute tone.
Típo, *sm.* Type, pattern, mould.
Tipografía, *sf.* 1. Printing. V. *Imprenta.* 2. Typography.

Tipográfico, ca, *a.* Typographical.
Tipógrafo, *sm.* Printer.
Tiquis Miquis, Barbarous words used to deride affected expressions.
Tíra, *sf.* 1. A long and narrow stripe. 2. A kind of light dart or arrow. 3. (Naút.) Fall. *Tira de un aparejo*, Fall of a tackle. *Tira de un aparejo real*, A winding tackle-fall. *Tira del aparejo de la gata*, The cat-tackle-fall. *Tira de las aparejuelas de portas*, Port-tackle-fall. *Tiras*, Fees at the clerk's office in appeal causes.
Tirabála, *sf.* Pop-gun which boys are used to play with.
Tirabótas, *sf.* Boot-hook for pulling on boots.
Tirabregüéro, *sm.* Truss, used to keep up ruptures.
Tirabuzón, *sm.* Cork-screw.
Tiracuéllo y Tiracól., *sm.* A kind of sword-belts worn by officers.
Tiráda, *sf.* 1. Cast, throw; the act of throwing. 2. Distance of one place from another. 3. Process or space of time. *De una tirada*, At one stretch. *Caminó seis leguas de una tirada*, He travelled six leagues at one stretch.
Tiradéra, *sf.* 1. Strap. 2. Indian arrow.
Tirádo, da, *pp.* of *tirar. Andar alguna cosa muy tirada*, (Met.) To be difficult to find, to be sold dear.
Tiradór, ra, *s.* 1. Thrower, one who throws or casts; drawer. 2. Fowler, a good marksman. 3. An iron button fixed to a door, whereby it is opened or shut. 4. (Impr.) Pressman. *Tirador de oro*, Gold-wire drawer.
Tiralíneas, *sm.* Instrument for drawing lines neatly.
Tiramiénto, *sm.* Tension, act of drawing.
Tiramíra, *sf.* A long narrow path; a long ridge of mountains.
Tiramollár, *va. Tiramollar un aparejo*, (Naút.) To overhaul a tackle. *Tiramollar las amuras y escotas*, (Naút.) To overhaul the sheets and tacks.
Tiranaménte, *ad.* Tyrannically.
Tiranía, *sf.* 1. Tyranny, despotic government. 2. Exorbitant price of goods or merchandise. 3. Ascendency of some passion.
Tiranicaménte, *ad.* Tyrannically, violently.
Tiránico, ca, *a.* Tyrannical, despotic.
Tiranización, *sf.* Tyranny, despotism, domination.
Tiranizadaménte, *ad.* Tyrannically.
Tiranizár, *va.* To tyrannise, to domineer; to usurp; to extort, to sell too dear.
Tiráno, na, *a.* Tyrannical, tyrant.
Tiráno, *sm.* 1. Tyrant, a despotic ruler. 2. Merchant or trader, who sells his goods at an exorbitant price. 3. Ruling passion.
Tiránte, *sm.* 1. Joist which runs across a beam. 2. Trace, which serves to draw a coach or other carriage. *Á tirantes largos*, With long traces. 3. Brace of a drum.—*a.* Extended, drawn; tightly or firmly bound. *Traer á tener la cuerda tirante*, To use too much rigour.
Tirantéz, *sf.* 1. Length of a thing which runs in a straight line. 2. Tenseness, rigidity.
Tirapié, *sm.* Stirrups or strap, with which shoe-makers make their work fast.
Tirár, *va.* 1. To throw, to cast, to dart. 2. To imitate, to resemble. 3. To attract, to draw

towards one; to incline to, to tend. 4. To induce by compulsion. 5. To hurt, to injure, to thwart. 6. To tug, to pull; to draw. 7. To discharge fire-arms. 8. To earn, to acquire. 9. To enlarge, to extend. 10. To lavish. 11. (Impr.) To print sheets. 12. To draw metal into slender threads. 13. V. *Quitar*. 14. To receive or take an allotted part. *Tirar á la mar*, (Naút.) To throw overboard; to stand out to sea. *Tirar las riendas*, To subject. *A' todo tirar*, To the utmost; to the greatest extent. *Tirar largo ó por lo largo*, To tell pleasant stories. *Tirar coces*, To kick, to rebel. *Tirar alguno la barra*, (Fam.) To sell things as dear as possible. *Tira y afloxa*, Boyish play; (Met.) Blowing hot and cold; ordering and counter-ordering.—*vn*. 1. To direct one's course, to take the road. 2. To endure, to remain.—*vr*. To retire, to withdraw or separate one's self. *A' mas tirar*, At most, at the utmost.

Tiratíte ó Tiracabéza, *sf*. Forceps, instrument used in midwifery.

Tiréla, *sf*. A striped stuff.

Tiréta, *sf*. Ribbon or thong of leather, to tie up breeches.

Tirícia, *sf*. Jaundice. V. *Ictericia*.

Tirílla, *sf*. A small stripe of linen; a piece of backstitched linen.

Tirillo, *sm*. A small shot.

Tiritáña, *sf*. A sort of thin silk; thin woollen cloth; a thing of little value or importance.

Tiritár, *vn*. To shiver, to shake with cold.

Tiritóna, *sf*. Shivering, shaking with cold.

Tíro, *sm*. 1. Cast, throw, shot. 2. Mark, aim. 3. Mark made by a throw. 4. Charge, shot; gun which is discharged. 5. Theft. *Le hicieron un tiro de cien guineas*, They robbed him of one hundred guineas. 6. Prank, imposition. 7. Set of coach-horses or mules. 8. Trace of coach-harness. 9. Space between the shoulders, measured by tailors. 10. Serious physical or moral injury. 11. Rope which pulls up the materials used in building. 12. Disease in horses which makes them bite the manger. *Tiros*, Sword-belts. *Estar á tiro de cañon*, To be within cannon-shot. *Hacer tiro*, To incommodate, to prejudice. *Errar el tiro*, To miss one's shot; to be deceived or mistaken.

Tirocínio, *sm*. First attempt, essay, or trial.

Tirón, *sm*. 1. Tyro; beginner, novice, apprentice. 2. Pull, haul, tug. 3. V. *Estiron*. 4. Time. V. *Vez*. *De un tiron*, At once, at a stroke. *No lo sacará de tres tirones*, He will not obtain it easily.

Tironiáno, *a*. Applied to Tiro's method of abbridging.

Tiroriro, *sm*. (Joc.) Sound of a musical wind-instrument; the instrument itself.

Tirotear, *vn*. 1. To blow wind instruments. 2. To shoot at random.

Tirotéo, *sm*. 1. Blast or sound of a wind instrument. 2. Act of shooting at random.

Tirría, *sf*. Aversion, antipathy, dislike.

Tírso, *sm*. Wand covered with ivy-leaves, used in sacrifices to Bacchus. V. *Tallo*.

Tisána, *sf*. Ptisan, a medical drink.

Tiséra, *sf*. (Ant.) V. *Tixera*.

Tísica ó Tísis, *sf*. Phthisis, consumption.

Tísico, ca, *a*. Phthisical.

Tisú, *sm*. Tissue, silk stuff interwoven with gold and silver.

Títere, *sm*. 1. Puppet a small image made of paste. 2. Dwarf, a ridiculous little fellow.

Titeréro, ra, *s*. V. *Titiritero*.

Titeretiría, *sf*. Puppet-shop.

Titerísta, *sm*. Puppet-show man.

Tití, *sm*. A very small monkey.

Titilación, *sf*. Titillation, tickling.

Titilár, *va*. 1. To titillate, to tickle, to affect with a prurient sensation by slight touches. 2. To please by slight gratification.

Titímalo, *sm*. (Bot.) Spurge. Euphorbia *L*.

Titiritáyna, *sf*. Confused noise of flutes or festive amusements.

Titiritéro, *sm*. Puppet-player, one who directs a puppet-show.

Títo, *sm*. 1. (Bot.) A kind of kidney-beans. Lathyrus cicera *L*. 2. Close-stool.

Titubeánte, *pa*. Staggerer; hesitating; groping.

Titubeár, *vn*. 1. To threaten ruin; applied to buildings. 2. To stutter, to stammer. 3. To vacillate, to doubt, to hesitate; to be staggered; to feel, to grope.

Titubéo, *sm*. Vacillation, wavering in what one says or thinks; making trials or essays.

Tituládo, *sm*. Person having a title.

Titulár, *a*. Titular, distinguished by a title.—*va*. To title, to give a title or name.—*vn*. To obtain a title from a king or other sovereign.

Titulíllo, *sm*. A petty title. *Andar en titulillos*, To stick at trifles.

Titulizádo, da, *a*. Titled, distinguished.

Título, *sm*. 1. Title, dignity, appellation of honour; titled person; inscription. 2. Cause, motive, pretext. 3. Title, ground or foundation of a claim or right. 4. Legal instrument, authority. *A' titulo*, On pretence, under pretext.

Tixéra, *sf*. 1. Scissors, a pair of shears or blades moveable on a pivot. 2. Carpenter's horse, cooper's mare, used for holding the wood while dressing; any instrument in the form of an X. 3. Shearer, one who shears sheep. 4. A small channel or drain. 5. Brace put across under the body of a coach, to give it an equal motion. *Buena tixera*, A great eater; good cutter. 6. Detracter, murmurer. 7. First feather in a falcon's wing. *Tixeras*, Beams put across a river to stop the timber floating in it. *Hacer tixera*, To twist the mouth; applied to horses.

Tixeretáda ó Tixeráda, *sf*. A cut with scissors.

Tixerétas, *sf. pl*. 1. A small pair of scissors. 2. Tendrils, the tender tops of vines, which cling to any thing within their reach. 3. Earwigs, insects which penetrate the ears.

Tixeretázo, *sm*. A cut with scissors.

Tixeretеár, *va*. 1. To cut with scissors. 2. To dispose of other people's affairs according to one's own will and pleasure.

Tixerílla y Tixeruéla, *sf*. Small tendril of vines.

Tíza, *sf*. Whitening, a kind of chalk or pipe-clay, used by silversmiths.

Tízna, *sf*. Matter for staining or blackening.

Tiznár, *va*. 1. To smut, to stain. 2. To tarnish, to blot.

Tízne, *s. com*. Soot which sticks to frying-pans or kettles.

Tiznón, *sm*. A large spot, soil or stain.

Tízo, *sm.* Half-burnt charcoal.
Tizón, *sm.* 1. Half-burnt wood. 2. Smut in corn; this is a contagious disease which may be obviated by washing and cleaning the seed: it exists in the pistil, style, and stigma or female organs which are unable to fulfil their functions, while the stamens, anthers, and pollen are found perfect, lying around the putrid and swollen stigma, consisting of black powder. 3. (Met.) Spot, stain, disgrace. 4. That part of a hewn stone which is concealed in the wall.
Tizóna, *sf.* Sword of the Cid, Ruy Diaz.
Tizonáda, *sf.* Stroke with a half-burnt stick.
Tizonázo, *sm.* Stroke with burning charred wood. *Tizonazos*, (Joc.) Hell fire.
Tizoncíllo, *sm.* A small burning coal; a little smut in corn.
Tizoneár, *va.* To stir up a fire; to lay or arrange wood or coals for lighting a fire.
Tizonéra, *sf.* Heap of ill-burnt charcoal.
Tizonéro, *sm.* Poker, an instrument for stirring the fire.
Tmésis, *sf.* (Gram.) Figure in poetry which divides a compound word into two.
To! *interj.* 1. A word used to call a dog. 2. Oh, expressing our knowledge of any thing.
Toálla y Toája, *sf.* 1. Towel, a cloth for wiping the hands. 2. A silk cover thrown over bolsters.
Toalléta, *sf. dim.* Napkin.
Tóba, *sf.* 1. (Bot.) Cotton thistle. Onorpordon acanthium *L.* 2. (And.) Stalk of a thistle given to asses. 3. Calcareous matter which collects on the teeth. 4. Tophus, a soft spongy stone.
Tobája ó Tobálla, *sf.* Towel. V. *Toalla.*
Toballéta ó Tobelléta; *sf.* Napkin.
Tobéra, *sf.* Iron pipe, through which the nozzle or extremity of a pair of bellows is thrust in iron-works. [foot to the leg.
Tobíllo, *sm.* Ankle, the joint which joins the
Tóca, *sf.* A thin stuff; a kind of head-dress.
Tocádo, *sm.* Ornament, dress; a set of ribbons for garnishing any dress. *Tocado de monja*, A nun's hood or head-dress.
Tocádo, da, *a.* Touched; contaminated; infected. *Estar tocado*, To be begun to rot or putrefy.
Tocadór, *sm.* 1. One who beats or touches. 2. Handkerchief tied round the head. 3. Toilet, a lady's dressing case or table. 4. Dressing-room. 5. Key for tuning musical instruments.
Tocamiénto, *sm.* Touch; inspiration. [to.
Tocánte, *a.* Respecting, relative.—*ad.* In order
Tocár, *va.* 1. To touch, to exercise the sense of feeling; to attain or reach with the hand. 2. To play on a musical instrument. 3. To toll, to ring a bell. 4. To try metals on a touch-stone; to touch, to magnetize; to examine, to prove. 5. To treat of, to discuss any matter lightly. 6. To know a thing certainly; to inspire, to move, to persuadé. 7. To strike slightly, to sound any thing. *No tocar pelota*, (Fam.) Not to hit the mark, to err totally. 8. To communicate or infect; to chastize. 9. To comb and dress the hair with ribbons.—*vn.* 1. To appertain, to belong. 2. To interest, to concern; to be a duty or obligation; to import. 3. To fall to one's share or lot. 4. To touch, to be contiguous to; to arrive in passing. 5. To be allied or related. *Tocar de cerca*, (Met.) To be nearly related. 6. To infest, to contaminate. *Tocar á la puerta*, To knock or rap at the door. *Tocar á la bomba*, (Naút.) To ring for pumping ship. *Tocar á mudar la guardia*, (Naút.) To ring for relieving the watch. *Tocar en un puerto*, (Naút.) To touch at a port. *Tocar la diana*, (Mil.) To beat the reveille. *Tocar la generala*, (Mil.) To beat the general. *A' toca teja*, Ready money, money in hand. *Tocar á alguno*, (Met.) To tempt or stimulate any one. —*vr.* To be covered, to put on the hat.
Tocáta, *sf.* Concert. [sake.
Tocáyo, ya, *a.* Having the same name, name-
Tochár, *va.* (Arag.) To bar a door with a pole.
Tochedád, *sf.* Clownishness, rusticity, ignorance, want of education.
Tócho, *sm.* 1. Pole. 2. Bar of iron.
Tócho, cha, *a.* Clownish, unpolished, coarse, homespun.
Tochúra, *sf.* Waggishness, sarcastic gaiety.
Tocinéro, ra, *s.* Porkman, one who sells pork or bacon.
Tocíno, *sm.* 1. Bacon, salt pork. 2. Hog's lard. *Témpano de tocino*, Flitch of bacon. *Tocino rancio*, Rank pork.
Tocón, *sm.* Stump of a tree; stump of an arm or leg.
Todavía, *ad.* 1. Notwithstanding, nevertheless. 2. Yet, still. 3. V. *Siempre.*
Tódo, da, *a.* All, entire. *Todo un Dios*, The whole power of God, used to indicate great difficulty. *Todos la matamos*, We are guilty of the same fault. *Con todo eso*, Notwithstanding, nevertheless. *Todo á la banda*, (Naút.) Hard over. *Todo el mundo abaxo*, (Naút.) Down all hands. *Me es todo uno*, It is all one to me. *A' todo*, At most. *Del todo*, Entirely, quite. *En todo y por todo*, Wholly, absolutely. *En un todo*, Together, in all its parts. *Ser el todo*, To be the principal or chief.—*sm.* 1. Whole, composition of integral parts. 2. (Geom.) A greater quantity compared with a less.
Toésa, *sf.* Toise, fathom; a French measure.
Tófo, *sm.* Tumour in the belly of cattle.
Tóga, *sf.* Gown; toga, dignity of counsellor.
Togádo, da, *a.* Applied to those who wear gowns.
Togíno, *sm.* (Naút.) Notch or knob to secure any thing from moving in a ship; pieces of wood on the sides of a vessel used as steps.
Tohálla, *sf.* Towel. V. *Toalla.*
Toláno, *sm.* Tumor or swelling in horses' gums. *Tolanos*, (Fam.) Short hair on the neck.
Tólda, *sf.* (Naút.) Awning.
Toldadúra, *sf.* Hanging of stuff to shelter from the heat, or moderate the light.
Toldár, *va.* V. *Entoldar.*
Toldéro, *sm.* (And.) Retailer of salt.
Toldílla, *sf.* Round-house.
Toldíllo, *sm.* Covered sedan-chair.
Tóldo, *sm.* 1. Awning. 2. (And.) Shop where salt is retailed. 3. Ostentation, pomp. *Toldo del alcazar*, (Naút.) Quarter-deck awning. *Toldo del combés*, Main-deck awning. *Candeleros de los toldos*, (Naút.) Stanchions of the awnings.
Tolerábl e, *a.* Tolerable, supportable.

Tolerablemente, *ad.* Tolerably.

Toleráncia y Toleración, *sf.* Patience, toleration, permission; tolerance, indulgence.

Toleránte, *a.* Tolerant; applied to a government which tolerates the freedom of worship.

Tolerantísmo, *sm.* Free exercise of all worship and religious opinions.

Tolerár, *va.* To tolerate, to suffer, to permit; to indulge.

Tolétes, *sm. pl.* (Naút.) Tholes, pins driven into the upper edge of a boat, to which the oars are fastened by means of a strop.

Tolladár, *sm.* V. *Atolladéro.*

Tolle Tolle, (Lat.) Confused noise of the populace.

Tollecér, *va.* (Ant.) V. *Tullir.*

Tollér, *va.* (Ant.) V. *Quitar.*

Tóllo, *sm.* 1. (Ict.) Spotted dog-fish. Squalus catulus *L.* 2. Cave or hollow for concealing sportsmen in wait of game. 3. Bag. V. *Atolladero.*

Tolóndro ó Tolondrón, *sm.* 1. Lump or contusion arising from a blow or stroke. *A' topa tolondro*, Inconsiderately, rashly. 2. A giddy, hare-brained fellow.

Tolondrón, na, *a.* Giddy, hare-brained; foolish. *A' tolondrones*, Precipitately, giddily, inconsiderately, interruptedly; with contusions or bruises.

Tolónes, *sm. pl.* V. *Tolano.*

Tólva, *sf.* Hopper, the box or trough, into which corn is put to be ground.

Tolvanéra, *sf.* Cloud of dust raised by whirlwinds.

Tóma, *sf.* 1. The act of taking or receiving. 2. Capture, conquest. 3. Portion of any thing taken at once. *Toma de razon*, Entry of receipts, bills of sale, &c. in books of accounts; counting-house journal, account or memorandum book. *Una toma de tabaco*, A pinch of snuff. *Una toma de quina*, A dose of bark. 4. Opening into a canal or drain.

Tomáda, *sf.* Conquest, capture.

Tomadéro, *sm.* 1. Handle, haft. 2. Opening into a drain.

Tomádo, *sm.* Ornamental plait or fold in cloths.

Tomadór, ra, *s.* 1. Taker, one who takes or receives. 2. Dog that finds or fetches the game. *Tomadores*, (Naút.) Rope-bands.

Tomadúra, *sf.* Catch, seizure, gripe.

Tomajón, na, *a.* Taking or accepting easily or frequently.

Tomár, *va.* 1. To take, to receive, to catch, to seize, to grasp, to recover. 2. To occupy, to exercise, to take possession of; to apply one's self to any business. 3. To understand, to apprehend; to interpret, to perceive. 4. To buy, to purchase. 5. To copy, to imitate. 6. To cover; applied to a stonehorse. 7. To eat or drink any thing. 8. To intercept, to take by stealth, to rob. 9. To invade, to surprise. *Tomarle á uno el sueño*, (Fam.) To be attacked by sleep. 10. To choose, to select. 11. To wish, to desire. 12. To take into company. 13. To undertake. *Tomar á cuestas*, To take upon one's self. 14. (Naút.) To arrive in port or at an anchoring place. 15. To experience effects. *Tomar frio* To catch cold. *Tomar cuentas*, To audit accounts. *Tomar el fresco*, To take the air. *Tomar viento*, (Naút.) To trim the sails to the wind. 16. Joined with some nouns it signifies the same as the verb from which they spring. *Tomar resolucion*, To resolve. *Tomar la pluma, aguja*, &c. To write, to sow, &c. *Tomar muger*, To marry. *Tomar la puerta*, To get away; to be off. *Tomar puerto*, (Naút.) To get into a port.—*vr.* 1. To get rusty or musty. 2. To suffer cold, heat, or grief. 3. To be attacked or affected anew. *Tomarse con alguno*, To pick a quarrel with one. *Tomarse con Dios*, To contend with God, to persevere obstinately in evil. *Tomarse del vino*, To get into liquor. *Tomarse de colera*, To fly into a passion.

Tomáte, *sm.* (Bot.) Tomato, or Tomate, a very nutritious fruit, although, like the potato, belonging to a poisonous genus of plants; it is sometimes absurdly and indecently called after the French, love-apple. Solanum lycopersicum *L.*

Tomatéra, *sf.* Plant bearing tomates; it is very like the potato, and belongs to the same genus.

Toménto ó Tomiénto, *sm.* Coarse tow.

Tomillár, *sm.* Bed of thyme.

Tomíllo, *sm.* (Bot.) Thyme. Thymus vulgaris *L.* *Tomillo perruno.* V. *Abrótano.* *Tomillo salsero*, (Bot.) Sweet marjoram, downleafed white flowered thyme. Thymus zygis *L.*

Tomín, *sm.* 1. Third part of a drachm, Spanish weight. 2. (Amer.) Real.

Tominéjo, *sm.* Least humming-bird. Trochilus minimus *L.*

Tomíza, *sf.* Bass rope.

Tómo, *sm.* 1. Bulk or body of any thing. 2. Importance, value, consequence. *Es cosa de mucho tomo*, It is a matter of great consequence. 3. Tome, volume. *De tomo y lomo*, Of weight and bulk; of consideration or importance.

Tomón, na, *a.* Accepting. V. *Tomajon.*

Ton, *sm.* Motive, occasion. V. *Tono. Sin ton ni son*, Without motive or cause, without rhyme or reason; unreasonably, inordinately.

Tóna, *sf.* (Gal.) Surface of any liquid.

Tonáda, *sf.* Tune, a musical composition.

Tonadíca, ó Tonadílla, *sf.* A short tune or song.

Tonánte, *pa.* (Poét.) Thundering; applied to Jupiter.

Tonár, *vn.* (Poét.) To thunder, to emit a thundering noise.

Tondíno, *sm.* (Arq.) Moulding on the astragal of a column.

Tondír, *va.* (Ant.) V. *Tundir.*

Tonél, *sm.* 1. Cask, barrel. 2. (Naút.) An ancient measure of ships; ten *toneles* make twelve *toneladas.*

Toneláda, *sf.* 1. Tun, a measure or weight of twenty hundred weight; collection of casks in a ship. *Baxel de quinientas toneladas*, (Naút.) A ship of five hundred tuns burthen. Tonnage-duty.

Tonelería, *sf.* 1. Trade or business of a cooper; shop or workshop of a cooper. 2. Quantity of water-casks for a ship.

Toneléro, *sm.* Cooper.

Toneléte, *sm.* 1. Ancient armour passing from

the waist to the knees. 2. Little butt or barrel.

Tónga y Tongáda, *sf.* Cloak. V. *Capa.*

Tónico, ca, *a.* Tonic, strengthening.

Tonillo, *sm.* Disagreeable monotonous tone in reading or speaking.

Tóno, *sm.* 1. Tone, modulation or inflexion of the voice; mode or manner of doing a thing. 2. Tune, a musical composition. 3. (Med.) Tone or vigour of body.

Tonsúra, *sf.* 1. Tonsure, the first clerical degree of the Roman Catholic church. 2. The act of cutting hair or wool.

Tonsurár, *va.* 1. To give the first clerical degree. 2. To cut the hair, to cut off the wool.

Tontáda, *sf.* Nonsense, a foolish speech or action.

Tontaménte, *ad.* Foolishly, stupidly.

Tontázo, za, *a. aum.* Doltish, very stupid.

Tontreár, *vn.* To talk nonsense, to act in a foolish manner.

Tontería, Tontedád y Tontéra, *sf.* Foolishness, ignorance; nonsense.

Tontíco, llo, *sm.* 1. A little dolt. 2. Hoop, a part of a lady's dress.

Tónto, ta, *a.* Stupid, foolish, ignorant. *Hacer el tonto,* To play the fool. *Tonto de capirote,* Great fool, idiot. *Tonto en vísperas,* (Fam.) Applied to one in a procession without taking part in it or knowing what to do.

Toñína, *sf.* (And.) Fresh tunny-fish.

Topácio, *sm.* Topaz, a precious stone.

Topáda, *sf.* V. *Topetada.*

Topadízo, za, *a.* V. *Encontradizo.*

Topadór, *sm.* 1. Encounterer, one who butts or strikes against another. 2. He who too readily accepts a bet at cards.

Topár, *va.* 1. To run or strike against. 2. To meet with by chance. 3. To depend upon, to consist in. *La dificultad topa en esto,* The difficulty consists in this. 4. To accept a bet at cards.—*vn.* To butt or strike with the head. *Tope donde tope,* (Fam.) Strike where it will.

Toparquía, *sf.* Seignory, jurisdiction, or lordship.

Tópe, *sm.* 1. Top, the highest point or part. 2. Butt, the striking of one thing against another. 3. Rub, the point in which any difficulty consists. 4. Obstacle, impediment. 5. Scuffle, quarrel. 6. The highest point of a mast. *Tope de un tablon,* (Naút.) Butt-end of a plank. *Tope de la arboladura,* Mast-head. *Á tope ó al tope,* Juncture, union or incorporation of the extremities of things. *Al tope,* Conjointly, contiguously. *Hasta el tope,* Up to the top.

Topéra, *sf.* Mole-hole.

Topetáda, *sf.* Butt, a stroke given with the head by a horned animal.

Topetár, *va.* To butt, to strike with the head; to offend, to encounter.

Topetón, *sm.* Collision, encounter, blow.

Topetúdo, da, *a.* Applied to animals accustomed to butt or strike with their head.

Tópico, ca, *a.* Topical, belonging to a particular place.

Topinária, *sf.* V. *Talparia.*

Topinéra, *sf.* V. *Topera.*

Topíno, *sm.* (Med.) Bubo, tumour.

Tópo, *sm.* 1. Mole, a little beast that works under ground. *Talpa L.* 2. Stumbler, one who stumbles or strikes against any thing. 3. A league and a half among the Indians.

Topografía, *sf.* Topography, a description of particular places.

Topograficaménte, *ad.* Topographically.

Topográfico, ca, *a.* Topographical.

Topógrafo, *sm.* Topographer.

Tóque, *sm.* 1. Touch, the act of touching. 2. Ringing of bells. *Toque á muerto,* Passing-bell. 3. Essay, trial, test. 4. Experience, proof. 5. Touchstone. 6. Moment, point; crisis. 7. Aid, assistance or inspiration by God. 8. Blow given to any thing. *Toque de luz,* Light in a picture. *Dar un toque,* To give one a trial in any business.

Toqueádo, *sm.* Sound of a stroke with the hands or feet.

Toquería, *sf.* 1. Collection of women's head-dresses. 2. Business of making women's veils.

Toquéro, *sm.* Veil-maker, one who weaves or makes veils for nuns; head-dress-maker.

Toquílla, *sf.* 1. Small head-dress of gauze, small veil. 2. Ribbon or lace round the crown of a hat.

Tóra, *sf.* 1. Tribute paid by Jewish families. 2. Book of the Jewish law. 3. Figure of a bull in artificial fire-works.

Torácico, ca, *a.* Thoracic, belonging to the breast.

Toráda, *sf.* Drove of bulls.

Torál, *a.* Main, principal.

Torál, *sm.* (And.) Yellow wax in cakes unbleached. *Torales,* Boxes filled with pitch

Toráx, *sm.* Chest, breast, thorax.

Torázo, *sm.* Large bull.

Torbellíno, *sm.* Whirlwind; a boisterous, restless person; multitude.

Torcáz, *a.* Applied to wild pigeons which are grey with white necks.

Tórce, *sf.* Link of a chain or collar.

Torcecuéllo, *sm.* (Orn.) Wry-neck. Yunx torquilla *L.*

Torcedéro, *sm.* Twisting-mill, an engine for twisting.—ra, *a.* V. *Torcido.*

Torcedór, ra, *s.* 1. Twister, a spindle for twisting thread. 2. Any thing which causes displeasure or grief.

Torcedúra, *sf.* 1. Twisting, the act of twisting. *Quitar la torcedura de un cable,* (Naút.) To untwist a cable. 2. A light, paltry wine, made of water poured into the press after the grapes have been pressed.

Torcér, *va.* 1. To twist, to form by complication or convolution; to double, to curve. 2. To deviate from the right road, to leave the paths of virtue; to turn, to deflect. 3. To put a wrong construction on any thing; to pervert, as judges do justice. 4. To dissuade, to induce to change an opinion. 5. To impugn, to refute. *Torcer las narices,* To turn up the nose in disgust. 6. To twist threads or ropes. *Torcer la llave,* To turn the key, to lock.—*vr.* 1. To change a resolution, favourable for others. 2. To be dislocated; to be sprained. 3. To be pricked, to turn sour; applied to wine. 4. To deceive at gaming. *Torcer la cabeza,* (Met.) V. *Enfermar.*

Torcída, *sf.* 1. Wick, twisted cotton put into lamps and candles. 2. Daily allowance of meat given to labourers in oil-mills.
Torcidaménte, *ad.* Obliquely, tortuously.
Torcidíllo, *sm.* A kind of twisted silk.
Torcído, *sm.* 1. A kind of sweet-meat, which is twisted. 2. Light, bad wine.
Torcijón, *sm.* Gripes, pains in the bowels.
Torcimiénto, *sm.* Turning; deviation; circumlocution.
Torculádo, *sm.* Female screw.
Tórculo, *sm.* A small press; a rolling press for prints.
Tordélla, *sf.* Large kind of thrush.
Tordíga, *sf.* Neats' leather for coarse shoes.
Tordíllo, lla, *a.* Of a thrush-colour, greyish, between black and white.
Tórdo, *sm.* 1. (Orn.) Thrush, throstle. Turdus musicus *L.* *Tordo de agua*, (Orn.) Reed thrush. Turdus arundinaceus *L.* *Tordo loco*, (Orn.) Solitary thrush. Turdus solitarius *L.* 2. (Ict.) Sea-thrush, wrass. Labrus turdus *L.*
Tórdo, da, *a.* Speckled black and white.
Toreadór, *sm.* Bull-fighter on horseback.
Toreár, *vn.* 1. To fight bulls on horseback. 2. To let a bull to cows.—*va.* (Fam.) To burlesque, to mock; to make bulls.
Toréo, *sm.* Art or practice of fighting bulls.
Toréro, *sm.* Bull-fighter on foot.
Torés, *sm.* (Arq.) Torus, large ring or round moulding at the base of a column.
Toréte, *sm.* 1. A small bull. 2. (Fam.) A difficult point, an intricate business.
Tórga, *sf.* Yoke put on the necks of hogs.
Toríl, *sm.* Place where bulls are shut up until they are brought out.
Toríllo, *sm.* 1. Little bull. 2. Dowel, round pin which holds together the felloes of a coach or cart wheel, or any timber-work. 3. Frequent subject of conversation.
Toriondéz, *sf.* The cow's desire of the bull.
Toriόndo, da, *a.* Applied to black cattle rutting.
Torloróto, *sm.* A shepherd's pipe or flute.
Torménta, *sf.* 1. Storm, tempest; hurricane. *Correr tormenta*, (Naút.) To run before the wind in a storm. 2. Adversity, misfortune.
Tormentadór, ra, *s.* V. *Atormentador.*
Tormentár, *vn.* To be agitated violently; to suffer a storm.
Tormentário, ria, *a.* Gunnery; applied to the artillery.
Tormentíla, *sf.* (Bot.) Tormentil, septfoil. Tormentilla *L.*
Tormentín, *sm.* (Naút.) A small mast on the bowsprit.
Torménto, *sm.* 1. Torment, pain, anguish; affliction. 2. Rack, torture. 3. (Mil.) Battering ordnance. *Tormento de toca*, Ancient mode of torturing, by making the victim drink strips of thin gauze and water; tedious affliction.
Tormentóso, sa, *a.* Stormy, boisterous, turbulent; easily dismasted; applied to a ship.
Tórmo, *sm.* Tor, a high pointed insulated rock.
Tórna, *sf.* 1. Restitution. *Tornas*, (And.) Coarse straw; recompense, restitution. 2. Return. V. *Tornada.* 3. Drain of water for irrigation.
Tornabóda, *sf.* Day after a wedding.
Tornáda, *sf.* Return from a journey.
Tornadízo, za, *a.* y *s.* Turncoat, deserter.
Tornádo, *sm.* Tornado. *Tornado de viento*, Whirlwind.
Tornadúra, *sf.* 1. Return; recompense. 2. Land measure of ten feet.
Tornaguía, *sf.* Return of a permit received from the custom-house.
Tornájo, *sm.* Trough. V. *Dornajo.*
Tornapúnta, *sf.* (Arq.) Stay, prop. V. *Puntal.*
Tornár, *vn.* To return, to restore.—*va.* 1. To return, to make restitution. 2. To turn; to repeat. 3. To defend, to protect. *Tornar cabeza á alguna cosa*, To attend to any thing, to consider, to be attentive. *A tornapeon ó á tornayunta*, (Fam.) Mutually and reciprocally.
Tornasól, *sm.* 1. (Bot.) Turnsol. Heliotropium europæum *L.* 2. Changeable colour of stuff, arising from the different manner in which the light is reflected.
Tornasolár, *va.* To cause changes in colour.
Tornatíl, *a.* Turned, made by a turner or with a wheel.
Tornaviáge, *sm.* Return-voyage.
Tornavirón, *sm.* V. *Torniscon.*
Torneadór, *sm.* 1. Turner, one who turns or works on a lathe. 2. Tilter, one who performs at tournaments.
Torneánte, *pa.* Tilting, turning, revolving.
Torneár, *va.* 1. To form or shape by turning on a lathe. 2. To put into a circular motion. 3. To tilt, to fight at tournaments.—*vn.* To meditate, to revolve in the mind.
Tornéo, *sm.* 1. Tournament, a combat on horseback; public festival of knights. 2. Dance performed in imitation of tournaments.
Tornéra, *sf.* Door-keeper of a nunnery.
Tornería, *sf.* Turning, the act of forming or shaping by turning on a lathe.
Tornéro, *sm.* 1. Turner, one whose profession is to work or turn on a lathe. 2. Messenger or servant of a nunnery.
Tornés, sa, *a.* Applied to money made at Tours. *Libra tornesa*, Livre Tournois.
Tornilléro, *sm.* Deserter.
Tornillo, *sm.* 1. Screw, or male screw. 2. Desertion, the flight of a soldier, who flies from his colours. 3. Hog's trough.
Torniquéte, *sm.* Tourniquet, a chirurgical instrument.
Torniscón, *sm.* Blow in the face with the back of the hand.
Tórno, *sm.* 1. Wheel, any circular body turning round on its axis; axle-tree. 2. Circumvolution, gyration. 3. Bidding at a sale or letting of lands. 4. Kind of horizontal wheel or box revolving on an axis, containing various compartments, and used in nunneries to present refreshments at a blind window. *En torno*, Round about. *Torno de hilar*, Spinning-wheel. *Torno con sus aspas*, Windlass.
Tórno ó Tornéo, *sm.* Art of turning, turnery.
Tóro, *sm.* 1. Bull, the male of the cow. Bos taurus *L.* *Toro Mexicano*, Bison. V. *Bisonte.* *Correr toros*, To fight bulls. 2. (Arq.) Ogee moulding.
Torόndo y Torondón, *sm.* V. *Tolondro.*
Toronjíl y Toronjína, *s.* (Bot.) Balm-gentle. Melissa officinalis *L.*
Torόnja, *sf.* (Bot.) Citron; kind of quince.

Toroñjo, *sm.* (Bot.) Citron-tree.

Toróso, sa, *a.* Strong, robust.

Torozón, *sm.* Gripes, severe pains in the bowels.

Tórpe, *a.* 1. Slow, dull, heavy; stupid, rude. 2. Lascivious, unchaste, obscene. 5. Indecorous, disgraceful, infamous.

Torpedád, *sf.* Dulness, rudeness. V. *Torpeza.*

Torpédo, *sm.* (Ict.) Electric ray, cramp-fish. Raia torpedo *L.*

Torpeménte, *ad.* Obscenely, basely; slowly.

Torpéza, *sf.* 1. Heaviness, dulness, rudeness, slowness. 2. Impurity, unchastity, lewdness. 3. Uncleanliness, want of ornament or culture; rudeness, ugliness. 4. Base infamy, turpitude.

Torpór, *sm.* Torpor, numbness, want of motion.

Torquáta, *sf.* V. *Toza.*

Torrár, V. *Tostar.*

Tórre, *sf.* 1. Tower, a high polygonal building which serves as a defence; turret, embattled tower. 2. Steeple of a church, in which bells are hung. 3. Country-house with a garden. 4. Rook, a piece at chess. *Torre de costa,* Watch-tower. *Torre de viento,* Castle in the air. *Torre de luces,* (Naút.) Light-house. *Torre albarrana,* Turret, watch-tower.

Torreár, *vn.* To fortify with towers or turrets.

Torrefacción, *sf.* Torrification, roasting.

Torrejón, *sm.* Ill-shaped turret.

Torrentáda, *sf.* Sweep of a torrent, impetuous current carrying every thing before it.

Torrénte, *sm.* 1. Torrent, a violent and rapid stream; an impetuous current. 2. Abundance, plenty. 3. Strong coarse voice.

Torreón, *sm.* Rondel, a round tower.

Torréro, *sm.* Bailiff or steward of a country-house and garden.

Torreznáda, *sf.* Plentiful dish of rashers.

Torreznéro, *sm.* A lazy fellow, who sits continually over the fire.

Torrézno, *sm.* 1. Rasher, a slice of bacon. 2. A voluminous book or pamphlet.

Tórrido, da, *a.* Torrid, parched, hot.

Torríja, *sf.* Slice of bread, fried in white wine, eggs, and butter or oil.

Torrontéro ó Torrontéra, *s.* Heap of earth on a declivity.

Torrontés, *sf.* A kind of white grapes.

Tórta, *sf.* 1. A round cake made up of various ingredients. *Tortas y pan pintado,* These are trifles to the fatigues yet to come; said to persons who complain of trifles. 2. Cake of wax set out to be bleached.

Tortáda, *sf.* A kind of large pie.

Tortéla, *sf.* (Bot.) Hedge-mustard.

Tortéra, *sf.* 1. Pan for baking tarts or pies. 2. Knob at the end of a twisting spindle.

Tortéro, *sm.* Knob of a spindle for twisting.

Tortílla ó ta, *sf.* 1. A little cake. *Hacerse tortilla,* To break into small pieces, to cake. *Volverse la tortilla,* (Met.) To turn the scale, to take a course contrary to that expected. 2. Omelet, pancake, eggs beaten up and baked in a frying-pan.

Tórtis, Twisted ornament; used only in the adverb, *De tortis,* Flowered letter, with which chapters are commenced in printing.

Tórtola, *sf.* (Orn.) Turtle-dove. Columba turtur *L.*

Tortólico, *a.* Innocent, candid, inexperienced.

Tórtolo, *sm.* (Orn.) Cock or male turtle-dove.

Tortóres, *sm. pl.* (Naút.) Fraps. *Dar tortores á un navio,* (Naút.) To frap a ship.

Tortozón, *sm.* Kind of large grapes.

Tortúga, *sf.* Tortoise. Testudo *L.*

Tortuosaménte, *ad.* Tortuously.

Tortuosidád, *sf.* Tortuosity, flexure.

Tortuóso, sa, *a.* Tortuous, winding, turning.

Tortúra, *sf.* 1. Tortuosity, flexure. 2. Rack, torture. V. *Question.*

Torvísco, *sm.* (Bot.) Flax-leaved daphne. Daphne gnidium *L.*

Tórvo, va, *a.* Torvous, stern, severe.

Torzál, *sm.* Cord, twist; union, intertexture.

Torzón, *sm.* V. *Torozon.*

Torzonádo, da, *a.* Contracted or twisted; applied to animals diseased in the bowels.

Torzuélo, *a.* *Halcon torzuelo,* The third hawk which leaves the nest.

Tos, *sf.* Cough, a convulsion of the lungs.

Toscaménte, *ad.* Coarsely, rudely.

Toscáno, na, *a.* 1. Tuscan; applied to an architectural order. 2. Native of Tuscany.

Tósco, ca, *a.* 1. Coarse, rough, unpolished. 2. Ill-bred, uninstructed.

Tosecílla, *sf. dim.* Slight cough.

Toseгóso, sa, *a.* Coughing much.

Tosér, *vn.* To cough; to feign a cough.

Tosidúra, *sf.* The act of coughing.

Tosigár, *va.* V. *Atosigar.*

Tósigo, *sm,* 1. Poison, especially that which is extracted from the yew-tree. 2. Grief, pain, anguish, vexation.

Tosigóso, sa. *a.* 1. Poisonous, venomous. 2. Coughing, having a cough.

Tosquedád, *sf.* Roughness, coarseness; rudeness.

Tostáda, *sf.* Slice of toasted bread.

Tostádo, da, *a.* Of a lively light-brown colour.

Tostadór, ra, *s.* 1. Toaster, one who toasts. 2. Toaster, the instrument on which any thing is toasted.

Tostár, *va.* To toast, to dry any thing at the fire until it is brown. *Tostar café,* To roast coffee.

Tostón, *sm.* 1. Sop, made of toasted bread and oil; roasted Spanish pea. 2. Any thing too much toasted. 3. Testoon, Portuguese silver coin containing 100 reis, and equal to 6 3-4d. sterl. 4. Kind of missile weapon. 5. In South America, a *real de á quatro,* or 4 silver reals; i. e. half a dollar or half an ounce. *Tostones,* Sucking pigs.

Totál, *sm.* Whole, totality.—*a.* General, universal, total.

Totalidád, *sf.* Totality, whole quantity.

Totalménte, *ad.* Totally.

Totilimúndi, *sm.* Rareeshow, a shew carried about in a box.

Totovía, *sf.* (Orn.) Wood-lark. Alauda arborea *L.*

Toucán, *sm.* (Orn.) Toucan. Rhamphastos *L.*

Tóxico, *sm.* V. *Tósigo.*

Toxínes, *sm. pl.* (Naút.) Belaying cleats, pieces of wood, having one or two projecting ends, whereby ropes are fastened. *Toxines de las peñoles de las vergas,* (Naút.) Cleats of the yard-arms.

Tóxo, *sm.* (Bot.) Species of broom.

Toysón, *sm.* V. *Tuson.*

Tóza, *sf.* 1. (Ar.) V. *Tocon.* 2. Piece of the bark of a tree.

Tozál, *sm.* (Ar.) Height, eminence.

Tozár, *vn.* 1. To butt, to strike with the head, 2. To contend foolishly.

Tózo, za, *a.* (Pint.) Low in stature.

Tozoláda ó Tozolón, *s.* Stroke or blow on the neck.

Tozúdo, da, *a.* V. *Obstinado.*

Tozuélo, *sm.* Fat part of the neck.

Trába, *sf.* 1. Ligament, ligature, the instrument with which one thing is united to another; cord with which the feet of cattle are tied. 2. Obstacle, impediment, hinderance. 3. Trammel, fetter, shackle. 4. Steps taken to obstruct justice. 5. (And.) Cross bar in the frame which encloses the stones in a horse-mill. 6. Each one of the arms of a fowling net. 7. Piece of cloth uniting the two parts of a scapulary worn by some religious.

Trabacuénta, *sf.* 1. Error, mistake. 2. Difference, dispute, controversy.

Trabadéro, *sm.* The small part of animals' feet.

Trabádo, da, *a.* 1. Robust, strong. 2. Having two white fore-feet, or two white feet on one side; applied to a horse.

Trabadúra, *sf.* Union, junction.

Trabajadaménte, *ad.* V. *Trabajosamente.*

Trabajádo, da, *a.* 1. Wrought; applied to metals. 2. Tired, weary; exhausted with fatigue. [person.

Trabajadór, ra, *s.* Labourer, an assiduous

Trabajár, *vn.* 1. To work, to be engaged in some work or business; to be diligent. 2. To endeavour, to make an effort, to contend for; to labour, to toil; to solicit, to procure. 3. To support, to sustain; applied to building or machinery. 4. To nourish and produce; applied to the earth.—*va.* 1. To work, to form, to execute. 2. To work the ground, to cultivate the soil. 3. To molest, to vex, to harass.

Trabájo, *sm.* 1. Work, labour, toil. 2. Obstacle, impediment, hinderance, difficulty. 3. Trouble, hardship, want, indigence. *Trabajos*, Poverty, misery. 4. Work, a writing on any subject; thing wrought. *Dia de trabajo*, Working-day. *Sacar á uno de trabajos*, To extricate one from troubles and difficulties.

Trabajosaménte, *ad.* Laboriously, difficultly.

Trabajóso, sa, *a.* 1. Laborious, elaborate. 2. Imperfect, defective.

Trabál, *a.* Applied to clasp nails.

Trabamiénto, *sm.* Act of joining or uniting.

Trabánco, *sm.* Piece of wood attached to a dog's collar to prevent him from putting down his head.

Trabár, *va.* 1. To join, to unite; to connect. 2. To dispute, to quarrel, to scuffle. *Trabarse de palabras*, To have words, to argue, to dispute or disagree. 3. To seize, to take hold of. 4. To censure, to blame. 5. To fetter, to shackle. 6. To thicken, to inspissate. 7. To set the teeth of a saw. *Trabar plática*, To chatter together. *Trabar batalla*, To combat, to fight. *Trabarse la lengua*, To lose the use of speech.

Trabazón, *sf.* Juncture, union; connexion.

Trábe, *sf.* Beam.

Trabéa, *sf.* A long gown.

Trabílla, *sf.* 1. A small clasp or tie. 2. Stitch, falling from the needle in knitting stockings.

Trabón, *sm.* 1. Fetter of a horse's foot, to keep him quiet in the stable. 2. Cross-planks in oil mills.

Trabúca, *sf.* Cracker, a kind of artificial fire-work, which bursts with a loud noise.

Trabucación, *sf.* Confusion, mistake.

Trabucadór, ra, *s.* Disturber. [takes.

Trabucánte, *pa.* Preponderating; causing mis-

Trabucár, *va.* 1. To derange, to throw into confusion, to confound, to perturbate. 2. To interrupt a conversation, to cut the thread of a discourse.—*vn.* To stumble, to tumble.—*vr.* To equivocate, to mistake.

Trabucázo, *sm.* 1. Shot with a blunderbuss. 2. A sudden fright.

Trabúco, *sm.* 1. Catapult, a battering engine used by the ancients. 2. Blunderbuss, a short wide-mouthed gun. 3. Piedmont measure of 9 geometric feet. *Trabuco naranjero*, Kind of cannon. V. *Naranjero.*

Trabuquéte, *sm.* Machine used by the ancients to throw large stones.

Tráca, *sf.* (Naút.) Streak or strake, the uniform range of the planks or boards of a ship. *Traca de palmejares*, (Naút.) Strake of the ceiling or foot wailing.

Tracamundána, *sf.* A ridiculous change of trifles or things of no value.

Tracción, *sf.* Attraction.

Trácia, *sf.* The Thracian stone, a fossil to which medical virtues are ascribed.

Trácias, *sm.* North-north-west wind.

Tracísta, *sm.* Projector, schemer; intriguer.

Trácto, *sm.* 1. Space of time. 2. Versicles sung at mass between the epistle and gospel.

Tradición, *sf.* 1. Tradition, an account delivered orally from age to age. 2. (For.) V. *Entrego.*

Tradicionál, *a.* Traditional, by tradition.

Traducción, *sf.* 1. Version, translation, interpretation. 2. A rhetorical figure, by which the same word is used in different senses.

Traducír, *va.* 1. To translate, to interpret in another language. 2. To change, to truck.

Traductór, ra, *s.* Translator.

Traedízo, za, *a.* That which may be drawn; tractable. [carrier.

Traedór, ra, *s.* One who brings or carries,

Traér, *va.* 1. To fetch, to bring, to carry, to conduct. 2. To draw, to attract. 3. To come, to handle, to manage. *Traer bien la espada*, To handle the sword dexterously. 4. To bind, to oblige, to compel. 5. To prevail upon, to persuade. 6. To be engaged in, to carry on. 7. To use, to wear. *Traer medias de seda*, To wear silk stockings. 8. To cause, to occasion, to contract; to exercise, to agitate, to vex. 9. It is sometimes used in preference to *llegar*, as *Sacamos frio y traemos calor*, We went out in cold and returned in warm weather. V. *Sacar. Traer perdido á alguno*, To be deeply in love; to be the ruin or destruction of a person.—*vr.* To dress one's self, to appear. *Traerse bien*, To be of a good appearance. *Traer á consequencia*, To place any thing in a situation which enhances or diminishes its value.

Trafagadór, *sm.* Trafficker, dealer.

Trafagánte, *pa.* Trafficker; trading.

Trafagár, *vn.* 1. To traffic, to carry on trade or commerce. V. *Traficar.* 2. To travel, to make journeys.

Tráfago, *sm.* 1. Traffic, commerce, trade. 2. A careful management of affairs and concerns.

Trafagón, na, *a.* Active, industrious, deeply engaged in trade and commerce.

Trafalmējo, ja, *a.* Bold, intrepid, audacious.

Traficación, *sf.* Traffic, trade, commerce.

Traficánte, *pa.* y *s.* Merchant, dealer, trader.

Traficár, *vn.* 1. To traffic, to carry on trade and commerce. 2. To travel, to journey.

Tráfico, *sm.* Commerce, traffic, trade.

Trafúlla, *sf.* Cheating, defrauding, swindling.

Tragacánta, *sf.* 1. (Bot.) Goat's thorn. Astragalus tragacantha *L.* 2. Tragacanth, a gum oozing out of the bark of the above-mentioned shrub.

Tragacéte, *sm.* Javelin, a missile weapon used by the Moors.

Tragadéro, *sm.* 1. Œsophagus, gullet. 2. Pit, gulph, abyss. *Tragadero de un puerto*, (Naút.) Mouth of a harbour. *Estar en el tragadero del mar*, (Naút.) To be in the trough of the sea, or in the midst of two waves.

Tragadór, ra, *s.* Glutton, voracious person.

Tragaféés, *sm.* Traitor, one who betrays his trust.

Tragahómbres, *sm.* (Fam.) Bully, hector.

Tragaldábas, *sm.* Glutton, gormandizer, a voracious eater.

Tragaléguas, *sm.* A great walker, one who walks much and fast.

Tragalúz, *sf.* Sky-light.

Tragamállas, *sm.* 1. Impostor, cheat, swindler. 2. Glutton, gormandizer.

Tragantáda, *sf.* A large draught of liquor.

Tragánte, *pa.* Swallowing, guzzling.—*sm.* 1. Sluice, mill-dam. 2. *Tragante del baupres*, (Naút.) Pillow of the bowsprit. *Tragante de pedrero*, (Naút.) Stock or crotch of a swivel gun.

Tragantón, na, *s.* 1. Glutton, a voracious eater. 2. The act of swallowing or forcing down the throat. 3. (Met.) Difficulty of believing any extraordinary thing.—*a.* Gluttonous, voracious.

Tragár, *va.* 1. To swallow, to take down the throat. 2. To eat much and quick, to eat voraciously. 3. To swallow up, to engulph. 4. To receive or believe without examination. —*vr.* To dissemble, to play the hypocrite; to pocket an affront. *Tragar el anzuelo*, (Met.) To allow one's self to be deceived. *No poder tragar á alguno*, To abhor or dislike one.

Tragázo, *sm. aum.* A large draught.

Tragazón, *sf.* Voracity, gluttony.

Tráge, *sm.* 1. Garb, the usual mode of dress in a province or country. 2. Mask, a dress used for disguise. 3. Simulation, hypocrisy, colour, pretence. 4. A complete dress of a woman. *Trage de á caballo*, Riding-dress. *Trage de mar*, (Naút.) Slops.

Trageár, *va.* To dress or clothe in a manner suitable to one's rank or condition.

Tragédia, *sf.* 1. Tragedy, a dramatic representation of a serious action. 2. Any mournful or dreadful event. *Parar en tragedia*, To have a fatal issue or end.

Tragélafo, *sm.* Kind of animal between a goat and deer.

Trágico, ca; y **Tragediόso, sa**, *a.* Tragic, disastrous.

Tragicaménte, *ad.* Tragically.

Tragicomédia, *sf.* Tragi-comedy, a drama composed of merry and serious events.

Tragílla, *sf.* A kind of harrow without teeth for levelling the ground.

Tragín, *sm.* Carriage. V. *Tragino y Trafago.*

Tragināánte, *sm.* Carrier.

Traginár, *va.* 1. To carry or transport goods from one place to another. 2. To travel.

Tragineríá, *sf.* Carrying trade.

Traginéro, *sm.* Carrier.

Tragíno, *sm.* Carriage, the act of carrying or transporting goods or merchandise from one place to another.

Trágio, *sm.* (Bot.) Bastard dittany.

Trágo, *sm.* 1. (Bot.) Satyrion. 2. Draught of liquor. 3. Calamity, adversity, misfortune. *A' tragos*, By degrees, slowly, gently.

Tragón, na, *a.* Gluttonous, voracious, ravenous.

Tragón, *sm.* Glutton. Ursus gulo *L.*

Tragonía y **Tragonería**, *sf.* Gluttony.

Tragopána ó **Tragopánade**, *sf.* Fabulous bird.

Tragoríga̋no, *sm.* (Bot.) Syrian herb, mastic.

Traguíco, llo, to, *sm. dim.* of *trago.*

Traición, *sf.* Treason, the want of fidelity or loyalty to the sovereign. *Alta traicion*, High treason. *A' traicion*, Treacherously.

Traída, *sf.* Carriage, the act of fetching or carrying any thing from one place to another.

Traído, da, *a.* 1. Brought, fetched, carried. 2. Used, worn, second hand.

Traidór, ra, *s.* Traitor; treacherous beast.

Traidór, ra, *a.* Treacherous.

Traidoraménte, *ad.* Treacherously.

Traílla, *sf.* 1. Leash, a cord or leather thong, by which a dog is led. 2. Pack-thread. 3. Instrument for levelling the ground.

Traillár, *va.* To level the ground.

Traína, *sf.* Train of gunpowder.

Traíña, *sf.* Jack, a small bowl. V. *Boliche.*

Traíte, *sm.* Act of raising a bur or nap on cloth.

Trálla, *sf.* Cord, basswood rope.

Tráma, *sf.* 1. Weft or woof, the thread or yarn which crosses the warp. 2. Deceit, imposition, fraud, plot. 3. Kind of weaving silk.

Tramadór, ra, *s.* 1. Weaver. 2. Plotter; artful contriver.

Tramár, *va.* 1. To weave, to throw the woof across the warp. 2. To plot, to contrive artfully, to form crafty designs.

Trámite, *sm.* Path; procedure, proceedings.

Trámo, *sm.* 1. Piece, morsel. 2. Piece of ground separated from another. 3. Flight or pair of stairs from one landing place to another.

Tramójo, *sm.* 1. Part of grain, which the reaper holds in his hand. 2. Band for tying the sheaf. 3. Fright, fear. *Pasó ó mamó el tramojo*, He experienced a dreadful alarm; he met a severe misfortune, or swallowed a bitter draught.

Tramón, *sm.* The shortest wool which remains

in the comb during the act of combing.
Tramontána, sf. 1. The north wind. 2. Vanity, pride, haughtiness. *Perder la tramontana*, (Met.) To become mad with passion.
Tramontáno, na, a. Transmontane, beyond the mountains.
Tramontár, vn. To pass to the other side of the mountains.—va. To assist, to relieve.—vr. To fly, to escape.
Tramóya, sf. 1. Scene, theatrical decoration. 2. Craft, wile, artifice, artful trick.
Tramoyísta, sm. 1. Artist who paints scenes and decorations for the theatre. 2. Impostor, swindler.
Trámpa, sf. 1. Trap, snare; moveable part of a counter; trap-door. *Caer en la trampa*, To fall into the snare, to be deceived by artifice. 2. Fraud, deceit, stratagem. 3. Debt fraudulently contracted. *Trampa adelante*, Deceitful procrastination; applied to persons who go borrowing with one hand to pay with another.
Trampál, sm. Quagmire; a dirty or muddy place.
Trampantójo, sm. Trick played before one's eyes.
Trampázo, sm. The last twist of the cord, employed to rack or torture an offender.
Trampeadór, ra, s. Borrower, swindler, cheat.
Trampeár, vn. To borrow or obtain money on false pretences, to swindle one out of his money.—va. To impose upon, to deceive.
Trampílla, sf. 1. A slight fraud, a petty imposition. 2. Small hole in the floor of an upper story through which a door or shop can be watched.
Trampísta, sm. Cheat, impostor, swindler, sharper.
Trampóso, sa, a. Deceitful, swindling; cheater.
Tránca, sf. 1. Bar, a piece of wood, laid across a door or window, to hinder entrance. 2. (Naút.) Cross-bar.
Trancáda, sf. V. *Tranco*.
Trancádo, sm. A small harpoon for catching eels.
Trancahílo, sm. Knot in thread or ropes.
Trancaníles, sm. pl. (Naút.) Water-ways; long pieces of timber serving to connect the sides of a ship with the decks, and forming a kind of channel for carrying off the water from the latter through the scupper-holes. *Trancaniles reservados ó interiores*, Under water-ways.
Trancár, va. To barricade. V. *Atrancár*.
Trancázo, sm. Blow with a bar.
Tránce, sm. 1. Peril, danger. 2. A critical moment; the last stage of life. 3. Sale of a debtor's property to satisfy his creditors. *A' todo trance*, Resolutely.
Trancelín, sm. A gold or silver hatband, garnished with jewels.
Tranchéte, sm. A broad curvated knife, used for pruning, &c.; shoemaker's heel-knife.
Tráncho, sm. (Gal.) V. *Alacha*.
Tránco, sm. 1. A long step or stride. 2. Threshold of a door. *En dos trancos*, Briefly, swiftly. *A' trancos*, In haste, in a trice.
Trangállo, sm. Yoke fixed on shepherd's dogs' necks, during the brooding-time of game.
Tranquéra, sf. Palisade, palisado.
Tranquéro, sm. Jamb or lintel of a door or window, made of stone.
Tranquilaménte, ad. Quietly, in a peaceful manner, tranquilly.
Tranquilár, va. 1. To quiet, to appease, to tranquillize. 2. To balance accounts.
Tranquilidád, sf. Tranquillity, rest, peace, repose.
Tranquilizár, va. To calm, to appease, to quiet, to tranquillize.
Tranquílla, sf. 1. A small bar. 2. Trap, snare, artful stratagem.
Tranquílo, la, a. Tranquil, calm, quiet, undisturbed.
Trans, prep. (Lat.) Used in composition, and signifying over, beyond.
Transacción, sf. Composition of a difference, accommodation, adjustment.
Transalpíno, na, a. Transalpine, beyond the Alps.
Transbisabuélo, la, s. V. *Tatarabuelo*.
Transbordár, va. (Naút.) To shift the cargo of a ship on board of another vessel.
Transcendéncia, sf. Transcendency; perspicacity, penetration.
Transcendentál, a. Transcendental.
Transcendénte, pa. That which transcends, transcendent.
Transcendér, vn. 1. To transcend, to transmigrate. 2. To be transcendent; to extend itself. 3. To emit or exhale a sweet scent or pleasing smell or odour.—va. 1. To be transcendental. 2. To conceive, to perceive or understand quickly and clearly.
Transcribír, va. To transcribe, to copy.
Transcúrso, sm. Course or process of time.
Tránseat, A Latin word, signifying Let it pass.
Transeúnte, a. Transient, soon past, soon passing; transitory; passenger.
Transferidór, ra, s. One who transfers.
Transferír, va. 1. To move, to remove, to transport. 2. To transfer, to convey, to make over; to defer. 3. To employ a word figuratively or in a figurative sense.
Transfigurábie, a. Changeable, that can be transformed.
Transfiguración, sf. Transformation, transfiguration.
Transfigurár, va. To transfigure, to transform.—vr. To be transfigured; to lose form or figure; to be metamorphosed.
Transfixión, sf. The act of piercing from side to side.
Transfíxo, xa, a. Transfixed, pierced through with any instrument.
Transflorár, va. (Pint.) To copy any picture or drawing at a side-light.
Transfloreár, va. To enamel, to inlay, to variegate with colours.
Transfolládo, da, a. (Albeyt.) Applied to tumours round a horse's legs.
Transformación, sf. Transformation.
Transformadór, ra, s. One who transforms.
Transformamiénto, sm. Transformation.
Transformár, va. 1. To transform, to transmute; to metamorphose. 2. To gain such an ascendency in another's affections, that it almost changes his or her character.—vr. To assume different sentiments or manners.
Transformatívo, va, a. That possesses power to transform.
Transfregár, va. To rub.

Transfretáno, na, *a.* Transmarine.
Transfretár, *va.* To cross an arm of the sea.
Tránsfuga ó Tránsfugo, *sm.* Deserter, fugitive.
Transfundír, *va.* To transfuse; to communicate.
Transfusión, *sf.* Transfusion; communication.
Transgredír, *va.* To transgress, or violate a law or rule.
Transgresión, *sf.* Transgression, violation of [a law.
Transgresór, ra, *s.* Transgressor, one that breaks or violates a law.
Transición, *sf.* Transition.
Transído, da, *a.* 1. Worn out with anguish, consumed by grief. 2. Avaricious, sordidly penurious.
Transigír, *va.* To accommodate differences; to settle disputes on friendly terms.
Transitár, *vn.* To travel, to go on a journey; to pass by any place.
Transitívo, va, *a.* Transitive, that passes or is transferred from one to another.
Tránsito, *sm.* 1. Passage, the act of passing from one place to another. 2. Inn, a house for the accommodation of travellers. 3. Road, way. 4. Change, removal. 5. Death of holy persons.
Transitoriaménte, *ad.* Transitorily.
Transitório, ria, *a.* Transitory, perishable.
Translación, *sf.* 1. Translation, removal, the act of removing; promotion of a bishop. 2. Translation, version. 3. Metaphor, figurative expression.
Translaticiaménte, *ad.* Metaphorically.
Translatício, cia; y Transláto, ta, *a.* Metaphorical.
Transmaríno, na, *a.* Transmarine, lying on the other side of the sea.
Transmigración, *sf.* Transmigration, the removal of a whole family, or several families, from one country to another. *Transmigracion pitagórica,* Transmigration of souls, according to the opinion of Pythagoras.
Transmigrár, *vn.* To transmigrate, to pass from one country to another.
Transmisíble, *a.* Transmissible.
Transmisión, *sf.* Transmission, the act of transmitting from one place to another.
Transmitír, *va.* To transfer, to make over.
Transmontár, *va.* V. *Trasmontar.*
Transmutáble, *a.* Transmutable, changeable.
Transmutación, *sf.* Transmutacion, the act of changing or converting into another nature or substance.
Transmutár, *va.* To transmute.
Transmutatívo, va; ó Transmutatório, ria, *a.* That which has the power of transmuting.
Transpadáno, na, *a.* Being beyond the Po.
Transparéncia, *sf.* Transparency, clearness; power of transmitting light.
Transparentárse, *vr.* 1. To be transparent. 2. To shine through; applied to light.
Transparénte, *a.* Transparent; having the power of transmitting light.—*sm.* Glass-window.
Transpiráble, *a.* Perspirable. [perspiration.
Transpiración, *sf.* Transpiration, insensible
Transpirár, *vn.* To transpire, to evaporate insensibly through the pores.
Transplánte, *sm.* V. *Trasplante.*

Transportación, *sf.* Transportation, conveyance, carriage, removal.
Transportamiénto, *sm.* 1. Transportation, carriage. 2. Rapture, ecstasy; rage.
Transportár, *va.* 1. To transport, to convey, to remove. 2. (Mús.) To change the key.—*vr.* To be in a transport; to be out of one's senses.
Transpórte, *sm.* Transport, transportation. *Bazel de transporte,* (Naút.) Transport or transport-ship, a vessel fitted out to carry stores and soldiers.
Transportín, *sm.* A thin and small mattress, put between other mattresses to make the bed more even.
Transposición, *sf.* Transposition.
Transterminánte, *pa.* Transgressing the limits.—*sm.* Travelling flock of sheep.
Transterminár, *va.* To pass from the limits of one jurisdiction to another; to trespass.
Transubstanciación, *sf.* Transubstantiation.
Transubstanciál, *a.* That which is converted into another substance.
Transubstanciár, *va.* To convert entirely into another substance or nature.
Transverberación, *sf.* V. *Transfixion.* [teral.
Transversál, *a.* Transversal, transverse, colla-
Transversalménte, *ad.* Transversally.
Transvérso, sa, *a.* Transverse. [*Trance.*
Tránza, *sf.* Peril, danger, critical moment. V.
Tranzadéra, *sf.* Knot of plaited cords or ribands.
Tranzár, *va.* 1. To plait or weave cords or ribands; to braid. 2. To cut, to truncate. 3. V. *Rematar.* [cut or cleared for fuel.
Tranzón, *sm.* Part of a forest which has been
Trápa, *sf.* Noise made by stamping with the feet, or bawling. *Trápas,* (Naút.) Relieving ropes or relieving tackle: they are furnished with two pendants, and used for heaving down a vessel which is to be careened. *Trapas de las velas,* Spilling lines, ropes fastened to the main and fore-sail.
Trapacear y Trapazár, *vn.* To deceive by falsehoods and artful contrivances.
Trapacería, *sf.* Fraud, deceit. V. *Trapaza.*
Trapacéro, ra, *a.* Cheating, deceitful. V. *Trapacista.*
Trapacéte, *sm.* Waste-book, the book in which merchants and traders make their first entries.
Trapacísta, *sm.* y *a.* Impostor, cheat, sharper, swindler; deceiver; fraudulent, false.
Trapájo, *sm.* Rag, tatter.
Trapajóso, sa, *a.* Ragged, tattered.
Trápala, *sf.* 1. A violent noise made by stamping with the feet, or bawling.—*s. com.* Garrulous loquacious babbler.
Trapaleár, *vn.* To be loquacious or garrulous; to babble.
Trapalóno, na, *a.* Loquacious; babbler, prater.
Trapáza, *sf.* Fraud, a deceitful trick.
Trapázo, *sm.* A large rag.
Trápe, *sm.* Buckram.
Trapécio, *sm.* (Geom.) Trapezium, an irregular figure of four unequal sides.
Trapería, *sf.* 1. Street inhabited by woollen-drapers. 2. Frippery, rag-fair, the place where rags and old clothes are sold. 3. Woollen-draper's shop.
Trapéro, ra, *a.* Dealing in rags or frippery.

Trapiche, *sm.* A small sugar-mill, or engine for bruising and squeezing the sugar-cane.

Trapíllo, *sm.* 1. Courtier of a vulgar woman. 2. Little rag. *De trapillo,* Decent or domestic clothing.

Trapisónda, *sf.* Bustle, noise, confusion.

Trápo, *sm.* 1. Cloth. 2. Rag, tatter. 3. Sails of a ship. *A' todo trapo,* With all might; (Naút.) All sails set. *Poner como un trapo,* To reprimand severely.

Tráque, *sm.* Crack, the noise made by a bursting rocket, or the priming of a gun. *Traque barraque,* (Vulg.) At all times, with whatever motive.

Traquéa, *sf.* 1. Windpipe, trachea. 2. Lungs [of plants.

Traquear, *vn.* To crack, to make a loud noise.—*va.* 1. To frequent, to handle a thing much. 2. To shake, to agitate, to move to and fro.

Traquéo, *sm.* 1. Noise or report of artificial fire-works. 2. The act of shaking or moving to and fro.

Traqueteár, *va.* To trace, to track.

Traquetéo, *sm.* Trace; noise.

Traquiartéria, *sf.* V. *Traquea.*

Traquído, *sm.* Noise or report of fire-arms.

Trás, *prep.* After, behind, besides. *Tras una puerta,* Behind a door. *Tras de venir tarde,* Besides coming late. In composition it is equivalent to *trans,* as *traspasar.*—*sm.* (Fam.) 1. Breech, bottom. 2. Blow or stroke attended with noise. *Tras, tras,* Repeated strokes or noise. *Trastras,* The last but one, in boys' plays. *Ir ó andar tras alguno,* To go in pursuit of one, to seek diligently; to follow after one. *No tener tras que parar,* To be extremely poor.

Trasabuélo, la, y Trasagüélo, la, V. *Tatarabuelo.*

Trasalcóba, *sf.* Alcove behind the principal recess.

Trasanteáyer, *ad.* V. *Anteanteayer.*

Trasañéjo, ja, *a.* Three years old; particularly applied to wine.

Trasbisniéto, ta, *s.* V. *Tataranieto.*

Trásca, *sf.* Leather thong.

Trascábo, *sm.* Trip, a trick by which a wrestler supplants his antagonist, and brings him to the ground.

Trascantón, *sm.* 1. Stone placed at the corner of a street. 2. Porter who stands at the corner of a street and waits for employment. *Dar trascanton ó trascantonada,* To hide one's self behind a corner.

Trascartárse, *vr.* To remain behind; applied to a card, which had it come sooner, would have won the game.

Trascartón, *sm.* Drawing of a winning card after the game is lost.

Trascendentál, *a.* V. *Transcendental.*

Trascendér, *vn.* 1. To transcend, to go beyond. 2. To exhale or emit a strong scent or odour. —*va.* To penetrate, to discover, to comprehend.

Trascendído, da, *a.* Acute, endowed with great penetration.

Trascól, *sm.* (Ant.) Woman's train.

Trascolár, *va.* (Med.) 1. To strain, to percolate. 2. (Vulg.) To pass over a mountain.

Trasconejárse, *vr.* 1. To squat; applied to game which is pursued by dogs. 2. To sheer off, to escape.

Trascordárse, *vr.* To forget, to lose the memory of.

Trascóro, *sm.* Space or part of a church at the back of the choir.

Trascorrál, *sm.* 1. Back-court or back-yard. 2. (Joc.) Breech, buttocks.

Trasdobladúra, *sf.* Treble, triple.

Trasdoblár, *va.* To treble, to multiply by three.

Trasdóblo, *sm.* Treble, triple. V. *Triple.*

Trasdós, *sm.* (Arq.) Inner side or back of hewn stones in buildings.

Trasegadór, *sm.* One who racks wine.

Trasegár, *va.* 1. To overset, to turn topsy-turvy. 2. To decant, to rack wine, to pour it into another vessel.

Trasañaladór, ra, *s.* One who alters marks.

Traseñalár, *va.* To alter or blot out the mark, and make a new one.

Trasera, *sf.* Back or posterior part.

Traséro, ra, *a.* Remaining behind, coming after.

Traséro, *sm.* Buttock, rump, the back part of animals. *Traseros,* (Joc.) Ancestors, forefathers, predecessors.

Trasfojár, *va.* To run over the leaves of a book. V. *Trashojar.*

Trasfundición, *sf.* Transfusion. V. *Transfusion.*

Trásgo, *sm.* 1. Goblin, hobgoblin, sprite. V. *Duende.* 2. A lively, restless, noisy boy.

Trasguár, *vn.* To play the hobgoblin.

Trasguéro, *sm.* One who imitates the tricks of hobgoblins and sprites.

Trashoguéro, *sm.* 1. Iron plate, placed at the back part of a fire-place or hearth. 2. Block of wood placed against the wall to keep in the fire.

Trashoguéro, ra, *a.* Idling, loitering the whole day near the fire-place.

Trashojár, *va.* To run over the leaves of a book.

Trashumánte, *pa.* Flock of sheep which pasture in the north of Spain in summer, and in the south in winter. *Trashumantes,* Travelling sheep.

Trashumár, *va.* To drive sheep to or from the common pasture-grounds or the mountains in spring and autumn.

Trasiégo, *sm.* 1. Removal, the act of moving things from one place to another. 2. The act of decanting liquors from one vessel into another.

Trasijádo, da, *a.* Lank, meager; thin flanked.

Trasijár, *vn.* To grow thin or meager.

Traslación y Trasladación, *sf.* V. *Translacion.*

Trasladadór, ra, *s.* Translator, one who translates from one language into another.

Trasladánte, *pa.* Translator, transcribing.

Trasladár, *va.* 1. To move, to remove, to transport. 2. To translate, to turn into another language. 3. To transcribe, to copy a writing.

Trasládo, *sm.* 1. (For.) A copy. 2. Imitation, resemblance, likeness.

Traslapár, *va.* V. *Solapar.*

Traslatívo, va, *a.* Metaphorical.

Trasloár, *va.* To bestow fulsome praise.

Traslucído, da, *a.* Transparent, clear, pellucid.

Traslucíénte, *a.* Translucent, transparent.

Traslucírse, *vr.* To be transparent; to shine through; to conjecture, to infer.

Traslumbramiénto, *sm.* The state of being dazzled by excessive light.

Traslumbrárse, *vr.* 1. To be dazzled with excessive light. 2. To vanish, to disappear.

Traslúz, *sm.* Light which passes through a

transparent body; (Pint.) transverse light.

TRASMÁLLO, *sm.* Trammel; iron handle of a hammer.

TRASMÁNO, *sm.* Second player at a game of cards. *A' trasmano,* Out of the right way; not within the common intercourse of life.

TRASMAÑÁNA, *sf.* The day after to-morrow.

TRASMARÍNO, NA, *a.* V. *Transmarino.*

TRASMATÁR, *va.* To outlive; (Joc.) To persuade one's self of having to enjoy a longer life than another.

TRASMINÁR, *va.* To undermine, to excavate, to dig under ground.—*vn.* To emit a strong scent.—*vr.* To pierce, to penetrate.

TRASMONTÁR, *va.* To pass to the other side of the mountain. V. *Tramontar.*

TRASMÓTA, *sf.* After wine, made by water poured on the pressed grapes.

TRASMUDÁR, *va.* 1. To move, to remove, to transport from one place to another. 2. To change the affections or inclinations; to convert. 3. To turn topsyturvy. V. *Trasegar.*

TRASMUTÁBLE, *a.* V. *Transmutable.*

TRASMUTACIÓN, *sf.* V. *Transmutacion.*

TRASMUTÁR, *va.* To alter, to change.

TRASNOCHÁDA, *sf.* 1. Last night. 2. Watch, the act of watching or sitting up a whole night. 3. (Ant.) Military surprise or nocturnal attack.

TRASNOCHÁDO, DA, *a.* Having watched the whole night; tired or fatigued from having sat up a whole night.

TRASNOCHADÓR, RA, *s.* Night-watcher.

TRASNOCHÁR, *vn.* To watch, to sit up a whole night.

TRASNOMBRÁR, *va.* To change or confound [names.

TRASNOMINACIÓN, *sf.* V. *Metonimia.*

TRASOÍR, *va.* To mistake, to misunderstand.

TRASOJÁDO, DA, *a.* Having sunken or hollow eyes; emaciated, worn out.

TRASOÑÁR, *vn.* To dream, to fancy erroneously.

TRASORDINÁRIO, RIA, *a.* Extraordinary.

TRASPADÁNO, NA, *a.* y *s.* Living beyond the Po.

TRASPÁGINA, *sf.* Back page.

TRASPALÁR, *va.* 1. To shovel, to remove with a shovel from one place to another. 2. To move, to remove. 3. To dig or hoe under a vine; to clear the ground of grass.

TRASPAPELÁRSE, *vr.* To be mislaid among other papers; applied to a writing which cannot be found.

TRASPASACIÓN, *sf.* (For.) Conveyance, transfer.

TRASPASÁDO, DA, *pp.* Transfixed.

TRASPASAMIÉNTO, *sm.* 1. Transgression or violation of the law; trespass. 2. Transfer, the act of conveying or making over. V. *Traspaso.*

TRASPASÁR, *va.* 1. To pass over, to go beyond; to cross. 2. To be touched with compassion, to be afflicted.—*va.* 1. To remove, to transport. 2. To run through with a pointed weapon, to transfix; to introduce with great force. 3. To cross a river. 4. To return, to repass. 5. To transgress, to violate a law. 6. To exceed the proper bounds; to trespass. 7. To transfer, to make over.

TRASPÁSO, *sm.* 1. Conveyance, transfer. 2. Grief, anguish. 3. Trespass, transgression or violation of a law; treachery.

TRASPÉCHO, *sm.* Bone on the back of a cross-bow, as an ornamental guard on the stock.

TRASPEYNÁR, *va.* To comb again what had been combed before.

TRASPIÉ, *sm.* 1. Trip, a trick by which a wrestler supplants his antagonist, and brings him down to the ground. *Echar ó dar traspies,* To supplant by artifice, to live by tricks. 2. Slip, stumble.

TRASPILÁSTRA, *sf.* (Arq.) V. *Contrapilastra.*

TRASPILLÁRSE, *vr.* To grow thin, to be emaciated.

TRASPINTÁR, *va.* To know from the cards drawn those that are to follow.—*vr.* To be disappointed; to turn out contrary to one's expectation.

TRASPLANTÁR, *va.* To transplant, to remove plants from one soil into another; to migrate.

TRASPLÁNTE, *sm.* Transplantation.

TRASPONEDÓR, RA, *s.* Transplanter, one who transplants.

TRASPONÉR, *va.* 1. To remove, to transpose, to transport. 2. To take a circuitous road in order to get out of sight. 3. To hide, to conceal. 4. To transplant.—*vr.* 1. To be drowsy or sleepy. 2. To set below the horizon; applied to the sun and planets.

TRASPONTÍN, *sm.* (Fam.) V. *Trasero.*

TRASPORTAMIÉNTO, *sm.* V. *Transportamiento.*

TRASPORTÁR, *va.* V. *Transportar.*

TRASPUÉSTA, *sf.* 1. Transport, removal. 2. Corner or turning of a mountain, which serves for a lurking-place. 3. Flight, disappearance. 4. Back-yard or court; back-door; out offices at the back of a dwelling-house.

TRASPUÉSTO, TA, *pp. irreg.* Transported.

TRASQUÁRTO, *sm.* Back-room.

TRASQUÉRO, *sm.* Leather-cutter, one whose profession is to cut out strong leather thongs.

TRASQUILADÉRO, *sm.* Place where sheep are shorn.

TRASQUILADÓR, *sm.* Shearer, one who shears.

TRASQUILADÚRA, *sf.* The act of shearing.

TRASQUILÁR, *va.* 1. To shear sheep; to cut the hair in an irregular manner; to clip the hair without order. 2. To clip, to curtail, to diminish.

TRASQUILIMÓCHO, CHA, *a.* (Joc.) Close shorn [or cropped.

TRASQUILÓN, *sm.* 1. Cut of the shears; as much wool or hair as is cut off by one snap of the shears or scissors. *A' trasquilones,* Irregularly, rudely, in an ugly manner. 2. Part of one's fortune, which has been clipped or lost through the fraudulent proceedings of others.

TRASTÁNO, *sm.* (Ant.) V. *Zancadilla.*

TRÁSTE, *sm.* 1. Fret, a thing tied round the neck or handle of a guitar, to distinguish the points of the diapason. 2. A small glass or cup, kept in wine-cellars for the use of wine-tasters. 3. V. *Trasto. Sin trastes,* Without head or tail; in a disorderly manner.

TRASTEÁDO, *sm.* Number of strings tied round the neck of a lute or guitar.

TRASTEADÓR, RA, *s.* A noisy fellow, who throws every thing into disorder and confusion; one who in a blusterous manner removes furniture from one room into another.

TRASTEÁNTE, *pa.* Dexterous performer on the [guitar.

TRASTEÁR, *va.* 1. To tie frets round the neck or handle of a guitar. 2. To remove furniture from one part of a house to another. 3. To play well on the guitar. 4. To talk upon a subject in a smart and lively manner.

Trastejadór, *sm.* Tiler, one whose profession is to cover houses with tiles.

Trastejadúra, *sf.* V. *Trastejo.*

Trastejár, *va.* To tile; to cover with tiles; to repair. *Por aqui trastejan,* Thither they repair; applied to debtors who flee the sight of their creditors.

Trastéjo, *sm.* Tiling, the act of covering houses with tiles.

Trastéra, *sf.* Lumber-room.

Trastería, *sf.* 1. Heap of lumber. 2. A ridiculous or foolish action.

Trasterminánte, *sm.* Travelling flock of sheep.

Trasterminár, *va.* V. *Transterminar.*

Trastesádo, da, *a.* Hardened, solid.

Trastiénda, *sf.* 1. Back-room behind a shop. 2. Prudence, precaution, forecast.

Trásto, *sm.* 1. Furniture, all sorts of moveables or goods put in a house for use or ornament. 2. Useless person, puppy. *Trastos excusados,* Useless lumber. *Trastos,* Useful arms, as sword, dagger, &c.

Trastornáble, *a.* 1. Moveable; easily turned topsyturvy. 2. Fickle, restless.

Trastornadór, ra, *s.* Disturber, a turbulent person.

Trastornadúra, *sf.* Overturning, inversion, perversion.

Trastornamiénto, *sm.* Act of overturning, inverting.

Trastornár, *va.* 1. To turn upside down, to invert, to overthrow; to confuse, to perplex the mind. 2. To persuade, to prevail upon.

Trastórno, *sm.* The act of turning upside down.

Trastrabádo, da, *a.* Applied to a horse with the far hind foot and the near fore foot white.

Trastrígo, *sm.* Wheat of the best quality.

Trastrocamiénto, *sm.* Transposition, inversion, change of order.

Trastrocár, *va.* To invert or change the order of things.

Trastruéco y Trastruéque, *sm.* Inversion, change of order.

Trastuélo, *sm. dim.* Little useless person.

Trastumbár, *vn.* To throw down, to overturn, to overset.

Trasudadaménte, *ad.* With sweat and fatigue.

Trasudár, *va.* 1. To sweat, to perspire. 2. To apply one's self to some business with assiduity and care.

Trasudór, *sm.* A gentle sweat.

Trasuntár, *va.* 1. To copy, to transcribe. 2. To abridge, to make shorter in words.

Trasuntivaménte, *ad.* Compendiously.

Trasúnto, *sm.* 1. Copy, transcript. 2. Likeness, close resemblance. *El es un trasunto de su padre,* He is the picture of his father.

Trasvenárse, *vr.* 1. To be forced out of the arteries or veins; applied to blood. 2. To be spilled, to be lost by shedding.

Trasvertér, *vn.* To overflow, to run over the brim of a vessel.

Trasvinárse, *vr.* 1. To leak, to ooze out of a vessel; applied to wine. 2. To be guessed, surmised or supposed.

Trasvolár, *vn.* To fly across.

Tratáble, *a.* Tractable, ductile, flexible.

Tratadíllo, co, to, *sm.* A brief tract or treatise.

Tratadísta, *s. com.* Author of treatises.

Tratádo, *sm.* Treaty; treatise.

Tratadór, ra, *s.* Mediator, arbitrator, umpire.

Tratamiénto, *sm.* 1. Treatment, usage, manner of using. 2. Compellation, style of address.

Tratánte, *sm.* Dealer in provisions, who buys by wholesale and sells by retail. *Tratante de caballos,* Dealer in horses, horse-jockey.

Tratár, *va.* 1. To touch, to handle. 2. To treat on a subject, to discuss; to confer, to consult. 3. To traffic, to trade. 4. To manage, to conduct. 5. To use, to treat. 6. (Met.) To study or be careful to attain an object.—*vr.* To entertain a friendly intercourse; to be on terms of friendship and intimacy; to live well or ill. *Tratar con dios,* To meditate, to pray. *Tratar verdad,* To profess or love the truth.

Tratíllo, *sm.* A peddling trade.

Tráto, *sm.* 1. Treatment, usage, behaviour, conduct; manner, address. 2. Trade, traffic. 3. Friendly intercourse; criminal conversation between man and woman. 4. Treachery, infidelity. 5. Religious meditation, prayer. 6. Compellation; style of address. *Trato de cuerda,* Punishment by suspending the criminal by the hands tied behind his back; in this state he is raised up and let fall again in the air; (Met.) bad conduct with any one.

Travérsas, *sf. pl.* (Naút.) Back-stays.

Través, *sm.* 1. Inclination to one side, bias. 2. Misfortune, calamity, adversity. 3. (Fort.) Traverse, an outwork with a ditch and parapet to defend a narrow pass. *De través al través,* Across, athwart. *Por el través,* (Naút.) On the beam. *Por la proa del través,* (Naút.) Before the beam. *Por la popa del través,* (Naút.) Abaft the beam. *Por el través de las barbas,* (Naút.) Athwart hawse. *Viento por el través,* (Naút.) Wind on the beam. *Por el través de Margate,* (Naút.) Abreast of Margate. *Ir al traves,* To go to any place not to return; applied to Spanish ships.

Travesáño, *sm.* 1. Cross-timber. V. *Atravesaño.* 2. Long bolster of a bed.

Travesár, *va.* To cross. V. *Atravesar.*

Traveseár, *vn.* 1. To be uneasy; to run to and fro in a restless manner; to traverse. 2. To jest, to joke. 3. To lead a debauched life; to behave improperly.

Traveséro, *sm.* Bolster of a bed.

Traverséro, ra, *a.* Transverse, across. *Flauta traversera,* A German flute.

Travesía, *sf.* 1. Oblique or transverse position or manner. 2. Distance, road, passage. *Hacer buena travesia,* (Naút.) To have a fine passage. 3. Fortification with traverses. 4. Money won or lost at gambling. 5. (Naút.) Side wind.

Travesío, ía, *a.* 1. Traversing; applied to cattle that traverse the limits of their pasture. 2. Transverse, oblique or lateral wind.

Travesío, *sm.* Place where persons or things cross; transitory place.

Travestído, da, *a.* Disguised.

Travesúra, *sf.* 1. The act of running to and fro in a restless manner. 2. Prank, ludicrous trick. 3. Penetration, lively fancy; sprightly conversation. 4. Wickedness, obscenity.

TRAVIÉSA, *sf.* 1. Oblique position, passage. V. *Travesía.* 2. Wager or bet laid by bystanders at card-tables.

TRAVIÉSO, SA, *a.* 1. Transverse, oblique. 2. Restless, uneasy; turbulent, noisy. 3. Lively, playful. 4. Intemperate, lewd, debauched. *Ser de mesa traviesa,* To be an old member of a corps or society.

TRAYCIÓN, *sf.* Treason, disloyalty. *A' traycion,* Treasonably. *La traycion aplace, mas no el que la hace,* (Ref.) Men love the treason, but they hate the traitor.

TRAYCIONÉRO, RA, *a.* Treasonous.

TRAYDÓR, RA, *a.* 1. Treacherous, perfidious, false. 2. Insidious, deceitful; applied to animals.—*sm.* Traitor.

TRAYDORAMÉNTE, *ad.* Treasonably, treacherously.

TRAYDORCÍCO, CA; LLO, LLA; TO, TA, *a. dim.* of [*traydor.*

TRAYÉNTE, *pa.* Bringer, conductor.

TRÁZA, *sf.* 1. First sketch or draught, trace, outline. 2. Plan, scheme, project; means. 3. Arrangement, proportion, symmetry. 4. Appearance, aspect, prospect. *Tiene la traza de un picaro,* He has the looks of a rogue.

TRAZÁDO, DA, *a.* Traced, outlined. *Bien ó mal trazado,* Person of a good or bad disposition or figure.

TRAZADÓR, RA, *s.* Planner, one who draws the [first sketch or plan.

TRAZÁR, *va.* 1. To contrive, to devise, to plan, to project. 2. To draw the first sketch or plan.

TRÁZO, *sm.* 1. Sketch, plan, design, project. 2. Moulding. V. *Linea.* *Trázos,* (Pint.) Folds of the drapery.

TRAZUMÁRSE, *vr.* To leak, to ooze. V. *Rezumarse.*

TREBÁLLA, *sf.* Sauce for goose, consisting of almonds, garlic, bread, eggs, spices, verjuice, sugar, and cinnamon, mixed together.

TRÉBEDES, *sf. pl.* Trevet, a tripod.

TREBEJÁR, *vn.* To play merry tricks, to jest, to sneer, to scoff.

TREBÉJO, *sm.* 1. Top, play-thing. 2. Fun, jest, joke.—*pl.* 1. Men, the pieces of a chess-board. 2. Implements, tools of any art or trade.

TREBELIÁNICA ó QUARTA TREBELIÁNICA, *sf.* The fourth part of an estate, to be deducted by the fiduciary heir, who holds it in trust for another.

TREBÓL, *sm.* (Bot.) Trefoil, clover. Trifolium *L.* *Trebol real,* (Bot.) Melilot. Trifolium italicum vel melilotus *L.*

TRÉCE, *a.* 1. Thirteen, ten and three. *Estarse en sus trece,* To persist, to execute with perseverance. 2. Thirteenth. V. *Decimotercio.*—*sm.* 1. The character or cipher 13. 2. One of the 13 governors in some ancient cities. 3. In the order of *Santiago* or St. James, one of the 13 knights nominated to a general chapter.

TRECEMESÍNO, NA, *a.* Thirteen months old.

TRECENÁRIO, *sm.* Number of thirteen days dedicated to any object.

TRECENÁTO ó TRECENÁZGO, *sm.* Office in the order of Santiago for which 13 knights are chosen.

TRECÉNO, NA, *a.* Thirteenth, the ordinal number [of thirteen.

TRECÉSIMO, MA, *a.* Thirtieth, the ordinal number of thirty.

TRECHÉL, *sm.* (Bot.) Red or brown wheat. Triticum subrubrum *L.*

TRÉCHO, *sm.* Space, distance of time or place. *A' trechos,* By intervals.

TRECIÉNTOS, TAS, *a.* Three hundred.

TRÉFE, *a.* 1. Lean, thin, meager. 2. Spurious, adulterated. 3. Afflicted with a consumption.

TREFEDÁD, *sf.* Consumption, hectic fever.

TRÉGUA, *sf.* Truce, cessation of hostilities; rest, repose.

TRÉINTA, *a.* Thirty, thrice ten.

TREINTANÁRIO ó TREINTENÁRIO, *sm.* Space of thirty days; thirty masses said for a person deceased.

TREINTAÑÁL, *a.* Containing thirty years.

TREINTÉNA, *sf.* The thirtieth part. [of thirty.

TREINTÉNO, NA, *a.* Thirtieth, the ordinal number

TRÉJA, *sf.* Mode of playing at billiards.

TREMADÁL, *sm.* V. *Tremedal.*

TREMEBÚNDO, DA, *a.* Dreadful, frightful.

TREMEDÁL, *sm.* Quagmire, a marshy ground.

TREMÉNDO, DA, *a.* 1. Tremendous, dreadful, terrible, formidable. 2. Awful, grand; worthy of respect and veneration.

TREMÉNTE, *pa.* Trembling.

TREMENTÍNA, *sf.* Turpentine, a resinous substance, obtained from the turpentine tree.

TREMÉR, *vn.* To tremble. [old.

TREMÉS ó TREMESÍNO, NA, *a.* Three months

TREMIÉLGA, *sf.* (Ict.) Electric ray. V. *Torpedo.*

TREMÍS, *sm.* Ancient gold coin.

TREMÓ, *sm.* Ornament in the manner of a frame, put round looking-glasses fixed in walls.

TREMOLÁNTE, *pa.* Waving in the air.

TREMOLÁR, *va.* (Naút.) To hoist the colours, jacks or pendants.—*vn.* To shiver; to be moved by the air.

TREMOLÍNA, *sf.* Rustling of the wind; bustle, confused noise.

TREMÓR, *sm.* Trembling.

TREMULAMÉNTE, *ad.* Tremblingly.

TREMULÁNTE, TREMULÉNTO, TA; Y TRÉMULO, LA, *a.* Tremulous, trembling.

TRÉN, *sm.* 1. Travelling equipage, train, retinue. 2. Show, pomp, ostentation.

TRÉNA, *sf.* Scarf, sash. 2. Garland of flowers. 3. (Cant.) Prison, jail. 4. Burnt silver.

TRENÁDO, DA, *a.* Reticulated, formed of network or platted strands.

TRÉNCAS, *sf. pl.* Two pieces of wood put across in a bee-hive. *Meterse hasta las trencas en algun negocio,* To be deeply implicated or involved in an affair.

TRENCELLÍN, TRENCÍLLA Y TRENCÍLLO, *s.* Hatband of gold or silver, garnished with jewels.

TRENCÍCA, LLA, TA, *sf. dim.* of *trenza.*

TRENCILLÁR, *va.* To garnish with a band of gold or silver lace and jewels.

TRENÉO, *sm.* Sledge.

TRÉNOS, *sm. pl.* Lamentations.

TRÉNQUE, *sm.* Mole or bank to turn off the current of a river.

TRENTÉNO, NA, *a.* (Ant.) V. *Trienteno.*

TRÉNZA, *sf.* Braided hair, platted silk.

TRENZADÉRA, *sf.* Tape. V. *Trenzadera.*

TRENZÁDO, *sm.* Braided hair.

TRENZÁR, *va.* To braid the hair.

TRÉO, *sm.* (Naút.) Square-sail, cross-jack-sail.

TRÉPA, *sf.* 1. Climbing, the act of climbing. 2. Edging sewed to clothes by way of ornament. 3. Flogging, lashing, beating. *Trepas,* Artful tricks, wiles, cunningness; malice; subtlety.

Trepacabállos, *sm.* (Bot.) Star-thistle, star knap-weed. Centaurea calcitrapa *L.*

Trepádo, da, *a.* Strong, robust.

Trepádo, *sm.* Edging sewed on clothes.

Trepadór, ra, *s.* Climber; a climbing place.

Trepanár, *va.* To trepan, to perforate with a trepan.

Trépano, *sm.* 1. Trepan, an instrument with which surgeons cut out round pieces of the skull. 2. Borer, piercer, a kind of drill used by stone-cutters. 3. Mould or frame used in paper-mills.

Trepánte, *a.* Wily, artful, crafty.

Trepár, *vn.* To climb; to creep upon supports; applied to ivy and other similar plants.—*va.* 1. To ornament with edging. 2. To trepan.

Trepidación, *sf.* Dread, fear, trepidation.

Trepidánte, *a.* V. *Temeroso y Tremulo.*

Trépido, da, *a.* Tremulous.

Tres, *a.* 1. Three, an unequal number, consisting of two and one. 2. Third. V. *Tercero.*—*sm.* 1. The character or figure 3. *Con dos treses,* With two threes. 2. Counters, any coin given to children as play-things; card with three spots. 3. Magistrate of a city which is governed by three magistrates. *Capitulo tres,* Third chapter. *Tres veces,* Three times, very.

Tresañéjo, ja, *a.* Three years old; done three years ago.

Tresdoblár, *va.* To triple. V. *Triplicar.*

Tresdóble, *sm.* The state or quality of being threefold.

Tresíllo, *sm.* Ombre, a game at cards played by three.

Tresmesíno, na, *a.* V. *Tremesino.*

Tresnál, *sm.* Collection of triangular plots of ground disposed for irrigation.

Trespasár, *va.* (Ant.) V. *Traspasar.*

Tresquiladéro, *sm.* Shearing place. V. *Trasquiladero.*

Tresquiladúra, *sf.* V. *Trasquiladura.*

Tresquilár, *va.* To shear. V. *Trasquilar.*

Trestánto, *sm.* V. *Triplo.*—*ad.* Three times as much.

Trestíga, *sf.* (Ant.) V. *Cloaca.*

Tréta, *sf.* 1. Thrust in fencing. 2. Trick, wile, artifice.

Tréudo y Tréudes, *s.* Trevet. V. *Trebedes.*

Treznár, *va.* (Arag.) V. *Atresnalar.*

Tría, *sf.* Frequent entering and going out of bees in a strong hive.

Triáca, *sf.* Theriaca, treacle; any antidote, preservative, or preventive.

Triacál, *a.* Made of treacle, theriacal.

Triangguládo, da, *a.* Made in the shape of a triangle.

Trianggulár, *a.* Triangular, forming three angles.

Triangularménte, *ad.* In a triangular form.

Triánguulo, la, *a.* Triangular.

Triánggulo, *sm.* Triangle, a figure of three sides and three angles. *Triangulo quadrantal,* Spheric triangle having one or more sides quadrants. *Triangulo ambligonio, escaleno, esférico, isóceles, ortogonio, ú oxígonio,* An obtuse-angled, scalene, spheric, isosceles, rectangled, or acute-angled triangle. *Triangulo austral y boreal,* (Astr.) Southern and northern triangle, constellations so called.

Triaquéra, *sf.* Vessel for theriaca or other medicine.

Triaquéro, *sm.* Chemist and druggist, who retails theriaca, treacle, and other medicaments.

Triár, *vn.* To go out and in frequently, as bees in a beehive; to work, as bees.

Triário, *sm.* Veteran Roman soldier forming a reserve corps in rear.

Tribáquio, *sm.* Foot of Latin verse consisting of three short syllables.

Tribón, *sm.* A triangular musical instrument.

Tríbu ó Tribu, *s. com.* Tribe.

Tribuír, *va.* To attribute. V. *Atribuir.*

Tribulación, *sf.* Tribulation, affliction.

Tribulánte, *pa.* Afflicting.

Tribulár, *va.* To afflict. V. *Atribular.*

Tríbulo, *sm.* 1. (Bot.) Caltrop. V. *Abrojo.* 2. Condolence, expression of grief, lamentation.

Tribúna, *sf.* Tribune, gallery or pew in a church.

Tribunádo, *sm.* Dignity of tribune.

Tribunál, *sm.* 1. Hall, where judges meet to administer justice. 2. Tribunal, court of justice.

Tribunáli (Pro), *ad.* 1. In halls and public courts with the dress and accompaniments of a judge. 2. In a decisive tone, decisively.

Tribúnico, ca; y Tribunício, cia, *a.* Belonging to a tribune.

Tribúno, *sm.* Tribune, a magistrate of ancient Rome.

Tributación, *sf.* 1. Tribute, contribution. V. *Tributo.* 2. Alienation of property.

Tributár, *va.* 1. To pay taxes or contributions. 2. To pay homage and respect. 3. To mark the limits of sheep-walks. 4. To put on a trevet.

Tributário, ria, *a.* Liable to pay taxes on contributions, tributary.

Tribúto, *sm.* 1. Tax, contribution. 2. V. *Censo.* 3. (Arag.) Trevet. 4. (Cant.) Courtezan, handsome prostitute.

Trica ó Trícas, *s.* Quibbles, sophisms, captious reasoning, cavillation.

Tricenál, *a.* Continuing thirty years.

Tricentésimo, na, *a.* Containing three hundred.

Tricésimo, ma, *a.* Thirtieth, the ordinal number of thirty.

Tricípite, *a.* Three-headed.

Triclínio, *sm.* Dining-room of the ancient Romans.

Tricolór, *a.* Tricoloured.

Tricórne, *a.* Three-horned, having three horns.

Tridénte, *a.* Having three teeth.—*sm.* Trident; fishing instrument.

Tridentífero, ra, *a.* Bearing a trident.

Triduáno, na, *a.* Tertian, consisting of three days.

Tríduo, *sm.* Space of three days.

Triebál, *a.* Triennial, lasting three years; happening once in three years.

Triénio, *sm.* Space of three years.

Trieñál, *a.* Triennial.

Trifáuce, *a.* (Poét.) Three-throated.

Trífido, da, *a.* (Poét.) Three-cleft, open in three parts.

Trifólio, *sm.* Trefoil. V. *Trebol.*

Trifórme, *a.* Having three different forms or shapes.

Trigáza, *sf.* Short straw of wheat.

Trigésimo, ma, *a.* Thirtieth, the ordinal number of thirty.

Trigélla y Trígola, *sf.* (Ict.) Red sur-mullet. Mullus barbatus *L.*

Tríglifo, *sm.* (Arq.) Triglyph.

Trígo, *sm.* (Bot.) Wheat. Triticum *L. Trigo de las indias.* V. *Maiz. Echar por esos trigos,* To speak without thinking. *Trigos,* Crops; corn-fields.

Trígono, *sm.* 1. (Astr.) Three celestial signs. 2. (Geom.) Radius of the signs.

Trigonometría, *sf.* Trigonometry, the art of measuring triangles.

Trigonométrico, ca, *a.* Trigonometrical.

Trigueño, ña, *a.* Swarthy, of a brownish colour.

Triguéra, *sf.* 1. (Bot.) Common wheat-grass. Triticum repens *L.* 2. Canary seed.

Trigueró, ra, *a.* Growing among wheat.

Trigueró, *sm.* 1. Sieve for sifting corn. 2. Corn-merchant, corn-factor.

Trilíngüe, *a.* Talking three languages.

Trílla, *sf.* 1. (Ict.) Red sur-mullet. Mullus barbatus *L.* 2. A sort of harrow used for separating corn from chaff. 3. The act or time of thrashing.

Trilladéra, *sf.* A kind of harrow used to separate corn from chaff.

Trilládo, da, *a.* 1. Thrashed, beaten. 2. Trite, stale, hackneyed. *Camino trillado,* Beaten track; common routine.

Trilladór, *sm.* Thrasher.

Trilladúra, *sf.* Act of thrashing.

Trillár, *va.* 1. To thrash, to separate corn from the chaff; to tread out corn. 2. To beat, to abuse. 3. To frequent, to visit often; to repeat.

Tríllo, *sm.* A kind of harrow, used in Spain for thrashing or separating corn from the chaff.

Triméstre, *sm.* Space of three months.

Trimiélga, *sf.* V. *Torpedo.*

Trín, *sm.* A sort of linen manufactured in Piedmont.

Trinácrio, ia, *a.* (Poét.) Sicilian.

Trinádo, *sm.* Trill, shake, quaver, tremulous sound.

Trinár, *vn.* To trill, to quaver, to shake the voice; to speak in a tremulous voice.

Trínca, *sf.* 1. Assemblage of three things, or persons of the same class or description. 2. (Naút.) Any cord or rope used for lashing or making fast. *A' la trinca,* (Naut.) Close-hauled. *Trincas,* (Naút.) Seizings. *Trincas del bauprés,* (Naut.) Gammoning of the bow-sprit. [turn or knot.

Trincafía, *sf.* (Naut.) Closehitch, a kind of

Trincafiár, *va.* (Naút.) To marl.

Trincapiñónes, *sm.* Rake, a dissolute youth.

Trincár, *va.* 1. To break, to chop, to divide into small pieces. 2. To leap, to skip, to hop. 3. (Naút.) To keep close to the wind. *Trincar los cabos,* (Naút.) To fasten the rope-ends. *Trincar las puertas,* (Naút.) To bar in the port-lids.

Trinchánte, *sm.* 1. Carver, one who carves at table. 2. Carving-knife. 3. Yeoman of the mouth.

Trinchár, *va.* To carve, to cut up, to divide meat; to dispose or decide with an air of authority.

Trinchéas, *sf. pl.* Trenches, entrenchments.

Trincheár, *va.* To entrench. V. *Atrincherar.*

Trinchéra, *sf.* (Fort.) Trench, entrenchment, ditch cut in the earth to cover the troops from the enemy's fire. *Ramal de trinchera,* (Fort.) Boyau.

Trincherár, *va.* (Fort.) To entrench, to make trenches or entrenchments.

Trinchéro y Trinchéo, *sm.* Wooden plate on which meat is cut and eaten at table; trencher.

Trincherón, *sm.* Dish or large trencher.

Trinchéte, *sm.* Knife used by shoe-makers; chisel used by stone-cutters. V. *Tranchete.*

Trínoos, *sm.* (Orn.) Kind of stork like a swan.

Trinéo, *sm.* Sledge, sled.

Trinidád, *sf.* Trinity, the incomprehensible union of three persons in the Godhead. *Meterse en trinidades,* To endeavour to find out what is impossible to be known.

Trinitário, ria, *a.* Trinitarian.

Trinitária, *sf.* (Bot.) Three-coloured violet; pansy, heart's ease. Viola tricolor *L.*

Tríno, na, *a.* Containing three distinct things.

Tríno, *sm.* (Astr.) 1. Trine. 2. Trill. V. *Trinado.*

Trinómio, *sm.* (Alg.) Number produced by the addition of three incommensurable quantities.

Trinquetáda, *sf.* (Naút.) Sailing under the foresail.

Trinquéte, *sm.* 1. (Naút.) Foremast, foresail; trinquet. 2. Tennis, a game played with balls. *A' cada trinquete,* At every step.

Trinquetílla, *sf.* (Naút.) Fore-stay-sail.

Trío, *sm.* 1. Working of bees in a hive. 2 Trio, musical composition.

Triónes, *sm.* (Astr.) Stars, called Charles's Wain.

Trípa, *sf.* 1. Gut, tripe, intestine. 2. Female belly big with young; belly or wide part of vessels. *Tripas,* Core, the inner part of some fruit; intestines. *Tripas del jarro,* (Joc.) The wine contained in a jar. *Tripas del cagalar,* Rectum.

Tripartído, da, *a.* Divided into three parts.

Tripartír, *va.* To divide into three parts.

Tripartíto, ta, *a.* Tripartite, divided into three parts.

Tripástos, *sm.* Pulley with three sheaves.

Trípe, *sm.* Shag, a kind of woollen cloth.

Tripería, *sf.* Shop where tripes are sold; a heap of tripes.

Tripéro, ra, *s.* One who sells tripes. *Tripéro,* Woollen belt to keep the belly warm.

Tripicalléro, ra, *s.* Dealer in tripes.

Tripílla, *sf.* A small gut.

Tripitrápe, *sm.* 1. (Fam.) Heap of old furniture and lumber. 2. Confusion of thoughts or ideas.

Tripitrópa, *sf.* (Fam.) Convulsion of the intestines or bowels.

Tríple, *a.* Triple, treble.

Tríplica, *sf.* (For.) Rejoinder.

Triplicár, *va.* 1. To multiply by three, to make threefold. 2. (For.) To rejoin.

Tríplice, *a.* Treble, including any quantity three times. [things.

Triplicidád, *sf.* Triplicity, union of three

Tríplo, la, *a.* Treble.

Trípode, *sf.* Tripod.—*s. com.* Tripod.

Trípói, *sf.* Tripoli.

Tripólio, *sm.* (Bot.) Sea starwort. Aster tripolium *L.*

Tripón, na, *a.* Having a large gut or paunch.

Triptóngo, *sm.* Triphthong, coalition of three vowels to form one sound.

Tripudiánte, *pa.* Dancer.
Tripudiár, *vn.* To dance.
Tripúdio, *sm.* Dance, ball.
Tripúdo, da, *a.* Gorbellied, big-bellied.
Tripulación, *sf.* (Naút.) Crew of a ship.
Tripuládo, da, *a.* (Naút.) Manned, equipped. *Navío tripulado con seis cientos hombres*, (Naút.) Ship manned with six hundred men.
Tripulár, *va.* 1. (Naút.) To man ships. 2. To interpolate, to mix.
Triquéte, *sm.* V. *Trinquete.* *A' cada triquéte*, At every stir or step.
Triquiñuéla, *sf.* (Fam.) Cheat, defraud; applied either to dealing or gaming.
Triquitráque, *sm.* 1. Crack, clack, clattering, clashing. 2. Rocket, serpent, artificial firework.
Triréme, *sf.* (Naút.) Trireme, galley with three ranks of oars on each side.
Tris, *sm.* 1. Noise made by the breaking of glass. 2. Trice, a short time, an instant. *Venir en un tris*, To come in an instant. *Estar en un tris*, To be on the verge of; to be on the point of.
Trísa, *sf.* (Ict.) V. *Sábalo.*
Triságio, *sm.* Angelic chorus of holy, holy, holy; any festivity repeated three days.
Trisarquía, *sf.* Triumvirate, the joint government of three persons.
Trísca, *sf.* Noise made by treading on any thing which breaks under the feet; any noise.
Triscadór, ra, *s.* 1. A noisy, rattling person. 2. (Cant.) Turbulent refractory person.
Triscár, *vn.* 1. To stamp, to make a noise with the feet. 2. To caper, to frisk about.—*va.* To mix; to join, to unite. V. *Trabar.*
Trisecár, *va.* To divide into three equal parts.
Trisección, *sf.* Trisection.
Trisílabo, ba, *a.* Consisting of three syllables.
Tristácho, cha, *a.* Sorrowful, melancholy.
Tríste, *a.* Dull, sad, mournful; wretched, unfortunate; abject, mean, low; without vivacity or cheerfulness.
Tristéga, *sf.* Shore, drain, conduit.
Tristél, *sm.* (Ant.) V. *Clister.*
Tristeménte, *ad.* In a sad mournful manner.
Tristéza, *sf.* Grief, affliction.
Tristícia, Tristúra, y Tristór, (Ant.) V. *Tristeza.*
Tristrás, *sm.* 1. V. *Trastras.* 2. (Fam.) Disgusting repetition of the same thing.
Trisúlco, ca, *a.* Having three points.
Tritíceo, ea, *a.* Triticean, belonging to wheat, wheaten.
Tritón, *sm.* Triton, a sea-demigod.
Tritón, *sm.* Musical interval of three tones.
Trituración, *sf.* Trituration, levigation, pulverization.
Triturár, *va.* To triturate, to reduce to powder, to grind, to pound, to comminute.
Triunfadór, ra, *s.* Conqueror, victor, one who triumphs.
Triunfál, *a.* Triumphal.
Triunfalménte, *ad.* Triumphally.
Triunfánte, *a.* Triumphant, pompous, magnificent.
Triunfanteménte, *ad.* Triumphantly.
Triunfár, *vn.* 1. To conquer, to gain a victory. 2. To triumph, to celebrate a victory; to conquer the passions. 3. To make an idle show of grandeur and wealth. 4. To trump at cards.
Triúnfo, *sm.* 1. Triumph, victory; conquest; trophy. 2. Slap with the back of the hand. 3. Trump, a card of a privileged suit.
Triunviráto, ó do, *sm.* Triumvirate.
Triunvíro, *sm.* Triumvir.
Triviál, *a.* 1. Frequented, beaten; applied to a road or path. 2. Trivial, vulgar, common.
Trivialidád, *sf.* Trivialness, vulgarity.
Trivialménte, *ad.* Trivially.
Trívio, *sm.* Cross-road, the point where three roads meet.
Tríza, *sf.* 1. Mite, a small part or particle. 2. Cord, rope.
Troa, *sf.* (Ant.) V. *Hallazgo.*
Trocáble, *a.* Changeable, that can be changed.
Trocadaménte, *ad.* Contrarily, falsely.
Trocádo, *sm.* Change, small coin.
Trocádo, da, *a.* Changed, permuted. *A' la trocada ó trocadilla*, In the contrary sense; in exchange.
Trocadór, ra, *s.* One who exchanges or permutes.
Trocamiénto, *sm.* V. *Trueque.*
Trocár, *va.* 1. To exchange, to barter, to truck; to change, to permute; to equivocate. 2. To vomit, to throw up from the stomach.—*vr.* 1. To be changed or reformed. 2. To exchange seats with another.—*sm.* **Trocar**, a surgical instrument for tapping patients in the dropsy.
Trocatínta, *sf.* A ridiculous barter, or exchange.
Trocatínte, *sm.* Mixed colour, changing colour.
Trocáyco, *a.* Trochaic; consisting of trochees.
Troceár, *va.* To divide into pieces.
Trocéo, *sm.* (Naút.) Parrel.
Trócha, *sf.* A narrow path, which runs across a high road.
Trochemóche (A'), *ad.* Helter-skelter, in confusion and hurry.
Trochuéla, *sf. dim.* A little path.
Trociscár, *va.* To make troches or lozenges.
Trocísco, *sm.* Troche, lozenge, a medicine prepared as a cake with sugar and flour or paste.
Trócla, *sf.* V. *Polea.*
Tróco, *sm.* (Ict.) V. *Rueda.*
Trofeísta, *sm.* Conqueror, victor.
Troféo, *sm.* Trophy, colours or other things taken from an enemy, and treasured up in proof of victory; emblem of triumph; victory. *Trofeos*, Trophies, military insignia.
Troglodíta, *sm.* Troglodyte, a savage, barbarous man; an inhabitant of caves; a voracious eater.
Trómpa, *sf.* 1. Trumpet, a musical wind-instrument. *Trompa de caza con círculos*, A French horn, or hunting horn. *Trompa marina*, A marine trumpet; a musical instrument having only one chord and played with a bow. 2. Proboscis, the snout or trunk of an elephant. 3. A large top. *A' trompa tañida*, At the sound of the trumpet; inconsiderately, rashly. *A' trompa y talega*, Helter-skelter, in confusion and hurry.
Trompáda, *sf.* 1. Blow given with a top. 2. (Naút.) Falling foul or on board of another vessel.
Trompár, *va.* To cheat, to deceive.—*vn.* To whip a top; to play at chess.

Trompázo, *sm.* 1. Blow given with a top or trumpet. 2. Misfortune, adverse accident.
Trompeár, *vn.* To whip a top, to play at chess.
Trompéro, *sm.* 1. Top-maker, one who makes tops for boys. 2. Cheat, impostor.
Trompéro, ra, *a.* Deceptious, false, deceiving.
Trompéta, *sf.* 1. Trumpet, a musical wind-instrument. 2. Trumpet-shell. Buccinum *L. Pobre trompeta*, An idle vulgar prattler.—*sm.* Trumpeter, one who sounds the trumpet.
Trompetázo, *sm.* (Joc.) Stroke with a trumpet.
Trompeteár, *vn.* To sound the trumpet.
Trompetería, *sf.* Pipes of an organ.
Trompetéro, *sm.* Trumpeter; trumpet-maker.
Trompetílla, *sf.* 1. A small trumpet. 2. An instrument in the shape of a horn or trumpet, to help the hearing. 3. Trunk or sting of gnats, and other similar insects.
Trompezár, *vn.* V. *Tropezar.*
Trompicár, *vn.* To stumble frequently; to falter.—*va.* 1. To obtain in an irregular manner an employment, which in justice belonged to another. 2. To trip, to occasion stumbling.
Trompíco, *sm. dim.* A small top.
Trompicón, *sm.* Stumbling. V. *Tropezon.*
Trompillár, *vn.* To stumble; to falter.
Trómpo, *sm.* 1. Man at chess. 2. Whipping-top. *Ponerse como un trompo*, (Met.) To be as full as a top; to eat or drink to satiety.
Trompón, *sm.* A big top. *A' trompon ó de trompon*, In an irregular or disorderly manner.
Tron, *sm.* Report of fire-arms.
Tronáda, *sf.* Thunderstorm.
Tronadór, ra, *s.* 1. Thunderer, thundering. 2. Squib, cracker, rocket; cohorn.
Tronánte, *pa.* Thundering.
Tronár, *vn.* To thunder, to make a noise like thunder, or the discharge of guns.
Troncál, *a.* Belonging to the trunk or stock, or proceeding from it.
Troncalidád, *sf.* Lineage, race, family.
Troncár, *va.* 1. To truncate, to mutilate, to cut off. 2. To interrupt a conversation, to cut the thread of a discourse.
Tronchádo, *a.* (Blas.) Applied to a shield having a diagonal bar.
Tronchár, *va.* To cut by the trunk or root; to break with violence.
Troncházo, *sm.* A large stalk; a blow with a stalk or stem.
Tróncho, *sm.* Sprig, stem or stalk of garden plants. *Bravo troncho de mozo*, (Fam.) Stout well-disposed youth.
Tronchúdo, da, *a.* Having a long stem or stalk.
Trónco, *sm.* 1. Trunk, the body of a tree. 2. Stock, the origin of a family. 3. Trunk, the body of an animal without the head and limbs. 4. An illiterate, despicable, and useless person. 5. Hind pair of horses in a coach.
Trónco, ca, *a.* Truncated, cut, mutilated.
Troncón, *sm.* A large stalk or trunk; a large log of wood.
Tronéra, *sf.* 1. (Art.) Embrasure of a battery. 2. Dormer, a small sky-light. 3. A harebrained foolish person. 4. Paper cracker; squib. 5. (Mil.) Loop-hole. *Troneras*, Holes and pockets of truck and billiard-tables.
Tronerár, *va.* V. *Atronerar.*

Trónga, *sf.* Woman of pleasure, prostitute.
Tronído, *sm.* Thunder. V. *Trueno.*
Tronitóso, sa, *a.* Resounding, thundering.
Tróno, *sm.* Throne, an elevated imperial or royal seat; the seat of an emperor or king; royal dignity; seat of the image of a saint. *Tronos*, Thrones, seventh choir of angels.
Tronquísta, *sm.* Coachman that drives a pair of horses.
Tronzár, *va.* 1. To shatter, to break into pieces. 2. To plait, to fold.
Trónzo, za, *a.* Having one or both ears cut off.
Trópa, *sf.* 1. Troops, soldiers. 2. Troop, a small body of horse. 3. Crowd, multitude; heap or mass. 4. Beat to arms. *Tropa de marina*, Marines. *Levantar las tropas*, To raise the camp. *En tropa*, In crowds, without regularity and order.
Tropél, *sm.* 1. Noise made by a quick movement of the feet. 2. Hurry, bustle, confusion. 3. Heap of things, confusedly tumbled together. 4. (Mil.) Ancient troop. *De tropel*, In a tumultuous and confused manner.
Tropelía, *sf.* 1. Precipitation, hurry, confusion. 2. Vexation, oppression, injustice.
Tropellár, *va.* To trample, to tread under foot. V. *Atropellar.*
Tropezadéro, *sm.* A slippery place; a bad, uneven road or path.
Tropezádo, da, *a.* Stumbled, obstructed. *Conserva tropezada*, Conserve made of very small pieces.
Tropezadór, ra, *s.* Tripper, stumbler
Tropezadúra, *sf.* Stumbling, obstructing, entangling.
Tropezár, *vn.* 1. To stumble, to trip in walking. 2. To be detained or obstructed. 3. To slip or slide into crimes or blunders. 4. To wrangle, to dispute.—*va.* 1. To discover a fault or defect. 2. To meet accidentally or casually.—*vr.* To stumble, to cut the feet in walking; applied to horses. *Sin tropezar en barras*, Inconsiderately, rashly.
Tropezón, na, *a.* Stumbling, tripping frequently. *A' tropezones*, With a variety of impediments and obstructions.
Tropezón, *sm.* 1. V. *Tropiezo.* 2. Act of tripping.
Tropezóso, sa, *a.* Apt to stumble or trip.
Trópico, *sm.* Tropic, the extreme limit of the sun's northern or southern declension from the equator.
Trópico, ca, *a.* 1. (Astr.) Tropical. 2. (Ret.) Containing tropes.
Tropiézo, *sm.* 1. Stumble, trip. 2. Obstacle, obstruction, impediment. 3. Slip, fault, error. 4. Difficulty, embarrassment. 5. Quarrel, dispute.
Tropílla, *sf.* A small body or detachment of troops.
Trópo, *sm.* Trope, a rhetorical change of a word from its original meaning.
Tropología, *sf.* Tropology, a moral discourse.
Tropológico, ca, *a.* Tropological, belonging to tropology.
Tróque, *sm.* Exchange, barter.
Troquél, *sm.* Die or dye, a solid piece of steel, in which a hollow figure is engraved.
Troquéo, *sm.* Trochee, a foot used in Latin

poetry, consisting of a long and short syllable.

Troquílo, *sm* (Arq.) Trochilus, concave moulding next the torus.

Trotáda, *sf.* Stretch, route, way.

Trotadór, ra, *s.* Trotter.

Trota Conventos, *sf.* (Fam.) V. *Alcahueta.*

Trotár, *vn.* To trot; to move swiftly, to be in haste.—*va.* To make a horse trot.

Tróte, *sm.* Trot, a jolting pace of a horse. *A' trote,* In a trot; in haste or hastily.

Trotéro, *sm.* V. *Correo.*

Trotíllo, *sm.* A light trot.

Trotón, na, *a.* Trotting high; spoken of a horse.—*sm.* V. *Caballo.*

Trotonería, *sf.* A continual trot.

Tróva, *sf.* Metrical composition. V. *Verso.*

Trovadór, ra, *s.* 1. Versifier, poet. 2. Finder.

Trovár, *va.* 1. (Arag.) To find by chance or accidentally. 2. To versify, to make verses. 3. To imitate a metrical composition by turning it to another subject. 4. To invert or pervert the sense of any thing.

Trovísta, *sm.* Finder, one that finds; versifier.

Trox ó Tróxe, *sf.* 1. Granary, a store-house for grain. 2. Congregation of the faithful; the church.

Tróxa ó Troxáda, *sf.* Knapsack, a bag in which soldiers carry their stores.

Troxádo, da, *a.* Contained in a knapsack.

Troxecíllo, *sm.* Kind of seat or compartment made of bricks about 18 inches high, on which the Franciscan friars sleep.

Troxéro, *sm.* Storekeeper, guard of a granary.

Tróya, *sf.* Troy. *Aquí fué Troya,* Here was Troy; applied to the site of any memorable place.

Troyáno, na, *a.* Trojan, native of Troy.

Tróza, *sf.* 1. (Naút.) Parrel. 2. Trunk of a tree sawn into boards.

Trozéo, *sm.* (Naút.) Rope which keeps the yard firm to a mast.

Trózo, *sm.* 1. Piece or part of any thing cut off. 2. (Naút.) Junk, ends of old cables cut into small pieces for making oakum. 3. (Mil.) Division of a column, forming the van or rear guard.

Trucár, *vn.* To play the first card.

Trúcha, *sf.* 1. (Ict.) Trout. Salmo trutta *L.* 2. Crane. V. *Cabria. O' ayunar ó comer trucha,* Either to fast or eat trout; neck or nothing.

Truchimán, na, *a.* Fond of business, or of making agreements.

Truchuéla, *sf.* (Ict.) Small cod-fish. V. *Abadejo.*

Trucidár, *va.* To kill, to destroy.

Trúco, *sm.* A skilful push at trucks. *Trucos,* Trucks, a game somewhat resembling billiards.

Truculéncia, *sf.* Truculence, ferocity.

Truculénto, ta, *a.* Truculent, fierce, cruel.

Trué, *sm.* A sort of fine white linen, manufactured at Troyes. The Madrid-traders call it *Troé.*

Truéco, *sm.* Exchange, barter. V. *Trueque. A' trueco ó en trueco,* In exchange.

Truéno, *sm.* 1. Thunder; report of fire-arms; a loud noise like thunder. 2. Ancient piece of artillery.

Truéque, *sm.* 1. Exchange, barter. 2. V. *Vómito.*

Trués, *sm. pl.* Linens or cloth made at Troyes.

Trúfa, *sf.* 1. Imposition, fraud, deceit. 2. (Bot.) Truffle. Tuber *L.*

Trufadór, ra, *s.* Fabulist, fabler, story-teller, liar.

Trufaldín, na, *a.* Dancing or playing in low farcical representations.

Trufár, *va.* (Ant.) To tell stories, to deceive. V. *Mentir.*

Truféta, *sf.* A sort of linen.

Truhán, na, *s.* Buffoon, low jester.

Truhanaménte, *ad.* Jestingly, buffoon-like.

Truhaneár, *vn.* To banter, to jest, to play the buffoon.

Truhanería ó Truhanáda, *sf.* Buffoonery, low jests, scurril mirth.

Truhanésco, ca, *a.* Belonging to a buffoon.

Truhaníllo, lla, *s.* A mean petty buffoon.

Trúja, *sf.* (And.) Place where olives are kept before being pressed in the mill.

Trujál, *sm.* 1. Oil-mill. 2. Copper, in which the materials for the manufacturing of soap are prepared. V. *Lagar.*

Trujaléta, *sf.* Vessel in which the juice of olives falls from the mill.

Trujamán, *sm.* 1. Dragoman, interpreter. 2. Broker, factor, one that buys or sells goods for another.

Trujamaneár, *vn.* 1. To interpret, to act as interpreter. 2. To exchange, barter, buy or sell goods for others; to act as a broker or factor. 3. To play the buffoon.

Trujamanía, *sf.* Brokering, brokerage.

Trujimán, na, *s.* V. *Trujaman.*

Trúlla, *sf.* 1. Noise, bustle; multitude. 2. Mason's level.

Trúllo, *sm.* 1. (Orn.) Teal. Anas coccea *L.* 2. Kind of vat for pressed grapes.

Truncadaménte, *ad.* In a truncated manner.

Truncamiénto, *sm.* Truncation, the act of truncating or maiming.

Truncár, *va.* To truncate, to maim; to mutilate a discourse.

Trúnco, ca, *a.* V. *Tronco.*

Trúque, *sm.* A game at cards.

Truquéro, *sm.* Keeper or owner of a truck-table.

Tú, *pron. pers.* Thou; used in the familiar style of friendship.—*a.* Thy, thine. V. *Tuyo. A' tú por tú,* Thee for thee; disrespectful or vulgar language. *Salta tú y dámela tú,* Juvenile play of thread-needle.

Tuáutem, *sm.* (Fam.) Principal person, leader, mover, author; essential point.

Tubérculo, *sm.* (Med.) Tubercle in the lungs.

Tuberósa, *sf.* (Bot.) Tuberose, oriental hyacinth. Hyacinthus orientalis

Tuberosidád, *sf.* Tuberosity.

Tuberóso, sa, *a.* Tuberous.

Túbo, *sm.* Tube. V. *Cañon.*

Tuciorísta, *s. com.* One who follows the safest doctrine.

Tudél, *sm.* A metal pipe with a reed put into a bassoon.

Tudésca, *sf.* (Bot.) V. *Maravilla. Lengua tudesca,* German language.

Tudésco, *sm.* 1. A kind of wide cloak. V. *Capote.* 2. German, native of Germany.

Tuéce ó Tuéca, *s.* Cavity made by wood-lice in timber.
Tuéra, *sf.* (Bot.) Coloquintida, bitter apple. Cucumis colocynthis *L.*
Tuérca, *sf.* Nut or female screw.
Tuérce, *sm.* V. *Torcedura.*
Tuéro, *sm.* Dry wood cut for fuel.
Tuertaménte, *ad.* V. *Torcidamente.*
Tuérto, ta, *a.* Blind of one eye; squint-eyed. *Á tuertas*, On the contrary, on the wrong side; obliquely.
Tuérto, *sm.* Wrong, injury. *Tuértos*, Pains in the bowels after child-birth; they are more commonly called *entuertós*. *Á tuerto ó á derecho*, Right or wrong; inconsiderately.
Tuétano, *sm.* Marrow, an oleaginous substance contained in the bones; pith of trees.
Tufaráda, *sf.* A strong scent or smell.
Túfo, *sm.* 1. A warm vapour or exhalation arising from the earth. 2. A strong and offensive smell. 3. Locks of hair which fall over the ear. 4. High notion, lofty idea, vanity.
Tugúrio, *sm.* Hut, cottage.
Tuición, *sf.* Tuition; protection.
Tuitívo, va, *a.* Defensive, that which shelters or protects.
Tulípa, *sf.* (Bot.) A small tulip.
Tulipán, *sm.* (Bot.) Tulip. Tulipa *L.*
Tullído, da, *a.* Crippled.
Tullidúra, *sf.* Dung of birds of prey.
Tullimiénto, *sm.* Contraction of the nerves.
Tullír, *vn.* To emit dung; applied to birds; to ill-treat.—*vr.* To be crippled or maimed.
Túmba, *sf.* 1. Tomb, sepulchral monument, vault. 2. Roof of a coach. 3. Tumble. V. *Tumbo.*
Tumbadéro, ra, *a.* Tumbler; falling. *Tumbaderas redes*, Drop-nets for catching wild animals.
Tumbadíllo, *sm.* (Naút.) Round-house, cuddy.
Tumbádo, da, *a.* Vaulted, arched.
Tumbága, *sf.* Pinchbeck or tomback; toy made of pinchbeck.
Tumbagón, *sm.* Any large piece made of tomback or pinchbeck; bracelet set with stones.
Tumbár, *va.* 1. To tumble, to throw down. 2. To surprise with a joke or jest. 3. To inebriate, to make drunk. *Tumbar un navio*, (Naút.) To heave a ship down.—*vn.* 1. To tumble, to fall down. 2. (Naút.) To heel, to lie along, to have a false list; applied to a ship.—*vr.* To lie down to sleep.
Tumbílla, *sf.* Horse for airing bed-linen.
Túmbo, *sm.* 1. Tumble, fall. 2. An important point, a matter of consequence. 3. Book containing the privileges and title-deeds of monasteries, &c. *Tumbo de olla*, What remains in the pot after the meat is taken out. *Tumbo de dado*, Imminent peril.
Tumbón, *sm.* 1. Coach, trunk with an arched roof or lid. 2. V. *Tuno.*
Tumbonbár, *vn.* 1. To vault, to make arches. 2. V. *Tunar.*
Tumefacción, *sf.* Tumefaction, swelling.
Tumefacérse, *vr.* To tumefy, to swell.
Túmido, da, *a.* 1. Swollen, inflated. 2. Pompous, elevated; applied to the style.
Tumór, *sm.* 1. Tumor, a morbid swelling. 2. Tumor, affected pomp, false magnificence.
Túmulo, *sm.* Tomb, sepulchral monument; funeral pile.
Tumúlto, *sm.* Tumult, uproar; mob.
Tumultuación, *sf.* Tumult, mob.
Tumultuánte, *pa.* Tumultuating.
Tumultuár, *vn.* To raise a tumult, to stir up disturbances, to excite commotions.
Tumultuariaménte, *ad.* Tumultuously.
Tumultuário, ria, *a.* Tumultuary, exciting disturbances or commotions.
Tumultuosaménte, *ad.* Tumultuously.
Tumultuóso, sa, *a.* Tumultuous.
Túna, *sf.* 1. (Bot.) Indian fig, the fig of the *Cactus opuntia.* 2. An idle and licentious life.
Tunál, *sm.* (Bot.) Indian fig-tree. Cactus opuntia *L.* V. *Nopal.*
Tunánte, *a.* Leading a licentious life; vagrant.
Tunantería, *sf.* Debauchery, idleness, vagrancy and libertinism.
Tunár, *vn.* To lead a licentious, lazy, vagrant life.
Túnda, *sf.* 1. The act of shearing cloth. 2. A severe chastisement or punishment.
Tundénte, *a.* Doing injury to some part of the body without drawing blood; raising a tumor.
Tundición, *sf.* Shearing of cloth.
Tundidór, *sm.* Shearer of cloth. *Banco del tundidor*, Shearing-board.
Tundidúra, *sf.* The act of shearing.
Tundír, *va.* 1. To shear, to cut the pile of cloth. 2. (Fam.) To cudgel, to flog, to inflict punishment.
Tundízno, *sm.* Shearings cut off from cloth.
Túnica, *sf.* 1. Tunic, a garment without sleeves worn by the ancients. 2. A woollen shirt worn by some religious persons under their clothes. 3. Tunicle, pellicle, or integument which covers the shells of fruit, or the eyes. 4. A long wide gown.
Tunicéla, *sf.* Garment worn by bishops; wide gown.
Túno, *sm.* Vagrant, libertine. V. *Tunante.*
Túpa, *sf.* Satiety, the act of glutting one's self, repletion.
Tupé, *sm.* Toupet.
Tupír, *va.* To press close.—*vr.* To stuff or glut one's self with eating and drinking.
Túra, *sf.* (Ant.) V. *Dura y Sopilote ó Gallinaza.*
Turár, *vn.* (Ant.) To continue in the natural state.
Túrba, *sf.* 1. Crowd, confused multitude. 2. Turf, a sod, peat, blackish earth which is used for fuel.
Turbación, *sf.* Perturbation, confusion, disorder; the act of exciting disturbances and commotions.
Turbadaménte, *ad.* In a disorderly manner.
Turbadór, ra, *s.* Disturber, one who excites disturbances, perturbator.
Turbál, *sm.* Turf-bog, peat-moss; collection of peat or fuel.
Turbamiénto, *sm.* (Ant.) V. *Turbacion.*
Turbamúlta, *sf.* Crowd, multitude.
Turbánte, *sm.* 1. Turban or turbant, the head-dress worn by the Turks. 2. Disturber.
Turbár, *va.* To disturb, to alarm, to trouble; to surprise.—*vr.* To be uneasy or alarmed; not to have a composed mind.
Turbatívo, va, *a.* Troublesome, that which disturbs or alarms.

Turbiaménte, *ad.* Obscurely; confusedly.
Túrbido, da, *a.* Muddy, turbid. V. *Turbio.*
Turbiedád, *sf.* Muddiness; turbidness; obscurity.
Turbinádo, da, *a.* Turbinated, twisted, spiral formed; applied to shells.
Turbiníta, *sm.* (Cón.) Wreath shell, spiral shell. Turbo *L.*
Turbíno, *sm.* Powder made of the root of turbith.
Túrbio, bia, *a.* 1. Muddy, disturbed, troubled. 2. Unhappy, unfortunate. 3. Dark, obscure; applied to language. *A' turbio correr ó quando todo turbio corra,* (Fam.) However bad or unfortunate it may be or happen.
Turbión, *sm.* 1. A heavy shower of rain. 2. Hurricane; violent concussion of a multitude of things.
Turbít, *sm.* (Bot.) Turbith. Convolvulus turpethum *L. Turbit mineral,* (Farm.) Turbith mineral, yellow oxide or subsulphat of mercury.
Turbonáda y Turbionáda, *sf.* Waterspout.
Turbón, *sm.* V. *Turbion.*
Turbuléncia, *sf.* 1. Turbidness, muddiness. 2. Turbulence, confusion, disorder, disturbance.
Turbulentaménte, *ad.* Turbulently.
Turbulénto, ta, *a.* 1. Turbid, not clear, thick, muddy. 2. Turbulent, confused, disorderly, tumultuous.
Túrco, ca, *a.* Turkish, peculiar to the Turks.
Turdíga, *sf.* Piece of new leather, about a foot in width, of which the poor in Spain make the coarse shoes, called *Abarcas.*
Turdión, *sm.* Ancient Spanish dance.
Turgéncia, *sf.* 1. Swelling, tumour. 2. Ostentation, vanity, loftiness, pride.
Turgénte, *a.* Turgent, swelling, tumid, protuberant.
Turíbulo, *sm.* Incensory, a vessel in which incense is burnt.
Turiferário y Turibulário, *sm.* The acolothist, who carries the incensory.
Turificación, *sf.* Incensing, perfuming with incense.
Turificár, *va.* V. *Incensar.*
Túrma, *sf.* Testicle. *Túrma de tiérra,* (Bot.) Truffle. Tuber cibarium *With.*
Turnár, *vn.* To alternate, to go or work, by turns.
Túrnio, nia, *a.* Squint-eyed; torvous, of a stern countenance.
Túrno, *sm.* 1. Turn, successive or alternate order; change, vicissitude. 2. (Naút.) Time, in which a sailor or party of sailors is employed in some particular business. *Relevar el turno á la bomba, ó á sondaleza,* To spell the pump or the lead. *Al turno,* By turns. *Por su turno,* In his turn.
Turón, *sm.* A kind of field-mouse. Mus silvaticus *L.*
Túrpe, *a.* (Ant.) V. *Torpe.*
Turquésa, *sf.* 1. Mould for making pellets or balls to be thrown from a cross-bow. 2. Turkois, a precious stone of a beautiful blue colour.
Turquesádo, da, *a.* Of the turkois colour.
Turquésco, ca, *a.* Turkish. *A' la turquesca,* In the Turkish manner.
Turquí ó Turquíno, na, *a.* Of a deep blue colour.
Turrár, *va.* To toast, to roast.
Turrón, *sm.* Sweetmeat made of almonds, pine-kernels, nuts and honey.
Turronéro, *sm.* One who makes or retails the sweetmeat, called *Turron.*
Tursión, *sm.* Fish resembling a dolphin.
Turulés, *sm.* Kind of strong grapes.
Turumbón, *sm.* Contusion on the head.
Tus ó Túso, *interj.* A word used for calling dogs.
Tusilágo, *sm.* (Bot.) Colts-foot. Tusilago farfara *L.*
Túso, sa, *s.* Name given to dogs.
Tusón, *sm.* 1. Fleece, the wool shorn from a sheep. 2. (And.) Colt which is not yet two years old. *Orden del tuson de oro,* Order of the Golden Fleece.
Tusóna, *sf.* Strumpet, having her head and eyebrows either shaved, as a punishment, or lost by disease.
Tútano, *sm.* Marrow. V. *Tuétano.*
Tuteár, *va.* To thou, to treat with familiarity.
Tutéla, *sf.* Guardianship, tutelage, protection. *Tutela dativa,* (For.) Guardianship appointed by a court.
Tutelár, *a.* Tutelar, tutelary; defensive, protecting.
Tutéo ó Tuteamiénto, *sm.* Thouing, the act of treating one in a familiar manner.
Tutía, *sf.* Tutty. V. *Atutia.*
Túto, ta, *a.* Safe. V. *Seguro.*
Tutór, ra, *s.* Guardian, tutor; protector.
Tutoría, *sf.* Tutelage, guardianship.
Tutríz, *sf.* Tutoress, governess.
Túyo, ya, *pron. pos.* Thine. *Ese sombrero es tuyo,* That hat is thine. *Tuyos,* Friends and relations of the party addressed.

THE *u* is the 24th letter in the Spanish alphabet; it loses its sound after *q* and *g*, and becomes a liquid, except where it is followed by an *e*, as in *quaderno, guarismo*, or when marked with a diæresis, as in *agüero*, when it retains its proper sound. Great care should be taken never to confound *u* and *v* in Spanish, as they differ not only in sound but in import, as *desuelo* and *desvelo.*

U', *conj. disj.* A disjunctive particle used in the place of *ó*, to avoid cacophony, when the following word begins with an *o* (or formerly with a *d*); *e. g. Lacre ú oblea,* Sealing-wax or wafer.
U', *interj.* Ah! alas!
Ubérrimo, ma, *a.* Very fruitful; extremely plentiful and abundant.
U'bi, *sm.* Place, room, sphere.
Ubicación, *sf.* Actual existence in a determinate place or space.
Ubicárse, *vr.* To be in a determinate space.
U'bio, *sm.* V. *Yugo.*
Ubiquidád, *sf.* Ubiquity, omnipresence.
Ubiquitário, *sm.* Ubiquitary; ubiquitarian.

U'BRE, *sf.* Dug or teat of female animals.
UBRÉRA, *sf.* Thrush, ulcerations in the mouth of sucking children.
UCÉ, *s. com.* Your honour or worship. V. *Vuesamerced.*
UCÉNCIA, *s. com.* Your excellency. V. *Vuecelencia.*
UESNORUÉSTE, *sm.* V. *Oesnorueste.*
UESSUDUÉSTE, *sm.* V. *Oesudueste.*
UÉSTE, *sm.* 1. West. 2. Zephyr, west-wind.
UFANAMÉNTE, *ad.* Ostentatiously, boastfully.
UFANÁRSE, *vr.* To boast, to be haughty or elated.
UFANÉZA Y UFANÍA, *sf.* 1. Pride, haughtiness. 2. Joy, gaiety, pleasure, satisfaction.
UFÁNO, NA, *a.* 1. Proud, haughty, lofty, arrogant. 2. Gay, cheerful, joyful, content.
U'FO (A'), *ad.* In a spunging manner; parasitically.
UGIÉR, *sm.* Usher, porter.
U'LCERA, *sf.* Ulcer, a sore or festered wound.
ULCERACIÓN, *sf.* Ulceration, the breaking out into ulcers.
ULCERÁR, *va.* To ulcerate, to disease with sores.
ULCERATÍVO, VA, *a.* Causing ulcers.
ULCERÓSO, SA, *a.* Ulcerous, afflicted with ulcers.
ULMÁRIA, *sf.* Meadow sweet, queen of the meadows. Spiræa ulmaria *L.*
ULTERIÓR, *a.* Ulterior, posterior.
ULTIMADAMÉNTE, *ad.* Ultimately.
ULTIMÁDO, DA, *a.* Finished, ultimate.
U'LTIMAMÉNTE, *ad.* Lastly, finally.
ULTIMÁR, *va.* To end, to finish.
ULTIMIDÁD, *sf.* Ultimity, the last stage.
U'LTIMO, MA, *a.* 1. Last, latest, hindmost. 2. Highly finished, most valuable. 3. Remote; extreme. 4. Final, conclusive, ultimate. *Estar á lo último,* To understand completely; to be expiring. *Por último,* Lastly, finally. *Ultimo entre todos,* Last of all, last among them all.
U'LTIMAS, *sf. pl.* Last or end syllables.
U'LTRA, *ad.* Besides, moreover.
ULTRAJADÓR, RA, *s.* One who outrages or insults.
ULTRAJAMIÉNTO, *sm.* Outrage, affront, injury.
ULTRAJÁR, *va.* To outrage, to offend, to treat injuriously; to despise, to depreciate.
ULTRÁJE, *sm.* Outrage, contempt, injurious language.
ULTRAJOSAMÉNTE, *ad.* Outrageously.
ULTRAJÓSO, SA, *a.* Outrageous, scornful.
ULTRAMÁR, *a.* 1. Ultramarine, beyond the seas, foreign. 2. (Pint.) Ultramarine, blue colour.
ULTRAMARÍNO, NA, *a.* Ultramarine.
ULTRAMARÍNO, *sm.* Ultramarine, the finest blue colour, produced by calcination from the lapis lazuli.
ULTRAMÁRO, *sm.* Ultramarine colour.
ULTRAMONTÁNO, NA, *a.* Ultramontane, beyond the mountains.
ULTRAPUÉRTAS, *sm.* Place situated without the gates.
ULTRÍZ, *sf.* Avenger; Divine Justice.
ULTRÓNEO, NEA, *a.* Spontaneous, voluntary.
U'LULA, *sf.* (Orn.) Owl. V. *Autillo.*
ULULÁTO, *sm.* Howl, screech, hue-and-cry.
UMBÉLAS, *sf. pl.* Umbels, the extremities of the stalks of plants, such as mountain-parsley, which serve in Spain as tooth-picks.
UMBILICÁDO, DA, *a.* Navel-shaped.
UMBILICÁL, *a.* Umbilical, belonging to the navel.
U'MBLA, *sf.* (Ict.) Fish of the salmon family found in the lakes of Switzerland and Italy. Salmo umbla *L.*
UMBRA, (Ant.) V. *Sombra.*
UMBRÁL, *sm.* 1. Threshold, the step under a door or gate; lintel, architrave. 2. Beginning, commencement, rudiment.
UMBRALÁR, *va.* To lay down the ground-timber of a door or gate; to place an architrave.
UMBRÁTICO, CA, *a.* Umbrageous, shady, yielding shade.
UMBRATÍL, *a.* Umbratile; resembling.
UMBRÍA, *sf.* Umbrosity, shadiness; a shady place.
UMBRÍO, BRÍA, *a.* Umbrageous, shady.
UMBRÓSO, SA, *a.* Shady, yielding shade.
UN, *a.* One; used for *uno,* but always before words; it is also used before verbs occasionally to give force and energy to an expression.
UNÁNIME, *a.* Unanimous.
UNANIMEMÉNTE, *ad.* Unanimously.
UNANIMIDÁD, *sf.* Unanimity, conformity of sentiments or opinions.
U'NCIA, *sf.* 1. An ancient coin, the value of which is not known. 2. Ounce, the sixteenth part of a pound, and sometimes the twelfth. V. *Onza.*
UNCIÓN, *sf.* 1. Unction, the act of anointing. 2. Extreme or last unction, the rite of anointing in the last hours. *Unciones,* Course of salivation, a method of cure practised in venereal cases.
UNCIONÁRIO, RIA, *a.* Being under salivation, salivating; place of salivating.
UNCÍR, *va.* To yoke oxen or mules for labour.
UNDÁNTE, *a.* (Poét.) V. *Undoso.*
UNDECÁGONO, *sm.* Undecagon, a polygon of eleven sides or angles.
UNDÉCIMO, MA, *a.* Eleventh.
UNDÉCUPLO, PLA, *a.* Eleven times as much.
UNDÍSONO, NA, *a.* Billowy, sounding like waves.
UNDÓSO, SA, *a.* Wavy, rising in waves, playing to and fro as undulations.
UNDULACIÓN, *sf.* Undulation, a tremulous motion observable in liquids.
UNDULÁR, *vn.* To rise or play in waves.
UNDULATÓRIO, RIA, *a.* Undulatory.
UNGARÍNA, *sf.* A kind of Hungarian dress.
U'NGAROS, *sm. pl.* Tanners, who make use of lime and bark-powder to abridge the process of tanning.
UNGÍDO, *sm.* Anointed of the Lord, king, sovereign.
UNGIMIÉNTO, *sm.* Unction, the act of anointing.
UNGÍR, *va.* To anoint, to consecrate.
UNGÜENTÁRIO, RIA, *a.* Preparing sweet-scented ointment or perfumes.
UNGÜENTÁRIO, *sm.* Perfume-box, in which sweet-scented ointments are kept; anointer.
UNGÜÉNTO, *sm.* 1. Unguent, ointment, liniment. 2. Perfume, balsam. *Ungüento de Mexico,* (Joc.) Money, cash. *Ungüento cetrino,* Ointment made of ceruse, camphor and oil mixed with citron juice, used to take freckles off the face, or remove cicatrices.
UNÍBLE, *a.* That which may be united.
U'NICAMÉNTE, *ad.* Only, simply.
UNICÁULE, *a.* Having but one stalk; applied to plants.
UNICIDÁD, *sf.* Singularity, distinctive quality.

U'nico, ca, *a.* Singular, alone, that of which there is but one; rare, excellent.
Unicórnio, *sm.* 1. Unicorn, animal having one horn. 2. (Min.) Ceratites.
Unidád, *sf.* 1. Unity, the state of being one. 2. Unit, the least number or the root of numbers. 3. Principle of dramatic writing, by which the unity of time and place is preserved. 4. Conformity, union.
Unidaménte, *ad.* Jointly, unanimously.
Unificár, *va.* To unite into one.
Uniformár, *va.* To make uniform.
Unifórme, *a.* Uniform, of an even tenour.
Unifórme, *sm.* (Mil.) Uniform, regimentals.
Uniformeménte, *ad.* Uniformly.
Uniformidád, *sf.* Uniformity, resemblance, even tenour.
Unigénito, *a.* Only begotten; applied to an only son, or the Son of God.
Unión, *sf.* 1. Union, the act of joining two or more; the state of being joined, conjunction. 2. Conformity, resemblance. 3. Concord, conjunction of mind, sentiments, or opinion. 4. Composition resulting from the mixture of several ingredients; physical or chemical union. 5. Consolidation of the lips of a wound. 6. Alliance, confederacy. 7. Contiguity, nearness of situation. 8. Symmetry, harmony. 9. Incorporation; sameness, similarity. 10. Hoop, ring. *Uniónes*, Pearls, perfectly like each other. *Union hypostática*, Hipostatic union of the divine Word and human nature.
Unír, *va.* 1. To join, to unite. 2. To mix, to incorporate. 3. To bind, to tie. 4. To approach, to bring near; to aggregate. 5. To conform. 6. To consolidate.—*vr.* 1. To join, to associate, to be united; to adhere, to concur; to associate. 2. To be contiguous, close, near.
Unisón, *sm.* Unison, musical consonance.
Unisonáncia, *sf.* Uniformity of sound; monotony, want of variety in cadence.
Unísono, na, *a.* 1. Unison, sounding alone. 2. Having the same sound.
Unísono, *sm.* Unison, a single unvaried note.
Unitívo, va, *a.* Unitive, having the power of uniting.
Unitóso, sa; y **Unituóso, sa**, *a.* Fit for being joined or united.
Univálvo, vá, *a.* Univalve; applied to shells.
Universál, *a.* Universal, general, extending to all; learned, well-informed.
Universalidád, *sf.* 1. Universality, extension to the whole. 2. Generality of information.
Universalménte, *ad.* Universally, generally.
Universidád, *sf.* 1. Universality, generality. 2. University, a place where all the arts and faculties are taught and studied. 3. Body of masters and students, assembled in a determinate place to teach and study arts and sciences. 4. Corporation, community. 5. The whole circle of nature; the vegetable, animal, or mineral kingdom. *Universidades*, Cities, towns, or other corporations.
Univérso, *sm.* Universe, the general system of created things or beings.
Univérso, sa, *a.* Universal.
Univocación, *sf.* Univocation.

Univocaménte, *ad.* Univocally, unanimously.
Univocárse, *vr.* To have the same meaning.
Unívoco, ca, *a.* 1. Univocal, having the same meaning. 2. Unanimous; like, resembling.
U'no, *sm.* 1. One, the element or root of all numbers. 2. One, any individual; intimate friend, another self.
U'no, na, *a.* 1. One; closely resembling the same; sole, only. 2. It is used relatively or to supply a name, as *Uno dizo*, It was said, or one said. *Uno á otro*, One another, reciprocally. *Todo es uno*, It is all the same; it is foreign to the point. *Uno á uno*, One by one. *Uno por uno*, One and then another; used to mark the distinction more forcibly. *Ya uno ya otro*, By turns. *Una por una*, At all events, at any rate, certainly. *Una y no mas*, Never, no more. *A' una*, Jointly, together. *Ser para en uno*, To be well matched; applied to a married couple. *Ir á una*, To amount to the same.
Untadór, ra, *s.* Anointer, one who anoints; surgeon who administers or performs mercurial frictions.
Untadúra y **Untamiénto**, *s.* Unction, the act of anointing.
Untár, *va.* 1. To rub over with unctuous matter, to anoint. 2. To suborn, to bribe. *Untar las manos*, To grease the hands, *i. e.* to bribe. 3. To varnish a piece of painting. *Untar el carro*, (Fam.) To bribe. *Untar el casco ó los cascos*, To flatter, to wheedle, to cajole. *Untar la mollera*, To be slow or dull of comprehension.—*vr.* 1. To be greased with unctuous matter. 2. To embezzle, to appropriate by breach of trust.
Untáza, *sf.* Grease. V. *Enxundia*.
U'nto, *sm.* 1. Grease, unctuous matter; fat of animals. 2. Unguent, ointment. *Unto de rana ó de México*, Bribe, money given to suborn.
Untóso, sa; y **Untuóso, sa**, *a.* Unctuous, greasy.
Untuosidád, *sf.* Unctuosity, unctiousness, oiliness, greasiness.
Untúra, *sf.* 1. Unction, the act of anointing. 2. Matter used in anointing.
U'ña, *sf.* 1. Nail, the horny substance at the ends of the fingers and toes. 2. Hoof, claw, or talon of beasts. 3. Pointed hook of instruments. 4. Part of the trunk of a felled tree, which still sticks to the root. 5. Crust growing on sores or wounds. 6. Excrescence or hard tumour on the eye-lids. 7. Dexterity in stealing or filching. 8. Curved beak of a scorpion. *De uñas á uñas*, From head to foot. *Hincar ó meter la uña*, To overcharge, to sell at an exorbitant price. *Mostrar las uñas*, To be inexorable. *Mostrar la uña*, To show one's teeth, to discover one's foibles. *Quedarse soplando las uñas*, To bite one's thumbs, to be disappointed. *Tener uñas algun negocio*, To be arduous or extremely difficult; applied to a task or business. *Uña olorosa*, Shell used in pharmacy. *Sacar las uñas*, (Fam.) To avail one's self of every means in any difficulty. *Uña de caballo*, (Bot.) Coltsfoot.
Uñáda, *sf.* Impression made with the nail, scratch.

Uñaráda y **Uñarázo**, *s.* Scratch, laceration with the nail.

Uñáte, *sm.* 1. The act of pinching with the nail. 2. V. *Uñeta*.

Uñáza, *sf. aum.* Large nail.

Uñéro, *sm.* A callous excrescence growing at the root of a nail.

Uñéta, *sf. dim.* 1. Little nail. 2. Chuck-farthing, a play among boys.

Uñidúra, *sf.* The act of yoking oxen or mules for labour.

Uñír, *va.* To yoke. V. *Uncir*.

Uñíta, ca; y **Uñuéla**, *sf. dim.* of *uña*.

Uñóso, sa, *a.* Having long nails or claws.

U'pa, *sf.* Up, up; a term used to make children get up from the ground. V. *Aupa*.

Upár, *vn.* To endeavour to get up.

Urácho, *sm.* (Anat.) Urachus, a membrane which passes from the top of the bladder to the umbilicus. This term has been erroneously defined even by the Academy as signifying the urethra, and by others as the ureter, prostate gland, &c.

Uránia, *sf.* Urania, the muse of astronomy.

Uranografía, *sf.* Description of the heavens.

Uranóscopo, *sm.* (Ict.) Star-gazer. Uranoscopus scaber *L.*

Uráño, na, *a.* Coy, reserved, timid; wild, untamed. V. *Huraño*.

Urbanaménte, *ad.* Courteously, politely.

Urbanidád, *sf.* Urbanity, civility, politeness.

Urbáno, na, *a.* 1. Peculiar to towns or cities. 2. Courteous, civil, polite, well-bred.

U'rca, *sf.* 1. (Naút.) Hooker, dogger; a pink-built, and sloop-rigged vessel. 2. (Naút.) Storeship. 3. (Ict.) Species of whale. V. *Orca*.

U'rce, *sm.* (Bot.) Heath. V. *Brezo*.

Urchílla, *sf.* Archil or orchil, a violet colour, used by dyers.

Urdidéra, *sf.* 1. Woman who warps. 2. A warping frame.

Urdidór, ra, *s.* 1. Warper. 2. Warping-mill.

Urdidúra, *sf.* The act of warping.

Urdiémbre y **Urdímbre**, *s.* Chain, warp, the threads which are extended lengthwise for the loom.

Urdír, *va.* To warp, to dispose the threads lengthwise for the loom. 2. To contrive.

Urétera, *sf.* (Anat.) Urethra, urinary canal.

Uréteres, *sm. pl.* Ureters, canals which convey the urine from the kidneys to the bladder.

Urético, ca, *a.* Belonging to the urethra.

Urgéncia, *sf.* Urgency, pressure of difficulty, necessity, want; obligation.

Urgénte, *a.* Urgent, pressing.

Urgenteménte, *ad.* Urgently.

Urgír, *vn.* To be urgent, to require a speedy cure or immediate execution; to be actually obliged.

Uríco, *sm.* Natron, carbonate or subcarbonate of soda; it is found in a valley of Maracaybo in Venezuela, at the bottom of a small lake.

Urína, *sf.* Urine. V. *Orina*.

Urinál, *a.* Urinary, urinous.—*sm.* Urinal.

Urinário, ria, *a.* Urinary, belonging to urine.

U'rna, *sf.* 1. Urn, the vessels in which the ashes of burnt bodies were formerly put. 2. Glass-case, in which small statues or images are kept. 3. Urn used by painters and sculptors to represent rivers.

Urníca, lla y ta, *sf.* A small urn.

Urnición, *sf.* (Naút.) Top-timbers.

U'ro, *sm.* A kind of wild ox. Bos urus *L.*

Urogállo, *sm.* (Orn.) Bird like a cock.

Urráca, *sf.* (Orn.) Magpie. Corvus pica *L.*

U'rsa, *sf.* She-bear. V. *Osa*.

Urúca, *sm.* (Bot.) Hart-leaved bixa or anotta. Bixa orellana *L.*

Usación, *sf.* Use, the act of using.

Usadaménte, *ad.* According to custom.

Usádo, da, *a.* 1. Used, worn out. 2. Experienced, skilful. *Al usado*, At usance, at the time fixed for the payment of bills of exchange, by the custom of the place on which they are drawn.

Uságe, *sm.* Usage, custom. V. *Uso*.

Uságre, *sm.* A kind of breaking out in the faces of children.

Usánza, *sf.* Usage, use, usance, custom.

Usár, *va.* 1. To use, to employ for some purpose, to make use of. 2. To practise, to perform, by custom or habit. 3. To exercise or perform an employment or office. 4. To enjoy any thing. 5. To communicate, to treat or use familiarly.—*vr.* To be in use or fashion.

Uséncia, *s. com.* Your reverence, a contraction of *vuestra reverencia*; an appellation of honour used to address clergymen.

Useñoría, Usía, ó Usiría, *s. com.* Your lordship or ladyship, a contraction of *vuestra señoría*.

U'sgo, *sm.* V. *Asco*.

Usiér, *sm.* Usher, porter. V. *Uxier*.

Usitádo, da, *a.* Frequently used.

U'so, *sm.* 1. Use, employment, service. 2. Usufruct; enjoyment. 3. Use, custom, style, general practice, habit, fashion, mode. 4. Usance, a time prefixed for the payment of bills of exchange, by the custom of the place on which they are drawn. 5. Office, exercise; wearing. 6. Frequent continuation, constant use; assiduousness. *Andar al uso*, To conform to the times, to temporize. *A' uso ó al uso*, According to custom.

Ustága, *sf.* (Naút.) Tye.

Ustéd ó **Vd.**, *s. com.* You, a contraction of *vuestra merced*; a general term used to address persons both in conversation and in writing.

Ustión, *sf.* Ustion, the act of making medical preparations by burning.

Usuál, *a.* 1. Usual, accustomed. 2. Tractable, social. *Año usual*, Current year.

Usualménte, *ad.* Usually.

Usuário, ria, *a.* Having the sole use of any thing.

Usucapión, *sf.* (For.) Usucaption.

Usucapír, *va.* To acquire the right of property of any thing, by the possession thereof during a space of time prescribed by law.

Usufrúcto, *sm.* Usufruct, profit, advantage; enjoyment.

Usufructuár, *va.* 1. To possess or enjoy the usufruct of any thing. 2. To render productive or fruitful.

Usufructuário, ria, *a.* Possessing or enjoying the usufruct of any thing.

Usúra, *sf.* 1. Interest, money paid for the use

of money lent or advanced. 2. Gain, profit. 3. Usury, unlawful interest.

Usuráe ó Usureár, vn. To lend money on interest; to practise usury; to reap benefit.

Usurariamente, ad. Usuriously, interestedly.

Usurário, ria, a. Belonging to interest or usury; practising usury.

Usuréro, ra, s. Usurer, money-lender.

Usuréro, ra, a. Usurious; excessive profit.

Usurpación, sf. Usurpation, an illegal seizure or possession.

Usurpadór, ra, s. Usurper, one who seizes or possesses that to which he has no right.

Usurpár, va. 1. To usurp, to possess by force or intrusion, to seize without right; to assume or usurp another's office, dignity, or employment. 2. To make use of a word in the room of another, or in another sense.

Ut, sm. Ut, the first of the musical notes.

Utensílio, sm. Utensil, an instrument for any use. *Utensilios*, (Mil.) Articles which the tenant of a house is to furnish the soldier quartered with him.

Uterál, a. Uterine, belonging to the womb.

Uteríno, na, a. 1. Uterine, belonging to the womb. 2. Born of the same mother, but having a different father.

U'tero, sm. Uterus, womb, the place of the fœtus in the mother.

U'til, a. Useful, profitable.—sm. Utility, advantage.

Utilidád, sf. Utility, profit; usefulness.

Utilizár, vn. To be useful, to yield profit.—vr. 1. To reap benefit or profit; to take advantage of or profit by. 2. To interest or concern one's self in some business.

Utilménte, ad. Usefully.

Utópia, sf. Utopia, imaginary country.

Utréro, ra, s. Bull or heifer between two and three years old.

Ut súpra, ad. As above.

U'va, sf. 1. Grape, the fruit of the vine, or Vitis vinifera *L.* 2. Bunch of grapes. 3. Tippler, one fond of drinking. *Hecho una uva*, Very drunk. 4. Wart on the eye-lid. 5. Fruit or berry of the barberry bush. 6. Tumour on the epiglottis. *Uva de Corinto*, (Bot.) Currants. *Uva pasa*, Raisins. *Uva de gato ó canilla*, White stone-crop. Sedum album *L.* *Uva espina ó crespa*, Gooseberry. Ribes grossularia *L.* *Uva lupina ó verca*, Wolf-berries. Aconitum Lycoctonum *L.* *Uva de raposa*, Nightshade. Solanum nigrum *L.* *Uva taminea ó taminia*, Lousewort.

Uváda, sf. 1. Plenty or abundance of grapes. 2. (And.) Kind of land-measure.

Uvaguemaéstre, sm. (Mil.) Officer who commands the train of baggage-waggons.

Uvál, a. Belonging to grapes.

Uváte, sm. Conserve made of grapes.

Uvayéma, sf. Species of wild vine.

U'vea, sf. Uvea, the third or outermost coat of the eye.

Uvéro, sm. Retailer of grapes.

Uvílla, ta, sf. A small grape.

Uziér, sm. Porter, groom-porter, gentleman-usher. *Uzier de armas*, Gentleman-usher of the king's arms. *Uzier de saleta*, Hall-keeper.

U'zas, sf. Kind of Brazilian club.

VAC VAC

THE pronunciation of *v* (which is the 25th letter), in the Spanish language is the same as in English, and somewhat softer than *b*, with which it was formerly often confounded. It is now generally used instead of *b* in words derived from other languages, or where foreign words are written with a character convertible into *v*, as *profectus*, makes *provecho;* but *vendicion*, selling, *bendicion*, blessing, &c. follow their Latin origin. *V.* is used in contractions for *vuestra*, your; *vd.* or *vm.* you; *V. M.* your Majesty; *V. S.* your Lordship or Ladyship; *V. R.* your reverence, &c.

Váca, sf. 1. Cow, the female of a bull. *Vaca de leche*, Milk-cow. 2. Beef, the flesh of black cattle. *Solómo de vaca*, Sirloin of beef. 3. (And.) Joint stock of two gamblers or partners in gambling. 4. (Ict.) Sea-cow. V. *Manati.* *Vaca de la boda*, He to whom every one applies in distress. *Vaca de San Anton*, (Ent.) Lady-cow, lady-bird. Coccinella septempunctata *L.* If this very common European insect be rubbed between the finger and thumb, and the finger then applied to an aching tooth, it gives immediate and effectual relief. *Vaca Marina*, (Ict.) Kind of whale, sea-cow.

Vacación, sf. Vacation, intermission of judicial proceedings, or any other stated employment; recess of courts of law and public boards.

Vacáda, sf. Drove of cows.

Vacáncia, sf. Vacancy.

Vacánte, a. Vacant, empty, disengaged.—sf. 1. Vacation; vacant office or time. 2. Rent fallen due during the vacancy of a benefice.

Vacár, vn. 1. To cease, to stop; to be vacant; to suspend any business. 2. To devote one's self to a particular thing; to follow a business.—va. To vacate an office.

Vacatúra, sf Vacancy.

Vacía, sf. Basin. V. *Bacia.*

Vaciadéro, sm. Drain, sink.

Vaciadízo, za, a. Cast, moulded.

Vaciádo, sm. 1. Form or image, moulded or cast in plaster of Paris, or wax; excavation. 2. (Arq.) Cavity in a pedestal below its ornamental mouldings.

Vaciadór, sm. Moulder, one who casts or moulds; one who evacuates, hollows, or makes empty.

Vaciamiénto, sm. Casting, moulding; evacuating, hollowing.

Vaciár, va. 1. To empty, to evacuate, to exhaust, to clear. *Vaciar el costal*, To tell all that one knows, to divulge the whole secret. 2. To mould, to form, to model. 3. To fall into, to discharge itself; applied to rivers. 4. (Arq.) To excavate. 5. To explain at large. —*vn.* 1. To fall, to decrease; applied to waters. 2. Not to make a good use of one's time. 3. To fade, to lose colour or lustre.—*vr.* 1. To be spilt, to be emptied; applied to liquors. 2. To tell or divulge what should be kept secret. 3. To empty, to be vacant.

Vaciedád, *sf.* 1. Emptiness, void, vacuity. 2. An inconsiderate or arrogant speech; obscene language.

Vaciéro, *sm.* Shepherd, whose sheep are all dry or barren.

Vacilación, *sf.* 1. Vacillation, the act or state of reeling or staggering. 2. Perplexity, irresolution.

Vacilár, *vn.* To vacillate, to reel, to stagger; to be doubtful or perplexed; to wander or be confused.

Vacín, *sm.* Basin. V. *Bacin.*

Vacío, cia, *a.* 1. Void, empty; vacuous. 2. Unoccupied, disengaged; idle; fruitless. 3. Concave, hollow. 4. Defective, deficient. 5. Vain, arrogant, presumptuous. 6. Not with young; applied to cattle. 7. Unloaded or empty; applied to horses, carts, &c.

Vacío, *sm.* 1. Void, empty space, vacuum. 2. Mould for casting metal. 3. Vacancy, place or employment unfilled. 4. Concavity, hollowness. 5. Blank, space unfilled in a book or writing. 6. Ullage of a cask or other vessel. 7. Spanish step in dancing. 8. Animal not with young. 9. Vacuity, cavity. 10. Flank, hollow part between the ribs and thigh of animals. *De vacio,* Empty; unemployed. *En vacio,* In vacuum.

Vacísco, *sm.* Fragments in quicksilver mines.

Váco, ca, *a.* Vacant.

Vacuidád, *sf.* Vacuity, emptiness.

Vacúna, *sf.* Ulcer on cow's teats, cow-pock.

Vacunación, *sf.* Vaccination; an effectual antidote to small-pox.

VACUNADO'R, *sm.* Vaccinater, he who communicates the cow-pock.

Vacunár, *va.* To vaccinate, to inoculate with the cow-pock to prevent the natural pox.

Vacúno, na, *a.* Belonging to black cattle.

Vácuo, a, *a.* Vacant; unoccupied. V. *Vacante.*

Vácuo, *sm.* Vacuum, a void or empty space.

Váde, *sm.* Case, portfolio in which school-boys keep their papers.

Vadeáble, *a.* 1. Fordable. 2. (Met.) Conquerable, superable, possible to be overcome.

Vadeár, *va.* 1. To wade, to pass a river without swimming or boats. 2. To conquer, to overcome, to surmount. 3. To sound, to try, to examine.—*vr.* To conduct one's self.

Vademécum, *sm.* Any thing portable. V. *Vade.*

Vadéra, *sf.* Ford, a shallow part of a river.

Vádo, *sm.* 1. Ford, a broad, shallow, level part of a river. 2. Expedient; resource. *No hallar vado,* To be at a loss how to act.

Vadóso, sa, *a.* Shoally, shallow.

Váfe, *sm.* Bold stroke or undertaking.

Váfo, *sm.* 1. V. *Vaho.* 2. Gust, violent blast.

Vagabúndo, da, *a.* Vagabond, idle vagrant.

Vagaménte, *ad.* In a vague, unsettled, or indeterminate manner.

Vagamundeár, *vn.* (Fam.) To rove or loiter about, to act the vagrant.

Vagamúndo, da, *a.* Vagabond, loitering about; not having any fixed abode.

Vagáncia, *sf.* Vagrancy.

Vagánte *pa.* Vagrant.

Vagár, *vn.* 1. To rove or loiter about; to wander, to range through unknown roads or fields. 2. To be unoccupied, to be at leisure, to be idle; to have time and opportunity to do any thing. 3. To revolve in the mind. 4. To be loose and irregular, or without the necessary order and disposition.—*sm.* 1. Leisure, freedom from business. 2. Slowness, indolence. *De vagar,* Slowly.

Vagarosaménte, *ad.* Vagrantly.

Vagoróso, sa, *a.* Errant, vagrant.

Vagázo, *sm.* Skin or peel of pressed grapes.

Vagído, *sm.* Cry of a child; a convulsive sob.

Vágo, ga, *a.* 1. Errant, vagrant. 2. Restless, uneasy. 3. Vague, wavering, fluctuating, unsettled. 4. V. *Vaco. Voz vaga,* A vague report. *En vago,* Unsteadily, unfirmly; unsuccessfully, in vain, vaguely.

Vágo, *sm.* 1. Uncultivated plot of ground. 2. Vagabond.

Vagueación, *sf.* Restlessness, levity, unsteadiness; flight of fancy.

Vagueánte, *pa.* Vagrant, wandering.

Vagueár, *vn.* To rove, to loiter. V. *Vagar.*

Vaguedád, *sf.* Levity, inconstancy.

Vaguído, *sm.* 1. Giddiness, the state of being giddy or having a sensation of circular motion. 2. Risk, peril, danger.

Vaguído, da, *a.* Giddy; perplexed.

Vahanéro, ra, *a.* Idle, knavish.

Vahár, *vn.* To exhale, to emit steam or vapour.

Vaharáda, *sf.* The act of emitting steam, vapour, or breath.

Vaharéra, *sf.* 1. Thrush, superficial ulcerations in the mouth of sucking children. 2. (Extrem.) An unripe melon.

Vaharína, *sf.* (Fam.) Steam, vapour, mist.

Vaheár, *vn.* To exhale, to emit steam or vapour.

Vahído, *sm.* Vertigo, giddiness.

Váho, *sm.* Steam, vapour of any thing moist and hot.

Vahúno, na, *a.* Savage, low, wild. V. *Bahuno.*

Vaída, *sf.* (Arq.) Vault or arch in the shape of a semicircle, and cut into 4 vertical planes, every pair of which are parallel.

Vaído, *sm.* Cry of children, a convulsive sob.

Vaivasór, *sm.* Gentleman, nobleman.

Val, *sm.* 1. Vale, dale, valley; it is a contraction of *valle,* and much used in composition. 2. (Mur.) Sewer, drain, sink. 3. Ancient contraction of *vale;* from *valer.*

Valár, *a.* Relating to a rampart, enclosure, or hedge.

Valár, *vn.* (Obsol.) To bleat. V. *Balar.*

Vále, *sm.* 1. Farewell, a parting compliment, adieu. 2. Bond or promissory note. *Vales reales,* Government bonds, exchequer-bills. 3. Note of pardon given to school-boys by the master. 4. First or single hand at cards. *El ultimo vale,* The last farewell; the point of death.

Valedéro, ra, *a.* Valid, efficacious, binding.
Valedór, ra, *s.* Protector, defender.
Valentácho, *sm.* Hector, bully, braggadocio.
Valentía, *sf.* 1. Valour, courage, gallantry, bravery. 2. Feat, a glorious or heroic exploit. 3. Brag, boast. 5. Fire or liveliness of imagination. 5. (Pint.) An uncommon dexterity in imitating nature. 6. An extraordinary or vigorous effort. 7. A public place where mended old shoes are sold in Madrid. *Hambre y valentía*, Misery and ostentation, or pride and poverty. *Pisar de valentía*, To strut, to walk with affected dignity, vigour, or strength.
Valentísimo, ma, *a. sup.* Most valiant; perfect or consummate in any art or science.
Valentón, *sm.* Braggadocio, bragger, hector.
Valentán, na, *a.* Arrogant, vainglorious.
Valentonáda ó **Valentóna**, *sf.* Brag, boast.
Valentonázo, *sm.* Bully, boaster. V. *Valenton.*
Valentoncíllo, lla, *a. dim.* A little vain or presumptuous.
Valéo, *sm.* 1. Kind of shrub used for brooms. 2. Round mat; shaggy mat.
Valér, *vn.* 1. To be valuable, meritorious, deserving. 2. To be saleable or marketable, to bear a certain price. 3. To prevail; to avail. 4. To serve as an asylum or refuge. 5. To be valid or binding; to be a head or have authority; to have power, to be able. 6. To be worth, to yield, to produce. 7. To amount to. 8. To be in favour, to have influence or interest. 9. To be equivalent to. 10. To have course, to be current; applied to different coins.—*va.* To protect, to patronise, to defend, to favour.—*vr.* 1. To employ, to make use of. 2. To avail one's self of, to have recourse to. *Vale dios*, By chance, fortuitously. *Valgate ó valgate Dios*, Exclamation of surprise and disapprobation. *Valgame Dios*, Good God! expression of surprise and disgust. *Mas vale ó valiera*, It is better, it would be better. *No valer un diablo.* (Fam.) To be very despicable and worth nothing.—*sm.* Value. *Menos valer*, Loss of the privileges of nobility or other rights; (Met.) Mark of infamy, contempt, disgrace, or disrespect.
Valeriána, *sf.* (Bot.) Valerian. Valeriana *L.*
Valerosaménte, *ad.* Valiantly, courageously.
Valeróso, sa, *a.* 1. Valiant, brave, courageous. 2. Peaceful, strong, active; powerful.
Valetudinário, ria, *a.* Valetudinarian, sickly, infirm of health.
Valía, *sf.* 1. Appraisement, valuation. 2. Credit, favour, use. 3. Party, faction. *A' las valias*, At the highest price which a commodity fetches in the course of the year.
Validación, *sf.* Validity or force of an act.
Validaménte, *ad.* In a solid or binding manner.
Validár, *va.* To give validity, to render strong, firm, or binding.
Validéz, *sf.* Validity, stability.
Válido, da, *a.* 1. Relying upon, confident of. *Valido de favor*, Confident of favour. 2. Favoured, regarded with peculiar kindness; accepted, esteemed. 3. Universally respected. 4. Valid, binding. 5. Strong, powerful. 6. Availed.
Valído, *sm.* Cry of sheep, bleating.
Valiénte, *a.* 1. Strong, robust, vigorous, powerful. 2. Valiant, spirited, brave, courageous, active, strenuous; efficacious, valid. 3. Eminent, excellent. 4. Great, excessive. *Hace un valiente frio*, It is excessively cold. 5. V. *Valenton.*
Valiénte, *sm.* Bully, hector, braggadocio.
Valienteménte, *ad.* 1. Vigorously, strongly. 2. Valiantly, courageously, strenuously. 3. Superabundantly, excessively. 4. Elegantly, nicely, with propriety.
Valimiénto, *sm.* 1. Use, the act of using or employing. 2. Utility, benefit, advantage. 3. A temporary or gratuitous contribution. 4. Interest, favour, protection, support.
Valióso, sa, *a.* Rich, wealthy; very valuable.
Valíza, *sf.* (Naút.) Beacon, buoy, or ton, pointing out sand-banks or shoals to pilots or navigators. *Valiza terrestre*, Landmark.
Válla, *sf.* 1. Intrenchment; space or ground surrounded with stakes or palisadoes. 2. Barrier, barricade.
Valladár, *sm.* (Gal.) V. *Vallado.*
Valladeár, *va.* To enclose with stakes, pales, or palisadoes. V. *Vallar.*
Valládo, *sm.* Enclosure with stakes or palisadoes, paling.
Vallár, *va.* To fence, to hedge, to enclose with pales, stakes, or palisadoes.
Válle, *sm.* 1. Vale, dale, valley. 2. The whole number of villages, places, and cottages situated within a district or jurisdiction. *Hasta el valle de Josafat*, Unto the valley of Jehoshaphat, *i. e.* until the day of judgment. [valley.
Vallecíco, llo, to; y **Valléjo**, *sm.* A small
Vallejón, *aum.* y **Vallesuélo**, *sm. dim.* of
Vallíco, *sm.* V. *Joyo.* [*vallejo.*
Valón, na, *a.* Native of the Netherlands; Waloon.
Valóna, *sf.* A plaited piece of linen or muslin hanging from the collar of a boy's shirt. *A' la valona*, In the Waloon style.
Valónes, *sm. pl.* A sort of trousers or wide breeches formerly worn in Spain.
Valór, *sm.* 1. Value, price; equivalency. 2. Validity, force. 3. Activity, power; valour, fortitude. 4. Income, revenue. *Relaciones de valores*, Account of rates. [lue.
Valorár ó **Valoreár**, *va.* To appraise, to va-
Valoría, *sf.* Value, price, worth.
Valúa, *sf.* V. *Valia.*
Valuación, *sf.* Appraisement, valuation.
Valuár, *va.* To rate, to value, to appraise.
Válvula, *sf.* Valve, the flexible part in the piston of a pump; any thing which opens and shuts, an aperture.
Vanaglória, *sf.* Vaingloriousness, boast, brag.
Vanagloriárse, *vr.* To be vainglorious, to boast of, to plume one's self with; to be elated with pride.
Vanagloriosaménte, *ad.* Vaingloriously.
Vanaglorióso, sa, *a.* Vainglorious, conceited, proud, boastful.
Vanaménte, *ad.* 1. Vainly, uselessly; without profit or advantage. 2. Superstitiously, in a superstitious manner. 3. Without ground or foundation. 4. Arrogantly, presumptuously, proudly; in a vain presumptuous manner.
Vandaliáno, na, *a.* Andalusian, native of Andalusia.
Vándalo, la, *s.* Vandal, one of a northern race which entered Spain in the 5th century.

Vandóla, sf. (Naút.) Jurymast. *En vandolas,* Under jurymasts.
Vanzár, vn. To talk nonsense.
Vanguárdia, sf. Vanguard.
Vanidád, sf. 1. Vanity, want of solidity or substance. 2. Ostentation, pageantry, vain parade. 3. Nonsense, an empty unmeaning speech. 4. Inanity, vacuity. 5. Illusion, phantom.
Vanidóso, sa, a. Vain, showy.
Vaniloqüéncia, sf. Verbosity, pomposity.
Vanilóqüio, sm. Vaniloquy.
Vanilóquo, üa, a. Vain, useless language.
Vanistório, sm. Ridiculous, affected vanity.
Váno, na, a. 1. Vain, wanting solidity or firmness. 2. Inane, empty. 3. Useless, fruitless. 4. Arrogant, haughty, presumptuous. 5. Insubstantial, without foundation, groundless. *En vano,* In vain, wantonly, unnecessarily.
Váno, sm. (Arq.) Vacuum in a wall, as the windows, doors, &c.
Vapór, sm. Vapour, steam, breath; frenzy.
Vaporáble, a. Vaperous, fumy, capable of evaporating.
Vaporación, sf. Evaporation, the act of flying away in fumes or vapours.
Vaporár, Vaporeár y Vaporizár, va. 1. To evaporate. V. *Evaporar.* 2. To form vapour.
Vaporóso, sa, a. Vaperous, fumy.
Vapulación y Vapulamiénto, s. Whipping, flogging.
Vapulár, va. (Joc.) To whip, to flog.
Vapuléo, sm. (Joc.) Whipping, flogging.
Vaqueár, va. To cover cows with the bull.
Vaquería, sf. Herd or drove of black cattle.
Vaqueríles, sm. pl. Winter pasture for cows.
Vaquerillo, sm. Boy who attends cows.
Vaqueríza, sf. Stable for black cattle in winter.
Vaqueríżo, za, a. Relating or belonging to cows.—sm. V. *Vaquero.*
Vaquéro, sm. 1. Cowherd, neatherd, cowkeeper. 2. Jacket or long loose dress worn by women and children.
Vaquéro, ra, a. Belonging to cowherds.
Vaquéta, sf. 1. Sole leather, tanned cow or ox-hides. 2. Ramrod. V. *Baqueta.*
Vaqueteár, va. To flow with leather thongs.
Vaquetéo, sm. Flogging, running the gauntlet.
Vaquílla ó Vaquíta, sf. A small cow, a young cow, a heifer.
Vára, sf. 1. Rod, a long slender twig. 2. Pole, staff. 3. Rod, verge, wand, an emblem of public authority; to its upper end is fixed a cross, on which oaths are administered. 4. Yard, an instrument for measuring; a measure of three feet. 5. Herd of forty or fifty head of swine. 6. Perch or roost of a falcon. 7. Chastisement, rigour. 8. Jurisdiction, authority. *Vara alta,* Sway, high hand. *Vara de pescar,* Fishing-rod. *Varas,* Shafts of a coach. *Varas de luz,* Meteors. *Vara de José,* (Bot.) Tuberosa. Polyanthes tuberosa *L.*
Varadéros, sm. pl. (Naút.) Skids or skeeds. V. *Posteleros.*
Varádo, a. V. *Listado.*
Varadór, sm. (Naút.) Voyal, a hawser bent to the cable for heaving in the anchor.
Varál, sm. 1. A long pole or perch. 2. A tall slender person.
Varapálo, sm. 1. A long pole or perch; switch. 2. Blow or stroke with a stick or pole. 3. Grief, trouble, vexation.
Varár, va. (Naút.) To launch a new-built ship. —vn. 1. (Naút.) To ground, to get on shore, to be stranded. 2. To be stopped.
Varascéto, sm. Treillage, a contexture of reeds, used in gardens.
Varázo, sm. Stroke with a pole or stick.
Varbásco, sm. V. *Verbasco.*
Varchílla, sf. Measure of grain, which contains the third part of a *fanega.*
Vardásca, sf. A thin twig.
Vardascázo, sm. Stroke with a small twig or switch.
Vareadór, sm. One who beats down with a pole or staff.
Vareáge, sm. Retail-trade, the act of selling by the yard; measuring by the yard.
Vareár, va. 1. To beat down the fruit of trees with a pole or long rod. 2. To cudgel, to beat with a staff or pole. 3. To wound bulls or oxen with a goad. 4. To measure or sell by the yard.—vr. To grow thin or lean.
Varejón, sm. A thick pole or staff.
Varénga, sf. (Naút.) Floor-timber. *Varenga de plan,* (Naút.) Midship floor-timber. *Varenga de sobreplanos,* (Naút.) Floor-rider.
Varengáge, sm. (Naút.) Collection of floor-timbers.
Varéo, sm. Measurement, act of measuring.
Varéta, sf. 1. A small rod or twig. 2. Lime-twig for catching birds. 3. Stripe in any kind of stuff different in colour from the ground. 4. A smart or piquant expression. 5. A circuitous manner of speech. *Irse de vareta,* (Fam.) To have a diarrhœa. *Gorrion con vareta,* (Joc.) A little man with a long sword.
Vareteár, va. To variegate stuffs with stripes of different colours.
Variáble, a. Variable, changeable; mutable.
Variableménte, ad. Variably.
Variación, sf. 1. Variation, the act of varying. 2. Change, mutation. *Variacion de la aguja,* (Naút.) Variation of the compass or magnetic needle from the true north point towards east or west.
Variádo, da, a. Variegated.
Variaménte, ad. Variously, differently.
Variánte, sf. Various readings in different editions of a work.—pa. Varying, deviating.
Variár, va. To change, to alter; to variegate. to diversify.—vn. 1. To vary. 2. (Naút.) To cause a deviation of the magnetic needle from the true north point.
Várice y Varíz, sf. Dilatation of a vein.
Varicóso, sa, a. Afflicted with a dilatation of the veins.
Variedád, sf. Variety, particular distinction; change, inconstancy, variation.
Variegádo, da, a. Variegated, stained with different colours.
Varilarguéro, sm. Bull-fighter with a long pike.
Varílla, sf. 1. A small rod; a curtain-rod. 2. Spindle, pivot. 3. Switch. *Varillas,* Jaw-bones; frame of a sieve or strainer. 4. Rib of a fan.
Varilláge, sm. Collection of ribs of a fan.
Vário, ria, a. 1. Various, divers, different. 2. Inconstant, variable, changeable. 3. Vague, undetermined. 4. Variegated. *Varios,* Some.

Varío, *sm.* (Ict.) Pink, menow or minnew. Cyprinus phoxinus *L.*

Varón, *sm.* 1. Man, a human being of the male sex. 2. A male human being, grown up to the state of manhood, which is considered from 30 to 45 years. 3. Man of respectability. 4. (Ant.) Baron, a degree of nobility. V. *Baron. Buen varon*, A wise and learned man; (Iron.) A plain artless being. *Varon del timon*, (Naút.) Rudder-pendant.

Varóna, *sf.* (Ant.) Masculine woman.

Varonía, *sf.* Male issue; male descendants.

Varonìl, *a.* Male, manly; spirited.

Varonilménte, *ad.* Manfully, in a manly manner.

Varráco, *sm.* V. *Verraco.*

Varraqueár, *vn.* To grunt like a boar.

Vasálla, *sf.* Vassal, a female subject.

Vasallàge, *sm.* 1. Vassalage, the state of a vassal; submission, dependence. 2. Liege money, a tax paid by vassals to their lord.

Vasállo, *sm.* 1. Vassal, subject; one who acknowledges a superior lord. 2. Feudatory.

Vasállo, lla, *a.* Subject, relating to a vassal. *Mal vasallo*, Disobedient, unsubjected.

Vasár, *sm.* Buffet on which glasses or vessels are put.

Vascongádo, da, *a.* Belonging to Biscay.

Vascuénce, *sm.* Biscay-dialect or language; any jargon not easily understood.

Vasculár, *a.* Vascular, consisting of vessels.

Vasculífero, ra, *a.* Vasculiferous, containing seed vessels.

Vásculo, *sm.* Vessel, any cylindrical part of the animal body.

Vasculóso, sa, *a.* Vascular, containing vessels.

Vaséra, *sf.* Buffet, a kind of cupboard.

Vasíja, *sf.* 1. Vessel in which liquors are kept. 2. Collection of vessels in a cellar for keeping liquors. *Vasija que rezuma*, A leaky cask.

Vasijílla, ta, *sf.* A small vessel.

Vasíllo, to, *sm. dim.* A small glass or cup. *Vasillo*, Cell or comb of bees.

Váso, *sm.* 1. Vessel, a concave piece of any matter for holding liquors; vase. 2. (Naút.) Room or capacity of a ship; a vessel. 3. Talent, genius. 4. (Astr.) Crater, a southern constellation. 5. Horse's hoof. 6. Vessel, vein or artery. 7. Receptacle, capacity of one vessel to contain another. *Vaso de barro*, The human body; an earthen vessel. *Vasos*, Close-stools, chamber-pots.

Vástago, *sm.* Stem, bud, shoot.

Vastedád, *sf.* Vastness, immensity, vast extent.

Vásto, ta, *a.* Vast, huge, immense.

Váte, *sm.* (Poét.) Bard, druid.

Vaticinadór, ra, *s.* Prophet, diviner.

Vaticinánte, *pa.* Foreteller; divining.

Vaticinár, *va.* To divine, to foretel.

Vaticínio, *sm.* Divination, prediction.

Vatídico, ca, *a.* (Poét.) Prophetical.

Vaxílla, *sf.* 1. Table-service. 2. Plate won at horse races.

Váya, *sf.* Scoff, jest.—*interj. Vaya*, Go!

Váyna, *sf.* 1. Knife or scissors'-case; scabbard of a sword. *Vayna abierta*, Scabbard of a large sword which covers only one-third of it, in order to be easily drawn. 2. Pod, the capsule of legumes, the case of seeds. 3. (Naút.) Bolt-rope-tabling, a broad hem made at the bottom or foot and skirts of sails, to which the bolt-rope is fastened. *De vayna abierta*, Hastily; boldly.

Vaynázas, *sm.* (Fam.) A humdrum, dull or dronish person.

Vaynéro, *sm.* Scabbard-maker.

Vaynìca, y lla, *sf.* 1. A small pod or shell. 2. A back-stitch near the seam at the edging of clothes. 3. (Bot.) Vanilla. Epidendrum vanilla *L.*

Vayvén, *sm.* 1. Fluctuation, vibration. 2. Unsteadiness, inconstancy. 3. Risk, danger. 4. (Naút.) Cord or rope of different thickness.

Véase, See; a direction of reference.

Vecéra, *sf.* Drove of swine and other animals.

Vecería, *sf.* Herd of swine.

Vecéro, ra, *a.* y *s.* 1. One who performs alternately or by turns. 2. Applied to trees which yield fruit one year and none another.

Vecinál, *a.* Belonging to the neighbourhood.

Vecinaménte, *ad.* Near, contiguously.

Vecindád, *sf.* 1. Population, the inhabitants of a place. 2. Vicinity, contiguity. 3. Right of an inhabitant, acquired by the residence in a town for a time determined by law. 4. Affinity, similarity, proximity. *Hacer mala vecindad*, To be a troublesome neighbour.

Vecindádo, *sm.* Vicinity, neighbourhood.

Vecindár, *va.* V. *Avecindar.*

Vecindário, *sm.* 1. Number of inhabitants of a place. 2. Roll or list of the inhabitants of a place. 3. Neighbourhood, vicinity; right acquired by residence.

Vecíno, na, *a.* 1. Neighbouring, living in the neighbourhood; near, proximate. 2. Like, resembling, coincident.

Vecíno, *sm.* 1. Neighbour, inhabitant, housekeeper. 2. Denizen. *Medio vecino*, He who in a parish distinct from his residence, paying half the contributions, enjoys the right of depasturing his cattle on the commons.

Vectigáles, *sm. pl.* Toll, duty paid on goods, which are carried from one place to another.

Véda, *sf.* Prohibition, interdiction.

Vedádo, *sm.* Warren, park, enclosure for game.

Vedamiénto, *sm.* Prohibition.

Vedár, *va.* 1. To prohibit, to forbid. 2. To obstruct, to let, to impede; to suspend or deprive.

Vedegámbre, *sm.* (Bot.) Hellebore.

Vedéja, *sf.* V. *Guedeja.*

Vedíja, *sf.* 1. Entangled lock of wool. 2. Tuft of entangled hair, matted hair. 3. Scrotum.

Vedijéro, ra, *s.* Collector of the loose locks of wool at shearing.

Vedijílla, ta, ca, *sf.* A small lock of wool.

Vedijúdo ó Vedejúdo, da; y Vedijóso, sa, *a.* Having entangled or matted hair.

Vedriádo, da, *a.* Glazed. V. *Vidriado* y *Vidrioso.*

Vedúño, *sm.* Quality of vines or grapes. V. *Viñedo.*

Veedór, ra, *s.* 1. Spy, one who pries into the actions of others. 2. Overseer, inspector. 3. Caterer, provider of provisions. 4. Principal equerry to the king after the equerry in chief. (Mil.) Inspector.

Veeduría, *sf.* Place or employment of an overseer or inspector; the inspector's office.

Véga, *sf.* An open plain; a tract of level and fruitful ground.
Vegáda, *sf.* Time, turn. *A' las vegadas*, At times; by turns.
Vegetabilidád, *sf.* Vegetability.
Vegetáble y Vegetál, *a.* Vegetable.
Vegetación, *sf.* Vegetation, the power of producing growth in plants.
Vegetánte, *pa.* Vegetating.
Vegetárse, *vr.* To vegetate.
Vegetatívo, va, *a.* Vegetative.
Vegéto, ta, *a.* Robust, vigorous, active.
Vegílla, *sf.* V. *Vigilia.*
Veguér, *sm.* (Arag.) Magistrate of a certain district.
Veguería y Veguerío, *s.* (Arag.) Jurisdiction of the magistrate, called *Veguér.*
Veheméncia, *sf.* Vehemence, violence, impetuosity; efficacy, force.
Veheménte, *a.* Vehement, violent, forcible, impetuous; persuasive, vivid.
Vehementeménte, *ad.* In a vehement or forcible manner.
Vehículo, *sm.* Vehicle.
Veintávo, *sm.* The twentieth part of any thing.
Veínte, *a.* Twenty. V. *Vigésimo. A' las veinte*, Unseasonably.—*sm.* 1. Number or cipher 20. 2. Pin standing alone in front of the nine-pins.
Veintén, *sm.* Twenty reals.
Veinténa, *sf.* The twentieth part; a score.
Veintenár, *sm.* V. *Veintena.*
Veintenário, ria, *a.* Containing twenty years.
Veinténo na; y Veintésimo, ma, *a.* (Ant.) Twentieth, the ordinal number of twenty. *Veinteno*, Applied to cloth containing 2000 threads in the warp.
Veinteñál, *a.* Lasting twenty years.
Venteochéno, na, *a.* Applied to warp consisting of 2800 threads.
Ventesenéno, na, *a.* Applied to the warp of cloth having 2600 threads.
Veinticínco, *a.* Twenty-five.
Veintidós, *a.* Twenty-two.
Veintidoséno, na; y Veintedoséno, na, *a.* 1. Applied to cloth, the warp of which contains 2200 threads. 2. Twenty-second.
Veintinuéve, *a.* Twenty-nine.
Veintiócho, *a.* Twenty-eight.
Veintiquatréno, na, *a.* Twenty-fourth.
Veintiquatría, *sf.* Office of a *Veintiquatro*, or magistrate of some towns in Andalusia.
Veintiquátro, *sm.* Magistrate of some towns in Andalusia.—*a.* Twenty-four.
Veintiséis, *a.* Twenty-six.
Veintisiéte, *a.* Twenty-seven.
Veintitrés, *a.* Twenty-three.
Veintiúna, *sf.* The game of Twenty-one.
Veintiúno, na, *a.* Twenty-one.
Veisle, lo, See it.
Vejancón, na, *a.* Decrepit, worn out with age; peevish from old age.
Vejarrón, na, *a.* Very old.
Vejestório, *sm.* Old trumpery; a petulant old man.
Vejéte, *sm.* 1. A ridiculous old man. 2. Actor of an old man.
Vejéz, *sf.* 1. Old age, the last stage of life. 2. Decay, the state of being worn out. 3. Imbecility and peevishness of old age. 4. A trite or stale story.
Vejezuéla, *sf.* An old hag.
Vejón, na, *s.* Very old person.
Vejóte, *sm.* An old man.
Véla, *sf.* 1. Watch, forbearance of sleep, attendance without sleep. 2. Watchfulness, vigilance. 3. Watchman, night-guard. 4. Pilgrimage. V. *Romería.* 5. Candle. *Velas sumergidas*, Dipped candles. *Velas amoldadas*, Mould candles. 6. A horse's ear; act of raising the ears. 7. Awning. 8. Sail, ship. 9. Night-work. 10. (Naút.) Sail, the expanded canvass which catches the wind, and carries on the vessel in the water. *Vela mayor*, Main-sail. *Vela de trinquete*, Fore-sail. *Vela de mesana*, Mizen. *Vela de gavia*, Main-top-sail. *Vela de velacho*, Fore-top-sail. *Vela de sobremesana*, Mizen-top-sail. *Vela de juanete mayor*, Main-top-gallant-sail. *Vela de juanete de proa*, Fore-top-gallant-sail. *Vela de periquito de sobremesana*, Mizen-top-gallant-sail. *Vela de cebadera*, Sprit-sail. *Vela de sobre-cebadera*, Sprit-sail-top-sail. *Vela seca*, Cross-jack-sail. *Vela de estay*, Stay-sail. *Vela de maricangallo*, Driver. *Vela de senda*, Try-sail. *Vela de congreja*, Broom-sail. *Velas de proa*, Head-sails. *Velas de popa*, After-sails. *Velas mayores*, Courses. *Vela baradera*, Drabbler. *Vela de cruz*, A square-sail. *Vela de lastrar*, Port-sail. *Caida de una vela*, Drop or depth of a sail. *Grotil de una vela*, Head of a sail. *Vela encapillada*, Sail blown over the yard. *Vela aferrada*, Furled sail, a sail which is taken in. *Vela cazada*, Trimmed sail. *Vela larga ó desaferrada*, Unfurled sail. *Vela cargada arriba ó sobre las candalizas*, A sail hauled up in the brails. *Vela tendida*, Taught or full sail. *Vela desrelingada*, Sail blown from the bolt-rope. *Vela en facha*, Backed sail. *Vela que flamea*, Sail which shivers in the wind. *Vela quadrada*, Square sail. *Marear una vela*, To set a sail. *Hacerse á la vela*, To set sail. *Llevar poca vela*, To carry an easy sail. *Hacer fuerza de vela*, To crowd sail. *En vela*, Vigilantly, without sleep. *A' la vela*, Prepared, equipped, ready. *A' vela y pregon*, Auction by inch of candle. *Tender las velas ó velas*, (Met.) To seize an opportunity for attaining any object; to dilate a subject, to embellish a discourse with figurative language.
Velácho, *sm.* (Naút.) Fore-top-sail.
Velación, *sf.* Watch, the act of watching. *Velaciones*, Nuptial benedictions.
Veláda, *sf.* Watch. V. *Velacion. Veladas*, Wakes.
Veládo, *sm.* (Fam.) Husband, married man.
Veladór, ra, *s.* 1. Watchman, night-guard, watcher. 2. Careful observer, vigilant keeper, spy. 3. A large wooden candlestick, used by tradesmen to work at night; table or bench on which a night-light is placed.
Veláje, *sm.* (Naút.) Sails in general. V. *Velamen.*
Velámbres, *sm. pl.* Nuptial benedictions.
Velámen, *sm.* (Naút.) Sails in general; set of sails; trim of sails. *Arreglar el velamen*, (Naút.) To trim the sails. *Estar con un mismo velamen*, (Naút.) To be under the same sails.

Velár, *vn.* 1. To be watchful, to wake, not to sleep. 2. To keep guard or stand sentinel by night. 3. To observe attentively; to watch carefully. 4. (Naút.) To appear, to show itself above the water as rocks. 5. To assist by turns before the holy sacrament when it is manifested. *Velar las escotas,* (Naút.) To stand by the sheets.—*va.* 1. To guard, to watch or keep. 2. To marry, to give the nuptial benediction. 3. To attend the sick or deceased at night.

Velárte, *sm.* Sort of fine broad cloth.

Veleidád, *sf.* 1. Velleity, the lowest degree of desire; feeble will. 2. Levity, inconstancy, fickleness.

Veleidóso, sa, *a.* Feeble-willed, inefficacious, inconstant, fickle.

Velejár, *vn.* (Naút.) To make use of sails.

Velería, *sf.* A tallow-chandler's shop.

Veléro, *sm.* 1. Tallow-chandler. 2. Pilgrim.

Veléro, ra, *a.* Swift sailing; applied to a ship.

Velésa, *sf.* (Bot.) Leadwort. Plumbago europea *L.*

Veléta, *sf.* Weather-cock; fickle person.

Veléte, *sm.* A light thin veil.

Velfálla, *sf.* A sort of linen.

Velicación, *sf.* (Med.) Vellication, stimulation.

Velicár, *va.* To vellicate, to twitch.

Velílla, *sf.* A small candle.

Velíllo, to, co, *sm. dim.* 1. A small vail. 2. Embroidered gauze.

Velláco, (Ant.) V. *Bellaco.*

Vellecíllo, *sm.* A small fleece.

Velléra, *sf.* Woman who takes off the soft hair growing on women's faces, women's barber.

Vellído, da, *a.* Downy, villous.

Véllo, *sm.* 1. Down, soft hair on parts of the skin where no strong hair grows. 2. The downy matter which envelopes some seeds or fruit. 3. Short downy hair of brutes.

Vellocíno, *sm.* Sheep's skin with the wool on.

Vellón, *sm.* 1. Fleece, as much wool as is shorn from one sheep; flock or lock of wool. 2. Copper coin of the province of Castile: it is also used like the English word *sterling.*

Vellonéro, *sm.* Collector of the fleeces at shearing.

Vellóra, *sf.* (And.) Knot or lump taken off woollen cloth.

Vellorí ó Vellorín, *sm.* Broad cloth of the natural colour of wool.

Vellorita, *sf.* (Bot.) Cowslip. Primula veris *L.*

Vellósa, *sf.* (Cant.) Coarse cloth or rug worn by mariners.

Vellosidád, *sf.* Downiness.

Vellosílla, *sf.* (Bot.) Creeping mouse-ear, mouse-ear hawkweed. Hieracium pilosella *L.*

Vellóso, sa, *a.* Downy, villous.

Vellúdo, da, *a.* Downy.

Vellúdo, *sm.* Shag, velvet.

Vellutéro, *sm.* Velvet-worker.

Vélo, *sm.* 1. Veil, curtain. 2. Pretence, pretext, cloak, mask. 3. Veil, female dress worn by nuns; the novices wear white veils, the professed black ones. 4. Piece of white gauze thrown over a couple at marriage, it falls on the man's shoulders and on the woman's head, at the same time a purple sash or ribbon is placed on the shoulders of both. 5. Feast at the profession of a nun, or at taking the veil. 6. Confusion, obscurity, perplexity, any thing which impairs the sight or intellect. *Correr el velo,* To pull off the mask. *Tomar el velo,* To become a nun.

Velocidád, *sf.* Velocity, quickness, nimbleness, readiness.

Velón, *sm.* Lamp in which oil is burnt.

Veloséra, *sf* Wooden lamp-stand or bracket.

Velonéro, *sm.* Lamp-maker.

Velóz, *a.* Swift, nimble, active.

Velozménte, *ad.* Swiftly.

Véna, *sf.* 1. Vein, a blood-vessel, which leads the blood back to the heart. 2. Fibre of plants. 3. Hollow cavity. 4. Vein or course of metal in a a mine. 5. Tendency or turn of mind or genius. *Vena poética,* A poetical vein. 6. Diverse quality or colour of earth or stones; stripes in stones; mineral water found under the ground. *Hallar á alguno de vena,* To find one in a favourable disposition. *Dar en la vena, ó hallar la vena,* To hit upon the right means. *Ganado en vena,* Cattle not castrated.

Venáblo, *sm.* Javelin, a short spear formerly used in hunting wild boars.

Venadéro, *sm.* Place much frequented by deer.

Venádo, *sm.* Deer, a kind of stag.

Venáje, *sm.* Current of a stream.

Venál, *a.* 1. Venal, belonging to the veins, contained in the veins. 2. Marketable, saleable. 3. Mercenary, prostitute.

Venalidád, *sf.* Venality, mercenariness, prostitution.

Venalogía, *sf.* Treatise of the veins.

Venático, ca, *a.* Having a vein of madness.

Venatório, ria, *a.* Venatic, used in hunting.

Vencedór, ra, *s.* Conqueror, victor.

Vencéjo, *sm.* 1. String, band. 2. (Orn.) Swift, black-martin. Hirundo apus *L.*

Vencér, *va.* 1. To conquer, to subdue; to prevail. 2. To surmount, to overcome, to clear. 3. To gain a law-suit. 4. To bend, to turn down. 5. To prevail upon, to persuade. 6. To suffer, to tolerate or bear with patience. 7. To incline, to twist any thing.—*vn.* 1. To obtain a place from which emoluments arise. 2. To gain, to succeed.—*vr.* To be master of one's passions; to govern one's desires.

Vencíble, *a.* Vincible, conquerable; superable.

Vencída, *sf.* Victory. *Llevar de vencida,* To prove victorious.

Vencído, da, *a.* Due, payable; conquered. *Ir alguno de vencida,* To begin or be about to be conquered. *Llevar á alguno de vencida,* To begin to conquer one.

Vencimiénto, *sm.* 1. Victory, conquest. 2. Bent, the act of bending or turning down. 3. Maturity of a bill of exchange, period of falling due. *Vencimiento de plazo,* (Com.) A bill due.

Vénda, *sf.* Fillet, a band tied round the head; a diadem. V. *Venta.*

Vendáje, *sm.* 1. Commission on the sale of goods disposed of by a factor or agent. 2. Ligature made with a fillet.

Vendár, *va.* 1. To tie with a band or fillet. 2. To hoodwink, to darken or cloud the understanding.

Vendavál, *sm.* A strong wind south by west.

Vendedéro, ra, *s.* One employed in selling any thing.

Vendedór, ra, *s.* Seller, trader.

Vendehúmos, *sm.* He who boasts his influence with persons in power to sell it to expectants; literally, a smoke-seller.
Vendéja, *sf.* A public sale.
Vendér, *va.* 1. To give or transfer any thing for a price. 2. To expose to sale. 3. To prostitute, to devote to crimes for a reward. 4. To render dear or difficult. 5. To persuade, to delude with false pretences. 6. (Met.) To betray faith, confidence, or friendship. *Vender salud*, (Fam.) To be or to appear very robust. *Vender juncia*, (Fam.) To boast of what one ought not, or of what in reality he has not. *Vender humos*, (Met.) To boast of great influence with men in power to swindle expectants. *Vender por mayor*, To sell in the lump or by wholesale. *Vender palabras*, To deceive by fair words.—*vr.* 1. To brag or boast of talents or merits one does not possess. 2. To devote one's self to the service of another. *Venderse caro*, To be of difficult access. *Venderse barrato*, To make one's self cheap. *Venderse ropa*, (Fam.) To be very cold.
Vendeháche, *sm.* (Mil.) Vender, dealer.
Vendíble, *a.* Saleable, marketable, vendible.
Vendíca y ta, *sf. dim.* Small fillet or diadem.
Vendicatívo, va, *a.* (Ant.) V. *Vengativo.*
Vendición, *sf.* Sale, the act of selling.
Vendído, da, *a.* Sold. *Estar vendido*, To be duped, to be exposed to great risks. *Estar como vendido*, To be disgusted in the company of those holding opposite sentiments or of strangers.
Vendímia, *sf.* 1. Vintage, the time in which grapes are gathered. 2. Large gain or profit.
Vendimiádo, da, *a.* Gathered vintage. *Como por viña vendimiada*, Easily, freely, without difficulty.
Vendimiadór, ra, *s.* Vintager, one who gathers the vintage or produce of vines.
Vendimiár, *va.* 1. To vine or gather the vintage. 2. To enjoy unlawful perquisites; to reap benefit or profit unjustly. 3. (Fam.) To kill, to murder.
Véndo, *sm.* List of cloth.
Veneficiár, *va.* 1. To bewitch, to injure by witchcraft. 2. (Ant.) To reap benefit from. V. *Beneficiar.*
Venefício, *sm.* 1. Charm, witchcraft; the act of bewitching. 2. (Ant.) Benefit, favour. V. *Beneficio.*
Venéfico, ca, *a.* Poisonous; using witchcraft.
Venenár, *va.* To poison. V. *Envenenar.*
Venenário, *sm.* Apothecary. V. *Boticario.*
Venenífero, ra, *a.* (Poét.) V. *Venenoso.*
Venéno, *sm.* 1. Poison, venom; any thing hurtful or injurious to health. 2. Medicine, medicament. 3. Poisonous mineral ingredients, used in the composition of paints or dyestuffs. 4. Wrath, fury, passion. 5. Bad, insipid taste. 6. (Met.) Any thing pernicious to morals and religion.
Venenosidád, *sf.* Poisonousness, the quality of being poisonous or venomous.
Venenóso, sa, *a.* Venomous, poisonous.
Venéra, *sf.* 1. Porcelain shell, or Mediterranean scallop, Ostrea jacobæa *L.* worn by pilgrims, who return from St. Jago or Santiago in Galicia. 2. Badge worn by the knights of military orders. 3. Vein of metal in a mine; spring of water.
Venerábles, *a.* Venerable, worthy of veneration; epithet of respect to ancient ecclesiastics of distinguished virtue; title given by the king to prelates.
Venerablemènte, *ad.* In a venerable manner; with respect or veneration.
Veneración, *sf.* 1. Veneration, profound respect. 2. Worship.
Veneradór, ra, *s.* Venerator, worshipper.
Venerándo, da, *a.* Venerable.
Veneránte, *pa.* Venerator, worshipping. [ship.
Venerár, *va.* To venerate, to respect, to wor-
Venéreo, rea, *a.* Venereous, venereal.
Venéro, *sm.* 1. A vein of metal in a mine; origin, root; a spring or source of water. 2. Radius or horary line of sun-dials.
Veneruéla, *sf.* A small Porcelain shell. V. *Venera.*
Vengadór, ra, *s.* Avenger, revenger.
Vengáble, *a.* Worthy of revenge, that may be revenged.
Vengála, *sf.* 1. A kind of thin gauze or veil. 2. (Mil.) A slender cane, or staff used by captains.
Vengancílla, *sf.* A slight revenge.
Vengánza, *sf.* Revenge, return of an injury.
Vengár, *va.* To revenge, to return an injury. —*vr.* To be revenged on.
Vengativamènte, *ad.* Revengefully.
Vengatívo, va, *a.* Revengeful, vindictive.
Vénia, *sf.* 1. Pardon, forgiveness. 2. Leave, permission. 3. Royal license, granted to minors to manage their own estates. 4. Bow with the head.
Veniál, *a.* Venial, pardonable.
Venialidád, *sf.* Venialness, state of being excusable.
Venialmènte, *ad.* In a pardonable manner.
Venída, *sf.* 1. Arrival; return, regress. 2. Overflow of a river. 3. Attack in fencing. 4. Impetuosity, rashness.
Venidéro, ra, *a.* Future, that will be hereafter.
Venidéros, *sm. pl.* Posterity.
Venído, da, *a.* Come. *Venido del cielo*, Come from heaven; expressing the excellence of any thing.
Venílla, ca, ta, *sf.* A small vein.
Venímo, *sm.* Bile, a sore angry swelling.
Venívo, na, *a.* Venomous, poisonous.
Venír, *vn.* 1. To come, to draw near. *Ven acá*, (Fam.) Come hither; used to call the attention and advise any one. 2. To happen, to pass. 3. To follow, to succeed. 4. To spring from, to be occasioned by; to infer, to deduce; to originate in, to proceed from. 5. To appear before a judge; to come into court. 6. To assent, to submit, to yield to another's opinion. 7. To answer, to fit, to suit. 8. To grow, to shoot up. 9. To make an application, to ask. 10. To occur, to be presented to the memory or attention. 11. To resolve, to determine. 12. To attack, to assault. 13. (Arit.) To result. 14. To be of one's party or opinion; to accompany. 15. To fall, to be overset. 16. Used impersonally, Come here, take this. 17. To succeed finally. *Vino á conseguir la plaza*, He obtained the place. *Vino á morir*, He has

just died. Here it is an auxiliary with the preposition *á* after it; in this case it sometimes signifies either the actual action of the following verb, or the state of readiness for action, as *venir baylando*, To dance; *venir á cuentas*, To calculate, to count. 18. To change the state or quality. 19. To be transferred, to pass from one to another. 20. To adduce; to produce. 21. To excite, to effect; to attain a degree of excellence or perfection. 22. Used to express politely satisfaction or pleasure at the arrival of any one; to welcome. *Vengamos al caso*, Let us come to the point. *Venir á menos*, To decay, to decline. *Venir de perilla*, To come at the nick of time.—*vr.* 1. To ferment, to attain perfection by fermentation, as bread or wine. It is often used the same as the neuter verb *venir*. *Venirse á buenas*, To be on good terms. *Venirse á casa*, To come home. *Venirse durmiendo*, To fall asleep.

Venóra, *sf.* (Ar.) Range of stones in a drain or trench.

Venóso, sa, *a.* Veiny, full of veins.

Vénta, *sf.* 1. Sale, the act of selling, market, vent. 2. A poor inn on roads far from towns or villages. *Hacer venta*, To halt or stop at a poor inn; to invite a passenger or traveller to dinner. *Ser una venta*, To be a dear place. *Estar de ó en venta*, (Fam.) To be on sale; applied to a woman who stands much at a window to see and be seen. 3. (Met.) Open place exposed to the inclemency of the weather.

Ventadór, *sm.* V. *Aventador*.

Ventája, *sf.* 1. Advantage, preference; additional pay. 2. Odds given at play.

Ventajosaménte, *ad.* Advantageously.

Ventajóso, sa, *a.* Advantageous, comparatively superior.

Ventálla, *sf.* Valve. V. *Válvula*.

Ventálle, *sm.* Fan. V. *Abanico*.

Ventána, *sf.* 1. Window, an aperture in a building, by which air and light are introduced. 2. Window-shutter. 3. Nostril, the cavity in the nose. 4. Any of the corporal senses of hearing or seeing. *Hacer la ventana*, To be constantly at the window; applied to women who show themselves at the window to their courtiers. *Tener ventana al cierzo*, To be elated with pride.

Ventanáge, *sm.* Number of windows in a building.

Ventanázo, *sm.* Slap of a window.

Ventaneár, *vn.* To frequent the window, to gaze repeatedly from the window.

Ventanéro, ra, *a.* Window-gazers; persons who are constantly at the window.

Ventanéro, ra, *sm.* Glazier, one whose trade is to make glass windows.

Ventaníca y Ventanílla, *sf.* A small window.

Ventaníco y llo, *sm.* A small window-shutter.

Ventarrón, *sm.* Violent wind.

Ventár y Venteár, *vn.* y *a.* 1. To blow, to move with a current of air. *Ventea muy fresco del N. O.* (Naút.) It blows very fresh at N. W. 2. To smell, to scent, to perceive by the nose. 3. To investigate, to examine. 4. To dry, to expose to the air.—*vr.* 1. To be filled with wind or air. 2. To break wind.

Venteadúra, *sf.* Split made in timber by the wind.

Ventéo, *sm.* Venthole in a cask.

Ventéro, ra, *s.* Keeper of a small inn.

Ventiléra, *sf.* A sort of leather case or purse fastened to a belt.

Ventilación, *sf.* Ventilation; discussion.

Ventilár, *va.* 1. To ventilate, to fan with the wind; to winnow, to fan. 2. To examine, to discuss.—*vn.* To move with a current of air, to circulate; applied to the air.

Ventísca, *sf.* Storm, attended with a heavy fall of snow.

Ventiscár, *vn.* To blow hard, attended with snow.

Ventísco, *sm.* V. *Ventisca*.

Ventiscóso, sa, *a.* Windy, stormy, tempestuous.

Ventisquéro, *sm.* 1. Place where heaps of snow are thrown together by the wind. 2. Storm, attended with snow.

Ventoléra, *sf.* 1. Gust, a sudden blast of wind. 2. Vanity, pride, loftiness. 3. V. *Regilera*.

Ventolína, *sf.* (Naút.) Light variable wind.

Ventór, *sm.* Pointer, a dog that points out the game; a fox-hound.

Ventorrillo y Ventórro, *sm.* A petty inn or tavern near a town.

Ventósa, *sf.* 1. Cupping-glass, a glass used by scarifiers to draw out the blood by rarefying the air. 2. Vent, air-hole, spiracle. *Pegar una ventosa*, To trick or swindle one out of his money.

Ventoseár y Ventoseárse, *vn.* y *r.* To break wind.

Ventoséro, ra, *a.* Fond of cupping.

Ventosidád, *sf.* Flatulency, windiness.

Ventóso, sa, *a.* 1. Windy; flatulent. 2. Pointing; applied to a pointer dog. 3. Vain, inflated. 4. Windy, tempestuous.

Ventráda, *sf.* Brood of young brought forth at once.

Ventrál, *a.* Belonging to the venter; ventral.

Ventrécha, *sf.* Belly of fishes.

Ventregáda, *sf.* Brood, litter; abundance.

Ventréra, *sf.* Roller or girdle which encircles the belly.

Ventrículo, *sm.* 1. Ventricle, the stomach. 2. Any of the cavities of the heart or brain.

Ventríloquo, *sm.* Ventriloquist.

Ventrón, *sm.* *aum.* of *vientre*.

Ventrúdo, da; y **Ventróso, sa**, *a.* Big-bellied, having a big venter or belly.

Ventúra, *sf.* 1. Luck, a favourable chance, fortune. 2. Contingency, casualty. *Buena ventura*, Good fortune told by gipsies and other vagrants. *Por ventura*, By chance. *Probar ventura*, To try one's fortune. 3. Risk, danger. *A ventura*, At a venture, at hazard; without much consideration. *La ventura de garcia*, (Irón.) Misfortune.

Venturéro, ra, *a.* 1. Casual, incidental. 2. Lucky, fortunate. 3. Vagrant, idle, adventurous.

Venturéro, *sm.* Fortune-hunter, adventurer.

Venturílla, *sf.* Good luck.

Venturína, *sf.* A precious stone of a yellowish brown colour.

Ventúro, ra, *a.* Future; that which will be hereafter; or that which is to come.

Venturón *sm.* Great luck.

Venturosaménte, *ad.* Luckily, fortunately.

Venturóso, sa, *a.* Lucky, fortunate.

Vénus, *sf.* 1. (Astr.) Evening star, a planet; Venus. 2. A beautiful charming woman. 3. Venery, carnal or sensual pleasures. 4. (Quim.) Copper. *Monte de venus*, (Quirom.) Small eminence in the palm of the hand at the root of any of the fingers.

Venustidád, *sf.* Beauty, gracefulness.

Venústo, ta, *a.* Beautiful, graceful.

Vénza, *sf.* Scarfskin, used by gold-beaters.

Ver, *va.* 1. To see, to perceive by the eye. 2. To observe, to consider, to reflect. 3. To see, to visit. 4. To foresee, to forecast. 5. To fancy, to imagine; to judge. 6. To find out, to discover; to explore. 7. To be present at the report of a law-suit. 8. To experience. 9. To examine. 10. To see at a future time. 11. Used with the particle *ya* it is generally a menace, as *ya verá*, you shall see. *Ver venir*, To await the resolution or determination of another person. *Ser ó estar de ver*, To be worth while seeing. *No poder ver á alguno*, To abhor or detest one. *Al ver*, On seeing a thing. *A' mi ver*, In my opinion, or as far as I can see. *A' ver, ó veamoslo*, Let us see it. *A' mas ver*, Farewell, until we see you again. *Ver las estrellas*, (Fam.) To be deeply afflicted with grief. *Ver tierras ó mundo*, To travel. *Tener que ver una persona con otro*, To have relation or connexion; to have carnal communication.—*vr.* 1. To be seen; to be in a place proper to be seen; to be conspicuous. 2. To find one's self in a state or situation. *Verse pobre*, To be reduced to poverty. *Verse negro*, To be in great want or affliction; to be greatly embarrassed. 3. To be obvious or evident. 4. To concur, to agree. 5. To represent the image or likeness, to see one's self in a glass. 6. To know the cards, at play. *Verse en ello*, To consider, to weigh in the mind. *Verse con alguno*, To have a crow to pluck with one. *Ya se ve*, It is evident; (Irón.) Likely indeed that such a thing should happen. *Verse ó irse viendo*, To discover, to view what should be concealed. *Verse y desearse*, To have very great care, anxiety, and fatigue in executing any thing.

Ver, *sm.* 1. Sense of the sight or seeing. 2. Light, view, aspect, appearance.

Véra, *sf.* (Extrem.) Edge, border. V. *Orilla*. *Veras*, Truth, reality, earnestness. *De veras*, In truth, really; joking apart; in all earnest. *Con muchas veras*, Very earnestly.

Veracidád, *sf.* Veracity, honesty of report.

Veranáda, *sf.* Summer season.

Veranadéro, *sm.* Place where cattle pasture in summer.

Veranár y Veraneár, *vn.* To spend or pass the summer season.

Veranéo y Veranéro, *sm.* Place where cattle graze in summer.

Veraníco y Veranillo, *sm.* A short summer.

Veraniégo, ga, *a.* 1. Belonging or relating to the summer season. 2. Thin or sickly in summer. 3. Imperfect, defective.

Veráno, *sm.* 1. Summer season. 2. (Ant.) Spring.

Verátro, *sm.* V. *Eléboro*.

Veráz, *a.* Veracious, observant of truth.

Verbál, *a.* Verbal; oral. *Copia verbal*, A literal copy.

Verbalménte, *ad.* Verbally, orally.

Verbásco, *sm.* (Bot.) Great mullein. Verbascum thapsus *L.*

Verbásculo ó Gordolobíllo, *sm.* (Bot.) Mullein. Verbascum lichnitis *L.*

Verbéna, *sf.* (Bot.) Vervain. Verbena officinalis *L.* *Coger la verbena*, (Met.) To rise early to take a walk.

Verberación, *sf.* Verberation; the act of the wind or water striking against any thing.

Verberár, *va.* To verberate, to beat, to strike, to dart against; applied to wind and water.

Verbigrácia, *ad.* For example, for instance.

Vérbo, *sm.* 1. Word, term, expression, mental image. 2. (Gram.) Verb, one of the parts of speech. 3. (Teol.) Word, second Person of the Holy Trinity. 4. (Lóg.) Verb or word which unites the predicate with the subject. *Verbos*, Swearing, angry expressions; abusive language. *Echar verbos*, To curse, to swear. *De verbo ad verbum*, (Lat.) Word for word, literally.

Verbosidád, *sf.* Verbosity, exuberance of words.

Verbóso, sa, *a.* Verbose, exuberant in words, prolix.

Verdácho, *sm.* A kind of gritty green earth, used by painters.

Verdád, *sf.* 1. Truth, veracity, reality. 2. Truth, verity, clear expression; certain existence of things. 3. A sort of delicate paste. 4. Axiom, maxim, truism. 5. Virtue of veracity or truth. *Verdad de perogrullo*, A notorious truth. *Verdad es que, ó es verdad que*, The truth is that. *Tratar verdad*, To love truth. *A' la verdad ó de verdad*, Truly, in fact, in truth. *Es verdad*, It is true.

Verdaderaménte, *ad.* Truly, in fact, indeed.

Verdadéro, ra, *a.* True, real, sincere, ingenuous.

Verdál, *sm.* Green gage, a sort of green plum.

Verdásca, *sf.* V. *Vardasca*.

Vérde, *sm.* 1. Green, the colour of herbs and plants. 2. Verdigrise, colour made of an oxide of copper. 3. Youth, the early stage of life. 4. Person in the bloom of age. 5. Green barley or grass, given in spring to horses or mules in order to purge them. *Darse un verde*, To amuse one's self. *Verde forzado*, Green made by mixing blue and yellow.—*a.* 1. Green, of the colour of plants. 2. Unripe, immature, not perfect; fresh. 3. Young, blooming. *Viejo verde*, A boyish old man.

Verdéa, *sf.* A sort of Florence white wine.

Verdeár, *vn.* To grow green, to get a greenish colour.—*va.* To collect grapes and olives to sell them.

Verdeceledón, *sm.* Sea-green, a colour made of light blue and straw colour.

Verdecér, *vn.* To grow green.

Verdecíllo, *sm.* (Orn.) Greenfinch. Loxia chloris *L.*

Verdecíllo, lla, *a. dim.* Greenish, inclined to green.

Verdeesmeralda, *a.* Emerald green.

Verdegáy, *sm.* A light bright green.

Verdegueár, *vn.* To grow green.

Verdéja, *a.* V. *Verdal.*
Verdemár, *sm.* Sea-green, a colour used by painters.
Verdemontáña, *sf.* Mountain-green, a green mineral colour, imported from Hungary.
Verdéte, *sm.* Verditer.
Verdevejíga, *sf.* Sap-green, a sort of deep coloured green.
Verdezól, *sm.* Kind of green shell-fish.
Verderón, *sm.* (Orn.) The yellow-hammer.
Verdéte, *sm.* V. *Cardenillo.*
Verdezuélo, *sm.* V. *Verdecillo.*
Verdín y Verdína, *s.* 1. Unripeness, immaturity. 2. Sea-weed, pond-weed, duck-meat. *Verdin*, Oxide of copper.
Verdinégro, gra, *a.* Of a deep green colour.
Verdíno, na, *a.* Of a bright green colour.
Verdiséco, ca, *a.* Pale green.
Verdolága, *sf.* (Bot.) Purslain. Portulaca *L.*
Verdón, *sm.* (Orn.) Greenfinch. Loxia chloris *L.*
Verdór, *sm.* 1. Verdure, herbage, green colour of plants. 2. Acerbity, the unpleasant taste of unripe fruit. 3. Vigour and strength of the animal body. *Verdores*, Youth, age of vigour.
Verdóso, sa, *a.* Greenish.
Verdóyo, *sm.* A green mouldy substance growing on walls.
Verdugádo, *sm.* Under petticoat formerly worn by women.
Verdugál, *sm.* Young shoots growing in a wood after cutting.
Verdúgo, *sm.* 1. The young shoot of a tree. 2. Tuck, a long narrow sword. 3. Hangman, the public executioner. *Pagar los azotes al verdugo*, To return good for evil. 4. Mark of a lash on the skin. 5. Things which afflict the mind. 6. Very cruel person. 7. (Arq.) Row of bricks in a stone or mud wall. 8. Small ring for the ears, hoop. 9. (Mil.) Leathern whip.
Verdugón, *sm.* A long shoot of a tree; a large mark of a lash.
Verduguíllo, *sm.* 1. A small shoot of a tree. 2. Blight, mildew, rust. 3. A small narrow razor. 4. A long narrow sword. 5. (Ant.) Ring.
Verduléro, ra, *s.* Green-grocer, one who sells greens and herbs.
Verdúra, *sf.* 1. Verdure; all sorts of greens and culinary vegetables or garden stuff. *Verduras*, Foliage in landscapes and tapestry. 2. Vigour, luxuriance.
Verduríta, *sf.* Slight herbage, paucity of vegetation.
Veréda, *sf.* 1. Path, narrow way. 2. Circular order or notice sent to several towns or places. 3. Route of travelling preachers.
Veredário, ria, *a.* Hired; applied to horses, carriages, &c.
Veredéro, *sm.* Messenger sent with orders or despatches.
Veredílla, ta, ca, *sf.* A very narrow foot-path.
Vérga, *sf.* 1. Yard, organ of generation in male animals. 2. Nerve or cord of the cross-bow. 3. (Naút.) Yard, a round piece of timber which supports the sails and derives its particular name from the sail it supports. *Verga seca*, Cross-jack-yard. *Poner las vergas en cruz*, To square the yards.
Vergájo, *sm.* Pizzle.
Vergél, *sm.* 1. Flower-garden; a beautiful orchard. 2. Any thing pleasing to the sight.
Vergéta, *sf.* A small twig.
Vergetádo, da, *a.* (Blas.) Vergette, paley, having the field divided by several small pales.
Vergonzánte, *a.* Bashful, shamefaced.
Vergonzosaménte, *ad.* Shamefully.
Vergonzocíco, ca; llo, lla; to, ta, *a. dim.* Diffident.
Vergonzóso, sa, *a.* 1. Shamefaced, modest. 2. Shameful. *Partes vergonzosas*, Privy parts.
Vergóña, *sf.* (Ant.) V. *Vergüenza.*
Vergueár, *va.* To beat with a rod.
Vergüénza, *sf.* 1. Shame. 2. Bashfulness, modesty; diffidence. 3. A base action. 4. Regard of one's own character; dignity, honour. 5. (Ant.) Curtain before windows or doors. *Perder la vergüenza*, To become abandoned. *Es una mala vergüenza*, It is a shameful thing. *Vergüenzas*, Privy parts.
Verguér ó Verguéro, *sm.* (Ar.) Kind of high constable.
Verguéta, *sf.* A small switch or rod.
Verguílla, *sf.* Gold or silver wire without silk.
Vericuéto, *sm.* A rough rugged road. *Vericuetos*, Strange or ridiculous ideas.
Verídico, ca, *a.* Veridical, telling truth.
Verificación, *sf.* Inquiry, examen; confirmation by argument or evidence.
Verificár, *va.* To verify, to confirm, to prove true.—*vr.* To prove true, to accomplish.
Verificatívo, va, *a.* Tending to prove.
Veríno, *sm.* 1. A fine sort of tobacco which grows at Verino, in South America. 2. (Burg.) Pimple, small pustule.
Verisímil, *a.* Probable, likely.
Verisimilitúd, *sf.* Verisimilitude, probability.
Verisimilménte, *ad.* Probably.
Vérja, *sf.* Grate of a door or window.
Vermiculación, *sf.* Vermiculation.
Vermiculár, *a.* Vermiculous, full of grubs.
Vermiculár, *va.* To vermiculate, to ornament parts of an edifice with worm-like figures.
Vermifórme, *a.* Vermiform.
Vermífugo, *a.* (Med.) Vermifuge, anthelmintic.
Verminóso, sa, *a.* Full of grubs.
Vermíparo, ra, *a.* Vermiparous, producing worms.
Vermívoro, ra, *a.* Vermivorous.
Vernál, *a.* Vernal, belonging to the spring.
Véro, ra, *a.* True, real. *De veras*, In truth.
Véro, *sm.* (Blas.) Cup or bell-formed vase on a shield.
Verónica, *sf.* 1. Image of Jesus Christ represented on a handkerchief, or other things. 2. (Bot.) Speedwell. Veronica officinalis *L.*
Verosímil, *a.* Verisimilar. V. *Verisimil.*
Verosimilitúd, *sf.* Verisimility. V. *Verisimilitud.*
Verráca, *sf.* (Naút.) A kind of tent pitched on shore by sailors for sheltering stores or utensils.
Verráco, *sm.* Boar, the male of a swine.
Verraqueár, *vn.* To grunt like a boar.
Verriondéz, *sf.* 1. Rutting time of boars and other animals. 2. Withering state of herbs.
Verrióndo, da, *a.* 1. Foaming like a boar at the rutting time. 2. Withering, flaccid.

Verrocál, *sm.* A craggy rocky place. V. *Berrocal.*
Verrucária, *sf.* (Bot.) Wart-wort. Euphorbia helioscopia *L.*
Verrúga, *sf.* Wart.
Verrugóso, sa, *a.* Warty, covered with warts.
Verruguiénto, ta, *a.* Full of warts, warty.
Verruguílla, ca, ta, *sf.* A small wart.
Versádo, da, *a.* Versed, conversant. *Versado en diferentes lenguas*, Conversant in different languages.
Versalílla, *sf.* (Impr.) Small capital letter.
Versár, *vn.* To whirl, to turn round rapidly.—*vr.* To be versed or conversant; to grow skilful in the management of some business or other.
Versatíl, *a.* Versatile; changeable, variable.
Versecíllo, *sm. dim.* of *verso.*
Versería, *sf.* Park of small artillery.
Verséte, *sm. dim.* Small piece of artillery.
Versícula, *sf.* Place where the choir-books are placed.
Versiculário, *sm.* One who takes care of the choir-books.
Versículo, *sm.* 1. Versicle, a small part of the responsory which is said in the canonical hours. 2. Verse of a chapter.
Versificadór, ra, *s.* Versifier, versificator.
Versificár, *va.* To versify, to make verses.
Versíllo, *sm.* A little verse.
Versión, *sf.* Translation, version.
Versísta, *sm.* Versifier, verseman, versificator; one who writes blank verse.
Vérso, *sm.* 1. Verse, a line consisting of a certain succession of sounds and number of syllables. 2. Culverin of a small bore, now disused. 3. Joke, witty saying, jest. 4. (Gal.) Cradle. *Verso de arte mayor*, Verse of 12 syllables.
Vertébra, *sf.* Vertebre, one of the joints of the back-bone.
Vertebrál, *a.* Vertebral, belonging to the joints of the back-bone.
Vertedéro, *sm.* Sewer, drain.
Vertedór, ra, *s.* 1. Nightman, one who empties the common sewer. 2. Conduit, sewer. 3. (Naút.) Scoop, a wooden shovel for throwing out water; used in boats.
Vertéllos, *sm. pl.* (Naút.) Trucks, pieces of wood with a hole in the middle to form the parrels.
Vertér, *va.* 1. To spill, to shed. 2. To empty or clear vessels. 3. To translate writings from one language into another. 4. To divulge, to publish, to reveal what was kept secret. 5. To exceed, to abound.
Vertibilidád, *sf.* Versatility, vertibleness.
Vertíble, *a.* Moveable, changeable, variable.
Verticál, *a.* Vertical, placed in the zenith.
Verticalménte, *ad.* Vertically.
Vértice, *sm.* Vertex, zenith, the point over the head; crown of the head.
Verticidád, *sf.* The power of turning; rotation.
Vertiénte, *sm.* Waterfall, cascade.—*pa.* Flowing.
Vertiginóso, sa, *a.* Giddy, troubled with giddiness.
Vértigo, *sm.* Giddiness.
Vertimiénto, *sm.* (Ant.) Effusion.

Véspero, *sm.* Vesper, the evening star.
Vespertíllo, *sm.* Bat. V. *Murciélago.*
Vespertína, *sf.* Evening discourse in universities.
Vespertíno, na, *a.* Vespertine, happening or coming in the evening.
Vespertíno, *sm.* Doctrinal sermon preached in the evening.
Vesquír, *vn.* (Ant.) V. *Vivir.*
Véste, *sf.* Clothes, garments. V. *Vestido.*
Vestíbulo, *sm.* Vestibule, portal.
Vestído, *sm.* 1. Dress, wearing apparel, clothes, garments. 2. Ornament, embellishment. *Vestido usado*, Second-hand clothes. *Vestido de corte*, Court-dress. *Vestido y calzado*, Without labour.
Vestidúra, *sf.* 1. Dress, wearing apparel. 2. Vesture, robe of distinction.
Vestígio, *sm.* 1. Vestige, footstep; ruins, remains of buildings. 2. Memorial, mark, sign, index. *Vestigio horizontal ó vertical*, In stone-cutting, the horizontal or the vertical figure of the shadows formed by the sun's perpendicular rays.
Vestíglo, *sm.* Horrid and formidable monster.
Vestiménta y Vestiménto, *s.* Clothes, garments. *Vestimentas*, Ecclesiastical robes.
Vestír, *va.* 1. To clothe, to dress, to cover or adorn the body with clothes. 2. To deck, to adorn. 3. To make clothes for others. 4. To cloak, to disguise. 5. To instruct, to inform, to advise. 6. To roughcast the walls of a building. 7. To affect a passion or emotion. 8. To give liberally, to make liberal presents. 9. (Met.) To embellish a discourse. *Vestir el proceso*, To carry on a suit according to law.—*vn.* To go well dressed.—*vr.* 1. To be covered; to be clothed. *El cielo se vistió de nubes*, The sky was overcast with clouds. *La primavera viste los campos*, Spring clothes the fields. 2. To be elated or puffed up with pride. 3. To dress one's self on rising after sickness.
Vestuário, *sm.* 1. Vesture, all the necessaries of dress. 2. Vestry, place where clergymen dress. 3. Money given to ecclesiastics for dress and stipend to assistants. 4. Green-room, dressing-room, in a theatre. *Vestuarios*, Deacon and sub-deacon who attend the priest at the altar.
Vestúgo, *sm.* Stem or bud of an olive.
Véta, *sf.* 1. Vein of ore, metal or coal in mines. 2. Vein in wood or marble. 3. Stripe of a different colour in cloth or stuff. *Descubrir la veta*, To discover one's sentiments or designs.
Vetádo, da; y Veteádo, da, *a.* Striped, veined, streaky; having veins or stripes.
Veteár, *va.* To variegate, to form veins of different colours.
Veteráno, *a.* Experienced, veteran, long practised; particularly applied to soldiers.
Vetílla, ca, *sf.* A small vein; a narrow stripe.
Vetústo, ta, *a.* (Ant.) Very ancient.
Vexación, *sf.* Vexation, molestation.
Vexámen, *sm.* Taunt, scurrilous criticism or censure.
Vexaminísta, *sm.* Censor, critic.

Vezár, *va.* 1. To vex, to molest, to harass. 2. To scoff, to censure, to ridicule.

Vexíga, *sf.* 1. Bladder, the vessel which contains the urine. 2. Blister, a pustule raised on the skin; any slight elevation on a plain surface.—*pl.* 1. Pustules of the small-pox. 2. Windgalls, an infirmity incident to horses. *Vexiga deperro*, (Bot.) Winter-cherry. Physalis sommifera *Cavan.*

Vexigación, *sf.* Vesication, blistering.

Vexigatório, ria, *a.* Blistering, raising blisters.

Vexigázo, *sm.* Blow with a bladder full of wind. *Dar en vexigazo*, To trick, to cheat.

Vexigón, *sm. aum.* Large bladder or blister.

Vexigüéla ó Vexiguílla, ca, ta, *sf.* Small bladder.

Vexiguéro, *sm.* 1. Spectator, by-stander, who bets at a gaming-table, but does not play. 2. Collector of rents.

Vexílo, *sm.* Standard, banner.

Vexéce, *sf.* (Ant.) V. *Vejez.*

Vez, *sf.* 1. Time, turn, alternate succession. 2. Epoch or epocha, a fixed time. 3. Draught, the quantity of liquor drank at once. 4. Herd of swine belonging to the inhabitants of a place. 5. United with *cada*, it intimates repetition, viz. *Una vez*, Once. *Á la vez ó por vez*, Successively, by turns. *De una vez*, At once. *Mas de una vez*, More than once. *En vez*, Instead of. *Tal vez*, Perhaps; seldom, once in a way. *Tal qual*, On a singular occasion or time. *Veces*, Power or authority committed to a substitute. *Hacer las veces de otro*, To supply one's place. *Á veces*, Sometimes, by turns.

Vezár, *va.* To accustom, to habituate. V. *Avezar.*

Vézo, *sm.* 1. Custom, habit. V. *Costumbre.* 2. Blubber-lip, a thick lip. V. *Bezo.*

Vía, *sf.* 1. Way, road, route. V. *Camino.* 2. Way, mode, manner, method, procedure. 3. Profession, calling, trade, line of business. 4. Post-road. 5. Passage, gut in the animal body. 6. Spiritual life. *Por via*, In a manner, or form. *Via reservada*, Office of a secretary of state and foreign affairs. *Via recta*, By the direct way. *Via Crucis sacra*, Calvary, a place having paths, stations for crosses, altars, &c. in imitation of Christ's journey on Mount Calvary. *Via purgativa*, (Teol.) First stage of a soul to perfection, by washing away its sins with tears. [treadles.

Viadéra, *sf.* Part of the loom close to the

Viadór, *sm.* Passenger, traveller.

Viáge, *sm.* 1. Journey, tour, voyage, travel. 2. Way, road. 3. (Arq.) Deviation from a right or straight line. 4. Gait, the manner and air of walking. 5. Excursion; errand. 6. Load, carried from one place to another at once. 7. Quantity of water which comes from the general reservoir, to be divided into various particular channels or conduits. *Buen viage*, Good journey or voyage; expression of indifference whether a thing is lost or not; it is also used on throwing dead bodies into the sea, and signifies rest in peace. *Viage redondo*, Voyage round the world.

Viagéro y Viajadór, *sm.* Traveller, passenger.

Viajánte, *pa.* Traveller, voyager.

Viajár, *vn.* To travel, to perform a journey or voyage.

Viajáta, *sf.* (Joc.) Looseness, diarrhœa.

Viál, *a.* Wayfaring; belonging to a journey

Viánda, *sf.* 1 Food, viands, meat, victuals. 2 (Met.) The eucharist, as food for the soul.

Viandánte, *sm.* Traveller, passenger.

Viandéra, *sm.* Waiter, who serves viands or puts them on the table.

Viaráza, *sf.* 1. Looseness, diarrhœa. 2. A rash and inconsiderate action.

Viarécta, *ad.* Straight along, straight forward.

Viático, *sm.* 1. Viaticum, provision for a journey. 2. The last rite, used to prepare the passing soul for its departure.

Vibdo, da, *a.* (Ant.) V. *Viudo.*

Víbora, *sf.* Viper. Coluber berus *L.* [viper.

Viborézno y Viboríllo, lla, *s.* Young small

Viborézno, na, *a.* Viperine, viperous.

Vibración, *sf.* Vibration, the act of moving or being moved with quick reciprocation or return.

Vibránte, *pa.* Vibrating, undulating. [turn.

Vibrár, *va.* 1. To vibrate, to brandish, to move to and fro with quick motion. 2. To throw, to dart.—*vn.* To vibrate, to play up and down or to and fro.

Vibúrno, *sm.* (Bot.) Wayfaring-tree, mealy guelder-rose. Viburnum lantana *L.*

Vicaría, *sf.* 1. Vicarship; vicarage; office and jurisdiction of vicar. 2. The second superior in a convent of nuns. *Vicaría perpetua*, Perpetual curacy.

Vicariáto, *sm.* Vicarage, the dignity of a vicar; the district subjected to a vicar.

Vicário, ria, *a.* Vicarial.—*s.* 1. Vicar, deputy, one who performs the functions of another in ecclesiastical affairs. 2. He who exercises the authority of the superior of a convent in his absence; one who transacts all ecclesiastical affairs as substitute of a bishop or archbishop. *Sacar por el vicario*, To convey a woman into a place of safety, by ecclesiastical authority, against the will of her parents or guardians, where she may freely declare her consent to a marriage. *Vicario, via de coro*, Choral vicar, superintendent of the choir. *Vicario general*, Vicar general, an ecclesiastical judge appointed to exercise jurisdiction over a whole territory in opposition to a *vicario pedáneo*, who has authority over a district only.

Více, Vice, used in composition to signify deputy, or one of the second rank.

Vicealmiránta, *sf.* The galley next in order to that of the admiral.

Vicealmirantázgo, *sm.* Office or rank of vice-admiral.

Vicealmiránte, *sm.* Vice-admiral.

Vicecamaréro, *sm.* Vice-chamberlain.

Vicecancillér, *sm.* Vice-chancellor.

Viceconsiliário, *sm.* Vice-counsellor.

Vicecónsul, *sm.* Vice-consul.

Viceconsuládo, *sm.* Vice-consulate.

Vicediós, *sm.* Sovereign pontiff.

Vicegerénte, *a.* Vicegerent.

Vicelegádo, *sm.* Vicelegate.

Vicelegatúra, *sf.* Office and jurisdiction of a vicelegate.

Vicenál, *a.* Arrived at the age of twenty years

Vicepatróno, *sm.* Vice-patron.

Viceprepósito, *sm.* Vice-president, vice-provost.
Vicepresidénte, *sm.* Vice-president.
Viceprovíncia, *sf.* Collection of religious houses which are not erected into a province, but occasionally enjoy that rank.
Viceprovinciál, *sm.* Vice-provincial.
Vicerrectór, *sm.* Vice-rector.
Vicerrectoráto y Vicerrectoría, *s.* Vice-rectorship.
Vicesenescál, *sm.* Vice-seneschal or steward.
Vicesimário, ria, *a.* Vicenary, relating or belonging to twenty.
Vicésimo, ma, *a.* Twentieth, the ordinal number of twenty.
Vice vérsa, *ad.* On the contrary; to the contrary.
Vícia, *sf.* Tare. V. *Arveja.*
Viciár, *va.* 1. To vitiate, to mar, to spoil or corrupt. 2. To counterfeit, to adulterate. 3. To forge, to falsify. 4. To annul, to make void. 5. To deprave, to pervert. 6. To put a false construction on a passage or expression.—*vr.* To deliver one's self up to vices; to become too much attached to any thing.
Vicicilín, *sm.* (Orn.) A small American bird which seldom perches or sits, and is seen pecking flowers on the wing. V. *Resucitado.*
Vício, *sm.* 1. Viciousness, faultiness. 2. Vice, moral corruption; evil habits. 3. Artifice, fraud, craft. 4. Excessive appetite, extravagant desire. 5. Deviation from rectitude, defect or excess. 6. Luxuriant growth. *Los sembrados llevan mucho vicio*, The corn-fields are luxuriant. 7. Forwardness or caprice of children, arising from too much indulgence in their education. *De vicio*, By habit or custom, without necessity or cause. 8. Viciousness of horses or mules.
Viciosaménte, *ad.* Viciously, in a vicious manner; falsely.
Vicióso, sa, *a.* 1. Vicious or vitious; given to vice. 2. Luxuriant, overgrown, vigorous. 3. Abundant; provided; delightful.
Vicisitúd, *sf.* Vicissitude, return of the same things in the same succession; successive or alternate order of events.
Vicisitudinário, ria, *a.* Changeable, variable.
Víctima, *sf.* Victim; sacrifice.
Victimário, *sm.* Servant who attended the sacrificing priest.
Victór, *sm.* 1. Shout, cry of acclamation, Long live! V. *Vítor.* 2 Public rejoicing in honour of the achiever of some glorious deed. 3. Table or tablet, on which is written a short eulogy of the hero of a festival.
Victoreár, *va.* To shout, to huzza. V. *Vitorear.*
Victória, *sf.* Victory, triumph, conquest; superiority, advantage over an opponent.—*interj.* Victory.
Victoriál, *a.* Relating to victory.
Victoriosaménte, *ad.* Victoriously, in a victorious manner.
Victorióso, sa, *a.* 1. Victorious. 2. Title given to warriors.
Vicúña, *sf.* Vigogne, a wild animal in South America, from which the celebrated Vigogne wool is obtained. Camelus vicugna *L.*
Vid, *sf.* 1. (Bot.) Vine. Vitis *L.* 2. Navel-string.
Vída, *sf.* 1. Life, union and co-operation of the soul and body; living or continuance in life. 2. Space or duration of life. 3. Livelihood, means of living. 4. Conduct, behaviour, deportment, way or manner of life; state, condition. 5. History or memoirs of any one's actions during life. 6. Aliment necessary to preserve life. 7. (Met.) Life, any thing very animating and agreeable. *Vida mia ó mi vida*, My life; expressions of endearment. *A vida*, With life. *No dexar hombre á vida*, Not to leave a living soul. 8. State of grace, eternal life. 9. Principle of nutrition, vital motions or functions; any thing which contributes to support life. 10. (For.) The determined number of 10 years. *Agua de la vida*, Brandy. *Buscar la vida*, To earn an honest livelihood; to scrutinize the life of another. *Dar mala vida*, To treat very ill. *Darse buena vida*, To give one's self up to the pleasures of life; to conform one's self to reason and law. *De por vida*, For life, during life. *En mi vida ó en la vida*, Never. *Hacer vida*, To live together as husband and wife. *Perdona-vidas*, Hector, bully. *Ser de vida*, To give hopes of life.
Vidénte, *pa.* He who sees, seeing; a seer.
Vidriádo, *sm.* Glazed earthenware.
Vidríado, da, *a.* V. *Vidrioso.*
Vidriár, *va.* To varnish, to glaze earthenware.
Vidriéra, *sf.* 1. A glass window. 2. A glass case or cover. *Licenciado vidriera*, Nickname for a person too delicate or fastidious.
Vidriería, *sf.* Glazier's shop, a shop where all sorts of glass-wares are sold.
Vidriéro, *sm.* Glazier, a dealer in glass.
Vídrio, *sm.* 1. Glass, an artificial transparent substance, made by fusing alkaline salts and flint or sand together. 2. Vessel or other thing made of glass. 3. Any thing very nice and brittle. 4. A very touchy or irascible person. 5. (Poét.) Water.
Vidrióso, sa, *a.* 1. Vitreous, brittle. 3. Slippery. 3. Peevish, touchy, irascible. 4. Very delicate.
Viduál, *a.* Belonging or peculiar to widowhood.
Vidúño y Viduéño, *sm.* Peculiar quality of grapes or vines.
Viejázo, *sm.* An old man worn out with age.
Viejecíto, ta; Viejezuélo, la, *a.* Somewhat old.
Viéjo, ja, *a.* 1. Old, stricken or much advanced in years. 2. Ancient, antiquated. 3. Applied to a youth of judgment and knowledge beyond his years. *Cuento de viejas*, Old woman's story. *Perro viejo*, (Fam.) A keen, clever experienced person.
Viéjos, *sm. pl.* The hair on the temples.
Viéldo, *sm.* A winnowing fork. V. *Bieldo.*
Vientecíllo, *sm.* A light wind.
Viénto, *sm.* 1. Wind, a violent course or agitation of the air. 2. Windage of a gun, the difference between the diameter of the bore and that of the ball. 3. Scent by which the dogs pursue the game. 4. Nape-bone of a dog, which stands prominent between the ears. 5. Vanity, petty pride. 6. Rope or cord, by which any thing is suspended in the air. 7. Any very light thing. 8. Any thing that violently agitates the mind. 9. That which assists or contributes to any end. 10. (Cant.) Propagator of evil reports. *Viento de bolina*, (Naút.) A scant wind. *Viento contrario*, Foul wind *Viento galerno*,

A fresh gale. *Vientos generales*, Trade-winds. *Viento en popa*, Wind right aft. *Viento derrotero*, Wind on the beam. *Quitar el viento á un baxel*, To becalm a ship. *Dar con la proa al viento*, To throw a ship up in the wind. *El viento refresca*, (Naút.) The wind freshens. *Cosas de viento*, Vain, empty trifles. *Moverse á todos vientos*, To be fickle, changeable, or wavering. *Dar el viento*, (Met.) To presume, to conjecture truly.

VIÉNTRE, *sm.* 1. Belly, that part of the animal body which reaches from the breast to the thighs, containing the bowels. 2. Fœtus enclosed in the womb; pregnancy, the state of being with child. 3. That part of any thing which swells out into a larger capacity; the belly or widest part of vessels. 4. The body, or more essential part of any instrument or act. 5. The mother, excluding the father. 6. Intestines of animals. 7. Stomach, when speaking of a great eater. *El parto sigue el vientre*, The offspring follows the womb, respecting slavery or freedom. *Reses de vientre*, Breeding cattle, such as are big with young.

VIENTRECÍLLO, *sm.* Ventricle, any small cavity in the animal body, especially those of the heart.

VIÉRNES, *sm.* 1. Friday, the sixth day in the week. 2. Fast-day, any day of abstinence, when meat is not to be eaten. *Cara de viernes*, A wan, thin face. *Viernes Santo*, Good-Friday.

VÍGA, *sf.* Beam, a large and long piece of timber. *Viga de largar*, Beam with which grapes or olives are pressed.

VIGÉSIMO, MA, *a.* Twentieth, the ordinal number of twenty.

VÍGIA, *s.* 1. (Naút.) The look out. 2. V. *Atalaya*. 3. Act of watching.

VIGIÁR, *vn.* (Naút.) To look out, to watch for any thing at sea.

VIGILÁNCIA, *sf.* Vigilance, watchfulness.

VIGILÁNTE, *a.* Watchful, vigilant, careful.

VIGILANTEMÉNTE, *ad.* Vigilantly.

VIGILÁR, *vn.* To watch over, to keep guard.

VIGILATÍVO, VA, *a.* That which makes watchful.

VIGÍLIA, *sf.* 1. The act of being awake, or on the watch. 2. Lucubration, nocturnal study. 3. Vigil, a fast kept before a holiday; service used on the night before a holiday. 4. Watchfulness, want of sleep. 5. Watch, limited time for keeping guard. 6. Office of the dead, to be sung in churches.

VIGÓR, *sm.* Vigour, strength, force, energy; activity, liveliness, briskness.

VIGORÁR, *va.* To strengthen, to invigorate.

VIGORNÉTA, *sf.* Silversmith's anvil. V. *Bigorneta*.

VIGÓRNIA, *sf.* V. *Bigornia*.

VIGOROSAMÉNTE, *ad.* Vigorously.

VIGOROSIDÁD, *sf.* Vigour, might, strength, force.

VIGORÓSO, SA, *a.* Vigorous, strong, active, powerful.

VIGÓTAS, *sf. pl.* (Naút.) Dead-eyes, small blocks which have eyes or holes but no sheaves.

VIGUERÍA, *sf.* (Naút.) All the beams of a ship; the timber-work of a vessel.

VIGUÉTA, *sf.* A small beam.

VIHUÉLA, *sf.* Guitar, a stringed musical instrument.

VIHUELÍSTA, *sm.* Player on the guitar.

VÍL, *a.* 1. Mean, despicable, sordid, low, servile. 2. Worthless, infamous, ungrateful, vile.

VILÁNO, *sm.* Bur or down of the thistle. V. *Milano*.

VILÉZA, *sf.* 1. Meanness, lowness, vileness, depravity. 2. A disgraceful action, an infamous deed; turpitude. 3. Rabble, mob.

VILIGACIÓN, *sf.* V. *Administracion*.

VILIPENDIÁR, *va.* To contemn, to revile.

VILIPÉNDIO, *sm.* Contempt, disdain.

VÍLLA, *sf.* 1. Town which enjoys by charter some peculiar privileges. 2. (Ant.) Country-seat. 3. Corporation of magistrates of a privileged town.

VILLADIÉGO, *sm.* *Coger las de villadiego*, To run away, to pack off bag and baggage.

VILLÁGE, *sm.* Village; hamlet.

VILLANÁGE, *sm.* VILLANAGE, the middling class or rank of society in villages; peasantry opposed to the nobility.

VILLANAMÉNTE, *ad.* Rudely, boorishly.

VILLANCÉJO Y VILLANCÉTE, *sm.* V. *Villancico*.

VILLANCHÓN, NA, *a.* Clownish, rustic, rude.

VILLANCÍCO, *sm.* A metric composition, sung in churches on certain festivals. *Villancicos*, Hackneyed answers, frivolous excuses.

VILLANCIQUÉRO, *sm.* One who composes small metric compositions, to be sung in churches.

VILLANERÍA, *sf.* 1. Lowness of birth, meanness. V. *Villanía*. 2. Middling classes of society. V. *Villanage*.

VILLANÉSCO, CA, *a.* Rustic, rude, boorish, coarse.

VILLANÍA, *sf.* 1. Lowness of birth, meanness. 2. Rusticity, inurbanity; indecorous word or act.

VILLÁNO, NA, *a.* 1. Belonging to the lowest class of country people. 2. Rustic, clownish. 3. Worthless, unworthy. 4. Villanous, wicked.

VILLÁNO, *sm.* 1. A kind of Spanish dance. 2. A false, vicious horse. 3. Villain, a rustic, an unsociable villager. *Villano harto de ajos*, (Fam.) Rude ill-bred forward bumpkin.

VILLANÓTE, *a. aum.* of *villano*, Highly rude.

VILLÁR, *sm.* 1. Village, a small place of a few houses or cottages. V. *Village*. 2. Billiards, a game.

VILLÁZGO, *sm.* 1. Charter of a town, containing the privileges of the place. 2. Tax laid upon towns.

VILLÉTA, *sf.* A small town or borough.

VILLÉTE, *sm.* Note, billet. V. *Billete*.

VILLÍCA, TA, *sf. dim.* Small town.

VILLIVÍNA, *sf.* A kind of linen.

VILLORÍA, *sf.* Farm-house.

VILLORÍN, *sm.* A sort of coarse cloth.

VILLORÍO, *sm.* A rotten borough; a miserable little place.

VILLORÍTA, *sf.* (Bot.) Colchicum, meadow saffron.

VILMÉNTE, *ad.* Vilely; in a mean, base, or illiberal manner.

VÍLO, A word only used adverbially; as *En vilo*, In the air; (Met.) Insecurely.

VILÓRDO, DA, *a.* Slothful, lazy, heavy.

VILÓRTA, *sf.* 1. Ring made of twisted willow. 2. A kind of cricket, played in Old Castile.

VILTÓSO, SA, *a.* (Ant.) V. *Vil*.

VÍMBRE, *sm.* (Bot.) Osier. V. *Mimbre.*
VIMBRÉRA, *sf.* V. *Mimbrera.*
VINAGÉRA, *sf.* Vessel in which wine and water are served at the altar for the mass.
VINÁGRE, *sm.* 1. Vinegar, wine grown sour; acetous acid. 2. Acidity, sourness. 3. (Met.) A person of a peevish or fretful temper. 4. Change for the worse, or from good to bad.
VINAGRÉRA, *sf.* Vinegar-cruet.
VINAGRÉRO, *sm.* Vinegar-merchant.
VINAGRÍLLO, *sm.* 1. Weak vinegar. 2. A kind of cosmetic lotion, used by women. 3. Rose-vinegar; snuff mixed with rose-vinegar, or prepared with that vinegar.
VINAGRÓSO, SA, *a.* Sourish; peevish, fretful.
VINARIÉGO, *sm.* Vintager, one who possesses a vineyard, cultivates vines, and gathers the grapes.
VINÁRIO, RIA, *a.* Belonging to wine.
VINATERÍA, *sf.* Place where wine is retailed; wine-trade.
VINATÉRO, *sm.* Vintner, wine-merchant.
VINÁTICO, CA, *a.* (Ant.) Belonging to wine.
VINÁZA, *sf.* Last wine drawn from the lees.
VINÁZO, *sm.* Very strong wine.
VINCAPERVÍNCA, *sf.* V. *Clematide.*
VINCULÁBLE, *a.* That may be entailed.
VINCULACIÓN, *sf.* Entail, act of entailing.
VINCULÁR, *va.* 1. To entail an estate. 2. To ground or found upon; to assure. 3. To continue, to perpetuate. 4. To secure with chains.
VÍNCULO, *sm.* 1. Tie, link, chain. 2. Entail, an estate entailed or settled with regard to the rule of its descent. 3. Charge or encumbrance laid upon a foundation.
VINDICACIÓN, *sf.* 1. Revenge, the act of avenging one's wrongs. 2. The act of giving every one his due.
VINDICÁR, *va.* 1. To vindicate, to revenge, to avenge. 2. To claim, to reclaim. 3. To assert, to defend.
VINDICATÍVO, VA, *a.* 1. Vindictive, revengeful. 2. Defensive, vindicatory.
VINDÍCTA, *sf.* Vengeance, revenge. *Vindicta publica*, Public vengeance, the atonement which crimes should pay to public justice as an example.
VINÍCO, LLO, TO, *sm. dim.* Small or light wine.
VINIÉBLA, *sf.* (Bot.) Hound's tongue. Cynoglossum officinale *L.*
VÍNO, *sm.* 1. Wine, the fermented juice of the grape. *Vino arropado*, Ropy wine. *Vino por trasegar*, Unracked wine. *Vino clarete*, (Rioja) Claret or pale red wine. *Vino de agujas*, Sharp rough wine. *Vino de cuerpo*, A strong-bodied wine. *Vino gota*, Mother-drop, or virgin wine, which flows spontaneously from the grape without pressure. *Vino doncel*, Sweet clear wine. *Vino tinto*, Red wine. *Una buena cosecha de vino*, A good vintage. 2. Preparation of fruit or vegetables by fermentation, called by the general name of *wine*. 3. Any thing which intoxicates, or deprives of the use of reason. *Vino de pasto*, Wine for daily use.
VINOLÉNCIA, *sf.* Temulency, inebriation with liquor.
VINOLÉNTO, TA, *a.* Temulent, inebriated.
VINOSIDÁD, *sf.* Quality of being vinous, or consisting of wine, vinosity.
VINÓSO, SA, *a.* 1. Vinous, having the qualities of wine, consisting of wine. 2. Temulent, inebriated.
VÍÑA, *sf.* 1. Vineyard, a ground planted with vine. 2. (Met.) Catholic church. *Como hay viñas*, As sure as fate. *Viñas*, (Cant.) Escape, flight. *De mis viñas vengo*, (Met.) A familiar excuse for absence.
VIÑADÉRO, *sm.* Keeper of a vineyard.
VIÑADÓR, *sm.* Cultivator of vines.
VIÑÉDO, *sm.* Country or district abounding in vineyards.
VIÑÉRO, *sm.* Vintager who owns and cultivates vineyards.
VIÑÉTA, *sf.* Vignette, flower, or other small picture, placed at the top of a page, or beginning and end of a chapter.
VIÑÍCA, TA, Y VIÑUÉLA, *sf. dim.* of *Viña.*
VIÓLA, *sf.* 1. Viol, a 6-stringed musical instrument, resembling a fiddle or violin, but larger. *Viola de amor*, A 12-stringed viol. 2. (Bot.) Violet. Viola *L.* V. *Alhelí.*
VIOLÁCEO, EA, *a.* Violaceous, violet-coloured.
VIOLACIÓN, *sf.* Violation, the act of violating or profaning.
VIOLÁDO, DA, *a.* 1. Having the colour of violets; made or confectioned with violets. 2. Violated.
VIOLADÓR, RA, *s.* Violator; profaner.
VIOLÁR, *va.* 1. To violate or transgress a law, to offend. 2. To ravish, to commit a rape, to violate a woman. 3. To spoil, to tarnish. 4. To profane or pollute the church.
VIOLÁRIO, *sm.* (Arag.) Annual pension given to any religious by the possessor of his paternal property.
VIOLÉNCIA, *sf.* 1. Violence, impetuousness, compulsion, force, violent and unnatural mode of proceeding. 2. Wrong construction, erroneous interpretation. 3. Rape, a violent defloration. 4. Excessiveness, intenseness, of cold, &c.
VIOLENTAMÉNTE, *ad.* Violently, forcibly.
VIOLENTÁR, *va.* 1. To enforce by violent means, to make use of violence; to violate. 2. To put a wrong construction on a passage or writing, to interpret erroneously. 3. (Met.) To open or break any thing by force, to enter any place against the will of its proprietor.—*vr.* To be violent.
VIOLÉNTO, TA, *a.* 1. Violent, impetuous, boisterous, irascible; forced, unnatural, contrary to the regular mode. 2. Strained, absurd, erroneous; applied to construction or interpretation. *Poner manos violentas*, To lay violent hands on any clergyman or person who enjoys ecclesiastical rights.
VIOLÉRO, *sm.* (Ant.) V. *Guitarrero.*
VIOLÉTA, *sf.* (Bot.) Violet. Viola *L.*
VIOLÍN, *sm.* 1. Violin, fiddle, a 4-stringed musical instrument. 2. Fiddler, musician.
VIOLINÉTE, *sm.* A pocket-violin, used by dancing-masters.
VIOLINÍSTA, *sm.* Player on the violin or fiddle.
VIOLÓN, *sm.* 1. Bass-viol, a musical stringed instrument. 2. Player on the bass-viol.

VIOLONCÍLLO, *sm.* Small bass-viol, or player on it.
VIPERÍNO, NA, *a.* Belonging to vipers.
VIQUITÓRTES, *sm. pl.* (Naút.) Quarter-gallery knees, curvated pieces of timber which form the quarter-gallery of a ship.
VÍRA, *sf.* 1. A kind of light dart or arrow. 2. Stuffing laid between the upper leather and inner sole. 3. Welt of a shoe.
VIRÁDA, *sf.* (Naút.) Tacking.
VIRADÓR, *sm.* (Naút.) Top-rope. V. *Birador.*
VIRÁR, *va.* (Naút.) To tack. V. *Birar.*
VIRATÓN, *sm.* A kind of large dart or arrow.
VIRAZÓNES, *sm. pl.* (Naút.) Land and sea breezes blowing alternately.
VIRÉO, *sm.* V. *Virio.*
VIRÉY, *sm.* Viceroy, he who governs in place of the king, with royal authority.
VIRÉYNA, *sf.* Lady of a viceroy.
VIREYNÁTO Y VIRÉYNO, *sm.* Viceroyship, the dignity or administration of a viceroy; duration of this office.
VÍRGEN, *s.com.* 1. Virgin, a woman unacquainted with men; man who has not been connected with woman. 2. Any thing in its pure and primitive state, untouched, uncultivated. *Cera virgen,* Virgin wax. *Plata virgen,* Native silver. 3. One of the upright posts, between which the beam of an oil-mill moves. 4. The holy Virgin Mary; image of the Virgin. 5. A nun. *Virgenes,* Nuns, religious women who have taken the vow of chastity.
VIRGINÁL, *a.* Virginal, belonging to virgins.
VIRGÍNEA, *sf.* (Bot.) Virginia tobacco. Nicotiana tabacum *L.*
VIRGÍNEO, NEA, *a.* Virginal.
VIRGINIDÁD, *sf.* Virginity, maidenhead.
VÍRGO, *sm.* 1. (Astr.) Sign of the zodiac. 2. Virginity.
VÍRGULA, *sf.* A small rod; slight line.
VIRGULÍLLA, *sf.* 1. Comma, a small stroke or point, serving to denote the distinction of clauses; it is called *coma* in printing and *tilde* in writing. 2. Any fine stroke or light line.
VIRGÚLTO, *sm.* Shrub, a bush, a small tree.
VIRÍL, *sm.* 1. A clear and transparent glass. 2. A small box with two plates of glass, in which the host is exposed to public view.
VIRÍL, *a.* Virile, manly.
VIRILIDÁD, *sf.* 1. Virility, manhood. 2. Vigour, strength.
VIRÍLLA, TA, *sf. dim.* of *vira.* *Virilla,* Ornament of gold or silver formerly worn in shoes.
VIRILMÉNTE, *ad.* In a manly manner.
VIRío, *sm.* (Orn.) Canary-bird.
VIRIPOTÉNTE, *a.* Marriageable; applied to women.
VIRÓL, *sm.* (Blas.) V. *Perfil.*
VIRÓLA, *sf.* (Naút.) Ring, hoop. V. *Birola.*
VIROLÉNTO, TA, *a.* Diseased with the small-pox, pock-pitted, or marked with the small-pox.
VIRÓN, *sm. aum.* Large dart.
VIROTÁZO, *sm. aum.* of *virote,* Wound inflicted with a dart or arrow.
VIRÓTE, *sm.* 1. Shaft, dart, arrow. 2. Spark, a showy, vain young man, who loiters idly about; inflated person. 3. Card of invitation, note, billet. 4. A long iron rod fastened to a collar on the neck of a slave, who shows an intention of running away. 5. (And.) Vine, which is three years old. *Traga virotes,* A starched coxcomb. 6. (Naút.) An indented piece of timber used in the poop of a ship. 7. Carnival trick. *Mirar por el virote,* (Met.) To be attentive to one's own concerns or convenience.
VIROTÓN, *sm. aum.* Large dart or arrow.
VIRTUÁL, *a.* Virtual.
VIRTUALIDÁD, *sf.* Virtuality, efficacy.
VIRTUALMÉNTE, *ad.* Virtually, in effect though not formally.
VIRTÚD, *sf.* 1. Virtue, efficacy, power. 2. Vigour, courage. 3. Power of acting. 4. Virtue, moral goodness, integrity, rectitude. 5. Power of motion or resistance; natural faculty. 6. Habit, disposition, virtuous life. 7. In mechanics, the moving power. 8. In the sacraments, their efficacy and value. *En virtud de,* In virtue of. *Virtudes,* The fifth of the nine choirs in which the celestial spirits are divided. *Hacer virtud,* To do well. *Varita de virtudes,* Juggler's wand.
VIRTUOSAMÉNTE, *ad.* Virtuously.
VIRTUÓSO, SA, *a.* 1. Virtuous, morally good. 2. Powerful, vigorous.
VIRUÉLA, *sf.* Pock, a pustule raised on the skin, commonly called small-pox. *Viruelas locas,* Good or favourable small-pox. *Viruelas bastardas,* Chicken-pox.
VIRULÉNCIA, *sf.* Virulence.
VIRULÉNTO, TA, *a.* 1. Virulent, Malignant. 2. Purulent, sanious.
VÍRUS, *sm.* (Med.) Virus, poison, contagion.
VIRÚTA, *sf.* Shaving, a thin slice of wood pared off with a plane.
VISÁGE, *sm.* Grimace, distortion of the face; VISAGE. *Hacer visages,* To make wry faces.
VISÁGRE, *sf.* Hinge. V. *Bisagra.*
VISÁL, *sm.* (Ant.) V. *Visera.*
VISÁNTE, *sm.* (Cant.) The eye.
VISÁR, *va.* To examine a document.
VÍSCERAS, *sf. pl.* Intestines, bowels.
VÍSCO, *sm.* V. *Liga.*
VISCOSIDÁD, *sf.* Viscosity, glutinousness; glutinous or viscous matter.
VISCÓSO, SA, *a.* Viscous, glutinous, tenacious.
VISÉRA, *sf.* 1. Visor, that part of the head-piece or armour for the head which covers the face. 2. Box with a spy-hole, through which a pigeon-keeper observes the motions of the pigeons.
VISIBILIDÁD, *sf.* Visibility, the state or quality of being perceptible to the eye.
VISÍBLE, *a.* Visible, perceptible to the eye; that which is so certain and evident that it admits of no doubt.
VISIBLEMÉNTE, *ad.* Visibly, clearly; evidently.
VISIÓN, *sf.* 1. Sight, vision; object of sight. 2. Vision, the act of seeing. 3. A frightful, ugly, or ridiculous person. 4. Phantom, apparition. 5. Spiritual vision, revelation, prophecy; beatifical vision. *Ver visiones,* To be led by fancy, to build castles in the air. *Vision beatifica,* Celestial bliss.
VISIONÁRIO, RIA, *a.* Visionary, affected by phantoms; not real.
VISÍR, *sm.* Vizier, the prime minister of the Turkish empire.
VISÍTA, *sf.* 1. Visit, the act of going to see ano-

ther; visit to a temple, or a patient. 2. Person who goes on a visit, visitor. 3. Search, judicial survey, inquest. 4. Visitation, inquisition. 5. Recognition, register; examination. 6. House in which the tribunal of ecclesiastical visitors is held. 7. Apparition or visible appearance to any one. 8. (Teol.) Visitation of God. 9. Body of ministers who form a tribunal to inspect the prisons; visit to prisons. *Visita de cárcel*, Brief view of the charges against prisoners, drawn up by a judge at certain periods. *Visitas*, Frequent visits, haunt.

Visitación, *sf.* Visitation, act of visiting, visit.

Visitadór, ra, *s.* 1. Visiter, one who visits another often. 2. An occasional judge, searcher, surveyor. *Visitador de registro*, (Naút.) Searcher of goods on board of ships; tide-waiter.

Visitár, *va.* 1. To visit, to pay a visit, to go to see; to visit a temple or church; to visit a patient as physician. 2. To make a judicial visit, search, or survey; to try weights and measures. 3. To search ships; to examine prisons. 4. To travel, to traverse many countries. 5. To inform one's self personally of any thing. 6. To appear, as a celestial spirit. 7. To frequent any place. 8. To visit religious persons and establishments as an ecclesiastical judge. 9. (Teol.) To send any special counsel from heaven. 10. (For.) To make an abstract of the charge against a prisoner at visitation.—*vr.* 1. To try a criminal offence. 2. To absent one's self from the choir for some time. *Visitar los altares*, To pray before each altar for some pious purpose.

Visitíca, lla, *sf. dim.* of *visita.*

Visívo, va, *a.* Having the power of seeing.

Vislumbrár, *va.* 1. To have a glimmering sight of any thing; not to perceive it distinctly. 2. (Met.) To know imperfectly, to conjecture by some indications.

Vislúmbre, *sf.* 1. A glimmering light, a faint glimpse at a distance. 2. Conjecture, surmise. 3. Imperfect knowledge, confused perception. 4. Appearance, slight resemblance. 5. Projecting part of any thing which is scarcely discovered.

Víso, *sm.* 1. Sight, act of seeing. 2. Prospect, an elevated spot, affording an extensive view. 3. Lustre, the shining superficies or surface of things; brilliant reflection of light. 4. Colour, cloak, pretence, pretext. 5. Apparent likeness, not a real resemblance; aspect, appearance. *A' dos visos*, With a double view or design. *Al viso de*, At the sight of. *Viso de altar*, Small square embroidered cloth placed before the eucharist.

Visogódo, da, *a.* y *s.* Visigoth, West-goth.

Visójo, ja, *a.* Squint-eyed. V. *Bisojo.*

Visóño, ña, *a.* Raw, unexperienced. V. *Bisoño.*

Visoréyno, *sm.* (Ant.) V. *Vireynato.*

Visório, ria, *a.* Belonging to the sight.

Visoréy, *sm.* Viceroy. V. *Virey.*

Víspera, *sf.* 1. Evening before the day in contemplation or question; the last evening before a festival. 2. Forerunner, prelude. 3. Immediate nearness or succession.—*pl.* 1. Vesper, one of the parts into which the Romans divided the day. 2. Vespers, the evening service. *En vísperas de*, At the eve of. *Vísperas Sicilianas*, Sicilian vespers, a threat of general punishment.

Vísta, *sf.* 1. Sight, the faculty or power of seeing; the act of seeing; vision. 2. Aspect, appearance. 3. Prospect, landscape, object of sight. 4. Apparition, appearance. 5. Organ of sight, the eye. 6. Meeting, interview. 7. Clear knowledge or perception. 8. Relation, respective connexion, comparison. 9. Intent, purpose. 10. First stage of a suit at law. 11. Opinion, judgment. 12. Revision of a sentence. 13. Look, simple view. 14. (Ant.) V. *Visera*. *A' vista de*, In the presence of; in consideration of. *A' vista de ojos*, At a glance. *A' la vista*, On sight, immediately: before, near, or in view; carefully observing, seeing, or following. *Conocer de vista*, To know by sight. *Echar una vista*, To look after. *Tener vista*, To be showy; to be beautiful. *Hacer la vista gorda*, To wink, to connive. *En vista de*, In consequence of; in consideration of. *Comer y tragar con la vista*, (Met.) To have a fierce and terrible aspect.—*pl.* 1. Meeting, conference, interview. 2. Presents made to a bride by a bridegroom the day preceding the nuptials. 3. Lights, windows in a building, balconies, virandas. 4. Prospect, an extensive view.—*sm.* Place or employment of a surveyor at the custom-house.

Vistázo, *sm.* Vast view, extensive glance.

Vistíllas, *sf. pl.* Eminence affording an extensive prospect, views.

Vísto, ta, *a.* Obvious to the sight, clear. *Visto bueno*, Pay the bearer; put to accounts after being examined. *Visto es ó está*, It is evident. *No visto*, Extraordinary, prodigious. *A' escala vista*, Openly, without defence.

Vistosaménte, *ad.* Beautifully, delightfully.

Vistóso, sa, *a.* Beautiful, delightful.

Vistóso, *sm.* (Cant.) V. *Sayo y ojo.*

Visuál, *a.* Visual, belonging to the sight.

Visúra, *sf.* Minute inspection of any thing.

Víta, *sf.* (Naút.) Cross-beam on the fore-castle, to which the cables are fastened when the ship is lying in port.

Vitál, *a.* Vital, belonging or necessary to life.

Vitalício, cia, *a.* Lasting for life; during life. *Pension vitalicia*, Annuity, pension. *Empleo vitalicio*, Employment or place of life.

Vitalidád, *sf.* Vitality, power of subsisting in life.

Vitándo, da, *a.* That ought to be shunned or avoided.

Vitéla, *sf.* 1. Calf. 2. Vellum, calf-skin.

Vitelína, *a.* Of a dark yellow colour; applied to the bile.

Vitór, *interj.* Shout of joy; Long live!

Vitór, *sm.* 1. Triumphal exclamation; public rejoicing. 2. Tablet containing some panegyrical epithets to a hero.

Vitoreár, *va.* To shout, to huzza, to address with acclamations of joy and praise.

Vitória, *sf.* Victory, triumph. V. *Victoria.*

Vitorióso, sa, *a.* Victorious.

Vítre, *sm.* Thin canvass.

Vítreo, trea, *a.* Vitreous, glassy; consisting of glass, resembling glass.

Vitrificación, *sf.* Vitrification, the act of converting into glass.
Vitrificár, *va.* To vitrify, to change into glass.
Vitriólico, ca, *a.* Vitriolic.
Vitriólo, *sm.* Vitriol, a saline and transparent substance, soluble in water, fusible and calcinable by fire.
Vituálla, *sf.* Victuals, viands, food, provisions; abundance of food.
Vitualládo, da, *a.* Victualled, stored or provided with victuals.
Vítula, *sf.* V. *Becerra.*
Vítulo Marino, V. *Becerro marino.*
Vitulíno, na, *a.* Belonging to a calf.
Vituperáble, *a.* Vituperable, blame-worthy.
Vituperación, *sf.* Vituperation, the act of blaming.
Vituperadór, ra, *s.* A blamer, a censurer.
Vituperár, *va.* To vituperate, to censure, to decry.
Vitupério, *sm.* 1. Vituperation, blame, censure; reproachful language. 2. Infamy, disgrace.
Vituperiosaménte, *ad.* Opprobriously.
Vituperosaménte, *ad.* Reproachfully.
Vituperóso, sa, *a.* Opprobrious, reproachful.
Viúda, *sf.* Widow, a woman whose husband is dead.
Viudál, *a.* Belonging to a widow.
Viudedád, *sf.* 1. Widowhood. 2. Dowry. 3. Usufruct enjoyed during widowhood of the property of a deceased person.
Viudéz, *sf.* Widowhood.
Viudíta, *sf.* A spruce little widow.
Viúdo, *sm.* Widower, a man whose wife is dead. —*a.* Applied to birds that pair or marry.
Vivác ó Viváque, *sm.* Town-guard to keep order at night; bivouac, night-guard.
Vivacidád, *sf.* Vivacity, liveliness, briskness, activity, vigour; brilliancy.
Vivaménte, *ad.* In a brisk or lively manner; to the life, with a strong resemblance.
Vivandéro, *sm.* (Mil.) Sutler, one who follows an army and sells provision.
Viváque, *sm.* A small guard-house.
Vivár, *sm.* Warren, a kind of park for the breeding of rabbits or other animals.
Vivarácho, cha, *a.* Lively, smart, sprightly.
Vivário, *sm.* Fish-pond.
Viváz, *a.* 1. Lively, active, vigorous. 2. Ingenious, acute, witty.
Vivéra y Vivéro, *s.* Warren; fish-pond; vivary.
Víveres, *sm. pl.* Provisions, store of provisions for an army or fortress.
Vivéza, *sf.* 1. Liveliness, vigour, activity. 2. Celerity, briskness. 3. Ardour, energy, vehemence. 4. Acuteness, perspicacity, penetration. 5. Witticism, an ingenious saying. 6. Great likeness, strong resemblance. 7. Lustre, splendour, brightness. 8. Grace and brilliance in the eyes. 9. Inconsiderate word or action.
Vividéro, ra, *a.* Habitable, capable of being dwelt in.
Vividór, ra, *s.* 1. One who lives long, a long liver. 2. An œconomist, one who manages his concerns with care, and knows and practises the methods of frugality and profit.
Viviénda, *sf.* 1. Dwelling-house, apartments, lodgings. 2. (Ant.) Mode of life.
Viviénte, *pa.* Living, animated.
Vivificación, *sf.* Vivification, the act of giving life, animating or enlivening.
Vivificadór, ra, *s.* One who vivifies, animates or enlivens.
Vivificánte, *pa.* Vivifying.
Vivificár, *va.* To vivify, to make alive, to animate, to enliven; to comfort, to refresh.
Vivificatívo, va, *a.* Having the power of giving life, animating or comforting.
Vivífico, ca, *a.* Vivific, giving life, making alive.
Vivíparo, ra, *a.* Viviparous, bringing the young alive; opposed to *oviparous.*
Vivír, *vn.* 1. To have life, to live, to be in a state of animation; to enjoy life. 2. To continue, to last. 3. To have the means of supporting life. 4. To live; emphatically, to enjoy happiness. 5. To pass life in a certain manner, either good or ill. 6. To be remembered, to enjoy fame. 7. To be, to exist; to be present. 8. To inhabit, to reside. 9. To temporize. 10. To guard the life. 11. To have eternal life. *Viva vd. mil años ó muchos años,* Live many years; or, I return you many thanks; expression of courtesy. *Quien vive?* (Mil.) Who is there? *Viva,* An exclamation of joy and gratitude. *Vive,* An exclamatory oath generally accompanied with another word.
Vívo, va, *a.* 1. Living, enjoying life, active. 2. Lively, efficacious, intense. 3. Disencumbered, disengaged. 4. Alive, kindled; applied to things burning. 5. Acute, ingenious; hasty, inconsiderate; diligent, nimble; pure; clean. 6. Constant, enduring. 7. Vivid, florid, excellent. 8. Very expressive. 9. Blessed. *Al vivo,* To the life; very like the original. *En vivo,* Living. *Viva voz,* By word of mouth. *Cal viva,* Quick lime. *Carne viva,* Quick flesh, in a wound. *Ojos vivos,* Very bright lively eyes.
Vívo, *sm.* 1. The strongest, thickest, and most solid part of things. 2. (Arq.) Any prominent part of a building which juts out beyond the level surface. 3. Mange, the itch or scab in dogs. 4. Edging, border. 5. He who lives in the grace of God.
Vizcácha, *sf.* A large kind of hare, Peruvian hare. Lepus viscaccia *L.*
Vizcondádo, *sm.* Viscountship, the dignity or title of a viscount.
Vizcónde, *sm.* Viscount.
Vizcondésa, *sf.* Viscountess, the lady of a viscount.
Vocé, *sm.* A contraction of *Vuesamerced ó usted.*
Vocablíco, llo, to, *sm. dim.* of *vocablo.*
Vocáblo, *sm.* Word, term, diction.
Vocabulário, *sm.* 1. Vocabulary, dictionary, lexicon. 2. Person who announces or interprets the will of another.
Vocabulísta, *sm.* (Ant.) V. *Vocabulario.*
Vocación, *sf.* 1. Vocation, calling by the will of God. 2. Trade, employment, calling. 3. V. *Advocacion y Convocacion.*
Vocál, *a.* Vocal, belonging to the voice, modulated, uttered by the voice, as opposed to mental.
Vocál, *sf.* Vowel.
Vocál, *sm.* Voter, one who has the right of voting in a congregation or assembly.

Vocalménte, *ad.* Vocally, in words, articulately.
Vocatívo, *sm.* (Gram.) Vocative, the fifth case in the declination of nouns.
Vocеadór, ra, *s.* Vociferator.
Vocеár, *va.* To scream, to bawl, to cry out, to clamour.—*va.* 1. To publish in a loud voice, to proclaim; to call to; applied occasionally to inanimate things, which manifest something. 2. To shout, to huzza; to applaud by acclamation; to boast publicly. 3. To plead, to persuade, to incline. 4. To defend in public. *Vocear á un baxel*, (Naút.) To hail a ship.
Vocería, *sf.* Clamour, a loud cry; defence.
Vocéro, *sm.* Advocate.
Vociferación, *sf.* Vociferation, clamour, outcry, boast, brag.
Vociferadór, ra, *s.* Boaster, bragger.
Vociferánte, *pa.* Vociferating; caller.
Vociferár, *vn.* To vociferate, to bawl, to proclaim in a loud voice.—*va.* To boast, to brag loudly or publicly.
Vocína, *sf.* (Naút.) Speaking trumpet used on board of ships.
Vocinglеár, *va.* To shout, to cry out.
Vocinglería, *sf.* 1. Clamour, outcry, a confused noise made by many voices. 2. Loquacity, too much talk.
Vocingléro, ra, *a.* Brawling, prattling, chattering.—*sm.* Loud babbler.
Voláda, *sf.* (Ant.) V. *Vuelo.*
Voladéra, *sf.* One of the floats or pallets of a water-wheel.
Voladéro, ra, *a.* Volatile, flying, fleeting.
Voladéro, *sm.* Precipice, abyss.
Voladízo, za, *a.* Projecting from a wall.
Voladór, ra, *a.* 1. Flying, running fast. 2. Pending or hanging in the air. 3. Blowing up by the force of gunpowder; applied to artificial fire-works.—*s.* Flier; volatile thing or person.
Voladór, *sm.* 1. (Ict.) Flying-fish. 2. (Gal.) Fox, coxcomb.
Volándas ó en Volándas, *ad.* In the air.
Volandéra, *sf.* 1. (In Oil-mills) Runner, the stone which runs edgewise upon another stone. 2. A vague or flying report, lie. 3. Wash of an axle-tree, nave-box of a wheel. 4. (Impr.) Moveable ledge on a galley against which types are arranged.
Volandéro, ra, *a.* 1. Suspended in the air, volatile. 2. Fortuitous, casual. 3. Unsettled, fleeting, variable, volatile.
Volánte, *a.* Flying, fluttering, unsettled.—*sm.* 1. An ornament of light gauze hanging down from women's head-dress. 2. Screen put before a candle. 3. Shuttle-cock, a cork stuck with feathers, and driven by players from one to another with battledoors. 4. Balance of a watch; fly of a jack. 5. Pulsation of the arteries. 6. (Mil.) Orderly man. 7. Livery servant or footboy who runs before his master. 8. Noise made in shutting or locking a door. V. *Taque.* 9. Coining-mill, or that part of it which strikes the dye. *Papel volante*, Short writing or manuscript easily disseminated; it generally contains some satire or libel. *Sello volante*, Open seal on a letter that those to whose care it is directed may read it.

Volantón, *sm.* A fledged or full-feathered bird able to fly.
Volapié (Á), *ad.* Half running, half flying.
Volár, *vn.* 1. To fly, to move through the air with wings; to move swiftly. 2. To vanish, to disappear on a sudden. 3. To rise in the air like a steeple or pile. 4. To make a rapid progress in studies; to subtilize, to refine sentiments; to move with rapidity or violence. 5. To project, to hang over, to jut out. 6. To execute with great promptitude and facility; to extend, to publish any thing rapidly.—*va.* 1. To rouse the game. 2. To attack by a bird of prey. 3. To blow up, to spring or discharge a mine. 4. (Met.) To irritate, to exasperate. 5. To ascend high. *Volar la mina*, To discover any secret business. *Como volar*, It is as impossible as it is to fly. *Echar á volar*, (Met.) To disseminate, to give any thing to the public. *Sacar ó salír á volar*, To publish, to expose. *Voló el pollo ó golondrino*, (Fam.) It escaped from between the hands. *Volar los escotines de juanetes*, (Naút.) To let fly the top-gallant sheets.
Volatería, *sf.* 1. Fowling; sporting with hawks. 2. Fowls, a flock of birds. 3. The act of finding or discovering by chance. 4. A vague or desultory speech; idle or groundless ideas. —*ad.* Fortuitously, adventitiously.
Volátil, *a.* 1. Volatile, flying or moving through the air; changeable, inconstant. 2. (Quím.) Passing off by evaporation.
Volatília, *sf.* (Ant.) Flying bird.
Volatilidád, *sf.* Volatility; quality of flying away by evaporation.
Volatilizár, *va.* To volatilize, to make volatile.
Volatín, *sm.* Rope-dancer.
Volatizár, *va.* (Quím.) To volatilize.
Volavérunt, Lat. (Joc.) Either lost or stolen.
Volcán, *sm.* 1. Volcano, a burning mountain. 2. Excessive ardour; violent passion.
Volcanéjo, *sm. dim.* Small volcano.
Volcár, *va.* 1. To overset, to turn one side upwards. 2. To make dizzy or giddy. 3. To make one change his opinion. 4. To tire out one's patience with pranks and buffoonery or scurrile mirth.
Volcár, *vn.* 1. To throw any thing up in the air so as to make it fly. 2. (Naút.) To overset a ship.
Voléo, *sm.* 1. Blow or stroke given to a ball in the air before it comes to the ground. 2. Step in a Spanish dance. *De un voleo, ó del primer voleo*, At one blow; at the first blow; in an instant.
Volición, *sf.* Volition, the act of willing; the power of choice exerted.
Volitívo, va, *a.* Having the power of volition.
Volquеárse, *vr.* To tumble, to wallow. V. *Revolcarse.*
Voltariedád, *sf.* Levity, inconstancy, volatility.
Voltário, ria, *a.* Fickle, variable, inconstant.
Volteadór, *sm.* Tumbler, one who shows or teaches postures and feats of activity.
Volteár, *va.* 1. To whirl, to turn round rapidly; to roll, to move by quick rotation. 2. To overturn, to overset. 3. To change the order, place, or state of things.—*vn.* To tumble, to exhibit postures and feats of agility.
Voltejár, *va.* (Ant.) V. *Voltear.*

VOLTEJEÁR, va. 1. To whirl. V. *Voltear*. 2. (Naút.) To tack in order to avoid a current.
VOLTERÉTA Y VOLTÉTA, sf. 1. A light spring or tumble in the air. 2. The act of turning up the card which makes trump.
VOLTÚRA, sf. (Ant.) V. *Mozela*.
VOLUBILIDÁD, sf. Volubility; inconstancy, fickleness, changeableness.
VOLÚBLE, a. Voluble, inconstant, fickle.
VOLÚMEN, sm. 1. Volume, size, bulkiness; corpulence. 2. Volume, tome, book. 3. Body of laws.
VOLÚMINE, sm. (Ant.) Volume, book.
VOLUMINÓSO, SA, a. Voluminous; of a large bulk or size.
VOLUNTÁD, sf. 1. Will, choice, arbitrary determination; faculty of receiving or rejecting any notion. 2. Divine determination. 3. Good-will, benevolence, kindness, affection. 4. Desire, pleasure; free-will, volition, election, choice, assent. 5. Disposition, precept; intention, resolution. *De voluntad, ó de buena voluntad*, With pleasure, gratefully.
VOLUNTARIAMÉNTE, ad. Spontaneous, voluntarily, without compulsion.
VOLUNTARIEDÁD, sf. Free-will, spontaneousness, freedom from compulsion.
VOLUNTÁRIO, RIA, a. Voluntary, spontaneous.
VOLUNTÁRIO, sm. Volunteer, a soldier who serves without compulsion.
VOLUNTARIOSAMÉNTE, ad. Spontaneously, selfishly.
VOLUNTARIÓSO, SA, a. Selfish; one who merely follows the dictates of his own will; desirous.
VOLUPTUOSAMÉNTE, ad. Voluptuously.
VOLUPTUÓSO, SA, a. Voluptuous, luxurious, given to excess of pleasures; sensual.
VOLÚTA, sf. Volute, an ornament of the capitals of columns.
VOLVÉR, va. 1. To turn, to give turns. 2. To direct, to aim; to remit; to send back a present. 3. To return, to restore. 4. To translate from one language to another. 5. To change the outward appearance of things; to invert, to change a thing from one place to another. 6. To vomit, to throw up victuals. 7. To make one change his opinion; to convert, to incline. 8. To return a ball. 9. To reflect a sound. 10. To turn away, to discharge. *Volver el rostro*, To flee, to run away, to evade; to pay attention by turning to look at one, or to show contempt by turning away. 11. To re-establish, to replace in a former situation. 12. To plough land a second time. 13. To resume the thread of a discourse interrupted. 14. To reiterate, to repeat. 15. (Ant.) To mix. *Volver la puerta*, To shut the door. *Volver la tortilla*, To turn the tables or scales. *Volver por sí*, To defend one's self; to redeem one's credit. *Volver á uno loco*, To confound one with arguments, to vanquish one so that he appears stupid.—*vn.* 1. To return, to come again or back to the same place. 2. To turn out of the road or straight line. 3. To repeat, to reiterate; in this sense it is accompanied by *á*. 4. To stand out for a person; to undertake his defence; to defend; here it is used with *por*. 5. To regain, to recover. *Volver sobre sí*, To reflect on one's self; to make up one's losses. *Volver en sí*, To recover one's senses. —*vr.* 1. To turn, to grow sour. 2. To turn towards one. 3. To retract an opinion, to change. *Volverse blanco*, To become white. *Volverse el cuajo*, To let the milk run from the mouth; applied to a child when its head is too low. *Volverse loco*, To be deranged, to become a fool.
VOLVÍBLE, a. That may be turned.
VOLVIMIÉNTO, sm. Act of turning.
VÓLVO Ó VÓLVULO, sm. Iliac passion.
VÓMICA, sf. Encysted tumour in the lungs.
VÓMICO, CA, a. That which causes vomiting.
VOMITÁDO, DA, a. Meager; pale-faced.
VOMITADÓR, RA, s. One who vomits.
VOMITÁR, va. 1. To vomit, to throw up from the stomach. 2. To foam, to break out into injurious expressions. 3. To reveal a secret, to discover what was concealed. 4. To pay what was unduly retained. *Vomitar sangre*, To boast of nobility and parentage.
VOMITÍVO, VA, a. Emetic, vomitive.
VÓMITO, sm. 1. The act of vomiting or throwing up from the stomach. *Volver al vomito*, To relapse into vices. 2. Matter thrown up from the stomach. *Provocar á vómito*, To nauseate, to loathe; used in censuring indecent or coarse expressions, or to contemn any thing.
VOMITÓN, NA, a. Often throwing up milk from the stomach; applied by nurses to a sucking child.
VOMITÓNA, sf. (Fam.) Violent vomiting and throwing up from the stomach after eating heartily.
VOMITÓRIO, sm. Passage or entrance in Roman theatres.
VOMITÓRIO, RIA, a. Vomitive, emetic.
VORACIDÁD, sf. 1. Voracity, voraciousness. 2. (Met.) Destructiveness of fire, &c.
VORÁGINE, sf. Vortex, whirlpool.
VORAGINÓSO, SA, a. Full of whirlpools.
VORÁZ, a. 1. Voracious. 2. Extremely irregular or disorderly; excessively destructive.
VORAZMÉNTE, ad. Voraciously.
VORMÉLA, sf. Kind of spotted weasel.
VORTANQUÍ, sm. Sapan-wood.
VÓRTICE, sm. Whirlpool, whirlwind, hurricane. *Vórtice aéreo*, Whirlwind, water-spout.
VORTIGINÓSO, SA, a. Vortical, having a whirling motion.
VOS, pron. You, ye. V. *Vosotros*. Used as respectful to persons of dignity, and by superiors to their inferiors.
VOSCO, (Ant.) i. e. *Con vos*, With you.
VOSEÁRSE, vr. To treat each other with you or ye.
VÓSO, SA, a. (Ant.) V. *Vuestro*.
VOSÓTROS, TRAS, pron. pers. pl. You, ye.
VOTACIÓN, sf. Voting, act of voting.
VOTÁDO, DA, pp. Devoted. *Votado á cristo ó á dios*, Wedded to an opinion, obstinate persistence in a notion or sentiment.
VOTADÓR, RA, s. One who vows or swears.
VOTÁNTE, a. Having the power of voting in a corporation or assembly.
VOTÁR, va. 1. To vow, to make vows. 2. To vote, to give a vote or suffrage; to give an opinion. 3. To curse, to utter oaths.—*vn.* 1. To dart, to launch. V. *Botar*. 2. To swear to celebrate a festival, or defend a mystery.

Votívo, va, *a.* Votive, given by vow.

Vóto, *sm.* 1. Vow, any promise made to the Divine Power; offering made to God or a saint. 2. Vote, suffrage; voter. 3. Opinion, advice, voice. *Voto de calidad,* A decisive vote. 4. Wish, desire. 5. Supplication to God. 6. Angry oath or execration. 7. Vow taken by a religious on professing a monk or nun. *Voto en cortes,* Deputy or representative of a town in the *cortes,* or assembly of the states of the kingdom. *Voto á dios,* A menacing oath. *Voto ó tal,* (Fam.) A mixed oath indicating disgust and vengeance.

Votla, a word used in playing, signifying a bar or objection.

Voz, *sf.* 1. Voice, the sound emitted by the mouth; sound in general. 2. Clamour, outcry. *Dar voces,* To cry. 3. Word, term, expression. 4. Power or authority to speak in the name of another. 5. Vote, suffrage; right of suffrage; opinion expressed. 6. Rumour, public opinion. 7. Motive, pretence, pretext. 8. Word, Divine inspiration. 9. (Gram.) Voice, active, passive, or medial. 10. (Mús.) Vocal music; treble, tenor; tune corresponding to the voice of a singer. 11. Order, mandate of a superior. 12. (For.) Life. *Voz activa,* Right or power of voting. *Voz pasiva,* Right or qualification to be elected. *Tomar voz,* To acquire knowledge, to reason; to confirm or support any thing by the opinions of others. *A' media voz,* With a slight hint; with a low voice, in a submissive tone. *A' una voz,* Unanimously, with common consent. *A' voces,* Clamorous cry, loud voice. *A' voz en grito,* In a loud voice. *Es voz comun,* It is generally reported. *En voz,* Verbally; (Mús.) In voice.

Voznár, *vn.* To cry like swans, to cackle like geese.

Vueceléncia, *s. com.* A contraction of *vuestra excellencia,* your excellency.

Vuélco, *sm.* Eversion, overturning.

Vuélo, *sm.* 1. Flight, the act of flying. 2. Wing, the limb of a bird by which it flies. 3. Part of a building which projects beyond the wall. 4. Width or fulness of clothes. 5. Ruffle, ornament of lace or plaited linen set to the wristband of a shirt. 6. Space flown through at once. 7. Elevation or loftiness in discoursing or working. 8. Leap or bound in pantomimes. *A' vuelo, ó al vuelo,* Flying, expeditiously. *Coger al vuelo,* To catch flying.

Vuélta, *sf.* 1. Turn, the act of turning, gyration; turn of an arch; circumvolution; circuit. 2. Requital, return, recompense; regress. 3. Iteration, repetition, rehearsal. 4. Back side, wrong side. 5. Whipping, flogging, lashing on the backside. 6. Turn, inclination, bent. 7. Ruffle. V. *Vuelo.* 8. (Naút.) Hatch. 9. Turn, change of things. 10. Trip, excursion, a short voyage. 11. Reconsideration, recollection. 12. Land once, twice, or thrice laboured. 13. Wards in a lock or key. 14. Order of stitches in stockings. 15. Roll, envelope. 16. Unexpected sally or witticism. 17. Surplus money to be returned in dealing. 18. (Ant.) Dispute. 19. (Mús.) Number of verses repeated. *A' la vuelta,* At your return; that laid aside; about the time; upon. *La vuelta de,* Towards this or that way. *Vuelta dada con los cables,* (Naút.) Turn in the hawse. *Media vuelta en los cables,* (Naút.) Elbow in the hawse. *Dar una vuelta,* To make a short excursion; to clean any thing; to examine a thing properly. *Dar vuelta con un cabo de labor,* (Naút.) To belay a running rope. *Andar en vueltas,* To shuffle, to make use of subterfuges. *Dar vueltas,* To walk to and fro on a public walk; to seek any thing; to discuss repeatedly the same topic. *A' vuelta ó á vueltas,* Very near, almost; also, with another thing, otherwise. *Tener vueltas alguno,* To be inconstant or fickle. *Tener vuelta,* (Fam.) An admonition to return any thing lent.—*interj.* Return; let him return or go back the same way.

Vueltecíca, lla, ta, *sf. dim.* of *vuelta.*

Vuélto, ta, *pp. irreg.* of *volver.*

Vuésa, *a.* Contracted from *vuestra,* and used before *merced, eminencia,* &c.

Vuesamercéd, *sf.* You sir, you madam; your worship, your honour; a contraction of *vuestra merced,* a title of courtesy given to a person who has no right to that of *vueseñoría ó vuestra señoría,* your lordship.

Vuesarcéd, *sf.* Contraction of *vuesamerced.*

Vueseñoría, *sf.* Contraction of *vuesta señoría.*

Vuéstro, tra, *a. pron.* Your, yours. It is used by subjects to a sovereign or by a sovereign to a subject. *Muy vuestro,* Entirely yours. *Vuestra señoría,* Your lordship or ladyship.

Vulgácho, *sm.* Mob, populace, the dregs of the people.

Vulgádo, da, *a.* (Ant.) Vulgar.

Vulgár, *a.* Vulgar, common, ordinary; vulgar or vernacular dialect, as opposed to the learned languages; without any specific peculiarity.—*sm.* The vulgar.

Vulgaridád, *sf.* Vulgarity; manners or speech of the lowest people; vulgar effusion.

Vulgarizár, *va.* 1. To make vulgar or common. 2. To translate from another idiom into the common language of the country.—*vr.* To become vulgar.

Vulgarménte, *ad.* Vulgarly, commonly, among the common people.

Vulgáta, *sf.* Vulgate, Latin version of the Bible.

Vúlgo, *sm.* 1. Multitude, populace, mob. 2. Way or manner of thinking of the populace. 3. Universality or generality of people. 4. (Cant.) Brothel. V. *Mancebía.*

Vulneráble, *a.* Vulnerable, that may be wounded.

Vulneración, *sf.* The act of wounding or vulnerating.

Vulnerár, *va.* 1. (Ant.) To wound. V. *Herir.* 2. To violate a law. 3. To injure the character or reputation.

Vulnerário, ria, *a.* 1. Vulnerary, useful in the curing of wounds. 2. (For.) Applied to an ecclesiastic who has wounded or killed any one.

Vulnerário, *sm.* Clergyman, guilty of having killed or wounded a person.

Vulpéja, *sf.* A bitch-fox.

Vulpíno, na, *a.* Vulpine, crafty, deceitful.

Vúlto, *sm.* 1. Volume; bulk, any thing bulky. V. *Bulto.* 2. Face.

Vultúrno, *sm.* Hot wind which rises with the sun at north-east, and comes round with it.
Vúlva, *sf.* Matrix, womb.
Vúsco, *pron.* (Ant.) *Con vusco,* With you.
Vustéd, *sm.* You, you sir, your honour, your worship; a contraction of *vuestra merced.* V. *Vuesamerced.*

THE *x* is the 26th letter in the Spanish alphabet, and is a semi-vowel, taken from the Romans, among whom it had in general the power of the two consonants *c* and *s*. This sound is preserved in Spanish, when it is followed by a consonant, or a vowel marked with a circumflex, as *extremo, exîstencia;* but otherwise it is converted into a strong guttural sound, scarcely to be distinguished from the Spanish *j* before all the vowels, or *g*, before *e* and *i*, when strongly pronounced. In some provinces of Spain, however, it is sounded only by a strong emission of the breath, like the English *h* in *here*. In several words it has been supplanted by *ch* and *ll*, as *chapeo* was originally written *xapeo*, and *zaga*, changed into *chaga*, and now *llaga*. It is also used at the end of many words pronounced gutturally, instead of *g* or *j*, which can terminate no Spanish word whatever; and is retained in the plural, as *carcax, carcaxes; dixe, dixes; relox, reloxes.*

X has been substituted by the Spaniards for *s* of the Latins, as *inserere* is made *inxerir, sapo, xabon,* &c. and for the two *ss* of the Italians, as in *basso,* which is become *baxo.*

Xa, *ad.* V. *Ya.* Used in Galicia, and the *x* pronounced soft, almost like *ch.*
Xabalcón y Xabalón, *sm.* Bracket, purlin.
Xabalconár y Xabalonár, *va.* To support by brackets the roof of a house.
Xabardíllo, *sm.* Company of strolling players. V. *Jabardillo.*
Xábeba ó Xábega, *sf.* A Moorish wind instrument, somewhat like a flute.
Xábega ó Xábega, *sf.* Sweep-net, a large net for fishing.
Xabeguéro, ra, *a.* Belonging to a sweep-net.—*sm.* Fisherman who fishes with a sweep-net.
Xabéque, *sm.* (Naút.) Xebec, a small three-masted vessel, navigated in the Mediterranean, and on the coasts of Spain and Portugal.
Xáble, *sm.* Circular groove in the staves of casks, which receives the bottoms and heads.
Xabón, *sm.* 1. Soap, a substance used in washing made of alkaline salt and unctuous matters. 2. (Met.) Any saponaceous mass or matter. *Xabon de palencia,* (Vulg.) Batlet, used by washer-women to wash linen. *Xabon de piedra,* Castile-soap, (Fam.) Smart stroke with a batlet. *Dar un xabon,* To reprimand severely.
Xabonádo, da, *a.* Soap, cleaned with soap.
Xabonádo, *sm.* 1. Wash, the act of washing with soap. 2. Parcel of linen washed with soap.
Xabonár, *va.* 1. To soap, to clean with soap. 2. (Fam.) To reprimand severely.
Xabonadúra, *sf.* The act of washing. *Xabonaduras,* Suds, a lixivium made of soap and water.
Xaboncíllo, Xabonéte ó Xabonéte de Olor, *sm.* Wash-ball.
Xabonéra, *sf.* 1. Box or case for a wash-ball. 2. (Bot.) Soapwort.
Xabonería, *sf.* Soap manufactory.
Xabonéro, *sm.* Soap-boiler, one who manufactures soap for sale.
Xácara, *sf.* 1. A sort of romance, generally celebrating the feats of some distinguished person. 2. A kind of rustic tune for singing or dancing; a kind of dance. 3. Company of young men who walk about at night-time singing *xácaras.* 4. Molestation, vexation. 5. Idle talk or prattle, story, tale; fable, lie, vain-glorious fiction.
Xacarandína ó Xacarandana, *sf.* 1. Low foul language; the language of ruffians and prostitutes' bullies. 2. Singing of *xácaras* or boastings. 3. (Cant.) Assembly of ruffians and thieves.
Xacareár, *vn.* 1. To sing *xácaras.* 2. To go about the streets singing and noising. 3. To be troublesome and vexatious.
Xacaréro, *sm.* 1. Ballad-singer. 2. Wag, a merry, droll, facetious person.
Xacarílla, *sf. dim.* of *Xácara.*
Xácaro, *sm.* Boaster, bully. *A' lo xácaro,* In a boastful or bragging manner.
Xácaro, ra, *a.* Belonging to boasters, or noisy singers. [rest.
Xacéna, *sf.* Girder, a beam on which the joists
Xachalí, *sm.* (Bot.) Tree in New Spain, which bears the fruit called *Xagua.*
Xáco, *sm.* A short jacket. V. *Xaque.*
Xáda, *sf.* (Arag.) V. *Azada.*
Xadiár, *va.* (Arag.) To dig up with a spade.
Xága, *sf.* Wound. V. *Llaga.*
Xágua, *sf.* Fruit of a tree in Cuba.
Xaguadéro, *sm.* (Ant.) V. *Desaguadero.*
Xalápa, *sf.* Jalap, a medical drug.
Xaleár, *va.* To halloo, to encourage the dogs, to chase with shouts.
Xalés, *sm.* Coarse linen, pack-cloth.
Xallúlo, *sm.* (And.) Bread toasted in the ashes.
Xálma, *sf.* A Moorish pack-saddle. V. *Enxalma.*
Xalméro, *sm.* Pack-saddle-maker.
Xalóque, *sm.* South-east wind. V. *Siroco.*
Xalxacóte, *sm.* (Bot.) Guava, a kind of South American pear tree, the leaves of which are used for curing the itch and cutaneous diseases. Psidium pyriferum *L.*
Xamacúco, *sm.* V. *Zamacuco.*
Xamár, *va.* To call. V. *Llamar.*
Xamborliér, *sm.* (Ar.) V. *Camarero.*
Xambrár, *va.* (Ar.) V. *Enxambrar.*
Xaméte, *sm.* A sort of stuff, formerly worn in Spain.
Xamúga ó Xamúgas, *sf.* A kind of side-saddle for women.

Xamuguílla, *sf. dim.* Small side-saddle. [car.
Xamuscár, *va.* To singe, to scorch. V. *Chamus-*
Xándalo, la, *a.* Having the gait and dialect of an Andalusian, particularly in giving the *la* a strong guttural sound.
Xáno, na, *a.* (Gal.) V. *Llano.*
Xántio, *sm.* (Bot.) Lesser burdock.
Xantolína, *sf.* 1. Persian worm seed. 2. Lavender-cotton, female wormwood. Santolina *L.*
Xapeléte, *sm.* An ancient covering for the hat, having the shape of a cap. V. *Chapelete.*
Xapóypa, *sf.* A kind of pancake.
Xapurcár, *va.* (Bax.) To stir up dirty water.
Xáque, *sm.* 1. Braggart, boaster. V. *Xeque.* 2. Move at the game of chess. *Xaque y mate,* Check-mate. 3. Saddle-bag. 4. Sort of smooth combing of the hair. *Xaque de aqui,* Away from here, avaunt!
Xaqueár, *va.* To give or make check-mate.
Xaquéca, *sf.* Megrim, head-ach.
Xaquél, *sm.* Chess-board.
Xaqueládo, da, *a.* Checkered.
Xaquéro, *sm.* Fine toothed comb.
Xaquéta, *sf.* Jacket, a short loose coat.
Xaquetílla, *sf.* A small jacket.
Xaquetón, *sm. aum.* 1. A large wide coat. 2. Great swaggerer, boaster.
Xáquima, *sf.* Headstall of a halter.
Xaquimázo, *sm.* 1. Stroke with tho headstall of a halter. 2. Displeasure; an unfair trick, ill turn.
Xára, *sf.* 1. (Bot.) Cistus or rock rose, labdanum-tree. Cistus ladaniferus *L.* 2. A kind of dart or arrow. *Xara cerval,* (Bot.) Round leafed cistus. Cistus globularifolius *L.*
Xarábe, *sf.* Sirup or sirop, the juice of fruit or herbs boiled with sugar; any sweet beverage.
Xarabeárse, *vr.* To use sirups.
Xarál, *sm.* 1. Place planted with the cistus or labdanum shrub. 2. A very intricate or puzzling point.
Xaramágo, *sm.* (Bot.) Hedge mustard.
Xarameño, ña, *a.* Applied to bulls reared on the banks of *Xarama.* [others.
Xaramúgo, *sm.* Small fish used as bait for
Xarapóte, *sm.* (Arag.) V. *Xarope.* [drugs.
Xarapoteádo, da, *a.* Stuffed with medical
Xarapoteár, *va.* (Arag. y And.) To stuff or fill with medical drugs.
Xaraquí ó Xaraquo, *sm.* Place for a recreating walk.
Xaráyz, *sm.* Pit for pressing grapes.
Xarázo, *sm.* Blow or wound with a dart.
Xárcia, *sf.* 1. Parcel or bundle of a variety of things laid by for use. 2. (Naút.) Tackle, rigging and cordage belonging to a ship. 3. A complete fishing-tackle. *Xarcia de primera suerte,* (Naút.) Cordage of the first quality *Almacen de xarcias,* (Naút.) Rigging-house, store-house for rigging. *Xarcias de respeto,* (Naút.) Spare rigging. *Tablas de xarcia,* (Naút.) Suit or set of rigging.
Xaréta, *sf.* 1. Seam, edge of clothes. 2. (Naút.) Netting of a ship.
Xarífe, *sm.* Sheriff. V. *Xerife.*
Xarífo, fa, *a.* Showy, full dressed, adorned.
Xaropár, Xaropeár, ó Xarapoteár, *va.* To stuff or fill with medical drugs; to give any liquor as a medical draught.

Xarópe, *sm.* 1. Medical draught or potion. 2. Any kind of bitter drink or beverage.
Xarragín, *sm.* (Ant.) Place having gardens and pleasure grounds.
Xárro, *sm.* (Bax. y Ar.) Bawler.
Xástre, *sm.* (Ant.) V. *Sastre.*
Xatéo, téa, *a.* Chasing the fox; applied to fox-dogs.
Xáto, *sm.* (Gal.) A yearling calf; *x* is pronounced soft.
Xáu, *interj.* A word used to encourage bulls and other animals. *Xau, xau,* Clamorous applause, confused acclamations.
Xaurádo, da, *a.* (Ant.) Desolate, afflicted, disconsolate.
Xauria, *sf.* Pack of hounds.
Xáuto, ta, *a.* (Ar.) Insipid, without salt.
Xazílla, *sf.* Vestige, mark, trace.
Xéa, *sf.* Import-duty formerly paid for all goods imported from the Moorish dominions.
Xébe, *sm.* V. *Alumbre.*
Xeféra ó Xéra, *sf.* Piece of drained marshy ground.
Xéfe, *sm.* Chief, head, superior. *Xefe de las caballerizas,* Master of the horse. *Xefe de esquadra,* (Naút.) Rear-admiral.
Xélfe, *sm.* A negro slave.
Xemál, *a.* Being a span wide or long.
Xéme, *sm.* 1. Span, the space from the end of the thumb to the end of the little finger. 2. A woman's face.
Xenábe ó Xanábe, *sm.* Mustard. V. *Mostaza.*
Xéno, na, *a.* (Ant.) V. *Lleno.*
Xépe, *sm.* V. *Alumbre.*
Xéque, *sm.* 1. An old man; a governor or chief among the Moors. 2. Portmanteau. V. *Xaque.*
Xéra, *sf.* 1. Extent of ground which can be ploughed in a day with a pair of oxen. 2. V. *Gira.*
Xerapellína, *sf.* An old ragged suit of clothes.
Xerezáno, na, *a.* y *s.* Native of or belonging to Xerez de la Frontera. *Vino de Xerez,* Xerez wine, vulgarly corrupted into *Sherry.*
Xérga, *sf.* 1. Coarse frieze; any coarse cloth. 2. Jargon, gibberish, unintelligible talk. V. *Gerigonza.* 3. Large sack. *Estar ó poner una cosa en xerga,* (Met.) To block out, to be begun but not finished.
Xergón, *sm.* 1. Large coarse pillow or sack filled with straw or paper cuttings. 2. Suit of clothes ill made. 3. An ill-shaped person. 4. (Fam.) Paunch, belly. *Llenar el xergon,* To eat heartily.
Xerguílla, *sf.* A sort of serge made of silk or worsted.
Xerífe, *sm.* Title or appellation of honour among the Moors.
Xerigónza, *sf.* Jargon, gibberish. V. *Gerigonza.*
Xerínga, *sf.* 1. Syringe, a pipe through which any liquor is squirted. 2. (Fam.) Importunity, vexation, trouble.
Xeringación, *sf.* Act of giving an injection; injection or matter injected.
Xeringár, *va.* 1. To syringe, to spout by a syringe. 2. To give or administer an injection. 3. To importune, to trouble, to vex.

Xeringázo, *sm.* The act of syringing; injection.
Xeringuílla, *sf.* (Bot.) Pipe-tree. Mabea taquari *L.*
Xeroftalmía, *sf.* (Cir.) Xerophthalmy, dry disease of the eye.
Xervílla, *sf.* A kind of shoes worn by servant maids.
Xervilléro, *sm.* (Ant.) V. *Zapatero.*
Xéta, *sf.* Bristle. V. *Seta ó Geta.*
Xetár, *va.* (Arag.) To dissolve in a liquid.
Xéto, *sm.* (Arag.) An empty bee-hive rubbed with honey to attract the bees.
Xía, *sf.* A sort of black mantle or cowl. V. *Chia.*
Xíbia, *sf.* (Ict.) Cuttle-fish. Sepia *L.*
Xibión, *sm.* Cuttle-fish bone used by gold and silversmiths.
Xícara, *sf.* Chocolate-cup.
Xicarílla, ta, *sf.* Small chocolate-cup.
Xífa, *sf.* Refuse of slaughtered beasts.
Xiferáda, *sf.* Stroke with a butcher's knife.
Xifería, *sf.* Slaughtering, the act of killing beasts for the shambles.
Xiféro, ra, *a.* Belonging to the slaughter-house.
Xiféro, *sm.* 1. Butcher's knife. 2. Butcher.
Xifía, *sf.* (Ict.) Xiphias, the sword-fish. Xiphias gladius *L.*
Xilguéro, *sm.* (Orn.) Linnet.
Xilobálsamo, *sm.* (Bot.) Tree which yields the balm of Gilead.
XilóstEo, *sm.* (Bot.) Pyrenees honeysuckle, upright honeysuckle. Lonicera pyrenaica et Xylosteum *L.*
Ximenzár, *va.* (Arag.) To ripple flax or hemp.
Xímio, mia, *s.* Ape, monkey. V. *Simio.*
Xinglár, *vn.* (Bax.) To cry.
Xión, *sm.* (Cant.) Yes. V. *Si.*
Xiquilíte *sm.* (Bot.) Plant from which a blue colour is made in America.
Xíride, *sf.* (Bot.) Stinking sword grass.
Xísca, *sf.* (Bot.) Coarse cane.
Xitádo, da, *a.* Ejected, cast out.
Xitár, *va.* (Arag.) To emit, to turn out.
Xitallár, *sm.* A place full of broom or cytisus.
Xitállo, *sm.* (Bot.) Prickly broom, hairy cytisus. Cytisus hirsutus *L.*
Xo, *interj.* V. *Jo ó Cho.*
Xorgolín, *sm.* (Cant.) Companion or servant to a bully or ruffian.
Xuagárzo, *sm.* (Bot.) Prickly cytisus.
Xubéte, *sm.* A kind of ancient armour.
Xúcla, *sf.* One of the seven vowel marks used by the Arabs.
Xúgo, *sm.* 1. Sap, juice of plants. 2. (Met.) Marrow, pith, substance of any thing.
Xugosidád, *sf.* Sappiness, succulence, juiciness.
Xugóso, sa, *a.* Sappy, juicy, succulent.
Xúgue, *sf.* Filthiness.
Xúlo, *sm.* Bell-wether, a sheep which leads the flock. V. *Manso.*
Xurél, *sm.* (Ict.) Godget, fish like gudgeon.
Xúta, *sf.* (Orn.) Kind of American duck

YA YAN

Y is the 27th letter in the Castilian alphabet, and was derived from the Greeks: it serves both as a consonant and a vowel; as a consonant, when followed by a vowel, as in *mayo*; and as a vowel it serves for a conjunctive particle, instead of the ancient *é*, (which is a contraction of the Latin *et*) except when followed by a word that begins with an *i*, or *y* before a consonant, in which case the ancient *é* is retained. Formerly it was used in all words derived from the Greek; but that practice is deemed pedantic, and *pyra, lyra,* &c. are now written *pira, lira.*

Y, And, a conjunction, is pronounced like the English *e;* when a consonant, it has nearly the same sound as in English. It is frequently used in interrogatives, as *ó ¿ tú, donde has estado ?* And thou, where hast thou been? *y bien?* And well then? *ó y que tenemos con eso ?* And what is that to us? Generally it is a copulative conjunction, as *Alonso, Fernando, y Manuel,* Alphonsus, Ferdinand, and Emmanuel.
Y, *ad.* (Ant.) There. V. *Allí.*
Ya, *ad.* 1. Already, now. 2. Presently, immediately. 3. Finally, ultimately. 4. At another time, on another occasion.—*part. dist.* Now. *Ya esto, ya aquello,* Now this, now that. *Ya que,* Since that, seeing that. *Ya si,* When, while, if.—*interj.* Used on being brought to recollect any thing. *No se acuerda vd. de tal cosa? Ya, ya,* Do not you remember such a thing? Yes, yes. *Ya se ve,* Yes, forsooth! it is clear; it is so.
Yáca, *sf.* (Bot.) A large-leaved Indian tree.
Yacénte, *a.* Jacent, vacant. *Herencia yacente,* Inheritance not yet occupied.
Yacér, *vn.* 1. To lie, to be stretched out. 2. To be fixed or situated in a place; to exist. 3. To sleep with a woman.
Yach ó Yate, *sm.* (Naút.) Yacht.
Yaciénte, *pa.* Extended, stretched; applied to honey-combs.
Yacíja, *sf.* 1. Bed, a place of repose. 2. Tomb, grave. *Ser de mala yacija,* To be a vagrant or of low sentiments and manners; to be restless; to have a bad bed.
Yactúra, *sf.* Loss.
Yágre, *sm.* A kind of sugar, extracted from the palm or cocoa-tree.
Yámbico, ca, *a.* Iambic; applied to a Latin verse.
Yámbo, *sm.* An iambic foot.
Yánta, *sf.* (Ant.) Dinner, mid-day meal.

YANTÁR, *va.* (Ant.) To dine. V. *Comer.*
YANTÁR, *sm.* 1. Viands, food. 2. A kind of king's taxes.
YÁRDA, *sf.* An English yard.
YÁRO, *sm.* (Bot.) Yarrow. Arum *L.*
YÉCO, CA, *a.* V. *Lleco.*
YÉDGO, *sm.* (Bot.) V. *Yezgo.*
YÉDRA, *sf.* (Bot.) Ivy. Hedera felix *L.*
YÉGUA, *sf.* Mare, the female of a horse. *Yegua paridera,* A breeding mare. *Yegua de vientre,* Mare fit to breed.
YEGUÁDA ó YEGÜERÍA, *sf.* Stud, a herd of breeding mares and stallions.
YEGUÁR, *a.* Belonging to mares.
YEGÜÉRO ó YEGÜERÍZO, *sm.* Keeper of breeding mares.
YEGÜEZUÉLA, *sf. dim.* Little mare.
YÉLMO, *sm.* Helmet, a part of the ancient armour.
YÉLO, *sm.* Frost; ice. *Bancos de yelo,* Flakes of ice.
YÉMA, *sf.* 1. Bud, gem, button, first shoot of trees. 2. Yolk, the yellow part of an egg. 3. Centre, middle. *En la yema del invierno,* In the dead of winter. *Dar en la yema,* (Met.) To hit the nail on the head; to touch the critical point. *Yema del dedo,* Fleshy tip of the finger. 4. (Joc.) Ace of diamonds in cards.
YÉNTE, *pa.* of *Ir.* Going, one that goes.
YÉRBA, *sf.* 1. Herb, a generic name given to all the smaller plants. 2. Flaw in the emerald which tarnishes its lustre. 3. Poison given in food; poisonous plant. *Pisar buena ó mala yerba,* To be of good or bad temper. *Yerba piogera ó piojenta,* Lousewort. Pedicularis myriophylla *L.* *Yerba benedicta,* V. *Valeriana.* *Yerba buena,* Mint. *Yerba cana,* Groundsel, ragwort. Senecio *L.* *Yerba de ballesteros,* White hellebore. *Yerba de cuajo,* V. *Cuajo.* *Yerba de la cabeza,* Tobacco. *Yerba del bazo ó cerval,* Spleenwort. *Yerba del espiritu santo,* V. *Angélica.* *Yerba de los lazarosos ó leprosos.* V. *Betónica.* *Yerba estrella,* Swine's cress, mouse-tail. *Yerba mora,* A species of nightshade, or variety of the egg-plant. Solanum melongena *L.* *Yerba puntera.* V. *Siempreviva.* *Yerbas del señor san Juan,* Odoriferous herbs ripe for sale on St. John's day. *Barro de yerbas,* Mug or jug made of perfumed clay with the figures of herbs upon it. *En yerba,* Greenly, tenderly; applied to fruits or seeds. *Queso de yerba,* Cheese made of vegetable runnet. *Sentir nacer la yerba,* Used to indicate one's vivacity or quickness; to be insensible.—*pl.* 1. Greens, vegetables; all kinds of garden stuff. 2. Grass of pasture land for cattle. *Otras yerbas,* (Joc.) Et cetera; used after several epithets.
YERBECÍCA, LLA, TA, *sf. dim.* of *Yerba.*
YERMÁR, *va.* To dispeople, to lay waste.
YÉRMO, *sm.* Desert, wilderness, waste country. *Padre del yermo,* Ancient hermit.
YÉRMO, MA, *a.* Waste, desert, uninhabited. *Tierra yerma,* Uncultivated ground.
YERNALMÉNTE, *ad.* (Joc.) In the manner of a son-in-law.
YERNÁR, *va.* (Joc.) To make one a son-in-law by force.
YERNECÍLLO, *sm.* A worthless petty son-in-law.
YÉRNO, *sm.* Son-in-law, the husband of one's daughter. *Engaña-yernos,* Baubles, gewgaws, trifles. *Ciega yernos,* Showy trifles.
YÉRO, *sm.* V. *Yerro.*
YÉRRO, *sm.* 1. Error, mistake, inadvertency; fault. 2. (Iron.) V. *Hierro.* *Yerros,* Faults, defects, errors. *Yerro de imprenta,* Erratum, literal error.
YÉRTO, TA, *a.* Stiff, motionless, unpliant, inflexible; rigid, tight. *Quedarse yerto,* (Met.) To be petrified with fear; to be immoveable with astonishment.
YÉRVO É YÉRO, *sm.* (Bot.) Tare, vetch, tares. Ervum *L.*
YESÁL ó YESÁR, *sm.* Gypsum-pit, a place where gypsum is dug.
YÉSCA, *sf.* 1. Spunk, tinder. *Yescas,* Any thing excessively dry or combustible. 2. Fuel, incentive or aliment of passion.
YESÉRA, *sf.* Kiln, where gypsum is calcined, and prepared for use.
YESERÍA, *sf.* Building constructed with gypsum.
YESÉRO, RA, *a.* Belonging to gypsum.
YESÉRO, *sm.* One that prepares or sells gypsum.
YÉSGO, *sm.* (Bot.) Dwarf elder. Sambucus ebulus *L.*
YÉSO, *sm.* Gypsum, sulphat of lime. *Yeso mate,* Plaster of Paris. *Yeso blanco,* Whiting.
YESÓN, *sm.* Partition-wall made of gypsum.
YESQUÉRO, *sm.* Tinder-box.
YÉZGO, *sm.* (Bot.) Dwarf elder. V. *Yesgo.*
YO, *pron. pers.* I. *Yo mismo,* I myself. Pronounced with emphasis, *yo* is an exclamation of contempt, of surprise, and negation; of commanding and of threatening; it is also a sign of majesty, as, *Yo el rey,* I the king.
YOGÁR ó YOGUÍR, *vn.* (Ant.) 1. To copulate, to come together as different sexes; to yoke. 2. To be detained, to make a stay.
YOLÁNTE, *sf.* Female proper name, the same as *Violante.*
YÓLE, *sm.* (Naút.) Yawl.
YÚCA, *sf.* (Bot.) Adam's needle; the root of this plant is farinaceous, and eaten like potatoes. Yucca *L.*
YUGÁDA, *sf.* Extent of ground which a yoke or pair of oxen can plough in a day.
YÚGE, *sm.* (Ant.) V. *Juez.*
YÚGO, *sm.* 1. Yoke, a frame of wood with bandage placed on the neck of draught-oxen. 2. Nuptial tie, with which a new-married couple is veiled; marriage ceremony. 3. Authority, power. 4. Confinement, prison, yoke. 5. Kind of gallows under which the Romans passed their prisoners of war. 6. (Naút.) Transom, a beam which lies across the sternpost. *Yugo de la caña,* (Naút.) Countertransom. *Yugo de la cubierta,* (Naút.) Deck-transom. *Yugo principal,* (Naút.) Wing-transom. *Sacudir el yugo,* To throw off the yoke.
YUGUÉRO, *sm.* Ploughman, ploughboy.
YUGULÁR, *a.* (Ant.) Jugular.
YUNGÍR, *va.* (Ant.) V. *Uncir.*

Yúnque, *sm.* 1. Anvil. 2. Constancy, fortitude. *Estar al yunque*, To bear up under the frowns of fortune; to bear impertinent or abusive language.
Yúnta, *sf.* 1. Couple, pair, yoke. 2. V. *Yugada.*
Yuntár, *va.* (Ant.) V. *Juntar.*
Yuntería, *sf.* Place where draught-oxen are fed.
Yuntéro, *sm.* V. *Yuguero.*
Yúnto, ta, *a.* Joined, united, close. V. *Junto. Arar yunto*, To plough together.
Yusáno, na, *a.* (Ant.) Inferior, lower.
Yuséra, *sf.* The horizontal stone in oil-mills which lies under the roller.
Yusión, *sf.* Precept, command.
Yúso, *ad.* (Ant.) V. *Debazo.*
Yuxtaposición, *sf.* Juxtaposition.
Yuyúba, *sf.* V. *Azufayfa.*

ZAF ZAH

THE *z* is sounded in Spanish like the English *th* in *think*, before all vowels; at the end of words it is pronounced as in English. Latin words terminating in *x* take *z* in Spanish, as *lux, luz; velox, veloz*. In the plural and in compound words it is superseded by *c*, as *paz* makes *paces, pacifico, apaciguar.*
Za, *interj.* A word used to frighten dogs.
Zabída y Zabila, *sf.* (Bot.) Aloes. Aloe spicata *L.*
Zabórda y Zabordamiénto, *s.* (Naút.) Stranding; the act of getting on shore.
Zabordár, *vn.* (Naút.) To touch ground, to get on shore, to be stranded; applied to a ship.
Zabórdo, *sm.* (Naút.) Stranding, the act of getting on shore.
Zábra, *sf.* (Naút.) A small vessel, used on the coast of Biscay.
Zabucár, *va.* To move, to shake, to agitate. V. *Bazucar.*
Zabullída, *sf.* Dipping, ducking.
Zabullidúra, *sf.* Submersion, ducking.
Zabullimiénto, *sm.* V. *Zambullidà.*
Zabullír, *va.* To plunge, to immerge, to put under water.—*vr.* 1. To plunge suddenly under water, to sink. 2. To lurk, to lie concealed.
Zacapéla ó Zacapélla, *sf.* Uproar, yell, noisy bustle.
Zacatín, *sm.* A small miserable place.
Zaceár, *va.* To frighten dogs away by crying [za.
Zadoríja, *sf.* (Bot.) Horned cumin. Hypecoum procumbens *L.*
Zafáda, *sf.* 1. Flight, escape. 2. (Naút.) The act of lightening the ship.
Zafár, *va.* 1. To adorn, to embellish; to disembarrass. 2. (Naút.) To lighten a ship.—*vr.* 1. To escape, to run away. 2. To avoid, to decline; to excuse; to free one's self from trouble. *Zafarse de los bazos*, (Naút.) To get clear of the shoals.
Zafaráncho, *sm.* 1. (Naút.) The state of being clear for action fore and aft. *Hacer zafarancho*, (Naút.) To make ready for action. 2. Moving, change.
Zafaréche, *sm.* (Ar.) V. *Estanque.*
Zafarí, *sm.* A sort of pomegranate, with quadrangular seeds or grains.
Zafariche, *sm.* (Ar.) Shelf for holding water vessels.
Zafería, *sf.* A small village, a farm-house.
Zafiaménte, *ad.* Clownishly.
Zafiedád, *sf.* Clownishness, rusticity.
Záfio, fia, *a.* Clownish, coarse, uncivil.
Zafío, *sm.* (Ict.) V. *Safio ó Congrio.*
Zafír ó Zafíro, *sm.* Sapphire, a precious stone of a blue colour.
Zafiríno, na, *a.* Being of the colour of a sapphire.
Záfo, fa, *a.* 1. Free, disentangled, empty. 2. (Naút.) Clear.
Zafón, *sm.* V. *Zahon.*
Zafrán, *sm.* (Ant.) V. *Azafran.*
Zága, *sf.* 1. Load packed on the back part of a carriage. 2. The extremity behind. 3. (Mil.) V. *Retaguardia.*—*sm.* The last player at a game of cards.—*ad.* V. *Detras. A' zaga ó en zaga*, Behind.
Zagál, *sm.* 1. A stout, spirited young man. 2. Swain, a young shepherd subordinate to the chief herd; subordinate coachman. 3. Under petticoat.
Zagála, *sf.* Lass, girl; a young woman.
Zagaléjo, ja, *s.* A young shepherd or shepherdess.
Zagaléjo, *sm.* An under petticoat.
Zagalíllo y Zagalíto, co, *sm.* A little shepherd.
Zaguán, *sm.* Porch, the entrance of a building.
Zaguanéte, *sm.* 1. Small entrance of a house. 2. A small party of the king's lifeguards.
Zaguéra, *sf.* (Ant.) V. *Retaguardia.*
Zaguéro, ra, *a.* Going or remaining behind.
Zahareño, ña, *a.* 1. Haggard, wild, intractable; applied to birds. 2. (Met.) Sour, haughty, indocile.
Zaharrón, *sm.* (Ant.) V. *Moharrache.*
Zahén, *a. Dobla zahen ó zahena*, A Moorish gold coin.
Zaheridór, ra, *s.* Censurer, one who blames or reproaches.
Zaherimiénto y Zahério, *sm.* Censure, blame.
Zaherír, *va.* To censure, to blame, to reproach; to upbraid.
Zahína, *sf.* Kind of tares sown in Andalusia. *Zahinas*, A kind of light and soft fritters, puff-cakes. *Zahinas de levadura*, Froth of barm.
Zahinár, *sm.* Land sown with *zahina.*
Zahón, *sm.* A kind of wide breeches.
Zahonádo, da, *a.* Of a dark colour, brownish.
Zahondár, *va.* To dig the ground, to penetrate. V. *Ahondar.*

Zahóra, *sf.* (Manch.) Luncheon among friends, with music.

Zahorár, *vn.* To have a repast with music.

Zahorí, *sm.* Vulgar impostor pretending to see hidden things, although in the bowels of the earth, if not covered with blue cloth.

Zahórra, *sf.* (Naút.) Ballast. V. *Lastre.*

Zahumár, *va.* To fumigate, to smoke. V. *Sahumar.*

Zahumério, *sm.* V. *Sahumerio.*

Zahúrda, *sf.* 1. Pigsty, hogsty. 2. A small, dirty, miserable house.

Zalá, *sf.* A kind of religious adoration paid by the Moors to God and their prophet Mohammed in the morning. *Hacer la zalá*, To pay homage.

Zalagárda, *sf.* 1. Ambuscade, ambush. 2. Gin, trap, snare. 3. Sudden attack, surprise. 4. Mock-fight; vulgar noise. 5. (Fam.) Malicious cunning.

Zaláma y Zalamería, *sf.* Flattery, adulation.

Zalaméro, ra, *s.* Wheedler, flatterer.

Zaléa, *sf.* An undressed sheepskin.

Zaleár, *va.* 1. To move any thing with care from one place to another. 2. To frighten dogs. V. *Zacear.*

Zaléma, *sf.* Bow, courtesy.

Zaléo, *sm.* 1. Skin of a beast lacerated by the wolf, which the herd carries to his master as an excuse; undressed sheepskin. 2. The act of shaking or moving to and fro.

Zallár, *va.* To direct and level a piece of warlike arms.

Zalmedína, *sm.* (Arag.) Magistrate with civil and criminal powers.

Zalóma, *sf.* (Naút.) Singing out of seamen when they haul with a rope.

Zalomár, *vn.* (Naút.) To sing out.

Zalóna, *sf.* A large earthen jar.

Zamacúco, *sm.* 1. Dunce, dolt, a stupid person. 2. Temulency, inebriation.

Zamánza, *sf.* (Fam.) Drubbing, flogging, castigation.

Zamárra, *sf.* Dress worn by shepherds, and made of undressed sheepskins.

Zamarreár, *va.* 1. To shake, to drag or pull to and fro. 2. To pin up close in a dispute. 3. (Met.) To drag, to ill-treat.

Zamarríco, *sm. dim.* de *Zamarro*, A portmanteau or bag made of a sheepskin, having the wool inside.

Zamarrílla, *sf.* 1. A short loose coat made of sheepskins. 2. (Bot.) Poley, mountain germander. Teucrium polium *L.*

Zamárro, *sm.* 1. A shepherd's coat made of sheepskins. 2. Sheep or lambskin. 3. Dolt, a stupid person. *Barbas de zamarro*, Nickname for persons having large irregular beards.

Zamarrón, *sm. aum.* of *Zamarra ó Zamarro.* [A large sheepskin.

Zamarrúco, *sm.* (Orn.) Titmouse. Parus pendulinus *L.*

Zambaígo, ga, *a.* y *s.* Son or daughter of an Indian by a negro woman, or by a negro man and Indian woman.

Zambapálo, *sm.* Ancient dance.

Zambárco, *sm.* A broad breast-harness for coach-horses and mules.

Zámbo, ba; y **Zambaígo, ga**, *a.* 1. Bandy-legged. 2. Applied to the son of a negro by an Indian woman, or vice versa.—*sm.* An American wild animal, resembling a dog with the head of a horse.

Zamboá, *sf.* 1. (Bot.) A sweet kind of quince-tree. Pyrus cydonia *L.* 2. Citron-tree.

Zambómba, *sf.* A kind of rustic drum.

Zambómbo, *sm.* Clown, rustic, an ill-bred person.

Zamborondón, na; y **Zamborotúdo, da**, *s.* Clownish, clumsy, ill-shaped.

Zámbra, *sf.* 1. A Moorish festival or feast, attended with dancing and music. 2. Shout, noisy mirth. 3. Kind of Moorish boat.

Zambucár y Zambucárse, *vn.* y *r.* To be hidden, to be concealed; to hide one's self.

Zambúco, *sm.* Squatting, the act of lying close to the ground, withdrawn from the sight; hiding, concealing.

Zambullída, *sf.* 1. Dipping, ducking, submersion. 2. In fencing, thrust on the breast.

Zambullír, *va.* y *r.* To plunge into water, to dip, to dive.

Zamoráno, na, *s.* Native of Zamora.—*a.* Belonging to Zamora. *Gayta Zamorana*, Kind of bagpipe, a musical instrument.

Zampabóllos, *sm.* (Fam.) Glutton. V. *Zampapalo.*

Zampáda, *sf.* Act of concealing, or putting one thing within another.

Zampár, *va.* 1. To conceal in a clever manner; to thrust one thing into another, so as to be covered by it and withdrawn from light. 2. To devour eagerly.—*vr.* To thrust one's self suddenly into any place.

Zampalimósnas, *sm.* A sturdy beggar.

Zampapálo y Zampatórtas ó Bodígos, *sm.* 1. A glutton, a greedy devourer of victuals. 2. Clown, rustic.

Zampeádo, *sm.* (Arq.) Wood-work and masonry in marshy foundations.

Zampóña, *sf.* 1. A rustic instrument, a kind of bagpipe. V. *Pipitaña.* 2. A poetical vein; genius or talent for poetry. 3. (Madrid) A poor person belonging to a workhouse; a term of derision. 4. Frivolous saying.

Zampoñeár, *vn.* 1. To play the bagpipe. 2. (Met.) To be prolix and frivolous in conversation, to prose. *Marear, zampoñear, ó empreñar la gata*, (Fam.) To be tiresome and prolix in gossiping.

Zampuzár, *va.* 1. To plunge, to dip, to dive, to put under water. 2. To hide, to conceal.

Zampúzo, *sm.* Immersion, submersion, concealment.

Zamúro, *sm.* (Orn.) Carrion-vulture. Vultur aura *L.*

Zanahória, *sf.* (Bot.) Carrot. Daucus carota *L.* *Zanahorias*, Deceitful caresses.

Zanahoriáte, *sm.* V. *Azanoriate.*

Zánca, *sf.* 1. Shank, that part of the leg of a fowl or bird which extends from the claws to the thigh. 2. A long shank or leg. 3. Large pin. *Zancas de araña*, Shifts, evasions, subterfuges.

Zancáda, *sf.* Stride, a long irregular step. *En dos zancadas*, Expeditiously, speedily.

Zancadílla, *sf.* 1. Trick, deceit, craft; act of supplanting. 2. (Naút.) Elbow in the hawse.

Zancádo, da, *a.* Insipid.

Zancajeár, *va.* To run about the streets bespattering the legs with dirt and mud.
Zancajéra, *sf.* Coach-step. [*joso.*
Zancajiénto, ta, *a.* Bandy-legged. V. *Zanca-*
Zancájo, *sm.* 1. Heel-bone of the foot. 2. The hind part of a shoe or stocking, which covers the heel. 3. A short ill-shaped person. 4. An ignorant stupid person. *No llegar al zancajo*, (Met.) To be widely distant or very far from attaining any thing.
Zancajóso, sa, *a.* 1. Bandy-legged. 2. Wearing dirty stockings with holes at the heels. 3. Clumsy, awkward, unhandy.
Zancarrón, *sm.* 1. The bare heel-bone. 2. Any large bone without flesh. 3. A withered, old, ugly person. 4. An ignorant pretender at any art or science. *Zancarron de Mahoma*, (Joc.) Mohammed's bones, which are at Mecca.
Záncos, *sm. pl.* 1. Stilts, supports on which boys raise themselves and walk; sticks with supports for the feet about their middle, having one end strapped to the thighs, and by means of which herds follow cattle through rivers and over moors. 2. Dancers or walkers on stilts. 3. (Naút.) Flag-staffs. *Poner á alguno en zancos*, (Met.) To favour one in obtaining fortune. *Subirse en zancos*, To be haughty and elated with good fortune.
Zancúdo, da, *a.* Long-shanked, having long thin legs.
Zandália, *sf.* Sandal.
Zandía, *sf.* (Bot.) Water-melon. V. *Sandía.*
Zandiál, *sm.* Place where water-melons are cultivated.
Zanéfa, *sf.* A printed border. V. *Cenefa.*
Zánga, *sf.* Ombre played by four.
Zangáda, *sf.* Raft or float made of cork.
Zangála, *sf.* Buckram, a sort of linen stiffened with gum.
Zangamánga, *sf.* Falsehood, tending to deceive or defraud a person.
Zanganáda, *sf.* Dronish or sluggardly act.
Zangandóngo y Zagandúllo, *sm.* 1. Idler, a lazy person, who affects ignorance and want of abilities, that he may not be obliged to work. 2. Dolt, an ignorant, stupid, awkward person.
Zanganeár, *vn.* To drone, to live in idleness.
Zángano, *sm.* 1. (Ent.) Drone, a bee which makes no honey. 2. Sluggard, idler, sponger.
Zangarílla, *sf.* A small watermill for grinding wheat on the banks of rivers in Estremadura.
Zangarilléja, *sf.* Trollop, a dirty lazy girl.
Zangarreár, *vn.* To scrape a guitar.
Zangarriána, *sf.* 1. An infirmity of the head, incident to sheep. 2. Sadness, melancholy.
Zangarullón, *sm.* A tall, sluggish, lazy lad.
Zangoloteár y Zangoteár, *va.* To move in a violent yet ridiculous manner.
Zangolotéo, *sm.* A violent yet ridiculous waddling; a wagging motion or movement.
Zangudnga, *sf.* A feigned disease; a fictitious disorder.
Zanguángo, *sm.* (Fam.) Lazy fellow who always finds pretexts to avoid working.
Zanguávo, *sm.* Tall idler that pretends to be ill, silly, or unable to work.
Zánja, *sf.* 1. Ditch, trench, train. 2. Foundation; fundamental principle. *Abrir las zanjas*, To lay the foundation of a building; to begin any thing.
Zanjár, *sm.* Pit or excavation dug in the ground.—*va.* 1. To open ditches or drains, to excavate. 2. To lay a foundation; to establish. 3. To terminate a business amicably.
Zanjíca, lla, ta, *sf. dim.* Small drain; slender foundation.
Zanjón, *sm.* A deep ditch; a large drain.
Zanjoncíllo, *sm.* A small drain or trench.
Zanqueadór, ra, *s.* 1. One who waddles or shakes from side to side in walking. 2. A great walker, one who walks much.
Zanqueamiénto, *sm.* The act of waddling or shaking from side to side in walking.
Zanqueár, *vn.* To waddle, to trot or run about; to walk much and fast.
Zanquilárgo, ga, *a.* Long-shanked.
Zanquíllas y Zanquítas, *sf. pl.* Thin long shanks or legs.
Zanquituérto, ta, *a.* Bandy-legged.
Zanquiváno, na, *a.* Spindle-shanked.
Zápa, *sf.* 1. Spade, an instrument for digging. 2. (Ict.) Dogfish. V. *Melgacho.* 3. Shagreen, a skin made rough in imitation of sealskin. 4. Kind of carving in silver. *Caminar á la zapa*, (Mil.) To advance by sap or mine.
Zapadór, *sm.* (Mil.) Sapper, one who works at saps or mines.
Zapár, *vn.* To sap, to mine.
Zaparráda, *sf.* A violent fall.
Zaparrastrár, *vn.* To trail, to drag along on the ground; applied to gowns or clothes.
Zaparrastróso, sa, *a.* 1. Dirty from trailing or dragging along on the ground. 2. Ill-made, badly done.
Zaparrázo, *sm.* 1. A violent fall, attended with great noise. 2. (Fam.) Calamity, misfortune.
Zapáta, *sf.* 1. A piece of sole leather put on the hinge of a door to prevent its creaking. 2. A kind of coloured half-boots. 3. Bracket of a beam. 4. (Naút.) Shoe. *Zapata de un ancla*, (Naút.) Shoe of an anchor. *Zapata de la quilla*, (Naút.) The false keel.
Zapatázo, *sm. aum.* 1. Large shoe. 2. Blow with a shoe. 3. Fall; the noise attending a fall. 4. Clapping noise of a horse's foot.
Zapateádo, *sm.* A kind of dance.
Zapateadór, ra, *s.* Dancer, who beats time with the sole of his shoe.
Zapateár, *va.* 1. To kick or strike with the shoe. 2. To lead by the nose. 3. To beat time with the sole of the shoe. 4. To hit frequently with the button of the foil. 5. To strike the ground with the feet; used of rabbits when chased.—*vr.* To oppose with spirit; not to give up a contested point; to resist in debating.
Zapatéo, *sm.* Act of making shoes.
Zapatéra, *sf.* 1. A shoemaker's wife. 2. Olive spoiled in the pickle.
Zapatería, *sf.* 1. Trade of a shoemaker; a shoemaker's shop. 2. Place or street which contains a number of shoemakers' shops. 3. Shoemaking business. *Zapatería de viejo*, A cobbler's stall.
Zapaterílllo, lla, *s.* A petty shoemaker.
Zapatéro, *sm.* Shoemaker. *Zapatero de viejo*, Cobbler.

Zapatéta, *sf.* Slap on the sole of a shoe.—*interj.* Oh! an exclamation of admiration.

Zapatíco, to y llo, *sm.* A nice little shoe.

Zapatílla, *sf.* 1. Pump. 2. Piece of shamois or buckskin put behind the lock of a gun or pistol. 3. Button at the end of a foil. 4. Exterior hoof of animals.

Zapatilléro, *sm.* Shoemaker who makes pumps and children's shoes.

Zapáto, *sm.* Shoe, a cover of the foot. *Zapato botin*, A half boot. *Zapato ramplon*, Thick-soled coarse shoe. *Zapato de madera*, A wooden shoe. *Zapato de tierra*, Earth or clay which sticks to the shoes. *Andar con zapatos de fieltro*, To proceed with great caution and silence. *Zapatos papales*, Clogs.

Zapatón, *sm.* 1. A large clumsy shoe. 2. A wooden shoe.

Zapatúdo, da, *a.* 1. Wearing large or strong shoes. 2. Large hoofed or clawed; applied to beasts.

Zápe, *interj.* A word used to frighten cats away; exclamation of aversion, or of negation at cards.

Zapeár, *va.* To frighten cats away by crying *zape*.

Zapíto, *sm.* Milk-pail.

Zapóte, *sm.* (Bot.) Sapota-tree. Achras sapota *L. Zapote mamey*, Sweet sapota. Achras mammosa *L.*

Zapuzár, *va.* To duck. V. *Chapuzar.*

Záque, *sm.* 1. Bottle or wine-bag made of leather. 2. Tippler, drunkard.

Zaqueár, *vn.* To rack, to defecate; to draw off liquor from one vessel into another.

Zaquizamí, *sm.* 1. Garret. 2. A small dirty house.

Zár, *sm.* Czar, the emperor of all the Russias.

Zára, *sf.* (Bot.) Indian corn, maize. V. *Maiz.*

Zarabánda, *sf.* 1. Saraband, a lively dance and tune. 2. Bustle, noise.

Zarabandísta, *s. com.* Dancer.

Zarabutéro, ra, *a.* V. *Embustero.*

Zaradión y Zaradíque, *sm.* Medicine for dogs, especially for curing the mange.

Zaragatóna, *sf.* (Bot.) Flea-wort. Plantago psyllium *L.*

Zaragocí, *sm.* Kind of plum.

Zaragüélles, *sm. pl.* A sort of drawers or wide breeches; a large pair of breeches ill made.

Zaramágo, *sm.* (Gal.) V. *Xaramago.*

Zaramagullón, *sm.* (Orn.) Didapper, minute merganser. Mergus minutus *L.*

Zarambéque, *sm.* A kind of merry tune and noisy dance.

Zaramúllo, *sm.* Busybody; a vain meddling person.

Zaránda, *sf.* Screen or frame for sifting earth or sand.

Zarandadór, *sm.* Sifter of wheat.

Zarandájas, *sf. pl.* 1. Trifles, worthless scraps or remnants. 2. Odds given at the game of trucks.

Zarandajíllas, *sf. pl. dim.* Little trifles.

Zarandalí, *ad.* Applied to a black spotted dove.

Zarandár y Zarandeár, *va.* 1. To winnow corn with a sieve. 2. To stir and move nimbly. 3. To separate the precious from the common.

Zarandéo, *sm.* Act of sifting or winnowing.

Zarandéro, *sm.* V. *Zarandador.*

Zarandíllo, *sm.* 1. A small sieve or riddle. 2. One who frisks nimbly about.

Zarangúllo, *sm.* Mixture of pepper, tomates, &c.

Zarapallón, *sm.* A shabby dirty fellow.

Zarapatél, *s.* A kind of salmagundi made up of various ingredients.

Zarapéto, *sm.* (Fam.) Intriguer, a crafty person.

Zarapíto, *sm.* (Orn.) Whimbrel, curlew-knot. Scolopax phæopus *L.*

Zaratán, *sm.* Cancer in the breast.

Zaráza, *sf.* Chintz, a fine cotton cloth. *Zarazas*, Paste made of pounded glass and poison for killing dogs.

Zarceár, *va.* To clean pipes or conduits with briérs.—*vn.* To move to and fro.

Zarcéro, ra, *a.* Fit to pursue the game among briers; applied to pointers.

Zarcéto, ta, *s.* (Orn.) Widgeon. V. *Cerceta.*

Zarcíllo, *sm.* 1. Ear-ring. 2. Tendril, the clasp of a vine or other climbing plant. 3. (Arag.) Hoop of a butt or barrel.

Zárco, ca, *a.* Of a light blue colour, applied to the eyes; clear and pure, applied to water.

Zarevítz, *sm.* The first born son of the emperor of Russia, and heir apparent to the throne.

Zargatóna, *sf.* V. *Zaragatona.*

Zariáno, na, *a.* Belonging to the Czar.

Zarítza ó Zarína, *sf.* Queen of the emperor of Russia; empress, czarina.

Zárja, *sf.* Reel, an instrument for winding silk.

Zárpa, *sf.* 1. Weighing anchor. 2. Dirt or mud sticking to the skirts of clothes. 3. Superior thickness of foundation walls. 4. Claw, the foot of a beast or bird armed with sharp nails. *Echar la zarpa*, To gripe, to claw. *Hacerse una zarpa*, To wet one's self extremely.

Zarpár, *va.* (Naút.) To weigh anchor. *El ancla está zarpado*, (Naút.) The anchor is a-trip.

Zarpastróso, sa, *a.* Ragged, dirty.

Zarpázo, *sm.* Sound of a body falling on the ground.

Zarpóso, sa, *a.* Bespattered with mire or dirt.

Zarracatería, *sf.* Deceitful flattery.

Zarracatín, *sm.* Haggler, miser.

Zarramplín, *sm.* Calkin of a horse's shoe

Zarramplináda, *sf.* Sound of calkins.

Zarrapástra, *sf.* Dirt or mire sticking to the skirts of clothes.

Zarrapastrón, na, *s.* Tatterdemalion, a ragged fellow.

Zarrapastrosaménte, *ad.* Raggedly.

Zarrapastróso, sa, *a.* Ragged, dirty, uncleanly.

Zárria, *sf.* 1. Dirt or mire sticking to clothes 2. Leather thongs for tying on *abarcas.*

Zarriénto, ta, *a.* Bespattered with mud or mire.

Zárrio, *sm.* V. *Charro.*

Zárza, *sf.* 1. (Bot.) Common bramble. Rubus *L.* 2. (Toledo) Company of fellowship porters, who assist at the edicts or decrees for burning, issued by the Inquisition. *Zarzas*, Thorns, difficulties.

Zarzagán, *sm.* A cold north-east wind.

Zarzaganéte, *sm. dim.* A light north-east wind.

Zarzaganíllo, *sm.* A violent storm at north east

Zarzahán, *sm.* A kind of striped silk.
Zarzaidéa, *sf.* (Bot.) Raspberry-bush. Rubus idæus *L.*
Zarzál, *sm.* Place full of briers or brambles.
Zarzamóra, *sf.* (Bot.) Blackberry-bush. Rubus fruticosus *L.*
Zarzaparílla, *sf.* (Bot.) Sarsaparilla. Smilax sarsaparilla *L.*
Zarzaparillár, *sm.* Plantation of sarsaparilla.
Zarzaperrúna, *sf.* (Bot.) Dog-rose. Rosa canina *L.*
Zarzarósa, *sf.* (Bot.) Dog-rose. V. *Zarzaperruna.*
Zárzo, *sm.* Hurdle, a texture of canes, sticks, or twigs. *Menear el zarzo,* (Fam.) To threaten to beat or chastise.
Zarzóso, sa, *a.* Full of brambles or briers.
Zarzuéla, *sf.* Play of two acts.
Zas, Zas, Words used to express the sound of repeated blows; raps at a door.
Zascandíl, *sm.* 1. An unforeseen accident. 2. A crafty impostor or swindler. 3. An upstart proud person of mean sentiments and extraction.
Záta y Zátara, *sf.* Raft, a frame or shoal made by laying pieces of timber across each other.
Zatíco, *sm.* A small bit of bread.
Zatiquéro, *sm.* Pantler, an officer of the king's household who keeps the bread.
Záto, *sm.* Morsel or piece of bread.
Zayár, *va.* (Naút.) To bowse, to haul a tackle.
Zay'da, *sf.* (Orn.) A variety of the African heron, having a blue head and long pendent crest; it is easily domesticated, and delights to perch on the top of farm-houses. Ardea caspica *L.*
Zay'no, na, *a.* 1. Of a chestnut colour; applied to a horse. 2. Vitious, treacherous, wicked; insidious. *Mirar de zayno,* To look sideways; to cast an insidious glance.
Zazahán, *sm.* Sort of flowered silk.
Zazosíto, ta, *a. dim.* of *Zazoso.*
Zazóso, sa, *a.* Pronouncing an *s* instead of a *c.* V. *Ceceoso.*
Zéa, *sf.* 1. Hip-bone. V. *Cea.* 2. (Bot.) Spelt-corn. Triticum spelta *L.*
Zébra, *sf.* Zebra. V. *Cebra.*
Zéda, *sf.* Sound of the letter *z* in Spanish.
Zedílla, *sf.* The ancient letter which was formed of a c and a comma under it, thus ç.
Zedoária, *sf.* (Bot.) Zedoary.
Zez, *a.* V. *Zahen.*
Zeladór, *sm.* 1. Zealot, one passionately ardent in any cause. 2. Overseer, superintendent.
Zelár, *va.* 1. To watch, to be attentive, to be vigilant or carefully observant. 2. To observe the actions of others, to spy, to explore. 3. To be jealous. 4. To engrave. V. *Celar.*
Zeléras, *sf. pl.* (Ant.) V. *Zelos.*
Zélo, *sm.* 1. Zeal, careful observance. 2. V. *Luxuria.* 3. Rut, the appetite for generation in animals. 4. Religious zeal.—*pl.* 1. Apprehensions, suspicions, fears. 2. Jealousy. *Pedir zelos,* To be jealous. *Dar zelos,* To occasion or excite suspicion.
Zelosaménte, *ad.* Zealously.
Zelóso, sa, *a.* 1. Zealous, carefully observant. 2. Jealous. 3. Rutting, hot. 4. Excessively careful or anxious.

Zelotípia, *sf.* Jealousy.
Zenít, *sm.* Zenith, the point over-head, opposite the *Nadir.*
Zenzalíno, na, *a.* Belonging to gnats.
Zenzálo, *sm.* Gnat.
Zequí, *sm.* European gold coin formerly used in Africa.
Zéquia, *sf.* Canal for irrigating lands. V. *Azequia.*
Zéro, *sm.* Zero, the cipher, nought. V. *Cero.*
Zéta, *sf.* Name of the letter z. V. *Zeda.*
Zilórgano, *sm.* A kind of musical instrument.
Zimosímetro, *sm.* Kind of thermometer.
Zimotécnia, *sf.* (Quim.) Treatise on fermentation.
Zínco, Zinc, ó Zínque, *sm.* Zinc or zink, a whitish metal.
Zínga, *sf.* (Naút.) V. *Singladura.*
Zipizápe, *sm.* A noisy scuffle with blows.
Zirigáña, *sf.* Adulation. V. *Chasco y Friolera.*
Zis Zas, (Fam.) Words expressing the sound of repeated blows or strokes.
Zítara, *sf.* A thin wall. V. *Asitara.*
Zizáña, *sf.* 1. (Bot.) Darnel. Lolium temulentum *L.* 2. Discord, disagreement; any thing injurious. 3. Vice mixed with good actions. *Sembrar zizaña,* To sow discord.
Zizañadór, ra, *s.* V. *Zizanero.*
Zizañár, *va.* To sow discord or vice.
Zizañéro, *sm.* Makebate, a breeder of quarels.
Zócalo, *sm.* Socle or zocle, a flat square member under the base of a pedestal.
Zocáto, ta, *a.* Over-ripe; applied to cucumbers which grow yellow.
Zóclo, *sm.* V. *Zueco.*
Zóco, *sm.* 1. A wooden shoe. V. *Zueco.* 2. Plinth.
Zocóba, *sf.* 1. (Bot.) Herb in South America used as an antidote to poisons. 2. Tree in New Spain yielding fine yellow wood.
Zodiáco, *sm.* (Astr.) Zodiac, the course of the sun through the twelve signs.
Zófra, *sf.* A Moorish kind of carpet.
Zollipár, *vn.* To sob, to sigh with convulsive sorrow.
Zollípo, *sm.* Sob, a convulsive sigh.
Zolócho, cha, *a.* Stupid, silly.
Zóma, *sf.* A coarse sort of flour. V. *Soma.*
Zómpo, pa, *a.* Clumsy, awkward.
Zóna, *sf.* 1. Zone, girdle. 2. Zone, a division of the terraqueous globe.
Zoncería, *sf.* Insipidity, want of taste and relish.
Zonzaménte, *ad.* Insipidly.
Zónzo, za, *a.* 1. Insipid, tasteless. 2. Stupid, thoughtless. *Ave zonza,* (Fam.) Careless, inert simpleton.
Zonzorrión, na, *s.* A very dull and stupid person.
Zoófago, *sm.* Insect which sucks the blood of animals.
Zoofíto, *sm.* Zoophyte, a body between a plant and animal, the link which unites the animal and vegetable kingdoms.
Zoofórica, *a.* Zoophoric; applied to a column bearing an animal.
Zoografía, *sf.* Zoography, description of animals.
Zoolatría, *sf.* Worship of animals.
Zoología, *sf.* Zoology, treatise of animals.

Zópas ó Zopítas, *sm.* Nickname to a person pronouncing z for s.
Zopilóte, *sm.* (Orn.) Carrion-vulture. Vultur aura *L.*
Zopénco, ca, *a.* Very stupid.—*sm.* (Burl.) [Block.
Zopetéro, *sm.* V. *Ribazo.*
Zopísa, *sf.* Pitch scraped from the bottom of ships; pitch mixed with wax.
Zópo, pa, *a.* Lame, maimed.
Zópo, *sm.* A clumsy stupid fellow.
Zoquéte, *sm.* 1. Block, a short piece of timber. 2. Bit or morsel of bread. 3. A rude, thick, sluggish, ugly little person; a dolt. 4. Belfry. 5. A short thick stick used in bending or twisting ropes. *Zoquete de cuchara,* (Naút.) Scoop-handle.
Zoqueteria, *sf.* Heap of blocks, plank-ends or short pieces of timber.
Zoquetéro, ra, *a.* Beggarly, poor, indigent, asking charity.
Zoquetíco y **Zoquetíllo**, *sm.* A small morsel of bread.
Zoquetúdo, da, *a.* Rough, ill-finished.
Zoríta, *sf.* (Orn.) Stock dove, wood-pigeon. Columba oenas *L.*
Zórra, *sf.* 1. Fox. Canis vulpes *L.* 2. Prostitute, strumpet. *Zorra corrida,* Artful street-walker. 3. Drunkenness, inebriation. 4. A sly crafty person. *Caldo de zorra,* A false appearance. 5. Low strong car for heavy goods. 6. V. *Sorra. Tener zorra,* (Met.) To have the head-ache; to be melancholy. *A' la zorra candilazo,* Address with which one cunning person deceives another knowing one, diamond cut diamond.
Zorrastrón, na, *s.* Crafty, cunning, roguish person.
Zorrázo, *sm. aum.* 1. A big fox. 2. A very artful fellow; a great knave.
Zorréra, *sf.* 1. Fox-hole. 2. A smoking chimney, a smoky kitchen or room. 3. Heaviness of the head, drowsiness.
Zorrería, *sf.* 1. Artfulness of a fox. 2. Cunning, craft, knavery.
Zorréro, ra, *a.* 1. Slow, tardy, inactive; lagging, loitering behind. 2. (Naút.) Sailing heavily; applied to a ship which is a bad sailer. 3. Applied to large shot. 4. Cunning, capricious.
Zorréro, *sm.* 1. Terrier, a dog which follows foxes and other game under ground. Canis Gallicus *L.* 2. Keeper of a royal forest.
Zorrílla, *sf.* 1. A little bitch fox. 2. Hoiden, an ill-taught awkward girl. 3. A kind of unguent. [fox.
Zorríllo y **Zorruélo**, *sm. dim.* Whelp of a
Zorríta, *sf. dim.* Little bitch fox.
Zórro, *sm.* 1. A male fox. 2. One who affects simplicity or silliness for the purposes of fraud and imposition. 3. Terrier. V. *Zorrero. Estar hecho un zorro,* To be extremely drowsy or heavy with sleep. *Zorros,* Fox-skins; fox-tails used in dusting furniture.
Zórro, ra, *a.* V. *Zorrero.*
Zorroclóco, *sm.* 1. (Mur.) A thin paste rolled up in a cylindric shape. 2. A dronish, humdrum, heavy fellow; one who feigns weakness to avoid work. 3. Caress, demonstration of love or friendship. V. *Arrumaco.*
Zorronglón, na, *a.* Slow, heavy, lazy.

Zorruéla, *sf.* A little bitch-fox. V. *Zorrilla.*
Zorrúllo, *sm.* A cylindrical piece of timber.
Zorrúno, na, *a.* Vulpine, belonging to a fox.
Zorzál, *sm.* 1. (Orn.) Thrush. Turdus musicus *L.* 2. (Ict.) Wrasse. Labrus tinca *L.* 3. Artful, cunning man.
Zorzaléña, *sf.* Applied to a small round kind of olives.
Zorzalíco, llo, to, *sm. dim.* of *Zorzal.*
Zostér, *sf.* Shingles, a kind of tetter that spreads itself around the loins. [son.
Zóte, *sm.* Ignorant, stupid, dronish, lazy per-
Zóylo, *sm.* A malicious or invidious critic or censurer.
Zozóbra, *sf.* 1. Uneasiness, anguish, anxiety. 2. (Naút.) A foul or contrary wind. 3. An unlucky cast of the die.
Zozobránte, *pa.* Anxious, dangerous.
Zozobrár, *vn.* 1. (Naút.) To be weather-beaten; to sink, to founder. 2. To be in great danger. 3. To grieve, to be in pain; to be afflicted.
Zúa ó **Zúda**, *sf.* Persian wheel. V. *Azuda.*
Zúbia, *sf.* Drain, channel for water.
Zúcio, cia, *a.* V. *Sucio*
Zuéco, *sm.* 1. A wooden shoe. 2. A sort of shoe with a wooden or cork sole. 3. A plain, simple style.
Zúfre, *sm.* Sulphur. V. *Azufre.*
Zufrír, *va.* To suffer. V. *Sufrir.*
Zuíza, *sf.* 1. A party of young men at a feast. 2. Quarrel, dispute.
Zuizón, *sm.* (Naút.) A half pike, used in boarding.
Zulacár, *va.* To anoint or cover with bitumen.
Zuláque, *sm.* 1. Bitumen. V. *Betun.* 2. (Naút.) Stuff, a composition of quick-lime, fish-oil, tar, and other ingredients, with which the bottom of ships is paid.
Zúlla, *sf.* 1. (Bot.) French honey-suckle. Hedysarum coronarium *L.* 2. (Vulg.) Human excrements.
Zullárse, *vr.* To go to stool, to break wind behind.
Zulléneo, ca; y **Zullón**, na, *a.* Breaking wind behind; flatulent.
Zullón, *sm.* The act of breaking wind, flatulence. [mach.
Zumacál ó **Zumacár**, *sm.* Plantation of su-
Zumacár, *va.* To dress or tan with sumach.
Zumáque, *sm.* 1. (Bot.) Sumach-tree. Rhus coriaria *L.* 2. (Joc.) Wine. *Ser aficionado al zumaque,* To be fond of wine, to be addicted to drinking.
Zumacáya y **Zumáya**, *sf.* (Orn.) The common owl, barn-owl. Strix flammea *L.*
Zúmba, *sf.* 1. A large bell, used by carriers. 2. Joke, jest; facetious raillery.
Zumbár, *vn.* 1. To resound, to emit a continued harsh sound; to hum. 2. To be near a certain time or place. *El no tiene aun cincuenta años, pero le zumban,* He is not yet fifty years old, but very near that age.—*va. y r.* To jest, to joke. *Hacer zumbar las orejas,* (Fam.) To make one feel by a smart reprehension. *Ir zumbando,* To go with great violence and celerity.
Zumbél, *sm.* 1. (Fam.) Frown, an angry mien or aspect. 2. (And.) Cord with which boys spin tops.

Zumbído y Zúmbo, *sm.* Humming, a continued buzzing sound.
Zumbón, na, *a.* Waggish, casting jokes. *Cencerro zumbon,* Bell placed on the head of the leading horse or mule in carts.
Zumbón, *sm.* Pigeon with a small maw.
Zumiénto, ta, *a.* Juicy, succulent.
Zumíllo, *sm.* (Bot.) Deadly carrot. Thapsia villosa *L.*
Zúmo, *sm.* 1. Sap, juice, liquor, moisture; it is properly the juice obtained by expression; that obtained by boiling is *zugo.* 2. Wine, the juice of grapes. 3. Profit, utility. *Zumo de cepas ó parras,* (Joc. y Fam.) Juice of the grape.
Zumóso, sa, *a.* Juicy, succulent. [V. *Ceño.*
Zúño, *sm.* Frown, angry mien or countenance.
Zúpia, *sf.* 1. Wine which is turned, and has a bad taste and colour; any liquor of a bad taste. 2. Refuse, useless remains.
Zúra y Zurána, *sf.* Stock-dove. V. *Zorita.*
Zurcidéra, *sf.* Bawd, pimp.
Zurcído, *sm.* Stitching, uniting, fine-drawing.
Zurcidór, ra, *s.* 1. Fine-drawer, one whose business is to sew up rents. 2. Pimp, procuress.
Zurcidúra, *sf.* Fine-drawing, the act of sewing up rents.
Zurcír, *va.* 1. To darn, to sew up rents, to fine-draw. 2. To join, to unite. 3. To patch up in haste. 4. To hatch lies. *Zurcir voluntades,* To unite, to agree, to join issue; to pander.
Zurdeár, *vn.* To be left-handed. [ed.
Zurdíllo, *sm.* One who is somewhat left-hand-
Zúrdo, da, *a.* Left-handed. *No ser zurdo,* To be very clever. *A' zurdas,* The wrong way.
Zuríta, *sf.* (Orn.) Stock-dove. V. *Zorita.*
Zuríza, *sf.* Quarrel, dispute. V. *Zuiza.*
Zúro, ra, *a.* Belonging to a stock-dove.
Zúrra, *sf.* 1. The act of tanning or currying leather. 2. (Ant.) Fox. 3. Flogging, drubbing, castigation. 4. Toil, drudgery. 5. Quarrel, dispute. 6. A severe reprimand. *Zurra al cáñamo,* (Fam.) An expression used to stimulate the punishment of any one, or to indicate obstinate perseverance in any thing.
Zúrra, *interj.* A term expressive of displeasure or anger.
Zurráco, *sm.* (Joc.) Cash.
Zurrádo, da, *a.* Curried, dressed. *Salvo el zurrado,* (Fam.) V. *Salvo el guante.*
Zurradór, *sm.* 1. Leather-dresser, currier, tanner. 2. One who flogs or chastises.
Zurrápa, *sf.* 1. Lees, sediment, dregs. 2. Any thing vile or despicable. *Con zurrapas,* In an uncleanly, dirty manner.
Zurrapílla, *sf.* Small lees in liquor.
Zurrapóso, sa; Zurrapiénto, ta, *a.* Full of lees and dregs.
Zurrár, *va.* 1. To curry, to dress leather. 2. To flog, to chastise with a whip. 3. To contest, to urge with vehemence. 4. To get one's theme done by others; applied to school-boys.—*vr.* To have a sudden call of nature; to dirty one's self. *Zurrar el bálago,* (Fam.) To beat, to strike, to bruise, to cudgel. *Zurrar la badana,* (Fam.) To ill-treat.
Zurriága, *sf.* 1. Thong, a long leather strap; a whip for tops. 2. (Orn.) Lark. V. *Calandria*
Zurriagár, *va.* To flog, to chastise with a whip.
Zurriagázo, *sm.* 1. A severe lash or stroke with a whip. 2. Unexpected ill treatment; unfortunate calamity or misfortune.
Zurriágo, *sm.* Whip for inflicting punishment.
Zurriár, *vn.* 1. (Vulg.) To hum, to buzz. 2. To speak in a harsh and violent tone.
Zurribánda, *sf.* 1. Repeated flogging or chastisement with a whip. 2. A noisy quarrel.
Zurribúrri, *sm.* Ragamuffin, a vile despicable person.
Zurrído y Zúrrio, *sm.* 1. Humming, buzzing 2. Confused noise or bustle.
Zurrír, *vn.* To hum, to buzz, to tinkle.
Zurrón, *sm.* 1. Bag or pouch in which shepherds carry their provisions. 2. Rind of some fruits. 3. Chaff, husks of grain. 4. Amnion or amnios, the innermost membrane with which the fœtus in the womb is covered. 5. Bag, sack, purse, tumour.
Zurróna, *sf.* Prostitute who ruins her gallants.
Zurroncíllo, *sm.* A small bag.
Zurronéro, *sm.* One who makes bags or sacks.
Zurrucárse, *vr.* To experience a sudden call of nature; to dirty one's self.
Zurrúsco, *sm.* A slice of bread which is over-toasted.
Zurugía, *sf.* (Ant.) V. *Cirugia.*
Zurujáno, *sm.* (Ant.) V. *Cirujano.*
Zurúllo, *sm.* Rolling-pin, any cylindrical piece of wood.
Zurumbét, *sm* (Bot.) Large East Indian tree.
Zutaníco, llo, *sm. dim.* of *Zutano.*
Zutáno, na, *s.* Such a one. *Zutano y fulano,* Such and such a one.
Zuzár, *va.* To set on dogs. V. *Azuzar.*
Zúzo, *interj.* A word used to call or set on a dog.
Zuzón, *sm.* (Bot.) Spatlin poppy, catchfly. Silene behen *L.*
Zygofillón, *sm.* (Bot.) Beancaper. Zygophillum *L.*

FIN DEL TOMO PRIMERO.

CPSIA information can be obtained
at www.ICGtesting.com
Printed in the USA
BVHW09*1108160818
524721BV00010B/212/P